10,710

DICTIONARY OF TWENTIETH-CENTURY MUSIC

Board of Advisors

DICTIONARY OF TWENTIETH-CENTURY MUSIC

Edited by JOHN VINTON

THAMES AND HUDSON · LONDON

First published in Great Britain in 1974 by
THAMES AND HUDSON LTD, LONDON

Published in the United States of America by
E. P. Dutton & Co Inc. under the title

Dictionary of Contemporary Music

Printed in the United States of America
ISBN 0 500 01100 1

Preface

In the spring of 1966 Jeanne Bernkopf, then an editor at E. P. Dutton, and Eric Salzman began work on this dictionary. During the next several months an advisory board was formed and some of the signed articles were commissioned. The initial plans called for a shorter and more informal book than the one you have in hand, but as the nature of the opportunity became clear, the goals and scope expanded. The National Endowment for the Humanities in Washington provided money for additional editorial help so that the project could continue at the expanded level, and in January 1968 I began work as Eric's associate editor. When the pressure of other commitments (principally composition) necessitated his resignation a year later, the editorship was turned over to me. Further increases in scope followed, principally with regard to the number of unsigned articles. New subsidies were obtained from the Mary Duke Biddle Foundation, the Martha Baird Rockefeller Fund for Music, the Ford Foundation, and from E. P. Dutton as well. The company, I might add, consistently maintained a laissez-faire policy toward the manner in which the manuscript was prepared. How remarkable this is in modern publishing was brought home to me by the questions of an editor from another firm: "Who keeps track of what you're doing? Whom do you report to at the end of the week?" Far from being watchdogs, my editors at Dutton's, Jeanne Bernkopf and later Marian Skedgell, were the most patient of advisors.

The quality of help Eric and I have had still amazes me. Anyone who has needed a part-time secretary will know what a blessing it is to find someone who is not only interested in your work but committed to it. I have had three such people: Muriel Potter, Patricia Guadagno, and Wendy Workman. Their efficiency—and company—have spoiled me for life. Donna Kerber helped to set up the procedures for obtaining information for the unsigned articles and began the operation of gathering this material and writing it up. She was succeeded by Cheryl Seltzer, who is widely known for her work as a pianist and concert arranger and who is equally skilled as an investigator and writer. I had the benefit of her help for over a year. Finally, I owe many thanks to Judith Kipnis. She joined the project in January 1970, at first as a part-time editorial assistant along with Mrs. Seltzer and then full time, remaining through the last and most crucial months of manuscript preparation. I wish I had half her conscientiousness, facility, and energy.

Even without complete knowledge of other projects of similar scope, I am certain that no editor has received more generous and knowledgeable advice than I. Wherever the book may be weak, the cause is not in the advice received but in the execution of it. My advisory board helped in all phases from raising money to suggesting subjects for articles and recommending authors. Similar kinds of advice have come from the authors themselves, almost all of whom have given far more information and guidance than the topics of their articles might suggest. I am grateful to Anna Maria Salehar and Cynthia Read for their help with translations from Russian. Donna Bloom and Don E. Gardner helped solve the bibliographical problems that inevitably arise in a project such as this. Milton Babbitt, H. Emerson Myers, and James Seawright kindly allowed me to use their definitions of "attack," "decay," "envelope," "event," and "synthesizer," originally published in the November 1968 issue of *Music Educators' Journal*. The following individuals have responded to various questions of mine; I hope they will find that their ideas have been put to good use:

Fedele d'Amico, Tadeusz Baird, Cathy Berberian, Carlos Chávez, Brian Cherney, Edward T. Cone, Ingolf Dahl, Edison Denisov, Wayne Dirksen, Jeff Duncan, Allen F. Edwards III, Guillermo Espinosa, Lejaren Hiller, Robert Holton, Robert C. Jones, Deborah Jowitt, André Jurres, Michael Kirby, John Kirkpatrick, Lothar Knessl, François Lesure, Anders Lönn, Per Olof Lundahl, James Lyons, Keith MacMillan, Robert A. Moog, Leo Normet, Juan Orrego-Salas, Yannis A. Papaïoannou, Benjamin Patterson, W. Stuart Pope, Michael Rudd, Susana Salgado, Makoto Shinohara, Claudio Spies, Davidson Taylor, Ruth Watanabe, Edward N. Waters, Reynold Weidenaar, Robert Zolnerzak.

I also want to thank the composers' associations and music information services in various countries for their help in locating individuals and in supplying a multitude of factual details. The most frequently consulted have been:

American Music Center, Canadian Music Centre, Centre Belge de Documentation Musicale, Cuban Mission to the United Nations, Czechoslovak Music Information Center, Donemus Foundation, Finnish Music Information Center, Swedish Society of Composers and Publishers, Swiss Music Library, Union of Soviet Composers.

Music publishers, too, were extremely patient and helpful, and the staff of the Music Division of the New York Public Library was, as always, a generous source of dependable information.

Finally, there are the several hundred composers whom my assistants and I corresponded with and who responded so kindly to a multitude of questions about their music and careers. I have had the pleasure of meeting some of them, and I hope I will come to know more of them in the future. Truly the network of relationships this book brought into being will always remain the most pleasant memory of my work.

SCOPE. On the face of it "contemporary music" should probably include all music of the present day and of the last several decades. This book, however, is confined to concert music in the Western tradition. Such a distinction may already be overly parochial, owing to the availability of all the world's contemporary musics and the eclecticism in contemporary listening habits. In terms of sound alone the distinction is suspect: Frederic Rzewski told me of playing, without identification, a tape of late 1960s American jazz to an audience of musicians in Venice. No one had the impression he was hearing jazz; to the contrary, some thought it was a new piece by Stockhausen. Yet human limitations (principally my own experience) and the need to be realistic about the size of the book have made it necessary to confine most of the coverage of jazz and popular music to general articles under those titles. Likewise, Asian music and folk music are each confined to general surveys, which are further limited to the relation these musics have to contemporary Western concert music.

Different concepts of "contemporary" were applied in the different types of articles. There was one overall consideration, however: What questions are readers (principally in the U.S.) likely to have about the subject? More specifically: (1) The articles on individual people are restricted to composers. The selection was based on current public interest. This means: Who is being performed both in his home area and abroad, and/or who is being commissioned to write music, and/or who is being recorded, and/or who is being published, and/or who commands the attention and respect of fellow composers and other observers of contemporary musical developments? Information of this sort was gathered from many dozens of books and periodicals from around the world (dating principally from the 1950s and 60s) and from inquiries among my advisors and authors. A rough chronological guide evolved after the first 200–300 selections, namely that a composer should be born after 1880 and/or live after 1930. The exceptions to this rule that are nevertheless included are notable: Busoni, Debussy, Janáček, Mahler, Satie, and several others. In making selections I tried to disregard my own tastes and to rely on what others, especially composers, say is significant. At least a hundred more composers ought to be included here, but sufficient information could not be obtained to warrant an article. (2) The surveys of technical and special subjects focus not so much on the actual state of affairs as on what is new and/or distinctive in this century. Thus the article on form does not discuss 20th-century modifications of the sonata-allegro scheme but concentrates instead on approaches to form that depart from 18th- and 19th-century practice. Some important areas have had to be omitted: the role of broadcasting is one, a survey of functional music (for theater, films, television, etc.) is another, music criticism is a third. The reason is that qualified authors were not available. Broadcasting, however, is taken up in several of the articles on countries, most notably Germany. Considering the level of thought in the field of criticism, it is perhaps not surprising that a sensitive and knowledgeable surveyor could not be found. (3) The surveys of countries cover the entire 20th century with emphasis on new and recent developments. (4) The selection of terms to be defined was based on current usage in the U.S. and is restricted to terms that are new or have new meanings in this century. Private jargon that has not found wide acceptance is not included.

Readers of dictionaries sometimes assume that the length of an article is directly related to the importance of its subject. My own criteria are different, though not unrelated: What needs to be said about the subject? How much space is needed to say it clearly? Many readers also assume that reference works contain The Truth. This may be possible if one is merely defining a word according to some current local usage. Art and people are a different matter. Perhaps a better way to use this book is to regard it as a slice of history reported in large part by some of its makers.

EDITORIAL STYLE. The spelling, capitalization, and word order of names follows the composer's own usage. This explains the apparent discrepancy between "de Grandis" and "Van Vactor" and between Wladimir Vogel's first and last name. If I know that a composer does not use one of his names professionally, it is placed within parentheses. Where a last name is composed of more than one word, the name is alphabetized either by the main word or, in the case of double names, the first word; thus, the articles about Diether de la Motte and Peter Maxwell Davies both appear under "M". Diacriticals are not taken into consideration in the alphabetization. Birth dates are according to the Gregorian calendar; the following months are always abbreviated: Jan (January), Feb (February), Sept (September), Oct (October), Nov (November), Dec (December).

Dates in the lists of principal compositions are of composition unless otherwise noted. The instrumentation is not spelled out if it is a standard combination; thus, a violin sonata is understood to be for violin and piano and a symphony, for orchestra. Deviations from standard practice are spelled out. Publisher's names, which follow the dates of composition, provide the reader with information as to the availability of a work. In many cases the work is not for sale but only for rent, and in some cases the music is merely "available from" rather than "printed by" the organization named. (Inquiries about unpublished works should be made directly to the composer, perhaps in care of one of his publishers.) Recordings are named for tape music.

In the lists of writings and in the bibliographies, the most concise manner of citation consistent with clarity was used. This leads to inconsistencies of citation from one periodical to another, but not to an inability to locate the material. Page numbers are always preceded by a colon, which serves to distinguish them from volume numbers. Where I was not familiar with a periodical and its manner of numbering volumes and pages, I included extra information to avoid possible difficulty in locating the material (by giving both volume number and date of publication, for example). Because of the length of its title and frequency with which it is cited, one periodical title is always abbreviated: *Perspectives*, which stands for *Perspectives of New Music*. Because this dictionary is written primarily for English-language readers, published English translations of books and articles are usually listed instead of the foreign-language originals.

In general, cross references to articles on individual composers are made only in the discussions of musical developments within individual countries. To have used cross references in more places than this would have cluttered the text with false leads that do not contain significant information regarding the topic at hand. References are made by means of an asterisk before the name under which the article is alphabetized, as in Claude *Debussy. The asterisk is used at the main discussion of a composer's work and not necessarily at the first mention of his name.

SOURCES OF INFORMATION.   In the case of signed articles, the author's research materials are in his own possession. In many instances, if the composer is living, the author consulted with his subject to insure against error. In the case of unsigned articles, most information was obtained from the composers themselves; others who helped are acknowledged at the end of the article. All material sent for the dictionary (usually including much more information than could be used) is in my possession and may be consulted by other researchers. Where a composer has commented on his own music, the remarks are either quoted directly or paraphrased. It should be remembered that while much authentic and relevant information can be obtained in the manner used here, composers are seldom trained bibliographers. A few inaccuracies, even in regard to dates of composition, are inevitable.

This dictionary and the people who wrote it have made me more aware than ever that we live in one of the great moments of world music. We all take for granted the rubbing together of old and new, of familiar and exotic, yet these forces have given us an unprecedented variety of musical artists and artistic productions. I can think of no other time when the human mind has been treated to such a feast. It is indeed a time to eat and be merry.

John Vinton

New York, June 1971

ACA	American Composers Alliance, New York	Barry	Barry & Cía., Buenos Aires
AMC	American Music Center, New York	Basart	Basart, Amsterdam
		Belaiev	Mitrofan Belaiev, Bonn
AME	American Music Edition, New York	Belmont	Belmont Music Publishers, Los Angeles
AMP	Associated Music Publishers, New York	Belwin	Belwin, Inc., c/o B-M
		Bennington	Bennington College (Choral) Series, c/o Broude-A
A-R	A-R Editions, New Haven	Berandol	Berandol Music, Toronto
Ahn & Sim	Ahn & Simrock, Berlin-Wiesbaden	Berben	Edizioni Berben, Ancona
		Billaudot	Editions G. Billaudot, Paris
Albert	J. Albert, J. Albert & Son, Sydney	Birchard	C. C. Birchard, c/o S-B
		Birnbach	Richard Birnbach, Berlin
Alkor	Edition Alkor, Cassel	Blanck	Ediciones de Blanck, Havana
Alsbach	G. Alsbach, Amsterdam	Bloch	Bloch Publishing Co., New York
L'Amicale	L'Amicale, Paris		
Amphion	Editions Amphion, c/o Ricordi	Boelke	Boelke-Bomart, Hillsdale, N. Y.
Apogee	Apogee Press, c/o World Library	Böhm	Anton Böhm und Sohn, Augsburg
Arión	Colección Arión, Mexico City	Boileau	Ediciones Boileau, Barcelona
Armónico	Ediciones Armónico, Barcelona	Boosey	Boosey & Hawkes, London-New York, etc.
Arrow	Arrow Music Press, Inc. This was a cooperative press whose publications are now in the catalogs of various publishers; for details contact Boosey	Bornemann	S. Bornemann, Paris
		Bosse	Edition Bosse, Regensburg
		Boston	Boston Music Co., Boston
		Bosworth	Bosworth & Co., Ltd., London
		Bote	Bote & Bock, Berlin
		Bowdoin	Bowdoin College Music Press, Brunswick, Maine
Ars Viva	Ars-Viva-Verlag, Mainz		
Artia	Artia, Prague	Breitkopf	Breitkopf & Härtel, Wiesbaden
Artisjus	Hungarian Copyright Office, Budapest	Breitkopf-L	Breitkopf & Härtel, Leipzig
Ascherberg	Ascherberg, Hopwood & Crew, London	Broadman	Broadman Press, Nashville
		Brockhaus	Max Brockhaus, Lörrach, Germany
Ashley	Ashley Publications, New York	Broekmans	Broekmans & van Poppel, Amsterdam
Augener	Augener, c/o Galliard		
Augsburg	Augsburg Publishing House, Minneapolis	Broude-A	Alexander Broude, New York
		Broude-B	Broude Bros., New York
Autograph	Composers' Autograph Publications, Redondo Beach, Calif.	Brown	Robert B. Brown Music Co., Los Angeles
Avant	Avant Music, c/o WIM	Bruzzichelli	Aldo Bruzzichelli Editore, Florence
BCMA	British and Continental Music Agencies Ltd., London		
		CBDM	Centre Belge de Documentation Musicale, Brussels
B-M	Belwin-Mills Publishing Corp., New York		
		CCM	Ediciones del Consejo Central de la Música, Barcelona
BMIC	BMI Canada, Ltd., c/o Berandol		
Bárd	Bárd, Budapest	CFE	Composers Facsimile Editions, c/o ACA
Bärenreiter	Bärenreiter-Verlag, Cassel		

ČHF	Český Hudební Fond (a rental library), Prague	DILIA	Czechoslovak Literary and Theater Agency, Prague
ČHIS	Československé Hudební Informační Středisko (Czech Music Information Center), Prague	DSS	Društvo Slovenskih Skladateljev [Society of Slovenian Composers], Ljubljana
CIRM	Centre International de Recherche Musicale, Paris	DVM	VEB Deutscher Verlag für Musik, Leipzig
CM	Le Chant du Monde, Paris	Demets-Eschig	Demets-Eschig, c/o Eschig
CMC	Canadian Music Centre, Toronto	Disney	Walt Disney Music Publishers, Los Angeles
CMP	Contemporary Music Project of the Music Educators' National Conference, c/o University Microfilms, Ann Arbor, Mich.	Ditson	Oliver Ditson Co., c/o Presser
		Doblinger	Ludwig Doblinger, Vienna-Munich
		Donemus	Donemus Foundation, Amsterdam
CNC	Consejo Nacional de Cultura, Havana	Dow	Dow Music Publishers, New York
CP	The Composers Press, Inc., c/o Southern-S	Duchess	Duchess Music Corp., c/o MCA
CPE	Composer-Performer Edition, Davis, Calif.	Durand	Durand, Paris
Cambridge	Cambridge Univ. Press, London	EAMI	Editorial Argentina de Música Internacional, Buenos Aires
Cameo	Cameo Music Co., Los Angeles	ECA	Edición Culturales Argentinas, Buenos Aires
Carisch	S. A. Carisch, Milan		
Carvalho	Carvalho Ltd., Lisbon	ECIC	Editorial Cooperativa Interamericana de Compositores, Montevideo
Catalunya	Comissariat de Propaganda de la Generalitat de Catalunya, Barcelona	ECM	Ediciones Cubanas de Música, Havana
Celesta	Celesta, Berlin		
Chalet	Editions du Chalet, Lyon	EFM	Editions Françaises de Musique, Paris
Chappell	Chappell & Co., New York-London	EGREM	Empresa de Grabaciones y Ediciones Musicales, Havana
Chester	J. & W. Chester, London		
Chikuma	Chikuma Shobo, Tokyo	EM	Edition Modern, Munich
Choudens	Editions Choudens, Paris	EMB	Editio Musica, Budapest
Christlieb	Christlieb Products, Sherman Oaks, Calif.	EMM	Ediciones Mexicanas de Música, Mexico City
Clivis	Ediciones Clivis, Barcelona		
Cole	M. M. Cole Publishing Co., Chicago	EMT	Editions Musicales Transatlantiques, Paris
Colfranc	Colfranc, c/o B-M	ERM	Editions Russes de Musique, c/o Boosey
Colombo	Franco Colombo, c/o B-M		
Concordia	Concordia Music Publishing House, St. Louis	ES	Editura de Stat, Bucharest
		ESCR	Editura Societatii Compozitorilor Romini, Bucharest
Continuo	Continuo Music Press, c/o Broude-A		
Coppenrath	Alfred Coppenrath, Altötting, Germany	ESEP	Ediciones de la Secretaría de Educatión Pública, Mexico City
Cos Cob	This was a cooperative press whose publications are now in the catalogs of various publishers; for details contact Boosey	ESPLA	Editura de Stat Pentru Literatură si Artă, c/o Muzicală
		E-V	Elkan-Vogel Co., c/o Presser
Costallat	Editions Costallat, Paris	Eastman	Eastman Publications, c/o Fischer
Cramer	J. B. Cramer & Co., London		
Cranz	Edition August Cranz, Brussels-London, etc.	Eberle	Josef Eberle, Vienna
		Eck en Zocn	G. H. van Eck en Zoon, The Hague
Crescendo	Crescendo Music Corp., Naperville, Ill.	Elkan	Henri Elkan, Philadelphia
Cserépfalvi	Cserépfalvi, Budapest	Engstrøm	Engstrøm & Sødring, Copenhagen
Curci	Edizioni Curci, Milan		
Curwen	J. Curwen & Sons, London	Enoch	Enoch & Cie., Paris

Enosis	Enosis Ellinon Mousourgon [Greek Composers Association], Athens	Gulbenkian	Gulbenkian Foundation, Lisbon
Erdo	Erdo-Kleider, Berlin	Gutheil	Gutheil Edition, c/o Boosey
Eschig	Max Eschig, Paris	Gwynn	Gwynn Publishing Co., Llangollen, Wales
Eulenburg	Ernst Eulenburg, Ltd., London-Zurich, etc.	HGZ	Hrvatski Glazbeni Zavod
Evett	Evett & Schaeffer, Paris		[Croatian Music Publishers], Zagreb
Experimental	Experimental Music Catalogue, London	Hamelle	Hamelle & Cie., Paris
		Hansen-W	Wilhelm Hansen, Copenhagen
FBC	Finnish Broadcasting Company, Helsinki	Hänssler	Hänssler Verlag, Stuttgart-Hohenheim
FE	Facsimile Editions, Northridge, Calif.	Hargail	Hargail Music Press, New York
		Harms	Harms, Inc., c/o Warner
Faber	Faber Music Ltd., London	Harris	Frederick Harris Co., Oakville, Canada
Famous	Famous Music Corp., New York	Heinr.	Heinrichshofens Verlag, Wilhelmshaven-Locarno
Fazer	Edition Fazer, Helsinki	Helgafell	Helgafell, Reykjavík, Iceland
Fema	Fema Publications, c/o Crescendo	Helios	Helios Music Edition, c/o Mark Press
Fidula	Fidula Verlag, Boppard, Germany	Henmar	Henmar Press, c/o Peters
Fischer	Carl Fischer, New York	Henn	Adolphe Henn, c/o Henn-Chapuis
Fischer-J	J. Fischer and Brother, c/o B-M	Henn-Chapuis	Editions Henn-Chapuis, Geneva
Fitzsimons	H. T. Fitzsimons Co., Chicago	Henschel	Henschelverlag, East Berlin
Flammer	Harold Flammer Inc., c/o Shawnee	Heugel	Heugel, Paris
		Heuwekemeijer	Heuwekemeijer, Amsterdam
Fleisher	Edwin A. Fleisher Music Collection, c/o Free Library of Philadelphia	Highgate	Highgate Press, c/o Galaxy
		Hinrichsen	Hinrichsen Edition, London
		Hofmeister	VEB Friedrich Hofmeister Musikverlag, Leipzig
Foetisch	Foetisch Frères S. A., Lausanne	Hohner	Matth. Hohner, Trossingen, Germany
Fog	Dan Fog, Copenhagen		
Forlivesi	Forlivesi, Florence	Hope	Hope Publishing Co., Chicago
Fortin	Fortin, Paris	Hotta	Hotta Gakufu, Tokyo
Fortissimo	Fortissimo Verlag, Vienna	Howeg	Frank Howeg, Hinwil, Switzerland
Fox	Sam Fox Publishing Co., New York	Hudební matice	Hudební Matice Umelĕcké Besedy [Music Publishers of the Society of Arts], c/o Supraphon
Frank	Frank Music Corp., New York		
Freeman	H. Freeman & Co., Brighton, England	Hug	Hug & Co., Zurich
G & C	G & C Music Corp., c/o Chappell	IEM	Instituto de Extensión Musical, Santiago
GEMEN	Gabinete dos Estudios Musicais da Emissora Nacional, Lisbon	IEPT	Ipourghion Ethnikis Pedias ke Thriskevmaton [Ministry of National Education and Religions], Athens
GUP	Gallery Upstairs Press, Buffalo	IIM	Instituto Interamericano de Musicología, Montevideo
Gaetanos	Gaetanos, Athens	IM	Internationale Musikbiblio-thek, East Berlin
Galaxy	Galaxy Music Corp., New York		
Galliard	Galliard, Great Yarmouth, England	IMI	Israel Music Institute, Tel Aviv
		IMP	Israel Music Publications, Tel Aviv
Gate	Gate Music Ltd., London		
Gehrman	Carl Gehrmans Musikförlag, Stockholm	Impero	Impero Verlag, Wilhelmshaven
		Imudico	Musikforlaget Imudico, Copenhagen
General	General Music Publishing Co., New York	International	International Music Co., London
Gerig	Hans Gerig, Cologne		
Gray	H. W. Gray Co., c/o B-M	Ione	Ione Press, Inc., c/o Schirmer-E

JAZU	Jugoslavenska Akademija Znanosti i Umjetnosti [Yugoslav Academy of Science and Art], Zagreb
Jobert	Société des Editions Jobert, Paris
Joshua	Joshua Music Corp., New York
Juilliard	Juilliard Edition, c/o Kalmus
KLHU	Státní Nakladatelství Krásné Literatury Hudby a Umění [State Publishing House for Literature, Art, and Music], c/o Supraphon
Kahnt	C. F. Kahnt, Lindau-Bodensee-Leipzig
Kalmus	Edwin F. Kalmus, Commack, N. Y.
Kawai	Kawai-Gafuku Co., Tokyo
Kigen	Kigen, Tokyo
King	Robert King Music Co., North Easton, Mass.
Kistner	Kistner & Siegel & Co., Lippstadt, Germany
Kjos	Neil H. Kjos Music Co., Park Ridge, Ill.
Lawson	Lawson-Gould, c/o Schirmer-G
Leduc	Leduc, Paris
Leeds	Leeds Music Corp., c/o MCA
Lemoine	Lemoine, Paris
Lengnick	Alfred Lengnick Ltd., South Croydon, England
Leuckart	F. E. C. Leuckart, Munich
Levain	Editions du Levain, Paris
Levant	Levant Music, c/o Presser
Lienau	R. Lienau, Berlin
Litolff	Collections Litolff, c/o Peters
Litolff-L	Collections Litolff, Leipzig
Lundquist	Abraham Lundquist Music Publishing Co., Stockholm
Lyche	Harold Lyche & Co., Drammen-Oslo
Lyra	Lyra Music Co., New York
McG-M	McGinnis and Marx, New York
MCA	MCA Music, New York
MH	Musikk-Huset, Oslo
MIC	Music Information Center, Helsinki
MJQ	MJQ Music, New York
MK	Magyar Kórus, Budapest
MP	Music Press, c/o Presser
MSC	Music Sales Corp., New York
McLaughlin	McLaughlin & Reilly Co., c/o S-B
Malcolm	Malcolm Music, c/o Shawnee
Maretti	R. Maretti, Montevideo
Mark Press	Mark Press Co., Marquette, Mich.
Marks	Edward B. Marks Music Corp., New York

Mathot	Mathot, c/o Salabert
Melody	Melody, Athens
Menningarsjoður	Menningarsjoður, Reykjavík, Iceland
Mercury	Mercury Music Corp., c/o Presser
Meridian	Société des Nouvelles Editions Méridian, Paris
Merion	Merion Music Corp., c/o Presser
Merrymount	Merrymount Music, c/o Presser
Merseburger	Merseburger Verlag, Berlin
Metropolis	Editions Metropolis, Antwerp
Mezhkniga	Mezhdunarodnaya Kniga (the Soviet music exporting agency), Moscow
Mills	Mills Music, Inc., c/o B-M
Moeck	Moeck Verlag, Celle
Möseler	K. H. Möseler-Verlag, Wolfenbüttel
Mowbray	Mowbray Music Publishers, c/o Presser
Muraille	Edition Muraille, Liège
Musicus	Edition Musicus, New York
Muzfond	Muzfond S.S.S.R., Moscow
Muzicală	Editura Muzicală, Bucharest
Muzyka	State Music Publishers, Moscow
NHK	Nippon Hōsō Kyōkai [Japan Broadcasting Corp.], Tokyo
NI	Naouka i Izkoustvo, Sofia
Nakas	Philip Nakas, Athens
Nakladni	Nakladni Zavod, c/o SKJ
Napoleão	Edition Arthur Napoleão, Rio de Janeiro
Neue Musik	Verlag Neue Musik, East Berlin
New Music	New Music Edition, c/o Presser
New Valley	New Valley Music Press, Northampton, Mass.
New World	New World Music Corp., New York
Nordiska	Nordiska Musikförlaget, Stockholm
Norsk	Norsk Musikforlag, Oslo
Novello	Novello & Co., Sevenoaks, England
ORTF	Office du Radio et Télévision Française, Paris
Oertel	E. G. Oertel, Brussels
L'Oiseau	L'Oiseau Lyre, Monaco
Okra	Okra Music Corp., c/o Seesaw
Olivan	Olivan Press, London
Ongaku	Ongaku no Tomo-sha [Friend of Music], Tokyo
Orbis	Orbis, c/o Supraphon
Otago	Univ. of Otago Press, New Zealand
Oxford	Oxford Univ. Press, London-New York-Toronto, etc.

PAU	Pan American Union, Washington	SC	Izdatyelstvo "Sovyetskii kompozitor" [Soviet Composer Publishers], Moscow-Leningrad
P-M	Pathé-Marconi, Paris		
PWM	Polskie Wydawnictwo Muzyczne [Polish Music Publishers], Cracow-Warsaw	SHF	Slovenský Hudobný Fond (a rental library), Bratislava
Panton	Union of Czechoslovak Composers, Prague	SHV	Státní Hudební Vydavatelství [State Music Publishers], c/o Supraphon
Paramount	Paramount Music Corp., c/o Famous	SK	Školska Knjiga, Zagreb
Paterson	Paterson's Publications, London	SKJ	Savez Kompozitora Jugoslavije [Union of Yugoslav Composers], Belgrade
Peer	Peer International Corp., c/o Southern	SM	Süddeutscher Musikverlag Willy Müller, Heidelberg
Pelikan	Muzikverlag zum Pelikan, Zürich	SNKLHU	Státní Nakladatelství Krásné Literatury, Hudby a Umění [State Publishers of Literature, Music, and Fine Arts], c/o Supraphon
Percus	Music for Percussion, New York		
Peters	C. F. Peters Corp., Frankfurt-New York, etc.		
Peters-L	Peters, Leipzig	SPAM	Society for the Publication of American Music, c/o Presser
Phillippo	Phillippo Editions, Paris		
Piedmont	Piedmont Music Co., c/o Marks	SPN	Státní Pedagogické Nakladatelství [State Educational Publishing House], Prague
Pioneer	Pioneer Editions, c/o ACA		
Polytone	Polytone Music, Sepulveda, Calif.	STA	STA Private Edition, Sherman Oaks, Calif.
Portucalense	Editora Portucalense, Porto, Portugal	STIM	Svenska Tonsättares Internationella Musikbyrå [Swedish Society of Composers and Publishers], Stockholm
Presser	Theodore Presser Co., Bryn Mawr, Pa.		
Pro musica	Pro musica Verlag, Leipzig		
Pro musica viva	Pro musica viva, Ljubljana	SUDM	Samfundet til Udgivelse af Dansk Musik [Society for Publication of Danish Music], Copenhagen
Prosveta	Prosveta, Belgrade		
Prowse	Keith Prowse, London		
public	the work is in the public domain and has been printed by more than one publisher	SVKL	Slovenské Vydavatelstvo Krásné Literatury [Slovak Publishing House for Literature], now Tatran, Bratislava
Remick	Remick Music Corp., c/o Warner	SY	Suomen Yleisradio [Finnish Broadcasting Co.], Helsinki
Ricordi	G. Ricordi, Milan-Paris-Buenos Aires, etc.	S-Z	Edizioni Suvini-Zerboni, Milan
Rivers	Two Rivers Press, Northampton, Mass.	Salabert	Editions Salabert, Paris
		De Santis	De Santis, Rome
Robbins	Robbins Music Corp., New York	Sassetti	Sassetti & Co., Lisbon
Rochester	Rochester Music Publishers, Fairport, N.Y.	Schirmer-E	E. C. Schirmer Music Co., Boston
Rogers	Winthrop Rogers, London	Schirmer-G	G. Schirmer, Inc., New York
Rongwen	Rongwen Music, Inc., c/o Broude-B	Schola Cantorum	Editions de la Schola Cantorum, Paris
Rouart-Lerolle	Rouart-Lerolle, Paris	Schott	B. Schotts Söhne, Mainz-Brussels, etc.
Rózsavölgy	Rózsavölgy & Co., Budapest	Schwann	Schwann, Düsseldorf
SA	Society of Authors, Lisbon	Seesaw	Seesaw Music Corp., New York
SANU	Srpska Akademija Nauka i Umetnosti [Serbian Academy of Science and Art], Belgrade	Sénart	Maurice Sénart, Paris
		Shawnee	Shawnee Press, Inc., Delaware Water Gap, Pa.
S-B	Summy-Birchard Co., Evanston, Ill.	Sidem	Editions Sidem, Geneva
SBK	Union of Bulgarian Composers, Sofia	Sifler	Paul J. Sifler Publications, Hollywood

Sikorski	Hans Sikorski, Hamburg	UM	University Microfilms, Ann Arbor, Mich.
Simrock	N. Simrock, Hamburg		
Sirius	Sirius Verlag, Berlin	UME	Union Musical Española, Madrid
Skandinavisk	Skandinavisk Musikforlag, Copenhagen		
Smith	R. Smith & Co., London	UNEAC	Unión Nacional de Escritores y Artistas de Cuba, Havana
Sonido 13	Ediciones Sonido 13, Mexico City	USC	Soyuz Kompozitorov S.S.S.R., [Union of Soviet Composers], Moscow
Sonzogno	Casa Musicale Sonzogno, Milan		
Southern	Southern Music Publishing Co., New York	Ukraine	Muzitchna Ukraina, Kiev
		unpub.	unpublished
Southern-S	Southern Music Co., San Antonio	VNM	Verlag Neue Musik, East Berlin
Stainer	Stainer and Bell, London	Vaga	Vaga, Vilna
Suecia	Edition Suecia, Stockholm	Van Rossum	Wed. J. R. Van Rossum, Utrecht
Supraphon	Editio Supraphon, Bratislava-Prague		
		Viking	Viking Musikvorlag, Copenhagen
TMP	Transcontinental Music Publishing Co., New York	Vikingsprents	Tonlistarutgafa Vikingsprents, Reykjavík, Iceland
Templeton	Templeton Publishing Co., c/o Shawnee	Vitale	Irmãos Vitale, São Paulo-Rio de Janeiro
Tempo	Tempo Music Publications, Chicago	Volkwein	Volkwein Bros., Pittsburgh
Tenuto	Tenuto Publications, Bryn Mawr, Pa.	WIM	Western International Music Co., Los Angeles
Thompson	Gordon V. Thompson, Toronto	Wai-te-ata	Wai-te-ata Press, New Zealand
		Warner	Warner Bros. Music, New York
Tonger	P. J. Tonger, Rodenkirchen/ Rhein	Warny	Jens Warny, Copenhagen
Tonos	Tonos Verlag, Darmstadt	Waterloo	Waterloo Music Co., Waterloo, Canada
Trio	Trio Music Co., New York		
Tritone	Tritone Press, c/o Presser	Weinberger	Josef Weinberger Ltd., London
Tyssens	Edgard Tyssens, Liège	Weintraub	Weintraub Music Co., c/o MSC
UCP	Univ. of Calif. Press, Berkeley-Los Angeles	Westerlund	R. E. Westerlund, Helsinki
ÚDLT	Ústřední Dům Lidové Umělecké Tvořivosti [Center for Folk Art], Prague	Western	Western Music Library, Chicago
		Williams	Joseph Williams Ltd., c/o Galliard
UE	Universal-Edition, Vienna-London, etc.	Witmark	M. Witmark & Sons, c/o Warner
UKH	Udruženje Kompozitora Hrvatske [Association of Croatian Composers], Zagreb	World Library	World Library of Sacred Music, Cincinnati
		Zanibon	Guglielmo Zanibon, Padua
UKS	Udruženje Kompozitora Srbije [Union of Serbian Composers], Belgrade	Zen-On	Zen-On, Tokyo

[prepared with the help of Neil Ratliff]

DICTIONARY OF
TWENTIETH-CENTURY
MUSIC

Abríl, Antón García, see under García-Abríl

Absil, Jean (Nicolas) (b. Bonsecours, Belgium, 23 Oct 1893), studied at the Royal Conservatory of Brussels (1913, 1917; composition, orchestration with Paul Gilson; counterpoint, fugue with Léon Dubois; harmony, Martin Lunssens; piano, Raymond Moulaert; organ, Desmet). He was director of the Academie de Musique "Jean Absil" in Etterbeek (1922–64) and professor of harmony and fugue at the Royal Conservatory of Brussels (1930–59) and at La Chapelle Musicale "Reine Elisabeth" in Waterloo.

PRINCIPAL COMPOSITIONS: *La Mort de Tintagiles*, symphonic poem, Op. 3 (1923–26); *Rhapsodie flamande* for orchestra or band, Op. 4 (1928); *3 Impromptus* for piano, Op. 10 (1932, Schott); *Violin Concerto*, Op. 11 (1933); *String Trio No. 1*, Op. 17 (1935, CBDM); *String Quartet No. 3*, Op. 19 (1935, CBDM); *Symphony No. 2*, Op. 25 (1936, CBDM); *Peau d'Ane*, 3-act pantomime, Op. 26 (1937, CBDM); *Sonatine* for piano, Op. 27 (1937, Schott); *Piano Concerto*, Op. 30 (1937, Bosworth); *Piano Quartet*, Op. 33 (1938, CBDM); *String Trio No. 2*, Op. 39 (1939, Chester); *Alcools* for soprano, alto, tenor, bass, Op. 43 (1940, Lemoine); *Serenade* for orchestra, Op. 44 (1940, Bosworth); *String Quartet No. 4*, Op. 47 (1941, CBDM); *Les Bénédictions*, cantata for chorus, orchestra, Op. 48 (1941); *Symphonic Variations*, Op. 50 (1942); *Les Chants du mort*, cantata, Op. 55 (1943); *Rumanian Rhapsody* for violin, orchestra, Op. 56 (1943, UE); *Symphony No. 3*, Op. 57 (1943); *Grande Suite* for piano, Op. 62 (1944, Schott); *Fansou, ou le chapeau chinois*, lyric comedy, Op. 64 (1944); *Le Zodiaque*, symphonic variations with piano, chorus, Op. 70 (1949); *Le Miracle de Pan*, ballet, Op. 71 (1949); *Phantasmes* for alto, piano, alto saxophone, percussion, Op. 72 (1950); *Les Voix de la mer*, 3-act opera, Op. 75 (1951); *Les Météorores*, ballet, Op. 77 (1951); *Rites* for band, Op. 79 (1952); *Mythologie*, suite for orchestra, Op. 84 (1954); *Divertimento* for 4 saxophones, chamber orchestra, Op. 86 (1955); *Suite bucolique* for string orchestra, Op. 95 (1957); *Silhouettes* for flute, piano, Op. 97 (1957, Lemoine); *Rhapsody No. 5* for 2 pianos, Op. 102 (1959, CBDM); *Violin Concerto No. 2*, Op. 124 (1964); *Piano Concerto*, Op. 131 (1967); *Asymétries* for 2 pianos, Op. 136 (1968); *Suite No. 2* for cello, piano, Op. 141 (1968); *Symphony No. 4*, Op. 142 (1969).

BIBL.: René Bernier, "Hommage à J. A.," *L'Ethnie française* 1968/5:46–47; Joseph Dopp, "Le Style dans la musique de J. A.," *Revue musicale* (Oct 1937):231–41 and (Dec 1937):411–20; Remy Dubois, "L'Inspiration chez J. A.," *Le Flambeau* (Brussels, 16 July 1939):63–79; Richard de Guide, "J. A.," *Musica* (Paris, Nov 1956): 5–9; ——, *J. A.: Vie et œuvre* (Tournai 1965); C. Höweler, *Sommets de la musique* (Brussels 1947):15–19; Edward Lockspeiser, "Opinion about J. A.," *The Listener* (Nov 1954); Albert Vander Linden, "Portrait de J. A.," *L'Ethnie française* 1968/5:48–49.

SEE ALSO Belgium.

Adamis, Michael (George) (b. Piraeus, Greece, 19 May 1929), studied theology at the Univ. of Athens (1948–54). He attended Athens Conservatory (1947–51), the Piraeus Conservatory (1951–56, Byzantine music with J. Margaziotis), and the Hellenic Conservatory (1956–59, theory and composition with J. A. Papaïoannou). He then studied at Brandeis Univ. in Mass. (1962–65; composition with Arthur Berger, Byzantine musicology with Kenneth Levy), where he was also associated with its electronic music studio. Adamis founded the Greek Royal Palace's Boys' Choir and served as its director from 1950 to 1967. In 1958 he founded the Athens Chamber Choir, which he currently directs. He taught Byzantine music and directed the choir at the Greek Theological School in Brookline, Mass. during 1961–62 and since 1968 has been choral director at Pierce College in Greece. Adamis wrote his earlier works using an extended tonality and in 1959 began using a free 12-tone system. In *Anakyklesis* (1964) he was concerned with an "interrelation between different ranges of sounds," and in his subsequent works he has worked largely with sound textures and less with pitch in an harmonic-melodic context.

PRINCIPAL COMPOSITIONS: *Liturgikon Concerto* for oboe, clarinet, bassoon, string orchestra (1955);

3

2 *Pieces* for violin, piano (1958); *Variations* for string orchestra (1958); *Suite in rythmo antico* for piano (1959); *Fones* for chorus; poem by Cavafy (1959, published in *Eniochos*, Athens, June 1960); *Duo* for violin, piano (1961); *Sinfonia da camera* for flute, clarinet, horn, trumpet, percussion, piano, string orchestra (1961); *3 Pieces* for double bass, piano (1962, EM); *Anakyklesis* for flute, oboe, celesta, viola, cello (1964, EM); *Pieces 1–2* on 2-track tape (1964); *Proshemata* for female reciter, 2-track tape; poems by E. Mahaira (1964); *Epitymbio* for piano (1965, published by Gerig in *Contemporary Greek Piano Music* I); *Minyrismos* on 2-track tape (1966); *Pröpotike* for flute (piccolo), metal percussion instruments, drums (1965); *Apocalypse* (*The Sixth Seal*) for chorus, narrator, piano, 2 4-track tapes (1967); *Metaschematism* [Transformations] on 2 4-track tapes (1967); *Byzantina Pathe* [Byzantine Passion] for 8 soloists, 4 choruses, percussion (1967); *Genesis* for 3 choruses, reciter, 2-track tape, painter, dance; poem by S. Beiles and A. Rooney (1968); *Mirolo* for 4 men's voices, percussion, tape (1970).

PRINCIPAL WRITINGS: "Dodecaphthogi musiki," *Eniochos* (Athens, June 1960):35; "Neotropi melodiki kataskevi" *Epoches* (Athens, August 1966): 154–55; review of Oliver Strunk's *Specimina notationum antiquiorium*, *Epeteris Byzantinon Spoudon* (Athens, 1966):433; "Catalogos ton cheirographon tis Bibliothekis Panayiotou Gritzani, Apokeimenon nyn en ti iera Metropoli Zakynthou [Catalogue of Manuscripts in Zante]," *ibid.* (1966): 313–65.

SEE ALSO Greece.

Adaskin, Murray (b. Toronto, 28 March 1906), studied violin in Paris with Marcel Chailley (1929) and in Toronto with William Primrose (1937) and Kathleen Parlow (1941–43). He studied composition in Toronto with John Weinzweig (1944–48) and in the U.S. with Charles Jones (1949, 50, 53, 54) and Darius Milhaud (1949, 50, 53). He was music director of the Empire Theater in Toronto (1927–31) and violinist with the Toronto Symphony (1926–63). He has taught at the Univ. of Saskatchewan since 1952, where he has been composer-in-residence since 1968.

PRINCIPAL COMPOSITIONS: *Violin Sonata* (1946); *Suite for Orchestra* (1947–48); *Ballet Symphony* (1950–51); *Sonatine baroque* for solo violin (1952, Ricordi); *Serenade concertante* for small orchestra (1954, Ricordi); *Grant, Warden of the Plains*, opera; libretto by Mary Elizabeth Bayer (1966); *Qalala and Nilaula of the North* for woodwinds, strings, percussion; based on Eskimo tunes from Rankin Inlet (1969); *Diversion for Orchestra* (1969); *Night Is No Longer Summer Soft* for student band (1970); *Fanfare for Orchestra* (1970); *Divertimento No. 4* for trumpet, orchestra (1970); *Trio* for flute, cello, piano (1970). List to 1961: *Composers of the Americas* 8:9–11.

BIBL.: "Portrait of M. A.," *Musicanada* (May 1967):8–9; Richard Savage, "M. A., Composer, Performer, Gentleman," *The Canadian Composer* 10:4.

SEE ALSO Canada.

Adler, Samuel (b. Mannheim, Germany, 4 March 1928), studied composition privately with Herbert Fromm (1943–47). He attended Boston Univ. (1946–48, BM; composition with Hugo Norden, musicology with Karl Geiringer and Paul Pisk, violin with Wolf Wolfinsohn) and Harvard Univ. (1948–50, MA; composition with Walter Piston, Paul Hindemith, and Randall Thompson, musicology with A. T. Davison and Tillman Merritt). He also studied composition with Aaron Copland and conducting with Serge Koussevitzky at Tanglewood in 1949 and 1950. Entering the Army in 1950, Adler organized and conducted the Seventh Army Orchestra in Germany. Concurrently he guest conducted European orchestras and ballet and opera companies. From 1953 to 1966 he was musical director of Temple Emanu-el in Dallas, Texas, where he also organized and conducted the Dallas Chorale (1954–56), conducted the Dallas Lyric Theater (1955–57), was instructor of fine arts at the Hockaday School (1957–66), and professor of composition at North Texas State Univ. (1958–66). Since 1966 he has been professor of composition at the Eastman School of Music.

PRINCIPAL COMPOSITIONS (published by Oxford unless otherwise noted): *Symphony No. 1* (1953, Presser); *Violin Sonata No. 2* (1956); *Symphony No. 2* (1957, Presser); *Shir chadash*, synagogue service (1960, TMP); *Symphony No 3*, "Diptych," for large wind orchestra (1960, Peters); *Southwestern Sketches* for wind ensemble (1961); *The Vision of Isaiah*, cantata for bass, chorus, orchestra (1962, Southern); *Sonata breve* for piano (1963); *B'shaaray t'filah*, synagogue service (1963, TMP); *String Quartet No. 4* (1963, Mills); *Requiescat in pace* for orchestra (1963); *Trio* for violin, cello, piano (1964); *Shiru ladonay*, synagogue service (1965, TMP); *Violin Sonata No. 3* (1965); *Symphony No. 4* (1967); *The Binding*, oratorio (1967); *Concerto* for winds, brass, percussion (1968); *From Out of Bondage*, cantata for soloists, chorus, brass quintet, percussion, organ (1968); *String Quartet No. 5* (1969); *A Whole Bunch of Fun*, secular cantata for mezzo-soprano or baritone, 3 choirs, orchestra (1969).

PRINCIPAL WRITINGS: "An Urgent Need in Today's Synagogue Music," *Journal of the Central Conference of American Rabbis* (Jan 1963):27–30; "Problems of Teaching Composition in our Colleges Today," *American Music Teacher* 13/2:18–19; "Music in the American Synagogue," *American*

Choral Review 6/3:7–9 and 6/4:3–6; "Choral Music in the Liturgy: Comments on a Jewish Sacred Service," *ibid.* 10/3:128–30; "The Contemporary Music Project and Curriculum Change," *Music Educators Journal* (Sept 1968):36–38, 123; *Anthology for the Teaching of Choral Conducting* (New York 1970).

BIBL.: Robert Douglass, "*The Binding*," *American Choral Review* 10/4:194–96; Aron M. Rothmüller, *The Music of the Jews* (South Brunswick, N. J., 1967):247–48; "American Composer Sketches: S. A.," *Music Educators Journal* (March 1967):41–45.

SEE ALSO Liturgical Music: Christian; Liturgical Music: Jewish.

Aguilar-Ahumada, Miguel (b. Huara, Chile, 12 March 1931), studied in Santiago at the Conservatorio Popular (1949–50) and the National Conservatory (1951–55; composition with Jorge Urrutia-Blondel, analysis with Domingo Santa Cruz, music history with Juan Orrego-Salas) and in Cologne at the Hochschule für Musik (1963–65, conducting with Wolfgang von der Nahmer). He has taught history, analysis, and harmony at the Modern School of Music in Santiago (1954–55), at the Conservatorio de la Sinfónica in Concepción (1956–63), the Univ. of Concepción (since 1965), and the Univ. of Chile in Chillán (since 1969). He performs contemporary piano music professionally. His music to 1954 was much influenced by Schoenberg, Berg, Stravinsky, Bartók, and Hindemith; thereafter Webern was the principal influence. His first work using serial procedures is the second *Microscopia* (1955); the first using aleatory ones, *Texturas* (1965).

PRINCIPAL COMPOSITIONS (published by IEM): *Piano Sonata No. 1* (1952); *Fragment on Kafka's "The Castle"* for piano (1954); *Obertura al Teatro Integral* for orchestra (1954); *Septet* for wind quintet, double bass (1954); *2 Microscopias* for piano (1955); *Simetrías* for piano (1958); *Concerto* for winds, strings (1958); *6 Children's Songs* for soprano, clarinet (1958); *Missa "Maria Zart"* for soprano, clarinet, bass clarinet, trumpet, trombone (1961); *Umbral y ambito* for chamber orchestra (1962); *Texturas* for piano, concrete sounds on tape (1965); *Composición con 3 sonidos* for glasses containing liquid, balloons, tape of the sounds of a cow (1965); *Fantasía a 3* for speaking chorus, vocal soloist, piano, sounds on tape of an orchestra tuning up (1967); *Tour Eiffel* for soprano, clarinet, trumpet, trombone, violin, viola, double bass, xylophone, cymbals, wood block; text by Vicente Huidobro (1967); *Canción de Marcelo Cielomar* for soprano, clarinet, trumpet, trombone, violin, viola, double bass; text by Huidobro (1969); *La puerto abierta hacia la noche* for soprano, piano; text by Huidobro (1969); *Música aleatoria 1969* for orchestra. List to 1967: *Composers of the Americas* 14:19–20.

PRINCIPAL WRITINGS: "El fundamento tradicional de la armonía Strawinskyana," *Revista musical chilena* 46; "La evolución estilística en la Obra de René Amengual," *ibid.* 47; "La crisis estilísticas de Igor Strawinsky," *ibid.* 50.

SEE ALSO Chile.

Ahrens, Joseph (Johannes Clemens) (b. Sommersell, Westphalia, Germany, 17 April 1904), studied at the State Academy of Church and Educational Music in Berlin (1925–28) with Alfred Sittard (organ, improvisation) and Wilhelm Middelschulte (organ, composition). At the same time he studied choral singing at the Benedictine Abbeys of Gerleve and Beuron. Since 1928 he has taught Catholic church music at the Hochschule für Musik, Berlin, where he became a professor in 1936. Ahrens was organist at St. Hedwig's Cathedral from 1934 until World War II, after which he became organist and choir director at Salvator College in Berlin. He composes mainly church music. He often uses intervals as the basic material of a composition as, for example, the diminished ninth in his *Toccata eroica* or the augmented seventh in the *Dorian Toccata*. Ahrens's music also relates to his religious beliefs; contrapuntal textures, for instance, are equated with the realm of spiritual contemplation.

PRINCIPAL COMPOSITIONS: ★ For organ: *Toccata eroica* (1932, Schott); *Ricercare in A Minor* (1934, Böhm); *Canzone in C-Sharp Minor* (1943, Böhm); *Partita "Lobe den Herren"* (1947, Schott); *Das heilige Jahr* (1948–50, Böhm); *Triptychon über B-A-C-H* (1949, Schott); *Concerto* for organ, winds (1954–58, SM); *Cantiones gregorianae* (1957, Schott); *Trilogia sacra*: part 1, "Domus Dei," for organ; part 2, "Regnum Dei," for baritone, flute, oboe, English horn, clarinet, horn, bassoon, double bass; part 3, "Civitas Dei," for organ (1959, 1959, 1960; SM); *Verwandlungen I, II, III* (1963, 1964, 1965; Schott). ★ For chorus (published by SM unless otherwise noted): *Missa gotica* (1947, Schwann); *Missa hymnica* (1948); *Missa salvatoris* (1949); *St. Matthew Passion* (1950); *Christmas Gospel According to St. Luke* (1952); *6 Latin Motets* (1953, 1956); *St. John Passion* (1961); *Missa dodekaphonica* for high and low voices with organ or flute, oboe, English horn, clarinet, bassoon, trumpet, trombone, double bass (1966).

BIBL.: Wilfried Brune, "*Missa dodekaphonica* von J. A.," *Musica Sacra* (Cologne) 1968/3:114–18; ——, "Profile: J. A. 65 Jahre," *Musica Sacra* 1969/3:107–11; Werner David, "Das Orgelschaffen von J. A.," *Musik und Altar* 1948:59–63 and 1949:54f.; Walter Kaempfer, "Profile: J. A.," *Musica Sacra* 1964/5:138–40; Wilhelm Koch, "Chormusik als Gotteslob, zum Chorschaffen von

J. A.," *Musik und Altar* 1953:10–13; Otto Riemer, "Musik der Verkündigung, zum Schaffen von J. A.," *Musica* (Cassel) 1957/7–8:396–99; Johanna Schell, "J. A. zum 60 Geburtstag; Weg, Werk, und Bedeutung," *Katholische Kirchenmusik* (St. Gall) 1964/2:78–83; Rudolf Walter, "J. A., der Schöpfer eines neuen Orgelstils," *Musik und Altar* 1948:63–68; ——, "J. A.: *Das heilige Jahr*," *Musik und Altar* 1952:159–64, 191–94.

Akiyama, Kuniharu (b. Tokyo, 22 May 1929), studied French literature at Waseda Univ. in Tokyo (1947–51, surrealist writings with André Breton) and contemporary music with John Cage and Iannis Xenakis. He has taught music in Tokyo at the Kuwazawa Design School (since 1961) and Zokei Univ. (since 1967). He writes music and art criticism for several Japanese periodicals. In 1967 he helped organize Cross-talk, a U.S.–Japanese performing-arts series.

PRINCIPAL COMPOSITIONS: *Torawareta Onna* [Sound Poem] on tape (1952, the Sony Co.); *Nihiki no sanma* [2 Mackerel Pike], film score on tape (1961); *Mado* [The Window] for flute; score for the film by Yoji Kuri (1962); *Hiho 19* [Arcana 19] for soprano, vibraphone, piano, percussion, glass bottles and other objects (1962); *A'chi wa ko'chi* [That Way Is This Way], for alto, brass ensemble, tape; score for the film by Kuri (1963); *Shokuji no tame no ongaku* [Music for Meals] on tape using stone instruments; prepared for the athletes' cafeteria at the 1964 Olympics (1964); *Chokoku-ten no tame no ongaku* [Music for a Sculpture Exhibit] for organ, tape (1966); *Tsubure kakatta migime no tameni* [For the Dimming Right Eye], tape music and human body sounds; score for the film by T. Matsumoto (1968); *Kane no ongaku* [Music for Bells], sounds of stone instruments and glass bottles on 4-channel tape (1970); *Onara no uta* [Music for Farting], score for Kuri for clarinet, trumpet, trombone, tuba (1971).

PRINCIPAL WRITINGS: "Schönberg to ware ware [Schoenberg and Us], program book of Jikken Kobo (June 1952); "Nihon no sakkyokukai no seishinteki jokyo" [The Mental Situations of the Japanese Composers' World], *Ongaku-geijutsu* (Dec 1966):6–13; "Iannis Xenakis . . . Towards Metamusic," *Bijutsu techo* (Sept 1969):30–53; "John Cage and . . . Philosophy of Actions," *ibid.* (Dec 1970):210–32.

SEE ALSO Japan.

Akutagawa, Yasushi (b. Tokyo, 12 July 1925); studied at the Tokyo Music School (1943–49; composition with Kunihiko Hashimoto, orchestration with Akira Ifukube, conducting with Nobori Kaneko, piano with Motonari Iguchi). Since 1956 he has been conductor of the Tokyo Symphony Orchestra and since 1969, of the New Symphony Orchestra. He has been president of the Japan Conference of Music since 1966 and secretary of the Japanese Federation of Composers since 1970.

PRINCIPAL COMPOSITIONS: *Music for Orchestra* (1950, Crescendo); *Triptyque* for string orchestra (1953, Muzyka); *Symphony No. 1* (1954); *Symphony for Children*, "Twin Stars," for narrator, orchestra (1957); *Erolla Symphony* (1958); *Dark Mirror*, opera (1960); *Music for Strings* for 2 string quartets, double bass (1962, Ongaku); *Negativ* for string orchestra (1966); *Sinfonia ostinata* (1967); *L'Orphée de Hiroshima*, television opera (1967); *Concertino ostinato* for cello, orchestra (1969); *Ballata ostinata* for orchestra (1970).

PRINCIPAL WRITINGS: *Watashi no ongaku-dangi* [Music Lectures] (Tokyo 1959); *Ongaku no genba* [The Music Scene] (Tokyo 1962); *Ongaku o aisuruhito ni* [For Music Lovers] (Tokyo 1967).

SEE ALSO Japan.

Albright, William (b. Gary, Ind., 20 Oct 1944), studied at the Juilliard School (1959–62; composition with Hugh Aitken, piano with Rosetta Goodkind), at the Univ. of Mich. (1963–70; composition with Ross Lee Finney, Leslie Bassett; organ with Marilyn Mason), and at the Paris Conservatory (1968–69, composition with Olivier Messiaen). He also studied privately in Paris with Max Deutsch. Since 1970 he has taught composition at the Univ. of Mich., where he is associate director of the Electronic Music Studio. He has given many organ and piano recitals of contemporary music in the U.S. and Europe. Popular music and jazz, along with his work in theater and films, have influenced his music.

PRINCIPAL COMPOSITIONS: *Chorale-Partita in an Old Style* for organ (1963, E-V); *Foils* for wind ensemble (1963–64, E-V); *Salvos* for flute, clarinet, bassoon, violin, viola, cello, percussion (1964); *Juba* for organ (1965, E-V); *2 Pieces for 9 Instruments* for flute, clarinet, bass clarinet, strings, piano percussion (1965–66); *Pianoàgogo* for piano (1965–66, Jobert); *Pneuma* for organ (1966, E-V); *Caroms* for flute, bass clarinet, trumpet, double bass, piano, celesta, percussion (1966, Jobert); *Tic* for soloist, 2 jazz-rock improvisation ensembles, films, tape (1967); *Organbook* for organ (1967, Jobert); *Beulahland Rag* for narrator, jazz quartet, improvisation ensemble, tape, film, slides (1967–69); *Alliance* for orchestra (1967–70, Jobert); *Grand Sonata in Rag* for piano (1968); *Marginal Worlds* for winds, strings, piano, 2 percussionists (1969–70, Jobert).

Aleatory Music, see Indeterminacy; see also Notation, Performance

Alexander, Josef (b. Boston, 15 May 1910), studied at the New England Conservatory (1923–26; piano, harmony with Julius Chaloff; theory with Frederick S. Converse) and at Harvard Univ. (1934–39; composition with Walter Piston, orchestration with Edward B. Hill, orchestration with Hugo Leichtentritt, musicology with Willi Apel). He also studied composition in Paris with Nadia Boulanger (1939) and at Tanglewood with Aaron Copland (1940). He has taught at the St. Rosa Convent in Chelsea and Malden, Mass. (1932–34), Boston College (1932–34), Harvard Univ. (1938–42), and Brooklyn College (since 1943). He taught piano and composition privately during 1927–37 and has been a professional pianist since 1922.

PRINCIPAL COMPOSITIONS: *Piano Concerto* (1938, Fleisher); *String Quartet* (1940); *Piano Quintet* (1942); *Piano Trio* (1944); *Epitaphs* for orchestra (1947, Fischer); *Wind Quintet* (1949); *Symphony No. 1*, "Clockwork," for string orchestra (1951, Fischer); *Piano Quartet* (1952); *Canticle of Night* for low voice, orchestra (1953); *Symphony No. 2* (1954, Fischer); *3 Symphonic Odes* for men's voices, orchestra (1956, Fischer); *Clarinet Sonata* (1957, General); *Songs for Eve* for soprano, harp, English horn, violin, cello (1957, General); *4 (Movements) for 5 (Brass)* (1958, Southern); *Concertino* for trumpet, strings (1959, Shawnee); *Trombone Sonata* (1959, General); *Celebrations* for orchestra (1960, General); *Symphony No. 3* (1961, General); *Nocturne and Scherzo* for violin, piano (1963, General); *3 Pieces for 8* for flute, clarinet, trumpet, violin, cello, double bass, piano, percussion (1965, General); *Duo Concertante* for trombone, percussion, orchestra (1965, General); *Quiet Music* for strings (1965–66, General); *Symphony No. 4* (1968); *4 Preludes on Playthings of the Wind* for high voice, chorus, 2 trumpets, 2 horns, 2 trombones, tuba, piano (1969–70).

Alfvén, Hugo (b. Stockholm, 1 May 1872; d. Falun, 8 May 1960), studied violin at the Stockholm Royal Conservatory (1887–91) and with Lars Zetterquist (Stockholm) and César Thomson (Brussels). He also studied composition with Johan Lindegren in Stockholm and, during 1896–1903, in several European countries under Swedish government scholarships. During 1890–97 he was a violinist in the Royal Court Orchestra. He was music director of the Univ. of Uppsala orchestra during 1910–40 and also conducted a number of choruses, among them O. D. (1910–47) and Allmänna Sången (1919–31, 1934–38). His music is in the late romantic tradition. He frequently used Swedish folk material, and his *Midsummer's Vigil* was the first orchestral work in Sweden to do so.

PRINCIPAL COMPOSITIONS: *Violin Sonata in C Minor*, Op. 1 (1896, Lundquist); *Symphonies Nos. 1–5*: No. 1 in F Minor, Op. 7 (1897, Gehrman); No. 2 in D, Op. 11 (1898–99, Hansen-W); No. 3 in E, Op. 23 (1905, Gehrman); No. 4 in C Minor, Op. 39 (1918–19, UE); No. 5 in A Minor (1942–52, Suecia); *Skärgårdsbilder* [Pictures from the Skerries] for piano (1902, Nordiska); *Herrens bön* [The Lord's Prayer], cantata for soloists, chorus, orchestra, Op. 15 (1903, Suecia); *Midsommarvaka* [Midsummer's Vigil], rhapsody No. 1 for orchestra, Op. 19 (1904, Hansen-W); *En skärgårdssägen* [A Tale of the Skerries], symphonic poem, Op. 20 (1905, Gehrman); *Festpel* [Festival Music] for orchestra (1907, Lundquist); *Uppsalarapsodi*, rhapsody No. 2 for orchestra, Op. 24 (1907, Lundquist); *7 Dikter* [7 Poems] for voice, piano, Op. 28 (1908, Lundquist); *Gustaf Frödings jordafärd* for men's chorus, Op. 29 (1911, Lundquist); *Herr Sten Sture* for men's chorus, orchestra, Op. 30 (1912, Musikaliska Konstføreningen); *Uppenbarelsekantat* [Revelation Cantata] for soloists, chorus, orchestra, Op. 31 (1913, Musikaliska Konstføreningen); *Sveriges flagga* [Sweden's Flag] for men's chorus (1916, Gehrman); *Lindagull* for men's chorus (1923, Gehrman); *Bergakungen* [The Mountain King], ballet pantomime (1923, Gehrman); *Cantata for the Uppsala Univ. Jubilee* for soloists, chorus, orchestra, Op. 45 (1927, Suecia); *Vi*, incidental music for the play by Nordström (1932, Gehrman); *Gryning vid havet* [Dawn at Sea] for men's chorus (1933, Gehrman); *Cantata for the Riksdag Jubilee* for soloists, chorus, orchestra, Op. 51 (1935, Musikaliska Konstføreningen); *Dalarapsodi*, rhapsody No. 3 for orchestra, Op. 48 (1937, Hansen-W); *The Prodigal Son*, ballet pantomime (1957, Suecia). A complete thematic index by Jan Olof Ruden was published in 1972 in Stockholm.

PRINCIPAL WRITINGS: *Memoires*: vol. 1, *Första satsen* (Stockholm 1946); vol. 2, *Tempo furioso* (1948); vol. 3, *I dur och moll* (1949); vol. 4, *Finale* (1952).

SEE ALSO Scandinavia.

Allende (-Sarón), **Pedro Humberto** (b. Santiago, Chile, 29 June 1885; d. Santiago, 17 August 1959), studied at the National Conservatory in Santiago (1899–1908, violin with Aurelio Silva). He taught violin and general musical subjects at a number of secondary schools in Santiago; during 1918–46 he taught composition and harmony at the National Conservatory. He helped organize the teaching of music in Chile's primary and secondary schools and was active in many music organizations, especially those concerned with folk music research.

PRINCIPAL COMPOSITIONS: *Paisaje chileno* for chorus, orchestra; text by Carlos Mondaca (1913); *Escenas campesinas chilenas*, symphonic suite (1913–14, IEM); *Concerto sinfónico* for cello, orchestra (1915, IEM); *El encuentro* for 2 sopranos, piano; text by Mondaca (1915, Sénart); *Debajo de un limón verde* for soprano, alto, piano; text by Max Jara (1915, Sénart); *12 Tonadas* for piano (1918–22, Durand; Nos. 10–12 for orchestra, 1925, Sénart); *La voz de las calles*, symphonic poem (1920, IEM); *Oda a España* for baritone, chorus, orchestra; text by Samuel Lillo (1922); *9 Studies* for piano (1922–36, some published by Sénart); *Se bueno* for chorus, text by the composer (1923); *Mientras baja la nieve* for voice, piano; text by Gabriela Mistral (1925); *El surtidor* for voice, piano; text by Mistral (1925); *A las nubes* for voice, piano; text by Mistral (1925); *Miniaturas griegas* for piano (1928, Sénart); *La despedida* for 2 sopranos, alto, orchestra; poem by Ildefonso Pereda Valdes (1933); *Luna de la media noche* for soprano, orchestra; poem by Manuel Magallanes Moure (1937); *Violin Concerto* (1940, IEM); *En una mañanita* for soprano, orchestra; poem by Tegualda Allende Ponce (1945); *String Quartet in the Dorian Mode* (1945). Complete list: *Composers of the Americas* 2:5–15.

PRINCIPAL WRITINGS: *Metodología original para la enseñanza del canto escolar* (Santiago 1922); *Conferencias sobre la música* (Santiago 1918);"La musique populaire chilienne," in *Art populaire . . . di 1er congrès international des arts populaire, Prague, 1928* (Paris 1931):118–23; "Chilean Folk Music," *Bulletin of the Pan American Union* (Sept 1931):917–24; "El ambiente a través de los años," *Aulos* (1 Oct 1932).

BIBL.: Carlos Isamitt, "Anotaciones alrededor de H. A. y su obra," *Boletín latino-americano de música* (April 1946):237–46; Alfonso Leng, "P. H. A.," *Antártica* (August 1945):81–84; *Revista musical chilena*, special issue on Allende (Sept 1945); Nicolas Slonimsky, "H. A., First Modernist of Chile," *Musical America* (August 1942):5f.; Robert Stevenson, "La música chilena en la época de Santa Cruz," *Boletín interamericano de música* (Sept 1968):5–7; Vicente Salas-Viú, *La creación musical en Chile* (Santiago, c.1952):115–29.

[prepared with the help of Tegualda and Ikela Allende Ponce]

SEE ALSO Chile.

Alpaerts, Flor (b. Antwerp, 12 Sept 1876; d. Antwerp, 5 Oct 1954), studied composition at the Royal Flemish Conservatory with Jan Blockx. He taught theory, counterpoint, and fugue at the Conservatory beginning in 1903 and was director of the institution during 1933–41. He also conducted concerts at the Royal Zoological Society during 1919–51 and the Royal Flemish Opera during 1922–23. During 1919–54 he was artistic director of the Peter Benoit Fonds, where he supervised the edition of several of Benoit's works. He was among the first of the Belgian impressionists (*Pallieter*, 1921), and his expressionistic *James Ensor Suite* (1929) proved to be an important turning point in Belgian music.

PRINCIPAL COMPOSITIONS: *Psyche*, symphonic poem (1900, CBDM); *Herleving*, symphonic poem (1903, CBDM); *Symphonisch Gedicht* for flute, orchestra (1903, CBDM); *Karakterstuk* for trumpet, orchestra (1904, CBDM); *2 Pièces* for piano, violin, cello (1906, CBDM); *Lentesymphonie* (1906, CBDM); *Cyclus Liefdeliederen* for voice, piano; texts by G. Priem (1907, Metropolis); *Salome*, incidental music to the play by Oscar Wilde (1907, CBDM); *Shylock*, 3-act opera; libretto by H. Melis after Shakespeare (1910–13, CBDM); *8 Little Songs* for soprano, piano; texts by V. Delamontagne (1914, Metropolis); *Avondmuziek* [Evening Music] for 2 flutes, 2 oboes, 2 clarinets, 2 bassoons (1915, Metropolis); *Children's Songs*, vol. 1, for medium voice, piano; French texts by Eug. Van den Bosch, English texts by J. Sears (1915–16, Schott); *Vlaamse Idylle* for orchestra (1920, CBDM); *La Brabançonne*, Belgian national anthem (1920, CBDM); *Pallieter*, symphonic poem (1921, Schott); *Benedictus Deus* for chorus, chamber orchestra (1926, CBDM); *Thijl Uilenspiegel*, symphonic poem (1927, Schott); *Avondindruk*, symphonic poem (1928, Schott); *Zomeridylle* (1928, Schott); *James Ensor Suite* for orchestra (1929, Schott); *Jonker Krekel van Klaverghem* for soprano, tenor, chorus, piano; text by P. de Mont (1932, CBDM); *String Quartets Nos. 2, 4* (1944, 1950; CBDM); *Violin Concerto* (1948, CBDM).

PRINCIPAL WRITINGS: *Muzieklezen en Zingen*, a solfège text in 5 vols. (Antwerp, n.d.).

BIBL.: A. Corbet, *F. A.* (Antwerp 1941).

Alsina, Carlos Roqué (b. Buenos Aires, 19 Feb 1941), studied liberal arts at the Bartolomé Mitre College in Buenos Aires (1954–58) and music privately with Benjamin E. Olsson (piano, 1946–50) and Theodor Fuchs (piano, counterpoint, analysis, conducting, 1951–59). He also studied with Francisco Kröpfl at the Estudio de Fonologia Musical of the National Univ. in Buenos Aires (1962–64). He was a member of the Agrupación Nueva Música during 1959–64 and an assistant conductor at the Teatro Colón during 1960–64. In 1964 he went to Germany where he was assistant conductor at the Deutsche Oper in Berlin in 1966 (during these years he became acquainted with the music of Luciano Berio). He was a member of the Center of the Creative and Performing Arts at the State Univ. of N.Y. at Buffalo during 1966–68 and taught contemporary piano music there in 1967. Since 1969 he has been a member of the European improvisation group New Phonic Art. He has concertized as a pianist since 1964 in South America, Europe, and the U.S.

PRINCIPAL COMPOSITIONS (published by S-Z unless otherwise noted): *4 Klavierstücke* for piano (1958, 1960, 1965, 1969; Nos. 3 and 4 published by S-Z); *Wind Quintet*, Op. 9 (1961, unpub.); *3*

Pieces for string orchestra, Op. 13 (1964, unpub.); *Funktionen* for flute, clarinet, bassoon, trumpet, violin, cello, piano, 2 percussionists, Op. 14 (1965, unpub.); *Consecuenza* for trombone, Op. 17 (1966, Bote); *Auftrag* for flute, clarinet, bassoon, horn, violin, viola, cello, double bass, percussion (1967); *Trio 1967* for cello, trombone, percussion (1967, Bote); *Textes 1967*, theater piece for soprano, flute, trumpet, trombone, violin, cello, double bass, piano, percussion (1967, unpub.); *Symptom* for orchestra, Op. 21 (1969, Bote); *Rendez-vous* for clarinet/saxophone, Alpine horn/trombone, piano, piano/organ/percussion (1970); *Consecuenza II* for solo voice (1971); *Schichten* for chamber orchestra, Op. 27 (1971).

PRINCIPAL WRITINGS: "Kann ein Komponist vom Komponieren leben?" *Melos* 36:153–54; "Selbstportrait," *Begegnung*, supplement for the Donaueschingen Musiktage (Oct 1970):20–21.

Amenábar, Juan (b. Santiago, Chile, 22 June 1922), began music studies as a teenager and took courses in civil engineering at the Univ. of Chile (1940–45) followed by composition and orchestration with Jorge Urrutia-Blondel at the National Conservatory (1948–52) and electronic music with Werner Meyer-Eppler, also at the Conservatory (1958). His interest in electronic music dates back to 1953–56, when he was chief music programmer for Radio Chilena. He organized an Experimental Workshop at the Univ. of Chile in 1956 and the following year produced the first Latin American tape composition, *Los peces*. He works in his own studio, the only one in Chile designed specifically for composition. He has contributed new music to the field of Catholic liturgical music. He teaches composition privately and is active as a lecturer on and promoter of new music, especially electronic music. He composes "to order" with a particular duration, sound medium, and performance situation in mind and uses whatever style and technique will best fulfill the intended function of a piece. A concern with the social role of art has led him to write many uncomplicated choral and instrumental pieces for home performance.

PRINCIPAL COMPOSITIONS: *Ronda* for chorus; text by the composer (1950, IEM and PAU); *Mi novia, madre* for chorus; text by Z. Brncic (1950, IEM); *Suite* for piano (1952, IEM); *A la orilla del estero* for chorus; text by M. Arteche (1952, IEM and PAU); *La tortuga* for chorus; text by R. Alberti (1952, IEM and PAU); *Voz marinera* for chorus; text by Alberti (1953, IEM); *Toccata* for organ (1955, IEM); *Tonada y zapateo* for flute, violin, piano, percussion (1955); *Los peces* on tape; based on the Fibonacci series (1957); *Pater noster* for chorus; Spanish text (1962); *Feedback* for violin (1964, IEM); *Cantos de Alicia* for alto, recorder, harpsichord, string sextet; text by Alicia Morel (1964); *Misa litúrgica* for man's voice, chorus, instrumental ensemble, guitar ad lib; Spanish text (1964, IEM); *Sol de Septiembre*, martial hymn for men's chorus, instrumental ensemble, percussion; text by Arteche (1964); *Padre nuestro IV* for voice, guitar (1965); *Sanctus* for woman's voice, jazz ensemble (1968); *Klesis* on tape (1968, recorded by Astral); *El vigía del personaí*, ballet score on tape (1968); *Música continua* on tape (1969); *Laudes* for unison chorus (1970); *Divertimento cordoves* for percussion, instrumental ensemble, tape (1971).

PRINCIPAL WRITINGS: *Introducción a la música cinematográfica* (Univ. of Chile Film Institute 1958); "Creación de un laboratorio de música electrónica para la U. de Chile," *Revista musical chilena* 60:50ff.

SEE ALSO Chile.

Amengual-Astaburuaga, René (b. Santiago, Chile, 2 Sept 1911; d. Santiago, 2 August 1954), studied at the Chilean National Conservatory in Santiago (1923–35; composition with Pedro Humberto Allende-Sarón, piano with Rosa Renard and Alberto Spikin). He taught at the Liceo "Manuel de Salas" in Santiago from 1940 and from 1945 at the National Conservatory, of which he was also the director until his death.

PRINCIPAL COMPOSITIONS: *Burlesca* for piano (1932–38, Schirmer-G); *Transparencias* for piano (1938, *Boletín latino-americano de música* 4: supplement); *Sonatina* for piano (1939, ECIC); *Introducción y allegro* for 2 pianos (1939); *String Quartet No. 1* (1941, IEM); *Piano Concerto* (1941–42, IEM); *El vaso* for soprano, chamber orchestra (1942, IEM); *Violin Sonata* (1943–44); *Harp Concerto* (1943–50, IEM); *Little Suite* for flute, piano (1945, IEM); *2 Short Preludes* for piano (1950); *Wind Sextet* (1953–54).

PRINCIPAL WRITINGS: "La música vocal [de Pedro Humberto Allende-Sarón]," *Revista musical chilena* (Sept 1945):37–47; "El sentido dramático de Santa Cruz en sus obras para piano," *ibid.* (Dec 1951):90–119.

BIBL.: Miguel Aguilar, "La evolución estilística en la obra de R. A.," *Revista musical chilena* (Oct 1954):9–17; Juan Orrego-Salas, "El concierto para arpa y orquesta de R. A.," *ibid.* (spring 1950): 54–64; Vicente Salas-Viú, *La creación musical en Chile, 1900–1951* (Santiago, c.1952); ——, "La obra de R. A. del neoclasicismo al expresionismo," *Revista musical chilena* (Oct 1964):62–72.

Americas, see Argentina, Brazil, Canada, Chile, Mexico, United States

Amram, David (Werner) (b. Philadelphia, 17 Nov 1930), studied piano, trumpet, and French horn as a child. He entered Oberlin Conservatory in 1948 and transferred to George Washington Univ. in 1949, where he earned a BA in history (1952). He composed incidental music for plays at Ford's Theater in Washington (1951–52) and formed his own jazz group at this time. In 1955–56 he attended the Manhattan School of Music (composition with Vittorio Giannini, French horn with Gunther Schuller) and played in jazz bands. Amram was music director of the New York Shakespeare Festival (1956–67, music for 28 productions), the Phoenix Theater, New York (1958–60), and the Lincoln Center Repertory Theater (1963–65). He was composer-in-residence at the New York Philharmonic (1966–67). He is primarily self-taught in composition and is strongly influenced by the spontaneity of jazz. Like many jazz musicians, he has learned how to compose by improvising on the spot.

PRINCIPAL COMPOSITIONS (published by Peters unless otherwise noted): *Trio*, for tenor saxophone, horn, bassoon (1958); *Overture and Allegro* for solo flute (1959); *Discussion* for flute, cello, piano, percussion (1960); *Sonata* for piano (1960); *Violin Sonata* (1960); *Shir l'erev shabat* for tenor, chorus, organ (1961); *String Quartet* (1961); *2 Anthems* for chorus (1961); *Dirge and Variations* for violin, cello, piano (1962); *May the Words of the Lord* for chorus, organ (1962); *3 Songs for Marlboro* for horn, cello (1962); *Thou Shalt Love the Lord, Thy God* for chorus, organ (1962); *The Wind and the Rain* for viola, piano (1963); *After the Fall*, incidental music for the Arthur Miller play (1963); *A Year in Our Land*, cantata for soloists, chorus, orchestra (1964); *Sonata* for solo violin (1964); *Let Us Remember*, cantata for soloists, chorus, orchestra (1965); *The Final Ingredient*, opera (1965); *By the Rivers of Babylon* for soprano, women's voices (1966); *Fanfare and Processional* for brass quintet (1966); *King Lear Variations* for wind orchestra (1966); *Three Dances* for oboe, strings (1966); *Songs from Shakespeare* for voice, piano (1968); *Twelfth Night*, opera; libretto by Joseph Papp and the composer (1968); *Woodwind Quintet* (1968); *3 Songs for America* for baritone, quintet, string quintet; texts by John F. Kennedy, Martin L. King, Robert F. Kennedy (1969); *Triptych* for solo viola (1969).

PRINCIPAL WRITINGS: *Vibrations* (New York 1968).

Amy, Gilbert (b. Paris, 29 August 1936), began piano at six and had secondary schooling in a Paris lycée, earning the baccalauréat and a national award in philosophy in 1954. From 1956 until 1960 he studied at the Paris Conservatory (analysis with Olivier Messiaen, composition with Darius Milhaud). In 1956 he met Pierre Boulez and began composing under his guidance while studying harmony and piano with Yvonne Loriod. From 1959 until 1961 he attended the Darmstadt summer courses. In 1962 he made his debut as a conductor and was appointed assistant music director of the Odéon Théâtre de France. He took Boulez's conducting class in Basel in 1965, and in 1967 succeeded Boulez as director of the Domaine Musical in Paris. By that time Amy's works were being played throughout the world, and he had toured extensively as a conductor, directing his own and other contemporary works.

Amy has retained in all his works the rigorous spirit of his early training in the post-World War II school of serialism. His first works, although still under the influence of Boulez, reflect this orientation and already give evidence of two main features of his style: clear, constantly polyphonic writing and subtle instrumentation. His subsequent evolution has generally coincided with that of European serialism; in the *Piano Sonata* (1957–60) he, like other serial composers at that time, investigated processes ranging from the generalized series to mobile form. During this period he also completed *Cantate brève* and *Mouvements*, both in strict serial technique, and started *Inventions*, based on new considerations of the problem of equivalences. Still another direction was evidenced in *Antiphonies*, composed during 1960–63 but actually contemplated since 1958 when he heard Stockhausen's *Gruppen* and turned his attention to acoustic and spatial factors. In *Diaphonies* (1962) appeared a new poetic element which has become one of the outstanding characteristics of his later orchestral works, *Strophe*, *Trajectoires*, and *Chant*. The orchestral sonority is both refined and sumptuous. Serial principles no longer apply to single elements but to whole areas, which permits a large-scale conception. Mobile form processes appear locally to ensure greater flexibility but do not govern the overall form, which remains generally closed. Works since 1968 have continued to follow this direction with emphasis on the poetic element.

PRINCIPAL COMPOSITIONS (published by Heugel): *Cantate brève* for soprano, flute, xylorimba, vibraphone; texts by García-Lorca (1957); *Piano Sonata* (1957–60); *Mouvements* for 17 instruments (1958); *Inventions* for flute, piano/celesta, harp, vibraphone/marimba (1959–61); *Antiphonies* for 2 orchestras (1960–63); *Epigrammes* for piano (1961); *Diaphonies* for 2 groups of 12 instruments (1962); *Alpha-Beth* for wind sextet (1963–64); *Iriade* for orchestra, after a mescaline-inspired text by Henri Michaux (1963–64); *Cahiers d'épigrammes* for piano (1964); *Cycle* for 6 percussionists (1964–65); *Strophe* for soprano, orchestra; poems by René Char (1965–66); *Trajectoires* for violin, orchestra (1966); *Relais* for 5 brasses (1967); *Chant* for orchestra (1967–68); *Cette Etoile enseigne à s'incliner* for 7 men's voices, tape, instruments (1970); *Jeu* for 1–4 oboes (1970); *Récitatif, air et variation* for 12 solo voices (1970).

PRINCIPAL WRITINGS: "Richard Wagner" and other articles, *Encyclopédie de la musique* (Paris 1958–61); "L'Espace sonore," *Esprit*, special issue on music (Jan 1960):75–89; "Sur Quelques Problèmes récent . . . et futurs," *Phantomas* (Belgium, Jan 1960):33–36; "Musique pour 'Misérable Miracle' d'Henri Michaux," *Tel Quel* (spring 1964):83–93; "Redécouvrir l'Ecoute," *Preuves* (Nov 1965):29–31.

BIBL.: Maurice Faure published an interview with Amy in *Les Lettres nouvelles* (Jan 1961):165–74.

Betsy Jolas

Analysis, see Theory

Andrico, Michel (Jean) or **Andricu, Mihail** (b. Bucharest, 22 Dec 1894), studied at the Bucharest Conservatory (1904–13, 1919–20; composition with Alphonse Casteldi, violin with R. Klenek). During 1913–14 and 1920–22 he consulted with Vincent d'Indy and Gabriel Fauré in Paris. He taught chamber music and later composition at the Bucharest Conservatory (1926–59) and was vice president of the Rumanian Composers Union (1947–56). He was also music critic for *Le Moment* in Bucharest. His music combines the "character and atmosphere" of Rumanian folk music with classic forms.

PRINCIPAL COMPOSITIONS: *4 Novelettes* for piano quintet, Op. 4 (1925, Hamelle); *Chamber Symphonies Nos. 1–2*, Opp. 5, 98 (1926, ESPLA; 1962); *Octet* for clarinet, bassoon, horn, string quintet, Op. 8 (1928, ESPLA); *Piano Sonata*, Op. 12 (1929, Hamelle); *String Quartet*, Op. 14 (1930, ESPLA); *Taina*, 3-act ballet, Op. 17 (1932); *3 Pièces* for piano, Op. 18 (c.1933, Hamelle); *4 Esquisses* for piano, Op. 19 (c.1933, Hamelle); *3 Capriccios* for orchestra, Op. 24 (1936); *Suita pitorească* for orchestra, Op. 25 (1938); *Symphonies Nos. 1–9*: No. 1, Op. 30 (1943); No. 2, Op. 46 (1946, ES); No. 3, Op. 54 (1949, ESPLA); No. 4, Op. 76 (1954, Muzicală); No. 5, Op. 78 (1955); No. 6, Op. 82 (1957, Muzicală); No. 7, Op. 85 (1958); No. 8, Op. 91 (1960); No. 9, Op. 101 (1962, ESCR); *Violin Sonata*, Op. 33 (1944, ESCR); *Trio* for oboe, clarinet, bassoon, Op. 34 (1944); *Suite No. 3* for orchestra, Op. 38 (1946); *Sinfoniettas Nos. 3, 6, 7*, Opp. 45, 101, 102 (1946, 1962, 1963); *Piano Sonata,*

Op. 55 (1950, Salabert); *Suite* for piano, Op. 81 (1957, ESCR); *Violin Concerto*, Op. 93 (1960, Muzicală); *6 Portraits* for orchestra, Op. 114 (1969).

Andriessen, Henrik (b. Haarlem, 17 Sept 1892), studied at the Amsterdam Conservatory (1914–16; piano, organ with Jean de Pauw; composition, Bernard Zweers). He has been organist at St. Joseph's Church, Haarlem (1916–34) and at Utrecht Cathedral (1934–38). During 1937–49 he was director of the Utrecht Conservatory and during 1949–57 of the Royal Conservatory in the Hague. He taught at the Univ. of Nÿmegen (1952–63). Andriessen has made notable contributions to Roman Catholic church music. His compositions are based on traditional formal concepts and usually incorporate broad, flowing melodic lines that often resemble those of Franck and the French impressionists. Rhythm tends to be metrical and regular and harmony tonal with occasional whole-tone chords or parallelisms in the impressionist manner. During the 1930s Andriessen worked with nontertial harmonies, and during the 1950s he wrote several works based on 12-tone themes.

PRINCIPAL COMPOSITIONS (published by Donemus unless otherwise noted): *Choral No. 1* for organ (1913, Van Rossum); *Toccata* for organ (1913, Van Rossum); *Magna res est amor* for soprano, orchestra or organ (1919, Van Rossum); *Miroir de peine*, song cycle for soprano, string orchestra or organ (1923, Van Rossum); *Cello Sonata* (1926); *Sonata da chiesa* for organ (1927, Van Rossum); *Missa simplex* for chorus (1927, Van Rossum); *Passacaglia* for organ (1929, Van Rossum); *Symphony No. 1* (1930); *Violin Sonata No. 2* (1933); *3 Pastorales* for mezzo-soprano, piano (1934, Van Rossum); *Variations on a Theme of Kuhnau* for orchestra (1935); *Missa Christus Rex* for double chorus, organ (1938, Van Rossum); *Piano Trio No. 2* (1939); *Sinfonia per organo* (1940, Van Rossum); *2 Madrigali* for chorus, strings (1940); *Te Deum laudamus No. 1* for chorus, orchestra or organ (1943, Van Rossum); *Variations on a Theme of Couperin* for flute, harp, strings (1944); *Philomela*, opera; libretto by Jan Engelman (1949–50); *Concerto* for organ, orchestra (1950); *Wind Quintet* (1951); *Symphonic Etude* for orchestra (1952); *3 Canzone* for chorus (1958); *Veni Creator* for chorus, orchestra (1960); *De Spiegel uit Venetië*, opera (1964); *Piano Sonata No. 2* (1966); *Petit Concert spirituel* for flute, oboe, violin, cello (1966).

PRINCIPAL WRITINGS: *César Franck* (Stockholm 1947); *Over Muziek* (Utrecht 1950); *Muziek en Musikaliteit* (Utrecht 1952); *De Gedachtegang in de Muziek* (Utrecht 1963).

BIBL.: Thurston J. Dox, "H. F. A.: His Life and Works," (PhD diss., Eastman School, 1970);

Wouter Paap, *Moderne Kerkmuziek in Nederland* (Bilthoven 1941); ——, "H. A.," *Mens en Melodie* 7:236–37; ——, "H. A.," *ibid.* 17:261–62; Joseph Wouters, "H. A.," *Sonorum Speculum* 7:1–11.
[prepared with the help of Thurston J. Dox]
SEE ALSO Liturgical Music: Christian.

Andriessen, Louis (b. Utrecht, 6 June 1939), studied composition with his father, Hendrik, and later (1957–62) with Kees van Baaren at the Royal Conservatory in the Hague. He studied privately with Luciano Berio in Milan and Berlin (1962–65). Further influences on Andriessen have been Stockhausen, Cage's theories, and Stravinsky. He is writing a book on Stravinsky, chapters of which have appeared in *De Gids* (on Stravinsky's relationship to Gesualdo, Machaut, Webern, and others). Andriessen has composed theater and film scores and since 1968 has served as musical advisor to the Globe theater group of Amsterdam, where he lives as a free-lance composer.
PRINCIPAL COMPOSITIONS: *Séries* for 2 pianos (1958, Donemus); *Percosse* for flute, trumpet, bassoon, percussion (1958); *Nocturnen* for soprano, chamber orchestra (1959, Donemus); *Paintings* for flute, piano (1961, Moeck); *Ittrospezione II* for orchestra (1963, Donemus); *Registers* for piano (1963, Peters); *Sweet* for recorder (1964, Schott); *Double* for clarinet, piano (1965, Donemus); *Souvenirs d'enfance* for piano(s) (1966, Querido, Amsterdam); *Anachronie I* for orchestra (1967, Donemus); *Contra Tempus* for 23 musicians (1968, Donemus); *Reconstructie*, a political opera, in collaboration with the composers Reinbert de Leeuw, Misja Mengelberg, Peter Schat, Jan van Vlijmen; libretto by Hugo Claus and Harry Mulisch (1969); *Anachronie II* for oboe, chamber orchestra (1969); *Hoe het is* for electronic improvisation group, 52 solo strings (1969).
PRINCIPAL WRITINGS: "Mendelsohn, frisdranken en de avant-garde," *De Gids* (Oct 1966):331–34; "G. de Machaut en de Messe de Nostre Dame," *ibid.* (Jan 1968):53–58; "Carlo Gesualdo di Venosa," *ibid.* (April 1968):256–61; "Perséphone," *ibid.* (May 1968):329–32; "De tÿd in tegenspraak," *ibid.* (Aug 1968):178–81.
BIBL.: Lidy van Marissing, "Componist L. A.: '. . . ik praat veel met Bach . . .'," *De Volkskrant* (Amsterdam, 9 April 1969); Aad van der Mÿn, "Je comporeert omdat je het niet laten kan!", *Het Parool "Extra"* (Amsterdam, 23 Dec 1966); E. Vermeulen, "Compositions by L. A. and Peter Schat Incorporating Quotations," *Sonorum Speculum* 35:1–12; ——, "In den Niederlanden reicht die Generation von 1930 der Generation von 1880 die Hand," *Melos* (Jan 1969):10–14; condensations of 4 reviews appeared as "Opera: *Reconstruction*," *American Musical Digest* 1/1:12–16.
SEE ALSO Netherlands.

Angerer, Paul (b. Vienna, 16 May 1927), studied 1943–46 at the Vienna Hochschule für Musik (composition with Friedrich Reidinger) and at the Vienna Conservatory (violin with Franz Bruckbauer, piano with Viola Thern). He has been violist with the Orchestre de la Suisse Romande (1949–53) and the Vienna Symphony (1953–57). During 1964–66 he was kapellmeister at the State Theater in Bonn; during 1966–68, musical director of Ulm Theater; and since 1967, opera director of the Salzburg Landestheater. He has also been kapellmeister and composer at the Vienna Burgtheater since 1960. He plays the harpsichord and the recorder in baroque chamber groups. In his early music he was influenced by the work of Hindemith. He has composed for both the stage and television and edited many classical chamber works.
PRINCIPAL COMPOSITIONS (published by Doblinger unless otherwise noted): *Music* for viola (1948); *Wen der Himmel retten will, dem gibt er die Liebe*, oratorio for soloists, chorus, chamber orchestra; text by Lao-tse (1949, unpub.); *Music for Orchestra* (1950, unpub.); *Konzertantes Quartett* for oboe, horn, viola, cello (1951); *Serenata* for violin, viola, horn, bassoon (1951); *Duo* for alto recorder, viola (1952, unpub.); *Trio* for recorder, viola d'amore, lute (1953, unpub.); *Musica examinata* for cello, piano (1953); *Agamemnon muss sterben*, dramatic cantata for speaker, mezzo-soprano, tenor, baritone, 2 choruses, chamber orchestra, percussion; text by Rudolf Bayr (1954, unpub.); *Musica ad impulsum et pulsum* for strings, percussion (1955); *Musica fera* for orchestra (1956, unpub.); *Toccaten* for harpsichord (1957); *Gloriatio* for bouble bass, chamber orchestra (1957); *Die Passkontrolle*, TV opera; libretto by Friedrich Kühnelt (1959, unpub.); *Concerto* for piano, string orchestra (1962); *Viola Concerto* (1962); *Chanson gaillarde* for oboe, cello, harpsichord (1963); *Cogitatio* for wind quintet, strings (1964); *Inklination der Ariadne des Monteverdi* for orchestra (1967); *Hotel Comédie*, musical; libretto by W. Schneyder after Goldoni (1970, unpub.).
PRINCIPAL WRITINGS: "Die Bühne als raumschaffendes Element," *Maske und Kothurn* 11/4.

Anhalt, István (b. Budapest, 12 April 1919), began music lessons at the age of six. He later studied at the Royal Academy of Music (1937–41, composition with Zoltán Kodály) and the Paris Conservatory (1946–48; piano with Soulima Stravinsky, conducting with Louis Fourestier, János Ferencsik). He also studied composition with Nadia Boulanger (1946–48). In 1949 Anhalt emigrated to Canada, where he taught at McGill Univ., Montreal, becoming chairman of the music department in 1963. In 1969–70 he was visiting professor at the Univ. of Buffalo. In addition to many works for traditional media, Anhalt has written electronic music, and in 1959 he helped organize the first public concert of electronic music in Canada.

PRINCIPAL COMPOSITIONS: *Funeral Music* for flute, clarinet, bassoon, horn, 2 violins, 2 violas, 2 cellos (1951); *Piano Sonata* (1951); *Trio* for violin, cello, piano (1953, BMIC); *Comments* for contralto, violin, cello, piano; text from *Montreal Star* (1954); *Fantasia* for piano (1954); *3 Songs of Death* for chorus; text by Sir William Davenant, Robert Herrick (1954); *Symphony No. 1* (1958, BMIC); *Electronic Music Compositions Nos. 2* ("Sine Nomine II"), *3, 4* (1959, 1960, 1961); *Cento* for 12 speaking voices and 2-track tape (1967, BMIC); *Symphony of Modules,* for orchestra, 2 2-track tapes (1967). List to 1961: *Composers of the Americas* 8:14–15.

BIBL.: J. Beckwith, "Composers in Toronto and Montreal," *Univ. of Toronto Quarterly* 26:47–69; —— "Recent Orchestral Works by Champagne, Morel, and A.," *Canadian Music Journal* 4/4:44–48.

SEE ALSO Canada.

Antheil, George (b. Trenton, N. J., 8 July 1900; d. New York, 12 Feb 1959), studied first with Constantine von Sternberg and later with Ernest Bloch. In the early 1920s he concertized in Europe as a pianist, often shocking audiences by introducing his own compositions, bearing such titles as *Airplane Sonata* and *Mechanisms*. He returned to the U.S. permanently in 1933 and settled three years later in Hollywood, where he wrote numerous film scores.

Antheil's extensive and varied musical output encompasses many short piano works, several sonatas, symphonies, concertos, two string quartets, five ballets, seven operas, incidental music, and assorted choral works. His literary accomplishments were nearly as diverse. Under his own name and various pseudonyms he wrote a detective mystery, a prophetic account detailing the future course of World War II, a study of glandular abnormalities among criminals, and an autobiography. A number of his articles appeared in *Esquire*. His journalistic contributions ranged from interpreting the war news to supplying a daily advice-to-the-lovelorn column.

Antheil began his career as an avowed iconoclast. The work that did most to establish his reputation was *Ballet mécanique*. First conceived in 1923 for five pianolas and assorted percussion to accompany an abstract film by Fernand Léger, he soon revised it as an independent work for eight pianos, a pianola, eight

xylophones, two electric doorbells, and the sound of an airplane propeller. The first complete performance (Paris 1926) caused a riot. For the well-publicized American premiere in New York the following year, the composer agreed to double the number of pianos, add such noisemakers as anvils, buzzsaws, and automobile horns, and employ an actual airplane propeller on stage for its visual and psychological effect. In a final revision, completed in 1953, he omitted the pianola, reduced the pianos to four, provided prerecorded tapes of jet engines, and cut the total length by half. According to his later statements, *Ballet mécanique* was never intended to glorify machines as commonly supposed but instead to be a study in which "time-space" principles replaced tonality as the basis of formal organization. Its occasional tone clusters in the pianos and characteristically Stravinskian rhythmic ostinatos, displacement of regular accents, and rapidly shifting meters indicate some of the stylistic milieu with which Antheil associated himself. Syncopations and other jazz-influenced rhythms appear most prominently in his *Symphony No. 1* (1922), *Jazz Symphonietta* (1926), and the opera *Transatlantic* (1928–29), which employs such unconventional stage settings as a Child's Restaurant and an extended aria delivered by the prima donna from her bathtub.

From the 1930s on Antheil displayed more conservative tendencies. His music from these years abounds in melodic lyricism superimposed over a clearly defined tonal base. A strongly linear texture is replete with canons, fugues, and other contrapuntal devices. There are frequent thematic recurrences from previous sections or movements, revealing his later preoccupation with traditional formal procedures. Influences of Stravinsky are still evident, the most notable being rhythmic ostinatos, displacement of regular accents, and consonant chords containing a single dissonant note.

PRINCIPAL COMPOSITIONS (list prepared with the help of Elisabeth B. Antheil; works published by Weintraub unless otherwise noted): *Airplane Sonata* for piano (1922); *Sonata sauvage* for piano (1922); *Symphony No. 1* (1922); *Violin Sonata No. 1* (1923); *Jazz Symphonietta* for 22 instruments (1926); *Ballet mécanique* (1923–24; revised 1953, Templeton); *Transatlantic*, 3-act opera; libretto by the composer (1928–29, UE); *Helen Retires*, 3-act opera; libretto by John Erskine (1931); *Dreams, ballet*; choreography by George Balanchine (1935); *Course*, dance score; choreography by Martha Graham (1936); *Symphonies Nos. 4–6* (1942, Boosey; 1947–48, Leeds; 1948); *McKonkey's Ferry Overture* for orchestra (1948); *Piano Sonata*

No. 4 (1948); *Serenade* for string orchestra (1948); *Songs of Experience* for voice, piano; poems by William Blake (1948); *Volpone*, 3-act opera; libretto by Alfredo Perry after Ben Jonson (1950); *8 Fragments from Shelley* for chorus (1951); *Capital of the World*, ballet after Ernest Hemingway; choreography by Eugene Loring (1953, Schirmer-G); *Cabezza de vacca*, cantata; text by Allan Dowling (1955–56, Templeton).

PRINCIPAL WRITINGS: *Bad Boy of Music* (Garden City, N. J., 1945).

BIBL.: Gilbert Chase, *America's Music*, 2nd ed. (New York 1966):572–75; Ezra Pound, *A. and the Treatise on Harmony* (Chicago 1927); Randall Thompson, "G. A.," *Modern Music* 8:17–28.

Thomas E. Warner

SEE ALSO Opera, Orchestration, United States.

Antoniou, Theodore (b. Athens, 10 Feb 1935), studied at the National Conservatory, Athens (1947–58, composition with Manolis Kalomiris), the Hellenic Conservatory, Athens (1958–61, composition and orchestration with Yannis Papaïoannou), the Hochschule für Musik, Munich (1961–65, masterclass with Günther Bialas), the Studio for Electronic Music, Munich (1964–65, Josef Anton Riedl), and at Darmstadt (1963, 1966). He has taught at the National Conservatory, Athens (1956–60), and at Stanford Univ. (since 1969). In Athens he was active as a conductor and promoter of new music. His own works combine conventional and electronic media to explore "extremely abstract relationships, such as the movements of sounds, the possible combinations of a dialogue, the several ways of playing an instrument . . . problems of space, sound, movement, and event."

PRINCIPAL COMPOSITIONS (published by Bärenreiter unless otherwise noted): *Concertino* for piano, strings, percussion (1962); *Epilogue* for mezzo-soprano, speaker, oboe, horn, guitar, piano, double bass, percussion; text by Homer (1963); *Jeux* for cello, strings (1963); *Micrographies* for orchestra (1964); *Kontakion* for vocal soloists, chorus, strings; text by Romanos (1965); *Violin Concerto* (1965); *Sil-ben* for piano (1965, Gerig); *Lyrics* for violin, piano (1967); *Clytemnestra*, ballet (1967); *Events* for violin, piano, orchestra (1967–68); *Climate of Absence* for medium voice, oboe, chamber ensemble; text by O. Elytis (1968, unpub.); *Katharsis* for flute, chamber ensemble, electronic organ, tape (1968, unpub.); *Events II* for orchestra (1969, unpub.); *Cassandra*, sound action for dancers, actors, orchestra, tape, lights, projections (1969, unpub.); *Events III* for chamber ensemble, tape (1969, unpub.).

PRINCIPAL WRITINGS: "Ó neos synthetis ē paixnidi tes alētheias" [The Young Composer or

the Game of Truth], *Epoches* (April 1966):348f.; "Theatro kinematografos kai synchroni moussiki" [Film and Contemporary Music], *ibid.* (Aug 1966): 16off.; "Ó Antoniou milaei gia tā ergā tou" [Antoniou Speaks About His Works], *Lyrikos Kosmos* (Nov 1966):11ff., 29f.; "Ï nea moussiki kai tō koino" [New Music and the Audience], *Ethnos* (27 July 1967); "New Music in the U.S.A.," *Athens Daily Post* (8 Sept 1967); "New Music in the U.S.A.," *Washington Evening Star* (1 Jan 1968); "Über den Griechischen Komponisten N. Skalkottas," *Schweizerische Musikzeitung* (May–July 1969):136–40.

BIBL.: K. Hashagen, "T. A.," *Musica* (Cassel, Aug 1968):276–78; Irving Lowens, "An Hour with A.," *Washington Sunday Star* (12 Oct 1969).

SEE ALSO Greece.

Apergis, Georges A. (b. Athens, 23 Dec 1945), studied composition privately with Yannis Papaïoannou in 1964. He is a free-lance composer living in Paris.

PRINCIPAL COMPOSITIONS: *Color Music* for 10 instruments in a medium range and 9 in a medium-low range (1966–69); *Lioretto* for orchestra (1968); *Music for an Orange Girl* for chamber orchestra (1968); *Plastic Piece 1* for 2 orchestras (1968); *Quadrat* for 4 double basses (1969); *Variations sur un portrait de Bach* for any instrument (1970); *Apua micans* for any instruments, singers, actors, dancers, lights, etc. (1970); *Entretiens* on tape (1970); *Music Box* for harpsichord (1970); *Simata* for prepared piano (1970); *Oedipe* for orchestra (1970); *Vesper Oratorio* for vocal soloists, chamber orchestra (1970); *Symplexis* for 20 jazz soloists, orchestra (1970).

SEE ALSO Greece.

Aponte-Ledée, Rafael (b. Puerto Rico, 15 Oct 1938), studied at the Madrid Conservatory (1957–64; composition with Cristóbal Halffter, other subjects with Francisco Calés Otero, Enrique Massó, and Emilio López) and the Di Tella Institute in Buenos Aires (1965–66, 1969; composition with Alberto Ginastera and Gerardo Gandini), where he worked at the Electronic Music Studio. He has been active in the Fluxus group since 1967 as codirector, composer, and conductor, and his music has been influenced by the work of Gandini, John Cage, and Earle Brown.

PRINCIPAL COMPOSITIONS: *Presagio de pájaros muertos* for actor, tape (1966); *Impulsos . . . in memoriam Julia de Burgos* for orchestra (1967, Peer); *Epíthasis* for 3 oboes, 2 trombones, double bass, 3 percussionists (1968); *La Ventana abierta*, 1st version for 3 mezzo-sopranos (singing phonemes), 2 flutes, violin, cello, piano/celesta, percussion (1968), 2nd version for 3 mezzo-sopranos, flutes, clarinet in A, trumpets in D and C, horn, 2 percussionists, guitar, piano/celesta, 2 string quartets (1969); *Tentativas* for violin, chamber orchestra, tape (1969); *Aquí presente* for 5 trumpets (1969).

Apostel, Hans-Erich (b. Karlsruhe, 22 Jan 1901), studied at the Munz Conservatory in Karlsruhe (1915–19) and privately in Vienna with Arnold Schoenberg (1921) and Alban Berg (1925–35). In 1920 he served as a conductor at the Badisches Landestheater in Karlsruhe, and from 1921 until the war he taught music privately in Vienna and performed as a concert accompanist. He was a reader for Universal Edition from 1930 until the war. Since 1945 he has devoted himself exclusively to composition.

PRINCIPAL COMPOSITIONS (published by UE unless otherwise noted): *String Quartet No. 1*, Op. 7 (1935, unpub.); *Kubiniana*, 10 pieces for piano, Op. 13 (1945–50); *Haydn Variations* for orchestra, Op. 17 (1949); *Ballade* for orchestra, Op. 21 (1955); *String Quartet No. 2*, Op. 26 (1956); *Rondo ritmico* for orchestra, Op. 27 (1957); *Piano Concerto*, Op. 30 (1958); *5 Austrian Miniatures* for orchestra (1959); *Ode* for alto, orchestra; text by the composer (1961–62); *String Quartet No. 3*, "6 Epigrams," Op. 33 (1962); *Festive Music* for wind orchestra (1962, Doblinger); *Chamber Symphony*, Op. 41 (1966).

PRINCIPAL WRITINGS: *Ethik und Ästethik der Musik* (Vienna 1970).

BIBL.: Harald Kaufmann, *H.-E. A.* (Vienna c.1965).

Applebaum, Louis (b. Toronto, 3 April 1918), attended the Royal Conservatory of Music, Toronto, where he studied with Boris Berlin, Healey Willan, Leo Smith, and Ernest MacMillan. He earned a MusB degree from the Univ. of Toronto in 1940. He studied composition privately in New York with Roy Harris and Bernard Wagenaar (1940–41). He has worked for the National Film Board of Canada as a composer (1941), music director (1942–46), and consultant (1949–53). During 1946–47 he composed film scores in Hollywood, and since 1953 he has written incidental music for the stage productions at Stratford, Ontario. He has founded and directed the Stratford, Ontario, Music Festival and the International Conference of Composers, also in Stratford. He was president of Group Four Productions during 1960–66 and is a member of the board of directors of the Canadian Music Centre. Electronics and the music of Stravinsky have had the greatest impact on his development.

PRINCIPAL COMPOSITIONS: *Tomorrow the World*, film score (1944); *Story of GI Joe*, film score (1945); *Dreams that Money Can Buy*, film score (1948); *Lost Boundaries*, film score (1948); *Variations on a Theme from a Film Score* for string quartet, oboe (1948); *Cry of the Prophet* for baritone, piano; text from *Jeremiah* (1951); *4 English Carols* for chorus with orchestra or piano (1951); *French-Canadian Carols* (also called *Suite*) for chorus, orchestra or piano (1951); *Teresa*, film score (1951); *The Whistle at Eaton Falls*, film score (1951); *3 Stratford Fanfares* (1953, Leeds); *Dark of the Moon*, ballet suite (1954; revised and titled *Barbara Allen*, 1960); *Suite of Miniature Dances* (1958); *Ride a Pink Horse*, musical comedy (1962); *Concertante* for orchestra (1967); *Terre des hommes*, fanfare (1967); *Royal Ceremonial*, fanfare (1967); *Song for the National Arts Centre* for children's choir, band (1967). List to 1965: *Composers of the Americas* 10:13–19.

PRINCIPAL WRITINGS: "Film Music," *Music in Canada* ed. by Ernest MacMillan (Toronto 1955): 167–76; "Foreword," *The Modern Composer and His World* ed. by John Beckwith and Udo Kasemets (Toronto 1961):5–9; "Stratford's Music Festival," *The Stratford Scene 1958–68* ed. by Peter Raby (Toronto 1968):58–76.

Archer, Violet (Balestreri) (b. Montreal, 24 April 1913), studied at the McGill Conservatory (1930–36; composition with Claude Champagne, Douglas Clarke) and at the Yale Univ. School of Music (1947–49; composition with Paul Hindemith, Richard Donovan). She also studied composition privately in New York with Béla Bartók in 1942. She has taught at McGill Univ. (1944–47), Cornell Univ. (1952), and at the Univ. of Alberta (1948–49 and since 1962), where she is chairman of the Division of Theory and Counterpoint. During 1950–53 she was composer-in-residence at North Texas State Univ.

PRINCIPAL COMPOSITIONS: *The Bell* for chorus, orchestra; poem by John Donne (1949); *Fanfare and Passacaglia* for orchestra (1949, BMIC); *Piano Concerto* (1956); *Divertimento* for orchestra (1957, BMIC); *Apocalypse* for soprano, chorus, brass, timpani (1958); *Violin Concerto* (1959); *3 Sketches for Orchestra* (1961, BMIC); *Divertimento* for brass quintet (1963); *Prelude-Incantation* for orchestra (1964); *Sing, the Muse* for chorus; poems by Shakespeare, Marston, Drummond, Raleigh (1964); *Horn Sonata* (1965); *Cantata sacra* for vocal soloists, chamber orchestra; text by the composer (1967); *Sinfonietta* (1968); *Sinfonia* (1970); *Clarinet Sonata* (1970). List to 1963: *Composers of the Americas* 9:9–12.

Ardévol, José (b. Barcelona, 13 March 1911), began composing as a child and studied composition, conducting, and piano with his father, Fernando Ardévol, and (in 1930) conducting with Hermann Scherchen. He also studied liberal arts at the Univ. of Barcelona. In 1930 he emigrated to Cuba. He taught music history and esthetics at the Havana Municipal Conservatory (1936–41) and composition at the Univ. of Havana (1945–50) and at the Univ. of Oriente (1949–51). He played a prominent part in the Cuban revolutionary movement and in the reorganization of musical culture under the Fidel Castro government. During 1958–59 he directed the National Music Committee of the revolutionary underground. During 1959–65 he conducted the orchestras of the Ministry of Education Radio Network, edited the music journal *Revolución*, and was National Director of Music for the government. He has taught composition at the Amadeo Roldán Conservatory since 1965 and at the National School of Music since 1968, while holding a variety of government posts. The nationalist and neoclassic orientation in his music of the 1930s and 40s gave way in the early 50s to the influence of Webern. In 1967 he began using aleatory procedures as well.

PRINCIPAL COMPOSITIONS: *Study in the Form of a Prelude and Fugue* for percussion (1933, Percus); *Suite* for percussion (1934, Percus); *3 Ricercari* for string orchestra (1936); *Música de cámara* for 6 instruments (1936, PAU and Peer); *Sonate a tres Nos. 1–6* (1937, 1938, 1942, 1942, IIM and Southern; 1943, 1946); *Concerto* for 3 pianos, orchestra (1938); *Piano Sonatas Nos. 1–3* (1944; No. 3, IIM and Southern); *Symphony No. 2*, "Hommage to Falla" (1945, Southern); *Symphony No. 3* (1946, Southern); *Suites cubana Nos. 1–2* for orchestra (1947, Southern; 1949); *Cello Sonata* (1948); *Sonata* for solo guitar (1948, Southern and UNEAC); *Sonatina* for cello, piano (1950, Ricordi); *Symphonic Variations* for cello, orchestra (1951, Southern); *El son*, "Capriccio concertante" for violin, orchestra (1952); *Versos sencillos* for voice, orchestra; text by José Martí (1952); *Wind Quintet* (1957); *Música* for chamber orchestra (1957, Southern); *String Quartet No. 3* (1958, published by the National Library in Havana); *Cantos de la Revolución* for chorus; texts by Cuban poets (1962, EGREM); *3 Short Pieces* for violin or cello, piano (1965); *Música* for guitar, chamber orchestra (1967); *Movimiento sinfónicos Nos. 1–2* (1967, 1969); *Che Comandante*, cantata for 3 vocal soloists, chorus, orchestra; text by Nicolas Guillén (1968); *Tensiones* for piano, left hand (1968); *Lenin*, cantata for 6 vocal soloists, chorus, orchestra; text by Lenin and Félix Pita Rodríquez (1970). List to 1959: *Composers of the Americas* I:4–14.

PRINCIPAL WRITINGS: *Música y revolución*, a collection of essays (Havana 1966).

Arel, Bülent (b. Istanbul, 23 April 1919), studied at the Ankara State Conservatory (1940–47, composition with N. Akses, piano with Ferhunde Erkin, conducting with Ernst Praetorius, 20th-century music with Edward Zuckmayer) and sound engineering in 1951 with Jozé Bernard and Willfried Garret. During 1951–59 he worked at Radio Ankara as a sound engineer and during 1962–65, as Western music program director. He worked at the Columbia-Princeton Electronic Music Center during 1959–61 and in 1962. He has taught theory at the Istanbul Municipal Conservatory (1947–50), harmony at the Ankara State Conservatory (1951–59), piano and music history at the Ankara State Teachers' College (1951–59), and composition and electronic music at Yale Univ. (1961–62, 1965–71), Columbia Univ. (1970–71), and the State Univ. of N. Y. at Stony Brook (since 1971). Before 1957 he wrote "symphonic works in a neoclassic style under the influence of Ravel and Stravinsky." Since then he has used 12-tone techniques and, most recently, free atonal pitch relations. His electronic pieces are composed "of mostly individually composed sounds" subjected to "classic electronic studio techniques."

PRINCIPAL COMPOSITIONS: *Piece for Unaccompanied Viola* or for solo violin (1957); *Music for String Quartet and Tape* (1958, revised 1962); *6 Bagatelles* for strings (1958); *Short Study* on tape (1960); *Electronic Music No. 1* (1960, recorded by Son Nova Records); *Impressions of Wall Street* on tape (1961); *Music for a Sacred Service* on tape (1961, Son Nova Records); *The Scapegoat*, tape score for the play by John F. Matthews (1961, excerpt recorded by Son Nova Records); *Stereo Electronic Music No. 1* on 5-, or 4-, or 2-track tape (1961, Columbia Records); *For Violin and Piano* (1966, CRI Records); *Interrupted Preludes* for organ (1967); *Short Piece* for orchestra (1967); *Mimiana I*, "Flux," tape score for dance with film; choreography by Mimi Garrard (1968); *Mimiana II*, "Frieze," dance score on tape; choreography by Garrard (1969); *Capriccio for T.V.* with video-tape dance sequences filmed by James Seawright (1969); *Stereo Electronic Music No. 2* on 4- or 2-track tape (1970, 2-track version recorded by CRI).

SEE ALSO Electronic Music: Notation.

Argentina is the leading musical country of South America. The active economy of the country is largely responsible for this situation in that it has helped the arts to flourish at home and has made it possible for Argentina to participate in world musical developments. Many Argentine musicians have been able to go to Europe or the U.S. to study, and Buenos Aires, particularly the Colón Theater, has long been a regular stop on the international circuit of touring artists. Furthermore throughout the century there has been a stream of musician-immigrants from Europe; as in the U.S., these newcomers have broadened and enlivened the musical life of the country.

Argentina's largest city, Buenos Aires, is the musical capital both of the country and of the continent. A large proportion of Argentina's musicians live there, including most of her composers, and this is where opportunities for employment and for the performance of new music are best. Other musical centers are developing. In Rosario, for instance, the Instituto Superior de Música at Del Litoral Univ. now offers instruction in performance and composition along with seminars and courses in electronic and concrete music. In Córdoba, one of the important central cities, there is an experimental group in the Escuela de Bellas Artes. In October 1966 it sponsored the Primeras Jornadas de Música Experimental [First Sessions of Experimental Music], in which there were concerts of native and foreign music (recordings of the works performed were issued by Jornadas Música Experimental, Córdoba).

Until World War II most serious Argentine composers traveled to Europe to study. More recent generations have studied within the country, which now offers good training, mainly on the private rather than the institutional level. Some composers study at the National Conservatory or the Municipal Conservatory in Buenos Aires, but most younger ones find the atmosphere there too conservative. An educational advance was made in 1962 when Alberto Ginastera (b. 1916) founded the Latin American Center for Advanced Musical Studies at the Di Tella Institute. The Center offers seminars with such diverse international figures as Copland, Maderna, Messiaen, Nono, Ussachevsky, among others, and it houses a laboratory for electronic music. It gives concerts of works by faculty and students and sponsors an annual festival, mostly of chamber music, in cooperation with the ISCM. Finally, it offers two-year fellowships biannually to 12 Latin-American composers, of which four are usually Argentines. (In Argentina, the only other fellowships for composers have been the Europe Prize, which, until 1920, allowed several composers to study abroad, and the Fund for the Arts, which currently offers a one-year fellowship every other year.)

Only a small proportion of new Argentine music is published; the major firms who handle music are Editorial Argentina de Música and Barry & Cía, both of Buenos Aires. In regard to performances of new works, the problems of the composer have remained fairly constant throughout the century and are comparable to conditions elsewhere: performances of music by older composers writing in familiar styles are more easily obtained than those of music by younger men writing in radical styles. The latter must usually be arranged with private funds and through the personal effort of a few performers. (A special condition existed until 1955 under the Perón regime, when a native work was required on all concert programs. Although this law encouraged creativity, it also opened the door to many amateurs, whose music lowered the general level of what was performed.) The larger organizations that present 20th-century music are based at the Colón Theater: the ballet and opera companies and the two symphonic groups, the Orquesta Estable del Teatro Colón, and the Orquesta Filarmónica. In previous years the latter orchestra introduced the work of many composers who wrote in nationalistic styles drawing on local legends and musical idioms. Nowadays one can frequently hear what is currently in common use—music built around the manipulation of sonorities, with emphasis on chord clusters and irregular rhythmic patterns. Foreign conductors often introduce works from Europe and the U.S. In general the composer earns his living by performing, teaching, and giving lectures and radio programs. He is still considered an amateur who composes on weekends and who must sometimes earn his living outside the field of music. The situation may change in coming years as younger men take on significant administrative posts, but the change will be slow.

Younger composers tend to band together to provide performances of their works. An important group early in the century was the Grupo Renovación, most of whose members wrote in a nationalistic style, later in a neoclassic one; an exception was Juan Carlos *Paz (1901–72), who was working with dodecaphonic techniques. The music of this group, much of it published by the group itself and by Editorial Argentina de Música, constitutes an important source of information about Argentine music up to 1930. The group disbanded in 1931. Paz formed another group in 1937, then known as Conciertos de Nueva Música and called since 1950 Agrupación Nueva Música. It offers advanced Argentine and foreign chamber works. The music of its members reveals a taste for atonality with a strong emphasis on dodecaphonic and serial techniques. The group has presented many works from Central Europe and the U.S. In 1957 the Asociación de Jóvenes Compositores de la Argentina was created to perform and promote its members' music. During its first ten years it gave more than 50 chamber concerts, five symphonic concerts, and many radio broadcasts. It has also arranged for the publication and recording of its members' music (publishers: Editorial Argentina de Música and Ricordi Americana; record company: Club Internacional del Disco). The Agrupación Euphonía is a small group of composer-performers created in 1959 by Gerardo *Gandini (b. 1936) and Armando Krieger (b. 1940); in 1962 its name was changed to Agrupación Música Viva. It holds concerts and lectures containing both foreign and native music, and it has taken the step, unprecedented in Argentina, of commissioning works to be performed at its concerts. It has collaborated with other institutions in Chile and Uruguay and with the contemporary music festivals held in Tucumán, Argentina (in 1963), and in Lomas de Zamora, Argentina (in 1964). The music of its members is largely post-Webernian, but being a group of composer-performers, it values experimentation, particularly with regard to unusual ways of producing sounds with instruments and to the use of delicate sonorities extracted from clusters.

Two individuals deserve mention because of their work with contemporary music. The composer and conductor Juan José *Castro (1895–1968) used the now disbanded Asociación del Profesorado Orquestal ensemble to introduce the great works of this century in Argentina. His premieres of Argentine works included the *Panambí Suite* of Ginastera. The pianist Jorge Zulueta (b. 1934) is unique in his devotion to new Argentine music. His recordings for Club Internacional del Disco include all styles and phases of music in the country.

Until recently nationalism was the predominant style. It led to tonal music colored with the pentatonic scales of folk styles. The folk character of symphonic and chamber works was often enhanced by programmatic depictions of legends, both native and Spanish. The rhythmic patterns of native music appeared frequently: *gato*, a fast 6/8 dance; *chacareras*, a slower 6/8 dance; *vidalas*, a wailing song, also 6/8; *triste*, a sorrow song in 3/4; *malambo*, a strong, male dance in 3/4; and the urban *tango* as played by an *orquesta típica*, consisting of *bandoneon* (a kind of accordian), violin, piano, and singer. This phase of Argentine music is well illustrated by *El tarco en flor* [The Flowering Tarco], a symphonic poem by Luis Gianneo (1897–1968), and by the *Variaciones concertantes* for orchestra by Alberto *Ginastera (b. 1916). The nationalistic approach was also successfully used in stage works that depicted legends of the Guarani Indians, early Hispanic adventurers, or the lonely lives and fierce battles of the gauchos in the pampas. An example of this is *Huemac*, an opera and ballet by Pascual de Rogatis (b. 1882) based on a legend of the Araucanian Indians and incorporating war dances in local rhythms, as well as melodic lines derived from Araucanian songs.

Some Argentine composers began to turn away from folk elements and toward the neo-classic style about 1930. Some still tried to blend in elements of Spanish influence or of the popular tango, but the use of contrapuntal textures and classical forms gave their music a wider international appeal than the purely nationalistic compositions mentioned above. Examples are *3 pinturas de Paul Klee* or *Variaciones olímpicas* for orchestra by Roberto Garcia Morillo (b. 1911), *Preludio y toccata* by José Maria Castro (1892–1964), and *Música* for strings by Roberto *Caamaño (b. 1923). The operas *Bodas de sangre* [Blood Wedding] and *Proserpina y el extranjero* [Proserpine and the Foreigner] by Juan José Castro show his devotion to Spanish music, particularly to Falla.

Newer compositional techniques have also been adopted by Argentines. The first to use dodecaphony and serialism was Paz, whose taste for experimentation has led him most recently into open forms (for instance, in his polyrhythmic *Música* for piano and orchestra, 1963). Ginastera, who had mixed Argentine and pre-Columbian elements in his *Cantata para America mágica* (1960), became more experimental in his microtonal *Violin Concerto* (1963). César Franchisena (b. 1922) has done valuable acoustical experiments and translated them into his works. In his *Visiones siderales* for piano (1954) he extended the dodecaphonic system by superimposing "levels of perception"—clusters of cluster chords, for instance, where one chord is masked by another, or the use in some passages of tempos faster than the normal capacity of perception.

There is also experimentation with new notational systems and microtones. Antonio *Tauriello (b. 1931) uses microtonal intervals within the tempered scale and has developed a special notational system that makes scores such as *Transparencias* for six instrumental groups (1965) look and sound like abstract designs. I have been working in this area, too, but microtonal structures in my music are outside the framework of the tempered scale, incorporating all possible frequencies. At times these frequencies are so close together that they produce "beats"; at other times they may form dense microtonal clusters that sound like colored noise. I use a three-line notational system together with colored ink. In such works as *Strobo I* for double bass, percussion, lights, audience, and electronic sounds (1967–68), the performer is asked to produce sounds lower or higher than the normal register of his instrument. He does this by "untuning" the instrument, by amplifying weak, otherwise inaudible, overtones, and producing noises in unusual ways.

An interest in electronic music has been stimulated by the laboratory for electronic music at the Di Tella Institute and by some of the Argentines who have been living abroad. Mario Davidovsky (b. 1934, living in New York) is well known for his combinations of electronic and instrumental sounds. Edgardo Cantón (b. 1934, living in Paris) is interested in musique concrète; his *Voix Innouies* (1966) contains thick masses of colored noise that seem to merge into nothingness. Other composers are more interested in experiments with theatrical music. Mauricio *Kagel (b. 1932, living in Cologne) in *Sur scène* (1959–60) and Carlos* Alsina (b. 1941) in *Trío* for trombone, cello, and percussion (1967) make the visual element as important as the sound. Gandini has achieved a joyous humor, particularly in his *Ládieu* for piano, vibraphone, 3 percussion players, and conductor (1967).

BIBL.: Juan Carlos Paz, *Introducción a la música de nuestro tiempo* (Buenos Aires 1955); Pola Suarez Urtubey, *Alberto Ginastera* (Buenos Aires 1967).

Alcides Lanza

Argento, Dominick (Joseph) (b. York, Pa., 27 Oct 1927), studied at the Peabody Conservatory (1947–51, 1953–54; composition with Hugo Weisgall, Nicholas Nabokov, Henry Cowell; piano with Alexander Sklarewski), the Cherubini Conservatory, Florence (1951–52; composition, Luigi Dallapiccola; piano, Pietro Scarpini), and at the Eastman School (1955–57; composition, Bernard Rogers, Howard Hanson, Alan Hovhaness). Since 1958 he has taught at the Univ. of Minnesota. A major influence on his recent development has been composing incidental

scores for stage productions by Tyrone Guthrie in Minneapolis (1965–69).

PRINCIPAL COMPOSITIONS (published by Boosey): *The Boor*, opera (1957); *6 Elizabethan Songs* for high voice, piano (1958); *Colonel Jonathan the Saint*, opera (1958–61); *Christopher Sly*, opera (1963); *The Masque of Angels*, opera (1964); *Royal Invitation, or Homage to the Queen of Tonga* for chamber orchestra (1964); *The Mask of Night*, variations for orchestra (1965); *The Shoemakers' Holiday*, opera (1966); *The Revelation of St. John the Divine*, rhapsody for tenor, men's chorus, brass, percussion (1966); *A Nation of Cowslips*, song cycle for chorus (1968); *Letters from Composers*, song cycle for tenor, guitar (1969); *Bravo Mozart!*, concerto for oboe, violin, horn, orchestra (1969).

SEE ALSO Opera.

Arizaga, Rodolfo (b. Buenos Aires, 11 July 1926), studied law at the National Univ. of Buenos Aires and music at the Conservatory there (1935–43) and went to Paris to study with Nadia Boulanger, Olivier Messiaen, and Ginette Martenot. He has taught at the National Univ. in Rosario (1960–61) and at the Universidad del Salvador in Buenos Aires (1967–69). He has also been music critic for *Clarin* in Buenos Aires (1946–64) and for *Primera Plana* (since 1964) and has written reviews and articles for a number of other Argentine publications as well. His first works were neoclassic in orientation; some were composed under the influence of Spanish impressionism. After studying with Messiaen he modified his techniques, and beginning with the *String Quartet No. 1* (1968) he has used any system or approach that best suits his needs. In some works he has allowed the performers various kinds of choice, sometimes through the medium of graphic notation.

PRINCIPAL COMPOSITIONS: *Martirio de Santa Olalla* for alto, 6 instruments (1952, EAMI); *Passacaglia* for string orchestra (1953, EAMI); *Delires*, cantata for soprano, women's chorus, orchestra (1957); *Piano Concerto* (1963); *Prometeo 45*, 1-act "poema dramático"; text by the composer (1962); *Música para Cristóbal Colón* for orchestra (1966, EAMI); *Misa angelica* for 6 solo voices, chorus (1966); *String Quartet No. 1* (1968); *El ombligo de los limbos, la momia y una encuesta* for alto, tenor, narrator, organ, percussion (1969); *Hymnus* for string orchestra (1971).

PRINCIPAL WRITINGS: *Manuel de Falla* (Buenos Aires 1961); *Juan Jóse Castro* (Buenos Aires 1963); *Enciclopedia de la música argentina* (Buenos Aires 1971).

BIBL.: "Los compositores argentinos: R. A.," *La Prensa* (Buenos Aires, 13 Feb 1968); Jacobo Romano, "Músicos de hoy: R. A.," *Buenos Aires musical* (15 Dec 1968).

Arnell, Richard (Anthony Sayer) (b. London, 15 Sept 1917), studied at the Univ. College School and the Royal College of Music (1935–39, composition with John Ireland). In 1939 he moved to New York. He was the BBC's North American music consultant during 1943–45. He returned to London in 1947 and was appointed professor of composition at Trinity College in 1948. In 1964–65 he founded *Composer* magazine. Arnell was a Fulbright exchange lecturer at Boudoin College, Nebraska (1967–68), and an exchange professor at Hofstra Univ., N.Y. (1968–69).

PRINCIPAL COMPOSITIONS (published by Hinrichsen unless otherwise noted): *The Land*, film score (1940, unpub.); *Harlequin in April*, ballet (1951); *Lord Byron*, symphonic portrait (1952); *Landscapes and Figures* for orchestra (1956); *Symphony No. 5* (1957); *Moon Flowers* opera (1958); *Robert Flaherty—Impression* for orchestra (1960); *Piano Concerto No. 2* (1966–67); *The Food of Love*, orchestral overture (1968).

Arnold, Malcolm (Henry) (b. Northampton, England, 21 Oct 1921), studied at the Royal College of Music (1938–40; composition with Gordon Jacob, conducting with Constant Lambert, trumpet with Ernest Hall). He was a trumpeter in the London Philharmonic (1940–42, 1946–48) and BBC Symphony (1945–46). Since then he has been a free-lance composer and conductor.

PRINCIPAL COMPOSITIONS (with dates of composition unless otherwise noted): ★ Concertos (with orchestra unless otherwise noted): for horn, strings (1944, Lengnick); clarinet, strings (1949, Lengnick); piano duet, strings (published 1951, Lengnick); oboe, strings (1952, Paterson); flute, strings (1954, Paterson); harmonica (1954, Paterson); horn (1956, Paterson); organ (1960, Paterson); guitar (1961, Paterson); 2 violins, strings (1962, Faber); 2 pianos (1969, Faber). ★ Other works: *Beckus the Dandipratt*, comedy overture (1943, Lengnick); *Viola Sonata* (1947, Lengnick); *Violin Sonatas Nos. 1–2* (1947, Lengnick; 1953, Paterson); *The Smoke*, overture (1948, Lengnick); *English Dances* for orchestra (1950, Lengnick); *Symphonies Nos. 1–6* (published 1952, Lengnick; 1953, 1958, 1960, 1961, Paterson; 1967, Faber); *Homage to the Queen*, ballet (1953); *Trio* for flute, viola, bassoon (1954, Paterson); *Tam O'Shanter*, overture (1955, Paterson); *Solitaire*, ballet (1956); *Quintet* for flute, horn, bassoon, violin, viola (1960, Paterson); *Quintet* for 2 trumpets, horn, trombone, tuba (1961, Paterson); *Peterloo*, overture (1968, Faber).

BIBL.: R. Murray Schafer, *British Composers in Interview* (London 1963).

Arrigo, Girolamo (b. Palermo, Sicily, 2 April 1930), studied at the Bellini Conservatory in Palermo (1950–54) and privately with Max Deutsch in Paris (1954–57). He lives in Paris and is a free-lance composer. Dante and Karl Marx have been important influences on his development.

PRINCIPAL COMPOSITIONS: *2 Epigrammi* for soprano, mezzo-soprano, tenor, baritone, bass; texts by Michelangelo (1956, Heugel); *String Trio* (1957, Bruzzichelli); *3 Occasioni* for soprano, 32 instruments; texts by Eugenio Montale (1958, Heugel); *Fluxus* for 9 instruments (1959, Bruzzichelli); *4 Occasioni* for 7 voices, horn, viola, mandolin, guitar, celesta; texts by Montale (1959, Bruzzichelli); *Serenata* for guitar (1960, Heugel); *Epitaffi* for chorus, orchestra; texts by Michelangelo (1961, Ricordi); *Episodi* for soprano, flutist; texts by Sappho, Stesichorus, Anacreon (1963, Heugel); *Thumos* for winds, percussion (1964, Heugel); *Shadows* for orchestra (1965, Bruzzichelli); *Petit Requiem pour une troisième possibilité* for 9 instruments (1967, Bruzzichelli); *Infrarosso* for 16 instruments (1967, Bruzzichelli); *Seven Against Thebes*, incidental music for the play by Euripedes (1968); *Eclatement* and *Funerailles* for 6 horns, 6 trombones (1969, Ricordi); *Orden*, a collage opera consisting of the following: "E venne la notte" for soprano, 2 mezzo-sopranos, baritone; "Acte d'anticipation" for 12 voices; "Le Soleil et la mort" for 12 men's voices, text by Pierre Bourgeade; "Chant de l'exode" for baritone, Hammond organ, 2 horns, text by Bourgeade; "Jinete del pueblo" for soprano, mezzo-soprano, baritone, cello, double bass, 2 percussionists, text by Rafael Alberti; "Adios recuerdos" for 2 sopranos, mezzo-soprano, tenor, baritone, bass, 4 trombones, text by Miguel Hernandez; "Dalla nebbia verso la nebbia" for 6 cellos, 6 double basses (1969, Ricordi); *L'Illusion comique*, incidental music for the play by Corneille (1970); *La Nuit bulgare*, film score (1970).

Arutiunian, Aleksander (Grigor) (b. Yerevan, Armenia, 23 Sept 1920), studied at the Yerevan State Conservatory (1936–41, composition with V. Talian, piano with O. Babassian). During 1946–48 he studied privately in Moscow with H. Litinski, Nikolai Peiko, Victor Zuckerman, and Rogal-Levitzki. During this time he became acquainted with Miaskovski, Shostakovich, Kabalevsky, and Khatchaturian, all of whom had a great influence on his further development. He has been director of the Armenian Philharmonic Society since 1954. Since 1957 he has been a member of the board of directors of the U.S.S.R. Composers Union and, since 1955, of the Armenian Composers Union.

PRINCIPAL COMPOSITIONS: *Piano Concerto* (1941); *Overture No. 1*, "Ours Is the Right Cause" (1942); *Overture No. 2*, "Concertante" (1944); *Polyphonic Partita* for piano (1945); *Triumphal March* for orchestra (1947); *Solemn Ode* for orchestra (1947); *Symphonic Poem in Memory of Colonel Zakiyan*, composed with E. Mirzoyan (1948); *Cantata about the Motherland* (1949); *Festive Overture* (1949); *Cantata about Lenin*, composed with E. Mirzoyan (1950); *Concerto* for coloratura soprano, orchestra (1950); *Trumpet Concerto* (1950); *Concertino* for piano, orchestra (1951); *Dance Suite* for orchestra (1953); *Symphony No. 1* (1958); *Tale about the Armenian People*, vocal-symphonic poem (1961); *Horn Concerto* (1962); *Sayat-Nova*, opera (1963–69); *Concerto* for flute, oboe, clarinet, horn, trumpet (1964); *Symphoniette* for chamber orchestra (1966).

PRINCIPAL WRITINGS: Arutiunian has written reports for Yerevan periodicals on Shostakovich's concerts in Yerevan, Aram Khachaturian's 60th birthday, and Benjamin Britten's visit to Armenia.

Ascone, Vicente (b. Siderno, Italy, 16 August 1897), moved to Montevideo with his family when still a child and studied harmony and composition there with Luis Sambucetti and trumpet with Aquiles Gubitesi. He has taught at the Verdi Institute in Montevideo and the Municipal Music School of Paysandú (1963–68). He is presently director and professor of composition at the Municipal Music School in Montevideo. He has been a trumpeter with the SODRE Orchestra, director of the Montevideo Municipal Band (1940–54), and continues to appear as an orchestral conductor.

PRINCIPAL COMPOSITIONS: *Suite uruguaya* for orchestra (1926); *Paraná Guazú*, 4-act opera (1930); *Acentos de America* for orchestra (1940); *Rapsodié criolla* for piano, orchestra (1944); *Sobre el Rio Uruguay* for orchestra (1946); *Symphonies Nos. 1–3* (1948, 1955, 1964); *String Quartets Nos. 1–2* (1948, No. 2 undated); *3 Estampas campesinas* for orchestra (1960); *Politonal* for piano, orchestra (1967); *Trumpet Concerto* (1969); *Violin Concerto* (1970). Ascone has also written 6 ballets, 5 operas, and many songs; list to 1970: *Composers of the Americas* 16.

BIBL.: *Compositores musicales uruguayos* (Montevideo 1969); Roberto Lagarmilla, *Compositores uruguayos* (Montevideo 1970); Susana Salgado, *Breve historia de la música culta en el Uruguay* (Montevideo 1971).

[prepared with the help of Susana Salgado]

Ashley, Robert (b. Ann Arbor, Mich., 28 March 1930), attended the Univ. of Mich. (1948–52, MusB with a major in theory; 1957–60, composition and acoustics), and the Manhattan School of Music (1952–54, MusM, major in piano and composition). During 1958–66 he and the composer Gordon Mumma operated the Cooperative Studio for Electronic Music in Ann Arbor, and from 1960 to 1961 he was a research assistant in acoustics at the Univ. of Mich. He collaborated with the painter-sculptor Milton Cohen during 1958–64 on "Space Theater" programs combining projections and amplified sound. Ashley has toured with the program "New Music for Pianos" (1961–68) and with the Sonic Arts Group (since 1966). He has directed the ONCE Group, a multimedia ensemble based in Ann Arbor, since 1963, and was coorganizer of the ONCE Festival (1961–68). In 1969 he became director of the Mills College Center for Contemporary Music. He has produced film sound tracks, and acknowledges "the very strong influence of film form and the manner of film production (group effort directed toward an abstract goal)."

PRINCIPAL COMPOSITIONS: *Sonata* for piano (1959); *The 4th of July* on monaural tape (1960, CPE); *Maneuvers for Small Hands* for piano (1961); *Detroit Divided* on 4-channel tape (1962); *Trios* (*White on White*) for various instruments (1963, CPE); *in memoriam . . . Esteban Gomez*, (quartet) for any instruments (1963, CPE); *in memoriam . . . John Smith*, (concerto) for any instruments (1963, CPE); *in memoriam . . . Crazy Horse*, symphony (1963, CPE); *in memoriam . . . Kit Carson*, opera (1963, CPE); *The Wolfman* on monaural tape (1964, CPE; ESP record 1009); *The Wolfman* for amplified voice, tape (1964 CPE; recording included in the periodical *Source*, vol. 4); *Kittyhawk* (*An Antigravity Piece*), electronic music theater (1964, *Tulane Drama Review* vol. 10, no. 2); *Combination Wedding and Funeral*, electronic music theater (1964, *Tulane Drama Review* vol. 10, no. 2); *Quartet* for any number of instruments (1965, published in *Selmer Bandwagon* vol. 13, no. 5); *Untitled Mixes* on tape (1965, ESP record 1009); *She Was a Visitor* for speaker, chorus (1967, CPE); *That Morning Thing*, electronic music theater (1967); *The Trial of Anne Opie Wehrer and Unknown Accomplices for Crimes against Humanity*, electronic music theater (1968); *Purposeful Lady Slow Afternoon*, electronic music theater (1968, Time record); *The Wolfman Motorcity Revue*, electronic music theater (1968).

PRINCIPAL WRITINGS: Articles on the ONCE Group in *Tulane Drama Review* 10:187–202, *Arts in Society* (spring 1968):86–89, and *Source* 3:19–22.

BIBL.: H. Wylie Hitchcock, "Current Chronical," *Musical Quarterly* (April 1962):244–48; Udo Kasemets, "Current Chronical," *ibid.* (Oct 1964):515–19; Gordon Mumma, "Technology in the Modern Arts: Music and Theater," *Chelsea* 20–21:99–110; ——, "The ONCE Festival and How It Happened," *Arts in Society* (summer 1967):381–98; Robert Sheff and Mark Slobin, "Music Beyond the Boundaries," *Generation* (Univ. of Mich., fall and winter 1965):27–65, 55–95.

SEE ALSO Instrumental and Vocal Resources, Mixed Media, Performance, Prose Music, Text Setting and Usage, United States.

Asian Music and Western Composition. From the rise of polyphony to the decline of romanticism, Asian music played an insignificant role in the musical world of the West, providing at best decorative features in the days of Turkish marches and *Scheherazade*. In the present century, however, Asian music has emerged as an influence of growing significance on the development of Western music. The turning point took place almost a century ago when Debussy became disillusioned with Wagner, was drawn toward symbolism and impressionism, and was exposed to an Indonesian gamelan at the 1889 International Exhibition in Paris.

EARLY 20TH-CENTURY PARALLELS. When Debussy spoke of Javanese music as being based on a counterpoint beside which that of Palestrina pales, he revealed himself as having perceived not only the multilayer structure in gamelan music but also its rhythmic intricacy, neither of which was suspected by his fellow composers. A gamelan composition is based on the principle that a nuclear theme is played simultaneously with several layers of elaboration on the theme in different registers and at different paces. Instruments with characteristic timbres are assigned to specific registers for particular types of elaboration. (The gamelan principle is not unique to Southeast Asia. For instance, the Korean *Hyang ak*—court music for an orchestra of winds, strings, and percussion—employs a similar principle of simultaneous elaborations.) The sonority of the Debussyian orchestra is largely the admixture of a number of melodic, rhythmic, registral, and timbral variants of a single linear movement; in this respect it is similar to gamelan sonority and may, in view of Debussy's comment, have been a conscious adaptation. For an example one need hardly look beyond one score, *La Mer*, with such passages as at rehearsal Nos. 5, 14, 54–55, and 62–63. Another common characteristic of Asian music is the subtle use of indefinite-pitched percussion, and Debussy may also have been the first Western composer to recognize the lyrical qualities of the percussion. The opening "Scherzando" of *Jeux* may well be the first conscious step in the West in using percussion according to Asian standards; witness the simple figure on the tambourine and cymbal, which answers the same figure played *sul ponticello* by muted violas. Asian influence is again suggested by a comment of Debussy, that beside Asian percussion instruments those of the West produce the noise of a traveling circus. (Whether Debussy based his whole-tone scale on the *slendro* scale—a pentatonic scale of seemingly equidistant intervals that are in fact minutely different from each other—is a matter of historical interest but of less consequence conceptually.)

The mystic or emotive power in music has been the subject of serious investigations in China and India. Western composers, too, have been attracted to the idea. Scriabin was devoted to theosophy and to his dream of creating a pantheistic "Mystery," but apparently this did not lead him to any genuine insight into Asian music. The serialized aspect of his "mystic chord" has no real relation to the Indian raga. His idea of correlating pitches in the order of the cycle of fifths to the color spectrum is obviously related to the belief, almost universal among ancient civilizations as well as in medieval Europe, in correlating musical tones to the seasons, cardinal points, substances, and other natural phenomena. One wonders, though, whether Scriabin was aware of the Indian concept of equating scale tones to specific colors and emotions or the Chinese concept by which such associations are also extended to timbre (an important classical Chinese concept is that timbre and pitch are the two primary resources in music). Two other composers of this generation who were also attracted to Eastern philosophy and theosophy were the Englishmen Gustav Holst and Cyril Scott. Despite their interest in scalar material, harmony, and rhythm, however, the Eastern influence in their music produced no more than a superficial exoticism.

Two major composers who began their careers at the turn of the century had contacts with Eastern music and were at first primarily known for their assimilation of folk and exotic elements: Stravinsky and Bartók. Some of the Russian folk music Stravinsky knew was of Asian origin, and the influence of that great orientalist, Rimsky-Korsakov, must not be underestimated. Much has been said of the rhythm, orchestral sonority, and melodic material that characterize the preneoclassic Stravinsky. The source of some of his ideas cannot be satisfactorily ascertained, particularly in view of his reticence on this subject. Nevertheless it is inconceivable that he was immune to the types of Asian music that permeated plebeian musicmaking in the Russia he knew. A likely example of conscious reference to some Asian technique is the opening of *Les Noces*; here the use of grace notes with intervals larger than a second produces a sliding attack that is typical of certain Asian singing styles.

With Bartók there is no ambiguity as to his involvement in serious studies of musical cultures of non-Western origin; he studied not only East European folk music but also Arab and Turkish music. In him we have a unique example of how successfully ethnomusicological inquiries by a composer can influence his own esthetics and techniques. Even more significant than his assimilation of the materials he studied is his attitude toward such inquiries: In studying non-Western music one must consider the character and tradition of its culture as well as all the inherent qualities of the material itself, not all of which are perceptible or definable according to established Western concepts. In musical terms this would include at least the awareness of the tuning system, instrumental characteristics or vocal qualities employed, performing technique, inflection in pitch and rhythm, as well as theoretical and philosophical ramifications. Even if Bartók did not fully explore certain intrinsic qualities of the music he studied, such as microtonal inflection, his melody, harmony, rhythm, and instrumental idiom were fundamentally the result of his ethnomusicological studies. While these Bartókian features have been imitated extensively, the promising path his attitude pointed to has remained largely untrodden by composers to this day.

Two other composers of the same generation, Webern and Varèse, came from an emphatically Western tradition and were not exposed as young men to any notable Eastern influences, yet the style of each echoes Eastern concepts. Webern's concern with clarifying motivically generated structures with highly variegated textures meticulously defined in regard to articulation, timbre, register, duration, etc., reminds one of certain types of Asian music in which the shifting melodic structure would seem either static or erratic were it not similarly defined. The music for *ch'in* (a Chinese zither), for example, is impossible to understand if one recognizes only that it is in a sort of variation form and is based on a single mode, usually pentatonic. The meaning of the music derives from the great variety in articulation, the almost continuous change in timbre, the pitch inflections, and the diverse types of vibratos employed. Nor can Webern, particularly in his preserial works (e.g., *6 Bagatelles*, Op. 9, and *3 Little Pieces* for cello and piano, Op. 11), be understood purely in terms of pitch relationship. His concern with all the definable physical characteristics of individual tones is conceptually and esthetically in sympathy with important categories of Asian music. Varèse's concept of music as "organized sound" and of sound as "living matter," which in itself is of historic consequence, is

again a modern Western parallel of a pervasive Chinese concept: that each single tone is a musical entity in itself, that musical meaning lies intrinsically in the tones themselves, and that one must investigate sound to know tones and investigate tones to know music.[1] This concept, often shrouded in poetic and mystic metaphors, is fundamental to many Asian musical cultures. It is manifest in the great emphasis placed on the production and control of tones, often involving an elaborate vocabulary of articulations, modifications in timbre, inflections in pitch, fluctuations in intensity, vibratos, and tremolos as in *ch'in* music. Another example is the solo music for such wind instruments as the Japanese *shakuhachi* (an end-blown flute) and the Korean *piri* (a double-reed instrument), in which the lip aperture and air pressure are meticulously regulated to achieve such a vocabulary. Such concentration on the values of a single tone is the antithesis of traditional Western polyphonic concepts, in which the emphasis on multilinearity and reliance on equal temperament make the application of such values limited and subordinate. In wishing to "liberate sound" from "mechanical restrictions" and to replace the "interplay of melodies" by a "melodic totality,"[2] Varèse was referring to sound in the Confucianist sense—that which one must investigate as the first step toward music. This perception of music is fundamentally non-Western but has now come to be accepted as characteristically 20th century. While Varèse was more concerned with complex aggregates of sounds than individual ones, with the growth potential of the interval components of nuclear ideas than with continual melodic movement, his music suggests a strong affinity with Asian music. This affinity is strikingly demonstrated by a curious coincidence between the opening of *Intégrales* and that of the *ha* movement of a *togaku* composition (Japanese court music of Chinese origin). The trumpets and the E♭ clarinet have the same function as the *ryuteki* (a transverse flute) and the *hichiriki* (a double-reed instrument), carrying the linear material that represents the nuclear idea of the work. The piccolos and the B♭ clarinet provide sonorities in the upper register as does the *sho*

[1]Cf. *Yüen Chi*, a Confucianist classic on music; Needham: 126ff. (see bibl.); R. H. van Gulik, *The Lore of the Chinese Lute* (Tokyo 1940): 22–26.

[2]Cf. Chou Wen-chung, "Open Rather than Bounded," *Perspectives* 5/1: 1–6; Edgard Varèse, "The Liberation of Sound" ed. by Chou, *Contemporary Composers on Contemporary Music* ed. by E. Schwartz and B. Childs (New York 1967): 196–208.

(a mouth organ). The trombones provide sonorities in the lower register as do the *koto* (a zither with movable bridges) and the *biwa* (a lute). The percussion ensemble adds a fourth stratum of sonority and rhythm comparable to the drums in *togaku*. In both cases, each stratum is of a specific timbre, has a specific function, moves within a specific register, and yet is closely related to the same linear material.

Such close parallels with Asian concepts were not characteristic of another revolutionary, Schoenberg. The function of a 12-tone set has sometimes been compared to that of an Indian raga, but any similarities are strictly one-dimensional. To begin with, the transposition and transformation of the set have no parallel in the use of a raga. While the fact that a raga has both a pitch content and a motive content is perhaps comparable to the pitch content and the partitioning of a set, the ordering in a raga takes place largely within each motive. Essentially, improvisation on a raga is more a permutation of motives than an ordering of pitches. On the other hand, each tone in a raga is regarded as having its own specific expression within the expressive context of the raga. (In *Brihaddesi* the Indian sage Matanga defines the word *svara*—tone—as "that which shines by itself" and the meaning of the term as "the sound that generates an expression.") The expression of individual tones is emphasized systematically by the use of *gamakas*, often translated as ornaments but involving far more than the external embellishment of an existing melody with simple devices. *Gamakas* have their own expressive values and are assigned to specific tones according to the tones' structural relationship within a raga. Moreover the execution of a *gamaka* can be highly intricate, involving subtle inflections in pitch, timbre, and loudness. This emphasis on expressive as well as structural functions of single tones and short motives is foreign to Schoenberg's ideas. Finally a raga functions with a tala, which specifies the time units to be employed, their groupings, and the stresses. (The influence of the tala concept on Olivier Messiaen's rhythmic concept, evolved in the 1930s, will be noted later. Milton Babbitt's application of the set operations to rhythmic organization since the late 1940s represents an independent Western development that is conceptually unrelated to the tala.)

At the time when serialism and neoclassicism were still incipient, a third movement emerged, microtonalism. Speculations and experiments in microtonal tuning and usage in Western music can be traced back to the renaissance, but it was not until the 1920s, when composers such as Alois *Hába became persistent and productive, that a microtonal movement could be said to have begun. The movement, which spread from Russia (Ivan Wyschnegradsky) to Mexico (Julián Carrillo), was in part stimulated by an increasing awareness of non-Western music, especially Arab fretting systems, the Indian system of 22 *srutis* to the octave, the pitch inflections so prominent in most non-Western cultures, and the various multiple-division systems investigated in China. While Hába became interested in quarter tones as a result of exposure to Slovak folk music, the American Harry Partch and some other prominent microtonalists were fully aware of the various Chinese, Indian, and Arab systems. Still others made studies of other Asian tunings.

DEVELOPMENTS IN THE U.S. Harry Partch's dedication to his 43-tone, just-intonation system is concomitant with his emulation of characteristically non-Western sound qualities and Eastern performance techniques and philosophies of music. Born in Oakland, Calif., he has been much exposed to Asian music and theater. With him we come to a group of American composers who either came from the West Coast or had connections with Asia, who learned from Eastern music, and who have helped make the U.S. the center of activities in assimilating non-Western musical ideas and practices. These composers include Henry Cowell, Alan Hovhaness, Lou Harrison, Colin McPhee, and John Cage. There are many possible causes for the central role of the U.S. in recent years: its geographical proximity with Asia, the presence of Asians and Africans in the population, the long history of intercommerce unhampered by overt political and cultural colonization, the rise of ethnomusicological studies, the permanent residence or frequent visits of many Asian composers and musicians, and finally the evangelistic work of the composers mentioned.

Serious concern with Asian music on the part of American composers was shown from the turn of the century, for example by John Alden Carpenter and Charles Griffes, who were led via impressionism to a kind of orientalism that was, despite its inconsequential character, responsible for some of their more successful efforts. Another American, Henry Eichheim, actually traveled in East Asia studying and collecting musical material and instruments. As early as the 1920s he was using Asian instruments and authentic material in his orchestral works. Unfortunately, despite his sincerity and personal experience, his works are merely experimental and technically crude. The Franco-American composer, Dane Rudhyar, was strongly influenced by Scriabin but is a more knowledgeable student than he of Eastern philosophy and mysticism. His criticisms in the 1920s of traditional Western concepts of music parallel those of Varèse except for Rudhyar's reference to Asian ideas and psychic power. He claimed that the Western composer is not concerned with "the single tones which will be heard" but only with the pitch relationship based on "soundless abstractions of tone, the musical notes," which are not precisely defined as sound in terms of its physical and emotive attributes. On the contrary, he maintained, every tone heard is "a complex entity," and in Asian music one is indeed "confronted with living tones."[3] This clearly reflects the Chinese and Indian concepts referred to previously. Rudhyar was not the first to have recognized this quality in Asian music. Earlier, among others, Edward MacDowell correctly surmised that to the Chinese "the texture of a sound is to be valued." But he interpreted this in a negative way: "sound without music" that lacks "some quality which will remove it from the purely sensuous."[4] The MacDowell misconception remains to this day as a principal obstacle for many in understanding either Asian or contemporary music.

The West Coast group, strongly influenced by Asian music, soon emerged as an important facet in contemporary American music. Cowell was the foremost of this group. Growing up in California, he was fully exposed to Asian cultures. He later traveled widely in Asia and elsewhere, studying the music of various cultures and collecting material. Eventually he became the chief publicist for Asian music in this country, arousing interest among composers and laymen alike. He advocated a "world music," firmly believing in a synthesis of East and West; indeed his early use of tone-clusters and his exploration of tone qualities to be obtained inside the piano may have been the result of his early exposure to Asian music. In his works, however, while achieving a level of sophistication unmatched by his predecessors, his assimilation of Asian concepts and practices failed to rise above the simplism that characterized American music of the 1930s and 40s.

The position of Hovhaness is essentially the same as that of Cowell, although his esthetic

response to the material he learned from the East is deeper and his technique more advanced. His stylistic revaluation in the late 1940s was due basically to his Armenian ancestry, his study of Central Asian melodic procedures, and his disillusion with contemporary preoccupation with the "artifice" in music. His recent works tend to be influenced more by his contacts with East and South Asian music.

Harrison and Cage both started on the path of "orientalization" early in their careers. But, as sensitive as some of their early works are, such as the gamelan-inspired *Double-Music* written in collaboration, their music contains a tint of neo-chinoiserie. The adoption of Indian, Indonesian, or Japanese melodic or rhythmic treatment in Western notation for Western instruments—disregarding such life-giving elements in the original models as constant subtle modifications in pitch, rhythm, and timbre, the emphasis on the production and control of tones, the value placed on the expressive as well as the structural functions of single tones—is not really different from the 19th-century practice of forcing an oriental melody into tonal harmony. In recent years, however, Harrison has been studying the instruments and music of several Asian cultures and has apparently developed new insights. In combining his use of just intonation with microtones played on Asian instruments and in exploring the potentials rather than merely borrowing the procedures of Asian music, he has embarked on a new and promising path. The presence of Asian instruments in his recent works is at least more conceptually integrated than it is in works of others, such as Cowell and Hovhaness, where novelty tends to take precedence despite a genuine love for the instrument in question.

Aside from his early interest in Eastern music, Cage, the most influential of the West Coast group, is particularly notable for his adaptation of certain philosophical ideas from the East, which has stimulated significant debate on the meaning of composition and performance. There is, however, a need for clarification in regard to how his interpretation of these ideas corresponds to the original. The prepared piano was invented out of necessity (to provide percussion sounds without the instruments) for *Bacchanale* (1938); nevertheless, its sound qualities are akin to such pitched percussion instruments as the *saron*, *gender*, and *ranat ek* commonly employed in gamelans. In the composer's most important work for prepared piano, *Sonatas and Interludes* (1946–48), he made an "attempt

---

[3] Dane Rudhyar, *Art as Release of Power* (New York 1930): 22–23, 27.

[4] Edward MacDowell, *Critical and Historical Essays* ed. by W. J. Baltzell (Boston 1912): 263.

to express in music the 'permanent emotions' of Indian tradition."[5] Here Cage is apparently referring to the *sthayi bhava*, the primary states of mind. In art the *bhavas* are the seed that bring about the *rasa*, the esthetic response aroused by emotions that are suprasensuous. In Indian theory each of the 22 *srutis* has its own emotive value, and the *rasa* of a raga is determined by the *sruti* content of its scale tones as well as by the emphasis given to certain tones and motives; that is, the question of emotion is a structural matter that functions at various levels in a composition. Whether Cage's piano preparation can be equated with the Indian concept of seeding the material with appropriate sounds is a debatable point.

Cage later turned his attention to *I Ching* and Zen and evolved the chance operations first used in 1951 in *Music of Changes* and *Imaginary Landscape No. 4*. *I Ching* is a book of philosophy based on the principle of *I*, which originates from the interaction of the two cosmic forces of *yin* and *yang* and is manifest in natural phenomena, human events, and states of mind. It is also a book used for divination and for oracular pronouncements. Its foundation is a system of eight symbolic images called *kua* (trigrams). Each of these images consists of three lines, each representing one of the two polar opposites, *yin* and *yang*. The images represent the forces that interact with each other in a state of perpetual transformation and superimposition and germinate all things in the universe. The meaning of each of the 64 resultant composite images, called hexagrams, is revealed through a metaphoric text. As philosophy, the *I* principle refers, on one level, to simplicity from which complexity evolves; on another level, phenomena out of complexity; on still another level, conglomeration and dispersion of phenomena; and finally, invariability. It is the idea of invariability that makes the reading of the text of a hexagram a source of wise counsel, as the interaction of a given set of objective events and subjective states of mind is predictable.

A hexagram is arrived at by means of involved numerical operations with the aid of 49 yarrow stalks, a procedure that is regarded as being numerologically related to the cosmic forces. This procedure is not based on causality, nor is it merely a matter of chance, since the interpretation of the text is a crucial step involving the complex interdependence of the interpreter's culture, experience, knowledge, and emotions. Thus, arriving at a hexagram is a supraconscious act that is meaningful only if it is followed by a conscious act of interpreting the text. Cage's application of *I Ching* does not take the text into consideration but merely translates each hexagram into a preassigned musical value.[6] In this regard the use of a computer for applying the digital principle of *I Ching* in *HPSCHD* (1967–69), a joint work with Lejaren Hiller, has not changed Cage's position. Taking a scientific rather than a philosophical view, one could regard *I Ching* as a "cosmic filing-system" based on binary arithmetic or as a "repository of concepts" to which all events and processes in nature can be referred.[7] In this sense, Iannis *Xenakis's idea of a "stochastic music" is closer to the concept of *I Ching* than Cage's; and when György *Ligeti speaks of "global categories" involving the interrelationship of "register and density, distribution of various types of movement and structure," and of "compositional design of the *process* of change,"[8] he too is closer to applying the principle of events and processes in *I Ching*.

In regard to Zen, Cage says in the foreword to *Silence* that he frees it of "any responsibility" for his actions. Nevertheless Zen is frequently referred to or inferred in his lectures, and even the title *Silence* is clearly a reference to Zen as the philosophy of silence, that is to *wu* (no-thing-ness), which cannot be expounded upon. But the "subconscious" and the "unconscious" referred to by Cage in discussions of indeterminacy (*Silence*: pp. 35–40) are psychological and psychoanalytic concepts unrelated to *wu nien* (no-thought), the Zen idea of unconsciousness. His philosophy of silence, chance, and indeterminacy is actually a modern American product for which certain external aspects of the Eastern originals served as the stimulant lending a mystic aura of orientalism. Nevertheless the neoexoticism in Cage may be serving the same purpose as a *kung an* in Zen, which is a seemingly senseless and enigmatic dialogue or story that is used to bring about Zen enlightenment by blocking the mind.

DEVELOPMENTS IN EUROPE. In addition to his impact in the U.S., Cage provoked a controversy in Europe in the mid-1950s, eventually causing his philosophy to become highly influential. That Karlheinz Stockhausen and

[5]Robert Dunn, *John Cage Catalogue* (New York 1962):17.

[6]John Cage, *Silence* (Middletown, Conn. 1961): 57–59.

[7]Joseph Needham, *Science and Civilisation in China*, vol. 2 (Cambridge, England 1954):304–45.

[8]György Ligeti, "Metamorphoses of Music Form," *Die Reihe*, English ed., 7:5–19.

Pierre Boulez, the two pacesetters in Europe at the time, both reacted with such a sense of immediacy demonstrates, on the one hand, the need for rejuvenating ideas and on the other, that existing musical concepts and techniques had been exploited to such an extent in Europe that musicians there were ready to entertain ideas fundamentally opposed to their own tradition. Cage's influence on Stockhausen was progressive, from performer choice in *Klavierstück XI* (1956) to an almost Cage-like theater piece, *Originale* (1961), to the realization procedures in the electronic *Microphonie I* (1964). Boulez criticized Cage for his "adoption of a philosophy tinged with orientalism that masks a basic weakness in compositional technique." Rejecting Cage's use of chance as "through inadvertence," he proposed to "absorb" it and to "integrate chance into the notion of structure itself."[9] He used the Latin-derived term "aleatory" to denote this concept of chance, perhaps to remove any tinge of orientalism. He also cited the performance practice of Indian ragas (without, however, fully appreciating the esthetic and technical factors that control the improvisational procedures) in suggesting the use of structural "formants" as a new compositional principle to absorb chance. This, he felt, would retain the "closed cycle" principle of occidental music while introducing the "open development" concept of the Orient. Not surprisingly, the source of inspiration for Boulez's first work using the formant principle, the *Piano Sonata No. 3* (1957), was not Eastern but Mallarmé (also the inspiration behind the first work of Debussy to reflect Asian concepts and techniques, *Prélude à l'après-midi d'un faune*). In regard to performance practices called for in aleatory music, varying from the controlled open form of Boulez to the decontrolled indeterminacy of Cage, it should be noted that the improvisation involved is very different from that employed in Eastern music. First of all, not many types of Eastern music actually employ improvisation. Secondly, in some types the only improvisatory aspect is in an "elastic" as opposed to a "plastic" realization of the composed work. Finally, in the performance of a raga, where the art of improvisation is the kernel of the music, the performer must have been trained in the centuries-old tradition of the music and be thoroughly immersed in the material at hand: the tonal structure of the raga, the expressive values of the constituent *srutis*, the meaning of the

motivic fragments, the *gamakas* to be applied on certain tones, the manner in which the tala is to be elaborated, how the various forms of augmentation and diminution are permutated, when variants of the tala may be used, which other talas it can be combined with, and above all how these interacting factors are coordinated and musical events evolved according to the character and the structure of the raga and the tala and according to certain formal schemes. Clearly then this Indian art is highly disciplined, far from being "uncontrolled," "unconscious," or "nonrational," as is commonly assumed when it is cited as precedent in support of aleatory practices. The Asian concept of improvisation, which could doubtless enrich contemporary Western music, is yet to be understood and studied seriously by Western composers.

It is significant that both Boulez and Stockhausen studied with Olivier Messiaen, the only major composer since Bartók to have successfully integrated what he learned from a non-Western culture with his own tradition (plainsong, Bach, and Debussy) without debasing the ideas acquired. The most significant aspect of Messiaen's career as teacher is the wide dissemination of his rhythmic theory, which resulted from his fascination with Indian music and his ruminations on the structure of some ancient Indian talas. His fundamental principles, such as "rhythms with added values" and "more complex forms" of augmentation or diminution, were inspired by the tala concept and its performance practice in which polyrhythmic and polymetric schemes may arise out of refined subdivisions of the time units, temporary superimposition of another tala, and augmentation or diminution in what appear as complex ratios in the Western musical tradition. These principles, already emerging in some works of the mid-1930s, were first systematically employed in the *Quatour pour la fin du temps* (1941) and described in the book, *The Technique of My Musical Language*.[10] Eventually they led to Messiaen's serialization of rhythmic values in *Mode de valeurs et d'intensités* (1949).

Indian influence on Messiaen is not limited to rhythm. While he learned from the "expressive melodic contours" of Gregorian chant, he was also attracted to the "exquisite, unexpected melodic contours" of Indian music. As he has pointed out, some of his meditative organ works based on Christian mysticism, such as *La Nativité du Seigneur*

[9]Pierre Boulez, "Alea" trans. by D. Noakes and P. Jacobs, *Perspectives* 3/1:42–53.

[10]Olivier Messiaen, *The Technique of My Musical Language*, trans. by J. Satterfield (Paris 1950).

(1935) and *Les Corps glorieux* (1939), not only feature Indian-inspired rhythm but "Indian melodic color"[11] as well. Even his use of bird-song is not unrelated to Indian procedures in melodic elaboration and transformation. For example, the variations on the call of a blackbird in "Amen des anges . . ." from *Visions de l'Amen* (1943) are reminiscent of the improvisatory executions of raga motives. Even more intriguing is Messiaen's penchant for verbal imagery in prescribing the character of his rhythmic, melodic, harmonic, and timbral ideas. This not only echoes the Indian concept of *rasa* but also finds a distant precedent in Chinese *ch'in* music, in which each finger technique and tone quality has a specific poetic and pictorial reference that defines the state of mind needed to express the meaning of the musical event. Some of Messiaen's images have close counterparts in *ch'in* imagery: "bee in the flower" / "butterfly over flowers"; "distant carillon" / "fading reverberations of a temple bell"; "a gust of wind" / "like the sound of wind". In all, Messiaen's music, thinking and teaching represent a major step in the integration of Western and non-Western musical concepts and techniques.

DEVELOPMENTS IN ASIA. A movement toward such an integration has also taken place in Asia in recent decades. Most notable among a number of prominent Asian composers who are at the center of this movement is the Korean Isang Yun, now living in Germany. His works, such as *Re-ak* for orchestra (1966) and *Om mani padme hum* for soprano, baritone, chorus, and orchestra (1964), are outstanding among attempts by composers with a similar aspiration. The East Asian elements in Yun's music include philosophy, formal ideas, structural principles, and sound material; above all is his meticulous attention to the articulation, propagation, and termination of single tones. In Japan a host of composers, such as Kazuo Fukushima, Toshi Ichiyanagi, Toshiro Mayuzumi, and Joji Yuasa, have written music that not only bears strong Western influence (ranging from serialism to electronic procedures, from Varèse to Cage) but is also permeated with such traditions as Zen, calligraphy, *shakuhachi* music, and Buddhist chanting. Toru Takemitsu of Japan and José Maceda of the Philippines have written the most successful examples thus far of music that either combines Eastern and Western instruments or is written for Asian instruments according to contemporary Western principles. In *November Steps* (1967) and

other works, Takemitsu has blended the two types of sonorities with remarkable success. However, the difference in attitude in the production and control of tones between the Western orchestra and the Japanese solo instruments remains a fissure in sound (which may perhaps be accepted as one of the compositional concepts employed). Though he is a less experienced composer, Maceda's attempts, such as *Kubing* (1966) and *Ugma Ugma* (1963), successfully explore the sonorities of Asian instruments, predominantly percussion, and of voices singing words taken from various Asian languages. The music is organized according to principles neither traditionally Eastern nor alien to the spirit of the East. His interest in phonemics is in the tradition of such categories of Asian vocal music as the Japanese *gidayu* and the Korean *pan sori*, in which individual speech sounds are often transformed into musical events according to their timbral values as well as the dramatic context of the words. (Similar use of phonemes by Luigi Nono, Luciano Berio, Salvatore Martirano, and other Western composers are far less successful.) So far the only Westerner who could have reciprocated these Asians' endeavor was the late Colin McPhee. A Canadian-American and a student of Varèse, he lived in Bali for many years, devoting himself to a thorough study of gamelan music. But aside from *Tabuh Tabuhan* (1936), which is only an adaptation of authentic Balinese material for the orchestra, McPhee did not produce any works that reflect his remarkable knowledge of Balinese music.

CONCLUSIONS. At the beginning of this century Gustav *Mahler used translated Chinese poems for his *Das Lied von der Erde*, a choice that surely affected his musical material and orchestral sonorities. The work is a spiritual summation of his time and a farewell to life on earth, and if Mahler is indeed a key link between the romantic era and our own, the last figure of the orthodox tradition in Western music, then perhaps it is more than symbolic that his "farewell" should have taken on an Asian accent. Perhaps he closed the door on musical regionalism—unobserved and not quite intentionally. Perhaps too Messiaen, Bartók, and others, each faithful to his own tradition and yet in quest of new pastures, have opened the gate for the confluence of musical currents, Western and non-Western—not quite unobserved but certainly not unintentionally.

BIBL.: Chou Wen-chung, "Single Tones as Musical Entities: An Approach to Structured Deviations in Tonal Characteristics," *American Society of*

[11]*Ibid.*: 33.

University Composers Proceedings 3 (1970); A. H. Fox-Strangway, *The Music of Hindostan* (London 1914); R. H. van Gulik, *The Lore of the Chinese Lute* (Tokyo 1940); Mantle Hood, "Music, The Unknown," *Musicology* (1963); William Malm, *Japanese Music and Musical Instruments* (Tokyo-Rutland, Vt. 1959); ———, *Music Cultures of the Pacific, the Near East, and Asia,* (Englewood Cliffs, N. J. 1967); Colin McPhee, *Music in Bali* (New Haven 1966); Joseph Needham, "Sound," *Science and Civilisation in China,* vol. 4, part 1 (Cambridge, England 1962); Curt Sachs, "The Lore of Non-Western Music," *Some Aspects of Musicology* (New York 1957); Egon Wellesz, ed., *Ancient and Oriental Music,* vol. 1 of *The New Oxford History of Music* (London 1957).

Chou Wen-chung

SEE ALSO Dance, Instrumental and Vocal Resources, Israel, Japan, Jazz, Rhythm.

Asriel, Andre (b. Vienna, 22 Feb 1922), studied at the State Academy in Vienna (1935–38; theory with Richard Stöhr, piano with Grete Hinterhofer), the Royal College in London (1939, piano with Frank Merrick), the Hochschule für Musik in Berlin (1947–49; composition with Hermann Wunsch, piano with Franz Rössler), and at the German Academy of the Arts in East Berlin (1950–51). He also studied composition privately in London with Ernst H. Meyer (1942) and piano there with Franz Osborn (1944–45). He has taught at the Hanns Eisler Hochschule since 1950. Until 1960 he performed publicly as an accompanist. Since 1942 he has written many political songs and since 1956 scores to over 30 films and documentaries. Influences on his music have ranged from Bach to Eisler and include jazz and folk music.

PRINCIPAL COMPOSITIONS: *Piano Sonata* (1953, Pro Musica); *6 Lieder* for medium voice, piano; texts by Bertolt Brecht (1954, Litolff-L); *8 Liebeslieder* for medium voice, piano; texts by Jens Gerlach (1955, Litolff-L); *Songs und Balladen,* vols. 1–2, for medium voice, piano (1957, 1964; Litolff-L); *Der Frieden,* musical theater; libretto based on Aristophanes (1962); *4 Inventions* for trumpet, trombone, orchestra (1963, Neue Musik); *Suite in Scat* for chorus, 3 rhythm sections (1965); *Polly,* musical theater; libretto based on John Gay (1965, Henschel); *6 Fabeln nach Aesop* for chorus (1967); *Faust I,* musical theater; libretto after Goethe (1968); *Serenade for Nonet* for winds, strings (1969).

PRINCIPAL WRITINGS: *Jazz* (Berlin 1966).

Asuar, José Vicente (b. Santiago, Chile, 20 July 1933), studied engineering at the Catholic

Univ. of Chile (1952–58) and at the Technische Univ. in Berlin (1959–60, information theory with Fritz Winckel) and music at the National Conservatory in Santiago (1952–58; composition with Jorge Urrutia-Blondell, orchestration with Juan Orrego-Salas) and the Berlin Hochschule für Musik (1959–60, composition with Boris Blacher). He also attended the seminars of Boulez, Stockhausen, Maderna, and Ligeti at the Darmstadt summer courses (1960–62) and was coached in electronic music by Werner Meyer-Eppler in Berlin in 1958. During 1958-59 he was director of the electronic music studio at the Catholic Univ. of Chile, during 1960–62 he organized the electronic music studio at Karlsruhe, and during 1965–68 he directed the Estudio de Fonologia Musical at Caracas. He has been director of the department of sound technology at the Univ. of Chile since 1969.

PRINCIPAL COMPOSITIONS: *Encadenamientos* for flute, bassoon, violin, cello (1957); *Variaciónes espectrales* on tape (1959); *Preludio la noche* on tape (1962); *Estudio aleatorio* on tape (1962); *Heterofonias* for orchestra (1965); *Octeto* for 4 flutes, 4 percussionists (1966); *La noche II* on tape (1966); *3 Ambientes sonoros* on tape (1968); *Guararia reparo* for Venezuelan Indian instruments, tape (1968); *Imagen de Caracas* for voices, instruments, tape (1968).

PRINCIPAL WRITINGS: *Generación mecanica y electronica del sonido musical* (thesis, Catholic Univ., Santiago, 1958); "Y . . . sigamos componiendo," *Revista musical chilena* 83:55–100; "Mi fin es mi comienzo," *ibid.* 89:43–78; "Fatalidades," *ibid.* 107:33–45.

SEE ALSO Chile.

Atonality, the absence from music of those pitch relations that 1) establish a key center (i.e., a tonality) or 2) are associated with the tonic-dominant tonal system. The absence of (2) helps to distinguish atonal music from passages of highly chromatic music that can be related, directly or indirectly, to a single tonality.

SEE ALSO Harmony and Counterpoint.

Attack, those amplitude characteristics having to do with the beginning of a sound or signal (sometimes called growth).

©*Music Educators Journal* (Nov 1968)

Atterberg, Kurt (Magnus) (b. Gothenburg, Sweden, 12 Dec 1887), studied civil engineering at the Royal Institute of Technology, Stockholm (1907–11), and music at the Stockholm Conservatory (1910–11, composition and instrumentation with A. Hallén). He considers himself largely self-taught, however. In 1912 he made his conducting debut in Gothenburg and during 1913–22 was conductor at the Royal Dramatic Theater, Stockholm. Since then he has conducted European orchestras in concerts featuring Swedish music. He has held several organizational posts and in 1914 and 1918 helped found the Society of Swedish Composers, of which he was chairman during 1924–47. Between 1912 and 1968 he worked in the radio division of the National Patent and Registration Office and during 1919–57 wrote musical criticism for the *Stockholm-Tidningen*. Atterberg's music uses traditional forms and borrows extensively from Swedish folk materials. His output includes five operas, three ballets, and chamber works, in addition to the instrumental pieces listed below.

PRINCIPAL COMPOSITIONS (published by Breitkopf unless otherwise noted): *Symphonies Nos. 1–8*, Opp. 3, 6, 10, 14, 20, 31, 45, 48 (1909–11; 1911–13, Nordiska; 1914–16; 1918; 1919–22; 1927–28, UE; 1942, Suecia; 1944, Suecia); *Violin Concerto in E Minor*, Op. 7 (1913); *Cello Concerto in C Minor*, Op. 21 (1917–22); *Horn Concerto in A* (1926); *Piano Concerto in B-Flat Minor*, Op. 37 (1927–35); *Symphony No. 9 in B-Flat Minor*, "Sinfonia visionaria," for mezzo-soprano, baritone, chorus, orchestra (1955–56, Suecia).

SEE ALSO Scandinavia.

Austin, Larry (b. Duncan, Okla., 12 Sept 1930), studied at North Texas State Univ., San Antonio College, Mills College, and the Univ. of Calif. at Berkeley. Since 1958 he has been professor of music at the Univ. of Calif. at Davis. In 1967 he cofounded and became editor of *Source*, a periodical devoted to music of the avant-garde.

The years before 1958 were devoted to composition training and to extensive performance as a modern-jazz improviser on trumpet and string bass. This background led to several works involving both jazz and concert techniques, culminating in *Improvisations for Orchestra and Jazz Soloists* (1961). The work does not focus so much on mixing disparate idioms as on using a fluent improvisatory language as a compositional element, bringing spontaneity and immediacy to the music. The experience gained in works such as this encouraged Austin and his colleagues at the Univ. of Calif. to form in 1963 the New Music Ensemble, a group of composer-performers

engaged in group improvisation and in the performance of new music. Over the next four years Austin applied improvisation techniques to a concept of form that he calls "open style," which was fully established in *Open Style for Orchestra with Piano Soloist* (1965). In this work a specified latitude of choice is available to the performers, who rely on a system of analog notation, using coordinates 1 centimeter apart, to control and coordinate the flow of the music. The rhythm is nonmetrical.

Later works have used open form processes combined with modern technological and theatrical resources. These works incorporate multiple visual and aural effects produced by live and taped electronic sounds, instruments and voices, films, lights, mirrors, actions, and television. Austin has described his theater piece *The Magicians* (1968): ". . . I don't wish it to be considered a piece of music. If one needs terms of reference . . . it might be considered a *time object*. . . . I wanted to take music out of the context of a dramatic flow of consequential events and to lose, as much as possible, the sense of time."

PRINCIPAL COMPOSITIONS: *Improvisations for Orchestra and Jazz Soloists* (1961, MJQ); *Continuum* for 2–7 instruments (1964); *Piano Variations* (1964, MJQ); *A Broken Consort* for 7 instruments (1964, MJQ); *Open Style for Orchestra with Piano Soloist* (1965, CPE); *The Maze*, theater piece in open style for 3 percussionists, tapes, machines, projections (1965, CPE); *Accidents* for electronically prepared piano, mirrors, actions, black light (1967, CPE); *Bass*, theater piece in open style for string bass, player, tape, film (1967, CPE); *Brass* for electronically amplified and modified brass instruments, film, slides (1967, CPE); *The Magicians* for children, live and taped electronic sounds, black light, slides, films (1968, CPE); *Piano Set* in open style (1968, CPE); *Transmission One*, video-audio electronic composition for color television broadcast (1969, video tape available from CPE); *Agape*, electronic masque for soloists, dancers, rock band, celebrants, tapes, projections (1970, CPE).

PRINCIPAL WRITINGS: "Preface," "Conversation," *Source* I/I:I, 3–37, 104–08; "Preface," *Source* I/2:I–3; "Events/Comments," *Source* 3/I: 75; "Is the Concerto Dead? Yes," *New York Times* (1 Sept 1968); "Music and Light," *Arts-canada* (Dec 1968); "Music is Dead, Long Live Music," *New York Times* (6 July 1969).

BIBL.: Gilbert Chase, "Improvisation and Open Style," *America's Music* (New York 1966):673–76; ——, "Toward a Total Theater," *Arts in Society* (spring 1969):25–39; Tod Dockstader, "Source," *Musical Quarterly* (Oct 1968):549–53; John Gillespie, "The Avant-Garde: L. A.," *The Musical Experience* (New York 1968):424–25.

Barney Childs

SEE ALSO Mixed Media, Performance, United States.

Australia. Truly contemporary music has arrived in Australia only since the 1960s, although it made sporadic appearances before this in some of the ideas (rather than the works) of Percy *Grainger (1882–1961); in Raymond Hanson (b. 1913), who has written in a post-Hindemithian style; in Margaret *Sutherland (b. 1897), the grand old lady of modern music in Australia; in John Antill (b. 1904), the only Australian composer to utilize Aborigine sources successfully; and in Robert Hughes (b. 1912), who has written in a postimpressionist idiom. In Europe, which has had a new-music movement since early in the century, composers such as Schoenberg, Stravinsky, Bartók, Hindemith, Berg, Varèse, and Webern are an acknowledged part of history. To the average concertgoer in Australia, these composers still represent avant-garde (unpleasant) music. Audiences seem to be maturing in other ways, however; for instance, letters to the press attacking various appraisals by critics indicate that some listeners are starting to form their own opinions.

Australia's strongly traditional heritage was transplanted from England by many visiting and resident English musicians and by Australians trained in England. Among the latter were Dorian Le Galliene (1915–63), educated at the Royal College of Music in London; William G. James (b. 1895); Miriam Hyde (b. 1913), another Royal College student known for her piano miniatures and concertos; Frank Hutchens (1892–1965), who studied at the Royal Academy and is also best known for his piano pieces; Roy Agnew (1893–1944), who studied at the Royal College, and English-born Fritz Hart (1874–1949) and Edgar Bainton (1880–1956), all three of whom were prolific composers and prominent educators. Probably the only prominent Australian composer with few ties to England was Alfred Hill (1870–1960), who nevertheless represents a continuation of the European romantic tradition. Although Australia's geographic isolation has contributed to the late arrival of new music, it is noteworthy that England, from which so much of her cultural heritage derives, also long resisted new trends despite its own proximity to the European continent.

In the 1950s, when most of the younger composers now gaining prominence were trained, the music textbooks in use were by Victorian English gentlemen. Music history ended with Vaughan Williams and Debussy, harmony and counterpoint began with Palestrina and ended with Elgar. Analysis took no cognizance of such 20th-century European approaches as that of Schenker. The primary and high schools, in general, still do not bring the student in contact with contemporary music in a really creative way. Only recently have state education authorities appreciated the importance of having a fully trained musician in the schools, and even today music may be taught by someone who merely has a free period and who leads class singing or plays records and reads the liner notes. Higher music education has been conducted in the conservatories, which have emphasized performance training, and in the universities, which have emphasized the academic musical subjects. These distinctions are beginning to break down, and the greater financial stability of the universities will probably bring them out on top. The development of the Canberra School of Music (founded 1965), which is modeled on the Juilliard School in New York, may point toward a flexible type of tertiary institution, amalgamating the best of both existing systems. In the meantime, although the conservatories remain conservative both in class courses and in student recital programming, many universities have been appointing younger composers to their staffs in recent years. This has given the universities a strong injection of vital, creative courses as well as outlooks aimed towards new music (though a paradox remains in that the universities depend on conservatory-trained students to perform new music). Some universities are also sponsoring performances, as well as the commissioning of both local and overseas works.

Major influences on music education in Australia are the yearly examinations in instruments and theoretical subjects that are administered by the Australian Music Examinations Board. Tens of thousands of candidates at every grade level are tested each year, and some educational institutions use the results as entrance qualifications. The board's repertory listings are overwhelmingly conservative, and only recently, in the higher grades, have a few modern works crept in (more contemporary music will probably be listed in the future).

Among the encouraging signs for new music are developments at the Australian Broadcasting Commission. There are now many broadcasts of important new-music events from around the world, and even radical Australian works appear in live and recorded broadcast concerts. In addition, the commission has recently begun processing stereo records of new Australian works and making them available for sale to educational institutions. Government support came in 1968 via the

Commonwealth Assistance to Australian Composers (CAAC), which is administered by a committee in the Prime Minister's Department. The budget for 1971 was about 30,000 Australian dollars. Funds are used to subsidize publications and performances of new music and to help composers during the time they need to complete a project. The program plans to subsidize recordings and has already begun issuing surveys of Australian music both on tape and in score, which are sent to major libraries all over the world. Australian publishers, partly as a result of CAAC subsidies, now issue not only short works aimed at the educational market but large-scale works as well; only a few years ago the more advanced composers had little chance of publication. A final encouraging note is the fact that there is a sympathetic press, centered mainly in Sydney, while press interest in new music in other cities ranges from moderately high in Canberra and Melbourne to very low in Brisbane. Fortunately the most informed and constructive critics are on the large and strategically located newspapers.

Among the prominent composers at work today are Nigel *Butterley (b. 1935), Peter *Sculthorpe (b. 1929), Donald *Hollier (b. 1934), Richard Meale (b. 1932), Felix *Werder (b. 1922), and myself (b. 1934). Together we represent a wide variety of approaches. Butterley is fond of setting sacred texts or being inspired by near-sacred material; *Laudes* (1963), for example, contains musical impressions of four European churches and *In the Head the Fire* (1966) contains sacred texts from several sources. Butterley has thus been represented at times as a mysticoreligious composer, but he rejects this label, citing instead his efforts to reach a broad public, not "a small band of initiates." Indeed he uses a more flamboyant and theatrical approach in such works as *The Tell-Tale Heart* (1961), an opera after Poe, and particularly in *Interactions* for painter, piano, and orchestral groups (1967).

An intensity of emotion pervades much of the music by Sculthorpe and myself. In Sculthorpe one usually senses feelings of loss, loneliness, and grief. His music is strongly sensual, exploring coloristic devices and new sound possibilities. It generally hovers between the extremes of static sound and a sort of cultivated primitivism, which may have stemmed from his love of Bartók but now seems linked with his interests in Indonesian music. The searing sounds in the *Sun Music* series for orchestra and for voices and instruments (1965–68) may also have had their beginnings

in his interest in the Bloch of *Schelomo* and *Voice in the Wilderness*. Busoni's idealism and German expressionism have led me to use musical theater to intensify already extreme emotional states and to open the doors of perception to a dimension inaccessible in everyday life. My opera *Fall of the House of Usher* (1965) explores the macabre and horrific, while another, *Lenz* (1970), veers between ecstatic mysticism and blasphemy. My piano music owes much of its inspiration to the great pianists of the past, Liszt, Busoni, Bartók. In addition, the music of Bloch has always moved me deeply. A recent *Concerto* for wind quintet and orchestra shows new kaleidoscopic tendencies in color change. Hollier, who recently returned from England, shares my enthusiasm for the theater, not only as a composer (*Orpheus and Eurydice*, 1969) but also as an operatic coach and touring accompanist. Even his instrumental works have a dramatic air about them, for he loves to compose on huge sheets of drawing paper and he determines the physical layout of his performers with an eye to appearance.

The rich tradition of European art and thought are strongly evident in Werder's music. Philosophy, in fact, may have had a greater effect on his music than anything else, although he admits to having been "strongly influenced in my early years by Hebraic modes (as well as Persian and Sumerian); today I have dropped the modes but still retain the speech rhythms." His esthetics are based on such sources as Aristotle's *Poetics* and Lessing's *Laokoon*; even the structure of some pieces is founded on philosphic concepts. He defines art as a "communication of a 'Feeling'" and sees himself as a poet in that he uses music as a language to communicate "feeling." Significantly he teaches and lectures a great deal and is one of our important critics. His nine string quartets are the most ambitious and consistently successful Australian essays in that genre.

All of us acknowledge a large debt to Europe: Sculthorpe and myself as mentioned; Werder, whose philosophical ties have been mentioned and who has also drawn on Monteverdi, Gluck, the Gabrielis, on Mozart ("for content"), on Handel and Bartók ("for technique"), and on Schoenberg, whose 12-tone method appears in many works of the 1960s; Hollier, whose studies in England toward a doctorate revealed (or reinforced) such possibilities as the freedom of ornamentation in early music and the grand gesture in the romantic cadenza; and Meale, who has been successively interested in the theories and music of such seminal figures as Bartók, Martinů, Hindemith, Messiaen, Boulez, and Xenakis. Meale, the possessor of an exceptionally lucid mind, is very much interested in the intellectual processes of making music and tends to absorb the structural and logical processes of his sources rather than the sounds characteristically associated with them. Hollier, on the other hand, engages in daring juxtapositions, for instance aleatory music and strict counterpoint akin to Bachian double fugues (*Piano Concerto, Piano Sonata*, both 1966). As for the Eastern influences that have recently begun to affect our music, Sculthorpe and Meale are perhaps the most striking exemplars. The former has been drawn to Indonesian and Japanese music and the latter toward Japanese dramatic construction and terminology, though characteristically he is interested in the structures and disciplines rather than in specific sounds. The only new-music trend that is not significantly reflected in Australia is the use of electronic apparatus. Equipment is still scarce, and there are few experienced practitioners where it is available.

BIBL.: Anne Boyd, "Not for Export," *Musical Times* (Nov 1970):1097–1100; Roger Covell, *Australia's Music, Themes of a New Society* (Melbourne 1967); ——, "Music in Australia," *Current Affairs Bulletin* 32/8; Andrew McCredie, *Catalogue of 46 Australian Composers & Selected Works* (Canberra 1969); ——, *Musical Composition in Australia* (Canberra 1969); Larry Sitsky, "Emergence of New Music in Australia," *Perspectives* 4/1; ——, "New Music," *Current Affairs Bulletin* 46/8; ——, "New Music in Australia," *Hemisphere* (Canberra) 13/11.

Larry Sitsky

Austria and Germany. There were few restrictions on international travel at the turn of the century, and although the Viennese circle around Arnold *Schoenberg (1874–1951) developed independently of international influences, the middle European musical environment was characterized generally by intensive international exchange. Until World War I the gathering place for composers was Vienna; thereafter Berlin was the more prominent city. The name of Schoenberg is closely associated with both. In 1904 Alban *Berg (1885–1935) and Anton *Webern (1883–1945) began studying with him in Vienna. In 1907 his *Chamber Symphony* of the previous year had its first performance there, and although it remained within the bounds of tonality it evoked a furor. Similar outrage followed a concert by the Schoenberg circle in 1912. Such

opposition, which showed the lingering influence of Eduard Hanslick, the conservative critic who had died in 1904, bound Schoenberg and his pupils more closely together. One of their few influential advocates was Gustav *Mahler (1860–1911), director of the Vienna Hofoper until 1907, to whom the developing style of the Schoenberg circle was slightly indebted. In 1909 the publishing house Universal Edition was founded in Vienna by Emil Hertzka. His first contracts were signed with Mahler, Franz Schreker, and Schoenberg; the enterprise quickly gained wider significance, publishing the most important composers in Germany, Czechoslovakia, Hungary, and Italy.

Schoenberg moved to Berlin in 1911, where he came in contact with the group of artists known as Der Blaue Reiter and including Wassily Kandinsky, Franz Marc, and others. The 1912 edition of the *Blaue Reiter Almanack* included musical compositions by Schoenberg, Berg, and Webern (Schoenberg, of course, was also a serious painter). In October 1912 *Pierrot lunaire* was first performed in Berlin; again Schoenberg's music caused public consternation, but this time it was tinged with admiration and a tour through several German cities followed. During the war Schoenberg, Berg, and Webern were occasionally required to perform military service and were also experiencing technical problems in composition; both of these factors brought a temporary halt to their production.

After the war avant-garde art experienced a period of unusual receptivity on the part of the Austrian and German governments and their local cultural ministries. Even conservative patrons of the arts were drawn into the overall trend, whose motto might have read: Be youthful and progressive at any price, or at least look that way. A major development was the founding in Vienna of the Society for Private Musical Performances. The idea was Schoenberg's, largely the result of unpleasant experiences with the general public. The group believed that even the best intentioned connoisseur could achieve understanding of new music only through repeated attendance at first-class performances. Consequently members of the society, under the direction of the best conductors and composers, were required to participate in up to 30 rehearsals per work. There were concerts every week, and over 200 pieces by all the important contemporary composers were presented before financial problems forced the society out of existence in 1921. Similar groups emulated the society's activity in Hamburg, Berlin, and

Frankfurt. In 1919 two important monthlies began publication, *Musikblätter des Anbruch*, put out by Universal Edition in Vienna and lasting until 1937, and *Melos*, published in Berlin under the editorship of Hermann Scherchen, the conductor and lifelong advocate of new music; *Melos* still publishes despite a period of suppression during 1936–46.

Up to 1919 the advocacy of the avant-garde in Germany had been in the hands of the Allgemeinen Deutschen Musikvereins, founded in 1861 by Franz Liszt and Franz Brendel. A new direction was established within the group in 1919 when Hans *Tiessen (1887–1971) and Georg Schunemann (1884–1945) were elected to the jury that selected works for the society's annual festival. Tiessen was close to the Melos group, and Schunemann, a scholar, was involved in the development of a progressive musical education. At the 1920 festival in Weimar, they presented Schoenberg's radically new *Orchestral Pieces*, Op. 16. The society continued to produce festivals until its dissolution in 1937. Other organizations came into being: Scherchen founded his Neue Musikgesellschaft in Berlin in 1919. In the south German town of Donaueschingen, Prince Egon zu Fürstenberg produced an annual festival for new chamber music; it was here that Paul *Hindemith (1895–1963) first gained widespread attention with a performance of his *Second String Quartet*. Edgard *Varèse (1885–1965) arrived in Berlin in 1922 and organized several progressive composers into a German branch of his International Composer's Guild, forerunner of ISCM, which was formed in Salzburg later that year during a four-day festival of chamber music by 54 composers from 15 countries. The organization then made its headquarters in London with Edward J. Dent, the scholar and journalist, as its first president; it produced festivals in various European cities until the outbreak of World War II.

Berlin in the 20s drew all shades of avant-gardists, and most of the better composers taught there. Franz Schreker (1878–1934) came from Vienna in 1920 to be director of the Musikhochschule. He was one of the few middle Europeans able to develop a harmonic and orchestral style that could approach the sensuality of French impressionism. The vocal lines in his operas often approach an Italian bel canto. His operas, the symbolic expression of an erotic-mystic *art nouveau* (e.g., *Der ferne Klang*, 1912), competed for a while with the operas of Richard *Strauss (1864–1949), but by 1930 they were all but forgotten. Ernst *Krenek (b. 1900), one of Schreker's pupils,

attracted some attention at an early age with his recklessly atonal music. His jazz opera, *Jonny spielt auf* (1925–26) became an international hit. Krenek later felt himself drawn toward the Schoenberg school and adopted the 12-tone technique. Another of Schreker's pupils, the Czech Alois *Hába (1893–1972), developed a quarter-tone system. Ferruccio *Busoni (1866–1924), who had envisioned both a third-tone and a sixth-tone system in his 1906 *Entwurf einer neuen Ästhetik der Tonkunst*, came to Berlin in 1920 to take over a masterclass in composition at the Akademie der Künste; after his death he was replaced by Schoenberg. In 1927 Hindemith received a teaching assignment at the Staatlichen Hochschule für Musik.

Progressive forces were also at work in Berlin theaters. In 1923 Erich Kleiber became General Music Director of the Staatsoper; his premiere of Berg's *Wozzeck* in 1925 achieved international acclaim. 1927 saw the opening of the Krolloper under the artistic direction of Otto Klemperer; it lasted only four years but became in this short period a showplace for the best directors, set designers, and conductors. There was scarcely a single avant-garde idea that failed to achieve notice there. Perhaps the greatest success of the Krolloper was the premiere of the *Dreigroschenoper*, a piece of social criticism by Bertolt Brecht and Busoni's student, Kurt *Weill (1900–50).

A broad discussion of music as a social force was initiated in 1921 with the posthumous publication of *Die rationalen und soziologischen Grundlagen der Musik* by Max Weber. Brecht and Weill intended to lead the general public to a critical consideration of social problems, and to this end Weill developed an intentionally uncomplicated style based on popular dance music and jazz (which began to have an impact in Europe in the 20s). This easy-going style found further expression in the worker's songs and cantatas of Hanns *Eisler (1898–1962), another of Schoenberg's students. Social-minded groups were also to be found in the *Jugendbewegung* [Youth Movement]. Before World War I this had been an anti-city, back-to-nature clique (Der Wandervogel, led by Hans Breuer), which sought in nature something akin to a paradise lost. Under the impact of the music educator Fritz Jöde and others, it was opened to broader segments of the population. Singing and instrumental groups were established all over Germany, and respectable composers began writing music for them in a popular, slightly neobaroque style, called *Gebrauchsmusik* or

Sing- und Spielmusik. Hindemith involved himself for a while with the cultivation of music among the young and composed for laymen and even children (the opera *Wir bauen eine Stadt*). Musical scholars also supplied material; they helped revive older folksongs, 16th-century madrigals, the renaissance recorder and medieval fidel and other earlier forms and instruments. The *Jugendbewegung* served in this revival of folk music and music of the 16th–18th centuries and made noteworthy contributions to music education. Nevertheless the movement often subordinated musical quality to a feeling of community "togetherness," and the emphasis on national folklore helped bring certain groups to the point where they could be integrated into National Socialism. More advantageous reforms were instituted by the Social Democrat and educator Leo Kestenberg, a pupil of Busoni. As head of the music section of the Prussian Ministry of Science, Art, and Popular Education, he introduced new concepts in music education from kindergarten through the university. Music teachers, for example, were expected to have pedagogical and psychological training as well as musical, and to this end new examination procedures were introduced. The effects of his ideas are still being felt.

National Socialism was victorious in Germany in 1933, and music could not avoid being drawn into the ensuing political struggles. In fact the Nazi ideology already had precursors on the musical scene. Wagner had written on "Das Judentum in der Musik" in 1850, and in 1917 Busoni was attacked in "Futuristengefahr" by Hans *Pfitzner (1869–1949), who taught alongside Busoni and Schoenberg at the Berlin Akademie der Künste. Both writings anticipated the "final solution to the Jewish problem." During the Nazi period music was centrally directed from the Reichsmusikkamer, a section of Joseph Goebbel's propaganda ministry, of which the first president was Richard Strauss. Avantgarde, socialist, and especially "non-Arian" musicians were dismissed from their positions and had to emigrate. This was the fate of such composers as Schoenberg, Hindemith, Weill, and Eisler, of reformers like Kestenberg, and of conductors such as Bruno Walter and Otto Klemperer. The government prohibited all foreign music, thereby pulling Germany out of the international current for 12 years. The music of the National Socialists was characterized by fanfares and drums used to heighten the effect of mass demonstrations. After 1945 all of the less significant composers who had

been writing specifically National Socialist music were forgotten.

Not every noted composer had the possibility or the desire to emigrate. Various ways and means existed to make life in the Third Reich tolerable. Some composers chose to withdraw from musical life, and they ceased to publish. Others of a more traditional musical orientation continued to be performed, even though they were not necessarily in agreement with the national ideology (e.g., Rudolf *Wagner-Regeny, 1903–69, whose operas tend toward the humanistic and socially critical and who was therefore accepted in East Germany after the war). Still other composers wrote proregime music on occasion (e.g., Werner *Egk, b. 1901, who wrote music for the Olympic Games of 1936, for a Hitler Youth film, etc.). No composer of importance, however, continued to collaborate for the entire 12 years. Some well-known musicologists were occupied with research on racial questions (e.g., Friedrich Blume, who wrote *Das Rasseproblem in der Musik*, 1938). Considered in purely materialistic terms, the musical life in Germany during the war and in such occupied cities as Amsterdam, Paris, and Prague, was one of great brilliance. German music, of course, held sway and was performed by many prominent artists.

The progressive musical trends in middle Europe before World War 11 were shaped primarily by Schoenberg and Hindemith. The background of Schoenberg's innovative thinking includes the chromatic harmony and continuous, proselike, asymmetric forms of Liszt and Wagner and the contrapuntal textures of Brahm's chamber music. Schoenberg began to loosen the bonds of tonality by using wholetone scales, fourth chords, and complex polyphony in which chords are the chance confluence of freely moving tonal lines. The definitive break came in 1908 with the nontonal "Du lehnest wider eine Silberweide" from *Buch der hängenden Gärten*, Op. 15. Timbre was emancipated from its traditional function as a support for melody, form, and the like, in the principle of *Klangfarbenmelodie*, first presented in the Op. 16 orchestral pieces (1909) and further developed by Webern in his Opp. 6 and 10 (1910, 1911–13). *Erwartung* is noteworthy for its use of interval constellations (e.g., fourths together with sevenths), large and small melodic ranges, and extreme dynamic contrasts to convey the emotional tension of an expressionist text. Form was reduced in the Op. 19 piano pieces to a small time span, derived in part from Mahler's use of single intervals as the basis for a long work. Webern pushed the idea to an extreme in his Opp. 9 and 11 (1913, 1914), and once said that a piece should be over once all 12 tones had been heard. Finally the 12-tone method appeared in Schoenberg's 5 *Pieces* for piano, Op. 23 (1920–23), following a decade of experiments and anticipations. The concept of a rapid circulation of all 12 chromatic pitch classes was not exclusive to Schoenberg but was in the air; as early as 1919 J. M. *Hauer (1883–1959) was writing 12-tone music in Vienna using, however, unordered collections of pitch classes in a modelike fashion rather than in strictly serialized successions. After a period of greatly reduced forms, Schoenberg found new possibilities for formal expansion in the use of texts and of baroque procedures (passacaglia, canon, etc.); unlike the German neobaroque composers, however, Schoenberg and his school never copied baroque melodic patterns.

Until 1945 Schoenberg's 12-tone technique was adopted by only the small circle associated with him. In his own works the musical material was dictated by a basically melodic conception and was then developed into a row. Berg's rows sometimes contain triads that facilitate reminiscences of tonal relations. Webern thought in terms of strict internal structures and anticipated some of the serial applications made later to durations, dynamics, and timbres. Eisler, who occasionally wrote 12-tone music after 1924, preferred an antiromantic approach and strove for easy comprehensibility, clear rhythms, and transparent textures. Krenek began to use the 12-tone technique about 1930 in an undogmatic, relatively uncomplicated, and melodious style.

Hindemith's career began in an opera-house orchestra, and his work before World War I stemmed from Schreker and Strauss and from Reger, with whom he shared a taste for Bach-like polyphony and chromatic harmony that compresses all 12 tones into the smallest possible time span. After the war he became fiercely antiromantic; his marionette play *Nusch-Nuschi*, Op. 20 (1920) contains a vicious parody of King Mark in Wagner's *Tristan*. The Bach ideal remained, however, as can be seen in the *Cello Sonata*, Op. 11, No. 3 (1919), which follows Bach's *Partita in E* for solo violin as a model but nevertheless breaks all melodic bounds, ranging through two and three octaves. (A strong pro-Bach influence at this time was the 1917 book *Grundlagen des linearen Kontrapunkts* by the Swiss theorist Ernst Kurth, which praised the "kinetic energy" of Bach's melodies.) In Hindemith's *Das Marienleben* (1922–23) a new idea of style was achieved, neoclassicism. Busoni explained

his own concept of "young classicism" in a 1920 letter to the music critic Paul Bekker: "the mastery of the results of previous experiments—their transformation into good and stable forms." Some characteristics of Hindemith's style can be described in terms of further quotations from Busoni's letter: 1) "a return to melody . . . which dominates all the parts . . . and generates the harmony . . . in short, a perfectly evolved polyphony"; 2) an "absolute" view of music "divested of all sensuous elements and of any subjectivity whatever"; 3) a preference for baroque forms and techniques (ostinato, passacaglia, fugue, concerto, number opera, etc.); 4) pulsating, motoric, baroquelike rhythms; and 5) an expanded tonality based on the overtone series.

After the Nazis came to power the Protestant church became somewhat of an enclave for composers in the Third Reich. Hindemith's influence, even after he emigrated in 1937, continued to be felt in pupils of his such as Harald *Genzmer (b. 1909). Many other composers independently arrived at a similar style. Hugo *Distler (1908–42), Ernst *Pepping (b. 1901), and Johann Nepomuk *David (c. 1895) exemplify the Protestant church composers whose styles included references to the ecclesiastical modes, polyphonic techniques (such as parallel fourths and fifths) derived from medieval music, an harmonic asperity resulting from linear voice leading, figurative representation of texts after the baroque ideal of Schütz, Bach, and others, and formal schemes and procedures from before 1750. Among other composers of the pre-1945 period, Egk and Carl *Orff (b. 1895) have a certain popular South German atmosphere. Both show a strong talent for the theater; Orff in particular brought new stimulus to dance and theater with his use of elementary rhythms and static melodic patterns of extreme simplicity.

Gottfried Eberle
(trans. from German by James Rogers)

SINCE 1945. Austria has continued to be the home of one of the world's great publishing houses, Universal Edition, and it still supports an active concert and festival life. It has long since ceased to be a leading creator of new music, however. As Rudolf Klein observed in 1965, "After a promising breakthrough in the 20s came a period of stagnation, which has today most probably reached its lowest point. Although it was Austria's privilege to be the country where such masters as Schoenberg, Berg, and Webern, who shaped the lineaments of the music of our century, were born, lived, and created, many changes have since taken place. The few Austrian composers of some importance now live abroad, those who stayed at home have put their pens down in disappointment. Austria is gradually becoming a vast music museum" (*Musical Quarterly* 51:190). Among the significant younger composers today are Friedrich *Cerha (b. 1926) and Kurt *Schwertsik (b. 1935). Roman *Haubenstock-Ramati (b. Poland, 1919) and György *Ligeti (b. Transylvania, 1923) also make their home in the country.

In Germany the first postwar task was to acquaint the population with what had been going on in the rest of the musical world since 1933, when National Socialist cultural politics had forced an isolationist position on the country. There was an equal need to find young composers—if indeed there were any— and give them a chance to be heard. It was a while before local government agencies could meet these needs, and initially three institutions undertook the task of recultivating modern music: the Darmstadt summer courses, the Donaueschingen festival, and the various radio stations with their concert series and night programs.

The Darmstadt courses began in 1946 with support from the city of Darmstadt (then 90 percent destroyed), the state government of Hessen, and the American military. After 1948 additional assistance was provided by the federal government, surrounding cities and states, German and foreign radio stations, and German industry. In 1947 the Internationale Musikinstitut Darmstadt was founded in connection with the courses. It eventually assumed their organizational direction and in 1960 became the secretariat of the German section of the ISCM. Today the institute possesses Germany's largest collection of documents relating to new music. Beginning in 1958 important lectures began to be published in the annual *Darmstädter Beiträge zur neuen Musik*. Since 1961 the courses have had an orchestra, the Internationales Kammerensemble Darmstadt, conducted by Bruno *Maderna (b. 1920) and consisting of specialists in new music from several countries. Until 1970 the courses took place for two weeks each year; since then they have occurred biennially, though expanded in length to at least three weeks. The person chiefly responsible for their success was Wolfgang Steinecke (1910–61), their director until his death; he was succeeded by Ernst Thomas (b. 1916).

Originally the courses were planned to fill a specifically postwar German need: Information about new music was directed to practicing musicians and teachers and to future critics, theoreticians, and representatives of theater and radio. All of these participants were in effect being trained to inform others. The first consideration was performance— concerts, courses in interpretation, and master classes; there were only a few lectures in which individual trends in modern composition were explained. The emphasis started to shift as non-German composers began attending to explain their own innovations and spheres of interest. From Paris came René *Leibowitz (b. 1913) in 1948 and Olivier *Messiaen (b. 1908) in 1949. Varèse and Krenek came from the U.S. in 1950. They presented their own compositions and those of their students; underlying theories were discussed in personally directed seminars. As early as 1949 these participants began drawing students from outside Germany, and in that year the name was changed from Vacation Courses for International New Music to International Vacation Courses for New Music. By the 1960s 75 percent of the participants were non-German. In 1950 the course offerings began to shift from interpretation to theory, reflecting the change in interest from practical performance applications to the analysis of new compositional methods. Logic demanded that the results of theoretical seminars appear on ensuing Darmstadt concert programs. At first the works of young composers were presented in semiprivate studio performances, later publicly. By the mid-50s the courses had become the most important forum for contemporary music in the world. The developments at Darmstadt, which have reflected all the newest trends in music, can be divided into four phases:

1. The years 1946–52 were a period of recapitulation. 1946 and 1947 centered on Hindemith and, to a lesser extent, early and middle Stravinsky and Les Six. A 1948 presentation of the Schoenberg *Piano Concerto* stole the wind from the neoclassicist's sails, and thereafter the younger participants seemed to be interested in nothing but dodecaphony. An examination of the work of Béla Bartók in 1950 came too late to have any practical results.

The most influential teacher during these years was Wolfgang *Fortner (b. 1907), whose own work was then undergoing a transformation from the esthetics of baroque "objectivity" through 12-tone to serial composition. A whole list of new names appeared. In 1946 Hans Werner *Henze (b. 1926) first displayed the talent and amazing productivity that was to make him a symbol of new German music. Others included Hans Ulrich *Engelmann

(b. 1921) and, somewhat later, Bernd Alois
*Zimmermann (1918–70). In 1952 Karlheinz
*Stockhausen (b. 1928) introduced ideas that
were to be decisive for the second phase
of the courses; his colleagues were Karel
*Goeyvaerts (b. 1923) from Belgium, Luigi
*Nono (b. 1924) from Italy, and Pierre
*Boulez (b. 1925) from France.

2. The second phase, 1953–58, began with
an anniversary concert commemorating the
70th birthday of Anton Webern. Boulez,
Nono, Goeyvaerts, and Stockhausen explained the significance of his music and discussed the effects of his later work on their
own production. The past was closed; the
younger generation had assumed the leadership. They were concerned with expanding on
Webern's legacy, first by serializing the basic
parameters, then the higher, composite levels
of composition, and arriving finally at a more
flexible technique of "group composition."
Boulez, Nono, and Stockhausen, together with
Maderna, quickly assumed teaching positions.
They were joined later by Henri *Pousseur
(b. 1929) and Luciano *Berio (b. 1925). At
first they conducted workshops, then analysis
seminars and composition courses.

3. The years 1958–63 spelled the end of serial
composition. Already in 1957 Boulez had
delivered his famous lecture on controlled
chance and Stockhausen had presented his
open-form *Klavierstück XI.* John *Cage
(b. 1912), who was then well on the way to an
indeterminate music, taught a course in 1958;
this too may have influenced the fate of serial
thought. At the same time, Stockhausen,
already a spokesman for the most recent trends,
had developed conceptions of sound and form
based on the principle of a continuum rather
than discrete quantities. The new Polish music
as developed by Krzysztof *Penderecki (b.
1933), which was better known at Donaueschingen, and the sound designs of Ligeti
were introduced in these years. The visualizing
and theatricalizing of music reached a high
level in the work of Mauricio *Kagel (b. 1932),
who had been composing in Cologne since
1957; his chamber piece *Sur Scène* (1959–60)
had its premiere in Bremen in 1962 and was
performed at Darmstadt the following year. It
became significant that the newer composers
on the scene represented not so much general
trends as individual modes of expression:
Niccolò *Castiglioni (b. 1932) and Sylvano
*Bussotti (b. 1931) from Italy and two Ger-
mans, Johannes G. *Fritsch (b. 1941), a
student of Stockhausen, and Helmut *Lachenmann (b. 1935), a student of Nono.

4. The individualism and pluralism that

developed in Darmstadt in the early 60s began
to cause much confusion and to endanger the
possibility of any sort of systematic instruction.
Beginning in 1964 an attempt was made to
solve these problems by holding more general
discussions on current questions in contemporary music. Theoreticians and composers,
among them Kagel, Ligeti and Dieter *Schnebel (b. 1930), explored problems in notation,
form, and music theater. They were continuing a Darmstadt tradition begun in the 50s
when Theodor W. Adorno (1903–69) lectured
on criteria for new music. The direction of the
time, however, was not along such lines, nor
was this approach helped by the orientation
toward electronic and computer-based music,
which developed during 1964–66 under the
influence of Josef Anton Riedl (b. 1929),
director of the now defunct Munich Studio
for Electronic Music. The growth of pluralism
continued: collage techniques, group improvisation, texture composition, live electronics,
prose music. At the same time, and partly
because of the increasing numbers of students,
the give-and-take atmosphere of previous
seminars was replaced by monologues, the
individual instructor talking about his own
interests. Music students were no exception to
the growing worldwide distrust of authority,
and individual teachers were in some cases
openly challenged. Thomas's decision to cancel
the 1971 courses and resume them on a
biennial basis only was symptomatic of the
overall confusion.

The Cologne Courses for New Music, run
by the Rhenish Music School in Cologne since
1963, have tried to avoid the difficulties at
Darmstadt. The number of participants is
limited, and instruction is spread out over a
three-month period. Theory and practice are
more closely related. Students in interpretation courses must also take the composition
course and its complementary lectures and
seminars. The overall esthetic position is
determined by the course director, Stockhausen during 1963–68 and Kagel since then.
The theoretical instruction has now been
limited to such topics as "Musik und Bild"
(1969) and "Musik als Hörspiel" (1970).

Unlike most other series devoted to new
music, the Donaueschingen Festivals have a
history of several decades. The Chamber Music
Festivals for the Advancement of Contemporary Music had a great influence in the 20s;
they were planned and financed by the Gesellschaft der Musikfreunde Donaueschingen and
the princes of Fürstenberg. The concerts, as
revived in 1950, are now organized principally
by the Southwest German Radio of Baden-

Baden, and until his death in 1970, Heinrich Strobel, music director of the radio, had complete control of programing and commissioning. Events are concentrated over one weekend, usually at the end of October. Unlike Darmstadt, the Donaueschingen Festival works from the premise that its audience will consist of internationally established critics, composers, publishers, and radio music directors. It is probably the world's most publicized platform for new music.

Also unlike Darmstadt, Donaueschingen programs contain many examples of earlier 20th-century music, so that Stravinsky, the Vienna school, Hindemith, Bartók, and Varèse mingle with music of the 60s and 70s. The programs also include the middle generation, now greatly outnumbered by younger composers at Darmstadt: Messiaen, Fortner, Karl Amadeus *Hartmann (1905–63), Boris *Blacher (b. 1903). The dominating force has nevertheless been that of the avant-garde, but with the important difference that Strobel restricted his selection to the most successful representatives: Henze, Stockhausen, Nono, Zimmermann, and then with increasing regularity Boulez, who made his international conducting debut at Donaueschingen in 1958. Later serial attempts to use spatial factors as a basic parameter of composition were introduced here. Stockhausen's *Gruppen* for 3 orchestras and Boulez' *Poésie pour pouvoir* were performed in 1958, Pousseur's *Rîmes pour différentes sources sonores* and Berio's *Allelujah II* in 1959. Strobel's first great success came in 1960 with the premiere of Penderecki's *Anaklasis*; thereafter German radio was deluged with Polish cluster music. Another triumph came in 1961 with the premiere of Ligeti's *Atmosphères*. Strobel had less success when he introduced Haubenstock-Ramati, Giselher *Klebe (b. 1925), Jacques *Wildberger (b. 1922), and Iannis *Xenakis. The concrete music of Pierre *Schaeffer and Pierre *Henry, introduced in 1953, and Cage's music for prepared piano, introduced in 1954, all proved to be about a decade ahead of their time. In the final analysis the significance of Donaueschingen has been less in forwarding the development of new music than in making its better exponents more widely known. In this function it continues to make a major contribution.

The widespread presence of new music in the cultural life of West Germany is largely due to the ten German radio stations and to the competition among them. They are publicly owned but administered autonomously. Each has a music section with a special department for new music, eight have their own orchestras, and four have choruses. New music, often commissioned by the stations, averages about four hours of broadcast time per week on each station and is frequently discussed on night programs. Among the most important commentators have been Adorno, Heinz-Klaus Metzger and Hans G. Helms and the composers Wolf Rosenberg (b. 1915), Herbert *Brün (b. 1918), and Schnebel.

The Hessian Radio in Frankfurt coordinates its Festival of New Music with the Darmstadt summer courses, and the Southwest Radio in Baden-Baden actually organizes the Donaueschingen festivals. The Bavarian Radio in Munich began a Musica Viva series in October 1945 under the direction of K. A. Hartmann. It consists of eight evenings per season and has until recently been devoted to the "classicists" of modern music: Stravinsky, Bartók, Hindemith, and Milhaud, and to a lesser extent Schoenberg and Berg. The younger generation—at least those who had achieved some standing elsewhere—began to appear in 1952: Henze, Klebe, Zimmermann, Stockhausen, Nono in 1960, and later on Boulez. Even when Wolfgang Fortner became director after Hartmann's death, the station continued to show little interest in experimental music.

The Northwest German Radio in Hamburg, which became independent of the Northwest German Radio in Cologne in 1955, has pursued a more experimental policy than Munich. In 1951 Herbert Hübner presented the first in his series, "das neue werk." At first the plan was to examine the newest developments in art, literature, and music in conjunction with the Hamburg Free Academy of the Arts. This quickly led to an eight-program series emphasizing music by the younger generation. Every attempt was made to include all new trends, even though such comprehensiveness could not avoid some music that was mediocre. The first decade concentrated on the Italian avant-garde and on Klebe and Henze among the Germans. After 1960 Hübner played at least one Polish work on every second concert and began to move in the direction of the Boulez school, as had Strobel in Donaueschingen. He also presented music of the older generation, including the Vienna school. He was responsible for the concert premiere of Schoenberg's *Moses und Aron* in 1954 and for the first survey of his total legacy in 1958. On the Cologne station a "Neue Musik" series began in 1951 under Eigel Kruttge. In 1953 this too became an eight-program series (retitled "Musik der Zeit") with programing similar to Hamburg. When the Cologne radio established its electronic music studio, the series began to take on a personality of its own, later intensified when Otto Tomek became director in 1960. Tomek stood apart from the Boulez school and from the limited horizon this esthetic had forced on the Hamburg radio and on Donaueschingen, and he was thus free to examine most of the nonvisual works of Kagel, new American music, and Stockhausen's latest works.

The most significant accomplishment of the German stations is the Bremen Tage pro Musica Nova, begun in 1962 by Hans *Otte (b. 1926), music director of the station. This biennial festival not only presents new music but stimulates further development through commissions that focus specifically on the most current problems in new music. Several important works were written for it, including three from 1961–62 that marked the beginning of a post-serial renaissance in organ music: Ligeti's *Volumina*, Kagel's *Improvisation ajoutée*, and *Interferences* by Bengt *Hambraeus. Kagel's theater concept found its first success in Bremen. Cage and Schnebel were played there, along with Luc *Ferrari (b. 1929) and Guiseppe G. *Englert (b. 1927). In 1970 Otte even took into account the politicalization of music that was occupying many participating composers and performers.

The "Third Program" of German television in Hamburg and Cologne has also contributed to the history of contemporary music by presenting a number of important compositions and producing documentaries on current composers and festivals. In addition they have given Kagel the opportunity to express his ideas in film under optimum conditions.

Local concert organizations began to follow the initiative of the radio stations in the 50s. Works by some younger composers found their way into the programs of municipal orchestras, and by now almost every large city also has a separate series devoted to new music. One program is of international significance, Josef Anton Riedl's "Neue Musik München." This began under the sponsorship of the Munich Jugendkulturwerk and has pursued the most advanced trends: Stockhausen, Kagel, Schnebel, and the Cage school. The series has also begun to question the concert form itself, mixing presentation and commentary, introducing film and theater, and concentrating finally on mixed-media productions. Also in the 50s the major opera houses (Hamburg, Berlin, Cologne, and Stuttgart) began departing from the "star system" and from totally sung operas. They introduced the new music-

theater concepts and emphasized acting ability, thus making possible fine productions of *Wozzeck*, *Lulu*, and *Moses und Aron* (now part of the standard repertory) and also encouraging younger composers to experiment with a genre that was becoming socially and artistically questionable. Henze and Klebe composed several operas in a relatively conventional idiom; the more radical efforts have included Zimmermann's *Die Soldaten* (1958–60), Dieter *Schönbach's (b. 1931) multimedia *Geschichte von einem Feuer* (1967–68), and Kagel's *Staatstheater* (1970–71).

The German recording industry has followed the demands of a relatively broad interest in new music. An initial project, however, met with failure, the "Musica Nova" series of Deutsche Gramaphon Gesellschaft (DGG), which based its repertory selection on frequency of performance rather than quality. In 1960 Werner Goldschmidt founded the Wergo Co., which has been producing a "Studio-Reihe neuer Musik" with fully documented critical commentaries. The series began with Schoenberg, Stravinsky, and Prokofiev but was soon redirected to radically modern music. It was then bought by the publishers B. Schott in 1970. The catalog now consists of over 60 titles, and the success of the venture has prompted DGG to introduce a series, "Avantgarde," concentrating on the most radical trends. It should be pointed out that such developments as these affect, in turn, the nature of new music. Many composers after 1945 believed that esthetic change would have political and social consequences, and their belief drove forward many of the forces for change in postwar music. However, when the class that continues to have economic control over the course of society begins to accept new music, to play it, to distribute it, then the music itself loses its aggressiveness (which is a matter of context). It loses its raison d'être as well, for although the upper classes may suspect that new music has some merit, they also know that they can prove their power and show their liberality if they accept criticism. Thus, rather than helping to destroy the power of the upper classes, new music begins to affirm it, and the impetus that brought the music into being is dissipated.

Although new music is well established in Germany—certainly more solidly than anywhere else—this does not mean that a composer can make a decent living from his music. There are many commissions available, but they rarely come frequently enough to provide a suitable monthly income. Henze is an exception. Composers who perform their own works fare better. Stockhausen conducts and does his own mixing in live electronic works; Kagel does his own directing. Both also hold teaching positions. Schnebel makes his living as a Protestant theologian. Many members of the younger generation work at jobs having little to do with their principal interest. The more fortunate teach instruments or theory at a conservatory or do free-lance work for the radio stations.

In music written immediately after the war some specifically German concerns came to the surface. For example, 12-tone technique was used by younger composers not as a means for constructing tightly integrated, panthematic structures but rather as an escape hatch from the rigid diatonic thinking of Hindemith. It was a way to construct broad, nontonal, freely moving thematic shapes, to achieve rich, iridescent chords encompassing all chromatic possibilities. The most important examples are Henze in his early work (especially the *Violin Concerto* of 1947), Zimmermann (his 1951 *Symphony*), and middle-period Fortner (the *White Rose* ballet, 1950). There is a romantic and particularly German dodecaphony here, a concentration on what Schoenberg considered to be only one approach among many—the separation of melody and harmony, of theme and accompaniment. Thus while row forms were followed quite strictly in regard to a melody, vertical structures were often formed without regard to "correct" pitch-class ordering. This and other postwar German music is noteworthy for its subjectivity, especially when compared with Hindemith. After 1950, however, when the encounter with Webern began in earnest, German musicians fell in line with international trends, with which they have been united ever since.

Hansjörg Pauli
(trans. from German by James Rogers)

SEE ALSO Electronic Music: History and Development; Israel; Liturgical Music: Christian; Opera; Theory.

Avidom, Menahem (b. Stanislaw, Poland, 6 Jan 1908), studied at the American Univ. of Beirut (1926–28) and the Paris Conservatory (1928–31, composition with Henri Rabaud). During 1945–52 he was secretary general of the Israel Philharmonic Orchestra. Since 1955 he has been Director General of the Israel Performing Rights Society; he is also chairman of the Israel Composers' League. The main influences on his music have been French impressionism, Oriental folklore, and 12-tone and serial techniques.

PRINCIPAL COMPOSITIONS: *Concerto* for flute, strings (1944, IMP); *Symphonies Nos. 1, 2, 5, 7*: No. 1, "A Folk Symphony" (1946, IMP); No. 2, "David" (1949, IMP); No. 5, "The Song of Eilat" (1956, IMP); No. 7, "The Philharmonic" (1960, Mills); *Alexandra*, 3-act opera (1953, IMI); *String Quartet No. 2* (1960, Mills); *12 Changing Preludes* for piano (1960, Vechinuch); *Enigma* for 5 winds, piano, percussion (1962, IMI); *B-A-C-H Suite* for winds, strings, piano, percussion (1965, IMP).
SEE ALSO Israel.

Avni, Tzvi (Jacob) (b. Saarbrücken, Germany, 2 Sept 1927), studied at the Israel Academy of Music in Tel Aviv (1953–58; composition, theory with Mordecai Seter), at Tanglewood (1963; composition with Aaron Copland, Lucas Foss), and Columbia Univ. (1963–64; electronic music with Vladimir Ussachevsky). He also studied composition and orchestration privately in Tel Aviv with Paul Ben-Haim (1954–56). Since 1961 he has been director of AMLI (Americans for a Music Library in Israel). During 1966–70 he was editor of *Guitite*, the bimonthly of Musical Youth in Israel. During 1958–68 he arranged over 100 Israeli folksongs for the radio.

PRINCIPAL COMPOSITIONS (published by IMI): *Summer Strings* for string quartet (1962); *Vocalise* on tape (1964, recorded by Turnabout); *Meditations on a Drama* for chamber orchestra (1966); *Collage* for voice, flute, percussion, electric guitar (1967); *5 Pantomimes* for flute, clarinet, horn, trumpet, viola, double bass, piano, percussion (1968).
SEE ALSO Israel.

Avshalomov, Aaron (b. Nikolaevsk, Siberia, 12 Nov 1894; d. New York, 26 April 1965), studied at the Zurich Conservatory (1913–14). He was head librarian of the Municipal Library of Shanghai (1928–c. 43) and conductor of the Shanghai City Government Symphony Orchestra (c.1943–46). In his music he was especially interested in integrating Chinese melodic and rhythmic characteristics with Western forms and instrumentation. His *Peiping Hutungs* (1932) is a symphonic sketch of street life in a Chinese city.

PRINCIPAL COMPOSITIONS (published by ACA unless otherwise noted): *Kuan Yin*, opera (1925, unpub.); *The Soul of Ch'in*, pantomime ballet (1926); *The Peiping Hutungs* for orchestra (1932, Ricordi); *Last Words of Tsin Wen* for soprano, orchestra (1933); *Yang Kwei Fei*, opera (1933, unpub.); *Piano Concerto in G* on Chinese themes (1935); *Symphonies Nos. 1–3* (1938, 1948, 1949).
BIBL.: *ACA Bulletin* (May 1962).

Avshalomov, Jacob (b. Tsingtao, China, 28 March 1919), studied in China with his father, Aaron, privately in Los Angeles with Ernst Toch (1938), and at Reed College, Portland, Ore. (1939–41), the Eastman School (1941–43, composition with Bernard Rogers), and Tanglewood (1946, composition with Aaron Copland). He taught at Columbia Univ. (1947–54) and has since been conductor of the Portland Junior Symphony. Some of his early works (e.g., *The Taking of T'ung Kuan*), have oriental flavors, the result of his boyhood in China. Other influences include renaissance madrigals and motets.

PRINCIPAL COMPOSITIONS (dates unavailable): *Phases of the Great Land* for orchestra (Highgate); *Sinfonietta* (ACA); *Slow Dance* for orchestra (Merion); *Symphony*, "The Oregon" (ACA); *The Taking of T'ung Kuan* for orchestra (ACA); *City Upon a Hill* for narrator, chorus, orchestra, liberty bell; text by William Blake (ACA); *How Long, O Lord*, cantata for alto, chorus, orchestra (Marks); *Inscriptions at the City of Brass* for female narrator, chorus, orchestra without strings; text from the Arabian Nights (ACA); *Prophecy* for tenor, chorus, organ; text from Isaiah (Ione); *Tom O'Bedlam* for chorus, oboe, tabor, jingles; anonymous 17th-century text (Ione); *Disconsolate Muse* for flute, piano (AMP); *Evocations* for clarinet (or viola), piano (ACA); *Sonatine* for viola, piano (Merrymount); *The Little Clay Cart*, incidental music for orchestra (ACA).

Ayala-Pérez, Daniel (b. Abalá, Yucatán, Mexico, 21 July 1906), studied at the State Music School in Mérida, Yucatán (1921–27), and at the National Conservatory in Mexico City (1929–33; composition with Carlos Chávez; theory with Pedro Michaca; violin, conducting with Silvestre Revueltas; other subjects with Julián Carrillo, Manuel M. Ponce, and José F. Vázquez). From 1933 to 1967 he was professor of music education at the National Institute of Fine Arts in Mexico City. As an emissary of the Institute he was director of the Dept. of Cultural Esthetics in Morelia, Michoacán (1938–39); director of the State Conservatory of Music in Mérida, Yucatán (1942–54); and founder and director of the Veracruz Institute of Fine Arts (1955–70). In 1942 he founded the Orquesta Típica "Yukalpeten" and the Yucatán Symphony Orchestra in Mérida, which he directed, along with the State Musical Band, until 1954. Ayala-Pérez has been influenced by the mythology and musical culture of the Mayan Indians and other native Mexican groups. His music draws on indigenous scales and rhythms and occasionally makes use of native instruments.

PRINCIPAL COMPOSITIONS: *El grillo* for soprano, clarinet, violin, piano, seed rattle (1931–32); *Uchben x'coholte* [An Ancient Cemetary] for soprano, chamber orchestra; Mayan text (1931–32; second version as a 2-act ballet for soprano, chamber orchestra, winds, 1936); *U kayl chaac* [Mayan Rain Song] for soprano, chamber orchestra with native percussion; Mayan text (1934); *Tribu*, symphonic poem for orchestra (1934); *Panoramas de Mexico*, suite for chamber orchestra (1936; arranged for string quartet, *3 Folklore Miniatures*, 1954); *El hombre Maya*, ballet suite for orchestra (1939); *Symphony No. 1* (1946); *Mi viaje a Norteamerica*, suite for orchestra (1947); *Acuarela nocturna* for orchestra (1948); *Suite Veracruz* for orchestra (1957).

SEE ALSO Mexico.

Van Baaren, Kees (b. Enschede, Netherlands, 22 Oct 1906; d. Oegstgeest, Netherlands, 2 Sept 1970), studied in Berlin during 1924–27 at the Sternsche Konservatorium and the Hochschule für Musik (composition with Friedrich Koch, piano with Rudolf Breithaupt). He also studied composition privately in Rotterdam with Willem Pijper, who was the major influence on his development as a composer. During 1947–53 he was director of the Amsterdam Musiklyceum; during 1953–57, of the Utrecht Conservatory; and during 1957–70, of the Royal Conservatory at The Hague. Early influences on his style came from Debussy and especially Pijper. His music of the 1930s and 40s was basically neoclassic, after which he came under the influence of Schoenberg and the Viennese 12-tone composers (he was the only Dutch composer of his generation to do so). He always displayed a penchant for contrapuntal textures. During the 60s he grew closer to Webern's style, as manifest in his fondness then for brevity, asymmetrical melodic and rhythmic units, pointillistic sound textures, and sophisticated handling of serial techniques.

PRINCIPAL COMPOSITIONS: (published by Donemus): *Piano Sonatina* (1948); *Muzikaal Zelfportret* for piano (1954); *Variazioni* for orchestra (1959); *Wind Quintet*, "Sovraposizioni II" (1963); *Piano Concerto* (1964); *Musica* for orchestra (1966).

PRINCIPAL WRITINGS: "Kompositionsunterricht und Theorieunterricht," *Kongressbericht der 3. Direktiorenkonferenz* (Cologne 1960):29–34.

BIBL.: Jackson Hill, *The Music of K. v. B.* (PhD diss., Univ. of N. C., 1970); Jos Wouters, "Composers' Gallery: K. v. B.," *Sonorum Speculum* 16:1–14.

[prepared with the help of Jackson Hill]
SEE ALSO Netherlands.

Babbitt, Milton (b. Philadelphia, 10 May 1916), grew up in Jackson, Miss., where he began music studies (violin, clarinet) at age four and at the same time developed an interest in mathematics under the guidance of his father, a mathematician. His undergraduate studies (at the Univ. of N. C., Univ. of Pa., and New York Univ.) were divided between music and mathematics, and his principal teachers were Philip James and Marion Bauer, whose classes at N. Y. U. attracted a number of "advanced" young composers during the 1930s. After graduation Babbitt worked with Bauer as a critic for the *Musical Leader* and at her suggestion studied with Roger Sessions, first privately and then as a graduate student at Princeton Univ., where he was also appointed to the faculty. During World War II his work was mainly in mathematics, in Washington and as an instructor at Princeton. Immediately after the war his first major contributions to musical thought began to appear, most notably a study of the formal properties of the 12-tone system, an analytical study of the Bartók quartets, and a number of compositions in which the conceptual and technical insights of his theoretical and analytical works were projected compositionally. The concept of musical articulation through which this projection took place was that which later became known in the popular press as "total serialization." After a short career as a composer of popular songs and musical comedies, Babbitt returned in 1948 to the Princeton music department, where he is now Conant Professor of Music. His activity as a teacher of composers and theorists has been at least as conspicuously significant a medium for the development, formulation, and communication of his musical concepts and insights as have been the traditional media of creative musical intellection. In 1952 he was on the faculty of the Salzburg Seminar in American Studies; in 1957 and 1958 at the Berkshire Music Center; in 1959 and 1960 at the Princeton Seminar in Advanced Musical Studies; in 1964 at the Darmstadt summer courses. In the early 1950s Babbitt became interested in the compositional possibilities of the Mark I electronic music synthesizer being built by RCA engineers at the David Sarnoff Research Center in Princeton. He was a consultant in the construction of an improved Mark II synthesizer, which became a principal basis for the establishment of the Columbia-Princeton Electronic Music Center, for which Babbitt has been on the committee of direction since its inception in 1959. Since then he has written several tape works and works for live performers and tape.

The significance of Babbitt's work in the theoretical reconstruction and compositional extension of the 12-tone syntax of Schoenberg and Webern, in the reformulation of the conceptual and empirical basis of musical tradition, and in his articulation of the explicit relation of the study and invention of musical structure to the whole spectrum of contemporary intellectual development, amounts virtually to a second 20th-century musical revolution. Schoenberg, Stravinsky, and Schenker, the principal architects of the first such revolution, reaffirmed, reconstructed, or replaced those musical "universals" on which musical thought had long rested, but which no longer accounted for compositional developments within the same tradition. Babbitt, with all of the developments of 20th-century scientific, philosophical, and linguistic study at his disposal, was the first to recognize the relativistic nature of such constructs as tonal functions and 12-tone relations. From this followed the further recognition that a musical composition might be understood as representing a set of interdependent empirical-rational choices out of a vast domain of possibility (and hence as representing a potential for uniqueness in musical identity far greater than had ever before been envisioned). In being so understood, moreover, a composition could come to be perceived, in a more than metaphorical or honorific way, as a unique and complex instance of rational thought within an empirical domain. Thus for Babbitt the force of any "musical systems" was not as universal constraints for all music, but as alternative theoretical constructs, rooted in a communality of shared empirical principles and assumptions validated by tradition, experience, and experiment.

Under such an interpretation, the invention of musical systems themselves becomes an act of composition rather than its invariant context. Even more significant for the music-conceptual scheme of the newer musical "revolution" is that the absence of universals virtually necessitates the notion of a composition as a "total structure"—that is, as a multiple integrated set of determinate, particular relations among all its discernible components. For since no principles external to the contents of a work can provide it with

musical identity, no less comprehensive a notion of musical structure could suffice to account for the unique experiences and qualities associated with particular musical works, even in a superficial sense. Thus some of the most far-reaching and powerful contemporary notions of "musical structure" originated with Babbitt, quite apart from the particular systematic and structural inventions originated in his compositional and theoretical works.

These inventions themselves, of course, are the principal substance of Babbitt's creative accomplishment. But their individual ingenuity, which is their most often acknowledged and most frequently emulated aspect, is perhaps accountable for the unique character of Babbitt's works than is the depth of creative discovery, examination, and reconstruction of resources of musical coherence, and of unprecedented numbers of levels of musical structure, all of which may be observed in practice to make a significant difference for the special experienced identities of musical works that the totality of his inventions represent. Thus, one may say that not only has Babbitt found unique ways to think about musical things, he has uniquely found musical things to think about, and unique ways to represent his thoughts in both verbal and musical formulations. And perhaps most significant, he has uniquely conceived each aspect of that thought in a context of significant and continuous interconnection with every other aspect of it.

To give even a minimal account of the nature of Babbitt's work, one has to go beyond the mere citation of individual attributes to the demonstration, however sketchy, of the significant interlinking of such attributes into a consequential chain whose totality constitutes a particular musical conception. For convenience in facilitating such a demonstration (i.e., rather than to create or resolve any substantive music-theoretical issues), it seems useful to distinguish three hierarchically connected music-conceptual levels on which Babbitt's inventions can be ranged: the *structure* of a given musical system, the *compositional resources* of that system, and the *realizations* of such resources as individual "compositional ideas" of individual works. In the first instance one is concerned with that collection of functions (e.g., scale-degree, fifth, triad, etc., in the tonal system; set, trichord in the 12-tone system), their relations (e.g., tonic, dominant, dissonance-consonance, etc., in the tonal system; transposition, retrograde inversion, order adjacency in the 12-

tone system), and the properties of these relations. These functions constitute a set of dispositions to perceive acoustical events in certain ways as one would use a notion of "English" to hear speech sounds in a particular way and "French" to hear such sounds in a different way. The contents of one such set, then, may be considered to provide a *syntax* in terms of which musical ideas may be articulated; and hence, one may designate this level as the *syntactical* level of musical structure.

The compositional resources of such a syntax may be considered to consist in possibilities of association, connection, differentiation, and dimensionality available through the selective, ordered juxtaposition of particular functions and relations contained in the syntax. Such possibilities, of course, result from the relational properties embedded in the system itself; but they are not themselves part of the system nor is their exploitation in a given composition prescribed or entailed by the system, which is merely a reference for anything which might in fact be present. Familiar examples of such compositional resources are prolongations or triads by arpeggiation or *linearization*, as well as modulations, cadences, or *Ursätze* in tonal music. Finally the utilization of such resources in a particular ordering and by means of particular acoustical events in individual musical works constitutes the level of musical realization, the level at which specific composition and analysis may be said to take place.

For Babbitt, the study of the music of Schoenberg and Webern may well have provided the point of departure for his own original musical constructions. One can visualize how, in the early 1940s, he observed that the compositional connections—harmonic, contrapuntal, and phraseological—in works of Schoenberg and Webern could be regarded as projections of original musical continuities in a traditional sense (hence, as 12-tone *compositions*) through the ingenious exploitation of properties inherent in the structures of the particular 12-tone sets on which those works were based, as they related to the transformational array of sets generated by the structure of the 12-tone system (hence, as *12-tone* compositions).

To take a single example: the observation that the phraseology of the second movement of Webern's Op. 27 is defined by an obvious two-part counterpoint, immediate repetitions of single pitches, and large-scale repetitions of simultaneously attacked pitches is connected with the observation that this pattern is generated by a two-part counterpoint of set forms,

such that the particular choice of intervals within the set, transpositional relations of simultaneous sets, and relations of successive transpositions of set pairs all have crucial and interrelated significance in providing the resources for the projected associations. A further observation on the music of Schoenberg reveals the congruence of phraseological and textural articulation with a harmonic association in which completions of 12-pitch-class aggregates in the total texture articulate simultaneous contrapuntal unfoldings of distinct set forms. This procedure, too, is discovered to be possible because of properties intrinsic to the structure of the particular set within the range of relations "prescribed" by the system. For given particular sets, particular intervals of transposition, inversion, and retrogression will make possible counterpoints where presentations of two or more sets simultaneously will result in nonduplications of pitch classes over segments of the sets.

Now both the duplication within a segmented counterpoint in Webern and the nonduplication in Schoenberg are seen to derive from a similar property, that of the *content invariance* of certain segments of sets given the existence of certain interval properties. Thus for example, if the first and second members of a certain set are related by a given interval (say a semitone, as C and D♭), and if there are two other adjacent elements in the set related by the same interval (say, D and E♭), then a transposition of the set by the interval between the first and second semitone-pairs (here two semitones) will result in the appearance of the pitch classes of the second semitone-pair (D and E♭) in the order position of the first semitone pair (i.e., as the first and second elements). Moreover a transposition by the inversion of the same interval (i.e., by 10 semitones) will result in the appearance of the first semitone pair (C and D♭) in the order position of the second pair. This property can be extended to segments of any size, such that the structure of the set can insure that various transpositions will have various degrees of pitch-class duplication or nonduplication, which then become an available resource for compositional articulation. The generalization of this property is greatly assisted by the discovery that the intuitive notion of interval identity is representable, with satisfactory results, as equal differences (i.e., pitches that lie equal numbers of semitones apart are heard as determining equivalent intervals), so that transposition can be represented by the arithmetic operation of addition, applied to numbers representing semitone (-class) relations of pitch (-classes).[1] Thus the powerful resources of mathematics in the investigation of relational properties can be invoked to discover musically intuitive resources of association. Such, and strictly such, is the role of mathematics in Babbitt's musical thought.

Our example proceeds: Just as transposition can be represented as addition of a "constant," so inversion can be represented as complementation or subtraction from a "constant" (i.e., the octave as a "quantity" of 12 semitones). And so too can retrogression be represented as order-position complementation (so that a first pitch class of a set appears in the last order position of the retrograde of the set, etc.) and retrograde-inversion as both pitch-class position and order-position complementation (so that the complement of the first pitch class of a set appears in the last order position). And properties of interval invariance under these transformations are also discovered and generalized to reveal the particular relation of set structure to compositional possibility.

Thus emerges a notion of *segmental invariance* as a compositional resource of 12-tone-systematic music. And the special case of nonduplication of pitches over stretches of set counterpoints is generalized as a notion of *combinatoriality*. And the prevalence of combinatorial construction as a structural principle of Schoenberg's music is formulated, as the prevalence of controlled segmental duplication in Webern, giving special musical meaning to the set-shapes and choices of transpositions in the small and the large in their music —thus articulating both significant individuating characteristics for each of the pieces involved and for the "styles" of the two composers and rooting these differences in a common resource of musical relation.

These notions, moreover, are highly suggestive to further development in composition. For example, Schoenberg's simultaneous counterpoints of half-set segments containing no duplications suggests the possibility of connecting successive sets such that the two adjacent halves do not contain any duplications either. Thus is created a new articulative resource, known as *secondary set formation* (see the first of the *3 Compositions for Piano* for instances of secondary sets). And Webern's notions of duplications, such that his sets tend to be constructed out of internal segments related to each other by the same relations

(transposition, inversion, retrograde-inversion, retrogression) as those by which whole sets are related suggests the development of sections of pieces by the extension of parts of sets into locally "whole" sets by means similar to "derived sets" (examples of derived sets may be observed at the openings of the *String Quartet No. 2* and *Composition for 4 Instruments*). And noticing that what is true of elements of sets adjacent in order may be extended to relations of elements not adjacent in order suggests that a "counterpoint" made up from the presentation of a single set by stratification of its elements through different registers can be related to other such "counterpoints" in significant ways through the understanding and control of set structure. Thus are conceived various partitionings of a set in presentation (as for example in the presentation of a set succession C, D♭, D, E♭, a "correspondence" can be set up by presenting C and D in a low register, D♭ and E♭ in a high one so that the temporal successions C, D♭, D, E♭ is partitioned into two registral successions C D and D♭ E♭, thus giving two significant *motivic levels*). One way of realizing such a resource of partitioning is that through suggestive presentations of *background sets*, significant instrumental and registral lines may be generated so as also to present 12-tone sets; thus the notion of *set completion*, derived initially from Schoenberg's counterpoint, can function on yet another time and function level of musical structure.[2] (See, for example, the set partitionings in the opening bars of *Relata I*.)

The resources of pitch association in music are, of course, realized through time. All musical structure is thus in a fundamental sense rhythmic structure. So the differentia among time intervals may also be structured through a syntax, that is, in a globally consistent way rather than in a locally determined, articulative manner. And similarly the other traditional musical differentia (dynamics, timbres) are also subjectible to structuring in this sense, such that a single succession may represent simultaneously a multiplicity of interrelated functions, a counterpoint of counterpoints in different dimensions, in which a single pitch attack may represent part of a pitch line delineated by time adjacency, as well as parts of different pitch lines delineated by registral adjacency, timbral identity, dynamic identity, etc.

---

[1] Babbitt devised the terms *pitch class* and *interval class* to represent the traditional notions of the functional equivalence of octave-related pitches and intervals.

[2] The notion and utilization of sets that represent each interval class as well as each pitch class uniquely is another of Babbitt's inventions (see, for example, *3 Compositions for Piano*).

But since durational structure is primarily defined by pitch functions, and since its properties are not inherent in the sense that pitch properties are, one's *durational syntax* is more variable from piece to piece than one's *pitch syntax*. Thus *sets* defined by successions of different-sized bundles of evenly spaced attacks (articulated by phrasing, accentuation, etc.: *3 Compositions for Piano*, I), or defined by successions of "time intervals" between attacks (*Composition for 4 Instruments*), or defined by variable articulations of the time contents of a fixed "measure" (*Composition for Tenor and 6 Instruments, All Set, Partitions*, opening of *Relata I*, and most subsequent compositions) might function to generate the *durational counterpoint* of a piece.

The complexity and subtlety with which chains of musical reasoning are realized in Babbitt's actual compositions virtually preclude their explicit exemplification to any revealing extent in a limited context such as this. The notions already mentioned are only a tiny subset of those he has originated and realized musically in a variety of ways so great as to necessitate deep study of many scores for the acquisition of even a superficial sense of their musical scope. Nevertheless a schematic registral representation of the first four "harmonic" (pitch) aggregates of *Partitions for Piano* may prove suggestive (Ex. 1); notice in particular pitch and interval contents of registral lines, dimensions of registral lines in each partition and in each pair of partitions (they all sum to 6 in pairs), contents of total-successional lines, harmonic content of local groups, and registral successions across set-counterpoint boundaries, which by virtue of

AGGREGATES	REGISTERS		NUMBER OF ELEMENTS
I	1	E (E)(E)	1
	2	B (B) (B) D---Bb	3
	3	Eb Ab F#−F(F)C#	5
	4	C G−A (A)	3
II	1	C# F (F)F#G#D#(D#)	5
	2	A G (G) C (C)	3
	3	E	1
	4	Bb D B	3
III	1	A (A) D C	3
	2	F# (F#)C#(C#) Eb E	4
	3	Bb G B	3
	4	F Ab	2
IV	1	B G (G)Bb(Bb)	3
	2	Ab F(F)(F)(F)	2
	3	C D (D D) (D)A(A)(A)	3
	4	E Eb Db Gb	4

Ex. 1.

the contents and dimensions of the individual partitions result in the presentation of a linear aggregate (set) in each registral voice.

The compression and ramification in this partial representation of a fragment and the narrow conceptual slice offered in the narrative account preceding may be taken as indicators of the protean scope of Babbitt's work. Even at this early date that work appears to have extended the musical universe in a multitude of directions and respects and has taken it near to the bounds of human conceptual and perceptual capacity, while taking it near as well to the heights of contemporary intellectual accomplishments.

PRINCIPAL COMPOSITIONS (published by AMP unless otherwise noted): *3 Compositions for Piano* (1947, Boelke); *Composition for 4 Instruments* for flute, clarinet, violin, cello (1947–48, New Music); *Composition for Viola and Piano* (1950); *The Widow's Lament in Springtime* for soprano, piano; poem by William Carlos Williams (1950, Boelke); *Du* for soprano, piano; poem by August Stramm (1951, Boelke); *Woodwind Quartet* (1953); *String Quartet No. 2* (1954); *2 Sonnets* for baritone, clarinet, viola, cello; poems by G. M. Hopkins (1955); *Semisimple Variations* for piano (c.1956, Presser); *All Set* for alto saxophone, tenor saxophone, trumpet, trombone, double bass, drums, vibraphone, piano (1957); *Partitions* for piano (1957, Lawson); *Composition for Tenor and 6 Instruments* for tenor, flute, oboe, violin, viola, cello, harpsichord (1960); *Sounds and Words* for soprano, piano (1960, Marks); *Composition for Synthesizer* on tape (1961–63); *Philomel* for soprano, recorded soprano, synthesized accompaniment on tape (1963–64); *Relata I* for orchestra (1965); *Sextets* for piano, violin (1966); *Post-Partitions* for piano (1966); *Ensembles for Synthesizer* on tape (c.1967); *Correspondences* for string orchestra, synthesized sounds on tape (1967); *Relata II* for orchestra (1968); *String Quartet No. 3* (1969–70); *Phonemena* for soprano, piano (1969–70). List to 1966: *Composers of the Americas* 12:13–15.

PRINCIPAL WRITINGS: "The String Quartets of Bartók," *Musical Quarterly* 35:377–85; "Some Aspects of Twelve-Tone Composition," *The Score and IMA Magazine* (June 1955):53–61; "Who Cares if You Listen?" *Contemporary Composers on Contemporary Music* ed. by E. Schwartz and B. Childs (New York 1967):244–50; "Twelve-Tone Invariants as Compositional Determinants," *Problems of Modern Music* ed. by P. H. Lang (New York 1960):108–21; "Electronic Music, The Revolution in Sound," *Columbia Univ. Magazine* (spring 1960):4–8; "Set Structure as a Compositional Determinant," *Journal of Music Theory* 5:72–94; "Past and Present Concepts of the Nature and Limits of Music," *International Musicological Society Congress Report, New York 1961*:398–403; "Twelve-Tone Rhythmic Structure and the Electronic Medium," *Perspectives* 1/1:49–79; "Remarks on the Recent Stravinsky," *ibid.*

2/2:35–55; "The Synthesis, Perception, and Specification of Musical Time," *Journal of the International Folk Music Council* 16:92–95; "An Introduction to the R.C.A. Synthesizer," *Journal of Music Theory* 8:251–65; "The Use of Computers in Musicological Research," *Perspectives* 3/2:74–83; "The Structure and Function of Musical Theory," *College Music Symposium* 5:49–60; "Edgard Varèse: A Few Observations of His Music," *Perspectives* 4/2:14–22; "Three Essays on Schoenberg: Concerto for Violin and Orchestra, Das Buch der hängenden Gärten, Moses und Aron," *Perspectives on Schoenberg and Stravinsky* ed. by B. Boretz and E. Cone (New York 1968):47–60; "Relata I," *The Orchestral Composers Point of View* ed. by R. S. Hines (Norman, Okla. 1970):11–38; "Contemporary Musical Composition and Musical Theory: A Contemporary Intellectual History," *Perspectives in Musicology* ed. by B. Brook, E. Downes, and S. Van Solkema (New York 1971).

Benjamin Boretz

SEE ALSO Asian Music and Western Composition; Electronic Music: History and Development; Electronic Music: Notation; Mathematics; Musicology and Composition; Performance; Rhythm; Serialism; Text Setting and Usage; Texture; Theory; 12-Tone Techniques; United States.

Bacewicz, Grażyna (b. Łódź, Poland, 5 Feb 1913; d. Warsaw, 17 Jan 1969), studied at the Warsaw Conservatory, receiving two diplomas in 1932 (composition with Kazimierz Sikorski, violin with Jozef Jarzębski). She studied composition in Paris with Nadia Boulanger (1933–34) and violin with A. Touret and Karl Flesch. Mrs. Bacewicz was a professional violinist until 1955. She also taught harmony and counterpoint at the Łódź Conservatory (1934–35, 1945) and composition at the State Academy of Music in Warsaw (from 1966 until her death). She was vice president of the Polish Composers' Association during 1962–69.

PRINCIPAL COMPOSITIONS (published by PWM unless otherwise noted): *String Quartets Nos. 1–7* (1938; 1942; 1947; 1950, Tyssens; 1955; 1960; 1965, Moeck and PWM); *Symphonies Nos. 1–4* (1943, unpub.; 1950; 1952; 1953); *Violin Sonatas Nos. 1–5* (1945, 1946?, 1947, 1951, 1955); *Concerto for String Orchestra* (1948); *Violin Concertos Nos. 3–7* (1948; 1952; 1954; 1958, unpub.; 1965); *Piano Quintet* (1952); *Piano Sonata No. 2* (1953); *10 Studies* for piano (1957); *Music for Strings, Trumpets, and Percussion* (1958); *Sonata* for solo violin (1958); *The Adventures of King Arthur*, comic radio opera (1959); *Pensieri notturni* for chamber orchestra (1961); *Concerto for Orchestra* (1962); *Cello Concerto No. 2* (1963); *Quartet* for 4 cellos (1964); *Musica sinfonica in tre movimenti* (1965);

Contradizione for chamber orchestra (1966, Moeck and PWM); *Concerto* for 2 pianos, orchestra (1966); *In una parte* for orchestra (1967); *Viola Concerto* (1967–68, Curci and PWM); *4 Capriccios* for solo violin (1968); *Pożądanie* [Desire], ballet in honor of Picasso (1968).

Bäck, Sven-Erik (b. Stockholm, 16 Sept 1919), attended the Royal Music Academy in Stockholm (1938–43; violin, viola with Charles Barkel). He studied composition with Hilding Rosenberg (1940–45), attended the Schola Cantorum Baseliensis (1948, 1950; medieval and renaissance music with August Wenzinger and Ina Lohr), and the Accadèmia di Santa Cecilia in Rome (1951–52, composition with G. Petrassi). Bäck was a member of the Kyndel Quartet (1940–44), the Barkel Quartet (1944–53), and was conductor of the "Chamberorchestra 1953" (1953–57). He is a member of the Swedish Royal Academy of Music, and since 1959 has been director and teacher at the Swedish Radio Music School at Edsberg Castle. In addition to the compositions listed below, he has composed many ballet, film, and theater scores.

PRINCIPAL COMPOSITIONS (published by Hansen-W unless otherwise noted): *String Quartet Nos. 1–3* (1945, 1947, 1949); *Expansive Preludes* for piano (1949); *Sonata* for flute (1949); *Kattresan* [Cat's Journey], "Concerto per bambini," for children's choir, 2 recorders, violin, percussion (1952); *Sinfonia da camera* (1955, STIM); *Tranfjädrarna* [Crane Feathers], chamber opera (1957); *Ett spel om Maria. Jesu Moder*, oratorio for soloists, choir, children's choir, organ, orchestra (1958); *Gästabudet* [The Banquet], chamber opera (1958); *13 Motets* for chorus (1959–69); *A Game Around a Game* for strings, percussion (1959); *Fågeln* [The Bird], chamber opera (1962); *Favola* for clarinet, percussion (1962); *Intrada* for orchestra (1964); *Movimento (Rôles)* for orchestra (1966); *O altitudo* for organ (1966). List of compositions, 1945–66: *Nutida Musik* 3–4:20–25.

PRINCIPAL WRITINGS: "Karl-Birger Blomdahl och S.-E. B.," *Prisma* 1948/1:94–98; "Tranfjädrarna," *Modern nordisk musik* ed. by Bengtsson (Stockholm 1957):196–203; *Musikaliske Selvportraetter* ed. by T. Meyer and J. Möller-Marein (Copenhagen 1966):80–87.

BIBL.: Ingemar Bengtsson, "S.-E. B. och Ingvar Lidholm," *Melos* (Dec 1956):345–49; Karl-Birger Blomdahl,"Sonat för soloflöjt,"*Prisma* 1950/1:80; Andrew McCredie, "S.-E. B., A New Mind in Swedish Music," *The Chesterian* 1959/33:114–27; Bo Wallner, *Vår tids musik i Norden* (Stockholm 1968):183–205, English trans. (London 1971). Four articles · about Bäck appeared in *Nutida musik* 3–4:2–30.

SEE ALSO Scandinavia.

Bacon, Ernst (b. Chicago, 26 May 1898), studied at Northwestern Univ. (1915–18, theory with P. C. Lutkin), Chicago Univ. (1919–20, theory with A. Oldberg and T. Otterstroem), and the Univ. of Calif. He studied piano privately in Chicago with Alexander Raab (1916–21) and in Vienna in 1924 with Malwine Bree and Franz Schmidt. He studied theory privately in Vienna in 1924 with Karl Weigl and in San Francisco in 1928 with Ernest Bloch; he also studied conducting with Eugene Goossens in 1926 in Rochester. He conducted several orchestras in San Francisco during 1934–37 while he was supervisor of the Federal Music Project there; he also wrote criticism for *The Argonaut* (1933–35). He has taught at several schools, including Converse College in S. C. (1938–45) and Syracuse Univ. (1945–63). He has performed in Europe and the U.S. as pianist and conductor and has lectured at many U.S. colleges.

PRINCIPAL COMPOSITIONS: *10 Songs* for voice, piano; poems by Goethe, Eichendorff, Whitman, Lenau, Rückert, Lecher, Lillie (1928); *Songs of Eternity*, 4 songs for baritone, orchestra; poems by Emily Dickinson and Walt Whitman (1932); *Black and White Songs*, 5 songs for baritone, orchestra (1932); *Twilight*, 3 songs for low voice, orchestra; poems by Whitman (1932); *Midnight Special*, 4 songs for medium voice, orchestra (1932); *My River*, 5 songs for medium voice, orchestra; poems by Dickinson (1932); *Symphonies Nos. 1–4*: No. 1 (1932); No. 2 (1937, AMP); No. 3, "Great River," for narrator, orchestra; poem by Paul Horgan (1956); No. 4 (1962–63); *Ecclesiastes*, oratorio for soprano, bass, chorus, orchestra (1936); *A Tree on the Plains*, 2-act music play; libretto by Horgan (1940, revised 1962); *6 Songs* for medium or low voice, piano; poems by Sandburg, Whitman, Dickinson (1942, New Music); *5 Poems* for soprano, piano; poems by Dickinson (1943, Schirmer-G); *Along Unpaved Roads* for medium or low voice, piano (1944, Mercury); *From Emily's Diary* for soprano, alto, women's chorus, orchestra; text by Dickinson (1945, Schirmer-G); *Piano Quintet* (1946); *Cello Sonata* (1946); *The Lord Star*, cantata for bass, chorus, brass, strings, organ; poem by Whitman (c.1950, piano score published by Mercury); *String Quintet* (1951); *By Blue Ontario*, oratorio for alto, bass-baritone, chorus, orchestra; poem by Whitman (1958); *Riolama*, concerto for piano, orchestra (1964); *The Last Invocation*, requiem for chorus, orchestra; poems by Whitman, Dickinson (1968–71).

PRINCIPAL WRITINGS: *Words on Music* (Syracuse 1960); *Notes on the Piano* (Syracuse 1963).

Badings, Henk (b. Bandung, Indonesia, 17 Jan 1907), studied mine engineering and geology at the Technical Univ. in Delft,

Netherlands (1924–30), and is self-taught as a composer. He has taught historical geology at the Technical Institute (1931–34), composition at the Rotterdam Conservatory (1934–37) and the Hochschule für Musik in Stuttgart (since 1962), and acoustics at the Univ. of Utrecht (since 1961). During 1937–41 he was codirector of the Music Lyceum in Amsterdam and during 1941–44, director of the State Conservatory in The Hague. He devoted himself exclusively to composing during 1944–61. In 1962 he was guest professor at the Univ. of Adelaide in Australia. The music of Arthur Honegger, Darius Milhaud, and Paul Hindemith have influenced his development as a composer. In many works from about 1924 on he used an "octotonic" scale of alternating whole and half steps. His instrumentation to about 1940 tended to be heavy and dark and the melodic lines long and broadly contoured. Thereafter he preferred lighter textures. About 1952 he began to work with new tunings (including a 31-tone scale) and electronic sound sources (eventually including computers). *Genesis* for 5 tone-generators (1958) treats both time and pitch in free, unfixed ways.

PRINCIPAL COMPOSITIONS (published by Donemus unless otherwise noted): *Symphonies*: No. 2 (1932, Schott); No. 3 (1934, UE); No. 5 (1949, Schott); No. 6, "Psalm," for chorus, orchestra (1953); No. 7, "Louisville" (1954); No. 8, "Hannover" (1956); No. 9 for string orchestra (1960); No. 12, "Sinfonische Klangfiguren" (1964); *Violin Sonatas Nos. 1–3* (1933, Schott; 1939, Schott; 1952); *Piano Sonatas Nos. 1, 2, 6* (1934, Schott; 1941, Schott; 1947); *Largo and Allegro* for string orchestra (1935, UE); *Piano Sonatine No. 1* (1936, Schott); *String Quartets Nos. 2, 4* (1936, Schott; 1966); *Symphonic Variations 1* (1936, UE); *Tragic Overture* for orchestra (1937, UE); *Theme and Variations* for piano (1938, UE); *Balletto grottesco* for piano 4-hands (1939, UE); *Piano Concerto No. 1* (1939); *Symphonic Prologue* (1942, UE); *Violin Concerto No. 4* (1947); *Apocalypse*, oratorio for vocal soloists, chorus, orchestra (1948); *Ballade* for flute, harp (1950); *Symphonic Variation 2*, "Ballade" (1950); *6 Images* for chorus; texts by A. Baud (1950, EFM); *3 Ballades* for women's chorus (1950, EFM); *Sonatas Nos. 2–3* for solo violin (1951; 1951, Schott); *Sonata No. 2* for solo cello (1951); *Viola Sonata* (1951); *Saxophone Concerto* (1951); *Organ Concerto* (1952); *Piano Quintet* (1952); *Octet* for clarinet, bassoon, horn, string quartet, double bass (1952); *Overture No. 5*, "For a Holland Festival," for orchestra (1954); *Cello Concerto No. 2* (1954); *Double Concerto No. 1* for 2 violins, orchestra (1954); *Orestes*, radio opera (1954, unpub.); *Kain*, ballet on 2-track tape (1956, unpub.); *Flute Concertos Nos. 1–2* (1956; 1963, Peters); *Cantata 5*, "Laus pacis," for soprano, men's chorus, wind orchestra (1956); *Evolutionen*, ballet on 1- or 2-track tape (1958, unpub.); *Genesis*,

ballet on tape (1958, unpub.); *Salto Mortale*, chamber opera for TV (1959, unpub.); *Capriccio* for violin, 2-track tape (1959); *Martin Korda D.P.*, dramatic choral opera for soprano, alto, tenor, bass, chorus, orchestra (1960); *Sonata No. 2* for 2 violins in 31-tone temperament (1963); *Double Concerto No. 3* for 2 pianos, orchestra (1964); *Lucebert-Lieder*, 3 songs for men's chorus, tape (1964); *Pittsburgh Concerto* for orchestra, 2-track tape (1965, Peters); *6 Lechler Leider* for voice, piano (1966); *Concerto* for harp, wind orchestra (1967, Peters); *Triple Concerto No. 2* for 3 horns, wind orchestra, tape (1970, unpub.); *Ballade van die bloeddorstige Jagter* for vocal soloists, chorus, orchestra, tape (c. 1970?, unpub.); *Kontrapunkte* for piano, tape; composed in collaboration with Hellmut Schoell (1970, recorded by Kulturringkonzerte 73).

BIBL.: Sylvia van Ameringen, "H. B.," *Musica* 1953/10:430–34; Jos Wouters, "H. B.," *Sonorum Speculum* 32:1–23.

SEE ALSO Netherlands.

Baird, Tadeusz (b. Grodzisk, Poland, 26 July 1928), studied at the State Music Academy in Warsaw (1947–51, composition with Kazimierz Sikorski) and Warsaw Univ. (1948–52, musicology with Zofia Lissa). Until the late 1950s Baird's music followed in the late-romantic tradition, and the penchant for lyricism then evident has continued to the present. He began using 12-tone procedures about 1956 and with the *4 Songs* of 1966 began to explore the structural potentials in sound textures. The *Sinfonia brevis* is a fully developed example of this latter approach.

PRINCIPAL COMPOSITIONS (published by PWM; copublishers also noted): *Symphony No. 1* (1950); *Colas Breugnon* for flute, chamber orchestra (1951); *Concerto for Orchestra* (1953); *Cassation* for orchestra (1956); *4 Love Sonnets* for baritone, chamber orchestra; poems by Shakespeare (1956); *String Quartet* (1957); *4 Essays* for orchestra (1958); *Espressioni varianti* for violin, orchestra (1959); *Egzorta* [Exhortation] for narrator, chorus, orchestra (1960); *Erotica*, 6 love songs for soprano, orchestra; poems by M. Hiller (1961); *Variations without a Theme* for orchestra (1962, Schott); *Epiphany Music* for orchestra (1963); *Songs of the Trouvères* for mezzo-soprano, 2 flutes, cello; medieval French texts (1964); *4 Dialogues* for oboe, chamber orchestra (1964, Schott); *Jutro* [Tomorrow], musical drama (1966); *4 Songs* for mezzo-soprano, chamber orchestra; texts by Vesne Parun (1966, Chester); *4 Novelettes* for chamber orchestra (1967, Chester); *5 Songs* for mezzo-soprano, chamber orchestra; texts by Halina Poswiatowska (1967–68, Chester); *Sinfonia brevis* (1968, Chester); *Symphony No. 3* (1968–69, Chester).

BIBL.: T. Marek, "Samtida polska tonsättare," *Musikrevy* 15:194 and 20:214; K. H. Wörner, "Poland," *Musical Quarterly* 48:112–13; Tadeusz

A. Zielínski, "Wokol problematyki ekspresji," *Ruch muzyczny* 5:5–6. Reviews of Baird's music have appeared in the Polish journals *Muzyka* (1956) and *Ruch muzyczny* (1958, 1960, 1963). SEE ALSO Dance, Poland.

Ballet, see Dance

Ballif, Claude (b. Paris, 22 May 1924), studied during 1942–51 at the Bordeaux Conservatory (composition with J. F. Vaubourgoin), the Paris Conservatory (composition with Noël Gallon, Tony Aubin, and Olivier Messiaen), and the Berlin Hochschule für Musik (composition with Boris Blacher and Josef Rufer). In 1953 he graduated from the Univ. of Berlin. He taught at the Institutes Françaises in Berlin and Hamburg during 1955–58. During 1959–61 he worked with the Groupe de Recherches Musicales at the French Radio in Paris. He has taught analysis and musicology at L'Ecole Supérieure Technique des Industries Audio-Visuelles (1962–63) and at L'Ecole Normale (1963–65) and pedagogy at the Reims Conservatory (since 1964).

PRINCIPAL COMPOSITIONS: *Pièces détachées* for piano, Op. 6 (1952–53); *Antienne No. 1 à la Ste. Vierge* for 6 vocal soloists, 8 instruments, Op. 7 (1952, revised 1965); *Airs comprimés* for piano, Op. 5 (1953); *String Trio*, Op. 16 (1956); *Piano Sonata No. 2*, Op. 19 (1957); *Voyage de mon oreille* for orchestra, Op. 20 (1957, Bote); *Phrases sur le souffle*, vocalises for alto, 8 instruments, Op. 25 (1958); *Quintette avec flûte* for flute, oboe, string trio, Op. 24 (1958); *Flute Sonata*, Op. 23 (1958); *Mouvement pour 2* for flute, piano, Op. 27 (1959, Bote); *Ceci et cela* for orchestra, Op. 26 (1959, revised 1965); *Double Trio* for flute, oboe, cello and violin, clarinet, horn, Op. 35 (1961); *A cor et à cri* for orchestra, Op. 39 (1962); *Imaginaire I* for flute, clarinet, trumpet, trombone, violin, cello, harp, Op. 41 (1963).

PRINCIPAL WRITINGS: *Introduction à la métatonalité* (Paris 1956); "Triste exotisme," *La Revue musicale* (1961); "L'Usage des instruments dans la musique contemporaine," *Cahiers d'études de la radio* (Paris, 1963); "Matière, mouvement, musique," *La Revue musicale* (1963); "Les Modes de mouvement," *Entretiens sur le temps* (Mouton, 1967); "Points, mouvement," *La Revue musicale* (1968):53–75; "Un sens des sons," *Revue d'esthétique* 1968/2–3; "L'Ars nova en France," *Encyclopédie des musiques sacrées*, vol. 2 (Paris 1968); *Berlioz* (Paris 1968).

BIBL.: *C. B.; Essais, Etudes, Documents*, special number of *La Revue musicale* 263 (1968); *C. B., Journée du 7 Mars 1968 l'A. R. C.*, supplement to *La Revue musicale* 263.

Banks, Don (b. Melbourne, Australia, 25 Oct 1923), attended the Melbourne Univ. Conservatorium of Music (1947–49, composition with A. E. H. Nickson and Dorian Le Gallienne) and studied privately with Matyas Seiber (London, 1950–52) and Luigi Dallapiccola (Florence, 1952–53). He is active in England as a free-lance composer and has written many film and television scores. He founded the Australian Musical Association in London, was chairman of the Society for the Promotion of New Music (1967–68), and serves on the Executive Committee of the British Society for Electronic Music. The analytical procedures and theories of Milton Babbitt have exerted a decisive influence on Banks since he and Babbitt first met in 1952. Another important influence is Banks's experience as a jazz pianist and arranger, mainly in Australia. This involvement has lead in recent years to some third-stream compositions (such as *Settings from Roget*).

PRINCIPAL COMPOSITIONS (published by Schott): *Sonata* for violin, piano (1953); *Three Studies* for cello, piano (1954); *Sonata da Camera* (1961); *Horn Trio* (1962); *Horn Concerto* (1965); *Settings from Roget* for jazz singer, jazz quartet (1966); *Assemblies* for orchestra (1966); *Tirade*, triptych for mezzo-soprano, piano, harp, 3 percussion (1968); *Violin Concerto* (1968).

PRINCIPAL WRITINGS: "Composers' Forum" (*re* the *Violin Concerto*), *Musical Events* (London, August 1968):8–9.

BIBL.: William Mann, "The Music of D. B.," *Musical Times* (August 1968):719–21; Francis Routh, *Contemporary British Music* (London 1970).

Banshchikov, Gennadii Ivanovich (b. Kazan City, U.S.S.R., 9 Nov 1943), attended the Moscow Conservatory (1961–64, composition with S. Z. Balecanyan) and the Leningrad Conservatory (1965–69, composition with B. A. Arepot). His development has also been influenced by German music, principally that of Richard Strauss and Arnold Schoenberg. In addition to the compositions listed below, he has written many scores for radio and television.

PRINCIPAL COMPOSITIONS: *Cello Concertos Nos. 1–5*: No. 1 with chamber orchestra (1962); No. 2 (1963); No. 3 for solo cello (1965); No. 4, "Duodecimet," for cello, 11 instruments (1966); No. 5 (1970); *Piano Concerto* with chamber orchestra (1963); *Zodniye* [The Architects], cantata for bass, male chorus, orchestra; text by D. Kedrin (1964); *To the Memory of F. G. Lorca*, cantata for chorus, chamber orchestra (1965); *Symphony* (1967); *Lyubov i Silin*, opera; libretto by S. Volkov after the play by K. Prutkoff (1968); *Piano Sonata*

(1969); *Cello Sonata* (1969); *How Ivan Ivanovitch quarreled with Ivan Nikiforovich*, opera; libretto after Gogol (1971).

Barati, George (b. Györ, Hungary, 3 April 1913), studied at the Ferenc Liszt Conservatory in Budapest (1932–38, composition with Leo Weiner and Zoltán Kodály) and at Princeton Univ. (1939–43, composition with Roger Sessions). He was first cellist of the Budapest Symphony and at the Municipal Opera House (1935–38) and has played in the San Francisco Symphony Orchestra (1946–50) and the California String Quartet (1947–50). During 1939–43 he was conductor of the Princeton Chamber Ensemble, which he founded; during 1948–52, of the Barati Chamber Orchestra of San Francisco; and during 1950–67, of the Honolulu Symphony Orchestra. His music has been influenced by his contacts with Bartók and Kodály in Budapest and by performing in orchestras under many distinguished conductors.

PRINCIPAL COMPOSITIONS: *String Quartets Nos. 1–2* (1944, 1962; ACA); *Prisma* for harp (1948, Peer); *2 Piano Pieces* (1948, ACA); *Chamber Concerto* (1952, Peters); *Sonata* for violin (1956, Peters); *Cello Concerto* (1957, Peters); *Configuration* for orchestra (1957, Peer); *The Dragon and the Phoenix* for orchestra (1960, Peters); *Quartet* for flute/alto flute, oboe (English horn), double bass (cello), harp (1964, Peters); *Symphony* (1964, Peters); *The Waters of Kane* for chorus, orchestra (1964, ACA); *Polarization* for orchestra (1965, Peters); *Octet* for flute, oboe, bassoon, string quartet, harpsichord (1967, Peer); *Triple Exposure* for cello (1967, Peters); *Hawaiian Bird-Catching Song* for children's chorus, percussion (1969); *Festival Hula*, symphonic dance (1969); *The Feather Cloak*, opera; libretto by Reuel Denney (1970); *2 Pieces* for guitar (1970); *South Seas' Suite* for guitar, orchestra (1970).

PRINCIPAL WRITINGS: "Mathematics and Music," *Congress on Mathematics Report* (Honolulu 1964) and *Music Journal* (Nov and Dec 1966).

Barbe, Helmut (b. Halle, 28 Dec 1927), studied at the Berlin Church Music School (1946–52; theory with Ernst Pepping; organ, piano with Herbert Schulze; choral conducting with Gottfried Grote) and conducting privately with Theodor Jakobi (1953–54). Since 1950 he has been organist and choir director at St. Nicholas' Church in Spandau and since 1955, a harmony and orchestration teacher at the Berlin Church Music School. He has directed the Berlin Studentenkantorei (1965–68) and the student Kammerchore (since 1968). His compositions have been strongly influenced by the music of Stravinsky and Webern.

PRINCIPAL COMPOSITIONS: *Ich will dem Herren singen*, motet for chorus (1955, Merseburger); *Passion Motet* for chorus (1955, Merseburger); *Magnificat 1956*, concerto for chorus, 11 winds, low strings, organ, timpani (1956, Hänssler); *Gesang des Abgeschieden*, 5 songs for baritone, piano; poems by Georg Trakl (1957); *Canticum Simeonis*, concerto for tenor, chorus, strings, celesta, organ, percussion (1958, Hänssler); *Ostergeschichte* for alto, baritone, chorus, orchestra (1961, Hänssler); *Missa brevis* for chorus, 2 flutes, oboe, English horn, bassoon, cello (1961, Hänssler); *Organ Sonata 1964* (1964, Hänssler); *Chinesische Impressionen* for chorus, text by Li Tai Pe translated by Klabund (1964, Bärenreiter); *Psalm 90*, motet for chorus (1965, Bärenreiter); *Requiem* for soprano, flute, oboe, bassoon, viola, cello, double bass (1965, Hänssler); *Violin Concerto* (1966, Sikorski); *Ye Shall Have a Song*, cantata for women's chorus, oboe, horn, harp (1967, Hänssler); *5 Songs* for soprano, piano (1969); *Aus des goldenen Stadt* for piano trio (1969); *Jeruschalajim*, concerto for high voice, organ (1969, Hänssler); *Psalm 42*, sacred concerto for tenor, organ (1970, Hänssler); *Hovs Hallar*, concerto for organ, 12 solo strings, percussion (1970); *Magnalia D*, biblical scenes for baritone, chorus, organ (1971).

BIBL.: S. Günther, "Jüngstes Kirchenmusicalisches Schaffen, H. B.," *Gottesdienst und Kirchenmusik* (1962): 87–91; H. G. Schönian, "H. B.," *ibid.* (1960): 85ff.

SEE ALSO Liturgical Music: Christian.

Barber, Samuel (b. West Chester, Pa., 9 March 1910), began piano lessons at six and composing a year later. At 14 he entered the Curtis Institute in Philadelphia, where his principal studies were in composition (with Rosario Scalero), piano (with Isabelle Vangerova), and singing (with Emilio de Gogorza). From 1931 to 1933 he taught piano at Curtis, and since then he has earned his living principally from his music.

Barber ranks with Aaron Copland and George Gershwin as one of the most frequently performed of American composers. His songs, choral pieces, and piano and chamber music have become part of the repertory of American performers. His idiom is in what is generally regarded as the mainstream of musical tradition. The earliest works, such as the popular *Cello Sonata* (1932), are quite conservative, post-romantic in harmony. After about 1939 (the break is audible in the *Violin Concerto* of that year), his harmony became much more dissonant. His music, however, has remained tonal though with varying degrees of freedom. Sometimes it is anchored only to a single tone or chord; sometimes it reverts to the highly organized tonality of tradition. Counterpoint is important and handled with ease (the last movement of the *Piano Sonata* (1949) is a whirlwind fugue). Rhythms are interesting and varied. The orchestral works are alive with color. Barber's American background is capitalized on in *Excursions* (1944), four piano pieces treating popular American music (boogie-woogie, blues, folksong, barn dance), and *Souvenirs* (1952), a set of ballroom dances of c.1914. The songs range from short lyrical pieces to big dramatic works; in mood they vary from gentle, sometimes highly sophisticated humor to stark tragedy. They are marked by the literary quality of the texts (Joyce, Rilke, Yeats, G. M. Hopkins, among others), by the skilled writing for the voice, and by the sensitive prosody—the music of *Hermit Songs* (1953), for example, fits the natural pronunciation of the words so closely that no time signatures are needed or used. Barber's ability to sustain a lyric mood successfully far beyond the confines of a song is shown in the 18-minute *Knoxville, Summer of 1915* (1947).

PRINCIPAL COMPOSITIONS (published by Schirmer-G): *Cello Sonata* (1932); *String Quartet in B Minor* (1936; slow movement arranged for string orchestra, *Adagio for Strings*); *Reincarnations* for chorus (1936–40); *Essay for Orchestra No. 1* (1937); *Violin Concerto* (1939); *A Stop Watch and an Ordnance Map* for male chorus, timpani; text by Stephen Spender (1940); *Essay for Orchestra No. 2* (1942); *Capricorn Concerto* for flute, oboe, trumpet, strings (1944); *Excursions* for piano (1944); *Cello Concerto* (1945); *Cave of the Heart*, dance; choreography by Martha Graham (1946; originally titled *The Serpent Heart*; the orchestral suite titled *Medea*); *Knoxville, Summer of 1915* for soprano, orchestra; text by James Agee (1947); *Piano Sonata* (1949); *Souvenirs* for orchestra (1952); *Hermit Songs* for voice, piano; medieval Irish texts (1953); *Prayers of Kierkegaard* for chorus, orchestra (1954); *Vanessa*, 4-act opera; libretto by Gian Carlo Menotti (1957–58); *Toccata festiva* for organ, orchestra (1960); *Piano Concerto* (1962). List to 1959: *Composers of the Americas* 5:16–21.

BIBL.: Nathan Broder, *S. B.* (New York 1954); Russell E. Friedewald, *A Formal and Stylistic Analysis of the Published Music of S. B.* (PhD diss., State Univ. of Iowa, 1957).   Nathan Broder

SEE ALSO Dance, Opera, United States.

Barce, Ramón (b. Madrid, 16 March 1928), studied at the Univ. of Madrid (1950–56), where he earned a PhD in linguistics and at the Madrid Conservatory (1954–57, composition with Gerardo Gombau). In 1958 he founded the group Nueva Música in Madrid, and in 1967 he became editor of *Sonda*, a journal of contemporary music, and director of the Sonda concert series.

PRINCIPAL COMPOSITIONS: *Canciones de la ciudad* for soprano, flute, bass clarinet, bassoon, timpani, viola, cello; texts by Elena Andrés (1959); *Estudio de sonoridades* for piano (1962); *Parábola* for wind quintet (1963); *Objetos sonoros* for chamber orchestra, percussion (1964); *Abgrund Hintergrund*, theater piece (1964); *Alfa* for string orchestra (1965); *Nueve preludios* for piano (1965); *Coral hablado* for 6 men's voices (1965); *Concierto de Lizara No. 2* for percussion, winds (1966); *Las cuatro estaciones* for orchestra (1967); *Canadá-trío* for flute, piano, percussion (1968); *Obertura fonética* for wind sextet (1968); *Concierto de Lizara No. 1* for oboe, trumpet, percussion, string orchestra (1969); *Música fúnebre* for flute, oboe, clarinet, strings, percussion (1969).

PRINCIPAL WRITINGS: "Relatividad de la fijación musical," *Atlántida* (Madrid) 4:422–27; "Control, supercontrol, infracontrol," *Atlántida* 15:306–15; "Hacia cero: del sonido al rito," *Décollage* (Cologne) 4; "Nuevo sistema atonal," *Atlántida* 21:330–43; "Grafización," *Sonda* (Madrid) 2:11–18; "Comentarios a la estética de Lukács," *Sonda* 5:9–18. Barce also edited a Spanish edition of Schoenberg's *Style and Idea* (Madrid 1964).

BIBL.: Tomas Marco, "Nuevo sistema musical," *S. P.* (Madrid, 31 July 1966):53f.; Jacobo Romano, "Músicos de hoy: R. B.," *Buenos Aires musical* (16 May 1966):3.

SEE ALSO Spain.

Barkauskas, Vytautas (b. Kaunas, Lithuania, 25 March 1931), studied physics and mathematics at the State Pedagogical Institute in Vilna during 1949–53 and music there at the Talat-Kelpša College of Music (1949–53) and at the Lithuanian State Conservatory (1953–59; composition with Antanas Račiunas, orchestration with Eduardas Balsys, harmony with Zigmas Aleksandravičius). He was an adviser to amateur composers for the music department of the Lithuanian Folk Art Institute during 1958–61 and has since taught theory at the Lithuanian State Conservatory. His music has been influenced by new music presented at the Warsaw Autumn festivals and the Zagreb Music Biennials. His *Poezija* cycle uses a free treatment of the 12-tone system. *Intimate Composition*, which is concerned primarily with sound textures, incorporates aleatory processes. *3 Aspects* is a polystylistic synthesis.

PRINCIPAL COMPOSITIONS: *Symphonies Nos. 1–2* (1963, 1971); *Poezija* [Poetry], cycle for piano (1964, Muzyka); *Concertino* for 4 chamber groups (1966); *Variations* for 2 pianos (1967, SC); *Žodis revoliucijai*, cantata for narrator, chorus, orchestra; text by Antanas Drilinga (1967, Muzyka); *Intimate Composition* for oboe, 12 strings (1968); *3 Aspects* for orchestra (1969); *Contrast Music* for 4 flutes, cello, percussion (1969); *Sonata pathetique* for piano (1969); *Pro memoria*, 3 movements for flute, bass clarinet, piano (harpsichord), 5 percussionists (1970); *Monologue* for oboe (1970, Peters-L); *La vostra nominanza e color d'erba*, music mirage for chamber chorus, string quintet (1971).

Barlow, Wayne (b. Elyria, Ohio, 6 Sept 1912), studied at the Eastman School (1930–37, composition with Edward Royce, Bernard Rogers, Howard Hanson) and at the Univ. of Southern Calif. (1935, composition with Arnold Schoenberg). He has taught at Eastman since 1937 and is director of the Electronic Music Studio there. Since 1945 he has been organist and choirmaster at St. Thomas Episcopal Church in Rochester.

PRINCIPAL COMPOSITIONS: *The Winter's Passed* for oboe, strings (1938, Fischer); *The 23rd Psalm* for chorus, organ or orchestra (1944, Fischer-J); *Mass in G* for chorus, orchestra (1950); *Night Song* for orchestra (1957); *Missa Sancti Thomae* for chorus, organ (1959, Gray); *Sinfonia da camera* for orchestra (1962); *Hymn Voluntaries for the Church Year* for organ (1963, Concordia); *Trio* for oboe, viola, piano (1964); *Dynamisms* for 2 pianos (1967); *Elegy* for viola, piano or orchestra (1967); *Wait for the Promise of the Father*, cantata for chorus, orchestra (1968); *Concerto* for saxophone, band (1970); *Psalm 97* for chorus, organ, tape (1970, Hope).

PRINCIPAL WRITINGS: *Foundations of Music* (New York 1953); "Crisis!", *Music Journal* (Feb 1962):27; "Of Choral Music for the Church," *The Choral Journal* (April 1964); review of William Austin's *Music in the Twentieth Century* in *Music Educators' Journal* (Nov 1967):119; "Electronic Music: Challenge to Music Education," *Electronic Music Review* (April 1968):40 and *Music Educators' Journal* (Nov 1968):66.

Barraqué, Jean (b. Paris, 17 Jan 1928), studied with Jean Langlais and then Olivier Messiaen (1948–51). He belonged to the French radio's Groupe de Recherches Musicales from 1951 to 1953. In 1961 under the sponsorship of Etienne Souriau, he joined the Centre National de la Recherche Scientifique to pursue research in musical esthetics.

Barraqué is a modern romantic, an heir to the Beethoven tradition; he feels that "our century requires grandeur and even grandiloquence." Most of his output, which is still rather small, borders on the opera form; the huge cycle *The Death of Virgil* is dramaturgical in nature but involves no scenic action. The composer has a marked predilection for the soprano voice and for the piano. One or the other or both are found in all his works previous to the *Concerto*, and for both his writing is purposefully difficult. As an inheritor of the 12-tone Viennese school, he has remained faithful to the serial system, contributing to its further development the procedures of "proliferating series" (two series interacting to produce a third, etc.). He combines complex polyphonic textures with "irrational" rhythms based on uneven values and constantly changing tempos. A vehement tone and a quest for the paroxysmal, which does not exclude deliberately exaggerated effects, alternate and at times coexist with a nocturnal, dreamlike poetry in which silence plays a crucial role. He is a determined adversary of those who would deprive art of its sacred qualities, and his style is opposed to everything in contemporary music that may be regarded as experimental, including collage and aleatory procedures.

PRINCIPAL COMPOSITIONS (published by Bruzzichelli): *Piano Sonata* (1950–52); *Séquence* for voice, percussion, vibraphone, celesta, piano, harp, violin, cello; text from Nietzsche (1950–55); *Le Temps restitué* for soprano, chorus, orchestra; text by Broch (1957–69); *... au-delà du Hasard* for 4 instrumental ensembles, 1 vocal ensemble; text by the composer (1959); *Chant après chant* for 6 percussionists, voice, piano; text by the composer, Hermann Broch (1966); *Concerto* for clarinet, vibraphone, 6 instrumental ensembles (1968). (Except for the *Concerto*, all the works composed after 1956 are part of or are related to the large-scale cycle *The Death of Virgil*.)

PRINCIPAL WRITINGS: "Résonances privilégiées," *Cahiers de la Compagnie Madeleine Renaud Jean-Louis Barrault* (Paris 1954):27–37; "Des Gouts et des couleurs," *Domaine musical* (Paris) 1:14–23; *Debussy* (Paris 1962); "Propos impromptu," *Courrier musical de France* 26:75–80.

BIBL.: André Hodeir, *Since Debussy* (New York 1961):161–203; *Histoire de la musique* (vol. 3 of the *Encyclopédie de la Pléiade*, Paris 1963):1253.

André Hodeir

Barraud, Henry (b. Bordeaux, 23 April 1900), studied at the Paris Conservatory (1926–27, fugue with Georges Caussade) but was expelled by the director, Rabaud, who, according to Barraud, considered his compositions a bad influence on the other students. He then studied privately with Paul Dukas and Louis Aubert. During 1934–37 he was music director for the 1937 Paris Exposition. He was program manager and music director for the French Radio-Television network during 1944–65. His musical style has been influenced by wide-ranging interests including Gregorian chant, Notre Dame organa, Josquin des Prez, Monteverdi, and such contemporary composers as Debussy, Stravinsky, Schoenberg, and Webern.

PRINCIPAL COMPOSITIONS: *4 Preludes* for string orchestra (1935–37, Leduc); *La Farce de Maître Pathelin*, 1-act comic opera; libretto by Gustave Cohen (1937–38, Boosey); *Piano Concerto* (1939, Boosey); *Offrande à une ombre* for orchestra (1941–42, Boosey); *Le Testament de François Villon*, cantata for tenor, chorus, harpsichord (1945, Durand); *Le Mystère des Saints Innocents*, oratorio for narrator, baritone, chorus, orchestra; text by Charles Péguy (1946, Boosey); *Numance*, lyric tragedy in 2 acts; libretto by Salvador de Madriaga (1949–52, Boosey); *Images pour un poète maudit*, suite for chamber orchestra (1954, Salabert); *Te Deum* for chorus, 16 wind instruments (1955, Ricordi); *Symphony* for string orchestra (1955–56, Boosey); *Symphony No. 3* (1956–57, Boosey); *Lavinia*, 3-act opéra bouffe; libretto by Félicien Marceau (1958–59, Boosey); *Rapsodie cartésienne* for orchestra (1959, Boosey); *Rapsodie dionysienne* for orchestra (1961–62, Boosey); *Divertimento* for orchestra (1962, Boosey); *Concerto* for flute, string orchestra (1962, Boosey); *Symphonie concertante* for trumpet, orchestra (1965–66); *3 Etudes* for orchestra (1967–68, EFM); *Une Saison en enfer* for orchestra (1968–69, Boosey); *Variations à treize* for chamber orchestra (1969, Boosey).

PRINCIPAL WRITINGS: *La France et la musique occidentale* (Paris 1956); *Berlioz* (Paris 1966); *Pour Comprendre les musiques d'aujourd'hui* (Paris 1968); *Les Huit Chefs d'oeuvre de Théâtre Lyrique* (Paris 1971).

BIBL.: *Hommage à H. B.*, special edition of *La Table ronde* (July 1961); Antoine Goléa, *20 Ans de musique contemporaine* (Paris 1962).

SEE ALSO France.

Barroso, Sergio-Fernández (b. Havana, 4 March 1946), studied at the Amadeo Roldán Conservatory (1951–66, piano with César Pérez Sentenat, organ with Manuel Suarez) and at the Prague Music Academy (1966–68; composition with Vaclav Dóbias, instrumentation with Vaclav Zich, analysis with Karel Janeček). Since 1968 he has taught counterpoint and fugue at the National School of Arts and the Roldán Conservatory and has been music advisor to C.M.B.F. Radio. He is also director of the music department of the Havana National Library "José Martí." His musical development has been influenced by ancient Eastern literature and its parallels in pre-Columbian America. He is interested in music of a dramatic character with emphasis on rhythm and color.

PRINCIPAL COMPOSITIONS (published by EGREM): *Oda al soldado muerto* for orchestra (1967); *Oboe Concerto* (1967–68); *Concerto* for 2 pianos (1 on tape), 3 percussionists, audience in 2 groups (1968); *Plasmasis*, ballet for 2 dancers on tape; choreography by Alicia Alonso (1970); *La casa*, ballet after García-Lorca for winds, percussion, speaking voices, tape; choreography by Alonso (1970); *Concerto* for guitar, "orquesta fonatoria" (1970).

Bárta, Lubor (b. Ludná, Czechoslovakia, 8 Aug 1928), attended Charles Univ. in Prague (1946–48, musicology, esthetics) and the Prague Academy of Musical Arts (1948–52, composition with Jaroslav Řídký). He is active in Prague as a composer and pianist. The primary influences on his composition have come from Stravinsky, Bartók, Hindemith and Martinů.

PRINCIPAL COMPOSITIONS (published by Supraphon unless otherwise noted): *Viola Concerto* (1957, ČHF); *Piano Concerto* (1959); *Violin Sonata No. 2* (1959); *Piano Sonata No. 2* (1961); *Ludi* for chamber orchestra (1964); *4 Compositions* for oboe (or clarinet), piano (1965); *8 Compositions* for piano (1965); *Sonata* for guitar (1965); *4 Children's Choruses*; text by Z. Kriebl (1965); *Flute Sonata* (1966, Panton); *String Quartet No. 3* (1967); *Wind Quintet No. 2* (1969, ČHF); *The Bitter Summer* (Symphony No. 2) (1969, Panton); *Violin Concerto No. 2* (1970, unpub.).

BIBL.: *Contemporary Czechoslovak Composers* (Prague 1965):37–38.

SEE ALSO Czechoslovakia.

Barth, Hans (b. Leipzig, 25 June 1897; d. Jacksonville, Fla., 8 Dec 1956), moved to the U.S. with his family when he was still a child. He studied composition at the Leipzig Conservatory with Carl Reinecke. He was director of the Yonkers, N.Y., Institute of Musical Art and the National School for Musical Culture in New York City and taught piano at the Mannes School and the Miami Conservatory in Fla. (1948–56). In 1928 he and George Weitz built a portable 1/4-tone piano, for which he composed a number of pieces.

PRINCIPAL COMPOSITIONS: *Miragia*, comic opera, Op. 2 (1916, revised 1931); *Concerto* for 1/4-tone piano, orchestra, Op. 11 (1928); *Piano Sonatas Nos. 1–2*, Opp. 7, 14 (1929; 1932, AMP); *Quintet* for strings, 1/4-tone piano (1930); *Concerto* for 1/4-tone piano, string orchestra, Op. 15 (1930); *Suite* for 1/4-tone strings, brass, kettledrums

(1930); *Suites Nos. 1–2* for piano, Opp. 20, 23 (1938, 1941); *Symphony No. 1*, "Prince of Peace," for orchestra, Op. 25 (1940); *10 Etudes* for 1/4-tone piano, orchestra (1942–44); *Symphony No. 2* (1948).

PRINCIPAL WRITINGS: *Technic*, a piano teaching manual (New York 1949).

SEE ALSO Microtones.

Bartholomée, Pierre (b. Brussels, 5 August 1937), studied at the Brussels Royal Conservatory (1953–58, harmony and counterpoint with Léon Stekke, Jean Louël, and Arsène Souffrian; chamber music with Rodolphe Soiton; piano with André Dumortier). He also studied piano privately with Wilhelm Kempf. In 1960 he was a producer for the music division of Belgian Television. During 1960–61 he taught harmony at the Music Academy in Ixelles and during 1961–67, piano at the Uccle Academy of Music in Belgium. He performs as a pianist and conductor and directs the instrumental ensemble Musiques Nouvelles. The principal influence on his musical thinking has been that of Henri Pousseur. Other influences have included Boulez and Berio and music of the 16th–17th centuries.

PRINCIPAL COMPOSITIONS: *Chanson* for cello (1964, UE); *Cantate aux Alentours* for mezzo-soprano, bass, flute, harp, 2 violas da gamba, Hammond organ, 2 percussion groups, electronic amplification (1966); *Tombeau de Marin Marais* for violin, 2 violas da gamba, harpsichord (1967, UE); *La Ténèbre souveraine* for 5 vocal soloists, double chorus, orchestra (1967); *Récit* for organ (1970); *Harmonique* for orchestra (1970, UE).

SEE ALSO Belgium.

Bartók, Béla (b. Nagyszentmiklós, Hungary—now Sînnicolau Mare, Rumania, 25 March 1881; d. New York, 26 Sept 1945), came of a musical family and showed an early aptitude for piano and composition. His first public concert, in a small country town in 1892, included a piano piece of his own called *The Danube*, which described the course of the river through various countries. Moving in 1894 to Pozsony (now Bratislava), he studied with the conductor László Erkel (son of the finest 19th-century Hungarian opera composer, Ferenc Erkel) until 1899, when he entered the Royal Academy of Music in Budapest to study composition with Hans Koessler and piano with István Thomán (a Liszt pupil). He was quickly recognized as an outstanding pianist, but made little headway in composition until 1902, when the first performance in Budapest of Strauss's *Thus Spake Zarathustra* stimulated and released his imagination. Inspired by Strauss's example and by the movement for national independence then stirring, he wrote a large-scale symphonic poem *Kossuth* (1903) dealing with the events of the 1848 uprising. It was performed in Budapest and Manchester in 1904.

In 1905 Bartók became aware of Hungarian peasant music, which is different from what had previously been known as Hungarian folk music. He also came into contact with his fellow composer Zoltán Kodály, who had independently made the same discovery. Together they published in 1906 a collection of 20 Hungarian folksongs with piano accompaniment. Under Kodály's influence Bartók became acquainted at this time with the music of Debussy. In 1907 he was appointed a professor of piano at the Royal Academy of Music in Budapest. For the next ten years he assiduously collected and studied the folk music of Hungary and neighboring peoples, especially the Rumanians and Slovaks, who had large national minorities within the frontiers of pre-1919 Hungary. His own music was not received well, and after 1911 he withdrew from public musical life and worked on folk music. His first book, on Rumanian folksongs in Hungary, was published in Bucharest in 1913.

The tide of recognition began to turn in Bartók's favor after his ballet *The Wooden Prince* (1914–16) was produced at the Budapest Opera House in 1917. Its success was so great that his opera *Bluebeard's Castle* (1911), formerly rejected, was produced the following year. Universal Edition of Vienna, the leading publishers of advanced music, contracted to publish his works. He was commissioned to write a work for the celebrations of the 50th anniversary of the union of Buda and Pest (*Dance Suite*, 1923), which was quickly taken up by orchestras all over the world. Another of his major ethnographical works appeared in German in the same year, followed by his study of Hungarian folk music in Hungarian in 1924, in German in 1925, and in English in 1931. During these years he resumed his career as a concert pianist, and a spate of new piano works, written in 1926 for his own use, initiated a new and prolific period of composition. In 1934 he was released from his duties as a piano teacher and given a salaried position at the Hungarian Academy of Sciences, where he prepared for publication the vast mass of Hungarian folk music collected by himself and others. During the next few years his renown as a composer was such that he wrote almost exclusively on commission.

At the outbreak of war in 1939 Bartók began to think of leaving Europe, and after a concert tour to the U.S. (his second) in spring 1940 he emigrated there with his wife and their son in October. He did not settle easily in his new environment, for his music was not widely performed, concert engagements for himself and his wife were not abundant, and his health was failing. During 1941–42 he worked at Columbia Univ. on the Milman Parry collection of Serbo-Croatian folk music. He produced no new compositions until a commission from the Koussevitzky Music Foundation resulted in the *Concerto for Orchestra* (1943). Two other large works followed (including a sonata for unaccompanied violin commissioned by Yehudi Menuhin); at his death Bartók also left behind the first draft of a *Viola Concerto*.

Bartók's Op. 1 was a *Rhapsody* for piano and orchestra, and his swansong was a concerto for the same medium. His output includes three other major works for piano and orchestra, a sonata for piano solo and one for two pianos and percussion, as well as nearly 400 smaller piano pieces in various collections, including two for educational purposes: *For Children* (85 pieces) and *Mikrokosmos* (153 pieces). His greatest achievement in any one medium were the six string quartets, spaced out over his mature career. He understood the violin well and worked with a number of well-known violinists (Hubay, Vecsey, Stefi Geyer, Arányi, Szigeti, Székely, Gertler, and Menuhin). For this instrument he wrote two concertos, two rhapsodies, four sonatas, and a set of 44 short duos based on folk music. His three works for the stage, all written in his 30s, show dramatic talent but the setbacks they encountered, owing to the lurid subject of the *Mandarin* and the political associations of Béla Balázs, librettist of the first two, discouraged him from further attempts. Like several other leading composers he wrote no mature symphony, but produced two important orchestral works in his later years, both distinguished by their imaginative and effective concertolike use of the orchestra (*Music for Strings, Percussion and Celesta*, and the *Concerto for Orchestra*). He wrote one major choral work and several sets of songs, but his vocal music is the least important part of his output.

His early works, after the revelation of Strauss in 1902, reflect the ripe, post-romantic harmony of this composer. From 1904, the

year of the *Rhapsody*, Strauss's influence gave way to that of Liszt, whose principle of thematic transformation Bartók adhered to all his life, especially in the years 1928–36. The characteristic rhapsody form (a slow movement followed by a fast one), used by Liszt, also continued to attract him throughout his career (*Violin Sonata No. 2, String Quartet No. 3*, the original two-movement conception of *Contrasts*). After his discovery of Hungarian folk music (from 1906 on), he began to make use of such folk characteristics as continually varied repetitions of small motives, the descending perfect fourth and major second in the melody at cadences, modal harmony, including pentatony, and the lack of an upbeat in the rhythm, which derives from the accentuation of the Hungarian language. These were integrated with such advanced harmonic procedures as extreme chromaticism, bitonality, and cluster chords. He first achieved a perfect synthesis in *Bluebeard's Castle* (1911). Even at the time of his most intensely expressionist works, around 1920, elements of folk music remained, for instance, the dancelike rhythms of the finale of the *Violin Sonata No. 1* and in the actual folk tunes that form the basis of the *Improvisations*, Op. 20. When Bartók abruptly turned to neoclassicism five years later, folksong still turned up, as in the principal melodic motive of the finale of the *Piano Sonata* (1926). His two *Rhapsodies* for violin and orchestra (1928) were largely based on folk tunes.

Bartók was quick to perceive new developments in the work of his contemporaries and quick to apply them to his own work. Stravinsky's new directions in particular were a recurrent stimulus to him. His ballets *The Wooden Prince* (1914–16) and *The Miraculous Mandarin* (1918–19) were responses to *Petrushka* and *The Rite of Spring*. His first two piano concertos were strongly influenced by Stravinsky's works in this medium—not by Stravinsky's particular brand of neoclassic tonality, which Bartók never imitated, but by his neoclassic ideal as a revolt against expressionism, his noncantabile linear piano writing, and his dry, brittle, harsh instrumental sound with its emphasis on winds in preference to strings. Bartók was also keenly aware of Schoenberg's endeavor, and he was sympathetic to his preoccupation with total thematic unity, but except for flirtations with atonality in the two violin sonatas and with a 12-tone melody in the *Violin Concerto No. 2* (1937–38), he took no steps along the 12-tone path of Schoenberg. He sought instead his own solution, derived from the Lisztian concept of thematic transformation. The *String Quartet No. 4* (1928) comes close to the kind of total thematic integration Schoenberg sought. Bartók's tonal writing might be described as *polymodal* in that it incorporates a variety of modes or modal inflexions on a common tonic.

Bartók's exploration of symmetry and inversion for harmonic as well as formal organization is related to the ideal of total thematic unity and to Schoenberg's attempt to establish by this means a valid alternative to tonality as a method of large-scale musical organization. The seeds may be found in Bartók's earliest works, for instance in *Kossuth*, where the distorted "Gott erhalte" theme appears simultaneously with its own inversion. Similar mirror writing applied to harmony as well as melody is found in the two sonatas for violin and piano. The same principle pervades the *String Quartet No. 4*, from the formation of the thematic nucleus expounded at the beginning of the slow movement to the five-movement arch form in which the last two movements are a kind of inverted recapitulation of the first two. In the *String Quartet No. 5* (1934) the principle of symmetrical inversion (in the melody, counterpoint, and form) is still more comprehensively applied. In the matter of thematic integration this work is more relaxed, and thereafter Bartók began to compose more freely again.

It is with Stravinsky and Schoenberg that Bartók is to be ranked among his contemporaries. He has not had such a far reaching or powerful influence on the course of music in the 20th century owing partly to temperament and partly to his particular national circumstances. Born into a country that had not yet produced a great nationalist composer and having a virgin folk music to draw on, he was able to develop in a direction not available to most of his contemporaries. And as a pioneer and explorer of new possibilities he excelled in the individual application and adaptation of innovations made by others rather than in breaking entirely new ground himself, except in his experiments with symmetry, which he magnificently exploited and seemingly exhausted in a handful of masterpieces.

PRINCIPAL COMPOSITIONS (published by UE unless otherwise noted; some works have been published by more than one firm, but only one of them is listed here): *Kossuth*, symphonic poem (1903, ZK); *Rhapsody* for piano, orchestra, Op. 1 (1904, Rozsavölgyi); *Scherzo* for piano, orchestra (1904, ZK); *Suite No. 1* for orchestra, Op. 3 (1905, Rozsavölgyi); *Suite No. 2* for orchestra, Op. 4 (1905–07; revised 1920, 1943); *20 Hungarian Folksongs* for voice, piano (Nos. 1–10 arranged by Bartók, 11–20 by Kodály; 1906, Rozsavölgyi); *Violin Concerto [No. 1]* (1907–08, ZK); *8 Hungarian Folksongs* for voice, piano (1907–17); *14 Bagatelles* for piano, Op. 6 (1908); *String Quartets Nos. 1–6* (1908–09; 1915–17; 1927; 1928; 1934; 1939, Boosey); *For Children* for piano (1908–09, revised 1945); *A kékszakállú herceg vára* [Duke Bluebeard's Castle], 1-act opera, Op. 11; libretto by Béla Balázs (1911); *Allegro barbaro* for piano (1911); *4 Pieces* for orchestra, Op. 12 (1912, orchestrated 1921); *The Wooden Prince*, 1-act ballet (1914–16); *Suite* for piano, Op. 14 (1916); *5 Songs* for voice, piano, Op. 15 (1915–16); *3 Studies* for piano, Op. 18 (1918); *A csodálatos mandarin* [The Miraculous Mandarin], 1-act pantomime, Op. 19; scenario by Menyhért Lengyel (1918–19, revised and orchestrated 1924, finale revised c. 1935); *Improvisations on Hungarian Peasant Songs* for piano, Op 20 (1920); *Violin Sonatas Nos. 1–2* (1921, 1922); *Dance Suite* for orchestra (1923); *Piano Sonata* (1926); *Out of Doors* for piano (1926); *Piano Concerto No. 1* (1926); *9 Little Piano Pieces* (1926); *Mikrokosmos* for piano (1926–39, Boosey); *Rhapsodies Nos. 1–2* for violin, orchestra (1928); *20 Hungarian Folksongs* for voice, piano (1929); *Cantata Profana: The 9 Enchanted Stags* (1930); *Piano Concerto No. 2* (1930–31); *44 Duos* for 2 violins (1931); *27 Choruses* for children's or women's voices (1935); *Music for Strings, Percussion and Celesta* (1936); *Sonata for 2 Pianos and Percussion* (1937); *Violin Concerto [No. 2]* (1937–38, Boosey); *Divertimento* for string orchestra (1939, Boosey); *Concerto for Orchestra* (1943, Boosey); *Sonata* for solo violin (1944, Boosey); *Piano Concerto No. 3* (1945, Boosey).

PRINCIPAL WRITINGS: *Die Volksmusik der Rumänen von Maramures* (Munich 1923); *Hungarian Folk Music* (London 1931); *Die Melodien der rumänischen Colinde* (Vienna 1935); *La Musique populaire des hongrois et des peuples voisins* (Budapest 1937); *Serbo-Croatian Folk Songs* (New York 1951); *Rumanian Folk Music* ed. by B. Suchoff (The Hague 1967).

BIBL.: Ferenc Bónis, ed., *B. B. His Life in Pictures* (London 1964); Agatha Fassett, *The Naked Face of Genius* (Boston 1958); Erich Kapst, "Stilkriterien der polymodal-chromatischen Gestaltungsweise im Werk B. B.," *Beiträge zur Musikwissenschaft* 1970/1:1–28; Ernő Lendvai, "Duality and Synthesis in the Music of B. B.," *New Hungarian Quarterly* 3; Serge Moreux, *B.* (London 1953); Halsey Stevens, *The Life and Music of B. B.*, paperback ed. (New York 1969); John Vinton, "B. on his own Music," *Journal of the American Musicological Society* 19:232–43; ——, "Toward a Chronology of the Mikrokosmos," *Studia Musicologica* 6:41–70.

                                                      Colin Mason

SEE ALSO Asian Music and Western Composition, Dance, Claude Debussy, Folk Resources, Form, Harmony and Counterpoint, Hungary, Instrumental and Vocal Resources, Melody, Microtones, Opera, Orchestration, Popular Music, Rhythm, Texture, Theory.

Bartolozzi, Bruno (b. Florence, 8 June 1911), studied violin with Carlo Nucci at the Cherubini Conservatory (1926–30) and devoted a large portion of his early years to performing. He attended the Conservatory again (1946–49) to study composition with Paolo Fragapane; he also studied conducting at the Chigi Academy, Siena (1953), with Alceo Galliera. Bartolozzi began teaching at the Cherubini Conservatory in 1965. R. S. Brindle (*Musical Quarterly* 49:98) has compared Bartolozzi to Dallapiccola, saying that "there is the same ability to create evocative lyricism, to produce subtle orchestral colors, and to form a smooth harmonic flow within 12-tone usage."

PRINCIPAL COMPOSITIONS: *Concerto for Orchestra* (1952, S-Z); *Sentimento del sogno* for soprano, orchestra; text by Giuseppe Ungaretti (1952, Bruzzichelli); *Serenata* for violin, guitar (1952); *3 Pieces* for guitar (1952); *2 Studi* for violin (1952); *Divertimento* for chamber orchestra (1953, S-Z); *Concerto* for violin, strings, harpsichord (1957); *Estri del fa diesis* for piano (1959); *String Quartet* (1960, Bruzzichelli); *Concertazioni* for bassoon, strings, percussion (1963); *Concertazioni* for oboe, several instruments (1965); *Collage* for oboe (1967); *The Hollow Man* for any woodwind (1967); *3 Recuerdos del cielo* for voice, several instruments; text by Rafael Alberti (1967); *Concertazioni a quattro* for flute, oboe, clarinet, bassoon (1968, S-Z).

BIBL.: Reginald Smith Brindle, "Current Chronicle. Italy," *Musical Quarterly* 49:98–101; ——, "Current Chronicle. Italy," *ibid.* 52:106–09. SEE ALSO Instrumental and Vocal Resources.

Bartoš, Jan Zdeněk (b. Dvůr Králové nad Labem, Czechoslovakia, 4 June 1908), studied at the School for Music Teachers (USČUH) in Prague (1933–35), Prague Conservatory (1935–39; composition with Otakar Šín, conducting with Method Doležil), and at the graduate school of the Conservatory (1939–43; composition with Jaroslav Křička). He studied the violin privately as a child and during 1925–29 with Karel Hršel in Hradec Králové. He has played the violin in orchestras and, during 1929–31, as a soloist. During 1945–56 he was a member and later director of the Department of Music of the Ministry of Schools and Culture in Prague. He was editor-in-chief of the music publishing division of the State Publishers of Literature, Music, and Fine Arts (SNKLHU) during 1956–58. Since 1958 he has taught composition and theory at the Prague Conservatory.

PRINCIPAL COMPOSITIONS: *Má pout* [My Pilgrimage], meditation for mezzo-soprano, viola, piano, Op. 28 (1943, Pazdírek); *Concertino* for bassoon, orchestra, Op. 34 (1943, Panton); *Sonatina* for viola, piano, Op. 46 (1947, SNKLHU); *Běžec míru* [Runner of the Peace Race] for narrator, baritone, chorus, orchestra, Op. 47 (1948); *Prokletý zámek* [The Accursed Castle], 1-act comic opera, Op. 54 (1951, DILIA); *String Quartets Nos. 5, 6, 8, 9:* No. 5, Op. 66 (1952, SNKLHU); No. 6, "In miniatura," Op. 72 (1956, SNKLHU); No. 8, Op. 86 (1960); No. 9, Op. 95 (1963); *Útok na nebe* [The Attack on Heaven], 4-act opera, Op. 71 (1953–54); *Meditace na Štursova "Raněného"* [Meditation on Štursa's "The Wounded Soldier"] for mezzo-soprano, string orchestra, Op. 76 (1956, SHV); *Symphonies Nos. 2–4:* No. 2, "Da camera," for chamber orchestra, Op. 78 (1956, SNKLHU); No. 3 for string orchestra, Op. 101 (1964–65, Supraphon); No. 4, "Concertante," for oboe d'amore, string orchestra, Op. 126 (1968); *Piano Sonata No. 2,* "Giocosa," Op. 82 (1959, SNKLHU); *Poselství* [The Mission], cantata for narrator, women's chorus, string orchestra, piano, organ, Op. 84 (1960); *Komenský* [Comenius], cantata for baritone, women's chorus, 2 oboes, 2 horns, 2 bassoons, piano, Op. 90 (1961); *Král maněže* [King of the Circus], ballet pantomime, Op. 94 (1963, DILIA); *Concerto da camera* for oboe, strings, Op. 97 (1963); *Preludia* for flute, piano, Op. 98 (1964, Panton); *Mirella,* ballet, Op. 105 (1965); *Viola Concerto,* Op. 106 (1966); *Inventions* for bass clarinet, string orchestra, Op. 107 (1966); *Sonety o Praze* [Sonnets of Prague] for narrator, tenor, harp, string orchestra, Op. 108 (1966); *Concerto* for accordion, string orchestra, Op. 112 (1966); *Divertimento No. 4* for oboe, clarinet, bassoon, piano, Op. 113 (1966); *Divertimento No. 5* for wind quintet, Op. 114 (1966); *Rhapsody* for brasses, Op. 115 (1966); *Horn Concerto,* Op. 119 (1967); *String Trio,* Op. 123 (1968); *Divertimento No. 8* for viola, horn, piano, Op. 128 (1968); *Suite* for clarinet, piano, Op. 129 (1968); *Z Petrarkových sonetů Lauře* [From Petrarch's Sonnets for Laura] for tenor, bass, oboe, violin, cello, harpsichord, Op. 131 (1969); *Trio Sonata* for 2 violins, piano, Op. 134 (1970).

PRINCIPAL WRITINGS: *Národní zpěvníček* [Little Folksong Book] (Prague 1947); *Zpěvníka naší tělovýchovy* [Songbook for Our Sportsmen] (Prague 1953); *Ctení o hudebních formách* [Readings on Musical Forms] (Prague 1960); *O vývoji hudebních forem a žánrů* [The Development of Musical Forms and Genres] (Prague 1964); *Hudba volá SOS* [Music Calls SOS] (Prague 1968).

Bassett, Leslie (Raymond) (b. Hanford, Calif., 22 Jan 1923), attended Fresno State College, Calif. (1940–47), the Univ. of Mich. (1947–49 and 1953–56, composition with Ross Lee Finney), and the Ecole Normale de Musique in Paris (1950–51, composition with Honegger). He also studied with Nadia Boulanger, with Roberto Gerhard (1960), and electronic music with Mario Davidovsky (1964). In 1952 he began teaching at the Univ. of Mich. He was a fellow at the American Academy, Rome (1961–63). Bassett considers his contacts with young composers at the Univ. of Mich. and during the two years he spent in Rome as the most stimulating factors in his development as a composer.

PRINCIPAL COMPOSITIONS: *Trio* for viola, clarinet, piano (1953, ACA-CFE); *5 Pieces* for string quartet (1957, Galaxy); *To Music* for solo voice (1962, Galaxy); *String Quartet No. 3* (1962, ACA-CFE); *Variations* for orchestra (1963, Peters); *Designs, Images, and Textures* for orchestra (1964, Peters); *3 Studies in Electronic Sounds,* on tape (1965); *Notes in the Silence* for chorus, piano; text by Hammarskjöld (1966); *Triform,* on tape (1966); *Nonet* for 4 winds, 4 brass, piano (1967, Peters); *Colloquy* for orchestra (1968, Peters); *Music for saxophone, piano* (1968, Peters); *Collect* for choir, tape (1969, Peters).

BIBL.: Ross Lee Finney, "L. B.," *BMI Many Worlds of Music* (July 1966):16.

SEE ALSO Liturgical Music: Christian.

Baur, Jürg (b. Dusseldorf, Germany, 11 Nov 1918), attended the Staatliche Musikhochschule in Cologne (1937–40; composition and theory with Philipp Jarnach, piano with Karl Hermann Pillney, protestant church music and organ with Michael Schneider) and the Univ. of Cologne (1948–52, musicology with K. G. Fellerer). Baur became acting director of the Robert Schumann Conservatory, Dusseldorf, in 1956 and since 1965 has served as director. During 1952–60 he was kantor and choir director at the Pauluskirche, Dusseldorf, and since 1959 has been a guest lecturer at the Evangelischen Landeskirchenmusikschule. Baur's early compositional development was influenced by Reger, Hindemith, and Bartók, the string quartets of the latter two being of particular significance. Subsequently he was drawn to Schoenberg's 12-tone techniques and around 1960 to serialism.

PRINCIPAL COMPOSITIONS (published by Breitkopf unless otherwise noted): *Toccata* for organ (1950); *Concerto* for viola, chamber orchestra (1951–52); *String Quartet No. 3* (1952); *Sinfonia Montana* (1953); *Concerto* for mixture trautonium, string quartet (1955, Peters); *Concerto for Strings* (1957, Peters); *Sonata* for 2 pianos (1957); *Konzertante Musik* for piano, orchestra (1958); *Quintetto sereno* for 5 winds (1958); *Du selber bist das Rad,* 3 motets for chorus; texts by Angelus Silesius (1959, Peters); *Metamorphosen* for piano trio (1960, Peters); *Concerto romano* for oboe, orchestra (1960); *Incontri,* 3 pieces for flute (alto recorder), piano (1960); *Herz, stirb oder singe,* song cycle for high voice, piano (or chamber orchestra); texts by

Jimenez (1960, Peters); *Divertimento,* 3 fantasies for harpsichord, percussion (1961–62); *Mutazioni* for flute or alto recorder (1962); *Romeo and Juliet,* "Visionen" for orchestra (1962–63); *Piccolo mondo,* music for an imaginary ballet, for orchestra (1963); *Dialoge* for cello, piano (1963); *3 Fantasies* for guitar (1964); *6 Bagatelles* for clarinet (1964); *Heptameron* for piano (1964–65); *Lo specchio* for orchestra (1965–66); *Pentagramm,* concerto for wind quintet, orchestra (1966); *Mit wechselndem Schlüssel,* song cycle for low voice, piano; texts by Celan (1967); *Perché,* fragments for soloists, chorus, orchestra; texts by Ungaretti (1968); *Abbreviatüren* for 13 strings (1969).

PRINCIPAL WRITINGS: "Über Anton Weberns 'Bagatellen für Streichquartett'," *Neue Wege der musikalischen Analyse* (Berlin, Merseburger, 1967); articles on pedagogy and theory in *Musik im Unterricht* and *Melos* (1960–65).

BIBL.: Hanspeter Krellmann, *Ich war nie Avantgardist* (Wiesbaden, Breitkopf, 1968).

Bautista, Julián (b. Madrid, 21 April 1901; d. Buenos Aires, 8 July 1961), studied at the Madrid Conservatory (1912–21; composition with Conrado del Campo, piano with Pilar Fernández de la Mora, violin with Julio Francés). He taught at the Madrid Conservatory (1936–39), the National Conservatory in Buenos Aires, and the Conservatory of San Juan, Puerto Rico, but devoted most of his time to private teaching.

PRINCIPAL COMPOSITIONS: *Juerga,* 1-act ballet (1921); *Colores,* 6 pieces for piano (1921–22); *Sonatina* for string trio (1924); *Prelude and Dance* for guitar (1928); *Obertura para una ópera grotesca* for orchestra (1932); *3 Ciudades* for voice, orchestra (1937); *Spanish Fantasia* for clarinet, orchestra (1945–46); *4 Poemas galegos* for voice, flute, oboe, clarinet, viola, cello, harp; text by Lorenzo Varela (1946, EAMI); *Romance del Rey Rodrigo* for chorus (1956); *Sinfónia breve* (1956, Ricordi); *String Quartet No. 3* (1958, Ricordi).

BIBL.: Gilbert Chase, *The Music of Spain* (New York 1959):203–05; Roberto García Morillo, "J. B.," *Revista musical chilena* (August 1949); 26–43; Alberto Ginastera, "Notas sobre la música moderna argentina," *ibid.* (Oct 1948): 26–27; Federico Sopeña, *Historia de la música española contemporanea* (Madrid 1958):198.

Bax, Arnold (Edward Trevor) (b. Streatham, England, 8 Nov 1883; d. Cork, Ireland, 3 Oct 1953), studied at the Royal Academy of Music (1900–05. theory with Frederick Corder, piano with Tobias Matthay). He was independently wealthy and devoted himself solely to composition. In 1942 he was appointed Master of the King's Music. His early work was influenced by Irish folklore, and his later by the moods of the northern landscape and by heroic tragedy.

PRINCIPAL COMPOSITIONS (published by Chappell unless otherwise noted): *In the Faery Hills*, tone poem for orchestra (1909); *2 Russian Tone Pictures* for piano (1911, unpub.); *Piano Quintet* (1914–15); *Violin Sonatas Nos. 2–3* (1915, 1927); *The Garden of Fand*, tone poem for orchestra (1916); *Tintagel*, tone poem for orchestra (1917); *String Quartets Nos. 1–3* (1918, 1924, 1936); *Piano Sonatas Nos. 1–4* (1919, 1919, 1925, 1932); *The Truth about the Russian Dancers*, ballet; scenario by J. M. Barrie, choreographed by Tamara Karsavina (1920, unpub.); *Mediterranean* for piano or orchestra (1920); *Viola Sonata* (1921); *Mater ora filium* for double chorus (1921); *Quintet* for oboe, string quartet (1923); *Legend* for viola, piano (1929); *Symphonies Nos. 3, 4, 6, 7* (1929, 1931, 1934, 1939); *Overture to a Picaresque Comedy* (1930); *Concerto* for flute, harp, oboe, strings (1934); *Concerto* for bassoon, harp, string sextet (1936); *Violin Concerto* (1937); *Legend Sonata* for cello, piano (1943); *Epithalamium* for chorus, organ; text by Edmund Spenser (1947); *Fanfares for the Royal Wedding* (1947, unpub.); *Concerto* for piano left-hand, orchestra (1949); *Coronation March* (1953, unpub.).

PRINCIPAL WRITINGS: *Farewell My Youth*, an autobiography (London 1943).

BIBL.: Edwin Evans, "A. B.," *Musical Quarterly* 9:167–80; Aloys Fleischmann, "A. B.," *Recorded Sound* (Jan–April 1968):273–76; R. L. E. Foreman, "A. B., A Discography," *loc. cit.*:277–83; ——, "The Unperformed Works of Sir A. B.," *Musical Opinion* (July 1966):598–99; Colin Scott-Sutherland, "The Symphonies of A. B.," *Music Review* 23:20–24; ——, "Some Unpublished Works of A. B.," *ibid.* 24:322–26; B. Thistlethwaite, *The Bax Family* (London 1936).

SEE ALSO Great Britain.

Bayle, François (b. Tamatave, Madagascar, 27 April 1932), studied literature and mathematics at the Univ. of Bordeaux and music at the Paris Conservatory (1959, composition with Olivier Messiaen). He worked with Pierre Schaeffer at the composition studio of the Groupe de Recherches Musicales during 1960–62 and has been working for the studio since 1966. The feeling of independence from other contemporary developments that Bayle finds in the studio and the spirit of discovery that surrounds its leader, Pierre Schaeffer, have been the principal influences on his music.

PRINCIPAL COMPOSITIONS: *Points critiques* for horn, piano, cello, percussion (1960); *Trois-Portraits-de-l'oiseau-qui-n'existe-pas*, film score (1962); *L'Archipel* for string quartet, tape (1963, recorded by Philips); *Pluriel* for 19 instruments, loudspeakers (1963, EFM); *Fautrier l'enragé*, film score (1963); *L'Oiseau chanteur*, musique concrète

(1963, recorded by Philips); *Galaxie*, film score (1964); *Lignes et points*, musique concrète film score (1964); *Espaces inhabitables*, musique concrète (1966–67, recorded by Philips); *Portrait-poème de Léonor Fini*, film score (1968); *Jeïta ou Murmure des eaux*, musique concrète (1969–70, recorded by Philips); *L'Expérience acoustique*, musique concrète (part 1, 1970; part 2, 1971; parts 3–5 in process).

PRINCIPAL WRITINGS: "Expérience collective, création solitaire," *Le Monde* (4 Feb 1971):13; "De l'Expérience musicale à l'expérience humaine," an article by Pierre Schaeffer containing a section by Bayle, *Revue Musicale* (May 1971).

BIBL.: Pierre Schaeffer, *Solfège de l'objet sonore* (Paris 1966); ——, *La Musique concrète* (Paris 1967):117–18.

Be-bop, see Jazz

Becerra-Schmidt, Gustavo (b. Temuco, Chile, 26 August 1925), studied at the Univ. of Chile (graduated 1949) and the National Conservatory (composition with P. H. Allende and Domingo Santa Cruz, conducting with Armando Carvajal, musicology with Vicente Salas-Viú). He has taught composition and analysis at the Univ. of Chile since 1947. During 1959–63 he was director of the Instituto de Extensión Musical at the Univ., and he was artistic director of the university's television station during 1963–64. Since 1968 he has been secretary general of the faculty of music, dance, and theater. In addition to the compositions listed below he has written nearly 40 scores for theater and films.

PRINCIPAL COMPOSITIONS (published by IEM unless otherwise noted): *Piano Concerto* (1958); *String Quartets Nos. 4–7* (1958; 1959; 1960; 1961, unpub.); *Trio* for flute, violin, piano (1958, Peer); *Saxophone Quartet* (1959); *Symphony No. 3* (1960, unpub.); *Guitar Concertos Nos. 1–2* (1964, 1968); *Juegos*, 12 ball games for piano, ping-pong balls, brick, tape (1966, unpub.); *Macchu Picchu*, oratorio for chorus; poem by Pablo Neruda (1966); *Llanto por el Hermano solo* for chorus; poem by Fernando González (1966); *Responso para José Miguel Carrera* for voice, wind quintet, piano, percussion (1967); *Morula, gastrulay blastula* for piano, tape (1968, unpub.); *Spij, spij*, polacca for voice, guitar (1969, unpub.). List to 1962: *Composers of the Americas* 8:19–24.

PRINCIPAL WRITINGS: "La crisis de la enseñanza de la composición en occidente," a series of 9 articles published in *Revista musical chilena*, vols. 12–13.

BIBL.: Luis Merino Montero, "Los cuartetos de G. B.," *Revista musical chilena* (April 1965):44–78.

[prepared with the help of Alcides Lanza]

SEE ALSO Chile.

Beck, Conrad (b. Lohn, Schaffhausen, Switzerland, 16 June 1901), attended Zurich Conservatory (1921–24; composition with Volkmar Andreae, counterpoint with Reinhold Laquai). During 1924–35 he lived in Paris, where he studied orchestration with Jacques Ibert. From 1938 to 1966 he was music director of the Basel radio. Beck's development was influenced especially by the guidance he received in Paris from Honegger, Roussel, and Nadia Boulanger, and by his association there with Bohuslav Martinů, Marcel Mihalovici, Tibor Harsanyi, and Alexander Tcherepnin. He has made extensive studies of old folksongs and has arranged many, especially from Switzerland and Alsace.

PRINCIPAL COMPOSITIONS (published by Schott unless otherwise noted): *String Quartet No. 3* (1926); *Concertino* for piano, orchestra (1927); *La Mort d'Oedipe*, cantata for soprano, tenor, baritone, chorus, organ, 2 trumpets, 2 trombones, timpani; text by René Morax (1928); *Concerto* for string quartet, orchestra (1929); *Es kommt ein Schiff geladan*, motet (1930); *Little Suite* for string orchestra (1930); *Symphony No. 5* (1930); *4 Women's Choruses* (1931); *Innominata* for orchestra (1931); *Oratorio on Sayings of Angelus Silesius* (1933–34, unpub.); *String Quartet No. 4* (1934); *Serenade* for flute, clarinet, string orchestra (1935); *Chamber Concerto* for violin, chamber orchestra (1936); *Chamber Cantata on Sonnets of Louiza Labé* for soprano, flute, piano, string orchestra (1937); *Flute Concerto* (1941, unpub.); *String Trio No. 2* (1946); *Viola Concerto* (1949); *Der Tod zu Basel*, miserere for soprano, bass, narrators, chorus, orchestra (1956); *Hymn* for orchestra (1952); *Concertino* for clarinet, bassoon, orchestra (1954); *Herbstfeuer*, 6 songs for alto, chamber orchestra; poems by Ricarda Huch (1956); *Aeneas Silvius Symphony* (1956–57); *Sonatina* for orchestra (1958); *Suite Concertante* for winds, percussion, double bass (1961); *String Quartet No. 5* (1962–63); *Concertino* for oboe, orchestra (1963–64); *Concertato* for orchestra (1963–64); *Hommages* for orchestra (1965–66); *Die Sonnenfinsternis*, cantata for alto, flute, clarinet, harpsichord, string orchestra; text by Adalbert Stifter (1967); *Clarinet Concerto* (1968); *Fantasie* for orchestra (1968–69).

PRINCIPAL WRITINGS: "Die Folklore und die Musik unserer Zeit," *Schweizerische Musikzeitung* (March 1955):89–94; "Der Tod zu Basel," *The Composer's Point of View* ed. by R. S. Hines (Norman, Okla., 1963):125–37.

BIBL.: Ernst Mohr, "Zum Kompositionsstil von C. B.," *Schweizerische Musikzeitung* 1961/3:25–28; Aloys Mooser, "Le Concerto de C. B.," *Dissonances* 1930/12; ——, "St. Jacob an der Birs, de C. B.," *ibid.* 1944/11–12; Leo Schrade, "Laudatio zum Kunstpreis der Stadt Basel, 23. 3. 64," *Neue Zeitschrift für Musik* 1964/7–8:308–09; Willi Schuh, *Schweizer Musik der Gegenwart* (Zurich 1948); ——, *Von neuer Musik* (Zurich 1955).

SEE ALSO France, Switzerland.

Becker, Günther (Hugo) (b. Forbach, Germany, 1 April 1924), studied at the Badische Hochschule für Musik in Karlsruhe (1946–49). He began private composition lessons in 1949 with Wolfgang Fortner, continuing to study with him at the Nordwestdeutsche Musikakademie in Detmold (1953–56), where he also studied choral conducting with Kurt Thomas and theory and conducting with Gerhard Nestler. During 1949–53 Becker was a ballet accompanist and a composer-pianist for a political-satire cabaret. He taught music at the Greek National School in Anavryta (1956–58) and the Goethe Institute in Athens (1957–68). In 1962 he founded the Studio for New Music in Athens. He returned to Germany in 1968 and lives in Essen as a free-lance composer. In 1969 he founded the ensemble Gruppe MHz, which consists of electrified and electronically regulated instruments.

PRINCIPAL COMPOSITIONS (published by Gerig unless otherwise noted): *Diaglyphen* for chamber orchestra (1962, Peters); *String Quartet No. 1* (1963); *Nacht- und Traumgesänge* for chorus, orchestra; text by Odysseas Elytis (1964); *Stabil-instabil* for orchestra (1965); *Correspondances I* for instruments of the clarinet family, chamber orchestra (1966); *Serpentinata* for wind quintet (1968); *Correspondances III* for electronically controlled double-bass and electrically modulated viola (1969); *Meteoron* for electronic sounds, organ, percussion (1969).

PRINCIPAL WRITINGS: *Neue griechischer Volksmusik* (Cologne 1967).

BIBL.: U. Stürzbecher, *Werkstattgespräche mit Komponisten* (Cologne 1969).

SEE ALSO Greece.

Becker, John J(oseph) (b. Henderson, Ky., 22 Jan 1886; d. Wilmette, Ill., 21 Jan 1961), earned a diploma from the Krueger Conservatory in Cincinnati (1905) and a doctorate of music from the Wisconsin Conservatory (1923). His principal teachers were Alexander von Fielitz (1907–08; theory, harmony, conducting), Carl Busch (1908; conducting, composition), and Wilhelm Middelschulte at the Wisconsin Conservatory (composition, counterpoint). He was professor of composition and piano at North Texas College (1906–14), director of music at the Univ. of Notre Dame (1918–28), chairman of the fine arts department at the College of St. Thomas in St. Paul (1928–33), the Minnesota state director for the Federal Music Project (1935–41), and professor and composer in residence at Barat College, Lake Forest, Ill. (1943–57). He also taught composition at the Chicago Musical College (1949–50). During 1936–40 he was associate editor of *New Music Quarterly*.

Becker's earliest compositions, principally songs and piano pieces, were written under the influence of Von Fielitz and are in a romantic-impressionist idiom. His study of 16th-century choral literature under Middelschulte found expression in a large body of church music and in a mature style in which the Netherlands polyphonic style is converted into a personal, dissonant idiom. His doctoral study, a comparison of 19th-century German literature and music, laid the ground for his later preoccupation with the stage, particularly with new forms that fuse music, poetry, dance, mime, and color. Around 1927 his music underwent a radical change towards a more complex dissonant idiom, undoubtedly owing to his new contact with Cowell, Ives, Riegger, Ruggles, and other experimentalists, many of whose works he conducted in St. Paul during the 1930s. (Becker and the composers named all shared a pioneering spirit and have been categorized by some as the "American Five.") The foremost characteristics of Becker's new style are: use of percussion sonorities; use of the piano as a percussion instrument; unconventional abstract musical forms and patterns, often indicated by the title *Soundpiece*; massed chordal effects in which the resulting overtones serve to blend the disparate textures; and an orchestration in which doubling is minimized and instruments of widely differing timbre are combined and contrasted. His stage works and symphonies of the 1930s and 40s, many containing a message of social protest, point toward mixed-media theater.

PRINCIPAL COMPOSITIONS: *Symphonies Nos. 1–3, 5–7*: No. 1, "Etude primitive" (1915); No. 2, "Fantasia tragica" (1920); No. 3, "Symphonia brevis" (1929, Peters); No. 5, "Homage to Mozart" (1942, ACA); No. 6, "A Symphony of Democracy," with narrator, chorus (1942, ACA); No. 7 with narrator, singing and speaking choruses (1953–54, unfinished); *2 Poems of Departure* for soprano, piano (1927, ACA); *Piano Concerto*, "Concerto Arabesque" (1930, New Music); *Dance Figure* for singer, dance group, orchestra (1932); *4 Songs from the Japanese* for soprano, piano (1934, ACA); *Horn Concerto* (1933); *Mockery*, scherzo for piano, dance orchestra (1933, ACA); *Missa symphonica* for men's chorus (1933, CFE); *Abongo* for percussion orchestra, 2 solo dancers, dance group (1933, Autograph Editions); *Concertino pastorale* for 2 flutes, orchestra (1933); *A Marriage with Space* for solo and mass recitation, solo dancer, dance group, orchestra; text by Mark Turbyfill (1933–35); *Psalms of Love* for

soprano, piano (1935, CFE); *Soundpieces Nos. 1–6, 8*: No. 1 for piano, strings (1935, ACA); No. 2, "Homage to Haydn," for string quartet or string orchestra (1936, Merion); No. 3 for violin, piano (1936, Peters); No. 4 for string quartet (1937, Merion); No. 5 for piano (1938, Merion); No. 6 for flute, clarinet (1941, Peters); No. 8 for string quartet (1959, unfinished); *Vigilante* for dancer, piano, 5 percussionists (1938); *When the Willow Nods*, incidental music to the play by Alfred Kreymborg (1940, ACA); *Privilege and Privation*, 1-act opera; libretto by Kreymborg (1939); *The Snow Goose: A Legend of World War II* for orchestra (1944); *Moments from the Liturgy* for women's voice, narrator, vocal soloist, singing and speaking choruses (1948); *Julius Caesar* for orchestra, score for the film by David Bradley (1949); *Madeleine et Judas*, incidental music for the drama by Raymond Bruckberger (1958); *At Dieppe*, 4 songs for soprano, piano (1959, CFE).

PRINCIPAL WRITINGS: "Wilhelm Middelschulte, Master of Counterpoint," *Musical Quarterly* 14: 192–202; "Fine Arts and the Soul of America," *Religious Education* (Nov 1930); "Henry Cowell: Musical Explorer," *Northwest Musical Herald* (Nov 1932):4; "Charles E. Ives: Musical Philosopher," *ibid.* (Jan 1933):5; "Wallingford Riegger," *ibid.* (March 1933):6 and *Bulletin of the American Composers Alliance* 9/3:13–14; "Imitative versus Creative Music in America," *American Composers on American Music* ed. by H. Cowell (Stanford, Calif 1933):188–90; "Finding a Personal Orchestral Idiom," *Musical America* (Feb 1950):126–27, 256; "Essays Before a Sonata," *Music News* (Feb 1950):22–23.

BIBL.: Gilbert Chase, *America's Music* (New York 1955):578–80; Henry Cowell, "Current Chronicle: New York," *Musical Quarterly* 39: 426–29; ———, "J. B.: A Crusader from Kentucky," *Southern Literary Messenger* (Oct 1939):657–59; ———, "J. J. B.," *American Composers on American Music* (Stanford, Calif., 1933):82–84; John W. Downey, "Homage to J. J. B.," *Focus Midwest* (July 1962):18–19; Don C. Gillespie, *The Music of J. J. B.* (PhD diss., Univ. of N.C., in progress); Wallingford Riegger, "J. J. B.," *Bulletin of the American Composers Alliance* 9/1:2–7.

Don C. Gillespie

SEE ALSO Dance, Mixed Media.

Beckwith, John (b. Victoria, British Columbia, Canada, 9 March 1927), studied at the Univ. of Toronto (BM, 1947; MM, 1961) and privately with Alberto Guerrero (piano, 1945–50) and Nadia Boulanger (composition, Paris, 1950–52). He was public relations director of the Royal Conservatory in Toronto during 1948–50 and instructor in musical theory, 1955–65. He has been a member of the faculty of music of the Univ. of Toronto since

1952; he became dean in 1970. He has worked for the Canadian Broadcasting Corp. as a script writer (1953–55), writer and organizer of a music series (1955–61), and occasional broadcaster of musical documentaries, lectures, and reviews (since 1959). He was a founding member and secretary (1953–59) of the Canadian League of Composers. During 1962–67 he was on the board of directors of the Ten Centuries Concerts in Toronto. His "early works imitated (sometimes unconsciously) models such as Satie, Ravel, Copland, Hindemith. My early orientations seem French and North American at the same time. Many pieces with literary subjects or texts, both then and now, have a primitive regional identification. Since the *Study for String Trio No. 3* (1955) serialism plays a strong technical role. Stravinsky and Ives are reflected in various aspects. Since *A Message to Winnipeg* (1960) collage-like techniques have influenced the formal organization of many pieces."

PRINCIPAL COMPOSITIONS: *Music for Dancing* for 2 pianos (1948) or orchestra (1949) or chamber orchestra (1959, BMIC); *The Great Lakes Suite* for soprano, baritone, cello, clarinet, piano; poems by James Reaney (1949); *4 Songs to Poems by e. e. cummings* for soprano, piano (1950); *Woodwind Quartet* (1951); *3 Studies* for string trio (1955–56); *Night Blooming Cereus*, 1-act opera for 8 singers, chamber orchestra; libretto by Reaney (1953–58); *Concerto Fantasy* for piano, orchestra (1958–59); *A Message to Winnipeg*, musical collages for 3 speakers, clarinet, violin, piano/celesta, percussion; text by Reaney (1960); *12 Letters to a Small Town*, musical collages for 4 speakers, flute/piccolo, oboe, piano/harmonium, guitar; texts by Reaney (1961); *A Chaucer Suite* for alto, tenor, baritone (1962); *Flower Variations and Wheels* for orchestra (1962); *Wednesday's Child*, musical collages for 4 speakers, soprano, tenor, flute, piccolo, viola, piano, small harpsichord, celesta, percussion; written for a radio documentary by Reaney (1962); *Concertino* for horn, orchestra (1963); *Jonah*, chamber cantata for alto, tenor, bass-baritone, bass, chorus, horn, clarinet, strings, timpani (1963, BMIC); *The Trumpets of Summer*, choral suite for male speaker, 4 vocal soloists, chorus, flute, bassoon, trumpet, cello, harp, percussion; text by Margaret Atwood (1964); *Canada Dash, Canada Dot*, words-and-music collage for speakers, vocal soloists, chamber orchestra; texts by Reaney; part 1, "The Line Across," part 2, "The Line Up and Down," part 3, "Canada Dot" (1965–67); *Sharon Fragments* for chorus; texts by David Willson (1966, Waterloo); *Place of Meeting* for male speaker, tenor, blues singer, chorus, orchestra; text by Dennis Lee (1966–67); *Circle, with Tangents* for harpsichord, 13 strings (1967, BMIC); *The Sun Dance* for 2 sopranos, alto, tenor, 2 basses, 4 small choruses, large chorus, 13 percussion instruments (1968); *Gas!* for 20 speakers

(1969). List to 1959: *Composers of the Americas* 8:27–28.

PRINCIPAL WRITINGS: "Composers in Toronto and Montreal," *Univ. of Toronto Quarterly* 26/1; "Jean Papineau-Couture," *Canadian Music Journal* 3/2; "Alberto Guerrero" and "Notes on Some New Music Heard on CBC Radio," *ibid.* 4/2; "Recent Orchestral Works by Champagne, Morel, and Anhalt," *ibid.*, 4/4; coeditor with Udo Kasemets, *The Modern Composer and His World* (Toronto 1961); "A Stravinsky Triptych," *Canadian Music Journal* 6/4; "Schoenberg Ten Years After," *Canadian Forum* (Nov 1961); "Notes on *Jonah*," *Alphabet* (London, Ont.) 8; "The Bernstein Experiment," *Canadian Forum* (April 1964); "A 'Complete' Schoenberg," *ibid.* (Jan 1967). Beckwith has also contributed to the *Canadian Annual Review* ed. by Saywell (Toronto 1961–64); reviewed concerts for *The Globe & Mail* (1948–49, 1953–54) and *The Toronto Daily Star* (1959–62, 1963–65); and written program notes for the Univ. of Toronto concert series (1956–68), Ten Centuries Concerts (1962–67), and the Toronto Symphony (since 1966).

BIBL.: "J. B., a Portrait," *Musicanada* 6:8–9.
SEE ALSO Canada.

Bedford, David (Vickerman) (b. London, 4 August 1937), studied at Lancing College in Sussex (1951–55) and the Royal College of Music (1956–60, composition with Lennox Berkeley). In 1960 he studied composition privately in Venice with Luigi Nono, and in 1961 he worked for a few weeks at the Electronic Music Studio of the RIA in Milan. He has taught at secondary schools in London and at Queen's College (since 1968). As a student he was influenced by the music of Schoenberg. He is especially interested in educational music for pupils with little or no musical knowledge. In the late 1960s he made some pop-music arrangements.

PRINCIPAL COMPOSITIONS (published by UE): *Piece for Mo* for 3 violins, cello, double bass, accordian, vibraphone, percussion (1963); *2 Poems* for chorus, texts by Kenneth Patchen (1963); *A Dream of the 7 Lost Stars* for chorus, chamber orchestra; poem by Patchen (1964–65); *Music for Albion Moonlight* for soprano, flute, clarinet, violin, cello, piano, melodica; poem by Patchen (1965); *That White and Radiant Legend*, for narrator, soprano, flute, clarinet, oboe, bassoon, violin, viola, cello, double bass; poem by Patchen (1966); *Trona for 12* for winds, strings (1967); *18 Bricks Left on April 21st* for 2 electric guitars (1967); *Five* for string quintet (1967); *Gastrula for Orchestra* (1968); *The Tentacles of the Dark Nebula* for tenor, string ensemble; text from the story "Transience" by Arthur C. Clarke (1969). His educational music includes *Whitefield Music II* for 6–36 players, each with 2 instruments (one capable of sustained sounds), and *An Exciting New Game for Children of All Ages* for any number of players, any number of instruments, one die, and a counter.

SEE ALSO Great Britain.

Beecroft, Norma (Marian) (b. Oshawa, Ontario, Canada, 11 April 1934), studied at the Toronto Conservatory (1950–58; composition with John Weinzweig, piano with Weldon Kilburn) and the Accadèmia di S. Cecilia in Rome (1959–61, composition with Goffredo Petrassi). She attended summer courses at Tanglewood (1958, composition with Aaron Copland and Lukas Foss), Darmstadt (1960, 1961; composition with Bruno Maderna), and the Dartington School of Music in Devon, England (1961, composition with Maderna). She also worked with Myron Schaeffer at the Univ. of Toronto Electronic Music Center during 1962–63 and with Mario Davidovsky at the Columbia-Princeton Electronic Music Center during the summer of 1964. She was a television script assistant for the Canadian Broadcasting Corp. during 1954–57 and 1962–63 and was a producer for CBC radio, 1963–69. Since 1969 she has been writer and commentator for the weekly CBC radio series "Music of Today." Miss Beecroft has held several administrative posts including president of the Ten Centuries Concerts in Toronto (since 1964).

PRINCIPAL COMPOSITIONS (available at CMC unless otherwise noted): *3 Pezzi brevi* for flute with harp or piano or guitar (1960–61, UE); *Improvvisazioni concertanti* for flute, orchestra (1961); *Contrasts for 6 Performers* for oboe, viola, harp, marimba, vibraphone, percussion (1962); *From Dreams of Brass* for narrator, soprano, chorus, orchestra, tape; text by Jane Beecroft (1963–64); *Elegy* and *2 Went to Sleep* for soprano, flute, percussion, tape; poems by Leonard Cohen (1966–67); *Undersea Fantasy*, electronic music on tape for a puppet show (1967); *The Living Flame of Love* for chorus, poem by St. John of the Cross (1967, Waterloo); *Rasas for 7 Performers* for flute, piano, harp, percussion, violin, viola, cello (1969).

BIBL.: J. S. Weissmann, "Current Chronicle, Italy," *Musical Quarterly* 49:243–44; "Miss N. B.; Well-travelled Composer," *Canadian Composer* (May 1966):4, 40, 46; "A Conversation with N. B.: The New World of Electronic Music," *ibid.* (Oct 1967):34, 36, 46; "Women on the Go 1967," *Chatelaine Magazine* (July 1967):40; "N. B.," *Musicanada* (May 1969):10, 11.

Beeson, Jack (Hamilton) (b. Muncie, Ind., 15 July 1921), studied at the Univ. of Toronto (1938; piano, theory); the Eastman School (1939–44, composition with Bernard Rogers and Howard Hanson); Columbia Univ. (1945–46, musicology); and composition informally with Béla Bartók (1944–45). He wanted to become an opera composer from about age 12 and began by sketching in that year a verse libretto based on Shelley's *The Cenci.* He was an accompanist and conductor with the opera workshop at Columbia Univ. during 1944–48. His best known opera, *Lizzie Borden.*(1965), based on a famous murder in Boston in 1892, was performed at the New York City Opera during the spring season of 1965. Beeson began teaching at Columbia Univ. in 1945, where he is MacDowell Professor of Music and was chairman of the music department. He has also been an officer of several music organizations.

PRINCIPAL COMPOSITIONS: *Jonah*, opera; libretto by composer (1950); *Hello Out There*, opera; libretto by composer (1953, Mills); *The Sweet Bye and Bye*, opera; libretto by Kenward Elmslie (1956, Boosey); *Symphony No. 1 in A* (1959, MCA); *Transformations* for orchestra (1959, MCA); *Commemoration* for band (1960); *Fanfare* for brass, winds, percussion (1963); *Lizzie Borden*, opera; libretto by Kenward Elmslie (1965, Boosey); *My Heart's in the Highlands*, opera; libretto by composer (1969).

PRINCIPAL WRITINGS: "Magic, Music, and Money," *Columbia University Forum* 2/1:30–35 and *The Columbia University Forum Anthology* (New York 1968):22–30; "Grand and Not So Grand," *Opera News* 27/9:8–13 and *Contemporary Composers on Contemporary Music* ed. by Elliott Schwartz and Barney Childs (New York 1967): 316–24.

SEE ALSO Opera.

Beglarian, Grant (b. Tiflis, Georgia, U.S.S.R., 1 Dec 1927), received his early musical education in Teheran, Iran, and came to the U.S. in 1947. He attended the Univ. of Mich. (1947–51, 1954–58, DMA; composition with Ross Lee Finney, viola with Paul Doktor, musicology with Hans David and Louise Cuyler). In 1961, after considerable free-lance work composing, editing, copying, playing in orchestras, and conducting, he founded and was the first president of Music Book Associates. He was director of the Contemporary Music Project of the Ford Foundation during 1961–69 and since 1969 has been dean of the Univ. of Southern California School of Performing Arts.

PRINCIPAL COMPOSITIONS: *Violin Sonata* (1949); *Cello Sonata* (1951); *9 Duets for Violins* (1955, Fischer); *12 Hungarian Folk Songs* for orchestra

(1957); *Divertimento for Orchestra* (1957–58, Piedmont); *Chamber Music* for bassoon, string trio (1959); *Nurse's Song* for orchestra (1960, CMP); *Sinfonia* for orchestra (1961, CMP); *Woodwind Quintet* (1966, Piedmont); *A Hymn for our Times* for 1, 3, or 6 bands (1968, Piedmont); *. . . And All the Hills Echoed* for bass, organ, timpani, chorus or audience (1968, Piedmont). List to 1968: *Composers of the Americas* 14:23–24.

PRINCIPAL WRITINGS: "The Composer in Public School," *Fine Music* (Cleveland, 24 April 1960); "The Musical Experience in Contemporary Education," *Proceedings of the International Seminar on Teacher Education in Music* (Ann Arbor, August 1966):96–104; "Music, Education, and the University," *Bulletin of the National Association of Schools of Music* (1966) and *Music Educators' Journal* (Feb 1967):51–63; "Focus on the Arts: A Crisis in Values," *Elementary School Principal* (Oct 1967): 8–13; "Music in Contemporary Education," *College Music Society Symposium* (Fall 1967):29–35, 85–88; "The Education of the American Composer," *Encyclopedia of Education* (New York, 1971).

Bekku, Sadao (b. Tokyo, 24 May 1922), studied theoretical physics at Tokyo Imperial Univ. (1943–46) and composition at the Paris Conservatory with Darius Milhaud and Olivier Messiaen (1951–54). Since 1961 he has been professor of composition at Toho Gakuen Univ. His harmonic style, though based on a chromatic-modal system, is fundamentally tonal.

PRINCIPAL COMPOSITIONS: *Symphony* (1961, Ongaku); *San-nin-no onna-no monogatasi* [A Story of 3 Women], 3-act opera; libretto by Matsuko Suzuki after a Kyogen play (1965); *Arima-no Miko* [Prince Arima], 3-act opera; libretto by Tadashi Matsubara after Tsuneari Fukuda (1967); *Violin Concerto* (1969, NHK); *Viola Concerto* (1971, NHK).

SEE ALSO: Japan.

Belgium. The diversified musical life of present-day Belgium is probably representative of what is taking place in most of the Western world. Musical theaters, which in the 19th century played a dominant role not only in Brussels but in all the larger provincial towns, have now almost disappeared. During the 1960s the Brussels opera house (known as Théâtre de la Monnaie) seemed to reverse this trend owing primarily to the choreographer Maurice Béjart, whose Ballets du 20ᵉ Siècle attracted a large public (although I would say his efforts represent a crude vulgarization of modern art). As for the traditional opera repertory, even such stars as Wieland Wagner and Karl Boehm have been able to provide only a provisional postponement of the inevitable decline. A desire for national prestige explains the subsidies granted to an enterprise like the Opéra de Wallonie, which has its home in Liège and tours the important southern cities (similar enterprises exist in the Flemish regions to the north).

Until recently the great private concert societies, particularly the Société Philharmonique of Brussels, were growing in popularity. Thanks in part to the interest in music stimulated by the Jeunesses Musicales' activities (begun during World War II), these societies had recruited a growing public from among the less wealthy classes. The repertory was kept within narrow limits, however, both of time (Bach to Ravel) and musical complexity. Nowadays there seems to be less interest, principally because of the spread of phonograph records (aided by loan institutions such as the Discothèque Nationale), broadcasting (the Belgian state radio carries much concert music, including 20th-century and Belgian music), a growing interest among younger students and the intelligentsia for modern and even experimental music (seldom heard in traditional concert programs), and renewed interest, even among the educated classes, for the popular musics of the world, especially Anglo-Saxon folk, rock, pop, and jazz. Attempts to restructure the concert societies are still only tentative in nature.

Education programs and organizations in Belgium date from the 19th century; even then they were somewhat removed from the living art of music. Today almost nothing about them except instruction in the most technical aspects of performance can still be defended. For a long time composition has not been taught in the conservatories, and the teaching of theory, harmony, counterpoint, and fugue bears no relation to serious current composition. Nevertheless, this sort of teaching lives on, kept alive no doubt because it is one of the few sources of revenue for many professional musicians, particularly composers.

Contemporary Belgian composers, even the most individualistic of them, all link themselves to one or more of the major international currents, and in general Belgian concert music differs only in nuances from that of the neighboring countries, especially France and the Netherlands. Some composers are among the leaders of new trends, but more frequently they follow them or merely repeat formulas. With few exceptions their production is usually characterized by some delay. Thus until the end of World War I the most advanced Belgian music was still largely dominated by Wagner (or at least Wagnerism) and parallel movements including Franckism, especially in the Walloon regions. The dominant figure within the country at that time was Paul *Gilson (1865–1942), a student of François Gevaert. Gilson gained attention before the war but became even more important thereafter as he devoted himself to teaching and formed a circle of musicians who became the core of official modern Belgian music. Gilson transmitted the heritage of Wagner, Strauss, and the late-19th-century Russians to his students. He also let them be exposed to other influences, even the more recent ones that he himself did not care for, such as his French contemporaries Debussy and Ravel. Gilson's students gained considerable craftsmanship in 19th-century techniques but did not involve themselves in their music and used certain eccentric features to merely decorate what was basically a superficial expression. That they soon came to represent an official Belgian school is shown by the careers of two of them, Marcel *Poot (b. 1901) and Gaston Brenta (1902–69). In 1925 both were among the founders of the Synthétistes, a group of Gilson's pupils. During 1949–66 Poot was director of the Brussels Conservatory and for many years head of SABAM, the Belgian authors rights society. Brenta was music director of the French-language section of the Belgian radio from the end of World War II until his death. Other composers who have held positions of influence and who have participated on official committees, juries, and the like, include Raymond Moulaert (1875–1962), Francis de Bourguignon (1890–1961), and particularly Jean *Absil (b. 1893), one of the best known of Belgian composers and an active teacher. Their works and those of their friends and students (Raymond *Chevreuille, b. 1901; Victor *Legley, b. 1915; Marcel *Quinet, 1915–71) have supplied many entries for the Queen Elisabeth contests and similar established events. This circle also molds the activities of the official publishing agency, the Centre Belge de Documentation Musicale, which is patterned after the Donemus Foundation in the Netherlands (few Belgians are published abroad). The music of all these composers possesses a certain homogeneousness recalling neoclassicism or neoromanticism mixed in differing degrees with the more obvious features of Ravel, Stravinsky, Honegger, Hindemith, and some traits of the Viennese 12-tone masters. Their music has little influence on developments in the international scene and is seldom performed abroad.

Next to this rather academic activity a more experimental spirit has always existed in one form or another. Between the wars this spirit was centered in the work of three musicians, Albert Huybrechts (1899–1938), Paul Collaer (b. 1891), and André *Souris (1899–1970). Huybrechts was a student of Joseph *Jongen (1873–1953), who like Gilson was a dominant force for postromantic and impressionist Belgian music. When he was only 27 he won two distinctions in the U.S.: first prize at the Ojai Valley Festival and the Elizabeth Sprague Coolidge Prize. Most of Huybrecht's works, including the most important ones, were played only after his death and are still rarely heard either in Belgium or abroad. His music was always imbued with intense emotions; it coupled influences from Ravel at his most innovative with an atonality akin to Berg.

Collaer was trained as a chemist, but his passion for music caused him to dedicate himself more and more to this art. He is an indefatigable explorer, defending the new vistas revealed by adventurous composers. He worked as a pianist, a lecturer, a concert organizer, and orchestral conductor in Brussels. In 1922 he founded the Concerts Pro Arte in collaboration with the string quartet of the same name; for 12 years these concerts were a forum for the most modern music of the time: Milhaud, Stravinsky, the Viennese (including Webern), and others. In 1933 the Pro Arte Concerts were absorbed by the Philharmonic Society, and they soon disappeared altogether. Collaer, however, entered the state radio and soon became music director of the Flemish section. Until well after World War II he used this position to forward his knowledge and love of contemporary and older music; he himself conducted the first performances in Belgium of some of Webern's late works as well as the first postwar performance of Monteverdi's *Orfeo*. Now Collaer devotes himself almost exclusively to ethnomusicological research.

Souris, a student of Gilson, was never inclined to orthodoxy. His early compositions were marked by his passion for Debussy, then still a controversial figure, and he soon became involved with the Correspondance group of surrealist and dada writers and artists. He participated not only in the artistic work of the group but in its concern for a social morality in the entire structure of society. He limited himself at the time to a few inventions of the most corrosive antiart, collages, false commonplaces, and the like, and even retired for awhile to his native province to conduct a town band. For several years beginning during World War II he directed the musical studio of the Seminaire des Arts in Brussels, a private undertaking located in the Palais des Beaux-Arts that made new poetry, painting, films, and music available to the general public. There Souris presented and analyzed music from medieval times to the present and re-awakened many minds to contemporary music.

Since about 1950 the younger generations of composers and their public have been turning toward the future, toward the discovery of new possibilities, of a new musical language incorporating in some renewed way a dialogue with the immediate past and with popular, ancient, and other musics. My own activities in this regard included helping to found the Brussels electronic music studio in 1958. At first the studio was a private institution; later it received support from the government. In 1970 its activities were absorbed by the Center for Musical Research in Liège, which is supported by the government, the city of Liège, Liège Univ., and the French-language Belgian radio. It conducts not only electroacoustical but also theoretical research and experimentation concerning new types of performance and listening. As a collaborator in organizing new music broadcasts at the radio since 1956, I have been able to initiate many activities there and elsewhere oriented toward recent music. At present the radio has three program channels with regional as well as national centers of production. The studios in Liège are doing by far the most advanced work. In addition since 1964 the radio has held an exceptional biannual series in Brussels, Reconnaisance des Musiques Modernes, under Georges Caraël, music director for the radio's third program.

Concerts of new music occur principally in Brussels, Liège, and the university center of Louvain near Brussels. In Brussels the association Musiques Nouvelles was founded in 1962. It organizes concerts in collaboration with the radio, the Philharmonic Society, and other organizations; it also initiated a program of conferences and seminars which are now incorporated in the Centre de Sociologie de la Musique of the Univ. of Brussels. An ensemble called Musiques Nouvelles was also founded in 1962; it is under the direction of Pierre *Bartholomée (b. 1937), who with Philippe *Boesmans (b. 1936) is one of the two outstanding younger composers from the southern region. In Liège there is a Jeunesses Musicales and a series called Concerts Froidebise, named after Pierre Froidebise (1914–62), an organist of wide culture, one of the best Belgian musicans during the 1940s and 50s, and a man who inspired many younger Liège musicians, including myself. The Festival des Flanders in Ghent and other cities is active in the northern Flemish half of the country and has some chapters that emphasize modern music. Finally in 1963 a second studio of electronic music came into existence, the Institute for Psychoacoustics and Electronic Music. It is sponsored by the Dutch-language section of the radio and the Royal Univ. of Ghent, where the studio is located. Its music director until 1970 was the composer Louis de *Meester (b. 1904); responsibility for its operation is now divided between the musicologist Herman Sabbe and the composer Lucien *Goethals, who are overseeing various types of practical and theoretical research. Among the composers who have worked there are David van de Woestijne (b. 1915), who comes from an important family of Flemish painters and writers, and Karel *Goeyvaerts (b. 1923), whose *Sonata for 2 Pianos* (1950–51) anticipated the serialism that Boulez explored in his *Structures*. Goeyvaerts was also an important influence on the young Stockhausen. His music today is much more eclectic than before.

BIBL.: *Het Instítoot voor Psychoakoestiek en Elektronische Muziek* (Ghent 1966); *Music in Belgium* (Brussels 1964); *Le Studio de musique électronique de Bruxelles* (Brussels 1963); Robert Wangermee, *La Musique belge contemporaine* (Brussels 1959).

Henri Pousseur

Benguerel (i Godo), **Xavier** (b. Barcelona, 9 Feb 1931), studied composition and counterpoint in Barcelona with Cristófor Taltabull (1954–60) but is primarily self-taught. He has been mainly influenced by the music of Schoenberg and contemporary German composers. His music is strongly contrapuntal and often incorporates 12-tone procedures.

PRINCIPAL COMPOSITIONS: *Cantata d'amic i amat* for voice, chorus, flute, oboe, clarinet, bassoon, horn, trombone, percussion; poem by Ramón Lull (1959, Armónico); *Successions* for wind quintet (1960, EM); *Concerto* for 2 flutes, strings (1961, Bärenreiter); *Duo* for clarinet, piano (1963, Seesaw); *Violin Concerto* (1965, Seesaw); *Estructura IV* for piano (1966, Seesaw); *Symphony for Small Orchestra* (1966); *Festival Symphony* (1966, EM); *Paraules de cada dia* for voice, flutes, clarinets, harp, vibraphone, piano, celesta, percussion (1967, EM); *Music for 3 Percussionists* (1967, Moeck); *Symphony for Large Orchestra* (1968, Moeck); *Test Sonata* for small orchestra (1968, Moeck); *Music* for oboe, chamber orchestra (1968, Moeck); *Musica riservata* for 11 solo strings (1969, Schott); *Joc* for flute, oboe, clarinet, piano, violin, viola, cello, percussion (1969, Moeck); *Dialogue Orchestrale* (1969, Schott); *Organ Concerto* (1970, Schott); *Consort Music* for 11 strings (1970).

BIBL.: René Leibowitz, "La música de X. B.," *Serra d'or* (Barcelona) 101:68–70; Wolf-Eberhard von Lewinski, "Vier katalanische Komponisten in Barcelona," *Melos* 38:92–103; Josef Soler, "La Música de X. B.," *Imagen y Sonido* 67:50f., —— "X. B.," *Heterofonia* (Mexico City) 4:15ff.

Ben-Haim, Paul (b. Munich, 5 July 1897), attended the State Academy of Music in Munich (1915–16, 1918–20; composition with Friedrich Klose, piano with Bertold Kellermann). He studied conducting privately with Hugo Roehr. Ben-Haim was an assistant conductor at the Munich State Opera (1920–24) and a conductor at the Augsburg Opera House (1924–31). He then taught, conducted, and composed in Munich until 1933, when he emigrated to Israel and continued these activities there. The decisive influence on his work "came from the folkloristic musical tradition of the Jews and Arabs in the lands of the Near and Middle East. . . . I began to study this material [in Europe] in the 20s." He studied it firsthand after he emigrated to Israel, "noting down traditional melodies, arranging and performing them in many public concerts in Palestine, Lebanon, Syria, and Egypt."

PRINCIPAL COMPOSITIONS (published by IMP unless otherwise noted): *Symphonies Nos. 1–2* (1939–40, 1943–45); *Sonatina* for piano (1946); *From Israel*, suite for orchestra (1951); *Sonata* for solo violin (1951, unpub.); *3 Songs without Words* for voice with chamber orchestra or piano (1952); *Serenade* for flute, violin, viola, cello (1952); *The Sweet Psalmist of Israel*, "3 Symphonic Movements" (1953); *Dance and Invocation* for orchestra (1960); *3 Psalms* for soloists, chorus, orchestra or organ (1962); *The Eternal Theme*, "Music for Orchestra" (1966); *Kabbalat Shabbat* (Friday evening service) for soloists, chorus, organ or orchestra (1966–67).

BIBL.: *P. B.-H.* (Tel Aviv: IMP, 1967).

SEE ALSO Israel.

Bennett, Richard Rodney (b. Broadstairs, Kent, England, 29 March 1936), studied at the Royal Academy of Music in London (1953–56)

with Lennox Berkeley and Howard Ferguson. During this time he completed many works, including the *Piano Sonata* and two of his four string quartets. He then spent two years as a pupil of Pierre Boulez in Paris. Since 1958 he has lived in London, earning his living mainly as a composer of film music. During 1970–71 he was visiting professor at the Peabody Institute in Baltimore.

Bennett is a "12-tone composer" who has written fluently in this idiom from an early stage in his career. His works include three operas (a fourth is in process), two symphonies, a piano concerto, and four string quartets, as well as several works for miscellaneous chamber ensembles and for piano. He has composed 33 film scores since 1955 and has also written music for educational purposes, for radio, television, and the theater.

Although the works of Webern provided his first introduction to 12-tone music, he has not been directly influenced by the Viennese school. In the early works, such as the *Piano Sonata* (1954), the logical unwinding of the tone row did not preclude the use of tonal harmonic materials and traditional rhythmic structures. A radical change took place in the works for one and two pianos that date from his study years in Paris. In these, serial control was applied to many elements—pitch, attack, dynamics, and durations. These works, however, were interim experiments, uncharacteristic in their rhythmic complexity and harmonic asperity and in their relatively obscure formal outlines, which followed the 1950s practice in their dependence on precompositional formulas. The works written within a few years of his return to London (*Calendar, The Approaches of Sleep*, and *Winter Music*, all 1960) reveal little of his "Paris" style. Instead, they return to a line of development suggested by the early student works. Although rhythm continued to have an independent existence and did not merely underline melodic and harmonic contours, the underlying pulse again became strongly defined. The most recent works place increasing emphasis on an internal rhythmic structure that contributes independently to the overall cohesion. Moreover, the harmony is enriched by passing tonal implications (as in *The Music that Her Echo Is*) and by the possibilities resulting from a freer application of 12-tone procedures, e.g., not avoiding serial "false relations." His vivid orchestration stems from the expressive needs of the music and not from an exploration of peripheral techniques and unusual groupings of instruments.

PRINCIPAL COMPOSITIONS (published by UE unless otherwise noted): *Piano Sonata* (1954)s *Calendar* for chamber ensemble (1960, Mills); *The Approaches of Sleep* for 4 voices, 10 instrumente (1960, Mills); *Winter Music* for flute, piano (1960, Mills); *The Ledge*, chamber opera (1961, Mills); *Nocturnes* for chamber orchestra (1962, Mills); *London Pastoral* for tenor, chamber orchestra (1962, Mills); *Oboe Sonata* (1962, Mills); *Fantasy* for piano (1962, Mills); *5 Studies* for piano (1962–64); *Jazz Calendar* for 12 players (1963); *The Mines of Sulphur*, 3-act opera; libretto by Beverley Cross (1963–65); *String Quartet No. 4* (1964); *Aubade* for orchestra (1964); *Sonata No. 2* for solo violin (1964); *Symphonies Nos. 1–2* (1965, 1967); *Epithalamion* for chorus, orchestra (1966); *Penny for a Song*, opera (1966); *The Music that Her Echo Is*, cycle for tenor, piano (1967); *Wind Quintet* (1967–68); *All the King's Men*, opera for children (1968); *Piano Concerto* (1968); *5 Impromptus* for guitar (1968); *Capriccio* for piano 4-hands (1968); *Crazy Jane* for soprano, clarinet, cello, piano (1968–69); *Victory*, 3-act opera (1968–69); *Jazz Pastoral* for voice, jazz orchestra (1969); *Oboe Concerto* (1969–70); *Guitar Concerto* with chamber ensemble (1970); *Party Piece* for young pianist, small orchestra (1970); *Devotions* for chorus (1971); *The House of Sleeps* for 6 male voices (1971).

PRINCIPAL WRITINGS: "A Composer on his Opera," *Music and Musicians* (Sept 1961):18, 38; "In Search of Pierre Boulez" (Susan Bradshaw, coauthor), *Music and Musicians* (Jan 1963):10–13 and (August 1963):14–18, 50; "Symphony," *Musical Events* 21/2:9. Bennett also translated with Bradshaw *Boulez on Music Today* (London 1971).

Susan Bradshaw

SEE ALSO Great Britain; Liturgical Music: Christian.

Bennett, Robert Russell (b. Kansas City, 15 June 1894), studied piano with his mother and other instruments with his father, who was a professional instrumentalist and teacher. He also studied composition in Kansas City with the Danish composer Carl Busch. He moved to New York in 1916 and led army bands during World War I. In 1922 he began orchestrating and arranging Broadway musicals and revues, a field he has dominated ever since. During 1926–32 he left Broadway to study for four years in Paris with Nadia Boulanger and to travel and compose in Europe.

In addition to scores and arrangements for musicals, films, and television, Bennett's output includes three operas and many orchestral works. They reveal a comprehensive grasp of musical styles, both past and present; in fact Bennett incorporates so wide a range of stylistic elements in his music that one might

not know from one piece to the next that they were written by the same person. An extremely agile musician, he is often able to compose directly on score paper without making preliminary drafts or short scores. (His perspicacity is also revealed in his ability to recite the records of baseball players and race horses.) Bennett's orchestrations and arrangements of Broadway musicals have done much to raise the standards of the genre. His overtures, underscoring, and dance sequences, for instance, were the first in which counterpoint and other procedures of symphonic development replaced mere repetitions of tunes and accompaniments.

PRINCIPAL MUSICAL ARRANGEMENTS: Bennett has done what is called the "musical arrangements" for well over 200 musicals. The most successful have been (with composer and date of composition): *Rose-Marie* (Rudolf Friml, 1924); *Sunny* (Jerome Kern, 1925); *Showboat* (Kern, 1927); *The Cat and the Fiddle* (Kern, 1931); *Music in the Air* (Kern, 1932); *Face the Music* (Irving Berlin, 1932); *Roberta* (Kern, 1933); *On Your Toes* (Richard Rodgers, 1936); *Louisiana Purchase* (Berlin, 1939); *Panama Hattie* (Cole Porter, 1940); *Oklahoma!* (Rodgers, 1943); *The Gay Divorcee* (Porter, 1944); *Carousel* (Rodgers, 1945); *Annie Get Your Gun* (Berlin, 1946); *South Pacific* (Rodgers, 1948); *Kiss Me Kate* (Porter, 1948); *The King and I* (Rodgers, 1951); *My Fair Lady* (Frederick Loewe, 1956); *The Sound of Music* (Rodgers, 1959); *Camelot* (Loewe, 1960).

PRINCIPAL CONCERT COMPOSITIONS (for orchestra unless otherwise noted): *Rondo Capriccioso* for 4 flutes (1916, N.Y. Flute Club); *Abraham Lincoln* (1931, Harms); *Sights and Sounds* (1934, Harms); *Organ Sonata in G* (1934, Arrow); *Maria Malibran*, 3-act opera (1935); *Hollywood*, scherzo for orchestra (1937); *8 Etudes* (1938); *Hexapoda* for violin, piano (1940, Chappell); *Song Sonata* for violin, piano (1947, Chappell); *Suite of Old American Dances* for band (1949, Chappell); *Concerto grosso* for wind quintet, wind orchestra (1957, Henmar); *Symphonic Songs* for band (1959, Chappell); *Stephen Collins Foster*, commemoration symphony for orchestra, chorus (1959, Chappell); *Ohio River Suite* (1959, Henmar); *Symphony* (1963).

Hershy Kay

Bentoiu, Pascal (b. Bucharest, 22 April 1927), studied composition in Bucharest with Michael Jora (1943–48). During 1953–56 he worked as a researcher at the Folklore Institute in Bucharest. His music is "a synthesis of modal, tonal, and serial idioms" and includes jazz and tape works. He has written incidental music for over 20 plays.

PRINCIPAL COMPOSITIONS (published by Muzicală unless otherwise noted): *String Quartet*, Op. 3

(1953, unpub.); *Piano Concerto No. 1*, Op. 5 (1954); *Luceafărul* [The Evening Star] for orchestra, organ, Op. 7 (1957); *Violin Concerto*, Op. 9 (1958); *Piano Concerto No. 2*, Op. 12 (1960); *Violin Sonata*, Op. 14 (1962); *L'Amour médecin*, opera, Op. 15; libretto by the composer after Molière (1964); *Symphony* for 3 saxophones, orchestra, Op. 16 (1965); *Hamlet*, opera for soloists, chorus, orchestra, tape, Op. 18 (1966–69); *Iphigenia's Sacrifice*, opera for soloists, women's chorus, organ, percussion, Op. 17; libretto by the composer (1968).

PRINCIPAL WRITINGS: "Consideraţiuni asupra ritmului şi notaţiei melodiilor de joc româneşti" [Considerations on the Rhythmic and Melodic Notation of Rumanian Folk Dances], *Revista de folclor* (Bucharest) 1956/1–2:36–67; "Câteva aspecte ale armoniei în muzica populară din Ardeal [Some Aspects of Harmony in the Folk Music of Ardeal], *Studii de muzicologie* (Bucharest 1965): 147–214; "Mihail Jora," *ibid.* (1966):109–32.

BIBL.: Lucian Grigorovici, "Bukarester Oper zeigt Molière in moderner Tracht," *Melos* (Sept 1967):316–17.

Bentzon, Niels Viggo (b. Copenhagen, 28 August 1919), studied at the Royal Danish Conservatory (1939–43; theory with Knud Jeppesen, piano with Christian Christiansen, organ with Emilius Bangert). He is self-taught as a composer. Since 1949 he has taught composition and theory at the Royal Danish Conservatory. His compositions have been influenced by his interest in jazz and popular music and by the work of Hindemith, Schoenberg, and Bartók.

PRINCIPAL COMPOSITIONS (published by Hansen-W): *Toccata* for piano, Op. 10 (1940); *String Quartets Nos. 1–9*: No. 1, Op. 9 (1940); No. 2, Op. 39 (1944); No. 3, Op. 72 (1951); No. 4, Op. 95 (c.1954); No. 5, Op. 105 (1956); No. 6, Op. 124 (c.1959); No. 7, Op. 165 (c.1965); No. 8, "Dartmouth Quartet," Op. 228 (c.1967); No. 9, Op. 232 (c.1968); *Passacaglia* for piano, Op. 31 (1944); *Partita* for piano, Op. 38 (1945); *Piano Sonata No. 3*, Op. 44 (1946); *Symphonies Nos. 4, 5, 7, 8, 10*: No. 4, "Metamorphosen," Op. 55 (1948–49); No. 5, "Ellipsen," Op. 61 (1950); No. 7, "De tre versioner," Op. 83 (c.1952); No. 8, "Sinfonia discreta," Op. 113 (c.1957); No. 10, "Den hymniske," Op. 150 (1963); *Metafor*, ballet, Op. 58 (1950); *Piano Sonata No. 5*, Op. 77 (1951); *Kurtisanen*, ballet, Op. 89 (c.1952); *Symphonic Variations*, Op. 92 (1953); *Piano Concerto No. 4*, Op. 96 (1954); *Cello Concerto No. 1*, Op. 106 (1956); *Brilliantes concertino on Mozart's "Ein Mädchen oder Weibchen"* for piano, orchestra, Op. 108 (1956); *Concerto for Strings*, Op. 114 (c.1957); *Concerto* for 6 percussionists, Op. 115 (c.1957); *Wind Quintet No. 5*, Op. 116 (c.1958); *Mutations for Orchestra*, Op. 123 (c.1959); *Rhapsody* for piano, orchestra, Op. 131 (1961); *Ostinato for*

Orchestra, Op. 133 (1961); *Violin Concerto No. 2*, Op. 136 (1961); *Døren* [The Door], ballet, Op. 141 (1962); *Faust III*, opera, Op. 144 (c.1962); *Flute Concerto*, Op. 147 (c.1963); *Piano Concerto No. 5*, Op. 149 (1963); *Meet the Danes* for orchestra, Op. 153 (1964); *Jenny von Westphalen*, ballet, Op. 177 (1965); *Piano Sonata No. 8*, Op. 193 (c.1966); *Jubilaeumsballet 800*, Op. 207 (1967); *Die Serapionsbrüder* for piano, Op. 254 (c.1969); *Napolean Sonata* for piano, Op. 263 (c.1969); *Rossini Sonata* for piano, Op. 264 (c.1969); *Devrient Sonata* for piano, Op. 265 (c.1969).

SEE ALSO Scandinavia.

Berezowsky, Nicolai (Tikhonovich) (b. St. Petersburg, 17 May 1900; d. New York, 27 August 1953), studied at the Imperial Capella in St. Petersburg (1908–17) and emigrated to the U.S. in 1922, where he attended the Juilliard School (composition with Rubin Goldmark, violin with Paul Kochanski). In Russia he had been a violinist in the Bolshoi Theater Orchestra and musical director of the School of Modern Art in Moscow. During 1923–29 he was a violinist with the N. Y. Philharmonic and during 1935–40, a member of the Coolidge Quartet of the Library of Congress. He was an assistant conductor for CBS Radio during 1932–36 and 1941–c.46.

PRINCIPAL COMPOSITIONS (published by Boosey unless otherwise noted): *Symphonies Nos. 1–4*, Opp. 12, 18, 21, 27 (1925, ERM; 1929; 1936; 1943, unpub.); *Theme and Variations* for clarinet, piano, strings (1926, ERM); *Suite hebraïque* for orchestra (1928); *Violin Concerto*, Op. 14 (1930, ERM); *Concerto lirico* for cello, orchestra, Op. 19 (1934); *Viola Concerto* (1941); *Clarinet Concerto*, Op. 28 (1941); *Harp Concerto*, Op. 31 (1944, E-V); *Gilgamesh*, cantata for narrator, vocal quartet, chorus, orchestra, Op. 32 (premiere 1947, Levant); *Sextet Concerto* for string orchestra (1951, AMP); *Babar the Elephant*, children's opera, Op. 40 (premiere 1953, Fischer).

BIBL.: Alice Berezowsky, *Duet with Nicky* (Philadelphia 1943); Robert Ward, "N. B.," *ACA Bulletin* 3/4:20 and *Juilliard Review* 1954:26–29.

Berg, Alban (b. Vienna, 9 Feb 1885; d. Vienna, 24 Dec 1935), began composing songs on romantic texts as a teenager. He had little formal musical training until he began studying privately with Arnold Schoenberg (1904–12); his evolution entirely under one mentor is almost unique in musical pedagogy. While a student of Schoenberg he developed a lifelong friendship with his fellow pupil Anton Webern and became involved with artistic and intellectual circles in Vienna, counting among his acquaintances the artists of the Vienna Sezession, the poet Peter Altenberg, the satirist Karl Kraus, and especially Gustav Mahler. Berg married in 1911 and began that year to work at Universal Edition preparing piano reductions and analytical guides, notably for Schoenberg's *Gurrelieder*. He was drafted into the Austrian army in 1915 and did chiefly office work until the armistice. Thereafter and until it was discontinued in 1923, he collaborated with Schoenberg in founding and running the Vienna Society for Private Musical Performances. During these years he also began to teach privately. The premiere of *Wozzeck* at the Berlin Opera in 1925, together with subsequent productions elsewhere in Europe, made Berg famous and enabled him to devote himself almost exclusively to composition. His death at 50 occurred before he could finish orchestrating the last act of *Lulu*.

All of Berg's works are characterized by a large conception. Even in those pieces that can be called short (Opp. 4, 5), there is always great density and compression of musical gesture. (By contrast, in most of Webern's brief works the textures and overall shapes and sizes of musical events seem appropriate to a small conception, however intricate the structure.) Berg thus faced two major problems: creating large-scale forms without the benefit of traditional tonal supports, and devising large structures when the very idea of large-scale symphonic music had apparently been exhausted in the works of Mahler.

Berg's large forms often suggest specific classical forms or traditional simple outlines. The arch form is especially common as an underlying principle. The beginning and end of the *Altenberg Lieder*, Op. 4, for instance (first song, bars 14–15; fifth song, last six bars), contain a two-chord progression and its reversal. The second and fourth songs begin and end with the same note in the accompaniment. The middle song begins and ends with the same chord. In later works Berg made much use of the arch form's logical extension, the strict palindrome (for example, the second part of *Der Wein*, the Allegro misterioso of the *Lyric Suite*, the film music in act II of *Lulu*). Other traditional formal models in Berg include fugue (*Wozzeck* II/2), theme and variations (*Chamber Concerto*, movement I; *Wozzeck* III/1), and passacaglia (*Altenberg Lieder*, No. 5; *Wozzeck* I/4). In all of these, only the broadest outlines of the classical conception remain, and new constraints replace the old. For instance, in the *Altenberg Lieder* passacaglia, three themes share an equal responsibility for supporting the piece; in the

Wozzeck passacaglia the truly thematic material is not the basis for each variation, and the ground bass (though it can hardly be called that) is more of an abstract formulation, a punctuating device, than a thematic idea.

In the more symphonic of Berg's movements overall forms may have less specific outlines. An example is the "March," the third of the *3 Pieces* for orchestra. There is no march form, of course, but rather a march style. The formal considerations of Berg's march are based on an energetic succession of musical events that occur as the result of a process of melodic and motivic development (as in Beethoven, but even more as in the first movement of Mahler's *Sixth Symphony*); within this process there are motivic mileposts (e.g., bars 45–46 and 160) that tie the movement cyclically to the other two pieces in the set. In short, the overall form of this march is not so much a large structure per se as it is the outward manifestation of internal relationships of smaller structures; the same is true of other movements of Berg's music in which the named genre has no fixed outline (e.g., the "Rhapsody" that constitutes *Wozzeck* I/2).

Wozzeck, a pathbreaking work, cleaves to some operatic traditions in its use of leitmotivs and self-contained numbers (military march, lullaby, waltz, etc.); in addition, Berg acknowledged his debt to Debussy's *Pelléas et Mélisande*, with its relatively large number of short scenes separated by substantial orchestral interludes. The work contains two wholly original devices: the casting of each scene as a self-contained musical piece of some named form or genre, and the use in some scenes of microstructural procedures that do not contribute to the larger form but are instead manifestations of Berg's search for the most intrinsic and fundamental kinds of structure (a search shared by Schoenberg and Webern and culminating in the 12-tone method). The first scene of act II exemplifies both of these points: the larger form is that of a sonata allegro, and the principal harmonic and melodic materials derive from specific source chords.

The basic unit of Berg's microstructure is the motive, with all the protean flexibility that a motivic usage can entail. Motives appear as themes, as in the *Piano Sonata*, and as leitmotivs, as in the operas. They may appear simultaneously as themes and as the substructure of the accompaniment, as in the outer sections of the first of the *Altenberg Lieder*, where the entire pitch substance is motivically organized. A motive may be a small referential unit, a cell, or a chord or something like a series in miniature that does not exist in any exclusively thematic form, as in the second of the *Altenberg Lieder* or in *Wozzeck* II/1. The motive may also be a group of short melodic figures constantly changing but always related by a common interval content, as in the *3 Pieces* for orchestra. The "Inventions" in act III of *Wozzeck* contain examples of what a motive may be: a melody, a single pitch class, a rhythm, or a chord. Rhythmic motives are a pervasive feature from Op. 3 (1910) on. In *Wozzeck*, the *Chamber Concerto*, the *Lyric Suite*, *Lulu*, and the *Violin Concerto*, there are prominent rhythmic motives, often manipulated independently of pitches, as in medieval isorhythmic procedures. (In the Allegro misterioso of the *Lyric Suite*, all rhythmic details derive from a specific couple of *Hauptrhythmen*, themselves derived from the melodic structure of the series employed.) In the 12-tone works, all of Berg's motivic practices became integrated with his unique conceptions of dodecaphonic writing. In *Lulu*, for instance, the leitmotiv idea is extended to include special 12-tone sets associated with individual characters in the drama.

Berg's harmony can be called "tonalistic" in that it is often oriented towards a tone center (as opposed to a key center) that cannot be defined according to classical harmonic relationships but whose existence answers an analogous need. The most obvious example is the murder scene in *Wozzeck* (III/2), the "Invention on a Tone." The pitch-class B, present in every bar in a variety of registers, acts as an interior pedal point in an ebb and flow of more or less distantly related harmonies. Berg's vertical structures, considered by themselves, run the gamut from simple triads to 12-tone aggregates. They may result from the confluence of independent voices, they may be simple verticalizations of linear motives, or they may themselves be generated by a specific procedure (as in the 12-tone chord of superposed perfect fourths in Op. 6, No. 2, bar 66); vertical structures may also be "Berg chords," having a tonic or dominant or occasionally polytonal appearance but with their direction obscured by foreign tones (as with many chords in Mahler's last works). Most important of all, vertical structures generate and are generated by their own context, which exhibits a fine balance between the linear and vertical dimensions and contains reminiscences of a dissolved classical tonality. (Except in a few special cases, the practices of Schoenberg and Webern demonstrate no comparable approach to the vertical dimension.) That Berg's harmonic context is never-

theless regulated by the exigencies of motivic organization is one of his most remarkable technical achievements.

Berg's textures typically emphasize the polarity of melody and accompaniment, or melody and bass, or melody with other voices in counterpoint and accompaniment. A particularly common device is the "wedge" formed by two chromatically converging or diverging melodic lines, one or both of which may be thickened with parallel moving chords. The principle of sliding chromaticism, as in Chopin's *E-Minor Prelude*, and sometimes the principle of classical harmonic sequence are related to these procedures and play a considerable part in Berg's harmony. Dense, florid counterpoint of the type that abounds in Schoenberg or Webern is comparatively rare in Berg and occurs only momentarily; in such instances, Berg's harmony is likely to lose its tonalistic balance. (Dense textures in Schoenberg and Webern usually result from an aggregate of single lines—long lines in Schoenberg and short ones in Webern—whereas Berg's textures usually consist of an aggregate of melody plus chordal layers within which one or two melodic lines stand out.)

Of Berg's major works, only *Der Wein*, *Lulu*, the *Violin Concerto*, and parts of the *Lyric Suite* relate in any consistent way to Schoenberg's 12-tone method. Berg's use of 12-tone procedures was hardly a conversion to Schoenbergian orthodoxy but rather a continuation of his own earlier practices, and from the start his procedures differed in a number of particulars from those of his teacher. The first movement of the *Lyric Suite*, for instance, uses three related but different series, in contrast to Schoenberg's practice of using only one. Furthermore Berg usually presented a linear statement of a series in an individualized melodic form and avoided permutations of the row that would destroy the distinctive melodic and rhythmic contours. Thus he used the inversion of a row (which retains the melodic contour, though in mirror form) but rarely the retrograde and retrograde inversion. An exception is the use of retrograde forms in the "return" part of a palindrome, in which the entire musical structure is retrograde.

Notably in *Lulu*, Berg used a special disposition of 12-tone rows on a equal footing with serial uses, namely the partitioning of a series into two or more unordered tropes (such as two hexachords) in which the pitch-class content of each trope, and not the serial order of pitches within the trope, is the defining factor. This kind of procedure, first devised by

J. M. Hauer, is a nonlinear way of defining a harmonic or melodic pitch hierarchy. (Of Schoenberg's 12-tone works, only the *Ode to Napoleon*, Op. 41, makes use of unordered hexachordal tropes.) The trope thus becomes a referential unit comparable to the scale in tonal music; indeed, in Berg's works it is a means for accommodating the region between tonality and atonality, as well as for bridging serial and nonserial structure. For example, the three series of the first movement of the *Lyric Suite* are all specific orderings of the same pair of hexachordal tropes, which in their simplest form are the first six degrees of the C-major and F♯-major scales (bar 33). Berg's striving for a systematic 12-tone tonality reached its most dramatic results in the *Violin Concerto*, whose series unfolds as a progression of major and minor triads related by the cycle of fifths, plus a fragment of a whole-tone scale (movement I: solo violin, bars 15–18). By way of confirming the tonal connotations of this series, Berg introduced into this work a Carinthian folksong and Bach's harmonization of the chorale *Es ist genug*.

As far as the abstract consideration of the 12 tones of the chromatic scale is concerned, Berg actually anticipated Schoenberg as a 12-tone (but not as a 12-tone serial) composer. The earliest and most striking examples are in the *Altenberg Lieder*, in which a 12-tone melody exists in two different thematic forms (the prelude to the first song, beginning in bar 9, and the second of the three passacaglia themes in the fifth song, beginning in bar 5). The *3 Pieces* for orchestra and *Wozzeck*, both antedating Schoenberg's invention, contain similar isolated examples. Outwardly the function of the "twelveness" of these structures is in part to maintain an active change in pitch classes, illustrating Berg's appreciation of at least one aspect of the need to preserve chromatic totality in an atonal idiom.

Berg's preoccupation with numbers in music was an abstraction of an entirely different order. One example is in *Wozzeck* III/1, whose variations are each seven bars long, except for variation 2 (two bars adding up to seven beats), variation 6 (five bars adding up to 14 beats), and the final variation (21 bars including the interlude, with the descent of the curtain occupying seven beats). The most extreme example of this kind of construction is the *Lyric Suite*, where metronome markings, bar numbers at principal points of articulation, and total numbers of bars in each movement are mostly multiples of 23, Berg's fateful number.

One other aspect of Berg's music deserves mention, his predilection for quotation. This was either a private conceit, such as the use of Schoenberg's changing chord (from the *5 Pieces* for orchestra, Op. 16) in *Wozzeck* (I: bar 520), or something more outspoken, such as the *Tristan* quotation in the last movement of the *Lyric Suite*. The practice took on special significance in *Lulu*, where Berg underlined his identification with the composer Alwa by quoting short extracts from *Wozzeck* and the *Lyric Suite*.

Berg's music is characteristically closer to the spirit of the 19th century than is either Schoenberg's or Webern's. The principal source of this kinship was certainly Berg's reverence for Mahler's art. Mahler had succeeded in transforming the Beethovenian "bold gesture" and the *Tristan*-like "endless melody" into a highly individual and entirely valid basis for symphonic composition, and, among the three Viennese revolutionaries, it was Berg who carried the Mahlerian *Gemüt* into the 20th century. By contrast Schoenberg was, in the works of his early maturity, much closer in spirit to Wagner and Brahms, while Webern in his early works owed more directly to Schoenberg than to anyone else. It is significant that whereas Schoenberg and Webern embraced a neoclassic spirit of economy in their later works, Berg remained virtually independent of this trend and pursued a personal revolution in form, the significance of which is only recently being appreciated.

PRINCIPAL COMPOSITIONS (published by UE): 7 *Early Songs* for high voice with piano or orchestra (1905–08, orchestrated 1928); *Piano Sonata*, Op. 1 (1907–08); *4 Songs* for medium voice, piano, Op. 2; poems by Hebbel, Mombert (1909–10); *String Quartet*, Op. 3 (1910); *5 Orchestral Songs on Picture Postcard Texts of Peter Altenberg* for orchestra, Op. 4 (1912); *4 Pieces* for clarinet, piano, Op. 5 (1913); *3 Pieces* for orchestra, Op. 6 (1914); *Wozzeck*, 3-act opera after Büchner, Op. 7 (1917–22; *3 Excerpts from Wozzeck* for voice, orchestra, 1924); *Chamber Concerto* for piano, violin, 13 winds (1923–25; slow movement arranged as *Trio* for clarinet, cello, piano, 1935); *Lyric Suite* for string quartet (1925–26; *3 Movements from the Lyric Suite* for string orchestra, 1928); *Der Wein*, concert aria for soprano, orchestra; text by Baudelaire (1929); *Lulu*, 3-act opera after Wedekind's *Erdgeist* and *Büchse der Pandora* (1929–35; acts I–II published; 5 excerpts for voice and orchestra, called *Lulu Symphony*, arranged 1934, include two portions of the otherwise unpublished third act).

PRINCIPAL WRITINGS: *Guide to Schoenberg's Gurrelieder* (Vienna 1913); *Short Thematic Analysis of Schoenberg's Pelleas und Melisande*, Op. 5 (Vienna 19—?); *Thematic Analysis of Schoenberg's Chamber Symphony*, Op. 9 (Vienna 19—?); "What is Atonality?", *Music Since 1900* by N. Slonimsky (New York 1937):565–71. Many of Berg's important writings are printed in Redlich and Reich (see bibl.).

BIBL.: George Perle, *Serial Composition and Atonality*, 3rd ed. (Berkeley-Los Angeles 1971); Hans F. Redlich, *A. B.: Versuch einer Würdigung* (Vienna 1957); ——, *A. B.: The Man and His Music*, a condensed translation of the former (New York 1957); Willi Reich, *A. B.: Bildnis im Wort* (Zurich 1959); ——, *A. B.: mit Bs eigenen Schriften* ... (Vienna 1937; the English translation, New York 1965, is of an abridged version of the book and is not recommended).

Mark DeVoto

SEE ALSO Austria and Germany, Dance, Expressionism, Instrumental and Vocal Resources, Jazz, Mixed Media, Opera, Orchestration, Performance, Text Setting and Usage, Texture, 12-Tone Techniques.

Berg, Gunnar (b. St. Gall, 11 Jan 1909), began to study music in 1931 and later became a piano student of Hermann D. Koppel and during 1944–47 of Elisabeth Jürgens. He also studied briefly at the Royal Danish Conservatory. In 1948 he went to Paris, where he studied with Arthur Honegger but soon came under the influence of Olivier Messiaen. Beginning in 1952 he attended the Darmstadt summer courses, where he was especially influenced by the music of Anton Webern and Karlheinz Stockhausen. He is a free-lance composer. His own music is serially organized.

PRINCIPAL COMPOSITIONS: *Holzschnitte* for voice, piano (1938–41); *Feldspath*, suite for piano (1944); *Hymnos* for string orchestra (1946); *Cosmogonie* for 2 pianos (1952); *Essai accoustique 3* for piano, orchestra (1954); *El triptico gallego* for orchestra (1957); *Gaffky's*, 10 collections for piano (1958–59, No. 1 published by Fog); ... *pour clarinette et violon*, 37 "views" (1959); ... *pour piano et orchestre* (1959); *Uculang* for piano, orchestra (1967); *Random* for cello, percussion (1968); *Tronqué* for xylophone, cello, piano (1969).

BIBL.: Mogens Andersen, "G. B.," *Dansk Musiktidsskrift* 36:221–23; ——, "G. B. og hans galiciske triptyk" [G. B. and His Galician triptych], *Nutida musik* 1962–63/5:18–23; Bo Wallner, *Music of Our Time in Scandinavia* (Stockholm-London 1971).

[Prepared with the help of Ib Planch Larsen]

Berg, Josef (b. Brno, Czechoslovakia, 8 March 1927), studied composition at the Brno Conservatory with Vilém Petrzelka and musicology at the Univ. of Brno. During 1950–53 he worked in the music education department of the Czech Radio in Brno and wrote music criticism and theoretical articles for a number of newspapers and journals. His early music was influenced largely by Moravian folk music. Since 1959 he has used 12-tone and other techniques emanating from Cologne.

PRINCIPAL COMPOSITIONS: *Sextet* for harp, piano, string quartet (1959); *Songs of the New Werther* for bass-baritone, piano; text by the composer (1962, Supraphon); *Nonet* for 2 harps, harpsichord, piano, percussion (1962, Supraphon); *The Return of Odysseus*, chamber opera for narrator, female dancer, soprano, baritone, bass clarinet, tuba, violin, piano, percussion; libretto by the composer (1962, ČHF and Supraphon); *Sonata in modo classico* for harpsichord, piano (1963, ČHF); *European Tourism*, chamber opera for vocal sextet, bass clarinet, ionica, guitar, piano, harpsichord, percussion; libretto by the composer (1963, ČHF); *Organ Music on a Theme of Giles Binchois* (1964); *The Drinking Horologe*, madrigal; text by Omar Khayyam (1964, ČHF); *Euphrides in Front of the Gates of Tymenas*, chamber opera for actor, tenor, 2 ballerinas, tuba, tape; libretto by the composer (1964); *String Quartet* (1966, Panton); *Johanes Docior Faust*, opera, libretto by the composer (1966, DILIA); *2 Canti* for baritone, instrumental ensemble, organ, metronome; Latin text by J. Novák (1966); *Breakfast at Slankenwald Castle*, scene from a puppet comedy for 4 narrators, baritone, clarinet, horn, bassoon, violin, viola, cello (1966, ČHF); *O Corino*, homage to classicism for 4 vocal soloists, classical orchestra; text by Theophile de Viau (1967, ČHF); *Oresteia* for narrator, vocal quartet, instrumental ensemble; text by Aeschylus and the composer (1967, ČHF).

SEE ALSO Czechoslovakia.

Bergamo, Petar (b. Split, Yugoslavia, 27 Feb 1930), studied at the Belgrade Music Academy (1954–60, composition with Stanojlo Rajičić). He has taught composition at the Belgrade Music Academy since 1966. His music has moved from a late-romantic emotionalism to the use of contemporary harmonic techniques within the context of traditional formal structures.

PRINCIPAL COMPOSITIONS: *Variazioni sul tema interrotto* for piano (1957); *String Quartet* (1958); *Navigare necesse est*, overture-fantasy (1960); *Symphonies Nos. 1–2* (1961, 1963); *Musica concertante* for orchestra (1962); *Concerto abbreviato* for clarinet (1966); *I colori argentei* for chamber ensemble (1968); *Ritrovari per 3* for violin, cello, piano (1969); *Steps*, ballet (1970).

BIBL.: Vlastimir Peričić, *Composers in Serbia* (Belgrade 1969).

Berger, Arthur (Victor) (b. New York, 15 May 1912), began to study music seriously at 18 when he transferred from the City College of

New York to New York Univ., where he was a pupil of Vincent Jones. About this time he was strongly attracted to the music of Arnold Schoenberg but found 12-tone techniques too difficult to separate from the Viennese ethos, which he found overbearing, and he gave up composition for several years. Only 2 Episodes for piano has been retained from the early period. Berger attended Harvard Univ. (1934–37), where he studied principally with Walter Piston. He worked with Nadia Boulanger in Paris (1937–39), and his intensive study of the music of Stravinsky eventually led him to return to composition, this time in a more diatonic, neoclassic style. His first works in this vein were 3 Songs of Yeats (1939) and the Woodwind Quartet (1941), both written while he was teaching at Mills College. Berger returned to Harvard in 1941 for more graduate study and became the moving spirit behind a group of composers in Boston with a similar neoclassic, Stravinskian orientation, including Irving Fine and Harold Shapero. He wrote for the New York Sun (1945–48) and was associate music critic of the New York Herald Tribune (1948–53). He has also written for the Boston Transcript and Saturday Review and has been editor of Listen Magazine, the Musical Mercury (1934–37), and was cofounder and editor (1962–63) of Perspectives of New Music. Since 1953 he has taught at Brandeis Univ.

Berger's output consists primarily of chamber and piano music; there is only a small amount of vocal and large orchestral music. Its special qualities derive in part from a peculiarly American rhythm of syncopations and pauses combined with a careful attention to detail, craftsmanship, and order. These qualities are most obvious in the neoclassic works, from the Woodwind Quartet to Polyphony (1956) but are also present in the serial works that followed, e.g., the transitional Chamber Music for 13 Players (1956), which marked the return to 12-tone procedures abandoned after 1933. The use of register as a primary shaping force contributes to an open, transparent sound and to a fragmentation that gives single lines the impression of being polyphony. This exploitation of register, which is characteristic of serialism in general, prompted one critic to refer to Berger's neoclassic music as "white-note Webern."

PRINCIPAL COMPOSITIONS: Woodwind Quartet in C (1941, Peters); Serenade concertante for violin, woodwind quartet, orchestra (1944; revised 1951, Peters); Duos 1–2 for violin, piano (1948, 1950; ACA); Duo for cello, piano (1951, ACA); Ideas of Order for orchestra (1952, Peters); Polyphony for orchestra (1956, ACA); Chamber Music for 13 Players (1956); String Quartet (1958); Chamber Concerto (1960); 3 Pieces for 2 pianos (1961); Septet for flute, clarinet, bassoon, violin, viola, cello, piano (1966); 5 Pieces for piano (1969).

PRINCIPAL WRITINGS: "Form is Feeling," Modern Music 22; Aaron Copland (New York 1953); "Stravinsky and the Younger American Composers," The American Composer Speaks ed. by G. Chase (Louisiana State Univ. 1966); "Notes on the Plight of the American Composer," Culture for the Millions? ed. by N. Jacobs (New York 1961); "Problems of Pitch Organization in Stravinsky," Perspectives 2/1:11–42; "New Linguistic Modes and the New Theory," Perspectives 3/1:1–9; "Introduction," Aesthetic Analysis by D. W. Prall (New York 1967).

BIBL.: Henry Cowell, "Current Chronicle" (on Ideas of Order), Musical Quarterly 39:429–32; Peggy Glanville-Hicks, "A. B.," ACA Bulletin (1953); Karl Kohn, "Current Chronicle" (on 3 Pieces for 2 pianos), Musical Quarterly 50:229–32; John MacIvor Perkins, "A. B.: The Composer as Mannerist," Perspectives 5/1:75–92; George Perle, "Current Chronicle" (on String Quartet), Musical Quarterly 46:521–23; David Stock, "Reports on New Music" (on Septet), Perspectives 7/1:143.'

David Stock

SEE ALSO United States.

Berger, Jean (b. Hamm, Germany, 27 Sept 1909), studied musicology with Heinrich Besseler and Egon Wellesz at the Universities of Heidelberg and Vienna (1928–32) and composition with Louis Aubert in Paris (1932–35). He was a choral conductor, arranger, and concert accompanist during 1932–46, engaging in many worldwide tours and taking part in premiere performances of works by Pierre Capdevielle, André Jolivet, Nicolas Obouhov, and others. He has taught at Middlebury College in Vt. (1948–59), the Univ. of Ill. (1959–61), the Univ. of Colo. (1961–68), and Temple Buell College in Denver (since 1968). His experiences as a performer and his musicological studies, particularly in medieval and early 17th-century music, have contributed to his development as a composer. He writes primarily for amateur musicians.

PRINCIPAL COMPOSITIONS: Brazilian Psalm for chorus (1941, Schirmer-G); Vision of Peace for chorus (1948, Broude-B); Magnificat for soprano, flute, percussion, chorus (1960, Sheppard); Psalm 57 for chorus, brass quartet (1960, Presser); The Fiery Furnace, dramatic cantata for vocal soloists, chorus (1962, Schirmer-G); A Song of Seasons for vocal soloists, chorus, melodica, small percussion (1967, Sheppard); The Pied Piper, a play with music for vocal soloists, several choruses, small orchestra (1968, Schirmer-G). Berger has also made editions of works by Giuseppe Torelli, Giacomo Perti, and other 17th-century Bolognese composers.

PRINCIPAL WRITINGS: "The Sacred Works of G. Perti (1661-1756)," *Journal of the American Musicological Society* 17:370–77.

BIBL.: Douglas Pritchard, "The Choral Style of J. B.," *American Choral Review* (Sept 1965):4ff.

SEE ALSO Liturgical Music: Christian.

Berger, Theodor (b. Traismauer an der Donau, Austria, 18 May 1905), studied at the Music Academy in Vienna (1926–32; composition with Franz Schmidt; counterpoint, Hubert Kessler; conducting, Erich Wolfgang Korngold). He considers himself mainly self-taught, however, and describes his music as influenced by the great composers of the past and conditioned by practical requirements. He works as a free-lance composer and conductor and has also lectured over German radio.

PRINCIPAL COMPOSITIONS: *Malinconia* for 27-voice string orchestra (1933, UE); *Cronique symphonique* for orchestra (1940, UE); *Homeric Symphony* for orchestra (1948, Sikorski); *Concerto-manuale* for 2 pianos, metalophone, marimbaphone, percussion, string orchestra (1951, Sikorski); *Sinfonia parabolica* for orchestra (1956, Sikorski); *Sinfonia Jahreszeiten* for orchestra (1958, Sikorski); *Frauenstimmen im Orchester* for women's chorus, harp, string orchestra (1959, Sikorski); *Violin Concerto* (1964, UE).

Bergman, Erik (Valdemar) (b. Uusikaarlepyy, Finland, 24 Nov 1911), studied at Helsinki Univ. (1931–33; musicology with Ilmari Krohn, literature with Yrjö Hirn), the Sibelius Academy in Helsinki (1931–38; composition with Erik Furuhjelm, Bengt Carlson; piano with Ilmari Hannikainen), and the Hochschule für Musik in Berlin (1937–39, composition with Heinz Tiessen). During 1949–50 he studied 12-tone and serial techniques with Wladimir Vogel in Switzerland. He has been a music critic for *Nya Pressen* (1945–47) and *Hufvudstadsbladet* in Helsinki (since 1947). He has also been a professor of composition at the Helsinki Academy since 1963. In Helsinki he has conducted several choral groups since 1933 and has written for numerous periodicals, as well as lecturing on the radio. He has traveled extensively to study folk music, particularly to North Africa and the Near East (areas whose literature he has used in his vocal works).

PRINCIPAL COMPOSITIONS: *Sonatine* for piano, Op. 36 (1950, Gehrman); *Rubaiyat* for baritone, men's chorus, orchestra, Op. 41; text by Omar Khayyàm (1953); *Med dig* [With You] for medium voice, piano, Op. 45; texts by Karin Boye, Bertil

Malmberg, Erik Lindorm, Pår Lagerquist (1956, Fazer); *Svanbild* for baritone, men's chorus with solo quartet, Op. 47b (1958, Fazer); *Aubade* for orchestra, Op. 48 (1958, Fazer); *Aton* for baritone, speaker, chorus, orchestra, Op. 49; poem by Akhnaton (1959); *4 Galgenlieder* for 3 speakers, speaking chorus, Op. 51b; poems by Morgenstern (1960, Fazer); *Simbolo* for orchestra, Op. 52 (1960, Hansen); *Concertino da camera* for flute, clarinet, bass clarinet, percussion, piano, violin, viola, cello, Op. 52 (1961); *Sela* for baritone, chorus, chamber orchestra, Op. 55; text from the Psalms (1962); *Fåglarna* [The Birds] for baritone, men's chorus with 5 solo voices, percussion, celesta, Op. 56; text by Solveig von Schoultz (1962, Fazer); *Circulus* for orchestra, Op. 58 (1965); *Springtime* for baritone, chorus, Op. 60; texts by von Schoultz (1966); *Nox* for baritone, chorus, flute, English horn, percussion (1970, Fazer).

BIBL.: Erik Bergman, Kaj Chydenius, and Kari Rydman, "E. B.," *Suomen Säveltäjiä* ed. by Einari Marvia (Helsinki 1966) 2:366–76; Timo Mäkinen and Seppo Nummi, "Today and Tomorrow," *Musica fennica* (Helsinki 1965):87–92; Seppo Nummi, "E. B.'s nyimpressionism," *Modern musik* (Stockholm 1967):59–64; Denby Richards, *The Music of Finland* (London 1968), ch. 8, pp. 27–30; Bo Wallner, "Scandinavian Music After the Second World War," *Musical Quarterly* (1965); ——, "Uppbrott från nationalismen i Norge och Finland," [Quitting Nationalism in Norway and Finland], *Vår tids musik i Norden* (Stockholm 1968):239–44.

Bergsma, William (b. Oakland, Calif., 1 April 1921), attended Stanford Univ. (1938–40), and the Eastman School (1940–44; composition with Howard Hanson, orchestration with Bernard Rogers). From 1946 to 1963 he was at the Juilliard School, first as an instructor and then as chairman of the composition department and associate dean. In 1963 he became director of the School of Music at the Univ. of Washington.

PRINCIPAL COMPOSITIONS: *String Quartets Nos. 1–3* (1942, Galaxy; 1944, Hargail; 1953, Fischer); *6 Songs*, poems by e. e. cummings (1945, Fischer); *The Fortunate Islands* (1947; revised 1956, Fischer); *Tangents* for piano (1951, Fischer); *The Wife of Martin Guerre*, 3-act opera; libretto by Janet Lewis (1956, Galaxy); *Concerto for Wind Quintet* (1958, Galaxy); *Fantastic Variations*, on a theme from Wagner's opera *Tristan und Isolde* for viola, piano (1961, Galaxy); *Confrontation from the Book of Job* for chorus, 22 instruments or orchestra (1963, Galaxy); *Violin Concerto* (1965, Galaxy). List to 1960: *Composers of the Americas* 6:9–14.

BIBL.: Richard F. Goldman, "The Wife of Martin Guerre," *Musical Quarterly* 42:391–94; Abraham Skulsky, "The Music of W. B.," *Juilliard Review* (spring 1956):12–26.

Berio, Luciano (b. Oniglia, Italy, 24 Oct 1925), comes from a family of musicians and first studied music with his father, an organist and composer. He graduated from the Music Academy in Milan in 1951, where he had studied composition with Giorgio Ghedini and Giulio Paribeni. In 1951 he studied serial techniques with Luigi Dallapiccola at Tanglewood. In 1955 he and Bruno Maderna founded the electronic Studio di Fonologia at the Italian Radio in Milan, where Berio remained until 1961. In 1958 he began his association with the summer courses at Darmstadt, where many of his works have been performed and where he has given lectures and seminars. He is married to the soprano Cathy Berberian, for whom he has written several works, including *Chamber Music* (1952), *Omaggio a Joyce* (1958), *Visage* (1961), *Sequenza 3* (1963), and *Prière* (1968). Berio has lived in the U.S. since 1962 and now teaches composition at the Juilliard School.

Berio's output until 1962 was largely determined by three trends in contemporary music: serialism, the application of electronic technology, and indeterminacy. *Chamber Music* (1952) is instructive of his approach to serialism. The first part follows 12-tone procedures strictly, the second is not serial but a rhythmic study on a single note (A), and the third contains subtle melodic and timbral imitations among the cello, clarinet, and harp which presage the highly pointillistic use of sound in Berio's last major serial piece, *Serenata I* (1958). In this latter work Berio reintroduced virtuosity by giving the flute an impressive part. Serial procedures were applied to tone color as well as to pitch and duration. *Thema*, "Omaggio a Joyce" (1958), a musique concrète work on tape, was created under the influence of Stockhausen's *Gesang der Jünglinge* (1955–56). The composer took an excerpt from *Ulysses* and had Miss Berberian recite it in English, French, and Italian. After studying the sonorous possibilities of the three versions, he chose the English and, by means of electronically produced transformations, constructed a "choral-instrumental" work from the sounds of that version. By using two tape tracks, Berio was able to create an interplay of moving and stationary sounds, thereby widening compositional possibilities. *Différences* (1958–59) contains both live and prerecorded instrumental sounds, thereby reestablishing contact with the normal background of listeners (among other works to do this is Varèse's *Déserts* and Stockhausen's *Gesang der Jünglinge*). After this Berio began working with performer choice as a compositional element. Indeterminate and nonperiodic rhythms occur in the first *Sequenza* (for flute, 1958), where proportional notation is used to indicate relative durations; because relative distances in the notation keep changing, no one pulse can maintain itself throughout the piece. A significant esthetic point here is that although the composer has set up the conditions within which a work of art can exist, it is always a performance rather than the wishes of the composer that will determine the success of the piece. In *Circles* (1962) the singer and instrumentalists may perform either the notated pitches or approximations, either following a strict pattern or not. The interplay of spaces in *Différences* is here applied to free vs. precisely controlled passages, including interpenetrations such as the interpretation of some "free" passages according to predetermined rhythms and pitches. Moreover the singer conducts the instrumental ensemble at times, not by following a score but according to her perception of the impact her interpretation is having on the audience.

Since 1962 Berio's thinking has been more eclectic and more personal. One is now aware of a large "work in progress," of the reuse and further development from one piece to another of schemes, concepts, sound patterns, and the like. This process can be likened to human memory in its ability to enlarge on an immediate fact of life (examples include *Sequenza 6*, *Chemins 2*, and *Chemins 3*). The trilogy *Epiphanie* (1961), *Laborintus II* (1965), and *Sinfonia* (1968) illustrates Berio's most recent development. *Epiphanie* consists of an instrumental cycle (extracted from *Cahiers 1–3* for orchestra, 1959–61) and a vocal cycle for soprano or mezzo-soprano on texts by Proust, Joyce, Machado, Sanguineti, Simon, and Brecht. This is an aleatory work not in its notation but in its structure, for each cycle can be combined differently according to the conductor's wishes. The selected succession will enhance either the apparent heterogeneity or the dialectical unity of the various poetic situations. Although the piece does not use any serial or electronic devices, it shows their influence in terms of rhythmic impulse, pitch arrangement, blending of tones, and use of the voice. *Laborintus II*, written for the seventh centenary of Dante's birth, establishes a link with the medieval mystery and morality plays. Texts from Dante, T. S. Eliot, and Ezra Pound blend with street cries, exclamations, syncopated words, interjections, and the like; and musical references to the madrigal and to contemporary sounds (clusters, glissandi, etc.) blend with allusions to free jazz of the 1960s. Berio sometimes used serial procedures and also made references to works of his own (the flute part recalls *Serenata I* and *Tempi concertati*, while the harp part evokes *Circles* or *Différences*). This is a new expressionism that abandons all rules and appeals more to the sensibility than to the intellect. As a study in various kinds of codes, *Laborintus II* is surpassed by *Sinfonia*. The second part of this work is an homage to Martin Luther King, whose name is fragmented, with each segment being associated with a specific instrument. References to water pervade the score: the text in the first part quotes from a Brazilian myth on the origin of water (as recounted in Claude Levi-Strauss's book *Du Cru et du cuit*), and the music in the third part contains quotations from Debussy's *La Mer*, Wagner's *Das Rheingold*, and the Scherzo from Mahler's *Second Symphony*. There are other musical references in the score, from Bach to Vinko Globokar and including some to Berio's own music (the piano part relates to *Sequenza 4*, some of the chord spacings recall *Epiphanie*, and the use of the voice derives from *Laborintus II*). In all, this is a work that cannot be fully comprehended in any one performance, a fact that Berio has said is one of its fundamental attributes.

Further uses of vocal sound and combinations of live and prerecorded sound appear in *Cela veut dire que . . .* (1969–70). This work uses various vocalized sounds as part of its thematic material (recurring nasalized sounds, for instance). The text, excerpts from French, Italian, and Yugoslav folklore, is performed by a live chorus, which is juxtaposed with a tape prepared from recordings of choral sounds and seven vocal sounds voiced in seven ways. The constant presence of the interval B–F links the vocal and electronic developments. (A revised version of the piece was performed in Rome, June 1970; there, traditional musical elements—a small orchestra— and choreographic and visual elements were added.)

PRINCIPAL COMPOSITIONS: ★ Serial works: *2 Pieces* for piano, violin (1951, S-Z); *Chamber Music* for soprano, clarinet, cello, harp; poems by James Joyce (1952, S-Z); *Nones* for orchestra (1954, S-Z); *Serenata I* for flute, 14 instruments (1957, S-Z). ★ Electronic works: *Mutazioni* on tape (1956, S-Z); *Thema*, "Omaggio a Joyce," on 2-track tape (1958, S-Z); *Différences* for flute, clarinet, viola, cello, harp, and tape (1958–59, S-Z); *Visage* on tape (1961). ★ Aleatory works: *Sequenza 1* for flute (1958, S-Z); *Tempi concertati* for flute, violin, 2 pianos, chamber ensemble (1960, UE); *Epiphanie* for soprano, orchestra; texts from Proust, Montale, Joyce, Eliot, Machado, Simon, Brecht (1961, UE); *Circles* for soprano, harp, 2 percussion ensembles; poems by e. e. cummings (1962, UE). ★ Eclectic works: *Sequenza 3* for woman's voice (1963, UE); *Laborintus II* for voices,

instruments, reciter, tape; text by Edoardo Sanguineti (1965, UE); *Sequenza 4* for piano, *5* for trombone, *6* for viola (1966, UE); *Sinfonia* for orchestra, organ, harpsichord, piano, chorus, reciters (1968); *Cela veut dire que . . .* for chorus, tape (1969–70). ★ Other works: *Sincronie* for string quartet (1962, UE); *Chemins 2* for viola, 9 instruments (1967, UE); *Chemins 3* for viola, 9 instruments, orchestra (1968).

PRINCIPAL WRITINGS: "Poesia e musica, un' esperienza," *Incontri musicali* 3 (Milan, 1959); "Façon de parler," *Preuves* (Paris, 1961); "Du Geste et de Piazza Carità," *Cahiers de la Compagnie Madeleine Renaud, Jean-Louis Barrault* 41 (1963).

Jacques M. Poissenot

SEE ALSO Austria and Germany, Dance, Instrumental and Vocal Resources, Italy, Melody, Microtones, Mixed Media, Opera, Performance, Text Setting and Usage.

Berkeley, Lennox (Randal) (b. Oxford, England, 12 May 1903), attended Gresham's School in Holt, Norfolk, and Merton College at Oxford and studied composition privately with Nadia Boulanger in Paris (1927–33). He was on the staff of the BBC music division (1942–45) and was professor of composition at the Royal Academy of Music, London (1946–68).

PRINCIPAL COMPOSITIONS (published by Chester unless otherwise noted): *String Quartet No. 1* (1936, Boosey); *Serenade* for strings (1939); *String Quartet No. 2* (1940); *Divertimento* for chamber orchestra (1942); *6 Preludes* for piano (1942); *Piano Sonata* (1943); *Symphony No. 1* (1943); *String Trio* (1944); *3 Mazurkas* for piano (1944); *4 Poems of St. Teresa* for contralto, strings (1947); *Symphony No. 2* (1952); *Nelson*, 3-act opera (1953); *A Dinner Engagement*, 1-act opera (1954); *Ruth*, 1-act opera (1956); *Missa brevis* for chorus (1959); *Winter's Tale*, suite for orchestra (1960); *Ronsard Sonnets* for tenor, orchestra (1963); *Mass for 5 Voices* (1964); *Castaway*, 1-act opera (1966); *Oboe Quartet* (1967); *Signs in the Dark* for chorus, strings; text by Laurie Lee (1967); *Magnificat* for chorus, orchestra (1968); *Symphony No. 3* (1969).

BIBL.: R. Murray Schafer, *British Composers in Interview* (London 1963).

Berlinski, Herman (b. Leipzig, 18 August 1910), studied at the Leipzig Conservatory (1928–32; piano with Otto Weinreich, harmony with Siegfried Karg-Elert), the Ecole Normale in Paris (1934–38; piano with Alfred Cortot, composition with Nadia Boulanger), and at the Seminary College of Jewish Music in New York (1953–60). He was organist at Temple Emanu-El in New York during 1954–63 and has since been Minister of Music at the

Washington (D.C.) Hebrew Congregation. His early works (now lost) were composed under the predominating influences of the time: Stravinsky, Schoenberg, Bartók, and Hindemith. The Nazi persecutions and a period of years as a refugee intensified his awareness of his existence as a Jew and led him to a deep involvement with sacred and secular Jewish music. His religious works are dominated by a concern for their liturgical function and the need for direct communication.

PRINCIPAL COMPOSITIONS: *Sinfonias Nos. 1–7* for organ: No. 1, "From the World of my Father" (1938); No. 2, "Holydays and Festivals" (1954, Mercury); No. 3, "Sounds and Motions" (1963, Gray); No. 4 with orchestra (1968); No. 5 (1971); No. 6 with strings, percussion (1969); No. 7, "David and Goliath," with male soloist (1944, revised 1971); *Symphonic Visions* (1949); *Avodat Shabbat: Sacred Service 1958* for soloists, chorus, orchestra (1957, Mercury); *Kiddush Ha-Shem* for soloists, chorus, orchestra (1960); *Litanies for the Persecuted*, cantata for alto, narrator, organ (1960); *The Baltimore Cantata* for soloists, chorus, orchestra (1967); *Job*, oratorio for soloists, chorus, orchestra (1971).

PRINCIPAL WRITINGS: "The Religious Composer and the Crisis in Contemporary Music," *American Guild of Organists Quarterly* (July 1960); "In Search of Criteria," *ibid.* (April 1965); "Pop, Rock and Sacred Music," *Music, Magazine of the A.G.O.* (Nov 1970, Jan 1971).

BIBL.: Mildred Kayden, "H. B.," *American Composers Alliance Bulletin* 8/3.

SEE ALSO Liturgical Music: Jewish.

Bernal-Jiménez, Miguel (b. Morelia, Michoacan, Mexico, 16 Feb 1910; d. New Orleans, 12 July 1956), studied organ, composition, and Gregorian chant at the Pontifical Institute of Sacred Music in Rome (1928–33). He edited the journal *Schola cantorum* for several years beginning in 1945. During the last four years of his life he was dean of the music faculty of Loyola Univ. in New Orleans, where he also wrote for the periodical *Cecilie*. In Mexico he helped bring advanced compositional techniques to the field of liturgical music.

PRINCIPAL COMPOSITIONS (most dates not available): *3 Cartas para México* for orchestra; *Cuarteto colonial* for string quartet; *Suite michoacana* for orchestra; *La divina filotea* for chorus, soloists, orchestra; *Navidad en Pátzcuaro*, ballet; *Los 4 galanes de Juana*, ballet; *Tingambato*, ballet (premiere 1941); *Noche en Morelia*, symphonic poem (premiere 1941); *Tata Vasco*, opera (1941). Bernal-Jiménez also wrote two settings of the Mass for voices and organ and several organ sonatas.

[prepared with the help of Esperanza Pulido]

Bernier, René (b. St.-Gilles-lez-Bruxelles, 10 Sept 1905), studied at the Brussels Conservatory (harmony, counterpoint with Raymond Moulaert, Henry Sarly, Frederic Rasse; musicology with Ernest Closson; piano with Charles Scharrès) and composition privately with Paul Gilson. During the early 1930s he was a member of the artists' group Les Synthétistes and later in the decade of the movement La Sirène. During World War II he was music critic for *L'Etoile belge* and *L'Eventuel*, and he has since written articles on music for French, English, and Polish periodicals as well. Since 1945 he has been inspector of music education in French-speaking Belgium. He has also taught at the conservatories of Liege (1946–47) and Mons (since 1948) and served on various composition and performance juries in Europe. His development as a composer was influenced by the neoclassic movement in France and by the encouragement of Albert Roussel and Louis Aubert.

PRINCIPAL COMPOSITIONS: *Trio* for flute, cello, harp (1942, CBDM); *Liturgies* for voice, string orchestra (1946, Salabert); *Sortilèges ingénus*, 14 songs for women's chorus, orchestra or piano (1947, Cranz); *Du Coq à l'ane* for chorus (1951, Salabert); *Le Tombeau devant l'escaut*, symphonic poem (1952, Leduc); *Le Bal des ombres*, ballet (1954, Bizet); *Incantations* for chorus (1955, EFM); *Symphonietta* for string orchestra (1957, Cranz); *Hommage à Sax*, concertino for alto saxophone, orchestra (1958, Leduc); *Reverdies*, "ou de diverses manières concertantes de 'sonner' le printemps," for clarinet, chamber orchestra (1960, Leduc); *Offrande à Erard* for harp (1962, Leduc); *Tanagras*, ballet (1969).

BIBL.: "Entretien avec R. B." (Brussels radio, July 1963); "Hommage à R. B." (Brussels radio, 29 Sept 1968); "Entretien entre R. B. et Daniel-Lesur" (French television, 16 March 1961); "R. B., créateur race," *L'Ethnie française* 4: 33–35; "Visite au musicien R. B." (Brussels radio, 25 Dec 1951).

Bernstein, Leonard (b. Lawrence, Mass., 25 August 1918), began to develop his musical gifts after the age of ten, when by chance his family acquired a piano. His subsequent musical ambitions were discouraged by his father, a Russian-Jewish immigrant who in the "old country" had held musicians in low esteem. His father did, however, promote a love for Jewish tradition, profoundly affecting several of his son's compositions. Moreover the sermons of Rabbi H. H. Rubenowitz (Temple Mishkan Tefila, Boston) enthralled the youngster, foreshadowing his clear expository style as an author. Bernstein is probably the first internationally known musician to be wholly the product of American schooling. He graduated from Boston Latin School in 1935, Harvard Univ. in 1939 (A. Tillman Merritt, theory; Walter Piston, fugue; Edward B. Hill, orchestration), and the Curtis Institute in 1941 (Fritz Reiner, conducting; Randall Thompson, orchestration; Isabelle Vengerova, piano). Keyboard studies had begun under Helen Coates (later his secretary) and Heinrich Gebhard. In the summers of 1940–43 he studied at Tanglewood, where he became assistant to Serge Koussevitzky, some of whose flamboyant conducting style and sense of mission he assimilated. He credits his English teacher at Boston Latin, Phillip Marson, with introducing him to the wonder of language, and David W. Prall at Harvard with broadening his literary interests. Significantly his compositions display a penchant for using texts or some form of program. As he wrote in the foreword to *The Age of Anxiety*, "I have a deep suspicion that every work I write, for whatever medium, is really theater music in some way."

Bernstein became assistant conductor of the New York Philharmonic in 1943 and on 13 November made a spectacular debut, substituting on short notice for the ailing guest conductor Bruno Walter. Thereafter he toured widely with other orchestras, conducting and sometimes doubling as piano soloist. From 1945 to 1948 he headed the New York City Center Orchestra, presenting many novelties. In 1951 he married the Chilean actress Felicia Montealegre (they have two daughters and a son). He taught part-time at Brandeis Univ. (1951–55) and during the summers at Tanglewood, where he succeeded Koussevitzky in the conducting department. During his 40s (1958–68) he was music director of the Philharmonic. His programs included much contemporary music, about 200 works, with emphasis on the so-called French school (early and middle Stravinsky, Copland, and disciples of Nadia Boulanger). He showed less sympathy toward the Viennese school of Schoenberg and his followers and gave little support to younger composers of any persuasion (which was not true when he lead the City Center orchestra). His natural talents as a teacher have found greatest fulfillment on television. This began in 1955 with seven appearances on the "Omnibus" series, then with the Philharmonic (until 1962) in 15 programs for adults. Since 1958 he has also undertaken "Young People's Concerts," making a major contribution to American culture. His "Omnibus" scripts

became a best-seller when published as part of *The Joy of Music* (1959).

Bernstein is one of the few composers who is equally at home in the popular theater and concert hall. Stylistically he has been a consolidator rather than an innovator and as such is a true eclectic. His prominent influences have been Stravinsky, Copland, and Shostakovich, and the lesser ones Strauss, Mahler, Hindemith, and Berg. Added to this are jazz and Latin-American idioms and the occasional use of 12-tone procedures (but always in the context of tonality, which the composer feels "is built into the human organism"). In his operetta *Candide* he indulged his eclectic proclivities to the hilt, for the globe-trotting plot allowed him to parody many national styles. But even in his early, Hindemithian *Clarinet Sonata*, this aspect of his personality emerged in jazzy passages. Although there is an element of Shostakovich in the *Jeremiah Symphony*, the individuality becomes considerably stronger. Adolescent memories of Jewish songs are evoked: prayer cadences, Bar Mitzvah cantillation, and traditional Biblical chant.

Rhythm in Bernstein's music is particularly striking, showing a predilection for syncopations, cross-rhythms, and asymmetric meters in slow and fast tempos. His melodies place architectonic importance on short motives and intervals, with a large work sometimes exploiting one basic interval (perfect fifth in *Wonderful Town*, minor seventh in *Candide*, tritone in *West Side Story*). Also he has favored motives in which an ascending or descending interval is preceded or followed by a single step up or down (e.g., fa-mi-do or do descending to mi-re). His orchestration displays a conspicuous use of solo piano, brass in high registers, and large virtuoso percussion sections. The stage works contain an unusual degree of formal cohesion. The one-act opera *Trouble in Tahiti* (1951–52), a satire on suburbia, is symmetrically organized into seven scenes. The ballet *Fancy Free*, with its piquant 1940s jazz, is a set of seven vignettes organized in rondo design. Its transformation into *On the Town* was the first Broadway musical to contain as many as eight dance episodes within the standard two-act format. The ballet *Facsimile* is actually an A-B-A symphonic movement in which all the melodic material grows out of the opening phrases. Bernstein has also cultivated a concatenation technique of melodic variation with musical ideas evolving from each other (as in the metamorphosis: warm-worm-word-cord-cold). His second symphony, *The Age of Anxiety*, is the first work to use this procedure. In the film score to *On the Waterfront*, a barbaric fugato for percussion is gradually transmuted into a lyric love theme through such chain-reaction devices.

In his works Bernstein has shown great concern with the unrest of mid-20th-century life. Much of the subject matter of *On the Waterfront* is of violence. *The Age of Anxiety* and *Trouble in Tahiti* treat the neuroses of contemporary society. His most popular work, *West Side Story*, deals with urban social problems. The third symphony, *Kaddish*, uses a spoken text by the composer about existential despair, in juxtaposition to the Jewish prayer of mourning. Still, this general preoccupation with *angst* is tempered by the optimism and simplicity in the Hebrew settings of the *Chichester Psalms*.

The composer is a man of immense energy who works best when great and not necessarily compatible demands are made on him. His second musical, *Wonderful Town*, was written in only one month. Many of his best works have been completed under pressure. Indeed two of the most disparate ones were composed simultaneously: *Candide* and *West Side Story*. His versatility and originality have made him a cultural hero around the world. Critics, particularly in the 1950s, have often questioned his wide-ranging activities and his involvement with both the commercial stage and the concert hall. They have said he would become a better musician if he concentrated on only one musical discipline to the exclusion of the others. The fact is that had he followed their advice, he would have ceased to be himself.

PRINCIPAL COMPOSITIONS (published by Schirmer-G unless otherwise noted): *Clarinet Sonata* (1941–42, Witmark); *Symphony No. 1*, "Jeremiah" (1941–44, Harms); *7 Anniversaries* for piano (1942–43, Witmark); *I Hate Music*, 5 kid songs for voice, piano; text by the composer (1943); *Fancy Free*, suite for orchestra from the ballet (1944); *On the Town*, musical (1944); *La Bonne Cuisine*, 4 recipes for voice, piano (1945); *Hashkivenu* for cantor solo, chorus, organ (1945, Witmark; republished by Schirmer-G); *Facsimile*, choreographic essay for orchestra (1946); *Symphony No. 2*, "Age of Anxiety," for piano, orchestra (1947–49); *4 Anniversaries* for piano (1948); *Prelude, Fugue, and Riffs* for large dance band (1949); *2 Love Songs* for voice, piano; texts by Rilke (1949); *5 Anniversaries* for piano (1949–51); *Trouble in Tahiti*, 1-act opera (1951–52); *Wonderful Town*, musical (1953); *Serenade* for violin, string orchestra, percussion; after Plato's Symposium (1954); *On the Waterfront*, symphonic suite from the film score (1955, final version 1960); *The Lark*, incidental music for the play by Jean Anouilh as adapted by Lillian Hell-

man (1955); *Candide*, comic operetta (1956); *West Side Story*, musical (1957); *Symphony No. 3*, "Kaddish," for woman narrator, soprano, boys' chorus, chorus, orchestra (1961–63); *Chichester Psalms* for countertenor, chorus, orchestra (1965); *Mass*, "Theater Piece for Singers, Players, and Dancers"; libretto by Stephen Schwartz and the composer (1970–71). List to 1957: *Composers of the Americas* 6:17–21; list to 1963: Gottlieb 1964 (see bibl.).

PRINCIPAL WRITINGS: *The Joy of Music* (New York 1959); *Leonard Bernstein's Young People's Concerts for Reading and Listening* (New York 1962); *The Infinite Variety of Music* (New York 1966).

BIBL.: David Drew and Hans Keller, "L. B.," *Score* (June 1955):77–84; Irving Fine, "Young America: B. and Foss," *Modern Music* 22:238–43; Jack Gottlieb, "The Choral Music of L. B. (Reflections of Theater and Liturgy)," *American Choral Review* (summer 1968); ——, "L. B.: Kaddish Symphony," *Perspectives* 4/1:171–75; ——, *The Music of L. B.: A Study of Melodic Manipulations* (DMA thesis, Univ. of Ill., 1964); William Hamilton, "On the Waterfront," *Film Music* (Sept 1954):3–14.

Jack Gottlieb

SEE ALSO Dance; Liturgical Music: Jewish; Musical; Popular Music.

Beurle, Jürgen (b. Ludwigsburg, Germany, 27 Feb 1943), studied at the Hochschule für Musik in Stuttgart (1962–67, composition with E. Karkoschka), the Univs. of Stuttgart and Tübingen (1965–69; philosophy, philology), and the Rijksuniversiteit in Utrecht (1969–70, electronic and computer composition with G. M. Koenig). In 1967 he worked with Stockhausen at the Darmstadt summer courses. He has also been influenced by the work of John Cage.

PRINCIPAL COMPOSITIONS: *Sinus* for soprano, baritone, violin, viola, percussion (1966, Moeck); *Variable Realisationen* for any 1–4 performers (1967, Moeck); *Statischdynamisch* for orchestra (1967–68, Ahn & Sim); *Diaphon* for voice, percussion (1967–68, Moeck); *Objets* for chorus, chamber ensemble, 2 tape recorders (1968, Moeck); *Conditional* for voice, piano, 3 tape recorders (1968–69, Moeck); *Madrigal* for soprano, 2 choruses, percussion, 5 tape recorders, audience (1969); *Neuril* for 2 performers using 4-track tape recorders (1970); *Differenz* for 5 groups of performers (1970).

Binkerd, Gordon (Ware) (b. Lynch, Neb., 22 May 1916), studied at Wesleyan Univ. in S. D. (1933–37), the Eastman School (1940–41; composition with Bernard Rogers), and at Harvard Univ. (1946–49; composition with

Walter Piston). He was professor of composition and theory at the Univ. of Ill. during 1949–71. Since retiring he has devoted himself exclusively to composing.

PRINCIPAL COMPOSITIONS (published by Boosey): *Cello Sonata* (1952); *Symphony No. 1* (1955); *Piano Sonata* (1955); *Symphony No. 2* (1957); *String Quartet No. 1* (1958); *Movement for Orchestra* (1960); *String Quartet No. 2* (1962); *The Recommendation* for chorus; poem by Robert Crashaw (1962); *Jesus Weeping* for double chorus; poem by Henry Vaughan (1964); *A Christmas Caroll* for double chorus; poem by Robert Herrick (1964); *Shut Out that Moon*, song cycle for soprano, piano; text by Thomas Hardy (1966); *Nocturne* for chorus, cello; poem by William Carlos Williams (1966); *Autumn Flowers* for chorus; text by Jones Very (1966); *In a Whispering Gallery* for chorus; text by Hardy (1966); *The Fair Morning* for soprano, piano; text by Very (1969); *3 Songs* for mezzo-soprano, piano: "How Lilies Came White," poem by Herrick; "Upon Parting," poem by Herrick; "Never the Nightingale," poem by Adelaide Crapsey (1970).

BIBL.: David Cohen, "Music from the Radical Center," *Perspectives* (fall 1964): 131–35; Dorothy V. Hagan, "G. B.," *American Composers Alliance Bulletin* (Sept 1962): 1–6; Howard Smither, "Current Chronicle," *Musical Quarterly* (1963): 237–40.

Birtwistle, Harrison (b. Accrington, Lancashire, England, 15 July 1934), first studied clarinet and then attended the Royal Manchester College (composition with Richard Hall) and the Royal Academy in London. He took up school teaching and during 1962–65 was Director of Music at Cranborne Chase School near Salisbury; here in 1964 he directed the first Summer School for Music. He lived in the U.S. during 1966–68, spending the first year as a visiting fellow at Princeton Univ. With Peter Maxwell Davies he formed the Pierrot Players in London for the performance of new chamber music that involves a theatrical dimension.

Refrains and Choruses (1957) departed significantly from the European mainstream of the time, which it superficially resembles; in its processes of growth from a single note, its many homophonic passages, and its persistent use of repeated notes, unison sounds, and octave relationships, it foreshadowed important traits of the composer's more mature style. In 1959 the *Monody for Corpus Christi* marked a strengthening of Birtwistle's melodic gifts and an inclination towards greater complexity. Massive octave sonorities have an important formal function in *Chorales* (1962–63) and the *3 Movements with Fanfares*

(1964); both works also juxtapose complex polyphony with simpler material in homophonic rhythms. *Tragoedia* (1965) contains a dramatic atomization of rhythm into repeated notes and ostinato figures. The opera *Punch and Judy* (1966–67) has a curiously infantile libretto that contributes to the overall effect of a grotesque and nightmarish ritual drama. Various types of ostinato dominate the work, contrasting with gradually more sustained irruptions of lyrical writing that culminate in a love duet. Later works, such as the *Cantata* (1969) and *Medusa* (1969–70), continue to emphasize sound textures and to engender formal shapes concentrically with ideas growing one out of another.

PRINCIPAL COMPOSITIONS (published by UE): *Refrains and Choruses* for flute, oboe, clarinet, bassoon, horn (1957); *Monody for Corpus Christi* for soprano, flute, violin, horn; medieval carol texts (1959); *Precis* for piano (1959); *The World is Discovered* for chamber ensemble (1960); *Chorales for Orchestra* (1962–63); *3 Movements with Fanfares* for chamber orchestra (1964); *Entr'actes and Sappho Fragments* for soprano, flute, oboe, violin, viola, harp, percussion (1964); *Tragoedia* for wind quintet, harp, string quartet (1965); *Ring a Dumb Carillon* for soprano, clarinet, percussion; text by Christopher Logue (1965); *The Mark of the Goat*, dramatic school-cantata for variable orchestration (1965–66); *The Visions of Francesco Petrarca*, 7 sonnets for baritone, chamber ensemble, school orchestra (1966); *Verses* for clarinet, piano (1966); *Punch and Judy*, full-evening opera in 1 act; libretto by Stephen Pruslin (1966–67); *Nomos* for 4 amplified wind instruments, orchestra (1968); *Cantata* for soprano, flute/piccolo, clarinet, violin/viola, cello, piano/celesta, glockenspiel; tombstone inscriptions and ancient Greek texts (1969); *Medusa* for chamber ensemble (1969–70); *Nenia on the Death of Orpheus* for soprano, 3 bass clarinets, piano, crotales; text arranged by Peter Zinovieff (1970); *Meridian* for mezzo-soprano, chorus, 3 English horns, 3 bass clarinets, 2 percussion, 2 harps, horn, cello; text by Thomas Wyatt and Logue (1970–71); *Prologue* for tenor, bassoon, 2 trumpets, horn, trombone, violin, double bass; Greek texts in English translation (1971); *An Imaginary Landscape* for orchestra (1971).

BIBL.: *A Couple of Things about Harry*, BBC television documentary (1971).

Bill Hopkins

SEE ALSO Great Britain.

Blacher, Boris (b. Newchwang, China, 6 Jan 1903), the son of German-Russian parents, attended the German school in Newchwang, the Russian Realgymnasium in Irkutsk (1914–17), and the Gymnasium in Charbin (1919–21).

As a child he studied piano and violin. He began working at the Irkutsk opera house in 1917 and for the Charbin orchestra in 1919. In 1922 he moved to Berlin with his mother, where he studied architecture and mathematics at the Technische Hochschule and, beginning in 1924, composition with Friedrich Ernst Koch. Blacher earned his living in Berlin by copying music, making arrangements for café orchestras, and composing for films. In 1945 he became professor of composition at the Berlin Hochschule and during 1953–70, its director.

In addition to incidental music for theater, film, and radio, Blacher has composed orchestral pieces, three piano concertos for his wife Gerty Herzog, chamber music, and stage works. His melodic style is mostly diatonic and limited to small intervals; neither the large leaps and frequent changes of register typical of the Schoenberg school nor chromaticism are present. Blacher's harmony is basically tonal. Triads, however, are often strung together freely without regard to tonal functions, and different keys are employed simultaneously, resulting in polytonality.

Blacher's music is often built from short motives of rhythm and tone color. The *Concertante Musik* (1937) begins with a rhythmic motive in two bassoons, from which the rest of the piece evolves. Tone colors in the work recur in a systematic order throughout the composition: bassoon, horn, strings, bassoon, violin, strings, flute, bassoon with strings, clarinet, bassoon with strings, oboe, etc. He has used the 12-tone method in his ballet *Lysistrata* (1950) and again in *Rosamunde Floris* (1960). More characteristic are "variable meters," a rhythmic process he developed in 1950 consisting of systematic changes of meter (2/8, 3/8, 4/8, 5/8 . . . , 6/8, 5/8, 4/8, 3/8 . . . , 2/8, 9/8, 3/8, 8/8, 4/8, 7/8 . . . , etc.). Variable meters first appeared in the *Ornamente* (1950).

Beginning in 1929 Blacher began using jazz styles and idioms. A slow fox trot and a Charleston occur in *Jazzkoloraturen*, Op. 1. The *Concertante Musik* (1937) employs syncopation similar to the jazz of about 1930. A jazz quartet (vibraphone, double bass, percussion, piano) appears in *2 Poems for Jazz Quartet* (1958) and *Rosamunde Floris*. In 1962, following experiments and lectures at the Technical Univ. in Berlin, Blacher began composing electronic spatial compositions such as the opera *Zwischenfälle bei einer Notlandung* (1966). Among Blacher's students are Gottfried von Einem, Giselher Klebe, and Isang Yun.

PRINCIPAL COMPOSITIONS (published by Bote):

Jazzkoloraturen for soprano, alto, saxophone, bassoon, Op. 1 (1929); *5 Sinnsprüche Omars des Zeltmachers* for voice, piano, Op. 3 (1931); *Fest im Süden*, dance drama, Op. 6; scenario by Ellen Petz (1935); *Concertante Musik* for orchestra, Op. 10 (1937); *2 Sonatinas* for piano, Op. 14 (1940); *Violin Sonata*, Op. 18 (1941); *Der Grossinquisitor*, oratorio for baritone, chorus, orchestra; text by Leo Borchard after Dostoevski (1942); *Romeo und Julia*, opera (1943); *Die Flut*, 1-act chamber opera, Op. 24; libretto by Heinz von Cramer (1946); *Variations on a Theme by Paganini* for orchestra, Op. 26 (1947); *Die Nachtschwalbe*, dramatic nocturne in 1 act, Op. 27; libretto by Friedrich Wolf (1947); *Piano Concerto No. 1*, Op. 28 (1947); *Preussisches Märchen*, ballet in 5 scenes, Op. 30; scenario by Cramer (1949); *Hamlet*, ballet, Op. 35; scenario by Tatjana Gsovsky (1949); *Lysistrata*, ballet, Op. 34; scenario by the composer (1950); *Ornamente* for piano, Op. 37 (1950); *Piano Concerto No. 2*, Op. 42 (1952); *Abstrakte Oper*, opera in 7 scenes, Op. 43; idea and text by Werner Egk (1953); *Ornament* for orchestra, Op. 44 (1953); *Träume vom Tod und vom Leben*, cantata for tenor, chorus, orchestra, Op. 49; poem by Hans Arp (1955); *Der Mohr von Venedig*, ballet, Op. 50; scenario by Erika Hanka (1955); *Rosamunde Floris*, 2-act opera, Op. 60; libretto by Gerhart von Westerman after Georg Kaiser (1960); *Variations on a Theme by Muzio Clementi*, piano concerto No. 3, Op. 61 (1961); *Tristan*, ballet; scenario by Gsovsky (1965); *Zwischenfälle bei einer Notlandung*, "reportage" for tape, instruments, singers; libretto by Cramer (1965); *Zweihunderttausend Taler*, 3-act singspiel; libretto by the composer after Sholem Aleichem (1968).

BIBL.: H. H. Stuckenschmidt, *B. B.* (Berlin 1963).

H. H. Stuckenschmidt
(trans. from German by Jeanne Wolf)

SEE ALSO: Austria and Germany, Opera, Rhythm.

Blanco, Juan (b. Havana, 29 June 1920), studied traditional composition at the Havana Municipal Conservatory and at the Univ. of Havana with Harold Gramatges and José Ardévol. He is self-taught in contemporary techniques and electronic music. Since 1969 he has been music advisor to the Casa de las Américas in Havana. He has written articles and criticism for Cuban magazines and newspapers. In addition to the works listed below he has composed several dozen scores for theater, films, and dance.

PRINCIPAL COMPOSITIONS: *Música para danza* on tape (1961); *Ensamble V* on tape (1962–63); *Estudios I–II* on tape (1962–63); *Estructuras* on tape (1962–63); *Texturas* for orchestra, tape (1963–64); *Episodios* for orchestra (1964); *Contrapunto espacial I* for organ with 3 wind groups, 4 percussion groups distributed throughout the space to make triangular and rhomboidal floor patterns

(1965–66); *Poema espacial No. 3*, "Viet-Nam," sound-light composition for 4 tape tracks distributed live to 37 loud speakers (c.1968–); *Contrapunto espacial II*, "Erotofonías," for 60 strings divided into 20 groups, 5 percussion groups, guitar, alto saxophone, 3 tape tracks derived from recitations of the Song of Solomon (1968); *Poema espacial No. 4*, "Mella," sound-light composition for 3 tape tracks distributed live to 11 loud speakers (1969); *Contrapunto especial III*, "Sí, nó: ¿y qué?" for 20 actors, 24 instrumental groups distributed throughout the performance area, 2 tapes (1969); *Contrapunto espacial IV*, "Boomerang," for 10 actors, 5 instrumental groups, tape (1970). Blanco also composed tape music for the Cuban Pavilions at Expo '67 and Expo '70.

Blatný, Pavel (b. Brno, Czechoslovakia, 14 Sept 1931), studied at the Brno Conservatory (1950–55, composition with Th. Schaefer), the Univ. of Brno (1953–58, musicology with J. Racek and B. Štědroň), the Prague Music Academy (1955–58, composition with P. Bořkovec), and the Berklee School of Music in Boston (1968, jazz composition). He attended the Darmstadt summer courses during 1965–69. He is a free-lance composer and conductor. Since 1964 he has produced music programs for Brno Television. In 1968 and 1969 he lectured on composition at the Remscheid summer courses in Germany. During the 1950s he was influenced by the work of Stravinsky, Martinů, and Prokofiev, and later in the decade particularly by neobaroque and neorenaissance styles. Since 1960 he has explored a variety of contemporary processes (including 12-tone, serial, aleatory, and electronic), as well as those of modern jazz.

PRINCIPAL COMPOSITIONS: *Concerto for Chamber Orchestra* (1957, ČHF); *Trio* for flute, bass clarinet, piano (1961, ČHF); *Concerto for Jazz Orchestra* (1962–64, Supraphon and EM); *Study* for 1/4-tone trumpet, jazz band (1965, Supraphon); *Pour Ellis* for trumpet, jazz band (1965, Supraphon); *10′30″* for orchestra (1965, Supraphon); *D-E-F-G-A-H-C* for jazz band (1968, Supraphon); *Večer Tříkrálový*, musical after Shakespeare's *Twelfth Night* for vocal soloists, large jazz band or piano (1969).

PRINCIPAL WRITINGS: "Z bloku vytrženo," *Opus Musicum* (Czechoslovakia) 1969/8:245.

BIBL.: Jindra Bártová, *Tři mladí z Brna* [3 Young Men from Brno], *Hudební rozhledy* 1966/5:134; Lubomír Dorůžka, "Who Is P. B.?" *Jazz Forum* (Warsaw, Nov 1970); Antonín Matzner, "Třetí proud a P. B." [The Third Stream and P. B.], *Hudební rozhledy* 1965/4:162; ——, "P. B. — Third Stream Compositions," *Melodie* 1969/7:222; Ivan Poledňák, "P. B.: Skladby třetíno proudu" [P. B.: Third Stream Compositions], *Hudební*

rozhledy 1970/6:285; Dietrich Zimmerle, "Komponist und Jazz," *Jazz Podium* (Germany) 1969/1:21.

Bliss, Arthur (b. London, 2 August 1891), studied at Pembroke College, Cambridge Univ. (graduated 1913) and at the Royal College of Music in London (1914; composition with Charles Stanford). He also received help from Ralph Vaughan Williams and Gustav Holst. He was director of the Overseas Music Service of the BBC during 1942–44. In 1950 he was knighted and in 1953 appointed Master of the Queen's Musick.

PRINCIPAL COMPOSITIONS (published by Novello unless otherwise noted): *A Colour Symphony* (1921–22, Curwen; revised 1932, Boosey); *Ballads of the 4 Seasons* for voice, piano (1923); *Pastoral: Lie Strewn the White Flocks* for mezzo-soprano, chorus, flute, string orchestra, timpani (1928); *Morning Heroes*, symphony for narrator, chorus, orchestra (1930); *Clarinet Quintet* (1931); *Things to Come*, film score for orchestra (1934–35); *Music for Strings* (1935); *Checkmate*, 1-act ballet (1937); *Piano Concerto* (1938); *String Quartet in B Flat* (1941); *Miracle in the Gorbals*, ballet; choreography by Robert Helpmann (1944); *Adam Zero*, ballet; choreography by Helpmann (1946); *The Olympians*, 3-act opera; libretto by J. B. Priestley (1948–49); *String Quartet No. 2* (1950); *The Enchantress*, scena for alto, orchestra; text adapted from Theocritus (1952); *Song of Welcome* for soloists, chorus, orchestra; text by C. Day Lewis (1954); *Violin Concerto* (1955); *Meditations on a Theme of John Blow* for orchestra (1955); *Edinburgh*, overture for orchestra (1956); *Discourse for Orchestra* (1957, recomposed 1965); *Tobias and the Angel*, 2-act opera, libretto by Christopher Hassall (1960); *The Beatitudes*, cantata for soprano, tenor, chorus, orchestra, organ; text arranged by Hassall and the composer (1962); *Mary of Magdala*, cantata for alto, bass, chorus, orchestra; text adapted by Hassall (1963); *A Knot of Riddles* for baritone, winds, harp, string quartet; text from the Exeter Book (1963); *The Golden Cantata* for tenor, chorus, orchestra; text by Kathleen Raine (1964).

PRINCIPAL WRITINGS: "Aspects of Contemporary Music," *Musical Times* (April 1934):401; "Some Answers to Some Questions," *Music* (Dec 1951):17; ["British Musicians' Visit to Russia"], *The Times* (1 June 1956):11; "Gerald Finza," *The Times* (3 Oct 1956):13; "Let Us Take the Initiative," *The Composer* (fall 1964):3; "Verdi—a symposium," *Opera* (Feb 1951):111; "Arnold Bax, 1881–1953," *Music & Letters* (Jan 1954); "Great Music Should Be Seen as well as Heard," *TV Times* (31 Jan 1964):6; *As I Remember* (London 1970).

BIBL.: David Cox, "A View of B.'s Music," *The Listener* (18 Nov 1965):818; K. E. Eggar, "The Orchestral Works of A. B.," *Music Student* (Sept

1921); Alan Frank, "Sir A. B.," *Modern British Composers* (London 1943); Michael Kennedy, "Two British Composers," *Halle* (Dec 1956):1.
[prepared with the help of Laurence Swinyard]

Blitzstein, Marc (b. Philadelphia, 2 March 1905; d. Fort-de-France, Martinique, 22 Jan 1964), was born into a wealthy family and derived much of his tenderness and savage satirical sense from childhood experiences. His grandmother was a banker who held the family purse strings and made her grandson beg for money to take piano lessons (this despite his precocity—he started piano study at three). Some of his most sardonic stage portraits are those of wealthy art patronesses. Blitzstein attended the Univ. of Pa. and the Curtis Institute (piano with Alexander Siloti, 1923–25; composition with Rosario Scalero, 1924–26). He also studied with Nadia Boulanger in Paris (1926) and Arnold Schoenberg in Berlin (1927). Returning to New York in 1931, when the Depression was at its height, he soon felt that the political left was the only hope for the U.S. Looking to the working people as the future audience for the modern composer, he abandoned the chamber-music genres of his Paris years and turned toward the popular theater. In 1936 he wrote his masterpiece, *The Cradle Will Rock*, dealing with the conflict between a steel baron and a burgeoning labor union. It enjoyed a long and profitable run on Broadway. This was followed in 1937 with a radio song-play, *I've Got the Tune*, also with a prolabor plot. During 1942–45 Blitzstein served with the air force in England. After the war he wrote several stage works, including incidental scores for plays. Except for his adaptation of the *3-Penny Opera*, he did not repeat his earlier success in the popular musical theater; he seemed to be making a promising turn in the direction of serious opera in the years before his death, however.

The 1920s Paris school, particularly the neoclassicism of Stravinsky, influenced Blitzstein's early music. Like many pupils of Boulanger, he became adept at a "white-note" diatonic style sprinkled with dissonance. His political orientation after 1931 gave his music the profile and direction it had lacked before. The mature works are characterized by crisp diatonic melodies with a touch of jazz or pop idiom joined to sophisticated harmonies, often containing dissonances, polychords, polyrhythms, and polytonality. The songs sometimes embrace deliberate banalities, parodying commercial commonplaces. Simple tunes, on the other hand, occasionally appear in highly sophisticated contexts—theme-and-variations,

chorale prelude, etc. This musical idiom has had a strong influence, notably on Leonard Bernstein and (indirectly) even on some rock musicians of the 1960s. Most of the composer's papers and musical manuscripts have been placed in the Center for Theater Research of the Univ. of Wis.

PRINCIPAL COMPOSITIONS (published by Chappell unless otherwise noted): *Triple Sec*, 1-act opera-farce; libretto by Ronald Jeans (1928, ms. at Univ. of Wis.); *The Cradle Will Rock*, opera; libretto by the composer (1936, ms. at T. Witmark Music Library); *I've Got the Tune*, 1-act radio song-play; text by the composer (1937, ms. at Univ. of Wis.); *The Spanish Earth*, film score composed with Virgil Thomson (1938, Brandon Film Library); *Native Land*, film score (1941; suite for orchestra, *Movie Music*, 1941); *No for an Answer*, opera; libretto by the composer (1941); *Freedom Morning*, symphonic poem (1943); *The Airborne Symphony* (1945, ms. at Univ. of Wis.); *The Guests*, ballet; choreography by Jerome Robbins (1948); *Regina*, opera; libretto by the composer after Lillian Hellman's *The Little Foxes* (1948–49); *3-Penny Opera*, an adaptation of the Brecht-Weill work (1951, unpub.); *This is the Garden*, cantata; text by the composer (1957); *Lear: A Study* for orchestra (1958); *Idiots First*, 1-act opera; libretto by the composer after Bernard Malamud (unfinished). Complete list: *Composers of the Americas* 5:29–33.

Elie Siegmeister

SEE ALSO Musical, Opera, Popular Music, United States.

Bloch, Ernest (b. Geneva, 24 July 1880; d. Portland, Ore., 15 July 1959), studied in Geneva during his teens with Louis Rey (violin) and Emile Jaques-Dalcroze (composition). Between 1897 and 1899 he studied in Brussels under Ysaÿe (violin) and Rasse (composition), the latter a pupil of Franck. In 1900 he studied at Frankfurt with Ivan Knorr, who, Bloch said, was responsible for teaching him to develop his own musical personality. During 1901–03 he was in Munich, where he took a few lessons from Ludwig Thuille. Following a year in Paris, he returned to Geneva in 1904, where he married, entered his father's clock business, conducted symphonic concerts at Neuchâtel and Lausanne (1909–10), and lectured on esthetics at the Geneva Conservatory (1911–15); he composed in his spare time.

In 1916 Bloch came to the U.S. as conductor for the dancer Maud Allan. During 1917–20 he taught first at the David Mannes School of Music in New York and then privately and also conducted American orchestras in his own works. In 1919 he was awarded the Coolidge Prize for his *Viola Suite*; then, during 1920–25, he served as the first director of the

Cleveland Institute of Music, and in 1924 he became a U.S. citizen. During 1925–30 he headed the San Francisco Conservatory.

He lived principally in Switzerland during 1930–39, with occasional trips to European cities to conduct his own works. In 1939 he returned to the U.S., settling in 1941 at Agate Beach, Ore. Shortly thereafter he became professor of music at the Univ. of Calif. at Berkeley, where he taught summer courses until his retirement in 1952. His death resulted from cancer.

Bloch's many honors included the first Gold Medal in Music by the American Academy of Arts and Sciences (1947) and an unprecedented two New York Music Critics Circle Awards in one year (1952) for chamber music (*String Quartet No. 3*) and symphonic music (*Concerto grosso No. 2*). He wrote more than 30 works for orchestra and chamber orchestra, many with solo instrument(s), and a large amount of solo and chamber music. There is also an opera and a *Sacred Service* for the Reformed Jewish Temple.

Bloch's student pieces were somewhat undisciplined, often too expansive for the material they contained. The *Symphony in C-Sharp Minor* (Munich 1901) reveals the influence of R. Strauss in matters of melodic and harmonic construction and orchestration, and the symphonic poems *Hiver—Printemps* (Paris 1904) reflect Debussy's influence in the use of color per se, particularly in the woodwind and harp solos and the closing reflective coda.

In *Macbeth*, a lyric drama in seven scenes produced at the Opéra Comique in November 1910, Bloch combined elements of Wagnerian music drama, Debussy's *Pelléas et Mélisande*, Mussorgsky's *Boris Godunov*, and characteristics of his own mature writing: frequent changes of meter, tempo, and tonality; the melodic use of augmented and perfect fourths at crucial moments; open fifths and fourths; cross-relations; modal flavor; a darkly hued instrumentation; many repeated-note patterns; and cyclic form, a technique undoubtedly developed through study with Rasse. Bloch's use of cyclic structures diverges from the Franckian school in that thematic material is not molded to fit a preconceived form; rather the form evolves from the thematic material, considerably enhanced by the kaleidoscopic use of orchestral color.

With the "Jewish cycle" (1911–16), a series of epics inspired by scripture, he achieved a musical identity. The "oriental" or quasi-Hebraic atmosphere of the cycle is heightened by many augmented seconds and by passages employing celesta and harps. The Scotch-snap rhythm and its reverse is so prominent that it has been called the "Bloch rhythm." Although little use was made of authentic Hebraic thematic material (the symphony *Israel* is an exception), some Bloch mannerisms take on a new meaning in the context of the cycle; for example, the repeated-note patterns and augmented and perfect fourth "calls" in *Schelomo* resemble the call of the shofar on the High Holy Days, while the unfettered rhythmic flow is similar to that of Hebrew chant.

Bloch's obeisance to the neoclassic movement appeared during the 1920s in such compositions as the two violin sonatas, the *Piano Quintet No. 1* with its quarter tones in the first and last movements, and in the *Concerto grosso No. 1*. During the 1930s he returned again to large-scale works, producing the monumental *Avodath Hakodesh*, a Jewish *Sacred Service*, and the *Violin Concerto* with its American Indian motto.

The Agate Beach creations were a summation of the composer's career. Less personal and rhetorical than those of earlier years, some of them may be categorized as neoclassic (*Concerto grosso No. 2*), some as neoromantic (*Concerto symphonique*), and others as abstract or expressionistic (*Sinfonia breve*, which employs 12-tone themes).

Bloch taught his students (Roger Sessions, Quincy Porter, Frederick Jacobi, Isadore Freed, Halsey Stevens, Bernard Rogers, and others) to develop and create according to their own individual gifts and personalities. He did not found any schools of composition, and he molded his own style from existing musical ingredients. He stated that most of his works were inspired by poetic or philosophical ideas, and he proclaimed the primacy of melody in his creative thinking. He felt that if listeners were not moved by what they heard, the music was without value.

PRINCIPAL COMPOSITIONS (published by Schirmer-G unless otherwise noted): *Macbeth*, opera (1904–09, S-Z); *Prelude and 2 Psalms* for soprano, orchestra (1912–14); *Israel* for 5 solo voices, orchestra (1912–16); *3 Jewish Poems* for orchestra (1913); *Schelomo*, "Hebraic Rhapsody," for cello, orchestra (1915–16); *Suite* for viola with piano or orchestra (1919); *Violin Sonata No. 1* (1920); *Piano Quintet No. 1* (1921–23); *Baal Shem* for violin with piano or orchestra (1923, Fischer); *Violin Sonata No. 2*, "Poème mystique" (1924, Leuckart); *Concerto grosso No. 1* (1924–25, Birchard); *Avodath Hakodesh* [Sacred Service] (1930–33, Broude-B); *Piano Sonata* (1935, Carisch); *Voice in the Wilderness*, symphonic poem for orchestra, cello (1936); *Violin Concerto [No. 2]* (1937–38, Boosey); *String Quartet No. 2* (1945, Boosey); *Concerto symphonique* for piano, orchestra (1947–48); *String Quartet No. 3* (1952); *Concerto grosso No. 2* (1952); *Sinfonia breve* (1952); *Symphony for* trombone, orchestra (1954, Broude-B); *Symphony in E Flat Major* (1954–55); *Piano Quintet No. 2* (1957, Broude-B); *Suites Nos. 1–2* for solo violin (1958, Broude-B). Complete lists: *Composers of the Americas* 9:21–32; David Z. Kushner, *Catalogue of E. B.'s Works* (Radford, Va., 1968); ——, "Catalog of the Works of E. B.," *American Music Teacher* 18/4:21–23.

PRINCIPAL WRITINGS: "E. B. Surveys the Problem of Music Education," *Musical America* (21 May 1921):3, 40; "Man and Music," *Musical Quarterly* 29:374–81; "Thoughts at 70," *Etude* (Feb 1951):9–10, 57.

BIBL.: Ernest Chapman, "E. B. at 75," *Tempo* 35:6–12; Joan Chissell, "Style in B.'s Chamber Music," *Music and Letters* 24:30 ff.; Alex Cohen, "E. B.," *The Music of E. B.* (New York 1956): 44–59; Guido Gatti, "E. B.," *Musical Quarterly* 7:20–38; David Z. Kushner, "A Commentary on E. B.'s Symphonic Works," *Radford Review* 21:99–137; ——, "A Singular E. B.," *Music Journal* (Jan 1970):40, 51, 53; ——, *E. B. and His Symphonic Works* (Ann Arbor: Univ. Microfilms, 1968); ——, "E. B.: Teacher-Thinker," *American Music Teacher* 18/1:29–30; Dika Newlin, "The Later Works of E. B.," *Musical Quarterly* 33:443–59; Roger Sessions, "E. B.," *Modern Music* 5/1: 3–11; Howard Taubman, "E. B. at 70—A Musician Apart," *New York Times Magazine* (16 July 1950):17–19; Maria Tibaldi-Chiesa, *E. B.* (Turin 1933).

David Z. Kushner

SEE ALSO Liturgical Music: Jewish; Microtones; Switzerland.

Blomdahl, Karl-Birger (b. Vaxjo, Sweden, 19 Oct 1916; d. Stockholm, 14 June 1968), studied composition with Hilding Rosenberg during the late 1930s and early 40s and traveled in France and Italy during 1946–47. He was a member of the Monday Group, which paved the way for modern music in Sweden after World War II. Under Blomdahl's chairmanship (1950–54) the chamber-music society Fylkingen was reorganized into Sweden's most important forum for contemporary music. During 1960–64 he was professor of composition at the Royal Academy of Music in Stockholm and subsequently director of the music department of the Swedish Radio, where he was also one of the initiators of EMS, an electronic music studio.

Blomdahl made his debut as a composer in 1938 with a series of instrumental works. Written largely under the influence of Hindemith's *Unterweisung im Tonsatz*, they exhibit a linearity and an energetic, baroquelike pulsation. A second phase was inaugurated around 1950 when the composer created a series of ballets and large-scale vocal works in collaboration with the choreographer Birgit Åkesson and the poet Erik Lindegren. Though tonality plays an important role in many instances, these works are largely constructed according to serial principles. In his *Third Symphony*, "Facetter" [Facets] (1950), Blomdahl modified Schoenbergian 12-tone procedures through a tonal and rhythmic organization of material reminiscent of Bartók, notably the *Fourth String Quartet*, which had great influence on Blomdahl during the late 40s. His vocal music received its decisive impetus from Swedish lyric poetry of the 1940s. The text for *I speglarnas sal* [In the Hall of Mirrors] (1952) is taken from Lindegren's collection *Mannen utan väg* [The Man without a Road] (1942), itself a modern masterpiece. For it Blomdahl used various declamatory vocal styles, including recitative, simple homophonic choral writing, and choral speech, often highlighting the phonological characteristics of the text. In *Anabase* he further explored these techniques, although in the opera *Aniara* (1959) he used a less radical style. The orchestral work *Forma ferritonans*, written in 1961 for the opening of the iron works at Oxelösund, is constructed from chemical number and letter symbols. The work parallels avant-garde tendencies of the early 1960s in its use of timbre and volumes (e.g., Ligeti and Penderecki) and is a musical counterpart of processes in the iron industry. "The composer lets a sound—or rather a cluster—grow out of the depths toward a tremendous climax, only to break up into small particles, which in their turn coalesce toward the end into an evocative waltz" (Wallner in *Perspectives*: 187). During 1962–64 Blomdahl completed his second opera, *Herr von Hancken*, in which he partly reshaped his orchestration techniques to underline the dramatic content of the plot. By using such devices as small group formations in which various instruments are treated soloistically, he achieved diversified timbres in which the boundaries between percussion and non-percussion sounds are often obscured. The result is a harsh, ascetic, intricate style unique in the composer's output. In his electronic composition *Altisonans* (1966), he made use of environmental sounds (bird calls, signals from passing satellites) and subjected them to various electronic treatments.

PRINCIPAL COMPOSITIONS (published by Schott unless otherwise noted): *Concerto grosso* for chamber orchestra (1944, Nordiska); *Dance Suite No. 1* for flute, violin, viola, cello, percussion; choreography by Birgit Åkesson (1949, Suecia); *Symphony No. 3*, "Facetter" (1950); *I speglarnas sal* [In the Hall of Mirrors] for soloists, chorus, orchestra; 9 sonnets from Erik Lindegren's

Mannen utan väg [The Man without a Road] (1951–52); *Chamber Concerto* for piano, woodwinds, percussion (1953); *Sisyphos*, choreographic suite for orchestra; choreography by Åkesson (1954); *Trio* for clarinet, cello, piano (1955); *Anabase* for soloists, chorus, orchestra; poem by S.-J. Perse (1955–56); *Minotauros*, choreographic suite for orchestra; choreography by Åkesson (1957); *Aniara*, 2-act opera; libretto by Lindegren after Harry Martinsson (1959); *Forma ferritonans* for orchestra (1961); *Spel för 8* [Game for 8], choreographic suite for chamber orchestra; choreography by Åkesson and Kåre Gundersen (1962); *Herr von Hancken*, 3-act opera; libretto by Lindegren after a novel by Hjalmar Bergman (1962–64); *Altisonans* on tape (1966). List 1938–57: *Modern nordisk musik* (Stockholm 1957): 167; annual lists 1958–68, *Swedish Journal of Musicology* 40–50.

PRINCIPAL WRITINGS: "Facetter . . . ," *Modern nordisk musik* ed. Ingmar Bengtsson (Stockholm 1957):168–76; "Ich war in Moskau und Leningrad," *Melos* (1960):208–12; "Princetonföreläsningar om text och musik" [Princeton Lectures on Text and Music], *Nutida musik* 1960–61/4:21–25; "Aniara," *The Modern Composer and His World* ed. by J. Beckwith and U. Kasemets (Toronto 1961):102–06; "Forma ferritonans," *Nutida musik* 1961–62/3:19.

BIBL.: R. K. Aiken, *K.-B. B.* (master's thesis, Univ. of Cincinnati, 1968); I. Bengtsson, "Den unga svenska musiken" [The Young Swedish Music], *Prisma* 1948/6:23–33; B. Hambraeus, "Conversation with K.-B. B.," *Swedish Music Past and Present* (1967, special edition of *Musikrevy*): 86–88; Ruth K. Inglefield, "K.-B. B.," *Musical Quarterly* 58:67–81; G. Larsson, "Form och livserfarenhet" [Form and Life Experience], *Nutida musik* 1962–63/2:6–10; H. H. Stuckenschmidt, "B.'s 'Herr von Hancken': Bittere Zauber-Buffa," *Melos* (1965):408–11; B. Wallner, "*Aniara*: Revue vom Menschen in Zeit und Raum," *Melos* (1960):76–79; ——, "K.-B. B.," *Melos* (1956):342–45; ——, "K.-B. B.," *Perspectives* 7/2: 186–89; ——, *Vår tids musik i Norden* (Stockholm 1968), English trans. (London 1971).

Erik Kjellberg
SEE ALSO Opera, Scandinavia.

Blues, see Jazz

Blum, Robert (Karl Moritz) (b. Zurich, 27 Nov 1900), studied at the Zurich Conservatory (1919–23; composition with Volkmar Andreae, counterpoint with Philipp Jarnach, piano with Carl Baldegger) and the Prussian State Academy of the Arts in Berlin (composition with Ferruccio Busoni). Since 1925 he has been conductor of the Orchestergesellschaft Baden and of many choral groups. He has also taught composition and counterpoint at the Zurich Music Academy since 1943. His style has been influenced by an acquaintance with music from the 15th–18th centuries, especially Bach and Mozart, and by Busoni, Schoenberg, and Webern. In addition to the works listed below, he has written over 100 scores for films of all types (industrials, documentaries, features, etc.).

PRINCIPAL COMPOSITIONS: *Psalm 23, "Der Herr ist mein Hirte"* for alto, chamber orchestra (1923); *Amarapura*, ballet music derived from Blum's 2-act opera (1924); *Partita No. 1* for orchestra (1929); *Der Maler*, dramatic cantata; text by the composer (1929); *Von der Erlösung durch den Geist in Jesu Christo*, cantata for chorus, string orchestra (1933, EM); *Das Sankt Galler Spiel von der Kindheit Jesu* for alto, chorus, orchestra; text by Hans Reinhart (1934, Hug); *String Quartet No. 1* (1934–35); *Im Aargöi sind zwöi Liebi*, dialect song play; text by Adolf Haller (1935); *Partita No. 2* for orchestra (1936, EM); *Jä — soo!*, film score (1936, Präsens-Film); *Landammann Stauffacher*, film score (1941, Präsens-Film); *Lamentatio angelorum* for flute, clarinet, oboe, horn, string quintet (1942, Bärenreiter); *Passionskonzert* for string orchestra, organ obbligato (1943); *Der Streiter in Christo Jesu* for soprano, chamber orchestra (1943, EM); *Lobgesang aus der Offenbarung Johannis* for 12-part chorus, chamber orchestra (1945); *Marie Louise*, film score (1945; Präsens-Film, suite published by Sidem); *Partita No. 3* for orchestra (1951, EM); *Heidi*, film score (1952, Präsens-Film); *Viola Concerto* (1953); *Overture of Swiss Folk Melodies* for winds (1954); *Concerto for Orchestra* (1955); *Vogel Juchei*, 36 dialect songs for chorus; texts by Georg Thürer (1958, Hug); *Symphony No. 4* (1959); *Frühmorgens wenn die Sohn aufgeht* for chamber ensemble (1959); *Die Käserei in der Vehfreude*, film score (1959, Neue-Film AG.); *Wir danken dir, Herr Jesu Christ*, chorale partita for wind or string quintet or chamber orchestra (1959); *Oboe Concerto* (1960); *4 Psalms* (146, 130, 84, 117) for soprano, chorus, string orchestra (1960); *Erzengel Michael*, oratorio for vocal soloists, chorus, orchestra, organ (1961); *Triple Concerto* for violin, oboe, trumpet, orchestra (1963); *Concerto* for wind quintet, harp, string orchestra, timpani (1964); *Der Tod des Agamemnon* for vocal soloists, men's chorus, orchestra; text by the composer (1965); *Symphony No 5* for chamber orchestra (1965); *Divertimento on a 12-Tone Row* for wind and string quintets (1966). Complete list in Fierz.

BIBL.: Gerold Fierz, *R. B.* (Zurich 1967).

Blumenfeld, Harold (b. Seattle, 15 Oct 1923), studied at the Eastman School (1941–43; composition with Bernard Rogers), Yale Univ. (1946–49; composition, theory with Paul Hindemith), and Zurich Univ. and Conservatory (1948–49; musicology with A. Cherbuliez). He also studied conducting at Tanglewood with Leonard Bernstein, Robert Shaw, and Boris Goldovsky (summers 1947–49). Blumenfeld teaches at Washington Univ. in St. Louis, where he has held the rank of professor since 1951. He was cofounder in 1960 of the New Music Circle of St. Louis and its director during 1962–64. In 1963 he began directing the Washington Univ. opera studio and was also director of the St. Louis Opera Theater (1964–67). Blumenfeld's early music is neoclassic in style with a strong emphasis on the melodic element. In his later works, although the melodic aspect remains dominant, he is also concerned with the "vertical expansion and compression of materials and their juxtaposition and overlapping."

PRINCIPAL COMPOSITIONS: *Elegy for the Nightingale* for baritone, chorus, orchestra (1955); *Amphitryon 4*, opera; libretto by composer after Molière (1956–62, MCA; orchestral suite, *Symphony Amphitryon 4*, 1966); *Contrasts* for orchestra (1958); *Miniature Overture* (1962, MCA); *Transformations* for piano (1964); *Expansions* for woodwind quintet (1965); *The Road to Salem*, television opera; libretto by Gale Hoffman (1966–69, MCA); *Movements* for brass (1967).

PRINCIPAL WRITINGS: "Weisgall's *Nine Rivers from Jordan*," *Lincoln Center Journal* (Oct 1968): 3–4; "Horspfal versus The Homespuns," *Cultural Affairs* (New York) 5:18–23; "Battle of Baby Doe," *Opera News* (8 March 1969):8–10.

Boatwright, Howard (Leake) (b. Newport News, Va., 16 March 1918), studied composition with Paul Hindemith at Yale Univ. (1945–48). He has taught violin at the Univ. of Texas (1943–45) and theory at Yale (1948–64) and has been dean of the music school of Syracuse Univ. since 1964. His activities as a professional string player and conductor have included numerous concerts in the U.S. and Europe, some in conjunction with his wife, soprano Helen Boatwright, and many devoted to music of the 18th century and earlier. He was music director of St. Thomas's Church in New Haven during 1949–64 and wrote a large number of liturgical works at that time. Five summers at the camp of the Country Dance Society of America in Mass. (1956–61) provided the raison d'être for a series of vocal works based on Anglo-American folksongs.

PRINCIPAL COMPOSITIONS: *Trio* for 2 violins, viola (1948, New Valley); *Variations* for chamber orchestra (1949, Oxford); *Serenade* for 2 strings, 2 winds (1952, Oxford); *The Women of Trachis* for women's chorus, chamber orchestra; text by Sophocles, trans. by Ezra Pound (1955); *Mass in C* for chorus, organ (1958, Oxford); *Clarinet Quartet* (1958, Oxford); *The Passion according to St.

Matthew for vocal soloists, chorus, organ (1962, Schirmer-E); *Canticle of the Sun* for soprano, chorus, orchestra; poem by Francis of Assisi (1963, Schirmer-E); *Music for Temple Service* for baritone (cantor), chorus, organ (1964, Schirmer-E); *The Ship of Death* for vocal quartet, string quartet; text by D. H. Lawrence (1966); *The Lament of Mary Stuart* for soprano, harpsichord, cello ad lib; text from the Carissimi cantata (1968).

PRINCIPAL WRITINGS: "Quincy Porter," *ACA Bulletin* 3:2–8; *Introduction to the Theory of Music* (New York 1956); "Untempered Intonation in the West," *Journal of the Music Academy* (Madras) 31:113–37; *A Handbook on Staff Notation for Indian Music* (Bombay 1960); "Paul Hindemith as a Teacher," *Musical Quarterly* 50:279–89; "Ives' Quarter-tone Impressions," *Perspectives* 3/2:22–31; *Indian Classical Music and the Western Listener* (Syracuse Univ. 1966); "Quincy Porter, *String Quartet No. 7*," notes for the recording by Owl Records (1967). Boatwright has also edited *Essays Before a Sonata and Other Writings* by Charles Ives (New York 1962).

BIBL.: Janet Knapp, "H. B., An American Master of Choral Music," *American Choral Review* (Oct 1963):1–4.

Boesmans, Philippe (b. Tongeren, Belgium, 17 May 1936), attended the Conservatory of Liège (1954–62, piano with Robert Leuridan and Stephan Askenase, composition with Pierre Froidebise and Henri Pousseur). Since 1962 he has been on the musical staff of Belgian radio and television. His compositions emanate from the post-Webern serial tradition. Beginning with his composition *Sonance* (1964) he has attempted to reintegrate consonant harmonic and melodic materials within a basically atonal framework.

PRINCIPAL COMPOSITIONS: *Sonance* for 2 pianos (1964); *Impromptu* for 23 instruments (1965); *Corrélation* for clarinet, 2 ensembles (1967, Jobert); *Explosives* for harp, 10 instrumentalists (1968, Jobert); *Verticales* for orchestra (1969); *Blocage* for voice, chorus, ensemble (1970).

SEE ALSO Belgium.

Bogusławski, Edward (b. Chorzów, Poland, 22 Sept 1940), studied at the Katowice Music College (1959–66, composition with B. Szabelski, theory with J. Gawlas) and composition with Roman Haubenstock-Ramati in Vienna in 1967. He has taught theory, solfège, and orchestration at the Katowice Music College since 1963.

PRINCIPAL COMPOSITIONS (published by PWM): *Sygnały* for orchestra (1966); *Apokalypsis* for narrator, chorus, orchestra (1967); *Metamor; phoses* for oboe, clarinet, violin, viola, cello (1967)-

Canti for soprano, orchestra (1970); *Per pianoforte* (1971, PWM and Schott); *Concerto* for oboe, oboe d'amore, English horn, musette, orchestra (1971); *Intonazioni* for orchestra (1971).

BIBL.: Janusz Ekiert, "B. en zijn Poolse tijdgenoten," *Ouverture* (Rotterdam, 3 Nov 1967):19; Tadeusz Kaczyński, "Sibelius, Bartók, B.," *Ruch Muzyczny* 1966/5:9. Individual works are discussed in the program books of the Warsaw Autumn Festivals of 1964, 1967, and 1968.

du Bois, Rob (Louis) (b. Amsterdam, 28 May 1934), is the son of an amateur violinist and was self-taught in music except for some piano lessons as a child. He did not attend his first concert until the age of 16. His university training was in law, and he works for BUMA, the Dutch performing rights association. His music has explored some chance techniques and has utilized unusual instrumental playing devices. For instance, *Spiel und Zwischenspiel* for recorder (1962) uses overblowing and multitones. *Music for Solo Flute* (1961) alternates written-out movements with five schemes, each containing five groups of notes; the entire work can vary in length from four and a half to eight minutes.

PRINCIPAL COMPOSITIONS (published by Donemus unless otherwise noted): 7 *Pastorales*: No. 1 for oboe, clarinet, harp (1960); No. 2 for recorder, flute, guitar (1963); No. 3 for clarinet, bongos, double bass (1963); No. 4 for guitar (1963); No. 5 for string quartet (1964–66); No. 6 for piano (1963–66); No. 7 for recorder (1964, Moeck); *Muziek voor Altblokfluit* [Music for Alto Recorder] (1961, Schott); *Rondeaux* for piano 4-hands (1963–64); *Words* for mezzo-soprano, flute, cello, piano (1966); *Pour 2 Violons* (1966); *Because Going Nowhere Takes a Long Time* for voice, flute (or clarinet), piano (1967); *Trio à cordes* (1967); *Music for a Sliding Trombone* (1968); *Reflexions sur le jour où Perotin le Grand ressuscitera* for wind quintet (1969); *Souvenir pour violon* (1969); *A Flower Given to My Daughter* for orchestra (1970); *Midas*, ballet (1970).

Bolcom, William (Elden) (b. Seattle, 26 May 1938), attended the Univ. of Wash., first privately, then as a regular student (1949–58; composition with George Frederick McKay and John Verrall, piano with Berthe Jacobson). He then studied at Mills College, Oakland, Calif. (1958–59; MA, 1961; composition with Milhaud), the Paris Conservatory (1959–61; composition with Milhaud and Jean Rivier, esthetics with Olivier Messiaen, counterpoint with Simone Plé-Caussade), and Stanford Univ. (1961–64; composition with Leland

Smith). He has taught at the Univ. of Wash. (1965–66) and at Queens College in New York (1966–68). He was visiting critic in musical theater at the Yale Drama School (1968–69) and composer-in-residence at the New York Univ. School of the Arts (1969–70). Of special significance to Bolcom's development have been Milhaud's "openness," George Rochberg, and Boulez's 1960 lectures at Darmstadt. His compositions have incorporated a wide variety of influences and techniques ranging from serialism to popular music, improvisation, collage, and microtones. *Session 2*, for example, uses "bits of everything from B. Marini to Beethoven to wild chromatic-1960's to bits of waltzes."

PRINCIPAL COMPOSITIONS: *String Quartet No. 6* (1958–59); *12 Etudes* for piano (1959–66, Merion); *Fantasy-Sonata* for piano (1960–62); *Dynamite Tonite*, pop opera for actors, 11 instruments; libretto by Arnold Weinstein (1960–66, Trio); *Décalage* for cello, piano (1961–62); *Octet* for flute, clarinet, bassoon, violin, viola, cello, bass, piano (1962); *Session 1* for flute, oboe/English horn, bassoon, trombone, viola, cello, percussion (1965, Presser); *String Quartet No. 8* (1965); *Session 2* for violin, viola (1966, Presser); *Fives* for violin, piano, 2 string quintets, string orchestra (1966); *Session 3* for E-flat clarinet, violin, cello, piano, percussion (1967); *Black Host* for organ, percussion, tape (1967); *Session 4* for clarinet, 2 violas, cello, trombone, harp, piano, 2 percussionists, tape (1967, Presser); *Dream Music No. 2*, epitaph for Frank O'Hara, for percussion quartet (1966–67); *Greatshot*, actors' opera; libretto by Weinstein (1967–69); *14 Piano Rags* (1967–70); *Praeludium* for organ, vibraphone (1969); *Dark Music* for tympani, cello (1969–70).

Bondon, Jacques (Laurent Jules Désiré) (b. Boulbon, France, 6 Dec 1927), studied at the Paris Conservatory (1948–53; composition with Darius Milhaud and Jean Rivier, harmony with Georges Dandelot, counterpoint and fugue with Charles Koechlin). In 1963 he formed L'Ensemble Moderne de Paris, of which he is president. During 1963–65 he was a member of the music committee of the French Radio-Television Network, and he has been a member of the Commission Nationale de la Musique Populaire of the Ministry of Arts and Letters since 1970. In his compositions he strives to be free of all technical formulas and to achieve maximum flexibility in structure and rhythm.

PRINCIPAL COMPOSITIONS: *Le Taillis ensorcele* for 2 orchestras (1957, Heugel); *Kaleïdoscope* for wind quintet, trumpet, trombone, 2 cellos, double bass, harp, ondes Martenot, 2 percussion (1957,

EMT); *String Quartet No. 1* (1959, EMT); *Giocoso* for violin, string orchestra (1960, EMT); *Musique pour un autre monde* for orchestra (1962, Choudens); *La Nuit foudroyée*, 4-act opera (1963, Choudens); *Fleurs de feu*, fireworks ballet for orchestra (1965, EMT); *Concerto de Mars* for guitar, orchestra (1966, Eschig); *Concerto de moulines* for violin, orchestra (1966, Eschig); *Suite pour Xº jeux* for chorus, orchestra; composed for the Winter Olympics in Grenoble (1967, Eschig); *Sonata pour un ballet* for wind quintet, trumpet, trombone, double bass, 2 percussion (1968, Choudens); *Le Soleil multicolore* for flute, viola, harp (1969, Eschig); *Lumières et formes animées*, concerto for string orchestra (1970, Eschig); *Ana et l'albatross*, 4-act opera; libretto by Yves Mauffret (1970, Eschig).

PRINCIPAL WRITINGS: "Manifeste," *Combat* (Paris, 5 April 1955); "Pour Sortir de l'impasse," *Opera* (Paris, Dec 1970).

BIBL.: Pierre Ancelin, "Entretien avec J. B.," *Les Lettres Françaises* (15 Oct 1964); Marie-José Chauvin, "Entretien avec J. B.," *Le Courrier Musical de France* 29; Luc-André Marcel, "J. B.," *Cahiers du Sud* 360 (1961):304; Jean Roy, "J. B.," *Présences contemporaines* (Paris 1962).

Boretz, Benjamin (b. New York, 3 Oct 1934), studied at Brooklyn College, Brandeis Univ., and Princeton Univ. He has taught at several schools, principally New York Univ. (1964–69) and Columbia Univ. (1969–72). He has been associate editor and, later, editor of *Perspectives of New Music* (since its inception in 1962) and music critic for the weekly *The Nation* (1962–69).

PRINCIPAL COMPOSITIONS: *Concerto grosso* for chamber orchestra (1954–55); *Partita* for piano (1955); *Divertimento* for chamber ensemble (1955); *Violin Concerto* (1956–57); *String Quartet* (1957–58); *John Donne Songs* for soprano, piano (1960–61); *Brass Quintet* (1962–63); *Group Variations I* for chamber ensemble (1964–67); *Group Variations II* for computer-synthesized tape (1968–70).

PRINCIPAL WRITINGS: "Roger Sessions," *Musical Quarterly* (April 1960); "Serial Composition and Atonality by George Perle," an article-review, *Perspectives* (spring 1962); "American Music," *Cimaise* (Paris, July 1964); "The Crisis in Musical Discourse," *Bericht über den 9. International Kongress* (Salzburg 1964); "The Conceptual Framework of Postwar American Music," prepared for the U.S. Information Agency (1965); "The Theoretical Character of Musical Entities," *Proceedings of the American Society of University Composers* (1968); "Meta-Variations: Studies in the Foundations of Musical Thought," *Perspectives* (1970–71, published in installments); "Nelson Goodman's *Languages of Art* from a Musical Point of View," *Journal of Philosophy* (August 1970).

Bořkovec, Pavel (b. Prague, 10 June 1894), studied composition privately with J. B. Foerster and Jaroslav Křička and at the Prague Conservatory with Josef Suk. He was a free-lance composer until 1946, after which he taught composition at the Prague Academy of Music and Dramatic Arts until 1964. In the late 1920s he was a leading figure in moving Czech music from late romanticism into a neoclassic expression.

PRINCIPAL COMPOSITIONS: *String Quartets Nos. 1, 2, 4, 5* (1924, 1928, 1947, 1961; Supraphon); *Old Chinese Poetry* for men's chorus; Chinese poetry in Czech translation (1925, Hudební Matice); *Symphony No. 1* (1926–27, ČHF); *Start*, symphonic allegro (1929, ČHF); *Piano Concertos Nos. 1–2* (1931, 1949–50; Supraphon); *Sonata* for viola solo (1931); *7 Songs* for soprano, piano; poems by Vítězslav Nezval (1931, orchestrated 1936; Hudební Matice); *Capricious Songs* for baritone with piano or chamber orchestra; poems by Goethe and Villon (1931–32, Hudební Matice); *Wind Quintet* (1932, Hudební Matice and ČHF); *Violin Concerto* (1933, ČHF); *Violin Sonatas Nos. 1–2* (1934, Panton; 1956, Supraphon); *Partita* for orchestra (1936, Panton); *Folk Sayings* for chorus, piano; texts by Karel Jaromír Erben (1936); *The Satyr*, opera in 5 scenes; libretto by Otakar Fischer after Goethe (1937–38, DILIA); *The Pied Piper*, ballet; scenario by the composer (1939, Supraphon); *2 Compositions* for piano (1941, Hudební Matice); *Concerto grosso* for 2 violins, cello, orchestra (1941–42, Supraphon); *Nonet* for wind quintet, 4 strings (1941–42, Hudební Matice and ČHF); *Sonatina* for violin, piano (1942, Hudební Matice); *Symphonietta No. 1* for chamber orchestra (1944, Panton); *Tom Thumb*, opera in 5 scenes; libretto by František Kubka (1945–47, DILIA); *6 Songs* for children's or women's chorus, texts by Jaroslav Seifert (1949, Orbis); *Cello Concerto* (1950–51, ČHF); *Symphonies Nos. 2–3* (1955, Supraphon; 1960, Panton); *Madrigals about Time* for chorus, texts by Hana Prošková (1958); *Animals* for mezzo-soprano, piano; texts by Prošková (1961); *Dreams*, 7 songs for low voice, orchestra; texts by Prošková (1962, ČHF); *Silentium turbatum* for alto, electric guitar, orchestra; texts by Prošková (1964–65, Supraphon); *Intermezzo* for horn (cello), piano (1965, Panton); *Symphonietta No. 2* for orchestra (1968, Panton).

BIBL.: Jaroslav Kasan et al., *P. B., His Personality and Work* (Prague 1964).

SEE ALSO Czechoslovakia.

Bornefeld, Helmut (b. Stuttgart-Untertürkheim, 14 Dec 1906), studied in Stuttgart at the Adlerschen Conservatory (1924–28) and the Staatliche Musikhochschule (1928–31; 1935–37; composition, piano, organ). During 1931–36 he directed a chamber choir and a group of instrumentalists in Esslingen. Since 1937 he has restored over 100 historic organs in Germany and has contributed articles on organ restoration and church music to German periodicals. In 1946 he and Siegfried Reda organized the summer Heidenheimer Workshop for New Church Music, with which he was associated until 1960. Since 1937 he has been director of music and organist at St. Paul's in Heidenheim-Brenz.

PRINCIPAL COMPOSITIONS: *Choralwerk* (1940–59, Bärenreiter); *Stern und Blume*, songs for chorus (1941–59, Bärenreiter); *Momento mori* for medium voice, organ (1954, Bärenreiter); *Hirtenlieder* for medium voice, organ (1955–57, Bärenreiter); *Psalm der Nacht* for soprano, organ (1965, Hänssler); *Organ Sonata* (1965–66, Hänssler); *Patmos* for baritone, organ, percussion; poem by Hölderlin (1969, Hänssler); *Introduction and Capriccio* for trumpet, timpani, organ, brass (1969, Hänssler); *Trivium* for recorder, gamba, keyboard instrument (1969, Hänssler); *Tympanon* for timpani (1970, Hänssler); *Canticum canticorum*, dialogue for organ, percussion (1970, Hänssler).

PRINCIPAL WRITINGS: *Das Positiv* (Cassel 1947); *Orgelbau und neue Orgelmusik* (Cassel 1952); *Orgelspiegel* (Cassel 1966).

BIBL.: Martin Rössler, "H. B.—*Orgelspiegel*," *Württenburger Blätter für Kirchenmusik* (1966/4); Joachim Widmann, "H. B.," *Gottesdienst und Kirchenmusik* (1963/2).

Boskovich, Alexander Urijah (b. Cluj, Transylvania, 16 August 1907; d. Tel Aviv, 6 Nov 1964), studied at the Vienna Academy of Music (1924–29; composition with Richard Stöhr, piano with Victor Ebenstein) and in Paris with Paul Dukas and Nadia Boulanger (composition) and Alfred Cortot (piano). He was active as a conductor and pianist. During 1930–38 he conducted the Cluj State Opera and the Goldmark Symphony. He moved to Palestine in 1938 and taught at the Academy of Music in Tel Aviv during 1945–64. During 1955–64 he was also music critic for the Israeli paper *Ha'aretz* and the author of many articles on the problems of Jewish music. He was a serious student of Jewish mysticism, particularly the Kabbala and Hassidic literature. The Hebrew language and the cantillation of the Bible inspired some aspects of meter and surface rhythm in his music. The *Concerto da camera*, which includes parts for four percussionists, combines these concerns with serial techniques.

PRINCIPAL COMPOSITIONS: *The Golden Chain*, suite for orchestra (1937, IMI); *Violin Concerto* (1942); *Oboe Concerto* (1943, revised 1960; IMP); *Adonai ro'i* [The Lord Is My Shepherd], for alto (baritone), orchestra (1946); *Semitic Suite* for orchestra (1946–47, IMP); *Piccola Suite* for flute,

snare drum, string orchestra (1956–57); *Psalm* for violin, piano (1957); *Cantico di ma'aloth* [Song of Ascent] for orchestra (1960, IMP); *Daughter of Israel*, cantata for tenor, chorus, orchestra; text by Chaim N. Bialik, with excerpts from the Bible and Hebrew liturgy (1960); *Piece for Oboe and Harpsichord* (1961–62); *Lament* for violin (cello), piano (1962); *Concerto da camera* for violin, 10 instruments (1962); *Ornaments* for flute, orchestra (1964).

PRINCIPAL WRITINGS: "La Musique israélienne contemporaine et les traditions ethniques," *Journal of the International Folk Music Council* 16:39–42.

BIBL.: Max Brod, *Die Musik Israels* (Cassel 1971). [prepared with the help of Miriam Boscovich]

SEE ALSO Israel.

Botto, Carlos (Vallatino) (b. Viña del Mar, Chile, 4 Nov 1923), studied at the National Conservatory of the Univ. of Chile (1948–52; composition with Gustavo Becerra-Schmidt, Domingo Santa Cruz, and Juan Orrego-Salas; piano with Herminia Raccagni). He studied composition privately in the U.S. with Luigi Dallapiccola. He has taught at the Chilean National Conservatory since 1952 and was its director during 1961–68. During 1954–58 he was also program annotator for the I.E.M. concerts at the Univ. of Chile. Since 1969 he has taught composition at the Catholic Univ. of Chile. He describes his music as a conjunction of impressionism and expressionism, influenced by the works of Berg, Debussy, and Bartók.

PRINCIPAL COMPOSITIONS: *Variations* for piano, Op. 1 (1948, revised 1966); *10 Preludes* for piano, Op. 3 (1950–52, IEM); *String Quartet*, Op. 5 (1951–54); *Pedagogical Diversions* for piano, Op. 6, 155 instructional pieces for children (1955–59); *Cantos al amor y a la muerte* for tenor, string quartet, Op. 8a (1956, PAU); *3 Capriccios* for piano, Op. 10 (1959); *Cantos de amor y soledad* for voice, piano, Op. 12; poems by James Joyce (1959–62); *Academias del jardin*, song cycle for voice, piano, Op. 16; poems by Polo de Medina (1959–62); *Fantasia* for viola, piano, Op. 15 (1961–62); *Partita* for piano, Op. 22 (1967). List to 1967: *Composers of the Americas* 14:27–29.

SEE ALSO Chile.

Boucourechliev, André (b. Sofia, Bulgaria, 28 July 1925), studied at the State Academy of Music in Sofia (1946–49), the Ecole Normale de Musique in Paris (1949–51; theory, piano with Reine Gianoli), the Saarbrucken Conservatory (1955, piano with Walter Gieseking), and at the summer courses at Darmstadt (1958–62). He has been associated with the Studio di Fonologia of the Italian radio in

Milan (1957–58) and the Groupe de Recherches Musicales of the French radio (1959–60). During 1954–60 he taught piano classes at the Ecole Normale. He has been music critic for *Nouvelle Revue française* (1957–63), *Preuves* (1963–68), *La Quinzaine Littéraire* (1968–69), and *Reforme* (since 1967). He became a French citizen in 1956. His *Archipels* are open-form mobile works that are generally performed in two or more versions per concert.

PRINCIPAL COMPOSITIONS: *Piano Sonata* (1959); *Texte I* on tape (1959, recorded by Philips); *Texte II* on tape (1960, recorded by Boite à Musique); *Grodek* for voice, flute, 3 percussionists (1963, UE); *Musiques nocturnes* for clarinet, harp, piano (1966); *Archipel 1* for 2 pianos, 2 percussionists (1967, UE); *Archipel 2* for string quartet (1968); *Archipel 3* for piano, 6 percussionists (1969); *Archipel 4* for piano (1970).

PRINCIPAL WRITINGS: *Schumann* (Paris 1956, New York 1960); *Chopin* (Munich 1962, New York 1963); *Beethoven* (Paris 1963); "La Musique sérielle aujourd'hui," *Preuves* nos. 177–81 and 188; "Stravinsky un et multiple," *Stravinsky* (Paris 1967):149–73; "Architectures de pénombre," *Schumann* (Paris 1970); "Transmutations," *Beethoven*, a special issue of *L'Arc* (Aix-en-Provence 1970):49–56. He has also contributed to the 2nd edition of *The Harvard Dictionary of Music*.

SEE ALSO France.

Boulanger, Nadia (b. Paris, 16 Sept 1887), was born into a family of musicians, several members of which taught at the Paris Conservatory. She studied at the conservatory herself (composition with Gabriel Fauré, organ with Charles Widor) and won a Prix de Rome in 1908 with the cantata *La Sirène*. She taught harmony classes at the Ecole Normale during 1920–39. In 1921 she began teaching at the American Conservatory at Fontainebleau, becoming director of the school in 1950. Since 1945 she has taught a class in accompaniment at the Paris Conservatory. She also holds Wednesday afternoon classes at home, at which she plays and discusses new and older music. Her chief fame is as a teacher of composers. Her students have included a large number of Americans, and she has visited the U.S. both to teach (at Wellesley College, Radcliffe College, the Juilliard School) and to conduct the Boston Symphony (1938), New York Philharmonic (1939), and other orchestras.

Boulanger first gained prominence as a teacher in the early 1920s. American musicians at the time still felt the need to complete their education in Europe. Before World War I they tended to go to Germany, but afterwards Paris held a greater attraction. Paul Dukas, who taught composition at both the Paris Conservatory and the Ecole Normale, recommended Boulanger to the newly arrived Americans, as did European students of hers at the new school at Fontainebleau. The fact that such prominent Americans as Walter Piston and Aaron Copland spoke highly of her when they returned to the U.S. was important in her career. It was also in her favor that she spoke English and that during the 1920s and 30s she was at the crest of her physical and intellectual powers.

Her teaching concentrated on the analysis of music past and present and on counterpoint exercises, beginning with elementary two-part, note-against-note writing. She spent considerable time analyzing Bach, Mozart, and Beethoven; in regard to more recent works, those of Fauré and Stravinsky were especially important to her, but such composers as Sibelius, Bartók, Hindemith, Schoenberg, Ives, and Vaughan Williams were of little or no interest. In dealing with student compositions she would read through a new score at the piano, criticizing what she found weak and replaying passages that were "tellement extraordinaire." Except in cases where the music diverged too radically from her own tastes, she grasped quickly and accurately the essence of a student composition. If convinced of the rightness of a new idea, she was capable of a real enthusiasm; in the 1960s she began to be receptive to some avant-garde ideas.

She impressed students with her intimate knowledge of a large body of music and with her well-trained ear and adeptness of "fixed-do" solfège. She was particularly sensitive to rhythm and phrasing in performance and to overall architectural construction in composition. Probably the most decisive factor in her success was her personal dedication to music as an art. For her, great music demanded an almost religious awe, and her zeal and self-confidence fired many students with a sense of purpose they had never experienced before. She made it clear that what still remained for a student to do was always far more than what he had done already. On the other hand, she also believed that the seeming miracle of inevitability in an acknowledged masterpiece followed principles equally possible of attainment in a student work. Thus the accomplishment of even her simplest counterpoint exercise was a step toward artistic perfection. Her dynamism tended toward the domineering, especially as she grew older, and some of her more individualistic students fought with her (or left her classes). She demanded a large production and was inclined to be satisfied with a well turned-out piece however imitative it might be. Some of her students have since been criticized for producing music too similar in style, but others—including her most famous ones—have not been accused of this.

[prepared from remarks by Josef Alexander, Aaron Copland, Tudor Ciortea, Harrison Kerr, Robert Moevs, Walter Piston, Joel Spiegelman, and John Vincent]

SEE ALSO Education for the Professional.

Boulez, Pierre (b. Montbrison, France, 26 March 1925), first studied mathematics; following this and until 1945 he studied composition with Olivier Messiaen. During 1944–45 he studied counterpoint with Andrée Vaurabourg-Honegger and 12-tone technique with René Leibowitz. In 1946 Boulez became a conductor and composer at the Theatre Marigny, where he, Jean-Louis Barrault, and Madeleine Renaud founded the Domaine Musical concert series in 1953. Boulez himself first came to international attention in 1951 when *Polyphonie X* was premiered at the Donaueschingen Musiktage. Since 1958 Boulez's principal residence has been Baden-Baden. He conducted a master class in composition at the Basel Musikakademie during 1960–63 and in the spring of 1963 held a guest professorship at Harvard Univ. He belongs to the teaching staff of the International Ferienkurse für Neue Musik in Darmstadt. Since the early 1960s he has been more active as a conductor than as a composer. He has been permanent guest conductor of the Cleveland Orchestra and chief conductor of the BBC Orchestra in London. In the fall of 1971 he became music director of the New York Philharmonic and of the BBC Orchestra in London.

Two-thirds of Boulez's compositions are instrumental works, mostly for chamber ensembles. The remaining third of his compositions are vocal works for the concert hall. So far there are no stage works. His style stems basically from four composers: Schoenberg, as founder of the 12-tone method; Webern, as a model of succinctness and as a precursor of total serialism; Messiaen, as an innovator in the field of serialism and in the treatment of rhythm; and Debussy, as a model for a treatment of form that is divorced from traditional formulas and also for his use of color, particularly orchestral mixtures, and the seemingly free flow among nuances of expression. An example of the interaction of

these influences is the *Sonatine* (1946), the form of which is based on Schoenberg's *Chamber Symphony*, Op. 9. It contains pointillistic sounds in the piano part that are reminiscent of Webern. The suppleness of melodies in slow passages reflects the impressionist tradition, while the influence of Messiaen is evident in the precise construction of sound and rhythm cells and in the interlinking tone and rhythm rows.

Works of the late 40s and early 50s reveal a desire to expand on what the two immediately preceding generations had achieved. For instance, the widely spaced intervals in the cantata *Le Visage nuptial* (1946–47) recall Webern; at the same time the piece reaches out in new directions by employing choral speech, whispering, crying, and spoken glissandos. The first movement of *Structures I* for two pianos (1951–52) illustrates the directions Boulez pursued in terms of serialism. In addition to a row of 12 tones, the work employs a row of note values from a 32nd note to a dotted quarter (= 1–12 32nd notes). There is a row of 12 dynamic levels from pppp to FFFF and a row of 10 articulations from extremely short staccato to legato. The forms and transpositions of the pitch row are balanced symmetrically, e.g., the original row in piano 1 sounding simultaneously with its inversion in piano 2, or the original row being transposed to each successive tone of the inversion and the inversion being transposed to each successive tone of the original. The four principal forms of the pitch row are piled on top of one another until a six-voice texture is formed; each pitch series as it enters is combined with a different set of dynamic levels and articulations. Whereas in the first movement a particular articulation is always linked with the same dynamic level, in the third movement the same articulation is combined with various dynamic levels and vice versa. The overall sound of the work is pointillistic, and most of the musical syntax differs radically from that of traditional music. In place of themes or motives there are isolated, precisely constructed sound events and their negative, silence. The varying densities of events take the place of harmonic tensions, and instead of a pulse one experiences a kaleidoscopic sequence of varying time values. In terms of the performing medium (two pianos), it is interesting to note that Boulez withdrew an earlier and equally rigorous serial work, *Polyphony X* (1951), which was composed for 18 solo instruments. That work demonstrated to the composer that complex serial music is not suited to mixed instrumental ensembles because differences in construction and playing technique make it impossible to maintain articulations, dynamic levels, and the like, with precision when they are passed from one instrument to another.

Boulez has used electronic apparatus and media in a few works. For a short while at the beginning of the 1950s he experimented with musique concrète and produced two works, both called *Study*. In his largest electronic work, *Poésie pour pouvoir* (1958), he combined concrete and electronic sounds with orchestra. The orchestra is divided into three sections under two conductors, and an 8-track tape is played over 84 loudspeakers that are placed around the hall. The tape parts are complex mixtures of readings from the surrealist poet Henri Michaux. The loudspeakers create an aural spiral of which the audience is sometimes inside and sometimes outside, seeming either to follow the sounds or to be followed by them. Boulez stands somewhat aloof from this composition today; although it was a daring work, the first large-scale experiment in combining electronic and traditional sound sources, the composer does not feel that the technical resources then available permitted him to realize on tape what he had in mind.

About 1957 Boulez, along with other European composers, began to use indeterminacy, partly as a result of John Cage's activities in Europe and partly as a reaction to the rigidity of serialism. Boulez's thinking was also influenced by the novels of James Joyce and Stéphane Mallarmé (*Un Coup de dés*, the sketches for *Le Livre*) and by Indian music, with its controlled chance resulting from the alternation of composed and improvised music. In the *Piano Sonata No. 3* (1956–57) chance is involved on several levels: The overall form is mobile; the five movements can be played in any order except for the third, which must always be in the center. The order and other details of sections within movements are also variable. The work is set up so that single choices affect the course of the rest of the movement; in some cases a particular section must follow the one already played, while in other cases the performer may choose from among several sections. A parallel to mobile form is found in the way Boulez exploits the sound resources of the piano, both in the *Third Sonata* and later in *Structures II* (1956–61). These works contain many pedal and resonance effects that cause the sound profiles to change constantly, to both build and dissolve at the same time, and to be reflected in their own echoes.

The five-part Mallarmé portrait *Pli selon pli* is a culmination of much of Boulez's style.

Its nucleus was *2 Improvisations on Mallarmé* (1957), from which it grew over a period of five years (the title, roughly equivalent to "bit by bit," refers to the growth process). All five movements contain poems or text segments from Mallarmé, often transformed from linear-structured phrases and verses into segments of sound and declaimed in every way from speech to ornate melody. The approach to text setting here can also be seen in *Le Marteau sans maître* (1953–55). The overall form is circular, a design that has occupied Boulez since the *Third Sonata*. The three central movements, which make use of various degrees of chance, are flanked by "Don" and the finale, "Tombeau"; the structure of "Don," according to the composer, is derived from "Tombeau." "Don" also includes some of the sound profiles and text segments of the central sections. In a gesture that welds the arms of the circle together, the final fortissimo chord of "Tombeau" is identical with the opening exclamaton of "Don." Improvisation takes three different forms in the central sections: in the first section nothing is left to the performers' choice, although the contours of the voice part occasionally sound improvised; the second section contains an interplay of freedom and restraint in that the breath control of the singer determines the phrasing of the instrumental parts; in the third section there are composed variants from which the conductor chooses. The style and techniques in *Pli selon pli* have influenced numerous composers, particularly Jean Claude Eloy and Gilbert Amy. The concept of multiple paths through a network of music appears in the middle movement of Heinz Holliger's *Trio* for oboe or English horn, viola, and harp (1966), as well as in works by other composers.

Since the late 1950s, when Boulez expanded his conducting activities, his rate of composition has slackened, and he has begun to rewrite earlier works. He has also adhered more closely to the concept of a "work in progress," an idea that can be traced back in Boulez at least as far as *Structures*. The idea is that a composition is never finished in a definitive form but always remains open to further creation and elaboration.

PRINCIPAL COMPOSITIONS: *Sonatine* for flute, piano (1946, Amphion); *Piano Sonata No. 1* (1946, Amphion); *La Visage nuptial* for soprano, alto, women's chorus, orchestra; poems by René Char (1946–47; revised 1951–52, Heugel); *Piano Sonata No. 2* (1947–48, Heugel); *Livre pour quatour* for string quartet (1948–49, Heugel; version for string orchestra, *Livres pour cordes*, 1968–69, Heugel); *Le Soleil des eaux*, cantata for soprano, men's chorus, orchestra; text by Char (2 versions, 1948–58, 1965); *Polyphonie X* for 18 solo instruments (1951); *Structures I* for 2 pianos (1951–52, UE); *Le Marteau sans maître* for alto, 6 instruments; text by Char (1953–55, UE); *Piano Sonata No. 3* (1956–57, UE); *Structures II* for 2 pianos (1956–61, UE); *Pli selon pli*, portrait of Mallarmé for soprano, orchestra (1957–62, portions published by UE); *Poésie pour pouvoir* for tape, 3 orchestras; text by Henri Michaux (1958); *Figures-Doubles-Prismes* for orchestra (1963–68, UE); *Eclat-Multiples* for orchestra (1965–71, UE); *Domaines* for clarinet, several instruments (1968, UE); *Cummings ist der Dichter* for 16 solo voices and instruments (1970, UE).

PRINCIPAL WRITINGS: *Notes of an Apprenticeship* (New York 1968); *Thoughts on Music* (Cambridge, Mass., 1970).

Josef Häusler

(trans. from German by Jeanne Wolf)

SEE ALSO Asian Music and Western Composition, Austria and Germany, France, Harmony and Counterpoint, Instrumental and Vocal Resources, Orchestration, Performance, Rhythm, Serialism, Switzerland, Text Setting and Usage.

Bozay, Attila (b. Balatonfüzfó, Hungary, 11 August 1939), studied composition with Ferenc Farkas at the Academy of Music in Budapest during 1958–62. Until 1967 he worked at the Hungarian Radio compiling orchestral programs, after which he lived in Paris for a year on a Hungarian state grant. He is currently a free-lance composer in Budapest.

Bozay's output to date consists mainly of chamber music and works for solo instruments. Like his fellow graduates of the 1960s, he did not write exclusively in a folkloristic style but turned immediately to more contemporary idioms, particularly dodecaphony and, to a lesser extent, serialism. He has shown an interest in combining older and newer trends. For instance, his *Variations* for piano (1964) uses the four-line structure, the short-long dotted rhythms, and the descending melodic lines of Hungarian folk music, as well as clusters and tone rows. Another amalgamation can be seen in the *Pezzo sinfonico*, written in Paris (1967); in this work the one-movement format (and apparently the programmatic allusions) of a 19th-century symphonic poem are combined with serial procedures and an emphasis on percussion instruments. Bozay's style also emphasizes long-spanning melodic arches (reminiscent of Berg), folk-derived rhythmic pulsations (reminiscent of Bartók), and contrasting sound textures.

PRINCIPAL COMPOSITIONS: *Papirszeletek* [Slips of Paper], song cycle for soprano, clarinet, cello (1962, EMB); *Wind Quintet* (1962, EMB); *Kiáltások*

[Outcries] for tenor, chamber ensemble (1963); *String Quartet* (1964, EMB); *Variations* for piano (1964, EMB); *Pezzo concertato* for viola, orchestra (1966, EMB); *Pezzo sinfonico* for orchestra (1967, EMB).

Péter Várnai

(trans. from Hungarian by Egon Kenton)

Braga-Santos, Joly (b. Lisbon, 14 May 1924), studied at the Lisbon Conservatory (1934–43: composition with Luis de Freitas-Branco, also privately with Freitas-Branco until 1945), the Venice Conservatory (1948, conducting with Hermann Scherchen), in Gravesano, Switzerland (1957–58, electronic music and acoustics), and the Rome Conservatory (1959–60, composition with Virgilio Mortari). He conducted the Oporto Radio Symphony Orchestra during 1955–59. In 1961 he became assistant conductor of the National Broadcasting Symphony Orchestra. He was one of the founders of the organization Portuguese Musical Youth. The two major influences on his style have been the modality of ancient Portuguese folk music and the Portuguese polyphonists of the 16th and 17th centuries. Since 1961 his music has grown increasingly chromatic and atonal.

PRINCIPAL COMPOSITIONS: *Symphonic Overtures Nos. 1–3* (1945; 1947; 1954, Sassetti); *Symphonies Nos. 1–5* (1946, 1948, 1949, 1950, 1966); *Elegy to Vianna da Motta* for orchestra (1948, Sassetti); *Symphonic Variations on an Alentejo Theme* (1950; version for dance, 1965); *Concerto for String Orchestra* (1950, Sassetti); *Viver ou morrer*, one-act opera (1952); *Merope*, 3-act opera (1959, Sassetti); *Viola Concerto* (1960, Sassetti); *Divertissement* for orchestra (1961, Sassetti); *3 Symphonic Sketches* (1962, Sassetti); *Symphonietta* for chamber orchestra (1963, Sassetti); *Requiem for Pedro de Freitas-Branco* for vocal soloists, chorus, orchestra (1964, Gulbenkian); *Double Concerto* for violin, cello (1966, SA); *Concertant Variations* for harp, orchestra (1967, Gulbenkian); *Trilogia das barcas*, three-act opera (1969, Gulbenkian).

Brant, Henry (Dreyfus) (b. Montreal, 15 Sept 1913), studied with his father, a professional violinist, and as early as 1921 was playing homemade instruments in a backyard orchestra for which he composed his first experimental music. He attended the McGill Univ. Conservatorium (1926–29) and in 1929 moved with his family to New York City, where he continued his studies at the Institute of Musical Art (1929–34; composition with Leonard Mannes, piano with James Friskin) and at the Juilliard School (1932–34, composition with

Rubin Goldmark). He also studied composition privately with Wallingford Riegger (1930,) 1931) and George Antheil (1934, 1935) and conducting with Fritz Mahler (1938, 1939). During the 1930s he earned his living as an orchestrator and arranger for such musicians as Andre Kostelanetz and Benny Goodman. In the 40s he also composed and conducted for radio, ballet, and films in New York, and during the 50s and 60s he extended these activities to Hollywood and Europe. Such practical experiences as these gave him an intimate knowledge of instruments, instrumental technique, and orchestration. He has taught composition and orchestration at several schools, among them Columbia Univ. (1945–52), Juilliard (1947–54), and Bennington College (since 1957). In his teaching and conducting he was among the early proponents of such innovators as Charles Ives and Harry Partch, and he was among the first to put into practice (in his classes) the concept of group-composing, in which as many as 20 student composers collaborate in the production of a single large work.

Brant's output comprises over 80 orchestral, chamber, choral, and solo instrumental pieces, in addition to music for films and theater. His music shows great sensitivity towards sound per se. He has used nonconventional sound sources, such as kitchen hardware (*Music for a Five and Dime Store*, 1931); extensions of familiar instruments, such as his concept of an eight-member string family based on violin proportions (*Consort for True Violins*, 1966) and *Angels and Devils* (1931), a flute concerto with an orchestra of piccolos, flutes, and alto flutes; orchestras of pitched and unpitched percussion (*Origins*, 1952); and choral heterophony both declaimed and sung (*December*, 1955). In the early 1950s he began using antiphonal textures involving the entire area of a concert hall (*Antiphony 1* for five separated orchestral groups, 1953). The concept has been expanded in such works as *Millennium 2* (1954), in which the audience is completely surrounded by brass and percussion; *The Grand Universal Circus* (1956), in which unrelated music-dramatic events take place simultaneously in different parts of the theater; *Voyage 4* (1963), in which the vertical wall space as well as the space below the floor is occupied by performers; and *Windjammer* (1969), in which the players walk through the hall according to specified routes, while performing continuously.

Contrast of all kinds is central to Brant's thinking. "By 1950," he has written, "I had come to feel that single-style music, no matter how experimental or full of variety, could no longer evoke the new stresses, layered insanities, and multidirectional assaults of contemporary life on the spirit. Perhaps if the music itself were many layered, multidirectional, and hammered together out of irreconcilable elements, it could speak more expressively of the human predicament. This straightforward solution presented itself: To pit against each other two (preferably more) entirely different kinds of music—a combination, say, as heterogeneous as something suggesting a Dixieland band versus a Balinese gamelan versus a military cortège" (liner notes for the Desto all-Brant recording). It was to clarify and heighten such contrasts that he began to explore the spatial separation of sound sources; he now considers the spatial plan of each work an essential part of its internal grammar. Since the 50s each of his pieces has comprised "at least two distinct ensemble groups, each of which keeps to its own style, highly contrasted to the styles of the other groups, retains its own rhythmic, harmonic, and instrumental scheme consistently throughout, and is assigned to its own specific, isolated position in the concert hall. There is no interchange of style or material from group to group." To achieve "an elaborate but natural-sounding complexity," he avoids all unusual technical difficulties in the individual parts (except when writing solos for particular virtuosos), and to this same end he began in 1951 to call for "controlled improvisation," leaving pitch choices to the performers but specifying tone quality, range, dynamics, articulation, and rhythmic character. This he found made complex textures instantly playable. He has also used similar procedures to allow for controlled rhythmic improvisation.

Brant is a skilled flutist, keyboard performer, and percussionist; he also collects and performs on non-Western wind and percussion instruments. The elaborate organ cadenzas in the recordings of *Kingdom Come* (1970, Desto recording) and *Hieroglyphics 3* (1958, CRI) are played by him, likewise the 11 bravura instrumental parts which make up *Machinations* (1970, Desto).

PRINCIPAL COMPOSITIONS (published by MCA Music; all works from 1953 on specify various separated groupings of instruments): *Angels and Devils*, concerto for 11 flutes (1931, revised 1956); *Origins*, percussion symphony (1952); *Antiphony 1* for 5 separated orchestral groups, 5 conductors (1953); *Ceremony*, triple concerto for violin, oboe, cello, soprano, alto, tenor, bass, divided orchestra, piano 4-hands (1954); *Millennium 2* for soprano, brass, percussion (1954); *December*, cantata for 2 speakers, soprano, tenor, large and small choruses, orchestra (1955); *Encephalograms 2* for soprano, piccolo, oboe, clarinet, harp, percussion, organ, piano (1955); *Labyrinth 1* for 4 woodwinds, brass or for string orchestra, 4 solo women's voices ad lib (1955); *On the Nature of Things* for orchestra (1956); *The Grand Universal Circus*, spatial theater piece for 8 singing and speaking voices, 32 choristers, 16 instruments (1956); *Hieroglyphics 3* for solo viola, harp, timpani, chimes, celesta, harp, optional voice, and organ (1957); *Mythical Beasts* for mezzo-soprano, chamber orchestra (1958); *The Children's Hour* for 6 vocal soloists, chorus, 2 trumpets, 2 trombones, organ, jazz drums, percussion (1958); *Dialogue in the Jungle* for soprano and tenor singers and declaimers, winds, percussion (1959); *The Crossing* for violin, cello, oboe (soprano saxophone), glockenspiel, voice (1959); *Atlantis* for speaker, mezzo-soprano, chorus, orchestra, band, percussion—4 separated groups (1960); *The Fire Garden* for soprano, chorus, flute, piccolo, harp, piano, percussion (1960); *Violin Concerto with Lights* (1961); *Fire in Cities* for chorus, orchestra, 2 pianos—3 separated groups, 3 conductors; text by the composer (1961); *Barricades* for oboe (soprano saxophone), piano, hand organ (clarinet, bassoon, trombone), strings, xylophone, piccolo, tenor (1961); *Headhunt* for solo trombone, bassoon, bass clarinet, double bass (cello), chimes, timpani (1962); *Vovage 4* for 3 orchestral groups, 3 conductors (1963); *Millennium 4* for 2 trumpets, horn, trombone, euphonium (1963); *Verticals Ascending* for 2 orchestral groups, 2 conductors (1967); *Kingdom Come* for 2 orchestras, organ (1970); *Machinations* for E♭ flute, ceramic flute, double flageolet, double ocarina, organ, harp, percussion (1970). List to 1960: *Composers of the Americas* 6:24–36.

PRINCIPAL WRITINGS: "Space as an Essential Aspect of Musical Composition," *Contemporary Composers on Contemporary Music* ed. by E. Schwartz and B. Childs (New York 1967):221–42.

BIBL.: Henry Cowell, "Current Chronicle," *Musical Quarterly* 40/3; Stewart Sankey, "H. B.'s Grand Universal Circus," *Juilliard Review* (fall 1956):21–37; Theodore Strongin, "Composers on Main Street," *ACA Bulletin* 12/1:1–6.

John Vinton

SEE ALSO Dance, Instrumental and Vocal Resources, Orchestration.

Braun, Peter Michael (b. Wuppertal, Germany, 2 Dec 1936), studied at the Städtisches Konservatorium in Dortmund (1948–56), the Staatliche Hochschule für Musik, Cologne (1956–59, 1965–68; composition with Frank Martin, Bernd Alois Zimmermann; conducting, Wolfgang von der Nahmer; electronic music, Herbert Eimert), and at the Nordwestdeutsche Musikakademie, Detmold (1959–61, composition with Giselher Klebe). He is working as a free-lance composer, pianist, and lecturer. His music has been influenced by Debussy's refinement of tone color and juxtapositions of sound and silence, Stockhausen's group-composition techniques and use of synthetic noise, and Ligeti's concepts of texture and use of clusters.

PRINCIPAL COMPOSITIONS (published by Gerig unless otherwise noted): *Trio* for violin, cello, piano (1958, unpub.); *4 Pieces* for chamber orchestra (1958–59); *Thesis-Medium* for piano (1960, revised 1967); *Essay* for oboe (1960); *Monophonie* for Spanish or electric guitar (1961–67); *Wind Sextet, after a picture by Georges Mathieu* for flute, oboe, clarinet, trumpet, horn, bassoon (1961); *Ereignisse, "Hommage à Edgard Varèse,"* on tape (1966–68, unpub.); *Transfer* for orchestra (1967–68); *Variété* for orchestra (1968–69).

PRINCIPAL WRITINGS: "Max Reger—Musiker des 20. Jahrhunderts," *Neue Zeitschrift für Musik* 5:175–78.

Brazil ranks with Argentina, Chile, and Mexico as one of the most musically developed countries in Latin America. The biggest musical centers of the country are Rio de Janeiro and São Paulo, the capitals of the union's most industrialized states. There is also intense musical activity in other state capitals, such as Recife, Salvador, Belo Horizonte, Curitiba, Brasília, and Pôrto-Alegre. Brazil's musical life is thus more decentralized than that of Argentina or Mexico (where it is almost totally concentrated in Buenos Aires and Mexico City), and in this respect Brazil is comparable to the U.S. The Brazilian composer, however, cannot earn a living from his music alone and usually supports himself by teaching or working for the various cultural organizations and universities.

Most of the official (subsidized) orchestras, opera houses, and concert societies confine their repertories to European works written c.1750–c.1920. Some change may be forthcoming at the Municipal Theater in Rio; Britten's *Peter Grimes* was produced there in 1967 and Berg's *Lulu* in 1970. Other new operas have been promised for the near future.

After 1940 some isolated modern-music groups began to be formed, mainly in Rio and São Paulo. They were all short-lived. The first and most important was the Grupo Música Viva (1940–48), whose founders were the German composer H. J. Koellreutter (b. 1915) and his Brazilian disciples Cláudio Santoro (b. 1919) and César Guerra-Peixe (b. 1914). Koellreutter had brought dodecaphony to Brazil when he came in 1938 (he remained until 1960), and the group used the 12-tone method as its alternative to the nationalism then rampant in the country. Its activities, centered in Rio, included concerts of works by Schoenberg, Berg, Webern, and youthful works by its members and other new talents from Brazil and South America, public lectures and radio programs, exchanges of scores with European and Latin American groups, and even publishing a magazine. After the group fell apart Santoro and Guerra-Peixe embraced nationalism. Koellreutter, however, moved to the northeastern state of Bahia and created the Free Music Seminars of Bahia Univ.; there until 1960 he continued his fight for contemporary music. During this same period he also conducted the International Summer Courses at Teresópolis, a popular mountain resort town outside Rio. Younger Brazilian composers who attended these courses had the benefit of such instructors as Ernst Krenek and Wolfgang Fortner.

No other groups of young composers were formed until after 1960. Those who preferred non-nationalist approaches were discouraged by the indifference shown their works, and they lived almost in hiding; some observors have even concluded that Brazil somehow lacked the generation of composers that should have come to light at this time. After 1960 the Grupo Música Nova was organized in Santos, a coastal city in the state of São Paulo; the Grupo Musical Renovador appeared in Rio; the Sociedade Pró-Música Brasileira appeared in the city of São Paulo; and the Grupo de Compositores da Bahia appeared in Bahia. Only the first and last of these, which became affiliated with universities, have survived; their founders were all disciples of the Swiss composer Ernst Widmer (b. 1927), a pupil of Willy Burkhard at the Zurich Conservatory who has lived in Brazil since 1956.

The Santos group holds yearly festivals of contemporary music that have featured recent works of Stockhausen, Pousseur, Ligeti, Nono, Berio, and others. The Bahia group, consisting of about five composers, has presented works by its members in annual festivals since 1966 and has made plans to increase its scope by including works from the rest of Brazil, the Americas, and Europe. Another group that has been working for contemporary music is Juventude Musical Brasileira led by Eleazar de Carvalho, musical director of the Rio-based Brazilian Symphony. This group was responsible for two Festivals of Avant-Garde Music (1962, 1966) and for the First Inter-American Festival of Rio de Janeiro (1967)

at which some important works of the Americas had their premieres. In 1969 De Carvalho helped Cláudio Santoro organize the first Festival of Avant-Garde Music of the Americas, performed by the Brazilian Symphony with financial backing from the state government. One of the founders of the earlier Grupo Música Viva, Edino Krieger, persuaded the Guanabara state government to create in 1969 the first Guanabara Music Festival, which was the greatest stimulus ever given younger Brazilian composers. Held in Rio, it presented 16 premieres of Brazilian works (chosen in competition), eight of them by composers who had never before heard their music performed. The second Guanabara Music Festival (1970) presented 24 premieres, including works from Brazil, other Latin American countries, and the U.S. In March 1971 several groups of Brazilian composers from different areas founded the Brazilian Society of Contemporary Music, now affiliated with the ISCM, to promote the performance of new music. The society has also established a Brazilian Information Center to distribute scores and tapes.

The radio station of the Ministry of Education and Culture gives generous support to contemporary music. Its broadcasts reach all parts of the country and a large portion of the rest of Latin America. Once a week there is a program devoted entirely to the music of our time. The station exchanges tapes with other broadcasters around the world, with festival organizers, and also in conjunction with UNESCO's annual International Rostrum of Composers. Thus Brazilians can hear new foreign works almost as soon as they are first presented abroad. This station was also the first broadcasting organization in Brazil to commission composers of both the older and younger generations. The resulting compositions are regularly presented by the station's orchestra, chorus, wind quintet, and chamber ensemble. Educational television only recently appeared in Brazil, but it is soon expected to have a nationwide network carrying significant music programs.

Little music is printed in Brazil outside of teaching pieces and other easy-to-play compositions. A few ambitious programs for the printing of symphonic works have been started from time to time, but none has lasted long. The outlook for recordings is better: the Ministry of Educational Radio is producing a comprehensive survey of Brazilian music with special emphasis on contemporary developments. The first records appeared in 1970 and 12 more LPs followed in 1971.

All Brazilian institutions where composition is taught are associated with the Ministry of Education or with a university. The oldest and most conservative is the School of Music of the Univ. of Rio, founded in the 19th century as the National Music Institute. It ignores modern music altogether. So do the Brazilian Conservatory of Music in Rio and the Drama and Music Conservatory in São Paulo. The better composers turn away from all three and pursue advanced study under private instructors (usually foreigners temporarily established in the country, like Koellreutter, Lamberto Baldi, Krenek, and Fortner) or abroad. A few schools are more forward looking. At Bahia University's Free Music Seminars, composition is taught with excellent results under the direction of Widmer. Another example is the Pro Arte Music Seminars in Rio founded by Koellreutter. Camargo Guarnieri (b. 1907) holds private courses in São Paulo, but his students tend to follow their master's nationalistic ideas and to repudiate more current outlooks. Opportunities for Brazilians to study abroad usually come from foreign institutions. In 1958 Edino Krieger went to London at the invitation of the British Council. In 1962 Gilberto Mendes, Rogerio Duprat, and Damiano Cozzela attended the summer course at Darmstadt, where they worked with Pousseur, Boulez, and Stockhausen. In 1963–64, thanks to a Rockefeller Foundation grant, I attended courses at the Torcuato Di Tella Institute in Buenos Aires, and in 1964 Santoro spent a year in West Berlin on a Ford Foundation fellowship. The Ministry of Foreign Relations has financed travel by composers to international festivals where their works were being presented. All of these contacts, coming about mostly since 1960, have helped to break down the isolationism that had previously blocked musical growth in Brazil.

Until his death, Heitor *Villa-Lobos (1887–1959) dominated Brazilian music and thereby maintained the country's taste for nationalism. There is a vast store of folk material for such music to draw upon. The four ethnic strains that provide the most important musical resources are the Portuguese with their European culture; the African slaves with their percussion instruments and mystical-religious songs and superstitions; and, to a lesser extent, the Spaniards who conquered neighboring countries; and the Indians. The enormousness of Brazil's territory and the roughness of her terrain resulted in the scattering and isolation of these groups over the centuries so that only

now a gigantic road-building program has begun to reestablish communication. In the north and northeast (and particularly in those states that are rich in folklore: Ceará, Rio Grande do Norte, Paraíba, Pernambuco, and Bahia), there is a song type using pentatonic scales, lowered sevenths, and raised fourths; these scale formations probably originated after the Jesuits introduced Gregorian chant in the 1500s. The Negro slaves who came to this region brought a rhythmic, syncopated music extraordinarily varied in its accent patterns and using an abundance of drums. It changes its name from place to place depending on the dialect spoken (*maracatu, catimbó,* or *macumba* in Pernambuco and Paraíba; *candomblé* in Bahia). The popular urban music of Brazil, such as the samba of Rio, was born from various folk elements, standardized to fit commercial purposes. In the south, especially in the lowermost state of Rio Grande do Sul, the music resembles Argentine folk varieties. There in pampa country one finds the typically gaucho rhythmic forms in 6/8 meter that do not appear elsewhere.

Of the nationalist composers only Villa-Lobos achieved a complete fusion of the various elements that make up Brazil's musicality. Even in his output, however, European and Brazilian elements are not always integrated. The symphonies, concertos, and sonatas contain isolated folk references within a traditional context. His other works fuse European, African, and Indian elements completely, particularly the *Nonetto,* the *Chôros,* the *Proles do Bébé,* the *Descobrimento do Brasil,* and the *Bachianas brasileiras.* So organic is the fusion in these works that the *Chôros,* particularly their orchestration, could influence a composer like Messiaen, far removed in many ways from Villa-Lobos. Francisco Mignone (b. 1897) went through several phases before he arrived at a combination of Afro-Brazilian elements. At present he is experimenting with dodecaphony and applying it to choral works such as *Pequeno oratório de Santa Clara* (1962) and a series of Masses. Oscar Lorenzo-Fernandez (1897–1948) initiated a sort of national neoclassicism with sonata form as its basic element. His *Trio brasileiro* (1923) typifies his use of folk or popular themes treated according to sonata procedures. Camargo *Guarnieri (b. 1907) has also tried to fuse ethnic and classic elements. The refined, strongly musical results he has achieved can be seen in his *String Quartet No. 3,* *Symphony No. 4,* and *Piano Concerto No. 3* (all 1962–64).

As is true elsewhere, younger composers in

Brazil are making use of the whole gamut of contemporary techniques and procedures. Nationalism is now a movement of the past. Yet younger composers seem to retain a Brazilian identity in their musical exuberance, their fondness for colorful orchestration and novel uses of percussion, and in the constant rhythmic impulse in their music unconsciously derived from their daily contact with the drum beats that furnish a background for the mystical-religious practices of a large part of the population. These traits are most prominent among composers in Rio and Bahia. Those of São Paulo City and Santos are closer to Stockhausen, Boulez, and Pousseur and to the techniques acquired by most of them during apprenticeships at Darmstadt. Three of the latter have worked with new types of notation allowing various kinds of performance freedom within a conditioned framework. These are Gilberto *Mendes (b. 1922), Rogério *Duprat (b. 1932), Damiano Cozzella (b. 1929), and Olivier Toni (b. 1926). José-Antonio *Prado (b. 1943) stands apart from this group; he uses techniques learned in France under Messiaen, and his music often has a strong mystical flavor. In Rio Cláudio *Santoro (b. 1919) renewed his pre-1948 interest in dodecaphony around 1960 and in the late 60s began working with proportional notation. Beginning in 1963 Edino *Krieger (b. 1928) began blending a previous interest in dodecaphony with a neoclassicism that had been largely influenced by Hindemith. His most recent works explore new uses of instruments and sound textures. My own development began within a nationalistic context and moved about 1963 to serial procedures. In 1967 I began working with proportional notation designed to yield clusters and sound blocks.

BIBL.: Vasco Mariz, *Figuras da música brasileira contemporánea*, 2nd ed. (Pôrto, Portugal 1970); ——, *Música brasileña contemporánea* (Rosario, Argentina, 1952).

Marlos Nobre

(trans. from Portuguese by Luiz-Flavio de Faro)

Bridge, Frank (b. Brighton, England, 26 Feb 1879; d. Eastbourne, 10 Jan 1941), studied composition with Charles Stanford at the Royal College of Music (1899–1903). He played in the Joachim and the English String Quartets as violist (1906–15) and conducted professionally before World War I; later he devoted himself to composition and to some

private teaching. About 1920 he broke with his earlier competent but conventional style: "Balanced sentences were broken up, melodic lengths reduced. Preponderance of augmented intervals over minor, major and perfect removed the whole implications of major and minor triads and their inversions. The fringes of polytonality were touched. . . . Continuity of the classical sort was inevitably replaced by a procession of shorter spans, swiftly changeable in mood, pace and intensity." He continued to exhibit a "love of swift and impatient climaxes, the lure of beauty of sound for its own sake" (Howells: 214; see bibl.). He also introduced polytonality into his chamber works in the 1920s.

PRINCIPAL COMPOSITIONS (published by Augener unless otherwise noted): *Phantasy Quartet* for piano quartet (1910); *The Sea*, suite for orchestra (1910–11, Stainer); *Love Went A-Riding* for voice, piano (1914, Rogers); *2 Poems* after Richard Jefferies for orchestra (1915); *Piano Sonata* (1921–24); *String Quartets Nos. 3–4* (1926, 1937); *There Is a Willow Grows Aslant a Brook* for chamber orchestra (1927); *Piano Trio No. 2* (1929); *Violin Sonata* (1930, Galaxy); *Phantasm*, rhapsody for piano, orchestra (1931, Galaxy); *The Christmas Rose*, children's opera (1932, Galaxy); *Rebus*, overture (1940, Boosey).

BIBL.: Benjamin Britten, "Early Influences: a Tribute to F. B. (1879–1941)," *Composer* 19:2–3; Edwin Evans, "Modern British Composers: F. B.," *Musical Times* (Feb 1919):55–61; Herbert Howells, "F. B.," *Music and Letters* 22:208–15; P. J. Pirie, "A Note on F. B.," *Tempo* 66–67: 27–32.

Brindle, Reginald Smith, see under Smith Brindle

Britain, see Great Britain

Britten, (Edward) **Benjamin** (b. Lowestoft, Suffolk, England, 22 Nov 1913), showed exceptional musical promise from his earliest years and took music lessons during school vacations with Harold Samuel (piano) and Frank Bridge (composition). He began study at the Royal College of Music in 1930 (piano with Arthur Benjamin, composition with John Ireland) but found the atmosphere stultifying. He left in 1934 and was soon offered a permanent contract by Ralph Hawkes, the publisher, and a job by the G.P.O. Film Unit. During 1935–39 he wrote music for over 20 films, an experience that taught him adaptability, economy, and speed.

In spring 1939, discouraged by political events, he went to Canada for a few months, then settled in Amityville near New York City. He returned to England in March 1942 and spent the remainder of the war giving concerts. He then settled in his native Suffolk. In 1947 he founded the English Opera Group and in 1948 the Aldeburgh Festival, which has since been held annually. He has toured widely as conductor and pianist.

Britten is predominantly a vocal composer. His output to 1970 included 11 operas, 13 song cycles, 10 works in cantata form, as well as numerous single songs, choruses, and vocal works that defy classification. His instrumental works avoid well-tried forms in favor of new ones, and although he is generally least successful when he attempts a prolonged essay without words, his *Cello Symphony* (1963) overcame this difficulty.

His early works already showed the eclecticism that was to be a hallmark of his style. He could impart the same clarity of thought to the complicated *Sinfonietta* (1932), influenced by Stravinsky and Schoenberg, as to the simple and diatonic *Hymn to the Virgin* (1930). The dominant figures of the early 20th century have had far less influence on him than have certain of the great composers of the past and his own teacher Frank Bridge. From Bridge, a hard taskmaster, he learned the necessity of complete technical assurance. Britten acknowledges Bridge too as the source of his own polytonality, and one might add that Bridge did not, as many teachers might have done, discourage his pupil's innate romanticism. The older composers whom Britten admires include Purcell, Mozart, Schubert, Verdi, and Mahler. They are all melodists whose music has great aural appeal, and the same quality is present in Britten's music. He has never abandoned the natural harmonic system and the scales that grow from it, without which melodies in the traditional sense cannot be written. (This is one reason for his popularity.)

Like Stravinsky before 1950, Britten has always reserved the right to use the simplest diatonic harmonies, to which he imparts a flavor of his own (especially through hints at the Lydian fourth and the Aeolian seventh and through combinations of tonic and dominant harmonies, the latter perhaps borrowed from Stravinsky). This, together with his occasional use of extreme chromaticism (and even of free serial techniques in *Cantata Academica, War Requiem,* and *The Turn of the Screw*), gives him a large harmonic vocabulary that enables him to depict the widest range of emotional meanings, a goal to which he holds fast.

Britten's greatest facility is for creating compositions that are unique in form and conception and consequently easily memorable (another reason for his popularity). Original ideas, such as the combination of the Requiem Mass with Wilfred Owen's war poems in the *War Requiem* or the foundation of the guitar *Nocturnal* on a piece by Dowland, seem to come more readily to him than to other composers. These works also illustrate two notable stylistic traits. One is the use of two distinct and contrasting elements in a single work, the alternation of which is a favorite formal device and one that makes for easy comprehension on first hearing. The other stylistic trait is the incorporation of other composers' music, e.g., of Dowland in *Lachrymae,* of Purcell in *The Young Person's Guide,* of plainsong in the church operas and *A Ceremony of Carols,* and of the canon *Sumer Is Icumen In* in the *Spring Symphony.* By this and by his many arrangements of Purcell, Rossini, and folksongs, he has disdained an isolationist position while paradoxically anticipating some procedures of more experimental composers.

Virtually all Britten's compositions were written with specific artists and a specific event in mind, although they prove to be entirely adaptable to other situations. The singing of tenor Peter Pears has inspired Britten's finest works for solo voice (e.g., *Serenade, Nocturne, Canticles 1* and *3*) and dominates all the operas. (Pears and Britten have also given excellent performances of lieder by Schubert and others.) The playing of cellist Mstislav Rostropovich drew from Britten a sonata, a symphony, and two cello suites. Despite his appreciation of professionals, Britten has always encouraged amateurs, especially children, and many of his works are either designed for amateur performance (e.g., *Noye's Fludde, Let's Make an Opera*) or have prominent parts for boys' voices (e.g., *A Midsummer Night's Dream, The Golden Vanity*).

Britten's contributions to English musical life, his enrichment of so many musical genres, and his restoration of English opera (beginning with *Peter Grimes*) have done more than anything else to raise his country's musical standing in the eyes of the world. The renaissance that grew up under Vaughan Williams, Holst, and Walton may be said to culminate in him. His influence in England has been strong, especially on composers such as

Richard Rodney Bennett, Nicholas Maw, and Gordon Crosse but also on more radical composers (Peter Maxwell Davies, Harrison Birtwistle, David Bedford, Roger Smalley) who share his concern with amateurs and his capacity for imparting to each work a distinct personality.

PRINCIPAL COMPOSITIONS (those through Op. 69 published by Boosey, thereafter by Faber): *Sinfonietta* for chamber orchestra, Op. 1 (1932); *A Boy Was Born*, choral variations for men's, women's, and boys' voices, Op. 3; anonymous 15th- and 16th-century texts (1932–33, revised 1955); *Our Hunting Fathers*, symphonic cycle for soprano, orchestra, Op. 8; text by W. H. Auden (1936); *Variations on a Theme of Frank Bridge* for strings, Op. 10 (1937); *Piano Concerto No. 1*, Op. 13 (1938, revised 1945); *Violin Concerto*, Op. 15 (1939, revised 1958); *Les Illuminations* for high voice, strings, Op. 18; text by Arthur Rimbaud (1939); *Sonfonia da Requiem* for orchestra, Op. 20 (1940); *7 Sonnets of Michelangelo* for tenor, piano, Op. 22 (1940); *String Quartet No. 1 in D*, Op. 25 (1941); *A Ceremony of Carols* for treble voices, harp, Op. 28 (1942); *Rejoice in the Lamb*, festival cantata for soloists, chorus, organ, Op. 30 (1943); *Serenade* for tenor, horn, strings, Op. 31 (1943); *Peter Grimes*, 3-act opera, Op. 33; libretto by Montagu Slater after a poem of George Crabbe (1945); *The Holy Sonnets of John Donne* for high voice, piano, Op. 35 (1945); *String Quartet No. 2 in C*, Op. 36 (1945); *The Rape of Lucretia*, 2-act opera, Op. 37; libretto by Ronald Duncan after the play of André Obey (1946, revised 1947); *The Young Person's Guide to the Orchestra*, variations and fugue on a theme of Henry Purcell for narrator, orchestra, Op. 34; text by Eric Crozier (1946); *Albert Herring*, 3-act opera, Op. 39; libretto by Crozier after a story by Guy de Maupassant (1947); *Saint Nicholas*, cantata for tenor, chorus, 4 boy singers, string orchestra, piano duet, percussion, organ, Op. 42; text by Crozier (1948); *Spring Symphony* for soprano, alto, tenor, chorus, boys' choir, orchestra, Op. 44 (1949); *The Little Sweep*, opera from *Let's Make an Opera*, Op. 45; libretto by Crozier (1949); *Billy Budd*, 2-act opera, Op. 50; libretto by E. M. Forster, Crozier after Melville (1951, revised 1960); *Canticle II, Abraham and Isaac* for alto, tenor, piano, Op. 51; text from the Chester miracle play (1952); *Winter Words* for high voice, piano, Op. 52; text by Thomas Hardy (1953); *Gloriana*, 3-act opera, Op. 53; libretto by William Plomer (1953); *The Turn of the Screw*, 2-act opera, Op. 54; libretto by Myfanwy Piper after James (1954); *The Prince of the Pagodas*, ballet, Op. 57; choreography by John Cranko (1956); *Songs from the Chinese* for high voice, guitar, Op. 58; Chinese texts translated by Arthur Waley (1957); *Noye's Fludde*, the Chester miracle play set for soloists, chorus, chamber ensemble, children's orchestra, Op. 59 (1957); *Nocturne* for tenor, 7 instruments, string orchestra, Op. 60 (1958); *6 Hölderlin-Fragmente* for voice, piano, Op. 61 (1958); *Cantata academica, carmen basiliense* for soloists, chorus, orchestra, Op. 62 (1959); *Missa brevis in D* for boys' voices, organ, Op. 63 (1959); *A Midsummer Night's Dream*, 3-act opera, Op. 64; libretto by the composer and Peter Pears after Shakespeare (1960); *Cello Sonata in C*, Op. 65 (1961); *War Requiem* for soloists, chorus, orchestra, chamber orchestra, boys' choir, organ, Op. 66; text by Wilfred Owen and traditional (1961); *Symphony for Violoncello and Orchestra*, Op. 68 (1963); *Cantata misericordium* for tenor, baritone, chorus, string orchestra, piano, harp, timpani, Op. 69; Latin text by Patrick Wilkinson (1963); *Curlew River*, parable for church performance for soloists, chorus, flute/piccolo, horn, viola, double bass, harp, percussion, chamber organ, Op. 71; text by William Plomer (1964); *Songs and Proverbs of William Blake* for baritone, piano, Op. 74 (1965); *Voices for Today*, anthem for chorus, boys' chorus, organ, Op. 75 (1965); *The Poet's Echo*, 6 songs for high voice, piano, Op. 76; poems by Pushkin translated by Pears (1966); *The Burning Fiery Furnace*, parable for church performance for soloists, chorus, chamber ensemble, Op. 77; libretto by Plomer (1966); *The Prodigal Son*, parable for church performance for soloists, chorus, chamber ensemble, Op. 81; libretto by Plomer (1967). List to 1963: *B. B.: A Complete Catalogue of His Works* (London 1963).

PRINCIPAL WRITINGS: *On Receiving the First Aspen Award: A Speech* (London 1964); *The Rape of Lucretia: A Symposium* (London 1948).

BIBL.: Michael Dawney, "Some Notes on Britten's Church Music," *Tempo* 82:13ff.; Peter Evans, "Sonata Structures in Early Britten," *Ibid.*: 2–13; J. W. Garbutt, "Music and Motive in *Peter Grimes*," *Music and Letters* 44:334ff.; Anthony Gishford, ed., *Tribute to B. B. on his 50th Birthday* (London 1963); Imogen Holst, *B.* (London 1966); Patricia Howard, *The Operas of B. B.* (New York 1969); Michael Hurd, *B. B.* (London 1966); Hans Keller, "B. and Mozart," *Music and Letters* 29:17 ff.; Heinrich Lindlar, ed., *B. B.* (Bonn 1954); ——, ed., *B. B.: Das Opernwerk* (Bonn 1955); Donald Mitchell and Hans Keller, eds., *B. B.: A Commentary on his Works* (London 1952); *Tempo* 66–67, a 50th birthday issue; Eric Walter White, *B. B.: A Sketch of his Life and Works* revised ed. (Berkeley-Los Angeles 1970); Percy M. Young, *B.* (London 1966).

Joscelyn Godwin

SEE ALSO Great Britain; Liturgical Music: Christian; Opera; Text Setting and Usage.

Brncic, Gabriel (Oliverio) (b. Santiago, 16 Feb 1942), studied engineering at the Univ. of Chile (1960–64) and music at the National Conservatory (1950–64; composition with Gustavo Becerra-Schmidt, oboe with Gaetano Girardello, viola with Zoltan Fisher) and at the Torcuato Di Tella Institute in Buenos Aires (1965–66; composition with Alberto Ginastera, analysis with Gerardo Gandini, electronic composition with Francisco Kröpfl). Since 1967 he has assisted Kröpfl at the Institute.

PRINCIPAL COMPOSITIONS: *Octet* for brasses (1966); *Dialexis* for 9 percussionists (1966); *Momento, mortus est!* for violin, clarinet, electronic sounds on tape (1967); *Quodlibets 1–24* for various instrumental groups, tape (1967–69); *Viola Concerto* (1967); *Juegos* for string quintet (1967); *¡Volveremos a las montañas!*, third version for electronic sounds on tape (1968); *Puerto Montt* for woman's voice, chorus, chamber orchestra, piano, electronic sounds on tape (1969).

PRINCIPAL WRITINGS (unpublished): *Teoría de la interelación paramétrica* (1966); *Tesis sobre estructura y forma musical contemporánea* (1967–69); *Comentarios acerca de la improvisación colectiva actual* (1969).

Brott, Alexander (b. Montreal, 15 March 1915), studied at the Quebec Academy of Music (1931–32), McGill Univ. (1930–35), and the Juilliard School (1935–39; composition with Bernard Wagenaar, violin with Sascha Jacobsen, conducting with Willem Willeke). He has taught composition, conducting, orchestration, and violin at McGill Univ. since 1939 and is currently chairman of the instrumental department. He was concertmaster and assistant conductor of the Montreal Symphony during 1945–58. In 1939 he founded the McGill Chamber Orchestra and in 1960, the Montreal Pops Orchestra, both of which he directs. He has conducted for the CBC since 1948, and has appeared as guest conductor in Europe, Mexico, Israel, and Russia.

PRINCIPAL COMPOSITIONS (published by CMC): *Songs of Contemplation* for soprano, strings (1940); *From Sea to Sea* for orchestra (1946); *Concordia* for orchestra (1947); *Critics' Corner* for string orchestra (string quartet), percussion (1950); *Violin Concerto* (1950); *Vignettes* for piano (1952); *Sept for 7* for narrator, strings, winds (1955); *Arabesque* for cello, orchestra (1958); *3 Astral Visions* for string orchestra (1960); *Vision of the Dry Bones* for baritone, piano, strings (1960); *Spheres in Orbit* for orchestra (1961); *3 Acts for 4 Sinners* for saxophone quartet (1961); *Triangle, Circle, 4 Squares* for strings (1963); *Centennial Colloquy* for 13 winds (1967); *Centennial Celebration* for narrator, 2 soloists, women's chorus, strings (1967); *Paraphrase in Polyphony*, on a Beethoven canon, for orchestra (1967); *Mini-Minus* for chamber orchestra (1968); *The Young Prometheus* for orchestra, 12 preludes and fugues orchestrated from Beethoven's sketches (1969); *7 Minuets, 6 Canons* for orchestra, orchestrated from Beethoven's sketches (1969); *Spasms for 6* for 6 percussionists (1970); *The Emperor's New Clothes* for narrator, orchestra;

text based on Hans Christian Andersen (1970). List to 1960: *Composers of the Americas* 6:39–41.

PRINCIPAL WRITINGS: *"The Young Prometheus," The Montreal Star* (15 Nov 1969): 17, 20.

Brower, Leo (b. Havana, 1 March 1939) studied during 1959–60 at the Juilliard School, (composition with Vincent Persichetti and Stepan Wolpe) and the Hartt College of Music (composition with Isadore Freed, medieval and renaissance music with Joseph Iadone). During 1960–61 he was a music assistant at Radio Havana, and during 1960–62 he directed the music department of the Instituto de Arte Industria Cinematograficos (IAIC). He also taught harmony, counterpoint, and composition at the National Conservatory in Havana (1961–67). Since 1969 he has been director of the experimental music department of the IAIC. He has received stipends from the Cuban government for work as a concert guitarist (1961–67) and composer (since 1967). In his various professional posts he has played and conducted music by Ives, Cage, Kotoński, Nono, Kagel, Cardew, among other contemporary composers. His musical development has been influenced by this music and by general concepts in the arts, for example the style of Paul Klee and the writings of M. Ghyka and Iannis Xenakis. The social goals of the Cuban revolution have also been an important factor. Most of his work from 1956 to 1962 (over 50 pieces) stemmed from nationalist musical concerns. Contacts with members of the contemporary Polish school (1961), Luigi Nono (1967), and Hans Werner Henze (1969–70) helped stimulate the adoption of contemporary techniques. His *Sonograma I* (1963) was the first piece of indeterminate music in Cuba. He has composed scores for over 40 films and has worked with pop art and mass media productions.

PRINCIPAL COMPOSITIONS: *3 Danzas concertantes* for guitar, string orchestra (1958, Neue Musik); *Variantes* for percussionist (1962); *Sonograma I* for prepared piano (1963); *Sonograma II* for orchestra (1964, Schott); *2 Conceptos del tiempo* for 10 players (1965, EGREM); *Hommage to Mingus*, arioso for jazz combo, orchestra (1965); *Conmutaciones* for prepared piano, 2 percussionists (1966, UNEAC); *Tropos* for orchestra (1967); *La tradición se rompe . . . pero cuesta trabajo* for orchestra (1967–69); *Sonograma III* for 2 pianos (1968, EGREM); *5 Epigrams* for cello (violin), piano (1968); *The Kingdom of This World* for woodwind quintet (1968, Schott); *Rem tene verba sequentur* for string quartet (1969); *Cantigas del tiempo nuevo* for actors, children's chorus, piano, harp, 2 percussionists (1969); *Exaedros* for any 6 players or multiples of 6 players (1969).

PRINCIPAL WRITINGS: *Sintesis de la armonia contemporanea*, vol. I (Havana, EGREM, 196?); "La vanguardia en la música cubana," *Música* (Havana) 1:2–6; "Improvisation in 'Open Forms'," *Ibid.* (1970); "La vanguardia de la música cubana," *Sonda* (Madrid, 1970).

BIBL.: Alejo Carpentier, "Un concierto joven," *El Mundo* (Havana, summer 1966); Juan Vicente Melo, "Urge que Mexico conozca la nueva música cubana," *Siempre!*, supplement (Mexico City, 18 Jan 1967):9–10.

Brown, Earle (b. Lunenburg, Mass., 26 Dec 1926), studied mathematics and engineering at Northeastern Univ., Boston. He attended the Schillinger House School of Music in Boston (1946–50) and studied composition, orchestration, style, and Schillinger techniques with Roslyn Brogue Henning. During 1950–52 he was an authorized teacher of the Schillinger techniques of arranging and composition in Denver. Along with John Cage and David Tudor, he was an associate member of the Music for Magnetic Tape project in New York (1952–55). During 1955–60 he produced the Contemporary Sound Series for TIME Records. He received a Guggenheim Fellowship for 1965–66 and has received many commissions from orchestras and festivals throughout the world. He held the Alton Jones Chair of Composition at the Peabody Conservatory in Baltimore during 1968–70.

Brown's music is largely the result of his association with a variety of arts, particularly the visual arts. Major influences have been the spontaneous improvisatory quality of Jackson Pollock's paintings and the mobile sculpture of Alexander Calder. The purpose of Brown's work is to create a compositional environment that is not fixed but can be shaped and reshaped according to whatever poetic expression the moment requires. Brown believes that if the performer is given a chance to actively participate in creating the work, the music will be more exciting and more intense.

The first published works, written 1950–52, are 12-tone serial compositions based on Schillinger techniques. They involve total organization but are not dependent on the unit 12. In *3 Pieces* and *Perspectives* there are several rhythmic cells, each consisting of specific pitch curves and rhythmic designs. Individual cells are superimposed on other cells, with the density of texture dependent on pitch permutations, e.g., the repositioning of

rhythmic values, the replacing of pitches by rests, and the transposition, absence, or displacement of pitch material. Since rhythm is the foundation and the governing force of the cell, pitch-curve changes are dependent on changes in the rhythmic contour. *Music for Violin, Cello and Piano* has a pointillistic texture that emphasizes the similarities of certain sound qualities among the three instruments (pizzicato on the cello, for instance, related to plucking with the finger inside the piano). A later work, *Pentathis* (1957) also uses Schillinger techniques.

Brown's first graphic scores were produced in 1952–53. Three such scores in *Folio* were the first examples of time notation (now called proportional notation), which does not divide time into precise metrical units but into relative durations whose lengths are suggested by the relative spacing of the notational symbols. In *December 1952* from *Folio*, Brown abandoned the concept of written pitches and constructed a design consisting of lines in differing positions and lengths; these are the stimulus for an improvisation by any group of musicians for any period of time. The first open-form work, aside from a brief experiment for piano by Henry Cowell, was Brown's *25 Pages* for 1–25 pianos (1953). Here the performer or performers are allowed to organize the pages in whatever order they wish. In addition the work is an example of space-time notation: the pitches and durations are specified but, because of the absence of clefs, the pages can be performed either side up.

Random sampling tables were used for *Indices* (1954) to determine the pitches, the groupings, and the instrumentation, as well as the placement of these elements in the total time of the work. The work is based on the probabilities inherent in statistical thinking. The end work might also be called "discontinuous" because each pitch, dynamic, etc., results from a random sampling process and therefore is conceived without relation to or dependence on other pitches, dynamics, etc.

The instrumental works of 1961–63 further develop the open-form and time-notation techniques. Written events, which the conductor may interpret in a percussive or sustained manner, speeded up or slowed down, are written on separate pages. The conductor is free to choose the sequence, juxtaposition, and timing of the events. In *Available Forms II* there are 2 conductors, each conducting 49 instruments. Because neither conductor predetermines what the other shall be doing, two or more different events from two different pages may occur simultaneously. Mobile structures within closed forms appeared in the *String Quartet 1965* and *Corroboree* (1964), in which the performers follow a given sequence of events, the internal details of which may be varied according to the performer's choice. In contrast, *9 Rarebits* (1965) and *Event: Synergy II* (1967–68) are in open form with the sounds specified but the sequence of events not predetermined. The latter uses both graphic and conventional notation.

PRINCIPAL COMPOSITIONS: *3 Pieces* for piano (1951, Schott); *Perspectives* for piano (1952, Schott); *Music for Violin, Cello and Piano* (1952); *Folio*, consisting of 3 works for any number of instruments: *November 1952, December 1952, 1953* (1952–53, AMP); *25 Pages* for 1–25 pianos (1953); *Indices* for chamber orchestra (1954); *Pentathis* for flute, bass clarinet, trumpet, trombone, harp, piano, violin, viola, cello (1957, Schott); *Available Forms I* for 18 musicians on specified instruments (1961, AMP); *Available Forms II* for 98 musicians on specified instruments, 2 conductors (1962, AMP); *Novara* for flute, bass clarinet, trumpet, piano, 2 violins, viola, cello (1962, UE); *From Here* for 20 musicians on specified instruments, 4 optional choruses (1963, UE); *Corroboree* for 3 pianos (1964, UE); *String Quartet 1965* (1965, UE); *9 Rarebits* for 1–2 harpsichords (1965, UE); *Event: Synergy II* for chamber orchestra (1967–68, UE). List to 1965: *Composers of the Americas* 12:18–21.

Sarah S. Meneely

SEE ALSO Indeterminacy, Notation, Rhythm, United States.

Brün, Herbert (b. Berlin, 9 July 1918), attended the Jerusalem Conservatory (1936–38, composition with Stefan Wolpe) and Columbia Univ. (1948–49). During 1945–63 he worked as a free-lance composer, living primarily in Israel and Germany and writing for the theater, radio, and television. He was a writer and lecturer for the German Broadcasting Co., lectured at the Darmstadt summer courses, and made two lecture tours in the U.S. Since 1963 he has been teaching and conducting research at the Univ. of Ill., and in 1969–70 he taught at Ohio State Univ. During 1955–61 Brün conducted research in Paris, Cologne, and Munich on the utilization of electro-acoustics and electronic sound production in musical composition, and in 1963 he extended this research to computer-assisted composition. He has used computers in a number of his compositions since this time. In recent years he has also become increasingly aware of the "political significance of musical ideas—an awareness that keeps growing the more I teach, the more I hear and listen, the more I compose."

PRINCIPAL COMPOSITIONS: *String Quartet No. 1* (1953, IMP); *Trio* for flute, clarinet, bassoon (1953); *String Quartet No. 2* (1957); *Anepigraphe* on tape (1958, EM); *Mobile for Orchestra* (1958, Tonos); *String Quartet No. 3* (1961, Tonos); *Wayfaring Sounds* on tape (1962, EM); *Futility 1964*, electronic sounds and voice on tape (1964); *Gestures for 11* for chamber ensemble (1964, Apogee); *Sonoriferous Loops* for flute, trumpet, double bass, xylophone, marimba, percussion, 2-track tape (1964); *Trio* for flute, double bass, percussion (1964); *Gesto* for piccolo, percussion (1965); *Non sequitur VI* for flute, cello, harp, piano, percussion, 2-track tape (1966); *Trio* for trumpet, trombone, percussion (1966); *3 Pieces* for solo percussion (1967); *Infraudibles*, computer music on tape (1968); *Mutatis mutandis*, composition for interpreters (1968); *Nonet* for chamber ensemble (1969).

PRINCIPAL WRITINGS: "Against Plausibility," *Perspectives* 2/1:43–50; "Betrachtungen eines Beteiligten," *Forum* 130 (Vienna, 1965):598–99; "Ersättning eller analogi?" [Substitute or Analogy?], *Nudita musik* 7 (Stockholm, 1966):27–31; "Chaos and Organization," *Institute of Contemporary Arts Bulletin* 166 (London, 1967):8–11; "Muzyka i informacja," *Res facta* 3 (Crakow, 1969):172–91; "Infraudibles," *Music by Computers* ed. by H. von Foerster and J. Beauchamp (New York 1969):117–21; "mit verdorrten Zungen," *Musik auf der Flucht vor sich selbst* (Munich 1969):45–54; "From Musical Ideas to the Computer and Back," *The Computer and Music* ed. by H. B. Lincoln (Ithaca 1970):23–36; ". . . to hold disclosure, at least with a computer . . .," *The New Music* ed. by Colin Mason (London 1970); "Composition with Computers," *Cybernetic Serendipity* ed. by J. Reichardt (New York 1969):20ff.; *Über Musik und zum Computer* (Karlsruhe 1970).

BIBL.: Burt J. Levy, "H. B.: Three Works for Percussion," *Perspectives* 8/1:136–38.

SEE ALSO Austria and Germany.

Brunswick, Mark (b. New York, 6 Jan 1902; d. London, 26 May 1971), received his early musical training from Rubin Goldmark in New York (1918–23). He then studied counterpoint, fugue, and composition with Ernest Bloch in Cleveland (1923–24) and composition with Nadia Boulanger in Paris (1925–29). A further influence was his contact with Roger Sessions beginning in Cleveland in 1924. Brunswick was head of the theory and composition department of New York's Greenwich House Music School during 1938–43. During 1946–67 he was a professor at the City College of New York and until 1965 chairman of the music department.

PRINCIPAL COMPOSITIONS (published by CFE unless otherwise noted): *2 Movements* for string quartet (1925, UE); *Lysistrata Suite* for mezzo-soprano, women's chorus, orchestra (1930);

Fantasia for viola (1932, Rivers); *A Fragment of Sappho* (= 2nd movement of *Eros and Death*) for chorus (1932, UE); *Symphony in B Flat* (1945); *Eros and Death*, choral symphony for mezzo-soprano, chorus, orchestra; texts by Lucretius, Sappho, Emperor Hadrian (1932, 1950–54; unpub.); *7 Trios* for string quartet (1956); *Quartet* for violin, viola, cello, double bass (1957); *Septet* for wind quintet, viola, cello (1958); *5 Madrigals* for chamber chorus, viola, cello, double bass (1958–66); *The Master Builder*, opera after Ibsen (1959– ; Act I, CFE); *4 Songs*; texts by the composer (1964); *Air with Toccata* for string orchestra (1967).

PRINCIPAL WRITINGS: "Roger Huntington Sessions," *Modern Music* 10/4:182–87; "After Munich," *Ibid.* 16/1:3–9; program notes for the third concert in the New Friends of Music series (New York 1940–41); "Tonality and Perspective," *Musical Quarterly* 29:426–39; "Beethoven's Tribute to Mozart in *Fidelio*," *Ibid.* 31:29–32.

BIBL.: Miriam Gideon, "The Music of M. B.," *ACA Bulletin* 13/1:1–10; Gerald Warfield, "An Interview with M. B.," *Contemporary Music Newsletter* (New York) 3/3–4:1–2.

Bruynèl, Ton (b. Utrecht, 26 Jan 1934), studied at the Utrecht Conservatory (composition with Henk Badings and Kees van Baaren, piano with Wolfgang Wijdeveld). He has worked at the electronic music studios of Utrecht Univ. and the Technical Univ. at Delft. In 1957 he established a studio of his own in Utrecht.

PRINCIPAL ELECTRONIC COMPOSITIONS: *Resonance I*, theater piece in collaboration with the Eleo Pomare dance group, sculptor Chinkichi Tajiri, painter Sam Middleton (1960–62); *Reflexen*, Burmese-drum sounds on tape (1961); *Collage Resonance II* on tape, created in collaboration with poet Gerrit Kouwenaar (1963); *Reliëf* for organ, 4-track tape (1965, Donemus); *Mobile* on 2-track tape (1965, Donemus); *Milieu* for organ, 2-track tape (1965); *Freem*, film score (1965); *Arc* for organ (2 players), 4-track tape (1966–67, Donemus); *Décor*, ballet score on tape (1967–68); *Mécanique* for wind quintet, 2-track tape (1968, Donemus); *Signs* for wind quintet, 2-track tape (1968–69, Donemus).

Bucchi, Valentino (b. Florence, 29 Nov 1916), studied at Florence Univ. (1935–39, music history with Fausto Torrefranca) and the Cherubini Conservatory in Florence (1935–40, composition with Luigi Dallapiccola and Vito Frazzi). During 1938–42 he was a critic for *La Nazione* in Florence. He has taught at the Florence Conservatory (1945–52, 1954–57) and the Venice Conservatory (1952–54) and is director of the Morlacchi Conservatory

in Perugia (since 1957) and a member of the council of the Accademia Chigiana in Siena (since 1968). During 1958–60 he was artistic director of the Accademia Filarmonica Romana and during 1963–65, of the Teatro Comunale in Bologna. Since 1969 he has been a musical consultant for Radio Italiano. He is predominantly a composer for the theater, and his work has been influenced by his studies of medieval dramatic compositions and baroque opera.

PRINCIPAL COMPOSITIONS: *4 Liriche* for soprano, piano (1934–40, S-Z); *Il giuoco del Barone*, 1-act opera (1936–37, revised 1955; S-Z); *Sonatina* for piano (1938, S-Z); *3 Poesie di G. Noventa* for soprano, piano (1940, S-Z); *5 Madrigali*, "La dolce pena," for soprano, 2 flutes, 2 trumpets, 2 violas, cello, double bass, harp (1947, S-Z); *Pianto delle creature*, cantata for voice, orchestra (1947, Carisch); *Il cielo è rosso*, film score (1949); *Cori della pietà morta* for chorus, orchestra (1949–50, S-Z); *Ballata del silenzio* for orchestra (1951, S-Z); *Febbre di vivere*, film score (1953); *Il contrabasso*, 1-act "opera grottesca" (1953–54, S-Z); *Racconto siciliano*, ballet for 4 dancers, 2 pianos (1955, Carisch); *String Quartet* (1956, Carisch); *Mirandolina*, "balletto giocoso" (1956–57, Carisch; *Suite* for orchestra, 1958, Carisch); *Concerto in rondò* for piano, orchestra (1957, Forlitesi); *Concerto lirico* for violin, string orchestra (1958, Carisch); *Una notte in paradiso*, 1-act "cantofavola" (1960, Carisch); *Banditi e orgosolo*, film score (1961); *Fantasia* for strings (1963, Carisch); *Concerto grottesco* for double-bass, strings (1966–67, Ricordi); *Il coccodrillo*, 4-act opera (1968–69, Ricordi); *Concerto* for solo clarinet (1969, Ricordi); *Lettres de la religieuse portugaise* for soprano (1970, Ricordi). Bucchi has also made arrangements of older music: *Li Jeus de Robin et de Marion* based on Adam de la Halle (1951–52, S-Z); *Laudes evangelii*, "choreographic mystery" based on 13th-century laude for soloists, chorus, orchestra (1952, Carisch); *L'Orfeo* based on Monteverdi (1966, Carisch).

PRINCIPAL WRITINGS: *L'Orfeo di Claudio Monteverdi* (Florence 1949); "Seraphita," *La rassegna musicale* 31:438–42.

BIBL.: Fedele D'Amico, *I casi della musica* (Milan 1962):30–33 et passim; Augusto Hermet, *Poesia e poetica musicale di V. B.* (Florence 1954); Leonardo Pinzauti, *Il Maggio Musicale Fiorentino dalla prima alla trentesima edizione* (Florence 1967); Renato Sabatini, *Medaglioni musicali umbri: V. B.* (Perugia 1968); *Soggetti di opere liriche scelte e riassunte*, vol. I (Turin 1959):54–57.

Bucci, Mark (b. New York, 26 Feb 1924), studied at St. John's Univ., Brooklyn, N.Y. (1941–42), the Juilliard School (1947–51; composition with Vittorio Giannini, Frederick Jacobi), Tanglewood (1949, composition with

Aaron Copland), and the Columbia-Princeton Electronic Music Center (1967–69; electronic composition with Vladimir Ussachevsky, Mario Davidowsky). He also studied privately with Tibor Serly (1944–46). He was brought up in a family of theater musicians and describes his work as influenced by his home environment and by the music of Bartók and Puccini.

PRINCIPAL COMPOSITIONS: *13 Clocks*, a musical based on Thurber (1952, Frank); *Triad*, 3 1-act operas; librettos by the composer ("The Dress," 1953; "Sweet Betsy from Pike," 1953; "Tale for a Deaf Ear," 1957; Frank); *Concerto for a Singing Instrument* for any voice or instrument, string orchestra, harp, piano (1960, Frank); *The Wondrous Kingdom*, "Flora and Fauna," for chorus; texts by Blake, Emerson, George Herbert (1962); *The Hero*, 1-act opera based on Frank D. Gilroy's "Far Rockaway"; libretto by David Rogers (1965); *A Time to Play*, score for the film by Art Kane (1967); *The Mouse that Roared*, musical based on the novel by Leonard Wibberley; book by Christopher Sergel, lyrics by David Rogers (1969).

PRINCIPAL WRITINGS: "A Permanent Rainbow," *American Record Guide* 25/3:192–93; "A Self-portrait," *Festival Theatre Student Study Series* (San Anselmo, Calif., 1966–67), syllabus 3:13–18.

Bucht, Gunnar (b. Stocksund, Sweden, 5 August 1927), studied musicology at Uppsala Univ. (1947–53) and composition privately with Karl-Birger Blomdahl (1947–51), Carl Orff (1954), Goffredo Petrassi (1954–55), and Max Deutsch (1961–62). He taught musicology at Stockholm Univ. during 1965–69. Since 1970 he has been cultural attaché at the Swedish Embassy in Bonn.

PRINCIPAL COMPOSITIONS (available from STIM and as noted): *Symphonies Nos. 1–6* (1952; 1953; 1954; 1957–58, Suecia; 1960; 1961–62); *La fine de diaspora* for chorus, orchestra; text by Quasimodo (1958); *Tronkrävarna* [The Pretenders], 2-act opera; libretto after Ibsen (1962–65); *Jerikos murar* [The Walls of Jericho], 1-act oratorio-opera (1966–67); an electronic version on tape prepared 1970); *Symphonie pour la musique libérée* on tape (1969).

BIBL.: Gunnar Larsson, "G. B. och traditionen" [G. B. and Tradition], program book for the Stockholm Royal Opera (10 Sept 1966):7–12.

SEE ALSO Scandinavia.

Büchtger, Fritz (b. Munich, 14 Feb 1903), studied at the Hochschule für Musik in Munich (1921–28; Anton Beer-Walbrunn, composition; Wolfgang von Waltershausen, theory; Sagerer, organ; Knappe, conducting). During 1922–31 he organized and conducted four Festivals of New Music, presenting works by Bartók, Egk, Hindemith, Schoenberg, Krenek, and Stravinsky, among many others. In 1927 he founded the Munich Society for Contemporary Music, which he headed until 1933. In 1947 he founded the Studio for New Music in Munich. During the Nazi period (1931–48), he wrote only tonal works, but in much of his music before and since he has combined tonality and 12-tone procedures.

PRINCIPAL COMPOSITIONS: *3 Motets after St. John* for chorus, Op. 33 (1947, Müller); *Der weisse Reiter*, oratorio after the Apocalypse of St. John for baritone, chorus, orchestra, Op. 34 (1948, Möseler); *Music for String Quartet No. 1*, Op. 36 (1948, Möseler); *Orpheus*, 4 songs for medium voice, piano, Op. 41; poems by Rilke (1950); *Concerto for String Orchestra*, Op. 42 (1950, Möseler); *Das gläserne Meer*, oratorio after the Apocalypse of St. John for baritone, chorus, orchestra, Op. 43 (1953); *Klaviermusik No. 1* (1953, Möseler); *The Resurrection according to St. Matthew* for chorus with orchestra (or strings), organ (1954, Bärenreiter); *Die Varklärung*, chamber oratorio for baritone, women's chorus, strings (1957, Bärenreiter); *Concerto for Orchestra* (1957, Sirius); *String Quartet No. 2* (1958, Bärenreiter); *Christmas Oratorio* for voice, flute, oboe, strings, (1959, Bärenreiter); *Die Traumstadt* for 5 choirs (1961, Bärenreiter); *Johannes der Täufer*, oratorio for baritone, choir, orchestra (1962, Bärenreiter); *Rilke-Chöre* for chorus (1962); *Chansons irrespecteuses* for high voice, piano (1962); *Violin Concerto* (1963, Möseler); *2 szenische Kantaten* for 4 soloists, chorus, orchestra; texts by Thornton Wilder (1964–65); *Stufen* for orchestra (1966); *String Quartet No. 3* (1967); *3 Ballads after François Villon* for baritone, piano (1968); *3 Songs after e. e. cummings* for soprano, piano (1968); *Strukturen* for 4 woodwinds, strings (1968); *Schichten und Bögen* for orchestra (1969).

BIBL.: Hermann Pfrogner, "Der Musiker F. B. Auf der Suche nach der Harmonie der Zwölftonwelt," *Die Kommenden* 11:20; Erich Valentin, "Von der Sieben zur Zwölf. Porträt der Komponisten F. B.," *Neue Zeitschrift für Musik* 119:119f.

SEE ALSO Liturgical Music: Christian.

Budd, Harold (b. Los Angeles, 24 May 1936), attended Los Angeles City College (1957–59, theory with H. Endicott Hanson), San Fernando Valley State College (1961–63; composition with Aurelio de la Vega; analysis, esthetics, and music psychology with Gerald Strang), and the Univ. of Southern Calif. (1963–66, composition with Ingolf Dahl). Since 1970 he has been teaching at the Calif. Institute of the Arts. Early influences on Budd were jazz, the music of Morton Feldman and John Cage, and graphic arts, especially Mark Rothko and the minimalists of the 1960s. The composer is "very interested in the idea of making pretty things with a kind of radical simplicity. Consequently, much of my music is extremely quiet, and very little happens (in terms of old-time virtuosity—but it does, I think, call for a lot of spiritual virtuosity)." His works *Noyo* and *November* are mobile. In *Noyo*, each player begins at a place of his own choosing and moves in his own time; "all sounds are very quiet, all durations (including silence) are long." His *California 99* is a collaborative work. He asked eight composer-performers to write 36 "events," which he then "choreographed" to produce the piece. *Couer d'Orr* is an organ tape, with a D-flat major chord on one channel and B major on the other, "to be used as the matrix for any number of live, ritual-like performances."

PRINCIPAL COMPOSITIONS: *Noyo* for piano, vibraphone, chimes (1966); *November* for double bass, tape (prerecorded double bass) (1967, score page in *Esquire* magazine, May 1970); *Mangus Colorado* for 4 or more electronically modified gongs (1969, *Source* magazine 6); *California 99* for trumpet, alto saxophone, tuba, piano, double bass, percussion, trombone, tenor saxophone (1969); *Vittorio* for electronically modified gong, carillon (chimes), flügelhorn, string quartet, female speaking voices (1969); *Couer d'Orr* for tape, soprano saxophone, and/or voices (1970); *The Candy-Apple Revision*, D-flat major chord for any sound source (1970).

BIBL.: David Ahlstrom, "Footnotes 4 Mr. T.," *The Composer* 2/1:28; David Cope, *New Directions in Music* (Dubuque, Iowa, 1971).

Burian, Emil František (b. Pilsen, Czechoslovakia, 11 June 1904; d. Prague, 9 August 1959), studied at the Prague Conservatory (1920–27, composition with Josef B. Foerster). His career was closely associated with the theater. In 1928 he was an actor and program director for the Umělecká Beseda in Prague. During 1929–30, 1932, and 1945–46 he was director and manager of the National Theater in Brno. In 1933 he founded "D," a Prague avant-garde theater, which he directed until 1941 (when he was imprisoned by the Nazis) and during 1945–49. He also composed film scores and directed films. He was editor-in-chief of the weekly *Kulturní politika* during 1946–49. His work was influenced by Negro jazz and spirituals and Czech folksong. In 1927 he developed the "voice band" for choral recitation.

PRINCIPAL COMPOSITIONS: *Alladin a Palomid*, fairy opera after Maurice Maeterlinck (1923); *From Youth* for string sextet (1924); *Mastičkář*

[The Quack], opera buffa (1925); *Fagot a flétna* [The Bassoon and the Flute], ballet (1925); *American Suite* for 2 pianos (1926); *Dřevění vojáčci* [Wooden Soldiers], ballet (1926); *Manéž* [The Menagerie], ballet (1927); *Autobus*, ballet (1927); *Bubu z Montparnassu* [Bubu from Montparnasse], jazz opera (1927); *String Quartets Nos. 1–8* (1927–51); *Variations on Folk Songs* for wind quintet (1928); *Wind Quintet* (1933, Orbis); *Maryša*, opera in 5 scenes based on the play by the brothers Mrštík (1938, Supraphon); *Lost Serenade* for violin, piano (1940); *Accordian Concerto* (1949).

PRINCIPAL WRITINGS: *O moderní ruské hudbě* [Modern Russian Music] (Prague 1926); *Polydynamika*, a collection of essays (Prague 1926); *Sborová recitace a scénická hudba* [Choral Recitation and Incidental Music] (Prague 1927); *Jazz* (Prague 1928); *Černošské tance* [Negro Dances] (Prague 1929).

BIBL.: Bohumil Karásek, "E. F. B.," *Hudební věda* (1968):522–47; ——, "V boji pokrokové umění" [The Struggle for Progressive Art], *Hudební rozhledy* (1953):636–39; ——, "Burianovské reminiscence" [Reminiscences of B.] *ibid.* (1964): 444–46; Adolf Scherl, "E. F. B.—dramatik," *Česká literatura* 8:267–90; —— and Milan Obst, *K dějinám čěské divadelní avantgardy, Jindřich Hondl—E. F. B.* (The History of the Czech Theater Vanguard . . .] (Prague 1962).

SEE ALSO Czechoslovakia.

Burkhard, Willy (b. Leubringen, Switzerland, 17 April 1900; d. Zurich, 18 June 1955), studied at the Leipzig Conservatory (1921; composition with Sigfrid Karg-Elert, piano with Robert Teichmüller) and the Munich Conservatory (1922–23, composition with Walter Courvoisier). He also studied composition privately in Paris with Max d'Ollone. He taught harmony at the Bern Conservatory (1929–33) and composition at the Zurich Conservatory (1942–55). During 1926–33 he conducted the Bern Münsterchors and Lehrergesangvereins Lyss and the Orchestervereins Langenthal. He aimed at a regeneration of liturgical music and of vocal and instrumental polyphony; in this he sought models in renaissance and baroque music, especially the church music of Schütz and J. S. Bach. Among contemporary figures, the influences of Scriabin, the French impressionists, Stravinsky, and Bartók were strongest.

PRINCIPAL COMPOSITIONS (published by Bärenreiter unless otherwise noted): *Herbst*, cantata for soprano, violin, cello, piano, Op. 36; text by Christian Morgenstern (1932, Schott); *Fantasie* for string orchestra, Op. 40 (1934, Schott); *Das Gesicht Jesajas*, oratorio for soprano, tenor, bass, chorus, organ, orchestra, Op. 41 (1934–35, Hug and Bärenreiter); *Die Versuchung Jesu*, cantata for low voice, organ, Op. 44 (1936); *Die Verkündigung Mariae*, motet for chorus, Op. 51 (1938, Hug); *Ein feste Burg ist unser Gott*, fantasy and chorale for organ, Op. 58 (1939); *Hymnus* for orchestra, Op. 57 (1939, UE); *Concertino* for cello, string orchestra, Op. 60 (1940, UE); *Christi Leidensverkündigung*, cantata for tenor, small chorus, organ, Op. 65 (1942); *String Quartet No. 2* in 1 movement, Op. 68 (1943); *Violin Concerto*, Op. 69 (1943, UE); *Symphony* in 1 movement, Op. 73 (1944); *Violin Sonata*, Op. 78 (1946); *Lyrische Musik in memoriam Georg Trakl* for flute, viola, cello, piano, Op. 88 (1949–51); *Messe* for soprano, bass, chorus, chamber orchestra, Op. 85 (1950–51); *Fantasia mattutina* for orchestra, Op. 83 (1950); *Cello Sonata*, Op. 87 (1951); *Choraltriptychon* for organ, Op. 91 (1953); *6 Preludes* for piano, Op. 99 (1953–55); *Die Sintflut*, cantata for chorus, Op. 97 (1954–55); *Suite* for solo flute, Op. 98 (1955). A *Werkverzeichnis* is published by the Willy Burkhard Gesellschaft in Bern.

PRINCIPAL WRITINGS: "Grenzen des musikalischen Hörens," *Schweizerische Musikzeitung* (15 Nov 1937); "Versuch einer kritischen Auseinandersetzung mit der Zwölftontechnik," *ibid.* (1 March 1954).

BIBL.: Ernst Mohr, *W. B.* (Zurich 1957); Walter Tappolet, *Evangelische Kirchenmusik: Die Briefe von W. B. an Walter Tappolet* (Zurich 1964); Hans Zurlinden, *W. B.* (Zurich-Stuttgart 1956).

[prepared with the help of Fritz Indermühle]
SEE ALSO Switzerland.

Burt, Francis (b. London, 28 April 1926), studied composition with Howard Ferguson at the Royal Academy of Music, London (1948–51), and with Boris Blacher at the Hochschule für Musik, Berlin (1951–54). He has lived in Vienna since 1956. Burt has written many works for Austrian and German theaters and television. Although a former student of mathematics and physics, he does not try "to systematize my musical language but to broaden it—to make it capable of expressing a variety of emotions." While stationed in Nigeria with the British army (1946–47), he observed the kinesthetic reactions evoked in listeners by Ibo drumming. He believes that similar principles of spontaneous reaction and involvement should pervade theater music.

PRINCIPAL COMPOSITIONS (published by UE unless otherwise noted): *Volpone*, 4-act opera after the play by Ben Jonson (1952–58, revised 1960–61); *Iambics* for orchestra, Op. 5 (1953, Bote); *The Skull*, cantata for tenor, piano or orchestra, Op. 6 (piano version 1953–54, orchestra version 1955); *Espressione orchestrale* for orchestra (1958–59); *The Golem*, 1-act ballet (1959–63); *Fantasmagoria per orchestra* (1963); *Barnstable, oder Jemand auf der Dachboden*, 1-act opera after the play by James Saunders (1967–69, Bärenreiter).

BIBL.: Franz Endler, "Kopf und Herz im Gleichgewicht," *Die Presse* (Vienna, 2–3 Oct 1965).

Bush, Alan (Dudley) (b. London, 22 Dec 1900), studied at the Royal Academy of Music (1918–22; composition with Frederick Corder, piano with Tobias Matthay) and the Univ. of Berlin (1929–31; musicology with Johannes Wolf, Friedrich Blume). He also studied composition privately with John Ireland (1922–27). He has taught harmony and composition at the Royal Academy since 1925. From 1925 on he conducted amateur working-class choruses in England, Belgium, and France, and during 1944–54 he directed the Workers' Music Association Singers. In 1938 he founded the London String Orchestra, which he conducted until 1950. His music has been influenced by the working-class movement in Great Britain; the amateur and professional music life of the Soviet Union, which he has visited several times; his acquaintance with Hanns Eisler and his colleagues Ernst Hermann Meyer and Georg Knepler; and by the theoretical writings of Ernst Haeckel, Marx, Engels, and Lenin. He has appeared as a pianist and conductor throughout the world.

PRINCIPAL COMPOSITIONS: *Dialectic* for string quartet, Op. 15 (1929, Boosey); *Piano Concerto* with baritone, chorus, Op. 18 (1934–37, Galliard); *Symphonies Nos. 1–3*: No. 1 in C, Op. 21 (1939–40, Galliard); No. 2, "The Nottingham," Op. 33 (1949, Galliard); No. 3, "The Byron," Op. 53 (1959–60); *Lyric Interlude* for violin, piano, Op. 26 (1944, Galliard); *The Press Gang*, children's opera; libretto by Nancy Bush (1946, Workers Music Association and Hofmeister); *3 Concert Studies* for piano trio, Op. 31 (1947, Novello); *Violin Concerto*, Op. 32 (1948, Galliard); *Wat Tyler*, opera; libretto by Nancy Bush (1948–50, Novello and Henschel); *Concert Suite* for cello, orchestra, Op. 37 (1952, Galliard); *The Spell Unbound*, children's opera; libretto by Nancy Bush (1953, Novello); *Men of Blackmoor*, opera; libretto by Nancy Bush (1954–55, Galliard and Henschel); *Dorian Passacaglia and Fugue* for orchestra, Op. 52 (1959, Novello); *Variations, Nocturne, and Finale on an English Sea Song* for piano, orchestra, Op. 60 (1960, Novello); *The Ferryman's Daughter*, children's opera; libretto by Nancy Bush (1961, Novello); *The Sugar Reapers or Guyana Johnny*, opera; libretto by Nancy Bush (1961–64, Henschel); *Prelude, Air, and Dance* for violin, string quartet, percussion, Op. 61 (1963–64, Novello); *Joe Hill: The Man Who Never Died*, opera; libretto by Barrie Stevens (1965–68); *Time Remembered* for chamber orchestra, Op. 67 (1968); *Scherzo* for wind orchestra, percussion, Op. 68 (1969, Novello); *Serenade* for string quartet, Op. 70 (1969).

PRINCIPAL WRITINGS: *In My Seventh Decade* (London 1971).

BIBL.: Ates Orga, "A B.: Musician and Marxist," *Music and Musicians* (August 1969); R. Murray Schafer, *British Composers in Interview* (London 1963); Ronald Stevenson, "A. B.: Committed Composer," *Music Review* 25:323–42.
SEE ALSO Great Britain.

Busoni, Ferruccio (Benvenuto) (b. Empoli, Italy, 1 April 1866; d. Berlin, 27 July 1924), pursued the careers of composer and pianist from an early age. His father, a clarinettist, and his mother, a pianist, both encouraged these pursuits, and he was launched on a professional career at seven, touring extensively and astounding audiences as performer, improviser, and composer. Because of this existence, he was largely self-taught as a composer, although he did spend a year with Wilhelm Mayer-Remy at Graz in 1880–81. The constant necessity of earning money to support the rest of the Busoni family led to a series of teaching posts: Helsingfors in 1889, Moscow in 1890, and Boston during 1891–94. He returned to Europe in 1894 and lived almost continuously in Berlin until his death. There, his activities gradually shifted from piano playing to composition and some conducting. His personality and interests widened, and he became a champion of new music. His master classes at Weimar (1901, 1902), although officially based on piano playing, were actually a free meeting place for young performers and composers. During World War I he refused to live in any of the belligerent countries and settled in Zurich. His opera *Arlecchino*, a satire on war, dates from this time. The war left him broken in spirit and health; he played less and less and concentrated his remaining energies on the opera *Doktor Faust*, which he left incomplete at his death.

Busoni's music includes four operas, solo vocal and choral works, some chamber music, a vast quantity of piano music, and orchestral and concerted works. The early music, culminating in the mammoth *Piano Concerto* (1904), is of a traditionally oriented romantic nature with liberal injections of classical forms and polyphonic techniques. The *Elegien* (1907) and *An die Jugend* (1909), both for piano, heralded a revolution in his thinking. Taking late Liszt as a point of departure, these works move into a characteristic Busonian disembodied world—a curious mixture of impressionism, aloofness, and withdrawal from "reality." The seventh *Elegie*, which also exists in orchestral form (*Berceuse*), is one of the earliest examples of that tenuous style of scoring later associated with Webern and his imitators. Expanded tonality and polarized tonality (an extremely saturated chromaticism that revolves around a pivotal tone) were explored in some of the *Piano Sonatinas*; the second of these achieves an absence of regular pulse, as well as utilizing a modern notational technique that does away with natural signs. The *Indianisches Tagebuch* for piano (1915), especially No. 2 of the cycle, contains a Bartók-like usage of primitive rhythms and folk melodic elements in "barbaric" style. The orchestral *Indianisches Tagebuch* (1915), especially "Dance of the Spirits," is a virtuoso demonstration of chamber ensemble playing akin to that of later avant-garde composers. In *Turandot* (1917) he anticipated Bartók and Messiaen in the structural use of exotic scales, while his introduction of old forms and procedures in *Doktor Faust* (1916–   ) paralleled Berg's *Wozzeck*. His unperturbed mixing of styles, especially apparent in the operas, is a prominent feature in much new music today.

Busoni as a musical thinker predicted and theoretically stipulated many later developments. In his *Sketch for a New Esthetic of Music* (1900) he discussed the use of microtones, electronic technology, and exotic scales. Elsewhere (*The Unity of Music*, *The Essence of Music*) he set down the theoretical prerequisites for 12-tone music, for the abolition of "consonance" and "dissonance." He also invented a new organic system of notation for the piano that did away with accidentals and other anomalies foreign to the keyboard (Breitkopf published the Bach *Chromatic Fantasy* in this notation in 1910). His concept of "young classicism" was misunderstood in his day and forgotten with Stravinsky's neoclassicism; he was referring to the attitude and spirit in which classical music is written, anticipating the thoughts of many composers today: "The mastery, sifting, and exploitation of all the achievements of past experiments and their embodiment in fixed and beautiful forms" (Vogel, see bibl.: 170).

PRINCIPAL COMPOSITIONS (published by Breitkopf): *Konzertstück* for piano, orchestra, Op. 31a (1890); *Violin Concerto*, Op. 35a (1987); *Piano Concerto* with men's chorus, Op. 39 (1904); *Elegien* for piano (1907); *Berceuse élégiaque* for orchestra, Op. 42 (1909); *An die Jugend* for piano (1909); *Fantasia nach Bach* for piano (1909); *6 Sonatinas* for piano (1910–21); *Die Brautwahl*, opera; libretto by the composer after E. T. A. Hoffmann (1911); *Nocturne symphonique*, Op. 43 (1912); *Fantasia contrappuntistica* for piano; based on Bach (1912); *Indianische Fantasie* for piano, orchestra, Op. 44 (1913); *Rondo Arlecchinesco* for orchestra, Op. 46 (1915); *Indianisches Tagebuch* for orchestra, Op. 47 (1915); *Indianisches Tagebuch* for piano (1915); *Arlecchino*, 1-act opera, Op. 50; libretto by the composer (1916); *Doktor Faust*, opera; libretto by the composer (begun 1916, completed 1925 by Philipp Jarnach); *Turandot*, 2-act opera; libretto by the composer after Gozzi (1917); *Concertino* for clarinet, small orchestra, Op. 48 (1919); *Sarabande and Cortège* for orchestra, Op. 51 (1919); *Divertimento* for flute, orchestra, Op. 52 (1920); Tanwalzer for orchestra, Op. 53 (1920); *Romanza e scherzoso* for piano, orchestra, Op. 54 (1921); *Toccata* for piano (1922); *10 Variations on a Chopin Prelude* for piano (1922); *Klavierübung* for piano; based on Bach (10 vols. published 1925). Busoni also transcribed, edited, or arranged for piano a large quantity of music by other composers, principally Bach, Mozart, and Liszt.

PRINCIPAL WRITINGS: *Entwurf einer neuen Ästhetik der Tonkunst* (Trieste 1907; American ed., *Sketch of a New Esthetic of Music*, New York 1911); *Gesammelte Aufsätze: Von der Einheit der Musik* (Berlin 1922; English ed., *The Essence of Music and Other Papers*, London 1957); *Versuch einer organischen Klavier-Notenschrift* (Wiesbaden 1910); "Lehre von der Übertragung von Orgelwerken auf das Klavier," appendix to the Breitkopf edition of Bach's *Well Tempered Klavier*, book 1; *Über die Möglichkeiten der Oper und über die Partitur des "Doktor Faust"* (Wiesbaden 1926; English ed. in *The Essence of Music . . .*). Busoni also published the librettos of his operas and the other librettos he wrote but did not use himself.

BIBL.: N. Barinova, *Vospomiuaniye o Hoffmane i F. B.* (Moscow 1964); Gerda Busoni, *Erinnerungen an F. B.* (Berlin 1958); Emil Debusmann, *F. B.* (Wiesbaden 1949); Edward J. Dent, *F. B.* (London 1933); Bernard van Dieren, *Down Among the Dead Men* (London 1935); Remo Giazotto, *B.: La vita nell'opera* (Genoa 1947); Guido Guerrini, *F. B.: La vita, la figura, l'opera* (Florence 1944); Hanspeter Krellman, *Studien zu den Bearbeitungen F. B.* (Regensburg 1966); Hugo Leichtentritt, *F. B.* (Wiesbaden 1916); Siegfried F. Nadel, *F. B.* (Wiesbaden 1931); Edgard Refardt, ed., *Briefe B.s an Hans Huber* (Zurich 1939); Arnolfo Santelli, *B.* (Rome 1939); Gisela Selden-Goth, *F. B.* (Leipzig 1922); ——, "F. B., un profilo," *Historiae musicae cultores* 20 (1964); ——, *25 B.-Briefe* (Vienna 1937); Larry Sitsky, "B. and the New Music," *Quadrant* (Sydney) 33; ——, "F. B.'s 'Attempt at an Organic Notation for the Pianoforte,' and a Practical Adaptation of it," *Music Review* 29/1; ——, "The Six Sonatinas for Piano of F. B.," *Studies in Music* (West Australia) 2; K. S. Sorabji, *Around and About Music* (London 1932); H. H. Stuckenschmidt, *F. B.* (London 1970); Wladimir Vogel, "Impressions of F. B.," *Perspectives* 6/2:167–73.

Larry Sitsky

SEE ALSO Austria and Germany, Microtones, Opera, Rhythm, Switzerland, Theory.

Bussotti, Sylvano (b. Florence, 1 Oct 1931), composed and studied violin as a child. He entered the Cherubini Conservatory in his native city in 1940 (harmony and counterpoint with Roberto Lupi, violin with Giovacchino Maglioni, piano with Luigi Dallapiccola). He won a violin scholarship in 1943 but left the conservatory without taking the final examination. After several years of self-instruction, he spent 1957–58 in Max Deutsch's free class for composition and musical analysis in Paris. Between 1961 and 1969 he won several prizes at the ISCM and Venice Biennale festivals, traveled in the U.S. on an invitation from the Rockefeller Foundation, and from 1965 on, organized performances in theaters, clubs, and avant-garde festivals with his own group, "L'opera." He also staged and designed sets for operas by Puccini, Debussy, Stravinsky, Ghedini, Malipiero, and others. His activities include painting (exhibitions in many galleries throughout Europe) and writing on music.

Bussotti has composed mainly for the voice, for solo instruments, and for nonstandard chamber groups. First influenced by Webern and serial music as a whole, he also owes much to John Cage, particularly in such experimental compositions as *5 Piano Pieces for David Tudor* (1959) and *Julio organum Julii* for organ (1963). He does not use predetermined formal schemes but creates larger forms through an accumulation of details, e.g., *Il nudo* is a collection of four, well characterized fragments, each of which plays an architectural and expressive role in the work, itself a kind of summary of the larger *Torso*. There are also many subtle relationships between the various works based on Braibanti poems. Some of his works "elaborate, comment, or reflect" upon earlier ones, e.g., *Solo, Rara*, and *La Passion selon Sade*. Many of them quote from each other and contain a wealth of private references and enigmatic symbols. Bussotti uses timbre to achieve complex, tenuous, lacelike textures. His work in the visual arts has led him to invent new methods of graphic notation, and each page of his music has a striking and unique visual appearance. This "music for the eye" augments "music for the ear" but never takes precedence over it, for beauty of sound remains his chief concern. His music expresses a neohumanism, emphasizing in particular man's sensuality and eroticism; this contrasts strongly with the more abstract approaches in much of contemporary music.

PRINCIPAL COMPOSITIONS: *5 Piano Pieces for David Tudor* (1959, UE); *7 Fogli*: No. 1, "Couple," for flute, piano; No. 2, "Coeur," for percussion; No. 3, "Per 3," for piano; No. 4, "Lettura di Braibanti," for voice; No. 5, "Mobile-Stabile," for guitar, voice, piano; No. 6, "Manifesto per Kalinowski," for chamber orchestra, voice; No. 7, "Sensitivo," for violin (1959, UE); *Phrase à 3* for string trio (1960, UE); *Pour Clavier* for piano (1960, UE); *Torso* for voices, orchestra (1960–63, Moeck); *Memoria* for voices, orchestra (1962, Bruzzichelli); *La Passion selon Sade*, "staged concert" for voice, instruments, narrator (1965–66, Ricordi); *5 Frammenti all'Italia*: Nos. 2, 4 for chorus; Nos. 1, 3, 5 for vocal sextet (1966, Ricordi); *The Rara Requiem* for voices, chamber orchestra (1969, Ricordi).

PRINCIPAL WRITINGS: *Nouvelle Musique: essai* (Aix en Provence 1961); *Sensitivo: Analysis* (Brussels 1961); "Extramusicale," *Il Ponte* (Florence, 1964); "Il gioco nella musica," *Almanacco Bompiani* (Milan, 1966). Bussotti has also written reviews and articles for *Marcatré* (Rome, 1964–65) and *Discoteca* (Milan, since 1966).

BIBL.: Alberto Arbasino, *Grazie per le magnifiche rose* (Milan 1965):482; Mario Bartolotto, *Fase seconda* (Turin 1969):201;——, Piero Capponi, "Dialogo sull'arte atemporale," *Nutida Musik* (1967).

Henry-Louis de La Grange

SEE ALSO Austria and Germany, Italy, Rhythm.

Butterley, Nigel (Henry) (b. Sydney, 13 May 1935), studied at the New South Wales Conservatorium (1952–55; composition with Alex Burnard, Raymond Hanson, Noel Nickson). He also studied piano privately with E. Saadforth Hooper (1941–50) and Frank Warbrick (1950–55) and composition with Priaulx Rainier in London (1962).

PRINCIPAL COMPOSITIONS (published by Albert): *In the Head, the Fire* for narrator, tenor, baritone, chorus, wind instruments, piano, organ, percussion (1966); *Meditations of Thomas Traherne* for children's recorder group, orchestra (1968); *Exploration* for piano, orchestra (1970); *Violin Concerto* (1970).

PRINCIPAL WRITINGS: "Composing 'Religious' Music," *Crux* (Melbourne) 72/2:4–5.

SEE ALSO Australia.

Butting, Max (b. Berlin, 6 Oct 1888), studied musicology at the Univ. of Munich (1908–13) and composition with Friedrich Klose at the Munich Conservatory (1908–13). He also studied composition privately with Walter Courvoisier. During the 1920s and early 30s he began composing for radio and teaching courses in radio composition at the Charlotten-

burg Hochschule and the Klindworth-Scharwenka Conservatory. He was inactive during 1933–45. In 1948 he became music director for the East Berlin radio and in 1950 a founding member of the German Academy of the Arts in East Berlin, for which he served in various executive posts until 1959.

PRINCIPAL COMPOSITIONS: *Symphonies Nos. 1–10*: No. 1, Op. 21 (1922); No. 2, Op. 29 (1924, UE); No. 3, Op. 34 (1925, UE); No. 4, Op. 42 (1940, Peters-L); No. 5, Op. 43 (1943, Peters-L); No. 6, Op. 44 (1945, Peters-L); No. 7, Op. 67 (1949, Peters-L); No. 8, Op. 84 (1952, Peters-L); No. 9, Op. 94 (1956); No. 10, Op 108 (1963); *Kleine Stücke* for string quartet, Op. 26 (1925, Schott); *15 Short Piano Pieces*, Op. 33 (1925, UE and Peters-L); *Piano Trio*, Op. 54 (1947, Peters-L); *Das Memorandum* for vocal soloists, chorus, orchestra, Op. 52 (1947–48); *String Quartets Nos. 5–10*: No. 5, Op. 53 (1947, Peters-L); No. 6, Op. 90 (1953, Peters-L); No. 7, Op. 95 (1957); No. 8, Op. 96 (1957); No. 9, Op. 97 (1957); No. 10, Op. 118 (1971); *Nach dem Krieg*, 4 cantatas for chorus, chamber orchestra, Opp. 59, 61–63 (1948); *Hauskonzert bei Langners* for flute, violin, cello, piano 4-hands, Op. 65 (1949, Peters-L); *Sonatine* for string orchestra, Op. 68 (1949, Peters-L); *Overture* for orchestra, Op. 69 (1949, Peters-L); *Kleine Kammermusik* for flute, horn, violin, cello, Op. 70 (1949, Peters-L); *Die Lügengeschichte vom schwarzen Pferd*, cantata for baritone, chorus, chamber orchestra, Op. 71; text after A. Eckener (1949, Sikorski); *Flute Concerto*, Op. 72 (1950, Peters-L); *Spielereien*, inventions for piano, Op. 74 (1950, Peters-L); *Festschrift für Bach*, 6 inventions for flute, violin, English horn, viola, bassoon, cello, Op. 77 (1950, Peters-L); *La serenata gentile*, octet for flute, oboe, bassoon, piano, string quartet, Op. 80 (1951, Peters-L); *Piano Sonata*, Op. 82 (1951, Peters-L); *Sonatine für Gretl* for piano, Op. 87 (1952, Peters-L); *Symphonic Variations*, Op. 89 (1953, Peters-L); *Ballade* for orchestra, Op. 91 (1954, Peters-L); *5 Serious Pieces* (after Dürer) for orchestra, Op. 92 (1955, Sikorski); *Diarium*, 40 studies for piano, Op. 93 (1956, Peters-L); *Plautus im Nonnenkloster*, opera; libretto by C. F. Meyer and H. Zinner (1959, Peters-L and Henschel); *Sinfonietta in 3 Movements*, Op. 100 (1960, IM); *Klavierstücke*, Op. 102 (1961, Peters-L); *Wochenend Konzert* for orchestra, Op. 104 (1962, IM); *Symphonic Rhapsody*, Op. 106 (1962); *4 Movements* for wind quintet (1962); *4 Lieder and an Epilogue* for voice, piano (1962, IM); *Serenade* for orchestra, Op. 107 (1963); *Piano Concerto*, Op. 110 (1964); *Triptychon* for orchestra, Op. 112 (1967); *Stationen* for orchestra, Op. 118 (1970).

PRINCIPAL WRITINGS: coauthor, *Musikgeschichte* (Berlin 1955).

C

Caamaño, Roberto (b. Buenos Aires, 7 July 1923), studied at the National Conservatory in Buenos Aires (1939–46; composition with Athos Palma, piano with Amelia Cocq de Weingand and Fritz Masbach). He has performed professionally as a pianist, and during 1949–52 he taught piano at the Escuela Superior de Música of the Univ. del Litoral. He has taught harmony, form, and Gregorian chant at the Institute of Sacred Music in Buenos Aires since 1955 and piano and orchestration at the National Conservatory since 1956. He was appointed artistic director of the Teatro Colón in 1960.

PRINCIPAL COMPOSITIONS: *2 Cantos gallegos* for voice, piano, Op. 3; texts by Rosalía de Castro (1945, Ricordi); *3 Cantos de Navidad* for voice, piano, Op. 4; texts by Lope de Vega (1946, Barry); *6 Preludes* for piano, Op. 6 (1947, Barry); *Psalm 149* for female soloist, chorus, orchestra, Op. 7 (1948, Barry); *Suite* for string orchestra, Op. 9 (1949, Barry); *Psalm 114* for chorus, Op. 10 (1950, Barry); *Prelude, Adagio, and Fugue* for orchestra, Op. 11 (1951, Barry); *Lamento en la tumba de Manuel de Falla* for voice, piano, Op. 13 (1952, Ricordi); *Gregorian Variations* for piano, Op. 15 (1953, Ricordi); *American Variations* for orchestra, Op. 16 (1953, Barry); *2 Cantares galaico-portugueses del siglo 13* for voice, piano, Op. 18 (1954, Ricordi); *Bandoneon Concerto*, Op. 19 (1954); *Magnificat* for chorus, orchestra, Op. 20 (1954, Barry); *Piano Concerto*, Op. 22 (1957, Barry); *Música* for string orchestra, Op. 23 (1957, Barry); *Piano Quintet*, Op. 25 (1962). List to 1962: *Composers of the Americas* 8:43–44.

PRINCIPAL WRITINGS: "Encuesta: El Conservatorio Nacional; Contesta; R. C.," *Buenos Aires Musical* No. 352 (1966):3; "The Colon Theater in Buenos Aires," *Inter-American Music Bulletin* 54:1–10.

BIBL.: A. T. de Atchabahian, "R. C. (el talento en la joven generación de compositores)," *Clave* (Nov 1961):9–10; Roberto García Morillo, "La música en la Argentina," *Nuestra música* 7/26 (1952):104.

Cage, John (b. Los Angeles, 15 Sept 1912), studied piano with Richard Buhlig (Los Angeles 1932) and composition with Henry Cowell (New York 1933–34) and Arnold Schoenberg (Los Angeles 1935–37). He organized percussion ensembles and concerts starting in 1936 on the West Coast and in the Northwest. During 1937–39 he worked at the Cornish School in Seattle as a dance-class accompanist; he also organized a percussion group there, gave a series of exhibitions of paintings, and taught briefly a music composition course for dancers. He taught at the School of Design in Chicago (1941–42), after which he moved to New York, where he organized concerts (percussion, prepared piano, dance) and began his collaboration with the dancer Merce Cunningham. He studied Erik Satie and Anton Webern and attended lectures on Zen by Daisetz Suzuki in the late 1940s and early 50s. In 1950 he began his association with the pianist David Tudor. In 1952 he organized the Project of Music for Magnetic Tape, the first American group for the production of tape music; early participants in the Project included Earle Brown, Morton Feldman, and myself. During the summers of 1948–52 he was active at Black Mountain College, N. C. There, in 1952, he and the Cunningham dance group put on Cage's *Theater Piece*, which was probably the first happening and mixed media event in the U.S.

Cage came to know the artists Robert Rauschenberg in 1950 and Jasper Johns in 1953, both of whose work is congenial. Beginning in 1954 he made regular tours giving lectures and concerts and appearing with the Cunningham Dance Co., of which he is musical director. He became an expert mycologist and, about 1959 or 1960, a founding member of the New York Mycological Society; he was a teacher of the subject at the New School in New York during 1956–60. He conceived and helped organize the Foundation for Performance Arts and the Merce Cunningham Foundation. He took up the study of Buckminster Fuller in 1950 and Marshall McLuhan in 1959. In 1960, when he was a Fellow of the Center for Advanced Studies at Wesleyan Univ., he came to know N. O. Brown. During 1965–68 he was regularly in the company of Marcel Duchamp. Since 1966 he has been composer-in-residence at the Universities of Ill., Calif. at Davis, Cincinnati, and Wesleyan.

Few works in Cage's output fit into any traditional category or genre. His music, in fact, is characterized by the constant appearance of new techniques, ideas, and qualities, and by an effort to change all of these once they seem adequately represented. Piano and percussion music predominate, and, starting in the 1950s, tape music, live electronic music, and works for unspecified sound sources and numbers of players. There is also taped material for a lecture and seven lectures accompanied by directions on how they are to be read (in ways similar to musical performance).

The earliest pieces are chromatic, confined to ranges of 25 notes, and are usually in three-part counterpoint with repetitions of individual notes as far apart as possible. They are static and spare and contrast with the more dramatic and propulsive character of the pieces that followed in 1935–38. The latter are 12-tone works that use fixed patterns of tone-row fragments and rhythms, tending to ostinatos (e.g., *Metamorphosis* for piano).

A long involvement with percussion music and consequently with rhythm began in 1934. Cage developed the idea of a rhythmic structure in which there is a proportional relationship between phrase lengths and the lengths of the larger parts of a whole composition. Though akin to Schoenberg's idea of an harmonic integration of all details in a composition with the whole, this structural principle shifted its basis from pitch to duration and hence to the basic components in music of sound and silence. Applied first in *First Construction (In Metal)* (1939), it was variously used until 1956, accommodating a variety of materials. The earlier percussion music used ostinatos and rhythms often highly elaborated by shifting accents, gruppettos, and their various superpositions, producing complex cross-rhythms. Cage was among the first modern composers to elaborate the use of asymmetric rhythms composed of sequences of notes running counter to the beat (gruppettos such as seven or five or nine in the time of four), in addition to the more usual devices of syncopation and asymmetric rhythmic phrasing by means of shifting accents on an otherwise regular beat. The general sound in these works tends to be constant, keeping within a fixed range of movement and timbre, and not developing. Metal instruments are used for clangorous and festive or hard and mechanical qualities (e.g., *Imaginary Landscape No. 3*);

wood and skin are used for more private and mysterious music (e.g., *Amores*). Cage's interest in percussion—and in sounds not conventionally regarded as musical—was shared with Edgard Varèse and distantly recalls the projects for noise music of the Italian futurists. Cage's sonorities are new, however, partly because of the rarer and invented instruments used, such as marimbula, button and cup gongs, tin cans, automobile brake drums, gong in water, flower pots. At this time Cage also began working with electrically derived sound sources, such as frequency recordings on variable speed turntables (*Imaginary Landscape No. 1*, 1939). Later his use of electricity was continued with radios (*Imaginary Landscape No. 4*, 1951), phonograph cartridges and amplifiers (*Cartridge Music*, 1960), contact microphones (e.g., *Music for Amplified Toy Pianos*), and complex electronic circuitry (*Variations V–VII*).

The need for percussion sounds where only a piano was available occasioned the invention of the prepared piano in 1938. The piano's sounds were altered by means of screws, bolts, pieces of rubber, wood, and other material set between given strings, making available to a keyboard player gamuts of finely differentiated sounds, both multiple and complex in pitch (including microtonal intervals) and indefinitely pitched (thudlike, rattling, etc.). This unconventional use of an instrument recalls Henry Cowell's use of actions directly on the piano strings and his new playing techniques for producing tone clusters. Later, as in *Music for Piano* (1953–56), Cage used direct plucking and muting of the piano strings by hand and striking of the piano body and frame. The extension as far as possible of the sound-producing capacities of conventional instruments was worked out particularly in *26′ 1.1499″ for a String Player* (1955), where the notation prescribes the physical actions required of the player rather than the resulting sound. In general the instrumentalist here is encouraged to become like a percussionist, ready for special notations and for the exercise of practical agility. The music for prepared piano (1938–54) shares rhythmic qualities with the percussion music, especially ostinatos, but also brings in melody and resonance effects. It culminated in the 70-minute cycle of *Sonatas and Interludes* (1946–48, the first in a series of extended pieces such as *Music for Piano*, versions of *Variations*, *HPSCHD*, which can run for several hours). This cycle, like all the works from 1938 on, is intended to express dramatic and contemplative states, both traditional and private, particularly the so-called permanent emotions of traditional Indian esthetic theory (the heroic, erotic, wondrous, mirthful, odious, sorrowful, fearful, angry, and their common tendency toward the tranquil). There is also an interest in expressing the quality of the seasons (*The Seasons, String Quartet in Four Parts, Winter Music*).

The objectifying of feelings begun in the prepared-piano music became in 1951 an objectifying of music itself through the use of chance in the process of composition (the Indian esthetic now began to give way to the often alogical flavor of Zen). Finding that the pursuit of expressiveness failed in communication and led only to self-enclosure, Cage used chance as a way of liberation, both psychological and technical, from self, taste, imagination, musical tradition, and ingrained compositional habits. The application of chance to music was supported by the idea (found expressed by the authority on Indian esthetics, Ananda Coomaraswamy) that art imitates nature in her manner of operation and by the sense (related to Zen) that any separation of art and life, the latter characterized by nature and chance, is unreal and impractical. At this time Cage also experienced in an anechoic (reverberation-free) chamber that there is no such thing as complete silence for the human ear, and he decided that the understanding of music as a duality of sound and silence was mistaken (there are always sounds to be listened to). Cage now felt no preference for musical (intended) sounds over others. The point of a musical performance became for him the activity of performers and the attention of listeners. Silence, as the absence of musical or performed sounds within a composition, now became prominent in his work and is radically represented by *4' 33"* (1952). This piece calls for no sounds at all to be played, illustrating that there are in any case sounds to be heard. Because the performer(s) still need to make some indication that a piece is being performed, the work created a performance situation that led directly to an understanding of music as theater.

The transition to procedures using chance began with the use of gamuts of single tones, intervals, and aggregates produced by one or more instruments, out of which melodic lines were made, mostly diatonic and static (e.g., *String Quartet*, 1950). Elements of a gamut were then set out on charts and their sequence on a chart was determined by moves as in magic squares (*16 Dances, Concerto for Prepared Piano and Orchestra*). For the piano solo *Music of Changes* (1951), charts were made

with 64 elements in each. This was suggested by the ancient Chinese oracle book, *I Ching*, in which 64 sets of texts are used for consultation according to a selection process that involves the tossing of yarrow stalks or coins. Cage made a chart for each aspect of sound—pitch (including noise or silence), duration, amplitude—and for tempos and superpositions of sequences (up to eight). Tossing coins then established the combinations of all these. The whole was set out in a predetermined (not by chance) rhythmic structure. The treatment of note rhythms also marked a change. Durations were notated graphically (a quarter-note equal to $2\frac{1}{2}$ cm.) and, being often irrational (e.g., 1/2 plus 4/7ths of an eighth-note plus 1/3rd of a quarter), became completely fluid; all regular pulse was gone.

Thereafter, ways and degrees in which chance or indeterminate elements made up a composition or, further, a performance were elaborated. Imperfections in the music paper were marked and chance operations were used to determine how many would be sounds and in what way. Superimposed staves located pitches or noises. The performer(s) determined tempo, durations, dynamics, and the superposition or overlap of pages (*Music for Piano*, consisting of isolated single sounds; *Winter Music*, mostly chord aggregates with associated harmonics; and, with restrictions and complications, a series of pieces whose titles were timing indications, such as *34' 46.776" for a Pianist*). Star locations on an astronomical atlas replaced paper imperfections as the markings given to be overlayed by templates in *Atlas eclipticalis*. None of these pieces is structured as a whole. Varying amounts of material can be used for any performance (e.g., any number of pages from 4 to 84 of *Music for Piano*), and there are no scores and no fixed relations of parts within a score. Pieces are no longer compositions in the sense of delimited objects, but are processes without preset beginning or end. As such, like their parts, they can themselves be combined and superimposed (e.g., *Aria* with *Fontata Mix* or any part of *Concert*).

Indeterminacy with respect to performance reached a set of limits in *Variations I–VII. I–IV* (1958–63) and *VI* (1966) consist of transparent plastic sheets inscribed with lines, points or circles, accompanied by instructions telling how these can be interpreted to furnish material for performance by any number of players using (except in *VI*) any sound producing means. In *Variations I* five lines refer to parameters of sound, and points of varying sizes refer to events of varying complexity. The sheets are overlaid in any way and the perpendicular distances from points to lines indicate a degree with respect to the parameter a line refers to, e.g., a point close to a line referring to frequency might equal a low pitch, or a point at a medium distance from a line for timbre might equal a medium complexity of overtone structure. The performer decides which lines refer to which parameters and the scale on which readings are made, e.g., for pitch, the range within which determinations apply. *Variations III* refer to impingements of sounds and actions, *IV* to the location in space of sounds. *VI* calls for the assembling of electronic sound systems (no sounds per se are specified). *V* and *VII* have no musical score. Instead the performer of *V* is supplied with a general description of past performances; one contained dance by Merce Cunningham, film material by Stan Vanderbeek, special electronic equipment including electric eyes so that the movements of the dancers would trigger sound sequences, television material by Nam June Paik, and lighting and scenery by Robert Rauschenberg. *Variations VII* was produced at an Experiments in Arts and Technology festival and used sounds transmitted from outside the performance building. These pieces in the *Variations* series (such as *4′ 33″*) represent a logical and graphic extreme, a paring down of notation to a point where almost nothing appears to be indicated. They are at once transparent and ambiguous and fluid. Indeterminate as they are in this way, however, they do not allow a performer simply to improvise at the moment of performance (though circumstances might arise during a performance requiring a player to vary or alter his course). They require specific decisions and preparations before they can be performed.

Cage's concern with theater goes back to 1935 with his earliest pieces for film, theater, and dance. It appeared within a musical composition in *Water Music* (1952) in which a pianist also uses a radio, whistles, water containers, a deck of cards, and a large score mounted like a poster. Here the visual element of a musical performance became part of its unique quality, not a distraction. The concern with theater was also an explicit acceptance by Cage of the public and social character of music, which suggested that music is not a score to be read nor sounds to be heard but the physical activity itself from which sounds result or which invite one's attention to any sounds whatever. Here and in the other ways outlined above, Cage has introduced new areas to music: the use of percussion and noise (appearing especially in the later 1950s in

Europe in such pieces as Pierre Boulez's *Marteau sans maître* and in Karlheinz Stockhausen's *Zyklus*); chance or indeterminacy in composition and performance (e.g., in Stockhausen); new notation (the use of graphic notation in the U.S. and Europe); intermedia and happenings (e.g., in the work of Robert Ashley, Mauricio Kagel, Allan Kaprow, and George Brecht); live electronic music (e.g., Larry Austin, David Behrman, Alvin Lucier, and Gordon Mumma). These influences have not always been specific or direct. Cage, by his persistent experimental activity (and publicizing), stands as an example and encouragement for others to proceed in new ways. He has thus affected in a general way the work of Morton Feldman, LaMonte Young, Cornelius Cardew, Toshi Ichiyanagi, and myself, among other and younger composers.

PRINCIPAL COMPOSITIONS (published by Peters): *Metamorphosis* for piano (1938); *First Construction (In Metal)* for percussion sextet (1939); *Imaginary Landscape No. 1* for 2 variable-speed phonoturntables, frequency recordings, muted piano, cymbal (1939); *She Is Asleep* for 12 tom-toms, voice, prepared piano (1943); *A Book of Music* for 2 prepared pianos (1944); *The Seasons* for orchestra (1947); *Sonatas and Interludes* for prepared piano (1946–48); *String Quartet in 4 Parts* (1950); *Concerto for Prepared Piano and Chamber Orchestra* (1951); *Music of Changes* for piano (1951); *Imaginary Landscape No. 4* for 12 radios, 24 players, conductor (1951); *Water Music* for pianist with accessory instruments (1952); *Williams Mix* for 8-track tape (1952); *4′33″* (tacet) for any instrument(s) (1952); *Music for Piano 4–84* for 1–84 pianist(s) (1953–56); *34′46.776″ for a Pianist* for prepared piano (1954); *26′1.1499″ for a String Player* (1955); *Winter Music* for 1–20 pianist(s) (1957); *Variations I* for player(s) on any kind and number of instruments (1958); *Concert for Piano and Orchestra* for piano, 1–13 instrumental parts (1957–58); *Fontana Mix, a)* a score for the production of 1 or more tape track(s) or for any kind and number of instrument(s), or *b)* prerecorded tape material to be performed in any way (1958); *Aria* for any voice (1958); *Cartridge Music*, amplified small sounds or amplified piano or cymbal (1960); *Theatre Piece* for 1–8 performers (1960); *Music for Carillon No. 4* (1961); *Variations II* for player(s) using any sound-producing means (1961); *Atlas eclipticalis* for orchestra of 86 instrumental parts (1961–62); *Variations III* for any number of people performing any actions (1963); *Variations IV* for any number of players, any sounds (1963); *Variations VI* for a plurality of sound systems (1966); *HPSCHD* for 1–7 harpsichord players, 1–51 tape machines; in collaboration with Lejaren Hiller (1967–69); *Cheap Imitation* for piano (1969). Lists to 1962: *J. C. Catalogue* (New York, Henmar Press, 1962); *Composers of the Americas* 8:49–58.

PRINCIPAL WRITINGS: *Notes*, pamphlet with the recording of the 25-year retrospective concert of

Cage's music (New York, George Avakian, 1958); *Silence* (Middletown, Conn., 1961); *A Year from Monday* (Middletown 1967); interview with J. C. and Lejaren Hiller about *HPSCHD*, *Source* 4.

BIBL.: Cornelius Cardew, "Notation—Interpretation, etc.," *Tempo* (summer 1961): 21–23; Henry Cowell, "Current Chronicle: New York," *Musical Quarterly* 38:123–34; H. Wiley Hitchcock, *Music in the United States* (Englewood Cliffs, N. J., 1969): 214–15, 241–44; Richard Kostelanetz, ed., *J. C.* (New York 1970); Wilfrid Mellers, *Music in a New Found Land* (New York 1965):177–88; Heinz-Klaus Metzger, "John Cage o della liberazione," *Incontri musicali* (Milan, August 1959):16–31; ——, "Über die Verantwortung des Komponisten," *Collage* (Palermo 1965):70–76; Eric Salzman, *Twentieth Century Music* (New York 1967):164–69; Dieter Schnebel, "L'Avicenna di Bloch, Cage e il rapporto forma-materia nella nuova musica," *Il Verri* (Milan 1969):61–67; Virgil Thomson, "America's Musical Maturity," *Yale Review* 51: 66–74; Calvin Tomkins, *The Bride and the Bachelors* (New York 1968):69–144; Christian Wolff, "New and Electronic Music," *Audience* (Cambridge, Mass.) 5/3 (1958); ——, "On Form," *Die Reihe*, English ed., 7:26–31; Peter Yates, *Twentieth Century Music* (New York 1967):231–36, 291–92, 303–12, 333–34.

                                                                                 Christian Wolff

SEE ALSO Asian Music and Western Composition; Austria and Germany; Dance; Electronic Music: History and Development; Form; Happening; Indeterminacy; Instrumental and Vocal Resources; Microtones; Mixed Media; Performance; Prose Music; Recording; Rhythm; Text Setting and Usage; Texture; Tuning and Temperament; United States.

Le Caine, Hugh (b. Port Arthur, Ontario, 27 May 1914), studied physics until 1939 at Queen's Univ. in Kingston and during 1948–52 at the Univ. of Birmingham in England. He worked for the National Research Council of Canada during 1940–48 and since 1952 has researched and developed electronic equipment there. He has invented a variety of electronic instruments and equipment. His first (1937) embodied a new, more flexible means of organ tone generation in which free reeds, instead of valves, control the air supply and the electrical output is controlled by the voltage applied to the reed by a keying system; the instrument was developed to measure very small currents in the nuclear physics laboratory. Over the next 30 years he developed a number of touch-sensitive keyboard devices, including printed-circuit keyboards (1962) and printed-circuit hand controllers for the spatial projection of sound (1964). His polyphone (1970) is a polyphonic keyboard instrument with touch-sensitive keys and independently tunable oscillators (with waveforms also independently adjustable), each covering the audible range and capable of frequency modulation. In 1959 he helped set up the first Canadian electronic music studio (at the Univ. of Toronto) and in 1964, the second (at McGill Univ.). In 1961 he developed special equipment for the studio at Hebrew Univ. in Jerusalem. He has taught seminars on electronic music at the Univ. of Toronto and at McGill Univ. since 1966.

PRINCIPAL COMPOSITIONS: *Dripsody* on tape (1955, recorded by Folkways); *99 Generators* for touch-sensitive organ keyboard (1956); *Invocation* on tape (1957); *A Noisome Pestilence* on tape (1958); *Textures* on tape (1958); *The Burning Deck* on tape (1958); *Alchemy* using a printed circuit keyboard (1964); *Perpetual Motion* on tape, composed with the aid of a computer (1970).

[prepared with the help of Lowell Cross]

Calabro, Louis (b. Brooklyn, N.Y., 1 Nov 1926), did graduate study at the Juilliard School (1948–53, composition with Vincent Persichetti). Since 1955 he has been teaching composition at Bennington College.

PRINCIPAL COMPOSITIONS: *Divertimento* for woodwind quintet (1954, E-V); *String Quartet No. 1* (1954); *Piano Sonata No. 1* (1954); *Young People's Sonatine* for piano (1955, E-V); *Suite of 7* for piano (1956, E-V); *Macabre Reflections*, 6 songs for mezzo-soprano, piano; poems by Howard Nemerov (1956, E-V); *Symphony No. 2* for strings (1957); *Motet in 42 parts* for chorus, brass; poem by G. M. Hopkins (1957); *Dynamogeny*, sonata for viola, piano (1958); *Ceremonial March* for brass, percussion (1958, E-V); *Metaphors* for 50-part chorus; poem by Wallace Stevens (1959); *Rain Has Fallen* for women's chorus; poem by James Joyce (1959); *10 Short Pieces* for strings (1961, E-V); *Symphony No. 3* (1962, E-V); *Dadacantatadada* for blues singer, orchestra (1964); *Great Society* (1965); *Diversities* for piano (1966, E-V); *Epitaphs* for orchestra, chorus (1967); *Piano Variations* (1968); *String Quartet No. 2* (1968); *The Child Sleeps* for chorus (1968, E-V); *Environments* for clarinet, 12 brasses (1969, E-V); *Latitude 15.09°N (Longitude 108.5°E)*, oratorio for alto chorus, orchestra (1970).

Camargo Guarnieri, Mozart, see under Guarnieri, (Mozart) Camargo

Canada. The first native Canadian composer is thought to have been a Jesuit priest, Charles-Amador Martin (1648–1711), from whom a Gregorian-chant composition survives, a prose in honor of the Holy Family. Subsequent landmarks include the first North American opéra-bouffe, *Colas et Colinette* (1788) by Joseph Quesnel (1749–1809), and orchestral music, piano works, and an operetta by Calixa Lavallée (1842–91), the most versatile and gifted of pre-20th century Canadian composers. French and English musical traditions were dominant during the generations of Guillaume Couture (1851–1915) and Healey Willan (1880–1968). Finally during the late 1930s and early 40s some outstanding native talents appeared who rejected this dominance.

A need for government and institutional support for music was felt in the 1940s, and positive responses to this need materialized during the next decade. In 1951 the *Report of the Royal Commission on National Development in the Arts, Letters, and Sciences* (called the Massey Report after the commission chairman, the Rt. Hon. Vincent Massey) was published. Its main practical effects for music were the establishment in 1957 of the Canada Council to administer federal support for the arts, humanities, and social sciences, and through the Council the establishment in 1959 of the Canadian Music Centre. An independent event, but one related to the overall feeling of rebirth, was the founding of the Canadian League of Composers in 1951. The Canada Council has given scholarships to young musicians and leave-fellowships and short-term work grants to established older ones. It has also given grants to performing organizations, sometimes for the specific purpose of commissioning and/or performing new works. The Canadian Music Centre was established to promote Canadian music and to provide a reference and loan collection of scores and recordings; by 1970 the collection included some 4,000 works by about 130 composers. The League, which began with 15 members, had 52 by 1970. During the 1950s established composers, among them John Weinzweig, Murray Adaskin, Barbara Pentland, and István Anhalt, moved into key teaching posts in Canadian universities, bringing with them contemporary techniques and a professional orientation. Before their arrival music had generally been geared to the conservative and craft-oriented examination system prevalent in British and U.S. universities in the 19th and early 20th centuries. By 1970 about two dozen universities were offering professional degrees in music education, performance, musicology, and composition. Another evidence of expanding activity came in 1958 when the Univ. of Toronto Electronic Music Studio was founded, the second such studio in North America. Subsequently studios were founded at McGill Univ. in Montreal, at Simon Fraser

Univ. in Burnaby, British Columbia, and at the Univ. of British Columbia in Vancouver. Some composers put together studios of their own, of which those of Otto Joachim in Montreal, and Samuel Dolin in Toronto were among the first.

During the 1960s attention was focused on Canadian music through commissions for new works to inaugurate several performing arts centers and, in 1967, to commemorate the centennial of Canadian Confederation and Expo 67, the world's fair at Montreal. At least 140 works were commissioned for the events of 1967, some of which turned out to be far more than *pièces d'occasion*: in the orchestral category, John Weinzweig's *Concerto* for harp and chamber orchestra, Otto Joachim's *Contrasts*, and Bruce Mather's *Orchestral Piece 1967*; in chamber music, Barbara Pentland's *Trio con Alea* and R. Murray Schafer's *Requiems for the Party Girl*; and in stage works, Harry Freedman's ballet *Rose Latulippe* and Harry Somers's opera *Louis Riel*. In addition to bringing such works as these to light, the wave of commissions in 1967 seems to have reinforced the practice of commissioning as a part of Canadian cultural life.

In Canada, as in the world at large, performances of new music are generally dependent on the efforts of individual musicians. Only a few Canadian orchestras have featured large amounts of 20th-century music. The Vancouver Chamber Orchestra plays from the modern repertory regularly, and the Winnipeg Symphony Orchestra included much contemporary music during 1958–68, when it was under the leadership of Victor Feldbrill. Among other conductors, Meredith Davies (in Vancouver, 1963–71) and Seiji Ozawa (in Toronto, 1965–69) have programmed new and avant-garde music, including that of Canadians. The Ten Centuries Concerts, a Toronto series managed by a group of local composers and orchestral players during 1962–67, presented unfamiliar music for smaller media from all eras, including some daring innovations from the contemporary repertory. The composer Udo Kasemets founded the Isaacs Gallery Ensemble, which presented mixed-media concerts intermittently in Toronto during 1965–69. Other centers for new music are the concerts of the Société de Musique Contemporaine du Québec (founded 1966 by Serge Garant), an annual three-day festival at Niagara-on-the-Lake, Ont. (begun 1970), and New Music Concerts in Toronto (begun 1972).

The vast geographical distances and relatively sparse population in Canada create great communications problems. No agency does more to promote new music than the Canadian Broadcasting Corporation, whose federally supported radio and television networks are a major means of coordinating and unifying the various regions and cultural groups in the country. In the years following World War II, the CBC supported composers mainly by giving national broadcasts of their works. As early as 1948 a library of transcriptions of Canadian music was started, amounting to about 300 works by 1969, and in 1967 some of these transcriptions began to be released by commercial record companies. In the early 70s the CBC began making its own recordings for commercial release. During the postwar years the CBC also compiled and published the first two editions (1947, 1952) of a *Catalogue of Canadian Composers*. During 1952–65 the CBC Symphony Orchestra in Toronto gave regular public and broadcast concerts in which new repertory, local and international, was given prominence. One effect, among others, was to acquaint Toronto orchestral players with new music. Under the direction of the composer Pierre Mercure, a CBC television series in the late 1950s and early 60s, "L'Heure du Concert," stressed the modern repertory. The CBC Vancouver Chamber Orchestra continues to program new works. Owing to all these activities, Canadian works of merit seldom go long without at least one performance. Furthermore composers have access to a nationwide audience, not just a local one, and they can tape performances of their works for private study and use. Since 1960 the CBC has been commissioning music at the rate of six to 20 or more works per season. Included are folk music arrangements, chamber works, orchestral pieces, musicals, and operas.

Aside from commercial releases of CBC transcriptions, nothing approaching an adequate coverage of Canadian music exists on records. In 1955 it was found that only two of the several discs produced up to that time were still available. By 1969 some 150 Canadian pieces were available to Canadian buyers. This repertory embraced a fair cross-section of the newer output but contained serious gaps as regards the composers included. The *Schwann Long Playing Record Catalog* for March 1969 included works by 11 contemporary Canadians but omitted such distinguished figures as Jean Papineau-Couture, Barbara Pentland, R. Murray Schafer, Gilles Tremblay, John Weinzweig, and Healey Willan. Part of the difficulty is that decisions about what should be recorded are made abroad, particularly in the U.S., where information about Canadian music is

scarce. Furthermore when a new and worthwhile Candian work is recorded, there is usually great difficulty in obtaining the foreign distribution and promotion that would make the recording commercially successful.

Although Canada's dozen-odd music publishing firms are of modest size, they have published most major composers of all esthetic persuasions. The major houses are Leeds, Ricordi, Boosey and Hawkes, Gordon V. Thompson (all in Toronto), Southern and Archambualt (in Montreal), Waterloo (in Waterloo, Ontario), and BMI Canada (in Toronto; the publishing activities of the organization were turned over to Berandol in 1969). Especially notable is the BMI Canada "Canavangard" series under the editorship of Udo Kasemets. In 1969 the Canada Council initiated 20,000-dollar annual subsidies to music publishers, a program that corresponds to its long-standing support of special projects in book publishing. Canadian music is less well served by critical writings. Books and articles by qualified writers are rare, and competent journalism almost equally so. The *Canadian Music Journal* (1955–62) was founded by the Canadian Music Council and discontinued because needed subsidies were withdrawn. The semi-annual *Cahiers de musique du Canada/ Canada Music Book* (begun 1970) revived the idea of an independent professional journal. *The Music Scene* (founded 1965) and the *Canadian Composer* (founded 1967) are organs of the performing-rights organizations BMI Canada and the Composers', Authors', and Publishers' Assoc. of Canada, respectively, and contain useful information. Another source is *Musicanada*, published by the Canadian Music Centre during 1967–70.

Since the 1930s Canadians have composed works in virtually every current international idiom; variety, in fact, is one of the chief features of Canadian music. In few Western countries have older styles been upheld with such skill as in the large output of Healey *Willan (1880–1968). His 14 settings of the *Missa brevis* (1932–63) show little evidence of contact with Canadian or international currents but contain a unique mixture of renaissance polyphony, early-20th-century modal harmony, Irish keening, and the reticence of Anglo-Catholic plainchant. Two organ works separated by 43 years, the *Passacaglia and Fugue No. 2* (1959) and the *Introduction, Passacaglia, and Fugue* (1916), both attest to Willan's command of full organ sonorities and post-Mendelssohn chromatic counterpoint. The earlier works of Claude *Champagne (1891–1965) recall the colorful folklorism of composers such as Falla; the *Symphonie gas-pésienne* (1945), for instance, is a musical travelogue through the Gaspé region in eastern Quebec. Later Champagne moved into more experimental areas, especially in the *String Quartet* (1956) and *Altitude* (1959) for chorus and orchestra, both of which show the atonal linearity of Schoenberg and the ecstatic and fervid textures of Messiaen.

Most composers of the 1910–30 generation were rather quick to adapt to and adopt international trends. Murray *Adaskin (b. 1906) relates to Milhaud in his early music, Jean *Papineau-Couture (b. 1916) to Stravinsky, Barbara *Pentland (b. 1912) to Hindemith and Copland. *Le Diable dans le beffroi* (1942) a tone poem by Jean Vallerand (b. 1915) is modeled on Dukas, while the violin and cello sonatas of John *Weinzweig (b. 1913) draw on the Jewish expressive vein that was also explored by Bloch. Each of these composers has also moved into other areas, such as serialism, the use of electronic apparatus, indeterminacy, and explorations of sound textures and sonorities. Weinzweig was the first Canadian to adopt the 12-tone method (in a short piano piece of 1939, composed, according to the composer, in response to a first hearing of Berg's *Lyric Suite*). Weinzweig's serial structures make use of a slow exposure technique by which, for example, notes 1–3 are set in motion for a few bars, then note 4, then 5 and 6, etc., until the whole repertory is established; the economic but kinetic character of his rhythmic style has been described by one critic as "pokes in the midriff." Similar features can be seen also in the music of such pupils of his as Harry *Somers (b. 1925) and Harry *Freedman (b. 1922). Weinzweig's later music includes intricate hexachord manipulations and a severely economical pointillism along with novel tone qualities, such as those resulting from unusual fingerings and tonguings in the clarinet part of the *Divertimento No. 4* (1968). In his *Harp Concerto* (1967) the timbres of the solo part are serialized. Some of his larger works (*Wine of Peace*, 1957; *Dummiyah*, 1969) contain social and political comment. Pentland has moved through post-Webern serialism (*Symphony for 10 Parts*, 1957) to semifree assemblages like the *Trio con Alea* for strings (1966) and notated-rubato studies à la Elliott Carter, such as the *Septet* for organ, brasses, and strings (1967). Somers has essayed in turn neoclassic fugal processes (*Symphony No. 1*, 1951), spatial-antiphonal orchestration (*Stereophony*, 1962), indeterminacy (*Evocations* for voice and piano, 1966), and theater pieces (*Improvisation*, 1968).

Papineau-Couture was attracted to serial composition by way of the cyclic-variation processes he employed in such pieces of the mid-1950s as the *Psaume CL*. In each of the later series of five *Pièces concertantes* (1957–63) for various orchestral ensembles, mirroring or additive phrases or the use of fan shapes became a single, central principle of development. Further constructional maneuvers occur in the *Sextuor* (1967), in which all lines, after reaching a central point in time, are played in exact reverse. Comparable tendencies occur in the later work of Pierre *Mercure (1927–66), whose *Lignes et pointes* (1965) is a 24-unit serial work, and in such Varèse-inspired instrumental pieces as *L'Etoile noire* (1962) and *Neumes d'espace et reliefs* (1967) by François *Morel (b. 1926).

In their imaginative extensions of texture and sonority, the pieces by Mercure and Morel are comparable to Somers's *5 Concepts for Orchestra* (1961), each of which examines a different musical facet, such as dynamic cross-fading or fast ornamentation, and Weinzweig's *Divertimento No. 4* for clarinet and strings, a brief but exhaustive display of color and pitch changes on the clarinet (including glides and quarter tones). Various works by Bruce *Mather (b. 1939), Gilles *Tremblay (b. 1932), and Serge *Garant (b. 1929) reflect the exploitation of timbres and rhythmic freedom by such Europeans as Boulez and Berio. Their command of the newer percussion devices is shown in their use of special objects for beating or scraping (knitting needles on drums, double-bass bows on cymbals, etc.), special ways of relating body to instrument (knuckles, flat of the hand, elbow, forearm), new instruments or new attack points for old ones, and detailed seating plans to allow one player easy access to numerous timbres. Mather used a conventional orchestra in his *Orchestra Piece 1966* with its gradually expanding interludes for piano, mandolin, and harp. Tremblay combined the ondes Martenot with a delicate percussion battery and three solo voices in *Kékoba* (1965); in this work he incorporated a wide gamut of ondes timbres that are untapped in most European music for the instrument. Garant's *Anerca* (1961–63), set to translated Eskimo texts, reminds one of Boulez's *Le Marteau sans maître*; his *Phrases 2* (1968) for orchestra, in which the players speak and shout phrases by Che Guevara as they play, is aligned with Weinzweig's social-political music in purpose and with the later works of George Crumb in technique.

The first work by a Canadian to employ indeterminacy was probably the *Nonet* (1959–

60) of Otto *Joachim (b. 1910). In the second movement the choice and order of the given musical components is left to the performers; the first movement, which is fully notated, is recorded on tape during each performance, and the tape is played backwards as the third movement. In Joachim's *Illumination I* (1965), lights are aimed at each music stand and varied in intensity by the leader at a dimmer-board; the fluctuations in intensity determine such features as the speed, loudness, and prominence of each part in the texture. His *Contrasts* for full orchestra also employs controlled choice; pitches and most tone colors are specified, while the durations of notes and of sections are only roughly indicated. Udo *Kasemets (b. 1919) has embraced indeterminacy wholeheartedly; his theatrical and gamelike pieces derive from *I Ching* and other sources, and his scores often resemble scripts or choreographic scenarios more than musical notation. His *Variations (on Variations [on Variations])* (1966) are variations by the performers on variations by Kasemets on a poetic text that is itself variational, centering around different associations of the same few words and syllables.

Quotation, both in the dislocating sense of Satie and in the newer sense of George Rochberg, Berio, and others, may be observed in its Canadian guise in my own words-and-music collages (*The Line Across*, 1965, uses a galop by Lavallée with Lavallée's name as the central text element) and in some recent works by R. Murray *Schafer (b. 1933). Schafer's *Gitā* for chorus, brasses, and tape (1967), which is based on a Sanskrit text, quotes from a Heinrich Schütz motet, while his *Son of Heldenleben* (1968) for orchestra superimposes mid-century percussion sounds on several passages from the Richard Strauss tone poem played simultaneously.

Jazz is cultivated in the larger Canadian cities, and its influence shows in the country's composed concert music, as well as in third-stream compositions. Weinzweig's music often reveals his retention of the "swing" of 1930s jazz; the word *swing*, in fact, is a recurrent rhythmic indication in his scores as late as the *Divertimento No. 4* (1968). Jazz timbres, rhythms, and structure are overt in works of Freedman, such as the *Woodwind Quintet* (1962) and *Armana* for orchestra (1967). Third-stream works are most evident from the Toronto group centered around the jazz composer, author, and teacher Gordon Delamont (b. 1918) and particularly the composer Norman *Symonds (b. 1920). Symonds's *Concerto grosso* for jazz quintet and symphony

orchestra (1958) is more natural than such parallel European works as those of Rolf Liebermann, in which the jazz element is more superficially imitated and more crudely contrasted with the concert-symphonic vocabulary.

In the field of electronic music Canadians have played a noteworthy role. As early as the late 1930s the experimental filmmaker Norman McLaren was drawing soundtracks on film by hand. From about 1948 Hugh Le *Caine (b. 1914), an inventor in the fields of physics and electronics, worked on electronic devices and brief electronic compositions at the National Research Council in Ottawa; his *Dripsody* (1955) is an early example of concrete music; a single drip of water formed the basic sound resource. Other examples include the short inventions (1964–70) of Gustav Ciamaga (b. 1930) and four *Electronic Compositions* (1959–62) by István *Anhalt (b. 1919). Combinations of live and prerecorded sounds in Canadian music date from Garant's *Nucléogamme* (1954) and include Anhalt's *Cento* (1967) for tape and 12 solo speaking voices, his *Symphony of Modules* (1967) for orchestra (involving controlled chance) and stereo tape, and *Tétrachromie* (1963) by Mercure, in which a stereo tape part is combined with a wind trio and a four-man percussion group, the aim being to create sound images corresponding to a prearranged scheme of changing color patterns (a latter-day "color-symphony" à la Scriabin). An application of the electronic experience to conventional media can be heard in the third movement of the *Symphony No. 3* (1968) of Clermont *Pepin (b. 1926), with its wide clusters, bizarre registral switches, and free (nonrepetitive and nonmotivic) rhythms. Anhalt perhaps anticipated such applications in the long-sustained and carefully controlled densities of his *Symphony No. 1* (1958).

Opportunities for the production of new operatic and other stage works have increased in recent years; 1967 saw 20 new works produced. The recent repertory ranges from Willan's Delius-like *Deirdre* (1946), based on the Irish legend, through my own *Night Blooming Cereus* (1958), a "rural-Ontario 'Winter's Tale'" (as one critic put it), to the experimental works of Schafer and Gabriel Charpentier (b. 1925). Schafer's *Loving/Toi* (1964–65), a bilingual television opera in which the composer had Charpentier as colibrettist and Mercure as producer, uses advanced film techniques, modern mime and dance movement, and a musical vocabulary incorporating the new vocal virtuosity, both prerecorded and live sounds, aleatoric percussion parts, among other techniques, to express the theme of feminine elusiveness. Charpentier's *An English Lesson* (1968) is a chamber opera for speakers, singers, and instrumental ensemble on a text consisting entirely of French words and phrases commonly used in English (rendezvous, savoir faire, etc.); his *Orphée* (1969) retells the legend with audience participation, a rock-and-roll orgy, and a male lead who performs to his own accompaniment on folk instruments (wood flute, bagpipes, hurdy-gurdy). The most successful operatic venture of recent seasons is Somers's *Louis Riel* (1967), based on the life of a half-breed Canadian rebel of the 1860s–80s. The work combines a bilingual libretto, adaptations of 19th-century popular tunes, Canadian Indian motives, elaborate stereophonic effects, and, in some sections, prerecorded sound.

A leitmotiv in 20th-century Canadian culture is the longing for separate artistic identity (or identities). This is no belated quest for nationalism. Rather it corresponds to the impulse that drives Japanese composers of today to reexamine their dying classical traditions amid their involvement with post-Webernism, electronics, etc. Canadians, habitually sceptical about their own artistic achievements, have been slow to define what musical threads might lend a local touch to their handling of global movements. On the one hand, of course, such indigenous accents are implied in the character of the best works by the country's best composers. On the other, a renewed interest in ethnomusicology may be on the brink of revealing hitherto little understood facets of Canadian musical culture. In the 1920s and 30s composers such as Sir Ernest MacMillan, Hector Gratton, and Claude Champagne were much concerned with the country's indigenous and imported folk music; but such preoccupations virtually disappeared from view in the work of succeeding generations. The 1960s inaugurated a swing back, if not to folk music, at least to studies of music in relation to the Canadian environment that may in time be more useful for composers. The groundwork was well laid by Marius Barbeau (1885–1969), who beginning in the first decade of the 20th century studied French-Canadian music and the musics of many native Indian tribes. To Barbeau's pioneering efforts were added the field researches of Helen Creighton in the Atlantic Provinces, Kenneth Peacock, and others. Current projects of the federal Museum of Man include the collecting of songs among several dozen ethnic groups that have contributed to the complex Canadian pattern, from the Mennonites of rural Alberta to the older-established segments of urban Montreal's Jewish community.

BIBL.: John Beckwith and Udo Kasemets, eds., *The Modern Composer and His World* (Toronto 1961); Lowell M. Cross, *A Bibliography of Electronic Music*, revised ed. (Toronto 1970); Andrée Desautels, "Les Trois Ages de la musique au Canada," *La Musique* ed. by N. Dufourcq (Paris 1965); Helmut Kallmann, ed., *Catalogue of Canadian Composers*, revised ed. (Toronto 1952); ———, *A History of Music in Canada 1534–1914* (Toronto 1960); Annette Lasalle-Leduc, *La Vie musicale au Canada français* (Quebec 1964); Ernest MacMillan, ed., *Music in Canada* (Toronto 1955); Julian Park, ed., *The Culture of Contemporary Canada* (Ithaca, N. Y., 1957); Malcolm Ross, ed., *The Arts in Canada* (Toronto 1958); *34 Biographies of Canadian Composers* (Montreal; CBC, 1964); Arnold Walter, ed., *Aspects of Music in Canada* (Toronto 1969). Since 1963 catalogs of Canadian music have been published by the Canadian Music Centre in Toronto.

John Beckwith

Cardew, Cornelius (b. Winchcombe, Gloucestershire, England, 7 May 1936), received his musical education as a chorister at Canterbury Cathedral (1943–50) and at the Royal Academy of Music in London (1953–57). He studied electronic music in Cologne (1957–58) and was assistant to Karlheinz Stockhausen (1958–60), during which time *Carré* for choruses and orchestras was produced as a collaborative effort. He also studied with Goffredo Petrassi in Rome (1964–65). Since 1960 he has performed, lectured, and taught in Britain, Europe, and the U.S. He lives in London.

Cardew's early pieces, mostly for piano, employ serial techniques and follow the style of piano music being written at that time by Boulez and Stockhausen, though the writing is somewhat freer. The music is carefully conceived for the instruments used (for instance, the notation of harmonics and decay of sounds in *February Pieces*). The influence of John Cage began to show around 1960, when Cardew's notation became more graphic and the form of his music tended to indeterminacy with respect to instrumentation, duration, etc. This trend culminated in *Treatise* (1963–67), a 193-page graphic score without instructions, to which the performer reacts freely. The more recent pieces employ a mixture of musical, verbal, and graphic elements, e.g., *Schooltime Compositions* (1967–) or *The Great Learning*, part I (1968), in which the score includes the Chinese characters of the text for which a chorus, playing whistles, improvises sound equivalents.

The earlier music demands considerable technical skill of the performers. In contrast the newer pieces can be played by non-musicans. They require no less expertise, however, for the performer must constantly be aware that he is part of a group activity and must act accordingly; his difficulties are mental and social rather than physical and individual. The concept of the performer as a member of society, not as an insulated music-making machine, is a logical extension of Cage's recent views on composing; it also stems, in Cardew's case, from a wide experience of improvised music (notably with the AMM group in London and with the Scratch Orchestra, which he founded in 1969). This experience has considerably influenced his thinking, and it is here too that his influence on younger composers, especially in Britain, has been greatest.

PRINCIPAL COMPOSITIONS: *String Trio* (1957, Hinrichsen); *2 Books of Study for Pianists* (1958, Hinrichsen); *Autumn '60* for orchestra (1960, UE); *Octet '61 for Jasper Johns* for unspecified instruments (1961, Hinrichsen); *Ah Thel* for mixed chorus (1962, Novello); *Treatise* for unspecified performing medium (1963–67, GUP); *Solo with Accompaniment* for unspecified instruments (1964, UE); *3 Winter Potatoes* for piano (1965, UE); *Schooltime Compositions* for unspecified performing medium (1967– , GUP); *The Great Learning* for various performers (parts 1–7, 1968–70).

PRINCIPAL WRITINGS: "The Unity of Musical Space," *New Departures* (1959, No. 1):53–56; "Notation, Interpretation, Etc.," *Tempo* 58:21; "Report on Stockhausen's *Carré*," *Musical Times* (Oct 1961):619 and (Nov 1961):698; "Contemporary Music," *Westermann's Concert Guide* ed. by Gerhard von Westermann and translated by Cardew (London 1963):422–45; "A Scratch Orchestra: Draft Constitution," *Musical Times* (June 1969):617–19; *Treatise Handbook* (Buffalo 1970).

BIBL.: Justin Conolly, "C.'s 'The Great Digest'," *Tempo* 86:16–17; Brian Dennis, "C.'s 'The Great Learning'," *Musical Times* (Nov 1971); Edward Greenfield, "Shoot the Pianist, Not the Composer," *The Guardian* (5 August 1967):4; G. W. Hopkins, "Potatoes," *Musical Times* (August 1967):739; Roger Smalley, "A Beautiful Score," *ibid.* (May 1968):462.

Christopher Hobbs

SEE ALSO Great Britain, Performance, Prose Music, Rhythm.

Cardoso, Lindembergue (Rocha) (b. Livramento, Brazil, 30 June 1939), studied at the Music Seminary of the Univ. of Bahia (1959–70; composition with Ernst Widmer). He conducted the S. Bento Chorale during 1966–70, and during 1968–70 he taught at the Musical Institute in Bahia. He has played saxophone for the Itapoan Television Network (1960–62) and bassoon in the Symphony Orchestra of Bahia Univ. (since 1968). In 1966 he helped found the Grupo de Compositores da Bahia. His music has been influenced by his researches into folk and popular idioms and by works from the Darmstadt summer courses, which he has heard at the yearly festivals of the Escola de Musica e Artes Cênicas of Bahia Univ.

PRINCIPAL COMPOSITIONS: *A festa da Canabrava* for orchestra (1966); *O fim do mundo* [The End of the World] for chorus, winds, percussion (1966); *Missa nordestina* for chorus (1967); *Piano Trio* (1967); *Minisuite* for wind ensemble (1967); *Caricaturas* for percussion (1967); *Via sacra* for orchestra (1968); *O boi Espaço* [The Bull Espaço], ballet for voices, flute, clarinet, bassoon, timpani, percussion, guitar; choreography by Lia Robato (1968); *Procissão das carpideiras* [Procession of the Weepers], for mezzo-soprano, women's chorus, orchestra (1969); *Captações* for voices, winds, strings, radios, electronic apparatus (1969); *Serestachôrofrevo* for orchestra (1969); *Espectros* [Ghosts] for chorus, orchestra (1970); *Dois* [Duo] for soprano, bassoon (1970); *Aleluia* for chorus (1970); *Wind Quintet* (1970); *Morte, paixão e vida no ano de Aquarius* [Death, Passion, and Life in the Year of Aquarius], ballet for voices, flute, brass, folk percussion, piano, electric guitar, electronic apparatus; choreography by Robato (1970).

Carlstedt, Jan (Axel) (b. Orsa, Sweden, 15 June 1926), studied at the Royal Academy of Music in Stockholm (1948–52, composition with Lars-Erik Larsson) and at the Royal College of Music in London (1952–53; composition with Herbert Howells). He also studied privately in Italy during 1954–55 and later in Czechoslovakia and Spain. In 1960 he founded the contemporary music society, Samtida Musik, in Stockholm and in 1961, Musik för Ungdom, the Swedish branch of Jeunesses Musicales. During 1961–63 he was secretary of the Society of Swedish Composers; he became treasurer in 1969. Since 1970 he has been a board member of the Swedish Society of Composers, Authors, and Publishers. His music has been somewhat influenced by his studies of folk music from Sweden and southern and eastern Europe and by the symphonic music of Shostakovich and Britten.

PRINCIPAL COMPOSITIONS (published by Suecia unless otherwise noted): *Symphonies Nos. 1–2* (1952–54, 1968); *String Quartets 1–3* (1952, 1966, 1967); *String Trio* (1955); *Sonata* for string orchestra (1956, Hansen-W); *Sonata* for solo violin (1959); *Divertimento* for oboe, violin, viola, cello (1962); *Cello Concerto* (1970).

SEE ALSO Scandinavia.

Carneyro, Claudio (b. Porto, Portugal, 27 Jan 1895; d. Porto, 18 Oct 1963), studied at various times in Porto with Carlos Dubbini (violin) and Lucien Lambert (composition) and in Paris during 1923–24 with Charles-Marie Widor and Paul Dukas (composition). He taught composition at the Municipal Conservatory in Porto (1934–58) and was director there (1955–58). He was a member of the Office for Portuguese Musical Studies of the National Radio Network during 1942–49 and musical consultant for the Northern Regional Radio during 1943–51. In 1946–47 he founded the Porto Chamber Orchestra. His work was strongly influenced by his interest in Portuguese folk music.

PRINCIPAL COMPOSITIONS: *Improviso sobre uma cantiga do Povo* for violin, piano (1925); *Partita* for string trio (1928–35, Gulbenkian); *3 Poemas en prosa* for piano (1930, Sassetti); *Cantares*, 6 short songs for voice, piano, on medieval Portuguese poems (1931); *Momento* for string orchestra (1933, Gulbenkian); *Pavana e galharda* for string orchestra (1939); *Khroma* for viola, orchestra (1941); *O simbolismo Cristão na cantiga poplar* for women's voices (1941, Portucalense); *Catavento* for piano, chamber orchestra (1942); *5 Short Pieces* for mezzo-soprano (baritone), orchestra (1942); *20 Harmonizations of Portuguese Folksongs* (1942, GEMEM); *Nau Catrineta*, ballet on a Portuguese legend (1944); *String Quartet in D Minor* (1957, Gulbenkian); *Harpa eolia* for piano (1948, Sassetti); *Dizem* for women's chorus, text by Fernando Pessoa (1948); *Portugalesas*, suite for orchestra (1949); *Orações populares*, 6 pieces for women's chorus (1951); *Roda dos degredados* for violin, orchestra (1960); *Bagatella* for 2 pianos (1961); *Bailadeiras* for orchestra (1962); *Gradualis* for orchestra (1962).

PRINCIPAL WRITINGS: *Pregoes* [On Portuguese Street Cries] (Porto 1936); *Bi-centenario de Mozart* (Porto 1950); "Em memoria de Carlos Dubbini," *Boletim camara municipal do Porto* 18:1–2; "Analise de O cravo bem temperado'," *Arte musical* (August 1965):752–57. Carneyro also wrote program notes for the Porto branch of Circulo de Cultura Musical.

BIBL.: *Arte musical* (August 1965); Vasco Mariz, "C. C.," *Comercio de manhã* (Rio de Janeiro 1949). Program notes by João de Freitas-Branco have appeared in Gulbenkian Festival program booklets (1961–68).

[prepared with the help of Katherine Carneyro]

Carrillo, Julián (b. Ahualulco, San Luis Potosí, Mexico, 28 Jan 1875; d. San Angél, 9 Sept 1965), studied at the Academy of Don Flavio F. Carlos in his native state (1885–90) and at the National Conservatory with Pedro Manzano (violin), Melesio Morales (composition), and Francisco Ortega y Fonseca (acous-tics). During this period Carrillo coined the term *sonido 13* [13th sound], referring to a specific microtonal pitch, the first two-octave harmonic on the fourth string of the violin. To Carrillo this was the first pitch to lie outside the traditional tuning system of 12 semitones to the octave; he later applied the term to his entire microtonal system, which he codified during the late teens and early 20s. Championed by Porfirio Díaz, Carrillo continued his training in Europe during 1899–1904, first at Leipzig (theory with K. Reinecke, composition with S. Jadassohn, conducting with A. Nikisch and H. Sitt, violin with H. Becker) and then at the Ghent Conservatory under A. Zimmer (violin).

During 1906–24 Carrillo was engaged in public service. Among other activities he founded the Beethoven Orchestra and String Quartet in Mexico City (1909), was president of the International Congress on Music in Rome (1911), was director of the National Conservatory in Mexico (1913, 1920–24), and founded and conducted the Symphony Orchestra of America in New York (during World War I). During the last 40 years of his life he worked out the potentialities of the *sonido 13* system in terms of theory, musical instruments, notation, and composition. In 1926 Leopold Stokowski began championing Carrillo's microtonal works with a performance of his first *Sonata casi fantasia* in 4ths, 8ths, and 16ths of a whole tone. Throughout the 1930s Carrillo and Stokowski toured Mexico (Chihuahua, Tabasco, Durango, Jalapa, and other states) with the newly formed Sonido 13 Orchestra. In 1947 Carrillo built his first piano tuned in 3rds of a whole tone; 15 differently tuned pianos (from 3rds to 16ths of a whole tone) were built by the German firm of Carl Sauter and displayed at the Brussels World's Fair in 1958 (many of Carrillo's instruments are now at the Univ. of Ill.). In the 1960s the Philips Company in Paris recorded some 40 works with Carrillo conducting the Lamoureux Orchestra. Carrillo's esthetic of newness in music through an emphasis on sound per se has influenced Latin Americans of the younger generation, among whom are Mario Davidowsky and Mauricio Kagel of Argentina and Leon Schidlowsky and Samuel Claro of Chile.

Carrillo's works using traditional tuning include 15 orchestral, 10 dramatic, 20 chamber, and 20 solo compositions. His output in the *sonido 13* system consists of 14 orchestral, 3 dramatic, 30 chamber, and 32 solo compositions. The works written at the turn of the century (such as the *Symphony No. 1*) are in the style of Brahms; during 1911–22 Carrillo wrote atonal music. When he took up his *sonido 13* idiom in 1922 (beginning with the *Preludio a Colón*), he returned to tonality with strong impressionist overtones. (Tonality was possible to maintain because all of Carrillo's microtones are equally tempered subdivisions of traditionally tuned whole tones.) Probably because of the newness of the *sonido 13* sound, Carrillo remained conservative in terms of tonality, as well as in terms of form, melody, meter, texture, and other musical elements. Some of his orchestral works employ a concept he called *metamorfoseador* [metamorphosis], by which the baroque concerto-grosso medium is used with the concertino in *sonido 13* and the ripieno in traditional tuning; an example is *Horizontes* (1950).

PRINCIPAL COMPOSITIONS (published by Sonido 13): In traditional tuning: *Symphony No. 1 in D* (1901); *Symphony No. 2 in C* (1908); *4 Atonal String Quartets* (1917–20); *Impresiones de la Hubana*, suite for orchestra (1928); *Xochimilco*, nocturne for orchestra (1935). ★ In *sonido 13* tuning: *Preludio a Colón* for small orchestra in 4ths, 8ths, 16ths of a tone (1922); *3 Colombias* for orchestra in 4ths, 8ths, 16ths (1926–30); *Fantasia Sonido 13* for small orchestra in 4ths, 8ths, 16ths (1931); *Preludio 29 de Septiembre* for piano in 30ths (1949); *Horizontes*, prelude for small orchestra in 4ths, 8ths, 16ths, accompanied by an orchestra tuned in conventional semitones (1950); *6 Casi Sonatas* for violin in 4ths (1957–59); *4 Casi Sonatas* for viola in 4ths (1957–59); *6 Casi Sonatas* for cello in 4ths (1959); *Balbuceos* for piano in 16ths (1959); *6 String Quartets* in 4ths (1958–64); *Misa de la restauración* in 4ths for men's voices a cappella (1962); *2 Violin Concertos* in 4ths (1964). Complete list of compositions and theoretical writings in Benjamin (see bibl.).

PRINCIPAL THEORETICAL WRITINGS: *Pre-Sonido 13: Analisis físico-musical* (New York 1926); *Leyes de metamorfosis musicales* (New York 1927); *Génesis de la revolución musical del sonido 13 . . .* (San Luis Potosí 1940); *Sonido 13: Fundamento científico e histórico* (Mexico City 1948); *Dos leyes de física musical* (Mexico City 1956); *Sistema general de escritura musical* (Mexico City 1957).

BIBL.: Gerald R. Benjamin, "J. C. and *Sonido Trece*," *Yearbook, Inter-American Institute for Musical Research* (Tulane Univ.) 3:33–68; Jean-Etienne Marie, "J. C.," *Nouvelles de Mexique* (Mexican Embassy in Paris) 43–44:3–10.

Gerald R. Benjamin
SEE ALSO Mexico, Microtones.

Carter, Elliott (Cook, Jr.) (b. New York, 11 Dec 1908), began to write music while still in high school and showed his first essays to Charles Ives, whose music he admired. Ives encouraged him to study music seriously and wrote a recommendation for him to Harvard Univ., where Carter majored in literature. In his senior year he turned to music and began study with Walter Piston. During 1932–35 he studied in Paris with Nadia Boulanger. On his return to the U.S. he was musical director of Ballet Caravan until 1940. He has taught at the Juilliard School and at several universities, principally Columbia, Yale, Cornell, and the Mass. Institute of Technology. The beginning of Carter's international fame came with the *String Quartet No. 1* (1951). Since then he has worked slowly, producing an important work every two or three years.

The neoclassicism in Carter's early music had an engaging fluency and above all a rhythmic vitality still characteristic of his writing. Looking back today one can see that the *Piano Sonata* (1945–46) marked a new beginning, a break not only with Carter's own previous work but with the other music of his time. The two innovations of the *Piano Sonata* are a new way of characterizing the harmonic structure of a work and a new conception of meter. The harmonic material of the sonata was inspired by the character of the instrument—its timbre, resonance, and even its mechanical properties—although this is true only if one considers the instrument as playing a heuristic and not a determinative role. The harmony derives from the overtone series and the overtone resonance of a concert grand piano. Not only the possibilities of making silently depressed notes resonate but the quality of sound that overtones produce in combination are used as a basis of the harmonies and, to some extent, of the melodic curve. Octave doubling becomes a functional harmony, not merely a reinforcement. From this comes the character of the music, its harsh brilliance, and the inevitable clang of bare fifths and octaves. The basic chord, which is built of successive fifths (B-F♯-C♯-G♯-D♯-A♯), resolves naturally to a B-major or A♯-major triad, and the opening of the *Sonata* immediately states an opposition between B and A♯ that runs through the entire work.

The metrical innovation is the combination of a steady rhythm with a continuously and rapidly changing pulse (there is a precedent for this in Bartók's *Etude* for piano No. 3, but there the idea is only briefly developed). The changes of time signature are so frequent (on an average of every two bars) that they were omitted from the score of the first movement as printed. The import of this innovation becomes clear only in the work that followed, the *Cello Sonata* (1948), with the development of "metric modulation," the establishment of a new tempo out of the development of a cross-rhythm within the old tempo. The point of this technique is neither the change of tempo nor the cross-accents but the clear sense of the simultaneous existence of two tempos—two rhythmic worlds in fact. In the end all the various tempos of a single work can be heard as specific divisions of one all-embracing conception.

In the *Sonata for Flute, Oboe, Cello, and Harpsichord* (1952), Carter's most immediately enchanting work, the instruments are each individually characterized, and their interaction is the collision of separate and impenetrable identities. The rhythm and tone color prevent an immediate blend of sound, and the unity is found only when one has accepted the articulated oppositions. The music attains the state of a true dialectic in which the play of musical ideas is as important as the ideas themselves. The movement is not linear, and the overlapping of the dialogue creates a fluidity that is genuinely new in music because it represents an interpenetration not of voices but of textures that are firmly outlined and never lose their separate identities.

In two works in particular, the *String Quartet No. 1* (1951) and the *Variations for Orchestra* (1955), the sense of rhythmic, textural, and instrumental identity is placed in the service of a dramatic esthetic best called by the old-fashioned term of the "sublime." In keeping with the grandeur of style, the *Quartet* renounces all color effects that do not spring directly from the melodic lines. The rhythmic impetus even absorbs the use of speech rhythms; here as always, recitative is a dramatization of an individual voice, but in the *Quartet* it does not represent a slackening of the larger organizing movement. The controlled flow of a *parlando* line is equally evident in the *Variations*, particularly in the unison string passages with which the third and seventh variations open.

At first the overlapping and superimposition of different rhythmic systems required a simplification of interior rhythm so that each system could be easily identified (Carter's rhythms are always designed to be heard events). In most cases this entailed an equalization of rhythm so that steady patterns were dovetailed and irregularities only gradually introduced. With the fourth of the *Variations*, however, the opposing patterns were introduced into a scheme of continuous deceleration and, with variation six, continuous acceleration. This technique was expanded in the *Double Concerto* for harpsichord, piano, and two chamber orchestras (1961). In this work

for 18 players, a sustained, cantabile slow movement is played by the winds and brass, with the strings pizzicato, the harpsichord and piano staccato, and a great variety of percussion instruments for four players delicately executing a continuous and steadily accelerating movement—a constantly changing filigree work imposed like a grid upon the lyrical background. This genuinely coloristic use of rhythm is followed by a duet in perpetual motion for both soloists in different rhythms (eight notes in the harpsichord to nine in the piano), where the doubling of the melody produces a staggered rhythmic effect like a controlled rubato. The orchestra and harpsichord make a long ritardando while the piano speeds up to the limit of the instrument's (and player's) capacities, dying away into a blurred murmur that continues to echo against the ever slower beats of the crotales and harpsichord. The wit of this work is evident throughout, starting with the controlled rise of the musical ideas in gradually defined fragments from the pure percussion sonority of the opening and ending with their disintegration after the massive climax that starts the coda. The complicated rhythms are not cross-rhythms but cross-tempos, for the divisions prevent the listener from assuming a basic pulse at the beginning of each measure. One hears clearly and easily as many as four rates of speed equally balanced.

With the *Double Concerto* the harmonic and rhythmic aspects of Carter's language derive the one from the other even more closely than before. This is achieved by what might be called a syncopated periodic pattern. In the piano cadenza, for example (bar 528), major ninths occur on every seventh note of a rapid tempo and major sevenths at every ninth note; a few bars later major thirds are introduced at every fifth note. The fascinating combinations that result as these series start together, move apart, and come together again are clearly audible. The *String Quartet No. 2* (1959) already exploits this conception by using different intervals to characterize and isolate each instrument, once again creating a play of opposing forces. In this quartet and in the *Double Concerto*, the composer emphasizes the high degree of characterization by a wide spacing on the stage so that each instrumentalist may be seen and heard as an independent unit.

The *Piano Concerto* (1966) carries this conception forward even more imaginatively: the concerto idea of a single voice against a mass is heightened paradoxically by fragmenting the orchestra and also by adding a concertino group to the piano solo. The fragmentation of the orchestra increases the sense of mass because it is used to form tone clusters. At certain points every member of the orchestra plays a different note in an enormous, monolithic cluster that fills the entire musical space. In a similar way the extra solo voices dramatize the isolation of the piano.

The *Concerto for Orchestra* (1969) shows Carter's most ambitious grasp of simultaneous large-scale rhythmic levels. Here we are dealing not with cross-tempos but with cross-movements, for the four movements exist simultaneously. Two of them are in a steady tempo: one, played by cello, piano, and harp, is forceful and heavy; the other, played by double bass, tuba, and trombones, is an impassioned recitative. The other two change gradually as the work proceeds: one, played mainly by flutes and violins, from extremely fast fluttering to sustained chords; the other, played by violas, trumpets, and oboes, from slow chords to extremely rapid notes. The movements are presented separately, juxtaposed and superimposed in a way that retains their integrity and yet forms a single dramatic progression. It is less the originality of the idea than the success with which it has been carried out that makes Carter today the composer who has done so much to enlarge our conception of musical time and its relation to harmonic space.

PRINCIPAL COMPOSITIONS (published by AMP unless otherwise noted): *Pocahontas*, ballet; choreography by Lew Christensen (1937–39); *Symphony No. 1* (1942); *Holiday Overture* for orchestra (1944, revised 1961); *Piano Sonata* (1945–46, Mercury); *The Minotaur*, ballet; choreography by John Taras (1947); *Cello Sonata* (1948); *8 Etudes and a Fantasy* for woodwind quartet (1949–50); *String Quartet No. 1* (1951); *Sonata for Flute, Oboe, Cello, Harpsichord* (1952); *Variations for Orchestra* (1955); *String Quartet No. 2* (1958–59); *Double Concerto* for harpsichord, piano, 2 chamber orchestras (1961); *Piano Concerto* (1966); *Concerto for Orchestra* (1969). List to 1959: *Composers of the Americas* 5:31–35.

PRINCIPAL WRITINGS: various articles in *Modern Music* (1937–46); "Gabriel Fauré," *Listen* (May 1945): 8–9, 12; "Walter Piston," *Musical Quarterly* 32:354–73; "La Musique aux Etats-Unis," *Synthèses* (Brussels, May 1954): 206–11; "The Rhythmic Basis of American Music," *Score* (June 1955): 27–32; "Music of the Twentieth Century," *Encyclopedia Britannica* (Chicago 1957) 16:16–18; "Shop Talk by an American Composer," *Musical Quarterly* 46:182–201; "The Milieu of the American Composer," *Perspectives* I/1:149–51; "Expressionism and American Music," *ibid.* 4/1:1–13; "A Further Step," *The American Composer Speaks* ed. by G. Chase (Baton Rouge, La., 1966). Complete list to 1957 in Edmunds.

BIBL.: John Edmunds, *Some 20th-Century American Composers*, vol. 1 (New York 1959); William Glock, "A Note on E. C.," *Score* (June 1955): 27–32; Richard Franko Goldman, "Current Chronical—New York," *Musical Quarterly* 46: 361–64; Michael Steinberg, "E. C.s 2 Streichquartett," *Melos* (Feb 1961):35–37; Kurt Stone, "Current Chronical—New York," *Musical Quarterly* 55:559–72; Igor Stravinsky and Robert Craft, *Dialogues and a Diary* (New York 1963):47–48.

Charles Rosen

SEE ALSO Dance, Notation, Orchestration, Rhythm, United States.

Cary, Tristram (Ogilvie) (b. Oxford, 14 May 1925), is the son of novelist Joyce Cary. He had music lessons from his mother but did not decide on a career in music until after he began service in the navy in 1942. He studied science and philosophy at Christ Church, Oxford (1942, 1946–47) and music at the Trinity College of Music (1948–50, composition with George Oldroyd). He began experimenting with electronics and music in 1947 (work with radar in the navy had introduced him to electronics) and by 1949 he was producing musique concrète on primitive disc equipment. His first electronic scores date from 1952–55. From 1950 on he did lecture and concert work and soon after began composing for films, radio, and television. He has his own electronic studio (it was the first in Great Britain) and in 1968 founded a studio at the Royal College of Music, where he teaches. Since 1969 he has also been director of a design and manufacturing concern, Electronic Music Studios, Ltd.

PRINCIPAL CONCERT WORKS: *Three Threes and One Make Ten*, concerto grosso for 5 winds, 5 strings (1961, Novello); *Sonata for Guitar Alone* (1961, Novello); *3 4 5*, electronic score (1967, Galliard); *Birth is Life is Power is Death is God is . . .*, electronic score (1967, Galliard); *Narcissus* for flute, tape recorder (1968, Galliard); *Continuum* electronic score (1969, Galliard); *Peccata mundi* for narrator, chorus, orchestra, 4 tape tracks; text by the composer (1969–70, Galliard); *Trios* for synthesizer, 2 turntables (1971, Electronic Music Studios, Ltd.).

PRINCIPAL FILM SCORES: *The Ladykillers* (1955); *The Little Island* (1958); *Sammy Going South* (1963); *Sources of Power*, a multiscreen film for the industrial section of the British Pavilion at Expo '67 in Montreal; Cary also prepared all of the other sound segments used in the industrial section (1967).

PRINCIPAL RADIO AND TELEVISION SCORES (for the BBC): *The Japanese Fishermen* (1955); *East of the Sun and West of the Moon* (1959); *The Children of Lir* (1959); *They Met on Good Friday* (1959); *The Infernal Machine* (1960); *The Ballad of Peckham*

Rye, 2nd version (1962); *Jane Eyre* (1963); *The Ha-Ha* (1963); *Madame Bovary* (1964); *The Rhyme of the Flying Bomb* (1964; concert suite, 1964); *Die Ballade von Peckham Rye* (1965, prepared for Austrian television and the NWDR); *Leviathan '99* (1968; concert suite, 1971).

PRINCIPAL WRITINGS: "Sproggletaggle," *Composer* (Jan 1966): 6–9; "Superserialismus—Is There a Cure?" *Electronic Music Review* (Oct 1967): 7–9; "Electronic Music, Its Creation, Protection and Exploitation," *Performing Right* (May 1970): 7–12; "Electronic Music, Background to a Developing Art," *Audio Annual* (1971): 42–49.

BIBL.: Hugo Cole, "His Monster's Voice." *Guardian* (9 July 1971): 8.

SEE ALSO Great Britain.

Casanova, André (b. Paris, 12 Oct 1919), studied law at the Faculté de Droit in Paris (1937–40) and Aix-en-Provence (1941). He studied music at the Ecole Normale de Musique, Paris (1942–43) and with René Leibowitz (1944–47). He teaches piano privately in Paris and was a member of the music committee of the French Radio during 1963–65. He regards Nietzsche and Wagner as the main influences on his musical development.

PRINCIPAL COMPOSITIONS: *Divertimento* for flute, oboe, clarinet, bassoon, violin, cello, piano, mezzo-soprano; text by J. Supervielle (1954, Jobert); *Ballade* for clarinet, chamber orchestra (1954–55, Ricordi); *Notturno* for piano, percussion, strings (1958–59, Ricordi); *Cavalier seul*, cantata for baritone, string quartet; text by Jean Moal (1960, Ricordi); *Capriccio* for oboe, orchestra (1960, Jobert); *Anamorphoses* for tenor saxophone, harp, percussion, strings (1961–62, Jobert); *Redoutes*, 5 songs for soprano, bass, orchestra; texts by J. Moal (1962, Choudens); *Concertino* for piano, chamber orchestra; arranged for orchestra alone by André Jouve (1962, Jobert); *Violin Concerto* (1963, Jobert); *Suite* for string orchestra (1964, Amphion); *Dithyrambes* for tenor, orchestra; text by Nietzsche (1964); *La Clé d'argent* for soprano, tenor, baritone, orchestra; text by Moal after Villiers de l'Isle-Adam (1964–65); *String Trio* (1966); *Serenade* for flute, instrumental ensemble (1966); *4 Intermezzi* for piano (1967); *Règnes*, 3 allegories for soprano, orchestra; text by Moal (1967); *Strophes* for xylophone, timpani, strings (1968); *Prelude* for string orchestra (1968); *Concerto* for oboe, harp, brass sextet, percussion (1968); *3 Poems of R. M. Rilke* for chorus (1968); *Hauteclaire, ou le bonheur dans le crime*, lyric drama in prologue, 3 acts; libretto by Bernard George after Barbey d'Aurevilly (1969).

PRINCIPAL WRITINGS: During 1955–56 Casanova wrote many articles on music for the French monthly *Preuves*. In addition, an interview with him appeared as "La Musique et l'équation," *Cahiers universitaires* 27: 58ff.

BIBL.: Luc-André Marcel, "A. C.," *Cahiers du sud* 380: 288–300; Lucien Rebatet, "La *Ballade* d'A. C.," *Ecrits de Paris* 68: 90–92.

Casella, Alfredo (b. Turin, 25 July 1883; d. Rome, 5 March 1947), was the son of Carlo Casella, a cellist, and Maria Bordino, an amateur pianist from whom he received his first piano training. There was considerable chamber-music playing in the Casella home, which provided the composer with what was an atypical (i.e., non-operatic) musical environment for an Italian of that time. When he was 12, his mother sent Casella to Paris where he attended the Conservatory for six years as a pupil of Louis Diémer (piano), Xavier Leroux (harmony and counterpoint), and Gabriel Fauré (composition). In 1902 he started his career as a concert pianist and the following year published his first chamber works. In 1912 he conducted the Concerts Populaires at the Trocadero Theater in Paris, and during 1912–15 he taught a piano class at the Paris Conservatory, originally as a substitute for Cortot. From 1915 to 1923 he taught piano at the Liceo Musicale di Santa Cecilia in Rome, all the while maintaining an active concert career as a soloist, a chamber musician, and conductor. In 1917 he founded the Italian Society for Modern Music through which he introduced the Italian public to contemporary Italian and foreign music, previously almost unknown in Italy. In 1924, with Gabriele D'Annunzio and Gian Francesco Malipiero, he founded the Corporazione delle Nuove Musiche, which later became a section of ISCM. His piano teaching positions included a master class at the Accadèmia di Santa Cecilia in Rome (1932–47) and summer courses at the Accadèmia Musicale Chigiana in Siena (1933–42). In 1939 he founded the Siena Weeks, a festival that concluded the summer courses and which still exists; it featured Italian baroque music, much of which Casella himself unearthed and edited (he was particularly interested in Vivaldi). He died after several years of illnesses resulting orginally from an intestinal occlusion.

Casella was a versatile composer who wrote in almost all mediums of musical expression: opera and ballet, chamber and orchestral genres, piano and organ works, and sacred music. His style is rather difficult to describe, for as Edward Dent has said, he helped his young countrymen to find a style for themselves but had difficulty finding one of his own. His early works were influenced by Debussy, Stravinsky, and Mahler, the latter of whose music he conducted in Paris early in the century when it was still largely unknown there. He once declared that he could become anything as a composer except a romantic (this in spite of his love of Chopin). He hated both Debussy's whole-tone scale and the ninth chords of late romantic music. He was tempted by dodecaphony, but his Italian nature, he said, prevented his from making it his own language however much he admired it. About 1920 he identified himself with the neo-classic movement, and his "definitive" style, to use his own words, was made of "a natural-ness and a simplicity that are the result of painful and wearisome assimilations and re-nunciations, and not outbursts of ingenuities and amateurisms." Perhaps his greatest achievement resulted from his activities on be-half of new music, for he paved the way for the renaissance of Italian symphonic and chamber music that returned Italy to the forefront of European musical developments.

PRINCIPAL COMPOSITIONS: *Toccata* for piano (1904, Ricordi); *Italia*, rhapsody for orchestra (1909, UE); *Suite in C* for orchestra (1909–10, UE); *Il convento veneziano*, choreographic comedy in 2 acts (1912–13, Ricordi); *Notte di maggio* for voice, orchestra (1913, Ricordi); *2 Chansons anciennes* for voice, piano (1913, Mathot); *Pupazzetti*, 5 easy pieces for piano 4-hands (1915, Ricordi); *Sonatina* for piano (1916, Ricordi); *A notte alta*, poem for piano (1917, transcribed for piano, orchestra, 1921; Ricordi); *12 Pezzi infantili* for piano (1920, UE); *3 Canzoni trecentesche* for voice, piano (1923, Ricordi); *Concerto for String Quartet* (1923–24, UE); *La giara*, choreographic comedy in 1 act (1924, UE); *Partita* for piano, orchestra 1924–25, UE); *Concerto romano* for organ, orchestra (1926, UE); *Scarlattiana*, divertimento for piano, 32 instruments on music of D. Scarlatti (1926, UE); *Cello Sonata in C* (1926, UE); *Serenade* for clarinet, bassoon, trumpet, violin, cello (1926, UE); *Violin Concerto in A Minor* (1928, UE); *La donna serpente*, fairy opera in 3 acts (1928–31, Ricordi); *Introduction, Choral, and March* for brass, percussion (1931–35, UE); *La favola d'Orfeo*, 1-act chamber opera (1932, Carisch); *Symphony* for piano, cello, clarinet, trumpet (1932, Carisch); *Introduction, Aria, and Toccata* for orchestra (1933, Ricordi); *Concerto* for piano, violin, cello, orchestra (1933, Ricordi); *Cello Concerto* (1934–35, Ricordi); *Symphony, Arioso, and Toccata* for piano (1936, Carisch); *Il deserto tentato*, 1-act mystery (1936–37, Ricordi); *Concerto for Orchestra* (1937, Ricordi); *Sonata a 3* for piano, violin, cello (1938, Ricordi); *Symphony* (1939–40, Ricordi); *La camara dei disegni*, 1-act children's ballet for chamber orchestra (1940, UE); *Paganiniana*, divertimento for orchestra (1942, UE); *La rosa del sogno*, 1-act ballet on music of Paganini (1942–43, UE); *6 Studies* for piano (1942–44, Curci); *3 Canti sacri* for baritone, organ (1943, S-Z); *Concerto* for strings, piano, timpani, percussion (1943, UE);

Missa Solemnis "Pro Pace" for soprano, baritone, chorus, orchestra (1944, UE). A complete list of works in D'Amico and Gatti (see bibl.).

PRINCIPAL WRITINGS: *The Evolution of Music Through the History of the Perfect Cadence* (London 1923); *Igor Strawinski* (Rome 1928); *21+26*, a collection of articles (Rome 1930); *Il pianoforte* (Rome–Milan 1937); *I segreti della giara*, an auto-biography (Florence 1941; an English translation, *Music in My Time*, published Norman, Okla., 1955); *John Sebastian Bach* (Turin 1942); *Strawinski* (Brescia 1947); *Beethoven Intimo* (Florence 1949); *La tecnica dell'orchestra contemporanea* (Milan 1950).

BIBL.: F. D'Amico, "C. dieci anni dopo," *Il contemporaneo* (Rome, 16 March 1957); ——, "Sulla *Messa* di C.," *La rassegna musicale* (Rome, April 1952); —— and G. M. Gatti, *A. C.* (Milan 1958); M. Castelnuovo-Tedesco, "C. e il suo terzo stile," *Il pianoforte* (Turin, August 1925); L. Cortese, *A. C.* (Genoa 1930); H. Fleischer, *La musica contemporanea* (Milan 1938); M. Glinski, "A. C.," *Revue musicale* 208 (1948); G. Graziosi, "C., Malipiero e i giovani," *La ruota* (Rome, May 1940); D. de' Paoli, *La crisi musicale italiana* (Milan 1939); B. Rondi, *La musica contemporanea* (Rome 1952):83–87; N. Slonimsky, "Modernist Speaks for the Ancients," *Boston Evening Transcript* (28 May 1929); R. Vlad, "Riflessi della dodecafonia," in "C., Malipiero, and Ghedini," *La rassegna musicale* (March 1957).

Enrique Solares

SEE ALSO Italy; Liturgical Music: Christian; Musicology and Composition; Opera.

Cassuto, Alvaro (Leon) (b. Porto, Portugal, 17 Nov 1938), studied composition with Artur Santos and Fernando Lopes Graça (Lisbon Conservatory, 1955–59), E. G. Klussmann (Hochschule für Musik, Hamburg, summer 1960), and with Ligeti and Stockhausen (Darmstadt, summer 1961). He studied con-ducting with Hubert Ahlendorf, Herbert von Karajan (Berlin, summer 1960), Pedro de Freitas-Branco (Lisbon, 1960–63), and Franco Ferrara and Jean Fournet (Hilversum, summer 1966). In 1964 he earned a PhD in law from the Univ. of Lisbon. He was assistant con-ductor of the Gulbenkian Chamber Orchestra, Lisbon, 1965–68, and of the Little Orchestra Society, New York, 1968–69. In 1971 he be-came permanent conductor of the Lisbon Radio Orchestra. He has contributed many articles to the Portugese periodical *Arte musicale* during 1959–64 and has prepared programs for the national radio station in Lisbon during 1960–68. Cassuto was the first Portuguese composer to write 12-tone music. Since 1961 his approach has broadened to en-compass the use of tone color as a primary structural element; he has been particularly influenced by Penderecki's use of tone clusters for string instruments.

PRINCIPAL COMPOSITIONS (published by Schirmer-G): *Sinfonia breve No. 1* for orchestra (1959); *Sinfonia breve No. 2* for orchestra (1960); *Variations for Orchestra* (1960); *Permutazioni* for divided orchestra (1962); *In memoriam Pedro de Freitas-Branco* for orchestra (1963); *Canticum in Tenebris* for soloists, chorus, orchestra (1968); *Evocations* for orchestra (1970); *Circle* for orchestra (1971).

Castelnuovo-Tedesco, Mario (b. Florence, 3 April 1895; d. Hollywood, 16 March 1968), studied at the Cherubini Royal Institute in Florence (1913–18, composition with Ildebrando Pizzetti, piano with Edgardo Del Vallee de Paz). He emigrated to the U.S. in 1939, where he taught theory and composition at the Los Angeles Conservatory from 1942 and composed many film scores. The composer's style was often likened to the countryside around Florence; Guido Gatti has remarked on the "soft undulating lines, all delicately traced by the whole gamut of colors, grays and greens of every value." The composer was also attracted to Spanish folk music and Jewish liturgical chant.

PRINCIPAL COMPOSITIONS: *Coplas* for voice, piano, Op. 7 (1915, Forlivesi); *Il raggio verde* for piano, Op. 9 (1916, Forlivesi); *La mandragola*, 3-act musical comedy, Op. 20; text by Macchiavelli (1920–23, UE); *33 Shakespeare Songs* for voice, piano, Op. 24, 12 vols. (1921–25, Chester); *Alt Wien* for piano, Op. 30 (Forlivesi, 1923); *Piano Concerto in G*, Op. 46 (1927, UE); *Aucassin et Nicolette* for voice, instruments, marionettes, Op. 98 (1938); *Guitar Concerto*, Op. 99 (1939, Schott); *Sacred Service* for baritone, chorus, organ, Op. 122 (1943, Leeds); *Sonata* for violin, viola, Op. 127 (1945, Mercury); *All's Well that Ends Well*, opera (1956); *The Merchant of Venice*, opera (1958); *Saul*, oratorio, Op. 191 (1960); *The Song of Songs*, scenic oratorio (1963).

PRINCIPAL WRITINGS: "The Composer Speaks," *The New Book of Modern Composers* ed. by David Ewen (New York 1961):111–12.

BIBL.: Gastone Rossi-Daria, "M. C.-T.," *The Chesterian* (Jan 1926):114–19; "Voci aggiunte e rivedute per un dizionario di compositori viventi," *La rassegna musicale* 23:42–53.

SEE ALSO Liturgical Music: Jewish.

Castiglioni, Niccolò (b. Milan, 17 July 1932), studied until 1953 at the Verdi Conservatory in Milan (piano with Friedrich Gulda, composition with Giorgio Federico Ghedini) and later at the Mozarteum in Salzburg (composition with Boris Blacher). Since 1958 he has also frequented the summer courses at Darmstadt.

He concertized extensively in Europe as a pianist and since 1966 has been associated as a composer with several U.S. universities, including the Univ. of N. Y. at Buffalo (1966–67), the Univ. of Mich. (1967), and the Univ. of Wash. (1968–69). An early work that he has since repudiated, *Apreslude* for orchestra (1959), was written under the influence of Mahler; *A Solemn Music II* (1964–65) shows the influence of Boulez.

PRINCIPAL COMPOSITIONS: *Inizio di movimento* for piano (1958, S-Z); *Cangianti* for piano (1959, S-Z); *Tropi* for flute, clarinet, violin, cello, percussion (1959, S-Z); *Gymel* for flute, piano (1960, S-Z); *Rondels* for orchestra (1960–61); *Synchromie* for orchestra (1962–63); *Consonante* for flute, 12 instruments (1963, Schott); *A Solemn Music II* for soprano, chamber orchestra; text by John Milton (1964–65, Schott); *Ode* for 2 pianos, wind orchestra, percussion (1966–67); *Granulation* for 2 flutes, 2 clarinets (1967); *Symphony in C* for chorus, orchestra; text by Jonson, Dante, Shakespeare, Keats (1968–69).

SEE ALSO Austria and Germany, Instrumental and Vocal Resources, Italy.

Castro, Juan José (b. Buenos Aires, 7 March 1895; d. Buenos Aires, 3 Sept 1968), began music studies in Buenos Aires and went to Paris in 1920 to work with Vincent d'Indy (composition) and Edouard Risler (piano). He also studied violin. He embarked on the career of conductor in 1928, when he organized the Orquesta Renancimento in Buenos Aires. From then until his death he conducted 642 concerts with orchestras in 19 countries, performing a repertory of 589 works. His many conducting posts included the Filarmonica de La Habana in Cuba (1947–48), the Orquesta del Sodre in Montevideo (1949–51), the Victorian Symphony Orchestra in Melbourne (1951–53), and the Sinfónica Nacional in Buenos Aires (1955–60). In 1959 he became director of the Puerto Rico Conservatory.

Castro's output includes six large stage works (two ballets and four operas); suites, symphonies, and symphonic poems for orchestra; choral and solo vocal works; and chamber and solo piano music. The style of these works is not easily categorized, for Castro was cosmopolitan both as a person and as a composer. His harmonic vocabulary, for example, drew on everything from major triads to polytonal chords to unresolved dissonances and strict serialism. His music may, in fact, have a more distinctive sound to an Argentine listener, who has a background of largely nationalistic music, than to a European, who is more accustomed to music drawing on eclectic sources. Nationalism in Castro generally takes the form of rhythmic or harmonic patterns based on folk sources (Spanish as well as Argentine) rather than of direct quotation. In the fourth movement of his *String Quartet*, for instance, he suggests a country atmosphere by using the rhythms of one of the most characteristic dances of the Argentine pampas, the *pericón*. Similarly tango elements appear in the first movement of the *Sinfonía argentina* and elsewhere. In the Garcia-Lorca operas he used some popular melodies actually chosen by the poet, who wanted to convey through their presence some of the flavor of the locales in which his plays are set.

PRINCIPAL COMPOSITIONS: *Sinfonía bíblica* for chorus, orchestra (1932); *Sinfonía argentina* for orchestra (1934); *6 Canciones de Garcia-Lorca* for voice, piano (1938); *3 Canciones cordobesas* for voice, piano (1939, EAMI); *Piano Sonata* (1939); *Sinfonía de los campos* for orchestra (1939); *Offenbachiana*, ballet (1940, Ricordi); *Toccata* for piano (1940, EAMI); *Piano Concerto* (1941, Ricordi); *Tangos* for piano (1941, EAMI); *String Quartet* (1942); *La zapatera prodigiosa*, 2-act opera; libretto by Garcia-Lorca (1943, Ricordi); *Martín Fierro*, cantata for baritone, chorus, orchestra; text by José Hernandez (1944); *Intrata y danza rustica* for violin, piano (1946, EAMI); *El llanto de las sierras* for orchestra (1947); *Proserpina y el extranjero*, 3-act opera; libretto by Omar del Carlo (1951, Ricordi); *Bodas de Sangre*, 3-act opera; libretto by Garcia-Lorca (1952, Ricordi); *Sonatina española* for piano (1953, UE); *Corales criollos No. 3* for orchestra (1953, UE); *Cosecha negra*, 3-act opera; libretto by the composer (1961); *Suite introspectiva* for orchestra (1961); *Epitafio en ritmos y sonidos* for chorus, orchestra (1961); *Violin Concerto* (1962). List to 1953: *Composers of the Americas* 4:9–15.

BIBL.: Rodolfo Arizaga, *J. J. C.* (Buenos Aires 1963); Kurt Pahlen, *La opera* (Buenos Aires 1958); ——, *La música sinfónica* (Buenos Aires 1963); *Revista ars* (special issue, Buenos Aires 1969).

Rodolfo Arizaga
(trans. from Spanish by Alcides Lanza)

SEE ALSO Argentina.

Caturla, Alejandro García, see under García-Caturla

Cazden, Norman (b. New York, 23 Sept 1914), studied at the Juilliard School (1927–39; piano with Arthur Newstead, Ernest Hutcheson, composition with Bernard Wagenaar), The City College of N. Y. (1938–43), and Harvard Univ. (1943–47; composition with Walter Piston, Aaron Copland). He has taught piano at Juilliard (1934–39) and other musical subjects at Vassar College (1947–48,

1956), Peabody Institute (1948–49), the Univ. of Mich. (1949–50), the Univ. of Ill. (1950–53), the New School for Social Research (1956–58), and the Univ. of Maine at Orono (since 1968). In his teens and twenties he concertized as a pianist in the Eastern U.S. He was assistant music director of radio station WNYC in New York during 1941–42 and music director of WLIB in 1942. During 1942–43 he was music director for the Humphrey-Weidman Repertory Dance Co. He has collected Catskill Mountain folk music and has organized folk festivals in the area; some of his music reflects this interest.

PRINCIPAL COMPOSITIONS: *7 Compositions* for piano, Op. 21 (1933–39); *Sonatina* for piano, Op. 7 (1935); *String Quartet*, Op. 9 (1936); *Concerto for 10 Instruments*, Op 10 (1937, MCA); *Piano Sonata*, Op. 12 (1938); *3 Chamber Sonatas* for clarinet, viola, Op. 17 (1938); *Quartet* for clarinet, strings, Op. 23 (1939); *Variations* for piano, Op. 26 (1940, Presser); *Horn Sonata*, Op. 33 (1941); *Flute Sonata*, Op. 36 (1941); *Suite* for violin, piano, Op. 43 (1943); *Symphony*, Op. 49 (1948, MCA); *3 Ballads* for orchestra, Op. 52 (1949, MCA); *3 New Sonatas* for piano, Op. 53 (1950, No. 3 published by Lawson); *Suite* for brass sextet, Op. 55 (1951, AMP); *Dingle Hill*, play with music for soloists, chorus, orchestra, Op. 70; libretto by Norman Studer (1958, MCA); *Quintet* for oboe, strings, Op. 74 (1960); *Sonatina* for piano, Op. 88 (1964); *Chamber Concerto* for orchestra, Op. 94 (1965, MCA); *Woodwind Quintet*, Op. 96 (1966); *Piano Trio*, Op. 97 (1969). List to 1969: *Composers of the Americas* 15:47–54.

PRINCIPAL WRITINGS: *Musical Consonance and Dissonance* (PhD diss., Harvard Univ., 1948); "Towards a Theory of Realism in Music," *Journal of Aesthetics & Art Criticism* 10:135–51; "Folk Idiom vs. Synthetic Language for the Composer," *American Music Teacher* (May 1952):2–18; "Tonal Function and Sonority in the Study of Harmony," *Journal of Research in Music Education* 2:21–34; "Hindemith and Nature," *Music Review* 15:288–306; "Realism in Abstract Music," *Music & Letters* 36:17–38; "Staff Notation as a Non-musical Communications Code," *Journal of Music Theory* 5:113–28; "The Thirteen Tone System," *Music Review* 22:152–71; "How to Compose Non-music," *Journal of Music Theory* 5:287–96; "Composing with a Clob: A Minor History Retold," *Music Review* 28:232–46; "The Second Note Is Free," *ibid.* 30:237–42.

BIBL.: *Composers of the Americas* 15 (Washington 1971); Herbert Haufrecht, "The Writings of N. C.," *ACA Bulletin* 8/2:2–9.

Cerha, Friedrich (Paul) (b. Vienna, 17 Feb 1926), attended the Vienna Akademie für Musik (1946–51; violin with Vasa Prihoda, composition with Alfred Uhl) and Vienna Univ. (1946–50, PhD; musicology, philosophy,

German philology, music education). As a violinist and conductor Cerha has been active in the performance of contemporary music throughout Europe. He is director of the instrumental ensemble "die reihe," which he co-founded in 1958. In 1960 he became a professor at the Vienna Akademie, where he teaches courses on new music and its interpretation and on the composition of electronic music.

PRINCIPAL COMPOSITIONS (published by UE unless otherwise noted): *2 Éclats en reflexion* for violin, piano (1956, EM); *Formation et solution* for violin, piano (1956, EM); *Espressioni fondamentali* for orchestra (1956–57, Bärenreiter); *Relazioni fragili* for harpsichord, chamber orchestra (1957, EM); *Enjambements* for flute, violin, percussion, trumpet, trombone, double bass (1959); *Mouvements* for chamber orchestra (1960); *Intersecazioni* for violin, orchestra (1960–61); *Spiegel I–VII* for orchestra, tape (1960–68); *Exercises* for baritone, reciter, chamber orchestra (1962–67); *Symphonien* for winds, timpani (1967); *Catalogue des objets trouvés* for chamber ensemble (1968).

PRINCIPAL WRITINGS: "Die Wiener Schule und die junge Generation," *Die Wiener Schule* (Vienna: Österreichische Musikzeitschrift, 1961):43–54; partial reprint in *Aufforderung zum Misstrauen* (Salzburg 1967):162–72; "Zu 'Spiegel'," notes for a *Musica Viva* concert (Munich, 13 Dec 1963); "Texttreue oder Sinntreue," *Österreichische Musikzeitschrift* 22/12:726–33; "Zu meiner Musik und einigen Problemen des Komponierens heute," *Beiträge '68/69 Österreichische Gesellschaft für Musik*:56–62; reprint in *Protokolle 68* (Vienna 1968):22–30.

BIBL.: J. Häusler, "F. C.," *Donaueschinger Blätter 1964*; Harald Kaufmann, "Antecknigar om F. C.," *Nutida musik 4* (1965–66):23–25; György Ligeti, "C.: *Relazioni fragili*," notes for a "die reihe" concert (Vienna, 16 May 1960); Karlheinz Roschitz, "F. C., Portrait eines Komponisten," *Österreichische Gesellschaft für Musik* (Nov–Dec 1964):1–2; Kent Sobotik, "F. C.," *Dialog* (Vienna: Institute of European Studies, 1963):12–14.

SEE ALSO Austria and Germany.

Cervetti, Sergio (b. Dolores, Uruguay, 9 Nov 1941), studied at the Peabody Conservatory (1963–67; composition with Stefan Grove, Ernst Krenek; conducting, László Halász). He was composer-in-residence of the Berlin Cultural Exchange Program (1969–70), during which time he and the dancer Kenneth Rinker founded the Berlin Dance Ensemble. During his attendance at seminars in contemporary music given at the Festival of Interamerican Music, Caracas (May 1966), he became interested in the work of Penderecki, Stockhausen, and Xenakis. His work in Berlin with dancers led him to concentrate on music for the stage in which is incorporated any and all sound

elements (folklore, pop, noise, silence, etc.). More recently (in *Peripetia*, 1969) he has applied cybernetics to musical composition. During 1970–72 he was in New York, where he worked at the Columbia-Princeton Electronic Music Studio and taught at Brooklyn College.

PRINCIPAL COMPOSITIONS: *5 Episodes* for piano, cello, violin (1965, Moeck); *6 Sequences for Dance* for cello, piano, horn, celesta, electric guitar, flute, percussion (1966, Moeck); *Orbitas* for orchestra, percussion (1967); *Zinctum* for string quartet (1967, Moeck); *Hay Wagon* for 10 voices, electric guitar, accordian, orchestra (1968); *Pulsar* for brass sextet (1969); *Prisons No. 1* for singers, dancers, 2 trombones, double bass, electric guitar, electronic organ, percussion (1969); *Lux lucet in tenebris*, motet for chorus (1969); *Peripetia* for singers, orchestral players (1969); *4 Fragmentos de Pablo Neruda* for soprano, oboe, guitar, cello, percussion (1970); *Prisons No. 2* for electronic sounds on 2-channel tape, speaking choir, orchestra (1970–71).

PRINCIPAL WRITINGS: "Kann ein Komponist vom Komponieren leben?" symposium, *Melos* 36:155–56.

BIBL.: Alan Kriegsmann, "Local Avant-Garde Composer Is Heading for West Berlin," *Washington Post* (22 Dec 1968) G:10; Washington Roldán, "En el buen camino," *El pais* (13 Nov 1967); ——, "El universalismo de America," *Facetas* (USIA, Uruguay) 2/1.

Chaikovsky, Boris (Alexandrovich) (b. Moscow, 10 Sept 1925), studied piano and composition at the Gnesin Music School and at the Moscow Conservatory (c.1948–49; composition with N. Myaskovsky, Dmitri Shostakovich, and Vissarion Shebalin). In his music during the 1950s he often used folk melodies from Russia and elsewhere.

PRINCIPAL COMPOSITIONS (information not available on post-1962 works): *Sonatina* for piano (1944); *Sonata* for solo cello (1946); *Symphonies Nos. 1–2* (1947, 1962); *The Star*, opera based on a story of World War II by Kazakevich (1949); *Fantasia on Russian Folk Themes* for orchestra (1950); *Slavic Rhapsody* for orchestra (1951); *Piano Sonata* (1952); *Sinfonietta* (1953); *Piano Trio* (1953); *Capriccio on English Themes* for orchestra (1954); *String Quartets Nos. 1–2* (1954, 1961); *String Trio* (1955); *Concertino* for clarinet, orchestra (1957); *Cello Sonata* (1957); *Overture on the 40th Anniversary of the October Revolution* (1957); *Violin Sonata* (1959); *Piano Quintet* (1962). Chaikovsky has also written a number of film scores.

Champagne, Claude (b. Montreal, 27 May 1891; d. Montreal, 21 Dec 1965), studied at the Dominion College of Music in Montreal until

1906 and at the National Conservatory (1906–09). During 1921–28 he was in Paris working for the Canadian Archives and studied composition with André Gedalge and Raoul Laparra and violin with Jules Conus. He taught composition at McGill Univ. (1932–41) and at the Conservatoire de la Province de Québec (1942–62), which he helped found. In 1945 he was a guest lecturer at the Rio de Janeiro Conservatory. Some of his music incorporates elements of French-Canadian folk music.

PRINCIPAL COMPOSITIONS: *Hercule et Omphale*, symphonic poem (1918); *Prélude et filigrane* for piano (1919, BMIC); *Suite canadienne* for chorus, orchestra (1928, Durand); *Dance villageoise* for violin, piano and other media (1929, BMIC); *Habanera* for violin, piano (1930); *Berceuse* for chamber orchestra (1938); *Quadrille brésilien* for piano (1942, BMIC); *Images du Canada français* for chorus, orchestra (1943); *Symphonie gaspésienne* (1945); *Concerto in D Minor* for piano, chamber orchestra (1950); *Messe breve* for 3 solo voices (1951, BMIC); *Paysana* for chamber orchestra (1953); *String Quartet* (1956); *Altitude*, symphonic poem for chorus, ondes Martenot, orchestra (1959, BMIC). Champagne also wrote a number of undated songs and madrigals with French texts and made arrangements of French-Canadian folksongs. List to 1959: *Composers of the Americas* 6:44–46.

BIBL.: Thomas Archer, "C. C.," *Canadian Music Journal* (winter 1958):3–10; "C. C.," *Canadian Composers* (Montreal 1964):24–27; Marvin Duchow, "C. C.," *Music Scene* (Sept 1968):7; Arnold Walter, ed., *Aspects of Music in Canada* (Montreal 1968):99–105.

[prepared with the help of Sister Anne Walsh]
SEE ALSO Canada.

Chance, see Indeterminancy; see also Notation, Performance

Chanler, Theodore (Ward) (b. Newport, R. I., 29 April 1902; d. Boston, 27 July 1961), studied at the Cleveland Institute (1920–22, composition with Ernest Bloch), Oxford Univ. (1923–25), and with Nadia Boulanger in Paris. He was a critic for the *Boston Herald* in 1934. During 1945–47 he taught at the Peabody Conservatory.

PRINCIPAL COMPOSITIONS: *Nocturne* for violin, piano (1925); *Violin Sonata* (1927); *8 Epitaphs* for medium voice, piano; texts by Walter de la Mare (1937, Arrow); *3 Epitaphs* for the same (1940); *4 Rhymes from "Peacock Pie"* for voice, piano; texts by De la Mare (1940, AMP); *The Second Joyful Mystery*, fugue for 2 pianos (1942–43, AMP); *The Children* for children's chorus or solo voice,

piano; text by Leonard Feeney (1945, Schirmer-G); *The Pot of Fat*, chamber opera (premiere 1955).

PRINCIPAL WRITINGS: "Poetry and Music," *Modern Music* 18:232–34; "Words and Musical Form," *ibid.* 20:226–28; "Form Is Line," *ibid.* 22:21–22.

BIBL.: Robert Tangeman, "The Songs of T. C.," *Modern Music* 22:227–33.

Chant, Michael H. (b. Wakefield, Yorkshire, England, 9 Jan 1945), studied at Wakefield Cathedral under the organist and choirmaster Percy George Saunders (1959–63). He has a degree in mathematics and works in a tax office in London. In 1969 he initiated a continuing composition called *Private Company* to which some 20 musicians have contributed. "Music," according to the aims of the Company, "means some rite involving monodic temporal divisions and/or continuous activity. The results of the investigations of the members will be sold to the public."

PRINCIPAL COMPOSITIONS: *Sonata audia-organica* for double bass (1966); *Reductions* for piano (1967); *Merrion Music* for 3 or more players of portable instruments (1967); *Harmonium Piece* for 2 American organs, church bell, documentation in collaboration with Hugh Shrapnel (1970).

PRINCIPAL WRITINGS: "Responses to Virtues, for Theorizing," *Treatise Handbook* by Cornelius Cardew (Buffalo 1970):xxi.

SEE ALSO Great Britain.

Chávez (-Ramírez), **Carlos** (b. Mexico City, 13 June 1899), comes from a family of professional people. He began composing as a child and later studied harmony with Juan B. Fuentes and piano with Pedro Luis Ogazon. His first major work, a symphony, dates from 1915. He traveled in Europe (1922–23) and the U.S. (1923–24, 1926–28) and in 1928 assumed two positions that initiated a quarter century of intense involvement on his part in the development of Mexican music and musical life. He became that year the conductor of the orchestra of the Mexico City Musicians' Union (soon after given the name Orquesta Sinfónica de México) and director of the National Conservatory. The orchestra, which he conducted until 1948, became known for its wide-ranging repertory that included a large number of new Mexican works. The conservatory, where he remained until 1935, became a major training center for professional musicians. During 1933–34 he was chief of the Department of Fine Arts in the Secretariat of

Education, and in 1947 he founded the National Institute of Fine Arts, serving as its director until 1952. Since 1935 he has made yearly visits to the U.S., and after 1952 he expanded his activities as a conductor, touring throughout the world. In 1960 he founded a composer's workshop at the National Conservatory and remained as its director until 1965.

Chávez's mature works include some 15 for orchestra, including three concertos; six stage works; 20 chamber works, including three string quartets and six piano sonatas; and a number of large choral works and shorter solo vocal and instrumental pieces. Perhaps the most significant characteristic of this music is its use of strongly marked linear textures. A typical example occurs at rehearsal No. 1 in the *Sinfonía de Antígona* (1933), where strings in a high register are set against winds in midrange, the juxtaposition being underscored by the use of fourths and fifths in the former and seconds and sevenths in the latter. The *Soli* series (1933–66), mostly for winds, exemplifies Chávez's ability to use reduced instrumental forces to produce sparse and unusual timbral mixtures. The symphonies contain similarly sparse textures, usually in divertimento-like passages and sometimes in a concertato style akin to Bach's *Brandenburg Concertos*. Passages that evoke a prehistoric time may appear, but in unexpected places; for example, in the passacaglia of the *Symphony No. 6* (1961) or in the sustained call of an Indian flute (simulated by piccolo), which closes the Introduction to the *Symphony No. 3* (1951) and becomes a central motif of the Allegro.

Much of the vigor in Chávez's works (for example, the *Sinfonía india*, 1935) derives from their percussive rhythms and dexterous combinations of timbres (including native instruments). Such pieces have the obsessive, magical appeal of aboriginal dances. In later music, however, this association no longer holds, as exemplified by the abstract designs of the *Toccata* (1942), the first all-percussion work to enter the international repertory, and *Tambuco*, also for percussion (1964), in which silence is as important as sound and rhythms intertwine in non-repetitive, spiral-like shapes (a conception of sound and form that parallels some of the developments in electronic music). In *El fuego nuevo* (1921), a ballet on an Aztec ritual, Chávez aimed at a simple and concisely expressed primitivism. In this and other works, such as the ballets *Los 4 soles* (1925), *H.P.* (1926), and *Xochipilli* (1940), he rarely quoted folk material but concentrated instead on evoking the atmosphere of prehispanic myths and traditional rituals. His relationship to native materials is quite different from some earlier Mexican composers who used folklore to supposedly reinstate a distinctively Mexican music but who actually wrote musically uninteresting works based largely on Creole and Mestizo materials. Chávez has never been an assiduous collector of folk material, nor does he claim for his music a specifically Mexican character.

Form and structure in his music have always depended on the expressive needs of individual works. Thus the *Sinfonía india* is based on a classical symphonic scheme (telescoped into one movement) but the *Violin Concerto* (1948) follows a mirror form: ABCD-DCBA. More recently he has eschewed repetition and symmetry in favor of nonrepetitive, ongoing processes in which motives derive one from another. (This approach is discussed in his *Musical Thought*, 1961.) In the *Invention* for piano (1958) there are similarities among motivic shapes, but there are few repetitions of melody, rhythm, or harmony. An example of a rhythmic recurrence comes in the third section, where groups of two and three notes are occasionally set off by rests from the ongoing flow. Similar processes, together with Chávez's usual concern with conciseness, clarity, and originality in the handling of instrumental timbres, can be seen in *Resonancias* (1964), *Tambuco* (1964), *Clio* (1969), and *Discovery* (1969).

PRINCIPAL COMPOSITIONS: *El fuego nuevo*, Aztec ballet; scenario by the composer (1921); *String Quartets Nos. 1–3* (1921, 1932, 1943); *Sonatina* for violin, piano (1924, Mills); *Sonatina* for cello, piano (1924, Mills); *Sonatina* for piano (1924, Boosey); *Energía* for piccolo, flute, bassoon, horn, trumpet, trombone, viola, cello, double bass (1925, Mills); *Los 4 soles*, Indian ballet; scenario by the composer (1925); *Caballos de vapor*, "H. P.," ballet; scenario by the composer (1926, Boosey); *Sonata* for 4 horns (1929, Mills); *Todo* for medium voice, piano; poem by Ramón López Velarde (1932, Boosey); *Symphonies Nos. 1–6*: No. 1, "Sinfonía de Antígona" (1933, Schirmer); No. 2, "Sinfonía india" (1935, Schirmer); No. 3 (1951, Boosey); No. 4, "Sinfonía romántica" (1953, Mills); No. 5 for string orchestra (1953, Boosey); No. 6 (1961, Mills); *Soli Nos. 1–4*: No. 1 for oboe, clarinet, trumpet, bassoon (1933, Boosey); No. 2 for wind quintet (1961, Mills); No. 3 for bassoon, trumpet, viola, timpani, orchestra (1965, Mills); No. 4 for brass trio (1966); *10 Preludes* for piano (1937, Schirmer-G); *Piano Concerto* (1938, Schirmer-G); *Toccata* for percussion (1942, Mills); *La hija de Cólquide*, ballet for wind and string quartets (1943, Mills); *Violin Concerto* (1948, Mills); *The Visitors*, 3-act opera; libretto by Chester Kallman (1953); *Inventions Nos. 1–3*: No. 1 for piano (1958, Boosey); No. 2 for violin, viola, cello (1965, Mills); No. 3 for harp (1967, Mills); *Resonancias* for orchestra (1964, Mills); *Tambuco* for 6 percussion (1964, Mills); *Clio*, symphonic ode (1969, Schirmer-G); *Discovery* for orchestra (1969, Schirmer-G).

PRINCIPAL WRITINGS: *Toward a New Music: Music and Electricity*, trans. by H. Weinstock (New York 1937); *Musical Thought* (Cambridge, Mass. 1961).

BIBL.: Aaron Copland, *Our New Music* (New York 1941, revised ed. 1968); ———, *Music and Imagination* (Cambridge, Mass. 1952); Henry Cowell, "C.," *The Book of Modern Composers* ed. by E. D. Ewen (New York 1942); Roberto García Morillo, *C. C.* (Mexico City 1960); Paul Rosenfeld, *Discoveries of a Music Critic* (New York 1936); ———, "El americanismo de C. C.," *Música* (Mexico City, Feb 1931); Nicolas Slonimsky, *Music of Latin America* (New York 1945); Herbert Weinstock, "C. C.," *Musical Quarterly* 22:425ff., revised version, *Composers of the Americas* 3:60–73.

Gloria Carmona
(trans. from Spanish by Alcides Lanza and César Rennert)

SEE ALSO Dance, Mexico, Popular Music.

Chemin-Petit, Hans (b. Potsdam, 24 July 1902), studied at the Hochschule für Musik in Berlin (1920–26; composition with Paul Juon, cello with Hugo Becker). Since 1929 he has been a professor at the Hochschule, where he was assistant director during 1965–68. During 1939–44 he was conductor of the Cathedral Choir in Magdeburg and since 1944, of the Philharmonic Choir in Berlin. He has been a member of the Academy of Arts in Berlin since 1964, becoming director in 1968. He cites Wilhelm Furtwängler, Fritz Busch, Siegmund von Hausegger, and Siegfried Ochs as the major influences on his development.

PRINCIPAL COMPOSITIONS: *Der gefangene Vogel*, chamber opera (1927); *3 Songs* for alto, piano; texts by Ricarda Huch (1928, Lienau); *3 Claudius Motets* for chorus (1933, Merseburger); *Prologue for Orchestra*, quadruple fugue (1939, Lienau); *2 Choral Motets* (1939, Merseburger); *Vom Abend bis zum Morgen* for women's choir; poem by Eichendorff (1942, Bote); *Trio in the Old Style* for oboe, clarinet, bassoon (1943, Lienau); *Concerto for Orchestra* (1944, Lienau); *Kleines Triptychon*, songs for soprano, piano (1945, Lienau); *Wind Quintet* (1948, Lienau); *Symphony in C* (1949); *Psalm 90* for baritone, chorus, orchestra (1953, Bote); *Psalm 150* for chorus, orchestra (1954, Bote); *2 Solo Recorder Sonatas* (1958, 1960, Sikorski); *König Nicolo*, opera; libretto after Wedekind (1959, Bote); *Prooemion* for chorus, organ, percussion; poem by Goethe (1960, Merseburger); *Aus dem Buch Hiob*, cantata for alto, recorder, viola (1960, Lienau); *Psalm 98* for chorus, orchestra (1961, Bote); *Intrada e passacaglia*, parergon to the opera *König Nicolo* (1962–63, Bote);

Concerto for organ, string orchestra, timpani (1963, Merseburger); *Toccata and Passacaglia* for piano (1967, Celesta); *Symphonic Cantata* for alto, chorus, orchestra (1967, Bote); *Music for Orchestra* (1968); *Die Komödiantin*, comic opera; libretto after Coubier (1968, Erdo); *Introit and Hymn* for chorus, organ, brass, timpani (1969, Merseburger); *Die Rivalinnen*, comic chamber opera; libretto by Loredano (1970).

BIBL.: O. Soehngen, *Laudatio aus Anlass der Ernennung zum Ehrenmitglied des Philharmonischen Chores Berlin* (Berlin, Merseburger, 1967).

Chennevière, Daniel, see Rudhyar, Dane

Chevreuille, Raymond (b. Brussels, 17 Nov 1901), graduated from the Music School of St. Josse Ten Noode in Brussels in 1918, after which he took courses at the Brussels Conservatory, studying harmony with Gabriel Minet and François Rasse. He is mainly self-taught in composition. During 1936–59 he was a sound engineer for Brussels Radio and Television and during 1956–63, director of music programing there. Since then he has devoted himself exclusively to composition.

PRINCIPAL COMPOSITIONS (available from CBDM): *String Quartets Nos. 1–6*, Opp. 1, 5, 6, 13, 23, 32 (1930, 1934, 1934, 1939, 1942, 1945); *Piano Trio*, Op. 8 (1936); *Piano Concertos Nos. 1–3*, Opp. 10, 50, 88 (1937; 1951, Schott; 1968); *Symphonies Nos. 1–7*, Opp. 14, 30, 47, 54, 60, 67, 84 (1939, 1944, 1951, 1952, 1954, 1957, 1964); *Cello Concertos Nos. 1–2*, Opp. 16, 87 (1940, 1965); *Violin Concertos Nos. 1–3*, Opp. 19, 56, 86 (1941, 1953, 1965); *Evasions*, cantata for soprano, chamber orchestra; text by Maurice Careme, Op. 25 (1942); *Saisons*, cantata for baritone, chamber orchestra; text by Joseph Weterings, Op. 26 (1943); *Concerto* for string trio, orchestra, Op. 29 (1943); *Double Concerto* for viola (saxophone), piano, orchestra, Op. 34 (1946); *Concerto for Orchestra*, Op. 37 (1947); *Horn Concerto*, Op. 43 (1949); *Barbe Bleue*, symphonic tale, Op. 42 (1949); *D'un Diable de briquet*, symphonic tale for radio after Andersen, Op. 45 (1950); *Récit et air gai* for clarinet, piano, Op. 46 (1950); *Atta Troll*, 1-act chamber opera after Heinrich Heine, Op. 51 (1952); *5 Bagatelles* for string quartet, Op. 53 (1952); *Trumpet Concerto*, Op. 58 (1954); *Symphony* for chamber orchestra, Op. 68 (1958); *Carnaval à Ostende*, symphonic suite in honor of the painter James Ensor, Op. 72 (1959); *Concerto grosso* for 2 trumpets, orchestra, Op. 77 (1961); *Concerto* for flute, chamber orchestra, Op. 79 (1961); *Bruegel, peintre des humbles*, symphonic suite, Op. 82 (1963); *Concerto* for clarinet, string orchestra, timpani, percussion, Op. 89 (1968).

SEE ALSO Belgium.

Chiari, Giuseppe (b. Florence, 26 Sept 1926), studied piano with Vittoria Senatori in Florence (1949–54). He concertizes as a pianist in Europe. During 1962–65 he was a member of the avant-garde music theater group in Florence, Gruppo 70, and he is associated with the Fluxus movement in Germany. Many of his works make use of theatrical elements.

PRINCIPAL COMPOSITIONS: *Intervalli* for piano (1952–57); *Gesti sul piano* (1962); *Lettera* for orchestra (1962); *Le corde* for 2 pianos (1962); *Per arco* for cello (1962); *Canzone* for orchestra (1962–70); *Teatrino* for actor-pianist (1963); *La strada* for actor-instrumentalist(s) (1965, CPE); *Opera*, "Don't Trade Here," for actor-musician(s) (1965, published in *Musica senza contrappunto*; see principal writings); *Quel che volete* for a few instruments (1965, CPE and *Source* 1); *Beethoven* for orchestra (1965–70); *Piano Concerto* (1966); *La folla solitaria* for narrators, chorus (1967); *Il silenzio* on tape, in collaboration with Micholo Borelli (1967); *Ave Maria* for cello (1968, published in *Musica senza contrappunto*); *Sonata* for voice, piano (1968, published in *Musica senza contrappunto*).

PRINCIPAL WRITINGS: *Musica senza contrappunto* (Rome 1969). Chiari has also written numerous articles for *Marcatré* (Rome).

BIBL.: John Gruen, *The New Bohemia* (New York 1966).

SEE ALSO Performance, Prose Music, Rhythm.

Childs, Barney (b. Spokane, Wash., 13 Feb 1926), became interested in new music while in high school through reading Henry Cowell's *New Music Quarterly*. His predoctoral academic training was in English (at the Univ. of Nev. and Oxford Univ.). He began composing at 23 but received no formal composition instruction until studying with Leonard Ratner (1952–53) at Stanford Univ., where he wrote a PhD dissertation on poetry and music in the madrigal. He studied with Carlos Chávez and Aaron Copland at Tanglewood (summers 1953,1954) and with Elliott Carter (1954–55). During 1956–69 he taught English at the Univ. of Arizona and English and music at Deep Springs College, Nev.; during 1969–71 he taught at the Wis. College-Conservatory.

Childs's earliest works, influenced by Hindemith, Ruggles, and Chávez, emphasize contrapuntal designs, conventional forms, and a harmonic system developed from the dissonant relationships implied in simultaneous major and minor thirds (*Quartet* for clarinet and strings, 1953). After 1954 an interest in the music of Ives and Carter led to an increasing use of continuous motivic expansion, sometimes incorporating American Indian melodies. He has never used serialism.

Since 1961 he has been concerned with indeterminacy and with the total world of "real" sound (as opposed to synthesized or live electronic sound). His works have included an increasing range of unconventional musical materials: nonpitched and unorthodox sounds from conventional instruments, performer's voices, and performer-chosen quotations from disparate sources. His use of tape is usually limited to such real-life material as radio announcements, amateur musicians practicing, and readings from musical instrument advertisements. He uses indeterminacy within larger fixed forms and gives performers choices ranging from the manner of articulating a line of given pitches to improvisation. His search for a self-generating musical structure culminated in the *Nonet* (1967), in which each player assembles and organizes his own part before a performance from categories of sound material provided him; he then places his sounds in the performance at whatever points he pleases within his own specified "time blocks."

PRINCIPAL COMPOSITIONS: *Sonata* for solo clarinet (1951, Tritone); *Bassoon Sonata* (1953, Tritone); *Bass Quintet* (1954, CFE); *Septet* for instruments, voices (1958); *Welcome to Whipperginny* for percussion nonet (1961); *Interbalances IV* for trumpet, optional speaker (1962, Tritone); *Music for 2 flute players* (1963, Merion); *Jack's New Bag* for 10 players (1966, CPE); *Nonet* (1967, CFE); *The Bayonne Barrel and Drum Company* for solo wind, 16 players (1968, CFE); *Keet Seel* for chorus, text by the composer with quotations from 16th-century writers (1970, ACA); *Clarinet Concerto* (1970, ACA); *When Lilacs Last in the Dooryard Bloom'd* for vocal soloists, chorus, band; poem by Walt Whitman (1970–71).

PRINCIPAL WRITINGS: "The Beginning of the Apocalypse?" *Kulchur* (New York) 15:48–56; "Young Performers and New Music," *Music Educators' Journal* 51/1:40–42; "The Newest Minstrelsy," *Bandwagon* 15/5:4–7; "Articulation in Sound Structures," *Texas Studies in Literature and Language* 8:423–45; "Indeterminacy and Theory," *The New Music* ed. by G. Battcock (New York 1971).

BIBL.: Peter Horwath, "Amerikas 'New Music': Eine Unterhaltung mit dem Komponisten B. C.," *Neue deutsche Hefte* 108:69–82.

Ben Johnston

Chile. The first generation of important Chilean composers was born in the 1880s and 90s. At that time and for at least three decades thereafter, the country's musical life was centered at the Teatro Municipal in Santiago, which had been founded in 1857 and was devoted almost exclusively to European opera performed by European singers and conductors. The beginnings of an expanded musical life occurred in 1917 when the Sociedad Bach was founded by Domingo *Santa Cruz, (b. 1899), then a law student at the Univ. of Chile in Santiago. The society was composed of university students, and its initial purpose was to perform choral music of the late renaissance and baroque periods. After 1924, however, it led the way in redirecting the entire musical life of the country. Under its prodding a state agency was set up in 1927 to oversee musical and other artistic activities. In 1930 all its services were brought under the aegis of the Faculty of Fine Arts at the Univ. of Chile (where Santa Cruz was teaching music history and analysis), which meant that state involvement in music was in the hands of artists and largely free of political pressures. The society produced concerts where the works of renaissance polyphonists were heard for the first time, along with the important works by Bach (the *Christmas Oratorio* in 1925) and contemporary compositions by Falla, Respighi, and Chilean composers. The society also established a music conservatory where new ideas, methods and programs were studied as an alternative to the old conservatory training. The music magazine *Marsyas* (1927–28) was the society's official organ.

Until 1928 professional music education was the province of the National Conservatory (founded 1849), which was devoted mainly to preparing singers and instrumentalists for Italian opera performances. In that year the conservatory was reorganized with Armando Carvajal (b. 1893) as director, and it adopted the reforms of the Sociedad Bach conservatory; in 1930 it was absorbed by the university under the Faculty of Fine Arts. In 1948 the Faculty itself was divided into Faculties of Music and of Visual Arts with the Music Faculty incorporating the National Conservatory, the Instituto de Investigaciones Musicales (with research programs in folk and concert music), and the Instituto de Extensión Musical. The latter had been created in 1940 by congress to promote the development of music throughout the country and incorporated into the university in 1942. It has under its jurisdiction the National Symphony (founded 1941), National Ballet (1945), the Univ. of Chile Choir (1945), the *Revista musical chilena* (1945), and several chamber groups. The institute has offered an impressive series of premieres of music from all times, including all the works of Chilean composers. It has published and recorded some Chilean works and published articles about Chilean

music in the *Revista*. In 1947 it established the Chilean Music Festivals, held every two years in Santiago and restricted to music that has not been performed before. The festivals are open to all native composers and to foreign-born composers who have lived at least five years in the country. The pieces that receive the top prizes are incorporated in the institute's regularly sponsored concerts. Composers may submit unpublished works to another biennial competition, "Premios por obra," in which cash awards are made by a jury of 3–5 composers, critics, and musicologists. In 1967 the institute established a noncommercial radio station at the Univ. of Chile, over which Chilean music is broadcast every day.

Among other organizations that have contributed to the development of music in Chile is the Asociación Nacional de Conciertos Sinfónicos, established in 1931 by Carvajal and Santa Cruz. In its eight years of existence this association performed nearly all the contemporary Chilean repertory, as well as many works by Albeniz, R. Strauss, Prokofiev, Hindemith, Debussy, Ravel, Stravinsky, Respighi, Falla, Casella, Dukas, among other contemporary composers. The private organizations include the Sociedad Nueva Música in Santiago (founded 1943), the Grupo Tonus (1949), and the binational institutes, mainly the Goethe Institute and the Chile-North American Institute. The local affiliate of ISCM is the Asociación Nacional de Compositores (established 1936 and now including 32 members), which itself has organized many concerts of contemporary music. A Philharmonic Orchestra was established in 1955 by Juan Matteucci under the aegis of the Municipal Theater of Santiago, which later added a ballet company and a chorus. Juan Orrego-Salas (b. 1919) created the first university-sponsored choral group in 1938 at the Catholic Univ. in Santiago; in 1959 he founded a music department there that includes a music school, a chamber orchestra, and a Musica Antiqua group. Similar projects have arisen at the Univ. of Concepción in Concepción and the Univ. Austral de Valdivia and at campuses of the Univ. of Chile elsewhere in the country, mainly Arica, La Serena, Temuco, and Osorno. Although composers today cannot earn their living solely from their music, there are many opportunities for them to combine creative work with teaching, performance, or administration.

The first decades of this century saw an extension of the European romantic tradition in native Chilean works, including those by Luigi S. Giarda (1868–1952), Javier Rengifo

(1884–1958), Roberto Puelma (b. 1893), and Salvador Candiani (1917–1969). The country's first internationally known composer was Enrique *Soro (1884–1954), who studied at the Milan Conservatory on a scholarship from the Chilean government and was published by Ricordi in Milan and G. Schirmer in New York. At a time when opera was the preferred genre with Chilean audiences, he chose to write chamber and orchestral works in the romantic tradition of Schumann and Tchaikovsky. He was a prominent teacher and from 1919 until the reorganization of 1928, director of the National Conservatory. Pedro Humberto *Allende-Sarón (1885–1959) and Alfonso *Leng (b. 1894), who belong to Soro's generation, were both trained in Chile. The former is known especially for his use of native rhythms within an impressionist context. The latter, a pupil of Soro, wrote a symphonic poem in 1920, La muerte de Alsino, that exemplifies German romanticism in Chile; his musical catalog covers more than 50 years of creative activity. Of the other successful composers of this generation, Acario *Cotapos (1889–1969) and Carlos *Isamitt (b. 1887) are noteworthy for the advanced stylistic positions they took. Cotapos was self-taught, and his radical outlook, especially his colorful imagination and his free use of every new technique and style, has influenced many younger composers. Isamitt's Friso araucano for orchestra (1931), using native Araucanian Indian rhythms, was one of the last deliberately nationalistic works in Chile; he was also the first Chilean to use 12-tone techniques (beginning in 1939). Among other nationalist composers are Carlos Lavin (1883–1962), Samuel Negrete (b. 1893), Juan Casanova Vicuña (b. 1894), Jorge Urrutia-Blondel (b. 1905), René *Amengual-Astaburuaga (1911–1954), Ramon Campbell (b. 1911), and Carvajal.

Santa Cruz has already been discussed as the leading force behind Chile's present-day music life. His compositional style evolved in the 1930s from an expressionist sort of writing toward neoclassicism with atonal leanings. His chamber and symphonic works are closely related to European music of the time, especially Hindemith, and are far removed from nationalistic concerns. Santa Cruz's pupil, Gustavo *Becerra-Schmidt (b. 1925) has taught at the Univ. of Chile since 1947. His music covers a wide spectrum of genres and styles from the academic outlook of his first works to avant-garde, aleatory, and electronic works. Among his best-known pieces are six string quartets and three symphonies. Juan *Orrego-Salas (b.

1919), who is among the most widely known Chilean composers, has written a large number of chamber and symphonic works. His Canciones castellanas (1947) and his first symphonies reveal a neoclassic tendency somewhat akin to the later works of Bartók and Falla. Later he became less attached to functional harmony (Symphony No. 4, 1966; Piano Sonata, 1967), and in the Missa in tempore discordiae (1969) he used aleatory procedures. Other composers of expressionist and neoclassic tendencies include Alfonso *Letelier (b. 1912) and Carlos Riesco (b. 1925).

León *Schidlowsky (b. 1931) studied in Europe during 1952–55 and has used serial and more recently aleatory procedures. Such works as the symphony La noche de cristal (1961), Llaqui [Sadness] (1965), dedicated to the revolutionary poet Javier Heraud, who was assassinated in 1963, and Nueva York (1965), dedicated to "my black brothers of Harlem," testify to a profound concern for political, religious, and social conditions. Such composers as Eduardo *Maturana (b. 1920), Abelardo Quinteros (b. 1923), Roberto Falabella (1926–58), Leni Alexander (b. 1924), Roberto Escobar (b. 1926), Juan Allende-Blin (b. 1928), Fernando *Garcia (b. 1930), Miguel *Aguilar-Ahumada (b. 1931), and Enrique Rivera (b. 1941) have also used serial techniques.

As elsewhere, a number of composers follow an eclectic inspiration, not adhering to any particular style or technique. These include Carlos *Botto (b. 1923), Darwin Vargas (b. 1925), and Miguel *Letelier-Valdés (b. 1939). The avant-garde and experimental approach to composition can be found in many works by the younger composers already mentioned as well as in Celso *Garrido-Lecca (b. Peru, 1926), Tomas Lefever (b. 1926), Juan *Amenábar (b. 1922), and José Vicente *Asuar (b. 1933).

BIBL.: Samuel Claro, Panorama de la música contemporánea en Chile (Santiago 1969); Roberto Escobar and Renato Yrarrázaval, Música compuesta en Chile 1900–1968 (Santiago 1969); María Ester Grebe, "León Schidlowsky Gaete: Síntesis de su trayectoria creativa (1952–1968)," Revista musical chilena (April 1968):7–52; Eugenio Pereira-Salas, "El centenario del Teatro Municipal 1857–1967," Revista musical chilena (June 1957): 30–35; ——, "La música chilena en los primeros cincuenta años del siglo XX," ibid. (summer 1950–51):63–78; Vicente Salas-Viú, La creación musical en Chile 1900–1951 (Santiago 1952); Domingo Santa Cruz, "El Instituto de Extensión Musical, su origen, fisonomía y objeto," Revista musical chilena (Sept 1960):7–38; Robert Stevenson, "Chilean Music in the Santa Cruz Epoch," Inter-American Music Bulletin 68:1–18.

Juan Pablo Izquierdo and Samuel Claro

Chou Wen-chung (b. Chefoo, China, 29 June 1923), studied at the National Chungking Univ., Chungking, China (1941–45), the New England Conservatory of Music (1946–49; composition with Carl McKinley, Nicolas Slonimsky), and Columbia Univ. (MA, 1954; composition with Otto Luening). He also studied composition with Bohuslav Martinů (1949) and Edgard Varèse (1949–54). He has taught composition and theory privately since 1955 and lectured at Brooklyn College (1961–62) and Hunter College (1963–64) in New York. He joined the music faculty of Columbia Univ. in 1964. He has been on the boards of several contemporary music societies, including CRI, and is a founding member of the American Society of University Composers. In much of his music Eastern and Western elements are coordinated. His *All in the Spring Wind* (1952–53) and *And the Fallen Petals* (1954) combine "line, mass, and their interaction, together with such elements as articulation, duration, intensity, and timbre . . . into an integrated body of sound that ebbs and flows —in the manner of a tonal brushwork in space." Since 1960 he has adapted principles from the *I Ching*, Chinese calligraphy, and ancient Chinese instrumental music in his works.

PRINCIPAL COMPOSITIONS (published by Peters unless otherwise noted): *Landscapes* for orchestra (1949); *Seven Poems of T'ang Dynasty* for high voice, instruments (1951–52, Presser); *All in the Spring Wind* for orchestra (1952–53); *And the Fallen Petals* for orchestra (1954); *Metaphors* for wind orchestra (1960–61); *Cursive* for flute, piano (1963); *Riding the Wind* for wind orchestra (1964); *Yü Ko* for 9 players (1965); *Pien*, concerto for piano, winds, percussion (1966); *Yün* for winds, 2 pianos, percussion (1969). List to 1969: *Composers of the Americas* 15:226–29.

PRINCIPAL WRITINGS: "A Varèse Chronology," *Perspectives* 5/2:7–10; "Open Rather than Bounded," *ibid.* 5/2:1–7; "Varèse; A Sketch of the Man and his Music," *Musical Quarterly* 52:151–70; "Towards a Re-Merger in Music," *Contemporary Composers on Contemporary Music* ed. by Elliott Schwartz and Barney Childs (New York 1967): 309–15; "East and West, Old and New," *Asian Music* (New York) 1/1:19–22.

SEE ALSO Asian Music and Western Composition.

Christou, Yannis (b. Heliopolis, Egypt, 9 Jan 1926; d. Athens, 8 Jan 1970), was the son of an industrialist. He attended Victoria College, Alexandria (1938–44), and King's College, Cambridge Univ. (1938–44; philosophy with L. Wittgenstein, Bertrand Russell), and studied composition with Hans Redlich at Letchworth (1945–48) and orchestration in Rome and Genoa with F. Lavagnino (1949–50). He also studied psychology with Karl Jung in Zurich in 1948. During 1949–50 he studied music at the summer courses of the Acadèmia Musicale Chigiana in Siena. He was influenced by the philosophical ideas of his elder brother, Evanghelos, a psychoanalyst and disciple of Jung. After working with 12-tone and serial techniques (1948–58), he began investigating other methods, including the use of electronic sounds, and established his own electronic studio in Athens. He invented a musical notation in 1965 that incorporates stage action, which he felt should be part of a musical composition. During 1965–66 he sketched some 140 rites, called *Anaparastasseis* or "reenactments," 35 of which he considered completed. (Unfortunately, the notation is not decipherable; it consists largely of notes and sketches to be filled in by the composer and performers during rehearsals and performances.) Christou's outlook became gradually more metaphysical and mystical, as can be seen in the prefaces to his works. His death resulted from an auto accident.

PRINCIPAL COMPOSITIONS: *Phoenix* for orchestra (1948–49, Ricordi); *Symphony No. 1* (1951, De Santis); *Latin Liturgy* for chorus, brass, percussion (1953); *6 Songs on Poems by T. S. Eliot* for mezzo-soprano, orchestra (1955, Impero); *Patterns and Permutations* for orchestra (1960); *Toccata* for piano, orchestra (1962); *Tongues of Fire*, oratorio for Pentecost for 3 vocal soloists, chorus, orchestra (1964); *Mysterion*, oratorio for speakers, 3 choruses, orchestra, tapes, actors (1965–66, Chester); *The Persians*, music for the play by Aeschylus (1965); *Praxis for 12* for 11 strings, piano; performable in a version for string orchestra, piano (1965–66, Chester); 140 *Anaparastasseis* [Reenactments] for various instruments (1965–66; *Anaparastassis I* and *Anaparastassis III*, "The Pianist," pub. by Chester); *Epicycle* for "continuum" and ensemble, a modifiable synthesis of a constant and an aleatoric group (1967, Chester); *The Strychnine Lady* for viola, 5 actors, instrumental ensembles, tapes, playthings, red cloth (1967, Chester); *Enantiodromia* for orchestra (1968, Chester); *Oedipus Rex*, music for Sophocles' tragedy, on tape; *Oresteia*, unfinished opera (1967–70).

BIBL.: Günther Becker, "In Memoriam J. C., ein Überblick über das nachgelassene Werk," *Frankfurter Allgemeine Zeitung* (26 March 1970); Piero Guarino, "Compositeurs d'Egypte: J. C.," *Rhythme* (Alexandria, Oct 1954):5; John G. Papaioannou, 'O Y. C. ki'ē metaphysikè ēs mousikēs [Y. C. and the Metaphysics of Music] (Athens, Hellenic Assoc. for Contemporary Music, 1970).

[prepared with the help of George Leotsakos]
SEE ALSO Greece.

Chromaticism, the use in tonal music of a (relatively) large number of pitches outside the scale of the prevailing key center(s).

Cikker, Ján (b. Banská Bystrica, Czechoslovakia, 29 July 1911), studied at the Prague Conservatory (1930–31, 1933–34; composition with Jaroslav Křička) and at the Prague Academy of Music (1934–36, composition with Vítězslav Novák). He also studied conducting with Felix Weingartner in Vienna during 1936–37. He has taught composition at the Prague Conservatory and Music Academy since 1939. During 1945–48 he was also director of the opera department of the Slovak National Theater in Bratislava. Initially his music was a synthesis of Slovak folk-music elements and European concert traditions. Later on he was drawn to the expressionistic music drama stemming from Berg.

PRINCIPAL COMPOSITIONS: *String Quartets Nos. 1–2* (1935); *Leto*, symphonic poem (1941, Simrock); *Concertino* for piano, orchestra (1942, Simrock); *Vojak a matka*, symphonic poem (1943); *Slavonic Suite* for orchestra (1943, Simrock); *Ráno* [Morning], symphonic poem (1946, SHF); *Spomienky* [Reminiscence], suite for orchestra (1947, Bärenreiter); *Vlčie diery* [Wolves' Den], film score (1948); *Juro Jánošík*, opera (1954, SVKL and Alkor); *Dramatic Fantasy* for orchestra (1957, SHF); *Beg Bajazid* [Prince Bajazid], opera (1957, SHF and Alkor); *Meditácia Blaženi sú mŕtvi* [Blissful Are the Dead] for orchestra (1962, Bärenreiter); *Vzkriesenie* [The Resurrection], opera after Tolstoy (1962, SHF and Alkor); *Mister Scrooge*, opera after Dickens (1963, SHF and Alkor); *Orchestral Studies for the Stage* (1964, Panton); *Hra o láske a smrti* [The Play of Love and Death], opera after Romain Rolland (1969, Bärenreiter); *Hold L. v. Beethovenovi* [Homage to Beethoven] for orchestra (1970).

BIBL. Jozef Šamko, *J. C.* (Bratislava 1955).

SEE ALSO Czechoslovakia.

Ciortea, Tudor (b. Brașov, Rumania, 28 Nov 1903), studied at the Gheorghe Dima Conservatory in Cluj, Rumania (1923–24, piano with Ilie Sibianu), the Ecole Normale de Musique, Paris (1927–28; composition with Paul Dukas; musical form and analysis with Nadia Boulanger), and at the Conservatory of Music in Bucharest (1930–31; composition, Nonna Otescu; folk music, Constantin Brăiloiu). Since 1949 he has been teaching composition and form at the Ciprian Porumbescu Conservatory in Bucharest.

PRINCIPAL COMPOSITIONS: *Cello Sonata* (1946, Muzicală); *7 Songs* to poems by Mihai Eminescu

(1951, ESPLA); *String Quartet No. 2* (1953, ESPLA); *Piano Quintet* (1957, Muzicală); *Passacaglia and Toccata* for orchestra (1957); *Concerto for String Orchestra* (1958, Muzicală); *Piano Sonata No. 3* (1959, Muzicală); *Flute Sonata* (1959, Muzicală); *Octet*, "Din isprăvile lui Păcată" for wind quintet, viola, cello, piano (1961); *Clarinet Sonata* (1962); *Trumpet Sonata* (1963); *Songs* for voice, piano (1964, Muzicală); *4 Ballads* for women's chorus; poems by Garcia-Lorca (1965, Muzicală); *Cîntece de gheișe* [Geisha Songs] for 3 women's voices, cello, piano; traditional Japanese texts (1966); *Trei istorioare despre vint* [. . .About the Wind] for voice, flute, piano; poem by Garcia-Lorca (1967); *Balada fiului pierdut* [Ballad of the Lost Son] for 3 women's voices, clarinet, cello, harp (1968); *4 cintece maramureșene* (4 Songs from Maramures) for piano (1969).

PRINCIPAL WRITINGS: "Sonata a III a pentru vioară și pian de George Enescu" [Sonata No. 3 for violin and piano by George Enescu], *Muzica* (Bucharest) 1955/5:37–44; *Cvartetele de Beethoven* [The Quartets of Beethoven] (Bucharest 1968).

BIBL.: Wilhelm Georg Berger, *Ghid pentru muzica instrumentală de cameră* [Guide to Instrumental Chamber Music] (Bucharest 1965):366–68; Andrei Porfetye, "*Octet* pentru suflători, violă, violoncel și pian de T. C." [*Octet . . .* by T. C.], *Muzica* 1962/8:13–16; ——, "T. C.," *ibid.* 1964/5–6:19–28.

Clarke, Henry Leland (b. Dover, N.H., 9 March 1907), studied piano as a child with Ruth Olive Roberts, attended Harvard Univ. (BA, 1928; MA, 1929; PhD, 1947; composition with Gustav Holst, 1932) and the Ecole Normale de Musique, Paris (1929–31, composition with Nadia Boulanger). He studied privately with Hans Weisse, New York (1933–34). Clarke was an assistant in the music division of the New York Public Library (1932–36) and a teaching assistant at Bennington College, Vt. (1936–38), where he studied with Otto Luening. During 1938–42 he was head of graduate studies at Westminster Choir College. He has also taught at the Univ. of Calif., Los Angeles (1947–48, 1949–58, summer 1962), Vassar College (1948–49), and the Univ. of Wash. in Seattle (since 1958).

PRINCIPAL COMPOSITIONS (published ACA-CFE unless otherwise noted): *Gloria in the 5 Official Languages of the United Nations* for chorus, orchestra (1950); *No Man Is an Island* for men's chorus, piano or band (1951, Leeds); *The Loafer and the Loaf*, chamber opera (1951); *Monograph* for orchestra (1952); *Love-in-the-World* for tenor, women's voices, piano (1953, Mercury); *Wonders Are Many* for tenor, baritone, men's chorus (1954, Mercury); *Saraband for the Golden Goose* for orchestra or woodwind quintet (1957); *Points*

West for band (1960); *Encounter* for viola, or-
chestra (1961); Lysistrata, opera (1969).
PRINCIPAL WRITINGS: "The Basis of Musical
Communication," *Journal of Aesthetics and Art
Criticism* 10:242–46; "Toward a Musical Period-
ization of Music," *Journal of the American
Musicological Society* 9:25–30; "The Abuse of the
Semitone in Twelve-Tone Music," *Musical
Quarterly* 45:295–301.
BIBL.: John Verrall, "H. L. C." *ACA Bulletin*
9/3:2–5.

Clementi, Aldo (b. Catania, Italy, 25 May
1925), studied with Alfredo Sangiorgi, a pupil
of Schoenberg, and with Goffredo Petrassi.
Clementi's earliest works derived from neoclassic Stravinsky. From Sangiorgi he gained
an interest in 12-tone techniques; beginning
with the *Concertino* for 9 instruments (1956)
chromatic elements began to penetrate the
diatonic harmonies and pointillistic textures
began to appear. Like Webern, Clementi also
began to cultivate brevity (many of his pieces
from the late 1950s and 60s are 5 to 10 minutes long). In the *3 Studi* (1956–57) and subsequent works, the example of Stockhausen
can be felt in the use of "group composition"
processes. The construction is a succession of
brief episodes, or phrases, juxtaposed in col-
lagelike fashion and not related as antecedents
and consequents, developments, or repetitions.
Works of the early 1960s began to incorporate
an indeterminacy of detail within fixed gestures.
As described by Mario Bortolotto (*Musical
Quarterly* 51:72), *Informel No. 3* (1963) consists of a dense 72-part counterpoint in which
there are 43 rhythmic units, each of which is
assigned to a particular sound. Having written
the score, the composer eliminated some
portions by drawing curved lines over the
music.
PRINCIPAL COMPOSITIONS (published by S-Z): *3
Studi* for chamber orchestra (1956–57); *Episodi* for
orchestra (1958); *Ideogrammi I* for 16 instruments,
percussion (1959); *Ideogrammi II* for flute, 17 instruments (1959); *Triplum* for flute, oboe, clarinet
(1960); *Collage I*, action-music in 1 act with
visuals by Achille Perilli (1961); *Informels Nos. 1–3*:
No. 1 for 12 percussion and keyboard players
(1961); No. 2 for 15 players (1962); No. 3 for
orchestra (1963); *Collage II* on tape (1962);
Intavolatura for harpsichord (1963); *Variante B*
for orchestra (1964); *Reticolo: 11* for 11 instruments (1966); *Silben* for women's voices, 4 instruments (1966); *Concerto* for wind orchestra, 2
pianos (1967).
BIBL.: Mario Bortolotto, "A. C.," *Melos* 30:
364–69.
SEE ALSO Italy.

Cluster (Tone Cluster), a chord or sonority
most of the members of which are a major or
minor second apart.
BIBL.: Henry Cowell, *New Musical Resources*
(finished 1919; published New York 1929):117–38;
Mauricio Kagel, "Tone Clusters, Attacks, Transitions," *Die Reihe*, English ed., 5:40–55; James
Tenney, *Meta (+) Hodos* (New Orleans 1964).
SEE ALSO Harmony and Counterpoint, Notation.

Coates, Eric (b. Hucknall, Nottinghamshire,
England, 27 August 1886; d. Chichester, 21
Dec 1957), studied privately in Nottingham
with Ralph Horner (composition) and George
Ellenberger (violin) and attended the Royal
Academy of Music in London (1906; composi-
tion with Frederick Corder, viola with Lionel
Tertis, piano with Hartley Braithwaite). He
was violist with the Hambourg, Cathie, and
Walenn Quartets and the Queen's Hall Orches-
tra (1912–18).
PRINCIPAL COMPOSITIONS: *Stonecracker John* for
voice, piano (undated, Boosey); *Miniature Suite*
for chamber orchestra (1911, Boosey); *From the
Countryside*, suite for orchestra (1914, Boosey);
The 3 Bears, fantasy for orchestra (1926, Chappell);
Sleepy Lagoon, valse serenade for orchestra (1930);
London Suite for orchestra (1933, Chappell); *Saxo-
Rhapsody* for alto saxophone, orchestra (1936,
Chappell); *4 Centuries Suite* for orchestra (1941,
Boosey).
PRINCIPAL WRITINGS: *Suite in 4 Movements*, an
autobiography (London 1953).
BIBL.: J. Frank, "A Tribute to E. C.," *Musical
Opinion* (Feb 1958):317f.; R. Wimbush, "E. C.
1886–1957," *The Gramophone* 35:351–52.

Coelho, Ruy (b. Alcacer do Sal, Portugal, 3
March 1892), studied at the Lisbon Conservatory (composition with Antonio Eduardo da
Costa Ferreira and Tomas Borba, piano with
Rey Colaco), in Berlin (1910–13; composition
with Engelbert Humperdinck, Max Bruch,
Arnold Schoenberg), and at the Paris Conservatory (composition with Paul Vidal). He
has concertized as a pianist (since 1914) and
conductor (since 1917) and has also written
criticism for the Lisbon newspapers *Diario de
noticias* and *Diario de manhã*. Portuguese folk
and popular music have been strong influences
on his compositions.
PRINCIPAL COMPOSITIONS (dates are of first performance): *Piano Concertos Nos. 1–2* (1909, 1948);
Violin Sonatas Nos. 1–2 (1910, 1924); *Princesa dos
sapatos de ferro*, ballet (1912); *Symphonias camo-
neanas Nos. 1–5* (1912, 1917, 1943, 1951, 1966);
Piano Trio (1916); *Canções de saudade e amor* for

voice, piano (1917); *Crisfal*, 1-act opera; libretto by Afonso Lopes Vieira (1920); *Rosas de todo o ano*, opera (1921); *Nun'alvarez*, symphonic poem (1922); *Rainha santa*, ballet (1926); *Portuguese Suites Nos. 1–2* for orchestra (1926, 1928); *Inês de Castro*, 3-act opera (1927); *Petites Symphonies Nos. 1–2* (1928, 1957); *Entre-giestas*, 3-act opera (1929); *A feira*, ballet (1930); *Tá-mar*, 3-act opera (1938); *Don João IV*, 3-act opera (1940); *Don Sebastião*, ballet (1943); *Auto da barca do inferno*, opera (1950); *Arraial na ribeira*, ballet (1951); *Inês Pereira*, 3-act opera (1952); *Oratorio fatima* (1960); *Orfeu em Lisboa*, 3-act opera (1963); *Oratorio da paz* (1967); *La belle dame sans péché*, opera (1968); *Sinfonia d'alem mar* (1969); *Auto da barca da gloria*, opera (1970).

Cohn, Arthur (b. Philadelphia, 6 Nov 1910), attended the Combs Conservatory of Music, Philadelphia (1920–28), and studied privately in Philadelphia with William F. Happich (composition, 1929–32) and Sascha Jacobinoff (violin, 1930–31). Chamber music studies were with Emil Folgmann at the Univ. of Penn. (1930–31). He did graduate work at the Juilliard School (1933–34, composition with Rubin Goldmark, score reading with George Volkel). Cohn was curator and director of the Fleisher Music Collection at the Philadelphia Free Library (1934–52) and head of the music division (1946–52). He directed the Univ. of Penn. Museum Concerts (1949–56) and served as executive director of the Settlement Music School in Philadelphia (1952–56). He was head of symphonic and foreign music at Mills Music Co. during 1956–66, after which he became director of serious music at MCA Music. Since 1942 he has conducted the Symphony Club of Philadelphia and since 1958, the Haddonfield, N. J., Symphony Orchestra. He conducted the Philadelphia Little Symphony (1952–56), the Philadelphia Orchestra children's concerts (1954, 1956), and the Columbia Univ. Orchestra (1966–67). He has written criticism for the *American Record Guide, Modern Music, Tempo, Philadelphia Art and Music,* and the *Rochester Times-Union.*

PRINCIPAL COMPOSITIONS: *6 String Quartets* (1928, 1930, 1932, 1935, 1935, 1945); *Suite in E Minor* for violin, piano (1932); *Retrospections* for string orchestra (1933); *Music for Brass Instruments* for 4 trumpets, 3 trombones (1935, Southern); *4 Preludes* for string orchestra, a revised version of the *String Quartet No. 1* (1937, Mills); *Suite* for viola, orchestra (1937, Mills); *Machine Music* for 2 pianos (1937); *Piano Preludes* (1939); *4 Symphonic Documents* for orchestra (1939, Mills); *Music for Ancient Instruments* (1939); *Quintuple Concerto* for 5 ancient instruments, modern orchestra (1940, Mills); *Histrionics* for string orchestra, a revised version of the *String Quartet No. 4* (1940, Mills); *Flute Concerto* (1941, Mills); *Hebraic Study* for solo bassoon or bassoon, piano (1944, Vogel); *Declamation and Toccata* for solo bassoon or bassoon, piano (1944, Vogel); *Quotations in Percussion* for 103 instruments, 6 players (part 1, 1958; part 2, 1959; Mills); *Kaddish* for orchestra (1964, Mills).

PRINCIPAL WRITINGS: "Addenda," *The Collector's Haydn* (Philadelphia 1960); *The Collector's 20th-Century Music in the Western Hemisphere* (Philadelphia 1961); *20th Century Music in Western Europe* (Philadelphia 1965); *Musical Quizzical* (New York 1969).

Colgrass, Michael (Charles) (b. Chicago, 22 April 1932), attended the Univ. of Ill. (1950–54, percussion with Paul Price, composition with Eugene Weigel), Tanglewood (summers 1952, 1954; composition with Lukas Foss), and Aspen (summer 1953; composition with Darius Milhaud). He moved to New York in 1956, where he studied privately with Wallingford Riegger (1958–59) and Ben Weber (1959–62). He is a free-lance percussionist and has played with concert and theater orchestras, dance and opera companies, jazz bands, and other groups. His performing experience has made him sensitive to the needs of performers, and he often writes with specific players in mind. Since 1965 he has leaned toward the theater and has been writing his own poetry and scripts; consequently his "work is increasingly influenced by literary ideas as opposed to strictly musical ones." His style emphasizes lyrical melody and the development of rhythmic ideas and draws on the eclecticism of his background as a performer.

PRINCIPAL COMPOSITIONS (published by MCA unless otherwise noted): *3 Brothers* for percussion (1950, Percus); *Chamber Music* for 4 drums, string quintet (1953); *Chamber Music* for percussion quintet (1954, Percus); *Inventions on a Motive* for percussion quartet (1955, Percus); *Variations* for 4 drums, viola (1957, Percus); *Wind Quintet* (1962); *Light Spirit* for flute, viola, guitar, percussion (1963); *Rhapsody* for clarinet, violin, piano (1963); *Rhapsodic Fantasy* for solo percussion, orchestra (1965); *As Quiet As* for orchestra (1966); *Virgil's Dream* for 4 actor-singers, 4 mime-musicians (1967); *The Earth's a Baked Apple* for orchestra, chorus (1968).

PRINCIPAL WRITINGS: "Fear and the Creative Process," *ACA Bulletin* 8/4:21–22; "A Composer Who'll Try Anything—Once," *New York Times* (17 Nov 1968), section D:25, 40.

BIBL.: Robert T. Jones, "Composing Has Its Rewards," *New York Times* (1 April 1969):50.

SEE ALSO Dance.

Collage, a juxtaposition of independent styles. The juxtaposition may be a simultaneity and/or a succession. In music for a large and potentially diverse medium, such as orchestra or magnetic tape, the separate styles are usually composed of many contrasting features of timbre, rhythm, melody, harmony, etc.; in music for a simpler medium, such as a solo instrument, the juxtaposition will necessarily be accomplished in less elaborate ways, for instance with shifts in rhythm and tonality. The significant factor is that the juxtaposition involves coherent units of sound that are themselves the product of separate musical elements. Thus a passage in which two or more key centers occur simultaneously but which maintains the same basic rhythmic and melodic character throughout may be polytonal but is probably not also a collage.

In traditional music, collage is most familiar in operatic scenes where music from onstage is interrupted by music from offstage in a different key, tempo, timbre, etc. There the collage of styles is heard as a momentary clash or dissonance, which is soon resolved. In a true collage situation the juxtaposition is not treated as a dissonance needing resolution but as a norm. The first composer to conceive of collage in this manner was Charles *Ives (1874–1954), who arrived at the concept about 1909 after having used polytonality, polyrhythms, quotations from existing popular and concert music, spatially separated sound sources, and other techniques now associated with collage textures. Although collage in the visual arts has a fairly continuous history, beginning with the dada movement (c.1916–22), collage in music ceased in the mid-20s, when Ives stopped composing, and was not taken up again until the 1960s.

SEE ALSO Texture.

Combinatoriality, see 12-Tone Techniques

Complementation, see 12-Tone Techniques

Computer Applications. Composers have used computers in two basic ways: as aids for precompositional calculations and as generators of electronic sound. The former application has been explored by Lejaren Hiller, Iannis Xenakis, and others; the latter was initially made possible by a program, Music IV, de-veloped in 1960 by Max V. Matthews of Bell Telephone Laboratories. Computers have also been used recently to analyze individual works, to study particular past styles of composition, to study tuning and temperament, and to study and invent notational systems.

PRECOMPOSITIONAL USES. Hiller's original approach was to take a set of a priori compositional rules (including those of Fux governing 16th-century modal counterpoint and others derived from 20th-century serial music) and to use the computer to "compose" passages that conform to those rules. The rules used in his first computer-generated piece, the *Illiac Suite for String Quartet* (1957), were essentially restrictive: at each point the program excluded all notes that would violate any of the rules, and the machine then chose at random from among the remaining possibilities. The results thus incorporated random selection processes into the familiar styles dictated by the chosen rules, and the piece can be considered as a study in degrees of randomness. In the last movement of the *Illiac Suite* and in *Computer Cantata* (1963), Hiller began to approach the problem of decision making, i.e., of programming a musical ear into the computer. Notes (or durations, dynamics, etc.) were not chosen at random but according to weighted probabilities. Each decision was dependent on a certain number of previous decisions. To take a simple example, a note was chosen according to the implications of the previously chosen note; those implications were in the form of a set of probabilities incorporated into the rules of the program, which dictated which note was most likely to follow a given note, which was next most likely, etc. Each decision could, of course, be made to depend upon any number of previous (or future) decisions with any degree of complexity in the system of probabilities. At first Hiller used simple systems of weights, but in later works, such as *Algorithms I–II* (1968–69), he was able to achieve more genuinely musical results by weighting his probabilities according to the principles of information theory and by utilizing complex serial procedures. Hiller's results show that a composer can become well enough acquainted with the correlation between the probabilities he chooses and the results he obtains and with the interrelationship between statistical weights assigned to the various musical parameters to be able to select these weights creatively and sensitively. Having achieved this ability, he could make the selection of probabilities the principal compositional decision for a given work. Although details might have to be corrected in the end product, the sound ideal, as specified by the program, would be realized. The results achieved by Robert H. McMahan, who has approximated the late piano music of Brahms, indicate that a computer can faithfully reproduce (and therefore specifically alter) a given style of music by analyzing and then imitating it. (The analysis, however, must go beyond the merely statistical, and McMahan's work indicates that this is possible.)

The work of Xenakis is similar to that of Hiller, except that he is concerned more with sound structures than with compositional methods. Xenakis utilizes a variety of mathematical concepts, and when one such concept involves considerable calculation, he uses the computer as a tool. For example, in *Metastaseis* for orchestra of 61 players (1953–54) he used it to calculate patterns of glissandos traveling at different varying rates with constantly changing directions and frequent collisions. In *Eonta* for piano and 5 brasses (1963–64) he used probability theory, somewhat as Hiller does, to create "stochastic" sound structures. In general, he determines fixed sound structures in his programs but allows for a variety of realizations within the restrictions of the program.

SOUND GENERATION. The Music IV program of Matthews has been adapted to acommodate various esthetics ranging from the compositional interrelationship of a multitude of sound parameters (as practiced at Princeton Univ.) to the search for new timbres (as carried on at Stanford Univ.). One of the more sophisticated music programs developed from the original Music IV was produced under the direction of composers John Chowning and Leland Smith and programmer David Poole at Stanford. The program represents symbolically what amounts to the numerical equivalent of the sound-producing circuitry found in a typical electronic music studio. By means of punch cards or a teletype keyboard the composer "tells" the computer how to connect this circuitry and what values to use in determining every aspect of the sound that will result. The machine then calculates an array of numbers that represents the sound wave of the desired sonority (25,000 numbers per second of sound give a very close approximation of an actual continuous wave form). This array is then converted into voltage, amplified, and presented through loudspeakers. The advantages over using the actual electrical components as in the usual electronic studio include the computer's greater accuracy and versatility and the composer's ability to design new circuitry numerically in a matter of minutes rather than having to actually construct new

equipment. Many computers are equipped with a screen on which the composer may see pictures of the wave forms with which he determines his basic sounds, attack-decay envelopes, probability distributions, loudness functions, etc. These waves are produced by a variety of means and may even be drawn by hand on the surface of the screen. The most spectacular of many special features of the Stanford program is the creation of the illusion that a sound is traveling in the space behind the speakers according to a path prescribed by the composer. This is done automatically by the program, which numerically simulates the Doppler shift, reverberation, change of volume, stereo directionality, and loss of high frequencies experienced as sound sources travel great distances. Thus the composer can bring the spatial factor under his control and with only four speakers arranged in a tetrahedron can make a sound seem to originate from any position in an auditorium.

Computer technology is expanding rapidly, as is composers' understanding of this technology. In the last few years there have been as many advances in the potentials of computer music systems as there have been completed pieces. Thus the relatively small number of computer pieces (by Hiller, Gerald Strang, Smith, Hubert S. Howe, J. K. Randall, Jean-Claude Risset, Charles Dodge, Barry Vercoe, and others) should not be taken as an indication of any lack of achievement in the medium. The following brief survey provides an indication of recent advances, concentrating on two types of research, that devoted to making computer technology more accessible to composers and that concerned with expanding the possibilities of the medium (in neither case should this survey be considered exhaustive). In the first category are the FORTRAN version of Music IV (Godfrey Winham); real-time sound generation, i.e., elimination of the often considerable delay between specifying a sound and hearing it (John Clough's Interactive Realtime Music Assembler, or IRMA); streamlined languages for sound synthesis (Vercoe's MUSIC 360, Matthews's Music V, and Howe's MUSIC 7); streamlined language for composition (Jack P. Citron's MUSPEC). In the second category are the synthesis of speech, which can then be used and altered as a type of electronic sprechstimme (Winham, Randall, Dodge, and Wayne Slawson); the creation of imperfection in computer-generated sound so that a more lifelike quality of sound is achieved (Strang, Chowning, Arthur Layzer, Arthur Roberts); interfacing between a computer and an electronic music studio, so that, for example, a small computer might control a Moog synthesizer (Matthews).

BIBL.: "Computer Performance of Music," a series of 7 articles, *American Society of University Composers Proceedings* 1:27–55; J. L. Divilbiss, "Realtime Generation of Music with a Digital Computer," *Journal of Music Theory* 8:99–111; Heinz von Foerster and James W. Beauchamp, eds., *Music by Computers* (New York 1969); Hubert S. Howe, Jr., "A General View of Compositional Procedure in Computer Sound Synthesis," *American Society of University Composers Proceedings* 3:98–108; ——, "Music and Electronics, a Report," *Perspectives* 4/2:68–75; Gerald Lefkoff, ed., *Computer Applications in Music* (Morgantown, W. Va. 1967); Harry B. Lincoln, ed., *The Computer and Music* (Ithaca, N.Y. 1970); Max V. Mathews et al., *The Technology of Computer Music* (Cambridge, Mass., 1969); James C. Tenney, "Sound-Generation by Means of a Digital Computer," *Journal of Music Theory* 7:24–71; Iannis Xenakis, *Musiques formelles* (Paris 1963); R. Kh. Zaripov, "Cybernetics and Music," trans. by Michael Kassler, *Perspectives* 7/2:115–54.

Jonathan D. Kramer

SEE ALSO Theory.

Concrete Music, see Musique Concrète. See also Electronic Music: History and Development.

Cone, Edward Toner (b. Greensboro, N. C., 4 May 1917), studied at Princeton Univ. (1935–39, 1941–42; composition with Roger Sessions, musicology with Roy Welch, Oliver Strunk) and at Columbia Univ. (1939–41; musicology with Paul Henry Lang). He has taught at Princeton Univ. since 1947.

PRINCIPAL COMPOSITIONS: *Symphony* (1952); *Elegy* for orchestra (1953); *Nocturne and Rondo* for piano, orchestra (1956); *Prelude, Passacaglia, and Fugue* for piano (1957); *Violin Concerto* (1958); *Music for Strings* (1965); *String Sextet* (1966); *Variations* for orchestra (1969).

PRINCIPAL WRITINGS: "Analysis Today," *Problems of Modern Music* (New York 1960):34–50; "Music: A View from Delft," *Musical Quarterly* 47:439–53; "Beyond Analysis," *Perspectives* 6/1: 33–51; *Musical Form and Musical Performance* (New York 1968). Cone was also an editor and contributor to *Perspectives on Schoenberg and Stravinsky* (Princeton 1968).

BIBL.: Robert Morgan, "E. T. C.'s *String Sextet*," *Perspectives* 8/2.

Constant, Marius (b. Bucharest, 7 Feb 1926), studied at the Bucharest Conservatory, the Paris Conservatory, and the Ecole Normale

de Musique (1946–49; composition with Olivier Messiaen, Nadia Boulanger, and Arthur Honegger; conducting with Jean Fournet). He was a member of the musique concrète laboratory Club d'Essai during 1947–52. In 1967 he lectured at Stanford Univ., and in 1970 he taught at the International Conductors' Course of the Netherlands Radio in Hilversum, specializing in avant-garde repertory. During 1963–71 he was the president and music director of Ars Nova, a Paris orchestra for the performance of modern music. His contacts with George Enescu during World War II affected his subsequent musical development.

PRINCIPAL COMPOSITIONS (published by Salabert unless otherwise noted): *24 Preludes* for orchestra (c.1958, Ricordi); *Turner*, 3 essays for orchestra (1961, Ricordi); *Chants de Maldoror* for dancer-conductor, narrator, 23 improvisors, 10 cellos; texts by Isidore Ducasse (1962, Ricordi); *Eloge de la folie*, ballet; choreography by Roland Petit (1966); *Paradise Lost*, ballet; choreography by Petit (1967); *Chaconne et marche militaire* for orchestra (1968); *Winds* for chamber wind orchestra, double bass (1968); *5 Chants et 1 vocalise* for soprano, orchestra; texts by Lou Bruder (1968); *14 Stations* for percussion, 6 instruments (1970); *Equal* for 5 percussionists (1970); *Candide*, mimodrama (1970); *Prayer Wheels* for harpsichord (1970).

SEE ALSO France.

Constantinescu, Dan (b. Bucharest, 10 June 1931), studied at the Bucharest Conservatory (1950–55, composition with Leon Klepper and Mihail Jora). He has taught harmony there since 1957. His music has been influenced by the late works of Enescu and by Messiaen, Webern, and Boulez.

PRINCIPAL COMPOSITIONS: *Divertimento in the Classical Style* for string orchestra (1954); *Ballad* for orchestra (1955); *Partita* for orchestra (1957); *Piano Sonata* (1961, Muzicală); *Violin Sonata* (1962, Muzicală); *Flute Sonata* (1963, Muzicală); *Concerto* for piano, string orchestra (1963, Muzicală); *Trio* for piano, violin, clarinet, percussion (1964); *Cello Sonata* (1964); *Clarinet Sonata* (1965); *Variations* for violin, viola, cello, piano (1966, Muzicală); *String Quartet* (1967); *Sinfonia da camera* for violin, viola, cello, flute, bass clarinet, trumpet, piano, percussion (1968); *Sinfonia concertante* for orchestra (1970).

BIBL.: Articles on Constantinescu's music have appeared in *Revista muzica* (Bucharest) 1958/12, 1960/10, 1965/8, 1967/4, and 1968/5.

Constantinidis, Yannis (b. Smyrna, Turkey, 21 August 1903), studied harmony and counterpoint in Dresden with Josef Gustav Mraczek

(1922–23) and in Berlin with Paul Juon (1923–25); he also studied in Berlin with Karl Rössler (1923–25, piano), Karl Ehrenberg (1925–26, conducting), and Kurt Weill (1926–27, composition). He has worked in Athens for HMV Records (1934–46) and for Columbia Records (1935–46). He was a musical advisor for Athens radio during 1939–59.

PRINCIPAL COMPOSITIONS: *5 Tragoudia tis agapis* [5 Love Songs] for voice, piano (1931); *20 Tragoudia tou Ellinikou laou* [20 Greek Folksongs] for voice, piano (1935–45); *Du Dodecanèse* [From Dodecanes], songs and dances for piano (1944–46); *Suite* for violin, piano (1948, Enosis); *Suites Dodecanesienne Nos. 1–2* for chamber orchestra (1948, 1949); *44 Paedika kommatia* [44 Children's Pieces] for piano (1948–50, published as *Greek Miniatures* by Rongwen); *8 Danses des îles grecques* for piano (1951, No. 2 published by Gerig in *Contemporary Greek Piano Music*); *3 Sonatinas* for piano (1952–53).

Conyngham, Barry (b. Sydney, 27 August 1944), studied at the Univ. of Sydney (composition with Peter Sculthorpe) and privately in Tokyo with Toru Takemitsu. During 1962–65 he was a professional jazz pianist and band leader. During 1969–70 he taught at the Univ. of New South Wales and at the National Institute of Dramatic Art in Sydney. He has composed a number of film scores and in 1969 was composer for the Australian Commonwealth Film Unit presentation at Expo '70 in Osaka. Since 1966 he has worked in close association with the Australian composer Richard Meale.

PRINCIPAL COMPOSITIONS (published by UE unless otherwise noted): *Dialogues* for string trio (1966, unpub.); *Farben* for double chorus (1967, unpub.); *Crisis: Thoughts in a City* for string orchestra, percussion (1968–69); *5 Windows* for orchestra (1969); *Horizon*, 9-track film score for Expo '70 (1969, unpub.); *Three* for string quartet, 2 percussionists (1969); *Edward John Eyre* for actors, female voice, wind quintet, string orchestra (1970); *Ice Carving* for orchestra of violins (1970); *Water . . . Footsteps . . . Time* for piano, harp, guitar, double bass, tam-tam, double orchestra (1970).

BIBL.: Suzanne Gartener, "Writing for Schools: B. C.," *Music Now* 3 (1971).

Copland, Aaron (b. Brooklyn, N. Y., 14 Nov 1900), is the son of Lithuanian Jewish parents. His father, whose original name was Kaplan, had immigrated to the U.S. from Russia via Scotland and owned a department store in Brooklyn. Although young Copland took piano lessons from age 13, it was not until his 17th year that he began to study theory (in Brooklyn with Rubin Goldmark) and to seriously compose. In 1921 he left for France, where he enrolled at the new American Conservatory at Fontainebleau. His teacher in composition was an uninspiring academician, Paul Vidal; however, Copland was greatly impressed with a harmony teacher at Fontainebleau, Nadia Boulanger, and in the fall of 1921 moved to Paris to study composition privately with her. He returned to the U.S. in 1924 and, during a summer spent in Pennsylvania as pianist in a hotel trio, began to compose a work for organ and orchestra requested by Mlle. Boulanger for her 1925 American concerts. The result was the *Symphony* for organ and orchestra, premiered in January in New York under Walter Damrosch and repeated the next month in Boston under Serge Koussevitzky. These performances gained for Copland some notoriety as a dissonant modernist and, more importantly, resulted in an orchestral commission from Koussevitzky. Copland fulfilled it with *Music for the Theater*, and both this work and the subsequent *Piano Concerto* received Koussevitzky performances, marking the beginning of Copland's long association with the conductor.

Copland received Guggenheim fellowships (the first given a composer) in 1925 and 1926 and an RCA recording award in 1929 and gave lectures at the New School for Social Research in New York during 1927–37. He revisited Europe in 1926, 1927, and 1929, and in 1931 he lived for a time in Morocco. During the 30s he made three extended visits to Mexico, partly at the instigation of Carlos Chávez, who conducted the premiere of his *Short Symphony* there in 1934. In 1941 and 1947 he toured several Latin American countries under auspices of the U.S. State Dept. Since 1956 he has toured as a conductor in the U.S., Europe, Australia, Japan, Israel, and the Soviet Union. He has twice replaced Walter Piston at Harvard Univ. (1935, 1944), and during 1951–52 he was Charles Eliot Norton professor there. In addition, he taught composition at Tanglewood (1940–65), where he exerted considerable influence on a generation of American composers. His activities on behalf of new and American music have included cofounding the Copland-Sessions Concerts in New York (1928–31) and participation in a festival of contemporary music at Yaddo in Saratoga Springs, N. Y. (1932); membership on the board of the League of Composers; founding the Cos Cob Press (which published many American works); involvement with the American chapter of ISCM; and founding of the American Composers Alliance in 1937.

Although Copland produced his first composition at nine (a song now lost), he wrote nothing further until he was 16. Between 1917 and 1920 he composed several works which, though well-made, exhibit only slight individuality; among them are *4 Moods* (*Esquisses*) for piano (one of which contains the first appearance in his music of jazz rhythms), and his first published scores, the Debussian *Cat and the Mouse* for piano and *Old Poem* for voice and piano. The first mature work is *As It Fell Upon a Day* (1923); this and other works of 1922–25 show a strong reaction against romanticism and a more-than-passing acquaintance with the music of Debussy, Roussel, and especially Stravinsky. They have lean textures, clear formal shapes, angular melodies, a considerable amount of dissonance, jarring rhythms (polyrhythms in the finale of the *Dance Symphony*), and ostinatos.

In 1925 Copland decided that his output was "too European in derivation," and he decided to introduce jazz elements in an effort to "Americanize" his music. This resulted in the cautiously jazzy *Music for the Theater* and the blatantly jazzy *Piano Concerto*, as well as (to a lesser extent) the more grandiose *Symphonic Ode*. After 1930 however, he largely abandoned jazz, though its influence continued to be felt in the rhythmic life of many works. Instead, he embarked on a more serious, even austere, mode of expression that resulted in such works as the *Piano Variations*, *Short Symphony*, and *Statements* for orchestra. The *Piano Variations* (1930) is illustrative of this new direction: Practically every chord and figuration is a direct outgrowth of a terse seven-note theme. Notable also is the serial device of octave displacement, which functions both melodically and harmonically, and the often declamatory rhetoric (declamation has always played an important role in his music, from the early *Grogh* to the *Connotations* for orchestra, 1961–62). The influence of Bartók is evident in the percussive treatment of the piano.

During this time of experimentation the idea of an "American sound" was never far from Copland's thoughts. In addition he began to feel "an increasing dissatisfaction with the relations of the music-loving public and the living composer." He finally decided to try reaching a larger audience by simplifying his style. In 1936 he produced the orchestral fantasy *El salón méxico*, based on popular Mexican themes, and its success provided the impetus for a long line of compositions in what

he has described as his "more accessible style," including the ballets, several suites, and other works. In these scores such diverse ingredients as New England hymnody, North and Latin American musical folklore, and jazz are combined with unadorned parallel triads, descending thirds and diatonic blends, colorful orchestration, unusual vertical chord spacing, and an overall emphasis on economy. *Appalachian Spring* (1944) is typical, containing the plainest of harmonic and melodic materials (e.g., the Shaker hymn "Simple Gifts") transformed by a sensitive use of tone color and octave displacement and by a fertile variation technique. Along with the "accessible" works, Copland has continued to produce abstract, often severe, music aimed at smaller audiences, and his output since 1936 has run in two continuing and parallel lines that are closely related and that occasionally merge (as in the *Third Symphony*, 1946). This situation accounts for the appearance, within two years of each other, of such dissimilar works as the simple, dominant-tonic *Old American Songs* (1950–52) and the complex, serially oriented *Piano Quartet* (1950). In the latter work, which is based on an 11-note row, Copland fully utilized 12-tone technique for the first time. Tendencies in this direction were apparent as early as 1927 in an experimental 12-tone song and especially in the 1930 *Piano Variations*, with its concentration on a 7-tone thematic cell. His later exploration of the technique (in the *Piano Quartet*; *Piano Fantasy*, 1955–57; *Connotations*, 1961–62; and *Inscape*, 1967) was stimulated by postwar developments in this area; as in the case of Stravinsky, he was able to approach serialism in an individual manner.

PRINCIPAL COMPOSITIONS (published by Boosey unless otherwise noted): *Passacaglia* for piano (1922, Sénart); *As It Fell Upon a Day* for voice, flute, clarinet; text by Richard Barnefield (1923); *Symphony* for organ, orchestra (1924); *Dance Symphony* (1925); *Music for the Theater* for orchestra (1925); *Piano Concerto* (1926); *Symphony No. 1* (1928); *Symphonic Ode* (1928, revised 1955); *Vitebsk*, study on a Jewish theme for violin, cello, piano (1929); *Piano Variations* (1930); *Short Symphony* (Symphony No. 2) (1933); *Statements* for orchestra (1934); *El salón méxico* for orchestra (1936); *Sextet* for string quartet, clarinet, piano (1937); *The Second Hurricane*, high school opera; libretto by Edwin Denby (1937); *Billy the Kid*, ballet; choreography by Eugene Loring (1938); *An Outdoor Overture* for orchestra (1938); *Quiet City* for trumpet, English horn, string orchestra (1940); *Our Town*, film score for the play by Thornton Wilder (1940); *Piano Sonata* (1941); *Lincoln Portrait* for narrator, orchestra (1942); *Rodeo*, ballet; choreography by Agnes de Mille (1942); *Fanfare for the Common Man* for brass, percussion (1942); *Danzón cubano* for orchestra (1942–44); *Violin Sonata* (1943); *Appalachian Spring* for 13 instruments, ballet; choreography by Martha Graham (1944; suite for orchestra, 1944, rescored for 13 instruments, 1970); *Symphony No. 3* (1946); *In the Beginning* for mezzo-soprano, chorus (1947); *The Red Pony*, film score (1948); *Concerto* for clarinet, string orchestra with harp, piano (1948); *Piano Quartet* (1950); *Old American Songs* for voice, piano (1950–52); *12 Poems by Emily Dickinson* for medium voice, piano (1950); *The Tender Land*, opera; libretto by Horace Everett (1954; orchestral suite, 1957); *Canticle of Freedom* for chorus, orchestra; poem by John Barbour (1955); *Piano Fantasy* (1955–57); *Orchestral Variations* (1957); *Dance Panels* for orchestra (1959, revised 1962); *Nonet* for strings (1960); *Connotations* for orchestra (1961–62); *Emblems* for band (1964); *Music for a Great City* for orchestra (1964); *Inscape* for orchestra (1967); *Duo* for flute, piano (1970–71). List to 1961: *Composers of the Americas* 1:28–35.

PRINCIPAL WRITINGS: *What to Listen for in Music* (New York 1938); *Our New Music* (New York 1941; revised ed., *The New Music*, 1968); *Music and Imagination* (Cambridge, Mass., 1952); *Copland on Music* (New York 1960).

BIBL.: Arthur Berger, *A. C.* (New York 1953); Edward T. Cone, "Conversation with A. C.," *Perspectives* 6/2:57–72; William Flanagan, "A. C.," *Hi-Fi Stereo Review* (June 1966):43–54; Peter Garvie, "A. C.," *Canadian Music Journal* (winter 1962):3–12; Richard Franko Goldman, "A. C.," *Musical Quarterly* 47:1–3; Wilfrid Mellers, *Music in a New Found Land* (London 1964):81–101; Bryan Northcott, "C. in England," *Music and Musicians* (April 1969):34–36; Phillip Ramey, "With Copland in London," liner notes for the recording *Copland Conducts Copland* (Columbia MS 7223); Paul Rosenfeld, *Musical Impressions*, reprint (New York 1969):248–56; Julia Smith, *A. C.* (New York 1955); *Tempo* 95 (special Copland issue); Virgil Thomson, *American Music Since 1910* (New York 1971):49–59.

Phillip Ramey

SEE ALSO Dance, Folk Resources, Instrumental and Vocal Resources, Jazz, Opera, Popular Music, Rhythm, United States.

Cordero, Roque (b. Panama, 16 Aug 1917), attended Hamline Univ., St. Paul, Minn. (1943–47, composition with Ernst Krenek) and Tanglewood (summer 1946, conducting with Stanley Chapple). He also studied conducting with Dimitri Mitropoulos in Minneapolis (1944–46) and with Leon Barzin in New York (1947–48). He was director and teacher, National Institute of Music in Panama (1953–64) and artistic director and conductor of the National Orchestra of Panama (1964–66). Since 1966 he has been professor of music and

assistant director of the Latin-American Music Center at Indiana Univ. Since 1946 he has composed with 12-tone procedures almost exclusively. Ronald Sider has said of the *Violin Concerto*: "A characteristic melodic pattern is the upward leap of a major seventh. Ostinato patterns are common. Solos for timpani assume considerable importance, with rhythms generally complex. The violin writing is virtuosic" (*Inter-American Music Bulletin* 77:14).

PRINCIPAL COMPOSITIONS (published by Peer unless otherwise noted): *Symphonies Nos. 1–3* (1945, 1956, 1965); *Sonatina* for violin, piano (1946); *Symphonic Movement* for string orchestra (1946); *Quintet* for flute, clarinet, violin, cello, piano (1949); *Introduccion y allegro burlesco* for orchestra (1950, unpub.); *Duo 1954* for 2 pianos (1954); *Adagio tragico* for string orchestra (1955); *String Quartets Nos. 1–2* (1960; 1968, unpub.); *Mensaje funebre* for clarinet (1961); *Violin Concerto* (1962); *Cello Sonata* (1963); *Circunvoluciones y moviles* for 57 players (1967, unpub.); *Permutaciones 7* for clarinet, trumpet, tympani, violin, viola, double bass, piano (1967); *Concertino* for viola, string orchestra (1968, unpub.); *Paz, Paix, Peace* for 4 trios, harp (1969, unpub.). List to 1962: *Composers of the Americas* 8:61–64.

PRINCIPAL WRITINGS: "El folklore en la creacion musical panameña," *Revista universidad* (Panama) 31:103–13; "Nacionalismo versus dodecafonismo?," *Revista musical chilena* 13/67:28–38; "Relaciones de la educacion musical con los conservatorios de música," *ibid.* 18/87:63–67; *Curso de solfeo* (Buenos Aires 1963); "El publico y la música viva," *Interamerican Monograph Series* (Bloomington) 1:57–63; "La música en Centro America y Panama," *Journal of Interamerican Studies* (Miami) 8:411–18.

BIBL.: Gilbert Chase, "Composed by C.," *Music of the Americas* 10/6:7–11; Roberto García-Morillo, "R. C., valor autentico de la música latino-americana," *La nacion* (Buenos Aires, 10 April 1958):5; Juan Orrego-Salas, "R. C., un musico de America," *Zig-Zag* (Santiago, 10 June 1960):60–61; Ronald Sider, "R. C., the Composer and his Style . . .," *Inter-American Music Bulletin* 61:1–17; Magdalena Vicuña, "R. C., gran figura de la música americana," *Revista musical chilena* 14/71:183–85.

Coria, Miguel Angel (b. Madrid, 24 Oct 1937), attended the Royal Conservatory in Madrid (1955–61; harmony, counterpoint, and fugue with Angel Arias; orchestration with Gerardo Gombau, piano with Pedro Lerma). In 1966–67 he studied with Gottfried Michael Koenig and Jaap Vink at the electronic studio of the Univ. of Utrecht. He was harpsichordist with the Aula de Música chamber orchestra in Madrid during 1964–65. In 1964, with the composer Luis de Pablo, he founded the Alea Electronic Music Studio. Coria was musical commentator for the Spanish radio during 1964–66 and since 1968 has been composing scores for a series of science programs on television.

PRINCIPAL COMPOSITIONS: *Imágenes* for flute, oboe, vibraphone, violin, viola (1963); *Vértices* for flute, oboe, clarinet, bass clarinet, harp, celesta, vibraphone, 2 violins, viola, cello (1964, revised 1968); *Frase* for piano (1965, revised 1968); *Volúmenes* for flute, harp, celesta, piano, 2 violins, viola, cello (1966–67); *Collage* on tape (1966–67); *Joyce's Portrait* for soprano, 2 flutes, 2 horns, celesta, harp, 2 violins, viola, cello (1968); *Lúdica I* for orchestra (1968–69); *Lúdica III* for chamber orchestra (1969); *Lúdica IV* for piano solo, flute, clarinet, horn, trombone, 2 violins, viola, cello (1969).

PRINCIPAL WRITINGS: "El teórico" [on Paul Hindemith], *Arriba* (Madrid, 12 Jan 1964):26; "Anton von Webern, dodecafonismo serialista" (unpub. lecture, 1964); "Sistema tonal y sistema atonal" (unpub. lecture, 1966); program notes, 4th Pan American Festival of Music (Washington 1968); program notes, Concert of the Alea group (Madrid, 14 April 1969).

BIBL.: Arthur Custer, "Contemporary Music in Spain," *Musical Quarterly* 51:59; Federico Sopeña, "Música contemporánea en cantar y tañer," *A B C* (Madrid, 19 Dec 1963); ——, "Estrenos españoles en la bienal," *ibid.* (4 Dec 1964); Vicente Salas-Viú, "La joven generación de compositores españoles en la bienal," *El mercurio* (Santiago, Chile, 10 Feb 1965).

SEE ALSO Spain.

Corigliano, John (b. New York, 16 Feb 1938), attended Columbia College (1955–59, composition with Otto Luening) and the Manhattan School of Music (1962–63, composition with Vittorio Giannini). He also studied composition privately with Paul Creston in 1959. Corigliano has worked for radio and television stations in New York: as programer and writer for radio station WQXR (1959–61) and WBAI (1962–64) and since 1960 as assistant director of musical programs at CBS-TV. He was music director of the Morris Theatre in New Jersey (1962–64) and composed incidental scores for its 1964 and 1965 productions. He is president of Music For The Theatre, a rental library of incidental music tapes and scores, which he founded in 1966. In 1968–69 Corigliano taught composition and orchestration at the National Cathedral College of Church Musicians in Washington. In 1969 he was arranger of rock music for Kama Sutra and Mercury records and began using

the Moog Synthesizer for commercials for Centaur Productions.

PRINCIPAL COMPOSITIONS (published by Schirmer-G unless otherwise noted): *Petit fours* for voice, piano (1958, unpub.); *Kaleidoscope* for 2 pianos (1959); *Fern Hill* for chorus, orchestra; poem by Dylan Thomas (1960); *What I Expected Was . . .* for chorus, brass, percussion; text by Stephen Spender (1961); *Violin Sonata* (1963); *The Cloisters* for voice, orchestra (1965); *Elegy* for orchestra (1965); *Tournaments Overture* for orchestra (1967); *Piano Concerto* (1967); *Christmas at the Cloisters* for chorus, piano (1968); *Poem in October* for tenor, flute, oboe, clarinet, string quartet, harpsichord (1969). List to 1963: *Composers of the Americas* 9:40.

BIBL.: David Hall, liner notes for the recording of the *Violin Sonata* (CRI SD-215); James Lyons, liner notes for the *Piano Concerto* (Mercury SR-90517).

Cortés, Ramiro (b. Dallas, 25 Nov 1933), studied at Yale Univ. (1953–54, composition with Richard Donovan), the Univ. of Southern Calif. (1954–56, composition with Halsey Stevens and Ingolf Dahl), the Juilliard School (1960–61, composition with Víttorio Giannini), and in Rome (1956–58, composition with Goffredo Petrassi). During 1963–66 he was a computer programmer. He has taught at the Univ. of Southern Calif. since 1966 and is active as a pianist and conductor at the Univ. and at Monday Evening Concerts in Los Angeles. His study during the late 1950s of the serial music of Stravinsky and Dallapiccola led to a "turning point" in his own music, and until the late 1960s he used serial procedures. His *Quintet* (1967–68) is not serial but does avoid the repetition of a tone before all others of the chromatic scale have been used. Often in his music similar rhythmic and melodic shapes are juxtaposed and superimposed in a free contrapuntal fashion.

PRINCIPAL COMPOSITIONS: *Divertimento* for woodwind trio (1953; revised 1957, Peer); *Missa brevis* for women's chorus, piano (1954, Presser); *Suite* for piano (1955, E-V); *Nocturnal upon S. Lucy's Day* for tenor, string quartet; poem by John Donne (1957, revised 1966); *Chamber Concerto* for cello, 12 winds (1958, revised 1961); *Trio* for violin, cello, piano (1959, revised 1965); *The Eternal Return* for orchestra (1963, revised 1966); *Concerto* for violin, string orchestra (1965); *Duo* for flute, oboe (1967); *The Brass Ring* for 2 trumpets, 3 trombones (1967); *Woodwind Quintet* (1967–68, E-V); *Homage to Jackson Pollack* for viola (1968); *Charenton*, suite of variations for chamber orchestra (1968–70).

Cotapos, Acario (b. Valdivia, Chile, 30 April 1889; d. Santiago, 22 Nov 1969), lived in New York during 1917–27, where he studied privately and associated with the avant-garde group of Edgard Varèse, Aaron Copland, Henry Cowell, and Darius Milhaud. He was one of the founders of the International Composers Guild, later named the League of Composers. From 1927 to 1939 he lived in Paris and Madrid and wrote his most important compositions. He returned to Chile in 1940 to become secretary of the National Conservatory, a post he held until 1946. From 1949 until his death he was supervisor of the Instituto de Extensión Musical of the Univ. of Chile.

PRINCIPAL COMPOSITIONS (published by IEM unless otherwise noted): *Le Détachement vivant* for 28 instruments (1917, unpub.); *Philippe L'Arabe* for baritone, instruments (premiere 1918, unpub.); *4 Symphonic Preludes* (1923); *Sonata-Fantasia* for piano (premiere 1924); *Voces de gesta* for orchestra (1930); *El pajaro burlon* for orchestra (1932); *Imaginacion de mi pais* for orchestra (1950); *Balmaceda* for narrator, orchestra; text by the composer (1955); *Fantasia* for piano, harpsichord, 8 instruments (1956, unpub.).

BIBL.: The April 1961 issue of *Revista musical chilena* is devoted to Cotapos.

SEE ALSO Chile.

Counterpoint, see Harmony and Counterpoint

Cowell, Henry (Dixon) (b. Menlo Park, Calif., 11 March 1897; d. Shady Hill, N. Y., 10 Dec 1965), spent his boyhood near San Francisco and in Kansas, Oklahoma and Iowa. Cowell said that the traditional music he heard in these areas, as well as Asian classical music, remained permanent influences in his musical thinking. He was first a violinist, appearing publicly at age six, but it was a composer-pianist that he made his debut in San Francisco on 12 March 1912, creating a minor scandal with his advanced compositions. His first burst of professional activities came in the 1920s. He made five tours of Europe during 1923–33 and began a series of domestic tours which continued for 25 years. It was at this time that friendships began with European colleagues such as Béla Bartók and Alban Berg. A renowned champion of American composers, in 1927 he founded New Music, a society for the publication and recording of contemporary works. Major scores of Charles Ives, Carl Ruggles, Virgil Thomson, and many other North and South American composers were printed by New Music Edition; a few European masters such as Webern and Schoenberg were also included. Cowell remained closely involved with the venture until its catalog was taken over by Theodore Presser in the early 60s.

In 1928 Cowell became the first American composer to be invited to appear in the Soviet Union; he performed in Moscow, and some of his piano music was published by the state publishing house. His long career as a pedagogue, begun as an itinerant piano teacher when he was a boy, was established in 1928 at the New School for Social Research in New York; he remained as director of musical activities there until 1963. He also lectured for over 30 years in universities all over the U.S., Europe, and Asia. His last major teaching post was at Columbia during 1951–65. Three of the students who had private lessons with Cowell were George Gershwin, Lou Harrison, and John Cage.

Cowell, who had an abiding interest in the music of other cultures, especially those of Asia, studied non-European musical systems at the Univ. of Berlin in 1932–33. His private study of Eastern music was extensive, and he traveled in Turkey, Lebanon, Pakistan, India, Japan, and Iran, where he spent several months in 1957 as a consultant on broadcasting for the Iranian government. During 1937–41 he was incarcerated in San Quentin prison, having been sentenced on a "morals" charge in Calif. without trial and without the presence of a defense attorney. He transformed this potentially shattering experience into one of productivity: with no encouragement and little practical assistance, he gave music lessons to his fellow inmates, organized a band, and studied and composed. Pressure from members of the professional music community led to a pardon at the request of the prosecuting attorney.

Cowell moved in 1941 to White Plains, N. Y., as secretary to Percy Grainger. Subsequently he devoted his full time to the business of composing, performing, teaching, writing, and securing performances of his and other American composers' music. In 1941 he married Sidney Robertson, the writer and folksong collector, and during World War II took on the post of Senior Music Editor of the Overseas Division of the Office of War Information. The last nine years of his life were plagued with seriously debilitating illnesses (including cancer) which did not, however, stop him from continuing his teaching and other professional activities whenever possible.

Cowell's approach to all the basic elements of music was highly individual, even radical. As early as 1916 he began his ambitious theoretical work *New Musical Resources* (he finished the book in 1919 with the help of his English teacher S. S. Seward, but it was not published until 1930.) His first piano pieces for public performance, such as *The Tides of Manaunaun* (1912) and *Advertisement* (1914), contained what he called "tone-clusters," groups of adjoining notes struck simultaneously with the fist, the palm, or the forearm. These works were not mere experiments but rather assured works with carefully calculated effects and even a special system for notating clusters. He continued to work intermittently with the tone-cluster idea in other piano, chamber, and orchestral music. In the piano works the clusters were used both as huge blocks of sound moving up and down the keyboard and as subdued atmospheric effects in combination with melodic lines. In the ensemble works the cluster effect was often achieved by having individual instrumental lines converge to create massive chords.

Cowell's second major innovation, beginning in 1923, was a further exploitation of the sound resources of the grand piano. He left the bench to pluck, strum, sweep, and stop the piano strings in ways similar to stringed-instrument technique. *Aeolian Harp* (1923) is played with one hand silently depressing the keys while the other manipulates the strings. *The Banshee* (1925) is played throughout on the strings with an assistant holding down the damper pedal. *Sinister Resonance* (1925) is played on the keys in the conventional manner but with a simultaneous stopping and muting of the strings by hand. Elsewhere the bass strings are struck with a mallet.

Another innovative concept that Cowell developed in several scores beginning in the 1930s was that of indeterminacy, in which the composer relinquishes control over the final form or even content of a work. In Cowell's case, he occasionally wrote varying lengths of music for a piece and suggested that the performers assemble them in any order, excluding or repeating sections at will; this he called "elastic" form. In other instances during his career he instructed that a certain number of measures should be improvised by the performer; at the end of one ensemble work, the performers are to "continue to improvise ad lib."

To demonstrate the combination of complex rhythms, Cowell conceived a keyboard percussion instrument which he called the "rhythmicon." It was constructed by Leon

Theremin in 1931. Cowell himself referred to his invention as a machine rather than a musical instrument, yet he subsequently featured it prominently in at least one composition (*Rhythmicana*, 1931).

A number of Cowell's works grew out of his interest in Asian culture. He did not so much quote existing traditional materials as use characteristic rhythms, scale systems, and melodic patterns. He also used the Indian tablatarang and jalatarang and other Eastern instruments in combination with conventional Western instruments. In the last years of his life he composed two concertos for the Japaanese koto and (Western) orchestra. Cowell felt no restraint in using musical ideas from foreign cultures, and he also reached into the folk music of his own heritage. His family was Irish, and marching along throughout his whole career is a parade of banshees, leprechauns, and fiddlers playing jigs and reels in all manner of contexts (from piano solos to full orchestra and band works). Like many other American composers of his generation, he also produced works that consciously exploited the American scene and the American musical past. His interest in antique Americana came into full bloom with the *Hymn and Fuguing Tune* series (1944–64) inspired by the modal folk hymns of William Walker and the southern tradition Cowell had heard among relatives in Oklahoma and Kansas as a boy. As in rural tradition, Cowell's works in this genre begin with a slow choralelike section, which leads to a fugal section in a faster tempo. He used doubled parallel fourths, fifths, and octaves, and occasional free-moving dissonances, all of which are characteristic of the originals. These works are interesting not only for their beauty and originality but also as examples of the restoration of an older, all-but-forgotten style within a contemporary framework.

Like a number of other major figures in 20th-century music (Schoenberg, Stravinsky, and Ives are three), Cowell produced a body of work encompassing such great variety of expression as to confound both his friends and enemies. In evaluating his musical significance, one must beware of one of the standards of conventional criticism, consistency. While it is natural to seek to understand the phenomena in art and in life, to fix them in the mind, and to classify them, human nature, especially in the creative artist, is devious, contradictory, and full of inconsistency. It is therefore of doubtful value to reject new artistic products of a particularly rich and soaring imagination because they frustrate a sense of order or do not behave as one imagined they would or do not fit a convenient label. What Cowell embodies is versatility and eternal enterprise. His works are, in fact, a metaphor of that profoundly American ideal, freedom of choice. To look closely at all of his many musics is to be confronted with the image of a vivid, prismatic personality. Always, however, there is a prevailing spirit: it appears in the inquisitive, ingenuous child prodigy of little conventional education superbly tinkering with music in the early years of the century as though it were a wondrous new toy; it appears also in the elder statesman, the seasoned professional artist and teacher who, even in infirmity, seemed boyish and always surprised. His world of musical creativity was one of adventure and necessity, and one in which he moved calmly and with delight. It is for others to fit the pieces of the puzzle together. What concerned Cowell, as he said, was "to write as beautifully, as warmly, and as interestingly as I can."

PRINCIPAL COMPOSITIONS: *The Tides of Manaunaun* for piano (1912, Breitkopf and AMP); *Advertisement* for piano (1914, Breitkopf and AMP); *Antimony* for piano (1914, Breitkopf); *Dynamic Motion* for piano (1914, Breitkopf); *Quartet Romantic* for 2 flutes, violin, viola (1915); *Cello Sonata* (1915); *String Quartets Nos. 1–5*: No. 1, "Pedantic" (1916, AMP); No. 2 (1926, AMP); No. 3, "Mosaic" (1934, AMP); No. 4, "United Quartet" (1936, Peters); No. 5 (1956, Peters); *6 Ings* for piano (1916, Breitkopf); *Amiable Conversation*, "Scherzo amiable," for piano (1917, Breitkopf); *Symphonies Nos. 1–20*: No. 1 (1918); No. 2, "Anthropos" (1938); No. 3, "Gaelic" (1942, AMP); No. 4, "Short Symphony" (1946, AMP); No. 5 (1948); No. 6 (1951, Peters); No. 7 (1952, AMP); No. 8, "Choral," for chorus, orchestra (1952); No. 9 (1953); No. 10 (1953, AMP); No. 11, "The 7 Rituals of Music" (1953, AMP); No. 12 (1956, AMP); No. 13, "Madras," for orchestra with tablatarang and jalatarang (1958, Peters); No. 14 (1960, AMP); No. 15, "Thesis for Orchestra" (1960, AMP); No. 16, "Icelandic" (1962, AMP); No. 17 (1962, Peters); No. 18 (1964, Peters); No. 19 (1964, AMP); No. 20 (1965, Peters); *The Snows of Fujiyama* for piano (1922, Breitkopf); *Aeolian Harp* for piano (1923, Bechstein Saal and AMP); *Ensemble* for 2 violins, viola, 2 cellos, 3 thundersticks (1924, Brietkopf); *Piece for Piano with Strings* for piano (1924, AMP); *The Banshee* for piano (1925, Bechstein Saal and AMP); *Reel*, "Lilt of the Reel," for piano (1925, Muzyka); *7 Paragraphs* for string trio (1925, Peters); *Sinister Resonance* for piano (1925, AMP); *Piano Concerto* (1928, Sénart); *Suite* for solo string, percussion piano, chamber orchestra (1928; utilizes *Banshee, Leprechaun, Fairy Bells*); *Tiger* for piano (1928, Muzyka); *Polyphonica* for orchestra (1930, AMP); *Synchrony* for orchestra (1930, Adler and Peters); *Rhythmicana* for rhythmicon, orchestra (1931); *Sound-form for Dance* for flute, clarinet,

bassoon, Western and Asian percussion (1936); *American Melting Pot* for orchestra (1937); *Old American Country Set* for orchestra (1937, AMP); *Ritual of Wonder* for trumpet, piano, percussion (1937); *3 Antimodernist Songs* for voice, piano (1938, No. 2, Peters); *The Coming of Light* for chorus (1938, Flammer); *A Curse and a Blessing* for band (1938); *Celtic Set* for band (1939, Schirmer-G); *Hilarious Curtain Opener and Ritournelle* for piano (1939, NME); *Tales of Our Countryside* for piano, orchestra (1939, includes *Tides of Manaunaun*; AMP); *Ancient Desert Drone* for orchestra (1940, AMP); *Shoonthree* for band (1940, Mercury); *Little Concerto* for piano, band (1942, AMP); *Animal Magic* for band (1944, Leeds); *Hymn and Fuguing Tunes Nos. 1–18* for various solo instruments and ensembles (1944–64); *Violin Sonata* (1945, AMP); *The Donkey* for voice, piano (1946, MP); *The Little Black Boy* for voice, piano (1947, Peters); *O'Higgins of Chile*, opera (1947, unfinished); *Saturday Night at the Firehouse* for orchestra (1948, AMP); *Fiddler's Jig* for violin, string orchestra (1952, AMP); *Persian Set* for chamber orchestra with tar (1956, Peters); *A Thanksgiving Psalm from the Dead Sea Scrolls* for men's chorus, orchestra (1956, AMP); *Homage to Iran* for violin, piano (1957, Peters); *Ongaku: Music, or the Art and Science of Sound* for orchestra (1957, AMP); *Percussion Concerto* (1958, Peters); *Antiphony* for 2 orchestras (1959, Peters); *Chiaroscuro* for orchestra (1960, AMP); *Accordion Concerto* (1960); *Harmonica Concerto* (1960); *Edson Hymns and Fuguing Tunes* for chorus, orchestra or organ (1960, AMP); *Koto Concertos Nos. 1–2* (1962, AMP; 1965, Peters); *The Creator* for vocal soloists, chorus, orchestra (1963); *Harp Concerto* (1965); *Piano Trio* (1965, Peters). List to 1955: *Composers of the Americas* 2:28–35; to 1959: Weisgall; to 1962: Gerschefski (see bibl.).

PRINCIPAL WRITINGS: "The Process of Musical Creation," *American Journal of Psychology* 37; *New Musical Resources* (New York 1930, reprinted 1969); *American Composers on American Music: A Symposium* (Stanford, Calif. 1933; reprinted New York 1962); *The Nature of Melody* (written late 1930s, unpub.); *Charles Ives and His Music* prepared in collaboration with Sidney Robertson Cowell (New York 1955, reprinted 1969).

BIBL.: Henry Brant, "H. C., Musician and Citizen," *Etude* (Feb, March, April 1957); Edwin Gerschefski, "H. C.," *ACA Bulletin* 3/4, with supplement to list of works, 10/4; Hugo Weisgall, "The Music of H. C.," *Musical Quarterly* 45.

Richard Jackson

SEE ALSO Asian Music and Western Composition, Dance, Instrumental and Vocal Resources, Notation, Recording, Tuning and Temperament, United States.

Crawford Seeger, Ruth (b. East Liverpool, Ohio, 3 July 1901; d. Washington, 18 Nov 1953), attended the American Conservatory in Chicago (1920–29), where she studied piano and composition and also taught. She studied composition in New York in 1929 with Charles Seeger, whom she married in 1931. The family moved to Washington in 1935. There, from 1937 on, she made several thousand transcriptions of American folk music from recordings at the Library of Congress and composed piano accompaniments for some 300 of them. She also developed teaching methods for children utilizing folk music. She brought an adventurous mind to composition, which is especially evident in the serial-like devices in her *String Quartet* (1931).

PRINCIPAL COMPOSITIONS: *Suite* for flute, oboe, clarinet, horn, bassoon, piano (1927); *Suite No. 2* for piano, strings (1929); *5 Songs* for voice, piano; poems by Carl Sandburg (1929); *Etude in Mixed Accents* for piano (1930, New Music); *String Quartet* (1931, New Music); *2 Ricercari* for voice, piano (1932); *Suite* for wind quintet (1952). Mrs. Seeger also edited or arranged 8 volumes of folksong, among them: *American Folk Songs for Children* (1948), *Animal Folk Songs for Children* (1950), *American Folk Songs for Christmas* (1953), and *Let's Build a Railroad* (1954). List to 1952: *Composers of the Americas* 2:38–40.

Creston, Paul (b. New York 10 Oct 1906), studied piano (1921–25) and organ (with Pietro Yon, 1925–26) in New York. He decided on a career in composition at 26 and taught himself by studying Bach, Scarlatti, Chopin, Debussy, and Ravel, with "assistance from Beethoven, Mozart, Brahms, Scriabin, and Stravinsky." He was a theater organist for silent films during 1926–29 and organist at St. Malachy's church in New York during 1934–67. He has taught at Swarthmore College (1956), at the N. Y. College of Music (1963–67), and at Central Wash. State College (since 1967), where he is currently composer-in-residence. He has lectured at many other colleges in the U.S. and the Near East. The philosophy of Pythagoras and Walt Whitman and the poetry of Rabindranath Tagore "have been the most powerful forces" in his life and music.

PRINCIPAL COMPOSITIONS: *3 Chorales from Tagore* for chorus, Op. 11 (1936, Schirmer-G); *Suite* for viola, piano, Op. 13 (1937, Schirmer-G); *Suite* for violin, piano, Op. 18 (1939, Schirmer-G); *Saxophone Sonata*, Op. 19 (1939, Shawnee); *2 Choric Dances* for orchestra, piano, Op. 17b (1940, Schirmer-G); *Symphonies Nos. 1–5*: No. 1, Op. 20 (1940, Schirmer-G); No. 2, Op. 35 (1944, Schirmer-G); No. 3, Op. 48 (1950, Shawnee); No. 4, Op. 52 (1951, Fischer); No. 5, Op. 64 (1955, Fischer); *Concertino* for marimba, orchestra, Op. 21 (1940, Schirmer-G); *Concerto* for saxophone with orchestra, Op. 26a, or band, Op. 26b (1941,

Schirmer-G); *Psalm 23* for voice, piano, organ (orchestra), or for voice, chorus, piano, Op. 37 (1945, Schirmer-G); *Piano Concerto*, Op. 43 (1949, Shawnee); *Missa solemnis* for chorus with organ or orchestra, Op. 44 (1949, Mills); *Concerto* for 2 pianos, orchestra, Op. 50 (1951, Fischer); *Suite* for flute, viola, piano (1952); *The Celestial Vision* for men's chorus, Op. 60 (1954, Shawnee); *Celebration Overture* for band, Op. 61 (1954, Shawnee); *Dance Overture*, Op. 62 (1954, Shawnee); *Violin Concerto No. 1*, Op. 65 (1956, Fischer); *Toccata* for orchestra, Op. 68 (1957, Schirmer-G); *Suite* for organ, Op. 70 (1957, Fischer); *Fantasia* for organ, Op. 74 (1958, Fischer); *Accordian Concerto*, Op. 75 (1958, Fischer); *Prelude and Dance* for band, Op. 76 (1959, Fischer); *Janus* for orchestra, piano, Op. 77 (1959, Fischer); *Violin Concerto No. 2*, Op. 78 (1960, Fischer); *3 Narratives* for piano, Op. 79 (1962, Mills); *Isaiah's Prophecy*, Christmas oratorio, Op. 80 (1962, Fischer); *Corinthians 13* for orchestra, Op. 82 (1963, Mills); *Metamorphoses* for piano, Op. 84 (1964, Mills); *Choreografic Suite* for orchestra, piano, Op. 86a (1965, Mills); *Pavane Variations* for orchestra, piano, Op. 89 (1966, Schirmer-G); *Chthonic Ode* for orchestra, piano, Op. 90 (1966, Schirmer-G); *Anatolia*, "Turkish Rhapsody," for band, Op. 93 (1967, Shawnee); *Kalevala*, fantasy on Finnish folksongs for band, Op. 95 (1968, Schirmer-G); *The Northwest* for chorus, orchestra, Op. 98 (1969, Mills). List to 1959: *Composers of the Americas* 4:61–69.

PRINCIPAL WRITINGS: "The Crime Against Music," "Is Dancing Art?" "The Three S's of Dance and Music," *Dance Lover's Magazine* (1923); "First (and Last) Performances," *Music Publishers' Journal* (Oct 1944); "Listening to the Composer's Music," *Music Journal* (March 1956); *Principles of Rhythm* (New York 1964); "Music and the Mass Media," *Music Educators' Journal* (March 1970).

BIBL.: Henry Cowell, "P. C.," *Musical Quarterly* (Oct 1948):533–43; Madeleine Goss, "P. C.," *Modern Music-Makers, Contemporary American Composers* (New York 1952):371–82; Howard Mitchell, "The Hallmark of Greatness," *Musical Courier* (15 Nov 1956).

Cross, Lowell (Merlin) (b. Kingsville, Texas, 24 June 1938), studied English, mathematics, and music at Texas Technological College (1956–64), where he established an electronic music studio in 1961, and music at the Univ. of Toronto (1964–68; electronic music with Myron Schaeffer, Gustav Ciamaga; media, technology with Marshall McLuhan). During 1967–68 he taught electronic music at the Univ. of Toronto and was a research associate at the electronic music studio there. During 1968–70 he taught at Mills College and was artistic director of the Tape Music Center. He became an artist in residence at the Center for New Performing Arts at the Univ. of Iowa in

1971. In 1970 he was guest consultant at the National Institute of Design at Ahmedabad, India, and since 1969 he has been a consulting artist-engineer for Experiments in Art and Technology, Inc., New York. During 1963–65 he developed the "stirrer," a 4-channel input/output device for directing and mobilizing sounds in space. Since 1965 he has been introducing electronic visual techniques, including color and monochrome television and laser devices, into musical performance. In 1968 he built an electronic chessboard for John Cage's *o'oo" II*, and, with Carson Jeffries, he invented the laser deflection system used in the Pepsi-Cola Pavilion at Expo '70 in Osaka.

PRINCIPAL COMPOSITIONS: *0.8 Century* on tape (1962); *3 Etudes* on tape (1965; 4-channel version, 1968); *Video II (B)* for tape, audio system, television (1965–66); *Video II (C)* for tape, audio system, color television (1965–68); *Musica instrumentalis* for acoustical stereophonic instruments, monochrome and color television (1966–68, Berandol); *Video III* for phase-derived audio system, monochrome and color television; composed with David Tudor (1968); *Video II (L)* for tape, krypton ion laser, X-Y deflection system (1969); *Video/Laser I* for phase-derived audio system, krypton ion laser, X-Y deflection and color modulation system, monochrome and color television; composed with Tudor (1969); *Video/Laser II* for a variety of signal sources, krypton ion laser, 4 X-Y deflection systems, audio system, monochrome and color television, translucent plastics; composed with Carson Jeffries and Tudor (1970).

PRINCIPAL WRITINGS: *A Bibliography of Electronic Music*, revised ed. (Toronto 1970); "The Stirrer," *Source* 4:25–28; "Electronic Music, 1948–1953," *Perspectives* 7/1:32–65; "Laser Deflection System," *E.A.T. Proceedings No. 8*: appendix D; "Audio/Video/Laser," *Source* 7–8.

BIBL.: *Canavanguard* 1:37–41; "New Tools for Art," *Art & Man* (Washington) 1/4:14–15; *Source* 4:27; Calvin Tomkins, "Onward and Upward with the Arts—E.A.T.," *New Yorker* (3 Oct 1970): 83ff.

SEE ALSO David Tudor.

Crosse, Gordon (b. Bury, England, 1 Dec 1937), attended Oxford Univ. (1958–63; harmony, counterpoint with Bernard Rose; music history with Egon Wellesz; medieval music with Frank Harrison). During 1961–63 he researched early 15th-century music. In 1962 he studied composition with Goffredo Petrassi at the Accadèmia de Santa Cecilia, Rome. Crosse worked for the eastern region of the Workers' Educational Association (1963–64) and taught at Birmingham Univ. in the extramural department (1964–66) and the music department

(as a Haywood Fellow, 1966–69). Since 1969 he has been a Fellow in Music, Univ. of Essex. Important influences on his music have included his study of medieval music and his association with the theater in Oxford, for which he composed incidental scores.

PRINCIPAL COMPOSITIONS (published by Oxford): *Elegy* for small orchestra, Op. 1 (1959); *Concerto da camera* for violin, winds, brasses, percussion, Op. 6 (1962); *Carol* for flute, piano, Op. 7 (1962); *Meet My Folks!*, "Theme and Relations," for speaker, children's chorus, children's percussion band, oboe, clarinet, bassoon, horn, trumpet, cello, piano, 3–4 percussionists, Op. 10; poems by Ted Hughes (1964); *Changes*, a nocturnal cycle for soprano, baritone, chorus (optional children's chorus), orchestra, Op. 17 (1965); *Purgatory*, opera, for baritone, tenor, women's voices, orchestra, Op. 18; based on the Yeats play (1966); *Ceremony* for cello, orchestra, Op. 19 (1966); *The Grace of Todd*, 1-act opera, Op. 20; libretto by David Rudkin (1966–67).

Crumb, George (b. Charleston, W. Va., 24 Oct 1929), attended Mason College (BM, 1950) and the Univ. of Ill. (MM, 1952). He entered the Univ. of Mich. in 1954, where he studied composition with Ross Lee Finney. During the summer of 1955 he studied with Boris Blacher at the Berkshire Music Center and continued with him at the Berlin Hochschule für Musik until 1956. After receiving a DMA from Michigan (1959), he began teaching at the Univ. of Colo. In 1964–65 he was a Creative Associate at the Center of the Creative and Performing Arts in Buffalo, and in 1965 he moved to the Univ. of Penna. He has received many commissions and prices, including the 1968 Pulitzer Prize for *Echoes of Time and the River*.

Crumb's mature style, which was first manifest in the *5 Pieces for Piano* (1962), does not follow an established convention or "ism." It possesses an unpretentious musicality best expressed in the composer's remark that "music can exist only when the brain is singing." The influence of Webern is evident in the economy and compactness of musical gesture. The unfolding of arhythmic musical lines, often modal and chantlike, along with the use of spare but lush impressionistic sonorities are reminiscent of Debussy, mildly seasoned with 13th-century organum. The use of exotic percussive effects are evocative of oriental theater and dance (water gong, fifth-partial piano harmonics "like tiny bells," piano strings struck with the palm of the hand, pitched antique cymbals, and the like). There is a strong sense of harmonic stability in spite of the fact that the harmony does not function tonally; the treatment of dissonance is free and unordered. Where an 18th-century composer would have used different rates of harmonic rhythm to vary the apparent speed of his music, Crumb uses different vertical and horizontal densities. His music has an improvisatory quality, so that when sections occur in which there are aleatoric features, the dividing line may be imperceptible to the listener; thit characteristic also results from the fact that Crumb treats aleatoric sections as extensions of the adjacent passages.

PRINCIPAL COMPOSITIONS (published by Mills unless otherwise noted): *String Quartet* (1954); *Sonata* for solo cello (1955, Peters); *Variazioni* for orchestra (1959); *5 Pieces* for piano (1962); *Night Music I* for soprano, piano, celesta, percussion (1963); *Night Music II* for violin, piano (1964); *3 Madrigals*, book I, for soprano, vibraphone, string bass; book II, for alto flute, flute in C, piccolo, percussion (1965); *Echoes I*, "11 Echoes of Autumn, 1965," for alto flute, clarinet, piano, violin (1966); *Echoes II*, "Echoes of Time and the River," 4 processionals for orchestra (1967); *Songs, Drones, and Refrains of Death* for baritone, electric guitar, electric double bass, electric piano (doubling an electric harpsichord), 2 percussionists; poems by García-Lorca (1968); *Madrigals, Book III* for soprano, harp, percussionist; poems by García-Lorca (1969); *Madrigals, Book IV* for soprano, flute (doubling alto flute, piccolo), harp, double bass, percussionist; poems by García-Lorca (1969). List to 1969: *Composers of the Americas* 15:57–59.

BIBL.: Detailed articles on individual works have appeared as follows: on *Night Music I* (*Perspectives* 3/2:143–51), on *Echoes of Time and the River* (*Musical Quarterly* 54:83–87), on *11 Echoes of Autumn* (*ibid.* 55:280–84).

Richard Wernick

SEE ALSO Instrumental and Vocal Resources, Orchestration, Text Setting and Usage.

Cruz, Domingo Santa, see under Santa Cruz

Cruz, Ivo (b. Corumba, Brazil, 19 May 1901), studied law at the Univ. of Lisbon (1920–24) and music at the Trappsche Musikschule in Munich (1925–30, conducting with August Reuss) and the Univ of Munich (1927–30). He also studied composition privately until 1924 in Lisbon with Tomás de Lima and Tomás Borba and in Munich with Richard Mors (1925–30). He has founded several musical organizations in Lisbon: the Renascimento Musical (1923), a society for the revival of early Portuguese music; the Duarte Lobo choral society (1930); the Lisbon Philharmonic

(1936), which he conducts; and the Pro Arte touring orchestra (1951). Since 1938 he has been director of the National Conservatory in Lisbon. He has edited Portuguese music of the 16th–19th centuries.

PRINCIPAL COMPOSITIONS: *Aguarelas* [Water Colors] for piano (1922, Sassetti); *Violin Sonata* (1922, Sassetti); *Canções perdidas* [Lost Songs] for voice, piano (1923); *Motivos luzitanos* [Lusitanian Themes] for orchestra (1928); *Triptico* for soprano (tenor), orchestra (1941); *Pastoral*, ballet in 3 scenes (1942; *Ritornello e danças* transcribed for 2 pianos, 1953, Sassetti; the same transcribed for 2 guitars by Emilio Pujol, 1962, Eschig; the same for band by Silva Dionisio, 1967); *Os amores do poeta* [The Poet's Love] for high voice, orchestra (piano); text by Camões (1942, Sassetti); *Baladas lunaticas* [Lunatic Ballads] for voice, piano; text by Afonso Lopes Vieira (1944); *Portuguese Concerto No. 1* for piano, orchestra (1945); *Portuguese Concerto No. 2* for piano, orchestra (1946, Sassetti); *Sinfonia de Amadis* for orchestra (1952; *Cortege and Dance* transcribed for 2 pianos, 1958); *Idilio de Miraflores* [Miraflores's Idyll] for orchestra (1952); *Homenagens* [Homages] for piano (1955, Sassetti); *Caleidoscopio* for piano (1957); *Suite* for piano (1960); *Sinfonia de Queluz* for orchestra (1964); *Canções profanas* [Profane Songs] for voice, piano (1968; No. 1, "O sol é grande," transcribed for violin or cello, piano).

Cugley, Ian (Robert Sebastian) (b. Melbourne, 22 June 1945), studied at the Univ. of Sydney (1963–67; composition with Peter Sculthorpe and Peter Maxwell Davies, technical subjects with Ian Spink and Donald Peart). He has taught at the New South Wales Conservatory (1967) and the Univ. of Tasmania (since 1967) and directed a number of student and church choruses and orchestras. Since 1967 he has been a percussionist with the Tasmanian Symphony Orchestra. He has drawn inspiration from Bartók and Webern and to a lesser extent from Indian and Japanese music. His conversion to the Catholic faith at 20 focussed his interests on early Western music and on the ritual and liturgical use of music.

PRINCIPAL COMPOSITIONS: *Pan, the Lake* for flute, horn, cello, kulintang gongs, percussion, strings (1965, Albert); *Prelude for Orchestra* (1965, Albert); *Sonata* for flute, viola, guitar or harp (1966); *Alma redemptoris mater* for children's chorus, amateur instrumental ensemble, flute, string quartet (1967); *3 Pieces* for chamber orchestra (1968, Albert); *5 Variants* for string orchestra (1969); *The 6 Days of Creation* for soprano, alto, flute, clarinet, horn, trombone, viola, cello, harp; text by James McAuley (1969).

PRINCIPAL WRITINGS: "Peter Sculthorpe—An Analysis of His Music," *ARNA* (Sydney Univ., 1967):48–56; "Creativity and Musical Standards,"

Tasmanian Journal of Education 3/2:38–50; "Irkanda to Ketjak," *Togatus* (Univ. of Tasmania, 23 April 1969):8–9; "The Contemporary Composer in Education," proceedings of the UNESCO seminar on music in tertiary education, Brisbane, August 1969.

BIBL.: Robina Rathbone, "Asia's Influence on Australia's Music," *Hemisphere* 14/12:26–30.

Culmell, Joaquín Nin, see under Nin-Culmell

Custer, Arthur (b. Manchester, Conn., 21 April 1923), studied engineering at the Univ. of Hartford (1940–42) and music at the Univ. of Conn. (1946–49, BA), the Univ. of Redlands in Calif. (1949–51, MM, composition with Paul Pisk), and the Univ. of Iowa (1956–59, PhD, composition with Philip Bezanson). He also studied composition with Nadia Boulanger during 1960–62. Custer taught at Kansas Wesleyan Univ. (1952–55), where he was chairman of the division of fine arts, and the Univ. of Omaha (1955–58). From 1959 to 1962 he was supervisor of music for the U.S. Air Force in Spain. As music consultant to the U.S. Information Agency in Madrid (1960–62), he gave lectures, conducted, and helped organize concerts of American music. He was assistant dean of fine arts at the Univ. of Rhode Island (1962–65) and during 1963–65 was vice president of the R. I. Fine Arts Council, president of the R. I. Music Teachers Assoc., and vice president of the Eastern Division of the Music Teachers National Assoc. He was dean of the Philadelphia Musical Academy (1965–67) and from 1967 to 1970, director of the Metropolitan Educational Center in the Arts in St. Louis, where he also wrote program notes for the 1967–69 seasons of the St. Louis Symphony and directed the St. Louis New Music Circle. In 1970 he became director of the Arts in Education Project of the Rhode Island Council on the Arts.

PRINCIPAL COMPOSITIONS (published by Joshua unless otherwise noted): *Colloquy,* string quartet no. 1 (1961, Merion); *Sinfonia de Madrid* (1961, Marks); *Cycle* for flute (piccolo), alto saxophone, bass clarinet, trumpet, violin, viola, cello, double bass (1963); *Songs of the Seasons* for voice, chamber orchestra or piano (1963); *Concertino for Second Violin and Strings,* string quartet no. 2 (1964); *Two Movements* for wind quintet (1964); *Three Love Lyrics* for tenor, flute, viola, harp (1965); *Permutations* for violin, clarinet, cello (1967); *Concerto* for brass quintet (1968); *Found Objects I* for chorus, tape (1968); *Found Objects II,* "Rhapsodality Brass!" for orchestra (1969); *Interface I* for string quartet, 2 recording engineers

(string quartet no. 3) (1969); *Rhapsodality Brown!* for piano (1969). List to 1969: *Composers of the Americas* 15:62–67.

PRINCIPAL WRITINGS: "La música norteamericana contemporanea," *La estafeta literaria,* Madrid (15 August 1961):16–17; (1 Sept 1961):14–15 and (15 Sept 1961):15–16; "Contemporary Music in Spain," *Musical Quarterly* (Jan 1962):1–18; "Fuentes de la música popular norteamericana," *La estafeta literaria* (15 Dec 1962):9–10; "American Conductors Take Note: Odón Alonso, Today's Music Today," *ACA Bulletin* (Dec 1962): 13-14; "Contemporary Music in Spain," *Musical Quarterly* (Jan 1965):44–60; "Current Chronicle: Philadelphia," *Musical Quarterly* (April 1967): 251–59; "The 'Coreness' of Music: Questions, Observations, and an Impudent Proposal," *Music Educators Journal* (April 1968):30–33, 141; "I Hate Music: Advice to College Freshmen," *American Music Teacher* (May 1968):42–43; "Current Chronicle: Edwardsville," *Musical Quarterly* (Oct 1968):538–41.

BIBL.: Paul A. Pisk, "Current Chronicle," *Musical Quarterly* (July 1963):359–60.

Cybernetics, see Computer Applications; Electronic Music: Apparatus; Electronic Music: History and Development

Czechoslovakia. Czech and Slovak music have grown from an ancient and rich tradition in which both Western and Eastern influences converged. There is immense musical activity today as shown by the book, *Contemporary Czechoslovak Composers* (Prague 1965), which lists 363 composers. This enthusiasm for music is based on several factors: the value placed on music as a manifestation of national life, the people's Slavonic musical talent, and a rich heritage of professional and folk music. The latter is represented by hundreds of songs and dances, especially from Slovakia, Moravian Slovakia, Wallachia, and Southern Bohemia. Some of this music is very old and follows the medieval modes, is rich in syncopation and metric variability, and has interesting instrumental accompaniments (violin, viola, double bass, clarinet, dulcimer, shepherd's pipe, bagpipe, etc.).

The capital city of Prague is the natural center of Czechoslovak culture. A busy and varied musical life also exists in Bratislava, the capital of Slovakia; in Brno, the main city in Moravia; in the cities of Ostrava, Plzeň, Košice, and in many smaller towns. As many as 70 festivals, concert series, and concert-music competitions take place every year. The Prague Spring Festival (founded 1946) is the most prominent, owing to its size and the many foreign participants who come from both East and West. It is held from about May 12 to June 4 and includes, in addition to theater performances, some 25 symphonic and 25 chamber concerts. More than 20 local and foreign orchestras, opera companies, and chamber and vocal ensembles perform some 150 compositions. About one-third of the music is from the 20th century, and half of this is Czech and Slovak. The Bratislava Music Festival takes place during April–June and displays a similar character. The Ostrava Musical May lasts over a month. The autumn International Music Festival in Brno lasts a week and is organized along special themes ("Musica Antiqua," "Leoš Janáček et Musica Europaea," "Musica Vocalis," etc.). Other festivals include the Expositions of Experimental Music in Brno (lasting several days), the Choral Music Festival in Jihlava (which includes a competition for new choral music), the Courses for Contemporary Music at Smolenice, the "weeks of new music by Czech and Slovak composers," the International Interpretation Courses of music by Janáček and Martinů at Luhačovice Spa, and many others. All such enterprises are supported directly or indirectly by state or regional authorities. Public attendance has decreased somewhat in recent years, but it is still good.

Efforts during the 19th century toward a national theater and opera have resulted today in 13 permanent opera groups working all year long. The most prominent are the National Theater in Prague (founded 1883 and consisting of two opera houses), the Slovak National Theater in Bratislava (founded 1886), the State Theater in Brno (1882), the Zdeněk Nejedlý Theater in Ostrava (1907), and the Josef Kajetán Tyl Theater in Plzeň. There are also opera studios at the Music Academies, experimental theaters such as the State Ballet Studio in Prague, and many "Theaters of Music," which have come into existence since 1949 and give programs primarily of recorded music, often combined with live commentary, slides, films, or performances by actors or dancers. There are several dozen professional instrumental and choral ensembles, including 19 major orchestras (of which the Czech Philharmonic, founded 1896, and the Slovak Philharmonic, founded 1949, are the best known). Other significant ensembles include the Philharmonic (formerly the Czech) Choral Ensemble, the Moravian Teachers' Choral Association, the Smetana Quartet in Prague, and the Janáček Quartet in Brno. A few ensembles specialize in contemporary music, and the others may devote as much as a third of

their programs to the 20th century. About 300 premieres of local works take place annually. (This would perhaps be a good record in another country of comparable size, but in Czechoslovakia it represents only a small proportion of the new music that is written each year.) Czechoslovak radio (founded 1923) broadcasts about 4,000 hours of concert music per year, of which about 900 hours are devoted to recent Czech and Slovak works. Contemporary foreign music is broadcast for up to two hours daily, and special local and foreign festival concerts and other events may also be broadcast. Television broadcasts include concert and theater performances.

Czech publishing houses have been reorganized several times since World War II. At present all scores, recordings, and books on music are issued through two agencies: Supraphon, the state publishing house; and Panton, the publishing house of the Guild of Czeckoslovak Composers. Foreign trade is handled by Artia and, for musical instruments, by Musicexport. The work of the publishing houses reflects public musical interest: popular music is in the majority, and concert music in the familiar idioms, both older and more recent, comes next. There are, however, specialized editions and recordings of avant-garde works. Composers may have their works published either directly or on recommendation of committees of the Composers' Guilds. Because the production capacity of the two publishing houses is insufficient, most contemporary compositions are issued in facsimile by the archives of the musicians' organizations (the music funds). The several periodicals published earlier in the century have now been replaced by *Hudební rozhledy* (Music Perspectives, founded 1948), the journal of the Guild of Czech Composers; *Slovenská hudba* (Slovak Music, founded 1957), the journal of the Guild of Slovak Composers; *Opus musicum* (founded 1969); and several specialized periodicals devoted to musicology and to popular and dance music. The specialized music journals devote about one-third of their space to discussions of new music. Another journal of the Guild of Czech Composers, *Konfrontace* (Confrontation, founded 1969), and a series of Supraphon called *Nové cesty hudby* (The New Ways of Music, founded 1964) both contain theoretical studies, analyses, specimens of experimental scores, and the like.

Public music training, which begins at the primary and secondary levels of general education, is supplemented at nearly 350 People's Arts Schools (with departments for music, drama, literature, visual arts, and dance).

Professional training is given first in six-year programs at seven secondary music schools (the conservatories) and then in four or five-year programs at the Prague Academy of Music and Dramatic Art, the Higher School of Music and Dramatic Art in Bratislava, and at the Janáček Academy of Music and Dramatic Art in Brno. Musicologists and teachers for the basic education schools attend the various universities. Composers working toward an academy diploma must acquire theoretical and practical knowledge of all basic forms and techniques of composition, including contemporary techniques. Conductors must usually include at least one contemporary work in their full-length examination concerts. In 1969 the Janáček Academy initiated an elective two-year postgraduate program in experimental music. Students may make educational trips to other countries lasting from several months to several years. Most of these are made under exchange agreements with other socialist countries; however, musicians also take part in important music enterprises elsewhere. Young composers are most attracted to the summer courses at Darmstadt, to the ISCM festivals, to the Warsaw Autumn Festival, the Zabreb Bienale, and to such artistic centers as Paris, Munich, and Milan.

Most professional composers, performers, and writers on music (in both the popular and concert fields) belong to either the Czech or Slovak sections of the Guild of Czechoslovak Composers (founded 1949), which has replaced a number of previous organizations, some dating back to the 19th century. The Guild promotes the development of music life along lines established by state cultural policy. The Czech Music Fund in Prague and the Slovak Music Fund in Bratislava engage in many activities: they help young artists, especially by giving scholarships; they subsidize competitions; they maintain such cultural institutions as the Janáček Museum in Brno; they also commission works, give non-interest loans, provide work space and instruments, maintain vacation homes, copy music for their archives (the Czech archives has over 4,000 works), issue publicity materials, etc. They are supported from state funds and from a fixed percentage of the royalty and performance fees earned by their members. Through these organizations and through teaching and other professional activities, the economic position of the Czechoslovak composer is secure.

Musical development in Czechoslovakia has always responded to artistic trends from other parts of the world. Exceptions to this rule occurred during the two world wars, when international contacts were disrupted, and during the late 1940s and early 50s, when the principle of "socialist realism" was oversimplified by authorities to mean adapting the arts to the demands of popular taste and using only traditional means of expression inherited from the 19th century or earlier. (One result of this misinterpretation was Václav Dobiáš's cantata *Buduj vlast, posílíš mír* [Build Your Country to Strengthen Peace], 1950, written in imitation of Smetana's style.) Speaking of more normal conditions, however, it is Leoš *Janáček (1854–1928) who has been the inspiration behind modern Czech and Slovak music. His mature output was based on an intimate experience of Moravian-Slovak folk music and on a thorough investigation of psychological processes, especially as manifested in what he called the "melody of speech." He was misunderstood for a long time because he gave up the traditional techniques of development in favor of the repetition and transformation procedures of folk music. He used short rhythmic-melodic motifs derived from folk music and speech inflections and also employed such folk characteristics as modal harmony, heterophony, montagelike phrase sequencing, and sound layers in bright instrumental colors. Many listeners interpreted such features as a primitivism lacking technical skill, and production of an enthusiastic folklorist who remained in artistic isolation (somewhat later, Béla Bartók met with similar reactions). Janáček's most important pupils (including Vilém Petrželka, 1889–1967; Jaroslav Kvapil, 1892–1958; and Osvald Chlubna, b. 1893) worked primarily during the first third of the century. Their music is actually closer to that of Vítězslav *Novák (1870–1949) and Josef *Suk (1874–1935), two composers who emphasized technical virtuosity within traditional means, polyphonic textures, grandiose sound, and other features of late romanticism (especially R. Strauss) and impressionism. Both composers, but especially Novák, also drew on folk sources, but they favored a romantic stylization of such material over the simpler and more authentic treatment of Janáček. A long line of composers carried the Novák-Suk tradition well into the 1950s and even down to the present day. The influence of their music, combined with that of choral music by Josef Bohuslav Foerster (1859–1951) and orchestral music by Otakar Ostrčil (1879–1935) can be heard in Pavel *Bořkovec (b. 1894), Alexander *Moyzes (b. 1906), Eugen *Suchoň (b. 1908), and Jan *Cikker (b. 1911). The last three are also noteworthy for their contributions to the tradition of a Slovak national music.

The leading Czech neoclassicist was Bohuslav *Martinů (1890–1959), who studied with Albert Roussel in Paris and who spent much of his professional life outside his native country. The first performance in Prague (in 1924) of his orchestral rondo *Half Time* was the first manifestation of the neoclassic movement in the country. Iša *Krejčí (1904–68) and Emil František *Burian (1904–59) were Martinů's leading followers. Burian was also noteworthy for his use of choral speech set to music (he founded a "voice band" in 1927), of jazz, and of varying types and forms of art in the scenic design of theater works. Alois *Hába (1893–1972) was a major force throughout the world in the development of music using microintervals, both as a composer and as a designer and builder of instruments. In 1923 he founded a composition department for quarter-tone and sixth-tone music at the Prague Conservatory, and from 1945 to 1951 he headed a similar department at the Academy of Musical Arts in Prague. His *New Theory of Harmony in the Diatonic, Quarter-, Sixth-, and Twelfth-Tone Systems* was published in 1927. He also wrote atonal and 12-tone works and, as one of the leading modern artists of the world, he helped Czech music absorb the influence of Schoenberg's ideas. Other composers of this time include Klement *Slavický (b. 1910), Andrej *Očenáš (b. 1911), and Dezider *Kardoš (b. 1914).

In 1956, after the 20th Congress of the Communist Party of the Soviet Union, political tensions decreased and both a broad stylistic spectrum and contacts with foreign countries were again made possible. The eagerness of Czech composers to revive and review all 20th-century trends and to complete their knowledge of the most recent developments was like an explosion. Schoenberg, Berg, Webern, Bartók, Honegger, Hindemith, Prokofiev, Milhaud, Shostakovich, and Messiaen were revived and rediscovered. Their music as well as that of Orff, Britten, Varèse, Cage, Boulez, Nono, Stockhausen, Pierre Schaeffer, Xenakis, Ives, Lutosławski, and others initiated an unprecedented creative surge in the late 1950s. The conflict of traditional and modernistic views and the questions of purpose in music raised by the new techniques and the new experimental attitude toward art are still with us today. The important thing is that all things are again possible.

The heritage of Czech composers working today includes their Slavonic sensitivity and hot temper, which appears particularly in melody, rhythm, and the use of dynamics; a taste for the richness and abundance of tone colors in programmatic music; and a sense of order and craftsmanship inherited from neighboring Germany. Although it is unfair to single out a few of the dozens of active composers in Czechoslovakia today, the following remarks will at least indicate the range of style in new music. The leading figures are Miloslav *Kabeláč (b. 1908) and Jan *Kapr (b. 1914). Kabeláč is distinguished by the economy and concentration in his music and by his use of elements from non-European and ancient cultures. Kapr has worked in concrete and electronic music and believes in an eclectic approach to determining the style of a work; his theoretical treatise *Konstanty* (The Constants, Prague 1967) deals with the problems of selecting elements from a variety of stylistic sources. Both composers have worked with new notational methods. Neoclassicism stemming from Martinů is represented by the music of his pupil, Jan *Novák (b. 1921); the neoromantic and impressionist approaches are followed by a number of composers born principally in the 1920s, including Petr *Eben (b. 1929). Most composers of the younger and middle generations combine a modal or serial approach to harmony with aleatory elements and the use of layered timbral planes. The less radical of them—those who follow an evolutionary path stemming from Stravinsky, Honegger, Bartók, Prokofiev, and classical 12-tone music—include Vladimír *Sommer (b. 1921), Ilja *Hurník (b. 1922), Otmar *Mácha (b. 1922), Viktor *Kalabis (b. 1923), Svatopluk *Havelka (b. 1925), Jindřich *Feld (b. 1925), Jaromír *Podešva (b. 1927), Lubor *Bárta (b. 1928), and Zdeněk *Pololáník (b. 1935). A more radical approach to harmony, serialism, the mixing of stylistic elements, use of instruments, and building of forms can be found in Josef *Berg (b. 1927), Miloslav *Ištvan (b. 1928), Ilja *Zeljenka (b. 1932), Jan *Klusák (b. 1934), Luboš *Fišer (b. 1935), and the author (b. 1929). The most recent experimental trends —including work with recorded and live electronic sound (especially in Bratislava, Plzeň, and Brno), new concepts in music theater, happenings, graphic notation, collages of sound, visual, and other elements, team-productions, and computer music—have been cultivated by Zbyněk *Vostřák (b. 1920), Alois *Piňos (b. 1925), Marek *Kopelent (b. 1932), Jozef *Malovec (b. 1933), and Ladislav *Kupkovič (b. 1936).

BIBL.: *Československý hudební adresář 69* (Prague 1969); *Československý hudební slovník osob a institucí*, vols. 1–2 (Prague 1963, 1965); Pavel Eckstein, *Die tschechoslowakische zeitgenössische Oper / The Czechoslowak Contemporary Opera* (Prague-Bratislava 1967); Čeněk Gardavský, ed., *Contemporary Czechoslovak Composers* (Prague-Bratislava 1965); Vladimír Helfert, *Česká moderní hudba* (Olomouc 1936); Ivan Hrušovský, *Slovenská hudba v profiloch a rozboroch* (Bratislava 1964); Vladimír Lébl and Ladislav Mokrý, "O současném stavu nových skladebných směrů u nás" [On the State of New Compositional Tendencies Here], *Nové cesty hudby* I (Prague 1964): 11–35; Jan Matějček, *Music in Czechoslovakia* (Prague 1967); *La Musique tchécoslovaque* (Prague 1946); Jan Racek, *Česká hudba* (Prague 1958); Ladislav Šíp, *Zur Geschichte der tschechischen und slowakischen Musik*, vol. 2 (Prague 1959); Jiří Svoboda, Jan Trojan, *Vývoj české a slovenské hudby* (Prague 1967).

Ctirad Kohoutek

D

Dahl, Ingolf (b. Hamburg, 9 June 1912; d. Frutigen, Switzerland, 7 August 1970), studied at the Music Academy in Cologne (1930–32, composition with Philipp Jarnach), the Univ. of Zurich (1932–36), Zurich Conservatory (1932–35; conducting with Volkmar Andreae, piano with Walter Frey), and with Nadia Boulanger in 1944 in California. He left Europe in 1938. During 1942–45 he was a radio conductor and arranger in Hollywood. He conducted for the Monday Evenings Concerts in Los Angeles and during 1964–66 was music director of the Ojai Music Festival. He taught at the Univ. of Southern Calif. beginning in 1945 and conducted the Univ. Symphony Orchestra during 1945–60 and 1968–69. Dahl was mainly interested in instrumental music. The dissonant and polyphonic style of his early work began to change in the direction of internal clarification (open textures, firmly controlled tonality, supple rhythms, and virtuoso instrumental writing) under the influence of the American environment. From the *Piano Quartet* (1957) on he turned toward the serialization of melodic-harmonic materials.

PRINCIPAL COMPOSITIONS: *Allegro and Arioso* for woodwind quintet (1942, McG-M); *Music for Brass Instruments* for brass quintet (1944, Witmark); *Concerto a tre* for clarinet, violin, cello (1946, Boosey); *Duo* for cello, piano (1946); *Divertimento* for viola, piano (1948, Presser); *Concerto* for alto saxophone, wind orchestra (1949, MCA); *Quodlibet on American Folk Tunes* for 2 pianos 8-hands (1953, orchestrated 1965; Peters); *Sonata seria* for piano (1953, Presser); *The Tower of St. Barbara* for orchestra (1954, Shawnee); *Piano Quartet* (1957); *Sonata pastorale* for piano (1959, Southern); *Serenade for 4 Flutes* (1960, Boosey); *Sinfonietta* for concert band (1961, Broude-A); *Piano Trio* (1962, Southern); *Aria sinfonica* for orchestra (1965, Broude-A); *Duo concertante* for flute, percussion (1966, Broude-A); *Variations on a Theme by C. P. E. Bach* for string orchestra (1967, Broude-A); *A Cycle of Sonnets* for baritone or alto, piano (1968); *Sonata da camera* for clarinet, piano (1970); *Elegy Concerto* for violin, chamber orchestra (1970).

PRINCIPAL WRITINGS: "Stravinsky in 1946," *Modern Music* 23; "The Technique of Cartoon Music," *Film Music Notes* 8/5; "Stravinsky on Film Music," *Musical Digest* (Sept 1946); "The Reconstruction of J. S. Bach's *Violin Concerto in D Minor*," preface to the Boosey edition (1959); "The Composer as Teacher," *College Music Symposium* (fall 1970). Dahl was also cotranslator of Stravinsky's *Poetics of Music* (Cambridge, Mass. 1947).

SEE ALSO United States.

Dallapiccola, Luigi (b. Pisino, Istria, Austria-Hungary—now Yugoslavia, 3 Feb 1904), attended the local Italian gymnasium, 1914–21, where his father was principal and professor of Greek and Latin. From early 1917 to late 1918 his parents, politically suspect as Italians during the war, were forced to live in Graz, where he continued his studies. Private lessons in theory and piano had started as early as 1912 and in composition in 1914. In 1922 he moved to Florence, his permanent residence ever since, and began to study piano with Ernesto Consolo. The next year he joined a class in harmony and counterpoint at the Conservatorio L. Cherubini and soon came under the tutelage of the composer Vito Frazzi. In 1931 he received his *diploma di composizione* and succeeded Consolo on the staff of the conservatory. He became *professore di piano complementare* in 1934 and retained this position until 1967. In 1938 he married Laura Coen Luzzatto.

By the mid-1930s Dallapiccola was recognized by knowledgeable observers as one of the most talented composers of the new Italian generation. During the 40s, his work made a significant place for itself on the European musical scene and from the early 50s on gained international acceptance. Germany, where he has received various official honors, and the U.S. have provided the majority of his commissions and premières. He has taught at the Berkshire Music Center (1951), Queens College, New York (1956, 1959), the Univ. of Calif. at Berkeley (1962), the Instituto Torcuato di Tella in Buenos Aires (1964), Dartmouth

163

College (summer 1969), and at the Aspen Music School (1969). Among his pupils are Luciano Berio, Donald Martino, Salvatore Martirano, and Henry Weinberg.

Dallapiccola's output to 1968 comprises 17 works for voice and instrumental ensemble (chiefly small), nine works for chorus (occasionally with soloists) and instrumental ensemble (chiefly large), and four operas (including a mystery play); in addition, there is music for orchestra, solo instruments (with and without accompaniment), and a ballet, as well as songs, a cappella choruses, and both recastings and arrangements of 17th- and 18th-century masters.

All of Dallapiccola's early compositions (1925–30), except for a few pages, have remained in manuscript. Publication began with works completed in 1932. From then on until the early 1940s his work passed through a period of rapid growth. It received stimulation from the Italian contemporary idiom, to which G. F. Malipiero, Casella, and the more traditional Pizzetti were contributing, and from French music, especially the harmony of Ravel (Schoenberg's *Pierrot Lunaire* had impressed Dallapiccola as early as 1924 but had no immediate effect on his writing). In keeping with European tendencies, he also used early genres and procedures (madrigal comedy, baroque dances, passacaglia), and at times extensive ostinato figuration. From the beginning he showed a preference for the voice, especially the high solo voice with chamber ensemble. His melodic lines, distinguished in later years by their *espressivo* style, were at first fluent and elegant, often retracing the modal and pentatonic contours of 16th-century music. After 1934–35 his lines gained in intensity through the inclusion of larger and firmer intervals and of chromaticism. A synthesis of early attempts was attained in *Canti di prigionia* (1938–41), Dallapiccola's first work of consequence. Its theme, human suffering and liberation, was taken up again in *Il prigioniero* (1944–48) and *Canti di liberazione* (1951–55).

In 1942, under the impact of Schoenberg and his circle, Dallapiccola adopted dodecaphony (the first Italian composer to do so), and he has adhered to it almost exclusively. His mastery of dodecaphonic procedures, though he had written isolated 12-tone passages from the mid-1930s on, matured slowly, and for several years his music even retained traces of the tonality of the past. The new orientation enriched his melodic style with tritones, sevenths, and ninths, as well as his chord structure, which even when untraditional as

total sound had been marked by audible traditional intervals or intervallic combinations. He was also encouraged to follow his native bent towards complex polyphony. Dallapiccola has availed himself not only of the ordinary tone row but of two special variants: the all-interval row, which consists of all the intervals within one octave (*Quaderno musicale di annalibera* and *Canti di liberazione,* both based on the same row, and *Piccola musica notturna*); and a symmetrical one (*Cinque canti, Requiescant,* and *Dialoghi*), whose second half is the retrograde inversion of the first. After 1950 he began to observe Schoenbergian discipline in restricting himself to a single row within each composition.

From 1953 on Dallapiccola developed what he called a "floating rhythm," in which a regular pulse is frequently obscured by sequences of dotted notes and by triplets of changing duration. This type of rhythm, most distinct in pianissimo passages, has at times so permeated the texture of a work that few tones of the different voice parts coincide. A new phase opened with the *Cinque canti* of 1956. Under the influence of Anton Webern, the melodic line was split into groups often containing no more than two or three tones. In spite of such intervals as ninths and major sevenths, melodic coherence remained unimpaired; so did the strict auditory control of pitches, in contrast to current trends.

In setting his texts, usually of very high quality, the composer has not merely conveyed their overall character but suggested an eloquent reading by means of pauses, changing speeds, and groupings of words. He has also followed the practice of the late renaissance and the baroque of singling out details of the text and intensifying them with aural and even visual equivalents (e.g. at the end of movement III the score of *Cinque canti* is arranged like a cross with two arms stretched over the horizontal beam). Finally as a means of emphasis he has quoted from himself by applying to a thought in the text the music which had accompanied an identical or similar thought in an earlier work.

Though heir to the intricacies of the 12-tone procedures developed by Schoenberg, Berg, and Webern, Dallapiccola has exploited the sensuous qualities of sound more insistently than they. Thus as an admirer of Bellini and Verdi (and Monteverdi) he has created vocal lines containing elements of the *bel canto* (and pre-*bel canto*) tradition. Similarly in his orchestration he frequently includes harp, celesta, and vibraphone, not only for the sake of delicate "pedal" effects but to add luster to the total sound. He is also fascinated (and at times inspired) by late Debussy and the fragility of his scores but responds to dramatic moments in texts with massive, even turbulent sonorities.

PRINCIPAL COMPOSITIONS (published by S-Z unless otherwise noted): *Volo di notte*, opera; libretto by the composer after Saint-Exupéry (1937–38, Ricordi; second ed., UE); *Canti di prigionia* for chorus, several instruments (1938–41, Carisch); *Marsia*, ballet (1942–43, Carisch); *Cinque frammenti di Saffo* for soprano, chamber orchestra; translations by Quasimodo (1942); *Sex carmina Alcaei* for soprano, several instruments; translations by Quasimodo (1943); *Due liriche di Anacreonte* for soprano, 2 clarinets, viola, piano; translations by Quasimodo (1944–45); *Il prigioniero*, opera; libretto by the composer after P. A. Villier de l'Isle-Adam and Charles de Coster (1944–48); *Ciaccona intermezzo e adagio* for cello (1945, UE); *Due studi* for violin, piano; version for orchestra, *Due pezzi per orchestra* (both versions, 1946–47); *Quattro liriche di Antonio Machado* for soprano, piano (1948; for soprano, chamber orchestra, 1964); *Tre poemi* for soprano, chamber orchestra; poems by Joyce, Michelangelo, Manuel Machado (1949, Ars Viva); *Job*, mystery play for narrator, solo voices, chorus, orchestra; libretto by the composer (1949–50); *Canti di liberazione* for chorus, orchestra; texts from Castellio, Exodus, St. Augustine (1951–55); *Quaderno musicale di Annalibera* for piano (1952, unpub.; revised, 1953; version for orchestra, *Variazioni per orchestra*, 1953–54); *Goethe-Lieder* for mezzo-soprano, 3 clarinets (1952–53); *Piccola musica notturna* for orchestra (1954, Ars Viva); *An Mathilde*, cantata for soprano, orchestra; poems by Heine (1955); *Cinque canti* for baritone, 8 instruments; translations from early Greek poets by Quasimodo (1956); *Concerto per la notte di natale dell'anno 1956* for chamber orchestra with soprano; poem by Jacopone da Todi (Dec 1956–58); *Requiescant* for chorus, orchestra; texts by St. Matthew, Wilde, Joyce (1957–58); *Dialoghi* for cello, orchestra (1959–60); *Ulisse*, opera; libretto by the composer (1960–68); *Preghiere* for baritone, chamber orchestra; text by M. Mendes in an Italian translation (1962); *Parole di San Paolo* for medium voice, several instruments (1964); *Sicut umbra* for mezzo-soprano, 12 instruments; poems after Job by Juan Ramón Jiménez (1970); *Tempus destruendi—Tempus aedificandi* for chorus; Latin texts by Paulino di Aquileia and Dermatus (1971, 1970). List of works, 1925–64: *Quaderni della rassegna musicale* (Turin) 2:141–50; list of 12-tone works, 1942–57: Nathan 1958 (see bibl.).

PRINCIPAL WRITINGS: "Notes on the Statue Scene in Don Giovanni," *Music Survey* (London) 3:89–97; "On the Twelve-Note Road," *ibid.* 4:318–32; "The Genesis of the *Canti di Prigionia* and *Il Prigioniero*: An Autobiographical Fragment," *Musical Quarterly* 39:355–72; "My Choral Music," *The Composer's Point of View* ed. by R. S. Hines (Norman, Okla., 1963):151–77; "Begegnung mit Anton Webern," *Melos* 32:115–17;

"Encounters with Edgard Varèse," *Perspectives* 4/2:1–7; "Words and Music in Nineteenth Century Italian Opera," *ibid.* 5/1:121–33; "Nascita di un libretto d'opera [*Ulisse*]," *Nuova rivista musical italiana* 2:505–24 (German trans., *Melos* 35:265–78); *Ferruccio Busoni scritti e pensieri* ed. by L. D. and Guido M. Gatti (Florence 1941; second ed. 1954). List of writings, 1935–64: *Quaderni della rassegna musicale* 2:111–16.

BIBL.: Fedele d'Amico, "L. D.," *Melos* 20:69–74; Ulrich Dibelius, "L. D.," *ibid.* 31:81–87; Hans Ulrich Engelmann, "D.'s *Canti di liberazione*," *ibid.* 23:73–76; Massimo Mila, "*Il Prigioniero* di L. D.," *Rassegna musicale* (Rome) 20:303–11; Hans Nathan, "The Twelve-Tone Compositions of L. D.," *Musical Quarterly* (1958): 289–310; ——, "L. D.: Fragments From Conversations," *Music Review* (1966):294–312; John M. Perkins, "D.'s Art of Canon," *Perspectives* 1/2:95–106; *Quaderni della rassegna musicale* 2 (1965); Roman Vlad, *L. D.*, English translation (Milan 1957); Jacques Wildberger, "D.'s *Cinque canti*," *Melos* 26:7–10. Extensive bibl. to 1964: *Quaderni della rassegna musicale* 2:151–53.

Hans Nathan

SEE ALSO Italy, Opera, 12-Tone Techniques.

Dan, Ikuma (b. Tokyo, 7 April 1924), studied at the Tokyo Music Academy (1942–44, 1945–46; composition with Kanichi Shimofusa and Saburo Moroi, harmony and orchestration with Kunihiko Hashimoto) and the Military Band School (1944–45). He tours as a conductor, chiefly of his own music. Since 1967 he has presented a weekly series of pops concerts with the Yomiuri Orchestra on Nihon television. He taught at the Tokyo Music Academy during 1947–50 and during 1947–53 wrote music for radio dramas at the NHK radio. Since 1954 he has been music director and composer (four scores per year) for the Toho Motion Picture Co.

PRINCIPAL COMPOSITIONS: *Symphonies Nos. 1–5* (1949–50, 1955–56, 1960, 1964–65, 1965); *Yuzuru* [The Twilight Heron], opera (1950–51, orchestration revised 1956; Boosey); *Kikimimi-Zukin* [The Listening Cup], 3-act opera (1954–55); *Yang Kweifei*, opera (1957–58); *Dan Ikuma Kakyoku Shu*, 50 collected songs (published 1958, Ongaku); *Chanchiki* [Cling-Clang], opera (1961–63); *Misaki no Haka* [The Tomb on the Cape] for chorus (1963–64, Ongaku); *Kaze ni Ikiru* [In the Midst of the Wind], suite for chorus (1964, Ongaku); *Concerto Grosso for Strings* (1965); *Divertimento* for chorus (published 1969, Kawai); *Nihon Shinsho* [Ode to Japan], cantata (undated).

PRINCIPAL WRITINGS: *Asa no Kuni, Yori no Kuni* [Morning Country, Night Country], travel essays (Tokyo 1957); *Pipe no Kemuri* [Pipe Smoke], vols. 1–5 (Tokyo 1965, 1967, 1967, 1969, 1970).

SEE ALSO Japan.

Dance. Relationships between music and dance in the 20th century have been subject to continual challenge and reform. Dance, as a result, has had profound effects upon the music of the era. This situation contrasts markedly with that of the 19th century when it was expected of ballet music that it should be wholly subservient to the requirements of the dance. As Deryck Lynham has observed, "The music was written to the order of the choreographer, who all too frequently had little or no knowledge of orchestration, whilst the composer was barely acquainted with the scenario. There had to be so many bars in a given mood for this dance and so many for that, now a polka and then a galop or mazurka or other familiar dance rhythm."[1] Even the ballet music of Tchaikovsky, which is exceptional in its excellence, had to be written according to specific recipes provided by his choreographers.

A turning point arrived in 1899. During this one year the ballerina Carlotta Grisi died, the original Giselle and one of the adornments of the romantic era; Anna Pavlova (1881–1931), soon to be heralded by the West as one of the most impressive emissaries of a new ballet generation, made her debut at the Maryinsky Theater in St. Petersburg; the impressario Serge Diaghilev (1872–1929) began publishing the journal *Mir iskusstva* [The World of Art], in which he and his circle of insurgent intellectuals and artists demanded a new dramatic integrity for ballet and a new dignity and depth for its music; and lastly, an American girl of 21, Isadora Duncan (1878–1927) began her crusade in Europe for a personal dance expression freed from past conventions, performed barefoot and corsetless, exalted in theme, its fundamental motor impulses rooted in the music of the masters. Soon thereafter in the U.S., Ruth St. Denis (1877–1968), later joined by Ted Shawn (1891–1972), provided the initial impetus for what was to become a new, distinctively American dance tradition. The currents set in motion by these pioneers and their disciples drew dance into renewed contact with the mainstream of musical development (a contact that had lain severed since the time of Beethoven's *The Creatures of Prometheus*, choreographed by Salvatore Vigano in 1801).

INFLUENCES OF DANCE ON MUSIC. From the most general standpoint, the prevailing direction in both arts has been toward a broad expansion of esthetic horizons and, as an immediate corollary, uninhibited exploration of

[1]Deryck Lynham, *Ballet Then and Now* (London 1947):112.

new materials, techniques, textures, forms, and styles. Emancipated concepts of melody, harmony, and tonality, along with multiple refinements in musical sonority, rhythm, and texture have been either suggested or buttressed by analogous advances in choreography, e.g., liberated shape, flow, and dynamics of movement. Impressionism, for instance, found a dual outlet and embodiment in Fokine's choreography for *Daphnis and Chloë* and in the Ravel score commissioned by Diaghilev (premiere 1912). So too primitivism found a generative impulse in the ballet *Le Sacre du printemps* (Nijinsky-Stravinsky, 1913) as well as in the earliest of the ballets Diaghilev asked Prokofiev to compose, never realized on stage but later incorporated into the *Scythian Suite*, Op. 20 (premiere 1916). Neoclassicism crystallized in such Stravinsky dance scores as *Pulcinella* (1919–20) and *Renard* (produced 1922), both created for Diaghilev's Ballets Russes with choreography by Massine and Nijinska, respectively. Surrealism and dada assumed musical and choreographic guise in the series of Erik Satie ballets, starting with *Parade* (1917, choreographed by Massine), composed both for Diaghilev's company and for the Paris-based Ballets Suédois under the impresario Rolf de Maré (1886–1964); these ballets involved such illustrious collaborators as Picasso, Picabia, Cocteau, and René Clair. The nationalist movement has found expression in scores from around the world (the most familiar to U.S. audiences is perhaps Aaron Copland's *Appalachian Spring* for Martha Graham, 1944). Aleatoric procedures applied to the invention or performance of music and dance made their first appearance side by side in the joint productions of Merce Cunningham and John Cage during the early 1950s. In fact, with the exception of dodecaphony and serialism, a majority of the century's salient musical innovations arose in the context of dance and in certain instances even owed their inspiration to dance.

Dance has also left its imprint on musical physiognomy in less direct ways. The venerable practice of modeling musical works on dance forms or rhythms (in compositions not intended for dance performance) has continued unabated, e.g., in Ravel's *Valses nobles et sentimentales*, Bartók's *Rumanian Dances*, or in the many dance movements in the works of Berg and Schoenberg. In a few cases entire works have been dictated by choreographic principles or ideas. Aaron Copland's *Grogh* (1922) is a borderline example: conceived as a ballet and inspired by a film (Friedrich Murnau's *Nosferatu*, 1922), it had no prospects of being realized on stage, but ballet was in the air and Copland was attracted by its combination of symphonic and programmatic elements (parts of the score were later absorbed into *Cortège macabre*, 1923, and *Dance Symphony*, 1925, the latter title illustrating a fusion that is characteristically modern). Related instances are the two installments of Louis Gruenberg's *Music for an Imaginary Ballet* (1929, 1945), Henry Brant's work of the same title (1947), and Stravinsky's *Dances concertantes* (1941–42), conceived as an abstract orchestral piece but containing such specifically choreographic movements as "Marche," "Pas d'action," and "Pas de deux." William Schuman's *Judith* (1949) was written to be performed in the concert hall as a "dance concerto," the solo dancing by Martha Graham serving as a sort of instrumental surrogate; Morton Gould's *Tap Dance Concerto* (1952) is a kindred case.

Stravinsky is the most striking example of a composer whose music has been very largely molded by dance images, themes, and concepts. His ballet *Apollo musagetes* (1927–28) is an archetypical example. The composer chose the classical subject, bringing to fruition "an idea that had long tempted" him. His remarks about the growth of his conception reveal the extent to which choreographic images determined not only the general character but the smallest details of the musical form and instrumentation. "When, in my admiration for the beauty of line in classical dancing, I dreamed of a ballet of this kind, I had specially in my thoughts what is known as the 'white ballet,' in which to my mind the very essence of this art reveals itself in all its purity. I found that the absence of many-colored effects and of all superfluities produced a wonderful freshness. This inspired me to write music of an analogous character. It seemed to me that diatonic composition was the most appropriate for this purpose, and the austerity of its style determined what my instrumental ensemble must be. I at once set aside the ordinary orchestra because of its heterogeneity, with its groups of string, wood, brass, and percussion instruments. I also discarded ensembles of wood and brass, the effects of which have really been too much exploited of late, and I chose strings. . . . The taste for melody per se having been lost, it was no longer cultivated for its own sake, and there was therefore no criterion by which its value could be assessed. It seemed to me that it was not only timely but urgent to turn once more to the cultivation of this element from a purely musical point of view. That is why I was so much attracted by the idea of writing music in which everything should revolve about the melodic principle. And then the pleasure of immersing oneself again in the multi-sonorous euphony of strings and making it penetrate even the furthest fibers of the polyphonic web! And how could the unadorned design of the classical dance be better expressed than by the flow of melody as it expands in the sustained psalmody of strings?"[2]

Through commissions alone, dance has had a great impact on musical composition. Major dance companies and choreographers have often provided composers with their first public recognition. Diaghilev alone, for example, commissioned Stravinsky, Debussy, Ravel, Falla, Milhaud, Poulenc, Richard Strauss, Satie, Prokofiev, Auric, Rieti, and Sauguet, among others. Martha Graham has ordered scores from Hindemith, Riegger, Cowell, Antheil, Diamond, Copland, Barber, Chávez, Menotti, Schuman, Dello Joio, Persichetti, Hovhaness, Surinach, Starer, El-Dabh, and others. Among the composers who wrote special works for Doris Humphrey were Adolph Weiss, Dane Rudhyar, Paul Nordoff, Norman Lloyd, Henry Cowell, Lionel Nowack, Wallingford Riegger, and Otto Luening. Individual patrons have also prompted important compositions, e.g., Princess Edmond de Polignac, who commissioned Stravinsky's *Renard* (1916, produced 1922 with choreography by Nijinska); Elizabeth Sprague Coolidge who commissioned the same composer's *Apollo* (1927–28, first performed with choreography by Adolph Bolm; also choreographed the same year by George Balanchine); and Ida Rubinstein who commissioned Ravel's *Bolero* (1928, choreography by Nijinska).

Through the appeal and panache of theatrical presentation, dance has afforded some composers a broader and more sympathetic audience than they might otherwise have enjoyed. Stravinsky has acknowledged the effect of Diaghilev's personal faith and encouragement on his own career. Critic Peter Yates, referring to the collaboration between John Cage and Merce Cunningham, notes that "Cage had not been able, before this association, to command a public. With Cunningham, he was able to bring his inventions before audiences, which, although not unaware of his presence and influence, need not commit themselves to accept or reject him. This continuity of appearances . . . turned back the repeated rejections, the mockery, which might have overcome him."

[2]Igor Stravinsky, *An Autobiography*, paperback ed. (New York 1962):135–36.

Dance has also served to illuminate or clarify abstruse musical relationships by bringing them to the surface of visual and kinesthetic awareness. In 1963 George Balanchine choreographed Stravinsky's *Movements for Piano and Orchestra* (composed 1958–59), prompting the composer to comment: "To see Balanchine's choreography . . . is to hear the music with one's eyes. . . . The choreography emphasizes relationships of which I had hardly been aware—in the same way—and the performance was like a tour of a building for which I had drawn the plans but never explored the result."[3] Allied examples include the following: Bolm's dance version of Schoenberg's *Pierrot lunaire* (produced as early as 1926; later settings by Eleanor King, Robert Joffrey, Glen Tetley, and others), Antony Tudor's *Pillar of Fire* (1942, set to Schoenberg's *Verklärte Nacht*), José Limón's *The Exiles* (1950, set to Schoenberg's *Kammersymphonie No. 2*), Anna Sokolow's dance version of Berg's *Lyric Suite* (1953), Herbert Ross's *Los caprichos* (1949, set to Bartók's *Contrasts*), Martha Graham's setting of Varèse's *Intégrales* (1934), Gerald Arpino's *Incubus* (1962, set to Webern's *5 Pieces for String Quartet*), Balanchine's *Ivesiana* (1954), the same choreographer's setting of Xenakis's *Metastaseis* and *Pithoprakta* (1968), and the 2-part choreography of *Episodes* by Balanchine and Graham (1959, set to Webern's instrumental music).

METHODS OF COLLABORATION. Composers and choreographers have worked together or separately, in intimate contact or in total isolation, and with widely varying degrees of influence over each other's efforts. Fokine, in his memoirs, described half a dozen different approaches he employed in setting his dances to music. Alwin Nikolais has proclaimed, "music first, after, with, without, by chance and often by the grace of God."[4] For *Undertow* (1945), choreographer Antony Tudor communicated instructions to composer William Schuman over the telephone and by letter giving a general description of mood, atmosphere, and the length of sections, but no hint of the ballet's plot (which is indicative of what Tudor has generally considered a desirable degree of correspondence between music and dance). The idea for *Parade* (1917) was proposed neither by its composer, Satie, nor by the choreographer, Massine, but by Jean Cocteau, who also took a hand in the choreography along with Massine and the set designer, Picasso, while Satie worked on his score. Martha Graham advised Norman Dello Joio regarding the music for *Diversion of Angels* (*Seraphic Dialogue*, 1948) that "the texture should be like soft flesh," after which they pursued their tasks separately, not viewing each other's work until both score and choreography were complete. Sometimes the choreographer's work is finished even before the composer begins. Wallingford Riegger, who wrote the music for Graham's *Bacchanale* (1931), has expressed his astonishment at finding the dancers assembled at a preliminary meeting with the finished choreography ready for demonstration. Lucia Dlugoszewski, resident composer with the Erick Hawkins company, customarily starts writing when Hawkins's designs are done. In the case of Merce Cunningham and John Cage, music and dance are often composed independently and not executed together until the first public performance. A number of choreographers and composers have proceeded similarly; thus composer Luciano Berio and choreographer Ann Halprin worked entirely independently on *Esposizione* (1963), and the cast did not hear the music until opening night.

In some cases, close working relationships have evolved, resulting in a reciprocal transfer of creative ideas. Describing an early prototype of this kind of collaboration, Dane Rudhyar has written: "I may have the distinction of being the first modern composer to have worked satisfactorily for and with a dancer of the modern, abstract type on what can be called a modern dance recital. This was in 1913–14 in Paris. The dancer was Valentine de Saint-Point and the results were performed in April 1917 at the Metropolitan Opera in New York. . . . We discussed the structural abstract pattern of the composition, its main accents and tempos, basic rhythms, crescendos and decrescendos and the relative approximate length of its several parts. Then each of us went to work. I came with pencil sketches of music, she with half-finished dances, the basic themes-movements of which were all set, the exact development of these themes being left loose and elastic. In a few hours the dance and music were practically completed, with finishing touches and adjustments evolving through rehearsals"[5] (the Rudhyar works were his *Visions végétales* and *Poèmes ironiques*). In another representative instance, choreographer Doris Humphrey and composer Norman

[3] Hubert Saal, "Stravinsky's Alter Ego," *Newsweek* (19 Jan 1970):80.

[4] A. J. Pischl and Selma Jeanne Cohen, eds., "Composer/Choreographer," *Dance Perspectives* 16:36.

[5] Dane Rudhyar, "The Companionate Marriage of Music and Dance," *Dance Observer* 5/3:37.

Lloyd began work on *Lament for Ignacio Sanchez Mejias* (premiere 1946) separately, after six months' discussion of the overall conception. "We decided," Lloyd relates, "that I should write the music for the opening and closing sections of the poem while Miss Humphrey would work out the big dance section in the middle of the piece. After several weeks we came together, I to play the music, she to show me her dance. We changed creative places, and I went to work on the middle section, while she began to choreograph the beginning and ending."[6] At one point, Lloyd drastically revised his initial segment in response to the choreographer's advice.

Among the more unusual working relationships between choreographers and composers are the following: John Herbert McDowell wrote a new score (1967) for Paul Taylor's *From Sea to Shining Sea*, which previously had been set to Ives (1965). When performance rights were suddenly withdrawn for the Ravel music originally used with Gerald Arpino's *Sea Shadow* (1962), Michael Colgrass composed a new score literally overnight (1966), working with a filmed version of the dance. The score for *Les Mariés de la Tour Eiffel*, choreographed in 1921 by Jean Börlin and Jean Cocteau for Les Ballets Suédois, is a pastiche in which all of Les Six with the exception of Louis Durey took a hand. In 1961 for *Performance*, José Limón commissioned eight composers to write variations on a theme by William Schuman On occasion, composers have invented choreography of their own; in a score composed in 1957 for Jean Erdman, Ezra Laderman indicated phrasing and dynamics for the dance between the staves of music. Choreographer Alwin Nikolais has composed his own electronic music for the great bulk of his dance works. The interpenetration of the two arts has culminated in recent years in an actual exchange of roles between dancer and musician, choreographer and composer. Examples can be found among the dance works of Cunningham, Ann Halprin, the Judson Dance Theater, and others.

Variety has characterized not only collaborative approaches to music and dance, but also of choices of musical materials, which have reflected and reinforced the 20th-century quest for original, unconventional sonority. Examples include the use of silence (e.g., Doris Humphrey's *Water Study*, 1928, and *Drama of Motion*, 1930; Paul Taylor's *Untitled Duet*, 1956; Jerome Robbins's *Moves*, 1959; Merce

Cunningham's *Open Session*, 1964); verbal accompaniment (Cunningham's *How to Pass, Kick, Fall and Run*, 1965, with readings from John Cage); pure percussion sound (many early instances in the works of Mary Wigman and the Denishawn troupe); electrical or mechanical sounds, such as recorded time signals (Taylor's *Epic*, 1957) or a metronome (Midi Garth's *Anonymous*, 1954); medleys or collages (the tape collage by Eric Salzman and Archie Shepp for Daniel Nagrin's *The Peloponnesian War*, 1968; J. H. McDowell's score for Taylor's *Public Domain*, 1969); and electronic music of every description (probably the earliest instance was Cunningham's *Collage*, 1952, choreographed to parts of the Pierre Schaeffer-Pierre Henry *Symphonie pour un homme seul*).

This century has also witnessed significant changes in the degrees of correlation between music and dance. The dramatic theme, phrasing, dynamics, and most importantly, the rhythm of modern choreography have been liberated from musical domination. This departure from older practice has freed composers from the obligation to write music that accords with the dance at every instant. Some choreographers (e.g., Ruth St. Denis in her "music visualization" phase) have still occasionally enforced a rigorous parallelism (sometimes referred to as "mickey-mousing," from a similar custom in animated film scores). Otherwise, the gamut has run from a free but still relatively taut correspondence (typical of the works of Balanchine) to a looser association in which music and dance share a "mood" but have only the broadest rhythmic outlines in common (as in many works by Martha Graham, Paul Taylor, and Antony Tudor), to a use of music as an "environment" that occasionally has a direct effect on the movement (as in many works by Anna Sokolow), to an unbound coexistence in time with music and dance proceeding simultaneously but autonomously (exemplified in many of the Cunningham-Cage collaborations).

1900–29. Though borderlines cannot be precisely fixed, the first phase of 20th-century dance may be said to have ended with the death of Diaghilev. The period was largely characterized by reaction to the ideals and idioms of romanticism on the one hand and by a vigorous exploration of new resources and styles on the other. The predominant figures in the dance world were Isadora Duncan, the Diaghilev entourage, Rudolf von Laban (1879–1958), Mary Wigman (b. 1886), and the Ballet Suédois company of Rolf de Maré, all working mostly in Europe, and

[6]Norman Lloyd, "Composing for the Dance," *Juilliard Review* 8/2:4.

Ruth St. Denis and Ted Shawn in the U.S. The key composers were Stravinsky and Satie.

Duncan had virtually no direct influence on music. Indirectly, however, by her rejection of the subordinate, stereotyped role music played in 19th-century ballet, by the primacy she assigned to music as the motivation for her dance creations, and through her use of musical works of seriousness, complexity, and depth, she helped to set the stage for the rejuvenated partnership of composer and choreographer. Through her influence on Fokine, too, she helped to extend the realm of "dance music" far beyond the confines of ready-made accompaniment. The musical legacy of the continental pathfinders of the modern-dance movement—Von Laban and his pupil Wigman—was also of an indirect kind, stemming mainly from their exploratory outlook, and from the work of their numerous students (Wigman's pupils included Margaret Wallman, who taught at the Denishawn school for a time, and Hanya Holm, who in turn instructed Alwin Nikolais, Valerie Bettis, and Glen Tetley). The work of other dance pioneers, such as Maud Allan (1883–1956) and Loie Fuller (1862–1928) had only negligible consequences for music. One other figure deserves mention, the theorist-pedagogue-composer Emile Jaques-Dalcroze (1865-1950), who had a deep effect on Marie Rambert, Nijinsky, Wigman, Holm, Uday Shankar, and Kurt Jooss, among others, and whose importance reached far beyond his immediate circle.

Diaghilev galvanized a wholesale reformation of ballet, for which purpose he convened under one banner the most imposing constellation of choreographic, scenic, and musical artists the world has yet seen and then set forth deliberately to foster revolutionary musical developments within the context of dance. The early Diaghilev-engineered collaborations between Fokine and Stravinsky (*The Firebird*, 1909–10; *Petrushka*, 1910–11) and Nijinsky and Stravinsky (*Le Sacre du printemps*, 1911–13) signaled the dawning of a new esthetic era. Fokine's "five principles" (published in a letter to the London *Times*, 6 July 1914) codified the new aims (Fokine had been thinking along such lines at least as early as 1904) and specifically courted their realization in musical terms. The first four principles call for a revitalized approach to choreography in defiance of the conventions of the Imperial Russian ballet and demand "a new form corresponding to the subject, the most expressive form possible" for each new choreographic project. The fifth principle asks for an alliance with other arts "only on the condition of complete equality" without imposing "any specific 'ballet' conditions on the composer or the decorative artist," but allowing "complete liberty to their creative powers."

Stravinsky and his collaborators were one principal axis of new activity. Another centered around Satie and Les Six, who worked with Diaghilev's choreographers and Les Ballets Suédois (1920–25); especially important were those works of theirs that prefigured the pop-art, parodistic, and antiart tendencies of recent years. Another influential figure was the German choreographer Kurt Jooss (b. 1901), who, like Wigman, was a pupil of Von Laban. For his first independent company, the Neue Tanzbühne at Münster, he created ballets to music by Egon Wellesz (*A Persian Ballet*, produced 1924) and Hindemith (*Der Dämon*, 1925; the same score was used by José Limón in *The Demon*, 1963). For a later company, Ballets Jooss, Frederick A. Cohen (1904–67) served as "house composer" (one of the earliest cases of such a close, exclusive relationship between a composer and a single dance company). Among Cohen's scores is the expressionist, antiwar Jooss ballet *The Green Table* (1932).

In the U.S. a significant, indigenous musical repertory for dance did not begin to develop until the 1920s and had to wait for the second generation of native choreographers and dance companies for its first full flowering. St. Denis and Shawn, like Duncan, bequeathed no palpable musical literature to posterity, though they did commission and use music by such Americans as Deems Taylor, Charles Wakefield Cadman, and a host of lesser known figures. Nevertheless they were not without effect in the musical realm. Louis Horst (1884–1964), musical director of the Denishawn School during 1915–25, was to become the guiding spirit for several generations of dancers and musicians, particularly during his years of association with Martha Graham and with the foremost centers of modern-dance activity. Moreover, the Hindu, American Indian, Chinese, Japanese, Javanese, Egyptian, Persian and other ethnic dances of Denishawn, though of questionable authenticity, did assist in the liberation of 20th-century music from the parochialism of earlier European tradition. Also the Denishawn offspring (Horst, Graham, Humphrey, Weidman, and others) soon set forces in motion that would continue to provide American composers their first worldwide recognition.

1930–50. The second major evolutionary phase, extending to about 1950, saw a decisive shift from Europe to the U.S. as far as new developments and dominant trends were concerned. Diaghilev's choreographers and dancers were dispersed in several directions after his death. His surviving associates spurred the creation of new musical repertory in England (Ninette de Valois, Marie Rambert, and dancers Alicia Markova and Anton Dolin), France (Serge Lifar, choreographer and ballet master of the Paris Opéra, 1930–44 and 1947–58), and the U.S. (George Balanchine, director of the New York City Ballet and its predecessors; Mikhail Mordkin, whose own company evolved into the present American Ballet Theater). The various "Ballet Russe" companies (1932–63) were dominated on the choreographic side by Michel Fokine (1880–1942), Leonide Massine (b. 1896), and David Lichine (b. 1910). The Russian ballet under the Soviet regime, though it has remained closer to the Imperial tradition than ballet in other countries, also enriched musical literature, most notably in the scores of Shostakovich, Prokofiev, Kabalevsky, and Khachaturian.

Stimulated by European examples, native Americans began to establish classical ballet companies. The earliest included the Philadelphia Ballet (1934–42), the Page-Stone Ballet (1938–41, progenitor of the Chicago Opera Ballet), and the San Francisco Ballet, which crystallized from the San Francisco Opera Ballet under the stewardship of Willam Christensen in 1937. Most of the scores commissioned by these companies were by American composers, and many were based on American programmatic material. During the same period American modern dancers began to gain a foothold on university and college campuses (usually in the physical education department), which led to the dissemination of new concepts over a broad geographical area. Several summer programs at schools and colleges also evolved into important centers of creative activity where choreographers and dancers met and worked with some of the country's leading musicians.

By the mid-50s the rise of major American ballet and modern dance companies had led to a massive new repertory of musical works for dance, composed both by native and immigrant composers, among them Stravinsky, Copland, Riegger, Schuman, Hindemith, and Virgil Thomson. Louis Horst, musical director for Ruth St. Denis and the Denishawn Dancers (1915–25), for Martha Graham (1926–48), and founder of the important periodical *Dance Observer* (1933–64), played a crucial role as a patron saint of the American modern dance

movement. Distinctively American dramatic and musical material began to pervade dance composition as typified in *The Shakers* (D. Humphrey-traditional tunes, 1931), *American Provincials* (Graham-Horst, 1934), *Hear Ye, Hear Ye* (Ruth Page-Aaron Copland, 1934), *Union Pacific* (Massine-Nicolas Nabokov, 1934), *Frontier* (Graham-Horst, 1935), *Pocohantas* (Lew Christensen-Elliott Carter, 1936), *Billy the Kid* (Eugene Loring-Copland, 1938), *City Portrait* (Loring-Henry Brant, 1938), *Filling Station* (L. Christensen-Virgil Thomson, 1938), *Square Dances* (Humphrey-Lionel Nowack, 1939), *Rodeo* (De Mille-Copland, 1942), *Song of the West* (Humphrey-Roy Harris, 1942), *Appalachian Spring* (Graham-Copland, 1944), and *Fancy Free* (Jerome Robbins-Leonard Bernstein, 1944). Dance also found a new outlet and musical partnership in the stage musical; among the pacesetting examples were *On Your Toes* (Rodgers and Hart, choreography by Balanchine, 1936), *Oklahoma* (Rodgers and Hammerstein, dances by De Mille, 1943), *Annie Get Your Gun* (Irving Berlin-Helen Tamiris, 1946), and *Kiss Me, Kate* (Cole Porter-Hanya Holm, 1948). Even earlier dance and music had begun to conjoin in new ways in motion pictures. Some notable instances include the surrealist fantasy *Ballet mécanique* (directed by Fernand Léger with accompanying music composed by George Antheil, 1924) and *Skeleton Dance*, the first of Walt Disney's "silly symphonies" (1929).

Elements of Latin, Afro-Cuban, and Afro-American jazz began to be absorbed into the mainstream of Western music and dance. This began well before 1930, resulting in such fusions as Satie's *Parade* (choreography by Massine, 1917), Stravinsky's *L'Histoire du soldat* (original staging and choreography by Georges Pitöeff, 1918), Milhaud's *La Création du monde* (choreography by J. Börlin, 1923), John Alden Carpenter's *Krazy Kat* (choreography by A. Bolm, 1922), the same composer's *Skyscrapers* (choreography by Sammy Lee, 1926), and William Grant Still's *Lenox Avenue* ("a series of choreographic street scenes" originally composed 1937). Many Negro choreographers in the 1930s, in both ballet and free-dance idioms, drew on the multiple strands of Afro-American music and formal concert music. One of the earliest was Hemsley Winfield (1907–34), who in 1931 formed the first Negro dance company in the U.S., the Negro Concert Dancers, with a St. Denis protégé, Edna Guy. Winfield also choreographed and danced the solo role in Louis Gruenberg's opera *The Emperor Jones* (premiere 1933). Another important Winfield work was *Shingandi* (1930), an "African" ballet with music by David Guion (b. 1895).

Another significant development that cuts across the borderlines of chronological phases deserves mention—the close ties from the early part of the century onward between dancers and American composers of a radical, experimental turn of mind, starting with Henry Cowell (1897–1965). A number of Cowell's most novel ideas were incorporated in dance works. *The Banshee* (1925), which deals with sounds made by striking and plucking the piano strings, was used for dance as early as 1928 by Doris Humphrey. His concept of "elastic form," a predecessor of indeterminacy, found application in his score for Martha Graham's *Immediate Tragedy* (1937); the idea involved the writing of a given musical phrase in alternate versions of differing length, the choice and sequence of their use being left to the choreographer. Many of his other innovations (the use of unusual percussion instruments, the borrowing of sonorities and melodic modes from non-Western sources, the use of polyrhythms and of rhythmic patterns derived from numerical ratios in overtone frequencies, etc.) are imbedded in the numerous scores he composed for Doris Humphrey, Charles Weidman, Elsa Findlay, Sophia Delza, Tina Flade, Hanya Holm, Bonnie Bird, Erick Hawkins, Gertrude Lippincott, Jean Erdman, and others. Other nontraditional American composers whose music has found important dance outlets include John J. Becker (*Abongo* for 29 percussion instruments, 1933; *A Marriage with Space* for solo and mass recitation, solo and group dancers, orchestra, 1933–36), Adolph Weiss (*The Libation Bearers*, a choreographic cantata for chorus, vocal soloists, solo dancer, orchestra, 1920; also music for Doris Humphrey), Dane Rudhyar (*The Call*, 1929; *Breath of Fire*, 1930; *Dances of Women*, 1930; and other works for Humphrey plus music for Ruth St. Denis), Russian-born Joseph Schillinger (works for Mildred Strauss, Sophia Delza, Pauline Koner, and others during the 1930s), Russian-born Leo Ornstein (*Poems of 1917* for Martha Graham, 1928), George Antheil (*Course* for Graham, 1936), Harry Partch (*The Bewitched*, 1955, used by Alwin Nikolais), Alan Hovhaness (*Ardent Song* for Graham, 1954), Henry Brant (*City Portrait*, 1939, and *The Great American Goof* for Eugene Loring, 1940), and Lou Harrison (*Green Mansions, Johnny Appleseed, Solstice*, and other works, which have been used by several choreographers). In a related category are the Austrian-born Ernst Krenek (*Jest of Cards*, 1957, and other ballets), German-born

Stefan Wolpe (*The Man from Midian* for Eugene Loring, 1942), and Elliott Carter (*The Ball Room Guide*, 1937, and *Pocohantas*, 1937–39 for Lew Christensen; *The Minotaur* for John Taras, 1947). Since Winfield's time many distinguished black dancer-choreographers have pursued similar paths, though from quite different and varying vantage points. Among the most noteworthy have been Pearl Primus, Katherine Dunham, Syvilla Fort, Alvin Ailey, Geoffrey Holder, Donald McKayle, Talley Beatty, and Eleo Pomare.

A younger generation began to emerge whose ideas led into the next evolutionary phase: Martha Graham's former pupils and collaborators, Anna Sokolow, Paul Taylor, Erick Hawkins, and Merce Cunningham; José Limón, scion of the Humphrey-Weidman troupe; and Alwin Nikolais, whose principal teacher was Hanya Holm. Sokolow has used jazz (*Rooms*, 1955, score by Kenyon Hopkins; *Session for Six*, 1964, score by Teo Macero) and music of highly inventive sound textures (*Memories*, 1968, score by Tadeusz Baird; *Steps of Silence*, 1968, score by Anatol Vieru). Taylor has employed scores by John Cage, Morton Feldman, Gunther Schuller, Richard Maxfield, Lou Harrison, John Herbert McDowell, and others; he has also used electronic tape scores, recordings of heartbeats (*Panorama*, 1957), and total silence. Erick Hawkins has commissioned scores from Riegger, Cowell, Hunter Johnson, Bohuslav Martinů, and Robert Evett, among others, but since 1951 has worked almost exclusively with Lucia Dlugoszewski, whose original percussion orchestra complements the floating, weightless, stress-free idiom of his dance movement. Limón, like Sokolow, has relied mostly on preexisting scores, though Norman Dello Joio wrote *Variations on a Theme* (1956) for his *There Is a Time*. In his early work Nikolais used preexisting scores, occasionally also collaborating with composers, as in *8 Column Line* (1939) to music by Krenek and *The Bewitched* (1957) to music by Harry Partch. Since 1956 he has composed his own concrete or synthesized tape scores.

SINCE 1950. Many younger choreographers during the 1950s reacted against a hardening of styles and methods that had occurred during the 40s, and their innovations affected the relations between dance and the other arts, particularly music. The first conspicuous manifestations came in the early 50s as the entente between John Cage (b. 1912) and Merce Cunningham (b. 1921) gathered momentum. The simultaneous application of chance procedures to both music and choreography in *16 Dances for Soloist and Company of 3* (1951) was the first in a series of collaborative breakthroughs. The Cunningham Dance Co. itself was formed in 1952 with Cage as musical director and Robert Rauschenberg as scenic artist. Cage and Cunningham strive towards a nonlinear, "presentational" (as opposed to "representational") dance, antihistrionic and nonmimetic in form with neither art imposing demands or restrictions upon the other. As Cage has said, "There is simply an activity of movement, sound, and light." This contrasts not only with the dramatic representation in much ballet but with earlier modern dance, which merely adjoined psychological dimensions to conventional narrative and incorporated such devices as abstraction and symbolism. In eschewing the linearity of earlier dance and music, along with dramatic plot, character, period, and atmosphere, Cunningham's choreography and Cage's music evolved away from the orderly progression of well-defined ideas and approached instead what might be termed discontinuous adjacencies or disjunctive abstraction. "Discontinuity," Cage wrote in 1958, "has the effect of divorcing sounds from the burden of the psychological intentions." For similar reasons Cunningham has used nonsequential, nonmimetic movement to divest dance of specific narrative or emotional connotation. Another motivation for the discontinuity was to permit a more direct apprehension of sounds and movements for their own sake, unimpeded by extrinsic references. This paring down of artistic substance to unvarnished, atomic constituents has taken place in all the arts ("minimal art"); it has the effect of isolating the elements in a given series (thereby cancelling or obliterating connections) and, together with the lack of "development," has given rise to a new species of temporal experience in music and dance, one that substitutes an ongoing stasis, a sense of unchanging persistence, for the traditional mode of continual progression.

A number of other significant general trends have emerged from the Cage-Cunningham partnership. Foremost is the use of chance or random procedures in creation and performance. Another is the simultaneous involvement of several, independently acting arts within the context of a single artwork—in other words, the inter-, multi-, or mixed-media phenomenon. At first sight it might appear that the multimedia concept runs contrary to the intended autonomy of music and dance in the Cage-Cunningham collaborations. This is not the case, however. The older ideal of an integrated totality of arts, subsumed under a single controlling theme (stemming mainly from Wagner, Appia, and Craig), has its nearest contemporary analog not in the multimedia art of Cage, Cunningham, and their collaborators, but in the morphologically unified "total theater" of Nikolais. With Cage and Cunningham, the separate media are given equal weight and retain distinct, even discordant identities. They coexist and may even interact, but they never fuse into an amalgam. They remain simultaneous but isolated constituents of a pluralistic whole. An additional trend can be seen in the growing enlargement of the permissable spectrum of musical sound and dance movement. Cage has resorted to every kind of sound source from mundane "noise" to electronically generated or modified sound. At the same time Cunningham has explored the dance potential of a whole range of movement, both commonplace and invented, formerly excluded from the vocabulary of the art. The modeling of sound and movement forms on those encountered in prosaic, "everyday" experience is one aspect of a still more inclusive trend—towards the eradication of the borderlines between art and nonart, or between art and "life." Perhaps the most comprehensive embodiment of all these trends was reached in *Variations V* (1965) with choreography by Cunningham, electronic music by Cage (determined to a certain variable extent by the effect of the dancers' motions upon on-stage antennas and photoelectric cells), film and slide projections by Stan Vanderbeek, electronic devices by Robert Moog and Billy Kluver, and distorted television images by Nam June Paik—combining chance, electronics, multimedia, and quotidian elements (the piece ended with Cunningham riding around the stage on a bicycle). Cunningham has referred to the work as "a galaxy of events where everything interacts."

The two main focal points of new activity, in addition to the continuing Cage-Cunningham collaboration, were centered around Cunningham's contemporary Ann Halprin, working with her own troupe in relative isolation on the West Coast, and those (mainly pupils and adherents of Cunningham) who founded the Judson Dance Theater at New York's Judson Memorial Methodist Church in 1962. The enlargement of the sound and movement spectrum was pushed to the ultimate limits, with the help of unfettered esthetics and a rapidly developing audio-visual technology. Thus Cage's assertion in 1958 that the "present nature of music" was based primarily on "an acceptance of all audible phenomena as material proper to music" was echoed a decade later by critic Jill Johnston, who noted that the most revolutionary tenet of "the new dance" is that "any sort of movement, or action, and any kind of body (nondancer as well as dancer) was acceptable as material proper to the medium."[7] Similarly the tendency towards nonlinear, disjunctive abstraction was carried to extremes. Cage's dictum in 1954 that "the feeling we are getting nowhere" is "a pleasure which will continue" surfaced again in Ann Halprin's remarks about her *Esposizione*: "the whole dance—it took forty minutes—was a series of false beginnings. Nothing ever got anywhere";[8] the same motif is even more forcefully articulated in the description by Judson vanguardist Yvonne Rainer (who studied with Halprin, among others) of her *Parts of Some Sextets* (1965, no music): "Its repetition of actions, its length, its relentless recitation, its inconsequential ebb and flow all combined to produce an effect of nothing happening. The dance 'went nowhere,' did not develop, progressed as though on a treadmill or like a 10-ton truck stuck on a hill: it shifts gears, groans, sweats, farts, but doesn't move an inch."[9]

The antiart proclivities and the quest for the commonplace led in the new dance both to the participation of nondancers (often including musicians and other artists outside the dance domain) and to the discarding of costumes and even practice clothes (the latter already in common use in the Graham era) in favor of street dress or in some cases nudity. At the same time the proscenium stage and enclosed formal spaces of all kinds began to be rejected in favor of open, unconfined interiors (gymnasiums, museums) or workaday, outdoor settings (streets, parks). In place of "musical accompaniment," choreographers began to refer to "ambient sound," and to construe the aural component of their choreography as simply one (often dispensable) dimension of a sensory totality. Sonic collage, usually on tape, has become a frequent mode of approach to "music" for dance. Multimedia presentations have proliferated, and the distinctions between "dance recital," "musical concert," "theatrical performance," and "happenings" or "events" have grown harder to define.

Working collaborations between composers and choreographers have declined in number, partly because of economic factors and partly because of the availability and versatility of tape recorders and the access to vast repertoires of recorded music and sound. Many younger choreographers devise their own tape collages. Perhaps this recent attitude toward music, like the bare stages and costumeless dancers, is part of a trend among dancers to reassert the self-sufficiency of their art.

In spite of the foregoing there are a number of esthetic "resonances" between some new choreography and new music. Yvonne Rainer has interested herself in what she calls "found movement" (i.e., walking, running, skipping, and the like) and has been investigating the effects of reversing or contradicting conventional patterns of energy distribution within a series of movements. In describing her *The Mind Is a Muscle, Trio A* she has noted that "one of the most singular elements in it is that there are no pauses between phrases. . . . The end of each phrase merges immediately into the beginning of the next with no observable accent. . . . Another factor contributing to the smoothness of the continuity is that no one part of the series is made any more important than any other. . . . A great variety of movement shapes occur, but they are of equal weight and are equally emphasized."[10] Several musical analogs suggest themselves, primarily the idea of equal pitch distribution in 12-tone methodology. Describing another aspect of the same work, she states that "small discrepancies in the tempo of individually executed phrases" result in three simultaneous solo performances seeming to be "constantly moving in and out of phase and in and out of synchronization."[11] There is a close correspondence here to the phase-displacement techniques in the "extended-time" pieces of such composers as Steve Reich, Terry Riley, David Rosenboom, Larry Austin, and others. Finally, group improvisation in music has exact counterparts in the work of many dancers.

Though ballet choreography has continued to rely to varying degrees on traditional principles, a number of ballet choreographers have kept pace with the century's rapidly evolving musical syntax. Balanchine, as a preeminent example, latched onto the new

[7]John Cage, *Silence* (Middletown, Conn., 1961):84; Jill Johnston, "Which Way the Avant Garde?", *New York Times* (11 August 1968):D24.

[8]Ann Halprin, "Yvonne Rainer Interviews A. H.," *Tulane Drama Review* 10/2:151.

[9]Yvonne Rainer, "Some Retrospective Notes on a Dance for 10 People and 12 Mattresses Called *Parts of Some Sextets*, Performed at the Wadsworth Atheneum, Hartford, Connecticut, and Judson Memorial Church, New York, in March, 1965," *Tulane Drama Review* 10/2:178.

[10]Yvonne Rainer, "A Quasi Survey of Some 'Minimalist' Tendencies in the Quantitatively Minimal Dance Activity Midst the Plethora, or an Analysis of Trio A," *Minimal Art* ed. by Gregory Battcock (New York 1968):269–70.
[11]*Ibid.*:272.

technology in 1961 with *Electronics*, with a synthesized tape score by Remi Gassmann and Oskar Sala, the first electronic score composed for ballet in the U.S. And since Stravinsky's score for *Agon* (1953–57), written for ballet and one of the composer's earliest forays into 12-tone processes, Balanchine has followed his collaborator into almost every turn of his serial ventures. In Europe the French choreographer Maurice Béjart utilized musique concrète as early as 1954 in his *Symphonie pour un homme seul* (the music by Pierre Schaeffer and Pierre Henry, 1949–50). The rock-music idiom has been used in dance and has even been replenished by such dance commissions as Robert Joffrey's multimedia *Astarte* (1967), with music by the rock ensemble Crome Syrcus, slide and film projections by Gardner Compton, costumes by Hugh Sherrer, and sets and lighting by Thomas Skelton.

PROSPECTS. If the term *dance* is extended to cover the arts of movement or motion in their broadest possible signification, then a vast new terrain may present itself for creative musical and choreographic enterprise. Music has already undergone such a transformation with the advent of electronically synthesized tape music, in which the mediation of human performers is dispensed with and the composer's conception is translated directly into finished and unalterable form. As esthetics, cybernetics, and audio-visual technology move towards a point of intersection, dance too may evolve along similar lines. Working with electrocybernetic devices, choreographers may soon be able to realize movement designs directly, in three dimensions, without the intervention of live dancers. There is already a long tradition of kinetic and luministic art, stretching from Marcel Duchamp's *Mobile: Bicycle Wheel* of 1913 and the related experiments of Rodchenko, Gabo, Man Ray, Moholy-Nagy, and others, through such unclassifiable spectacles as Oskar Schlemmer's *Triadic Ballet* (1922) and Alexander Calder's *Circus* (1926), as well as the latter's motorized *Dancing Torpedo Shape* (1932), and up through such creations as Otto Piene's *Light Ballet* (1939), Frank Malina's environmentally activated light capsule, *Entrechats II* (1966), and a number of Jean Tinguely's servomechanical contraptions—for example, his *Radio Sculpture with Feathers* (1962), which uses electrical feedback from a radio receiver to regulate both a feather's giddy undulations and the receiver's tuning control. Experimental films frequently border on a kind of abstract visual choreography, and a host of new technological fields, such as computer-display graphics,

videographic cinema, and three-dimensional motion-picture holography, offer potential routes to entirely new fusions of sound and motion. In some respects the works of Nikolais might be regarded as a harbinger of cybernetic choreography.

In Stanley Kubrick's film *2001: A Space Odyssey* (1968), one can see perhaps the first glimmerings of what music and dance might come to mean in an intergalactic context, i.e., in the film's whimsical marriage of cosmic choreography with both the traditional strains of Strauss and the esoteric yammerings of György Ligeti. More recently an actual example of extraterrestrial "dance" with interplanetary sonic counterpoint took place in the 1969 moonwalk—the astronauts' movements shaped by the moon's distinctive gravitational characteristics and accompanied by sound transmission across gaping caverns of space and time.

BIBL.: George Amberg, *Ballet in America* (New York 1949); Verna Arvey, *Choreographic Music: Music for the Dance* (New York 1941); *Ballet Review* 1/6 (devoted to the Judson Dance Theater); Carolyn Brown, "On Chance," *Ballet Review* 2/2: 7–25; Anatole Chujoy and P. W. Manchester, *Dance Encyclopedia*, 2nd ed. (New York 1967); *Dance Perspectives* 34 (devoted to Merce Cunningham); Robert Dunn, ed., *John Cage Catalogue* (New York 1962); S. L. Grigoriev, *The Diaghilev Ballet 1909–1929* (London 1960); Martin Howe, "Erik Satie and His Ballets," *Ballet* 5/8:25 and 6/1:25; Jill Johnston, "Dance," *The New American Arts* ed. by R. Kostelanetz (New York 1965); Deryck Lynham, *Ballet Then and Now: A History of the Ballet in Europe* (London 1947); John Martin, *The Modern Dance* (New York 1933, reprinted 1965); Olga Maynard, *American Modern Dancers* (Boston 1965); A. J. Pischl and Selma Jeanne Cohen, "Composer/Choreographer," *Dance Perspectives* 16; *Stravinsky and the Dance* (New York 1962); Calvin Tomkins, *The Bride and the Bachelors* (New York 1965); Eric Walter White, *Stravinsky: The Composer and His Works* (Berkeley-Los Angeles 1966).

Alan and Sali Ann Kriegsman
SEE ALSO Mixed Media, Musical.

Daniel-Lesur, see under Lesur, Daniel-

David, Johann Nepomuk (b. Eferding, Austria, 30 Nov 1895), was a choir boy at the Stift St. Florian during 1905–10 and later studied at the Vienna Music Academy (1920–23, composition with Josef Marx). He has taught in the Volksschule in Wels, Austria (1923–34), the Leipzig Staatliche Hochschule (1942–45), and the Stuttgart Staatliche Hochschule (1948–63). In the early 1930s he directed the chorus of the Landeskonservatorium in Leipzig, and for a short time after World War II he was director of the Mozarteum in Salzburg. He has drawn inspiration from renaissance and baroque composers, particularly Josquin, Ockeghem, Schütz, and Bach. In 1953 he began using 12-tone techniques. He has edited works by Bach, Krebs, and Mozart.

PRINCIPAL COMPOSITIONS (published by Breitkopf): *Stabat Mater* for chorus (1927); *Chaconne in A* for organ (1927); *Fantasia super "L'Homme armé"* for organ (1929); *Introduction and Fugue on "Jerusalem, du hochgebaute Stadt," Toccata on "Lobe den Herrn, den mächtigen Konig," Partita on "Mit Fried' und Freud' ich fahr' dahin," Fantasia on "Ein feste Burg ist unser Gott,"* from 5 books of organ chorales (1932–35); *String Trio in G Minor* (1935); *Partitas Nos. 1–2* for orchestra (1935, 1939); *Ich wollt, dass ich daheime wär*, chorale motet for chorus; text by Heinrich von Laufenberg (1936); *Symphonies Nos. 1–8* (1936, 1938, 1940, 1945, 1951, 1954, 1956, 1964–65); *Duo concertante* for violin, cello (1937); *Kume, kum, geselle min*, divertimento on old folksongs for orchestra (1938); *Und ich sah einen neuen Himmel*, motet for chorus (1939); *Es sungen drei Engel ein' süssen Gesang*, sacred concerto for organ (1941); *Trio* for flute, violin, viola (1942); *Sonata* for solo flute (1942); *Sonata* for solo violin (1943); *Sonata* for solo viola (1943); *Variations on an Original Theme* for recorder or flute, lute (1943); *Sonata* for flute, viola (1943); *Sonata* for solo cello (1944); *Sonata* for 2 violins (1945); *Partita on "Unüberwindlich starker Held, Sank Michael"* for organ (1945); *Die Welt ist Gottes Haus*, motet for chorus; text by Theophrastus Paracelsus (1945); *3 Tierlieder* for chorus (1945); *4 String Trios* (1–2, 1945; 3–4, 1948); *Ut queant laxis*, hymn for chorus after Guido d'Arezzo (1946); *Partita on "Es ist ein Schnitter"* for organ (1947); *Victimae pascale laudes*, motet for chorus (1948); *Partita on "Da Jesus an dem Kreuze stund"* for organ (1952); *Partita on "Lobt Gott, ihr frommen Christen"* for organ (1952); *German Mass* for chorus (1952); *Violin Concertos Nos. 1–2* (1952, 1957); *Missa choralis* for vocal quartet (1953); *Sinfonia preclassica super nomen H-A-S-E* (1953); *Sinfonia breve* (1955); *Partita on "Innsbruck, ich muss dich lassen"* for organ (1955); *Requiem chorale* for soloists, chorus, orchestra (1956); *Empfangen und genährt*, motet for chorus; text by Matthias Claudius (1956); *Komm Trost der Nacht, o Nachtigall*, motet for chorus; text by H. J. Ch. von Grimmelshausen (1956); *Ezzolied*, oratorio for soloists, chorus, orchestra (1957); *Partita on "Aus tiefer Not"* for organ (1959); *Magische Quadrate*, symphonic fantasy (1959); *Spiegelkabinett*, waltzes for orchestra (1960); *Psalm 139, "Herr, du erforschest mich,"* for chorus (1961); *Maria, durch den Dornwald ging*, motet for chorus (1962); *Toccata and Fugue* for organ (1962); *Fantasias on "Mitten wir im Leben sind," "Maria durch den Dornwald ging," "Wenn mein Stündlein vorhanden ist"* for organ (1962); *Sonata* for 3 cellos (1962); *Maget und muoter*, motet for soprano, chorus; text by Walther von der Vogelweide (1966); *O, wir armen Sünder*, cantata for alto, chorus, organ; text by Hermann Bonn (1966); *Mass* for 4 high voices (1968); *Nun komm der Heiden Heiland* for organ (1969); *Concerto* for violin, cello, small orchestra (1969); *Partita* for organ (1970).

BIBL.: Hans Georg Bertram, *Material, Struktur, Form . . .* (Wiesbaden 1965); Rudolf Klein *J. N. D.* (Vienna 1964).

SEE ALSO Austria and Germany; Liturgical Music: Christian.

Davies, Hugh (Seymour) (b. Exmouth, Devon, England, 23 April 1943), studied at Oxford Univ. (1961–64; music history with Frank Harrison, harmony and counterpoint with Edmund Rubbra). During 1964–66 he was assistant to Karlheinz Stockhausen and a member of his live electronic music group. He was a concert organizer for the Arts Laboratory of London during 1967–69 and since 1967 has been director of the Electronic Music Workshop at the Univ. of London. He builds his own instruments and electronic equipment and uses them in the ensemble The Gentle Fire and in the Music Improvisation Co., a free jazz group. He has been concerned with reaching larger audiences than normally hear new music and with involving listeners in music in a positive way.

PRINCIPAL COMPOSITIONS: *Contact* for piano (1963); *Vom ertrunkenen Mädchen* for soprano, flute, clarinet, piano (1964); *Quintet* for 5 performers, 5 microphones, sine/square-wave generator, 4-channel switching unit, potentiometers, 6 loudspeakers (1967–68); *Kangaroo* for organ (1968); *Interfaces* for 2 performers with 2 stereo tapes, photocell divider, potentiometers, 4 loudspeakers, or for 6 performers with the same equipment plus amplified objects, 2 oscillators, 2 ring modulators (1967–68); *Shozyg I / Shozyg II / Shozyg I + II* for specially constructed stereophonic instruments with ad lib filtering or ring modulation (1968); *Spring Song* for springboard, a specially constructed amplified instrument (1970). Davies has also built instruments called Culinary Shozyg (1969–70) and Sho(zyg?) (1970); in collaboration with John Furnival he built instruments and "feelie boxes" called Lazy Garlic—Shozyg IV (1969), The Jack and Jill Box (1969–70), and Moral Music with Water (1969–71).

PRINCIPAL WRITINGS: "A Discography of Electronic Music and Musique Concrète," *Recorded Sound* 14 (1964):205–24 and 22–23 (1966):69–78; "die Reihe reconsidered," *Composer* 15:20–22 and 16:17–21; *International Electronic Music Catalog*

(Cambridge, Mass. 1968); "Working with Stock-hausen," *Composer* 27 (1968):8–11.
SEE ALSO Great Britain.

Debussy, (Achille) Claude (b. St.-Germain-en-Laye, near Paris, 22 August 1862; d. Paris, 25 March 1918), had little formal education as a child. Achille Arosa, an intimate of his aunt's whose brother was Gauguin's patron, met the boy and sparked his enthusiasm for painting. Another important figure in his early development was Antoinette Flore Mauté, Paul Verlaine's mother-in-law, who gave him piano lessons about 1870–71. He entered the Paris Conservatory in 1872 (theory with Albert Lavignac, piano with Antoine Marmontel, composition with Ernest Guiraud). In 1880 and 1881 he accepted summer employment as a pianist to Nadezhda von Meck, Tchaikovsky's patron, and visited Russia and much of Europe. In 1882 he failed to win the Prix de Rome, but in 1884 he succeeded with the cantata *L'Enfant prodigue* and spent the next two years at the Villa Medici in Rome. There he met Franz Liszt, who probably encouraged him to hear music by Lassus and Palestrina; he also heard *Lohengrin* there, and followed this by visits to Bayreuth in 1888 and 1889 to hear *Tristan*, *Meistersinger*, and *Parsifal*. Finally in 1889 he heard a Javanese gamelan at the Paris Exhibition. His associations with painters and poets, however, were to influence his thinking more than his friendships with musicians.

Debussy married Rosalie Texier in 1899 and left her in 1904 to live with Emma Bardac, whom he married in 1908; their daughter, Claude-Emma, was born in 1905. To support his family he toured England, the continent, and Russia to conduct his music and began writing criticism under the pen name M. Croche. The publisher Jacques Durand also helped by arranging for a regular stipend beginning in 1905. Nevertheless financial problems were a source of great difficulty for the rest of his life. His death resulted from cancer, which apparently had been the cause of ill health from about 1910.

Harmony in Debussy's music often presupposes the chord as an object chosen for the sonorous values in its resonances, registration, and scoring. Most chords are based on superpositions of thirds, thus permitting the resonance of the open fifth (often occurring as a pedal point) as well as access to the triad, which can then be used for repose without sounding inappropriate. Many chords are derived from or imply modes that have weak tonal functions —with a lowered seventh or raised fourth, with no intervallic differentiation in the case of the whole-tone scale, with an ambiguous tonic and absent seventh in the case of the pentatonic. Debussy often used these and other chords in a tonally nonfunctional manner by shifting them in parallel blocks to different pitch levels or juxtaposing them with other chords chosen for contrast rather than resolution. By extension, melodic modes were chosen for their special characteristics, and modulation was effected by shifting to new pitch levels without regard to the dominant-tonic functions that might be implied in the material; again, contrasts were chosen without regard to tonal functions. Perfect cadences were largely abandoned, and plagal ones occur hardly more frequently.

From early in his career Debussy was aware that his harmonic concepts demanded new forms; the traditional schemes that had evolved from tonal practices would not adequately contain his harmonic materials. His thinking in this regard was reflected in the general artistic change from fixed to fluid forms at the turn of the century. Poetry, painting, and, especially in France, Art Nouveau architecture and design all shared in this search. Debussy's forms tend to be a series of waves, large crests whose principal themes recede into the background and continue as ostinatos while other versions of themselves or new material is superposed. Motives may have antecedents, but they do not demand consequents as do the bipartite themes of earlier music. Although the thematic repertory in most of the large-scale works is fairly limited, alterations in texture and rhythm disguise thematic identities so that they often become mere suggestions of themselves. Because all pitches are subject to chromatic alteration, motives having a common derivation may finally refer to each other by shape alone. Juxtapositions are not prepared, and bridge passages may be abandoned or only fleetingly suggested. Many of the early pieces have a symmetrical shape with an emotional peak about two-thirds of the way through, usually in a central section that is based on its own thematic material. This is followed by a return to the thematic or motivic vocabulary of the beginning. Rarely, however, does the return function as a literal recapitulation; in the effort to localize the sensation of the moment, the material undergoes constant and radical transformation. Motivic reuse represents a commentary or gloss, not a variation or development.

In his desire to constantly vary his material, Debussy evolved an extraordinary vocabulary of timbre, which assumes a structural importance often equal to that of the pitch components in a given work. The uniqueness of individual orchestral works is largely the result of a specific sound ideal. Most pieces have a unique effective instrumentation. Where this is not the case, characteristic doublings may occur: the mixture of horns and low violins at the end of *L'Après-midi d'un faune*; the English horn and two cellos in *La Mer*; the piccolo and harp scales in *Jeux*. A device related to doubling is the superposing of melodic material in differing articulations and speeds so that concurring pitches are intensified; compare for instance the 16 bars after No. 55 in *La Mer*, the sixth bar after No. 50 in *Jeux*, and the opening of the *Sonata* for flute, viola, and harp. As a result of such devices, each fragment in a structural mosaic may have its own color, unique to that passage and to that piece.

Debussy objected to Strauss's homogeneous orchestration, comparing it to "an American cocktail with 18 ingredients," in which multiple doublings obscure the characteristics of individual instruments. In Debussy even the strings often play divisi (which is one reason that textures are transparent and can be superposed without obscuring each other). His doublings, when they do occur, are used much less for reinforcing the sound than for changing the timbre. Instruments sometimes double each other octaves apart, the higher one creating a new set of upper partials. Unusual registers are exploited, notably the low register of the flute; the harp and percussion are often elevated to new solo roles. The pulverized orchestra that results does not "play itself" the way a Ravel orchestra does; continuous attention to balance is needed. Similarly, the complex resonances in Debussy's piano writing demand careful use of the pedals, the damper pedal in particular, so that minute gradations in resonance will permit the clear articulation of faster moving parts over sustained bass lines.

Like timbre, rhythm and tempo in Debussy often function to characterize pieces and local events. Succeeding "waves" may create layers of rhythm as motives crest, turn back on themselves, and become rhythmic backdrops for other material; often the backdrop is composed of nervous, propulsive ostinatos, the new material of langorous and rubato rhythms. In the vocal music a closely woven motivic play in the instrumental part(s) may be juxtaposed with vocal lines whose rhythms and melodic contours preserve the less rigid linguistic properties of the text. Rapid ornamental melismas break through regular rhythmic textures, frequent changes of tempo occur, and the directive "rubato" appears often in opposition to a fixed tempo.

As with the symbolist poets of the second half of the 19th century, especially those he set to music (Verlaine, Baudelaire, and Mallarmé), Debussy expressed a new and vast repertory of emotional states, often furtive and fleeting, often mixing pain and pleasure, often stated by suggestion and experienced in moments of extreme condensation and compression. From the beginning he was considered a revolutionary, but he was seemingly outdistanced, even in his own lifetime, by Stravinsky and Schoenberg. Paradoxically Stravinsky's music of the early teens contains much of Debussy's enlargement of the diatonic-modal repertory and techniques of structural articulation (even if Stravinsky's music is conceived in larger blocks, more highly differentiated from each other). Schoenberg and his pupils, who seemed not to regard Debussy seriously, could hardly have been unaffected by his attention to timbre and to his compression of form. Those composers who were influenced by the harmonic lushness and instrumental shimmer of the impressionism Debussy was supposed to represent, lacked the intellectual sensitivity and rigor to realize vital and coherent works. Perhaps only Bartók successfully exploited some of the radical elements in Debussy (but only in his works of the late teens and early twenties). A major obstacle in the public acceptance of Debussy's music was its very sensuousness. His "nature" pieces, for instance, invite delight, not the terror and awe of man pitted against a powerful antagonist. It was difficult for many to ally joyful and accepting voluptuousness with profundity. Even those musicians who accorded him a sense of formal design were slow to acknowledge any spiritual depth. As Artur Schnabel is reported to have said, "His music gives me great esthetic satisfaction but not that ethical emotion that I expect from great musical works." Until recently his music was generally relegated to the end of concert programs where it was intended to provide relief from the spiritual weight of the great masterpieces. Since World War II his art has undergone a reevaluation. His nonlinear, nondevelopmental concept of time and form stands behind the "open" and "moment" forms of Boulez and Stockhausen. His structuring of timbre and rhythm in planes has become an important feature in much recent music (as has his spatial concept of sounds coming "from a distance"). As Stravinsky commented shortly before his death in 1971, Debussy "is in all senses the century's first musician."

PRINCIPAL COMPOSITIONS (published by Durand; many are in the public domain): *Printemps* for women's chorus (1882); *L'Enfant prodigue*, cantata (1884); *Printemps*, symphonic suite (1886–87); *La Damoiselle élue*, cantata for soloists, chorus, orchestra; text by Rossetti (1887–89); *2 Arabesques* for piano (1888); *Petite Suite* for piano duet (1889); *5 Poèmes de Baudelaire* for voice, piano (1890); *Suite bergamasque* for piano (1890–1905); *L'Après-midi d'un faune* for orchestra (1892–94); *String Quartet in G Minor* (1893); *Pelléas et Mélisande*, opera; libretto by Maurice Maeterlinck (1893–95, revised c.1897); *Nocturnes* for orchestra (1895–99); *Pour le piano* (1896–1901); *3 Chansons de Bilitis* for voice, piano (1897); *Estampes* for piano (1903); *La Mer*, 3 symphonic sketches for orchestra: "De l'Aube à midi sur la mer," "Jeux de vagues," "Dialogue du vent et de la mer" (1903–05); *Images* for piano (I: 1903–05, II: 1907); *Danse sacrée et danse profane* for harp, strings (1904); *Children's Corner*, suite for piano (1906–08); *Images* for orchestra: "Gigues," "Iberia," "Rondes de printemps" (1906–12); *Rhapsody* for clarinet, piano (1909–10); *3 Chansons de Charles d'Orléans* for chorus (1908); *3 Ballades de François Villon* for voice, piano (1910); *Preludes* for piano (I: 1910, II: 1910–13); *Le Martyre de St. Sébastien*, mystery play for vocal soloists, chorus, orchestra; text by Gabriele d'Annunzio (1911); *Syrinx* for flute (1912); *Jeux*, ballet; scenario by Nijinsky (1912–13); *3 Poèmes de Stéphane Mallarmé* for voice, piano (1913); *En Blanc et noir* for 2 pianos (1915); *Cello Sonata* (1915); *Sonata* for flute, viola, harp (1915); *Etudes* for piano (1915); *Violin Sonata* (1916–17).

PRINCIPAL WRITINGS: Several volumes of letters have appeared: to Jacques Durand (Paris 1927), to Paul-Jean Toulet (Paris 1929), to André Messager (Paris 1938), to Robert Godet and G. Jean-Aubry (Paris 1942), to Pierre Loüys (Paris 1945), to Gabriele d'Annunzio (Paris 1948), to André Caplet (Paris 1957), to his wife Emma (Paris 1957), to Louis Laloy (*La Revue de musicologie* 1962). About a third of his criticisms are included in *M. Croche, the Dilettante Hater* (New York 1928).

BIBL.: Jean Barraqué, *D.* (Paris 1962); *Debussy et l'évolution de la musique au XXᵉ siècle*, conference report (Paris 1965); Marcel Dietschy, *La Passion de C. D.* (Neuchâtel 1962); Herbert Eimert, "D.'s Jeux," *Die Reihe* 5; Edward Lockspeiser, *D.: His Life and Mind*, 2 vols. (London 1962, 1965); Wilfrid Mellers, *Caliban Reborn* (New York 1967); Eric Salzman, *Twentieth Century Music* (Englewood Cliffs, N. J., 1967).

Paul Jacobs

SEE ALSO Asian Music and Western Composition, Dance, Folk Resources, France, Harmony and Counterpoint, Impressionism, Jazz, Melody, Opera, Orchestration, Rhythm, Text Setting and Usage, Theory, Tuning and Temperament.

Decay, those amplitude characteristics having to do with the ending of a sound or signal.

© *Music Educators Journal* (Nov 1968)

Delannoy, Marcel (François Georges) (b. La Ferté-Alais, France, 9 July 1898; d. Paris, 14 Sept 1962), studied architecture at the Ecole des Beaux-Arts and was self-taught in music with coaching in harmony and theory from his wife, Lisette Claveau, and from Jean Gallon and André Gedalge. Arthur Honegger also encouraged and advised him. According to Ewen (see bibl.) "in his earlier works Delannoy leaned towards impressionism. Beginning with his *Quartet* he veered towards neoclassicism . . . fully crystallized in the opera *Ginevra* . . . in which the idioms of Cimarosa and Pergolesi are given contemporary treatment." He believed that the ecclesiastical modes and international folklore would be the most viable bases for any new systems of music.

PRINCIPAL COMPOSITIONS: *Le Poirier de Misère*, opera (1923–25, Heugel); *String Quartet in E* (1928–30, Durand); *Le Fou de la dame*, ballet cantata (1927–28, Heugel); *Philippine*, operetta (1928–35, Eschig); *La Pantoufle de vair*, ballet (1931, Eschig); *Symphonies Nos. 1–2* (1932, Sénart and Salabert; 1954, Salabert); *Ginevra*, comic opera (1938–42, Eschig); *Puck*, opera (1943–45, Méridian); *Concerto de mai* for piano, orchestra (1949, Eschig); *Suite à chanter* for mezzo-soprano, strings, piano, celesta (1949–55, Eschig).

PRINCIPAL WRITINGS: *Honegger* (Paris 1953).

BIBL.: André Boll, *M. D.* (Paris 1957); René Dumesnil, "M. D.," *Revue musicale* No. 127:31–44; David Ewen, *European Composers Today* (New York 1954):39–40; Guy Ferchaut, "M. D.," *Melos* 18:214–17; A. Machabey, *Portraits de trente musiciens français* (Paris 1949):55–58.

SEE ALSO France.

Delius, Frederick (b. Bradford, Yorkshire, 29 Jan 1862; d. Grez-sur-Loing, 10 June 1934), was born into a family of wool merchants who, though musical, insisted on a business career for their son. During 1884–85 Delius lived on an orange plantation in Florida where an American organist, Thomas F. Ward, gave him a basic training in composition. In 1886 he entered the Leipzig Conservatory. The musical instruction was little to his purpose, but he met Grieg in Leipzig and thereafter continued to associate with Scandinavian writers and artists. One of these, the Norwegian painter Jelka Rosen, became his wife, and in 1888 they settled at Grez-sur-Loing near Fontainebleau, where they remained for the rest of his life.

Delius was a solitary individualist in his art as in his life, indifferent to the music of most other composers. Late Wagner, Grieg, and (perhaps) Debussy played some part in the formation of his style, which is marked by an extreme chromaticism of harmony (character-ized by frequent descending minor sevenths), a delicate feeling for orchestral textures (in which solo woodwinds are employed with poignant effect), a preference for slow tempos, and a general lack of metric pulse. These qualities combine to create an atmosphere of sadness, regret, and languor with occasional interludes of ecstatic vigor. He expressed him-self most convincingly in tone poems and orchestral rhapsodies (*On Hearing the First Cuckoo in Spring*, *Brigg Fair*), free variation forms (*Brigg Fair*, *Dance Rhapsody No. 1*), and choral works (*Appalachia*, *Sea Drift*, *A Mass of Life*). His *Violin Concerto* (1916) is successful in spite of his limitations in dealing with classical sonata structures, for instead of trying to achieve the usual dramatic contrasts of a sonata form he composed a sustained and lyric rhapsody. The most important of his early compositions were first performed in Germany. Recognition in England did not begin until the 1920s and was chiefly brought about by Thomas Beecham. In his later years, though blind and paralyzed, he was able to continue composing with the help of an amanuensis, Eric Fenby.

PRINCIPAL COMPOSITIONS (published by Boosey unless otherwise noted; list prepared by Robert Threlfall of the Delius Trust): *Florida*, suite for orchestra (1887, revised 1889); *Irmelin*, 3-act opera (1890–92); *The Magic Fountain*, 3-act opera (1894–95, unpub.); *Koanga*, 3-act opera (1895–97); *Piano Concerto* (1897, revised 1906–07); *Norwegian Suite* for orchestra (1897, unpub.); *Paris, the Song of a Great City*, nocturne for orchestra (1899, UE); *A Village Romeo and Juliet*, opera in 6 scenes (1900–01); *Life's Dance* for orchestra (1901; re-vised 1912, Oxford); *Appalachia*, orchestral varia-tions with chorus (1902); *Sea Drift* for baritone, chorus, orchestra; poem by Walt Whitman (1903); *A Mass of Life* for soloists, chorus, orchestra; text by Nietzsche (1904–05); *Songs of Sunset* for soprano, baritone, chorus, orchestra (1906–07); *Brigg Fair*, an English rhapsody for orchestra (1907); *In a Summer Garden* for orchestra (1908); *Dance Rhapsodies Nos. 1–2* for orchestra (1908, UE; 1916, Galliard); *Fennimore and Gerda*, opera in 11 pictures (1909–10); *The Song of the High Hills* for chorus, orchestra (1911, UE); *Arabeske* for baritone, chorus, orchestra (1911); *2 Pieces*, "On Hearing the First Cuckoo in Spring," "Summer Night on the River," for small orchestra (1911–12, Oxford); *North Country Sketches* for orchestra (1913–14, Galliard); *Requiem* for soprano, baritone, chorus, orchestra (1914–16); *Concerto* for violin, cello, orchestra (1915–16, Galliard);

Violin Concerto (1916, Galliard); *Eventyr*, "Once Upon a Time," for orchestra (1917, Galliard); *A Song before Sunrise* for small orchestra (1918, Galliard); *Hassan*, incidental music (1920–23); *Cello Concerto* (1921); *A Song of Summer* for orchestra (1929); *Songs of Farewell* for chorus, orchestra (1930).

BIBL.: Thomas Beecham, *F. D.* (London 1959); Frank Howes, *The English Musical Renaissance* (London 1966); Arthur Hutchings, *D.: A Critical Biography* (London 1948); Rachel Lowe, "The D. Trust Manuscripts," *Brio* (spring 1961); Christopher Redwood, "Fennimore and Gerda," *Composer* (spring 1968).

Michael Graham-Dixon

SEE ALSO Great Britain, Impressionism, Melody.

Del Tredici, David (Walter) (b. Cloverdale, Calif., 16 March 1937), attended the Univ. of Calif. at Berkeley (1955–59, B.A., composition with Arnold Elston, Seymour Shifrin), and Princeton Univ. (1959–60, 1963–64; compo-sition with Roger Sessions, Earl Kim). He studied piano privately with Bernhard Abram-owitsch in Berkeley (1953–59) and Robert Helps in New York (1962–64). He was active as a pianist on the West Coast, making five solo appearances with the San Francisco Symphony. In 1958 while attending the Aspen School of Music, he attended classes of Darius Milhaud, who encouraged him to compose. Del Tredici was Fromm pianist at Tanglewood (1964, 1965) and resident composer at the Marlboro Festival (1966, 1967). Since 1967 he has been on the music faculty of Harvard Univ.

PRINCIPAL COMPOSITIONS: *6 Songs* for voice, piano; texts by James Joyce (1959); *String Trio* (1959); *Scherzo* for piano 4-hands (1960); *Fantasy Pieces* for piano (1962, Boosey); *I Hear an Army* for soprano, string quartet (1964, Boosey); *Night Conjure-Verse* for soprano, countertenor (mezzo-soprano), string quartet, horn, piccolo, flute, oboe, clarinet, bass clarinet, bassoon (1965); *Syzygy* for amplified soprano, horn, tubular bells, string sextet, wind octet, 2 trumpets (1966, Boosey); *The Last Gospel* for amplified soprano, amplified rock group (2 electric guitars, 2 saxophones), chorus, orchestra (1967); *Pop-pourri* for amplified soprano, amplified rock group (2 electric guitars, 2 saxophones), chorus, orchestra (1968, Boosey); *Scene and Arias from Alice in Wonderland* for soprano, orchestra (1969).

Dello Joio, Norman (b. New York, 24 Jan 1913), began his musical training under his father, an organist who had emigrated from Italy in the early 1900s, and continued organ lessons with his godfather, Pietro Yon (1930–32). He attended the Institute of Musical Art in New York (1933–38) and studied composition at the Juilliard School with Bernard Wagenaar (1939–41) and at Yale Univ. with Paul Hindemith (1941–43). He taught composition at Sarah Lawrence College during 1945–50 and joined the composition faculty at the Mannes College in 1958. In the 1960s and early 70s he was chairman of the Contemporary Music Project, sponsored by the Ford Foundation. In 1972 he became Dean of Fine Arts at Boston Univ.

Dello Joio's output consists of numerous short piano works, three piano sonatas, songs, chamber music for various combinations of string and woodwind instruments, incidental music for theater and television, band music, dance scores, four operas, solo concertos for such unusual instruments as the harp and harmonica, several symphonies, and a large number of choral compositions. His music exhibits a strikingly lyric inventiveness resulting from long-breathed diatonic and modal melodies. Gregorian chant has profoundly colored his melodic writing, and elements of Italian grand opera and jazz rhythmic patterns are also present. In addition to melody, his style emphasizes a rhythmic vitality and a diatonic harmonic idiom that incorporates carefully controlled dissonances. Textures are usually polyphonic, and formal structures display a clarity of organization. Variation techniques are prominent, especially in the works of 1946–57.

PRINCIPAL COMPOSITIONS (list prepared by the composer): *The Mystic Trumpeter* for chorus, horn (1943, Schirmer-G); *Piano Sonata No. 2* (1943, Schirmer-G); *Trio* for flute, cello, piano (1944, Fischer); *Diversion of Angels*, dance score; choreography by Martha Graham (1945, Fischer); *On Stage*, dance score; choreography by Michael Kidd (1945, Schirmer-G); *A Jubilant Song* for female or mixed chorus, piano (1946, Schirmer-G); *Piano Sonata No. 3* (1947, Fischer); *Variations, Chaconne, and Finale* for orchestra (1947, Fischer); *Seraphic Dialogue*, dance score; choreography by Graham (1948, Fischer); *Song of the Open Road* for chorus, trumpet, piano; poem by Walt Whitman (1949, Fischer); *A Psalm of David* for chorus, piano, brass, percussion, strings (1950, Fischer); *The Triumph of Saint Joan*, 1-act opera (1951, Fischer; symphony of the same name, 1951, Fischer); *Lamentation of Saul* for baritone, orchestra (1954, Fischer); *Meditations on Ecclesiastes* for string orchestra (1956, Fischer); *There Is a Time* for string orchestra, dance score; choreography by José Limón (1956, Fischer); *To St. Cecilia*, cantata for chorus, piano or brasses (1957, Fischer); *Fantasy and Variations* for piano, orchestra (1961, Fischer); *Variants on a Mediaeval Tune* for band (1963, Marks); *The Louvre*, inci-

dental score for the NBC television documentary (1965, Marks); *Antiphonal Fantasy* for organ, brass, strings (1966, Marks); *Colloquies* for violin, piano (1966, Marks); *Proud Music of the Storm* for chorus, brass, organ; poem by Whitman (1967, Marks); *Songs of Walt Whitman* for chorus with piano or orchestra (1967, Marks); *Time of Snow*, dance score; choreography by Graham (1968, Marks); *Years of the Modern* for chorus, percussion, brass (1968, Marks); *Capriccio on the Interval of a 2nd* for piano (1969, Marks); *Homage to Haydn* for orchestra (1969, Marks); *Mass* for chorus, organ, brass (1969, Marks); *Songs of Abelard* for band (1969, Marks). List to 1962 in Downes (see bibl.); to 1964: *Composers of the Americas* 9:43–50.

BIBL.: Edward Downes, "The Music of N. D. J.," *Musical Quarterly* 48:149–72; Madeleine Goss, *Modern Music-Makers* (New York 1952):432–46.

Thomas E. Warner

SEE ALSO Dance, Opera.

De Marchena-Dujarric, Enrique (b. Santo Domingo, 13 Oct 1908), studied law at the Univ. of Santo Domingo. He attended the Liceo Musicale in Santo Domingo (1918–22) and studied privately with Flérida Nolasco (piano, 1918–21), Esteban Peña Morell (composition, 1922–24, 1928), Luis E. Mena (instrumentation, 1928–29), and Enrique Casal Chapí (composition, orchestration, 1942–44). He has been delegate and ambassador from the Dominican Republic to the United Nations (1947–60), ambassador to Switzerland and Germany (1966–69), and Undersecretary of State (1945–47) and Minister of Foreign Affairs (1955–56) of the Dominican Republic. During 1941–47 and 1954–56 he taught legal subjects at the Univ. of Santo Domingo. During 1929–42 and 1968–70 he was a music critic for *Listin Diario*. He has lectured on Dominican folklore in the U.S., Europe, and Japan. He describes his music as mostly impressionistic in style.

PRINCIPAL COMPOSITIONS: songs for students; texts by Ramón Emilio Jimenez (1940); *12 Images* for piano (1940–45); *Rainbow*, symphonic poem (1944); *2 Heroic Pieces* for military band (1944); *Violin Concerto in D* (1945); *Suite de imagenes* for orchestra (1945); *Cradle Song* for voice, piano (1945); *10 Preludes* for piano (1945–50); *Impressions* for piano (1945–60); *Concertino* for flute, orchestra (1946); *2 Preludes* for organ (1948); *Divertimento* for oboe, orchestra (1954); *3 Poems* for orchestra (1965); *20 Love Songs* for high voice, piano; texts by Dominican poets (1966–69).

PRINCIPAL WRITINGS: *Música de America* (Santo Domingo 1942); *Del areito de anacaona al poema folklorico* (Santo Domingo 1942).

BIBL.: Jacob Coopersmith, "Music in the Dominican Republic," *Musical Quarterly* 31 (1945).

Denisov, Edison (b. Tomsk, Siberia, 6 April 1929), studied mathematics at the Univ. of Tomsk (graduated 1951). Dmitri Shostakovich persuaded him to give up mathematics and study composition, and he attended Moscow Conservatory (1951–56; composition with Vissarion Schebalin, Nicholas Peiko; analysis with Victor Tsukkerman; counterpoint with Semion Bogatyrev, piano with Vladimir Belov). Since 1959 he has taught at Moscow Conservatory, and during 1968–70 he worked at the Experimental Studio of Electronic Music in Moscow. His music has also been influenced by his study of folk music during travels through Russian villages.

PRINCIPAL COMPOSITIONS: *Music for 11 Instruments* for winds, timpani (1961); *Canti di Catull* for bass, 3 trombones (1962); *Concerto* for flute, oboe, piano, percussion (1963, UE); *Solntse inkov* [Incan Son] for soprano, flute, oboe, trumpet, horn, violin, cello, 2 pianos, percussion; poem by Gabriela Mistral (1964, UE); *Italyanskie pesni* [Italian Songs] for soprano, flute, violin, horn, harpsichord; poems by Alexander Blok (1964); *Crescendo e diminuendo* for harpsichord, 12 strings (1965); *Plachi* [Tears] for soprano, piano, 3 percussionists; Russian folk texts (1966, UE); *5 Geschichten vom Herrn Keuner* for tenor, piccolo, clarinet, E-flat alto saxophone, trumpet, trombone, piano, double bass, percussion; text by Bertolt Brecht (1966); *3 Pieces* for piano 4-hands (1967); *Ode* for clarinet, piano, percussion (1968); *Romanticheskaia muzyka* [Romantic Music] for oboe, harp, string trio (1968, UE); *Osen* [Autumn] for 13 voices; text by V. Khlebnikov (1968); *String Trio* (1969); *Wind Quintet* (1969); *Peinture* for orchestra (1970); *Penie ptits* [Song of the Birds] for harpsichord, tape (1970).

PRINCIPAL WRITINGS: *Strunnie kvartety B. Bartók* [The String Quartets of B. Bartók], *Muzyka i sovremyennost'* 3; *Zametki ob orkestrovke D. Shostakovich* [Notes on Shostakovich's Instrumentation], *Dmitri Shostakovich* (Moscow 1967): 439–99; *Dodekaphonie i problemi sovremennoi kompozitorskoi tekhniki* [Dodecaphony and Technical Problems of Contemporary Composition], *Muzyka i sovremennost'* 4:478–525; *Stabilnie i mobilnie elementy muzykal'noi formi i ikh vzaimodeistie* [Stable and Mobile Elements of Form and Their Interaction], *Problemy muzykalnikh form i zhanrov* (Moscow 1970).

SEE ALSO Notation, Soviet Union.

Denmark, see Scandinavia

Dennis, Brian (Jonathan Charles) (b. Marple, England, 24 May 1941), studied at the Royal College of Music (1961–65, composition with Peter Racine Fricker and John White, singing with Hervey Alan and Mark Raphael) and the Cologne Courses for New Music (1965–66, composition with Karlheinz Stockhausen, Luciano Berio, Henri Pousseur, and Earle Brown). He has taught at the Shoreditch School in London (1966–69), St. Mark and St. John's College, a teacher-training college in Chelsea (1969–71), and London Univ. (since 1971). His music has been influenced by his work with children and older students and by a continuing interest in painting and other contemporary arts.

PRINCIPAL COMPOSITIONS: *Pounding Silk Floss* for 12 percussionists (1966); *Programmes* for 2 pianos, 2 percussionists, tape echo (1968); *Aquarelle*, children's piece for piano, 6 percussionists (1968); *Tetrahedron*, children's piece for organ, percussion (1968); *Abstract* for organ, electronic piano, vibraphone, marimba (1969); *Tune Patterns* for orchestra (1969–70); *Patterns 1, 2, 3*, children's pieces (1969–70); *24 Linked Piano Pieces* (1970); *Estuary* for dancers, chorus, string orchestra, percussion (1971); *Chromatic Chime Machine*, children's piece (1971).

PRINCIPAL WRITINGS: *Experimental Music for Schools* (London 1969).

SEE ALSO Great Britain.

Density, the quantity, closeness, and/or complexity of sounds in a texture. Density is relative and depends, among other factors, on the pitch range and timespan of a texture, as well as on the overtone spectra of component sounds. A very dense texture, for example, could result from only a few sounds provided that they occupy a narrow pitch range (e.g., as in a cluster of minor seconds) or are sounded for only a brief instant, or embody a complex overtone structure (e.g., as with sounds produced by double basses in their lowest register).

Dessau, Paul (b. Hamburg, 19 Dec 1894), studied at the Klindworth-Scharwenka Conservatory in Berlin (1910–12, violin with Florian Zajic) and with Eduard Behm and Max Loewengard (piano and composition). He was a coach at the Hamburg State Theater (1913–14) and conductor at the Cologne Opera (1918–23) and the Städtische Oper in Berlin (1926). He has written much music for theater and films. His work has been influenced by his association with Otto Klemperer, Arthur Nikisch, and Arnold Schoenberg.

PRINCIPAL COMPOSITIONS: *Piano Sonata* (1914); *Lyrisches Intermezzo* for alto, piano (1919, DVM); *Concertino* for flute, clarinet, horn, violin (1925,

Schott); *String Quartets Nos. 1–5* (1932, Peters; 1942–43; 1943–46; 1948; 1955, Breitkopf-L); *Die Thälmann-Kolonne* for voice, piano; text by Karl Ernst (1936; published in *20 Lieder*, Thüringer Volksverlag, and in *Wir singen* 5:74–75, Hofmeister); *Deutsches miserere* for vocal soloists, chorus, children's chorus, orchestra, organ, trautonium; text by Brecht (1944–47); *Die Verurteilung des Lukullus*, opera in 12 scenes; libretto by Brecht (1949, revised 1951, 1960; Henschel, Ars Viva, Peters-L); *Lilo Hermann*, melodrama for sprechstimme, small chorus, flute, clarinet, trumpet, violin, viola, cello (1953, Neue Musik); *Orchestermusik Nos. 1–3*: No. 1 (1955, Peters-L); No. 2, "Meer der Stürme" (1967, Peters-L); No. 3 (1970, Peters-L); *In memorium Bertolt Brecht* for orchestra (1957, Peters-L); *Puntila*, opera in 13 scenes and an epilogue; libretto by Peter Palitzsch and Manfred Wekwerth after Brecht (1957–59, Henschel, Bote); *Jüdische Chronik* for speaker, baritone, chamber chorus, chamber orchestra (1960); *Appell der Arbeiterklasse*, oratorio for alto, tenor, chorus, orchestra; text by various authors (1961); *Requiem für Lumumba* for speaker, soprano, baritone, chorus, chamber ensemble (1963); *Bach-Variationen* for orchestra (1963, Peters-L); *Quattrodrama 1965* for 4 cellos, 2 pianos, 2 percussionists (1965, Bote); *Mozart-Adaptationen* for orchestra (1965, Peters-L); *Lanzelot*, opera in 15 scenes; libretto by Heiner Müller (1969, Henschel). ★ Incidental music to plays by Brecht: *Mutter Courage und ihre Kinder* (1946, Henschel and Thüringer Volksverlag); *Der gute Mensch von Sezuan* (1947, Henschel); *Mann ist Mann* (1951); *Ker kaukasische Kreiderkreis* (1953–54, Henschel); *Coriolan*, Shakespeare's play trans. by Brecht (1964).

BIBL.: F. Hennenberg, *Dessau, Brecht: Musikalische Arbeiten* (East Berlin 1963); ——, *P. D.* (Leipzig 1965).

[prepared with help of Günter Mayer]

Devčić, Natko (b. Glina, Croatia, Yugoslavia, 30 June 1914), attended the Zagreb Academy of Music (1933–39, composition with Franjo Dugan, piano with Antonija Geiger-Eichorn and Svetislav Stančić). He subsequently studied composition with Joseph Marx at the Vienna Academy of Music in 1949–50 and with Jean Rivier at the Paris Conservatory in 1955. In 1953 he attended the Salzburg Seminar in American Studies (contemporary American music with Edward Cone) and in 1965, the Darmstadt summer courses (instrumentation techniques with Pierre Boulez). During 1967–68 he worked with Mario Davidovsky at the Columbia-Princeton Electronic Music Center. Since 1962 he has been head of the composition department at the Zagreb Academy. Devčić's study of Istrian folk music and the writings of Stockhausen

have been especially significant to his development.

PRINCIPAL COMPOSITIONS: *Istrian Suite* for orchestra (1948, SK); *Ballade* for piano, orchestra (1953, UKH); *Labinska vještica* [The Witch of Labin], opera (1957, UKH); *Concertino* for violin, chamber orchestra (1958, Gerig); *Ševa* [The Lark], cantata for female speaker, baritone, chorus, orchestra; text by Skender Kulenović (1960); *Koraci* [Steps], 5 movements for piano (1960, Gerig); *Prologue* for winds, percussion (1965, Gerig); *Microsuite* for piano (1965, Gerig); *Structures transparentes* for harp (1966, Gerig); *Fibula* for 2 orchestras (1967); *Columbia 68* on tape (1968); *Igra riječi* [Play of Words] for 2 speakers, chorus, instrumental ensemble, tape (1969); *Concerto* for chamber ensemble (1969).

PRINCIPAL WRITINGS: "Razmišljanja o suvremenoj glazbi nakon povratka s američkih studija" [Reflections upon Contemporary Music after Returning from American Studies], *Telegram* (Zagreb, 23 August 1968); "O elektronskoj glazbi i oko nje" [About Electronic Music], *ibid.* (30 August 1968); "Od pastirskog instrumenta do suvremenih struktura" [From Shepherd's Instrument to Modern Structures], unpub. lecture given May 1969.

BIBL.: Milo Cipra, "N. D.: Ševa, kantata na riječi Skendera Kulenovića," *Zvuk* 57:198–209.

DeVoto, Mark (Bernard) (b. Cambridge, Mass., 11 Jan 1940), studied at Harvard Univ. (1957–61; composition with Walter Piston, harmony with Daniel Pinkham, counterpoint with Randall Thompson) and Princeton Univ. (1961–64; composition with Roger Sessions, theory with Earl Kim, Milton Babbitt, and Edward T. Cone). He has taught at Reed College in Portland, Ore. (1964–68) and at the Univ. of N. H. (since 1968). He edits the *Newsletter* of the International Alban Berg Society and is also a free-lance writer and a professional electrician.

PRINCIPAL COMPOSITIONS: *Planh* for 6 voices, flute, oboe, clarinet, trombone, harp (1960); *Night Songs and Distant Dances* for orchestra (1962); *3 Edgar Allan Poe Songs* for soprano, concertina, guitar, harpsichord, 8 flutes (1967, revised 1970); *The Distinguished Thing*, concerto No. 3 for piano, 12 instruments (1968); *Fever-Dream Vocalise* for soprano, flute, cello, piano, percussion (1968).

PRINCIPAL WRITINGS: "Some Notes on the Unknown *Altenburg Lieder*," *Perspectives* 5/1: 37–74.

Diamond, David (Leo) (b. Rochester, N. Y., 9 July 1915), began violin lessons at seven and started composing in his early teens. He studied composition with Bernard Rogers at the

Eastman School (1933–34) and attended the New Music School and Dalcroze Institute in New York (1934–35; composition with Roger Sessions, Dalcroze subjects with Paul Boepple). He continued private studies with Sessions during 1936–37. Thanks to a patron, Cary Ross, he traveled to Paris in 1936, where he met André Gide, Albert Roussel, Maurice Ravel, Charles Despiau, and Charles Munch, and where he composed *Psalm* for orchestra, the first work to bring him national attention. He studied there with Nadia Boulanger (1937, 1938). During the 1940s he lived principally in the U.S., did much composing, and received many commissions and awards. During 1953–65 his home was Florence. He returned to the U.S. in 1965 and was chairman of the composition department of the Manhattan School of Music (1965–67). Since 1967 he has lived in Rochester.

Diamond is a contemporary classicist whose symphonies, string quartets, and songs are the central works in a very large and varied output. Clear structures are often based on traditional contrapuntal and sonata-allegro procedures but architectonically proportioned into unusual one or two-movement divisions. Fugues and variations occur frequently. His lyric gift, often intense, somewhat austere and romantically tinged, has evolved with his harmonic idiom from early diatonic-modal features to a more chromatic, nontonal style. A string player himself, his quartets are always idiomatically written for the instruments.

PRINCIPAL COMPOSITIONS (published by Southern unless otherwise noted): *Psalm* for orchestra (1936); *TOM*, ballet; scenario by e. e. cummings (1936); *Concerto for String Quartet* (1936); *Violin Concertos Nos. 1–3* (1936, 1947, 1967); *Cello Sonata* (1936, Presser); *Variations* for small orchestra (1937); *Quintet* for flute, string trio, piano (1937); *Heroic Piece* for small orchestra (1938); *Elegy in Memory of Ravel* for brass, harps, percussion (1938); *Music* for double string orchestra, brass, timpani (1938); *Cello Concerto* (1938); *Quartet* for violin, viola, cello, piano (1938); *Symphonies Nos. 1–8* (1940; 1942; 1945; 1945, Schirmer-G; 1964; 1951, Harms; 1959; 1960); *Concerto for Small Orchestra* (1940); *String Quartets Nos. 1–10* (1940, 1943, 1946, 1951, 1960, 1962, 1963, 1964, 1966, 1966); *The Dream of Audubon*, ballet; scenario by Glenway Wescott (1941); *Concerto* for 2 solo pianos (1942); *Music for Shakespeare's The Tempest* (1944, Chappell); *Rounds* for string orchestra (1944, E-V); *Violin Sonata* (1946, Schirmer-G); *Music for Shakespeare's Romeo and Juliet* (1947, Boosey); *Piano Sonata* (1947); *Chaconne* for violin, piano (1948); *L'Ame de Debussy*, cycle for voice, piano; text by Debussy (1949); *Piano Concerto* (1950); *Chorale* for chorus; text by James Agee (1950);

Quintet for 2 violas, 2 cellos, clarinet (1950); *Mizmor L'David*, sacred service for tenor, chorus, orchestra or organ (1951, Mills); *The Midnight Meditation*, cycle for voice, piano; text by Elder Olson (1951); *Piano Trio* (1951); *Sinfonia concertante* (1954); *Sonata* for solo violin (1954); *Sonata* for solo cello (1956); *The World of Paul Klee* for orchestra (1957); *Woodwind Quintet* (1958); *Nonet* for 3 violins, 3 violas, 3 cellos (1961); *This Sacred Ground* for baritone, chorus, children's chorus, orchestra (1962); *We Two*, cycle for voice, piano; text by Shakespeare (1964); *Choral Symphony: To Music* for tenor, bass-baritone, chorus, orchestra (1967); *Hebrew Melodies*, cycle for voice, piano; text by Byron (1967); *Music for Chamber Orchestra* (1969). List to 1968: *Composers of the Americas* 13:29–48.

PRINCIPAL WRITINGS: "From the Notebook of D. D.," *Music Journal* (April 1964):24–25, 57–59.

BIBL.: Richard D. Freed, "Music is D.'s Best Friend," *New York Times* (22 August 1965), section X:11; Madeleine Goss, *Modern Music Makers* (New York 1952):448–60. Reviews of individual works appeared in *Modern Music*, 1936–49.

Francis Thorne

SEE ALSO Dance.

Dianda, Hilda (b. Cordoba, Argentina, 13 April 1925), studied composition with Honorio Siccardi in Buenos Aires (1942–48) and G. F. Malipiero in Venice (1949–50) and conducting with Hermann Scherchen in Venice (1949–50). In 1959 she worked with the Groupe de Recherches Musicales at the French Radio in Paris and at the R.A.I. Electronic Music Studio in Milan. She attended the Darmstadt summer courses in 1960 and 1961. Since 1967 she has taught composition and orchestration at the Univ. of Cordoba, where she also directs the chamber orchestra.

PRINCIPAL COMPOSITIONS: *String Quartets Nos. 1, 3* (1947; 1962–63, ECA); *Canciones de amor desesperado* for alto, flute, viola, cello; texts by Silvina Ocampo (1950); *La Flauta de jade* for voice, piano; Chinese text in French translation (1951); *Música para arcos* for string orchestra (1952); *Concertante* for cello, winds, double bass, percussion (1952); *Concerto* for violin, string quintet (1954); *Estructuras Nos. 1–3* for cello, piano (1960, PAU); *Diedros* for flute (1962, EAMI); *Canciones* for soprano, guitar, vibraphone, 3 percussionists; poems by Rafael Alberti (1962); *Percusión 11* for 11 percussionists (1962, EAMI); *Núcleos* for strings, 2 pianos, 10 percussionists (1963, EAMI); *Resonancias 1* for 5 horns (1964); *Resonancias 2* for piano (1964); *Resonancias 4* for clarinet, trumpet, cello, 2 percussionists (1964); *Resonancias 3* for cello, orchestra (1965, Schott); *a 7* for cello, 5 tapes (1966); *Resonancias 5* for 2 choruses (1967–68); *Ludus 1* for orchestra (1968, Schott); *Ludus 2* for 11 instruments (1969); *Ludus 3* for organ (1969); *Divertimento a 3* for 3 percussionists (1969–70, Schott); *Impromptu* for string orchestra (1970, Schott). List to 1963: *Composers of the Americas* 9:53–56. PRINCIPAL WRITINGS: *Música en la Argentina de hoy* (Buenos Aires 1966). BIBL.: *Composers of the Americas* 9:51–56.

Dimov, Bojidar (b. Lom, Bulgaria, 31 Jan 1935), studied at the State Conservatory in Sofia (1956–58, composition with Wesselin Stojanov) and at the Music Academy in Vienna (1958–64, composition with Karl Schiske, conducting with Friedrich Cerha). He also attended the Darmstadt summer courses (1961, 1966, 1967; Stockhausen and others) and the Cologne Courses for New Music (1969, Mauricio Kagel). Since 1970 he has taught theory and new music in Cologne at the Rheinischen Musikschule and at the Pädagogischen Hochschule and has conducted "trial and error," a new-music ensemble which he founded.

PRINCIPAL COMPOSITIONS: *Compositions Nos. 1–3:* No. 1 for piano (1963, EM); No. 2 for string sextet (1964, UE); No. 3 for wind quintet (1967–68, EM); *Incantations Nos. 1–3* for soprano, chamber ensemble (1963, 1967, 1971; EM); *Continuum 2,* "Trauerminuten für Dana Košanovà," for chamber orchestra (1968–69, Gerig); *Raumspiel* for piano, chamber ensemble, conductor (1969–70, Gerig); *Invocation,* "Kunst-Wettspiel" in 7 circles for 2 soloists or 2 improvisation ensembles, public (1970–71); *Symphonies,* "To the memory of Igor Stravinsky," for high voice, chamber orchestra (1971); *Dual* for oboe (English horn), clarinet (bass clarinet), horn, piano, guitar (electric guitar), violin, cello, conductor (1971).

PRINCIPAL WRITINGS: "Webern und die Tradition," *Österreichische Musikzeitschrift* (1965); "10 Jahre im Schatten der Wiener Staatsoper," *Nutida musik* (1968–69); "Praktische Fernseharbeit in Köln," *Melos* (July 1970).

Distler, Hugo (August) (b. Nuremberg, 24 June 1908; d. Berlin, 1 Nov 1942), studied at the Dupont Private Music School in Nuremberg as a child and at the Landeskonservatorium in Leipzig (1927–31; composition, theory with Hermann Grabner; organ with Günther Ramin; piano with C. A. Martienssen). He was organist at St. Jacob's Church in Lübeck during 1931–37 and taught composition, organ, and choral conducting at the Hochschulen für Musik in Stuttgart (1937–40) and Berlin (1940–42); he also directed the Berlin State and Cathedral Choirs. Distler

gave many concerts as organist, harpsichordist, and choir director. His church music was influenced by his association with Karl Staube, Cantor of St. Thomas's in Lübeck, and by the Lübeck church music tradition (Schütz, Buxtehude, Bach) and its two famous organs, built in 1557 and 1636.

PRINCIPAL COMPOSITIONS (published by Bärenreiter unless otherwise noted): *German Choral Mass,* Op. 3 (1931, Breitkopf); *Der Jahrkreis,* 52 short motets, Op. 5 (1932); *Choralpassion* for 2 soloists, chorus, Op. 7 (1932); *Organ Partitas,* Op. 8, "Nun komm der Heiden Heiland" (1933) and "Wachet auf, ruft uns die Stimme" (1935); *The Christmas Story* for 4 soloists, chamber chorus, Op. 10 (1933); *Geistliche Chormusik,* 9 motets, Op. 12 (1934–41); *Concerto* for harpsichord, string orchestra, Op. 14 (1935); *Neues Chorliederbuch* for chorus, Op. 16 (1937); *Mörike-Chorliederbuch,* 48 choral settings, Op. 19 (1939); *String Quartet in A Minor,* Op. 20 (1939–40).

PRINCIPAL WRITINGS: "Die Orgel unserer Zeit," *Musica* 1:147–53; "Vom Geiste der neuen evangelischen Kirchenmusik," *Zeitschrift für Musik* 102:1325–29; *Die beiden Orgeln in St. Jakobi in Lübeck nach dem Umbau 1935* (Lübeck 1935); "Gedanken zum Problem der Registrierung alter, speziell Bachscher Orgelmusik," *Musik und Kirche* 20:101–06; "Über seine *Spielstücke für Positiv,*" *Neues Musikblatt* (June 1939):3–4 and *Hausmusik* 16/6:159–61; *Funtionelle Harmonielehre* (Cassel 1940); "J. S. Bach's *Dorische Toccata und Fuge,*" *Musik und Kirche* 12:49–57.

BIBL.: W. Bieske, "Die Orgelwerke H. D.s," *Musik und Kirche* 22:177–81; W. Blankenburg, "Neue Kultmusik; zum Erscheinen der liturgischen Sätze von H. D. über altevangelische Kyrie- und Gloriaweisen," *ibid.* (1936):247–53; H. Bornefeld, "H. D.," *Musica* 1:142–47; G. Grusnick, "H. D.s *Choralpassion,*" *Musik und Kirche* 5:39–43; ———, "Wie H. D. Jakobiorganist in Lübeck wurde," *Musik und Kirche* 28:97–107; W. Oehlmann, "Das Chorwerk H. D.s," *Die Musikpflege* (1943): 5–12; L. Palmer, *H. D. and His Church Music* (St. Louis, 1967); U. von Rauchhaupt, *Die vokale Kirchenmusik H. D.s* (Gütersloh 1963); H. Schmozi, "Die Wort-Ton-Verhältnisse in D.s *Choralpassion,*" *Musica* 7:556–61.

[prepared with the help of Waltraut Distler]

SEE ALSO Austria and Germany; Liturgical Music: Christian.

Dixieland, see Jazz

Dlugoszewski, Lucia (b. Detroit, 16 June 1931), studied physics and mathematics at Wayne State Univ. (1946–49) and piano at the Detroit Conservatory (1940) and the Mannes

School of Music (1950–51). She also studied piano privately in New York with Grete Sultan (1950–53) and composition with Edgard Varèse (from 1951). Since 1960 she has taught intermittently at New York Univ. and the New School for Social Research. Her principal work is with the Foundation for Modern Dance, sponsor of the Erick Hawkins Dance Co., for which she has been a teacher and composer since 1960. In her compositions, many of them written for the dance, she works with sound textures for their own sake and for their potential in expanding self-awareness. She has developed over 100 pitched and unpitched percussion instruments made of glass, plastic, wood, paper, and metal, on which she herself performs. The most elaborate of these is the timbre piano (invented 1951), which, in addition to a keyboard, uses bows and plectra made of a variety of materials. In 1958 she began to put together an orchestra of 100 percussion instruments made of glass, wood, paper, metal, skin, and plastic. The initial impetus was to provide a vocabulary of sounds with no preset emotional associations. Her ideas have been influenced by Oriental philosophies and by the work of F. S. C. Northrop.

PRINCIPAL COMPOSITIONS: *Piano Sonatas 1–3* (1949, 1950, 1950); *Moving Space Theater Piece for Everyday Sounds* (1949); *Melodic Sonata* for piano (1950); *Sonata* for solo flute (1950); *Transparencies for Everyday Sounds 1–50* (1951); *Everyday Sounds for e. e. cummings* (1951); *Orchestra Structure for the Poetry of Everyday Sounds* (1952); *4 Transparencies*: No. 1 for harp, No. 2 for flute, No. 3 for harp and violin, No. 4 for string quartet (1952); *Desire* for voice, timbre piano, "theater structure" for the Living Theater's production of the play by Picasso (1952); *Ubu Roi*, theater structure for the Living Theater for orchestra of everyday sounds (1952); *Variations on Noguchi*, opera of everyday sounds and voices for the film by Menken-Maas (1953); *Tiny Opera* for 4 poets, moving voice, dancers, piano (1953); *Moving Theater Piece* for many players (1953); *Silent Paper Spring and Summer Friend Songs* (1953–70); *Archaic Timbre Piano Music* (1953–56); *Arithmetic Points* for orchestra (1955); *Instants in Form and Movement* for timbre piano, chamber orchestra (1957); *Music for Small Centers* for piano (1958); *Music for Left Ear* for piano (1958); *Suchness Concert* for invented percussion orchestra (1958–60); *Flower Music* for string quartet (1959); *Music for Left Ear in a Small Room* for piano (1959); *Rates of Speed in Space* for ladder harp quintet (1959); *Delicate Accidents in Space* for unsheltered rattle quintet (1959); *Concert of Man Rooms and Moving Space* for flute, clarinet, timbre piano, 4 unsheltered rattles in various locations (1960); *Women of Trachis*, structure for Ezra Pound's translation of the play by Sophocles

for flute, moving clarinet, timbre piano, separated unsheltered rattles (1960); *Guns of the Trees* for chamber ensemble; score for the film by Jonas Mekas (1961); *Archaic Aggregates* for timbre piano, ladder harps, tangent rattles, unsheltered rattles, gongs (1961); *White Interval Music* for timbre piano (1961); *4 Attention Spans* for orchestra (1964); *Orchestral Radiant Ground* (1964); *Quick Dichotomies* for 2 trumpets, clarinet, invented percussion (1965); *Swift Music* for 2 timbre pianos (1965); *Music for Left Ear in a Small Room* for clarinet (1965); *Suchness with Radiant Ground* for clarinet, percussion duo (1965); *Percussion Flowers* (1965); *Percussion Kitetails* (1965); *Percussion Airplane Hetero* (1965); *Beauty Music* for clarinet, timbre piano, percussion (1965); *Music for Left Ear in a Small Room* for violin (1965); *Beauty Music II* for chamber orchestra, invented percussion (1965); *Beauty Music III* for chamber orchestra, timbre piano (1965); *Hanging Bridges* for string quartet (1967); *The Heidi Songs*, opera; libretto by John Ashbery (1967–70); *Leap and Fall, Quick Structures* for 2 trumpets, clarinet, 2 violins, percussion (1968); *Hanging Bridges* for orchestra (1968); *Naked Swift Music* for violin, timbre piano, invented percussion orchestra (1968); *Kitetail Beauty Music* for violin, timbre piano, invented percussion (1968); *Skylark Concert*, an evening of music for chamber orchestra (1969–70); *Theatre Flight Nageire* for sound and movement of a clarinet, timbre piano, invented percussion orchestra (1969–70); *Naked Quintet* for brass quintet (1970); *Space Is a Diamond* for trumpet (1970); *Velocity Shells* for timbre piano, trumpet, invented percussion (1970); *Swift Diamond* for timbre piano, trumpet, invented percussion (1970); *Sabi Music* for violin (1970); *Pure Flight* for string quartet (1970); *John Ashbery Poetry* for narrator, chamber orchestra, movement (1970); *Parker Tyler Language* for voice, chamber orchestra, movement (1970); *A Zen in Ryoko-In*, score for the film by Ruth Stephan for invented percussion orchestra (1971).

PRINCIPAL DANCE SCORES (for Erick Hawkins): *Openings of the Eye* for flute, percussion, timbre piano (1952); *Here and Now with Watchers* for timbre piano (1954–57); *8 Clear Places* for 100-piece invented percussion orchestra (1958–61); *To Everyone Out There* for orchestra (1964); *Geography of Noon* for invented percussion orchestra (1964); *Cantilever II* for piano, orchestra (1964); *Lords of Persia* for 2 trumpets, clarinet, invented percussion orchestra (1965); *Dazzle on a Knife's Edge* for timbre piano, orchestra (1966); *Tight Rope* for chamber orchestra (1968); *Lords of Persia II* for chamber orhcestra (1968); *Agathlon Algebra* for orchestra, timbre piano (1968); *Black Lake* for orchestra, timbre piano, invented percussion orchestra (1969); *Lords of Persia III* for chamber orchestra (1971); *Of Love . . . or he is a cry, she is his ear* for brass quintet, invented percussion orchestra (1971).

PRINCIPAL WRITINGS: "Notes on New Music for the Dance," *Dance Observer* (Nov 1957); "American Poems and Drawings," *A New Folder*

(1959); "And What Is the Avant-Garde?" *Dance Observer* (Nov 1960); "2 New York Composers," *Wagner Literary Magazine* (1961); "Music Sound," *Jubilee* (Feb 1962); "Composer Choreographer," *Dance Perspectives* (1963).

BIBL.: John Gruen, "L. D. Surfacing," *Vogue* (1 Oct 1970); Allen Hughes, "And Miss D. Experiments—A Lot," *New York Times Magazine* (7 March 1971).

[prepared with the help of Mary Jane Ingram]
SEE ALSO Dance.

Dockstader, Tod (b. St. Paul, 20 March 1932), studied art and general subjects at the Univ. of Minn. and began making films there. He produces tape music in his home studio in Westport, Conn., while earning a living as a film writer and editor, cartoonist, photographer, recording engineer, and industrial designer. Varèse's *Poème*, along with his attitude toward music as sound, have been influential on Dockstader's thinking.

PRINCIPAL COMPOSITIONS (on tape): *8 Electronic Pieces* (1959–60, recorded on Folkways FM3434); *Traveling Music* (1960, recorded on Owl ORLP-6); *Luna Park* (1961, recorded on Owl ORLP-6); *Apocalypse* (1961, recorded on Owl ORLP-6 and 7); *Drone* (1962, Owl ORLP-7); *Water Music* (1963, Owl ORLP-7); *Quatermass* (1964, Owl ORLP-8); *2 Moons of Quatermass* (1964); *Telemetry Tapes* (1965); *Omniphony I*; prepared in collaboration with James Reichert (1966–67, Owl ORLP-11); .*Counter.* (1969); *Whitewater* (begun 1970).

PRINCIPAL WRITINGS: "Inside Out: Electronic Rock," *Electronic Music Review* (Jan 1968); "Source," *Musical Quarterly* (Oct 1968):549–53.

Dodecaphony, see Serialism, 12-Tone Techniques

Dodge, Charles (b. Ames, Iowa, 5 June 1942), studied at the Univ. of Iowa (1960–64, composition and theory with Richard Hervig), Columbia Univ. (1964–70; composition with Jack Beeson, Chou Wen-chung, and Otto Luening; electronic music with Vladimir Ussachevsky), Princeton Univ. (1966–67, computer music programming with Godfrey Winham), and Tanglewood (1964, composition with Gunther Schuller and Arthur Berger). He has taught at Columbia Univ. (1967–69, 1970–71), and at Princeton Univ. (1969–70). Among other administrative posts, he has been an executive of the American Composers Alliance since 1967 and its president since 1971.

PRINCIPAL COMPOSITIONS (published by ACA): *Folia* for flute, bass clarinet, English horn, tuba, violin, viola, piano, 2 percussionists (1965); *Rota* for orchestra (1966); *Changes*, computer synthesized sounds on tape (1967–70, recorded by Nonesuch Records); *Earth's Magnetic Field*, a realization in electronic sound on tape of an index of the sun's radiation on the magnetic field of the earth (1970, Nonesuch Records); *Humming*, computer synthesized vocal and electronic sounds on tape (1971).

Döhl, Friedhelm (b. Göttingen, Germany, 7 July 1936), studied at the Musikhochschule in Freiburg (1956–64; composition with Wolfgang Fortner, piano with Carl Seemann), at the Univ. of Freiburg (1956–62), and at the Univ. of Göttingen (1962–64). He has taught composition and theory at the Robert Schumann Conservatory in Düsseldorf (1965–67) and at the Free Univ. of Berlin (since 1969).

PRINCIPAL COMPOSITIONS: *Piano Sonatas Nos. 1–4:* No. 1, "Rondos" (1959); No. 2, "Szenen" (1960); No. 3, "Spiegelungen" (1961); No. 4, "Passages" (1962, Gerig); *Oktett 1961*, "Varianti" (1961); *Canto W* for flute (1962); *Klangfiguren* for wind quintet (1962, Gerig); *Improvisation I* for organ (1962); *Kartenspiele* for 2 violins (1962); *Ovulapis*, reflexes for flute, piano (1962, Bosse); *Albumblätter* for 1–10 flutes (1963); *Sybille*, fragment after Hölderlin for baritone, flute, viola, cello, piano (1963); *7 Haiku* for soprano, flute, piano (1963, Gerig); *Tich Yuang Tuc*, epitaph for soprano, clarinet, wind quartet, piano, percussion (1963, Gerig); *Sternverdunkelung*, cantata for 2 choruses, baritone, organ, chamber ensemble (1963); *Julianische Minuten* for flute, piano (1963, Bosse); *Toccata* for flute, trumpet, harpsichord, piano (1964, Gerig); *Tappeto*, impressions after the poetry of Giuseppe Ungaretti for cello, harp (1967, Gerig); *Melancholia*, "Magische Quadrate" for soprano, chorus, orchestra (1968, Gerig); *Pas de Deux* for violin, guitar (1969, Gerig); . . . *wenn aber . . .*, 9 fragments for baritone, piano (1969, Gerig).

PRINCIPAL WRITINGS: "Wege der neuen Musik," *Neue Zeitschrift für Musik* 126:105–08; "Sinn und Unsinn musikalischer Form," *Terminologie der Neuen Musik* (Berlin 1965):58–69; *Weberns Beitrag zur Stilwende der neuen Musik* (PhD diss., Univ. of Göttingen, 1966).

Donatoni, Franco (b. Verona, 9 June 1927), studied harmony privately with Piero Bottagisio (1944–45) and attended the Verdi Conservatory in Milan (1946–48), the G. B. Martini Conservatory in Bologna (1948–51, composition with Lino Liviabella and Ettore

Desderi), and the Accadèmia di S. Cecilia in Rome (1952–54, composition with Ildebrando Pizzetti). He also attended the Darmstadt summer courses in 1954, 1958, and 1961. He has taught harmony, counterpoint, and composition at the G. B. Martini Conservatory (1954–55), the Verdi Conservatory in Milan (1955–67 and since 1969), the Verdi Conservatory in Turin (1968–69), and the Accadèmia Musicale Chigiana, Siena (since 1970). The influences on his work have included Goffredo Petrassi (until 1951), Béla Bartók (until 1954), Schoenberg and Webern (until 1956), Pierre Boulez (until 1957), Karlheinz Stockhausen (until 1961), John Cage (until 1964), Gustav Mahler (until 1970).

PRINCIPAL COMPOSITIONS (published by S-Z unless otherwise noted): *String Quartet* (1950, Zanibon); *Concertino* for strings, brass, percussion (1952, Schott); *Sinfonia* for strings (1953, Boosey); *Divertimento* for violin, orchestra (1953–54, Schott); *5 Pieces* for 2 pianos (1954, Zanibon); *Composition in 4 Movements* for piano (1955, Schott); *3 Improvisations* for piano (1957, Schott); *String Quartet No. 2* (1958); *Serenata* for soprano, chamber orchestra; poem by Dylan Thomas (1958–59); *For Grilly*, improvisations for flute, clarinet, bass clarinet, violin, viola, cello, percussion (1960); *Sezioni*, improvisations for orchestra (1960); *Doubles*, esercizi for harpsichord (1961); *Puppenspiel* for orchestra (1961); *Per orchestra* (1962); *String Quartet No. 4*, "Zrcadlo" (1963); *Puppenspiel No. 2* for flute, piccolo, orchestra (1965); *Etwas ruhiger im Ausdruck* for flute, clarinet, violin, cello, piano (1967); *Souvenir*, chamber symphony, Op. 18, for 15 instruments (1967); *Solo* for 10 strings (1969); *Doubles II* for orchestra (1969–70); *Secondo estratto* for piano, harp, harpsichord (1970).

PRINCIPAL WRITINGS: "Teatro musicale oggi," *Il verri* (Milan) 16; "Penteo, o dell'apparenza," *ibid.* 30; *Questo* (Milan 1970).

BIBL.: Mario Bortolotto, *Fase seconda; studi sulla nuova musica* (Turin 1969); Antonino Titone, "F.D.," *Collage* (Palermo) 8.

SEE ALSO Italy.

Donner, Henrik Otto (b. Tampere, Finland, 16 Nov 1939), studied at the Sibelius Academy in Helsinki (1959–63, composition with Nils-Erik Fougstedt and Joonas Kokkonen) and at the Stichting Gaudeamus in Bilthoven (1963, electronic composition with Gottfried Michael Koenig). He attended the Darmstadt summer courses (1962–64) and studied composition privately in Vienna with György Ligeti (1963). During 1968–69 he was music director and conductor for the theater department of the Finnish Radio, and in 1969 he became director of an experimental music group there. He has been conductor of the male chorus Akademiska Sångföreningen since 1969. He is also active as a jazz musician. His music has been influenced by his work with Ken Dewey and Terry Riley in the field of theater and happenings and by his work with the Lilla Teatern in Helsinki.

PRINCIPAL COMPOSITIONS: *Cantata profana* for soprano, tenor, baritone, chamber ensemble (1962); *Ideogramme 2* for chamber orchestra, tape (1963); *For Emmy 2* for chamber orchestra (1963); *Moonspring, or Aufforderung zum . . . , or Symphony No. 1* for string orchestra, organ (1964); *To Whom It May Concern* for orchestra, jazz drums (1966); *Heracle*, incidental music for a TV production of Euripedes's play (1966); *The Cyclops*, TV score for Euripedes's play (1967); *XL* for soprano, chamber orchestra; text by Ezra Pound (1969). Donner has also composed numerous film scores.

BIBL.: Einari Marvia, *Suomen säveltäjiä*, vol. 2 (Porvoo 1966); Timo Mäkinen and Seppo Nummi, *Musica fennica* (Helsinki 1965):107–08; Erkki Salmenhaara, *Vuosisatamme musiikki* [The Music of Our Century] (Helsinki 1968):22off.; Bo Wallner, *Vår tids musik i Norden* (Stockholm 1968), English trans. (London 1971).

Donovan, Richard (Frank) (b. New Haven, 29 Nov 1891; d. New Haven, 22 Aug 1970), attended the Yale School of Music (1912–14, 1922) and the Institute of Musical Art in New York (1914–18). He also studied organ with Charles Widor in Paris. He was music director of the Taft School in Watertown, Conn. (1920–23) and taught at Smith College (1923–28). He then taught at the Institute for Musical Art (1925–28) and Finch College (1926–40) in New York City, where he was also active as a choral conductor and church organist. In 1928 he began teaching at Yale and was professor of theory from 1947 to 1960. In New Haven he was organist and choirmaster at Christ Church from 1928 to 1965, conducted the Bach Cantata Club during 1933–44, and was associate conductor of the New Haven Symphony during 1936–51. Donovan was a member of the executive board of New Music publishers and of the board of the American Composers Alliance, for the latter of which he served as president during 1961–62.

PRINCIPAL COMPOSITIONS (published by ACA unless otherwise noted): *How Far Is It to Bethlehem?* for women's chorus, organ (1927, Kalmus); *Chanson of the Bells of Oseney* for women's chorus, piano (1930, Galaxy); *Suite No. 1* for piano (1932, New Music); *Sextet* for flute, oboe, clarinet, bassoon, horn, piano (1932); *4 Songs* for soprano, string quartet (1933); *Piano Trio* in one movement (1937, Arrow); *Ricercare* for oboe, string orchestra (1938, Boosey); *Serenade* for oboe, violin, viola, cello (1939, New Music); *Fantasy on American Folk Ballads* for male chorus, piano 4-hands or orchestra (1940, Fischer-J); *Suite* for oboe, string orchestra (1944–45); *Hymn to the Night* for women's chorus (1947, Fischer-J); *2 Choral Preludes on American Folk Hymns* for organ (1947, Mercury); *Good Ale* for male chorus, piano (1947, Fischer); *How Should I Love?* for women's chorus, piano (1947, Mercury); *Passacaglia on Vermont Folk Tunes* for orchestra (1949); *4 Songs on English Texts* for medium voice, piano (1950, New Valley); *Terzetto* for 2 violins, viola (1950, New Valley); *Suite No. 2* for piano (1953); *Woodwind Quartet* (1953); *4 Songs to Nature* for women's chorus, piano (1953, AMP); *Mass* for unison voices (or optional 2 and 3 parts), organ, 3 trumpets, timpani (1955); *Antiphon and Chorale* for organ (1955); *Adventure* for piano (1956); *5 Elizabethan Lyrics* for high voice, string quartet (1957); *Music for 6* for oboe, clarinet, trumpet, piano, violin, cello (1961, Peters); *Magnificat* for male chorus, organ (1961, A-R). List to 1965: *Composers of the Americas* 15:92–95.

BIBL.: Alfred Frankenstein, "R.D.," *ACA Bulletin* 1956/4.

[prepared with the help of Grace R. Donovan]

Dragatakis, Dimitris (b. Platanousa, Epirus, Greece, 22 Jan 1914), attended Athens Conservatory (1932–46; violin with G. Psillas, harmony with Leonidas Zoras, counterpoint and fugue with M. Kalomiris). He taught violin at the conservatory during 1940–51 and was violinist in the orchestra of the Athens National Opera from 1944 to 1969. Dragatakis's earlier music was oriented toward the Greek "national school." Since 1958 his compositions have been influenced first by neoclassicism and then by the 12-tone Viennese school.

PRINCIPAL COMPOSITIONS: *Essay* for orchestra (1954); *String Quartets Nos. 1–4* (1957, 1958, 1960, 1967); *Lyric Sketches* for string orchestra (1958); *Violin Sonatas Nos. 1–2* (1958, 1961); *Symphonies Nos. 1–4* (1959, 1960, 1964, 1966); *Trio* for 2 violins, viola (1960); *Suite* for double string quartet (1961); *Sonatinas Nos. 1–2* for piano (1961, 1963); *Songs* on poems of F. Agoules and V. Theodorou (1961, Enosis); *Trio* for oboe, clarinet, bassoon (1962); *Chamber Concerto* for clarinet, strings (1962); *Trio* for horn, trumpet, trombone (1963); *Dedication*, variations on a theme of M. Kalomiris for flute, oboe, clarinet, trumpet, 2 violins, cello, piano (1963); *Ballet Suite No. 1* (1963); *Woodwind Quintet* (1964); *Ulysses and Nausicaä*, ballet suite No. 2 for 11 instruments (1964); *Ballet Suite No. 3* for 12 instruments (1964); *Concertino* for horn, chamber orchestra (1965); *Differences* for violin, flute, oboe, clarinet, horn, cello, percussion (1965); *String Trio* (1965); *4 Sketches* for 3 string groups (1966, 1967, 1967, 1968); *Reference to Electra* for soprano, viola, horn, piano (1969); *Ballet Suite*

No. 4 for flute, oboe, horn, santuri, percussion, piano, sung and spoken vocal effects (1969).

SEE ALSO Greece.

Driessler, Johannes (b. Friedrichsthal/Saarbrücken, Germany, 26 Jan 1921), attended the Saarbrücken Conservatory (1930–39; piano with Ferdinand Krome; organ, choral conducting, counterpoint with Karl Rahner; theory with Fritz Neumeyer), the Cologne Musikhochschule (1939–40; organ with Michael Schneider, piano with Hans Haass, composition with Wilhelm Maler), and the Univ. of Cologne (1939–40; musicology with Ernst Bücken and K. G. Fellerer). He taught at the Landerziehungsheim Schondorf in Ammersee, Bavaria (1945–46) and since then has been professor at the Nordwestdeutsche Musikakademie in Detmold.

PRINCIPAL COMPOSITIONS (published by Bärenreiter unless otherwise noted): *Christe eleison*, Passion motet, Op. 9 (1948); *Dein Reich komme*, oratorio, Op. 11 (1948–49); *De profundis*, oratorio for soloists, chamber chorus, large chorus, winds, piano, timpani, Op. 22 (1950–52); *Gaudia mundana*, oratorio, Op. 19 (1951); *Piano Concerto*, Op. 27 (1953); *20 Orgelsonaten durch das Kirchenjahr*, Op. 30 (1954–55); *Altenberg Mass* for 7-voice chorus, 10 winds, Op. 33 (1954); *Cello Concerto*, Op. 35 (1954); *Der grosse Lobgesang* for soprano, chorus, winds, Op. 45 (1958–59); *Ikarus*, choral symphony for vocal soloists, chorus, orchestra, Op. 48 (1959–60, Breitkopf); *Concerto* for string trio, orchestra, Op. 54 (1963, Breitkopf); *Dum spiro spero*, "Symphony No. 1," Op. 55 (1964, Breitkopf); *Dum ludo laudo*, "Symphony No. 2," Op. 60 (1966, Breitkopf); *Amo dum vivo*, "Symphony No. 3," Op. 63 (1969, Breitkopf).

SEE ALSO Liturgical Music: Christian.

Druckman, Jacob (b. Philadelphia, 6 June 1928), studied at the Juilliard School (1949–54, 1955–56; composition with Bernard Wagenaar, Vincent Persichetti, Peter Mennin), the Ecole Normale de Musique in Paris (1954–55, composition with Tony Aubin), Tanglewood (1949, 1950; composition with Aaron Copland), and at the Columbia-Princeton Electronic Music Center (1965–66). He taught part-time at Bard College in New York State during 1961–67. Since 1957 he has taught "literature and materials of music" at Juilliard and since 1967 has been an associate of the Columbia-Princeton Electronic Music Center.

PRINCIPAL COMPOSITIONS: *Dark upon the Harp* for mezzo-soprano, brass quintet, percussion (1962); *The Sound of Time* for soprano, orchestra; texts by Norman Mailer (1965); *Animus I* for trombone, tape (1966); *String Quartet No. 2* (1966, MCA); *Incenters* for 13 players (1968, MCA); *Animus II* for mezzo-soprano, 2 percussionists, tape (1969, MCA); *Animus III* for clarinet, tape (1969, MCA).

PRINCIPAL WRITINGS: "Stravinsky's Orchestral Style," *Juilliard Review* (spring 1957):10–19.

Dujarric, Enrique de Marchena-Dujarric, see under De Marchena

Duke, Vernon, see Dukelsky, Vladimir

Dukelsky, Vladimir (Alexandrovitch), also known as Vernon Duke (b. Parafianovo, Russia, 10 Oct 1903; d. Santa Monica, Calif., 16 Jan 1969), studied at Kiev Conservatory (1915–18, composition with Reinhold Glière). He left Russia in 1920 and lived for brief periods in Turkey, the U.S., and France. During 1923–28 he was commissioned by Diaghilev to write several ballets. He emigrated permanently to the U.S. in 1929. At the suggestion of George Gershwin, he chose a pen name for his popular stage works. He also composed film scores for MGM and Warner Bros.

PRINCIPAL COMPOSITIONS: *Zephyr and Flore*, ballet (1925, ERM); *Piano Concerto in C* (1926, Heugel); *Symphonies Nos. 1–3* (1927, ERM; 1928, revised 1968; 1950, Fischer); *Mistress into Maid*, opera (1928, revised 1958); *Epitaph*, cantata for soprano, chorus, orchestra (1931, revised 1962); *Ballade* for piano, orchestra (1931–43, Fischer); *Walk a Little Faster*, musical (1932); *Jardin Public*, ballet (1934); *Ziegfield Follies*, musicals (1934–35); *Dédicaces* for piano, soprano obbligato, orchestra (1937, revised 1965); *The End of St. Petersburg*, oratorio for soprano, tenor, baritone, chorus, orchestra (1938); *Cabin in the Sky*, musical (1940); *Banjo Eyes*, musical (1941); *Violin Concerto* (1942, Fischer); *Cello Concerto* (1942, Fischer); *The Lady Comes Across*, musical (1942); *Jackpot*, musical (1942); *Tars and Spars*, musical (1944); *La Bal des Blanchisseuses*, ballet (1947, Fischer); *Violin Sonata* (1949, Ricordi); *Two's Company*, musical (1952); *Ode to the Milky Way* for woodwinds, horns, timpani (1954, Ricordi); *String Quartet in C* (1955, Ricordi); *Littlest Revue*, musical (1955); *Variations on an Old Russian Chant* for oboe, strings (1955); *Sonata* for harpsichord or piano (1955, Broude-B); *Emperor Norton*, ballet (1957); *Time Remembered*, musical (1957); *In American*, 10 songs (1967).

PRINCIPAL WRITINGS: *Passport to Paris* (Boston 1955); *Listen Here!* (New York 1963).

[prepared with the help of Kay McCracken Duke]

SEE ALSO Musical.

Duprat, Rogério (Ronchi) (b. Guanabara, near Rio de Janeiro, Brazil, 7 Feb 1932), studied philosophy at the Univ. of São Paulo (1950–54) and music at the Conservatório Heitor Villa-Lobos in São Paulo (1952–60; composition, harmony with G. Olivier Toni; Claudio Santoro; cello with Varoli) and at the Darmstadt summer courses (1962; classes with Stockhausen, Boulez, Ligeti, Pousseur). During 1953–63 he was a cellist in the São Paulo Municipal Orchestra. In 1956 he founded the São Paulo Chamber Orchestra, which he conducted until 1962. Since then he has composed for films, taught at the Univ. of Brazil (1964–65), and conducted and arranged music for records and television.

PRINCIPAL COMPOSITIONS: *String Quartet* (1958); *Concertino* for oboe, horn, strings (1958); *Lírica* for viola, clarinet, strings (1959); *Variations* for 7 winds, 5 strings, percussion (1959); *Organismo*, on a poem by Decio Pignatari, for 5 woodwinds, string quartet, celesta, vibraphone, percussion (1961); *Mbáepu* for bassoon, trombone, violin, mandolin, xylophone (1961); *Antinomies I* for orchestra (1962, PAU); *Experimental Music* on tape using the IBM 1620 computer (1963); *Proseta unbica* for ambulant orchestra (1964, UE); *Ludus mardalis 1–2* on tape, prepared with Damiano Cozzella (1967); *Concêrto alimentar* [Feeding Concerto] for kitchen and bathroom fixtures and utensils, electric appliances, food and beverages; mixed-media event for television with home audience participation (1969); *Concêrto de bandeirolas*, television event for silent musicians with flags, sounds on tape (1969).

PRINCIPAL WRITINGS: Duprat et al., "Manifesto música nova," *Invenção* (June 1963):5–6; "Em tôrno do pronunciamento," *ibid.*:7–11; interviews in *O estado de S. Paulo* 10/10, 22/4; *Folha de S. Paulo* 26/10; *Folha de tarde* 29/11; *Tribuna de Santos* 41/1.

SEE ALSO Brazil.

Dupré, Marcel (b. Rouen, 3 May 1886; d. Meudon, near Paris, 30 May 1971), studied at the Paris Conservatory (1903–14; composition, fugue with Charles-Marie Widor; organ with Alexandre Guilmant; piano with Louis Diémer). He also studied organ privately with Guilmant during 1897–1908. He became assistant organist at St. Sulpice in Paris in 1906 and principal organist in 1934 upon Widor's retirement. During 1925–54 he taught organ at and during 1954–56 was director of the Paris Conservatory. He wrote eight books on organ playing and composition and also prepared editions of the organ works of Bach, Handel, Mendelssohn, Schumann, and Franck.

PRINCIPAL COMPOSITIONS (for organ unless otherwise noted): *3 Preludes and Fugues* (1912, Leduc);

De profundis, oratorio for soloists, chorus, organ, orchestra (1919, Leduc); *15 Antiphons* (1920, Gray); *Variations on a Noel* (1922, Leduc; *Suite bretonne* (1923, Leduc); *Symphonie-passion* (1924, Leduc); *Le Chemin de la croix* (1931, Durand); *79 Chorales* (1931, Gray); *3 Preludes and Fugues* (1939, Bornemann); *Evocation* (1941, Bornemann); *Le Tombeau de Titelouze* (1942, Bornemann); *La France au Calvaire*, oratorio for soloists, organ, orchestra (1952, Bornemann); *Quartet* for violin, viola, cello, organ (1958); *3 Fugues modales* (1968, Bornemann).

PRINCIPAL WRITINGS: *Traité d'improvisation à l'orgue* (Paris 1925); *Méthode d'orgue* (Paris 1927); *L'Harmonie* (Paris 1934); *Le Contrapoint* (Paris 1935); *La Fugue* (Paris 1936); *Exercices d'improvisation* (Paris 1936).

BIBL.: R. Delestre, *L'Oeuvre de M. D.* (Paris 1952); Bernard Gavoty, *M. D.* (Monaco 1955).

SEE ALSO Liturgical Music: Christian.

Duration, see Rhythm

Durey, Louis (b. Paris, 27 May 1888), received his musical education in Paris from Léon Saint-Requier, with whom he studied from 1907 to 1914. He was one of Les Six and the earlier Nouveaux Jeunes group. He was secretary general of the Fédération Musicale Populaire beginning in 1937 and became president in 1956. He also wrote numerous articles and reviews for *Europe, Musique soviétique, L'Humanité*, etc., and prepared several editions of Janequin's chansons. In his youth Durey was especially attracted to the music of Debussy; in 1914 he became acquainted with part of Schoenberg's *Book of the Hanging Gardens*, and his *L'Offrande lyrique*, written the same year, was according to Frédéric Robert "the first French music influenced by Schoenberg."

PRINCIPAL COMPOSITIONS: *L'Offrande lyrique* for voice, piano, Op. 4; poems of R. Tagore trans. by André Gide (1914); *2 Pieces* for piano 4-hands or orchestra, Op. 7 (1916, 1918, Eschig); *Eloges* for vocal quartet, chamber orchestra, or for chorus, orchestra, Op. 8; poems by Saint-Léger Léger (1916–17, 1962); *Images à Crusoé* for voice, piano, or for voice, flute, clarinet, celesta (harp), string quartet, Op. 11; poems by Saint-Legér Léger (1918, Chester); *La Bestiaire* for voice, piano, Op. 17; poems by Apollonaire (1919, Chester); *6 Madrigaux de Mallarmé* for voice, piano, or for voice, wind quartet, piano, Op. 22 (1919); *Le Printemps au fond de la mer* for voice, 10 winds, Op. 24; poem by Jean Cocteau (1920); *Sonatina* for flute, piano, Op. 25 (1920–25, Editions Ouvrières); *Cantata de la prison* for voice, piano (orchestra), Op. 32; poems by Apollinaire (1922–23; orchestral version, CM); *Le Dit des arbres* for

voice, flute, clarinet, bassoon, piano, string quartet, Op. 33; poems by Rémy de Gourmont (1922–23); *L'Occasion*, 1-act "lyric-comedy" after Mérimée, Op. 34 (1923–25); *3 Sonatinas* for piano, Op. 36 (1926, Heugel); *String Quartet No. 3*, Op. 39 (1927–28, CM); *Vergers* for voice, piano, Op. 42; poems by Rilke (1931–32, CM); *3 Chansons musicales* for chorus, Op. 55; poems by Garcia-Lorca (1948, CM); *La Longue Marche* for tenor, chorus, orchestra, Op. 59; text by Mao Tse-Tung (1949, CM); *Paix aux hommes par millions* for soprano, chorus, orchestra, Op. 60; poem by Mayakovsky (1949, CM); *Ile-de-France*, overture for orchestra, Op. 78 (1954–55, CM); *Trio-Serenade* for string trio, Op. 79 (1955); *10 Choeurs de métiers* for vocal quartet, 2 flutes, clarinet, violin, piano, celesta, Op. 82; poems by Jean Marcenac (1956–57, CM); *Concertino* for piano, 7 winds, double bass, timpani, Op. 83 (1956–57); *Les Soirées de Valfère* for wind quintet, Op. 96 (1963, Braun); *Cantate de la rose et de l'amour* for soprano, piano (string orchestra), Op. 104; poems by Louis Emié (1965); *Sinfonietta* for strings, Op. 105 (1965–66, EMT); *Autoportraits* for piano, Op. 108 (1967).

BIBL.: Frédéric Robert, *L. D.* (Paris 1968).

Durkó, Zsolt (b. Szeged, Hungary, 10 April 1934), studied composition with Ferenc Farkas at the Academy of Music in Budapest (1956–60) and with Goffredo Petrassi in Rome (1961–63). He lives in Budapest.

Durkó's music is primarily contrapuntal, and it often consciously draws on medieval procedures. Individual voices, for instance, are constructed more with horizontal designs than with vertical confluences in mind. *Fioriture* (1966–67) is based on a repeating cantus firmus over which florid variants of a countermelody are heard. The composer has also found inspiration in the medieval taste for altering and/or recombining a restricted number of melodic units (as represented, for instance, in the 13th-century lai and in organum). Contrasts in Durkó's music are achieved primarily through juxtapositions of solo and tutti textures and juxtapositions of short sections, some being rhapsodic and others being tightly knit from short motives or intervals and rhythmic cells. Tone color itself plays more of a supportive than a structural role. Hungarian folk music, especially the ancient dirges and the early 19th-century *verbunkos* dances, underlies some aspects in works such as *Fioriture* and *Una rapsodia ungherese* (1964). In the late 1960s, e.g., in *Altamira* (1968), tone color began to have a more important structural function than before, and another trend became apparent—an attraction toward melody in the classic sense.

PRINCIPAL COMPOSITIONS (published by EMB and Boosey unless otherwise noted): *Episodi sul tema B-A-C-H* for orchestra (1963); *Organismi* for violin, orchestra (1963–64); *Psicogramma* for piano (1964); *Una rapsodia ungherese* for 2 clarinets, orchestra (1964); *String Quartet No. 1* (1966); *Fioriture* for orchestra (1966–67); *Dartmouth Concerto* for soprano, chamber ensemble (1967); *Altamira* for orchestra (1968); *Cantilene* for piano, orchestra (1969, unpub.); *String Quartet No. 2* (1969, unpub.); *Concerto* for 12 flutes, orchestra (1970, unpub.).

BIBL.: Stephen Walsh, "An Introduction to the Music of Zs. D.," *Tempo* 85.

Péter Várnai
(trans. from Hungarian by Egon Kenton)

SEE ALSO Hungary.

Duruflé, Maurice (b. Louviers, France, 11 Jan 1902), studied at the Paris Conservatory (1919–22, composition with Paul Dukas, organ with Charles Tournemire and Louis Vierne). He has been assistant organist at Ste.-Clothilde in Paris (1919–29) and chief organist at Notre Dame Cathedral (1930–31) and at St.-Etienne-du-Mont in Paris (since 1930). He has taught organ and harmony at the Paris Conservatory since 1943.

PRINCIPAL COMPOSITIONS (published by Durand): *Scherzo* for organ (1926); *Prelude, Recitative, and Variations* for flute, viola, piano (1928); *Prelude, Adagio, and Chorale Variations on "Veni creator spiritus"* for organ (1930); *Suite* for organ (1934); *3 Dances* for orchestra (1936); *Prelude and Fugue on the Name Alain* for organ (1942); *Requiem* for mezzo-soprano, orchestra (string orchestra), organ (1947); *Andante and Scherzo* for orchestra (1954); *4 Motets* (on Gregorian melodies) for chorus (1960); *Mass "Cum jubilo"* for baritone, baritone chorus, orchestra (string orchestra), organ (1966).

SEE ALSO Liturgical Music: Christian.

Dutilleux, Henri (b. Angers, France, 22 Jan 1916), attended the Paris Conservatory (1932–38; music history with Maurice Emmanuel; harmony with Jean Gallon; counterpoint, fugue with Noël Gallon; composition with Henri Busser). He was choral director at the Paris Opéra (1942–43) and director of services for music programs at the French radio (1944–63). He began teaching composition at L'Ecole Normale de Musique in Paris in 1961 and became president there in 1969. The major influences on Dutilleux's development have come from Debussy, Ravel, and Roussel, and from Stravinsky and Schoenberg. He is an admirer of Chopin and Berlioz. He also credits the visual arts (the films of Renoir, Bergman, and Fellini and the works of Fra Angelico, Rodin, and Van Gogh) and literature (Shakespeare and Baudelaire) with having shaped his musical thinking. He has received many honors, including the Prix de Rome and membership in the Legion d'honneur.

PRINCIPAL COMPOSITIONS: *Piano Sonata* (1946–48, Durand); *Symphony No. 1* (1949–51, Amphion); *3 Sonnets de Jean Cassou* for baritone, orchestra (1953); *Le Loup*, ballet; choreography by Roland Petit (1953, Ricordi); *Symphony No. 2,* "Le Double" (1956–59, Heugel); *Metaboles* for orchestra (1962–65, Heugel); *Cello Concerto* (1967–69, Heugel).

PRINCIPAL WRITINGS: "Confidences d'H. D. sur sa deuxième Symphonie," *Journal musical français* (4 Jan 1966):4; "Face à face," *Le Figaro littéraire* (24–30 June 1968):15.

BIBL.: Antoine Goléa, *20 Ans de musique contemporaine* II (Paris 1962):159–64; Nicole Hirsch, "H. D.," *Diapason* 127:40–42; Jean Roy, *Présences contemporaines* (Paris 1962):159–64.

SEE ALSO France.

Dyad, a collection of two pitch classes considered either as a simultaneity or as a succession. The term occurs most frequently in reference to segments of 12-tone sets.

Eastern Music, see Asian Music and Western Composition, Japan

Eben, Petr (b. Žamberk, Czechoslovakia, 22 Jan 1929), studied at the Prague Academy of Music (1948–54, composition with Pavel Bořkovec, piano with František Rouch). He has taught musicology at Charles Univ. in Prague since 1955 and performs professionally as a pianist, especially in chamber ensembles. An interest in Silesian folksongs has combined with plainchant and medieval music to influence his development as a composer.

PRINCIPAL COMPOSITIONS: *6 Piesní milostných* [6 Love Songs] for voice, harp (piano); medieval texts (1951, SHV); *Zelená se snítka* [There Greens a Twig], song cycle for children's chorus (1953, SHV); *Starodávné čarovéní milému* [The Lover's Magic Spell], cantata for female soloists, chorus (1957, Supraphon); *Láska a smrt* [Love and Death], song cycle for chorus (1958, SHV); *Nedělní hudba* [Sunday Music] for organ (1958–59, SHV); *Piano Concerto* (1961, Panton); *Písně nelaskavé* [Unkind Songs] for alto, viola (1964, Panton); *Ubi caritas et amor*, antiphon for 5-voice chorus (1964, Bärenreiter); *Laudes* for organ (1964, Panton); *Ordo modalis* for oboe, harp (1964); *Apologio Sokratus*, oratorio for soloists, chorus, orchestra (1964, SHV); *Wind Quintet* (1965, SHV).

PRINCIPAL WRITINGS: with Jarmil Burghauser, *Čtení a hra partitur* [How to Read and Play Scores] (Prague c.1960).

SEE ALSO Czechoslovakia.

Eckhardt-Gramatté, S. C. (Sophie-Carmen or Sonia) (b. Moscow, c.1902), spent her childhood in England and France and received early piano training from her mother, a former pupil of Anton Rubinstein. She studied violin and piano at the Paris Conservatory, chamber music with Vincent d'Indy at the Schola Cantorum, violin privately with Jacques Thibaud in Paris and Bronislav Hubermann in Berlin, and composition with Max Trapp at the Berlin Academy of Arts. She also discussed orchestration and other musical topics with Casals, Honegger, and Scherchen, beginning in the 1920s. She made her debut on both violin and piano in Berlin at 11, and pursued an active solo career on both instruments until the early 30s, when her attention turned more toward composition. She was married to the German Expressionist painter Walter Gramatté (who died in 1929), and later to the art historian and critic Ferdinand Eckhardt. Her present home is in Winnepeg, Canada.

PRINCIPAL COMPOSITIONS: *Suite No. 3* for piano (1924); *10 Caprices* for solo violin (1924–34, No. 3 published by Simrock); *Concerto* for solo violin (1925, CMC); *Suite No. 3,* "Mallorca Suite," for solo violin (1926, Eschig); *Suite No. 6,* "3 Klavierstücke," for piano (1928–51, CMC); *String Quartets Nos. 1–3* (1938; 1946; 1964, CMC); *Symphony in C* (1939, CMC); *String Quartet No. 2,* "Hainburger" (1943); *Duo for 2 Violins No. 1* (1944, CMC); *Wind Quartet* for flute, B♭ clarinet, tenor clarinet (A clarinet), bass clarinet (bassoon) (1946, CMC); *Markantes Stück* for 2 pianos, orchestra (1946–50); *Ruck-Ruck-Sonata* for clarinet, piano (1947); *Violin Concerto No. 2* (1948–52, CMC); *Triple Concerto* for trumpet, clarinet, bassoon, strings, timpani (1949, UE); *Bassoon Concerto* (1950, CMC); *Suite No. 5,* "Klavierstück," for piano (1950); *Concerto for Orchestra* (1953–54, CMC); *Duo concertante* for flute, violin (1956, CMC); *Duo concertante* for cello, piano (1959, CMC); *Wind Quintet* (1963, CMC); *Nonet* for flute, oboe, clarinet, bassoon, horn, violin, viola, cello, double bass (1966–67, CMC); *Piano Trio* (1966–67, CMC); *Symphony Concerto* for piano, orchestra (*Piano Concerto No. 3*) (1966–67, CMC); *Suite* for flute, clarinet, bassoon (1967, CMC); *Suite No. 4* for solo violin (1968, CMC).

BIBL.: Jean Sangwine, "S. C. E.-G. Composer," *Chatelaine* (Canada, Sept 1967):43; Ken Winters, "The Same Moon and Stars: E.-G. in Profile," *Winnepeg Free Press* (17 Feb 1962); "E.-G.," *The Canadian Composer* (Sept 1969):9–11; "S. C. E. -G: A Portrait," *Musicanada* (Oct 1969):8–9.

Economics, see Publishing; see also articles on individual countries

Eder, Helmut (b. Linz, 26 Dec 1916), studied at the Bruckner Conservatory in Linz (1946–48), the Munich Hochschule (1953–54, composition with Carl Orff), and the Stuttgart Hochschule (1954, composition with Johann Nepomuk David). He also studied conducting with Fritz Lehmann. He has taught at the Mozarteum in Salzburg since 1967.

PRINCIPAL COMPOSITIONS: *Symphonies Nos. 1–3* (1950; 1953, EM; 1959–60, Bärenreiter); *Moderner Traum*, ballet; choreography by Andrej Jershik (1956); *Ödipus*, opera (1959); *Concerto* for 2 pianos, orchestra, Op. 30 (1961, Bärenreiter); *Concerto a dodici* for strings, Op. 38 (1963, Doblinger); *Anamorphosen*, ballet; choreography by Jean-Pierre Genet (1963); *Violin Concertos Nos. 1–2*, Opp. 29, 41 (1963, EM; 1966, Doblinger); *Der Kardinal*, TV opera (1964); *Oboe Concerto*, Op. 35 (1964, Bärenreiter); *Die irrfahrten des Odysseus*, ballet; choreography by Erich Walter (1965); *Bassoon Concerto*, Op. 49 (1967, Doblinger); *Organ Concerto*, Op. 50 (1969, Doblinger); *Weisse Frau*, opera (1969); *Konjugationen 3*, TV opera (1969); *Metamorphosen über ein Fragment von Mozart* for orchestra (1970, Doblinger).

Education for the Nonprofessional. Music has had a part in European education since classical Greek times, when music and poetry were considered disciplines for training the soul. During the middle ages and renaissance, the "common" man perpetuated his musical heritage through the troubadours, folk culture, and the mastersinger guilds that eventually grew into the conservatories of the 18th century; the aristocratic classes cultivated music within the church and as one of the liberal arts. During the Reformation, music became a part of the instruction in court and church schools, given impetus by the advent of printing and the subsequent wide distribution of hymn books and, later, tune books. Musical literacy became a desired product of schooling because it allowed a more complete realization of hymns in the divine service. Amateur music making took on important status in aristocratic homes during the 17th and 18th centuries, while the rise of instrumental music and opera increased the need for trained musicians. In response there developed a conservatory system in Europe for the training of professionals and emphasizing performance and a theoretical knowledge of music. During the 19th century, state supported elementary schools required musical training as a part of the basic literacy of the populace and as a means for continuing national cultural heritages. In the universities, music was studied as a philosophical and historical discipline in the humanities. In most of Europe, this system remained intact into the 1950s. One exception is Russia where, after the Revolution of 1917, mass music education was developed to preserve the indigenous culture and to perpetuate the ideals of the revolution through song and art. At the same time in Hungary, such composers as Bartók and Kodály were looking to folk music as a means for developing mass music education through singing. In the U.S., singing schools were developed in the 1700s to improve congregational and choir singing. These were usually taught by conservatory-trained musicians and were based on European models. From this same background came the conventions and festivals of singing teachers. In 1834 Lowell Mason, working at the Hawes School in Boston, introduced music into the general-education curriculum, thus establishing a system to develop musical literacy in everyone.

1900–50. In the U.S. by the turn of the century, the emergence of professional orchestras, opera companies, and bands contributed to a growing professional climate and gave evidence of an increasing national interest in music. Even small towns were being offered a wide range of music and entertainment through tours booked by the Chautauqua Circuit (c.1903–c.1925). Singing institutes were often established by music publishing houses to train musicians in teaching methods. Eventually these institutes became the basis for music offerings in the normal schools for teacher training. These schools trained school music teachers to meet state certification requirements, while the conservatories concentrated on developing professional performers. Professional organizations were founded—the Music Teachers National Association in 1876 and the Music Educators National Conference in 1907, and by the early 1900s music was an accepted part of the public school curriculum and more professional musicians were becoming teachers.

A major impetus for American school music was the progressive education movement, based in a pragmatic philosophy with which the performance aspects of music were highly compatible. School music was said to possess many nonmusical attributes, such as building character, citizenship, health, and even today music is often supported in the schools for these reasons. The inclusion of instrumental instruction is one of America's unique contributions. It first came into the schools with the formation of orchestras made up of students who had received their training through private instruction outside the school, but, as in many other areas of the curriculum, those aspects that had been the purview of the home or church soon were taken over into the curriculum. Many school programs for teaching performance on instruments were established by musicians in the employ of band-instrument and uniform manufacturers. These would go into a community school system and promise to develop a band within one year's time, with the understanding that the school would then be obligated to purchase instruments and uniforms. Soon the school would hire a permanent instrument teacher. Local, state, and national music festivals and contests became a popular part of the school-music movement by the late 1930s, but the number of such programs was so large after World War II that national-level contests had to be abandoned. By the 1940s most schools required music experiences for all students throughout the first seven or eight grades, after which music became an elective with primary emphasis on performance. In response to the need for better professional education of teachers and performing musicians, many universities and conservatories developed to a position where they could favorably compete with the established institutions of Europe.

1950-70. By the early 1950s several factors were influencing music education in Europe: the occupation forces, particularly those of the U.S. with their Armed Forces schools; the developing trade and exchange of ideas between Western countries; the shrinking world of communication and transportation; various government sponsored cultural exchange programs and educational visits; and in 1953 the founding of the International Society for Music Education under the auspices of UNESCO. All these activities gave rise to a similarity in educational thinking throughout many European countries.

The Soviet government takes the music education of all citizens as a major part of its educational responsibility. As in many European countries, music is compulsory in grades one–seven and optional in grades eight–ten. Most activity consists of choral singing, theoretical rudiments, and the study of selected compositions. Highly talented students may be transferred in the eighth year to schools specializing in education in the arts. Young people and adults may take part in advanced nonprofessional, government-supported, music education programs outside the classroom. The major Russian composers, such as Kabalevsky and Shostakovich, have helped guide their country's music education and have provided music specifically for school use. Great stress has been given to the idea of developing higher spiritual values through music experiences.

Most other countries in East Europe have developed similar programs, stressing music's role in the child's esthetic, technical, physical, and intellectual growth. They have also emphasized music's ability to soften the academic atmosphere and to enhance a sense of patriotism. Yugoslav education trains children to be actively involved in creating music and in forming judgments; it is less concerned with abstract theory and verbal history. Balkan isorhythms and melismatic melody are used in a spiral curriculum designed to inculcate concepts regarding the nature of music. In Hungary, the work started by Bartók and brought to its acme by Kodály is based on singing rooted in the use of folk-music elements and the active involvement of students. Its methodology uses solmization, hand signals, and the development of an inner listening ability, all of which has led to a degree of musical literacy and enjoyment unprecedented in modern music education. Proponents of the Kodály system feel that it encourages exemplary emotional and spiritual characteristics in children, thus favorably affecting their academic achievement, character, and personality development.

Some areas of Western Europe seem to have clung to past traditions longer than other areas. Music in the schools is comprised primarily of singing experiences for the first six years and of elective extracurricular organizations and special conservatory education for the talented. Notable exceptions occur, particularly in the work of Carl Orff in Munich, beginning in the 1920s. His method, codified in *Das Schulwerk*, teaches through creative exercises and improvisation. He built easy-to-play pitched and unpitched percussion instruments, to be augmented by clapping, knee slapping, and rhythmic speech. His creative experiences with music first make use of the pentatonic scale to encourage students to improvise without imitating familiar music; gradually other scale tones are added to provide a full major-minor vocabulary. This approach has been an important stimulus to the incorporation of student creativity in music education. In England such composers as George Self, Brian Denis, and Ronald Senator have been working to develop methods for greater student creativity. Their methods involve creative experimentation based on contemporary music techniques. They stress unusual sound sources and the relinquishing of strict controls over the elements of improvisation and composition. In Canada, the U.S., and Australia, similar experiments are also in use.

The Scandinavian countries insure that music is available to everyone. In Sweden, for example, there are some 350 municipal music schools supported by the state for those who want practical training. Swedish television offers courses for the nonmusician, particularly adults and teenagers. School teaching is assigned to "practical music teachers," who receive their training in music and the procedures of music education from the state at no cost (they tend not to receive much general education, but this is gradually changing). The practical musician-teachers not only teach in the public schools but also work with churches and hospitals, much in keeping with the European tradition of the "town musician."

Most non-European countries with deep European roots have modeled their education on European principles, but the mid-1900s witnessed a desire for more individuality and for greater use of indigenous resources. The most recent example of this is in Australia, where a Society for Music Education was established in 1967. Its purpose is to encourage and advance the growth of a national system of music based on the latest philosophies and methodologies. Likewise, in Canada the post-World War II years have seen a rapid rise in the use of native music. In 1962 the composer John Adaskin began assembling contemporary Canadian music for school use. R. Murray Schafer's informal texts of diarylike lesson plans and strategies are a model of contemporary didactic writing.

Music education in Japan is controlled by the state through the use of authorized textbooks. Since World War II education has expanded under Western influence, and many of those who train teachers and shape education programs have themselves been trained abroad. Most public school programs emphasize memorization, singing, and the playing of instruments such as recorder, harmonica, and tuned percussion. Performance is a prime tool and principal objective, although further Western influences have brought a greater stress on relating music to other subject areas and more progressive modes of training children in the processes of music. The Suzuki method of string training develops violin skills in children through rote teaching and increased aural sensitivity. The key to the pedagogy is cooperation between parents and student and between students and teacher, not individual competitiveness as is often the case in the West.

The late 1950s were crisis years in U.S. music education, but from the experiences of these years have evolved some important positive trends. Increased school enrollments after World War II caused shortages in classrooms and teachers, particularly at first on the grade-school level, where music instruction was being provided by a general classroom teacher with the support of occasional visits by a musically trained specialist. Even throughout the 60s, grade-school music often depended on the interest and expertise of individual classroom teachers, some of whom with a particular interest or ability in music would serve several classrooms in a building. At the end of the 50s the Russian launching of Sputnik focused the nation's attention on science. The humanities and in particular the arts suffered a period of neglect, although many organizations, including the American Association of School Administrators, strongly supported a balanced education. In the face of increasing academic and science oriented workloads, existing goals in music education, which emphasized performance and entertainment, could no longer be supported. Educators now turned their attention towards music as a humanistic discipline, towards understanding the nature of the musical process and the components of music experiences. Many sought help from abroad in the methods of Kodály, Orff, and Suzuki. New education technologies also came into play. But most important a number of seminars and conferences at this time made recommendations that are now being implemented and that hold great promise for the future.

At the end of the 1950s the Ford Foundation, following the suggestion of composer Norman Dello Joio, established a program for placing young composers in residence in the public schools, where they wrote music for the school's performing groups. This program was called the Contemporary Music Project. It gave students a chance to observe composers at work, but it also quickly revealed how uninformed most teachers were in regard to contemporary music techniques. At this point a series of experiments in curriculum revision began. In 1963 a seminar at Yale Univ., "Music in Our Schools," recommended that more "comprehensively competent musicians" be the aim of teacher education. A Northwestern Univ. seminar on "Comprehensive Musicianship" in 1965 recommended that general music education in the freshman and sophomore college years synthesize the components of musicianship (listening and analysis, performance, and composition) and no longer offer them in a compartmentalized fashion. Beginning in 1967 the Juilliard Repertory Project collected music for use through grade six that includes contemporary, folk, and non-Western materials, and the Manhattanville Music Curriculum Project developed a curriculum in which students create their own music, analyze, and evaluate it. Thus a pattern of decisions had been set, all of them involving the concept of "comprehensive musicianship" as the basis for music education. In 1969–70 this concept was fully articulated in a recommendation by an MENC commission on teacher education: "Music educators need to demonstrate at least a minimum knowledge of and competence to teach in all musics, and cannot be restricted in their training to the styles represented by a few hundred years of Western art music. The enormity of the task of becoming competent to function within the whole spectrum of music dictates the need for a new set of tools. Music educators need something more than performance skills. They must develop a comprehensive musicianship which, coupled with an open-mindedness toward the use of any sounds combined in a musical context, will enable them to address themselves to any music they encounter."

Music education at the beginning of the 1970s finds itself in a position similar to that of most of society. It is overwhelmed by the rapidity with which change and evolving ideas have struck. The way in which music teachers respond to the needs of society will depend greatly on the type of college education provided the musician in the future. This in turn will depend on whether the music-education profession seeks an understanding of the whole art of music and its processes or whether it continues to fragment and compartmentalize the development of music and musicianship and lose its relevancy to the everyday life of Western man.

BIBL.: Edward Bailey Birge, *History of Public School Music in the United States* (Washington 1928, 1966); *Comprehensive Musicianship* (Washington 1965); Karl Ernst, ed., *Music in General Education* (Washington 1965); Nelson Henry, ed., "Basic Concepts in Music Education," *The 57th Yearbook of the National Society for the Study of Education* (Chicago 1958); Max Kaplen, *Foundations and Frontiers of Music Education* (New York 1966); Bonnie Kowall, ed., "Perspectives in Music Education," Music Educators' National Conference *Source Book 3* (Washington 1966); Egon Kraus, ed., *The Present State of Music Education in the World* (Cologne 1960); Charles Leonhard and Robert House, *Foundations and Principles of Music Education* (New York 1959); Claude V. Palisca, *Music in Our Schools, A Search for Improvement*, Office of Education Bulletin No. 28 (Washington 1964).

Robert J. Werner

Education for the Professional. The professional musician is one who earns some portion of his livelihood in the field of music: the composer, performer (including the conductor), theorist, historian, and educator. All of these roles can of course be blended into a single individual, and most professional musicians enact all during some parts of their careers. It is this multiplicity of necessary operational skills that poses one of the complexities of the education process for the musician. The category "educator" currently subsumes in many careers all of the other four categories, and only a small number of composers, performers, and conductors do not enjoy some remuneration from private or institutional teaching. Professional training in music has always been dominated by the face-to-face master-apprentice relationship. Only recently have modern economics and technology begun to depersonalize the educational process and lead to group strategies.

NONINSTITUTIONAL TRAINING. The professional musician is not usually a "late bloomer." The optimum age of initiation into music is probably four to six, which is when the attribute called "talent" usually surfaces. The early education that follows usually is one of rather narrow skill development, i.e., learning to play an instrument. The nature of the human maturation process precludes serious vocal training until after the voice has reached its physiological adulthood, but many professional singers have early training that is similar to that of the incipient instrumentalist. In the U.S. the professional musician's initial training and that of the eventual amateur are about the same. Both spend their precollege years in the same treadmill of practice, music lessons, and recitals, and they participate together in the same musicmaking groups in public and private schools. Although some countries, such as the Soviet Union and Hungary, provide channels through which the highly talented can be discovered and separated for specialized programs, the cultivation of a musical elite is mostly a fortuitous process through childhood and adolescence. For this reason parental concern and patience is the most crucial factor in the flowering of musical talent in the 6–16 age span.

Many unscheduled, noncurricularized events provide insights and attitudes equal in significance to those obtained from established educational processes: youthful jazz and rock groups, chamber ensembles of various dimensions, accordion bands, singing groups, church choirs, and other performance involvements that develop outside the usual educational restraints. The motivated young musician in a large urban area has no difficulty joining in—or initiating—these kinds of learn-by-doing events. Their common emphasis on action rather than elegance provides a setting within which individual fluency and corporate joy are more readily obtainable than in the more highly controlled institutional situations.

INSTITUTIONALIZED TRAINING. Formal training today can be said to begin at college age or, when the student is fortunate, in the secondary school. Some private and public high schools in the U.S. offer exceptionally rewarding work for the musically talented, and what is said below about conservatory and college training can be understood to apply to a limited degree to such exceptional secondary schools.

Since as early as the 15th century, youth of evident musical talent utilized the conservatory (Latin, *conservatorium*) as a preprofessional workshop. Originally a site where orphaned boys could learn to read and sing to the glory of God, this early manifestation of the trade school preserved and nurtured the choral tradition of the Roman Catholic church and in the process trained singers and composers within a tradition that touted excellence and total professional commitment to the art. By the mid-18th century the conservatory in the modern sense outgrew the exclusive choral tradition, changing its image and goals with the time and achieving a more balanced instrumental and vocal program. Several modern conservatories, such as the Conservatoire de Musique in Paris, were founded in the latter part of the 18th century, and the major North American institutions followed a century or more later. The university, which in Europe dates back to the 12th century, traditionally has sponsored the historical and conceptual aspects of music, leaving performance problems to the conservatory. This schism between "tradesman" and "scholar" has now begun to disappear in some U.S. schools, however (see below).

THE PROFESSIONAL CURRICULUM. Performance by singing or playing an instrument constitutes the main thrust of studies in the conservatory and college during baccalaureate studies, even though many students have decided by this time that teaching will be their principal occupation. In North America, choral and instrumental ensembles of various types provide a semblance of professional context for training musicians and for entertaining the college community. A student's other training consists of work in three main areas: 1) basic skills of musical performance that are related to no particular performance medium;

2) the syntactic or structural aspects of music, usually called *music theory*; and 3) a historical perspective of the whole art, but especially the "classical" music cultivated by Western European aristocracy between 1700 and 1900. Although the actual substance and teaching strategies for this training varies, its essential features are controlled in most U.S. schools by the accreditation practices of the National Association of Schools of Music, which was created in 1924 by Howard Hanson of the Eastman School of Music and consisting of administrators from the accredited schools. Indirect influence over curricula is also exerted by such groups as the College Music Society, Music Teachers National Association, and Music Educators National Conference.

BASIC SKILLS. The skills development of musicians normally centers around activities and drills called *ear training*. These have to do with perceptual processes most relevant to music, namely hearing, recalling, and reporting (verbally or in musical notation) what is heard. In the U.S. this training has for many years occurred within a dictation-response format in which the teacher performs isolated musical patterns and the pupil notates what he hears. (More recently recorded excerpts and programmed instructions have begun to replace the teacher in this process.) The subject matter in these drills usually consists of melodies of simple pitch and rhythmic constitution and brief progressions of functional harmony typical of music composed during 1700–1850. In some situations the procedure has assumed the character of highly automated, assembly-line techniques: music materials are chosen for their compatibility with the teaching system rather than for their relevance to musical understanding; pitch-interval recognition replaces work with musical patterns; the solitude of the work carrel replaces the social interchange of the classroom; and the piano or electronic organ becomes a sole purveyor of all musical messages.

Sight singing, or *solfège* (*solfeggio*), has long been a major part of skill development. Its main function is to develop the visual-aural imagery required to decipher musical notation and translate it into sound. American institutions also emphasize "keyboard skills" (which is often a euphemism for "beginner's piano"). The aim is to equip students to realize scores and improvise settings of simple melodies at the piano. Although many consider this to be an essential professional skill, numerous famed musicians, including Berlioz, Koussevitzky, and Toscanni, could not perform with any finesse at the piano.

A final required general skill is the ability to read and write music notation with reasonable facility. This the musician needs unless his professional role will allow him to rely on improvisation or rote learning (which is the case with many successful pop stars). Notation skills are usually taught within the context of general theoretical studies and of necessity within the dictation processes of the aural skills classes.

Since about 1950 there has been widespread interest in integrating development of the basic skills with remaining aspects of the curriculum. Many educators have questioned the wisdom of accepting students for professional training who do not already possess these skills or, if accepted, of teaching skills as isolated matters removed from their relevancy to conceptual musical substance. Some notable schools, such as Juilliard, and projects, such as the Contemporary Music Project, have attempted to integrate teaching processes. It has been discovered, for example, that a student can develop effective aural acuity within a course in music history provided that specific perceptual goals dominate his study (which must involve tightly guided listening) rather than secondary data, such as biography. Similarly the intricacies of music notation can be learned most meaningfully in a learn-by-doing process in which the student's preoccupation is not learning to write notes on paper but rather creating his own music as an expression of himself.

MUSIC THEORY. The first genuine music theorist of published record was Aristoxenus, a pupil of Aristotle. Numerous other illustrious men, including Descartes, Leibniz, and Helmholtz, have tried to unravel the mysteries of musical syntax, to parse the sentences of musical rhetoric. Only a highly filtered residue of this musicophilosophical dialectic seeps into the training of most musicians. The substantive basis of college and conservatory courses called "music theory" has been generalizations about tonal harmony inferred from a narrow segment of musical practice in Western Europe. In addition students usually study the contrapuntal processes of 16th-century church polyphony and 18th-century counterpoint, such as Bach's. The educational premise for teaching so little was that thorough indoctrination in the music of a single type—if that type had retained its validity for contemporary audiences—would enable the student to cope with any music. This view began to dim during the late 1940s and early 50s (more than 20 years after Schoenberg's method was devised) as dodecaphonic music became widely accepted.

Shattered faith in the universal applicability to all music of treasured rules of harmony led many educators toward a reappraisal of the musical basis. A first product was a letting down of stylistic barriers, the sampling of other kinds of music in order to establish a firmer foundation for the music learning process. One of the main conclusions reached by the Seminar in Comprehensive Musicianship at Northwestern Univ. in April 1965 was that the teaching procedures and subject matters of contemporary music theory were in need of immediate and thorough overhaul.

In the more progressive colleges and conservatories of the U.S., the scene is primarily one of transition. The main change is the adoption of an "all-elements" basis for teaching musical structure, a basis that utilizes music from a wide variety of ages and cultures as an approach to an understanding of music syntax, replacing past emphasis on the single element of harmony with attention to all the musical parameters that can potentially shape a musical structure.

HISTORICAL STUDIES. The study of music as history is not necessarily a music experience. Courses designed for the professional often are concerned more with biographical and output data on composers than with the musical artifacts themselves. It is assumed, however, that the true professional must know the past of his art—the goals and aspirations of its practitioners and the human contexts within which they worked. The assumption is untestable, and few professionals challenge it.

In many professional schools the student is occupied for two years with studies of an essentially historical cast. The earlier year is usually called "Introduction to Music," "Music Literature," etc. Later, usually in the senior year, there is a course called "Music History." The logic behind this plan appears to have been sound: the student would become acquainted in the early course with a large portion of the concert-music repertory and, in the later one, shape his knowledge into a meaningful perspective of historical evolution. Yet in many schools the two years are difficult to tell apart. Both begin with a chronological survey of what little is known of Greek music of ancient times and continue as far as the instructor can get in two semesters. This usually means that Wagner becomes "recent" music for most graduates, if indeed they get beyond Tchaikovsky or Brahms. The result is a less than satisfactory grasp of historical succession, primarily because the learner has no adequate opportunity to make intimate and thorough contact with whole pieces of music.

Furthermore students tend to emerge from their baccalaureate studies with no notion of what music of recent or ancient times is like nor why it might be different from Handel or Brahms. Only in rare instances do classes have truck with such exotica as South African drumming, the Japanese koto, East Indian ragas, or Javanese gamelans. And only in the most avant-garde circles of academia is American jazz a serious topic comparable, say, with the isorhythmic motet or the birth of Florentine opera.

Since 1965 some of the leading colleges and conservatories in the U.S. have begun to integrate the initial course in music literature (with its intended emphasis on the repertory of our culture) with the syntactical matters of the traditional theory course. A notable forerunner of this shift was the "Literature and Music" format adopted in the late 40s at Juilliard during the leadership of William Schuman. The "L&M" process is a totally integrated course incorporating historical, theoretical, and performing operations. The demands on the single teacher are gargantuan, but a healthy relevance is achieved between the various musicianly roles which in the past have been represented by different courses and different instructors. Many schools first attempted instructional integration during 1966 under the auspices of the Institutes for Music in Contemporary Education, a phase of the Contemporary Music Project under grants from the Ford Foundation and the Music Educators National Conference. A number of these curricula remain in operation today in their original or in slightly revised forms.

CONSERVATORY VS. UNIVERSITY. As suggested above, the conservatory and university traditionally have maintained somewhat different professional goals, although since the third decade of this century both have trained professional musicians. The primary thrust of the conservatory has been to train composers, performers, or conductors. In a sense the conservatory has acted as an artistic trade school, nurturing the talented for narrowly defined professional roles, which it was presumed demanded extraordinary depth at the expense of breadth of vision. Until within the last decade, the typical major orchestra or opera company in the U.S. was populated almost exclusively by musicians who had been trained in a conservatory here or in western Europe, and the concert circuits were worked by the products of Curtis, Juilliard, Peabody, Oberlin, and the New England Conservatory. Furthermore, the generation of U.S. composers born around the turn of the century

was almost exclusively the tutorial product of one French mentor, Nadia Boulanger, and those who were not were either self-taught or had studied with a west European at one of the same conservatories that produced the concert artists. During this era the role of the university was primarily that of developing musicians who would teach: professor-scholars for the college and university circuit and music teachers for the primary and secondary grade schools. Professional music education thus took the form of a three-tiered hierarchy in which the conservatory was the pinnacle, preparing the "doers" of the music world; the university trained musical scholars; and the lowest stratum, the college music department, graduated the high-school band directors and general music teachers, who it was assumed followed this profession only by default.

The grip of the conservatory on the musically talented, a condition passed on untested from such revered but antiquated models as the Paris Conservatory, did not weaken until mid-century. At that time state universities suddenly emerged as a potential force in the country's musical life, leading to an amalgamation of the two roles of performer-specialist and scholar-generalist. The way was paved by such schools as Indiana Univ. and the Univ. of Southern Calif., where former members of major orchestras and opera companies and renowned concert artists joined forces with scholars and educators. Professional and social changes helped the amalgamation. First, the commercial concert world was crumbling. Where previously scores of singers and players could be maintained on community circuits throughout the country, by 1960 the impact of competing interests, such as television and professional sports, had reduced the concert world to a relative wasteland. Second, the flush financial state of some state universities immediately after World War II and their desire to expand, combined with the new accessibility via jet travel of the small hamlets where most state universities have been planted, made it possible for schools in once-remote Indiana or Wisconsin or Texas to lure the most illustrious names of the concert world. Thus the university suddenly acquired the prestige formerly found only in the major conservatories. For the first time single music education institutions could boast of the combined forces of performer, scholar, and educator. This fusion constitutes the major advance in professional education during this century as well as the first genuine change from European models.   William Thomson

SEE ALSO Performance.

Edwards, Ross (b. Sydney, 23 Dec 1943), attended the New South Wales Conservatory (1959–62), the Univ. of Sydney (1963), and the Univ. of Adelaide (1966–69; composition with Richard Meale, Peter Maxwell Davies, Šandor Veress). He also studied composition privately with Richard Meale in 1963 and worked with Maxwell Davies in London in 1970. Although never officially his pupil, Edwards has been influenced by the Australian composer Peter Sculthorpe.

PRINCIPAL COMPOSITIONS (published by Albert): *Quem quaeritis*, a nativity play for performance by children and adults for soprano, alto, baritone, chorus, organ, trumpet, wind and percussion chamber orchestra (1967); *String Quartet* (1968–69); *Etude* for orchestra (1969); *Monos I* for cello (1970).

PRINCIPAL WRITINGS: "Nigel Butterley's *In the Head the Fire*," *Music Now* (Australia) 1/2 (1969): 6–11.

Egge, Klaus (b. Gransherad, Norway, 19 July 1906), studied composition privately with Fartein Valen and piano with Nils Larsen. He attended the Oslo Conservatory (graduated 1929 with a major in organ) and the Berlin Hochschule für Musik (1937–38, composition and conducting with Walter Gmeindls). During 1930–45 he taught music at a secondary school; he has written music criticism since then. He has occupied many official posts, including the presidency of the Norwegian Composers' Society (since 1945). His work to about 1940 was nationalistic. Compositions such as the *First Symphony* (1942) and *Second Piano Concerto* (1944) are rooted as well in Bachian polyphony. Beginning in the late 1940s he has been concerned with the structural uses of orchestral timbre and with more complex rhythms. His *Symphonies Nos. 4–5* (1967, 1969) use serial (but not 12-tone) techniques.

PRINCIPAL COMPOSITIONS (published by Lyche): *Piano Concertos Nos. 1–2* (1937, 1944); *Sveinung Vriem*, symphonic epic for vocal soloists, chorus, orchestra (1938–39); *Symphonies Nos. 1–5*: No. 1 (1942); No. 2 (1947); No. 3 (1957); No. 4, "Sinfonia sopra B-A-C-H, E-G-G-E" (1967); No. 5, "Sinfonia dolce quasi passacaglia" (1969); *Violin Concerto* (1953): *Cello Concerto* (1966).

BIBL.: Ingmar Bengtsson, ed., *Modern nordisk musik* (Stockholm 1957); Olav Gurvin, *Norske saerdrag i musikken* (Oslo 1940); Bo Wallner, *Vår tids musik i norden* (Stockholm 1968), English trans. (London 1971).

SEE ALSO Scandinavia.

Egk, Werner (b. Auchsessheim, Bavaria, Germany, 17 May 1901), is the son of a public school teacher. He attended the St. Stephan gymnasium in Augsburg and thereafter was self-taught. He was attracted to the professions of musician, painter, and writer, but, after a year of study and travel in Italy, he decided on music. He has been a free-lance composer and conductor most of his life. During 1937–41 he was also Kapellmeister at the Berlin State Opera and during 1950–53, director of the Berlin Musikhochschule. Both as an unofficial spokesman and as president of the German Music Council (since 1968), he has worked on behalf of author's rights and the improvement of social conditions for musicians.

Egk is primarily a man of the theater, both as a conductor and composer. His stage works, for which he writes his own scenarios and librettos, deal with major figures of history and legend: Faust, Don Juan, Columbus, Peer Gynt, Casanova. An uncompromising man, he has sometimes met with censorship. His oratorio *Furchtlosigkeit und Wohlwollen* (1931) was reviled as degenerate pacificism. The troll scene in *Peer Gynt* (1938) contains a satire on the Nazi regime, which caused the opera to be banned. The Bavarian Minister of Culture banned the Faust ballet *Abraxas* (1948) on grounds of obscenity. Egk has expressed such qualities as irony, wit, and sarcasm, qualities rarely found in German music and probably resulting in Egk's case from his enthusiasm for Voltaire and rationalism. His music is generally polytonal and polyrhythmic, and there is no evidence of 12-tone influences. The emphasis on rhythmic and orchestral color stems from the early influence of Stravinsky. To this is added a typically Swabian-Bavarian taste for craftsmanship and conciseness.

PRINCIPAL COMPOSITIONS (published by Schott): *Furchtlosigkeit und Wohlwollen*, oratorio for tenor, chorus, orchestra (1931); *Columbus*, radio opera (1932, stage version 1951); *Die Zaubergeige*, 3-act comic opera based on Pocci (1935); *Peer Gynt*, 3-act opera based on Ibsen (1938); *Joan von Zarissa*, ballet based on the Don Juan legend; choreography by Lizzie Maudrik (1940); *La Tentation de St. Antoine* for alto, string quartet, string orchestra; 18th-century texts (1946); *Abraxas*, ballet after Heine; choreography by Marcel Luipart (1948); *Französische Suite* for orchestra; based on Rameau (1949); *Chanson et romance* for coloratura soprano, orchestra; text by Paul le Silentiaire (1953); *Irische Legende*, opera after Yeats (1955); *Der Revisor*, 5-act comic opera after Gogol (1956); *Variations on a Caribbean Theme* (1959; ballet version, *Danza*, 1960); *Die Verlobung in San Domingo*, opera after Kleist (1963); *Casanova in London*, ballet; choreography by Janine Charrat (1969); *Orchestra Sonata No. 2* (1968).

PRINCIPAL WRITINGS: *Musik-Wort-Bild*, a collection of essays (Munich 1960).

BIBL.: Ernst Krause, *W. E.* (East Berlin 1971); Karl Schumann, *Gedächtnisprotokoll* (Munich 1971).

Karl Schumann

SEE ALSO Austria and Germany.

Ehrlich, Abel (b. Cranz, Germany, 3 Sept 1915), studied at the Music Academy in Zagreb (1934–38), at the Music Academy in Jerusalem (1939–44; counterpoint, harmony with S. Rosowsky), and at the Darmstadt summer courses (1959, 61, 63, 67), where he first met Pousseur, Stockhausen, and Nono. Since 1964 he has taught composition at the Israel Music Academy in Tel Aviv. Until about 1955 his music was largely influenced by his study of Near Eastern folk music, particularly its multi-layered rhythms, elasticity of melodic intervals, and the timbres and "breathing" rhythms of cantillation. Since then he has explored serial procedures.

PRINCIPAL COMPOSITIONS: *String Quartets Nos. 1–6*, Opp. 64, 70, 79, 130, 181, 201 (1946; 1947; 1952; 1962, IMI; 1967; 1969); *Bashrav* for violin, Op. 86 (1953, IMP); *Work for Orchestra*, Op. 99 (1957); *Mikhtav hizkiyah* [The Writing of Hiskia], for soprano, violin, oboe, bassoon, Op. 128 (1962, IMI); *Sharharit* for piano, Op. 137 (1963); *Yarëah pagum* [Damaged Moon] for alto, flute, piano, Op. 146 (1964); *Al t'hiyu kha-avotekhem* [Don't Be as Your Fathers] for chorus, Op. 148 (1964, IMI); *Woodwind Quintets Nos. 1–4*, Opp. 159, 199, 208, 212 (1966, 1969, 1970, 1970); *Quartet* for 4 percussionists, Op. 189 (1968); *Quintet* for oboe, horn, piano, percussion, cello, Op. 192 (1968).

BIBL.: Iain Kendell, "New Music," *The Chesterian* (winter 1960).

SEE ALSO Israel.

Eimert, Herbert (b. Bad Kreuznach, Germany, 8 April 1897), studied at the Cologne Musikhochschüle (1919–24) and at the Univ. of Cologne (until 1930), where he majored in musicology. He worked at the West German Radio in Cologne during 1927–33 and was a music critic for the *Kölnischen Zeitung*, 1936–45. Beginning in 1945 he directed night music programing at the Cologne Radio; in 1951 he established an electronic music studio there, which he directs. He was coeditor of *Die Reihe* during 1955–62.

PRINCIPAL COMPOSITIONS: *String Quartet No. 1* (1925); *Tanzmusik* for saxophone, flute, mechanical instruments (1926); *String Quartet No. 2* (1944); *Glockenspiel* on tape (1953, UE; recorded by DGG); *Etüden über Tongemesche* on tape (1953–54, UE; recorded by DGG); *5 Stücke* on tape (1955–56, UE; recorded by DGG); *Epitaph für Aikichi Kuboyama* for sprechstimme, harmonica, electronic sounds on tape (1960–62, UE; recorded by Wergo).

PRINCIPAL WRITINGS: *Atonale Musiklehre* (Leipzig 1924); *Musikalische Formstrukturen im 17. und 18. Jahrhundert* (Augsburg 1932); *Lehrbuch der Zwölftontechnik* (Wiesbaden 1950); *Grundlagen der musikalischen Reihentechnik* (Vienna 1964).

SEE ALSO Mathematics.

Einem, Gottfried von (b. Bern, 24 Jan 1918), studied composition with Boris Blacher (1941–43) and theory and counterpoint with Johann Nepomuk David. He was choral coach for the Berlin Staatsoper (1938–43). Public recognition first came in 1944 when his ballet *Prinzessin Turandot* was premiered in Dresden. In 1947 the premiere of his opera *Dantons Tod* took place at the Salzburg Festival, where his second opera *Der Prozess* was given its first performance in 1953. Einem was a lecturer at the Vienna Konzerthaus Gesellschaft (1946–66), as well as a member of the Board of Directors of the Salzburg Festival (1946–51) and later of the Festival's Artistic Council (1953–66). Since 1963 he has taught composition at the Akademie für Musik und darstellende Kunst in Vienna.

Einem's special talent is opera, in which medium he is the most successful European composer after Berg and Strauss (*Dantons Tod*, for instance, has been produced nearly 40 times in Europe). His output includes four operas, five ballets, more than a dozen orchestral works, two choral works, songs, and chamber music. The early music (through *Dantons Tod*, 1944–46) made use of polytonality, polyrhythms, and sharp contrasts in tone color. Here Stravinsky's influence predominated. Beginning with the *Meditations* for orchestra (1954), Einem has shown an increasing concern for clarity of tonality and formal structure. His use of orchestral color has become more transparent and richer in nuance. Melody, even in purely instrumental works, has grown more cantabile. The use of contrapuntal textures for dramatic and psychological portrayal, already apparent in *Dantons Tod*, has grown more prominent. These stylistic changes resulted largely from Einem's work at the Salzburg Festival and his consequent close study of Mozart (*Der Zerrissene*, 1961–64, is one of the best expressions of this newer style). In spite of his success, Einem's influence on younger composers is slight, for they consider him conservative. He is sought after as a teacher, however, not least because he does not try to force his own ideas on his students.

PRINCIPAL COMPOSITIONS: *Prinzessin Turandot*, ballet, Op. 1; choreography by Tatjana Gsovsky (1942–43, Bote); *Concerto for Orchestra*, Op. 4 (1943, Bote); *Dantons Tod*, opera, Op. 6; libretto by Boris Blacher and the composer (1944–46, UE); *Hymnus an Goethe* for alto, chorus, orchestra, Op. 12 (1949, UE); *Rondo vom goldenen Kalb*, ballet, Op. 13; choreography by Helga Swedlund (1950, Schott); *Der Prozess*, opera, Op. 14; libretto by Blacher and Heinz von Gramer after the novel by Kafka (1950–52, Schott); *Meditations* for orchestra, Op. 18 (1954, Schott and UE); *Piano Concerto*, Op. 20 (1955, Bote); *Symphonische Szenen* for orchestra, Op. 22 (1956, Schott); *Ballade* for orchestra, Op. 23 (1957, Schirmer-G); *Medusa*, ballet, Op. 24; choreography by Erika Hanka (1957, Bote); *Dance-Rondo* for orchestra, Op. 27 (1959, AMP); *Philadelphia Symphony*, Op. 28 (1960, Boosey); *Von der Liebe*, lyric fantasies for voice, orchestra, Op. 30 (1961, Boosey); *Der Zerrissene*, opera, Op. 31; libretto by Blacher (1961–64, Boosey); *Kammergesänge*, 8 songs for medium voice, small orchestra, Op. 32 (1965, UE); *Der Besuch der alte Dame*, opera; libretto by Friedrich Dürrenmatt (1970, Boosey).

PRINCIPAL WRITINGS: *Das musikalische Selbsportrait von Komponisten, Dirigenten, Sängerinen und Sänger unserer Zeit* (Hamburg 1963).

BIBL.: Dominik Hartmann, *G. v. E.* (Vienna 1968).

Dominik Hartmann
(trans. from German by Jeanne Wolf)

Eisler, Hanns (b. Leipzig, 6 July 1898; d. Berlin, 6 Sept 1962), grew up in Vienna, was in the military (1916–18), and then began studying at the Vienna Conservatory. During 1919–23 he was a student of Arnold Schoenberg. In 1925 he moved to Berlin. In spite of the fact that his chamber music was successful in Venice, Donaueschingen, Baden-Baden, and Berlin, he felt unfulfilled. He began searching for a new public, and by 1927 his compositional style began to reflect the needs of the revolutionary workers' movement (he had been sympathetic to socialist ideas from early in his life). In collaboration with Bertolt Brecht and Ernst Busch, beginning in 1929, he wrote political songs, choruses, and theater, film, and orchestral music, all in a vigorous *Kampfmusik* style. In 1933 the Hitler regime forced him into exile. After giving concerts in Austria, Holland, and Belgium, and composing film and theater music in Paris, Eisler began working with Brecht in Denmark in 1934. This was interrupted by film music in London, a concert tour to the U.S. in 1935, and a period writing

songs for the International Brigades in Spain in 1937.

Eisler moved to the U.S. in 1938, where he taught at the New School for Social Research in New York, the Univ. of Southern Calif., and elsewhere. In 1940–43 he directed practical and theoretical experiments to apply modern music to motion pictures (an account of these experiences is contained in his *Composing for the Films*, 1947). During his exile he composed vocal and instrumental music, including much chamber music. In 1947 the U.S. congressional House Un-American Activities Committee exerted pressure to have Eisler blacklisted and deported. After an international protest he was allowed to leave America peacefully in 1948.

Eisler lived in Vienna and then moved in 1950 to Berlin. He wrote songs, cantatas, and music for film and theater in a new, popular style, now following national traditions much more than in preceding periods. This was another way by which his music reflected the needs of the antifascist, democratic movement (1945–52) and the revolutionary socialist movement and society (post 1952) in the German Democratic Republic. After his death a Hanns Eisler Archives was established at the Deutsche Akademie der Künste, where Eisler had held master classes in composition.

Eisler's output centers on his vocal works and theater and film music. He wrote more than 600 vocal pieces: revolutionary songs, lieder, chansons, solo and choral ballads, folk-like songs, etc., along with choruses, chamber cantatas, and symphonic compositions for voices and orchestra. He composed music for nearly 40 stage works and more than 40 films. His instrumental music includes eight orchestral suites, two symphonies, various orchestral pieces, and much chamber music. He contributed to a Marxist theory of music in numerous speeches and articles on the crisis of late bourgeois musical culture and on the role of music in the development of socialism.

Eisler used an extraordinary variety of composing techniques of the past and present. In most cases the songs and other music of the *Kampfmusik* type include elements of modality, jazz, and modern music. The formal structure is based on a free variation and combination of simple melodic-harmonic units, using the techniques of pairing, transposition, sequence, and contrast (the *Solidaritätslied*, 1930, is a good example). The melodies are diatonic, and the rhythmic pulse is clearly articulated. Harmony is quasitonal and dominated by various nonfunctional progressions. It is worth noting that triads, diatonic melodies, and repeated rhythmic patterns in Eisler sound unusual and striking because they do not follow conventional patterns. In other types of music Eisler used more advanced materials, especially dissonant chromaticism and 12-tone techniques. His *Quintet*, Op. 70 (1941–44), contains such advanced resources. The instrumental works, especially the 12-tone compositions, reveal Eisler's preference for continuous forms with freely conceived structures (suite, rhapsody, choral variation, prelude, invention, etude, and the like).

PRINCIPAL COMPOSITIONS (published by Breitkopf-L unless otherwise noted): ★ For vocal soloists, chorus, orchestra: *Die Massnahme*, Op. 20; text by Brecht (1930, UE); *Deutsche Sinfonie*, Op. 50; text by Brecht (1935–37, IM and Breitkopf-L); *Lenin-Requiem*, text by Brecht (1937). ★ For voice, orchestra: *Die Teppichweber von Kujan-Bulak*; text by Brecht (1957); *Ernste Gesänge* (1962). ★ For voice, small orchestra: *4 Balladen*, Op. 22 (1927–30); *6 Lieder*, Op. 28 (1928); *6 Balladen*, Op. 18 (1929–30, UE); *Solidaritätslied*, Op. 27; text by Brecht (1930); *Einheitsfrontlied*; text by Brecht (1934, IM and Breitkopf-L); *Ballade von der Judenhure Marie Sanders*; text by Brecht (1935); *Auferstanden aus Ruinen*, national anthem of the D.D.R.; text by Becher (1949, IM and Verlag "Lied der Zeit," Berlin); *Kinderlieder*; text by Brecht (1949). ★ For voice, several instruments: *Palmström*, 5 pieces for sprechstimme, piccolo, flute, clarinet in A, violin, viola, cello, Op. 5; text by Morgenstern (1924, UE and Breitkopf-L); *Die Weissbrotkantate* for voice, piano (2 clarinets, viola, cello); based on an Italian peasant legend (1937); *Kriegskantate* for voice, 2 clarinets, viola, cello; text by Eisler (1937); *Die Zuchthauskantate* for voice with piano (2 clarinets, viola, cello); text by Eisler (1937). ★ For voice, piano: *6 Lieder*, Op. 2 (1922, UE and Breitkopf-L); *Zeitungsausschnitte*, Op. 11 (1922–26); *4 Wiegenlieder für Arbeitermütter*, Op. 23; text by Brecht (1932); *2 Elegien*; text by Brecht (1937); *Die Hollywood-Elegien*; text by Brecht and the composer (1942–44); *6 Hölderlin-Fragmente* (1943); *Neue deutsche Volkslieder*; text by Becher (1950, DVM); *Lieder nach Texten von Kurt Tucholsky* (1959–61); ★ For chorus: *4 Stücke*, Op. 13 (1928, UE and Breitkopf-L); *2 Männerchöre*, Op. 17 (1929, Hug and Breitkopf-L); *2 Männerchöre*, Op. 35; text by Brecht and Kraus (1929, Hug and Breitkopf-L); *2 Stücke*, Op. 21; text by Brecht (1931, UE and Breitkopf-L); *Gegen den Krieg*, cantata in variation form, Op. 51; text by Brecht (1936); *Woodbury-Liederbüchlein* for 3-part children's or women's chorus (1941). ★ Music for theater: *Die Mutter* by Gorki and Brecht (1931); *Die Rundköpfe und die Spitzköpfe* by Brecht (1934, Henschel); *Durcht und Elend des III. Reiches* by Brecht (1945); *Galileo Galilei* by Brecht (1946); *Höllenangst* by Nestroy (1948, unpub.); *Hamlet* by Shakespeare (1954, unpub.); *Winterschlacht* by Becher (1955, *Winterschlacht-Suite* published by Neue Musik); *Tage der Kommune* by Brecht (1956,

portions published by Breitkopf-L); *Die Geschichte der Simone Machard* by Brecht (1957, portions published by Breitkopf-L); *Schweyk im zweiten Weltkrieg* by Brecht (1942–57). ★ Film music: *Niemandsland* by Frank (1931; portions published in the *Orchestra Suite No. 2*, Op. 23, UE); *Kuhle Wampe* by Brecht and Dudow (1932; portions published in the *Orchestra Suite No. 3*, Op. 26, UE); *Zuidersee* by Ivens (1933, unpub.); *400 Millionen* by Ivens (1938, unpub.); *Forgotten Village* by Steinbeck and Klein (1941, unpub.); *Hangmen Also Die* by Brecht and Lang (1943, unpub.); *None but the Lonely Heart* by Odets (1944, unpub.); *Belami* by Pozner and Daquin (1955, unpub.); *Puntila* by Brecht, Pozner, Wieden, and Cavalcanti (1956, portions published by Breitkopf-L); *Nuit et brouillard* by Resnais (1956, unpub.). ★ Orchestral music: *Kleine Sinfonie*, Op. 29 (1931–32, Neue Musik); *5 Orchesterstücke* (1938); *Kammersinfonie* (1940, Neue Musik); *Rhapsodie* for large orchestra, soprano (1949, Peters-L); *Sturm-Suite* (1957, Neue Musik). ★ Chamber music: *Piano Sonata No. 2*, Op. 6 (1924); *8 Klavierstücke*, Op. 8 (1926, Litolff-L); *Prelude and Fugue on B-A-C-H* for string trio, Op. 46 (1936, music supplement of *Musica Viva* 1936/11); *Violin Sonata*, "Reisesonate" (1937, Litolff-L); *String Quartet* (1937, Litolff-L); *Nonet No. 2* for flute, clarinet, bassoon, trumpet, percussion, 3 violins, double bass (1939, Neue Musik); *Theme and Variations* for piano (1940); *Septet No. 1*, variations on American nursery songs for flutes, clarinet, bassoon, string quartet, Op. 92a (1941, Neue Musik); *Quintet* for flute, clarinet, violin/viola, cello, piano, Op. 70 (1941–44, Litolff-L); *Piano Sonata No. 3* (1943, Litolff-L); *Septet No. 2* for flute, clarinet, bassoon, string quartet (1947, Neue Musik). Complete list: N. Notowicz and J. Elsner, *H. E. Quellennachweise* (Leipzig 1966).

COLLECTED WRITINGS: *Reden und Aufsätze* (Leipzig 1961); *Sinn und Form*, Sonderheft Hanns Eisler (Berlin 1964).

OTHER WRITINGS: "Avantgarde-Kunst und Volksfront," with Ernest Bloch, *Die neue Weltbühne* (Prague 1938):1568–73; *Composing for the Films* (New York 1947); *Johannes Faustus* (Berlin 1952); "Über die Dummheit in der Musik," *Sinn und Form* 10:442–45, 541–45, 763–66.

BIBL.: H. A. Brockhaus, *H. E.* (Leipzig 1961); P. Dessau and F. Goldmann, "Versuch einer Analyse zu H. E.s Kantate *Die Teppichweber von Kujan-Bulak*," *Sinn und Form*, Sonderheft H. S.: 219–27; J. Elsner, *Zur vokalsolistischen Vortragsweise der "Kampfmusik" H. E.s* (Leipzig 1970); E. Klemm, "Bemerkungen zur Zwölftontechnik bei E. und Schönberg," *Sinn und Form* (1964):771–84; G. Mayer, "Zur Dialektik des musikalischen Materials," *Deutsche Zeitschrift für Philosophie* (Berlin) 1966/11:1367–88; N. Notowicz, "E. und Schönberg," *Deutsches Jahrbuch für Musikwissenschaft 1963*:7–25; H. H. Stuckenschmidt, "H. E.," *Musikblätter des Anbruch* (1928):163–67.

Günter Mayer
(trans. from German by Jeanne Wolf)

SEE ALSO Austria and Germany.

Eisma, Will (b. Soengailiat, Indonesia, 13 May 1929), studied at the Rotterdam Conservatory (1948–53; composition with Kees van Baaren, violin with Jewsey Wulf) and the Accadèmia di S. Cecilia in Rome (1959–61, composition with Goffredo Petrassi). He is a professional violinist. During 1953–59 he played with the Rotterdam Philharmonic Orchestra and since 1961, with the Radio Chamber Orchestra in Hilversum. His childhood in Southeast Asia may have influenced his music; World War II, he feels, certainly did. The works below of 1959–60 are 12-tone; those of 1961–65, serial and postserial; and the later ones, "free style."

PRINCIPAL COMPOSITIONS (published by Donemus unless otherwise noted): *Concerto I* for chamber orchestra (1958, unpub.); *Sonata* for clarinet, horn, violin, viola, cello (1959, unpub.); *Concertino for Chamber Orchestra* (1959); *Concerto III* for orchestra (1960); *Concerto* for 2 violins, orchestra (1961); *2 madrigali* for violin, piano (1962); *Volumina* for orchestra (1964); *Diaphora* for 15 strings, harpsichord, percussion (1964); *Archipel* for string quartet (1964); *Fontemara* for wind quintet (1965); *Nonlecture IV* for violin (1967); *Elaborated Relaxation*, electronic sounds on tape (1967, unpub.); *Pages from Albion Moonlight* for 2 mezzo-sopranos, baritone, chorus, orchestra (1968); *Newsreel*, electronic sounds on tape (1969, unpub.); *5 Roses for Diana* for 16 winds (1969); *Stripped of Outer String Quotes*, electronic sounds on tape (1969, unpub.).

Electronic Music: Apparatus and Technology. The history of electronic music apparatus can be traced back at least to Thaddeus Cahill's Telharmonium (1906), to the electronic musical instruments of the Europeans Theremin, Trautwein, and Martenot (1920–30), as well as to the many electronic organs that have been produced since the invention of the vacuum tube. Only since 1950, however, has electronics had a significant impact on serious music, at first mostly through the medium of "tape music" (music manipulated with, recorded on, and played back from magnetic tape) and more recently through live performances with electronic musical instruments and special apparatus.

Some of the landmark technical developments have been 1) commercialization of the audio tape recorder (c.1950); 2) the RCA Synthesizer (1954); 3) development of high speed digital/analog equipment and the Bell Telephone Laboratories computer program for sound generation (1961); 4) the voltage-control concept and the modular approach to electronics systems made possible by the availability of cheap semiconductors (1963). The latter development soon made possible the marketing of *synthesizers* by several firms.

While technology has changed considerably over the years, the production of an electronic-music composition has always consisted of a number of steps in *signal manipulation*, by which a signal is eventually manifested as sound produced by a loudspeaker. The four basic types of signal manipulation are 1) signal generation, 2) signal modification, 3) signal storage, and 4) signal combining and synchronization.

The typical electronic music studio of the 1950s and early 60s contained signal generators or other signal sources, signal modifiers, audio tape recorders, patching and mixing equipment, and a two-channel amplifier/speaker system. Most equipment was manually controlled. Starting in the mid-1960s there was a rapid transformation to the use of voltage-controlled sound synthesizers, while simultaneously there was much experimentation with digital computer synthesis. During 1969–71 several groups began experimenting with the use of *minicomputers* to program voltage-controlled synthesizers.

SIGNAL GENERATORS. The following descriptions apply to electronic apparatus in use in electronic music studios during the 1950s and early 60s. All are still in use, but many now allow voltage control of certain parameters. A *generator* produces an electrical signal or *waveform* of a predefined nature. Usually there are one or more parameters pertaining to the signal that can be adjusted by means of knobs or switches on the front panel of the instrument.

Waveform generators (oscillators). A waveform is the graph of a single vibration of a periodic or quasi-periodic signal (see Fig. 1). A periodic signal is one that repeats itself at a regular rate, called the rate of oscillation or *frequency*. The listener perceives frequency as pitch. The amplitude of the waveform is the maximum excursion of the signal from its average value. The listener perceives amplitude as loudness or volume. In an electronic waveform generator the signal is a periodic electrical vibration. The variable parameters are amplitude and frequency, which the composer must be able to manipulate independently of each other. A typical manually controlled generator provides controls for continuous change of frequency and amplitude over several restricted ranges and for switching between the ranges of these parameters. One early type of generator, however, called the *beat generator*, allowed a complete continuous

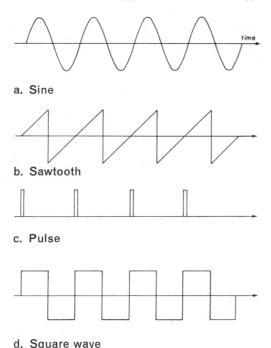

a. Sine

b. Sawtooth

c. Pulse

d. Square wave

Fig. 1 Basic Waveforms

sweep of frequency over the entire audible range.

The basic waveforms used in electronic music systems are the sine, sawtooth, pulse, and square waves (see Fig. 1). The sine wave is the most basic signal, containing only one wave component; no other signals can be extracted from it. Sawtooth, pulse, and square waves are composed of infinite numbers of sine waves with integrally related (*harmonic*) frequencies and differing amplitudes.

A plot of the amplitudes vs. the frequencies of the constituent sine waves of the tone is called the *spectrum* of the tone. The listener interprets a spectrum as tone color. The sine wave has a pure, penetrating sound, much like a French horn in its high register. The square wave has a hollow, clarinetlike tone. In the medium and high registers, the sawtooth and pulse waves have a "buzzlike" quality; in the lower register they sound like a bass trombone.

Noise generators. Noise signals, unlike periodic waveform signals, never repeat themselves. Although completely random, they can be characterized in terms of statistical averages. Moreover it is possible to characterize noises in terms of sine waves that are infinitesimally close in frequency. The most basic noise signal is *white noise*, which contains sine waves at all frequencies with equal amplitudes.

Paradoxically each individual wave has an infinitesimal amplitude. The sound of white noise resembles the rushing of a water fall. A white noise generator has a single output with no controls.

Inharmonic generators. Signals generated by these devices are not intended to be periodic. They are composed of nonintegrally related frequencies. The sounds produced may be bell-like or metallic in quality. In contrast to periodic tones, it is usually desired that the listener easily hear out some of the individual frequencies of the sound. But if the frequencies are sufficiently close together (dense), it is impossible to hear separate frequencies, and the sound approaches that of colored noise (noise whose constituent sine waves have unequal amplitudes). For complete flexibility all the constituent waveforms of the signal must be variable in frequency and amplitude.

Other signal sources. Signals produced by sources other than electronic apparatus have been used extensively. One obvious source is the acoustical environment. "Live" or musique concrète sounds can be picked up by microphones and manipulated like any electrical signal. Also an antenna can be used to pick up radio noise, and other types of transducers can be used to pick up other kinds of signals.

SIGNAL MODIFIERS (SIGNAL PROCESSORS, SIGNAL TRANSFORMERS). A signal modifier changes one or more attributes of a signal. Certain parameters define the modification process. These can be adjusted by means of knobs or switches provided on the front panel of the instrument.

A *filter* acts on an input electrical signal to modify the amplitudes of the individual sine waves (the spectrum) of the signal. It does not change the frequencies (pitches) of the waves, nor does it create any new frequencies. A filter is classified in terms of its frequency response characteristic: *low-pass*, *high-pass*, *band-pass*, and *band-stop* are the most common. The low-pass filter allows all waves whose frequencies are below a certain cutoff frequency to pass unaltered; it reduces the amplitudes of waves above the cutoff frequency. A high-pass filter passes unaltered only those frequencies above its cutoff frequency. The band-pass filter passes only those waves within a specified band of frequencies grouped about a center frequency. The band-stop filter rejects all waves within the defined frequency band. Usually the composer can adjust the cutoff frequencies, center frequencies, and bandwidths of a filter. However, the cutoff ratios and roll-off rates, which define the sharpness of transition between the frequency regions where waves are passed and where they are rejected, are usually fixed for a given filter.

Filters are used primarily to give variety in tone color to signals (it is this feature that is exploited in electronic organs). No amount of filtering of a sine wave will produce anything other than a sine wave, but filtering of pulse, sawtooth, and square waves can produce many different tone qualities. A secondary use of filters, particularly of narrow bandwidth, band-pass types, is to extract pitches (frequencies) from signals that contain many spectral components. When white noise is passed through a filter, the spectrum of the resulting sound conforms exactly to the filter characteristic. Since white noise is infinitely dense in sine waves, a narrow bandwidth, band-pass filter produces a noise with more-or-less definite pitch, akin to a cluster of sine waves. As the bandwidth becomes narrower, the output signal approaches a sine wave, although instead of having a constant amplitude, as a sine wave does, its amplitude fluctuates randomly.

A *spectrum shaper* consists of a number of band-pass filters with contiguous pass bands whose outputs are applied to attenuators and then combined to form the output signal. The input signal is applied simultaneously to all of the band-pass filters. A large variety of frequency characteristics and, correspondingly, a large variety of tone colors is obtainable.

A *reverberator* generates a combination of the original signal and many time-delayed versions or *echoes* of it. Usually the echoes die away, but for special effects they can be made to increase. With a simple reverberator the echoes are evenly spaced in time, having amplitudes that decrease with time. This type of reverberation can easily be produced with a feedback-connected tape recorder. However, monotonous chains of echoes result from this scheme unless several simple reverberators with different, carefully chosen delay times are combined. Near-natural reverberation can be achieved more easily by hybrid electrical-acoustical devices such as echo chambers, metal springs, thin parallel metal plates, or wire baskets acting in combination with speakers and microphones. These devices can produce more complex (and unpredictable) reflections than sophisticated all-electronic systems (such as those using digital memory techniques), but the control of some reverberation parameters, which may lead to unusual and interesting effects, is sacrificed.

A *modulator* operates on two input signals to produce a third signal. This signal is not a mere combination of the original signals but a completely new signal that preserves some of the characteristics of the original ones. An *amplitude modulator* superimposes the amplitude variations of one input signal upon the other.

A *ring modulator* (analog multiplier) is used to combine several signals so that the output consists of sums and differences of all the input frequency components. It is most frequently used to enhance or completely refashion the timbre of sounds that already have distinctive complexities built into them (e.g., with regard to rhythms and attacks). *Phase modulators* (PM modulators, doppler-effect modulators) produce a different effect, which with regard to sine wave signals is the same as *time modulation*. (If a sine tone were played back on a tape recorder with its speed alternating back and forth between, say, 7 and 8 inches per second, the sound would waver in pitch and the result would be a time-modulated sine tone.)

Frequency shifters (*Klangunwandlen*) are used to alter the frequencies of sound material. Although frequencies are shifted by this device, pitch transposition in the musical sense is not accomplished. Frequencies are shifted by a fixed amount so that tones that were originally harmonic (containing integrally related frequencies) usually become inharmonic (with nonintegrally related frequencies). This is in contrast to normal transposition where all frequencies are multiplied by the same factor, and harmonicity and pitch intervals are preserved.

SIGNAL STORAGE DEVICES: TAPE RECORDERS. The most practical medium for electrical signal storage is magnetic tape. Any kind of music can be recorded on tape for subsequent listening. However, because of the flexibility of tape recorders for erasing, recording, and editing, composers can make use of the tape medium in the same sense that painters make use of canvas and paint. With most electronic music it is usually expedient to tape record intermediate results in order to break up the construction of complex compositions into smaller, more amenable steps. One method for using tape is as follows: discrete sound events are recorded, spliced together, and then combined by simple addition with a mixer circuit (see signal routing). By repeating this process an entire composition can be built up from a number of basic sounds. At any point one or more of the tape tracks may be subjected to signal modification, such as reverberation.

Unlike all-electronic apparatus, which usually requires little care, tape recorders require regular maintenance. Moreover the technique of tape recording is often imprecise, because there are many ways (often not well understood) that a tape recording system can contaminate a signal. Although recent improvements in tape recording technology, including that of the tape itself, now enable almost perfect recordings, the cost of very high quality machines ($5,000 or more per recorder) plus the fact that at least three recorders are needed for flexible tape music operation (two for playback of separately produced tracks and one for recording the result) limit their availability to only a few studios. Most studios use professional quality, 2-channel tape recorders, and many have 4-channel machines as well; 8- or even 16-track recorders may be widely used soon. In 1967 Dolby Laboratories began marketing an electronic device to reduce the noise introduced by tape recorders (principally hum, print-through, and hiss); use of this device has resulted in a substantial improvement in tape recording quality, and it has been widely adopted.

Variable-speed tape recorders and time-rate changers. Tape machines can be used to modify signals as well as to store them. By changing the speed of the tape in relation to the playback head, corresponding changes can be made in pitch and tempo. While with simple, fixed-head equipment it is impossible to have one change without the other, more elaborate, rotating head equipment allows the two to be altered separately, albeit with some distortion of the signal. By combining tape delay and periodic tape speed changes, it is possible to produce a sound modification process called *phasing*. This is essentially a time-variant filtering process.

SIGNAL ROUTING: MIXERS, SWITCHES, AND PATCH BOARDS. The final step in music realization, as well as one of the intermediate ones, is the routing of signals to their final destinations, often the tracks of a master tape, of which at the present time there are usually two or four. The combining of several signals onto one or more tracks is accomplished by a *mixer*. A mixer has several inputs and usually a fewer number of outputs, which are called channels. The channels may correspond to the tracks on the master tape or to the loudspeakers used to monitor the sounds as they are created. With one type of mixer, input attenuators are provided to control the amplitude (volume) of each of the signals before they are combined with the others. The outputs of the attenuators may be connected by means of switches to any combination of the output channels. Also the absolute levels of the

output channels containing the combined signals are controlled by separate, master level attenuators. A more elaborate mixer substitutes *pan pots* or *joy sticks* for channel switches so that a different amount of each signal can be sent to each channel, and thus arbitrary distributions of the input signals between the channels can be achieved. For a manually operated studio, attenuators perform a crucial role in the realization process, since they are not only used for setting levels but also for producing crescendos and decrescendos during the generation of sound tracks. Therefore high quality attenuators that allow production of fast level changes without accompanying noise are essential.

For each step in the process of composition, electric cords need to be connected between instruments. As the number of inputs and outputs increases, however, the cords cross over the controls of the instruments and each other and become unwieldy. One device for systematizing the interconnections is the telephone patchboard. All inputs and outputs are permanently wired to specific locations behind the patch field, and connections between the patch positions are made via patch cords. More sophisticated systems are also in use. For example, some patchboards can be removed and replaced by any one of several preconnected patchboards. Another type uses patch plugs that are inserted in matrix locations, each of which corresponds to a particular input/output combination.

DEVELOPMENTS SINCE THE MID-1960s. During the mid-60s several modifications and additions were made to electronic music apparatus to give the composer greater freedom and flexibility. With previous equipment it was not possible to control parameters such as frequency and amplitude quickly and accurately. Changes in volume were restricted to those that could be produced by the manual manipulation of control knobs. In the 60s, *voltage control*, the use of special, often subaudible electrical signals, began to replace the human hand as the vehicle of control. New signal generators and signal modifiers were created that could respond to control signals. Special *envelope generators* were built to provide signals for the control of the attack and decay of sounds. It became possible to hook devices together so that all of them could be activated by pushing a single button. This enabled composers to produce single sounds with complexities comparable to those of conventional musical instruments. Other improvements during the 60s made the creation and manipulation of several layers of sound easier. While during the 50s a large amount of tape splicing and montaging was necessary, now several methods of program control were devised, including computer control, that would automatically produce rhythmic sets of events and complex event changes. Several manufacturers, starting with R. A. Moog, Inc. (1964), began supplying integrated packages of voltage-controlled circuit modules called *synthesizers*. For the first time almost all of the circuits required for electronic music synthesis were provided in single, moderately priced packages. Multitrack tape recorders became more common, making it easier to synchronize separate lines of music. Finally the digital computer, potentially the most flexible musical instrument, was programmed for complete sound synthesis, and *computer music* was established as an electronic music medium in its own right.

Voltage-controlled devices and devices for producing control signals. Three basic types of voltage-controlled devices are manufactured: the voltage-controlled amplifier, the voltage-controlled oscillator, and the voltage-controlled filter. All of these devices can be linked together, enabling the output of one to be used either as a signal or control input to any of the others. Other devices are used solely to produce control signals.

The voltage-controlled amplifier, like the ordinary amplifier, alters the amplitude (volume) of the input signal. However, the amplification or *gain* of this device can be controlled using external signals. The voltage-controlled oscillator performs like an ordinary waveform generator, except that frequencies (pitches) are determined by one or more external control voltages. In a similar manner, a voltage-controlled filter can be used for the external manipulation of the bandwidth, center frequency, or cutoff frequency of sounds. Any of these devices can be hooked up to various other, manually controlled devices such as a keyboard, a *linear controller* (where the lateral position of the finger along a conducting metal strip corresponds to pitch or amplitude), or a *contact board* (where the finger makes contact between two conductors). They also may be connected to any other device producing control signals, including devices like themselves.

The envelope generator produces controls for the attack and decay of sounds. The general pattern of an envelope signal may be described by a voltage that starts from zero, reaches a maximum value, and decreases to zero again. The importance of this type of signal can be appreciated from the fact that all musical instrument tones have distinctive amplitude-versus-time curves of this sort. The most

common envelope characteristic used in sound synthesis consists of an *exponential* attack followed by a constant steady state and an exponential decay (Fig. 2a). Others utilize *linear* attack and linear decay (Fig. 2b), *scooped* exponential attack (Fig. 2c), *overshoot* attack (Fig. 2d), and immediate decay (percussive) (Fig. 2e). The attack time and other parameters can be manually or voltage controlled. The envelope generator requires a trigger signal to tell it when to begin its attack and when to begin its decay

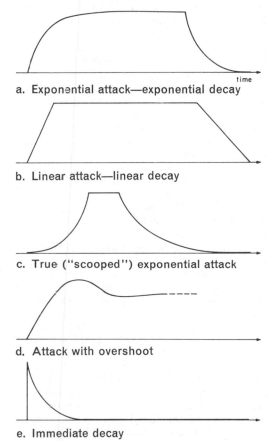

a. Exponential attack—exponential decay

b. Linear attack—linear decay

c. True ("scooped") exponential attack

d. Attack with overshoot

e. Immediate decay

Fig. 2 Characteristic envelopes

Voltage-controlled oscillators, amplifiers, and filters, together with a keyboard and some envelope generators, can be connected to perform as a monophonic musical instrument or tape-music signal source.

Frequency modulators. Frequency modulation results when the frequency of one voltage-controlled oscillator is controlled with the combination of a constant voltage (which establishes the average frequency) and a signal from another waveform generator. Several categories of effects, such as vibrato, trill, warble, buzz, and clangerous-tone, can be produced, depending on the modulating signal used. Since the resulting sound depends on a number of factors, including the amplitude, waveform, and frequency of the modulating signal, a large range of sonorities is possible with this simple arrangement.

Nonlinear processors (function generator). Unlike filters and reverberators, which are linear processors, a nonlinear processor may produce frequencies not present in the inputs. Or the output may be a control signal derived from the input. A special nonlinear processor called a *derivative synthesizer* was built in 1967 by Eric Gschwandtner of the Wurlitzer Co. It can produce a rich variety of tone colors, and, when linked with other devices, can be used to produce complex sounds closely resembling, for instance, clarinet or trumpet tones. Another nonlinear device, the *envelope follower*, is used to superimpose attack-decay characteristics of available sound materials onto other sounds. Still another device, the *amplitude filter*, allows a sound to be produced only when it exceeds a certain volume.

Timbre synthesizers. Several methods have been introduced to change the waveforms of periodic (harmonic) signals in order to produce new tone colors. Four of them are direct waveform synthesis, modulation synthesis, subtractive synthesis, and additive synthesis. In direct waveform synthesis, a signal is produced by controlling the amplitudes of individual equally spaced points on a waveform graph. With modulation synthesis, a periodic tone is modulated by another tone to create a new one. With subtractive synthesis, new colors are created by passing a periodic wave through a filter that enhances or subdues certain frequencies. With additive synthesis, any arbitrary spectrum comprising a limited number of harmonics can be generated by superimposing individual sine waves. Harmonic synthesizers that have been built include a seven-harmonic generator by Cahill (1906) that uses electrical dynamos, a 100-harmonic generator by Fletcher (1940) that uses sine waves recorded on separate tracks of a magnetic drum, and an electronic six-harmonic generator built by this writer (1964). The last-named, which is housed in the Experimental Music Studio at the Univ. of Ill., provides for independent voltage control of the fundamental frequency and six harmonic amplitudes. It can be actuated by a keyboard and can produce a variety of attacks and tone colors.

PROGRAM CONTROL OF SOUND SYNTHESIS EQUIPMENT. A large variety of sounds can be produced with configurations of voltage-controlled circuits driven by a keyboard or other *actuator*, and these sounds can be recorded on tape and combined in any manner by tape splicing. However, splicing is a cumbersome process. It can be eliminated by providing an automatic means for control-voltage generation, signal combination, and signal synchronization, several kinds of which have been used from the mid-1950s to the present.

Paper-tape generation of control voltages. Manually controlled apparatus, which was used exclusively in the 50s, can be automatically and dynamically manipulated by means of relays and servo motors. Already in the 50s punched paper tape was being used to program relays and motors. When fed into a tape reader the information on it was converted to establish connections between pieces of equipment and to control the values of musical parameters. This method was used for the RCA Synthesizer built by H. F. Olson in 1954 (the Mark II version of which was obtained by the Columbia-Princeton Electronic Music Center' in 1959). Although its originators felt that this machine could produce any sound, this has not been borne out. (Another system of the same general type was built about 1959 by Helmut Klein at the Siemens Electronic Music Studio in Munich.) A system for paper-tape control of voltage-controlled devices, the *coordinome*, was developed in 1966 by Emmanuel Ghent and Stein Raustein of New York Univ., assisted by Robert Moog.

Graphic control. Another control technique involves the conversion of spatial graphs into time graphs by means of light beams that scan a drawn graph. The light is converted into appropriate electrical control signals that are applied as control signals to various voltage-controlled devices. This kind of system allows the composer to control parameters continuously rather than in discrete steps, as with punched paper tape; he is therefore able to achieve greater nuances of expression. Despite the obvious attractiveness of this approach, however, this type of equipment is not in wide use because of technical limitations and cost.

The sequencer. Another important control device is the *sequencer*, first manufactured by Buchla Associates of Berkeley, Calif. It allows the composer to program the characteristics of several successive sound events; he can modify the durations and control voltages for each event easily. Although the device is limited by the finite number of different events that can be programmed, by combining two or more sequencers it is possible to produce pseudo-random sequences of events. This device is often used with another device called a *random voltage generator*, which can be used to produce series of random pitches.

Control by digital computer. A digital computer can be used to solve many of the problems inherent in noncomputer control systems. For instance, the main problem in programming voltage-controlled equipment by means of punched paper tape stems from the absence of a memory in the system for storing information until it is needed; each parameter must be spelled out in complete detail every time it is required. A small digital computer with a moderate-sized memory can supply this missing link. It can also be used to interpret compact symbolic scores (of the composer's invention) and convert these into the appropriate control voltage changes; thus it can relieve the composer of most of the detailed specifications for parameters. Groups that are presently experimenting with computer control of analog equipment are Electronic Music Studios Ltd., London (Peter Zinovieff); Bell Telephone Laboratories, Murray Hill, N.J. (Max Mathews); and the Univ. of Ill. Experimental Music Studio (Edward Kobrin).

Complete sound synthesis with digital computer. Although a system of analog apparatus allows the composer direct access to the sound-producing elements and enables him to experiment with sounds before actually realizing a composition, such a system lacks universality. It cannot produce every imaginable audio signal nor, therefore, every imaginable sound (although large varieties of sound are possible with large analog systems). On the other hand, the digital computer with the proper peripheral equipment is a universal sound-generating apparatus. It can generate the sample points in digital form for any waveform, and high speed equipment can convert sequences of such sample points into continuous signals so as to cover the entire audible range of frequencies. Of course, computer programs are needed to compute the sample points that are to be converted into sound, and the universality of the sound production will always be limited to that of the programs. Furthermore composers still do not have the information they need to produce precisely all the sounds they might imagine. (Research to analyze and synthesize acoustical musical instrument tones, which are highly complex, may provide the key to an adequate description of timbres.)

In 1961 a flexible program for computer sound generation was written by Max Mathews of Bell Telephone Laboratories. By means of this program (currently called Music V) analog circuits such as voltage-controlled oscillators, filters, and envelope generators are simulated within the computer. Signals are computed in digital form, which, when generated at a later time, are close approximations of comparable analog signals. With this program it is not only possible for the composer to use simulated circuits that have already been programmed, but also for him to program his own original designs. The Bell Labs program has been adopted at a number of computer installations in the U.S. where the necessary digital-to-analog conversion equipment is available. Stanford University's system is described in the article Computer Applications.

Flexible as they are, computers have several disadvantages: Being a serial machine, the computer performs one calculation at a time; if anything happens to interrupt the calculations, it may lose its place and much of the calculations may be lost. Also the signals generated by computers are only approximations of the intended signals, both in time and amplitude. Lack of perfection in amplitude approximation gives rise to a noise behind the signal, although with a well-designed system it is usually hardly noticeable. In addition the finite time between calculated points on the signal waveform may result in a distorted version of the intended signal (by the *foldover effect*). The serial nature of the computer poses a further problem, for the amount of computer time required to calculate a given sound is proportional to and is typically much greater than the length of the sound itself. Since computer time is scarce and expensive, composers often have had to work during low-demand hours, such as midnight to 8 A.M. (These problems hopefully will diminish as faster and cheaper computers become available.) Because computers remove the composer a step away from sound itself and because they require from him a certain amount of computer programming, most composers prefer the electronic tape studio or live electronic performance. Perhaps the greatest challenge before electronics technologists in the field of music is to develop new systems that successfully combine the flexibility and universality of the digital computer with the immediacy of the analog systems.

BIBL. (in chronological order): Benjamin F. Miessner, "Electronic Music and Instruments," *Proceedings of the Institute of Radio Engineers* 24:1427–63 (1936); H. F. Olson, H. Delar, "Electronic Music Synthesizer," *Journal of the Acoustical Society of America* 27:595–612 (1955); Hugh Le Caine, "Electronic Music," *Proceedings of the Institute of Radio Engineers* 44:457–78 (1956); Eric Salzman, "From Composer to Magnetron to You," *High Fidelity* (August 1960):89–92; Max V.

Mathews, "An Acoustical Compiler for Music and Psychological Stimuli," *Bell System Technological Journal* 40:677–94 (1961); Oskar Sala, "Mixture: Trautonium and Studio Technique," *Gravensano Blatter* 6:53–60 (1962); Hugh Le Caine, "A Tape Recorder for Use in Electronic Music Studios and Related Equipment," *Journal of Music Theory* 7:83–97 (1963); Lejaren Hiller and James W. Beauchamp, "Research in Music with Electronics," *Science* 150:161–69 (1965); James W. Beauchamp, "Additive Synthesis of Harmonic Musical Tones," *Journal of the Audio Engineering Society* 14:332–42 (1966); Robert A. Moog, "Electronic Music: Its Composition and Performance," *Electronics World* (Feb 1967):42–46; *Electronic Music Review* 1–7 (Trumansburg, N.Y., 1967–69); Peter J. Schuyten and Stephen W. Fields, "Signal Gains for Electronic Music," *Electronics* (29 April 1968):93–97; *Music by Computers* (New York 1969); Max V. Mathews, *The Technology of Computer Music* (Cambridge, Mass., 1969); Peter Zinovieff, "A Computerized Electronic Music Studio," *Electronic Music Reports* 1:5–22 (Utrecht, 1969); *Synthesis* 1– , (Minneapolis, 1971–).

James Beauchamp

Electronic Music: History and Development. By now more than 10,000 electronic compositions have been produced by more than 2,000 composers using equipment that includes over 500 permanent electronic music studios not used for other purposes. Electronic sounds have been used in virtually every conceivable context in Western civilisation for which music is employed: radio and television advertising jingles and station identification signals, films, Catholic Masses, and children's fairy-story records are among the less predictable. Pop and jazz musicians perform on synthesizers or feed their instruments through ring modulators, frequency dividers, or tape-delay systems. In some schools students are producing short electronic studies in their early teens, and the more scientifically minded are building simple equipment. Already several hundred electronic music synthesizers are in use around the world.

COMPOSITIONAL APPROACHES. *Electronic music* originally referred only to sounds synthesized electronically, as opposed to *musique concrète*, which designated music using normal musical and everyday sounds recorded via microphone; in most countries today the term *electronic music* covers the whole range of sound material, musical styles, and esthetics.

The basic compositional procedures differ little from those of instrumental and vocal music: A composer selects the material he considers suitable for the composition he has in mind (inspired either in terms of the pre-determined instruments/equipment for which the work is to be composed, or freely, in which case he must find the most appropriate instrumentation). He explores the potentialities inherent in this material, develops it, modifies it, and integrates all the elements into a finished structure. The processes involved in assembling an electronic composition consist basically of sound generation (using oscillators or acoustic sounds introduced by means of microphones), sound modification (using filters, modulators, reverberation, tape treatments, etc.), and sound storage and reproduction (tape, amplifiers, and loudspeakers).

Precursors of electronic music techniques go back to the beginning of the 20th century. Each closely followed the invention and development of particular items of equipment: telephone, microphone, loudspeaker, oscillator, phonograph record, and film soundtrack. The main fields of early exploration involved manipulation of records, hand-drawn film soundtracks (especially by the Canadian film maker Norman McLaren), and electric musical instruments (such as the Theremin and ondes Martenot). Most work before 1948 (by Varèse, Hindemith, Toch, Milhaud, and others) consisted only of experiments; the chief exception was John Cage, whose first three *Imaginary Landscapes* (1939–42) include records played at variable speeds, audio oscillators, and an amplified coil of wire.

Electronic music proper came into existence in 1948 with the first musique concrète studies of Pierre Schaeffer, a French sound engineer and radio producer. He was followed very soon afterwards by composers in several other countries, in some cases without knowledge of Schaeffer's work. A decisive impetus came from the perfection and commercial availability of the tape recorder around 1948. Musique concrète existed for three years, however, before tape recorders superceded the record players initially used by Schaeffer, whose original reluctance to make the changeover was later overcome by the realisation that the medium would not have developed much further without the transfer to tape. The precision with which sounds can be edited and dissected on tape enabled composers to think freely in the medium, limited only by the amount and quality of the equipment available (generally no greater a restriction than that imposed by the commissioning of a work for specified instruments).

Schaeffer's first works were all entitled *Study* and were mostly simple collages based on sounds such as those recorded at a railway station, from a saucepan, and at the piano.

Methods of sound modification consisted only of various disc treatments, including the *sillon fermé* (closed groove disc "loop"). Pierre Henry joined Schaeffer in 1949 and introduced greater musical sophistication into the techniques of musique concrète, as in their joint 20-minute *Symphonie pour un homme seul* (1949–50). The sounds they used became more divorced from the associations implicit in their origins, and the structures became more expansive, incorporating textures and combinations that instrumentalists would not have been able to sustain. Between 1951 and 1953 a number of guest composers worked at the studio Schaeffer and Henry established. Among these were Pierre Boulez, Olivier Messiaen, and Karlheinz Stockhausen, all of whose more purist approach to sound forced them to reject Schaeffer's esthetic and indeed his considerable library of recorded sounds. They preferred to use a minimum of very abstract sound materials and to develop them in a highly organic way.

Two other studios were established during this period, one at the NWDR (now WDR) radio in Cologne, directed by Herbert Eimert, the other at Columbia Univ. in New York, directed by Vladimir Ussachevsky and Otto Luening. Composers who worked at the Cologne studio included Stockhausen, Karel Goeyvaerts, Henri Pousseur, Gottfried Michael Koenig, and Bengt Hambraeus. They built up their compositions from pure sine waves, the main sound source of early electronic compositions, applying serial techniques derived from Webern to various parameters. In general they avoided pitch systems possible on conventional instruments. The most significant of these first electronic pieces were Stockhausen's *Studies I–II* (1953–54), the second of which was also the first electronic work to be fully notated in score form and published (see Electronic Music: Notation). Early works from New York showed a less abstract and extreme attitude toward sound material, using instrumental sounds such as those of piano, flute, and percussion. Luening and Ussachevsky collaborated on *Rhapsodic Variations* for tape and orchestra (1953–54), one of the earliest works to combine tape with live performance; *A Poem in Cycles and Bells* for the same forces (1954) was based on the tape pieces *Fantasy in Space* and *Sonic Contours* by Luening and Ussachevsky, respectively.

Early electronic music tended to explore the extremes of concrete and electronic sound materials and to concentrate primarily on tape treatments as a way of modifying and combining sounds. It was not until the mid 50s-that composers first began to use electronic transformation equipment such as filters and ring modulators to any extent. This was accompanied by an increasing tendency to combine sounds from different sources and often to transform the original material beyond recognition. Indeed some entirely electronic works give the impression of being partially concrete and vice versa. Stockhausen's *Gesang der Jünglinge* (1955–56) adds a boy's treble voice, sometimes fragmented, transposed, and superimposed on itself, to a full range of electronic sounds and treatments. Iannis Xenakis's *Analogique A + B* (Paris, 1958–59) combines nine string instruments with a tape built up entirely from sine waves. Ussachevsky's *Piece for Tape Recorder* (1956) mixes instrumental, electronic, and concrete sounds. Between 1956 and 1960 most studios adopted two-channel tape recording equipment for the spatial projection and movement of sound, and between 1960 and 1962 the largest studios expanded to four-channel installations. Cologne bypassed the two-channel stage altogether, and its first productions for standard four-channel equipment date from 1958: György Ligeti's *Artikulation* (1958), Mauricio Kagel's *Transición I* (1958–60), and Stockhausen's *Kontakte* for tape alone or in combination with piano and percussion (1959–60); in addition, Stockhausen's *Gesang der Jünglinge* was reduced to a four-channel version from the original five.

Until 1960 virtually all electronic music was stored on magnetic tape and could only be performed by replaying the tape. The procedures involved in building up the final composition, layer by layer and stage by stage, are time consuming and require much uncreative tape editing. A composer generally needs technical assistance or else must become his own technician. Around 1960 two other aspects of electronic music began to be developed, both of which simplify or even eliminate these procedures: 1) the generation of electronic sounds by means of integrated systems, controlled either manually (voltage-controlled electronic music synthesizers such as the Moog and Buchla in the U.S., the Synket from Italy, and the more recent American ARP and English VCS-3, or "Putney") or semiautomatically (computer systems with associated sound-generating equipment either commercial or custom built); and 2) live electronic performance, which features the real-time operation of equipment in a concert situation, combining the three stages of producing a tape composition into a simultaneous presentation and interaction of processes and usually bypassing tape storage altogether. Integrated studios or synthesizers can enable a composer to record a complex work directly on tape in real time. This generally occurs, however, only after hours or days of preparation, and it would seem that most composers take as much time to compose an electronic work as they would an instrumental work of equivalent complexity and length. As of 1970 there were still comparatively few important synthesizer compositions; Morton Subotnick, who was instrumental in the development of the Buchla, has produced three for records, including *Touch* (1969). The same assessment applies to computer music, where much of the work has been done in the form of experiments by scientists. Best known in this field is Max Mathews of the Bell Telephone Laboratories (where composer James Tenney worked 1961–64); the computer programs developed there have been adapted and used in many other centers, such as at Princeton Univ. by a group headed by James K. Randall (*Lyric Variations* for violin and tape, 1966–68). Both synthesizers and computer systems are likely to become much more sophisticated in the next few years, including for example the replacement of many of the knobs on synthesizers by finger-controlled, touch-sensitive devices for live performance operation.

THE MAJOR STUDIOS. The early works of Schaeffer and Henry were produced on equipment at the drama department of the French Radio in Paris. Their success led to the setting up of a permanent studio in 1951 with the newly introduced tape recorders and a variety of sound modification equipment. The Westdeutscher Rundfunk (WDR) studio in Cologne and the Columbia Univ. studio in New York were both begun in 1951 on an improvised basis and more permanently established in 1953. These three studios have always been considered the leading centers.

In 1958 Schaeffer reorganized the Paris studio under the name Groupe de Recherches Musicales. Xenakis produced several works there (1957–62), as have François Bayle (*Espaces inhabitables*, 1966–67), Ivo Malec (*Cantata pour elle* for soprano, harp, tape, 1966), Bernard Parmegiani (*Violostries* for violin, tape, 1963–64; in collaboration with the violinist Devy Erlih), and Luc Ferrari (*Und so weiter* for amplified piano, tape, 1965–66). The number of works produced in Cologne has always remained small because composers are invited to work for several months on a composition (some studios allow only a few days), and a second working area was not installed until 1966. Recent productions include Stockhausen's *Hymnen* (1966–67; there is also a

version for 6 performers and tape, and one of the 4 "regions" that make up the nearly 2-hour-long work can be combined with orchestra), which is based on recordings of national anthems, often highly processed and modified, much as he used folk music from different countries in *Telemusik* (1966, NHK Radio, Tokyo).

A grant from the Rockefeller Foundation enabled the Columbia Univ. studio to be expanded in 1959 into the Columbia-Princeton Electronic Music Center. One of its several composition studios is devoted to the RCA electronic music synthesizer Mark II, a special-purpose sound-generating computer system with which Milton Babbitt has worked (*Philomel* for soprano, tape, 1963–64). Varèse realized the final version of *Déserts* (for wind, percussion, tape) at the Columbia-Princeton center in 1960–61 (originally produced at the French Radio in 1954). Many other American and foreign composers have worked there, including the Argentine-born Mario Davidovsky (*Synchronisms Nos. 1–3* for instruments, tape, 1963–65).

Electronic music has developed in virtually every country where Western music is predominant, taking a characteristic form reflective of the local cultural, social, and economic situation. Thus in Europe and Japan most studios are at radio stations, where much of the essential equipment is already in daily use; in the U.S. and Canada, where broadcasting is a profit-oriented industry, and recently in Britain and Latin America, most studios are at universities. Among the major studios established at radio stations during the 50s are those in Milan (Luciano Berio: *Omaggio a Joyce*, 1958; *Visage*, 1961; both based on the voice of Cathy Berberian), Tokyo (Toshiro Mayuzumi, Makoto Moroi), Warsaw (Włodzimierz Kotoński, Krzysztof Penderecki), and London (BBC Radiophonic Workshop; mainly music for radio and television but also Roberto Gerhard's *Collages* for orchestra, tape, 1960). University studios include those founded at Urbana, Ill. by Lejaren Hiller and at Toronto by Myron Schaeffer; other studios include the state-supported Apelac studio in Brussels (Henri Pousseur: *Rimes pour différentes sources sonores* for 3 orchestral groups, tape, 1958–59; *3 Visages de Liège*, 1961), which is now at Liège Univ.; and two studios founded by industries, Siemens & Halske in Munich (Josef Anton Riedl) and Philips in Eindhoven (Henk Badings; guest composer Varèse: *Poème électronique*, 1957–58), of which the latter was dismantled in 1960 and its equipment installed at Utrecht Univ. (G. M.

Koenig). Pierre Henry left the French radio studio in 1958 and set up the privately sponsored Studio Apsome in Paris (*Le Voyage*, 1961–63). A number of other privately owned studios were also established during the 1950s, mostly on a small scale. By the mid-60s private studios were as numerous as officially sponsored ones, and many are now very adequately equipped.

During the 1960s the most widespread activity was in the U.S. Over 200 studios were functioning there in 1970, divided fairly equally between institutions and private persons. Some of the best known of the newer studios are at Princeton Univ. (computer music group, separate from the Columbia-Princeton Center), Yale and Brandeis Universities, the Univ. of Calif. at Davis and at San Diego, and Mills College. Subotnick and Walter Carlos each maintain sizeable private studios. In the late 1950s Robert Ashley and Gordon Mumma established a private studio in Ann Arbor, Mich., and Subotnick, Ramon Sender, and Pauline Oliveros did likewise in San Francisco, but both were dispersed in the late 60s. Subotnick is now working at the studio of the Calif. Institute of the Arts in Los Angeles.

Other major studios include: the installation at the Torcuato di Tella Institute in Buenos Aires, at the Scriabin Museum in Moscow (directed by Yevgeny Murzin, inventor of the ANS sound synthesizer), the private studio of the Tokyo engineer Jyunosuke Okuyama (where Toshi Ichiyanagi and Toru Takemitsu work), the private studios of Dick Raaijmakers, Jan Boerman and Ton Bruynèl in Holland, Pietro Grossi's S2FM in Florence, Stockholm Radio (Knut Wiggen, director; Bengt Hambraeus, Karl-Birger Blomdahl), Prague and Bratislava radio stations, the Rundfunk- und Fernsehtechnisches Zentralamt in East Berlin (Gerhard Steinke, director), the Technical Univ. in West Berlin (Fritz Winckel, director; Boris Blacher), Ghent Univ., and the private computerized studio of Peter Zinovieff in London (where Harrison Birtwistle has worked). With increasingly lower prices and higher quality equipment and the advent of special-purpose electronic music synthesizers, not to mention the difficulty of finding an institutional studio in which to work, a young composer may now invest in an integrated studio installation of his own, just as he might buy a top-quality grand piano—and at a comparable price.

Electronic music techniques have also been applied to other arts. The poets Paul de Vree (Belgium), Ferdinand Kriwet (West Germany), and Bernard Heidsieck (France)

have explored treatments and degrees of intelligibility of texts, which may also exist in printed versions, while the French poets Henri Chopin and François Dufrêne have exploited the special qualities of vocal sounds, usually avoiding word associations altogether. The equipment used to produce sound poetry ranges from actual electronic music studios to a single domestic microphone and tape recorder. Sculptors are increasingly incorporating audio oscillator circuits into kinetic sculptures, often in connection with lights and with overall control affected by movements of spectators in the vicinity. In some cases a composer has collaborated with the sculptor, as with several sound environments produced by Toshi Ichiyanagi in Japan.

LIVE ELECTRONIC MUSIC. This more recent development in electronic music involves the simultaneous transformation during performance by electronic equipment of sounds from any or any combination of the following four sources: conventional instruments; specially constructed or adapted instruments, sometimes with built-in microphones; sounds prerecorded on tape; and electronically generated sounds. The first of these is used in works such as Stockhausen's *Mixtur* for orchestra, sine-wave generators, and ring modulators (1964) and *Mikrophonie II* for chorus, Hammond organ, and ring modulators (1965), as well as in interpretations by David Tudor and others of various scores by Cage, such as *Electronic Music for Piano* (1964). In Stockhausen's *Mikrophonie I* for tamtam, microphones, filters, and potentiometers (1964), the tamtam is treated in such a way that it effectively becomes a completely new instrument. Cage's *Cartridge Music* (1960), the first substantial work to use live electronic techniques, uses contact microphones and record-player cartridges to amplify "small," otherwise inaudible sounds, a technique much used today and in some cases extended to the amplification of small sounds produced on conventional instruments. In such pieces the amplification of these sounds may be the only way in which they are transformed. Kagel has built new performance instruments, often amplified (*Unter Strom*, 1969), as have other composers, and even purely acoustic instruments often show that their development owes much to electronic music. Prerecorded tapes may contain unprocessed or only partially processed sounds (e.g., as a method of introducing sounds into a concert hall from a source that cannot itself be brought in). The final category not only includes live performance on electronic music synthesizers but also the use of acoustic feedback, as in Robert Ashley's *The Wolfman* (1964), where feedback is "modulated" by the mouth movements of an amplified vocalist. Live electronic transformation equipment has been devised by Jyunosuke Okuyama and used in several works by Ichiyanagi (*Situation*, 1966) and Roger Reynolds (*Ping*, 1968). Gordon Mumma develops special circuitry as an integral part of each composition, as in *Hornpipe* (1967) for modified French horn. Such equipment frequently uses voltage-control and/or computer-type logic circuitry.

Synthesizers have been used not only as self-contained instruments but also to modify instrumental or vocal sounds in live performance. Because they can be connected to a keyboard, except for the Buchla synthesizer, synthesizers have been treated by a number of pop and jazz musicians as if they were special organs with additional sound effects. During 1970, Moog and ARP introduced smaller, performance versions with a built-in keyboard, the former of which has been used by the jazz keyboard player Sun Ra.

Two important aspects of live electronic music are the emphasis it places on the composer-performer (an increasingly rare figure in the 19th and early 20th centuries) and the introduction into electronic music of the hazards and revelations of performance situations. Further, instrumental and electronic sounds can be integrated more effectively in a live situation than when instruments are combined with prerecorded sounds on tape (even when an instrument is confronted with a treated version of itself on tape, the tape cannot react to the live sound). The range of interaction between instrumental and live electronic sounds and treatments is considerable, for equipment knobs, switches, slide controls, and foot pedals can be performed on with as much precision and subtlety as conventional instruments. Also techniques apparently only possible on tape have subsequently been applied to live situations; Terry Riley, for example, has developed a performance technique based on a fixed interval tape-delay system (*Dorian Reeds*, 1966), and Steve Reich has transferred and adapted phasing techniques to instrumental works (*4 Organs*, 1970). Several performance groups in Europe and the U.S. concentrate on live electronic techniques, and a substantial repertory is growing up. In the future the term *electronic music* will probably refer primarily to live performance and *tape music* will be considered as a special case involving processes too complex to be realized on the spot.

BIBL.: Lowell Cross, *A Bibliography of Electronic Music* revised ed. (Toronto 1970); ——, "Electronic Music, 1948–53," *Perspectives* 7/1:32–65; Hugh Davies, *International Electronic Music Catalog* (Cambridge, Mass., 1968); *Music Educators' Journal* (Nov 1968), a special issue also reprinted by the Music Educators National Conference as *Electronic Music*.

Hugh Davies

SEE ALSO Dance, Indeterminacy, Instrumental and Vocal Resources, Microtones, Mixed Media, Orchestration, Rhythm.

Electronic Music: Notation. The purpose of preparing a score for a musical work has always been to provide a means of communicating specifically musical ideas to a performer whose task is then to read these instructions and interpret them in performance. For works that use live instruments coordinated with electronic sounds, some kind of score for the electronic events is needed to facilitate coordination; likewise for electronic works whose final realization occurs in live performance, instructions to the performer-technician(s) are needed. For those other electronic works whose "performance" is an integral part of the composer's work, i.e., those pieces whose compositional ideas have been realized and frozen on magnetic tape, which then requires only playback to be heard, there is no need for a score since there is no intermediary performer between the composer and his audience. In some instances composers have prepared scores anyway for purposes of copyright, personal satisfaction, or with the intent of making recreation of the work possible. (Universal Edition in Vienna and PWM in Cracow have published graphic scores and realization scores, one of which is entirely verbal.)

Electronic scores can be grouped in two general categories according to purpose: 1) realization scores, which provide all the technical data required to produce the piece; 2) representational scores, designed to be followed by a score reader and most often encountered in works for tape and live performers. (There are instances of realization scores, such as Karlheinz Stockhausen's *Studie 2*, that can be followed to some degree; however, the complexity of the sound material limits the possibility of a score reader being able to "hear" the piece on the basis of information in the score.) The encoding systems used in electronic scores transmit two kinds of data in varying degrees: 1) technical information (frequency and intensity values, transformation processes, and the like), and 2) descriptive information (formal or informal schematic symbologies and/or verbal commentary characterizing various sound types). In the broadest sense, machine-coded programs, such as punched paper tapes and computer programs, can be considered as "scores" for the pieces so realized; the same is true of encoding systems whose elements are primarily verbal descriptions and/or electronic circuits indicating the nature of sound generation and transformation. Closer to the usual concept of a score are those instances of notations based on extensions of traditional methods, as well as schematic graphic methods analogous to those present-day scores where the indications are primarily suggestive rather than prescriptive or that serve to describe resultant textures rather than component parts. In graphic notations of electronic music the traditional concepts of vertical and horizontal axes for frequency (or pitch) and time scales, respectively, are retained. For a multichannel work, each channel may have a separate system on the page, allowing the spatial distribution of events to be projected. Other scores provide separate strata for different sound sources, i.e., basic "instrumental"-like categories akin to the disposition of the traditional orchestral score; the simplest categorization would separate pitched and nonpitched sounds. In addition specific timbral categories or modes of sound production can be designated by unique symbols and used in conjuction with timbral score stratification.

In the temporal domain, scores of nonmetrically conceived pieces use proportionate or "time" notation, in which the lengths of symbols indicate durations in fractions of seconds. For dynamic (loudness) indications, traditional symbols may be used; however, realization scores often have a separate intensity vs. time graph coordinated with the frequency-time stratum to indicate decibel levels and shapes of amplitude envelopes.

The notation of frequency has presented the most complex problems; as the quantity and complexity of the sound materials and how they change increase, the ability of any notation to communicate detailed information diminishes. For a tempered-pitch rooted work, such as Milton Babbitt's *Philomel*, traditional short-score notation suffices (no attempt being made to specify electronic timbres). In instances of nontempered pitches, staff notation can only approximate the true sounds, as in Bülent Arel's *Stereo Electronic Music No. 1* (Arel's score is notable for its detail and the symbology used in projecting various aspects of the material, both with respect to sound makeup and perceptual qualities). Realization scores, such as Ex. 1, use a true frequency scale rather than pitch references for the vertical axis. As pitched sounds become more noiselike, the limitations of staff notation become more apparent, for only general areas of prominent frequencies can be indicated. Realization scores can account for such sounds with greater precision, but, as mentioned before, the ability of a score reader to deduce the sonic character of such events is severely limited.

Two kinds of notational practice are shown in Ex. 1 and 2. Stockhausen's *Studie 2* (Ex. 1) is concerned exclusively with sine-tone mixtures whose frequency components can be exactly stipulated. Because of the limited nature of the material, a maximum amount of information can be conveyed directly by the scales used. The upper part of the score is a frequency-time system above a time line in which the distances between event terminals are indicated in centimeters of tape (the tape proceeds at the rate of 76.2 cm. per sec.). Although many tone mixtures are employed, each contains five tones in exact ratios such that the height of the rectangles indicating the sound events specify the mixture type as well as the internal frequency components. (These components can be deduced by dividing the enclosed vertical dimension into four equal sections and reading the five frequencies directly from the scale at the left.) For each sound there is a corresponding amplitude envelope, indicated on the intensity-time system beneath the time line; one can observe, for instance, that the first three sounds have envelope shapes that can be characterized as "decrescendo," "crescendo," and "steady-state," respectively.

In contrast to *Studie 2*, the material of Stockhausen's *Kontakte* (Ex. 2), while derived from limited resources, is of a considerably more varied nature. The excerpt shown (between 16′ 33.6″ and 17′ 0.5″) is from the score prepared for the version with piano and percussion; it is an example of representational notation (a realization score also exists). The instumental parts, which appear beneath the score of the tape part, are not shown. The various symbols stratify the timbral components, which range from events with specific rhythmic patterns (some of whose sounds have envelopes suggested) to general textural indications. One can read relative pitch heights within the various patterns but can make no such correspondences among patterns, since there is no single frequency scale

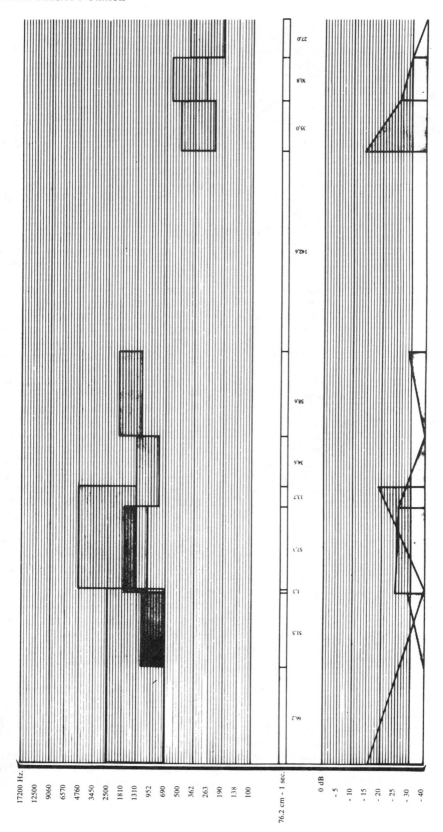

Ex. 1 Karlheinz Stockhausen, *Studie II*, p. 1

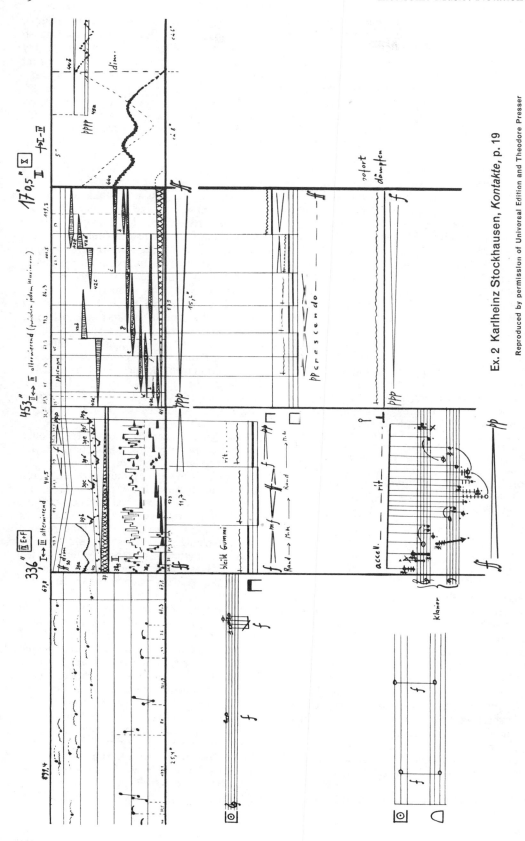

Ex. 2 Karlheinz Stockhausen, *Kontakte*, p. 19

but rather an arbitrary division of the vertical axis to allow separation of the various musical lines. Traditional dynamic markings can be noted. (The Roman numerals refer to speakers I-IV distributed around the hall; the boxed Roman numeral refers to the particular "moment" (formal division) in the score. Numbers and letters adjacent to sound symbols indicate compositional makeup. The arabic numerals toward the top designate tape lengths in centimeters; the 11,7″ and 15,2″ are sectional time indications.)

Attempts to provide general means for symbolically representing electronic sounds include a system proposed by the present writer that can be used for analytic purposes as well as in conjunction with a graphic score. The technique lies in the application of a descriptive formula to characterize sounds or groups of sounds; the terms of this formula refer to timbral aspects, envelope, and further modifications to the sound. The formula can incorporate symbols to denote various operations on sound components so that the nature of any substantial changes in timbre, pitch, etc., can be conveyed. While not directed specifically to the problems of score preparation, use of this system supplements graphic symbols by describing in a concise manner the nature of the sounds suggested graphically.

BIBL.: Herbert Eimert, F. Enkel, and Karlheinz Stockhausen, *Problems of Electronic Music Notation* trans. by D. A. Sinclair (Ottawa 1956); Brian Fennelly, *A Descriptive Notation for Electronic Music* (PhD diss., Yale Univ. 1968); Erhard Karkoschka, *Das Schriftbild der Neuen Musik* (Celle 1966); Karlheinz Stockhausen, *Texte 1-2* (Cologne 1963, 1964).

Brian Fennelly

Elgar, Edward (William) (b. Broadheath, Worcester, England, 2 June 1857; d. Worcester, 23 Feb 1934), the fourth of seven children of an organist and music-shop proprietor, was entirely self-taught and gained practical experience as organist, violinist, and conductor of local orchestras and choirs. His early efforts at composition were ignored by the public, but after his marriage in 1889 he produced a series of choral works that won him national fame. With his orchestral *Enigma Variations* (first performance conducted by Hans Richter in London, 1899) he achieved European recognition. His setting of Cardinal Newman's *Dream of Gerontius* was a failure at its first performance at Birmingham under Richter in 1900 but

later had a great success in Düsseldorf. Knighted in 1904, Elgar dominated English musical life until his death and was lavishly honored. He produced a series of orchestral works between 1908 and 1920 which many consider to be his masterpieces. After his wife's death in 1920, coinciding with the emergence of a postwar England with which he felt out of sympathy, he went into semiretirement, writing little but often conducting his own works in concert and for recordings. From 1924 until his death he was Master of the King's Music.

Elgar was the first unmistakable, original genius in English music since Purcell, a fact that was recognized by Europeans more quickly than by his fellow countrymen. No other English composer of his time could equal him for virtuosity of orchestration nor appeal to so wide an audience. His style was romantic and its formation was strongly influenced by the composers whose music he played and studied as a youth, notably Mendelssohn, Spohr, and Gounod. In his early music he derived a placid melodic style from Mendelssohn and a fondness for consecutive triads in root position from Gounod. His chromaticism borrowed Spohr's descending cadences of thirds or sixths over a tonic pedal; later on the influence of Wagner's chromatic apparatus was undeniable.

The Elgar style derives from several melodic, harmonic, and rhythmic characteristics. He used rising sevenths in his melodies, often combining them with a falling sixth. His tunes also contain frequent leaps to accented passing tones, which give them their urgency and upward sweep. A restlessness, an extension of his personality, is created by constant rubato, frequent changes of dynamics, and strongly accented rhythmic patterns (often dotted figures). He was a tonal composer even though the tonality is often made vague by an extensive use of chromaticism. Some of his most beautiful music resulted from simple diatonic procedures. Though he abhorred the modality of folksong, he made striking use of flattened sevenths and the descending minor melodic scale to convey nostalgia—a "sadly merry" feeling, to use his own words. He constantly used wide-interval sequences as a means of modulation, which enabled him to extract as much as he wanted from the major-minor system even though other composers of the time were finding its possibilities exhausted. The vividness of his orchestration was achieved through sonorous string writing (derived, he said, from Handel), brilliant writing for brass, and many episodes of counterpoint for woodwind. He used a method of symphonic development in which thematic material, often short, was not developed logically but by revealing unsuspected contrapuntal relationships and highlighting significant intervals.

Because of his ability to write in a melodic style for stately occasions and because of his music's opulent sound, Elgar is often characterized as a pompous laureate, a judgment that led to the denigration of his work in the 1920s and later. He was actually a complex, hypersensitive person, however. His psychological uncertainty affected nearly all his work, manifesting itself in the restlessness of rhythm mentioned above and in the sudden veering from moods of opulent, extrovert grandeur to nostalgia and a longing for "what might have been." Such contrasts are especially evident in the two symphonies and two concertos. At the same time, there was an English reticence in his expression, which may explain why his music is rated higher today in the land of his birth than elsewhere.

PRINCIPAL COMPOSITIONS (published by Novello unless otherwise noted): *The Wand of Youth Suites Nos. 1–2*, Opp. 1a, 1b (composed originally c.1867, revised 1907, 1908); *Serenade in E Minor* for strings, Op. 20 (1888–92, Breitkopf); *Froissart Overture*, Op. 19 (1890, unpub.); *The Black Knight*, cantata, Op. 25 (1893); *King Olaf*, cantata, Op. 30 (1894–96); *Organ Sonata in G*, Op. 28 (1895, Breitkopf); *Sea Pictures*, song cycle, Op. 37 (1897–99, Boosey); *Caractacus*, cantata, Op. 35 (1898); *Enigma Variations* for orchestra, Op. 36 (1898–99); *The Dream of Gerontius*, oratorio, Op. 38 (1899–1900); *Pomp and Circumstance Marches Nos. 1–2*, Op. 39 (1901, Boosey); *Cockaigne Overture*, Op. 40 (1901, Boosey); *Introduction and Allegro* for string quartet, string orchestra, Op. 47 (1901–05); *The Kingdom*, oratorio, Op. 51 (1901–06); *Coronation Ode* for vocal soloists, chorus, orchestra, Op. 44 (1902, Boosey); *The Music Makers* for alto, chorus, orchestra, Op. 69 (1902–12); *The Apostles*, oratorio, Op. 49 (1903); *In the South Overture*, Op. 50 (1903–04); *Symphony No. 2 in E♭*, Op. 63 (1903–10); *Symphony No. 1 in A♭*, Op. 55 (1907–08); *Violin Concerto in B Minor*, Op. 61 (1909–10); *Falstaff*, symphonic study, Op. 68 (completed 1913); *The Spirit of England* for vocal soloists, chorus, orchestra, Op. 80 (1915–17); *Violin Sonata in E Minor*, Op. 82 (1918); *String Quartet in E Minor*, Op. 83 (1918); *Piano Quintet in A Minor*, Op. 84 (1918–19); *Cello Concerto in E Minor*, Op. 85 (1919); *Severn Suite* for band, Op 87 (1930, Smith); *Nursery Suite* (1931, Prowse). Complete list in Kennedy (see bibl.): 275–305.

PRINCIPAL WRITINGS: *Letters to Nimrod* ed. by P. Young (London 1965); *A Future for English Music and Other Lectures by E. E.* ed. by Young (London 1968).

BIBL.: Michael Kennedy, *Portrait of E.* (London 1968); Basil Maine, *E.: His Life and Works* (London 1933); Diana M. McVeagh, *E. E.: His*

Life and Music (London 1955); W. H. Reed, *E. as I Knew Him* (London 1936); Percy M. Young, *E., O.M.* (London 1955).

Michael Kennedy

SEE ALSO Great Britain.

Eloy, Jean-Claude (b. Rouen, 15 June 1938), studied at the Paris Conservatory (1953–61, composition with Darius Milhaud, ondes Martenot with Maurice Martenot), at the Darmstadt summer courses (1957, 1960), and with Pierre Boulez in Basel (1961, 1962), where he met Stockhausen. During 1966–68 he taught at the Univ. of Calif. at Berkeley; in general, however, he lives as a free-lance composer. He considers *Equivalences* (1963) as particularly representative of his music of the last decade.

PRINCIPAL COMPOSITIONS: *L'Herbe du Songe*, song cycle for soprano, piano; poems by Yvan Goll (1959); *3 Pieces* for piano (1959); *Encore une aube* for soprano, piano (1959); *Stèle pour Omar Khayyam* for soprano, piano, harp, percussion (1960); *Chamber Cantata* for soprano, piano, harp, 2 ondes Martenots, percussion (1960); *Piece* for solo flute (1961); *Etudes I–II* for flute, harp, cello (1961); *Chants pour une ombre* for soprano, 9 instruments (1961); *Etude III*, symphony No. 1 (1962, Heugel); *Equivalences* for 18 instruments (1963, Heugel); *Poly-chronies* for winds, piano, harp, percussion (1964); *Macles* for 6 instrumental groups (1967); *Amas* for piano (1970); *Faisceaux-Diffractions* for 28 instrumentalists (1970).

PRINCIPAL WRITINGS: "Musiques d'Orient, notre univers familier," *La Musique et la vie* 2 (ORTF, Paris, 1969); "L'Improvisation: refuge, utopie ou nécessité?", excerpts in *The World of Music* 1970/3. Eloy also wrote program notes for the Domaine Musical concerts in Paris, 1962–66.

BIBL.: Jacques Treboutat and Pierre Vozlinsky, *Un Homme et sa musique*, television film (1966, broadcast over the French Television Network 1967).

SEE ALSO France, Mathematics.

Enescu, George (Enesco, Georges) (b. Liveni-Virnav, now named George Enescu, Dorohoiŭ, Rumania, 19 August 1881; d. Paris, 4 May 1955), started playing the violin at four and began to compose a year later. At seven he enrolled for a preparatory year at the Vienna Conservatory, and he started his higher studies there in 1890, having already made his first public appearance as a violinist at a concert in Slanic-Moldova shortly before his eighth birthday. Although he was regarded as a mature artist by the time he was thirteen, he went to the Paris Conservatory in 1895 for further violin studies. Once in Paris, he concentrated mainly on composition and studied with Massenet and Fauré. A concert in Paris in 1897 was devoted entirely to his works, and a year later the Colonne Orchestra played his Op. 1, *Rumanian Poem*. At this time Enescu began his association with leading instrumentalists of the day. With the pianist Alfred Cortot he played the premiere of his *Violin Sonata No. 1* in 1898; as a pianist he and Jacques Thibaud gave the first performance of the *Violin Sonata No. 2* in 1900 (the latter work Enescu regarded as the earliest in which he found his true direction). Besides performing as a violinist and pianist, he was also active as a conductor, and he remained so until 1951, undertaking frequent foreign tours and giving many first performances of contemporary works. For the rest he divided his time between Paris and Bucharest, teaching in both. Yehudi Menuhin, Arthur Grumiaux, Ivry Gitlis, and Roman Totenberg were among his pupils. Ill health eventually forced him to give up playing, and he devoted the last four years of his life to composition.

Enescu wrote some 40 major compositions, with chamber and piano music predominating over orchestral. The orchestral works are mostly of great textural complexity and consequently are difficult to balance, which may explain why they are rarely performed outside Rumania. His only opera, *Oedip*, is generally considered his masterpiece. Enescu's style evolved principally from three sources: Rumanian folk music, the preclassic era (especially Bach), and late romanticism. French impressionism played a smaller role, while Wagner's influence is often detectable, as in the *Symphony No. 1* (1905) and in the highly chromatic harmonies in the *Chamber Symphony* (1954), which also has echoes of early Schoenberg. Enescu was never interested in innovation for its own sake, and he remained an adherent to the tonal tradition. In the *Violin Sonata No. 3* (1926), however, he came close to Bartók in his treatment of folklike material by using an adventurous harmonic idiom that includes clusters. In general, works such as the *Suite No. 2* for orchestra, with their blend of preclassicism and massive orchestration, tend to be less successful than the smaller essays in which Enescu looked to his native country for inspiration.

PRINCIPAL COMPOSITIONS: *Poème roumain* for orchestra, Op. 1 (1897, Enoch); *Suite dans le style ancien* for piano, Op. 3 (1897); *Violin Sonatas Nos. 1–3*, Opp. 2, 6, 25 (1897, 1899, 1926; Enoch, Nos. 2 and 3 also ESPLA); *Symphonie concertante* for cello, orchestra, Op. 8 (1901, Enoch and ESPLA);

Rumanian Rhapsodies Nos. 1–2 for orchestra, Op. 11 (1901, 1902, Enoch and ESPLA); *Symphonies Nos. 1–3*, Opp. 13, 17, 21 (1905, Enoch and ESPLA; 1913, Muzicală; 1919, revised 1921, Muzicală); *Dixtuor* for winds, Op. 14 (1906, Muzicală); *Suite No. 2* for orchestra, Op. 20 (1915, Salabert and Muzicală); *String Quartets Nos. 1–2*, Op. 22 (1921, 1952, Salabert and Muzicală); *Piano Sonatas Nos. 1–3*, Op. 24 (1924, Enoch and ESPLA; 1937, Salabert; 1935, Salabert and Muzicală); *Oedip*, lyric tragedy in 4 acts, Op. 23; libretto by Edmond Fleg (1932, Salabert and Muzicală); *Cello Sonata No. 2*, Op. 26 (1935, Salabert and Muzicală); *Suite villageoise* for orchestra, Op. 27 (1938, Muzicală); *Piano Quintet*, Op. 29 (1940, Muzicală); *Piano Quartet*, Op. 30 (1944, Salabert and Muzicală); *Vox maris*, symphonic poem for tenor, chorus, orchestra, Op. 31 (1950, Salabert and Muzicală); *Chamber Symphony* for 12 solo instruments, Op. 33 (1954, Salabert and Muzicală). Complete list in Tudor.

BIBL.: Andrei Tudor, *E.* (Bucharest 1958).

Malcolm Rayment

Engel, Lehman (b. Jackson, Miss., 14 Sept 1910), studied at the Cincinnati College Conservatory (1926–29) and the Juilliard School (1930–34; composition with Rubin Goldmark). He also studied composition privately with Roger Sessions in 1935. During 1949–52 he was musical director of the State Fair Musicals in Dallas and during 1962–65, of the Musical and Dramatic Theater Academy of America. In 1960 he founded the BMI Musical Theatre Workshop, which he has directed since then. He has written extensively for films, television, radio, and theater and has conducted a number of musicals on Broadway. He has also contributed many articles on musical theater to U.S. newspapers and magazines.

PRINCIPAL COMPOSITIONS: *The Pierrot of the Minute*, 1-act opera for soprano, mezzo-soprano (1927); *The Chinese Nightingale*, cantata for 2 sopranos, 2 tenors, bass, chorus, orchestra (1928); *Medea*, opera-ballet (1932); *Excerpts from Job* for tenor, chamber orchestra (1932, New Music); *String Quartet* (1933); *Piano Sonata* (1938, Arrow); *Sinfonietta No. 1* for chamber orchestra (1938); *The Gates of Paradise*, variations for piano (1941; *Boletín latino-americano de música*, Oct 1941:21); *Viola Concerto* (1945); *Cello Sonata* (1945, SPAM); *Symphony No. 1* (1945); *Symphony No. 2* (1945); *Overture for the End of the War* (1946); *The Creation* for narrator, orchestra (1946, AMP); *Dialogue* for violin, viola (1950); *Music for the Classical Tragedy*, incidental music to Shakespeare's *Hamlet, Julius Caesar, Romeo and Juliet, Macbeth* (1953, Flammer); *Malady of Love*, opera for soprano, baritone, 2 mimes (1954, Flammer); *Violin Sonata* (1955); *The Soldier* for mezzo-soprano, tenor, baritone, 3 speakers, chamber orchestra, child mime (1955, Chappell); *Jackson*, overture (1961). Engel has also edited an anthology of choral music: *Renaissance to Baroque*, 7 vols. (New York 1931–69).

PRINCIPAL DANCE SCORES (with choreographer): *Ceremonials* (Martha Graham, 1932); *Driver of the Storm Winds* (Edwin Strawbridge, 1932); *Ekstasis* (Graham, 1933); *Transitions* (Graham, 1934); *Crystal* (Tashimira, 1934); *Songs of the Night* (Harry Losée, 1935); *Marching Song* (Graham, 1935); *Parade* (Gene Martel, 1935); *Traditions* (Charles Weidman, José Limón, William Matons; 1935); *Imperial Gesture* (Graham, 1935); *Phobias* (Gluck Sandor, Felicia Sorel; 1936); *The Shoe Bird* (Rex Cooper, 1967).

PRINCIPAL WRITINGS: *Planning and Producing the Musical Show* (New York 1957); *The American Musical Theater: A Consideration* (New York 1967); *Words with Music* (New York 1972).

Englemann, Hans Ulrich (b. Darmstadt, 8 Sept 1921), studied at the Städtische Akademie für Tonkunst in Darmstadt (1932–42) and at Goethe Univ. in Frankfurt (1946–52), where he followed a general arts program. He studied composition privately with Wolfgang Fortner in Heidelberg (1946–49) and 12-tone techniques at seminars in Darmstadt with René Leibowitz (1948) and Ernst Krenek (1950). Since 1945 he has composed for radio, theater, and films and has written many articles on opera, theater music, contemporary composers, and modern theory for *Melos* and concert program booklets. During 1954–61 he was art adviser and composer for the Darmstadt Landestheater. Since 1969 he has been a professor at the Staatlicher Hochschule für Musik in Frankfurt. His work has been influenced by his contacts with Varèse (1950), Dallapiccola (1955), and the conductor Hermann Scherchen (1947, 1948), as well as by his practical work as a stage assistant and composer for the theater.

PRINCIPAL COMPOSITIONS: *Toccata* for piano, Op. 1 (1947, Schott); *Doctor Faust's Hollenfahrt*, 1-act opera, Op. 4 (1949–50, Ahn & Sim); *Composition in 4 Parts* for soprano, flute, piano, vibraphone, xylophone, percussion, Op. 11 (1953, Ahn & Sim); *Strukturen* for orchestra, Op. 15 (1954, Ahn & Sim); *Die Mauer*, cantata for vocal soloists, actors, chorus, orchestra, Op. 15 (1954–55); *Nocturnos* for soprano, orchestra, Op. 18 (1958, Ahn & Sim); *Variante* for flute, Op. 20 (1959, Ahn & Sim); *Ezra Pound Music* for chamber orchestra, Op. 21 (1959, Ahn & Sim); *Trias* for piano, orchestra, tape, Op. 24 (1962, Ahn & Sim); *Duplum* for 2 pianos, Op. 29 (1965, Tonos); *Der Fall Van Damm*, 3-act opera, Op. 30 (1966–67, Gerig); *Ophelia*, theater piece, Op. 36 (1968, Bosse).

PRINCIPAL WRITINGS: *Béla Bartók's "Mikrokosmos"* (PhD diss., Würzburg 1952); "Fragen serieller Kompositionsverfahren," *Bericht über den Internationalen Musikwissenschaftlichen Kongress* (Cassel 1962):375–79.

BIBL.: W. E. Lewinski, "H. U. E.," *Theaterheft der Städt Bühnen* (Essen), No. 17; Eric Sarnette, "H. U. E.," *Musique et radio*, No. 10; Ursula Stürtzbecher, "H. U. E.," *Werkstattgespräche* (Cologne 1970).

SEE ALSO Austria and Germany.

England, see Great Britain

Englert, Giuseppe (Giorgio) (b. Florence, 22 July 1927), attended the Zurich Conservatory (1945–48, composition with Willy Burkhard) and studied organ privately in Paris with André Marchal (1949–56). He attended the Darmstadt summer courses several times during 1955–66. From 1957 to 1962 he was organist and assistant to André Marchal at Sainte-Eustache in Paris. He was codirector of Le Centre de Musique in Paris (1964–68) and since 1970 has been teaching at the Centre Experimental Universitaire de Vincennes in Paris. In recent years Englert has been interested in combining instrumental, vocal, electronic, and theatrical elements, and in collective works in which "all participants share the responsibility as authors." He has collaborated in such productions as *Peppermint* (at Le Centre de Musique, 1968), *Intervention* (at the Sion Festival, 1969), and *Cartoline* (at the Autunno Musicale di Como, 1969).

PRINCIPAL COMPOSITIONS: *Au Jour ultime liesse* for alto, alto flute, clarinet, bass trumpet, 2 violas, double bass (1961–63); *Les Avoines folles* for string quartet (1962–63, Peters); *Fragment* for orchestra (1964, Peters); *Aria* for timpani and a few instruments (1965, Peters); *La Joute des lierres* for string quartet (1965–66); *Le Roman de Kapitagolei* for orchestra (1966–67, Peters); *Recit et aria* on tape, for the dance "Expansion-Transformation"; choreography by Jean Cébron (1967, Peters); *Tarok*, musical game for 3–6 string instruments (1967); *July 68* on 4-track tape (1968); *Vagans animula* for organ, tape (1969).

BIBL.: Heinz-Klaus Metzger, "G. G. E.," *Züricher Almanach* (1968):23–28.

SEE ALSO Austria and Germany, Switzerland.

Englund, Einar Sven (b. Ljugarn, Gotland, Sweden, 17 June 1916), studied at the Sibelius Academy in Helsingfors (1935–41; composition with Selim Palmgren, Bengt Carlsson;

orchestration, Leo Funtek; piano, Martti Paavola) and at Tanglewood (1949, composition with Aaron Copland). Since 1950 he has been a free-lance conductor, pianist, and music reviewer for the Finnish Radio and Television Network and since 1956, music reviewer for *Hufvudstadsbladet* in Helsingfors. He has taught composition at the Sibelius Academy since 1958. His music has been influenced by the work of Stravinsky and by his study of folklore, for which he has traveled extensively in middle and eastern Europe. He has written many compositions for radio and television plays.

PRINCIPAL COMPOSITIONS: *Piano Quintet* (1941); *Symphony No. 1* (1946); *Epinikia*, symphonic poem (1947); *Symphony No. 2* (1948); *Suite* for orchestra from incidental music to *Kiinan muuri* [The Great Wall of China] by Max Frisch (1949); *Introduzione e toccata* for piano (1950, Fazer); *4 Dance Impressions* for orchestra (1954); *Cello Concerto* (1954); *Valkoinen peura* [The White Reindeer], suite for orchestra from the film (1954); *Odysseus*, suite for orchestra from the ballet (1959); *Sinuhe*, suite for orchestra from the ballet (1965); *Nocturne* for piano (1966); *Sonatine in D Minor* for piano (1968, Fazer); *Chaconne* for chorus, trombone, double bass (1969, Fazer); *Introduzione e toccata* for violin, piano (1970); *Symphony No. 3* (1970).

PRINCIPAL WRITINGS: "Jean Sibelius, 1893–1905," *Hufvudstadsbladet* 8/10 (1967):9; "Väinö Raitio, ett tonsättaröde" [V. R., A Composer], *ibid.* 29/10 (1968).

BIBL.: Seppo Numi, Modern musik (Stockholm 1967):50–54, 97–99.

Enríquez, Manuel (b. Ocotlán, Mexico, 17 June 1926), studied at the Guadalajara Conservatory (1942–50) and at the Juilliard School (1955–57; composition with Peter Mennin, violin with Ivan Galamian, chamber music with William Primrose). In 1971 he worked at the Columbia-Princeton Electronic Music Center. He has been assistant concertmaster of the National Symphony Orchestra of Mexico since 1958 and has taught composition at the National Conservatory since 1968. Early in his career his work was influenced by Miguel Bernal Jiménez; later his acquaintance with Stefan Wolpe inspired him to compose in "a very contemporary language."

PRINCIPAL COMPOSITIONS: *Violin Concertos Nos. 1–2* (1955; 1966, EMM); *Symphonies Nos. 1–2* (1956, 1962); *Transición* for orchestra (1965, EMM); *Trayectorias* (1967, Schott); *String Quartet No. 2* (1967, UE); *Ambivalencia* for violin, cello (1967, UE); *Si libet* for orchestra (1968, EMM); *Ixamatl* for orchestra (1969, Schott); *Móvil I* for piano (1969, UE); *Móvil II* for violin (1969, UE); *Diptico I* for flute, piano (1969, UE); *Concierto*

para 8 for clarinet, bassoon, trumpet in C, trombone, violin, double bass, percussion, conductor (1969, UE). List to 1969: *Composers of the Americas* 15:98–100.

PRINCIPAL WRITINGS: "Panorama de la composición en México," *Nutida musik* (Stockholm, April 1970).

BIBL.: J. Antonio Alcaraz, "La obra de M. E.," *Espejo* 5; Esperanza Pulido, "M. E.," *Heterofonías* 2/11.

SEE ALSO Mexico.

Envelope, those characteristics of amplitude that determine the growth and decay of a signal. The contours of a sound or sounds include such variables as the rate of attack time, attack height, frequency, timbre, sustain level, rate of initial decay, and also the rate of final decay.

© *Music Educators Journal* (Nov 1968)

Erb, Donald (James) (b. Youngstown, Ohio, 17 Jan 1927), studied at Kent State Univ., Ohio (1947–50, composition with Harold Miles), the Cleveland Institute of Music (1950–53, composition with Marcel Dick), Indiana Univ. (1961–64, composition with Bernard Herdew), and privately in Paris with Nadia Boulanger (1952). He has taught at the Cleveland Institute of Music (1953–61, since 1966), Indiana Univ. (1961–62, 1963–64), Bowling Green State Univ., Ohio (1964–65), and the Case Institute of Technology in Cleveland (1965–67). He has been composer-in-residence for the public schools in Bakersfield, Calif. (1962–63) and the Dallas Symphony (1968–69). Since 1966 he has also co-directed Portfolio, a contemporary music series in Cleveland.

PRINCIPAL COMPOSITIONS: *Correlations* for piano (1959); *Music for Violin and Piano* (1959); *String Quartet No. 1* (1960); *Sonneries* for brass choir (1961); *Four for Percussion* (1962); *Compendium* for band (1962); *Dance Pieces* for violin, piano, trumpet, percussion (1963); *Cummings Cycle* for chorus, orchestra (1963, AMP); *Hexagon* for flute, alto saxophone, trumpet, trombone, cello, piano (1963); *Antipodes* for string quartet, percussion (1963); *Symphony of Overtures* (1964, Highgate); *VII Miscellaneous* for flute, double bass (1964); *Fallout?* for narrator, chorus, string quartet, piano (1964); *Reticulation* for band, tape (1965); *Phantasma* for flute, oboe, double bass, harpsichord (1965); *Concert Piece I* for band (1966); *Diversion for 2* for trumpet, percussion (1966); *Percussion Concerto* (1966); *String Trio* for violin, electric guitar, cello (1966); *Summermusic* for piano (1966); *Kyrie* for chorus, piano, percussion, tape (1967);

Reconnaissance for violin, double bass, piano, 2 Moog synthesizers (1967); *Christmasmusic* for orchestra (1967); *3 Pieces* for brass quintet, piano (1968); *In No Strange Land* for tape, trombone, double bass (1968); *The Seventh Trumpet* for orchestra (1969).

Erbse, Heimo (b. Rudolstadt, Germany, 27 Feb 1924), studied at the Musikhochschule in Weimar (1945–47) and at the Hochschule für Musik in Berlin (1950–52, composition with Boris Blacher). During 1947–50 he was an opera producer in Jena, Meiningen, and Sondershausen. Since then he has been a freelance composer.

PRINCIPAL COMPOSITIONS: *Sonata* for 2 pianos, Op. 3 (1951, Bote); *String Quartet*, Op. 5 (1951, Bote); *Capriccio* for piano, string orchestra, percussion, Op. 4 (1952, Bote); *Piano Sonata*, Op. 6 (1952, Bote); *Ekstato* for piano, Op. 7 (1953, Bote); *Piano Trio*, Op. 8 (1953, Bote); *Impression* for orchestra, Op. 9 (1954, Bote); *Präludium* for orchestra, Op. 10 (1954, Peters); *Dialog* for piano, orchestra, Op. 11 (1955, Bote); *3 Songs after Eichendorff*, Op. 12 (1955, Peters); *Sinfonietta giacosa* for orchestra, Op. 14 (1956, Peters); *Julietta*, 4-act opera, Op. 15 (1956–57, Peters); *Ruth*, ballet, Op. 16 (1958, Bote); *3 Songs after Mörike*, Op. 17 (1959, Peters); *Tango Variations* for orchestra, Op. 18 (1959, Peters); *Pavimento* for orchestra, Op. 19 (1960, Peters); *Quartet* for flute, oboe, clarinet, bassoon, Op. 20 (1961, Peters); *3 Songs after Celan*, Op. 21 (1962, Peters); *Piano Concerto*, Op. 22 (1962, Bote); *Symphony in 4 Movements*, Op. 23 (1963, Bote); *Der Herr in Grau*, 2-part opera, Op. 24 (1965–66, Bote); *Flute Sonata*, Op. 25 (1966, Bote); *Das Hohelied Salomos* for soprano, baritone, piano or orchestra, Op. 26 (1967, Peters); *Orchestra Songs* for baritone, orchestra, Op. 27; text from Trakl (1968, Peters); *Symphony No. 2* (1969–70).

Erickson, Robert (b. Marquette, Mich., 7 Feb 1917), began playing the piano at five, learned to read music about two years later, and began violin at ten. He also composed while still a child but did not decide to become a composer until his mid-20s. He met his principal teacher, Ernst Krenek, in 1936, by which time he was already working with 12-tone techniques (he was finished with serialism by 1943). He received an MA from Hamline Univ. (St. Paul, Minn.) in 1947, taught at St. Catherine College in St. Paul (1947–53), and then moved to Calif., where he has taught at the San Francisco Conservatory (1957–66) and the Univ. of Calif. at San Diego (since 1966).

Between 1936 and the mid-50s Erickson was combining atonality with a "rather rigorous imitative counterpoint" (his description). His book *The Structure of Music: A Listener's Guide to Melody and Counterpoint* (published 1955) "purged him of the contrapuntal obsession." The *String Quartet No. 2* (1957) marked the beginning of a new interest in timbre, which reached a highpoint in the 1967 *Ricercar à 3* for three double basses (two of which are prerecorded on tape). This piece uses no bowed sounds but explores various kinds of pizzicato combined with glissandos, drones, percussive sounds, etc., all of which give it an oriental color. An interest in improvisation and in new ways of dealing with rhythm also characterize the post-1957 works. The *Duo* for violin and piano (1959) incorporated new rhythmic concepts as outlined in Erickson's "Time Relations" article: "I wanted a quality of motion less tempo-bound than what I had previously composed. I had always used accelerando and ritardando in my music to ameliorate the 'tickiness' of a rigidly held unit and to help establish the fluidity of motion which I wanted; and for the *Duo* I hit upon the compositional idea of combining certain musical events in disjunct but commensurable tempos, which sometimes would integrate with each other without any single tempo dominating, and at other times would be connected by means of accelerando and ritardando. What this turned out to be was a field of tempos. . . . During the composition of my *Chamber Concerto* . . . I found myself working with a larger number of tempos and counters . . ., turning away from hierarchical rhythmic relationships toward a rhythm of constantly emerging and changing patterns of relationship." Improvisation was introduced in the last movement of the *Chamber Concerto* (1960), where one or more instruments are instructed to "improvise in the style of the composition" while the other instruments play composed parts. This movement was a study piece for the *Piano Concerto* (1963), in which the improvisation called for from the soloist requires as much virtuosity as do the written-out sections. At the urging of his students Pauline Oliveros and Ramon Sender, Erickson began in 1964 to work with tape. In this idiom he usually uses concrète-music processes, beginning with sounds ranging from bells to ocean waves. These are recorded, filtered, tuned, and manipulated into multilayered textures. *Pacific Sirens* (1968) is an example: "The tape portion of the music was produced from a tape recording of ocean waves electronically filtered to make 16 different pitch bands, which were retuned, equalized, and remixed to produce the performance tape. The players play into the wave sounds, sometimes matching and sometimes counterpointing the sounds on tape, to produce a continuous, seamless siren song."

Vocal and speech sounds entered Erickson's instrumental music after 1965. In *General Speech* (1969) a trombonist colors and articulates some notes by voicing syllables into the instrument. Other notes are colored by changing the shape and volume of the mouth cavity, talking through the instrument, swallowing air, or controlling the air supply in other ways.

Erickson has constructed a number of instruments for use in his works. In the article "Instruments for *Cardenitas*" he has explained how he composed the instruments and the work simultaneously: "The special value in such an approach is that the composer is able to compose the whole chain: he is able to compose on the micro-level of the sounds; he is able to specify his sounds precisely; and his players are not aware of external control." An important point about Erickson's instruments is that performers can play them using techniques that are either simple or already known to them.

PRINCIPAL COMPOSITIONS: *Variations for Orchestra* (1957); *String Quartet No. 2* (1957); *Duo* for violin, piano (1959, Presser); *Chamber Concerto* (1960, Presser); *Ramus*, toccata for piano (1962); *Concerto* for piano, 7 instruments (1963, Presser); *Ricercar à 5* for trombone, tape (1966, recorded by A.R.); *Roddy* on tape using the sounds of rods (1966); *Ricercar à 3* for double bass, tape (1967, recorded by Ars Nova); *Down at Piraeus* for chorus, tape (1967); *Cardenitas 68* for singer, 6 instrumentalists (1968); *Do It* for double chorus, speaker, gongs, drone (1968); *Pacific Sirens* for tape, 10–14 instruments (1968); *High Flyer* for amplified flute (1969); *General Speech* for trombone; text from Douglas MacArthur (1969).

PRINCIPAL WRITINGS: *The Structure of Music: A Listener's Guide to Melody and Counterpoint* (New York 1955); "Time Relations," *Journal of Music Theory* (winter 1963); "Varèse and the Music of the Sixties," *Composer* (Feb 1970); "Instruments for *Cardenitas*," *Source* 5:26–29.

Bertram Turetzky

Escher, Rudolf (George) (b. Amsterdam, 8 Jan 1912), moved to the Netherlands in 1921, having spent his early childhood in Java. He studied at the Toonkunst Conservatorium in Rotterdam (1931–37; counterpoint with J. H. Besselaar, composition with Willem Pijper) and at the Technical Univ. in Delft (1959–60), where he attended lectures on electronic studio equipment. During 1945–46 he contributed articles on music and art to *De Groene*

Amsterdammer, and from 1955 to 1962 he was a program annotator for the Concertgebouw Orchestra. In 1960 he worked in the Studio for Electronic Music in Delft and in 1961 at the Studio for Electronic Music at the State Univ. of Utrecht. During 1960–61 he also lectured on contemporary music at the Study Center for Contemporary Music of the Amsterdam Conservatory, and since 1964 he has taught and done research at the Institute for Musical Science at the State Univ. of Utrecht. He conceives of music as a means of communication and expression rather than merely a technical exercise. In his own work he has been concerned with the use of intervals in creating melody, harmony, and rhythmic structures.

PRINCIPAL COMPOSITIONS (published by Donemus unless otherwise noted): *Musique pour l'esprit en deuil* for orchestra (1941–43); *Arcana musae dona*, suite for piano (1944, Broekmans); *Nostalgies* for tenor, chamber orchestra; poems by Jean-Marie Levet (1951); *Chant du désir* for mezzo-soprano, piano; poems by Louise Labé (1951); *Le Tombeau de Ravel* for flute, oboe, violin, viola, cello, harpsichord (1952); *Le Vrai Visage de la paix* for chamber chorus; poem by Paul Eluard (1953); *Songs of Love and Eternity* for chamber chorus; 6 poems by Emily Dickinson (1955); *Ciel, air et vents* for chamber choir; poems by Ronsard (1957); *Symphony No. 2* (1958, revised 1964); *Summer Rites at Noon* for 2 orchestras facing each other (1962–69); *Quintetto a fiati* for flute, alto flute, oboe d'amore, clarinet, bass clarinet, bassoon, horn (1966–67); *Univers de Rimbaud*, cycle 1, for tenor, chamber orchestra (1969).

PRINCIPAL WRITINGS: "Maurice Ravel," *Groot Nederland* (July 1939):52–73; "Muziekleer" [Musical Science], *Erste Nederlandse Systematisch Ingerichte Encyclopaedie*, vol. 2:507–36; "Debussy: *Pelléas et Mélisande*," program book of the Holland Festival (15 June 1948); "Raoul Dufy, Schilder van het Musiceren" [R. D., painter of music-making], catalog of the Dufy Exposition (Arnheim 1956); "Variaties op een Visioen" [Variations on a Vision], *Algemeen Handelsblad* (3 June 1961), supplement:1–2; "Claude Debussy, musicien français," *ibid.* (6 Jan 1962), supplement: 3; "Ravel in de twintigste Eeuw" [Ravel's Place in the 20th Century], *Het Residentie-Orkest* (The Hague) 4/1:4–7, 4/2:16–21.

BIBL.: "R. E.: *Musique pour l'esprit en deuil*," *Sonorum Speculum* 20:15–33; "R. E.: *Quintetto a fiati*," *Sonorum Speculum* 34:24–34; "R. E.: *Songs of Love and Eternity*," program book of the Holland Festival (15 June 1968).

Escobar, Luis Antonio (b. Villapinzón, Columbia, 14 July 1925), studied at the National Univ. of Columbia (1944–47, composition with Egisto Giovanetti), the Peabody Conservatory (1947–50, composition with Nicolas Nabokov), Columbia Univ. (1950–51), the Salzburg Mozarteum (1951, composition with Boris Blacher), and the Berlin Hochschule für Musik (1951–53, composition with Blacher). He has taught history, orchestration, harmony, and composition at the Conservatory of the Columbia National Univ. (1954–57) and at Javeriana Univ. (1957, 1962). He was president of the Columbian Symphony during 1960–63, and in 1966 he founded the Columbian Philharmonic. During 1960–63 he was director of the cultural division of the Ministry of National Education. He was Second Secretary at the Columbian Embassy in Bonn during 1967–70.

PRINCIPAL COMPOSITIONS: *Violin Sonatinas Nos. 1–2* (1947, 1954); *Piano Sonatinas Nos. 1–5* (1950, 1952, 1954, 1956, 1959); *String Quartets Nos. 1–3* (1950, 1951, 1970); *Concertino* for flute, orchestra (1951); *Symphony No. 1* (1954); *Avirama*, ballet; scenario by the composer (1955); *Tío conejo zapatero*, ballet mimodrama; book by Enrique Buenaventura (1955); *Hymn of the Univ. of the Andes* for soprano, chorus; text by Eduardo Carranza (1956); *Cantata campesina* for chorus, orchestra (1956); *La princesa y la arveja*, children's opera (1957); *Flute Sonatina* (1957); *Concerto* for harpsichord, string orchestra (1958); *Piano Concerto* (1959); *Pequeña sinfonía* (1960); *Cánticas de cantas colombianas* for chorus, orchestra (1960); *Preludes* for percussion and piano, ballet; choreography by George Balanchine (1960); *Los hampones*, opera for soprano, baritone, bass, percussion, choruses, piano (celesta or harp); libretto by Jorge Gaitán Durán (1961); *Juramento a Bolívar*, symphonic poem for chorus, orchestra (1966); *Rondas y canciones infantiles* for children's chorus (1966). List to 1963: *Composers of the Americas* 8:65–70.

Eshpai, Andrei (Jakolevich) (b. Kozmodemjansk, U.S.S.R., 15 May 1925), studied at the Moscow Conservatory (1948–56; composition with I. Ja. Miaskovsky, E. K. Golubev, and N. I. Khachaturian; piano with B. B. Sefrenitsky). During 1963–70 he taught composition at the Moscow Conservatory. He concertizes as a pianist throughout the U.S.S.R.

PRINCIPAL COMPOSITIONS (available from Mezhkniga): *Piano Sonata* (1948); *Symphonic Dances* (1950); *Hungarian Melodies* for violin, orchestra (1952); *Piano Concerto* (1954–55); *Violin Concerto* (1956); *Symphonies Nos. 1–3* (1959, 1961–62, 1965–66); *Violin Sonatas Nos. 1–2* (1966, 1971); *Concerto for Orchestra* (1967); *Cantata*; text by V. Maiakovsky (1968); *Festival Overture* for chorus, 12 violins, 8 cellos, 6 harps, 4 pianos, orchestra (1970). Eshpai has also composed scores for over 30 films and for many television shows.

Esplá, Oscar (Emigdio) (b. Alicante, Spain, 5 August 1886), studied philosophy and engineering at the Univ. of Barcelona (1903–11). He studied composition privately in Meiningen and Munich with Max Reger in 1912 and in Paris with Camille Saint-Saëns in 1913. During 1931–34 he was president of the Junta Nacional de Música y Teatros Liricos. He has been director of the Madrid Conservatory (1936–39) and of the Oscar Esplá Conservatory in Alicante (since 1958). His music has been influenced by Debussy and Stravinsky, and he has made use of the popular music of the Mediterranean coast of Spain in some compositions.

PRINCIPAL COMPOSITIONS: *Impresiones musicales* for piano (1905); *El sueño de Eros*, symphonic poem (1912, UME); *Poema de niños*, suite for orchestra (1913, Eschig); *Violin Sonata* (1915); *Nochebueno del diablo* for dancers, vocal soloists, chorus, orchestra (1924, Eschig); *Misterio de Elche*, restoration of a 13th-century liturgical drama (1924); *Don Quijote velando las armas*, symphonic episode (1925, Eschig); *Levante* for piano (1927); *Canciones playeras* for soprano, orchestra or piano (1928); *Confines* for chamber orchestra (1928); *La pájara pinta* for orchestra or piano (1930, UME); *3 Movements* for piano (1930); *La balteira*, opera-ballet (1934); *Sonata del sur* for piano, orchestra (1945, UME); *Lirica española*, 5 exercise books for piano (1960–62); *Sinfonía aitana* (1963, UME); *Psalm 129* for vocal soloists, chorus, orchestra (1965, UME); *Cantata* in commemoration of the 20th anniversary of the proclamation of the Rights of Man by the U. N., for narrator, baritone, chorus, orchestra (1968, UME); *Plumes au vent*, opera (1969).

PRINCIPAL WRITINGS: *El arte y la musicalidad* (Alicante 1919); "Sobre la ópera," *Polyphonie* (Paris 1947):26–42; "Vues sur l'art," *Journal de psychologie* (Oct 1947):403–24; "Función musical y música contemporánea," (lecture published by the Real Academia de Bellas Artes, San Fernando, 1955); "En torno a la vocación musical," *Revista de psicología general y aplicada* (Madrid, Oct 1961):801–34. Esplá has also written numerous articles on esthetics for *A B C* (Madrid) since 1950.

BIBL.: Henri Collet, *L'Essor de la musique espagnole* (Paris 1928); Antonio Iglesias, *La música de piano de O. E.* (Madrid 1965); Federico Sopeña, "Ayer y hoy de O. E.," *Atlántida* (Madrid, Jan 1968):94ff.; Karel Willems, *Un Grand Musicien espagnol, O. E.* (Amsterdam 1952).

SEE ALSO Spain.

Estrada, Carlos (b. Montevideo, 15 Sept 1909; d. Montevideo, 7 May 1970), studied in Montevideo with Adelina Pérez Montero (piano), Carlos Correa Luna (violin), Manuel Fernández Espiro (harmony and counterpoint), and Padre Ochoa (Gregorian chant) and at the

Paris Conservatory (1938; composition with Roger Ducasse, Henri Busser; conducting with Albert Wolff, Paul Paray). In 1936 he founded the Chamber Orchestra of Montevideo, which he directed until 1938, and in 1959 he established the Municipal Symphony Orchestra. He taught harmony at the Univ. of Montevideo (1950–56) and at the National Conservatory.

PRINCIPAL COMPOSITIONS: *Suites Nos. 1–2* for string orchestra (1937, 1961); *Daniel*, oratorio for vocal soloists, orchestra (1942); *L'Annonce faite à Marie*, music drama (1943); *Concertino* for piano, orchestra (1944); *Les Uns et les autres*, music drama (1950); *Symphonies Nos. 1–2* (1951, 1967); *Robaiyat* for soprano, orchestra (1955). Estrada has also written numerous works for voice and piano, chorus, piano solo, organ, and chamber ensembles. Complete list: *Composers of the Americas* 16.

BIBL.: *Compositores musicales uruguayos* (Montevideo 1969); Roberto Lagarmilla, *Compositores uruguayos* (Montevideo 1970); Susana Salgado, *Breve historia de la música culta en Uruguay* (Montevideo 1971).

[prepared with the help of Susana Salgado]

Ethnomusicology, see Asian Music and Western Composition, Folk Resources

Etkin, Mariano (Josué) (b. Buenos Aires, 5 Nov 1943), studied privately (including composition with Guillermo Graetzer, 1963–64), and at the Torcuato di Tella Institute (1965–66; composition with Alberto Ginastera, Maurice Le Roux, Earle Brown, Iannis Xenakis, Mario Davidovsky, Roger Sessions). In Europe he has studied electronic music with Gottfried M. Koenig at the Utrecht State Univ. (1968–69) and conducting. He worked with Luciano Berio at the Juilliard School in New York (1969–70). He is active throughout Argentina as a pianist and conductor of contemporary music.

PRINCIPAL COMPOSITIONS: *3 Pieces* for piano (1959); *Variantes* for flute (1960); *3 Parábolas* for chamber ensemble (1963); *Elipses* for string orchestra (1964); *Entropías* for 7 brasses (1965); *Homenaje a Filifor forrado de niño* for flute, piccolo, clarinet, Eb clarinet, 2 percussionists (1966); *Estáticamóvil I* for 3 double basses, 2 trombones, harmonium, piano, 2 percussionists (1966); *Estáticamóvil II* for violin, viola, cello (1966); *Soles* for flute, horn, double bass (1967); *Distancias* for piano (1968); *Juego uno* for 2 trombones (1969); *Muriendo entonces* for viola and double bass with contact microphones, horn, trombone, tuba, 2 percussionists (1969); *IRT-BMT* for flute, double bass (1970).

BIBL.: "Músicos de hoy: M. E.," *Buenos Aires musical* 415 (1970):5.

Etler, Alvin (Derald) (b. Battle Creek, Iowa, 19 Feb 1913), studied at Western Reserve Univ. (1931–36, composition with Arthur Shepherd), the Cleveland Institute of Music (1931–36; oboe with Bert Gassman and Philip Kirchner), and the Yale Univ. School of Music (1942–44, composition with Paul Hindemith). He played in theater orchestras as a child and during 1938–40 was an oboist with the Indianapolis Symphony. He has taught at Yale Univ. (1942–46, 1965–66), Cornell Univ. (1946–47), the Univ. of Ill. (1947–49), Mt. Holyoke College (1953, 1960), and at Smith College (since 1949). Since 1968 he has been chairman of the Governing Committee of the Hampshire College Electronic Workshop. His development has been influenced by the Viennese school and by the "electronic gadgets" of Dayton C. Miller, the Cleveland musical instrument collector. He uses "serialistic techniques both loosely and strictly though not exclusively. Tonal centers have never been entirely abandoned. New sounds and pitch materials creep in where circumstances dictate. The color of jazz is never far beneath the surface. Aleatoric methods are almost entirely ignored, since control of tension through purposeful handling of all parameters is an ever present shape determinant."

PRINCIPAL COMPOSITIONS (published by AMP unless otherwise noted): *Wind Quintet Nos. 1–2* (1955, 1957); *Sonatina* for piano (1955, Broude-A); *Concerto in One Movement* for orchestra (1957); *Concerto* for violin, wind quintet (1958); *Elegy* for small orchestra (1959); *Ode to Pothos* for chorus (1961); *Triptych* for orchestra (1961); *Concerto* for wind quintet, orchestra (1961); *Concerto* for clarinet, trumpets, trombones, percussion, double basses (1962); *Brass Quintet* (1963); *String Quartets Nos. 1–2* (1963; 1965, Broude-A); *Concerto* for brass quintet, string orchestra, percussion (1967, Broude-A); *Convivialities* for orchestra (1968, Broude-A); *Concerto* for string quartet, orchestra (1968, Broude-A); *Clarinet Sonata No. 2* (1969, Broude-A).

Europe, see Austria and Germany, Belgium, Czechoslovakia, France, Great Britain, Greece, Hungary, Italy, Netherlands, Poland, Scandinavia, Soviet Union.

SEE ALSO Education for the Nonprofessional;

Electronic Music: History and Development; Liturgical Music: Christian; Liturgical Music: Jewish; Mixed Media; Opera; Performance; Recording.

Evangelatos, Antiochos (b. Lixourion, Cephalonia, Greece, 7 Jan 1904), studied law at the Univ. of Athens (1920–21), philosophy at the Univ. of Leipzig (1922–24), and music at the Musikhochschule in Leipzig (1924–28, composition with Max Ludwig) and the Basel Conservatory (1931, conducting with Felix Weingartner). Since 1932 he has been director and professor at the Hellenic Conservatory in Athens. He has conducted the National State Opera since 1940; during 1954–59 he was music director of Athens Radio.

PRINCIPAL COMPOSITIONS: *Symphony No. 1* (1929); *Epitaph* for chamber orchestra (1930); *Suite in D Minor* for orchestra (1933); *Overture for a Drama* for orchestra (1937); *The Young Maiden and Death* for voice, orchestra (1940); *Variations and Fugue on a Greek Folksong* for orchestra (1947–48, Schott); *Coasts and Mountains of Attica* for orchestra (1953); *Piano Concerto* (1959–60); *Symphony No. 2* (1967–68).

Evangelisti, Franco (b. Rome, 21 Jan 1926), studied engineering at the Univ. of Rome (1944–48) and composition at the Univ. of Freiburg (1954–56). In Rome he studied privately with Daniele Paris (1948–53; technical subjects, organ), Valentina Dobici (1949, solfège), and De Russis (1952–53, Gregorian chant). During 1952–60 he attended the Darmstadt summer courses, where he worked with Ernst Krenek and René Leibowitz. He became interested in electronic music through meetings with Werner Meyer-Eppler. In 1959 he organized the Palermo Festival for new music. In 1961 he founded in Rome an association for new music, Nuova Consonanza, and in 1964–65, an improvisation group of the same name. During 1968–69 he lectured on electronic music at the Accadèmia di S. Cecilia.

PRINCIPAL COMPOSITIONS: *4!*, 4 fattoriale for violin, piano (1954–55); *Ordini* for orchestra (1955, Tonos); *Poiezioni sonore* for piano (1955–56, Tonos); *Incontri di fasce sonore* on tape (1956–57, UE); *Random or Not Random* for orchestra (1956–62, Peters); *Proporzioni* for flute (1958, Bruzzichelli); *Campi integrati* on tape (1959); *Aleatorio* for string quartet (1959, Tonos); *Spazio a 5* for vocal sounds, 5 percussionists, electronic equipment (1959–61, Tonos); *Condensazioni* for orchestra (1960–62, Peters); *Die Schachtel*, action mimoscenica after Franco Nonnis for 7–10 mimes,

chamber orchestra, projections (1962–63, Peters).

PRINCIPAL WRITINGS: Evangelisti has written and lectured over Italian and German radio on electronic music, group improvisation, open form, and other avant-garde topics. His printed writings include: "Verso una composizione elettronica," *Ordini* (Rome, July 1959):48–54; "Risultati del Congresso per la musica elettronica a Venezia 1960," *La Biennale di Venezia* 44–45 (1961):31; "Espacio para la música," *Acenta cultural* (Madrid, March 1961):47; "Für eine neue Form der elektronischen Komposition," *Römische Reden* (Munich, 1965):114; "Improvisazione di gruppo," *Melos* (March 1966).

BIBL.: Mario Bortolotto, *Fase seconda, studi sulla nuova musica* (Turin 1969):193–200; Paolo Emilio Carapezza, "La nuova musica dopo la quarta settimana di Palermo," *Collage* 1:45–47; Ulrich Dibelius, *Moderne Musik 1945–1965* (Munich 1966).

SEE ALSO Italy.

Event, a single, perceptually separable musical entity in all of its dimensions, i.e., pitch, duration, loudness, timbre, and the like.

© *Music Educators Journal* (Nov 1968)

Evett, Robert (b. Loveland, Col., 30 Nov 1922), studied at Colorado College (1941–46, composition with Roy Harris) and at the Juilliard School (1951–52; composition with Vincent Persichetti, choral conducting with Margaret Hillis). He was music critic for *The New Republic* during 1952–54 and books and arts editor during 1954–67. During 1967–69 he was associate editor of *The Atlantic Monthly,* and he continues to write articles on music for both magazines. He identifies himself with the baroque era and describes his music as well made and adhering to conservative principles.

PRINCIPAL COMPOSITIONS: *Cello Concerto* (1954); *Piano Concerto* (1957); *Harpsichord Concerto* (1961, Peters); *Harpsichord Sonata* (1961); *Symphony Nos. 1–3* (1963, 1965, 1965); *Anniversary Concerto 75* for orchestra (1963); *Lauds* in honor of St. Ignatius of Loyola for men's chorus, orchestra, harpsichord (1964); *Office of Compline* for 3-part chorus (1966); *Fantasia on a Theme by Handel* for piano, violin, cello (1966); *Bassoon Concerto* (1969). List to 1965: *Composers of the Americas* 10:30–34.

BIBL.: Irving Lowens, "Current Chronicle," *Musical Quarterly* (Jan 1964).

SEE ALSO Dance.

Exoticism, see Asian Music and Western Composition, Folk Resources

Experimental, "an act of which the outcome is unknown" (John Cage, *Silence*: 13). In the past, musical "experiments" have generally been precompositional acts, as evidenced for example in Ferruccio Busoni's definition of neoclassicism: "the mastery, sifting, and exploitation of all the achievements of past experiments and their embodiment in fixed and beautiful forms" (quoted by Wladimir Vogel, *Perspectives* 6/2:170). In the view of Cage and others, experiments need not be tampered with ("sifted" and "exploited"); they are valuable as they are and can, in fact, free music from such limiting determinants as individual taste and memory.

Expressionism. The term *expressionism* is used today by art historians and critics to refer to certain German painters of the early 20th century, particularly the "Blaue Reiter" group that was active in Munich from about 1909. This group received its principal leadership from Wassily Kandinsky, a founder of abstract painting and a close friend of Arnold Schoenberg, some of whose paintings he reproduced in the Blaue Reiter yearbook of 1911 (the anthology also included scores of songs by Schoenberg, Berg, and Webern). In the decade before World War I, the association of artists and intellectuals in Germany and Austria, of whose work the Blaue Reiter collection was only one manifestation, was tremendously fruitful. The beginnings of nonrepresentational painting and the influence of the ideas of Sigmund Freud had immediate effects on Schoenberg's music. The two main characteristics of German expressionist painting—the avoidance of representational forms or classical draftsmanship or both, and the tendency toward association with exaggerated psychological states—have a close counterpart in the anticlassical aspects of Schoenberg's early atonal works. The monodrama *Erwartung* (1909, text by Marie Pappenheim) is one of Schoenberg's most important works in this respect, because of its neurotically motivated scenario and its extirpation of all vestiges of classical musical structure; the monomania of the story is continuous, and the music is without a single thematic device—melodic, harmonic, or rhythmic. In a later stage work on his own text, *Die glückliche Hand* (1910–13) and in the cycle *Pierrot Lunaire* (1912, texts after the French of Albert Giraud), Schoenberg reintroduced some degree of formal design but without reducing the level of morbidity. On the other hand, in his purely instrumental works of the period (e.g., *Piano Pieces*, Opp. 11 and 19) there is a variable complement of perceptible form and no overt psychological element. All these tendencies, with increasing refinements, persisted in Schoenberg's music in later years and, though in different ways, in Berg's and Webern's. Considered as a whole, the formal attitudes (including the very conceptions of tonality and atonality) of Schoenberg and his two famous pupils are as broadly variable as those of the "expressionist" painters, which range from Piet Mondrian's severely formalized but abstract designs to Oskar Kokoschka's nonclassical forms but representational images.

Historically expressionism as an art movement has no counterpart in music. Painters calling their work "abstract" increased in numbers after World War I and came to represent a predominant tendency; in the years just before World War II a movement called "abstract expressionism" sprang up, chiefly in the U.S., in which a number of artists recaptured some of the principles of the early years of German expressionist painting. In music, however, the three Viennese composers fought a lonely battle for many years against the 19th-century romanticism from which they had sprung, against a rising tide of neoclassicism (which was not without its effects on them), and especially against the minions of Hitler who tried to exterminate their art. Not until after World War II could their music be widely heard and accepted on its own terms, and by then those terms were no longer a vital force; the intervening years had obscured their historical and intellectual significance. It was also only in the postwar years that the work of some lesser figures, particularly in the U.S., began to be recognized as a parallel trend to Viennese expressionism. The works of Carl Ruggles (b. 1876) are the most typical of this independent American expressionism; they are marked by complex textures, atonal harmony, and autonomous, nonclassic form. (Certain short works by Charles Ives may be thought of in this category, but only with reservations; Ives here, as in almost everything, was a law unto himself.)

BIBL.: B. S. Myers, *The German Expressionists* (New York 1957); Peter Selz, *German Expressionist Painting* (Berkeley, Calif., 1957).

Mark DeVoto

SEE ALSO Form.

Ezaki Kenjiro (b. Tainan, Formosa, 27 Nov 1926), studied at Nihon Univ. in Tokyo (1953–57, composition with Kiyohiko Kijima) and at the Experimental Music Studio of the Univ. of Ill. and the Columbia-Princeton Electronic Music Center (1965–66, electronic music with Vladimir Ussachevsky). He has had his own electronic music studio in Tokyo since 1966 and has been chairman of the Association of Sound Designers since 1968. For the 1970 Exposition, Fujitsu Limited commissioned him to prepare computer music using the FACOM-270-30. In 1971 he lectured on composition at the Univ. of Tokyo.

PRINCIPAL COMPOSITIONS: *Moving Pulses* for 3 voices, percussion (1961, Ongaku); *Discretion* for female voice (1962, Ongaku); *Concretion* for string trio (1962, S-Z); *Contention* for woman's voice, guitar (1963, Casa de la Guitarra, Tokyo); *Presage* for orchestra (1964); *Nodule* for guitar (1964, S-Z); *Music* for guitar, electronic sounds on tape (1967, Casa de la Guitarra); *Ensemble* for piano, 2 playback devices (1967).

PRINCIPAL WRITINGS: "Gendai-ongaku to Electronics" [Contemporary Music with Electronics], *Stereo* (Tokyo) 97 (1970):126–32; "Gendai-ongaku to Computer" [Contemporary Music with Computers], *Ongaku Geijutsu* 28/13:46–49.

SEE ALSO Japan.

F

Fabini, (Félix) **Eduardo** (b. Solís de Mataojo, Uruguay, 18 May 1882; d. Montevideo, 17 May 1950), studied at La Lira Conservatory in Montevideo (c.1897–1900; violin and harmony with Romeo Masi, Virgilio Scarabelli, Miguel Ferroni, and Italo Casella) and at the Brussels Royal Conservatory (1900–03) with César Thomson and August de Boeck. Until 1914 he concertized as a violinist in Latin America and played with the Uruguayan Chamber Music Association. He also appeared as an accompanist in vocal recitals.

PRINCIPAL COMPOSITIONS: *Campo* for orchestra (1910–22, Ricordi); *La isla de los ceibos* for orchestra (1924–26, Maretti); *La patria vieja* for soprano, chorus, orchestra (1925); *Melga sinfónica* for orchestra (1931); *3 Tristes* for piano (premiere 1935, 1936; No. 1 published by Palacio de la Música in Montevideo, No. 2 by Schirmer-G). Fabini also composed numerous chamber works and songs; complete list: *Composers of the Americas* 2:53–57.

BIBL.: *Compositores musicales uruguayos* (Montevideo 1969); Roberto Lagarmilla, *E. F.* (Montevideo 1954); ——, *Compositores uruguayos* (Montevideo 1970); Susana Salgado, *Breve historia de la música culta en el Uruguay* (Montevideo 1971).

[prepared with the help of Susana Salgado]

Falik, Jurii (Alexandrovich) (b. Odessa, 30 July 1936), studied at the Leningrad Conservatory (1955–64; composition with Balkashin and Boris Arapov, cello with Schtrimer and Mstislav Rostropovich). He has taught cello, instrumentation, and score reading at the Leningrad Conservatory since 1964 and has performed in the U.S.S.R. as a cellist and conductor.

PRINCIPAL COMPOSITIONS: *String Quartets Nos. 1–2* (1955, 1965); *Concertino* for oboe, chamber orchestra (1961); *Partita* for organ (1965); *Wind Quintet* (1967, Muzyka); *Oresteia*, ballet after Aeschylus (1968); *Music* for string orchestra (1968); *Symphony* for string orchestra, percussion (1969, Muzyka); *A Capella Choruses* (1969–70); *Concerto for Orchestra* based on the Till Eulenspiegel legends (1971, Muzyka); *Skomorokhi*

[Minstrels], concerto for 4 winds, 2 brass, 18 percussion (1971, SC).

BIBL.: A. Stratievsky, "Tragedica prodolzhaetsia" [The Tragedy Continues], *Sovetskaia muzyka* 1969/6.

Falla, Manuel de (b. Cádiz, Spain, 23 Nov 1876; d. Alta Gracia, Argentina, 14 Nov 1946), studied at the Royal Conservatory in Madrid (1897–99, composition with Felipe Pedrell, piano with José Tragó). During 1907–14 he lived in Paris, where he became friends with Debussy, Dukas, Ravel, and Roussel. He performed as a pianist and conductor, chiefly of his own music. He moved to Argentina in 1939. His work was strongly influenced by the native songs and dances of Spain and, after the mid-20s, by Spanish 18th-century harpsichord music.

PRINCIPAL COMPOSITIONS: *La vida breve*, 2-act opera; libretto adapted by P. Milliet after C. Fernández-Shaw (1904–05, Eschig); *Noches en los jardines de España* for piano, orchestra (1911–15, Eschig); *7 Spanish Songs* for voice, piano; folk texts (1914–15, Eschig); *El amor brujo*, gypsy ballet; scenario by Gregorio Martinez-Sierra (1914–15, Chester); *El corregidor y la molinera*, pantomime in 2 scenes; scenario by Martinez-Sierra (1916–17); *El sombrero de tres picos*, ballet in 2 scenes; choreography by Léonide Massine (1918–19, Chester); *Fantasia baetica* for piano (1919, Chester); *El retablo de Maese Pedro*, marionette opera in 1 act; text adapted by the composer from Cervantes (1919–22, Chester); *Concerto* for harpsichord, flute, oboe, clarinet, violin, cello (1923–26, Eschig); *Soneto a Córdoba* for soprano, piano; text by Luis de Góngora (1927, Oxford); *Atlántida*, scenic cantata; text by J. Verdaguer (begun 1926, completed by Ernesto Halffter; Ricordi).

PRINCIPAL WRITINGS: *Escritos sobre música y músicos* ed. by F. Sopeña (Buenos Aires 1950).

BIBL.: Rodolfo Arizaga, *M. de F.* (Buenos Aires 1961); Suzanne Demarquez, *M. de F.* (Paris 1963); Julio Jaenisch, *M. de F. und die spanische Musik* (Zurich 1952); *Musica d'oggi* 5 (1962) special issue devoted to Falla; Jaime Pahissa, *M. de F.: His Life and Works* trans. by J. Wagstaff (London 1954); Kurt Pahlen, *M. de F. und die Musik in Spanien* (Olten 1953).

SEE ALSO Dance, Popular Music, Spain.

Farkas, Ferenc (b. Nagkanizsa, Hungary, 15 Dec 1905), attended the Academy of Music, Budapest (1923–28, composition with Leo Weiner, Albert Siklós) and the Accadèmia di S. Cecilia, Rome (1929–31, composition with Ottorino Respighi). Farkas was coach and conductor at the Budapest Municipal Theater (1927–29) and was composer and conductor for the Sascha Filmstudio, Vienna (1933–34) and Nordisk Films, Copenhagen (1935–36). He taught theory and composition at the Budapest Municipal Music School during 1935–41, after which he was professor of composition at the Conservatory of Music, Kolozsvár (1941–43) and its director (1943–44). In 1944–45 Farkas was assistant director of the chorus of the Hungarian State Opera, Budapest. In 1946 he organized the Conservatory of Music at Székesfehérvár, serving as director for two years. Since 1949 he has been professor of composition at the Academy of Music, Budapest.

PRINCIPAL COMPOSITIONS (published by EMB unless otherwise noted): *Quaderno romano* for piano (1931); *Concertino* for harp, orchestra (1937, revised 1956; UE); *A bűvös szekrény* [The Magic Cupboard], 2-act opera (1942, UE); *Musica pentatonica* for string orchestra (1945, Sidem); *Cantata lirica* for choir, orchestra (1946); *Gyümölcskosár* [Fruit Basket], song cycle for voice, instrumental ensemble or piano (1946); *March Suite* for chamber orchestra (1947); *Prelude and Fugue* for orchestra (1947, Mills); *Furfangos diakok* [The Sly Students], ballet (1949, EMB and Boosey); *Concertino* for harpsichord, string orchestra (1949, UE); *Csinom Palkó*, musical play (1950, EMB and Henschel); *Serenade* for wind quintet (1951); *Ouverture symphonique* for orchestra (1952); *Antiche danze ungheresi* for wind quintet (1953); *Calendar*, duet-cycle with ensemble (1955, UE); *2 Aquarelles* for piano (1955); *Correspondances* for piano (1957, Mills); *Hybrides* for piano (1957, Mills); *Cantus pannonicus* for soprano, choir, orchestra (1959); *Piccola musica di concerto* for string orchestra (1961, Schott); *Sonata a due* for viola, cello (1961); *3 Masses* for choir, organ (1962, 1964, 1968, unpub.); *Ballade* for cello, piano (1963, Boosey); *Vidróczki*, 3-act opera (1964); *Trittico concertato* for cello, string orchestra (1965); *Concerto all'antica* for baryton (viola da gamba), string orchestra (1965, UE); *Laudatio Szigethiana*, oratorio (1966); *Waiting for the Spring* for baritone, choir, orchestra (1967); *Sérénade concertante* for flute, string orchestra (1967); *Hommage à Alpbach*, song-cycle for voice, piano (1968, unpub.).

BIBL.: József Ujfalussy, *F. F.* (Budapest 1969).

SEE ALSO Hungary.

Feld, Jindřich (b. Prague, 12 Feb 1925), studied the violin with his father and later attended the Prague Conservatory (1945–48;

composition with Emil Hlobil, violin with his father), the Prague Academy of Music (1948–52, composition with Jaroslav Řídký), and the Charles Univ. (1945–52; musicology, esthetics, philosophy). Feld has taught privately and written for radio, films, and television. He was also a visiting lecturer in composition at the Univ. of Adelaide, Australia (1968–70). He has contributed many articles on contemporary music to the Czech periodical *Hudební rozhledy*.

PRINCIPAL COMPOSITIONS: *Flute Concerto* (1954, SHV); *4 Pieces* for flute (1954, Leduc); *2 Compositions* for cello, piano (1954–55, Panton); *Concerto in C* for chamber orchestra (1956–57, SHV); *Postman's Tale*, children's opera (1956, DILIA); *Rhapsody* for violin, orchestra (1956, SHV); *Flute Sonata* (1957, Leduc); *Cello Concerto* (1958, Panton); *Bassoon Concerto* (1958–59, Leduc); *Chamber Suite* for nonet (1960, Leduc); *Suite* for chamber string orchestra (1960–61, Leduc); *String Quartet No. 3* (1962, EM); *3 Frescoes* for orchestra (1963, SHV); *Concert Music* for oboe, bassoon, orchestra (1964, Sonzogno); *String Quartet No. 4* (1965, SHV); *Serenata giocosa* for chamber orchestra (1966, EM); *3 Inventions* for chamber choir (1966); *Symphony No. 1* (1966–67, SHV); *Suite* for accordian (1967, Hohner); *Wind Quintet No. 2* (1968, SHV).

SEE ALSO Czechoslovakia.

Feldman, Morton (b. New York, 12 Jan 1926), studied composition with Wallingford Riegger and Stefan Wolpe. The esthetic principles of his music were shaped by his close association in New York with John Cage, Earle Brown, Christian Wolff, and David Tudor in the early 1950s. He lives in New York and lectures extensively in America and abroad.

Feldman's main concern has been to develop new kinds of sound relationships. The techniques he has evolved to do this include some types of indeterminacy, and, early in his career, graphic notation. Both of these first appeared in music in his *Projections* (1950–51). These works divide the gamut of each player's instrument into high, middle, and low registers and allow the player to select pitches within the specified register. Durations in the notated score are indicated by the relative length of horizontal rectangles placed over short vertical strokes that mark a steady pulse. Using generally quiet sounds, the pieces explore the nuances of various instrumental combinations, contrasting timbres, and registers as in Varèse but without that composer's use of preselected pitches. The notation furnishes a blueprint for planes of timbre that are extended horizontally and interrelated in time.

Vertical as well as horizontal sound relationships are exploited in *Marginal Intersection* for orchestra (1951). Individual sonorities are sometimes specified, such as solo horn against a brass line in which all players choose from among specified pitches during a graphically indicated duration. Additional planes of sound are provided by two electric oscillators that generate very low and high frequencies, barely audible pressures that the instrumental sounds bounce from.

The very low dynamic levels that Feldman favors and the absence of metered rhythm may give some listeners the impression of a totally static music. This is not the case, however. In the score for *The Swallows of Salangan* (1960) the pitches are lined up, resembling a series of chords, but the durations of the pitches are selected by each performer. The pitch changes that produce successive "chords" do not occur simultaneously so that the piece is heard as a shifting mass of sonorities having no precise rhythmic articulations. One senses movement because of the emergence of carefully planned momentary polarities and even passing suggestions of tonalities. It is a significant esthetic point that the perception of such movement is physical, not intellectual as in traditional music. *In Search of an Orchestration* (1967) discards these polarities and exploits instead the wide range of changing timbres available in the orchestral medium. *First Principles* (1966–67) contains definite changes from one kind of sound to another, but, though measured, these articulations are very broadly (and irregularly) spaced so that they cannot be precisely discerned. Instrumental resources in the piece are divided into groups, each with its own pattern of articulations. Thus cross-rhythms occur, though they use longer durations than do the polymetric cross-rhythms in Ives and others.

In evaluating Feldman's influence, it is essential to point out that for him sounds come first in the creative process and technical procedures come second. Feldman himself feels that most composers who claim to follow him have turned his techniques into mere sound-producing processes; they are not themselves motivated by the inner conception of sound that has generated his own technical innovations.

PRINCIPAL COMPOSITIONS (published by Peters): *Projection I* for cello (1950); *Marginal Intersection* for orchestra (1951); *Atlantis* for chamber orchestra (1959); *The Swallows of Salangan* for chorus, 23 instruments (1960); *First Principles* for large instrumental ensemble (1966–67); *In Search of an Orchestration* for orchestra (1967).

PRINCIPAL WRITINGS: "Predetermined/Indetermined," *Composer* (fall 1966); "Boola Boola," *Composer* (winter 1966–67); "Conversations without Stravinsky," *Source* 2; "An Interview with Robert Ashley," *Contemporary Composers on Contemporary Music* ed. by E. Schwartz and B. Childs (New York 1967): 362–66; "Varken-eller," *Nutida musik* 11; "Give My Regards to Eighth Street," *Art News Annual* (1968).
BIBL.: David Behrman, "What Indeterminate Notation Determines," *Perspectives* 3/2:58–73; Peter Dickinson, "F. Explains Himself," *Music and Musicians* (July 1966): 22–23; Wilfred Mellers, *Music in a New Found Land* (London, 1964); Knut Wiggen, "Ett kapitel ur en bok man aldrig hinner skriva," *Nutida musik* 11.

Barney Childs

SEE ALSO Dance, Indeterminacy, Rhythm, United States.

Fellegara, Vittorio (b. Milan, 4 Nov 1927), studied mathematics and physics at the Univ. of Milan (1945–50) and music at the Verdi Conservatory in Milan (composition with Luciano Chailly, diploma in 1951). During 1956–59 he was secretary of the Accadèmia Filarmonica Romana, and since 1959 he has been secretary of the Italian section of ISCM. He has taught composition at the Donizetti Institute in Bergamo since 1960. His music has been influenced at different periods by the work of Hindemith (1948–54); Petrassi (1955–57), and Nono (1958–59).

PRINCIPAL COMPOSITIONS (published by S-Z): *Otteto* for winds (1953); *Concerto breve* for chamber orchestra (1956); *Sinfonia* (1957); *Requiem di Madrid* for chorus, orchestra; text by García-Lorca (1958); *Dies irae* for chorus, 6 trumpets, cymbals, percussion; text by García-Lorca (1959); *Serenata* for chamber ensemble or chamber orchestra (1960); *Variazioni*, "Frammenti II," for chamber orchestra (1961); *Mutazioni*, ballet in 6 scenes (1962); *Epitaphe* for 2 sopranos, flute, timpani, percussion, vibraphone, piano, celesta; text by P. Eluard (1964); *Cantata* for 2 women's voices, orchestra; text by G. Leopardi (1966); *Madrigale* for vocal quintet, chamber orchestra; anonymous medieval German texts (1968).
BIBL.: Armando Gentilucci, "Avanguardia e impegno: rapporto dialettico" [The Avant-garde and Engagement: a dialectical report], *La musica moderna* (Milan) 100:49–58; Luigi Pestalozza, "Castiglioni, Donatoni, e F.," *La biennale di Venezia* 62:55–58; ———, "V. F.," *Nutida musik* 10.

Fennelly, Brian (b. Kingston, N.Y., 14 Aug 1937), attended Yale Univ. (1963–68; composition with Mel Powell; theory with Donald

Martino, Allen Forte, George Perle; analysis with Mel Powell, Gunther Schuller). Since 1968 he has been on the faculty of New York Univ. During 1965–67 he was an editorial assistant for the *Journal of Music Theory,* and since 1969 he has been coeditor of the *Contemporary Music Newsletter.*

PRINCIPAL COMPOSITIONS (available at ACA): *Wind Quintet* (1967); *Divisions for a Violinist* for solo violin (1968); *Evanescences* for alto flute, clarinet, violin, cello, tape (1969).

PRINCIPAL WRITINGS: "A Descriptive Language for the Analysis of Electronic Music," *Perspectives* 6/1:79–95; "Structure and Process in Webern's Opus 22," *Journal of Music Theory* 10/2:300–28; a review of *Serial Composition* by R. Smith Brindle, *ibid.* 11/2:288–91.

SEE ALSO Electronic Music: Notation.

Fernández, Oscar Lorenzo (b. Rio de Janeiro, 4 Nov 1897; d. Rio de Janeiro, 27 August 1948), attended medical school and entered the National School of Music in 1917 (piano with Henrique Oswald, composition with Francisco Braga). He taught at the National School of Music from 1925 and in 1936 became director of the Brazilian Conservatory, which he had helped found. In 1930 he founded the review *Illustracão musical.* As a conductor he helped promote Brazilian nationalist music.

PRINCIPAL COMPOSITIONS: *Trio brasileiro* for violin, cello, piano (1924, Ricordi); *Canção sertaneja* for voice, piano; text by Eurico Góes (1924, Vitale); *Suite sinfônica* on 3 Brazilian folk tunes for orchestra (1925, Southern); *Suite* for wind quintet (1926, AMP); *Imbapara,* American Indian tone poem for orchestra (1928, Southern); *Toada* for voice, piano; text by Mario de Andrade (1928, Vitale); *3 Studies in the Form of a Sonatina* for piano (1929, Ricordi); *Reisado do pasoreio,* suite for orchestra (1930, Southern and Ricordi); *Malazarte,* 4-act lyric drama (1931–32); *Valsa suburbana* for piano (1932, Ricordi); *Cantigas de minha terra* for chorus (1935, Vitale); *Suites brasileiras Nos. 1–3* for piano (1936–38, Vitale); *3 Invenções seresteiras* for clarinet, bassoon (1944, *Boletín latino-americano de música*); *2 Invenções seresteiras* for flute, clarinet, bassoon (1944, Southern); *Symphony No. 1* (1945, Southern); *Symphonic Variations* for piano, orchestra (1948, Southern). Complete list: *Composers of the Americas* 7:9–16.

PRINCIPAL WRITINGS: "O canto coral nas escolas" [Choral Singing in the Schools], *Revista brasileira de música* 5/2:25–35; "A contribuição harmonica de Villa-Lobos para a musica brasileira" [Villa-Lobos's Harmonic Contribution to Brazilian Music], *Boletín latino-americano de música* 6:283–300.

BIBL.: Eurico Negueira França, *L. F.: Compositor brasileiro* (privately printed 1959); Albert

T. Lupert, "L. F. and Camargo Guarnieri: Notes Toward a Mid-century Appraisal," *Conference on Latin American Fine Arts, June 14–17, 1951,* *Proceedings* (Austin, Texas, 1952):98–114.

Ferrari, Luc (b. Paris, 5 Feb 1929), studied at the Versailles Conservatory (1946–48), the Ecole Normale de Musique in Paris (1948–50; Alfred Cortot, piano; Arthur Honegger, composition), and at a master class in composition given by Olivier Messiaen (1953). He became associated with the Groupe de Musique Concrète at the French Radio in 1958. When the group dissolved later that year, Pierre Schaeffer and he refounded it as the Groupe de Recherche Musicale, of which Ferrari was a director until 1966. During 1960–62 he taught musique concrète for the GRM and was a professor at the Rheinische Musikschule at Cologne during 1964–66. In 1965–66 he produced and directed for French television a series of documentary films on contemporary music. He has lectured at the Stockholm Electronic Studio of the Swedish Radio (1966), the German Film and Television Academy in Berlin (1967), and at McGill Univ. (1969).

PRINCIPAL COMPOSITIONS: *Visage I* for piano (1956); *Visage II* for brass, percussion (1956); *Visage IV,* profile for 10 instruments (1957–58); *Visage V,* musique concrète on tape (1958–59, recorded by Philips); *Tête et queue du dragon,* musique concrète on tape (1959–60, recorded by Philips); *Tautologos I* on tape (1961, recorded by Boite à Musique); *Tautologos II,* musique concrète on tape (1961, recorded by Boite à Musique); *Flashes* for 14 instruments (1963); *Heterozygote* on tape, "musical drama for concert or stage, or musical anecdote" (1963, recorded by Philips); *Symphonie inachevée* for orchestra (1963–66, Moeck); *Music Promenade* for 4 tape recorders (1964–69, recorded by Wergo); *Und so weiter* for piano, tape (1965–66, recorded by Wergo); *Société II,* "Et si le piano était un corps de femme" for 4 soloists, piano, percussion, 16 instruments (1967, Moeck); *Interrupteur* for 9 instruments (1967, Moeck); *Les Jeunes Filles,* "Société III," on 16-mm. film, written and directed by the composer (1967); *Société IV,* "Méchanique collectivité individu," for orchestra (1967); *Société V,* "Participation or Not Participation," for 6 percussionists, actor, audience (1967–69); *Société VI,* "Liberté, liberté cherie," action for audience (1969); *Tautologos III,* "Vous plairait-il de tautologuer avec moi?", for any group of instruments (1969).

BIBL.: Hansjörg Pauli, notes for the Wergo record SP-835-485; Pierre Schaeffer, *La Musique concrète* (Paris 1969):108–14; ——, *Le Traité des objets musicaux* (Paris 1966).

SEE ALSO Austria and Germany.

Ficher, Jacobo (b. Odessa, Russia, 15 Jan 1896), studied at the Imperial Conservatory in St. Petersburg (1912–17; violin with Leopold Auer, S. Korguiev). In 1919 he was appointed concert-master of the Leningrad State Opera Orchestra, but never took up the post. In 1923 he settled in Buenos Aires, where in 1929 he founded the contemporary music group Grupo Renovación. In 1939 he became conductor of the General Society of Musicians' Symphony Orchestra. He founded the Argentine Composers League in 1947. Since 1956 he has taught composition at La Plata Univ., the National Conservatory of Music in Buenos Aires, the Municipal Conservatory Manuel de Falla, and the Arts Institute of the Teatro Colón.

PRINCIPAL COMPOSITIONS: *Poema heroico* for orchestra, Op. 7 (1927, revised 1934); *Sulamita*, tone poem for orchestra, Op. 8 (1927, revised 1960); *String Quartet No. 1*, Op. 9 (1927, revised 1947); *Obertura patética* for orchestra, Op. 11 (1928, revised as *Exodus* 1960); *Violin Sonata No. 1*, Op. 15 (1929, revised 1960); *3 Symphonic Sketches*, Op. 17 (1930); *Sinfonía de cámara* for chamber orchestra, Op. 20 (1932); *Symphony No. 2*, Op. 24 (1933); *Colombina de hoy*, 1-act ballet for 2 pianos, Op. 25 (1933); *Los invitados*, 1-act ballet, Op. 26 (1933); *Piano Trio*, Op. 30 (1935); *String Quartet No. 2*, Op. 35 (1936); *Symphony No. 3*, Op. 36 (1938–40); *Melchor*, 3-act ballet for chorus, 14 strings, Op. 40; text by César Tiempo (1938–39); *El organillero* for bass, orchestra, Op. 41; text by Leónidas Barletta (1940); *3 Dances in Popular Argentine Style* for piano, Op. 43 (1941, EAMI); *Piano Sonata No. 1*, Op. 44 (1941, Fischer); *Violin Concerto*, Op. 46 (1942); *Golondrina*, 3-act ballet, Op. 47 (1942); *Cello Sonata*, Op. 48 (1943); *Piano Sonata No. 2*, Op. 49 (1943); *Gaucho*, film suite for orchestra, Op. 51 (1944); *Psalm 119* and *Pulvis eris et pulvis reverteris* for tenor, women's chorus, orchestra, Op. 52 (1944); *Piano Concerto*, Op. 53 (1945); *Violin Sonata No. 2*, Op. 56 (1945); *6 Fables* for piano, Op. 59 (1946, Southern) or chamber orchestra (1951); *Serenata* for string orchestra, Op. 61 (1947, EAMI); *Symphony No. 5*, "Así habló Isaías," Op. 63 (1947); *Hamlet Symphony*, Op. 67 (1948); *Salmo de alegría*, cantata, Op. 69; text by Rafael Alberti (1949, Radio Nacional de Argentina, Buenos Aires); *2 Poems of Longfellow* for voice, piano, Op. 70 (1949); *Piano Sonata No. 3*, Op. 71 (1950, EAMI); *Piano Sonata No. 4*, Op. 72 (1950, Ricordi); *String Quartet No. 4*, Op. 73 (1952); *El oso*, 1-act chamber opera, Op. 75; libretto based on Chekhov (1952); *Suite* for chamber orchestra, Op. 78 (1953); *Piano Concerto No. 2*, Op. 81 (1954); *Overture to Don Segundo Sombra*, Op. 82 (1954); *Pedido de mano*, 1-act chamber opera, Op. 84; libretto after Chekhov (1955–56); *Concerto* for harp, chamber orchestra, Op. 85 (1956); *Symphony No. 6*, Op. 86 (1956); *Piano Sonata No. 5*, Op. 87 (1956); *Rapsodia* for

chorus, saxophone quartet, Op. 88 (1956); *Saxophone Quartet*, Op. 89 (1957, Southern); *Oda a la libertad* for narrator, orchestra, Op. 90; text by José Isaacson (1957); *Mi Aldea*, cantata for soprano, alto, tenor, chamber orchestra, Op. 91; text by Manuel Rugeles (1958); *Epopeya de mayo*, symphony no. 7, Op. 92 (1958–59); *Violin Sonata No. 3*, Op. 93 (1959); *Variations and Fugues on a Theme of Mozart* for orchestra, Op. 95 (1961); *Piano Quintet*, Op. 96 (1961); *Piano Sonata No. 6*, Op. 97 (1961); *Festival Overture*, Op. 98 (1962); *Piano Sonata No. 101* (1964); *Piano Concerto No. 3*, Op. 103 (1964); *4 Sonetos de amor* for chorus, Op. 104; texts by Manuel Rugeles (1964); *Symphony No. 8*, Op. 105 (1965); *Flute Concerto*, Op. 107 (1968); *Wind Quintet*, Op. 108 (1969); *Kadish*, cantata for soprano, alto, tenor, bass, chorus, orchestra, Op. 112 (1969). List to 1956: *Composers of the Americas* 2:60–69.

BIBL.: Rodolfo Arizaga et al., "Homenaje a J. F.," *Davar* 110:101–11; *Composers of the Americas* 2:58–69; Nicolai Malko, *A Certain Art* (New York 1966):208, 219; Boris Zipman, *J. F.* (Buenos Aires 1966).

Filter, an electronic device that permits the selective transmission of specified frequencies of the input signal by the attenuation of undesired frequencies. Filters are used primarily to give variety in tone color to signals.

SEE ALSO Electronic Music: Apparatus and Technology.

Fine, Irving (b. Boston, 3 Dec 1914; d. Natick, Mass., 23 August 1962), attended Harvard Univ., 1933–39, and became closely associated during those and succeeding years with Serge Koussevitzky, Aaron Copland, and Igor Stravinsky. Following a year of study abroad with Nadia Boulanger, he returned to Harvard as director of the Glee Club (1939–46) and assistant professor of music (1946–50). In 1950 he moved to Brandeis Univ., where he became chairman of the School of Creative Arts.

Fine was not prolific, partly because of his administrative and teaching duties and partly because he was by nature a composer who preferred to work slowly. He was a neo-classicist by temperament as well as training and had a deep personal commitment to the esthetic values of the 18th century. Even after 1952, when he became interested in 12-tone techniques, his music reflected a style and a feeling of order and control closer to Mozart (by way of Stravinsky) than Schoenberg or Berg. He valued elegance and refinement and generally felt that his melodic lyricism, rhythmic grace, and carefully controlled dissonance were best expressed through the medium of chamber ensembles. However, his last work, the *Symphony* (1960–62), demonstrated his ability to compose for large orchestra with the same facility and transparency of his earlier works. In a personal way he anticipated the practice of many younger composers today of employing peripherally melodic and harmonic materials derived from 12-tone rows (or portions of rows) in an undoctrinaire manner almost antithetical to the raison d'être of dodecaphony. Fine made it a practice to point out in program notes (e.g., *String Quartet* and *Mutability*) that his use of 12-tone material was secondary to considerations of form, tonality, and harmonic rhythm.

PRINCIPAL COMPOSITIONS: *3 Choruses from "Alice in Wonderland"* for chorus; No. 3 also for men's chorus (1942, Witmark); *Partita* for wind quintet (1948, Boosey); *The Hour Glass* for chorus; poems by Ben Jonson (1949, Schirmer-G); *Notturno* for strings, harp (1950–51, Boosey); *Mutability*, 6 songs for mezzo-soprano, piano; texts by Irene Orgel (1952, Mills); *Serious Song*, a lament for string orchestra (1955, Broude-B); *Fantasia* for string trio (1956, Mills); *Romanza* for wind quintet (1958); *Symphony* (1960–62, Mills). List to 1960: *Composers of the Americas* 6:57–61.

PRINCIPAL WRITINGS: "Young America: Bernstein and Foss," *Modern Music* (May 1945); "Story of 20th-Century Music," *Book of Knowledge* (New York 1948). Fine also wrote articles and reviews for *Modern Music, Musical America, New York Times, Notes*, and other periodicals.

Richard Wernick
SEE ALSO United States.

Fine, Vivian (b. Chicago, 28 Sept 1913), studied piano at the Chicago Musical College (1919–22) and attended the American Conservatory in Chicago (1925–31; composition with Adolf Weidig and Ruth Crawford Seeger), and the Dalcroze School in New York (1935–36). She studied piano with Abby Whiteside (1937–45), composition with Roger Sessions (1934–42), and orchestration with George Szell (1943). From 1931 she was active as a performer of contemporary piano music. In addition to extensive private teaching, she has been on the faculties of New York Univ. (1945–48), the Juilliard School (1948), the State Univ. College at Potsdam, N. Y. (1951), and Conn. College School of Dance (1963–64). She was musical director of the Bethsabee de Rothschild Foundation from 1955 to 1961 and has been teaching at Bennington College since

1964. She was a founder of the American Composers Alliance and served as vice president during 1961–65. Special influences on her compositional development have included her piano studies during 1924–31 with Djane Lavoie-Herz, a pupil and disciple of Scriabin; the interest shown in her work by Henry Cowell, Dane Rudhyar, and Imre Weisshaus during 1929–31; and from 1931, her association in New York with young composers sponsored by Aaron Copland.

PRINCIPAL COMPOSITIONS: *4 Pieces for 2 Flutes* (1930); *4 Songs* for voice, strings (1933, New Music); *The Race of Life*, ballet for piano, percussion; choreography by Doris Humphrey (1937, orchestrated 1938; orchestral version with slides of drawings by James Thurber, 1961); *4 Elizabethan Songs* for voice, piano (1937–41); *Sonatina* for oboe, piano (1939); *Suite in E♭* for piano (1940); *Concertante* for piano, orchestra (1944); *Capriccio* for oboe, string trio (1946); *The Great Wall of China* for voice, flute, cello, piano (1947, New Music); *Divertimento* for cello, percussion (1951); *Violin Sonata* (1952); *A Guide to the Life Expectancy of a Rose* for soprano, tenor, flute, clarinet, violin, cello, harp (1956); *String Quartet* (1957); *Valedictions* for soprano, tenor, chorus, chamber orchestra (1958); *Alcestis* for orchestra, ballet; choreography by Martha Graham (1960); *Fantasy* for cello, piano (1962); *Quintet* for string trio, trumpet, harp (1967); *Paean on the sound "I"* for narrator, speaking and singing choruses, 12 brass instruments (1968–69).

PRINCIPAL WRITINGS: an untitled article on the subject of composers and choreographers, *Dance Perspectives* 16 (1963):8–11.

BIBL.: Doris Humphrey, "Music for an American Dance," *Bulletin of the American Composers Alliance* 8/1 (1958); Wallingford Riegger, "Music of V. F.," *ibid.*; William T. Upton, "Aspects of the Modern Art-Song," *Musical Quarterly* (Jan 1938).

Finney, Ross Lee (b. Wells, Minn., 23 Dec 1906), began cello and piano lessons as a child and played chamber music with other members of his family and professionally. He attended the Univ. of Minn. (1924–25, composition with Donald Ferguson) and Carleton College in Minn. (1925–27). He studied with Nadia Boulanger in Paris (1927–28, also during other summers) and with Alban Berg in Vienna (1931–32). In addition he attended Harvard Univ. (1928–29), and also studied with Roger Sessions intermittently during 1929–48. He taught at Smith College 1929–48, and since then has been at the Univ. of Mich. His other activities have included conducting, lecturing, singing (in Europe), founding the Valley

Music Press (now New Valley), the Smith College Music Archives, and establishing the electronic music studio at the Univ. of Mich. The strongest influences on his development have come from Boulanger and her student group of 1927–28, from Roger Sessions, and from Alban Berg (whose full effect Finney felt only after 1945). At least since 1950 Finney has been concerned with combining tonal functions with 12-tone techniques and serialism. This aspect of his thinking has rarely been taken note of but is considered by the composer to be basic.

PRINCIPAL COMPOSITIONS: *Poems by Archibald MacLeish* for voice, piano (1935, AME); *Bleheris* for tenor, orchestra (1937, Peters); *Piano Sonata No. 3* (1942, New Valley); *Symphonies Nos. 1–3* (1942, 1959, 1960; Peters); *Hymn, Fuguing, and Holiday* for orchestra (1943, Fischer); *Piano Sonata No. 4* (1945, Mercury); *String Quartets Nos. 4, 6, 7, 8* (1947, Schirmer-G; 1950, Peters; 1955, New Valley; 1960, New Valley); *Spherical Madrigals* for chorus (1947, Peters); *3 Love Songs* for high voice, piano (1948, New Valley); *Cello Sonata No. 2* (1950, New Valley); *Quintet* for piano, strings (1953, Peters); *Violin Sonata No. 3* (1955, New Valley); *Variations* for orchestra (1957, Peters); *Fantasy in 2 Movements* for violin (1958, Peters); *String Quintet* (1958, Peters); *Still Are New Worlds* for chorus, narrator, orchestra (1962, Peters); *Divertissement* for clarinet, violin, cello, piano (1964, Bowdoin); *Percussion Concerto* (1965, Peters); *Nun's Priest's Tale* for chorus, vocal soloists, narrator, folk singer with electric guitar, small orchestra (1965, Peters); *The Martyr's Elegy* for tenor, chorus, orchestra (1966, Peters); *Symphony Concertante* (1967, Peters). List to 1966: *Composers of the Americas* 11:24–32.

PRINCIPAL WRITINGS: *Analysis and the Creative Process* (Claremont, Calif., Scripps College, 1959); "The Composer Must Rebel," *Pan Pipes* (Jan 1969):3–6.

BIBL.: Paul Cooper, "The Music of R. L. F.," *Musical Quarterly* 53:1–21; R. S. Hines, ed., *The Orchestral Composer's Point of View* (Norman, Okla., 1970); Henry Onderdonk, "Aspects of Tonality in the Music of R. L. F.," *Perspectives* 6/2:125–45.

SEE ALSO Musicology and Composition, United States.

Fišer, Luboš (b. Prague, 30 Sept 1935), attended the Prague Conservatory (1952–56) and the Prague Academy of Musical Arts (1956–60), where he studied composition with Emil Hlobil. He works as a free-lance composer in Prague, writing functional music (for television, radio, and films) in addition to concert music.

PRINCIPAL COMPOSITIONS: *Piano Sonatas Nos. 1, 3, 4* (1955, Supraphon; 1960, Panton; 1964, Panton); *Ruce* [The Hands], sonata for violin,

piano (1961, Supraphon); *Chamber Concerto* for piano, ensemble (1964); *Patnáct listů podle Dürerovy Apokalypsy* [15 Prints after Dürer's Apokalypse] for orchestra (1965, Supraphon); *Caprichos* (after Goya) for large chorus, chamber chorus (1966, Supraphon); *Pieta* for 9 instruments (1967); *Requiem* for soprano, baritone, chorus, orchestra (1968, Supraphon); *Double* for orchestra (1969); *Lamentation over the Destruction of Ur* for double chorus, percussion (1969).

SEE ALSO Czechoslovakia.

Fitelberg, Jerzy (b. Warsaw, 20 May 1903; d. New York, 25 April 1951), began music studies with his father, a conductor, and continued after 1920 at the Hochschule für Musik in Berlin (composition with Walter Schrecker). He also studied with Walter Gmeindl at the Berlin Academy of Music. In 1933 he emigrated to Paris and in 1940, to the U.S. Most of his output consisted of non-programmatic, instrumental music in the classic forms.

PRINCIPAL COMPOSITIONS: *String Quartet No. 2* (c.1928, UE); *Concerto for String Orchestra* (1928, UE); *Violin Concertos Nos. 1–2* (1928, Omega; 1935, Eschig); *Suite No. 2* for orchestra (1928, UE); *Sonata* for 2 pianos, 2 violins (1938, Chester); *Serenade* for violin (viola), piano (1943, Southern); *Nocturne* for orchestra (c.1944, AMP); *String Quartet No. 5* (1945); *Symphony No. 1* (1946, Marks).

BIBL.: Emilia Elsner, "J. F.," *Chesterian* (Sept 1939):14–19.

Flanagan, William (b. Detroit, 14 August 1926; d. New York, c.31 August 1969), studied journalism for two years at the Universities of Detroit and Mich. and music at the Eastman School (composition with Burrill Phillips, Bernard Rogers) and Tanglewood (1947, 1948; composition with Arthur Honegger, Samuel Barber, Aaron Copland). He also studied composition privately in New York with David Diamond. He was a music reviewer for *The New York Herald Tribune* and a contributing editor of *Stereo Review*; he also wrote many articles for the *Partisan Review*, *Musical Quarterly, Notes,* and other periodicals. Before his death (by suicide) he was working on a book on American composers.

PRINCIPAL COMPOSITIONS: *Divertimento* for string quartet (1947, ACA); *Piano Sonata* (1950, Peer); *A Concert Ode* for orchestra (1951, Peer); *Time's Long Ago*, cycle of 6 songs for soprano, piano; texts by Herman Melville (1951, Peer); *Bartleby*, 1-act opera; libretto by James Hinton, Jr., and Edward Albee (1952–57, ACA); *The Weeping*

Pleiades, song cycle for baritone, flute, clarinet, violin, cello, piano; texts by A. E. Housman (1953, Peer); *The Lady of Tearful Regret*, dramatic narrative for coloratura soprano, baritone, flute, clarinet, string quartet, piano; text by Albee (1959, ACA); *Moss*, song cycle for soprano, piano; text by Howard Moss (1959–62; Nos. 1–4, Peters; No. 5, Peer); *Narrative* for orchestra (1965, ACA). Flanagan also composed 13 other songs for voice and piano and incidental music to 4 plays by Albee. List to 1965: *Composers of the Americas* 12:30–34.

BIBL.: Peter Reilly, "W. F.," *Stereo Review* 21/5:134; Lester Trimble, "W. F. (1923–1969): An Appreciation," *Stereo Review* 23/5:118.

Fleming, Robert (James Berkeley) (b. Prince Albert, Sask., Canada, 12 Nov 1921), attended the Royal College of Music in London (1937–39; piano with Arthur Benjamin, composition with Herbert Howells) and the Royal Conservatory in Toronto (1941–42, 1945–46; composition with Healey Willan, organ with Frederick Sylvester, conducting with Ettore Mazzoleni). A staff composer of the National Film Board of Canada in Montreal since 1946 and its music director since 1958, he has written over 200 documentary film scores.

PRINCIPAL COMPOSITIONS: *Sonatina* for piano (1940, Oxford); *Secrets* for voice, piano (1941, Oxford); *Shadow on the Prairie* for orchestra, ballet suite (1953); *Ballet Introduction*, suite for orchestra (1960); *Concerto '64* for piano, orchestra (1964); *Tuba Concerto* (1966); *Confession Stone* for voice, piano (1966, Leeds); *String Quartet* (1969). List to 1965: *Composers of the Americas* 12:37–49.

Flothius, Marius (Hendrikus) (b. Amsterdam, 30 Oct 1914), studied with Arend Koole (1928–30, piano) and Hans Brandts Buys (1930–37; piano, theory) and at Utrecht Univ. (1932–34; musicology with Albert Smijers) and Amsterdam Univ. (1934–37, 1964–66; musicology with Karel Bernet Kempers). During 1937–42 and 1953–55 he was assistant manager of the Concertgebouw Orchestra; he has been artistic director since 1955. He has also been a music critic for the Amsterdam *Het Vrije Volk* (1945–53) and librarian of the Donemus Foundation (1946–50). His music has been influenced by his musicological studies of Monteverdi and Mozart and by the compositions of Debussy, Bartók, Willem Pijper, and Bertus van Lier.

PRINCIPAL COMPOSITIONS (published by Donemus): *Sonnet* for mezzo-soprano, orchestra, Op. 9 (1939–40); *Dramatic Overture*, Op. 16 (1943–46); *Flute Concerto*, Op. 19 (1944); *Sonata* for violin, Op. 23, No. 3 (1944–45); *Concerto* for horn, chamber orchestra, Op. 24 (1944–45); *To an Old Love* for mezzo-soprano, orchestra; text by Ellen Marsh; Op. 32 (1947–48); *Love and Strife*, cantata for alto, flute, oboe d'amore, viola, cello, Op. 34; texts by Kathleen Raine (1949); *Pour le Tombeau d'Orphée* for harp, Op. 37 (1950); *Partita* for violin, piano, Op. 38, No. 1 (1950); *Concerto* for violin, chamber orchestra, Op. 39 (1950); *Sonata da camera* for flute, harp, Op. 42 (1951); *String Quartet*, Op. 44 (1951–52); *Negro Lament* for alto, alto saxophone, piano, Op. 49; texts by Langston Hughes (1953); *Fantasia* for harp, chamber orchestra, Op. 51 (1953); *Clarinet Concerto*, Op. 58 (1957); *Symphonic Music*, Op. 59 (1957); *Odysseus and Nausikaä*, madrigal for speaker, vocal quartet, harp, Op. 60; text by Homer (1960); *Espressioni cordiali* for string orchestra, Op. 63 (1963); *Hymnus* for soprano, orchestra, Op. 67 (1965).

PRINCIPAL WRITINGS: *Contemporary English Composers* (Amsterdam 1949); *Mozarts Bearbeitungen eigener und fremder Werke* (Salzburg 1969).

BIBL.: Wouter Paap, "Nederlandse componisten van deze tijd, XV. M. F.," *Mens en Melodie* 6/1: 4–9; ——, *Music in Holland* (Amsterdam c.1961):44.

Floyd, Carlisle (b. Latta, S. C., 11 June 1926), studied at Converse College, Spartanburg, S. C. (1943–45) and Syracuse Univ. (1945–46, 1948–49; composition, piano with Ernst Bacon). He has studied piano privately with Sidney Foster (1949–50) and Rudolf Firkusny (Aspen, Colo., 1952, 1955). Since 1947 he has taught at Florida State Univ.

PRINCIPAL COMPOSITIONS (published by Boosey unless otherwise noted): *Slow Dusk*, 1-act opera (1949); *Susannah*, 2-act opera (1955); *Pilgrimage*, cantata for voice, orchestra (1956); *Piano Sonata* (1957); *Wuthering Heights*, opera (1959); *The Mystery*, song cycle for voice, orchestra (1960); *The Passion of Jonathan Wade*, opera (1962); *The Sojourner and Molly Sinclair*, 1-act opera (1963); *Markheim*, 1-act opera (1966); *Introduction, Aria, and Dance* for orchestra (1967, Presser); *Of Mice and Men*, opera (1969, Colombo).

SEE ALSO Opera.

Folk Resources. Although Western composers have always made use of so-called folk materials, the tendency has become steadily more pronounced in the last hundred years. Two different phenomena are involved: 1) Nationalism, in which a composer draws on musical traditions from his own geographical area. From earliest childhood, all composers are subject to the unconscious assimilation of indigenous musical ideas; we are not concerned here with this naturally absorbed material but rather with the conscious discovery and use of national material. 2) Exoticism, in which a composer reaches outside his own area for new materials and new methods. This tendency, though it is centuries old, has been accelerated in the 20th century in part by the worldwide spread of fast systems of communication and by the growth of the discipline of ethnomusicology (itself a symptom of exoticism) and its use of field recording equipment.

Nationalism and exoticism tend to be fostered by different social and intellectual conditions. Nationalistic music, for example, tends to be valued in countries just emerging from a condition of political or cultural domination or dependence; it is in part a result of pride in a newly discovered national identity. Exoticism tends to occur in more developed countries, those in which a large quantity of highly respected music is available, most of which adheres to commonly held principles; thus exoticism may indicate a restlessness among creative people, a need to stretch the imagination toward new challenges. Despite their differences, nationalism and exoticism today are kindred insofar as they both represent a rejection of what the composer experiences as imposed or infertile musical values. There are, of course, overlappings of these phenomena. The most frequent occurs when the nationalistic composer who seeks for roots in what he considers to be the purest traditions of his racial or national group turns to what is for him the exotic area of peasant art of the distant past. Béla Bartók is perhaps the most striking example, but Wagner's use of legend and saga, Scott's glorification of medieval Scotland, and European musicological probings into the art of the Middle Ages also exude the spirit of what might be termed "indigenous exoticism."

In the late 18th century, "Turkish" music and exotic opera plots gave evidence that Europe was beginning to feel the pull of distant lands. The colonial powers became fascinated by the cultures of conquered lands and subject peoples. Evidence of this occurs in the ethnomusicological activities of La Borde, Amiot, and even Rousseau (whose example of Chinese music in his *Dictionary* was used by Weber and copied from the latter's music by Hindemith). The effect of this on the substance of music remained almost nil, for composers were not yet ready to forsake the idea that only European music manifested truly artistic standards and values. Berlioz, for instance, said that Chinese music was "grotesque and abominable." Rather than allowing the underlying principles of their music to be transformed by the borrowed material, 19th-century composers generally confined their exoticism to programmatic music about the exotic lands, with perhaps an occasional bit of pentatonicism added on. ("Hungarian" music of the time made a slightly more organic use of the borrowed material, even if it was gypsy music and not peasant music that was borrowed.) This sort of exoticism came more or less to an end with the literary and musical chinoiserie of Mahler's *Das Lied von der Erde*.

Debussy, in many ways quintessentially French, was a dedicated exoticist who was fascinated by the music of Southeast Asia as presented at the Paris Exhibitions of 1889 and 1900. His enthusiasm for and understanding of the music is quite clear from his own words, "Javanese music is based on a type of counterpoint by comparison with which that of Palestrina pales." (Some appearances in his music of principles akin to those of East Asia are cited in the article Asian Music.) The impulse toward exoticism is even clearer in Debussy's "Spanish" music. Spanish themes, both literary and musical, had appeared in the music of several earlier French composers and writers, but it was Debussy who gained what Manuel de Falla referred to as an "impressive" understanding of Spanish style (in "La Puerta del Vino" from *Preludes*, book 2, and "La Soirée dans Granade" from *Estampes*). The confluence of composition and musicology is aptly illustrated here, for Debussy based his music on material he studied in the folksong collections of Felipe Pedrell. Pedrell, the editor of the collected works of Victoria, utilized Spanish themes in his operas; as the teacher of Albeniz, Granados, and Falla, he was highly influential in the production of a Spanish national music.

Nationalistic composers of the 19th century introduced metrical shifts, new polyphonic combinations, new sonorities, drones, modal melodies, and the like into the concert hall. In the early 1910s Bartók, Ives, Kodály, Stravinsky, and Vaughan Williams often frightened audiences with the explosive energy of their folk sources. In *The Firebird* Stravinsky quoted peasant songs drawn from Rimsky-Korsakov's collection; in *Petrouchka* he not only quoted several songs but suffused the entire work with the sounds of Russian folk polyphony and Russian peasant life. Indeed, in these stage works as well as later in *Les Noces,* we have almost the impression of a kind of musical anthropology. The short diatonic melodies, the shifting metrical patterns, the drones, the harmonic style of the polyphony are all modeled on the sounds of peasant music. It is unimportant whether a given melody is a folk tune or not, for, as Bartók said, the composer "completely absorbed the idiom of peasant music, which has become his mother tongue."

Nationalistic tendencies were given theoretical and philosophical backing mainly by Bartók and Vaughan Williams. The latter, for example, thought of even Bach as a national composer because of his deep love for the German chorale. Bartók reasoned that since the great musical tradition of the Hungarian people was preserved in the songs of the people rather than in the notated works of composers, it was necessary for the Hungarian musician to study and absorb peasant music in order to understand his own heritage. He cited Kodály's *Psalmus Hungaricus* as an outstandingly successful example of this kind of absorption. He also felt that one had to absorb folk music on the spot, that it was not sufficient to study the material in archives and museums.

In the U.S. a number of composers (led by Arthur Farwell) attempted, in the first decade of the 20th century, to create a native music based largely on the thematic and rhythmic structure of American Indian music; Farwell's Wa-Wan Press was the main vehicle for dissemination of harmonized piano "transcriptions," songs, and fantasies by such composers as Harvey Loomis, Carlos Troyer, and Farwell himself. Later Charles Wakefield Cadman, Arthur Nevin, and Henry Gilbert took up the cudgel, but the movement was short-lived. It did, however, serve the purpose of accustoming the musical public to shifts of meter and uncommon melodic styles. The music of Ives provides a striking example of the results that can be achieved when a composer is truly steeped in his native traditions. Ives, like Stravinsky, produced a kind of musical anthropology. Massed heterophonic singing at camp meetings, late-finishing brass-band players, the simultaneous performance of two tunes at a parade—these characteristics, which earlier generations considered crudities, were perceived by Ives to be not only an essential aspect of the American musical tradition but valuable as sound ideals. Copland, early in his career, expressed his desire to be an American composer by writing compositions that utilized jazz sonorities, rhythms, and melodic inflections; later he turned to well-known tunes in such works as

The Second Hurricane, the *Outdoor Overture,* and *John Henry.* The vogue of jazz was extremely widespread after World War I, both among composers such as Stravinsky and Milhaud, to whom it was exotic, and among those such as Copland, to whom it was native. This was one case, however, where an essential ingredient in the borrowed material, the free and creative interplay among a group of *improvising* musicians, was not utilized. This characteristic of jazz performance began to enter concert music in the 1950s in "third-stream" compositions, which pitted jazz against traditional concert performance practice, often using a concerto-grosso format. The concept of music as a performance rather than a notated composition entered the concert world in the 1960s with the rise of indeterminate performance works (see Indeterminacy, Performance).

Nationalistic and folkloristic opera, particularly the works of Mussorgsky and Borodin, was profoundly influential on early 20th-century composers; though nationalistic opera continues to be composed even today, its force is far from potent. Among operas that had elements tending toward the "musical anthropology" mentioned earlier are Falla's *La vida breve* and Vaughan Williams's ballad opera *Hugh the Drover.* Other examples that draw scenic, musical, and literary materials from folk life are Kodály's *Háry János* and Weinberger's *Švanda.* The exotic plot, though it has suffused the entire history of opera, lost ground; in such works as Puccini's *Turandot* and Holst's *Savitri* Chinese and Hindu musical materials are but little apparent.

Several attitudes toward folk resources exist simultaneously today. Particularly in Central and South America, a relatively new sense of national identity (and the presence of previously untapped folk materials) continues to inspire a purely nationalistic music. Although younger composers in these countries were turning away from the nationalistic esthetic by the 1960s, many musicians of the middle and older generations have retained this point of view, forming one of the last outposts of musical nationalism in the West. The demands of political leaders in the Soviet Union and the countries of Eastern Europe have caused nationalism to exist beyond what would probably have been a shorter lifespan. There too, many younger composers since the 1960s have adopted a more eclectic outlook. There is a tendency, especially in Western Europe and North America, to abandon folk sources altogether in favor of an "international" vocabulary based after World War II on

12-tone and serial techniques and expanded in the 1960s to include aleatory, collage, electronic, and other procedures. Alongside all these tendencies, many Western composers are searching the exotic regions for philosophical and technical guideposts. Thus Messiaen has used the Indian tala system to extend the somewhat meagre rhythmic resources of Western music and in his *Turangalíla* symphony has recreated the sonority of the gamelan (as did his pupil Boulez in *Le Marteau sans maître*). Finally there are composers at work in most countries who are trying to synthesize the traditional expression of their own area and the methods and materials of the international vocabulary. As in the past, the effect of nationalism or exoticism on the course of music history will probably depend not on the raw material that is brought to light but on what individual composers do with it. If someone with a keen mind, such as Bartók, exploits effectively the principles that underlie a body of folk music, then a new way of thinking may be picked up and used by others. If, however, the composer merely fills out an existing system of thought with folk colors, the result may be appealing for a time but will probably have no further life.

BIBL.: Béla Bartók, "The Influence of Peasant Music on Modern Music," *Béla Bartók, A Memorial Review* (New York 1950); Manfred Bukofzer, "The New Nationalism," *Modern Music* 23:243–47; N. Curtis, "A Plea for Our Native Art," *Musical Quarterly* 6:175–78; Alfred Einstein, "National and Universal Music," *Modern Music* 14:3–11; Charles Seeger, "Tradition and the (North) American Composer," *Music in the Americas* ed. by George List and Juan Orrego-Salas (The Hague 1967):195–212; Ralph Vaughan Williams, *National Music* (London 1935).

Theodore C. Grame

SEE ALSO Asian Music and Western Composition; Hungary; Japan; Jazz; Liturgical Music: Jewish; Melody; Musical; Musicology and Composition; Popular Music; Rhythm.

Form. In the most general sense form consists of shape (contour, the variation of some attribute of a thing in space or time) and structure (the disposition of the parts of a thing, relations of one part to another and to the whole). In music, shape is the result of changes in time of some attribute or parameter of sound, while structure has to do with various relations between sounds and sound configurations at the same or at different moments in time. (The term *form* will not be used in this discussion in the restricted sense of

a fixed or standard scheme of relationships, as in *sonata form*.)

Shape and structure imply at least two hierarchical levels of organization and perception (*whole* and *part*), and usually more than two (since sound configurations that are parts of the larger whole may themselves contain parts). Any thorough description of the form of a piece of music must therefore include descriptions of form at several hierarchical levels. This is true of pre-20th century music as well but has been obscured by the fact that much of the detailed *infrastructure* of that music was taken for granted (e.g., instrumental timbres, diatonic pitch relations, periodic rhythms, etc.). Since 1900, however, changes have occurred at all hierarchical levels, and the infrastructure can no longer be ignored.

In addition to shape and structure, there is a third factor that determines form. A description of the shape (or sometimes the structure) of a formal unit at one of these hierarchical levels frequently involves certain statistical characteristics (the average value and range of each important parameter) of the formal units at the next lower level. There are thus three aspects of form to consider at each hierarchical level: the structural (internal relations), the morphological (shape), and the statistical (state or condition).

These relations between state, shape, and structure at adjacent hierarchical levels are, incidentally, relevant to the old problem of form vs. content. A little reflection will show that the "content" of a formal unit at a given hierarchical level is determined by the structural, morphological, and statistical properties (i.e., the *form*) of each of its component units at the next lower level. Conversely, formal properties at one hierarchical level become the "content" of formal units at the next higher level. This is not always obvious at intermediate levels, but what we do finally call "content" is the result of "forms" at a level below the first one we have agreed to deal with formally. (Form vs. function posits a similarly artificial distinction — the reverse of the form/content distinction, but one which may also be resolved via the concept of hierarchical levels.) We shall find inconsistencies in the historical development of new forms at various levels simultaneously ("old wine in new bottles," and vice versa), but it is no longer necessary to treat form and content as fundamentally different things.

In what follows, new formal conditions in 20th-century music will be described at each of these hierarchical levels. For the smallest "indivisible" sound units at the first hierarchical level, the word *element* will be used. Singular configurations of elements, forming the units at the second hierarchical level, will be called *clangs*. For a unit at the third hierarchical level, consisting of a cohesive group of clangs, the word *sequence* will be used. Whether a given sound or sound configuration is to be considered an element, a clang, or a sequence depends on many variable factors—both objective and subjective. Most commonly an element will be a single tone, but it might be a trill, a chord, a glissando, or a more complex noise. Perhaps the most important variable factor is the musical content itself. In a very dense texture, an "indivisible" element might actually be a complex sound configuration. On the other hand in a very sparse texture, especially at a slow tempo, a single tone might be perceived as a clang. Although the clang is often equivalent to the *motive* or *phrase* of traditional music, it should be understood here to include any collection of sound elements perceived as a primary aural gestalt.

THE FIRST HIERARCHICAL LEVEL: SOUND ELEMENTS. Changes have occurred in the larger framework (scales and tuning systems) within which pitches are selected and interrelated. After two centuries of a music whose elements consisted of tones and chords based on a diatonic/triadic, 12-tone, equal-tempered tuning system, there now exist: 1) chromatic and other nondiatonic pitch-scales that are still within the older tuning system (Debussy, Scriabin, Schoenberg); as well as 2) different tuning systems [e.g., quarter-tone and sixth-tone temperaments (Ives, Hába), simple-ratio or *just* scales (Partch), and free, indeterminate pitch "gamuts" (Cage, musique concrète)]; and 3) harmonic (i.e., chordal) structures based on 1 or 2 above or otherwise non-triadic.

In addition there have been important changes at the element level with respect to timbre, including: 1) an increased use of new timbres produced by unusual playing techniques on conventional instruments (e.g., bowing at the bridge, flutter-tonguing, etc.); 2) further extensions of the range of timbres via the development of new instruments, including electronic devices (Russolo, Varèse, Partch, Cage); 3) the use of tone clusters and other dense, "dissonant" chords (Ives, Cowell, Bartók) and complex "aggregates" (Cage); and 4) a more frequent use of noises (i.e., sounds without salient pitch) as elements structurally equivalent to tones and chords, rather than as secondary, supportive, or merely "background" elements (Varèse, Cage, musique concrète, etc.).

In some cases (e.g., concrete music and much of Cage's later work), the elements so frequently lack pitch saliency that the very notions of scale and tuning system become irrelevant. Here the conventional distinction between musical and nonmusical sounds breaks down completely. In the light of the changes that have taken place in music since 1900, it is evident that any sound is potentially musical, i.e., any sound may function as an element in the musical fabric, and this in a way that is structurally equivalent to any other sound.

It is of interest to note here that formal changes at this first level have profoundly influenced, and been influenced by, changes in the medium (the development of new instruments, playing techniques, and notation). The most obvious example of this is electronic music, but this is only the latest of a series of changes in the medium that began as early as 1910.

THE SECOND HIERARCHICAL LEVEL: THE CLANG. At the next higher level, where the smaller sound elements are grouped into clangs (meaning any collection of sound elements perceived as a primary aural gestalt), important structural changes have occurred with respect to tonality and rhythm. It is at this level that key-defining pitch relations begin to be manifested in pre-20th century (as well as later tonal) music, and the avoidance or "transcendence" of such pitch relations is characteristic of much of the new music since 1900. This is of structural (as distinct from merely textural) significance, if only because it removes a powerful means of relating one part to another and of providing both continuity (via similarity) and variety among musical configurations at the clang level and higher. One example of the tendency to avoid key-defining pitch relations is found in the early melodic writing of Schoenberg, Berg, and Webern, and later in the work of Ruggles: the avoidance of an early repetition of a previously heard pitch or its near octaves. In the later 12-tone method of Schoenberg, this tendency actually became a systematic procedure which, together with a number of others, was intended to replace the cohesive and structural functions of the earlier tonal system.

Rhythmic structure at the clang level has changed since 1900 from simpler, periodic rhythms based on units of two and three, toward more complex—and even completely aperiodic and indeterminate—rhythms with varying unit durations.

Another important change at the clang level

has been a greater use of parameters other than pitch and time to give shape to a clang, especially intensity and timbre. In earlier music both intensity and timbre are usually constant within each clang, tending to vary only from clang to clang or even only from sequence to sequence. The frequent use of crescendo and decrescendo markings in Webern's Op. 5 or Op. 9, for example, indicates the greater importance of intensity as a shaping factor within each clang. And the alternation of instrumental timbres on the same pitch or nearby pitches, as in Schoenberg's Op. 16, No. 3, or Op. 21, No. 4, exemplify a similar use of timbre.

THE THIRD HIERARCHICAL LEVEL: THE SEQUENCE. At the next higher level, that of sequences (meaning a series of several clangs perceived as a larger, if looser, gestalt), quite a number of new formal conditions have arisen. It is at this third hierarchical level that structure in its fullest sense (relations between parts that are themselves complex) first becomes really important. Among the new developments are the following: 1) New (and some very old) kinds of shape variations of the basic, "thematic" clangs (e.g., inversion, retrograde, octave transposition, etc., as in Schoenberg and Webern); 2) A new importance of parameters other than pitch and time in determining shape relations between the clangs in a sequence (which follows from their use in giving shape to each clang as noted earlier); 3) A use of both *heteromorphic* sequences, in which no two clangs have or are derived from the same shape (as in some early Schoenberg and Webern, as well as Cage after 1951), and *isomorphic* sequences, in which all the clangs are identical (Satie's *Cinéma*, for example). In most sequences, clangs tend to be interrelated in a way that might be called *metamorphic;* completely isomorphic or heteromorphic sequences are the exception, even in 20th-century music; 4) The absence (in nontonal music) of conventional cadence formulas to define the end of a sequence. Just how the perceptual boundaries of the sequence are created in the absence of tonal conventions is a problem of closure in *gestalt* perception and will not be dealt with here except to say that in general the same *gestalt* factors of cohesion and segregation are involved at the sequence level as at the clang and element levels—primarily temporal proximity and parametric similarity.

It was noted earlier that the medium is of special importance in its influence upon, and in its being influenced by, formal conditions at the first hierarchical level. At the clang and sequence levels, it is compositional method that seems to play a similar role. Developments 1 and 2 above will be recognized as two aspects of serial technique, and it is at these levels that the effects of serial methods have been most noticeable. This applies to other methods too, including those based on chance.

HIGHER LEVELS OF ORGANIZATION: SECTIONS, MOVEMENTS, THE WHOLE PIECE. Between the sequence and the whole piece the question arises as to the actual number of hierarchical levels that are relevant to the musical experience. This depends on the piece itself. In much earlier music there are well-defined sections and often movements, thus interposing two distinct hierarchical levels between those of the sequence and the whole piece. In much 20th-century music, on the other hand, there is no reason to consider any intermediate levels between these two—that is, the next larger grouping of sequences that is relevant to perception and analysis is the whole piece itself. In general, however, where there are intermediate levels, their formal characteristics are similar to those of the sequence or of the whole piece. More specifically, what has already been said about sequences will apply also to sections, and the observations that follow on whole pieces will apply to movements.

The absence in nontonal music of conventional cadence formulas to effect closure, mentioned earlier with respect to sequences, applies to the whole piece as well (and to any intermediate levels). The piece, of course, has its automatically defined "boundaries" simply by virtue of its starting and stopping (though just how coherent a gestalt it is will depend on many other factors as well). Again the same *gestalt* factors of cohesion and segregation are involved at this large-form level as at all lower levels. In addition a number of other devices have been used by 20th-century composers to effect or reinforce a sense of closure. They include: 1) A return to some point of departure and/or a resolution of some kind of tension. These are equivalent to conventional formal situations when the point of departure and return is a key center and the resolution is achieved harmonically, but both return and resolution may be realized in a number of other ways not involving conventional tonality (e.g., Bartók, *Music for Strings, Percussion and Celeste*, first movement). 2) Reaching a limit beyond which the preceding process cannot continue (Ives, *The Housatonic at Stockbridge,* or *A Farewell to Land*). This is usually an upper or lower limit on some parametric scale and might be called an intrinsic limit to distinguish it from 3 below. 3) The arbitrary stopping of a process, which might also be called reaching an extrinsic limit (e.g., the time allotted for a particular performance of a piece of indeterminate duration). The effect here is as though looking at a landscape through an open window: the perceptual boundaries are defined "arbitrarily" by the window, rather than being inherent or "intrinsic" to the process ("landscape") itself. Music that ends this way often begins this way also, and we might call this a "windowed" form of closure (or *gestalt* boundary-definition in general). It is frequently found in Cage's music since 1951.

The first of these three types of closure assumes that the piece has begun by establishing some clear point of departure, which is then followed by an excursion or deviation. This suggests a kind of arch form, familiar from 19th-century music. The second implies that most of the piece has been moving in a given direction, which has finally brought it to some intrinsic limit, and we might call this a *ramp* form. The third, on the other hand, assumes the precedence of a relatively static or statistically homogeneous condition, creating a "flat" large-form shape that might be called *ergodic,* borrowing a term from mathematics meaning a process whose statistical properties as a whole are the same as the statistical properties of each part at the next lower hierarchical level. The arch and ramp shapes are thus *nonergodic,* but they are only two especially clear and simple examples of nonergodic shapes. There are others, though they are usually combinations of arch and ramp shapes.

The most important morphological distinction here is that between ergodic and nonergodic, but these terms refer to the shape of a piece in some parameter, as distinct from relations between the parts of a piece. They may thus serve to describe the morphological aspect of a whole piece, but they tell us nothing about structure. For this, other terms will be needed which can distinguish among various types of large-form structure. Returning to the original definition of structure as "relations between sounds and sound configurations," let us consider how many different kinds of relationship are possible. There are, first of all, simple parametric relations: higher/lower, louder/softer, faster/slower, and the like. These have already been subsumed in the definition of shape. The simplest kind of relation that is uniquely structural would involve comparisons between two or more shapes at the next lower hierarchical level and specifications of their relative positions in time.

The first question in the determination of structure would thus be: Is this clang (or sequence, or section) identical in shape to some previous clang (or sequence, or section), or is it of different shape? If the two gestalt units thus compared are not identical, are they still morphologically similar in some way or in some degree? That is, are they "related" by some perceptible process of transformation by which one might be considered to have been derived from the other? And finally, if they are so related, what type of transformation or variation is involved in this apparent derivation?

In answering these questions, the three terms that were used to describe types of structure at the sequence level will be found useful: *isomorphic* (identity of shape), *heteromorphic* (complete dissimilarity of shape), and *metamorphic* (partial similarity of shape or relation via transformation). These terms may be applied in fact to structure at any hierarchical level beyond the first, since structure only exists, by definition, when the parts of a thing themselves contain parts. Applied to the highest level then, we may begin with the following breakdown of structural types. When no morphological similarities at all are perceptible in a piece of music (as in some of the earlier works of Schoenberg and Webern, as well as many of the more recent works of Cage), the structure may be called heteromorphic. When there are perceptible morphological relations of various kinds in a piece (as in most music), the structure may be called metamorphic. And if a piece consists of nothing but the repetition of one morphological entity, at whatever level, it may be called isomorphic (with respect to that level and with respect to that parameter that determines the shape of the repeated unit). This last is obviously rare, though Ravel's *Bolero* provides one example of a structure that is essentially isomorphic at the section level (and with respect to the parameters pitch and note duration, if not others). Other manifestations of such a structure at other levels and in other parameters are certainly conceivable if not common occurrences in 20th-century music.

We thus have as our starting-point three types of structure at the large-form level (as well as at lower levels): isomorphic, metamorphic, and heteromorphic. By far the most common type of structure is the metamorphic, and within this type there are obviously a very large number of possible structures, reflecting the multiplicity of types of morphological transformation that can be perceived. A partial list of such transformations would have to include: permutations of the temporal order of the gestalt units at the next lower hierarchical level, whether elements, clangs or sequences, perhaps even sections; interval expansions and contractions; extensions and truncations (both horizontal and vertical); insertions and deletions of lower-level gestalt units (again both horizontally and vertically), including all varieties of "ornamentation"; the mirror transformations (inversion, retrograde, retrograde-inversion) of 12-tone and later serial music; and finally various less systematic distortions or parametric shifts of lower-level gestalt units that preserve only the general topological features of the larger unit's shape.

In most cases a combination of several of these types of transformation will be heard in any given piece of music, so they do not provide a basis for characterizing the structure of a whole piece, with the possible exception of permutation. Many of the works of Stravinsky, for example, seem to involve little more than permutations of the temporal order of a relatively fixed set of clangs (e.g., the "Danse Sacrale" in *The Rite of Spring*, or the second of the *3 (4) Etudes for String Quartet (Orchestra)*. Sometimes this kind of permutation process is applied to sequences, rather than clangs, as in the same composer's *Symphonies of Wind Instruments*. Such a process is analogous to a kaleidoscope, in which all of the perceived forms are the result of the continually varied juxtaposition of a fixed set of gestalt units at the next lower level. The fact that so many 20th-century pieces proceed in this way suggests that the *permutational structure* should be considered a basic structural type within the larger category of metamorphic structures (other examples: Messiaen, *Catalogues des oiseaux*; Cage, *Music of Changes*.)

There is another large class of structures that use a much wider range of transformations, though also including permutation. These can be called *developmental structures*. Whereas the permutational structures were compared to a kaleidoscope, the developmental structures might be compared to the growth of a flower or a tree. More generally these developmental structures proceed like some natural process in which the gestalt units at the lower level undergo perceptible changes also, as well as creating changing shapes at the higher level. Among such developmental structures, we might further distinguish two basic types, according to the apparent direction of the morphological changes, i.e., whether essentially from simple to complex (as in the sonata-allegro form and much music of the 19th and 20th centuries) or in some other

direction, including no direction at all. The "Emerson" movement of Ives's *Concord Sonata* (as Cowell pointed out) seems to begin with everything at once, in a deliberately not-so-clear profusion, followed by a progressive clarification of this initial material, in which one after another of a set of four or five basic thematic "ideas" is singled out (extricated from the more complex fabric) and subjected to transformations of various kinds. The process seems to involve a kind of extractive variation, in contrast to the expansive variation of, say, Beethoven, Brahms, or Bartók.

At this highest of the several hierarchical levels of organization and perception, in place of medium or method, certain esthetic concerns seem to have the most influence on musical form. This is especially true of one aspect or manifestation of esthetic concerns, the *experiential model,* by which is meant conscious and unconscious assumptions about the function of a piece of music and about the nature of the musical experience itself. The model, of course, also affects musical form at other lower levels, but it is at the large-form level that the idea of a model underlying musical forms becomes most useful. In pre-20th-century music the model invariably has to do with song and dance forms (the "colloquial" language of folk music). In addition there is a large body of music whose overall form suggests, explicitly or implicitly, a rhetorical model, often superimposed upon or incorporating the basic elements of the song/dance model.

The song/dance model is manifested at the large-form level primarily in the orderly recurrence of sections (supported, of course, at the lower levels by all of the basic conventions of pre-20th-century music mentioned earlier). With a few notable exceptions (e.g., some of Ives's pieces and the later works of Webern), there has been a tendency to avoid the repetition or recurrence of whole sections in new music since 1900, even when there is a clear-cut sectional structure. The song/dance model, therefore, has not survived very well the changes that have occurred in 20th-century music; it has largely disappeared from concert music, remaining primarily only in popular genres and functional music.

The same cannot be said of the rhetorical model, however. It is most clearly expressed in traditional sonata-allegro form, with its statement, development, and recapitulation, and its excursion away from and back to a tonic. Again this large-form model is supported at lower levels by variation processes and by tonal conventions. (At this point it can be seen that the first of the two types of developmental structure described earlier—involving a movement from simple to complex—should be called a *rhetorical developmental structure;* other developmental structures would then be called *nonrhetorical developmental.*)

In late 19th-century program music and in impressionism certain new models began to be used (e.g., natural processes or events, life situations, place characteristics, and the like). But these often tended to be completely conscious and explicit and to be superimposed upon or assimilated within the conventions of the traditional song/dance and rhetorical models. New experiential models in 20th-century music include the following: 1) subconscious, irrational thought-processes, as in Viennese expressionism. While still related to the older rhetorical model in its implication that some kind of idea (or "thought process") is being communicated, the actual form is radically changed by the shift from rational to irrational, from the clear, orderly exposition and development of the musical ideas to a more mysterious, often apparently chaotic series of fragments. (It is significant that this development in music coincided historically with Freud's work in psychology, including the psychoanalytic technique of free association, and James Joyce's stream-of-consciousness prose.) Among the effects this model had on form were the heteromorphic (athematic) sequence-structure mentioned earlier and the development of what might be called the *short-form,* involving extreme condensation and often, though not always, extreme complexity in comparison to earlier music. 2) Memory-processes (as in many pieces by Ives). Although similar in many ways to 1 this model involves the "irrational" juxtaposition and superimposition of otherwise "rational" clangs and sequences, or fragments of these, and a deliberate stylistic eclecticism. Ives used many other models, of course, including the song/dance and rhetorical models, and perhaps no single piece expresses only the memory-process model, but such a model is nevertheless relevant to many of his pieces, especially the two *Orchestral Sets.* 3) Physical processes (Varèse, Cage). Since Cage's work in the 1950s, this model often involves chance methods and situations that are indeterminate in various ways and in varying degrees. Among the formal results of this model are the ergodic form (with "windowed" boundaries) mentioned earlier and a kind of "environment music" (Cage, *Variations IV*), in which some physical process is not only the model but actually becomes the source or controlling agent of the sounds themselves.

The first two of these new models usually give rise to structures that are developmental, even when they are nonrhetorical, with the exception of a few cases in which the structures are completely heteromorphic (e.g., Schoenberg's *Herzgewächse,* Op. 20, or the first of the *6 Kleine Klavierstücke,* Op. 19). The third model on the other hand most often gives rise to permutational structures, since it often involves a situation in which, in some senses at least, all the possibilities are given at the outset and what happens later on results simply from the permutation of this set of possibilities.

Of the three extra-formal factors that have been mentioned as contributing to and resulting from changes of form at various hierarchical levels (medium, method, and model), this last was actually the first to change (in late 19th-century program music and impressionism). This was followed by the changes in method, resulting from the breakdown of the tonal system around the turn of the century, and finally by the changes in the medium, beginning around 1910. The major changes in these broad, form-influencing factors have thus been, from the standpoint of hierarchical levels, from the top down. The reason for this order of events seems to be that as we move from higher to lower hierarchical levels, we move from musical realms that were at the time more consciously controlled, more subject to individual stylistic variation, and less predetermined culturally toward realms that were more highly predetermined, less subject to individual stylistic variation, and therefore less consciously controlled.

James Tenney

BIBL.: Earle Brown, "Form in New Music," *Source* 1:46–51; *Form in der Neuen Musik* (vol. 10 of *Darmstädter Beiträge zur Neuen Musik*); Henri Pousseur, "The Question of Order in New Music," *Perspectives* 5/1:93–111; James Tenney, *Meta (+) Hodos* (New Orleans 1964).

SEE ALSO Dance, Indeterminacy, Melody, Popular Music, Serialism, Text Setting and Usage, Texture, Theory.

Fortner, Wolfgang (b. Leipzig, 12 Oct 1907), studied at the Leipzig Conservatory (composition with Hermann Grabner) and obtained a teacher's diploma in 1931. He has taught composition and theory at the Church Music Institute in Heidelberg (1931–54), at the Nordwestdeutsche Musikakademie in Detmold (1954–57), and at the Staatliche Musikhochschule in Freiburg im Breisgau (since 1957). He founded the Heidelberg

Chamber Orchestra in 1935, and, after 1945, directed the Musica Viva concerts in that city. He directed similar series in Freiburg and at the Bavarian Radio in Munich. Since 1946 he has also lectured at the summer courses in Darmstadt.

Fortner's output in the 1930s and early 40s was conditioned by two trends of the time, the revival of interest in church music in Germany and the neoclassic (or more properly neobaroque) movement. In works from this period, many of which were for church use, there are echoes of Hindemith's precise but tonally free counterpoint and of Stravinsky's rhythmic drive. Beginning in the mid-40s the 12-tone method began to affect Fortner's style, as in the 12-tone passacaglia theme from *Chamber Music* for piano (1944). His *Symphony* (1947), with its new instrumental combinations, was the real turning point, however. Not wishing to be confined to any compositional systems, Fortner began using free adaptations of the 12-tone method involving, for instance, the interpolation of many segments of a row transposed to different pitch levels. His style since then has encompassed the motoric rhythms of the *Movements* for piano and orchestra (1953), the hollow sonorities and intensely emotional text of *The Creation* (1954), and a continuing interest in mirror forms and other kinds of symmetry.

PRINCIPAL COMPOSITIONS (published by Schott unless otherwise noted): *Fragment Maria*, cantata for soprano, 8 solo instruments (1929); *String Quartet No. 1* (1929); *Grenzen der Menschheit* for baritone, chorus, orchestra; poem by Goethe (1930); *Toccata and Fugue* for organ (1930); *3 geistliche Gesänge* for chorus (1932); *Concerto for organ*, string orchestra (1933); *Eine deutsche Liedmesse* for chorus (1934); *Preamble and Fugue* for organ (1935); *Concerto for String Orchestra* (1935); *String Quartet No. 2* (1938); *Piano Concerto* (1942); *Violin Concerto* (1946); *Symphony* (1947); *String Quartet No. 3* (1948); *Fantasy on B-A-C-H* for 2 pianos, 9 solo instruments, orchestra (1950); *The White Rose*, ballet (1950); *Mitte des Lebens*, cantata for soprano, flute, clarinet, horn, violin, harp (1951); *Isaaks Opferung*, oratorio-scene for alto, tenor, bass, 40 solo instruments (1952); *Movements* for piano, orchestra (1953); *The Creation*, cantata for medium voice, orchestra (1954); *Corinne*, opera buffa (1958, unpub.); *Chant de Naissance* for soprano, chorus, violin, orchestra (1958); *Bluthochzeit*, opera; text after García-Lorca (1957); *In seinem Garten liebt Don Perlimplin Belisa*, opera; text after García-Lorca (1962); *Die Pfingstgeschichte nach Lukas* for tenor, chorus, 11 instruments, organ (1963); *Triplu* for orchestra, piano obbligato (1966).

PRINCIPAL WRITINGS: Fortner has written many essays on the theory and esthetics of new music for *Melos*.

BIBL.: Ulrich Dibelius, *Moderne Musik 1945–1965* (Munich 1966): 34–42; Hans H. Stuckenschmidt, *Oper in dieser Zeit* (Verber 1964): 97–102; Karl H. Woerner, *Neue Musik in der Entscheidung* (Mainz 1956): 101–04; Winfried Zillig, *Variationen über neue Musik* (Munich 1959): 257–59.

Siegfried Günter
(trans. from German by Jeanne Wolf)
SEE ALSO Austria and Germany, Opera.

Foss, Lukas (b. Berlin, 15 August 1922), graduated from the Curtis Institute in Philadelphia in 1940 (composition with Scalero, piano with Vengerova, conducting with Reiner). He was subsequently a student of Koussevitzky and Hindemith and later (1944–50) pianist for the Boston Symphony. In 1953 he joined the faculty of the Univ. of Calif. at Los Angeles, where he organized the experimental Improvisation Chamber Ensemble (1957). During 1963–70 he was conductor of the Buffalo Symphony and codirector of the Buffalo Center of the Creative and Performing Arts.

His more than 40 published works include 3 operas, 16 orchestral works (symphonies, concertos, ballets, etc.), 6 works for chorus and orchestra, and music for smaller instrumental groups, solo piano, and chorus. Stylistically they divide into two idioms: traditional (1940–59) and experimental. The most notable features of the earlier style are their technical facility and spontaneous lyricism. The melodies typically are additively constructed motive by motive in a classical manner, producing a context of balance and homogeneity against which asymmetrical phrases, sudden contrasts, and unexpected juxtapositions stand out. The rhythm has a consistent pulse that is, however, frequently subject to shifting accents and changing meters. There is a predilection for complex contrapuntal development and cyclical forms. The harmonic style shows the influences of Hindemith, Copland, and Stravinsky, all assimilated into a markedly individual style that is particularly evident in the vocal music (*The Prairie*, 1942; *Song of Songs*, 1946; *Griffelkin*, 1955).

After five years of experiments in chamber improvisation, Foss emerged in the 1960s (*Time Cycle*, 1960) as a major influence in the new surge of American experimental music, providing a focus for the merging tendencies of indeterminacy, intuition, and technical methodology. *Echoi* (1961–63), one of the most significant works of contemporary American chamber music, contains in germinal form many of the ideas and techniques that were extended and developed in subsequent works. It introduces a great degree of rhythmic complexity and flexibility, blurring the line between coordinated and noncoordinated rhythm, audible and inaudible, as music emerges and submerges from and into inaudibility (*Echoi IV; Baroque Variations*, 1967). In *Echoi* Foss also began the move toward a gradually increasing use of indeterminacy, which he developed in later works into a method by which performers can extract from a score many possible but precalculated combinations of events. In both *Elytres* (1964) and *Fragments of Archilochos* (1965) the performance schemes are outlined in accompanying graphs. The works are divided into a series of phrases (events) and the orchestra into separate groups of instrumental "forces." The scores are totally notated, and each different performance is obtained from the various deletions and/or combinations of phrases suggested by the guide. Depending on how the instrumental forces are assigned and at what point the conductor chooses to begin and end the work, any one of hundreds of performance possibilities may result. In another vein the *Cello Concert* is so constructed as to offer the soloist at one point a choice of three different orchestral accompaniments. The two that are not chosen then combine to form the accompaniment to the next movement. Thus while the solo part remains the same, it is altered in meaning and quality by its contextual setting.

Composition by deletion became a favored technique of Foss in the 1960s, first appearing in the precompositional phase of *Echoi,* in which serial methods served to obtain a scaffolding of raw materials from which the composer then selected and composed in a free and willful manner. Subsequently deletion was used on the compositional level in *Elytres* and *Fragments*, as described above; in the *Baroque Variations* the idea was carried into a new realm, operating, as it were, on a postcompositional basis to form a composition fashioned completely from preexisting works, the entire conception deriving from the manner in which selection and deletion occurred.

The majority of works of 1960–68 concentrate on smaller instrumental groups, often featuring electronically suggested mannerisms, not only in the use of prerecorded tape and amplification but more interestingly through the live simulation on instruments of electronic effects, such as speed distortion (*Baroque Variations*) mechanical replay (*Echoi IV*), and

tape superimposition (*Cello Concert,* 1966; *Baroque Variations*). In *Echoi* and works thereafter the latter idea of musical superimpositions is extended so that the various techniques frequently begin to approximate techniques used in other arts. Gestures, words, and notes achieve an equality and are used interchangeably (*Paradigm*, 1968). A musical situation itself becomes a drama of instruments acting and reacting to one another as adversaries in a play. A disruptive musical idea superimposes itself on another, not in the contrapuntal sense of blending with it but in the contrary sense of clashing with it, forcing the other into a struggle to maintain an independent identity. The later works contain many examples of this type of confrontation: the annihilation of the piano by the timpani in *Echoi III*; the cello grappling with a prerecorded "rival" cello in the *Cello Concert*; the wall of sound through which another music tries to emerge (*Non-Improvisation,* 1967). Superimposition is also used in another way, where the idea is of combining but not uniting several different "musics" in a coexistence as it were, each drawing significance from proximity to the other, from the intentionally nonperfect union that contains, however, potentially perfect points of contact.

The recent music of Foss is conspicuous in its use of borrowed material and in its use of music as metaphor—of the past and as commentary on the present, a music about music (a children's tune in *Echoi*; a Bach *Sarabande* in the *Cello Concert*; Bach, Handel, and Scarlatti in the *Baroque Variations*; tonality within atonality, tonality as symbol). The past here is not repeated, but neither is it destroyed; it is as though from a new vantage point everything has again become possible.

PRINCIPAL COMPOSITIONS: *4 2-Voiced Inventions* for piano (1937, Schirmer-G); *The Prairie*, cantata for chorus, soloists, orchestra (1942, Schirmer-G); *Song of Songs*, cantata for soprano, orchestra (1946, Fischer); *The Jumping Frog of Calaveras County* for 7 characters, chamber orchestra, optional chorus (1949, Fischer and Lienau); *A Parable of Death* for narrator, tenor, chorus, orchestra (1952, Fischer); *Griffelkin*, 3-act opera (1955, Fischer); *Psalms* for chorus with orchestra or 2 pianos (1956, Fischer); *Time Cycle*, 4 songs for soprano with orchestra or clarinet, cello, percussion, piano/celesta (1960, Fischer); *Echoi* for clarinet, cello, percussion, piano (1961–63, Fischer and Schott); *Elytres* for flute, violins, piano, harp, percussion (1964, Fischer and Schott); *Fragments of Archilochos* for countertenor, speakers, choruses, mandolin, guitar, percussion (1965); *Cello Concert* for cello, orchestra, tape (1966, Fischer); *Baroque Variations* for orchestra (1967, Fischer and Schott); *Paradigm* for percussion, guitar, and 3 other instruments chosen from a given list (1968). List to 1960: *Composers of the Americas* 7:19–23.

BIBL.: Eric Salzman, "The Many Lives of L. F.," *Saturday Review* (25 Feb 1967):73–76.

Lita Dubman

SEE ALSO Performance.

Frame Notation, see Notation

France. Until World War I the principal outlets for new compositions were the symphonic associations in Paris (Société des Concerts du Conservatoire, Concerts Colonne, Lamoureux, or Pasdeloup), the Ballet Russe, the lyric theaters in Paris and in the provinces, and the presentations of the Théâtre des Arts, which were under the patronage of Jacques Rouché. Chamber music was presented by two societies: La Société National, which had been founded by César Franck and was oriented toward students of the Schola Cantorum; and La Société de Musique Independante, to which belonged Ravel, Florent Schmitt, and students of Gabriel Fauré's classes at the Paris Conservatory. Stage works were in a fortunate position because pieces having any success at the Paris Opéra or Opéra-Comique were assured productions in the prospering provincial theaters. Most of the important French composers of the time were products of Fauré's composition courses at the Paris Conservatory. This institution had a strong rival in the Schola Cantorum, founded in 1896 and run by Vincent d'Indy. In contrast with teaching methods at the Conservatory, which emphasized harmony above all other disciplines, d'Indy followed an historical approach; his pupils began with counterpoint and arrived at harmony only after long studies in linear writing. D'Indy had a dogmatic spirit, and few of his pupils gained the prominence of Fauré's.

During 1919–29 French musical life flourished in an extraordinary manner. The number of composers and virtuosos in Paris was quite large, and one could count on at least five or six concerts a day in the various theaters and concert halls. Publishers welcomed new music. Jacques Rouché, who had become head of the Paris Opéra, was quick to find a place for the works of new composers, as was the Opéra-Comique. A new generation of young musicians appeared, rallying around the writer-esthete Jean Cocteau and around Erik Satie, who paradoxically lived his entire musical career as an outsider. These young musicians engendered extreme curiosity not only from an immense public but also from the sophisticated and fashionable Parisian society that frequented several notable salons, including that of the composer and patron the Princesse de Polignac. A private organization, the Walter Straram Orchestra, which consisted of the best instrumentalists in Paris, gave evening concerts attended by a public that was even more sophisticated than the audiences attracted by the symphonic associations, which played on Sunday afternoons. Straram presented works by all the young composers of that time. During this period there was also a brilliant night life in the various cabarets, where all the artists of Paris, and from everywhere else, gathered; the most famous cabaret was Le Boeuf sur le Toit. Furthermore there were weekly meetings of the *Revue musicale,* a journal founded in 1919 and directed by the musicologist Henri Prunières. These were informal gatherings at which music was occasionally played. (At one I remember hearing Alfred Cortot and a celebrated violinist sightread a piano-violin adaptation of a new piece by Milhaud, *Le Boeuf sur le toit.*) It would have been unthinkable for a virtuoso or visiting composer not to attend these meetings.

All of this changed rather suddenly with the economic collapse of 1929. The publishing houses became much more cautious. Audiences for the Sunday concerts thinned out. The power of the symphonic associations became concentrated in the hands of committees of instrumentalists, who kept a wide eye on the receipts and who balked at the authority (and wider vision) of conductors when it came to setting up programs. The result was a lowering in the quality of the new works selected and a growing (and justifiable) suspicion on the part of audiences toward all new or unfamiliar music. After the Concerts Straram disappeared in 1933 with the death of their founder, there was a kind of respite in the fight over who would play new works. The Orchestre Symphonique de Paris assumed priority. It was founded in 1929 by Ernest Ansermet and Louis Fourestier and later conducted by Pierre Monteux. As an example of Monteux's programs, I recall one in March 1934 that included premieres of a Milhaud work, of a Roussel, of Marcel Delannoy's *Symphony,* and of my own *Poème.* Charles Munch founded a second defender of contemporary music in 1935, the Orchestre Philharmonique. Furthermore in 1935 the French radio, under the guiding hand of Emmanuel Bondeville, engaged several large symphonic groups: four from Paris and others from Lille, Strasbourg, Lyon, Nice, Marseilles, Toulouse, Bordeaux, and Rennes. The Paris Opéra and Opéra-Comique continued to put on new works, but after 1936, when a wave of general strikes occurred that lead to social reforms, the expenses incurred by these theaters became so great that state intervention was necessary in order to save them. The two houses were united in 1938 under the direction of Rouché; although the subsidies were generous, this arrangement brought on formidable control by the Minister of Finances.

In order to give people a chance to hear contemporary music written for chamber ensembles, the most prominent French and foreign composers in Paris (from Milhaud and Honegger to Prokofiev and Martinů) founded the Triton association. Until his death, the composer P. O. Ferroud (1900–36) took the initiative in this group; thereafter I took charge with the aid of another composer, Jean Rivier (b. 1896). We offered all kinds of contemporary music from Ravel, Roussel, and Stravinsky to Webern. I was also put in charge of the music section of the 1937 Paris Exposition, for which scores were commissioned from Milhaud, Honegger, Ibert, Delannoy, Messiaen, Koechlin, and others to accompany gigantic "festivals of light" presented in the evenings on the Seine to audiences of some 200,000. For the Exposition the Comédie des Champs-Élysées was turned into an experimental lyric theater for the presentation of more intimate events. *Vénitienne* by Rivier, *Philippine* by Delannoy, *Les Invités* by Harsanyi, and *Le Poule noire* by Rosenthal were among the works presented. The project attracted such directors as Louis Jouvet, Gaston Baty, and Marcel Herrand and might have outlasted the Exposition had not World War II interrupted all such activities.

During the occupation of France, Paris maintained a brilliant musical life, but it was German, not French. After the liberation of Paris in 1944, musical activities began to revolve around the Radiodiffusion Française, of which I was music director from 1944 until 1965. The radio had a number of important organizations at its disposal: four orchestras in Paris, to which was added an ensemble for avant-garde music in 1962, the Musica Nova group (now called Ars Nova) under the direction of composer Marius Constant (b. 1925); six orchestras in the provinces; a chorus of 120; and a children's chorus. The old symphonic associations survived but with increasing financial problems; they concen-

trated almost exclusively on the traditional repertory. The Réunion des Théâtres Lyriques (the combined Paris Opéra and Opéra-Comique) has had seven directors since Rouché left about 1945. The administrative apparatus established in 1938 and the control exercised by the Minister of Finances caused this enterprise to fall into a state of semiparalysis with programing limited to a few prestige pieces and a few premieres of ballets and operas (Milhaud's *Bolivar*, Tomasi's *L'Atlantide*, Barraud's *Numance*, Poulenc's *Dialogue des Carmélites*, and Honegger's *Jeanne d'Arc au Bûcher*).This situation led to a grave crisis in 1970, when the Opéra was closed. It reopened the following season with new regulations and new work contracts; Rolf Liebermann was scheduled to become manager in 1973 with Georg Solti as music director. The radio was the only organization to make a major policy of the performance of contemporary music. Although the 12-tone composers in France, whose central figure was Pierre Boulez, found an outlet in the Musica Nova group at the radio, they began to polarize the interests of Parisian society in a manner not known since the demise of the salons earlier in the century. This polarization had begun several years before with the establishment of the Domaine Musical, a concert-giving organization under the sponsorship of the actor-director Jean-Louis Barrault. For many years it was led by Boulez; now Gilbert Amy (b. 1936) is director. The huge success of the Domaine Musical in the mid-1960s encouraged the formation of other avant-garde groups, which soon rivaled each other in ardor and enthusiasm.

In the late 1960s the radio began to decline as a central force in French music, and another official initiative came on the scene. It is the post of Director of Music within the Ministry of Cultural Affairs, established in 1966. The office is directed by the composer Marcel Landowski (b. 1915). In 1967 it founded the Orchestre de Paris, which inherited some musicians from the defunct Société des Concerts. The office intends to decentralize musical life by placing lyric theaters and large orchestras in other cities (Lyons, in 1969, was the first to get an orchestra). Music schools and conservatories are also being established outside Paris. At present the Paris Conservatory is the only college-level music school in France, and preparatory training can be obtained only at a few private schools (the Schola Cantorum, the École Normale de Musique, two or three conservatories such as the one at Versailles, and others) or from private teachers, including, of course, the most famous, Nadia Boulanger. Although teaching on the professional level is improving, a serious problem remains in regard to music education among the general public, which is neglected both at the primary and secondary levels. The Jeunesses Musicales de France has tried to fill in this gap; it organizes concerts throughout the country and publishes a paper read by more than 100,000 people. However, only governmental efforts will be able to accomplish what is necessary.

The decentralization of musical life since World War II has manifested itself in the establishment of several music festivals in the provinces. The state and particularly the French radio have subsidized these, the latter lending its orchestras. Some festivals, such as the one at Aix-en-Provence, are monopolized by traditional music, but a large place has been made for contemporary works at the festivals of Strasbourg, Besançon, and Bordeaux. Music of the extreme avant-garde fills the entire program of the Royan Festival (founded 1963). None of the contemporary-music groups, including the festivals, discriminates either for or against French composers, although permanent conducting positions are almost always held only by Frenchmen.

Composers who are either French or who are living in France can always have their works performed somewhere in the country. With two or three exceptions, however, none can earn his living from his music alone, particularly since the record industry seems loathe to record contemporary music in any great quantity. Composers earn their living by teaching, working in administrative positions, composing for films, conducting, writing criticism, and similar occupations. Some commissions come from the state, the radio, or from abroad, and some musicians who have specialized in the ballet can earn a fairly sizeable income thanks to several small, itinerant ballet companies, such as those of Boris Kochno, Jean Babilée, or Roland Petit, which prospered after 1945 but seem to be declining now.

Most of the important composers during the pre-World War I period studied with Fauré at the Paris Conservatory. Their music was brilliant, colorful, filled with orchestral virtuosity in the tradition of Berlioz or Chabrier. These composers were subtle harmonists who were less interested in scholarly contrapuntal techniques than in felicitous combinations of sound. Chords were considered for their own value and for the pleasure they could procure for the ear. Each

instant of musical duration thus took on an absolute value independent of the structural continuity into which it was integrated. Even so there still existed a feeling for the beauty of an overall, linear design. Such characteristics can be found in the music of Paul Dukas (1865–1935), Maurice *Ravel (1875–1937), and Florent Schmitt (1870–1958) and in other gifted musicians such as Charles *Koechlin (1867–1951), Louis Aubert (1877–1967), Roger Ducasse (1873–1954), among others. Albert *Roussel (1869–1937), who was to become one of the most important of all these, did not begin composing until he was thirty and had not yet written his major works. Towering above all these figures was Claude *Debussy (1862–1918). Although older than any of them, he carried music further than they and brought about a disintegration of the tonal system and a dissolution of sounds and timbres that prefigured the music of Webern and, later on, Boulez.

A new generation made a rather noisy entrance after 1919. The greatest amount of attention was accorded Les Six, four of whose members went on to hold important places in the musical world: Darius *Milhaud (b. 1892), Arthur *Honegger (1892–1955), Francis *Poulenc (1899–1963), and Georges Auric (b. 1899). Another group formed somewhat later called itself L'École d'Arcueil, after the suburb where its spiritual leader, Erik *Satie (1866–1925), lived; its outstanding members were Roger Desormière (1898–1962), better known as a conductor, and Henri *Sauguet (b. 1901). The Triton group mentioned earlier came on the scene in 1932; its members included Milhaud, Honegger, Poulenc, Bohuslav *Martinů (1890–1959), Prokofiev, Ibert, Jean *Rivier (b. 1896), P. O. Ferroud (1900–36), Marcel *Delannoy (1898–1962), Claude Delvincourt (1888–1954), Henri *Tomasi (1901–71), Jean Françaix (b. 1912), Conrad *Beck (b. 1901), and Manuel *Rosenthal (b. 1904), and myself (b. 1900). In 1935 four composers already known in musical circles formed "La Jeune France": André *Jolivet (b. 1905), Olivier *Messiaen (b. 1908), Daniel *Lesur (b. 1908), and Yves Baudrier (b. 1906). This group possessed the financial means, at least at first, to present its members in several symphonic concerts. Georges *Migot (b. 1891) and Edgard *Varèse (1885–1966) both had strong ties with the group, the latter having an enormous influence on Jolivet.

The French temperament being individualistic, one should not think of these groups as "schools." Actually they merely represented coalitions of interest and friendship. If there is a common element in the work of these composers vis-à-vis the older generations, it would be the abandonment of an impressionistic esthetic and the espousal of art for art's sake, such as one finds in Ravel (*La Valse,* for instance). There is also a great concern for clarity and for communicating to the listener the intimate feelings of the composer, even if the latter inclination was carried, as with Jolivet, to the formation of a neoprimitive, incantatory style. Each of these musicians was aware of the crisis in the traditional tonal system. Some sought a solution through the use of chromaticism, occasionally pushed to the extreme, or through polytonality (especially Milhaud). They were all aware of experimentation with quarter-tones and 12-tone procedures, but they believed these to be leading to an impasse, and they avoided them in their own works. Another characteristic of the interwar period was a taste for large-scale musical frescoes (Milhaud, *Les Choéphores*; Honegger, *Le Roi David, Judith*; among others). A few great lyrical works, whose esthetic was equally grand, were put on at the Paris Opéra: *Salamine* by Maurice Emmanuel (1862–1938), *Oedipe* by George Enescu (1881–1955), *Maximilien* by Milhaud, *La Chartreuse de Parme* by Sauguet, and others. Finally it was during this period that Roussel proved himself to be one of the greatest composing talents of his generation. Unlike most of his contemporaries, he developed a harmonic style that was closely associated with contrapuntal techniques (he was, in fact, a product of the Schola Cantorum and not of the Paris Conservatory).

After the war the generation that had manifested its talents in the Triton concerts continued to produce works at a rapid rate. Several younger composers joined their ranks, including Maurice *Ohana (b. 1915), Serge *Nigg (b. 1924), Jean-Louis *Martinet (b. 1912), Henri *Dutilleux (b. 1916), and Marius *Constant (b. 1926). Messiaen, who had developed a system of rhythm and harmony based on Indian musical practice, began to have a wide influence in the postwar years. He is one of the few composers who has successfully integrated concepts from Western and Asian music. He attracted a new generation of composers to his classes at the Paris Conservatory, among whom were Stockhausen and Boulez, but many of these soon rallied around another (private) teacher, René *Leibowitz (1913–72). Leibowitz championed 12-tone techniques, and under his guidance and the leadership of Pierre *Boulez (b. 1925) serialism

began to spread. With Anton Webern as their model, Boulez and his adherents arrived at a pointillistic manner of expression, of which Boulez's *Le Marteau sans maître* provided an example that has been imitated the world over. In the late 1960s serialism began to decline as an exclusive approach to composition, and many once serial composers were turning to aleatory procedures. The four *L'Archipels* (1967–70) by André *Boucourechliev (b. Bulgaria, 1925) are perhaps the most convincing aleatory works to be produced in France in recent years. Other composers who are more or less committed to this direction include Jean-Claude *Eloy (b. 1938), Betsy *Jolas (b. 1926), Jean-Pierre *Guézec (1934–71), and Paul *Méfano (b. 1937). Young audiences have been attracted to works of Iannis *Xenakis (b. Rumania, 1922), who has lived in France since 1948.

France has also been a principal center for work in the field of electronic music. Again it was the French radio that fostered developments, in this case by providing facilities, beginning in 1948, for the musique-concrète works of Pierre *Schaeffer (b. 1910) and others. Among the most recent trends, the John Cage "school" has made some inroads, but it remains to be seen whether Frenchmen, for whom dada and surrealism are old hat, will find any new and lasting values in this type of music.

Henry Barraud
(trans. from French by Royal S. Brown)

SEE ALSO Dance; Electronic Music: History and Development; Opera.

Franco, Johan (b. Zaandam, Netherlands, 12 July 1908), studied liberal arts at the First College of The Hague (1923–28) and music privately with Willem Pijper (1928–33). He emigrated to the U.S. in 1934 and became a citizen in 1942. He is a free-lance composer.

PRINCIPAL COMPOSITIONS (published by CFE): *String Quartets Nos. 1–6* (1931, 1940, 1949, 1950, 1953, 1960); *7 Epigrams* for wind quintet (1932); *Symphonies Nos. 1–5* (1933, 1939, 1940, 1950, 1958); *Concerto lirico No. 1* for violin, chamber orchestra (1937); *6 Partitas* for piano (1940–52); *Sonata* for solo violin (1944); *Theme and Variations* for piano (1944); *2 Sonatas* for solo cello (1950, 1951); *As the Prophets Foretold*, cantata for 4 vocal soloists, brass, carillon (1956); *3 Prayers* for guitar (1959, Berben); *Songs of the Spirit* for high voice, wind quintet or piano (1959); *Redemption Triptych* for piano (1960); *Supplication, Revelation, Triumph* for orchestra (1961–67); *Concerto lirico No. 2* for cello, orchestra (1962); *Sonata* for solo tenor saxophone (1964); *12 Words* for low voice, piano (1965); *Concerto lirico No. 3* for piano, chamber orchestra (1967); *Sayings of the Word* for medium voice, piano (1968); *Concerto lirico No. 4* for percussion, chamber orchestra (1970); *American Folksong Suite* for guitar (1970, Berben); *4 Pieces* for guitar (1970, Berben). Franco has also written a large number of pieces for carillon.

BIBL.: William B. Hoskins, "J. F.: The Music and the Man," *ACA Bulletin* 8/3.

Freed, Isadore (b. Brest-Litovsk, Russia, 26 March 1900; d. Rockville Center, near New York, 10 Nov 1960), emigrated to the U.S. as a child and studied 1914–18 at the Univ. of Pa. and the Philadelphia Conservatory. He studied piano with Adele Margulies in New York (1918–20), George Boyle in Philadelphia (1920–23), Joseph Weiss in Berlin (1924), and Josef Hofmann in Philadelphia (1924). He studied composition with Ernest Bloch in New York (1918–21) and with Vincent d'Indy at the Schola Cantorum in Paris (1929–30). He has taught at the Curtis Institute (1924–25), Temple Univ. (1937–47), and the Hartt College of Music (from 1944). During 1930–33 he conducted the Concerts Spirituels in Paris and during 1934–36, the Philadelphia Chamber Orchestra, which he founded.

PRINCIPAL COMPOSITIONS: *String Quartets Nos. 1–3* (1925, 1930, 1936); *Vibrations*, ballet in 7 scenes (1927); *Homo sum*, 1-act opera for 4 voices, chamber orchestra (1930, Templeton); *Jeux de timbres*, symphonic suite (1931, Eschig); *Triptyque*, suite for strings (1932, Eschig); *Sacred Service for the Sabbath* for chorus, organ (1937, Bloch); *Viola Rhapsody* for viola, orchestra (1939, Fischer); *Violin Concerto* (1939, Templeton); *Horizons* for orchestra (1941); *Postscripts* for women's chorus, piano (1942, Fischer); *Triptych* for violin, viola, cello, piano (1943, Schirmer-G); *The Princess and the Vagabond*, opera (1948, Templeton); *Woodwind Quintet* (1949); *Symphony No. 2* for brasses (1951, Templeton); *Cello Concerto* (1952, Templeton); *Sonatina* for oboe, piano (1954).

PRINCIPAL WRITINGS: *Harmonizing the Jewish Modes* (New York 1958). Freed also edited a volume of biographies, *Contemporary Piano Music* (Bryn Mawr, Penna., c.1959).

SEE ALSO Liturgical Music: Jewish.

Freedman, Harry (b. Lodz, Poland, 5 April 1922), attended the Royal Conservatory of Music in Toronto (1945–50, composition with John Weinzweig, oboe with P. W. Bauman). He also studied composition with Aaron Copland and Olivier Messiaen at Tanglewood in 1949. During 1941–43 Freedman was active as a jazz clarinetist and as an arranger for jazz bands in Ottawa and Winnipeg. Since 1946

he has played the English horn in the Toronto Symphony. In 1962 Freedman helped organize the "Ten Centuries Concerts," a Toronto series devoted to unfamiliar music. He was host and commentator for a children's television show in 1961 and for the CBC's "Thursday Music" radio program during 1968–69. Since 1969 he has been a director of the Composers, Authors, and Publishers Assoc. of Canada. In addition to the works listed below, Freedman has composed many scores for television, radio, and films.

PRINCIPAL COMPOSITIONS: *5 Pieces* for string quartet (1948–49, CMC); *Suite* for piano (1949–50, CMC); *Tableau* for string orchestra (1952, Ricordi); *2 Vocalises* for soprano, clarinet, piano (1953, CMC); *Images*, musical impressions of 3 Canadian paintings, for string orchestra (1957–58; scored for full orchestra, 1959, BMIC); *Symphony No. 1* (1960, BMIC); *Wind Quintet* (1961, CMC); *Tokaido* for chorus, wind quintet; Japanese poems (1964, CMC); *Fantasy-Allegro* for string orchestra (1964, CMC); *Totem and Taboo* for chorus (singing only vowel sounds), piano (1965); *Rose Latulippe*, ballet; choreography by Brian Macdonald (1966, CMC); *A Little Symphony* (1966, Leeds); *Anerca* for soprano, piano; Eskimo poems (1966, CMC); *Tangents* for orchestra (1967, Leeds); *Poems of Young People* for alto, piano; texts by Toronto school children (1968); *Toccata* for soprano, flute (1968); *5/13*, ballet for chamber orchestra, tape; choreography by Macdonald (1969). List to 1962: *Composers of the Americas* 8:73–74.

BIBL.: John Beckwith, "Composers in Toronto and Montreal," *University of Toronto Quarterly* 26:55–56; Udo Kasemets, "New Music," *Canadian Music Journal* 5:50–51.

Freitas, Frederico (Guedes) **de** (b. Lisbon, 15 Nov 1902), studied at the National Conservatory in Lisbon (1919–24, composition with A. E. da Costa Ferreira, piano with Aroldo Silva, violin with Alexandre Bettencourt, musicology with L. Freitas-Branco). During 1930–40 he was artistic manager for His Master's Voice in Portugal. He began conducting the Emissora National Orchestra in Lisbon in 1935, and has also conducted the Lisbon Choral Society (1940–47), which he founded, and the Oporto Symphony (1949–53). He teaches various music subjects at the Liceu de Camões and the Liceu de Gil Vicente and composition at the Center for Gregorian Studies. Debussy and Schoenburg have been the most prominent influences on his music. His *Sonata* of 1923 contains the first use of polytonality by a Portuguese composer.

PRINCIPAL COMPOSITIONS: *Sonata* for violin, cello (1923); *Dança* for piano (1923, Sassetti); *Ingenui-*

dades for piano (1924, Sassetti); *Boas noites* for voice, piano; poems by João de Deus (1924); *A lenda dos bailarins*, symphonic poem (1926); *Nocturno* for cello, piano (1926); *Missa solene* for vocal soloists, chorus, orchestra (1940); *Dança da Menina Tonta*, ballet (1941); *Imagens de terra e do mar*, ballet (1943); *Piano Sonata* (1944); *Ciranda* for piano (1944, Schott); *Quarteto concertante* for 2 violins, 2 cellos, string orchestra (1945); *Violin Sonata* (1946); *String Quartet* (1946); *6 Pieces* for piano (1946, Hansen-W); *Nazaré*, ballet (1948); *Wind Quintet* (1950); *Theme and Variations* for piano (1954); *Missa "Regina mundi"* for chorus (1954); *Flute Concerto* (1955); *Igreja do mar*, radio opera (1957); *O eremita*, 1-act opera (1957); *Don João e a Mácara,* radio opera (1960); *Symphony*, "Os Jerónimos" (1962); *Organ Sonata* (1963). Freitas has also made many arrangements of traditional Portuguese music.

PRINCIPAL WRITINGS: "Canções tradicionais Portuguesas do cielo da Quaresma e Páscoa" [Traditional Portuguese Songs for the Season of Lent and Easter], *Panorama* (March 1967): 21ff.; "Viana da Mota, pianista cosmopolita e compositor Lusitano" [Viana da Mota, Cosmopolitan Pianist and Portuguese Composer], *Panorama* (Dec 1968): 5ff.

Frequency, the number of sound waves per second of a vibrating body, or, in the context of electronic music (where the term is more frequently encountered in contemporary music), the vibrations per second of an electric signal. Frequency usually determines pitch.

Fribec, Krešimir (b. Daruvar, Croatia, Yugoslavia, 24 May 1908), studied composition with Zlatko Grgošević in Zagreb (1936–37). He was on the musical staff of Radio Zagreb during 1943–64. Fribec is one of the few exponents of musical expressionism in Croatia. In his use of 12-tone techniques, he has stressed harmonic rather than polyphonic elements, an approach that he compares to such French composers as Jolivet and Boulez.

PRINCIPAL COMPOSITIONS: *Vibracije* [Vibrations], ballet (1955, EM); *Krvava svadba* [Blood Wedding], opera after García-Lorca (1958); *Ritmi drammatici* for instrumental ensemble (1960, UKH); *Assonance* for piano (1961); *String Quartets Nos. 1–6* (1962, 1964, 1966, 1967, 1968, 1969); *Galeotova pesam* [Song of Galeot], rhapsody for orchestra (1965, UKH); *Lamento* for strings (1967); *Violin Concerto* (1968); *Heliofonia* for orchestra (1969); *Grčka trilogija* [Greek Triology], ballet after Oedipus, Antigone, Prometheus (1969).

BIBL.: Krešimir Kovačević, *Hrvatski kompozitori i njihova djela* [Croation Composers and Their Works] (Zagreb 1960): 156–63.

Fricker, Peter Racine (b. London, 5 Sept 1920), started his studies at the Royal College of Music, which were interrupted by World War II, and began in 1946 to study composition with Mátyás Seiber. In 1951 he began teaching at the College and during 1953–64 succeeded Michael Tippett as music director of Morley College. Since then he has taught at the Univ. of Calif. at Santa Barbara, where he is now department chairman.

Fricker has written in all the standard genres except staged opera. During the 1950s he also composed music for seven films and six radio programs, including two radio operas, as well as the ballet *Canterbury Prologue*. The impression that his music made in England during the late 40s was of uncompromising dissonance and harsh strength. He was the first postwar British composer to assimilate the discoveries of the chief European composers of the previous half century and synthesize them into a personal style. This style includes, but is not limited by, the linear counterpoint and tenuous relationship to a key center of Bartók, the serial techniques of the 12-tone composers, and the clarity and transparency of Stravinsky. If any aspect can be said to be particularly "English," it is the overall sonority, the interest in writing idiomatically for instruments to make them sound at their best. This tendency is strikingly apparent as early as the *Wind Quartet* (1947), for example, the treatment of the flute in the "Badinerie." The *3 Scenes* for orchestra (1966), written for performance by massed orchestras from California high schools, includes a finale that concentrates attention on various instruments and sections in succession and lets each sound to best advantage. In the *Magnificat* (1968), the vocal solos seem to have been designed for the voices of the specific singers scheduled for the premiere.

The *4 Sonnets for Piano* (1955) make strict use of 12-tone technique, but Fricker's serialism is more often occasional and free. Sometimes a serial approach to rhythm occurs (*Episodes 2* for piano, 1969), another time improvisation (*Threefold Amen*, 1966). Frequently the approach is one in which small cells are manipulated by various permutations of pitches (i.e., No. 6 of *12 Studies* for piano, 1961). The opening song of the cycle *O longs desirs* for soprano and orchestra (1963) begins in the strings with a passage in which alternate vertical intervals grow larger by half-steps. This gradual expansion in interval size is reflected in the vocal line. Although to the analyst Fricker's music may seem intellectually conceived, the speed at which he composes shows that involved processes are part of his natural musical thinking. To the listener his music has strong emotional qualities, as evidenced in the *Symphony No. 4.*

PRINCIPAL COMPOSITIONS (published by Schott unless otherwise noted): *Wind Quintet*, Op. 5 (1947); *3 Sonnets* for tenor, 7 instruments, Op. 7 (1947); *String Quartet in 1 Movement*, Op. 8 (1947); *Symphony No. 1*, Op. 9 (1948–49); *Prelude, Elegy and Finale*, Op. 10 (1949); *Violin Concerto No. 1*, Op. 11 (1949–50); *Violin Sonata*, Op. 12 (1950); *Symphony No. 2*, Op. 14 (1950–51); *Viola Concerto*, Op. 18 (1951–53); *String Quartet No. 2*, Op. 20 (1952–53); *Piano Concerto*, Op. 19 (1952–54); *Violin Concerto No. 2*, "Rapsodia concertante," Op. 21 (1953–54); *Dance Scene* for orchestra, Op. 22 (1954); *Horn Sonata*, Op. 24 (1955); *The Tomb of St. Eulalia*, elegy for countertenor, viola da gamba, harpsichord, Op. 25 (1955); *Litany* for double string orchestra, Op. 26 (1955); *Choral* for organ (1956); *Cello Sonata*, Op. 28 (1956); *The Vision of Judgment*, oratorio for soprano, tenor, chorus, orchestra, Op. 29; poem by Cynewulf (1957–58); *Octet* for flute, clarinet, bassoon, horn, violin, viola, cello, double bass, Op. 30 (1957–58); *Variations* for piano, Op. 31 (1957–58); *Toccata* for piano, orchestra, Op. 33 (1958–59); *Pastorale* for organ (1959); *Serenade No. 1* for flute, clarinet, bass clarinet, viola, cello, harp, Op. 34 (1959); *Trio* for flute, oboe, piano, Op. 35 (1959); *Symphony No. 3*, Op. 36 (1960); *12 Studies* for piano, Op. 38 (1961); *Cantata* for tenor, chamber ensemble, Op. 37; text by Wm. Saroyan (1961–62); *O longs desirs*, 5 songs for soprano, orchestra, Op. 39; text by Louise Labe (1963); *Symphony No. 4*, Op. 43 (1964–66); *Ricercare* for organ, Op. 40 (1965); *4 Dialogues* for oboe, piano, Op. 41 (1965, Oxford); *Fantasy* for viola, piano, Op. 44 (1966); *3 Scenes* for orchestra, Op. 45 (1966, unpub.); *The Day and the Spirits* for soprano, harp, Op. 46; primitive texts (1966–67, unpub.); *7 Counterpoints* for orchestra, Op. 47 (1967, unpub.); *Ave maris stella* for male voices, piano, Op. 48 (1967, unpub.); *Episodes 1* for piano, Op. 51 (1967–68, unpub.); *Magnificat* for vocal soloists, chorus, orchestra, Op. 50 (1968, unpub.); *6 Pieces* for organ, Op. 53 (1968, Augsburg); *Toccata*, "Gladius Domini," for organ, Op. 55 (1968, unpub.); *Some Superior Nonsense* for tenor, flute, oboe, cello, harpsichord, Op. 56; texts by Morgenstern (1968, unpub.); *Episodes 2* for piano (1969, unpub.); *Praeludium* for organ, Op. 60 (1970, Oxford); *Paseo* for guitar, Op. 61 (1970, Faber); *The Roofs* for coloratura soprano, percussionist, Op. 62; text by W. S. Merwin (1970, unpub.).

PRINCIPAL WRITINGS: "The Vision of Judgement," *The Composer's Point of View* ed. by R. S. Hines (Norman, Okla., 1963):181ff.; an essay on his orchestral music, *The Orchestral Composer's Point of View* ed. by Hines (Norman 1970):76ff.; "F. Himself talks to Tom Sutcliffe," *Music and Musicians* (August 1970):34–36.

BIBL.: Alun Hoddinott, "P. R. F.," *Music and Musicians* (August 1970):30–34; Colin Mason, "F., P. R.," *Grove's Dictionary of Music and Musicians* (New York 1955) 3:498–500 and 10:176–77; R. Murray Schafer, *British Composers in Interview* (London 1963):137–46; Denis Stevens, "R. F.," *Music 1952* ed. by A. Robertson (London 1952); Hugh Wood, "English Contemporary Music," *European Music in the 20th Century* ed. by H. Hartog, revised ed. (London 1961):161–64.

Douglass Green

SEE ALSO Great Britain.

Friedman, Ken(neth) (Scott) (b. New London, Conn., 19 Sept 1939), studied liberal arts at Calif. Western Univ. (1965), Shimer College in Ill. (1965–66), and San Francisco State College (1966–71, composition with Richard Maxfield). He has been a member and director of the Fluxus group since 1966 and has been a consultant and, in 1971, general manager for the Something Else Press. Since 1966 he has also free-lanced as a teacher, writer, and editor (primarily for underground papers), designer, college teacher, Unitarian minister, conference leader, and media consultant. He considers "Zen and worship the root of my musical experience and training; I consider the calligraphy and visuality of a written score as beautiful as its sounds; I consider not melody but sound-formation and have as great an interest in rhythm as I do in melodic line.... In 1967 I quit reading and writing standard notation altogether and devoted myself to configurations of sound."

PRINCIPAL COMPOSITIONS: *Piece for 6 Instruments in 5 Minutes* (1965–66, published in John Cage's *Notations*); *Portfolio* (1965–66, Gnu Music Co., Berkeley); *Score 59* for any instrument (1967, Fluxus West); *2 Short Pieces* for any instrument(s), telephone (1967, ED912, Milan); *Piece for Winds* (1967); *2 Scores* for unspecified orchestra (1967–70, Gnu); *True Religion* for autoharp (1968); *S. S. B.* for piano (1970); *The Violent Pilgrim* for piano (1971).

PRINCIPAL "EVENTS, PERFORMANCES, ACTIONS": *Jesus Saves but Moses Invests* (Santa Barbara 1964); *The Truly Incredible Friedman* (San Diego 1964, 1965); *Transportation and You* (Los Angeles 1965); *Chesterfield for Peace* (Orange County 1965); *Christmas Tree Events* (Manhattan Beach 1965); *Come ze Revolution* (Pasadena 1965); *Ibn Ibrahim Ensemble* (Mt. Carroll, Ill., 1966); *The Arabic Embassy Scandal* (Redlands, Calif., 1966); *Rama Lama* (Camp de Benneville Pines 1966); *Allah Sings* (Ithaca College, N. Y., 1966); *Selling Piece* (Marblehead Unitarian Church 1966); *Vhen I Shpeak* (New London, Conn., 1966); *Nabaschwijli Events* (San Diego 1966); *Festival* (La Mesa, Calif., 1966); *Street Pieces* (San Diego 1966); *Chants* (Fluxus West, San Francisco 1967); *Fluxtapes* (Fluxus West 1967); *Keeping Together Man-*

ifestation (San Francisco State College 1967); *KTM Instant Theater* (Phoenix, San Francisco, Berkeley 1967); *Rock Placement* (San Diego 1967); *Reception* (Lindbergh Field, San Diego, 1967); *20 Gallons* (Western College for Women, Ohio, 1967); *Bird in Flight* (San Diego, New York, Boston 1967); *Fol de Nuit* (San Francisco, Boston 1967); *The 5-foot Bed* (Fluxus, New York, 1967); *Curry Nimble's Nomination* (Omaha Unitarian Church 1967); *San Jose Action Theatre* (San Jose 1968); *Setup for Captain Ohio* (San Francisco 1968); *Instant Theatre* (Camp de Benneville Pines 1968); *Platebusters* (San Francisco 1968); *Flux Mountain Concert* (Big Bear, Calif., 1968); *Fluxus Talk Show* (KFMB, San Diego, 1968); *Ubu Amos Tap Dance* (Pacific Beach, Calif., 1968); *Poolside Sunlight* (Santa Fe 1968); *Instant Theatre* with Dick Kossow (Santa Fe 1968); *The Funeral* (Santa Fe 1958); *The Last Service* (Santa Fe 1968); *Kosher-Nostra Supper* (Champaign, Urbana, Ill., 1968); *286* (San Francisco, San Diego 1968); *Aktual/Events in Motion* (San Diego 1968); *The Monkey's Night Out* (San Diego 1969); *Cruising for Burgers* (Boston 1969); *Pagings* (Boston, San Francisco 1969); *Zen Softball* (Berkeley 1970); *Fur Vostell* (San Francisco, Cologne 1970); *Krishna Bless My Openings* (Richmond, Calif., 1970); *Charles Van Damme Family* (1970).

Fritsch, Johannes G. (b. Bensheim-Auerbach, Germany, 27 July 1941), attended the Univ. of Cologne (1961–65, musicology, sociology, philosophy) and the Cologne Hochschule für Musik (1961–65, viola, composition). Since 1964 he has been violist of the Stockhausen Ensemble, and since 1965 he has been teaching theory at the Cologne Conservatory. He has been associated with the electronic music studio of the Westdeutscher Rundfunk since 1964.

PRINCIPAL COMPOSITIONS: *Duett für Bratsche* for viola, tape (1961); *Zeichen*, String Quartet No. 1 (1963); *Nachtmusik*, String Quartet No. 2, for violin, viola, cello, double bass (1963); *Madrigal triste* for oboe, tape (1963); *Filigranfalter* for high voice, 12 strings (1963); *Fabula rasa* for 4-track tape (1964); *Piano Trio No. 1* (1964); *Ikonen* for 3 pianos (1964); *Concerto da camera* for violin, 12 strings (1964); *Partita* for viola, contact microphones, tape machines, filters, potentiometers (1965–66, EM); *Modulation I* for violin, viola, cello, double bass, piano (1966); *Modulation II* for 13 instruments, electronic equipment, and the optional use of a tape of *Modulation I* (1966); *Akroasis* for orchestra (1966–68); *Concerto battuto* for percussion, 3 string trios, double bass (1967); *Modulation III*, *Modulation V*, "Musik für Räume und Plätze," on 2 or more stereo tapes (1968); *Modulation IV* on 4-track tape (1968); *Singspiel* for 3 actors, 2 musicians (1969).

SEE ALSO Austria and Germany.

Frohne, Vincent (Sauter) (b. La Porte, Ind., 26 Oct 1936), studied composition with Donald H. White at De Pauw Univ. (1954–58), Wayne Barlow and Howard Hanson at the Eastman School (1958–63), Darius Milhaud at the Aspen Summer Music Festival (1957), Leon Kirchner at the Berkshire Music Center (1959), and Boris Blacher at the Hochschule für Musik in Berlin (1960–61, 1962–63). In 1962–63 he studied information theory and studio technique with Fritz Winckel at the Berlin Studio for Electronic Music of the Technische Universität. Since 1968 he has been director of the concert series "Chamber Music of the 20th Century" in Berlin and has performed as pianist in his own works and as a conductor of chamber groups. His music since 1959 "has been serial, although not in the style of Webern . . . The 12 tones are treated unequally so that a few tones often establish tonal centers" (though functional harmony is not present). He uses developing variation as in Debussy and Bartók; orchestral sound and "the harmonic material play a much larger role in the form" than is the case with most serial composers. "Although most of the pieces are written in 4/4, a sense of meter is almost never apparent."

PRINCIPAL COMPOSITIONS (published by Bote unless otherwise noted): *Study* for clarinet, Op. 17 (1960); *Piano Sonata*, Op. 21 (1962, unpub.); *Adam's Chains*, song cycle for soprano, orchestra, Op. 22 (1963–64); *Ordine II* for orchestra, Op. 25a (1965); *Sonata* for solo cello, Op. 26 (1966, unpub.); *String Quartet No. 1*, Op. 28 (1967); *Pendulum* for flute, piano, Op. 29 (1968); *Sacred Songs of William Blake* for mezzo-soprano, speaker, chamber ensemble, Op. 30 (1969).

BIBL.: Wolfgang Becker, program notes for *Adam's Chains, Philharmonische Blätter* (Berlin) 4 (1968–69):2; Alan Kriegsman, "Intriguing Mix of Old, New," *Washington Post* (11 April 1969): B-12.

Fuleihan, Anis (b. Kyrenia, Cyprus, 2 April 1900; d. Stanford, Calif., 11 Oct 1970), came to the U.S. in 1915 and attended the Von Ende School of Music in New York (1915–16) but was mainly self-taught as a composer. He was active as a pianist beginning in 1919 and as a conductor from the mid-30s; he also taught piano privately in New York until the mid-40s. He taught piano and composition at Indiana Univ. during 1947–51 and was director of the Beirut National Conservatory (1953–60). He founded and conducted the Orchestre Classique of Tunis (1962–65) under the auspices of the U.S. State Dept. During 1967–68 he was visiting lecturer at Illinois Univ. Fuleihan's early recollections of and subsequent research into Mediterranean music were influential on his development as a composer.

PRINCIPAL COMPOSITIONS (published by Southern unless otherwise noted): *To the Young Prince* for voice, piano (1925, MCA); *My Achmed Has Gone to Give Battle* for voice, piano (1928); *Mediterranean* for orchestra (1932); *Preface to a Child's Storybook* for orchestra (1932); *Symphony No. 1* (1936); *Concerto No. 1* for piano, string orchestra (1936); *Piano Concerto No. 2* (1936); *Fiesta* for orchestra (1939); *Symphonie concertante* for string quartet, orchestra (1940); *Concerto* for 2 pianos, orchestra (1940); *Piano Sonatas Nos. 1, 2, 9* (1940, 1943, 1962); *String Quartets Nos. 1–5* (1940, 1948, 1957, 1959, 1965); *Air and Fugue on White Keys* for piano (1940); *3 Cyprus Serenades* for orchestra (1941); *Invocation* for orchestra (1941); *Epithalamium* for piano, string orchestra (1941, Schirmer-G); *Divertimento No. 2* (1942); *Etude: Melody for Winds* for wind orchestra (1943, Schirmer-G); *Etude: Staccato and Legato* for orchestra (1943, Schirmer-G); *Concerto* for violin, piano, orchestra (1943); *Rhapsody* for cello, string orchestra (1945, Boosey); *Toccata* for piano, orchestra (1959, unpub.); *Pour les cordes* for string orchestra (1961, unpub.); *Violin Sonata* (1961, unpub.); *Piano Trio* (1968, Boosey).

[prepared with the help of Arthur Cohn]

Futurism, a movement in the arts that originated in Italy and emphasized dynamic force and motion (and in music, noise), partly as a glorification of modern industrial technology. The movement was given musical direction by the musician Francesco Pratella (1880–1955) and the painter Luigi Russolo (1885–1947). Pratella conceived his music for standard instruments, as in his *Musica futurista per orchestra,* which was given in Rome in February and March 1913. Russolo thought in terms of sounds other than those of conventional instruments. He issued a monograph in Milan (*L'arte dei rumori*) just after Pratella's Rome concerts in which he advocated the use of noises in musical composition and classified noises into six groups. His treatise "implied that although sound itself was limited only by the physiology of the ear and cóntained an infinite number of graduations of tone, pattern, and quality, only a small part of that infinite field of sound was acceptable in Western culture as 'music.' Russolo wanted all sound to be possible material for music." He

also advocated a break from dance-derived (metrical) rhythm (Kirby: 33–34; see bibl.). To accomplish these ends Russolo developed a series of instruments called *intonarumori* [noise intoners]. "All were rectangular wooden boxes with funnel-shaped acoustical amplifiers, or megaphones, projecting from the front. The boxes, averaging about two-to-three feet in height, and the megaphones varied in size, but the general appearance was the same. They were 'played' by means of a protruding handle that moved in a slot in the top or side of the instrument. Inside the *intonarumori* were various motors and mechanisms" that produced clanks, hisses, buzzes, hums, and other noises. Two of Russolo's works for *intonarumori* were performed in a London concert of 1914, *The Awakening of a Great City* and *A Meeting of Motorcars and Aeroplanes.* (Russolo also developed a notation for his instruments; it retained staves as in traditional notation but elongated the noteheads into lines that move through the staves and are not restricted to the 12 discreet pitches of the equal-tempered chromatic scale.) In the 1920s he built a series of noise-making keyboard instruments, called *psofarmoni,* which in some ways anticipated the prepared piano of John Cage.

Futurism lost its vitality in the other arts by 1918. In music it was especially significant for the publicity it gave to a new concept of compositional material, i.e., sound that may have no definite pitch and is noteworthy primarily for its timbre(s) or texture. Although there is no direct line from futurism to electronic and other recent music that exploits sound textures (indeed composers such as Debussy and Ives, who also used sound textures as primary structural material, preceded futurism), the movement brought this concept further into the general consciousness.

BIBL.: Rosa Trillo Clough, *Futurism* (New York 1961); Lowell Cross, "Electronic Music, 1948–1953," *Perspectives* 7/1:32–65; Nicholas Gatty, "Futurism, A Series of Negatives," *Musical Quarterly* 2:9–12; Michael Kirby, *Futurist Performance* (New York 1971); Maurice Lemaître, "Introduction," *L'Art des bruits: Manifeste futuriste 1913* by Luigi Russolo (Paris 1954); Wilibald Nagel, "Musica futuristica," *Die Musik* (1915):3ff.; John C. G. Waterhouse, "A Futurist Mystery," *Music and Musicians* (April 1967):26–30. Several writings of the futurists are translated in Kirby and in Nicolas Slonimsky, *Music Since 1900,* 4th ed. (New York 1971).

Gaburo, Kenneth (Louis) (b. Somerville, N. J., 5 July 1926), studied composition at the Eastman School (1943, 1946–49; with Bernard Rogers), the Accadèmia di Santa Cecilia in Rome (1954–55, with Goffredo Petrassi), and the Univ. of Ill. (1955–62, with Burrill Phillips and Hubert Kessler). He has taught at Kent State Univ. in Ohio (1949–50), McNeese State College in Louisiana (1950–54), the Univ. of Ill. (1955–68), and the Univ. of Calif. at San Diego (since 1968). In 1964 he formed the New Music Choral Ensemble, formerly based at the Univ. of Ill. and currently in La Jolla, Calif. The group performs 20th-century repertory and experiments in extending the vocal medium through improvisation, electronics, the incorporation of theater elements such as physical movement, facial expression, spoken effects, and audience-performer interaction. Gaburo's music has been influenced by his involvement with electronics and his performing experience as a conductor. "The more recent 'inter-disciplinary' attitude as reflected on campuses has been a main motivation," especially linguistics, mathematics, logic, philosophy, theater, and literature.

PRINCIPAL COMPOSITIONS: *Elegy* for chamber orchestra (1954–56, Presser); *Bodies*, an opera for actors, concrete score on tape; libretto by the composer (1956–57); *Line Studies* for flute, clarinet, trombone, viola (1956–57); *Antiphony V* for piano, tape (1959–69); *Shapes and Sounds* for orchestra (1960); *Two* for mezzo-soprano, alto flute, double bass (1962, Presser); *Antiphony III (Pearl White Moments)* for 16 singers, tape (1962–63); *Exit Music I: The Wasting of Lucrecetzia* on tape (1964, recorded by Nonesuch); *Exit Music II: Fat Millie's Lament* on tape (1965, recorded by Nonesuch); *Lemon Drops* on tape (1965, recorded by MGM Heliodor); *For Harry* on tape (1965, MGM Heliodor); *Lingua I–IV*, a 6-hour theater (1965–70): I, "Poems and Other Theaters," consists of "Inside" for double bass, "The Flight of Sparrow" for actor and tape, "Dante's Joynt" for voice, tape, and projections, "Mouthpiece" for trumpet and projections, "Glass" for vocal quartet and percussion, and "Poesies" for 7 sculptured humans and tape; II, "Maledetto," for 7 virtuoso speakers; III, "In the Can," a dialectic mix in 3 rounds for 40 actors, audience, multimedia; IV, "The Flow of $((i))^2$," for assorted phenomena; *Circumcision* for 3 groups of men's voices (1966); *Antiphony IV (Poised)* for piccolo, trombone, double bass, tape, amplification equipment (1966–67).

BIBL.: John Cage, *Notations* (New York 1967); Virgil Thomson, *American Music since 1910* (New York 1971); liner notes for Nonesuch record H-71198.

SEE ALSO Instrumental and Vocal Resources, Microtones, Musicology and Composition.

Gagnebin, Henri (b. Liege, 13 March 1886), studied at the Geneva Conservatory (1906–08; composition, organ with Otto Barblan; piano with Oscar Schulz) and at the Schola Cantorum in Paris (1908–16; composition with Vincent d'Indy; organ with Abel Decaux, Louis Vierne; piano with Blanche Selva; Gregorian chant with Amédée Gastoué). He also studied privately in Lausanne (1903–05; harmony with Justin Bischoff; piano with Auguste Laufer) and in Berlin (1905–06). During 1910–16 he was organist at the (Lutheran) Church of the Redemption in Paris and during 1916–25, at Saint-Jean in Lausanne. He taught music history at Lausanne Conservatory during 1918–25 and organ and history at Neuchâtel Conservatory during 1924–25. He was director of the Geneva Conservatory during 1925–57 and dean of the piano faculty there during 1957–61. In 1938 he founded the International Performance Competition in Geneva. He has performed as an organist in concerts in Switzerland and has contributed articles on music to Swiss journals since 1918. He has transcribed and edited several volumes of medieval music. He considers himself a classicist and, as a young man, was influenced in his harmonic thinking by the French impressionists.

PRINCIPAL COMPOSITIONS: *Piano Sonata in A Minor* (1909); *Symphony No. 1 in B Minor* (1911); *Les Vierges folles*, symphonic poem (1913); *Violin Sonata in E* (1915, Rouart-Lerolle and Salabert); *Ouverture française* for orchestra (1915); *String Quartet No. 1 in F Minor* (1917, Henn); *Jour de fête*, overture for orchestra (1918); *Symphony No. 2 in F Minor* (1921); *Pastorale* for flute, clarinet, bassoon, harp (1921); *Cello Sonata in A* (1922, Sénart and Salabert); *String Quartet No. 2 in E-Flat Minor* (1924, Lemoine); *String Quartet No. 3 in F-Sharp Minor* (1927, Lemoine); *Saint François d'Assise*, oratorio for tenor, baritone, chorus, orchestra, organ; text by Paul Budry (1933, Henn); *Suite for the Instruments of the Orchestra* (1936, Leduc); *Les Vanités du monde*, oratorio for soprano, baritone, chorus, orchestra, organ; text by Jules Balliods (1938, Henn); *Abraham sacrifiant*, musique de scène for chorus; text from Théodore de Bèze (1939); *3 Tableaux symphoniques d'après F. Hodler* (1942); *Trio in D* for flute, violin, piano (1941, Curci); *Jedermann*, musique de scène for soloists, chorus, orchestra; text by Hofmannsthal (1942); *Chant pour le jour des morts et la toussaint*, oratorio for soprano, baritone, chorus, string orchestra, organ; text by Balliods (1943, Henn); *4 Toccatas* for piano (1944, 46, 58, 58; Henn); *Sonata d'église pour le jour de Pâques* for trumpet, organ (1945, Schola Cantorum); *Le Voile rose*, musique de scène for solo voice, chorus, children's chorus, harmonium; text by Mme. Bachofen (1945); *Psalm 100* for chorus, organ (1947); *Printemps*, ballet (1948); *Psalm 139* for chorus, orchestra (1948); *L'Aube*, musique de scène for solo voice, chorus, children's chorus, harmonium (1949); *Suite No. 1 on Huguenot Psalms* for orchestra (1950); *Piano Concerto* (1951, Ricordi); *Toccata in F* for organ (1955, Doblinger); *Symphony No. 3 in E* (1955); *Les Mystères de la foi*, oratorio for soloists, chorus, piano or orchestra; text by Francis Jammes (1958, Henn); *Divertimento* for winds, percussion (1959); *Fantaisie* for piano, orchestra (1960); *Quartet* for flute, violin, cello, piano (1961); *Sonata da chiesa per la Natale* for oboe, organ (1961); *Psalm 104* for soloists, chorus, orchestra (1962, Henn); *Partita on a noël* for organ (1965); *Rhapsody* for flute, harp (1966); *Suite No. 2 on Huguenot Psalms* for orchestra (1966); *Messe latine sur vieux noëls* for chorus, organ (1966, Henn); *Sans blâââgue*, suite for orchestra (1967); *Dialogue and Passacaglia* for organ (1967); *String Trio* (1968); *Cantate psalmique* for chorus, 8 brasses (1969, Cantate Domino); *Le Chant nuptial* for women's chorus, chamber orchestra (1969); *Sonata da chiesa per il Venerdì Santo* for cello, organ (1969); *Wind Octet* (1970); *3 Dances* for piano (1970); *Brass Quintet* (1970). List to 1966 published by the Swiss Music Archives (Zurich 1966).

PRINCIPAL WRITINGS: *Etude sur la Messe en si min de Bach* (Lausanne 1923); *Fritz Bach, sa vie et son œuvre* (Neuchâtel 1935); *La Restauration du psautier huguenot* (Paris 1937); articles in *La Musique en Suisse Romande de 1900 à 1950* (Zurich 1950); "La Musique dans l'histoire de Genève," *Livre d'or du bimillénaire de Genève* (Geneva 1942); *Entretien sur la musique* (Geneva 1945); "Jaques-Dalcroze compositeur," *Emile Jaques-Dalcroze* (Neuchâtel 1965):159–288; *Musique mon beau souci* (Neuchâtel 1968).

BIBL.: Samuel Baud-Bovy, "H. G.," *40 Con-temporary Swiss Composers* (Amriswil 1956):54–60; Claude Desclouds, "H. G.," *6 Compositeurs jurassieurs* (Porrentruy 1966); Kathleen Healy Harper, *Pièces d'orgue sur les psaumes huguenots* (Masters thesis, Union Theological Seminary, 1965); Peter Mieg, "H. G.," *La Musique en Suisse Romande de 1900 à 1950* (Zurich 1950).

SEE ALSO Switzerland.

Gál, Hans (b. Brunn, near Vienna, 5 August 1890), studied at the Univ. of Vienna (1908–13; composition with E. Mandyczewski, piano with Anka Landau, Richard Robort). He taught at the Univ. of Vienna (1919–29) and at the Univ. of Edinburgh (1945–65). During 1929–33 he was director of the Municipal College of Music in Mainz. He has performed as a pianist since 1910 and as a conductor since 1921 and was coeditor of the complete edition of Brahms.

PRINCIPAL COMPOSITIONS: *String Quartets Nos. 1–3*: No. 1, Op. 16 (1916, Simrock), No. 2, Op. 35 (1929, Schott), No. 3, Op. 95 (1969, Simrock); *Der Arzt der Sobeide*, opera, Op. 4 (1918, UE); *Die heilige Ente*, opera, Op. 15 (1923, UE); *Divertimento* for 8 winds, Op. 22 (1924, Leukart); *Das Lied der Nacht*, opera, Op. 23 (1926, UE); *Symphonies Nos. 1–3*: No. 1, Op. 30 (1927, Simrock), No. 2, Op. 53 (1943, Breitkopf), No. 3, Op. 62 (1952, Breitkopf); *Ballettsuite*, Op. 36 (1929, Schott); *Zauberspiegel*, suite for chamber orchestra, Op. 38 (1930, UE); *Violin Concerto*, Op. 39 (1931, Breitkopf); *Die beiden Klaas*, Op. 42 (1933, Schott); *Concertino* for piano, string orchestra, Op. 43 (1934, Simrock); *Serenade* for string orchestra, Op. 46 (1937, Novello); *De profundis*, cantata for 4 soloists, chorus, orchestra, organ, Op. 50 (1937, Breitkopf); *Concertino* for violin, string orchestra, Op. 52 (1939, Bärenreiter); *Cello Concerto*, Op. 67 (1944, Breitkopf); *Lilliburlero*, variations for orchestra, Op. 48 (1945, Novello); *Piano Concerto*, Op. 57 (1947, Breitkopf); *Concertino* for organ, string orchestra, Op. 55 (1948, Nordiska); *Mäander*, suite for orchestra, Op. 69 (1955, Novello); *Lebenskreise*, cantata for 4 soloists, chorus, orchestra, Op. 70 (1956, Bärenreiter); *24 Preludes* for piano, Op. 83 (1960, UE); *Concertino* for cello, string orchestra, Op. 87 (1965, Simrock); *Idyllikon* for small orchestra, Op. 79 (1969, Boosey); *Triptych* for orchestra (1970).

PRINCIPAL WRITINGS: *The Golden Age of Vienna* (London 1948); *Johannes Brahms* (London 1963); *Richard Wagner* (Frankfurt 1963); *The Musician's World* (London 1965); *Franz Schubert, oder Die Melodie* (Frankfurt 1970).

BIBL.: Wilhelm Waldstein, *H. G.* (Vienna 1965).

Galindo (-Dimas), **Blas** (b. San Gabriel, now Ciudad Venustiano Carranza, Jalisco, Mexico,

3 Feb 1910), attended the Conservatorio
Nacional de Música de México (1931–44,
piano with Manuel Rodríguez Vizcarra; harmony, counterpoint with José Rolón; composition with Carlos Chávez; analysis with
Candelario Huizar; music history with Ernesto
Enríquez; acoustics with Daniel Casteñeda).
He also studied with Aaron Copland at Tanglewood (1941–42). During 1947–61 Galindo was
director of the Conservatorio Nacional, where
he had been teaching various musical subjects
since 1942.

PRINCIPAL COMPOSITIONS: *Jicarita* for voice,
orchestra (1939); *Sones de Mariachi* for orchestra
(1941, EMM); *Madre mía cuando muera* for voice,
orchestra (1944); *Arrullo* for voice, orchestra
(1944); *5 Preludes* for piano (1945, EMM); *Violin
Sonata* (1945, EMM); *Cello Sonata* (1948, EMM);
Poema de Neruda for string orchestra (1948); *El
sueño y la presencia*, ballet (1951); *Sinfonía breve*
for string orchestra (1952, Peer); *7 Pieces* for piano
(1952, EMM); *Hermana, hazme llorar* for voice,
piano (1954); *Symphony No. 2* (1957 EMM);
Homenaje a Juárez, cantata for vocal soloists,
narrator, chorus, orchestra (1957); *Suite* for violin,
piano (1957, EMM); *Flute Concerto* (1960); *Piano
Quintet* (1960, EMM); *A la independencia*, cantata
for vocal soloists, chorus, orchestra (1960); *Piano
Concerto No. 2* (1961, EMM); *4 Pieces* for orchestra (1961); *Violin Concerto* (1962); *3 Pieces* for
clarinet, orchestra (1962); *Overture* for organ,
orchestra (1963); *3 Pieces* for horn, orchestra
(1963); *Letanía erótica para la paz* for vocal
soloists, chorus, organ, narrator, orchestra (1963–
65); *Wind Quintet* (1967). List to 1965: *Composers
of the Americas* 11:35–46.

PRINCIPAL WRITINGS: "Candelario Huizar," *Revista nuestra música* 2:57–64; "Compositores de
mi generación," *ibid.* 3:73–81.

BIBL.: Carlos Chávez, "B. G.," *Revista nuestra
música* 1:7–13; Salomón Kahan, "B. G.," *Fascina-
ción de la música* (Mexico 1964):447–54.

SEE ALSO Mexico.

Gandini, Gerardo (b. Buenos Aires, 16 Oct
1936), studied composition with Alberto Ginastera in Buenos Aires (1956–59) and Goffredo
Petrassi in Rome, where he attended the
Accadèmia di S. Cecilia (1966–67). He taught
composition at the Catholic Univ. in Buenos
Aires beginning in 1958 and at the Torcuato
di Tella Institute beginning in 1960. In 1970
he joined the staff of the American Opera
Center at the Juilliard School. He has performed as a pianist in concerts of new music
in South America, the U.S., and Europe, and
his concert activity has been an important
influence on his development as a composer.

PRINCIPAL COMPOSITIONS: *Concertino* for clarinet,
strings, percussion (1960); *Variations* for orchestra

(1964); *Cadencias I* for violin, orchestra (1966);
Cadencias II for chamber orchestra (1967, Barry);
Música nocturna for flute, piano, string trio (1967,
PAU); *Ládieu* for piano, vibraphone, 3 percussionists, conductor (1967, UE); *Soria Moria* for
variable instrumental ensemble (1968); *Contrastes*
for 2 pianos, orchestra (1968); *Fases* for clarinet,
orchestra (1969); *Fantasie-impromptu* for piano,
orchestra (1970); *Piange e sospira* for flute, violin,
clarinet, piano (1970).

SEE ALSO Argentina.

Garant, Serge (b. Quebec City, 22 Sept 1929),
studied composition in Montreal with Claude
Champagne (1949–50). During 1951–52 he was
in Paris studying counterpoint with Mme.
Arthur Honegger and attending the classes of
Olivier Messiaen, where he met Pierre Boulez
and Karlheinz Stockhausen. After he returned
home he became active as a pianist and
arranger for Radio Canada. Since 1966 he
has taught composition and analysis at the
Univ. of Montreal and has been musical
director of the Société de Musique Contemporaine du Québec. He is increasingly active
as a conductor of contemporary music.

Garant's works are notable in reconciling
a rigorous logic, which incorporates total
serialism, and an impression of great freedom
and spontaneity. He is very sensitive to timbre,
weight, and contrast of density. While his
overall designs show a certain antidramatic
restraint, there is an explosive vitality in the
rhythmic detail. *Offrande I* (1969) is typical of
his recent work. It consists of a short introduction followed by a theme, the opening of
the ricercar from Bach's *Musical Offering* in
Webern's orchestration; ten variations, of
which the fourth uses the modulating canon
of the model and the fifth uses Bach's canon
at the unison; and a coda, which uses Bach's
canon by augmentation and contrary motion.
(The Bach quotations are presented as in the
original, never in a deformed manner.) The
bond between Bach's and Garant's music is a
symbolic, numerical one. In the precompositional stage the numeric series 3, 4, 1, 9, 8,
2, 5 was formed from the number of semitones
between the pitches of Bach's theme, repetitions of numbers being omitted. This series
formed the top line of a table of seven lines
which reads the same horizontally and vertically. A second table was formed by the sums
of the terms of the first table taken by twos.
These numbers were arranged in numeric
order (1, 2, 3, 4, 5, 8, 9) and applied to
durations, dynamics (seven levels from ppp to
fff), tempos (MM=64, 66, 68, 70, 72, 78, 80

or 96, 93, 90, 87, 84, 72, 69), percussion timbres (from claves, the dryest sound, to gong, the most resonant), and to densities within a certain duration. The basic harmonic fields are the seven notes of the theme that produced the original numeric series (C, E♭, G, A♭, B, A, F) and the other five complementary notes. By a multiplication process involving these two groups and five smaller divisions of a row, itself generated from the two basic groups, the 40 pitch complexes of the work were obtained.

PRINCIPAL COMPOSITIONS: *Asymétries No. 1* for piano (1958); *Asymétries No. 2* for clarinet, piano (1959); *Anerca* for soprano, flute, clarinet, bassoon, harp, percussion, violin, viola, cello (1961–63, Berandol); *Cage d'oiseau* for soprano, piano (1962); *Pièce pour piano No. 2* (1962); *Ouranos* for orchestra (1963); *Ennéade* for orchestra (1964); *Phrases 1* for alto, piano, percussion (1967); *Phrases 2* for 2 orchestras (1968); *Jeu à 4* for 16 instruments (1968); *Amuya* for 20 instruments (1968); *Offrande 1* for 20 instruments, prerecorded soprano voice (1969); *Offrande 2* for orchestra (1970); *Offrande 3* for 2 harps, 2 percussion, 3 cellos, piano (1971).

Bruce Mather

SEE ALSO Canada.

García, Fernando (b. Santiago, Chile, 4 July 1930), studied at the National Conservatory in Santiago (1955–57, trombone with Abraham Rojas) and composition privately with Juan Orrego-Salas (1951–56), Carlos Botto (1956–57), Gustavo Becerra-Schmidt (1957–60). He has taught at the Conservatorio de Ñuñoa (1954–56), the Conservatorio Independencia (1957–59), the Escuela Moderna de Música (1959–61), and the Univ. of Chile (since 1961). During 1958–60 he was trombonist in the Professors Symphony Orchestra of the Ministry of Education. He has also written articles and criticism for a number of Latin American newspapers and journals.

PRINCIPAL COMPOSITIONS (published by IEM unless otherwise noted): *Estáticas* for piano (1961); *América insurrecta* for narrator, chorus; text by Pablo Neruda (1962); *Estáticas* for orchestra (1963); *Sombra del paraíso* for tenor, clarinet, bassoon, violin, cello, percussion (1963); *Urania* for orchestra (1965); *La tierra combatiente* for 3 narrators, orchestra; text by Neruda (1965); *Sebastián Vásquez* for 2 narrators, soprano, orchestra; text by A. Sabella (1966); *4 Poemas concretos* for tenor, string quartet (1966); *La arena traicionada* for orchestra (1967); *Firmamento sumergido* for orchestra (1968); *Romerías* for piano (1968); *Los héroes caídos hablan* for 3 narrators, speaking chorus, orchestra; texts by Soviet fighters

(1968); *Cantos de Otoño* for tenor, piano; texts by A. Sabella and García-Lorca (1970, unpub.).

PRINCIPAL WRITINGS: García wrote an article on Chilean music for a book on the culture of Chile (published Moscow 1968).

SEE ALSO Chile.

García-Abríl, Antón (b. Teruel, Spain, 19 May 1933), studied at the Valencia Conservatory (1947–53, composition with Manuel Palau), the Madrid Conservatory (1953–57, composition with Julio Gomez), the Accadèmia Chigiana in Siena (1955–56, composition with Vito Frazzi, conducting with Paul von Kempen, film music with Francesco Lavagnino), and the Accadèmia di S. Cecilia in Rome (1964, contemporary music with Goffredo Petrassi). He has taught at the Madrid Conservatory since 1957. Many of his scores have been written for theater, films, and television.

PRINCIPAL COMPOSITIONS: *Concerto for String Instruments* (1962, UME); *Piano Concerto* (1963, UME); *Homenaje a Miguel Hernandez* for bass with wind quintet, 2 pianos or with orchestra (1964); *Cantico della creature* for vocal soloists, chorus, orchestra; text by St. Francis of Assisi (1964, UME); *Don Juan*, ballet; choreography by Antonio Gades and José Granero (1965); *3 Pieces* for double quintets, percussion (1968).

BIBL.: Antonio Fernandez-Cid, *Canciones de España* (Madrid 1963); Tomás Marco, *Música española de vanguardia* (Madrid 1970).

SEE ALSO Spain.

García-Caturla, Alejandro (b. Remedios, Cuba, 7 March 1906; d. Remedios, 12 Nov 1940), attended law school in Cuba and served as a judge in the town of Remedios until his murder by a criminal he was about to sentence. He began composing as a child and studied composition in Havana with Pedro Sanjuán and in Paris in 1928 with Nadia Boulanger. In 1932 he founded the Orquesta de Conciertos, a chamber orchestra in Caibarién, which he conducted. According to Carpentier (see bibl.), García-Caturla was attracted to the music of 19th-century Cuban composers, which fuses European concert elements, French melody, recollections of *tonadillas*, and Negro rhythms. He rarely quoted folk material but instead reworked melodic, harmonic, or rhythmic characteristics to form a synthesis of his own. The rhythmic life of *La rumba*, for example, forms "a general vibration, a series of gusts of sound" which a rumba dancer would have trouble fitting his steps to.

PRINCIPAL COMPOSITIONS: *Chamber Concerto* (1926); *3 Danzas cubanas* for orchestra (1927,

Sénart); *Obertura cubana* for orchestra (1927); *String Quartet* (1927); *Danza lucumí* for piano (1928); *Danza del tambor* for piano (1928); *Yamba-Ó* for orchestra, after Alejo Carpentier (1928–31); *Bembé* for winds, piano, percussion (1929; orchestrated 1932, Sénart); *2 Poemas afro-cubanos* for voice, piano; texts by Carpentier (1929, Sénart); *Son* for piano (1930, Ediciones de la Revista Musicalia, Havana); *Comparsa* for piano (1930, New Music); *Suite cubana No. 1* for piano, 8 winds (1931, New Music); *El caballo blanco* for chorus (1931, IIM and Southern); *La rumba* for voice ad lib., orchestra; text by José Zacarías Tallet (1933); *Sonata corta* for piano (1934, New Music); *Sabás* for voice, flute, oboe, clarinet, viola, cello; text by Nicolás Guillén (1937); *Canto de cafetales* for chorus (1937, IIM and Southern); *Son in F Minor* for piano (1939, Fischer); *Berceuse campesina* for piano (1939, Fischer). Complete list: *Composers of the Americas* 3:90–95.

PRINCIPAL WRITINGS: "Posibilidades sinfónicas de la música afrocubana," *Musicalia* 2/7:15–17; "The Development of Cuban Music," *American Composers on American Music* ed. by H. Cowell (Stanford, Calif., 1933):173–74.

BIBL.: Alejo Carpentier, *La Música en Cuba* (Mexico City 1946):244–51; Henry Cowell, "Roldán and Caturla of Cuba," *Modern Music* 18:98–99; María Muñoz de Quevedo, "A. G.-C.," *Boletín latino-americano de música* 5:611–18; Adolfo Salazar, "La obra musical de A. C.," *Revista cubana* (Jan 1938):5–43; Nicolas Slonimsky, "Caturla of Cuba," *Modern Music* (Jan 1940):76–80.

Garrido-Lecca, Celso (b. Piura, Peru, 9 March 1926), studied at the National Conservatories in Lima and Santiago, Chile (composition with Free Focke, theory and harmony with André Sas, form and counterpoint with Rodolfo Holzmann and Domingo Santa Cruz, orchestration with Aaron Copland). He has been composer and musical advisor at the Theater Institute of the Univ. of Chile, where he has also taught composition.

PRINCIPAL COMPOSITIONS: *Orden* for piano (1954); *Música para teatro* for wind quintet (1956); *Divertimento* for wind quintet (1957); *Canciones de Hogar* for soprano, clarinet, cello, piano (1958); *Música* for 6 instruments, percussion (1959); *Sinfonía* (1960); *Laudes* for orchestra (1962); *String Quartet* (1963); *Elegía a Machu Picchu* for orchestra (1965); *Intihuatana* for string quartet (1967); *Antares* for 2 string quartets, double bass (1968). ★Principal theater and film scores: *La violación de Lucrecia* (André Obey); *El alcalde de Zalamea* (Calderon de la Barca); *La fierecilla domada* (Shakespeare); *El angel que nos mira* (Thomas Wolff); *El baile de Ladrones* (Jean Anouilh); *Un caso interesante* (D. Buzàtti).

SEE ALSO Chile.

Gebrauchsmusik, most often translated "music for use" or "utilitarian music." The term refers to works of the 1920s and 30s written for special purposes, such as radio or films, or for nonprofessional performers; the latter classification was also referred to as *Gemeinschaftmusik* or *Sing- und Spielmusik* [music to be sung and played]. *Gebrauchsmusik* was cultivated by several younger composers of the time who were dissatisfied with the cliquishness of the avant-garde and wanted to reach wider audiences. The concept was also related to a broader cultural pattern, especially in Germany, where the trend "towards a polyphonic style gave rise to a new type of music-making, cultivated especially by the youth, and distinguished from the usual orchestral styles in that every voice has an importance of its own, i.e., all voices are equal, forming a new *Gemeinschaft* (community) in which new joy is found. . . . The main emphasis in the new youth is put less on listening to compositions written for the concert hall than on making music themselves. Correspondingly, it is no longer the virtuoso who plays the leading role, but the group, the community."[1] Although *Gebrauchsmusik* ceased to be a vital movement by the end of World War II, the feeling of a dichotomy between professional concert life and everyday experience has remained an issue and has continued to inspire redefinitions of composer-performer-audience roles (see Indeterminacy, Performance).

BIBL.: Hermann Closson, "The Case against Gebrauchsmusik," *Modern Music* 7:15–19; Paul Hindemith, *A Composer's World* (Cambridge, Mass., 1952):viii; John Tasker Howard, *This Modern Music* (New York 1942):158–71; Rudolph Weingartner, "Gebrauchsmusik as a Reaction to the Nineteenth Century," *American Music Teacher* (March 1953):2ff.

Generator, a device that produces an electrical signal or waveform of a predefined nature. Usually there are one or more parameters (such as frequency and amplitude) pertaining to the signal which can be varied either by manual adjustment of knobs or switches on the front panel of the device or through some means of external programming (such as voltage-control). While in the strict sense the term "oscillator" refers specifically to that part of a generator which produces a repetitive

1. A letter from the publisher B. Schott to Nicolas Slonimsky, 16 June 1936, quoted in the latter's *Music Since 1900* (New York 1937):572–73.

waveform, it is often used interchangeably with "generator."

SEE ALSO Electronic Music: Apparatus and Technology.

Genzmer, Harald (b. Blumenthal, near Bremen, 9 Feb 1909), attended the Berlin Musikhochschule (1928–29, 1931–34; composition with Paul Hindemith, orchestration with Curt Sachs, music history with Georg Schünemann). Upon completion of his studies he served as a coach at the Breslau Opera, and from 1938 until the early 40s he taught theoretical subjects and ensemble at the Volksmusikschule in Berlin-Neukölln; during this period he wrote numerous compositions for amateurs. He became interested in electronic music in 1938 when he began working with the trautonium virtuoso Oskar Sala, for whom he wrote two concertos. Genzmer has been professor of composition at the Hochschule in Freiburg-im-Breisgau (1946–57) and the Munich Hochschule (since 1957). He is also music director of the Bavarian Academy of Fine Arts.

PRINCIPAL COMPOSITIONS (published by Peters unless otherwise noted): *Trautonium Concerto* (1939, Ries & Erler, Berlin); *Violin Sonata No. 1* (1943, Schott); *Flute Sonata No. 2* (1945, Schott); *Piano Concerto* (1948, Schott); *String Quartet No. 1* (1949, Schott); *Concerto* for mixtur-trautonium, orchestra (1952, Schott); *Violin Sonatina* (1953, Schott); *Cello Sonata* (1953, Schott); *Violin Sonata No. 3* (1954); *Sinfonietta* (1955, Schott); *Viola Sonata No. 2* (1955, Bärenreiter); *5 Choruses on Texts by Jacques Prévert* for 4–10 mixed voices (1956–57, Schott); *Wind Quintet* (1956–57); *Südamerikanische Gesänge* for 4–9 mixed voices (1957, Schott); *Symphonies Nos. 1–2* (1957, 1958; Schott); *Prologue for Orchestra* (1959, Bärenreiter); *Concerto da camera* for violin, orchestra (1959, Schott); *Jiménez Cantata* for soprano, chorus, orchestra (1962); *Nonet* for oboe, clarinet, bassoon, horn, string quartet, double bass (1962); *5 Songs on Texts of Luis de Camões* for baritone, piano (1962–63); *10 Preludes* for piano (1962–63); *Concertino No. 2* for piano, string orchestra (1963); *Kammermusik* for clarinet, violin, cello, piano (1964); *Piano Trio* (1964); *Concerto* for harp, string orchestra (1965); *Introduction and Adagio* for string orchestra (1965); *Irische Harfe* for 4–8 mixed voices (1965); *Trumpet Sonatina* (1965); *Der Zauberspiegel*, ballet; scenario by Hans Stadlmair (1965); *Advent Concerto* for organ (1966); *Viola Concerto* (1967); *Englisch Horn*, 8-part cycle for men's chorus (1968, Schott); *Schiller Cantata* for high voice, male chorus, orchestra (1968); *Die Tageszeiten* for organ (1968); *Concerto* for trumpet, string orchestra (1968).

PRINCIPAL WRITINGS: "Der Komponist über sein Werk: H. G., *Englisch Horn*," *Der Chordirigent* (B. Schott, Jan 1969): 7–9.

BIBL.: Erich Valentin, "Lieder der Welt: das Chorschaffen H. G.," *Der Chordirigent* (Jan 1969): 1–6.

SEE ALSO Austria and Germany.

Gerhard, Roberto (b. Valls, Catalonia, Spain, 25 Sept 1896; d. Cambridge, England, 5 Jan 1970), studied with Granados and Pedrell in Barcelona and with Schoenberg in Vienna and Berlin (1924–28). He returned to Barcelona in 1929 and at the beginning of the Spanish Civil War moved to England, where he became a naturalized citizen. For the first 15 years of his life in England he was neglected by all but a handful of admirers. He remained without a publisher until the mid-1950s, and it was only when he was approaching his 70th birthday that he began to win recognition as one of the outstanding composers of his generation.

Everything Gerhard wrote after he left Schoenberg's masterclass was recognizably his own. His apprentice works were not without individuality, but the earliest of them, the López Picó song cycle and the *Piano Trio* (both 1918), were overindebted to Ravel and Debussy. Much more indicative of the future was the work that persuaded Schoenberg to admit Gerhard to his masterclass, the *7 Hai-Ku* of 1922. In a BBC radio program note (c.1966) the composer said of the *Hai-Ku*: "I was concerned with inventing melodic line and harmonic texture directly from the twelve-tone fund, without leaning on familiar scales or chord-combinations. A difference from Schoenberg or Webern is that conjunct motion and the smaller intervals predominate in the line-drawing; by contrast, the harmonic texture is predominantly wide-meshed. These were early preferences, a matter of taste which for me has not changed with time."

What did change through Schoenberg's teaching were Gerhard's structural methods. Entirely new and Schoenbergian in the *Wind Quintet* of 1928 was the serial basis and therefore the polyphony (the *Hai-Ku* and the earlier works were homophonic). The series, however, is not 12-tone, and the polyphony sometimes gives way to tune-and-accompaniment textures, even to simple ostinato. The "early preference" for conjunct motion and whole-tone segments was now confirmed by the example of Schoenberg's own *Wind Quintet* (Op. 26, 1924), but despite the Schoenbergian absence of functional tonality, there are

strong tonal echoes. While the treatment of
sonata form and "developing variation"
(Schoenberg's term) reflect the Viennese tradition as interpreted by Schoenberg, numerous
melodic and rhythmic inflections proclaim the
composer's Spanish origin (although in repudi-
ating the Parisian affiliations of contemporaneous Spanish music, Gerhard had volun-
tarily isolated himself from his compatriots).

During the 1930s Gerhard studied the early
Spanish polyphonists, wrote little, and left
more than one major work unfinished.
Emigration seemed to unleash his creative
powers, for between 1940 and 1947 he wrote
far more music than he had in the previous
two decades. All of it was directly or indirectly
connected with his Spanish past, via the bridge
of Schoenberg. In 1947 he completed his
Sheridan opera, *The Duenna*. Like Stravinsky's opera *The Rake's Progress*, it ended and
summarized a central period in the composer's
development. In it a frankly Spanish idiom was
associated with a synthesis of almost all the
forms (neoclassical or Viennese) and harmonic
styles (tonal, bitonal, nontonal, and 12-tone
serial) hitherto characteristic of Gerhard's
music.

After *The Duenna* came a fallow period of
three years. Gerhard was now engaged in a
radical reassessment of his hitherto equivocal
relationship to the Schoenbergian revolution.
He immersed himself in Schoenberg's recent
works and reexamined the long-neglected
serial heterodoxies of J. M. *Hauer and Alois
*Hába. His cogitations led to and were en-
riched by an intensive exploration of certain
literary and philosophical fields: such writers
as William James, Alfred North Whitehead,
and Bertrand Russell, on the one hand, and
Albert Camus and Simone Weil on the other.

If the major works of the 1940s were the fulfillment of Gerhard's destiny as a distinguished
national figure, those that followed were of a
higher order. Gerhard's creative regeneration
and his emergence as a European master were
heralded by his *Concerto for Piano and Strings*
(1951). Apart from the little *Impromptus* (1950),
the *Concerto* was his first consistently 12-tone
work and also the first in which he renounced
"classical" 12-tone technique. The liberties,
again for the first time, were Schoenbergian
rather than Bergian (*cf.* Schoenberg's *Ode to
Napoleon* and earlier works such as the *Suite*,
Op. 29, and *Von Heute auf Morgen*). The
traditions of early Spanish keyboard music
were drawn upon, and the Spanish feeling,
though still unmistakable, was universalized.

Gerhard's *Symphony No. 1* (1952–53), one of
the finest symphonies of the postwar period,
was less overtly Spanish than the *Piano
Concerto*. Technically it still owed something
to Schoenberg, but formally it broke away
from Austro-German symphonism: although
there was still a trace of sonata thinking in the
first movement, the argument was no longer
thematic and formal symmetries were discarded. In the later works of the 50s Gerhard's
so-called "athematicism" (a term coined by
Hába) became even more rigorous. Admittedly
there are vestiges of classical form in the
Nonet (1956) and quasithematic elements (including a Spanish folktune) in the *Harpsichord
Concerto* (1955–56), but the series was now the
real arbiter of the form. The *Symphony No. 2*
(1959) was even stricter in its avoidance of
melodic signposts, and indeed of any linear independence. Furthermore contrasts of character within each of the four movements were
kept to the barest minimum. In this symphony
the danger of monotony, already apparent in
those parts of the *Harpsichord Concerto* that
recall Hauer's hexachordal "tropings," was
not altogether avoided. Gerhard reacted
accordingly. In his *Symphony No. 3* ("Collages," 1960), he restored some degree of
traditional line drawing. Moreover, and this
was fundamental, he reverted to his earlier
principles of character contrast, adapting them
to a one-movement form divided into many
balancing and interlocking spans. Such forms
recurred in all Gerhard's subsequent works.
What did not recur, but remained formally and
texturally influential, was the collage of orchestral music and electronic tape sound, the
latter acting upon and reacting to the former.
Gerhard's researches into the uses of electronic
tape had arisen from his creative experience in
the *Symphony No. 1*, where at times the orchestra seemed already to be hankering after
multitrack tape and the nirvana of white
noise. In that sense *Collages* was a fission-
fusion experiment, as well as the expression of
a philosophical idea that is both existentialist
and religious. It is a work that had to be written
in order to pave the way for its greater successors, the *Concerto for Orchestra* (1965) and
the *Symphony No. 4* ("New York," 1967).
Here, the formal and antiformal functions of
tape sound were fulfilled by the orchestra
alone, and the kind of characteristic detail
reintroduced in the *Symphony No. 3* was
greatly enriched.

In so far as Gerhard remained a Spanish
composer, by his sixties he had surpassed the
achievement of Falla, his most notable predecessor. In so far as he had become an international one, he was a leader even when (indeed, particularly when) he appeared to be

following his juniors (for instance, Nono, Boulez, or Ligeti). Like Stravinsky and Messiaen he acknowledged innovating talent or genius wherever he found it, but ultimately was incapable of following anything but the promptings of his inner ear. Temperamentally his music has affinities with Bartók's (the elemental ferocity and the luminous mysticism that goes with it) and perhaps also with Busoni's (the sense of spiritual and cultural exile, the Faustian "Traum der Jugend"). Among Schoenberg's European pupils his position was unique in two respects: His mature art owed nothing to Mahler or to Central European expressionism, and his finest achievements belonged to the age inaugurated by Boulez and his manifesto, "Schoenberg est mort."

PRINCIPAL COMPOSITIONS: *L'Infantament meravellos de Shahrazade* for voice, piano; poems by López Picó (1918, UME); *Piano Trio* (1918, Sénart); *7 Hai-Ku* for voice, 5 instruments (1922, Mills); *Wind Quintet* (1928, Mills); *Ariel*, ballet (1934); *Don Quixote*, ballet (1940–41, Prowse); *Hommaje a Pedrell*, symphony (1941); *Violin Concerto* (1942–45, Mills); *Pandora*, ballet (1944–45); *The Duenna*, 3-act opera after Sheridan (1945–47); *Impromptus* for piano (1950, Prowse); *Concerto for Piano and Strings* (1951, Mills); *Symphony No. 1* (1952–53, Mills); *Concerto for Harpsichord, Strings, and Percussion* (1955–56, Mills); *String Quartet No. 1* (1955–56, Prowse); *Nonet* for 8 winds, accordion (1956, Mills); *Symphony No. 2* (1959, Mills); *Symphony No. 3*, "Collages," for tape, orchestra (1960); *String Quartet No. 2* (1960–62, Oxford); *Hymnody* for 11 players (1963, Oxford); *The Plague* for speaker, chorus, orchestra; text after Camus (1963–64, Oxford); *Concerto for Orchestra* (1965, Oxford); *Epithalamion for Orchestra* (1966, Oxford); *Symphony No. 4*, "New York" (1967, Oxford); *Libra* for flute, clarinet, violin, guitar, piano, percussion (1968, Oxford); *Leo*, chamber symphony for 10 players (1969, Oxford).

David Drew

SEE ALSO Great Britain, Spain.

Turtle Bay (1937–40) Music Schools in New York, at Converse College, Spartanburg, S. C. (1940–59), the Univ. of N. Mex. (1959–60), and the Univ. of Georgia (since 1960). He has written articles on music for a number of professional journals.

PRINCIPAL COMPOSITIONS (published by CFE unless otherwise noted): *Saugatuck Suite*, Op. 6, for piano; Nos. 2, 3, 4, 6, also for orchestra and No. 6 also for band (1931); *Meeting at Night, Parting at Morning* for women's chorus, Op. 8, No. 2; text by Robert Browning (1932); *Statement, Aria, and Development* for violin, piano, Op. 12 (1934); *8 Variations* for piano, Op. 14 (1934); *Piano Quintet*, Op. 16 (1935); *Streamline* for band, Op. 17 (1935, Witmark); *Lai*, for women's chorus, Op. 20, No. 1; text by Mary Barnard (1936); *New Music* for piano, Op. 23 (1937); *Fanfare, Fugato, and Finale* for orchestra, Op. 24 (1937); *8 Variations* for string quartet, Op. 25 (1937); *Septet* for brasses, Op. 26 (1938); *On His Blindness* for women's chorus, Op. 31, No. 1; text by John Milton (1941); *Half Moon Mountain* for baritone, women's chorus, orchestra, Op. 33; text by Robert Hagy (1947–48, AMP); *The Lord's Controversy with His People* for baritone, women's chorus, small orchestra, Op. 34, No. 1; text by William Barton (1947–49); *The Salutation of the Dawn* for chorus, orchestra, Op. 37; Sanskrit texts (1952); *100 Variations* for solo violin, Op. 38 (1952); *6 Songs* for women's or children's chorus, piano, Op. 39; texts by Carl Sandburg (1953, 1961); *Toccata and Fugue* for orchestra, Op. 40 (1953–54, revised 1957–58); *Piano Trio*, Op. 43 (1955–56, revised 1959–60); *Rhapsody* for violin, cello, piano, Op. 46 (1963, ACA); *24 Variations* for cello, Op. 50 (1963, ACA); *Celebration* for violin, orchestra, Op. 51 (1964, ACA); *Psalm 100* for chorus, Op. 53 (1965, ACA); *Border Raid* for chorus, Op. 57, No. 1 (1965); *And Thou Shalt Love the Lord* for chorus, Op. 57, No. 2 (1965, Merion); *12 Etudes* for piano, Op. 58 (1966, ACA); *Homage à Chopin*, Op. 60 (1966, ACA).

PRINCIPAL WRITINGS: *Anyone Can Compose* (c.1952, unpub.).

BIBL.: Donald McRae, "E. G.," *ACA Bulletin* 10/1:1–7.

Germany, see Austria and Germany

Gerschefski, Edwin (b. Meriden, Conn., 10 June 1909), studied at Yale Univ. (1926–31, piano with Bruce Simonds) and the Tobias Matthay Pianoforte School in London (1931–32). He also studied piano with Artur Schnabel in Como, Italy (1935) and composition with Joseph Schillinger in New York (1935–37). He has taught at the Yorkville (1933–37) and

Gershwin, George (b. Brooklyn, N. Y., 26 Sept 1898; d. Hollywood, 11 July 1937), first showed an interest in music in 1910 when his family bought an upright piano. In 1912, after an unproductive series of piano lessons with neighborhood teachers, he became a student of Charles Hambitzer, who broadened his musical horizons by introducing him to the works of Chopin, Liszt, and Debussy. Gershwin subsequently studied theory and harmony with Edward Kilenyi and Rubin Goldmark, counterpoint with Henry Cowell, and theory, composition, and orchestration with Joseph Schillinger.

From the start Gershwin liked popular music and jazz. At 15 he left high school, where his grades were not good, to become a pianist and song "plugger" at Remick's, a publisher of popular music. His first song was published in 1916 and his first complete score for a musical comedy, *La La Lucille*, followed in 1919. Also early in his career Gershwin began to write "serious" music—a brief, naive movement for string quartet, *Lullaby* (1919), and a short jazz opera, *Blue Monday Blues* (1922), subsequently renamed *135th Street*. The acclaim accorded the 1924 premiere of the *Rhapsody in Blue* marked the beginning of Gershwin's reputation as a composer for the concert hall. The 1920s and 30s saw a long line of successful songs and musicals and several film scores, nearly all of them with lyrics by George's brother, Ira, as well as concert works for orchestra and the opera *Porgy and Bess* (1934–35). Along with his ever-increasing eminence as a composer during those years, Gershwin frequently appeared in public as pianist and conductor of his own music. At his death, of a brain tumor, he left behind some unpublished music from which Ira Gershwin, by adding lyrics, has fashioned a number of posthumous songs, including scores for two films, *The Shocking Miss Pilgrim* (1946) and *Kiss Me, Stupid* (1964).

Gershwin's musical style for both his popular and serious works is essentially the same. The harmony in both cases ranges from the diatonic to the chromatic, generally avoiding extreme dissonances. A noticeable characteristic of Gershwin's diatonic harmony is the quick, successive shifts from the tonic to neighboring tonalities, usually a half step or a whole step away (such as C-B♭-B-C). His chromatic harmony, with its emphasis on stepwise inner-voice movement, also makes frequent unprepared tonal shifts. There is an American flavor in his use of parallel sixths and tenths, which are evocative of jazz, and in his frequent "oom-pah" accompaniments, which recall dance and jazz bands; both mannerisms probably resulted from the composer's habit of composing quickly at the piano. Jazz "blue notes" in melodies, particularly flattened thirds and sevenths, and syncopations of all kinds are additional Americanisms. Other elements of the Gershwin style include a natural flair for imitative counterpoint (e.g., the four-part free canon in the finale of the *Concerto in F*), as well as a use of literal melodic-motivic repetitions, rhythmic ostinatos, numerous sequences, and disjunctive pauses.

Gershwin's large-scale compositions may be thought of as extensions of his popular songs. While the latter, because of their brevity, are excellent examples of their kind, the symphonic pieces contain many structural deficiencies that resulted from Gershwin's rather limited experience in expanding musical materials. However, the tunes in these works are usually so outstanding that they often compensate for other inadequacies. One might thus be tempted to describe Gershwin's orchestral pieces as consisting of attractive tunes separated by filler material, though such a description is, of course, an oversimplification. No matter how these symphonic pieces are evaluated, they alone set Gershwin apart from other distinguished Tin Pan Alley figures who are known only for their popular songs. Although Gershwin is one of America's most famous composers, his influence on others has been relatively small. His work is such a personal expression that even the numerous technical deficiencies in his serious compositions have come to be accepted as part of the Gershwin sound. Furthermore his music was unquestionably the product of a particular era in that it captured the essence of the 1920s, the so-called Jazz Age, and the 30s.

PRINCIPAL COMPOSITIONS: ★Songs: Gershwin wrote hundreds of songs, of which many—such as *Swanee*, *The Man I Love*, *Embraceable You*, *Fascinating Rhythm*, *'S Wonderful*, *Oh Lady Be Good*, *Liza*, and *I Got Rhythm*—have become extremely popular. ★Musicals: *George White's Scandals* (annual revues, 1920–24); *Sweet Little Devil* (1924); *Primrose* (1924); *Lady Be Good* (1924); *Tell Me More* (1925); *Tip-Toes* (1925); *Oh, Kay* (1926); *Strike Up the Band* (two versions, 1927, 1930); *Funny Face* (1927); *Rosalie* (1928); *Treasure Girl* (1928); *Show Girl* (1929); *Girl Crazy* (1930); *Of Thee I Sing* (1931); *Pardon My English* (1933); *Let 'Em Eat Cake* (1933). ★Film scores: *Delicious* (1930); *Shall We Dance*, *A Damsel in Distress*, *The Goldwyn Follies* (1936–37). ★Concert music (published by New World): *Rhapsody in Blue* for piano, orchestra (1924); *Piano Concerto in F* (1925); *An American in Paris* (1928); *Second Rhapsody* for orchestra with piano (1931); *Cuban Overture* (1932); *"I Got Rhythm" Variations* for piano, orchestra (1934); *Porgy and Bess*, opera (1934–35).

BIBL.: Merle Armitage, ed., *G. G.* (New York 1938); Leonard Bernstein, "A Nice G. Tune," *The Joy of Music* (New York 1959):52; Vernon Duke, "G., Schillinger, and Dukelsky," *Musical Quarterly* 33:102–15; Vladimir Dukelsky (Vernon Duke), *Passport to Paris* (Boston 1955); David Ewen, *A Journey to Greatness* (New York 1956);

Ira Gershwin, *Lyrics on Several Occasions* (New York 1959); Isaac Goldberg, *G. G.* (New York 1958); ――, *Tin Pan Alley* (New York 1960); Edward Jablonski and Lawrence D. Stewart, *The Gershwin Years* (New York 1958); Oscar Levant, *A Smattering of Ignorance* (New York 1940); Henry Osborne Osgood, *So This Is Jazz* (Boston 1926); Robert Payne, *G.* (New York 1960); Paul Rosenfeld, *Discoveries of a Music Critic* (New York 1936); Paul Whiteman, *Jazz* (New York 1926).

Charles Schwartz

SEE ALSO Jazz, Musical, Opera, Popular Music, United States.

Ghedini, Giorgio Federico (b. Cuneo, Italy, 11 July 1892; d. Genoa, 25 March 1965), studied privately in Turin with Evasio Lovazzano (piano and organ) and S. Grossi (cello) and at the Liceo Musicale in Bologna (graduated 1911, organ with Enrico Bossi). He taught composition at the Liceo Musicale in Turin (1918), the Parma Conservatory (1938–41), and the Milan Conservatory (from 1941).

PRINCIPAL COMPOSITIONS: *Partita* for orchestra (1926, Ricordi); *Concerto grosso* for orchestra (1927, S-Z); *Concerto a cinque* for wind quintet, strings (1930, Leeds); *Pezzo concertante* for 2 violins, viola obbligato, orchestra (1931, Ricordi); *Lectio libri sapientiae*, sacred cantata for voice, trumpet, piano, strings (1938, Zerboni); *La pulse d'oro*, 1-act opera; libretto by T. Pinelli (1939, Ricordi); *Architettura*, concerto for orchestra (1940, Ricordi); *Concerto spirituale* for 2 sopranos and 9 instruments or women's chorus and chamber orchestra (1943, S-Z); *Piano Concerto* (1946, Ricordi); *Il belprato*, concerto for violin, strings (1947, Ricordi); *Concerto funebre per Duccio Galimberti* for tenor, bass, 2 trombones, strings, timpani (1948, S-Z and Leeds); *Billy Budd*, 1-act opera; libretto by Quasimodo after Melville (1949, S-Z and Leeds); *L'alderina*, concerto for flute, violin, orchestra (1951, Ricordi); *L'olmeneta*, concerto for 2 cellos, orchestra (1951, Ricordi); *La via della Croce*, opera (premiere 1961).

BIBL.: R. Amadei, "Intorno ad alcune opere di G. F. G.," *Musica d'oggi* 8/8–10:237–42; Angiola Maria Bonisconti, "Il teatro musicale di G. F. G.," *ibid.* 4:194–200; ――, "Jorge F. G.," *Revista musical chilena* (August 1964):20–29; John S. Weissmann, "La musica di G. e il suo significato europeo," *Musica d'oggi* 4:201–05.

SEE ALSO Italy.

Ghent, Emmanuel (b. Montreal, 15 May 1925), attended McGill Univ. (1942–46) and studied composition privately with Ralph Shapey during 1961–63. He has been associated with the Columbia-Princeton Electronic Music Center since 1966 and has been working at the computer-controlled electronic music studio of Bell Telephone Laboratories in Murray Hill, N. J., since 1968.

PRINCIPAL COMPOSITIONS: *Quartet* for flute, oboe (English horn), clarinet, bassoon (1960, Oxford); *Entelechy* for viola, piano (1963, Oxford); *Dithyrambos* for brass quintet (1965, Oxford); *Hex, an Ellipsis* for trumpet, ensemble, 4-track tape (one track contains signals to the performer) (1966); *Helices* for violin, piano, tape (1969); *Battery Park* on tape, including "L'Après-Midi d'un Summit Meeting," "Galloping Pentagonism," "Our Daily Bread" (1969–70).

PRINCIPAL WRITINGS: "Programmed Signals to Performers: A New Compositional Resource," *Perspectives* 6/1:96–106; "The Coordinome in Relation to Electronic Music," *Electronic Music Review* 1 (1967):33–43.

Giannini, Vittorio (b. Philadelphia, 19 Oct 1903; d. New York, 28 Nov 1966), studied at the Royal Conservatory in Milan (1911–14), the Juilliard School (1925–30; composition with Rubin Goldmark, violin with Hans Letz), and the American Academy in Rome (1932–36). He taught composition and orchestration at several schools, including Juilliard (from 1940). His music is consistently tonal and reflects a taste for baroque textures and forms and for the late romantic esthetic, especially the chamber music of Brahms and Fauré. His operas derived from the Italian *verismo* tradition.

PRINCIPAL COMPOSITIONS: *String Quartet* (1930, Birchard); *Piano Quintet* (1930, SPAM); *Lucedia*, 3-act opera (1934, Drei Masken Verlag, Berlin); *Requiem* for vocal soloists, chorus, orchestra (1936, UE); *The Scarlet Letter*, 4-act opera (1937, Ahn & Sim); *Beauty and the Beast*, radio opera (1938, Ricordi); *Concerto grosso* for string quartet, string orchestra (1946, E-V); *Trumpet Concerto* (1947, Remick); *Variations on a Cantus Firmus* for piano (1947, E-V); *Frescobaldiana* for orchestra (1948, Ricordi); *The Taming of the Shrew*, opera after Shakespeare (1950, Ricordi); *Canticle of Christmas* for baritone, chorus, orchestra (1951, Colombo); *Prelude and Fugue* for string orchestra (1955, Chappell); *Canticle of the Martyrs* for chorus, orchestra (1956, Moravian Music Fund); *Symphony No. 3* for band (1959, Colombo); *Praeludium and Allegro* for band (published 1959, Ricordi); *The Medead*, monodrama for soprano, orchestra (1960, Colombo); *Psalm 130*, concerto for double bass or cello, orchestra (1963, Colombo); *The Servant of 2 Masters*, opera (premiere 1967).

PRINCIPAL WRITINGS: "Shakespeare's Musical Taming," *Music Journal* (June 1958):8, 25.

BIBL.: M. L. Mark, "The Band Music of V. G.," *Music Educators' Journal* (April 1969):77–80;

Robert Parris, "V. G. and the Romantic Tradition," *Juilliard Review* (spring 1957):32–46; Max de Schauensee, "The Gianninis," *Opera News* (11 April 1964):14–16.

Gideon, Miriam (b. Greeley, Colo., 23 Oct 1906), attended Boston Univ. (1922–26, BA) and Columbia Univ. (1942–46, MA; medieval music with Eric Hertzmann, musicology with Paul Henry Lang) and studied composition privately in New York with Lazare Saminsky (1931–34) and Roger Sessions (1935–43). She has been on the music faculty of Brooklyn College (1944–54) and City College, N. Y. (1947–55, since 1971) and has taught at the Jewish Theological Seminary since 1955 and at the Manhattan School of Music since 1967.

PRINCIPAL COMPOSITIONS (published by CFE): *Lyric Piece* for string quartet (1941); *Lines from "The Hound of Heaven"* for voice, oboe, string trio (1945); *String Quartet* (1946); *Sonata* for viola, piano (1948); *Sonnets from Shakespeare* for voice, trumpet, string quartet (1950); *Symphonia brevis* for orchestra (1953); *Fortunato*, opera in 3 scenes (1954–56, piano score published by CFE); *Sonata* for cello, piano (1961); *The Condemned Playground* for soprano, tenor, flute, bassoon, string quartet; texts by Horace, Milton, Gary Spokes (translated into Japanese by Satoka Akiya), Baudelaire, Millay (1963); *Questions on Nature* for voice, oboe, piano, glockenspiel, tam-tam; text by Adelard of Bath (1964); *The Habitable Earth*, cantata for soloists, chorus, piano, oboe; text from Proverbs (1965); *Spiritual Madrigals* for men's voices, viola, cello, bassoon; texts by Rilke, Heine, the 13th-century minnesinger Trimperg (1965); *Rhymes from the Hill* for voice, clarinet, cello, marimba; texts by Christian Morgenstern (1968); *Sabbath Morning Service* for soloists, chorus, organ, ensemble (1969–71, unpub.). *The Seasons of Time* for voice, flute, cello, piano, celesta; ancient Japanese poetry (1970, General).

PRINCIPAL WRITINGS: "The Music of Carlos Chávez," *New Book of Modern Composers* ed. by D. Ewen (New York 1961):122–30; "The Music of Mark Brunswick," *ACA Bulletin* 13/1:1–10.

BIBL.: David Ewen, *Composers Since 1900* (New York 1969):221–23; Burt Korall, "M. G.," *BMI News* . . . (New York, June 1963):31–33; Hans Nathan, "The U.S. of America," *History of Song* ed. by Denis Stevens (New York 1961):452–53; George Perle, "The Music of M. G.," *ACA Bulletin* 7/4:2–9; Lazare Saminsky, *Living Music of the Americas* (New York 1949):106–10; Albert Weisser, "Interview with M. G.," *Dimensions in American Judaism* (New York, spring 1970):38–40.

Gielen, Michael Andreas (b. Dresden, 20 July 1927), studied analysis and composition with E. Leuchter in Buenos Aires (1942–49) and analysis with Josef Polnauer in Vienna (1950–53). A further influence was Gielen's uncle, the composer-pianist Edward Steuermann. Gielen was a conductor at the Vienna State Opera (1952–60) and first conductor of the Royal Opera of Stockholm (1960–65). Since 1969 he has been music director of the Belgian National Orchestra in Brussels.

PRINCIPAL COMPOSITIONS: *Variations* for string quartet (1949); *4 Poems of Stefan George* for chorus, 19 instruments (1955–58, UE); *Variations* for 40 instruments (1959, UE); *Ein Tag tritt hervor*, "Pentaphonie," for obbligato piano, vibraphone, marimbaphone, electric guitar, harmonium, ondes Martenot, 5 groups of 5 musicians each; text by Pablo Neruda (1960–63, Gerig); *die glocken sind auf falscher spur*, melodramas and interludes for 6 musicians (female singer, speaker, cellist, guitarist, pianist, percussionist), tapes; poems by Hans Arp (1967–69, Gerig).

BIBL.: Friedrich Saathen, "Current Chronicle," *Musical Quarterly* 44:516–19.

Gilbert, Anthony (b. London, 26 July 1934), studied at Morley College in London (1958–62; harmony, counterpoint, and music history with Anthony Milner, composition with Alexander Goehr). He has lectured in composition at Goldsmiths' College of the Univ. of London since 1969; during 1970–71 he was Granada Fellow in the Arts at the Univ. of Lancaster. Since 1965 he has been an editor for contemporary music at Schott's in London.

PRINCIPAL COMPOSITIONS (published by Schott): *Sinfonia* for chamber orchestra, Op. 5 (1965); *Regions* for 2 chamber orchestras, Op. 6 (1966); *Sonata No. 2* for piano 4-hands, Op. 8 (1967); *Brighton Piece* for 2–3 percussionists, clarinet, high horn, small trumpet, trombone, cello, Op. 9 (1967); *9 or 10 Osannas* for clarinet, horn, violin, cello, piano, Op. 10 (1967); *Spell Respell* for electric bassett clarinet, piano, Op. 14 (1968); *Mother* for chamber ensemble with electronic devices, Op. 15 (1969); *The Scene-Machine*, 1-act opera; libretto by George McBeth (1970).

BIBL.: G. W. Hopkins, "The Music of A. G.," *Musical Times* (Oct 1968):907–10.

SEE ALSO Great Britain.

Gilboa, Yaakov (b. Košice, Czechoslovakia, 2 May 1920), studied at the Jerusalem Academy of Music (1944–47; composition with Josef Tal, Paul Ben-Haim), the Cologne Courses for New Music (1963, composition with Karlheinz Stockhausen), and the Darmstadt summer courses. He is a clerk for the municipality of Tel Aviv and teaches and lectures on music in his free time. His early compositions were "postromantic, influenced by Schoenberg, Hindemith, and Stravinsky, and the so-called 'Mediterranean style'." After 1963 he began to combine the techniques acquired at Cologne and Darmstadt with such Eastern characteristics as heterophony and polyrhythm. Most of his works are short and mosaiclike in structure.

PRINCIPAL COMPOSITIONS: *Safiah* [Wild Flowers] for mezzo-soprano, horn, harp, string orchestra (1957); *Avim holfoth* [Passing Clouds] for mezzo-soprano, clarinet, cello, piano (1958); *Sonnetoth erev* [Evening Sonnets] for alto, piano (1958); *Shiva harakim ketanim* [7 Little Insects], piano pieces for children (1959); *Violin Sonata* (1960); *Shteym esrrey halonoth Chagall beyerushalaym* [The 12 Chagall Jerusalem Windows] for 7 women's voices, baroque ensemble (1964, IMP); *Gewishim* [Crystals] for 5 players (1968, IMP); *Telalim* [Dew] for children's speaking chorus, harp (1968, IMP); *Dardarim* [Thistles], theater piece for 3 vocal soloists, 4 players (1969, IMP); *Pastellim* [Pastels], duo for piano (1969, IMP); *Ofakim bekahol wessagol* [Horizons in Blue and Violet], dance score for 6 players (1970, IMP).

BIBL.: Willi Tappolet, "La découverte de musique en Israel," *Liaisons* (Geneva, May–June 1968):4.

SEE ALSO Israel.

Gillis, Don E. (b. Cameron, Mo., 17 June 1912), studied at Texas Christian Univ. (1931–35; composition with Keith Mixson) and North Texas State Univ. (1943; composition with Roy T. Wills, Wilfred Bain). During 1932–35 he was staff trombonist for radio station WBAP in Fort Worth, Texas. He was director of the band at Texas Christian Univ. and of the orchestra at Southwestern Baptist Seminary (1935–42) and is chairman of the arts division of Dallas Baptist College (since 1968). During 1944–54 he worked for the National Broadcasting Co., producing the NBC Symphony radio broadcasts (with Toscanini) and other programs. He was executive vice president of the Interlocken Music Camp during 1958–61. He has conducted on the radio and for films, the stage, and concerts. In his youth "the band, the square dance, the hymntune, and early jazz were very much a part of my environment. . . . I am fundamentally a melodist. . . . I have not embraced any particular school of writing but have been influenced orchestrally by . . . R. Strauss, Sibelius, and Debussy. . . . My greatest enjoyment in composition is writing for the stage." His output includes 25 works for band, including an opera.

PRINCIPAL COMPOSITIONS: *The Raven* for narrator, orchestra (1937); *This Is Our America* for baritone, chorus, orchestra or band (1941, Mills); *Short Overture to an Unwritten Opera* (1945, Boosey); *Symphony No. 5* (1945); *Portrait of a Frontier Town*, symphonic suite (1946, Boosey); *Symphony 5 1/2, "A Symphony for Fun"* (1947, Boosey); *The Alamo*, symphonic poem (1947); *Symphony No. 6, "Mid-Century U.S.A."* (1947–48); *Symphony No. 8, "A Dance Symphony"* (1949); *Shindig*, ballet (1949); *Symphony No. 1 for Band* (1949); *Tulsa, "A Symphonic Portrait in Oil"* (1950); *The Man Who Invented Music* for narrator, orchestra (1950); *Rhapsody* for harp, orchestra (1952); *The Coming of the King* for chorus (1954, Mills); *Pep Rally*, 2-act opera for band (1956); *5 Acre Pond*, poem for oboe, orchestra (1957); *The Libretto*, 1-act comic opera (1958); *Men of Music* for band (1958, Volkwein); *The Land of Wheat*, suite for band (1959); *Star Valley Junction*, opera (1961–62); *Ceremony of Allegiance* for narrator, band (1964, Kjos); *7 Golden Texts* for narrator, chorus, band or orchestra (1965); *World Première*, 1-act comedy (1966–67); *The Gift of the Magi*, 1-act opera (1966); *The Nazarene*, 1-act opera (1967–68, Broadman); *Piano Concerto No. 2* (1967); *Symphony No. 10, "Big D"* (1967); *Toscanini: Portrait of a Century* for narrator, orchestra (1967); *Rhapsody* for trumpet, orchestra (1969).

PRINCIPAL WRITINGS: *The Unfinished Symphony Conductor* (Austin 1967).

Gilson, Paul (b. Brussels, 15 June 1865; d. Brussels, 3 April 1942), studied harmony and counterpoint privately with Charles Duyck and composition at the Brussels Conservatory (1887) with François Gevaert. He began to teach harmony at the Brussels Conservatory in 1899 and at the Antwerp Conservatory in 1904. During 1920–40 he was mentor to the new generation of Belgian composers, with some of whom he founded Les Synthétistes in 1925. During 1906–14 he was music critic for the journal *Le Soir*, and in 1924 he founded *La Revue musicale belge*, for which he wrote until 1940. He was inspector general of music education in Belgium during 1908–30. His music was influenced principally by the Russian Five, as well as by Wagner and Brahms.

PRINCIPAL COMPOSITIONS: *Danse et rapsodie écossaises* for orchestra (1885–86, Muraille); *Fanfare inaugurale* for orchestra (1887, Breitkopf); *Sinaï*, cantata for vocal soloists, chorus, orchestra; text by J. Sauvenière (1889); *Rapsodie canadienne* for orchestra (1891, Breitkopf); *3 Mélodies populaires flamandes* for strings (1891); *La Mer*, symphonic sketches for orchestra (1892, Breitkopf); *Chansons écossaises* for voice, orchestra; texts by Leconte de Lisle (1892–98, Salabert); *Alvar* for voice, orchestra; text by E. Bède (1893); *Francesca da Rimini*, oratorio for vocal soloists, chorus, orchestra; text by J. Guillaume (1894, Schott); *Gens de mer*, opera after Victor Hugo (1895, Oertel); *Cantate inaugurale*, military music for chorus (1896, Schott); *Hymne à l'art* for vocal soloists, chorus, orchestra; text by Em. Vossaert (1897); *La Captive*, ballet (1899–1900); *Princesse Rayon de Soleil*, opera; libretto by P. de Mont (1901, Oertel); *Suite rustique* for piano (1902, Cranz); *Variations symphoniques* for brass instruments (1903); *Par les routes* for piano (1914, Cranz).

PRINCIPAL WRITINGS: *Histoire de la musique et des musiciens belges*, in collaboration with René Lyr (Paris 1914); *Le Tutti orchestral* (Brussels 1921); *Notes de musique et souvenirs* (Brussels 1942).

BIBL.: Gaston Brenta, *P. G.* (Brussels 1965); A. Corbet, "P. G.," *Music and Letters* 27; "P. G.," *Jeugd en Muziek* (Jan 1955); *La Revue musicale belge*, special issue (June 1935).

[prepared with the help of CBDM]

SEE ALSO Belgium.

Ginastera, Alberto (b. Buenos Aires, 11 April 1916), studied in his native city at the Williams Conservatory (1928–35) and at the National Conservatory (1936–38; harmony with Athos Palma, counterpoint with José Gil, composition with José André). Public recognition first came in November 1937 when Juan José Castro conducted the premiere of the ballet suite *Panambí* in Buenos Aires. Ginastera received a Guggenheim fellowship in 1942 for travel to the U.S. but, because of the war, was unable to make the trip until 1945. He lived in New York during 1945–47, composing and acquainting himself with music training programs in universities and music schools in the East and Midwest. Since 1948 he has been teaching and composing primarily in Argentina but often on commission from other countries. In 1962 he organized and became director of the Center for Advanced Musical Studies at the Torcuato di Tella Institute in Buenos Aires. Now the leading center in Latin America for the study of composition, it provides Latin American students with opportunities to experiment freely and to consult with composers from all parts of the world.

The Inter-American Music Festivals in Washington, D.C. have provided a forum for much of Ginastera's international reputation. For the first festival (1958) the Elizabeth Sprague Coolidge Foundation commissioned his *String Quartet No. 2*. For the second (1961) the Fromm and Koussevitzky Foundations commissioned the *Cantata para América mágica* and *Piano Concerto No. 1*, respectively. Other Washington commissions have been the operas *Bomarzo* and *Beatrix Cenci* (for the Washington Opera Society) and the cantata *Bomarzo* (for the 13th festival in 1964 of the Coolidge Foundation).

Ginastera's works can be divided into those in a nationalistically oriented style (to c.1960) and those in more advanced idioms. In the former group belong seven solo piano compositions, two string quartets, several string duos, three series of songs for voice and piano, four orchestral works, and two ballets. The latter group includes cantatas, operas, and concertos. Considering the great success of his vocal and operatic works, Ginastera could now be said to occupy in the New World the position that Henze or Britten hold in Europe.

Throughout his career Ginastera has tended to use traditional formal schemes and to emphasize percussion instruments, dense orchestral textures (especially prominent in *Panambí*, 1935–37, among the earlier works), and forceful rhythms, including rhythmic patterns associated with or derived from folk music. He has also used microtones frequently, the most effective use occurring in the *Violin Concerto* (1963). The strong rhythmic appeal in the string quartets (1948, 1958) and other earlier works has been compared to Bartók, as have Ginastera's uses of folk-music elements divorced from a nationalistic context (*Piano Sonata*, 1952). The example of Villa-Lobos, the most influential Latin American composer of the 1940s and 50s, may also have affected Ginastera's thinking along these lines. Symmetrical arch forms, another Bartók feature, help give coherence to the opera *Don Rodrigo* (1964) and other works. In only a few of the earlier works did he use specific popular dances; two examples are the *5 Canciones populares argentinas* (1943), and *Estancia* (1941), one of the more popular ballets in Argentina. Harmony throughout the earlier works tended to be highly dissonant and polytonal.

Ginastera used 12-tone procedures in some of the earlier works, such as the *Piano Sonata*, and began using them extensively beginning with the *String Quartet No. 2* (1958) and the *Cantata para América mágica* (1960). Dodecaphony is never used to the exclusion of other procedures, however; the quartet blends dodecaphonic and microtonal sections, while the cantata contains both serialized and, toward the end, aleatoric rhythms. In the cantata, which uses about 50 different percussion instruments, additive rhythms and polyrhythmic cells are enriched by what Ginastera calls "the insertion of irrational values inside other irrational values." When the desired effect finally becomes too complex to notate, aleatoric procedures take over. Such rhythmic processes have continued in the more recent works (both *Bomarzo*s and the *Violin Concerto*). Also noteworthy in the cantata, because of its continuing importance, is Ginastera's expressionist treatment of the voice. Large and unusual intervals, such as 11ths, occur, along with 12-tone rows and microtonal effects, including the use of sprechstimme. Such characteristics can be found even in the choral parts of the operas, for instance in a passage in *Bomarzo* where the chorus sings the word "love" in more than 40 languages.

PRINCIPAL COMPOSITIONS: *Panambí*, ballet and orchestral suite, Op. 1 (1935–37, Barry); *Estancia*, ballet and dance suite, Op. 8 (1941, Barry); *String Quartet No. 1*, Op. 20 (1948, Barry); *Piano Sonata*, Op. 22 (1952, Barry); *Variaciones concertantes* for chamber orchestra, Op. 23 (1952, Boosey); *String Quartet No. 2*, Op. 26 (1958, Barry); *Cantata para América mágica* for voice, percussion orchestra, Op. 27; texts from pre-Columbian Indian sources (1960, Barry and Boosey); *Piano Concerto No. 1*, Op. 28 (1961, Barry and Boosey); *Violin Concerto No. 1*, Op. 30 (1963, Boosey); *Don Rodrigo*, 3-act opera, Op. 31; libretto by Alejandro Casona (1964, Boosey); *Sinfonia "Don Rodrigo"* for soprano, orchestra (1964, Boosey); *Bomarzo*, cantata for speaker, male voice, chamber orchestra, Op. 32; texts by Manuel Mujica Láinez (1964, Boosey); *Bomarzo*, 3-act opera, Op. 34 (1966, Boosey); *Estudios sinfónicos* for orchestra, Op. 35 (1967–68, Boosey). List to 1961: *Composers of the Americas* I: 39–42; list to 1966 in Urtubey.

BIBL.: Pola Surez Urtubey, *A. G.* (Buenos Aires 1967).

Alcides Lanza

SEE ALSO Argentina, Opera.

Glanville-Hicks, Peggy (b. Melbourne, Australia, 29 Dec 1912), started composition lessons with Fritz Hart at age 15. She studied at the Melba Conservatory (1929–31) and the Royal College of Music, London (1932–36, composition with Ralph Vaughan Williams, piano with Arthur Benjamin and Constant Lambert, conducting with Sir Malcolm Sargent). She also studied with Egon Wellesz in Vienna and Nadia Boulanger in Paris. She lived in New York during 1942–59 and during part of this period was a critic for the *New York Herald Tribune*, as well as a contributor to various musical and general periodicals and to *Grove's Dictionary of Music and Musicians*. She directed the Composers Forum concert series (1948–60). These concerts enabled her to revive such works as George Antheil's *Ballet mécanique* and Paul Bowles's opera, *The Wind Remains*. She received a Fulbright fellowship and a Rockefeller grant in 1959–60 to study the demotic music of Greece and to restudy the musical systems of India. Since 1959 she has lived in Athens. She reports that "some years ago . . . , a conviction grew that in melody and rhythm we find perennial elements, but that in harmony . . . we had exhausted the vein and come to an impasse in our current total dissonance. Accordingly, I demoted the harmonic element to a minor and occasional role, developing a new kind of melody-rhythm structure." She has used oriental and ancient modes, sometimes combining them with serial procedures.

PRINCIPAL COMPOSITIONS (dates of composition not available): ★ Operas: *The Transposed Heads*, 6-scenes; libretto by Thomas Mann (AMP, premiered 1954); *Nausicaa*, 3-acts; libretto by Robert Graves (Colfranc, premiered 1961). ★ Ballets: *Saul and the Witch of Endor* for trumpet, percussion, strings; choreography by John Butler (Peters); *Tragic Celebration*, choreography by Butler (Peters); *A Season in Hell* after a poem by Rimbaud; choreography by Butler (composed 1965). ★ For orchestra: *Etruscan Concerto* for piano, chamber orchestra (Peters); *Concerto romantico* for viola, orchestra (Peters); *Letters from Morocco* for tenor, orchestra; text from letters of Paul Bowles. ★ Chamber works: *Sonata* for piano, 5 percussionists (AMP); *Concertino da camera* for flute, clarinet, bassoon, piano; *Harp Sonata* (Weintraub). List to 1967: *Composers of the Americas* 13:55–59.

Glière, Reinhold (Moritzovich) (b. Kiev, 11 Jan 1875; d. Moscow, 23 June 1956), studied at the Kiev Music School (1891–94) and the Moscow Conservatory (1894–1900; composition with Anton Arensky, Sergei Taneyev, and Mikhail Ippolitov-Ivanov). He also studied composition in Berlin with Julius Conus (1905–07). He was director and professor of composition at the Kiev Conservatory (1913–20) and then taught on the Moscow Conservatory faculty. He toured extensively as a conductor. After the Revolution he sought to place his talent in the service of the Soviet people. His German romantic and Russian nationalist orientation agreed with official Soviet policies on music, and by 1950 he was one of the most popular and highly honored Soviet composers.

PRINCIPAL COMPOSITIONS (available from Mezhkniga unless otherwise noted): *String Quartets Nos. 1–4* (1900, 1905, 1928, 1948); *Symphony No. 3*, "Ilya Murometz," Op. 42 (1909–11, Jurgenson);

March of the Red Army for wind orchestra (1924); *Shakh Senem*, opera (1923–25, revised 1934; overture published by Leeds); *The Red Poppy*, ballet (1926–27, revised 1949); *Harp Concerto*, Op. 74 (1938); *Concerto* for soprano, orchestra, Op. 82 (1942–43); *Cello Concerto*, Op. 87 (1945–46); *The Bronze Horseman*, ballet (1948–49). Glière also wrote over 200 piano pieces and 150 songs.

PRINCIPAL WRITINGS: "Pis'ma k M. R. Renkvist" [Letters to M. R. Renkvist], *Sovetskaia muzyka* (Oct 1965):29–38 and (Nov 1965):58–70.

BIBL.: Igor F. Belza, *R. M. G.* (Moscow 1962); Boris S. Iagolim, *R. M. G., Bibliography* (Moscow 1964); Stanley Krebs, *Soviet Composers and the Development of Soviet Music* (New York 1970); G. Litinsky, "G. pedagogg," *Sovetskaia muzyka* 1961/25:109–14; Rena Moisenko, *Realist Music* (London 1949):88–96.

SEE ALSO Soviet Union.

Globokar, Vinko (b. Anderny, France, 7 July 1934), studied at the Ljubljana Conservatory in Yugoslavia (1949–54, trombone with Karas), the Paris Conservatory (1955–59, trombone with Lafosse and Masson), and composition privately with René Leibowitz (1959–63) and Luciano Berio (1965). Since 1968 he has taught trombone at the Cologne Musikhochschule and composition and trombone at the Kurse für Neue Musik there.

PRINCIPAL COMPOSITIONS (published by Peters): *Plan* for zarb (Persian drum), 4 instruments of the performers' choice (1965); *Voie* for 3 choruses, 3 orchestral groups; text by Mayakovski (1965–66); *Accord* for soprano, 5 instrumentalists (1966); *Traumdeutung* for 4 choruses; text by Edoardo Sanguineti (1967); *Fluide* for 9 brasses, 3 percussionists (1967); *Etude pour folklora I* for chamber orchestra (1968); *Etude pour folklora II* for orchestra (1968); *Correspondences* for 4 instrumentalists (1969); *Discours III* for 5 oboes (1969).

PRINCIPAL WRITINGS: "Problem instrumentalnega in glasbenega teatra" [Problems of Instrumental and Musical Theater], *Muzikolośki zbornik* (Ljubljana) 4:132–37; "Neue Entwicklungsmöglichkeiten der Blasinstrumente," *Sonda* (Madrid), vol. 5; "Vom Standpunkt eines Interpreten," *Melos* 36:513; "Vom Reagieren," *ibid.* 38:59–62.

BIBL.: Dragotin Cvetko, "Les nouvelles orientations dans la musique slovène contemporaine," *Le Livre slovène* (Jan 1966):28; ——, "Pogovor o novi glasbi" (Discussion about New Music), *Slowenian hebdomadary* (10 May 1969):268; Erika Jirku, "Rijeć kao mogućnost muzike" [The Word as Musical Possibility], *Croatian hebdomadary Telegram* (9 May 1969):20.

Glodeanu, Liviu (b. Dîrja-Cluj, Rumania, 6 August 1938), studied at the Cluj Music School (1950–55), the Cluj Conservatory

(1955–57, counterpoint with Dorin Pop, harmony with Liviu Comes), and the Bucharest Conservatory (1957–61, composition with Marţian Negrea, form with Tudor Ciortea). He was a researcher at the Folklore Institute of the Rumanian Academy during 1961–63. Since then he has been artistic advisor of the Bucharest Philharmonic Orchestra. Many of his works aim for an archaic expression akin to primitive rituals and incantations, and he retains features of ancient Rumanian folk music even when using serial or aleatory procedures.

PRINCIPAL COMPOSITIONS: *The Young Dead Soldiers*, cantata for mezzo-soprano, men's chorus, orchestra; text by Archibald MacLeish (1958); *4 Madrigals* for chorus, chamber ensemble (1958–65, Muzicală); *3 Songs* for mezzo-soprano, flute, piano; texts by García-Lorca (1960); *Piano Concerto* (1960); *Suite* for children's chorus, wind instruments, percussion (1961, Muzicală); *Mouvement symphonique* (1961, Muzicală and Bärenreiter); *Prelude, Chorale, and Fugue* for piano (1962); *Flute Concerto* (1962, Muzicală); *Invenţiuni* [Inventions] for wind quintet, percussion (1963, Muzicală); *Piano Sonata No. 2* (1963, Muzicală); *Ulisse* for high voice, orchestra (1967); *Etudes* for orchestra (1967); *Zamolxe*, opera; libretto after Lucian Blaga (1968–69); *String Quartet No. 2* (1970); *Ricercare* for orchestra (1970).

PRINCIPAL WRITINGS: "Apartenenţa compozitorului la cultura naţională" [The Composer's Affiliation with National Culture], *Muzica* (March 1966); "Rolul folclorului în creaţie" [The Role of Folklore in Artistic Creation], *Muzica* (July 1966).

BIBL.: George Balan, "L. G.," *Contemporanul* (8 March 1963); Iancu Dumitrescu, "Ipostaze în creaţia românească" [Apostasy in Rumanian Artistic Creation], *Romania literară* (4 Dec 1969); Walter M. Klepper, "Concertul pentru flaut şi orchestră de L. G." [The Flute Concerto of L. G.], *Muzica* (Dec 1966):10–16; Elena Zottoviceanu, "Privire asupra noii creaţii romaneşti pentru pian" [Observations on New Rumanian Compositions for Piano], *Studii şi cerectări de istoria artei* 1963/1:28–31.

Goehr, Alexander (b. Berlin, 10 August 1932), is the son of Walter Goehr, a conductor who pioneered in performing the works of Schoenberg; the family settled in England in 1933. Goehr studied with Richard Hall at the Royal Manchester College, with Olivier Messiaen at the Paris Conservatory (1957), and privately with Yvonne Loriod (also 1957). He produced orchestral concerts for the BBC (1960–68) and was composer in residence at the New England Conservatory (1968–69) and a teacher at Yale Univ. (1969–70). In 1967 he formed the Music Theatre Ensemble, a group of singers, actors, dancers, mimes, and instrumentalists that has premiered his recent theater pieces.

The work which first gained Goehr wide recognition was *The Deluge* (1957–58), a cantata after Leonardo da Vinci. Its dramatic incisive lines are those of a composer who had rejected the pointillistic influence of Webern. The music's great flexibility results partly from Goehr's virtuoso handling of the vocal soloists and instruments and partly from his fluent use of linear serialism. Virtuoso scoring is also a feature of the divertimentolike *Suite* for chamber ensemble, Op. 11 (1961), but this work evinces a freer use of motivic elements. Goehr has spoken of his interest in using repetition as a means of clarifying formal structures, and repeated ideas or even whole structural blocks tend to proliferate in his later works. The *Little Music for Strings* (1963) relies on four-part, triadically based chords and on patterned, even thematic material. An increasing literalness of repetitions can be traced in both symphonic and dramatic works. The *Violin Concerto* (1961–62) uses much conventional concerto material (above all in cadenza figurations). *Hecuba's Lament* (1959–61), the offspring of a projected opera, contains an embryonic motivic technique that later reached fulfillment in the opera *Arden muss sterben* (1966). The varied background of Goehr's music is illustrated by *Triptych* (1968–70), a set of three theater pieces, and the *Concerto for 11 Instruments* (1970). The former draws on biblical texts, Plato, and 12th-century Hebrew sources, which are related through singing, choral speech, and narration; mime is used to convey the composer's interpretation of the texts. The *Concerto* uses a 19th-century Russian Jewish wedding band instrumentation and a formal scheme similar to Beethoven's *Piano Sonata*, Op. 101.

PRINCIPAL COMPOSITIONS (published by Schott): *Piano Sonata*, Op. 2 (1951–52); *Fantasia* for orchestra, Op. 4 (1954, revised 1958); *The Deluge*, cantata for soprano, alto, flute, horn, trumpet, harp, violin, viola, cello, double bass, Op. 7; text after Leonardo da Vinci (1957–58); *Sutter's Gold*, cantata for bass, chorus, orchestra, Op. 10 (1959–60); *Suite* for flute, clarinet, horn, harp, violin/viola, cello, Op. 11 (1961); *Hecuba's Lament* for orchestra, Op. 12 (1959–61); *Violin Concerto*, Op. 13 (1961–62); *2 Choruses*, Op. 14; texts by Milton and Shakespeare (1962); *Little Symphony*, Op. 15 (1963); *Little Music for Strings*, Op. 16 (1963); *5 Poems and an Epigram of William Blake* for chorus, Op. 17 (1964); *Pastorals* for orchestra, Op. 19 (1965); *Piano Trio*, Op. 20 (1966); *Arden muss sterben*, 3-act opera, Op. 21; libretto by Erich Fried after an anonymous 16th-century play (1966); *String Quartet No. 2*, Op. 23 (1967); *Romanza* for cello, orchestra, Op. 24 (1968); *Triptych*, 3-part theater

piece for actor, 2 mimes, 5 singers, instrumental group: part 1, "Naboth's Vineyard," Op. 25 (1968); part 2, "Shadowplay-2," Op. 30 (1970); part 3, "Sonata about Jerusalem," Op. 31 (1970); *Konzertstück* for piano, orchestra, Op. 26 (1969); *Nonomiya* for piano, Op. 27 (1969); *Paraphrase* for clarinet, Op. 28 (1969); *Symphony in 1 Movement*, Op. 29 (1970); *Concerto for 11 Instruments*, Op. 32 (1970).

BIBL.: R. Murray Schafer, *British Composers in Interview* (London 1963).

Bill Hopkins

SEE ALSO Great Britain, Opera.

Goethals, Lucien (Gustave Georges) (b. Ghent, Belgium, 26 June 1931), studied at the Royal Conservatory in Ghent (1947–56, orchestration with Norbert Rosseau). He studied electronic composition with Louis de Meester in 1962 at the Electronic Music Institute of the Rijksuniversiteit and with Gottfried Michael Koenig at the Stifting Gaudeamus courses at Bilthoven in 1963. He also attended the Darmstadt summer courses in 1963. Since then he has been a composer-programmer at the Electronic Music Institute. In 1964 he helped found Spectra, a Belgian group for the study and performance of contemporary music.

PRINCIPAL COMPOSITIONS: *2 Cristaux* for piano (1961); *Etude 1*, electronic music on 1-track tape (1962); *Etude 3*, electronic music on 1-track tape (1963); *Dialogos* for wind quintet, 2 string quintets, string orchestra, percussion, 4-track tape (1963); *Pentagone* for piano (1963); *Etude 5* on 1-, 2-, or 4-track tape (1964); *Endomorphie 1* for violin, piano, 1-track tape (1964, *Documenta musicae novae* 1969/2); *Cellotape* for cello with contact microphone, piano, 1-, 2-, or 4-track tape (1965, *Documenta musicae novae* 1969/2); *Movimientos y acciones* for flute, violin, viola; harp, percussion; clarinet, violin, cello (1965); *Sinfonia en gris mayor* for 2 orchestras, percussion ensemble, 2 1-track tapes (1966); *Endomorphie 2* for flute, oboe, clarinet bassoon, horn, trumpet, trombone, tuba, 2 1-track tapes (1966); *2 Mélodies* for mezzo-soprano, flute, violin, cello; texts by Jan Van der Hoeven (1966); *Vensters* for 2 narrators, 3–4 percussion, 3–4 1-track tapes (3–4 projectors optional); percussion solo, piano, cello, stereo tape (1967); *Contrapuntos* for 1 stereo tape to 12 1-track tapes (1967); *Mouvement* for string quartet, 2 1-track tapes (1967); *Enteuxis* for string orchestra, oboe, flute (1968); *Quebraduras* for piano, violin, viola, cello (1969); *Ensimismamientos* for piano, violin, cello, bassoon, contact microphones, tape (1969); *Soliloquios* for violin (1969); *Studie 6*, electronic music on 1-track tape (1969); *Cáscaras* for mezzo-soprano, flute, clarinet, violin, cello, piano; text by Claudio Rodriquez (1970).

BIBL.: Herman Sabbe, *L. G.: Le constructivisme*

bifonctionnel, Yearbook of the Institute for the Psychoacoustics of Electronic Music (Ghent 1967):35–59.

Goeyvaerts, Karel (b. Antwerp, 8 June 1923), attended St. John Berchmans College in Antwerp (1940–42), Antwerp Conservatory (1942–47), and the Paris Conservatory (1947–51; composition with Darius Milhaud, analysis and music esthetics with Olivier Messiaen). He worked at the Electronic Music Studio of the German Radio in Cologne during 1953–59, and has been teaching composition at the Antwerp Conservatory since 1966. "[My] extensive analysis of the works of Anton Webern brought me in the late 1940s to an enlarged application of serial techniques." His *Sonata* for 2 pianos (1950–51) was probably the first totally serial structure; it had a great influence on Stockhausen, among others. His electronic *Composition No. 5* (1953) was one of the first works produced solely from sine waves.

PRINCIPAL COMPOSITIONS: *3 Lieder per sonare a venti-sei* for 26 solo instruments (1948–49); *Sonata* for 2 pianos (1950–51, Ghent Univ.); *Composition No. 5*, electronic music on tape (1953); *Composition No. 6* for 15 instruments, 180 sound objects (1953); *Jeux d'été* for 3 orchestral groups (1961); *Parcours* for 2–6 violins (1967); *Mass in Memory of John XXIII* for chorus, 10 winds (1968); *Active-Reactive* for 2 oboes, 2 trumpets, piano (1968); *Catch à 4*, "Action for 4 Strolling Musicians," for 4 musicians playing different instruments of their choice (1969).

PRINCIPAL WRITINGS: "The Sound Material of Electronic Music," *Die Reihe*, English ed., 1:35–37.

SEE ALSO Austria and Germany, Belgium.

Goldstein, Malcolm (b. Brooklyn, N. Y., 27 March 1936), studied violin with Antonio Miranda and liberal arts and music at Columbia Univ. (1952–60). During 1959–61 he was a research assistant at the Columbia-Princeton Electronic Music Center. He has taught at Columbia Univ. (1961–65), the New England Conservatory (1965–67), the New School for Social Research in New York (1963–65, 1967–69), and at Dickinson College, Pa. (1969–71). He has played the violin professionally, done choreography and dancing with the Judson Dance Theater in New York and the Dance Circle of Boston, and worked as a musician-engineer for the Merce Cunningham Dance Co. His music has been influenced by a wide range of listening from Machaut and Monteverdi to Ives, Varèse, and Cage.

PRINCIPAL COMPOSITIONS; *Das Erwachen* for soprano, chamber orchestra; text by Rilke (1959); *Paradoxes* for violin, trumpet, bassoon, cello (1962); *Stillpoint* for brass quintet (1962); *Emanations* for violin, cello (1962); *It seemed to me . . .*, a tape collage (1963); *Judson #6 Piece* on tape (1963); *Ludlow Blues* for winds, tape (1963); *Majority—1964* for string trio, piano (1964); *Overture and Illuminations from Fantastic Gardens* for 3–5 voices, piano; text by Rimbaud (1964); *Passages* for string quartet (1967); *death: the act or fact of dying* for reader(s), text from the dictionary (1967); *Sheep Meadow*, tape collage (1967); *State of the Nation*, environment of magnetic tape loops, audience (1967; published in *12 Evenings of Manipulations*, Judson Gallery Publications, N. Y., 1967); *Images from Cheng Hsieh*, tape collage (1967); *Sheet Metal* on tape (1967); *Book of the Dead* for winds, percussion (1968); *for several people, together* (1969); *frog pond at dusk* for variable possibilities (1970).

PRINCIPAL WRITINGS: "Blueberry Picking," *The New Music* ed. by Gregory Battcock (New York 1972).

SEE ALSO Texture.

Goleminov, Marin (b. Küstendil, Bulgaria, 28 Sept 1908), studied at the Sofia Conservatory (1927–31, violin with T. Tortchanov), the Schola Cantorum in Paris (1931–34, composition with Vincent d'Indy and Paul Dukas, conducting with M. Labaye), and the Akademie der Tonkunst in Munich (1938–39, composition with Josef Haas, conducting with Hans Knappe). He was a member of the Avramov Quartet during 1935–38. He has conducted throughout eastern Europe and was director of the Sofia National Opera. Since 1947 he has taught composition at the Sofia Conservatory. His work has been influenced by Bulgarian folk music and by his commitment to national socialism.

PRINCIPAL COMPOSITIONS (published by NI unless otherwise noted): *String Quartets Nos. 1, 3, 4, 5* (1934; 1944; 1967, SBK; 1969, SBK); *Loud Gidia* for chorus (1935, 1946); *Nestinarka*, ballet after K. Petkanov (1940); *Nestinarka Suite* for orchestra (1941); *Symphonic Variations on a Theme by D. Christov* (1942); *National Heroes* for chorus (1944); *Stara planina* for chorus (1945); *Wind Quintet No. 2* (1947); *Prelude, Aria, and Toccata* for piano, orchestra (1947, 1954); *5 Sketches* for string quartet (1948); *Haidouk's Love* for voice, piano (1949); *He Feigned* for chorus (1949); *Cello Concerto* (1949–50); *Oak* for voice, piano (1950); *Spring Song* for voice, piano (1950); *The Blackberry* for chorus (1950); *My Love, She Was Weeping* for voice, piano (1952); *Haidouk's Nights* for chorus (1952); *Song* for chorus (1953v); *Iailo*, 3-act opera; libretto by M. Petkanova (1958); *Poem* for orchestra (1959); *You Will Leave Me* for voice, piano (1959); *Concerto* for string quartet, string orchestra (1963); *Symphonies Nos. 1–3*

(1963; 1967; 1970, SBK); *Trio* for oboe, clarinet, bassoon (1964); *Yearning for the Sun* for children's chorus (1965, unpub.); *Small Is My Country* for chorus (1965, unpub.); *Nature,* 5 impressions for high voice, piano (1968, SBK); *Violin Concerto* (1968, unpub.).

PRINCIPAL WRITINGS: *Towards the Source of Bulgarian Musical Composition* (privately published 1937); *Instrumentation* (Sofia 1947); *Problems of Orchestration,* 2nd ed. (Sofia 1966).

Gombau, Gerardo (b. Salamanca, Spain, 3 August 1906), attended the Univ. of Salamanca (1916–23) and the Madrid Conservatory (1920–22; piano with José Balsa and José Tragó, violin with Cecilio Görner, composition with Conrado del Campo). Further work was undertaken in piano with Aroca, Alexander Uninsky, and Andrade de Silva, and in conducting with Del Campo, Pérez Casas, Erich Kleiber, and Sergiu Celibidache. He taught piano at the Salamanca Conservatory during 1935–43, and since 1945 has been on the faculty of the Madrid Conservatory (courses in composition and piano accompaniment). In 1942 he founded the Salamanca Symphony Orchestra, conducting it until 1947, and he has guest-conducted several other European orchestras. Since 1962 he has served as advisor to the Sociedad General de Autores de España and since 1969 has been a member of the Consejo Asesor of the Comisaría General de la Música.

PRINCIPAL COMPOSITIONS: *Don Quijote velando las armas,* symphonic poem (1945); *Apunte bético* for harp (1948, Northern Calif. Harpists' Assoc.); *Sonata para orquesta de cámara* (1952); *Romance del duero* for voice, piano; text by G. Diego (1954, UME); *Calatañazor* for voice, piano; text by Diego (1954, UME); *7 claves de Aragón* for voice, chamber orchestra; text by S. Galindo Herrero (1955); *Cantiga da Vindima* for voice, piano; text by Delgado Gurriarán (1958, UME); *La hortelana del mar* and *El cazador y el leñador* for voice, piano; texts by R. Alberti (1959); *3 piezas de la "Belle Epoque"* for guitar (1959); *Scherzo* for voice, chamber orchestra; text by José Hierro (1960); *No son todos ruiseñores* for voice, clarinet, guitar; text by Góngora (1961); *Música para voces e instrumentos* for chorus, orchestra (1961); *Sonorización heptáfona* for harp (1963); *Texturas y estructuras* for wind quintet (1963); *Tú me levantas, tierra de Castilla* for voice, piano; text by Unamuno (1964); *Dedicatoria* for violin, piano (1966); *Música para 8 ejecutantes* for flute, clarinet, trumpet, trombone, 2 percussionists, viola, cello (1966); *Cantata para la inauguración de una Losa de Ensayo* for vocal soloists, orchestra (1967); *Música 3 + 1* for string quartet (1967); *Experiencias electro-acústicas,* concrete and electronic sounds on tape (1968); *Alea 68* for instrumental ensemble, tape (1968); *Policromía* for 4 saxophones, orchestra (1969); *Ostinati* for piano 6-hands (1969).

PRINCIPAL WRITINGS: "Las *Variaciones* Op. 31 de Schoenberg," *Estafeta literaria* (15 Jan 1960); "Albéniz: las influencias," *ibid.* (1 July 1960); "La *Sonata del Sur* de Oscar Esplá," *ibid.* (15 July 1960); "La *Sonatina para Flauta y Piano* de Pierre Boulez," *ibid.* (15 Jan 1961); "Bajo el signo de la ruptura tonal," *Aulas* (Madrid Servicio de Educación y Cultura) 12 (Feb 1964):24–25; "El piano, Webern y sus *Variaciones* Op. 27," *ibid.* 30–31 (1965):28–30. Gombau has also given numerous lectures and radio talks, including "Stravinsky" (1963), "Los cuartetos de Schoenberg" (1964), "Iannis Xenakis" (1964), "Dos improvisaciones sobre Mallarmé de P. Boulez" (1966), "Jean Barraqué's *Chant aprés chant*" (1967), and "El 'serialismo' francés" (1968).

BIBL.: Antonio Fernández Cid, *Canciones de España* (Madrid 1963); ——, *La música y los músicos españoles en el siglo XX* (Madrid 1963):77; Arthur Custer, "Contemporary Music in Spain," *Musical Quarterly* 48:13–15; ——, "Contemporary Music in Spain," *ibid.* 51:55–56; Manuel Valls-Gorina, *La música española después de Manuel de Falla* (Madrid 1962); Tomás Marco, "G. G.," *Imagen y sonido* 56 (Feb 1968):46–47.

SEE ALSO Spain.

Gonzalo, Gisela Hernandez, see under Hernandez-Gonzalo

Goossens, Eugene (b. London, 26 May 1893; d. London, 13 June 1962), came from a family of conductors and studied at the Royal College of Music (1907–10; violin with Achille Rivarde; composition with Charles Wood, Charles Stanford). He was violinist (1911–15) and assistant conductor (until 1920) with the Queen's Hall Orchestra, after which he formed his own orchestra. During 1923–31 he conducted the Rochester Philharmonic; during 1931–46, the Cincinnati Symphony; and during 1947–56, the Sydney Symphony in Australia. He was director of the New South Wales Conservatory during 1947–56.

PRINCIPAL COMPOSITIONS: *Fantasy* for string quartet, Op. 12 (1915, Chester); *String Quartets Nos. 1–2* (1915, Chester; 1942, Boosey); *Kaleidoscope,* 12 pieces for piano, Op. 18 (1918, Chester); *Philip II,* incidental music to the play by Verhaeren, for chamber orchestra, Op. 22 (1918, Chester); *Piano Quintet,* Op. 23 (1919, Chester); *Silence* for chorus, Op. 31 (1922, Chester); *Sinfonietta,* Op. 34 (1922, Chester); *Oboe Concerto,* Op. 45 (1927, Curwen); *Judith,* 1-act opera, Op. 46; libretto by Arnold Bennett (1927, Chester); *Concertino* for string octet, Op. 47 (1930, Chester); *6 Songs from*

"Chamber Music" for voice, piano, Op. 51; texts by James Joyce (1930, Curwen); *Don Juan de Mañera*, 4-act opera, Op. 54; libretto by Bennett (1930, Chester); *Symphonies Nos. 1–2* (1940, 1942–44; Fischer); *Apocalypse*, oratorio, Op. 64 (1950–54, Boosey).

PRINCIPAL WRITINGS: "Modern Developments in Music," *Proceedings of the Musical Association* (1922):57–76; *Overture and Beginners*, an autobiography (London 1951).

BIBL.: *Canon* (July 1952), a Goossens commemorative issue; "E. G., a Revaluation," *Chesterian* (Jan, April 1954); "The Unconventional Composer," *Music and Musicians* (9 April 1961); J. Carmichael, "Sir E. G.," *ibid.* (28 April 1960); Robert Hull, "E. G.," *Music and Letters* 12:345–53.

Gotovac, Jakov (b. Split, Yugoslavia, 11 Oct 1895), studied music privately in Split (1913–18; composition with Antun Dobronić, Josip Hatze, C. M. Hrazdira) and at the Musikhochschule in Vienna (1920–21; composition with Joseph Marx). He was conductor and chorus master at the Croatian National Theater in Zagreb during 1923–58. His music is nationalistic in orientation and influenced by Russian and Slavic composers.

PRINCIPAL COMPOSITIONS: *2 Anakreontske pjesme* [2 Anacreon Songs] for baritone, piano (1918); *Jadovanka za teletom* [Elegy for a Dead Calf] for chorus (1924, Breitkopf); *Koleda*, a peasant ritual in 5 parts for men's chorus, 3 clarinets, 2 bassoons, timpani (1925, Schott); *Simfonijsko kolo* [Symphonic Reel] for orchestra (1926, Schott); *Dubravka*, pastoral opera (1928); *Morana*, opera (1930, Henschel); *Ero s onoga svijeta* [Ero, the Joker], opera (1935, UE); *Orači* [The Ploughmen] for orchestra (1937, Schott); *Pjemsa i ples sa Balkana* [Balkan Song and Dance] for string orchestra (1939, Schott); *Rizvan-aga* for baritone, orchestra; text by Mažuranić (1939, Schott); *Pjesme cežnuća* [Songs of Desire] for mezzo-soprano, chamber orchestra (1939, Schott); *Guslar* for orchestra (1940, Schott); *Intima*, 5 songs for baritone, piano (1945); *Kamenik* [The Quarry], opera (1946); *Mila Gojsalića* [Mila, the Heroine from Poljiza], opera (1951, DSS); *Zvonimirova ladja* [King Zvonimir's Ship] for chorus (1952); *Gjerdan* [The Necklace], play with music (1955); *Stanac*, opera (1958, DSS); *Dalmaro*, opera (1964); *Peter Svačić*, opera-oratorio (completed 1969).

Gottlieb, Jack (b. New Rochelle, N. Y., 12 Oct 1930), studied with Karol Rathaus, Irving Fine, Aaron Copland, Boris Blacher, and Burrill Phillips, and earned a DMA from the Univ. of Ill. in 1964. He was a vocal conductor while studying at the Univ. of Ill. and

was an assistant to Leonard Bernstein at the New York Philharmonic (1958–66); he is also Bernstein's literary editor. He taught at Loyola Univ. in New Orleans (summer 1966) and at the Institute in Judaic Arts, Warwick, N. Y. (1966–67). In 1970 he became music director of Congregation Temple Israel in St. Louis.

PRINCIPAL COMPOSITIONS: *Hoofprints*, 3 songs for soprano, piano; text by Tennessee Williams (1954; revised 1963); *String Quartet* (1954); *Tea Party*, movement I from *A Symphony of Operas*; text by Horace Everett (1955, Boosey); *Piano Sonata* (1960); *In Memory Of . . .*, cantata for chorus, vocal soloist, organ; text by Moses Ibn Ezra (1960, Boosey); *Twilight Crane*, fantasy for woodwind quintet (1961, Schirmer-G); *Songs of Loneliness* for baritone, piano (strings, percussion, piano); text by Constantine Cavafy (1962); *Public Dance*, movement II from *A Symphony of Operas* (1964); *Shirei ahavah l'Shabbat* [Love Songs for Sabbath], service for cantor, chorus, organ, female speaker, dancers, optional percussion (1965, Presser); *Articles of Faith* for orchestra, voices (1965, Presser); *Now: Golden Gate*, film score for woodwind quintet, percussion, cello (1967); *Haiku Souvenirs*, 5 songs for voice, piano; text by Leonard Bernstein (1967); *Church or Synagogue Psalms* for chorus, organ, 2 flutes, percussion (1967); *The Silent Flickers*, 12 diversions for piano 4-hands (1967); *The Song of Songs, which Is Solomon's*, synagogue opera (1969–); *New Year's Service for Young People* for 2-part chorus, organ (1970). List to 1963: *Composers of the Americas* 9:76–78.

PRINCIPAL WRITINGS: *The Music of Leonard Bernstein: A Study of Melodic Manipulations* (PhD diss., Univ. of Ill., 1964); "Leonard Bernstein. *Kaddish Symphony*," *Perspectives* 4/1:161–75; "A Joyless Noise?", *Conservative Judaism* 22/2:55–72; "The Choral Works of Leonard Bernstein. Reflections of Theater and Liturgy," *American Choral Review* 10:155–77.

Gould, Morton (b. Richmond Hill, N. Y., 10 Dec 1913), began playing the piano and composing at four and soon won acclaim for his ability to improvise. He studied at the Institute of Musical Art in New York at eight; his subsequent studies were with Vincent Jones (composition) and Abby Whiteside (piano). During his teens he frequently appeared as a pianist playing the standard repertory, his own compositions, and improvisations. In 1934 he produced and conducted a series of weekly radio programs for the Mutual Broadcasting System, which were followed in 1943 by a series for the Columbia Broadcasting System. Many of his lighter works were introduced on those programs. In recent years he has combined composing with frequent guest appearances as a conductor of his own and other composers' music.

The bulk of Gould's large output is for orchestra. His theater music includes two Broadway musicals, three motion picture scores, music for a 39-part TV documentary, and two ballets. In addition there are many works for piano, chamber groups, and concert band. In many of the earlier works, popular American music is fused with highly formalized structures: jazz is exploited in such compositions as *Chorale and Fugue in Jazz*, *4 American Symphonettes*, *Derivations*, and *Interplay*. Folklore and folksong influences appear in such pieces as *A Foster Gallery*, *Columbia*, *A Lincoln Legend*, and *Fall River Legend*. In later works Gould has concentrated on abstract as opposed to programmatic or popular works. His style has become more contrapuntal and dissonant, and more complex in its treatment of musical materials. The *Jekyll and Hyde Variations* (1955), *Dialogues* (1956), and *Prisms* (1962) use dodecaphonic procedures. *Venice* (1966) deals with problems of texture and balance arising from the use of two separated orchestras. *Vivaldi Gallery* (1967) incorporates features of 17th-century music, such as its canonic and linear textures and its block-sectional concept of sound. Throughout his career Gould has been a skillful orchestrator, sensitive to color and texture and original in his combinations of instruments. Recordings of Gould's music are extremely numerous and often feature the composer as conductor.

PRINCIPAL COMPOSITIONS: ★ For orchestra: *Chorale and Fugue in Jazz* (1932, Fischer); *Symphonette No. 2* (1936, Mills); *Little Symphony* (1936, Mills); *Piano Concerto* (1937, Mills); *Spirituals* for string choir, orchestra (1937, Mills); *Symphonette No. 3* (1939, Mills); *A Foster Gallery* (1940, Mills); *Latin-American Symphonette* (1940, Mills); *A Lincoln Legend* (1941, Mills); *Symphony No. 1* (1943, Mills); *Interplay* for piano, orchestra (1943, Mills); *Viola Concerto* (1943, Mills); *Viola Concertette* (1943, Mills); *Symphony No. 2* on marching tunes (1943, Mills); *Concerto for Orchestra* (1944, Mills); *Harvest* for vibraphone, harp, strings (1945, G&C and Chappell); *Minstrel Show* (1946, G&C); *Symphony No. 3* (1946, G&C); *Serenade of Carols* (1948, G&C); *Family Album* (1950, G&C); *Dance Variations* for 2 pianos, orchestra (1952, G&C); *Inventions* for 4 pianos, orchestra (1953, G&C); *Jekyll and Hyde Variations* (1955, G&C); *Dialogues* for piano, strings (1956, G&C); *Declaration Suite* (1957, G&C); *Rhythm Gallery* for narrator, orchestra (1958, G&C); *Festive Music* for off-stage trumpet, orchestra (1964, G&C); *Columbia* (1966, G&C); *Venice*, audiograph for two orchestras (1966, G&C); *Vivaldi Gallery* for string quartet, divided orchestra

(1967, G&C); *Troubador Music* for 4 guitars, orchestra (1968, G&C). ★ For concert band: *Jericho* (1939, Mills); *Ballad* (1945, G&C); *Symphony*, "West Point" (1951, G&C); *Santa Fe Saga* (1955, G&C); *Derivations* for clarinet, band (1955, G&C); *St. Lawrence Suite* (1958, G&C); *Prisms* (1962, G&C). ★ Ballet: *Interplay* (1943, Mills); *Fall River Legend* (1947; suite, 1947, G&C). ★ Films: *Delightfully Dangerous* (1944); *Cinerama Holiday* (1954; suite, 1954, G&C); *Windjammer* (1957). ★ Television: *World War I* (1964, for CBS). ★ Musicals: *Billion Dollar Baby* (1944, Chappell); *Arms and the Girl* (1948, Chappell). List to 1958: *Composers of the Americas* 6:70–76.

Sol Berkowitz

SEE ALSO Dance.

Grabovsky, Leonid (Aleksandrovich) (b. Kiev, 28 Jan 1935), studied at the Kiev Conservatory (1954–59; harmony with N. Vilinsky; counterpoint, fugue, composition with L. Revutsky; orchestration, composition with B. Liatoshynsky) and taught there from 1966 to 1968. He has been writing music for various Kiev film studios. The primary influences on his musical development have been Stravinsky, Bartók, Schoenberg, Varèse, Webern, the Polish avant-garde, the ideas of Stockhausen and Xenakis, the music of Cage and Feldman, and the prose scores of George Brecht.

PRINCIPAL COMPOSITIONS: *4 Ukrainian Songs* for chorus, orchestra (1959, Muzyka); *Symphonic Frescos* for orchestra (1961, Ukraine); *Trio* for violin, double bass, piano (1964); *Pasteli* [Pastels] for mezzo-soprano, violin, viola, cello, double bass; text by P. Tychyna (1964); *Iz iaponskikh khokku* [From Japanese Haiku] for tenor, flute, piccolo, bassoon, xylophone (1964); *Konstanty* [Constants] for 4 pianos, 6 percussionists, violin (1964–66); *A Little Chamber Music* for 15 strings (1966); *Homöomorphy I–III* for piano (1968–69); *More* [The Sea] for narrator, chorus, organ, orchestra; text from Saint-John Perse (1968–70); *Vizerunki* [Ornaments] for oboe, viola, harp (1969).

PRINCIPAL WRITINGS: "O moem uchitele," [About My Teacher (B. Liatoshynsky)]," *Sovetskaia muzyka* 1969/2:47–51. Grabovsky also translated into Ukrainian Ernst Krenek's "Zwölfton-Kontrapunkt-Studien," *Ukraïns'ke muzikoznavstro* [Ukrainian Musicology] 1968/4.

BIBL.: Grigorii Golovinsky, "Smelo samobytno," [Boldly, Originally]," *Sovetskaia muzyka* 1962/10: 35–39; Yulii Malishev, "Simfonichni freski L. G.," *Ukraïns'ke muzikoznavstro* 1966/3:113–26.

SEE ALSO Soviet Union.

Graça, Fernando Lopes, see under Lopes-Graça

Grainger, Percy (Aldridge) (George Percy) (b. Brighton, Australia, 8 July 1882; d. White Plains, N. Y., 20 Feb 1961), received formal keyboard instruction from Louis Pabst (Melbourne, 1893–95), James Kwast (Frankfurt, 1895–99), and Ferruccio Busoni (Berlin, two weeks in 1903). He studied composition with Iwan Knorr (Frankfurt, 1895–97, 1899). In 1901 he settled in London and pursued an international concert career. He also collected 500 British folksongs, introducing the use of a wax cylinder phonograph in Britain for this purpose (the *Journal of the Folk-Song Society*, 3/12, contains a portion of his findings). In 1914 he emigrated to the U.S. With Dom Anselm Hughes he edited the series *English Gothic Music* (1936–1950).

Grainger wrote over 400 compositions in almost every medium. His most popular works, those based on folk or borrowed material, are brief, simple in texture, diatonic, and essentially *Gebrauchsmusik* (e.g., *Shepherd's Hey*, 1908–13). His original music (not based on folk or borrowed material) used some compositional techniques that did not gain currency until much later: polytonality (*Gumsucker's March*, 1914), indeterminacy (*Random Round*, 1912–15; see also his article "The Impress of Personality in Unwritten Music," *Musical Quarterly* 1:431–33), microintervals (*Free Music*, 1935), and complex rhythms (*Hill Song No. 1*, 1901–02). *The Warriors* (1913–16) requires three conductors and mallet percussion.

The instrumental compositions exhibit complex rhythms, innovative harmonies, and sweeping countermelodies. Line, texture, and intervals were the main considerations: "I want the music, from first to last, to be ALL THEME and never thematic treatment," he wrote. He possessed unusual facility in choral writing and often accompanied the voices with "large chamber music" (6–24 players). His music is unpretentious and reflects his democratic attitudes and love of nature. The use of unusual orchestral instruments and a penchant for indicating tempo and dynamics with slang terms have perhaps contributed to its neglect, but his wind music has had considerable influence on the development of contemporary band literature.

Grainger's final years, aside from concert tours, were spent in attempts to develop an electronic device that would realize his concept of "free music," i.e., freer rhythms, gliding intervals, and greater dissonance. A museum which he founded in Melbourne in 1935 houses his collection of music and memorabilia; the Library of Congress also has a large Grainger collection.

PRINCIPAL COMPOSITIONS: *Kipling "Jungle Book" Cycle*, 14 pieces for small chorus, chamber orchestra (1898–1945, Schott); *Hill Song No. 1* for chamber orchestra (1901–02; rescored 1921, UE); *British Folk Music Settings*, 43 pieces (1901–50, some unpub., others Fischer, Schirmer-G, Schott); *Irish Tune from County Derry* (1901) for strings (Schott) or band (Fischer) or chorus (Schirmer-G); *Lads of Wamphray* for band (1905, Fischer); *Walking Tune* for woodwind quintet (1905, Schott); *Hill Song No. 2* for 22 winds (1907, Leeds); *English Dance* for orchestra (1906–09, Schirmer-G); *Brigg Fair* for tenor, chorus (1908, Schott); *In a Nutshell Suite* for orchestra, piano, Deagan percussion instruments (1908–16, Schirmer-G); *Colonial Song* (1911–12) for 3 strings, harp, orchestra (Schott) or band, 2 optional voices (Fischer); *My Robin Is to the Greenwood Gone* for 8 instruments or solo piano or violin, cello, piano (1912, Schott); *Children's March* for piano, band (1913–16, Schirmer-G); *The Warriors* for orchestra, 3 pianos (1913–16, Schott); *The Marching Song of Democracy* for organ, chorus, orchestra (1915–16, Schott and UE) or band, chorus (1948, Schott, UE); *Danish Folk Music Settings*, 13 pieces (1922–46, Schirmer-G); *Free Music* for string quartet (1935); *Lincolnshire Posy* for band (1937, Schott); *English Gothic Music*, 13 pieces for chorus, optional organ and instruments (1936–50, Schirmer-G).

PRINCIPAL WRITINGS (in addition to those already cited): "Arnold Dolmetsch: Musical Confucius," *Musical Quarterly* 19:187–98; *Music: A Commonsense View of All Types* (Melbourne 1934); "Foreword," *The Band's Music* by Richard Franko Goldman (New York 1938); "Culturizing Possibilities of the Instrumentally Supplemented A Cappella Choir," *Musical Quarterly* 27:160–64; "The Specialist and the All-Round Man," *A Birthday Offering* ed. by Gustave Reese (New York 1943); "About Delius," *Frederick Delius* by Peter Warlock (New York 1952).

BIBL.: Thomas Armstrong, "The Frankfort Group," *Proceedings of the Musical Association* 85:1–16; Richard Franko Goldman, "P. G.'s 'Free Music'," *Juilliard Review* 2:37–47; Charles W. Hughes, "P. G., Cosmopolitan Composer," *Musical Quarterly* 23:127–36; D. C. Parker, *P. A. G.: A Study* (New York 1918); Cyril Scott, "P. G., The Music and the Man," *Musical Quarterly* 2:425–33; Thomas C. Slattery, *The Wind Music of P. A. G.* (PhD diss., Univ. of Iowa, 1967).

Thomas C. Slattery

Gramophone see Recording

Granados (y Campiña), **Enrique** (b. Lérida, Spain, 27 July 1867; d. on board a ship in the English Channel, 24 March 1916), studied at the Barcelona Conservatory (c.1883–87; composition with Felipe Pedrell, piano with Francisco Jurnet, Joan Baptista Pujol) and privately in Paris during 1887–89 with

Charles Bériot. In 1900 he established a piano institute, the Academia Granados. He also concertized in Europe and the U.S. as a pianist and conductor.

PRINCIPAL COMPOSITIONS (many dates unavailable): *12 Spanish Dances* for piano (1892, UME); *María del Carmen*, 3-act opera; libretto by José Feliú y Codina (premiere 1898); *Goyescas, or Los majos enamorados* for piano (1911, International); *Goyescas*, 2-act opera; libretto by Fernando Periquet y Zuaznabar (premiere 1916, Schirmer-G); *6 Pieces on Popular Spanish Songs* for piano (UME); *Allegro de concierto* for piano (UME); *4 Tonadillas en estilo antiguo* for voice, piano (UME); *7 Canciones amatorias* for voice, piano (UME); *Intermezzo from Goyescas* for orchestra (1911); *Violin Sonata*; *Valses poéticos* for piano (UME).

BIBL.: G. Jean Aubry, "E. G.," *Musical Times* (1 Dec 1916); Antonio Fernandez Cid, *G.* (Madrid 1956); Henri Collet, *Albeniz et G.* (Paris 1926); Ann Livermore, "G. and the 19th Century in Spain," *Music Review* 7:80–87; E. L. Mason, "E. G.," *Music and Letters* 14:231–38; *Revista musical catalana*, memorial issue (15 June 1916).

[prepared with the help of Antonio Carreras]

de Grandis, Renato (b. Venice, 24 Oct 1927), studied at the Cesare Pollini Conservatory in Padua (1942–50), the Benedetto Marcello Conservatory in Venice (1950–51; composition with Gian Francesco Malipiero, Sante Zanon; conducting with Nino Sanzogno), the Accademia Musicale Chigiana in Siena (1951–54, conducting with Paul van Kempen), and at the Darmstadt summer courses (1959–61). He is a free-lance composer, writer on music, and teacher of composition and currently lives in Darmstadt. His music has been influenced by his study of 17th- and 18th-century music (including that of his ancestors Vincenzo and Pietro Francesco de Grandis) and of advanced techniques, particularly those of John Cage.

PRINCIPAL COMPOSITIONS: *La fanciulla del lago*, 1-act mimodrama for mime, orchestra (1949); *6 Piano Sonatas* (1952–58); *Il gave* and *Il pastore*, 1-act operas (1953–54); *Il cieco di Hyuga*, noh-play in 1 act for vocal soloists, chorus, flute, celesta, harp, harpsichord, double bass, 3 percussionists (1959, Tonos); *La comedia veneziana*, cantata for soprano, bass, chorus, harmonica, mandolin, piano, double bass, percussion (1960, 1969; Schott); *Study* for flute, piano (1960, Tonos); *Cadòre* for orchestra (1961–62, Bärenreiter); *Canti sulle pause* for tenor saxophone, trombone, violin, celesta, vibraphone, percussion (1961, Tonos); *Gloria al re*, 3-act opera farce (1962, Gerig); *Virelai* for clarinet, harmonica, harp, celesta, harpsichord, double bass, percussion (1964) or violin, viola, cello, harp, celesta, harpsichord, percussion (1966); *Toccata a doppio coro*

figurato for 2 pianos (1965, Gerig); *Storia marina*, cantata for vocal soloists, double chorus, orchestra (1966); *3 Canzoni da battello* for soprano, oboe, horn, celesta, harp, piano, strings (1966–67, Gerig); *Salterio popolare*, 35 songs for voice, piano (1967–68, Tonos); *Gloria* and *Sanctus* for chorus (1968); *Cantata ciozota* for soprano, flute, mandolin, harp (1968); *La Rossiniana*, divertimento for orchestra (1968, Tonos; adapted for ballet 1969); *5 Toccatas* for piano (1968, 1969; Tonos); *Serenades Nos. 2–3*: No. 3 for tenor, flute, 2 keyboard instruments, double bass, percussion (1969); No. 2 for cello (1970); *Feste sull'acqua*, suite for orchestra (1970, Schott).

PRINCIPAL WRITINGS: "Musik in Hannover zur Leibnizzeit," *Leibniz* (Hanover 1966):117–27; "Über das Wesen der Oper," *Lob der Provinz* (Darmstadt 1967):389–94; "Musiktheater heute," "Monteverdi," "Rossini," 3 conferences broadcast by the Hessischer Rundfunk, Frankfurt (1965, 67, 68).

BIBL.: A. Fichera, "*Der Blinde von Hyuga*," "R. de G.," program book of the Bonn State Theater (April 1969); Helmut Haack, "Einige Bemerkungen zu R. de G.'s *Rossiniana*," program book of the Würtemberg State Theater, Stuttgart (Oct 1970); Wulf Konold, "Der Weg des R. de G. zu einer neuen Kantabilität," *Melos* 38:1–6. Articles on individual works have appeared in *Melos* (1967/9, 1969/9, 1970/5) and *Opera* (July 1969).

Graphic Notation (Graphics), drawn visual analogs used to communicate a composer's intentions with regard to the sounds and textures he wants in a piece of music or to suggest the outlines or conditions within which a performance may occur. The earliest example of a graphic score seems to have been *Projections* (1950–51) by Morton Feldman.

SEE ALSO Notation.

Great Britain. In 1900 England was truly a land without music. The situation is exemplified by Edward *Elgar (1857–1934): he had already proved his genius with the concert overture *Froissart* (1890) and the *Enigma Variations* (1898–99), but the indigenous pundits were either repelled or merely uninterested, and it was left to Richard Strauss and north Germany to draw England's attention to its remarkable and indeed unique inventor of music.

During the first half of the century the teaching of music and associated disciplines (history, appreciation, etc.) remained almost universally outdated and often incompetent. The main centers of teaching were the Royal

College of Music, the Royal Academy of Music, Trinity College London, the Royal Manchester College of Music, and several of the universities, notably Oxford, Cambridge, and Durham. The universities paid most attention to academic aspects and theory generally while the other establishments concentrated mainly on practical musicmaking. Very few teachers knew or understood any music later than Brahms, nor for the most part did they make any effort to do so. In the late 1930s most English students were still being taught what their predecessors had been taught in 1900 with the result that Bartók and Stravinsky were practically unknown and members of a student orchestra at the Royal College could and did rehearse a Brahms symphony without knowing or taking the trouble to find out which of the four it was.

It is equally uninspiring to survey the professional concert scene at the beginning of the century. Standards of performance appear to have been inconsistent and mostly lamentable. Sir Henry Wood (1869–1944), along with the Promenade Concerts and the New Queen's Hall Orchestra, both in London, made by far the most substantial and consistent effort to bring about an improvement. Later the formation of the BBC Symphony in 1931 with Sir Adrian Boult (b. 1889) as its permanent conductor, the creation of the London Philharmonic in 1932 by Sir Thomas Beecham (1879–1961), and Toscanini's guest appearances with the BBC Orchestra brought to London a standard of professional performance previously unknown in the country. The little significant activity that took place outside London included the various regional orchestras of the BBC, Glyndebourne from 1934 to 1939, and the Halle Orchestra, which at times presented some of the famous international artists of the period. In the autumn of 1939, in the space of a few weeks, all that had been achieved was jettisoned in what now seems to have been near panic. With the exception of the phoenix-like Halle Orchestra under Sir John Barbirolli (1899–1970), professional music had reached a new, possibly all-time low by 1945. Queen's Hall had been destroyed in 1941, orchestras decimated or disbanded, and teaching establishments mostly stripped to the bone of any kind of talent. Indeed, it looked for a time like the end of the road.

Of the composers who represented the best in English music before 1945, Elgar was of course the commanding international figure. His purely musical sensitivity has yet to be matched by any English composer. A charac-teristic reluctance to reveal his innermost feelings sometimes led to bursts of grandiose and bombastic orchestral cover for what he believed his audience should have to work to understand. Frederick *Delius (1862–1934) contributed a subtle imagination conditioned by his European parentage and his aversion to petty, parochial triviality. He had the good fortune to attract the services of Beecham and to a lesser extent Barbirolli as interpreters. Much of his music is nostalgic and literally out of this world, but the forthright character of the first *Dance Rhapsody* and the relentless vigor of the first movement of *A Mass of Life* show the reverse of the coin. Gustav *Holst (1874–1934) is the only other English composer of the early period for whom international stature can be claimed. His style was individual, eclectic, and often aloof, and his personality seems often to withdraw, leaving the listener with an enigma which, however, can at times fascinate. Of his comparatively small output, only *The Planets* is regularly performed today.

Ralph *Vaughan Williams (1872–1958) came to be idolized by much of the English musical establishment during the last 25 years of his life; perhaps they recognized in his music a reflection of their own parochial derivations and tendencies. Little of Vaughan Williams's work has thrived on the international scene. The *Symphonies 4–6*, with their sturdy and forthright, if at times unimaginative and inflexible, idiom indicate what he might have become had he emancipated himself from the influence of folklore and those inhibitions which so often are the bane of British artists. Arnold *Bax (1883–1953) was an industrious composer who left seven symphonies as the foundation of a large miscellaneous output; hardly any of this music figures in public programs, however. He called himself a "brazen romantic" and regarded his music as the expression of emotional states, which of course is now out of line with fashion. John *Ireland (1879–1962) studied composition under C. V. Stanford, from whom he acquired the traditional technical foundation of the period. He wrote mostly in the smaller forms and was primarily a miniaturist. William *Walton (b. 1902) put himself in the forefront of English composers at age 27 with his *Viola Concerto*. He has always been a slow worker, and his output has remained comparatively small. Edmund *Rubbra (b. 1901) was born of poor working-class parents in Northampton and had no background of privilege or wealth from which to launch himself. In 1916 he organized a concert of works by

Cyril Scott (1879–1971), which encouraged the older composer to propose lessons, a turning point in Rubbra's career. Three tough, cogent symphonies in three years (1936–39), together with an effective orchestration of the Brahms-Handel *Variations*, set a high standard that has subsequently varied little.

It is perhaps typical of the English musical tradition that from among the various composers discussed, no typical national style of composition can be formulated. Delius and Holst had the common factor of a German background, but otherwise we have here a collection of individuals who cannot be welded into a community. Ireland, faithfully reproducing Stanford's voice, is the closest to being a true "establishment" figure. With the partial exceptions of Alan *Rawsthorne (b. 1905–71), Michael *Tippett (b. 1905), Benjamin *Britten (b. 1913), and Walton as a young man, none of the older-generation composers classifies technically as a progressive, though the emotional depths plumbed by Elgar at his best have for this writer no parallel in any other music. (Only Walton seems to have absorbed any Elgarian characteristics.)

Geoffrey Sharp

SINCE 1945. The end of World War II, almost coinciding with the production in London of Benjamin Britten's first opera *Peter Grimes* (June 1945), heralded a new era in British music, which was naturally fostered by the return to normal conditions of musical life. Hitherto the revival in English music, which had begun half a century before with Elgar, had made little impact elsewhere though it had aroused much interest in Britain itself. Elgar, Delius, Holst, and Walton had won only limited acceptance outside Britain, Vaughan Williams (the dominant figure between the world wars) even less. Now, almost overnight, Britten established himself as a composer of world significance and placed his country on the international operatic map for the first time. His ability to create music drama from a wide range of situations, his musical invention, and his technical resource were confirmed in the operas that followed and in his large output in other, chiefly vocal, media. He is still the dominant figure in British music.

Of the composers who have followed Britten's operatic lead, the most striking is Michael *Tippett (b. 1905). His style (nurtured by such varied influences as the Elizabethan madrigal, Purcell, the Negro spiritual, Stravinsky, and Hindemith) was already evident in the *Concerto for Double String Orchestra* (1938–39), the oratorio *A Child of our Time* (1939–41),

and three string quartets. His operas are musically rich but theatrically less accessible than Britten's, owing chiefly to the intellectual concentration of the libretti, all written by the composer. His three symphonies (1944–71), *Piano Concerto* (1953–55), and *Concerto for Orchestra* (1962–63) also reveal a melodic profusion, rhythmic vitality, and textural complexity.

Modern British composers, steeped like their predecessors in a long and rich literary tradition, have done much of their best work in the vocal media. Alan *Rawsthorne (1905–71) stood slightly apart from his colleagues in his preference for the instrumental media. Most noteworthy are his three symphonies (1950–64), *Piano Concerto No. 2* (1951), which is among the best British works in this medium, and chamber music. A composer whose development owed much to foreign influence is Lennox *Berkeley (b. 1903), who studied in Paris with Nadia Boulanger. Humphrey *Searle (b. 1915) and Peter Racine *Fricker (b. 1920) were among the earliest British composers to adopt the serial idiom; their music forms a link between Britten and Tippett and the younger generation.

Although the country's musical institutions have yet to respond to a corresponding degree, the last 25 years are most noteworthy for the abundance of varied musical talent that has emerged. The first attempts to bring the country to an awareness of what was happening on the European continent were made by the postwar wave of Schoenberg enthusiasts such as Erwin Stein, Matyas Seiber, and Hans Keller. Seiber (1905–60) was an influential teacher at Morley College in London, while Keller still works at the BBC and as a freelance lecturer and writer. Morley College has always been the home of the liveliest institutionalized composition teaching in London. Seiber, Tippett, Fricker, and Alexander *Goehr (b. 1932) all taught there, and the course is now being run by Cornelius *Cardew (b. 1936). Some colleges and universities are developing music faculties along American lines with artists and ensembles in residence and rudimentary electronic studios. The most advanced in all respects is York Univ., run by the composer and teacher Wilfrid *Mellers (b. 1914), followed closely by the universities of Southampton, East Anglia, and Cardiff. The institutionalized teaching of new music is perhaps best developed at the primary-school level. Many composers, for example Peter *Maxwell Davies (b. 1934), David *Bedford (b. 1937), George Self (b. 1936), Brian *Dennis (b. 1941), and Elis *Pehkonen (b. 1942), have contributed and gained much in school jobs. More important than any single indigenous institution have been the personalities of the distinguished continental teachers and composers (Petrassi, Messiaen, Stockhausen, Berio, Nono, and Maderna, among others) to whom British composers have flocked or who have visited the Dartington Summer School of Music, which used to be a powerhouse of new ideas and creative activity. More recently important figures such as Babbitt and Pousseur have been attracted by the new Composers' Weekends organized in London by the Society for the Promotion of New Music.

The Royal College of Music and Goldsmiths' College, both in London, are developing electronic facilities, but the largest and most sophisticated studio is located in a living-room in southwest London. This belongs to Peter Zinovieff (b. 1933), who together with the electronic composer Tristram *Cary (b. 1925) has formed Electronic Music Studios Ltd., which produces a wide range of equipment. This company is something of an oasis, however, for nowhere in Britain is there a studio comparable to those in Cologne, Paris, Warsaw, or New York. The large resources of the BBC's long-established Radiophonic Workshop are reserved for the production of incidental music and sound effects for television and radio. For these reasons, the most important single group of composers to emerge since the war, the so-called Manchester school of Harrison *Birtwistle (b. 1934), Goehr, and Maxwell Davies has, unlike its counterparts in most other countries, had little to do with electronics.

The situation of the composer today is clearly better than it was earlier in the century, but with few exceptions no younger composer lives from composition alone. Teaching is the most common means of livelihood. Some composers hold BBC production posts, some (about three at any one time) are composers-in-residence at a university or college, some work in publishing, writing, and criticism, while a few earn very good incomes by composing for films and television. The main channels of musical communication connecting Britain with the European continent and the Americas tend to work well in one direction only. The music of Britten, Tippett, Walton, and Bennett is certainly widely known, but most of the world seems largely unaware that experimental and avant-garde activity exists in England. An important reason for this is financial. Whereas the BBC can play tapes from continental stations gratis, a continental station wishing to play a BBC tape must, in accordance with a musicians' union ruling, pay a full fee to all players involved in the recording.

Performances are more frequent and prompt than previously. The BBC began to play an important role in this regard when the Tuesday Invitation Concerts were begun in 1959 by William Glock (b. 1908). By dint of his catholicity of taste and untiring effort, he has done more than any other single person to break down the insularity which still bedevils British taste and attitudes. Glock was also responsible for developing the BBC's summer Promenade Concerts, in which a good deal of recent music is played to huge audiences, for directing the Dartington Summer School, and for editing the short-lived periodical *The Score*. (*Tempo*, published by Boosey & Hawkes, is now the only magazine in Britain devoted to new music.) The development of new music is in general hampered by a lack of money among the promotional organizations, despite government subsidies. This is the main reason why electronic and mixed-media music has not flourished. The Music Now organization in London fights on, promoting mixed-media events by Cardew, the Scratch Orchestra, and such visitors as Sun Ra and the Sonic Arts Union of New York. Music theater has been sponsored by the under-financed Focus Opera Group, which has mounted Ligeti's *Aventures*, Kagel's *Sur scène*, and Cardew's *Schooltime Compositions*. Operatic resources, though abundant in terms of singers and players, have until now been reserved for the relatively conventional works of Richard Rodney *Bennett (b. 1936), Malcolm *Williamson (b. 1931), and Nicholas *Maw (b. 1935), none of which makes extraordinary demands on a house equipped for romantic opera. Maxwell Davies's challenging *Taverner* (completed 1970) has had to wait years for the promise of a production at Covent Garden (which came from the new directors Colin Davis and Peter Hall), while the three recent operas of Elizabeth *Lutyens (b. 1906) are still not being produced. Chamber opera fares better, as evidenced by the most recent operatic essays of Benjamin *Britten (b. 1913) and by Birtwistle's two works in the genre. And German opera houses have proved enterprising; Hamburg has produced Goehr's *Arden muss sterben* and the *Hamlet* of Humphrey *Searle (b. 1915), later produced at Covent Garden, and Cassel has produced *The Scene Machine* by Anthony *Gilbert (b. 1934).

Festivals continue to proliferate all over the British Isles, but few have a distinctive character and few are a force in new music. The most significant in this regard is the English

Bach Festival (founded 1962), which has regularly featured a high proportion of important contemporary music. Its visitors have included Messiaen, Barraqué, Stockhausen, Amy, and Xenakis. The Aldeburgh Festival (1946) is primarily a platform for its founder, Benjamin Britten, and a focus for virtuoso performers from all over the world. The Cheltenham Festival (1945) has become identified with the music, often symphonic, of conservative composers such as Fricker, Searle, Edmund *Rubbra (b. 1901), and Robert Simpson (b. 1921).

The most interesting concerts in recent years have been given by small groups organized to play music under the composer's direction. Consciously or not, they have sometimes achieved something of the atmosphere and spontaneity of environmental rock concerts, which for the past six years have been an exciting feature of the contemporary music scene. Certainly there has been a new attempt in concert music to exploit the theatricality of such musicmaking. Successful in this regard have been the Pierrot Players (founded 1967 and now called The Fires of London) of Maxwell Davies and Birtwistle and the Music Theatre Ensemble (1967) of Goehr. In 1965 Cardew joined a free improvisation group, AMM, and in 1969, together with Michael *Parsons (b. 1938) and Howard *Skempton (b. 1947), he formed the Scratch Orchestra, now 80 strong. This amorphous anti-orchestra meets regularly to play, plan, and improvise for audiences or for their own enjoyment, in town halls, in the open air, on public transport, etc. The results are often incoherent but they constantly provoke thought about concerts and the social role of musicmaking. The orchestra's vitality is evident in the fact that it has already spawned offspring: the Promenade Theatre Orchestra of John White (b. 1936) and Christopher *Hobbs (b. 1950), which has returned to strictly notated scores played on toy and mechanical instruments; the Private Company of Michael *Chant (b. 1945); and the Wood and Metal Band of Hugh *Shrapnel (b. 1947). Intermodulation, founded 1970 by Roger Smalley (b. 1943) and myself (b. 1943), and The Gentle Fire, founded 1968 by Hugh *Davies (b. 1943) and Richard Orton (b. 1940), both perform live electronic compositions by their members, by Stockhausen, and by the American avant-garde.

Almost every stylistic trend in contemporary music has been reflected in British works since the war. Although British music has not instigated any developments and although the general tendency among composers is to tone down influences from outside, this is not to deny the high quality of much of the work done within the received idioms. The conservative wing of British composers is tonality bound. It is represented by the symphonies of Simpson and Rubbra, the operas of Alan *Bush (b. 1900), and the cantatas of Anthony *Milner (b. 1925). Significantly less dogmatic in regard to tonality is the sparse idiom of Britten's late music. Michael Tippett's rate of development continues to increase as he grows older. The toughening of his idiom in the warlike *King Priam* (1958–61) has been succeeded by its concentration in the psychological kaleidoscope of *The Knot Garden* (1967–70). Roberto *Gerhard (1896–1970) likewise became gradually less derivative and more questing as he grew older, as evidenced in his *Concerto for Orchestra* (1965) and *Symphony No. 4* (1967). A more orthodox post-Schoenberg serial language has been cultivated by Lutyens, who has written in every conceivable genre, and by Searle, primarily in symphonies and operas. Perhaps as a reaction to orthodox serialism, four younger composers, Bennett, Maw, Williamson, and Thea *Musgrave (b. 1928)—who should not be thought of as a "group"—have developed free, pragmatic idioms in which tonal structures often play a basic role. A younger composer of roughly this same orientation is John *Tavener (b. 1944), whose flair for drama and color is apparent in music bearing the marked imprint of Messiaen, Stravinsky, and the Polish school. Maxwell Davies, Birtwistle, and Goehr have all evolved highly individual techniques, the most individual being that of Maxwell Davies. Medieval and renaissance procedures (cantus firmus, troping, parodying, etc.) pervade even his early music, and recent works contain extraneous stylistic references of all kinds. His techniques had an early influence on Smalley, who uses renaissance material in his own *Missa brevis* (1967) and then reworks his own transformation of the material in the *Missa parodia I–II*. As indicated above, Smalley's interest has turned to live electronics and controlled improvisation, as in his *Pulses* (1969) for brass and percussion.

Tim Souster

SEE ALSO Electronic Music: History and Development, Opera.

Greece. In 1830 Greece gained independence from the Turks, whose rule for three and a half centuries had inhibited the growth of hellenism in every cultural field. By then the only forms of music known in Greece were Byzantine chant, with its characteristic modes and rhythms, and folk music, with quasi-modal scales, distinctive five- and seven-beat rhythms, and numerous native instruments (violin; sandoúri, a kind of dulcimer; lute; líra, a kind of fiddle; clarino, a clarinet; zournas, a kind of oboe; flutes; bagpipes; etc.). The only part of Greece to avoid the Turkish yoke, the Ionian Islands in the west, had been occupied by the Venetians (1386–1797), French (1797–1814), and English (1814–64). The islands had always been in close touch with Italy, which influenced Ionian folk music, and there, in the 19th century, emerged the first group of Greek composers, the so-called Ionian School. These composers were educated in Italy and left mostly operas in Italian styles. The most important of those who lived into the 20th century were Spiro Samaras (1861–1917), whose operas were successful in Italy, and Dionyssios Lavrangas (1860–1941), founder of what was replaced by the State Opera (1939). After 1840 Italian opera groups began visiting Athens and later other cities, and the lasting significance of the Ionian School is that it did much to introduce Western music to the rest of Greece. In 1871 the teaching of music, which had been private, was undertaken by the Athens Hodeion [School of Music], now a semigovernmental institution. There music instruction was put on a methodical and professional basis for the first time in Greece, and the students formed an orchestra that has given public concerts since 1893 and has finally developed (1942) into the so-called Athens State Orchestra.

The main musical centers today are Athens (about 2.5 million residents) and Salonica in the north (about 545,000). Of the four major educational institutions, three are in Athens (with branches in most of the important provincial towns): the Athens School of Music; the Hellenic School of Music, established 1899; and the National School of Music, founded in 1926 by Manolis Kalomiris, the father figure in Greek music. In spite of their names, the last two institutions are private. The Salonica State School of Music, founded 1915, is the only Greek institution of this kind fully subsidized by the state. Salonica is also the home of the Macedonian School of Music, founded 1926. These schools do not always take modern or avant-garde techniques into consideration, so that talented young composers and performers must continue their studies abroad, often with the help of state, private, or foreign scholarships.

Dimitri Mitropoulos (1896–1960) conducted the present Athens State Orchestra during 1927–39, but after the war the programing and performances deteriorated. The orchestra shares its musicians with the Radio Symphony Orchestra, founded 1938 almost exclusively for broadcasting, or the opera orchestra. It gives about 35 concerts a year and makes some effort to present all trends in Greek music, including (sporadically) advanced ones. The Salonica State Orchestra (founded 1959) gives 30 concerts a year and plays from the traditional repertory. Since 1955 the National Tourist Organization has sponsored the summer Athens Festival (one and a half to two months long), which is held in the open-air Roman theater under the Acropolis. The Festival favors music above all the arts and has greatly contributed to raising public taste by acquainting Greek listeners with the highest international standards in symphonic and chamber music, opera, and ballet. The Festival has occasionally programed Greek and foreign avant-garde music and dance, but in recent years only established cultural values have been favored.

The National Broadcasting agency (founded 1937) has helped spread Western concert music in Greece, and since 1954 the third program broadcasts five to six hours of concert music every day. The television stations (founded 1967) are still developing from an experimental stage. Up to now the publishing of scores (or recordings) has been limited. In 1948–52 the French Institute in Athens printed a few works by composers of the older generation. During the mid-50s to mid-60s the Ministry of Education published a fairly wide ranging selection of works by Greeks. More recently avant-garde Greek composers have been published by foreign companies: Universal Edition (Skalkottas), Gerig, Edition Modern, Boosey & Hawkes (Xenakis), Chester (Christou), Bärenreiter (Antoniou), among others.

The circumstances outlined above provided the understructure for the so-called Greek "national school" of composers, whose activities covered roughly the first half of the century. Though never widely known abroad, the output of this school has had considerable impact at home. Manolis *Kalomiris (1883–1962), often regarded as the founder of the school, left 14 textbooks and 222 opuses. His whole output was based on the folklore of modern hellenism. His veneration of folk music helped principally to enrich his melodic lines. Moving between Wagnerism and the 19th-century Russian school, he attained, especially in his orchestral scores, a style characterized by thick polyphonic textures, colorful orchestration, and an exuberant, overwhelming sense of dramatic impact and melodic pathos. Mario *Varvoglis (1885–1967), who studied at the Paris Conservatory and with Vincent d'Indy, combined folk-derived melodic material with a French taste for balance, clarity of texture and form, and harmonic precision, often imbued with a gentle poetic or pastoral feeling. Emilio *Riadis (1886–1935), from Salonica, was a disciple of Ravel and Charpentier and is known mainly for his songs. Set to modern Greek (including his own) and sometimes French verses, they have folk-derived vocal lines and inventive piano accompaniments in which exquisite arabesques bathe the listener in a dreamy atmosphere of Oriental sensualism. The last widely known member of the National School is Petro *Petridis (b. 1892). He turned not only to folklore but, even more than Kalomiris, to Byzantine chant and the medieval modes. A French critic once noted that "his solid counterpoint leaves a strange sense of classicism, which his frequent and cleverly calculated harmonic daring does not disturb."

The transition from nationalism to more recent trends is represented in the work of Mitropoulos and Nikos *Skalkottas (1904–49). Mitropoulos left few works, and they have been overshadowed by his fame as a conductor. He was the first Greek composer, however, to use post-Debussy techniques, at least in some of his compositions. Skalkottas, a student of Schoenberg during 1927–31, was the first 12-tone composer in Greece (although this became known only after his death). From 1933 on he lived in isolation in Athens unaware of subsequent developments in music. After 1938 he shifted toward a free atonal style and seemed almost to be reinventing music for himself. With great insight he combined 12-tone and atonal melodic structures with traditional metrical rhythms and forms. There is now an archives of Skalkottas's manuscripts in Athens, and as additional works are brought to light he emerges as perhaps Greece's greatest composer.

Just after World War II what was wrongly considered a second Greek national school seemed to be forming, represented by Manos Hadjidakis (b. 1925), Mikis Theodorakis (b. 1925), and to a lesser degree Arghyris *Kounadis (b. 1924). They turned to an urban folksong type, the *rebetiko* (scorned until then by serious composers), and also wrote successfully for dance, encouraged by the Helleniko Hereodrama, a private dance group founded in 1950 by Mrs. Rallou Manou that commissions young composers. The main legacy of this group of composers has been in the popular field (such as the Broadway musical *Ilya Darling* and the films *Never on Sunday* and *Zorba the Greek*). In other ways this kind of music has been eclipsed by more recent developments.

SINCE 1960. Through private initiatives several conditions arose in the 1960s that benefited new Greek music. The musicologist John G. Papaioannou was already giving many lectures on Skalkottas and on modern music, thereby helping to prepare a public for new music. In 1962 he and the German composer Günter *Becker founded the Studio for New Music at the Athens Goethe Institute, which has since organized 45 concerts in which more than 20 Greek works have been premiered. Also in 1962 Hadjidakis financed a competition for young composers at the Athens Technological Institute. This competition brought to public attention many young composers, some of whom were living abroad: Xenakis, Logothetis, Nikos Mamangakis (b. 1929), Antoniou, Ioannidis, Tsouyopoulos, and others. Since 1963 many contemporary Greek works have been performed at the English Bach Festival, held in Oxford and London and run by the Greek harpsichordist Lina Lalandi. In 1964–67 Hadjidakis founded, trained, and directed the Experimental Orchestra of Athens, which was supported for a while by the city itself. This ensemble participated in three Athens Festivals (1964–66), and although it was short-lived (it gave less than 20 concerts) it premiered at least 15 Greek works. The Hellenic Association for Contemporary Music (HACM) was founded in 1965 in cooperation with the Greek section of ISCM. It organized three Hellenic Weeks for Contemporary Music (1966, 1967, 1968) under the aegis of the National Tourist Organization and, in 1971, the Ford Foundation. Forty Greek works were presented, 21 of which had been composed or commissioned for the festivals. In 1967 Antoniou founded the Hellenic Group for Contemporary Music, an ensemble that has given 20 concerts of advanced and experimental works, 80 percent Greek or world premieres. In Salonica the Univ. of Salonica Chamber Choir and Instrumental Ensemble often includes 20th-century music in its concerts. Its director since 1958 has been Yannis Mandakas, who since 1965 has also been co-director (with Uwe Martin) of the Studio for New Art at the Salonica Goethe Institute. This studio has organized concerts with German ensembles and some Greek soloists, presenting music ranging from Schoenberg to Stockhausen and Josef-Anton Riedl.

In spite of these favorable conditions, it is still difficult for a composer to earn his living in Greece. He can teach, of course, and there are opportunities to compose stage music (mostly for ancient tragedies) or film scores, or he may devote some of his time to writing popular music. Commissions from the various institutions and festivals in Greece are not numerous. Most composers live abroad, some dividing their activities between Greece and their adopted home.

The most active composers of the newest Greek music share a tendency to immediately assimilate and recast whatever the changing image of world music offers. Parallel with this is each composer's personal concern with novelty and originality, a concern that is often fruitful. Yannis *Papaïoannou (b. 1910), president of HACM, has taught many of the composers cited below and is the only teacher of 12-tone and serial techniques in Greece. Combining arresting melodies with formal balance, he has passed from nationalism toward neoclassicism, atonal harmony, and 12-tone procedures. Lately he has explored a style of archaic austerity in which eerie polyphonic webs produce a kind of pointillism. Equally smooth has been the transition of Yorgo *Sicilianos (b. 1922) from neoclassicism in the 1950s to serialism in the 60s. Dimitri *Dragatakis (b. 1914), self-initiated in contemporary idioms, started from a Shostakovich-like neoclassicism and gradually developed toward a free atonal style in which shrewdly calculated effects often stem from a sense of drama and contrast. Anestis *Logothetis (b. 1921), who lives in Vienna, is working with graphic notation of various kinds. Arghyris Kounadis, director at the Musikhochschule in Freiberg, has used both serial and aleatory procedures.

The early death of Yannis *Christou (1926–70) robbed Greece of a major musician. His early (serial) compositions revealed an unusually acute capacity for allowing musical materials to generate forms: musical cells proliferate, giving birth to living organisms of sound. Later his wide philosophical learning, his studes of ancient and oriental cultures, and his interest in psychoanalysis led him to regard his music as a means for releasing psychic energy, of setting free the most primeval emotions. This exploration culminated in a series of awe-inspiring stage rites, akin to psychodramas. Michael *Adamis (b. 1929) has a small electronic studio in Athens; his earlier works were 12-tone. Yannis *Ioannidis (b. 1930) is a thoughtful, mature artist now living in Caracas. George *Tsouyopoulos (b. 1930), who lives in Munich, is little known in

Greece; he has sometimes ornamented serial approaches with quotations from traditional music. Theodore *Antoniou (b. 1935) has sought to organize the avant-garde sound of the 1960s into clearcut forms. An ever-present element of archaic, ageless melody, sharply contrasting with the surrounding, rough-sounding material, gives his works a sense of human dignity. Georges *Apergis (b. 1945), now living in Paris, has an extremely musical nature; his music blends disparate materials to produce vividly colorful results. Two other composers who live in Paris, Yorgo Kouroupos (b. 1942, a disciple of Olivier Messiaen) and Kyriakos Sfetsas (b. 1945, a disciple of Max Deutsch), had important works presented at the 1971 Hellenic Week for Contemporary Music. These composers, together with a third newcomer to the festival, Stephanos Vassiliadis (b. 1933, a disciple of Yannis Papaïoannou), will probably gain wider attention in the years to come. (We have not dealt here with Iannis *Xenakis, b. 1922, who is a figure of universal importance and whose career has been made primarily abroad.) These and perhaps another dozen fine composers are remarkably productive, and together they constitute a musical force which, for the first time in modern Greece, has reached international proportions.

BIBL.: F. Anoyanakis, "I Moussiki stin neoteri Hellada" [Music in Modern Greece], a supplement to *Historia tis Moussikis* [History of Music] by Karl Nef (Athens 1958):547–611; ——, *Katalogos Ergon Manoli Kalomiri (1883–1962)* [Catalog of the Works of Manolis Kalomiris . . .] (Athens 1964); John G. Papaioannou, "Nikos Skalkottas," *Music in the 20th Century* ed. by H. Hartog (London 1957):336–45; ——, program notes for the Hellenic Weeks for Contemporary Music (Athens 1966, 1967, 1968, 1971).

George Leotsakos

Green, Ray (b. Cavendish, Mo., 13 Sept 1909), studied at the San Francisco Conservatory (1927–33, composition with Ernest Bloch, Gregorian chant with Guilio Silva) and the Univ. of Calif. at Berkeley (1933–35, composition with Albert Elkus, fugue with E. G. Stricklen). He had also studied privately with Elkus during 1929–33. During 1939–41 he was supervisor and director of the Northern Calif. Federal Music Project Chorus in San Francisco; during 1946–48 he was chief of the Music Division of the Veterans Administration in Washington; and during 1948–61, executive secretary of the American Music Center in New York. He was music director and manager for the May O'Donnell Dance Co. in

New York during 1940–61. In 1951 he founded the publishing house American Music Edition. His music has been much influenced by early American hymn-tune harmony and counterpoint and by the rhythmic vitality of jazz. His vocal works of the 1930s and later are based on renaissance, especially English, models. In 1960 he installed an electronic music studio in his home in New York.

PRINCIPAL COMPOSITIONS (dates do not include subsequent revisions; published by AME unless otherwise noted): *Quartet*, 4 preludes for piano (1931); *5 Epigrammatic Romances* for string quartet (1933); *String Quartet* (1933, unpub.); *An American Agon*, sonata for piano (1933); *Break of Day*, madrigal for chorus (1933); *Sea Calm*, ¼-tone madrigal for 5 men's voices; text by Langston Hughes (1934); *Sonata brevis* for piano (1934, unpub.); *4 Short Songs* for soprano, piano; text by Carl Sandburg (1934); *Holiday for 4* for clarinet, bassoon, viola, piano (1935, Arrow); *Festival Fugues*, an American toccata for piano (1936); *Pieces for Children: and for grown-ups to make a note of* for piano (1936); *3 Inventories on a Texas Tune* for piano, percussion (1936, unpub.) or orchestra (1939, unpub.); *Adam lay i-boundyn*, madrigal for 4 voices (1937); *Care away, away, away*, madrigal for 4 voices (1937); *3 Fragments for Electra* for flute (1937, unpub.), revised as *3 Dance Energies* (1950); *Of Pioneer Women . . .*, dance score; choreography by May O'Donnell (1937, unpub.); *American Document*, dance score for 2 pianos, drums; choreography by Martha Graham (1938, unpub.); *Lullay myn lyking* for chorus (1939); *So Proudly We Hail*, American dance saga; choreography by O'Donnell (1940, unpub.); *Songs to Children's Poems* for voice, piano (1940); *On American Themes*, dance score; choreography by O'Donnell and José Limón (1941, unpub.); *Concertante* for viola (or clarinet), piano (1941); *Dance Theme and Variations* for piano (1943); *Suspension*, dance score; choreography by O'Donnell (1943, unpub.); *Hymn Tunes for Strings* for string quartet (1944); *Symphony No. 2* (1945); *Concertante* for viola, orchestra (1946); *Sunday Sing Symphony* (1946); *Short Sonatas Nos. 1–12* for piano (1949–70); *Folksong Fantasies* for trumpet, band (1949); *Lonesome Valley*, rhapsody for harp, orchestra (1950); *Corpus Christi* for soloist, chorus; early English text (1950); *3 Choral Songs* for women's chorus; text by Emily Dickinson (1950); *Duo concertante* for violin, piano (1950); *Dance Sonata* for 2 pianos, choreography by O'Donnell (1953); *Dance Sonata No. 2* for piano, choreography by O'Donnell (1957); *The Queen's Obsession* for piano, tape (1959, unpub.); *Hymn Tune Set* for 2 pianos (1960); *Piano Books for Young People*, 6 vols. (1961).

Griffes, Charles T[omlinson] (b. Elmira, N. Y., 17 Sept 1884; d. New York, 8 April 1920), received encouragement from his hometown piano teacher, Mary Broughton, whose financial assistance enabled him to study in Berlin during 1903–07 with Rüfer and Humperdinck. From 1908 until his death he taught in a private boys' school in Tarrytown, N. Y.

At Tarrytown Griffes composed many short piano pieces, songs, a piano sonata, a string quartet, several orchestral tone poems, and a few works using exotic materials, including a dance pantomime incorporating Japanese melodies. The bulk of his most characteristic works appeared 1912–18. He used such exotic elements as Japanese and American Indian tunes or Oriental scale formations but never abandoned the traditional framework of Western harmony and rhythm. He absorbed strong influences from Debussy, Stravinsky, Busoni, Mussorgsky, and Scriabin. From the impressionists he adopted melodic chromaticism, chains of parallel chords, especially 9ths and 11ths, quickly shifting tonal centers, rapid alternation of irregular meters, and programmatic titles. Both polymetric and polytonal passages appeared briefly in the late works. His *Piano Sonata* (1918–19), with its violently alternating moods, epitomizes his later style. Strong harmonic influences of Scriabin are evident, notably tritonal and augmented chordal structures, which when combined with insistent rhythmic ostinatos and biting cross rhythms of three against two, produce a savage effect. Judging from this work, which was revised a year before his death, Griffes was well along the way to becoming an important experimental composer.

PRINCIPAL COMPOSITIONS (published by Schirmer-G unless otherwise noted): *Tone Images* for mezzo-soprano, piano, Op. 3; texts by Oscar Wilde and W. E. Henley (1912); *3 Tone Pictures* for piano, Op. 5 (1914); *Fantasy Pieces* for piano, Op. 6 (1914); *4 Roman Sketches* for piano, Op. 7: "The White Peacock," "Nightfall," "The Fountain of the Acqua Paola," "Clouds" (1916); *2 Sketches* for string quartet, based on American Indian themes (1916–18); *The Kairn of Koridwen*, dance drama for 5 woodwinds, celesta, harp, piano (1916, unpub.); *Shojo*, Japanese dance pantomime for 4 woodwinds, 4 strings, harp, percussion (1917, unpub.); *3 Poems by Fiona MacLeod* for high voice, piano, Op. 11 (1918); *Poem* for flute, orchestra (1918); *Piano Sonata* (1918–19); *Nocturne for Orchestra* (1919); *The Pleasure Dome of Kubla Khan*, symphonic poem for orchestra (1919). Complete list in Anderson.

BIBL.: Donna K. Anderson, *The Works of C. T. G.: A Descriptive Catalogue* (PhD diss., Indiana Univ., 1966); Marion Bauer, "C. T. G. as I Remember Him," *Musical Quarterly* 29: 355–80; Daniel Boda, *The Music of C. T. G.* (PhD diss., Florida State Univ., 1962); Gilbert Chase, *America's Music*, 2nd ed. (New York 1966):517–

20; Edward M. Maisel, *C. T. G.* (New York 1943); William T. Upton, "The Songs of C. T. G.," *Musical Quarterly* 9:314–28.

Thomas E. Warner

SEE ALSO Asian Music and Western Composition, Impressionism, United States.

Grosskopf, Erhard (b. Berlin, 17 March 1934), studied medicine and philosophy at Goethe Univ. in Frankfurt (1955–57). Subsequently he attended the Berliner Kirchenmusikschule (1957–59), the Berlin Hochschule für Musik (1959–64, composition with Ernst Pepping, orchestration with Boris Blacher, analysis with Josef Rufer), and the Technische Universität in Berlin (1959–61, electronic studio techniques, mathematics, physics). Grosskopf was lecturer in theory at the Städtisches Konservatorium in Berlin during 1964–66. Since 1969 he has been associated with the electronic music studio of Utrecht State Univ.

PRINCIPAL COMPOSITIONS (published by Bote unless otherwise noted): *Sonata No. 1* for violin, cello, piano (1965); *Sonata No. 2* for solo violin (1965); *Sonata No. 3* for flute, violin, viola, cello (1967); *Sonata Concertante No. 2* for violin, orchestra (1967); *Nexus* for flute, percussion, tape; alternate version in collaboration with B. Damke includes visual effects (1968); *Flecktreue Raritätenkunst P*, concerto for clarinet, 8 instruments, live electronic sounds (1969); *Dialectics* for 4- or 7-track tape, flute (violin), clarinet (viola), trombone (double bass) (1969, unpub.).

Group Composition, a concept of structure introduced by Karlheinz *Stockhausen in his *Klavierstücke I–IV* (1952–53). A *group* is a segment of time usually containing more than one pitch. Each segment has some distinguishing characteristic (e.g., a particular dynamic level among all the pitches or a process of change as from soft to loud) that allows the composer to subject groups to various processes, such as serial ordering and transformation.

Group Improvisation, see Performance

Groven, Eivind (b. Laardal, Norway, 8 Oct 1901), studied at Oslo Conservatory during 1923–25 and is self-taught in composition. A collector of Norwegian folk music, he has combined this material with traditional concepts of form. In the early 20s he invented an organ that automatically produces nontempered intervals.

PRINCIPAL COMPOSITIONS (dates are of first performance): *Mot ballade* for chorus, orchestra; text after Hans Kinck (1933); *Brudgommen* [The Bridegroom] for soprano, 2 altos, tenor, chorus, orchestra; text by Ingeborg Hagen (1933); *Moen* [The Heath] for soprano, orchestra; text by Kinck (1934); *Renaissance*, symphonic poem (1935); *Historiske syner* [Historic Visions], symphonic poem (1936); *Fjelltonar* [Tunes from the Hills], symphonic poem for hardanger fiddle, chamber orchestra (1939); *Moderens korstegn* [The Mother's Sign of the Cross] for soprano, chamber orchestra; text by Henrik Wergeland (1942); *Neslandskyrkja* [The Nesland Church] for soprano, chamber orchestra; text by M. B. Landstad (1942); *Den tyngste sorg og møda* [The Heaviest Sorrow] for soprano, chamber orchestra; text by Ivar Aasen (1946); *Solstemning* [Sun-mood] for solo flute or flute, piano (1946, Lyche); *På hospitalet om natten* [In the Hospital at Night] for soprano, chamber orchestra; text by Wergeland (1946); *Ivar Aasen Suite* for soprano, bass, men's chorus, orchestra; texts by Aasen (1946); *Symphony No. 2*, "Midnattstimen" [The Midnight Hour] (1946); *Symphony No. 1*, "Innover viddene" [Toward the Mountains] (1948); *Piano Concerto No. 1* (1950); *Hjalarljod*, festival overture (1950, Lyche); *Symfoniske slaater*, 3 Norwegian folk dances for orchestra (1956); *Olav Liljukrans* for chorus (1960, Huset); *Balladetone* for 2 hardanger fiddles (1963); *Regbogen* [Rainbow] for 2 hardanger fiddles (1963); *Margjit Hjukse* for chorus, hardanger fiddle (1964, MH); *Draumkvaede* for soprano, tenor, baritone, chorus, orchestra; traditional text (1965); *Faldafeykir* for orchestra (1967).

PRINCIPAL WRITINGS: *Naturskalaen* [The Natural Scale] (Skien 1927); *Temperering og remstemning* [Temperament and Modal Tuning] (Oslo 1948; English ed. 1970); *Eskimomelodier fra Alaska* [Eskimo Melodies from Alaska] (Oslo 1955); *Renstemningsautomaten* [A Machine for Modal Tuning] (Oslo 1968).

SEE ALSO Scandinavia.

Gruenberg, Louis (b. Brest-Litovsk, Russia, 3 August 1884; d. Beverly Hills, Calif., 9 June 1964), arrived in the U.S. in 1885, studied in New York (1892–1903, piano with Adele Margulies) and Germany (1904–08, composition with F. E. Koch, piano with Ferruccio Busoni). During 1912–19 he taught at the Vienna Conservatory and concertized in Europe as a pianist. In 1919 he gave up his concert career and returned to the U.S. During 1934–37 he taught composition at the Chicago Musical College. In addition to the works listed below, he composed many film scores.

In the *National Cyclopedia of American Biography*, Mrs. Gruenberg observes: "In earlier years, when his use of folk music accorded with contemporary tastes, his work was best known for its powerful primitive style. Due to changing tastes and his complete withdrawal from public life, Gruenberg's work was rarely performed in the last 20 years of his life."

PRINCIPAL COMPOSITIONS: *Violin Sonatas Nos. 1-3* (1912; 1924, UE; 1950); *Piano Concertos Nos. 1-2* (1914; 1938, revised 1963); *Hill of Dreams* for orchestra (1919); *Vagabondia* for orchestra (1922); *4 Indiscretions* for string quartet (1922, UE); *Daniel Jazz*, for vocal soloist, 8 instruments; text by Vachel Lindsay (1924, UE); *Animals and Insects* for voice, piano (1924, UE); *Enchanted Isle* for orchestra (1925); *Jazz Suite* for orchestra (1925); *4 Songs* for voice, piano (1925, UE); *Creation* for vocal soloist, 8 instruments; text after a Negro spiritual (1925, UE); *20 Negro Spirituals* for voice, piano (1926, UE); *Jack and the Beanstalk*, children's opera; libretto by John Erskine (1930, Birchard); *Symphonies Nos. 1-4* (1930, revised 1963; 1941, last revision 1963; 1941, revised 1964; 1946, revised 1964); *4 Diversions* for string quartet (1930); *Emperor Jones*, opera; libretto after Eugene O'Neill (1932); *Serenade to a Beauteous Lady* for orchestra (1934); *Green Mansions*, radio opera; libretto after W. H. Hudson (1937); *Piano Quintet* (1937); *String Quartet No. 2* (1937); *5 Variations on a Popular Theme* for string quartet (1942); *Violin Concerto* (1944); *Music to an Imaginary Ballet* for orchestra (1945); *Music to an Imaginary Legend* for orchestra (1945); *Americana* for orchestra (1947); *Volpone*, opera (1948-50); *Antony and Cleopatra*, opera (1955-62); *A Song of Faith*, oratorio for narrator, vocal soloists, chorus, orchestra (1959-62); *6 Winter Songs* for voice, piano (1963); *Prose Songs* for voice, piano; traditional Chinese texts (1963).

PRINCIPAL WRITINGS: *Conversations with Myself*, unpublished journal.

[prepared with the help of Irma Gruenberg]
SEE ALSO Dance, Opera, United States.

Guarnieri, (Mozart) **Camargo** (b. Tieté, Brazil, 1 Feb 1907), studied privately in São Paulo with Lamberto Baldi (1926-32, composition), Mario de Andrade (1928-45, composition), and Antonio de Sá Pereira (1925-28, piano) and during 1938-39 in Paris with Charles Koechlin (counterpoint, esthetics) and François Rühlmann (conducting). During 1927-38 he taught at the São Paulo Conservatory and during 1960-61 served as its director. In 1945 he founded the Brazilian Academy of Music. Currently he teaches orchestration, composition, and conducting at the Santos Conservatory of Music and at the Conservatory of the State Univ. at Goiás. His music is largely

nationalistic and makes extensive use of polyphonic textures.

PRINCIPAL COMPOSITIONS: *Sonatina No. 1* for piano (1928, Ricordi); *Violin Sonata No. 1* (1930, AMP and Ricordi); *Piano Concerto No. 1* (1931); *Cello Sonata* (1931); *Ponteios* for piano, books 1-5 (1931-35, 1947-49, 1954-55, Ricordi; 1956-57, 1958-59); *A morte do aviador*, cantata for soprano, chorus, orchestra; text by Mario de Andrade (1932); *Pedro Malazarte*, 1-act comic opera; libretto by Andrade (1932); *String Quartet No. 1* (1932); *Violin Sonata No. 2* (1933); *Sonatina No. 2* for piano (1934); *Sonatina No. 3* for piano (1937, AMP and Ricordi); *Violin Concerto No. 1* (1940); *Symphony No. 1* (1944); *String Quartet No. 2* (1944); *Symphony No. 2* (1944); *Piano Concerto No. 2* (1946, AMP); *Sonatina* for flute, piano (1947, MP); *Violin Sonata No. 3* (1950); *Chôro* for violin, orchestra (1951); *Symphony No. 3* (1952); *Variations on a Northeastern [Brazilian] Theme* for piano, orchestra (1953); *Violin Concerto No. 2* (1953); *Cello Sonata No. 2* (1955); *Chôro* for clarinet, orchestra (1956); *Chôro* for piano, orchestra (1956); *Violin Sonata No. 4* (1956, Ricordi); *Séca*, cantata for voice, chorus, orchestra; text by Sylvia Celeste de Campos (1957); *Sonatina No. 4* for piano (1958, AMP and Ricordi); *Violin Sonata No. 5* (1959); *Colóquio,* cantata for voice, chorus, wind quintet, percussion; text by Ernesto Guerra da Cal (1959); *Um homem só*, 1-act opera; libretto by Gianfrancesco Guarnieri (1960); *Concertino* for piano, chamber orchestra (1961); *Chôro* for cello, orchestra (1961); *Sonatina No. 5* for piano (1962, Ricordi); *String Quartet No. 3* (1962); *Violin Sonata No. 6* (1963); *Symphony No. 4*, "Brasília" (1963, AMP); *Piano Concerto No. 3* (1964); *Sonatina No. 6* for piano (1965); *Guanábará*, cantata for narrator, baritone, chorus, orchestra; text by Cecília Meireles (1965); *Seresta* for piano, chamber orchestra (1965); *Homenagem a Villa-Lobos* for wind orchestra (1966); *Sequência, Coral e Ricercare* for chamber orchestra (1966); *Piano Concerto No. 4* (1968); *O caso do vestido*, cantata for mezzo-soprano, orchestra; text by Andrade (1969). List to 1959: *Composers of the Americas* 4:28-49.

BIBL.: Guillermo Rendón, "M. C. G.," *Acteon* (Bogotá) 1:19-23.

SEE ALSO Brazil.

Gubaidulina, Sofia (Asgatovna) (b. Tsistopol', Tataria, U.S.S.R., 24 Oct 1931), studied at the Kazan music academy (1946-49, theory with Nazib Zhiganov, piano with Maria Piatnitskaia), the Kazan Conservatory (1949-54, composition with Albert Leman, piano with Leopold Lukomsky and Grigory Kogan), and the Moscow Conservatory (1954-63, composition with Nikolai Peiko and Vissarion Shebalin). During 1963-64 she was an accompanist at the Moscow Theater Institute. She has been a composer with the Studio of Documentary Films (1963–67), the Studio of Art Films in Odessa (1964–69), the Theater on Taganka in Moscow (1966), the Studio of Animated Cartoons (since 1968), and the Moscow Soviet Theater (since 1970). Since 1968 she has worked at the Electronic Music Studio in Moscow. Her compositional development has been influenced by the music of Webern and by the mystical and social philosophies of Nikolai Berdyaev.

PRINCIPAL COMPOSITIONS: *Fatseliia* for soprano, orchestra (1956); *Piano Quintet* (1957, Muzyka); *Intermezzo* for 8 trumpets, 16 harps, percussion (1961); *Ciaccona* for piano (1962, SC); *Allegro rustico* for flute, piano (1963, SC); *5 Etudes* for double bass, harp, percussion (1965); *Piano Sonata* (1965); *Sonata* for percussion (1966); *Noch' v Memfis* [Night in Memphis] for alto, men's chorus, chamber orchestra (1968); *Detto* for organ (1969); *Rubaiiat* for baritone, chamber ensemble (1969); *Vivente—non vivente* on tape; composed with the aid of a computer (1969–70); *Concorcantsa* for chamber ensemble (1971).

BIBL.: Victor Bobrovsky, "Otkroite vse okna" [Open All the Windows], *Sovetskaia muzyka* 1962/2: 23–28; Valentina Kholopova, "Obnovlenie palitry" [Renewing the Palette], *ibid.* 1968/7:28–30; Václav Kučera, "Nové proudy sovetske hudbe" [New Works of Soviet Music], *Edice přátel hudby* (Prague 1967).

Gudmundsen-Holmgreen, Pelle (b. Copenhagen, 21 Nov 1932), attended the Royal Danish Conservatory (1953–58, music history and theory with Finn Høffding, Svend Westergaard). He was a stage manager at the Royal Theater during 1959–64. Since 1967 he has taught composition at the Conservatory of Jutland. Influences on his early style were Bartók, Stravinsky, and the Danish composer Vagn Holmboe. In 1959 he was attracted to serialism. Since 1964 his music has tended toward "simplicity and absurdity." *Tricolore* for orchestra, his simplest piece, consists of three unchanging chords repeated in simple rhythmic patterns of long durations. In his "most absurd piece," *Je ne me tairai jamais. Jamais.*, "short and simple motives of extremely different character are repeated, confronted, and sabotaged."

PRINCIPAL COMPOSITIONS: *Chronos* for chamber orchestra (1962, SUDM); *Collegium Musicum Concert* for chamber orchestra (1964); *Frère Jacques* for chamber orchestra (1964); *Repriser* for chamber orchestra (1965, SUDM); *Symphony* (1962–65); *Signals* for orchestra without strings (1966); *5 Pieces* for orchestra (1966); *Je ne me tairai jamais. Jamais.*, for narrator, 12 voices, oboe, bassoon, 2 trombones, percussion, electric

organ, mandolin, viola, bass (1966); *Tricolore* for orchestra (1967); *String Quartet No. 4* (1967, Hansen); *Piece by Piece* for chamber orchestra (1968, Hansen); *Pictures at an Exhibition* for piano (1968); *Infantile Music* for 6–100 players (1968); *Kadence* for band (1969); *Preludin and Fuck* for brass band (1969).

PRINCIPAL WRITINGS: "Omkring Repriser," *Dansk Musiktidsskrift* 1966/2:54–55; "Film og Musik," *ibid.* 1969/1:9–12.

BIBL.: Jan Maegaard, "Det Forudbestemte og det Tilfaeldige" [Predetermination and Indeterminacy], *Dansk Musiktidsskrift* 1962/4:102–04; Poul Nielsen, "Omkring den ny Enkelhed" [The New Simplicity], *ibid.* 1966/5:138–42; ——, "Den demokratiske Daemon," *Nutida musik* 1968–69/1:61–64.

Guerra-Peixe, César (b. Petrópolis, Brazil, 18 March 1914), studied at the National Music School of the U.F.R.J. in Guanabara (1932–33; harmony with A. França, violin with Paulina D'Ambrósio), the Brazilian Music Conservatory in Guanabara (1940–43, composition with Newton Pádua), and the Comissão Paulista de Folclore in São Paulo (1953; folk music with Rossini Tavares de Lima). He also studied 12-tone techniques and composing for radio with H. J. Koellreutter in Guanabara (1943–45) and composition with Edoardo de Guarnieri (1956). During 1930–40 he was a violinist in small orchestras, and during 1963–68 he played in the National Symphony Orchestra of the Radio of the Ministry of Education and Culture. He was an arranger for various radio stations and record companies during 1940–60, and since 1967 he has been director and arranger of music for Tupi Television in Rio de Janeiro. He has taught composition privately at the Pro Arte Musical Seminary in Rio (1963–70) and at the Musical Seminary of the Museum of Art and Sound in Guanabara (since 1968). Under Koellreutter's guidance and until 1949 he produced atonal and 12-tone works. Thereafter he strove for a more nationalistic style, using native materials and avoiding any avant-garde techniques (serial, aleatory, electronic, etc.) that would not complement folk materials.

PRINCIPAL COMPOSITIONS: *Música Nos. 1–2* for piano (1945–47); *Pequeno duo* for violin, cello (1946, ECIC); *Symphony No. 1* (1946); *Duo* for flute, violin (1947); *String Quartet No. 1* (1947, ECIC); *Divertimento No. 2* for string orchestra (1947); *Suite No. 2,* "Nordestina," and *Suite No. 3,* "Paulista," for piano (1954, Ricordi); *Symphonic Suites Nos. 1–2* (1955); *Ponteado* for orchestra (1955); *Symphony No. 2,* "Brasília" (1960); *Sonata* for solo violin or guitar (1969); *4 Prelúdios* for solo violin or guitar (1970).

PRINCIPAL WRITINGS: "Um século de música no Recife," *Diário de Pernambuco* (Recife 1952); *Maracatus do Recife* (São Paulo 1956); "Os Cabocolinhos do Recife," *Revista brasileira de folclore* 15; "Rezas-de-defunto," *ibid.* 22; "Zabumba, orquesta nordestina," *ibid.* 26.

BIBL.: Vasco Mariz, *Música brasileña contemporanea* (Rosario, Argentina, 1952); Rossini Tavares de Lima, *Pequeno guia do ouvinte de música erudita* (São Paulo-Rio de Janeiro 1955).

Guézec, Jean-Pierre (b. Dijon, France, 29 August 1934; d. Paris, 10 May 1971), studied at the Paris Conservatory (1954–62; composition with Darius Milhaud, Jean Rivier; analysis, Olivier Messiaen) and at Tanglewood (1963). From 1969 he was professor of analysis at the Paris Conservatory. He explored new concepts of musical form and texture, usually using a different combination of instruments in each work. He compared his approach to the paintings of Mondrian with lines and shapes "projected into time and colored with sound."

PRINCIPAL COMPOSITIONS (published by Salabert): *Architectures colorées* for winds, brass, strings, percussion (1964); *Ensemble multicolore* for winds, brass, strings, percussion (1965); *Assemblages* for winds, brass, percussion (1967); *Textures enchaînées* for winds, brass, harp, percussion (1967); *Successif-simultané* for 12 strings (1968); *String Trio* (1968); *Reliefs polychromés* for 12 vocalists (1969); *Forme-couleurs* for 2 harps, chamber ensemble (1969); *Couleurs juxtaposées* for percussion (1969).

BIBL.: Martine Cadieu, "Entretiens avec J.-P. G.," *Les Lettres françaises* 1271:16–23; Marie-José Chauvin, "Entretiens avec J.-P. G.," *Le Courrier musical de France* 23:164–72; Maurice Fleuret, "Plaidoyer pour une musique pure," *Nouvel Observateur* 139:36.

SEE ALSO France.

Gutchë, Gene (b. Berlin, 3 July 1907), studied at the Univ. of Minn. (1948–50; composition with Donald Ferguson, James Aliferis) and at the State Univ. of Iowa (1950–53; composition, conducting, Philip Greeley Clapp). He came to the U.S. in 1925 and for much of his life has earned his living in various commercial businesses. In 1953 he became a free-lance composer. His music makes use of traditional forms and genres and of such contemporary resources as microtones, polytonality, and 12-tone procedures. Gutchë always aims at communicating to a wide audience.

PRINCIPAL COMPOSITIONS: *Centennial String Quartet*, Op. 12, No. 3 (1951, ACA); *Symphony No. 3*, Op. 19 (1952, Fleisher); *Rondo capriccioso* for chamber orchestra, Op. 21 (1953, Fleisher); *Piano Concerto*, Op. 24 (1955, Fleisher); *Piano Sonata*, Op. 6, No. 3 (1958, Highgate); *Holofernes* for orchestra, Op. 27, No. 1 (1958, Highgate); *Judith* for chamber orchestra, Op. 27, No. 2 (1959, Fleisher); *Concertino for Orchestra*, Op. 28 (1959, Fleisher); *String Quartet No. 4*, Op. 29, No. 1 (1960, ACA); *Symphony No. 4*, Op. 30 (1960, Fleisher); *Timpani concertante* for orchestra, Op. 31 (1961, Fleisher); *Piano Sonata*, Op. 32, No. 1 (1961, Highgate); *Piano Sonata*, Op. 32, No. 2 (1962, Highgate); *Symphony No. 5*, Op. 34 (1962, Highgate); *Bongo Divertimento* for percussion, orchestra (1962, Highgate); *Violin Concerto*, Op. 36 (1962, Fleisher); *Genghis Khan* for orchestra, Op. 37 (1963, Highgate); *Raquel* for orchestra, Op. 38 (1963, Highgate); *Rites in Tenochtitlan* for piano, orchestra, Op. 39, No. 1 (1965, Fleisher); *Hsiang Fei* for orchestra, Op. 40 (1965, Highgate); *Gemini* for piano 4-hands, orchestra, Op. 41 (1965, Fleisher); *Aesop Fabler Suite* for orchestra, Op. 43 (1966, Fleisher). List to 1968: *Composers of the Americas* 15:113–17.

PRINCIPAL WRITINGS: "Hodeir, Experiment or Art?" *St. Paul Pioneer and Dispatch* (26 Feb 1961), theater section, p. 6; "Age of Consent," *ibid.* (1 Dec 1963), theater section, p. 6, and *Music Today* 8/5:4; "Pandora's Music Box," *Music Educators' Journal* 52/4:113; "American Culture," *Minneapolis Sunday Tribune* (6 March 1966), arts section, p. 1; "Decline of a Revolution by Design," *Music Journal* 24/10:26, 53; "Formula in Aesthetics," *Music Journal* 27/7:102; "Taste Is an Octopus," *Music Journal* 27/1:36–37, 64.

BIBL.: Peter P. Jacobi, "G. G., Worker, Not Academician," *Christian Science Monitor* (9 Sept 1964); ——, "Contemporary Music and the Society It Does Not Belong To," *Tri-Quarterly* 5:160–75; John Sherman, "G. G.," *BMI Many Worlds of Music* (Dec 1966):9.

Gutiérrez-Heras, Joaquín (b. Tehuacán, Mexico, 28 Sept 1927), studied at the Conservatory in Mexico City (1950; composition with Blas Galindo, Rodolfo Halffter), the Paris Conservatory (1952–53, composition with Jean Rivier, analysis with Olivier Messiaen, counterpoint with Georges Dandelot), and at the Juilliard School (1960–61; composition with William Bergsma, Vincent Persichetti). In 1957 he helped found the group Nueva Música de México. During 1966–70 he was director of Radio Universidad de México.

PRINCIPAL COMPOSITIONS: *Divertimento* for piano, orchestra (1949); *Variations on a French Song* for harpsichord (1960); *Chamber Cantata on Poems by Emilio Prados* for soprano, 2 flutes, harp, 4 strings (1961); *Los cazadores*, symphonic scene (1962); *Woodwind Trio* (1965); *Sonata simple* for flute, piano (1965, EMM).

PRINCIPAL FILM SCORES: *Remedios Varo* (1965); *Pedro Paramo* (1966); *Pax* (1967); *Olympic Games in Mexico* (1969).

PRINCIPAL WRITINGS: "Music in Transition," *Atlantic Monthly* (March 1964): 112–17.

SEE ALSO Mexico.

Guyonnet, Jacques (b. Geneva, 20 March 1933), studied at Geneva Univ. (1953–56, classics), the Geneva Conservatory (1950–58; composition, piano, conducting), and the Darmstadt summer courses (1958, 1960, composition and conducting with Pierre Boulez). During 1959–61 he wrote a music column for the *Geneva Tribune*. In 1961 he founded the Geneva concert society, Studio de Musique Contemporaine, which he directs, and in 1967 he organized the Electronic Music Studio A.R.T. (Art, Recherche, Technique). He has toured as a lecturer and conductor in Europe, the U.S., and Latin America.

PRINCIPAL COMPOSITIONS (published by the A.R.T. studio unless otherwise noted): *En 3 Eclats!* for piano, chamber orchestra (1964); *Stèle in memoriam J. F. K.* for chamber orchestra, tape (1964, unpub.); *Chronicles de 1964 à 1971* for piano (1964–71); *L'Approche du caché I and II*: No. 1 for cello, 6 instruments (1966); No. 2 for mezzo-soprano, chamber orchestra, optional tape (1967); *7 Portes du temps* for orchestra (1966–69); *Entremonde,* dance score for flute, piano, 4 percussion, tape (1967, unpub.); *Let there Be Events* for 17 instrumental soloists (1968–71); *Good Grief, Jerry!*, a mobile piece for soprano, 17 instrumentalists, optional tape (1970); *Images 60/70*, pop-electronic dance score on tape (1970–71); *A Single Requiem* for vocal soloists, chorus, orchestra (1971).

PRINCIPAL WRITINGS: "Structure et communication," *Cahiers Renaud-Barrault* 41 (1963); *Les Charactères du son: Vers une nouvelle conception du temps musical* (Neuchâtel 1964); *Réformer l'enseignement musical* (Paris c.1965); "D'Est en Ouest," *Preuves* (Jan 1966); "Pour une Politique de la musique," *Journal de Genève* (29 Oct and 19 Nov 1966).

H

Haas, Joseph (b. Maihingen, Germany, 19
March 1879; d. Munich, 31 March 1960),
studied composition with Max Reger in
Munich during 1904–08 and organ with Karl
Straube in Leipzig. He taught composition at
the Stuttgart Conservatory (1911–21), the
Institute of Church Music in Munich (1926–
44), and the Munich Hochschule für Musik
(1921–50).

PRINCIPAL COMPOSITIONS (published by Schott
unless otherwise noted): *Violin Sonata*, Op. 21
(1909, Rahter); *String Quartet*, Op. 50 (1919,
Wunderhorn-V); *Eine deutsche Singmesse* for
chorus, organ, Op. 60 (1924, unpub.); *Ein Frei-
heitslied*, Op. 78 (1929, unpub.); *Speyerer Domfest-
messe* for chorus, winds, organ, Op. 80 (1930);
Die heilige Elisabeth, oratorio for narrator, soprano, chorus, children's and men's choruses,
orchestra, Op. 84; text by W. Dauffenbach (1931);
Christnacht, Christmas cantata for narrator, vocal
soloists, chorus, orchestra, Op. 85 (1933); *Das
Lebensbuch Gottes*, oratorio for soprano, alto,
women's and mixed choruses, orchestra, Op. 87;
text by Angelus Silesius (1934); *Tobias Wunderlich*,
3-act opera, Op. 90; libretto by H. H. Ortner and
L. Andersen (1937); *Das Lied von der Mutter*,
oratorio for soprano, baritone, children's, men's,
and mixed choruses, orchestra, Op. 91; text by
Willi Lindner (1939); *Die Hochzeit des Jobs*, 4-act
opera, Op. 93; libretto by L. Andersen (1944);
Te Deum for chorus, orchestra, Op. 100 (1946);
Das Jahr im Lied, folksong oratorio for narrator,
vocal quartet, chorus, orchestra, Op. 103 (1952);
Die Seligen, oratorio for soprano, baritone,
choruses, orchestra, Op. 106 (1957); *Deutsche
Kindermesse*, Op. 108 (1958, unpub.). List to 1953:
K. G. Fellerer, *Catalogue of Works* (Haas Society
1953).

PRINCIPAL WRITINGS: *Max Reger* (Bonn 1949);
Reden und Aufsätze (Mainz 1964).

BIBL.: *Festgabe J. H.* (Mainz 1939); Kurt
Honolka, "J. H.'s Gebrauchsmusik," *Das viel-
stimmige Jahrhundert* (Stuttgart 1960): 221–24;
Karl Laux, *J. H.* (Berlin 1954); Franz Josef
Wehinger, "Traurigsein hebt keine Not," *J. H.,
Leben und Werk* (Karlsruhe 1959); *Zeitschrift für
Musik*, special issue, 115/3.

Hába, Alois (b. Vizovice, Moravia, 21 June
1893: d. Prague, Nov. 1972), was the son of a
folk musician and grew up in a district rich in
folk music. He began composing at 15 and then
studied with Vitězslav Novák at the Prague
Conservatory (1914–15) and with Franz
Schreker in Vienna (1918–20) and Berlin (1920–
22). He came to know Schoenberg's works in
Vienna while a proofreader at Schoenberg's
publisher, Universal Edition, as well as through
Schoenberg's private concerts. In Berlin he
associated with the circle of young modernists
around Busoni and also studied oriental music
at the phonograph archives of Carl Stumpf and
Erich von Hornbostel. Following their example,
he developed his own archives of recorded
Moravian and Slovak folksong in the department of quarter-tone and sixth-tone music,
which he founded and directed at the Prague
Conservatory (1923–51). After 1951, when the
department was closed, he devoted himself
exclusively to composition.

After the formation of an independent
Czechoslovakia in 1918, many Czech composers sought a "new" music. Hába's most
significant activities were with microtonal
resources. He has written quarter-tone, sixth-
tone, and most recently fifth-tone works, all
for a variety of instruments. He has also
developed a theory of harmony in quarter-
tone, sixth-tone, and 12-tone systems and has
designed quarter-tone and sixth-tone instruments (three types of piano, a harmonium,
trumpets, clarinets). The Czech musical tradition has always been a decisive factor in his
style. He does not usually quote folk melodies,
but in many works (Opp. 6, 41, 82) he has
used modal turns of phrase and characteristic
folk rhythms, much as Janáček and Novák
did. He often incorporates such elements into
more complicated harmonic and polyphonic
structures, sometimes alongside aggressive
dissonances, such as minor seconds and
ninths and major sevenths (Opp. 8, 83, 86).
His athematic method of building musical
sentences and paragraphs recalls Schoenberg's
middle period (*Erwartung*), and some of his
12-tone works compare favorably with those
of the modern Viennese school (Opp. 40, 46,
92, 95, among others). Hába does not, however, abandon tonality, for many successions

of tones and chords contain features of functional harmony, e.g., successions of dominants of various keys with the tonics unstated.

PRINCIPAL COMPOSITIONS: *String Quartet*, Op. 4 (1920, UE); *6 Pieces* for piano, Op. 6 (1920, Hudební Matice); *String Quartet* in ¼-tones, Op. 7 (1920, UE); *Symphonic Fantasia* for piano, orchestra, Op. 8 (1920, ČHF); *Fantasia* in ¼-tones for violin, Op. 9a (1921, UE); *String Quartet No. 3* in ¼-tones, Op. 12 (1922, UE); *Chor-Suite* in ⅓-tones (1922, UE); *String Quartet No. 5* in ⅙-tones, Op. 15 (1923); *Suite No. 3* for ¼-tone piano, Op. 16 (1923, UE); *Fantasia No. 2* for ¼-tone piano, Op. 19 (1924, UE); *Suite* for ¼-tone clarinet, ¼-tone piano, Op. 24 (1925); *Fantasia* for viola, ¼-tone piano, Op. 32 (1928); *Fantasia* for cello, ¼-tone piano, Op. 33 (1928); *Matka* [The Mother], opera in ¼-tones, Op. 35; libretto by the composer (1929–30, DILIA); *Fantasia* for nonet, Op. 40 (12-tone work; 1931–32, SHV); *Fantasia* for nonet, Op. 41 (7-tone work; 1932); *Cesta života* [The Way of Life], symphonic fantasia, Op. 46 (1933–34, Panton); *Nová země* [The New Land), opera, Op. 47; text by F. Pujman after the novel by F. Gladkov (1935–36); *Přijd království Tvé (Nezaměstnaní)* [Thy Kingdom Come (The Unemployed)], opera in ⅙-tones, Op. 50; libretto by the composer (1939–42); *Suite* for ¼-tone guitar, Op. 54 (1943); *Sonata* for ¼-tone piano, Op. 62 (1945, ČHF); *String Quartet No. 7*, Op. 73 (1951, SNKLHU); *String Quartet No. 9*, Op. 79 (1952); *Nonet No. 3*, Op. 82 (1953, SNKLHU); *Violin Concerto*, Op. 83 (1954, ČHF); *Suite* for cello in ⅙-tones, Op. 85a (1955, ČHF); *Viola Concerto*, Op. 86 (1955–56, ČHF); *Suite* for violin in ⅙-tones, Op. 85b (1956, ČHF); *String Quartet No. 11* in ⅙-tones, Op. 87 (1957–59, SHV); *String Quartet No. 12* in ¼-tones, Op. 90 (1960, SHV); *String Quartet No. 13*, Op. 92 (1961, SHV); *String Quartet No. 14* in ¼-tones, Op. 94 (1963, Panton); *String Quartet No. 15*, Op. 95 (1963); *String Quartet No. 16* in ⅕-tones, Op. 98 (1967).

PRINCIPAL WRITINGS: *Von der Psychologie der musikalische Gestaltung, Gesetzmässigkeit der Tonbewegung und Grundlagen eines neuen Musikstils* (Vienna 1925); "Grundlagen der Tondifferenzierung und der neuen Stilmöglichkeiten in der Musik," *Von neuen Musik* (Cologne 1925): 52–58; *Neue Harmonielehre des diatonischen, chromatischen, Viertel-, Drittel-, Sextel- und Zwölftonsystems* (Leipzig 1927); "Die entgültige Lösung des Problems des Vierteltonflügels," *Auftakt* 6:23–26; "Die vier ätherischen Bilderkräfte in der Musik und in der Musikentwicklung," *Die drei. Monatschrift für Anthroposophie Dreigliederung und Goetheanismus* 9:288–313; "Schönberg und die weiteren Möglichkeiten der Musikentwicklung," *Arnold Schönberg zum 60. Geburtstag* (Vienna 1934): 15–17.

BIBL.: Jan Matejiček, "A. H.," *Tschechische Komponisten von Heute* (Prague 1957): 84–87; Willi Moellendorf, "A. H., Op. 7, Streichquartet im Vierteltonsystem," *Melos* 3:150–51; Erwin Schulhoff, "Wie spielt man auf dem Vierteltonklavier?" *Auftakt* 6:106–09; Jiří Vysloužil, "A. H. als Kompositionslehrer," *Sborník prací filosofické fakulty brněnské university* 14:379–87; ——, "K. Hábovu postavení ve vyvoji české a evropské moderní hudby" [H.'s Position in the Development of Czech and European Modern Music], *Hudební věda* 2:567–84 (includes summary in German); ——, "H.'s Idea of Quarter-tone Music," *Hudební věda* 5:466–72; ——, "Arnold Schoenberg und die tschechische Musik," *Aspekte der neuen Musik* ed. by W. Burde (Cassel 1968): 58–67; George Whitman, "A. H., Seminal Works of Quartertone Music," *Tempo* 80:11–15.

Jiří Vysloužil

SEE ALSO Austria and Germany, Czechoslovakia, Instrumental and Vocal Resources, Microtones, Theory.

Hába, Karel (b. Vizovice, Moravia, 21 May 1898), studied at the Prague Conservatory (1918–23; composition with Vítězslav Novák, violin with Jan Mařák and Karel Hoffmann). He wrote for and edited the National Radio Journal during 1929–50 and was a violist with the Czech Philharmonic Orchestra, 1929–36. He taught pedagogical methods at Charles Univ. during 1950–63. Some of his music from the mid-20s explores ¼-tone resources, but he did not pursue this line of development as did his brother, Alois.

PRINCIPAL COMPOSITIONS (dates are approximate): *String Quartets Nos. 2–4*: No. 2, Op. 5 (1924, Hudební matice); No. 3, Op. 27 (1944, SNKLHU); No. 4, Op. 48 (1970, Panton); *Violin Concerto*, Op. 6 (1926); *Trio* for violin, cello, ¼-tone piano, Op. 8 (1926); *Septet*, Op. 16, for clarinet, horn, bassoon, violin, viola, cello, piano (1928–29); *Jánosík*, opera; libretto by Antonín Klášterský (1929–32); *Cello Concerto*, Op. 18 (1934); *Duo* for violin, cello, Op. 19 (1935); *Stará historie* [Old History], opera; libretto by Ferdinand Pujman (1937–40); *Symphonies Nos. 1–2* (1939, 1955); *Piano Trio*, Op. 24 (1940, Hudební matice); *Nonet*, Op. 32, for wind quintet, string trio, double bass (1948); *O Smolíčkovi* [About Smolitschek], children's radio opera, Op. 33; libretto by V. Čtvrtek (1949); *Budovatelům Ostravska* [To Those Who Build Up Ostrava], cantata for soprano, tenor, baritone, chorus, orchestra, Op. 34 (1951, Panton); *Trio* for 2 violins, viola, Op. 35 (1952); *Nejmenším zpěváčkům* for voice, piano, Op. 37 (1955, SHV); *Kalibův zločin*, opera; libretto after K. V. Rais (1956–60); *Děti zpívají* [Children's Songs] for voice, piano, Op. 38 (1956, SHV); *15 Concert Etudes* for violin, Op. 40 (1957, SHV); *Valašské písně* [Songs from Moravia] for voice, piano (1957, SNKLHU); *Z dětského světa* [From a Child's World] for voice, piano, Op. 41 (1960, SHV); *Sonatina* for 3 violins, Op. 42a (1960, SNKLHU); *Sonatina* for 3 clarinets, Op. 42b (1960, SNKLHU); *3 Instructive Duos* for 2 violins, Op. 44 (1968, Panton).

PRINCIPAL WRITINGS: *Škola čtvrttónové houslové hry* [Violin Method in the Quarter-Tone System] (1927, unpub.); *Moderní houslová technika* [Modern Violin Technique], 2 vols., Op. 12 (Prague 1928).

SEE ALSO Czechoslovakia.

Hachimura, Yoshio (b. Tokyo, 10 Oct 1938), studied harmony, counterpoint, and fugue with Yuzuru Shimaoka at the Tokyo Univ. of Arts (1957–61) and composition privately with Yoshiro Irino (1960–63). Since 1961 he has been a lecturer at the Toho Gakuen School of Music. The traditional arts of Japan, together with the music of contemporary Japanese composers, have been formative influences on his development. Debussy, Scriabin, Messiaen, and Ligeti have also been major influences.

PRINCIPAL COMPOSITIONS (published by Ongaku unless otherwise noted): *Improvisation* for piano, Op. 1 (1957); *1 Hour at Every Breath* for soprano, flute, clarinet, tenor saxophone, vibraphone, 2 percussion, violin, Op. 3 (1960); *Improvisation* for violin, piano, Op. 4 (1964); *Constellation* for violin, vibraphone, tubular chimes, piano, Op. 5 (1969); *Meditation Higan-Bana* for piano, Op. 6 (1969, Shunju Sha); *Shigarami No. 2* for noh-kan, 3 shakuhachis, 2 samisens, Op. 7 (1970); *The Garden of Love* for chorus, Op. 8; text by William Blake (1971, unpub.).

BIBL.: Kôji Sano, liner notes for *The Works of Y. H. and Shukô Mizuno* (Toshiba record TA-7030).

SEE ALSO Japan.

Haieff, Alexei V. (b. Blagoveschensk, Siberia, Russia, 25 August 1914), studied at the Juilliard School (1934–38, composition with Rubin Goldmark and Frederic Jacobi) and privately with Constantin Shvedoff in New York (1933–34) and Nadia Boulanger in Cambridge, Mass., and Paris (1938–39). He has taught at the Univ. of Buffalo (1962, 1964) and the Carnegie-Mellon Institute (1962–63). During 1952–53 and 1958–59 he was composer-in-residence at the American Academy in Rome and during 1967–70, at the Univ. of Utah. He has appeared as guest conductor with the Woody Herman Band (1946) and the Buffalo Philharmonic Orchestra (1964).

PRINCIPAL COMPOSITIONS (published by Chappell unless otherwise noted): *Symphonies Nos. 1–3* (1942, unpub.; 1957, 1961); *Divertimento* for chamber orchestra (1944–46, Boosey); *Sonata* for 2 pianos (1946); *Violin Concerto* (1948, unpub.); *Piano Concerto* (1949–50, Boosey); *String Quartet No. 1* (1951, Belaieff); *Eclogue* for harp, string

orchestra (1953–54); *Piano Sonata* (1955); *Saints' Wheel* for piano (1960); *Cello Sonata* (1963); *Eloge* for 9 instruments (1967, unpub.); *Holy Week Liturgy* for chorus (1968–69, unpub.); *Caligula* for baritone, orchestra (1970, unpub.).

Halffter, Cristóbal (b. Madrid, 24 March 1930), studied at the Madrid Conservatory (1948–51, composition with Conrado del Campo). He also studied privately in Spain with Alexandre Tansman. During 1955–63 he conducted the Orchestra Manuel de Falla, and toured as a conductor in Europe, the U.S., and Latin America. During 1965–66 he was music director of the Madrid Radio Symphony Orchestra. He taught at the Madrid Conservatory during 1962–66 and was its director from 1964.

PRINCIPAL COMPOSITIONS (published by UE): *Espejos* for 4 percussionists, tape (1963); *Secuencias* for orchestra (1964); *Simposion* for vocal soloists, chorus, orchestra (1966); *Lineas y puntos* for wind instruments, tape (1966); *Anillos* for orchestra (1968); *Yes, Speak Out, Yes*, cantata for vocal soloists, chorus, orchestra (1968); *Fibonacciana* for flute, string orchestra (1969); *String Quartet II* (1970); *Noche pasiva del sentido* for soprano, 2 percussionists; text by St. John of the Cross (1970).

BIBL.: Tomás Marco, *La música española de vanguardia* (Madrid 1970).

SEE ALSO Mathematics, Spain.

Halffter, Ernesto (Alberto) (b. Madrid, 16 Jan 1905), studied at the Colegio Alemán in Madrid (1911–21) and privately with Manuel de Falla in Granada (1922–26) and Maurice Ravel in Paris (1936). In 1931 he founded the Seville Conservatory of which he was director until 1936. During 1942–52 he taught at the Instituto Español in Lisbon. Since 1966 he has been musical advisor for the Spanish Television network. He has conducted in both Europe and America and is an honorary conductor of the Madrid Symphony Orchestra.

PRINCIPAL COMPOSITIONS: *Sinfonietta* (1924, Eschig); *Sonatina*, ballet (1928, Eschig); *Dulcinea*, ballet (1940); *Cojo enamorado*, ballet (1954, UME); *Fantasia galaica*, ballet (1955, Colombo); *Rapsodia portuguesa* for piano, orchestra (1962, Eschig); *Canticum in memorium P. P. Johannem XXIII* for soprano, baritone, chorus, orchestra (1964, Colombo); *Entr'acte*, chamber opera (1964, Colombo); *Elegia for Prince Pierre de Polignac* for chorus, orchestra (1966, Colombo); *Psalms* for vocal soloists, chorus, orchestra (1967, Colombo); *Guitar Concerto* (1969).

SEE ALSO Spain.

Halffter, Rodolfo (b. Madrid, 30 Oct 1900), is self-taught in composition except for 3 months study with Manuel de Falla in Granada (1938). In 1939 he moved to Mexico. He has worked for the Secretariat of Public Education there since 1941 and has taught music analysis at the National Conservatory since 1944. In 1940 he organized *La Paloma Azul*, a dance group directed by Anna Sokolow. He directed the journal *Nuestra música* during 1946–52 and in 1946 founded the publishing house Ediciones Mexicanas de Música, of which he is manager. During 1959–64 he was director of the music department at the National Institute of Fine Arts. His early compositions stem from the tradition of Falla. He began using 12-tone techniques in *3 Hojas de álbum* (1953), which was the first 12-tone work written in Mexico.

PRINCIPAL COMPOSITIONS: *Suite* for orchestra, Op. 1 (1924–28, CCM); *Marinero en tierra* for voice, piano, Op. 27; text by Rafael Alberti (1925, Ricordi); *2 Sonatas de El Escorial* for piano, Op. 2 (1928, UME); *Giga* for guitar, Op. 3 (1930, Eschig); *Impromptu* for orchestra, Op. 6 (1931–32); *Preludio y fuga* for piano, Op. 4 (1932, UME); *Obertura concertante* for piano, orchestra, Op. 5 (1932, CCM); *Clavileño*, opera buffa, Op. 8 (1934–36); *Don Lindo de Almeria*, ballet, Op. 7 (1935; *Suite*, 1935, EMM); *Divertimento* for 9 instruments, Op. 7a (1935); *Danza de Avila* for piano, Op. 9 (1936, Fischer); *Pequeñas variaciones elegiancas* for piano, Op. 10 (1937, Catalunya); *Violin Concerto*, Op. 11 (1939–40, EMM); *Pastorale* for violin, piano, Op. 18 (1940, EMM and Southern); *La mandrugada del panadero*, ballet, Op. 12 (1940; *Suite*, 1940; EMM); *2 Sonetos* for voice, piano, Op. 15; texts by Sister Juana Inés de la Cruz (1940–46, EMM); *Homenaje a Antonio Machado* for piano, Op. 13 (1944, EMM); *La nuez* for 3-voice children's chorus, text by Alfonso del Rio (1944, ESEP); *Elena la traicionera*, ballet, Op. 14 (1945); *Piano Sonata*, Op. 16 (1947, EMM); *3 Epitafios* for chorus, Op. 17; text by Cervantes (1947–53, EMM and Southern); *11 Bagatelas* for piano, Op. 19 (1949, EMM); *2-Part Invention on C-H-A-V-E-Z* for piano (1949, unpub.); *Piano Sonata No. 2*, Op. 20 (1951, PAU); *3 Sonatas de Antonio Soler* for orchestra (1951, Arión); *Obertura festiva*, Op. 21 (1952, Arión); *3 Hojas de álbum* for piano, Op. 22 (1953, UME); *3 Pieces* for string orchestra, Op. 23 (1954, Arión); *String Quartet*, Op. 24 (1957–58, EMM); *Tripartita* for orchestra, Op. 25 (1959, Arión and Ricordi); *Cello Sonata*, Op. 26 (1960, EMM); *3 Movements* for string quartet, Op. 28 (1962, EMM); *Música* for 2 pianos, Op. 29 (1965, EMM); *Piano Sonata No. 3*, Op. 30 (1967, EMM); *Desterro* for voice, piano, Op. 31; text by Xosé M. Alvarez Blázquez (1967, EMM); *Pregón para una pasqua pobre*, Op. 32, for chorus, trumpets, trombones, percussion (1968). List to 1954: *Composers of the Americas* 2:85–89.

BIBL.: "Twelve-Note Music in Mexico," *The Times* (London, 22 August 1955); Michael Greet Field, "Two-World Composer," *Americas* 7/10:10–14.

SEE ALSO Mexico, Spain.

Hall, Pauline (b. Hamar, Norway, 2 August 1890; d. 24 Jan 1969), studied in Norway (1910–12) with Catharinus Elling and later (1912–14) in Paris and Dresden. She was music critic for the Oslo newspaper *Dagbladet* during 1934–64 and was president of the Norwegian section of ISCM, 1938–61.

PRINCIPAL COMPOSITIONS: *Verlaine Suite* for orchestra (1929); *Suite* for flute, oboe, clarinet, bassoon, horn (1945, Lyche); *Julius Caesar*, suite for orchestra (1950); *Kongsemnerne* [The Pretenders] for orchestra, incidental music for the Ibsen play (1958); *Little Dance Suite* for oboe, clarinet, bassoon (1960); *4 Tosserier* for soprano, clarinet, bassoon, horn, trumpet; text by Halfdan Rasmussen (1961); *Variations on a Classical Theme* for flute (1961); *The Marquise*, ballet (1964).

SEE ALSO Scandinavia.

Hambraeus, Bengt (b. Stockholm, 29 Jan 1928), studied at the Univ. of Upsala (1947–56; musicology with Carl-Allan Moberg) and at the Darmstadt summer courses (1951, Wolfgang Fortner; 1952, Olivier Messiaen; 1953–54, Ernst Krenek). He also studied organ privately with Alf Linder (1944–48). During 1948–56 he was librarian and secretary at the musicological institute of the Univ. of Upsala. Since 1957 he has been a member of the editorial board of *Nudita musik* and on the staff of the Swedish Broadcasting Corporation (1965–68, director of chamber music division; since 1968, production director). He has composed at the Studio for Electronic Music of the Westdeutscher Rundfunk in Cologne (1955); the Studio di Fonologia, Radio Audizioni Italiane in Milan (1959); and at the Studio for Electronic Music in Munich (1963). He has lectured frequently over the Swedish Broadcasting Network and at institutions in Sweden and Finland and has written numerous articles on musicology and contemporary music for Swedish periodicals.

PRINCIPAL COMPOSITIONS: *Rota* for 3 orchestras, 2-track tape (1956–62); *Constellations I–III* for organ, tape; II is for tape only (1958–61, recorded by Philips); *Introduzione-Sequenze-Coda* for 3 flutes, 6 percussionists, electronic amplification (1958–59, Hansen-W); *Mikrogram* for alto flute, viola, vibraphone, harp (1961, Suecia); *Interferences* for organ (1961–62); *Transfiguration* for orchestra (1962–63, Hansen-W); *Responsorier* for solo voice, 2 organs, chorus, chimes (1964); *Fresque sonore* on tape (1965–67, recorded by Swedish Discophil).

PRINCIPAL WRITINGS: "Klangproblem i 1600–1700-talens orgelkenst," *Svensk tidskrift för musikforskning* (1950); "Preludium-Fuga-Toccata-Ciacona" (on Buxtehude's organ music), *ibid.* (1957); *Codex carminum gallicorum* (a study of MS VH 87 Bibl., Upsala Univ. Library; Stockholm 1961); "Om notskifter," *Paleografi-traditionförnyelse* (Stockholm 1970).

SEE ALSO Austria and Germany, Scandinavia.

Hamilton, Iain (b. Glasgow, 6 June 1922), moved from Scotland to London in 1929, was educated at Mill Hill School, and started to train as an engineer. In 1947 he won a scholarship to the Royal Academy of Music, from which he graduated in 1951. For the next decade he was active in all branches of London musical life as composer, teacher, lecturer, pianist, and member of numerous committees, including chairmanship of the British section of ISCM. In 1962 he was composer-in-residence at Tanglewood and began teaching at Duke Univ. in N. C., where he became chairman of the music department in 1966. He now divides his time between the university and New York City.

A prolific composer, Hamilton writes in all media but shows a bias toward orchestral and chamber music. In the first category belong two symphonies, five concertos, two overtures, and sundry other works. His chamber music includes two string quartets, a quintet and a sextet, and a number of instrumental sonatas, plus compositions for piano and organ. He has written two operas, *The Royal Hunt of the Sun* and *Agamemnon*, and, earlier, a ballet, *Clerk Saunders*. There are film scores, notably *Seawards Go the Great Ships*.

Hamilton belongs to the group of continental-oriented British composers who came to the fore in the early 1950s, before the generation of Maxwell Davies, Birtwistle, and Goehr. During his formative years Hindemith, Bartók, and Stravinsky were the dominant influences, and his early compositions were praised for their thrusting vigor, seriousness, dark-tinged scoring, formal innovations, and individual flavor of rhetorical and sometimes harsh beauty. By the late 1950s Hamilton had become a serialist, as in the *Sinfonia* for two orchestras, and had thereby moved ahead of British taste. Since his move to the U.S., literary and dramatic preoccupations have

come increasingly to the fore, as in his operas and the mixed-media *Pharsalia*; a new-found interest in the voice is illustrated by *Dialogues* for coloratura soprano. Coexistent with and to some extent conditioned by these new concerns has been a withdrawal in instrumental pieces since the *Sextet* (1962) from a position of extreme austerity and abstractionism. The solo sonatas of the mid-60s, for instance, reflect an increasing interest in the technical and expressive capacities of individual instruments, particularly woodwinds.

PRINCIPAL COMPOSITIONS: *Symphony No. 2* (1950–51, Schott); *Violin Concerto* (1952, Schott); *The Bermudas* for baritone, chorus, orchestra (1956, Schott); *Cello Sonata* (1958–59, Schott); *Sinfonia* for 2 orchestras (1958, Schott); *Piano Concerto* (1959–60; revised 1967, Schott); *Arias* for small orchestra (1962, Schott); *Cantos* for orchestra (1964, Schott); *Dialogues* for coloratura soprano, small ensemble (1965, Schott); *Sonata* for flautist, piano (1966, Presser); *Threnos—In Time of War* for organ (1966, Presser); *Agamemnon*, 2-act opera (1967–69, Presser); *The Royal Hunt of the Sun*, 2-act opera (1967–69, Presser); *Pharsalia*, a dramatic commentary for chamber ensemble (1968, Presser); *Circus* for 2 trumpets, orchestra (1969, Presser); *Epitaph for This World and Time* for 3 choruses, 2 organs (1970, Presser); *Voyage* for horn, orchestra (1970, Presser); *Alastor* for orchestra (1970, Presser).

PRINCIPAL WRITINGS: "Webern and Berg" and "Swiss Music," *European Music in the 20th Century* ed. by H. Hartog (London 1957); "Art and Responsibility," *Duke Univ. Alumni Register* (April 1963); "Reflections of a British Composer in America," *Perspectives* 5/1:134–38. Hamilton also wrote many articles on 19th- and 20th-century topics for *Listener* (London, BBC) during 1957–60.

BIBL.: William Mann, "I. H.'s Road to Serialism," *London Times* (5 Oct 1959); Colin Mason, "The Recent Music of I. H.," *Listener* (24 Oct 1957); Anthony Milner, "Some Observations on the Music of I. H.," *Musical Times* (July 1956). R. Murray Schafer, *British Composers in Interview* (London 1963).

Christopher Grier

Hamm, Charles (Edward) (b. Charlottesville, Va., 21 April 1925), studied at the Univ. of Va. (1943–47; counterpoint, theory with Randall Thompson, musicology with Stephen Tuttle) and Princeton Univ. (1947–50, 1957–59; composition with Edward Cone, Bohuslav Martinů, musicology with Arthur Mendel, Oliver Strunk). He has taught music history, theory, and composition at the Cincinnati Conservatory (1950–57) and at Newcomb College of Tulane Univ. (1959–63) and musicology at the Univ. of Ill. (since 1963).

PRINCIPAL COMPOSITIONS: *Prelude and Fugue* for 2 pianos (1962); *Mobile* for piano, tape (1963); *Canto* for narrator, singer, instruments (1963); *Portrait of John Cage* for piano, 4 tapes (1963); *Round* for any number and combination of voices or instruments (1964); *Something Else for Ellsworth Snyder* for pianist (1967).

PRINCIPAL WRITINGS: *A Chronology of the Works of Guillaume Dufay* (Princeton 1964); *Opera* (Boston 1965); "The American Composer and Opera," *The American Composer Speaks* ed. by Gilbert Chase (Baton Rouge 1966). Hamm has also edited the complete works of the 15th-century English composer, Leonel Power (1969).

SEE ALSO Musicology and Composition.

Hanell, Robert (b. Tschoschl, Czechoslovakia, 2 March 1925), studied music privately with his father, an organist. During 1945–55 he conducted orchestras at Zwickau, Meiningen, Gera, and Görlitz. He was musical director of the Komische Oper in East Berlin during 1955–65, as well as guest conductor at the Staatsoper there. Since 1965 he has been chief conductor for the East German Radio.

PRINCIPAL OPERAS (published by Henschel unless otherwise noted): *Der Bettler von Damaskus* (1947); *Die Gnomenwette* (1949); *Cecil* (1951, unpub.); *Die Spieldose* (1957); *Dorian Gray* (1962); *Oben und unten*, a singspiel (1964); *Esther* (1966); *Griechische Hochzeit* (1969).

Hanson, Howard (b. Wahoo, Neb., 28 Oct 1896), came of Scandinavian ancestry (his parents emigrated from Sweden in their early years). He studied composition with Percy Goetschius at the Institute of Musical Art in New York and later with Arne Oldberg at Northwestern Univ. He won the American Prix de Rome in 1921 and spent three years at the American Academy in Rome. In 1924, when he was barely 28, he became director of the Eastman School of Music in Rochester, N. Y., retaining this post for 40 years. In 1925 he inaugurated a series of American music festivals in Rochester at which he conducted a great number of new works of all stylistic types, an achievement unique in American music. In 1961–62, under the auspices of the U.S. State Department, he conducted the Eastman School Philharmonia Orchestra in Russia, Europe, and north Africa. As the teacher of two generations of American composers, he has contributed greatly to the national standards of musical excellence in the U.S.

Although he recognizes the validity of different idioms and techniques, Hanson believes that romantic ideals should be the animating force of all music. He is primarily a symphonist and finds his natural language in instrumental composition. He has been described as an American Sibelius, and indeed there are considerable areas of consanguinity between the two composers. Both write music rooted in folk inflections, specifically those of the north, without however resorting to actual quotations from popular melodies. Both explore the inner spiritual world of man; both are universal in their appeal.

Hanson's style is firmly anchored in tonality, but his harmonies are enhanced by euphonious dissonances; he often uses bitonal combinations of two major triads at the distance of a tritone between their tonics. Asymmetrical rhythms and compound meters impart an energetic quality to his music. In his orchestration he shows a predilection for the somber sonorities of low instrumental registers, especially in slow movements. In this he and Sibelius are again similar. Hanson's individuality reveals itself in the peculiarly American spaciousness of his melodic structures, a grandeur of symphonic design in the cyclic formation of thematic materials, and the vivacity of rhythmic patterns that naturally yield themselves to fugal developments. Although he does not hesitate to append explicit programmatic subtitles to his symphonies, he shows great interest in advanced techniques of abstract composition. His ability to expand the intellectual horizons of musical composition beyond his own practice is shown by his theoretical treatise, *Harmonic Materials of Modern Music: Resources of the Tempered Scale* (New York 1960), in which he systematically tabulates technical devices employed by contemporary composers.

PRINCIPAL COMPOSITIONS (published by Fischer unless otherwise noted): *Concerto* for organ, strings, harp (1921); *Symphonies Nos. 1–6*: No. 1, "Nordic" (1923); No. 2, "Romantic" (1930, Birchard); No. 3, inspired by Swedish sources (1938, Birchard); No. 4, "Requiem" (1943); No. 5, "Sinfonia Sacra" (1955, Birchard); No. 6 (1968); *Lux aeterna*, symphonic poem with viola obbligato (1923, Schirmer-G); *Pan and the Priest*, symphonic poem with piano obbligato (1926, Birchard); *String Quartet* (1926, Birchard); *The Lament of Beowulf* for chorus, orchestra (1926, Birchard); *Merry Mount*, opera (1933, Harms); *3 Songs from "Drum Taps"* by Walt Whitman for chorus, baritone, orchestra (1935); *Piano Concerto* (1948); *The Song of Democracy* for soloists, chorus, orchestra (1957); *Mosaics* for orchestra (1957); *Song of Human Rights*, cantata (1963). List to 1959: *Composers of the Americas* 5:38–45.

BIBL.: E. Royce, "H. H.," *American Composers on American Music* ed. by Henry Cowell (Stanford 1933); B. Tuthill, "H. H.," *Musical Quarterly* (April 1936).

Nicolas Slonimsky

SEE ALSO Liturgical Music: Christian; Opera; United States.

Happening, a theater genre that developed principally among artists and sculptors associated with the Reuben Gallery in New York, c.1959–63, at which time the term itself came into use. The genre has a compartmentalized structure in which self-contained theatrical units (consisting of actions, images, sounds, etc., alone or in combination) are presented in sequence and/or simultaneously. When performers in a happening carry out an assigned task, they are appearing as themselves in the present time and present place; they are not, as in traditional theater, playing the role of a character other than themselves. Among the early examples are various events that took place at the Bauhaus during the 1920s and one that was staged in 1952 at Black Mountain College in N. C. The latter was a collaborative work by composer John Cage, dancer Merce Cunningham, painter Robert Rauschenberg, pianist David Tudor, and others; it incorporated music, dance, painting, poetry readings, actions, recordings, films, and slides.

BIBL.: Al Hansen, *A Primer of Happenings & Time/Space* (New York 1965); Michael Kirby, *Happenings* (New York 1965); Richard Kostelanetz, ed., *The Theatre of Mixed Means* (New York 1968).

SEE ALSO Indeterminacy, Mixed Media.

Harbison, John (b. Orange, N. J., 20 Dec 1938), attended Harvard College (1956–60), the Hochschule für Musik in Berlin (1960–61), and Princeton Univ. (1961–63, composition with Earl Kim, Roger Sessions). He was composer in residence, Reed College, Ore. (1968–69) and began teaching at the Mass. Institute of Technology in 1969. In the latter year he also became music director of the Cantata Singers in Boston. A jazz player from 1952 to 1965, his musical development has been shaped by this experience and by his activities as a string-quartet player and conductor of new music.

PRINCIPAL COMPOSITIONS: *Sinfonia* for violin, double orchestra (1963); *Confinement* for 12 players (1965); *Shakespeare Series* for soprano, piano (1965); *Cantata Sequence*, 3 cantatas for soprano, various instrumental combinations; texts by Emily Dickinson (1965–68); *Violin Concerto* (1967); *Parody-Fantasia* for piano (1968); *Serenade* for flute or piccolo, clarinet, bass clarinet, violin, viola, cello (1968); *String Trio* (1969).

Harman, Carter (b. Brooklyn, N. Y., 14 June 1918), attended Princeton Univ. (1936–40, composition with Roger Sessions), and Columbia Univ. (1947–49, composition with Otto Luening). In the summers of 1934–36 Harman studied at the Ernest Williams Band and Orchestra School, Saugerties, N. Y. While Harman was in college, Milton Babbitt introduced him to the potentialities of manipulating sound after it has been recorded on a film sound track (the precursor of magnetic tape); his first experiments with tape composition were in 1954 under the guidance of Emory Cook, an electronics and sound engineer. Basic skills of musical journalism were learned from Howard Taubman, formerly music critic for the *New York Times*. Harman was a music reporter and record reviewer for the *Times* (1947–52) and was music editor of *Time Magazine* (1952–57). He was location recording engineer for the film *Lord of the Flies* (1962) and during 1958–67 was engineer for recording the Casals Festival in Puerto Rico. From 1960 to 1969 he was president of the West Indies Recording Corporation, San Juan. Since 1967 he has been executive vice president and producer of Composers Recordings Inc. in New York.

PRINCIPAL COMPOSITIONS: *Blackface*, ballet (1947); *Circus at the Opera*, children's opera (1951); *The Food of Love*, opera (1951); *Hymn to the Virgin* for chorus (1952, AMP); *You and I and Amyas*, a round for 3 voices (1952).

PRINCIPAL WRITINGS: *A Popular History of Music* (New York 1956, 1969); "Revolt of the Composers," *Atlantic Monthly* (Sept 1968): 129–32; "How Electronic Music Got that Way," *ibid.* (Dec 1968): 138–43.

Harmonic, an overtone or partial, i.e., one of the frequency components of a complex sound. The frequency of a harmonic is an integral (whole-number) multiple of the fundamental frequency.

Harmony and Counterpoint. The rise of new harmonic phenomena in the early 20th century was conditioned by developments at the end of the 19th. Traditional harmony had been based on the triad as the fundamental consonance and on the mechanics of tonality. These offered extensive possibilities for musical expression, the full utilization of which led eventually to the disintegration of the tonal system itself. Especially important in this regard were the condensation of modulatory passages, chromatic harmony, and the use of increasing numbers of transitional dissonances. Around 1900 the traditional division into consonances and dissonances was abandoned in such works as Debussy's *Nocturnes*, *Pelléas et Mélisande*, *Pour le piano*, *Estampes*, and *Masques* and Ravel's *Jeux d'eau*, *String Quartet*, *Sonatine*, and *Miroirs*. In avant-garde works around 1910 the triad was abandoned as the fundamental consonance. Such works as Bartók's *14 Bagatelles*, Prokofiev's *4 Piano Pieces* and *Suggestion diabolique*, Stravinsky's *Petruchka*, Schoenberg's *3 Piano Pieces*, and Webern's *5 Movements* for string quartet showed that any combination of sounds could function as a basic, stable chord requiring no resolution. The 20th-century composer soon had at his disposal a broad spectrum of sound combinations, differing greatly in color and expressiveness.

CHORD TYPES. The character of a 20th-century composition is determined in large part by the range of pitch combinations a composer uses and by the extent to which he stresses some over others. The quality or individuality of a combination is determined by its component intervals and their spacing and by the relative number of "stable" and "unstable" pitches it contains ("stability" being determined by the way the composer uses the various pitches). Within the equal-tempered system, the chords in use in 20th-century music can be classified into four types according to their interval structure: 1) Chords made of thirds, including tritones, sevenths, and ninths, all of which can be arranged as a series of triads. This type of combination was inherited from the 19th century. 2) Chords composed of fourths or fifths in both simple arrangements (G-C-F-B♭, C-G-D, etc.) and in inversions (F-G-B♭-C, G-C-D, etc.). 3) Whole-tone chords consisting of clusters of major seconds (C-D, C-D-E, etc., including all six tones in the whole-tone scale) and of all other combinations derived from this scale (C-D-F♯-B♭, C-E-G♯, etc.). 4) Chords built from the 12-tone chromatic scale, including clusters of minor seconds and other combinations derived from this scale and not included among the preceding types (C-F♯-B, C-D♭-G-A♭, etc.). It should be emphasized that the use of freely devised vertical combinations in a composition does not rule out the existence of a harmonic context in which differentiations occur. In some contexts, chords (mostly belonging to the first three types above) are used as stable combinations, as pillars of the chosen harmonic system, while other chords (mostly belonging to type four) are used as transitional tensions on the way to a resolution (a function similar to dissonance in traditional harmony).

Ex. 1. Béla Bartók, *Sonata for 2 Pianos and Percussion*, I: 33–36
Quoted by permission of Boosey & Hawkes, Universal Edition, and Theodore Presser

An example of such differentiation occurs in Ex. 1: triads and fourth chords are used to support the melodic line, while other chords (×) are used as transitional sounds; the latter are harsher than the former, owing to the minor seconds they contain (one member of which appears not only in the melody but doubled an octave below).

ORGANIZATION OF THE SOUND MATERIAL. The sound material employed in a composition is linked with the overall harmonic organization of that composition. In earlier music the material was regulated by the principles of tonality, including the hierarchical arrangement of chords around a tonic. Twentieth-century music has not completely abandoned tonal arrangements, although they now usually appear in modified forms. A connection with traditional tonal techniques appears primarily when there is an emphasis on a central pitch or chord (both functioning as the tonic) to which other, tension-producing pitches or chords are opposed. Twentieth-century composers also use diatonic arrangements that may suggest specific keys (at least locally). However, the traditional functional chain, which combined all confluences of sound in accordance with tonal principles, has been broken. Instead there may be immediate juxtapositions of tonally remote pitches, chords, and chord groups. Such juxtapositions may give rise to a new hierarchy of tensions analogous to the gravitational pull of dominant-tonic relationships. The greatest degree of tension in such cases is caused by tritone relationships (for example, F♯ when C has been established as the "center of gravity," or a group of tones such as F♯-C♯-D♯ when another group, C-G-A, is the established center). As in the tonal system, these tensions can apply both horizontally (melodically) and vertically (harmonically). In Ex. 2 the tonal

Ex. 2. Sergei Prokofiev, "Gavotte," No. 3 from *4 Pieces* for piano, Op. 32: 1–8
Quoted by permission of Boosey & Hawkes

center is F♯ minor, and there are deflections toward C and B♭ major. For Bartók the tritone opposition was especially important, both in terms of melodic material, which often oscillates between remote diatonic regions (from an A region to a G♯ region in Ex. 3, and in

Ex. 3. Béla Bartók, *The Miraculous Mandarin*, clarinet part: [13]
Quoted by permission of Boosey & Hawkes, Universal Edition, and Theodore Presser

terms of chord relations (for example, the opposition of B♭ as a center and E as a deflection in the Op. 14 *Suite*, or the limitation of harmonic material in the *Bagatelle No. 13* to E♭-minor and A-minor triads). Dominant-tonic relationships are replaced by tritone relationships, even in final cadences, in such works as the *Fifth String Quartet*, the *Music for Strings, Percussion, and Celeste*, and *Sonata for 2 Pianos and Percussion*.

Modality is another kind of harmonic organization. Here all vertical combinations in a composition (or portion thereof) are based on a selected group of pitch classes (a *scale*). All pitches in a modal scale are equal; there are no built-in oppositions and hierarchies as in tonality. Instead, vertical com-

binations are all drawn from a single, static harmonic field and are therefore homogeneous in harmonic color and "weight." A composer may choose to emphasize one pitch over others (one pitch, for example, may serve as a closing tone, or *finalis*, as in Ex. 5), or he may simultaneously impose other harmonic structures (tonal tensions, ostinatos, etc.) on a modal field, but the field, by itself, always remains antihierarchical and tensionless.

Various modal arrangements have been used in the 20th century: 1) seven-tone diatonic scales without chromatic tones (Ex. 4); 2)

Ex. 4. Igor Stavinsky, *Petrouchka*, tableau IV: 1–5
Quoted by permission of Boosey & Hawkes

pentatonic scales, from which various chords can be built, primarily the fourth and fifth chords of type 2 above (Ex. 5); 3) whole-tone

Ex. 5. Béla Bartók, *Dance Suite*, III: 1–8
Quoted by permission of Boosey & Hawkes, Universal Edition, and Theodore Presser

scales, which lead to the major-second combinations and other chords of type 3 above (Ex. 6); 4) artificial scales of the composer's

Ex. 6. Claude Debussy, *Piano Prelude No. 2*, "Voiles": 56–59
Quoted by permission of Editions Durand

invention, such as are prominent in Messiaen
—in Ex. 7, chords are formed from the tones

Ex. 7. Olivier Messiaen, No. 5 from *20 Regards
sur l'Enfant Jésus* (right hand of piano II
part): 1–5

of the scale D-E♭-F♭-F-A♭-A-B♭-C♭, which
consists of two identical segments of three half-
steps and a minor third each); 5) 12-tone
modality, in which all tones of the chromatic
scale are used in quick enough succession to
keep the listener aware of the total chromatic
field. The distinctive harmonic color of this
last type results from the continuous change
of chordal material and the predominance of
the fourth chord-type above (Ex. 8; Schoen-

Ex. 8. Arnold Schoenberg, No. 2 from *Piano
Pieces,* Op. 11 : 9–13

berg's later 12-tone method, from Op. 23 on,
provided a more complete realization of the
potentials of the 12-tone scale).

METHODS OF STABILIZATION. Harmonic organization, of whatever type, necessitates some
kind of design for stabilization. In modal

Ex. 9. Sergei Prokofiev, No. 12 from *Visions
fugitives,* Op. 22: 16–19

contexts, stabilization is achieved through the
exploitation of the selected scalar material.
Stabilization can also be achieved through
consistency of movement, for example consistent half-step movement of voices within
chords as in Ex. 9. Such procedures can impart
regularity and order to even the most unconventional chord sequences. Repetition also
produces stability. One type, the parallel
movement of the same chord configuration
to various pitches, appears in Ex. 10. Stability

Ex. 10. Claude Debussy, *Piano Prelude No. 19,*
"La Terrasse des audiences du clair de
lune" : 3–4

can be created among different chord configurations if the interval structure is the same.
Bartók used this device in the third movement
of his *Piano Sonata,* where except for three
brief passages only fourths and seconds (with
inversions) are used; likewise the last part of
No. 5 from the *Improvisations,* Op. 20, contains only tritones and major seconds (again
with inversions of the latter). The major
sevenths and major and minor ninths in Ex.
11 create a similarly homogeneous, stable
feeling.

Ex. 11. Anton Webern, *Variations for Piano,*
Op. 27 : 1–6

In non-12-tone and nonmodal music, the
simplest and most widespread means of
stabilization is the ostinato, the constant repetition of a motive and/or chord sequence

having a small number of component pitches (Ex. 12; an ostinato, however, can be more

Ex. 12. Sergei Prokofiev, No. 3 from *Visions fugitives*, Op. 22 : 13–16
Quoted by permission of Boosey & Hawkes

Ex. 13. Sergei Prokofiev, No. 14 from *Visions fugitives*, Op. 22 : 2–5
Quoted by permission of Boosey & Hawkes

complex, as in Ex. 13, which contains moving tones). Ostinatos usually stabilize one layer of sound, which then becomes a fulcrum for other, freely moving sounds. Most often ostinatos appear as accompaniments to melodies, which form continuously varying confluences with them. Because repeating sounds quickly establish themselves as a norm or anchor, ostinatos can create varying levels of tension and stability among pitches and thereby establish a system of hierarchies throughout an entire sound field. In Ex. 12 the repeated second G-A occurs on strong beats and is doubled an octave above; it is established as a harmonic center. The repeated C♯-D♯ interval occurs on weak beats and is not doubled; it is thus made to occupy an "inferior" position in the hierarchy of stable sounds. In Ex. 14 the harmonic center is the stable D♯-F interval in the lower staff. G is the strongest pitch beneath this interval, owing to its rhythmic placement and the fact that

Ex. 14. Sergei Prokofiev, No. 5 from *Sarcasms*, Op. 17 : 59–65

it precedes the other remaining pitches. The treble part consists of two chords, the first of which is the stronger since it occupies the stronger rhythmic position and doubles the central pitches of the lower part. The "foreign" tones in these chords have tension levels of their own; the B, which is constantly present and does not change register (unlike the D♯, which does change octaves) is the most stable. The freest—and least stable—tones in the passage are those in the mid-range. In ways such as this, ostinato procedures offer an alternative to tonal harmonic centricity, an alternative that is structured entirely by the composer.

SOUND LAYERS. The layering of sound is a frequent phenomenon in 20th-century harmony. In ostinato procedures, the layers are often related through tones stressed in common (for instance, the F and D♯ in Ex. 14). However, the layers may each follow different organizational principles, and the resulting confluences may be a fortuitous outcome of contrapuntal encounters among the layers. Layering may occur even where only one tonal center is present. In Ex. 15 the upper layer is

Ex. 15. Igor Stravinsky, *Piano Sonata*, I : 15–18
Quoted by permission of Boosey & Hawkes

organized in parallel thirds, the lower one in arpeggiated triads. Together the two layers form confluences which the ear can easily comprehend, not because they follow any external rules of traditional harmony but because each layer possesses an inner consistency. Layers may also be built of different modal materials or even show clear tonal features, which may result in bimodality or bitonality. In Ex. 16 there is a juxtaposition

Ex. 16. Karol Szymanowski, No. 18 from *Mazurkas*, Op. 50 : 96–101

Quoted by permission of Universal Edition and Theodore Presser

of the Lydian mode on B and of an ostinato made of fifths in C; one appreciates the naturalness and order of the separate layers and, hopefully, also savors the sounds that result from their combination. Bitonal passages in Milhaud are typically the result of two layers in different tonalities. Two layers are combined in many of Bartók's *Mikrokosmos* pieces, and often each layer is restricted in pitch-class content. In No. 109, for example, G♯, A, D, and E♮ are used in the left hand and B, C, F, and G♭ in the right. Within layers, all the previously described methods of harmonic stabilization can be used.

THE LIMITS OF HARMONY. One can speak of harmony only when the sound material of a composition is composed primarily of discrete pitches that are organized into intervals and larger vertical combinations according to a perceived system. Since 1950 much music has been written in which the element of harmony in this sense plays a small or negligible role. In the serial music of Boulez, Stockhausen, and others, vertical combinations tend to be subordinate to serial operations and are often little differentiated from one another. Harmony here is reduced to an even, static color, and other musical elements provide material for the artistic shaping and differentiation that exists in the work. In clusters, such as those in some passages of Penderecki, one can speak of a selection of intervals, but this is only one factor among others of equal or greater importance, including the breadth and density of the cluster and its register. In music where nonpitched sounds are used, harmony can no longer be said to exist. Other aspects of sound, such as overtones, envelopes, densities, intensities, durations, are the important elements.

COUNTERPOINT. Composers in the 20th century (as those in the 19th) have created no new contrapuntal forms or procedures. Rather

they have continued to utilize such traditional devices as imitation, inversion, retrograde, stretto, etc. Only the following have changed: 1) the pitch content of a work, 2) the interval structure of individual voices, and 3) the choices of vertical sound combinations (confluences). In the last category considerable freedom prevails, for the obliteration of the traditional boundaries between consonance and dissonance has opened up limitless possibilities for combining voices. Composers usually compensate for weakened harmonic ties with sharpened contours of pitch and rhythm in individual voices. Thus attention is concentrated far more than a century ago on the structure and flow of individual voices as well as on thematic and rhythmic interrelationships. (The term *linear counterpoint* is often applied to this kind of writing.) Confluent sounds are often fortuitous, although rarely completely so. Although the sequence of vertical intervals may not be a matter of basic importance (as they were, for example, with Bach), composers today usually try to achieve a vertical sound context that corresponds to the melodic character of the voices. This situation is illustrated in Ex. 17. The

Ex. 17. Béla Bartók, *String Quartet No. 4*, I : 11–12

Quoted by permission of Boosey & Hawkes, Universal Edition, and Theodore Presser

upper voice, which has a distinct interval structure (consistent half-step movement) and a clear-cut rhythmic profile, is counterpointed with the lower voice through imitation and inversion procedures. This results in several different confluences, among them traditional consonances. However, the high proportion of harsh intervals creates an overall sound context in the phrase that enhances the strident energy of the separate voices.

Linearity is not an invariable characteristic of 20th-century polyphony. There are works in which the harmonic element, strongly emphasized, is based on a careful choice of confluences. This phenomenon is most often linked with the application of traditional harmonic devices. In addition, however, it may also result from: 1) the coordination of the interval structure of confluences with the interval makeup of individual voices, or 2) the limitation of confluences to one selected type. In Ex. 18 both individual voices and confluences are structured in fourths. The greatest

Ex. 18. Paul Hindemith, Fugue No. 4 from *Ludus tonalis*: 9–14

Quoted by permission of B. Schott and Belwin-Mills

agreement between counterpoint and harmony in 20th-century music occurs in a context of 12-tone modality, for here the modally stabilized pitch material automatically creates definite harmonic consequences.

BIBL.: Béla Bartók, "Problem der neuen Musik," *Melos* (1920); Wilfrid Dunwell, *The Evolution of 20th-Century Harmony* (London 1960); Paul Hindemith, *The Craft of Musical Composition* (New York 1941, revised 1945); Y. Kholopov, *Sovremennye cherty garmonii Prokof'eva* [Modern Traits in Prokofiev's Harmony] (Moscow 1967); Ernst Kurth, *Romantische Harmonik und ihre Krise* (Berlin 1923); Joseph Machlis, *Introduction to Contemporary Music* (New York 1961); Olivier Messiaen, *Technique of My Musical Language* (Paris 1950); Vincent Persichetti, *20th-Century Harmony* (New York 1961); F. Reuter, *Praktische Harmonik des 20. Jahrhundert* (Halle 1952); Rudolph Reti, *Tonality-Atonality-Pantonality* (London 1958); G. Welton Marquis, *20th-Century Music Idioms* (Englewood Cliffs 1964).

Tadeusz A. Zieliński
(trans. from Polish by Ludwik Krzyżanowski)

SEE ALSO Asian Music and Western Composition, Form, Melody, Microtones, Musicology and Composition, Popular Music, Serialism, Texture, Tuning and Temperament.

Harris, Roy (b. Lincoln County, Neb., 12 Feb 1898), spent his formative years in suburban Los Angeles, where during the mid-1920s he was a pupil principally of Arthur Farwell and also of Modest Altschuler and Arthur Bliss. In 1926, shortly after the Andante from an early unfinished symphony was conducted in Rochester, N.Y., by Howard Hanson, he began study with Nadia Boulanger in Paris and obtained two consecutive Guggenheim

Fellowships. In 1929 he returned to the U.S., where the *Piano Sonata* (1928), *Concerto* for clarinet, piano, and string quartet (1927), and the *String Quartet No. 1* (1930) (all products of his stay in Paris) began to be heard. Serge Koussevitzky commissioned and premiered in Boston (Jan 1934) his *Symphony 1933* (properly No. 1), which launched his reputation as America's leading modern symphonist. The remainder of the decade saw a steady stream of ambitious works, culminating in the *Symphony No. 3* (1937), probably the most frequently performed American symphony. Since that time Harris has taught and lectured at numerous colleges, conducted his own works, organized music festivals, traveled to the U.S.S.R. under auspices of the U.S. State Department, and written a host of compositions in various forms (including over 110 commissions). He is now composer in residence at the Univ. of Calif. at Los Angeles.

The fact that Harris came to the formal study of music somewhat late in life helps account for the striking originality of his style. He has been praised for his melodic gifts, but in fact the range of his melodic invention is rather circumscribed, and he is no purveyor of easy tunes with sequential repetitions. Although some of his themes are highly chromatic (a few are made up of all 12 tones in the scale, as in the *Piano Quintet*, 1936) and although others are only fragmentary motifs (*Piano Sonata*), for the most part long-lined melody plays an essential role. It is both the seed and a dynamic principle of growth, constantly evolving in a kind of continuous variation and sometimes employing interpolations of notes or the juxtaposition of sharply contrasted materials (*Symphony No. 9*, 1962). The basically diatonic character of Harris's melody is derived from Anglo-Saxon hymns and the rural American folk melos, with which all his music is permeated (*Symphony No. 4*, 1939). But Harris has infused this regional material with his own assimilation of classical procedures, such as passacaglias, chorales, fugues, cancrizans, and the like (*Symphony No. 5*, 1942). Another characteristic of many Harris themes is a penchant for falling intervals having a yearning, plangent quality. Striving, desolation, exuberance, and ultimate triumph are among the principal psychological forces behind such features.

Harmonically Harris is almost always tonal, but frequently he makes use of polychords in dissonant combinations, fourths and fifths predominating and giving his music a broad, open feeling. The triad and the ancient modes play an important role (*String Quartet No. 3*,

1937); in fact the composer has compiled systematic inventories of these and other musical devices, seemingly in an effort to rationalize his own intuitive compositional methods. His rhythms are asymmetrical, full of unexpected accents and unusual cadences that contribute to sudden shifts of dynamics and mood (*Symphonies Nos. 7* and *9*). His orchestration emphasizes the various instrumental choirs as collective units in an antiphonal manner (*Symphony No. 3*). He uses a type of quasilinear counterpoint modeled after Bach and the renaissance Flemish masters (*Symphony No. 5*). Although his contrapuntal writing may not be orthodox in terms of strictly independent lines, it would seem that his polyphonic manner is a complex product of all the above factors working in close conjunction.

From the beginning Harris has been intent on creating a new type of 20th-century music in the large-scale forms of the past, and it is here that his talents seem most at home. His many programmatic and occasional pieces tend toward the inconsequential or banal, and it is significant that he has written no operas and few theater works of any kind. His output, like that of most prolific composers, has been uneven, owing in part to a lack of self-criticism. In some of his most recent works he has tended to lapse into old formulas and unconscious self-quotation. It should be borne in mind, however, that one cannot fully appreciate a new Harris score in one exposure, for his blend of the intellectually formidable and the emotionally compelling, with little regard for purely coloristic considerations, makes for a music that is often quite difficult. His influence on the development of American symphonic and chamber literature is incalculable. Without the example he set with his early works, the whole school of classically oriented American figures (Piston, Schuman, Gould, Mennin, among others) would be unthinkable. Since the end of World War II changes in musical fashion have overtaken Harris and the kind of music associated with his name. In addition, there has been a reaction against some of the exaggerated claims made for him during the 1930s. At its best, however, which is more often than currently assumed, Harris's work embodies a vision of human life that is at once tragic and affirmative. Like his counterparts, Sibelius, Janáček, and Saeverud, he has fused national idioms with traditional forms to express universal meanings.

PRINCIPAL COMPOSITIONS (list prepared with the composer's help): *Concerto* for clarinet, piano, string quartet (1927, Cos Cob); *Piano Sonata* (1928, Cos Cob and Arrow); *String Quartets Nos. 1–3* (1930; 1933, Schirmer-G; 1937, Mills); *String Sextet* (1932, Flammer); *Symphonies Nos. 1–12* (1933, Schirmer-G; 1934, Schirmer-G; 1937, Schirmer-G; 1939, Schirmer-G; 1942, Mills; 1944, Mills; 1951, AMP; 1962, AMP; 1962, AMP; 1965, AMP; 1967, AMP; 1969, AMP); *When Johnny Comes Marching Home* for orchestra (1934, Schirmer-G); *Songs for Occupations* for chorus (1934, Schirmer-G); *Piano Trio* (1934, published in *Modern Music*); *Prelude and Fugue* for string orchestra (1936, Schirmer-G); *Symphony for Voices* (1936, Schirmer-G); *Piano Quintet* (1936, Schirmer-G); *Time Suite* (1936, Schirmer-G); *Soliloquy and Dance* for viola, piano (1938, Schirmer-G); *String Quintet* (1939); *Challenge 1940* for baritone, chorus, orchestra (1940, Mills); *American Creed* for orchestra (1940, Mills); *Ode to Truth* for orchestra (1941, Mills); *Piano Concerto* with band (1942, Mills); *Violin Sonata* (1942, Mills); *Cantata* for chorus, organ, brass (1943, Mills); *Mass* for men's chorus, organ (1943, Schirmer-G); *Piano Concerto No. 1* (1945); *Concerto for 2 Pianos* (1946, Fischer); *Kentucky Spring* for orchestra (1949, Mills); *Cumberland Concerto* (1951, Mills); *Piano Concerto No. 2* (1953, AMP); *Abraham Lincoln Walks at Midnight*, chamber cantata (1953, AMP); *Fantasy* for piano, orchestra (1954, AMP); *Psalm 150* for chorus (1955, Golden Press); *Folk Fantasy for Festivals* for piano, chorus (1956, AMP); *Give Me the Splendid Silent Sun*, cantata (1959, AMP); *Canticle to the Sun*, cantata (1961, AMP); *Epilogue to Profiles in Courage: JFK* for orchestra (1963, AMP); *Salute to Youth* for orchestra (1963, AMP); *Duo* for cello, piano (1964, AMP); *Horn of Plenty* for orchestra (1964, AMP); *Piano Sextet* (1968, AMP); *Concerto for* amplified piano, brasses, percussion (1968, AMP).

BIBL.: Aaron Copland, "R. H.," *Our New Music* (New York 1941); Henry Cowell, "R. H.," *American Composers on American Music* (Palo Alto, Calif., 1933); Robert Evett, "The Harmonic Idiom of R. H.," *Modern Music* (spring 1946); Arthur Farwell, "R. H.," *Musical Quarterly* (1932); Arthur Mendel, "R. H.'s *Piano Quintet*," *Modern Music* (fall 1939); Nicolas Slonimsky, "R. H.," *Musical Quarterly* (1947), revised version in *Etude* (Dec 1956 and Jan 1957).

Paul A. Snook

SEE ALSO Dance, Popular Music, United States.

Harrison, Lou (b. Portland, Ore., 14 May 1917), attended San Francisco State College and studied with Henry Cowell (1934–35). During this period he began composing percussion works, some for concerts organized in collaboration with John Cage. He also began working with dancers as a composer, accompanist, and as a dancer himself. He taught at Mills College during 1936–39, and accompanied dance classes there and in Los

Angeles, to which he moved in 1941. While in Los Angeles he studied with Arnold Schoenberg. Harrison moved to New York in 1943, where he met Virgil Thomson and earned his living as a critic, copyist, and as a composer for dance. He edited for publication several major works by Charles Ives, among them the *Piano Sonata No. 1* and the *Symphony No. 3*, which he conducted at its first performance (1947). He returned to California in 1953 (where he met Harry Partch) and did various odd jobs. In the 1960s he intensified his activities as a designer and builder of instruments. He visited Japan, Korea, and Taiwan in 1961–62 on a Rockefeller Fellowship. In 1967 he began teaching at San Jose State College.

A melodist in all forms, Harrison adapts to his purpose melodic usages of Schoenberg and some aspects of serial and aleatory procedures. During his early years, while working as a dance-studio accompanist, he composed a great variety of vocal, dance, and instrumental music, which has supplied many movements of more recent compositions (in this practice he resembles Ives). Some of his music is intended for performance in just intonation. He often emulates medieval and renaissance polyphony and the practices of Asian cultures. Gamelan-like rhythms occur in the *Suite* for violin, piano, and small orchestra and in the *Concerto in Slendro*; Western and Asian instruments are combined in several works from the 1960s. He has used such nonstandard sound sources as brake drums, coffee cans, and flower pots, demonstrating a subtle awareness of unexpected sound relationships. A favorite instrument, the "tack piano," appears in such works as *Solstice* and the *Symphony on G*. He is a student of Esperanto and prefers this language for his vocal works because of its open vowels.

PRINCIPAL COMPOSITIONS: *6 Cembalo Sonatas* (1934–43, NME); *Suite for Symphonic Strings* (1936–60, Peters); *Mass* for vocal soloists, trumpet, harp, strings (1939–49, Peer); *Canticles Nos. 1, 3* for percussion orchestra (1940, 1941; Percus); *Suite* for piano (1943, Peters); *Schoenbergiana* for string sextet (1945, arranged for woodwind sextet by Robert Hughes); *Suite No. 2* for string orchestra (1948, Merrymount); *Symphony on G* (1948–61, Peer); *Solstice* for flute, oboe, trumpet, celesta, tack piano, 2 cellos, double bass (1950, Peer); *Suite* for violin, piano, small orchestra (1951, AMP); *Rapunzel*, opera; text by William Morris (1954, Peer); *4 Strict Songs* for 8 baritones, orchestra (1955, AMP); *Concerto* for violin, percussion orchestra (1959, Peters); *Concerto in Slendro* for violin, celesta, percussion (1961, Peters); *Moo gung kwa, Se tang ak* for classical Korean court orchestra (1961); *3 Psaltery Pieces*

(1961–62, 1964, 1966–69); *Nova Odo* for orchestra, chorus, special instruments (1962); *Pacifika Rondo* for chamber orchestra of Western and Asian instruments (1963); *Political Primer* for vocal soloists, chorus, orchestra (c.1965); *Peace Piece One* for chorus; text from the Metta Sutra (1968); *Young Caesar*, puppet opera (1970). List to 1963: *Composers of the Americas* 8:89–93.

PRINCIPAL WRITINGS: During 1943–47 Harrison wrote articles and reviews for the *New York Herald Tribune*, *Listen*, *Modern Music*, and other periodicals.

Peter Yates

SEE ALSO Asian Music and Western Composition, Dance, Instrumental and Vocal Resources, Microtones, Tuning and Temperament.

Hartig, Heinz (Friedrich) (b. Cassel, 10 Sept 1907; d. Berlin, 16 Sept 1969), attended the Cassel Conservatory (piano, theory), the Berlin Hochschule für Musik (*Schulmusik*), and the Univ. of Vienna (musicology). He also studied composition briefly with Boris Blacher during the winter of 1946–47. During World War II he was harpsichordist in the Collegium Musicum of Hermann Diener. Around 1948 he became acquainted with Paul Dessau and was a conductor of Brecht theater productions in Berlin. From 1951 he taught composition at the Berlin Hochschule. Wolfgang Burde has described Hartig's early compositions as a synthesis of neoclassic elements and Blacher's variable meters. With *Perché* (1958) he began to employ Schoenberg's 12-tone techniques and with the *Variationen* (1962), serial principles. He always placed emphasis on the formal principles of repetition and variation, especially in his later work, when he was concerned with more athematic structures.

PRINCIPAL COMPOSITIONS (published by Bote unless otherwise noted): *Variations en métres variables* for piano, Op. 12 (1951); *Der Trinker und die Spiegel*, 5 chansons for baritone, piano; text after W. Mehring, Op. 16 (1953); *Perché*, lament for chorus, guitar, Op. 28 (1958); *Schwarze Sonne*, ballet, Op. 31 (1958); *Messe nach einem Feuersturm* for baritone, chorus, orchestra; text after Dylan Thomas, Op. 32 (1960); *Escorial*, chamber opera after de Ghelderode, Op. 36 (1961); *Variationen über einen siebentönigen Klang* for orchestra, Op. 39a (1962); *3 Songs* for baritone, orchestra; text after G. Benn and W. Schwarz, Op. 40 (1964); *Wohin?*, oratorio for soprano, baritone, bass, 2 choruses, orchestra, tape, Op. 41 (1963–64, unpub.); *Komposition in 5 Phasen* for cello, chorus, orchestra, tape, Op. 44 (1966, unpub.); *Immediate* for flute, clarinet, piano, 2 cellos, Op. 45 (1966); *Composizione per 2* for cello, piano, Op. 47 (1968); *Composizione per 5* for flute, oboe, string trio, Op. 50 (1968); *Concerto strumentale* for violin, orchestra, Op. 48 (1968–69).

BIBL.: Wolfgang Burde, *H. F. H.* (Berlin 1967).

Hartley, Walter Sinclair (b. Washington, 21 Feb 1927), studied at the Eastman School (1947–53; composition with Bernard Rogers, Howard Hanson; piano with José Echániz). He has taught at the National Music Camp, Interlochen, Mich. (1956–64); at Davis and Elkins College, Elkins, W. Va. (1958–69), where he was head of the Music Dept.; and at the State Univ. College, Fredonia, N. Y. (since 1969). He is also a professional pianist. Busoni, Honegger, Bartók, Stravinsky, and Hindemith were the major influences on his music. He uses traditional forms, contrapuntal textures, and a free tonal orientation and is especially attracted to wind instruments.

PRINCIPAL COMPOSITIONS: *Triptych* for orchestra, Op. 12 (1951, Fema); *Piano Concerto*, Op. 17 (1952, Fema); *Chamber Symphony*, Op. 22 (1954, Galaxy); *Scenes from Lorca's "Blood Wedding,"* Op. 26, for orchestra (1956, Fema) or piano (unpub.); *Divertimento* for cello, wind quintet, Op. 28 (1956, Fema); *Concerto for 23 Winds*, Op. 29 (1957, Rochester); *Sonata concertante* for trombone, piano, Op. 32 (1958, Fema); *String Quartet No. 2*, Op. 49 (1962, Galaxy); *Sinfonia No. 3* for brass choir, Op. 57 (1963, Tenuto); *Duo* for alto saxophone, piano, Op. 60 (1964, Tenuto); *Sinfonia No. 4* for winds, Op. 64 (1965, MCA); *Concerto* for alto saxophone, band, Op. 69 (1966, Tenuto); *A Psalm Cycle* for medium-high voice, flute, piano, Op. 73 (1967, Tenuto); *Tuba Sonata*, Op. 76 (1967, Tenuto); *Piano Sonata No. 2*, Op. 80 (1968, Tenuto).

BIBL.: Winston Morris and William Bell, "W. S. H.," *Encyclopedia of Literature for the Tuba* (New York 1967).

Hartmann, Karl Amadeus (b. Munich, 2 August 1905; d. Munich, 5 Dec 1963), received a traditional education at the Munich Musikakademie with Joseph Haas (1923–27). More important was his practical and theoretical study with Hermann Scherchen, who encouraged his individuality and helped him obtain first performances (Strasbourg, 1933; Prague, 1935) and composition prizes (Geneva, 1936; Vienna, 1937). During the Nazi regime he was compelled to withdraw from public notice, although he did not remain inactive. He continued to compose, and he studied during 1941–42 with Anton Webern in Vienna. After 1945 he destroyed many of his early works and began again, quickly gaining prominence as a creative artist and as a leader of the Musica Viva concert series in Munich.

The core of Hartmann's output is a series of eight symphonies. The first one resembles Mahler in the use of five movements and an alto solo, the later ones in the dominance of adagio movements. More evident is the heaviness of Bruckner's diction and Reger's technique of increasing contrapuntal density. In general, however, Hartmann's style is in the tradition of tonally free expressionism (as in Berg). His music encompasses brilliance alternating with Stravinsky-like dryness (*Symphony No. 5*), rhythmic procedures derived from Boris Blacher's "variable meters" (*Piano Concerto*), virtuoso gestures (in the concertos as well as in the fugal writing of the symphonies 3, 6, and 7), and, at the end, clarity of tone color (*Symphony No. 8* and *Gesangsszene*). A unison beginning is characteristic of Hartmann's compositions, after which an accumulation of polyphonic lines and an increasing dynamic level leads to emotionally charged climaxes. Thus, in spite of differing numbers of movements, each work tends to have a monolithic quality.

PRINCIPAL COMPOSITIONS (published by Schott): *String Quartet* (1934); *Des Simplicius Simplicissimus Jugend* (1934–35; first performed, 1949); *Symphony No. 1* (1937–40); *Concerto funebre* for violin and string orchestra (1939); *Symphony No. 2*, "Adagio" (1941–46); *Symphony No. 4* (1946–47); *String Quartet No. 2* (1948); *Symphony No. 3* (1948–49); *Symphony No. 5*, "Concertante" (1950); *Symphony No. 6* (1951–53); *Concerto* for piano, winds, percussion (1953); *Concerto* for viola, piano, winds, percussion (1954–55); *Symphony No. 7* (1958); *Symphony No. 8* (1962); *Gesangsszene* for baritone, orchestra; text by Giraudoux (1963, unfinished).

PRINCIPAL WRITINGS: *Kleine Schriften* ed. by Ernst Thomas (Mainz 1965).

BIBL.: Ulrich Dibelius, *Moderne Musik 1945–65* (Munich 1966); Elizabeth and Richard Hartmann, eds., *Epitaph* (Munich 1964); K. H. Ruppel, ed., *Musica Viva* (Munich 1959).

Ulrich Dibelius
(trans. from German by Jeanne Wolf)

SEE ALSO Austria and Germany.

Harutiunian, Aleksander Grigor, see under Arutiunian

Hashagen, Klaus (b. Semarang, Java, 31 August 1924), studied at the Northwest German Music Academy in Detmold (1946–50; composition with Günter Bialas, acoustics with W. Thienhaus). During 1951–66 he was a sound engineer and music editor for the Norddeutscher Rundfunk in Hanover. He has been director of the music division of the Bayerischen Rundfunks in Nuremberg since 1966.

PRINCIPAL COMPOSITIONS (dates not available): *Percussion I–IX*, electronic and concrete music on tape; *Pergiton I–IV* for guitar with percussion or tape and orchestra (No. IV recorded by Deutsche Grammophon); *Rondell* for wind quintet; *Campane e fiorituri* for wind quintet; *Colloquium* for wind quintet; *Perpetuum mobile* for 4 clarinets; *Scènes fugitives* for string quartet; *Mobile Szenen I–III* for percussion with orchestra or piano or chamber ensemble and tape; *Transposition-Improvisation* for percussion, tape; *Giorno per giorno*, cantata for soprano, flute, harpsichord, percussion, tape; *Bau des Tempels* for narrator, chamber ensemble, tape; *Davids Dankgesang* for narrator, chorus, tape; *Der vergessene Mond*, cantata for mezzo-soprano, chamber ensemble; *Manasses Gebet* for men's chorus, tape; *Studien für 5 Gruppen* for 5 chamber orchestras; *Studien für 4 Streichquartette*; *Gesten* for recorder, tape (Moeck); *Toccata* for piano (Bosse); *Alphabetische Gesänge* for men's chorus, piano; *Die Tagesschau* in various versions for narrator, chorus, chamber ensemble, projections; *Cymbalon* for harpsichord, tape; *Inventions* for piano; *Divertimento on French Folksongs* for orchestra (Bärenreiter and Bosse); *Suite* for oboe, harpsichord; *Suite* for strings; *Meditation* for solo percussion; *Lieder eines Lumpen* for men's chorus, percussion; *Timbres* for organ; *Vitrum nostrum*, musical scene after Georg Forster for singers, instrumentalists; *3 Psalms of David* for chorus (Möseler); *Rezitationen des Schwarzen Orpheus* for narrator, jazz ensemble; *Duocordis* for 2 string instruments; *Viocela* for violin, harpsichord; *Gardinenpredigt eines Blockflötenspielers* for solo recorder (Hänssler); *Septalie* for any ensemble (Bosse); *Die 4 Apostel*, impression for narrator, women's voices, orchestra.

Haubenstock-Ramati, Roman (b. Cracow, 27 Feb 1919), studied musicology and philosophy at the Univ. of Cracow and was a composition student of Arthur Malawski (1935–38) and Josef Koffler (1939–40). He directed the music department of Radio Cracow (1947–50), and during 1950–56 was director of the state music library and professor of music at the academy in Tel Aviv. In 1957 he began working at the musique-concrète studio of the French radio in Paris, and in the same year became the reader for new music at Universal Edition in Vienna. Since 1968 he has been living in Vienna as a freelance composer.

Most of Haubenstock-Ramati's works are for orchestral and chamber ensembles, of which a few include voices. There are several theater pieces, including one opera. The influences of Stravinsky and Szymanowski dominated in the early compositions. In 1938 the composer became acquainted with scores of Anton Webern and began using 12-tone tech-

niques. Since that time he has been in the forefront of the European avant-garde. He has been especially concerned with new kinds of notation.' In 1959 he organized the first exhibit of musical graphics at Donaueschingen, and he has used combinations of exact and associative notation in his "mobiles" for various instruments. In *Tableau for Orchestra* the right-hand pages of the score contain the basic design graphically notated for the conductor; the left-hand pages contain a few important places in this design written out in detail. In addition each player has his own part. This notational method enables the composer to achieve full and highly detailed sound textures, while still permitting the conductor to have a readable score.

PRINCIPAL COMPOSITIONS (published by UE): *Les Symphonies de timbres* for orchestra (1956); *Chants et prismes* for orchestra (1957); *Sequences* for violin, orchestra in 4 groups (1957–58); *Interpolation*, mobile for flute (1958); *Liaisons*, mobile for vibraphone, marimbaphone (1958); *Mobile for Shakespeare* for voice, 6 players (1959); *Petite Musique de nuit*, mobile for orchestra (1959); *Decisions*, a file of graphic notations for various instruments (1959–68); *Credentials* or *Think, Think, Lucky* for sprechgesang, 8 players; text by Samuel Beckett (1960); *Jeux 6*, mobile for 6 percussionists (1961); *Vermutungen über ein dunkles Haus* for 3 orchestras, 2 of which are prerecorded on tape (1963); *Amerika*, opera in 2 parts; libretto by the composer after Kafka (1963–64); *Klavierstücke (1)* for piano (1964–67); *Comedie*, antiopera in 1 act; text from Beckett (1967); *Tableau I, II, and III* for orchestra (1967–71); *Symphonie "K"* for orchestra (1967); *Catch* for harpsichord (1968); *Jeux 2* for 2 percussionists; *Divertimento*, stage work for 2 percussionists, 2 actors, dancer (and/or mime) (1968); *Jeux 4* for 4 percussionists (1968); *Catch 2* for 1–2 pianos (1968); *Madrigal* for chorus (1970).

PRINCIPAL WRITINGS: "Notation: Material and Form," *Perspectives* 4/1:39–44; "Form," *Darmstädter Beiträge zur Neuen Musik* 10; "Zwischen Trenn und Computer," *Wort und Wahrheit* (Vienna, 1971).

BIBL.: Erhard Karkoschka, "R. H.-R. und der 27. Februar 1969," *Melos* 36:57–62. Reviews of individual compositions have appeared in *Melos* (1956, 58, 60, 61, 66), *Neue Zeitschrift für Musik* (1958), and *Musical Quarterly* (1961, 67).

Erhard Karkoschka
(trans. from German by Jeanne Wolf)

SEE ALSO Austria and Germany, Instrumental and Vocal Resources, Mixed Media, Notation.

Haubiel, Charles (Trowbridge), (b. Delta, Ohio, 30 Jan 1892), studied piano with Rudolph Ganz in Berlin (1911–13) and with Rosina and Josef Lhevinne in New York

(1920–26) and attended Mannes College (1919–24, composition with Rosario Scalero). He also studied orchestration with Modest Altschuler in New York (1948–52). Active for a time as a concert pianist, he then taught piano at Kingfisher College, Okla. (1913–15), the Musical Art Institute in Oklahoma City (1915–17), and the Institute of Musical Art, New York (1921–31). He taught music history at New York Univ. during 1923–47 and in 1935 founded the Composers' Press, of which he was president until 1967. He has been active as a writer and lecturer on music. Haubiel divides his output into three categories: neoclassic, romantic-impressionist, and Americana; he tends to agree with the description of John Tasker Howard (see bibl.) that his music is a combination of Brahms and Debussy.

PRINCIPAL COMPOSITIONS: *Suite passacaille* for 2 pianos (1917; recomposed 1931, CP); *Ariel* for piano (1919; revised 1930, Marks); *Gothic Variations* for violin, piano (1919; revised 1942, CP) or for violin, orchestra (1968, CP); *Portraits*, "Capriccio," "Idillio," "Scherzo," for piano (1919, CP) or orchestra (1934, CP); *L'amore spirituale*, 3 songs in canonic form for women's chorus, 2 pianos; texts by Oscar Wilde (1924, CP); *Echi classici*, string quartet no. 1 in C minor (1924, 1936; Southern-S); *Vox cathedralis*, chorale variations and fugue for organ (1925) or 2 pianos (1928) or orchestra (1938); *Metamorphoses*, 29 variations on "Swanee River" for piano (1926, CP); *Brigands Preferred*, 2-act musical satire; libretto by Martin Leonard (1927); *Karma*, symphonic variations on a theme by Handel (1928; orchestration revised under the title *Of Human Destiny*, 1968); *Duo-forms*, "Caprice in Waltz Form," "Serenade and Romance," "Scherzo-tarantelle," for cello, piano (1929, 1933, 1933; CP); *Salari*, "Dawn Mists," "Meridian," "The Plane Beyond," for piano (1932, 1956, 1934; CP) or orchestra (1933, 1936, 1936); *Incidental Music to "The Passionate Pilgrim"* (1934): "Elizabethan Songs" (CP), "Pastorale" for oboe, bassoon (Avant), "Romanza" for violin, cello, piano (CP), "Gay Dances" for violin, cello, piano (unpub.), "In Praise of Dance" for oboe, violin, cello, piano (one section published by Southern-S); *The Cosmic Christ*, cantata for high voice, piano; text by Mabel Struble (1937, CP; orchestrated 1948); *Miniatures* for string orchestra (1938, CP); *Vision of St. Joan*, cantata for soprano, alto, boys' chorus, adult chorus, orchestra; text by Hortense Flexner (1939, CP); *Nuances* for flute (violin) with piano (1940, CP) or with orchestra (1949); *Cello Sonata in C Minor* (1941, CP); *In the French Manner* for flute, cello, piano (1942, CP); *1865 A.D.* for orchestra (1943, revised 1958 and 1962; sketches for piano and for violin, piano, 1940, published by CP); *Violin Sonata in D Minor* (1945, CP); *Pioneers*, symphonic saga of Ohio (1946; revised 1956, 1960); *American Rhapsody* for orchestra or

soprano, men's chorus (1948; orchestrated 1962; piano reduction 1963, CP); *Pastoral Trio* for flute, cello, piano (1949, CP); *Sunday Costs 5 Pesos*, Mexican folk opera; libretto by Josephine Niggli (1949, revised 1954), arranged for performance with chamber orchestra (1968); *Epochs*, "Symmetry," "Nocturne," "En Saga," for violin, piano (1955, 1954, 1954; CP); *Heroic Elegy* for orchestra (1967).

PRINCIPAL WRITINGS: "Revolt Against Tradition in Musical Composition," *Musicology* (Middlebury, Vt.)i/1. During 1937–45 Haubiel published many lectures, prepared for radio station WNYC in New York, in *The Musician* (New York).

BIBL.: "C. H.," *Music of the West* (March, 1966); John Tasker Howard, *Our American Music* (New York 1954).

Hauer, Josef Matthias (b. Wiener Neustadt, Austria, 19 March 1883; d. Vienna, 22 Sept 1959), attended the Teacher's Training School in Wiener Neustadt and was self-taught in composition. He taught general subjects at the Volksschule in Krumbach (1902–04) and Catholic religious instruction at the Wiener Neustadt Volksschule (1904–14, 1919); he then retired on a pension. His compositions from 1910–19 use atonal pitch relations within a context of polyphonic textures. During these years he began associating colors and emotional affects with individual pitches and intervals. He came in contact with Arnold Schoenberg in 1918, and a piece of his was performed in an early concert by Schoenberg's Society for Private Musical Performances. In 1919, independently of Schoenberg, he developed a 12-tone method and composed his first 12-tone piece, *Nomos*, Op. 19. His method is based on 44 collections of the 12 pitch classes (called *tropes*), each subdivided into 6-note groups. It differs from Schoenberg's method in its rules for the circulation of pitches, including those governing movement between collections within the same piece. Hauer continued to explore the potentials of his method and after 1939 began to use the title *Zwölftonspiel* for almost all his works; this reflects his belief that "in my whole life I have written only one work," i.e., a multifaceted revelation of the related laws he had discovered.

PRINCIPAL COMPOSITIONS: (selected with the help of the Hauer Studio in Vienna; a number of teaching aids are available from the Studio to assist performers): ★ *Nomos* for piano 2-hands or 4-hands, Op. 1 (1912, Eberle); 7 *Little Pieces* for piano, Op. 3 (1913, Eberle); *Songs of Friedrich Hölderlin* for voice, piano, Op. 6 (1914, Eberle); *Nomos* for piano, string ensemble, Op. 19 (1919,

Eberle); *Hölderlin Songs* for medium voice, piano, Op. 21 (1922, Schlesinger, Berlin); *Piano Pieces with Superscriptions after the Words of Hölderlin*, Op. 25 (1923, Lienau); *Suite No. 7* for orchestra, Op. 48 (1926, UE); *Wandlungen*, chamber oratorio for 6 vocal soloists, chorus, orchestra, Op. 53; text by Hölderlin (1927, UE); *Der Menschen Weg*, cantata for 4 soloists, chorus, orchestra, Op. 67; text by Hölderlin (1934, revised 1952; UE); *Dance in Slow 3/4 Time* for 2 violins, 2 violas, piano (1958, Fortissimo); *Hausmusik* for piano 4-hands (1958, Fortissimo). ★ *Zwölftonspiel*: for orchestra (August 1940); for piano (Dec 1946, Fortissimo); for orchestra (Dec 1946); for piano 4 hands, tone row by Ernst Hartmann (Jan 1947, Fortissimo); for viola, harpsichord (April 1947); for violin, harpsichord; tone row by Maria Panzer-Spetlich (July 1948); for 5 violins (May 1950); for 2 violins, harpsichord (Feb 1955); for piano 4-hands, accordion (March 1955); for piano 4-hands (May 1955, Fortissimo); for piano (June 1955, Fortissimo); for harpsichord (June 1955, Fortissimo); for piano 4-hands (April 1956, Doblinger); for piano 4-hands (July 1956, Fortissimo); for piano 4-hands (July 1956, Fortissimo); for piano (Sept 1956, Fortissimo); for 2 violins, viola, cello (Jan 1957, Fortissimo); for 2 violins, viola, cello, piano 4-hands (April 1957, Fortissimo); for piano 4-hands (July 1957, Fortissimo); for violin, cello, piano 4-hands, accordion (Oct 1957, Fortissimo); for flute, bassoon (bass clarinet), string quartet (Jan 1958, Fortissimo); for chamber orchestra (May 1958, Fortissimo); for string sextet (May 1958, Fortissimo).

PRINCIPAL WRITINGS: *Über die Klangfarbe*, Op. 13 (Vienna 1918); *Vom Wesen des Musikalischen* (Leipzig 1920); *Deutung des Melos: Eine Frage an die Künstler und Denker unserer Zeit* (Leipzig 1923); *Vom Melos zur Pauke: Eine Einführung in die Zwölftonmusik* (Vienna 1925); *Zwölftontechnik: Die Lehre von den Tropen* (Vienna 1926). Hauer wrote many articles, especially during the 1920s, on atonality, 12-tone technique, and other topics for *Melos, Musikblätter des Anbruch, Neue Musik-Zeitung, Die Musik*, and other periodicals.

BIBL.: Karl Eschmann, *Changing Forms in Modern Music* (Boston 1945); Monika Lichtenfeld, *Untersuchungen zur Theorie der Zwölftontechnik bei J. M. H.* (Regensburg 1964); Walter Szmolyan, *J. M. H.* (Vienna 1965).

SEE ALSO Austria and Germany, 12-Tone Techniques.

Havelka, Svatopluk (b. Vrbice, Czechoslovakia, 2 May 1925), studied liberal arts and musicology at the Univ. of Prague and composition privately with Karel B. Jirák. He first gained experience as an arranger of folksongs and other material for the popular variety ensemble Nota in Ostrava. He has since written much film music in addition to the works listed below. The Czech writer Jiří

Pilka has compared Havelka's *Symphony No. 1* with Shostakovich and Prokofiev.

PRINCIPAL COMPOSITIONS: *Night Music* for orchestra (1944); *Songs from the Baroque* for medium voice, piano (1944); *Suite* for small orchestra (1947); *4 Suites on Moravian Folk Texts* for narrator, vocal soloists, chorus, chamber orchestra (1948, 49, 49, 51); *Spring*, vocal rhapsody for soloists, adult and children's choruses, orchestra (1949); *Symphony No. 1* (1956, Supraphon); *In Praise of Light*, cantata for soprano, alto, bass, chorus, orchestra (1960, Panton); *Heptameron*, "a poem to nature and love," for narrator, soprano, alto, bass, orchestra (1964, ČHF); *Foam*, on a poem of Hans M. Enzensberger, for orchestra (1965, Panton).

SEE ALSO Czechoslovakia.

Heiden, Bernhard (b. Frankfurt, 24 August 1910), studied at the Berlin Hochschule für Musik (1929–33, composition with Paul Hindemith, conducting with Prewer) and Cornell Univ. (1945–46, musicology with Donald Grout). He became a U.S. citizen in 1941. During 1938–39 he was a staff arranger for radio station WWJ in Detroit, and he conducted the Detroit Chamber Orchestra during 1942–43. He has taught composition at Indiana Univ. since 1946.

PRINCIPAL COMPOSITIONS (published by AMP unless otherwise noted): *Alto Saxophone Sonata* (1937, Schott); *Horn Sonata* (1939); *Incidental Music to "The Tempest"* (1941, unpub.); *String Quartets Nos. 1–3* (1947, 1951, 1963; unpub.); *Euphorion*, scene for orchestra (1949); *Concerto for Small Orchestra* (1949); *Sinfonia* for woodwind quintet (1949); *Divine Poems* for chorus; texts by John Donne (1949); *Quintet* for horn, string quartet (1952); *Violin Sonata* (1954); *Symphony No. 2* (1954); *Memorial* for orchestra (1955); *Serenade* for bassoon, string trio (1955); *Conspiracy in Kyoto*, film score (1955, unpub.); *Piano Trio* (1956); *Sonata* for piano 4-hands (1956); *Cello Sonata* (1958); *Viola Sonata* (1959); *The Darkened City*, opera (1961–62, unpub.); *Quintet* for oboe, string quartet (1963, unpub.); *Envoy* for orchestra (1963); *In memoriam* for chorus; text by Hal Borland (1964); *Woodwind Quintet* (1965, Broude-A); *Cello Concerto* (1967); *4 Dances* for brass quintet (1967, Broude-A); *Inventions* for 2 cellos (1967); *Horn Concerto* (1969); *Partita* for orchestra (1970); *Intrada* for alto saxophone, wind quintet (1970, Southern).

PRINCIPAL WRITINGS: "Hindemith's System—A New Approach," *Modern Music* 19:102–07.

Heider, Werner (b. Fürth/Bay, Germany, 1 Jan 1930), studied at the Privat-Musikschule in Nuremberg (1945–51, composition and

piano with Willy Spilling) and at the Musikhochschule in Munich (1951–52, composition
with Karl Höller, piano with Maria Landes-
Hindemith, conducting with Heinrich
Knappe). He has also frequently attended the
Darmstadt summer courses. Since 1962 he has
been director of the Colloquium Musicale and
the Nuremberg Jazz Collegium. In 1968 he
became conductor of the Ars Nova Ensemble
of Nuremberg.

PRINCIPAL COMPOSITIONS (published by Peters
unless otherwise noted): *4 Glimpses of Night* for
soprano, piano, orchestra; text by Frank Marshall
Davis (1958); *Modi* for piano (1959, Ahn & Sim);
Dialog for clarinet, piano (1960); *Inventio I* for
violin (1961, Ahn & Sim); *Inventio II* for clarinet
(1962, Ahn & Sim); *Konturen* for violin, orchestra
(1962–64); *Konflikte* for percussion ensemble
(1963); *Modelle* for dancers, chamber orchestra,
4 percussionists, harp, piano (1964); *Inventio III*
for harpsichord (1964); *Katalog* for recorder (1965,
Moeck); *Katalog* for vibraphone (1965, Moeck);
Strophen for clarinet, chamber orchestra (1965);
Picasso-Musik for mezzo-soprano, violin, clarinet,
piano; text by Picasso (1966); *-da-sein-Musik* for
20 winds; in memoriam Willy Spilling (1966);
Plan for strings (1966); *Passatempo* for clarinet,
bassoon, trumpet, trombone, violin, double bass,
percussion (1967); *Inneres* for organ (1967); *Land-
schaftspartitur* for piano (1968); *Edition*, a "basic
model" which is adapted by the composer on
order for instrumental and/or vocal ensembles of
5 or more performers (1968); *Programm I* for
harpsichord, tape (1969); *Bezirk* for piano, orchestra (1969); *Fauststück* for piano (1970, Gerig).

BIBL.: Erich Limmert, "Komponisten-Portrait
W. H.," *Musica* (March 1970); Rudolf Stöckl,
"Neue Klänge und Strukturen," *Das neue Erlangen*
(Dec 1968):916–22.

Heiller, Anton (b. Vienna, 15 Sept 1923),
studied music privately and attended the
Vienna Academy of Music (1941–42; piano,
harpsichord, and organ with Bruno Seidlhofer; theory with Friedrich Reidinger). He
is an organist, harpsichordist, and conductor,
and has been professor of organ at the Vienna
Academy since 1945. He is largely self-taught
in composition, and is known primarily for
his sacred vocal music.

PRINCIPAL COMPOSITIONS (published by Doblinger unless otherwise noted): *Messe in Mixolydisch*
for chorus, organ (1944, UE); *Organ Sonata No. 1*
(1945, UE); *Organ Sonata No. 2* (1947); *2 kleine
Partiten* for organ (1948, Ars Viva); *Ach wie
nichtig, ach wie flüchtig* for chorus (1949, UE);
Te Deum for chorus, organ, winds (1953, UE);
Psalmenkantate for vocal soloists, orchestra (1955,
UE); *François Villon*, ballade for soloists, chorus,
orchestra; text by Franz Krieg (1956); *In festo
corporis Christi* for organ (1957); *4 Sacred Motets*

for chorus (1959, UE); *Missa super modos duo-
decimales* for chorus, 2 oboes, English horn,
bassoon, violin, viola, cello (1960); *Kleine Messe
über Zwölftonmodelle* (1962); *Organ Concerto*
(1963); *Psalm 37* for chorus, orchestra (1963, UE);
Deutsches Ordinarium for chorus, orchestra or
organ (1965); *English Mass* for chorus, congregation, organ (1965, McLaughlin); *In principio erat
Verbum*, cantata (1965); *Fantasia super "Salve
Regina"* for organ (1966); *Deutsches Proprium* for
Trinity Sunday, for chorus, congregation, organ
(1967); *Ecce lignum crucis* for organ (1967, Oxford:
Modern Organ Music, Book 2); *Stabat mater* for
chorus, orchestra (1968).

PRINCIPAL WRITINGS: "Zum Tode Paul Hinde-
miths," *Katholische Kirchenmusik* (Switzerland,
March 1964):88.

BIBL.: Rudolf Klein, "A. H. auf dem Weg zur
Psalmenkantate," *Österreichische Musikzeitschrift*
(May 1955):150 ff.; Franz Kosch, "Ein öster-
reichischer Kirchenmusiker: Persönlichkeit und
Werk A. H.," *Die Furche* (16 March 1968).

SEE ALSO Liturgical Music: Christian.

Heininen, Paavo (Johannes) (b. Järvenpää,
Finland, 13 Jan 1938), studied at the Univ.
of Helsinki and the Sibelius Academy (until
1960) and at the Cologne Hochschule and the
Juilliard School. He was a pianist at the Finnish Opera during 1959–60 and has lectured
on theoretical subjects at the Sibelius Academy
(1962–63, since 1966) and the Turku Academy
of Music (1963–66).

PRINCIPAL COMPOSITIONS: *Toccata* for piano
(1956); *Sonatine* for piano (1957, Fazer); *Symphonies Nos. 1–3* (1958, revised 1960; 1962; 1969);
Preambolo for orchestra (1959); *Tripartita* for
orchestra (1959); *Concerto for String Orchestra*
(1959, revised 1963); *Quintetto* for flute, saxophone, piano, vibraphone, percussion (1961);
Canto di natale for soprano, piano; text by J. da
Todi (1961); *Soggetto* for orchestra with 14 solo
strings (1963); *Adagio*, "Concerto for Orchestra
in the Form of Variations" (1963, revised 1966);
Musique d'été for flute, clarinet, percussion, harpsichord, violin, cello (1963, revised 1967); *Piano
Concertos Nos. 1–2* (1964, 1966); *Discantus* for
alto flute (1965); *Arioso* for string orchestra (1967);
Cantico delle creature for baritone, organ; text
by Francis of Assisi (1968).

Helfritz, Hans (b. Hilbersdorf, Germany, 25
July 1902), studied at the Univ. of Berlin
(1927–29, music history with Curt Sachs), the
Berlin Hochschule für Musik (1927–29; composition with Max Butting, Heinz Tiessen,
Paul Hindemith), and at the Univ. of Vienna
(1930, composition with Egon Wellesz,
comparative musicology with Erich von

Hornbostel). During 1931–35 he recorded bedouin music in southern Arabia for Hornbostel; he lectured in the U.S. during 1937–38 on his Arabian expeditions. Now a citizen of Chile, he lived in that country during 1939–60 studied the folk music of Peru and Bolivia. and Since 1960 he has lived in the Balearic Islands and in Germany.

PRINCIPAL COMPOSITIONS: *Concertino* for harpsichord, chamber orchestra (1930); *Concertino* for piano, chamber orchestra (1945); *Tenor Saxophone Concerto* (1945, Ars Viva); *Concerto* for organ, string orchestra (1946, Ars Viva); *String Quartet* (1946); *Aru Amunyas* for piano, based on Bolivian folk music (1946); *Violin Sonata* (1947); *Suite* for flute, piano (1948); *China klagt*, 6 songs based on Chinese classical poetry for mezzo-soprano, piano (1950); *Lieder der Neger* for high voice, harp; text by Langston Hughes (1954); *Canciones corales sobre motivos religiosos de Bolivia* for women's chorus (1957, SM); *Dance Suite* for 2 flutes, 3 violins, cello, percussion; based on Inca tunes from Peru and Bolivia (1960, Pelikan); *5 Pieces* for organ (1965).

PRINCIPAL WRITINGS: *La Musique éthiopienne* (St.-Michel de Provence 1970), with recording by Harmonia Mundi.

BIBL.: Vincente Salas-Viú, *La creación musical en Chile 1900–1951* (Santiago de Chile 1952):209–14.

Hellermann, William (David) (b. Milwaukee, 15 July 1939), attended the Juilliard School (1963–65, fugue with Vittorio Giannini, composition with Stanley Wolfe), and Columbia Univ. (1965–69; composition with Chou Wen-chung, Otto Luening; electronic music with Vladimir Ussachevsky). During 1964–66 he studied composition and analysis with Stefan Wolpe in New York. He attended the summer seminars of Stockhausen, Ligeti, Kagel, and Brün at Darmstadt in 1966. At Tanglewood in 1967 he studied composition with Donald Martino and attended the seminars of Elliot Carter, Ross Lee Finney, and Seymour Shifrin. Hellermann has been teaching at Columbia Univ. since 1967. He has codirected two concert series, Columbia Composers (1965–68) and Composers' Group for International Performance (since 1967), and has been general manager of a third, Composers' Forum (since 1968). He performs as classical guitarist and conducts chamber ensembles.

PRINCIPAL COMPOSITIONS (published by ACA unless otherwise noted): *Inter-Polations* for piano (1966); *Poem* for soprano, flute, clarinet, cello, trombone (1967); *Resonata* for brass quintet (1967); *Formata* for trombone, flute, clarinet, percussion, piano (1967); *Ariel* on tape (1967); *Ek-Stasis* on tape (1968); *Mai '68*, electronic music for a theatre happening based on the May 1968 revolt in Paris (1968); *Time and Again* for orchestra (1969); *Accorda* for flute, oboe, clarinet, piano (1969, unpub.); *Exchanges* for solo guitar (1969, Ashley); *Ex-Tempore* for concert band (1969, unpub.); *perFORM* for amplified guitar, flute (1969, unpub.).

PRINCIPAL WRITINGS: Notes for the *Ariel* recording (Turnabout Records 34301); interview on WBAI-FM (New York 1969), available from the WBAI archives.

Helm, Everett (b. Minneapolis, 17 July 1913), studied at Carleton College (1930–34) and Harvard Univ. (1934–36, 1938–39; composition with Walter Piston, musicology with Hugo Leichtentritt). He also studied composition in Europe with Gian Francesco Malipiero (1936–37) and Ralph Vaughan Williams (1937, 1938) and musicology with Alfred Einstein (1936–38). In 1941 he worked informally with Darius Milhaud at Mills College. He has taught at the Longy School in Cambridge, Mass. (1939–41), Mills College (1941), Western College in Oxford, Ohio (1942–44), and the Univ. of Ljubljana, Yugoslavia (1966–68). During 1944–46 he traveled in Latin America on a U.S. State Department grant. During 1948–50 he was chief of the Theater and Music Branch in Hesse for the U.S. Military Government in Germany. He has been active as a music journalist since 1948 and was editor-in-chief of *Musical America*, 1961–63.

PRINCIPAL COMPOSITIONS: *Violin Sonata* (1938, Schott); *3 Gospel Hymns* for orchestra (1942, revised 1956; AMP); *Concerto for String Orchestra* (1950, Alkor); *Piano Concertos Nos. 1–2* (1951, Schott; 1956, Bote); *Adam and Eve*, a mystery for actors, chorus, chamber orchestra (1952, Ahn & Sim); *Concerto* for flute, oboe, bassoon, trumpet, violin, percussion, strings (1954, Schott); *Symphony* for string orchestra (1955, Schott); *The Seige of Tottenberg*, opera (1956, Bote); *Sinfonia da camera* for chamber orchestra (1961, Simrock); *String Quartet No. 2* (1962, Bote); *Woodwind Quintet* (1966, Schott); *Concerto* for double bass, strings (1968).

PRINCIPAL WRITINGS: "Heralds of the Italian Madrigal," *Musical Quarterly* (1941):306–18; "Secular Vocal Music in Italy," *New Oxford History of Music* 3 (London 1960):381–405; *Béla Bartók* (Hamburg 1965); *Composer, Performer, Public* (Paris 1969).

Helps, Robert (b. Passaic, N. J., 23 Sept 1928), studied at the Juilliard School (1937–43), Columbia Univ. (1947–49), and the Univ. of

Calif. (1949–51; composition, theory with Roger Sessions). He also studied privately with Sessions (1944–57) and with Abby Whiteside (1943–57, piano). He has taught piano at Princeton Univ. (1962–67), the San Francisco Conservatory (1967–69), Stanford Univ. (1967–68), Univ. of Calif. at Berkeley (1968–69), and at the New England Conservatory (1969–70). He is a professional pianist and plays much contemporary music.

PRINCIPAL COMPOSITIONS: 2 *Songs* for soprano, piano; texts by Herman Melville (1950); *String Quartet* (1951); *Fantasy* for piano (1952); *Adagio for Orchestra*, later included in Symphony No. 1 (1953); *Symphony No. 1* (1955, Marks); *3 Etudes* for piano (1956, Peters); *Piano Trio* (1957); *Image* for piano (1958, published by Lawson in the anthology New Music for the Piano); *Recollections for Piano* (1959, Peters); *Portrait for Piano* (1960, Peters); *Solo* for piano (1961); *Cortège* for orchestra (1963); *Serenade*: "Fantasy" for violin, piano; "Nocturne" for string quartet; "Postlude" for piano, violin, horn (1964); *Piano Concerto* (1966); *Saccade* for piano 4-hands (1967, Peters).

Henry, Pierre (b. Paris, 9 Dec 1927), studied at the Paris Conservatory (1937–47; composition with Olivier Messiaen, Nadia Boulanger, and Félix Passeronne). During 1949–58 he collaborated with Pierre Schaeffer, the French radio engineer who in 1948 had produced the first examples of musique concrète. During 1950–58 Henry was director of the Groupe de Recherches de Musique Concrète at the French Radio Television Network. In 1958 he founded the first private electronic studio in France, Apsome.

PRINCIPAL COMPOSITIONS (on tape): *Symphonie pour un homme seul*, composed in collaboration with Pierre Schaeffer (1949–50, final revision 1966); *Le Voile d'Orphée* (1953); *La Noire à soixante* (1961); *Le Voyage*, based on the Tibetan Book of the Dead (1961–63, recorded by Philips); *Variations pour une porte et un soupir* (1963, recorded by Philips); *La Reine verte* (1963, recorded by Philips); *Messe de Liverpool* (1967); *Apocalypse de Jean* (1968); episodes for the Maurice Béjart ballet *Messe pour le temps présént* (1970, recorded by Philips); *Ceremony* (1970); *Fragments pour Artaud* (1970); *Gymkhana* (1970).

SEE ALSO Austria and Germany; Dance; Electronic Music: History and Development; Recording.

Henze, Hans Werner (b. Gütersloh, Westphalia, 1 July 1926), began study at the Brunswick State Music School in 1942 but had to interrupt his studies when called to military service in 1944. Just after the war he became repetiteur at the Stadttheater in Brunswick, and in 1946 he continued his music studies, this time at the Kirchenmusikalisches Institut in Heidelberg. During 1946–48 he studied privately with Wolfgang Fortner. In 1947 and 1948 he attended the lectures of René Leibowitz on Schoenberg at the Darmstadt summer courses. In 1948 he worked at the Stadttheater in Constance, and in 1950 he became artistic and ballet director at the theater in Wiesbaden. In the meantime his fame as a composer had spread throughout Germany. In 1949 the theater in Heidelberg had produced his first opera, *Das Wundertheater*, and three years later Hanover produced his *Boulevard Solitude*. In 1953, after having won the Premio Italia with the radio opera *Ein Landartzt*, he renounced his work commitments and dedicated himself completely to composition. He moved to Italy, first to Naples and then in 1961 to the countryside near Rome. During 1961–67 he taught a composition course at the Mozarteum in Salzburg.

Henze's output includes opera, ballet, symphonic works, chamber music, and instrumental music with solo voices and with chorus. The abundance and multiformity of this production highlight two important aspects of his artistic personality: the fertility of his musical invention, and his rejection of any form of stylistic dogmatism. In the years immediately after World War II he was part of the avant-garde group of post-Schoenbergian musicians, but in the 1950s he rejected what he felt was this group's adherence to a disintegration of the means of musical expression. His rejection of radical positions was never total, however. He reaffirmed his ties with the whole European tradition, which is French and Italian as well as Germanic, and proceeded to assimilate the heritage of the 12-tone Viennese school, the rhythmic style of Stravinsky, the lyric cantabile lines of Italian music, and the French taste for irony and intellectual refinement. He was early recognized for his abilities as an orchestrator, and his use of 12-tone procedures never precluded the exploitation of instrumental colors or of melodic relations and harmonic tensions. Even the most frigid pointillism of the post-Webern school was transformed in his music into light and enchanting iridescences. He has made use of traditional formal schemes, particularly variations. During the 1960s he gradually renounced the use of 12-tone themes but retained inversion, retrograde, and other variation processes.

Henze's ability to translate into musical terms a psychological trait, a gesture, a poetic suggestion brought him to the theater, for which he has written his most successful works (*Elegy for Young Lovers*, 1959–61, and *The Bassarids*, 1965). His use of the voice is closer to Berg than to Schoenberg, and although he may write disjunct vocal lines, passages close to speech, and icy coloratura embellishments, he has never relinquished sensuous vocalism and song.

Henze's integration and refinement of the above technical resources reached their culmination about 1965. Since then he has tended toward a maximum variety of style, reflecting the social upheavals in this time and the new awareness of the vastness and variety of humanity. Thus popular tunes (*Sixth Symphony*, 1969), rock music, electronic sound, microtones, and clusters have found a place in his latest work.

PRINCIPAL COMPOSITIONS (published by Schott): *Symphony No. 1* (1947, revised 1963); *Das Wundertheater*, 1-act opera for actors; text after Cervantes (1948, revised 1964); *Symphony No. 2* (1949); *Symphony No. 3* (1949–50); *Piano Concerto No. 1* (1950); *Boulevard Solitude*, 2-act opera; libretto by Grete Weiss (1951); *König Hirsch*, 3-act opera (1952–55, revised 1962); *Ode to the Westwind* for cello, orchestra (1953); *Symphony No. 4* in 1 movement (1955); *5 neapolitanische Lieder* for medium voice, chamber orchestra (1956); *Concerto per il Marigny* for piano, 7 instruments (1956); *Ondine*, ballet; choreography by Frederick Ashton (1956–57); *Der Prinz von Homburg*, 3-act opera after Kleist (1958); *Kammermusik 1958* for tenor, guitar, 8 instruments (1958); *L'usignolo dell'imperatore*, ballet; choreography by F. Enriquez, F. Coba (1959); *Piano Sonata* (1959); *Elegy for Young Lovers*, 3-act opera; libretto by W. H. Auden, Chester Kallmann (1959–61); *Antifone* for orchestra (1960); *Symphony No. 5* (1962); *Novae de infinito laudes* for chorus (1962); *Los caprichos*, fantasia for orchestra (1963); *Cantata della fiaba estrema* for chorus, orchestra; text by E. Morante (1963); *Ariosi* for soprano, violin, orchestra; texts from Tasso (1963); *Being Beauteous* for coloratura soprano, harp, 4 cellos; text by Rimbaud (1963); *Der junge Lord*, 2-act opera; libretto by J. Bachmann (1964); *The Bassarids*, 1-act opera; libretto by Auden, Kallmann (1965); *Die weisse Rose* for chamber orchestra (1965); *Double Concerto* for oboe, harp, strings (1966); *Double Bass Concerto* (1966); *Fantasia for Strings* (1966); *Muses of Sicily*, concerto for chorus, 2 pianos, winds, timpani; Latin text from Virgil (1966); *Moralities*, 3 scenic cantatas; text by Auden (1967); *Piano Concerto No. 2* (1967); *Das Floss der Medusa*, "oratorio volgare e militare"; text by E. Schnabel (1968); *Symphony No. 6* (1969); *Versuch über Schweine* for voice, orchestra; text by G. Salvatore (1969); *El Cimarron*

for voice, flute, guitar, percussion; text by M. Barnet, H. M. Enzensberger (1970).

PRINCIPAL WRITINGS: *Undine, Tagebuch eines Ballets* (Munich 1959); *Essays*, a collection of lectures and articles from 1952–62 (Mainz 1964); untitled article, *Orchestral Composer's Point of View* ed. by R. S. Hines (Norman, Okla., 1970): 89–104.

BIBL.: Fedele d'Amico, *I casi della musica* (Milan 1962):181–84, 312–15, 450–56; Klaus Geitel, *H. W. H.* (Berlin 1968); Antoine Golea, *20 Ans de la musique contemporaine* (Paris 1962); Everett Helm, "6 Modern German Composers," *American-German Review* (1956–57):12–15; Rudolph Stephan, "H. W. H.," *Die Reihe*, English ed., 4:29–35; H. H. Stuckenschmidt, "H. W. H.," *Neue Zeitschrift für Musik* (1957):491–92; ——, *Oper in dieser Zeit* (Hanover 1964):105–14; ——, *Schöpfer der neuen Musik* (Frankfurt/Main 1958):290–301.

Franco Serpa
(trans. from Italian by Aliza Mandel)
SEE ALSO Austria and Germany, Opera.

Hernandez-Gonzalo, Gisela (b. Cárdenas, Cuba, 15 Sept 1912), studied at the Bach Conservatory (1930–35; music history, esthetics, and harmony with María Muñoz de Quevedo), the Havana Municipal Conservatory (1940–44, composition with José Ardevol), and the Peabody Institute (1944–47, composition with Gustav Strube, choral conducting with Theodore Chandler). She has been active as a choral conductor in Cuba and directed the Havana Chorale during 1947–53. During 1947–62 she taught various musical subjects at the Hubert de Blanck Conservatory in Havana. In 1949 she helped found the music publishers Ediciones de Blanck. Since the Revolution she has held a number of official posts with the National Cultural Council and the Ministry of Education. Since 1969 she has been a musical advisor for the Cuban Radio Network.

PRINCIPAL COMPOSITIONS: *Piano Sonata in C* (1942); *9 Songs* for voice, piano; texts by Mirtha Aguirre, García-Lorca, R. Tagore, J. R. Jiménez, D. M. Loynaz (1943–58, de Blanck); *Choral Suite* for chorus; texts by García-Lorca (1944, IIM); *Zapateo cubano* for piano (1954); *4 Cubanas* for piano (1957); *Suite coral* for chorus; texts by García-Lorca (1944, IIM); *5 Songs* for voice, piano; texts by F. García-Marruz, C. Solis, C. Vitier, A. Gaztelu, Lezama Lima (1964); *Tríptico* for chorus; texts by N. Guillén (1967, EGREM); *Diálogo de octubre* for 2 soloists, chorus, orchestra; text by Aguirre (1968–70); *3 Songs* for voice, piano; texts by A. Augier, N. Guillén, M. Brull (1969–70).

Herrmann, Hugo (b. Ravensburg, Germany, 19 April 1896; d. Trossingen, 7 Sept 1967), studied at the Stuttgart Conservatory (c.1917, piano and organ with Oskar Schroeter) and the Berlin Hochschule für Musik (c.1919, composition with Franz Schreker). During his conservatory years he worked as a teacher, organist, and choir director in Ludwigsburg, Stuttgart, and elsewhere. During 1923–25 he was organist at the Holy Redeemer Church in Detroit and for the Detroit Symphony. Returning to Germany, he concertized during 1925–35 as a pianist and organist and organized many choral societies, music festivals, and informal performing groups. During 1935–63 he was director of the Trossingen State Music School. His musical style was influenced by Catholic mysticism and the compositional techniques of the middle ages.

PRINCIPAL COMPOSITIONS (dates are of first performance unless otherwise noted): *Marionetten*, chamber cantata no. 1 for chorus, chamber orchestra, Op. 23 (composed c.1926); *String Quartets Nos. 1–5*: No. 1, Op. 2a (1926); No. 2, Op. 66 (1929); No. 3, "Frühling," Op. 101 (1939, Sikorski); No. 4 (composed 1941); No. 5, "Epiphanie" (composed 1957); *Requiem*, chamber cantata no. 2 for soloists, chorus, chamber orchestra, Op. 30 (composed 1927); *Galgenlieder*, chamber cantata no. 3 for alto, chorus, flute, saxophone, double bass, Op. 44; text by Christian Morgenstern (1928); *Symphonies Nos. 1–5*: No. 1, Op. 32 (1928, Bote); No. 2, Op. 56 (1929, Bote); No. 3 for boys' chorus, orchestra (composed 1950, Boosey); No. 4, adapted from *Paracelsus* (composed 1951, Sikorski); No. 5 after Dante's *Divine Comedy* (composed 1955, Sikorski); *Gazellenhorn*, chamber opera, Op. 43; libretto by E. Rupp (1929); *Chamber Cantata No. 4* for chorus, chamber orchestra, Op. 54; text by R. Dehmel (1929); *Vasantasena*, 2-act opera, Op. 70; libretto by L. Feuchtwanger (1930, Bote); *17 Choral Etudes* for chorus, Op. 72 (1930, Bote); *Laienchorschule für neue Musik* for chorus (composed 1930, Bote); *Violin Concerto*, Op. 75 (1931, Bote); *Harpsichord Concerto*, Op. 76 (1931, Bote); *Jesus und seine Jünger*, oratorio for 3 vocal soloists, chorus, orchestra, harpsichord, Op. 80 (1931, Bote; revised 1955); *Paracelsus*, 2-act opera, Op. 100; libretto by M. Sills-Fuchs (1943, Sikorski); *Des Friedens Geburt* for alto, bass, chorus, orchestra, harpsichord (composed 1946, Tonos); *Double Concerto* for harp, accordion, orchestra (composed 1951, Hohner); *Friedensfeier* for soprano, tenor, chorus, harp, double bass, celesta, vibraphone, timpani (composed 1957, Sikorski).

PRINCIPAL WRITINGS: "Neue deutsche Chorschulung und das zukünftige Chorwerk," *Die Musik* (March 1934); there is also an unpublished autobiography.

BIBL.: Armin Fett, ed., *H. H.: Leben und Werk* (Trossingen 1956); ——, *H. H.: Werkverzeichnis* (Hechingen, n.d.); *H. H. Werkverzeichnis* (Berlin, Bote, 1933); "Vater und Traeger der Harmonikamusik," *Trossinger Zeitung* (9 April 1968); Helmi Strahl, *An Assessment and Critical Edition of H. H.'s Songs*, (PhD diss., Univ. of Texas, in progress).

[prepared with the help of Clara Herrmann and Helmi Strahl]

Hexachord, Hexad, a collection of six pitch classes considered either as a simultaneity or as a succession. The terms occur most frequently in reference to segments of 12-tone sets. *Hexachord* in this sense is unrelated to the ancient and medieval concepts to which the term is also applied.

Hibbard, William (b. Newton, Mass., 8 Aug 1939), studied violin and composition at the New England Conservatory (to 1963) and the Univ. of Iowa (to 1967). He teaches at the Univ. of Iowa, where he is also director of the Center for New Performing Arts.

PRINCIPAL COMPOSITIONS: *Variations* for brass nonet (1960, AMP); *4 Pieces* for large chamber ensemble (1962); *Portraits* for flute, piano (1963, Ione); *String Trio* (1964, Ione); *Intersections 1–2* for woodwind quintet, piano, 5 percussion (1966); *Super flumina babylonis*, motet for 6 voices, string sextet (1968); *Stabiles* for 13 players (1969); *Variations* for cello (1970, Ione); *Reflexa* for soprano, 5 players (1970).

PRINCIPAL WRITINGS: "Some Aspects of Serial Improvisation," *American Guild of Organists Quarterly* (Oct 1966 and Jan 1967).

SEE ALSO Performance.

Hicks, Peggy Glanville, see under Glanville-Hicks

Hill, Edward Burlingame (b. Cambridge, Mass., 9 Sept 1872; d. Francestown, N. H., 10 July 1960), studied composition with John Knowles Paine at Harvard Univ. (1892–94) and with F. F. Bullard and George Chadwick in Boston. He also studied piano with Arthur Whiting in New York (1895–96) and composition with Charles Widor in Paris (1898). He taught orchestration, composition, and other subjects at Harvard during 1908–40; in 1921 he lectured on French music at the Univ. of Strassburg and the American Conservatory at

Fontainebleau. His students at Harvard included Virgil Thomson, Ross Lee Finney, and Leonard Bernstein.

PRINCIPAL COMPOSITIONS: *Stevensoniana Suites Nos. 1–2* for orchestra, Opp. 24, 29 (1916–17; 1921–22, Schirmer-G); *The Fall of the House of Usher*, symphonic poem, Op. 27 (1919–20); *Lilacs* for orchestra, Op. 33 (1927, Cos Cob); *Symphony in B♭*, Op. 34 (1927); *Sextet* for piano, winds, Op. 39 (1934, SPAM); *String Quartet in C*, Op. 40 (1935, arrangement for string orchestra published by Boosey); *Symphony No. 3 in G*, Op. 41 (1936); *Piano Quartet in A*, Op. 42 (1937); *Music for English horn, orchestra*, Op. 50 (1943).

PRINCIPAL WRITINGS: *Modern French Music* (Boston 1924).

BIBL.: David Ewen, ed., *American Composers Today* (New York 1949):125–27; John Tasker Howard, *Our Contemporary Composers* (New York 1941):56–59; George H. L. Smith, "E. B. H.," *Modern Music* 16:11–16.

Hiller, Lejaren (b. New York, 23 Feb 1924), developed an interest in both science and music at an early age. Childhood musical experiences included study of piano and theory and also cutting designs in player-piano rolls to produce musical compositions. He studied theory and composition at Princeton Univ. with Roger Sessions and Milton Babbitt, but his major field was chemistry. After earning his PhD in 1947, he worked as a research chemist for the DuPont Co. in Waynesboro, Va., also writing articles and a textbook in chemistry and obtaining several patents. His interest in music continued, and he composed many chamber and keyboard works and received his first public performance (of the *Suite* for small orchestra, 1951). He resigned from DuPont in 1952, traveled extensively in Europe, and then went to the Univ. of Ill. as a research associate in the chemistry department. Work with computer programming suggested analogies with the processes of musical composition, and in 1955–56, with Leonard Isaacson, he wrote programs that produced *Illiac Suite for String Quartet*, the first computer composition of consequence. He earned a master's degree in music in 1958 and joined the music faculty with responsibility for establishing and operating an Experimental Music Studio and developing cooperative research in electronics, computers, music, and acoustics. Contact with the theater department encouraged him to compose a series of stage works. Since 1968 he has been teaching composition at the State Univ. of N. Y. at Buffalo and codirecting with Lukas Foss the Center for the Creative and Performing Arts in Buffalo.

Hiller's compositions fall into three categories: abstract instrumental works, works for the stage, and pieces depending wholly or in part on computer and/or electronic techniques. Works of the first group (mostly written in the first part of his career) make use of traditional instruments and ensembles and such formal structures as sonata-allegro, variations, passacaglia, etc., reflecting the sympathies of his major teachers and also his own inclination toward logic and order. In later works various types of computer programs assume this same formal function, and electronic sound is combined with live performance (there are only a handful of pieces for electronic sound alone). In works of all types, Hiller lays out and applies a rigid structural principle, then overlays and even obscures it with unpredictable and fascinating detail. The theorist may concern himself with the modified song form of the second movement of the *Piano Sonata No. 1* or the passacaglia of the last movement of the *Symphony No. 2* and the mathematician with the computer programs of *Computer Cantata* or *HPSCHD*. The listener responds to the rich and unpredictable detail, the vitality and virtuosity, the asymmetries, and very often the aural and visual humor. Hiller frequently uses common and familiar musical material (Mozart, Ives, Appalachian ballads, the contrapuntal style of Palestrina), but only as chunks of building material that do not permeate, stylistically, the composition into which they are placed. The early stage works are in the nature of incidental music, dependent largely on the plays for which they were written for form and content. But in all works written since *Machine Music* (1964), elements of stage and concert music are blended so that visual and dramatic elements become an intrinsic part of the composition itself.

PRINCIPAL COMPOSITIONS: *Piano Sonatas Nos. 1–2* (1946, 1947); *Piano Concerto* (1949); *Suite* for small orchestra (1951); *Symphonies Nos. 1–2* (1953; 1960, Presser); *Illiac Suite for String Quartet*, computer program written in collaboration with Leonard Isaacson (1957, Presser); *5 Appalachian Ballads* for voice, guitar or harpsichord (1958); *Divertimento* for chamber ensembles (1959, Presser); *2 Electronic Theater Fantasies* (1959–60); *Quartet No. 4* for strings (1962, Presser); *7 Electronic Studies* on 2-track tape (1963); *Computer Cantata* for soprano, tape, chamber ensemble; composed in collaboration with A. Baker (1963, Presser); *Machine Music* for piano, percussion, tape (1964, Presser); *A Triptych for Hieronymus* for actors, dancers, acrobats, projections, tape, antiphonal instrumental groups (1966); *An Avalanche* for pitchman, prima donna, player piano, percussionist, prerecorded tape; text by Frank Parman (1968); *HPSCHD* for 1–7 harpsichords,

1–51 tapes; composed in collaboration with John Cage (1968, Peters); *Computer Music* for percussion, tape; composed in collaboration with G. Allan O'Conner (1968); *3 Rituals* for 2 percussionists, lighting expert (1969).

PRINCIPAL WRITINGS: "Some Structural Principles of Computer Music," *Journal of the American Musicological Society* 9; "Musical Composition with a High-Speed Digital Computer," written with Isaacson, *Journal of the Audio Engineering Society* 6; "Computer Music," *Scientific American* 201/6; *Experimental Music*, written with Isaacson (New York 1959); *Informationstheorie und Computermusik*, vol. 8 of the *Darmstädter Beiträge zur neuen Musik*; "Electronic Music at the University of Illinois," *Journal of Music Theory* 7; "Computer Cantata: An Investigation of Compositional Procedure," written with R. A. Baker, *Perspectives* 3/1; "Automated Music Printing," written with Baker, *Journal of Music Theory* 9; "An Integrated Electronic Music Console," *Journal of the Audio Engineering Society* 13; "Musical Applications of Electronic Digital Computers," *Gravesäner Blätter* 27–28:46–72; "Information Theory Analysis of Four Sonata Expositions," written with C. Bean, *Journal of Music Theory* 10; "Structure and Information in Webern's *Symphonie* Op. 21," written with R. A. Fuller, *Journal of Music Theory* 11.

Charles Hamm

SEE ALSO Computer Applications, Instrumental and Vocal Resources, Mathematics, Microtones, Mixed Media, Performance, Rhythm, United States.

Hindemith, Paul (b. Hanau, Germany, 16 Nov 1895; d. Frankfurt/Main, 28 Dec 1963), began the study of violin at nine. By the time he entered Hoch's Konservatorium at 14, he was already known in the Frankfurt area as an exceptionally precocious player. At the conservatory his efforts in composition came to the attention of his theory teacher, Arnold Mendelssohn (grand-nephew of Felix). From Mendelssohn and Bernhard Sekles, a German impressionist composer, he received his only formal instruction in composition. He served as concertmaster at the Frankfurt Opera from 1915 to 1923 (except for military service in 1917–18) and continued to compose. The first works to be published were written in 1917–18, and in 1919 Hindemith began a life-long association with the firm of B. Schott's Söhne.

Hindemith's professional chamber-music playing began with the quartet of his violin teacher, Adolph Rebner, and continued after 1922 with the Amar Quartet, in which he was violist. With the latter group he participated in the contemporary music festivals at Donaueschingen (1921–27) where he introduced his own early quartets as well as many new works by other composers. In 1927 he left Frankfurt to teach composition at the Staatliche Hochschule für Musik in Berlin. There he began his extensive researches in music theory and history as well as his performances of old music with students using authentic instruments.

In 1934 the Nazi regime denounced Hindemith as a "cultural bolshevik" and boycotted his works. He took a forced leave from the Hochschule during 1934–35 and completed his masterpiece, the opera *Mathis der Maler*. Pressure from the Nazis caused Hindemith to begin seeking opportunities outside of Germany. Between 1935 and 1937 he visited Turkey several times to help the government draw up a plan for developing musical life along Western lines. When he was finally forced to resign from the Hochschule in 1937, he moved to Switzerland and also made his first visit to America. After further visits in 1938–39, he moved to the U.S. early in 1940, assuming a professorship at Yale in the fall of that year which lasted until 1953.

The American years were spent in relative quiet since Hindemith did not maintain an active concert schedule. However, it was during this period, especially from 1945 to about 1952, that his teaching and music became a dominant influence on new music in America and Europe. In addition his Collegium Musicum at Yale, which gave concerts of old music, stimulated the development of other organizations of the type in America.

Hindemith reestablished contact with Europe with a series of tours beginning in 1947. In 1950 he began teaching at the Univ. of Zurich, alternating yearly with Yale, from which he finally resigned in 1953. In 1957 his monumental opera *Die Harmonie der Welt*, on which he had worked since the completion of *Mathis*, was produced in Munich. His last years were spent without teaching duties in composing and as a touring conductor.

Hindemith held to the main stream of European classical music, as did Johannes Brahms before him, being neither a simple-minded reactionary nor an over-enthusiastic progressive. Consequently, as the centrifugal force of new movements threw their protagonists further from the center, he became more isolated. A much sought after teacher from about 1930 to 1955, he ended his career scarcely noticed by young composers of the post-World War II period.

Hindemith's pattern of relating composition directly to practical realization was set early in life, for he began composing while learning to play the violin. His first pieces were E-string exercises modeled on those in Book I of De Beriot's *Violin Method*. Thereafter every new exposure to music became the source of a new piece.

The early published works (such as the Op. 11 sonatas in Eb and D for violin and piano and in F for viola and the *String Quartet in F Minor*, Op. 10) show influences of Strauss, Reger, and Debussy. After World War I Hindemith was again able to study new scores published outside Germany, and he underwent a rapid evolution toward newer styles. He was especially influenced by the early ballets of Stravinsky and the early string quartets of Bartók. By 1921, when he first took part in the Donaueschingen festivals, his own personality had fully emerged. In instrumental works of 1921–27, called *Kammermusik*, he revealed an immense kinetic rhythmic drive, a sense of humor not usual with German composers, a fondness for contrapuntal textures (somewhat reminiscent of the baroque), and in slow movements a lyrical gift that was to become increasingly significant in the further development of his style. The lyricism in the *Marienleben* (original version 1922–23) was particularly prophetic. The largest work of the period, the opera *Cardillac* (1926, revised 1952) was notable for turning away from the ideal of Strauss and Wagner toward a Mozartean emphasis on the purely musical side of opera.

Hindemith's activities in Berlin after 1927 were the basis of new stylistic developments. Confronted with students for the first time, he sought direct answers to direct questions as to how he went about the process of composition. The result, after thorough historical research to establish a background, was the first volume of *Unterweisung im Tonsatz* [The Craft of Musical Composition], published in 1937. Simultaneously his style grew to full maturity, culminating in *Mathis der Maler* (1934–35). Here and thereafter there was little of the brash humor, over-energetic rhythmic drive, and grinding dissonance of the 1920s. Lyricism became more prominent; the harmony, while not in a 19th-century style, grew smoother through meticulous control of dissonant tensions. A sense of security and completeness resulted from the reestablishment of controlled tonalities within a style that is nevertheless chromatic. Cadences, though rarely following the traditional dominant-tonic formulas, were used in their old function to mark divisions in the form. Having found his own solution to the problem of formal delineation within a chromatic style, Hindemith began a series of sonatas, which extended from the *Sonata in E* for violin and piano (1935) through the *Sonata* for bass tuba and piano (1955). Though not numbered as a series, the plan became evident as one by one each orchestral instrument, piano, harp and organ was accounted for. The concertos, symphonies, and chamber music other than sonatas written after 1935 also show a return to the principles of classical form-building, relying on clearly defined tonality, though not limited to the chord vocabulary nor the conventional progressions of traditional tonal harmony. Some of the finest of these works (for example, the ballet suite, *Nobilissima visione*, 1938, and the *Violin Concerto*, 1939) date from the period between the completion of *Mathis* (1935) and the emigration to the U.S. (1940), years during which his attention was not divided between composing and teaching.

Although there was no fundamental change of style during Hindemith's years in America, he reacted energetically to commissions from American orchestras and choral groups, and the character of some works reveals their American origins: for example, the *Symphonic Metamorphosis on Themes of Carl Maria von Weber* (1943), which contains a jazz fugato; and the requiem, *When Lilacs Last in the Dooryard Bloom'd* (1946), written on a Whitman text for Robert Shaw in specific response to the choral renaissance which took place during the 40s.

In addition to his principal works in the major categories, Hindemith (especially during the early years) wrote a number of experimental compositions, as well as pieces for children and amateurs. In the former class are several works from the Frankfurt and Berlin periods for player piano, mechnical organ, and an early electronic instrument, the trautonium, invented by Hindemith's pupil, Friederich Trautwein. Besides pieces for ensembles of trautoniums, he composed a *Konzertmusik* (1931) for trautonium and string orchestra, one of the earliest pieces to combine electronic and conventional instruments.

After assuming an active role at Donaueschingen as a protagonist for new music, Hindemith (along with Weill and others) reacted against the hermetic cliquishness of the avant-garde and began to speak in favor of music usable by ordinary players and singers (*gebrauchsmusik*, "music for use"). He wrote easy canons, pieces for string and brass ensembles, boys' choruses, a musical play for children (*Wir bauen eine Stadt*, 1930), and music for a day-long village festival (*Plöner Musiktag*, 1932). Unfortunately, the term *gebrauchsmusik* caught on too well and haunted him throughout his career. It was frequently misapplied to his music as a whole and wrongly taken to typify his outlook on the problem of artistic production.

At the present time Hindemith's music is neither new enough nor old enough to be fashionable. Nevertheless the solidity of his accomplishment continues to elicit frequent performances—even during that period after a composer's death when his works are likely to be neglected. His theories, which cost him much time and effort, relate less and less to evolving techniques, but as a composer he is assured an enduring place among the masters of Western music.

PRINCIPAL COMPOSITIONS (published by Schott; sonatas, songs other than major cycles, smaller instrumental and choral pieces, experimental, amateur, and teaching pieces are not included): *String Quartets Nos. 1–4*, Opp. 10, 16, 22, 32 (1918, 1922, 1922, 1923), and *Nos. 5–6* (1943, 1945); *Mörder, Hoffnung der Frauen*, 1-act opera, Op. 12; text by O. Kokoschka (1919); *Sancta Susanna*, 1-act opera, Op. 21; text by A. Stramm (1921); *Kammermusik No. 1 with Finale 1921*, Op. 24, No. 1 (1921); *Die junge Magd*, songs for alto, flute, clarinet, string quartet, Op. 23, No. 2; texts by G. Wakl (1922); *Kleine Kammermusik* for 5 winds, Op. 24, No. 2 (1922); *1922*, suite for piano, Op. 26 (1922); *Das Marienleben* for soprano, piano, Op. 27; texts by R. M. Rilke (1922–23, second version 1936–48); *Concerto for Orchestra*, Op. 38 (1925); *Cardillac*, 3-act opera, Op. 39; text by F. Lion after E. T. A. Hoffmann (1926, second version 1952); *Neues vom Tage*, 3-act comic opera; text by M. Schiffer (1928–29, second version 1953); *Hin und zurück*, 1-act sketch, Op. 45a; text by M. Schiffer (1929); *Konzertmusik* for viola, orchestra, Op. 48 (1930); *Konzertmusik* for strings, winds, Op. 50 (1930); *Das Unaufhörliche*, 3-part oratorio; text by G. Benn (1931); *Philharmonic Concerto*, variations for orchestra (1932); *String Trio No. 2* (1933); *Mathis der Maler*, symphony for orchestra (1934); *Mathis der Maler*, opera in 7 scenes; text by the composer (1934–35); *Der Schwanendreher*, concerto for viola, small orchestra (1935); *Symphonic Dances* for orchestra (1937); *Quartet* for piano, clarinet, violin, cello (1938); *Nobilissima visione*, dance legend with choreography by L. Massine; also a suite for orchestra (1938); *Violin Concerto* (1939); *6 Chansons* for chorus; texts by R. M. Rilke (1939); *Symphony in E♭* (1940); *The 4 Temperaments*, theme with 4 variations for piano, string orchestra (1940, ballet version 1946); *Cello Concerto* (1940); *13 Latin Motets* for high voice, piano (1941–60); *Ludus tonalis* for piano (1942); *Symphonic Metamorphosis on Themes of Carl Maria von Weber* for orchestra (1943); *Herodiade*, recitation after Mallarmé for chamber orchestra; also a ballet (1944); *Piano Concerto* (1945); *Sinfonia serena* (1946); *When Lilacs Last in the Dooryard Bloom'd*, requiem "for those we loved"; text by W. Whitman (1946); *Clarinet Concerto* (1947); *Apparebit repentina dies* for chorus, brass instruments; Latin

text before 700 A.D. (1947); *Septet* for winds (1948); *Concerto* for woodwinds, harp, orchestra (1949); *Horn Concerto* (1949); *Concerto* for trumpet, bassoon, string orchestra (1949); *Symphony in B♭* for band (1951); *Die Harmonie der Welt*, symphony (1951); *Ite, angeli veloces*, 3-part cantata; text by P. Claudel (1953–55); *Die Harmonie der Welt*, 5-act opera; text by the composer (1957); *12 Madrigals* for chorus; texts by J. Weinheber (1958); *The Long Christmas Dinner*, 1-act opera; text by T. Wilder (1960); *Organ Concerto* (1962); *Mass* for chorus (1963).

PRINCIPAL WRITINGS: *Unterweisung im Tonsatz*, 3 vols. (Mainz 1937, 1938, 1970); *The Craft of Musical Composition*, English translation of vols. 1–2 of the preceding (New York 1941, revised 1945); *A Composer's World* (Cambridge, Mass., 1952).

BIBL.: *H., Zeugnis in Bildern* (Mainz, 1955); *P. H., Die letzten Jahre* (1965); Heinrich Strobel, *P. H.* (Mainz, 1928, second ed. 1931, third ed. 1948). The definitive biography can be written only upon the release of Hindemith's papers and effects in 1973.

Howard Boatwright

SEE ALSO Austria and Germany, Dance, Harmony and Counterpoint, Jazz, Musicology and Composition, Opera, Performance, Popular Music, Rhythm, Switzerland, Text Setting and Usage, Texture, Theory.

Hobbs, Christopher (b. Hillingdon, Middlesex, England, 9 September 1950), attended the Royal Academy of Music in London (1967–69; composition with Cornelius Cardew, percussion with Patricia Brady). He is active in the performance and composition of experimental music and has been a member of the AMM and Scratch Orchestra performance groups in London since 1968. In 1969 he founded the Experimental Music Catalogue to distribute scores of new unpublished music. In addition to the *Word Pieces* listed below, he has written numerous works for specified instruments and indeterminate performance, mostly using random techniques of composition yielding results characterized by lack of contrast, development, progress, etc.

PRINCIPAL COMPOSITIONS: *Word Pieces*, 13 verbal pieces for various specified or unspecified performers (1966–69, Experimental).

PRINCIPAL WRITINGS: "Listen, Act," *ICA Magazine* (May 1968):8–9; program notes for recitals by John Tilbury.

SEE ALSO Great Britain.

Hodkinson, Sydney (P.) (b. Winnipeg, Canada, 17 Jan 1934), studied with Louis Mennini and Bernard Rogers at the Eastman School (1953–58), with Elliott Carter, Roger Sessions, and

Milton Babbitt at Princeton Univ. (1960), and with Leslie Bassett, Nicolò Castiglioni, and Ross Lee Finney at the Univ. of Mich. (1965–68). During 1955–58 he taught woodwinds in the public schools of Rochester and Brighton, N. Y. He has taught at the Univ. of Va. (1958–63) and the Univ. of Mich. (since 1968) and appears in concert as a conductor and clarinetist. During 1966–68 he conducted the Contemporary Directions Series and the Composers Forums in Ann Arbor, and since 1968 he has directed the Rockefeller New Music Project at the Univ. of Mich.

PRINCIPAL COMPOSITIONS: *Threnody* for orchestra (1957); *Stanzas* for piano trio (1959, Tritone); *Drawings*, set No. 1 for percussion quartet (1960, Percus); *Drawings*, set No. 3 for clarinet, drums (1961, Percus); *Lament for Guitar and 2 Lovers*, a fable for actors, dancers, musicians; libretto by Lee Devin (1962); *Mosaic* for brass quintet (1964); *Refractions* for piano (1965); *Drawings*, set No. 6 for violin, 3 clarinets (1965); *Taiwa*, a myth for actor, dancers, musicians; choreography by F. Coggan (1966); *Caricatures*, 5 paintings for orchestra (1966, Ricordi); *Interplay*, a histrionic controversy for 4 musicians (1966); *Armistice*, a truce for dancers, musicians (1966, BMIC); *Dissolution of the Serial* for piano and 1 instrument (1967); *Imagind Quarter*, an incentive for 4 percussionists (1967, BMIC); *Fresco*, a mural for orchestra (1968, Jobert); *Organasm*, a scenario for organ, assistants (1968, BMIC); *Arc*, aria with interludes for soprano, flute, piano, 2 percussionists (1969); *Ritual* for chorus (1970).

Høffding, Finn (b. Copenhagen, 10 March 1899), received most of his musical training privately in Copenhagen. He studied violin with Kristian Sandby (1911–21); organ with P. S. Rung-Keller (1919–21); harmony, counterpoint, and composition with Knud Jeppesen (1918–21); and music history (especially church music) with Thomas Laub (1920–21, 1922–23). In Vienna during 1921–22 he studied composition with Joseph Marx and took courses in piano and theory at the Academy of Music. He was professor of harmony, counterpoint, and composition at the Royal Academy of Music in Copenhagen from 1931 to 1969 and served as its vice chancellor in 1954–55. Høffding has been active in music education and has composed numerous works for amateurs and for educational purposes. During 1929–39 he was chairman of the Danish Musikpaedagogisk Forening. In 1931, together with Jørgen Bentzon, he founded the Copenhagen Folkemusikskole. His music has been influenced primarily by Nielson, Bartók, and Stravinsky.

PRINCIPAL COMPOSITIONS: *String Quartet No. 1 in D Minor*, Op. 2 (1920); *Sinfonia impetuosa*, Op. 3 (1923); *Il canto deliberato*, for coloratura soprano, chorus, orchestra, Op. 5; the text is in a language constructed by the composer and notated phonetically (1924); *String Quartet No. 2*, Op. 6 (1925, Hansen-W); *Kejserens Nye Klaeder* [The Emperor's New Clothes], Op. 8, opera after Andersen; libretto by the composer (1926; dance suite from the opera, Op. 9, 1929, Hansen-W); *Dialogues* for oboe, clarinet, Op. 10 (1927, Skandinavisk); *Kammermusik*, Op. 11, for soprano, oboe (English horn), piano; phonetic text as above (1927, Skandinavisk); *Symphony No. 3* for 2 pianos, orchestra, Op. 12 (1928, SUDM); *Kilderejsen* [The Trip to the Holy Spring], opera, Op. 16; libretto by Vilhelm Andersen after Ludvig Holberg (1931; dances from the opera, *Majfest*, Op. 44, Skandinavisk); *Sinfonia concertante* for piano, chamber orchestra, Op. 25 (1934, SUDM); *Eisenbahngleichnis* for chorus, piano, 3 saxophones, Op. 26; poem by Erich Kästner (1934); *Pasteur*, concert opera, Op. 27 (1935, Hansen-W); *Fem Svaner* [Swans of the North], cantata, Op. 28 (1937, Hansen-W); *Kristoffer Columbus*, cantata, Op. 29; poem by Johannes V. Jensen (1937); *Pans Fløjter*, Op. 30, for chorus, piano, flute; poem by Harald Herdal (1938, Hansen-W); *Evolution*, symphonic fantasy, Op. 32 (1939, SUDM); *Wind Quintet*, Op. 36 (1940, Skandinavisk); *Det Er Ganske Vist* [It's Perfectly True], symphonic fantasy after Andersen, Op. 37 (1943, SUDM); *Vår—Höst* for baritone, orchestra, Op. 40 (1944); *Via nova 1 and 2*, Opp. 50, 52, a piano method conceived as an introduction to modern music; prepared in collaboration with Birgitta Nordenfelt and with contributions by Vagn Holmboe, Herman Koppel, Ingvar Lidholm, Harald Saeverud, et al. (1951, 1952; Imudico, Gehrman); *The Arsenal at Springfield* for soloists, chorus, organ, orchestra, Op. 54; poem by Longfellow (1953, SUDM).

PRINCIPAL WRITINGS: *Harmonilaere* (Copenhagen 1933; enlarged ed., 1970); *Den Elementaere Hørelaere* (Copenhagen 1937); *Indførelse i Palestrinastil* (textbook on counterpoint, Copenhagen 1969).

SEE ALSO Scandinavia.

Hoffmann, Richard (b. Vienna, 20 April 1925), studied privately in Vienna with Aurel Nemes (violin, 1930–35) and Georg Tintner (composition, 1935). He emigrated to New Zealand in 1935 and attended the Univ. of New Zealand at Auckland (1942–45). During 1947–51 he studied with Arnold Schoenberg in Los Angeles and at the Univ. of Calif. During 1948–51 he was Schoenberg's secretary. In 1950 he filed the Schoenberg correspondence for the Library of Congress, and in 1961 he was appointed coeditor of the Schoenberg collected edition. Since 1954 he has taught at Oberlin College. He has also lectured on

Schoenberg's works in Europe, New Zealand, and the U.S. Out of his close association with Schoenberg grew his composition procedures which, though serial in method, use tone rows that are not necessarily 12-tone. Every element of his music—the intervals, meters, rhythms, timbres, and dynamics—is systematically organized.

PRINCIPAL COMPOSITIONS: *Piano Sonata* (1945–46); *String Quartets Nos. 1–2* (1947, 1950); *Violin Concerto* (1948); *Tripartita* for violin (1950); *Piano Quartet* (1950); *Fantasy and Fugue* for organ, in memoriam Arnold Schoenberg (1951); *Orchestra Piece* (1952, Heinr.); *Piano Concerto* (1953–54); *Cello Concerto* (1956–59); *Variations for Piano No. 2* (1957); *Orchestra Piece* (1961, UE); *String Trio* (1961–63, UE); *momento mori* for double men's chorus, orchestra, tape (1966–69).

Hoiby, Lee (b. Madison, Wis., 17 Feb 1926), studied at the Univ. of Wis. (1941–47, piano with Gunnar Johansen), Mills College (1947; piano, Egon Petri), and at the Curtis Institute (1948–52; composition, Gian Carlo Menotti). He is a free-lance composer and teaches privately.

PRINCIPAL COMPOSITIONS: *The Scarf*, 1-act opera (1955, Schirmer-G); *Piano Concerto* (1958); *Beatrice*, 3-act opera (1959); *A Hymn of the Nativity*, cantata for soprano, bass, chorus, orchestra (1960, Ricordi); *The Tides of Sleep*, symphonic song for low voice, orchestra (1961, Boosey); *Natalia Petrovna*, 2-act opera (1964, Boosey); *After Eden*, ballet (1966); *Landscape*, ballet (1968); *Summer and Smoke*, 2-act opera (1970).

Holland, see Netherlands

Hollier, Donald (Russell) (b. Sydney, 7 May 1934), studied at the New South Wales Conservatorium (1952–57; composition with R. Harson, piano with L. Geoffrey Smith, organ with E. J. Robinson), the Royal Academy of Music in London (1959–60; harmony, counterpoint with E. Thiman), and the National School of Opera, London (1960–61; coaching with Peter Gellhorn, Joan Cross). He has been director of music at Newington College, Sydney (1962–63), and head of academic studies at the Canberra School of Music (since 1968). He has also performed as an accompanist in Europe during 1964–67 and in Australia for the Australian Broadcasting System during 1968–70.

PRINCIPAL COMPOSITIONS: *In Praise of Music* for children's chorus, orchestra (1964, revised 1970); *Passion of Our Lord Jesus Christ*, opera-oratorio (1964–65); *Musick's Empire* for baritone, orchestra (1965); *Piano Quintet* (1966); *Concerto for organ, 18 strings* (1966); *Piano Concerto* (1966); *Piano Sonata* (1966); *Organ Sonata* (1966); *4 Songs of Dryden* for voice, piano (1966–67); *Concerto in Romantic Style* for guitar, flute, 2 violins, celesta (1967); *5 Songs* for high voice, cello, piano (1968); *Orpheus and Euridyce*, chamber opera for 3 soloists, 2 pianos, tape (1969); *Mass for chorus, organ* (1969); *Variations on a Theme of Sitsky* for violin, piano (1970).

BIBL.: Andrew McCredie, *Catalogue of 46 Australian Composers* (Sydney 1969); Larry Sitsky, "New Music," *Current Affairs Bulletin* (Univ. of Sydney) 46/3.

SEE ALSO Australia.

Holliger, Heinz (b. Langenthal, Switzerland, 21 May 1939), attended the conservatories in Bern and Basle (1955–59) and the Paris Conservatory (1962–63). He studied oboe (with Emile Cassagnaud, Pierre Pierlot), piano (with Yvonne Lefébure), and composition (with Sándor Veress, Pierre Boulez). Holliger was first oboist with the Basle Orchestra (1959–64). In 1966 he became professor of oboe at the Musikhochschule in Freiburg/Breisgau, Germany. Berio, Castiglioni, Klaus Huber, Krenek, Henze, Jolivet, Penderecki, Pousseur, Stockhausen, Veress, and others have written pieces for him.

PRINCIPAL COMPOSITIONS (published by Schott unless otherwise noted): *Erde und Himmel*, cantata for tenor and 5 instruments (1961); *Elis*, 3 nocturnes for piano (1961); *3 Liebeslieder* for alto, orchestra (1963); *Schwarzgewebene Trauer* for soprano, 3 instruments (1963); *4 Bagatelles* for soprano, piano (1963); *Glühende Rätsel* for alto and instrumentalists; text by Nelly Sachs (1964); *Der magische Tänzer*, 2 scenes for 2 singers, 2 dancers, 2 actors, choir, orchestra, tape; text by Nelly Sachs (1965); *Trio* for oboe, viola, harp (1966); *Siebengesang* for oboe, orchestra, voices, amplifiers (1967); *h* for wind quintet (1968); *Dona nobis pacem* for 12 unaccompanied voices (1968–69); *Pneuma* for 34 winds, organ, percussion, radios (1970); *Cardiophonie* for 1 wind player (1971).

BIBL.: Josef Hausler, "H. H.: Versuch eines Portraits," *Schweizerische Musikzeitung* (March 1967): 64–73.

SEE ALSO Switzerland.

Holmboe, Vagn (b. Horsens, Jutland, Denmark, 20 Dec 1909), studied at the Royal Conservatory in Copenhagen (1927–30, composition with Finn Høffding) and in Berlin with Ernst Toch (1931). During the 1930s and 40s he collected and wrote about Rumanian and Danish folk music. He also taught at the Royal Danish Institute for the Blind (1940–49) and wrote criticism for *Politiken*. During 1955–65 he taught at the Royal Conservatory.

PRINCIPAL COMPOSITIONS: *Requiem* for boys' chorus, chamber orchestra; text in German by Hebbel (1931); *Fanden og Borgmesteren* [The Devil and the Mayor], 1-act symphonic fairy play, Op. 23; text by Walter Kolbenhoff (1940); *Symphonies Nos. 4–9*: No. 4, "Sinfonia sacra," Op. 29 (1941, Hansen-W); No. 5, Op. 35 (1944, Viking); No. 6, Op. 43 (1947, Viking); No. 7, Op. 50 (1950, Viking); No. 8, Op. 56 (1951–52, Viking); No. 9, Op. 95 (1967–68, Hansen-W); *Lave og Jon* [Lave and Jon], 3-act opera; libretto by Lis Torbjørnsen (1946); *Suono da Bardo* for piano, Op. 49 (1949, Viking); *Chamber Symphonies Nos. 1–3*: No. 1, Op. 53 (1951, Viking); No. 2, "Elegi," Op. 100 (1968, Hansen-W); No. 3, "Frise," Op. 103 (1970, Hansen-W); *14 Motets* for chorus (1952–53, Viking); *Epitaph*, symphonic metamorphosis, Op. 68 (1956, Viking); *Kniven* [The Knife], 1-act chamber opera; libretto by the composer (1959–60); *Monolith*, symphonic metamorphosis, Op. 76 (1960, Hansen-W); *Epiloge*, symphonic metamorphosis, Op. 80 (1961–62, Hansen-W); *Requiem for Nietzsche* for baritone, tenor, chorus, orchestra, Op. 84; text by Thorkild Bjørnvig (1963–64, Hansen-W). Also among his principal works are 10 string quartets and 13 concertos for solo instruments and chamber orchestra (1939–56).

PRINCIPAL WRITINGS: "Den Rumaenske Folkemusic" [Rumanian Folk Music], *Dansk Musiktidsskrift* 9:214–19; "Gadesangen i København" [Street Cries of Copenhagen], *ibid.* 13:171–79; "Strejflys over Nogle Problemer i Dansk Musik" [Sidelights on Some Problems in Danish Music], *Prisma* 1950/2:57–61; "Tre symfonier" [3 Symphonies], in *Modern nordisk musik* ed. by I. Bengtsson (Stockholm 1957):152–66; *Mellemspil. Tre Musikalske Aspekter* [Interlude. 3 Musical Aspects] (Copenhagen 1961); "On Form and Metamorphosis," *The Modern Composer and His World* ed. by J. Beckwith and U. Kasemets (Toronto 1961):134–40.

BIBL.: Vagn Kappel, *Danish Composers* (Copenhagen 1967):68–83; Robert Layton, "V. H. and the Later Scandinavians," *The Symphony* ed. by R. Simpson (London 1967):230–43; Sven Lund, *La Vie musicale au Danemark* (Copenhagen 1962): 67–74; F. S. Petersen, "Status over et Halvsekel" [Status Over Half a Century], *Ny musik i Norden* (Stockholm 1953); Bo Wallner, "Modern Music in Scandinavia," *European Music in the 20th Century* ed. by H. Hartog (London 1957):133–34.

SEE ALSO Scandinavia.

Holst, Gustav (Theodore) (b. Cheltenham, 21 Sept 1874; d. London, 25 May 1934), came

from a family of several professional musicians. He studied with Charles Stanford at the Royal College of Music and afterwards became repetiteur and trombonist for the Carl Rosa Opera Co. Gradually he came to devote his life to music education: at professional music schools, as chorus master and conductor of amateur vocal groups, with music societies and orchestras. Two influences on his style were his studies of Sanskrit, which introduced him to Eastern thought, and his acquaintance with Cecil Sharp and Ralph Vaughan Williams, who encouraged an interest in English folksong and Elizabethan polyphony.

Holst's was a curiously ambivalent art. While not radical, it reveals many unconventional tendencies. His harmonic idiom largely eschewed chromaticism but made use of modal and oriental melodic designs. His use of quartal harmonic schemes and progressions and the clashes of suspension patterns in *The Hymn of Jesus* (1917) are the work of an original mind. The treatment of voices in the *Choral Symphony*, Op. 41 (1923–24) and the *Choral Hymns from the Rig Veda*, Op. 26 (1908–12) and the instrumental writing in *The Planets*, Op. 32 (1914–17) are likewise adventurous. The word-dominated rhythms of Elizabethan music are echoed in his preference for irregular rhythms such as 5/8 and 7/8. His chamber opera *Savitri*, Op. 25 (1908), is progressive in its chamber-music proportions and in its use of an Asian (Sanskrit) subject.

PRINCIPAL COMPOSITIONS: *A Somerset Rhapsody* for orchestra, Op. 21b (1906–07, Boosey); *Savitri*, chamber opera, Op. 25 (1908, Curwen); *Choral Hymns from the Rig Veda* for men's, women's, mixed choruses, orchestra, Op. 26 (1908–12, Stainer); *Hecuba's Lament* for mezzo-soprano, women's chorus, orchestra, Op. 31 (1911, Stainer); *The Planets*, suite for orchestra, Op. 32 (1914–17, Curwen); *The Hymn of Jesus* for chorus, piano, organ, orchestra, Op. 37 (1917, Stainer); *Ode to Death* for chorus, orchestra, Op. 38 (1919, Novello); *St. Paul's Suite* for strings, Op. 29 (1922, Curwen); *Fugal Concerto* for flute, oboe, strings, Op. 40, No. 2 (1923, Novello); *Choral Symphony No. 1* with soprano, chorus, Op. 41 (1923–24, Novello); *Egdon Heath* for orchestra, Op. 47 (1927, Novello); *Choral Fantasia* for soprano (semichorus), chorus, organ, instruments, Op. 51 (1930, Curwen).

BIBL.: Imogen Holst, *G. H.* (London 1938); ——, *The Music of G. H.* (London 1951); Frank Howes, *The English Musical Renaissance* (London 1966); Edmund G. Rubbra, *G. H.* (London 1947).

John S. Weissmann

SEE ALSO Asian Music and Western Composition, Great Britain, Impressionism.

Homs (Oller), **Joaquim** (b. Barcelona, 21 Aug 1906), studied engineering in Barcelona (1923–29) and has made a career as an industrial engineer. He studied cello privately with Fernando Pérez-Prió in Barcelona (1914–22) and taught himself piano and composition. During 1930–36 he studied with Roberto Gerhard. His compositions since 1954 have been largely based on 12-tone techniques emanating from Schoenberg.

PRINCIPAL COMPOSITIONS: *Duo* for flute, clarinet (1936, Boileau); *Sonata* for solo violin (1941, Seesaw); *String Quartet No. 3* (1950); *Trio* for flute, oboe, bass clarinet or bassoon (1954); *3 Impromptus* for piano (1955); *Music* for harp, flute, oboe, bass clarinet (1955); *Via Crucis* for speaker, string quartet, percussion (1956); *Les hores* for alto, flute, oboe, bass clarinet; poems by S. Espriu (1956); *Sextet* for string trio, woodwind trio (1959); *Inventions* for strings (1959, Boileau); *Impromptu No. 6* for piano (1960); *El caminant i el mur* for mezzo-soprano, piano; poems by Espriu (1962); *Invention* for orchestra (1964); *Music for 8* for piano, flute, clarinet, trumpet, violin, viola, cello, percussion (1964, Seesaw); *En la meva mort* for chorus (1966, Clivis); *String Quartet No. 6* (1966, Seesaw); *Preséncies* for orchestra (1967); *String Quartet No. 7* (1968, Moeck); *Woodwind Octet* (1968, Seesaw); *String Trio* (1968, Moeck); *Heptandre* for flute, oboe, clarinet, violin, cello, piano, percussion (1969).

BIBL.: Montserrat Albet, "La música de J. H.," *Imagen y sonido* 55 (Jan 1968); Sebastià Benet, "Entrevista amb J. H., compositor," *Serra d'or* 105 (June 1968); Wolf-Eberhard von Lewinski, "Vier katalanische Komponisten in Barcelona," *Melos* 38:92–103.

SEE ALSO Spain.

Honegger, Arthur (b. Le Havre, 10 March 1892; d. Paris, 27 Nov 1955), was of Swiss Protestant parentage and remained a Swiss national throughout his life. He first studied piano with his mother and began harmony at 13 with R. C. Martin and later violin with Lucien Capet. A performance of two Bach cantatas, which he heard when 15, made a lasting impression on him. During 1909–11 he studied at the Zurich Conservatory, where he came in contact with Bartók, and in 1911 he began study at the Paris Conservatory (counterpoint and fugue with André Gedalge, composition with Charles-Marie Widor, orchestration with Vincent d'Indy). In 1920 he came to the attention especially of French musicians when he and five other composers were grouped under the title Les Six. A year later international fame came with the premiere of his oratorio *King David* in Mezières,

Switzerland. He married the pianist Andrée Vaurabourg in 1926 and lived mostly in Paris. When asked whether he considered himself a Swiss or a French composer he would answer, "Je suis les deux."

Honegger's style was essentially choral, and his seven choral works are his most successful; there are, as well, 50 symphonic and chamber works, 13 for keyboard, 50 songs, 21 stage works, 8 for radio, and 44 for films. As his style developed he became the most individualistic and least Gallic of Les Six. In his early days he was involved with impressionism (*Pastorale d'été*, 1921), machine music (*Pacific 231*, 1924), and jazz (*Concertino* for piano and orchestra, 1925). He then moved toward a kind of neoromanticism that combined chromatic harmony (linking him to such composers as R. Strauss and Schoenberg) and a Wagnerian treatment of the orchestra, in which sound upon sound is piled up to reach dramatic peaks. A strong feeling for formal architecture and for counterpoint shows an influence from the late baroque, particularly J. S. Bach, whom he admired above all other composers. The emphasis on counterpoint lent itself to the use of long lines, as in Bach, and to much contrary motion, extensive use of melodic and rhythmic ostinatos, polychordal effects, and to polytonality, polyrhythms, and polymeters. There is a secure underpinning in his strong, baroquelike driving rhythms (Honegger particularly liked dotted rhythms, as in the French overture), in the fact that his music never loses sight of tonality, and in the procedure of often harmonizing melodies with the notes of the melody itself. As he told his students, "If your melodic or rhythmic design is precise and clear and commands the attention of the ear, the accompanying dissonances will never frighten the listener." He fitted words to melody in a rhythm and intonation close to ordinary speech (more so than Schoenberg did). Accented syllables are often short, producing a surprising kind of emphasis. Form is often baroquelike in its emphasis on rhythmic drive and the maintenance of consistent patterns to propel the music forward. Honegger used many two- and three-part forms, and in his symphonic pieces showed a liking for the arch form, ABCBA; frequently a return is stated in inversion. He explained his own aims as a composer with the words, "My inclination and my effort have always been to write music which would be comprehensible to the great mass of listeners and at the same time sufficiently free of banality to interest genuine music lovers."

PRINCIPAL COMPOSITIONS (published by Salabert unless otherwise noted): *Viola Sonata* (1920); *Sonatina* for 2 violins (1920); *Horace victorieux* for orchestra (1921); *King David*, oratorio (1921, orchestration revised 1923; Foetisch); *Sonatina* for clarinet, piano (1922, Rouart-Lerolle); *Un Cahier romand* for piano (1923); *Judith*, 3-act opera; libretto by René Morax (1925); *Antigone*, 3-act opera; libretto by Jean Cocteau (1927); *Symphony No. 1* (1930); *Cris du monde*, oratorio; text by René Bizet (1931); *Symphonic Movement No. 3* (1933); *Jeanne d'Arc au bûcher*, oratorio; text by Paul Claudel (1935); *String Quartet No. 3* (1937); *Symphony No. 2* for strings with trumpet ad lib. (1942); *Symphony No. 3* (1946); *Symphony No. 4* for chamber orchestra (1946); *Symphony No. 5* (1950); *A Christmas Cantata* (1953). Complete list in Tappolet; film music listed in Bruyr: 234–36 and Delannoy: 248–49 (see bibl.).

PRINCIPAL WRITINGS: *Incantation aux fossiles* (Lausanne 1948); *I Am a Composer*, trans. by W. O. Clough and A. A. Willman (New York 1966).

BIBL.: José Bruyr, *H. et son oeuvre* (Paris 1947); Leonard Burkat, "Current Chronicle," *Musical Quarterly* 38:118–23; M. F. G. Delannoy, *H.* (Paris 1953); H. E. Headley, *The Choral Works of A. H.* (PhD diss., North Texas State Univ., 1959); Allen Hughes, "H.—Death Was Often His Theme," *Musical America* (1 Jan 1956):7; ———, "Les Six," *Musical America* (15 Feb 1954):12, 128, 146; Jean Matter, *H. ou la quête de joie* (Lausanne 1956); Willy Tappolet, *A. H.* (Boudry-Neuchatel 1957).

James R. Hanna
SEE ALSO France, Jazz, Opera, Switzerland.

Hopkins, Bill (G. W.) (b. Prestbury, Cheshire, England, 5 June 1943), attended Worcester College in Oxford (1961–64; harmony and counterpoint with Edmund Rubbra, music history with Frank L. Harrison, 12-tone music with Egon Wellesz). He studied analysis with Olivier Messiaen at the Paris Conservatory in 1964 and privately with Jean Barraqué in 1965. Since 1965 he has worked as a free-lance writer on music and as a translator, proofreader, and editor. Of particular importance to his musical development are the prose writings (c.1945–50) of Samuel Beckett.

PRINCIPAL COMPOSITIONS: *2 Pomes* for soprano, bass clarinet, trumpet, harp, viola; texts by James Joyce (1964, UE); *Sensation* for soprano, tenor saxophone, trumpet, harp, viola; texts by Rimbaud and Beckett (1965); *Etudes en série* for piano (in 3 books, 1965–69; book 1 published by Schott); *Pendant* for violin (1968–69); *Comment on Rate* for 2 sopranos, alto, wind ensemble, violin, ondes Martenot, electronic organ; texts by William Faulkner and Beckett (1968–69).

PRINCIPAL WRITINGS: "Jean Barraqué," *Musical Times* (Nov 1966):952–54; "Debussy and Boulez," *ibid.* (August 1968):710–14.

Horst, Louis (b. Kansas City, 12 Jan 1884; d. New York, 23 Jan 1964), studied piano and violin in San Francisco and composition at the Vienna Conservatory (1925). During 1915–25 he was music director of the Ruth St. Denis and Denishawn dance companies, and during 1926–48 he was associated with the Martha Graham Dance Co. He taught at the Neighborhood Playhouse School of Theatre in New York (1928–64), Bennington College summer sessions (1934–45), the Juilliard School dance department (1951–64), and the Conn. College summer school (1948–63). He founded the magazine *Dance Observer* in 1934 and was its editor until his death.

PRINCIPAL DANCE SCORES: *Japanese Spear Dance* (choreographed by Ted Shawn, 1919); *Byzantine Dance* (Ruth St. Denis, 1925); *3 Poems of the East* (Martha Graham, 1926); *2 Balinese Rhapsodies* (Ruth Page, 1926); *Fragments: Tragedy and Comedy* (Graham, 1928); *Primitive Mysteries* (Graham, 1931); *Chorus of Youth* (Graham, 1932); *3 Tragic Patterns* (Graham, 1933); *American-Provincials* (Graham, 1934); *Celebration* (Graham, 1934); *Pleasures of Counterpoint No. 2* (Doris Humphrey, 1934); *Frontier* (Graham, 1935); *Horizons* (Graham, 1936); *Graduation Piece* (Pearl Lang, 1937); *Columbiad* (Graham, 1939); *Little Theodolina* (Nina Fonaroff, 1940); *El Penitente* (Graham, 1940); *Transformations of Medusa* (Jean Erdman, 1941); *Mountain White* (Agnes de Mille, 1941); *Yankee Doodle* (Fonaroff, 1942); *Born to Weep* (Fonaroff, 1946); *Tale of Seizure* (Yuriko, 1948).

PRINCIPAL WRITINGS: untitled essay on the subject of composers and choreographers, *Dance Perspectives* 19:6–8; *Modern Dance Forms in Relation to the Other Modern Arts*, prepared with C. Russell (New York 1967); *Preclassic Dance Forms* (New York 1968).

[prepared with the help of Alan and Sali Ann Kriegsman]
SEE ALSO Dance.

Horvath, Josef Maria (b. Pecs, Hungary, 20 Dec 1931), attended the Liszt-Ferenc Academy in Budapest (1949–56, piano with Peter Solymos, composition with Ferenc Szabó, folk-music studies with Zoltán Kodály, chamber music with András Mihály) and the Akademie Mozarteum in Salzburg (1957–59, piano with Kurt Leimer, composition with Cesar Bresgen). He has taught at the Mozarteum since 1963 and coorganized the Musica Nova concert series there. His early musical thinking, which was similar to that of Bartók, was reshaped through the influence of 12-tone and serial techniques and electronic music. These factors, together with his work on the esthetics of information theory, have contributed to the formation of a style that Horvath calls "*statistische-flexibel*." The term refers to the precise scaffolding of inner relationships, the details of which are left free to be shaped in a mutually compatible manner.

PRINCIPAL COMPOSITIONS: *4 Songs* for soprano, 4 instruments; texts by Hölderlin (1958, Peters); *Die Blinde* for mezzo-soprano, 2 sprechstimmen, 4 instruments (1959, Peters); *Messe* for chorus, orchestra (1959); *Entropia*, symphony for orchestra (1961); *Redundanz Nos. 1–3* for string quartet, wind octet (1966–68, Doblinger).

Hovhaness, Alan (b. Somerville, Mass., 8 March 1911), of Armenian and Scottish parentage, was exposed to further Armenian influences through contact with the priest-composer, Gomidas Vartabed. He studied composition with Frederick Converse at the New England Conservatory in Boston and later with Bohuslav Martinů at Tanglewood. During 1940–47 he lived in Boston composing, teaching, accompanying, and studying Eastern music. His first use of aleatoric procedures date from these years and can be found in *Lousadzak* (1944). He taught at the Boston Conservatory (1948–52), after which he made his home in New York and began to travel extensively, assisted at times by Fulbright, Guggenheim, and Rockefeller grants. Commissions have come from many lands, including three Eastern nations whose music he has studied closely, Japan, Korea, and India.

Few 20th-century composers have matched the volume and diversity of Hovhaness's output. His catalog contains over 230 works representing all the traditional media. In 1940 he destroyed most of his early music, which included 7 symphonies, 6 string quartets, several operas, and many piano pieces.

Hovhaness has developed a style that combines traditional Western materials with elements from other cultures, particularly those of Armenia, South India, and the Far East. His melodic and harmonic foundation is modal but often colored by chromaticism; mild dissonances usually result through concurring contrapuntal lines. The improvisatory melismas of ancient Armenian cantilation find echoes in his melodic lines and in the extended passages of unbarred and rhapsodic rhythms. A favorite melodic device is the repetition of motives or of single notes within phrases that are restricted in range and center around a single pitch. Other mannerisms, less typically Eastern, are frequent ostinato rhythms and pedal tones. For color he has employed such exotic instruments as the Chinese *ch'in*,

the Japanese *hichiriki*, the Korean *kayakeum*, and the Balinese gamelan orchestra. When employing traditional Western instruments he frequently emphasizes rapidly changing solo timbres over a sparse orchestral support.

PRINCIPAL COMPOSITIONS (list prepared by the composer, published by Peters unless otherwise noted): *Prelude and Quadruple Fugue* for orchestra (1936, revised 1954); *Lousadzak*, concerto for piano, strings (1944, Peer); *Tzaikerk* for chamber orchestra (1945, Peer); *Symphony No. 8*, "Arjuna" (1947); *Zartik Parkim*, concerto for piano, chamber orchestra (1948, Peer); *Symphony No. 9*, "St. Vartan" (1950, Peer); *Concerto No. 1*, "Arevakal," for orchestra (1951, AMP); *Khaldis*, concerto for piano, 4 trumpets, percission (1951, King); *Triptych* for soprano, chorus, chamber orchestra (1953, AMP); *Mysterious Mountain* for orchestra (1955, AMP); *Magnificat* for soloists, chorus, chamber orchestra (1958); *Meditation on Orpheus* for orchestra (1958); *Symphony No. 4* for wind orchestra, percussion (1959); *The Burning House*, 1-act opera; libretto by the composer (1960); *Koke no niwa* for English horn (B♭ clarinet), harp, percussion (1960); *Madras Sonata* for piano (1960); *Symphony No. 11*, "All Men Are Brothers," for orchestra (1960, revised 1969); *Symphony No. 12*, "Chorale," for chorus, chamber orchestra (1960); *Symphony No. 15*, "Silver Pilgrimage" (1962); *Variations and Fugue* for orchestra (1963); *Pilate*, 1-act opera; libretto by the composer (1964); *Symphony No. 17*, "Symphony for Metal Orchestra," for winds, percussion (1964); *Symphony No. 18*, "Circe," for orchestra (1964); *Fantasy on Japanese Woodprints* for xylophone, orchestra (1965); *Floating World* for orchestra (1965); *Symphony No. 19*, "Vishnu" (1966); *Fra Angelico* for orchestra (1967); *Mountains and Rivers without End* for 10 instruments (1968); *Requiem and Resurrection* for brass choir, percussion (1968); *Symphony No. 20 for Band* (1968); *Lady of Light* for soloists, chorus, chamber orchestra; text by the composer (1969). Selected list to 1952 in Daniel; list to 1964: *Composers of the Americas* 11:49–68; list of solo piano works to 1967 in Hinson.

BIBL.: Oliver Daniel, "A. H.," *ACA Bulletin* 2:3–7, 24; Maurice Hinson, "The Piano Works of A. H.," *American Music Teacher* 16:23ff., 44; Ned E. G. Will, Jr., "A. H.: East Meets West," *Music Journal* 21:30, 62, 74; "The Three Magi of Contemporary Music," *Tiger's Eye* (Westport, Conn.) 3:59–65.

Thomas E. Warner

SEE ALSO Asian Music and Western Composition, Dance, United States.

Hovland, Egil (b. Mysen, Norway, 18 Oct 1924), studied at the Oslo Conservatory (1946–49, composition with Bjarne Brustad, counterpoint with Per Steenberg, organ with Arild Sandvold). He also studied composition privately with Vagn Holmboe in Copenhagen and Luigi Dallapiccola in Florence. In 1957 he worked with Aaron Copland at Tanglewood. Since 1949 he has been organist and choirmaster of the Glemmen Church in Fredrikstad.

PRINCIPAL COMPOSITIONS: *Symphonies Nos. 1–2* (1952–53, 1954–55); *Concertino* for 3 trumpets, strings (1954–55); *Music for 10 Instruments* for wind quintet, strings (1957, Lyche); *Suite* for flute, strings (1959); *Lamenti* for orchestra (1963, Lyche); *Magnificat* for alto, alto flute, harp (1964, Norsk); *Varianti* for 2 pianos (1964, Norsk); *Wind Quintet* (1965, Norsk); *Elementa* for organ (1965, Norsk); *Fanfare and Chorale* for band or orchestra (1966, Norsk); *Variations* for oboe, piano (1968–69); *Symphony No. 3* for narrators, chorus; English text (1969); *Rhapsody 69* for orchestra (1969).

BIBL.: Bjarne Kortsen, *Modern Norwegian Chamber Music* (Haugesund 1965):31–38; ——, *Contemporary Norwegian Orchestral Music* (Bergen 1968):152–59.

SEE ALSO Scandinavia.

Howells, Herbert (Norman) (b. Lydney, England, 17 Oct 1892), studied at the Royal College of Music in London (1912–17, composition with Charles Stanford, counterpoint with Charles Wood, choral technique with Walford Davies, organ with Walter Parratt). He was organist at St. Mary's in Lydney (c. 1905), Salisbury Cathedral (1917), and St. John's College, Cambridge (1941–45). Since 1920 he has been on the faculty of the Royal College of Music and has served on the Associated Board of the Royal Schools of Music. He was director of music at Morley College, London (1925–28) and St. Paul's Girls' School (1936–62), and during 1954–64 he taught at the Univ. of London. He has been an adjudicator at many music festivals between 1920 and 1968.

PRINCIPAL COMPOSITIONS: *3 Rhapsodies* for organ (1915–16, Augener); *Piano Quartet in A Minor* (1916, Stainer); *Elegy* for viola, string quartet, string orchestra (1917, Boosey); *4 French Chansons* for voice, piano (1918, Chester); *Rhapsodic Quintet* for clarinet, strings (1919, Stainer); *Procession* for orchestra (1922, Ascherberg); *Lambert's Clavichord* (1927, Oxford); *In Green Ways* for high voice, piano (1915; revised 1928, Oxford); *Organ Sonata No. 2* (1933, Novello); *A Kent Yeoman's Wooing Song* for chorus (1933, Novello); *Pageantry Suite* for brass band (1934, R. S. Smith & Co.); *Hymnus paradisi* for chorus (1938, Novello); *Collegium regale Magnificat et Nunc dimittis* for chorus (1945, Novello); *Clarinet Sonata* (1946, Boosey); *St. Paul's Cathedral Magnificat et Nunc dimittis* for chorus (1951, Novello); *Missa sabrinensis* (1953, Novello); *De profundis* for organ (1960); *Howell's Clavichord Vols. 1–2* (1961, No-

vello); *Stabat Mater* for chorus (1963, Novello). ★ Undated works: *The House of the Mind*, motet for chorus (Novello); *Take Him, Earth, for Cherishing* for chorus (Novello); *Gavotte* for voice, piano (Oxford); *King David* for voice, piano (Oxford); *Come Sing and Dance* for voice, piano (Oxford); *3 Figures*, triptych for brass band (Weinberger).

PRINCIPAL WRITINGS: "The *Pastoral Symphony* of Ralph Vaughan Williams," *Music and Letters* 3:122–32; "Ralph Vaughan Williams' *Concerto Academico*," *The Dominant* (March 1925):24–28; "Charles Villiers Stanford," *Proceedings of the Royal Musical Association* 79/2:19–31; "Being British and Musical," *The London Times* (3 Jan 1952); "The Chamber Music of Arthur Benjamin," *Cobbett's Cyclopedic Survey of Chamber Music* (London 1963); "Hubert Hastings Parry," *Music and Letters* (April 1969).

BIBL.: "H. H.—His *In Gloucestershire* (String Quartet)," *Christian Science Monitor* (25 Dec 1920); Ernest Bradbury, "Pen Portrait of H. H.," *Musical Times* (April 1958); Edwin Evans, "Modern British Composers—VIII: H. H.," *ibid.* (Feb, March 1920); Gerald Finzi, "H. H.," *ibid.* (April 1954); Peter J. Hodgson, *The Music of H. H.* (PhD diss., Univ. of Colo., 1970); D. Hugh Ottaway, "H. H. and the English Revival," *Musical Times* (Oct 1967).

[prepared with the help of Peter J. Hodgson]

Hrisanide, Alexandru (Dumitru) (b. Petrila, Rumania, 15 June 1936), attended the Bucharest Conservatory (1953–64, composition with Mihail Jora, harmony with Paul Constantinescu, counterpoint with Zeno Vancea, form with Tudor Ciortea, piano with Florica Musicesco, and others). He studied composition with Nadia Boulanger at Fontainebleau and privately in Paris in 1965 and attended the Darmstadt summer courses in 1966 and 1967. He taught at the first Bucharest Academy of Music (1959–62) and since then has been on the faculty of the Bucharest Conservatory. He is active as a pianist throughout Europe and is also active as a critic and writer on musical subjects. The works of 1955–57 exhibit modal harmonic tendencies after the manner of Messiaen and make use of 12-tone techniques as well. The latter are applied to a Dorian theme in the *Passacaglia* and to Rumanian folksongs in the *Second Flute Sonata* and the *Clarinet Sonata*. The *Mers-Tefs* pieces use aleatory techniques.

PRINCIPAL COMPOSITIONS: *Piano Pieces Nos. 1–13* (1955–56; 1–7 published by Gerig); *Flute Sonatas Nos. 1–3* (1956; 1960–62, Muzicală; 1956); *Violin Sonata* (1957); *Trio* for violin, viola, bassoon (1958, Gerig); *String Quartet* (1958); *Passacaglia* for orchestra (1959); *Piano Sonatas Nos. 2–3* (1959,

1956–64; Gerig); *Vers-Antiqua (Hommage à Euri-pide)* for chamber ensemble of 22 players (1960); *Clarinet Sonata* (1960–62, Muzicală and Gerig); *Mers-Tefs 1* for violin (1960–68, Gerig); *Mers-Tefs 2* for 1–4 violins (1960–70, Muzicală and Gerig); *Volumes—Inventions* for cello, piano (1963, Muzicală and Salabert); *A la Recherche de la verticale* for oboe (1965, Gerig); *C'Etait Issu stellaire . . .*: part 1 for men's chorus, organ, trumpets, trombones, piano, percussion; text by Mallarmé (1965, Salabert); part 2, "Unda," for organ (1965, Salabert); *M.P.5* [Musique pour 5] for tenor saxophone (clarinet), violin, viola, cello, piano (1966, Salabert); *Ad perpetuam rei memoriam* for orchestra (1966, Ahn & Sim); *Directions* for flute, oboe, clarinet, bassoon, horn (1967–69, Gerig); *Musiques pour RA Nos. 1–6* on tape (1969–71; No. 4 consists of 2 different compositions, No. 6 of 3 different compositions); *Soliloquim + 11* for string quartet (1970, Gerig). Hrisanide has also edited a 2-volume anthology, *Neue rumänische zeitgenössische Klaviermusik* (1970, Gerig).

BIBL.: George Balan, "A. H.," *Contemporanul* (Bucharest, 25 Jan 1963); Costin Miereanu, "A. H.: *Ad perpetuam rei memoriam*," *Contemporanul* (Dec 1967); Radu Rupea, an interview with A. H., *Ateneu* (Bacau, Sept 1968).

Huber, Klaus (b. Bern, 30 Nov 1924), was trained as a school teacher and worked in this capacity in Zurich during 1946–47. He studied at the Zurich Conservatory (1947–49; theory, harmony, counterpoint with Willy Burkhard; violin with Stefi Geyer) and studied composition privately with Burkhard and later (1955–56) with Boris Blacher. He has taught violin at the Zurich Conservatory (1950–60), music history and literature at the Lucerne Conservatory (from 1960), and harmony and counterpoint at the Basel Conservatory (from 1961).

PRINCIPAL COMPOSITIONS: *Sonata da chiesa* for violin, organ (1953); *Concerto per la camerata* for recorder, flute, oboe, violin, cello, harpsichord (1954–55, Heinr.); *6 kleinen Vokalisen* for alto, violin, cello (1955; revised for violin, viola or clarinet, cello, 1962–63, Heinr.); *Oratio Mechtildis* for alto, chamber orchestra; text by Mechthild von Magdeburg (1956–57, Bärenreiter); *Antiphonische Kantate* for 2 choruses, orchestra; Psalm 123 (1956, revised for chamber ensemble 1957); *Des Engels Anredung an die Seele* for tenor, flute, clarinet, horn, harp; text by Johann Georg Albini (1957, UE); *Litania instrumentalis* for orchestra (1957, Bärenreiter); *2 Sätze* for 2 trumpets, 2 horns, 2 trombones, tuba (1957–58); *Auf die ruhige Nacht-Zeit* for soprano, flute, viola, cello; text by Catharina Regina von Greiffenberg (1958, Bärenreiter); *Soliloquia I–III* for vocal soloists, chorus, orchestra; texts by Aurelius

Augustinus (1960–62, 1959–60, 1960; Bärenreiter); *Noctes intelligibilis lucis* for oboe, harpsichord (1961); *Moteti cantiones* for string quartet (1962–63); *Tenebrae* for orchestra (1967).

SEE ALSO Switzerland.

Huber, Nicolaus A. (b. Passau, Germany, 15 Dec 1939), studied music education (1958–62) and composition (1962–67) at the State Music School in Munich, where his principal teachers were Oskar Koebel (piano) and Günter Bialas (composition). He also studied composition privately with Luigi Nono in Venice (1967–68). Huber taught at the Gymnasien in Nuremberg (1963), Aschaffenburg (summer 1964), Erlangen (1964–65), and Munich (1966–69). He worked with Josef A. Riedl at the Munich electronic music studio (1965–66). He moved to Dachau in 1968, where he teaches piano and composes. The most important influences on his development have come from Stockhausen and Ligeti and, previous to Ligeti, Debussy, Schoenberg, and Webern.

PRINCIPAL COMPOSITIONS (published by Bärenreiter unless otherwise noted): *Spektrale* for piano (1965, unpub.); *Mimus* for 2 trumpets, 2 trombones, 2 horns, piano, 2 percussionists (1965–66, Bosse); *Informationen über die Töne e-f* for string quartet (1965–66); *Chronogramm* for clarinet, violin, cello, piano (1966, Bosse); *Von . . . bis* for harmonium, viola, piano, percussion (1966); *Parusie* for orchestra, loudspeaker (1967); *Traummechanik* for percussionist, piano (1967); *Epigenesis I* for 4 recorder players (1968); *Epigenesis III* for 14 strings, percussion (1968); *Epigenesis II* for recorder player, tape (1969, unpub.); *Aion* for 4 groups of loudspeakers and odors (1969, unpub.).

Humel, Gerald (b. Cleveland, 7 Nov 1931), attended Oberlin Conservatory (1949–51, composition with Herbert Elwell; 1956–58, composition with Walter Aschaffenburg), Hofstra Univ. (1952–54, composition with Elie Siegmeister), the Royal College of Music, London (1954–56, composition with Herbert Howells), the Univ. of Mich. (1958–60, composition with Ross Lee Finney and Roberto Gerhard), and the Berlin Hochschule für Musik (1960–63, composition with Boris Blacher and Josef Rufer). Humel lives in Berlin, where he is a free-lance composer. In 1967 he became conductor of the Ensemble der Gruppe Neue Musik Berlin.

PRINCIPAL COMPOSITIONS SINCE 1960 (published by Bote unless otherwise noted): *Flute Concerto* (1961); *Jochem Wessels*, opera (1962–64, unpub.);

Erste Liebe, ballet (1965); *Herodias*, ballet (1966); *Symphony* for orchestra (1967–69); *Concerto* for wind orchestra (1968, Peters); *Flashes* for chamber ensemble (1968); *Temno* for cello, chamber ensemble (1969).

Hungary. Until the end of World War I, Hungary was ruled by the Hapsburg monarchy and musical taste was dominated by Brahms and Wagner. However, the latest symphonic poems of Richard Strauss were played in Budapest (they made a deep impression on *Bartók during his student years), and French trends were known, especially from 1907, when *Kodály returned from a sojourn in Paris, and after Debussy's concert in Budapest in Dec 1910. The influence of the developing second Viennese school began to be felt after 1910; the first Stravinsky premiere (*The Firebird*) took place in Budapest in March 1912.

The most important event for Hungarian music during this period was the publication in 1905 in the periodical *Ethnographia* of Kodály's first folk music collection. Gradually, on the basis of Hungarian folk music (and in Bartók's case Rumanian, Slovak, and some other folk music as well), a new Hungarian concert music was created. This new music began to flourish even before the end of World War I in Bartók's opera *Bluebeard's Castle*, his ballet *The Wooden Prince*, and his *String Quartet No. 2*, along with Kodály's chamber music and songs. The newer music, of course, was not often performed. Around 1911 it appeared mostly in special concerts organized by UMZE, the New Hungarian Music Association. There were also some noteworthy protagonists: the (Imre) Waldbauer Quartet, pianists Ernő Dohányi and Béla Bartók, Budapest Opera conductor Egisto Tango, the musicologist Antal Molnár, and the critic Béla Reinitz.

1920–45. At the beginning of this period Hungary had just lost more than half of the territory it previously controlled; because of this and other circumstances, it underwent great economic stress. The political leadership was chauvinistic, antisemitic, and from the 1930s on more and more fascist. These circumstances created an unfavorable climate for music. A number of talented musicians left the country, among them the conductors Antal Dorati, Eugene Ormandy, Georg Solti, and Zoltán Székely, first violinist of the Hungarian Quartet and the man to whom Bartók dedicated his *Violin Concerto*. No composer could earn his living by composing, and in the 40s

teaching by some composers was actually forbidden. In spite of all this Béla Bartók (1881–1945) and Zoltan Kodály (1882–1967) continued their fight for a new kind of Hungarian music. The characteristic features of the new music were determined by Kodály and his followers, who deliberately isolated themselves from neoclassicism and dodecaphony and promoted instead a nationalism based on Hungarian folk music. This style, which became very shallow during 1945–55, was characterized by pentatonic harmony with some modal coloring, melodies composed mostly of seconds and fourths, rhythmic formations inspired by Hungarian speech and poetry, and a high regard for the classic forms.

Bartók's approach differed from that of Kodály. His was a more cosmopolitan mind, and he drew inspiration from folk sources other than only Hungarian. In addition he did not use folk material so much for itself as for the more general guidelines it suggested in regard to new kinds of musical construction, e.g., retaining the shape of a motive' but altering its component intervals on repetition, or using major, minor, and other scale formations simultaneously (see Vinton in the bibl.). Owing in part to the wider applicability of Bartók's approach, he, more than his contemporaries, brought Hungarian music to international attention. Because of the intellectual rigor with which he applied folk-derived procedures, he also was the Hungarian composer who came closest to the new concepts of dissonance and consonance, form, and motivic construction of Stravinsky and Schoenberg, particularly during 1910–36. He kept abreast of world trends by studying these composers as well as Krenek, Hindemith, Honegger, Casella, Szymanovsky, Hába, and others. However, he taught only piano in Hungary, never composition, and thus had far less influence there than Kodály, who taught composition at the Budapest Academy from early in his career.

Other representatives of Hungarian music during these years included László *Lajtha (1892–1963), who furthered the French influence of Debussy, Ravel, and Roussel; Leo *Weiner (1885–1960), who combined a late romantic orientation with folklorism; Sándor *Jemnitz (1890–1963), a pupil of Reger; György *Kósa (b. 1897), a follower in these years of the young Schoenberg and of Bartók from before 1910; and from the 1930s Pál *Kadosa (b. 1903), a Kodály pupil also conversant with the Viennese school, Stravinsky's neoclassicism, and Bartók. The most talented of the Kodály circle were Ferenc *Szabó (b.

1902–1969), Endre *Szervánszky (b. 1911), and Ferenc *Farkas (b. 1905).

The widespread amateur choral movement, organized in these years, was the most effective propagator of new Hungarian music within the country. The spread of Hungarian music abroad and the interaction of local and foreign music was aided by the Modern Magyar Muzsikusok Csoportja [Modern Hungarian Musicians Group], founded 1928, which later absorbed another group, UMZE [New Hungarian Music Association], 1930–38, the Hungarian section of the ISCM. These groups organized one-composer evenings and other concerts devoted to contemporary music. In addition Hungarian works were appearing at international festivals and were being published by Universal Edition in Vienna (Bartók, Kodály, Kósa, Lajtha, among others) and by Schott in Mainz (Jemnitz, Kadosa, and others) and Leduc in Paris (Lajtha).

SINCE 1945. To an even greater extent than World War I, World War II and its aftermath left Hungary destitute. Nevertheless new economic and social measures taken after 1948 slowly benefited musicians and musical institutions. The Magyar Zenemüvészek Szövetsége [Association of Hungarian Musicians] was founded in 1949, replacing a similar association founded in 1945. It represents Hungarian musicians in international bodies such as the ISCM and is the chief advisor to Hungarian cultural authorities on musical matters. It publishes a monthly magazine, *Magyar Zene* [Hungarian Music], and holds monthly meetings in Budapest at which new Hungarian and foreign works are discussed. It also exchanges scores and tapes with foreign organizations. During 1945–53 the Bartók Szövetség [Bartók Association] was the central organization for a network of amateur choirs in schools and factories; it published a magazine called *Éneklő Nép* [Singing People] (1948–50).

The health and social needs of composers are handled by an organization founded in 1947 and now known as the Musical Department of the Art Foundation of the Hungarian Peoples Republic; it provides such benefits as health insurance, advances on royalties, vacation resorts, and costs for copying music. Editio Musica Budapest (founded 1950) publishes about 140 new Hungarian works annually, including joint publications with Boosey and Hawkes (35 a year), Doblinger, Peters, and Schott. Qualiton (founded 1951) issues recordings of 20–25 new Hungarian works annually. The national concert agency, Országos Filharmónia [National Philhar-

monia] (founded 1949) oversees about 2,000 concerts a year with a total attendance of about 100,000. Each season these concerts include 15–20 symphonic and 30–35 chamber works by contemporary Hungarians, half of which are premieres. The Hungarian radio broadcasts about 125 concerts of new music from international festivals each year as well as several new-music series. New Hungarian operas are shown principally at the two opera houses in Budapest, while new foreign operas are usually shown in Szeged, a city of 100,000 in the southeast (the opera houses in Pécs and Debrecen are also noteworthy). Opera attendance is about 1 million annually; Emil *Petrovics (b. Yugoslavia, 1930) and Sándor *Szokolai (b. 1931) are the leading composers of new Hungarian opera. The Pécs Ballet (the city, in the southwest, has a population of about 115,000) has been likened to the Diaghilev Ballet in that the director and choreographer Imre Eck (b. 1930) has personal contacts with composers and artists and draws them together.

The financial needs of musicians are insured by the government. Most composers have jobs in music and earn the greater part of their living from royalties; many composers, even some in their 30s, earn all their living by composing. The city councils, choral groups, and particularly the Hungarian radio all commission new works each year. Teachers of music are placed in the Academy of Music in Budapest or in the country's other six conservatories, eight music secondary schools, 500 music schools, and special music elementary schools (an institution unique in Hungary in which there are five or six singing classes a week). It is perhaps not surprising that overproduction of performers is a continuing problem.

Until about 1955 Kodály's music of 1910–30 continued to be the prevailing model for new works. Kodály's style satisfied the esthetic requirements, outlined by the Soviet official Andrei Zhdanov, that music should be accessible to the public at large. Its folk origins satisfied the widespread desire for a recognizably national music. Divertimentos, cantatas, and oratorios were the favored genres. Many works by Bartók were ignored because of their alleged "formalism"; only those with a direct folklore content or those dating from the composer's last years were accepted as suited to the Hungarian tradition. The most valuable works of this period were *Emlékezeto* [Memento] (1952) and *Föltárnadott a tenger* [In Fury Rose the Ocean] (1955) by Szabó; the *String Serenade* (1947–48) and *Concerto for*

Orchestra (1954) of Szervánszky; and the *Cantus Pannonicus* (1959) by Farkas.

During the mid-1950s the onesidedness of new music began to give way as Hungarian composers established contacts with other European centers and personalities and as foreign scores and recordings began flowing into the country. Esthetic principles were re-evaluated around 1957–58 with the result that composers could be more experimental and follow differing trends. Studying the Viennese 12-tone school (particularly Webern) and Stravinsky, Hungarian composers soon became familiar with newer techniques. Although most composers preferred to retain traditional forms along with folk-based harmonic, melodic, and rhythmic characteristics and the idea of thematic development, musical horizons were expanded. Instrumental, particularly chamber, music began to replace cantatas, oratorios, and songs as preferred genres. The decisive year was 1959 when Szervánszky wrote his *6 Orchestral Pieces* and György *Kurtág (b. 1926) his *String Quartet*. Szervánszky's piece is a treasure house of postwar avant-garde means: long-held durations, pointillism, unusual orchestral colors with emphasis on percussion, and the like. Kurtág's *Quartet* was written after a year in Paris with Messiaen; it is a free adaptation of Webern's idiom with a structure derived from interval combinations and row techniques. The influences of new Polish music and of the summer courses in Darmstadt became increasingly strong in the 1960s. Indeed within only five or six years Hungarians had absorbed post-Webern serialism along with many forms of indeterminacy and were again in the forefront of international developments.

The eclecticism of present-day Hungarian music can be indicated by some of the affinities it shows: Zsolt *Durkó (b. 1934), who studied with Goffredo Petrassi, leans toward Castiglioni, Donatoni, and the new Polish school; his works are often large scale both in length and in performing medium. Kurtág has favored a Webern-like asceticism in which thinly scored contrapuntal textures predominate. One of his most successful works, *Bornemisza Péter mondásai* [The Sayings of Péter Bornemisza] (1967), foreshadows a new synthesis in which Schütz (of the *Kleine Geistliche Konzerte*), Bach (fugal writing), Hungarian folk elements (especially pentatonic harmony), among other earlier elements, are united with Kurtág's own idiom stemming from Webern and Bartók. Rudolf *Maros (b. 1917) leans toward Nono, Boulez, and Ligeti, favoring music in which sound textures,

including clusters, are an important element. The only trends that have not been cultivated in Hungary are electronic music, owing to the lack of adequate studios, and those in which sounds and textures are the controlling elements, due to the value placed on traditional concepts of form as inherited from the Kodály school. Some Hungarian features continue to exist alongside the international vocabularies mentioned, e.g., rhythmic patterns derived from the Hungarian language, with its unvarying accent on first syllables, and characteristic timbres, as in Kurtág's *Duos* for violin and cimbalon (1961) or Durkó's *Hungarian Rhapsody* (1964). Bartók's works of the 1920s have reemerged as an important force. For example, the rustling, fantastic sounds in his "Notturno" find echoes in countless slow movements (Maros, *Euphonia No. 1*, 1963; Endre Székely, b. 1912, *Musica Notturna*, 1968), and his and Stravinsky's use of ostinato can be detected in many works by Kurtág. All of these characteristics appear to be developing into a new Hungarian school.

BIBL.: *Contemporary Hungarian Composers* (Budapest, published annually); László Eősze, *Zoltán Kodály* (Budapest and London 1962); Halsey Stevens, *The Life and Music of Béla Bartók*, revised ed. (New York 1964); John Vinton, "Bartók on His Own Music," *Journal of the American Musicological Society* 19:232–43; Percy M. Young, *Zoltán Kodály* (London 1964).

György Kroó

SEE ALSO Israel.

Hurník, Ilja (b. Ostrava, Silesia, Czechoslovakia, 25 Nov 1922), studied at the Prague Conservatory (1941–45, composition with Vítězslav Novák) and at the Prague Academy of Music (1948–51; piano with Vilém Kurz, I. Stepanova). A professional pianist, he specializes in the music of Janáček and the French impressionists. During 1968–69 he presented a series of lecture demonstrations on various musical subjects for the Czech Television Network. His music adheres to neoclassic ideals and makes use of baroque forms and Czech folk music.

PRINCIPAL COMPOSITIONS: *Maryka*, cantata for chorus, orchestra (1948, Panton); *Sonata da camera* for flute, oboe, cello, harpsichord (1952, SNKLHU); *Esercizi* for wind quartet (1958, UE); *Moments musicaux* for 11 winds (1962, Supraphon); *Ezop*, cantata for chorus, orchestra (1964, Supraphon); *Dáma a lupiči* [Lady Killers], opera (1966, Bärenreiter); *Mudrci a bloudi* [The Wise and the Foolish], opera (1969, Dilia).

PRINCIPAL WRITINGS (collected editions): *Trom-*

päter von Jericho (Prague 1966); *Die Gänse von Kapitol* (Prague 1969).

BIBL.: Jan Kluśak, "O pokorné hře" [About a Humble Play], *Hudební rozhledy* 17 (1964):1003.

SEE ALSO Czechoslovakia.

Husa, Karel (b. Prague, 7 August 1921), studied civil engineering at Prague Univ. (1939) and music at the Prague Conservatory (1940–45, composition with Jaroslav Ridky), the Academy of Music in Prague (1945–46), the Ecole Normale de Musique in Paris (1946–48, composition with Arthur Honegger, conducting with Jean Fournet), and at the Paris Conservatory (1948–49, conducting with Eugène Bigot). He also studied privately in Prague with Pavel Děděcek (composition, 1941–45) and in Paris with Nadia Boulanger (composition, 1947–48) and Andre Cluytens (conducting, 1946–48). During 1935–46 he studied painting privately. After moving to Paris in 1946 he conducted many European orchestras and recorded contemporary works. Since 1954 he has been professor of composition, orchestration, and conducting at Cornell Univ. and has conducted many orchestras in the U.S. He has published editions of works by Lully, Delalande, and Sir William Herschel. He cites Janáček, Bartók, Stravinsky, and, later, the Viennese School as influences on his music.

PRINCIPAL COMPOSITIONS: *Sonatina* for piano (1943, Boosey); *String Quartets Nos. 1–3* (1948, Schott; 1953, Schott; 1968, AMP); *Evocations of Slovakia* (1951, Schott); *Portrait* for string orchestra (1953, Schott); *Symphony No. 1* (1953, Schott); *4 Easy Pieces* for strings (1955, Schott); *8 Czech Duets* for piano 4-hands (1955, Schott); *Fantasies* for orchestra (1956, Schott); *Elégie* for piano (1957, Leduc); *Poem* for viola, chamber orchestra (1959, Schott); *Elégie et rondeau* for alto saxophone, chamber orchestra (1961, Leduc); *Mosaïques* for orchestra (1961, Schott); *Serenade* for wind quintet, string orchestra, xylophone, harp (1963, Leduc); *Concerto* for brass quintet, string orchestra (1965, Leduc); *2 Preludes* for flute, clarinet, bassoon (1966, Leduc); *Concerto* for alto saxophone, band (1967, AMP); *Music for Prague* (1968, AMP).

BIBL.: Shirley Fleming, "Musician of the Month: K. H.," *High Fidelity—Musical America* (August 1969):MA5.

I

Ibert, Jacques (b. Paris, 15 August 1890; d. Paris, 5 Feb 1962), studied at the Paris Conservatory (1909–13; composition with Paul Vidal, harmony with Emile Pessard, counterpoint with André Gedalge). He was director of the French Academy in Rome during 1937–60 and of the Paris Opéra during 1955–56.

PRINCIPAL COMPOSITIONS (published by Leduc unless otherwise noted): *Le Poète et la fée*, cantata (1919, unpub.); *La Ballade de la Geôle de Reading* for orchestra; after a poem of Oscar Wilde (1920); *Escales*, 3 pieces for orchestra (1922); *Jeux*, sonatina for violin (flute), piano (1923); *Angélique*, 1-act farce; libretto by Nino (1926, Heugel); *Le Roi d'Yvetot*, 4-act comic opera; libretto by Jean Limozin and André de la Tourrasse (1928, Heugel); *Symphonie marine* (1931); *Don Quichotte*, film score (1932); *Diane de Poitiers*, ballet for chorus, orchestra; scenario by Elisabeth de Gramont (1933–34); *Flute Concerto* (1934); *Le Chevalier errant*, choreographic epic after Cervantes for 2 narrators, chorus, orchestra; text by Alexandre Arnoux (1935); *Concertino da camera* for alto saxophone, 11 instruments (1935); *L'Aiglon*, 5-act music drama, composed with Arthur Honegger; libretto by Henri Cain adapted from Edmond Rostand (1937, Heugel); *String Quartet* (1937–42); *Le Petit Ane blanc* for voice, piano (orchestra); poems by Pierre Lorys (1940); *Louisville Concerto* for orchestra (1953); *Symphony No. 2, "Bostoniana"* (1955).

PRINCIPAL WRITINGS: "Le Cinéma et la musique," *Excelsior* (3 Nov 1933); "Le Film sonore, doléances et suggestions," *Revue musicale* (Dec 1934); "La Musique, langage universel," *Musica* (Chaix, April 1954); L'Avenir du théâtre lyrique," *Revue l'Opéra de Paris* 1959/18; "Introduction," *L'Histoire de la musique* by Robert Bernard (Paris 1961). Ibert also wrote articles on Rossini, *Musique* (15 Sept 1929); Roussel, *Revue musicale* (Nov 1937); Bartók, *Revue musicale* 224; and Honegger, *Inter-Auteurs* 121.

BIBL: Georges Auric, *Notice sur la vie et les travaux de J. I.* (Paris 1963); René Dumesnil, *La Musique contemporaine en France* (Paris 1930); Georges Favre, *Musiciens contemporaines* (Paris 1953); Jacques Feschotte, *J. I.* (Paris 1958); Arthur Hoérée, "J. I.," *Revue musicale* (July 1929); ——, "J. I.," *Eolus* (New York) 9/1; Paul Landormy, *La Musique française après Debussy* (Paris 1943).

Ikebe, Shinichiro (b. Mito City, Japan, 15 Sept 1943), studied at the Tokyo Univ. of Arts (1963–71 theory with Tomojiro Ikenouchi, composition with Akio Yashiro and Akira Miyoshi). He is a lecturer at the Tokyo Univ. of Arts and a free-lance composer of radio and theater music.

PRINCIPAL COMPOSITIONS: *Sonata* for solo violin (1965, Ongaku); *Crepa in 7 capitoli*, concerto da camera for violin, 3 violas, cello, double bass (1966, Ongaku); *2 Mouvements* for orchestra (1966); *Symphony* (1967, Ongaku); *Hiru no Tsuki*; poems by Bocho Yamamura (1967); *Lion* for 4×4 brass instruments, e.g., 4 trumpets, 4 horns, 4 trombones, 2 baritones, 2 tubas (1969); *Un-en* for 2 kotos, jyu-shichi-gen, strings (1970); *Sohmon* for chorus (1970, Ongaku); *The Death Goddess*, opera (1971); *Clipper by 9* for piccolo (flute), oboe, English horn, clarinet in E♭, 2 violins, viola, cello, double bass (1971).

SEE ALSO Japan.

Iliev, Constantin (b. Sofia, 9 March 1924), studied at the State Conservatory in Sofia (1942–46, composition with Pantcho Vladigerov, conducting with Marin Goleminov, violin with Vladimir Avramov) and the Prague Academy (1946–48, composition with Rzidki, 1/4-tone composition with Alois Hába, conducting with Vaclav Talich). He has been conductor of the Russe and Varna Orchestras in Bulgaria (1947–56) and the Sofia Philharmonic (since 1956). Since 1962 he has also taught conducting at the State Conservatory in Sofia. His early works were influenced by the compositions of Bartók and Stravinsky and the later ones by Schoenberg, Webern, and Messiaen.

PRINCIPAL COMPOSITIONS: *Symphonies Nos. 1–5* (1947, 1951, 1955, 1958, 1960); *String Quartets Nos. 1–4* (1949–54); *The Master of Bojana*, opera (1963, NI); *Reflections*, cantata for soprano, piano (1965); *Fragments* for orchestra (1968); *Tempi concertanti* for string quartet, string orchestra (1969). Iliev has also written a large number of chamber and choral works.

PRINCIPAL WRITINGS: *Lyubomir Pipkov* (Sofia 1960); "Izkustvoto na dirigenta"[The Conductor's Art], *Sbornik statii* (Sofia 1968).

Imbrie, Andrew W. (b. New York, 6 April 1921), studied piano with Leo Ornstein (1930–42), under whose influence he came to regard music as a communicative art, the origin of which is physical impulse. During 1938–48 he studied with Roger Sessions (privately, at Princeton Univ., and at the Univ. of Calif. at Berkeley). From Sessions came his practice of solving compositional problems contextually rather than by using predetermined forms or materials. Since 1948 he has taught at the Univ. of Calif. at Berkeley.

Imbrie's output is principally for symphonic and chamber ensembles. Maintaining a linear idiom (deriving from the later music of Schoenberg, where the harmony arises from the counterpoint), he has moved from the motoric and motivic music of his *First Quartet* (1942) toward a broader, nonmotivic manner, as in *Legend* (1959). In the latter the delineations of phrases and sections and the transitions between them are of primary importance. He has become increasingly concerned with how gestures influence the effect that each has. For example, the final sonority of the *Chamber Symphony* (1968), with its bass F♯, is particularly satisfying because of an earlier recurring melodic F♯. His "contextualism" is exemplified by his *Third Quartet* (1957), his most nearly 12-tone piece. Rather than selecting a row with interesting abstract properties, he employed one that provided a desired chord progression. Row forms were chosen to make pitches available as required by the context rather than to articulate hierarchical pitch areas (as in Schoenberg) or to give intriguing overlappings (as in Webern).

PRINCIPAL COMPOSITIONS (published by Malcolm unless otherwise noted): *String Quartets Nos. 1–4* (1942; 1953; 1957; 1969, unpub.); *Piano Sonata* (1947, New Valley); *Violin Concerto* (1951–54); *Serenade* for flute, viola, piano (1952); *Little Concerto* for piano 4-hands (1956); *Legend* for orchestra (1959); *Impromptu* for violin, piano (1960); *Christmas in Peebles Town*, opera in 4 scenes (1960, Peters); *Psalm 42* for male chorus, organ (1962); *Symphonies Nos. 1–3* (1965; 1969, unpub.; 1970, unpub.); *Cello Sonata* (1966); *Chamber Symphony* (1968). List to 1966: *Composers of the Americas* 12:69–72.

BIBL.: Martin Boykan, "A. I.: Third Quartet," *Perspectives* 3/1:139–46.

Jonathan D. Kramer

SEE ALSO United States.

Impressionism. The term *impressionism* is used by art historians and critics to categorize some of the techniques and sensibilities of a group of French painters of the last quarter of the 19th century (in particular Claude Monet, Edgar Degas, Pierre-Auguste Renoir, and Camille Pissarro). It has been borrowed by writers on music to categorize aspects of Claude Debussy's art and some similar aspects in the work of other composers. The borrowing has some justification. For instance, the paintings of the impressionists tend to avoid sharp outlines and uniform colors or color gradations; instead blurred outlines are the rule, along with careful juxtapositions of minute strokes of pure color that blend when viewed at a distance. Similarly Debussy's orchestration often relies on a massed complex of soft and subtly different instrumental details that unite and overlap to form a whole in which no detail predominates. The French painters, in their reaction against classical subjects and classical portraiture, preferred nonposed, nonsymbolic, nonliterary subject matter, relying chiefly on informal, snapshot-like views, landscapes, and portraiture in which essential qualities (impressions) rather than all-inclusive delineation are the principal visual motivation. By the same token Debussy's mature music is antiprogrammatic and eschews classical formal structures, thus existing at a greater remove than any other music of his time (and most since) from the literarily limned formal procedures of the German tradition. It is true that Debussy's later works (e.g., the *Préludes* for piano) sometimes bear descriptive titles, but the music itself indicates that the titles are more psychological than literary, for the music evokes rather than enacts. A piece such as "Clouds," the first of the orchestral *Nocturnes*, seems to have as its psychological basis the state of "cloud-ness" rather than "here is a cloud and here is what happens to it."

Debussy's disavowal of developmental forms, his nonreliance on classical harmonic motion, his enormously expanded harmonic vocabulary, and his subtly controlled and constantly differentiated sense of tonality had consequences in the first half of the 20th century at least as profound as Schoenberg's atonal revolution. The immediate results were the adoption of Debussy's harmonic discoveries and, to a lesser degree, of his formal freedoms by other composers who came to share with him the appellation "impressionist." Most notable among these was Maurice Ravel, whose piano works in his maturity (*Miroirs, Gaspard de la nuit*) show the influence of Debussy's harmony but actually anticipate by some years the expanded timbral resources of the piano that made Debussy's *Préludes* famous. Soon afterward Ravel's music moved away from the "character piece" genre, and he began to form his own harmonic style, chiefly along the lines of classical models and large symphonic forms antithetical to the autonomous formal designs of Debussy (because of this, Ravel would more properly be categorized as "neoclassicist"). In the few remaining years before World War I, Debussy's innovations in harmony and orchestration were a rallying point outside France, notably in short pieces of composers such as the American Charles Griffes and in the larger works of the Englishmen Gustav Holst and Frederick Delius. But except for a few isolated examples, the impressionist esthetic did not survive the impact of postwar pessimism, the rise of neoclassicism, and the explosive advent of Igor Stravinsky. In general, composers reacted against what they then felt to be the preciosity, Wagnerism, literary symbolism, and artnouveau decadence in impressionist music.

The so-called Russian impressionism of Alexander Scriabin presents a special and little understood case. Scriabin, like Debussy, was at first influenced by Chopin's harmonic idiom but soon developed a personal harmonic style that owed something to Debussy but evolved differently, though within the context of large, sprawling, autonomous forms. Scriabin's esthetic, compounded of Russian and French literary and mysticophilosophical conceits, is manifested in his music in ways less subtle and less refined than Debussy's. That Debussy's sensuous softness contrasts with Scriabin's bombast, and Debussy's simple and precise rhythms with Scriabin's complex and vague rhythms, and that at the same time both composers have so much in common harmonically, orchestrally, and formally, serve to show that impressionism has too often been used as a catch-all term, impeding rather than forwarding understanding.

BIBL.: J. Rewald, *The History of Impressionism* (New York 1946); R. H. Wzlenski, *Modern French Painters* (New York 1960).   Mark DeVoto

SEE ALSO Form.

Improvisation, see Indeterminacy, Jazz, Performance, Prose Music, Rhythm

Indeterminacy refers to musical material that is unpredictable before a performance. The term is also used for music that is predictable before performance but was composed through chance operations (with random or statistical procedures or both). The term *aleatory* is a pedantic synonym for indeterminacy introduced by Pierre Boulez but now used more frequently by writers than by composers. The techniques of indeterminacy and chance are used most often in music, but they have also been applied to other arts, especially those such as theater and dance that are involved with time.

The composer using indeterminacy may specify any degree of performer choice from arranging totally notated elements to extensive improvisation. He may ask that the performer work out all or part of the score ahead of the performance (perhaps by chance operations) from material and instructions he provides. He may also ask the performer to respond during a performance to instructions or diagrams, to actions and situations, either real and present or imagined. Free improvisation may be asked for in indeterminate scores, but this is a subordinate technique and not a compositional means.

ESTHETIC ASSUMPTIONS. Carried in logical order to their extreme, the esthetic assumptions of indeterminacy are:

1. Any sound or no sound at all is as valid, as "good" as any other sound.

2. Each sound is a separate event. It is not related to any other sound by any hierarchy. It need carry no implication of what has preceded it or will follow it. It is important for itself, not for what it contributes to a musical line or development.

3. Any assemblage of sounds is as valid as any other.

4. Any means of generating an assemblage of sounds is as valid as any other.

5. Any piece of music is as "good" as any other, any composer as "good" as any other.

6. Traditional concepts of value, expertise, and authority are meaningless.

The extent to which these assumptions have been accepted varies widely among composers. Total assumption of the position can produce the esthetic postulate that "art is simply that which is perceived esthetically" (Joseph Byrd). George Brecht's view is that "we can take an art attitude toward anything and thus we can do away with art as something special." One of Brecht's pieces is a small card bearing the title of the work *Concert for Orchestra* and the single word "exchanging." Henry Flynt's "concept art" produces compositions in which the material is simply a statement of the concepts behind the structures. At the other extreme, the processes of indeterminacy and chance operation are often assumed to be seemingly easy devices for making music sound (and look) "avant-garde," with no interest on the part of the composer in any of the esthetic assumptions. Indeterminacy may also appear as a philosophical position so interwoven with other views of the composer, perhaps political anarchism or Zen Buddism, that he sees his music solely as a polemic affirming his beliefs.

PRECURSORS. Several apparent precursors of indeterminacy can be cited: the cadenza of the 18th-century concerto, the realizing of a continuo from figured bass, Mozart's musical dice, and the like. More immediate would seem to be the dada movement (c.1916–22), a forceful and imaginative departure from accepted standards of what art was supposed to be and do. It often moved into what appeared to be contradiction, parody, and nonsense presented as serious art, sometimes by chance means. Despite similarity of approaches, however, indeterminacy and dada have a significant esthetic difference: dada was born of political revolt and was suprasatirical, what music critic Peter Yates terms "the prevailing negative," whereas indeterminacy began as an affirming creative rationale. Nevertheless many composers have found stimulus in the means and attitudes of dada: spontaneity, irreverence for the establishment, the use of chance, parody, the leveling of critical strictures about art—all these are compatible with the assumptions of indeterminacy.

Some music by Charles Ives, Henry Cowell, and Percy Grainger anticipated indeterminate approaches, and that of Satie and Varèse was influential in the denial of *affektenlehre*, the critical assumption codified in the 18th century that certain musical gestures, phrases, and sounds generate certain unfailing emotional responses. Not only dadaists (along with the Italian futurists) but many "experimental" American composers of the 1930s anticipated the "liberation of sound" in statement and example; indeterminacy fulfilled their predictions with both an esthetic and a means. Finally jazz, with its emphasis on expressive improvisation and inventive virtuosity, has been influential; significantly several younger indeterminate composers are skilled jazz instrumentalists.

DEVELOPMENTS SINCE 1950. In 1950 John Cage, who had been concerned with expanding the potential of sound resources and rhythmic structures, began to explore composition by chance operations, discovering through use of the Chinese *I Ching* [Book of Changes] a means by which this sort of composition could be developed. Three other composers were closely associated with Cage in New York during these early years. Morton Feldman began his development of the indeterminate assumptions with pieces that allowed the performer to choose the pitches he would play within limits furnished · by notation on graph paper. He moved on into an immediate "getting inside" the sound, "letting the sound be itself," by considering each sound-event as a separate sonorous entity with no implications concerning what would precede or follow it. Christian Wolff, just out of high school, was to develop during 1957–64 a tightly woven indeterminate notation that allows each performer choices in terms of what he hears (or does not hear) from other performers. Earle Brown, who first met Cage in Denver in 1951, was concerned, especially in the collection *Folio*, with "different invented notations of a highly ambiguous graphic nature, subject to numerous different but inherently valid realizations." The close friendship of these men at the time with painters (Philip Guston, Franz Kline, Mark Rothko, Jackson Pollock, later Robert Rauschenberg), dancers (especially Merce Cunningham), and pianist David Tudor anticipated the interaction of artists that was to be organic in later work. In the late 1950s and early 60s indeterminacy was developed in several directions:

1. In spring 1959 Cage began teaching at New York's New School for Social Research. He was not concerned with the means of composition; he taught by telling his class about his current projects and the ideas behind them and then encouraging the students to develop similar material in their own way. These classes included not only composers (Richard Maxfield, Toshi Ichiyanagi) and jazz musicians (Don Heckman, John Brooks) but also those whose interests were to develop in a synthesis of sound, action, and the written word (Dick Higgins, George Brecht, Al Hansen, Allan Kaprow, Jackson Mac Low; the last named had been using indeterminacy in language structure and chance in music in his own way since 1954).

2. In the late 1950s several young composers and artists on the West Coast became concerned with the new music. Many of them went to New York and studied at the New School in late 1960 with Richard Maxfield, who continued Cage's classes there: composers La Monte Young, Joseph Byrd, Terry Jennings; sculptors Robert Morris, Walter De Mari; dancer Simone (Morris) Whitman. Others from the Coast, though not in the class, were working with this group in concerts: composer Dennis Johnson, poet Diane

Wakoski. Composers Doug Leedy and Terry Riley remained in California but were to become part of the movement, as were New York composer Philip Corner, painter Larry Poons, and dancer Yvonne Rainer. The influential publication *An Anthology* (1963), edited by Young and Mac Low, provided an extensive selection of activity of this "second generation," as well as material by Cage and Brown.

3. Cage and Tudor introduced indeterminacy and chance in Europe in 1954 and 1958. Their work was regarded by the European establishment as trivial comedy. Mainstream European acceptance was slow, most composers regarding indeterminacy and chance as simply musical devices and ignoring the esthetic implications so vital in America. Some younger composers abroad have moved in a more direct line from Cage and his colleagues: Sylvano Bussotti, Cornelius Cardew, Giuseppi Chiari, Mauricio Kagel, Roland Kayn, György Ligeti, Bo Nilsson, Folke Rabe, Yannis Xenakis, and Americans living for long periods abroad, Frederic Rzewski, Allan Bryant, and Alvin Curran.

4. The Fluxus movement began in New York in 1961, growing particularly from the *Anthology* material and from a series of concerts at George Maciunas's AG Gallery. It turned from chance to an emphasis on notated instructions allowing extensive interpretational freedom and expanded to include artists abroad as well: Robert Filliou, Daniel Spoerri, Ben Vautier, and Benjamin Patterson in Europe, the Korean-German Nam June Paik, artists who had worked with the Gutai group in Japan, and the continental "concrete poetry" writers, notably Emmett Williams.

5. After about 1960 individuals and groups concerned with indeterminacy began to appear across North America. The ONCE group in Ann Arbor (Robert Ashley, George Cacioppo, Gordon Mumma, Roger Reynolds, Donald Scavarda, with film maker George Manupelli and environmentalist Milton Cohen) held annual festivals during 1960–65 that provided the principal outlet outside New York for music involving chance and indeterminacy as well as new approaches in electronic music and music-and-film. The San Francisco Tape Center, started in 1961 by composers Pauline Oliveros, Ramon Sender, and Morton Subotnick, technician William Maginnis, and projection artist Anthony Martin (later involving composers Riley and Steve Reich), concentrated on electronics and improvisation (Miss Oliveros began conducting night-school

classes in improvisation in 1960). In Davis, Calif., the New Music Ensemble (with Larry Austin, Richard Swift, and several younger composer-instrumentalists) developed a closely woven and sensitive group-improvisation technique. The New Music Workshop in Los Angeles and the Tucson New Art Wind Ensemble in Arizona were also contributory. Other composers included Philip Krumm, Jerry Hunt, and Houston Higgins in Dallas; Udo Kasemets in Toronto; and David Reck in Texas and New York. Lucia Dlugoszewski, accompanist for the dancer Erick Hawkins, devised and built her own pitched percussion instruments to embody a musical esthetic derived from Cage's prepared piano and proportional time structures. The Improvisation Chamber Ensemble, founded in 1957 by Lukas Foss, performed from fully written scores, at times using a graphic notation that allowed improvisation within fairly strict limits; it was not basically concerned with the assumptions of indeterminacy, however.

After about 1963, when indeterminacy and chance had ceased to be independent forces, their concepts of the "liberation of sound" continued to give direction to new music. Work in Cage's classes had generated a concern with theater pieces, works involving activity from the performer, with or without specified sound, the activity being stated beforehand or improvised in reaction to stipulated concepts. (There is no direct line of descent from "legitimate" theater to theater pieces, although they have since interacted. The latter were often influenced by what came to be known as *happenings*, developed independently by Al Hansen and painter Allan Kaprow at about the same time.) Richard Maxfield applied Cage's principles of "art as life" directly to composition, especially in electronic music, which he was the first to teach. Works of the West Coast "second generation" in New York led to what was later to be called *minimal art*, in which attention is directed to the simplest musical, verbal, or pictorial elements often extensively prolonged or repeated. Young's instruction pieces, cards stating activities, sounds, or concepts to be interpreted, were widely mailed and played before being published in *An Anthology*, stimulating widespread interest in the minimal and static. The Fluxus group explored "structure by intention": "You say what you intend and you leave the specific realization up to the performer."[1]

---

[1] Dick Higgins, *Postface* (New York 1964):29.

The later work of the New Music Ensemble and of Ashley and Mumma of ONCE explored live electronics, each performer controlling apparatus that altered his own sound or action. The new thing in jazz became a free improvisation with the traditional lines and changes abandoned for long sets in which each player, although sensitive to what he was hearing, played exactly what he felt moved to play. *Total theater* and *mixed media* influenced a range of activities from legitimate theater to the psychedelic light show. Rock music borrowed the use of new, unexpected, and unprepared sounds, live-electronic techniques, and unstructured forms. After 1965 a number of composers, many not previously concerned with indeterminacy, adopted what may be termed *polystylistics*, the use in their own music of other music, not simply as citation but as an organic structural feature. This other music, covering the entire range of history and culture, was used directly or altered, Ives-like; collaged or combined to generate much of a piece; or reworked and recomposed, usually using a single borrowed composition, into a completely new statement.

SUMMARY. The effects of indeterminacy have been reflected in notation, sound, musical roles, the relationship of music to other arts, and theory. The admissibility of any sound as musical material and the variety of indeterminate performance situations has resulted in many individual notational schemes; sometimes the *idea* of the piece, through the notation and without performance, *is* the piece. The variety of sound resources available to the composer has been expanded enormously, not only through the use of live electronic and tape techniques but also by exploration of unconventional sounds available from traditional musical instruments. The traditional distinctions between composer, performer, and audience have been blurred and in some areas dissolved. Although earlier composers have combined arts, present-day practice fuses them into mixed media in which not only previously separate forms of art but previously distinct styles are united. The esthetic assumptions behind indeterminacy have negated traditional theoretical concepts and values, leaving a vacancy that has yet to be filled. Contemporary approaches in redefinition of form and structure, systems analysis, linguistic and acoustic investigation, and the use of computers have already begun to suggest the outlines of a new theory.

BIBL.: ★ Backgrounds: Lejaren A. Hiller, Jr. and Leonard M. Isaacson, *Experimental Music* (New York 1959): 10–55; Hans Richter, *Dada: Art and Anti-Art* (New York 1965). ★John Cage and his circle: John Cage, "Interview with Roger Reynolds," *Contemporary Composers on Contemporary Music* ed. by E. Schwartz, B. Childs (New York 1967): 336–48; ———, *Silence* (Middletown, Conn., 1961); Morton Feldman, "Predetermined/Indetermined," *Composer* 19:3ff.; Richard Kostelanetz, *The Theatre of Mixed Means* (New York 1968):50–63; Calvin Tomkins, *The Bride and the Bachelors* (New York 1965):69–144. ★Second generation, New York: Al Hansen, *A Primer of Happenings & Time/Space* (New York 1965); Dick Higgins, *Postface* (New York 1964); Richard Kostelanetz, *op. cit.*: 183–218; Jackson Mac Low and La Monte Young, eds., *An Anthology* (New York 1963); *Tulane Drama Review* 10/2. ★Second generation, non-New York: "Groups," *Source* 3:15–27; Gordon Mumma, "The ONCE Festival," *Arts in Society* 4/2:380–98; Robert Sheff and Mark Slobin, "Music Beyond the Boundaries," *Generation* (Univ. of Mich.) 17/1:27–65, 17/2:55–95. ★Notation: John Cage, *Notations* (New York 1969); Cornelius Cardew, "Notation—Interpretation, etc.," *Tempo* 58:21–33; Erhard Karkoschka, *Das Schriftbild der Neuen Musik* (Celle 1966). ★Theory: David Behrman, "What Indeterminate Notation Determines," *Perspectives* 3/2:58–73; Earl Brown, "Form in New Music," *Source* 1:46–51; Barney Childs, "Indeterminacy and Theory," *The Composer* 1; Roger Reynolds, "Indeterminacy: Some Considerations," *Perspectives* 4/1:136–40; James Tenney, *Meta (+) Hodos* (New Orleans 1964). Ongoing activities have been covered in the bulletins of Experiments in Arts and Technology, Inc. (EAT) in New York and in the Fluxus *Newsletter* and publications of the Something Else Press, originally in New York and later relocated in Southern California.

Barney Childs

SEE ALSO Asian Music and Western Composition, Dance, Instrumental and Vocal Resources, Jazz, Notation, Orchestration, Performance, Rhythm, and articles on individual countries.

Information Theory, see Mathematics, Theory

Instrumental and Vocal Resources. The diversity of esthetics in the 20th century has resulted in a rapid expansion of compositional techniques of all kinds and particularly in the development of new sonic resources. The increased exploration of sound materials has been motivated by: 1) the continued refinement of the element of pitch and the continued elaboration of traditional coloristic devices; 2) the trend toward a globally and temporally eclectic music; and 3) the compositional use of noise and pitch approximation. Within each of these categories, composers have used essentially three techniques for the production of new sounds: 1) the use of nontraditional instruments; 2) the generation of new sounds on traditional instruments; and 3) the alteration of traditional instruments and the invention of new ones. These techniques are not, of course, creations of the 20th century. Many composers in the past have written for novel instruments, usually with theatrical or programmatic purposes in mind (Papageno's bells, the anvils of the *Ring*, Strauss's wind machine, etc.). The experiments of Monteverdi, Berlioz, and Rimsky-Korsakov exemplify previous attempts (which are now standard techniques) to produce new sounds by means of unusual playing techniques. The alteration or invention of instruments reached a peak in the 19th century: The invention of valves about 1815 changed the character of brass instruments; fingering systems for woodwinds were redesigned several times to extend ranges and improve flexibility and accuracy. The piano keyboard was lengthened, resonance increased, and the double escapement introduced. Even the kettledrum was radically altered with the introduction of the pedal tuning mechanism. New instruments were invented: saxtrombas, saxhorns, and saxophones by Adolphe Sax; tenor trumpets, euphoniums, and tubas by various people, including Wagner; and innumerable experiments of brief life and colorful nomenclature, such as ophicleides, kenthorns, and tenoroons. Only the string family remained essentially unchanged during the century. Virtually every alteration of traditional instruments was to improve their ability to accurately and swiftly generate the full spectrum of discrete chromatic pitches. The incorporation of novel instruments, the invention of new ones, and the development of new playing techniques were largely attempts to "color" pitches. Thus by the beginning of the 20th century composers had available a large number of instruments and instrumental techniques specifically designed to produce accurate pitches in a wide variety of timbres. Increasing their variety and sophistication still further was particularly the concern of composers interested in the continued refinement of music organized by discrete pitches.

ELABORATION OF TRADITIONAL COLORISTIC DEVICES. Although some 20th-century composers have attempted to widen the pitch spectrum itself by means of unorthodox tunings, most have confined their music to the traditional 12-tone scale. The latter group has typically expanded sound resources by elaborating on the 19th-century developments

mentioned. The desire to suggest programmatic or theatrical events is still a prime motivation for the use of nontraditional instruments. Respighi's recorded nightingale in *The Pines of Rome* and the airplane propellor in George Antheil's *Ballet mécanique* are examples. (Here and elsewhere specific composers and compositions are mentioned as examples only; they are not necessarily either the first or the best appearance of the phenomena under discussion.) The 1960s have seen an increased interest in theatrical music, the trend led by the Argentine composer Mauricio Kagel, whose instrumentation is often predominately motivated by a dramatic conception (as in *Die Himmelsmechanik*). More abstract instances of theatrical instrumentation occur in Kagel's *Match*, where police whistles are used to stop the action, and in Lejaren Hiller's *Machine Music*, in which the last movement includes sounds made by children's toys.

Much more extensive has been the continued evolution of playing techniques on conventional instruments. The initial motivation for many of these developments was once again pictorial or theatrical. Most of the effects for harp devised by Carlos Salzedo were given descriptive names and used for programmatic reasons in his *Modern Study of the Harp* (New York 1921). Novel keyboard techniques were often similarly motivated: the interior strumming first used in 1923 in Henry Cowell's *Aeolian Harp* or the enormous tone clusters of Charles Ives's *The Masses*. Because vocal music is almost invariably linked to a text, vocal techniques are especially likely to be used suggestively. Schoenberg's half-sung, half-spoken sprechstimme eventually became a cliché of the Viennese school, but when it appeared in *Pierrot Lunaire* it served the purpose of evoking an otherworldly, moonstruck atmosphere. More recently composers such as Henry Brant and Witold Lutosławski have utilized shouts, half-whispers, and whispers for dramatic reasons. Even in untexted music, such as Kagel's *Phonophonie* or György Ligeti's *Aventures*, the vocal effects are often theatrically motivated. Although these and other special techniques began as representational devices, many soon lost their pictorial associations and have been used simply for themselves. Kenneth Gaburo's *Antiphony III* is an example. Many other timbral subtleties have been achieved by transferring techniques from one instrument to another or by specifying playing techniques already used intuitively by performers.

For the woodwinds three kinds of timbral sophistication emerged within the framework of conventional sounds: the specification of articulation, the specification of harmonics, and the utilization of unusual embouchure techniques. Investigations into the first of these began in the 19th century when Strauss and Mahler both asked flutists to flutter-tongue. The 20th century has seen this technique expanded to oboe, as in Stravinsky's *Rite of Spring*; to clarinet, as in Strauss's *Don Quixote*; and to bassoon, as in Britten's *Sinfonia da Requiem*. Other more subtle articulations also began to be utilized in a precise way in this century. A more or less uniform notation for double and triple tonguing and the various degrees of legato tonguing began to emerge from the scores of Ravel, Stravinsky, Shostakovich, and others. A few identifiable techniques have appeared among the welter of articulations peculiar to jazz, such as the "slap-tongue" called for in numerous dance-band scores and in the concert-hall oriented music of George Gershwin, Aaron Copland, and Morton Gould. More recently composers have become interested in the subtle distinctions that result from the use of different consonants in articulating single notes. On wind instruments a tone initiated by the syllable "ta" is noticeably different from the same tone initiated by "ha," "cha," or even "da." This technique was used by players well before 1900, but the explicit notation appearing in David Gilbert's *Poeme VI* or Donald Martino's *Strata* for bass clarinet is unique to the 20th century. Woodwind harmonics have a similar history. Performers have long utilized the fact that notes in the higher registers can be produced as upper partials of several different fundamentals, but only in the 20th century have composers exploited the slight differences in color and intonation that result. Stravinsky was again a pioneer: in *The Rite of Spring* he asked for three flutes to play the C-major triad above the staff as partials of the low C (normally these pitches would be played as partials of G, C, and E, respectively). More recent composers have been still more explicit, using notated harmonics structurally, as in Niccolò Castiglioni's *Alef* for solo oboe, or even notating exact fingerings, as in Bruno Bartolozzi's *Collage*. A related effect for clarinet, stopping the tone holes and muting the bell, has been used by Martino in his *Concerto for Woodwind Quintet*. In addition to the foregoing, the players of some woodwind instruments can produce timbres radically different from the usual ones by altering their normal embouchure. Single-reed instruments can produce a soft, muted "subtone" or "echo tone" by partially stopping the reed with the tongue. The technique has been used by jazz saxophonists for years. Concert uses date back to Berlioz's *Damnation of Faust*, but the echo-tone effect has only appeared consistently since 1900, as in Berg's *4 Pieces* for clarinet and piano. An analogous effect is the flute "whistle tone," a soft, thin ethereal sound occurring only in the upper register and produced by a relaxed embouchure and an undirected air stream; instances occur in Roger Reynold's *Quick Are the Mouths of Earth*.

Unlike those for woodwinds, concert playing techniques for brasses have not expanded significantly during this century. There are a few exceptions: Flutter-tonguing (already used in the 1800s) became common in the music of Honegger, Stravinsky, Milhaud, and others. Half muting on the French horn, which lowers the pitch and produces a distant, clouded sound, has been used by several composers, notably Benjamin Britten in the *Serenade for Tenor, Horn, and Strings*. The most consistently used new procedure is really a matter of notation: composers are now inclined to ask for sound qualities descriptively, "brassy," "overblown," "biting," etc. A number of technical possibilities have remained virtually unexploited: the subtly different articulations produced by different attack consonants, the different intonations and timbres that result when pitches are produced as partials of different fundamentals, the colors and occasional eccentric or unpitched sounds that result when the valves are depressed only part way. Actually most major advances in brass technique have come in the field of jazz, where even the basic sound was altered, becoming more focused, more biting, less full. Jazz musicians use a large variety of pitch inflections, most of which are not notated but some of which bear descriptive terms: the "shake," a rapid oscillation of pitch; the "rip," a fast sharp glissando; the "smear," a flatted note slowly brought into tune; the "growl," a low, throaty tone in imitation of early blues singers; and a few others. Various composers have called for these, among them Stravinsky, Milhaud, Gershwin, and Gould.

Expansions in string technique have usually been based on techniques known in the 19th century. As with the woodwinds, much of the emphasis has been on the explicit notation of known techniques rather than on the invention of new ones. Many colors previously used by players for dramatic purposes began to be specified by composers and used for their compositional values; Schoenberg, Webern, and Bartók, for example, used harmonics, open strings, and specification of strings for specific pitches. The exact notation of bowing styles (spiccato, at the point, etc.) and locations (sul ponticello, sul tasto, etc.) is now common, and even the direction for bowing multiple stops is sometimes specified, as in the fourth movement of Bartók's *String Quartet No. 4* (bar 333). In addition, at least two new techniques were added in George Crumb's *Songs, Drones, and Refrains of Death*, where the violinist is instructed to bow behind the fingers on the fingerboard and to play with the bow hairs slack (both procedures produce a pale, tenuous sound with little resonance). Pizzicato techniques have undergone considerably more elaboration. Left-hand pizzicato, although known in the 19th century, was first used extensively by such composers as Stravinsky, Berg, and Bartók. Bartók is particularly noteworthy in this regard. His *Fourth Quartet* includes arpeggiated and nonarpeggiated pizzicato, instructions about where on the fingerboard the pizzicato is to be produced, strumming, and "snap pizzicato" in which the string rebounds off the fingerboard; his *Fifth Quartet* contains fingernail pizzicatos. Techniques involving various plectra such as guitar picks, ukelele picks, and plastics or metals of various kinds have also appeared in recent years; Crumb even asks for a pizzicato produced while wearing a thimble.

New techniques have appeared for the double bass (see Turetzky in the bibl.), partly because of the influence of jazz and partly because of the large number of interested virtuosos. Thumb pizzicato, pizzicato tremolo, and the "slap pizzicato" produced by the palm of the hand are examples. Pitches can also be produced if the string is simply pressed forcefully against the fingerboard by the left hand alone. Many of these techniques appear in George Perle's *Monody II* and Thomas Frederickson's *Music for Double Bass Alone* and for other strings in quartets by Michael von Biel and others. As with the brasses, composers have also described the desired effects: "mechanically," "nasally," "dry," or even, in the case of Charles Ives, "con fistiswatto."

Specific instructions for various kinds of vibrato and glissando have been used for all instruments as well as the voice during this century. Nonvibrato, already used by 19th-century composers, became common after 1900; the Bartók quartets offer many examples. But composers went still further. As early as 1932 Henry Brant specified speed and type of vibrato in his *Temperamental Mobiles* for solo flute. Kenneth Gaburo's *Antiphony III* and Edwin London's *Brass Quintet* combine vib-

rato controls with several trilling and tremolo effects, encompassing a large spectrum of pitch inflections. Subtle vibrato effects have long been an integral part of jazz, and recent jazz scores have begun to notate precisely the quality desired: Morgan Powell's *Odomtn* mixes lip, slide, narrow, wide, and nonvibrato all in the space of a few bars. Glissandos have also become relatively commonplace, as exemplified in the Bartók quartets. An unusual glissando effect, rarely used to date, can be produced on string instruments by fingering an artificial harmonic and keeping the distance between both fingers constant during the slide; the result is a series of broken glissandos generated by the different partials produced during the slide. Wind and brass glissandos range from the rough, "rip"-like effect on horn called for in *The Rite of Spring* to the smooth clarinet glide that opens Gershwin's *Rhapsody in Blue*. The latter effect is not easy to produce on winds and only recently has been used extensively in scores by Xenakis, Haubenstock-Ramati, and others. Very slow glissandos coupled with steady pitches can combine to produce beating effects, as in Xenakis's *Eonta*.

Eonta utilizes two other techniques that can be applied to virtually any instrument. Sounds played into an open piano with the dampers lifted produce a hazy reverberation; George Crumb, Robert Helps, Xenakis, and others have used this effect. The second technique can be traced from Gabrieli through Hectro Berlioz, Charles Ives, and Henry Brant, and involves the use of separate locations for different sound sources. In *Eonta*, the performers actually move about the stage, swinging the bells of their instruments; the procedure is exploited for both its sound and theatrical potentials. Less dramatic-oriented instances range from the spatial dialectic used in Brant's *Antiphony I* and Stockhausen's *3 Gruppen* through the isolation of individual players in Toshiro Mayuzumi's *String Quartet* to the total sound environment of a full-scale performance of the Cage-Hiller *HPSCHD*.

NEW AND ALTERED INSTRUMENTS. Most improvements in traditional instruments have been the work of instrument makers seeking to perfect acoustic characteristics or to facilitate fingerings. The addition of trill keys, the refinement of valves, and the perfection of alternative models, each with its own characteristics, are examples. Some changes have resulted from demands made by composers. Notes at the extremities of instrumental ranges could occasionally only be produced after physical alterations in the instruments.

Thus a low B♮ and then a low B♭ were added to the flute. Baritone saxophone players in jazz bands discovered they often needed a low C, which they first produced by muting the bell with their knee and later by adding a key. Extensions were made to produce the low A on bassoon called for in the Stravinsky *Mass* and the low G in his *Symphony in C*. Trombonists began using E tuning slides to produce the low B required by Stravinsky, Bartók, and others.

Mutes for changing the tone quality of instruments have a long history, specifically those used on string and brass instruments. Berlioz used a muted clarinet in *Lélio*. Other woodwinds have been muted in the 20th century: Stravinsky asks for muted oboe in *Petrouchka*, and Liadov opens his *Enchanted Lake* with muted bassoon. Jazz saxophonists have occasionally played into large inverted megaphones or inserted metal objects into the bell of their instruments to produce a buzzy sound. Jazz, in fact, has also been responsible for the enormous increase in the kinds of brass mute, undoubtedly because of the need to expand the limited number of timbres available in most jazz ensembles. The most generally known brass mutes are the straight, cup, Harmon, hat, wa-wa, bucket, whisper, and plunger. They appear in scores by Stravinsky, Copland, Gershwin, and Virgil Thomson, as well as in virtually all jazz charts. Mutes of a sort have even been applied to singers. In Ligeti's *Aventures* the singer is directed to stop his nose, to cover his mouth with his hands, and to use a megaphone to alter vocal timbres. In *L's GA* by Salvatore Martirano the vocalist breathes helium, which causes his voice to become high-pitched and pinched.

Twentieth-century musicians have also continued 19th-century attempts to invent new instruments. Most have not gained wide acceptance, as exemplified by Emmanuel Moor's double-keyboard piano or the eight-member acoustic string family built by Carleen Maley Hutchins and used in Henry Brant's *Consort for True Violins*. Attempts at new acoustic instruments have been made even recently, as with the violino grande constructed by the Swedish chemist Hans Olaf Hansson and scored for by Penderecki, Serocki, and others. Some conventional or established instrumental types have been constructed out of new materials in order to produce novel timbres. In this class are Carl Orff's stone glockenspiels, Gunnar Schonbeck's and Robert Ericson's marble marimbas, and Schonbeck's marble gongs, clarinets, and flutes.

Virtually all of the more successful new instruments have been either percussive or electronic. Foremost among the percussion is the vibraphone, which evolved from the marimba (the dates vary in reference sources from 1907 to the mid-20s). It was first popularized in jazz but eventually became an avant-garde cliché, especially after its extensive use in Boulez's *Le Marteau sans maître* (1953–55). The history of most other percussion instruments is less definite, and many are ad hoc creations assembled for a particular effect in a particular piece (two efforts by Allan Bryant and Robert Erickson are described in *Source* 3 and 5).

Electronic instruments fall into two large categories: those modeled after traditional instruments and those constructed on essentially new principles. The former have been chiefly associated with jazz and popular music, the latter with concert music. The impact of electronics on popular music began with the microphone, which made possible the balancing of a singer or soloist against a large band. Some electronic instruments, such as the electric guitar, electric bass, and some electric pianos, are basically outgrowths of this phenomenon in that they are essentially microphoned acoustic instruments. Others, such as the electric organ, generate sounds entirely by electronic means. With the advent of the rock idiom the production of volume and noise became crucial, and various distorting devices ("fuzz-tone," "wa-wa," and octave couplers) were added to the basic electroacoustic instruments. These are now available with normal microphone attachments so that virtually any instrument can be electronically amplified or distorted. Although such devices are now used almost exclusively in rock and jazz, it seems likely that other composers will turn to them increasingly in the future.

The possibility that electronics might form the basis for totally different instruments was first contemplated by Herrmann von Helmholtz, who built a number of simple generators in the mid-1800s. The first large-scale work began when in 1906 Thaddeus Cahill constructed his telharmonium, which was essentially a synthesizer that combined the discrete outputs of individual A.C. generators. It was large and cumbersome, and Cahill proposed transmitting its output via telephone wires. A much smaller and simpler instrument was the theremin, or aethereophone, invented by Leon Theremin around 1920. It has been used by Bohuslav Martinů, Varèse, and others, and in film scores such as those for *Spellbound* and *The Lost Weekend* by Miklós Rózsa. Its great deficiencies are its monochromatic color and the lack of any control over attack and decay. Despite this, however, it continues to be used, as in the rock musical *Hair*. Two other electronic instruments introduced in the 1920s also met with some success. Friedrich Trautwein's trautonium, first constructed about 1928, was a monophonic keyboard instrument that used a variable resistor to alter frequency. Although the basic sound material was a sawtooth generator, tuned circuits allowed for some color changes, thus overcoming one of the principal limitations of the theremin. A more advanced model, the mixturtrautonium, appeared about 1950 and featured multiple manuals, expanded coloristic possibilities, and movable keys that made possible glissandos and unusual tunings. Although compositions for the trautonium exist by Hindemith, Jürg Baur, and others, its greatest use has been in European film scores such as *Stahl* and *Berliner Kaleidoscop*. A second instrument constructed at the same time was Maurice Martenot's ondes Martenot, a sawtooth generator and variable resistor with a touch-sensitive keyboard and a direct connection to the resistor that made possible subtle dynamic changes as well as glissandos and vibratos. Its popularity has been mostly confined to France where Ibert, Honegger, Milhaud, and others have scored for it. Numerous other electronic instruments (the ondoline, the späraphon, the orgatron, the dynophone) have had only limited success. A recent addition is Robert Moog's synthesizer, used with studio tape equipment since the early 1960s. The advantage of the Moog equipment is that voltage-control devices can be used to define both precise overtone proportions and exact attack-decay envelopes. Thus an enormous variety of exact and reproducible timbres are available over the entire frequency spectrum. Its limitations are twofold: first, it remains a monophonic instrument in live performance; and second, it is not touch sensitive, meaning that the performer is confined to the envelope initially set up.

INSTRUMENTS AND NEW TUNING SYSTEMS. Composers interested in new tuning systems have had great incentive to invent and alter instruments. By their nature, strings are adaptable to alternate tunings, but pitched percussion, keyboard, and most winds require substantial alteration. Bartók, Varèse, Włodzimierz Kotoński, and others have used quarter tones occasionally as special effects. For such isolated instances normal instruments suffice, but an entire piece written in a quarter-tone idiom places a strain on even the best performer. For this reason the Czech composer Alois Hába, long a champion of quarter and sixth-tone systems, has had quarter-tone

clarinets, flutes, and trumpets and a sixth-tone harmonium constructed for his music. (The Italian composer and pianist Ferruccio Busoni anticipated Hába when he proposed a quarter-tone piano in his *Sketch of a New Esthetic of Music*, 1910.) Although Hába had a two-manual quarter-tone piano built for himself, he did not write much for it. Charles Ives evidently had an instrument like this in mind for two of the *3 Quarter-Tone Pieces*; in their final version, however, he asks that they be played on two pianos tuned a quarter tone apart (Hába himself did use such pairs). Julián Carrillo, the Mexican composer, subdivided the half-step still further into eighth and sixteenth tones. He devised a number of instruments to produce these pitches, including an extremely complicated harp, and also developed a complex numerical notation for them. Extensions of just or mean-tone intonations, which divide the octave into unequal parts, have been used by the American composer Benjamin Johnston and several Dutch composers, including Jan van Dijk, Hans Kox, and Henk Badings. Johnston either uses traditionally flexible instruments, as in his *String Quartet No. 2*, or retunes instruments of fixed pitch, as in the *Sonata for Microtonal Piano*. The Dutch also use traditional instruments, although a 31-tone organ has been built in Holland and a number of pieces written for it.

Perhaps the best known composer in the microtonal field is Harry Partch. Partch's system involves 43 tones per octave. He makes his own instruments, which he regards as an integral part of his compositions, both visually and aurally. With the exception of an "adapted viola" (a standard viola with a special fingerboard, held vertically when played) and the specially tuned reed organ called a chromelodeon, all of Partch's instruments are either plucked strings or percussion. Most of the latter employ either extreme ranges, as in his bass marimba, or highly unusual materials, such as the large Pyrex jars cut and tuned to form the cloud-chamber bowls. Another inventor of fanciful percussion instruments is Lucia Dlugoszewski, composer for the Erick Hawkins Dance Co.

ECLECTICISM AND NEW RESOURCES. Partch and Dlugoszewski are largely motivated by a desire to recapture the esthetic of ancient monophonic and Asian music. They are therefore a good example of another widespread trend in the 20th century, the incorporation of ideas, styles, and techniques from other cultures and times. Composers motivated by this eclecticism have drawn on three main sources: historical

Western musics, popular Western musics, and non-Western musics. The eclecticism has manifested itself both in the inclusion of instruments peculiar to other cultures and times and in the development of playing techniques that approximate their sound or sound capabilities.

Attempts to accurately perform baroque and renaissance music have produced a generation of virtuosos on early instruments, many of whom are also interested in new music. Composers have been quick to seize the opportunity this offers. The most striking revival has been that of the harpsichord. Interest generated by such players as Wanda Landowska and Ralph Kirkpatrick resulted in a large number of pieces, including Falla's *Concerto* and Elliott Carter's *Double Concerto*. More recently, commissions from the Swiss harpsichordist Antoinette Vischer have produced avant-garde pieces by Luciano Berio, Ligeti, and others, chief among them the Cage-Hiller *HPSCHD*. There has been a revival of interest in the lute and guitar among composers as diverse as Benjamin Britten and David Reck, sparked by performers such as Julian Bream and Stanley Silverman. The Dutch recorder player Frans Breuggen has had several works written for him, including a *Sequenza* by Berio. Prebaroque instruments have been employed, both individually, as in Rob du Bois's *Pastorale VII* for alto recorder, and collectively, as in Mauricio Kagel's *Music for Renaissance Instruments*.

Of the folk and popular Western musics, jazz has contributed the various playing techniques already mentioned, as well as numerous percussion instruments such as the vibraphone, hi-hat, and sizzle cymbal. Composers from Milhaud to Gunther Schuller have used these and other elements of recent popular music. Even outdated popular-music instruments have been employed, such as a player piano in Hiller's *Avalanche* or the out-of-tune honky-tonk piano in some of Peter Maxwell Davies' pieces. Other composers, such as Bartók, Stravinsky, and Ives, have turned to national or folk musics, occasionally incorporating folk instruments themselves. Stravinsky scored for cembalo in *Renard*. Carlos Chávez, who is well-known for his use of traditional Mexican string and percussion instruments, is one of many hundreds of Latin-American composers to use native instruments. Traditional instruments have also been used in imitation of folk effects, as in Copland's *Rodeo*, but this has only rarely involved the learning of new playing techniques.

A third source of instruments and techniques is non-Western music. In general, traditional Western playing techniques have not been adapted to produce non-Western effects. An exception is Henry Cowell's *Homage to Iran* (copyrighted 1959) in which piano strings are stopped in imitation of an Iranian drum. More usually non-Western influence has manifested itself in the organization or esthetic milieu of a piece, as in the Debussy *String Quartet* or the recent music of Terry Riley. The use of non-Western instruments, however, has been widespread. From India have come the sitar and tabla, popular among rock musicians such as George Harrison of the Beatles. Some popular musicians in the U.S. have used instruments of mixed heritage, like the "Hawaiian" guitar. Many Japanese and other Asian composers writing in essentially Western idioms have scored for their traditional instruments. The most numerous and influential imports into Western music have been percussion instruments: from Indonesia have come various xylophones, many of them used or adapted by Carl Orff, and numerous tuned gongs; from Africa, innumerable drums, particularly the Conga drum and log drum, and a few struck-string instruments; from Latin America, steel drums, bongos, timbales, claves, maracas, and gourds; from China, cymbals, wood blocks, wind chimes, and temple bells; from the West, cowbells, musical saws, washboards, ratchets, and sleigh bells. In fact, it is almost impossible to find a contemporary score using percussion that does not involve instruments of nonconcert and/or non-Western origin (see especially scores by Cowell, Lou Harrison, Colin McPhee, Amadeo Róldan, and Alex North).

It is worth noting that instrument builders in New York and Hollywood, in response to requests from composers and arrangers working in the fields of commercial functional music, have used non-Western instrumental models to make pitched, Western-oriented percussion instruments. The procedure is to take a single instrument, such as the African log drum, and to build a series of like instruments in graduated sizes tuned to Western equal temperament. In this way such instruments as log drums, lou-jons from China, boo-bams from South America, tom-toms, cow-bells, temple blocks, etc., have become available, each in an accurately tuned two-octave chromatic gamut. A related adaptation of non-Western sound sources is found in the instruments designed by Lou Harrison. Using as prototypes string and wind instruments of Chinese, Japanese, Korean, and Indonesian origin, he has constructed soprano, alto, tenor, and bass sizes and ranges without altering the basic design or timbre of the model. Some of Harrison's instrumental families retain the original tuning scheme while others are adapted to Western equal temperament.

NOISE AND PITCH APPROXIMATION. The increased interest in percussion has been the single most striking development in 20th-century sound resources. Notable milestones have been *The Rite of Spring*, Varèse's *Ionization*, and Stockhausen's *Zyklus*. Although many composers have exploited percussion as a result of their interest in eclecticism, others have done so more from an interest in the compositional use of noise. Many resources have been developed specifically in response to this latter concern, and even some of the timbral experiments mentioned earlier, such as flutter-tonguing and snap pizzicato, are reflections of it. Percussion instruments gathered from various cultures and times have been augmented by the use of found objects. Although Erik Satie scored for roulette wheels, office machines, and a "bouteillophone" in *Parade* (1917), the first extended compositional use of machinery and "junk" occurred some ten years earlier in the work of the Italian futurists. John Cage, Harry Partch, and Lou Harrison are more commonly recognized as the great pioneers in this area. Many of their innovations, such as automobile brake drums, inverted tin cans, and Pyrex jars, have since become standard percussion equipment. Experiments continue; Satie's use of bottles, for instance, has been greatly extended in the *Glass Concert* assembled by Anna Lockwood and described in *Source 5*.

Noisy or ambiguous sounds can also be produced on conventional instruments by the use of unconventional playing techniques. Again John Cage was a pioneer, as evidenced by the orchestral parts to his *Piano Concert*, which are essentially compilations of novelties he discovered by consultation with instrumentalists. Techniques of this sort yield three main types of material: percussive sounds, nonpercussive noise, and approximate or complex sounds. The most common percussive sounds on woodwinds are the key clicks exploited by Varèse in *Density 21.5*. Clicks can be "voiced" or "unvoiced," depending on whether a staccato note is sounding simultaneously; the pitch varies individually from key to key and over the entire instrument depending on the mouthpiece and embouchure used. Another possibility is to rattle the keys without closing them. A few other percussive effects can be produced by the embouchure alone; for example, tonguing the mouthpiece of the flute or the crook of the bassoon produces a dry, pizzicatolike sound. Unpitched air sounds are the outstanding source of nonpercussive noise on woodwind instruments. Again many refinements are possible, especially on the flute; the timbre varies according to the vowel formation inside the mouth, the pitch fingered on the instrument, and the direction of the air stream relative to the mouthpiece. Inhalation sounds are different from exhalation, and whispered words or word fragments produce various timbres. Other noises can be produced by scraping or rubbing the instrument or by means of muting.

Woodwind players can produce multiphonic sounds by aiming directly between two partials of a fundamental, thus producing both, by using unusual fingerings that break the air column into several component parts, and by singing through the instrument while producing a pitch. Although jazz players such as Eric Dolphy and John Coltrane may have been the first to employ such sounds consistently, the simplest type, which mixes partials, first appeared in a concert score in Luciano Berio's *Sequenza* for solo flute. More complex sounds are particularly numerous on double reeds and were pioneered in Bruno Bartolozzi's *Bassoon Concerto* and George Perle's *3 Inventions for Solo Bassoon*. More recently composers have begun scoring for such multiple stops, among them Berio, Martirano, and Roger Reynolds (see Bartolozzi 1967 in the bibl.). Most composers interested in multiple stops are also interested in the sounds that result from singing and playing at the same time. The vowel, range, and vibrato used all modify the result as does the breathiness of the played pitch and the type of attack. The interference patterns produced often result in three or more discernible pitches. Combining sung sounds with multiphonics and timbral inflections such as flutter-tonguing can produce sounds of formidable complexity and ambiguity.

One other source of extreme or approximate sounds is the radical alteration of embouchure. Reed instruments, if bitten, produce very high, barely controllable pitches and chords. Extremely relaxed embouchures have similar peculiar effects, resulting in indefinite pitches or multiphonics. The outstanding experimentation was done by jazz players such as Coltrane. The flute can be played with a trumpetlike embouchure, which produces a pitch approximately a sixth below the fingered note. And motion forward or backward on the reed or mouthpiece has considerable effect on the sound; this has been called for by Bartolozzi and others.

Brass instruments have similar capabilities. They can be tapped, scraped, or rubbed to produce percussive effects. Bells of brass instruments will vibrate to produce a pitch if rubbed along a hard surface. Striking the mouthpiece with the palm of the hand produces a pop whose pitch depends on the length of the tubing. Valves can be fluttered or rattled, either with or without air sounds. As with the woodwinds, much variety exists in the air sounds themselves depending on vowel formation, embouchure, and other factors. Multiple sounds can be produced either by aiming between the partials of a fundamental or by combining sung and played sounds. The former technique has been little used, but the latter was known as early as the 19th century; the cadenza of Weber's *Horn Concerto* calls for sounds produced this way, and the exact intonation required produces sum and difference tones, in effect generating chords. Berio uses sung and played sounds more freely in his *Sequenza* for solo trombone; a large collection of novel trombone effects can be found in Carlos Alsina's *Consecuenza*.

Percussive techniques on string instruments have a history dating back at least to the 17th century; in his *Battle Symphony* Heinrich Biber asked the violin section to tap their instruments with the bow. String instruments can also be rapped with knuckles, fingers, etc.; the rock guitarist Jimi Hendrix used to smash and burn his guitar. Less extreme examples of percussive string sounds can be found in the quartets by Von Biel and Ramon Sender. The strings of the double bass can also be played by being struck with mallets, as in Lou Harrison's *Labyrinth No. 3*. Sustained noise sounds can be produced by scraping or rubbing the body of the instrument. Bearing down with the bow produces an intense band of low noise; other approximate pitches can be produced by bowing behind or on the bridge. Bowing the body produces hissing sounds of various types; the tailpiece and even the peg of the cello can be bowed with interesting results. The most outstanding examples of expanded string techniques are found in music of Ligeti and Penderecki.

Percussive effects can be produced with the voice by means of tongue clicks, popping sounds by the lips or cheeks, and voiced or unvoiced plosives. Noise sounds can be produced by various shades of whispers, sustained consonants such as s, sh, z, etc., and rolled r's

and b's. Choruses can produce noiselike clusters by singing or humming randomly within fixed ranges. Squeaks of various kinds can be produced by the lips, tongue, and teeth, and whistles produced in several ways can complement pitched vocal effects such as falsetto. The vocal music of Ligeti, Kagel, Penderecki, and Pauline Oliveros is largely focused on techniques like these. Even vocal multiple stops are possible; the technique has long been known in some Asian cultures, and the jazz singer Ella Fitzgerald can produce them (she sings in octaves on the recording *Ella in Berlin*). Related sound sources are finger snaps, hand claps, stamping, and other sounds produced by nonvocal means. They have always been used as percussive accents in folk and popular music, but their use in Western concert pieces has begun only recently. (The use of language and pseudo-language, as in Kagel's *Phonophonie*, is discussed in the article Text Setting and Usage.) Finally vocal and related sounds can be combined with instrumental sounds, either by direct mixing as in some multiple sounds or by asking instrumentalists to vocalize. Much of Crumb's *Songs, Dances, and Drones of Death* relies on the latter, as do many pieces by Kagel, Reynolds, Hiller, and Robert Ashley.

Because few standards existed at the beginning of the century, virtually all percussion techniques constitute new instrumental resources. Striking the instrument is still the conventional mode of performance; now, however, composers increasingly specify the precise kind of mallet, attack, and location to be struck. The traditional mallets—stick, metal, wrapped, and sponge—have been augmented by glass, hard rubber, plastics, and cloth. These large categories have also been refined: thread-wrapped mallets, for example, produce different sounds depending on the size of the thread and the tightness of the wrapping. The traditional association of specific mallets with particular instruments has also broken down; it is not unusual to use triangle beaters on cymbals or drums, or timpani mallets on chimes. Traditional methods of attack have been refined and new ones have been developed, such as the rimshot, the brush, the cymbal scrape, etc. The location of the attack changes timbre; a cymbal struck on the edge sounds different from the same instrument struck near the center. Portions of instruments not traditionally struck have also been employed: for instance, the rims and sides of drums, the edges of gongs, and the frames of ideophones.

In addition, innumerable individual oddities have been discovered. The pitch of a vibraphone note can be bent slightly by pressing a hard object against the bar while striking. The pitch of any struck instrument changes when lowered into water; several composers, again led by Cage and Harrison, have called for "water gongs." Chimes produce very delicate, ethereal harmonics if struck on the top by glass mallets. Percussionists have also investigated the production of sounds by methods other than striking. A heavily rosined contrabass bow can be applied to almost any metallic instrument and is especially effective on cymbals and gongs. It is even possible to produce discrete pitches by damping cymbals at various nodes while bowing, as required in Roger Reynolds' *Ping*. Bass drums and other large membranophones produce groaning sounds if rubbed with hard rubber or a finger. And percussion instruments can be combined: a cymbal set on a kettledrum, a vibraphone struck with claves.

Perhaps the most famous expansion of playing techniques has occurred with regard to the piano. Since Henry Cowell's first experiments in the 1920s, many composers have used sounds produced on the inside of the instrument. The strings can be struck by mallets, beaters, or the fingers, or they can be plucked or pulled. Scraping lengthwise along bass strings produces a resonant, scratchy sound. Strings can be damped with the finger or with other objects or partially stopped at nodes to produce harmonics. They can even be completely stopped with a hard metal object to produce glissandos and vibratos. These and many other techniques appear in Crumb's *Night Music*, as well as in pieces by Cage, Busotti, Maderna, Reynolds, and others. Percussive sounds can also be generated without using the strings. The keys can be rattled softly, the keyboard lid can be slammed or struck, the top of the instrument rapped or hit with mallets. A particularly interesting set of sounds can be made by striking various parts of the interior frame with the dampers lifted; Benjamin Johnston's *Knocking Piece* is an example. (Similar kinds of sound can also be produced on the harpsichord, the harp, and the organ. Instances appear in the harp music of Bernard Rands and in organ pieces by Ligeti, Kagel, and Christian Wolff.) The most celebrated experiment has been the prepared piano. The insertion of objects into the interior of the instrument dates back at least to Ravel's *L'Enfant et les sortilèges* (1920–25), for which paper is woven into the strings. Various

attachments to produce twangy or buzzy sounds were popular during the days of the player piano. The term prepared piano, however, is normally applied to Cage's creation of 1938 in which small bits of paper, metal, rubber, screws, tacks, etc., were inserted between the strings. All of this transformed the monochromatic piano into a varied collection of timbres, pitches, and noises, as is evidenced by Cage's *Sonatas and Interludes*.

Other instruments have also been altered. Cage's trombone part in the *Piano Concert* includes several instances in which the player is directed to remove the outer slide. Wind players can remove the mouthpiece and use it as an instrument or even play what remains by the use of a brass-instrument embouchure. Gordon Mumma has experimented with the sounds produced by playing a French horn with a bassoon reed.

Recently composers interested in approximation and noise have been turning to live electronics. Again Cage was a pioneer, using a variable speed turntable and a test record in his *Imaginary Landscape No. 1*. He subsequently began using contact microphones and phonograph cartridges, and many of his lectures and performances during the 1950s employed various electronic distortions. Live electronics has since moved in two directions: the electronic modification of live instrumental sounds, and the designing of purely electronic events. Recent work in the former area was initiated with Stockhausen's *Mikrophonie I* and *II*, which use filters, potentiometers, and ring modulators to amplify and distort live sounds. Reynolds' *Ping* uses all of these devices, as well as a photocell mixer to distribute the sounds among the speakers. Franco Evangelisti, Ashley, and Oliveros are also working in this area, and collective work has been done by the Musica Elettronica Viva and Sonic Arts groups in Europe and the ONCE group in the U.S. The live use of purely electronic sounds is being investigated largely by young composer-engineers such as Gordon Mumma (working with the Merce Cunningham Dance Company), Alvin Lucier, and Gerald Shapiro. The most recent technical advance is the incorporation of small-scale digital switching devices by Martirano and David Rosenboom. Scores that are simply circuit specifications and descriptions of environments are becoming common (examples can be found in *Source*).

SUMMARY. The dominant motivation toward new sound resources at the present time is the interest in compositional uses of noise, complex sounds, and approximation. Three areas in particular seem most likely to be expanded rapidly in the immediate future: new wind-instrument sounds, new possibilities with percussion instruments, and live electronics. The development of each area will depend heavily on the continuing emergence of a new generation of virtuosos as exemplified by Severino Gazzelloni (flute), Stuart Dempster (trombone), Bertram Turetzky (double bass), Gerd Zacher (organ), and above all David Tudor (piano). The new virtuoso, in fact, is different from past performers in that he is above all a creator of new techniques. His job, as Tudor has observed, is to derive from the intentions of the composer an appropriate technique for every piece. He must be a virtuoso in invention as well as in execution. Thus, the distinction between performer and composer is being undermined, as is that between performer and audience: In Cage's *4′33″*, for instance, the audience performs as the performer(s) listen(s); in Haubenstock-Ramati's various *Mobiles* the performer composes; in Mumma's *Hornpipe* the composer performs.

The underlying thrust in much recent music and the common element in the motivations outlined at the beginning of this article is the integration of music with other categories of art and thought. The resources most likely to be crucial to future music may not be musical resources at all but rather the byproducts of attempts to interpenetrate music with other aspects of art and life. The spectrum of resources eventually available may therefore ultimately be coextensive with life itself.

BIBL.: Anthony Baines, *Woodwind Instruments and Their History* (London 1967); Bruno Bartolozzi, *New Sounds for Woodwind*, trans. and ed. by R. S. Brindle (London 1967); —— and Lawrence Singer, *Metodo per oboi* (Milan 1969); Alfredo Casella and V. Mortari, *La tecnica dell'orchestra contemporanea* (Milan 1950); Alan Douglas, *The Electrical Production of Music* (London 1957); Adriaan D. Fokker, *Neue Musik mit 31 Tönen* (Düsseldorf 1966); John C. Heiss, "For the Flute: A List of Double-stops, Triple-stops, Quadruple-stops, and Shakes," *Perspectives* 5/1:139–47; —— "Some Multiple Sonorities for Flute, Oboe, Clarinet, and Bassoon," *Perspectives* 7/1:136–42; Donald Martino, "Notation in General—Articulation in Particular," *Perspectives* 4/2:47–58; Werner Meyer-Eppler, *Elektrische Klangerzeugnung* (Bonn 1949); Harry Partch, *Genesis of a Music* (Madison, Wis., 1949); Karl Peinkofer and Fritz Tannigel, *Handbuch des Schlagzeugs* (Munich 1969); Gardner Read, *Thesaurus of Orchestral Devices* (New York 1953); Curt Sachs, *The History of Musical Instruments* (New York 1940); Reginald Smith Brindle, *Contemporary Percussion* (London 1970); *Source* magazine (Davis, Calif., 1967–); Michael Steinberg, "Some Observations on the Harpsichord in 20th-Century Music," *Perspectives* 1/2:189–94; Bertram Turetzky, "The Bass as a Drum," *Composer* (U.S.) 1/2:100ff.; ——, "A Technique of Contemporary Writing for the Contrabass," *Composer* 1/3:118ff.; Michael Vetter, "Apropos Blockflöte," *Melos* 35:461–68.

William Brooks

SEE ALSO Asian Music and Western Composition; Dance; Electronic Music: Apparatus and Technology; Folk Resources; Japan; Jazz; Musicology; Notation; Orchestration; Performance; Popular Music; Text Setting and Usage.

Ioannidis, Yannis (b. Athens, 8 June 1930), studied piano with Elli Farandatou and Spiros Farandatos in Athens (1946–55) and attended Athens Univ. (1948–51, law) and the Hochschule für Musik in Vienna (1955–63; composition with Otto Siegl, organ with Karl Walter, harpsichord with Eta Harich-Schneider). He taught at the Pierce College in Athens during 1963–68 and then moved to Venezuela, where since 1969 he has been music director of the Chamber Orchestra of the National Institute of Culture and Fine Arts in Caracas and professor of composition at the Intermusica Institute. He also performs professionally as an organist. His music is composed in "a free atonal idiom."

PRINCIPAL COMPOSITIONS: *Duo* for violin, piano (1962); *Symphonikó triptycho* for orchestra (1963); *Peristrofi* [Rotations] for string octet (1964); *3 Pieces* for piano (1965); *Versi* for clarinet (1967, Gerig); *Arioso* for string nonet (1967); *2 Pieces for Chorus*; texts by Rilke (1967); *Tropic* for orchestra (1968, Gerig); *Figuras* for string ensemble (1968); *Provolés* [Projections] for 19 instruments (1968); *Fragmento* for cello, piano (1969); *Metáplasis A* for orchestra (1969); *Actinia* for woodwind quintet (1969); *Metáplasis B* for orchestra (1970, Gerig).

PRINCIPAL WRITINGS: *Moussiki* [Music], a general history and theory text (Athens 1969).

BIBL.: John G. Papaioannou, program notes for the Hellenic Weeks for Contemporary Music (Athens 1966, 1967, 1969).

Ireland, John (Nicholson) (b. Bowdon, England, 13 August 1879; d. Sussex, 12 June 1962), studied at the Royal College of Music (1893–1901; composition with Charles Stanford, piano with Frederick Cliffs, organ with Walter Parratt) and the Univ. of Durham (graduated 1905). During 1904–26 he was organist at St. Luke's, Chelsea, London. He taught at the

Royal College of Music during 1923–39; his pupils included Benjamin Britten, Alan Bush, and Humphrey Searle. Peter Crossley-Holland (see bibl.) has pointed out that the use of modal scales and harmony, present in most of Ireland's music, stems from an acquaintance with Tudor music, plainsong, and to a lesser extent folk music. He learned much from Ravel and Stravinsky and was attracted to the magic and power of evocation in Arthur Machen's writings and in the vestiges of pagan history on the Channel Islands.

PRINCIPAL COMPOSITIONS: *Phantasy Trio* for violin, cello, piano (1906, Augener); *Violin Sonatas Nos. 1–2* (1908–09, Augener; 1915–17, Rogers); *Greater Love Hath No Man*, motet for soprano, chorus, organ (1912, Stainer); *Decorations* for piano (1912–13, Augener); *Sea Fever* for voice, piano; text by John Masefield (1913, Augener); *The Holy Boy* for piano (1917, Rogers), revised for violin, piano (1919, Rogers), revised for chorus (1941, Boosey), revised for string orchestra (1941); *Piano Sonata* (1918–20, Augener); *Mai-Dun* (1920–21, Augener); *Cello Sonata* (1923, Augener); *3 Songs* for voice, piano; texts by Thomas Hardy (1925, Cramer); *Piano Sonatina* (1926, Oxford); *We'll to the Woods No More*, song cycle for voice, piano; texts by A. E. Housman (1926–27, Oxford); *Piano Concerto* (1930, Chester); *A Downland Suite* for band (1932, Smith); *Legend* for piano, orchestra (1933, Schott); *A London Overture* (1936, Boosey); *These Things Shall Be* for baritone, chorus, orchestra (1936–37, Rogers); *Concertino pastorale* for string orchestra (1939, Boosey); *Sarnia, an Island Sequence*, for piano (1940–41, Rogers); *Satyricon*, overture for orchestra (1946, Williams); *The Overlanders*, film score (1946–47); *The Hills* for chorus (1953, Stainer); *Meditation on John Keble's Rogationtide Hymn* for organ (copyright 1959, Freeman); *A Sea Idyll* for piano (copyright 1960, Chester); *Sextet* for clarinet, horn, string quartet (copyright 1961, Augener); *Ballade of London Nights* for piano (no date, Boosey). Catalog: E. Chapman, *J. I.* (London, Boosey, 1969).

BIBL.: Joselyn Brooke, *The Birth of a Legend; a Reminiscence of Arthur Machen and J. I.* (London 1964); Peter Crossley-Holland, "J. I.," *Grove's Dictionary* ... (London 1954); John Longmire, *J. I., Portrait of a Friend* (London 1969); Murray Schafer, *British Composers in Interview* (London 1963):24–35; Nigel Townshend, "The Achievement of J. I.," *Music and Letters* 24:65–74.

SEE ALSO Great Britain.

Irino, Yoshiro (b. Vladivostok, U.S.S.R., 13 Nov 1921), studied economics at Tokyo Imperial Univ. (1941–43) and composition privately with Saburo Moroi. He has taught at the Toho-Gakuen Music School since 1961.

He has been using 12-tone techniques since 1951.

PRINCIPAL COMPOSITIONS: *String Sextet* (1950); *Sinfonietta* for chamber orchestra (1953, Ongaku); *Ricercari* for chamber orchestra (1954); *Double Concerto* for violin, piano, orchestra (1955, Ongaku); *Concerto grosso* for 2 groups of strings, 1 group of winds and percussion (1957); *Music* for violin, piano (1957, Ongaku); *Divertimento* for 7 winds (1958); *Music* for violin, cello (1959, Ongaku); *Sinfonia* (1959, Ongaku); *Partita* for wind quintet (1962); *Aya no tsuzumi* [Drum of Silk], television opera (1962); *Hontô no sorairo* [True Sky Blue], drama with music (1963); *Symphony No. 2* (1964, Peters); *3 Movements* for 2 kotos, 17-gen (1966); *Violin Sonata* (1968, Ongaku); *3 Movements* for cello (1969, Ongaku); *Trio '70 for H. R. S.* for flute/alto flute/bass flute/piccolo, violin, harpsichord/celesta (1970); *Globus* for horn, percussion (1971).

PRINCIPAL WRITINGS: Irino has prepared Japanese translations (from German) of Josef Rufer's *Komposition mit 12 Töne* and (from English) of René Leibowitz's *Schoenberg and His School*.

SEE ALSO Japan.

Isamitt, Carlos (b. Rengo, Chile, 13 March 1887), studied at the Santiago Normal School (theory and violin with Pedro Serosen) and at the National Conservatory (composition with Domingo Brecia, Pedro Humberto Allende). He also studied violin privately with Sante Lo Priore and drawing and painting at the Santiago School of Fine Arts, where he later served as a teacher and director. During 1924–27 he traveled in Europe as the Chilean representative to various congresses on the arts. He has taught music at the Pedagogical Institute and the National Conservatory and drawing and composition at the Advanced Institute of Physical Education. He was also artistic director of the Santiago primary schools. He has written many articles on music and the plastic arts for Latin American periodicals. He was the first Chilean composer to use 12-tone techniques (beginning in 1939).

PRINCIPAL COMPOSITIONS: *8 Tonadas chilenas* for voice, piano (1918–23); *String Quartet* (1925–28); *Frisco araucano* for voice, orchestra (1931, IEM); *Suite sinfónica* (1932, IEM); *Piano Sonata*, "Evocación araucana" (1932); *15 Cantos araucanos* for voice, piano (1932); *Estudios Nos. 2–7* for piano: Nos. 2–4 (1934–35); Nos. 5–7 (1938–39); *Mito araucano* for orchestra (1935, IEM); *3 Pastorales* for violin, piano (1939, ECIC); *2 Leyendas* for piano (1939); *Trawin ül* for baritone, clarinet, bassoon, 2 trumpets in D, cello, kettledrum (1941, *Boletín latinoamericano de música*, Montevideo); *Violin Concerto* (1943); *5 Cantos huilliches* for voice, piano (1945); *Suite* for cello, chamber orchestra (1950); *Suite* for flute (1953,

IEM); *Te Küduam mapuche* for voice, bassoon, kultrún; text by the composer (1958); *4 Movimientos sinfónicos* for orchestra (1960, IEM); *Concerto for harp*, chamber orchestra (1961, IEM). List to 1961: *Composers of the Americas* 13:62–71.

BIBL.: Raquel Barros and Manuel Dannemann, "C. I.: Folklore e indigenismo," *Revista musical chilena* 20/97:37–42; Samuel Claro, "La música de cámara de C. I.," *ibid*. 20/97:22–36; Magdalena Vicuña, "C. I.," *ibid*. 20/97:5–13.

SEE ALSO Chile.

Ishii, Kan (b. Tokyo, 30 March 1921), is the son of Bac Ishii, a pioneer of modern Japanese dance. He studied at the Musashino Music Academy in Tokyo (1939–43) and at the Hochschule für Musik in Munich (1952–54; composition with Carl Orff; conducting with Heinrich Knappe, Fritz Lehmann, Kurt Eichhorn). Since 1956 he has taught at Toho Music Univ. in Tokyo and since 1966, at the Aichi Univ. of Arts in Nagoya. He has directed the Tokyo-to Chorus League (during 1966–70) and the All Japan Chorus League (since 1970).

PRINCIPAL COMPOSITIONS: *Kare-ki to taiyo* [The Parched Tree and the Sun] for men's chorus (1955, Schott); *Marimo*, 3-act ballet (1962, Hotta); *En-no-Gyodja*, 3-act opera (1963, Hotta); *Kesa-to-Morito* [Kesa and Morito], 3-act opera (1968, Hotta).

PRINCIPAL WRITINGS: "*Salome*—Richard Strauss," *Geijutsu-shincho* (Sept 1954):164–70; "*Carmina Burana*—Carl Orff," *Ongaku Geijustu* (Feb 1955):27.

SEE ALSO Japan.

Ísólfsson, Páll (b. Stokkseyri, Iceland, 12 Oct 1893), studied at the Royal Conservatory in Leipzig (1913–18; theory with Hans Grisch, piano with Robert Teichmüller, music history with Stefan Krehl) and privately with Joseph Bonnet in Paris (organ, 1923–24). He was director of the Icelandic Conservatory (1930–57) and music director of the Icelandic State Radio (1930–59). He was also editor of the music journal *Heimir* (1935–37) and music critic for the Reykjavík paper *Morgunbaldið* (1940–60). He was organist at the Reykjavík Cathedral during 1939–68.

PRINCIPAL COMPOSITIONS: *Lofsöngur* [Anthem] for chorus, piano; text by Davíd Stefánsson (1929, Menningarsjóður); *Alþingishátíðarkantata* [Cantata for the Millennial Celebration of the Althing] for vocal soloists, chorus, orchestra; text by Stefánsson (1929); *Chaconna* for organ (1938, Lengnick); *Introduction and Passacaglia in F Minor* for organ (1938, Engstrøm); *Gullna hliðið* [The Golden Port], 4 songs for voice, piano or soloists, chorus, orchestra; text by Stefánsson

(1941, Víkingsprents); *Háskólakantata* [University Cantata] for vocal soloists, chorus, orchestra; text by Stefánsson (1961); *Variations on a Theme by Ísólfur Pálsson* for piano (1965).

BIBL.: Matthías Jóhannessen, *Hundaþúfan og hafið* [The Dog-Turf and the Ocean] (Reykjavík 1961); ——, *Í dag skein sól* [The Sun Shone Today] (Reykjavík 1964); *P. I.*, a festschrift (Reykjavík 1963).

Israel. The cultural climate of Israel is largely conditioned by two phenomena: the tension created in this land of immigrants as a result of different cultures living together; and the amalgamating factors of a common heritage, both national and historical, among the various groups and of the newly revived Hebrew language. In the early stages of Zionist settlement at the beginning of this century, music schools and instrumental ensembles were founded that performed music of the classical and romantic repertory. Among the large waves of immigrants in the 1930s were many highly skilled musicians who gave a strong impetus to Israel's musical life. The most important event of this period was the founding in 1936 of the Israel Philharmonic Orchestra, then called the Palestine Symphony Orchestra, by the violinist Bronislaw Huberman (1882–1947). Since its first concerts under Arturo Toscanini (beginning in 1936), the orchestra has been the best known musical body of the country. It has always included some works of local composers in its programs, and it is still the only outlet for those Israeli composers who write for large orchestra. In 1936 a somewhat smaller orchestra, the Israel Broadcasting Services Symphony, was founded. This group has presented many first performances of Israeli works, especially in its weekly broadcast concerts. The radio itself also broadcasts many vocal and chamber works, as well as radio operas by local composers. Opera activities are more limited, and only a few significant operas have been composed in Israel; among them are *Dan the Watchman* (1941) by Marc Lavry and *Alexandra* (1953) by Menahem *Avidom.

The foundations for music education began to take shape in the 1930s and 40s, so that when the state was formed in 1948 there were already two academies of music in Jerusalem and in Tel Aviv and a State Music Teachers Training College. The two academies, now named the Samuel Rubin Academies after the American who sponsors various musical institutions in Israel, have produced a whole generation of musicians, including composers.

At the Jerusalem Academy an electronic music studio has been established recently, and the Tel Aviv Academy is planning to open another. Courses in musicology are given at the Hebrew and Tel Aviv Universities.

The Israel Composers League, founded 1952, now includes 90 composers of concert music and 60 song writers. Since 1956 it has served as the Israeli section of the ISCM, which held its annual international conference in Israel in 1954. The activities of the league include composers' forums, concerts of contemporary music including electronic music, and the annual Israel Music Weeks, held in cooperation with various musical organizations, during which many old and new Israeli works are presented. The league also publishes a yearly bulletin devoted to current events and articles about Israeli compositions.

Commissions and prizes for new works come from several local sources. One of the foremost is the Israeli Composers Fund. This fund commissions several works annually. Recently it has commissioned works from both Israelis and non-Israelis for concerts of the Testimonium fund, established 1966 by Recha Freier to commemorate historical motifs epitomizing the Jewish past. The Israel Chamber Ensemble under Gary Bertini frequently commissions and performs new Israeli works. The America-Israel Cultural Foundation provides a year's grant to an Israeli composer every three years. The annual Israel Festival of Music and Drama, headed by A. Z. Propes, often includes new Israeli works, as does the International Harp Competition sponsored by the Ministry of Tourism every few years. This competition has encouraged many Israeli composers to write music for the harp, and some of their pieces are obligatory in the competition. The Israel Festival was also the first to conduct a seminar for young composers (in 1962); it was directed by Öedöen Partos and included the participation of ten young composers. In 1968 the Festival initiated a Composers Workshop in cooperation with the Israel Composers League and the America-Israel Cultural Foundation. The workshop presents several works commissioned for various chamber ensembles, especially by the younger generation of composers, and closes with a public concert of these works. Since its inception in 1964 the Batsheva Dance Co. has paid special attention to Israeli music; it has based many dance works on local scores, some commissioned. A younger company, Bat-Dor (founded 1968), is following a similar policy. The important music prizes in Israel are the annual prize of

the ACUM, the Israeli preforming rights society; the Engel Prize, presented by the city of Tel Aviv every two years; the Samuel Lieberson Prize given yearly since 1968 for a chamber work; and most important the Israel Prize, awarded every 3–4 years by the State of Israel.

Despite all the opportunities for the performance of new works by local composers, the possibilities are still comparatively few, especially for repeat performances. Because of the political situation and the resultant lack of cultural relationships with neighboring countries, Israeli composers have to look to more distant lands for foreign performances. Great progress has been made lately in this regard, due to the activities of the two main music publishers, both of which have representatives abroad: Israeli Music Publications, Ltd. (founded in 1949 and headed by its owner, Dr. P. E. Gradenwitz), and the Israel Music Institute (IMI). Supported by the government, the latter recently has become the publishing house for the newer works of the most representative composers of Israel. Its publications include more than 250 works. IMI also incorporates the Israel Music Information Centre and the Israel Music Centre, which has established a recording collection of all current Israeli works performed in the country. Another publisher, Hamerkaz Letarbut (sponsored by the workers union), is concerned mainly with vocal works. Recently the local branches of two U.S. companies, RCA and CBS, have begun to produce records of Israeli music. The Broadcasting Services also does its part to distribute Israeli music through its recording service and by submitting recordings to the International Rostrum in Paris and to the Italy Prize competition (Mordecai Seter's radio oratorio *Midnight Vigil* won the latter in 1962). In recent years Israeli performers, ensembles, and conductors have usually included Israeli works in their tour programs. As for their economic situation, most Israeli composers earn their living as teachers, librarians, administrators, radio programers, music critics, arrangers of light and folk music for radio, records, films, and the like. They compose in their spare time.

Israeli composers can be divided into two main groups: those of the older generation, who came to Israel as adults with well-defined, professional music backgrounds acquired in their countries of origin (mostly Germany, Poland, and Hungary); and the younger composers, who were either born in Israel or who came at an early age and received their basic music education in Israel, studying composition under the first group. Most of the latter went for some study abroad during the 1950s and 60s.

Most of the composers who came from Europe before World War II went through a period of adjustment to their new surroundings. They were affected by the wild, ancient landscape, the spirit of the bible, the rhythm of the newly revived Hebrew language, the idealization of a rural life that had been denied to Jews in the Diaspora, and the Middle Eastern melos, which they first became acquainted with in its authentic form from the Eastern Jews and the local Arabs. During the 1930s and 40s many of them collected and arranged Eastern folk melodies, and sooner or later their works showed an influence of these activities. Some of the more conspicuous folk features are florid melodic lines composed of small intervals, ancient modes, the various styles of bible cantillation, syncopated rhythms influenced by Mediterranean dances such as the Arabic *debka* and the Balkan *hora*, and musical textures with heterophonic ingredients. During the same period an Israeli "folksong" type was created by song writers who came to Israel at a young age and lived as pioneers. Their model and source of inspiration was Yoel Engel (1868–1927), the first professional composer who came to live in the new land. The best known composer of concert music of that time is Paul *Ben-Haim (b. Germany, 1897). His works are close to Bloch, Ravel, and Khatchaturian and have a strong pastoral-epic atmosphere. Usually he writes in the classical forms and genres. Some of the younger composers, such as Marc Lavry (Latvia 1903—Israel 1967), Menahem Avidom (b. Poland 1908), and Emanuel Amiran (b. Poland 1909), are also folklorists who have consciously tried to create an eastern Mediterranean style.

Some composers of the older generation continued to follow the paths of their earlier years in Europe, however. To these belong people such as Joachim Stutschewsky (b. Ukraine 1891), who bases his works mainly on the Jewish folklore of Eastern Europe, Erich Walter Sternberg (b. Germany 1891), and the younger Artur Gelbrun (b. Poland 1913), who both continue to compose in postromantic styles.

In the 1950s new directions began to acquire importance, as revealed in the works of Öedöen *Partos (b. Hungary 1907), Alexander Urijah *Boskovich (Transylvania 1907—Israel 1964), and Mordecai *Seter (b. Russia 1916). Folk elements still predominate, but there is a pronounced tendency among these composers to free themselves from the naive-dancelike-pastoral approach of their predecessors; they use folkloristic elements in a more dissonant, "dry," and personal manner. In the early 1960s serial elements began to appear in their works, sometimes as a result of a search for some possible common elements among serial techniques and the Oriental use of *maqamat* (modes): Partos, *Tehilim* string quartet (1960); Boskovich, *Concerto da Camera* (1962); Seter, *Judith* (1962). Ben-Zion *Orgad (b. Germany 1926), who is close in outlook to these composers, has combined serial ways of thinking in his recent music with an archaic biblical atmosphere inspired by the Canticles (*Mizmorim*, 1966).

During World War II and the War of Independence most composers were cut off from musical developments in the outside world, and only in the late 1950s did interest grow in the newer styles and techniques. This is particularly true of the younger generation of composers, such as Yehoshua *Lakner (b. Czechoslovakia 1924), Noam *Sheriff (b. Israel 1935), Ami *Maayani (b. Israel 1936), and myself (b. Germany 1927). We grew up and were educated in Israel, and our early works had a Middle Eastern and folkloristic background and approach. In the 1950s and 60s we studied in Europe or in the U.S., where we came in contact with newer trends. Our works of the mid-60s contain serial and aleatoric elements, tone clusters, microtones, and other ingredients from the present world of sound; we have also worked with electronic music. This style change has not, however, completely superseded our former approach, and even our recent works contain elements related to the Middle Eastern spirit: Lakner, *Mohamet's Dream* (1968); Sheriff, *Chaconne for Orchestra* (1968); Avni, *Meditations on a Drama* (1966); Maayani, *Microtonus* (1964–65). Although born abroad, Abel *Ehrlich (b. Germany 1915) has gone through a similar development, starting with his *Bashrav* for solo violin (1953) and extending into his *Radiations* for piano (1961). A reverse process occurred with Sergiu *Natra (b. Rumania 1924), who came to Israel after World War II as a dodecaphonist and here began to include Eastern motifs in his works (*Song of Deborah*, 1967). Among the younger generation there is also a group of composers who write in a more conservative dodecaphonic vein. To this group belong the Israeli-born Ram Da-Oz (b. 1929) and Asher Ben-Yohanan (b. 1929).

Josef *Tal (b. Poland 1910) combines musical ideas from the East with progressive Western styles. Many of his compositions are 12-tone. He is director of the Hebrew Univ. electronic music studio, which was the first such studio in Israel. Significantly, some of his electronic works have biblical themes (*Exodus*, 1960, and *Lament on the Death of Moses*). The most avant-garde trends in music are expressed in the works of composers like Yizchak *Sadaï (b. Bulgaria 1935), Yehuda *Yannai (b. Rumania 1937), and Yaakov *Gilboa (b. Czechoslovakia 1920), all of whom have been represented at recent ISCM festivals. Mention should also be made of Roman *Haubenstock-Ramati (b. Poland 1919), who is living now in Austria, where he has become a prominent figure in avant-garde circles. In conclusion it should be said that although some Israeli composers may lack close daily contact with developments abroad, many are up-to-date with events through radio, records, scores, and publications, which come in great profusion from all over the world. Others even see an advantage in their geographical isolation from the centers of musical fashion as they strive for a music that is both distinctive and new.

BIBL.: B. Bar-Am, ed., *20 Years of Israel Music* (Tel Aviv 1968); M. Brod, *Israel's Music* (Tel Aviv 1951); P. Gradenwitz, *Music and Musicians in Israel* (Tel Aviv 1952); ——, *The Music of Israel* (New York 1949); A. Holde, *Jews in Music* (New York 1959); A. Ringer, "Musical Composition in Modern Israel," *Musical Quarterly* 51:282–97; A. Rothmüller, *Die Musik der Jüden* (Zurich 1951); J. Shalita, *Jewish Music and Musicians* (in Hebrew, Tel Aviv 1960).

Tzvi Avni

SEE ALSO Liturgical Music: Jewish.

Ištvan, Miloslav (b. Olomouc, Czechoslovakia, 2 Sept 1928), attended the Janáček Academy of Music in Brno (1948–52, composition with Jaroslav Kvapil). He has taught at the Acaddemy since 1965 and since 1966 has been associated with the electronic music studio of Radio Brno.

PRINCIPAL COMPOSITIONS: *Piano Trio* (1958, Panton); *Balada o jihu* [Ballad of the South], 3 symphonic frescos after a song by Lewis Allan (1960, Supraphon); *String Quartet* (1963, Supraphon); *6 Studies* for chamber orchestra (1964, Panton); *Zaklínání času* [Incantation of Time] for two reciters, orchestra (1967); *Já Jácob* [I, Jacob], chamber oratorio for coloratura soprano, popsong tenor, reciter, flute, English horn, electric guitar, piano, electric organ, percussion, tape; Biblical text (1968).

PRINCIPAL WRITINGS: *Metoda montáže izolovaných prvků v hudbě* [The Montage Method of Isolated Elements in Music] (Prague 1969); Ištvan has also written many articles in *Hudební rozhledy*.

SEE ALSO Czechoslovakia.

Italy. Two factors have conditioned the evolution of music in 20th-century Italy: 19th-century opera and Fascism. Opera was virtually the sole artistic expression throughout the last century, blotting out other creative activities from the graphic arts to the theater and literature. This tradition swept on after Verdi's death (1901) and carried with it an entire generation of composers devoted almost exclusively to opera (Giacomo Puccini, 1858–1924; Umberto Giordano, 1867–1948; Ermanno Wolf-Ferrari, 1876–1948; Franco Alfano, 1876–1954; Ildebrando Pizzetti, 1880–1968; Riccardo Zandonai, 1883–1944), which meant that for some 35–40 years Italian music was dominated by an essentially 19th-century idiom, however much it may have been enhanced by greater harmonic freedom and richer orchestral colorings.

Verdi, as cosmopolitan a composer as he became, nevertheless sowed the first seeds of a musical nationalism, which, in practical terms, meant a deliberate resistance to foreign (Germanic) influences. Fascism (1922–45) turned this tendency into a policy, ultimately cutting a further generation of composers off from the international ferments that would have stimulated renewal and experimentation. The process did, however, have two important side effects: It raised the obliging composer to a position of prestige, and it led to a rediscovery of Italy's rich tradition of 17th- and 18th-century instrumental music. This rediscovery offered a valid "national" alternative for those composers seeking a way out of the marshlands of late veristic opera. The German alliance and World War II came just when the fruits of this evolution might have come to maturity. Fascism until then had always been much more elastic than Nazism in its approach to innovative art; indeed Fascism promoted modern music as an instrument of cultural propaganda, so that both Hindemith and Stravinsky, for example, were able to exert considerable influence on the rising generation of Italian composers, though the Viennese school had virtually no following until after the war. Mention must be made in passing of Ferruccio Busoni (1866–1924), the expatriate Italian composer who spent all his active musical life in Germany, thus unwittingly depriving Italy of what might have been a decisive influence at a decisive moment. His music, his teachings, his theorizing—keyed to the issues and moods of German music—had very little bearing on the course of contemporary music in Italy.

Most composers today are trained at one of the state conservatories that exist in all the larger cities, of which the Accademia di Santa Cecilia in Rome is the most important. Private music schools are rare, and private composition lessons even rarer. The aspiring composer must usually teach when his school days are over, and for this he needs the diploma of a state conservatory. Though the composition chairs are often held by reputable composers, the usual conservatory training tends to be traditional and academic. Many of the younger composers have turned to places such as Darmstadt or Cologne to round out their musical education.

The composer's opportunities for earning a living are limited mostly to teaching in the state conservatories or to working as consultants or employees at RAI, the government-owned radio. The various opera houses tend to appoint more or less established composers as artistic directors. Few if any active composers turn to music criticism or research as a source of income. Some conduct and some play instruments, though rarely on a regular professional concert level, and some write film music. Significantly the greater number of younger composers to emerge since World War II are financially independent.

On the whole new music is infrequently performed, especially in public concerts. By far the greatest opportunity for hearing new music and for getting it performed is offered by RAI. With its four orchestras (Milan, Turin, Rome, Naples) and ample financial resources, it ranges widely and often courageously through the contemporary repertory, occasionally commissioning new works. Milan radio has one of the finest electronic studios in Europe, the Studio Elettronico di Fonologia Musicale (founded 1955). Several organizations have also been important: the annual Festival Internazionale di Musica Contemporanea in Venice (founded 1930) has been a showcase of new music in Italy; the prestigious Pomeriggi Musicali of Milan (founded 1945); the short-lived but important Incontri Musicali of Milan (1956–59); the Accademia Filarmonica Romana (founded 1821) has always included contemporary music concerts in its annual series; the Società Italiana Musica Contemporanea (the Italian section of ISCM), which in its most active years (1950–67) sponsored concerts all over Italy, as well as three successful International Composition Contests. More recently the annual Palermo

Week (founded 1963), the Nuova Consonanza Group in Rome (founded 1961), the Società Cameristica Italiana of Florence (founded 1960), among others, have offered new music. The state-owned orchestras tend to be conservative (the Santa Cecilia Orchestra in Rome, the La Scala Orchestra in Milan, among others). Modern opera appears relatively frequently in the larger opera houses, which are state subsidized and obliged by law to stage a certain number of modern Italian works, but there is little public following. La Scala, the Fenice (Venice), the Communale (in Bologna and in Florence), and the San Carlo (Naples) are the most available to new stage works; the theaters in Rome, Turin, Genoa, and Palermo, among others, tend to be more conventional.

Almost all Italian composers since the war have had their works published by Suvini-Zerboni in Milan, some of them receiving a regular stipend from the publisher. Ricordi, the publishing giant of Italy, has until very recently resisted the more experimental and radical reaches of contemporary music. Smaller houses such as Carisch limit their present activities largely to representing foreign publishers. Some of the better-known young composers have contracts with foreign publishers. New Italian music has begun to appear on records only in recent years. RCA Italiana, for example, has issued a three-record set ("Musica Nuova"), as well as a record of improvisations by the Nuova Consonanza Group. The Italian labels Sugar Music, Arcophon, CBS Italiana, Vedette, and others, and some German, French, and American companies have also recorded modern Italian music.

Alfredo *Casella (1883–1947) was, if not the first, at least the most important Italian composer to realize that the cultivation of instrumental music was perhaps the only way out of the impasse of early 20th-century veristic opera. It was due almost exclusively to his example and to his teachings that the neoclassic period in Italian contemporary music came into being during the 1920s. One of the immediate effects was the reworking of old music into modern suites; typical of this are such works as *Rossiniana* (1925) or the *Antiche arie e danze per liuto* (1917, 1924, 1932) by Ottorino Respighi (1879–1936), where the original material is mostly transcribed for large modern orchestra, or Casella's *Scarlattiana* (1926) and *Paganiniana* (1942), where the originals are fused and recast (with some mild dissonance) for orchestra. On a more scholarly level are the editions of the works of Claudio Monteverdi, Antonio Vivaldi, and others by Gian Francesco *Malipiero (b. 1882). This tradition was continued in the next generation with such brilliant orchestral adaptations as *Tartiniana I & II* (1951, 1956) by Luigi *Dallapiccola (b. 1904). These excursions into old music did not leave a definitive neoclassic imprint on their composers' original works, though both Goffredo *Petrassi (b. 1904) in his *Partita* (1932) and Dallapiccola in his *Partita* (1932) and *Divertimento* (1934), among others, did attempt to adapt classical forms to contemporary uses. A much more apparent effect was the renewed interest in Gregorian chant and the old modes. This influence took both melodic and harmonic form and represented a further attempt to renew music within a national framework. For some composers this influence was permanent: Ildebrando *Pizzetti (1880–1968), for example, evolved a melodic and vocal style whose long, diatonic, vaguely oriental melodies, shorn of cadence, clearly reflect his fondness for plainsong (*La Pisanella*, 1913; *Violin Concerto in A*, 1944; *Preludio a un altro giorno*, 1952); G. F. Malipiero had frequent recourse to modal harmonies in his nine symphonies, together with some of the melodic feeling of Gregorian melismas; and Respighi wrote a violin concerto entitled *Concerto gregoriano* (1922), as well as a *Concerto in modo misolidico* (1924). Composers of the following generation found this path too limited. Their development enjoyed (with the help of Casella) the beneficial influence of Hindemith and Stravinsky, an influence which answered the mounting demand for a new instrumental style and new instrumental forms. It is worth noting that folk music played little or no part in the nationalistic sedimentation of music under Fascism. Casella, in his *Serenata* (1927) and in the ballet *La giara* (1924), among other works, utilized folk elements, but they were exceptions.

Virtually every notable 20th-century Italian composer has written at least one opera, very largely in an effort to bring a new instrumental awareness and a new vocal approach to the genre. Pizzetti became almost exclusively an opera composer, with eleven more or less "traditional" operas, from *Fedra* (1909–12) to *Murder in the Cathedral* (1958). Opera is one of the most important genres in the production of G. F. Malipiero, whose modernity often takes the form of a caustic irony in style and subject matter (*Torneo notturno*, 1931, and *Gli eroi di Bonaventura*, 1968). Respighi wrote nine richly orchestrated operas with an emphasis on the exotic and fabulous (*La campana sommersa*, 1927; *La fiamma*, 1934). Casella himself applied his brash instrumental textures and angular lines to opera (*La donna serpente*, 1928–31). The modernist operas of Giorgio Federico *Ghedini (1892–1965) temper Wagnerian leanings with a strong neoclassical sense of melodic and harmonic structure (*Maria d'Alessandria*, 1937; *Billy Budd*, 1949). In the immediately following generation, it was Dallapiccola more than any other who devoted his attentions almost exclusively to the singing voice and hence to opera, producing works (*Volo di notte*, 1940; *Il prigioniero*, 1944–48; *Job*, 1949–50; *Ulisse*, 1960–68) in which the severity of his serial and canonic techniques is softened by a sensitive use of the orchestra and by a lyrical and highly elastic molding of the voice that reveals the influence of Alban Berg. Petrassi, on the other hand, has written only two operas, of which *Il Cordovano* (1944–48) is a brilliant, virtuosic comic opera. Among the young composers Luigi *Nono (b. 1924) is one of the few to have devoted serious attention to the stage, though Luciano *Berio in *Allez Hop* (1959) and *Opera* (1969–70) and Bruno *Maderna in the mime opera *Hyperion* (1964) have opened up new directions. Nono's operas, like most of his other works, are presented as documents of social protest where an attempt is made to break down the traditional syntax of operatic form through the introduction of electronic tapes, projections, and instruments as protagonists on the stage, and where every possibility of the human voice is exploited (*Intolleranza*, 1960–61, and such staged works as *La fabbrica illuminata*, 1964, and *A floresta é jovem e cheja de vida*, 1966). An interesting attempt at a form of "total opera," involving sounds, words, lights, gestures, mime, dance, etc., is to be found in *Passion selon Sade* (1965–66) by Sylvano *Bussotti (b. 1931).

The marked interest in the singing voice on the part of many Italian composers has given rise to an adaptation of 16th- and 17th-century polyphonic chordal music sometimes called *neomadrigal*. Goffredo Petrassi was among the first to see the possibilities of early Italian polyphonic music, in particular that of the Roman school (Palestrina, among others). The influence of Casella, Hindemith, and Stravinsky (*Symphony of Psalms*), working on Petrassi's natural inclination, led to a series of large-scale works for chorus and orchestra mostly religious in theme and distinguished by a limpid, almost chaste orchestral texture, a masterly handling of the chorus, and a terse economy of thematic material (*Salmo 9*, 1934–36; *Magnificat*, 1939–40; *Coro di morti*, 1940–

41; *Noche oscura*, 1950–51). Dallapiccola's neomadrigal works are of equal stature, but, in contrast to the great liturgical models which inspired Petrassi, Dallapiccola turned to the preoperatic dramatic madrigals of the late 16th century (Orazio Vecchi, Adriana Banchieri, and others), recasting them in such works as the *Sei cori di Michelangelo Buonarroti il Giovane* (1933–36), the *Canti di prigionia* (1938–41), and the *Canti di liberazione* (1951–55), where the composer's grasp of subtle instrumental and vocal colors and his polyphonic voice-leading are placed at the service of an intensely personal musical expression. Venetian composer Luigi Nono looked to the 16th-century Venetian school (Andrea and Giovanni Gabrieli) for his neomadrigal works (*Il canto sospeso*, 1956; *Cori di Didone*, 1958). in which an underlying lyrical sensitivity sometimes yields to massed effects of polemical violence. The classical chamber madrigal (Monteverdi, Marenzio, and others) is the model of Italy's most recent neomadrigalist, Sylvano Bussotti, whose a cappella madrigals reveal a fertility of inventiveness and a poetic sensibility (*Ancora odoni i colli*, *La curva dell'amore*, *Rar'ancora*; 1967–68).

Mention should be made here of the postwar influence of Bartók on Italian music, an influence whose main expression is to be found in the music of Guido Turchi (b. 1916), particularly in the *Concerto breve* (1947) for string quartet or string orchestra and the *Piccola serenata notturna* (1950) for orchestra. Turchi later composed an opera, *The Good Soldier Sveik* (1962), in which there is a Hindemith neoclassicism. There are also strong Bartókian elements in Petrassi's *Fourth Concerto* (1954) and especially in his cantata *Noche oscura*, but these elements were abandoned in his later production. Not Bartókian but more middle European than other Italian composers' are the works of Mario Zafred (b. 1922), which show a certain post-Brahmsian fondness for the great classical instrumental forms (six symphonies, solo concertos, quartets and quintets), as well as for grand opera (*Hamlet*, 1961; *Wallenstein*, 1964) in the Germanic, but pre-Wagnerian tradition.

All the current trends have found expression in the works of the young Italian avant-garde composers, including experimentations in the field of electronic music. Rumanian-born composer Roman *Vlad (b. 1919) was perhaps the first to introduce the principles of the Viennese School into Italy about 1940–43, but by about the same time Luigi Dallapiccola had fully adopted the 12-tone method. Such a method proved antithetical to Goffredo Petrassi's

tastes, though he eventually incorporated many of its principles into his instrumental music (in the fourth of his eight concertos this absorption makes one of its first appearances), but he has never adopted it completely in the orthodox sense. Serial writing and post-Weberian experimentalism have been embraced by all the more significant postwar composers, many of whom came under the direct influence of composers such as Boulez and Stockhausen in Darmstadt or of pedagogues such as Scherchen in Switzerland. Franco *Evangelisti (b. 1926), for example, lived and worked for a number of years in Germany; he contributed a great deal to formulating a precise notation for avant-garde music and has been active in bringing contemporary Italian composers into the mainstream of European music. Aleatory music, while tested by many young composers, has one of its more extreme champions in Franco *Donatoni (b. 1927), who in such works as *Quartetto IV (Zrcadlo)* (1963) or *Black and White* for 37 string instruments (1964) determines the order in which various musical events are performed by chance or arbitrary selection. Less extreme but more influential has been Bruno *Maderna (b. 1920) whose compositions, conducting, and experimental and organizational activities placed him for a long time at the center of Italian musical life; for some years he worked with Luciano *Berio (b. 1925) in setting up an electronic studio at the Milan radio, in organizing concerts, and in editing an important, though short-lived music review, *Incontri Musicali*. Berio eventually moved to the U.S. in the early 1960s. Both Maderna and Berio are wide-ranging, post-Webernian eclectics; Maderna has developed a rather personal, delicately lyric style in such works as *Dimensioni III* (1963) and the *Oboe Concerto No. 2* (1967).

The influence of Stockhausen has been widespread, especially in the works of Aldo *Clementi (b. 1925), whose keen abstract pictorial sense has led to dense static curtains of sound with minute, almost imperceptible inner shifts and alterations of color (e.g., *Informel 3*, 1963; *Variante B*, 1964; *Reticolo: 11*, 1966). Collage techniques have recently been explored, particularly in the works of Niccolò *Castiglioni (b. 1932), first in the radio opera *Through the Looking Glass* (1961), then progressively on through his later compositions (*A Solemn Music II*, 1964–65): styles are juxtaposed, direct quotations are intermingled with flawless stylistic imitations of music from the past, hieratic repetitions recur like obsessions. Before this Castiglioni had proved to have one of the most imaginative and original orchestral palettes of his generation, which resulted in bold instrumental gestures and, typical of this period, shrill, stuttering rhythmical patterns in the extreme upper register reminiscent of Messiaen's "bird" pieces (see *Aprèsludes*, 1959; *Tropi*, 1959). Quarter-tone inflections are common in the works of many of the younger avant-garde composers, as are experimentations with rhythm and variable tempos.

As a footnote it is perhaps indicative of the current situation in Italy that Dallapiccola, Berio, and Castiglioni now live and work in the U.S., Maderna resides in Germany, and Evangelisti has ceased composing.

Robert Mann

SEE ALSO Opera.

Ives, Charles (Edward) (b. Danbury, Conn., 20 Oct 1874; d. West Redding, Conn., 19 May 1954), was the son of a town band leader, George Edward Ives, who had been well schooled in the European tradition but who also experimented with tone clusters, polytonality, quarter tones, and acoustics. This and his participation in both the vernacular (band and camp meeting) and genteel (church and musical soirée) traditions were prophetic of his son's fusion of widely disparate styles and techniques. In fact the father-son relationship was the greatest single formative factor in the development of the son's music and philosophy.

Charles began snare drum lessons at 7 and soon moved on to piano, organ, and composition. At 15 he began advanced organ studies and became organist at the Danbury Baptist Church. He remained at this job until 1893, during which time he was attending Danbury Academy where he was known as a good baseball and football player. He entered Yale Univ. in September 1894, preparing for a business career. In November his father died suddenly, and Charles turned for guidance to Horatio Parker, a good but conventional Victorian composer who was head of the Yale music department. Parker taught Ives harmony, counterpoint, and orchestration, but Ives's unwillingness to submit all of his creative energies to academic requirements in music led to an estrangement between the two. Ives continued his organ studies with Dudley Buck and worked as organist at New Haven's Church on the Green, where he probably first heard some of his choral music performed.

In 1898 Ives graduated from Yale and moved to New York. He became a clerk at the Mutual Life Insurance Co. and took jobs as organist at the First Presbyterian Church in Bloomfield, N. J., and later at the Central Presbyterian Church in New York City (remaining until 1902). In 1907 he and another insurance salesman, Julian Myrick, opened their own agency of the Washington Life Insurance Co. During 1902–17 Ives divided his energies between his business and composition, to the detriment of his health. His intense compositional activity almost ceased after the outbreak of World War I, and he spent the next four years gathering together some of his badly disorganized manuscripts and rearranging earlier works. In October 1918 he suffered a heart attack from which it took him almost a year to recover; later on he suffered from diabetes and cataracts. Starting in 1920 he began to publish some of his works privately, including *114 Songs* (published 1922), the *Concord Sonata*, and the accompanying *Essays*, which Ives had worked on as early as 1915 but to which he devoted concentrated energy only during his convalescence in 1918–19.

Ives retired from business in 1929, a rich man, and moved permanently to his farm in West Redding, secluding himself from the outside world (except for trips to Canada and Europe) for the rest of his life. From the time they were married in 1908, Mrs. Ives (née Harmony Twitchell) had supplied encouragement when the music world reacted with indifference to her husband's music. Now during his years of failing health, she handled family business, maintained his correspondence, and defended his solitude against all intrusions. During his active years Ives watotally ignored as a composer, but after retires ment his reputation began to grow. Although such men as Nicholas Slonimsky, Ives's friend the poet Henry Bellaman, and the French pianist E. Robert Schmitz figured prominently in this first recognition of Ives, his most important link with the musical world was Henry Cowell. Cowell published several of Ives's songs, chamber pieces, and his most complex score, the second movement of the *Symphony No. 4*, in the influential quarterly *New Music*, which he edited. Ives himself financed all such efforts on his behalf. (His opposition to the professional music world and his belief that all music is public domain led him to resolve not to secure copyrights for his music.) The major events in the emergence of Ives's music were: a performance in New York of the *Concord Sonata* by John Kirkpatrick in 1939; the receipt of the 1947 Pulitzer Prize after a performance of the *Third*

Symphony conducted by Lou Harrison; the premiere of the *Second Symphony* conducted by Leonard Bernstein in 1951; the publication of a catalog of manuscripts by Kirkpatrick in 1960, revealing for the first time the extent of Ives's output; and the premiere of the *Fourth Symphony* conducted by Leopold Stokowski in 1965. Publication and recording of Ives's important works began on a large scale only after 1954.

Ives's earlier style drew on four sources: 1) the American church and organ repertory, which is essentially straightforward and naive in technique but colored with late romantic chromaticism and the "elevated rhetoric" of French organ style; 2) the late 19th-century symphonic tradition of Brahms and Dvořák; 3) the American sacred and secular vernacular traditions, including revival hymns, patriotic and popular songs, dance music, and college songs; 4) the experimental attitude toward sound materials that Ives inherited from his father, together with a completely original method of merging diverse stylistic and acoustic materials. These elements have been listed approximately in the chronological order in which they dominated Ives's musical thinking, but at every point in his career they were all present.

The formative period (up to 1896) includes about 35 songs, many organ works, band marches, short piano pieces, fugal exercises, and choral anthems and canticles; many are either lost or in a fragmentary state. The culminating work is the *String Quartet No. 1*. The basic style is a watered-down chromatic harmony and foursquare rhythm typical of late 19th-century American church music, but it is occasionally distinguished by rapid and unconventional shifts in key, asymmetrical rhythms, the interjection of either quotation or parody of popular materials, a marked preference for contrapuntal textures, and a tendency to juxtapose incongruous musical elements. There are occasional harmonic oddities (such as the polytonal interludes in the *America Variations*) and a few works are wholly experimental (*A Song for the Harvest Season*, a fugue in four keys; *Psalm 67*, which is in two keys throughout).

During 1896–1905 Ives was working in larger, more ambitious genres, as evidenced by the first three symphonies and the violin sonatas. Although these, obviously, are outgrowths of the German tradition, they fail to conform to the conventions of sonata form. In the symphonies tonality remains functional. The first owes much to Dvořák and is rare for Ives in its lack of quotations. But even here the harmonic progressions move freely and unpredictably (in the opening few bars the theme moves from D minor through such remote keys as B minor and C minor before returning to a dominant seventh). There is greater originality of form in the *Symphony No. 2*. The first and fourth of its five movements are thematically related and introductory in character. The second is in a free ternary design rather than sonata form as such. The last evolves freely according to a dramatic structure based on the nature of quoted materials rather than thematic recurrence in and of itself. A group of transcribed organ settings of revival hymns, originally written for church services, comprises the material developed in the *Third Symphony*. In each of these symphonies the orchestra employed gets successively smaller.

The violin sonatas and *Piano Sonata No. 1* are more inventive formally. A typical movement (e.g., *Violin Sonata No. 2*: I) is based on a "verse-prose" scheme with sections of free or variable rhythm (prose) alternating with sections of steady meter (verse). The motivic material is drawn from a hymn and is presented in distorted fragments that gradually coalesce into a complete statement at the end. While Ives was developing this sort of thematic logic, he continued to broaden his stylistic flexibility by frequently borrowing complex variations of pulse from ragtime (*Piano Sonata No. 1*: II and IV). His greatest harmonic and contrapuntal inventiveness, however, occurs in the series of Psalm settings (mostly composed 1896–1900), where he explored almost every imaginable area of tonal organization: whole-tone scales (Psalm 100), quartal harmony (beginning of Psalm 14), polytonality (Psalms 67, 135), tone clusters and atonality (Psalm 90), and a 12-tone row (Psalm 25). The use of polyrhythms reached a peak of complexity in the second of the three *Harvest Home Chorales*, where three parts move in a note-to-note ratio of 9:6:4.

Around 1905–06 Ives broke completely with convention, and his music entered its mature phase. In 1906 he produced a number of works for varied ensembles ranging from a few instruments to chamber orchestra. In two of these pieces, *The Unanswered Question* (or "A Contemplation of a Serious Matter") and *Central Park in the Dark in the Good Old Summer Time* (or "A Contemplation of Nothing Serious"), different groups of the orchestra play in independent layers of rhythm and sonority, coinciding vertically in a random fashion. In *The Unanswered Question* the conductor is instructed to cue in the various parts of the texture at will, an early example of what became, 40 years later, one procedure of aleatory music.

All the techniques so far described reached their culmination in the large-scale works of this last period: the *Concord Sonata*, the *Holidays Symphony*, the two *Orchestral Sets*, and the *Fourth Symphony*. The second movement of the first *Orchestral Set* recreates a childhood experience: two bands, boosting rival baseball teams, come down from opposite ends of Main Street playing different marches in different keys and tempos. Each band is determined not to be disrupted or outshown by the other. Ives's ability to recreate such experiences of his early years can be attributed not only to great aural acuity and vivid memory, but even more to a philosophy and compositional technique that perhaps makes him such a uniquely American composer. Ives's own version of New England Transcendentalism is epitomized in his *Concord Sonata* and the *Essays*, which can be taken together as a musicopoetic entity. In these works he employs a syntax (the logical relationship of successive events) that, like his musical textures, is a piecing together of externally unrelated events that must be taken in the context of the whole to be comprehensible. It is appropriate therefore to describe Ives's mature compositional style as the first extensive musical application of collage technique.

A persistent source of criticism of Ives's music stems from his almost total isolation from an audience and from the professional world of music during his most productive years. Aaron Copland, for instance, said in 1934 that "weaknesses" in the *114 Songs* arise "from a lack of that kind of self-criticism which only actual performance and public reaction can bring." Yet Ives's isolation led not just to a failure to attune his aural imagination to the exigencies of orchestral balance, but to a freedom from convention as well. This is not to say that everything he wrote is equally successful. To the contrary, Ives's transcendental acceptance of all musical experience made him a somewhat careless editor of his work, and the charge of unevenness is justified. Nonetheless, whole generations of musicians have come under his influence. Henry Cowell's use of tone clusters, while independently derived, was encouraged and extended as a result of his close personal association with Ives. Elliott Carter's juxtapositions of rhythms can be traced back to his early acquaintance with the composer and his music. Lou Harrison's extensive use of per-

cussion instruments was foreshadowed in Ives's *Fourth Symphony*, fourth movement. Since World War II, John Cage, Karlheinz Stockhausen, and others have extended the revolutionary esthetic implications of Ives's procedures. His juxtapositions of styles and textures were the first extensive musical application of collage techniques, and the present-day use of noise and electronic collage springs from Ives, both technically and philosophically. The notational experiments of aleatory music arise out of a desire to involve the performer in the creative process much as Ives did when he invited performers to choose from among several versions of a passage (*Piano Sonata No. 1*), to distort rhythmic values (*Violin Sonata No. 3*), improvise extensions of phrases, or arrange a work for alternate combinations of instruments. The narrowing of distinctions between art and life, which many present-day composers are exploring, are very much a part of Ives. Indeed he even invited composers of the future to collaborate with him on an open-ended composition, a *Universe Symphony*, which would be performed outdoors by an unlimited number of people.

PRINCIPAL COMPOSITIONS: *Variations on America* for organ (1891 or 1892, Mercury); *Psalm 67* for chorus (1893 or 1894, AMP); *String Quartet No. 1*, "A Revival Service" (1896, Peer); *3 Harvest Home Chorales* for chorus, brass, organ (1898?–1902, Mercury); *Symphony No. 2* (1897–1902, Southern); *Piano Sonata No. 1* (1902–09, Peer); *Violin Sonata No. 2* (1903–10, Schirmer-G); *Orchestral Set No. 1*, "3 Places in New England" (1903–14, Mercury); *Symphony No. 3*, "The Camp Meeting," for small orchestra (1904–11, AMP); *New England Holidays*, "Washington's Birthday," "Decoration Day," "The Fourth of July," "Thanksgiving" (1904–13; AMP, Peer, AMP, Peer); *Central Park in the Dark* for chamber orchestra (1906, Boelke, AMP); *The Unanswered Question* for chamber orchestra (1906, Peer); *Set for Theater or Chamber Orchestra* (1906–11, NME); *String Quartet No. 2* (1907–13, Peer); *Robert Browning Overture* for orchestra (1908–12, Peer); *Piano Sonata No. 2*, "Concord, Mass., 1840–1860" (1909–15, AMP); *Symphony No. 4* with chorus (1909–16, AMP); *34 Songs* for voice, piano (1889–1921, NME); *3 Pieces* for 2 pianos tuned a $\frac{1}{4}$-tone apart (1923–24, Peters). Complete lists: Cowell, Kirkpatrick, and *Composers of the Americas* 2:92–100.

PRINCIPAL WRITINGS: *Essays before a Sonata, The Majority, and Other Writings by C. I.* ed. by H. Boatwright (New York 1970); *Autobiographical Memos* ed. by J. Kirkpatrick (New York 1971).

BIBL.: Elliott Carter, "The Case of Mr. I.," *Modern Music* 16:102ff.; Aaron Copland, "114 Songs," *Modern Music* 11:102ff.; Henry and Sidney Cowell, *C. I. and His Music*, 2nd ed. (New York 1969); David Hall, "C. I., an American

Original," *Hi-Fi/Stereo Review* (Sept 1964):142ff.; H. Wiley Hitchcock, *Music in the United States* (Englewood Cliffs 1969): ch. 7; John Kirkpatrick, *A Temporary Mimeographed Catalogue of the Music Manuscripts and Related Materials of C. E. I.* (Yale Univ. 1960); Dennis Marshall, "C. I.'s Quotations: Manner or Substance?", *Perspectives* 6/2:45–56; Wilfred Mellers, *Music in a New-Found Land* (London 1964); Frank R. Rossiter, *C. I. and American Culture: The Process of Development, 1874–1921* (PhD diss., Princeton Univ., 1970).

Laurence Wallach

SEE ALSO Dance; Folk Resources; Form; Jazz; Liturgical Music: Christian; Microtones; Orchestration; Text Setting and Usage; Texture; Theory; United States.

J

Jacob, (Dom Clément) **Maxime** (b. Bordeaux, 13 Jan 1906), studied at the Paris Conservatory (1927–28; harmony, counterpoint with André Gedalge) and privately with Charles Koechlin (1926–27) and Darius Milhaud (1926–30). In the mid-20s he was associated with several other French composers who called themselves L'Ecole d'Arcueil (the name was a tribute to Satie, who lived in Arcueil, a working-class suburb outside Paris). During 1925–28 Jacob conducted an orchestra in Vieux-Colombier. In 1930 he entered the Benedictine Order at the Abbey of En-Calat, where he has served as organist. He has given many organ recitals in France.

PRINCIPAL COMPOSITIONS: 15 *Piano Sonatas* (1929, 32, 34, 40, 41, 42, 43, 44, 44, 44, 45, 46, 47, 48, 49); *Organ Suite in C* (1939, Leduc); *Interludes liturgiques* for organ (1939, Leduc); 3 *Violin Sonatas* (1940, 44, 45); *Le Chemin de la Croix* for string orchestra (1946, Jobert); 2 *Cello Sonatas* (1946, 47; Jobert); *Feuillets d'album* for piano (1957, Jobert); *Piano Concerto* (1961, Jobert); 8 *String Quartets* (1961, 62, 63, 64, 65, 66, 67, 68–69); *Flute Sonata* (1966); *Les Hymnes* (Patrice de la Tour du Pin) for vocal soloists, chorus (1966, Levain); *Les Psaumes pour tous les temps* for soloists, chorus (1966, Editions ouvrières); *Livre d'orgue* (1967, Editions ouvrières); *Journal de mon âme* for piano (1968); *Misse syncopée* (1968). Jacob has also written about 400 *Mélodies* for voice, piano (1923–69, some published by Jobert) and many liturgical works (1966–69, published by Levain and Chalet).

PRINCIPAL WRITINGS: *L'Art et la grâce* (Paris 1939); *Souvenirs à 2 voix* (Toulouse 1969); "Le compositeur et la réforme liturgique," *Encyclopédie des musiques religieuses* (Paris c.1971).

BIBL.: Jean Roy, *Présences contemporaines . . .* (Paris 1962); ——, "M. J.," *Revue musicale* (July 1939):23–27.

Jacobi, **Frederick** (b. San Francisco, 4 May 1891; d. New York, 24 Oct 1952), studied in New York with Rubin Goldmark (composition), Ernest Block (composition), Paolo Gallico (piano), and Rafael Joseffy (piano), and at the Berlin Hochschule für Musik with Paul Juon (composition). He was an assistant conductor at the Metropolitan Opera (1914–17) and taught at the Juilliard School (from 1936) and the Julius Hartt School of Music in Hartford (from 1946). His music reflected both his Jewish background and his field research into the music of the Pueblo Indians.

PRINCIPAL COMPOSITIONS: *String Quartet* on Indian Themes (1924, SPAM and Schirmer-G); *Indian Dances* for orchestra (1927, UE); *Friday Evening Service* for baritone, chorus (1930–31, Bloch); *Cello Concerto* (1932, UE and AMP); *Piano Concerto* (1934–35); *Scherzo* for flute, oboe, clarinet, bassoon, horn (1936); *Violin Concerto* (1936–37, Leeds); *Hagiographa*, 3 biblical narratives for string quartet, piano (1938, Arrow); *Ode* for orchestra (1943, Boosey); *The Prodigal Son*, 3-act opera; libretto by Herman Voaden (1944, 4 dances published by Schirmer-G); *String Quartet No. 3* (1945, AME); *Concertino* for piano, string orchestra (1946, E-V); *Symphony in C* (1948).

PRINCIPAL WRITINGS: "F. J. on the Composer's Craft," *International Musician* (March 1949): 20–21.

BIBL.: David Diamond, "F. J.," *Modern Music* (March 1937); Olin Downes, "American Composer," *New York Times* (2 Nov 1952):sec. 2.

Janáček, **Leoš** (Eugen) (b. Hukvaldy, Czechoslovakia, 3 July 1854; d. Ostrava, 12 August 1928), was the son of a school master and organist and was surrounded by folk music from infancy. He learned to play the organ, but it was his fine voice that set him upon a musical career. When he was 11 it earned him a scholarship to the St. Augustine Abbey in Brno, where Father Pavel Křížkovský, a distinguished composer of church music and unaccompanied choral works, was in charge. In 1872 Janáček went to the Brno Teachers' Training College and in 1874 to the Prague Organ School. In 1876 he passed the state teachers' examination. He undertook brief periods of composition study at the Leipzig Conservatory (1879) and Vienna Conservatory (1880) but found both unhelpful, as he disliked the German approach (he particularly loathed "Wagnerian bombast"). He finally settled in

Brno and became the city's most active and influential musician.

In 1885 Janáček began his researches into Moravian folk music. These, together with his studies of the rhythms and pitch curves of speech, revealed the compositional path he was seeking, and he finally reached maturity as a composer in his mid-40s. The success of his opera *Jenufa* in Prague in the mid-1910s spurred the composer, then 62, to a tremendous burst of creative energy, and during the last 12 years of his life he wrote the majority of his most important compositions.

The main influences on Janáček during his formative years were Křížkovský and Dvořák. He took his teacher as a model when composing a cappella choruses; his *Lasské Dances* clearly owe much to Dvořák's *Slavonic Dances*. Like the majority of Moravian and Bohemian composers, Janáček adopted a predominantly Western approach, and it was only when he looked eastward that his creative personality developed. His melodic style derived from the folk music of eastern Moravia, a music that, with its modal tendencies and irregular phrase lengths, is far removed from the four-square folksongs of Bohemia. Taking his cue from Mussorgsky's speech rhythms, Janáček notated in sketch books short sentences and phrases he overheard in towns or in the countryside, paying particular attention to the moods in which the words were spoken. This study enabled him to develop a personal and natural style in vocal music generally and in opera in particular; it also influenced his approach to instrumental music, which is mostly built out of short phrases suggestive of vocal exclamations. While Janáček's early works might have been written by almost any minor central-European composer of the period, those of his middle period (c.1895–1916) display a highly personal dialect that became increasingly starker in its expression.

Janáček's originality sprang largely from his melodic material, consisting mainly of short pungent phrases that are subjected to sudden changes of mood and tonality. By means of simple but rarely obvious variational procedures, he built up a melodic fragment to a climax of great emotional intensity. His favorite devices included augmentation and diminution, the latter often giving rise to accompaniment figuration. Harmonically he was no innovator. Common chords, sevenths, ninths, and whole-tone combinations were usually sufficient for his needs, but these chords are often strangely spaced and frequently follow each other in unexpected sequences. He had a special predeliction for the second (or ninth) and, to a slightly lesser extent, the seventh degrees of the scale. Besides emphasizing them melodically, he came to regard them as consonances with (rather than additions to) the tonic, third, and fifth of the scale. Indeed, in the *Sinfonietta* and other compositions of his last years, the second sometimes replaces the tonic in the bass. Formal analysis of his music is often difficult because he dispensed with classical structures; the shape of a movement or work of his maturity, however, always gives the impression of deriving inevitably from the content. When writing for instruments he enhanced the impact of his music by overthrowing accepted procedures of orchestration, sometimes writing unplayable or nearly unplayable passages. He reveled in the extreme low notes of bass instruments, especially those of the trombone, as well as in the highest notes of certain treble instruments, and he often left a wide gap between these extremes. Janáček himself seems to have exhausted all the possibilities of his chosen style and to have left no room for important followers. Recently, however, some Czech composers, including Luboš Fišer, have benefited from his characteristic repetitions of brief but pungent phrases.

PRINCIPAL COMPOSITIONS (available from Supraphon unless otherwise noted): *Její pastorkyňa* [Her Foster Daughter], usually known as *Jenufa*, 3-act opera; libretto by Gabriela Preissova (1894–1903, revised 1906, 1911, 1916; Supraphon and UE]; *Po zarostlém chodníčku* [On an Overgrown Path], 15 pieces for piano (1901–08); *Piano Sonata*, "1.×.1905" (1905); *Kantor Halfar* for men's chorus (1906); *Maryčka Magdónova* for men's chorus (1906, revised 1907); *Sedmdesát tisíc* [Seventy Thousand] for men's chorus (1909); *V mlhách* [In the Mist], 4 pieces for piano (1912); *Věčné evangelium* [The Everlasting Gospel], cantata (1914); *Hradčanské písničky* [Songs of Hradčany] for women's chorus (1916); *Taras Bulba*, rhapsody for orchestra after the story by Gogol (1915–18); *Zápisník zmizelého* [The Diary of a Young Man Who Disappeared], song cycle for tenor, alto, 3 women's voices, piano (1917–19); *Káťa Kabanová*, 3-act opera; libretto by the composer after Ostrovsky's *The Storm* (1919–21, UE); *Příhody lišky bystroušky* [The Cunning Little Vixen], 3-act opera; libretto by the composer after Rudolph Těsnohlídek (1921–23, UE); *String Quartet No. 1* (1923); *Věc Makropulos* [The Makropulos Case], 3-act opera; libretto by the composer after Karel Čapek (1923–25, UE); *Mládí* [Youth] for wind sextet (1924); *Concertino* for piano, clarinet, flute, horn, 2 violins, viola (1925); *Capriccio* for piano left-hand, flute/piccolo, 2 trumpets, 3 trombones, tenor tuba (1926); *Sinfonietta* (1926, UE); *Glagolitic Mass* for vocal soloists, chorus, organ, orchestra (1926, UE); *String Quartet No. 2*, "Intimate Letters" (1928); *Z mrtvého domu* [From the House of the Dead], 3-act opera; libretto by the composer after Dostoevsky (1927–28, UE). Complete lists in Hollander and in Štědroň 1959 (see bibl.).

PRINCIPAL WRITINGS: *Uplná nauka o harmonii* [Complete Harmony Text] (Brno 1920). Janáček's correspondence with various individuals has been published; the most important are: with Max Brod (Prague 1953), with Gabriela Horvátová (Prague 1950), with Karel Kovařovic (Prague 1950), with Otakar Ostrčil (Prague 1948), with F. S. Procházka (Prague 1949), and with the librettists of *The Excursions of Mr. Broucek* (Prague 1950).

BIBL.: Max Brod, *L. J.* (Vienna 1956); Hans Hollander, *J., His Life and Works* (London 1963); Daniel Muller, *L. J.* (Paris 1930); Rosa Newmarch, *The Music of Czechoslovakia* (London 1942); Bohumir Štědroň, *L. J., Letters and Reminiscences* (Prague 1955); ——, *The Work of L. J.* (supplement to *Hudební rozhledy*, Nov 1959); Jaroslav Vogel, *L. J., His Life and Works* (London 1962).

Malcolm Rayment
SEE ALSO Czechoslovakia, Opera.

Janson, Alfred (b. Oslo, 10 March 1937), studied piano as a child with his mother. He played the accordion in Oslo cafés as a teenager and began appearing as a jazz pianist. He eventually had training in harmony and counterpoint with Bjørn Fongaard and in composition with Finn Mortensen. He began to compose seriously about 1962 and has since written many film and theater scores. He continues to tour as a concert and jazz pianist.

PRINCIPAL COMPOSITIONS (published by Hansen-W): *November 1962* for piano (1962); *Vuggesang* [Cradle Song] for 48 strings, soprano (1963); *Konstruksjon og hymne* [Construction and Hymn] for orchestra in 3 groups (1963); *The Balcony*, tape score for the play by Genet (1964); *Canon* for Hammond organ, piano, soprano, tenor saxophone, double bass, 2 percussionists, tape (1965, recorded by Philips); *Theme* for piano solo, chorus, organ, percussion (1966); *Nocturne* for 2 choruses, 2 cellos, 2 percussion groups, harp; text by Nietzsche (1967); *Mot Solen* [Toward the Sun], scenic poem for 2 saxophones, chorus, orchestra; inspired by the life of the Norwegian painter Edward Munch (1968); *I dag død, imorgen rosenrød* [Candy and Balloons], television musical; text by Anders Bye and Bengt Calmeyer (1969); *Röster i mänskligt landskap* [Voices in a Human Landscape], mass for chorus, 10 instruments, 3 actors; text by Elisabeth Hermodsson (1969); *Valse Triste* for jazz orchestra, tape (1970).

SEE ALSO Scandinavia.

Janssen, Werner (b. New York, 1 June 1900), studied at Dartmouth College (1918–19; harmony, counterpoint with Philip G. Clapp), and at the Academy of Santa Cecilia in Rome

(1930–33; orchestration with Respighi). During 1918–19 he studied theory and composition with Frederick S. Converse in Boston; during 1920–21, conducting with Felix Weingartner in Basel; and during 1921–25, conducting with Herman Scherchen in Strasbourg. He has been music director of the Baltimore Symphony (1937–39), of the Janssen Symphony in Los Angeles (1940–52); the Salt Lake City Symphony (1946–47), the Portland Symphony in Oregon (1947–49), and the San Diego Symphony in California (1952–54). During 1939–42 he was musical director for Walter Wanger Productions in Hollywood, and a significant part of his output has been film scores. He has also composed incidental music for plays, TV, and documentaries.

PRINCIPAL COMPOSITIONS: *New Year's Eve in New York* for orchestra, jazz band (1928, Birchard); *Obsequies of a Saxophone* for 6 winds, snare drum (1929); *Louisiana Symphony* (1929); *String Quartet No. 1*, "Kaleidoscope" (1930); *String Quartet No. 2* (1933); *Quintet for 10 Instruments* for winds, string quartet (1966).

Japan. As in politics and economics, Japan's cultural activity, including music, is centralized in Tokyo. There are six important orchestras in the city, half of which have toured successfully abroad. The important music schools number at least five. There are orchestras in a number of other cities, and activity does go on elsewhere. Osaka, for example, has advanced music schools of its own and sponsors each year the largest music festival in the country, the Osaka International Music Festival. Nevertheless it remains true that Osaka's composers and performers are unable to find recognition in Japan unless they are first recognized in Tokyo.

Japan's principal musical life follows a tradition (that of the West) that has been developing in the country for little more than a century. Western music was introduced at the beginning of the Meiji Period (1868–1912); before this, music in Japan stemmed solely from the ancient world of *kabuki* and *noh*, *gagaku* and *bunraku*. Especially since World War II it has been the Western rather than the Japanese tradition that has become a background to daily life, and now it is no longer a borrowed thing but deep within the roots of a personal tradition.

The first composers to introduce and absorb the European tradition (through the 19th century) were Kosaku Yamada (1886–1965) and, following in his footsteps, Kiyoshi Nobutoki (1887–1965). In 1930 the Shinko

Sakkyoku Renmei [New Composers' Federation] was founded with a core of 16 composers including Shukichi Mitsukuri (1895–1971), Meiro Sugawara (b. 1897), Yasuji *Kiyose (b. 1900), and Yoritsune Matsudaira (b. 1907). This group became the Japanese section of ISCM and eventually led in 1930 to the foundation of the Japan Contemporary Music Association (which in 1971 included 167 composers). The composers in the earlier group were much influenced by impressionism and neoclassicism, as well as by elements of Japan's folk traditions. Kiyose utilized the pentatonic scale found in Japanese folksong and *gagaku* in numerous songs and piano pieces. Matsudaira, the only prewar composer to join directly with the postwar generation in experimental composition, combined 12-tone techniques after World War II with *gagaku* themes. In each of his works (e.g., *Theme and Variations* for orchestra, 1951; *Saibara Metamorphoses,* 1953; *Umai, Sami* for orchestra, 1958; *Bugaku,* 1961) he has given a fresh and personal interpretation to elements of traditional Japanese music. The works mentioned were performed at ISCM festivals in the 1950s and 60s, thereby bringing his name to international attention. Lately he has used aleatory procedures in which the performer chooses from fragments of melody, mixing improvisatory elements with fully controlled events (e.g., *Somaksah* for flute, 1961; *Portrait* for 2 pianos, 2 percussionists, 1968).

The work of other prewar composers can be roughly divided according to their French or Austrian-German leanings. Paris-trained Tomojiro Ikenouchi (b. 1906) and Kishio Hirao (1907–54) are representative of the first group, Berlin-trained Saburo *Moroi (b. 1903) the second. Under training from Ikenouchi many other composers have followed in the French tradition, including Sadao *Bekku (b. 1922, the present chairman of the Japan Contemporary Music Assoc.), Teizo *Matsumura (b. 1928), Akio Yashiro (b. 1929), Makoto *Shinohara (b. 1931), and Akira Miyoshi (b. 1933). Moroi ceased composing in 1948; his students Yoshiro *Irino (b. 1921) and Minao *Shibata (b. 1916) went on to introduce atonal and 12-tone music, opening new possibilities for postwar Japanese composers. (Irino was the first Japanese composer to write 12-tone works.)

SINCE 1945. Immediately after the war the various types of composers organized a number of groups and had their works performed. Rather than joining directly with the prewar generation, however, the younger composers tried to work out their own expression through positive contact with new movements from abroad. Loosening themselves from the bonds of the country's long isolation and nationalist feelings and putting themselves in touch with the methodology and directions of new music in the West, they attempted to initiate a new sensibility.

An experimental group along these lines appeared in Tokyo in 1949, Jikken Kobo [Experimental Workshop]. It consisted of 14 composers, performers, poets, painters, and engineers who banded together to explore the area now known as mixed media. Completely unaware of Pierre Schaeffer's work in Paris, they put on performances of their own tape music combined with films and live music. They also stirred interest in new Western movements through all-Schoenberg concerts and other such programs. The members included composers Toru *Takemitsu (b. 1930), Joji *Yuasa (b. 1929), Hiroyoshi Suzuki (b. 1930), Keijiro Sato (b. 1926), Kazuo Fukushima (b. 1930), pianist Takahiro Sonada and myself, a poet and music critic. We were the spiritual progeny of Varèse, Cage, and Messiaen. As with the other composers in the group, Takemitsu attended no conservatory but was practically self-taught, studying privately with Kiyose and Fumio Hayasaka (1914–55). Hayasaka, who wrote music for the films of Akira Kurosawa, left a deep impression upon many younger composers. The influence of his Eastern esthetics can be felt in Takemitsu, but not in a merely nationalist, folk-oriented way. The use of nonvibrato and pizzicato in Takemitsu's *Dorian Horizon* for 17 strings, for example, suggests the resonance of the *shò* and the *shôko*; it would seem that he has discovered the "space" of *gagaku* as well. In *Water Music* there is a resonance close to the *tsuzumi,* and such works as *Eclipse* and *November Steps* actually use traditional Japanese instruments. Takemitsu is not interested in a nationalist "program music." "As far as I am concerned," he has said, "I must not be trapped by traditional instruments any more than by all other kinds of instruments existing in this world. In my own way I want to cultivate two different kinds of music to make a living order that combines the fundamentally different musical phenomena of the West and Japan." Toshiro *Mayuzumi (b. 1929) shares these concerns. His *Nirvana Symphony* (1958) is based on a frequency/amplitude analysis of the sounds made by the huge Buddhist temple bells in Japan (which he calls the "campanology effect"). He also built a musical structure out of *tendai shômyô,* a type of Buddhist chant. His tape pieces *Campanology* and *Aoi-no-Ue* use transformed sounds of bells and *noh*, respectively.

Mayuzumi has been working at the NHK electronic music studio, which was founded in 1955. He composed his first electronic work, *Study*, that year and in 1956 collaborated with Makoto *Moroi (b. 1930) on *Variations sur 7*. Recent work by younger composers has made use of a wide variety of techniques; the composers involved now constitute the main avant-garde group in Japan. *Assemblage* by Yori-Aki *Matsudaira (b. 1931, son of Yoritsune) explores relations between tape and live sound. The five-channel tape piece *Icon* by Yuasa was made exclusively from white noise. *Parallel Music* and *Shiki-Soku Ze-Ku* by Toshi Ichiyanagi (b. 1933) made use of chance operations in composition; his *Tokyo 1969* is a montagelike combination of spoken materials in several languages, popular music, and rock bands, all of which are modulated and mediated by various electronic processes, including a translation computer. *Phonogene* for 12 instruments and tape and *Omvilic des limbes after A. Artaud* by Yuji *Takahashi (b. 1938) incorporate processes derived from mathematics. Ichiyanagi, who studied under John Cage while in the U.S. during 1952–61, has been the chief proponent in Japan of Cage's ideas on indeterminacy. He is active both as a performer and as a composer and has produced a number of instrumental works in graphic notation, live electronic pieces, and recently other works involving environmental art and sound design. Takahashi, who has lived in the U.S. since 1966, is well known as a pianist. He studied under Iannis Xenakis and has used computers in plotting the deployment of sound groups, as in his *Orphika* for orchestra and *Nikite* for chamber ensemble. (Works using computers are still rare in Japan, owing to their unavailability to composers. The few composers who have been able to explore their potential include Ichiyanagi, Kenjiro *Ezaki, b. 1926, and Komei Hayama, b. 1932.)

During 1957–63 a Japanese version of the Darmstadt summer courses existed in the resort town of Karuizawa. It was a project of the Institute for 20th-Century Music, founded by seven musicians including Mayuzumi, Makoto Moroi, and the music critic Hidekazu Yoshida. The first of their festivals included works by Berg, Stockhausen, and Boulez, and subsequent festivals continued to introduce new trends from abroad. A group experimenting in improvisation and happenings was founded in Tokyo in 1960 under the influence of Cage, Ichiyanagi, and others. Called Group Ongaku, its central figures were Takehisa

Kosugi (b. 1938), Shūkō *Mizuno (b. 1934), and Chieko Shiomi (b. 1938). It disbanded in the mid-60s. Kosugi's subsequent work has gone beyond the traditional framework of music, and during a visit to the U.S. in 1965–66 he worked with Nam June Paik in the Fluxus group, giving performances employing small radio frequency oscillators and various kinds of activity. A group similar to Group Ongaku was formed in Tokyo in 1962 with Ichiyanagi and Takahashi as leaders. It was called New Direction and took up both Japanese and Western avant-garde work.

The next generation of composers includes Yoshio *Hachimura (b 1938), Teruyuki *Noda (b. 1940), Haruna *Miyake (b. c.1942), and Shinichiro *Ikebe (b. 1943); their common musical traits include the use of tone clusters and glissandos to create new harmonic structures and a certain academic tendency (including the use, for example, of the traditional Western formal schemes). It must be said that there is a wearing out of the experimental spirit among the young, partly because avant-garde music is shut out from the music academies, which refuse to have avant-garde composers on their staffs, and partly because of a continuation of the prewar folk-music movement and of an exclusively traditional training in the primary schools. There is, however, a movement with its roots in the nationalist tradition that shows considerable vitality. It is centered in the Yagi no Kai group, founded in Tokyo in 1953 and including Michio Mamiya (b. 1929) and Hikaru Hayashi (b. 1931). (Though not a member, Yasushi *Akutagawa, b. 1925, shares many of the group's attitudes.) The initial purpose of the group was to apply Bartók's approach to folk materials and to relate music to the problems of contemporary politics and life. The group's first works showed a strong influence from Bartók and the Soviet composers. Unlike the prewar folk-music-movement composers, the Yagi no Kai group wanted a new creativity of their own and were not looking just for musical motifs, such as folktunes; their search was for the wellsprings of Japanese folk energy, language, politics, and life. Like the avant-garde composers of Poland, they seem to be developing a new musical syntax. Hayashi's choral work *Atom Bomb Landscape*, for example, uses vocal clusters in setting the agonizing texts of a poet who died from the effects of radiation.

Only a handful of Japan's composers can earn a living solely from composing; most of these write for radio and television. The rest teach or hold other positions; a few are masters of ceremony on television. As elsewhere, the dissemination of new music through publication and performance is limited. Scores are published mainly by two firms, Ongakū no Tomo-sha [Friend of Music] and Kawai-Gakufu. The NHK Broadcasting Co. and the Japan Philharmonic Orchestra are commissioning and performing new works with increasing frequency; however, the proportion of contemporary works on the programs of other organizations is extremely small. Although there is no permanent opera house, two or three new operas are produced every year by such composers as Osamu Shimizu (b. 1911) and Ikuma *Dan (b. 1924), and Kan *Ishii (b. 1921) has introduced a number of scores for dance each year.

Smaller private organizations are the most active on behalf of new music. The introduction and performance of experimental works was undertaken by the Experimental Workshop in the early 1950s and, later in the decade, by the festivals of the Institute for 20th-Century Music. In the early 1960s the Sogetsu Art Center was the scene of activity for Ichiyanagi, Takahashi, and others in the New Direction group (now disbanded). At present the most forward-looking activity takes place in the Crosstalk performing series of the American Cultural Center and in the Japanese-German Festivals for New Music of the German Culture Center. The former was established in 1967 by Donald Albright (its director), Roger Reynolds, Joji Yuasa, myself, and a number of artists and film critics. In 1969 it invited composers from the Sonic Arts Union to Tokyo and sponsored a large Crosstalk Intermedia Festival. Since then there have been about four concerts a year weighted in favor of American and Japanese music but including other works as well. The German Center has held concerts each February since 1967, organized by Maki Ishii (b. 1936), who studied under Josef Rufer in Germany, Irino, and Fukushima. The Center sponsored a series on avant-garde piano works, inviting the Kontarsky brothers to perform, and has recently begun a composition contest. The Friends of 20th-Century Music, organized by Kunio Toda (b. 1914) and others, has sponsored four or five concerts yearly since 1968; the programs include a wide variety of works from throughout the century. Shin-ichi *Matsushita (b. 1922) and his pupil Eisei Tsuji (b. 1933) are leaders of the Osaka Autumn festivals.

Kuniharu Akiyama
(trans. from Japanese by Joseph Love)

SEE ALSO Education for the Nonprofessional.

Jaques-Dalcroze, Emile (b. Vienna of Swiss parents, 6 July 1865; d. Geneva, 1 July 1950), studied at the Geneva Conservatory (1875–87), the Vienna Conservatory (1887–91; composition with Robert Fuchs, theory with Hermann Grädener, piano with Adolf Prosniz), and composition at Vienna Univ. with Anton Bruckner and in Paris with Antoine-François Marmontal, Léo Delibes, and Gabriel Fauré. He developed a rhythmic approach to musical pedagogy based on body gestures and movement. During 1892–1910 he taught solfège and improvisation at the Geneva Conservatory. He then founded the first Dalcroze Institute in Hellerau, Germany; this closed in 1914, and he founded another in Geneva, which he directed until his death. He possessed a remarkable feeling of closeness with the people of French Switzerland, and many of his 600 songs, for which he wrote both words and music, became so popular that they were absorbed into the "folk music" of the area. He also composed several large patriotic stage works.

PRINCIPAL COMPOSITIONS: *Le Violin maudit*, 3-act opera; libretto by A. Pouthier (1893); *La Veillée*, oratorio; text by the composer and Jeanne Thoiry (1893); *Janie*, 3-act idyll; libretto by Ph. Godet (1894, Kistner); *Sancho Pança*, 4-act lyric comedy; libretto by Yves Plessis (1896, Henn); *Violin Concertos Nos. 1–2* (1902, 1911); *Le Festival vaudois*, 5-act popular spectacle (1903, Foetisch); *Le Bonhomme Jadis*, 1-act comic opera; libretto by Franc Nohain (1906, Heugel); *Les Jumeaux de Bergame*, 2-act opera (1908, Heugel); *Echo et Narcisse*, cantata; text by Jacques Chenevière (1912); *La Fête de Juin*, 4-act popular spectacle; libretto by D. Baud-Bovy and A. Malche (1914, Foetisch); *Les Premiers Souvenirs*, poème en images; text by Chenevière and the composer (1918); *La Fête de la jeunesse et de la joie*, song cycle with mimes, dancers; texts by Chenevière and P. Girard (1923, Foetisch); *Le Petit Roi qui pleure*, 3-act fairy opera; libretto by the composer (1932, Henn); *Le Joli Jeu des saisons*, 3-act opera; libretto by the composer (1934, Henn). In addition to these works, he composed many songs for voice or women's chorus and piano, chamber works, piano pieces, and orchestral tone poems.

PRINCIPAL WRITINGS: *Le Rythme, la musique et l'education* (Lausanne 1920, New York 1921); *Souvenirs, notes et critiques* (Geneva 1942); *Notes bariolées* (Geneva 1948).

BIBL.: *E. J.-D., l'homme, le compositeur, le créateur de la rythmique* (Neuchâtel 1965).

[prepared with the help of Henri Gagnebin]
SEE ALSO Dance.

Jazz came into being in the southern U.S. in the late 19th century and first blossomed in the vicinity of New Orleans at the turn of the 20th.

Contrary to popular belief, jazz does not owe its existence to any one culture or race, although the American Negro played the dominant role in the early years. Nourishment came from at least three continents: the additive rhythms of West African drumming, European functional harmony, American Gospel singing, and a blues scale whose origin has not yet been convincingly traced. All of these merged within the social milieu of the American South with its black fraternal organizations, public band concerts, minstrel shows, red light bistros, and Gospel churches. Certain musical characteristics, such as melodic improvisation to a harmonic scheme, rhythm-section continuo playing, instrumentation, intonation, a typical timbral concept, and other performance-practice features, have distinctions which, especially in combination, are peculiar to jazz. Other musical elements (for example, formal schemes and harmonic structure) are held in common with other Western musical types.

Jazz music was being performed long before it was given its generic name, for jazz was preceded by both ragtime (c.1890–c.1920) and blues (c.1900–   .), the former an instrumental style and the latter, at this time, a vocal style. Once the name came into common usage (1913–15 according to jazz musicians of that period), all other names became identifiers of substyles. The most important of these, in approximate chronological order, are ragtime, blues, Dixieland or New Orleans style, Chicago style, swing, be-bop, progressive, and the avant-garde styles of the 1960s (free jazz, electronic rock, raga rock, bosa nova, etc.). Although some of the early music was notated and published (T. M. Turpin's *Harlem Rag*, 1895; William H. Krell's *Mississippi Rag*, 1897; and W. Scott Joplin's *Maple Leaf Rag*, 1899), jazz has always been a performer's rather than a composer's music.

ORIGINS. Many jazz elements existed in music before the crystalization of the style called ragtime. Syncopated rhythms in the songs and dances of American blacks probably derived from African drumming and Afro-Caribbean dance rhythms. Field hollers, work chants, and spirituals were part of the American black slave tradition. Spirituals, such as "Swing Low, Sweet Chariot," "River Jordan," and "One More River to Cross," may have originally been West African boat songs reworked for Christianity. Civil War songs, blues, jigs, and reels were all in the air. Concert and marching bands were part of the Negro fraternal lodges of New Orleans, Memphis, and St. Louis in the 1870s and were also part of the musical entertainment in contemporary white society.

Ragtime (c.1890–c.1920) is a substyle whose chief characteristics are duple meter (2/4 or 4/4); functional harmony stressing tonic, dominant, subdominant, and applied dominants in a major tonality; compounded song-form structures with 16 or 32-bar periods and shorter introductions, vamps, and codas; a syncopated treble melody which operates in opposition to a harmonic and nonsyncopated bass line; and a bass line which moves approximately at half the speed of the melody. The chief ragtime syncopations occur on the second and fourth eighth notes in a 4/4 measure, while accented melody notes often, but not always, reinforce beats 3 and 4 (fifth and seventh eighth-notes).

The piano was the principal performing instrument of ragtime, but the style, since it was also suitable for other combinations, was frequently performed by brass bands. In the former instance, the pianist would play "stride," that is, he would use the left hand in a "downbeat-upbeat" manner in which beats 1 and 3 (in 4/4) were heavily accented single notes, octaves, or tenths, and beats 2 and 4 were unaccented triads. In the latter situation, the brass bass and bass drum would play only beats 1 and 3 while the harmony instruments, that is, melodic instruments of mid-range (euphoniums, alto horns, etc.) would fill in the chords on all the beats. The pianist's right hand and the treble melody instruments of the band (cornet, trumpet, clarinet, etc.) would create the characteristic syncopated melodies.

The ragtime pianist's touch was percussive, and the pedal was not used for legato effects. The pitch system of ragtime, in contrast to that of the blues and most other forms of jazz, was the equal-tempered scale. However, since much early ragtime was performed on old, out-of-tune upright pianos, a certain out-of-tuneness accompanied by mechanical noise became almost characteristic of the style.

Piano rags were performed solo, but often a small group of additional instruments, percussive or percussive-harmonic (trap drums, banjo, pizzicato double bass, etc.), were used. Ragtime is primarily an instrumental style, but a few rags, especially later ones, had texts and were sung.

While syncopation is the chief characteristic of ragtime melodies, these syncops were usually placed in simple proportion to the beat (usually 2:1). Rhythms of more complex proportions, although they do occur (e.g., *New Orleans Joys* by Jelly Roll Morton), are not typical. In other jazz styles, performers

Ex. 1a.

1	2	3	4	5	6	7	8	9	10	11	12
I ————————				IV ———	I ———			V ———		I ———	

Ex. 1b.

1	2	3	4	5	6	7	8	9	10	11	12
I	V7	I	I♭7	IV	II	III♯	VI	II7	V7	I ———	

B♭ Blues

1	2	3	4	5	6	7	8	9	10	11	12
B♭ F♯m7 BM7 Em7	A7 Dm7	Bm7 E7		E♭7	B♭°A7	B♭ Cm7	Dm7 G7	Cm7	F7	B♭ G7	Cm7 F7
(I)				(IV)		(I)		(II7)	(IV7)	(I)	

Ex. 1c.

tend never to play eighth-notes evenly but in trochaic groupings

(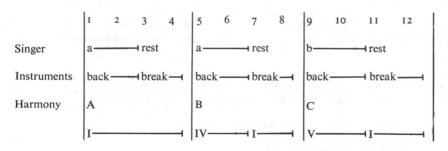).

In ragtime the even performance of eighth notes, regardless of accents or groupings, is the rule.

Since ragtime and blues were contemporaneous in the first decade of the century and since sound recordings of that period are not extant, it is difficult to determine exactly what and how the ensembles played. The "orchestras" are reported to have played both varieties of music in addition to other dances and marches. A typical ensemble, Buddy Bolden's, had seven players at one time: cornet, clarinet, violin, trombone, guitar, string bass, and trap drums. At another time, it still had seven members, but it used two clarinets and no violin. The most noted performers in this style were pianists Scott Joplin, James P. Johnson, and Jelly Roll Morton and cornettists Buddy Bolden, King Oliver, and Papa Celestin. Ben Harney can probably claim the distinction of being the first published jazz pedagogue. His *Ragtime Instructor* appeared in New York in 1897. Ragtime was prominent to about 1910, shared the limelight with the blues for a few years, and disappeared around 1920.

Blues (c.1900– .) refers to a style of music, a type of performance, a musical form, and a despondent state of mind. All these meanings have their origin in the vocal tradition of black work songs and spirituals. This vocal tradition has given it a character different from the instrumental style of ragtime. Formally its chief feature is a repeated chaconnelike harmonic structure of 12 bars duration in 4/4 time. This period is divided equally into three four-bar phrases, the first of tonic harmony, the second of subdominant and tonic harmony, and the last of dominant and tonic harmony. Ex. 1 presents the simple and two slightly embellished schemata.

The early blues had two traditions, urban and rural. The country blues frequently had different period lengths (from 8 to 16 bars), but the city blues used a standardized 12-bar form. Vocal blues most often overlaid an A-B-B′ harmonic structure with an a-a-b text and melody: $A\overset{a}{|}B\overset{a}{|}B'\overset{b}{}$ (see also Ex. 2). The two-

	1	2	3	4	5	6	7	8	9	10	11	12
Singer	a ——— rest				a ——— rest				b ——— rest			
Instruments	back ——— break ———				back ——— break ———				back ——— break ———			
Harmony	A				B				C			
	I ———————				IV ——♭——I———				V ——————I———			

Ex. 2.

line verse, rhymed or unrhymed, was often, but not always, in iambic pentameter. The first line (with repeat) functioned as an antecedent phrase and the second line as a consequent phrase.

Blues harmony was normally neither major nor minor, for the characteristic blues sound resulted from the simultaneous use of major and minor tonalities and nontempered scale intervals. The blues scale in the key of C (Ex. 3) often admitted A♭ as well as the

Ex. 3. Blues scale

indicated E♭ and B♭. These are the minor thirds of the major I, IV, and V harmonies. Although any chromatic note could be admitted, the flatted fifth, G♭, was also commonly stressed. All these notes were unstable in performance with regard to both intonation and function, and this quality was one of the leading features of the blues. Also, since blues stems from a vocal, rather than an instrumental tradition, portamentos, fall-offs, nonstandard vibratos, and nontempered tuning were also part of the melodic style.

Rhythmically blues again offered an interesting contrast to ragtime. Whereas the regular rhythmic line of ragtime, the standard against which a melody might syncopate, was an alternation of strong and light pulses, the regular rhythmic line of blues was a steady stream of strong pulses. Whereas the ragtime performer syncopated by hitting or accenting between beats or on less strong beats, the blues performer often syncopated by missing, not by hitting, a particular point in time. This improvisatory rhythmic style allowed great flexibility. The performer might start a melody at some interval after the harmonic framework had begun and then crowd in the words and music; or he might insert words or melismas into the melodic line at a whim, so that irregular note groups of five or seven might overlay two or three beats without any of the notes being coincident with a beat (Ex. 4).

The principal blues instrument was the voice, accompanied in the early days by guitar or piano. In instrumental ensembles, melody instruments other than the voice (trumpet, cornet, clarinet, trombone, saxophone, etc.) often developed a blues performance style that was an imitation or extension of the voice. "Bent" pitches, a variety of consonantal attacks and releases, and a cultivation of individual timbres or tone qualities were all part of the blues melodic style.

The nature of the blues framework, a short chaconne structure, made the blues admirably suited for the support of solo improvisation in either free melodic invention or theme and variation styles. The early improvisers seemed more concerned with the ornamentation of old melodies than with the creation of new ones. The usual place for a "flight of fancy" was the "break": a brief (usually two-bar) improvised instrumental cadenza could begin at the end of one chorus as the introduction to the next or as a "fill" between the three phrases of a melody (see Ex. 2). The *Memphis Blues* (written 1909, published 1912) and the *St. Louis Blues* (1914), both by W. C. Handy, were the first published blues to gain wide prominence. The earliest known, according to Jelly Roll Morton, was the anonymous *Mamie's Blues* of about 1900. Most early blues singers improvised their music during performances; the leading figures of the early period were Ma Rainey, Bessie Smith, Huddie Leadbelly Ledbetter, and Blind Lemon Jefferson.

Dixieland (c.1912– .) is an instrumental musical style that borrowed elements of ragtime and blues and added its own distinctive characteristics of group improvisation, continuo rhythm-section playing for the backing of solos, and a semistandard orchestration that defined the musical function of the several instruments involved. The Dixieland (also called New Orleans style or classic style) ensemble consisted of two sections, one primarily responsible for rhythm and harmony and the other for melodic improvisation. The normal instrumentation called for three melody instruments and two or three rhythm instruments. The ordinary basic three of the "front line," or melody section, were trumpet or

I'm gon-na find my — — self an - oth - er — man —

Ex. 4. Bessie Smith, "Cold in Hand Blues"
Quoted from Gunther Schuller's *Early Jazz* (New York 1968) by permission of Oxford University Press

cornet, clarinet, and slide trombone. The "back row," or rhythm-section, usually consisted of piano and/or banjo, trap drums, and sousaphone, tuba, or double bass played pizzicato. By 1920 a fourth member, the saxophone, had been added to the front line.

Group improvisation was facilitated by the tacit understanding among the musicians that they each had a specific musical role to perform as determined by their instrument. The trumpet played "lead," and his duty was to "rag" the melody, i.e., to play it in a syncopated but only slightly ornamented fashion. The clarinet was expected to create a fast moving, ornate, high obbligato. At times, and usually by agreement, the clarinet would play a part that paralleled the trumpet's melody in thirds and sixths. The trombone customarily played in a manner that has come to be described as "tailgate trombone" playing. In this it played a counter-melody to the trumpet, elaborating on a melodic line derived from the harmonic structure of the piece (the roots and fifths of the triads used). The part was thus both harmonic and melodic. It also had a rhythmic function of accenting the first and third beats of the 4/4 bar. This part was usually liberally salted with glissandos. The tenor saxophone played a "fill" role, adding missing triadic notes to provide sonority and volume; it was a nondescript counterpoint to either the trumpet or trombone part, and usually remained somewhat unobtrusive. If a combo had to be reduced in size, this part was the least vital and the first to go.

In the rhythm section, the piano was used like a ragtime piano with the right-hand syncopated melody omitted. Except during a piano solo, at which time the Dixieland piano could be distinguished from a ragtime piano, the Dixieland piano reinforced the harmonic structure by playing triads on the off beats with the right hand. A banjo often substituted for, or was used in addition to, the piano. The bass, whether brass or string, played brass-band or marching-band fashion as described under ragtime. The drummer reinforced the two-beat ragtime rhythm by playing the bass drum with a foot pedal on beats 1 and 3 and the snare and suspended cymbal on beats 2 and 4, thus creating the "boom-chuck" rhythm of ragtime and Dixieland. The hands of the drummer were free to use sticks or wire brushes on a variety of percussion instruments (snare drum, tom-tom, cowbell, wood block, suspended cymbals, etc.) in a free and ornamental manner.

The Dixieland band's repertory was heterogeneous, for anything could be molded into their style by the improvising musicians. Still, many numbers are specifically associated with Dixieland and are characteristic of the style: "Didn't He Ramble?", "When the Saints Go Marching In," "Muskat Ramble," "Dipper Mouth Blues," and "Willie the Weeper." Leading performers in the style were trumpeters Bunk Johnson, King Oliver, and Louis Armstrong; trombonists Kid Ory and Jack Teagarden; clarinetists Johnny Dodds and Jimmy Noone; soprano saxophonist Sidney Bechet; pianists Jelly Roll Morton, Lil Hardin Armstrong, and Earl Hines; banjo players Bud Scott and John St. Cyr; bassists Bill Johnson and Pops Foster; and drummers Baby Dodds and Zutty Singleton.

THE 1920S. During the 20s most of the leading figures of the earlier years were still alive and performing. Early in the decade, the most significant musical feature was the expansion of the role of the soloist. In the later years, the "big band," an ensemble composed of sections rather than individual instruments, began to develop. The jazz arranger and, with Duke Ellington, the jazz composer emerged. Whereas the Dixieland band had two sections, rhythm and melody instruments, the new bands had from three to five. Rhythm, brass, and reeds were basic; violins might be used; and the brass might be divided into trumpet and trombone sections. Although the repertory was not essentially different from that of the preceding years, the interpretation was different because the arrangers used the sections in new ways and redefined the role of the soloist.

The bands consisted of 10 to 20 players. A rhythm section of piano, bass, and trap drums was common to all groups. Guitar and banjo might be added, but they no longer could substitute for the piano. The saxophone section contained three to six members, and soprano, alto, tenor and baritone saxophones and clarinet all came into use as part of the saxophone choir. The most common function of this group was to back the remainder of the band with sustained chords, which were frequently played in similar motion and identical rhythm. At first the brass section had two trumpets and one trombone; this was later expanded to three or more trumpets (and in the 30s, three or more trombones), which could be used in a manner similar to that of the sax section. The soli concept emerged. Melodies were now played by an entire section either in unison or with a thickened line (chords moving in close position with the melody in the highest voice). Solos were still performed, but now they occurred in the

Ex. 5. Swing-band rhythm

middle of pieces, had length limits controlled by the arranger, and were often backed with riffs (repeated short melodic phrases) or section chords. Group improvisation was eliminated, and an enriched harmony (with four- and five-note chords rather than triads) and sectional antiphony were added.

Different bands each developed a distinctive sound. Fletcher Henderson, with arranger Don Redman, designed the most common big-band orchestration. Paul Whiteman created the "symphonic jazz" sound by using violins and classically schooled arrangers and composers. Duke Ellington, the first big-band jazz composer, also developed a distinctive sonority. Other methods of performance appeared (boogie-woogie piano playing, mutes used throughout the brass section); new dances came in and went out of fashion (Charleston, Black Bottom); other features too numerous to mention here also played a part in shaping 1920s jazz. The most influential leaders were those named above plus Bix Beiderbecke, who expanded the New Orleans tradition into Chicago style jazz, and Bennie Moton, who started the riffing Kansas City style jazz. Guy Lombardo, who crystallized the "sweet" commercial sound, is sometimes listed among jazz bands by writers on jazz but is never so categorized by other jazz musicians.

THE 1930S. Swing, Kansas City style, and Duke Ellington's orchestra style were the three most important trends of the 30s. The swing bands used the orchestration concepts developed by Fletcher Henderson and Don Redman in the 20s. They intensified the rhythmic pulse to a merged 4/4 and 2/4 by having the dummer "drive" the bass drum on every beat and "ride" a cymbal with a stick (Ex. 5). The thickened line, sax-section-soli melody accompanied by syncopated, staccato brass chords became the characteristic sound of swing (Ex. 6). It too was an outgrowth of functional instrumentation: melodic lines were for reeds; chords reinforcing the rhythm were for brass, except in solos. One important new instrument, the vibraphone, was added to rhythm sections. Swing bands highlighted precision, orchestration, and ensemble identity and minimized solo improvisation and individuality. Except in the cases of certain band leaders (those who could perform solo and whose musical identity in many ways became synonymous with that of the organization), solos in swing arrangements were often less than one chorus in length, sometimes only four or eight bars long. Within the section, specialization took place. The first trumpet played "lead," the high notes, and the tutti melodies. The second trumpet played solos; he was the improvising "jazzer." The third and fourth trumpets were "section men," often younger and less experienced players. Virtuosity began to be cultivated for its own

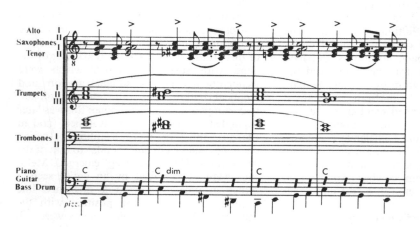

Ex. 6. Typical Benny Goodman orchestration

Ex. 7. Typical Duke Ellington orchestration

sake, and the leaders, Benny Goodman (clarinet), Jimmy Dorsey (alto saxophone), and Gene Krupa (drums), set new standards of technical proficiency. Other leading swing orchestras were those of Glenn Miller, Tommy Dorsey, and Artie Shaw.

Duke Ellington, a talented pianist and composer, used the swing band concept of orchestrated music, sectional sound, enriched harmonies, and thickened lines (Ex. 7). He also added one more dimension by capitalizing on the individual talents of the men in his orchestra, thereby bringing back to the big bands that element of individuality that had been minimized by the swing bands.

Kansas City style refers to the music of the bands of Bennie Moton and Count Basie. Primarily playing a blues repertory, they brought to the big band a new method of group improvisation by utilizing riffs, unison and harmonized, and percussive, syncopated brass chords (Ex. 8). Because the blues pattern is simple, sectional harmonization by ear in four or five parts was not difficult. Riffing became a follow-the-leader technique, and different members of the group could be featured as

Ex. 8. Typical Count Basie orchestration

improvising soloists. Sometimes no written arrangement was used, and often the notated arrangement merely consisted of a sketch for an introduction and a coda. Riffs and chording provided the orchestration, and improvisation provided the melody.

THE 1940s. Be-bop, the new jazz of the war years, was primarily a small combo manifestation. Although a few big bands played bop, the standard combination was a quartet or quintet of rhythm section and one or two solo instruments. Scat singing (vocalizing an instrumental line with nonsense syllables) was one of the features of this instrumental style (Ex. 9). Although blues remained the most

sha- baa- ba — doo-bee   ba – doo-bee-doo- nn — day

Ex. 9. Scat singing

common chaconne pattern in the be-bop repertory, complex chord sequences (ones that modulated frequently, were tonally ambiguous, used chromatic alterations, and involved 9ths, 11ths, 13ths and added tones) were favored as schemata for melodic improvisation. Complexity and virtuosity were a real part of this mannered style, and after-hours "jam" sessions tested the mettle of the participants. Chromatic melodies with asymmetrical phrases and elided cadences were often matched with impossibly fast tempos. Charlie Parker, alto saxophonist, dominated the movement both as musical and spiritual leader. Trumpeter Dizzy Gillespie and drummers Kenny Clarke and Max Roach were also important in the establishment of this substyle.

An important change in drumming technique occurred at this time. The bass drum was relieved of its old function of maintaining the beat in either two-beat Dixieland fashion (playing on beats 1 and 3) or in four-beat swing style (playing on every beat) and was given a highlighting role instead. In combination with the sticks, the bass drum would now be heard only in "fills," "bombs," and syncopated melodic underscoring. The same change occurred in be-bop piano technique. Accompanying no longer meant regular, on-the-beat chording but syncopated, irregular "comping." This left only the pizzicato string bass and the ride and sock cymbals maintaining the metrical structure. A new degree of concentration and perception

was required of the audience. A be-bop performance of a single work usually followed an exposition-improvisation-recapitulation pattern.

THE 1950s. Although a proliferation of substyles occurred during the 50s, the differences were more of degree than kind. Substantive stylistic change was less apparent than subtly shaded lines of demarcation. Two events gave birth to a new sound. "Cool" jazz originated with a Stan Getz tenor saxophone solo in *Early Autumn* and a Miles Davis record album *Birth of the Cool*. The timbre changed from a loud, biting sonority rich in overtones to a soft, breathy, flutelike sound. Vibratos changed from fast and wide to slow and narrow, sometimes disappearing altogether. In terms of harmony, melody, and rhythm, however, cool jazz was be-bop in a different timbral wrapping. Important figures, besides Getz and Davis, were Lee Konitz (alto saxophone), Dave Pell (tenor saxophone), Gerry Mulligan (baritone saxophone), Shorty Rogers (trumpet), John Lewis and Lennie Tristano (both piano).

"Hard-bop," or "funky-jazz," was be-bop with a new name. New stars, such as Horace Silver (piano) and Al Kohn (tenor saxophone), appeared, but new music did not. Dixieland had a revival, and Louis Armstrong again became prominent. The swing bands of Goodman and Dorsey continued to be popular. The big band tradition continued with Woody Herman and Stan Kenton. Not until the next decade did a new substyle appear.

THE 1960s. The novelty of the 60s was "free jazz," a music that has been claimed as a mode of expression for the black nationalism of the American Negro. It is a musical type that professes no stylistic norms. Chance, surprise, and unrelated individual utterances by instruments, standard or otherwise, are a part of the sound. Some unity is achieved through the use of quasiritornello techniques, tertian vertical structures (regardless of the expressed opinion of some adherents who claim they are playing atonally), semistandard instrumental combinations (reeds, brass, and rhythm sections), and repeated motivic ideas that emanate partly from the learned playing technique associated with each instrument. The new sound is achieved by breaking the rules, sometimes playing out-of-tune and as fast as possible, and maintaining no beat or pulse. Ornette Coleman (alto saxophone) and John Coltrane (tenor saxophone) were the two pioneers. Archie Shepp, Joseph Jarman, and a few others followed in their path.

Two new elements were introduced into the

jazz of the 60s, but their influence has been minimal thus far. The influence of Asian music, with its different scales and tunings, nonharmonic framework, and non-Western instruments and philosophy, has led to "raga jazz" or "raga rock." New electronic devices to create and alter sound have been used by both soloists and bands to augment or change the standard instrumentation.

INFLUENCES OF JAZZ ON CONCERT MUSIC. Few, if any, branches of 20th-century Western concert music can claim total insulation from the influence of jazz. Claude Debussy was formerly considered the first legitimate composer to embrace the new idiom. He did so as early as 1908 when he composed "Golliwog's Cakewalk" (*Children's Corner Suite*, 1906–08) for his daughter. The researches of John Kirkpatrick have disclosed, however, that Charles Ives composed a ragtime dance and thirteen ragtime pieces for theater orchestra between 1902 and 1904.

Maurice Ravel's *Violin Sonata* (1923–27) has a "Blues" movement, and in his *Piano Concerto* for the left hand (1930–31) jazz timbres, phrases, and rhythms abound. Neither is a jazz work; rather, they are, as are most of the works in this list, jazz influenced. Other Frenchmen to incorporate aspects of the idiom into their music were Darius Milhaud (*Le Boeuf sur le toit*, 1920, and the black ballet, *La Création du monde*, 1923) and Arthur Honegger (*Concertino* for piano and orchestra, 1924). The most obvious jazz features in these works are the syncopated jazz rhythms, but Milhaud's *Création* contains much more. The instrumentation, the blues harmonic progressions, and the ragtime tunes indicate a desire to genuinely merge jazz elements with the composer's own personal style. Erik Satie, too, composed a ballet, *Parade*, for Diaghilev in 1917 that contains the dance "Rag-Time du paquebot." Igor Stravinsky followed close on Satie's heels in 1918 with *L'Histoire du soldat* (one movement is entitled "Ragtime") and *Ragtime for 11 Instruments* and in 1919, *Piano Rag Music*.

In 1945 Stravinsky composed the *Ebony Concerto* for Woody Herman and his band. This work is interesting as an illustration of the real separation that can occur between concert music and jazz. Played by a jazz band and featuring a jazz clarinetist, the *Ebony Concerto* displays jazz elements but never "swings," largely because the neoclassic Stravinsky, using his peculiar brand of nonfunctional harmony, kept the music from driving toward cadential goals. It has the appearance but not the substance of jazz. In contrast Aaron Copland's *Concerto for Clarinet and String Orchestra* (1948), a work commissioned and first performed by the swing clarinetist Benny Goodman, speaks with authenticity to the jazz musician even though Copland's interest was not to write a jazz concerto. The composer's extensive experience with North and South American popular music and his long-standing interest in jazz (his *Concerto* for piano and orchestra of 1926 uses jazz mutes on the slide trombone and Dixieland rhythms throughout) must have been subconsciously present as he applied his conservatory training and creative gifts to the composition of this work. The melodic lines are at once classical and jazz. The syncopations arise out of the demands of the music and seem not to be imposed arbitrarily by the composer. A free-flowing, improvisatory character dominates the solo line throughout. Even without brass, saxophones, and rhythm section, this piece has the rhythmic and harmonic drive, the melodic grace, and the discreet dissonance of a genuine jazz work.

Jazz rhythms and harmonic treatment are to be found in Paul Hindemith's compositions of 1921–22, *Kammermusik No. 1* and *Suite for Piano* (movements "Ragtime" and "Shimmy"). Ernst Krenek wrote two "jazz" operas, *Der Sprung über den Schatten* (1924) and *Jonny spielt auf* (1925–26). The first opens with a foxtrot, has ragtime rhythms, and a number marked "Einleitung und Jazz." It is much more German expressionist than it is jazz. *Jonny*, whose hero is a Negro jazz fiddler, has numbers entitled "Shimmy," "Blues," "Spiritual," and calls for jazz instruments in the orchestra and on the stage; the jazz influence is much stronger in this work. Kurt Weill's *Mahagonny* (1927–29) and *Dreigroschenoper* (1927) are works with jazz characteristics. Three lesser composers of the period wrote serious jazz works that are of historical, if not musical interest today: John Alden Carpenter, *Concertino* for piano and orchestra (1915), *Krazy Kat* (ballet, 1922), and *Skyscrapers* (ballet, 1926); Louis Gruenberg, *The Daniel Jazz* (1924); and Constant Lambert, *Rio Grande* (1928).

During this period, some of the jazz musicians tried writing in the larger traditional forms. The most important were the three works of George Gershwin: *Rhapsody in Blue* (1924), *Concerto in F* (1925), and *Porgy and Bess* (1934–35).

Jazz also changed the nature of the American musical comedy. The earlier works (e.g., Victor Herbert, *Babes in Toyland*, 1903) were in Viennese operetta style, but Cole Porter,

Irving Berlin, Gershwin, Richard Rodgers, and many others used jazz and Tin Pan Alley ideas to mutate the operetta into the musical, a distinct genre.

Of the Viennese serialists, Alban Berg had the most profound interest in jazz. Anton Webern and his followers (e.g., Pierre Boulez) have incorporated some jazz instruments into their music (saxophone, vibraphone, muted brass), but that is all, and these could have come to their attention by some other route. Berg, however, in his opera *Lulu* (1929–35) used a jazz band on the stage to play two ragtime numbers and an English waltz. The music is Berg, not jazz, but the feeling is jazz, not concert.

Although a slowing down of jazz influence on concert music took place between late Gershwin (*Jazz Piano Preludes*, 1936) and the end of World War II, American concert composers of the 30s and 40s (Aaron Copland, Roy Harris, William Schuman, Virgil Thomson, and Walter Piston) kept one ear to their native music. Since World War II, cross-currents have been plentiful. Serious attempts at 12-tone jazz have been made by Robert Graettinger (*City of Glass*, 1948), Rolf Liebermann (*Concerto* for jazz band and orchestra, 1954), and Milton Babbitt (*All Set*, 1957). The *Symphony No. 9* (1956–57) of Ralph Vaughan Williams includes a "sax section" in the orchestration. There have also been jazz settings of the liturgy (Frank Tirro, *American Jazz Mass*, 1960) and jazz bands in church (Duke Ellington, *Sacred Concert*, 1961–). Jazz composers are writing in the larger traditional forms (Bill Russo, *3 Pieces for Blues Band and Symphony Orchestra*, 1968) and are joining the circle of the avant-garde (David Reck, *Blues and Screamer*, 1967). Two U.S. composers have successfully straddled the fence between "legitimate" music and jazz, Leonard Bernstein and Gunther Schuller; Schuller's third-stream music (*Transformation*, 1957) has become the symbol of the cross-fertilization of jazz and concert music, and the idea has reached as far as Eastern Europe in third-stream works of Pavel Blatný and others. Many techniques of vocal and instrumental production have been further expanded in recent years under the influence of jazz; an example is Karlheinz Stockhausen's *Momente* (1962–64), which calls for scat singing. Perhaps most important of all at the present time are uses of the group-improvisation principle by the various avant-garde performance groups. All such groups acknowledge the impetus they have received not only from jazz techniques but from the jazz concepts

of music as performance (rather than notated composition) and of performance as spontaneous (but disciplined) personal expression.

BIBL: ★ General: William Austin, *Music in the 20th Century* (New York 1966); Avril Dankworth, *Jazz: An Introduction to its Musical Basis* (New York 1968); H. Wiley Hitchcock, *Music in the United States* (Englewood Cliffs, N. J., 1969); Gunther Schuller, *Early Jazz: Its Roots and Musical Development* (New York 1968); James A. Standifer and Barbara Reeder, *Source Book of African and Afro-American Materials for Music Educators* (Washington 1972); Marshall Stearns, *The Story of Jazz* (New York 1964). ★ Special topics: Rudi Blesh, *Shining Trumpets* [Chicago style, Kansas City style, Ellington, swing] (New York 1958); —— and Harriet Janis, *They All Played Ragtime* (New York 1959); Leonard Feather, *Inside Be-bop* (New York 1949); Charles Keil, *Urban Blues* (Chicago 1966); Alan P. Merriam and Fradley H. Garner, "Jazz—The Word," *Ethnomusicology* 12:373–96.

Frank Tirro

SEE ALSO Folk Resources; Indeterminacy; Instrumental and Vocal Resources; Liturgical Music: Christian; Liturgical Music: Jewish; Musical; Orchestration; Performance; Popular Music; Rhythm; United States.

Jemnitz, Sándor (b. Budapest, 9 August 1890; d. Balatonföldvár, Hungary, 8 August 1963), studied at the Budapest Academy of Music with János Koessler; in Leipzig with Max Reger, Karl Straube, and Hans Sitt; and in Berlin (1921–24) with Schoenberg. During 1917–21 he was associated with several German opera companies. During 1924–44 he was music critic for the Budapest newspaper *Népszava*, and in 1945 he became a professor at the Béla Bartók Conservatory in Budapest.

PRINCIPAL COMPOSITIONS: *Violin Sonatas Nos. 1–3* (1921, 1923, 1925; Kistner); *Trumpet Quartet* (1925); *String Trios Nos. 1–2* (1925, Kistner; 1929, UE); *Duet Sonata* for viola, cello (1927, Schott); *Concerto for Chamber Orchestra* (1931); *Duet Sonata* for saxophone, banjo (1934); *Suites Nos. 1–2* for violin, piano (1952, 1953; EMB); *Concerto for String Orchestra* (1954). ★ 17 sonatas for solo instruments: for piano (1914, Wunderhorn; 1927, UE; 1929, UE; 1933, Rózsavölgyi; 1954, EMB); for violin (1922, Wunderhorn; 1932, Rózsavölgyi and NME; 1938, Rózsavölgyi); for cello (1933, Rózsavölgyi); for harp (1933); for double bass (1935); for trumpet (1938, Rózsavölgyi); for organ pedals (1941); for flute (1941); for viola (1941, Rózsavölgyi); for organ (1959, EMB; 1959).

PRINCIPAL WRITINGS: *Bachtól Bartókig* [From Bach to Bartók] (Budapest 1937); *Schumann élete leveleiben* [Schumann's Life in His Letters] (Budapest 1958); *Mendelssohn* (Budapest 1958); *Chopin* (Budapest 1960); *Mozart* (Budapest 1961).

SEE ALSO Hungary.

Jeney, Zoltán (b. Szolnok, Hungary, 4 March 1943), studied at the Liszt Academy in Budapest (1961–66, composition with Ferenc Farkas), and the Accàdemia di S. Cecilia in Rome (1967–69, composition with Goffredo Petrassi). Since 1969 he has been working under a grant from the Art Foundation of the Hungarian People's Republic. His musical thinking has been influenced by the works and writings of Pierre Boulex and Karlheinz Stockhausen, the theories of Paul Klee, and the poems and essays of the Hungarian poet Sándor Weöres.

PRINCIPAL COMPOSITIONS: *3 Songs on Poems of Apollinaire* for soprano, piano (1962); *5 Piano Pieces* (1962, EMB); *5 Songs on Poems of A. Jozsef* for soprano, clarinet, cello, harp (1963); *Igy jöttem* [Thus I Came], film score (1964); *Az áramlás szobra* [Stream Sculpture] for vocal quintet; text by Sándor Weöres (1965); *Omaggio* for soprano, orchestra; text by L. Szabó (1966); *Aritmie – Ritmiche* for flute, viola, cello (1967); *Soliloquium No. 1* for flute (1967, EMB and Boosey); *Wei wu wei* [Unintended Influence] for flute, clarinet, viola, cello, double bass, harp, piano, celesta, percussion (1968); *Capriccio*, film score (1969).

PRINCIPAL WRITINGS: *L'analisi della microstruttura del "Jeux" di Debussy* (1967, unpub.); "Soliloquium No. 1," program book of the Gaudeamus Festival (Bilthoven 1968); *Nyitászárási kombinációk és a trillabillentyük lehetséges kombinációi a Böhm-rendszerü fuvolán* [The Possible Combinations of Stops and Trill Stops on the Böhm Flute] (1970, unpub.).

BIBL.: Attila Bozay, *On Z. J.* (unpub.); László Somfai, "Young Hungarian Composers—Notes on the Works Introduced," *Magyar Zene* 1968/2:165–74.

Jeppesen, Knud (b. Copenhagen, 15 Aug 1892), studied at the Univ. of Copenhagen (musicology with Angul Hammerich) and also in Copenhagen with Carl Nielsen (composition and counterpoint) and Thomas Laub (musicology). He was a composer for the Elbing and Liegnitz state theaters in Germany (1912–14). He later attended the Univ. of Vienna (musicology with Gudo Adler, PhD in 1922). Jeppesen was organist at St. Stefan's church, Copenhagen (1917–31). He began teaching at the Royal Danish Conservatory in 1920 and was one of its directors (1932–47). He taught at the Univ. of Aarhus and directed its musical institute (1946–57). He edited *Acta musicologica* (1931–53) and was president of the International Musicological Society (1949–52).

PRINCIPAL COMPOSITIONS (published by Hansen-W unless otherwise noted): *Sjaellandsfar Symphony* (1938–39, unpub.); *Lave og Jon* for men's chorus, orchestra (1938); *Horn Concerto* (1942, unpub.); *Te Deum danicum* for soloists, chorus, orchestra (1946); *Rosaura*, 3-act opera (premiere 1950); *Aaret i Danmark*, 20 Danish songs for voice, piano (1953); *Prelude and Fugue in E* for organ (1953, Nordiska); *50 Koralforspil* for organ (1957); *Intonazione boreale* for organ (1958); *Domine, refugium factum es* for soprano, flute, violin (1959); *Passacaglia* for organ (1965); *Tvesang* for soloists, choir, orchestra (1965). List to 1956: *Natalicia musicologica K. J. septuagenario* (Copenhagen 1962):309–18.

PRINCIPAL WRITINGS: *The Style of Palestrina and the Dissonance* (London 1927); *Counterpoint* (New York 1939).

Joachim, Otto (b. Düsseldorf, 13 Oct 1910), studied at the Rhein Music School in Cologne (1928–31, violin with Hermann Zitzmann). During 1934–39 he lived and concertized in Malaya and China. In 1949 he moved to Canada, where he became a violinist in the Montreal Symphony and the Montreal String Quartet. In 1957 he was cofounder of the Société de Musique de Notre Temps, and in 1959 he became director of the Montreal Consort of Ancient Instruments, for which he has constructed a number of renaissance instruments. He has taught violin, viola, and chamber music at McGill Univ. (1956–64) and the Conservatory of Quebec Province (since 1956). In 1960 he established his own electronic music studio in Montreal using homemade equipment.

PRINCIPAL COMPOSITIONS: *Asia*, symphonic poem (1928–39); *3 Bagatelles* for piano (1939); *Music for violin, viola* (1953); *Cello Sonata* (1954, BMIC); *L'Eclosion* for piano (1954, BMIC); *March* for voice, piano; text by Ian Clark (1954); *Concertante No. 1* for violin, string orchestra, percussion (1955); *String Quartet* (1956, BMIC and AMP); *12 12-Tone Pieces* for children (1959, BMIC); *Nonet* for winds, strings, piano (1959–60); *Psalm* for chorus (1960, BMIC); *Saxophone Quartet*, "Interlude" (1960); *Fantasia* for organ (1961); *Concertante No. 2* for string quartet, string orchestra (1961–62); *Expansion* for flute, piano (1962, BMIC); *Divertimento* for wind quintet (1962); *Music for 4 Viols* (1962); *Dialogue* for viola, piano (1963); *Illumination I* for narrator, flutes, guitar, piano, 2 percussionists, light control; original text by Alfred Purdy (1965, BMIC); *Katimavik* on tape (1966–67); *Contrastes* for orchestra (1966–67, Ricordi); *Illumination II* for winds, 4 strings, piano, percussion, electronically manipulated lecture on Fourier theory, light control (1968–69); *Kinderspiel* for narrator, violin, cello, piano (1969–70). List to 1964: *Composers of the Americas* 10:37–39.

SEE ALSO Canada.

Johannsson, Bengt (Viktor) (b. Helsinki, 2 Oct 1914), studied at the Sibelius Academy in Helsinki (intermittently 1932–46; composition with Sulho Ranta, Selim Palmgren, Leo Funtek; cello with Yrjö Selin). Since 1952 he has been music supervisor of the Finnish Radio; he has also worked at the radio's electronic music studio. He has lectured on music history at the Sibelius Academy since 1965. He made his conducting debut in 1952. His orchestral, concerted, and chamber music of the 1940s and 50s was influenced by neoclassicism, particularly that of Sibelius and Stravinsky. Since 1965 he has been particularly interested in vocal music and in new choral techniques, including the use of speech.

PRINCIPAL COMPOSITIONS: *Missa sacra* for tenor, chorus, orchestra (1960, Westerlund); *3 Electronic Etudes* on tape (1960); *The Tomb of Akr Çaar* for baritone, chorus; text by Ezra Pound (1964, Fazer); *Triptych* for soprano, baritone, chorus (1965); *Requiem* for baritone, 2 choruses, 2 string orchestras, brass ensemble, timpani (1966); *3 Classic Madrigals* for chorus (1967, Fazer); *Cantata humana* for baritone, chorus, orchestra; text by Dag Hammerskjøld (1969); *3 Chansons* for baritone, piano (1969, Fazer).

BIBL.: Denby Richards, *The Music of Finland* (London 1968): 35–36.

Johannsson, Magnus Blöndal (b. Sólbakki, Iceland, 8 Sept 1925), studied at the Reykjavík Conservatory (1935–39, 1942–45) and the Juilliard School (1948–53). Since 1955 he has worked for the music department of the Iceland State Broadcasting Service. He conducted operas and musicals for the National Theater during 1964–70 and still does so for Iceland Television. His *Study* for sine tones and wind quintet (1957) was the first electronic work composed in Iceland.

PRINCIPAL COMPOSITIONS: *Duo Sonata* for oboe, clarinet (1954); *Cantata* for 2 voices, narrator, trumpet, piano (1954); *Study* for sine tones, wind quintet (1957); *Samstirni* on tape (1960); *Punktar* for orchestra, tape (1961); *15 Minigrams* for woodwind quintet (1961); *Dimensions* for violin (1963); *Sonorities* for piano (1963); *Frostrósir* [Frost Crystals], ballet for dancers, lights, tape, chamber orchestra (1968). Johannsson's film music includes three electronic scores for the documentaries *Eldar í öskju* [Askja on Fire] (1961); *Surtur fer sunnan* [Birth of an Island] (1964); *Með svigalaevi* [Sequel to Surtsey] (1965).

BIBL.: Aurelio De la Vega, "Regarding Electronic Music," *Tempo* (winter 1965–66): 4–5.

Johnson, David (Carl) (b. Batavia, N. Y., 30 Jan 1940), studied in the preparatory depart-ment of the Eastman School (1947–57), at Antioch College (1957–62; theory, composition), and Harvard Univ. (1962–64; composition with Leon Kirchner, Billy Jim Layton). He also studied composition with Nadia Boulanger in Paris (1964–65) and electronic music with Karlheinz Stockhausen and others in Cologne (1965–70). During 1966–67 he was an assistant at the WDR Electronic Music Studio in Cologne, and he taught electronic music at the Rheinische Musikschule in 1968 and worked for the German Pavilion at the World's Fair in Osaka in 1970. As of 1970 he was "no longer composing in the traditional sense. I am working toward the cyberneticization of music generation, soldering, and studying electronics."

PRINCIPAL COMPOSITIONS: *Recitativo, Aria, Chorale* for flute (1965–66); *3 Pieces* for string quartet (1965–66); *Piano Piece 1A* (1966); *Telefun* on tape (1968); *Ton-Audition* on tape (1968); *Music Makers*, live electronic improvisation (1969).

Johnson, Hunter (b. Benson, N. C., 14 April 1906), studied at the Univ. of N. C. (1924–26) and at the Eastman School (1927–29; composition with Bernard Rogers, piano with Sandor Vas). He has taught at the Univ. of Mich. (1929–33), the Univ. of Manitoba (1944–47), Cornell Univ. (1948–53), Univ. of Ill. (1959–65), and the Univ. of Texas (since 1966).

PRINCIPAL COMPOSITIONS: *Symphony No. 1* (1932); *Piano Concerto* (1936); *Piano Sonata* (1936–48, Presser); *For an Unknown Soldier* for flute, string orchestra (1938, New Valley); *Letter to the World*, dance for Martha Graham (1940; *Suite* from the dance score, 1958, Galaxy); *Deaths and Entrances*, dance for Graham (1943); *Music for String Orchestra* (1948, Galaxy); *Trio* for flute, oboe, piano (1954, Galaxy); *North State* for orchestra (1963, Galaxy); *Past the Evening Sun* for orchestra (1964, Galaxy).

BIBL.: Joseph Bloch, "Some American Piano Sonatas," *Juilliard Review* (fall 1956).

SEE ALSO Dance.

Johnson, Robert Sherlaw (b. Sunderland, England, 21 May 1932), studied at the Univ. of Durham (1950–53), the Royal Academy of Music in London (1953–57, piano with Max Pirani), and in Paris during 1957–58 with Nadia Boulanger (composition) and Jacques Février (piano). He lectured in music at the Univ. of York during 1965–70. Since 1970 he has been university lecturer at the Univ. of Oxford and fellow of Worcester College. Messiaen, Stockhausen, Boulez and Varèse have influenced his musical thought. The early works (to the *Piano Sonata No. 1*, 1963) show an interest in serialism that crystallized in subsequent pieces up to the strictly organized *Improvisations* (1966–67); in the latter, the performers may assemble the material in different ways. The *Second Piano Sonata* (1967) is based on more freely organized "group" structures and combines sounds produced from the keyboard with sounds produced directly inside the piano. Further timbral extensions occur in *Praises of Heaven and Earth* (1969), where instruments are combined with a prerecorded tape.

PRINCIPAL COMPOSITIONS: *Piano Sonata No. 1* (1963, Oxford); *Night Songs* for soprano, piano (1964); *Liturgia redemptionis nostrae*, chamber cantata for soprano, 9 instruments (1965); *Veni sancte Spiritus* for chorus, percussion (1965, Faber); *Sedit angelus* for chorus (1965, Novello); *String Quartet No. 1* (1966); *Improvisations 1–3* for violin, piano (1966–67); *Piano Sonata No. 2* (1967, Oxford); *The Resurrection of Fêng-Huang* for chorus (1968, Oxford); *7 Short Pieces* for piano (1968, Oxford); *Trika* for piano, orchestra (1968); *String Quartet No. 2* (1969); *Praises of Heaven and Earth* for soprano, piano, tape (1969, Oxford).

PRINCIPAL WRITINGS: "Olivier Messiaen," *Church Music* (June 1969).

BIBL.: Peter Aston, "R. S. J.," *Musical Times* (March 1968).

Johnston, Ben(jamin) (b. Macon, Ga., 15 March 1926), studied at the Cincinnati Conservatory (1949–50, composition with Mary Leighton), the Univ. of Calif. at Berkeley (1950); Mills College (1951–52; composition, orchestration, analysis with Darius Milhaud; piano with Alexander Libermann), the Univ. of Ill. (1953–55, piano with Claire Richards), and the Columbia-Princeton Electronic Music Center (1959–60; theory and techniques of electronic music with Otto Luening, Vladimir Ussachevsky). He also studied piano with John Powell in Richmond, Va. (1940–43); microtonal theory and instruments with Harry Partch in Gualala, Calif. (1950–51); and composition with John Cage in New York (1959–60). During 1946–48 he was a dance-band pianist. Since 1951 he has taught composition, theory, and acoustics at the Univ. of Ill. School of Music and Division of Dance. His music of the mid and late 1960s made use of instruments tuned in just intonation and in microtones. Nonstandard tunings were sometimes combined with the techniques of serialism (*String Quartets Nos. 1 and 2* are examples). Indeterminacy entered into some works; an entire movement of *Sonata for 2* is improvised within set rules.

PRINCIPAL COMPOSITIONS: *3 Chinese Lyrics* for soprano, 2 violins; texts by Rihaku, trans. by Ezra Pound (1955); *Night* for baritone, women's chorus, chamber ensemble; text by Robinson Jeffers (1955); *Gertrude, or Would She Be Pleased to Receive It?*, dance-opera for alto, tenor, soprano, small chorus, chamber ensemble; text by Leach (1956); *Gambit for Dancers and Orchestra* (concert version titled *Ludes for 12 Instruments*) for chamber ensemble; choreography by Merce Cunningham (1959); *9 Variations* for string quartet (1959); *5 Fragments* for alto, oboe, cello, bassoon; texts by Thoreau (1960); *Sonata for 2* for violin, cello (1960); *Ivesberg Revisited* and *Newcastle Troppo* for jazz band (1960); *A Sea Dirge* for mezzo-soprano, flute, violin, oboe; text by Shakespeare (1962); *Knocking Piece* for 2 percussionists, piano (1962, CPE); *Duo* for flute, double bass (1963, McG-M); *String Quartet No. 2* (1964); *Sonata for Microtonal Piano* (1965); *String Quartet No. 3* (1966); *Lament* for flute, trumpet, trombone, viola, cello, double bass (1966); *Quintet for Groups* for orchestra (1966); *Ci-Gît Satie* for chorus, double bass, drums (1967); *One Man* for trombone, percussion (1967); *Museum Piece*, sound track for a Smithsonian Institution orientation film (1968–69); *Auto Mobile*, sound environment on tape for an automobile exhibit, Smithsonian Institution (1968–69); *2 Oboes and 2 Tablas and 2 Banyas*, using 142-tone just-intonation scale (1969–70).

PRINCIPAL WRITINGS: "Report from Urbana," *Perspectives* 2/1:137–41; "Scalar Order as a Compositional Resource," *Perspectives* 2/2:56–76; "Proportionality and Expanded Pitch Resources," *Perspectives* 5/1:112–20; "Three Attacks on a Problem," *Proceedings of the American Society of University Composers* (1967):89–98.

BIBL.: Barney Childs, "B. J.'s *Quintet for Groups*," *Perspectives* 7/1:110–21.

SEE ALSO Instrumental and Vocal Resources, Microtones, Musicology and Composition.

Jolas, Betsy (b. Paris, 5 August 1926), studied at Bennington College (1945–46; harmony with Paul Boepple, organ with Karl Weinrich, piano with Hélène Schnabel) and at the Paris Conservatory (1948–55; composition with Darius Milhaud, analysis with Olivier Messiaen, counterpoint with Simone Plé Caussade). During the mid-1940s she sang with and accompanied the Dessoff Choirs in New York. Since 1955 she has been editor of *Ecouter aujourd'hui,* the periodical of the French Radio-Television Network. She has also contributed to *Preuves* and other journals.

PRINCIPAL COMPOSITIONS (published by Heugel): *L'Oeil égaré*, radio cantata; text by Victor Hugo (1961, EFM); *Dans la Chaleur vacante*, radio cantata for soloists, chorus, chamber orchestra; text by Bouchet (1963, EFM); *Mots* for 5 vocal soloists, chamber ensemble; text by the composer (1963); *Quatuor II* for coloratura soprano, violin, viola, cello (1964); *Motet II* for chorus, winds, strings; text by Jacques Dupin (1965); *J.D.E.* for winds, strings (1966); *4 Plages* for string orchestra (1967); *D'un Opéra de voyage* for winds, strings, harp, 6 percussionists (1967); *Tranche* for harp (1967); *Points d'aube* for alto, 13 winds (1968); *états* for violin, 6 percussionists (1969); *Diurnes* for chorus of 12–72 voices (1970); *Sonate à 12* for 12 solo voices (1970); *Lassus ricercare* for 10 instruments (1970).

PRINCIPAL WRITINGS: "Il Fallait Voter Seriel même si . . . ," *Preuves* 178:40–42.

BIBL.: Martine Cadieu, "Entretien avec B. J.," *Lettres françaises* (21 Feb 1968):18; Marie-José Chauvin, "Entretien avec B. J.," *Courrier musical de France* 27:162–73; Maurice Flueret, "La Musique au féminin," *Nouvel observateur* (6 April 1966): 37; Genêt (Janet Flanner), "Letter from Paris," *New Yorker* (11 May 1968).

SEE ALSO France, Orchestration.

Jolivet, André (b. Paris, 8 August 1905), was attracted to painting and literature as well as music and studied harmony and counterpoint with Paul Le Flem (1927–32) while completing a degree in literature at the Univ. of Paris. During 1928–30 he studied composition with Edgard Varèse, becoming that composer's only composition pupil. In 1936 he founded the group Jeune France with Olivier Messiaen, Daniel-Lesur, and Yves Baudrier; their common esthetic was a "return to the humane, a discarding of all artificial quests." During 1943–59 he was conductor and later music director of the Comédie-Française. In succeeding years he toured widely as a conductor and lecturer. He has been a technical advisor for music at the French Ministry of Cultural Affairs (1959–62), president of the Concerts Lamoureux (1963–68), and professor of composition at the Paris Conservatory (1965–70).

Jolivet's oeuvre consists primarily of orchestral and chamber works, including five symphonies, twelve concertos, a string quartet, and seven large works for solo instruments. He has also written choral and solo vocal pieces and stage works. A concern with sonority led him to explore bass resonances. Structural coherence came to depend not on melodic themes but on underlying intervals (an augmented fifth in the *String Quartet,* 1934, for example, wrestles throughout the work with a perfect fifth); rhythmic groups came to have a similar function as a basic element in the musical framework. All of these tendencies have led to polytonal and nontonal pitch relations; however, Jolivet does not adhere strictly to any procedures, neither tonality nor any of the 20th-century systems. The immediate popular success of *Les 3 Complaintes du soldat* (1940) and *Guignol et Pandore* (1943) gave some observers the impression that Jolivet was returning to a more traditional means of expression, more tonal or at least modal. This did not happen. He shares Varèse's interest in timbre, and Jolivet's exploitation of unusual instrumental possibilities, within the context of traditional playing techniques, has made him a skillful orchestrator. His attitude toward melody is that it is not so much an element to be developed as an embodiment of the character and unity of a work. The structural significance accorded the placement of pitches and intervals in Oriental melody, to which Jolivet is very sensitive, can be found in his own melodic lines, many of which are quite long.

PRINCIPAL COMPOSITIONS: *String Quartet* (1934, Heugel); *Mana* for piano (1935, Costallat); *5 Incantations* for flute (1936, Boosey); *5 Danses rituelles* for orchestra (1939, Durand); *Les 3 Complaintes du soldat* for voice, orchestra (1940, Durand); *Suite liturgique* for high voice, oboe, cello, harp (1942, Durand); *Dolorès ou le miracle de la femme laide*, opéra bouffe (1942, Durand); *Suite delphique* for 12 instruments (1943, P-M); *Guignol et Pandore* for orchestra (1943, Eschig); *Pastorales de Noël* for flute, bassoon, harp (1943, Heugel); *Poèmes intimes* for voice with piano or chamber orchestra (1944, Heugel); *Chant de Linos* for flute, violin, viola, cello, harp (1944, Leduc); *Serenade* for wind quintet (1945, Costallat); *Piano Sonata No. 1* (1945, UE); *Ondes Martenot Concerto* (1947, Heugel); *Concertino* for trumpet, strings, piano (1948, Durand); *Concerto* for flute, strings (1949, Heugel); *Piano Concerto* (1950, Heugel); *Concerto* for harp, chamber orchestra (1952, Billaudot); *Epithalame* for 12-part "vocal orchestra" (1953, P-M); *Symphony No. 1* (1953, Heugel); *Concerto* for bassoon, strings, harp, piano (1954, Heugel); *Trumpet Concerto No. 2* (1954, Heugel); *Suite transocéane* for orchestra (1955, Heugel); *3 Interludes de la vérité de Jeanne* for orchestra (1956, Salabert); *Piano Sonata No. 2* (1957, Heugel); *Suite française* for orchestra (1957, P-M); *Rhapsodie à 7* (1957, P-M); *Percussion Concerto* (1958, Salabert); *Symphony No. 2* (1959, Heugel); *Symphony for strings* (1961, Boosey); *Cello Concerto No. 1* (1962, Boosey); *Madrigal* for chorus, strings (1963, Boosey); *Symphony No. 3* (1964, Boosey); *Le Coeur de la matière*, cantata (1965, Billaudot); *Suite rhapsodique* for violin (1965, Boosey); *Suite en concert* for cello (1965, Boosey); *Suite en concert* for flute, percussion (1965, Billaudot); *12 Inventions* for 12 instruments (1966, Billaudot); *Concerto* for cello, strings (1966, Billaudot); *Cérémonial en hommage à Varèse* for 6 percussionists (1968); *Mandala* for organ (1969, Billaudot); *Songe à nouveau rêvé* for soprano, orchestra; text by Antoine Goléa (1970, Leduc); *Heptade* for trumpet, percussion (1971, Billaudot). List to 1968 published by Billaudot.

PRINCIPAL WRITINGS: "Le 'Canon de mon esthétique'," *Contrepoints* (Jan 1946); "A Propos du *Concerto pour ondes et orchestre*," *Revue internationale de musique* 10 (1951); *Ludwig Van Beethoven* (Paris, 1955); review of *Influence des musiques de tradition orale* by Gérard Michel, *Bulletin of the International Folk Music Council* 33 (Oct 1968).

BIBL.: Suzanne Demarquez, *A. J.* (Paris 1958); Antoine Goléa, *Esthétique de la musique contemporaine* (Paris 1954); Roland-Manuel, *Histoire de la musique*, vol. 2 of *Encyclopédie de la Pléiade* (Paris 1963); Gérard Michel, "A. J., Essai sur un systeme esthétique musical," *Revue musicale* (Jan 1947); Jean Roy, "A. J.," *Présences contemporaines* (Paris 1962); Abraham Skulsky, "A. J.," *Musical America* (June 1952); Dom Angelico Surchamp et al., *A. J.* (St. Léger-Vauban 1957).

Gérard Michel

SEE ALSO France.

Jones, Charles (William) (b. Tamworth, Ontario, Canada, 21 June 1910), moved to New York City where he attended the Institute of Musical Art (1928–32), graduating with a major in violin. He did graduate work at the Juilliard School (1935–39, composition with Bernard Wagenaar). He has taught at Mills College, Calif. (1939–44), at the Aspen Music School (summers 1951–present), and elsewhere. His output since 1936 has comprised more than 60 works, most of which are instrumental compositions. His music is basically lyrical as can be observed, for instance, in his melodic lines, which follow smooth-flowing, long-range contours even when chromaticism and jagged leaps are in abundance. He has never used 12-tone or serial procedures.

PRINCIPAL COMPOSITIONS: *String Quartets Nos. 1–5* (1936; 1944, Mercury; 1951; 1954; 1961); *Symphonies Nos. 1–4* (1939; 1957, Peters; 1962; 1965); *Piano Sonatas Nos. 1–2* (1946, 1950); *5 Melodies* for orchestra (1945, Marks); *Cassation* for orchestra (1948); *Sonata a tre* for piano trio (1952); *The Seasons*, cantata for soprano, baritone (in another version, tenor), speaker, 6 instruments (1959); *Ballade* for piano (1961); *Concerto* for 4 violins, orchestra (1963); *Piers the Plowman* for tenor, chorus, orchestra; Middle English texts by William Langland (1963); *I Am a Mynstral*, cantata for tenor, 5 players; text by Langland (1967); *Masque* for speaker, 12 players; text from Pope's *Rape of the Lock* (1968); *Anima* for soprano, piano, viola; texts by Langland (1968).

Jongen, Joseph (b. Liège, 14 Dec 1873; d. Sart-lez-Spa, 12 July 1953), studied at the Liège Conservatory (graduated 1897) and was director of the Royal Conservatory in Brussels during 1925–39.

PRINCIPAL COMPOSITIONS (published by CBDM unless otherwise noted): *Fantasie* on 2 Walloon noëls for orchestra, Op. 24 (1902, Durand); *Violin Sonatas Nos. 1–2*, Opp. 27, 34 (1903, Schott; 1909, Durand); *Lalla-roukh*, symphonic tableau, Op. 28 (1904, Chester); *S'arka*, 1-act ballet, Op. 36; scenario by Frans Thys (1910); *2 Rondes wallonnes* for piano, Op. 40 (1912, Durand); *Impressions d'Ardennes* for orchestra, Op. 44 (1913, Chester); *Caprice impromptu* for cello, piano, Op. 51, No. 2 (1916); *Epithalame et scherzo* for 3 violins, piano, Op. 49 (1917, Schott); *Tableaux pittoresques* for orchestra, Op. 56 (1917, Chester); *Les Fêtes rouges*, 3 songs for soprano, piano, Op. 57; texts by Frans Hellens (1917); *Poème heroïque* for violin, orchestra, Op. 62 (1919, Schott); *3 Etudes de concert* for piano, Op. 65 (1920, Bosworth); *Danse lente* for flute, harp, Op. 66 (1924, Chester); *2 Pièces en trio* for flute, cello, harp (1925, Schott); *Entrevisions* for soprano, piano, Op. 80; text by Charles van Lerberghe (1926); *Symphonie concertante* for orchestra with organ, Op. 81 (1926, Cranz); *Pièce symphonique* for piano, orchestra, Op. 84 (1928, Schott); *Habanera* for cello, piano, Op. 86 (1928); *2 Pièces* for 4 cellos, Op. 89 (1929); *Serenata* for violin, piano, Op. 89 bis (1929, Bosworth); *Passacaille et gigue* for orchestra, Op. 90 (1929, Cranz); *Suite No. 3* for orchestra, Op. 93 (1930); *Sonata eroica* for organ, Op. 94 (1930, Leduc); *2 Pièces en trio*, nocturnal elegy for violin, cello, piano, Op. 95 (1931); *24 Little Preludes* for piano, Op.116 (1941); *La Cigale et la fourmi* for children's chorus, chamber orchestra, Op. 118; text by La Fontaine (1941); *Il Etait une Bergère* for children's chorus, chamber orchestra, Op. 134 (1947); *String Trio*, Op. 135 (1948); *Cocass March, Petite Berceuse, and Divertissement* for piano 4-hands, Op. 139 (1949).

SEE ALSO Belgium; Liturgical Music: Christian.

Jora, Mihail (b. Roman, Rumania, 2 August 1891; d. Bucharest, 10 May 1971), studied at the Iaşi Conservatory (1909–11, theory with Sofia Teodoreanu) and the Leipzig Conservatory (1912–14; composition with Max Reger, harmony with Stephan Krehl, piano with Robert Teichmüller). During 1928–33 he was musical director of the Rumanian Broadcasting Corp. He taught composition at the Bucharest Conservatory (1929–62). He also concertized as a pianist and wrote musical criticism for the Rumanian press. The influences on his music included German neo-romanticism, the impressionism of Florent Schmitt, and Stravinsky.

PRINCIPAL COMPOSITIONS: *Suita mică* [Little Suite] for violin, piano, Op. 3 (1917); *Privelişti moldoveneşti* [Moldavian Landscapes], suite for orchestra, Op. 5 (1924, ESPLA and Muzicală); *String Quartet*, Op. 9 (1927, Salabert); *La piaţă* [To the Fair], choreographic tableau for orchestra, Op. 10 (1928, Muzicală); *Symphony in C*, Op. 17 (1937, Muzicală); *Piano Sonata*, Op. 21 (1942, ESPLA); *Variations of a Theme of Schumann* for piano, Op. 22 (1943, Muzicală); *Curtea veche* [The Ancient Court], Op. 24, ballet in 2 scenes (1948); *Poze şi pozne* [Portraits and Jokes], miniatures for piano, Opp. 25, 41, 48 (1948, ESPLA and Muzicală; 1959; 1963); *Viola Sonata*, Op. 32 (1952, ESPLA); *Ballade* for baritone, chorus, orchestra, Op. 37; text by Mariana Dumitrescu (1955, Muzicală); *Intoarcerea din adîncuri* [Return to the Abyss], 3-act ballet, Op. 39 (1958, Muzicală); *Sonatina* for piano, Op. 44 (1961, Muzicală); *Violin Sonata*, Op. 46 (1962); *String Quartet No. 2*, Op. 52 (1966). PRINCIPAL WRITINGS: *Moments muzicală* (Bucharest 1968). BIBL.: George Sbârcea, *M. J.* (Bucharest 1969). [prepared with the help of the Rumanian Composers Union]

Josif, Enriko (b. Belgrade, 1 May 1924), studied at the Belgrade Music Academy (1947–54, composition with Milenko Živković), the Vojislav Vučković Music School (1952, 53), the K. Stanković State Music School (1955–57), and the Accadèmia de S. Cecilia in Rome (1961–62, composition with Goffredo Petrassi). He has taught at the Belgrade Music Academy since 1965 and was president of the Association of Serbian Composers (1967–69). The predominant influences on his style have come from Debussy, Bartók, and Stravinsky. In addition, his music shows affinities to the counterpoint, rhythmic pulse, and instrumental forms of the baroque. He prefers not to publish his music.
PRINCIPAL COMPOSITIONS: *Parody Concerto* for violin, piano (1948); *Improvisations on a Folk Theme* for 14 winds (1948); *Sonata brevis* for piano (1949, SBK); *String Quartet* (1952); *Symphonietta* (1954); *Isečak* [A Piece] for narrator, soprano, piano 4-hands (1954); *Ciklus pesama* [Song Cycle] for soprano, piano (1954); *Sonata antica* for orchestra (1955); *Lyric Symphony* for 4 flutes, harp, strings (1956); *Oratorio profano da camera* for narrator, soprano, celesta, piano, percussion (1956); *Smrt Stefana Dečanskog* [The Death of Stefan of Dečane], motets for narrator, alto, bass, chorus, 16 instruments; medieval Serbian texts (1956, expanded and orchestrated 1970); *4 Priče* [4 Stories] for piano (1957); *4 Skice* [4 Sketches] for piano (1957); *Pesma nad pesmama* [The Song of Songs] for soprano, alto, tenor, women's chorus, chamber orchestra (1957); *Piano Concerto* (1959); *Rusticon* for alto, chorus, orchestra (1962); *3*

Psalma [3 Psalms] for piano (1963); *Snovidenja* [Dreams] for flute, harp, piano (1964); *Symphony in 1 Movement* (1965); *Divertimento* for wind quintet (1969); *Bird! Don't Drop Your Wings*, ballet; scenario by Vera Kostić after Tagore (1970). PRINCIPAL WRITINGS: "Contemporary Trends in Yugoslav Music," *Papers of the Yugoslav-American Seminar on Music* ed. by Malcolm H. Brown (Cambridge, Mass., 1968).

Josten, Werner (b. Elberfeld, Germany, 12 June 1885; d. New York, 6 Feb 1963), studied with Rudolph Siegel in Munich (harmony and counterpoint) and with Emil Jaques-Dalcroze in Geneva. He was assistant conductor at the Munich Opera during 1918–21, after which he emigrated to the U.S. and taught counterpoint and composition at Smith College (1923–49). His interest in 17th- and 18th-century opera led him to revive a number of stage works by Monteverdi, Handel, and Fux, which he presented at Smith College.
PRINCIPAL COMPOSITIONS: *Crucifixion* for bass, chorus (1915, Schirmer-G); *Ode for St. Cecilia's Day* for soprano, baritone, chorus, orchestra (1925, Schirmer-G); *Sacred Concertos Nos. 1–2* for piano, string orchestra (1925, Elkan); *Batoula*, ballet for chorus, orchestra (1930–31, suite published by Elkan); *Endymion*, ballet (1933, AMP); *Symphony for Strings* (1935, Elkan); *Violin Sonata* (1936, AME); *Symphony in F* (1936, Elkan); *Sonatina* for violin, piano (1939, AME and AMP); *Rhapsody* for orchestra (1957).
BIBL.: Philip Keppler, "Baroque Beachhead: Recollections of a Bold Venture," *Opera News* (1 Dec 1958): 30–33; *W. J., 1885–1963, A Summary of His Compositions with Press Reviews* (New York 1964).

Jyrkiainen, Reijo (Einari) (b. Suistamo, Finland—now U.S.S.R., 6 April 1934), studied at the Sibelius Academy (1956–63; composition with Joonas Kokkonen, orchestration with Nils-Eric Fougstedt) and at the Univ. of Helsinki (1958–63, musicology with Erik Tawaststjerna). He has attended the Darmstadt summer courses (1962–64) and visited electronic music studios in Bilthoven (1963) and Munich (1964). During 1957–66 he was controller of music recording for the Finnish Broadcasting Company. He was librarian of the Helsinki Philharmonic Orchestra and a teacher of contemporary-music history at the Sibelius Academy during 1966–67. Since then he has been director of serious music for Finnish television.

PRINCIPAL COMPOSITIONS: *Frammenti per il septetto d'archi* (1962); *For Four* for violin, clarinet, guitar, percussion (1963); *Contradictions* for flute, clarinet, piano, guitar, string quartet (1965); *Idiopostic* on tape (1966).

PRINCIPAL WRITINGS: "Orkesterimuunnelmissa, Op. 31" [Variations for Orchestra], *Dodekafonia Schoenbergin* (Helsinki 1962): 53–66; *Béla Bartókin jousikvartetot I–III* [Béla Bartók's String Quartets I–III] (diss., Univ. of Helsinki, 1966).

BIBL.: Denby Richards, *The Music of Finland* (London 1968): 55–56.

K

Kabalevsky, Dmitri (Borisovich) (b. St. Petersburg, 30 Dec 1904), moved with his family to Moscow in 1919, where he studied general subjects at the Scriabin Institute until 1922. During the next three years he continued working with his piano teacher at the Institute, V. Selivanov, played for silent movies, and taught young pianists, for whom he composed easy pieces. He studied at the Moscow Conservatory (1925–29, piano with Goldenweiser, composition with George Catoire and Miaskovsky) and began teaching there in 1932. He has held several prominent positions in Soviet music life, including editorship of *Sovetskaia muzyka* (the official organ of the Union of Soviet Composers), head of the music department of the Soviet Radio Committee, head of the music section of the Institute of Arts History in the Academy of Sciences, and secretary of the Union of Soviet Composers. He is often in the public eye leading delegations, writing articles for newspapers and journals, appearing on television, addressing factory workers, and presenting awards.

For Kabalevsky, music has been a means for reflecting the political and social aims of the Soviet Union. The opera *Colas Breugnon*, which deals with a Burgundian craftsman of the 17th century, has many interpolations of present-day proletarian concepts. In the *Symphony No. 1* the gloom representing Tsarist Russia is portrayed through the combination of double bass, cello, and bassoon. The *Symphony No. 3* is a requiem composed on the tenth anniversary of Lenin's death. Kabalevsky's other opera, the *Taras Family*, deals with partisan fighters in World War II.

The most prominent influences on his style have been those of Mussorgsky, Borodin, and Tchaikovsky. The symphonies and concertos are all conceived in the classic-romantic forms. Some chromaticism appears in the *Violin Concerto*. His lyrical, broad, emotionally evocative melodies and his use of the traditional forms and harmonies result in uncomplicated, aurally agreeable music that has an immediate appeal to the average listener. A certain amount of folk material is present: While composing *Colas Breugnon* he undertook a study of Burgundian folksong; however, although the mass scenes have a folklike flavor, he actually quoted only two Burgundian tunes. In the *Symphony No. 1* folk themes and folklike melody are used to portray Lenin and the people. The secondary theme in the first movement of the *Violin Concerto* is a popular Ukrainian folksong. In *The Golden Spikes* ballet he used Byelorussian folk material, and in *The Folk Avengers* the influence of Ukrainian music is evident (most of this material is taken from the Rimsky-Korsakov collection). Throughout his career he has worked with and for children, producing choral and piano pieces for them and dedicating his set of three concertos to youth. It is in these works that he has probably achieved his greatest musical success.

PRINCIPAL COMPOSITIONS (available from Mezhkniga unless otherwise noted): *Prelude* for piano, Op. 1 (1925); *2 Pieces* for cello, piano, Op. 2 (1927); *Children's Pieces* for piano, Op. 3 (1927, unpub.); *Songs* for voice, piano, Op. 4; text by Aleksandr Blok (1927?); *4 Preludes* for piano, Op. 5 (1929); *Piano Sonata*, Op. 6 (1929); *String Quartets Nos. 1–2*, Opp. 8, 44 (1928, 1945); *Piano Concertos Nos. 1–3*, Opp. 9, 23, 50 (1929, 1935, 1952); *Poem of Struggle* for chorus, orchestra, Op. 12; text by A. Zharov (1930); *Sonatina in C* for piano, Op. 13 (1930); *Galician Zhakeria* for vocal soloists, chorus, orchestra, Op. 15; composed for radio (1931, unpub.); *8 Songs* for children's chorus, piano, Op. 17 (1932); *Symphonies Nos. 1–3*, Opp. 18, 19, 22 (1932, 1934, 1934); *4 Preludes* for piano, Op. 20 (1933–34, unpub.); *Kola Briun'on* [Colas Breugnon] (original title, Master of Clamecy), 3-act opera, Op. 24; libretto by V. Bragin after Romain Rolland (1937); *The Comedians*, orchestral suite after Ostrovsky, Op. 26 (1938); *Vasilek* [Cornflower], ballet (1938); *Suite* for jazz orchestra, Op. 29 (1940, unpub.); *The Golden Spikes*, ballet (1940); *V ogne* [In the Flame, also called Near Moscow], opera, Op. 33; libretto by Solodar (1942, withdrawn); *3 Songs* for voice, piano, Op. 34; poems by Marshak (1941); *Narodnye mstiteli* [The Folk Avengers], suite for chorus, orchestra, Op. 36; text by E. Dolmatovsky (1942); *The Motherland Is Great*, oratorio (1942); *24 Preludes* for piano, Op. 38 (1943); *Piano Sonata No. 3*, Op. 46 (1946); *Sem'ia Tarasa* [The Taras Family],

4-act opera, Op. 47; libretto by S. Tsenin after
B. Gorbatov's *The Unsubdued* (1947); *Violin Concerto*, Op. 48 (1948); *Cello Concerto*, Op. 49 (1949);
Nikita Vershinin, opera, Op. 53; libretto by S.
Tsenin after Vs. Ivanov's *Armoured Train 14-69*
(1954); *Romeo and Juliet*, incidental music for
orchestra, Op. 56 (c.1955); *Lenintsy* [Lenin Lads
and Lasses], cantata for children's, youth, adult
choruses, Op. 63; text by E. Dolmatovsky (published 1960). ★Dates unavailable: *Songs for Morning, Spring, and Peace* for children's chorus,
orchestra, Op. 57; *Spring Sings*, 3-act operetta, Op.
58; *Rondo* for piano, Op. 59; *4 Rondos* for piano,
Op. 60; *In the Magic Forest* for narrator, chorus,
piano, Op.61; *A Game Chorus* for children, chorus,
piano, Op. 67; *Rondo* for violin, piano, Op. 69.

BIBL.: David Ewen, *The Complete Book of 20th
Century Music* (Englewood Cliffs, N. J., 1961);
Elena Grosheva, *D. K.* (Moscow 1956); Stanley
D. Krebs, *Soviet Composers and the Development
of Soviet Music* (New York 1970).

Larissa Janczyn
SEE ALSO Dance, Soviet Union.

Kabeláč, Miloslav (b. Prague, 1 August 1908),
studied at the Prague Conservatory (1928–34;
composition with K. B. Jirák, conducting with
P. Dědeček, piano with V. Kurz). He was
music director and conductor for Radio
Prague during 1932–41 and 1945–47. He has
taught composition at the Prague Conservatory
since 1958. His music has been influenced by
a wide range of interests, including Gregorian
chant, the folk music of primitive and Oriental
peoples, and contemporary techniques. Since
1966 he has been chairman of the Committee
for Non-European Music of the Oriental
Society.

PRINCIPAL COMPOSITIONS: *Passacaglia* for piano,
Op. 3 (1937); *Malá vánoční kantáta* [Little Christmas Cantata], Op. 4, nativity play for soprano,
men's voices, chamber ensemble; folk texts (1937);
Neustupujte! [Do Not Retreat!], Op. 7, cantata
for men's chorus, winds, percussion; folk texts
(1939, Supraphon, ČHF); *6 Choruses*, Op. 10, for
men's chorus; text by Jiří Wolker (1939–42); *Wind
Sextet*, Op. 8 (1940, SNKLHU and ČHF); *Symphonies Nos. 1–8*: No. 1 in D, Op. 11, for string
orchestra, percussion (1941–42, ČHF and Panton);
No. 2 in C, Op. 15 (1942–46, ČHF and Panton);
No. 3 in F, Op. 33, for organ, brass, timpani
(1948–57, SHV); No. 4 in A, "Camerata," Op. 36
(1954–58, ČHF and Panton); No. 5 in B Minor,
"Dramatica," Op. 41, for soprano, orchestra (1960,
SHV); No. 6, "Concertante," Op. 44, for clarinet,
orchestra (1961–62); No. 7, Op. 52, for speaker,
orchestra; text from the New Testament (1967–68,
ČHF); No. 8, "Antiphonies," Op. 54, for soprano,
chorus, percussion, organ (1969–70); *7 Pieces* for
piano, Op. 14 (1944–47, Hudební Matice); *Overture No. 2* for orchestra, Op. 17 (1947, Hudební

Matice); *Modré nebe* [The Blue Sky], cycle for
children's chorus, piano, Op. 19; texts by František
Hrubín (1950, SNKLHU); *Moravské ukolébavky*
[Moravian Lullabies] for soprano, chamber orchestra, Op. 20; folk texts (1951); *Mysterium času*
[The Mystery of Time], passacaglia for orchestra,
Op. 31 (1953–57, SNKLHU); *Dětem* [For Children], suite for chamber orchestra, Op. 22 (1955,
ČHF); *Sonatina* for oboe, piano, Op. 24 (1955,
Panton); *6 Lullabies* for alto, women's chorus,
instrumental ensemble, or alto, piano, Op. 29
(1955, SNKLHU); *8 Preludes* for piano, Op. 30
(1955–56, SNKLHU); *Ballad* for violin, piano, Op.
27 (1956, SNKLHU); *Suite* from incidental music
to Sophocles' *Electra*, Op. 28a, for alto, women's
chorus ad lib., orchestra (1956); *3 Melodramas* for
narrators, chamber orchestra, Op. 34b; for the
play, *Master of 9 Songs*, by Kuo-mo-zho (1957);
2 Fantasies for organ, Op. 32 (1957–58, SNKLHU
and Panton); *Přírodě* [To Nature], 6 choruses for
children's chorus, piano, Op. 35; texts by Hrubín
(1957–58, SHV); *Myslivecké písně* [Hunter's Songs]
for baritone, 4 horns, Op. 37; folk texts (1958–59);
Cizokrajné motivy [Themes from Foreign Lands]
for piano, Op. 38 (1959); *Small Suite* for piano
4-hands, Op. 42 (1960, SHV); *8 Inventions* for 6
percussionists, Op. 45 (1960–63, Panton); *Hamletovská improvizace* [Hamlet Improvisation] for orchestra, Op. 46 (1962–63, SHV); *Ohlasy dálav*
[Echoes from Far Away], 5 songs for alto, piano,
Op. 47 (1963); *4 Preludes* for organ, Op. 48 (1963,
Panton); *Zrcadlení* [Reflections], 9 miniatures for
orchestra, Op. 49 (1963–64, Panton); *Eufemias
Mysterion* [The Mystery of Silence] for soprano,
chamber orchestra, Op. 50; Greek text (1964–65,
SHV); *8 Ricercari* for 1–6 percussionists, Op. 51
(1966–67).

SEE ALSO Czechoslovakia.

Kadosa, Pál (b. Léva, Hungary, now Czechoslovakia, 6 Sept 1903), attended the Academy
of Music in Budapest (1923–27 piano with
Arnold Székely, composition with Zoltán
Kodály). Since 1945 he has been professor and
dean of the piano faculty at the Academy.
During 1953–57 and since 1963 he has also
served as president of the Hungarian performing rights society.

PRINCIPAL COMPOSITIONS (published by EMB
unless otherwise noted): *Piano Sonatas Nos. 1–4*
(1926; 1926–27, EMB and Schott; 1930, EMB and
Schott; 1959, EMB and Boosey); *Violin Sonata*
(1927, unpub.); *Piano Concertos Nos. 1–4* (1931,
1938, 1953, 1967); *Violin Concerto No. 1* (1932,
unpub.); *Divertimentos Nos. 1–2* (1933, 1934);
String Quartets Nos. 1–3 (1935, 1936, 1956); *Concerto* for string quartet, orchestra (1936); *Viola
Concerto* (1937); *Symphonies Nos. 1–8* (1942; 1948;
1957, EMB and Boosey; 1959; 1961; 1966; 1968,
EMB and Boosey; 1969, EMB and Boosey);
Partita for orchestra (1944); *Huszti Kaland*, 2-act

opera (1949–50, unpub.); *Flute Sonata* (1961); *Violin Sonata* (1962); *Pian' e forte* for orchestra (1962); 7 *Songs*; poems by Attila Jósset (1964).

BIBL.: Ferenc Bónis, *K. P.* (Budapest, EMB, c.1964).

SEE ALSO Hungary.

Kagel, Mauricio (b. Buenos Aires, 24 Dec 1932), studied literature and philosophy at the Univ. of Buenos Aires (1950–55) and music privately. In 1955 he began organizing concerts of old and new music for the university, and during the same year he was a choral coach and conductor at the Teatro Colón. In 1957 he moved to Cologne, where he worked at the Studio for Electronic Music; simultaneously he studied with Werner Meyer-Eppler at the Institute for Research in Phonetics and Communications in Bonn. Since 1958 he has been active as a conductor, writer, and lecturer in Europe and the Americas. Since 1963 he has been increasingly involved in the theater as a composer and as a director of his own works; he has been writing and directing television films since 1965.

While still in Argentina Kagel wrote both precisely structured pieces, such as the *String Sextet* (1953), and more freely organized and experimental works, such as *Tower Music* (1953). The *Sextet* combines independent rhythmic processes in different meters. *Tower Music* is a taped piece for 24 groups of loudspeakers; it was combined with lights projected from a steel tower built in 1954 for the Feria de America exhibition in Mendoza.

Kagel's most important works date from after his emigration to Europe. In terms of sound they range from the raucous to the delicate. *Anagrama* (1957–58) calls for screaming and yelling from singers, as well as equally wild noises from instruments. The performers in *Improvisation ajoutée* (1961–62) make an infernal noise on the organ and also laugh, cough, whistle, scream, and clap. *Sonant* (1960–   ) contains the instruction to "play as quietly as possible"; it calls for such delicate effects as the sound of balls thrown on a kettle drum and the sound of writing on top of a drumhead. Kagel's search for new sounds reached a climax in *Der Schall* (1968), in which exotic or primitive instruments may join with sounds made by feathers, steel, or any other source of interesting sound.

Visual and theatrical elements have gained increasing importance in Kagel's music. In *Pandorasbox* (1960–   ), a hand-organ player revolves on a music stool. In *Sur scène* (1959–60) a mime improvises gestures while the musicians play on keyboard and percussion instruments, a speaker delivers a lecture, and a singer delivers nonverbal commentaries. These activities, which have no external meaning, are comparable to the use of language in *Anagrama*, where the vocal sounds are based on transformations into nonsense of a Latin anagram. Relationships between sound and action are further explored in three works of 1962–65: *Antithèse*, *Phonophonie*, and *Tremens*. In the first of these, for actor and electronic sounds, one's hearing is supposed to be affected by seeing the actor listening to the electronic apparatus, handling it, fleeing from it, etc. In the second work, a singer plays four roles (singer, imitator, ventriloquist, and deaf-mute), the gestures and sounds of which form a kind of counterpoint. In *Tremens* an actor under the influence of drugs reacts spontaneously to what he hears.

The concept of music is stretched to an outer limit in such theater pieces as *Pas de cinq* (1965), in which five actors merely walk around the stage, and *Kommentar und Extempore* (1965–67). In the former the music consists of the various sound qualities and rhythms created by footsteps. In the latter, choreographed gestures are used in time, as though they were musical materials; in addition there are preset and improvised spoken materials. It is of interest that Kagel's films manipulate editing, camera angles, placement of performers, and other visual elements according to musical values such as rhythm, repetition, contrast, etc.

As already indicated, indeterminacy is involved in many works. Some portions of the score for *Transición II* (1958–59) are notated on moveable disks and staves so that varying pitches and sequences of pitches may result. In *Diaphonie* (1962–64) notes projected on a screen serve as the stimulus for "automatic" tone production. All of the players see the same images, but all do not produce the same tones; the result is a kind of heterophony. Another kind is achieved in a work called *Heterophonie* (1959–60) in which 20–42 soloists occasionally have the same direction, such as to play a high, long, and loud tone, but are free to choose the specific pitch, time value, and dynamic level. Kagel has sometimes reused his compositions. *Improvisation ajoutée* makes use of the parts for *Heterophonie*. Likewise the second organ work, *Phantasia mit Obbligatos* (1967) was inserted in *Halleluja* (1967–68).

PRINCIPAL COMPOSITIONS: *String Sextet* (1953); *Tower Music* for prerecorded concrete and instrumental sounds, light projections (1953); *Anagrama* for 4 solo voices, speaking choir, chamber ensemble (1957–58); *Transición I, II* for pianist, percussionist, prerecorded sounds (1958–60, 1958–59); *Sur scène*, chamber-music theater piece for speaker, mime, singer, 3 instrumentalists (1959–60); *Sonant* for guitar, harp, double bass, drums (1960–); *Pandorasbox-Bandoneonpiece* (1960–); *Metapiece/Mimetics* for piano (1961); *Heterophonie* for an orchestra of solo instruments (1959–60); *Improvisation ajoutée* for 3 organists (1961–62); *Antithèse* for actor, electronic and audience sounds (1962); *Diaphonie* for 2 projectors, chorus, orchestra (1962–64); *Phonophonie* for 2 voices, other undefined sound sources (1963–64); *Match* for 3 players on 2 cellos and percussion (1964); *Tremens*, scenic montage for 2 actors, electronically amplified instruments (1963–65); *Journal de théâtre*, "Pas de cinq," variable scene for 5 actors (1965); *Die Himmelsmechanik*, composition using visual images of suns, moons, clouds, etc. (1965); *Kommentar und Extempore*, soliloquies with gestures for 3 actors, singer, 7 brass instruments (1965–67); *Variactions* for 4 actors, 3 singers, tapes (1965–67); *Music for Renaissance Instruments* (1965–67); *String Quartet* (1966–68); *Phantasia mit Obbligatos* for 3 organists, tape (1967); *Montage* for various sound sources (1967); *Halleluja* for voices (1967–68); *Der Schall* for 5 players (1968). ★Films: *Antithèse* (1965); *Match* (1966); *Solo* (1966–67); *Halleluja* (1968).

PRINCIPAL WRITINGS: "Tone, Clusters, Attacks, Transitions," *Die Reihe* English ed. 5:40–55; "Translation-Rotation," *ibid.* 7:32–62; "Über das instrumentale Theater," *Neue Musik* (Munich, 1961); "Komposition-Notation-Interpretation," *Darmstädter Beiträge zur Neuen Musik* 9:55–63; ["Form"], *Ibid.* 10:51–56.

BIBL.: Mario Bortolotto, "Comédie á tiroir," *Il verri* (Milan) 14; ——, "Phantasiestücke après une lecture de Cage," *La Biennale di Venezia*, vol. 14, no. 52/53; Ulrich Dibelius, *Moderne Musik 1945–65* (Munich 1966):193–203; Marianne Kesting, "Musikalisierung des Theaters:Theatralisierung der Musik," *Melos* 36:101–08; Dieter Schnebel, *Das musikalische Theater des M. K.* (Cologne 1968); Hans Rudolf Zeller, "Komposition gegen Komposition," *Melos* 35:413–17.

Dieter Schnebel
(trans. from German by Jeanne Wolf)
SEE ALSO Austria and Germany, Instrumental and Vocal Resources, Mixed Media, Performance, Rhythm.

Kalabis, Viktor (b. Červený Kostelec, Czechoslovakia, 27 Feb 1923) studied musicology and psychology at Charles Univ. in Prague (1945–49) and music at the Prague Conservatory (1945–48, composition with Emil Hlobil) and at the Academy of Musical Arts in Prague (1948–52, composition with Jaroslav Řídky). Since 1953 he has been manager of the music department at Radio Prague.

PRINCIPAL COMPOSITIONS: *Concerto for Chamber Orchestra*, "Hommage à Stravinsky," Op. 3 (1948); *Cello Concerto*, Op. 8 (1951, SHV); *Piano Concerto*, Op. 12 (1954, Panton); *Symphony No. 1*, Op. 14 (1957, SHV); *Violin Concerto* (1959, SHV); *Symphony No. 2*, "Sinfonia pacis," Op. 18 (1961, SHV); *String Quartet No. 2*, Op. 19 (1962, SHV); *Chamber Music for Strings*, Op. 21 (1963, Panton); *Symphonic Variations* for orchestra, Op. 24 (1964, Panton); *Concerto for Orchestra*, Op. 25 (1966, Panton); *Accents* for piano, Op. 26 (1967, Supraphon); *Sonata* for violin, harpsichord, Op. 28 (1967, Supraphon); *Cello Sonata*, Op. 29 (1968, Supraphon); *Clarinet Sonata*, Op. 30 (1969, Panton).

SEE ALSO Czechoslovakia.

Kallstenius, Edvin (b. Filipstad, Sweden, 29 August 1881; d. 22 Nov 1967), studied natural sciences at Lund Univ. (1898–1903) and music at the Leipzig Academy (1904–07). During 1928–46 he was music librarian for the Swedish Broadcasting Corp. He was also a board member of the Society of Swedish Composers during 1928–46 and of the Swedish Performing Rights Society during 1932–57. He once stated that "my musical religion is called *harmony*—everything else takes second place." Counter-point is less emphasized. His earlier works showed a "kinship with late German Romanticism," and toward the end of his career he used serial techniques.

PRINCIPAL COMPOSITIONS: *Violin Sonata*, Op. 7 (1909, Hansen-W); *String Quartet No. 3*, Op. 8 (1913, Suecia); *En serenad i sommarnatten* [A Serenade in the Summer Night] for orchestra, Op. 10 (1918, Nordiska); *Piano Concerto*, Op. 12 (1922); *Sinfonietta No. 1*, Op. 13 (1923); *Symphony No. 1*, Op. 16 (1926); *Clarinet Quintet*, Op. 17 (1930, Suecia); *Dalarapsodi* for orchestra, Op. 18 (1931, Suecia); *Symphony No. 2*, Op. 20 (1935); *Musica gioconda* for string orchestra, Op. 27 (1942, Gehrman); *Passacaglia enarmonica* for orchestra, Op. 31 (1943); *String Quartet No. 5*, Op. 33 (1945); *Sinfonietta No. 2*, Op. 34 (1946); *Symphony No. 3*, Op. 36 (1948); *Cello Concerto*, Op. 40 (1951); *Symphony No. 4*, Op. 43 (1954); *Hymen, O Hymenaios* for soloists, chorus, orchestra, Op. 45 (1955); *Sinfonietta dodecitonica*, Op. 46 (1956); *String Quartet No. 7*, "Dodekitonico," Op. 49 (1957); *Sinfonietta semi-seriale*, Op. 50 (1958); *Trio svagante* for clarinet, French horn, cello, Op. 51 (1959); *Sinfonia su temi 12-tonici*, Op. 52 (1960); *Lyric Suite* for flute, saxophone, cello, Op. 55 (1962).

SEE ALSO Scandinavia.

Kalomiris, Manolis (b. Smyrna, Turkey, 14 Dec 1883; d. Athens, 3 April 1962), studied piano in Athens and Constantinople and attended the Vienna Conservatory (1901–06, composition with Hermann Grädener, piano with A. Sturm). He taught piano at the Obolenski Lyceum in Harkov, Russia, during 1906–10 and piano, harmony, and counterpoint at the Athens School of Music during 1911–19. In 1919 he founded the Hellenic School of Music and in 1926, the National School of Music, which he directed until 1948. During 1918–20 and 1922–37 he was inspector general of military music. Until 1957 he was also music critic for the paper *Ethnos*. He was president of the Union of Greek Composers, 1936–45 and 1947–57. His music was influenced primarily by Greek folksong, German music and the Wagner operas, and the Russian national school.

PRINCIPAL COMPOSITIONS: *Anatoliki zografià* [Sunrise Picture] for piano (1902, Christides in Constantinople); *3 Ballads* for piano (1906, Maretschek, Harkov; Nos. 1 and 3 published by Gaitanos); *Roméïki Souíta* [Greek Suite] for orchestra (1907; revised 1910, 1936); *I Eliá* [The Olive Tree] for women's chorus, orchestra; text by Costís Palamás (1907–09, revised 1944); *Ya ta Hellenopoula* [For Greek Children] for piano (1910–49; Gaitanos, Melody, and Cazazis); *Quintet with Song* for female voice, string quartet, piano; text by L. Mavilis (1912, 2nd movement published by Gaitanos); *Íamvi ké Anápesti* [Iambs and Anapests] and *Mayovótana* [Wild Herbs of May] for female voice, orchestra; texts by Palamás (1914, Sénart); *O Protomástoras* [The Master Builder], 2-part musical tragedy; libretto by Nikos Kazantzakis (1915, revised 1919, 1940; piano reduction, Gaitanos); *Tó Daktylídi tís Mánas* [Mother's Ring], 3-part music drama; libretto after Yannis Cambyssis (1917; piano reduction, Gaitanos); *Levendiá Symphony* [Valor Symphony] for chorus, orchestra (1920, revised 1937, 1952; IEPT); *String Trio* (1921, Sénart); *Quartet quasi fantasia* for harp, flute, English horn, viola (1921, revised 1954); *2 Rhapsodies* for piano (1921; Menestrel, Paris, and Constantinidis, Athens); *Rhapsody* for piano, orchestrated by Gabriel Pierné (1925); *I Eléftheri Poliorkiméni* [Besieged Yet Free] for female voice, chorus, orchestra; text by Dionyssios Solomos (1926); *Nissiótikes Zografiés* [Island Pictures] for violin, orchestra (1928, revised 1939; violin-piano score, Gaitanos); *I Symphonía tón Anídeon ké tón Kalón Anthrópon* [The Symphony of the Naive and Kind-Hearted People] for mezzo-soprano, chorus, orchestra (1931); *3 Hellenikí Horí* [3 Greek Dances] for orchestra (1934); *Piano Concerto* (1935); *Apó tá Lyriká toú Sikelianoú* [From the Lyric Verses of Sikelianos] for female voice, orchestra (1937); *St' Ossiou Loukà to Monastiri* [At the Ossios Loukàs Monastery] for narrator, orchestra; text by A. Sikelianos (1937); *Tríptycho* for orchestra (1937–40); *Preludes Nos. 1–5* for piano (1939, Gaitanos); *Minas o Rémbelos* [Minas the Rebel], tone poem for orchestra (1940); *O Thánatos tís Andrioménis* The Death of the

Valiant Woman], tone poem for orchestra (1943–45, published by the Institut Français in Athens); *Anatolí* [The Orient], 2-part musical fairy tale; libretto by the composer after Cambyssis (1945–48); *Violin Sonata* (1948, Melody); *Tá Xotiká Nerá* [The Shadowy Waters], opera; libretto after Yeats (1950–52); *Kontsertáki* [Concertino] for violin, orchestra (1955); *Symphony No. 3*, "Palamikí," for narrator, orchestra; text by Palamás (1955, IEPT); *Constantine Palaeologue*, 3-part musical legend after Nikos Kazantzakis (1961).

PRINCIPAL WRITINGS: *Wagner, o Dimiourgós toú Moussikoú Drámatos* [Wagner, the Creator of Musical Drama] (Athens 1953). Kalomiris also wrote many textbooks in Greek on theory, harmony, form, solfège, and organology.

BIBL.: F. Anoyanakis, *Kalálogos Érgon M. K. 1883–1962* [Catalogue of the Works of M. K.] (Athens 1964).

[prepared with the help of George Leotsakos]
SEE ALSO Greece.

Kapr, Jan (b. Prague, 12 March 1914), studied at the Prague Conservatory (1933–41; composition with Jaroslav Řídký, Jaroslav Křička). He was music director for the Czechoslovak Radio in Prague (1939–46), editor-in-chief at the music publishing house of Orbis, Prague (1950–54), and teacher of composition at the Janáček Academy in Prague (since 1961). During 1946–49 he wrote music criticism for various Czech periodicals, and since 1947 he has composed film music for Czechoslovakian Film Productions. In his music he has drawn on the modality of folk music and on such influences as Les Six, Suk, Martinů, and Stravinsky. He also uses the techniques of the 12-tone Viennese school and controlled chance.

PRINCIPAL COMPOSITIONS (published by Supraphon unless otherwise noted): *String Quartet No. 6* with baritone solo (1963); *Symphony No. 6* (1964); *Contraria Romana* for baritone, piano (1965, unpub.) or baritone, orchestra (1967, unpub.); *Dialogues* for flute, harp (1965); *String Quartet No. 7* (1965, unpub.); *Ciffres* for piano, percussion, tape (1966, Panton); *Oscillazione* for violin, clarinet, trumpet, piano, cello, percussion (1966, unpub.); *Exercises for Gydli* for soprano, flute, harp (1967); *Rotation 9* for violin, viola, cello, piano (1967); *Omaggio alla tromba* for 2 trumpets, wind ensemble, piano, timpani (1968); *Symphony No. 7*, "Krajina dětství" [Country of Childhood], for children's chorus, orchestra (1968); *Testimonies* for violin, cello, bass clarinet, piano (1970, unpub.).

PRINCIPAL WRITINGS: *Konstanty* [Constants] (Prague 1967); "J. K. o své VII. symfonii 'Krajina dětství'" [J. K. about His Seventh Symphony "Country of Childhood"], *Hudební rozhledy* (1969):652.

BIBL.: Jindra Bártová, "Konstanty, Šifry a J. K."

[Constants, Ciphers, and J. K.], *Hudební rozhledy* 1968/3:84–87; Bohumil Karásek, "Hamburgský týden" [The Week at Hamburg], *ibid.* 1969/14: 442; Milan Kuna, "Pod tíhou nového slyšení" [Under the Weight of New Hearing], *ibid.* 1968/8: 231; ——, "An Interview with J. K.," *Music News from Prague* 1969/4; Antonín Špelda, "Skladatelé o svém díle" [Composers on Their Work], *ibid.* 1968/18:553–55; "J. K.," Program book of the 43rd ISCM festival (Hamburg 1969): 31–32.

SEE ALSO Czechoslovakia.

Kardoš, Dezider (b. Nadlice, Czechoslovakia, 23 Dec 1914), studied composition at the Bratislava Academy of Music and Drama with Alexander Moyzes and the Master School of the Prague Conservatory with Vítězslav Novák and musicology at the Univ. of Bratislava. He worked for the Czech Radio at Prešov and Košice in eastern Slovakia, where he came in contact with the local folk culture. In 1951 he became director of folk music for the Czech Radio in Bratislava and later managing director of the Slovak Philharmonic. He teaches composition at the Higher School of Musical Arts. His symphonic and choral music is in the tradition of Bartók, Honegger, and Shostakovich.

PRINCIPAL COMPOSITIONS: *Suite* for piano, Op. 5 (1937); *Wind Quintet*, Op. 6 (1938); *Eastern Slovak Songs* for voice, piano, vols. 1–2, Opp. 9, 17 (1939, 1948); *Symphonies Nos. 1–5*: No. 1, Op. 10 (1942); No. 2, "On the Native Land," Op. 28 (1955); No. 3, Op. 33 (1961); No. 4, "Piccola," Op. 34 (1962); No. 5, Op. 37 (1963); *Bagatelles* for piano, Op. 18 (1948); *Peace Cantata* (1951); *Eastern Slovak Overture*, Op. 22 (1951); *Greetings to a Great Country*, Op. 25 (1953); *Compositions for Youth* for piano, Op. 27 (1956); *Concerto for Orchestra*, Op. 30 (1957); *Let's Help the Nightingale*, children's songs, Op. 31a (1959); *Heroic Ballad* for string orchestra, Op. 32 (1959); *Concert* for strings, Op. 35 (1963); *One-handed* for men's chorus, Op. 36a (1963); *2 Songs from Eastern Slovakia* for mixed chorus and female chorus, Op. 36b (1964).

SEE ALSO Czechoslovakia.

Karetnikov, Nikolai (Nikolaevich) (b. Moscow, 28 June 1930), studied in Moscow at the Central Music School (1942–48, composition with Vissarion Schebalin, piano with Ekaterina Nikolaeva) and the State Conservatory (1948–53, composition with Schebalin, technical subjects with Igor Sposokin and Victor Tsukkerman). Since 1958 he has composed many scores for television, films, and the

theater and performed as pianist and conductor of his own music in concerts and for films. He has also worked at the Electronic Music Studio of the A. Scriabin Music Museum in Moscow. His music was influenced first by Mussorgsky, Shostakovich, Wagner, and Mahler and later by Schoenberg and Webern. He now considers himself a strict serialist who deviates from this approach only in electronic music.

PRINCIPAL COMPOSITIONS: *Symphonies Nos. 1–4* (1951, 1956, 1959, 1963); *Julius Fuchik*, oratorio for soloists, chorus, orchestra (1953); *Dramaticheskaia poema* [A Dramatic Poem] for orchestra (1958); *Veter* [The Wind], film score (1958); *Mir vkhodiashchemu* [Peace to Him Who Enters], film score (1960); *Vanina-Vanini*, 1-act ballet after Stendhal; choreography by Natalia Kasatkina and Vladimir Vassiliev (1960); *Lento variacione* for piano (1961); *String Quartet* (1963); *Violin Sonata* (1963); *Skvernyi anekdot* [A Bad Joke], film score (1965); *Concerto for Winds* for band (1965); *Kroshka Tsakhes po prozvaniiu Tsinnober* [Klein Zack genannt Zinnober], 3-act ballet after E. T. A. Hoffmann; choreography by Kasatkina and Vassiliev (1967); *Chamber Symphony* for 19 players (1968); *Concert Piece* for piano (1969); *5 dukhovnykh pesnopenii* [5 Brass Melodies] for chorus, brass (1969); *4 Pieces* for flute, clarinet, bass clarinet, violin (1969); *Beg* [The Race], film score (1970).

Karkoff, Maurice (Ingvar) (b. Stockholm, 17 March 1927), studied at the Royal Academy of Music in Stockholm (1947–53, composition with Lars-Erik Larssen) and privately with Karl-Birger Blomdahl in Stockholm (1944–48) and Erland von Koch (1953–55), Vagn Holmboe (1956 in Copenhagen), Nadia Boulanger (1956–57 in Paris), André Jolivet (1957 in Paris), Wladimir Vogel (1959 and at other times in Ascona), and Alexander Boskovich (1963 in Tel Aviv). During 1962–66 he was assistant music critic for the *Stockholms Tidningen*. He has taught composition at the Borgarskola in Stockholm since 1965.

PRINCIPAL COMPOSITIONS: *Korta variationer* [Short Variations] for string quartet (string orchestra), Op. 9 (1953, Suecia); *Symphonies Nos. 1, 3, 4*: No. 1, Op. 17 (1955–56, Gehrman); No. 3, "Sinfonia breve," Op. 38 (1958–59, Gehrman); No. 4, Op. 69 (1963, Gehrman); *Violin Concerto*, Op. 22 (1956); *Piano Concerto*, Op. 28 (1957–60, Gehrman); *Cello Concerto*, Op. 31 (1958); *Quartet* for 2 trumpets, horn, trombone, Op. 33 (1958); *Trombone Concerto*, Op. 35 (1958); *2 Impressions* for flute, harp, Op. 36 (1958); *Little Serenade* for wind quintet, Op. 34 (1959); *Miniatyrsvit* [Miniatures] for piano, Op. 39 (1959, Gehrman); *Suite* for harpsichord, strings, Op. 67 (1962); *7 Pezzi* for orchestra, Op.

63 (1962, Suecia); *5 Tagore Songs* for tenor, piano, Op. 64 (1962); *Oriental Pictures* for orchestra (piano), Op. 66 (1965–66); *Nocturne* for clarinet, piano, Op. 81 (1966); *Metamorphoses* for orchestra, Op. 89 (1967); *4 Sacred Songs* for chorus, Op. 88 (1967); *Epitafium* for nonet or small chamber orchestra, Op. 93 (1968); *Quattro parti* for 13 brasses, percussion, Op. 94 (1968); *Sinfonietta grave* for orchestra, Op. 95 (1968–69); *Monopartita* for piano, Op. 99 (1969); *Sonata* for 2 trumpets, horn, 2 trombones, tuba, Op. 105 (1970).

Karkoschka, Erhard (b. Mährisch Ostrau, Czechoslavakia, 6 March 1923), attended the Stuttgart Hochschule für Musik (1946–53, composition with Karl Marx, conducting with Gustav Koslik), and the Univ. of Tübingen (1956–59, musicology with Walter Gerstenberg and Georg Reichert, also philosophy and comparative religion). Since 1958 he has taught harmony, theory, and composition at the Stuttgart Hochschule für Musik und Darstellende Kunst and since 1963 has directed the Ensemble Neue Musik Stuttgart. In 1964 he became a director of the Institut für Neue Musik und Musikerziehung in Darmstadt. He has given seminars at the Muzički Biennale Zagreb (1967), Royal Musikhögskolan Stockholm (1968), and the Internationalen Ferienkursen in Darmstadt (1968). The most important influences on Karkoschka's style have been the music of Webern and Messiaen and the ideas of John Cage.

PRINCIPAL COMPOSITIONS: *Kleines Konzert* for violin, chamber orchestra (1955, Bärenreiter); *Eine Suite vom Wind* for soprano, chorus (1955, Schott); *Polyphone Studie* for orchestra (1956, Bärenreiter); *desideratio Dei* for organ (1963, Tonos); *triptychon über B-A-C-H* for organ (1965, Tonos); *quattrologe* for string quartet (1966, Tonos); *4 stufen* for orchestra (1966, Ahn & Sim); *homo sapiens 1968* for 16 solo voices (1968, Moeck); *szene* for 2 cellos (1968, Tonos); *psylex* for soprano, flute, tape (1968, Bosse); *antimonie* for wind quintet (1969, Tonos).

PRINCIPAL WRITINGS: *Studien zur Entwicklung der Kompositionstechnik im Frühwerk Anton Weberns* (diss., Univ. of Tübingen, 1959); "Zur rhythmischen Struktur in der Musik von Heute," *Bericht über den Internationalen Musikwissenschaftlichen Kongress* (Cassel 1962):379–88; "Zum Terminus strukturell," *Terminologie der neuen Musik* (Berlin 1965):70–82; "Form und Formanalyse," *Probleme des musiktheoretischen Unterrichts* (Berlin 1967):40–63; *Neue Methoden der musikalischen Analyse und einige Anwendungen auf spätere Instrumentalwerke von Karl Marx* (Stuttgart 1967); *Notation in New Music* (London 1969); *Neue Musik in phänomenologischen Analysen* (Celle 1971).

Karyotakis, Theodore (Demosthenes) (b. Argos, Greece, 21 July 1903), attended the Greek Univ. (1920–25) and the Athens Conservatory (c.1921–23, piano and harmony). He studied privately with Dimitri Mitropoulos (c.1929–35, harmony and composition) and Marios Varvoglis (counterpoint and orchestration). He has been general secretary of the Union of Greek Composers since 1957, general secretary of the National Council of Music since 1966, and a member of the Council of the Athens State Orchestra since 1967. He divides his output into three periods: 1932–38, the agitated, intense style of his early years; 1938–60, a period during which a Greek national spirit is synthesized with prevailing contemporary idioms; 1960 to the present, 12-tone works.

PRINCIPAL COMPOSITIONS (some of the unpublished works are available from the Philip Nakas House in Athens): *Ballade* for piano, strings, percussion (1939, IEPT); *Rhapsody* for violin, orchestra (1940, IEPT); *Petite Symphonie* for strings (1943); *Epic Song* for orchestra (1944); *Violin Sonatas Nos. 1–2* (1945, 1955); *Variations* for piano (1946); *Divertimento* for orchestra (1948); *Love Songs* for mezzo-soprano, flute, harp (1948); *The Divine Gifts* for voice, piano (1949); *String Trio* (1952); *Song Cycles* for 1–2 voices, harp (1952); *Little Fires* for voice, piano (1955); *Serenata* for small orchestra (1955, IEPT); *Song of Songs* for narrator, vocal soloists, women's chorus, orchestra (1956); *String Quartet* with voice (1962); *Ethries* [Clear Sky], 10 songs for voice, clarinet, strings (1962); *Rhapsody* for cello, piano (1963); *Sonatina* for solo cello (1963); *Sonatina* for viola, piano (1963); *6 Songs* for voice, piano (1963); *Duos* for flute, viola (1963); *3 Compositions* for orchestra (1965); *9 Inventions* for violin, piano (1966); *Concerto for Orchestra* (1967); *Essay* for orchestra (1969); *Trio* for clarinet, viola, piano (1969); *Duos* for flute, clarinet (1969); *Orion*, 7 inventions for voice, violin (1969).

BIBL.: Andrea Karbone, "The Composer T. K.," 2 radio lectures published in the journal of the Athens Radio (18 June 1967).

Kasemets, Udo (b. Tallin, Estonia, 16 Nov 1919), studied at the Tallin Conservatory, the Stuttgart Hochschule für Musik, and the Darmstadt summer courses (1950, composition with Ernst Krenek). In 1951 he emigrated to Canada, where he has become one of the foremost promoters of avant-garde music. During the late 50s and early 60s he originated and directed various music series in Toronto including Musica Viva; the Toronto Bach Society; Men, Minds, and Music (contemporary music); and the Isaacs Gallery Mixed-Media Concerts and Ensemble, now the Synergetic Theater. In the early 60s he was music critic for the Toronto *Star*, and he has contributed music analyses to numerous journals. Since 1966 he has been editor of *Canavangard*, a series of avant-garde scores published by BMI in Canada. He has performed professionally as a pianist, organist, and conductor and has taught voice, theory, and piano. His music before 1960 was "essentially in a post-Schoenbergian, 12-tone idiom." Since then he has been concerned with music as performance, not merely the writing of a composition. According to Beckwith (see bibl.), his work has followed two paths: 1) musical and theatrical games, pieces involving social participation with little or no distinction between performer and nonperformer; and 2) pieces which retain a central basis in sound. In the first category is *Cumulus* (1963–64), notated as a maplike chart, and *Calceolaria* (1966), a folio of instructions, scenarios, and charts. Works of the second type are intended to yield new sound patterns; *Timepiece* (1964), for example, is notated with graphics that symbolize the broad contrasts a performer may strive for.

PRINCIPAL COMPOSITIONS: *Haiku* for voice, flute, cello, piano; classical Japanese poems trans. by Harold Henderson (1961, BMIC); *Squares* for piano duet (1962, BMIC); $\sqrt{5}$ for 2 performers using 2 pianos, percussion (1962–63, BMIC); *Trigon* for 1, 3, 9, or 27 performers—instrumentalists and/or vocalists and/or dancers (1963, BMIC); *Communications*, a "noncomposition" for speaker(s), singer(s), instrumentalists(s), dancer(s), etc.; text from e. e. cummings (1963, BMIC); *Cumulus* for any solo instrument or ensemble, 2 tape recorders (1963–64, BMIC); *Timepiece* for 1 performer using 1 or more instruments or sound-producing media (1964, BMIC); *Cascando* for 1–128 performers (1965, BMIC); *5PP*, 5 performance pieces for painters, props, electronic equipment, speakers, audience (1966, BMIC); *Calceolaria*, an "idea-score" yielding time/space variations on a floral theme by any number of performers using any media (1966, BMIC); *Contactics*, a "choreography" for musicians, audience (1966, BMIC); *Variations (On Variations [On Variations])* for singer, instrumentalist, 4 loudspeakers, 1 or 2 tapes (1966, BMIC); *Octagonal Octet and/or Ode* for 8 or fewer performers (1967, BMIC); *Octode*, graphic score for electronic realization (1967); *T¹*, computer-controlled multimedia, audience-participation piece (c.1968); *In memoriam Marcel Duchamp*, a cumulative realization using multiplications and divisions of *music for Marcel Duchamp* and 26 statements *re* Duchamp by John Cage (1969). List to 1960: *Composers of the Americas* 8:104–07.

PRINCIPAL WRITINGS: "18 Edicts on Education," *Source* 4.

BIBL.: John Beckwith, "K: Torrents of Reaction," *Music Scene* (Jan 1970).

SEE ALSO Canada.

Kašlík, Václav (b. Poličná, Czechoslovakia, 28 Sept 1917), studied until 1947 at Charles Univ., the Prague Conservatory, and the Prague Academy (1938–42, composition with Rudolf Karel, conducting with Václav Talich). He conducted at the Brno Opera (1942–45), was artistic director of the Opera "5 May" in Prague (1945–48), and has since been director of the Prague National Theater.

PRINCIPAL COMPOSITIONS: *Zbojnická balada* [The Brigand's Ballad], opera (1939–42, revised 1962–63, DILIA); *Don Juan*, ballet for organ, 2 pianos, string quartet, percussion (1940, arranged for orchestra c.1946; DILIA); *Jánošík*, ballet (1952] DILIA); *Vesnická symfonie* [Village Symphony, (1960); *Krakatit*, television opera after Karel Čapek (1960).

Kassern, Tadeusz (Zygfryd) (b. Lvov, Poland, 19 March 1904; d. New York, 2 May 1957), studied at the Polish Musical Society Conservatory in Lvov (1919–22) and the State Conservatory in Poznań (1922–26). He also studied law at Poznań Univ. (1922–26). In 1931 he studied music in Paris. He followed simultaneously the careers of jurist, composer, and critic. In 1948 he went to New York as a cultural attaché in the Polish consulate. He later left the consulate and was granted asylum in the U.S. He taught in New York at the Third Street Music School Settlement, 1951–57, and during 1954–57 was head of the composition department at the Dalcroze School of Music. He also lectured at the New School for Social Research. His early works were influenced by French impressionism and the style of Karel Szymanowski. After 1928, under the influence of neoclassicism and Bartók, he began to emphasize polyphonic textures and greater formal clarity. Ultimately he arrived at a kind of neoromanticism within classic forms.

PRINCIPAL COMPOSITIONS: *4 Songs* for voice, piano (1926, PWM); *Concerto* for soprano, orchestra (1928, PWM); *Children's Cantata* for soprano, chorus, orchestra (1931); *5 Ballads* for men's chorus (1933, PWM); *Flute Concerto* (1934); *Concertino* for flute, clarinet, bassoon (1936); *Dies irae*, symphonic poem (1936); *Sonatina* for piano (1936, PWM); *Double Bass Concerto* (1937, PWM);

Pastoral Suite for chamber orchestra (1937); *Piano Sonata No. 2* (1937, PWM); *4 Copernicus Motets* for boys' and men's choruses (1937, PWM); *Polish Folk Suite* for mezzo-soprano, male chorus (1938, PWM); *4 Songs* for voice, piano (1938, PWM); *Children's Suite* for 2 pianos (1940, PWM); *Concerto for String Orchestra* (1944, PWM); *Sonatina No. 2* for piano (1944); *Sonata brevis* for piano (1945, PWM); *Sonatina kolędowa* [Christmas Carol Sonatina] for piano (1945, PWM); *Concerto for oboe, string orchestra* (1946); *10 Folk Songs* for voice, piano (1947, PWM); *Sonatina* for flute, piano (1948); *The Anointed*, 4-act opera (1949); *4 Pieces* for piano (1949, Fischer); *Teen-Age Concerto* for piano, chamber orchestra (1952, Schirmer-G); *Sun-Up*, 1-act American folk opera; libretto after L. Vollmer (1952); *Sonatina on Foster Themes* for piano (1952); *Comedy of the Dumb Wife*, 1-act comic opera; libretto based on Anatole France (1953).

BIBL.: J. Reiss, *Muzyka Polska* (Cracow 1959). [prepared with the help of Michal Kondracki]

Kay, Ulysses (b. Tucson, Ariz., 7 Jan 1917), studied at the Univ. of Ariz. (1934–38), the Eastman School (1938–41; composition, orchestration with Bernard Rogers; composition, Howard Hanson), Tanglewood (1941), Yale Univ. (1941–42; composition, theory with Paul Hindemith), and Columbia Univ. (1946–49; composition, Otto Luening). He has been a music consultant for Broadcast Music, Inc., New York (1953–68) and has taught at Boston Univ. (1965), the Univ. of Calif. at Los Angeles (1966–67), and the Herbert H. Lehman College of the City Univ. of New York (since 1968).

PRINCIPAL COMPOSITIONS (published by Duchess unless otherwise noted): *10 Essays* for piano (1940); *Overture: Of New Horizons* (1944, Peters); *4 Inventions* for piano (1946); *Suite for Strings* (1947, Peters); *3 Pieces after Blake* for soprano, orchestra (1952); *Serenade for Orchestra* (1954, AMP); *The Juggler of Our Lady*, 1-act opera (1956); *Choral Triptych* for chorus, string orchestra (1962, AMP); *Fantasy Variations* for orchestra (1963); *Emily Dickinson Set* for women's chorus, piano (1964); *Markings* for orchestra (1966); *Symphony* (1967); *Stephen Crane Set* for chorus, 13 instruments (1967); *The Capitoline Venus*, 1-act opera (1970, MCA). List to 1961: *Composers of the Americas* 7:36–45.

SEE ALSO Liturgical Music: Christian.

Kayn, Roland (Wolfgang) (b. Reutlingen, Germany, 3 Sept 1933), studied during 1952–55 at the Hochschule für Musik in Stuttgart and the Kirchenmusikschule in Esslingen. He also attended the Hochschule für Musik,

Berlin (1956–58, composition with Boris Blacher). During 1959–62 he worked at various electronic studios (the Polish Radio in Warsaw with Josef Patkowski, the Westdeutscher Rundfunk in Cologne, and the Siemens Electronic Studio in Munich). In 1969 he was at the Studio di Fonologia of the Radio Audizioni Italiane in Milan, and in 1970 at the Institut voor Sonologie at Utrecht State Univ. He is a professional organist and cellist. His early works were influenced by Schoenberg and Varèse, his organ pieces by Messiaen. The serial techniques of his earlier works were later replaced by procedures derived in part from information theory. He now aims at "a redefinition of music through the construction and dissection of formal sound structures and the passing association of tonal materials."

PRINCIPAL COMPOSITIONS: *Aggregate* for brass, strings, percussion (1958, Sikorski); *Vectors I* for orchestra (1960, S-Z); *Schwingungen* for 5 sound groups (1961–62, Moeck); *Galaxis*, multiple sound structure for variable instrumental ensemble (1962, Moeck); *Allotropie* for multiple instrumental formations (1962–64, S-Z); *Signals* for 7 instrumental groups (1964–66, S-Z); *Entropy PE 31* on 4-track tape (1968); *Cybernetics III* on 4-track tape (1969, S-Z).

PRINCIPAL WRITINGS: "Scheda," *Collage* (Palermo) 7 (1967): 85ff.; "*Diffusions* for 1–4 electronic organs," published in Swedish in *Nutida musik* (Stockholm) 1967–68/7–8:25; "Erweiterungen und Grenzen des Instrumentalklangs," "Struktur und Klang in der Elektronischen Musik," and "Random or Not Random," 3 lectures prepared for the Norddeutscher Rundfunk, Hamburg (1959, 1961, 1964) and published in Polish in *Horyzonty muzyki* (Cracow, 1966).

BIBL.: Henryk Schiller, "*Allotropie* by R. K.," published in Polish in *Ruch muzyczny* (Warsaw) 1967/6:16ff.; Nicola Sgro, "R. K.: *Schwingungen*," *Collage* (Palermo) 1 (1963):33ff.

Kelemen, Milko (b. Podravska Slatina, Yugoslavia, 30 March 1924), studied composition and conducting in Zagreb (1945–52) and composition at the Paris Conservatory (1954–55) with Olivier Messiaen, Darius Milhaud, and Tony Aubin. He taught at the Zagreb Music Academy (1955–58) and then studied for two years in Freiburg with Fortner. After teaching again at the Zagreb Academy (1960–65), he moved to Munich, where he worked on electronic music. He moved to Berlin in 1967, where he is working under the auspices of Deutscher Akademischer Austauschdienst.

Kelemen's earliest works were in late-19th- and early 20th-century styles. They emphasized expressive melodies, chromatic harmonies, and varied rhythms and followed traditional formal schemes. During his study in Germany and until the mid-1960s, he began to abandon these traditional approaches and to use serial and pointillistic techniques; polyphonic structures prevailed. Polyphony, a new method of building chords, the use of fragmented melodies and of polyrhythms gave works of this period a different sound, which has now been modified by small microstructures and an ongoing form in which the structures develop out of each other. This has led to a new interest in the use of instrumental textures to emphasize the characteristics of melodic, chordal, and rhythmic structures. Folk elements from the composer's native region are a further feature of all Kelemen's compositions, including the most recent.

PRINCIPAL COMPOSITIONS: *Concert Improvisations* for string orchestra (1955, UE); *Adagio and Allegro* for string orchestra (1956, UE); *Concerto* for bassoon, string orchestra (1956, UE); *Dances* for baritone, string orchestra (1956, UE); *Concerto giocoso* for chamber orchestra (1957, Schott); *Constellations* for chamber orchestra (1958, Schott); *Skolion* for orchestra (1959, Schott); *Čovjek pred zrcalom* [The Man Before the Mirror], ballet (1959, Peters); *Transfigurations* for piano, orchestra (1960, Peters); *Equilibres* for 2 orchestras (1960, Peters); *Dessins commentées* for piano (1964, Peters); *Novi stanar* [The New Tenant], opera (1964, Peters); *Abbandonata*, ballet (1964, Peters); *Sub rosa* for orchestra (1964, Peters); *Les Mots*, cantata (1965, Peters); *Judita* on tape (1966); *Composé* for 2 pianos, 3 orchestras (1967, Peters); *Surprise* for string orchestra (1967, Peters); *Changeant* for cello, orchestra (1968, Peters); *Motion* for string quartet (1968, Peters); *The Pest*, opera (1968–69).

Dragotin Cvetko

Kelly, Robert (b. Clarksburg, W. Va., 26 Sept 1916), studied at the Curtis Institute (1939–42, composition with Rosario Scalero) and at the Eastman School (summers 1948–49, 1950–51; composition with Herbert Elwell). He also studied violin privately with Samuel Gardner (1935–36, Juilliard School) and Emil Heerman (1938–39, Cincinnati Conservatory). During 1946–70 he taught composition at the Univ. of Ill. The subject matter of some of his music derives from the writings of Kahlil Gibran: the First Symphony "is of brevity; the Second Symphony is of time (seasons of the year); the Third Symphony (*Emancipation Symphony*) is of freedom. . . . *The White Gods* is of man's relentless greed for wealth and power."

PRINCIPAL COMPOSITIONS (published by ACA unless otherwise noted): *A Miniature Symphony* (No. 1) (1948, Highgate); *Symphony No. 2* (1958, High-

gate); *Emancipation Symphony* (No. 3) (1961); *Concerto* for violin, cello, orchestra (1961); *The White Gods*, 3-act opera (1963–65); *Violin Concerto* (1968); *Diacoustics* for piano, percussion ensemble (1970). List to 1966: *Composers of the Americas* 13:74–80.

PRINCIPAL WRITINGS: *Theme and Variations*, a study of linear 12-tone composition (Urbana 1969).

Kelterborn, Rudolph (b. Basel, 3 Sept 1931), attended the municipal Musikakademie in Basel (1950–53, composition with Walther Geiser, theory with Gustav Güldenstein, conducting with Alexander Krannhals), the Mozarteum in Salzburg (1950, conducting with Igor Markevitch), and the Nordwestdeutsche Musikakademie, Detmold (1955; composition with Wolfgang Fortner, Günter Bialas). He taught theory and conducting in Basel (1950–55) and composition at the Nordwestdeutsche Musikakademie, Detmold (1960–68). In 1968 he became professor of composition and music analysis at the Zurich Musikhochschule and in 1969 editor-in-chief of *Schweizerische Musikzeitung*. He has appeared as guest conductor in Switzerland and Germany.

PRINCIPAL COMPOSITIONS (published by Bärenreiter unless otherwise noted): *String Quartet No. 2* (1956); *Missa* (1957); *Die Errettung Thebens*, opera (1960–62); *Metamorphosen* for orchestra (1960); *Lamentationes* for strings (1961); *String Quartet No. 3* (1962); *Kammersymphonie No. 2* for strings (1963, Bote); *Meditationen* for 6 winds (1964, Heinr.); *Der Traum meines Lebens verdämmert*, cantata (1965); *Die Flut*, oratorio (1965); *Monosonata* for piano (1965); *Kaiser Jovian*, opera (1965–66); *Miroirs* for winds, harp, piano, percussion, double basses (1966, Bote); *Fantasia a tre* for violin, cello, piano (1967); *Phantasmen* for orchestra (1967); *Symphony 1* (1967); *Musica Spei* for choir, organ, soprano (1968); *Octet 1969* (Bote).

BIBL.: Franzpeter Goebels, Dino Larese, *R. K.* (Amriswil 1969); Ernst Mohr, "Zur Kompositionstechnik R. K.s," *Musica* 14/5:281–85.

SEE ALSO Switzerland.

Kenins, Talivaldis (b. Liepaja, Latvia, 23 April 1919), studied at the State Conservatory in Riga (1940–44, harmony and counterpoint with Joseph Wihtol) and the Paris Conservatory (1945–50; composition with Tony Aubin; form, analysis, and esthetics with Olivier Messiaen). He has taught counterpoint and composition at the Univ. of Toronto since 1952 and is a music commentator for Radio Canada.

PRINCIPAL COMPOSITIONS (available from CMC unless otherwise noted): *String Quartet* (1948); *Christmas Chorale* for chorus (1948, Waterloo); *Septet* for winds, strings (1949); *Cello Sonata* (1950); *Piano Trio* (1952); *Piano Concerto*, "Duo" (1952); *To a Soldier*, cantata for vocal soloists, chorus, organ (1953, Kalnass, Chicago); *Violin Sonata* (1954); *Suite concertante* for cello, piano (1955); *Concertino* for 2 pianos (1956); *Daniel*, oratorio for vocal soloists, chorus, organ (1956, unpub.); *Piano Quartet* (1958); *Diversions* for cello, piano (1958); *Divertimento* for clarinet, piano (1959, Boosey); *Symphonies Nos. 1–3* (1959, 1968, 1970); *Piano Sonata* (1961, Harris); *Bonhomme* and *Ojibway Song*, 2 folk songs for chorus (1962, Harris); *Nocturne and Dance* for string orchestra (1963–69, Boosey); *Folk Dance, Variations, and Fugue* for orchestra (1964); *Concerto* for violin, cello, string orchestra (1965); *Little Suite* for string quartet (1965); *Concertante* for flute, piano (1966, Boosey); *Fantasy Variations* for flute, viola (1967); *Suite in D* for organ (1967); *Diversities*, 12 etudes for piano (1967, Leeds); *Carrion Crow, Maiden's Lament*, and *Land of Silver Birch*, 3 folk songs for men's chorus (1967, Thompson); *Concertino a cinque* for flute, oboe, viola, cello, piano (1968); *Piae cantiones novae* for chorus (1968, Waterloo); *2 Dialogues* for cello, piano (1968); *Psalm 150* for chorus (1970, Waterloo); *Gloria* for vocal soloists, chorus, orchestra (1970); *Lagalai* for chorus, instrumental ensemble (1970); *Partita breve* for viola, piano (1971). List to 1961: *Composers of the Americas* 8:110–12.

BIBL.: "Meet Your Fellow Members," *The Canadian Composer* 22: 4–5; "From Diplomat to Composer," *ibid.* 22:44–45; "T. K., A Portrait," *Musicanada* 18:8–9; Valentins Berzkalns, "T. K.," *Latvju muzika* (Kalamazoo, Mich.) 3:232–60.

Kennan, Kent (Wheeler) (b. Milwaukee, 18 April 1913), studied architecture and liberal arts at the Univ. of Mich. (1930–32) and composition there with Hunter Johnson. He attended the Eastman School (1932–34, 1935, 1936; composition with Howard Hanson; orchestration with Bernard Rogers). He won the Prix de Rome in 1936 and lived in Europe through 1939; while there, he studied composition briefly with Ildebrando Pizzetti in Rome. Kennan has taught composition, orchestration, and counterpoint, among other musical subjects, at Kent State Univ., Ohio (1939–40), the Univ. of Texas (1940–42, 1945–46, and since 1949), Ohio State Univ. (1947–49), and at Eastman (summers, 1954, 1956).

PRINCIPAL COMPOSITIONS: *Night Soliloquy* for flute with piano, or with strings and piano, or with wind ensemble (1936, Fischer); *Il campo dei fiori* for trumpet, orchestra (1937); *Nocturne* for viola, orchestra (1937); *Promenade* for orchestra (1938, Fischer); *Symphony* (1938); *3 Preludes* for piano

(1938, Schirmer-G); *Andante* for oboe, orchestra (1939); *Blessed Are They that Mourn* for chorus, orchestra (1939, Schirmer-G); *The Unknown Warrior Speaks*, for men's chorus (1944, Gray); *Sonatina* for piano (1946); *2 Preludes* for piano (1951, Lawson); *Theme with Variations* for organ (1952); *Sonata* for trumpet, piano (1956, Remick).

PRINCIPAL WRITINGS: *Orchestration Workbook* (New York 1952); *The Technique of Orchestration* (New York 1952, 1970); *Counterpoint* (New York 1959); *Counterpoint Workbook* (New York 1959); *Orchestration Workbook II* (New York 1969).

Kerr, Harrison (b. Cleveland, 13 Oct 1897), studied music privately in Cleveland (1913–20) and at the American Conservatory at Fontainebleau (1921, composition with Nadia Boulanger, piano with Isidor Phillip and Camille Decreus). He has taught at Greenbrier College (1927–28), the Chase School (1928–35) and the Univ. of Okla. (1949–68), where he was also Dean of the College of Fine Arts. During 1937–49 he was secretary of the American Composers Alliance; during 1940–47, executive secretary of the American Music Center. He has written many reviews and essays for *The New York Times, Musical America*, etc.

PRINCIPAL COMPOSITIONS: *6 Songs to Poems by Adelaide Crapsey* for voice, piano (1924–28, Marks); *Symphonies Nos. 1–3* (1927–29, Arrow; 1943–45, ACA; 1953–54, ACA); *Piano Sonatas Nos. 1–2* (1929, ACA; 1943, Arrow); *Notations on a Sensitized Plate* for voice, clarinet, piano, string quartet (1935, Merion); *Trio* for clarinet, cello, piano (1936, Merion); *String Quartet* (1937, Arrow); *Wink of Eternity* for chorus, orchestra (1937, ACA); *Piano Trio* (1938, ACA); *Dance Suite* for orchestra or for 2 pianos, percussion (1938, ACA); *Suite* for flute, piano (1940–41, Arrow); *Preludes* for piano (1943, ACA); *Overture, Arioso, and Finale* for cello with piano or orchestra (1944–51, ACA); *Violin Concerto* (1950–51, ACA); *Violin Sonata* (1956, ACA); *The Tower of Kel*, 4-act opera (1958–60); *Sinfonietta* for chamber orchestra (1968, ACA).

BIBL.: Gilbert Chase, *America's Music*, 2nd ed. (New York 1955):614–16; Alexander L. Ringer, "H. K., Composer and Educator," *ACA Bulletin* 8/2:10–16.

Ketting, Otto (b. Amsterdam, 3 Sept 1935), studied at the Royal Conservatory in The Hague (1952–58). During 1959–61 he played trumpet in the Residentie Orchestra of The Hague. He has taught composition at the Rotterdam Conservatory since 1967. His *Concertino* for orchestra and jazz quintet (1960) was the first Dutch composition combining jazz and concert styles. In his concert music he uses atonality, serialism, theatrical elements, and chance. His incidental music for Greek drama, Shakespeare, contemporary plays, and films is "in a more conventional, French oriented style."

PRINCIPAL COMPOSITIONS (published by Donemus unless otherwise noted): *Fanfares 1956* for brass, percussion (1956); *2 Canzoni* for orchestra (1957); *Concertino* for 2 trumpets, orchestra (1958); *Symphony No. 1* (1959); *Variazioni* for orchestra (1960); *Concertino* for jazz quintet, orchestra (1960); *Pas de deux* for 24 winds, cellos, percussion (1961); *Het laatste bericht* [The Last Message], ballet; choreography by Benjamin Harkarvy (1962); *Collage No. 9* for 16 brass, 5 percussionists (1963); *Alleman* [The Human Dutch], film score (1963, unpub.); *Interieur*, ballet; choreography by Jaap Flier (1963); *Collage No. 6* for jazz band, orchestra (1966); *The River Must Live*, film score (1966, unpub.); *Collage No. 7* for dancers, orchestra (1967); *A Set of Pieces* for flute, piano (1967); *Choreostruction*, ballet; choreography by Job Sanders (1967); *A Set of Pieces* for wind quintet (1968); *The Land Must Provide*, film score (1968, unpub.).

Khachaturian, Aram (Il'ich) (b. Tiflis, 6 June 1903), is the son of a bookbinder. He attended the Tiflis Commerical School, taught himself piano, and played tenor horn in the school band. In 1921 he was brought to Moscow by his brother Suren. In 1922 he entered the biology department of Moscow University and was accepted at the Gnessin School as a cello student. The following year he entered Mikhail Gnessin's composition course. He followed Gnessin to the Moscow Conservatory in 1929, studying with him there for one more year, then with Nicholas Miaskovsky and (for orchestration) with Sergei Vasilenko. His *First Symphony* (1934–35) was a diploma work. He continued into graduate school under Miaskovsky, serving as his assistant until 1937. Thereafter he taught in the Conservatory and in the Gnessin School.

Khachaturian has written three ballets, three symphonies, four concertos, three concerto-rhapsodies, some chamber music, a number of shorter works, incidental music, and film scores. His creative output diminished after the mid-1950s as he became increasingly occupied with official delegations, speech making, and conducting. Armenian by descent, he often uses Armenian tunes in his music but just as frequently has used Russian, Uzbek, Ukrainian, Georgian, or Azerbaidzhanian, all in the Rimsky-Korsakov tradition. The finale of his *Piano Trio* is based on an Uzbek folk tune, and the clarinet in the first movement imitates a *zurna*, a Transcaucasian wind in-

strument. The *Dance Suite* (1932–33), his first orchestral work, consists of five short dances in which Armenian, Georgian, and Uzbek tunes are used. His *First Symphony* has the improvisatory character of an *ashug* [bard] song, which is a Caucasian, usually Azerbadzhanian tale without set form. The use in this work of a massive orchestra and the handling of the ornamented melodic lines follows the 19th-century Russian tradition. In the third movement a Georgian *lezginka* is the basis for the development of intricate cross-rhythms.

The influence of contemporaries is strong in Khachaturian's music. Prokofiev's influence is discernible in his motoric ostinatos and tonal shifts; he has also learned well the style of Shaporin's lyricism, the intellectual coolness of Peiko, and the harmonic toughness of Shostakovich. He is a gifted orchestrator who understands the texture, color, and rhythmic possibilities of instruments.

PRINCIPAL COMPOSITIONS (available from Mezhkniga): *Symphonies Nos. 1–3* (1934–35, 1942, 1947); *Piano Concerto* (1936); *Pesn'ia Stalina* [Song of Stalin] for chorus, orchestra (c.1937); *Poema Stalina* [Poem of Stalin] for chorus, orchestra; text from the Azerbaidzhanian ashug Mirza from Tauza (1938); *Violin Concerto* (1940); *Gaiane*, 3-act ballet (1942; *Suites Nos. 1–3*, 1943); *Concerto* for violin, cello, orchestra (c. 1944); *Cello Concerto* (1946); *Traurnaia oda pamiati Vladimira Il'icha Lenina* [Funeral Ode to Lenin] from the film Vladimir Il'ich Lenin (1948); *Spartak*, 4-act ballet; scenario by N. Volkov after the Spartacus story (1950–56; *4 Suites*: Nos. 1–3, 1955; No. 4, 1966); *Grand Overture for the Opening of the 21st Party Congress* (1956); *Concerto-Rhapsody* for piano, orchestra (1961); *Ode of Joy* for chorus (1961); *Song to the Fatherland* for bass, orchestra (1961); *Concerto-Rhapsody* for violin, orchestra (1961–62); *Concerto-Rhapsody* for cello, orchestra (1963).

PRINCIPAL WRITINGS: "Kak Ia Ponimaiu Narodnost' v Muzyke" [How I Understand the Folk Element in Music], *Sovetskaia Muzyka* (May 1952).

BIBL.: Gerald Abraham, "A. K.," *Monthly Musical Record* (March 1942); Y. Y. Baynkop, *Sovetskie Kompozitory* (Leningrad 1938); Stanley D. Krebs, *Soviet Composers and the Development of Soviet Music* (New York 1970); Ivan Martinov, *A. K.* (Moscow 1947); Gustav Schneerson, *A. K.* (Moscow 1958).

Larissa Janczyn

SEE ALSO Dance, Soviet Union.

Khrennikov, Tikhon (Nikolaevich) (b. Yeletz, Russia, 28 May 1913), studied with Mikhail Gnessin at the Gnessin Music School (1929–32) and at the Moscow Conservatory (1932–36; composition with Vissarion Shebalin,

Henrich Neuhauz). He was musical director of the Central Army Theater during 1941–54. Since 1948 he has been first secretary of the Union of Soviet Composers. His music derives from the concert-music tradition of 18th- and 19th-century Russia and from Russian folk music.

PRINCIPAL COMPOSITIONS (available from Mezhkniga): *Piano Concerto No. 1* (1932–33); *Symphonies Nos. 1–2* (1933–35, 1940–41); *V buriu* [Into the Storm], 4-act opera; libretto by A. Faiko and N. Virta (1936–39); *Frol Skobeev*, 4-act comic opera; libretto by S. Tsenin after D. Averkiev (1945–50); *Mat'* [Mother], 4-act opera; libretto by A. Faiko after Gorky (1952–56); *Violin Concerto* (1959); *Chertei i odna devushka* [100 Devils and a Girl], operetta (1963); *Belaia noch'* [White Night], operetta (1967); *Bezrodnyi ziat'* [The Common Son-in-law], a revised version of *Frol Skobeev* (1967); *Mal'chik-velikan* [A Boy Giant], children's opera (1970); *Pervyi podvig* [First Exploit], ballet (1970).

BIBL.: V. F. Kucharsky, *T. K.* (Moscow 1957); I. Kremliev, *T. K.* (Moscow 1963); Ivan Martynov, *T. K.* (Moscow 1968).

SEE ALSO Soviet Union.

Killmayer, Wilhelm (b. Munich, 21 August 1927), studied at the Staatliche Hochschule für Musik in Munich (1952–53, composition with Carl Orff) and the Univ. of Munich (1950–53, musicology with Rudolf von Ficker). He also studied composition and conducting with Hermann Wolfgang von Waltershausen in Munich (1945–50). During 1961–65 he conducted ballet at the Bavarian State Opera in Munich.

PRINCIPAL COMPOSITIONS (published by Schott): *Lorca*, romances for soprano, piano, percussion (1955); *La buffonata*, ballet for dancers, soloists, chorus, orchestra (1958–60); *La tragedia di Orfeo*, ballet for the same (1961); *Sappho*, 5 songs for soprano, orchestra (1961); *Yolimba oder Die Grenzen der Magie*, opera (1963); *Une Leçon de Français* for chorus, wind instruments (1964); *7 Rondeaux* for 6 women's voices (1966); *3 Canti di Leopardi* for baritone, orchestra (1967); *Lauda* for chorus, orchestra (1967); *Pezzi e intermezzi* for piano, cello, orchestra (1968); *Sinfonie No. 1*, "Fogli," for orchestra (1968); *Sinfonie No. 2*, "Ricordanze," for 13 instruments (1969); *Preghiere* for baritone, orchestra (1969).

Kilar, Wojciech (Adam) (b. Lvov, Poland, 17 July 1932), studied at the Katowice State Academy of Music (1950–55, composition and piano with Bolesław Woytowicz), the Cracow State Academy of Music (1955–58, composition with Woytowicz), and the Darmstadt summer courses (1957). He also studied in Paris with Nadia Boulanger (1959–60). He is a free-lance composer and has written many scores for films and the theater. He also performs as a pianist in his own works.

PRINCIPAL COMPOSITIONS (published by PWM unless otherwise noted): *Little Overture* for orchestra (1955); *Symphonies Nos. 1–2*: No. 1 for string orchestra (1955, unpub.); No. 2 "Sinfonia concertante" for piano, orchestra (1956, unpub.); *Oda Béla Bartók in memoriam* for violin solo, brass, 2 groups of percussion (1957); *Concerto* for 2 pianos, percussion orchestra (1958, unpub.); *Herbsttag*, cantata for alto, string quartet; text by Rilke (1959, unpub.); *Riff 62* for 2 clarinets, 3 saxophones, 4 trumpets, 4 trombones, 36 violins, 12 double basses, piano, 2 percussion groups (1962); *Générique* for orchestra (1963); *Diphthongos* for chorus, strings, percussion, 2 pianos (1964); *Springfield Sonnet* for orchestra (1965); *Solenne* for soprano, strings, brass (1966); *Training 68* for clarinet, trombone, cello, piano (1968).

BIBL.: Ludwig Erhardt, *Muzyka Polska* (Warsaw 1968):186–87; Leon Markiewicz, "W. K.— En nutida komponist" [W. K.—A Modern Composer], *Nutida musik* (Stockholm) 1965–66/1–2: 18–21; Bogusław Schäffer, *Przewodnik koncertowy* [Concert Leaders] (Warsaw 1965):356–57.

Kirchner, Leon (b. Brooklyn, N. Y., 24 Jan 1919), began the study of piano at an early age and was performing publicly at 14. His family moved to California when he was nine, and it was in Los Angeles that he received most of his musical training. He studied with Stravinsky, Schoenberg, Toch, and Klemperer, among others, and in 1938 went to the Univ. of Calif. at Berkeley, where he studied with Albert Elkus and Edward Strickland (BA, 1940). He pursued further studies with Ernest Bloch and Roger Sessions in California and New York. He has taught at the Univ. of Southern Calif. (1950–54), Mills College (1954–60), and Harvard Univ. (since 1961). Since arriving at Harvard he has widened his activities as pianist, lecturer, and conductor (he is principal conductor of the Boston Philharmonic).

Kirchner's music has been described as "rhapsodic," "ecstatic," "restless," "urgent" —terms connoting a certain degree of emotional excitement. More important, they imply that the composer wishes his ideas to be received primarily in their immediacy of impact and only secondarily as shapes and arrangements. The music is carefully controlled but not according to systems: the harmonic language, for example, is reminiscent of Schoenberg and Berg, but there is no trace of 12-tone technique; movements fall into sections but do not correspond nor even provide analogies (largely because of the absence of repetition) to formal types. Although a neoclassic impulse in the earlier music led to readily perceivable sectional differentiations, the almost total absence of this impulse in later works, such as the *Third Quartet*, eliminates sectional opposition; despite tempo fluctuations and dynamic changes, the listener is aware only retrospectively of having been lifted from one state to another. The use of techniques to conceal technique is indicative of Kirchner's attempt to "involve the listener very directly with the organic growth of a work." Such growth is also ensured by the lack of sharp distinctions between declamatory and lyrical factors; lyricism is the basic impulse in the music, and the declamatory moments proceed naturally from it. This fact alone may have led Aaron Copland to characterize Kirchner's style as belonging to the "Bartók-Berg axis of contemporary music." The composer has written very little for voice but has been working intermittently since 1964 on an opera based on Saul Bellow's *Henderson, the Rain King*.

PRINCIPAL COMPOSITIONS (published by AMP unless otherwise noted): *Duo* for violin, piano (1947, Mercury); *Piano Sonata* (1948); *String Quartets Nos. 1-3* (1948, Mercury; 1958; 1966); *Piano Concertos Nos. 1-2* (1953, 1963); *Toccata* for strings, solo winds, percussion (1956); *Concerto* for violin, cello, 10 winds, percussion (1960). List to 1960: *Composers of the Americas* 7:48-49.

BIBL.: Alexander L. Ringer, "L. K.," *Musical Quarterly* 43:1ff.

Laurence D. Berman

SEE ALSO United States.

Kiyose, Yasuji (b. Usa City, Japan, 13 Jan 1900), coached in composition with Kosuke Komatsu (1926-27) and studied harmony and counterpoint with Klaus Pringsheim (1934-35). He teaches privately. His music has been influenced by traditional Japanese music and, among 20th-century European composers, by Debussy, Ravel, and Bartók.

PRINCIPAL COMPOSITIONS: *To an Ancient Time* for orchestra (1937); *Lento and Allegro* for flute, piano (1937); *Trio* for flute, clarinet, bassoon (1938); *Japanese Festival Dances* for orchestra (1940); *Violin Sonatas Nos. 1-3* (1941, 1948, 1950); *Piano Concerto* (1950); *String Trio* (1951); *Piano Trio No. 2* (1955); *Quintet* for woodwinds, harp (1957); *Unknown Soldiers*, requiem (1960, piano score published by Kawai-gakufu); *2 Movements* for violin, piano (1960, Ongaku); chamber music for traditional Japanese instruments: *Trio* (1964); *Octet* (1964); *Quintet* (1965); *Quartet* (1965). Kiyose has also written 2 volumes of songs (1921, 1966; Zenon-gakufu) and many choruses (1952-71, Kawai-gakufu).

SEE ALSO Japan.

Klangfarbenmelodie, a term coined by Arnold Schoenberg meaning "tone-color melody." It refers to the use of a succession of timbres as thematic material in a composition, analogous to the use of a succession of pitches for similar purposes in traditional music. Schoenberg first used the concept in the third of his *5 Pieces for Orchestra*, Op. 16 (1909), where the pitches in a chordal mass are filtered through various orchestral timbres; changes in timbre, along with changes in dynamics, durations, and other elements, constitute the shape or form of the piece. Schoenberg first used the term in print in his *Harmonielehre* (Vienna 1911).

BIBL.: Robert Beyer, "Die Klangwelt der electronischen Musik," *Zeitschrift für Musik* 113:74-79; ——, "Electronische Musik," *Melos* 21:35-39; ——, "Zur Situation der electronischen Musik," *Zeitschrift für Musik* 116:452-56; Robert Craft, "Anton Webern," *Score* (Sept 1955):9-22; René Leibowitz, "Alban Berg's Five Orchestral Songs . . . ," *Musical Quarterly* 34:487-511; ——, *Schoenberg and His School*, trans. by Dika Newlin (New York 1949):201-03 *et passim*; Herman Pfrogner, "Elektronik-Lust am Untergang," *Neue Zeitschrift für Musik* (Sept 1957):484-89.

Klebe, Giselher (Wolfgang) (b. Mannheim, 28 June 1925), studied composition with Kurt von Wolpurt at the Berlin State Conservatory and with Josef Rufer and Boris Blacher. He has taught composition at the Nordwestdeutsche Musikakademie in Detmold since 1967.

PRINCIPAL COMPOSITIONS (published by Bote unless otherwise noted): *Sonata* for 2 pianos, Op. 4 (1949, Schott); *Divertissements* for 5 winds, strings, percussion, Op. 5 (1949); *Die Zuitschermaschine*, metamorphosis on the picture by Klee for orchestra, Op. 7 (1950); *String Quartets Nos. 1-2*, Opp. 9, 42 (1950, 1963); *2 Nocturnes* for orchestra, Op. 10 (1951); *Symphony* for 42 strings, Op. 12 (1951, Schott); *Violin Sonata*, Op. 14 (1952, Schott); *Römische Elegien* for narrator, piano, harpsichord, double bass, Op. 15; text from Goethe (1952, Schott); *Der Räuber*, 4-act opera after Schiller, Op. 25 (1952-56); *Symphony No. 2*, Op. 16 (1953, Schott); *Rhapsody* for orchestra, Op. 17 (1953); *Signale*, ballet, Op. 21 (1955); *Elegia appassionata* for piano trio, Op. 22 (1955); *Raskolnikows Traum*, dramatic scene for soprano, clarinet, orchestra, Op. 23; text from Dostoevsky (1956); *Menagerie*, ballet, Op. 31 (1958); *Dir tödlichen Wünsche*, 3-act opera after Balzac, Op. 27 (1959); *Die ermordung Cäsars*, 1-act opera, Op. 32 (c.1960); *Alkmene*, 3-act opera, Op. 36 (1961); *Adagio and Fugue* on a theme from Wagner's Die Walküre for orchestra, Op. 37 (1962); *5 Songs* for medium voice, piano or orchestra, Op. 38 (1962); *Figaro lässt sich scheiden*, 2-act opera, Op. 40 (1962-63); *Missa "Miserere nobis"* for 18 winds, Op. 45

(1963–64); *Stabat Mater* for soloists, chorus, orchestra, Op. 46 (1964); *Introitus, Aria, and Alleluja* for organ, Op. 47 (1964); *2 Studies* for percussion, Opp. 30, 48 (1964); *Jacobowsky und der Oberst*, 4-act opera after Franz Werfel, Op. 49 (1965); *9 Duettini* for flute, piano, Op. 39 (1965); *Gebet einer armen Seele*, mass for chorus, organ, Op. 51 (1966, Bärenreiter); *Symphony No. 3*, Op. 52 (1967, Bärenreiter); *Piano Quintet*, "quasi una fantasia," Op. 53 (1967, Bärenreiter); *Das Märchen von der schönen Lilie*, 2-act opera after Goethe, Op. 55 (1967–68, Bärenreiter); *Scene and Aria* for 3 trumpets, 3 trombones, 8 cellos, 2 pianos, Op. 54 (1968, Bärenreiter).

PRINCIPAL WRITINGS: "Richard Wagner und die Kontinuität der abendländischen Musik," *Jahrbuch der Freien Akademie der Künste* (Hamburg, 1964); "Mathematik und Phantasie in der neuen Musik," *ibid.* (1965).

SEE ALSO Austria and Germany, Opera.

Klusak, Jan (b. Prague, 18 April 1934), studied at the Prague Academy of Music (1953–57; composition with Pavel Bořkovec, theory with Karel Janeček, film and theater music with Václav Trojan). He has worked with a number of Czech film directors as a composer and actor and has recently participated in events staged at a Prague studio for theater of the absurd.

PRINCIPAL COMPOSITIONS: *Čtyři malá hlasová cičvení* [4 Small Vocal Exercises] for narrator, 11 winds; texts by Franz Kafka (1960, Panton); *Obrazy* [Pictures] for 12 winds (1960, SHV); *Variations on a Theme by Mahler* for orchestra (1960–62, Panton); *Invention I* for chamber orchestra (1961, SHV); *Černé madrigaly* [Black Madrigals] for chorus; texts by František Halas (1961); *Sonata* for violin, winds (1964–65, SHV); *O sacrum convivium!*, concrete motet on tape (1968); *Invention VI* for wind quintet, violin, viola, cello, double bass (1969).

PRINCIPAL WRITINGS: "Výrazové možnosti nového slohu" [New Style and Its Expressive Possibilities], *Hudební rozhledy* 1962/15: 760–61 "Variations on a Theme by Mahler" (1968, unpub. lecture).

BIBL.: Eduard Herzog, preface to the SHV edition of *Obrazy* (1967); Vladimír Lébl, "O současném stavu nových skladebných směrů u nás" [The Present State of New Compositional Styles in Czechoslovakia], *Nové cesty hudby* (Prague 1964): 11–25.

SEE ALSO Czechoslovakia.

Kochan, Günter (b. Luckau, Germany, 2 Oct 1930), studied at the Berlin Hochschule für Musik (1946–50; composition with Hermann Wunsch, Boris Blacher) and the German Academy of the Arts in East Berlin (1950–53,

composition with Hanns Eisler). He has taught harmony, counterpoint, and composition at the Deutsche Hochschule für Musik "Hanns Eisler" in East Berlin since 1950 and has composed for films and television.

PRINCIPAL COMPOSITIONS: *Piano Concerto* (1957–58, Peters-L); *Sinfonietta* (1960, Peters-L); *Concerto for Orchestra* (1962, VNM); *Symphony* for chorus, orchestra (1962–64); *Divertimento*, "Variations on a Theme by Weber," for orchestra (1964, Peters-L); *3 Shakespeare Songs* for alto, orchestra (1964, Peters-L); *Die Asche von Birkenau*, cantata for alto, orchestra; text by Stephen Hermlin (1965, Neue Musik); *Symphony No. 2* (1968, DVM); *Der Prozess der Karin Lenz*, opera in 8 scenes (1968–70).

Kodály, Zoltán (b. Kecskemét, Hungary, 16 Dec 1882; d. Budapest, 6 March 1967), was the son of a railroad station master who was transferred frequently, permitting the young Kodály a unique opportunity to discover the differences in folksong repertory in different parts of the country, as well as the differences between the basic musical systems of Western concert music and the music of the Eastern peasants. His parents were good amateur performers on violin and piano, and the elder Kodály, as soon as he arrived in a new location, would organize a string quartet in which his children played when needed. The son began to compose at an early age and was awarded a scholarship to pursue his studies in Budapest. There he studied composition with Hans Koessler (1900–04) and at the same time earned a PhD degree in philology with a dissertation on the strophic structure of Hungarian folksongs.

In 1906 Kodály began collaborating with Béla Bartók in systematically collecting peasant songs by means of cylinder phonographs and pen. The first fruit of their work was a publication of 20 folksongs (1907), Nos. 1–10 edited by Bartók, 11–20 by Kodály. Their aim was scholarly accuracy and completeness plus a desire, through simple piano accompaniments, to bring this music closer to public taste as it then existed. In 1907 Kodály toured the big cities of western Europe and then settled down to teach composition at the Royal Academy of Music in Budapest, where he remained (with one interruption) throughout his life.

Kodály took a leading role in the founding of the New Hungarian Music Association and in drafting the plan published in *Ethnographia* in 1913 for collecting all folk material. (In 1934 the Hungarian Academy of Sciences adopted the plan and entrusted Bartók and Kodály with its realization. Vol. I, devoted to children's games, appeared in 1951, and five other volumes have since appeared). Meanwhile, Kodály's compositions were being performed publicly in western Europe and the U.S., although less frequently in Budapest (two concerts in 1910 and 1918). He became active as a music critic and essayist, publishing his first study of the role of the pentatonic scale in Hungarian folk music in 1917. His first major and universal success came with the performance of the *Psalmus hungaricus* in 1923. Two stage works, *Háry János* (1926) and *Székelyfonó* (1932), were even more successful. His other activities included training young students in the study of folk music, teaching school children to sing, and writing (he published nine scholarly essays during 1917–29 as well as music reviews). During 1926–28 he also organized music festivals in Hungary. Honors began to pour in, and whereas he was greeted by the critics with derision at the beginning of his career, he was lionized in the last three decades of his life.

Kodály believed firmly that music is primarily melodic and therefore singable and communal. He abandoned the Western orientation in concert music and turned instead to folk sources for the revitalizing of music in Hungary. He persuaded schoolteachers and the government to introduce singing in the schools and wrote simple pieces for children's choruses, for factory choirs, and for singing societies. Even his earliest pieces (before 1910), although somewhat rambling and lacking his later conciseness, reveal his intent to create a musical language with an authoritatively Hungarian flavor.

His style is primarily melodic, with the melody related to the Hungarian folk idiom, some of the characteristics of which are a prominence of the interval of the fourth, of the pentatonic scale, and of the falling fourth and rising whole tone in cadences His harmony is logically derived from the melodic characteristics. The structure of the whole is always clear and well proportioned; a formal balance is always observed. He avoided experiments with chromaticism, with the farther harmonic overtones, exotic scales, or nontraditional forms.

Kodály's lifelong friendship and collaboration with Bartók is extremely important. Bartók went much farther in experiments in style and form and gained much more international recognition. It is to Kodály's credit that he did not follow his friend on these paths but remained true to himself, to his more conservative nature. They respected each other, and their collaboration resulted in artistic achievements that made their period the most glorious in the history of Hungarian music.

PRINCIPAL COMPOSITIONS (published by UE unless otherwise noted): *Adagio* for violin, piano (1905, Rózsavölgyi); *Nyári este* [Summer Evening] for orchestra (1906); *20 Hungarian Folksongs* for voice, piano; Nos. 1–10 arranged by Bartók, 11–20 by Kodály (1906, Rozsnyai); *4 Songs* (1907, UE); *16 Songs*, Op. 1 (1907–09, Rózsavölgyi); *String Quartet No. 1*, Op. 2 (1908–09, Rózsavölgyi); *Piano Music*, Op. 3 (1909, Rózsavölgyi); *Cello Sonata*, Op. 4 (1909–10, Rózsavölgyi); *5 Songs*, Op. 9 (1910–18); *7 Songs* (1912–18); *Duo* for violin, cello, Op. 7 (1914); *Sonata* for solo cello, Op. 8 (1915); *Megkésett melódiák* [Belated Melodies] for voice, piano, Op. 6 (1916); *String Quartet No. 2*, Op. 10 (1916–18); *Serenade* for 2 violins, viola, Op. 12 (1919–20); *Psalmus hungaricus* for tenor, chorus, orchestra, Op. 13 (1923); *Székely Volksballaden und Lieder aus Transsylvanien*, 119 pieces (1919–20); *Székelyfonó* [The Spinning Room], lyric scenes based on Hungarian folksongs and dances (1924–32); *Háry János*, 3-act opera, Op. 15; libretto by B. Panlini, Z. Harsányi (1925–27); *Marosszéki táncok* [Dances from Marosszék] for orchestra (1930); *Galántai táncok* [Dances from Galanta] for orchestra (1933); *Budavári Te Deum* [Te Deum of Buda Castle] for vocal soloists, chorus, orchestra (1936); *Concerto for Orchestra* (1939, available from EMB); *Symphony* (1961). Kodály also wrote a large number of vocal and choral works for children and adults, all with Hungarian texts. Complete list in *Contemporary Hungarian Composers* (Budapest 1970).

PRINCIPAL WRITINGS: Kodály left an imposing amount of scholarly essays in ethnomusicology and music education, among them: *A magyar népdal strófaszerkezete* [The Strophic Structure of Hungarian Folksong] (Budapest 1905); *Ötfoku hangsor a magyar népzenében* [The Pentatonic Scale in Hungarian Folk Music] (Budapest 1917); *Erdélyi magyarság* [Hungarians of Transylvania], written in collaboration with Bartók (Budapest 1913); *Sajátságos dallamszerkezet a cseremisz népzenében* [Peculiar Melodic Structures in Cheremiss Folk Music] (Budapest 1934); *A magyar népzene* [Hungarian Folk Music] English trans., *Folk Music of Hungary* (New York 1960); *Visszatekintés* [Reminiscences] (Budapest 1965).

BIBL. (in English): L. Eősze, *Z. K., His Life and Works* (London 1962); P. Young, *Z. K.* (London 1964).

Egon Kenton

SEE ALSO Folk Resources; Hungary; Liturgical Music: Christian.

Koechlin, Charles (b. Paris, 27 Nov 1867; d. le Canadel, Var, 31 Dec 1950), studied widely and took music really seriously only at the age of 22. Thereafter he studied at the Paris Conservatory (1890–97) under Massenet, Gédalge, and Fauré, who particularly influenced him. He led a comfortable and comparatively uneventful life, composing, writing theoretical works, teaching, and lecturing, mostly on contemporary music. He was president of the French section of ISCM. Because of his almost complete immersion in his art, he sometimes appeared eccentric to outsiders, a fact reflected in his independent approach to composition.

Koechlin's output includes over 200 opus numbers with works in almost all genres; particularly noteworthy are the symphonic poems, the chamber and piano music, and the songs and choruses. The major influences were Franck (musical form), Fauré (exquisite craftsmanship), Debussy (harmony and color), Satie (free piano writing), and Stravinsky (orchestration), as well as the free and asymmetric melodies of plainsong and medieval music. His compositions are basically melodic, an obvious feature in the many choruses, songs, and monodies for solo wind instruments, but also present in the simpler, wholly diatonic piano pieces, e.g., the *Sonatines* and *Petites Pièces*. In addition to the presence of irregular melodies, the complex *Paysages et marines* for piano shows a medieval influence in its use of parallel fourths and fifths, which occur alongside chords of superimposed fourths and fifths. This combination of "ancient" and "modern" helps to give the music its strangely timeless character. Counterpoint, often present in the smaller works, takes on more importance in the chamber music, e.g., in the at times virtually atonal *Wind Trio*, Op. 92, and in the complex, polyphonic *Violin Sonata*. Much of the *Viola Sonata* (dedicated to his pupil Darius Milhaud) and *Paysages et marines* are bitonal. One can see Koechlin's full stature in the large orchestral works, particularly the cantata *L'Abbaye*, the *Second Symphony*, *Le Buisson ardent* (the last two using the ondes Martenot) and the Jungle Book symphonic poems. The last of these poems, *Les Bandar-Log*, ruthlessly parodies some of the inferior imitative composers of his time. Koechlin's music is fastidiously written, mostly very restrained and with no spectacular appeal. It follows no fashion or school in music. Because the larger works are rarely performed and very few published, his influence (except as a teacher) has been slight. The stature of his music must remain enigmatic until his works are more accessible.

PRINCIPAL COMPOSITIONS: *L'Abbaye*, sacred suite for solo voices, orchestra, organ: Part I, Op. 16 (1899–1902), Part 2, Op. 42 (1906–08); *3 Poèmes* for orchestra after Kipling, Op. 18 (1899–1910); *La Forêt*, symphonic poem; part I, Op. 25 (1897–1904), part 2, Op. 29 (1896–1907); *Jacob chez Laban*, biblical pastorale in I act, Op. 36 (1896–1908); *5 Chansons de Bilitis* for voice, piano, Op. 39 (1898–1908); *La Forêt païenne*, ballet, Op. 45 (1916–20); *String Quartet No. 1*, Op. 51 (1911–13, Salabert); *Flute Sonata*, Op. 52 (1913, Salabert); *Viola Sonata*, Op. 53 (1906–15, Salabert); *5 Mélodies sur les poèmes de la Shéhérazade de Tristan Klingsor* for voice, piano; set 1, Op. 56 (1914–16), set 2, Op. 84 (1922); *String Quartet No. 2*, Op. 57 (1915–16); *Oboe Sonata*, Op. 58 (1911–16, McG-M); *Paysages et marines* for piano, Op. 63 (c.1916, Salabert); *Violin Sonata*, Op. 64 (1916, Salabert); *Cello Sonata*, Op. 66 (1917, Salabert); *Horn Sonata*, Op. 70 (1918–25); *Bassoon Sonata*, Op. 71 (1919); *String Quartet No. 3*, Op. 72 (1921, Salabert); *Sonatas* for clarinet, piano or chamber orchestra, Opp. 85, 86 (1923, L'Oiseau); *Trio* for flute, clarinet, bassoon, Op. 92 (1924, Salabert); *La Course de printemps*, symphonic poem after Kipling, Op. 95 (1925–27); *3 Organ Sonatas*, Op. 107 (1929, L'Oiseau); *Hymne* for ondes Martenot, orchestra, Op. 110 (1939–42); *20 Chansons bretonnes* for cello with piano or chamber orchestra, Op. 115 (1934, Salabert); *L'Ancienne Maison de campagne*, suite for piano, Op. 124 (1932–33, L'Oiseau); *7 Stars Symphony*, suite for orchestra based on the characters of film stars, Op. 132 (1933); *Primavera* for flute, violin, viola, cello, harp, Op. 156 (1936); *Symphony of Hymns* for orchestra (1936); *Septet* for wind quintet, English horn, alto saxophone, Op. 165 (1937, L'Oiseau); *Le Buisson ardent*, symphonic poem; part I, Op. 171 (1938), part 2, Op. 203 (1945); *La Loi de la jungle*, symphonic poem after Kipling, Op. 175 (1939); *Les Bandar-Log*, symphonic poem after Kipling, Op. 176 (1939–40, Eschig); *Offrande Musicale sur le nom de B.A.C.H.* for organ, orchestra, Op. 187 (1942); *Symphony No. 2*, Op. 196 (1943–44); *Partita* for chamber orchestra, Op. 205 (1945, Salabert).

PRINCIPAL WRITINGS: *Etude sur les notes de passage* (Paris 1922); *A Summary of the Rules of Counterpoint* (Paris 1926); *Traité d'harmonie*, 3 vols. (Paris 1927–30); *Debussy* (Paris 1927); *Gabriel Fauré*, English ed. (London 1946); *Théorie de la musique* (Paris 1935); *Traité d'orchestration*, 4 vols. (1–2, Paris 1949).

BIBL.: M. D. Calvocoressi, "C. K.'s Instrumental Works," *Music and Letters* 5:357ff.; Wilfred Mellers, *Studies in Contemporary Music* (London 1947), ch. 5; Pierre Renaudin, *C. K.* (Paris 1952).

Niall O'Loughlin

SEE ALSO France.

Koellreutter, Hans Joachim (b. Freiburg, 2 Sept 1915), attended the Berlin State Academy of Music (1934–36, composition with Paul

Hindemith, conducting with Kurt Thomas and Hermann Scherchen, flute with Gustav Scheck, piano with C. A. Martienssen, musicology with Georg Schuenemann and Max Seiffert), and the Geneva Conservatory (1936–37, flute with Marcel Moyse). He taught at the Brazilian Conservatory in Rio de Janeiro (1937–52) and at the Institute of Music in São Paulo (1942–44). He was founder and head of the Free Academy of Music in São Paulo (1952–55) and the music department of Bahia Univ. (1952–62), and founded music schools in Piracicaba, Itabuna, and Feira de Santana, Brazil. He also was chief conductor of the Bahia Symphony Orchestra and served as general secretary and president of the Brazilian section of ISCM. During 1963–65 he was head of the program department of the Goethe Institute in Munich and from 1965 to 1969, director of the German Cultural Institute in New Delhi and representative of the Munich Goethe Institute for India, Ceylon, and Burma. During this time he founded and was principal of the Delhi School of Music. In 1969 he became director of the German Cultural Institute of the Goethe Institute in Tokyo and representative of the Munich Goethe Institute for Japan. In 1970 he began work organizing a music department for the new Campinas Univ. in São Paulo.

PRINCIPAL COMPOSITIONS: *4 Pieces* for orchestra (1937); *Flute Sonatas Nos. 1–2* (1937, 1939); *Violin Sonata* (1939); *Inventions* for oboe, clarinet, bassoon (1940); *Música 1941* for piano (1941, Peer and ECIC); *Variations* for flute, English horn, clarinet, bassoon (1941); *Intrata* for bass (1942); *Duo* for cello, piano (1943); *Nocturnes* for mezzo-soprano, string quartet (1943, ECIC); *Variations* for orchestra (1945); *Música concertante* for piano, 7 winds, percussion (1946); *Música* for orchestra (1947); *Música 1947* for string quartet (1947); *Chamber Symphony* (1948); *Diaton 8* for flute, English horn, bassoon, harp, xylophone (1955); *Systática* for flute, percussion (1955); *O Café*, choral drama; text by Mario de Andrade (1956); *Concretion* for orchestra (1960, EM); *Constructio ad synesin* for orchestra (1962, EM); *8 Haikai by Pedro Xisto* for baritone, flute, electric guitar, piano, gongs, cymbals, wood blocks, tam-tam (1963, EM); *Kulka-Chants* for soprano, piano (1964, EM); *Sunyata* for flute, chamber orchestra of Western and Indian instruments (1968); *India Report* for soprano, speaker, chamber chorus, speaking chorus, chamber orchestra of Western and Indian instruments (1969); *Composition 70* for sitar, chamber orchestra (1970); *Yugen* for soprano, Japanese instruments (1970).

PRINCIPAL WRITINGS: *Jazz Harmonia* (São Paulo 1969); *3 Lectures on Music* (Mysore 1968); *10 Lectures on Music* (New Delhi 1969); *History of Western Music* (New Delhi c.1970).

SEE ALSO Brazil.

Koenig, Gottfried Michael (b. Magdeburg, Germany, 5 Oct 1926), studied sacred music at the Staatsmusikschule in Brunswick (1946–47) and attended the Nordwestdeutsche Musikakademie in Detmold (1947–50, composition with Günther Bialas, piano with Natermann, analysis with Mahler, acoustics with Thienhaus), the Institute for Musical-Technical Formation at the Staatliche Hochschule für Musik in Cologne (1953–54), and Bonn Univ. (1963–64), where he studied the construction and programming of computers. He was an assistant at the Studio for Electronic Music of the Northwest German Radio, Cologne (1954–64), taught at the Staatliche Hochschule für Musik, Cologne (1958–64), and became artistic director at the Studio for Electronic Music, Rijksuniversiteit, Utrecht, in 1964. The ideas of T. W. Adorno have had the greatest impact on his thinking.

PRINCIPAL COMPOSITIONS: *Klangfiguren* on tape (1955–56, recorded by DGG); *Essay* on tape 1957–58, UE); *Wind Quintet* (1958–59, Tonos); *String Quartet* (1959, Tonos); *Piece for Orchestra No. 2* (1961–62, Tonos); *Terminus* on tape (1962); *Piece for Orchestra No. 3* (1963); *Project 1* (version 1) for 14 instruments (1967, Peters); *Project 1* (version 3) for 9 instruments (1967, Peters); *Terminus 2* on tape (1967, recorded by DGG); *Funktion Grün* on tape (1967, recorded by DGG); *Funktion Gelb* on tape (recorded by Wergo).

PRINCIPAL WRITINGS: In *Die Reihe* (English ed.): "Studio Technique," 1:52–54; "Bo Nilsson," 4:85–89; "Studium im Studio," 5:30–40; "Commentary," (German ed. 8:80–98. ★ "Via electronica," *Movens* (Wiesbaden 1960):161–68; "Serielle und aleatorische Verfahren in der electronischen Musik," *Die Sonde* (Bonn) 5/1:26–33; "The Second Phase of Electronic Music," *Vision 65* (New York 1966):169–83; "Notes on the Computer in Music," *The World of Music* 9/3:3–13; "Computer-Verwendung in Kompositionsprozessen," *Musik auf der Flucht vor sich selbst* ed. by U. Dibelius (Munich 1969).

BIBL.: Ulrich Dibelius, *Moderne Musik 1945–65* (Munich 1966):164–74; Nicole Lachartre, "Les Musiques artificielles," *Diagrammes du monde* (Monaco) 146:56–60.

Kohn, Karl (b. Vienna, 1 August 1926), studied at the N. Y. College of Music (1940–44, piano with Carl V. Werschinger, conducting with Julius Pruewer) and Harvard Univ. (1946–50, 1954–55; composition with Walter Piston; theory with Irving Fine, Randall Thompson, Edward Ballantine). He has taught at Tanglewood (1954, 55, 57) and at Pomona College in Calif. (since 1950). He performs as a pianist and conductor (especially medieval, renaissance, and 20th-century music). He has been on the board of directors for Monday Evening Concerts in Los Angeles since 1957 and has directed its Ensemble I since 1963.

PRINCIPAL COMPOSITIONS (published by Fischer unless otherwise noted): *3 Descants from Ecclesiastes* for chorus, piano or brass (1957); *Castles and Kings*, a children's suite for orchestra (1958); *3 Scenes* for orchestra (1958–60); *Sensus spei*, motet for chorus with piano and/or instruments (1961); *Concerto mutabile* for piano, chamber ensemble or orchestra (1962); *Capriccios* for harp, cello, flute, clarinet, piano (1962); *Serenade* for wind quintet, piano (1962, unpub.); *Interludes* for orchestra (1964); *Episodes* for piano, orchestra (1966); *Introductions and Parodies* for clarinet, bassoon, horn, string quartet, piano (1967, unpub.); *Rhapsodies* for marimba, vibraphone, percussion (1968, unpub.); *Impromptus* for 8 winds (1969, unpub.).

PRINCIPAL WRITINGS: "Richard Swift: *Concerto,*" *Perspectives* 2/1:90–102; "Current Chronicle," *Musical Quarterly* (Jan, July 1963; April 1964; Oct 1965; Jan, April 1966); *Music in American Life* (Chicago 1967).

BIBL.: Richard N. Loucks, "An Appreciation of K. K.," *Pomona Today* (July 1966):7–10; Lawrence Morton, "Current Chronicle," *Musical Quarterly* (April 1963):229–35; Pauline Oliveros, "K. K.: *Concerto mutabile,*" *Perspectives* 2/2:87–99; Leonard Stein, "New Music on Mondays," *Perspectives* 2/1:150.

SEE ALSO Performance.

Kohoutek, Ctirad (b. Zábřeh na Moravě, Czechoslovakia, 18 March 1929), attended the Conservatory of Brno (1946–49, composition and theory with Vilém Petrželka), the Janáček Academy of Music, Brno (1949–53, composition with Jaroslav Kvapil), the summer school at Dartington, England (1963), and the Darmstadt summer sessions (1965). He began teaching at the Janáček Academy in 1949 and became Dozent for composition and theory in 1965. Influenced by Moravian and Slovakian folklore and the classics of the 20th century, his development has moved from postromanticism to free modality, dodecaphony, and serialism. Beginning in the early 1960s his music and writings have pursued a concept that Kohoutek calls "planned" composition. According to this idea, the composer reaffirms the value of maintaining control over all aspects of a musical work from preliminary outlines and sketches to the smallest details of notation and performance. All old and new techniques (including modern technology) are available to the composer except those that

would remove some aspect of the final product from his control.

PRINCIPAL COMPOSITIONS: *Ukolébavka černošské mámy* [Lullaby of a Negro Mother], cantata for alto, chorus, orchestra; text by Jiří Navrátil (1951–52; version for alto, piano published by SHV); *Mnichov* [Munich], symphonic poem for orchestra (1953); *Festival Overture* for orchestra (1956); *Suite* for viola, piano (1957); *Violin Concerto* (1958); *String Quartet* (1959, SHV); *Suite* for wind quintet (1959, Panton); *Velký přelom* [The Great Revolution], symphony for orchestra (1960); *Balady z povstání* [Revolutionary Ballads], 2 cantatas; texts by Jarmila Urbánková (1960); *Symphonic Dances* for orchestra (1961); *Za život* [To Life] for 3 women's choruses; text by J. Urbánková, M. Kratochvílová, and J. Pilař (1960); *Pátý živel* [The Fifth Element], melodrama for narrator, orchestra; text by Oldřich Mikulášek (1962); *Rapsodia eroica* for organ (1963, Supraphon); *Symphonietta* for orchestra (1963); *Concertino* for cello, chamber orchestra (1964); *Inventions* for piano (1965, Panton); *Preludes* for chamber orchestra (1965); *Hudební oříšky* [Little Musical Nuts] for children's chorus (1965); *Memento 1967*, concerto for percussion, winds (1966, Supraphon); *Panychida letní noci* [Panychide of the Summer Night] for viola, piano, percussion, tape (1968); *Symphonic Rotations in 4 Scenes* for orchestra (1968–69).

PRINCIPAL WRITINGS: *Novodobé skladebné směry v hudbě* [Contemporary Directions in Musical Composition] (Prague 1965); *Projektová hudební kompozice* [Planned Composition] (Prague 1966); *Skladebné principy hudebních slohů* [Principles of Style in Early Composition] (Prague 1969).

BIBL.: Jiří Vysloužil, "Cesta slibně započatá," *Hudební rozhledy* 7:230–31.

SEE ALSO Czechoslovakia.

Kohs, Ellis (Bonoff) (b. Chicago, 12 May 1916), attended the Univ. of Chicago (1933–38, composition with Carl Bricken), the Juilliard School (1938–39, composition with Bernard Wagenaar, music pedagogy with Olga Samaroff Stokowski), and Harvard Univ. (1939–41; composition with Walter Piston, musicology with Hugo Leichtentritt, Willi Apel). He taught at Wesleyan Univ. during 1946–48, College of the Pacific during 1948–50, and became chairman of the theory department, Univ. of Southern Calif., in 1950.

PRINCIPAL COMPOSITIONS (published by Merrymount unless otherwise noted): *Concerto for Orchestra* (1941, ACA); *String Quartet No. 1* (1942); *Night Watch* for flute, horn, tympani (1943); *Sonatina* for bassoon, piano (1944); *Legend* for oboe, string orchestra (1946, AMP); *Passacaglia* for organ, strings (1946, Gray); *Piano Variations* (1946); *Sonatine* for violin, piano (1946–48); *Variations on "L'Homme armé"* for piano (1947);

Capriccio for organ (1948); *Toccata* for harpsichord or piano (1948); *String Quartet No. 2*, "A Short Concert" (1948, ACA); *Chamber Concerto for viola, string nonet* (1949); *Symphony No. 1* (1950, ACA); *Fatal Interview*, 5 songs for voice, piano; text by Edna St. Vincent Millay (1951, ACA); *Sonata* for clarinet, piano (1951); *3 Chorale Variations on Hebrew Hymns* for organ (1952); *Lord of the Ascendant* for 8 solo dancers, 7 solo voices, chorus, libretto by Dexter Allen (1955, ACA); *Symphony No. 2* (1956, ACA); *Psalm 23* for 4 vocal soloists, chorus (1957, ACA); *3 Songs from the Navajo* for chorus (1957); *Epitaph* for tenor, piano; text by George Santayana (1959, ACA); *Studies in Variation*, part I for woodwind quintet; part II for piano, strings; part III for piano; part IV for solo violin (1962, Cameo); *Sonata* for snare drum, piano (1966); *Amerika*, opera; libretto by the composer based on Kafka's novel (1966–69, Merion); *Duo for Violin and Cello after Kafka's "Amerika"* (1970). List to 1969: *Composers of the Americas* 15:120–26.

PRINCIPAL WRITINGS: "Thoughts from the Workbench," *ACA Bulletin* VI/1:3–5; *Music Theory* (New York 1961).

Kokkonen, Joonas (b. Iisalmi, Finland, 13 Nov 1921), attended the Sibelius Academy in Helsinki (1940–41, 1945–49; harmony with Selim Palmgren, piano with Ilmari Hannikainen, counterpoint and composition with Sulho Ranta), and Helsinki Univ. (1940–41, 1945–48; musicology with Toivo Haapanen). Kokkonen began teaching at the Sibelius Academy in 1948 and was a professor of composition there during 1959–65. He was also music critic of *Ilta-Sanomat* (1947–57) and *Uusi Suomi* (1957–63), and has been active as a pianist. In 1963 he became a member of the Finnish Academy.

PRINCIPAL COMPOSITIONS: *Music for String Orchestra* (1957); *String Quartet No. 1* (1959); *Lintujen Tuonela* [The Hades of the Birds] for solo voice, orchestra (1959); *Symphony No. 1* (1960); *Symphony No. 2* (1961); *Sinfonia da camera* for 12 strings or string orchestra (1962, SY); *Missa a cappella* (1963, Westerlund); *Opus sonorum* for orchestra (1964, SY); *String Quartet No. 2* (1966); *Laudatio Domini* for chorus (1966, Frazer); *Symphony No. 3* (1967, Frazer); *Symphonic Sketches* 1968); *Cello Concerto* (1969).

PRINCIPAL WRITINGS: "J. K.," autobiographical article in *Suomen Säveltäjiä* ed. by Einari Marvia (Helsinki 1966), vol. 2:463–77.

BIBL.: Timo Mäkinen and Seppo Nummi, "Today and Tomorrow," *Musica Fennica* (Helsinki 1965):92–97; Seppo Nummi, "J. K. och vår tids symfoni," *Finland i dag. Modern musik* (Stockholm 1967): 66–72; Ilkka Oramo, "J. K., Symphony Composer," *Finlandia Pictorial* 1963/6; Denby Richards, *The Music of Finland* (London

1968):40–42; Erkki Salmenhaara, "J. K., romantisoituva klassikko," *Suomen Musiikin Vuosikirja 1967–1968* (Helsinki 1968):68–81; Bo Wallner, *Vår tids musik i Norden* (Stockholm 1968):245–49, English trans. (London 1971).

Kolb, Barbara (b. Hartford, Conn., 10 Feb 1939), studied at the Hartt College of Music (1957–64, composition with Arnold Franchetti) and at Tanglewood (1960, 64, 68; composition with Lukas Foss, Gunther Schuller). During 1969–70 she lived at the American Academy in Rome as a recipient of the Rome Prize. In *Trobar Clus* 12 instruments are divided into four groups. "Repetition functions more through rotary recurrences of various groups of instruments than through a literal repetition of 'thematic' material. However, each group retains its own personality and proceeds in a continuous state of evolution. . . . One should feel a rather positive staticism. . . . The work should convey various statements which are complete unto themselves yet imply continuation."

PRINCIPAL COMPOSITIONS: *Chansons Bas* for voice, harp, 2 percussionists (1965, Fischer); *Figments* for flute, piano (1966, Fischer); *3 Place Settings* for narrator, clarinet, violin, double bass, percussion (1968, Fischer); *Crosswinds* for alto saxophone, winds (1968–69, Boosey); *Trobar Clus* for flute, trumpet, 2 trombones, violin, viola, cello, double bass, guitar, harpsichord, 2 percussionists (1970, Boosey); *Toccata* for harpsichord, tape (1971).

Komorous, Rudolf (b. Prague, 8 Dec 1931), studied at the Prague Conservatory (1946–52, bassoon with Karel Pivoňka), the Prague Academy of Musical Arts (1952–59, composition with Pavel Bořkovec, bassoon with Pivoňka), and at the Electronic Music Studio in Warsaw (1959). He was first bassoonist of the Prague Opera Orchestra during 1952–59 and 1961–68. During 1961–68 he also performed in the contemporary-music ensemble Musica Viva Pragensis, and during 1965–67 he was a member of the Prague group New Music. In 1954 he became a member of Šmidrové, a group of Czech artists. He taught bassoon and chamber music at the Central Conservatory of Peking, China, during 1959–61. In 1968 he emigrated to Canada. During 1969–70 he taught in the U.S. at Macalester College in St. Paul, Minn.

PRINCIPAL COMPOSITIONS (published by UE unless otherwise noted): *Sladká královna* [The Sweet

Queen] for bass harmonica, keyboard harmonica, piano, bass drum (1964); *Lady Whiterose*, chamber opera for 2 women singers, pigmy (1964–66); *Olympia* for acolyte bells, sleigh bells, nightingale, rattle, flexatone, bass harmonica, keyboard harmonica (1964); *Mignon* for any 4 strings (1965); *Náhrobek Malevičův* [The Tomb of Malevich], electronic music on tape (1965, recorded by Supraphon); *York* for flute, oboe, bassoon, double bass, mandolin, piano (1967); *Chmurný půvab* [Gloomy Grace] for 11 players, nightingale (1968); *Gone*, tape music for 2 bassoons, electronic sounds (1969, unpub.); *Bare and Dainty* for orchestra (1969, unpub.).

BIBL.: Eduard Herzog, "Avantgarde der Tschechoslowakei," *Begegnung: Zeitschrift für Literatur, Bildende Kunst, Musik, und Wissenschaft* (Sonderheft, Oct 1968): 5–9; Jan Kříž, *Šmidrové* (Prague 1970); Vladimír Lébl, "R. K.," *Sborník Pražské skupiny nové hudby* (Prague 1957).

Kondracki, Michał (b. Połtava, Ukraine, Russia, 5 Oct 1902), studied composition with Karol Szymanowski at the Warsaw Conservatory (1923–27) and with Paul Dukas and Nadia Boulanger in Paris (1928–30). In 1943 he emigrated to the U.S., where he is a freelance composer and teacher. Since 1945 he has contributed a column, "Letters from the U.S.," to the Warsaw journal *Ruch muzyczny*. Many of his works have drawn on Polish folk music and legend; the music of Scriabin, Roussel, Ravel, Stravinsky, and Prokofiev have also been major influences.

PRINCIPAL COMPOSITIONS: *Mała symfonja góralska* [Little Highlander Symphony] for 16 instruments (1930, PWM); *Partita* for orchestra (1930); *Metropolis*, symphonic ballet (1930); *Żołnierze* [Soldiers on Parade] for orchestra (1932, PWM); *Popieliny*, opera (1934); *Piano Concerto* (1935); *Concerto for Orchestra* (1936); *Baśń Krakowska* [Legend of Cracow], ballet (1937); *Mecz* [Soccer Match] for orchestra (1937); *Cantata ecclesiastica* for vocal soloists, chorus, orchestra (1937–38); *Toccata* for orchestra (1939); *Epitaphe* for orchestra (1940); *Symphony* (1942); *2 Brazilian Dances* for orchestra (1943); *Psalm* for orchestra (1945); *Nocturne* for harp, strings (1951); *Grotesque* for orchestra (1952); *Kolęda* [Canticle] for flute, chamber orchestra (1955); *Moods* for piano (1956); *Hymn to Aphrodite* for string orchestra (1957).

BIBL.: Stefan Jarociński, *Polish Music* (Warsaw 1965); Jozef Reiss, *Muzyka Polska* (Cracow 1959).

Kopelent, Marek (b. Prague, 28 April 1932), studied at the Prague Academy of Musical Arts (1951–55, composition with Jaroslav Řídký). Since 1956 he has been an editor of contemporary music for Supraphon, and since

1965, director of the ensemble Musica Viva Pragensis. He is also a member of the Prague avant-garde group New Music. He performs as a pianist, has composed for radio plays, experimental films, and poetry recitations, and has written many articles on contemporary music for Czech periodicals. About 1960, largely under the influence of Webern, he reevaluated his technical and esthetic approach. His *Third Quartet* is of "serial character" and has nonperiodic rhythms; it also allows some degree of performer choice. The text of *Matka* is a collection of variants on the title word, chosen for their phonetic-textural values. *Contemplation* is a nonserial study in sound textures. Theatrical gestures are used in the *Fourth Quartet*.

PRINCIPAL COMPOSITIONS: *String Quartets Nos. 1–4* (1954; 1955; 1963, UE and Supraphon; 1967); *Nenie with Flute* for 9 women's voices, flute, chamber ensemble (1960–61, Panton); *Canto intimo* for flute, vibraphone (1963, ČHF); *Matka* [Mother], fresco for flute, chorus (1964, Panton); *Music for 5* for oboe, clarinet, bassoon, violin, piano (1964, Gerig); *In Honor of Vladimír Holan* for nonet (1965, ČHF); *For Arnošt Wilde* for piano (1966); *Play* for string quartet (1965–66); *Contemplation* for orchestra (1966, Gerig and Supraphon); *Snehah* for soprano, jazz alto on tape, chamber ensemble (1967, Gerig and Supraphon); *Hallelujah!* for organ (1967, Gerig); *Bijoux de Bohême* for dulcimer or flute, dulcimer, vibraphone (1967, Gerig); *Accord and Disaccord* for 12 soloists, orchestra (1967–68).

SEE ALSO Czechoslovakia.

Koppel, Herman (David) (b. Copenhagen, 1 Oct 1908), studied at the Royal Academy of Music in Copenhagen (1926–29; composition with Rudolph Simonsen, Anders Rachlew). He concertizes as a pianist and has taught piano at the Royal Academy since 1949.

PRINCIPAL COMPOSITIONS: *String Quartets Nos. 1–4*: No. 1, Op. 2 (1928–29); No. 2, Op. 34 (1939, SUDM); No. 3, Op. 38 (1944–45, Hansen-W); No. 4, Op. 77 (1964, SUDM); *Symphonies Nos. 1–7*: No. 1, Op. 5 (1929–30); No. 2, Op. 37 (1943); No. 3, Op. 39 (1944–45, Hansen-W); No. 4, Op. 42 (1946); No. 5, Op. 60 (1955, SUDM); No. 6, Op. 63 (1957); No. 7, Op. 70 (1960–61); *Piano Concertos Nos. 1–4*: No. 1, Op. 13 (1931–32, Hansen-W); No. 2, Op. 30 (1936–37); No. 3, Op. 45 (1948, Imudico); No. 4, Op. 69 (1960, Imudico); *Variations on a Jewish Folk Dance*, Op. 17 (1932); *Suite* for piano, Op. 21 (1934, SUDM); *Clarinet Concerto*, Op. 35 (1941, SUDM); *Sextet* for winds, piano, Op. 36 (1942, SUDM); *Concerto* for violin, viola, chamber orchestra, Op. 43 (1947, Hansen-W); *5 Biblical Songs* for voice, piano, Op. 46 (1949); *4 Love Songs* for voice, piano, Op. 47

(1949, Imudico); *3 Psalms of David* for tenor, boys' chorus, orchestra, Op. 48 (1949, SUDM); *4 Songs with Old Testament Texts* for voice, piano, Op. 49 (1949); *Piano Sonata*, Op. 50 (1950); *Ternio* for violin or cello, piano, Op. 53 (1951, Imudico); *Cello Concerto*, Op. 56 (1952, SUDM); *Piano Quintet*, Op. 57 (1953, SUDM); *2 Biblical Songs* for soprano, orchestra (piano), Op. 59 (1955); *Divertimento pastorale* for oboe, viola, cello, Op. 61 (1955, SUDM); *Concertino* for string orchestra, Op. 66 (1958, SUDM); *42nd Psalm of David* for soprano, piano, Op. 68 (1960); *Variations* for clarinet, piano, Op. 72 (1961, Leduc); *Capriccio* for flute, piano, Op. 73 (1961, Leduc); *Moses*, oratorio, Op. 76 (1963–64); *Requiem*, Op. 78 (1965–66); *Macbeth*, Op. 79, opera (1967–68); *9 Variations* for violin, cello, piano, Op. 80 (1969).

SEE ALSO Scandinavia.

Korn, Peter Jona (b. Berlin, 30 March 1922), studied at the Beltane School in London (1934–36, composition with Edmund Rubbra), the Jerusalem Conservatory (1936–38, composition with Stefan Wolpe), the Univ. of Calif. at Los Angeles (1941–42, composition with Arnold Schoenberg), and the Univ. of Southern Calif. (1946–47, composition with Ernst Toch). During 1947–48 he was music director of the Coronet Theater in Los Angeles and during 1948–56, of the New Orchestra. He lectured on composition at the Univ. of Calif. at Los Angeles during 1964–65. Since 1967 he has been director of the Richard Strauss Conservatory in Munich.

PRINCIPAL COMPOSITIONS: *Concertino* for horn, double string orchestra, Op. 15 (1952, Boosey); *In medias res*, overture, Op. 21 (1953, Boosey); *Variations on a Tune from "The Beggars' Opera"* for orchestra, Op. 26 (1954–55, Simrock); *Symphony No. 3*, Op. 30 (1956; revised 1969, Simrock); *Das fremde Haus*, 3-act opera, Op. 35; libretto by composer after Johanna Spyri's *Heidi* (1961–63, Bote); *Wind Quintet*, Op. 40 (1966, Peters); *Exorcism of a Liszt Fragment* for orchestra, Op. 44 (1966–68).

PRINCIPAL WRITINGS: "The Changing of the (Avant) Garde," *Saturday Review* (14 Feb 1959): 63–66; "9 Fashionable Myths about Music and How to Explode Them," *Show* (Dec 1963); "Conversations with Schmilowitz," *High Fidelity* (Oct 1962):56; "Diary of a Young Man of Fashion," *High Fidelity* (Sept 1967):60; "Symphony in America," *The Symphony* ed. by R. Simpson (London 1967):ch. 32.

Kósa, György (b. Budapest, 24 April 1897), studied at the Budapest Academy of Music (1910–15; composition with Victor Herzfeld and Zoltán Kodály). He also studied piano

privately with Béla Bartók (1904–07) and Ernst Dohnányi (1916–17). During 1916–17 he was a coach at the Budapest Opera, and during 1920–21 he conducted at the Theatre Tripolis. From 1927 to 1962 he taught at the Budapest Academy. As a pianist he was especially noted for his Bach recitals. His music has been influenced by Mahler and by the ancient and modern poetry of many countries. He has been little affected by the 12-tone Viennese school and Bartók.

PRINCIPAL COMPOSITIONS: *6 Pieces* for orchestra (1920, UE); *String Quartets Nos. 1, 2, 3, 6* (1920 Hansen-W; 1929, EMB; 1933; 1959–60, EMB); *Laodameia*, cantata for alto, chorus, orchestra (1924); *3 Sad and 3 Gay Bagatelles* for piano (1924, UE); *Jutka Kinderstücke* for piano (1928, UE); *Easter Oratorio* for 7 vocal soloists, chorus, winds, strings (1932); *Trio* for 2 violins, viola (1946, EMB); *Mass No. I* for soloists, chorus, organ (1946); *Jutka Ballades* for piano (1946, EMB); *Fantasia on 3 Hungarian Folksongs* for orchestra (1948); *Andante and Vivace* for cello, piano (1948, EMB); *Tartuffe*, opera; text by Molière (1951); *Dance Suite* for orchestra (1951, EMB); *Angelus Silesius Songs* for voice, piano (1953); *14 Po-Chü-Yi Songs* for voice, piano (1954–56, EMB); *Das Lied vom ewigen Kummer*, ballet for chorus; text by Po-Chü-Yi (1955); *Märchenvogel*, children's pieces for piano (1957, EMB); *Symphony No. 8* (1959, EMB); *7 Rilke Songs* for voice, piano (1960); *Villon*, oratorio for baritone, chorus, orchestra (1960–61); *Ballads* for chorus; Transylvanian texts (1964, EM); *Manole* for vocal soloists, chorus, orchestra; Transylvanian texts (1965); *Miniatures* for harp trio (1965); *Requiem No. 2* for vocal soloists, chorus, orchestra (1966); *Orpheus* for 6 solo voices, alto flute, harp, string trio, timpani; text by Rilke (1967); *Cantata humana* for chorus, wind orchestra; text by Janus Pannonius (1967); *Christus*, chamber cantata for 8 vocal soloists, oboe, harp, string quartet (1969).

BIBL.: L. Fabian, "G. K.," *Musikblätter des Anbruch* (Vienna) 1926/8:2; Marianne Pándi, *K. G.* (Budapest 1966); L. Pollatschek, "G. K.," *Der Auftakt* (Prague) 1925/5:7.

SEE ALSO Hungary.

Kotoński, Włodzimierz (b. Warsaw, 23 August 1925), studied at the Warsaw Academy of Music (1945–51, composition with Piotr Rytel) and at the Darmstadt summer courses (1959–60). He also studied composition privately during 1950–51 with Tadeusz Szeligowski in Poznań. During 1951–59 he did research in Polish folklore at the State Institute of Art. In 1959 he went to Paris, where he became acquainted with Pierre Schaeffer and Olivier Messiaen. During 1966–67 he worked at the Electronic Music Studio of the Westdeutscher

Rundfunk in Cologne. He has worked at the Experimental Studio of the Polish Radio in Warsaw since its inception in 1958, and since 1967 he has taught electronic music at the Warsaw Academy. He was vice president of the Polish Composers' Union during 1963–66.

PRINCIPAL COMPOSITIONS (published by PWM unless otherwise noted): *Prelude and Passacaglia* for orchestra (1954, unpub.); *6 Miniatures* for clarinet, piano (1957, unpub.); *Kammermusik* for winds, brass, strings, guitar, harp, celesta, 4 percussionists (1958, Schott); *Musique en relief* for orchestra (1959, Schott); *Trio* for flute, guitar, percussion (1960); *Study on One Cymbal Stroke*, musique concrète on tape (1960); *Canto* for chamber orchestra (1961, Moeck); *Concerto per quattro* for harp, guitar, harpsichord, piano, chamber orchestra (1961–65); *Selection I* for 4 jazz players (1962); *Pezzo* for flute, piano (1962–64); *Musica per fiati e timpani* for woodwinds, 2 timpanists (1963); *Microstructures*, musique concrète on tape (1963, unpub.); *Monochromie* for oboe (1964); *Wind Quintet* (1964); *a battere* for guitar, viola, cello, harpsichord, 3 percussionists (1966, PWM and Moeck); *Klangspiele*, electronic music on 2 4-track tapes (1967); *Pour quatre* for clarinet, trombone, cello, piano (1968); *Music for 16 Cymbals and String Orchestra* (1969).

PRINCIPAL WRITINGS: *Goralski i Zbójnicki tańce Górali Podhalańskich* [Goralski and Zbojnicki Dances of the Podhale Highlanders] (Cracow 1956); *Instrumenty perkusyjne we współczesnej orkiestrze* [Percussion Instruments in the Modern Orchestra] (Cracow 1965), enlarged and revised as *Schlaginstrumente in modernen Orchester* (Mainz 1967).

Kounadis, Arghyris (Panos) (b. Constantinople, 14 Feb 1924), studied at Athens Conservatory (1941–53, interrupted by wars; piano with S. Farandatos), the Hellenic Conservatory in Athens (1953–55, composition with Yannis Papaïoannou), and at the Staatliche Hochschule für Musik in Freiburg (1958–61, composition with Wolfgang Fortner, conducting with Carl Ueter). During 1949–63 he composed music for the National Theater in Athens (classical dramas), as well as for other theaters, films, and the ballet. Since 1963 he has lectured in solfège and ear training at the Staatliche Hochschule für Musik in Freiburg, has been assistant to Wolfgang Fortner in the Musica Viva program at the Institute for New Music of the Hochschule, and has directed the Ensemble for New Music there. In his music he uses 12-tone techniques integrated freely with traditional Greek styles.

PRINCIPAL COMPOSITIONS: *Plans for a Summer* for soprano, piano; texts by G. Seferis (1949); *Moments musicaux* for violin, piano (1949,

Gaetanos); *Sinfonietta* (1951); *5 Compositions for Orchestra* (1957–58, EM); *5 Sketches* for flute (1958, EM); *Chorikon* for orchestra (1958, EM); *3 Nocturnes after Sappho* for soprano, flute, celesta, vibraphone, violin, viola, cello (1960, EM); *String Quartet* (1960, EM); *3 Poems of Constantine Kavafy* for soprano, flute, celesta, piano, guitar, cello (1961, Tonger); *Duo* for flute, violin (1962, EM); *Der Gummisarg*, 1-act opera (1962, Bote); *Epigramma I* for double chorus (1963, EM); *Triptychon* for flute, chamber orchestra (1963–64, Schott); *3 Pezzi per trio* for flute, cello, piano (1964, Tonger); *Epitymbion in memoriam Ch. E. Ives* for 6 percussionists, 13 flutes (1965); *Rhapsodia* for soprano, orchestra (1966, Bote); *Heterophonika idiomela* for orchestra (1967, Bote); *Epigramma II* for chorus (1968); *Rendering of 3 Poems by Miltos Sachtouris* for soprano, bass, piano (1968); *Wer Ohren hat zu hören, der möge hören* for 5 brasses (1969); *7 Ariettas from Kefallenia*, folk-music collection (Tonger).

SEE ALSO Greece.

Koutzen, Boris (b. Uman, Russia, 1 April 1901; d. Pleasantville, N. Y., 10 Dec 1966), studied violin as a child with his father and attended the Moscow Conservatory (composition with Reinhold Glière, violin with Leo Zetlin). He emigrated to the U.S. in 1923. During 1923–28 he was a violinist with the Philadelphia Orchestra and during 1937–45, with the NBC Symphony Orchestra; he also concertized as a soloist. He taught violin at the Philadelphia Conservatory (1925–62) and at Vassar College (1944–66), and in 1958 he organized the Chappaqua Chamber Orchestra north of New York, which he conducted until his death. His approach as a composer was that of a romanticist; his style has been described as almost exclusively polyphonic.

PRINCIPAL COMPOSITIONS (published by General): *Sonatina* for piano (1931); *Sonatina* for 2 pianos (1944); *Concerto* for flute, clarinet, bassoon, horn, cello, string orchestra (1934); *The Fatal Oath*, 1-act opera; libretto by the composer after Balzac (1938–54); *Holiday Mood* for violin, piano (1943); *Sonatina* for 2 pianos (1944); *Duo concertante* for violin, piano (1944); *Violin Concerto* (1946); *Piano Trio* (1948); *Morning Music* for flute, string orchestra (1950); *Eidolons* for piano (1953); *Divertimento* for orchestra (1956); *Rhapsody* for band (1959); *Concertino* for piano, string orchestra (1959); *Fanfare, Prayer, and March* for orchestra (1961); *Elegiac Rhapsody* for orchestra (1961); *You Never Know*, 1-act comic opera; libretto by the composer (1962); *Poem* for violin, string quartet (1963); *Melody with Variations* for violin or clarinet, piano (c.1964); *Pastorale and Dance* for violin, piano (c.1964); *Music for Violin Alone* (1966).

[prepared with the help of Paul Kapp]

Kraft, Leo (b. Brooklyn, N. Y., 24 July 1922), studied at Queens College (1940–45, composition with Karol Rathaus), Princeton Univ. (1945–47, composition with Randall Thompson), and in Paris with Nadia Boulanger (1954–55). He has taught at Queens College since 1947. The chief influence on his composition has been the need to clarify and organize his thoughts in teaching his students.

PRINCIPAL COMPOSITIONS (published by General unless otherwise noted): *Short Suite* for flute, clarinet, bassoon (1951); *Concerto No. 1* for flute, clarinet, trumpet, strings (1951, unpub.); *A Proverb of Solomon* for chorus, small orchestra (1953, Mercury); *Variations* for orchestra (1958, unpub.); *Partita No. 1* for piano (1958); *String Quartets Nos. 2–3* (1959, 1968; unpub.); *When Israel Came Forth* for chorus, Psalm 114 (1961, Presser); *Partita No. 2* for violin, viola (1961, unpub.); *English Love Songs* for high voice, piano (1961, unpub.); *5 Pieces* for clarinet, piano (1962); *3 Pieces* for orchestra (1963); *Fantasy* for flute, piano (1963); *Partita No. 3* for wind quintet (1964); *Statements and Commentaries* for piano (1965); *Trios and Interludes* for flute, viola, piano (1965); *Night Music* for orchestra (1965, unpub.); *Concerto No. 2* for 13 players (1966, unpub.); *Short Sonatas Nos. 1–2* for harpsichord (1968; 1970, unpub.); *Dialogues* for flute, tape (1968, unpub.); *Easy Animal Pieces* for piano (1968); *Spring in the Harbor*, chamber cycle for soprano, flute, cello, piano (1969, unpub.); *Concerto No. 3* for cello, winds, percussion (1969); *Dualities* for 2 trumpets (1970); *Pentagram* for alto saxophone (1971).

PRINCIPAL WRITINGS: *A New Approach to Ear Training* (New York 1967); "In Search of a New Pedagogy," *College Music Symposium* 8:109–16; "The Music of George Perle," *Musical Quarterly* (July 1971).

Kraft, William (b. Chicago, 9 June 1923), studied at various colleges including Columbia Univ. (1949–52; composition with Norman Lockwood, Henry Cowell, Jack Beeson, Otto Luening; counterpoint with Seth Bingham, Vladimir Ussachevsky). He also studied privately at the Juilliard School (1948–52, timpani with Saul Goodman, percussion with Morris Goldenberg) and at the Berkshire Music Center (1948, composition with Irving Fine, conducting with Leonard Bernstein). Since 1955 he has been principal timpanist and percussionist of the Los Angeles Philharmonic. He describes his compositions as having been influenced by his background as a jazz performer and arranger and by his acquaintance with Stravinsky and Varèse.

PRINCIPAL COMPOSITIONS: *3 Miniatures* for percussion, orchestra (1958, Mills); *Nonet* for brass, percussion (1959, WIM); *Concerto grosso* (1961,

Mills); *Derivations* for orchestra (1962–64, MCA); *Silent Boughs*, song cycle for soprano, string orchestra (1963, Mills); *Concerto* for 4 percussionists, orchestra (1964, Mills); *Configurations*, concerto for 4 percussionists, jazz orchestra (1965, MCA); *Momentum* for 8 percussionists (1966, SMC); *Double Trio* for prepared piano, piano, electric guitar, tuba, 2 percussionists (1966, MCA); *Contextures: Riots—Decade '60* for orchestra (1967, MCA); *Triangles*, concerto for percussion, 10 instruments (1968, MCA); *Games: Collage No. 1* for 2 antiphonal choirs, each of 11 brass, 2 percussion (1969).

PRINCIPAL WRITINGS: *Modern School for Snaredrum, with the Artist's Handbook* (New York 1955); "The Complete Percussionist," *The Ludwig Drummer 4/2.*

BIBL.: Martin Bernheimer, "The Composer Behind the Kettledrums," *Los Angeles Times* (31 March 1968), Calendar sec:36; Arther Cohn, "The True Essence of Percussion," *American Record Guide* 35/11:1062–63; Arthur Goldberg, "Noisemakers. No Not That, Too, Mr. Critic!" *Los Angeles Times* (9 April 1961).

Krejčí, Iša (b. Prague, 10 July 1904; d. 6 March 1968), attended Prague Conservatory (1923–29; composition with K. B. Jirák and Vítězslav Novák, conducting with Václav Talich). He conducted at the Bratislava Opera (1928–32) and was music director and conductor of Radio Prague (1934–45). During 1945–57 he was artistic director of the Olomouc Opera, and from 1957 until his death he served as conductor and dramaturge of the Prague National Theater. Václav Holzknecht cites Krejčí's admiration for Mozart and Smetana and has described his music as neoclassic. Although his style might be compared with Les Six in France (especially Poulenc), he actually developed independently of foreign influences. He had a strong interest in Czech folk music, especially in the chorales of the Bohemian Brethren.

PRINCIPAL COMPOSITIONS: *Little Ballet* for orchestra (1927–30, Panton); *Trio Divertimento* for piano, clarinet, string bass (1936, Hudební Matice); *Nonet* (1937); *Komenský Songs* for voice, piano (1938, SNKLHU); *Pozdvižení v Efesu* [Tumult in Ephesus], 2-act comic opera; libretto by Josef Bachtík after Shakespeare's *Comedy of Errors* (1939–43, SNKLHU); *Serenade* for orchestra (1947–50, Panton); *14 Variazioni sul un canto popolare* for orchestra (1948–50, SNKLHU); *String Quartet in D Minor* (1953, SNKLHU); *Symphony in D* (1954–55, ČHF); *Antigona*, 1-act opera after Sophocles (1959–62). Complete list in Holzknecht (see bibl.):283–90.

PRINCIPAL WRITINGS: "Dva náboženské momenty v moderní české hudbě" [Two Religious Moments in Modern Czech Music], *Listy hudební ma*-4 (1925); "B Martinů," *Auftakt* 8 (1928); *tice* "R. Wagner a dnešek" [R. Wagner and Our Time], *Klíč* 3 (1932–33); "L. Vycpálek," *Rytmus* 7 (1941–42); "Dnešní význam Smetanova novoromantismu" [The Significance Today of Smetana's Neoromanticism], *ibid.* 9 (1943–44); "Vlastní portrét" [Self-portrait], *idem.*

BIBL.: V. Helfert, *Česká moderní hudba* [Modern Czech Music] (Brno 1936):153; Václav Holzknecht, *Hudební skupina Mánesa* [The Musicians Associated with Mánes] (Prague 1969).

[prepared with the help of Václav Holzknecht]
SEE ALSO Czechoslovakia.

Krenek, Ernst (b. Vienna, 23 August 1900), began studies with Franz Schreker at the Vienna Academy of Music in 1916 and followed Schreker to Berlin (1920–23), when he became director of the State Conservatory there. Krenek visited Paris in 1924, where he became acquainted with the ideas of neoclassicism. During 1925–27 he was assistant to Paul Bekker, the general manager first at the State Opera at Cassel and then at Wiesbaden. Here he gained practical theater experience and wrote his most successful stage work, *Jonny spielt auf* (1925–26); this opera was produced in over 100 European opera houses, and its success enabled Krenek to devote his full time to composition. In 1928 he returned to Vienna and, partly by means of his personal acquaintance with Alban Berg and Anton Webern, began a systematic study of 12-tone technique. During 1930–33 he did extensive literary work, especially for the *Frankfurter Zeitung*. He emigrated to the U.S. in 1938 and was a professor at Vassar College (1939–42) and Hamline Univ. (1942–47). Since 1947 he has made his home in southern Calif., composing and writing. He has been a visiting professor at several universities and conservatories and has made frequent concert and lecture tours.

Krenek has written over 200 works, including 20 operas, seven string quartets, five symphonies, and other instrumental, vocal, and electronic works in various combinations. His literary works include prose, poetry, musicological studies, essays, and the libretti for most of his operas. An inquisitive musician, he has been stimulated by a wide variety of musical materials and points of view. He has never merely dabbled with new possibilities, however, but has always examined them thoroughly and left behind a significant body of work before turning in a new stylistic direction. His most successful works have generally fallen into one or both of two categories: 1) works of highly dramatic and/or lyrical quality (*String Quartet No. 7, Symphonic Elegy, 6 Motets, Quintina*); 2) works that have offered him an unusually great challenge, either because of their scope (*Lamentatio Jeremiae prophetae, Der goldene Bock*, which could also be included in the first category) or because of their experimental nature (*Flute Piece in 9 Phases, Sestina*).

His music may be roughly divided into five periods: 1) 1921–23, atonal; 2) 1924–26, neoclassic; 3) 1926–31, romantic; 4) 1931–56, 12-tone; 5) since 1957, serial. Though his earliest works reflect something of Schreker's post-impressionist style, Krenek became stylistically independent of his teacher during his study years in Berlin. He notes an influence of Bartók in his *String Quartet No. 1* (1921), and about the *Symphony No. 1* (1921) he comments that the liveliness of the music "was principally attained through relentless entries of vehement rhythmic figures and through abundant use of ostinato technique" (*Selbstdarstellung*: 13). The most important composition of the atonal period is the *Symphony No. 2* (1922), a three-movement work lasting 50 minutes. The music is highly dissonant, especially in the intense adagio movement. The use of motivic relationships as a source of unity hints at the direction the composer was to take several years later when he adopted the principles of 12-tone technique. His first theater works, *Die Zwingburg* (1922) and *Der Sprung über den Schatten* (1923), date from this period.

The Paris visit in 1924 led Krenek to conclude, much as Hindemith had, that music should serve the society for which it is written, should be "useful, entertaining, and practical" (*op. cit.*: 18). This resulted in shorter compositions for smaller ensembles and eventually in a new interest in tonality. The composer considers the *Concerto Grosso No. 2* (1924–25) to be the most important work of this period (*op. cit.*: 19).

The musical style of Krenek's jazz opera *Jonny spielt auf* (1925–26) manifests a kind of "Puccini lyricism" (*op. cit.*: 21). In the ensuing years his concern with tonality and simplicity evinced themselves in the opera *Leben des Orest* (1928–29), in which he attempted to reconcile romantic elements and grand-opera style with the jazz of *Jonny. Reisebuch aus den österreichischen Alpen* (1929), a cycle of 20 songs akin to Schubert's *Winterreise*, which Krenek admires, marked the culmination of his tonal-romantic phase.

The first work in which he employed the 12-tone technique throughout was the long and elaborate opera *Karl V* (1930–33). In the years following his emigration to the U.S., a rich creative period, he continued to employ 12-tone technique. One of his most important works was *Lamentatio Jeremiae prophetae* (1940–41), in which he applied for the first time what he called the "principle of rotation." This principle provides for the formation of serial variants through the systematic exchange of the pitches of a given series with their adjacent pitches. An example using a numerical series is: given series, 1-2-3-4-5-6; first rotation, 1-3-2-5-4-6; second rotation, 3-1-5-2-6-4; third rotation, 3-5-1-6-2-4; fourth rotation, 5-3-6-1-4-2; etc. The principle was applied in many subsequent works, notably the *String Quartet No. 7* (1943–44) which Krenek considers his most important work of these years (*op. cit.*: 48), and later in *Spiritus intelligentiae, Sanctus* (1956), his first electronic work, and *Kette, Kreis und Spiegel* (1956–57). His interest in serialism, in which elements in addition to pitch are serialized, culminated in *Sestina* (1957) and *Quaestio temporis* (1958–59). Some of Krenek's most recent works are notable for their lyrical qualities, for instance, the opera *Der goldene Bock* (1963–64), which is a summation of 40 years of opera writing, and *Quintina* (1965), which is rigorously organized but nevertheless more relaxed in feeling than some of his most experimental works.

PRINCIPAL COMPOSITIONS: *Symphonies Nos. 1–2*, Opp. 7, 12 (1921, 1922; UE); *String Quartets Nos. 1,7*, Opp. 6, 96 (1921, 1943–44; UE); *Concerto Grosso No. 2*, Op. 25 (1924–25, UE); *Jonny spielt auf*, 2-act opera, Op. 45 (1925–26, UE); *Leben des Orest*, 5-act opera, Op. 60 (1928–29, UE); *Reisebuch aus den österreichischen Alpen*, song cycle for medium voice, piano, Op. 62 (1929, UE); *Karl V*, 2-act opera, Op. 73 (1930–33, revised 1954; UE); *8-Column Line*, ballet score for chamber ensemble, Op. 85 (1939); *Lamentatio Jeremiae prophetae* for chorus, Op. 93 (1940–41, Bärenreiter); *Piano Sonata No. 3*, Op. 92 (1943, AMP); *Symphonic Elegy* for string orchestra (1946, E-V); *Pallas Athene weint*, 3-act opera (1952–55, Schott and UE); *Spiritus intelligentiae, Sanctus*, Pentecost oratorio on tape using voices and electronic sounds (1956, UE); *Kette, Kreis und Spiegel* for orchestra (1956–57, Bärenreiter); *Sestina* for soprano, violin, guitar, flute, clarinet, trumpet, percussion (1957, Bärenreiter); *Quaestio temporis* for orchestra (1958–59, Bärenreiter); *6 Motets* for chorus; text by Kafka (1959, Bärenreiter); *Flute Piece in 9 Phases* for flute, piano (1959, Bärenreiter); *Der goldene Bock*, opera (1963–64, Bärenreiter); *Quintina* for soprano, tape, chamber ensemble (1965, Bärenreiter); *Horizont umkreist* for orchestra (1967, Bärenreiter); *Das kommt davon oder: Wenn Sardakai auf Reisen geht*, opera (1969, Bärenreiter). A list, 1918–64, was published by UE in 1964; Knessl (see bibl.) contains a list to 1967.

PRINCIPAL WRITINGS: *Music Here and Now* (New York 1939); *Studies in Counterpoint, Based on the*

Twelve-Tone Technique (New York 1940); *Selbstdarstellung* (Zurich 1948; English translation, "Self-analysis," *New Mexico Quarterly*, 1953); *Johannes Ockeghem* (New York 1953). Krenek also edited the *Hamline Studies in Musicology* (St. Paul 1945, 1947).

BIBL.: Lothar Knessl, *E. K.* (Vienna 1967).

Charles Boone

SEE ALSO Austria and Germany, Dance, Jazz, Mathematics, Opera, Popular Music, Serialism, 12-Tone Techniques, United States.

Krieger, Edino (b. Brusque, Santa Catarina, Brazil, 17 March 1928), studied violin with his father, Aldo Krieger, and then attended the Rio de Janeiro Conservatory (composition with Hans Koellreutter), Tanglewood (1948, composition with Aaron Copland), the Juilliard School (composition with Peter Mennin), and the Royal College of Music in London (1955, composition with Lennox Berkeley). His works to about 1950 were impressionistic. Later he began using serial techniques, which he now combines with other contemporary resources and with some Brazilian folk elements.

PRINCIPAL COMPOSITIONS: *Improviso* for solo flute (1944); *Música 1945* for oboe, clarinet, bassoon (1945); *Sonatina* for flute, piano (1947); *Música da câmera* for flute, trumpet, violin, timpani (1948); *Música* for string orchestra (1952); *Música 1952* for piano (1952); *Sonata* for piano 4-hands (1953, Peer); *3 Canções de Nicolas Guillén* for baritone, piano (1953); *Suite* for string orchestra (1954); *Piano Sonatas Nos. 1–2* (1954, 1956); *Abertura* for orchestra (1955); *String Quartet No. 1* (1955, PAU); *Divertimento* for string orchestra (1959); *Brasiliana* for viola, string orchestra (1960); *Elementary Variations* for chamber orchestra (1964, Peer); *Natividade do Rio*, scenic oratorio for narrator, tenor, baritone, chorus (1965); *Ludus symphonicus* for orchestra (1966). Krieger has also composed a number of theater and film scores. List to 1966: *Composers of the Americas* 13:83–88.

SEE ALSO Brazil.

Kroeger, Karl (b. Louisville, 13 April 1932), attended the Univ. of Louisville (1950–54, 1956–59; composition with Claude Almand, George Perle), the Univ. of Ill. (1960–61, composition with Gordon Binkerd), and Brown Univ. (1969–71). During 1962–64 he was head of the American music collection, New York Public Library, and from 1964 to 1967 was Ford Foundation composer-in-residence in the Eugene, Ore., public schools. He taught at Ohio Univ. during 1967–68 and in 1968–69 was associated with the electronic music studio of the Univ. of Wis. He began teaching at Moorhead State College in Minn. in 1971.

PRINCIPAL COMPOSITIONS (published by Pioneer unless otherwise noted): *Sinfonietta* for orchestra (1958); *String Quartet No. 1* (1960); *Canzona No. 1* for brass sextet (1961, Tritone); *Concerto da camera* for oboe, strings (1961); *Partita* for brass quintet (1963, Tritone); *Duo concertante* for violin, cello (1963); *Suite* for orchestra (1965); *Sinfonietta* for string orchestra (1965); *Canzona No. 2* for brass sextet (1965, Tritone); *Dark of the Moon*, concert suite (1966); *String Quartet No. 2* (1966); *Canzona No. 3* for brass sextet (1967, Tritone); *Toccata* for clarinet, trombone, percussion (1968, Broude-A); *3 Studies* for electronic tape (1968–69, unpub.); *Fantasy* for brass quartet (1969); *Divertimento* for band (1970, Boosey).

PRINCIPAL WRITINGS: Since 1962 Kroeger has written reviews for *Notes*.

Kubik, Gail (Thompson) (b. South Coffeyville, Okla., 5 Sept 1914), studied at the Eastman School (1930–34; composition with Bernard Rogers, Edward Royce; violin with Samuel Belov; theory with Irvin McHose), the American Conservatory in Chicago (1935–36; composition with Leo Sowerby, violin with Scott Willits), and Harvard Univ. (1937–38, composition with Walter Piston). He has known Nadia Boulanger since 1937, and they have often exchanged ideas about music, including Kubik's own. He has taught composition, violin, and conducting for short periods at several schools. During 1940–41 he was staff composer and musical program adviser for NBC in New York. He was director of music for the Bureau of Motion Pictures of the Office of War Information during 1942–43, and during 1943–46 he composed and conducted scores for the U.S. Air Force Motion Picture Unit. He has continued to write many scores for radio, television, and films. Kubik feels that the essential expressivity of music lies in melody and that harmony, texture, color, etc., are important to the degree that they help set off the melodic line. His considerable involvement with functional music, which is written against a deadline, is relatively simple in texture, and is dramatic in tone, has greatly influenced his esthetic and technical orientation.

PRINCIPAL COMPOSITIONS: *In Praise of Johnny Appleseed* for bass-baritone, chorus, orchestra (1938, revised 1961; Colombo); *Celebrations and Epilogue* for piano (1938–50, Southern); *Song and Scherzo* for 2 pianos (1940, revised 1962); *Puck: A*

Legend of Bethlehem, radio score (NBC, 1940); *Violin Concerto* (1941, revised 1951; Chappell); *Sonatina* for piano (1941, Mercury); *Sonatina* for violin, piano (1941, SPAM); *Litany and Prayer* for men's chorus, brass, percussion (1943–45, Southern); *Thunderbolt*, film score (U.S. Army Air Force, 1943–45); *Memphis Belle: A War-Time Episode* for speaker, orchestra (1944); *A Mirror for the Sky*, folk opera (1946, excerpts published by Ricordi); *Piano Sonata* (1947, Southern); *Symphony in E Flat* (1947–49, Southern); *Soliloquy and Dance* for violin, piano (1948, Southern); *C-Man*, film score (Film Classics, 1949); *The Miner's Daughter*, film score (Columbia Pictures, 1950); *Gerald McBoing-Boing*, film score (Columbia Pictures, 1950; concert version for narrator, percussion, 9 instruments, 1950, Southern); *Fables in Song* for medium voice, piano; text by Theodore Roethke (1950–69); *Symphony concertante* for piano, viola, trumpet, orchestra (1952, revised 1953; Ricordi); *Thunderbolt Overture* (1953, Chappell); *Symphony No. 2 in F* (1955, Ricordi); *The Desperate Hours*, film score (Paramount Pictures, 1955); *Symphony No. 3* (1956); *Scenario for Orchestra* (1957, Paramount); *The Silent Sentinel*, TV score (CBS, 1958–59); *Sonatina* for clarinet, piano (1959); *Divertimento Nos. 1–2* for chamber ensembles (1959, MCA); *Scenes for Orchestra* (1962); *Intermezzo: Music for Cleveland* for piano (1967); *A Christmas Set* for chamber chorus, chamber orchestra; medieval texts (1968, MCA); *Prayer and Toccata* for organ, chamber orchestra (1969).

BIBL.: Nadia Boulanger and Edward Steuermann, record notes for Contemporary Records Inc. (Los Angeles) album M6006–S8006.

Kupferman, Meyer (b. New York, 3 July 1926), studied at Queens College (1943–45) and privately with Abram Klotzman (clarinet). He is self-taught in composition. Since 1951 he has taught composition and chamber music at Sarah Lawrence College. His music has been influenced by his experience as a jazz performer in the 1940s. Since 1947 he has been working with 12-tone materials (but not exclusively). He has written extensively for films and television.

PRINCIPAL COMPOSITIONS: *In a Garden*, 1-act opera; libretto by Gertrude Stein (1948, Mercury); *Divertimento* for orchestra (1948); *Libretto for Orchestra* (1949); *Variations* for piano (1950, General); *Chamber Symphony* (1950); *Little Symphony* (1952, Weintraub); *Doctor Faustus Lights the Lights*, 3-act opera; libretto by Gertrude Stein (1953); *Symphony No. 4* (1956); *Lyric Symphony* (1957); *Variations for Orchestra* (1957); *String Quartet No. 4* (1958); *Sonata on Jazz Elements* for piano (1958, General); *Cycle of Infinities* (all based on the same 12-tone row): No. 1

for flute (1961); No. 3, "Jazz Infinities," for saxophone, double bass, drums (1961); No. 6 for chorus (1962); No. 8 for string quartet (1963); No. 12 for chamber orchestra (1964); No. 18, *The Judgment*, 3-act opera for unaccompanied voices; libretto by Paul Freeman (1967); No. 20, *Schemata*, for orchestra (1967); No. 26, *Moonchild and the Doomsday Trombone*, for voice, oboe, chamber and jazz ensembles (1968); *Concerto* for cello, jazz band (1962); *Music from "Hallelujah the Hills"* for recorder (flute), harpsichord (1963, General); *Persephone*, ballet; choreography by Pearl Lang (1968).

BIBL.: Elliott Schwartz, "Current Chronicle," *Musical Quarterly* 51:683–85; Paul Turok, "*The Judgment*, a New Concept in Opera," *Music Journal* (May 1967):21–24.

Kupkovič, Ladislav (b. Bratislava, Czechoslovakia, 17 March 1936), studied at the State Conservatory in Bratislava (1950–55) and the Bratislava Music Academy (1955–61). During 1960–65 he played in the Slovakian Philharmonic Orchestra. Since then he has been a free-lance composer and conductor. His ensemble Hudba Dneška (Music of Today, founded 1963) has given concerts throughout central Europe. He has been working with collage techniques and with new concert environments (such as multiple-room works).

PRINCIPAL COMPOSITIONS (published by UE unless otherwise noted): *Mäso kríža* for trombone, 10 percussionists (1962); *Písmená* [Words] for 8 vocal soloists (1967); *Präparierte Texte 1–7* for various combinations (1968, unpub.); *Etude* for orchestra (1968, unpub.); *Dioe*, "orchesterspiele," with conductor (1968); *Musikalische Ausstellung* for chamber ensemble (1970, unpub.); *Notausgang* for orchestra (1970); *B.—Erinnerungen* for orchestra, tape (1970).

SEE ALSO Czechoslovakia.

Kuri-Aldana, Mario (b. Tampico, Mexico, 15 August 1931), studied at the Academia J. S. Bach in Mexico City (1948–51, piano with Carlos del Castillo), the National Univ. of Mexico School of Music (1952–60; composition with Estanislao Mejía, José F. Vásquez, Pedro Michaca, Juan D. Tercero), the National Institute of Fine Arts in Mexico City (1957–58, conducting with Igor Markevitch and Jean Giardino), the Torcuato di Tella Institute in Buenos Aires (1963–64; Alberto Ginastera, Riccardo Malipiero, Olivier Messiaen, Bruno Maderna, Aaron Copland, Gilbert Chase, Luigi Dallapicolla), and at the National Conservatory in Mexico City (1968, composition with Karlheinz Stockhausen). He also studied composition privately in Mexico City with Rodolfo Halffter and Luis Herrera de la Fuente. During 1955–65 he taught theory, harmony, and counterpoint at the Univ. of Mexico and during 1957–70 he taught at the National Univ. He conducted the Symphonic Band of the Ministry of Education during 1967–70 and has been a commentator on Latin American music for Radio Universidad since 1965. His compositions have been influenced by Latin American and other folk music, jazz, and by the works of Silvestre Revueltas and Carlos Chávez.

PRINCIPAL COMPOSITIONS: *Canto de 5-Flor* for cello, piano (1957); *3 Pieces* for oboe, string orchestra (1960, EMM); *The Four Bacabs*, suite for double wind orchestra (1960, Peters); *Cantares para una niña muerta* for chorus; texts by A. Khoury (1961, Ricordi); *Mascaras*, divertimento for marimba, wind orchestra (1962, Peters); *Xilofonias* for wind quartet, percussion (1964, EMM); *Candelaria*, suite for wind quintet (1965, Musica Rara); *3-Silvestre*, concerto for 9 instruments (1966); *Yellow Was the Color of Hope*, secular oratorio for mezzo-soprano, speaker, jazz band; text by Khoury (1966); *Symphony No. 2* for string orchestra (1967); *Lucero de Dios y Ave Maria* for chorus, organ (1969); *Spanish Songs* for mezzo-soprano, piano; texts by Spanish poets and Khoury (1970); *In memoriam* for baritone, chorus, concert band; text by Julio Cortázar and Khoury (1970).

PRINCIPAL WRITINGS: *Concepto mexicano de nacionalismo* (thesis, National Univ. of Mexico, 1962).

BIBL.: G. B. Foster, "Biografías de músicos mexicanos," *Carnet musical de X.E.L.A.* (Dec 1964):565–69; Salomón Kahan, "El compositor K.-A.," *Carnet musical de X.E.L.A.* (Nov 1963): 482–85; ———, *Fascinatión de la música* (Mexico City 1964):469–74; Alfred Rose, "Beca a M. K.-A.," *Carnet musical . . .* (Feb 1963):93–96.

SEE ALSO Mexico.

Kurtág, György (b. Lugos, Hungary, 19 Feb 1926), began piano lessons with his mother at five and later studied at the Budapest Academy of Music (1946–53, piano with Pál Kadosa, chamber music with Leo Weiner, composition with Sándor Veress and Ferenc Farkas). During 1957–58 he studied in Paris with Milhaud, Messiaen, and Marianne Stein. Since 1967 he has been teaching chamber music at the Academy. In 1971 he worked in West Berlin on a fellowship.

Kurtag's output since 1959 has been in the forefront of the Hungarian avant-garde. Up to 1962 this output consisted of three works for various chamber ensembles and a few solo pieces for piano, viola, and guitar; in 1968 Kurtág completed a concerto for soprano and piano, *Bornemisza Péter mondásai*. His pre-1959 works were in the then prevailing Bartók-Kodály style and included a viola concerto, piano pieces, vocal works, and incidental music.

The works since 1959 have used pitch serialism, although only rarely have they incorporated rows as large as 12 tones. These pieces have exhibited a Webern-like taste for short movements as well as an ability to state ideas fully with only a few tones; there is also a Webern-like feeling of inevitability in regard to the manipulation of other musical parameters. Rhythm is treated in a contrapuntal manner with no two voices moving in the same patterns. Melodies tend to emphasize wide intervals that reach beyond an octave, although narrow ranges are also exploited. Sound textures and colors are only rarely an important structural element. *Bornemisza . . .* marks a significant point in Kurtág's development because it is a large-scale work (40 minutes in length), with individual movements that are longer than some entire works of the 1959–62 period. In its opposition of vocal and instrumental resources, the piece recalls the ecclesiastical concerto style of Gabrieli, Schütz, and other 17-century composers.

PRINCIPAL COMPOSITIONS (published by EMB unless otherwise noted): *String Quartet* (1959); *Wind Quintet* (1959); *8 Piano Pieces* (1960, EMB and UE); *8 Duets* for violin, dulcimer (1961, EMB and UE); *Jelek* [Signs] for viola (1961); *Bornemisza Péter mondásai* [The Sayings of Peter Bornemisza], concerto for soprano, piano (1963–68, unpub.); *To the Memory of a Winter Sunset*, 4 fragments for soprano, violin, dulcimer (1969, unpub.); *4 Capriccios* for chamber ensemble (1971, unpub.).

Péter Várnai
(trans. from Hungarian by Egon Kenton)
SEE ALSO Hungary.

Kuusisto, Ilkka (Taneli) (b. Helsinki, 26 April 1933), is the son of an organist. He studied composition with Aarre Merikanto and Nils-Eric Fougstedt at the Sibelius Academy (until 1958) and sacred music under Seth Bingham at Union Theological Seminary in New York (1958–59). He has been organist of the Meilahti congregation in Helsinki, musical director at the Helsinki City Theater, and conductor of the South Finland Student Corporation Chorus and other groups.

PRINCIPAL COMPOSITIONS: *3 Introductions* for brass, chorus, organ (1956); *3 Chinese Songs* for soprano, flute, piano (1956); *Duo* for flute, cello (1957); *Valkeneva päivä* [A Lightening Day], cantata for vocal soloists, youth chorus, organ (1957, Westerlund); *Coelestis aulae nuntius* for trombone, organ (1959); *Rejoice, Young Man* and *As for Man, His Days are like Grass*, anthems for chorus with brass quartet in the first (1959); *Crucifixus* for baritone, string quartet; text by G. Rouault (1959); *Cassazione* for 2 clarinets, 2 horns (1961); *Ritmo acustico 1* for organ (1963, tape version 1963); *Effata* for dancer, chorus, tape, orchestra; composed with Reijo Jyrkiäinen, choreography by Heikki Värtsi (1963); *Sydämeni laulu* [The Song of My Heart] for soprano, bassoon, 3 horns, harp, strings (1965); *Jazzationes*, jazz suite for flute, tenor saxophone, piano, double bass, drums (1965); *Merellinen sarja* [Seaside Suite] for mezzo-soprano, piano; text by Jouni Lompolo (1966).

Labunski, Felix (b. Ksawerynow, Poland, 27 Dec 1892), studied theory with Lucian Marczewski (1922–23) and harmony with Witold Maliszewski (1923–24), both in Poland. He attended the Ecole Normale in Paris (1927–30; counterpoint, fugue, composition with Nadia Boulanger; orchestration with Paul Dukas) and continued private studies with Boulanger until 1932. In 1927 he cofounded the Association of Young Polish Musicians in Paris and served as its president (1930–33). He headed the concert-music department of the Polish Radio in Warsaw from 1934 to 1936, when he emigrated to the U.S. He taught at Marymount College in New York (1940–41), and joined the faculty of the Cincinnati College-Conservatory in 1945. From 1951 to 1964 he taught at the Univ. of Cincinnati.

PRINCIPAL COMPOSITIONS: *Triptyque champêtre* for orchestra (1931); *The Birds* for soprano, orchestra (1934); *String Quartet No. 1* (1935); *Gods' Man*, ballet (1937); *Suite* for string orchestra (1942); *Threnody*, "Homage to Paderewski," for piano (1941, Boosey); *Variations* for orchestra (1947); *There is No Death* for chorus, orchestra (1950); *Symphony in B* (1954); *Xaveriana* for 2 pianos, orchestra (1956); *Images of Youth*, cantata for children's chorus, soloists, orchestra (1956); *Piano Sonata No. 2* (1957); *Mass* for treble voices, organ (1958, World Library); *Diptych* for oboe, piano (1958); *Symphonic Dialogues* (1960); *String Quartet No. 2* (1962); *Canto di aspirazione* for orchestra (1963, Fischer); *5 Polish Carols* for organ (1966, World Library); *Polish Renaissance Suite* for orchestra (1967); *Intrada Festiva* for brass (1967); *Salut à Nadia* for brass (1967); *Music for Piano and Orchestra* (1968); *Salut à Paris* for orchestra (1968).

PRINCIPAL WRITINGS: "Karol Szymanowski," *Great Modern Composers* ed. by Oscar Thompson (New York 1941):353–66; "Music," *Poland* ed. by Bernadotte Schmitt (Berkeley 1945):323–27; "Discovering Special Creative Musical Talent," *Gifted Child Quarterly* (Cincinnati) 7/1:13–14.

BIBL.: David Ewen, "F. L.," *American Composers Today* (New York 1949):149–50; Bogusław Schäffer, *Leksykon Kompozytorow XX Wieku* (Cracow 1963):525–26.

Lacerda, Osvaldo (Costa de) (b. São Paulo, Brazil, 23 March 1927), studied at the Colegio Estadual "Presidente Roosevelt" (grad. 1946), the Law School at the Univ. of São Paulo (grad. 1961), and at the Carlos Gomez Conservatory of Music (grad. 1960). He also studied piano and harmony during 1943–52 and composition (1952–62) with M. Camargo Guarnieri. Since 1956 he has taught technical courses and composition both privately and at a number of conservatories in São Paulo and Santos. Since 1966 he has been associated with the Mozarteum Academy of Drama and Music in São Paulo and since 1969 with the Municipal Music School. During 1960–62 and since 1969 he has taught teacher-training courses for the São Paulo State Commission of Music. He has also lectured at the International Music Courses at Paraná during 1966–70. He believes with Vaughan Williams that music is "a national idiom universally understood. . . . What one has to do is to catch the essence of one's country's musical soul through the study of its folk and popular music." He has been influenced by the ideas of the Brazilian musicologist and esthetician Mario de Andrade.

PRINCIPAL COMPOSITIONS: *8 Variations on a Folk Theme* for violin, piano (1954); *Ponteios Nos. 1–5* for piano (1955–68, Ricordi); *5 Inventions in 2 Voices* for piano (1958, Ricordi); *Sonatina* for flute, piano (1959); *Suite No. 1* for piano (1961, Vitale); *Viola Sonata* (1962); *Variations and Fugue* for wind quintet (1962, PAU); *Piratininga*, suite for orchestra (1962); *Guanabara*, suite for band (1965); *Brasilianas Suites Nos. 1–3, 5* for piano (1965–69, Vitale); *3 Etudes* for 4 percussionists (1966); *Ferial Mass* for chorus (1966, Ricordi); *Mass in 2 Voices* for chorus, organ (1966, Vitale); *3 Psalms* (Nos. 22, 127, 129) for baritone, organ (1967, Vitale); *Santa Cruz Mass* for soloists, chorus, organ (1967, Vitale); *Sonata* for soprano recorder, piano (1967); *Proper for the Feasts of Our Lady* for baritone, violin or organ (1968, Vitale); *Brasiliana No. 4* for piano 4-hands (1968, Vitale); *Trilogia* for brasses (1968); *Dobrado ponto e maracatú* for brasses (1968); *3 Miniatures* for 4 percussionists (1968); *Invocação e ponto* for trumpet, strings (1968); *Seresta* for oboe, strings (1968); *Estudos Nos. 1–8* for piano (1969–70, Vitale); *Proverbs* for soprano, bass, chorus, strings, piano, percussion (1970). Lacerda has also written over 30 works for voice with piano or percussion and 17 choral works; his pedagogical methods include: *Curso preparatorio de solfejo e ditado musical* [Preparatory Course in Solfège and Musical Dictation] (São Paulo 1959); *Compendio de teoria elementar da musica* [Compendium of Elementary Music Theory] (São Paulo 1967). List of compositions to 1969: *Composers of the Americas* 15:129–41.

PRINCIPAL WRITINGS: "Constancias harmonicas e polifonicas da musica popular brasileira e seu aproveitamento na musica sacra" [Harmonic and Polyphonic Characteristics of Brazilian Folk and Popular Music and Its Use in Sacred Music] and "A criação do recitativo sacro brasileiro" [The Creation of Brazilian Sacred Recitative], *Musica brasileira na liturgia* (Petropolis 1969).

BIBL.: João Caldeira Filho, *A aventura da musica* (São Paulo 1969):132–35; Vasco Mariz, *A canção brasileira* [Brazilian Song] (Rio de Janeiro 1959): 126; ——, *Figuras da musica brasileira contemporanea* (Brasilia 1970):91–93, 198–203.

Lachenmann, Helmut Friedrich (b. Stuttgart, 27 Nov 1935), attended the Staatlich Hochschule für Musik in Stuttgart (1955–61; theory, counterpoint with Johann Nepomuk David; piano with Jürgen Uhde). He studied composition and analysis privately with Luigi Nono in Venice during 1958–60. In 1963 and 1964 he attended the Cologne Courses for New Music, studying with Stockhausen, Pousseur, and Rzewski. Since 1957 he has regularly attended the Darmstadt summer courses, studying with Nono, Stockhausen, Scherchen. In 1965 he worked at the Institute for Psychoacoustics and Electronic Music at the State Univ. in Ghent. During 1961–66 he was a guest lecturer at the Hochschule für Gestaötung in Ulm. Since 1966 he has taught at the Stuttgart Hochschule für Musik and since 1970, at the Pädagogischen Hochschule in Ludwigsburg.

PRINCIPAL COMPOSITIONS: *Echo andante* for piano (1962, Gerig); *Wiegenmusik* for piano (1963, Gerig); *String Trio* (1965, EM); *Scenario*, electronic sounds on tape (1965); *Interieur I* for percussion (1966, EM); *Trio fluido* for clarinet, viola, marimbaphone (1966, Gerig); *Consolation I* for 12 mixed voices, 4 percussionists (1967, Gerig); *Consolation II* for 16 mixed voices (1968, Gerig); *Notturno* for cello, chamber orchestra (1966–68, Gerig); *temA* for flute, voice, cello (1968, Gerig); *Air* for percussion, orchestra (1969, Gerig); *Pression* for cello (1969); *Guero* for piano (1969); *Dal niente* for clarinet (1970).

PRINCIPAL WRITINGS: "Klangtypen der neuen Musik," *Zeitschrift für Musiktheorie* 1:20–30; "Luigi Nono," radio lecture recorded for SDR (1969).

SEE ALSO Austria and Germany.

Laderman, Ezra (b. Brooklyn, N. Y., 29 June 1924), studied at Brooklyn College (1946–49), Columbia Univ (1950–52, composition with Otto Luening, prosody and opera with Douglas Moore) and privately with Stephan Wolpe. He was on the faculty of Sarah Lawrence College (1960–61, 1965–66) and was staff composer at the Bennington Composers' Conference (1967, 1968). He has contributed many articles on contemporary music to *The New York Times*.

PRINCIPAL COMPOSITIONS (published by Oxford unless otherwise noted): *Leipzig Symphony* (1945, unpub.); *Theme and Variations* for chamber ensemble (1954, unpub.); *Jacob and the Indians*, opera; libretto by Ernest Kinoy after S. V. Benet (1956–57, unpub.); *Sarah*, 1-act opera (1959, unpub.); *String Quartet No. 1* (1958–59); *Violin Sonata* (1958–59); *Goodbye to the Clown*, opera (1959–60, unpub.); *Stanzas for Chamber Orchestra* (1960); *The Eagle Stirred*, oratorio (1960–61, unpub.); *Violin Concerto* (1961); *Songs for Eve* for soprano, piano; text by Archibald MacLeish (1962–63); *The Black Fox*, film score (1963, unpub.); *Nonette* for chamber ensemble (1963); *Symphony No. 1* (1963–64); *String Quartet No. 2* (1964–65); *Shadows Among Us*, 2-act opera; libretto by Norman Rostin (1965–69); *The Trials of Galileo*, oratorio (1966–67); *Magic Prison* for 2 narrators, orchestra (1966–67); *Satire: Concerto for Orchestra* (1968); *Symphony No. 2*, "Luther" (1968).

SEE ALSO Dance.

Lajtha, László (b. Budapest, 30 June 1892; d. there, 16 Feb 1963), studied at the Budapest Academy with Viktor Herzfeld and at the Univ. of Sciences. In 1913 he became associated with the Budapest Ethnographic Museum and was later its music director. He taught at the National Conservatory in Budapest during 1919–49.

PRINCIPAL COMPOSITIONS (published by Leduc unless otherwise noted): *Des Esquisses d'un musicien* for piano (1913, Rószavölgi); *Piano Sonata* (1914, EMB); *Hungarian Folksong Arrangements* for voice, piano (1924, EMB); *String Quartets Nos. 3–10*: No. 3 (1929, UE); No. 4 (1930, Rózsavölgi); No. 5 (1934); No. 6 (1942); No. 7 (1950); No. 8 (1951); No. 9 (1953); No. 10 (1953); *Scherzo and Toccata* for piano (1930); *Sonatina* for violin, piano (1930); *Vocalise étude* for voice, piano (1930); *A hegylakók* [The Mountaineers] and *Esti párbeszéd* [Nocturnal Dialogue] for chorus (1932, Salabert); *Cello Sonata* (1932); *String Trios Nos. 2–3* (1932; 1945, UE); *Lysistrata*, ballet (1933); *Hortobágy Suite* for orchestra (1935); *Trios Nos. 1–2* for harp, flute, cello (1935, 1949); *Symphonies Nos. 1–9* (1936, 1938, 1948, 1951, 1952, 1955, 1957, 1959, 1961); *Divertissements Nos. 1–2* for orchestra (1936, 1939); *4 Madrigals* for chorus (1939); *Cello Concerto* (1940); *Les Soli* for orchestra (1941, UE); *3 Nocturnes* for chorus, orchestra (1941); *Le Bosquet des quatre dieux*, ballet (1943); *Capriccio*, ballet (1944, UE); *Sinfoniettas Nos. 1–2* (1946, 1956); *4 Hommages* for wind quartet (1946); *Quintet No. 2* for flute, violin, viola, cello, harp (1948); *Missa in tono phrygio* for chorus, orchestra (1950); *Ballada és verbunk* [Ballad and Recruiting Music] for chorus, orchestra (1951); *Missa* for chorus, organ (1952); *Magnificat* for women's chorus, organ (1954); *Sonate en concert* for flute, piano (1958); *2 Pieces* for flute (1958); *Sonate en concert* for violin, piano (1962). Lajtha also edited 8 collections of Hungarian folk music.

SEE ALSO Hungary.

Lakner, Yehoshua (b. Bratislava, Czechoslovakia, 24 April 1924), studied at the Jerusalem Conservatory (1942–43, composition with A. V. Boskovich and Öedöen Partos), the Israel Conservatory and Academy in Tel Aviv, Tanglewood (1952, composition with Aaron Copland), the Cologne Hochschule für Musik (1959–60, composition with Bernd Alois Zimmermann), the Electronic Music Studio of the Westdeutscher Rundfunk in Cologne (1959–60, electronic music with G. M. Koenig, Mauricio Kagel, Karlheinz Stockhausen), and the Darmstadt summer courses (1959, 1960, 1965). He studied piano privately in Tel Aviv with Frank Pelleg. Since 1950 he has taught at the Israel Conservatory and Academy, and since 1965 he has composed for the Theater an der Winkelwiese in Zurich.

PRINCIPAL COMPOSITIONS: *Flute Sonata* (1948, IMI); *Sextet* for woodwinds, piano (1951, IMI); *Toccata* for orchestra (1952, IMI); *Hexachords* for orchestra (1960, IMI); *Ballet for Rina Schönfeld* for flute, cello, piano, percussion (1962); *Chalomoh shel Muhamet* [Mohamet's Dream] for chorus, musique concrète on tape (1968). ★ Theater music (all musique concrète on tape): *Victor* (Vitroc) (1965); *Die Stühle* (Ionesco) (1966); *Nestroy Quodlibet* (1967); *Der Architekt und der Kaiser von Assyrien* (Arrabal) (1968); *Turandot* (Brecht) for voice (1969); *Die Nacht der Mörder* (Trians) (1969); *Jona* (Ionesco) (1970).

PRINCIPAL WRITINGS: "A New Method of Representing Tonal Relations," *Journal of Music Theory* (Nov 1960):194–209.

BIBL.: Articles about Lakner have appeared in *Das neue Israel* (Zurich, Jan 1966, Jan 1967, Sept 1968, March 1970).

SEE ALSO Israel.

Landowski, Marcel (b. Pont-l'Abbé, France, 18 Feb 1915), studied piano as a child with Marguerite Long and attended the Paris Conservatory (1935–37; composition with Henri Busser, conducting with Philippe Gaubert and Charles Munch). He also studied conducting privately with Pierre Monteux in Baux-de-Provence (1936). During 1946–51 he was music critic for *Opéra* and later contributed to *Demain* and *Paris-Comoedia*. Since 1962 he has been music director of the Comédie-Française. He has been Inspector Général of music education in France since 1964 and music director at the Ministry of Cultural Affairs since 1966. His friendships with Pierre Monteux and Arthur Honegger were important for his musical development.

PRINCIPAL COMPOSITIONS (published by Choudens unless otherwise noted): *Piano Concerto*, "Poème" (1939); *Rythmes du monde*, oratorio for narrator, 2 sopranos, chorus, orchestra; text by the composer (1939); *Le Rire de Nils Halérius*, 3-act opera; libretto by Gérard Caillet and the composer (1944–48, Choudens and SOFIRAD); *Cello Concerto* (1944–45); *Edina*, symphonic poem (1946); *Symphony No. 1*, "Jean de la Peur" (1949); *Le Fou*, 3-act opera; libretto by the composer (1949–54); *Le Ventriloque*, 1-act chamber opera; libretto by Paul Arnold and the composer (1954–55); *L'Opéra de poussière*, 2-act opera with prologue; libretto by Caillet and the composer (1958–62); *Symphonies Nos. 2–3* (1965).

BIBL.: Antoine Goléa, *M. L.* (Paris 1969).

SEE ALSO France.

Landré, Guillaume (b. The Hague, 24 Feb 1905; d. Amsterdam, 6 Nov 1968), studied law at the Univ. of Utrecht (1924–29) and composition privately with Willem Pijper (1924–29). He was music critic for the *Telegraaf* during 1929–31 and taught political science and commercial law at II Openbare Handelsschool in Amsterdam during 1930–47. During 1947–58 he was secretary of the Netherlands Arts Council. He also held posts in several music organizations, including the chairmanship of the Netherlands Composers' Society (1950–62). His compositions owed much to his study with Pijper. Often elegiac in mood, they make use of cyclical devices; in the last works 12-tone techniques are freely employed.

PRINCIPAL COMPOSITIONS (published by Donemus): *String Quartets Nos. 1–4* (1927, 1943, 1950, 1965); *Woodwind Quintets Nos. 1–2* (1930, 1960); *De Snoek* [The Pike], comic opera; libretto by Emmy van Lokhorst (1934); *Suite* for piano, strings (1936); *Cello Concerto* (1940); *Sinfonietta* for violin, orchestra (1941); *Piae memoriae pro patria mortuorum* for chorus, orchestra (1942); *Symphonic Music* for flute, orchestra (1947); *Symphony No. 3* (1951); *Chamber Symphony*

(1952); *Clarinet Concerto* (1957–58); *Concertante* for clarinet, double bass, orchestra (1959); *Sextet* for flute, clarinet, string quartet (1959); *Sonata* for chamber orchestra (1961); *Jean Levècq*, 1-act opera (1962–63); *La Symphonie pastorale*, opera; libretto by Claude Rostand after Gide (1964; *Interludes* from the opera, for orchestra, 1967); *Variazioni senza tema* for orchestra (1967).

[prepared with the help of Donemus]
SEE ALSO Netherlands.

organ (1967, Bornemann); *Livre oecuménique* for organ (1968, Bornemann).

BIBL.: Patrick Giraud, *Le Thème grégorien dans les oeuvres pour orgue de J. L.* (thesis, Gregorian Institute, Paris, and the Conservatory of Fribourg, Switzerland, 1964).

[prepared with the help of Marie-Louise Jaquet]
SEE ALSO Liturgical Music: Christian.

Language, see Text Setting and Usage, Theory

Langlais, Jean (François) (b. La Fontenelle, France, 15 Feb 1907), attended the Institut Nationale des Jeunes Aveugles (1917–30; counterpoint, composition, organ with André Marchal; piano with Blazy; harmony with Albert Mahaut, who was a pupil of César Franck) and the Paris Conservatory (1927, fugue with Noël Gallon; 1934, organ with Marcel Dupré and composition with Paul Dukas). He studied orchestration with the help of a fellow pupil, Olivier Messiaen. He has taught organ, composition, and choral singing at the Institut Nationale since 1931 and has been organist at the Basilica of Ste. Clotilde since 1945 and a teacher of organ and improvisation at the Schola Cantorum since 1961. Langlais has toured throughout the world as an organist and is best known for his organ compositions, most of which are collections of short pieces. The strongest influence on his development has come from his long association with Messiaen. He uses modal harmonies, often combined with Gregorian chant, and often borrows forms, genres, and technical procedures from the 17th and 18th centuries.

PRINCIPAL COMPOSITIONS: *Pièce* in free form for string quartet, organ (1935); *Symphony No. 1* for organ (1941–42, Philippo); *9 Pièces* for organ (1942–43, Bornemann); *Messe solennelle* for choruses, congregation, 2 trumpets, 2 trombones, organ (1947, Schola Cantorum); *Organ Concerto No. 1* (1949, Gray); *Hommage à Frescobaldi* for organ (1951, Bornemann); *Folkloric Suite* for organ (1952, Fitzsimons); *Organ Book* (1956, E-V); *La Passion* for vocal soloists, choruses, orchestra (1957); *Triptyque* for organ (1957, Novello); *Psalm 150* for 3 male voices, organ (1958, McLaughlin); *American Suite* for organ (1959, Gray); *Organ Concerto No. 2* (1961, Gray); *Essai* for organ (1962, Bornemann); *3 Solemn Songs* for choirs, congregation, 2 trumpets, 2 trombones, organ (1962–63, Schola Cantorum); *Homage to J.-Rh. Rameau* for organ (1963, E-V); *Poem of Life* for organ (1965, E-V); *Canticle of the Sun* for choruses, piano or organ (1966, E-V); *Poem of Happiness* for organ (1966, E-V); *Poem of Peace* for organ (1966, E-V); *Sonate en trio* for

Lansky, Paul (b. New York, 18 June 1944), studied at Queens College (1961–66; composition with George Perle, Hugo Weisgall; theory with Saul Novack) and at Princeton Univ. (1966–69; theory and composition with Edward Cone, Peter Westergaard, Milton Babbitt, J. K. Randall). During 1965–66 he was French hornist with the Dorian Woodwind Quintet. He has taught at Princeton since 1969.

PRINCIPAL COMPOSITIONS: *String Quartet* (1966–67); *Computer Piece* on tape (1967–68); *Piano Piece in 3 Parts* (1968); *2 Studies* for wind quintet (1969); *Short Serenade* for piano (1970).

PRINCIPAL WRITINGS: Concluding chapter in *Serial Composition and Atonality* by George Perle, 3rd ed. (Berkeley 1971).
SEE ALSO Texture.

Lanza, Alcides (Emigdio) (b. Rosario, Argentina, 2 June 1929), studied in Buenos Aires with Ruwin Erlich (piano), Roberto Kinsky (conducting), and Julián Bautista (composition). During 1963–64 he worked at the Torcuato di Tella Institute with Ginastera, Messiaen, Copland, Maderna, and Malipiero and during 1965, at the Columbia-Princeton Electronic Music Center with Ussachevsky. He also studied electronic engineering at the Technical School in Rosario. He was a coach and pianist at the Teatro de Colón during 1959–64. During 1965–70 he was a technician at the Columbia-Princeton Electronic Music Center. He has been active in promoting performances of contemporary music in Buenos Aires, New York, and other cities in the Americas.

PRINCIPAL COMPOSITIONS (published by Boosey unless otherwise noted): *Eidesis I* for orchestra (1963, EAMI); *Piano Concerto* (1964); *Cuarteto IV* for horns (1964); *Interferences I* for 2 groups of winds, electronic sounds on tape (1966); *Plectros II* for piano, electronic sounds on tape (1966); *Eidesis II* for brass, strings, percussion (1967);

Interferences II for percussion, electronic sounds on tape (1967); *Strobo I* for audience, double bass, percussion, electronic sounds on tape, lights (1967); *Cuarteto V* for strings (1967); *Ekphonesis I* on tape (1969, unpub.); *Ekphonesis III* for any 3 instruments, electronic sounds on tape (1969, unpub.).

PRINCIPAL WRITINGS: "A New Notational System," *Parametros* (Caracas, April 1969); "Consideraciónes sobre la música en su relación con el tiempo presente," *Revista de Letras* (Univ. of Puerto Rico) 1969/3:384–91; "Primer festival de música de las Americas," *ibid.* 1969/3:466–72.

SEE ALSO Argentina.

Larsson, Lars-Erik (b. Åkarp, Sweden, 15 May 1908), studied at the Royal Academy in Stockholm (1925–29, composition with Ernst Ellberg, conducting with Olano Morales). During 1937–53 he was a conductor for Radio Sweden. He taught composition at the Royal Academy during 1947–59 and during 1961–65 was director of music at the Univ. of Uppsala.

PRINCIPAL COMPOSITIONS (published by Gehrman unless otherwise noted): *Concerto Overtures Nos. 1–3*: No. 1, Op. 4 (1929); No. 2, Op. 13 (1934, UE); No. 3, Op. 34 (1948); *Princessan av Cypern* [The Princess of Cyprus], 4-act opera (1930–36, unpub.); *Sinfonietta* for strings (1932, UE); *Saxophone Concerto*, Op. 14 (1934); *Piano Sonatas Nos. 1–3*: No. 1, Op. 16 (1936, UE); No. 2, Op. 39 (1947); No. 3, Op. 41 (1950); *Pastoral Suite* for orchestra, Op. 19 (1938); *Intima miniatyrer* [Intimate Miniature] for string quartet, Op. 20 (1938); *Arresten på Bohus* [The Arrest on Bohus], 2-act opera bouffe (1938–39, unpub.); *Förklädd gud* [Disguised God] for soprano, baritone, chorus, orchestra (1940); *String Quartet*, Op. 31 (1944, Musikaliska Konstföreningen); *Cello Concerto*, Op. 37 (1947); *Music for Orchestra*, Op. 40 (1949); *Violin Concerto*, Op. 42 (1952); *12 Concertinos* for various solo instruments, string orchestra, Op. 45 (1953–57); *Missa brevis* for chorus, Op. 43 (1954); *Quartetto alla serenata* for string quartet, Op. 44 (1955); *Variations for Orchestra*, Op. 50 (1963); *Intrada solemnis* for vocal soloists, orchestra, Op. 51 (1964); *Soluret och urnan* [The Sundial and the Urn] for baritone, chorus, orchestra, Op. 53 (1966); *Quattro tempi*, divertimento for wind quintet, Op. 55 (1968).

SEE ALSO Scandinavia.

Latin America, see Argentina, Brazil, Chile, Mexico

Layton, Billy Jim (b. Corsicana, Texas, 14 Nov 1924), studied at the New England Conservatory (1945–48; composition with Carl McKinley, Francis Judd Cooke), Yale Univ. (1948–51, composition with Quincy Porter), and Harvard Univ. (1951–54, 1957–60; composition with Walter Piston; musicology with Otto Gombosi, Nino Pirrotta). He has taught at the New England Conservatory (1959–60), Harvard Univ. (1960–66), and the State Univ. of N. Y. at Stony Brook (since 1966). His work as a clarinetist, saxophonist, and arranger for jazz and dance groups during the 1940s was important in his musical development.

PRINCIPAL COMPOSITIONS (published by Schirmer-G): *5 Studies* for violin, piano, Op. 1 (1952); *An American Portrait*, symphonic overture, Op. 2 (1953); *3 Dylan Thomas Poems* for chorus, brass sextet, Op. 3 (1954–56); *String Quartet in 2 Movements*, Op. 4 (1956); *3 Studies* for piano (1957); *Divertimento* for violin, clarinet, bassoon, cello, trombone, harpsichord, percussion, Op. 6 (1958–60); *Dance Fantasy* for orchestra, Op. 7 (1964). List to 1950: *Composers of the Americas* 9:88–89.

PRINCIPAL WRITINGS: "The New Liberalism," *Perspectives* 3/2:137–42.

BIBL.: Gilbert Chase, *America's Music*, 2nd ed. (New York 1966):678–81; Wilfrid Mellers, *Music in a New Found Land* (London 1964): 229–34. The following reviews contain significant information: Richmond Browne (*Dance Fantasy*), *Perspectives* 4/1:161–70; Richard F. French (*String Quartet in 2 Movements*), *Musical Quarterly* 46:556–57.

SEE ALSO Musicology and Composition.

Lazarof, Henri (b. Sofia, Bulgaria, 12 April 1932), studied at the Sofia Academy (graduated 1948), the New Conservatory in Jerusalem (1949–52), the Accadèmia di S. Cecilia in Rome (1955–57), and Brandeis Univ. (1957–59). He has taught at the Univ. of Calif. at Los Angeles since 1962.

PRINCIPAL COMPOSITIONS: *Viola Concerto* (1959–60); *Concerto* for piano, 20 instruments (1960–61); *Inventions* for viola, piano (1962); *Quantetti* for piano, 3 prerecorded pianos on tape (1963); *Tempi concertati*, double concerto for violin, viola with flute, harp, xylophone, vibraphone, celesta, harpsichord, piano (1964); *Structures sonores* for orchestra (1966); *Rhapsody* for violin, piano (1966); *Espaces* for 2 flutes, 2 clarinets, 2 violas, 2 cellos, 2 pianos (1966); *Octet*, for wind quintet, bass clarinet, trumpet, trombone (1967); *Intonazione* for 2 pianos (1967); *Mutazione* for orchestra (1967); *Cello Concerto* (1968); *Omaggio*, chamber concerto for 19 players (1968); *Ricercar* for viola, piano, orchestra (1968); *Cadence 2* for viola, tape (1969); *Cadence 3* for violin, 2 percussionists (1970); *Textures* for piano, 5 instrumental ensembles (1970); *Continuum* for string trio (1970).

Le Caine, Hugh, see under Caine.

Lees, Benjamin (b. Harbin, China, 8 Jan 1924), attended the Univ. of Southern Calif. (1946–48, composition and theory with Halsey Stevens, piano with Marguerite Bitter). He also studied composition and orchestration with George Antheil (1949–54). For two years, 1950–52, he composed film scores and was pianist for the Eugene Loring Ballet School in Los Angeles. He was a visiting professor of composition at the Peabody Conservatory (1962–64, 1966–68) and a professor at Queens College, New York (1964–66). Lees states that "one of the predominant features of my music is a forward motion stemming from a very real rhythmic propulsiveness." This may result in frequent changes in meter. "Another aspect of my style is the development of motives or elements. . . . Once an idea is . . . stated, it will . . . be subjected to some kind of developmental treatment, no matter how minor. . . . I thrive on diversity. The tools of composition are everywhere for everyone to use . . . , and I have employed them all from a simple triad to controlled chaos."

PRINCIPAL COMPOSITIONS (published by Boosey): *Piano Concerto No. 1* (1954–55); *Symphony No. 2* (1957); *Violin Concerto* (1958); *Concerto for Orchestra* (1959); *Visions of Poets*, cantata for soprano, tenor, chorus, orchestra (1961); *Oboe Concerto* (1963); *Spectrum* for orchestra (1964); *Piano Sonata No. 4* (1964); *Concerto for string quartet, orchestra* (1964–65); *Piano Concerto No. 2* (1966); *Symphony No. 3* (1968). List to 1966: *Composers of the Americas* 12:86–89.

PRINCIPAL WRITINGS: "The American Composer. His Audience and Critics," *Music Journal* (March 1968): 37–86.

BIBL.: Deryck Cooke, "The Music of B. L.," *Tempo* (spring-summer 1959): 16–29; ——, "The Recent Music of B. L.," *Tempo* (spring 1963): 11–21.

de Leeuw, Ton (b. Rotterdam, 16 Nov 1926), studied music privately in Breda (1947–49; theory, piano with Louis Tosbosch), Paris (1949–50, orchestration with Thomas de Hartmann, analysis with Olivier Messiaen), and Amsterdam (1947–49, composition with Henk Badings; 1950–54, ethnomusicology with Jaap Kunst). During 1954–59 he was musical advisor to the Netherlands Radio Union and since 1966, a member of its advisory board. He was director of the Gaudeamus Foundation during 1958–61. He has taught composition, contemporary, and Asian music at the Conservatories of Amsterdam and Utrecht since 1960 and at the Univ. of Amsterdam since 1963. He has also lectured and conducted symposiums on contemporary and Asian music in Europe and India. While studying in Paris, he became interested in musique concrète through Pierre Schaeffer and in Schoenberg's 12-tone theories through René Leibowitz. He was also influenced by Willem Pijper's "germ-cell" principle of melodic motives, which he further developed rhythmically (the interest in rhythm was also stimulated by hearing non-European music on the radio). During 1957–60 de Leeuw worked at developing a "static" music, in which "all the musical bricks are directed to making possible a completely static equilibrium." During a trip to India in 1960 he heard "for the first time the rhythmic differentiation" and a highly sophisticated type of melodic-rhythmic development. He was also impressed by the "objectivity" of Eastern music as compared with Western music of the last few centuries, in which the composer is overly concerned with "wanting to be himself." In the *Symphonies of Winds* (1963) he began using proportional rhythmic notation in order to represent "a virtually unlimited scale of note values." In *De Droom* (1963) and *Haiku II* (1968) the texts are sometimes split into phonemes and used as a sound source. Movement by players to alter the spatial relationships of sounds occurs in the *Spatial Music* series (1966–68).

PRINCIPAL COMPOSITIONS (published by Donemus unless otherwise noted): *Hiob* [Job], radio oratorio for soloists, chorus, orchestra, tape (1956, unpub.); *Movements rétrogrades* for orchestra (1957); *String Quartet No. 1* (1958); *Antiphonie* for wind quintet, 4-track tape (1960); *Symphonies of Winds* for 29 wind instruments (1963, Peters); *De Droom* [The Dream], opera (1963); *Men Go Their Ways* for piano (1964); *String Quartet No. 2* (1964); *The 4 Seasons* for harp (1964); *Syntaxis I* on tape (1966); *Spatial Music I* for 32–48 players (1966); *Music for Violin* for 1 or 2 violins (1967); *Spatial Music IV* for 12 players (1968); *Haiku II* for soprano, orchestra (1968); *Lamento pacis* for chorus, 9 instruments (1969); *Litany of Our Time* for soprano, flute, double bass, harp, piano, percussion, live electronics (1970).

PRINCIPAL WRITINGS: "Mensen en Muziek in India," *Mens en Melodie* (May, July, August 1963); *Muziek van de Twintigste Eeuw* [Music of the Twentieth Century] (Utrecht 1964; "Introduction" printed in English translation in *Sonorum Speculum* 20: 1–14).

BIBL.: Jos Wouters, "Composers' Gallery: T. de L.," *Sonorum Speculum* 19: 1–26.

SEE ALSO Melody, Netherlands.

Legley, Victor (b. Hazebrouck, France, 18 June 1915), studied at the Brussels Conservatory (1933–35, composition with Jean Absil). During 1936–47 he was a violist with the Symphony Orchestra of the Netherlands International Radio, and since 1947 he has been music director of the Third Program for the Belgian Radio and Television Division. He has taught composition at the Brussels Conservatory since 1950 and at the Chapelle Royale Reine Elisabeth since 1955.

PRINCIPAL COMPOSITIONS (published by CBDM unless otherwise noted): *String Quartets Nos. 1–4*: No. 1, Op. 5 (1941, unpub.); No. 2, Op. 28 (1947); No. 3, Op. 50 (1956); No. 4, Op. 56 (1963); *Symphonies Nos. 1–5*: No. 1, Op. 10 (1942, unpub.); No. 2, Op. 29 (1947, unpub.); No. 3, Op. 42 (1953); No. 4, Op. 61 (1964); No. 5, Op. 64 (1965, unpub.); *Wind Trio*, Op. 11 (1942); *Violin Sonata*, Op. 12 (1943); *Viola Sonata*, Op. 13 (1943); *5 Mélodies françaises* for voice, piano, Op. 15 (1944); *Cello Sonata*, Op. 20 (1945); *Violin Concertos Nos. 1–2* (1947, 1967, both unpub.); *Piano Concerto*, Op. 39 (1952); *Clarinet Sonata*, Op. 40, No. 3 (1952); *Trumpet Sonata*, Op. 40, No. 6 (1953); *Little Carnaval Overture* (1954); *Serenade* for string orchestra (1957); *La Cathédrale d'acier* for orchestra, Op. 52 (1958); *Overture for a Comedy by Goldini*, "*Lo spirito di contraddizione*," Op. 53 (1958); *Wind Quintet*, Op. 58 (1961); *La Farce des deux nues*, 4-act opera; libretto after Herman Closseen (1966, unpub.); *Harp Concerto*, Op. 66 (1966, unpub.); *Paradise Regained* for orchestra (1968, unpub.); *3 Movements* for brass, percussion, Op. 76 (1969, unpub.); *Espaces* for string orchestra, Op. 77 (1970, unpub.); *Viola Concerto* (1971, unpub.).

PRINCIPAL WRITINGS: "Muziek en Radio" and "Actuele Aspecten voor een Compositieleer," papers published by the Royal Flemish Academy (1967, 1970).

SEE ALSO Belgium.

Lehmann, Hans Ulrich (b. Biel, Switzerland, 4 May 1937), studied at the Biel Conservatory (1956–60, diploma in cello), the Zurich Conservatory (1960–62, theory with Paul Müller-Zürich), the Basel Musik-Akademie (1960–63, composition with Boulez, Stockhausen), and the Univ. of Zurich (1960–67, musicology with Kurt von Fischer). Since 1964 he has been teaching music theory at the Basel Musik-Akademie and serving as president at the Basel section of ISCM. In 1969 he began teaching at the Univ. of Zurich.

PRINCIPAL COMPOSITIONS (published by Schott unless otherwise noted): *Quanti I* for flute, chamber orchestra (1962); *Régions* for flutist (1963, unpub.); *Episoden* for woodwind quintet (1963–64); *Mosaik* for solo clarinet (1964, unpub.);

Komposition für 19 for chamber orchestra (1964–65); *Noten* for organ (1964–66); *Spiele* for oboe, harp (1965); *Studien* for solo viola (1966); *Rondo* for soprano, orchestra; text by Helmut Heissenbüttel (1967); *Instants* for piano, strings (1969, unpub.); *Konzert* for 2 winds, strings (1969, unpub.).

PRINCIPAL WRITINGS: "Heissenbuttel als Komponist," *Begegnung* (1968): 19ff.

BIBL.: Mathias Knauer and Fritz Muggler, "Avantgardistische Schweizer Musik," *Österreichische Musikzeitschrift* 24/3: 172.

SEE ALSO Switzerland.

Leibowitz, René (b. Warsaw, 17 Feb 1913; d. Paris, 28 August 1972), lived primarily in Paris beginning in 1926. He studied with Anton Webern (1930–31; harmony, counterpoint), Arnold Schoenberg (1932, composition), and Pierre Monteux (1934–36, conducting). During 1946–54 he conducted at the French Radio, after which he toured throughout the world, specializing in the 12-tone repertory. He taught 12-tone techniques privately and was one of the foremost promoters of 12-tone music, both as a writer and teacher.

PRINCIPAL COMPOSITIONS: *String Quartets Nos. 1, 3, 6*, Opp. 3, 26, 65 (1939–40, 1951–52, 1965); *Symphony No. 4*, Op. 4 (1939–41, Schott); *Concerto* for violin, piano, orchestra, Op. 5 (1941–42, Boelke); *Concerto* for 9 instruments, Op. 10 (1943–44, UE); *Chamber Symphony*, Op. 17 (1946–48, Boelke); *Explanation of Metaphors*, Op. 15 (1947, Boelke); *Piano Trio*, Op. 20 (1950); *The City* for narrator, orchestra, Op. 24 (1951); *6 Pieces* for orchestra, Op. 31 (1954); *Piano Concerto*, Op. 32 (1954); *Viola Concerto*, Op. 35 (1954, Boelke); *Funeral Symphony* for vocal soloists, chorus, orchestra, Op. 33 (1954–55); *Sonata quasi una fantasia* for piano, Op. 44 (1957); *Humoresque* for 6 percussionists, Op. 46 (1957); *Overture* for orchestra, Op. 48 (1958); *5 Songs* for voice, piano, Op. 49 (1958); *Violin Concerto*, Op. 50 (1958); *Cello Concerto*, Op. 58 (1962); *Les Espagnols à Venise*, 1-act opera, Op. 60 (1962); *Toccata* for piano, Op. 62 (1964); *Suite* for violin, piano, Op. 66 (1965); *Rondo capriccioso* for piano, Op. 78 (1967); *Suite* for 3 instruments, Op. 81 (1968); *Labyrinthe*, 1-act opera, Op. 85 (1969).

PRINCIPAL WRITINGS: *Schoenberg and His School* (New York 1948); *Introduction à la musique de douze sons* (Paris 1949); *L'Histoire de l'opéra* (Paris 1957); *Thinking for Orchestra*, prepared in collaboration with Jan Maguire (New York 1961).

SEE ALSO Austria and Germany, France.

Leifs, Jón (b. Sólheimar, Iceland, 1 May 1899; d. Reykjavik, 30 July 1968), studied at the Leipzig Music Academy (1916–22; composition and conducting with Herman Scherchen;

theory with Paul Graener, Otto Lohse; piano with Robert Teichmüller). He was conductor for the Leipzig Volksakademie during 1923–24 and for the Icelandic Radio Network during 1935–37. Subsequently he was a free-lance composer who took an active part in advancing the music life of the country. From 1945 he was president of the Icelandic Composers Union and from 1948, of STEM, the Icelandic performing rights society. He collected Icelandic folksongs, and his own music was influenced by this interest.

PRINCIPAL COMPOSITIONS (some dates not available): *Trilogia piccola* for orchestra, Op. 1 (1919–24, Kistner); *Iceland Overture* for chorus, orchestra, Op. 9 (1926, Kistner); *Iceland Cantata* for chorus, orchestra, Op. 13 (1934, Kistner); *Saga Symphony*, Op. 26 (Kistner); *Baldr*, tone poem for orchestra, Op. 34; *Dettifoss* for baritone, chorus, orchestra, Op. 57 (1964); *Darraðarljóð* [War Ode] for chorus, orchestra, Op. 60 (1964); *Grógaldr* for alto, tenor, orchestra, Op. 62 (1965); *Edda Oratorium I–III* for vocal soloists, chorus, orchestra; *Requiem* for chorus; *String Quartets Nos. 1–3*. Leifs also wrote numerous songs and shorter choral works.

PRINCIPAL WRITINGS: *Islands künstlerische anregung* (Reykjavik 1951).

Leighton, Kenneth (b. Wakefield, England, 2 Oct 1929), studied classics and music at Queen's College, Oxford Univ. (1947–51) and composition with Goffredo Petrassi in Rome (1951). During 1953–56 he held a composing fellowship at the Univ. of Leeds. He has taught composition at the Univ. of Edinburgh (1956–68, since 1970) and at Worcester College, Oxford Univ. (1968–70). He is conductor and pianist with the Edinburgh Music Society Orchestra.

PRINCIPAL COMPOSITIONS (published by Novello unless otherwise noted): *Piano Concertos Nos. 1–3* (1951, 1960, 1969); *Violin Concerto* (1952); *Cello Concerto* (1955); *String Quartets Nos. 1–2* (1956, 1957; Lengnick); *The Light Invisible*, sinfonia sacra for tenor, chorus, orchestra (1958); *Piano Quintet* (1959); *Concerto* for large string orchestra (1961); *Mass* for soloists, double chorus, organ (1964, Oxford); *Symphony* (1964); *Piano Trio* (1965); *Et resurrexit* for organ (1966); *Fantasy*, "Conflicts," for piano (1967).

BIBL.: Ernest Bradbury, "K. L.'s *The Light Invisible*," *Musical Times* (August 1958); John V. Cockshoot, "The Music of K. L.," *Musical Times* (April 1957); Arthur Milner, "An Organ Work of K. L.," *Musical Opinion* (Oct 1964).

SEE ALSO Liturgical Music: Christian.

Leng, Alfonso (b. Santiago, Chile, 11 Feb 1894), is self-taught in composition. He be-

longed to the early-20th-century Group of Ten that helped modernize Chilean arts. He is an odontologist by profession.

PRINCIPAL COMPOSITIONS: *5 Dolores* for piano (1901–14); *Fantasía quasi sonata* for piano (1909); *10 Preludes* for piano (1919–32, IEM); *La muerte de Alsino*, symphonic poem (1920, IEM); *Fantasía* for piano, orchestra (1936, IEM); *Psalm 77* for vocal soloists, chorus, orchestra (1941); *Piano Sonata* (1950, PAU). Leng has also written some 15 songs for voice and piano to French, German, and Spanish texts. List to 1950: *Composers of the Americas* 15:158–60.

SEE ALSO Chile.

Leotsakos, George (b. Athens, 9 August 1935), studied at the Hellenic Conservatory in Athens (graduated 1964, composition with Yannis Papaïoannou) and privately with Papaïoannou beginning in 1952. During his music studies he worked as a journalist, and in 1960 he began work as a music critic. Since then he has written for the newspapers *Kathimerini* (1960–65), *Messimvrini* (1961–63), *Nea* (since 1965), and *Vima* (since 1969). During 1966–67 he broadcast a weekly program, "Music News from Around the World," over Athens Radio. He has promoted contemporary music and campaigned to reform Greek musical institutions. A major interest of his since 1955 has been Far Eastern music, particularly the music of Japan, and he has lectured extensively in Greece on this subject. He describes his music as "free, atonal."

PRINCIPAL COMPOSITIONS: *Petite Suite chevaleresque* for piano or harpsichord (1957; "Sérénade" is printed in *Neue Griechische Klaviermusik* 1, published by Göring); *12 Haiku* for woman's voice, piano; texts by Matsuo Bashô (1961); *7 Haiku* for woman's voice, piano; texts by Yosa Buson (1961); *5 Haiku* for woman's voice, piano; texts by Kobayashi Issa (1961); *Khmer* for flute (1963–65).

PRINCIPAL WRITINGS: "Bartók, génie discret," *Musique hongroise* (Paris 1962):72–74; "Protassis ya to Nôh" [Some Thoughts on Noh Theater], *Epoches* 29:1–8.

Lessard, John (Ayres) (b. San Francisco, 3 July 1920), studied at the Ecole Normale de Musique in Paris (1937–39; composition with Nadia Boulanger, Georges Dandelot). Since 1963 he has taught at the State Univ. of N. Y. at Stony Brook.

PRINCIPAL COMPOSITIONS: *Ariel* for voice, piano (1941, ACA); *Orpheus* for voice, piano (1944, Merrymount); *Bag of a Bee* for voice, piano (1949, ACA); *Interior* for voice, piano (1951, ACA);

When as in Silk My Julia Goes for voice, piano (1951, ACA); *Toccata in 4 Movements* for harpsichord (1951, ACA); *Wind Octet* (1952, ACA); *Cello Sonata* (1956, ACA); *Rose-cheekt Laura* for voice, piano (1960, Joshua); *Sinfonietta concertante* for orchestra (1961, Joshua); *Harp Concerto* (1963, Joshua); *12 Mother Goose Songs* for voice, string trio (1964, Joshua); *String Trio* (1963, Joshua); *Trio in 6 parti* for violin, cello, piano (1966, Joshua); *Quodlibets* for 2 trumpets, trombone (1967, Joshua); *Fragments from the Cantos of Ezra Pound*, cantata for baritone, flute, 2 trumpets, 2 horns, trombone, violin, viola, cello (1969, Joshua).

SEE ALSO United States.

Lesur, Daniel- (Jean Yves) (b. Paris, 19 Nov 1908), studied at the Paris Conservatory (1919–29, composition and organ with Charles Tournemire, harmony with Jean Gallon, counterpoint with Georges Caussade, piano with Armand Ferté). He was assistant organist at Ste. Clothilde during 1927–37. In 1936 he founded the group Jeune France with Olivier Messiaen, André Jolivet, and Yves Baudrier. He taught counterpoint at the Schola Cantorum during 1935–62 and was its director during 1957–61. He has worked for the French Radio since 1939, and for French Television since 1961; he has been music director of the latter since 1968. Since 1969 he has also been principal music inspector for the French Ministry of Cultural Affairs.

PRINCIPAL COMPOSITIONS: *Les Harmonies intimes* for medium voice, piano; text by the composer (1931, Salabert); *La Mort des voiles* for medium voice, piano; text by Paul Fort (1931, Salabert); *Scène de la Passion* for organ (1931, Leduc); *La Vie interieure* for organ (1932, Lemoine); *La Mouette* for medium voice, piano; text by Heinrich Heine (1932, Fortin); *Les Yeux fermés* for medium voice, piano; text by Heine (1932, Fortin); *Hymnes* for organ, 2 vols. (1935, Leduc; 1937–39); *Suite française* for orchestra (1935, Ricordi); *Passacaille* for piano, orchestra (1937, Billaudot); *Pastorale* for chamber orchestra (1938, EMT); *Ricercare* for orchestra (1939, Ricordi); *3 Poèmes de Cecile Sauvage* for medium voice, piano (1939, Ricordi); *Suite* for string quartet (1940, Costallat); *L'Enfance de l'art* for medium voice, piano; text by Claude Roy (1942, Ricordi); *Suite* for piano quartet (1943, Ricordi); *Variations* for piano, string orchestra (1943, Costallat); *Clair comme le jour* for medium voice, piano; text by Roy (1945, Ricordi); *Suite medievale* for flute, harp, string trio (1945–46, Durand); *Chansons cambodgiennes* for medium voice, piano (1946–47, Durand); *Berçeuses à tenir eveille* for high voice, piano; text by René de Obaldia (1947, Durand); *Pastorale variée* for piano (1947, Durand); *Ballade* for piano (1948, Durand); *Andrea*

del Sarto, symphonic poem (1949, Choudens); *Festival Overture* (1951, Ricordi); *L'Annonciation*, cantata for narrator, tenor, chorus, chamber orchestra; text by Loys Masson (1952, EMT); *La Cantique des cantiques* for chorus (1953, Durand); *Nocturne* for piano (1953, Broude-B); *Concerto da camera* for piano, chamber orchestra (1953, Ricordi); *Serenade* for string orchestra (1954, Ricordi); *Le Bal* for piano (1954, EMT); *Cantique des Colonnes* for women's chorus, orchestra; text by Paul Valéry (1954–57, Pathé-Marconi); *Le Bal du destin*, ballet (1956, EMT); *Symphonie de danses* for chamber orchestra (1958, Ricordi); *Messe du Jubilé* for chorus (1960, Ricordi); *3 Etudes* for piano (1962, Durand); *Fantaisie* for 2 pianos (1962, Ricordi); *Andrea del Sarto*, 2-act opera (1969, Choudens).

SEE ALSO France.

Letelier(-Llona), **Alfonso** (b. Santiago, Chile, 4 Oct 1912), studied at the National Conservatory of the Univ. of Chile in Santiago (1930–35, composition with Pedro Humberto Allende, piano with Raúl Hügel) and the Catholic Univ. of Santiago (1930–36, major in agronomy). In 1940 he founded the Escuela Moderna de Música in Santiago. He has taught composition at the National Conservatory since 1940 and was dean of the faculty of musical arts and sciences of the Univ. of Chile during 1952–62. Much of his music expresses the spirit and sometimes the letter of Chilean folklore. He has also been influenced by the religious mysticism and musical culture of the Spanish renaissance and by Gregorian chant. His harmonic vocabulary has ranged from traditional tonal materials to polytonality, atonality, and a free serialism. An emphasis on contrapuntal textures derives from Hindemith.

PRINCIPAL COMPOSITIONS (published by IEM unless otherwise noted): *8 Canciones* for chorus, Op. 9 (1934–39, ECIC); *La vida del campo* for piano, orchestra, Op. 14 (1937); *4 Canciones de Cuna* for vocal soloists, chamber orchestra, Op. 13 (1939, ECIC); *Sonetos de la muerte* for orchestra, Op. 18; texts by Gabriela Mistral (1943–47); *Variations on an Original Theme* for piano, Op. 22 (1948, Barry); *Viola Sonata*, Op. 19 (1949); *La historia de Tobías y Sara*, part 1, oratorio, Op. 26; text by Paul Claudel (1955); *Divertimento* for orchestra, Op. 25 (1955); *Suite Aculeu* for orchestra, Op. 27 (1955–56); *4 Pieces* for piano, Op. 33 (1965); *Estancias amorosas* for woman's voice, orchestra, Op. 34; poems by Carmen Valle (1966); *4 Preludios vegetales* for orchestra, Op. 35 (1966–68, unpub.); *2 Canciones de Stefan George* for voice, chamber orchestra, Op. 36 (1969, unpub.). List to 1956: *Composers of the Americas* 2:104–07.

PRINCIPAL WRITINGS: Letelier has published over 50 articles about Chilean composers and other musical topics in *Revista musical chilena*. He has also written for various Chilean newspapers.

BIBL.: *Revista musical chilena* 109 (special issue devoted to Letelier); Domingo Santa Cruz, "El compositor A. L.," *Revista musical chilena* (June 1967): 8–30.

[Prepared with the help of Magdalena Vicuña]

SEE ALSO Chile.

Letelier-Valdés, Miguel (Francisco) (b. Santiago, Chile, 29 Sept 1939); studied at the National Conservatory of the Univ. of Chile (1961–65; harmony, counterpoint, organ with Julio Perceval) and at the Latin American Center for Advanced Musical Studies in Buenos Aires (1965–66, composition with Alberto Ginastera). He studied privately in Buenos Aires with Maurice Le Roux (1965, film music) and Iannis Xenakis (1966, computer music), in Paris with Max Deutsch (1967, Mozart and Wagner operas), and in Hamburg with Diether de la Motte (1970, composition). He also studied organ in Buenos Aires with Hector Zeoli (1965–66), in Paris with Jean-Jacques Grünenwald (1967), and in Hamburg with Ulrich von Kameke (1969–70). He has given many organ recitals in South America and Germany. Since 1968 he has taught composition and organ at the National Conservatory of the Univ. of Chile. During 1968–69 he was music critic for *Política, economía, cultura* in Santiago. His music of the late 1960s began to reflect the influence of Berio, Ligeti, and the Polish school.

PRINCIPAL COMPOSITIONS: *3 Canciones* for chorus (1960, IEM); *Preludios breves* for guitar (1963, Ricordi); *Harpsichord Sonata* (1963); *Divertimento* for flute, oboe, clarinet, string quartet (1965); *Nocturno* for alto, clarinet, cello, piano, guitar (1966); *Instantes*, 5 pieces for orchestra (1966); *Fantasia* for woman's voice, piccolo, bass clarinet, trumpet, viola, double bass, piano, vibraphone (1969–70); *Concerto* for string orchestra, 2 pianos, percussion (1970); *Piece* for organ (1970).

PRINCIPAL WRITINGS: "Festival musical de Hannover" and "El arte de una fuga," *Revista musical chilena* 24/10:71–74.

BIBL.: Pablo Garrido, "M. L.," *La nacion* (Santiago, 15 June 1965): 2.

SEE ALSO Chile.

Levy, Edward I. (b. Brooklyn, N. Y., 2 May 1929), studied at the Contemporary Music School in New York (1949–51, analysis with Stefan Wolpe), the City College of New York (1953–57), and Princeton Univ. (1958–60; composition with Milton Babbitt, Roger Sessions, analysis with Earl Kim). He also studied composition privately with Ralph Shapey (1948–51) and Stefan Wolpe (1951–54). He has taught at the C. W. Post College of Long Island Univ. (1962–67) and at Yeshiva Univ. in New York (since 1967). The most important influences on his development have come from Wolpe and Babbitt. During his early teens he followed what was than modern jazz and learned a "sense of rhythmic flow, of phrasing, and preference for" certain chords from such musicians as Dizzy Gillespie and Charlie Parker. His music to about 1959 was based on selected motivic pitch groups, which determined the content of both lines and chords in a procedural context of developing variation. Since then his work has been 12-tone. His *Quintet* (1967) represents a merging of previous approaches, using among other procedures pitch source-groups derived from the intervals of the work's original set and projected so as to achieve contrasting "behaviors."

PRINCIPAL COMPOSITIONS: *2 Songs* for mezzo-soprano, piano; texts by García-Lorca (1951); *Clarinet Sonata* (1953–56); *String Quartet* (1958); *String Trio* (1959); *Trio* for clarinet, violin, piano (1961); *Images*, 3 songs for soprano, piano (1961); *Mobiles*, 5 short studies for piano (1963); *Piece in 1 Movement* for violin, piano (1964); *Quintet* for flute, alto saxophone, vibraphone, viola, double bass (1967); *Trio* for flute, cello, piano (1968); *Chamber Concerto* for 15 players (1968–69); *Psalm 147* for chorus, piano (1969); *Septet* for clarinet, bassoon, trumpet, horn, violin, cello, piano (1969).

PRINCIPAL WRITINGS: "Stefan Wolpe," *Perspectives* 2/1:51–65; *A Guide to Musical Analysis* (Univ. Microfilms 1967); "To Analyze Music, Sketch It," (author's title: "Uses of Musical Analysis"), *Music Educators' Journal* (Jan 1969): 39–40, 117–18; "Motivic Development Is How a Piece Moves" (author's title: "The Idea of Motivic Development"), *Music Educators' Journal* (Oct 1969): 30–34; "Compositional Technique and Musical Expressivity," *Journal of Research in Music Education* 18/1:3–15.

SEE ALSO Text Setting and Usage.

Lévy, Ernst (b. Basel, Switzerland, 18 Nov 1895), studied at Basel Univ. (1914–15, 1917; musicology with Karl Nef). He taught piano at the Basel Conservatory during 1916–20. During 1920–40 he lived primarily in Paris and taught at the Conservatory of La Chaux-de-Fonds, the State Music School in Biel, and privately in Basel. In 1941 he moved to the U.S., where he taught at the New England Conservatory (1941–45), Bennington College (1945–48), the Univ. of Chicago (1949), and the Mass. Institute of Technology (1954). He returned to Switzerland in 1966.

PRINCIPAL COMPOSITIONS: *Symphonies Nos. 1–15*: No. 1 (1916); No. 2 (1920); No. 3 for chamber orchestra (1922); No. 4, with dancers (1924); No. 5 for violin, trumpet, orchestra (1925); No. 6, "Sinfonia strofica" (1933–34); No. 7 (1936); No. 8 for wind orchestra, timpani, piano (1939); No. 9 for chorus, orchestra (1938); No. 10, "France" (1944); No. 11 (1949, Boosey); No. 12 for 3 vocal soloists, chamber orchestra (1951); No. 13 (1955); No. 14 (1962); No. 15 (1967); *4 Orchestral Suites*: No. 1, "Suite symphonique" (1925); No. 2, "über eine alte Volksrhymne" (1951); No. 3 (1957); No. 4 (1959); *Ode à la rose* for mezzo-soprano, orchestra; text by Pierre Ronsard (1925); *Cello Concerto* (1947); *Cantata No. 2* for women's or mixed chorus, chamber orchestra (1948); *Divertimento* for clarinet, piano (1952); *Cello Sonata* (1953); *Suite* for violin, cello (1956); *Piano Quartet* (1956); *String Quartet No. 3* (1958); *Sonatinas Nos. 1–2* for violin, piano (1962); *Trio* for clarinet, cello, piano (1963); *Suite* for viola (1963); *Sonata in 3 Parts* for 3 violins (1965); *Letzte Liebe* for soprano, string orchestra (1965); *Fantasia ricercante* for clavichord or piano (1966, Broude-A); *A Musical Gathering* for wind quintet, violin, viola, cello, double bass, piano (1969); *Sonata strofica* for flute, oboe, clarinet, horn, violin, viola, cello, double bass, piano, metallophones (1970).

PRINCIPAL WRITINGS: "Goethe's musiktheoretische Anschauungen," *Schweizerische Musikzeitung* 1952/10; "On the Proportions of the South Tower of Chartres Cathedral," *The Gothic Cathedral* ed. by Simson (New York 1956); "Essai sur la dodécaphonie," *Schweizerische Musikzeitung* 1966/6; *Tone, A Study in Musical Acoustics*, written with Siegmund Levarie (Kent, Ohio, 1968). Lévy and Levarie are also preparing a book, *Musical Morphology*.

BIBL.: Siegmund Levarie, "La musique d'E. L.," *Schweizerische Musikzeitung* (May 1968):178–87.

Lewis, Robert Hall (b. Portland, Ore., 22 April 1926), studied at the Eastman School (1945–51, 1954–55; composition with Bernard Rogers, trumpet with Sidney Mear), the Paris Conservatory (1952–53, conducting with Eugene Bigot), L'Ecole Monteux (summer 1954, conducting with Pierre Monteux), the Vienna Academy of Music (1955–57; composition with Karl Schiske, Ernst Krenek), Princeton Univ. (summer 1959), and the Université de Lille in London (1967). He also studied trumpet with Harry Glantz and Nathan Prager in New York (summers 1947–

48) and composition with Nadia Boulanger in Paris (1952–53) and Hans Erich Apostel in Vienna (1955–57). He has played trumpet in the Okla. City Symphony (1951–52) and the Rochester Philharmonic (1953–55), and taught at Goucher College (since 1957) and Johns Hopkins Univ. (since 1969). His "earlier music was concerned with a basic linear-developmental process in the serial manner. In recent years I have abandoned this approach for a music embracing larger and more varied conceptual gestures. Hence, the interplay of continuity-discontinuity, subtle contrasts of timbre and rhythm, and structural flexibility are more characteristic of my present style."

PRINCIPAL COMPOSITIONS: *String Quartets Nos. 1–2* (1956, 1962; Seesaw); *5 Songs* for soprano, clarinet, horn, cello, piano (1957); *Prelude and Finale* for chamber orchestra (1959, Presser); *5 Movements* for piano (1960, Seesaw); *Toccata* for violin, percussion (1963, Broude-A); *Designs* for orchestra (1963, Presser); *Symphony No. 1* (1964); *Music for 12 Players* for winds, strings, percussion, piano, harp (1965, Merion); *3 Pieces* for orchestra (1966); *Trio* for violin, clarinet, piano (1966, Doblinger); *Monophonies Nos. 1–4*: No. 1 for flute, No. 2 for oboe, No. 3 for clarinet, No. 4 for bassoon (1966, 68, 66, 67; Doblinger); *Music for Brass Quintet* (1966, Presser); *Concerto* for chamber orchestra (1967); *Diptychon* for orchestra (1967); *Sonata* for violin (1968, Seesaw); *Tangents* for double brass quartet (1968, Presser); *Divertimento for 6 Instruments* for flute, piccolo, clarinet, violin, cello, piano (1969); *Inflections Nos. 1–2*: No. 1 for double bass, No. 2 for violin, cello, piano (1969, 1970); *Serenades* for piano (1970).

PRINCIPAL WRITINGS: "*Night Music I* by George Crumb," *Perspectives* 3/2:143–51; "Report from Prague," *Perspectives* 6/1:153–55.

Lewkovitch, Bernhard (b. Copenhagen, 28 May 1927), studied at the Royal Danish Conservatory (1946–50) and privately in Paris in 1950. He has been organist and choral director of St. Ansgar's Cathedral (1947–50, 1951–63) and director of the Schola Cantorum in Copenhagen (since 1953) and music critic for the newspaper *BT* (since 1957). He is especially noted for his sacred choral music. During the 1960s his essentially traditional musical language was expanded to include serial processes, the use of choral speech, and other techniques.

PRINCIPAL COMPOSITIONS (published by Hansen-W): *Piano Sonata No. 3* (1950); *3 Psalms* for chorus, Op. 9 (1952); *Mass* for chorus, Op. 10 (1952); *3 Motets* for chorus, Op. 11 (1952); *Mass* for chamber chorus, winds, harp, Op. 15 (1954); *Improperia per voci* for chorus (1962); *Il cantico delle creature* for 8 voices; text by Francis of

Assisi (1962–63); *A Notre Dame*, 3 songs for Our Lady for chorus (1970); *Stabat Mater* for chorus (1970); *Sub vesperam* for chorus (1970).

SEE ALSO Liturgical Music: Christian, Scandinavia.

Ley, Salvador (b. Guatemala City, 2 Jan 1907), studied piano and theory in Guatemala during 1917–22 with Herculano Alvarado and Louis Roche. During 1922–34 he lived in Berlin, where he attended the Hochschule für Musik and studied piano privately with George Bertram (1922–30) and theory and composition with Wilhelm Klatte (1923–25) and Hugo Leichtentritt (1928–29). He also studied piano with Egon Petri in Zakopane, Poland, during the summer of 1931. Since 1926 he has been active as a concert pianist. During 1934–37 and again during 1944–53 he was director of the National Conservatory of Guatemala. He taught at the Westchester Conservatory near New York during 1963–70. His creative work was influenced by the cultural climate in Berlin during his stay there and by his association with such musicians as Artur Schnabel, Bruno Walter, Wilhelm Furtwängler, Otto Klemperer, and Edwin Fischer, as well as his acquaintance with the ideas of Busoni. He has written numerous articles for Guatemalan newspapers and has promoted Latin American music through lectures and intercultural programs.

PRINCIPAL COMPOSITIONS: *5 Songs to Poems by Enrique Gonzalez Martinez* for voice, piano (1940, *Copla triste* published by Marks); *6 Songs to Poems by Rainer Maria Rilke* (1942); *Serenade* for string orchestra (1949); *Obertura jocosa* for orchestra (1950); *Danza fantástica* for piano (1950, E-V); *Der Krieg* for voice, piano; text by Matthias Claudius (1950); *Piece* for viola, piano (1956); *Chamber Music 1 and 5* for voice, piano; texts by James Joyce (1958); *6 Songs to Poems by George Campbell* (1958); *Danza exotica* for piano (1959, Peer); *Semblanza* for piano (1959); *Lera*, 2-act opera; libretto by Campbell (1960); *Concertante* for viola, string orchestra (1962); *Suite* for flute, piano (1962); *Hymn to Being* for voice, piano; text by Campbell (1962); *Yo pienso en tí* for voice, piano; text by José Batres Montúfar (1963); *4 Pieces* for piano (1966); *Tarde del trópico* for voice, piano; text by Rubén Darío (1969); *We Face Each Other* for voice, piano; text by Campbell (1969); *The Serpent* for voice, piano; text by Theodore Roethke (1970). List to 1966: *Composers of the Americas* 12:92–98.

PRINCIPAL WRITINGS: "Cultural Aspects of Music Life in Guatemala," *Proceedings of the Conference on Latin American Fine Arts* (Austin, Texas, 1951):73–83.

Lidholm, Ingvar (Natanael) (b. Jönköping, Sweden, 24 Feb 1921), attended the Royal College of Music in Stockholm (1940–46) and studied composition privately with Hilding Rosenberg there and with Matyas Seiber in London (1954). During 1947–56 he was conductor of the Örebro Orchestra and during 1956–64, head of the Chamber Music Section of the Swedish Radio. Since 1965 he has taught composition at the Royal College of Music, Stockholm.

PRINCIPAL COMPOSITIONS: *Toccata e canto* for orchestra (1944, Gehrman); *Concerto for String Orchestra* (1945, Gehrman); *Flute Sonata* (1946, Nordiska); *Laudi* for chorus (1947, Gehrman); *Piano Sonata* (1947, Gehrman); *Music for Strings* (1952, Hansen-W); *4 Choral Pieces*; texts by Åke Nilsson (1953, Nordiska); *Concertino* for flute, oboe, English horn, cello (1954); *Ritornello* for orchestra (1955, UE); *4 Pezzi* for cello, piano (1955, UE); *Canto LXXXI* for chorus; text by Ezra Pound (1956, Nordiska); *A capella-bok* for chorus (1956–59, Nordiska); *Skaldens natt* [The Poet's Night] for soprano, chorus, orchestra (1958, Suecia and UE); *Mutanza* for orchestra (1959, UE); *Riter*, ballet, for winds, brass, percussion; libretto by Erik Lindegren, choreography by Birgit Åkesson (1959, UE); *Motus colores* for orchestra with electric guitar, electric mandolin, vibraphone (1960, Suecia and UE); *Poesis* for orchestra (1963, UE); *Nausikaa ensam* [Nausicaa Alone], scene for soprano, chorus, orchestra; text by Eyvind Johnson (1963, UE); *Holländarn* [The Dutchman], TV opera; libretto after Strindberg (1967).

PRINCIPAL WRITINGS: "Poesis for Orchestra," *3 Aspects of New Music* (Stockholm 1968):55–80 (reprinted in German, "Poesis für Orchester," *Melos* 36:63–76).

BIBL.: Bo Wallner, *Vår tids musik i Norden* (Stockholm 1968), English trans. (London 1971).

SEE ALSO Liturgical Music: Christian; Scandinavia.

Liebermann, Rolf (b. Zurich, 14 Sept 1910), studied law at the Univ. of Zurich, conducting with Hermann Scherchen, and composition with Wladimir Vogel. He was an assistant to Scherchen in Vienna beginning in 1937 but had to return to Switzerland during World War II, where he worked as a music critic and composer of popular pageants and songs. In 1945 he organized the orchestra of the Swiss Broadcasting Corp. and succeeded Scherchen as its director in 1950. He was music director of the North German Radio in Hamburg (1957–59), after which he became manager of the Hamburg State Opera.

PRINCIPAL COMPOSITIONS (published by UE): *Chinese Love Songs* for high voice, piano (harp), strings (1945); *Furioso* for orchestra (1947); *Piano Sonata* (1951); *Leonore 40-45*, opera; libretto by Heinrich Strobel (1952); *Penelope*, opera; libretto by Strobel (1954); *Concerto* for jazz band, orchestra (1954); *Die Schule der Frauen*, 1-act opera; libretto by Strobel after Molière (1955, later expanded to 3 acts; UE); *Geigy Festival Concerto* for Basel drum, orchestra (1958); *Les Echanges* for office machines, live or on tape (1964).

SEE ALSO Opera.

Ligeti, György (b. Diciosânmartin, Transylvania, 28 May 1923), studied with Ferenc Farkas and Sándor Veress at the Academy of Music in Budapest, where he later taught. Since 1956 his permanent residence has been Vienna. During 1957–58 he worked at the electronic studio in Cologne. Since 1959 he has lectured at the summer courses in Darmstadt, and since 1961 he has been teaching at the Academy of Music in Stockholm.

Atmosphères (1961), with its development of *Klangflächenkomposition* [composition with blocks of sound] marked a turning-point for new music both technically and esthetically, and it established Ligeti's position as a leader of the European avant-garde. The origins of his idea, which can be seen in a less developed form in *Apparitions* (1958–59), are to be found in his critical study of the theory and practice of serial technique, in the course of which he realized that serialism was leading to the disappearance of clear-cut intervals and rhythms. This conclusion led him in his own compositions to renounce individually perceptible intervals and rhythms (in fact, all identifiable outlines) and to concentrate exclusively on the creation of the sound itself, its coloration and density, its external volume, and its internal texture. The result of his complex interweaving of a large number of separate parts (*Mikropolyphonie*) is a shimmering fabric of densely saturated and apparently static polyphony in which the shape of the music derives from subtle changes in tone color, dynamics, densities, and similar elements.

This style, with its apparent lack of movement and incident, is in a sense counterbalanced by the two mime-dramas *Aventures* and *Nouvelles Aventures*. They incorporate a meaningless language based on phonetic sounds and are a music theater of the absurd, full of emotion and rich in associations. *Artikulation*, which also belongs to this group of pieces, is made up of small contrasting sound units put together like a mosaic; here the musical shape Ligeti imposes on the sound

material (electronically generated) reflects the characteristics of language. In the *Requiem*, the composer undertook a synthesis of the two techniques: aspects of the technique of *Atmosphères* can be seen in the oppressive and static Introitus and in the gently fluctuating Kyrie, while the expressive and dramatic Dies irae is clearly linked with the mosaic style of *Aventures*.

Since the mid-1960s Ligeti's work has shown an increasing tendency towards greater definition and distinctive shapes, especially in regard to harmony. In *Lontano*, for example, the construction is based on intervals and chords that gradually emerge out of a blurred harmony and gradually disappear again. The increased interest in harmony can also be seen in Ligeti's attempts to refine the gradations and shades of pitch within the traditional octave by using microtones, as in the *String Quartet No. 2* (where there are indefinite pitch variations within the semitone) and in *Ramifications* (where the strings are divided into two groups tuned slightly more than a quarter-tone apart). Although *Mikropolyphonie* remains the guiding principle in Ligeti's music, the textures since the late 60s have become more transparent, and from time to time fragmentary melodic and rhythmic shapes can now be discerned; this last approach is particularly suited to chamber music, as can be seen in the *Second String Quartet*, *10 Pieces for Wind Quintet*, and the *Kammerkonzert*.

PRINCIPAL COMPOSITIONS: *Artikulation*, electronic music on 4-track tape (1958, Schott); *Apparitions* for orchestra (1958–59, UE); *Atmosphères* for orchestra (1961, UE); *Volumina* for organ (1961–62, Peters); *Poème symphonique* for 100 metronomes (1962, instructions published in *Sonda* 2, Madrid, 1968); *Aventures* (1962) and *Nouvelles Aventures* (1962–65) for 3 singers, 7 players (Peters; libretto for the theatrical version of each, 1966, Peters); *Requiem* for 2 vocal soloists, 2 choruses, orchestra (1963–65, Peters); *Lux aeterna* for 16-part chorus (1966, Peters); *Cello Concerto* (1966, Peters); *Lontano* for orchestra (1967, Schott); *Continuum* for harpsichord (1968, Schott); *String Quartet No. 2* (1968, Schott); *10 Pieces for Wind Quintet* (1968, Schott); *Ramifications* for 12 solo strings or string orchestra (1968–69, Schott); *Kammerkonzert* for 13 players (1969–70, Schott).

PRINCIPAL WRITINGS: *Klasszikus összangsattan* [Classical Harmony Textbook] (Budapest 1954); *A klasszikus harmoniarend* [The System of Classical Harmony] (Budapest 1956); "Pierre Boulez: Decision and Automatism in Structure Ia," *Die Reihe*, English ed., 4:36–62; "Über die Harmonik in Weberns erster Kantate," *Darmstädter Beiträge zur Neuen Musik* 3:49–64; "Metamorphoses of Musical Form," *Die Reihe*, English ed., 7:5–19;

"Über musikalische Form," *Darmstädter Beiträge zur Neuen Musik* 10:23–35.

BIBL.: Ulrich Dibelius, "Reflexion und Reaktion: Über den Komponisten G. L.," *Melos* 37:89–96; Clytus Gottwald, "Lux aeterna: Ein Beitrag zur Kompositionstechnik G. L.s," *Musica* 25:12–17; Josef Häusler, "Interview mit G. L.," *Melos* 37:496–507; Harald Kaufmann, *Spurlinien* (Vienna 1969); ——, "Ls Zweites Streichquartett," *Melos* 37:181–86; ——, "Strukturen im Strukturlosen," *Melos* 31:391–98; Ove Nordwall, *Från Mahler till Ligeti* (Stockholm 1965); ——, "Der Komponist G. L.," *Musica* 22:173–77; ——, *L.-Monographie* (Mainz 1971); Erkki Salmenhaara, *Das musikalische Material und seine Behandlung in den Werken . . . von G. L.* (Helsinki-Regensburg 1969).

Monika Lichtenfeld
(trans. from German by Jeanne Wolf)

SEE ALSO Asian Music and Western Composition, Austria and Germany, Instrumental and Vocal Resources, Melody, Microtones, Orchestration, Rhythm, Text Setting and Usage.

Lilburn, Douglas (Gordon) (b. Wanganui, New Zealand, 2 Nov 1915), studied at Canterbury Univ. College (1934–36) and the Royal College of Music in London (1937–39, composition with Ralph Vaughan Williams). He has taught at Victoria Univ. in Wellington since 1949, where he helped establish an electronic music studio in 1966.

PRINCIPAL COMPOSITIONS: *Festival Overture* (1939); *Aotearoa Overture* (1940); *Landfall in Unknown Seas* for string orchestra (1942); *String Trio* (1945, Hinrichsen); *Chaconne* for piano (1946); *Diversions for String Orchestra* (1947, Oxford); *Elegy*, song cycle for voice, piano (1952); *Sings Harry*, song cycle for voice, piano (1954, Univ. of Otago Press, N.Z.); *Symphony No. 3* (1960, Faber); *Sonatina No. 2* for piano (1962, Wai-te-ata Press, N.Z.); *The Return* on tape (1965, recorded by Kiwi Records, N.Z.); *9 Short Pieces* for piano (1966, Albert).

Linguistics, see Theory

Linke, Norbert (b. Steinau/Oder, Germany, 5 March 1933), studied at the Hamburg Hochschule für Musik (1952–57, composition with Ernst Gernot Klussmann), at the Univ. of Hamburg (1952–57, music history with Heinrich Husmann), and at the Darmstadt summer courses (1962–64; composition with Karlheinz Stockhausen, Pierre Boulez, and György Ligeti). He has taught music at the Albert Schweitzer Gymnasium in Hamburg

since 1960, and since 1963 he has been a critic for *Die Welt, Melos,* and *Der neue Musikzeitung.* His musical development has passed from atonality to (in 1961) postserialism, then to composition centered on timbres and textures, graphic notation, and collage. Since 1965 he has followed a stylistic pluralism, in which these various techniques exist side by side and are integrated within a new formal framework.

PRINCIPAL COMPOSITIONS (published by Gerig): *Polyrhythmika Nos. 1–3* for piano (1961–68); *Varim I* for pianist, 2 percussionists (1962); *Konkretionen II* for string quartet (1962); *Canticum I–II* for chorus (1962–68); *Coloratura* for 3 flutes (1963); *Strati* for orchestra (1966); *Benn-Epitaph* for alto (baritone), clarinet, violin, cello, piano (1966); *Divisioni* for orchestra (1967); *Profit tout clair* for nonet of winds, strings (1967); *Brass Quintet* (1967); *Konkretionen IV* for trumpet, horn, timpani (1967); *Lyrical Symphony* for high voice, orchestra (1968); *Varim II* for soprano, piano, other instruments and electronic apparatus ad lib. (1968, unpub.; recorded by Deutsche Gramophon); *Rital* for organ (1969).

PRINCIPAL WRITINGS: *Die Orchesterfuge in Spätromantik und Moderne* (PhD diss., Univ. of Hamburg, 1959); "Kann ein Komponist vom Komponieren leben?" *Melos* (April 1969):162. ★ Program notes: Darmstadt summer courses (1963, 1964); Musica Nova, Bremen (1964)· Tage der neuen Musik, Hanover (1965, 1966, 1967); Bilthoven (1967, 1969); Zagreb Biennale (1967); and Ars Nova, Nuremberg (1969).

BIBL.: Ulrich Dibelius, *Moderne Musik, 1945–65* (Munich 1966):256.

Linn, Robert (b. San Francisco, 11 August 1925), studied at Mills College (1947, 1949; composition, orchestration with Darius Milhaud) and at the Univ. of Southern Calif. (1947–51; composition with Halsey Stevens, Roger Sessions; orchestration with Ingolf Dahl). During 1945–58 he was a jazz pianist and arranger. Since 1958 he has taught composition at the Univ of Southern Calif.

PRINCIPAL COMPOSITIONS: *String Quartet No. 1* (1952, AM); *Overture* for orchestra (1952, AM); *3 Madrigals* for vocal quartet; texts by James Joyce (1953, AM); *The Story Tellers of the Canterbury Tales,* film score (1953); *Quartet* for saxophones (1954, Avant); *Piano Sonata No. 1* (1955); *Adagio and Allegro* for chamber orchestra (1956); *Symphony in 1 Movement* (1956–60); *Anthem of Wisdom* for chorus, orchestra; text from Proverbs (1958, L-G); *Duo* for clarinet, cello (1959); *March of the Olympians* (1960, Disney); *Concerto grosso* for trumpet, horn, trombone, wind orchestra (1961); *The Hexameron* for 3 pianos, orchestra; reconstructed from the 1837 piano music of Liszt, Thalberg, Pixis, Herz, Czerny, Chopin (1962);

Brass Quintet (1963); *Woodwind Quintet* (1963, Pillin); *Piano Sonata No. 2* (1964); *Elevations* for wind orchestra (1964); *Dithyramb* for 8 cellos (1965); *Concertino* for violin, wind octet (1965); *Symphony for Strings* (1967–68); *The Pied Piper of Hamelin* for speaker, tenor, chorus, orchestra (1968–69); *Concerto* for clarinet, strings, percussion (1970).

Liturgical Music: Christian. The problem of style and materials in music for the church remains as elusive of solution as ever. The complexity of tonal and rhythmic materials in contemporary secular music places it beyond the reach of all but a few of those to whom the music of worship is entrusted. The problem is especially critical for choral literature, since the average church choir is composed largely of untrained volunteers who spend little more than an hour or two preparing each Sunday's music. The situation with respect to instrumental music is apt to be better, at least in urban churches that can afford to hire trained organists (and have a supply of such musicians at hand); but for the small congregation far removed from an urban center, the music program is likely to be minimal at best. The result has been the tacit acceptance on the part of the majority of composers writing for the church of certain stylistic boundaries beyond which the music will not be permitted to stray. This fact accounts for the resistance to stylistic change in sacred music and for its remarkably homogeneous nature. As in the past, there are composers today who specialize in church music; some are mentioned below. There are also composers whose reputations reside at least partly in their contributions to secular music but who have written music for the church. While many of the latter suffer a retrogression in style when they turn to sacred music, there are others, such as Vaughan Williams, Stravinsky, Penderecki, Britten, and Hanson, whose religious music represents no compromise in personal convictions.

1900–50. On 22 November 1903 Pius X issued his famous encyclical *Motu proprio*. The chief purpose of this document was to abolish the theatrical and secular styles of church music that had grown up during the 19th century. It also advocated a restoration of Gregorian chant and a return to the style of Palestrina as a model for figural music. The encyclical seems to indicate that the Cecilian Movement, started in Germany in the second half of the 19th century, had had little influence in improving musical conditions

in the Catholic church. As a matter of fact, alongside the editions of Palestrina begun by Franz Xavier Haberl, some rather dismal examples of church music were published by the Cäcilienverein. Conditions in Protestantism were no different.

The renaissance of church music got underway after World War I. In Germany, partly as a result of religious and liturgical revivals in both Catholic and Evangelical circles, the chorale and Gregorian chant became the focal points of the new music. Johann Nepomuk David's chief work, for example, is based on the chorale. Another important development in Europe, which was eventually to have considerable influence in the U.S., was the so-called *Orgelbewegung*, the revival of organ music of the baroque together with its principles of timbre and design (contrasting markedly with the pseudo-orchestral instrument that developed after 1750). New editions of the music were brought out by such people as Straube, Schweitzer, and Widor. The chief exponents of this type of organ construction were Marcussen, Kleis, Walker, Von Beckerath, Frobenius, and Flentrop. In the U.S. the movement began to be felt in the late 30s, but World War II, with its restriction on building materials and its military priorities, prevented progress until well into the 40s. The pioneers were the late Walter Holtkamp of Cleveland and Herman Schlicker of Buffalo. Since then many other builders have become interested in the movement.

In the U.S. education in church music contributed greatly to raising standards of performance and thus paved the way for composers of new music. In 1926 J. Finley Williamson founded the Westminster Choir College now located in Princeton, N. J. Two years later in New York, the School of Sacred Music at Union Theological Seminary was founded by Clarence Dickinson. In the midwest, a department of church music was started by Peter C. Lutkin at the music school of Northwestern Univ. These schools have been joined by smaller departments in many denominational colleges. Another organization that has raised standards is the American Guild of Organists (founded 1896). The ranks of Associate and Fellow member are conferred after rigid standards of performance and musical knowledge have been met. The Guild also certifies Choirmasters upon successful completion of an examination. Together with better performances and literature in the mass media (radio, recordings, television), all these agencies have paved the way for the new sacred music of first-rate composers.

A number of composers deserve mention for their work in the first half of the century (which continued beyond 1950 in some cases). In Germany Sigfrid Karg-Elert (1877–1933), building upon the tradition of Max Reger, composed a significant amount of organ music beginning in 1908. One of the most promising of German church musicians, Hugo *Distler (1908–42) unfortunately had his career cut short; a striking testimony to his sensitivity is his *Geistliche Konzerts* for soprano and orchestra (1937). The Hungarian Zoltán *Kodály (1882–1967) wrote at least three important sacred choral pieces: *Psalmus Hungaricus* (1923), *Te Deum* (1936), and *Missa brevis* (1945). The French composers Marcel *Dupré (b. 1886), Maurice *Duruflé (b. 1902), Jean *Langlais (b. 1907), Olivier *Messiaen (b. 1908), and Jehan Alain (1911–1940) have written significant organ music. Francis *Poulenc (1899–1963) wrote a number of sacred choral works, including a *Mass in G* (1937), *Motets pour un temps de pénitence* (1939), and *Stabat Mater* (1950), as well as a later *Office for Holy Saturday* (1961).

In the Low Countries Paul de Maleingreau (1887–1956) and Joseph *Jongen (1873–1953) of Belgium and Sam Dresden (1881–1957) and Hendrick *Andriessen (b. 1892) of Holland are important. In Denmark, Carl *Nielsen (1865–1931), while known principally for his symphonic music, served the cause of Danish church-music reform by writing a vast number of hymns beginning in 1902. Two expatriate Russians, Sergey *Rachmaninov (1873–1943) and Igor *Stravinsky (1882–1971) contributed significant sacred choral literature, the former his *Songs of the Church* for chorus (1920), composed for the all-night vigil, and the latter the *Symphony of Psalms* for chorus and orchestra (1930) and the *Mass* for winds and chorus (1944–48). Italy in the first half of the century is represented by Gian Francesco *Malipiero (b. 1882) in a large work for chorus and orchestra, *La cena* (1927), and by Alfredo *Casella (1883–1947) in his *Mass* (1944).The English composer Ralph*Vaughan Williams (1872–1958) wrote hymns for the hymnal of the Church of England, a *Festival Te Deum* (1937) and other canticles, and a *Mass in G Minor* (1923).

In Canada the development of church music is closely linked with Healey *Willan (1880–1968), who wrote anthems and service music for six decades; his published works number in the hundreds. Others active include Graham George, Alfred Whitehead, and W. H. Anderson. In the U.S. Charles *Ives (1874–1954) contributed several notable choral pieces, including 3 *Harvest Home Chorales* (c.1898–1902) and several Psalm settings. Of the latter, *Psalm 90* is particularly appealing. Bernard *Rogers (1893–1968) wrote three large works for chorus and orchestra, *The Raising of Lazarus* (1929), *The Exodus* (1933), and *The Passion* (1942), in addition to short anthems. Howard *Hanson (b. 1896) is known for his dramatic setting of *The Cherubic Hymn* for chorus and orchestra (1950) and for his settings of Psalms and other texts.

SINCE 1950. Church musicians in Germany and Austria were extremely active in the 1950s and 60s. Stylistically the great bulk of their music combines tertian and quintal harmonic materials in varying proportions ranging from nearly total use of traditional triads, seventh, and ninth chords to nearly complete dominance of quintal and quartal materials. Tonality, while an important organizing factor in most works, was occasionally relaxed, and there are many examples of polytonal choral writing. Scale materials are either largely seven-note diatonic, though not necessarily coupled with traditional tertian harmony, or what might be termed *expanded diatonic*, utilizing eight- or nine-note scale forms. Textures are most apt to be contrapuntal, balanced by syllabic, homophonic writing. The overall style represents a reaction against earlier tertian materials as well as a logical extension of them; the avoidance of tritone harmonies in much of the music suggests superficially the influence of Hindemith. The composers involved include Johann Nepomuk *David (b. 1895), Siegfried *Reda (1916–68), Distler, Ernst *Pepping (b. 1901), Johannes *Driessler (b. 1921), and Helmut *Barbe (b. 1927). More complex music is being written by such composers as Anton *Heiller (b. 1923), who is widely known in the U.S. as well as Europe; he uses extreme chromaticism, polychordal material, dissonant tertian and quintal harmony, and contrapuntal textures. Fritz *Büchtger (b. 1903) employs a 12-tone technique in a faintly tonal manner that relies on considerable unison choral writing and on help from the accompaniment to achieve a performable style.

Church music in England ranges from basically tertian materials in Benjamin *Britten (b. 1913) to pungent dissonances, tritone harmonies, and bitonal choral writing in Peter *Maxwell Davies (b. 1934). Richard Rodney *Bennett (b. 1936) uses tertian and quintal materials in sudden shifts of scale and cross relations. Modal and symmetrical scales appear in music by Kenneth *Leighton (b. 1929), along with rather dense tertian and quintal harmonies (many with tritones), remote chord connections, striking modulations, and polytonality. In the Low Countries Flor *Peeters (b. 1903) of Belgium is widely known for his organ and choral works based on tertian materials. Albert de Klerk (b. 1917) and Marius Monnikendam (b. 1896) of the Netherlands also stand out. The avant-gardist Henri *Pousseur (b. 1929) of Belgium has written settings of verses from the penitential Psalms; these are based on a 12-tone ordering of pitches and feature angular lines with leaps of the major seventh. Ingvar *Lidholm (b. 1921) of Sweden combines quartal and triadic materials, harmonic tension, and dissonance stemming from the linear movement of parts and polytonal lines. In Denmark Bernhard *Lewkovitch (b. 1927) blends mild dissonance with a predominantly tertian harmonic scheme; individual lines are carefully conducted, and frequent cross relations result from the flexible use of scale materials involving eight or nine tones in an expanded diatonic system.

Composers active in Canada since mid-century include Violet *Archer (b. 1913, best known for her symphonic and chamber music), Keith Bissell (b. 1912) and George Fox (b. 1911). Sacred music in the U.S. has attracted large numbers of composers, but the general artistic level is low. The work of all but a few seems aimed at an undiscriminating mass market. Some of the most effective examples are by composers whose reputations are based on their secular instrumental music. Tertian-quintal materials form the basis for the bulk of the best works. Utilizing these, together with modal and expanded diatonic scales, occasional chromaticism, and chord movement in seconds and thirds, often involving cross relations, are Daniel *Pinkham (b. 1923), Ned *Rorem (b. 1923), Ulysses *Kay (b. 1917), Samuel *Adler (b. 1928), and Ron *Nelson (b. 1929). More venturesome styles are exhibited by George *Rochberg (b. 1918) and Jean *Berger (b. 1909), both of whom employ somewhat more dissonance, including secundal harmony and polytonality. Richard Wienhorst (b. 1920), who writes sacred choral music nearly exclusively, frequently uses a style anchored in quartal and quintal foundations relieved by triads; the music is strongly diatonic, and vocal color plays an important role.

During the 1960s there was mounting pressure for the use of jazz, rock, and folk music in both Protestant and Catholic churches. Publishing houses and recording companies added popular-style church music to their catalogs. To some extent the translation of the Mass into the vernacular stimulated this movement within the Catholic church; however one of the earliest appearances of a jazz Mass was in an Anglican church in England. By the end of the decade the use of jazz and folk elements had spread throughout the Western church, including South America, although such use was apt to be limited to occasional services or to one out of several regular Sunday Masses or services. The appeal was mostly to young people. The jazz influence in Germany may be seen in Heinz Werner Zimmermann (b. 1930), whose diatonic style incorporates such characteristics as added-note chords, the variable seventh scale degree, parallel harmonies, and syncopation. Fr. Geoffrey Beaumont (b. 1904), a British priest of the Anglican church, is among the earliest composers of service music in a popular idiom; his 20th-Century Folk Mass was written in 1957. An American counterpart is the Rev. Ian Mitchell, an Episcopalian priest whose American Folk Song Mass is well known. Countless other settings of the liturgy, hymns, and anthems have been turned out in jazz, folk, and rock styles, including those by such notable figures as Vince Guaraldi, Dave Brubeck, and Duke Ellington. Alongside this acceptance of popular styles (albeit grudgingly) has come a tolerance for such instruments as the guitar, saxophone, drums, string bass, and other instruments that are typically associated with pop music. By the end of the decade electronic media had also arrived on the church scene. Leslie *Bassett (b. 1923), Richard Felciano (b. 1930), and Gregory Woolf (b. 1935) had turned out service music for voice and tape, and World Library Publications, Hope Publishing Co., and World Library of Sacred Music, among others, were looking for works in the new medium. All these developments prompted a response from the Vatican Congregation of Rites (1964) in the form of a 69-article instruction dealing with propriety in sacred music for Roman Catholic churches. Although the document dealt principally with congregational singing, it attempted also to come to grips with the question of musical style. In this it was less than successful, producing mostly vague generalities. In the matter of instruments, however, the instruction expressly prohibited the use of any that by common consent were suitable only to secular purposes. An interesting Catholic Mass that was produced in 1968 by the Philippine composer José *Maceda (b. 1917) may hold promise for future developments. Entitled Pagsamba or Music for a Religious Ritual, it is scored for over 200 musicians, some singing and others playing on native percussion instruments, including gongs. The musicians are scattered among the audience in a large circular hall, and the sound vocabulary includes (to use the composer's description) drones, "hanging melodies," opaque and transparent sound textures, screens, and diffusions. Observers at the premiere in Quezon City were struck by the feelings of wonder and awe evoked by the music, feelings usually absent when traditional concepts of musical syntax are combined with instruments associated with popular or folk musics.

BIBL.: ★ Books: Friedrich Blume, *History of Protestant Church Music*, English ed. (New York 1972); Leonard Ellinwood, *The History of American Church Music* (New York 1953); Winfred Douglas, *Church Music in History and Practice*, revised by L. Ellinwood (New York 1962), Erik Routley, *20th Century Church Music* (London 1964); Hans Klotz, *The Organ Handbook*, trans. by G. Krapf (St. Louis 1969); E. A. Wienandt, *The Anthem in England and America* (New York 1970); ——, *Choral Music of the Church* (New York 1965). ★ Periodicals: *Church Music* (St. Louis, 1964–); *Music* (American Guild of Organists, N. Y., 1967–); *Musik und Kirche* (Cassel, 1929–44, 1947–).

Wayne Barlow and M. Alfred Bischel

Liturgical Music: Jewish. The traditional elements of Jewish music include: 1) cantillation, the musical rendition of Biblical texts by a cantillator (*Baal korëh*); 2) prayer chants and modal improvisations (*Nuschaoth*), which may have originated with the poetic Hebrew liturgy of the middle ages and now constitute the main body of cantorial chant, distinct from cantillation of the Bible; 3) traditional sacred melodies (the *Missinai* tunes), which originated in medieval central Europe and consist of specific melodies used with liturgical texts on specific holidays; they are one of the few examples of congregational chant in Jewish music; 4) the music of the Hasidim, a religious sect that originated in eastern Poland in the early 18th century and sought to revive mysticism in Judaism, which they felt had become too exclusively verbal and logical; 5) Jewish folksong from the Orient, Spain, central Europe, Russia, and Poland. Jewish tradition distinguishes the holy (*kodesh*) from the everyday (*chol*). The use of secular music has always been considered corrupting, and normative Judaism has often reacted against its use. The only exception is the Friday Evening prayer, *L'cho dodi*, which is not scriptural and was written in the poetic form of a medieval love song.

Contemporary Jewish liturgical music stems from two 19th-century movements: the Reform movement in central Europe and the Haskala, the enlightenment movement in Russia. The Reform movement in Germany derived its impetus from a desire to relate Judaism meaningfully to the spiritual trends of the time and to assimilate the culture of the surrounding non-Jewish population. In the wake of 19th-century liberalism, Jews in central Europe had come into contact with all branches of learning, and Jewish composers had entered the world of Western music (under the influence of the romantic music then prevailing). German Jews tended to assimilate the musical expression of the Protestant church. They built large temples (which replaced room-sized synagogues), many with elaborate organs. They augmented the traditional cantor with choirs, and they hired professionals to create and perform new music. They discarded the heterophonic chanting of prayers characteristic of the Orthodox synagogue. Although some traditional Jewish musical elements were corrupted and even lost by these changes, a new solemnity and professionalism was gained. The composers Louis Lewandowski (1821–94) in Berlin and Solomon Sulzer (1804–90) in Vienna were notable products of the Reform movement.

BLOCH, SCHOENBERG, AND MILHAUD. Contemporary developments begin with the work of Ernest *Bloch, Arnold *Schoenberg, and Darius *Milhaud, for although they have not themselves written a great deal of liturgical music, their influence has been enormous. In their music they reestablished the role of the cantor on a new base of dignity and gave the choir and organ (and orchestra) an independent life and meaning of their own. They were, however, too individualistic to use traditional materials, and much of their melodic material is at variance with the traditional Jewish melos of eastern and central Europe. Bloch's main liturgical work, *Avodat ha-kodesh*, has a gesticular vehemence that evokes prophetic speech. Its mixolydian formulas are derived from medieval Christian church modes, and the polyphony harkens back to Palestrina and Lassus. Its inherent excellence, however, has brought it almost universal respect and acceptance among Jewish congregations.

Milhaud comes from an old Jewish Provençal family, and he has had a closer personal relationship with the liturgy than did Bloch. Even so, he uses a musical idiom typical only of Provence Jews, one which eastern and central Europeans find un-Jewish because of its transparent luminosity and Provençal folksiness. Milhaud's Sephardic (southern French-Spanish and Oriental) tradition was shared by Algazi and Mario Castelnuovo-Tedesco; present-day Israeli composers are inclined to follow him rather than other Europeans or Americans.

Schoenberg began with a deep sense of alienation from Judaism, and the bulk of his output has little to do with any of the basic elements of Jewish music. His return to Judaism in the 1930s impressed many young Jewish composers who might otherwise have abandoned the whole territory of religious music. Schoenberg's last works of Jewish import, such as the *Kol Nidre*, the *Warsaw Ghetto*, and *Psalm 130*, seem to reflect the experience of an alienated mind, even in spite of his reconversion.

SINCE 1945. After World War II the evolution of Jewish music became centered in the U.S. and Israel. The few Jewish congregations that remain in Germany consist of survivors of the Nazi concentration camps, most of whom are old and live defensively in an alien surrounding, preferring the old synagogue music they knew before the war. There are no new or young Jewish composers there. French Jewry has always been conservative in its preservation of traditional musical practices. The eastern Jewish emigration to France after the war is generally secular in its orientation. Of two notable French Jews, one, Darius Milhaud, has spent much of his time in the U.S., and the other, Leon Algazi, who was director of music of the Great Synagogue in Paris, was rarely heard from in his last years. In the Communist countries of eastern Europe, freedom of religion is severely limited, and liturgical expression has calcified. The Stalinist purges in Russia led to the discontinuance of Jewish music publication and the complete disappearance of many Jewish composers. These purges put an end to a brief renewal in Russian Jewish liturgical music, exemplified at its best by the *Unesane tokef* of Michael Milner (1883–c.1940) and the *Kaddish Symphony* of Alexander Krein (1883–1951).

Emigrants to the U.S. from eastern Europe and Russia brought a treasure house of secular folklore (the same material that was transforming European concert music in the first half of the century). The religious element slowly and steadily pushed the secular into the background, however, and it is within a liturgical Jewish context that the earlier emigrants are important. Lazare *Saminsky (b. Russia, 1882; d. U.S., 1959), music director

at Temple Emanu-el in New York from the mid-20s, had a keen awareness of the spatial dimensions of Temple Emanu-el. The traditional melismatic line of cantorial chant lost in his work some of its ornamentation; indeed, cantorial coloratura was completely eliminated. A harmonic structure evolved that corresponds well to the modal character of traditional melodic lines. Lazar *Weiner (b. Russia, 1897) has drawn at times from the secular traditions of eastern Europe. His personal affinity to the Yiddish language, which is capable of the utmost sensitivity and refinement, has given his work a particular warm, intimate quality not found in the somewhat cool and official "Temple-style" of Saminsky. The music of Isadore *Freed (b. Russia, 1900; d. U.S., 1960) has an endearing gentleness and devotional flavor. It uses little authentic Jewish material, for Freed is not at home with the free, improvising cantorial style of Russia; his tightly knit four-part harmonic progressions often evoke a modal Russian-Orthodox sound.

The emigrants from central Europe include Heinrich *Schalit (b. Austria, 1886), Herbert Fromm (b. Germany, 1905), and myself (b. Germany, 1910). Schalit fuses traditional south German Jewish elements into a modal mold; treated this way, the Jewish melos shows a surprising kinship to Gregorian chant. His music has a dignity and an objective quality quite different from the mysticism and emotional tension of eastern Jewry. Fromm's studies with Paul Hindemith trained him in a linear thinking which led to a subtle dissolution of symmetric rhythmic patterns and to a harmony that results from linear and modal thinking. This style is well suited to the character of Hebraic liturgical texts. There is an element of austerity in his music, however, that strikes many eastern Jews at first as arid. My own background is somewhat more eclectic. Polish ancestry places me close to Saminsky and Weiner, but my musical thinking was greatly influenced by Nadia Boulanger, with whom I studied in Paris, and by the Jeune France group, then dominated by Olivier Messiaen. The large number of purely instrumental works for organ in my liturgical output is a result of my career as a concert organist, a vocation still rare among Jewish composers.

The American-born (and/or American-educated) Jewish composer shares with most composers of his generation a sense of alienation toward religion in general and its forms of organization in particular. Consequently none devotes himself primarily to liturgical music. The liturgists of the older and middle generations have experienced Jewish existence in a different and more intense manner. They had to leave the countries of their origin and in many cases considered Jewish experience in their lives central and all-prevailing. Indeed this generation could not afford to be alienated from its own roots, for they presented the only valid cultural heritage available to them. The return to Judaism of Arnold Schoenberg demonstrates this in dramatic fashion. Hazzan (Cantor) David Putterman of the Park Avenue Synagogue in New York inaugurated a program of commissions in 1943 to interest more Jewish composers in the liturgy. In most cases he has commissioned mature composers who already have a stylistic orientation of their own and who in any case would not have been inclined to merely arrange traditional materials. A highly eclectic assortment of works has resulted, some of which are among those discussed below.

Samuel *Adler (b. Germany, 1928) is the son of a distinguished cantor. He was brought to the U.S. as a youngster and is a bridge between the older liturgists and the American-born generation. While music director at Temple Emanu-el in Dallas (1953–66), he wrote many liturgical works in a diatonic-linear style in which freedom of voice-leading produces dissonance. Leonard *Bernstein (b. 1918) has composed three large works of Jewish import. They were not meant to be liturgical, but two of them use traditional liturgical elements: cantillation of the Book of Lamentation in the *Jeremiah Symphony* and the idea of the Kaddish-Doxology, central to all Jewish liturgy, in the *Kaddish Symphony*. Only in the *Chichester Psalms*, written for performance in an English cathedral, did the composer use a more general idiom. Frederick *Jacobi (1891–1952), though American-born, belongs essentially to a European post-romantic tradition. His two *Friday Evening Services* engender a devotional atmosphere through free-flowing melodies and a feeling of gentility. Robert *Starer (b. Austria, 1924) is one of the major talents among present-day Jewish composers. During 1938–47 he lived in what is now the state of Israel, becoming closely involved with the country and with the Hebrew language. His *Friday Evening Service* is one of the few liturgical works in which melody is memorable without being vulgar, rhythm is virile without being motoric, and in which there is exuberance without hysteria. Yehudi *Wyner (b. Canada, 1929) is the son of Lazar Weiner and a student of Hindemith. His stylistic profile stands somewhat apart from his Judaic background, and his *Sacred*

Service is difficult for many congregations to grasp; its seriousness reveals a meditative and sophisticated mind, however. To date at least four services based on jazz and rock idioms have been widely performed in American synagogues: Charles Davidson's *And David Danced before The Lord*, Issachar Miron's *Rock and Rest*, Gershon Kingsley's *Rock Service*, and Raymond Smolover's *Rock Service*. Their appeal, of course, is to the young, whose alienation from Jewish institutions is of concern to the rabbinate. It remains to be seen, however, whether young people will accept an institution just because it attempts to speak to them musically in a familiar secular language.

BIBL.: A. Z. Idelsohn, *Jewish Music* (New York 1948); Aron M. Rothmüller, *The Music of the Jews* (Cranbury, N. J., 1967); Albert Weizzer, *The Modern Renaissance of Jewish Music* (New York 1954).

Herman Berlinski

SEE ALSO Israel.

Live Electronic Music, see Electronic Music: History and Development. See also Mixed Media.

Lloyd, Norman (b. Pottsville, Pa., 8 Nov 1909), studied theory and composition with Vincent Jones and Bertha Bailey at New York Univ. (1929–32), piano with Abbey Whiteside (1930–33), and composition with Aaron Copland (1936–37). He has taught at the Ernest Williams Band School (Brooklyn, 1934–35), New York Univ. School of Education (1936–45), Sarah Lawrence College (1936–48), and the Juilliard School (1946–63). He was dean of the Oberlin College Conservatory (1963–65), after which he became director of the arts program of the Rockefeller Foundation. During the 1930s and 40s he was pianist and composer for the dancers Martha Graham, Doris Humphrey, and Martha Hill. He describes his music as "modestly tonal."

PRINCIPAL COMPOSITIONS: *Valley of the Tennessee*, film score for chamber orchestra (1943, Office of War Information); *Lament for Ignacio Sanchez Mejias*, dance work for speaker-dancers, orchestra; choreography by Doris Humphrey (1946); *La Malinche*, dance work for soprano, trumpet, piano, percussion; choreography by José Limón (1949); *Restless Land*, choral ballet for chorus, piano, dance group (1950); *3 Pieces* for violin and piano (1950, AMP); *Moment in Love*, film score for string quartet (1956); *Piano Sonata* (1958, Mercury); *A Walt Whitman Overture* for band

(1960, Mercury); *Episodes* for piano (1960, Vogel); *The Ancient Egyptian*, film score (1962).

PRINCIPAL WRITINGS: *Golden Encyclopedia of Music* (New York 1968).

SEE ALSO Dance.

Lockwood, Normand (b. New York, 19 March 1906), studied elementary theory, form, and analysis at the Univ. of Mich. (1921–24) and composition with Ottorino Respighi (1926–27) and Nadia Boulanger (1927–29). He has taught at Oberlin College (1932–42), Columbia Univ. (1945–53), Union Theological Seminary (1945–54), Westminster Choir College (1948–50), Trinity Univ. in San Antonio (1953–55), and the Univ. of Denver (since 1961), where he is also composer-in-residence.

PRINCIPAL COMPOSITIONS: *Out of the Cradle Endlessly Rocking* for chorus; text by Walt Whitman (1939, Schirmer-G); *Carol Fantasy* for chorus, orchestra or band (c.1952, AMP); *Concerto* for organ, brasses (premiere 1952, AMP); *Prairie* for chorus, orchestra; text by Carl Sandburg (premiere 1953); *Tenting on the Old Camp Ground* for chorus (c.1953); *The Closing Doxology* for chorus, band (c.1953, Broude-B); *Elegy for a Hero* for chorus; text from Walt Whitman's "Memories of President Lincoln" (c.1954, Shawnee); *Light Out of Darkness* for baritone, chorus, orchestra (premiere 1957); *Clarinet Quintet* (premiere 1960); *Early Dawn*, opera; libretto by R. Russell Porter (premiere 1961); *Requiem for a Rich Young Man*, 1-act opera for 4 vocal soloists, 9 instruments; libretto by Donald Sutherland (premiere 1965); *The Dialogue of Abraham and Isaac* for tenor, piano; text from Sutherland's play, My Sister, My Spouse (premiere 1965); *Symphonic Sequences* (premiere 1966); *Oboe Concerto* (premiere 1968); *Choreographic Cantata* for chorus, organ, percussion, dance (premiere 1968, Augsburg); *Shine, Perishing Republic* for chorus, brass, violas, organ, percussion; text by Robinson Jeffers (premiere 1968).

Logothetis, Anestis (b. Burgas, Bulgaria, 27 Oct 1921), studied at the State Academy of Music in Vienna (1945–51; theory with Erwin Ratz and Alfred Uhl, conducting with Hans Swarovsky). In 1957 he studied for one month at the Studio for Electronic Music in Cologne with Gottfried M. König. He has continued work in this medium in Vienna, where he is a free-lance composer and teacher. His earlier compositions were influenced by Schoenberg and the Viennese School. Since 1959 he has been working with graphic and other notation.

PRINCIPAL COMPOSITIONS: *Agglomeration* for violin, string orchestra (1960, UE); *5 Portraits of Love*, ballet (1960, EM); *Katalysator* for horns

(1960, EM); *Kulmination I+II+III* for chamber orchestra (1961, EM); *Meditation* for any instruments or voices (1961, EM); *Mäandros* for orchestra (1963, UE); *Odyssee*, ballet (1963, UE); *Dynapolis* for orchestra (1963, UE); *Kentra* for chamber orchestra (1964); *Osculationen* for chamber orchestra (1964); *Ichnologia* for chamber orchestra (1964); *Labyrinthos* for any soloists, any chamber orchestra (1965, UE); *Orbitals* for chamber orchestra (1965); *Enòsis* for chamber orchestra (1965); *Diffusion* for chamber orchestra (1965); *reversible Bijunktion* for chamber orchestra (1965); *Desmotropie* for clarinet, piano (1965); *Enclaven* for any soloists, any orchestra (1966); *Desmotropie* for chamber orchestra (1967); *Polychronon* for chamber orchestra (1967); *Konvektionsströme* for orchestra (1968); *Styx* for orchestra of plucked-string instruments (1969).

PRINCIPAL WRITINGS: *Notation mit graphischen Elementen* (Salzburg 1967); "Gezeichnete Klänge," *Neues Forum* (Vienna) 183/1:177–79; "Kurze musikalische Spurenkunde," *Wort und Wahrheit* (Vienna) 2:131–36 and *Melos* 37:39–43.

BIBL.: Peter Gradenwitz, *Wege zur Musik der Gegenwart* (Stuttgart 1963):213–14; Erhard Karkoschka, *Das Schriftbild der Neuen Musik* (Celle 1966):80–81, 128–31; Karlheinz Roschitz, "A. L. und die 'Musikalische Graphik'," *Protokolle 69* (Vienna 1969):167–75.

SEE ALSO Greece.

Lombardo, Robert (b. Hartford, Conn., 5 March 1932), studied composition with Arnold Franchetti at the Hartt College of Music (1950–55), with Boris Blacher at the Berlin Hochschule für Musik (1958–59), and with Phillip Bezanson at the Univ. of Iowa (1959–61). He has taught theory at the Univ. of Iowa (1959–61) and the Hartt College (1963–64) and since then has been composer-in-residence and professor of composition at Roosevelt College in Chicago.

PRINCIPAL COMPOSITIONS: *I due orfani*, dramatic dialogue for 2 vocal soloists, chamber ensemble (1959); *Piano Variations* (1964); *Threnody* for string orchestra (1964); *5 Piccoli pezzi* for violin, piano (1965); *Nocturne* for double bass (1966); *Dialogues of Lovers* for baritone, 9 instruments (1966); *In memoriam* for bassoon, string trio (1967); *The Sorrows of a Supersoul*, 1-act comic opera (1967); *Aphorisms* for orchestra (1968); *Climbing for Tree Frogs*, love songs for soprano, harpsichord (1969); *Largo* for string quartet (1969); *Fantasy Variations* for cello (1969); *Fourplay* for violin, bassoon, percussion, harpsichord (1969).

London, Edwin (b. Philadelphia, 16 March 1929), attended Oberlin College (1948–52, French horn with Martin Morris), the Univ.

of Iowa (1952–54, 1958–60; composition with Philip Greeley Clapp, Phillip Bezanson), and the Manhattan School of Music (1956, French horn with Gunther Schuller). In 1956 he studied in New York with Luigi Dallapiccola. He also studied at the Aspen Music School (1960, composition with Darius Milhaud, conducting with Izler Solomon). During the summers of 1956–57 he was composer-conductor for the Toledo Shakespeare and Lyric Theater Festivals. He toured as a horn player in 1957 and in 1958 made musical arrangements for the Armando Trovajoli Orchestra in Rome. He taught at Smith College (1960–68) and conducted the Smith-Amherst Symphony Orchestra (1962–68), the Amherst Community Opera (1963–68), and the Hampshire Choral Society. In 1969 he became professor of composition at the Univ. of Ill. and guest conductor of the Hartt Chamber Players.

PRINCIPAL COMPOSITIONS: *Woodwind Quintet* (1958, MJQ); *Santa Claus*, mime opera for solo singers, dancers, chorus, small orchestra; text by e. e. cummings (1960); *3 Settings of Psalm 23* for women's, men's, and mixed choruses (1961, MJQ); *3 Symphonic Movements* for concert band (1962); *Sonatina* for viola, piano (1962, New Valley); *Brass Quintet* (1965); *Portraits of 3 Ladies* for narrator, mezzo-soprano, optional dancer, 14 instrumentalists, projections, electronic amplification (1967, Broude-A); *4 Proverbs* for soprano, women's chorus, 2 trumpets, bassoon (1968, Broude-A).

PRINCIPAL WRITINGS: Notes for the *Sonatina* recording (Advance Records, FGR-7).

SEE ALSO Instrumental and Vocal Resources, Mixed Media.

Lopatnikoff, Nikolai (b. Reval, Russia, 16 March 1903), studied music at the St. Petersburg Conservatory (until 1918, theory with Alexander Zhitomirsky) and the Helsinki Conservatory (1918–20, theory with Eric Furuhjelm) and civil engineering at the Technische Hochschule in Karlsruhe (1921–28). He also studied composition privately with Ernst Toch in Germany (1921). He lived in London during 1933–39, after which he moved to the U.S. He taught at the Carnegie-Mellon Institute in Pittsburgh during 1945–69. Contact with Hindemith and the Donaueschingen circle in south Germany during the 1920s had a considerable impact on his development.

PRINCIPAL COMPOSITIONS: *Sonata* for violin, piano, snare drum, Op. 9 (1926, ERM); *2 Pieces* for mechanical piano (1927, player rolls produced by Welte Mignon); *Symphony No. 1*, Op. 12 (1929, Schott); *Danton*, opera; libretto after Büchner

(1930–33); *Piano Concerto No. 2*, Op. 15 (1931, Schott); *Violin Concerto*, Op. 26 (1941, AMP); *Piano Sonata*, Op. 29 (1943, AMP); *Violin Sonata No. 2*, Op. 32 (1948, MCA); *Symphony No. 3*, Op. 35 (1954, MCA); *Variazioni concertanti* for orchestra, Op. 38 (1956, MCA); *Music for Orchestra*, Op. 39 (c.1957, MCA). List to 1965: *Composers of the Americas* 12:101–07.

BIBL.: Boris Pines, "N. L.," *Der Wihergarten* (Mainz 1930).

Lopes-Graça, Fernando (b. Tomar, Portugal, 17 Dec 1906), studied history and philosophy at the Universities of Lisbon (1928–31) and Coimbra (1932–34) and music at the National Conservatory in Lisbon (1923–31; composition with Tomás Borba; piano with Adriano Maréa, José Vianna da Motta; musicology with Luís de Freitas-Branco) and at the Sorbonne (1937–39, musicology). He also studied composition and orchestration privately in Paris with Charles Koechlin in 1938. He has performed professionally as a pianist in Europe and South America since 1920, concentrating on contemporary repertory. He taught piano and harmony at the Coimbra Music Institute during 1932–36 and at the Academy of the Friends of Music in Lisbon, 1941–54, where he was also artistic director. In 1942 he founded the Sonata concert series in Lisbon to present contemporary chamber music and was its director until 1961. He has also founded and directed several choral groups. Since 1960 he has been a director of the Portuguese folk-music recording project Antologia da Música Regional Portuguesa. During 1927–39 he was "hesitating between a nationalism more or less folkloristic and a neutral style, rather expressionistic." During 1940–59 he responded to the influences of Debussy, Ravel, Stravinsky, and Bartók, and afterwards became interested in a synthesis of these approaches. Since 1940 he has written 17 books on music, including general surveys, biographies of composers, discussions of Portuguese music, and a dictionary. He has also translated five books from English and French.

PRINCIPAL COMPOSITIONS: *Songs* for voice, piano; poems by A. Casais-Monteiro, Fernando Pessoa, José Régio, Carlos Queiroz, and Afonso Duarte (1931–36); *Piano Sonatas Nos. 1–4* (1931, 1939, 1952, 1961); *Pequeno cancioneiro do menino Jesus* [Little Songbook of the Child Jesus] for women's chorus, 2 flutes, string quartet, celesta, harp (1936); *La Fièvre du temps*, revue-ballet for 2 pianos (1938; orchestral suite, *A febre do tempo*, 1940); *Portuguese Folksongs*, 4 sets of 24 songs for voice, piano (1939–42, 1942–46, 1947–49,

1951–59); *Piano Concertos Nos. 1–2* (1940, 1952); *3 Portuguese Dances* for orchestra (1941, Schott); *História trágico-maritima* for baritone, women's chorus, orchestra; texts by Miguel Torga (1942); *Portuguese Folksongs* for chorus (11 sets, (1943–69); *Sinfonia per orchestra* (1944, S-Z); *Christmas Cantatas Nos. 1–2* for chorus; based on Portuguese carols (1945–50, 1960–61); *5 Estelas funerárias* [5 Funeral Steles] for orchestra (1948); *Peasant Suite No. 1* for orchestra (1950); *24 Preludes* for piano (1950–58); *4 Songs of Federico García-Lorca* for baritone, 2 clarinets, violin, viola, cello, harp, percussion (1953–54); *Album for the Young Pianist* (1953–54, Novello); *Concertino* for piano, strings, brass, percussion (1954); *Song of Love and Death* for piano, string quartet (1961, orchestrated 1962); *Poema de dezembro* for orchestra (1961); *Para uma criança que vai nascer* [For a Child about to Be Born] for string orchestra (1961, Jobert); *D. Duardos e Flérida*, cantata-melodrama for narrator, mezzo-soprano, alto, tenor, chorus, orchestra (1964–69); *Concerto da camera* for cello (1965, Jobert).

Lourié, Arthur (Vincent) (b. St. Petersburg, 14 May 1892; d. Princeton, N. J., 13 Oct 1966), studied piano at the St. Petersburg Conservatory. As a composer he was self-taught. He at first supported the Russian Revolution and was appointed by Lenin in 1918 to be director of the music section of the People's Commissariat of Education. Becoming disillusioned, he left Russia in 1921 and lived in Paris during 1923–40. In 1940 he moved to the U.S. Davenson (see bibl.) observes that Lourié's vocal and dramatic music is in the tradition of Mussorgsky and that the composer believed firmly in the primacy of melody. In his youth he experimented with some devices that became popular many decades later; his *Formes en l'air* (1915), for example, "scatter fragments of staves across the page," somewhat in the manner of a cubist design.

PRINCIPAL COMPOSITIONS: *Songs* for voice, piano; texts by Pushkin, Blok, and Akhmatova (1915–17); *Piano Gosse*, pieces for children (1917, ERM); *La Naissance de la beauté*, cantata for soprano, chorus of 6 sopranos, piano; text by Superville (1922, Fischer); *Dithyrambes* for flute (1923); *Grand gigue* for piano (1927, Rouart-Lerolle); *Sonate liturgique* for alto, wind ensemble (1928); *Concerto spirituale* for vocal soloists, chorus, orchestra, piano, organ (1929); *Symphonie dialectique*, symphony No. 1 (1930); *Le Festin pendant la peste*, opera; libretto by the composer after Pushkin (1933); *Procession* for 2 women's voices, piano; poem by Raïssa Maritain (1934); *La Flûte à travers le violon* for flute, violin (1935); *Kormtchaïa*, symphony No. 2 (1936); *El Cristo crucificado ante al mar* for voice, piano; sonnet by Bergamin (1938, Schirmer-G); *De ordinatione*

angelorum for chorus, 5 brasses; text by Thomas Aquinas (1942); *Concerto da camera* for chamber orchestra (1947, Rongwen); *The Mime* for clarinet (1956); *Le Maure de Pierre le Grand*, opera; libretto by the composer after Pushkin (1961). ★ Dates not available: *Berceuse* for piano (ERM); *Tu es Petrus*, motet for chorus.

PRINCIPAL WRITINGS: *Koussevitzky and His Epoch* (New York 1931); *Profanation et sanctification du temps* (Paris 1966).

BIBL.: C. Camajani, "The Music of A. L.," *Ramparts* (Menlo Park, Calif., Jan 1965); Henri Davenson, "A. L. (1892–1966)," *Perspectives* 5/2:166–69.

Lucier, Alvin (b. Nashua, N. H., 14 May 1931), studied at Yale Univ. (1950–56; composition with David Kraehenbuhl, Quincy Porter; theory with Howard Boatwright), at Brandeis Univ. (1958–60; composition with Harold Shapero, Lukas Foss, Boris Porena; analysis with Arthur Berger), and at the Darmstadt summer courses (1961, piano with David Tudor). During 1962–69 he was choral director and director of the Electronic Music Studio at Brandeis. Since 1970 he has taught at Wesleyan Univ. He has worked extensively with electronic apparatus, using a variety of sound sources and modification. In *Music for a Solo Performer*, three electrodes are attached to the scalp of a human performer. They pick up 10-cycle alpha brain waves, a low voltage signal that appears during nonvisual human mental activity. The signal is modified with amplifiers and filters and directed by a technical assistant to loudspeakers that activate sympathetic resonances in nearby percussion instruments. *Shelter* uses high-gain vibration pickups to sense human or other activity in the performing environment. Other processes are indicated in Lucier's list of compositions.

PRINCIPAL COMPOSITIONS: *Action Music for Piano* (1962, BMIC); *Song for Soprano* (1963, BMIC); *Composition for Pianist and Mother* for pianist, actress (1963, BMIC); *Elegy for Albert Anastasia* on tape (1965, BMIC); *Music for Solo Performer*, amplified alpha brain waves used to activate various standard and nonstandard percussion instruments (1965, CPE); *Shelter*, amplification of environmental sounds sensed by means of high-gain vibration pickups (1967); *Whistlers*, processing with electronic apparatus of the electromagnetic disturbances in the ionosphere known as "whistlers" (1967); *North American Time Capsule* for voices, vocoder (1967, BMIC); *Vespers*, performers doing various tasks in a dark space while using echo-location devices (1968); *Chambers*, an environmental sound composition for performers moving resonant environments (sea shells, tunnels, cupped hands, etc.) through other environments (streets, houses, etc.) (1968); *The Only*

Talking Machine of Its Kind in the World for speaker, tape (1969, CPE); *Hymn*, the building and amplification of a weblike structure; the length, weight, and density of strands determine pitch and timbre (1970); *Hartford Memory Space* for orchestra (1970, CPE); *I Am Sitting in a Room* for slides, tape (1970, CPE); *Signatures* for orchestra (1970).

PRINCIPAL WRITINGS: "A New Soundscape," *The Brandeis Justice* (1964); *"Music for Solo Performer,"* *Collage* (Palmero 1967) and *ICA Bulletin* (London 1967); "The Making of *North American Time Capsule,"* *Electronic Music Review* 5; "Music by Computers" (book review), *Music Educators' Journal* (Dec 1969); with J. Douglas Simon, *"Chambers,"* *Source* 5; *Chambers (Interviews on Music and Environment)*, a collection of prose scores and interviews (unpub.).

BIBL.: Gordon Mumma, "A. L.'s *Music for Solo Performer*," *Source* 3; Warren G. Ross, "Eeek Lunk Eeoww Clonk Thump Rrrooomm Oooop Noozle Lingg Clack Moooo Ugh Shoosh Izzle Clump," *The Scanner* (the Sylvania Co., May 1967); Ken Werner, "What's Happening in Electronic Music," *New England Teen Scene* (Oct 1967).

SEE ALSO Instrumental and Vocal Resources, Mixed Media, Performance, Prose Music.

Luening, Otto (b. Milwaukee, 15 June 1900), studied at the Academy of Music in Munich (1915–17), the Municipal Conservatory in Zurich (1917–20), and the Univ. of Zurich (1919–20). He also studied privately with Ferruccio Busoni and Philipp Jarnach. During his stay in Europe he performed as a flutist and conductor. He was executive director of the Eastman School's opera department (1925–28) and conductor of the Rochester American Opera Co. He has taught at the Univ. of Arizona (1932–34); Bennington College (1934–44), where he was chairman of the music department; Barnard College (1944–47); and Columbia Univ. (since 1949), where since 1959 he has been codirector with Babbitt and Ussachevsky of the Columbia-Princeton Electronic Music Center. He has been active in many organizations devoted to contemporary music, including the American Music Center (founder and chairman, 1940–60), American Composers Alliance (president, 1945–51), and Composers Recordings Inc. (chairman of the board since 1970).

Luening is among the dozen or so most important composers of the formative years in modern American music. His more than 275 works cover every medium, including tape and electronic music (in which he was a pioneer), and he has displayed the rare ability to collaborate with other composers. His early style was aggressively advanced, making use of polytonal, atonal, and near-serial techniques. His pronounced lyrical gift and flair for the evocative use of traditional harmonies appeared first in his *Fantasia for Orchestra* (1925) and climaxed with the opera *Evangeline* (1928–47). In 1928 he formulated what he calls "acoustic harmony," a principle involving the manipulation and reinforcement of overtones, which he still uses. He has written many works for specific performers and orchestras in which he reveals a keen understanding for individual talents, modest or advanced, and for the demands of the occasion. He was one of the earliest composers to use magnetic tape, first processing natural and man-made sounds, then turning to purely electronic sound sources. *Rhapsodic Variations* (1954), which he composed in collaboration with Ussachevsky, was the first work to combine tape-recorded sounds with live performers.

PRINCIPAL COMPOSITIONS (published by Highgate unless otherwise noted): *Sextet* for flute, clarinet, horn, violin, viola, cello (1918); *String Quartets Nos. 1–3* (1919, unpub.; 1922; 1928); *Coal Scuttle Blues* for 2 pianos, composed in collaboration with Ernst Bacon (1921, AMP); *Trio* for flute, violin, soprano (1924); *The Soundless Song* for soprano, string quartet, flute, clarinet, piano, dancers, lights (1924); *Symphonic Fantasia No. 1* (1924); *Serenade* for 3 horns, string orchestra (1927); *Evangeline*, 3-act opera; libretto by the composer (1928–32, revisions to 1947; unpub.); *2 Symphonic Interludes* (1935, Peters); *Fantasia brevis* for clarinet, piano (1936, New Music); *Sonatina* for flute, piano (1937); *Symphonic Fantasia No. 2* (1939–49); *Suite* for cello, piano (1946); *3 Nocturnes* for oboe, piano (1951); *Legend* for oboe, strings (1951); *Kentucky Concerto* for orchestra (1951); *Sonata* for bassoon (cello), piano (1952); *Trio* for violin, flute, piano (1952); *Music for Orchestra* (1952); *Fantasy in Space*, flute on tape (1952, recorded by Desto and Folkways); *Low Speed*, flute on tape (1952, recorded by Desto); *Invention*, flute on tape (1952, recorded by Desto); *Incantation* on tape, composed with Vladimir Ussachevsky (1952, recorded by Desto); *Trombone Sonata* (1953); *Poem in Cycles and Bells* for tape, orchestra; composed with Ussachevsky (1954, Peters; recorded by CRI); *Wisconsin Suite*, "Of Childhood Tunes Remembered," for orchestra (1955); *King Lear Suite* on tape, composed with Ussachevsky (1955, unpub.; recorded by CRI); *Of Identity* on tape, composed with Ussachevsky; choreography by Paul Curtis (1955, unpub.); *Theater Piece No. 2* for tape, voice, brass, percussion, narrator; choreography by Doris Humphrey and José Limón (1956, unpub.); *Serenade* for flute, strings (1957); *Sonata* for double bass (1958); *Back to Methuselah* on tape, incidental music for the play by Shaw; composed with Ussachevsky (1958, unpub.); *Synthesis* for orchestra, electronic sounds on tape (1960,

Peters; recorded by CRI); *Concerted Piece* for tape, orchestra; composed with Ussachevsky (1960, Peters; recorded by CRI); *Gargoyles* for violin, electronic sounds on tape (1961, Peters; recorded by Columbia); *Diffusion of Bells* and *Electronic Fanfare* on tape, composed with Halim El Dabh (1962, unpub.); *Moonflight*, flute on tape (1967); *Fantasy* for string quartet, orchestra (1969, Peters); *Sonata No. 3* for solo violin (1970–71, Peters). List to 1962: *Composers of the Americas* 7:52–62.

PRINCIPAL WRITINGS: "Some Random Remarks about Electronic Music," *Journal of Music Theory* 8:89–98; "An Unfinished History of Electronic Music," *Music Educators' Journal* (Nov 1968):42–49.

Carter Harman

SEE ALSO Dance; Electronic Music: History and Development; Recording; United States.

Lutosławski, Witold (b. Warsaw, 25 Jan 1913), comes from a family of scholars. His early studies included piano (with J. Śmidowicz), violin, and theory; further piano study was with J. Lefeld at the Warsaw Conservatory (1932–36). At the age of 15 he began studying composition with W. Maliszewski (a composer in the traditional manner with leanings toward Russian music), first privately and later at the conservatory. Simultaneously for a few semesters he studied mathematics at the Univ. of Warsaw. During 1932–55 he gave a few public piano performances, and occasionally since 1952 he has conducted his own compositions. He has also taught composition and analysis in the U.S. and Sweden intermittently since 1962, and he has given many lectures.

Lutosławski composes slowly with long breaks between compositions, and his works are noteworthy for the thoroughness with which compositional problems are handled. Most of his early work was destroyed in World War II; what remains follows traditional procedures in a somewhat academic manner. His lengthy *Symphony No. 1* (1941–47) was long considered too "intellectual" because it did not adhere to the neoclassicism that dominated Polish music of the time, but the short compositions based on folk music had great success. The 12 easy piano pieces *Melodie ludowe* (1945) followed Bartók's example in their dissonant melodic style filled with sevenths and tritones. This approach was later extended to larger works, such as the *Little Suite* for orchestra (1951) and the song cycle *Silesian Triptych* (1951). The most successful work of the folk-music period is the *Concerto for Orchestra* (1950–54), a large-scale piece

with a great deal of counterpoint and highly differentiated sonorities. The composer began using the 12-tone method in 1958, but this did not prove to be a fruitful approach, and he wrote only a few works during the next five years (many pieces were actually tonal). In the *3 Poems of Henri Michaux* (1963) he began using aleatory procedures in combination with such traditional processes and materials as ostinatos, static textures, and tonal-like harmonic patterns. In his music since then successive or simultaneous soundings of materials create various textural and harmonic structures in both fluid and metric rhythms.

PRINCIPAL COMPOSITIONS (published by PWM unless otherwise noted): *Symphonic Variations* (1936–38); *Symphony No. 1* (1941–47); *Melodie ludowe*, 12 easy piano pieces (1945); *Concerto for Orchestra* (1950–54); *Little Suite* for orchestra (1951); *Silesian Triptych* for soprano, orchestra (1951); *5 Songs* for woman's voice with piano or orchestra (1956–57, PWM and Moeck); *Muzyka żałobna* [Funeral Music] for strings (1958); *3 Postludes* for orchestra (1960); *Gry weneckie* [Venetian Games] for orchestra (1960–61, PWM and Moeck); *3 Poems of Henri Michaux* for chorus, orchestra (1963); *String Quartet* (1964, PWM and Chester); *Paroles tissées* for tenor, chamber orchestra (1965); *Symphony No. 2* (1965–67, PWM and Chester); *Livre pour orchestre* (1968, PWM and Chester); *Cello Concerto* (1970).

PRINCIPAL WRITINGS: *W. L.*, a collection of documents to 1966 ed. by S. Jarociński (Cracow 1967).

BIBL.: W. Brennecke, "Die Trauermusik von W. L.," *Fr. Blume Festschrift* (Cassel 1963); R. S. Hines, ed., *The Orchestral Composer's Point of View* (Norman, Okla., 1970); S. Jarociński, "The Music of W. L.," *Polish Perspectives* 6 (1958).

Bogusław Schäffer
(trans. from German by Jeanne Wolf)

Lutyens, (Agnes) **Elisabeth** (b. London, 9 July 1906), studied at the Royal College of Music (1926–30, composition with Harold Darke, viola with Ernest Tomlinson) and at the Ecole Normale de Musique (1922–23). She also studied privately in Paris with Georges Caussade in 1930. She has written over 100 scores for films and radio, as well as much incidental music for the theater. In 1931 she helped found the Macnaghten-Lemare Concerts in London, and in 1954 she founded the Composers Concourse there.

PRINCIPAL COMPOSITIONS: *Chamber Concerto*, Op. 8, No. 1 (1939, Mills); *3 Symphonic Preludes* (1942, Mills); *O Saisons, O Chaleaux* for soprano, mandolin, guitar, harp, string orchestra, Op. 13 (1946, Mills); *String Quartet No. 6*, Op. 25 (c.1952,

Mills); *Motet* for chorus, Op. 27; text by Wittgenstein (1953, Schott); *Valediction* for clarinet, piano, Op. 28 (1954, Mills); *Music for Orchestra*, Op. 31 1955, Mills); *De amore*, cantata for soprano, tenor, chorus, orchestra, Op. 39; text by Chaucer (1957, Schott); *6 Tempi for 10 Instruments* for wind sextet, string trio, piano, Op. 42 (1957, Mills); *Quincunx for Orchestra*, Op. 44 (1957, Mills); *Symphonies* for piano, winds, harp, percussion, Op. 46 (1961, Schott); *Catena*, cantata for soprano, tenor, 21 instruments, Op. 47 (1961–62, Schott); *Music for Orchestra II*, Op. 48 (1962, Schott); *5 Bagatelles* for piano, Op. 49 (1962, Schott); *String Quintet*, Op. 51 (1963, Schott); *Music for Orchestra III*, Op. 56 (1964, Schott); *String Trio*, Op. 57 (1964, Schott); *Scena* for violin, cello, percussion (1964, Schott); *Music for Piano and Orchestra*, Op. 59 (1964, Schott); *The Valley of Hatsu-se* for soprano, flute, clarinet, cello, piano, Op. 62; early Japanese poetry (1965, Olivan); *The Numbered*, 2-act opera, Op. 63; libretto by Minos Volanakis after Elias Canetti (1966–67, Olivan); *Akapotik Rose* for soprano, flute, 2 clarinets, violin, viola, cello, piano, Op. 64; text by Eduardo Paolozzi (1966, Olivan); *And Suddenly It's Evening* for tenor, chamber ensemble, Op. 65; text by Quasimodo (1967, Schott); *Scroll for Li-ho* for violin, piano, Op. 67, No. 2 (1967, Olivan); *Time Off? Not a Ghost of a Chance!*, charade in 4 scenes for actor, baritone, vocal quartet, chorus, 11 instruments, Op. 68; libretto by the composer (1967–68, Olivan); *Novenaria* for orchestra, Op. 67 (1968, Olivan); *Essence of Our Happinesses* for tenor, chorus, orchestra; texts from 9th-century Arabic sources, Donne, Rimbaud (1968, Olivan); *Horai* for violin, horn, piano, Op. 67, No. 3 (1968, Olivan); *The Tyme Doth Flete* for chorus, Op. 70; texts by Petrarch, Ovid (1968, Olivan); *Isis and Osiris*, lyric drama for 8 voices, small orchestra, Op. 74; libretto by the composer (1969, Olivan).

PRINCIPAL WRITINGS: An autobiography is scheduled for publication in London.

BIBL.: R. Murray Schafer, *British Composers in Interview* (London 1963).
SEE ALSO Great Britain.

Lybbert, Donald (b. Cresco, Iowa, 19 Feb 1923), attended Iowa State Univ. (1940–43, 1946), the Juilliard School (1946–48, orchestration and composition with Robert Ward and Bernard Wagenaar), and Columbia Univ. (1948–50; composition with Otto Luening, Elliott Carter). He also studied at the Fontainebleau School (1961, composition with Nadia Boulanger). During 1967–70 he was chairman of the music department at Hunter College in New York. Lybbert's music has been serially oriented since 1960. He also acknowledges the special influence of Messiaen: "Recondite or banal, I always feel prompted to steal from him." He has also worked in the Hunter College Electronic Studio, his interest being combinations of electronic sound and live performers.

PRINCIPAL COMPOSITIONS: *Uitstel Voor Monica*, 2-act opera (1953); *From Harmonium*, song cycle; poems by Wallace Stevens (1954, Merion); *Trio for Winds* for clarinet, horn, bassoon (1956, Peters); *Chamber Sonata* for viola, horn, piano (1957); *Concert Overture for Orchestra* (1958); *Leopardi Canti* for soprano, viola, flute, clarinet (1959); *Movement for Piano 4-Hands* (1960, Peters); *Austro Terris Influente*, 3 motets (1961, Mercury); *Sonata brevis* for piano (1962, Peters); *Praeludium for Brass and Percussion* (1963, Peters); *The Scarlet Letter*, 3-act opera (1964–67); *Lines for the Fallen* for soprano, 2 pianos tuned a quarter-tone apart (1968, Peters).

PRINCIPAL WRITINGS: *The Essentials of Counterpoint* (Norman, Okla., 1969).

Mc

McBride, Robert (b. Tucson, 20 Feb 1911), studied at the Univ. of Ariz. (1928–35, composition with Otto Luening). He has performed professionally as a clarinetist and oboist and has been a member of the Tucson Symphony Orchestra (1928–35) and the Univ. of Ariz. Woodwind Quintet (1963–67). He has taught theory and wind instruments at Bennington College (1935–46) and these subjects plus composition at the Univ. of Ariz. (since 1957). During 1946–57 he was composer-arranger for Triumph Films, New York.

PRINCIPAL COMPOSITIONS: (published by ACA and/or CFE unless otherwise noted): *Depression Sonata* for violin, piano (1933); *Prelude to a Tragedy* for orchestra (1935); *Fugato on a Well-known Theme* for orchestra (1935, Fischer); *Mexican Rhapsody* for orchestra (1935, Fischer); *Show Piece*, ballet excerpts for orchestra (1936); *Workout for Chamber Orchestra* (1936, AMP); *Prelude and Fugue* for string quartet (1936); *Oboe Quintet* (1936); *Workout* for oboe, piano (1936); *Tarry Delight* for high voice, piano; text by Ben Belitt (1939); *In the Groove* for flute, piano (1940, Mills); *Punch and the Judy* for orchestra (1943); *Aria and Toccata* for violin, piano (1946, Gate); *Concerto for Doubles* for saxophone, orchestra (1947); *Variety Day*, concerto for violin, orchestra (1948); *Jazz Symphony*, ballet (1953); *Fantasy on a Mexican Christmas Carol* for orchestra (1955); *School Bus* and *Tall-in-the-Saddle* for piano (1956, Merion); *Pioneer Spiritual* for orchestra (1956); *String Foursome* for string quartet (1957); *5 Winds Blowing* for wind quintet (1957); *Memorial* for organ (1958); *Vocalise* for chorus, piano 4-hands (1959); *Panorama of Mexico* for orchestra (1960); *Sunday in Mexico* for orchestra (1963, Peters); *Hill Country Symphony* (1964, Peters); *Country-Music Fantasy* for orchestra (1965, Peters); *Brooms o, Mexico* for soprano, chamber ensemble (1965; choreographed by Richard Holden, 1970); *Symphonic Melody* (1968); *Lament for the Parking Problem* for trumpet, horn, trombone (1968). List to 1963: *Composers of the Americas* 9:92–99.

McDowell, John Herbert (b. Washington, 21 Dec 1926), studied English literature at Colgate Univ. (1944–48) and music at Columbia Univ. (1953–57; composition with Otto Luening, Jack Beeson). He also studied composition with Roger Goeb and others at the Bennington Conference. During 1957–59 he edited the *Bulletin* of the American Composers Alliance. In 1952 he began composing for dance, theater, film, and television, and since the late 1950s has worked almost exclusively in these areas. Since 1959 he has staged happenings and theater events at the Living Theater, Judson Church, Cafe Cino, the Museum of Modern Art in New York, and elsewhere. He has acted in and directed over 50 plays in New York and choreographed 14 dances; in 1969 he helped found The New Gaity American Operetta Theater. He has taught at the American Dance Festival, Colgate Univ., New York Univ., and Russell Sage College, among others. He was one of the first U.S. composers of tape music (beginning in 1952). In the late 50s he began using (occasionally) chance procedures, performance by large groups of amateurs, and (rarely) serial techniques. His musical output totals more than 300 works.

PRINCIPAL COMPOSITIONS: *Suite* for harpsichord 4-hands (1954); *Vocalise for 7 Sopranos* (1954); *The Harbinger of Health* for soprano, piano (1955); *Disenchanted Songs* for baritone, piano (1955); *Good News from Heaven*, Christmas cantata for vocal soloists, chorus, orchestra (1956); *Missa brevis No. 2* for tenor, chamber orchestra (1957); *The Parlor Trick with Ferns*, concertinos for violin, bassoon, cello, chamber orchestra (1958); *Modulamen* for harpsichord, string quartet (1960); *4 Sixes and a Nine* for violin, bassoon, trumpet, cello, orchestra (1960); *Homage to Billy Sunday* for double bass, wind quintet (1961); *Dance concertante No. 3* for chamber orchestra (1961); *Canticle of Expectation* for men's chorus, organ, percussion (1962); *God Has Gone Up with a Shout* for brass, harp, organ (1964); *Oklahoma Danger Remark*, 1-act opera (1965); *Lyra Davidica*, Easter anthem for soprano, chorus, congregation, organ, harps, gong orchestra (1966); *Comes the Revolution* for cello, piano, tape (1969); *A Dog's Love*, opera; libretto by Michael Smith (1971); *Tumescent lingam*, theater piece for oboe, chorus, tape, rock group, 101 people, 1 dog, film, lights (1971). ★ Principal dance scores (with name of choreographer): *Tentative Changes* for viola (James

Waring, 1953); *At Home* for instruments, tape (Aileen Passloff, 1956); *Landscape* on tape (Waring, 1957); *Arena* for chamber orchestra (Passloff, 1958); *Insects and Heros* for orchestra (Paul Taylor, 1961); *Poet's Vaudeville* for soprano, chamber orchestra; texts by Diane di Prima (Waring, 1962); *Gigue, Saraband, and Twist* for chamber orchestra (Elaine Summers, 1963); *Fantastic Gardens*, in collaboration with other composers (Summers, 1964); *Good Times at the Cloud Academy* on tape (Waring, 1965); *From Sea to Shining Sea* for orchestra (Taylor, 1965); *Phantom of the Opera* for orchestra (Manhattan Festival Ballet, 1967); *Dark Psalters* for organ, strings, percussion (Manhattan Festival Ballet, 1968); *Screenplay* for orchestra (Netherlands Dance Theater, 1968); *Public Domain* on tape (Taylor, 1969); *Purple Moment* on tape (Netherlands Dance Theater, 1969); *Own Thing* on tape (Dorothy Vislocky, 1970); *Candide* for chamber orchestra (Richard Kuch, 1971); *Still Life* for chamber orchestra (Bertram Ross, 1971); *Tristan, Isolde, Aida, Hansel and Gretel* on tape (Don Redlich, 1971).

SEE ALSO Dance.

McPhee, Colin (b. Montreal, 15 March 1901; d. Los Angeles, 7 Jan 1964), studied composition with Gustav Strube at the Peabody Conservatory until 1921 and with Paul le Flem in Paris (1924–26) and Edgard Varèse in New York. He also studied piano with Arthur Friedheim in Toronto (1921–24) and Isidor Philipp in Paris (1924–26). During 1934–39 he lived in Bali, where he studied native music and drama. During 1939–45 he wrote the column "Scores and Records" for *Modern Music*. He taught in the Institute of Ethnomusicology at the Univ. of Calif. at Los Angeles during 1958–64. He considered himself "a conservative inasmuch as I believe that sound, well-balanced structure, rhythmic and metric vitality, and carefully planned continuity are the main factors which prevent a musical work from deterioration with age, provided the musical material itself is stated in terms of fresh and interesting resonance" (*ACA Bulletin* 5/1:19).

PRINCIPAL COMPOSITIONS: *Concerto* for piano, wind octet (1929, AMP); *Sea Shanty Suite* for baritone, men's chorus, 2 pianos, 2 sets of timpani (1929, Kalmus); *Invention and Kinesis* for piano (published 1930, New Music); *Tabuh-Tabuhan*, toccata for orchestra (1936, AMP); *Balinese Ceremonial Music* for flute, 2 pianos (1942, Schirmer-G); *Transitions* for orchestra (1951, AMP); *Symphonies Nos. 2–3* (1957, AMP; 1962, Peters); *Nocturne* for orchestra (1958, ACA); *Concerto for Wind Orchestra* (1959, Peters).

PRINCIPAL WRITINGS: *A House in Bali* (New York 1946); *A Club of Small Men* (New York 1948); *Music in Bali* (New Haven 1966).

BIBL.: Wallingford Riegger, "Adolf Weiss and C. McP.," *American Composers on American Music* ed. by Henry Cowell (New York 1962):36–42.

SEE ALSO Asian Music and Western Composition.

Maayani, Ami (Hay) (b. Ramat-gan, Israel, 13 Jan 1936), studied architecture at the Technion School in Haifa (1956–60), where he founded and conducted the Technion Symphony; music at the Jerusalem Academy (1950–53) and Columbia Univ. (1964–65, electronic music with Vladimir Ussachevsky); and philosophy at Tel Aviv Univ. (beginning in 1970). He also studied composition privately with Paul Ben-Haim during 1956–60. He has conducted the Israel Youth Orchestra (1953–57 and since 1971).

PRINCIPAL COMPOSITIONS: *Harp Concerto No. 1* (1960, IMI); *Maqamat* for harp (1961); *Toccata* for harp (1961, IMI); *Songs of King Solomon* for string orchestra (1962); *The Frame*, film score on tape (1964–65); *Microtonos,* film score on tape (1964–65); *Mismorim,* songs of thanksgiving and praise for high voice, chamber orchestra (1965); *Régalim —The Feasts of Pilgrimage* for high voice, orchestra (1966, IMI); *Improvisation variée* for flute, viola, harp (1966); *Harp Concerto No. 2* (1966); *Concerto for percussion, 8 winds* (1966, IMI); *Violin Concerto* (1967, IMI); *Cello Concerto* (1967, IMI); *2 Madrigals* for harp, woodwind quintet (1969); *Concerto* for 2 pianos, orchestra (1969); *Qumran,* symphonic metaphor (1970).

BIBL.: Yehuda Cohen, "Werden und Entwicklung der Musik in Israel," *Die Musik Israels* by Max Brod (Cassel 1971).

SEE ALSO Israel.

Maceda, José (b. Manila, 31 Jan 1917), studied at the Ecole Normale in Paris (1937–41, theory with Georges Dandelot, analysis with Nadia Boulanger, piano with Alfred Cortot), Queens College and Columbia Univ. in New York (1950–52, musicology), and several midwest U.S. universities and the Univ. of Calif. at Los Angeles (1957–58, 1961–63; ethnomusicology). He also studied piano with E. Robert Schmitz in San Francisco during 1946–49. In 1958 he worked briefly at the musique concrète studio of the French Radio in Paris. He has appeared professionally as a pianist (1940–57) and as a conductor of avant-garde and Asian music (since 1963).

During 1941–46 and 1953–60 he taught piano and theory at various secondary schools in Manila; since 1960 he has taught ethnomusicology at the Univ. of the Philippines. Maceda's continuing interest in electronic and avant-garde music and his long experience (since 1953) as a researcher in the music of Southeast Asia provide a background for his compositions since 1963 and the concerts of Asian and avant-garde Western music he has been conducting in Manila. He uses native instruments as well as the standard Western ones. *Kubing* uses vocal clicks, stops, plosives, vowel colors, glissandi, pitch levels, trills, whispers, and calls against the sound of zithers, jew's harps, buzzers, tubes, and slit drums.

PRINCIPAL COMPOSITIONS: *Ugma-Ugma* [Structures] for Asian instruments and voices using Asian techniques of vocal production (1963); *Agungan* [Gong Sounds] for 6 gong families (1966); *Kubing* [Music] for men's voices, bamboo percussion instruments (1966); *Pagsamba*, or *Music for a Religious Ritual,* for 241 vocalists and instrumentalists using Asian instruments scattered among the listeners in a circular hall (1968).

PRINCIPAL WRITINGS: "Philippine Music and Contemporary Aesthetics," *Cultural Freedom in Asia* (Tokyo and Rutland, Vt., 1956); *The Music of the Magindanao* (PhD diss., Univ. of Calif. at Los Angeles, 1964); "Background for New Music," program notes for A Concert of Asian and Avant-Garde Music (Manila 1964); "Qualidades latinas no Brasil e Filipinas," *Afro-Asia* (Univ. of Bahia, Salvador) 1:97–105; "Drone and Melody in Philippine Musical Instruments," proceedings of an International Conference of the Malaysian Society for Asian Studies (published Kuala Lumpur 1970).

SEE ALSO Asian Music and Western Composition; Liturgical Music: Christian.

Macero, Teo (b. Glens Falls, N. Y., 30 Oct 1925), studied at the Juilliard School (1947–53, composition with Henry Brant). During 1951–52 he taught part-time at Juilliard and during 1953–55, at the Institute for the Education of the Blind. He has been a producer, composer, conductor, and arranger at Columbia Records since 1955 and has written many scores for film and TV. He also concertizes as a saxophonist and conductor of jazz and contemporary music. Varèse, Riegger, Copland, and Cage have been the major influences on his own works.

PRINCIPAL COMPOSITIONS: *Session for 6*, dance score; choreography by Anna Sokolow (1954); *In Retrospect* for orchestra (1955–56); *Fusion* for orchestra (1956); *C* for alto saxophone, violin, viola, orchestra (1957); *Polaris* for orchestra (1960); *Torsion in Space* for orchestra (1961–62); *Time Plus,* dance score; choreography by Sokolow (1962); *Dylan,* musical (1964); *Pressure* for orchestra (1964); *Opus '65,* dance score; choreography by Sokolow (1965); *End of the Road,* film score (Allied Artists, 1969).

BIBL.: Felice Ascher, "An Interview with T. M.," *Film Library Quarterly* 2/2:9–12; Paul Turok, "T. M.," *BMI, the Many Worlds of Music* (Feb 1966):9.

SEE ALSO Dance, Orchestration.

Mácha, Otmar (b. Ostrava, Czechoslovakia, 3 Oct 1922), attended the Conservatory and Music Academy in Prague (1942–46, composition with Jaroslav Řídký). During 1945–62 he worked at Radio Prague, where contact with older colleagues (Miloslav Kabeláč and Klement Slavický in particular) and with new music from around the world were influential on his development as a composer. Since 1962 he has devoted full time to composition.

PRINCIPAL COMPOSITIONS: *Violin Sonata* (1948, Orbis); *The Testament of J. A. Comenius,* oratorio for mezzo-soprano, chorus, orchestra, organ (1952–55, SHV); *Ertappte Untreve,* opera for soprano, alto, tenor, bass, chamber orchestra (1956–57, Dilia); *Symphonic Intermezzi* for orchestra (1958); *Night and Hope,* symphonic poem for orchestra (1959, Supraphon); *The Lake Ukereve,* 5-act opera (1960–63, Dilia); *Bassoon Sonata* (1963, Panton); *Variations on the Subject and Death of Jan Řichlík* for orchestra (1965, Panton); *4 Monologs* for soprano, baritone, orchestra (1966, Panton); *Variants* for orchestra (1968).

SEE ALSO Czechoslovakia.

Maderna, Bruno (b. Venice, 21 April 1920), studied at the Milan Conservatory, the Accadèmia Chigiana in Siena, and at the Accadèmia di S. Cecilia in Rome (until 1940; composition with Alessandro Bustini, Giuseppe Mulè; conducting with Bernardino

Molinari). He has also studied conducting with Antonio de Guarnieri and Hermann Scherchen. He taught briefly at the Venice Conservatory and has been closely associated with the Darmstadt summer courses since 1951 (his home is in Darmstadt). He has led seminars there since 1954 and in 1961 founded the Darmstadt International Chamber Ensemble, which he conducts. He worked at the Electronic Music Studio of the Milan radio from its inception in 1955. He tours widely as a conductor. His music from the 1940s shows the influence of Bartók and also of Stravinsky. About 1951 he began writing serial music. His work in the electronic media has usually been in combination with live performance and, more recently, stage action. Salzman (see bibl.) has remarked that the electronic works "have the character of improvisations arising out of a direct and fresh experience of the materials." In *Hyperion,* in which stage action is included, a flutist "spends the first ten minutes of the work quietly unpacking piccolo, flute, alto flute, and bass flute; when he finally gets around to the actual act of performance, the sound that gushes forth is in fact an enormously amplified percussive fortissimo (on tape). The piece has a complex choral part—also on tape—with a babbling-of-tongues text made out of isolated words taken from many different languages. There is an instrumental ensemble part and, finally, a long and sensuous—almost Bergian—soprano song at the end."

PRINCIPAL COMPOSITIONS: (published by S-Z unless otherwise noted): *Serenata* for 11 instruments (1946, revised 1954; Bruzzichelli); *Introduction and Passacaglia* for orchestra (1947, Bruzzichelli); *Concerto* for 2 pianos, chamber orchestra (1948); *Musica su 2 dimensioni* for flute, 2-track tape (1952, revised 1958); *Flute Concerto* (1954, Schott); *Composizione in 3 tempi* for orchestra (1954); *Notturno* on tape (1956); *Syntaxis* on 2-track tape (1957); *Serenata 2* for 11 instruments (1957); *Continuo* on tape (1958); *Piano Concerto* (1959); *Dimensioni II,* "*Invenzioni su una voce,*" on 2-track tape (1960); *Concerto* for oboe, chamber ensemble, tape ad lib (1962, revised 1965; Bruzzichelli); *Dimensioni III* for soprano, flute, orchestra (1963); *Aria da Hyperion* for soprano, flute, orchestra (1964); *Aulodia per Lothar* for oboe d'amore, guitar ad lib (1965); *Stele per Diotima* for orchestra (1965); *Oboe Concerto* (1967); *Widmung* for violin (1967). ★ Composite works: *Hyperion,* theater piece (Dimensioni III + Aria da Hyperion + 2-track tape); *Hyperion II* (Dimensioni III + Cadenza for flute + Aria da Hyperion); *Hyperion III* (Hyperion + Stele per Diotima); *Dimensioni IV* (Dimensioni III + Stele per Diotima).

BIBL.: Josef Häusler, *Musik im 20. Jahrhundert* (Bremen 1969): 274–77; Giacomo Manzoni,

"B. M.," *Die Reihe* 4; Eric Salzman *Twentieth-Century Music* (Englewood Cliffs, N. J., 1967): 182–84.

SEE ALSO Austria and Germany, Italy, Orchestration, Performance.

Maegaard, Jan (Carl Christian) (b. Copenhagen, 14 April 1926), attended the Royal Danish Conservatory (1945–50, counterpoint with Knud Jeppesen, composition with Poul Schierbeck, orchestration with Jørgen Jersild, theory with Bjørn Hjelmborg) and the Univ. of Copenhagen (1951–57; musicology with Jens Peter Larsen, Nils Schiørring; esthetics, opera with Torben Krogh). In 1958–59 he studied music bibliography with Robert Nelson at the Univ. of Calif. at Los Angeles; research work undertaken in the Schoenberg Archives during the same year had a decisive influence on his development. Maegaard taught theory and music history at the Royal Danish Conservatory (1952–57); since 1959 he has been teaching musicology at the Univ. of Copenhagen. He is also a lecturer on 20th-century music for the Danish State Radio.

PRINCIPAL COMPOSITIONS: *Sonata* for bassoon, piano (1952); *Jaevndøgnselegi* [Elegy of Equinox] for soprano, cello, organ; poem by Ole Wivel, English translation by Eric Wahlgreen, J. Maegaard (1955, SUDM); *5 Preludes* for violin (1956–57, SUDM); *2 tempi* for orchestra (1958–61); *5 Pezzi* for piano (1959); *Trio-Serenade* for violin, cello, piano (1960, Engstrøm); *Chamber Concerto No. 2* for oboe, clarinet, bassoon, 15 strings; uses a variable form with the score fully notated but the sequence of sections and the option of using some portions left to the performer (1961, SUDM); *Oktomeri* for violin, piano (1962, SUDM); *Music for "Antigone"* for men's chorus, orchestra (1966); *Movimento* for clarinet, horn, string quartet, 2 percussionists, Hammond organ (1967).

PRINCIPAL WRITINGS: "Some Formal Devices in Expressionistic Works," *Dansk Aarbog for Musikforskning* (Copenhagen 1961):69–75; "A Study in the Chronology of Op. 23–26 by Arnold Schoenberg," *ibid.*, 1962:93–115; *Musikalsk modernisme* (Copenhagen 1964); *Studien zur Entwicklung des dodekaphonen Satzes bei Arnold Schönberg* (PhD diss., Univ. of Copenhagen, 1970).

SEE ALSO Scandinavia.

Mahler, Gustav (b. Kalischt, Austria—now Jihlava, Czechoslovakia—7 July 1860; d. Vienna, 18 May 1911), was the second of 14 children born to Marie Hermann and Bernhard Mahler, a Jewish distiller. As a child he showed extraordinary talent and took lessons from several local musicians. He studied at the Vienna Conservatory (1875–78) under Julius Epstein (piano), Robert Fuchs (harmony), and Franz Krenn (composition) and attended some of Anton Bruckner's lectures on harmony at the university. In 1880, after two years teaching privately in Vienna, he embarked on a conducting career, first in a tiny operetta theater near Linz (May–June 1880), later in Ljubljana (1881–82), Olomouc (1883), and Cassel (1883–85). At 25 he became a conductor at the Prague Opera, where his performances of Wagner, Mozart, and Beethoven's *Symphony No. 9* won great acclaim. He left after a conflict with his superior and during 1886–88 shared the post of chief conductor in Leipzig with Artur Nikisch, suffering greatly from the inevitable rivalry. Three unhappy love affairs inspired *Das klagende Lied* (1880), the *Lieder eines fahrenden Gesellen* (1884), and the *Symphony No. 1* (1888).

In 1888 the highly successful premiere in Leipzig of Weber's unfinished opera *Die drei Pintos*, which Mahler had completed, attracted attention from throughout Germany. In spite of this he left Leipzig because of a conflict with his superior and became director of the Budapest Opera. There he gave the Hungarian premieres of *Das Rheingold* and *Die Walküre* and produced one of the first veristic operas, *Cavalleria rusticana*. He was obliged to leave his post in 1891 because the new manager, a chauvinistic Hungarian nobleman, did not want a foreign-born director. Mahler's subsequent position as first kapellmeister of the Hamburg Opera (1891–97) had positive aspects: a major city, excellent singers, and contact with many great musicians. He also became a protégé of Hans von Bülow, replacing him at the head of the subscription concerts when Bülow retired. Yet Hamburg also had drawbacks: overwork (more than 150 performances conducted by him each season, not counting subscription concerts), insufficient rehearsal time, a mediocre orchestra, a director who cared only for the quality of the singing, and many conflicts with the star performers. In his free time he composed the *Wunderhorn Lieder* and the *Symphonies 2–3*.

In 1897, after his conversion to Catholicism, Mahler became first conductor, later director, of the Vienna Opera, largely thanks to the influence of Brahms and the critic Eduard Hanslick. His work there won him international recognition, particularly in the later years when he personally selected and trained a company of excellent singers and worked with the painter and set designer Alfred Roller. He also conducted the Vienna Philharmonic for three seasons, but his relationship with Viennese musicians was never warm: his artistic fanaticism, his "modern" interpretations, his drastic demands during rehearsal, and his stubborn character made many enemies in a city where tradition had become law and where art was mainly considered a pleasure to be enjoyed rather than a cause to be served. In 1901 he married Alma Schindler, daughter of the landscape painter Jakob and a musician and composer in her own right. She had a strong and possessive nature, and their union was stormy. Through Alma he met such men as the writer Gerhard Hauptmann and two musical revolutionaries, Alexander von Zemlinsky and Arnold Schoenberg, who became his close friends. During the Vienna years he devoted his vacation months to composing *Symphonies 4–8* and the *Rückert Lieder*.

Mahler resigned from the Vienna Opera in 1907 because of the conflicts and petty jealousies that had developed, making his situation impossible. He conducted at the Metropolitan Opera in New York (Jan 1908–March 1909), leaving when Italian musicians gained control of the organization and Arturo Toscanini became a conductor there. A committee of society women then reorganized the New York Philharmonic Orchestra for him. During his second season with the orchestra (1910–11) he fell dangerously ill, and conflicts with the board of directors and the hostility of a critic, Henry Krehbiel, added to his difficulties. He had been deeply affected in 1907 when a doctor diagnosed a serious heart condition, and his last symphonies and *Das Lied von der Erde* are grave reflections on the subject of death. His own death resulted from a throat infection that had begun in New York.

Mahler composed some 40 lieder, half of which have orchestral accompaniment, one cantata, and 11 symphonies (including *Das Lied von der Erde* and the unfinished tenth). Harmony is the least advanced element in this output. Its diatonicism is sharply opposed to Strauss's post-Wagnerian chromaticism. Nonetheless the chords of superimposed fourths in the *Symphony No. 7* heralded those of Schoenberg's *Kammersymphonie* and perhaps even inspired them. Also the first movement of the *Symphony No. 9* anticipates the downfall of the tonal system, for its tonality is treated as merely one color among many, not as a basis for the whole work. Mahler's composition is dominated by a polyphony that became increasingly complex in the later works with the result that chords formed by the meeting of voices often seem fortuitous. He even went so far as to "polyphonize" a melody by surrounding it with several closely imitative voices.

The rhythms are generally simple with a striking preference given to the march and ländler waltz. Mahler's fondness for the march is often attributed to childhood memories (military parades in Iglau), but they seem to have a symbolic value far beyond this—man's oppression by society, the unavoidable forces of destinity, the irreversibility of time. Marches do not have da-capo repeats and are thus opposed to the 3/4-time dances. The latter were increasingly frenzied and distorted in Mahler's later works, becoming a grotesque echo of daily reality. In his music, these simple rhythms finally blur into the polyphonic texture. At times they are brutally and deliberately cut short, at others the rhythmic progression is interrupted by long, static episodes in which everything dissolves and eventually re-forms.

Mahler's instrumentation has been discussed more than any other aspect of his music. Schoenberg was the first to underline the absurdity of praising it at the expense of his "musical" invention, for it is an integral part of the music, not an afterthought. It is, in fact, no less essential in Mahler than in Webern, and like Webern, Mahler often divided a melodic line among several different timbres. Mahler added new instruments to the orchestra—guitar, mandolin, celesta, cowbells—and employed traditional instruments in unusual registers. He also obtained new timbres by combining instruments in unusual ways. His instrumentation is clear, particularly in moments of ascetic spareness.

Mahler remained largely faithful to the classical and romantic symphonic forms, though he changed the order of movements, increased their number, and frequently abandoned the initial tonality in his finales. Yet it is in the area of form that his chief innovations are to be found. Adorno has shown how the breaks, digressions, intrusions, unexpected as they are, are never arbitrary even when they do not follow the usual patterns of musical logic. Adorno was also the first to speak of the "novelesque" dimension in Mahler's symphonies, based on a succession of individual events, a kind of "stream of consciousness," rather than a preconceived scheme. Like many present-day composers, Mahler treated the material for a work as an available whole and searched for its own inherent order. His most important innovations are the almost total suppression of literal repetition, the use of subtle variation procedures that renew a melody without losing its identity, and a new conception of the development section, which often destroys and dissolves rather than elaborates. In his ardent and romantic effort to express the whole of man in one symphonic universe, Mahler reached far into the future. He anticipated our present musical crisis: the decadence of form, the collapse of values, and the resulting malaise. In this respect he is akin to Kafka and Freud, who like himself were Bohemian Jews.

For many years Mahler's music was underrated, largely because of his double activity as interpreter and composer. It seemed impossible that a virtuoso conductor could also be a significant creator. A "creative impotence" was blamed for all that surprised and shocked in his "symphonic potpourris": the classical "reminiscences," the "quotations" from folk and street music, the abrupt changes of mood, the "banalities" and "sentimentality." No one denied his technical skill, but his detractors accused him of hiding his sterility behind a wealth of sound effects and vast orchestral resources. For years too Mahler's reputation suffered from the Bruckner-Mahler link, justified by only superficial likenesses, such as their shared nationality and the number and length of their symphonies. In all other ways the belated 18th-century church musician stood in opposition to the postromantic, whose acute sensitivity led him to foresee the great artistic upheavals of the 20th century. Finally, Mahler's contemporaries found much in his music provocative and shocking, most of all its basic paradoxes: tragedy/mockery, pathos/irony, nobility/vulgarity, gravity/humour, folklike simplicity/technical perfection, romantic and visionary mysticism/critical and modern nihilism. All these gave the impression that Mahler suffered from a split personality. Though some of these contradictions were already present in German romantic literature, especially in the tales of E. T. A. Hoffmann, they were not accepted in Mahler, yet these contrasts and inner conflicts now appear typically modern.

Although he was a postromantic who neither tried to revolutionize music nor to invent a new language, the revolutionaries who succeeded him in Vienna revered him, as can be seen in statements by Schoenberg, passages in Berg's music, and Mahler performances conducted by Webern. Some of the prophetic features of his music can be recognized instantly: a rich and subtle polyphony (later taken even further by the 12-tone composers), a daringly original orchestration, a tendency in

the last works towards a "total thematic" as advocated by Schoenberg (the use of the same motifs in principal and subsidiary parts), and the use of pre-Webernian evolutionary formal processes of "perpetual variation," using augmentation, diminution, inversion, and fragmentation. In light of the latest evolutions in music, Mahler appears even more prophetic. "Of all romantics, this arch-romantic has most to give to the music of the future," wrote Aaron Copland as early as 1941. Dieter Schnebel goes so far as to refer to the opening Andante of the *Ninth Symphony* as "the first work of new music," and he gives a detailed analysis of this "highly subjective musical prose," so full of unexpected twists and turns which nevertheless obey a secret logic of their own. Adorno also claims that "the substance of Mahler's music springs from the individual elements," that it reveals an entirely new conception of unity generated by the material itself and "concretely shaped in relation to the idea expressed." The relationship between Mahler's music and the tradition it is heir to is undoubtedly less harmonious than has been claimed. A daring distortion of inherited material pervades it rather than a nostalgia for the past. The material is manipulated for expressive ends or caricature. Music "reflects upon itself" and quotations take on a deeper, often personal meaning that may bear no relation to the material quoted. According to Luis de Pablo, Mahler went even further than Schoenberg in that he broke with the traditional concept of "beauty" and created a "polyphony of styles" in which the "ugly" and the "vulgar" play an essential part. Such eclecticism, so long condemned, is undoubtedly his most modern and prophetic trait.

PRINCIPAL COMPOSITIONS (published by UE unless otherwise noted): *Symphonies Nos. 1–10*: No. 1 in D (1888; a slow movement, "Blumine," was suppressed by Mahler and is published by Presser); No. 2 in C Minor for soprano, alto, chorus, orchestra (1888–94); No. 3 in D (1895–96); No. 4 in G for soprano, orchestra (1899–1900); No. 5 in C# Minor (1901–02, Peters); No. 6 in A Minor (1903–04, Kahnt); No. 7 in B Minor (1904–05, Bote); No. 8 in E♭ for 8 solo voices, children's chorus, double mixed chorus, orchestra (1906); No. 9 in D (1909); No. 10 in F# (1910; movements 1 and 3 completed, AMP; a complete "performing version" prepared by Deryck Cooke, published by Schott); *Das klagende Lied* for 3 solo voices, chorus, orchestra; text by the composer after the Grimms (1880; revised 1892, 1898); 5 *Lieder* for voice, piano (1880–83, Schott); 9 *Lieder aus "Das Knaben Wunderhorn"* for voice, piano (1888–92, Schott); 4 *Lieder eines fahrenden Gesellen* for voice, orchestra; texts by the composer (1884; orchestrated 1896, Weinberger); 10 *Lieder aus "Des Knaben Wunderhorn"* for voice, orchestra (1892–96); 7 *Lieder aus letzter Zeit* for voice, orchestra (1899–1902, Kahnt); 5 *Kindertotenlieder* for voice, orchestra; poems by Rückert (1901–04, Kahnt); *Das Lied von der Erde*, "a symphony" for tenor, alto (or baritone), orchestra; poems trans. from Chinese by Hans Bethge (1908). A complete edition, edited by Erwin Ratz, is being published by the Mahler Gesellschaft in Vienna.

PRINCIPAL WRITINGS: *Briefe (1879–1911)*, ed. by Alma Mahler (Vienna 1924); other letters included in Alma Mahler, *Memories and Letters* (New York 1946).

BIBL.: Theodor W. Adorno, *M., eine musikalische Physiognomik* (Frankfurt 1960); Natalie Bauer-Lechner, *Erinnerungen an G. M.* (Vienna 1923); Paul Bekker, *G. M.s Sinfonien* (Berlin 1921); Kurt Blaukopf, *G. M. oder der Zeitgenosse der Zukunft* (Vienna 1969); Neville Cardus, *G. M., His Mind and his Music*, vol. I (London 1965); J. B. Foerster, *Der Pilger* (Prague 1955); Ludwig Karpath, *Begegnung mit dem Genius* (Vienna 1934); Alma Mahler, *And the Bridge Is Love* (New York 1958); Donald M. Mitchell, *G. M., The Early Years* (London 1958); Dika Newlin, *Bruckner, M., and Schoenberg* (New York 1947); Hans F. Redlich, *Bruckner and M.* (London 1955); Willi Reich, ed., *G. M. im eigenen Wort, im Wort der Freunde* (Zurich 1958); Theodor Reik, *The Haunting Melody* (New York 1953); Alfred Roller, ed., *Die Bildnisse von G. M.* (Leipzig 1922); Arnold Schoenberg, Dieter Schnebel, Theodor Adorno, et al., *Über G. M.* (Tübingen 1966); Richard Specht, *G. M.* (Berlin 1913); Paul Stefan, ed., *G. M., ein Bild seiner Persönlichkeit in Widmungen* (Munich 1910); Bruno Walter, *G. M.* (New York 1958); ——, *Theme and Variations* (New York 1946).

Henry-Louis de La Grange

SEE ALSO Austria and Germany, Folk Resources, Orchestration.

Maler, Wilhelm (b. Heidelberg, 21 June 1902), studied music privately in Heidelberg with Hermann Grabner (1919–21), in Munich with Josef Haas (1921–23), and in Berlin with Philipp Jarnach (1923–25). He taught composition and theory in Cologne at the Rhein Music School and at the Staatliche Hochschule für Musik (1925–44). He was cofounder and director of the Nordwestdeutsche Musik Akademie in Detmold (1946–59) and director of the Staatliche Hochschule für Musik und Theater in Hamburg (1959–69). The principal influence on his style has been the new polyphony of the Hindemith school, 1920–35.

PRINCIPAL COMPOSITIONS (published by Schott unless otherwise noted): *Concerto* for harpsichord, chamber orchestra (1927); *Concerto grosso* (1928);

Orchesterspiel (1930); *St. George Cantata* for baritone, chorus, orchestra (1930); *6 dreistimmigen Spielmusiken* for any 3 instruments (1930); *Violin Concerto* (1932); *Inventions on Folksongs* for piano (1932); *4 Hölderlin Choruses* for chorus (1933); *der ewige strom*, oratorio; text by Andres (1934); *String Quartet in G* (1935); *3 Piano Pieces on Christmas Carols* (1936); *Flemish Rondo* for orchestra (1937); *Music for String Orchestra* (1937); *Piano Sonatas Nos. 1–3* (1939–45, SM); *Concerto* for piano trio, orchestra (1940); *kume geselle min,* cantata for soprano, chamber orchestra (1941, Tonger); *Der Mayen,* suite for piano (1942, Gerig).

PRINCIPAL WRITINGS: *Beitrag zur durmoll-tonalen Harmonielehre,* 6th ed. (Munich 1967). Maler has also written on music education and musical life for *Melos* and publications of the Deutscher Musikrat.

Malipiero, Gian Francesco (b. Venice, 18 March 1882), descended from an ancient and distinguished Venetian family; his mother was Countess Emma Balbi Valier. His grandfather (Francesco) composed operas, and his father, Luigi, was an amateur musician. During the winter of 1898–99 Malipiero studied at the Vienna Conservatory. In June 1899 he enrolled at the Liceo Musicale Benedetto Marcello in Venice, where he studied with M. E. Bossi and received his diploma in fugue in 1902. Further study with Bossi at the Bologna Liceo Musicale G. B. Martini led to a diploma in composition in 1904. Settling in Venice, Malipiero composed a number of works between 1905 and 1913 that he later destroyed or repudiated. During the winters of 1908–09 and 1909–10 he spent a few months in Berlin, where he audited lectures by Max Bruch (he was never a pupil of Bruch's). During this early period, Malipiero made important discoveries: "I went frequently to the Marciana Library to study the music of old composers who were practically unknown to my fellow students and teachers. I copied not only Monteverdi's works, but also many by Stradella, Galuppi, Nasco, Tartini, and others. From the very start I reacted instinctively against musical conditions in an Italy that was suffocated by the tyranny of 19th-century opera." In later years Malipiero edited many works by old Italian composers, including a complete edition of Monteverdi. From 1917 to 1921 he lived in Rome, after which he spent two years as professor of composition at the Conservatory of Parma. In 1923 he settled in Asolo, some 30 miles from Venice, where he still lives. By the mid-20s he was being performed frequently in France, Germany,

England, and America, as well as in Italy. From 1932 he gave master courses in composition at the Venice Conservatory, of which he was the director during 1939–52.

The catalog of Malipiero's works is extremely large and embraces all forms of composition. He was the first Italian for over a century to cultivate instrumental and symphonic music extensively, and in his stage works he broke radically with 19th-century concepts of *melodramma*, avoiding vocal display, high-note ostentation, set numbers, and standardized dramatic effects and assigning to the orchestra an integral part in the musical and dramatic development. The influence of early Italian music on his style accounts in part for its remarkable basic unity from 1913 to the present. In both operatic and concert works this style is marked by the consistent employment of light, transparent, nonacademic counterpoint that never obscures the leading melodic idea; a kind of melody that consists less in tunes that can be whistled than in combinations of motives and ideas that are moulded into long phrases; and the development of the musical material through free association and constant variation (never along sonata-form principles) in what Malipiero calls a "free conversation" that produces a cumulative formal structure, different in each work. An extended concept of tonality underlies all of Malipiero's works: the early ones betray the influence of Debussy; those of the 1920s were strongly attacked for their dissonant "modernism"; those of the 30s and 40s are frequently modal and predominantly diatonic; and the later works tend towards greater chromaticism and sharper dissonance, sometimes bordering on atonality. All of his music is marked by an "aristocratic" attitude, which avoids the commonplace and banal at the occasional risk of becoming esoteric. Speculative elements play no part in his work, which from first to last is expressive in intent.

Luigi Dallapiccola has called Malipiero "the greatest Italian composer since Verdi." The change in muscial climate following World War II and the vogue of serial techniques, which Malipiero finds incompatible with his own esthetic, have led to a neglect of his works, however. Signs of renewed interest are not wanting, and his recent operas have underscored his originality and his important place in 20th-century Italian music.

PRINCIPAL COMPOSITIONS (published by Ricordi unless otherwise noted): *Impressioni dal vero* for orchestra (1910–22, UE); *Poemi Asolani* for piano (1916, Chester); *Pause del silenzio* for orchestra (1917–26, UE); *L'Orfeide*, operatic trilogy: No. 1,

"La morte delle maschere" (1922); No. 2, "7 canzoni" (1919); No. 3, "Orfeo" (1920, Chester); *Rispetti e strambotti*, string quartet No. 1 (1920, Chester and UE); *3 Commedie goldoniane*, operas: 1. "La bottega del caffè" (1922); 2. "Sior Todaro Brontolon" (1922); 3. "Le baruffe Chiozzotte" (1920); *Stornelli e ballate*, string quartet No. 2 (1923); *La cena* for soloists, chorus, orchestra (1927, Birchard); *Torneo notturno*, opera (1929); *Concerti per orchestra* (1931); *Violin Concerto No. 1* (1932, Carisch); *Symphony No. 1*, "in quattro tempi come le quattro stagioni" (1933); *Piano Concerto No. 1* (1934); *Giulio Cesare*, opera (1935); *La Passione* for soloists, chorus, orchestra (1935); *Symphony No. 2*, "Elegiaca" (1936); *Piano Concerto No. 2* (1937, S-Z); *Cello Concerto* (1937, S-Z); *Antonio e Cleopatra*, opera (1937, S-Z); *Ecuba*, opera (1940, S-Z); *I capricci di Callot*, opera (1942, S-Z); *Vergilii Aeneis* for soloists, chorus, orchestra (1944, S-Z); *Symphonies Nos. 3–6*: No. 3, "delle campane" (1945); No. 4, "In memoriam" (1946); No. 5, "Concertante, in eco" (1947); No. 6, "degli archi" (1948); *Piano Concerto No. 3* (1948); *Sinfonia in un tempo* (1950); *Piano Concerto No. 4* (1950); *Sinfonia dello zodiaco* (1951); *Donna Urraca*, 1-act opera (1953); *Fantasie concertanti* for orchestra (1954); *Il Capitan Spavento*, 1-act opera (1955); *Dialoghi* for various combinations of instruments and voices (1956); *Piano Concerto No. 5* (1958); *Sinfonia per Antigedina* (1962); *Don Giovanni*, opera (1962); *Violin Concerto No. 2* (1963); *Symphony No. 8*, "Sinfonia brevis" (1964); *Piano Concerto No. 6*, "delle macchine" (1964); *Il Marescalso*, opera (1964, unpub.); *Le metamorfosi di Bonaventura*, opera (1965); *Symphony No. 9*, "dell' ahimè" (1966); *Don Tartuffo Bacchettone*, opera (1966); *Symphony No. 10*, "atropo" (1967); *Flute Concerto* (1968); *Gli eroi di Bonaventura*, opera (1968); *Symphony No. 11*, "delle cornamuse" (1970). Complete list to 1970 in Helm 1970.

PRINCIPAL WRITINGS: *The Orchestra* (London 1921); *I profeti di Babilonia* (Milan 1924); *Claudio Monteverdi* (Milan 1930); *La pietra del bando* (Venice 1945); *Stravinsky* (Venice 1945); *Cossi va lo mondo* (Venice 1946); *L'armonioso labirinto* (Milan 1946); *Il filo d'Arianna* (Milan 1966); *Di palo in frasca* (Milan 1967); *Da Venezia lontan* (Milan 1968). Malipiero has also written many articles.

BIBL.: F. d'Amico, "G. F. M.," *Melos* (Nov 1950); *L'approdo musicale* 9 (Jan 1960); M. Bontempelli, *G. F. M.* (Milan 1942); E. Helm, "G. F. M.," *Musical America* (April 1952); ——, "G. F. M., Intransigent Octogenarian," *Musical America* (April 1962); ——, "An Introduction to G. F. M.," *Soundings* (Cardiff, Wales, Oct 1970); *L'opera di G. F. M.*, essays by various authors (Treviso 1952); H. Prunières, "G. F. M.," *Musical Quarterly* (July 1920); ——, "G. F. M.," *Revue musicale* (Jan 1927).

Everett Helm

SEE ALSO Italy; Liturgical Music: Christian; Musicology and Composition; Opera.

Malipiero, Riccardo (b. Milan, 24 July 1914), studied at the Conservatories in Milan and Turin (1930–37) and at the Benedetto Marcello Conservatory in Venice (1937–39, composition with his uncle G. F. Malipiero). Since 1937 he has been a free-lance composer and writer on music. In 1949 he helped organize the first International Congress of 12-Tone Music in Milan.

PRINCIPAL COMPOSITIONS (published by S-Z): *Minnie la candida*, 2-act opera; libretto by Massimo Bontempelli (1942); *Violin Concerto* (1952); *Quintet* for piano, strings (1957); *Musica da camera* for wind quintet (1959); *6 Poesie di Dylan Thomas* for soprano, 10 instruments (1959); *String Quartet No. 3* (1960); *In Time of Daffodils* for soprano, baritone, flute, clarinet, bass clarinet, viola, double bass, guitar, percussion; text by e. e. cummings (1964); *Costellazioni* for piano (1965); *Carnet de notes* for chamber orchestra (1967); *Cassazione* for string sextet (1967).

PRINCIPAL WRITINGS: *G. S. Bach*, 2nd ed. (Brescia 1958); *C. Debussy*, 2nd ed. (Brescia 1958); *Guida alla dodecafonia* (Milan 1961).

BIBL.: Claudio Sartori, *R. M.*, trans. by R. Smith Brindle (Milan 1957); the same, in Italian, with a discussion of the works of 1957–64 by Piero Santi, *Due tempi di R. M.* (Milan 1964).

Malovec, Jozef (b. Hurbanovo, Czechoslovakia, 24 March 1933), studied at the Bratislava Academy of Music (1951–53, composition with Alexander Moyzes) and the Prague Academy (1953–57; composition with Jaroslav Řídký, Vladimír Sommer). He has been a program assistant for the music division of the Czech Radio at Bratislava since 1957, and in 1965 he helped establish its electronic music studio. His music was influenced first by Prokofiev and Shostakovich, later by Webern. He began composing electronic music for films in 1961 at the Bratislava Experimental Film Studio. In many of his works from 1960 on he uses 12-tone techniques.

PRINCIPAL COMPOSITIONS: *Piano Sonatinas Nos. 1–2* (1953, 1955); *Scherzo* for orchestra (1956); *Overture* for orchestra (1957); *2 Pieces* for chamber orchestra (1962); *Little Chamber Music* (1964); *Cryptogram* for bass clarinet, piano, percussion (1965, Supraphon); *Concert Music* for orchestra (1967, Supraphon); *Orthogenesis* on tape (1967, recorded by Turnabout); *Tmel*, synthesized and concrete sounds on tape (1968); *Punctum alpha*, electronic sounds on tape (1969); *Tabu*, electronic sounds on tape (1970).

PRINCIPAL WRITINGS: Malovec has written 2 articles on electronic music for *Slovenská hudba* (12/3 and 13/6–7).

BIBL.: Peter Faltin, "New Music in Slovakia," *Slovenská hudba* 11/8:341–47; Ivan Marton and

Ľubomír Chalupka, "Koncertná hudba pre orchester" [*Concert Music* for orchestra], *Hudobný zivot* 19:5.

SEE ALSO Czechoslovakia.

Mann, Robert (Wheeler) (b. Sandwich, Ill., 11 Sept 1925), studied at Butler Univ. in Indianapolis (1942–43), Indiana State Teachers' College (1944), the Chicago Conservatory of Music (1946–47), the New England Conservatory of Music (1947), the Univ. of Mich. (1947–48), and the Mozarteum in Salzburg (1948, composition with Frank Martin). He studied composition privately with Goffredo Petrassi in Rome (1948–52), where he makes his home. He was secretary general of ISCM during 1955–59 and treasurer during 1966–69.

PRINCIPAL COMPOSITIONS: *The Little Prince*, 1-act opera; libretto by the composer after St.-Exupéry (1951–52); *Spelt from Sibyl's Leaves* for chorus, orchestra; text by G. M. Hopkins (1953); *Night Songs* for voice, orchestra (1954); *The Scarlet Letter*, 4-act opera; libretto by the composer after Hawthorne (1955–58); *String Quartet* (1958); *Esercizi* for orchestra (1958); *Cantata* for soprano, keyboard instruments, percussion; text by Shelley (1960); *Anaglyphs* for piccolo, contrabassoon, guitar, 8 violas, 2 double basses, 5 percussionists (1961); *Symphony* (1969); *Song* for soprano, percussion; text by Shelley (1969).

Manzoni, Giacomo (b. Milan, 26 Sept 1932), studied music at the Milan Conservatory (1950–56) and the Darmstadt summer courses (1952–56) and foreign languages and literature at Bocconi Univ. in Milan (1950–55). He also studied piano privately in Milan with A. Mozzati. He has taught at the Milan Conservatory (1962–64, 1968–69) and the Bologna Conservatory (1965–68, since 1969). He has been music critic for *L'Unità* in Milan (1959–66) and an editor for *Il Diapason* (1956) and *Prisma* (1968–69) and has also translated from German a number of books by T. W. Adorno and Schoenberg.

PRINCIPAL COMPOSITIONS (published by S-Z unless otherwise noted): *Little Suite* for violin, piano (1952–55, unpub.); *Piano Album* (1956); *Fantasia, Recitative, and Finale* for orchestra (1956, unpub.); *Little Suite No. 2* for violin, piano (1956); *Prelude "Grave" by W. Currey, and Finale* for mezzo-soprano, clarinet, violin, viola, cello (1956, Ricordi); *3 Lyrics of P. Eluard* for soprano, flute, clarinet, trumpet, violin, cello (1958, unpub.); *Improvisations* for viola, piano (1958, unpub.); *5 Vicariote* for chorus, orchestra; Sicilian folk texts (1958); *La sentenza*, 1-act opera; libretto by E. Jona (premiere 1960); *2 Italian Sonnets* for chorus (1961, unpub.); *Don Chisciotte* for soprano, chamber chorus, orchestra; text by Nazim Hikmet (1961); *Studio per 24* for chamber orchestra (1962); *Studio 2* for orchestra (1962–63); *Atomtod*, 2-act opera; libretto by Jona (1964); *Studio 3* on tape (1964); *Scherzo* for voice, piano; text by Kurt Schwitters (1965); *Musica notturna* for 5 winds, piano, percussion (1966); *Insiemi* for orchestra (1967); *Ombre*, in memoriam Che Guevara, for chorus, orchestra (1968); *Quadruplum* for 2 trumpets, 2 trombones (1968); *Parafrasi con finale* for 10 instruments (1969); *Spiel* for 11 strings (1969); *Parole da Beckett* for 2 choruses, 3 instrumental groups, tapes (1970–71, Ricordi).

PRINCIPAL WRITINGS: "Luigi Dallapiccola," *Revista musical chilena* 85 (1963):50–72; *Guida all'ascolto della musica sinfonica* (Milan 1967); "Arnold Schönberg," *La musica moderna* (Milan) 4:97–160; "Edgard Varèse," *ibid.* 7:1–16; "Karlheinz Stockhausen," *ibid.* 7:17–32.

BIBL.: M. Baroni, "G. M.—Le ultime opere," *Notiziario* (Milan, April 1970); A. Gentilucci, "G. M.," *Nuova revista musicale italiana* 1968/6; "*Ombre* per il Che Guevara," *Utopia* (Bari) 1971/2:27–28.

Des Marais, Paul (b. Menominee, Mich., 23 June 1920), studied composition with Leo Sowerby in Chicago (1937–41), with Nadia Boulanger in Cambridge, Mass., and Paris (1941–42, 1949–50), and with Walter Piston at Harvard Univ. (1946–53). He has taught at Harvard Univ. (1953–56) and the Univ. of Calif. at Los Angeles (since 1956). His works to the mid-50s were neoclassic in orientation and strongly influenced by Stravinsky. Thereafter, though retaining a basis in tonal harmonic relationships, his music began to incorporate some serial techniques.

PRINCIPAL COMPOSITIONS: *Piano Sonatas Nos. 1–2* (1947, 1952); *Mass* for chorus (1949); *Suite for baritone, piano*; texts by Carol Hogben (1951); *Theme and Changes* for harpsichord (1953); *Motet* for voices, cellos, double basses; poems by George Herbert (1959); *Psalm 121* for chorus (1959); *Capriccio* for 2 pianos, percussion, celesta (1962); *Organum 1–6* for voices, organ, percussion (1963–); *Epiphanies,* chamber opera for 33 performers; film sequences by Dan McLaughlin, libretto by Harold Smith (1964–68), *Le Cimetière marin* for voice, keyboard instruments, percussion; text by Paul Valéry (1971).

PRINCIPAL WRITINGS: *Harmony: A Workbook in Fundamentals* (New York 1962).

Marchena-Dujarric, Enrique de, see under de Marchena

Marco, Tomás (b. Madrid, 12 Sept 1942), studied at the Univ. of Madrid (1959–64) and privately with Karlheinz Stockhausen (1962–66). In 1967 he collaborated with Stockhausen at Darmstadt on the collective composition, *Ensemble.* He has written criticism for *Diario SP* and *Melos* (1967–69), for the magazine *SP* (since 1962), and for the newspaper *Arriba* (since 1970). In 1967 he founded and became editor of *Sonda,* a review for new music. He has produced a contemporary music program on Spanish radio since 1967. Since 1965 he has explored relationships between music and language and music and theater. Some of his music since 1968 has been more "simplified" and has dealt with the implications in psychological perceptions of sound.

PRINCIPAL COMPOSITIONS: *Los Caprichos* for orchestra (1959–67); *Roulis-Tangage* for trumpet, cello, guitar/electric guitar, piano, vibraphone, 2 percussionists (1962–63); *Glasperlenspiel* for chamber orchestra (1963–64); *Paon* for 20 strings (1965); *Piraña* for piano (1965); *Albayalde* for guitar (1965, UE); *Jabberwocky* for actors, tenor, saxophone, piano, 4 percussionists, tape, 6 radios, lights, slides (1966); *Anna Blume* for 2 narrators, winds, 2 percussionists, tape (1967); *Cantos del pozo artesiano* for actress, 3 chamber ensembles, lights (1967, Salabert); *Aura* for string quartet (1968, Salabert); *Vitral* for organ, string orchestra (1968, Salabert); *Anábsis* for orchestra (1968–70); *Rosa-Rosae* for flute, clarinet, violin, cello (1969, Salabert); *Tea Party* for 4 vocal soloists, clarinet, trombone, cello, vibraphone (1969); *Mysteria* for chamber orchestra (1970); *Albor* for flute, clarinet, violin, cello, piano (1970).

PRINCIPAL WRITINGS: *Música de vanguardia española* (Madrid 1970).

SEE ALSO Spain.

Marescotti, André-François (b. Carouge, Switzerland, 30 April 1902), studied mathematics and technical subjects at the Technicum in Geneva and attended the Geneva Conservatory (1919–23, piano with Alexandre Mottu, organ with William Montillet, composition with Charles Chaix). He also studied privately with Jean Roger-Ducasse in Paris (1928–35). His various positions have all been in Geneva. In 1921 he became organist at the church of Compesières and was music director at Sacré-Coeur (1924–38). He began to teach composition and orchestration at the Geneva Conservatory in 1931 and succeeded Montillet as music director at St. Joseph's (1940–64). He has been active in many professional organizations and competitions.

PRINCIPAL COMPOSITIONS (published by Jobert unless otherwise noted): *6 Esquisses* for piano

(1922, Henn); *3 Noëls savoysiens* for chorus (1925–26, Henn); *3 Chants savoysiens* for chorus (1926, Henn); *3 Suites* for piano (1928, 1932, 1944); *Ouverture pour la comédie de celui qui épousa une femme muette* for orchestra (1930); *Prélude au Grand Meaulnes* for orchestra (1934); *Aubade*, symphonic poem (1936); *Où l'Etoile s'arêta*, theater music for chorus, orchestra (1938, Foetisch); *Fantasque* for piano (1939); *Croquis* for piano (1940); *Mouvement* for harp (1941); *3 Concerts carougeois* for orchestra (1941, 1958, 1964); *Reveillez-vous donc, pastoureaux* for 2 solo voices, chorus, orchestra or 1–3 solo voices, piano or organ (1944, Foetisch); *Vergers* for voice, piano (1945–46); *La Lampe d'Argiel*, oratorio for soloists, chorus, orchestra (1947, Henn); *Giboulées*, fantasy for bassoon, piano or chamber orchestra (1949); *Insomnies* for voice, orchestra or piano (1950–51); *3 Poèmes majeurs* for soprano, women's chorus, optional children's voices (1954, SOFIRAD); *Piano Concerto* (1956); *Hymnes* for orchestra (1963). List to 1963: Antoine Goléa, *A.-F. M.* (Paris, Jobert, 1963): 13–17.

PRINCIPAL WRITINGS: *Les Instruments d'orchestre* (Paris 1948–49); "Attitude du compositeur face aux tendances de la musique contemporaine," *Revue de théologie et de philosophie* (June 1960): 57–62.

SEE ALSO Switzerland.

Maric, Ljubica (b. Kragujevac, Yugoslavia, 18 March 1909), studied at the Belgrade Music School (1929–31) and the Prague Conservatory (1931–35, composition with Josef Suk, quarter-tone music with Alois Hába). During 1936–39 she taught at the Stanković Music School in Belgrade and during 1945–66, at the Belgrade Music Academy.

PRINCIPAL COMPOSITIONS: *String Quartet* (1940); *Wind Quintet* (1950); *Music for Orchestra* (1951); *Violin Sonata* (1953); *Pesme prostora* [Songs of Space], cantata for chorus, orchestra; texts from medieval Bogumili gravestones (1956); *Passacaglia* for orchestra (1958); *Muzika Oktoiha Nos. 1–3* [Oktoih Music, referring to a type of medieval Serbian folk singing] for orchestra (1958, 1959, 1962); *Byzantine Concerto* for piano, orchestra (1959); *Prag sna* [Threshold of Dreams], cantata for soprano, alto, chamber orchestra; surrealist poems by Marko Ristić (1961); *Ostinato super tema Oktoiha* [Ostinato on an Oktoih Theme] for chamber orchestra (1961); *Slovo svetlosti* [Sound of Light] for 6 narrators, chorus, orchestra; medieval Serbian poetry (1965).

PRINCIPAL WRITINGS: "Monotematićnost i monolitnost oblika fuge" [Monothematic and Monolithic Forms of the Fugue], *Spomenica akademije nauka i umetnosti* 26:147–51.

Marie, Jean-Etienne (b. Pont l'Evêque, France, 17 Nov 1917), studied at L'Ecole Superieure de Commerce in Rouen (1934–37), the Conservatory of Music in Caen (1938), the Univ. of Grenoble (1941–45, theology), and at the Paris Conservatory (1946–50, composition with Messiaen, Milhaud). During 1940–41 he was secretary of the Chamber of Commerce in Paris. Since 1949 he has been music director for French Radio and Television. In 1953 he traveled in Europe, Mexico, and the Near East as an envoy for the French Foreign Ministry. During 1960–70 he taught at the Schola Cantorum, and during 1961–70 he was a writer for *La Cinéma pratique*. In 1968 he founded the Centre International de Recherches Musicales. He has worked with combinations of live instruments and prerecorded electronic sounds, with microintervals, and with combinations of audio and visual effects. He has also used serial and, later, mathematically derived techniques of composition.

PRINCIPAL COMPOSITIONS: *Poems* for speaker, piano; texts by Eluard (1950); *Pieces for the Third Sunday in Lent* for chorus (1951, EFM); music for a film about the painter F. Desnos (1956); *Poesies* for chorus; texts by Shéhade (1957, EFM); *Polygraphie polyphonique No. 1* for violin in quarter tones, tape, film (1957); *Pentathle monogénique* for piano (1959); *Muerte del toro* on tape, music for a film by Mittanou (1961); *Images thanaïques* for orchestra, 2-track tape (1961, EFM); *Polygraphie No. 2* for 11 instruments, tape (1962, EFM); *Experience ambigüe* for 10 instruments, tape (1963, EFM); *Obediens usque ad mortem* for strings, winds, percussion (1966, Jobert); *Tombeau de Julian Carrillo* for 2 pianos, 2-track tape (1966, Jobert); *Appel au tiers monde*, ballet for speaker, tape; text by Cesaire (1968, Jobert); *Tlaloc* for orchestra, 3 2-track tapes (1968, Jobert); *Mimodrame 68* for singer, speaker, trumpet, trombone, percussion, dancer (1969); *Concerto milieu divin* for orchestra in 2 sections, harps tuned in 1/16 tones, 5 tapes (1969, CIRM).

PRINCIPAL WRITINGS: *Musique vivante* (Paris 1953); "Pour ou contre la musique à la télévision," *Cahiers de Radio Télévision* 14 (1959) and *Rundfunk und Fernsehen* (Hamburg) 3/4:247, 267; "Musique électronique," *Histoire de musique* (*Encyclopédie de la Pléiade*, Paris 1963):1418–67; "Situation de la musique en France," *Combats* (9–30 May 1967); "Resurgence du Pythagorisme," *Encyclopédie de musique religieuse* (Paris 1968); "Rêver la musique d'aujourd'hui," *Heterofonia* (Mexico City) 1–3; "Expériences d'électroacoustique musicale," *Revue musicale* 265.

BIBL.: "Musique experimentales," *Fontes artis musicae* (1965):214–22; B. Gavoty and D. Lesur, "Pour ou contre la musique moderne," *Nouvel observateur* (14 Feb 1967):195–201.

Mariétan, Pierre (b. Monthey, Switzerland, 23 Sept 1935), studied at the Geneva Conservatory (1959–60), the Basel Academy of

Music (1961–63, composition with Pierre Boulez and Karlheinz Stockhausen), the Cologne Hochschule für Musik (1960–62, composition with Bernd Alois Zimmermann, electronic music with Gottfried Michael Koenig), the Darmstadt summer courses (1960–61), and the Cologne Courses for New Music (1963–66, composition with Stockhausen and Henri Pousseur). Since 1961 he has concertized as a conductor. In 1966 he helped found and has since directed the Group d'Etude et de Réalisation Musicales, a Paris organization that sponsors new-music activities, including performances. In 1967 he helped organize audio-visual work teams for the Paris Biennial. He has taught composition seminars at Dartington, England (1967), and Sion, Switzerland (1968–70). At the suggestion of Stockhausen and Frederic Rzewski, he began in 1963 to explore some approaches of the U.S. avant-garde, especially as realized in music by John Cage, Earle Brown, Christian Wolff, Morton Feldman, and La Monte Young.

PRINCIPAL COMPOSITIONS: *Musiques* for various combinations of strings (1961–); *Récit suivi de légende* for soprano, flute, English horn, clarinet, horn, viola, harp, piano (1963–66, Jobert); *Caractères* for flute, viola, double bass (1963–); *Tempéraments* for orchestra (1964–65, revised 1969); *Circulaire* for 1–3 pianos, 1–12 hands (1966); *Forte-piano* for wind instrument, piano, electronic equipment (1966–68); *Marques* for cello, piano (1966); *Parts et ensembles* for flute, viola, double bass; clarinet, bassoon; piano, 3 percussionists (1967); *Initiales of Marsyas* for soprano, flute, saxophone, viola, trombone, cello, harp, piano (1967); *Systèmes* for piano(s) (1968); *Initiatives Nos. 1–2*, a plan of action for several instruments (1968); *Remémoration d'un ami commun* for violin, piano, tape (1969); *Scène* for woman's voice, conductor, winds, violin, cello, harp, piano, 2 percussion (1970); *MF/MP* for 4, 8, or 16 instruments, radio receiver (1970).

PRINCIPAL WRITINGS: "Kölner Kurse für neue Musik," *Revue musicale suisse* (Sept 1966); "Musique et architecture," *ibid.* (Nov 1966); "Etude pour un département de la musique dans la Maison de la Culture," *ibid.* (May 1968); "Milieu et environnement," *La Musique dans la vie* (OCORA-ORTF, Paris) 2 (Dec 1968).

SEE ALSO Switzerland.

Markowski, Andrzej (Jerzy) (b. Lublin, Poland, 22 August 1924), studied piano in Warsaw during 1938–44 and during 1946–55 attended the Trinity College of Music in London (composition with Alec Rowley) and the Warsaw Conservatory (composition with A. Malawski and P. Rytel, conducting with T. Wilczak and W. Rowicki). He participated in the Darmstadt summer courses in 1957 and 1958. He has been conductor of the Cracow Philharmonic (1959–64) and the Wroclaw Philharmonic (1965–68) and since 1968 has been assistant music director of the Warsaw National Philharmonic. In each positon he has introduced many contemporary works to Polish audiences. He has composed electronic and concrete music for over 15 films at the Warsaw Experimental Studio (his 1957 film score below was the first example of electronic music in Poland).

PRINCIPAL COMPOSITIONS: *Historia jednego myśliwca* [The Story of a Fighter Plane], film score for orchestra, electronic sounds (1957); *Życie jest piękne* [Life is Grand], film score for instruments, electronic sounds (1958); *Spacerek staromiejsui* [Promenade Through Old Town], film score for electronic and concrete sounds (1958); *Milcząca gwiazda* [Planet of Death], film score for orchestra, tape (1959–60); *Materia,* concrete film score based on recordings of 14 voices (1961); *Diabły* [The Devils], concrete film score based on the sounds of motors (1962); *Fantasmoskop*, ballet music for the film by K. Urbański for chamber orchestra, electronic sounds (1963–64); *Sonata Belzebuba,* film score (1967).

PRINCIPAL WRITINGS: *Paradoxes—Aphorisms—Apostrophes*, published in part in *Życie Warszawy* (April 1971).

Maros, Rudolf (b. Stachy, Czechoslovakia, 19 Jan 1917), studied composition with Kodály at the Academy of Music in Budapest (1939–42) and with Alois Hába in Prague (summer 1949). He began teaching orchestration and chamber music for winds at the Academy in 1949; he also teaches composition there. Since 1959 he has attended several summer courses at Darmstadt, and in 1971 he worked in West Berlin on a fellowship.

Maros has written instrumental music almost exclusively: many symphonic and chamber works, theater and film scores, three ballets, and some solo instrumental pieces. There are a few pieces for chorus and orchestra. At the beginning of his career he was strongly influenced by Kodály and composed in a folkloristic style. Even then, however, two characteristics emerged that were to become significant later: a sensitivity to timbre, and a high regard for purely musical (nonprogrammatic) relationships. These traits are especially evident in the works written since 1959. In that year he composed his first 12-tone pieces, including the *Ricercare*. Later he moved away from this constraint and began to build his compositions from the manipulation of small motivic units. The melodic and harmonic material in one movement of *5 Studii* (1960) is derived from the interval of a fourth enclosed within a fifth (C♯–F♯ within C–G); in another section of the piece the minor seconds in this configuration are emphasized. Works since the mid-60s have relied heavily on color, especially on the opposition and mixture of orchestral tone colors. The *Eufonias 1–3* (1963–65) employ shifting clusters in which all 12 tones of the chromatic scale sound simultaneously with their octave placement, spacing, and timbre changing. In such works as these, rhythm is fluid, dispensing with the periodic pulsations of the pre-Darmstadt music; the element of melody is almost nonexistent. More recent works, e.g., *Gamma* (1968), *Monumentum* (1969), and *Consort* (1970), combine rhythmic and melodic elements with shifts in timbre. Maros is attracted to mirror forms. The halves of a movement may contain a note-for-note mirroring of material, and in multimovement works the number of movements is often five, with the first and fifth and second and fourth corresponding in general character or mood.

PRINCIPAL COMPOSITIONS (published by EMB unless otherwise noted): *Musica leggiera* for wind quintet (1956); *Symphony for Strings* (1956, Mills and EMB); *Ricercare* for orchestra (1959); *5 Studii* for orchestra (1960); *6 Bagatelles* for organ (1961, Boosey and EMB); *Musica da ballo* for orchestra (1962); *Eufonias 1–3* (1963, 1964, 1965; Southern); *Musica da camera* for 11 players (1966, Southern); *Trio* for harp, violin, viola (1967, Southern); *Gamma* for orchestra (1968, Southern); *Monumentum* for orchestra (1969, Southern); *Consort* for wind quintet (1970, Southern); *Reflections*, ballet (1970, unpub.). Complete list to 1966: Péter Várnai, *M. R.* (Budapest 1967).

Péter Várnai
(trans. from Hungarian by Egon Kenton)
SEE ALSO Hungary.

Martín, Edgardo (b. Cienfuegos, Cuba, 6 Oct 1915), studied piano privately in Cienfuegos with Aurea Suárez (1925–35) and in Havana with Jascha Fischermann (1936–37), and composition with José Ardévol at the Havana Conservatory (1939–46). He also attended the Univ. of Havana (1937–41), where he sang in the Coral de la Habana under María Muñoz de Quevedo. He taught music history and esthetics at the Havana Conservatory, later called the Amadeo Roldán Conservatory (1945–68), at the National School of Arts (1968–69), and at the Univ. summer courses (1945–70). He was a music critic and contributor to the newspapers *Información* (1943–60), *Prensa Latina* (1960–63), and *Granma* (1966–67), and has been program annotator for a number of Cuban musical societies. While still at the university he became a member of the Grupo de Renovación Musical (1940–48) and later of the progressive artists society Nuestro Tiempo (1950–59). He collaborated with the 26th of July Revolutionary Movement, led by Fidel Castro, during 1953–59 and took part in the guerrilla fighting against Batista's troops. Under the Revolutionary Government he has served on a number of planning committees to reform music teaching in Cuba. In 1968 he founded the National Composers' Collective. Since 1967 he has received a monthly stipend to compose from the National Culture Council and since 1969, a stipend to write books on music. His music has been influenced by his acquaintance with Heitor Villa-Lobos, Aaron Copland, Paul Dessau, Camargo Guarnieri, Blas Galindo, and Luis de Pablo, among others.

PRINCIPAL COMPOSITIONS: *¡Ay, rostro y vista ... !* for 3-voice chorus; text by Petrarch (1942); *Variations* for harp (1944); *Concerto* for 9 winds (1944); *Fugues* for string orchestra (1947, PAU); *Concertante* for harp, chamber orchestra (1949); *6 Preludes* for piano (1949, Southern); *Los dos abuelos* for chorus, orchestra; text by Nicolás Guillén (1949); *2 Preludes* for piano (1950); *Soneras* for orchestra (1951, EGREM); *6 Villancicos cubanos* for chorus; texts by Dora Carvajal (1953); *4 Cantos de la Revolución* for high voice, piano; texts by Guillén and Pablo Armando Fernández (1962, EGREM); *Trío jagüense* for woodwinds (1963); *Variations* for guitar (1964, UNEAC); *7 Cantos del amor imposible* for high voice, piano; texts by the composer (1964, EGREM); *Así Guevara* for high voice, piano; text by Guillén (1967, EGREM); *Canto de héroes* for soprano, baritone, orchestra; text by Fernández (1967, EGREM); *String Quartets Nos. 1–2* (1967, UNEAC and EGREM; 1968, EGREM); *5 Cantos de Ho* for soprano, flute, viola, piano; texts by Ho Chi Minh (1969, EGREM); *Cuadros de Ismaelillo* for orchestra (1970, CNC). List to 1960: *Composers of the Americas* 7:65–67.

PRINCIPAL WRITINGS: "La música de cámara en Cuba, desde mediados del siglo XIX hasta nuestros días," *Pro-Arte Musical* (Havana, May 1954); "La influencia española en la música cubana," *Nuestro tiempo* (March 1958); "Penetración imperialista a través de la música," *Granma* (8 April 1967) and *El mundo* (Havana, 1 Oct 1967); *Panorama histórico de la música en Cuba* (Havana 1971); *Catálogo biográfico de compositores de Cuba* (Havana 1972?).

BIBL.: José Ardévol, "La creación musical en Cuba," *Unión* 1967/4: ——, *La música* (Havana 1969).

Martin, Frank (b. Geneva, 15 Sept 1890), began composing at age nine and on hearing Bach's *St. Matthew Passion* in 1902 resolved to be a composer. He studied privately with Joseph Lauber, then after 1911 was stimulated by Ernest Ansermet to explore various contemporary styles; however, he was mostly self-taught. After three years' military service he lived in Zurich (1918–20), where he published his earliest mature works. He visited Rome (1921–22) and Paris (1924–25) and returned to Geneva, where he studied eurhythmics and then taught at the Jaques-Dalcroze Institute (until 1938). He also directed the Technicum Moderne de Musique (1933–39). He moved to Amsterdam in 1946 to devote full time to composing but during 1950–57 commuted to Cologne as composition teacher at the Hochschule für Musik. Always a performer though never a virtuoso, he sang and played violin and piano at an early age and has continued to appear occasionally as a pianist or harpsichordist.

Martin has written for all media, large and small. There are many concerted works for various solo and ensemble combinations—notably the *Ballades* and the *Petite Symphonie concertante*—ten orchestral and ten chamber works, a few solo instrumental and vocal pieces, two operas, and five oratorios. In the oratorios he has most fully realized his Bach-inspired ideal. His music is not only idiomatic as Hindemith's or effective as Shostakovich's, but fresh and grateful as Ravel's (whom Martin acknowledges as an early model). Among his favorite rhythmic types are the march, chaconne, and gigue. Melodic rhythms, influenced by jazz, avoid any overreliance on the pulse of the accompaniment; typical melodies also avoid symmetry of phrases. Contrasts of rhythm and tempo mark the sections of his large forms; conventional formal patterns are seldom used. Martin's treatment of harmony is distinctive in that triads, conspicuously frequent, are related to each other less often by strong root progressions than through enharmonic double meanings. The triads both support and enrich melodies that use the whole chromatic scale. Sometimes a 12-tone melody suggests Schoenberg, whose technique Martin studied in the 1930s, but even these melodies, alongside quasimodal ones, fit into the distinctive harmony.

PRINCIPAL COMPOSITIONS (published by UE unless otherwise noted): *4 Sonnets à Cassandre* for mezzo-soprano, flute, viola, cello; poems by Ronsard (1921, Hug); *Mass* for double chorus (1922, Bärenreiter); *Trio on Irish Folksongs* for violin, cello, piano (1925, Hug); *Rythmes*, 3 symphonic movements (1926); *Violin Sonata* (1931); *La Nique à Satan* for choruses, baritone solo, winds, pianos, percussion, double bass (1931, Henn); *4 Short Pieces* for guitar (1933); *Piano Concerto [No. 1]* (1934); *Rhapsody* for 2 violins, 2 violas, double bass (1935, unpub.); *String Trio* (1936); *Symphony* (1937); *Ballade* for alto saxophone, strings, piano, percussion (1938); *Sonata da chiesa* for viola d'amore (flute), organ (strings) (1938); *Ballade* for flute (strings), piano (1939); *Ballade* for piano, orchestra (1939); *Ballade* for trombone, piano (orchestra) (1940); *Le Vin herbé*, oratorio after Joseph Bédier (1941); *Das Märchen vom Aschenbrödel*, ballet; scenario by Marie Eve Kreis (1941, Reiss); *Der Weise von Liebe und Tod des Cornets Christoph Rilke* for mezzo-soprano, small orchestra; text by R. M. Rilke (1943); *6 Monologe aus Jedermann* for baritone with piano (orchestra); text by Hofmannsthal (1943); *Passacaglia* for organ (strings or orchestra) (1944); *In terra pax*, oratorio for vocal soloists, 2 choruses, orchestra (1944); *Petite Symphonie concertante* for harp, harpsichord, piano, 2 string orchestras (1945); *8 Preludes* for piano (1948); *Golgotha*, oratorio for vocal soloists, chorus, orchestra, organ (1948); *Concerto for 7 winds*, strings, percussion (1949); *Ballade* for cello, piano (small orchestra) (1949); *4 Ariel Songs* for chorus; text by Shakespeare (1950); *Violin Concerto* (1951); *Concerto* for harpsichord, small orchestra (1952); *Der Sturm*, 3-act opera after Shakespeare's *The Tempest* (1955); *Etudes* for string orchestra (1956); *Ouverture en hommage à Mozart* (1956); *Ouverture en rondeau* (1958); *Psaumes* for choruses, orchestra, organ (1958); *Mystère de la Nativité* for at least 9 vocal soloists, 3 choruses, orchestra (1959); *3 Minnelieder* for soprano, piano; medieval German texts (1961); *Monsieur de Pourceaugnac*, opéra comique after Molière (1962); *Les Quatres Éléments*, symphonic etudes (1964); *Pilate*, cantata for vocal soloists, chorus, orchestra; text after Arnoul Gréban (1964); *Cello Concerto* (1966); *String Quartet* (1967); *Maria-Triptychon* for soprano, violin, orchestra (1968); *Erasmi monumentum* for orchestra, organ (1969); *Piano Concerto No. 2* (1969); *3 Danses* for oboe, harp, string orchestra (1970); *3 Poèmes de Villon* for 3 men's voices, 3 electric guitars (1971). Complete list to 1970 in Billeter (see bibl.).

PRINCIPAL WRITINGS: *The Composer's Point of View* ed. R. S. Hines (Norman, Okla., 1963): 196–205, 309–13; *Entretiens sur la musique* (Neuchâtel 1967); *The Orchestral Composer's Point of View* (Norman, Okla., 1970): 153–65. Extensive list: William Austin, *Music in the 20th Century* (New York 1966): 604.

BIBL.: Bernhard Billeter, *F. M. ein Aussenseiter der neuen Musik* (Frauenfeld 1970); Rudolf Klein,

F. M. sein Leben und Werk (Vienna 1960); ——, "F. M.s jüngste Werke," *Österreichische Musikzeitschrift* 20:483–86; Janet Eloise Tupper, *Stylistic Analysis of Selected Works by F. M.* (Ann Arbor, Univ. Microfilms, 1965).

William W. Austin

SEE ALSO Switzerland.

Martinet, Jean-Louis (b. Ste.-Bazeille, France, 8 Nov 1912), studied at the Paris Conservatory (1938–45, composition with Roger Ducasse, Olivier Messiaen; conducting with Louis Fourestier, Charles Munch, Roger Désormière; harmony, André Bloch; fugue, Charles Koechlin). In 1941 he was coached in Schoenberg's 12-tone theories by René Leibowitz. To further his study of the compositions of Schoenberg, Berg, and Webern, he spent three months in Vienna in 1949. Martinet has used 12-tone procedures sparingly, integrating them with a variety of more traditional techniques.

PRINCIPAL COMPOSITIONS: *Orphée*, symphonic poem (1944–45, Heugel); *Variations* for string quartet (1946, Heugel); *Prométhée*, symphonic fragments (1947, Heugel); *6 Songs* for chorus, orchestra; texts by René Char (1948, Heugel); *Episodes*, cantata for bass, chorus, orchestra (1949–50); *7 Poems by René Char* for vocal quartet, orchestra (1951–52, Heugel); *2 Images* for orchestra (1953–54, Schott); *Divertissement pastoral* for piano, orchestra (1955, EFM); *Mouvement symphonique* for string orchestra (1957, EFM); *Luttes* for orchestra (1958–59, EFM); *Les Douze*, cantata for speaker, chorus, orchestra; text by Alexandre Blok (1961, EFM); *Symphony*, "In memoriam" (1962–63).

PRINCIPAL WRITINGS: "Quelques Reflexions sur la musique," *L'Age nouveau* (May 1955).

SEE ALSO France.

Martino, Donald (James) (b. Plainfield, N. J., 16 May 1931), began music lessons at nine and started composing at 15. He attended Syracuse Univ. and Princeton Univ. and was a Fulbright scholar in Italy during 1954–56. His composition teachers have included Ernst Bacon, Milton Babbitt, Roger Sessions, and Luigi Dallapiccola. He has taught theory at the Third Street Settlement School in New York (1956–57), at Princeton (1957–59), and at Yale (1959–69), and composition at the Yale Summer School of Music and Art (1960–62), Tanglewood (1965–67, 1969), and the New England Conservatory, where he is chairman of the composition department.

Martino's music is characterized by its technical and intellectual rigor and by a flair for instrumental virtuosity (the composer is an excellent clarinetist). Both of these traits are always at the service of a traditional, virtually neoromantic expressivity that reveals itself in a dense polyphony that supports long, unbroken melodic lines, usually articulated by much use of tempo rubato. The early works (e.g., *Set for Clarinet*, 1954) tend to be more virtuoso and dramatic than the later ones, and they sometimes recall the rhythmic writing and short phrase structure of some of Bartók's fast movements (e.g., the opening of the *String Quartet No. 5*). Unlike most composers who have been associated with Princeton Univ., Martino turned to serial writing only after he had left the school. His early works (e.g., *Piano Fantasy*, 1958; *Trio*, 1959) lack dramatic elements and instead have a transparent and concentrated lyricism. The *Trio*, for instance, avoids all drastic changes of tempo, dynamics, or even texture, relying heavily on the interplay of short and graceful motives and on contrapuntal balances among the three instruments. Because they depend mostly on such small detail work and because of their extreme technical rigor, these are his most difficult works, both for the performer and the listener. They contain no obvious gestures or signposts, such as clearly defined foreground, thematic changes, or wide changes in texture, tempo, or dynamics. The return of dramatic and virtuoso elements is evident in the *Lieder* (1962), *Fantasy Variations* (1962), and *Piano Concerto* (1965). They contain dense polyphonic textures, the result of articulating long spans of time while maintaining a miniaturist's control of detail. Works of the late 1960s show a new balance and greater flexibility. In *Mosaic*, for example, the motivic work, constantly changing and inventive, never obscures the larger phrases, articulated by changes of sonority. The larger sections are more easily perceived on first hearing, and in subsequent ones more and more of the intricate detail can be grasped.

PRINCIPAL COMPOSITIONS (published by Ione unless otherwise noted): *A Set for Clarinet* (1954, McG-M); *Quodlibets for Flute* (1954, McG-M); *anyone lived in a pretty how town* for chorus, piano 4-hands (1955); *3 Songs* for voice, piano; poems by James Joyce (1956); *Portraits* for chorus, soloists, orchestra (1956); *7 Canoni Enigmatici* for any combinations of string quartet, clarinet quartet, or 2 violas and 2 cellos (1956); *Contemplations for Orchestra* (1957); *Quartet* for clarinet, strings (1957); *Piano Fantasy* (1958); *Trio* for violin, clarinet, piano (1959); *2 Lieder* for voice, piano; poems by Rilke (1962); *5 Frammenti* for oboe, double bass (1962); *Concerto for Wind Quintet*

(1964); *Parisonatina al' dodecafonia* for cello (1964); *Piano Concerto* (1965); *B, a, b, b, it, t* for clarinet (1966); *Strata* for bass clarinet (1966); *Mosaic for Grand Orchestra* (1967); *Pianississimo (A Sonata for the Piano)* (1970).

PRINCIPAL WRITINGS: "The Source Set and its Aggregate Formations," *Journal of Music Theory* 5; "Claudio Spies: Tempi," *Perspectives* 2/2: 112–24; "Notation in General—Articulation in Particular," *Perspectives* 4/2:47–58.

BIBL.: Henry Weinberg, "D. M.: Trio," *Perspectives* 2/1:82–90.

Alejandro Enrique Planchart
SEE ALSO Instrumental and Vocal Resources, Mathematics.

Martinon, Jean (Franisque-Etienne) (b. Lyons, 10 Jan 1910), studied at the Lyons Conservatory (1923–26, violin with Maurice Faudray) and the Paris Conservatory (1926–29; composition with Albert Roussel, Max d'Ollones, Vincent d'Indy; harmony with Jacques de la Presle; violin with Jules Boucherit; conducting with Roger Désormières, Charles Munch). He has concertized as a violinist and held many conducting posts, including assistant to Munch at the Société des Concerts in Paris (1944–46), president of the Concerts Lamoureux (1950–57), music director of the Chicago Symphony (1963–68), and music director of l'Orchestre National de l'O.R.T.F. (since 1968).

PRINCIPAL COMPOSITIONS: *Symphoniette* for string orchestra, piano, harp, percussion (1936, Salabert); *Domenon* for wind quintet (1938); *Psaume 136*, "Chant des captifs," for narrator, chorus, orchestra (1940–43, Billaudot); *Symphonies Nos. 2–4*: No. 2, "Hymne à la vie" (1942–44, Bärenreiter); No. 3, "Irlandaise" (1948, Choudens); No. 4, "Altitudes" (1965, Presser); *String Trio* (1943, Billaudot); *Concerto lyrique* for string quartet, chamber orchestra (1944, Schott); *String Quartets Nos. 1–2* (1946; 1966, Presser); *Hécube*, 2-act opera; libretto by Serge Moreux after Euripides (1949, EFM); *Le Lis de saron*, oratorio for vocal soloists, chorus, orchestra (1952, IMP); *Duo*, "Musique en forme de sonate" for violin, piano (1953, Schott); *Symphonie de voyages* for chamber orchestra (1956, Impero); *Violin Concerto No. 2* (1958, Schott); *Cello Concerto* (1963, Schott); *Hymn, Variations, and Rondo* for orchestra (1968, EFM). List to 1969: *Le Courrier musical de France* 26 (1969):141–43.

BIBL.: Jerzy Kosmala, *J. M.'s 'Concerto giocoso' for Violin and Orchestra, and Its Adaptation for the Viola* (thesis, Univ. of Ind., 1969).

Martinů, Bohuslav (Jan) (b. Polička, Czechoslovakia, 8 Dec 1890; d. Liestal, Switzerland, 29 August 1959), was the son of a cobbler and began violin lessons with a local tailor at six, his musical leanings being already apparent. Sometime between his tenth and twelfth years he began to compose; his first work was a string quartet. He entered Prague Conservatory in 1906, where he proved an unsatisfactory student and was expelled in 1910 for "incorrigible negligence" (he took more interest in the artistic life of Prague and in his own creative activities than in his counterpoint lessons). A year later he attempted the examination for state teaching certification, but he failed every subject and was pronounced unfit for a teaching career by Vitězslav Novák, one of the most influential Czech composers of the time. Even so Martinů took the exam again the following year, and this time he passed; until 1916, however, he could not find a teaching post. At that time he began work back in Polička. For the next four years he divided his time between his home town and Prague, playing second violin at times with the Czech Philharmonic Orchestra. In 1920 he became a full-time member of this orchestra, remaining with it for three years, during which he learned far more than any educational institution had been able to teach him. He owed much to Vaclav Talich, who was the orchestra's principal conductor. One of the works directed by Talich was Roussel's *Le Poème de la forêt*, which made such an impression on Martinů that he left Prague in 1923 to become Roussel's pupil in Paris. That same year Talich first conducted a short piece by Martinů in Prague, and thereafter few of his works had long to wait for a performance. Another champion of his music was Serge Koussevitzky, who gave *La Bagarre* in Boston in 1927 and *La Rhapsodie* the following year.

For 17 years Martinů lived frugally in Paris, devoting himself entirely to composition but returning home for a holiday each year. In the spring of 1941 he arrived in the U.S., having left most of his possessions behind. At the end of the war he hoped to return to Czechoslovakia to take up a position at the Prague Conservatory or some other important institution, but as no such post materialized, he never returned. He did, however, return to Europe in 1953 to spend the rest of his life mainly in France and Switzerland.

Martinů and Roussel were very much kindred spirits, especially in their classical outlook. Martinů found traditional forms well suited to his needs when writing instrumental music, and he was particularly drawn towards the concerto grosso. His huge output numbers about 385 compositions covering every category from opera to small piano pieces and including much chamber music for unusual instrumental combinations. As with Roussel's music, much of Martinů's is notable for its rhythmic energy (see the *Concerto* for double string orchestra, piano, and timpani, 1938). Although basically a diatonic composer, his harmonic range was wide. He could use simple progressions or bitingly dissonant ones equally effectively. Similarly, he was as much at home when writing in two parts, as in his *Madrigals* for violin and viola, as when producing complex polyphonic structures. Sometimes the latter defeat their own ends by bringing about thick and opaque textures, just as certain compositions for orchestra suffer from over-orchestration. Despite French influences and the relatively small effect of folk music on his works, Martinů always remained a thoroughly Czech composer and continued to set Czech texts and to produce works for home consumption throughout his long years of exile.

PRINCIPAL COMPOSITIONS: *Špaliček* [The Chap Book], 3-act ballet (1932, Orbis); *Sinfonia concertante* for 2 orchestras (1932, Schott); *Quintet No. 1* for strings, piano (1933, La Sirène Musicale, Paris); *Piano Concerto No. 2* (1934, Panton; revised 1944, Boosey); *Julietta,* 3-act opera after the play by Georges Neveux; libretto by the composer (1937, Boosey); *String Quartet No. 5* (1938, Supraphon); *Concerto Grosso* for orchestra (1938, UE); *3 Ricercari* for chamber orchestra (1938, Boosey); *Concertino* for piano, orchestra (1938, Panton); *Double Concerto* for 2 string orchestras, piano, timpani (1938, Boosey); *Cello Sonatas Nos. 1–2* (1939, Heugel; 1941, AMP); *Symphonies Nos. 1–5* (1942, 1943, 1944, 1945, 1946; all Boosey); *Concerto* for 2 pianos, orchestra (1943, AMP); *Quintet No. 2* for piano, strings (1944, AMP); *String Quartet No. 6* (1946, Supraphon); *Fantasies symphoniques,* symphony No. 6 (1953, Boosey); *Incantations* for piano, orchestra (1955–56, Bärenreiter); *Parables* for orchestra (1957–58, Bärenreiter); *Prophecy of Isaiah* for vocal soloists, male chorus, viola, trumpet, piano, timpani (1959, IMP). Complete list in Šafránek 1962.

BIBL.: Miloš Šafránek, *B. M.* (London 1946); —— *B. M.* (Prague 1962).

Malcolm Rayment
SEE ALSO Czechoslovakia, Dance.

Martirano, Salvatore (b. Yonkers, N.Y., 12 Jan 1927), studied at the Oberlin Conservatory (1947–51, composition with Herbert Elwell), the Eastman School (1952, Bernard Rogers), and the Cherubini Conservatory in Florence (1952–54, Luigi Dallapiccola). Prior to Oberlin he served in the U.S. Marine Corps as bandsman, and during 1946–47 he toured with dance bands, including those of Johnny Bothwell and Shorty Sherock. Since 1963 he has taught at the Univ. of Ill.

Martirano's works avoid duplications of medium. Student compositions aside, there is only one example each of a piece for orchestra, for a cappella chorus, for chorus and instruments, for piano, and for piano and voice; other pieces employ nonstandard chamber ensembles with and without pre-recorded tapes. Martirano also avoids redundance and reiteration within a work; lately he has eschewed the "writing" of music in favor of free-flowing spontaneities emanating from a computer-generated, real-time, electronic sound source. Among the structural principles Martirano has used are contrapuntal techniques associated with the Viennese dodecaphonists. The *Mass,* his first significant work, is an example; it also shows an affinity for the full, rich sound of the Palestrina choral style. *O O O O That Shakespeherian Rag* applies combinatorial techniques to a finite series of chords. The *Rag* is also interesting as an example of Martirano's occasional juxtaposition of popular and concert styles; here a jazz-like ensemble is used along with a chorus. The *Ballad* juxtaposes several popular songs (sung by an "amplified night club singer") with music for an instrumental ensemble in which pitches and registers are serially organized into a sound fabric that is almost a parody of serial music. The dramatic values in juxtapositions have been further explored in theater pieces written since the mid-1960s. A prerecorded tape in *Underworld* provides a background of serial music (mostly hexachord permutations) for nonserialized sounds and actions by live performers, including actors. Contemporary technological resources such as films, projections, television, electronic sound devices, and inflatable plastic objects were added to traditional performing resources for *L'sGA* and *Election Night Diversion.* The former uses helium gas, inhaled by an actor, to change the sounds of a normal voice into a thin, high-pitched parody of speech. This effect is combined with films of war and near-deafening prerecorded sounds (the time relationships of which are based on the Fibonacci series). Within this sound and visual setting, the text, one of the monuments of American political literature, seems like empty rhetoric.

PRINCIPAL COMPOSITIONS: *Sextet* for winds (1949); *Prelude* for orchestra (1950); *Variations* for flute, piano (1950); *String Quartet No. 1* (1951); *The Magic Stones,* chamber opera based on a tale from the Decameron (1951); *Violin Sonata* (1952); *A Cappella Mass* for chorus (1952–53, Schott);

Contrasts for orchestra (1954, Schott); *Chansons innocentes* for soprano, piano; poems by e. e. cummings (1957, Schott); *O O O O That Shakespeherian Rag* for chorus, instruments (1958, Schott); *Cocktail Music* for piano (1962, MCA); *Octet* for flute, clarinets, marimba, celesta, violin, cello, double bass (1963, MCA); *3 Electronic Dances* on tape (1963); *Underworld* for 4 actors, 4 percussionists, 2 double basses, tenor saxophone, 2-channel tape (1964–65, MCA); *Buffet* on tape (1965, MCA); *Ballad* for amplified night-club singer, instrumental ensemble (1966, MCA); *L'sGA* for gas-masked politico, helium bomb, 3 16mm movie projectors, 2-channel tape; text: the Gettysburg Address of Abraham Lincoln (1967–68, MCA); *The Proposal* for 2-channel tape, slides (1968, MCA); *Election Night Diversion,* an evening's entertainment created in collaboration with Edwin London (1968).

Edwin London

SEE ALSO Instrumental and Vocal Resources, Mixed Media.

Marttinen, Tauno (b. Helsinki, 27 Sept 1912), studied piano, conducting, and composition at the Viipuri Institute of Music and the Sibelius Academy. He is director of the Hameenlinna Institute of Music.

PRINCIPAL COMPOSITIONS: *Kokko, ilman lintu* [Eagle, Bird of the Air] for mezzo-soprano, orchestra; text from the Kalevala (1956); *Symphonies Nos. 1–4* (1958, 1959, 1963, 1964); *Linnunrata* [The Milky Way], variations for orchestra (1960); *Suite* for orchestra (1961); *Violin Concerto* (1962); *Rembrandt,* fantasy for cello, orchestra (1962); *Päällysviitta* [The Cloak], opera after Gogol (1962); *Gabbata* for tenor, baritone, narrator, 2 choruses, string orchestra; Biblical text (1962); *Pidot* [The Feast], song cycle for soprano (or tenor), orchestra (or piano) (1962, Westerlund); *Neljä yhteiskuntasatiiria* [4 Social Satires] for speaking chorus (1962–64); *Loitsu* [Incantation] for percussion trio (1963); *Piano Concerto* (1964); *Kihlaus* [The Engagement], opera; libretto by Aleksis Kivi (1964); 3 cantatas based on the Kalevala: *Lemminkäinen äiti Tuonelan joella* [Lemminkäinen's Mother at the River of Tuonela] for voice, orchestra (1964); *Lemminkäinen lähtö Pohjolaan* [Lemminkäinen Leaves for Pohjola] for mezzo-soprano, alto, baritone, bass (1965); *Lemminkäinen Pohjolassa* [Lemminkäinen in Pohjola] for alto, baritone, bass, chorus, orchestra (1965); *Fauni,* fantasy for orchestra (1965); *Apotti ja ikäneito* [The Abbot and the Old Maid], opera after Balzac (1965); *Hymy tikkaiden juurella* [Smile at the Foot of the Ladder], ballet after Henry Miller (1965); *Maailman luominen* [Creation of the World], symphonic poem (1966); *Cello Concerto,* "Dalai Lama" (1966); *Sammon synty* [Birth of Sampo] for men's chorus; text from the Kalevala (1966); *Kuoleman unia* [Dreams of Death],

song cycle for 2 solo voices, piano; text by Pirkko Jaakola (1966); *Mont St. Michel* for orchestra (1968); *Dorian Grayn muotokuva,* ballet (1969).

Marx, Karl (Julius) (b. Munich, 12 Nov 1897), attended the Hochschule für Musik in Munich (1920–24, composition with Anton Beer-Walbrunn, conducting with Siegmund von Hausegger, choral conducting with Eberhard Schwickerath) and studied composition and conducting privately with Carl Orff in 1920. He taught at the Munich Hochschule during 1924–39 and at the Hochschule für Musikerziehung in Graz, 1939–45. He conducted the Munich Bachvereins chorus (1928–39) and the madrigal choir of the Steinschen Musikschulwerks in Graz(1940–44). He was professor of composition at the Stuttgart Hochschule für Musik from 1946 to 1966 and headed its department of Schulmusik during 1955–63.

PRINCIPAL COMPOSITIONS (published by Bärenreiter unless otherwise noted): *Werkleute sind wir,* motet for chorus, Op. 6; poem by Rilke (1926–27, Breitkopf); *Violin Concerto in C,* Op. 24 (1935, Breitkopf); *18 Variations on an Old English Folksong* for 2 treble recorders, oboe, violin, viola, cello, Op. 30 (1937); *Rilke Cantata* for soprano, baritone, chorus, orchestra, Op. 43 (1920, 1942); *Und endet doch Alles mit Frieden* for 4 solo voices, chorus, orchestra, Op. 52 (1946–52); *Kammermusik* for flute, oboe, viola da gamba, harpsichord, violin, viola, cello, Op. 56 (1955); *Fantasia sinfonica,* Op. 67 (1967, revised 1969; unpub.).

PRINCIPAL WRITINGS: "Einführung in Béla Bartók, Musik für Saiteninstrumente, Schlagzeug u. Celesta," *Musikerziehung in der Schule* (Mainz 1956):216–32; "Über die zyklische Sonatenform," *Neue Zeitschrift für Musik* (1964):142–46; *Analyse der Klaviersonate B-dur KV 333 von W. A. Mozart* (Stuttgart 1966).

BIBL.: Erhard Karkoschka, ed., *Festschrift K. M.,* essays and analyses by former students together with a catalog of compositions, writings, discography (Stuttgart 1967).

Masson, Gérard (Marcel) (b. Paris, 12 Aug 1936), is largely self-taught in music. He studied composition with Karlheinz Stockhausen, Earle Brown, and Henri Pousseur at the Reinische Musikschule, Cologne (1965–66). The principal influences on his development have come from Wagner, Debussy, Varèse, and, among living composers, Stockhausen. Masson lives in Paris.

PRINCIPAL COMPOSITIONS (published by Salabert): *Pièces* for 14 instruments (1965); *Dans le deuil des vagues,* I and II, for orchestra (1966, 1968); *Ouest I* for 10 instruments and *Ouest II* for mezzo-soprano, 13 instruments; poems by Dominique Fourcade (1967, 1969).

PRINCIPAL WRITINGS: "Karlheinz Stockhausen," *Journal du Théâtre de la Ville* 3–4:43–44.

Mastrogiovanni, Antonio (b. Montevideo, Uruguay, 27 August 1936), studied at the National Conservatory in Montevideo (1963–68) and at the Torcuata Di Tella Institute in Buenos Aires (1969–70, analysis with Gerardo Gandini, composition with Francisco Kröpfl, electronic music with Fernando von Reichenbach). He also studied composition privately in Montevideo with Héctor Tosar. He has been technical director of the National Conservatory's music-publishing project since 1963.

PRINCIPAL COMPOSITIONS: *Contraritmos* for 2 string orchestras, percussion (1967); *Reflejos* for viola, cello, double bass, piano, celesta, harpsichord, harp (1969); *Secuencial I* for orchestra (1970); *Secuencial II* on tape (1970).

BIBL.: *Compositores Uruguayos* (Montevideo 1969); Susana Salgado, *Breve historia de la música culta en el Uruguay* (Montevideo 1971).

Mata, Eduardo (b. Mexico City, 5 Sept 1942), studied at the National Conservatory of Music in Mexico (1954–61, composition with Carlos Chávez, Julián Orbón; analysis with Rodolfo Halffter; conducting seminars with Erich Leinsdorf, Max Rudolf, Gunther Schuller). He was conductor of the Guadalajara Symphony during 1965–66 and has since been head of the concert department of the University of Mexico and conductor of its professional orchestra. Since 1971 he has also been teaching conducting at the National Conservatory. His current musical language is a free mixture of polytonal, 12-tone, serial, and aleatory techniques in which timbre and other textural elements are a major concern.

PRINCIPAL COMPOSITIONS: *Trio to Vaughan Williams* for clarinet, snare drum, cello (1957); *Piano Sonata* (1960); *Improvisación* for clarinet, piano (1961); *Symphony No. 1*, "Classical" (1962); *Debora*, ballet suite (1963); *Symphony No. 2*, "Romantic" (1963); *Los huesos secos*, ballet on tape (1963); *Improvisaciónes No. 1* for string quartet, piano 4-hands (1964); *Aires* for mezzo-soprano, 2 flutes, oboe, bassoon, 2 violas, cello, double bass; based on a 16th-century theme (1964, EMM); *Improvisaciónes No. 2* for strings, 2 pianos (one played by a percussionist) (1965, EMM);

Improvisaciónes No. 3 for violin, piano (1965, Southern); *Cello Sonata* (1966, Southern); *Symphony No. 3* for wind orchestra, horn (1966–67, Peters).

SEE ALSO Mexico.

Mathematics. In the past, such "mathematical" terms as second ("Second Symphony"), fifth ("parallel fifth"), passing tone (involving the geometrical notion of betweenness), and many others were found useful in discourses on music. More recently the logic of some mathematical systems has also been applied to analysis and composition. Periodicals such as *Perspectives of New Music*, the *Journal of Music Theory*, and *Die Reihe* may seem to the uninitiated more like collections of scientific articles than musical essays. Such material, however, reflects the widening attitudes of many composers who think in terms that are often better conveyed by graphs and number symbols than by traditional musical notation. The mathematics involved runs the gamut from simple numbers to such topics as set theory, information theory, and probability theory. Although it is still true that only a few musicians have had rigorous mathematical training, these few have often used the tools of the science to produce insightful and productive results.

Several types of activity are involved: 1) Investigations of the nature of sound and of sound-producing electronic instruments and circuitry, the physiology of the human ear, and the psychology of perception, all of which make use of the various sciences that involve mathematics. 2) Analysis of existing music by means of mathematical techniques. These investigations may suggest new modes of composition. 3) Studies of the materials of music, especially pitches, in the context of logical systems. This may be undertaken without regard to compositional applications, but in fields such as 12-tone music, where the theorists have generally also been the composers, such investigations have often suggested new modes of composition. 4) Music composition in which mathematical techniques are immediately brought to bear.

The present discussion focuses on the compositional applications of mathematics. It should be remembered that any system used in composition will control some facets of the music and not others; no system is used to generate meaningful music completely automatically. The value of mathematics is that it can provide new points of view for the composer, make available to him new aspects of his art, and suggest the means of controlling them.

NUMBER SYSTEMS. Numbers, like geometric figures, can stimulate the imagination and have always held an attraction for many composers. (Number systems, however, are not usually an instance of true mathematics.) The present-day popularity of numbers derives to a large extent from the concept of parameters, in which musical sounds are thought of as the sum of several components. In the view of many European composers, such as Karlheinz Stockhausen, the basic parameters are pitch, duration, intensity, timbre, and position in space. Americans, such as Milton Babbitt, tend to be less interested in the spatial aspect of music and to divide timbre into two components, overtone spectrum and attack-decay envelope. (In both views, such aspects of sound as register, density of attacks, rhythm, meter, instrumentation, etc., are regarded as derived from the other parameters according to the needs of the immediate musical context.) Once music had been reduced to several elements, numbers suggest themselves as a useful means by which to control the parameters, perhaps independently of each other. Jean-Claude Eloy, for example, derived the rhythms in *Macles* (1967) from an initial, arbitrary set of numbers, which were subjected to involved arithmetic and permutational computations. The basic esthetic in such a case is that number sequences give rise to combinations of parameter values that might not occur to the composer intuitively.

Some number systems are less "arbitrary" than others in that they have logical and/or perceptual bases. For example, many composers have been attracted to the Fibonacci series: 1, 2, 3, 5, 8, 13, 21, etc. (each number being the sum of the previous two). This set of numbers has been used to control durations of notes, lengths of sections, pitch structures, or density of attack points in the music of such diverse composers as Ernst Krenek (*Fibonacci Mobile*, 1964), Stockhausen (*Klavierstück IX*, 1954–55, revised 1961), Luigi Nono (*Il canto sospeso*, 1956), and Cristóbal Halffter (*Fibonacciana*, 1969). The independent use of the Fibonacci series by different composers implies that it has interesting inherent musical properties. There are, in fact, three separate properties of the series that can be perceived musically: It is a summation series; it approximates a sequence of terms in the ratio 2:3; and it approximates a series of golden means (of three consecutive terms, the largest is to the middle as the middle is to the smallest, to within one unit). These three aspects of the series are made audible in different ways in the works mentioned. (In addition, the position of formal articulations in some compositions of Bartók have been shown to follow the proportions of the golden mean.)

SET AND GROUP THEORIES. A set, quite simply, is any collection of objects. Set theory studies what can be said in the abstract about such collections and about the relationships between sets. A group is a set that also includes an operation that relates members of the set to each other. Set and group theories have been used to study music by considering the 12 chromatic pitches as a set or by considering the various transformations of a 12-tone row as the elements of a group. Such composers as Milton Babbitt and David Lewin, for example, have extended the implications of Schoenberg's 12-tone method into a 12 pitch-class system (referring to the 12 pitches without reference to an octave register). They have assigned the numbers 0–11 to the pitch classes and have then been able to work within an abstract conceptual system. Such a precompositional procedure enables composers to free themselves, when they deem it useful, from the aural connotations of musical pitches and notation and to work with their materials in purely logical ways. One result of such objectification of 12-tone composition has been the formulation of a basic row transformation beyond the processes of transposition, inversion, and retrogression used by Schoenberg (and rotation used by Krenek), namely multiplication by 5 or 7. In this new transformation, each integer is multiplied by 5 or 7 to produce a new sequence; a multiple of 12 is then subtracted from each member of the new series so as to produce a new series within the number range 0–11. The potentials in this calculation were discovered by Herbert Eimert and further developed by J. K. Randall, Hubert S. Howe, and Godfrey Winham. It formed the basis of Winham's "composition with arrays," in which the 12-tone system governs the harmonic as well as the contrapuntal aspects of the music (it was so used in his *Composition for Orchestra*, 1961–62). Because the mathematical treatment of 12-tone sets is abstract, it can be applied to parameters other than pitch, as in Winham's *Composition*. And although mathematical thinking is not a prerequisite for totally serialized music, mathematical models for the basic relations and operations of pitch sets can apply to duration, types of attack, etc., or, with the aid of precise electronic apparatus, to dynamics.

The 12-tone system is only one of several theories of sets. The theorist Allen Forte and composer Donald Martino have described the make-up of sets of pitches both in terms of pitch classes and intervals. Naturally, different means of defining pitch sets give rise to different types of relationships between sets. Forte feels that any two sets with the same total interval content can be considered equivalent. This means that some sets must be considered equivalent even though they are not related by transposition or inversion. There have also been other theories based on sets of tones. They have dealt with types of transformation of one set into another, different definitions of inclusion (when does one set contain another?), the statistical frequency of various pitch structures within the totality of all possible pitch sets, definitions of similarity of two sets, different degrees of similarity, meaningful permutations of ordered sets, generalizations to systems with other than 12 chromatic pitches, and other questions.

PROBABILITY THEORY. In mathematics a probability is a precisely calculated value indicating the likelihood of the occurrence of an event. In music, if a composer wishes to leave some factors to chance (either in composition or in performance), it is nevertheless possible for him to foresee the probable outcome (and make alternate plans if that outcome is not satisfactory). This concept is basic to the "stochastic" music of Iannis Xenakis. His major precompositional decisions concern large gestures, and the details contributing to these gestures are controlled only as a totality. The value of a single parameter at any instant is unpredictable, but it has a probability, determined by its context, so that the entire structure is anything but random. (His term "stochastic" comes from the Greek meaning "target" and was coined by the 18th-century Swiss mathematician Jacques Bernoulli, who promulgated the law of large numbers.) Xenakis considers his parameters as points moving in time. The life history of a sound can be represented by a graph of its constituent frequencies (the different tones present and their overtones) as they change in pitch and intensity along a time axis. The density of points on this graph, as well as the changes in density, is controlled statistically; no individual path is determined, but the total tendency of a texture is carefully calculated. Another innovation of Xenakis is the use of game theory in *Strategie* for two orchestras, each with its own conductor (1959–62). The composed sound structures that each conductor chooses to play are given points in relation to what his adversary chooses (both structures sounding simultaneously and the scoring procedure mathematically tested for fairness). Again the individual structures were composed using stochastic techniques.

INFORMATION THEORY. The mathematical laws governing the measurement and manipulation of information constitute information theory. The readiest application is in communications systems; it has recently been used in musical analysis. A body of music belongs to a style system which provides a context of expectations. Information is defined as the opposite of predictability. A completely predictable event, such as the final tonic of a tonal piece, is redundant; it contains no information. An unexpected event, such as a deceptive cadence, has high information content. Information theory attempts to discover how various style systems set up their implications and how individual pieces use the inherent properties of the style system. Since this analytic field is still little developed, it has not been used systematically and consciously by many composers. Lejaren Hiller has used some simple facets of information theory in programming computer-generated music, such as his *Computer Cantata* (1963).

TUNING AND TEMPERAMENT. 12-tone set theory is limited to the situation created by the 12 even-tempered chromatic pitches. The results of mathematical rigor within this system are indeed rich, but this does not mean that 12-tone equal temperament is the only viable pitch matrix. Although little has yet been done with the set theory of systems with more or less than 12 pitch classes, in either equal or unequal temperament, some composers and theorists have studied the nature of the traditional tuning system in order to arrive at basic principles that might be generalized. Harry Partch, for example, explains even temperament as an adjustment of the Pythagorean system, which results from combinations of ratios involving the numbers 1, 2, and 3. Partch himself does not accept the limit of 3, however; he works with ratios using 5, 7, 9, and 11, arriving at various scales, including one with 29 tones, which he fills in with additional pitches to produce a 43-tone scale (this is but one of many results of his researches into tuning and temperament). He has also demonstrated the musical feasability of his expanded scales by building instruments tuned in them and writing music for them.

BIBL.: Benjamin Boretz, "Meta-Variations: Studies in the Foundations of Musical Thought (I)," *Perspectives* 8/1 : 1–74; John Rothgeb, "Some Uses of Mathematical Concepts in Theories of

Music," *Journal of Music Theory* 10:200–15.
★ Set theory: Milton Babbitt, "Twelve-Tone Invariants as Compositional Determinants," *Problems of Modern Music* ed. by P. H. Lang (New York 1960):108–21; Allen Forte, "A Theory of Set-Complexes for Music," *Journal of Music Theory* 8:136–83; Hubert S. Howe, Jr., "Some Combinational Properties of Pitch Structures," *Perspectives* 4/1:45–61. ★ Probability theory: Lejaren A. Hiller and Leonard Isaacson, *Experimental Music* (New York 1959); Iannis Xenakis, *Musiques formelles* (Paris 1963). ★ Information theory: Edgar Coona and David Kraehenbuehl, "Information as a Measure of Structure in Music," *Journal of Music Theory* 2:127–61; Leonard B. Meyer, *Music, the Arts, and Ideas* (Chicago 1967): chs. 1–2; Richard Pinkerton, "Information Theory and Melody," *Scientific American* (Feb 1956): 77–86; Joseph E. Youngblood, "Style as Information," *Journal of Music Theory* 2:24–35. ★ Tuning and temperament: David Kraehenbuehl and Christopher Schmidt, "On the Development of Musical Systems," *Journal of Music Theory* 6: 32–65; Arthur Woodbury, "Harry Partch: Corporeality and Monophony," *Source* 2:91–93.

Jonathan D. Kramer

SEE ALSO Theory.

Mather, Bruce (b. Toronto, 9 May 1939), studied composition with Oskar Morawetz and John Beckwith at the Royal Conservatory in Toronto (1953–59), with Darius Milhaud and Olivier Messiaen in Paris (1959–62), and with Leland Smith at Stanford Univ. (1962–64). He has taught composition at McGill Univ. in Montreal since 1966 and has performed contemporary piano music for Ten Centuries Concerts in Toronto (1964–66) and La Société de Musique Contemporaine du Québec in Montreal (since 1966).

In most of Mather's works one finds the luxurious sonority of Berg, a lyricism recalling some of the more relaxed works of Boulez, and the restraint and understatement of Debussy. Regarding pitch organizations, Mather favors a procedure by which a sonic field is created consisting of 6 or 7 notes; these notes are then deployed in any order throughout a given section, almost like an oriental mode. Complex textures are often created by multiple echoing of a single line. Many passages of *Madrigal II* (1968), *Symphonic Ode* (1964), and *Ombres* (1967) are elaborated from such sonic fields (though this may not be immediately apparent, as the note groups tend to overlap), are extended by ornamentation using "nonharmonic" notes, or are diminished by "filtering" away some of the original notes. Mather's studies with Messiaen obviously suggested the use of such rhythmic techniques as the four-part

rhythmic canons in *Orphée* (1963), the free ostinato sections of *Madrigal II*, and the four simultaneous layers of tempo in *Fantasy* (1964). The supple grace with which he applies these techniques, however, is entirely his own.

PRINCIPAL COMPOSITIONS: *Cycle Rilke* for tenor, guitar (1959); *Mystras* for piano (1962); *Etude* for clarinet (1962); *Orphée* for soprano, piano, percussion (1963); *Fantasy* for piano (1964); *Symphonic Ode* for orchestra (1964); *La Lune mince* for chorus (1965); *Orchestra Piece 1966* (1966); *Ombres* for orchestra (1967); *Madrigal II* for soprano, alto, flute, violin, viola, cello, harp (1968); *Sonata* for 2 pianos (1970); *Musique pour Rouen* for 12 strings (1971); *Madrigal III* for alto, marimba, harp, piano (1971). List to 1968: *Composers of the Americas* 13:91–93.

R. Murray Schafer

SEE ALSO Canada.

Mathews, Max V. (b. Columbus, Neb., 13 Nov 1926), studied electrical engineering at the Calif. Institute of Technology (1946–50) and the Mass. Institute of Technology (1950–52, 1954). During 1933–41 he studied violin with Victor Hugo Jindra in Peru, Neb. Since 1955 he has been a member of the technical staff of Bell Telephone Laboratories.

PRINCIPAL COMPOSITIONS: *May Carol II* (1960, recorded by Decca); *Numerology* (1960, recorded by Decca); *The Second Law* (1961, Decca); *Masquerades* (1963, Decca); *Slider* (1965, Decca); *International Lullaby*, composed with O. Fujimura (1966); *Swansong* (1966, Decca).

PRINCIPAL WRITINGS: "Graphical Language for the Scores of Computer-Generated Sounds," written with L. Rosler, *Perspectives* 6/2:92–118, and *Music By Computers* ed. by H. VanFoerster and J. W. Beauchamp (New York 1969):84–114; "Control of Consonance and Dissonance with Nonharmonic Overtones," written with J. R. Pierce, *Music by Computers*: 129–32; *The Technology of Computer Music* (Cambridge, Mass., 1969); "GROOVE—A Program to Compose, Store, and Edit Functions of Time," written with F. R. Moore, *Communications of the ACM* (Dec 1970):715–21. Mathews has also written many other articles on the subjects of acoustic research and computer music.

Matsudaira, Yori Aki (b. Tokyo, 27 March 1931), studied biology at Tokyo Metropolitan Univ. (1948–57). He is self-taught in both piano and composition. Of the works listed below, the first four titles make use of serial procedures, the next four of aleatory procedures, and the last four of electronic and other nontraditional sound sources.

PRINCIPAL COMPOSITIONS (published by S-Z unless otherwise noted): *Variations* for violin, cello, piano (1957); *Velocity Coefficient* for flute, piano, percussion (1958, unpub.); *Orbits I, II, III* for flute, clarinet, piano (1960); *Configuration* for chamber orchestra (1961–63); *Instructions* for piano (1961, unpub.); *Co-Action* for cello, piano (1962); *Transient '64*, electronic sounds on tape (1964, unpub.); *Rhymes for Gazzelloni* for flute (1965–66); *Distributions* for string quartet, ring modulator (1967); *What's Next?* for soprano, 2 noise makers (1967, unpub.); *Alternations for Combo* for trumpet, double bass, piano, percussion, electronic apparatus (1967); *Assemblages* on tape (1968).

SEE ALSO Japan.

Matsumura, Teizo (b. Kyoto, 15 Jan 1929), studied harmony and counterpoint with Tomojiro Ikenouchi (1949–50, 1957–59). Since 1956 he has investigated ancient Asian cultures and philosophies of contemporary art under Akira Ifukube. He has lectured at the Tokyo Univ. of Arts since 1970 and also composes film and theater scores, the latter for Nissei Theater, where he is musical director. In his early years he was influenced by Maurice Ravel and Igor Stravinsky.

PRINCIPAL COMPOSITIONS (published by Ongaku): *Piano Quintet* (1962); *Symphony* (1965); *Prelude* for orchestra (1968).

BIBL.: The 1970/2 issue of *Ongaku-Geijutsu* (Tokyo) is devoted to Matsumura.

SEE ALSO Japan.

Matsushita, Shin-ichi (b. Osaka, 1 Oct 1922), studied at Kyushu Univ. (1942–46, conducting with Takashi Asahina). He has worked at the electronic music studio of Osaka Radio since 1959. Since 1965 he has divided his time between Osaka (where he teaches at the City Univ.) and Hamburg (where he teaches at the Univ. of Hamburg). In 1962 he organized the contemporary music festival "Autumn in Osaka," with which he is still associated. His music has been influenced by the writings of Josef Hauer and René Leibowitz and by his acquaintance with Cage, Stockhausen, and Xenakis.

PRINCIPAL COMPOSITIONS (published by Ongaku unless otherwise noted): *Le dimensioni,* symphony (1958–60, unpub.); *Canzona da sonare* for piano, percussion (1959); *Le Cloître noir* for voices, tape (1959); *Correlazioni per 3 gruppi* for orchestra (1960); *Musique* for soprano, chamber ensemble (1961); *Sinfonia vita* (1963, unpub.); *Spectra I, II* for piano (1963, 1967; UE); *Fresque sonore* for flute, oboe, clarinet, horn, harp, viola, cello (1966);

Astrale Atem for chamber orchestra (1968); *Kristalle* for piano quartet (1968).

PRINCIPAL WRITINGS: Matsushita has published articles on Penderecki, *Ongaku-Geijutsu* 32/6:8–17; Xenakis, *ibid.* 34/2:11–24; and Japanese music, *Encyclopedia Ricordi* (Milan 1962).

SEE ALSO Japan.

Matton, Roger (b. Granby, Quebec, 18 May 1929), studied at the Quebec Province Conservatory in Montreal with Claude Champagne and in Paris with Nadia Boulanger and Mme. Vaurabourg-Honegger. Since 1957 he has taught composition at Laval Univ. in Quebec, where he is also on the staff of the Archives du Folklore.

PRINCIPAL COMPOSITIONS: *Danse bresiliene* for 2 pianos or orchestra (1946); *Saxophone Concerto* (1948); *Pax,* symphonic suite (1950); *Suite on Gregorian Themes* for piano (1950); *Concerto* for 2 pianos, percussion (1954–55); *Escaouette,* suite of dances for vocal soloists, chorus, orchestra (1957); *L'Horoscope,* choreographic suite for orchestra (1958); *Mouvements symphoniques Nos. 1–2* (1960, 1962); *Concerto* for 2 pianos, orchestra (1964). List to 1964: *Composers of the Americas* 12:115–17.

Maturana, Eduardo (Araya) (b. Valparaíso, Chile, 14 April 1920), studied at the National Conservatory of the Univ. of Chile (1939–45, composition with Pedro Humberto Allende, violin and viola with Luis Mutschler, chamber music with Armando Carvajal). He has played viola in the Chilean Philharmonic Orchestra since 1955. He has also written program notes for the Chilean Philharmonic and Symphony Orchestras and has been a writer and photographer for Chilean periodicals. Writings by Juan Carlos Paz, René Leibowitz, Ernst Krenek, Herbert Eimert, and others initiated Maturana into 12-tone techniques, which appear in the piano pieces of 1947–48. He was the first Chilean to use them. He has since worked with musique concrète and aleatory processes.

PRINCIPAL COMPOSITIONS: *3 Poems* for string quartet (1946); *4 Pieces* for piano (1947–48); *Aforisticas* for piano (1947–48); *3 Short Pieces and a Chilean Air* for piano (1947–48); *Valses* for piano (1947–48); *Music* for flute, viola (1948); *Sonata* for viola (1948); *10 Micropiezas* for string quartet (1949–50, IEM; arranged for string orchestra, *Pieces for Orchestra*, 1965); *Sonatina* for flute (1952); *Introduction and Allegro* for chamber orchestra (1953); *Wind Trio* (1955); *4 Arias* for voice, oboe, cello, percussion (1959); *Wind Quintet* (1960); *Gamma I* for orchestra (1962); *3 Pieces for Orchestra* (1963–64); *Canciones* for tenor, piano (1964); *String Quartet* (1964, PAU); *Retrato, balada y muerte del poeta Teofilo Cid* for soprano, orchestra (1966); *Concertante* for horn, orchestra (1966); *5 Moviles* for string orchestra (1967); *Responso para el Comandante Che Guevara* for orchestra, tape (1968); *Canciones* for soprano, piano (1969); *Brass Quintet* (1970); *Elegias* for cello, orchestra (1970).

BIBL.: Pablo Garrido, "Biografía de E. M., músico chileno," *La hora* (30 May 1948); Robert Stevenson, "La música chilena en la época de Santa Cruz," *Boletín interamericano de música* (Sept 1968):5–7.

SEE ALSO Chile.

Maw, Nicholas (b. Grantham, Lincolnshire, England, 5 Nov 1935), attended the Royal Academy of Music (1955–58; harmony, counterpoint with Paul Steinitz; composition with Lennox Berkeley). He studied in Paris on a French government scholarship with Nadia Boulanger (1958–59) and Max Deutsch (1959). He taught composition at the Royal Academy of Music (1965–66) and was a Fellow Commoner in creative arts, Trinity College, Cambridge (1966–69). Maw credits the 20th-century Viennese and English schools of composition as having had the most influence on his style.

PRINCIPAL COMPOSITIONS (published by Boosey unless otherwise noted): *Nocturne* for mezzo soprano, small orchestra (1957–58, Chester); *Chamber Music* for wind-and-piano quintet (1962, Chester); *Scenes and Arias* for 3 women's voices, orchestra (1962, revised 1966); *One-Man Show*, opera; libretto by Arthur Jacobs (1963–64) *String Quartet* (1965); *Sinfonia* for small orchestra (1966); *The Voice of Love*, song cycle for mezzo-soprano, piano; poems by Peter Porter (1966); *Sonata* for strings, 2 horns (1967); *The Rising of the Moon*, opera; libretto by Beverley Cross (1967–69).

BIBL.: Susan Bradshaw, "N. M.," *Musical Times* 103:608–10; Bryan Northcott, "N. M.," *Music and Musicians* (May 1970):34–43, 82; Anthony Payne, "The Music of N. M.," *Tempo* 68:2–13; ———, "N. M.'s One-Man Show," *ibid.* 71:2–14; Stephen Walsh, "N. M.'s New Opera," *ibid.* 92.

SEE ALSO Great Britain.

Maxfield, Richard (Vance) (b. Seattle, 2 Feb 1927; d. Los Angeles, 1969), studied with Roger Sessions at the Univ. of Calif. at Berkeley and at Princeton Univ. He also worked with Aaron Copland at Tanglewood in 1953 and with Luigi Dallapiccola and Bruno Maderna in Italy, c.1954–56. He attended

John Cage's classes at the New School for Social Research in New York and in 1959–61 replaced Cage as the instructor. He also worked during these years as a free-lance audio engineer and technician. He taught at the San Francisco State College (1966–67) and was later a free-lance engineer and composer in southern California until his death (by suicide). Maxfield's music until the late 1950s was post-Webern serial. In 1958 he began electronic composition and later became the first teacher of electronic techniques in the U.S. In a formal statement written at age 35 and now in the possession of Virgil Thomson, Maxfield said of himself: "Much of his music has as its source material recorded sounds of the instrumentalists who in performance improvise with electronic tape (which is playing their earlier recorded sounds, now distorted by electronic manipulation). . . He is generally quite selective about his raw material and its alteration, but quite free with regard to placement (organization) of the finished product and the improvisation going on simultaneously."

PRINCIPAL TAPE COMPOSITIONS: *Cough Music* on tape (1959); *Fermentation* on tape (1960); *Perspectives* for violin, tape (1960); *Amazing Grace* on tape (1960); *Peripateia* for saxophone, violin, piano, 3 tape tracks (1960); *Piano Concert for David Tudor* for piano, tape (1961); *Perspectives II* (for La Monte Young) for violin or other bowed instrument, tape (1961); *Dishes* on tape (1961); *Clarinet Music* for 2 or more clarinets, tape (1961); *Steam* on 4 tape tracks (1961); *Dromenon* for instruments, tape (1961); *Toy Symphony* for flute, violin, toys, wooden boxes, ceramic vase, tape (1962); *Garden Music* on 2 tape tracks (1963); *Bacchanale* on 2 tape tracks (1963); *Bhagavadgita Symphony* (chapter 9) on 3 tape tracks (1963); *Electronic Symphony* on 2 tape tracks (1964); *Bacchanale II* on 2 tape tracks (1966); *Dream* on tape (1967). List to 1967: Hugh Davies, comp., *International Electronic Music Catalog* (Cambridge, Mass., 1968):177, 217–18.

PRINCIPAL WRITINGS: "Composers, Performance, and Publication" and "Music, Electronic and Performed," *Contemporary Composers on Contemporary Music* ed. by E. Schwartz and B. Childs (New York 1967):350–61.

[prepared with the help of Barney Childs]
SEE ALSO Dance, Indeterminacy.

Maxwell Davies, Peter (b. Manchester, England, 8 Sept 1934), studied during 1952–57 at the Royal Manchester College of Music and Manchester Univ. During 1957–59 he worked with Goffredo Petrassi in Rome. He was director of music at Cirencester Grammar

School (1959–62) and then went to Princeton Univ. for further study with Roger Sessions in 1962. He has lectured in Europe, Australia, and New Zealand, and was composer-in-residence at the Univ. of Adelaide in 1966. The following year he and Harrison Birtwistle formed a chamber ensemble in London, the Pierrot Players (reorganized in 1970 as The Fires of London), and many of Maxwell Davies's subsequent works have been premiered by the group.

Most of Maxwell Davies's works are for chamber ensembles of varying makeup but usually including, since 1964, a large battery of percussion. A keenly developed literary and historical sense pervades much of the music. *Prolation* (1959) extends a medieval principle of duration relationships to cover irregular values, and quotations of older music (ranging from medieval carols to Monteverdi) appear frequently in other works. The *8 Songs for a Mad King* (1969) is based on writings and court transcripts of King George III, and the inspiration behind *Vesalii icones* (1970) included both the anatomical drawings in Andreas Vesalius's textbook of 1543 and the 14 Stations of the Cross.

The instrumental works of the 1950s are noteworthy for their rhythmic complexity, but parallel with this Maxwell Davies developed a flowing style in his vocal works. The latter appears in the *String Quartet* (1961), based on Monteverdi's *Ave maris stella* and containing passages in which the performers can mold rhythms in their own way. Since about 1962 the composer has been occupied with an opera about the 16th-century composer John Taverner, and many compositions since then have been related to this project. In the first and second *Fantasias*, both based on an *In nomine* of Taverner (1962, 1964), sections in fixed tempos alternate with freer, proselike passages containing violent splashes of orchestral sound. The inclusion of tuned handbells in both works and the melodic use of timpani in the second give evidence of a growing interest in color. This trend was continued in such works as *Revelation and Fall* (1965), which uses a wide variety of conventional and unconventional percussion, and *L'Homme armé*, where stereo tape, preelectric gramophone horn, and player piano are combined with conventional sound sources. *8 Songs for a Mad King* and *Vesalii icones* combine stage action, principally by one performer, with vocal and instrumental sounds for the entire ensemble (many percussion, other sounds often produced through unconventional performing means). Structure in these works

follows the dramatic line of the text or scenario and consists of episodes and sound textures that mix original material in collage-like fashion with quotations from pop and concert music, both old and new, tonal and otherwise. The composer is continuing to explore the possibilities in new types of music theater and in electronic media.

PRINCIPAL COMPOSITIONS (published by Boosey unless otherwise noted): *5 Pieces* for piano (1956, Schott); *Alma redemptoris mater* for 6 winds (1957, Schott); *St. Michael Sonata* for 17 winds (1957, Schott); *Prolation* for orchestra (1959, Schott); *5 Motets* for vocal soloists, double chorus, instruments (1959); *Ricercar and Doubles* for 8 instruments (1959, Schott); *O magnum mysterium*, cycle of carols for chorus, instruments (1960, Schott); *String Quartet* (1961, Schott); *First Fantasia* for orchestra on an *In nomine* of John Taverner (1962, Schott); *Frammenti di Leopardi*, cantata for soprano, alto, instruments (1962, Schott); *Sinfonia* for chamber orchestra (1962, Schott); *John Taverner*, opera (c.1962–c.1968; revised 1970; unpub.); *Veni Sancte Spiritus* for vocal soloists, chorus, small orchestra (1963); *Second Fantasia* for orchestra on John Taverner's *In nomine* (1964); *Shakespeare Music* for chamber ensemble (1964); *Ecce manus tradentis* for chorus, 7 winds, harp, handbells (1965); *The Shepherd's Calendar* for young singers, instrumentalists; Goliard poems (1965); *Revelation and Fall* for soprano, chamber ensemble including 3 percussionists; text by Georg Trakl (1965); *Antechrist* for piccolo, bass clarinet, violin, cello, 3 percussionists (1967); *L'Homme armé* for flute/piccolo, clarinet, harmonium/harpsichord/player piano, percussionist, violin, cello, 2-track tape, pre-electric gramophone horn (1968); *Stedman Doubles* for clarinet, percussion (1968); *Stedman Caters* for flute/piccolo, clarinet, percussion, harpsichord, violin, cello (1968); *8 Songs for a Mad King* for actor-singer, flute/piccolo, clarinet, piano/harpsichord/dulcimer, violin, cello, percussion; text by Randolph Stow and King George III (1969); *St. Thomas Wake*, foxtrot for orchestra on a pavan by John Bull (1969); *Vesalii icones* for dancer-pianist, cello, instrumental ensemble; the dancer's role was created originally by William Louther (1970).

PRINCIPAL WRITINGS: "The Young Composer in America," *Tempo* 72.

BIBL.: R. Murray Schafer, *British Composers in Interview* (London 1963); Articles on individual works have appeared in *Tempo* 69, 70, 72, 73, 84, 87.

Bill Hopkins

SEE ALSO Great Britain; Liturgical Music: Christian; Opera.

Mayer, William (b. New York, 18 Nov 1925), attended Yale Univ. (1944, 1946–48), and the Mannes College of Music in New York

(1949–52, composition with Felix Salzer). He also studied composition with Roger Sessions at the Juilliard School (summer 1949) and privately with Otto Luening (1952–54) and studied conducting with Izler Solomon at the Aspen Music School in 1960. He attended the Bennington Composers Conference in 1951 and 1952 and has been working at the Columbia-Princeton Electronic Music Center since 1969. He taught composition and orchestration at Boston Univ. in 1966 and has lectured at the New School in New York. He served as chairman of the editorial board of Composers Recordings Inc. during 1967–70. His primary activity besides free-lance composing has been writing on contemporary music for the U.S. Information Agency. Mayer describes his music as often lyrical and "lontano" in mood. "This alternates with a strong rhythmic drive and an accent on two types of humor: joyful and sardonic. There is careful attention given to timbres, often delicate and transparent. Above all, there is a free use of compositional techniques and disparate material with the aim of synthesizing so-called opposites into a coherent whole." Mayer was influenced by the music he heard in his early twenties (Bartók, Stravinsky, and Barber especially) but cites as well his youthful love of show music, the songs of Jerome Kern, above all.

PRINCIPAL COMPOSITIONS (published by Fischer unless otherwise noted): *Songs* for voice, piano (1952–67; "Paradox" 1952, and "Barbara," 1963, published by Fischer); *Essay for Brass and Winds* for combined brass and woodwind quintets, percussion (1953, Boosey); *Hello, World!* for singer-narrator, orchestra (1956, Boosey); *Andante for Strings* (1956, MCA); *Concert Piece for Trumpet and Strings* with percussion (1957, Boosey); *Overture for an American* for orchestra (1958, Boosey); *2 Pastels for Orchestra* (1959, MCA); *Piano Sonata* (1960); *One Christmas Long Ago*, opera (1961, Galaxy); *Snow Queen*, ballet (1963; orchestral suite, *Scenes from the Snow Queen*, 1965–69); *Brass Quintet* (1964, unpub.); *Brief Candle*, micro-opera for small chorus, chamber orchestra (1965, Presser); *Octagon*, piano concerto (1965–66, MCA); *Letters Home* for chorus, orchestra; text from letters written by soldiers in Vietnam (1968, MCA); *Miniatures* and *News Items* for soprano, chamber ensemble (1968, Presser); *Eve of St. Agnes* for chorus, orchestra (1969); *Lines on Light* for chorus, piano (1970).

PRINCIPAL WRITINGS: "Chamber Opera: An American Evolution," *Music Journal* (Oct 1965): 36, 64–65; "Contemporary American Opera: A Survey of Its Development," lecture prepared for the U.S. Information Service (U.S. Govt. Printing Office, 1966); "Two Pastels for Orchestra," Program Booklet of the Cincinnati Symphony (3–4 Feb 1967):419–22.

BIBL.: Paul Affelder, "Letters Home," program notes in *Bravo* (Carnegie Hall, 1968).

Mayuzumi, Toshiro (b. Yokohama, Japan, 20 Feb 1929), studied composition with Tomojiro Ikenouchi at the Tokyo Univ. of Art (1945–51) and with Tony Aubin at the Paris Conservatory (1951–52). Since 1952 he has lived primarily in Japan, where in 1957 he founded a festival of contemporary music in Karuisawa. His musical development has been influenced by Oriental philosophy and Buddhism and by the work of Stravinsky and Messiaen.

PRINCIPAL COMPOSITIONS (published by Peters): *Sphenogrammes* for flute, alto saxophone, marimba, violin, cello, piano 4-hands, voice (1950); *Symphonic Mood* for orchestra (1950); *X, Y, Z*, musique concrète on tape (1953); *Bacchanale* for orchestra (1953); *Ectoplasme* for orchestra (1954); *Tonepleromas 55* for wind orchestra (1955); *Variations sur 7* on tape, in collaboration with Makoto Moroi (1956); *Pieces* for prepared piano, strings (1957); *Aoi-no-Ue* on tape (1957); *Microcosmos* for 7 players (1957); *Phonologie symphonique* for orchestra (1957); *Nirvana Symphony*, Buddhist cantata for male soloists and chorus, orchestra (1958); *Campanology* on tape (1959); *Mandala Symphony* (1960); *Bunraku* for cello (1960); *Prelude* for string quartet (1961); *Bugaku* ballet; choreography by George Balanchine (1962); *Samsara*, symphonic poem (1962); *Essay* for string orchestra (1963); *Pratidesana*, Buddhist cantata for male soloists and chorus, 3 horns, 4 percussionists, 2 pianos (1963); *The Birth of Music* for orchestra (1964); *Ritual Overture* for female voices (textless), winds (1964); *3 Hymns* on tape (1965); *The Bible*, score for the film by John Huston (1965); *Olympics*, ballet; choreography by Gerald Arpino (1965); *Reflections in a Golden Eye*, film score (1967); *Incantation* for orchestra (1967); *Mandala* for voice, electronic sounds on tape (1969); *Showa tempyo raku* for gagaku orchestra (1970).

[prepared with the help of Klaus Pringsheim]

SEE ALSO Asian Music and Western Composition, Japan, Microtones.

Medtner, Nicolai (Karlovich) (b. Moscow, 5 Jan 1880; d. London, 13 Nov 1951), studied at the Moscow Conservatory (1892–1900; composition with Sergei Taneyev and Anton Arensky, piano with Sapelnikov and Safonov). He taught piano at the Moscow Conservatory (1902–03, 1918–21) and concertized in Europe and the U.S. In 1921 he left Russia to live in France, Germany, and (after 1936) England. After World War II the Maharajah of Mysore created an endowment for the recording of his music. He was heavily influenced by

German romanticism, especially Brahms.
Ewen (see bibl.) says that "he believed in
singable melodies, well-sounding harmonies,
deeply felt emotions. Occasionally his writing
may get contrapuntally or rhythmically
complex."

PRINCIPAL COMPOSITIONS: *8 Mood Pictures* for
piano, Op. 1 (1902, No. 8 published by Jurgenson);
Violin Sonatas Nos. 1–3, Opp. 21, 44, 57 (1910,
ERM; 1924; 1936, Novello); *34 Fairy Tales* for
piano (1905–29; Op 8 published by Jurgenson;
Op. 9, Chester; Op. 14, Forberg; Opp. 20, 26, 34,
35, ERM; Opp. 42, 48, 51, Zimmermann); *Piano
Concertos Nos. 1–3*, Opp. 33, 50, 60 (1916–18,
Muzyka; 1926–27; 1942–43, Zimmermann); *Son-
ate-Vocalise* for voice, piano, Op. 41 (1921,
Zimmermann); *4 Sets of Romantic Sketches* for
piano, Op. 54 (1933, Zimmermann); *Piano Quintet
in C* (1940–50, Boosey). Medtner also wrote a
large number of songs.

PRINCIPAL WRITINGS: *The Muse and Fashion*,
essays trans. by Alfred Swan (Haverford, Penna.,
1951); *Povsednevnaia rabota pianista i kompozitora
Stranitsy iz zapissnykh knizhek* [The Late Work of
the Pianist and Composer, Stranitsy, from His
Notebooks] (Moscow 1963).

BIBL.: M. Boyd, "The Songs of N. M.," *Music
and Letters* 46:16–22; E. Dolinskaia, *N. M.*
(Moscow 1966); David Ewen, *European Composers
Today* (New York 1954):95–96; R. Holt, *M.
and His Music* (London 1948); ——, ed., *N. M.,
A Symposium* (London 1955); Leonid Sababeyeff,
Modern Russian Composers trans. by Judah A.
Joffe (New York 1927):129–43.

De Meester, Louis (b. Roeselare, Belgium,
28 Oct 1904), is self-taught in music. During
1933–39 he was director of the Meknès Conservatory in Morocco. He was a sound engineer for the Belgian Radio-Television Network
in Brussels during 1945–62. In 1962 he established the Institute for Psychoacoustics and
Electronic Music at the Rijksuniversiteit in
Ghent, and he directed the Institute until 1969.

PRINCIPAL COMPOSITIONS: *Magreb* for viola, orchestra (1946); *Capriccio* for orchestra (1948);
Sinfonietta buffa (1949, UE); *La Voix du silence*
for 2 narrators, baritone, women's chorus, children's chorus, flute, oboe, string orchestra; libretto
by Maurice Carême (1951); *Piano Concertos Nos.
1–2* (1952, 1956); *Musica per archi* (1955, Metropolis); *La Grande tentation de St. Antoine*, 1-act
opera buffa; libretto by Michel de Ghelderode
(1957); *Amalgames* for orchestra (1956); *Serenade*
for chamber orchestra (1959); *2 = trop peu, 3 = trop*,
1-act opera buffa for soprano, tenor, bass, orchestra (1966); *Paradÿsgeuzen* [Beggars in Heaven],
3-act opera; libretto by Gaston Martens. De
Meester's compositions also include chamber
music, songs, film and theater scores, and electronic music.

Méfano, Paul (b. Basra, Iraq, 6 March 1937),
attended the Paris Conservatory (1959–64,
composition with Darius Milhaud, analysis
with Olivier Messiaen), and the Basel Music
Academy (1962–64; composition and analysis
with Pierre Boulez, Karlheinz Stockhausen,
and Henri Pousseur; conducting with Boulez).
He attended the Darmstadt summer courses
in the mid-1960s, and during 1967–68 studied
Javanese and Balinese music at the Univ. of
Calif. at Los Angeles.

PRINCIPAL COMPOSITIONS: *Incidences* for piano,
orchestra (1960); *Quadrature* for 16 women's
voices, orchestra (1960); *Madrigal* for 3 sopranos,
piano, flute/piccolo, harp (or guitar), 4 percussionists (1962); *Mélodies* for soprano, chamber
ensemble (1962); *Paraboles* for dramatic soprano,
piano, chamber ensemble: poems by Yves Bonne-
foy (1964, Heugel); *Interferences* for horn, piano,
chamber ensemble (1966, Heugel); *Lignes* for bass,
3 horns, 3 trombones, bassoon, tuba, amplified
5-string double bass, 6 percussionists (1968,
Heugel); *Old Oedip* for male narrator, female
actress, contact amplifiers, ring modulator, tape
(1970), *La Cérémonie* for countertenor, baritone,
soprano, 12 speakers, orchestra; text by the composer (1970).

PRINCIPAL WRITINGS: "P. M." (an interview),
Courrier musical de France 1968/24:236–47; *Le
'Livre d'Orgue' de Messiaen* (unpub.); *Recherche
et esotérisme dans la messe de Guillaume de
Machaut* (unpub.).

BIBL.: Claude Samuel, *Entretiens avec Olivier
Messiaen* (Paris 1967):197.

SEE ALSO France.

Mellers, Wilfrid (Howard) (b. Leamington,
England, 26 April 1914), attended Leamington
College (1922–33), the Univ. of Cambridge
(1933–39, honors degree in English literature),
and the Univ. of Birmingham (DM, 1958).
He studied composition privately with Egon
Wellesz and Edmund Rubbra. He has taught
at Downing College, Cambridge (1945–48),
the education department of the Univ. of
Birmingham (1948–60), the Univ. of Pittsburgh in the U.S. (1960–63), and at the Univ.
of York (since 1964). Mellers' development
was conditioned in part by his literary training
and his interest in the theater. For the last
few years he has been especially interested in
interrelationships between concert music, jazz,
folk, and pop music; this is evident in two
large-scale works written 1968–69: *Life Cycle*,
a cantata for young people based on dance
songs of the Eskimos and the Gabon pygmies;
and *Yeibichai*, a cantata based on poems about
the "Wild West."

PRINCIPAL COMPOSITIONS (published by Novello unless otherwise noted): *String Trio* (1945, Lengnick); *Canticum incarnationis* for 6 voices (1960, Faber); *Spells* for soprano, flute (alto flute), oboe (English horn), viola, percussion (1960, Mills); *Alba* for flute, orchestra (1962, Mills); *Chants and Litanies of Carl Sandburg* for men's voices, piano, percussion (1962); *Trio* for flute, cello, piano (1962); *Lacrimae amoris* for countertenor, men's chorus (1963); *Rose of May: A Threnody for Ophelia* for speaker, soprano, flute, clarinet, string quartet (1964); *A May Magnificat* for mezzo-soprano, chamber orchestra (1966); *Noctambule and Sun-Dance* for woodwinds, brass, percussion, piano (1966); *Love Story* for soprano, countertenor, cello, harpsichord (1967); *Canticum resurrectionis* for 16 voices (1968, unpub.); *Life Cycle*, cantata for 3 choirs, 2 orchestras (1968, Cambridge); *Yeibichai*, cantata for chorus, orchestra, jazz trio, coloratura soprano, scat singer, tapes; poems by Gary Snyder (1968–69, unpub.); *Natalis invicti solis* for piano (1969); *The Word Unborn* for 16 voices, 6 instruments (1969, unpub.).

PRINCIPAL BOOKS: *Music and Society* (London 1946); *François Couperin and the French Classical Tradition* (London 1950); *Romanticism and the 20th Century*, from the series *Man and his Music* (London 1957); *Music in a New-Found Land* (London 1964); *Harmonious Meeting* (London 1965); *Caliban Reborn* (New York 1967).

SEE ALSO Great Britain.

Mellnäs, Arne (b. Stockholm, 30 August 1933), studied at the Royal Academy of Music in Stockholm (1953–63, composition with Karl-Birger Blomdahl, theory and music history with Bo Wallner) and the Berlin Hochschule für Musik (1959, composition with Boris Blacher). He also studied composition with György Ligeti in Vienna and Stockholm (1961–62) and electronic music with Gottfried Michael Koenig at Bilthoven (1962–63). He has taught theory at the Royal Academy in Stockholm since 1963. He has also worked at the San Francisco Tape Music Center (1964) and at the electronic music studio of the Swedish Broadcasting Corp. (since 1968). These experiences and meetings with Japanese avant-garde composers during a stay in Tokyo in 1964 have been major influences on his development.

PRINCIPAL COMPOSITIONS: *Collage* for orchestra (1962, Peters); *Tombola* for trombone, horn, electric guitar, piano (1963, Tonos); *Aura* for orchestra (1964, Hansen-W); *Gestes sonores* for any instrumental ensemble (1964, Hansen-W); *Succsim* for chorus (1965, Hansen-W); *Intensity 6.5* on tape, in memoriam Edgard Varèse (1966); *Fixations* for organ (1967, Peters); *Quasi niente* for 1–4 string trios (1968, Peters); *Kaleidovision*, electronic music on tape for a television ballet (1969); *Eufoni* on tape (1969); *Far Out*, text-sound composition on tape (1970); *Dream* for chorus, text by e. e. cummings (1970, Hansen-W); *Capricorn Flakes* for piano, harpsichord, vibraphone (1970, Peters); *Appassionato* on tape (1970).

PRINCIPAL WRITINGS: "Från gamla och nya världen" [From the Old and New Worlds], *Nutida musik* 1964–65/8:223–30; "Ur en kluddbok" [From a Sketch Book], *ibid.* 1965–66/1–2:42–45.

BIBL.: Bo Wallner, *Vår tids musik i Norden* (Stockholm 1968): 262–63, English trans. (London 1971).

SEE ALSO Scandinavia.

Melody. In the 18th and 19th centuries melody held a dominating position in relation to other musical elements. Composers often built their music around melodic themes whose contours and component motifs were chosen to produce a unique and memorable unit. In addition they used harmonic and metrical supports to give their themes stability and cohesion. Because of these factors, listeners came to focus a large part of their attention on the statement and development of melodic themes. The lack of melodic dominance is one of the most obvious features in much 20th-century music. Except in a few cases, however, it would not be accurate to say that the element of melody has been abandoned. Rather its internal characteristics and its relationship to other aspects of the musical fabric have changed.

Several broad tendencies in 20th-century music seem to be responsible for new melodic conceptions. These are 1) the abandonment of the traditional harmonic-metric base, 2) the use of modal and nontonal concepts, and 3) the realignment of musical elements into new hierarchies. An examination of several types of 20th-century melody will illustrate the effects of these tendencies and also indicate the range of melodic possibilities that have been explored by 20th-century composers.

Delius's song *Cynara* for baritone and orchestra (Ex. 1) is an example of traditional melody. None of the new tendencies mentioned above is present. The music is definitely tonal, melody is the main factor in the musical hierarchy, and the whole conception is based on a harmonic-metric substructure. Between the main cadences the harmony moves in softly fluctuating chords toward D (bars 4–5, 6–7, 13–14). The component phrases of the melodic line are placed between the cadential

Ex. 1. Frederick Delius, *Cynara*: 24–37
Quoted by permission of Boosey & Hawkes

posts. Although of secondary importance, the frequent occurrence of the three-note motif in bars 5, 7, 9, and 11 is indicative of a desire for fixed, recognisable units. Although this feature was an essential characteristic of traditional music, here we are far from the clarity of classical melody. The melodic phrases are irregular in length, and the last one ends purposely without cadential support (bar 12) in order to assure a continuous melodic flow throughout the piece. (It is this Wagnerian type of endless melody that led finally to Schoenberg's conception of melody as illustrated in the next example.) The traditional treatment of the text (the exploitation of normal speech accentuations and other syntactic properties and the melodic emphasis on important words) is also characteristic of this melody type.

An example of atonal melody before the introduction of the 12-tone technique is given in Ex. 2, taken from Schoenberg's *5 Pieces* for orchestra, Op. 16 (1908). There are no clearcut classical periods or phrases; instead

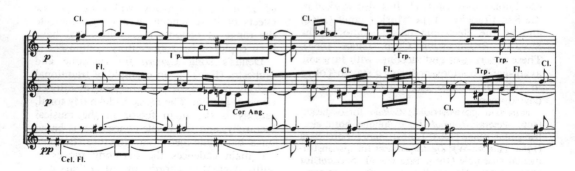

Ex. 2. Arnold Schoenberg, No. 2 from *5 Pieces for Orchestra*, Op. 16: 10–13
Quoted by permission of Henmar Press and C. F. Peters

Ex. 3. Igor Stravinsky, *Le Sacre du printemps*, rehearsal No. 10: 1–4
Quoted by permission of Boosey & Hawkes

there is a polymelodic texture in which short motifs are distributed throughout all parts, creating a continuous melodic flow. The delicate and refined orchestration shows how important tone color had become as an element independent of melody. (Schoenberg called such uses of timbre *Klangfarbenmelodie*). Melody is not fixed in a definite, recognisable shape but changes continuously from one form to another; it has lost its classical thematic function. There still remains a vestige of melodic consistency, however, in the repeated use of the same intervals and rhythmic patterns. Melody in this example moves more freely of harmonic or metric points of support. The F♯ in celesta and flute is not a tonal center but a kind of floating nucleus within the sound space that gives it an identifiable character. Such a phenomenon occurs often in atonality. Notice that in this early period of atonality the intervals are still small.

At about the same time as the Schoenberg example an entirely different type of melody came into being. An instance of it occurs in Ex. 3 from Stravinsky's *Le Sacre du printemps* (1911–13). Three short motifs occur simultaneously, moving freely against a chordal background. Although similar in some ways to the Schoenberg example, the differences are actually more striking. First of all there are fixed melodic units: the motifs are repeated

again and again with only slight changes. The instrumental colors also remain constant. Finally the motifs, which consist of a few notes circling around a melodic center, move not in an atonal but in an extended tonal field. The notes of the English horn (F-B♭-G) form a melodic nucleus that is one of the oldest melodic forms known to man; it is premodal, probably one of the basic elements of the later pentatonic scale. The A-clarinet motif, with its descending line and its repetitions, has an obviously archaic sound as well. Such melodic primitivism as this is as important to *Sacre* as are its rhythmic features. It is also representative of one of the main trends of this century in its search for modal and premodal elements. (In various forms melodic primitivism is also found in Debussy, Ravel, Milhaud, Orff, Bartók, Varèse, and others).

Music based on folk music is different from either Exx. 2 or 3. In general, folk-derived melodies are diatonic, they have clearcut phrase structures, meters, and rhythmic contours, and they possess a tonal or modal unity. As in Ex. 4, this kind of melody is close to the classic-romantic tradition; except for its local (national) color, Ex. 4 shares its basic features with all melodies that stem from that tradition. Although Ex. 4 needs no further comment, one type of folk-derived melody does, that stemming from American Negro

Ex. 4. Béla Bartók, *Music for Strings, Percussion, and Celesta*, violin part, IV: 5–13
Quoted by permission of Boosey & Hawkes

Ex. 5. Anton Webern, No. 1 from *3 Songs*, Op. 25: 1–5
Quoted by permission of Universal Edition and Theodore Presser

music and jazz. One of the earliest and best examples of such melodic derivation is Milhaud's *La Création du monde* with its blues notes, syncopations, and orchestral timbres inspired by jazz groups of the 1920s.

Where extended tonality is concerned, chromaticism may assume an important role. It is only in atonality, however, that chromatic notes are used as autonomous musical elements, not as notes derived from a diatonic scale. Twelve-tone techniques, the first systematic approach to atonality, postulate a row of 12 different chromatic notes from which all musical events, including melody and harmony, are derived. Although factors such as the contours and phrase lengths of a melody can coincide with corresponding properties of a row, the two are not identical. From Schoenberg via Webern to the generation of the 1950s, the row has been increasingly considered as a precompositional, structural base providing the raw material (sequence of notes, intervals) for both melody and harmony. Unlike early atonal melody (Ex. 2), Webern's song Op. 25, No. 1 (Ex. 5), uses relatively large intervals, which however remain subordinate to the overall contours of the melodic lines (this is true also of the short motifs that act as elements in larger phrase units). The row (the first 12 notes of the voice part) is responsible to a large extent for the high degree of intervallic consistency. Notice that the row does not coincide exactly with the phrase structure of the voice part. Similarly the piano motif marked A-B-C recurs in different parts of the row so that although the contour is the same the intervals are different. It is, as Webern took pride in pointing out, unity and variety at the same time. There is also a unity in the correspondences of intervals between the voice and piano so that, properly speaking, the traditional polarity of melody and accompaniment is abolished. The

voice line and the piano part have become different aspects of the same basic principle. (The use and treatment of text in this music is still quite traditional.)

The music of Messiaen takes yet a different path, and his later works in particular (from about 1950 on) have greatly influenced younger composers. His treatment of rhythm brought about the new type of melody shown in Ex. 6. The melodic unfolding is determined primarily by the treatment of rhythmic cells, which increase (A) and decrease (B) in duration. In spite of these changes, however, the music is essentially based on the principle of nondevelopment. The cells are juxtaposed as if they were unaffected by each other; they are not interlaced but autonomous. This approach is of utmost importance, for as a result the melody is a discontinuous process. The continuity, and therefore the potential unity, of traditional melody has been lost. Messiaen was not the first composer to think in this way, but he was certainly the most radical of the older composers to do so. Younger composers have continued in this direction, building their works by means of a more or less free system of permutative procedures.

A final step, leading toward melodic discontinuity, has been taken since the 1950s. Actually this step fulfills an old dream. It was anticipated by Debussy in his conception of music as "*le temps rythmisé,*" a flexible sound amalgam in which timbre, texture, rhythm, melody, harmony are all equally important as structural and expressive elements. Related to this is the athematic conception of Schoenberg in which melody is not fixed in a definite, recognisable shape. In other words, this dream is of a melody without thematic function, of lines merging into the musical flow, constantly changing, moving from one form into another. The 1950s saw an intense exploration of these

Ex. 6. Olivier Messiaen, *Livre d'orgue*, I: 1–7
Quoted by permission of Alphonse Leduc

conceptions among serial composers and in an even more direct way in the works of Iannis Xenakis. The abolition of fixed, recognizable pitches in the clusters and sound amalgams of Ligeti and others have gone the rest of the way by circumventing melody altogether. More recent trends (since 1960) are generally less rigorous. An example of new melodic shapes is the fragment from *Circles* (1960) by Luciano Berio given in Ex. 7. The melody is accompanied by harp and percussion, which play in fluid rhythmic patterns that fluctuate around C♯ (this may in part be an example of text illustration on the word "riverly"). The first of the two melodic phrases shown in the example moves in ever larger undulations towards C♯ via the first pitch, B, and C. The fundamental line B-C-C♯ (which Hindemith would have called a *Sekundgang*) contributes to the cohesion of the phrase. The second phrase revolves around C♯ as a melodic center (not to be confused with a tonal center). Surprisingly, then, this example of a more recent melody shows more than one traditional feature. Its relationship with the text is new, however. The symbols (♪ = approximate pitch, ♪ = on the breath, ♪ = spoken) and the elaborate differences in attacks and dynamics in the voice part serve two purposes: 1) they create a fusion of vocal and instrumental means (more obvious in other parts of the work), and 2) they create a new kind of close relationship between music and language. Berio is aiming here at a continuum between speaking and singing (a continuum stemming from Schoenberg's sprechgesang), and between word sounds and timbres. Music and language here penetrate each other in a new kind of fusion. These tendencies in recent music have given rise to still more highly differentiated ways of performing and to new kinds of notation.

BIBL.: Henry Cowell, *The Nature of Melody* (written late 1930s, unpub.); Ton de Leeuw, *Muziek van de Twintigste Eeuw* (Utrecht 1970).

Ton de Leeuw

SEE ALSO Asian Music and Western Composition, Jazz, Popular Music, Text Setting and Usage, Theory.

Mendes, Gilberto (Ambrósio García) (b. Santos, Brazil, 13 Oct 1922), attended Santos Conservatory (1941–48; harmony with Savino de Benedictis, piano with Antonieta Rudge) and studied with the Brazilian composers Claudio Santoro (1954) and G. Olivier Toni (1958–60). He attended the Darmstadt summer courses in 1962 and 1968, studying composition with Pierre Boulez, Henri Pousseur, and Karlheinz Stockhausen. He has taught music history and esthetics in Santos: at the Clube de Arte (1956), the Escola de Jovens (1966), and the Colégio Vocacional Stella Maris (since 1968). He has also lectured at the S. Paulo Goethe Institute and the Santos Ars Viva

Ex. 7. Luciano Berio, *Circles*, part II, voice part: 2–15
Quoted by permission of Universal Edition and Theodore Presser

Society. In the fall of 1970 he taught composition at Brasilia Univ. He is a writer on new music for the journals *O estado de São Paulo* and *A tribuna* (Santos). Since 1962 Mendes has organized the annual New Music Festival of the Santos Ars Viva Society. As a member of the New Music Group in São Paulo, he was coauthor (in 1963) of a manifesto "Música nova," "on behalf of a new Brazilian music . . . according to the modern theories of cybernetics, information, probability, quanta, semantics, and semiotics, structuralism, and human communication," and "against a poor musical nationalism, based only on folk music fitted in classical and romantic patterns." His thinking has been influenced by Erik Satie, John Cage, the pop artists Rauschenberg, Lichtenstein, Oldenburg, the movies of Godard, avant-garde writers Pound, cummings, Joyce, Kafka, and the Brazilian concrete poets Haroldo de Campos, Augusto de Campos, and Decio Pignatari.

PRINCIPAL COMPOSITIONS: *Ricercare* for 2 horns, strings (1960); *Music* for 12 different instruments (1961); *Música para piano No. 1* (1962, Ricordi); *Rotationis* for 13 different instruments (1962); *nascemorre* for voices, percussion, tape (1963, PAU and Southern); *cidade cité city* for 3 voices, percussion, piano, double bass, 3 phonographs, dust catcher, floor polisher, television, etc. (1964; *Invenção* review, S. Paulo); *blirium c-9*, aleatory music for various instrumental possibilities (1965, Ricordi); *Beba Coca-Cola* for 4 voices; poem by Decio Pignatari (1966); *Son et lumière* for piano sounds on tape, photographic flashes, and "a very beautiful woman pianist who walks like a mannequin" instead of playing the piano (1968); *Santos Foot-Ball Music* for piano, violin, viola, cello, double bass, clarinet, oboe, bassoon, flute, trumpet, trombone, bongos, 3-track tape including the broadcast of a football game, audience (1969).

PRINCIPAL WRITINGS: "Debussy," *Invenção* (S. Paulo, June 1963): 12–14; coauthor, "Música nova," *ibid.* 5–6, reprinted in *Revista musical chilena* (Dec 1963): 30–32; "De como a MPB perdeu a direção e continuou na vanguarda," *Balanço da bossa* (S. Paulo 1968): 121–28; "Música nuova brasiliana: dati e problemi," *Aut Aut* (Milan) 109–10: 206–12; "O som nôvo da música electrônica," *Shell em revista* 16 (1969): 28–31; "Darmstadt, do 'art nouveau' acs *Hymnen* de Stockhausen," *O estado de São Paulo* (1 Feb 1969); "Música de vanguarda das Américas," *ibid.* (21 June 1969); "Música nova Bohemica et Slovaca," *ibid.* (18 July 1970).

BIBL.: Augusto de Campos, *Balanço da bossa* (S. Paulo 1968): 7–11; Haroldo de Campos, *Arte no horizonte do provavel* (S. Paulo 1969): 22–23; Mauricio Lozano, "El grupo brasileño música nova," *Sonda* (Madrid) 1: 37–42, reprinted in *Melos* (April 1968): 141–44; Vasco Mariz, *Figuras da música brasileira contemporânea* (S. Paulo 1970); Decio Pignatari, "Vanguarda em explosão sonora," *Informação. Linguagem. Comunicação* (S. Paulo 1968): 127–34.

SEE ALSO Brazil.

Mennin, Peter (pseudonym of Peter Mennini) (b. Erie, Pa., 17 May 1923), attended Oberlin Conservatory (1941–42, composition with Normand Lockwood), and the Eastman School (1943–47, composition and orchestration with Bernard Rogers, composition with Howard Hanson). He taught composition at the Juilliard School (1947–58) and was director of the Peabody Conservatory (1958–62). Since then he has been president of the Juilliard School.

Mennin is primarily a symphonist; besides his seven symphonies to date, he has written several concertos. He has also written two string quartets, a violin sonata, an organ sonata, and some short piano pieces. His vocal music consists of four songs to poems by Emily Dickinson, cantatas, an opera, and considerable choral music. His melodies contain long-breathed cantabile lines that are both restrained in emotion and free of unessential decoration. Diatonically constructed, they often employ augmented seconds or diminished fifths. The metric organization is often free sounding and flexible with irregular and asymmetric rhythmic motives. The harmonic idiom is tonal and shuns excessive dissonance. The textures are usually polyphonic, and, although tonalities are carefully organized according to long-range goals, the momentary concurrences of polyphonic lines frequently create an illusion of considerable harmonic freedom. Preferring the characteristic registers of instruments, Mennin generally avoids extremes of range and also abstains from the exotic tone colors of unusual instruments. He is partial to solo oboe and flute timbres and tends to use orchestral colors to reinforce formal structure. He employs brass instruments both for coloristic potential and for rhythmic punctuation.

PRINCIPAL COMPOSITIONS (list prepared by the composer, music published by Fischer unless otherwise noted): *Concertino* for flute, strings, percussion (1945, Hargail); *Symphonies Nos. 3–7* (1946, Hargail; 1949; 1950; 1953; 1963–64; No. 4 "The Cycle," for chorus, orchestra); *The Christmas Story*, cantata for soprano, tenor, chorus, brass, timpani, strings (1949); *String Quartet No. 2* (1952); *Concertato*, "Moby Dick," for orchestra (1952); *Sonata Concertante* for violin, piano (1956); *Cello Concerto* (1956); *Piano Concerto* (1958); *Canto* for orchestra (1963); *Piano Sonata* (1967); *Cantata de virtute* for tenor, baritone, narrator, chorus, children's chorus, orchestra

(1968–69). List to 1954 in Hendl; to 1957: *Composers of the Americas* 5:48–52.

BIBL.: Walter Hendl, "The Music of P. M.," *Juilliard Review* 1:18–25.

Thomas E. Warner

Menotti, Gian Carlo (b. Cadegliano, Italy, 7 July 1911), studied at the Verdi Conservatory in Milan (1923–27), the Curtis Institute in Philadelphia (1928–33, composition with Rosario Scalero, piano with Vera Resnikoff). He taught composition at the Curtis Institute during 1948–55. In 1958 he founded the Festival of Two Worlds at Spoleto, Italy. He has been stage director for a number of operas at the Festival and at the Hamburg Opera, as well as for the premieres of his own operas, beginning with *The Medium* in 1946. He has written texts for his own vocal works, for Samuel Barber's *Vanessa* and *A Hand of Bridge*, and Lucas Foss's *Introductions and Goodbyes*. He has also written film scripts and two plays, *A Copy of Madame Aupic* (1959) and *The Leper* (1968), and has directed an Italian production of Anouilh's *Medea*. D'Amico (see bibl.) has observed that Menotti does not aim at "poetry" in his operas but at journalism in the best sense. Such works as *The Telephone*, *Amahl*, *The Saint of Bleecker Street*, and much of *The Consul* convey an immediate and familiar experience to the man-in-the-street. Although the structure of the operas is not based on a succession of arias but on the construction of larger scenes, care is always taken to assure the predominance of song and of the vocal lines.

PRINCIPAL COMPOSITIONS (dates are of first performance): *Pastorale* for piano, strings (1933); *Amelia Goes to the Ball*, 1-act opera (1937, Ricordi); *Poemetti*, children's pieces for piano (1937, Ricordi); *The Old Maid and the Thief*, opera in 14 scenes (1939, Ricordi); *The Island God*, 2-act opera (1941); *Sebastian*, ballet; choreography by Edward Caton (1944, suite published by Ricordi); *Piano Concerto* (1945, Ricordi); *The Medium*, 2-act opera (1946, Schirmer-G); *The Telephone*, 1-act opera (1947, Schirmer-G); *Errand into the Maze*, ballet; choreography by Martha Graham (1947); *The Consul*, 3-act opera (1950, Schirmer-G); *Amahl and the Night Visitors*, 1-act TV opera (1951, Schirmer-G); *Apocalypse* for orchestra (1951, Schirmer-G); *Violin Concerto* (1952, Schirmer-G); *Ricercare and Toccata* for piano (1953, Ricordi); *The Saint of Bleecker Street*, 3-act opera (1954, Schirmer-G); *The Unicorn, the Gorgon, and the Manticore*, ballet-opera for 6 dancers, chorus, 9 instruments; choreography by John Butler (1956, Ricordi); *Maria Golovin*, 3-act opera (1958, Ricordi); *Labyrinth*, 1-act TV opera (1963, Schirmer-G); *The Death of the Bishop of Brindisi*, cantata for mezzo-soprano, bass,

children's chorus, adult chorus, orchestra (1963, Schirmer-G); *The Last Savage*, 3-act opera (1963, Ricordi); *Martin's Lie*, 1-act church opera (1964, Schirmer-G); *Canti della Lontananza*, 7 songs for soprano, piano; texts by the composer (1967); *Help, Help, the Globolinks!*, 1-act opera (1968, Schirmer-G); *The Most Important Man in the World*, 3-act opera (1970).

BIBL.: Fedele D'Amico, "M.," *Encyclopédie de la musique Fasquelle* (Paris 1961), vol. 3:184; Winthrop Sargent, "Orlando in Mount Kisco," *New Yorker* (4 May 1963):49–89; Robert Tricoire, *G. C. M.* (Paris 1966).

SEE ALSO Dance, Musical, Opera.

Mercure, Pierre (b. Montreal, 21 Feb 1927; d. Paris, 27 Jan 1966), studied at Jean-de-Brébeuf College in Montreal until 1946, the Montreal Conservatory (1944–49, composition with Claude Champagne), in Paris during 1949–50 with Nadia Boulanger (composition), Arthur Hoérée (orchestration), and Jean Fournet (conducting), and at Tanglewood (1951, composition with Luigi Dallapiccola). During 1947–49 and 1950–52 he played bassoon in the Montreal Symphony. He then worked for the French television network of the CBC as chief producer of music programs. He was a dedicated avant-gardist concerned with finding new kinds of contrast in line, form, and sonority. As early as 1949 he and Gabriel Charpentier were experimenting in Paris with chance composition procedures and improvisation. At the same time he became interested in Pierre Schaeffer's new work there with musique concrète. Later on he studied electronic techniques with Richard Maxfield in New York. In 1961 he organized and directed the first International Week of Avant-Garde Music in Montreal. His death resulted from an automobile accident.

PRINCIPAL COMPOSITIONS: *Colloque* for voice, piano (1947, BMIC); *Kaleidoscope* for orchestra (1947–48, reorchestrated 1949; Ricordi); *Pantomime* for winds, brass, percussion (1948, Ricordi); *Dissidence*, 3 songs for soprano, piano; poems by Gabriel Charpentier (1955); *Cantate pour une joie* for soprano, chorus, orchestra; poems by Charpentier (1956, Ricordi); *Divertimento* for string quartet, string orchestra (1957); *Triptyque* for orchestra (1959, Ricordi); *Incandescence*, tape score for the François Riopelle Dance Group (1961); *Structures métalliques Nos. 1–2* on 4-track tape; based on metal sounds (1961); *Répercussions* on 3-track tape; based on the sounds of a Japanese carillon (1961); *Improvisation* on tape; based on piano sounds (1961); *Psaume pour Abri*, cantata for narrator, 2 choruses, strings, winds, harp, harpsichord, percussion, tape; poems by Fernand Ouellettes (1963); *Formes 64*, film score for concrete sounds with saxophone, trombone, tuba

(1964); *Lignes et points* for orchestra (1965); *Eléments III*, film score for concrete sounds with flute (1965).

BIBL.: Richard Hudson, "Canadian Contrasts," *Ricordiana* (Oct 1965):1-3; "Un musicien canadien P. M.," *ICI: Radio Culture Information* (20 Oct 1966):12-14.

[prepared with the help of Keith MacMillan]

Meriläinen, Usko (b. Tampere, Finland, 27 January 1930), studied at the music school in Tampere (1946-50) and at the Sibelius Academy (1951-55; composition and conducting with Aarre Merikanto, Leo Funtek). He also studied 12-tone techniques with Wladimir Vogel in Switzerland. He has been a choral conductor for the Finnish Opera, a piano and theory teacher at the Sibelius Academy and Tampere and Kuopio Schools of Music, and conductor for the Tampere Workers' Theater.

PRINCIPAL COMPOSITIONS: *Symphonies Nos. 1-2* (1953-55; 1964, Bote); *Partita* for brass (1954, King); *Piano Concertos Nos. 1-2* (1955, 1969); *Concerto for Orchestra* (1956); *Suite* for piano (1956); *Sonatina* for piano (1958); *Ruokojen kulkue* [Procession of Reeds], ballet (1960); *Piano Sonatas Nos. 1-2* (1960; 1966, Weinberger); *4 Songs* for soprano, piano; text by Pekka Lounela (1961); *4 Bagatelles* for string quartet (1962); *Riviravi*, piano pieces for children (1962, Fazer); *Chamber Concerto* for violin, 2 string orchestras, percussion (1962); *Epyllion* for orchestra (1963, Bote); *Impression* for chamber orchestra (1965, Bote); *String Quartet* (1965); *Hommage à Jean Sibelius* for violin, piano (1965); *Musique de printemps* for orchestra (1969).

Messiaen, Olivier (b. Avignon, 10 Dec 1908). His mother, the poetess Cécile Sauvage, wrote a book of verses, *L'Ame en bourgeon*, dedicated to the child she was expecting. His father, Pierre Messiaen, is a well-known translator of English authors, among them Shakespeare. One of the son's first pieces was written at age nine, *La Dame de Shalott* to a poem by Tennyson. At ten, through Jehan de Gibon, his music teacher in Nantes, he became acquainted with Debussy's *Pelléas et Mélisande*, which proved decisive in helping him determine his vocation. He entered the Paris Conservatory in 1919 and earned first prizes in harmony, counterpoint, and fugue (1926), piano accompaniment (1928), organ and improvisation (1929), music history (1929), and composition (1930). This last he studied in the classes of Jean and Noël Gallon, Georges Caussade, Estyle, Marcel Dupré, Maurice Emmanuel, and Paul Dukas. He has also studied Indian rhythmic processes, Greek

rhythm, plainchant, folk music, and various philosophies of time and duration. From early in his life he had been interested in nature. In some early works he began to quote birdsongs, and later he systematically notated the songs of the birds of France, classifying them by region and by the terrain they inhabit. This research culminated in the *Catalogue d'oiseaux* (1956-58).

Since 1931 Messiaen has been organist at the Church of the Trinity in Paris. In 1936 he became a professor at both the Ecole Normale de Musique and the Schola Cantorum and also founded the group Jeune France with André Jolivet, Daniel-Lesur, and Ives Baudrier. At this time he married the violinist Claire Desnos (their son, Pascal, is a professor of Russian).

Messiaen was imprisoned by the Germans for two years (during which time he composed and premiered the *Quatuor pour la fin du temps*) and on his release was appointed to the Paris Conservatory where he first taught harmony (from 1942), then musical analysis (from 1947) and composition (since 1966). Between 1943 and 1947 he gave private group lessons at the home of Guy-Bernard Delapierre, a musician he met while in captivity. He has also been asked to teach in Budapest (1947), Tanglewood (1948), Darmstadt (1950-53), and Saarbrücken (1953), and recent tours have taken him to Japan and North and South America. Among his pupils are Pierre Boulez, Yvonne Loriod, Jean-Louis Martinet, Maurice Leroux, Karlheinz Stockhausen, Serge Nigg, Michel Fano, Jean Barraqué, Pierre Henry, Chang Hao, Iannis Xenakis, Gilbert Amy, Makoto Shinohara, Alexander Goehr, Jean-Pierre Guézec, Raffi Ourgandjian, and Paul Méfano. Like Berlioz, he considers his true homeland to be the Alps of the Dauphiné. His statement, "I am not a French Cartesian" could equally apply to Berlioz, whom he admires greatly.

Messiaen's music moves around three poles: "the theological truths of the Catholic faith" (". . . the first aspect of my work . . . the only one perhaps that I will not regret at the hour of my death"); "the greatest theme of human love," that of Tristan and Isolde (*Harawi, Turangalîla, 5 Rechants*); and nature. All three "are summed up in only one idea: divine love!" (Samuel, ch. 1; see bibl.). For Messiaen "music was more than a work of art, it was a way of existing, an inextinguishable fire."[1]

His output can be divided into works for organ, piano, orchestra, and voice (the last

[1] Pierre Boulez, "Hommage à Messiaen," *Melos* (Dec 1958):387.

encompassing far fewer works than the others). In each domain the discoveries and inventions are numerous. The organ pieces, all of which Messiaen premiered, are religious in subject. They are especially noteworthy for their acoustic clarity, which is achieved, in spite of the reverberation time in church naves, through the use of contrasting timbres and a judicious distribution of sound in time. The piano is exploited through extensions of keyboard technique and the invention of new sonorities: the use of extreme registers, of chords that modify basic resonances, of the thumb on several notes at once, of clusters of chords, fast passages in permutation (*Ile de feu II*, p. 6), rapid groups in contrary motion ending strongly on the thumb, individuality of registers, etc. Above all, Messiaen has found in the pianist Yvonne Loriod, now his wife, not only an ideal interpreter but also a real collaborator who has done the fingerings for almost all the piano works. One can feel the importance in his work of such a skilled pianist. In his orchestral works the consciousness of timbre as structural material determines the use of color, which ranges from vibrating metals to the "European gamelan group" (vibraphone, marimba, xylophone, chimes, piano, gongs), through *Klangfarbenmelodie* groups, and huge polyphonic passages in which almost every instrument is a soloist (*Chronochromie*). Messiaen's sense of monumentality produces the vastness of certain evening-length works (*Turangalîla* in 10 movements; *La Transfiguration* in 14 parts), including some for piano (*20 Regards, Catalogue d'oiseaux*).

As in Debussy, form is always as varied as the material. Even if many refrain and strophic forms occur, the recurrences are often variations or, with more refinement, the continuation of previous passages (*Chronochromie, Catalogue d'oiseaux*). Events are sometimes grouped into a kind of mosaic of tempos, densities, timbres, etc. The nonlinear aspect of this conception reached an extreme in *Couleurs de la cité céleste* (1964), which Messiaen has likened to the rose window of a cathedral in that it could begin and end at any point.

Messiaen's harmony, at least in the early works, stems partly from Debussy: the use of dominant seventh or ninth chords of major and minor thirds; the same chords with added notes (sixth, augmented fourth), a harmonic parallel to "added values" in the rhythm; modal progressions of chords; and the use of natural resonances, especially distant harmonics, to alter timbres. Even more than from these traits, however, the distinctive color of Messiaen's music results from his use of limited-transposition modes (transposable only a few times before they return to their original pitches). The mode used controls both harmony and melody, and its interior symmetry is extended to other parameters. This extension, similar to certain Asian music (Bali, Java) appears as an authentic meeting of worlds following the example and implications of Debussy and Stravinsky; it is never done superficially in an exotic or banal manner. Again following the example of Debussy, the harmony has a coloristic rather than a functional role, isolating the pure instant; the static state of the instant often attains the ecstatic (*Couleur de la cité céleste, Et expecto resurrectionem mortuorum*). As in Varèse, harmony is often related to timbre: "Varèse has completely reconsidered harmony so that the concept of chords is replaced by sound complexes designed for maximum color and intensity" (Samuel: 205). Messiaen often uses pitched metal percussion (cymbals, gongs, tam-tam) to obtain striking textures. A subtle example can be found in the strophes of *Chronochromie* (from *chronos*, time; and *chroma*, color), where three "families of chords" are used to color the three superimposed lines of durations: 1) chord masses turning about a fixed center, 2) chords with contracted resonances, and 3) transposed inversions of complex chords on the same bass note.

In addition to the implications for melody of his harmonic thinking—for example, the frequent cadential use of the augmented fourth—Messiaen rooted many types of music in his melodic style. Such transplantation is characteristic: "Messiaen is a crucible of material in fusion," in Stockhausen's words.[2] The materials range from Gregorian chant to birdsong and include Mozart (whom he frequently analyzed for his classes), especially the accentuation group of anacrusis-accent-termination (*Chronochromie*, Introduction at No. 14); pentatonic music (second movement of *Les 3 Petites Liturgies*); Russian (descending fourths) and Peruvian folklore (*Harawi*); the supple curves of Indian music (*Turangalîla, 5 Rechants*); an enlarged *Klangfarbenmelodie* concept applied to single events or groups of events (*Chronochromie, Oiseaux exotiques, Livre d'orgue*); Stravinsky's generalised mobility of pitch, which is also found in nature where there are "no immobile pitches"; the monody of plainchant ("L'Abîme des ois-

[2] Karlheinz Stockhausen, "Hommage à Messiaen," *Melos* (Dec 1958): 392.

eaux" from the *Quatuor*, "Le Regard de l'esprit de joie" from *20 Regards*) along with some techniques of ornamentation and interpolation ("Par Lui tout a été fait" and the end of "Le Regard du silence" from *20 Regards*) and neumes applied to rhythmic values (*Neumes rythmiques*). Messiaen has also quoted plainchant as transformed (or "modulated" in the electronic meaning of that term) by contact with other material, such as another mode, a group of chords, or a group of timbres (the Alleluia quotations in *Couleur de la cité céleste*, rehearsal Nos. 8, 25, 41). Among Messiaen's personal melodic techniques are the regular and irregular expansion or contraction of intervals (*20 Regards*); the gradual modification of one melodic fragment while another remains constant, this being a melodic projection of a similar procedure in rhythm (piano part from the fifth movement of *Turangalîla*); and the changing of registers ("Danse de la fureur des 7 trompettes" from the *Quatuor*).

It is impossible to discuss Messiaen's use of birdsong from a purely intervallic point of view, owing to the blossoming multiplicity of intervals used by birds and the interpenetration of all musical parameters in their songs, which are so intimately connected with rhythm, timbre, and phoneticoharmonic features (*Réveil des oiseaux, Oiseaux exotiques,* and above all the fascinating thrush song in the "Antistrophes" of *Chronochromie* and the entire *Catalogue d'oiseaux*). It can be noted, however, that because birds do not sing in the 12-tone equal-tempered system and because they use microintervals, "translations" of their song was necessary: "For the melody and the rhythm I have always tried to notate with the utmost precision except for very small intervals and very short durations which are replaced by slightly larger intervals and durations, the others being impractical. But I always respect the scale of the different durations; the relations between pitches and durations stay the same with a slight change in tempo and register which, I repeat, does not destroy the relations" (Goléa:225–26). Messiaen has also explored the idea of melody in the negative, the use of chords whose component pitches drop out one by one in various rhythms, leaving a succession of silences (*Et expecto . . .*). The most far-reaching consequence of this enlarged concept of melody is the tendency to encompass all aspects of sound—the traditional aspect of pitch (still the most flexible), timbre, dynamics, tempos, etc.—through motion, which leads us to the cornerstone, rhythm.

Rhythm is the principal object of Messiaen's innovations and investigations. "I consider rhythm the prime and perhaps the essential part of music. . . . A rhythmic music is one that disregards repetition, squareness, and regular division, a music that is, in short, inspired by the movement of nature, a movement of free and uneven durations" (Samuel: 63–64). He shares this field of investigation with John Cage (a paradox considering the differences in their approach and techniques), and his work has been a starting point for other composers, most notably Boulez. The sources of Messiaen's treatment of rhythm are varied: 1) Ancient Greece. Here Messiaen was attracted to the implications in definitions by Plato and others of rhythm as order in movement. He was also impressed by the great variety obtainable in Greek meters simply from short and long durations and alternations of arsis and thesis. 2) Mozart's use of accentuation, which derives from speech. 3) Debussy's "love of nature, wind, and water," which led him to fluid rhythms, nonregularity in durations, and perpetual undulation (Samuel:70). 4) Stravinsky's use of variable rhythmic cells in *Le Sacre*. Messiaen has called these "*personnages rythmiques*" and has drawn parallels with the theater: a first cell acts (increases), a second is acted on (decreases), a third observes (remains the same). 5) Indian music. "I studied the 120 'deci-talas' that were collected in a slightly disorderly fashion by Cârngadeva [a 13th-century theorist] for so long a time that I finally discovered the different rhythmic rules proceeding from them . . ." (Samuel:81). 6) Schoenberg and Webern. Their serialization of pitch Messiaen applied also to durations, types of attack, and intensities (*Mode de valeurs et d'intensités*). In summary, "My rhythmical language is a mixture of all these elements: durations distributed in irregular numbers, an absence of even beats and of symmetrical measures, love for prime numbers, presence of nonretrogradable [palindrome] rhythms, and the action of *personnages rythmiques*. . . . All this evolves, is mixed, and superimposed" (Samuel:88).

The characteristic rhythmic techniques in Messiaen include the following: 1) the free multiplication of short values (e.g., 16th notes), which represent the primary unit; 2) the principle of the "added value"

(♫ ♫ ♩.);

3) irregular augmentations or diminutions

(♩ ♩ ♩ ♫);

4) rhythmic canons, often produced by the addition of a dot so that voices begin together and gradually pull apart from each other ("Regard du temps" and "Regard du silence" from 20 Regards); 5) palindrome rhythms

(♩♪♩♪♪♩♪♩♪♩♪♪♩♪)

from the eighth movement of *Turangalîla*); 6) rhythmic pedals (or isorhythms) in which the number of durations may not coincide with the number of "chords," thus creating new relations at each repetition (beginning of the *Quatuor*); 7) the addition to or subtraction from a series of durations of one value in each repetition

(♩♪♩♪♩♩♪♩♪♩♪♩♪♩♪♩♪)

♩♩♩.♩♩♪♩♪♩♪♪♩♪♩♪♩♪

etc., from the eighth movement of *Turangalîla*) or of one value in one duration of a group

(♫♫♫♪♫♪.│♫♫♫♪♫♪.│♫♫♫♪♫♪.│

from "Rousserolle effarvate" in the *Catalogue d'oiseaux*); 8) extensions of the *personnages rythmiques* concept, as in the central section of *Turangalîla*, where six are used, the three lower parts (horn, trombones) being retrogrades of the three upper parts (trumpets); another example is the second "Piece en trio," No. 5 from the *Livre d'orgue*, which Messiaen considers his "greatest rhythmic victory"; 9) evocations of the infinitely large, "the time of the planets," and the infinitely small, "the time of the atom," by means of extremely long and short durations ("Les Mains de l'abîme" from the *Livre d'orgue*); 10) "interversions" (Messiaen's term), or changes in the order of individual durations (*Chronochromie*, where 32 durations occur in symmetrical permutations) or of groups of durations (*Livre d'orgue*); 11) "sounds-durations," or association between pitches and durations ("Merle de roche" from *Catalogue d'oiseaux*, *Livre d'orgue*, *Chronochromie*); 12) "rhythmic metabol," or progressive transformation of one rhythm into another (7 *Haï-kaï*); 13) the changing of tempo for successive events so that each one has its own block of time ("Chocard des Alpes" and "Traquet stapazin" from the *Catalogue d'oiseaux*); 14) the inclusion in more recent works (7 *Haï-kaï*) of irrational values ("in which I was less interested before") and of a new conception of tempo by which not only the order of durations is changed but also the quality of a rhythm by means of accelerando or rallentando. All of these techniques stem from two different views of

time: quantitative time, which reached its summit in the *Livre d'orgue* (geometric time) and qualitative time, which reached its summit in the *Catalogue d'oiseaux* (the time of nature, of events, psychological and physiological time). It is the latter idea that Messiaen evokes when he alludes to "these great fields of long durations" and "a changing notion of time" (Samuel: 90). The synthesis of these two trends is undoubtedly the greatest accomplishment of *Chronochromie*, the "color of time."

Although Messiaen does not regard his *Mode de valeurs et d'intensités* (1949) as a great work, it was highly influential in the 1950s. Before it was published, Stockhausen is said to have listened to a recording of it several times in succession, and Boulez paid homage to it by deriving the 12-tone set of his *Structures* from it. In this work Messiaen separated four sound parameters from each other and applied a generalized serial technique to each: there are 36 pitches (in fixed registers), 24 durations, 12 attacks, and 7 intensities. This suggested to 12-tone composers that they should not confine their attention to pitch alone but deal with other parameters as well. The loosening here of traditional hierarchies among musical elements is part of a long-range trend that began before Messiaen in Berg and Varèse (variation of dynamics) and has continued after him in Boulez (variation of tempos, timbres, intensities), Stockhausen (application of abstract quantities to various parameters), and Xenakis (statistical variation processes).

A number of correspondences among various aspects of style and technique in Messiaen are readily apparent: added notes harmonically ↔ added values rhythmically; polymodality ↔ polyrhythms; symmetrical modes ↔ palindrome rhythms ("the charm of impossibilities and the relation between different subject matters," as he remarked in *The Technique of My Musical Language*). The concept of interrelationships (so close to Baudelaire) became especially important to Messiaen after he listened to certain birdsongs (i.e., the nightingale, thrush, mockingbird), in which each event is colored with a different timbre and where one can find influences and osmosis between sound and the surrounding shapes and movements (the melodic contour and the sea waves in "Le Courlis cendré" from *Catalogue d'oiseaux*). Recently Messiaen has tried to associate color and sound more closely (*Couleur de la cité céleste, Et expecto resurrectionem mortuorum*, and his recent monumental work *La Transfiguration de notre*

Seigneur Jésus-Christ). Thus the correspondences exist not only within the music itself but between life and music. This extends the implication of music through its cornerstone, movement. If one can use the meaningful word "poetry" in this same perspective, it is neither in a vague manner nor even because of the composer's "poetical" texts, but rather because of all these connections and relationships, rooted in life's pulsations and births, perceived at the heart of music itself.

PRINCIPAL COMPOSITIONS (published by Leduc unless otherwise noted): *Le Banquet céleste* for organ (1928); *Préludes* for piano (1929, Durand); *3 Mélodies* for soprano, piano (1929, Durand); *La Mort du nombre* for soprano, tenor, violin, piano (1929, Durand); *Diptyque* for organ (1929, Durand); *Les Offrandes oubliées* for orchestra (1930, Durand); *Apparition de l'Eglise éternelle* for organ (1931, Lemoine); *Thème et variations* for violin, piano (1931); *Hymne au Saint-Sacrement* for orchestra (1932, Broude-B); *L'Ascension* for orchestra (1932) or organ (1933); *Vocalise* for soprano, piano (1935); *La Nativité du Seigneur* for organ (1935); *Poèmes pour Mi* for soprano, piano; poems by the composer (1936, orchestral version 1937; Durand); *Fêtes des belles eaux*, sextet for ondes Martenot (1937, unpub.); *2 Monodies en quart de ton* for ondes Martenot (1938, unpub.); *Chants de terre et de ciel* for soprano, piano (1938, Durand); *Les Corps glorieux* for organ (1939); *Quatuor pour la fin du temps* for violin, clarinet, cello, piano (1941, Durand); *Rondeau* for piano (1943); *Visions de l'Amen* for 2 pianos (1943, Durand); *3 Petites Liturgies de la Presence divine* for women's chorus, piano, ondes Martenot, orchestra (1944, Durand); *20 Regards sur l'Enfant Jésus* for piano (1944, Durand); *Harawi, Chant d'amour et de mort* for soprano, piano (1945); *Turangalîla-Symphonie* for piano, ondes Martenot, orchestra (1946–48, Durand); *Cantéjodayâ* for piano (1948, UE); *5 Rechants* for 12-voice chorus (1948, Rouart-Lerolle); *4 Etudes de rythme*, "Ile de feu I," "Mode de valeurs et d'intensités," "Neumes rythmiques," "Ile de feu II," for piano (1949–50, Durand); *Messe de la Pentecôte* for organ (1950); *Livre d'orgue* for organ (1951); *Le Merle noir* for flute, piano (1952); *Timbres-durées*, musique concrète prepared in collaboration with Pierre Henry (1952, unpub.); *Reveil des oiseaux* for piano, orchestra (1953, Durand); *Oiseaux exotiques* for piano, 2 clarinets, xylophone, glockenspiel, percussion, small wind orchestra (1955, UE); *Catalogue d'oiseaux* for piano (1956–58, UE); *Chronochromie* for orchestra (1960); *Verset pour la fête de la dédicace* for organ (1960); *7 Haï-kaï* for piano, xylophone, marimba, orchestra (1963); *Couleurs de la cité céleste* for piano, winds, percussion (1964); *Et expecto resurrectionem mortuorum* for woodwinds, brass, metal percussion (1964); *La Transfiguration de Notre Seigneur Jésus-Christ* for piano, flute, clarinet, cello, xylorimba, vibraphone, marimba, chorus, orchestra (1965–69). Thematic catalog to 1964 in Samuel;

list of works to 1953 in Drew, to 1968 in Mari.

PRINCIPAL WRITINGS: *The Technique of My Musical Language*, English translation (Paris 1950); "La Nature, les chants d'oiseaux," *Guide du concert* (Paris, April 1959); *Conference de Bruxelles prononcée a l'Exposition Universelle de 1958*, includes English translation (Paris 1960); *Traité de rythme* (in preparation). Messiaen has also written didactic works on solfège (Paris 1935) and harmony (Paris 1939, 1953).

BIBL.: David Drew, "Messiaen, a Provisional Study," *Score* 10, 13, 14; Marcel Frémiot, "Le rythme dans le langage d'O. M.," *Polyphonie* (1949); Antoine Goléa, *Rencontres avec O. M.* (Paris 1961); "Hommage to M.," *Melos* (Dec 1958); Pierrette Mari, *O. M.* (Paris 1970); Claude Samuel, *Entretiens avec O. M.* (Paris 1967); Gilles Tremblay, "Oiseau-nature, M., musique," *Les Cahiers canadians de musique* (Montreal, spring-summer 1970); Stuart Waumsley, *The Organ Music of O. M.* (Paris 1969).

Gilles Tremblay

SEE ALSO Asian Music and Western Composition; Austria and Germany; Form; France; Harmony and Counterpoint; Liturgical Music: Christian; Melody; Rhythm.

Mestres-Quadreny, Josep M(aria) (b. Manresa, Spain, 4 March 1929), studied at the Univ. of Barcelona (1950–55, composition and other subjects with C. Taltabull) and is self-taught in contemporary techniques. A free-lance composer, he has been associated with the Electronic Music Laboratory of Barcelona since its establishment in 1968. His use of serialism, beginning in 1957, rapidly evolved toward procedures of continuous variation based on interval-duration relationships. In 1960 chance elements were introduced in his first mobile pieces. He has collaborated with artists and writers in Spain in the creation of theater works, sculpture-with-sound, and other types of "art objects." Since 1965 he has incorporated live electronic processes in some works. A development of the late 1960s was the exploration of computer-aided statistical procedures.

PRINCIPAL COMPOSITIONS: *Tramesa a Tàpies* for violin, viola, percussion (1961, Seesaw); *Concert per a representar*, music theater for voices, flute, clarinet, trumpet, trombone, double bass, percussion, tape; text by J. Brossa (1964); *3 Cànons en homenatge a Galileu* for piano or percussion, electronic equipment (1965, Seesaw); *Suite bufa*, music theater for mezzo-soprano, piano, electronic equipment; text by Brossa (1966, Seesaw); *Trio* (1968, Moeck); *Ibemia* for chamber orchestra (1969, Moeck); *Doble concert* for ondes Martenot, percussion, orchestra (1970, Seesaw).

BIBL.: Wolf-Eberhard von Lewinski, "Vier katalanische Komponisten in Barcelona," *Melos* 38:92–103.
SEE ALSO Spain.

Metric Modulation, a compositional technique for changing the pulse (not necessarily the meter) from one section of music to another. The term and the technique were introduced by Elliott Carter. In operation, the technique involves the introduction of a cross-rhythm within an established pulse rate (e.g., $\frac{4}{4}$ ♩♩♩♩♩); the new pulse rate (based on the new, shorter quarter-note value in this example) then becomes the norm for a succeeding section (which may be in any meter). SEE ALSO Elliott Carter.

Mexico. Music has not thrived as vigorously in Mexico as have the plastic arts, which are used to adorn even small villages with attractive mosaics, sculptures, and fountains. During the last 40 years, however, music life has improved. More and more Mexican musicians have received scholarships from foreign governments to study in Europe, the U.S., and Argentina, and foreign teachers have been invited by the Mexican National Conservatory and the Escuela de Música de la Universidad (both in Mexico City) with increasing frequency to give short courses in the different branches of music. Further stimulus from foreign lands has come in the form of outstanding orchestral musicians in two of Mexico City's three orchestras, the Sinfónica Nacional and the Sinfónica de la Universidad. The third orchestra is the Sinfónica de Bellas Artes; there are also orchestras in Guadalajara, Xalapa, Guanajuato, and Puebla. Carlos Chávez has been responsible for two important developments based on native talent. One of these is the Orquesta Sinfónica de México, which he founded in 1928 for the purpose of introducing modern music to the Mexican public and giving Mexican composers at least one opportunity to have their works performed. After 25 years Chávez disbanded this orchestra and formed a new one with more personal purposes. The new orchestra did not thrive long and was soon replaced by the present Orquesta Sinfónica Nacional, which has toured Mexico several times, as well as the U.S. and Europe. Outside of its regular seasons it gives students' concerts and has occasionally played in factories. Its present conductor is Luis Herrera de la Fuente. The other major Chávez contribution to Mexican music life is the Composer's Workshop at the National Conservatory, which he founded in 1960 and which ranks with the Center for Advanced Musical Studies in Buenos Aires as one of the two most important centers in Latin America for the study of composition. Its present director is a Chávez pupil and Workshop graduate, Héctor Quintanar (b. 1936), under whose supervision an electronic studio was partially installed in 1968 and completed in 1970.

As the above already indicates, Mexico City is the center of the country's music life. It is here that most musicians live, teaching at the music schools and playing for the orchestras, recording companies, theaters, and churches. It is here, too, that most performances of new music take place, though it must be remembered that new music fares no better in Mexico than it does elsewhere. Annual festivals of music are held in Mexico City and Puebla. In the former a festival of contemporary music is among the official events sponsored by the music department of the National Institute of Fine Arts. In the latter, the local government provides the funds. Other activities include concerts, ballet, and musical events for children (plays, puppet operas, and the like). Every Sunday the Town Hall sponsors open-air concerts, mostly of popular music, in the public parks. Of the two leading orchestras the Sinfónica de la Universidad plays much contemporary music to full houses on the university campus; its conductor Eduardo Mata (b. 1942) is a graduate of Chávez's Workshop. The Sinfónica Nacional is more conservative, but since 1962 it has been taking a prominent part in the contemporary music festivals. The Departamento de Difusión Cultural of the Univ. of Mexico sponsors two series of eight or more concerts each year, at which contemporary music is frequently presented. In its Casa del Lago (a "Little Trianon," built by Emperor Maximilian on the shores of Chapultepec Lake), music events take place every Saturday and Sunday. The National Conservatory sponsors a more ambitious series: its Sociedad de Conciertos del Conservatorio presented 21 Mexican works during 1968. This society was founded in 1967 by Francisco Savín (b. 1929), a leader of the avant-garde who studied in Czechoslovakia. Radio Universidad, the only Mexican station wholly devoted to cultural programing, broadcasts (locally) the university's concerts.

Concerts are also sponsored every year by the private Asociación Musical Manuel M. Ponce; since 1948, when it was founded, it has presented 16 one-composer programs of contemporary music. Its other activities include instrumental and choral concerts, lectures, chamber operas, among other events.

Only a small portion of new Mexican music is published, some by Ediciones Mexicanas de Música (founded in 1947 by Chávez, Halffter, and Bal y Gay) and others by foreign publishers. By 1970 Ediciones Mexicanas had 107 Mexican works in its catalog. Young composers often complain of the lack of opportunities, but they seldom band together for action (Mexican musicians are not gregarious by nature). Since 1935, when an organization of Chávez's pupils called Grupo de los Cuatro —Blas Galindo (b. 1910), José Pablo Moncayo (b. 1912), Salvador Contreras (b. 1912), and Daniel Ayala (b. 1908)—disbanded, no important groups have been formed. There is, however, a royalty collection agency, the Sociedad de Autores y Compositores, which in 1969 distributed 36 million pesos (almost 3 million dollars) in royalties among national composers and foreign collection organizations.

Nationalism dominated most contemporary Mexican music until the early 1940s, and it remained an important feature long thereafter. Manuel M. *Ponce (1886–1948) is known as the father of national Mexican music. His early works drew on Creole folk melodies charmingly harmonized. Later on he introduced these melodies into ballads, rhapsodies, and similar works, and also drew on Indian tunes and rhythms. He and José *Rolón (1883–1945), another nationalist-oriented composer, both studied in Paris in the late 1920s and early 30s and thereafter adopted some of the harmonic elements of the neoclassic movement, as well as certain impressionistic traits, such as whole-tone scales, undulating melodies, and disregard of traditional forms. Ponce's *Violin Concerto* (1943) contains many alterations of tonal chords, interwoven in the second movement with reminiscences of "Estrellita," and a final rondo full of vague remembrances of other Mexican songs and dances. Ponce's most lasting contribution lies perhaps in his more than 80 works for guitar, an instrument of which he had a thorough knowledge. Rolón went as far as using chord clusters and harsh clashes of seconds and open fifths, recalling certain characteristics of the *mariachis*. His last work, a *Piano Concerto* (1935), contains an inventive orchestration

based on traditional instrumental combinations and uses popular tunes and songs. Other Mexican composers of this generation tended to adhere to a romantic style of Massenet and Saint-Saëns.

Silvestre *Revueltas (1899–1940) is perhaps the best representative of the nationalist school and one of Mexico's most gifted musicians. His extensive use of ostinatos, which has been criticized by some listeners, may be seen as a reflection of the endless repeating of motives and themes in much indigenous Mexican music. His idiom shows influences from Stravinsky and Bartók. His melodies, mostly nationalistic, and his strong and fluid rhythms capture some of the jocular humor in the Mexican character, e.g., *Redes* (1935), *Música para charlar* (1942), *Sensemayá* (1938).

Many once-nationalist composers either abandoned that orientation or combined it with others. Carlos *Chávez (b. 1899) is not primarily a nationalist composer, although his *Sinfonía india* (1935) makes use of native melodies, as do *Los cuatro soles* (1926), *Xochipilli-Macuilxochitl* (1940), and other works. Folk elements have seldom been quoted by him, only suggested, and they have never precluded the use of other style features. *Antígona* (1933) contains contrapuntal textures emphasizing diatonic and modal harmonies. The *Piano Concerto* (1938) contains harsh dissonances, especially dense chords made up of perfect and augmented fourths. His latest works continue to explore a free atonal idiom and follow a "nonrepetition" principle (continuous transformation of melodic and rhythmic elements) that does not, however, totally abandon periodic rhythmic pulsations. Blas *Galindo (b. 1910), one of Chávez's early students, followed a nationalist orientation until his *Sones de mariachi* (1941). Thereafter he combined such Mexican traits as folk melodies and rhythms with other procedures, such as those proclaimed by Chávez. Galindo's idiom has become atonal, favoring formations of chords by fourths. One of his latest works, *Letanía Erótica para la Paz* (1964–65), contains a mixture of polytonality, atonality and electronic tapes. Rodolfo *Halffter (b. 1900) came to Mexico from Spain in 1939 and soon after became a Mexican citizen. As a composer, however, he has remained Spanish to the core. His early works, *Don Lindo de Almería* (1935), *Violin Concerto* (1939–40), among others, contain echoes of the refined popular idiom of his teacher, Manuel de Falla. Like Chávez in the field of Mexican music, Halffter seldom "quotes" Spanish folk tunes, but rather invents them. (Spanish and Mexican folk music of the Creole and Metis type have certain rhythmic characteristics in common, the former being much stronger, gayer, and richer in melody; but Mexico has nothing like the *cante jondo* Spain inherited from the Arabs, and Spain lacks the pentatonic scales of Indian music.) Halffter has preserved the rhythmic traits and gaiety of Spain, as well as the Madrilian *joie de vivre*. He began teaching composition at the National Conservatory in 1944 and since 1946 has been training his students in 12-tone and other serial procedures. No one had taught Schoenberg's method in Mexico before that, however, and young composers of the present day claim that this instruction comes too late to really interest them. Only Jorge González Avila (b. 1926), a pupil of Halffter, has remained faithful to this idiom. Beginning with *3 Hujas de album* for piano (1953) Halffter himself became a 12-tone composer. His *Piano Sonata No. 3* (1967), however, does not develop through a strict ordering of a 12-tone series but uses a freer manipulation of material combined with a Spanish pulse and typical good humor. His latest works, *Pregón para una Pascua pobre* (1968) and *Diferencias* (1970) show the same traits. Galindo's pupils and their contemporaries have likewise not been attracted by strict 12-tone writing; rather they prefer polytonality, atonality, and freer uses of serial techniques. In this group belong Leonardo Velázquez (b. 1935) and Mario *Kuri-Aldana (b. 1931). Both have used popular rhythms and native instruments, such as marimbas. Velázquez has, in addition, been trying his hand at every kind of contemporary technique. His *Variaciones para orquesta* (1961) is more "international" than his former works in that it does not contain national rhythms and melodies. Kuri-Aldana, however, retains some national characteristics; in *Xilofonías* (1965) he used traditional instruments to imitate native ones, as well as pentatonic harmonic material. Joaquín *Gutiérrez-Heras (b. 1927) avoids identification with styles and schools; his *Trio* for oboe, clarinet and bassoon (1965) is in a free atonal idiom.

Mexico has produced two notable innovators, Julián *Carrillo (1875–1965) and Augusto Novaro (1891–1960). Carrillo was among the earliest occidental composers to work with microtones. Unfortunately he loved exaggeration and claimed to have "conquered" 13,300 scales. He called his system of microtunings "Sonido 13" and said that it was equal to Colón's discovery of the New World. He had 12 microtone pianos built in Germany and made several recordings of his microtone

music in Paris. Novaro was a serious researcher in the field of acoustics and tuning. (He outlined his findings in *Teoria de la música*, published by himself in 1951.) Using an acoustical contrivance of his own invention, he built the four instruments of the string quartet, as well as guitars and novares (pianos that don't sound percussive). He also devised several kinds of piano tunings.

Avant-garde idioms have been explored by several composers of the 1960s. Manuel *Enríquez (b. 1926) is the foremost. He studied at the Juilliard School with Peter Mennin and afterwards began writing in a polytonal idiom, in which competing tonal poles produce a serial-like feeling. *Transición* (1965) marks a change from this orientation to aleatory and "ultratonal" writing, by which Enríquez means a fusion of tone, manipulation of materials, and color, as well as the highest possible degree of expression and communication. The *Violin Concerto* (1966) and the *String Quartet No. 2* (1967) are typical of this approach; in the former he fuses all the orchestral elements with those of the solo instrument (but without depriving the latter of a number of brilliant passages). He has since been combining traditional and graphic notation, and although he has not worked in electronic media, his *Si libet* (1968) imitates electronic sounds after the manner of Penderecki. Héctor *Quintanar (b. 1936), a Chávez pupil, has used the nonrepetition procedures of his teacher. His *Galaxias* for orchestra (1968) contains new instrumental effects, such as whistling through trumpets, horns, and trombones. In *Sideral I* (1968) he recorded and altered noises from a piano. Eduardo *Mata (b. 1942), a Workshop graduate, is one of the country's most brilliant young musicians. He has found inspiration in Stockhausen's music and has written serial works (*Piano Sonata*, 1960). Beginning with *Improvisaciónes No. 1* (1964) he abandoned serial writing for an atonal style of improvised character, based on rhythmic, dynamic, and other contrasts. His *Sinfonía No. 3* (1966–67) contains aleatory passages (with specified durations and pulsations) combined with more traditional procedures.

Opera has not been a successful genre among Mexican composers, although the National Institute's Opera Nacional in Mexico City usually offers two or three new operas each year, usually European. No Mexican work has gained international recognition, and it is perhaps indicative of the national situation that Chávez keeps reorchestrating his own opera *Panfilo and Lauretta* (begun in 1958) and has twice changed its title. Ballet on the other hand has given rise to many fine works, including those of Carlos Jiménez-Mabarak (b. 1916), the first Mexican composer to introduce electronic music to the country in 1960 by means of European tapes of the earliest experiments of Cage, Berio, and others. Other ballet composers—José Pablo *Moncayo (1912–58), composer of the internationally known *Huapango* (1941), Raúl Cosío (b. 1929), and others—are influenced by the nationalism of Chávez and Revueltas.

BIBL.: Otto Mayer-Serra, *Música y músicos de Latinoamérica* (Mexico City 1947); Roberto García Morillo, *Carlos Chávez* (Mexico City 1960); Robert Stevenson, *Music in Mexico* (New York 1952).

Esperanza Pulido

Meyer, Ernst Herrmann (b. Berlin, 8 Dec 1905), studied composition privately with Hanns Eisler and Walther Hirschberg and at the Berlin Hochschule für Musik (1930–31, radio and film music with Max Butting and Paul Hindemith). During 1926–30 he studied musicology at the universities of Berlin and Heidelberg, and in the early 30s he worked as a free-lance musicologist. During 1937–48 he lived in London, where he worked as a film technician and composer. Since 1948 he has taught musicology at Humboldt Univ. in East Berlin. His music, which observes the primacy of melody, has been influenced by the ideas of Marx, Lenin, and socialist realism.

PRINCIPAL COMPOSITIONS (published by Peters-L or Breitkopf-L): *Now, Voyager*, text by Walt Whitman (1946); *Symphony* for string orchestra (1946–58); *String Quartets Nos. 1–3* (1956, 1959, 1967); *The Gateway to Buchenwald* (1958); *Mansfelder Oratorium* (1960); *Sinfonie concertante* for piano, orchestra (1961); *Poem* for viola, orchestra (1962); *Violin Concerto* (1963); *Serenata pensierosa* for orchestra (1965); *Concerto grosso* for brass, strings, timpani (1966); *Symphony in B♭* (1967); *Harp Concerto* (1968); *Reiter der Nacht*, opera after Peter Abraham (1970–71). Meyer also wrote 16 cantatas during 1952–69.

PRINCIPAL WRITINGS: *English Chamber Music* (London 1946); *Musik im Zeitgeschehen* (Berlin 1952); *Aufsätze über Musik* (Berlin 1958).

Meyerowitz, Jan (b. Breslau, Germany, 23 April 1913), studied at the Berlin Hochschule für Musik (1930–33; composition with Walther Gmeindl, Alexander von Zemlinsky) and at the Accadèmia di S. Cecilia in Rome

(1933–37; composition with Alfredo Casella, Ottorino Respighi; conducting with Bernardino Molinari). He settled in the U.S. in 1946 and has been on the faculty of Tanglewood (1948–51), Brooklyn College (1954–61), and the College of the City of New York (since 1962). He has also lectured on Radio Munich and Radio Free Berlin.

PRINCIPAL COMPOSITIONS: *The Barrier*, 2-act opera; libretto by Langston Hughes (1949, Marks); *Eastward in Eden*, opera in 5 scenes; libretto by Dorothy Gardner (1951); *The Glory Round His Head*, Easter cantata for soloists, chorus, orchestra; text by Hughes (1953, Broude-B); *The 5 Foolish Virgins* for soloists, chorus, orchestra; text by Hughes (1953, Broude-B); *Robert Herrick Cantata* for soprano, chamber orchestra (1954); *Emily Dickinson Cantata* for soprano, orchestra (1954); *Symphony*, "Midrash Esther" (1954, Broude-B); *Esther*, 3-act opera; libretto by Hughes (1956, AMP); *e. e. cummings Cantata* for baritone, chamber orchestra (1956); *Port Town*, 1-act opera; libretto by Hughes (1958–60, Marks); *Godfather Death*, 3-act chamber opera (1960–61); *I rabbini* for soloists, chorus, orchestra; text from the Babylonian Talmud (1965); *6 Pieces* for orchestra (1965, Marks); *Winterballade*, 3-act opera; libretto by Gerhart Hauptmann (1966–67; published by the theater agency, Block Erben); *Sinfonia brevissima* (1967, Marks); *3 Romantic Pieces* for chamber orchestra (1969–70). In addition to these, Meyerowitz has written many songs and chamber works.

PRINCIPAL WRITINGS: *Arnold Schoenberg* (Berlin 1967); *Der echte jüdische Witz und seine Herkunft* (Berlin 1970).

BIBL.: Felix Greissle, "Current Chronicle," *Musical Quarterly* (April 1957).

Michalsky, Donal (b. Pasadena, Calif., 13 July 1928), studied clarinet with Kalman Bloch (1937–48) and attended the Univ. of Southern Calif. (1948–57, DMA 1965; composition, orchestration with Ingolf Dahl; theory with Halsey Stevens) and the State Academy of Music in Freiberg (1958, composition with Wolfgang Fortner). He also studied medieval notation with Carl Parrish in 1963. Since 1960 he has taught composition and music history at the Calif. State College at Fullerton.

PRINCIPAL COMPOSITIONS: *Divertimento* for 2 clarinets, bass clarinet (1952, Avant); *6 Pieces* for chamber orchestra (1954); *Sonata* for 2 pianos (1957); *Sonata concertante* for piano (1961); *Fantasies* for clavichord (1961); *Trio Allegro* for 2 clarinets, piano (1961); *Cantata da Requiem* (1962); *The Wheel of Time*, choral symphony for chorus, wind orchestra, percussion (1963–66); *Sinfonia concertante* for clarinet, piano, orchestra (1968); *5 Poets Plus* for soprano, flute (1969); *Song Suite* for piano (1970).

Microtones refer to all pitches that lie between the semitones of the 12-tone, equal-tempered tuning system. Microtones and microtonal variations of common intervals have been introduced into contemporary Western music in four principal ways: 1) through equal temperament within the octave; 2) through equal temperament within some other interval; 3) through extended just intonation; and 4) as components of noise and other "irrational" pitch elements. One form of equal temperament, first used in the early 20th century, begins with common 12-tone equal temperament. Each semitone is divided into two, three, or four equal parts, forming so-called quarter, sixth, or eighth tones. Although offering the advantage of including within their compass the standard occidental 12-tone scale, these microtonal scales otherwise diverge sharply from diatonic tuning, the acoustical basis of traditional Western music. Whereas 12 tones per octave derived by just tuning are almost the same as the 12 equally tempered tones, 24, 36, or 48 tones per octave have no such just-intonation equivalent. Since some other numbers of tones derived by just tuning can be equally tempered without grossly distorting the intervals, they have been proposed by several theorists. Two of the best known proposals in the 20th century are Joseph Yasser's (19 tones per octave) and Adriaan Fokker's (31 per octave). Both proposals are similar to the tripartite but actually untempered division of the whole tone proposed in 1922 by Ferruccio Busoni. There has also been a revival of interest in Gerhardus Mercator's (16th century) proposed temperament at 53 tones per octave. Except for the group of composers associated with Fokker in the Netherlands, not much music has been written using these temperaments for the obvious reason that both instrument design and performance practice stand in the way. The possibility of dividing some interval other than the octave into equal intervals was feasible only when music could be synthesized electronically. Since the electronic breakthrough, such scales have occasionally been used (Stockhausen's *Gesang der Jünglinge*; Mayuzumi's and Moroi's *Variations sur 7*). A systematic catalog of such scales is being assembled by Jozef Patkowski, head of the Experimental Music Studio of Radio Poland in Warsaw. Perhaps the most extensive use of them is in *HPSCHD*, composed on tape by John Cage and Lajaren Hiller with computers assisting in the derivation and realization of pitches. Harmonic progressions using scales based on just rather than tempered tuning yield microtones. For instance, in C major, with just triadic tuning, the A of the subdominant triad is approximately one-fifth of a semitone (a diatonic *comma*) lower than the A which is the ninth of the dominant triad. Also, the difference between enharmonic equivalents (G♯ and A♭) is approximately double the size of a comma, or about one-fifth of a whole tone.

USES IN COMPOSITION. Early 20th-century composers employed microtones for a variety of reasons. Charles Ives used them to get closer to the sounds he heard in his environment (bells, for example). Béla Bartók was approximating East European folk usages of pitch. Similarly Ernest Bloch sought an approximation of traditional Hebrew usages. But in the music of these composers, microtones are ornaments, the exception rather than the rule. Alois Hába, Ivan Wyschnegradsky, Julián Carrillo, and Hans Barth used them systematically. They were reacting to the postromantic breakdown of diatonic tonality and were seeking a fresh way to expand pitch resources. They obtained quarter or eighth tones by tuning 12-tone instruments at pitch distances of quarter or eighth tones, this being the easiest practical method for getting more notes per octave.

The greatest amount of recent composition with microtones has been done with just tuning. Harry Partch has rejected all kinds of temperament, has designed and built his own instruments, and has composed music for them. Although the number of pitches per octave on his "chromelodeon" keyboard, 43, has become associated with his music in general, each of his instruments actually has a different finite selection of pitches chosen from the potentially infinite tuning system he uses. By means of just intonation exhaustively using the intervals provided by the first 12 partials of the overtone series, he is able to extend his harmonic field as far as he chooses. (Analogously the modulations possible within the traditional diatonic system can extend infinitely far in either a sharp or a flat direction.) Lou Harrison, using a similarly derived pitch system, specifies adaptation of conventional instruments to play many-pitched just intonations, as does this writer. This is possible because performers have never abandoned just tuning of consonant intervals "by ear," because string and wind instruments permit flexible pitch control by the performer, and because many fixed-pitch instruments can be retuned as desired. The music of La Monte Young, rigorously based upon just tuning, is perhaps the purest example of such music in

Western art. Young's long-sustained, slowly changing harmonies allow for the precise perception of pitch intervals. Such music, scarcely concerned at all with the melodic use of pitch, is not even concerned with a "scale" in the conventional meaning of the term. However, its structure is based on pitch ratios, which themselves constitute a kind of scale.

Young's kind of "scale" is related to the concept of scalar order as defined through psychophysical research, notably that of S. S. Stevens. Measuring a given domain of perception may require a nominal, an ordinal, an interval, or a ratio scale. A nominal scale distinguishes only *same* and *different*. An ordinal scale also distinguishes *more than* and *less than*. An interval scale distinguishes equal increments of change between greater and less. A ratio scale provides analogous relationships between different scale positions. The most important measurable dimensions of music, pitch and duration, are capable of analysis by both interval and ratio scale. Since these kinds of scalar order provide statistically the highest potential for predictability, the traditional predominance of pitch and rhythm in nearly all the music of "high" cultures up to the 20th century is understandable. Recent musical preoccupation with less precisely differentiated aspects of sound reflects an interest in freer kinds of scalar order, as well as in more organized kinds. Many recent compositions introduce microtones either as components in sounds incorporated together by nominal scale ordering (e.g., the "notes" on Cage's prepared piano) or by ordinal scale ordering (cf. Christian Wolff's instructions to performers to select pitches closer together than semitones). Rhythm measured metrically (by equal time increments) uses only an interval scale. In its proportional aspect as variously used (for instance in works by Pierre Boulez, Luigi Nono, Stefan Wolpe, Elliott Carter, Henry Weinberg, and myself), it constitutes a ratio scale, thus providing in the time dimension the same infinite expansion from unity as do microtonal pitch-ratio scales.

The use of noise and natural-speech elements, coupled with the use of electronic musical synthesis, is bringing about a kind of music which simultaneously uses nominal, ordinal, interval, and ratio-scalar order in various perceptual domains (cf. works by Stockhausen, Luciano Berio, Kenneth Gaburo, and others). Nominal ordering, as in much indeterminate music, ordinal contouring, as in much "statistical" and "stochastic" music, interval ordering, as especially in serial composing, and ratio ordering, as discussed above,

all play a role. These techniques have been combined and applied to instrumental music (cf. especially orchestral works by Iannis Xenakis, Krzysztof Penderecki, György Ligeti, and others). Much recent electronic music similarly combines all types of scalar organization (e.g., Hiller's 7 *Electronic Studies*).

BIBL.: Gerald R. Benjamin, "Julián Carrillo and 'Sonido Trece'," *Yearbook, Inter-American Institute for Musical Research* (Tulane Univ.) 3:33–68; Howard Boatwright, "Ives' Quarter-Tone Impressions," *Perspectives* 3/2:22–31; Ferruccio Busoni, *Sketch of a New Esthetic of Music*, trans. by T. Baker (New York 1911); Julián Carrillo, *Sonido 13: Fundamento científico e histórico* (Mexico City 1948); Alain Daniélou, *Introduction to the Study of Musical Scales* (London 1943); ——, *Traité de musicologie comparée* (Paris 1959); Adriaan Fokker, *La Gamme, la musique, et le temperament égal* (n.p. 1951); Alois Hába, *Neue Harmonielehre des diatonischen, chromatischen, Viertel-, Drittel-, Sextel- und Zwölftonsystems* (Leipzig 1927); Ben Johnston, "Phase I-a," in collaboration with Edward Kobrin, *Source* 7; ——, "Proportionality and Expanded Musical Pitch Relations," *Perspectives* 5/1:112–20; ——, "Scalar Order as a Compositional Resource," *Perspectives* 2/2:56–76; Sigmund Klein, "Quarter-Tone Data," *Pro-Musica Quarterly* (March 1925); Thorvald Kornerup, *Acoustic Valuation of Intervals* (Copenhagen 1938); Richard Kostelanetz, chapter on La Monte Young, *The Theatre of Mixed Means* (New York 1968); Mayer J. Mandelbaum, *Multiple Division of the Octave and the Tonal Resources of 19-Tone Temperament* (PhD diss., Indiana Univ., 1961); "Microtonal Music in America," a forum, *Proceedings of the American Society of University Composers* 2; Ates Orga, "Alois Hába and Microtonality," *Musical Opinion* (July 1968):541–45; Harry Partch, *Genesis of a Music* (Madison, Wis., 1949); S. S. Stevens, "Mathematics, Measurement, and Psychophysics," *Handbook of Experimental Psychology* (New York 1951):1–49; George Whitman, "Seminal Works of Quarter-Tone Music," *Tempo* 80:11–15; Ivan Wyschnegradsky, "La Musique à quarts de ton et sa réalisation pratique," *Revue musicale* (Jan 1937):26–33; ——, "Quartertone Music, Its Possibilities and Organic Sources," *Pro Musica Quarterly* (Oct 1927):19ff.; Joseph Yasser, *A Theory of Evolving Tonality* (New York 1932).

Ben Johnston

SEE ALSO Asian Music and Western Composition, Instrumental and Vocal Resources, Jazz, Notation, Tuning and Temperament.

Miereanu, Costin (Adrian) (b. Bucharest, 27 Feb 1943), studied at the Bucharest Conservatory (1960–66; composition with Dan Constantinescu, Alfred Mendelsohn; orchestration with Aurel Stroe) and the Darmstadt summer courses (1967–69, composition with Karlheinz Stockhausen). He has been music editor of *Amfiteatru* (1966–68) and *Contemporanul* (since 1968); he has also written criticism for other Rumanian periodicals (since 1964). His serial music has been influenced by Webern and Boulez; later he began working with electroacoustics and with John Cage's aleatory procedures. Most recently he has explored action music and purely verbal scores.

PRINCIPAL COMPOSITIONS: *Donum sacrum Brancusi* for soprano, orchestra (1963, revised 1965; Schott); *Variantes* for clarinet (1964–66); *2 Madrigals* for chorus; texts by Adrian Maniu (1965); *Nacht* for mezzo-soprano, chorus; texts by García-Lorca (1965); *Monostructures I* for brass, strings (1966, Salabert); *Finis coronat opus* for piano, 6 instrumental groups (1966, Salabert); *Cadenza* for pianist(s) (1966); *Sursum corda* for piano, clarinet, violin, viola, cello (1966–67, Schott); *Couleurs du temps* for string orchestra or string quartet with tape or 2 string quartets, double bass (1966–68, Salabert); *Espace dernier* for chorus, 6 instrumental groups, tape; biblical text (1966–69, Salabert); *Musique poétique* for piano, 2 narrators ad lib. (1967); *Monostructures II* for brass, strings, tape ad lib. (1967, Salabert); *Lines* on tape, prepared in collaboration with Ben Bernfelding (1967–68); *Espaces II* for 20 strings, piano, tape (1967–69, Salabert); *! Black Against* on tape, prepared with Bernfelding (1968); *Espaces au-delà du dernier* for chamber ensemble (1968, Salabert); *Polymorphie 5 × 7*: concert version for chorus ad lib., variable ensemble, tape; stage version for actors, chorus, variable ensemble, tape (1968–69, Salabert); *Dans la Nuit des temps* for variable ensemble, tape (1968–69, Salabert).

PRINCIPAL WRITINGS: Miereanu has written a book on the origins of Rumanian concert music (Bucharest 1967) and articles on the Rumanian avant-garde (*Sonda* 1968/2), Berg's *Wozzeck* (*Secolul XX* 1965/3), and Webern and Georg Trakl (*Secolul XX* 1967/2).

BIBL.: Iancu Dumitrescu, "C. M.," *Luceafarul* (5 Feb 1968); Maurice Fleuret, "Les Marches du silence," *Le Nouvel Observateur* No. 229 (1969); ——, "L'Avalanche de Zagreb," *ibid.* No. 237 (1969); Doru Popovici, "C. M.," *Amfiteatru* 1966/3; ——, "C. M.," *La Musique corale roumaine* (Bucharest 1967). Discussions of his works have also appeared in the program books of the Bucharest Radio Symphony (21 Nov 1968), the Cluj Philharmonic (30–31 March 1968), the Bucharest Philharmonic (29 May 1968), and the Domaine Musical, Paris (21 April 1969).

Migot, Georges (Elbert) (b. Paris, 27 Feb 1891), studied harmony with J. Bouval and counterpoint with J. B. Ganaye and then attended the Paris Conservatory, where he studied composition with Charles Widor (beginning in 1913), music history with Maurice Emmanuel, orchestration with Vincent d'Indy, and organ with Guilmant and Gigout. Further musical associations were with Henry Expert and Nadia Boulanger. He also studied painting with Jules Emile Zingg. He presented weekly radio talks on "A Thousand Years of French Music" during 1936–39; from 1949 to 1961 was curator of the Paris Conservatory's museum of instruments. An interest in Asian music in the 1910s and later in French medieval polyphony were important influences on his compositional development. The harmonic vocabulary in his music is consistently modal, and harmony and rhythm derive from, rather than direct, an intertwining of melodic lines.

PRINCIPAL COMPOSITIONS (published by Leduc unless otherwise noted): *Le Paravent de laque aux 5 images* for 2 violins, viola, piano (1917); *7 Petites Images du Japon* for voice, piano or orchestra (c. 1917); *Trio* for violin, viola, piano (1919); *Symphonies Nos. 1–8, 10–12*: No. 1, "Les Agrestides" (1919–20); No. 2 (1927, EMT); No. 3 (1946–49); No. 4 (1946–49); No. 5 for winds (c.1955, unpub.); No. 6 for strings (1951, EFM); No. 7 for chamber orchestra (1953, unpub.); No. 8 for 10 winds (1954); No. 10 (1962, EFM); No. 11 for winds (1963, unpub.); No. 12, "Les Nombres" (1962, unpub.); *Hagoromo*, ballet (1920–21); *Suite pour violon récitant* with orchestra (1924); *2 Stèles* for low voice, harp, celesta, tam-tam, cymbals, double bass (1925); *Suite pour piano principal* with orchestra (1925–26); *Suite en concert pour harp* with orchestra (1926); *Le Rossignol en amour*, chamber opera (1926); *La Jungle* for organ, orchestra (1928); *Le Livre des danceries* for flute, violin, piano (1929); *Le Zodiaque*, 12 concert pieces for piano (1931–32); *Calendrier du petit berger* for piano (1932); *17 Poèmes du Brugnon* for voice, piano (1933); *Piano Trio* (1935); *Sermon sur la montagne*, oratorio (1936); *Livre d'orgue No. 1* (1937); *La Belle et la bête*, "opéra choréographique" (1938, unpub.); *Piano Sonata*, "Polonia" (1939); *La Passion*, 12 episodes for soloists, chorus, large orchestra (1941–42); *Flute Sonata* (1945); *La Retraite ardente* for voice, flute, violin, cello (1945, unpub.); *String Trio* (1945, unpub.); *L'Annonciation* for 2 soloists, women's chorus, string orchestra (1946, Edition Ouvrières, Paris); *Saint-Germain d'Auxerre* for 4 soloists, 3 choruses (1947); *Suite pour piano et choeur en vocalises* (1947–48); *La Mise au tombeau* for chorus, wind quintet (1949, unpub.); *Cantata d'amour* for soloists, chorus, orchestra (1950, unpub.); *5 Chants* for voice, string quartet (1951, unpub.); *Sonata* for solo violin (1951, unpub.); *Le Petit Evangéliaire* for 9 choruses (1952); *Requiem* (1953, Ouvrières); *La Resurrection* for 3 soloists, chorus, chamber orchestra (1953, unpub.); *La Nativité* for 3 soloists, chorus, flute, bassoon, string quartet (1954, Ouvrières); *Quartet* for flute, violin, cello, piano (1960, unpub.); *L'Ecclésiaste* for baritone, chorus, orchestra (1963, EFM); *In memoriam* for chorus, orchestra (1963, unpub.).

PRINCIPAL WRITINGS: *Essais pour une esthétique générale* (Paris 1920, 2nd ed. 1937); *Appoggiatures résolues et non résolues*, 3 parts (Paris 1922, 1923, 1931); *J.-Ph. Rameau et le génie de la musique française* (Paris 1930); *Les Ecrits de G. M.*, 3 vols. (Paris 1932); *Lexique de quelque termes utilisés en musique* (Paris 1947); *Poèmes*, 2 vols. (Geneva 1950–51); "Auto-portrait," *Journal musical français* (Feb 1969):24–25.

BIBL.: M. Henrion, "La musique vocale de G. M.," *Revue musicale* (Nov 1946); Marc Honegger, "G. M. et la musique religieuse," *Revue d'histoire et de philosophie religieuse* 1959/4; ——, "G. M.," *Réforme* (25 Feb 1961); Max Pinchard, *Connaissance de G. M.* (Paris 1959); Léon Vallas, *G. M.* (Paris 1923); P. Wolff, *La Route d'un musicien, G. M.* (Paris, Leduc, 1933).

[prepared with the help of Eleanor Foster]
SEE ALSO France.

Mihalovici, Marcel (b. Bucharest, 22 Oct 1898), studied privately in Bucharest and later in Paris (where he settled permanently) at the Schola Cantorum (1919–25; composition, conducting with Vincent d'Indy; Gregorian chant with Amédée Gastoué; violin with Nestor Lejeune). In 1932 he helped found the contemporary music society Triton. During 1959–62 he taught form and analysis at the Schola Cantorum. His music derives from the traditions of Enescu; neoclassic Stravinsky, Prokofiev, and Bartók; and Les Six.

PRINCIPAL COMPOSITIONS: *Sonatine* for piano (1922–23, UE); *Chansons et jeux* for voice, piano; Rumanian folk texts in French translation (1924, Eschig); *Sonatine* for oboe, piano (1924, Eschig); *Karagueuz*, ballet; scenario by M. Larionow (1926, Eschig); *3 Romances* for voice, piano; texts by Victor Hugo (1927–29, Salabert); *Cortège des divinités infernales* for orchestra (1928, Eschig); *L'Intransigeant Pluton*, 1-act opera; libretto by Regnard (1928, Eschig); *4 Caprices* for piano (1929, Eschig); *String Quartets Nos. 2–3* (1931, Eschig; 1946, Heugel); *Sonata* for 3 clarinets (1933, Salabert); *Divertissement* for orchestra (1934, Eschig); *Toccata* for piano, orchestra (1938–40, revised 1949; Heugel); *Violin Sonata No. 2* (1940–41, Heugel); *Ricercari* for piano (1941, Heugel); *Viola Sonata* (1942, Heugel); *Sonata* for violin, cello (1944, Amphion); *Symphonies pour le temps présent* for orchestra (1944, Eschig); *Contrerimes* for voice, piano; text by Paul-Jean Toulet (1944, Heugel); *Sappho*, music for the play by Edith Thomas (1946, EFM); *Phèdre*, opera in 5 scenes; libretto by Yvan Goll (1948–49, SOFI-RAD); *Sonata* for violin (1949, Heugel); *Sonata* for cello (1949, Heugel); *Le Paradis perdu*, music

for the play by Pierre-Jean Jouve (1951, EFM); *Sinfonia giocosa* (1951, Heugel); *Etude en 2 parties* for piano, instrumental ensemble (1951, Heugel); *Sinfonia partita* (1952, Heugel); *2 Poèmes* for chorus; text by Agrippa d'Aubigné (1952, SOFIRAD); *Mémorial*, 5 motets for chorus (1952, SOFIRAD); *Meurtre dans la cathédrale*, music for the play by T. S. Eliot (1952, EFM); *Sinfonia cantata* for baritone, chorus, orchestra (1953–63, Heugel); *Orphée*, music for the play by Jean Cocteau (1954, EFM); *Die Heimkehr*, 1-act opera; libretto by K. H. Ruppel (1954, revised 1955; Bote); *Elégie* for orchestra (1955, Bote); *Wind Trio* (1955, Ahn & Sim); *Thésée au labyrinthe*, ballet; scenario by Ruppel (1956, Heugel); *Alternamenti*, ballet; scenario by Claude Rostand (1957, Ricordi); *Ouverture tragique* (1957, Heugel); *Melusine*, music for the play by Goll (1957, EFM); *Abendgesang* for voice, piano; texts by Goll (1957, Schott); *Bassoon Sonata* (1958, Heugel); *Clarinet Sonata* (1958, Heugel); *Esercizio* for string orchestra (1959, Heugel); *Krapp (ou la dernière bande)*, 1-act opera after Samuel Beckett (1959–60, Heugel); *Sinfonia variata* (1960, Heugel); *Les Jumeaux*, 3-act opéra bouffe; libretto by Rostand (1961–62, Heugel); *Cascando*, music for the play by Beckett (1962, Heugel); *Musique nocturne* for clarinet (1963, Leduc); *Piano Sonata* (1964, Leduc); *Dialogues* for clarinet, piano (1964, Heugel); *Stances* for voice, piano; text by Mariana Dumitrescu (1964–68, ESCR); *Périples* for orchestra (1967, Heugel); *Symphony No. 5* (1967–68, Heugel); *Prétextes* for oboe, bass clarinet, chamber orchestra (1968, Heugel).

BIBL.: Georges Beck, *M. M., esquisse biographique* (Paris 1954); Claude Rostand, "Porträt M. M.," *Melos* 25:359–61.

Mihály, András (b. Budapest, 6 Nov 1917), studied at the Budapest Music Academy (1933–38; composition with István Strasset and Pál Kadosa, cello with Adolph Schiffer, chamber music with Leo Weiner). During 1948–49 he was general secretary of the Budapest Opera. He has taught chamber music at the Budapest Academy since 1950 and has been music adviser for the Budapest Radio since 1963. In 1968 he founded the Budapest Chamber Ensemble, of which he is conductor.

PRINCIPAL COMPOSITIONS: *Piano Trio* (1940); *String Quartets Nos. 1–2* (1942, 1960); *Symphonies Nos. 1–3*: No. 1, "Sinfonia da requiem" (1946); No. 2 (1950); No. 3 (1962, EMB and General); *Rhapsody* for viola, piano (1947, MK); *Serenade* for flute, clarinet, bassoon (1950); *Kedves Magyar Hazám* [Beloved Hungarian Fatherland], cantata (1952); *Cello Concerto* (1953, EMB); *Piano Concerto* (1954); *Fantasie* for wind quintet, string quartet, harp, celesta, percussion (1955, EMB); *Suite* for cello, piano (1957, EMB); *Chamber Music* for voice, piano; texts by James Joyce

(1958); *Piano Sonata* (1958); *Violin Concerto* (1959, EMB); *Emlék és intelem* [Recollection and Admonition] for chorus, orchestra; text by Zsuzsa Gál (1959, EMB); *1871*, cantata; text by István Raics (1960); *Ciacona* for piano (1961, EMB); *6 Songs* for voice, piano; poems by Attila József (1961, EMB); *3 Apocrypha* for 3 women's voices, clarinet, percussion (1962, EMB); *Mouvement* for cello, piano (1962, EMB); *Együtt es egyedül* [Together and Alone], 2-act opera; libretto by the composer after Miklós Hubay (1965); *As áhitat zsoltárai* [Psalms of Piety] for voice, piano; poems by Miklós Radnóti (1967, EMB); *3 Movements* for chamber ensemble (1968, EMB).

Milhaud, Darius (b. Aix-en-Provence, 4 Sept 1892) entered the Paris Conservatory in 1909, where he studied with André Gedalge and Charles Widor; the more influential was Gedalge. While a student he met the writer Paul Claudel, who engaged Milhaud as his secretary when he was appointed ambassador to Brazil. The two spent almost two years in Brazil (1917–18). In 1920 Milhaud became known as one of Les Six through a newspaper article by Henri Collet. During the 1920s and 30s he taught in Paris and traveled widely to lecture and to conduct and play his own works. In 1940 he emigrated to the U.S. He alternates one year at Mills College in Calif. with one year in Paris, where until the age of 70 he taught composition at the Conservatory.

Since the late 1920s Milhaud's health has been precarious. A rheumatic condition necessitates his use of a wheel chair, and from time to time his arms and hands give him great pain. In spite of this he is probably the most prolific composer of this century. Perhaps his determination to overcome his illness is a factor in his resolve never to refuse a commission and always to produce new works. His output encompasses a large spectrum of vocal and instrumental possibilities: more than a dozen operas, several ballets, over three dozen orchestral works including concertos, several dozen chamber works, and many vocal, choral, and solo instrumental pieces.

When he played an early work on his first encounter with Gedalge, the latter asked "Why did you use D♯ seventeen times on the first page?" Milhaud's subsequent training with Gedalge built up a great intolerance for this sort of monotony, not only as to the notes themselves but also in regard to rhythm and texture in general. Milhaud is also allergic to the variation form, and this is where his break with the dodecaphonists is most apparent.

From 1913 to 1922 he was occupied with an opera based on Claudel's translation of Aeschylus' *Oresteia*. This was the period of his studies and experiments in polytonality, which included superimposing various tonalities, examining all chords in their various inversions, and altering their modes from major to minor or vice-versa. In all these experiments, however, he maintained references to the "academic" treatment of tonal harmony as taught in conservatories. (It is interesting to note that almost all the well-known European composers born at the end of the 19th century have maintained a harmonic and contrapuntal order that can be analyzed by traditional methods.) In the opera *Les Choéphores* (1919), Milhaud used polytonality for dramatic tension. The work also contains striking uses of other procedures, for instance in the Exhortation, where passages for percussion and spoken chorus fragment words and sentences in a way that foreshadows language-conscious music of the late 1960s.

In 1917, seeking greater contrapuntal independence of voices and the elimination of musical development in the traditional sense, he wrote six chamber symphonies, all four minutes or less and using various groups of instruments. These works are comparable to the epigrammatic music of this period by Stravinsky and Webern. Having achieved contrapuntal melodic independence, the new goal was for rhythmic independence. He achieved this goal in the ballet *L'Homme et son désir* (1918), some sections of which, for percussion alone, are an evocation of the sounds of the Brazilian jungle. In these sections rhythmic patterns are stacked in a manner comparable to the stacking of tonalities.

Milhaud's immense facility with polytonality and counterpoint is perhaps best illustrated by the *5 Etudes* for piano and orchestra (1920), each piece of which has its own tone color and structure. The third is made up of four simultaneous fugues, one in A for winds, one in D♭ for brass, one in F for strings, and one for piano, the last named a two-part fugue combining the notes common to the other three tonalities. Another instance of his facility is the double string quartet which he wrote in 1948. Each four-part quartet can be played separately or the two can be played together as an octet. He wrote the work in a music notebook dating from 1848 in which each page contained eight blank staves.

In the field of electronic music there is a work on tape called *Etude poétique*, which was made in the Studio d'Essai in Paris. It is a montage of seven tapes. Six of them were separate recordings of six instrumentalists, each playing a phrase different in length and tempo from the others. The phrase was repeated over and over until Milhaud signaled that the last note was to be held and the passage thereby concluded. The seventh tape was a recording of two saxophones together with a mezzo-soprano and a reciter using texts from Claude Roy. The final montage is a stack of independent sound patterns.

PRINCIPAL COMPOSITIONS: Milhaud has written well over 400 works; of these he has chosen the following for this list: 3 operas on American subjects: *Christophe Colombo* (1928, UE), *Maxmilien* (1930, UE), and *Bolivar* (1943); *L'Homme et son désir*, ballet (1918, UE); *La Création du monde*, ballet (1923, Eschig); *Symphony No. 3*, "Hymnus ambrosianus" for chorus, orchestra (1946, Heugel); *Symphony No. 4* (1948, Salabert); *Piano Concerto No. 4* (1949, Heugel); *Violin Concerto No. 3*, "Concerto royal" (1958, Eschig); *Symphony No. 8*, "Rhodanienne" (1957, Heugel); *Pacem in terris* for chorus, orchestra; text from the encyclical by Pope John XXIII (1963, Salabert); *La Mère coupable*, opera based on the play by Beaumarchais (1964–65, Ricordi); *Symphony No. 10* (1960, Heugel). List (with many errors) to 1968: Roy (see bibl.).

PRINCIPAL WRITINGS: "La Mélodie," *Melos* 3:195ff.; "Polytonalité et atonalité," *Revue musicale* 4:29ff.; *Notes without Music* (London 1952); *Entretiens avec Claude Rostand* (Paris 1952).

BIBL.: Georges Beck, *D. M.* (Paris 1949, supplement 1956); David Drew, "Modern French Music," *European Music in the 20th Century* ed. by H. Hartog (London 1957); Colin Mason, "The Chamber Music of M.," *Musical Quarterly* 43; Jean Roy, *D. M.* (Paris 1968).

Charles Jones

SEE ALSO Dance; France; Harmony and Counterpoint; Jazz; Liturgical Music: Jewish; Melody; Mixed Media; Opera; Orchestration.

Miller, Edward (Jay) (b. Miami, 4 August 1930), studied at the Univ. of Miami (1948–53), the Hartt College of Music (1953–55; composition with Arnold Franchetti, Isadore Freed), the Berlin Hochschule für Musik (1956–58; composition with Boris Blacher, Josef Rufer), and at Tanglewood (1953, 1955; composition with Carlos Chávez, Blacher). He has taught composition and theory at the Hartt College since 1959.

PRINCIPAL COMPOSITIONS: *Reflections—At the Bronx Zoo* for orchestra (1965); *Orchestral Changes* for orchestra (1967); *Orchestral Fantasies* (1968); *The Young God*, opera (1968); *Anti-heroic Amalgam* for orchestra (1969); *The 7 Last Days* for chorus (1970).

Milner, Anthony (Francis Dominic) (b. Bristol, England, 13 May 1925), studied composition with Matyas Seiber (1944–48) and attended the Royal College of Music (1945–47, piano with Herbert Fryer, theory with R. O. Morris). He was a tutor in music history and theory at Morley College during 1946–62 and lectured at the Univ. of London and was director and harpsichordist of the London Cantata Ensemble, 1954–65. He has been teaching at the Royal College since 1961 and at King's College of the Univ. of London since 1965. He made lecture tours in the U.S. in 1964 and 1966. During the summers of 1965 and 1966 he was composer-in-residence at the School of Church Music at Loyola Univ. and lecturer at the Pius X School of Sacred Music, Manhattanville, New York, and in 1967 he lectured at the Sacred Music Workshop in Boystown, Omaha.

PRINCIPAL COMPOSITIONS (published by Novello unless otherwise noted): *Salutatio angelica*, cantata for alto, small chorus, chamber orchestra, Op. 1 (1948, UE); *Mass*, Op. 3 (1951); *Quartet* for oboe, strings, Op. 4 (1953); *The Song of Akhenaten* for soprano, chamber orchestra, Op. 5 (1954); *Benedic anima mea Dominum*, motet for double chorus, Op. 10, No. 1 (1954, UE); *Rondo saltato* for organ, Op. 6, No. 1 (1955); *The City of Desolation*, cantata for soprano, chorus, orchestra, Op. 7 (1955, UE); *The Harrowing of Hell*, cantata for bass soloists, chorus, Op. 9 (1956, unpub.); *St. Francis*, cantata for tenor, chorus, orchestra, Op. 8 (1956); *Our Lady's Hours*, song cycle for soprano, piano, Op. 11 (1957); *Cast Wide the Folding Doorways of the East* for chorus, Op. 12 (1957, UE); *Variations* for orchestra, Op. 14 (1958, UE); *The Water and the Fire*, oratorio for soprano, tenor, baritone, boys' choir, chorus, orchestra, Op. 16 (1960–61); *Divertimento* for string orchestra, Op. 18 (1961, UE); *Break to be Built, O Stone*, ceremonial ode for chorus, organ, orchestra, Op. 20 (1962, Oxford); *Sinfonia Pasquale* for string orchestra with optional winds, brass, Op. 21 (1963, UE); *Festival Te Deum* for chorus, orchestra or organ (1967); *Symphony No. 1*, Op. 23 (1968, UE); *Chamber Symphony* (1968, UE); *Roman Spring* for soprano, tenor, chorus, chamber orchestra (1969, UE).

PRINCIPAL WRITINGS: "Music in a Vernacular Liturgy," *English in the Liturgy* ed. by C. R. Cunliffe (London 1956):123ff.; "English Music," *European Music in the Twentieth Century* ed. by H. Hartog (London 1957):132ff.; "Radio and Gramophone," *Twentieth Century Music* ed. by R. Myers (London 1960):87ff.; "Music in Church, Hall, and Home," "The Baroque: Instrumental Music," chapters 5–6 of *Man and His Music* by Alec Harman and Wilfrid Mellers (London 1962); "Sixteenth Century Music," *The Pelican History of Music* ed. by D. Stevens and E. Robertson (London 1963):113ff.; "The Water and the Fire," *The Composer's Point of View: Twentieth-Century*

Composers' Essays on Choral Music ed. by R.
Hines (Norman, Okla., 1963); "The Music of
Michael Tippett," *Musical Quarterly* (Oct 1964):
423ff.; "The Musical Aesthetic of the Baroque,"
lecture (Hill Univ. Press, n.d.); *Music in Perfor-
mance* (London c.1971).
BIBL.: Ernest Bradbury, "The Progress of
A. M.," *Musical Times* (June 1963):405ff.
SEE ALSO Great Britain.

Miroglio, Francis (b. Marseille, 12 Dec 1924),
attended the Univ. of Aix-en-Provence—
Marseilles (1943–44, philosophy), the Marseilles Conservatory (1945–47, flute, solfège),
and the Paris Conservatory (1951–52, composition with Darius Milhaud). He subsequently
studied conducting with Paul Van Kempen
at the Accadèmia Chigiana in Siena, and with
Bruno Maderna at the Darmstadt summer
courses (1959–60). In 1965 he founded and
became director of the festival of contemporary music and art Nuits de la Fondation
Maeght in Saint Paul de Vence. In 1967 he
was a composer-in-residence in Berlin under
the auspices of the Ford Foundation. He has
composed several theater, ballet, television,
and film scores. Proceeding from serial techniques, Miroglio, through the influence of the
plastic arts, has sought a free use of temporal,
spatial, and timbral elements. All of his works
since 1962 are "musical mobiles"; his *Extensions II*, for example, uses 137 percussion
instruments in 22 interchangeable sequences.
Several of his works appear in alternate
scorings, or *"formations diverses."*
PRINCIPAL COMPOSITIONS: *Magies* for soprano,
10 instruments (1960, S-Z); *Espaces* for large
orchestra (1962, S-Z); *Espaces II* for wind orchestra, 2 harps, percussion (1962, S-Z); *Espaces III*
for string orchestra (1962, S-Z); *Espaces IV* for
tape, chamber ensemble (1962, S-Z); *Espaces V*
for chamber ensemble (1962, S-Z); *Soleils* for
piano (1962, S-Z); *Réseaux*, in 4 versions: harp
solo; harp, 9 instruments; harp, string quartet;
harp, 2 percussion groups (1964, UE); *Phases*, in
4 versions: flute, piano; flute, piano, string trio;
flute, piano, percussion trio; flute, piano, string
trio, percussion trio (1965, UE); *Projections* for
string quartet, with slides of the paintings of Miro
ad lib. (1966–67, UE); *Refractions* for violin, flute,
piano, percussion (1968, UE); *Tremplins* for 15–32
players; alternate versions with vocal quartet,
multiple strings; text by Jacques Dupin (1968–69,
UE); *Insertions* for harpsichord (1969, UE); *Extensions* for orchestra (1970, UE); *Extensions II*
for 6 percussionists; this work may also be played
as part of *Extensions* for orchestra (1970, UE).
PRINCIPAL WRITINGS: "Ad libitum," *The World
of Music* 1967/1:23.
BIBL.: Jean-Pierre Garnier, "Entretien avec
F. M.," *Le Courrier musical de France* 1967/17:4.

Mixed Media (Multimedia, Intermedia) is a
loosely applied term for theater works or
events that involve some merging of arts,
forms, techniques, means, and electronic
media, all directed at more than one of the
senses and generally involving some kind of
total surrounding (as opposed to the use of
only a proscenium stage). In contrast to traditional stage genres, which may also incorporate more than one art, mixed-media events
generally aim for some kind of spectator
involvement so that the presence or reactions
of the spectator have an influence over the
event. The range of activities included under
mixed media extend from *environments*, which
are nonlinear, nondevelopmental, and walk-
through events; to *happenings*, which are
simultaneous and/or sequential arrangements
of two or more actions, events, or perform-
ance-participation units; to *music theater*,
which tends to have a defined performance
time and space and to involve vocal and
instrumental performance as well as movement, electronics, and other elements. (Mixed-
media events may make little or no use of
music; the following discussion is restricted
to those manifestations in which music is a
central element.)
PRECEDENTS. The notion of a *Gesamtkunst-
werk* has, of course, figured in the field of
opera for the last four centuries. Its final
appearance in the conventional opera format
came in the music dramas of Wagner and his
successors. In reaction to the Wagnerian idea,
Stravinsky proposed a new approach in works
of 1915–34 such as *Renard, Les Noces, L'Histoire du soldat, Oedipus Rex,* and *Persephone,*
which mix acting, narration, mime, choral and
solo singing on parallel but intertwining planes
to create a theater of ritual and stylized form.
Other composers in the first half of this
century also attempted new kinds of music
theater. Schoenberg's *Pierrot lunaire* (1912),
written for an actress noted for her cabaret
appearances, is an early example. The notion
of a synesthetic artwork involving the audience
and using colored lights and perfume seems
to have been first invented by Scriabin. In the
1930s Edgard Varèse proposed works to both
Antonin Artaud and André Malraux involving
complex uses of technology and multiple
sensory impact. There were a number of
experimental uses of film in the 1920s: in
Alban Berg's *Lulu,* the Milhaud-Claudel
Christophe Colomb, and the Antheil-Léger
Ballet mécanique. A nonlinear format was
used in the Thomson-Stein *Four Saints in
Three Acts.* The advent of sound film opened
up new possibilities, such as a 1928 collage

soundtrack of city noises by Walther Ruttmann in Germany and in Canada, Norman McLaren's drawings on optical film soundtracks. In the U.S., John J. Becker produced a number of works during the 1930s with a mixture of light, mime, dance, and music, and many American composers have worked closely with dancers. Harry Partch has used his self-made instruments and microtonal idiom to produce ritualistic music events that employ mime, dance, speech, chant, song, and instrumental sounds.

EARLY DEVELOPMENTS. Mixed media developed and has continued to develop away from the confines of conventional music life. In 1952 John Cage and the dancer Merce Cunningham staged the first happening in the U.S. at Black Mountain College, N. C. It consisted of indeterminate events and activities within a determined time span and has been followed by many others, including Karlheinz Stockhausen's *Originale* (1961). (With Cage as music director, the Cunningham Dance Co. has continued to explore relationships between movement and sound, including the use of electric eyes and antennas on stage so that the movements of dancers trigger sound-producing apparatus.) Most subsequent happenings were initiated by artists, composers, poets, and others who were close to Cage in New York: Allan Kaprow (who in 1958–59 was the first to use the term *happening*), Dick Higgins, Claes Oldenburg, and many others. The genre has had a major impact on theater forms and staging techniques; in terms of mixed-media music events, it has tended to evolve in the direction of static, technology-oriented environmental forms.

During 1957–60 composer Henry Jacobs and film maker Jordan Belson conducted mixed-media concerts of various musics in the Morrison Planetarium in San Francisco. Nearly 50 speakers were installed around the room, permitting movement of sound in space, an aural equivalent of the movement of projections over the dome of the planetarium. In 1958 Jacobs and Belson put on similar concerts at the Brussels World's Fair. There too, one of the first mixed-media compositions was presented, the *Poème électronique* of Varèse and Le Corbusier. The latter, with architect-composer Iannis Xenakis, designed the physical environment, the pavilion of the Phillips Record Co., and the visuals. Varèse's tape music moved across the speakers on the interior surface of the structure, and the performance repeated in 8-minute cycles. (Since then, the fairs in New York, 1964, Montreal, 1968, and Osaka, 1970, have been major showcases for mixed-media compositions and environments.)

San Francisco continued to be influential in the early 1960s. Morton Subotnick, Ramon Sender, Pauline Oliveros, and others at the San Francisco Tape Center developed mixed-media events in collaboration with artists and film makers. Subotnick's work with visuals artist Anthony Martin was particularly important in pioneering mixes of film, projections through liquids, taped and live electronic music. Much of this work was accomplished with the help of Donald Buchla, an electronics engineer who has also designed a sound synthesizer. At the San Francisco Trip Festivals in the early 60s, rock musicians borrowed the idea of using environmental visuals with music; painter-film maker Andy Warhol was among the first, using films and projections with a rock group, The Velvet Underground, which he organized with composer John Cale (a Welsh disciple of Cage!). There has since been a good deal of interaction with the popular-music field, notably in the music of Frank Zappa (of the Mothers of Invention), Pink Floyd, and others; this has included mixed-media ideas about electronics, kinetic light, and theater.

Beginning in 1958, Ann Arbor, Mich., became a center of mixed-media experimentation through the activities of painter-sculptor Milton Cohen and later of the ONCE group, whose members included Cohen and composers Robert Ashley, George Cacioppo, and Gordon Mumma. Cohen creates environments as part of a genre he calls "space theater." Events within these environments combine sculpture, choreographed movement, projections, sound, group improvisation, and audience participation. ONCE Festivals took place annually during 1961–68 with Ashley as coorganizer.

CURRENT TRENDS. In the U.S. increasing work is being done with environments. These are usually nondirectional or nonlinear in form, i.e., without necessary beginning, middle, or end. They typically are static or steady-state events organized in long, slow, repeating cycles. Sometimes a maximum amount of detail is presented in a highly restricted, minimal field so that the averaging out of elements over any period of time yields the same statistical result. A common arrangement is for the visitor to enter, remain with, walk through, and leave the event at his own pace. Certain works of Cage (notably *Cartridge Music*, 1960, and the various *Variations*, 1958–66, several of which were used in dance and dance-theater works) provide prototypes.

The most extreme examples are those of La Monte Young (with visuals by Marion Zarzeela) in which single notes or intervals and single visual patterns can be sustained for many hours with only small internal variations. Terry Riley, Steve Reich, Philip Glass, and others have used live performance on specially designed electronic apparatus to produce, alter, or extend vocal and instrumental sound. Larry Austin's *The Maze* (1965) and *The Magicians* (1968) employ extended repeated elements in an open-ended theater format. Other composers, who may be less interested in the static quality of such environmental presentations, nevertheless work with similarly limited areas of experience, often marked by the use of electronic circuitry to produce as well as alter sounds in live performance and to extend sound into space. Gordon Mumma's electronic noise, produced through specially built circuits, Alvin Lucier's amplified or distorted sound pick-ups (brain waves, plate-glass windows, computer-compressed vocal babble), and Max Neuhaus's feedback systems are examples.

David Behrman and Robert Ashley have produced short amplified dramas with vocal and other sounds live and on tape. The environment format has sometimes been associated with composers (and visual artists) who can be described as minimalists. There is no necessary connection, however, between minimal art and environmental techniques. Quite the contrary; multimedia suggests multilayer experience, information overload, the electronic transmission of simultaneous messages from the Gobal Village. My own *Feedback* (1968), with visuals by Stan Vanderbeek, and my score for *Can Man Survive?*, a mixed-media exhibition at the American Museum of Natural History in New York (1969–70), use many disparate materials: the former, improvisation and performer-audience interaction with a variety of contrasting electronic and concrete elements; the latter, continuous-loop tape cartridges to create pools of sound that mixed and changed for each visitor as he moved through the environment. In Europe, the Musica Elettronica Viva, based in Rome but including the American Frederic Rzewski and Richard Teitelbaum, used live electronics to produce a kind of participatory theater, half environmental, half electronic ritual. More recently Stockhausen has organized similar ensemble events.

U.S. developments in new music theater have been centered in the universities. At the Univ. of Ill. Lejaren Hiller produced *A Triptych for Hieronymus* (1966) for actors, dancers, acrobats, projections, tape, and antiphonal instrumental groups and *An Avalanche for Pitchman, Prima Donna, Player Piano, Percussionist and Prerecorded Playback* (1968). Another Illinois composer, Salvatore Martirano, has produced several theater and mixed-media works including *Underworld* for dancers, instrumentalists, and 2-channel tape (1964–65) and *L'sGA* for narrator (wearing a gas mask and breathing helium), multiscreen films and projections, and tape (1967–68). Beginning with *Election Night Diversion* (1968) and *Lunar Landing* (1969), the Illinois group has experimented with interactions between "historical" events currently taking place and the emotional involvement of the audience. Among other resources in these works, they have used network and closed-circuit television to mix the event and the audience's participation in it. Other university centers include the Univ. of Calif. at San Diego, the Calif. Institute of the Arts in Los Angeles, the Univ. of Iowa, and the Univ. of Toronto. Many more are also developing programs. The character of all these music-theater forms depends on multiple layers of sound, of kinds of sound, of word, movement, light, and image; it is therefore maximal rather than minimal. Other examples are my *Verses and Cantos (Foxes and Hedgehogs)*, *The Nude Paper Sermon*, and *Creation*, all of which are mixes of spoken, sung, instrumental (renaissance instruments in the latter case), and taped electronic music interacting with staged movement, projections, audience involvement, and purely verbal elements. Electronic technology is used not only to provide new layers and new kinds of sound but also to project sound throughout the entire performer-audience space, to relate live, amplified, and pre-recorded sound, and to interrelate a variety of electronic-age experiences. This interplay of styles—of "ways of life"—helps integrate purely musical (or aural) structures and the other elements of the total experience and provides the basis for a truly contemporary theater.

Unlike recent work in the U.S., Europeans have tended to work within the proscenium theater (Stockhausen's *Originale* is among the exceptions). A number of composers have written theater and operatic works using the new language of the European avant-garde and sometimes extending the proscenium space with films, projections, audience interaction, and other techniques. Many such works make strong social statements, notably those of Luigi Nono. Luciano Berio's *Passaggio* (1963), written for the Piccola Scala, is antiopera; the heroine, a trapped, hunted figure, flees across the stage while the public, represented by the chorus placed in the audience, shouts her down. Other works of Berio include *Laborintus II* (1965), which incorporates dancers, instrumentalists, passages from Dante, tape, and the pop vocal group, the Swingle Singers. *Traces* (1964), a dramatic work dealing with the race issue, *Visage* (1961), a nonverbal vocal expression, and *Opera* (1970) merge older theater and dance forms with new means. Most of Berio's vocal works were written for Cathy Berberian, one of the principal figures in new European music theater. Among the other composers who have written dramatic or theater works for her are Sylvano Bussotti (*La Passion selon Sade*, 1965–66), and György Ligeti (*Aventures*, 1962, and *Nouvelles Aventures*, 1962–65). Another important composer is the Argentine Mauricio Kagel, who now lives in Cologne. His works include a number of original theater pieces generally involving actors as well as instrumentalists and electronics. Roman Haubenstock-Ramati's *Amerika* (1963–65) and Henri Pousseur's *Votre Faust* (1961–67) with open-form text (the audience votes on the direction the plot should take) have been produced in conventional opera houses.

PERSPECTIVES. Edwin London has observed: "When we look at the performing media of the past, crystallizing over a long period of time—the string quartet, the piano, the orchestra, etc.—we know that they once had a relevant social usage and function. They were not always art objects. Violins were used at dances, and pianos were in many homes where people did not necessarily think of themselves as Rubensteins; they simply enjoyed fooling around playing the piano. The fact that people have tape recorders, slide projectors, electric guitars and so forth in their homes today gives everyone the potential of becoming active [mixed-media] creators, if not great ones. Most people, particularly young ones, like to fool around generally, and it's from this play with the media, especially those having little continuity with or derivations from past 'musical' materials, which is producing a fresh approach" ("Panel Discussion":126; see bibl.). The intense developments over the last decade suggest that some form or forms of mixed media and environmental theater will provide a major focus of interest in coming years. The growth of a younger public, its orientation towards music and sound, its interest in new and alternate means of expression, and its acceptance of multilayer, multimedia experience as a natural and relevant contemporary

form provides the necessary work-performance-audience interaction for the development of a new art form. It seems likely that the future of such a complex performance medium lies largely with ensembles—groups or companies of performers, creators, and creative technicians working collaboratively. Sonic Arts, Musica Elettronica Viva, and some of the recent dance-music ensembles are forerunners. Early in 1970 I organized such an ensemble in New York, QUOG, and an increasing number of attempts in this direction are likely, many of them connected with the larger urban centers and universities but working outside of the established, institutionalized forms of music making and theater.

BIBL.: Gilbert Chase, "Toward a Total Musical Theatre," *Arts in Society* (spring 1969):25–38; Michael Kirby, *Happenings* (New York 1965); Richard Kostelanetz, *The Theatre of Mixed Means* (New York 1967); "Panel Discussion: Mixed-Media Composition" (remarks by Ross Lee Finney, George Cacioppo, Edwin London, Salvatore Martirano), *American Society of University Composers Proceedings* (1968):123–45; Eric Salzman, "The Revolution in Music," *New American Review* (April 1969):76–96; *Source* magazine (1967–); Gene Youngblood, *Expanded Cinema* (New York 1970).

Eric Salzman

SEE ALSO Dance, Indeterminacy, Japan, United States.

Mixer, an electronic device for combining several signals and routing them to one or more channels that may correspond to the tracks on a magnetic tape or to loudspeakers. A mixer has several inputs and usually a fewer number of outputs.

SEE ALSO Electronic Music: Apparatus and Technology.

Miyoshi, Akira (b. Tokyo, 10 Jan 1933), studied French literature at Tokyo Univ. (1951–55, 1957–60) and music at the Paris Conservatory (1955–57, composition with Raymond Gallois-Montbrun, harmony with Henri Challan). He has taught at Tōhō College since 1965 and at Tokyo Univ. of the Arts since 1966.

PRINCIPAL COMPOSITIONS: *Violin Sonata* (1954, Ongaku); *Symphonie concertante* for piano, orchestra (1954); *Sonata* for flute, cello, piano (1955, Ongaku); *Piano Sonata* (1958, Ongaku); *Ondine*, radio drama for actors, female narrator, women's chorus, orchestra, electronic and concrete sounds (1959, Ongaku); *3 Symphonic Movements* (1960,

Ongaku); *String Quartets Nos. 1–2* (1962, 1967; Ongaku); *Piano Concerto* (1962, Kawai); *Duel* for soprano, orchestra (1964, Ongaku); *Concerto for Orchestra* (1964, Ongaku); *Violin Concerto* (1965, Ongaku); *Torso III* for marimba (1968); *Metamorphosed Odes* for orchestra (1969); *8 Poems* for flute ensemble (1969); *Concerto* for marimba, string orchestra (1969); *Red Death I* for orchestra, electronic and concrete sounds on tape (1969); *Red Death II* for chorus, orchestra, electronic and concrete sounds on tape (1970); *Festival Overture* for orchestra (1970, NHK).

SEE ALSO Japan.

Mizuno, Shūkō (b. Tokushima City, Japan, 24 Feb 1934), studied theory and composition with Yoshio Hasegawa and Minao Shibata at the Tokyo Univ. of Arts (1957–61) but learned most of all from working during 1958–61 with Group Ongaku, a group-improvisation ensemble he organized. Presently he teaches at Chiba Univ. His music is based on a principle of "organized improvisation . . . mutual hearing and mutual responding."

PRINCIPAL COMPOSITIONS: *Kinkan-gun no tame no mittsu no jigen* [3 Dimensions for Brass Groups] for 4 trumpets, 4 horns, 4 trombones, tuba, 3 conductors (1961); *Koe no autonomy* [Autonomy for Voice] for 6 female soloists, female chorus (1964, Ongaku); *Orchestra 1966* (1966); *Provisional Color* for piano (1967, Ongaku).

PRINCIPAL WRITINGS: "Ongun-teki sahô e no shikô" [Reflections on Sound Group Composition], *Ongaku-Geijutsu* (1967):12–18 and (1968):50–53.

SEE ALSO Japan.

Mobile Form, see Open Form

Modern Dance, see Dance

Modulator, an electronic device for changing a characteristic of a waveform (such as its frequency or amplitude). The process of change is called *modulation*.

SEE ALSO Electronic Music: Apparatus and Technology.

Moeschinger, Albert (Jean) (b. Basel, 10 Jan 1897), studied piano and composition at the conservatories of Bern (1917–20), Leipzig (1920–22), and Munich (1923–24). He was professor of theory and piano at the Bern Conservatory during 1937–43. Since 1956 he has resided in Ascona (Tessin).

PRINCIPAL COMPOSITIONS: *Divertimento* for string trio, Op. 10 (1924, Hug); *Kleine Klavierstücke*, Op. 31 (1930); *Variations and Fugue on a Theme by Henry Purcell* for string orchestra, tympani (1933, Schott); *Violin Concerto*, Op. 40 (1934, revised 1950; Bärenreiter); *Tag unsres Volks*, cantata, Op. 46 (1938); *Fantasy* for string orchestra, Op. 64 (1943, Boosey); *Violin Sonata*, Op. 62 (1945, Hug); *Sonatina* for clarinet, piano, Op. 65 (1945, Boosey); *Symphonie à la gloire de . . .*, Op. 71 (1945); *Toccata No. 3* for piano, Op. 72 (1945, Bärenreiter); *Die kleine Meerjungfrau*, cantata (radio opera) after Andersen, Op. 75 (1947); *Symphony No. 2* for chamber orchestra, Op. 73 (1948, Boosey); *Trumpet Concerto*, Op. 78 (1954, Boosey); *Amor und Psyche*, ballet, Op. 79 (1954, Boosey); *Symphony No. 4*, Op. 80 (1956, Boosey); *Images* for flute, saxophone (clarinet), violin, cello, Op. 85 (1958, Billaudot); *Clarinet Sonata*, Op. 87 (1959); *5 Caprices* for flute, clarinet, bassoon (1960, Heinr.); *Labyrinth* for 3 women's voices, orchestra; text by Dante (1962); *Fantaisie concertante* for flute, clarinet, bassoon, orchestra, Op. 95 (1963); *Piano Concerto*, Op. 96 (1964, EM); *Extra muros* for wind orchestra, percussion, Op. 97 (1964); *Sonata in modo disinvolto* for cello, piano (1964); *Capriccio* for bassoon, orchestra (1964); *Toccata cromatica* for piano, wind orchestra, percussion, Op. 100 (1965); *Consort* for strings, Op. 99 (1966); *Ignis divinus*, ballet en concert, Op. 102 (1966); *Sarcasmes* for orchestra, Op. 101 (1967); *Concerto* for harpsichord, chamber orchestra (1967); *Concerto* for ballerina, saxophone, chamber orchestra, Op. 103 (1968); *Erratique* for orchestra (1969); *Eglogue, Variations, and Finale* for piano (1969); *Sonatina* for flute, piano (1969, Billaudot).

BIBL.: Hans Oesch, "A. M.," *Schweizerische Musikzeitung* (May 1957); ——, "Was hat uns A. M. zu sagen?" *ibid.* (Jan 1967); Paul Vosseler, "Zum 70. Geburtstag von A. M.," *Basler Nachrichten* (8 Jan 1967).

Moevs, Robert (Walter) (b. La Crosse, Wis., 2 Dec 1920), studied at Harvard Univ. (1938–42, 1951–52; composition with Walter Piston) and at the Paris Conservatory (1947–51, composition with Nadia Boulanger). During 1955–63 he taught at Harvard and since 1964, at Rutgers Univ. He has been influenced by the theoretical ideas of Pierre Boulez and describes his compositional procedure as "systematic chromaticism," a modification of serial techniques in which a pitch collection is systematically exhausted but not in a rigidly ordered way. Primary material, a configuration of intervals or motives (usually 3–4 pitches), is expanded or otherwise altered according to the needs of each piece. The procedure was first clearly arrived at in the *String Quartet*.

PRINCIPAL COMPOSITIONS: *Piano Sonata* (1949, Eschig); *Fantasia sopra un motivo* for piano (1951, Eschig); *14 Variations for Orchestra* (1952); *Duo* for oboe, English horn (1953, Eschig); *3 Symphonic Pieces* (1954–55, Fleisher); *String Quartet* (1957, Piedmont); *Attis* for tenor, chorus, orchestra, percussion (1958); *Itaque ut* for chorus (1959, Piedmont); *Concerto* for piano, orchestra, percussion (1960, 2nd movement 1968; Piedmont); *Variazioni sopra una melodia* for viola, cello (1961, Piedmont); *Et nunc, reges* for women's chorus, flute, 2 clarinets (1963, Schirmer-E); *Et occidentem illustra* for chorus, orchestra (1964, Piedmont); *Musica da camera* (1965, Piedmont); *Ave Maria* for chorus (1966, Harvard Univ.); *A Brief Mass* for chorus, organ, vibraphone, guitar, double bass (1968, Piedmont); *Heptáchronon* for cello (1969); *BACH Es ist genug* for organ (1970).

PRINCIPAL WRITINGS: "Some Observations on Instruction in Music Theory," *Symposium* 6:69–71; "Music and Liturgy," *Liturgical Arts* 38/1:4–9; "Intervallic Procedures in Debussy," *Perspectives* 8/1:82–101; "Mannerism and Stylistic Consistency in Stravinsky," *ibid.* 9/2; *Principles of Musical Analysis* (unpub.).

BIBL.: Bruce Archibald, "Composers of Importance Today: R. M.," *Musical Newsletter* (April 1971):19–21; Robert Erickson, "The Avant-Garde," *Notes* 24:800–01; Donal Henahan, "Reviews of Records," on *Musica da camera* and *Variazioni sopra una melodia, Musical Quarterly* 54:385–87; Roman Vlad, "Recensioni: Musica," *Rassegna musicale* 24:369.

Moment Form, a concept of structure devised by Karlheinz *Stockhausen. A *moment* is a segment of musical time, usually a few seconds to a few minutes in duration, that is defined internally by some constant (for example, the freezing of pitches in particular registers) or by some process (for example, the progressive subtraction of elements from a complex sound until silence results). The essential characteristic is that a moment is self-contained. What happens within the moments of a composition (and sometimes the proportional lengths of the various moments) is often more important than relationships between moments. In many moment-form works, such as Stockhausen's *Momente* (1962–64), the order of moments is indeterminant and may vary from one performance to another.

Mompou, Federico (b. Barcelona, 16 April 1893), studied at the Conservatorio del Liceo in Barcelona with Pedro Serra (solfège, piano)

and privately in Paris during 1911–13 with Isidore Philipp and Ferdinand Motte Lacroix (piano) and Marcel Rousseau (harmony and composition). He has lived in Paris (1921–41) and Barcelona (1914–20, since 1941). In his music he makes use of early Spanish forms and dances and has been a leading figure, along with Falla, in creating a Spanish school of composition.

PRINCIPAL COMPOSITIONS (prepared with the help of Luis de Pablo): *Scènes d'enfants* for piano (1915–18, Salabert); *Suburbis* for piano (1916–17, Salabert); *Cants màgics* for piano (1917–19, UME and Salabert); *Canción y danza Nos. 1–12* for piano: Nos. 1–4 (1918–28, UME and Salabert); Nos. 5–8 (1942–46, Salabert and Marks); Nos. 9–12 (1948–62, Salabert); *Fêtes lointaines* for piano (1920, Salabert); *Charmes* for piano (1920–21, Eschig); *3 Variations* for piano (1921, Eschig); *Combat del somni* for voice, piano; texts by José Janés (1942, 1946, 1948, 1951); *Llueve sobre el río* for voice, piano; text by J. R. Jiménez (1945); *Música callada* for piano (1959–67, Salabert); *Cantar del alma* for voice, piano; text by St. John of the Cross (undated, Salabert).

BIBL.: Santiago Kastner, *F. M.* (Madrid 1947); E. Vuillermoz, *Musiques d'aujourd'hui* (Paris 1923).

SEE ALSO Spain.

Moncayo, José (Pablo) (b. Guadalajara, Mexico, 29 June 1912; d. Mexico City, 16 July 1958), studied piano and composition privately in Mexico City, 1929–35, with Eduardo Hernández Moncada, Carlos Chávez, and Candelario Huízar. In 1942 he studied composition with Aaron Copland at Tanglewood. He was a pianist and percussionist with the Orquesta Sinfónica de México during 1932–44 and conductor of the Orquesta Sinfónica Nacional from 1949. In 1935 he, Blas Galindo, Salvador Contreras, and Daniel Ayala formed the Grupo de los Cuatro. Most of his music was based on diatonic and polytonal harmonies and was impressionistic in its use of timbre and parallel chords.

PRINCIPAL COMPOSITIONS: *Amatzinac* for orchestra (1935); *Huapango* for orchestra (premiere 1941); *Symphony* (1944); *3 Piezas* for orchestra (1947); *Sonata* for violin, cello; *Tierra de Temporal* for orchestra; *3 Piezas* for piano; *Homenaje a Cervantes* for orchestra.

[prepared with the help of Esperanza Pulido]
SEE ALSO Mexico.

La Montaine, John (b. Oak Park, Ill., 17 March 1920), studied in Chicago with Stella Roberts (composition) and Rudolf Gans (piano) and with Bernard Rogers and Howard Hanson (at the Eastman School), Bernard Wagenaar (at Juilliard), and Nadia Boulanger (in Fontainebleau). He was pianist with the NBC Symphony Orchestra during 1950–54 and taught at Eastman during 1964–65.

PRINCIPAL COMPOSITIONS (most dates of composition are not available; music can be obtained from Paul J. Sifler, Los Angeles, unless otherwise noted): *Song of the Rose of Sharon*, song cycle for soprano, orchestra, Op. 6 (Broude-B); *Piano Concerto*, Op. 9 (1958–59, Galaxy); *String Quartet*, Op. 16 (1960, Schirmer-G); *Wonder Tidings*, Christmas carols for chorus, organ, harp, percussion, Op. 23; *Woodwind Quartet*, Op. 24a; *Fragments from the Song of Songs* for soprano, orchestra, Op. 29 (Schirmer-G); *Novellis, Novellis*, pageant opera for Christmas, Op. 31 (1961, Schirmer-G); *Birds of Paradise* for piano, orchestra, Op. 34; *The Shephardes Playe*, Christmas opera, Op. 38 (1967); *Incantation* for jazz band, Op. 39; *Erode the Greate*, Christmas opera, Op. 40 (1969). List to 1963: *Composers of the Americas* 9:81–85.

Montsalvatge, Xavier (Bassols) (b. Gerona, Spain, 11 March 1912), studied at the Barcelona Municipal Conservatory (1923–36, composition with Enrique Morera and Jaime Pahissa). He has taught in Barcelona at the San Jorge Royal Academy of Fine Arts (since 1962), the Destino Seminary (since 1969), and the Municipal Conservatory (since 1970). Since 1962 he has also been an editor and music critic for the Barcelona newspaper *La vanguardia*. He became president of the advisory council of the music commission of the General Directorate of Fine Arts in 1970. Primarily self-taught as a composer, his music was influenced in the beginning by Stravinsky, Bartók, and the postimpressionist French composers. His early orientation was nationalistic; this gave way to polytonal, 12-tone, and postserial procedures.

PRINCIPAL COMPOSITIONS: *3 Divertimentos* for piano (1942, Southern); *Spanish Sketch* for violin, piano (1943, Southern); *El gato con botas*, opera (1948); *5 Canciones negras* for soprano, piano or orchestra (1950, Southern); *Concerto breve* for piano, orchestra (1953, Southern); *Partita* for orchestra (1958, UME); *Sonatine pour Yvette* for piano (1961, Salabert); *Una voce in off*, 1-act opera; libretto by the composer (1962); *Disintegracion morfologica de la "Chacona" de Bach* for orchestra (1963, UME); *Babel-1948*, 4-act opera; libretto by the composer (1968); *5 Invocaciones al Crucificado* for soprano, 12 instruments (1969, Southern and UME).

SEE ALSO Spain.

Montvila, Vytautas (b. Kaunas, Lithuania, 1 June 1935), studied bassoon at the Vilna Conservatory (1952–59) and composition with J. Juzeliunas at the Vilna State Conservatory (1959–64). He has been a sound engineer for Lithuanian Television since 1959.

PRINCIPAL COMPOSITIONS: *Bassoon Concerto* (1964); *Dramatic Poem* for orchestra (1965); *Cosmic Ballad* for piano (1966, Vaga); *Poem* for voice, piano (1966); *String Quartet* (1967); *Skambesiai* for piano, gongs, bells (1967); *Trikampiai* for flute, piano (1970, Vaga); *Gotika* for orchestra (1970); *Flute Concerto* (1971); *Chorai* for orchestra (1971).

SEE ALSO Soviet Union.

Moore, Douglas (Stuart) (b. Cutchogue, near New York, 10 August 1893; d. Greenport, N. Y., 25 July 1969), studied liberal arts and music at Yale Univ. (1911–17, composition with Horatio Parker). He also studied with Vincent d'Indy at the Schola Cantorum in Paris in 1921 and with Ernst Bloch at the Cleveland Institute of Music in 1924. He taught at Columbia Univ. beginning in 1926 and was chairman of the music department during 1940–62.

Moore's output includes seven major operas, three other stage works, and orchestral, choral, and chamber music. He was primarily a melodist whose melodic lines are sometimes short but are often expanded into set pieces or combined with countermelodies. His operas show a natural talent for unforced prosody and use extreme vocal and instrumental registers and wide melodic skips only when essential to the dramatic action. Sometimes the writing is unabashedly decorative, using arpeggios, passing tones, and suspensions in a conventional way and only to strengthen the melodic drive. The harmonic language is tonal with consonances predominating and dissonant contrasts used (at times with daring) to create dramatic tension. Chromatic and enharmonic tones often act as pivots for sudden changes to remote chords and keys. The harmonies are often in close position, but the spacing widens when countermelodies are added, enabling each melody to be heard clearly.

The rhythmic orientation in the operas stems from straight-forward, metric "Gay 90s" tunes, early 20th-century musical comedy, American folksong syncopation, ragtime and pop-music beats, waltz time, and sometimes hymns and marches. (The rhythmic impulses of song and dance also lie behind the purely instrumental music.) These ideas are often combined or contrasted with elastic, recitative-like speech rhythms in which there are rapid changes of meter. The operas are obviously American in character, but their recitatives and set pieces relate to 19th-century French opera and, to a lesser extent, 19th-century Italian traditions. They show little German and no Wagnerian influence. In their subjects and musical treatments, some of them (*The Devil and Daniel Webster, The Ballad of Baby Doe, Gallantry,* and *Carry Nation*) are notable examples of musical Americana. Many of the orchestral works (*The Pageant of P. T. Barnum, Farm Journal,* etc.) belong in the same category. Works such as the *Symphony in A* and the *String Quartet* follow traditional formal schemes more closely, but modify them when a scheme interferes with the melodic, lyric, or dramatic thrust of the music.

PRINCIPAL COMPOSITIONS: *The Pageant of P. T. Barnum,* suite for orchestra (1924, Eastman); *Violin Sonata* (1929); *String Quartet* (1933, SPAM); *White Wings,* 2-act opera; libretto by Philip Barry (1935); *The Headless Horseman,* 1-act high-school opera; libretto by Stephen Vincent Benet after Washington Irving (1936, Schirmer-E); *The Devil and Daniel Webster,* 1-act opera; libretto by Benet (1938, Boosey); *Dedication* for chorus (1938, Boosey); *Village Music,* suite for small orchestra (1941, Mercury); *Wind Quintet* (1942, SPAM); *In memoriam,* symphonic poem (1943, E-V); *Prayer for the United Nations* for alto, chorus, orchestra (1943, Gray); *Down East Suite* for violin with piano or orchestra (1944, Fischer); *Symphony in A* (1945, Schirmer-G); *Quintet* for clarinet, strings (1946); *Farm Journal,* suite for orchestra (1947, Fischer); *The Emperor's New Clothes,* 1-act opera for children (1948, Fischer); *Giants in the Earth,* 3-act opera; libretto by Arnold Sundgaard after O. E. Rölvaag (1950, Fischer); *Cotillion,* suite for orchestra (1952, Fischer); *Piano Trio* (1953, Galaxy); *The Ballad of Baby Doe,* 2-act opera; libretto by John Latouche (1956, Chappell); *Gallantry,* "A Soap Opera" in 1 act; libretto by Sundgaard (1957, Schirmer-G); *Wings of the Dove,* 2-act opera; libretto by Ethan Ayer after Henry James (1961, Schirmer-G); *The Greenfield Christmas Tree,* a Christmas entertainment for vocal soloists, chorus; libretto by Sundgaard (1962, Schirmer-G); *Carry Nation,* 2-act opera; libretto by William North Jayme (1966, Galaxy). Undated works: *God Rest You Merry Gentlemen* for chorus; *Perhaps to Dream* for women's chorus; *Simon Legree* for men's chorus, piano (all Fischer).

PRINCIPAL WRITINGS: *Listening to Music* (New York 1932, revised ed. 1937); *From Madrigal to Modern Music* (New York 1942). Moore also wrote articles and reviews for *Harper's, The Saturday Review,* and other general-interest magazines.

BIBL.: Otto Luening, "D. M.," *Modern Music* 20:248–53; Joseph Machlis, "D. M.," *American Composers of Our Time* (New York 1963):42–53;

——, "D. M.," *Introduction to Contemporary Music* (New York 1961):465–70; Elsa V. Posell, *American Composers* (New York 1963):137–41; Willard Rhodes, "D. M.'s Music," *Columbia Univ. Quarterly* 32:223–26.

Otto Luening

SEE ALSO Opera, United States.

Moran, Robert (Leonard) (b. Denver, 8 Jan 1937), studied 12-tone composition with Hans Erich Apostel in Vienna (1957–58) and attended Mills College (1961–63; composition with Darius Milhaud, Luciano Berio). Since 1964 he has performed as a pianist in avant-garde works and lectured in the U.S. and Europe on new music. He has been director of the West Coast Music Ensemble in San Francisco since 1968. He has worked in mixed media and often uses graphic notation.

PRINCIPAL COMPOSITIONS: *4 Visions* for flute, harp, string quartet (1963, UE); *Interiors* for chamber ensemble, or orchestra, or percussion ensemble (1964, Peters); *Bombardments No. 2* for 5 percussionists (1964, Peters); *Titus-No. 1* for amplified automobile, performers, stereo tape (1967, published in *Source* magazine, 1968); *Jewel-Encrusted Butterfly Wing Explosions* for orchestra in small groups, stereo tape, violinist-mummy, films, projections, theatrical actions (1967–68); *Bank of America Chandelier* for percussion quartet (1968); *Let's Build a Nut House* (Memoriam Paul Hindemith), chamber opera in 1 act (1969); *39 Minutes for 39 Autos,* a city-wide event that took place in San Francisco on 29 August 1969 utilizing automobile horns and lights, Moog synthesizer, tape, TV and radio broadcasting facilities, with home and office lights turned on and off on cue by the audience (see *Source* 9); *Hallelujah* for 20 marching bands, drum and bugle corps, choruses, carillons, organs, rock ensembles, blimp, spotlights, etc. (composed for performance in Bethlehem, Pa., by 75,000 people, 1970).

BIBL.: "Die geistige Welt," *Die Welt* (Hamburg, 30 May 1964); Johannes Berger, "Nachrichten aus den Staaten," *Frankfurter Rundschau* 63 (16 March 1970):15; Karlheinz Roschitz, "Zur Notation neuer Musik," *Österreichische Musikzeitschrift* (April 1967):189–205.

Morawetz, Oskar (b. Světlá nad Sázavou, Czechoslovakia, 17 Jan 1917), studied at Prague Univ. (1935–37; harmony, counterpoint with Jaroslav Krička; piano with Karel Hoffmeister). He emigrated to Canada in 1940 and attended the Univ. of Toronto (1942–44, piano with Alberto Guerrero). He has taught at the Royal Conservatory of Music in

Toronto (1946–56) and at the Univ. of Toronto (since 1952). He is self-taught in composition and has studied the music of most major composers since Bach (aided by a highly retentive memory). Among 20th-century composers, he especially admires Britten, Honegger, Stravinsky, Hindemith, Bartók, and Berg.

PRINCIPAL COMPOSITIONS: *String Quartet No. 2 in A* (1952–55); *Fantasy, Elegy, and Toccata* for piano (1958, Leeds); *Piano Concerto No. 1* (1962, Leeds); *Sinfonietta* for winds, percussion (1965, Leeds); *2 Preludes* for violin, piano (1965); *Concerto* for brass quintet, orchestra (1968, Leeds); *Memorial to Martin Luther King* for soloists, orchestra (1968); *Suite* for piano (1968, Leeds); *Reflections after a Tragedy* for orchestra (1969, Leeds); *Sinfonietta* for strings (1969, Leeds); *From the Diary of Anne Frank* for soprano, orchestra (1970). List to 1960: *Composers of the Americas* 6:79–82.

BIBL.: "O. M.," *Musicanada* (Dec 1969); "O. M.: An International Success," *The Canadian Composer* (March 1969):1–2.

Morel, François (d'Assise) (b. Montreal, 14 March 1926), studied at the Montreal Conservatory (1944–53, composition with Claude Champagne). He has earned his living as an arranger and as a composer of background scores for the theater and films. Probably the most important formative event in his life occurred in 1956, when he met several times with Edgard Varèse in New York. Although on the surface none of his works resemble Varèse, they reveal such Varèse-like features as an unusual sensitivity to instrumental sonority and color, a preference for masses of winds and percussion, a concentration on the instant as opposed to long developments, and a generally monorhythmic texture colored by changes of density. *Départ* (1969) is a typical work, although its unusual instrumentation is exceptional (12 strings, guitar, harp, 2 percussion). Its opening section consists of five very short events: a five-note phrase by the guitar; two notes by vibraphone played with a double-bass bow; a chord in the strings that is colored by nonvibrato playing by violas and cellos, *col legno* playing by two violins, and harmonics by two other violins with a percussive upbeat in the harp; a rapid figure by temple blocks; and finally a dry, ripped guitar chord. Although the work is only nine minutes long, there are no less than 15 sections arranged as a mosaic of seven slightly accompanied solos (for guitar, harp, vibraphone, cello), interspersed with chordal sections, as at the beginning of the work, and some mass

sections involving a heterophony of 12 different but equal parts. The dominant impression is of a delicate lacework that constantly renews itself.

PRINCIPAL COMPOSITIONS: *4 Chants japonais* for voice, piano (1949); *Etude de sonorités* for piano (1952, Berandol); *String Quartets Nos. 1–2* (1952, 1963); *Antiphonie* for orchestra (1953, Berandol); *Rituel de l'espace* for orchestra without violins (1958); *L'Etoile noire* for orchestra (1962, Berandol); *Wind Quintet* for 2 trumpets, horn, trombone, tuba (1962); *Alleluia* for organ (1967); *Novatook* for flute (1967); *Prisme-Anamorphose* for winds, percussion, harps, piano (1967); *Rythmologue* for 8 percussionists (1969); *Départ* for 12 strings, harp, guitar, 2 percussionists (1969); *Radiance* for small orchestra (1970).

Bruce Mather

SEE ALSO Canada.

Morgan, Robert P. (b. Nashville, 28 July 1934), studied at Princeton Univ. (1958–60; composition with Roger Sessions, analysis with Milton Babbitt, Edward Cone) and the Univ. of Calif. at Berkeley (1956–58, composition with Andrew Imbrie, piano with Bernard Abramowitch). He has taught at the Univ. of Houston (1963–67) and at Temple Univ. in Philadelphia (since 1967). He is a record critic for *High Fidelity* and an advisory editor of *Musical Newsletter*.

PRINCIPAL COMPOSITIONS: *Symphony* (1967); *Wind Quartet* (1969); *Interactions* for flute, piano (1970).

PRINCIPAL WRITINGS: "Edward T. Cone: String Sextet," *Perspectives* 8/1:112–25; "Bartók's String Quartets," *High Fidelity* (Sept 1970):58–61; "Towards a More Inclusive Musical Literacy: Notes on Easy 20th Century Piano Music," *Musical Newsletter* (Jan 1971):8–12.

Moroi, Makoto (b. Tokyo, 17 Dec 1930), attended the Tokyo Academy School of Music (now called Tokyo Univ. of the Arts; 1948–52, composition and theory with Tomojiro Ikenouchi). He has been a guest composer at the NHK (Japan Broadcasting Corporation) electronic music studio since 1956 and has taught at Osaka Univ. of the Arts since 1968. Influences on his development come from ancient Japanese shakuhachi music (for bamboo flute), Gregorian chant, and such Western composers as Bach, Beethoven, Schoenberg, Webern, Boulez, Stockhausen, and Ligeti.

PRINCIPAL COMPOSITIONS: *Partita* for flute (1951–52); *Composition* for orchestra (1951–53); *α and β* for piano (1953–54, Ongaku); *Développements raréfiants* for soprano, flute, bass clarinet, violin, cello, piano, 2 percussionists, claviolin (ondes Martenot); text by K. Kitasono (1957, Ongaku); *Die lange, lange Strasse lang* for 4 actors, tenor, choruses, orchestra, tape; text by Wolfgang Borchert (1961); *Suite concertante* for violin, orchestra (1963, Ongaku); *Chikurai*, 5 pieces for shakuhachi [bamboo flute] (1964, Ongaku); *Coachman Phaeton*, radio music drama for 4 actors, 2 sopranos, baritone, choruses, orchestra, tape (1965); *Piano Concerto No. 1* (1966, NHK); *Symphony*, with optional tape (1968, NHK); *Taiyō no Otozure* [Visit of the Sun] for baritone, women's chorus, orchestra (1969); *Les Farces* for violin (1970, Zen-On); *My "Izumo"* for vocal soloists, chorus, orchestra including electronic sounds on tape, traditional Japanese instruments (1970); *3 Mouvements concertants* for shakuhachi, percussion, 15 strings (1970–71, Zen-On).

SEE ALSO Japan, Microtones.

Moroi, Saburo (b. Tokyo, 7 August 1903), studied at Tokyo Univ. (1926–29, esthetics with Otsuka) and the Berlin Hochschule für Musik (1932–34, composition with Leo Schrattenholz, piano with Robert Schmidt). He was inspector of music and adult education for the Ministry of Education during 1946–64. During 1965–66 he was director of the Tokyo Metropolitan Symphony, and since 1967 he has been director of the Senzokugakuen Music Academy.

PRINCIPAL COMPOSITIONS: *Violin Sonata No. 2* (1931); *Piano Sonatas Nos. 1–2* (1933, 1940); *Piano Concerto in C* (1933); *Symphonies Nos. 1–5* (1934; 1938; No. 3 with organ, 1944; No. 4 with piano, 1951; 1970); *Viola Sonata* (1935); *Flute Sonata* (1937); *String Sextet* (1939); *Violin Concerto* (1939); *String Trio* (1940); *Suite* for piano (1942); *2 Symphonic Movements* for orchestra (1942); *Sinfonietta in B* (1943); *Visit of Sun*, fantasy oratorio; text by the composer (1968).

PRINCIPAL WRITINGS: *Ongaku kyoiku ron* [Music Education] (Tokyo 1947); *Kinō waseihō* [Harmony] (Tokyo 1948); *Beethoven* (Tokyo 1948); *Ongakujiten* [Music Dictionary] (Tokyo 1949); *Junsui taiihe* [Strict Counterpoint] (Tokyo 1949); *Romanha ongaku no chōrū* [Current Romantic Music] (Tokyo 1950); *Ongaku to shikō* [Music and Thinking] (Tokyo 1953). Moroi has also written analyses of Beethoven's string quartets and piano sonatas, as well as a five-volume history of musical forms.

Moross, Jerome (b. Brooklyn, N. Y., 1 August 1913), attended New York Univ. (1929–32) and the Juilliard School (1931–32). Between 1931 and 1950 he worked as a composer,

pianist, and orchestrator; subsequently he has devoted himself entirely to composition.

PRINCIPAL COMPOSITIONS (published by Chappell unless otherwise noted): *Paeans* for orchestra (1931, New Music); *Those Everlasting Blues.* for voice, chamber orchestra (1932, unpub.); *Beguine* for orchestra (1934, New Music); *Frankie and Johnny*, ballet suite (1937–38); *A Tall Story* for orchestra (1938, unpub.); *Susanna and the Elders*, 1-act ballet-opera; libretto by John Latouche (1940); *Symphony No. 1* (1940–41, unpub.); *Recitative and Aria* for violin, piano (1943, unpub.); *Willie the Weeper*, 1-act ballet-opera; libretto by Latouche (1945); *The Eccentricities of Davy Crockett*, 1-act ballet-opera; libretto by Latouche (1946); *Variations on a Waltz* for orchestra (1946, orchestrated 1968); *The Golden Apple*, 2-act opera; libretto by Latouche (1950–52); *Music for the Flicks*, suite for orchestra from 5 film scores (1952–65); *The Last Judgement*, ballet suite (1953); *Gentlemen, Be Seated!*, 2-act opera; libretto by Edward Eager (1955–57); *The Big Country*, film suite (1958); *Sonatina* for clarinet choir (1966); *Sonatina* for string bass, piano (1967); *Sonatina* for brass quintet (1968); *Sonatina* for woodwind quintet (1970).

Mortensen, Finn (Einar) (b. Oslo, 6 Jan 1922), studied privately with Erling Westher (1934–43, piano), Thorleif Eken (1941–42, harmony), Klaus Egge (1943–44, counterpoint), Reidar Furu (1945–48, double bass), and Niels Viggo Bentzon (1956, composition). He is basically self-taught in composition. In 1966 he visited Karlheinz Stockhausen's Cologne Electronic Music Studio. He has performed as a conductor, pianist, and double bass player. He was president of the Norwegian section of ISCM during 1961–64 and 1966 and director of the Norwegian State Concert Series during 1967–68. He has taught composition at the Oslo Conservatory since 1970. Bach, Bruckner, and Stockhausen have been the most important composers in his development.

PRINCIPAL COMPOSITIONS: *Wind Quintet*, Op. 4 (1951, Hansen-W); *Symphony*, Op. 5 (1953); *Sonata* for flute, Op. 6 (1953, Norsk); *Fantasia and Fugue* for piano (1958, Norsk); *Evolution* for orchestra, Op. 23 (1961, Norsk); *Tone Colors* for orchestra, Op. 24 (1962); *Piano Concerto*, Op. 25 (1963, Norsk); *Sonata* for 2 pianos, Op. 26 (1964); *Fantasia* for piano, orchestra, Op. 27 (1965–66); *Kammermusik*, Op. 31, for clarinet, bassoon, trumpet, trombone, percussion, violin, double bass (1968); *Impressions* for 2 pianos, Op. 32 (1970, Norsk).

PRINCIPAL WRITINGS: "Fartein Valens Fiolinkonsert," *Nutida musik* 3:14–17.

BIBL.: Bjarne Kortsen, *Modern Norwegian Chamber Music* (Haugesund 1965):52–95; ———,

Contemporary Norwegian Orchestral Music (Bergen 1968):294–99; Bo Wallner, *Vår tids musik i Norden* (Stockholm 1968):225–27, English trans. (London 1971).
SEE ALSO Scandinavia.

Morthenson, Jan W. (b. Oernskoeldsvik, Sweden, 7 April 1940), attended Uppsala Univ. (1961–66) and studied composition with Ingvar Lidholm (1960–61), G. M. Koenig (1961), and H. K. Metzger (1963–64); and with Luciano Berio and Karlheinz Stockhausen at the Darmstadt summer courses (1963). He was editor of the Fylkingen Bulletin of Art and Technology during 1966–68. In 1970 he lectured at the San Francisco Conservatory. He is a free-lance composer and television director.
PRINCIPAL COMPOSITIONS (published by Hansen-W unless otherwise noted): *Some of These . . .* for organ (1961); *Coloratura I–IV* for orchestra (1961–63, No. 1 unpub.); *Antiphonia I–III* for orchestra (1962, 1964, 1970); *Pour Madame Bovary* for organ (1962); *Eternes* for organ (1965); *Epsilon eridani* on tape (1967, unpub.); *Neutron Star* on tape (1967, unpub.); *Decadenza I* for organ, tape (1968); *Spoon River*, television program (1969, unpub.); *Decadenza II* for orchestra (1969–70); *Colossus* for orchestra (1970); *Farewell* for organ (1970); *Senza* for string orchestra (1970); *Ultra* on tape (1970, unpub.); *Supersonics*, television program (1970, unpub.); *Corona*, television program (1971, unpub.); *Sensory Project I–III* on tape (1971, unpub.); *Interferences I*, film score.
PRINCIPAL WRITINGS: *Nonfigurative Musik* (Stockholm 1964); "Science Fiction," *BLM* (Stockholm) 6:429–35.
BIBL.: Bo Wallner, *Vår tids musik i Norden* (Stockholm 1971), English trans. (London 1971).

Moser, Roland (Olivier) (b. Bern, 16 April 1943), studied at the Bern Conservatory (1962–66, composition with Sándor Veress), the Freiburg Hochschule für Musik (1966–69, composition with Wolfgang Fortner, conducting with Francis Travis, piano with Edith Picht-Axenfeld), and with Herbert Eimert at the Electronic Music Studio of the Cologne Hochschule für Musik (1969–70). He also attended the Darmstadt summer courses (1967–68). Since 1969 he has taught at the Conservatories of Winterthur and Lausanne. He plays in the contemporary music ensemble Neue Horizonte. His music has been influenced by his association with the group's leader, Urs Peter Schneider, as well as by the music of Webern, Feldman, Donatoni, Schnebel, and others.
PRINCIPAL COMPOSITIONS: *Pezzo* for flute, piano (1967, Ars Viva); *Ritornelle und Dialoge* for clarinet, trombone, violin, cello, piano, organ, 2 percussionists (1968); *Harmonies* for 2 pianos; based on a page by Franz Liszt and using "a technique of absurd serialism" (1834/1969); *Stilleben mit Glas*, electronic sounds on tape (1969–70); *Arbeit*, "Sisyphi in memoriam," for cello, tape recorder (1970); *Heinrich Heine* for mezzo-soprano, piano, instrumentalists (1970–).
BIBL.: Hans Humpert, "Elektronische Musik als Hochschulfach," *Melos* (Sept 1970):332–33; Kjell H. Keller, "*Harmonies* . . . von R. M.," *Der Bund* (16 April 1970):23.
SEE ALSO Switzerland.

Moss, Lawrence (b. Los Angeles, 18 Nov 1927), studied at Pomona College (1945–47), the Univ. of Calif. at Los Angeles (1947–49), the Eastman School (1949–50), the Univ. of Southern Calif. (1950–53, PhD 1957; composition with Leon Kirchner; composition, orchestration, conducting with Ingolf Dahl). During 1956–59 he taught at Mills College and during 1960–69, at Yale Univ. Since 1969 he has been chairman of the Division of Composition and Theory at the Univ. of Md. In 1957 he conducted the New Haven Opera Society as part of Project LEARN. His early works, principally the *Violin Sonata*, showed the influence of Kirchner. In the late 1960s he was exploring time relationships, particularly the polyphony of "time-affects" or moods.
PRINCIPAL COMPOSITIONS: *A Song of Solomon* for women's voices, piano (1956, Mercury); *Violin Sonata* (1959); *The Brute*, 1-act comic opera (1960, Presser); *4 Scenes* for piano (1961); *Scenes for Small Orchestra* (1961, Presser); *3 Rilke Songs* for soprano, piano (1963); *Music for 5* for brass quintet (1963, Merion); *Remembrances* for 8 instruments (1964, Presser); *The Queen and the Rebels*, opera (1965, Presser); *Windows* for flute, clarinet, double bass (1966); *Omaggio* for piano 4-hands (1966, E-V); *Patterns* for flute, clarinet, viola, piano (1967); *Exchanges* for 3 brasses, 3 woodwinds, percussion (1968); *Ariel* for soprano, orchestra (1969); *Elegy* for 2 violins, viola (1969); *Timepiece* for violin, piano, percussion (1970).
PRINCIPAL WRITINGS: "George Perle: String Quartet," *Perspectives* 3/1:136–39; "Last Year at Marienhöhe," *Perspectives* 3/2:170–72; "Schubert's *Moments Musicaux No. 1*: A Composer's Analysis," *Yale Journal of Music Theory* (fall 1968); "Toward a New Theater," *Perspectives* 8/1:102–05.
BIBL.: Elaine Barkin, "L. K. M.: 3 Rilke Songs . . .," *Perspectives* 6/1:144–52.
SEE ALSO Opera.

de la Motte, Diether (b. Bonn, 30 March 1928), studied at the Nordwestdeutsche Musikakademie in Detmold (1946–50, composition with Wilhelm Maler, piano with Conrad Hansen) and at the Darmstadt summer courses (composition with Wolfgang Fortner, Olivier Messiaen). During 1959–62 he was a reader for the music publishers B. Schott in Mainz. He has taught at the Evangelical School for Church Music in Düsseldorf (1950–59) and at the Hamburg Musikhochschule (since 1962).

PRINCIPAL COMPOSITIONS (published by Bärenreiter unless otherwise noted): *Concerto for Orchestra* (1963); *Symphony in 2 Movements* (1964); *Piano Concerto* (1965, Bote); *Symphonic Overture* (1966); *Flute Concerto* (1967); *Der Aufsichtsrat*, opera (1969); *Mixed Music II and III* on tape (1969, unpub.).

PRINCIPAL WRITINGS: *Musikalische Analyse*, 2 vols. (Cassel 1968).

BIBL.: Karl Grebe, "Musik für ein singendes Orchester – D. d. l. M.," *Musica* 4 (1967):155–58.

Moyzes, Alexander (b Kláštor pod Znievom, Czechoslovakia, 4 Sept 1906), studied as a child with his father, the composer Mikuláš Moyzes, and at the Prague Conservatory (1925–28; composition with Rudolf Karel, Otakar Šín; organ with B. A. Wiedermann; conducting with Otakar Ostrčil) and the Master School of the Conservatory (1929–30, composition with Vítězslav Novák). He taught composition at the Bratislava Academy of Music and Drama beginning in 1928 and later transferred to the Higher School of Musical Arts in Bratislava. For a while after World War II he was music director for Czech Radio in Bratislava. In his music he has aimed at a progressive Slovak art with wide international significance.

PRINCIPAL COMPOSITIONS (published by SHF unless otherwise noted): *Piano Sonata in E Minor*, Op. 2 (1927, revised 1942; Supraphon); *Symphonies Nos. 1–7*, Opp. 4, 16, 17b, 38, 39, 45, 50 (1928; 1942; 1942; 1947; 1948; 1951; 1955, Supraphon); *String Quartet*, Op. 7 (1928, unpub.); *Jazz Sonata* for 2 pianos, Op. 14 (1932); *Wind Quintet*, Op. 17 (1933, revised 1952); *Concertino* for orchestra, Op. 18 (1933); *Jánošík's Rebels*, overture, Op. 21 (1943); *Down the River Váh* for orchestra, Op. 26 (1945, Supraphon); *Poetic Suite* for violin, piano, Op. 35 (1948, Supraphon); *Znejú piesne na chotari* [Songs Resound in the Meadows], suite for soprano, tenor, chorus, orchestra, Op. 40 (c.1949, unpub.); *Dances from the Hron Region* for orchestra, Op. 44 (1950, Suraphon); *February Overture*, Op. 46 (1952, Suraphon); *Dances from Gemer*, suite for orchestra, Op. 51 (1955); *Violin Concerto*, Op. 53 (1958); *Ballad Cantata* for vocal soloists, chorus, orchestra,

Op. 55 (1958); *In Autumn*, song cycle for mezzo-soprano, piano, Op. 56; text by Ján Kostra (1960); *Duetto* for violin, piano (1961, unpub.); *Sonatina giocosa* for violin, string orchestra, harpsichord, Op. 57 (1962, Supraphon); *Morning Dew*, song cycle for mezzo-soprano, orchestra, Op. 59; text by Vojtěch Mihálik (1963, unpub.); *Small Sonata* for violin, piano, Op. 63 (c.1965); *The Brave King*, opera in 6 scenes with 2 ballets; libretto by the composer after Ján Hollý (1966); *Flute Concerto* (1966).

SEE ALSO Czechoslovakia.

Mumma, Gordon (b. Framingham, Mass., 30 March 1935), studied French horn and piano in Detroit (1949–52) and theory and composition at the Univ. of Mich. (1952–53). He cofounded and worked with the Cooperative Studio for Electronic Music in Ann Arbor, Mich. (1958–66) and was codirector of the ONCE Group and Festival there (1960–68). During 1962–63 he was a research assistant for the department of acoustics and seismics of the Institute of Science and Technology in Ann Arbor. Since 1966 he has been a composer and musician with the Merce Cunningham Dance Co. and the Sonic Arts Group in New York, and during 1969–70 he was a consultant artist and engineer for Experiments in Art and Technology, Inc., New York. He was one of the first composers to use live electronic-music processes. He designs circuitry that provides for a semiautomatic control system to integrate the compositional and performance aspects of any or all of the elements of musical sound, including the continuity of an entire composition. Decisions shared by the composer and performer in more traditional music are delegated among composer, live performer, and an electronic system that may employ computer logic. He uses the term *cybersonics* to denote this approach. His work has been influenced by the composers, dancers, and artists working with Merce Cunningham and by the compositions of Robert Ashley, Morton Feldman, and Christian Wolff.

PRINCIPAL COMPOSITIONS: *Gestures II* for 2 pianos (1958–62); *Megaton for William Burroughs* for 10 electronic, acoustical, and communications channels (1963); *Mographs* for various combinations of pianos and pianists (1962–64, BMIC and UE); *Music for the Venezia Space Theatre* for 4-channel tape, electronic apparatus (1964, Advance Records); *The Dresden Interleaf 13 February 1945* on 4-channel tape (1965, JME Records, Argentina); *Le Corbusier* for orchestra, organ, tape, cybersonic console (1965); *Mesa* for bandoneon with cybersonic console (1966, Odyssey Records); *Hornpipe* for horn, cybersonic console

(1967, Mainstream Records); *Digital Process* for acoustical and electronic instruments, digital control circuitry, tape, motion-picture projectors (1967–69); *Swarm* for violin, concertina, bowed crosscut saw, cybersonic modification (1968); *Runway* for cybersonic processing with digital control circuitry; prepared in collaboration with David Behrman (1968); *Beam* for violin, viola, cybersonic modification, digital-computer control (1969); *Conspiracy 8* for bowed crosscut saw, gate-controlled amplifiers with control oscillators, teletype and cathode-ray tube display, time-sharing digital computer with data-link, 7 auxiliary performers (1969–70).

PRINCIPAL WRITINGS: "An Electronic Music Studio for the Independent Composer," *Journal of the Audio Engineering Society* (July 1964):240–44; "The ONCE Festival and How It Happened," *Arts in Society* (Madison, Wis.) 4/2:381–98; *Creative Aspects of Live Electronic Music Technology*, Audio Engineering Society Preprint No. 550 (Oct 1967); *PDP-6 Computer Synthesis and Control of Musical Performance for the Cunningham Dance Company*, Steven Smolier, coauthor (Project Mac, Mass. Institute of Technology, 1968); "The Rhythm Studies of Conlon Nancarrow," *Source* (c.1971).

SEE ALSO Instrumental and Vocal Resources, Mixed Media, Performance, United States.

Musgrave, Thea (b. Edinburgh, 27 May 1928), studied at Edinburgh Univ. (1947–50; harmony, analysis with Mary Grierson; counterpoint, history of music with Hans Gal) and at the Paris Conservatory (1952–54, accompaniment with Nadia Boulanger). She also studied composition privately with Boulanger during 1950–54. During 1959–65 she lectured on music for the Extra-Mural Department of London Univ. Since then she has devoted herself exclusively to composing.

PRINCIPAL COMPOSITIONS (published by Chester): *Cantata for a Summer's Day* for vocal quartet, speaker, string quartet, flute, clarinet, double bass; also for flute, clarinet, string orchestra; texts by Hume and Lindsay (1954); *The Abbott of Drimock*, chamber opera for 7 singers, violin, cello, piano, celesta, percussion (1955); *5 Love Songs* for soprano, guitar; early English texts (1955); *Obliques* for harp, celesta, timpani, percussion, strings (1958); *A Song for Christmas* for high voice, piano (1958); *String Quartet* (1958); *Triptych* for tenor, orchestra; text by Chaucer (1959); *Colloquy* for violin, piano (1960); *Trio* for flute, oboe, piano (1960); *Monologue* for piano (1960); *Sir Patrick Spens* for tenor, guitar (1961); *The Phoenix and the Turtle* for small chorus, orchestra; text attributed to Shakespeare (1962); *Marko the Miser* for children to mime, sing, play; text by Afanasiev and Samson (1962); *The 5 Ages of Man* for chorus, orchestra; text by Hesiod-Lattimore (1963); *The Decision*, 3-act opera (1964–65); *Festival Overture*

for orchestra (1965); *Excursions*, 8 duets for piano 4-hands (1965); *Nocturnes and Arias* for harp, timpani, percussion, strings (1966); *Chamber Concerto No. 2* for 5 instruments (1966); *Chamber Concerto No. 3* for clarinet, bassoon, horn, string quartet, double bass (1966); *Concerto for Orchestra* (1967); *Impromptu* for flute, oboe (1967); *Music for Horn and Piano* (1967); *Memento creatoris* for chorus; text by Donne (1967); *Clarinet Concerto* (1968); *Beauty and the Beast*, ballet (1968–69); *Soliloquy* for guitar, tape (1969).

SEE ALSO Great Britain.

Musical, a theater genre that developed in the U.S. It combines a dramatic script with music, song lyrics, and (usually) dance. There are five general categories: 1) popular romance, 2) operetta, 3) folk musical, 4) revue, and 5) drama. The romance is by far the most prevalent type. It is a comedy, and the musical material is generally light and entertaining. *Call Me Madam* (Irving Berlin, 1950)[1] and *The Music Man* (Meredith Willson, 1951) are examples. The contemporary operetta is likely to have more demanding singing roles and a more fanciful plot than the romance. Examples are the fairy tale, *Finian's Rainbow* (Burton Lane, 1947) or the story of a wistful orphan in *Carnival* (Robert Merrill, 1961). The folk musical is inspired by the flavor of an ethnic culture. The score of *Fiddler on the Roof* (Jerry Bock, 1964) exploits Israeli musical elements, the story is typical of Jewish folk culture, and the choreography is based on characteristic folk dances. The folk-rock idiom in *Hair* (Galt MacDermott, 1967), together with the nudity and racial integration, reflected the hippie movement. Revues have topical lyrics and skits and, although frequently produced, are necessarily short lived; *Pins and Needles* (Harold Rome, 1937) and *Call Me Mister* (Rome, 1946) are among the few that could be revived today. Individual songs from revues often enjoy long popularity, as evidenced by "Easter Parade" and "Heat Wave" from *As Thousands Cheer* (Irving Berlin, 1933) and "April in Paris" from *Walk a Little Faster* (Vernon Duke, 1932). The drama is essentially an opera with popular appeal. The subject is more serious than that of a romance, and the music is usually more sophisticated, underscoring the dramatic situations more heavily and more continuously. The ending is seldom happy. *Street Scene* (Kurt Weill, 1947) fits this category, as do the Marc Blitzstein and Gian-Carlo Menotti

[1]The name of a musical is followed by the name of its composer and the date of first performance.

operas. Some works, of course, bridge these categories. *Brigadoon* (Frederick Lowe, 1947) combines the fanciful plot of an operetta with Scottish musical and choreographic elements as in a folk musical. *The King and I* (Richard Rodgers, 1951) has the exotic setting of a folk musical and the sad ending of a drama.

EARLY HISTORY. Precedents for the musical can be found as far back as mid-18th century American stage shows. The first staged musical effort that was completely American in origin was *The Archers* (Benjamin Carr, 1796), based on the story of William Tell (Mates: 3; see bibl.). An "extravaganza" called *The Black Crook* (Giuseppe Operti, 1866) had the first commercially successful long run and is often considered to be the father of the Broadway musical (Smith: 13–22, 56–61, 144). Other 19th-century "extravaganzas," "melodramas," "entertainments," etc., fulfilled the continuing need for staged musical entertainment. Until 1903 the comic opera-operetta was composed of self-contained musical pieces with dialogue between; it was in Victor Herbert's *Babes in Toyland* of that year that incidental and connecting music, an important feature of the modern musical, was first used. When *The Merry Widow* (Franz Léhar, 1905) was brought to America in 1907, the element of dance gained new stature; a long series of romantic ballroom-dance shows ensued, culminating in the romances of Fred and Adele Astaire during the 1920s and 30s. Two early spectaculars, *Around the World* (1911) and *The War of the Worlds* (1914), gave audiences a heightened taste for unusual scenic effects. The work in America of the director Max Reinhardt, the scenic designer Joseph Urban, and the various Ballet Russe companies were also significant for the developing musical (Smith: 196–98). Rudolph Friml in *High Jinks* (1913) and Sigmund Romburg in *The Passing Show* (1914) began to modernize the musical idiom of the operetta. At the same time George M. Cohan in *Hello Broadway* (1914) added ragtime elements from vaudeville to the romance, and Irving Berlin in *Watch Your Step* (1914) and later works added syncopation and other jazz elements.

In *Showboat* (1927) Jerome Kern and Oscar Hammerstein II evaluated the mood, pace, and placing of songs in terms of the dramatic values of the show, thereby anticipating the modern concept of a "program." This was also true of *Of Thee I Sing* (George Gershwin, 1931), which was the first musical to win the Pulitzer Prize for drama. In the topical revue *As Thousands Cheer* even the choreography was said to have been pertinent to the dramatic

situations (Smith: 280–83). Two other landmarks were *Porgy and Bess* (Gershwin, 1935) and *Lady in the Dark* (Kurt Weill, 1941), both of which integrated all elements of drama and music to a high degree.

STRUCTURE. The typical musical has two acts. Act 1 lasts about 90 minutes and act 2 about 45. (The total length is dictated by New York union regulations, which award orchestra musicians and stage hands an overtime payrate after 11:30 pm.) Because the first act must engage the interest of the audience and hold it through intermission, it usually contains the better musical material. *Reprises* (partial repetitions of material) are usually more numerous in the second act; they recall music from both acts and capitalize on the most appealing songs in the show. The new second-act material usually includes a song for the leading star, called the "11-o'clock spot." If music in the second act is effective and well placed ("programmed"), the audience will overlook the dramatic weaknesses that often occur there as issues raised in the first act are being resolved.

Two important structural concepts are the *program* and *layout* of a musical. The program is the placement of music to heighten dramatic situations and provide aural contrasts. For this, the mood, tempo, range, etc., of the music must be considered, along with the need for variety in solo, ensemble, and instrumental settings. In addition, the *song program* makes allowance for various song types: ballad or love songs, comedy songs, rhythm songs (called *upbeat* songs because of their fast, propulsive rhythm), light-hearted *charm* songs, and *scenes* (sequences of action or dialogue with musical background). The layout refers to the number of times a melody is recalled or repeated during a show. It depends on the quality and musical characteristics of the melody, its significance in the plot, and the relative importance of the character with whom it is identified.

Over the years the trend in song forms has been toward greater complexity. "Oh Promise Me" from *Robin Hood* (Reginald de Koven, 1890) was a strophic, pseudo-art song. "Harrigan" from *50 Miles from Boston* (George M. Cohan, 1907) was in a two-part form, AA', in which the second half was a slightly varied version of the first. The latter form continued to be used through the 1930s; in 1950 Frank Loesser capitalized on its then outdated nature by using it as one of the intentionally banal elements in "I Love You a Bushel and a Peck" (*Guys and Dolls*). The song form most frequently used nowadays begins with a free-form introduction (*verse*) and continues with 32 bars divided into four eight-bar sections, AABA (A is the principal theme or *refrain* and B is the contrasting theme or *release*). "I Feel Pretty" from *West Side Story* (Leonard Bernstein, 1957) expanded the length of this form to 64 bars. New material has sometimes been added to the AABA scheme: "My Heart Belongs to Daddy" from *Leave It to Me* (Cole Porter, 1938) is AABC; "Moonshine Lullaby" from *Annie Get Your Gun* (Irving Berlin, 1946) is ABA'C; "Soon It's Gonna Rain" from *The Fantastiks* (Harvey Schmidt, 1950) is AABAC. An example of extreme complexity is "Glitter and be Gay" from *Candide* (Leonard Bernstein, 1958): ABA-CRD(A)-CRD, in which R is recitative and (A) means that the A material appears not in the vocal line but in an instrumental interlude.

The quality that can be achieved within the usual song format is well illustrated by "Night and Day" from *The Gay Divorcée* (Cole Porter, 1944). The purpose of the music is to express the "torment" of love described in the lyrics. The verse combines a monotonous vocal line over a quasiostinato bass, thus depicting loneliness and longing. The remainder contains 16-bar units in an AABC format. A motive that appears at the beginning and end of A and at the beginning of B is developed in C to reach the climactic peak of the song. The regular beat and frequent syncopation, which place the work in the realm of popular music, tend to reinforce the mundane quality of the lyrics, but these features are overshadowed by the intricate use of motivic repetition and rhyme.

Ancestors of the musical had weak librettos, and it is largely the development of a good *book* (plot and dialogue), showing human beings in interesting situations, that has made the modern musical appealing. Although the libretto may be based on a novel or play, libretto writing did not develop from contemporary drama but grew in a trial-and-error fashion from productions of musicals themselves. There is usually a main plot with one set of characters and a counterplot with another overlapping set. The most successful works have given audiences a warm feeling of satisfaction, either because of the logical resolution of both plots (*Hello Dolly*, 1964; *Guys and Dolls*, 1950) or because human gallantry has won out (*Fiddler on the Roof*, 1966). Song lyrics, too, have been improving. One has only to compare the poems of a show like *Desert Song* (1926) with those of Oscar Hammerstein II in *Oklahoma!* (1943) and *Carousel*

(1945) or those of Alan J. Lerner in *Camelot* (1960) to see the increase in sensitivity, characterization, and verse technique.

Theater music is thought to follow the stereotyped harmonic formulas of popular music. Actually theater composers vary widely in harmonic style, agreeing only on the necessity for tonality. Irving Berlin and Vincent Youmans habitually employed a simple harmonic idiom; Jerome Kern and Cole Porter displayed a subtle use of altered chords and prepared dissonances; Marc Blitzstein and Leonard Bernstein have emphasized frequent melodic angularity with unprepared dissonance and "wrong-note" writing, particularly in their musical scenes. The controlling stylistic element, however, is always melody.

CREATIVE PROCEDURES. The musical differs from opera in many respects, for example, in its simpler style of music, its predominant use of ABA song forms, and its larger proportion of spoken dialogue. The most striking difference, however, is the manner in which it is created, for it is the product of a team of artists, not just of a composer and librettist. One or more writers devises the book; one or more others may write the song lyrics. The working relationship between composers and writers varies, as it does in opera; in some cases the words and in others the tunes are created first. The composer's contribution has the greatest impact on the final product, and his songs may remain popular for years after the complete stage work has closed. A good song can usually be updated to conform to any current style of accompaniment, whereas the stage work may soon be outdated because of its subject or staging techniques. Songs from the early George M. Cohan shows have turned up successfully in modern dress in the 1968 musical *George M.*, and Victor Herbert tunes still appear in pop concerts and movies.

The producer is the person on the creative team who gathers together the production and performance staffs and raises the money to produce the show ($800,000 or more in the early 1970s). The director and his staff determine the final program and layout on the basis of the psychological elements and entertainment values that become apparent in rehearsals and preopening performances. Changes are made up to opening night and sometimes beyond. The designer is responsible for sets and costumes; in some shows, such as *Man of La Mancha* (1967), he may create such a favorable environment that the dramatic elements appear to be better than they really are. Since *Oklahoma!*, most of the incidental and dance music has been fashioned to order (from the song composer's tunes) by other composers who are often unnamed. They work with the choreographer as dances are created and with the director as he requires musical underlay for scenes or changes of sets. Another expert or team of experts orchestrates the score during early rehearsals. The stars, of course, contribute their personalities to the production, and some decisions are made on the basis of what is most effective for a particular singer.

After four to five weeks of rehearsal and another five weeks of preopening performances, the musical opens on Broadway. If successful, it will play eight times a week for a year or more. By the time it opens it will be an expression not only of American attitudes and concerns but of a typically American faith in the efficiency of specialization and the wisdom of pooled judgment. The original Broadway production will be the basis of all others no matter where they occur.

MUSICALS DISTINGUISHED BY THEIR OVERALL EXCELLENCE: *Oklahoma!* (1943); *Carousel* (1945); *Annie Get Your Gun* (1946); *Kiss Me, Kate* (1948); *South Pacific* (1949); *Guys and Dolls* (1950); *The King and I* (1951); *My Fair Lady* (1956); *West Side Story* (1957); *Fiddler on the Roof* (1964).

BIBL.: Lehman Engel, *The American Musical Theater: A Consideration* (New York 1967); ——, *Words with Music* (New York 1972); Bernard Grun, *Kulturgeschichte der Operetta* (Munich 1961); Julian Mates, *The American Musical Stage before 1800* (New Brunswick, N.J., 1962); Leonard Allen Paris, *Men and Melodies* (New York 1954); Siegfried Schmidt-Joos, *Das Musical* (Munich 1965); Cecil Smith, *Musical Comedy in America* (New York 1950).

Carolyn Raney

SEE ALSO Dance, Jazz, Orchestration, Popular Music, United States.

Musicology and Composition. Composers have always been influenced by the music that is part of their environment, the music they hear, perform, and study. The present century differs from previous ones in the increasing variety of music available, a development in which musicologists have played a leading role. A distinction must be made between two different but related stages in this accumulation of repertory. The first, beginning in the 19th century, was a stagnation, the more-or-less permanent retention in performance of works that had achieved some success and popularity. This stage had little to do with musicology, resulting rather from complex sociological, intellectual, and economic factors that affected some of the other arts as well. The linking of most performances of orchestral, ensemble, and recital music to public, commercial occasions led inevitably to a decreasing role played by the composer, the private patron, and the trained amateur in determining what music was to be performed, and perhaps inevitably to a steady decrease in the number of new works played. A second stage, however, was closely linked to musicological work and would have been impossible without it. Many scholars of the 19th and 20th centuries have searched libraries and archives for works of previous centuries, compositions that had passed altogether out of the performance repertory and living memory. They have described these, analyzed them, and printed them in modern editions, transcribing them into modern notation when necessary to make them readily available to musicians of today. They have investigated performance practices and have studied and helped to reconstruct archaic instruments once used to play this music.

As resistance stiffened to the expansion of the repertory by the addition of any substantial body of new works, information about an older body of music (and the music itself) became increasingly available. This older music proved to be more acceptable to commercial audiences and to most performers. Music of increasingly remote times gradually became part of our 20th-century musical culture. Composers in their formative years heard and studied not only the music of their contemporaries and the immediate past, but also that of the previous six or eight centuries. They were thus exposed to a rich variety of compositional procedures and styles. Evidence of the effect on their music can be seen at every level of investigation and analysis, from the very titles of works (madrigal, passacaglia, fuguing tune, and other terms that had passed out of common usage) to the utilization of formal structures and procedures (the concerto-grosso principle, various sophisticated contrapuntal devices, and other methods of working with material practiced by composers of past centuries) and the use of various sonorities, textures, even harmonic structures that probably would not have suggested themselves had they not been observed in older music.

The extent of contact with older music and musicological work has varied greatly from composer to composer. Igor Stravinsky is an example of a composer with no formal musicological training and no extended contact with academic institutions or serious musicologists, but with a profound interest in a wide range of older music. He has drawn on elements of Eastern liturgical chant, Russian folk music, 14th-century Mass music, Gesualdo, Pergolesi, and the 18th-century symphonists—music available to him because of the work of musicologists. Paul Hindemith was associated with academic institutions for part of his life and was himself involved in editing, arranging, performing, and conducting music from the renaissance and later. His own works are endlessly indebted to this older music (structurally, harmonically, texturally, contrapuntally). At the other end of the scale are those composers who have engaged in serious research themselves. Anton Webern wrote a doctoral dissertation on some of the music of Heinrich Isaac, a prolific composer of the early 16th century, and made scholarly editions of it. Billy Jim Layton's dissertation dealt with Italian Mass music of the early 15th century. The proportional notation in which this music was written suggested the use of changing meters and tempos in his own 5 *Studies* for violin and piano; he has also used differentiated layers, usually based on a cantus firmus, and isorhythmic frameworks, both of which were suggested by early music. Early in the century, the music of an entire nation, Italy, was rejuvenated in large part by two composers, G. F. Malipiero and Alfredo Casella, who researched older styles and reapplied some of their principles and esthetic aims.

Musicologists have not concerned themselves solely with the discovery and editing of old music. The earliest definitions of the discipline embraced the systematic analysis of all music as an important area of musicological concern. While it is true that in most institutions today the rational and systematic investigation of the various elements of music has been split off from musicology and entrusted to theorists and composers, the origins of these procedures in musicological work and their relationship to other aspects of musicology are a matter of historical fact. Some would go so far as to define musicology as a method of working rationally with any aspect of any body of music and claim for musicology the entire range of systematic investigation, both historical and theoretical. The ever increasing involvement of composers (particularly in North America) with colleges and universities, their participation in the organization and teaching of courses in systematic analysis, and their own participation in research and scholarship can be considered as deeper involvement with ways of thinking about and dealing with music that originated with musicologists. The concept of music as a rational thing that can yield its secrets to intellectual analysis was first and most easily accepted for older music, but in time this notion was accepted by many as a valid and even necessary attitude toward newly composed or yet-to-be-composed music. The predominately rational approach to composition exemplified in the works of Roger Sessions, Ross Lee Finney, Milton Babbitt, and many others is in perfect consonance with what they have taught about music, both old and new. Countless other examples can be cited of composers who have integrated their creative work with research of one sort or another. The study of acoustics was first undertaken as a branch of musicology, and Ben Johnston's utilization of nontempered tunings in some of his compositions is a fruit of years of partially musicological study. Kenneth Gaburo's experiments with fragmentation of words and syllables in some of his vocal compositions have gone hand-in-hand with speculative studies of more general problems of text setting. Many composers, of course, have not accepted the notion of the relevance of a close familiarity with old music and the application of rational methodology to their own work. Such men as John Cage, Nam June Paik, and Terry Riley have worked more within the frame of reference of contemporary society, the music of their contemporaries, and other contemporary arts and sciences. Yet they too have a point of contact with musicology—through their ideas on esthetics, a field which the discipline also claims.

Charles Hamm

SEE ALSO Education for the Professional.

Musique Concrète, music prepared from recorded sounds. The term was coined in 1948 by Pierre Schaeffer, a broadcaster for the French radio; to him the term implied the assembling of music directly from concrete sound "objects" rather than the "abstract" creation of music through the medium of musical notation. The recorded sounds in musique concrète may be from the natural or man-made environment (e.g., birdsong, traffic noise, musical instruments). Although these sounds are generally modified by electronic means, in "strict" musique concrète usage they are not supposed to originate in electronic synthesis. (Schaeffer feels that electronic sound synthesis is an example of "abstract" composition because of its emphasis on separate parameters of sound, e.g., frequency, amplitude, duration, etc.). The distinction between musique concrète and electronically synthesized music was justified by compositional practice until the mid-1950s; since then composers have increasingly combined concrete and synthesized sound, as well as "live" and prerecorded sound. Now the term *electronic music* tends to be used for any music that involves electronic processing in composition.

BIBL.: Lowell Cross, "Electronic Music, 1948–1953," *Perspectives* 7/1:32–65; Pierre Schaeffer, *A la Recherche d'une musique concrète* (Paris 1952); ——, *Traité des objets musicaux* (Paris 1966); Peter Zinovieff, "Electronic Salutes Concrete," *Music and Musicians* (March 1969):30–31.

SEE ALSO Electronic Music: History and Development; Recording.

Nabokov, Nicolas (b. Lubcha, Minsk, Russia, 17 April 1903), studied composition privately in Yalta with Vladimir Rebikov (1920) and at the Stuttgart Academy of Music (1920–21) and the Berlin Hochschule für Musik (1921–23, Paul Juon). He also studied at the Sorbonne (1923–26). During 1926–33 he lived partly in Paris, partly in Germany, and taught composition, languages, and literature privately. His first important work, the ballet-oratorio *Ode*, was produced by Diaghilev's Ballet Russe de Monte-Carlo in Paris in 1928. In 1933 he emigrated to the U.S. He has taught at Wells College (1935–40), St. John's College (1940–44), the Peabody Conservatory (1948–50), the American Academy in Rome (1950–51), the City Univ. of N.Y. (1968), and since 1968 at the State Univ. of N. Y. in Buffalo. During 1944–47 he worked for the American Military Government in Berlin as assistant in charge of theater, film, and music and as cultural advisor to the U.S. ambassador. During 1947–48 he was requested by the U.S. Government to help establish the Russian section of *The Voice of America*. During 1951–66 he was Secretary General of the Congress for Cultural Freedom. He was cultural advisor to Berlin's mayor Willy Brandt during 1963–66. Since 1963 he has also been artistic director of the annual Berlin Festival of the Arts.

PRINCIPAL COMPOSITIONS: *Piano Sonata No. 1* (1926, Rouart-Le rolle); *Ode*, ballet-oratorio for soprano, alto, tenor, bass, chorus, orchestra; choreography by Leonide Massine (1928, ERM); *Symphonie lyrique* (1931, ERM); *Collectionneur d'echos* for soprano, chorus, 9 percussionists (1933, ERM); *Job*, cantata for 2 tenors, 2 baritones, bass, chorus (1933); *Union Pacific*, ballet; choreography by Massine (1933); *Symphony No. 2*, "Biblical" (1940, Belaiev); *Vie de Polichinelle*, ballet in 3 acts; choreography by Serge Lifar (1934); *Piano Sonata No. 2* (1940, Boosey); *The Return of Pushkin* for high voice, orchestra (1947, Belaiev); *La vita nova* for soprano, tenor, orchestra (1953); *Symboli Chrestiani* for baritone, orchestra (1956, Ricordi); *The Last Flower*, symphonic suite (1957); *Rasputin's End*, 3-act opera; libretto by Stephen Spender and the composer (1958, Ricordi); *4 Poems by Boris Pasternak* for baritone, orchestra (1959, Ricordi); *Studies in Solitude* for orchestra (1962, Ricordi); *5 Poems by Anna Akhmatova* from the cycle *Requiem*, for high voice, orchestra (1964); *Don Quixotte*, ballet in 3 acts; choreography by George Balanchine (1964–65, Belaiev); *The Wanderer*, ballet (1966); *Symphony No. 3*, "A Prayer" (1967, Belaiev); *Variations on a Theme by Tschaikovsky* for cello, orchestra (1968, Belaiev); *Love's Labour's Lost*, opera; libretto by W. H. Auden and Chester Kallmann (1970).

PRINCIPAL WRITINGS: *Old Friends and New Music* (Boston 1951).

SEE ALSO Dance.

Nationalism, see Folk Resources

Natra, Sergiu (b. Bucharest, 12 April 1924), studied at the Bucharest Music Academy (1945–52, composition with Leon Klepper). He was active in many Rumanian cultural organizations until 1961, when he emigrated to Israel. His music has been influenced by jazz, Stravinsky, Hindemith, and the 12-tone music of Schoenberg. During 1945–54 he followed the socialist-folkloristic trends in eastern Europe. Since 1961 he has absorbed influences from the Bible and the Hebrew language.

PRINCIPAL COMPOSITIONS: *Divertimento in Classical Style* for string orchestra (1943); *March and Chorale* for orchestra (1944); *3 Cortegii de stradă* [3 Street Corteges] for piano (1945, ESCR); *Suite for Orchestra* (1948, ESPLA); *Suita pentru copii* [Suite for Children] for piano (1949, ES); *Symphony* (1952); *Music for Violin and Harp* (1960, IMI); *Sinfonia for Strings* (1960, IMI); *Toccata for Orchestra* (1963); *Music* for harpsichord, flute, clarinet, 2 violas, cello, double bass (1964, IMI); *Sonatina* for harp (1965, IMI); *Music for Oboe and Strings* (1965, IMI); *Variations* for piano, orchestra (1966, IMI); *Leshónot haéysh* [Voices of Fire], ballet for chamber orchestra; scenario by Pearl Lang (1967, IMI); *Shírat Debórah* [Song of Deborah] for mezzo-soprano, chamber orchestra (1967, IMI); *Prelude* for narrator, orchestra (1968); *Commentary on Nehemiah* for baritone, chorus, orchestra (1968); *3 Sonatinas*: No. 1 for trombone, No. 2 for trumpet, No. 3 for oboe (1969); *Interlude* for harp (1970).

BIBL.: John Marson, "Harp Music," *Musical Times* (August 1966); Yehuda Kimmel, "S. N.: A Portrait," *Guitite* (Israel) 42:4–5; Alexander L. Ringer, "Musical Composition in Modern Israel," *Contemporary Music in Europe* (New York 1965): 295–96.
SEE ALSO Israel.

Nelson, Ron J. (b. Joliet, Ill., 14 Dec 1929), studied at the Eastman School (1947–56; composition with Howard Hanson, Bernard Rogers, Louis Mennini, Wayne Barlow) and at the Ecole Normale de Musique in Paris (1954–55, composition with Tony Aubin). He has taught at Brown Univ. since 1963 and is active as a choral conductor.

PRINCIPAL COMPOSITIONS (published by Boosey unless otherwise noted): *The Birthday of the Infanta*, opera (1956, Eastman); *Savannah River Holiday* for orchestra (1957, Fischer); *The Christmas Story*, cantata for narrator and chorus with brass, organ, timpani or with orchestra (1959); *Fanfare for a Festival* for chorus, brass, timpani (1960); *Triumphal Te Deum* for double chorus, brass, percussion (1962); *This Is the Orchestra* for orchestra (1963); *Jubilee* for orchestra (1963); *For Katherine in April* for orchestra (1964); *What is Man?*, oratorio for narrator, soprano, baritone, chorus with orchestra or with brass, percussion, organ (1964); *Vocalise* for women's chorus (1965); *God, Show Thy Sword* for chorus, organ, percussion (1968); *Trilogy: JFK—MLK—RFK* for orchestra (1969); *Rocky Point Holiday* for band (1969); *Meditation on the Syllable OM* for men's chorus (1970); *Alleluia, July 20, 1969* for chorus (1970).

SEE ALSO Liturgical Music: Christian.

Neoclassicism, an esthetic orientation that was in part responsible for the revival of forms, genres, and textures from instrumental music of the past, especially those of the 17th and 18th centuries. Neoclassicism was largely a reaction to late romantic, German-oriented music in which emotionalism and programmatic impulses outweigh considerations of formal clarity and balance. The period most generally labeled neoclassic extended from Stravinsky's *Pulcinella* (1919–20) to his *Rake's Progress* (1948–51), but there is much music both before and after that shows the impact of neoclassic thinking. The term is usually restricted to music that has its harmonic foundation in tonality; thus, although much 12-tone music emphasizes contrapuntal textures, old forms and genres, and craftsmanship, it is not labeled neoclassic. The broad ideal of neoclassicism was perhaps best expressed by Ferruccio Busoni: "the mastery, sifting, and exploitation of all the achievements of past experiments and their embodiment in fixed and beautiful forms" (quoted by Wladimir Vogel, *Perspectives* 6/2:170).

SEE ALSO Austria and Germany.

Netherlands. The Dutch are a sociable and civic-minded people, and their genius for cooperation shows itself in the particularly social art of music. Preeminent among organizations that have striven to make the lot of the contemporary Dutch composer easier is the Donemus Foundation, founded in 1947 "to promote the full development of Dutch music, in particular by offering support to Dutch composers." Donemus has addressed itself to the central problem affecting all modern composers, the dissemination of their work. It has built a microfilm collection of over 3,000 works by over 100 composers, printed copies of which can be made on order. The composer's royalty is 15 percent of the selling price for chamber music and two-thirds of the hire fee for orchestral material. Works are selected by an independent committee whose membership changes annually, and any work is released if a commercial publisher takes it on. In 1961 the foundation instituted the Donemus Audio-Visual Series: recordings of Dutch music, most of it contemporary, made from live performances and issued with scores and annotations in Dutch and English. Four records are released each year and sold at relatively low subscription rates. Donemus also maintains a reference library of nearly 4,000 contemporary Dutch works, with tape recordings of about 2,000 of them. Since 1958 it has published and distributed free of charge a journal called *Sonorum Speculum*, which documents the country's musical life. The Dutch government, the city of Amsterdam, the province of North Holland, and the Foundation for Netherlands Musical Interests all help to support Donemus.

The best known of the other Dutch musical foundations is Gaudeamus, which occupies a villa of the same name in Bilthoven, given to the Dutch people in 1945 by the German-born Walter Maas, who had been sheltered from the Nazis in Holland during World War II. Young composers are encouraged to stay at the villa to study and compose. Since 1947 special Music Weeks have been held there. Originally national in complexion, in 1951 they were made international in alternate years, and since 1959 an International Music Week has been held every year. Similarly a competition for interpreters of contemporary music, in which the entrants have to be under 35, began on a national basis in 1963, became European the following year, and has been international since 1965. Two composition prizes are also awarded each year in connection with the International Music Weeks, one for choral, chamber, orchestral, and electronic works by composers up to 35, the other for works in the field of music drama by composers up to 40. The foundation organizes chamber concerts, which include works by Dutch composers, and maintains a teaching studio for electronic music where Gottfried Michael Koenig (b. Magdeburg, Germany, 1926) has given annual courses. The ISCM has an active Dutch section, which was host to the society's annual festivals in 1933, 1948, and 1963.

The relationship between performing organizations and contemporary music shows much the same general pattern in the Netherlands as elsewhere. The country's leading orchestra, the Concertgebouw of Amsterdam, is conservative in its programming, though it has become more progressive since World War II; attempts have been made to broaden the repertory with special series of concerts featuring both modern and pre-19th-century music, but audience response has not usually been encouraging. Of the 14 other prominent professional orchestras (in a country of less than 13 million people), the Limburg Symphony Orchestra and the Radio Chamber Orchestra play the largest quantity of contemporary music, Dutch and foreign.

The Holland Festival, held every year from mid-June to mid-July in cities throughout the country, gives some encouragement to living composers. But on the whole the most active in this field among performing organizations are two chamber groups, the Gaudeamus String Quartet, connected with the Foundation, and the Danzi Quintet, founded in 1958 and probably the best wind quintet in the world; the latter specializes in the contemporary repertory.

Records tend to be expensive in the Netherlands, but they are available in great variety. Amsterdam in particular has several excellent specialist dealers, a thriving used-record shop in which contemporary items are often to be found, and unusually comprehensive record selections in the large stores. The presence in the Netherlands of one major international record company, Philips, has led to the recording of a number of contemporary Dutch works, though the company tends to be conservative in its repertory. The parent, Philips Electronics Company, maintains an electronic music studio at its Eindhoven headquarters. Work there is generally less forward-looking than that done in, say, Cologne, but this is a matter of the individual composers' predilections.

The propensity toward fruitful association is as notable in the creative as in the organizational field. Unlike the 20th-century composers of most countries, those in Holland tend to exhibit relatedness rather than extreme diversity of style. (Self-centeredness, especially of the Heaven-storming, metaphysical type, is not at all common in the Dutch, which is perhaps why musical composition did not flourish among them during the romantic period.) The tendency toward interrelationship was reinforced by the presence of one commanding figure, Willem *Pijper (1894–1947), the stamp of whose personality, imprinted both through his own music and through teaching, may be discerned in all 20th-century Dutch music.

Pijper was not the first Dutch composer to make an impact on the 20th-century musical world. He was preceded by Alphons Diepenbrock (1862–1921), whose work is still admired in Holland. But whereas Diepenbrock's music reflects the twin influences of Wagner and Debussy, Pijper, sharing the indebtedness to Debussy, replaces the Wagner influence with that of Mahler. It was this combination, reinforced by Pijper's strong interest in Dutch folk music (with its fondness for sturdily marked yet freely varied rhythms), that proved the really fecundating one for later composers.

Almost every Dutch composer of note studied either with Pijper or with one of his pupils. Among the first-generation pupils, Henk *Badings (b. 1907) has acquired the widest international reputation. His *Symphony No. 7* (1954) was written for the Louisville Orchestra, *No. 8* (1956) for the Norddeutscher Rundfunk in Hamburg. Most of his music is respectable rather than inspired. Impeccable technique and ingenious thematic development are applied to material that is itself often unmemorable. In this he resembles Reger, to whom, through Hindemith, his style may be traced. But it is his exhaustive treatment of small thematic units, allied with a Mahlerian crispness of orchestration, that links him to Pijper. These traits appear clearly in two of his best works, the *Symphony No. 3* (1934) and the *Concerto* for 2 violins and orchestra (1954). Like most of his works, they rely strongly on tonal centers. He has experimented with a scale of alternating whole and half tones, but even in his electronic compositions (most notably the *Capriccio for Violin and 2 Sound Tracks*, 1952) he retains a primarily tonal orientation.

Less well known outside the Netherlands, perhaps unjustly, are two other Pijper pupils, Guillaume *Landré (1905–68) and Hans Henkemans (b. 1913). Landré combined much musical administrative work with a large musical production. He was essentially a symphonist, and his symphonies (of which the third, 1950, best shows his qualities) are exceptionally clear-cut in form. Their distinction lies more in the refinement of Landré's ear and imagination than in any strongly personal expression, for Debussy stands behind his range of sonorities and Mahler behind his orchestration and his rhythmic penchant for stylized march measures (with fluid upbeat groups leading to emphatic first-beat stresses). Henkemans, a pianist with a high reputation for his playing of Debussy, has been influenced by the same two masters, but in his case the influences seem more completely digested. His best works show a stronger individuality than anything by Badings or Landré; their technical method is based essentially on the Pijperian germ-cell principle. His *Partita for Orchestra* (1960) is probably his most successful creation.

Unlike most of his compatriots, Kees van *Baaren (1906–70) has championed the use of 12-tone and serial methods. Pijper himself never used the 12-tone method, but he encouraged Van Baaren in the adoption of what seemed, for him, the right means of expression. It is probably Van Baaren's gift for variation techniques, shown most clearly in his *Variations* for orchestra (1959) but also implicit in the *String Quartet No. 2* of 1962 (subtitled "Sovraposizioni I"), that has made him a natural serial composer. This predilection sets him apart from Badings, Landré, Henkemans, and Pijper, who are all given to development rather than to variation.

As a teacher and as director of the Royal Conservatory in The Hague, Van Baaren provided a rallying point for the younger and more progressive composers. The liveliest among these are Peter *Schat (b. 1935), Jan van *Vlijmen (b. 1935), and Louis *Andriessen (b. 1939). (Schat also studied with Seiber and Boulez, and Andriessen with Berio.) These three are typical of the international avant-garde, but less extreme than some of its subgroups. Schat's *Improvisations and Symphonies* for wind quintet (1960), for instance, incorporates some aleatory techniques (allowing

the throw of dice to decide certain questions of sectional ordering), but also firmly controls the actual notes to be played by each performer.

Occupying an esthetically solid position between the traditionalists and the younger men are Luctor Ponse (b. 1914) and Ton de *Leeuw (b. 1926). Ponse was born in Geneva of Dutch parents and has lived in Holland since 1936. It is not only this background that suggests a link with Frank Martin (the Swiss composer who has lived in Holland since World War II), for the two also share an ability to produce shimmering sonorities within a framework of closely argued formal coherence. Works such as the *Concerto da Camera* with solo bassoon (1962), however, show that for Ponse, a Van Baaren pupil, the dodecaphonic element is of central importance, not tangential as it is for Martin. De Leeuw was at first a pupil of Badings. His mature music (dating from the early 1960s), however, reflects his later studies with Messiaen and of Indian music, for they display a mystical preoccupation with systematic and metaphysical aspects of rhythm. De Leeuw also shares with Boulez the feeling that modern Western music has become too much a vehicle for subjective expression and too little a shared experience; here too the importance of Indian music as a corrective is obvious.

The idea of a communal art, once again reflecting Dutch extroversion and sociability, has been carried further in the Netherlands than almost anywhere else. In 1966 the Holland Festival produced *Labyrinth*, an "opera of sorts" in which Peter Schat collaborated with a team of young artists ranging from text writer and director to costume designer, architect, choreographer, and filmmaker. Another operatic project, *Reconstruction* (1969), enlisted the talents of five composers, Schat, Van Vlijmen, Andriessen, Reinbert de Leeuw, and Misja Mengelberg. It was not a great success, but it may well indicate the direction of some future musical enterprises in Holland.

Bernard Jacobson

SEE ALSO Microtones.

Niculescu, Ştefan (b. Moreni, Rumania, 31 July 1927), studied at the Polytechnic School in Bucharest (1946–50) and the Bucharest Conservatory (1942–46, piano with Muza Ghermani Ciomac; 1951–57, composition with Mihail Andricu). He has also attended the Darmstadt summer courses beginning in 1966. During 1960–63 he was a research musicologist and teacher at the Institute for Art

History of the Rumanian Academy in Bucharest. He has taught composition and analysis at the Bucharest Conservatory since 1963 and composes film music for the Bucharest Cinema Studio and theater music for the National and Tîndărică Theaters. The works of Bartók, Enescu, Messiaen, and Webern have influenced his development.

PRINCIPAL COMPOSITIONS: *Clarinet Sonata* (1953–55, Muzicală); *Simfonia* (1955–57, Muzicală); *String Trio* (1957); *Cantata I* for women's chorus, orchestra (1959); *Cantata II* for tenor, chorus, orchestra (1960, Muzicală); *Scènes* for orchestra (1962, Salabert); *Symphonies* for 15 winds, brass, percussion (1963, Muzicală); *Inventions* for clarinet, piano (1964, Salabert); *Cantata III* for mezzosoprano, 5 winds (1965, Muzicală); *Hétéromorphie* for orchestra (1967, Ars Viva); *Formants* for 17 strings with or without other instruments (1968, Salabert); *Tastenspiel* for piano (1968); *Aphorismes d'Héraclite* for 20 soloists (1969, Salabert); *Wind Sextet* (1970, Muzicală); *Unisonos* for orchestra (1970, Ars Viva).

PRINCIPAL WRITINGS: "Importanţa ritmului în structura melodiei şi în stabilirea unei tipologii a creaţiei muzicale româneşti" [The Importance of Rhythm in Melodic Structure and in the Establishment of a Typology for Rumanian Music], *Muzica* (Bucharest): 1959/6:23–26; "Creaţia de cîntece a lui Mihail Jora" [Mihail Jora's Songs], *Studii şi cercetări de istoria artei* (Bucharest) 1963/2:385–409; "Eterofonia" [Heterophony], *Studii de muzicologie* (Bucharest) 5:65–67; "Aspecte ale gîndirii teoretice şi stilistice la Xenakis şi Boulez" [Aspects of the Theoretical and Stylistic Thought of Xenakis and Boulez], *Muzica* 1967/6:32–35. Among Niculescu's other articles are 7 on George Enescu.

BIBL.: George Draga, "'Cantata II' de S. N.," *Muzica* 1965/1; ——, "'Cantata III' de S. N.," *Muzica* 1965/7; Iancu Dumitrescu, "S. N.," *Luceafărul* (27 April 1968); Irina Odăgescu, "'Simfonia' de S. N.," *Muzica* 1962/11; Luminiţa Vartolomei, "Eteromorfie de S. N.," *Muzica* 1969/6.

Niehaus, Manfred (b. Cologne, 18 Sept 1933), studied at the Cologne Hochschule für Musik (1957–63, composition with Bernd Alois Zimmermann, violin with Franz Josef Maier) and philology at the Univ. of Cologne. During 1961–63 he was a teaching assistant at the Dörpfeld Gymnasium in Wuppertal. He was a stage manager at the Würtembergischen Landesbühne during 1963–65 and at the Kellertheater in Cologne during 1964–65. Since 1967 he has been a music producer for the West German Radio Network in Cologne, where he has written a number of radio and film scores. He also belongs to Gruppe 8 in Cologne, an association of composers.

PRINCIPAL COMPOSITIONS: *String Trio* (1959); *6 Pieces for Communion on Workdays* for organ (1959, Bosse); *Kantate den Hampelmännern* for vocal quartet, string orchestra, piano, percussion; text by Franz Wurm (1959–66); *Verkündigung* for soprano, harp with organ or with 2 pianos, harmonium, celesta, double bass (1960); *7 Haiku* for narrator, soprano, piccolo, violin, guitar, bells (1961); *Bartleby*, chamber opera (1961–66); *Duo* for violin, cello (1965); *Violin Concerto* (1965, Gerig); *Quintet* for oboe, Eb clarinet, Eb saxophone, hunting horn, tenor horn (1966); *Landkarte*, hommage à Nelly Sachs, for voice, 3 violins, viola, accordion (1966); *Hommage à Günter Eich* for soprano, countertenor, tenor, baritone, 3 violins, viola, percussion (1967); *Suite* for violin, guitar (1967); *Sequenzen und Blenden* for viola, percussion, 3–9 other players or tape (1967); *Die Pataphysiker*, musical farce (1968, Gerig); *Pop & Art* for orchestra (1968, Gerig); *Sextet* for clarinet, horn, bassoon, violin, viola, double bass (1968); *Scènes lyriques & électriques* for baritone ad lib., bassoon, cello, electric bass guitar (1968); *Maldoror*, scenes of evil; libretto by Alfred Feussner and the composer after Comte de Lautréamont (1969, Gerig); *Einige Anweisungen für die Mittellage* for electric guitar, viola, piano with 2 players (1969); *Die Badewanne*, radio comedy (1970); *Sinfonia* (1970, Gerig); *Trios I–II* (1970, Gerig); *Quartet mit Regler* (1970); *Streichquartett mit Negativform* (1970); *Rahmenstück* for chamber ensemble (1971); *Stadtmusik* for vocal soloists, chorus, winds, church bells (1971).

Nielsen, Carl (August) (b. Nørre Lyndelse, Fyn, Denmark, 9 June 1865; d. Copenhagen, 3 Oct 1931), studied at the Royal Conservatory in Copenhagen (1884–86; theory with Orla Rosenhoff, music history with Niels Gade). During 1889–1905 he was a violinist with the Royal Chapel Orchestra. He was a conductor at the Royal Theatre during 1908–14 and for the Copenhagen Musikföreningen during 1915–27. In 1931 he became director of the Royal Conservatory. His music emphasizes a clear and logical sense of form and development, derived in large part from Brahms. He used tonality and chromatic contrasts of tonalities for dramatic purposes: "Most of his mature works treat a chosen key as a goal to be achieved or an order to be evolved, and his final establishment of the key has all the organic inevitability . . . with which the flower appears at a plant's point of full growth" (Simpson:5; see bibl.).

PRINCIPAL COMPOSITIONS (published by Hansen-W unless otherwise noted): *Little Suite* for strings, Op. 1 (1888); *Symphonies Nos. 1–6*: No. 1, Op. 7 (1892); No. 2, "The 4 Temperaments," Op. 16 (1901–02); No. 3, "Sinfonia espansiva," for orchestra with wordless parts for soprano, baritone,

Op. 27 (1910–11, Kahnt and Engstrøm); No. 4, "The Inextinguishable," Op. 29 (1915–16); No. 5, Op. 50 (1921–22, Scandinavisk); No. 6, "Sinfonia semplice" (1924–25, SUDM); *Violin Sonatas Nos. 1–2*, Opp. 9, 35 (1895, 1912); *Hymnus amoris* for vocal soloists, chorus, orchestra, Op. 12 (1896–97); *Saul og David*, 4-act opera; libretto by Einar Christiansen (1898–1901); *Maskarade*, 3-act opera; libretto by Vilhelm Andersen after Ludwig Holberg (1904–06); *Violin Concerto*, Op. 33 (1911); *Pan og Syrinx* for orchestra (1917–18); *Songbook for the People's High Schools*, prepared with Thomas Laub, Oluf Ring, and Thorvald Aagaard (1922); *Danish Songbook*, with Håkon Andersen (1924); *Flute Concerto* (1926, SUDM); *Concerto for clarinet*, chamber ensemble, Op. 57 (1928, SUDM); *Commotio* for organ, Op. 58 (1930–31, SUDM).

PRINCIPAL WRITINGS: *Living Music*, trans. by Reginald Spink (London 1953); *My Childhood*, trans. by Spink (London 1953); *C. N.s Breve* ed. by Irmelin E. Møller and Torben Meyer (Copenhagen 1954); *Breve fra C. N. til Emil B. Sachs*, 2nd ed. (Copenhagen 1953).

BIBL.: Jürgen Balzer, ed., *C. N.: 1865–1965 Centenary Essays* (Copenhagen 1965); Ludwig Dolleris, *C. N. en musikographi* (Odense 1949); Dan Fog and Torben Schousboe, *C. N., kompositioner: en bibliografi* (Copenhagen 1965); Torben Meyer and Frede S. Petersen, *C. N., Kunsteren og Mennesket* (Copenhagen 1947); *Oplevelser og Studier Omkring C. N.*, a collection of memoirs (Copenhagen 1966); Robert Simpson, *C. N., Symphonist 1865–1931* (London 1952); Anne Marie Telmanyi, *Mit Barndomshjam* (Copenhagen 1965); Dean Clarke Wilson, *An Analytical and Statistical Study of the Harmony in C. N.'s 6 Symphonies* (PhD diss., Mich. State Univ., 1967).

SEE ALSO Liturgical Music: Christian, Scandinavia.

Nigg, Serge (b. Paris, 6 June 1924), studied at the Paris Conservatory (1941–46; composition, harmony with Olivier Messiaen; fugue, counterpoint with Simone Plé-Caussade). During 1945–48 he studied 12-tone techniques privately with René Leibowitz. Since 1967 he has been a music inspector for the Ministry of Cultural Affairs in France. After an initial interest in 12-tone techniques, he reacted strongly against such abstractions and emphasis on process and turned to a kind of neo-romanticism. Since 1956 he has been experimenting with syntheses of romantic expression and contemporary techniques.

PRINCIPAL COMPOSITIONS: *Timour*, symphonic poem (1944); *Variations* for piano, winds, horn, strings (1946, CM); *2 Pieces* for piano (1947, CM); *4 Mélodies sur des poèmes de Paul Eluard* for voice, piano (1948, Jobert); *Pour un Poet captif*, symphonic poem (1950, CM); *Billard*, ballet (1951,

P-M); *Petite Cantate des couleurs* for women's chorus; text by François Monod (1952, EFM); *Quintet* for flute, violin, viola, cello, harp (1952); *Piano Concerto* (1954, CM); *Violin Concerto* (1957, Jobert); *L'Etrange Aventure de Gulliver à Lilliput*, ballet for radio; text by Philippe Soupault after Swift (1958; concert version for 12 instruments, CM); *Musique funèbre* for string orchestra (1959, Billaudot); *Jérôme Bosch Symphony* (1960, Billaudot); *Concerto* for flute, string orchestra (1961, Jobert); *Histoire d'œuf* for 2 speakers, 6 percussionists, piano; text by Alain Trutat after Blaise Cendrars (1961); *Piano Sonata No. 2* (1964, Jobert); *Le Chant du dépossédé* for speaker, baritone, orchestra; text after Mallarmé (1964, Jobert); *Sonata* for violin (1965, Billaudot); *Visages d'Axel* for orchestra (1967, Jobert).

BIBL.: A. Goléa, "Panorama de la musique française moderne," *Tendances* (June 1960):21; Fernando Lopes-Graça, *Visita aos musicaos franceses* (Lisbon 1947); Claude Rostand, "Pour ou Contre la Musique contemporaine," *La Musique française contemporaine* (Paris 1952):118; Jean Roy, "Présences contemporaines," *Musique française* (Paris 1962).

SEE ALSO France.

Nikolais, Alwin (b. Southington, Conn., 25 Nov 1912), studied piano and organ as a child. He attended dance and music classes at the Bennington, Vt., School of Dance (summers, 1938–40; technique with Hanya Holm, Martha Graham, and Doris Humphrey; choreography with Holm and Louis Horst; history and criticism with John Martin; percussion and composition with Francesca Boas). During this period he also studied composition privately with a member of the Yale School of Music. He studied with Holm again at the Hanya Holm School of Dance, New York (1945–49). Nikolais directed the Hartford Parks Marionette Theater (1935–37) and the dance department of the Hartt School of Music (1939–42, 1946–48). He taught at the Henry Street Playhouse in New York City beginning in 1949 and formed a dance company there, originally using students as its core. In his dance accompaniments, Nikolais has attempted to move away from the stereotyped emotional responses he believes to be inherent in musical sound produced by conventional instruments. Instead he prefers abstract sound patterns produced by combinations of synthesized, instrumental and musique concrète sounds. Sound for him is one element in multimedia art works that also incorporate light, motion, costumes, and stage sets.

PRINCIPAL TAPE MUSIC: *Allegory* (1959); *Totem* (1960); *Facets* (1962); *Imago* (1963); *Galaxy* (1965);

Vaudeville of the Elements (1965); *Choros I* (1966); *Somniloquy* (1967); *Go 6* (1967); *Triptych* (1967); *Limbo* (1968).
SEE ALSO Dance.

Nikolov, Lazar (Kostov) (Burgas, Bulgaria, 26 August 1922), studied at the Sofia Conservatory (1942–46; composition with Dimitri Nenov, Pantscho Vladigerov) but is largely self-taught as a composer. He has taught at the Sofia Conservatory since 1961. With his *Concerto for String Orchestra* (1949) he abandoned folk-music idioms and gradually moved toward atonal pitch relations. Free uses of 12-tone techniques began in the late 50s. An increasing interest in the structural and expressive potentials of timbre and sonority led in the mid-60s to the use of aleatory procedures. In addition to the works listed below, he has written over 30 scores for films and plays.
PRINCIPAL COMPOSITIONS: *Piano Concertos Nos. 1–2* (1947–48, 1954–55); *Concerto for String Orchestra* (1949, NI and SBK); *Piano Sonatas Nos. 1–4* (1950, NI; 1951; 1955–56, NI; 1964); *Violin Concerto* (1951–52, NI); *Sonata for 2 pianos* (1952); *Symphonies Nos. 1–2* (1953, 1960–61); *Violin Sonata* (1953–54, NI); *Viola Sonata* (1955, NI); *Piano Quintet* (1958–59, NI); *Flute Sonata* (1962); *Clarinet Sonata* (1962); *Cello Sonata* (1962); *Prikovanijat prometey* [Prometheus Bound], chamber opera; libretto after Aeschylus (1963–69); *Concertino* for piano, chamber orchestra (1964, NI); *String Quartets Nos. 1–2*: No. 1, "Virtuosi irgi" (1964–65, Schott); No. 2 "Malak Requiem" (1970); *Symphonia* for 13 string instruments (1965); *Divertimento concertante* for chamber orchestra (1968); *Songs* for chorus, instrumental ensemble (1969–70).

Nilsson, Bo (b. Skelleftehamn, Sweden, 1 May 1937), is self-taught in music. He first came to international attention in 1956 when his *Frequenzen* was premiered at the Darmstadt summer courses. In most of his music until 1958 he used serial processes applied to individual pitches; thereafter he became one of the first composers to apply such processes to larger units, as in open-form structures.
PRINCIPAL COMPOSITIONS (dates from Häusler; see bibl.): *Frequenzen* for clarinet, flute, 2 percussion, vibraphone, xylophone, guitar, double bass (c.1956, UE); *Quantitäten* for piano (1958, UE); *Stunde eines Blocks* for soprano, 6 players; text by Yvvind Fahlström (1958–59, Nordiska); *20 Gruppen für Bläser* for piccolo, oboe, clarinet (1958–59, UE); *Und die Zeiger seiner Augen wurden langsam zurückgedreht* for soprano, alto, women's chorus, 4 loudspeakers, orchestra; text by Gösta

Oswald (1959, UE); *Ein irrender Sohn* for alto, alto flute, instruments; text by Oswald (1959, UE); *Mädchentotenlieder* for soprano, instruments; text by Oswald (1959, UE); *Reaktionen* for 4 percussionists (1960, UE); *Szene I–III* for chamber ensembles (1960, 1961, 1962; UE); *Entrée* for orchestra, tape; composed in collaboration with Karl-Erik Welin (1962–63, Nordiska); *Versuchungen* for orchestra in 3 groups (1963, Nordiska); *La Bran* for chorus, orchestra; text by Ilmar Laaban (1964, Nordiska); *Litanei über das verlorene Schlagzeug* for orchestra (1965, Nordiska).
BIBL.: Folke Hähnel, "B. N. und seine Attitüden," *Melos* 31:176–82; Josef Häusler, *Musik im 20. Jahrhundert* (Bremen 1969):294–96; G. M. Koenig, "B. N.," *Die Reihe 4*.

Nin-Culmell, Joaquín (Maria) (b. Berlin of Cuban parents, 5 Sept 1908), studied at the Schola Cantorum in Paris until 1930 (piano with Paul Braud) and at the Paris Conservatory until 1934 (composition with Paul Dukas, harmony and counterpoint with Jean and Noël Gallon). He also studied piano privately in Paris with Ricardo Viñes and Alfred Cortot and composition in Granada with Manuel de Falla. He has performed professionally as a pianist (1930–50) and as a conductor (since 1940) and has taught at Williams College in Mass. (1940–50) and at the Univ. of Calif. at Berkeley (since 1950).
PRINCIPAL COMPOSITIONS (published by Eschig unless otherwise noted): *Sonata breve* for piano (1932–33, Broude-B); *Piano Quintet* (1934–37, Boileau); *2 Poems of Jorge Manrique* for voice, string quartet (1934–36); *6 Variations on a Theme by Milan* for guitar (1945, UME); *Piano Concerto* (1946); *3 Poems of Gil Vicente* for soprano, piano (1950); *3 Traditional Cuban Folksongs* for chorus (1952, Broude-B); *24 Folksongs from Catalonia*, 2 vols. (1952–53, 1956–57); *48 Tonadas* for piano (1955–61, Broude-B); *El burlador de Sevilla*, ballet (1957–65); *12 Folksongs from Catalonia, Salamanca, and Andalucia* for voice, piano, 3 vols. (1960); *3 Old Spanish Pieces* for orchestra (1960); *Diferencias* for orchestra (1962); *Cello Concerto* (1962–63); *Suite* for cello (1964); *Cantata of Padre José Pradas* for alto, string quartet, harpsichord (1965); *Dedication Mass* for chorus, organ (1970, World Library); *2 Cuban Dances of Ignacio Cervantes* for guitar (undated).
PRINCIPAL WRITINGS: "La guitarra en la música española," *Revista hispánica moderna* (Columbia Univ.) 8 (1942):181–85; "El sentimiento religioso en Beethoven," *Revista lumen* (Havana, Jan 1944): 49–54; *4 Centuries of Music: An Exhibit*, prepared with Mary L. Richmond (Williamstown, Mass., May 1950); "Contemporary Caribbean Composers," *The Caribbean: Its Culture* ed. by A. C. Wilgus (Gainesville, Fla., 1955):31–42; "St. Mary's Dedication Mass," *Music* (New York, Feb 1971):37–39.

Nobre, Marlos (b. Recife, Brazil, 18 Feb 1939), studied at the Pernambuco Conservatory (1946–54, piano with Hilda Nobre, theory with Nysia Nobre) and the Instituto Ernani Braga in Recife (1955–59; harmony, counterpoint, fugue with Jaime Diniz). He studied composition at the 10th International Course at Terezópolis near Rio (1960, H. J. Koellreutter), the São Paulo Conservatory (1961–62, Camargo Guarnieri), and the Torcuata Di Tella Institute in Buenos Aires (1963–64; Ginastera, Messiaen, Dallapiccola, and R. Malipiero). In 1969 he worked at the Columbia-Princeton Electronic Music Center. He has been music coordinator for Rio's Secretary of Tourism since 1965 and cultural coordinator for the Ministry of Education Broadcasting Service since 1966. He has concertized as a pianist and conductor, principally in Brazil. His music was first influenced by the *Chôros* of Villa-Lobos and by Milhaud. After 1963 he began using serial techniques, but more in the "Latin" tradition of Dallapiccola and Berio than in the "Germanic" tradition of the Viennese school.

PRINCIPAL COMPOSITIONS: *Concertino* for piano, string orchestra (1959); *Piano Trio* (1960); *Theme and Variations* for piano (1961, Vitale); *3 Songs* for voice, piano (1962); *Sonata* for viola (1963); *Divertimento* for piano, orchestra (1963); *Rhythmic Variations* for piano, indigenous Brazilian percussion instruments (1963); *Ukrinmakrinkrin* for soprano, piccolo, oboe, horn, piano (1964, Southern); *Canticum instrumentale* for piccolo/flute, harp, piano, timpani (1967); *String Quartet No. 1* (1967); *Rhythmetron* for 32 percussion instruments; choreographed by Arthur Mitchell in 1969 (1968); *Tropicale* for piccolo, piccolo clarinet, piano, percussion (1968); *Concerto breve* for piano, orchestra (1969, Boosey); *Ludus instrumentalis* for chamber orchestra (1969); *Mosaico* for orchestra (1970); *Biosfera* for string orchestra (1970).

PRINCIPAL WRITINGS: "Problems of Notation," *Music in the Americas* (Univ. of Ind.) 1 (1965).

BIBL.: Vasco Mariz, *Figuras da música brasileira contemporânea*, 2nd ed. (Pôrto, Portugal, 1970).

SEE ALSO Brazil.

Noda, Teruyuki (b. Tsu, Japan, 15 June 1940), studied at the Tokyo Univ. of Arts (1960–67; harmony, counterpoint, and composition with Tomojiro Ikenouchi, Akio Yashiro, Yuzuru Shimaoka). He teaches at the University. Among European composers, Berg, Stravinsky, and Ligeti have had the greatest influence on his development.

PRINCIPAL COMPOSITIONS (published by Ongaku unless otherwise noted): *Piano Trio* (1963); *Symphony* (1966, unpub.); *Choral Symphony* (1968, unpub.); *Quintet*, "Mattinata," for marimba, 3 flutes, double bass (1968); *3 Developments* for piano (1969); *Dislocation* for orchestra (1969); *Eclogue* for flute, percussion (1970); *Mutation* for 4 Japanese instruments, orchestra (1971, unpub.).

PRINCIPAL WRITINGS: "The Possibilities of Japanese Instruments," *Ongaku-no-Tomo* (1970); "12 Tones and Dodecaphony," *Ongaku-Geijutsu* (1971).

SEE ALSO Japan.

Nono, Luigi (b. Venice, 29 Jan 1924), earned a law degree from the Univ. of Padua in 1946. During 1941–46 he was a nonmatriculated student at the Accadèmia Benedetto Marcello in Venice, and under the influence of Gian Francesco Malipiero he wrote his first compositions (later withdrawn). His second period of musical study took place during 1946–50 under Bruno Maderna and was based on the comparative analysis of compositional techniques of the middle ages and renaissance; in 1948 he also studied 12-tone techniques with Hermann Scherchen. After 1950 premieres of his works occurred under Maderna, Scherchen, and Rosbaud at the Darmstadt summer courses, in the concert series "das neue Werk" over Hamburg radio, and in Donaueschingen. From then on Nono quickly became internationally known as an exponent of the postwar avant-garde. He taught during 1957–60 at the Darmstadt courses and frequently after 1959 at the summer school in Dartington, England. He has made lecture tours throughout the world. In 1955 he married Schoenberg's daughter Nuria. He lives in Venice, where he divides his time between free-lance composing and political activities (he is one of the leaders of the Venice section of the Italian Communist Party).

During 1950–55 Nono composed mostly instrumental music. Between 1956 and 1963 he transferred his attention to the vocal genres, and since then he has worked almost exclusively in the electronic studio, employing in his tape compositions mostly sung and spoken vocal material. Nono's artistic development stems first of all from middle-European postwar developments: the expansion of pitch serialism from the late work of Anton Webern to the serialization of durations, intensities, timbres, and types of articulation. In this regard his music shares with other serial work of the 1950s the renunciation of the exposition and development of themes of a primarily melodic and rhythmic nature. No longer do lines and confluences determine the outward shape of the music but points of tone do.

Polifonica—Monodia—Ritmica (1951) is distinguishable from other serial compositions of this time in four principal ways: 1) The points of tone themselves are not important, but their relation to surrounding points is. Isolated prominent points come together to achieve structural groups, the constellations within the groups change, and the change of the constellations creates the form. 2) The serial principle is not transferred mechanically from pitch to the other parameters. Durations, intensities, and timbres are more simply organized, a reflection of the fact that their historical development is behind that of pitch. 3) Even though the basic material of the piece was given over to predetermining processes, the piece itself is not identical to the sum of segments of the set (as was sometimes the case in early serial pieces). 4) The material itself depends on prepared and discovered elements (behind *Polifonica—Monodia—Ritmica*, for instance, there is a Brazilian folksong).

Nono further separated himself from the systematic framework of "classical" serial style in *Incontri* (1955), a work that proved crucial in many respects. Pitches no longer stand freely in space nor come together in groups to create rhythmic designs; instead, they overlap each other forming bands of sound in which the stopping and starting of each tone (briefly touched or long held) changes the quality of the sound and articulates the passage of time. Rhythm, until now handled as a separate parameter and articulated through successions of impulse and rest, is now understood as a continuum and is no longer separable as before from the ongoing sonority. (Forty-five years earlier, Schoenberg, proceeding from another structural basis, had experimented with a similar thing in the third of his *5 Pieces for Orchestra*, Op. 16, and had called it *Klangfarbenmelodie*; in *Atmosphères*, 1961, György Ligeti is said to have proceeded from a stylistic basis similar to that of Nono.) Thereafter, in *Canto sospeso* and in later a cappella choruses, when Nono broke up texts into words, syllables, and phonemes and allowed these to wander through the voices (an innovation that is widely used today), he was merely expanding on the implications in *Incontri*, for word sounds had become an integrated component of the music. In structure, the vocal works hardly differentiate themselves from the previous instrumental pieces. Even the early electronic work *Omaggio a Emilio Vedova* (1960) includes extensions and refinements of processes in *Incontri* in that it exploits the possibilities of articulating a continually changing sound structure. The later electronic works also include concrete material (factory noises in *La fabbrica illuminata*, market cries and bells tolling in *Contrappunto dialettico*), elongated speech material, and non-European uses of the voice.

Nono's artistic development has never been separable from his political beliefs. Behind his renunciation of the esthetic play of isolated points of sound stands his renunciation of a social system that sees its goal in the self-entanglement of the individual. Behind his mistrust of mechanical serial procedures stands a mistrust of rigid, nondialectic thought. The texts that he set to music between 1950 and 1960 still reflect the European situation, especially the political standpoint of the Italian resistance, an historically determined antifascism. The opera *Intolleranza* made explicit his belief that the fight against the fascism of the Hitler period continues in the class struggle of the 1960s. In his electronic pieces the divergence from European vocal practices reflects a turn away from the central European elite, and the inclusion of concrete sounds and political texts reflects the conviction that one must build a bridge to those excluded for generations from the development of music. Nono's latest music is directed to the worker, farmer, and guerrilla, and not to the urban concertgoer.

PRINCIPAL COMPOSITIONS (published by Ricordi unless otherwise noted): *Polifonica—Monodia—Ritmica* for 5 winds, percussion, piano (1951, Schott); *Epitaph auf Federico García-Lorca*, parts 1–3: part 1, "España en el corazón," for soprano, baritone, chamber chorus, chamber orchestra (1951–52, Schott); part 2, "Y su sangre ya viene cantando," for flute, chamber orchestra (1952, Schott); part 3, "Memento," for female narrator, speaking chorus, chorus, orchestra (1952, Schott); *Incontri* for chamber orchestra (1955, Schott); *Il canto sospeso* for soprano, alto, tenor, chorus, orchestra; texts taken from the last letters of resistance fighters killed in battle (1956, Schott); *La terra e la compagna* for soprano, tenor, chorus, orchestra; text by Cesare Pavese (1957, Schott); *Cori di Didone* for chorus, percussion; text by Giuseppe Ungaretti (1958, Schott); *Composizione per orchestra 2*, "Diario polacco '58" (1959, Schott); *Sarà dolce tacere* for 8 solo voices; text by Pavese (1960, Schott); *Omaggio a Emilio Vedova* on tape (1960); *Intolleranza 1960*, opera for 5 singers, mime, chorus, orchestra; libretto by the composer after an idea of Angelo Maria Ripellino (1960–61, Schott); *Canti di vita e d'amore*, "Sul ponte di Hiroshima," for soprano, tenor, orchestra; texts by Günther Anders, Jesus Lopez Pacheco, Pavese (1962, Schott); *La fabrica illuminata* for soprano, tape; text arranged by Guiliano Scabia (1964); *A floresta é jovem e cheja de vida* for voices, clarinet, metal sheet, tape; text arranged by Giovanni Pirelli (1966); *Per Bastiana Tai-yang cheng* for orchestra, tape (1967); *Contrappunto dialettico alla mente* on stereo tape; text arranged by Nanni Balestrini (1968); *Musica-Manifesto No. 1*, parts 1–2: part 1, "Un volto, del mare," for voices, tape; text by Pavese (1969); part 2, "Non consumiamo Marx," for voices, tape; text arranged by the composer (1969); *Y entonces comprendió* for women's voices, chorus, tape, electronic equipment; text by Carlos Franqui (1969–70); *Voci destroying muros* for 4 sopranos, women's chorus, orchestra; text arranged by the composer (1970). Catalog, 1950–65, published by Schott; list of titles, 1950–68, included in the liner notes for the record "Luigi Nono" (Wergo 60038).

PRINCIPAL WRITINGS: "Geschichte und Gegenwart in der Musik von Heute," *Darmstädter Beiträge zur Neuen Music* 3; "Revolution und Musik," *Spandauer Volksblatt* (Berlin, 14 Sept 1969); "Entrevista con L. N.," *Rocinante* (Caracas, 26 Jan 1969); a conversation with Hansjörg Pauli in the latter's *Für wen komponieren Sie eigentlich?* (Frankfurt 1971).

BIBL.: Konrad Boehmer, "Über L. N.," liner notes for the record "L. N." (Wergo 60038); Ulrich Dibelius, *Moderne Musik 1945–1965* (Munich 1966):145–57; Massimo Mila, "La linea N.," *Rassegna musicale italiana* 30:297–311; Udo Unger, "L. N.," *Die Reihe* 4.

Hansjörg Pauli
(trans. from German by Jeanne Wolf)

SEE ALSO Austria and Germany, Italy, Mathematics, Mixed Media, Opera, Text Setting and Usage.

Nordheim, Arne (b. Larvik, Norway, 20 June 1931), studied at the Oslo Conservatory (1948–52; organ, piano, theory). He was a critic for *Dagbladet* in Oslo during 1960–68 and is now a free-lance composer. He has toured in various parts of the world as a lecturer and as a performer of live electronic works.

PRINCIPAL COMPOSITIONS (published by Hansen-W): *Epigram* for string quartet (1955); *String Quartet* (1956); *Aftonland*, song cycle for voice, chamber ensemble; text by Pär Lagerquist (1957); *Canzona* for orchestra (1960); *Katharsis*, ballet for orchestra, tape; choreography by Ivo Cramer (1962); *Partita* for viola, harpsichord, percussion (1963); *Epitaffio* for orchestra, tape (1963, recorded by Philips); *Favola*, musical play for TV for soprano, tenor, chorus, orchestra, electronic sound (1965); *Evolution*, electronic and concrete sound on 2-track tape (1966); *Respons 1* for 2 percussion groups, electronic sound (1966–67, recorded by Philips); *Signaler* for accordion, electric guitar, percussion (1967); *Eco* for soprano, children's and adult choruses, orchestra; text by Salvatore Quasimodo (1967); *Warszawa*, electronic and concrete sound on 4-track tape (1967–68); *Colorazione* for type X-66 Hammond organ, percussion, 2 tape recorders, amplifiers, loudspeakers (1968); *Solitaire*, electronic and concrete sound on 4-track

tape (1968, recorded by Philips); *Partita 2* for electric guitar (1969); *Lux et tenebrae*, electronic sound on tape (1970); *Floating* for orchestra (1970); *Pace*, electronic sound on tape (1970); *Osaka-Music*, electronic sound on tape (1970); *Dinosauros* for accordion, accordion sounds on tape (1970).

SEE ALSO Scandinavia.

Nordoff, Paul (b. Philadelphia, 6 June 1909), studied at the Philadelphia Conservatory (1923–27; chamber music, contemporary music, and piano with D. Hendrik Ezerman) and the Juilliard School (1928–33, composition with Rubin Goldmark, piano with Olga Samaroff). He taught composition at the Philadelphia Conservatory (1937–42) and Bard College (1949–57). Since 1959 he has been working exclusively in the field of music therapy for handicapped children.

PRINCIPAL COMPOSITIONS (dates not available): *Lost Summer* for mezzo-soprano, chamber orchestra; *Winter Symphony*; *Concerto* for violin, piano; *Gothic Concerto* for piano; *Lyric Sonata* for violin, piano; *Flute Sonata*; *The Story of Sweeney*, song cycle for voice, piano; *It's Been a Long, Hard Winter*, songs for voice, piano; poems by e. e. cummings. Nordoff has also collaborated with Clive Robbins on many pieces for handicapped children.

PRINCIPAL WRITINGS: *Music Therapy for Handicapped Children*, with Clive Robbins (Boston 1965); *Music Therapy in Special Education*, with Robbins (New York 1971).

SEE ALSO Dance.

Nørgård, Per (b. Gentofte, Denmark, 13 July 1932), studied at the Royal Danish Conservatory (1952–55; composition with Vagn Holmboe, Finn Høffding) and with Nadia Boulanger (1956–57). He has taught various musical subjects at the Conservatory of Fyn (1958–60), the Royal Danish Conservatory (1960–65), and the Jydske Conservatory at Aarhus (since 1965). Sibelius has been a strong influence on some of his music. Nørgård has exploited varied manipulations of short tonal motives, especially in contrapuntal textures. Beginning with *Fragment 6* (1959–61), he has also used serial processes and, later, graphic notation.

PRINCIPAL COMPOSITIONS (published by Hansen-W): *Quintet* for flute, violin, viola, cello, piano, Op. 1 (1951–52); *Sonata in 1 Movement* for piano, Op. 6 (1952, revised 1956); *Constellations*, concerto for 12 solo strings or 12 string groups, Op. 22 (1958); *Fragment 6* for 6 orchestral groups (winds, brass, percussion, harp, pianos, timpani) (1959–61); *4 Fragments* for piano (1960); *Fragment* for violin, piano (1961); *Nocturnes*, suite for soprano with piano or 19 instruments; Chinese texts in German translation (1961–62); *Prism*, song cycle for mezzo-soprano, tenor, baritone, flute, trombone, violin, cello, electric guitar, 2 percussionists; texts by Jørgen Sonne (1964); *Babel*, oratorio for 4 soloists (clown, rock singer, cabaret singer, conductor), chorus, orchestra (1966); *Luna* for orchestra (1967); *Voyage into the Golden Screen* for chamber ensemble (1968); *The Enchanted Forest* on tape (1968).

BIBL.: Bo Wallner, "Scandinavian Music after the Second World War," *Musical Quarterly* 50: 139–40; ——, *Vår tids musik i Norden* (Stockholm 1968), English trans. (London 1971).

SEE ALSO Scandinavia.

North, Alex (b. Chester, Pa., 4 Dec 1910), studied at the Juilliard School (1929–32, composition with Bernard Wagenaar) and the Moscow Conservatory (1933–34, composition with Anton Weprik). He also studied composition privately with Aaron Copland and Ernst Toch (1935–39). He has composed numerous scores for dance, theater, films, and television (including the 1949 "Billy Rose Show").

PRINCIPAL COMPOSITIONS: ★Concert music: *Quest* for chamber orchestra (1937); *The Hither and Thither of Danny Dither*, children's opera (1940, Marks); *Negro Mother Cantata* for chorus (1941); *Holiday Set* for chamber orchestra (1945); *Waltzing Elephant* for narrator, orchestra (1945); *Little Indian Drum* for narrator, orchestra (1946); *Morning Star Cantata* for chorus, 2 pianos, percussion (1946); *Revue* for clarinet, orchestra (1947, Mills); *Rhapsody* for piano, orchestra (1953); *Symphony* (1968). ★Dance scores (dates are of first performance): *War Is Beautiful* and *Façade— Exposizione italiano* (1937, choreography by Anna Sokolow); *American Lyric* (1938, Martha Graham); *Golden Fleece* (1941, Hanya Holm); *A Streetcar Named Desire* (1957, Valerie Bettis; published by Widmark); *Mal de siècle* (1958, Rosella Hightower and James Starbuck). ★Film scores (with name of film studio): *A Streetcar Named Desire* (1950, Warner Bros.); *Death of a Salesman* (1950, Columbia); *Viva Zapata* (1951, 20th Century-Fox); *Rose Tattoo* (1955, Paramount); *Spartacus* (1960, Universal); *Cleopatra* (1962, 20th Century-Fox); *Who's Afraid of Virginia Woolf* (1966, Warner Bros.); *Shoes of the Fisherman* (1968, Metro-Goldwyn-Mayer).

PRINCIPAL WRITINGS: *Music in Modern Media* (New York 1967).

SEE ALSO Orchestration.

Norway, see Scandinavia

Notation is designed to convey music by graphic means. The graphic signs and directions either symbolize pitches, durations, and other audible phenomena, or provide instructions for mechanical manipulations of musical instruments. Traditional notation, after having remained essentially unchanged for several centuries, became subject to various attempts at revision during the first half of the 20th century. These adjustments, extensions, and proposed innovations have become far more numerous and profound since about 1950, concomitant with the stylistic upheaval that has characterized concert music since then. The spectrum of recent music, ranging from uncompromising control over all compositional elements, as in total serialism, to unlimited ambiguity, as in some extreme examples of aleatory music, has caused a parallel development of notational signs and procedures, ranging from the greatest possible explicitness to complete freedom of interpretation. These notational changes evolved through adaptations and adjustments of traditional practices, through partial innovations to meet new musical demands that could no longer be expressed by traditional notational means, and through the invention of entirely new systems. The resulting profusion of new notational signs and methods has tended to impair composer-performer communication via notation, particularly when composers, unaware of each others' work, have used identical signs for different musical phenomena or different signs for identical effects. Although new notation is still unsettled and has few universally accepted standards, some typical signs and procedures can be singled out and some general trends and categories discerned. The following is a sampling of the most obvious notational problems and their most frequently encountered remedies.

NOTATION OF PITCHES. The traditional method of notating pitches was designed for diatonic music, i.e., music based on modes or scales that contain whole-tone and half-tone steps and in which tones outside the prevailing scale or key are in the minority. With the advent of atonal and of 12-tone music (in which all 12 tones are equidistant in the chromatic scale and are treated as equal in "weight") conventional pitch notation with its choice of accidentals and spellings, though technically still workable, became cumbersome and musically unrepresentative. Even so, it has not yielded thus far to any of the proposals for new systems. Even microtonal music has not brought with it notational innovations, for performers have found makeshift extensions of traditional means to be more practical.

In traditional notation (Ex. 1a) a natural sign or an accidental (except in the key signature) applies to the note it precedes and to all repetitions of that note within the measure. In highly chromatic music, such as that of the present era, performers often have difficulty remembering which notes they must continue to alter and which not. The two remedies in Exx. 1b and 1c are the most frequently employed; neither alters the essence of traditional pitch notation. Each note in Ex. 1b (except for repeated notes) is preceded either by a natural sign or by an accidental. While this method avoids the memory problem, it necessitates two pitch symbols for each note, the note-head and the sign preceding it. In Ex. 1c each accidental applies only to the one note it precedes (except for repeated notes); no natural signs are used. Exx. 1d–1f represent partial innovations in pitch notation. In Ex. 1d the five-line staff is retained but the black and white note-heads, instead of symbolizing durations, represent the black and white keys of the keyboard. Since the notes no longer indicate durations, rhythm must be notated by other means, in this case by the horizontal spacing of the notes (see the description of proportionate notation below). The conventional pitch and duration meanings of note-heads remain in Ex. 1e, but the number of staff lines is increased so that there is a line or space for each chromatic pitch, obviating accidentals. Several such systems have been proposed but none, including this one, is in practical use. In most of them the staff lines are grouped in some way for ease of orientation (cf. the systems by Velizar Godjevatz, Carl Johannis, Walter Steffens, and others). Whereas conventional notation makes no spatial distinction between whole and half steps, these systems provide true graphic equivalents for interval sizes. In Ex. 1f the number of staff lines is reduced and the spaces between them widened to accommodate more than one note-position. For greater clarity concerning the exact location of the notes in the spaces, identifying marks are often added to some or all of the note-heads. Ex. 1f is notated in a system proposed in 1925 by Arnold Schoenberg.

Early systems of microtonal notation (Alois Hába, Julián Carillo, etc.) have not survived. Others (such as Harry Partch's) are generally confined to the works of the innovator. The most common solution at present is to use conventional accidentals with alterations. Three kinds of alteration are shown in Ex. 2.

While tone clusters can be written by means of traditional notation, it is awkward to do so. Perhaps the most versatile alternative is that introduced by Henry Cowell (Ex. 3). Most other forms now in general use (Ex. 4) are similar to his. Sustained clusters, with or

Ex. 1a.

Ex. 1b.

Ex. 1c.

Ex. 1d.

Ex. 1e.

Ex. 1f.

without gradual changes in their width, are often notated as in Ex. 5.

NOTATION OF DURATIONS. The conventional method of notating durations was designed for music in which bipartite values predominate and note values are limited to the single geometric progression 1, 2, 4, 8, 16, etc., corresponding to whole notes and their division into halves, quarters, eighths, sixteenths, etc. Nonbipartite note values can only be indicated through appropriately adjusted bipartite values, such as by using prolongation dots, ties, numerals denoting triplets, quintuplets, and so forth. As rhythmic subtleties increased in music of the early 20th century, traditional notation began to show its limitations. More recently, when durations became an object of serial procedures and a largely pulseless music resulted, traditional notation became all but useless. The problem is particularly acute in music in which different rhythms, often extremely intricate to begin with, proceed simultaneously at different speeds so that contrasting strands of diverse meters and tempi cannot be coordinated by any common metric denominator. Traditional notation, lastly, becomes utterly helpless when called upon to indicate precisely controlled ritardando and accelerando passages, especially if such passages proceed simultaneously with any or all of the other aforementioned complexities.

Ex. 2.

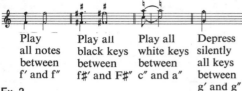

| Play all notes between f′ and f″ | Play all black keys between f♯′ and F♯″ | Play all white keys between c″ and a″ | Depress silently all keys between g′ and g″ |

Ex. 3.

Ex. 4.

Ex. 5.

*Violins divide up the cluster spectrum d′-g♯′ as evenly as possible, then move to the widest point of the cluster (at ⊕), where all half-tones between d′ and d″ are to be played, then continue, allowing gaps to form in the cluster as indicated.

**Double basses divide the cluster spectrum into quarter-tones and slide upwards, maintaining the original density.

One of the greatest difficulties in the performance of present-day music is keeping an ensemble together rhythmically. The performers cannot readily locate the coordinating metric pulses or beats in their music because such regular metric divisions (if they exist) usually lie obscured beneath highly fragmented and irregular rhythms. To ease this difficulty (at least in music rapid enough to permit the use of beamed note values), the beams are used not only to group notes together, as in conventional notation, but are also extended across rests in order to serve as brackets for complete metric beat units. Ex. 6a shows a rhythmic passage in conventional notation; Ex. 6b shows the same passage with extended beams indicating the beat units; in Ex. 6c short "rest stems" have been added to the beams for further clarification. Ex. 6d contains two often encountered new forms of time signatures that likewise show beat units (three dotted quarters) rather than mere note values (nine eighth-notes). Similar metric aids are often provided for conductors in the form of signs or numerals at the top of a score page (Ex. 7).

Ex. 6a. [musical notation]

Ex. 6b. [musical notation]

Ex. 6c. [musical notation]

Ex. 6d. [musical notation]

The procedures shown in Ex. 6, while useful in music in which one metric pulse governs all parts, are not capable of dealing satisfactorily with polymetrics that lack a common metric denominator, nor with precisely controlled ritardandos and accelerandos. Among the attempts to cope with these latter phenomena, while staying within the framework of conventional notation, is the use of constantly changing metronome marks (sometimes incorporating numbers not actually found on the metronome). One also finds less precise methods such as dotted arrows representing rubatolike acceleration or retardation, or alternating plus and minus signs denoting similarly alternating speed variations. The numerous instances of "metric modulation" in the scores of Elliott Carter and his followers also show the difficulty of indicating essentially simple but largely unconventional concepts by means of conventional notation. A new device that has gained fairly general acceptance is shown in Ex. 8. Here a free-rubatolike change in speed is indicated for a short phrase that occurs within a nonrubato context; the device is often combined with a horizontal spacing-out of the notes to imply the desired speed changes (Ex. 8b).

The most frequently used new method for dealing with durations is *proportionate notation*. This method, instead of employing durational symbols, transmutes durational proportions into the graphic equivalent of notes spaced out horizontally along the staff according to

Ex. 7a. [musical notation]

Ex. 7b. [musical notation]   ⊔ also is notated ↓↑

Ex. 7c. [musical notation]

[accel.] [rit.] [accel.] [rit.]

Ex. 8a.   Ex. 8b.   Ex. 8c.

Ex. 9a.

their durations (Exx. 1d, 5, and 8b). Metric pulses are generally indicated with bar lines or short strokes or wedges, but such indications are sometimes omitted to allow for greater rhythmic flexibility. In keyboard and ensemble music the vertical alignment of the notes shows how each part must proceed relative to the others; ensemble performers must therefore generally read such music from scores rather than from parts. Since proportionate notation obviates the use of traditional rhythmic symbols (white and black noteheads, flags, beams, etc.), these signs are often used to serve other purposes (beams to indicate phrasing, etc.). Ex. 9 shows a passage of music in conventional notation followed by three kinds of proportionate notation. In Ex. 9c, the most frequently used innovation, beams are placed between the notes and lengthened to indicate durations; in Ex. 9d the noteheads themselves are lengthened.

Although no substantial innovation in the use of symbols for durations has found acceptance, mention should be made of Henry Cowell's proposal in the early 1900s to increase the number of durational divisions of the whole note by adding third notes, fifth notes, etc. To identify the new units, Cowell borrowed the concept of shaped notes, which had been

Ex. 9b.

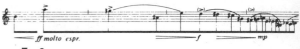

Ex. 9c.

Ex. 9d.

Ex. 9. Elliott Carter, *String Quartet No. 2*, II, cello part: 255–58
Quoted by permission of Associated Music Publishers

used in early American tunebooks to denote pitch. The system (Ex. 10), although perhaps the most comprehensive to have been developed, has remained a theory only. Even Cowell himself used it only once, to notate his piano piece *Fabric* (1917, published 1922 by Brietkopf Publications, Inc., New York, and included in the collection *Piano Music by Henry Cowell*, 1961).

NOTATION OF ARTICULATION, TIMBRE, DYNAMICS, ETC. With the abandonment of the conventional musical hierarchy of melody-rhythm-harmony, elements that used to be

o = ♩♩ whole-note into 2 (conventional notation)	⎾3⏋ o = ♩♩♩ whole-note into 3	o=♩♩♩♩ whole-note into 4	⎾5⏋ o = ♩♩♩♩♩ whole-note into 5	⎾6⏋ o=♩♩♩♩♩♩ whole-note into 6	⎾7⏋ o = ♩♩♩♩♩♩♩ whole-note into 7	etc.
1 whole-note o	1 whole-note o	see whole-note into 2	1 whole-note o	see whole-note into 3	1 whole-note o	
	1 2/3-note + 1 third-note △ ◿		1 4/5-note + 1 fifth-note □ ♩		1 4/7-note + 3 seventh-notes ◊ ♩♩♩	
2 half-notes ♩ ♩	3 third-notes ◿ ◿ ◿		2 2/5-notes + 1 fifth-note ♩ ♩♩		3 2/7-notes + 1 seventh-note ♩ ♩♩♩	
4 quarter-notes ♩♩ etc.	6 sixth-notes ◢ ◢ etc.		5 fifth-notes ♩ ♩ ♩ etc.		7 seventh-notes ♩♩ etc.	
8 eighth-notes ♪♪ etc.	12 twelfth-notes ♪ ♪ etc.		10 tenth-notes ♪♪ etc.		14 fourteenth-notes ♪ ♪ etc.	
etc.	etc.		etc.		etc.	

Ex. 10a.

Conventional notation: Cowell system:

Ex. 10b.

subordinate, such as timbre, articulation, and dynamics, rose in prominence and demanded greater notational precision. However, since each instrument has its own timbral and other characteristics and requires different manipulations, an enormous profusion of new devices to indicate playing techniques, attacks, timbres, etc., has come about. Only a few standard procedures have been agreed upon. Among them is the notation of sprechgesang in vocal music (Ex. 11) and the sign for "snap pizzicato" (Ex. 12) in string music. Several attempts

Ex. 11.

have been made to indicate exact dynamic degrees, mostly with the help of numerals in place of the imprecise *pp, mf, f, cresc.*, etc., of conventional notation. However, since exact dynamic degrees are extremely elusive except in electronic music, no standard procedures have evolved. Most other performance instructions continue to be indicated verbally, except in percussion music where pictorial abstractions are widely used to indicate instruments, beaters, and playing modes.

Ex. 12.

SOME NEW EXPLICIT NOTATIONAL SYSTEMS. Several entirely new systems have been proposed but none has found acceptance. Two such systems may be mentioned as typical of the chief trends. *Equiton* (Ex. 13) uses only two

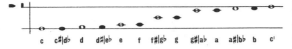

c   c#|db   d   d#|eb   e   f   f#|gb   g   g#|ab   a   a#|bb   b   c'

Ex. 13.

staff lines per octave. The twelve tones of the chromatic scale are notated with alternating black and white note-heads and without accidentals. Note-heads appear below, on, and above each staff line. Note-heads between the staff lines occur on three levels: close to the lower line, close to the upper line, and centered between the lines. For easy identification note-heads close to the staff lines (but not on them) have ledger lines drawn through them. The notation of durations is proportionate; bar lines and/or pulse strokes may be used. The

duration of each note lasts until the next note or a rest sign appears. Where contrapuntal textures make it desirable, straight or curved lines can be drawn from note to note to indicate voice leading (Ex. 14b). Durational beams may also be added as in Ex. 14c. Minor seconds involving two notes on the same level (not shown) are indicated by a single note-head half black and half white. Microtonal octave divisions (also not shown) are indicated with non-oval note-heads. (See also Rodney Fawcett, *Equiton*, 1958; Erhard Karkoschka," Ich habe mit Equiton komponiert," *Melos* 1962/7; ——, *Das Schriftbild der Neuen Musik*, Celle 1966.) *Klavarscribo* uses a staff in which the lines and spaces run vertically and are grouped according to the black and white keys of the keyboard (Ex. 15). No accidentals are needed since there is a note position for each black and white key. Black and white note-heads are used for easy identification with corresponding keys. The conventional up-and-down axis for pitches is changed to a left-right axis, also in accordance with the keyboard, and chords are thus notated horizontally. The music is read from top to bottom. The notation of durations is proportionate; bar lines are horizontal. (See also *Was ist Klavarscribo?* published anonymously and without date in Slikkerveer, Holland.)

NOTATION OF ALEATORY MUSIC. The deliberate imprecision of aleatory music never entered into the development of traditional notation. Neither the ornament signs of the baroque era nor the figured basses and their realization by continuo players nor the embellishments in the repeats of da capo arias can compare with the degree of interpretative license found in aleatory music. Aleatory music itself, moreover, covers a wide range from merely conditioned flexibility to total interpretative freedom. The most frequently encountered manifestations lie between the extremes. Such music is often called music of "controlled chance," i.e., music in which flexible (chance) passages alternate or are otherwise combined with precisely conceived music and are governed by certain composer-controlled directions. Its notation is often referred to as "frame notation," i.e., notation permitting free or flexible interpetation within a set, controlling framework.

The notational procedures for music of controlled chance depend on the kind and degree of interpretative freedom desired. For example, in Ex. 16 the pitches and the total duration (horizontal brackets) are specified while the succession and combination of pitches, the rhythm, tempo, dynamics,

Ex. 14a. Conventional notation

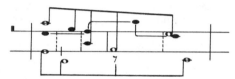

Ex. 14b. Equiton

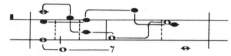

Ex. 14c. Equiton

Ex. 15.

articulation, etc., are not. The same applies to Ex. 17, except that here the lines between the notes indicate the desired succession of the given pitches; the performer chooses the opening pitch and the direction, clockwise or counter-clockwise. Unlike Exx. 16 and 17, Ex. 18 specifies the dynamics and the rhythm but leaves the choice of the pitches and tempo to the performer. The phrase is to be repeated for a total duration of 17 seconds. Ex. 19 provides a choice of three different passages that are placed one above the other. The notational approach is different in each segment of this example: The initial phrase shows specific pitches with proportionately notated durations; the upper choice contains mostly verbal instructions; the middle choice contains clusters; the bottom choice provides a nonspecific melodic contour combined with verbal instructions; the final segment contains a chord of specified pitches and dynamics but of indeterminate duration.

GRAPHICS. Ex. 20 shows one of the many forms of nonspecific notation called *implicative graphics* or *graphics*. In this example musical textures and gestures are implied by means of graphic analogs: Dense vs. empty fields imply sounds and activity vs. silence; bold dots vs. light dots imply dynamics; high versus low dots imply pitches, etc. The length of the frame represents the duration of the passage. Needless to say, graphics are not limited to dots. The choice of shapes is entirely free. Different shapes may or may not imply different musical concepts to different performers, and any shapes or devices will serve. Thus, Ex. 21 shows the approximate rise and fall of the voice and may also imply dynamic stresses (see also Exx. 24–25, and 19, bottom choice).

Graphics defy standardization. Ideally they are unique for each composition since they, along with the instructions (if any) for their performance, are an integral part of the composer's creative vision. The notation itself is, in fact, the only composer-controlled creative manifestation, a creation in a visual medium designed to inspire analgous (though

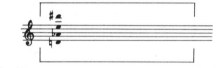

Ex. 16.

Ex. 17.

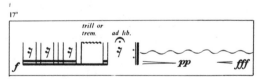

Ex. 18.

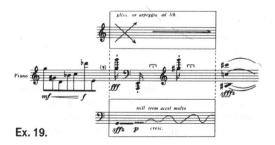

Ex. 19.

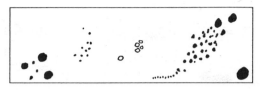

Ex. 20.

largely unpredictable) musical manifestations of an almost equally creative nature. Each performer is expected to realize the notation not only differently but differently at each performance. Even in the area of extreme indeterminacy, however, certain distinctions can be drawn, the most fundamental being that the majority of graphic scores adhere to the up-and-down axis for high and low pitches, the left-to-right axis for the sequence of events, and bold vs. light shapes for dynamic degrees. Completely indeterminate graphics dispense even with these vestiges of traditional notational concepts.

A SAMPLING OF SCORE PAGES. Precise (traditional) notation is represented by Ex. 22. Here

TIME WILL TELL... THE ACA-CACACA-DE-MY OF ANTROPO

Ex. 21. Roman Haubenstock-Ramati,
Credentials
Quoted by permission of Universal Edition and Theodore Presser

the notational problem is to present two different but simultaneously sounding meters. The time signature for all instruments is $\frac{5}{4}$ ($\downarrow = 175$), yet the music pulse of the second violin part is $\frac{4}{4}$ ($\downarrow = 140$). This example shows that traditional rhythmic notation is almost incapable of dealing with such a problem. The simple eighth beats of violin II are forced into grotesquely complex durational values so that they will fit into the metric structure of the other three instruments. Even these values are not precise, and an extra rhythm cue-line is required to show the true rhythm of the "uncooperative" part.

Ex. 23 contains *frame notation*. The pitch notation is conventional except that traditional clefs have been replaced by wedges that point to treble-clef G and bass-clef F. The notation of durations is proportionate. In the solo violin the durations of individual notes are indicated mostly by lengthened note-heads (note-lines) and the phrasing by beams. The solo violin begins with a triple stop, then plays a double stop (an open-string e″ plus b♭′) which slides upwards, etc. The horizontal lines above the solo-violin staff contain the following abbreviated instructions: A = *arco*; A + L = *col legno*; ep = *estremamente sul ponticello*; et = *estremamente sul tasto*; o = *ordinario*; nv = *non vibrato*; ev = *estremamente vibrato*. The lines below the solo-violin staff contain other playing instructions:

*Alternate rhythmic notation for violin II indicating how its part should sound, within itself. This alternate notation also indicates the correct length of resonance of each note, regardless of the note-values which appear in the actual performance part.

Ex. 22. Elliott Carter, *String Quartet No. 2*, II: 171–72
Quoted by permission of Associated Music Publishers

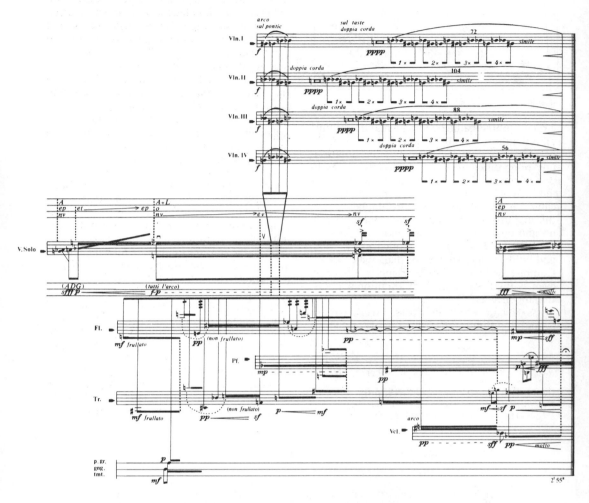

Ex. 23. Boguslaw Schäffer, *Imago musicae*, I: end
Quoted by permission of the composer

ADG = the strings on which to play the triple stop; and other instructions. Just before the end of the glissando, the flute enters on a low b, flutter-tongue, followed by the trumpet on g♯, also *frullato*. Later on, the flute plays a rather free tremolo, first on G′ and a′, then on g′ and a♭′, and finally on g′ and b♭′. The four accompanying violins first play four coordinated chords, then a sustained open-string a′, plus a number of four-note grouplets, each of which is repeated one to four times, and then *simile* until the first violin has played 72 notes, violin II 104, violin III 88, and violin IV 56 notes. The tempo is fast: 11 millimeters of score equal one beat at MM 56–66. All players must either use the full score or have explicit cues in their parts showing how their music fits into the total ensemble.

Ex. 24 contains two systems from a piece consisting of eleven systems of explicit notation interspersed with three "implicit areas" (the composer's term). The latter are left blank in the printed copies, and the graphics are subsequently drawn in by hand so that no two areas contain the same graphics, and no two copies of the piece are the same. The graphics may or may not be played by any or all performers. The music thus goes back and forth between events controlled by the composer and events that are largely unpredictable (including the possibility of complete silence). All systems, explicit as well as free, are played without interruption and have the same duration (not to exceed 15 seconds). The explicit systems have conventional pitch notation and proportionate durations ("time notation" is

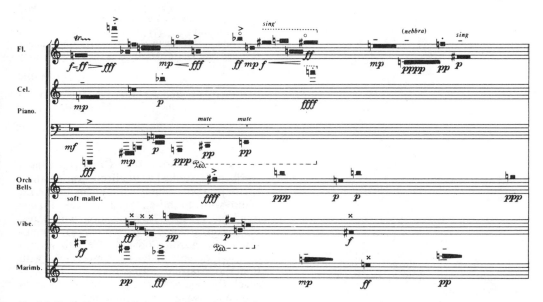

Ex. 24. Earle Brown, *Hodograph I*, systems 4–5
Quoted by permission of Associated Music Publishers

the composer's term). Some of the lengthened note-heads, in addition to indicating durations, show certain dynamics and articulations (see the fading notes of celesta and piano and the swell-fade shape of the vibraphone f).

Exx. 25 and 26 are entirely in graphic notation. Ex. 25 may be played by one or preferably two pianists, either as it is reproduced here or upside down. The performer(s) decide what the various graphics are to mean and then adhere to those decisions throughout the performance. However, the meanings should change from performance to performance. In addition to these options, the piece may be performed simultaneously with a prerecorded version, which may be electronically altered.

Ex. 26 is the keyboard part for a composition for prerecorded 2-track tape and harpsichord or prepared piano. The piece is in six sections of decreasing length (from 2′18″ to

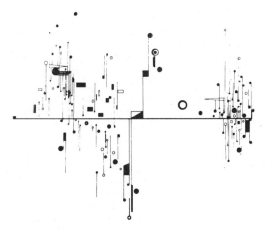

Ex. 25. Roman Haubenstock-Ramati, *Decisions*
Reproduced by permission of Universal Edition and Theodore Presser

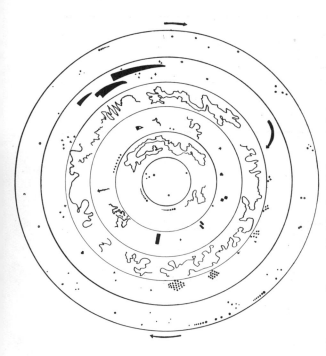

Ex. 26. Edison Denisov, *Chant des oiseaux*, harpsichord part

13″), which correspond to the six concentric bands in the notation. The tape was made entirely from bird sounds, which form an unmodified sound flow at the beginning and end; in sections 2–5 they become more distorted and sometimes, especially in the third section, take the form of dry, punctuated, harpsichordlike sounds. The keyboard player begins in the first band, just under the uppermost arrow. He proceeds around the band until he completes the circle, then drops down to the next band, and so on until he reaches the center. The graphics, according to the composer, signify "different colors," i.e., different registrations on the harpsichord or different kinds of objects inserted in the piano strings. The size of a sign represents "density" of sound. The composer suggests that dry sounds (such as the lute stop on the harpsichord) be used where short cross-marks appear and that clusters be played where there are solid blocks. The graphics further indicate that the keyboard sounds in bands 1 and 6 are to be discrete, highly punctuated points of timbre, whereas those in bands 3 and 5 are to form some kind of continuous flourish. Denisov's notation provides only general directions; the transference to specific sounds is left mostly to the imagination of the performer. As in

Ex. 25, the details of the keyboard part should change from performance to performance.

BIBL.: David Behrman, "What Indeterminate Notation Determines," *Perspectives* 3/2:58–73; Robert Erickson, "Time Relations," *Journal of Music Theory* 7:174–92; Erhard Karkoschka, "Darmstadt hilft der Notation neuer Musik," *Melos* 33:76–85; ——, *Das Schriftbild der Neuen Musik* (Celle 1966); Anestis Logothetis, *Notationen mit graphischen Elementen* (Salzburg 1967); J. M. Perkins, "Note Values, "*Perspectives* 3/2:47–57; Gardner Read, *Music Notation*, 2nd ed. (Boston 1969); Arnold Schoenberg, "Eine neue Zwölfton-Schrift," *Musikblätter des Anbruck* 7/1; Karlheinz Stockhausen, "Musik und Graphik," *Darmstädter Beiträge zur neuen Musik* 3; Kurt Stone, "Problems and Methods of Notation," *Perspectives* 1/2:9–31. *Darmstädter Beiträge zur neuen Musik* 9 is devoted entirely to notation.

Kurt Stone

SEE ALSO Electronic Music: Notation; Indeterminacy; Performance; Prose Music; Rhythm.

Novák, Jan (b. Nová, Říše, Czechoslovakia, 4 April 1921), studied at the Brno Conservatory (1940–46, composition with Vilém Petrželka, piano with František Schäfer), the Prague Academy (1946–47, composition with Pavel Bořkovec), and at Tanglewood (1947, composition with Aaron Copland). He also studied composition privately in New York with Bohuslav Martinů during 1947–48. He was a coach for one year at the Janáček Opera in Brno and also performed in a duo-piano team with his wife. He left Czechoslovakia in 1968 and now teaches piano at the municipal music school in Rovereto, Italy. His music has been affected by his interest in Latin metrics (he has written 2 books of Latin poetry, 1964 and 1966).

PRINCIPAL COMPOSITIONS: *Oboe Concerto* (1952, Supraphon); *Svatební košile* [The Spector's Bride], ballet (1954, Dilia); *Concerto* for 2 pianos, orchestra (1954, ČHF); *Passer Catulli* for bass, 9 instruments (1961, Supraphon); *Dido*, cantata-oratorio for narrator, mezzo-soprano, men's chorus, orchestra (1967) *Ignis pro Ioanne Palach*, cantata for chorus, orchestra; Latin text by the composer (1969, Zanibon); *Concentus Eurydicae* for guitar, string orchestra (1970, Zanibon); *Apicius modulatus*, kitchen recipes for voice, guitar (1970, Zanibon).

SEE ALSO Czechoslovakia.

Novák, Vítězslav (b. Kamenice, Czechoslovakia, 5 Dec 1870; d. Skutec, 18 July 1949), studied in Jindřichův Hradec with Vilém Pojman and at the Prague Conservatory (1889–92; composition with Karel Knittl, Karel Stecker, and Antonín Dvořák; piano with Josef Jiránek). He also studied law and philosophy at the Univ. of Prague (1889–95). He taught composition at the Prague Conservatory during 1909–39, and many of the succeeding generation of Czech composers were his pupils. His early music was in the tradition of Brahms and Dvořák; he quickly adopted a nationalist approach through the study of Moravian and Slovak folk music and the encouragement of Leoš Janáček.

PRINCIPAL COMPOSITIONS: *Piano Trio in G Minor*, Op. 1 (1892, SNKLHU); *Variations on a Theme by Schumann* for piano (1893, Orbis); *Ballad in E Minor* for piano, Op. 2 (1893, František A. Urbánek); *Piano Quartet in C Minor*, Op. 7 (1894, revised 1899; SNKLHU); *Piano Quintet in A Minor*, Op. 12 (1896, revised 1897, SNKLHU; *Songs on Moravian Folk Poetry* for voice, piano, Opp. 16, 17, 21 (1897–98, SNKLHU); *String Quartet in G*, Op. 22 (1899, SHV); *Sonata eroica* for piano, Op. 24 (1900, Orbis); *V Tatrách* [In the Tatras], symphonic poem, Op. 26 (1902, SHV); *Piano Trio in D Minor*, "Quasi una ballata," Op. 27 (1902, SNKLHU); *Slovak Suite* for chamber orchestra, Op. 32 (1903, SNKLHU); *String Quartet in D*, Op. 35 (1905, SNKLHU); *6 Men's Choruses*, Op. 37 (1906, Mojmír Urbánek); *Notturna* for voice, piano, Op. 39; text by German poets (1906–08, Simrock); *Bouře* [The Storm], sea fantasy for vocal soloists, chorus, orchestra, Op. 42; text by Svatopluk Čech (1908–10, UE); *Na domácí půdě* [On Native Soil], 8 choruses for men's chorus, Op. 44 (1911); *Exotikon*, suite for piano, Op. 45 (1911, UE); *Svatební košile* [The Spectre's Bride], ballad for vocal soloists, chorus, orchestra, Op. 48; text by K. J. Erben (1912–13, UE); *Karlštejn*, 3-act opera, Op. 50; libretto by Otakar Fischer (1914–15, UE); *6 Sonatinas* for piano, Op. 54 (1919–20, Orbis); *Lucerna* [The Lantern], 4-act fairy tale, Op. 56; libretto by Hanuš Jelínek (1919–22); *Dědův odkaz* [Grandfather's Legacy], 3-act opera, Op. 57; libretto by Antonín Klášterský (1922–25, piano score published by Hudební matice); *Signorina Gioventu*, ballet pantomime in 7 scenes, Op. 58; scenario after Čech (1926–28, Hudební matice); *Nikotina*, ballet pantomime in 7 scenes, Op. 59; scenario after Čech (1929, Hubební matice); *12 Lullabies* on *Moravian Folk Poetry* for women's chorus, Op. 61 (1931–32, Hudební matice); *Podzimní symfonie* [Autumn Symphony] for chorus, orchestra, Op. 62 (1931–34, Hudební matice); *South Bohemian Suite* for orchestra, Op. 64 (1936–37, Breitkopf); *In memoriam*, 4 songs for mezzo-soprano, string orchestra, harp, tom-tom, Op. 65 (1936–37, Hudební matice); *String Quartet in G*, Op. 66 (1938, Breitkopf); *De profundis*, symphonic poem for organ, orchestra, Op. 67 (1941, Hudební matice); *Cello Sonata*, Op. 68 (1941, SHV); *Svatováclavský triptych* [St. Wenceslaus Triptych] for orchestra, organ, Op. 70 (1941,

Hudební matice); *5 Mixed Choruses*, Op. 71 (1942, Hudební matice); *Májová symfonie* [May Symphony] for vocal soloists, chorus, orchestra, Op. 73 (1943, SHV).

PRINCIPAL WRITINGS: *Studie a vzpomínky* [Studies and Reminiscences] ed. by A. Srba (Prague 1932; supplements 1935, 1940); *O sobě a jiných* [About Myself and Others], 2 vols. (Prague 1946, 1969).

BIBL.: Igor Belza, *V. N.* (Moscow 1957); Alois Hába, *V. N.* (Prague 1940); Václav Holzknecht, *Národní umělec V. N.* [National Artist V. N.] (Prague 1948); Vladimír Lébl, *V. N. Život a dílo* [V. N. His Life and Works] (Prague 1964).

SEE ALSO Czechoslovakia.

Nowak, Lionel (b. Cleveland, 25 Sept 1911), studied at the Cleveland Institute of Music (1929–36, composition with Herbert Elwell, harmony with Roger Sessions, counterpoint with Quincy Porter). He was composer and music director for the Humphrey-Weidman Dancers (1938–42), a teacher at Converse College, S. C. (1942–46), at Syracuse Univ. (1946–48), and at Bennington College since 1948. He has also conducted and toured as a concert pianist. He has been involved in music-education programs at Bennington (summers, 1960, 1962), Yale Univ. (1963), and Manhattanville College. Since the mid-1950s his work has moved "toward the nonacademic serial side."

PRINCIPAL COMPOSITIONS (published by ACA unless otherwise noted): *Square Dances*, dance score for piano; choreography by Doris Humphrey (1938, unpub.); *Danzas mexicanas*, dance score for piano; choreography by José Limón (1939, unpub.); *On My Mother's Side*, dance score for piano; choreography by Charles Weidman (1939, unpub.); *The Green Land*, dance score for piano; choreography by Humphrey (1941, unpub.); *Flickers*, dance score for piano; choreography by Weidman (1942, unpub.); *House Divided*, dance score for piano; choreography by Weidman (1944, unpub.); *Story of Mankind*, dance score for orchestra; choreography by Humphrey (1946, unpub.); *Oboe Sonata* (1949); *Cello Sonata No. 2* (1951); *Diptych* for string quartet (1951, New Valley); *Trio* for clarinet, violin, cello (1951); *Quartet* for oboe, strings (1952); *Sonata* for solo violin (1952, New Music); *Wisdom Exalteth Her Children* for double women's chorus (1952, Bennington); *Trio* for violin, cello, piano (1954); *Fantasia* for piano (1954); *Duo* for viola, piano (1960); *Cello Sonata No. 3* (1960); *Concert Piece* for kettledrums, string orchestra (1961); *Soundscape* for piano (1964).

PRINCIPAL WRITINGS: "Composers on Main Street," a dialogue with Henry Brant, *ACA Bulletin* 12/1:1–8.

SEE ALSO Dance.

Number Systems, see Mathematics, Theory

Nystedt, Knut (b. Oslo, 3 Sept 1915), attended Oslo Conservatory (1931–40; composition with Per Steenberg, Bjarne Brustad; organ with Arild Sandvold). In 1947 he studied composition with Aaron Copland and organ with Ernest White in New York. Since 1946 he has been organist of the Torshov Church in Oslo and since 1950, conductor of the Norske Solistkor, which under his direction has made concert tours through Europe and the U.S. He has taught choral conducting at the Univ. of Oslo since 1964 and was composer-in-residence at Berea College, Ky., in 1968 and Augsburg College, Minn., in 1969.

PRINCIPAL COMPOSITIONS (published by Lyche unless otherwise noted): *String Quartet No. 1*, Op. 1 (1938, unpub.); *Spenningens Land* [The Land of Suspense] for orchestra, Op. 19 (1947); *String Quartet No. 2*, Op. 23 (1948); *Symphony for Strings*, Op. 26 (1950); *Concertino* for clarinet, English horn, strings, Op. 29 (1952); *Brenn-Offeret* [Burnt Sacrifice] for reciter, chorus, orchestra, Op. 36 (1954); *Fantasia Trionfale* for organ, Op. 37 (1955–69); *String Quartet No. 3*, Op. 40 (1956); *The 7 Seals*, visions for orchestra, Op. 46 (1958–60); *Pietà* for organ, Op. 50 (1961); *The Moment* for soprano, celesta, percussion, Op. 52; text by Kathleen Raine (1962, AMP); *De profundis* for chorus, Op. 54 (1964, AMP); *String Quartet No. 4*, Op. 56 (1966, unpub.); *Lucis creator optime* for soloists, chorus, orchestra, Op. 58 (1968, AMP).

BIBL.: Finn Benestad, "K. N. og hans nye storverk *Lucis creator optime*," *Norsk Musikktidsskrift* (March 1970): 1–7; Bjarne Kortsen, *Modern Norwegian Chamber Music* (Haugesund 1965): 96–111; ——, "To nye vokalverk av K. N.," *Norsk Musikktidsskrift* (Oct 1967): 149–52; ——, *Contemporary Norwegian Orchestral Music* (Bergen 1969): 317–33.

SEE ALSO Scandinavia.

Nystroem, Gösta (b. Silvberg, Sweden, 13 Oct 1890; d. Särö, near Gothenberg, 9 August 1966), studied composition with Andreas Hallén and during 1915–16 attended the Royal Academy of Music. He lived in Denmark during 1916–20, where he studied painting. During 1920–32 he lived in Paris and studied with d'Indy, Chevillard, and Sabaneyev. He then returned to Sweden, where he was music critic for *Göteborgs Handels- och Sjöfartstidning* during 1932–47 and curator of the Göteborg Art Society. Nystroem was a pioneer in modern Swedish music. After beginning in a "Nordic romantic" direction (Grieg, Sibelius, etc.), he became influenced during his Parisian period by impressionism, neoclassicism, Les Six, and Stravinsky. He preferred the symphonic medium. His work is characterized by formal balance, clearcut themes, and a delicate use of timbre.

PRINCIPAL COMPOSITIONS: *Concertos Nos. 1–2 for String Orchestra* (1930, 1955; Nordiska); *Symphonies Nos. 1–6*: No. 1, "Sinfonia breve" (1931, Nordiska); No. 2, "Sinfonia espressiva" (1935, Nordiska); No. 3, "Sinfonia del mare" (1948, Nordiska); No. 4, "Sinfonia Shakespeariana" (1952, Eriks); No. 5, "Sinfonia seria" (1963, Suecia); No. 6, "Sinfonia tramontana" (1965, Suecia); incidental music to Shakespeare's *The Tempest* and *The Merchant of Venice* (1934, 1936; Suecia); *Viola Concerto* (1940, Suecia); *Saenger vid havet* [Songs at Sea] for voice, piano (1942, Nordiska); *Sinfonia concertante* for cello, orchestra (1944, Nordiska); *Ungersvennen och de 6 prinsessorna* [The Young Lad and the 6 Princesses], ballet (1950, Suecia); *Violin Concerto* (1954, Suecia); *String Quartet* (1956, Nordiska); *Herr Arnes penningar*, opera (1958, Suecia); *Concerto ricercante* for piano, orchestra (1959, Nordiska).

BIBL.: Peter Louis Christensen, *The Orchestral Works of G. N.* (PhD diss., Univ. of Wash. 1961).

[prepared with the help of Per Olof Lundahl]

SEE ALSO Scandinavia.

O

Obradovií, Aleksandar (b. Bled, Yugoslavia, 22 August 1927), studied at the Belgrade Academy of Music until 1952 (composition with Mihovil Logar). During 1959–60 he studied in London with Lennox Berkeley, and during 1966–67 he worked at the Columbia-Princeton Electronic Music Center in New York. During 1953–54 he taught at the Stanković Graduate School of Music in Belgrade and since 1954, at the Belgrade Academy. His music makes use of polytonal and 12-tone techniques, with emphasis on formal architecture and opulent sound.

PRINCIPAL COMPOSITIONS: *Mala horska svita* [Little Choral Suite] (1948); *Marika* for chorus ·(1948); *Variations* for piano (1949); *Quintet* for flute, clarinet, string trio (1951); *Symphony No. 1* (1952); *Prelude and Fugue* for string orchestra (1954, SKJ); *Plameni vjetar* [Wind of Flame], song cycle for voice, orchestra (1955); *Concerto* for clarinet, string orchestra (1958, UKS); *Scherzo Overture* (1959); *Simfonijski epitaf* [Symphonic Epitaph], cantata for narrator, chorus, orchestra (1959, Prosveta); *Symphony No. 2* (1959–61, UKS); *Kroz svemir* [Through the Universe], symphonic suite (1959–61); *Kolo iz brigade* [Brigade Kolo] for chorus (1961); *Sequoia* for 2 voices, chamber ensemble (1964); *Epitaph H* for orchestra, stereo tape (1965); *Symphony No. 3* ,"Microsymphony," for orchestra, stereo tape (1967, UKS); *Electronic Toccata and Fugue* on tape (1967); *Sutjeska*, cantata for 2 narrators, chorus, orchestra (1968); *Microsonata* for clarinet (1969).

PRINCIPAL WRITINGS: "Verdi i njegova 'Travijata'" [Verdi and "La Traviata"], *Mladost* (March 1947); "O značaju Glinke i njegove opere 'Ivan Susanjin'" [The Significance of Glinka and His Opera "Ivan Susanin"], *Mladost* (May 1947); "Naše radiostanice i domaće muzičko stvaralaštvo" [Our Radio Stations and Our Composition], *Savremeni akordi* 2/4–5; "O posleratnom stvaranju srpskih kompozitora" [Composition in Serbia after the Second World War], *Zvuk* 1957/11–12; "Elektronska muzika" [Electronic Music], *Pro musica* 26; "Elektronski muzički centar u Njujorku" [The Electronic Music Center in New York], *Zvuk* 79 (1967); *Uvod u orkestraciju I–II* [Orchestration, vols. 1–2] (vol. 1, Belgrade 1971); *Elektronska muzika i elektronski instrumenti* [Electronic Music and Electronic Instruments] (unpub.).

BIBL.: Josip Andreis et al., *Historijski razvoj muzičke kulture u Jugoslaviji* [The Historical Development of Musical Culture in Yugoslavia] (Zagreb 1962): 708ff.; Vlastimir Peričić, *Muzički stvaraoci u Srbiji* [Composers in Serbia] (Belgrade 1968):351–56; Dušan Skovran, "Simfoniski epitaf A. O.," *Zvuk* 37–38 (1960); Jasna Šotra, "A. O.: *Epitaf H*," *Zvuk* 67 (1966).

Očenáš, Andrej (b. Selse, Czechoslovakia, 8 Jan 1911), studied at the Bratislava Academy of Music and Drama (composition with Alexander Moyzes, conducting with Jozef Vincourek) and the Master School of the Prague Conservatory (composition with Vítězslav Novák). He worked for the Czech Radio in Bratislava from 1939 and was music program director during 1956–62. He began teaching choral conducting at the conservatory in Bratislava in 1945 and took over the directorship of the institution and a composition class there in 1950.

PRINCIPAL COMPOSITIONS: *3 Songs* for soprano, orchestra (1938); *Suite No. 2* for piano (1938); *Margarita and Besná*, scenic cantata (1939); *At the Brigands' Ball*, ballet pantomime (1941); *Pictures of the Soul* for string quartet (1941); *Legends of the Native Land*, suite for orchestra (1943); *Song of the Green Mountains*, cantata (1943); *The Resurrection*, symphonic trilogy (1946, revised 1953); *To My People*, cycle of symphonic poems (1947); *A Year in the Village*, folksong arrangements (1948); *Cello Concerto* (1952); *A New Spring*, tone pictures for piano (1954); *Youthfulness*, suite for piano (1956); *Ruralia Slovacca*, cycle of symphonic poems (1957); *Marina*, love songs for chorus (1957); *Highland Songs*, ballet (1957); *Piano Concerto* (1959); *Song about the Communist Party in Slovakia* for chorus (1959); *Monuments of Glory*, symphonic tetralogy for tenor, children's and adult choruses, orchestra (1961); *Organ Pastels* (1961); *The Oravian Pastorale*, folksong arrangements (1961); *Concertino* for flute, piano (1961–62); *Concertino rustico* for cimbalom, strings, piano (1963); *As the Stars Are Falling*, cycle for chorus; text by Pavol Koyša (1963–64); *About Life*, cycle for men's chorus; poems by Ján Kostra (1964).

SEE ALSO Czechoslovakia.

Ohana, Maurice (b. Casablanca, 12 June 1915), studied literature and philosophy at the Sorbonne (1932–36) and attended the Schola Cantorum in Paris (1937–40, counterpoint with Daniel Lesur), and the Accadèmia di S. Cecilia in Rome (1944–46, piano with Alfredo Casella). He is mainly self-taught in composition. He is fond of Andalusian and African folk music, and his music for radio and his contact with electronic media have influenced his conception of sound.

PRINCIPAL COMPOSITIONS: *Llanto por Ignacio Sanchez Mejias* for speaker, baritone, chorus, chamber orchestra, harpsichord (1950, Billaudot); *Guitar Concerto* (1950–56, Amphion); *Cantigas* for chorus, 18 instruments (1953, Billaudot); *Etudes chorégraphiques* for 6 percussionists (1955, Schott); *Tombeau de Claude Debussy* for soprano, zither in $\frac{1}{3}$ tones, piano, chamber orchestra (1961, Amphion); *Improvisations* for flute (1960, Billaudot); *Signes* for flute, piano, zither in $\frac{1}{3}$ tones, percussion (1965, Amphion); *Synaxis* for 2 pianos, 4 percussionists, orchestra (1966, Amphion); *Syllabaire pour Phèdre*, chamber opera (1967, Amphion); *Cris* for chorus (1968, Salabert); *Chiffres de clavecin* for harpsichord, orchestra (1968, Salabert); *Silenciaire* for 6 percussionists, strings (1969, Salabert).

PRINCIPAL WRITINGS: "Bartók a nagyvilágban; Bartók és a müvésetek korszerű fejlödése," *ÚJ irás* 5:93–94.

SEE ALSO France.

Olah, Tiberiu (b. Arpasel, Rumania, 2 Jan 1928), studied at the Cluj Conservatory (composition with Eisikovits and Muresianu) and the Tschaikowsky Conservatory in Moscow (composition with Messner). He has taught composition at the Bucharest Conservatory since 1954. His music was influenced first by Stravinsky, Bartók, and the last works of Enescu, then by the Viennese school and the theories of Messiaen.

PRINCIPAL COMPOSITIONS: *Columna infinita* for orchestra (1962); *Cycle Brancusi* for various instrumental and vocal combinations (1962–68, Salabert and Schott); *Translations* for strings (1968, Salabert); *Music* for 13 instruments (1969, Salabert).

PRINCIPAL WRITINGS: A study by Olah of serialism in Webern's music of 1910 was published by the Rumanian periodical *Musica* in 1969.

Oliveira, Willy Corrêa de (b. Recife, Brazil, 11 Feb 1938), studied composition with Olivier Toni until 1961. He was music director and composer for Jotafilmes until 1964; during 1964–68, music and movie director for the

J. Walter Thompson publicity agency and during 1968–71, for the Mauro Salles publicity company. He has taught at the Lavignac Conservatory in Santos (1962), the Escola Superior de Propaganda (1969, information theory and poetics), and the Univ. of São Paulo (since 1969, theory). During 1955–59 his compositions were based on the modality of northeast Brazilian folk music, applied in a polyphonic context that often resulted in chromaticism. He then worked with 12-tone and serial techniques. His present work has been influenced by study with Henri Pousseur.

PRINCIPAL COMPOSITIONS: *Invention* for string trio (1957); *3 Canzonetti* for chorus (1957); *Paixão de Cristo*, cantata for vocal soloist, chorus, strings (1958); *Prelude and Fugue* for orchestra (1960); *Música para Marta* for 10 instruments (1961); *Semi di Zucca* for chorus (1963); *Homage to James Joyce* for narrator, 2 pianos, strings (1965); *Ouviver a música* for piano, chamber string orchestra (1965); *Divertimento* for female announcer, male speaker, string quartet, rock ensemble, orchestra (1967); *5 Kitsch* for piano (1967–68, Ricordi); *Um movimento* for chorus (1968, PAU); *3 Songs* for voice, piano (1969, Ricordi); *Life*, madrigal for chorus (1971, Ricordi).

PRINCIPAL WRITINGS: "Pensando o comunacação" [Thinking Communication], *Revista propaganda* (Jan 1966); "Música-Não Música-Anti Música," interview printed in *O Estado de São Paulo* (22 April 1967); "'Um movimento'," *Revista de vanguardia Invenção* 3.

Oliveros, Pauline (b. Houston, 30 May 1932), went to San Francisco in 1952, studied there with Robert Erickson, and worked as a freelance musician. She was involved with group improvisation from 1957 on and worked at the San Francisco Tape Center (1961–66). Her association with pianist David Tudor and dancer-choreographer Elizabeth Harris, beginning in 1963, reinforced her interest in the manipulation of sounds, musical and non-musical, and in collaborative performance. In 1966 she was appointed director of the Tape Music Center at Mills College, and in 1967 she began teaching electronic music at the Univ. of Calif. at San Diego.

Miss Oliveros wrote her pre-1963 music for conventional instruments using neither serialism nor indeterminacy. This music grew out of the freedom of sound she had gained in group improvisation: "I simply listened until I heard the next sound to write down." Later she explored mixed media, often using dancers, actors, live players, film, lighting, and tape music. Disliking the "visual vacuum" at performances of tape music alone, she began to make use of theatrical material, often improvised. From about 1966 her interest turned to multichannel tape interacting with live situations and theatrical forms. Her works of this type are long, often containing repeated and extended sonorities that are usually gradually altered. A reviewer's description of her pre-1963 pieces applies equally well to these later works: They unfold "without pretention, as a dramatic and unrestrained gesture through simple materials." Many of these works (e.g., *I of IV*) were composed directly on tape in real time (rather than through precomposition processes and synthesis), thus achieving a living musical process rather than a reworking of previously prepared raw materials. She is also concerned with live electronic performance in which electronic sounds or other sounds modified electronically are generated during performance. These sounds are dealt with instrumentally in keeping with her preference for "staying out of the studio and getting onto the stage." Unlike many mixed media composers of the late 1960s, her work shares with several West Coast contemporaries an unpretentious synthesis of diverse sonoric and theatrical elements without sensationalism and blatancy, relying more on a relaxed inventive temperament and a good-humored love of life.

PRINCIPAL COMPOSITIONS: *Sound Patterns* for chorus (1961); *Trio* for flute, piano, page turner (1961); *Pieces of 8* for woodwind octet, tape (1965); *George Washington Slept Here* for amplified violin, tape, projections, film, staging (1965); *I of IV* on tape (1966); *Big Mother Is Watching You* on tape (1966); *Beautiful Soop* on tape (1967); *Night Jar* for viola d'amore, tape, film, mime (1968); *Festival House* for orchestra, chorus, mimes, film, lighting (1968); *To Valerie Solanas and Marilyn Monroe in Recognition of Their Desperation* for orchestra, chorus, electronics, lights (1970); *Meditations on the Points of the Compass* for chorus (1970); *Sonic Meditations*, "for everybody" (1971–).

PRINCIPAL WRITINGS: "Karl Kohn: Concerto Mutabile," *Perspectives* 2/2:87–99; "Some Sound Observations," *Source* 3; "Tape Delay Techniques for Electronic Music," *The Composer* 2; "And Don't Call Them Lady Composers," *New York Times* (13 Sept 1970).

BIBL.: Morton Subotnick, "P. O.: Trio," *Perspectives* 2/1:77–82.

Barney Childs

SEE ALSO Instrumental and Vocal Resources, Mixed Media, Performance, Prose Music.

Open Form, a principle of structure in notated music according to which the sequence and/or makeup of segments at some level of the composition is variable. The principle was applied in some compositions by Charles Ives, Henry Cowell, and Percy Grainger early in the century but did not become widespread until John Cage promulgated the concept of indeterminacy after 1951. Earle Brown's *25 Pages* for 1–25 pianos (1953) seems to have been the first open-form work to stem from Cage.

The following examples indicate the variety of treatment that open-form music has encompassed: Brown's *25 Pages* consists of 25 pages of music that can be arranged in any order. A similar freedom of choice governs the order of sections in Karlheinz Stockhausen's *Klavierstück XI* (1956). The five movements of Pierre Boulez's *Piano Sonata No. 3* (1956–57) may be played in any order except for the third, which must remain at the center; in addition, the order of sections within movements is variable with each choice determining to varying extents the limits of future choices. Some portions of Mauricio Kagel's *Transición II* (1958–59) are notated on moveable disks and staves so that varying pitches and sequences of pitches may result. The sequence of sections in Stockhausen's *Zyklus* for percussionist (1959) forms a closed circle in that the order is predetermined and the performer chooses the point at which he will "enter" the circle and begin playing. Lukas Foss's *Elytres* (1964) and *Fragments of Archilochos* (1965) consist of phrases to be played by orchestral groups in sequences and combinations suggested to the performers by a guide.

In the 1950s some composers began using improvisation involving little or no precise musical notation. By the 60s improvisation was replacing open-form principles in the work of composers concerned with indeterminate performance. Music in this new context is thought of as a performance, and composition (as in jazz), the setting up of conditions in which the performance may occur. The conditions might be communicated graphically, as in Brown's *December 1952* (1952); verbally; partially in musical notation; or with combinations of all three, as in Christian Wolff's music of 1957–64. A culmination is represented by *HPSCHD* (1967–69) of Cage and Lejaren Hiller, a multimedia palette of sound and visual elements, both predetermined and indeterminate.

Opera. From the early 17th century much of the new in music appeared first in opera. This process ceased toward the end of the 19th century, and today opera is no longer at the focal point of contemporary music, neither for the composer nor for the educated musical public. Opera in the late 19th century, particularly in western Europe, was not receptive to new ideas largely because of two factors: 1) Opera had become ensconced in the bourgeois establishment, which increasingly resisted all change. 2) The field was dominated almost completely by Wagner and Verdi, who despite their differences shared a taste for an elaborate production apparatus, large orchestras and choruses, big voices, and the dramatic structure of the "well-made" play. That most turn-of-the-century opera composers and audiences were content to continue along the lines of these two masters is attested by the successful careers of Giacomo Puccini (1858–1924) and Umberto Giordano (1867–1948) in Italy; Jules Massenet (1842–1912), Vincent d'Indy (1851–1931), and Gustave Charpentier (1860–1956) in France; and Engelbert Humperdinck (1854–1921), Hans Pfitzner (1869–1949), and even Richard Strauss (1864–1949) in Germany. Such innovators as Debussy, Scriabin, and Schoenberg did not try out their new ideas first in opera, and later innovators, such as Webern and Varèse (like Scriabin), wrote none. Stravinsky's most radical and innovative work was theatrical, *Le Sacre du printemps,* but a ballet rather than an opera.

In the 19th century dozens of composers, including such major figures as Weber, Wagner, Rossini, and Verdi, earned their living almost entirely from their operas. This situation does not exist today with perhaps two exceptions, Gian-Carlo Menotti (b. 1911) and Benjamin Britten (b. 1913). Nevertheless, almost every major 20th-century figure has written at least one opera, and in the 1969–70 season alone over 80 new works were produced in Europe and the U.S. For many composers opera is still the best short cut toward establishing a reputation. Clearly this goal is more possible in a country such as Germany than in the U.S. Germany has some 70 tax-supported, year-round opera houses committed to the production of new works. Government subsidized radio and television networks share this commitment, and music publishing and recording companies are tied in as well. The U.S. has only a handful of bona fide professional opera companies, support for which is extremely difficult to sustain and must be obtained largely from private sources. Only one, the Metropolitan Opera Co. of New York, has a full season; this house has for years produced only a token number of contemporary works—the majority in the most conservative tradition. Some of the other companies have been more liberal in their attitude towards contemporary works, notably the New York City Opera Co., though generally the stylistic prejudice in favor of musically conservative works is everywhere in evidence. When contemporary works are produced by these other companies, the operas are frequently by non-Americans whose success has already been established elsewhere. By contrast, it is only on the rarest occasion that an American opera (other than Gershwin's *Porgy and Bess* and pieces by Menotti) is mounted in Europe.

LIBRETTOS. There are no patterns governing the relationship between librettos and music. Operas that employ conservative musical techniques may have forward-looking librettos, and vice-versa. In general, however, librettos have become less stereotyped, more adventuresome, and in themselves have attained a greater artistic parity vis-à-vis the music. Though the majority of opera texts continue along the dramaturgical patterns of previous centuries, these have frequently been recast and reworked. The most notable examples are the six librettos written by Hugo von Hofmannsthal (1874–1929) for Strauss. In literary terms all can be characterized as postromantic dramatic pieces, distinguished however by an extraordinary linguistic sensitivity that makes them the finest poetic librettos since those of Metastasio. They deal exclusively with women, and the Marschallin in *Rosenkavalier* is unquestionably one of the greatest characters in opera. Approaching the Hofmannsthal level are the librettos of W. H. Auden and Chester Kallman, of which *The Rake's Progress* (1951)[1] for Igor Stravinsky is the most successful. In it the authors deliberately recreated an 18th-century libretto with a Mozartian musical structure in mind. In part, this format was determined by Stravinsky, who wanted to write a numbers opera and not a music drama. This coincided with Auden's views about music theater as set forth in his many writings on this subject. *Elegy For Young Lovers* (1961) for Hans Werner Henze (b. 1926), although outwardly structured to resemble a numbers opera, functions much as an ordinary drama put together by the use of disjunct scenes. Given the ongoing French interest in librettos of high literary quality, it is no surprise that many major 20th-century French writers have produced works for the lyric theater. Equally typical is the preoccupation with classical antiquity, which the French have been reinterpreting for centuries; hence, Paul

[1] Unless otherwise noted, the dates given in this article are of first performance, not composition.

Claudel's adaptation of Aeschylus' Oresteia trilogy for Darius Milhaud (b. 1892), Paul Valéry's *Amphion* for Arthur Honegger (1892–1955), André Gide's *Persephone* for Stravinsky, as well as the several librettos by Jean Cocteau, notably *Antigone* for Honegger and *Oedipus Rex* for Stravinsky. Further major figures who have written for the musical theater include Gabriele D'Annunzio, who collaborated with Debussy and Ildebrando Pizzetti (1880–1968), and Luigi Pirandello, whose one libretto, *La favola del figlio cambiato,* was written for G. F. Malipiero (b. 1882).

Besides these specially created librettos, there continue to be numerous adaptations of significant literary works, from Japanese Noh plays to the philosophical plays of Heinrich von Kleist, from the novels of Dostoevsky and Tolstoy to the idea plays of Pirandello, from Shakespearian adaptations to the poetic drama of T. S. Eliot and García-Lorca, as well as adaptations of plays by Eugene O'Neill, William Saroyan, Tennessee Williams, and Arthur Miller. Such librettos demonstrate how avidly composers and librettists search for the unusual and provocative. One of the more unusual practices of some 20th-century composers is to take existing plays and transfer them almost verbatim into opera texts, thereby practically eliminating the libretto as such. This began with Debussy's setting of Maurice Maeterlinck's *Pelléas et Mélisande* and includes Strauss's version of Oscar Wilde's *Salome,* Berg's setting of Georg Büchner's *Wozzeck,* Marcel Mihalovici's setting of Samuel Beckett's *Krapp's Last Tape,* and my own verbatim setting of Yeats's *Purgatory.*

Though the didactic theater is an old European tradition reaching back to the middle ages and especially prominent in the 17th century, its association with the musical theater in the 20th century is novel. It is largely associated with texts created by Bertolt Brecht, particularly *Die Dreigroschenoper* (1928) and *Aufstieg und Fall der Stadt Mahagonny* (1930), both with music by Kurt Weill (1900–50). Brecht's superior theatrical technique and especially his insistence on maintaining an esthetic distance between audience and stage (which in his view was achieved most easily in opera), render these pieces immediately accessible and theatrically compelling. Marc Blitzstein (1905–64) is an important Brecht disciple in such works as *The Cradle Will Rock* (1937) and *No For An Answer* (1941), for which he wrote both texts and music.

Characteristically 20th-century theatrical modes—the abstract, the nonlogical, and the theater of the absurd—are also prominently represented in 20th-century librettos. The "absurd" theater is found as early as 1929 in Hindemith's setting of Marcellus Schiffer's sketch *Hin und zurück,* a tiny play in which the action moves forward to a climax and then reverses itself like a film run backwards. The "abstract" appears in Cocteau's words for Stravinsky's *Oedipus Rex* (1927). Translating the original French into Latin, a dead language that no one in a normal audience understands, forces the words to function purely for the sake of their aural values as sounds. The device of using a narrator to explain the story only points up the abstract quality of the piece. The most radically innovative librettos are those written by Gertrude Stein for Virgil Thomson (b. 1896). Words are strung together so that they lose their meaning in any logical sense and retain only their discrete connotations. Stein freely associated words that sound alike for their phonetic qualities as pure sound. Nevertheless these librettos do create a succession of feeling tones that differentiate the separate parts. From Stein it is a simple step to the texts of such quasioperatic works as *Passaggio* of Luciano Berio (b. 1925), in which words themselves are dissected and further broken up so that working theatrically with abstract sounds becomes total and complete.

MUSIC. Six composers stand out for their especially important contributions to 20th-century opera: Debussy, Strauss, Janáček, Schoenberg, Stravinsky, and Berg. In *Pelléas et Mélisande* (1902) Debussy turned away from all familiar 19th-century models, eschewing the grandiloquence of the German orchestra, the overpowering vocalism of the Italians, and the familiar "grandeur" of the French to return to the beginnings of the *dramma per musica* in which the word is predominant. The vocal style is that of French declamation at its most subdued. There are no separate lyrical moments, no arias, and no ensembles. The music, however, supports the play so as to bring out all its theatrical potential. Although quasi-Wagnerian leitmotivs are employed in the orchestra, they are not developed symphonically, nor does the music in any fashion fulfill the norms of tonal expectation. Furthermore the music never dominates except in the interludes covering scene changes; here it frequently refers to past or future action, thus providing a continuity to the series of small cinematographic scenes which make up the play. This same device was employed by other composers, including Berg in *Wozzeck* and Alberto Ginastera (b. 1916) in

Don Rodrigo. Although *Pelléas* remains unique, many echoes of it are heard in the single opera of Béla Bartók (1881–1945), *Duke Bluebeard's Castle* (1918).

With the production of *Salome* (1905) Richard Strauss (1864–1949) established his position as Wagner's successor and Germany's leading opera composer. For a time he belonged to the avant-garde, driving his post-Wagnerian chromaticism almost to its limits. This, however, he usually did only to highlight the more theatrical or the more violent psychological moments; in reality his predilection was for a thoroughly tonal music, securely grounded harmonically, that permitted him to spin out seemingly endless contrapuntal inner voices which do little more than provide internal motion. *Elektra* (1909), his first text by Hofmannsthal, is the apex of his radicalism, from whence he retreated, adapting simultaneously a neo-Mozartian and a neo-Johann Straussian stance in his most successful work, *Der Rosenkavalier* (1911). He underwent virtually no stylistic development thereafter. Strauss's postromanticism did not suit the temper of younger composers growing up in post-World War I Germany, and he had no direct successors. His opulent orchestral sound and the busyness of his part writing is discernable in such near contemporaries as Franz Schreker (1878–1934) and Erich Wolfgang Korngold (1897–1957) and in the work of younger composers in Germany and elsewhere.

In 1904, midway between the premieres of *Pelléas* and *Salome*, occurred the first production of *Její pastorkyně* [Her Stepdaughter], known abroad as *Jenufa*, by Leoš Janáček (1854–1928). This, the composer's third opera, was mounted in Brno, the provincial capital of Moravia, after having been rejected by the National Theater in Prague. So local was Janáček's reputation that *Jenufa* did not reach Prague until 1916 (from whence it went to Vienna in 1918 and Berlin in 1924). After World War II a Janáček revival took place, and today he is considered in Europe to be one of the chief operatic figures of our century. His mature operatic procedures are largely uninfluenced by any models. Basically he worked with small motivic formulas that bear a strong relationship to the speech accents and inflections of his local Czech dialect. His vocal lines have the character of highly stylized speech; he rarely employed folksongs. Harmonically, he moved about freely from a seeming tonality to a quasiatonality, often hovering midway for long stretches in an impressionist atmosphere. His highly unorthodox orchestration, full of instrumental arabesques, repeated figures, ostinatos, and generally rather sparse middle voices, highlights his ceaseless use of motives and constant timbral changes, which at first hearing can create the impression of discontinuity.

The monodrama *Erwartung* by Arnold Schoenberg (1874–1951) was written during this first decade, though not produced until 1924; *Die glückliche Hand* was also produced that year. Both the tonal crisis and the extreme psychological tension in Strauss's *Salome* and *Elektra* were forced on to an even more intense level in the Schoenberg operas. Three complete scenes of *Erwartung* are present in just 124 bars, and the music is surely the most complex written up to that time. It moves forward by means of constant motivic inventions, difficult to relate to each other and with no literal repetitions. Wagner's "unending melody" is still part of the esthetic, though differences between recitative and arioso are clearly discernable. The large orchestra is frequently used in a delicate, chamber-music fashion, as in Mahler. The music in his last (unfinished) opera, *Moses und Aron* (first produced in 1954) is completely 12-tone, and a huge apparatus is employed. The use of choruses is even more important and varied than in Mussorgsky's *Boris Godunov*. The opera's principal conflict, made evident by having Moses use sprechstimme and Aron sing, clearly raises the problem of the ethos view of music.

In the same year that Schoenberg wrote *Erwartung,* Igor Stravinsky (1882–1971) finished the opening act of his first theatrical work, *Le Rossignol* (completed five years later). In addition to this, he wrote two other works unmistakably classifiable as operas (pieces calling on the cooperation of music with both words and action), a one-act buffa *Mavra* (composed 1921) and *The Rake's Progress* (composed 1948–51). All his other vocal stage works separate the singers from the other participants (actors or dancers) or (in *Oedipus Rex* and *Persephone*) give the singers so little movement that the works can well be performed as costumed oratorios. All of the Stravinsky pieces bear his distinctive sonic imprint, resulting chiefly from the disposition of instrumental sound. The smaller works employing unusual instrumental forces have exercised an enormous influence and have been endlessly imitated, frequently with excellent results as in the recent mixed-media pieces by Peter Maxwell Davies (b. 1934) and Alexander Goehr (b. 1932). Various other elements of Stravinsky's manner have been picked up by other composers; Carl Orff (b. 1895), for example, uses obsessive repetitions of simple neomodal materials skillfully orchestrated. In moving away from a theater of pure music toward a more comprehensive theatrical conception, Stravinsky anticipated the present taste for mixed media and "total" theater.

Despite the widespread influence of the second Viennese School among composers, it has never achieved genuine popular acceptance save in the work of Alban Berg (1885–1935), especially his operas *Wozzeck* (1925) and *Lulu* (1937). Though employing first the free atonality and later the serial methods of the Schoenberg circle, Berg's music requires neither the sustained effort needed to follow Schoenberg's contrapuntal textures nor the intense concentration called for by Webern. Berg's music has an immediacy that makes it function dramatically, not to say theatrically. Of equal importance is his concern with tradition and the past. Though he knew full well that both operas were intrinsically revolutionary works of violent social protest, he nevertheless took great pains to fashion them in forms connected with and reminiscent of styles long neglected and almost abandoned. Realizing that these forms and devices were not perceptible in the theater and actually requesting audiences "to forget all theory and musical esthetics," he nevertheless felt it necessary to explain his procedures in public lectures and to call attention to them in the printed scores. From a purely theatrical point of view he differed radically from the other expressionists with whom he is associated. In works such as Ernst Krenek's (b. 1900) *Jonny spielt auf*, one is usually unpleasantly aware of the devices used to manipulate audience reactions. Berg, however, used the most subtle means to involve the audience, including such theatrical devices as controlling and precisely prescribing the timing of the "curtain music." His dramatic instincts led him to adopt a musical plan consisting of closed forms, each a separate entity somewhat in the fashion of 18th-century opera. Here again he showed his independence not only of Schoenberg but of the whole post-Wagnerian German tradition, which at that time still favored loosely constructed, through-composed works.

A number of other composers have also contributed to the course of 20th-century opera; they are discussed here in chronological order according to the production dates of their operas. Both operas by Maurice Ravel (1875–1937), the one-act buffa *L'Heure espagnole* (1911) and the adult fairy-tale *L'Enfant et les sortilèges* (1925) emphasize his independence of Debussy as well as his fundamentally classical bent. The atmosphere of the earlier work is at times impressionistic, though the vocal lines are occasionally quite Straussian. Ravel's classicism is especially evident in the clarity of texture and musical motion, the use of popular Spanish elements, and, in the later work, the witty succession of arias and ensembles. These works have been frequently performed and much imitated by other French composers. Also important to the development of the classic esthetic are the operas of Ferruccio Busoni (1866–1924). *Arlecchino* (1917), his second opera, is probably his best known work, though his unfinished *Doktor Faust*, produced in 1925 as completed by Philip Jarnach, is generally considered his masterpiece and regarded as the most searching musical reinterpretation of the Faust legend in our time.

Unlike France, Germany, and the Slavic countries, opera in Italy has depended principally on popular support. The narrowing of public taste to works in the two traditions of Verdi and Puccini made innovation there especially difficult. Nevertheless a group of younger composers, including Ottorino Respighi (1879–1936), Ildebrando Pizzetti (1880–1968), Gian Francesco Malipiero (b. 1882), and Alfredo Casella (1883–1947) challenged the established musical views. They sought first to reestablish some kind of instrumental tradition, which had all but disappeared, and later to build a new operatic style. Each achieved some local and international success during the 1920s and 30s, but few of their operas survived World War II. The *L'Orfeide* trilogy of Malipiero (1925) makes use of film, pantomime, multiple stages, and a host of other nonconventional theatrical devices. It is in these formal and technical features that interest chiefly lies; the music is basically conventional, employing a free diatonicism with an occasional use of dissonance.

The reputation of Arthur Honegger (1892–1955) as a dramatic composer was established overnight with the performance of his music for the biblical drama *Le Roi David* (1921). Like *L'Histoire du soldat*, this work was conceived originally for a small ensemble with spoken dialogue, dance, and mime, and constructed by juxtaposing tiny musical numbers of all types—solos, choruses, fanfares, marches, dances, etc. Only the concluding piece of each section was more elaborately extended. (The work was later rescored for large forces to become a concert piece.) The musical style belongs to the early neoclassicism of Les Six, tempered by Honegger's typical softness and purposeful simplicity. His most important opera, *Antigone*

(1927), is a through-composed work whose chief musical interest is given over to the orchestra. The voices employ a "melodic line created by the words," avoiding long held tones and extreme tessituras. The orchestral writing is dissonant with prominence given percussion. Though Darius Milhaud (b. 1892) has written more than a dozen operas, only *Le Pauvre Matelot* (1927) is an unqualified popular success. The music is in turn raucous, tender, playful, jazzily mocking, danceable, passionate, and somber, all purveyed by an endless melodic flow. The harmonic language is Milhaud s familiar polytonality, in this instance completely dominated by the melodic lines. The pitifully few performances his other major theater works have had make it almost impossible to assess their theatrical quality. *Les Choéphores* (composed 1916, staged 1935) contains prophetic uses of chorus and percussion: the chorus accompanies the spoken lines of a soloist with vowel sounds, grunts, shouts, squeaks, and only occasionally words. Similar effects are used in *Les Euménides* (composed 1922, concert performance 1927). *Agamemnon* (composed 1913, concert performance 1927) has a single singing role, Clytemnestra, accompanied by a large male chorus. *Christophe Colomb* (1930) employs the most diversified theatrical techniques, including film.

When the earliest operas of Paul Hindemith (1895–1963) were produced, he was in the foreground of Germany's avant-garde. Though he never allied himself with the Schoenberg circle, the free, vigorously chromatic, contrapuntal dissonances, driving rhythmic surge, and aggressive instrumental sound of his early works were easily mistaken as issuing from that esthetic. Actually in most of these pieces a tonal center is always present, though frequently covered up by the moving lines; the intensity and jagged profile were abandoned in later works. *Cardillac* (1926) is one of the earliest and best known revivals of the numbers opera. Each scene is self-contained and functions as a clearly organized musical unit. Though the music of *Mathis der Maler* (1938) has been known since the early 30s because of the popularity of the symphony drawn from the opera, the opera itself did not enter the repertory until after World War II. It does not seem to function altogether satisfactorily, not only because of the large forces required but because the different conflicts are neither clearly nor concisely presented. *The Long Christmas Dinner* (1961) repeats many of the procedures established in *Mathis*, particularly the use of well-known melodies employed as canti firmi in a quasichoral prelude manner. Its basic simplicity and tenderness and its extensive use of dramatic ensembles makes it a first-rate theater piece.

As with most Soviet music, only a few operas have penetrated the west, principally those by Sergei Prokofiev (1891–1953) and Dmitri Shostakovich (b. 1906). Prokofiev's first successes were *Love for 3 Oranges* (1921) and *The Fiery Angel* (1928). The former is brittle, satirical, witty, and detached, the latter markedly neoromantic. *Betrothal in a Monastery* (1947), known abroad as *The Duenna,* is completely tonal, diatonic, and simplified to the bone. The slight spice provided by Prokofiev's use of "wrong notes" remains. Less stageworthy, chiefly because of the scale of its subject matter, is his dramatization of Tolstoy's *War and Peace* (1955). It is a basically old-fashioned Russian opera with huge choral sections, battle scenes, and large ensembles. Shostakovich's first opera, *The Nose* (1930) was composed when the atmosphere in the Soviet Union was genuinely liberal. The absurd theatrical situation is depicted by one of the most ingenuous scores he has produced. In its tautness and wit it refers to Prokofiev's *Love for 3 Oranges*, though Shostakovich's music is more highly developmental and not nearly so fragmented. The orchestration is so effective it almost detracts from what is happening on stage. His second opera, *Lady Macbeth of Mtsensk,* was premiered in 1943 and later withdrawn on official orders. Shostakovich revised it during 1961–62 and retitled it *Katarina Ismailova*. The music, though basically tonal and far simpler than *The Nose,* is frequently brutal, lusty, and full of rhythmic energy. There are many discrete vocal numbers, but equally long sections weave the voice into an orchestral web. The musical material of each scene is developed symphonically. The interludes between scenes usually characterize the action and continue to develop material just heard. As in most Russian operas, great prominence is given choral scenes.

The early operas of Kurt Weill (1900–50), *Der Protagonist* (1926) and *Der Zar lässt sich photographiern*, and the ballet-opera *Royal Palace* (1927) belong to the music produced around the Schoenberg circle, despite the jazz interpolations and Spanish dance rhythms they contain. In 1927, after he began to collaborate with Bertolt Brecht, he abandoned his previous manner and tried to reconcile socially significant plays and "popular" music. Their first joint effort was the short singspiel *Mahagonny,* in which Weill set five poems from

Brecht's *Hauspostille*. This was to become the basis for the full-length *Mahagonny* of 1930, replete with ensembles and a difficult orchestral score. Their *Dreigroschenoper* (1928), an adaptation of the Gay-Pepusch opera first seen in London in 1728, consists of a succession of songs, deliberately simple, primitively harmonized, making use of only the most elemental dance rhythms, with the vocal parts well within the competence of normally musical actors. The orchestration is for small dance band. Throughout, one senses the hand of a theatrical craftsman. When Weill was forced to leave Germany, he emigrated to the U.S. and turned to the Broadway musical, to which he contributed such scores as *Knickerbocker Holiday*, *Lost in the Stars*, *Street Scene*, and *Lady in the Dark*. His only U.S. opera, *Down in the Valley*, was designed for student production. The career of Marc Blitzstein (who made an excellent English version of *The Three-Penny Opera*) parallels that of Weill; he too began with a theater of social consciousness and ended (less successfully) on Broadway.

After about 1935 artistic life in Europe slowed down and finally came to a near halt, but since 1945 the production of new operas has again proceeded vigorously. Many pieces written before 1945 have been reexamined and produced. The center of activity is again Germany, though the number of significant new composers and works from there is not as large as before. In fact, the first and most successful postwar opera composer is British, Benjamin Britten (b. 1913), and the widespread acceptance of his operas has made English a viable language for serious opera for the first time since Purcell's day. His musical style is predominantly tonal. There are frequent echoes of French impressionism, Stravinsky, and much Mahler, but the overall result is highly personal. It is based on triadic harmony (with myriads of cascading arpeggios), clear contrapuntal lines, and skillful orchestration. The arpeggios recur in every work and are used for the most diverse dramatic reason—from the storm music in *Peter Grimes* (1945) to the ghost music in *Turn of the Screw* (1954). Britten is especially fond of the harp, alto flute, bass clarinet, and above all the horn; these sounds immediately identify his orchestration. Fugal procedures crop up whenever he wants to be pompous, funny, or peculiarly English. His setting of English derives in part from his study of Purcell and in part from his long association with the tenor Peter Pears, his greatest and most constant interpreter. There are frequent verbal distortions and misplaced accents, but these are done deliberately by a master who knows what he is about. The subject most frequently found is the figure of the lonely or innocent person who is wronged. Another Englishman, Michael Tippett (b. 1905), has written three large operas, *The Midsummer Marriage* (1955), *King Priam* (1962), and *The Knot Garden* (1970). Each has highly complex librettos and somewhat inaccessible musical styles, neither of which promotes an immediate public response. Other English opera composers include Humphery Searle (b. 1915), Richard Rodney Bennett (b. 1936), Iain Hamilton (b. 1922), Alexander Goehr (b. 1932), and Nicholas Maw (b. 1935).

Somewhat paralleling Britten's success is the career of Hans Werner Henze (b. 1926), which was launched in 1949 with *Das Wundertheater*. Many of his works emit a hot-house type of distant intellectualism, which is difficult to reconcile with his recent political activity. His musical style stems from the new postwar serialism, and his dramatic subjects lead him to embrace expressionist techniques, including long chromatic lines. As in the work of all competent present-day composers, Henze's scoring is thoroughly expert. Other German opera composers, all older than Henze, include Wolfgang Fortner (b. 1907), Boris Blacher (b. 1903), Rolf Liebermann (b. 1910), Werner Egk (b. 1901), Giselher Klebe (b. 1925), and Bernd Alois Zimmermann (1918–70). Closely related to these is the Swede, Karl-Birger Blomdahl (1916–68), the Czech Jan Cikker (b. 1911), and the Yugoslav Milko Kelemen (b. 1924).

In France, only one composer besides Milhaud seems to have produced significant operas since World War II, Francis Poulenc (1899–1963). In Italy Luigi Dallapiccola (b. 1904) has carried forward the progressive aims of Malipiero and his associates. His work introduced serialism into Italy and gave it a personal flavor, undoubtedly emanating from Italian lyricism. Both *Volo di Notte* (not serial) and *Il Prigionero* have been widely and successfully produced. Luigi Nono (b. 1924) was originally identified with the 12-tone school. His one opera, *Intolleranza* (1960), has a contradictory mixture of styles and devices that does not make as clear an impression as his earlier, purely musical pieces. Other recent Italian opera composers include Riccardo Malipiero (b. 1914), Bruno Maderna (b. 1920), and Luciano Berio (b. 1925). Such avant-garde techniques as improvisation have been used by the Argentine Alberto Ginastera (b. 1916) and the Pole Krzysztof Penderecki (b. 1933), but the overall effect of their operas seems old-fashioned or at least less contemporary than Stravinsky's works of the early 20s—or even *Pierrot lunaire*.

U.S. OPERA. American opera has developed late and is generally removed from developments elsewhere. In other countries, tax-supported opera houses promote native talent not only at home but in foreign centers, where acclaim for a local product cannot help but impress the government officials who control the local budget. A subtle international network develops under these conditions (I'll produce your composers this year if you produce mine next year) from which the U.S. is excluded. Furthermore, lacking full tax support, American operatic life operates on popular support, which means that 1) as a rule only the safest operas are produced, and 2) the "best" house-filling personalities—singers, conductors, stage directors, and composers—must be used. In the case of singers, the application of these principles results in low production standards, since the most famous are always on the move and have only minimum rehearsal time to spend locally. It also means that local artists are underrated and overlooked, since they lack the drawing powers of the international stars. Hence American singers must go to Europe (where good singers are in short supply) to establish a reputation. Whatever the problems singers experience, American conductors and composers have considerably greater ones.

In addition to the few major opera companies, there are numerous smaller organizations, usually centered around a local orchestra. They normally have a small professional staff, do few productions, mostly import guest singers for the leading roles, and rarely mount fully integrated productions. Even more rarely do their repertoires venture beyond Puccini, and when they do their selection is not made on the basis of artistic challenge but with an eye for minimum musical demands and maximum (easy) accessibility. Most of these groups do not materially aid the development of opera in the U.S. There are also many opera workshops attached to educational institutions. Some, such as the American Opera Center at Juilliard and the Opera Department at the Univ. of Ind., have elaborate professional facilities. The majority of the others operate with limited means. Many were founded in the late 1930s and 40s by refugees from Hitler's Europe, who discovered that the small number of established groups in the U.S. could not absorb them. For a time it was believed that these workshops would become the spawning

ground for a genuine U.S. operatic tradition, and in the late 40s and 50s practically every composer in America tried to write an opera. Though these workshops continue to train good singers (mostly for nonexistent jobs), they have not as a rule encouraged new works, nor produced many, nor advanced the cause of U.S. opera in any significant way.

Considering the phenomenal increase in the number of American composers since 1950, it appears that the percentage writing opera is considerably smaller than it was 20 years ago. Only one American work has a secure place in the international repertory, *Porgy and Bess* (1935) by George Gershwin (1898–1937). Long produced as a musical, it is today considered *the* American folk opera. Five other Americans produced significant works prior to World War II: Louis Gruenberg (1884–1964), Douglas Moore (1893–1969), Virgil Thomson (b. 1896), Marc Blitzstein (1905–64), and Gian Carlo Menotti (b. 1911).

Thomson employed a unique, artificially simple, highly sophisticated style in his operas. The music uses triadic (but hardly functional) harmonies, irrationally but wittily juxtaposed scale passages, and melodic snips underlying vocal lines marked by the most polished English prosody since Purcell. Meyer Kupferman (b. 1926) also made a fine Gertrude Stein setting in his *In a Garden* (1949). Gruenberg's *The Emperor Jones* (1933) was successful both in the U.S. and abroad but failed to stay in the repertory. He was one of the first Americans to employ jazz in concert works. His operatic style is related to that of the Viennese expressionists without, however, being genuinely atonal. Moore's *The Devil and Daniel Webster* (1939) is the prototype of a whole series of American operas that still continues to appear. All share three distinguishing features: 1) their subject matter is American, drawn from history, folklore, or the life of a specific region or ethnic group; 2) their dramaturgy is usually straightforward; 3) their musical language is tonal and conservative, however different or personal the separate styles may be. In addition to other works by Moore, including his greatest success, *The Ballad of Baby Doe* (1956), the operas belonging to this category include: *The Mighty Casey* (1953) by William Schuman (b. 1910), *Hello Out There* (composed 1953), *Lizzie Bordon* (composed 1965), and *My Heart's in the Highlands* (composed 1969) by Jack Beeson (b. 1921), *The Tender Land* (1954) by Aaron Copland (b. 1900), *The Jumping Frog of Calavaras County* (1955) by Lukas Foss (b. 1922), *Susanna* (1955) by Carlisle Floyd (b.

1926), *The Crucible* (1956) by Robert Ward (b. 1917), *Mourning Becomes Electra* (commissioned 1961) by Marvin David Levy (b. 1932), and *Colonel Jonathan* (1971) by Dominick Argento (b. 1927). A traditional approach to dramaturgy and music is also characteristic of *The Ruby* (1955) and *The Trial at Rouen* (1956) by Norman Dello Joio (b. 1913), *The Wife of Martin Guerre* (1956) by William Bergsma (b. 1921), *The Scarf* (1958) by Lee Hoiby (b. 1926), *Vanessa* (1958) and *Antony and Cleopatra* (1966) by Samuel Barber (b. 1910), *Miss Julie* (composed 1964–65) by Ned Rorem (b. 1923), and the operas of Menotti. Although Leonard Bernstein (b. 1918) has written no full-scale operas, he has been a major force in the musical. His scores for *Candide* (1956) and *West Side Story* (1957) are musically highly challenging. His theatrical style owes much to the influence of Marc Blitzstein.

A few Americans have produced operas since World War II that do not belong in the above categories. These include: *The Trial of Lucullus* (1947) and *Montezuma* (1964) by Roger Sessions (b. 1896), *6 Characters in Search of an Author* (1959), *Athalia* (1964), and *9 Rivers from Jordan* (1968) by the present writer (b. 1912), *The Good Soldier Schweik* (1957) by Robert Kurka (1922–57), *The Alcestiade* (1962) by Louise Talma (b. 1906), and *The Visitation* (1966) by Gunther Schuller (b. 1925).

CONCLUSIONS. Despite the fact that opera is no longer at the center of contemporary music, practically every major 20th-century composer has tackled the genre at least once and a considerable number of masterpieces have been created in this century. The stylistic pluralism of our time is nowhere more apparent than in opera, and because of its theatricality it—together with films, dance, multimedia, etc.—remains a potentially effective vehicle for the dissemination of still other new musical procedures and techniques. By and large, opera is moving away from being primarily a musical experience toward some kind of total theater, a movement paralleled by the rise of multimedia. As for the future, it is clear that experimentation must continue and that new ideas must be explored in all areas, including television, which has been timorously conventional, and film, which has been strangely ignored. There are only two limitations, money and imagination. If the first is in short supply, the second can function for both; the reverse, however, is not true.

Hugo Weisgall

SEE ALSO Italy, and other articles on individual countries.

Orbón, Julián (de Soto) (b. Avilés, Spain, 7 August 1925), received his elementary music instruction in Spain at the Oviedo Conservatory (1935). He emigrated to Cuba with his father and studied piano with him during 1940–43 and harmony and counterpoint with José Ardevol. In 1946 he studied with Aaron Copland at Tanglewood. During 1946–60 he was director of the Orbón Conservatory in Havana, and during 1960–63 he taught in the composition workshop of the National Conservatory of Mexico. He now lives in New York. His music has been influenced by a wide range of musical and literary interests, including his friendship with Carlos Chávez and Heitor Villa-Lobos.

PRINCIPAL COMPOSITIONS: *Toccata* for piano (1942, Instituto Interamericano de Musicologia); *Homenaje a la tonadilla*, divertimento on themes by 18th-century Spanish composers for orchestra (1946, Southern); *Suite de canciones de Juan del Encina* for chorus (1947); *Preludio y danza* for guitar (1950, Colombo); *String Quartet* (1951, Southern); *3 Versiones sinfónicas* for orchestra (1953, Southern); *Himnus ad galli cantum* for soprano, flute, oboe, clarinet, string quartet, harp (1955, Broude-B); *Danzas sinfónicas* for orchestra (1956, Southern); *Concerto grosso* for string quartet, orchestra (1957–58, Boosey); *3 Cantigas del Rey* for soprano, string quartet, harpsichord (1960, Colombo); *Monte Gelboé* for tenor, orchestra (1962, revised 1964; Southern); *Partita No. 1* for harpsichord (1963, Southern); *Partita No. 2* for harpsichord, chamber ensemble (1963, Southern); *Partita No. 3* for orchestra (1965–66, Presser); *Introito* for chorus, orchestra (1967–68). List to 1960: *Composers of the Americas* 6:85–87.

PRINCIPAL WRITINGS: "Tradición y originalidad en la música hispanoamericana," *Revista del Conservatorio Nacional de México* (1962); "Dialogo con J. O.," *Exilio* (New York) 1969/2:5–13.

BIBL.: Alejo Carpentier, *La música en Cuba* (Mexico City 1946):259–62; Aaron Copland, *Copland on Music* (New York 1960); José Lezama Lima, "J. O.," *Tratados en La Habana* (Havana 1958):367–72.

Orchestration, also spoken of as "scoring," is the process of choosing the tone qualities to which each note in a piece of music is assigned for purposes of performance. It particularly deals with the simultaneous combination of contrasted and/or complementary timbres. (The terms *timbre*, *tone quality*, and *sonority* tend to be used synonymously by musicians.) Use of the term *orchestration* is generally limited to instrumental music, ordinarily with a minimum of two instruments. Live performance is assumed.

STANDARDIZED PERFORMING GROUPS. The symphony orchestra comprises a flute family (3–4 players), oboe family (3–4 players), clarinet family (3–4 players), bassoon family (3–4 players), French horns (4–8), trumpets (3–4), trombones (3–4), tubas (1–2), percussionists (4–5), violins (18–30), violas (6–12), double basses (4–10), harps (1–2) and keyboard players (1–2). This instrumentation was fixed by 1900 and is still standard throughout the world wherever concert music in the Western tradition is performed.

The "capsule symphony," or "little orchestra," enjoyed a vogue during the period of permanent radio orchestras in America (c.1930–55). The usual makeup was 1 flute, 1 oboe, 2 clarinets, 1 bassoon, 2 horns, 2 trumpets, 1 trombone, 1 percussionist, 1 pianist, 6–10 violins, 2–4 violas, 2–4 cellos, and 1–2 basses. The combination balances well, is capable of considerable variety of effect, and was often a point of departure for the makeup of theater orchestras and even of concert groups.

The small string orchestra is used principally for the performance of baroque music; its instrumentation is approximately 6 violins, 2 violas, 2 cellos, 1 double bass, and 1 keyboard player.

The chamber orchestra, while not standardized, is generally based on a one-of-each scheme, such as 1 flute, 1 oboe, 1 clarinet, 1 bassoon, 1 horn, 1 trumpet, 1 trombone, 1 piano, 1 percussionist, 1–2 violins, 1 viola, 1 cello, 1 double bass. This plan is the basis of instrumentation in much contemporary music and is sometimes the nucleus of pit orchestras in theaters.

The wind ensemble has a complete symphonic instrumentation but with the string section omitted.

The band contains an indeterminate number of piccolos, clarinets, trumpets, trombones, tubas, baritone horns, and percussion instruments. Any other standard wind instrument may be included, the number varying with each ensemble.

The jazz combo is made up of soloists, from 3 to about 7, of whom one is a pianist, percussionist, or bass player. The other primary instruments are clarinet, saxophone, trumpet and trombone.

The "big band" jazz ensemble consists of 4–5 saxophones (the players all doubling on clarinets), 3–4 trumpets, 2–4 trombones, 1 guitar, 1 double bass, 1 piano and 1 percussionist (the latter 4 known as the "rhythm section"). This kind of ensemble performs written-down jazz arrangements (derived from figurations characteristic of jazz improvisation). During the 1930s and 40s jazz-symphonic ensembles of 30–45 players were formed, principally for radio performance and for recording, the repertory being limited to arrangements of current popular material. These groups contained a saxophone section, a rhythm section, all the trumpet and trombone mutes associated with jazz playing, and always a number of musicians capable of improvising authentic jazz. There was also a string section, as well as representatives of all the normal symphonic woodwinds, brass, and percussion, plus harp.

The "rock" band includes 1–2 amplified guitars, 1 amplified bass, 1 electronic organ, 1 (often unamplified) percussionist, and frequently 1 or more solo voices or instruments, usually amplified or electronic.

ROLE OF THE ORCHESTRATOR. In most cases the composer of the music is also its orchestrator, and his plan of work usually involves one of the following procedures: 1) In a first draft he develops his musical material with respect to pitches, rhythms, modes of articulation, and dynamics, but without planning the choice of tone qualities. If the composer works at the piano (a common practice, especially prior to 1960), this first draft often consists of textures that a pianist's two hands can substantially encompass. In a second stage of work, the composer devotes himself entirely to the choice of timbres and timbre combinations. They may involve the transformation of "piano idiom" into orchestral idiom and the addition of material beyond that which the pianist's hands can manage (either new textures or, more commonly, octave duplications of pitches already present in the first draft). 2) Alternatively, the composer begins by devising a complete and detailed scheme of orchestral events (successions of timbral combinations) without inventing any specific melodic, rhythmic, or contrapuntal material. He then creates the actual musical ideas in terms of pitch and rhythm, keeping in mind the limitations imposed by the predetermined sonority scheme. This method, in placing emphasis on the direct creation of orchestral idioms, reduces the likelihood of "pianistic" textures (except in cases where keyboard idiom is essential to the musical style or to the timbral scheme). 3) The composer invents his musical material and conceives of its orchestral setting simultaneously.

On occasion the composer and the orchestrator may be two different people. This comes about when 1) a composer becomes interested in the orchestral possibilities of a nonorchestral work (an example is Schoenberg's orchestration of J. S. Bach's organ music); 2) a composer wishes to provide an alternative orchestral setting of a work by another composer which already exists in an original orchestral form (examples are Mozart's addition of new woodwind parts to Handel's oratorios and Rimsky-Korsakov's reorchestrations of Mussorgsky's operas); 3) a professional orchestrator assists a composer who is working against a deadline. In the last case, since many pages of full orchestral score must be produced in a limited time, the usual plan is for the composer to draft his musical material in compressed, unorchestrated form and then explain his orchestral scheme to the orchestrator, who, after making detailed notes, performs the actual task of writing out the score. The amount of orchestral detail left to the discretion of the orchestrator varies with each working arrangement, but the overall procedure outlined has been customary in the orchestration of Hollywood film music and Broadway musicals.

PRACTICES CARRIED OVER INTO THE 20TH CENTURY FROM PAST PERIODS. For the most part the orchestral customs and practices of the last 250 years still persist today; 20th-century orchestral changes and additions tend to be peripheral rather than fundamental, and almost all are still based on live performance. (The timbral combinations provided by computers, synthesizers, and other electronic devices require a new code of orchestration procedure, which has not yet been systematically formulated.) The principal categories of orchestration requiring live performers are the following:

Interchangeable orchestration, in which more than one scheme is provided for in the assignment of tone qualities, was common during the renaissance. Families of instruments (of the same kind) in graduated sizes and ranges were assumed (a family of viols, or recorders, or double-reeds, or trombones, etc.), and the music was playable by whichever family might be available; in some cases a group of voices was a possible alternative. Among 20th-century adaptations of this principle is the "cross-cuing" system in band music: many instrumental alternatives for individual parts are given, usually without regard for precise results in combination, and the overall result is frequently unbalanced, unclear, and nondescript in sonority (a score prepared in this way is also known as a *stock orchestration*). A more sophisticated application is the "free-form" approach of the 1960s, occasionally found in music for assorted chamber ensembles. Entire passages or textures of musical material, each for one or more instruments, may be added to the piece at the discretion of the conductor or performer, either vertically by superimposition or horizontally in a designated sequence. The reverse procedure, subtraction, may also be provided for. In both cases the timbral amalgam is not always specifically predictable in detail;

Homogeneous orchestration aims at a single, fused, overall timbre in textures that are usually homophonic. The contributions of individual participating tone qualities do not emerge separately but blend into a composite sonority amalgam. The operation known as *doubling* is frequently used; it involves the combining of two or more tone qualities at the unison, the octave, the "empty" double octave (a pair of notes two octaves apart with the middle octave-note missing), or the "filled-in" double octave (a pair of notes two octaves apart with the middle octave-note included— three notes in all). In large ensembles these doubling devices may serve to 1) provide opportunities for using the many available instruments even when the number of desired harmonic pitches is small; 2) provide additional weight or "thickness" of timbre, sometimes termed *functional doubling* (an example is 2–3 bassoons doubling, at the unison, a unison section of 10 cellos); 3) create new timbres by the unison amalgamation of congenial and/or complementary tone qualities, sometimes termed *expressive doublings* (an example is the unison of flute, bassoon, and clarinet). It must not be assumed that all instrumental timbres will mix or fuse, either at the unison or in harmony. For example, a violin and an unmuted trumpet will not fuse at the unison; both timbres will be heard separately. (The list of mixing and nonmixing tone qualities is long, intricate, and full of contradictions, and often only trial-and-error experimentation will teach the composer how to orchestrate with precision and control.) Another essential factor in homogeneous orchestration is *balance*. This means, first, that any timbre designated in the score is distinguishable by the ear; second, that a controlled proportion of degrees of prominence can be established in performance between the various tone qualities in use at any given moment. (Again, the study of which instruments will balance together and which will not is complex; only an exact knowledge of the smallest details involved can produce clear orchestral textures.) The methods and aims of homogeneous orchestration determined the orchestral practices of most composers in the late 18th century and in all of the 19th. They have persisted into the 20th but, in their application to dissonant harmonic textures, have resulted in unprecedented new sonorities; the scores of Debussy, Stravinsky, Milhaud, Hindemith, Shostakovich, Prokofiev, and Vaughan Williams come quickly to mind.

Polyphonic orchestration is applied principally to polyphonic music and involves assigning each linear constituent to its own distinctive tone quality so that musical contrasts already present in the polyphony are emphasized by contrasts in timbre. Characteristically, each line is assigned either to a single instrument only or to a unison of instruments of the same kind (the Bach choral works furnish many examples). True polyphonic scoring for large ensemble combinations was rare in the 19th century; exceptional instances can be found in Berlioz and Tchaikovsky. Composers in the latter part of the 19th century and into the 20th more commonly orchestrated their polyphony via the homogeneous orchestration method; Mahler symphonies and Strauss tone poems are examples. The effect of such procedure is to draw attention to the vertical, or harmonic, aspects of the polyphony at the expense of the horizontal, line-against-line contrasts. The 20th-century applications of this concept are discussed below under "Practices characteristic of the 20th-century."

Antiphonal or *spatial orchestration* adds the effects of spatial separation and distance to both homogeneous and polyphonic orchestration by dividing the performing forces into widely separated groups placed in the audience area as well as on stage. Multispatial, multiposition techniques were intrinsic to Venetian antiphonal music of around 1600, Giovanni Gabrieli being the key personality. The orchestral techniques of spatial antiphony went into a decline during the baroque, and from the early classical period only isolated examples have come down to us, such as Mozart's *Serenade* for four orchestras, K. 286. (The *echo* device is a primary ingredient in all the antiphonal music mentioned thus far.) Perhaps the only example of true spatial music in the 19th century is the "Tuba mirum" in Berlioz's *Requiem*, which is outstanding for the explicit precision of its spatial plan, the absence of echo technique, and the use of spatial antiphony to produce a harmonic rather than a polyphonic amalgam. Apparently, the next examples of antiphonal-spatial music occur in the 20th century: Charles Ives's *Unanswered Question* (1906) offers, possibly for the first time, a polyphonic organization of

spaces. There are independent texture continuities, each with its own pitch, rhythm, and timbre scheme, each texture assigned to a different physical locality in the hall. Such principles govern all of the spatial music of the present author (beginning in 1950) and apply substantially to some works of Karlheinz Stockhausen, such as *Gruppen* and *Carré* (1955–57, 1959–60). The spatial music discussed thus far assumes wide, maximal distances between participating groups, and spatial arrangement as an essential rather than optional factor in the music. A markedly different result is obtained in some works of Pierre Boulez and Iannis Xenakis, where large instrumental forces are positioned in a complex, unconventional manner but pressed into a concentrated space. A still different (and less pronounced) spatial effect obtains in some works of Elliott Carter, Bruno Maderna, Gunther Schuller, and Betsy Jolas; these use a "chamber-orchestra" polyphonic technique and spatial separations of instrumental groups but confine all the performing forces to the stage area. (It should be added that recordings of spatial music, when the playback system is limited to two channels, cannot give a realistic approximation of a composer's intentions unless the original plan is limited to two sound sources only.)

Spatial-motion orchestration is a familiar concept to anyone who has observed an outdoor street-band on parade or witnessed a choral procession in church. The device is occasionally encountered in the opera theater as an exit or entrance effect involving singers, though rarely instrumentalists. It is still undeveloped as a technique for concert-room music. There have been some small-group works in recent years in which musicians move short distances on stage while playing; these have usually been within the context of a theater event (and generally with inconclusive results for the listener). The present author has described experiments made to determine the principal limitations, possibilities, and ramifications involved when live performers move in indoor spaces.[1] The concept will probably find viable, practical solutions only when concert rooms are redesigned with wide passageways, ramps, and stages extending through every area of the sounding space, vertical as well as horizontal.

PRACTICES CHARACTERISTIC OF THE 20TH CENTURY. In general the 20th century has

[1] "Space as an Essential Aspect of Musical Composition," *Contemporary Composers on Contemporary Music* ed. by B. Childs and E. Schwartz (New York 1967): 223–42.

relied much more on the polyphonic orchestral method than did the 19th. Composers from Schoenberg, Berg, and Bartók up through the more recent work of Ligeti and Xenakis have achieved some of their most distinctive orchestral results through the exploration of new ways of orchestrating rhythmically complex polyphonic textures by the polyphonic handling of timbres. The *chamber-orchestra polyphonic method* is also a characteristic feature of 20th-century music. Examples can be found among all the composers mentioned thus far. Perhaps the most distinctive exploitation of the concept is the improvising jazz ensemble, which in its most characteristic form uses no written-down material whatever (though continuity plans can have a significant role in the textures developed). In some recent jazz all mechanical, repetitive, or symmetrical figurations formerly associated with the rhythm section are dispensed with, rhythmic noncoordination is introduced, and at times a totally uncompromising small-orchestra polyphony is achieved.

The vertical spacing of textures, together with the pitch ranges used, accounts for much of the characteristic sound of 20th-century orchestral music (quite aside from the choice or treatment of timbres). Prior to 1900 it was customary to 1) confine the main action of all orchestral music to a 5 1/2-octave middle range; 2) space all the notes in the vertical texture approximately the same distance apart with slightly wider spaces at the bottom; and 3) avoid, except in rare cases, the lowest and highest octave ranges heard by themselves; combinations of extreme high and extreme low with the middle range empty were almost unknown. In the 20th century 1) the total orchestral range has been extended a full 7 1/2-octave range and even more; 2) extreme highs and lows alone, and combinations of extreme high and low with no middle range have become common; and 3) irregular and complex vertical spacings are common, in which large vertical gaps in range may coexist with a bunching together of notes elsewhere in the texture.

A unique 20th-century development is what may be termed *heterogeneous orchestration*. The opposite of homogeneous orchestration, it deliberately superimposes contrasted and unrelated textures over the same octave range and in the same physical stage space with little or no regard either for timbral or dynamic balance or for preserving the identity of each texture, whether harmonic or contrapuntal. The intention is to produce a complex general impression. Ives's *The 4th of July* and the

scherzo movement from his *Fourth Symphony* contain many impressive passages of this kind. A distinction must be made between this kind of planned orchestral confusion and another concept of orchestration, very detailed in its indications of dynamic levels, which is sometimes encountered on the chamber-orchestra level. Implicit in these examples of prescribed dynamics is the assumption that every instrument can produce all the gradations *ppp* to *fff* on any note in its range and that every instrument can be made audible irrespective of the simultaneous dynamic levels of the other participating instruments. Both assumptions are, of course, contrary to actual possibility in unamplified live sound; consequently, in music orchestrated from this point of view the printed page may frequently indicate textural details which cannot reach the ear in performance.

Instant orchestration, or orchestration via planned improvisation, has been attempted in recent years with both large and small instrumental groups, vocal groups, and mixed groups. Considerable precision and control can be achieved, even without detailed written-down notation. After an explanatory and try-out session, brief verbal jottings for the performers, supplemented by visual signals and cues from the conductor, serve as reminders of ranges, tone qualities, dynamic schemes, general linear and rhythmic configurations, and sequences of events. Both noncoordinated rhythm and accompanied solos work with a natural ease in such arrangements, and coordinated rhythm is also possible. Much less practical is the predetermination of precise pitches, which tends to be time consuming and cumbersome in rehearsal and of doubtful unifying or identifying effect in performance.

As to the introduction of new live timbres into 20th-century orchestration, no instruments have become full-fledged members of the standard Western ensembles that were not already established there in the early years of the century. (Exceptions are found in jazz ensembles, which traditionally include both saxophones and the free and inventive use of many different trumpet and trombone mutes; even these, however, have not been carried over into symphonic groups, except as visitors.) What has taken place are the following: 1) Whereas Western orchestral organization had a rigidly exclusive makeup before 1900, any nonstandard instrument, singly or in small groups, is now freely admitted to the symphony orchestra as a temporary guest when required for a particular work. These guests may be in any category, from any culture or period of history, live, amplified, or electronic. 2) Keyboard instruments, while not yet permanent members of the orchestra, are now considered normal orchestral instruments, not just solo instruments. The combinatorial potentialities of the piano in this regard have been explored by such composers as Bartók, Stravinsky, and Shostakovich. The celesta often figures in combinations, the harpsichord occasionally, and the pipe organ much less frequently. 3) The percussion section now has access to an increased variety of definite-pitched instruments, although the number of players (3–5) remains at the 1900 norm. Pedal kettledrums are available in a variety of sizes with a total range of two octaves or more. The marimba-xylophone family covers a range of not less than five octaves, and the "bell quartet" of glockenspiel, chimes, vibraphone, and celesta is standard symphonic equipment. 4) The 20th-century orchestra has acquired some distinctive new sonorities by combining keyboard instruments and/or pitched percussion with strings and winds. String glissandos (bowed and plucked), string harmonics, and string *col legno* (using the wooden part of the bow) have contributed new timbres, particularly through discoveries by Debussy, Schoenberg, Bartók, and Stravinsky in combining these effects with woodwind, percussion, and keyboard timbres. However, they all represent additions to, rather than transformations of, the symphonic timbral vocabulary. Neither is the introduction of an unusual instrument or group of instruments a substantial new departure; the use of alto and bass flutes, oboe d'amore and baritone oboe, saxophones, or flugelhorns contributes only modifications of well-established patterns of tone quality. The idea of radically changing the fundamental timbre vocabulary of a large Western symphonic ensemble is still new; beginnings have been made by Varèse, Milhaud, Stravinsky, and George Antheil in writing for large groups of percussion with strings and winds omitted, and by George Crumb and myself in replacing some of the normal symphonic instrumental sections by nonstandard instruments.

JAZZ ORCHESTRATION. Since a saxophone group was always present in the big bands of the 1930s and 40s, it was possible to systematize many combinations involving saxophones, clarinets, trumpets, and trombones, the latter two being used both open and with a variety of mutes. The exploitation of timbral affinities between the four slightly improvising members of the rhythm section (chordal guitar, plucked bass, mid-range piano, and

percussion of indefinite pitch) also belongs to this period. In the large jazz-symphonic ensembles of this time, improvising was kept at a bare minimum and actual jazz ingredients were few, but full opportunities were provided for exploring every imaginable mixture between the tone qualities peculiar to jazz and those characteristic of symphonic writing. It would be fair to say that symphonic timbres produced the dominant sonority of such ensembles, and it is now fairly well agreed that authentic-sounding jazz cannot be extracted from a large string section or from groups of flutes, oboes, bassoons, or French horns. The most practicable way of combining the jazz and contemporary concert styles appears to be in concerto-grosso fashion, pitting a smaller real-jazz group against a larger orchestra playing nonjazz material. This procedure is found in works by Teo Macero and Rolf Liebermann.

ORCHESTRATION PLANNED SPECIFICALLY FOR RECORDING. During 1935–65 there was a continuous production of film scores in Hollywood, many of which were orchestrated for medium-to-large symphonic groups. Since this music was intended for optimum results on the sound track and not for live performance, the film studios established permanent recording installations with full-time technicians and highly sophisticated equipment. Intricate recording procedures were devised to permit artificial balances, for example a single, quiet low flute dominating a large brass section playing at full volume. Through an elaborate multimicrophone technique, unusual subtlety was developed in the precise articulation of specific timbral and textural detail, in the handling of echo and reverberation, and in giving the illusion of distance or "presence." The resourceful exploitation of such recording techniques reaches a highpoint in the film scores of Alex North. Aside from film music, the only other orchestral music ordinarily planned with recording techniques in mind is commercial background music for broadcast advertising on radio and television, and special arrangements of popular material distributed via disc. In these genres both small and medium-size combinations are common, and an unusual instrumentation is often chosen to exploit a particular recorded texture or device. Concert music designed primarily for recording is rare, probably because the expense of experimenting with each new recording setup makes the venture uneconomic except where a large volume of recording can be undertaken, as in the building of a large commercial-music

library. In another sense, all electronic composition in which actual live performance is not a
factor in the final result may be properly
considered concert music specifically planned
for recording; its designation as "orchestral"
or "chamber" would depend on the number of
musically independent participating channels
involved.

ORCHESTRATION INVOLVING MIXTURES OF
NORMALLY PRODUCED, AMPLIFIED, AND ELEC-
TRONICALLY PRODUCED SOUND. Considerable
experimentation is being undertaken with
these combinations, both in concert music and
theater music. When a live timbre is amplified
or if its timbre is electronically changed while
the musician is playing, both the original sound
coming directly from the instrument and its
amplified or altered form proceeding from a
loudspeaker can sometimes be heard simultaneously. The result is a kind of unison double
sound. Even if the original live tone quality is
inaudible and only the amplified or altered
timbre is heard, a comparison between the
unaltered-live and the amplified-live tone will
reveal the following differences: 1) In the
amplified or altered sound, a noticeable
proportion of the player's personal nuance in
dynamics and articulation is minimized or
neutralized. 2) The live sound diffuses itself
immediately in all directions; the amplified or
altered sound, if proceeding from the normal
single-direction speaker, is driven forward in a
compact blast. This may be tested by standing
behind the live player and walking around him,
then repeating this procedure with the loudspeaker. (The propane-flame speaker, now
under development, promises a solution to the
problem of achieving a wider, more lifelike
sound diffusion via speakers.) 3) When the
oboe, to take one example, plays, the standardized body of the instrument (plus the
reed) acts as its own "playback unit," retaining a considerable stability of projection
and quality under almost any acoustical circumstance. On the other hand, when amplified
instruments, fully electronic instruments or
conventional magnetic tapes are heard, the
sound arrives via amplifier and speaker,
neither one of fixed prescribed design or size,
and both subject to on-the-spot variations in
dial control in respect to frequency proportion
and decibel amount. These observations
indicate the kind of difficulties encountered in
trying to match or mix live with amplified,
altered, or fully electronic timbres. To date
only a few experiments have been undertaken
in amplifying or electrically altering the
timbres of a large number of live instruments
simultaneously (each instrument having its

own microphone connection). It is not possible
to predict that the simultaneous performance
of a number of different live instruments, all of
them with electronic alteration of their timbres,
will necessarily result in a satisfactory blend.
The timbral raw material involved is still the
original sound of each instrument and is still
subject to many of its original vagaries. Also,
the electronic changes will not affect all the
participating timbres in the same way (and for
reasons of musical variety it may not be
desirable that they should). Each combination
must therefore be tried and tested, as in
traditional types of orchestration.

In dealing with fully electronic performing
instruments, the timbral raw material common
to all is the electronically generated tone,
which tends to persist no matter how much
altered or transformed, and the risk is thus not
that of inadequate fusion of timbres but rather
that of insufficient variety of separate timbres
available for combination. The practical
course is to seek combinations involving the
most contrasted timbres available. One further
point concerns the combination of fully
electronic performing instruments with unaltered, unamplified live tone qualities. The
following are the operative factors to consider: 1) The closer an electronic timbre is
to the original oscillator tone (which has no
overtones), the more difficult will be its blend
with a live instrument such as the violin (every
note of which possesses its own complex set of
overtones, each sounding at a different
dynamic level). 2) Electronic instruments on
which vibrato is manually controllable (as on
the electronic cello) will mix with a live vibrato
much more closely than will electronic instruments having a built-in vibrato that is regular
and mechanical. 3) An electronic instrument
such as the ondes Martenot may possess one
speaker which includes a built-in gong,
another over which tuned strings are stretched;
its production of tone will obviously be more
composite, more diffused, more like that of a
live instrument than the direct blast coming
from an electronic instrument which uses only
electronically generated sound and projects
only through conventional single-direction
speakers. (Large groups of electronic performing instruments have not been assembled
to date; trios and quartets are occasionally
met with in commercial music, much less often
in the concert hall.)

Since the average number of recording
channels in electronic works is 3–8, the
orchestration aspects of electronic composition
via synthesizer are somewhat equivalent to
scoring chamber music. Around 1960 com-

posers of electronic music began the practice of taking a single instrument, such as the bassoon, and giving it specific musical material to be played normally. The composer would then record this material and subject it to electronic transformation to produce a variety of different tone qualities. These constituted the actual musical raw material out of which linear continuities with new pitch and rhythmic configurations were produced. It was evidently taken for granted that since all the sounds, however contrasted, originated in the live bassoon, all were automatically combinable. In more recent electronic music, in which all sounds originate in a synthesizer, the same misconception often persists, i.e., that all sounds originating in the same source will automatically combine when heard simultaneously. There exists as yet no canon of practice (comparable to Rimsky-Korsakov's *Principles of Orchestration*) indicating which sonorities in the electronic medium can be combined and balanced and which not. A musician's working classification of electronic timbres based on the detailed impressions made by their actual sounds (in terms analogous to the familiar categories of "openness," "nasality," "fullness," and "thinness") rather than on their mechanical or functional components ("envelope," "voltage," "decay," "trigger," etc.) still remains to be made.

Henry Brant

SEE ALSO Asian Music and Western Composition; Electronic Music: History and Development; Electronic Music: Notation; Instrumental and Vocal Resources; Jazz; Notation; Performance; Texture.

Orff, Carl (b. Munich, 10 July 1895), studied at the Akademie der Tonkunst in Munich and was active during 1915–19 as kapellmeister in Munich, Mannheim, and Darmstadt. He moved back to Munich in 1920, where he composed, taught, and studied early music, particularly that of the 16th century. The arrangements he made of works by Monteverdi (*Orfeo, Ballo dell' Ingrate, Lamento d'Ariana*) and the staged productions of Passions by Bach and Schütz that he conducted as director of the Munich Bachverein were influential on the development of his own theatrical style.

In 1924 Orff and Dorothee Günther founded the Günther School for gymnastics, dance, and music. Orff taught there and experimented with techniques of music education that emphasize a combination of music and movement. In collaboration with the piano maker

Karl Maendler he developed easy-to-play percussion instruments for use at the school and later used more sophisticated forms of these instruments in his concert works. Another result of his experiments was the *Schulwerk*, the first edition of which was prepared 1930–35 (it was revised 1950–54). The Günther School was disbanded in 1943, after which Orff remained in Munich, composing and teaching. He also held master classes in composition at the Hochschule für Musik there (1950–66).

In his early years Orff wrote many songs, cantatas, operas, theater scores, and orchestral and chamber works. After the first performance of his dramatic cantata *Carmina Burana* in 1937, he withdrew most of his early works and began to write exclusively for the theater. As it turned out, his style was definitely formed in *Carmina Burana*. Modifications of this style occurred in later works, in keeping with different subject matter, but no fundamental changes were made; nor did other stylistic currents in music have any effect. In 1943 and 1950 Orff wrote two other dramatic cantatas, *Catulli Carmina* and *Trionfo di Afrodite*, which, with the earlier work, form a stylistic and spiritual trilogy. After *Der Mond* (1937–38) and *Die Kluge* (1941–42), for which Orff wrote the librettos from fairy tales, he turned to dramas of antiquity. He set Sophocles' *Antigonae* (1947–48), using the German translation by Hölderlin; ten years later *Oedipus* (1958) followed, also in the Hölderlin version. In 1968 he completed *Prometheus*, which is based on Aeschylus's tragedy and uses the original Greek.

Orff has aimed toward a type of theater in which word, sound, scenic design, and movement are unified. Consequently it is not possible to judge his work solely against musical criteria. His melodies, for instance, grow from the text and are not an entity unto themselves. In the Greek tragedies recitation occurs for long stretches with only a sparse melodic movement that follows natural-speech inflections. Not until a dramatic climax occurs does the melody become more agitated, rising finally in ecstatic melismas. Rhythm in the voice parts is determined by the natural speech rhythms of the text. The instrumental accompaniments generally consist of terse motives based on dance rhythms, the motives being juxtaposed and grouped into large ostinato blocks. Climaxes are achieved through the repetition of these units. Ostinato blocks are an important structural feature in Orff, especially since traditional harmonic development may not be present. Most of Orff's scores call for a large orchestra, not for purposes of massive effects but rather to allow for widely differing tone colors. The entire orchestral force is used only for dramatic climaxes. As with rhythm, the sound textures may be organized into a series of static blocks that are important structurally. Intensity is altered by means of changes in the number of instruments in use rather than by means of changes in volume per se.

Orff has been influential chiefly as a teacher of young people. His *Schulwerk* is used in many countries, and its concepts have helped alter many traditional ideas of music education. Although Orff is an outstanding and successful composer, his work has remained outside the general course of 20th-century music history. Except for the fact that he has provided a musical-theatrical alternative to opera, he will probably have little effect on succeeding generations of composers.

PRINCIPAL STAGE WORKS (published by Schott): *Carmina Burana* (1935–36); *Der Mond* (1937–38); *Die Kluge* (1941–42); *Catulli Carmina* (1943); *Die Bernauerin* (1944–45); *Astutuli* (1945–46); *Antigonae* (1947–48); *Trionfo di Afrodite* (1950–51); *Oedipus, der Tyrann* (1958); *Prometheus* (1968). Complete list, 1912–55: Liess (see bibl.).

BIBL.: F. Etienne and P. Vanderschaeghe, *C. O.* (Handzame 1957); I. Kiekert, *Die musikalische Form in den Werken C. O.s* (Regensburg 1957); U. Klement, *Vom Wesen des Alten in den Bühnenwerken C. O.s* (Leipzig 1958); A. Liess, *C. O., Idee und Werk* (Zurich 1955); K. H. Ruppel, *C. O., ein Bericht in Wort und Bild* (Mainz 1955).

Ingeborg Shatz-Kiekert
(trans. from German by Jeanne Wolf)

SEE ALSO Austria and Germany, Education for the Nonprofessional, Instrumental and Vocal Resources, Melody.

Orgad, Ben Zion (b. Gelsenkirchen, Germany, 21 August 1926), studied violin privately with P. Kinari (1935–41) and R. Bergman (1941–47) and theory and composition with Paul Ben-Haim (1940–46). He attended the Israel Conservatory in Jerusalem (1946–47, composition with Josef Tal), Tanglewood (1949, 1952, 1961; composition with Aaron Copland), and Brandeis Univ. (1960–61; composition with Irving Fine, Harold Shapiro; musicology with Kenneth Levy). Since 1950 he has been supervisor of music education for the Israeli Ministry of Education and Culture. He describes the main influence on his music as "the life of the Jewish people."

PRINCIPAL COMPOSITIONS (published by IMI unless otherwise noted): *Ballade* for violin (1947,

Mercury); *Leave Out My Name* for mezzo-soprano, flute (1947, Mercury); *Hatzui Israel*, symphony for baritone, orchestra (1949–58); *The Story of the Spies*, biblical cantata (1950, Mercury); *O Lord, Our Lord*, motet for men's chorus (1951, IMI); *Isaiah's Vision*, biblical cantata (1952, Mercury); *Out of the Dust* for mezzo-soprano, string quartet (1955–56); *Monologue* for viola (1957, IMP); *Building a King's Stage* for orchestra (1957); *Music* for horn, orchestra (1959, IMP); *2 Preludes in an Impressionistic Mood* for piano (1961); *7 Variations on C* for piano (1961, IMP); *String Trio* (1961); *Tak'sim* for harp (1962, IMP); *Kaleidoscope* for orchestra (1965, unpub.); *Mizmorim*, cantata (1966); *Songs of an Early Morning* for mezzo-soprano, baritone, chamber orchestra; text by Amir Gilboa (1968); *First Watch* for string orchestra (1969, unpub.); *Melodic Dialogues on 3 Scrolls* for violin, oboe, percussion, string quartet, string orchestra (1969, unpub.); *Songs Without Words* for flute, clarinet, violin, cello, piano, percussion (1970, unpub.).

SEE ALSO Israel.

Oriental Music, see Asian Music and Western Composition, Japan

Ornstein, Leo (b. Krementchug, Russia, 2 Dec 1892), received his first piano lessons from his father, a cantor. About 1900 he entered the Imperial Conservatory in St. Petersburg and, while a student, coached singers at the Royal Opera. He emigrated to the U.S. in 1907, where he studied piano with Bertha Fiering-Tapper at the Institute of Musical Art in New York and attended Friends' Seminary. After his debut recital in New York in 1911 he concertized throughout North America, appearing with such orchestras as the New York Symphony, the Boston Symphony, and the Philadelphia Orchestra. In 1913 he concertized in Europe and lectured at the Sorbonne and Oxford Univ. Returning to the U.S. in early 1915, he gave a series of concerts in New York in which he introduced his own works, as well as those of Debussy, Ravel, Schoenberg, and Scriabin. He helped organize the League of Composers in 1923 and served on its board. About 1935 he ceased public performance in order to devote his time to compostion and teaching. He became head of the piano department of the Zeckwer Hahn School in Philadelphia. He subsequently established the Ornstein School of Music there, where he taught until his retirement about 1955. He also taught some courses at Temple Univ. Ornstein began to compose about 1913 and his early works, according to Henry Cowell (see bibl.) "startled the world with his unheard-of discords and his renunciations of form." As his wife has observed, his music is not restricted to any one style. "Some writing is almost as simple as folk music, although employing unusual intervals and scale lines. Other pieces are more atonal and more complex in structure than anything yet written. Most harmonies tend to be new and rhythms are frequently contrapuntal. There is a strong melodic content and structural form in everything, even the most controversial material, a mixture of clearly defined keys or tonalities with less anchored episodes."

PRINCIPAL COMPOSITIONS (most dates approximate): *Dwarf Suite* for piano (1912, Schott); *Wild Men's Dance* for piano (1912, Schott); *Impressions of Notre Dame and of the Tamise* for piano (1912, Schott); *3 Moods* for piano (1913); *Cello Sonata* (c.1916, Fischer); *Impressions of Chinatown* for piano (or orchestra) (1917, AMP); *Poems of 1917*, 10 pieces for piano (1917, Fischer); *Violin Sonata* (c.1917, Fischer); *Rhapsody* for cello, piano (c.1920); *Piano Sonata* (c.1920, Schirmer-G); *3 Russian Choruses* (1921, Fischer); *Piano Concerto* (premiere 1925); *Hebraic Fantasy* for violin, piano; written and performed in celebration of Albert Einstein's 50th birthday (1929); *Lysistrata Suite* for orchestra; incidental music for Norman Bel Geddes' production of the play (1933); *5 Songs* for voice, orchestra (piano); texts by Waldo Frank (1935); *6 Water Colors* for piano (c.1935, Fischer); *Nocturne and Dance of the Fates* for orchestra (1936); *String Quartet*, Op. 99 (c.1940); *Suicide in an Airplane* for piano (c.1940); *Nocturne* for clarinet, piano (c.1952, E-V); *Ballade* for saxophone, piano (c.1953); *20 Waltzes* for piano (1955-68); *Intermezzo* for flute, piano (1958); *Prelude and Allegro* for flute, piano (c.1958); *Tarantella* for piano (1958); *Prelude and Minuet in Antique Style* for flute, clarinet (c.1960). ★Undated compositions: *Piano Quintet*; *6 Preludes* for cello, piano; 6 volumes of children's solos and duets for piano (E-V, Schirmer-G).

BIBL.: Ch. L. Buchanan, "O. and Modern Music," *Musical Quarterly* (April 1918):174–183; Henry Cowell, *American Composers on American Music* (Stanford, Calif., 1933); Frederick Martins, *L. O.: The Man, His Ideas, His Work* (New York 1918); Paul Rosenfeld, *Musical Chronicle* (New York, 1923):220–27; ——, "Charles Martin Loeffler, L. O., Dane Rudhyar," *An Hour with American Music* (Philadelphia 1929):52–78.

SEE ALSO Dance.

Orrego-Salas, Juan (Antonio) (Santiago, Chile, 18 Jan 1919), studied composition privately as a youth with Humberto Allende and Domingo Santa Cruz. He received a baccalaureate in arts and letters (1938) and the degree *professor extraordinario* (1953) from the Univ. of Chile and also a professional degree in architecture (1943). Under Rockefeller and Guggenheim Fellowships (1944–46), he studied with Paul Henry Lang (Columbia Univ.), Randall Thompson (Princeton Univ.), and Aaron Copland (Tanglewood). He received a second Guggenheim Fellowship (1954–55) for independent study in the U.S. He was editor of the *Revista musical chilena* during 1949–61, after which he became director of the Latin American Music Center at Indiana Univ.

Orrego-Salas's output is divided about equally among vocal, chamber, and orchestral media. The vocal works, most of which employ Spanish texts, are significant since they clearly, although sparingly, reveal traits of Hispanic traditional and art music, such as flamencolike melodic arabesques and a vacillation between 3/4 and 6/8 meters. The instrumental solo and chamber works are cast mostly in baroque and classic forms. They are highly individualistic since a wide variety of media is represented and the melodic content is idiomatic to the instruments involved. The works for orchestra are generally more experimental in form and orchestration than the vocal or chamber pieces.

Melody in the early works was predominantly vocal in orientation. The influence of Falla and, in some compositions, Hindemith can be seen in those melodies in which lyricism is derived from smooth contours and rhythmic fluidity. With the loosening of the tonal regimen, melody became more instrumental in character, and irregular rhythmic groupings were more frequent. Twelve-tone melodies also appeared, but strict dodecaphonic principles were not applied. An additive procedure, in which melodic fragments are elongated in successive repetitions, is characteristic of later works. In the area of harmony, triadic structures and functional tonal relationships in the early works gave way to added-tone structures, quartal chords, clusters, and atonal relationships. Regular metrical sections were superceded by multimetric sections, such as might be found in Stravinsky, and sometimes by sections in free meter. Formally, procedures of thematic development and motivic recurrence were replaced by sections of freely varied motivic fragments and passage work, all of which depend largely on unusual orchestration for their effect. In essence, the later compositions have greater thematic unity and formal variety than the earlier ones.

PRINCIPAL COMPOSITIONS (published by Peer unless otherwise noted): *Cantata de Navidad* for soprano, chamber orchestra, Op. 13 (1945); *Canciones castellanas* for soprano, chamber orchestra, Op. 21 (1947, Barry); *Symphonies Nos. 1-4*, Opp. 26, 39, 50, 59 (1949, 1955, 1961, 1966); *El retablo del rey pobre*, opera-oratorio, Op. 27 (1949-52, IEM); *Piano Concerto*, Op. 28 (1950); *Concierto de cámara* for chamber orchestra, Op. 34 (1952); *Serenata concertante* for orchestra, Op. 40 (1955); *Duos concertante* for cello, piano, Op. 41 (1955); *String Quartet No. 1*, Op. 46 (1957); *El saltimbanqui*, ballet, Op. 48 (1959); *Concerto a 3* for violin, cello, piano, orchestra, Op. 52 (1962); *Sonata a 4* for flute, oboe, harpsichord, string bass, Op. 55 (1964); *Cantata* for soprano, baritone, men's chorus, orchestra, Op. 57 (1966); *Piano Sonata*, Op. 60 (1967); *Missa in tempore discordiae* for tenor, chorus, orchestra, Op. 64 (1969). List to 1962: *Composers of the Americas* 1:51-59.

PRINCIPAL WRITINGS: "The Young Generation of Latin American Composers. Backgrounds and Perspectives," *Inter-American Music Bulletin* 38:1-10; "Heitor Villa-Lobos: Man, Work, Style," *Inter-American Music Bulletin* 52:1-36; "An Opera in Latin America: *Don Rodrigo* by Ginastera," *Artes Hispanicas* 1/1:94-133.

John E. Druesedow, Jr.

SEE ALSO Chile.

Oscillator, see Generator

Otte, Hans (b. Plaven, Germany, 3 Dec 1926), studied at the conservatories of Weimar (1946-47) and Stuttgart (1948-50), at Yale Univ. (1950-51), composition with Paul Hindemith), and with Walter Gieseking in his master piano classes in Saarbrucken (1953-55). He has been music director of Radio Bremen since 1959.

PRINCIPAL COMPOSITIONS: *dromenon* for 3 pianos (1956-58); *tropismen* for piano (1959, UE); *tasso concetti* for female singer, flute, piano, percussion (1960, UE); *daidalos* for 2 pianos, 2 percussionists, guitar, harp (1961, UE); *ensemble* for strings (1962, Peters); *interplay* for 2 pianists (1963); *modell—eine probe aufs exempel*, music theater for female singer, male singer, 2 pianists (1963-65); *alpha-omega*, music theater for 2 dancers, 12 men's voices, 2 percussionists, organist (1964-65, Peters); *touches* for organ (1965); *passages* for piano, orchestra (1965); *nolimetangere*, music theater for actress, pianist, film, tape (1966-67); *buch für klavier* (1967); *buch für orchester* (1967); *comme il faut*, music theater for 4 actresses, projections, loudspeaker (1968-69); *live*, music theater for pianist (1969); *valeurs* for winds (1969); *nature morte—still leben*, film (1969).

PRINCIPAL WRITINGS: "Der Komponist und sein Modell," *Melos* 37/4:140-42.

SEE ALSO Austria and Germany.

Overton, Hall (Franklin) (b. Bangor, Mich., 23 Feb 1920; d. New York, 24 Nov 1972), studied at Aquinas College in Grand Rapids, Mich. (1938-40), the Chicago Musical College (1940-42, counterpoint with Gustave Dunkelberger), the Juilliard School (1948-50, composition with Vincent Persichetti), and the Aspen Summer School (1953, composition with Darius Milhaud). He also studied composition in New York in 1951 with Wallingford Riegger. He taught at the New School for Social Research in New York (1962-66) and at Juilliard (1960-72). During 1967-69 he was president of the American Composers Alliance. His music was influenced by his work from the late 1940s as a jazz pianist and arranger.

PRINCIPAL COMPOSITIONS: *The Enchanted Pear Tree*, 4-scene chamber opera; libretto by John Thompson after Boccaccio's *Decameron* (1949, CFE); *String Quartets Nos 1-3* (1950, CFE; 1954, Highgate; 1966, CFE); *Symphonic Movement* (1950, CFE); *3 Elizabethan Songs* for soprano, piano; texts by Ben Jonson (1953, CFE); *Symphony for Strings* (1955, Peters); *String Trio* (1957, CFE); *Polarities* for piano (1959, Lawson); *Viola Sonata* (1960, CFE); *Cello Sonata* (1960, CFE); *Symphony No. 2* (1962, Peters); *Pietro's Petard*, chamber opera for 2 sopranos, 2 tenors, 2 baritones, piano; libretto by Robert De Maria (1963); *Dialogue* for chamber orchestra (1963, CFE); *Sonorities* for orchestra (1964, MJQ).

BIBL.: David Cohen, "The Music of H. O.," *ACA Bulletin* (Dec 1962):8-12; Wilfred Mellers, *Music in a New-Found Land* (New York 1965):229-34.

Owen, Harold (John) (b. Los Angeles, 13 Dec 1931), studied at the Univ. of Southern Calif. (1953-57; composition with Ingolf Dahl, Halsey Stevens, and Ernest Kanitz). During 1959-60 he was composer-in-residence in Wichita, Kan., as part of the Ford Foundation-MENC Young Composer's Project. He was a vocalist and performer on renaissance instruments with the John Biggs Consort in Los Angeles during 1961-66 and has taught at the Univ. of Southern Calif. (1961-66) and the Univ. of Ore. (since 1966).

PRINCIPAL COMPOSITIONS: *Sonata* for 2 pianos (1954); *12 Concert Etudes* for clarinet (1955-63, Avant); *Clarinet Quintet* (1956); *Piano Concerto* (1956); *Chamber Music* for 4 clarinets (1960, Avant); *Metropolitan Bus Cantata* for chorus, piano 4-hands (1960, Avant); *Ouverture dans le style français* for organ (1964, Avant); *Sextet* for piano, woodwind quintet (1964); *Variation-suite* for orchestra (1964); *O Gracious God*, anthem for chorus (1965, Presser); *Canticle of the Sun* for vocal soloists, chorus, organ; text by Francis of Assisi (1966, CMP); *String Quartet* (1966).

P

Pablo, Luis de (b. Bilbao, Spain, 28 Jan 1930), earned a law degree from Madrid Univ. in 1952 and worked for Iberian Airlines during 1956–60. He received his first musical instruction as a child and audited harmony and counterpoint classes at the Madrid Conservatory (1953–55). After 1952 his encounters with Max Deutsch in Paris and Messiaen, Stockhausen, Boulez, and Ligeti at the Darmstadt summer courses redirected his musical thinking. He became involved in Spanish music life, until then hostile to the avant-garde, by founding the performance groups Tiempo y Música (1959) and Alea (1965), by taking over the direction of the Juventudes Musicales in 1960, and by arranging the first Biennial of New Music (Madrid 1964). Since 1960 he has been a free-lance composer.

Pablo's early works followed those of Falla and Bartók. He withdrew these and designated his first 12-tone piece, *Coral* (1953), as his Op. 1. During 1953–59 the influence of the Boulez circle predominated: in *Comentarios* (1956) he abandoned the serial determination of pitches, durations, and dynamics in favor of group-composition processes in which musical events consist not of individual tones but of groups of tones having a predominant characteristic (e.g., long durations, loudness) or incorporating a predominant process (e.g., increasing durations, increasing volume). This approach opened the door to aleatory processes, which first appeared in *Movil 1* (1957–58). Between 1959 and 1963 he worked with texture as a form-establishing element comparable to functional harmony in older music. In *Polar* for chamber ensemble (1961) he constructed textural developments by contrasting pointillistic structures and lines; in *Tombeau* (1962–63) he applied the same procedure to large orchestra. Simultaneously his music became more and more separated from the decorative character of many productions of the Boulez circle and took on aggressive, occasionally violent characteristics. From 1964 to 1968 he turned again to open forms: in the *Modulos* series he created five compositions in which either the overall form is established and the invention of details is left to the interpreters or the details are formulated and the interpreters assemble them according to given performance rules. Finding that he had been partly sacrificing the composer's responsibility over the musical material, he turned again to fully determined music. In *Heterogéneo* (1967–68) and *Quasi una fantasia* (1969), however, he began combining stylistically contradictory materials, "the fertilization of everything with everything, the complete and permanent interbreeding through all times and cultures." He has also begun using visual and theater elements in his music. Most recently he has been working in the medium of tape music and has founded a group for the improvisation of live electronic music.

PRINCIPAL COMPOSITIONS: *Coral* for woodwinds (1953); *Comentarios* for soprano, piccolo, vibraphone, double bass; text by Gerardo Diego (1956); *Movil 1* for 2 pianos (1957–58, Tonos); *Polar* for chamber ensemble (1961, Tonos); *Tombeau* for orchestra (1962–63, Tonos); *Modulos 1* for chamber ensemble (1965, Tonos); *Ejercicio* for string quartet (1965, Tonos; revised 1967 as *Modulos 4*, Salabert); *Iniciativas* for orchestra (1966, Tonos); *Modulos 2* for 2 chamber orchestras (1966, Tonos); *Modulos 3* for chamber orchestra (1967, Salabert); *Modulos 5* for organ (1967, Salabert); *Imaginario 2* for orchestra (1967, Salabert); *Heterogéneo* for Hammond organ, 2 speakers, orchestra (1967–68, Salabert); *Protocolo*, music theater for singers, dancers, chamber ensemble (1968, Salabert); *Parafrasis* for 24 instruments (1968, Salabert); *Quasi una fantasia* for string sextet, orchestra (1969, Salabert); *Por diversos motivos* for voices, projections, tape, chamber orchestra (1969, Salabert); *We* on tape (1969); *Tamaño natural* on tape (1970).

PRINCIPAL WRITINGS: *Aproximación a una estética de la música contemporánea* (Madrid 1968). Pablo has also translated into Spanish a work on Schoenberg and the writings of Webern.

BIBL.: Arthur Custer, "Contemporary Music in Spain," *Musical Quarterly* 50:44–60; Max Deutsch, foreword to *L. d. P.: Portrait d'un compositeur* (Darmstadt, Tonos, 1966); Jacobo Romano, "L. d. P.: Retrato de un compositor,"

Buenos Aires musical (1967); Eugenio de Vicente, "Neue Musik in Spanien," *Melos* (1965).

Hansjörg Pauli

SEE ALSO Spain.

Paccagnini, Angelo (b. Castano Primo, near Milan, 17 October 1930), studied at the Verdi Conservatory in Milan (1949–53, harmony with Bruno Bettinelli, composition with Bortone, clarinet and instrumentation with Giampieri, organ with Colonna) and worked during 1956–60 with Luciano Berio at the Studio di Fonologia of the RAI in Milan. He wrote radio and television music for the RAI during 1955–65 and has been chief of the Studio di Fonologia since 1968. In 1969 he established a course in electronic music at the Verdi Conservatory. He appears frequently as a conductor and in 1967 founded the renaissance ensemble Ars Antiqua di Milano, for which he transcribes older music, plays recorders and lute, and conducts.

PRINCIPAL COMPOSITIONS: *5 Cori di Euripide* for chorus (1952); *6 Tempi* for 2 pianos (1953); *4 Studi* for orchestra (1953); *String Quartet* (1956); *Variations* for piano I–II (1956, 1958); *Concerto* for violin, 6 instrumental groups (1958, UE); *Brevi canti* for mezzo-soprano, piano; text by P. Eluard (1958, UE); *Le sue ragioni*, 1-act opera (1959, UE); *Gruppi concertanti* for orchestra (1960, UE); *I dispersi*, ballet (1961, UE); *Sequenze e strutture*, electronic sounds on 4-track tape (1962, UE); *Actuelles* for soprano, speaking and singing choruses, orchestra (1963, UE); *Mosé*, stereophonic radio opera for vocal soloists, chorus, tape, orchestra (1963); *Il dio di oro*, radio opera for soprano, baritone, chorus, narrators, orchestra (1964); *Concerto No. 3* for soprano, orchestra (1965, UE); *Tutti la vogliono*, 3-act opera (1966); *Actuelles 1968* for soprano, tape, orchestra (1968, UE); *Partner*, electronic sounds on 4-track tape (1969, RAI, Milan); *Stimmen*, electronic sounds on 2-track tape (1969, RAI); *Concerto No. 4* for double string orchestra (1969, UE); *E' l'ora*, radio opera for soprano, narrators, tape, orchestra, electronic sounds (1970, RAI); *La misura il mistero*, stage opera for soprano, electronic sounds, 10 players (1970).

BIBL.: Armando Plebe, "Il caso Paccagnini," *Il portico* (Mantua, Feb 1967); Piero Santi, *Le sue ragioni* (Milan 1960).

[prepared with the help of Richard Bordoni]

Paik, Nam June (b. Seoul, Korea, 20 July 1932), studied at the Univ. of Tokyo (1952–56, esthetics with Y. Nomura), the Univ. of Munich (1956–57), the Freiburg Hochschule für Musik (1957–59, composition with Wolfgang Fortner), and the Univ. of Cologne (1958–62). He attended the Darmstadt summer courses during 1957–59, and in 1958 he worked at the Westdeutscher Rundfunk Electronic Music Studio in Cologne. He was associated with Galerie 22 and Mary Baumeister in New York during 1959–61 and has taken part in presentations of the New York Avant-Garde Festival since 1964. During 1961–64 he was an organizer for the Flexus group in Europe. He began experimenting with television as an art medium in the mid-1960s, was a consultant for communications research at the State Univ. of N.Y. at Stony Brook in 1968, and worked at WGBH-TV in Boston in 1970. Since 1970 he has been teaching intermedia and video-synthesis at the Calif. Institute of the Arts in Los Angeles. He outlines the following influences on his work: c.1952, Bartók, especially his *Piano Concerto No. 2*; c.1954, Schoenberg, especially his Op. 16; c.1956, Stockhausen, especially his *Klavierstücke II*; c.1958, Cage, especially his *Concert for Piano and Orchestra*, also Kurt Schwitters and Marcel Duchamp; c.1960, the Flexus group; c.1965, the cellist Charlotte Moorman.

PRINCIPAL COMPOSITIONS: *hommage à john cage* for 2 pianos (which are destroyed in the performance), 3 tape recorders, projections, live actions involving eggs, toy cars, motorbike (1959); *étude for pianoforte* involving the destruction of 2 pianos, cutting John Cage's necktie, and shampooing him without advance warning, "and quite much screaming and telephone call" (1960); *Simple* for actions, piano, 3 tapes (1961); *Sinfonie for 20 rooms*, a multiroom composition (1962, published in *Anthology*, New York 1963); *Moving Theater at Amsterdam*, a roving performance by members of the Flexus group that took place in various places in the city (1962); *2 Pieces for Alison Knowles* (1962, in *Decollage* No. 2); *EXPOSITION of Music*, an audience-participation sound environment created in about 20 rooms of a large villa, the Galerie Parnass in Wuppertal, Germany (1963); 3 pieces for Charlotte Moorman: *Cello Sonata* (1964); *Variation on a Theme by Saint-Saëns* (1965); *Opera sextronique* (1967); during the first performance in Town Hall, New York, 1967, Miss Moorman was arrested for having removed her brassiere; the performance was completed at another Town Hall concert in 1969; *Electronic Opera No. 1*, prepared at WGBH-TV in Boston with Fred Barzyk, David Altwood, Olivia Tappan (1968).

PRINCIPAL WRITINGS: Paik has published "compositions, essays, and ideas" in *Anthology* (New York 1963); *Decollage* (Cologne) Nos. 1–5; *Fluxus A* (Wiesbaden 1962); *Kalender* (Düsseldorf 1963, 1965); *Kikan* (Tokyo 1964); *Sogetzu Journal* (Tokyo 1963, 1964).

BIBL.: Earle Brown, "N. J. P.," *Anthology* ed. by La Monte Young and Jackson Maclow, 2nd ed. (New York 1970); John Cage, *A Year from Monday* (Middletown, Conn., 1968); John Gruen, *The New Bohemia* (New York 1967); Allan Kaprow, *N. J. P.* (Bonino Gallery, New York, 1968); Karlheinz Stockhausen, *Text II* (Cologne 1967); Gene Youngblood, *Expanded Cinema* (New York 1970).

SEE ALSO Dance, Prose Music.

Palmer, Robert (b. Syracuse, N.Y., 2 June 1915), studied composition with Bernard Rogers and Howard Hanson (Eastman School, 1934–39), Aaron Copland (Tanglewood, 1940), and Roy Harris (1939). He has taught composition at the Universities of Kansas (1940–43), Ill. (1955–56), and Cornell (since 1943). He has also been a visiting composer at many colleges in the U.S. His friendship with Quincy Porter during 1935–45 and that composer's "strongly integrated and personal harmonic language" influenced his harmonic style. Bartók's "realization of a fully integrated contemporary style has been a general ideal for many years. The melodic and formal ideas of Harris and the rhythms of Copland" have also affected his thinking.

PRINCIPAL COMPOSITIONS: *Piano Sonatas Nos. 1–2* (1938–46, 1942–48); *String Quartets Nos. 1–4* (1939; 1943–47; 1954, Peer; 1959); *3 Preludes* for piano (1941, New Valley); *Sonata* for 2 pianos (1944, Peer); *Toccata ostinato* for piano (1945, E-V); *Piano Quartet* (1947, SPAM); *Abraham Lincoln Walks at Midnight* for chorus, orchestra; text by Vachel Lindsay (1948, Peer); *Variations, Chorale, and Fugue* for orchestra (1947–54, Peer); *Chamber Concerto No. 1* for violin, oboe, strings (1949, Peer); *Piano Quintet* (1950, Peters); *Viola Sonata* (1951, Peer); *Wind Quintet* (1951); *Quintet* for clarinet, piano, strings (1952, Peer); *Sonata* for piano 4-hands (1952, Peer); *Slow, Slow Fresh Fount* for chorus; text by Ben Jonson (1953, Peer); *The Trojan Women* for women's chorus, winds, percussion; text from Euripides (1955); *Piano Trio* (1958); *Memorial Music* for chamber orchestra (1959–60, Peer); *Nabuchodonosor*, oratorio for tenor, baritone, men's chorus, brass, percussion (1960–64); *A Centennial Overture* (1965); *Symphony No. 2* (1966); *Choric Song and Toccata* for winds (1968–69); *Concerto* for piano, strings (1968–70).

PRINCIPAL WRITINGS: "Neglected Works," *Modern Music* 22/1:6–7; "Which Way Contemporary Music?" *Cornell Univ. Music Review* 11:3–13.

BIBL.: William Austin, "The Music of R. P.," *Musical Quarterly* (Jan 1956); Robert Evett, "How Right Is Right?" *Score Magazine* 12:33–37; Paul Rosenfeld, "R. P. and Charles Mills," *Modern Music* 20/4:264–65.

Panni, Marcello (b. Rome, 24 Jan 1940), studied at the conservatories in Milan (1959–60, conducting) and Rome (1961–63, composition with Boris Porena, conducting with Franco Ferrara), the Accadèmia Chigiana in Siena (1960, 1961; conducting with Sergiu Celibidache), the Accadèmia di S. Cecilia (1962, composition with Goffredo Petrassi), and the Paris Conservatory (1965–68, composition with Max Deutsch). Since 1968 he has been a guest conductor of European orchestras and festivals, and in 1970 he founded the Orchestra da Camera Nuova Consonanza in Rome.

PRINCIPAL COMPOSITIONS: *Arpège* for harp, 3 percussionists (1963, Peters); *Pretexte* for orchestra (1964, Peters); *Empedokles' Lied* for baritone, orchestra (1965, Peters); *D'Ailleurs* for string quartet (1966, S-Z); *Patience* for 1–72 voices, instruments (1966, Peters); *Après tout* for string trio, orchestra (1967–70, S-Z); *Déchiffrage* for instruments or solo organ (1968, Peters); *Agrémens* for string orchestra (1969, S-Z); *Domino*, "Clavierübung für Mariolina," for any keyboard instrument (1970, S-Z).

Panufnik, Andrzej (b. Warsaw, 24 Sept 1914), studied at the Warsaw Conservatory (1932–36, composition with Kazimierz Sikorski) and the Vienna State Academy (1937–38, conducting with Felix Weingartner). He also studied conducting in Paris with Philippe Gaubert (1939). During 1945–46 he was conductor of the Cracow Philharmonic and during 1946–47, of the Warsaw Philharmonic Orchestra. He emigrated to England in 1954. He was music director of the Birmingham Orchestra during 1957–59 and has often appeared as guest conductor in England and Europe. His earlier compositions were destroyed by fire in 1944. French (see bibl.) reports that his music is generally "founded on a kind of free tonality" that often "involves a major-minor duality. . . . The tendency to build passages or even whole works out of germ-cells of one, two or three intervals is a prominent feature of Panufnik's work, representing a self-imposed compositional discipline that he regards as absolutely necessary."

PRINCIPAL COMPOSITIONS (published by Boosey unless otherwise noted): *5 Polish Peasant Songs* for treble chorus, 2 flutes, 2 clarinets, bass clarinet (1940, reconstructed 1945, revised 1959); *Tragic Overture* (1942, reconstructed 1945, revised 1955); *6 Miniature Studies* for piano, books 1–2 (1947, revised 1955 and 1964); *Nocturne* for orchestra, piano (1947, revised 1955); *Lullaby* for 29 strings, 2 harps (1947, revised 1955); *Sinfonia rustica* (1948, revised 1955); *Heroic Overture* (1952, revised 1965); *Sinfonia elegiaca* (1957, revised 1966);

Autumn Music for 3 flutes/piccolo, 3 clarinets/bass clarinet, strings, percussion, vibraphone, celesta (1962); *Piano Concerto* (1962); *Sinfonia sacra* (1963); *Universal Prayer*, cantata for 4 soloists, chorus, 3 harps, organ; text by Alexander Pope (1968, unpub.); *Reflections* for piano (1968).

BIBL.: Peter French, "The Music of A. P.," *Tempo* 84:6–14; Barrie Hall, "A. P.'s *Sinfonia sacra*," *Tempo* 71:14–22.

Papaïoannou, Yannis (Andreas) (b. Cavala, Greece, 6 Jan 1910), studied at the Hellenic Conservatory (1929–34; theoretical studies with G. Sfakianakis, A. Contis; piano with M. Laspopoulou). He is primarily self-taught in composition but did study in Paris with Arthur Honegger in 1939. He has taught composition at the Hellenic Conservatory since 1954 and is president of the Hellenic Association for Contemporary Music and of the Greek section of the ISCM. He was the first composer in Greece to promote new-music resources. Twelve-tone writing appeared in his *Symphony No. 3* (1953) and was used strictly beginning 1961–62. He adapted total-serial procedures in the *Symphonies Nos. 4–5* (1963, 1964) and has since explored other advanced techniques. His work has been influenced by an interest in American, African, and Asian musics (including tribal music) and Byzantine chant.

PRINCIPAL COMPOSITIONS: *Odalisque* for piano (1937); *Chorographiko Preludio* for orchestra (1939); *Koursaros* [The Corsair] for orchestra (1940); *Poiema tou Dasous* [Poem of the Forest] for orchestra (1942); *Vassilis Arvanitis*, symphonic legend (1945); *Symphonies Nos. 1–5* (1946; 1951; 1953, IEPT; 1963, IEPT; 1964); *Triptucho* [Triptych] for string orchestra (1947); *O Orthros ton Psuchon* [The Matins of Souls], symphonic poem (1947); *Violin Sonata* (1947, Nakos); *2 Suites* for piano (1948, 1959); *Cheimoniatike Phantasia* [Winter Fantasy], ballet for flute, clarinet, violin, cello, piano; choreography by Mary Vruakou (1950); *Piano Concerto* (1950); *Pygmalion*, symphonic picture (1951); *Koursearikoi Choroi* [Corsair Dances] for orchestra or piano (1952); *Concerto for Orchestra* (1954, EM); *Suite* for violin, orchestra (1954); *Hellas*, symphonic poem after Shelley (1956); *Partita in modo antico* for piano (1957); *12 Inventions* for piano (1958); *Piano Sonata* (1958); *String Quartet* (1959); *Suite* for guitar (1960); *3 Suites* for orchestra: Nos. 1 and 2, "Eikones apo ten Asia" [Pictures from Asia]; No. 3, "Aiguptos" [Egypt] (1961); *Concertino* for piano, string orchestra (1962); *Archaic* for 2 guitars (1962); *Sonatina* for flute, guitar (1962); *Quartet* for flute, clarinet, guitar, cello (1962); *Wind Trio* (1962); *String Trio* (1963); *Oraculum* for piano (1965, Gerig); *E Kedeia tou Sarpedónos*

[Sarpidon's Funeral], cantata for narrator, soprano, chorus, chamber orchestra; poems by C. Cavafy (1965); *3 Byzantine Odes* for soprano, chamber ensemble (1966); *3 Tragoudia* [3 Songs] for mezzo-soprano, flute, oboe, viola, cello, piano, percussion; poems by Cavafy (1966); *Trio* for flute, oboe, guitar (1967); *Ta Vemata* [The Steps] for chorus, instrumental ensemble; poem by Cavafy (1967); *Symphonic Tableau* (1968); *Quartet* for oboe, clainet, viola, piano (1968); *3 Monologues of Electra* for soprano, instrumental ensemble (1968); *7 Piano Pieces* (1969); *Ainigma* [Riddle] for piano (1969); *5 Characters*, in memoriam Yannis Christou, for 2 trumpets, English horn, trombone, tuba (1970).

PRINCIPAL WRITINGS: "Paul Hindemith," *Epoches* 11:23–26; "Béla Bartók," *ibid.* 35:231–36; "Phantasia, Skephe kai Technike" [Imagination, Reflection, and Technique], *Annales d'Esthétiques* (Athens) 5:94–106.

SEE ALSO Greece.

Papineau-Couture, Jean (b. Montreal, 12 Nov 1916), studied with Léo-Pol Morin and Gabriel Cusson in Montreal and with Quincy Porter in Boston (1940). He also attended the Longy School in Cambridge, Mass., and the Univ. of Wis. and worked with Nadia Boulanger in Montecito, Calif. He taught at the Montreal section of the Province of Quebec Conservatory (1946–51) and thereafter at the Univ. of Montreal, where he has been dean since 1968. He has been active in promoting Canadian and contemporary music, holding such posts as president of the Canadian League of Composers (1957–59, 1963–66), director of the Canadian Music Council and Canadian Music Center (since 1945), and president of the Société de Musique Contemporaine du Québec (since its foundation in 1966).

Papineau-Couture is one of Canada's most prolific composers. His 60-odd works range from solo instrumental pieces to chamber music to symphonic and concerted works. Solo vocal and choral pieces are less numerous. He has not written operas or other stage works but has composed incidental music for five puppet shows. His first compositions (1942–48) are neoclassic—tonal, in traditional forms, and with much imitation and related contrapuntal devices. A period of experimentation followed (1949–56) in which Hindemith's concept of a "total chromatic" and Schoenberg's 12-tone technique led to atonality. The composer remained faithful to Hindemith; the spirit of the Schoenbergian technique, however, did not penetrate his music. In the *Suite* for violin, for example, 12-tone principles are employed with such richness of invention that the impression of rigidity often encountered in such music is replaced by a wide gamut of emotions. This kind of expression is also found in a few vocal works of the period, *Psaume CL* and *Mort*. The composer's mature works (since 1956) stem from Hindemith's approach to acoustics and the formation of chords, from Stravinsky's strong rhythmic impulse, and from Varèse's feeling for musical space. The technical means include simultaneous major and minor chords, successions of fourths and fifths, and percussive, rapid successions of 16th notes. The framework of each work is always logical, well planned, and, though still adhering to some traditional schemes (especially rondo), more personal and original than in the earliest pieces.

PRINCIPAL COMPOSITIONS: *Suite* for piano (1942, BMIC); *Concerto Grosso* for chamber orchestra (1943, revised 1955); *Quatrains* for soprano, piano; text by Francis Jammes (1947); *Tittle-tattle* for orchestra (1949); *Violin Concerto* (1951, BMIC); *String Quartet No. 1* (1953); *Psaume CL* for soprano, tenor, chorus, flute, bassoon, brass ensemble, organ (1954, BMIC); *Mort* for alto, piano; poem by François Villon (1956); *Suite* for violin (1956, Peer); *Pièces concertantes Nos. 1–5*: No. 1, "repliement," for piano, string orchestra (1957, BMIC); No. 2, "eventails," for cello, chamber orchestra without cellos (1959); No. 3, "variations," for flute, clarinet, violin, cello, harp, string orchestra (1959); No. 4, "additions," for oboe, string orchestra (1959); No. 5, "miroirs," for orchestra (1963); *Eclosion* for piano, violin, tape (1961); *3 Caprices* for violin, piano (1962, Peer); *Fantasy* for wind quintet (1963, BMIC); *Piano Concerto* (1965); *Viole d'amour* for chorus; text by Rina Lasnier (1966); *Sextet* for 3 reeds, 3 strings (1966–67); *Dialogues* for violin, piano (1967, Peer); *String Quartet No. 2* (1967); *Paysage* for 8 narrators, 8 singers, piano, 4 winds, harp, 5 strings, percussion; text by St. Denys Garneau (1968); *Oscillations* for orchestra (1969); *Nocturnes* for flute, clarinet, violin, cello, harpsichord, guitar, percussion (1969); *Contrastes* for voice, orchestra (1970); *Dyarchie* for harpsichord (1971). List to 1958: *Composers of the Americas* 5:59–62; list, 1942–59, Beckwith (see bibl.); selected list to 1963, *34 Biographies of Canadian Composers* (Montreal 1964):75f.

PRINCIPAL WRITINGS: "Que Sera la Musique canadienne," *Amérique française* (Oct 1942):24–26; "La Formation du compositeur," a lecture delivered at the International Composers' Conference (Stratford, Ontario, 8 August 1960); "Training of Composers," *The Modern Composer and His World* ed. by J. Beckwith and U. Kasemets (Toronto 1961):20–24; "Fragments de causerie sur Guillaume Couture," *Le Devoir* (Montreal, 2 June 1962).

BIBL.: John Beckwith, "J. P.-C.," *Canadian Music Journal* 3/2:4–21; Raoul Duguay, ed., "J. P.-C.," *Musiques du Kebek* (Montreal 1971):145–52.

Lyse Richer-Lortie

SEE ALSO Canada.

Papp, Lajos (b. Debrecen, Hungary, 18 August 1935), studied at the Liszt Academy in Budapest (1954–59, composition with Ferenc Szabó). During 1959–68 he taught theory and solfège at the Budapest School of Music. Since then he has been a free-lance composer.

PRINCIPAL COMPOSITIONS (several works are undated): *Variations* for piano (1959, EMB and Boosey); *3 Songs on Poems of Georg Trakl* for soprano, piano (1960, Boosey); *Cello Sonata* (1962, EMB); *4 Pieces* for cello (1963); *Improvisazione* for piano (1964, EMB and Boosey); *6 Bagatelles* for piano (1964, EMB); *Cello Concerto* (1965); *Dialogo* for piano, orchestra (1966, EMB); *Ricercare* for harp (EMB and Boosey); *Meditazioni in memoriam Milán Füst* for soprano, orchestra without strings; *9 Bagatelles* for harpsichord; *Kalevipoeg*, symphonic poem; *Miniatures* for cello, harp; *Quintet* for harpsichord, string quartet.

Parameter, a basic aspect of sound or of composition. The term came into use among musicians in the early 1950s along with the rise of electronic music, in which the separate aspects of a sound are usually independently controlled, and serialism with its independent serial ordering of values within such parameters as pitch class, loudness (also called intensity), duration, timbre, articulation, and position in space. The term is borrowed from mathematics where, however, it is not used as a synonym for dimension but indicates a place-holder for a constant (as in "sine nx," where n would be termed a parameter).

Parris, Robert (b. Philadelphia, 21 May 1924), studied at the Univ. of Penna. (1941–46), the Juilliard School (1946–48, composition with Peter Mennin), Tanglewood (1950, 51; composition with Jacques Ibert, Aaron Copland), and the Ecole Normale de Musique (1952–53, composition with Arthur Honegger), after which he settled in Washington, D.C. He has taught at the State Univ. of Wash. (1948–49) and George Washington Univ. (since 1963). During 1958–61 he wrote criticism for the *Washington Post*. He also teaches privately and is a pianist and harpsichordist.

PRINCIPAL COMPOSITIONS: *String Trio No. 2*, "Lament for Joseph" (1950, ACA); *Variations* for piano (1953, ACA); *Fantasy and Fugue* for cello (1954, Peters); *Alas, for the day*, cantata for chorus, organ or orchestra (1954, ACA); *Concerto* for 5 kettle drums, orchestra (1955, Peters); *Viola Concerto* (1956, ACA); *3 Passacaglias* for soprano, harpsichord, violin, cello; text by W. J. Smith and G. M. Hopkins (1957, ACA); *Trio* for clarinet, cello, piano (1959, ACA); *Violin Concerto* (1959, ACA); *The Leaden Echo and the Golden Echo* for baritone, orchestra; text by Hopkins (1960, ACA); *The Raids: 1940* for soprano, violin, piano; text by Edith Sitwell (1960, ACA); *Cadenza, Caprice, and Ricercare* for cello, piano (1961, ACA); *Lamentations and Praises* for 9 brasses, percussion (1962, Peters); *Trombone Concerto* (1964); *Sonata* for solo violin (1965, Peer); *The Phoenix*, concerto for kettledrums, orchestra (1969). List to 1965: *Composers of the Americas* 10:81–84.

PRINCIPAL WRITINGS: "French Fashions for the Spring," *Kenyon Review* (winter 1962):29–42.

Parsons, Michael (b. Bolton, England, 12 Dec 1938), studied philosophy at St. John's College of Oxford Univ. (1957–61) and composition with Peter Racine Fricker at the Royal College of Music in London (1961–62). During 1964–65 he did research on 16th-century Italian music and early opera, in particular the work of Emilio del Cavalieri. He met Cornelius Cardew in 1968, attended his class in experimental music at Morley College, and took part in performances of works by Morton Feldman, John Cage, Cardew, La Monte Young, and Terry Riley. He was a cofounder of the Scratch Orchestra in 1969. He has been a lecturer in music at Sir John Cass College of the City of London Polytechnic Univ. (1963–69) and at the Portsmouth College of Art (since 1970). He used serial techniques in his student works and then became interested in more open situations. "I like to work with a minimum of notation. A procedure is described, which defines the piece within certain limits (e.g., only these notes to be used in this order), but which may lead to different kinds of performance by leaving important features to depend on the people involved, the resources available, and the local situation. In recent compositions I have concentrated on limited musical material in the belief that over a length of time this can reveal a richness and variety of detail."

PRINCIPAL COMPOSITIONS (available from Experimental): *Mindfulness of Breathing* for low men's voices (1969); *Mindfulness Occupied with the Body* for chorus of at least 50 voices (1970);

Rhythm Studies for 2 pianos (1970); *Rhythm Studies* for drums (1970–71).

PRINCIPAL WRITINGS: "Sounds of Discovery," *Musical Times* (May 1968):429–30; "The Contemporary Pianist," a conversation with John Tilbury, *Musical Times* (Feb 1969):150–52.

SEE ALSO Great Britain.

Pärt, Arvo (b. Paide, Estonia, 11 Sept 1935), graduated from the Tallin Conservatory in 1963 (composition with Heino Eller). He is a freelance composer. His student works before 1960 were in a neoclassic style. Thereafter he began working with 12-tone techniques, *Klangfarbenmelodien*, clusters, and from 1964 on collage processes involving sharp contrasts of dynamics and style.

PRINCIPAL COMPOSITIONS: *Partita* for piano (1958, Muzfond); *Our Garden*, cantata for children's chorus (1959, SC); *Obituary* for orchestra (1960); *Pas du monde*, oratorio (1961); *Polyphonic Symphony* (1963); *Perpetuum mobile* for orchestra (1963, UE); *Syllabic Music* for 13 instruments (1964); *Collage on B-A-C-H* for chamber orchestra (1964); *Pro et contra*, concerto for cello, orchestra (1966); *Symphony No. 2* (1966); *Credo* for chorus, orchestra (1968).

SEE ALSO Soviet Union.

Partch, Harry (b. Oakland, Calif., 24 June 1901), the son of apostate missionary parents, grew up in southern Arizona where he "began playing reed organ, mandolin, cornet, violin, harmonica at five or six." He began composing seriously at 14 but burned everything, including a string quartet in just intonation, a symphonic poem, a piano concerto, and some 50 songs, about 1930. Since then he has "destroyed very little." He educated himself musically in public libraries and lists as influences on his work "Yaqui Indians, Chinese lullabies, Hebrew chants for the dead, Christian hymns, Congo puberty rites, Chinese music halls (San Francisco), lumber yards, and junk shops . . . Boris Godunov. . . ."[1] During the years 1923–28 he developed a unique philosophy, theory, and practice of music, which culminated in 1928 with the first draft of his book *Genesis of a Music* (published 1949). He received a Carnegie Corporation grant in 1934, but until 1943, when foundations, universities, and museums began contributing to his livelihood, he relied on

[1]Letter to the author, 1 June 1968.

limited private patronage and on hundreds of odd jobs. During part of the Depression he was a hobo. He managed to release privately a series of recordings (Gate 5 Records), which until 1966 were the only available versions of his music. A score of his was first published in 1967 in *Source* magazine.

Partch has created not only musical compositions but also the instruments for which they are written, the scale to which they are tuned, the theory behind the design of both music and instruments, and the very circumstances for making music. He calls this esthetic position "corporeal." In a fully realized Partch production there are spoken words wedded to music without the abstraction of singing; there is a dramatic story expressed through action, including actions by performing musicians and dancer-actor-singers; the setting includes, as sculptural objects, the handmade instruments themselves. Thus music functions as part of a many faceted work of art. One of the convictions that led him to create his own instruments (beginning in 1928) was his rejection of equal-tempered tuning, the basis of design of Western musical instruments since the 18th century. Building his musical theory, like most of those of Asia and of the ancient world, upon "just tuning," Partch has resumed and extended a tradition once considered lost in the West.

Partch's music is characterized by a predominance of plucked string and percussion timbres, which most of his own invented and adapted instruments provide. Pitch and rhythm characteristics are related to his theories. Melodically he uses a spectrum of finely graded microtonal scale steps commonly described as a 43-tone-per-octave scale; this enables him, among other things, to approximate speech melodies in notation. Harmonically his music employs not only all the chord structures of traditional music in uncompromised just tuning, but also utterly unfamiliar harmonies derived from relationships based upon use of the seventh and eleventh partials of the overtone series. Partch's rhythm employs a proportional system based upon superimposed metrical patterns timed at various speeds. His style is closer to recent avant-garde multimedia pieces than to more traditional music; however, his espousal of just intonation and the mathematics of rational proportion places him at sharp variance with proponents of noise and randomness, showing him to have more in common with Asian and African musics than with Western. This aspect of his work, together with his strongly metric rhythms and

his "corporeal" earthiness, gives his music an affinity for folk, rock, and jazz music. "I believe," he has said, "in musicians who are total constituents of the moment, irreplaceable, who may sing, shout, whistle, stamp their feet; in costume always, or perhaps half naked, and I do not care which half."[2]

INSTRUMENTS DESIGNED AND BUILT BY PARTCH: adapted viola (Santa Rosa, Calif.-New Orleans 1928–30); kithara I (Los Angeles 1938; rebuilt Urbana, Ill., 1959), guitar I (New York 1943), guitar II (Madison, Wis., 1945), chromelodeon I (Madison 1945), harmonic canon I (Madison 1945; rebuilt Urbana 1959), diamond marimba (Madison 1946), bass marimba (Gualala, Calif., 1949–50), marimba eroica (Oakland 1951; rebuilt Sausalito, Calif., 1954), cloud-chamber bowls (Gualala-Oakland 1950–51), spoils of war (Gualala-Sausalito 1950–55), harmonic canon II (Sausalito 1953), surrogate kithara (Sausalito 1953), kithara II (Sausalito 1954), bamboo marimba ("boo"; Sausilato 1955), bloboy (Evanston, Ill., 1958), chromelodeon II (Urbana 1959), crychord (Urbana 1959), mazda marimba (Urbana 1959), zymo-xyl (Petaluma, Calif., 1963), eucal blossom (Del Mar, Calif., 1964; rebuilt San Diego 1967), gourd tree (Del Mar 1964), quadrangularis reversum (Van Nuys, Calif., 1965), cone gongs (Venice, Calif., 1965), harmonic canon III ("blue rainbow"; Venice, Calif., 1965). ★ Small hand instruments: ugumbo (copy of a Zulu instrument), 2 waving drums, rotating drum, 2 belly drums, gourd drum, 6 pairs of bamboo claves, 4 pairs of eucal claves, 3 ektaras (copies or adaptations of Hindu instruments) (Venice-San Diego, Calif., 1965–67).

PRINCIPAL COMPOSITIONS: *17 Lyrics by Li Po, By the Rivers of Babylon, Potion Scene from Romeo and Juliet* (all 1930–33); *Barstow* (1941); *Dark Brother, U.S. Highball, The Letter, San Francisco Newsboy Cries* (all 1943); 2 settings from *Finnegan's Wake* (1944); *Intrusions* (1949–50); *Plectra and Percussion Dances* (1949–52); *Oedipus* (1951); *The Bewitched* (1955); *Windsong, Music Studio* (both 1958); *Revelation in the Courthouse Park* (1960); *Rotate the Body* (1961); *Water, Water* (1962); *And on the 7th Day Petals Fell in Petaluma* (1963–64, revised 1966); *Delusion of the Fury* (1963–66). List to 1958: *Composers of the Americas* 5: 65–68.

PRINCIPAL WRITINGS: *Genesis of a Music* (Madison, Wis., 1949).

BIBL.: Paul Earls, "H. P.: Verses in Preparation for 'Delusions of the Fury'," *Yearbook of the Inter-American Institute for Musical Research* (Tulane Univ.) 3:1–32; Wilfred Mellers, "An American Aboriginal," *Tempo* 64:2–6; Boris Kremenliev, "Ein Ritual von Traum und Wahn in Los Angeles," *Melos* 36:274–76.

Ben Johnston

SEE ALSO Asian Music and Western Composition, Dance, Instrumental and Vocal Resources, Mathematics, Microtones, Mixed Media, Tuning and Temperament, United States.

[2]Remark made for a BMI brochure, 1968, but not used there.

Partos, Öedöen (b. Budapest, 1 Oct 1907),
attended the Liszt Academy of Music (1918–
25; composition with Zoltán Kodály, violin
with Jenő Hubay). He was concertmaster of
several middle and eastern European orchestras during 1925–35 and taught violin and
composition in Baku in 1936–37. He moved to
Israel in 1938 and until 1956 was principal
violinist of the Israel Philharmonic. He has
been director of the Rubin Academy of Music
in Tel Aviv since 1951 and professor in the
musicology department of Tel Aviv Univ.
since 1961. Partos was influenced first by
Bartók, later by Hindemith, Messiaen, and
Oriental music.

PRINCIPAL COMPOSITIONS: (published by IMI
unless otherwise noted): *Concertino* for string
quartet (1932, IMP); *Yiskor* [In memoriam] for
viola, strings (1949, IMP); *Song of Praise*, viola
concerto (1949, IMP); *Ein gev*, symphonic fantasy
(1952, IMP); *Vision* for flute, piano, strings (1957,
IMP); *Viola Concerto No. 2* (1957, IMP); *Maqua-
mat* [Quintet] for flute, string quartet (1958, IMP);
Violin Concerto (1958) *Images* for orchestra
(1960); *Agada* [Legend] for viola, piano, percussion
(1960); *Tehilim* [Psalms], String Quartet No. 2
(1960); *Iltur* for 12 harps (1961); *Symphony
concertante* for viola, orchestra (1962); *Psalm* for
chorus, orchestra (1965); *Symphonic Movement*
(1965); *Nebulae* for wind quintet (1966).

BIBL.: Ishag Arazi, "Let This Land Be My
Land," *American String Teacher* (spring 1967);
Peter Gradenwitz, *Music and Musicians in Israel*
(Tel-Aviv 1959):73–78; ——, "Current Chron-
icle," *Musical Quarterly* 48:107–09; Alexander
Ringer, "Musical Composition in Modern Israel,"
ibid. 50:284–86.

SEE ALSO Israel.

Paz, Juan Carlos (b. Buenos Aires, 5 August
1901; d. Argentina, August 1972), was self-
taught in music and worked as a free-lance
composer, teacher, critic, and essayist. In
1930 he founded the Grupo Renovación and
in 1937, the Agrupación Nueva Música.
His compositional techniques developed
through four stages: during 1921–27 he was
influenced by baroque and classic forms
and used a tonal-chromatic harmonic style;
during 1928–33 he followed a polytonal,
neoclassic approach and was especially
influenced by Stravinsky and Honegger;
during 1934–50 he used 12-tone techniques
derived from Schoenberg and Webern; after
1955 he investigated the use of open forms,
relying more and more on intuition in his
choice and use of musical materials.

PRINCIPAL COMPOSITIONS: *3 Jazz Movements* for
piano (1932, EAMI); *3 2-Part Inventions* for piano

(1932, EAMI); *Concerto No. 1* for piano, flute,
oboe, clarinet, bassoon, trumpet (1932); *Concerto
No. 2* for piano, oboe, trumpet, 2 trombones,
bassoon (1935); *Composition on 12 Tones No. 3*
for clarinet, piano (1936, New Music); *Ritmica
ostinata* for orchestra (1942, EAMI); *Música 1946*
for piano (1946, Ricordi); *Dédalus* for piano, flute,
clarinet, violin, cello (1950, ECA); *Continuidad* for
orchestra (1960–61); *Invention* for string quartet
(1961); *Núcleos*, series 1 for piano (1962–64,
EAMI); *Music* for piano, orchestra (1963, PAU);
Concreción for flute, clarinet, bassoon, trumpet,
horn, trombone, tuba (1964); *Galaxia* for organ
(1964). List to 1956: *Composers of the Americas*
2:108–15.

PRINCIPAL WRITINGS: *La música de los Estados
Unidos* (Mexico City 1952, 2nd ed. 1958); *Introducción a la música de nuestro tiempo* (Buenos
Aires 1955); *Arnold Schoenberg o el fin de la era
tonal* (Buenos Aires 1958); *Alturas, tensiones,
ataques, intensidades* (Buenos Aires, in preparation). Paz also wrote some 200 essays on contemporary music and composers and related musical
subjects for Latin American journals.

BIBL.: Daniel Devoto, "La 'Agrupación Nueva
Música'," *Las Hojas* (Buenos Aires 1950); H.
Gallac, "La obra musical de J. C. P.," *Boletín
latino-americano de música* (Montevideo) 1 (1935);
Eduardo Keller, "J. C. P.," *Musica viva* (Rio de
Janeiro) 10–11 (1941); Jacobo Romano, *J. C. P.*
(in preparation); ——, "J. C. P., un revitali-
zador del lenguage musical," *Sonda* (Madrid) 1
(1967).

SEE ALSO Argentina.

Pedagogy, see Education for the Nonprofessional, Education for the Professional

Peeters, Flor (b. Tielien, Belgium, 4 July 1903),
studied at the Lemmen Institute in Mechelen
(1919–23; counterpoint, fugue with Lodewijk
Mortelmans; organ with O. Depuydt; Gregorian chant with Van Nuffel). He worked
privately for a short while with Marcel Dupré.
He has taught organ at the Lemmen Institute
(1923–52), the Royal Conservatory of Ghent
(1931–48), and the Royal Flemish Conservatory of Antwerp (1948–68), of which he was
also director during 1952–68. During 1935–48
he conducted a master class for organ and
composition at the Tilburg Conservatory in
Holland. He has been organist at Mechelen
Cathedral since 1923.

PRINCIPAL COMPOSITIONS: *Variations and Finale*
for organ, Op. 20 (1929, Schwann); *Mass for St.
Joseph* for chorus, organ, Op. 21 (1929, Schwann
and McLaughlin); *Toccata, Fugue, and Hymn on
"Ave maris stella"* for organ, Op. 28 (1931,
Lemoine); *Speculum vitae* for soprano, organ, Op.

36 (1935, Lemoine); *Flemish Rhapsody* for organ, Op. 37 (1935, Schott); *Elegie* for organ, Op. 38 (1935, Lemoine); *Psalm "Jubilate Deo"* for chorus, organ, Op. 40 (1936, McLaughlin); *Mére*, 6 songs for low voice, piano, Op. 41 (1936, Hewekemeijer); *Passacaglia and Fugue* for organ, Op. 42 (1938, Schott); *Ivory Tower*, 6 songs for high voice, piano, Op. 47 (1940, Peters); *Sinfonia* for organ, Op. 48 (1940, Lemoine); *6 Love Songs* for voice, piano, Op. 50 (1943, Peters); *Organ Concerto*, Op. 52 (1944, Peters); *Te Deum* for chorus, organ, Op. 57 (1945, Schwann and McLaughlin); *Missa festiva* for chorus, organ, Op. 62 (1947, Schwann); *Lied Symphony* for organ, Op. 66 (1948, Peters); *3 Preludes and Fugues* for organ, Op. 72 (1950, Schott); *Concerto* for organ, piano, Op. 74 (1951, Gray); *Missa jubilans* for chorus, organ, Op. 92 (1958, Peters); *Entrata festiva* for chorus, organ, Op. 98 (1959, Peters); *Hymn Preludes for the Liturgical Year* for organ, Op. 100 (1959–64, Peters); *Magnificat* for chorus, organ, Op. 108 (1962, McLaughlin); *6 Lyrical Pieces* for organ, Op. 116 (1966, Gray). Peeters has also composed an organ method in 3 vols., *Ars organi* (1952, Peters), and a book of teaching pieces, *Little Organ Book* (1953, McLaughlin). In addition, he has edited 12 volumes of early Dutch, English, and French organ music.

PRINCIPAL WRITINGS: "De toekomst van het Orgelspel in de Katholieke Eredienst" [Organ Pedal Technique in Playing in the Catholic Liturgy], *Musica sacra* (Mechelen, Dec 1961): 139–43; "Charles Tournemire, L'oeuvre d'orgue," *ibid.* (Sept 1964): 129–44; Choir Masters and Organists, Vatican Council II," *ibid.* 92: 100–04.

BIBL.: E. Donnell Blackham, *An Analytical Study of the Formal Treatment of the Cantus Firmus in 30 Chorale Preludes by F. P.* (Master's thesis, Brigham Young Univ., 1962); W. Giles, "The Organ Music of F. P., Opus 100," *Journal of Church Music* (Sept 1967): 8–10, 43; J. Lade, "The Music of F. P.," *The Listener* (August 1955); ——, "The Organ Music of F. P.," *Musical Times* (July 1968): 667–69; E. Paccagnella, "F. P. e la musica sacra moderna," *Ecclesiae* (Rome, Feb 1959); Piet Visser, *F. P., Organist* (Turnhout, Belgium, 1950).

SEE ALSO Liturgical Music: Christian.

Pehkonen, Elis (b. Swaffham, Norfolk, England, 22 June 1942), studied at the Royal College of Music (1960–64, composition with Peter Racine Fricker, piano with Angus Morrison) and privately with Richard Rodney Bennett). Since 1967, when he became a music teacher at the Cirencester School in Gloucestershire, he has been particularly involved in music for percussion and voices for young people. In 1968 he formed the Cirencester School Percussion Ensemble, composed of teenagers, which has toured in the south of England. As a composer he has been particularly influenced by Mauricio Kagel, Krzysztof Penderecki, and the writings of R. Murray Schafer; he feels no affinity with serial methods.

PRINCIPAL COMPOSITIONS: *Concerti with Orchestra* for piano, instrumental quintet, percussion, orchestra (1968, UE); *My Cats* for voices, percussion (1968, UE); *3 Symphonies for 10 Players* for piano, percussion (1968, Oxford); *Exeter Riddles* for baritone, piano (1969); *Sonata* for 2 trumpets (1969); *Gymels* for piano, percussion (1969); *The Music of Paradise* for 4 choirs, string ensemble, recorders, nightingale whistle, cymbal, auto harp (1971).

SEE ALSO Great Britain.

Peiko, Nikolai (Ivanovich) (b. Moscow, 25 March 1916), studied at the Music Academy of the Moscow Conservatory (1933–37, composition with T. I. Litinsky, harmony with I. Sposobin) and at the Moscow Conservatory (1937–40, composition with Nicolai Miaskovsky, analysis with Viktor Tsukkerman, analysis with N. Rakov). He has taught composition and orchestration at the Moscow Conservatory (1942–59) and at the Gnesin Conservatory (since 1954). His early music was influenced by Beethoven, German romanticism, and 19th-century Russian composers. In the 1930s he turned to Stravinsky, Prokofiev, Shostakovich, and other contemporary Russians. In the 60s he began working with 12-tone techniques within a tonal framework.

PRINCIPAL COMPOSITIONS: *Iz iakutskikh legende* [From Yakuts Legends], symphonic suite (1940–57); *Piano Concerto* (1943–47, arranged for 2 pianos, 1965; Muzyka); *Symphonies Nos. 1–5* (1945, SC; 1946, Muzyka; 1957, SC; 1965, SC; 1969); *Piano Sonata* (1946–50, Muzyka); *Iz russkoi stariny* [From Old Russia], symphonic suite (1948); *Moldavaskaia siuita* [Moldavian Suite] for orchestra (1949–50, Muzyka); *Sem' p'es na temy narodov USSR* [7 Pieces of Themes of the Peoples of the USSR], symphonic suite (1950, Muzyka); *Zhanna d'Ark*, ballet; scenario by V. Burmeister (1953–55; piano score, Muzyka; orchestra suite, SC); *Symphonic Ballad* (1956, SC); *Piano Quintet* (1961, Muzyka); *String Quartets Nos. 1–2* (1962, 1965); *Collected Songs* for voice, piano (published 1969, Muzyka).

PRINCIPAL WRITINGS: "27 simfoniia N. Ia. Miaskovsky" [The 27 Symphonies of N. Ia. Miaskovsky] and "Vospomonaniia ob uchitele" [Reminiscences about a Teacher], *Miaskovsky, stat'i pis'ma vospominaniia* [Miaskovsky, Letters, Reminiscences] (Moscow 1959).

BIBL.: G. Grigor'eva, *N. I. P.* (Moscow 1965); A. Kandinsky, *Balet "Zhanna d'Ark" N. I. P.* (Moscow 1958).

Peixe, César Guerra, see under Guerra-Peixe

Peixinho, Jorge (Manuel Rosado Marques) (b. Montijo, Portugal, 20 Jan 1940), studied at the Lisbon Conservatory (1951–58, piano with Fernando Laires), the Accadèmia di S. Cecilia in Rome (1960–61, composition with Boris Porena, Goffredo Petrassi, Luigi Nono), and the Basel Academy of Music (1962–63; composition with Pierre Boulez, Karlheinz Stockhausen; electronic composition with Gottfried Michael Koenig). He has taught courses in contemporary music and composition at the Academia de Amadores de Música in Lisbon (1962, 1971), the Society of Fine Arts in Lisbon (1964), the Oporto Conservatory in Brazil (1965–66), at Curitiba in Brazil (1970), and the Gulbenkian Foundation (1967–71). The study of Webern's music was a decisive influence on his development as a composer; Boulez and Nono were also influential during the years 1960–62, thereafter Stockhausen. Most recently he has been working with free collective improvisation.

PRINCIPAL COMPOSITIONS: *Políptico 1960* for chamber orchestra (1960); *Collage I* for 2 pianos (1962, revised 1965); *Diafonia 2* for harp, harpsichord, piano, celesta, metal percussion, 12 strings (1963); *Kinetofonias* for 25 strings, 3 tape recorders (1965); *Situações 66* for flute, clarinet, trumpet, viola, harp (1966); *Recitativo III* for flute, harp, percussion, tape recorder (1966–69); *Nomos* for orchestra (1967); *Eurídice reamada* for chorus, orchestra (1968); *As 4 estações* for trumpet, cello, harp, piano; all instruments amplified (1969–70); *CDE* for clarinet, violin, cello, piano (1970); *A pousasa das chagas*, film score (1970); *Almada— A Name of War* (1971). ★Principal theater scores: *Macbeth* (Shakespeare, 1964); *O gebo e a sombra* (Raúl Brandão, 1966); *A Foolish Diary* (Gogol, 1966); *The Four Seasons* (A. Wesker, 1969); *Nós não estamos algures*, audio-visual show (1969).

PRINCIPAL WRITINGS: "As novas correntes de vanguarda musical" [The New Ways of the Musical Avant-garde], *Jornal de letras e artes* (Lisbon 1964); "O 'Happening'" [The Happening], *Diário de Lisboa*; "'As 4 estações'," *Arte musical* (Lisbon, 1969); "A minha experiência com Stockhausen e a minha evolução eriadora" [My Experience with Stockhausen and My Creative Evolution], *Nutida musik* (Stockholm 1969).

BIBL.: E. M. de Melo e Castro, "A força do silêncio" [The Power of Silence], *Colóquio* (Lisbon, fall 1971).

Penderecki, Krzysztof (b. Dębica, Poland, 23 Nov 1933) took violin lessons as a child and studied composition with Artur Malawski and Stanisław Wiechowicz at the Music Acadmey in Cracow, from which he received a diploma in 1958. In 1959 he became an instructor of counterpoint and later of composition at the Academy. He gave lectures on composition at the Volkwang Hochschule für Musik in Essen (1966–68).

Penderecki's output consists mostly of vocal and orchestral music; there are only a few chamber works. With one exception (*Strofy* for soprano, instruments, narrator), the vocal music is scored for one or more choruses along with soloists, instrumental accompaniment, and sometimes a narrator. The tape music often includes human voices. String ensembles, sometimes with percussion, predominate in the instrumental works. The music for full orchestra includes several concerted works in which string instruments have most of the solo roles.

In the 1950s Penderecki used serial techniques in a manner close to the style of Pierre Boulez (*Strofy*, 1959, is a good example). He turned from this approach in 1960 and became one of the first composers to concentrate on experiments with new sonorities. In *Fluorescences* (1961) he used noises such as the sawing of wood, the sound of typewriters, and the rustling of parchment. In other works he introduced novel methods of sound production with string instruments, such as rubbing and striking the bow or hands over various parts of the instrument. In these and other ways he expanded the repertory of useable sounds to include knocking, rustling, screeching, hissing, etc. In addition he used traditional means of sound production to produce continuous glissandos that follow various patterns. There are also stationary and moving clusters in various lengths and widths. With wind instruments he has experimented with vowels sounded into the instrument. His choral music has included consonants rapidly articulated, along with hissing, whistling, etc. (*The Measures of Time and Silence*, 1960).

Thus after 1960 the controlling element in Penderecki's music became the spectrum of its sound. Although precisely defined formal outlines do not exist, some kind of cohesion is always present. Over small areas of music it results from the artistic placement of various points, lines, stripes, and other configurations of sound. Over larger areas it results from the juxtaposing of contrasting sound blocks and from gradual changes in sound production. In the *String Quartet* (1960), for instance, passages produced on the strings are juxtaposed with passages produced on the tailpiece. There is a long passage in which the noise of the hand hitting the strings (represented below by the letter *A*) gradually gives way to "normal" sounds (represented by *b*): AAAA AAAAAbAAbbbAAbAAbAAAbbbbAAbbA bbbAAbbbbAbbAbAbbbbbbbbb. Some of the most recent works contain traditional elements, such as melodic motives and triads and other chords (in the *St. Luke Passion*, 1963–65) and idiomatic virtuoso flourishes (in the concertos).

Penderecki is heir of the impressionistic tradition in his emphasis on attractive and subtly shaded sound. On the other hand, his music often uses harsh colors, irregularly spaced contrasts in loudness, and thick masses of sound in the orchestra or chorus to produce highly charged, dramatic effects (*Threnody*, 1960; *Canon*, 1962; *St. Luke Passion*; and other works). He is not attracted to theoretical schemes but seems to compose quite spontaneously. It is significant that he likes literary-dramatic subjects, which often stimulate him to produce interesting illustrative effects. His innovations have necessitated the invention of special notational signs to indicate novel sound production (e.g., on the tailpiece, on the bridge) and graphics to indicate clusters or glissandos that have elaborate shapes. His notation is always precise, although the execution of glissandos or of passages of rapidly changing noises will necessarily differ slightly from performance to performance.

PRINCIPAL COMPOSITIONS: *Psalmy Dawida* [The Psalms of David] for chorus, percussion (1958, Moeck); *Strofy* [Strophes] for soprano, narrator, 10 instruments (1959, PWM); *Anaklasis* for strings, percussion (1960, Moeck); *Wymiary czasu i ciszy* [The Measures of Time and Silence] for chorus, chamber ensemble (1960, Moeck); *Ofiarom hiroszimy—Tren* [To the Victims of Hiroshima—Threnody] for 52 strings (1960, PWM); *String Quartet* (1960, PWM); *Polymorphia* for 48 strings (1961, Moeck); *Psalmus* on tape (1961); *Fluorescences* for orchestra (1961, Moeck and PWM); *Canon* for 52 strings, 2 tapes (1962); *Stabat Mater* for 3 choruses (1962, PWM); *St. Luke Passion* for narrator, solo voices, orchestra (1963–65, Moeck and PWM); *Sonata* for cello, orchestra (1964, PWM); *Dies irae* for solo voices, choir, orchestra (1967, Moeck and PWM); *De natura sonoris* for orchestra (1967, Moeck and PWM); *Diably z Loudun* [The Devils of Loudun], opera; libretto after A. Huxley (1968, Schott).

BIBL.: Jan A. Kaluzny, "K. P. and his Contribution to Modern Musical Notation," *Polish Review* (N. Y.) 1963/3:86–95; Trygve Nordwall, "K. P.—studium notacji i instrumentacji" [Study in Notation and Instrumentation], *Res facta* (Cracow) 1968/2:79–112; K. P. and Tadeusz A. Zieliński, "Tonsattaren infor traditionen" [The Composer and Tradition], *Nutida musik* (Stockholm) 1963–64/1:14–17; Tadeusz A. Zie-

liński, "Technika operowania instrumentami smyczkowymi w utworach K. P." [P. 's Technique in Writing for String Instruments], *Muzyka* (Warsaw)48 /1:74–92.

Tadeusz A. Zieliński

SEE ALSO Austria and Germany, Harmony and Counterpoint, Instrumental and Vocal Resources, Microtones, Opera.

Pentland, Barbara (Lally) (b. Winnipeg, Canada, 2 Jan 1912), studied piano in Winnipeg and Montreal during 1921–29 and composition in Paris with Cécile Gauthiez, 1929–30. She attended the Juilliard School (1936–39; composition with Frederick Jacobi, Bernard Wagenaar) and Tanglewood (1941, 1942; composition with Aaron Copland). During 1943–49 she taught theory and composition at the Royal Conservatory in Toronto and during 1949–63, at the Univ. of British Columbia in Vancouver. Her music has been influenced by the works of Anton Webern and related developments in postwar Europe.

PRINCIPAL COMPOSITIONS: *Studies in Line* for piano (1941, BMIC); *Sonata Fantasy* for piano (1947); *Sonata* for violin (1950); *String Quartet No. 2* (1953); *Concerto* for piano, string orchestra (1955–56); *Symphony No. 3 for 10 Parts* for flute, oboe, horn, trumpet, strings, timpani, xylophone (1957, BMIC); *Toccata* for piano (1958, BMIC); *Symphony No. 4* (1959); *Duo* for viola, piano (1960); *Fantasy* for piano (1962, BMIC); *Piano Trio* (1963); *Trio con Alea* for violin, viola, cello (1966); *News* for virtuoso voice, orchestra (1968–70); *String Quartet No. 3* (1969); *Music of Now*, 3 books for piano students (1969–70). List to 1960: *Composers of the Americas* 6:90–94.

PRINCIPAL WRITINGS: "Canadian Music—1950," *Northern Review* 3/3:43–46.

BIBL.: "B. P.," *Canadian Composers* (Montreal 1964):76–79; Robert Turner, "B. P.," *Canadian Music Journal* (summer 1958):15–26.

SEE ALSO Canada.

Pepin, Clermont (b. St.-Georges-de-Beauce, Quebec, 15 May 1926), studied in Quebec with Georgette Dionne (piano and harmony), in Montreal with Claude Champagne (harmony) and Arthur Letondal (piano), at the Curtis Institute with Rosario Scalero (composition) and Jeanne Behrend (piano), at the Royal Conservatory in Toronto with Arnold Walter (composition) and Lubka Kolessa (piano), and in Paris during 1949–51 with Arthur Honegger, André Jolivet, and Olivier Messiaen. He teaches composition at the Quebec

Province Conservatory of Music and Drama in
Montreal.

PRINCIPAL COMPOSITIONS: *Piano Concertos Nos.
1–2* (1946, 1949); *Piano Sonata* (1947); *Symphonies
Nos. 1–2* (1948, 1957); *String Quartets Nos. 1–4*:
No. 1 (1948); No. 2, "Variations" (1956); No. 3,
"Adagio et fugue" (1959); No. 4, "Hyperboles"
(1960); *Suite* for piano (1950); *Guernica*, symphonic
poem (1952); *Les Portes de l'enfer*, ballet (1953);
Le Rite du soleil noir, symphonic poem (1955);
L'Oiseau-phenix, ballet; scenario by François
Bernier and Ludmilla Chiriaeff after a French
Canadian legend (1956); *Musique pour Athalie* for
woodwinds, brass (1956); *Monologue* for chamber
orchestra (1960–61). Pepin has also written some
two dozen piano pieces. List to 1960: *Composers
of the Americas* 6:97–100.

Pepping, Ernst (b. Duisburg, Germany, 9 Dec
1901), attended the Berlin Hochschule für
Musik (1922–26, composition with Walter
Gmeindl). Since 1934 he has taught composition at the Berlin Kirchenmusikschule, and
since 1953 he has also been a professor of
composition at the Berlin Hochschule.

PRINCIPAL COMPOSITIONS (published by Bärenreiter unless otherwise noted): *Kleine Messe* for
3-part chorus (1929); *90th Psalm* for chorus (1934,
Schott); *Lust hab' ich g'habt zur Musika*, variations
for orchestra (1936, Schott); *Piano Sonatas Nos.
1–3* (1937, Schott); *Deutsche Messe: Kyrie Gott
Vater in Ewigkeit* for chorus (1938, Schott);
Grosses Orgelbuch for organ (1939, Schott);
Symphonies Nos. 1–3 (1939, Schott; 1942, Schott;
1944); *Das Jahr* for chorus (1940, Schott); *Kleines
Orgelbuch* for organ (1940, Schott); *Lob der Träne*
for chorus (1940); *Der Wagen*, song cycle (1940–41,
Schott); *Organ Concertos Nos. 1–2* (1941, Schott);
Toccata and Fugue "Mitten wir in Leben sind" for
organ (1941, Schott); *Piano Sonata No. 4* (1945);
String Quartet (1943, Schott); *Phantasien* for piano
(1945); *Liederbuch nach Gedichten von Paul
Gerhardt* for voice, piano (1945–46); *Haus- und
Trostbuch* for voice, piano (1946); *Heut und Ewig*,
song cycle for chorus (1949); *Missa "Dona nobis
pacem"* for chorus (1949); *Passionsbericht des
Matthäus* for chorus (1950); *Piano Concerto*
(1950); *Te Deum* for soloists, chorus, orchestra
(1956); *2 Orchesterstücke* based on a chanson of
Binchois (1958); *Die Weinachtsgeschichte des
Lukas* for 4–7 mixed voices (1959); *Spandauer
Chorbuch*, an edition of the 2- to 6-part chorale
settings by Gottfried Grote (1960, Schott);
Johannes der Taufer, vespers for chorus (1962);
139th Psalm for alto, chorus, orchestra (1966);
Deines Lichtes Glanz, motet for chorus (1967);
Preludia-Postludia on 18 Chorales for organ (1968,
Schott).

PRINCIPAL WRITINGS: *Der Polyphone Satz*
(Berlin 1942).

SEE ALSO Austria and Germany; Liturgical
Music: Christian.

Performance. Discussing performance is
always difficult because of the evanescence of
the phenomenon. Even where recordings exist,
the evidence they provide is inconclusive, for
only recordings of live performances give an
accurate picture of what was actually happening at a given time. Moreover there are even
fewer qualified observers in this branch of
music than in the others; the few who know
rarely write, and the many who write usually
do not practise. It is almost impossible to
prove any assertion about performance or to
argue on the basis of accepted precepts. This
discussion, therefore, will not be an objective
summary of recent history but merely the
observations, reflections, and deductions of
two composers and practitioners.

GENERAL CONDITIONS. Variety of standards
and practices is the most basic general condition that pertains in the performance of
20th-century music. A good performance of
notated music has three main properties: 1)
Accuracy. Real accuracy would imply a
complete realization of the composer's intentions. What is meant here is only that the
minimum literal significance of the notation is
being translated into sound. Thus, accuracy
means that no explicit notational direction is
contravened. 2) Conceptual awareness. This
means that the performer is aware of the
implicit significance of the notation. He is
aware of the historical, conceptual, and
systematic framework of the piece he is playing.
3) Interpretation. This is an attitudinal matter,
suggesting that the performer strives to
identify his views with those of the composition he is realizing and thus become a "disembodied" medium for its projection. This
notion defines interpretation not as the addition of nuance (appropriate or otherwise) by
the performer, but as the discovery on increasingly profound levels of the composition's
structure.

The 20th century as a whole seems to have
a wider range of standards than any previous
era, and the spread seems to have constantly
increased (good performances getting better
and poor ones remaining about the same). The
main factors that contribute to this range are
familiarity with the music and size of the
performing medium. Premieres are usually
the poorest performances, for the work itself
and often its conceptual framework are
unfamiliar to its executants. The larger the
performing forces the worse the performance;
soloists and chamber musicians have both
greater capacities (as a rule) and greater
incentives to conscientious performance than
do rank and file members of a chorus or

orchestra. In the case of the largest forces (orchestras and opera troupes), performances tend to be very bad, not only because mass performance decreases the individual's concern and sense of participation but, more importantly, because the leadership (and hence the majority of the rank and file) of most of these institutions are tradition-oriented and ignorant of new music.

Time and place also contribute to the range in quality. It would be difficult if not impossible to find out precisely what early performances of the seminal literature of the century were like, unclouded by the distorted memories of apologists for the works themselves. Performance conditions in the Paris of Debussy and Stravinsky (1900–20) and the Vienna of Schoenberg, for instance, would reveal much of interest about the crucial works produced there; we might even be able to determine how performances affected compositional ideas. That Schoenberg found it necessary to found a Society for Private Performances in 1918 has always been taken to show the failure of established musical institutions to support new music. What has not been asked is how adequate his own performances were. This is the crucial point: not merely how the outside world treats a composer's new effort, but how he himself (or close colleagues) are able to project it. The evidence is not favorable. When Varèse was preparing the American premiere of *Pierrot lunaire*, Schoenberg told him that 100 rehearsals were required for the first performance. If this figure is accurate, it reveals that Schoenberg's players were hopelessly inadequate by present U.S. standards. (Parenthetically, we may note that Varèse's New York performing activity was like Schoenberg's in Vienna and reminds us that the same indifference to new music existed in the U.S.)

In regard to post-World War II music, performance standards in the U.S. and Europe appear to be quite different. With isolated exceptions, even European specialists in new music fall short of American standards of accuracy and comprehension. It would be interesting to know if this imbalance is more the result of a decline in European standards or an advance in American. Certainly the emigration of the major European composers to the U.S. before World War II offered an enormous stimulus to the growth of contemporary musical culture in America, just as their exodus left a vacuum in Europe.

In the U.S. standards are highest in large urban centers (particularly New York) and in the universities. Since 1960, and especially in the universities, there has been a reemergence of composer-performers working in collaboration with professional instrumentalists and singers. While there still remains an inverse relation between the size of an ensemble and the quality of performance it can produce, the values of the leadership do make an enormous difference. This explains the success of composer-directed groups in which the leadership has a personal stake in, and a unique comprehension of, the music being performed. In Europe older traditions have an inhibiting effect on the achievement of excellence by players. There, if a composer is involved in performance, he tends to function as an absolute authority. He may regard performance as a public-relations vehicle for the maintainance of his authority, and he may use the ensembles he directs primarily for professional advancement. Such attitudes discourage serious attention to the deeper properties of the piece being performed (or, be it said, composed). English standards, largely as a result of BBC patronage of contemporary music, are higher than those on the continent.

In regard to composer-directed performance, the achievements of several major composers are significant. Chief among them was Varèse, who after his arrival in New York in 1916 conducted the New Symphony Orchestra (founded 1919 specifically to perform contemporary music) and founded the International Composers Guild with Carlos Salzedo in 1921, which presented many U.S. premieres of Stravinsky, the Viennese, Bartók, Cowell, Ruggles, and others. Paul Hindemith was also active as a conductor and chamber musician. The present scene abounds with composers involved with performance. In Europe they usually serve as conductors; Pierre Boulez and Bruno Maderna are among the most significant. In the U.S. this activity is carried on mainly in university-based surroundings and includes as much instrumental performance as conducting. Among others who have been involved in this movement are Gunther Schuller, Lukas Foss, Ralph Shapey, Karl Kohn, William Hibbard, Harvey Sollberger, and myself.

In the U.S. there are notable ensembles of 6–24 performers in many universities: Columbia, Brandeis, Sarah Lawrence, the State Univ. of N. Y. at Buffalo and Stony Brook, the Univ. of Iowa, the Univ. of Wash., Mills College, the Univ. of Chicago, the Univ. of Houston, the Univ. of Calif. at Los Angeles, etc. There are also a few independent groups, the Monday Evening Concerts of Los Angeles being the oldest; the program content of such groups is widely varied, both in the U.S. and Europe. It is striking that even the most ideologically committed directors of these groups always include performances of the seminal literature as well as works of colleagues of divergent compositional views.

The commercial concert world stands in stark contrast to all these conditions. There is less incentive to conscientious performance since there is little sense of responsibility to the composer. Soloists and permanent chamber ensembles are by far the most conscientious, primarily because of a desire to uphold personal reputations. However, such performers' ideas of a good performance usually derive not from their discoveries about the nature of the piece but from previously learned abstractions about "expressing" generalities (including their own personalities), thus using the work as a vehicle for personal projection (composer-directed performance, it should be repeated, tends to regard the performer as a vehicle for expressing the work). Performances by orchestras and opera companies suffer not only from indifference among the players but from the preoccupation of conductors with public acclaim. Two recent exceptions are James Dixon, conductor of the State Univ. of Iowa orchestra, and Hans Rosbaud, late conductor of the Baden-Baden radio orchestra. Opera houses generally have the poorest standards partly for the reasons mentioned, partly because of the concentration on staging, and especially because performance levels in the standard literature are lower than those of orchestras. Economics are often cited to explain the underpreparation of post-1900 works in commercial institutions, but it is still true that available resources are often underutilized.

PERFORMANCE PROBLEMS IN THE SEMINAL LITERATURE. In Stravinsky from at least *Le Sacre* on, the major performance problem was thought to be rhythmic. This meant mainly changing meters, which once looked formidable on a page of score. However, since there is almost always a constant counting unit running through such changes, the problem was soon seen to be modest, and by mid-century it had disappeared as an issue altogether, even among musicians who do not specialize in 20th-century music. Indeed many present-day specialists have difficulty (especially in counting rests) negotiating the metric regularity of pre-20th century music. The Schoenberg (and Berg) repertory (especially orchestral) presents fewer meter changes, and the beats tend to be longer than in Stravinsky (and therefore easier to count in differing

quantities). The intrabeat milieu of Schoenberg, however, is more problematic than that of Stravinsky, and the interiors of Schoenberg's beats still tend to be messy. It is an interesting paradox: Stravinsky's rhythmic problems are external, they looked "modern," attention was paid to them, and they have been solved. Schoenberg's problems are more internal, they look more traditional, and they are still often ignored.

In the domain of instrumental balance (both orchestral and chamber), Stravinsky presents at this date no major problems. Serious questions of balance remain in Schoenberg and Berg, although in the chamber area the problems are understandably less severe. Webern is different. His texture and surface being simpler than those of the others, his problems have remained ones of conception and phrasing. He fares better conceptually now because his music has been studied, and better in terms of phrasing because of an increasing awareness of his debt to the traditional Viennese milieu (for example, his phrase relation, compressed, to Mahler).

Much of the seminal literature has been plagued by textual problems. Stravinsky has largely escaped this, but the Viennese (even Webern) have suffered from the perpetration of numerous errors in both chamber and orchestral publications. Though many of these are widely known, the publishers often seem unconcerned with revision and correction. Far worse is the case of Varèse, all of whose scores are riddled with errors (the published score of *Déserts* has almost 300!). With the Viennese there has even been suppression and falsification; the nonpublication of the allegedly fragmentary third act of *Lulu* is the most famous case.

In terms of notation, much that is considered traditional may actually be misleading, for many signs have changed their meaning without changing their form. When Schoenberg wrote

$$p \longrightarrow sf$$

in the *Violin Concerto* (1936), I suppose he meant sforzando within a forte context as we all do today. But when did it change? When Stravinsky wrote in the *Dumbarton Oaks Concerto* (1938)

for the strings, did he still mean

or did he intend the literal meaning of the signs as we take them today? Stravinsky presents primarily problems of underediting. The lack of articulation and dynamic indications, especially in his middle works, may have served his original purpose of discouraging "interpreters" by presenting neutral-looking pages. After only 30 years, however, this situation has begun to seriously obscure his intentions, and the problem will get worse.

As for Schoenberg's notation, how literally are his phrase directions to be taken as extensions of Wagnerian practice? (For that matter, how much do we know about Wagnerian practice?) What do his upbeat/downbeat signs really mean? Stress and prolongation vs. deemphasis and shortening? What does the sign Λ indicate? And what about sprechstimme? If the notes are not to be sung, what should be done with them? Glissandos to obscure the pitch? (Schoenberg apostles seemed to think not.) It seems almost like a performance direction arising out of hopelessness concerning singers, as much as out of the fact that *Pierrot lunaire* was commissioned by an actress. In any case, should one sing all the notes? In every case, after all, we are presented not with general linear contours but with specific pitches "not to be sung."

More recently, many composers have employed extensions of traditional notation rather than new notations to represent new compositional needs. An example is Stefan Wolpe, who has long employed beat-defying beamings and other notational complexities. A simple example is

$$\frac{2}{4} \; \gamma \; \overset{3}{\widehat{\Box\Box}} \; \gamma$$

I understand that he wants a sense of on-beat emphasis at the beginning of the triplet. But couldn't that be accomplished with a less eccentric combination of shifted barlines, accents, and subdivisions? An extreme instance arises in a passage for solo horn:

$$\frac{3}{4} \; \overset{\overset{4:3}{\overline{}}}{\overset{3}{\overline{}}} \; \acute{\Gamma} \; \acute{\Gamma} \; \acute{\Gamma}$$

It is hard to know what is meant here, since it equals nothing more than three quarter notes.

Babbitt and several other composers represent rhythm fairly clearly but are confusing in regard to articulation. Babbitt seems to use dynamics as articulative indications (stemming from the systematic use of dynamic levels to project different levels of compositional structure), but this often leaves the modes of attack and release unclear. Furthermore,

composers of this notational persuasion often feel that merely specifying a dynamic level for every event (which they do less precisely than appears on paper) will satisfy questions of phrasing. In other words, if the dynamic level of every event is specified, all larger groupings of events (phrases) will automatically fall into coherence. Such a procedure, unfortunately, depends on the assumption that dynamic levels are fixed quantities. Actually they are composite results of many factors (timbre, envelope, loudness, etc.), and they cannot be used in succession to indicate phrasing:

$$p \; mp \; mf \; f \; mf \; mp \; p$$

is not the same as

Attempts at new forms of notation (analog, graphic) are hard to evaluate since they are not neutral symbolic media for the expression of ideas but rather are wedded to ideological-compositional positions. They all have the effect of reducing rather than increasing the specificity of notation, which is opposed to the direction pursued by Western composers for at least 1,200 years. Also these means are expressive of compositional positions that themselves try to reduce the degree of predictable coherence a piece may possess. Therefore, it is not the notation but the compositional position that presents the performance problem.

SUMMARY AND PRESCRIPTIVES. Performance difficulties are of two kinds, psychological and physical. The psychological are also of two kinds, presentational and conceptional. Presentational problems indicate that the significance of the notation is not clear. For example, although the middle note in $\overset{3}{\sqrt{}}$ is halfway through the beat represented, its position on "and" is subsidiary in the notational presentation to its function in the triplet rhythm. Therefore it may be performed in the wrong place, as for instance if the performer unconsciously moves it nearer to the last member of the triplet in order to emphasize the qualitative, rather than the quantitative, aspects of the figure. When combined with $\sqrt{}$ as in , however, the displacement may be a serious error, especially if the mid-beat simultaneity is of special compositional importance. Conceptual troubles arise when the performer does not understand the framework of a piece. The player who looks for 19th-century rhetoric in the surface of 20th-century pieces provides a crude example. (Incidentally the idea that a notation sufficiently unambiguous to obviate the necessity of profound interpretation can exist is no more plausible than with any other language.) These two difficulties are always mixed. As can be inferred, it is almost always in the domain of time division that problems arise (indeed, this is true of all measured music).

The physical difficulties depend on the speed of events, their variability (in terms of dynamic levels and modes of articulation), and their distance from each other. Distance can be subdivided into four categories: 1) local-temporal, which concerns the execution of foreground rhythm; 2) large-scale temporal, which concerns the projection of the form and conception of the piece; 3) local-spatial, which concerns the execution of events within the same registral area (involving no change of hand position, string, overblowing, etc.); and 4) large-scale spatial, which concerns the execution of events in different registers (involving changes of hand position, string, overblowing, etc.).

What kinds of difficulties does 20th-century music present? Here one must speak very generally indeed, since 20th-century music is such a varied lot. Among the new demands being made of performers are ensemble phrasing and improvisation. The phrase structure of much recent music requires participation of more than one performer in the execution of single-line phrases. This requires a highly integrated ensemble performance, which previous music has not demanded (but which yields excellent results when applied to that music). The recent rise of indeterminant procedures cannot but lead to new types of performance (although they must be carefully distinguished from older types of improvisation, including traditional jazz, which proceeded according to highly developed conventions and traditions). In post-1945 Western music the major problems arise from demands (reaching a high point in Europe during the early 1950s and now abating) for speed of execution (especially of registrally dispersed events), for flexibility of rhythmic succession (especially internal rhythm, i.e., "irrational" beat divisions), and for highly varied dynamic levels and modes of articulation. It seems that the most difficult postwar music has already been written and that the present moment is witnessing a trend toward external simplification. Comparing

today's music with that of the 19th century, we can see that greater control is demanded (for the high-speed execution of varied events) but that less physical endurance is needed. Thus the overall level or quantity of demands has probably not changed.

The demands for flexibility and control, which are psychological, are in their nature temporary, for they disappear with familiarity and comprehension. But they persist today because the education of performers (both technical and conceptual) has generally not been revised since 1900. Of the four types of distance mentioned above, the only one addressed in present education is the local-spatial ("good" hand position, bow arm, vibrato, tone, etc.). This leaves 75 percent of the problems untended. Perhaps the best way to make up for the untended 75 percent would be to give each performer training in current composition; the postwar composer-performer reunion could aid in this effort since its advocates already know both worlds. The next step after this would be to suppress the reliance on the notion of "style." This notion creates a false (linguistically generated) dichotomy between "structure" and "manner," which in fact have no separate existence but only seem to separate themselves depending on the degree of generality of one's view at a given instant. They are one, and this oneness will be revealed to performer and hearer alike if they seek an understanding of compositional method through compositional activity, of the historical milieu through study of the works of 20th-century masters, and of the mechanics of playing through the exercise of instrumental and vocal skills.

Charles Wuorinen
(research assistance by Jeffrey Kresky)

INDETERMINATE PERFORMANCE. Since World War II, along with the continuing emphasis on technical proficiency in the performance of notated music, a radically new attitude toward performance has developed. In the case of older music of the classical European tradition, both increasing historical distance from the source and the proliferation of mass communication media have affected performance practice profoundly. The great performers of the past, so far as one can judge from the scanty evidence available, bent tradition to their will and subjected a text to their subjective expressive needs, treating it as an accompaniment to their solo. Most classical stars today limit themselves to the blind repetition of formulas acquired in the conservatories and executed with ruthless precision in concert halls designed to make a live performance sound like a stereo recording (nature imitating art). The illusionist techniques of recording have further widened the historical abyss that separates contemporary ears from the sounds of the past. Whereas the music of this century, in both composition and performance, could be said to be characterized by a process of increasing fragmentation, commercial recording uses this same process of analytic fragmentation to create the illusion of uninterrupted continuity of tradition. The microphones, the electronic doctoring-up, the splicing and editing done by unknown technicians, the bureaucratic hierarchy of the studio all combine to split time, space, matter, energy, and consciousness into separate fragments, reducing performer, listener, and indeed all living elements of the process of musical communication to a state of isolation and imprisonment. Both performing and listening thus become a solitary activity. This condition is of crucial importance when one considers that one of the most significant traditional functions of musical performance has been to bring people together to share in a common experience. There are signs, however, that alternatives to present-day classical performance practice may be available and that these may lead to a reburgeoning of the historical roots of our musical culture. Mauricio Kagel's *Ludwig Van* (1969), more an interpretation than a composition, represents a radically new approach to the performance of Beethoven. *HPSCHD* (1967–69) of John Cage and Lejaren Hiller, a performance-work whose complexity is perhaps unprecedented in the history of music, employs the computer as an instrument for a new interpretation of certain aspects of the music of Mozart. In some works by the Italian Giuseppe Chiari, such as *Beethoven's Moonlight Sonata* (1967), electronics and theater are used to disrupt the sense of order and continuity which the familiar sound of classical music habitually evokes. New modes of performance of the classics have been developed by the Scratch Orchestra of London. Michael Sahl's *Mitzvah for the Dead* (1966), Henri Pousseur's *Votre Faust* (1961–67), and Luciano Berio's *Sinfonia* (1968) all represent attempts to confront the closed stylistic universe of the classical performer with the possibility of a more fluid approach to the traditional literature.

In all of the above works the composer assumes the role of interpreter. The mobile relation of interpreter to text that is expressed in these pieces is not in itself an innovation but an extension of new compositional and performance procedures introduced in the 1950s and early 60s. The most important of these were the use of chance in composition and of improvisation in performance. The use of chance operations in composition necessarily led to new attitudes toward performance. As Cage wrote in his 1952 "Music of Changes," "Value judgments are not in the nature of this work as regards either composition, performance, or listening. The idea of relation (the idea: 2) being absent, anything (the idea: 1) may happen. A 'mistake' is beside the point, for once anything happens it authentically is" (*Silence*: 59). In the aleatory, graphic, and indeterminate music of the 50s the idea was that the performer participated in the operations of composition; he was "given a certain freedom" (Boulez, *Notes of an Apprenticeship*: 41), but with the composer still the boss. An early example is Karlheinz Stockhausen's *Klavierstück XI* (1956), which consists of a number of fragments in which pitches and rhythms are precisely notated by the composer but their chronological order is left to the performer. The tempo, phrasing, and dynamics are applied by the performer to each successive fragment according to rigid rules, depending on the order he has chosen. An extension of a similar technique can be found in Christian Wolff's *Duo for Pianists 2* (1958), the score of which consists of a number of fragments notated in such a way as to admit several possible versions of each to be worked out by the performers either prior to or during performance, depending on the degree of precision desired. The order of individual sections, instead of being chosen arbitrarily by the performers, simply "happens" in an unpredictable fashion as a result of a system of cues to which the performers respond. There is a basic difference in the criteria that govern a performer's choices in the two cases. With Stockhausen the appropriate attitude might be one of subservience; the performer might select a version that exhibited the encyclopedic nature of the composer's system with the greatest possible variety, arranging his material in all "parameters" from one extreme to another in the manner of serial music. He would, in effect, be finishing the composer's work for him, thereby displaying his own virtuosity but not exercising any real originality. With Wolff the use of indeterminacy in performance opens the work to external influences genuinely beyond the composer's intentions; it would be suitable for the performer to become the composer to the extent that he, too, would leave his decisions open and allow them to be governed by chance rather than by some rigid system or by the expressive inclinations of his own ego.

In the late 50s and early 60s the situation acquired a radical twist: largely under the influence of Cage, but also a result of developments in jazz, theater, and painting, a new art of performance made its appearance. The performance was the art, the collectively lived moment, the happening; a composition was not an eternal, Platonic model imperfectly mirrored in performance but more like preparation, rehearsal, setting up the stage and electrical equipment, phoning up musicians, and arranging concerts, etc. Whatever structures were built were like musical instruments, flexible and maneuverable, and the music was in the playing of them. Composition became the preparation of schemes for improvisation, the construction of platforms or scaffoldings from which the performer could take off and fly, or to which he could return as a point of rest. Structure became less visible and rational, more fluid and free. In compositions such as La Monte Young's *Poem for Tables, Chairs, Benches, Etc.* (1960–) and Cage's *Cartridge Music* (1960) and *Theater Piece* (1960), the performer made up his own time scheme and programed his own activities to fill it. Cornelius Cardew's *Octet '61* employs an ambiguous ciphered notation, the working out of which by each performer leads to unforeseeable combinations of events that could be produced neither by strict composition nor by free improvisation.

The youth movement, both in the U.S. and in Europe, provided fertile ground in the 60s for a rebirth of the art of performance. In and close to American universities, composers and performers busied themselves with the possibilities of live electronics and group improvisations: Foss, Austin, Ashley, Oliveros, Mumma, Behrman, Lucier, Young, Riley, Reich, and Glass all formed groups. The ONCE group in Ann Arbor and the New Music Ensemble in Davis, Calif., toured and performed for growing student audiences. The Sonic Arts Group, based in New York, does not deal directly with pure improvisation but has produced a number of works in which electronics are employed in a free and sometimes highly theatrical manner (Robert Ashley's *Frogs* and Alvin Lucier's *Vespers*, as well as compositions by Gordon Mumma and David Behrman). In the cities the new jazz musicians banded together to form large groups such as the Jazz Composers' Orchestra in New York and the AACM (Association for the Advancement of Creative Music) in Chicago. Many of these performers (Shepp,

Lacy, Cherry, Thicai, Silva, Jarman, Braxton) sought with varying degrees of success a more tolerant atmosphere across the Atlantic; and Europe, heated by the flames of youth politics and with a tradition for fostering the arts, provided in some ways a more fertile ground for the new music. "Free jazz" and improvising groups spread across the continent: NC (Nuova Consonanza) and MEV (Musica Elettronica Viva) in Rome, AMM in London, ICP (Instant Composers' Pool) in Amsterdam, QUAX in Prague. The Living Theater, driven from the U.S. by financial need, opened thousands of minds to new ideas on performance, collective improvisation, and audience participation. Of the European groups, AMM in London has concentrated mainly on pure improvisation. The MEV group, a traveling community of European and American musicians, has worked consistently and deliberately in the direction of anarchy. In *Sound Pool* (1968), social and musical structure were abandoned entirely. The "audience" was asked to bring sounds to be added to the "pool," and the activity of the group consisted mainly in catalyzing and sustaining a fountainlike feedback process of communication through pure sound spontaneously generated by the collective presence of masses of people.

The recent wave of interest in improvisation on the part of composers (many of whom are undeniably motivated by a concern with fashion) nevertheless reflects a genuine crisis of the art and a desire to reexamine its basic premises. Wherever the art of music is cultivated primarily by a specialized class of people known as "musicians," it has tended to develop an esoteric, competitive, and authoritarian character; it has become "classical," removed from the people. Musical performance, like athletics, has then been regarded as a competitive skill in which excellence consists in conforming to standards set by a competitive system. In a truly collective art form, individuality would flourish; the distinction between "classical" and "popular," like that between "composer" and "performer," would be abolished, but far from being destroyed in the process, each term would be assimilated into a higher unity. Good performers know that music is an active and not a passive experience; they know too that this act consists mainly of listening. Listening is an act of self-discipline. When the listener, i.e., the "audience," becomes performer, then it may be possible for music to become an art of collective self-discipline. Much music during the past decade shows a clear tendency in this direction. Attempts to induce immediate and radical change in the basic orientation of musical culture, in the spirit of Boulez's belief (expressed in 1948) that "music should be collective hysteria and spells, violently of the present time" (*Notes of an Apprenticeship*: 71), have not generally produced more than a minor disturbance of the established order. The orgiastic, Dionysian aspects of performance are not, nor have they ever been, the only nor even the principal features of musical culture. Nor is it thinkable or desirable that music should limit itself to the abstraction of pure improvisation, free of the ordering power of mind. The most extreme experiments in the abandonment of structure (e.g., Cage's *Musicircus* and MEV's *Sound Pool*) have shown that something more than absolute freedom is necessary if one wishes to avoid the alternative of terror. At the same time, they have helped begin the process of liberation.

Frederic Rzewski

SEE ALSO Asian Music and Western Composition; Education for the Professional; Electronic Music: History and Development; Indeterminacy; Instrumental and Vocal Resources; Jazz; Notation; Orchestration; Popular Music; Publishing; Rhythm.

Perkowski, Piotr (b. Oweczacze, Ukraine, 17 March 1901), studied at the Warsaw Conservatory (1923–25, composition with Roman Statkowski) and the Ecole de Science Politique in Paris (1926–28). He studied composition privately with Karol Szymanowski in Warsaw and with Albert Roussel in Paris. He was director of the Torun Conservatory during 1936–39 and taught composition at the Warsaw State Academy of Music during 1946–70, except for 1950–56 when he was dean of the Wroclaw Academy of Music. During World War II he organized Polish underground cultural activities and helped plan the reconstruction of Polish music life. In 1945 he organized the Union of Polish Composers and the Union of Polish Musicians and became director of music for the Ministry of Culture and Art. During 1946–49 he was president of the Council of Art Unions, and since 1965 he has been councilor for cultural development for the city of Warsaw. He has also held a number of other official posts. He was president of the Cracow Opera Association during 1951–56 and conducted the Orchestra of the Polish Radio during 1956–58. His music has been influenced by the ethos of Polish folk music and by his commitment to general humanistic values.

PRINCIPAL COMPOSITIONS (published by PWM unless otherwise noted): *Swantewit*, 3-act ballet (composed 1930, reconstructed 1945–48); *Sinfonietta* (1932, Eschig); *Szkice torunskie* [Torun Sketches] for orchestra (1938); *Warsaw Overture* for orchestra (1954, unpub.); *Nocturne* for orchestra (1955); *Klementyna*, 3-act ballet (1960–63); *Girlandy* [Garlands], radio opera (1961, unpub.); *Balladyna*, 2-act ballet (1961–64). Many of Perkowski's early works were lost during the war.

Perle, George (b. Bayonne, N. J., 6 May 1915), studied composition with Wesley LaViolette at De Paul Univ. (1934–38) and intermittently with Ernst Krenek during the early 40s. He has held a number of teaching posts, the most important being at the Univ. of Louisville (1949–57), Univ. of Calif. at Davis (1957–61), and Queens College in New York (since 1961). During 1971–72 he was Visiting Birge-Cary Prof. of Music at the State Univ. of N. Y. at Buffalo. He has also produced an important book on contemporary music (*Serial Composition and Atonality*), as well as over 40 scholarly articles.

In the 1930s Perle was among the first American composers to be attracted by the music and thought of Schoenberg, Berg, and Webern. The main stimulus to his composing, however, came not so much from the 12-tone system itself as from the type of systematic approach towards dodecaphonic music it represents. In 1939 he developed a "12-tone modal system" to join some of the methods of the 12-tone system with some of the properties of tonality. Basically this system creates a hierarchy among the notes of the chromatic scale so that they are all referentially related to one or two pitches which then function as a tonic note or chord in tonality. The system similarly creates a hierarchy among intervals and finally among larger collections of notes, "chords." The main debt of this system to the 12-tone system lies in its use of an ordered set to structure its relations. This set, however, does not necessarily control linear succession in the same way that a 12-tone set does. To date most of Perle's works use this system, most significantly, *3 Movements* for orchestra (1960), *String Quartet No. 5* (1960–67), *Cello Concerto* (1966), and *Serenade No. 2* (1968).

Dissatisfaction with certain limiting aspects of the system led Perle to use the 12-tone system on occasion (*3 Inventions* for piano, 1957) but more often to abandon precompositional constraints in favor of contextually derived procedures. The *String Quintet* (1958–59) and a series of works for solo instruments were written in this manner. "They are 'freely' or 'intuitively' conceived," according to the composer, "combining various serial procedures with melodically generated tone centers, intervallic cells, symmetrical formations, etc. A rhythmic concept, or rather ideal, toward which I progressed in these works was that of a beat, variable in duration but at the same time as tangible and coherent as the beat in classical music, and of an integration between the larger rhythmic dimensions and the minimal metric units."

Rather than as a means of writing different kinds of music, the several approaches Perle has used are methods of exploring the same kinds of ideas from different directions. What Perle has essentially been attempting is the creation of a musical language in which pitches have the same kinds of meaningful relations and inflections as they do in tonality, but which builds these properties among 12 pitches in the way tonality does among seven (the diatonic scale). In 1969, in collaboration with myself, he discovered that his 12-tone modal system contained the essential information with which to build a comprehensive musical system able to structure voice-leading and harmony on the large and the small in a compositionally meaningful way. The *String Quartet No. 6* (1969), *Toccata* (1969), and *Suite in C* (1970) use this new system.

PRINCIPAL COMPOSITIONS (published by Presser unless otherwise noted): *2 Rilke Songs* for voice, piano (1941, unpub.); *3 Sonatas* for solo clarinet (1943); *Hebrew Melodies* for cello (1945); *Solemn Procession* for band (1947); *Piano Sonata* (1950, Southern); *String Quintet* (1958–59); *Wind Quintets Nos. 1–3* (1959, 1960, 1967); *3 Movements* for orchestra (1960); *Monody 1* for flute (1960); *String Quartet No. 5* (1960–67); *Serenade No. 1* for viola, chamber ensemble (1962); *Monody 2* for double bass (1962); *3 Inventions* for bassoon (1962); *Short Sonata* for piano (1964); *Solo Partita* for violin, viola (1965); *Cello Concerto* (1966); *Serenade No. 2* for chamber ensemble (1968, unpub.); *String Quartet No. 6* (1969, unpub.); *Toccata* for piano (1969, unpub.); *Suite in C* for piano (1970, unpub.). List to 1970: *Composers of the Americas* 15:163–67.

PRINCIPAL WRITINGS: "The Chansons of Antoine Busnois," *Music Review* 11:89–97; "Theory and Practice in 12-tone Music," *Score* (June 1959):58–64; *Serial Composition and Atonality, An Introduction to the Music of Schoenberg, Berg, and Webern* (Berkeley–Los Angeles 1962); "*Lulu:* the Formal Design," *Journal of the American Musicological Society* 17:179–92; "*Pierrot Lunaire,*" *The Commonwealth of Music* ed. by G. Reese, R. Brandel (Glencoe, N. Y., 1965):307–

12; "The String Quartets of Béla Bartók," notes for a record album (Dover Publications 1967); "The Musical Language of Wozzeck," *Music Forum* 1:204–59; "Wozzeck: Ein zweiter Blick auf das Libretto," *Neue Zeitschrift für Musik* (5 May 1968):218–21; "Webern's Twelve-Tone Sketches," *Musical Quarterly* (Jan 1971): 1–25.

BIBL.: Leo Kraft, "The Music of G. P.," *Musical Quarterly* (April 1971); Henry Weinberg, "The Music of G. P.," *ACA Bulletin* (Sept 1962):6–11.

Paul Lansky

SEE ALSO Instrumental and Vocal Resources, Theory, 12-Tone Techniques, United States.

Perry, Julia (A.) (b. Lexington, Ky., 25 March 1924), attended Westminster Choir College in Princeton, N. J. (1943–48, composition with Switten). She studied counterpoint with Nadia Boulanger at Fontainebleau (summer 1952) and worked with Luigi Dallapiccola at Tanglewood (summer 1951) and in Italy (1952–53, 1955–56). During the summers of 1956–58 she studied conducting with Zecchi and Galliera at the Accadèmia Chigiana in Siena. In 1967 she taught at Florida A. & M. Univ. in Tallahassee and in 1969 was a visiting music consultant at the Atlanta Colleges Center.

PRINCIPAL COMPOSITIONS: *Stabat Mater* for mezzo-soprano, string quartet or string orchestra (1951); *Short Piece for Orchestra* (1952); *Symphony No. 1* (1959); *Symphony No. 3* (1962); *Violin Concerto* (1963); *Symphony No. 4* (1964); *The Selfish Giant*, opera-ballet (1964); *Piano Concerto* (1965); *Symphony No. 9* (1965–70); *Symphony No. 6* for band (1966, Fischer); *Symphony U.S.A.* for chorus, small orchestra (1967); *Symphony No. 8* (1968–69).

PRINCIPAL WRITINGS: "Compendium in Musical Perspective," (unpub. lecture, 1969); "Generation Gap in Popular Music Perspective," (unpub. lecture, 1969); *40 Studies for Classroom Musical Composition* (unpub. manuscript, 1969–70).

Persichetti, Vincent (b. Philadelphia, 6 June 1915), studied at Combs College, the Philadelphia Conservatory, and the Curtis Institute. His principal teachers were Russell King Miller (1924–36) and Roy Harris (1943) in composition, Fritz Reiner (1938–42) in conducting, and Olga Samaroff (1938–42) in piano. He is one of America's most influential composition teachers and has been on the faculties of the Philadelphia Conservatory (1942–62) and the Juilliard School (since 1947), where he is chairman of the composition department. He has been director of publications for the Elkan-Vogel Co. since 1952 and is also active as pianist, lecturer, conductor, and critic.

Persichetti's works number about 120 and include nine symphonies, 11 piano sonatas, 13 serenades for various instrumental combinations, some 70 songs, nine band works, three string quartets, two piano quintets, much other chamber and choral music, and works for the organ. He has a phenomenal natural musicality, closely resembling Hindemith's. He can improvise entire sonatas, read the most complex scores at sight, and in the classroom quote musical examples covering the entire range of musical literature from memory. Technical fluency is apparent from his earliest works, dated 1929. He has always written in whatever manner suits his particular conception at the time, from freely tonal through quasi-serial music, all with an equally sure hand. There has been no steady developing direction, though recently (*The Creation*, 1970) the music has become more introspective, complex, and adventuresome. His best music is fashioned from lyrical melodic lines or seminal motivic materials having their basis in diatonic harmony. Rhythmically much of the music has the familiar American drive, though when he writes slow music or becomes improvisational he becomes more personal and interesting. His music is always practical and as such is widely used and performed. The best insight into his style is provided by his own text, *Twentieth Century Harmony*, which is almost a codification of his materials.

PRINCIPAL COMPOSITIONS (published by E-V): *Harmonium*, song cycle for soprano, piano, Op. 50; poems by Wallace Stevens (1951); *Symphony No. 4*, Op. 51 (1951); *Piano Sonata No. 9*, Op. 58 (1952); *Symphony No. 5* for strings, Op. 61 (1953); *Piano Quintet*, Op. 66 (1954); *Symphony No. 6* for band, Op. 69 (1956); *String Quartet No. 3*, Op. 81 (1959); *Shimah b'koli*, Psalm 130, for organ, Op. 89 (1962); *Stabat Mater* for chorus, orchestra, Op. 92 (1963); *Piano Sonata No. 11*, Op. 101 (1965); *Mascarade* for band, Op. 102 (1965); *The Creation* for chorus, orchestra, Op. 111 (1970); *Symphony No. 9*, "Janiculum," Op. 113 (1971).

PRINCIPAL WRITINGS: *William Schuman*, written with Flora Rheta (New York 1954); *Twentieth Century Harmony* (New York 1961).

Hugo Weisgall

SEE ALSO Dance.

Petrassi, Goffredo (b. Zagarola, near Palestrina, Italy, 16 July 1904), entered the choir school of San Salvatore in Laura in 1913. In 1919 he began working in a Rome music store, where he could study the scores he was hired to keep in order and where he met many professional musicians, among them Alessandro Bustini who gave him piano lessons on Sundays. He began studying harmony with Vicenzo di Donati in 1925 and attended the Accadèmia di Santa Cecilia (1928–32). He has been teaching at that conservatory since 1934, and since 1936 has been active on various governmental commissions on music and in several private musical organizations in Italy. During 1954–56 he was president of the ISCM.

Petrassi's production is centered in seven concertos for orchestra, the *Flute Concerto* and *Estri*, and in his large choral works. He has written only a few piano pieces and songs. From the start his music was marked by technical mastery, clarity of form and texture, a highly developed feeling for timbre, and a natural musicality that is evident even in his most advanced works. His music from the 1930s displays enormous vitality in its driving rhythms and strident dissonances, which alternate with consonant passages. In their neoclassical traits these works show influences of Stravinsky, Hindemith, and Casella. During the 40s Petrassi wrote music marked by an increased sensitivity in the handling of musical materials, a turning inwards, and a new lyrical expressivity. One feels in this music not only the musician but also the philosopher. A number of compositions of this decade are (in the broad sense) religious in character, although not liturgical: the *Magnificat* (1939–40), the *Sacred Hymns*, and the *Coro di morti* (1940–41). The two operas are very different; *Il Cordovano* (1944–48) is a spirited opera buffa, while *Morte dell'aria* (1949–50) is a tragic, metaphysical work, somewhat in the Wagner tradition with hints of Schoenberg. Beginning in the third concerto for orchestra (*Récréation concertante*, 1953) he made free use of serial devices. He has remained true, however, to the humanistic tradition, creating music that is neither autobiographically personal nor speculatively "abstract" but which is oriented toward human expression and, in its detached atmosphere, sometimes borders on the metaphysical. The orchestral concertos Nos. 4–7 (1954–64) and *Estri* (1966–67) are characterized by an economy and concentration of musical ideas and means, an almost complete renunciation of thematic material in favor of motivic fragmentation, and a formal continuity that depends not on repetition or imitation but on the free association of logically and psychologically related sounds and silences in a structure that is never static.

PRINCIPAL COMPOSITIONS (published by S-Z unless otherwise noted): *Partita* for orchestra

(1932); *Concertos for Orchestra Nos. 1–7*: No. 1 (1933–34, Ricordi); No. 2 (1951); No. 3, "Récréation concertante" (1953); No. 4 for string orchestra (1954); No. 5 (1955); No. 6, "Invenzione concertata," for strings, brass, percussion (1957); No. 7 (1964); *Salmo 9* for chorus, orchestra (1934–36, Ricordi); *Piano Concerto* (1939); *Magnificat* for soprano, chorus, orchestra (1939–40, Ricordi); *Coro di morti* for men's voices, 3 pianos, brass, double bass, percussion (1940–41); *La follia di Orlando*, ballet in 3 scenes with recitatives for baritone (1942–43); *Ritratto di Don Chisciotte*, 1-act ballet (1945, UE); *Il Cordovano*, 3-act opera (1944–48); *Morte dell'aria*, 1-act tragedy (1949–50); *Noche oscura*, cantata for chorus, orchestra (1950–51); *String Quartet* (1956–57); *Serenata* for flute, viola, double bass, harpsichord, percussion (1958); *Trio* for violin, viola, cello (1959); *Flute Concerto* (1960); *Mottetti per la Passione* for chorus (1965); *Estri* for 15 instruments (1966–67).

BIBL.: Fidele d'Amico, *G. P.* (Rome 1942); Mario Bortolotto, "Il cammino di G. P.," *Quaderni della rassegna musicale* 1 (Turin 1964); ——, *Le Opere di G. P. 1957–1960* (Milan 1960); ——, "P.s Stil 1960," *Melos* 33:48–50; Everett Helm, "P. 'To Discover my Own Self'," *Christian Science Monitor* (17 June 1968); L. Pinzauti, "A colloquio con G. P.," *Nuova rivista musicale italiana* (1968):482–93; B. Porena, "I concerti di P.," *ibid.* (1967):101–19; John S. Weissmann, *G. P.* (Milan 1957); ——, "G. P. and his Music," *Music Review* 22:198–211. Bibl. 1926–69: Claudio Annibaldi, ed., *Catalogo bibliografico delle opere di G. P.* (Milan 1971).

Everett Helm

SEE ALSO Italy.

Petrić, Ivo (b. Ljubljana, Yugoslavia, 16 June 1931), attended the Academy of Music in Ljubljana (1953–58), where he studied composition and conducting. He lives in Ljubljana, where since 1962 he has directed the Slavko Osterc ensemble, which has given numerous performances of contemporary music throughout Europe. Petrić describes his earlier music as "neoclassical atonalism," influenced strongly by Hindemith and Bartók. After visiting new-music festivals in eastern Europe and becoming acquainted with the music of Lutosławski, Penderecki, and Ligeti, he began around 1961 to explore new types of sound (a "kind of new impressionism" including prepared instruments), new instrumental playing techniques, and indeterminacy.

PRINCIPAL COMPOSITIONS: *"Goga" Symphony* (1954); *Concerto grosso* for strings (1955); *Concerto* for flute, chamber orchestra (1955); *Symphony No. 2* (1957); *Concerto* for clarinet, chamber orchestra (1958, DSS); *Symphony No. 3* (1960); *Musique concertante* for woodwind quintet,

strings, timpani (1962, DSS); *Elégie sur le nom de Carlos Salzedo* for harp (1962, Pro Musica Viva); *Croquis sonores* for harp, chamber ensemble (1963, Pro Musica Viva); *Mosaiques* for clarinet, chamber ensemble (1964, DSS); *Symphonic mutations* (1964, DSS); *Epitaf* for harp, clarinet, violin, cello, strings, percussion (1965, DSS); *Jeux à 3* for cello, percussion, harp (1965, DSS); *Jeux à 4* for flute, E♭ clarinet, percussion, harp (1965, DSS); *Jeux* for voice, harp (1965); *Nuances en couleur*, chamber music for flute/piccolo, bassoon/contrabassoon, piano, harp, cello (1966, DSS); *Jeux II*, vocal and instrumental sounds on tape (1966); *Intarzije* [Inlaid Work] for chamber ensemble (1968, DSS); *Intégrals en couleur* for chamber orchestra (1968, DSS); *Lirizmi* for horn, piano (1969); *String Quartet 1969*, "à la mémoire de mon père" (1969); *3 Satires after Kriloff* for chorus, chamber ensemble (1970).

PRINCIPAL WRITINGS: "Razvoj glasbene misli 20. stoletja" [Development of Musical Meaning in the 20th Century], *Sodobnost* 10:385–96, 509–17, 612–21, 767–80; "Glasbena grafika—glasbeni jezik bodočnosti" [Musical Graphics—Musical Language of the Future], *ibid.* 11:151–58.

Petrides, Petro (John) (b. Nigdé, Turkey, 23 July 1892), studied law and political science at the Sorbonne (1911–14) and composition briefly with Albert Roussel (1919–20). As a composer he is mainly self-taught. During 1919–21 he lectured on the modern language and literature of Greece at the Sorbonne. He has been a music critic and contributor of articles on music for Greek, French, English, and American periodicals. The modal polyphony in his music is derived from folk music and Byzantine church music.

PRINCIPAL COMPOSITIONS: *Symphonies Nos 1–4*: No. 1, "Greek" (1926–28); No. 2, "Lyric" (1940); No. 3, "Parisian" (1941); No. 4, "Doric" (1943); *Greek Suite* for orchestra (1930, Schott); *The Modal Keyboard*, 12 suites for piano (1932); *Chorale and Variations on a Byzantine Theme Nos. 1–2* (1932, revised 1940; 1939); *Piano Concertos Nos. 1–2* (1934, 1936); *The Byzantine Offering*, prelude, aria, and fugue for orchestra (1934, revised 1935); *Ionian Suite* for orchestra (1937, Schott); *Digenis Akritas* for orchestra after a 7th-century Byzantine epic (1937–39); *Concerto for String Orchestra* (1939); *The Peddler*, ballet (1943); *Double Concerto* for 2 pianos, orchestra (1950); *St. Paul*, oratorio for vocal soloists, chorus, orchestra (1950); *Zefyra*, 3-act music drama (1957); *Requiem for the Emperor*, oratorio (1964).

SEE ALSO Greece.

Petrovics, Emil (b. Nagybecskerek, Yugoslavia, 9 Feb 1930), studied at the Liszt Conservatory in Budapest (composition with

Ferenc Farkas, music history with Dénes Bartha, folk music with Zoltán Kodály). He was music director of the Petöfi Theater in Budapest the five years it existed, during 1960–64. Since then he has taught general musical subjects at the Academy of Theater and Cinema Arts and also since 1969, composition at the Liszt Conservatory.

PRINCIPAL COMPOSITIONS (published by EMB unless otherwise noted): *Flute Concerto* (1957); *String Quartet* (1958); *Triangulum*, 3 studies for chorus (1958); *Négy önarckép álarcban* [4 Masked Self-Portraits] for harpsichord (1958); *C'est la Guerre*, 1-act opera (1961, Artisjus); *Lysistrata*, comic concert-opera for 2 sopranos, tenor, chorus, orchestra (1962); *Wind Quintet* (1964); *Passacaglia in Blues* for bassoon, piano (1964); *Sinfonia* for string orchestra (1964); *Jónás Könyve* [The Book of Jonah], oratorio for 2 tenors, baritone, chorus, orchestra (1966, unpub.); *Évszakok zenéje* [Music of the Seasons] for women's chorus (1967); *Crime and Punishment*, 3-act opera after Dostoevsky (1969, Artisjus).

PRINCIPAL WRITINGS: *Ravel* (Budapest 1958); "Dodekafonija u današnjoj madarskoj musici" [The 12-Tone Method in Contemporary Hungarian Music], *Zvuk* (Belgrade) 28–29:357–64; "Zeneszerzö és közönség" [The Composer and His Public], *Kortárs* (Budapest) 1963/5:718–20; "Hamburgi Jegyzatek" [Notes from Hamburg], *Magyar Zene* 1964/4:417–20; "De la musique associée à l'image," *Cinéma pratique* (Paris) 82:92–94.

BIBL.: Imre Fábián, "2 Opera Composers," *Tempo* 88:10–19; Imre Földes, "Beszélgetés P. E." [Conversations with E. P.], *Harmincasok* (Budapest 1969):125–45; György Kroó, "A 'C'est la Guerre' bemutatója az Állami Operaházban" [The First Performance of "C'est la Guerre" at the State Opera House], *Magyar Zene* 1962/2:132–42.

SEE ALSO Hungary.

Pfitzner, Hans (Erich) (b. Moscow, of German parents, 5 May 1869; d. Salzburg, 22 May 1949), achieved early recognition in Germany with his music drama *Der arme Heinrich* (1891) and the *Piano Trio in F* (1896). He held a municipal position in Strasbourg (1908–17), where he conducted the orchestra, headed the conservatory, and directed the opera. These years culminated in his masterpiece, the opera *Palestrina*. During the 1920s and early 30s, when he was teaching composition at the Music Academy in Munich, "Pfitzner Weeks" were celebrated frequently in German and Austrian cities, and many official honors were conferred upon him. The Third Reich bestowed the title *Reichskultursenator*, but his outspoken manner soon alienated him from the Nazi Party, and performances of his works

became infrequent (in some instances they were allegedly forbidden). The postwar years found him destitute until the Vienna Philharmonic provided financial support.

Pfitzner's output embraces five operas, 12 orchestral and concerted works, much chamber music, piano etudes, works for voice and orchestra, and 106 songs. An ardent defender of 19th-century musical values, whose models were Beethoven, Schumann, and Wagner, he opposed atonality and experimental trends. His expansive lyricism, chromatic richness framed by traditional cadences, and thematic transformation were often enlivened by contemporary resources such as dissonant counterpoint, nontriadic harmony, and unconventional rhythmic intricacies.

PRINCIPAL COMPOSITIONS: *Cello Sonata in F♯ Minor*, Op. 1 (1890, Breitkopf); *Der arme Heinrich*, opera; libretto by J. Grun (1891, Brockhaus); *Piano Trio in F*, Op. 8 (1896, Simrock); *Die Rose vom Liebesgarten*, opera; libretto by Grun (1897–1901, Brockhaus); *Das Christ-Elflein*, opera after I. V. Stach (1906, revised 1917, Brockhaus); *Piano Quintet in C*, Op. 23 (1908, Peters); *Palestrina*, opera; libretto by the composer (1912–15, Fürstner); *Von deutscher Seele*, cantata, Op. 28; text by J. v. Eichendorff (1921, Fürstner); *Piano Concerto in E♭* (1922, Boosey); *String Quartet in C♯ Minor* (1925, Boosey); *Violin Concerto in B Minor* (1925, Boosey); *Das dunkle Reich*, choral fantasy; composite text (1929, Brockhaus); *Das Herz*, opera, Op. 39 (1930–31, Boosey); *Symphony in C♯ Minor*, an adaptation of the string quartet (1932, Boosey); *Kleine Sinfonie*, Op. 44 (1939, Brockhaus); *Symphony in C* (1940, Boosey). Complete list in Grohe (see bibl.).

PRINCIPAL WRITINGS: *Gesammelte Schriften*, 3 vols. (Augsburg 1926–29); *Über musikalische Inspiration* (Berlin 1940).

BIBL.: Walter Abendroth, *H. P.* (Munich 1935); ——, *H. P.: Sein Leben in Bildern* (Leipzig 1941); ——, ed., *H. P.: Reden, Schriften, Briefe . . .* (Berlin 1955); ——, ed., *Mitteilungen der H. P.—Gesellschaft* (Munich 1954–); Julius Bahle, *H. P. und die geniale Mensch* (Constance 1949); Helmut Grohe, *H. P.: Verzeichnis sämtlicher im Druck erschienen Werke* (Munich n.d.); Karl Franz Müller, *In Memoriam H. P.* (Vienna 1950); Hans Rutz, *H. P.: Musik zwischen den Zeiten* (Vienna 1949); Ludwig Schrott, *Die Persönlichkeit H. P.s* (Zurich 1959); Erich Valentin, *H. P.: Werk und Gestalt eines Deutschen* (Regensburg 1939).

Donald G. Henderson

SEE ALSO Austria and Germany, Opera.

Philippot, Michel P(aul) (b. Verzy, France, 2 Feb 1925), earned his baccalaureate in mathematics and then attended the Paris Conservatory (1945–47) and the Professional

Training Center of the French Radio-Television Network (1948–49). He studied privately with René Leibowitz during 1945–49. He held the title of Professeur d'Education Musicale de la Ville de Paris during 1946–49, worked for the French Radio-Television Network as a sound engineer from then until 1959, and directed the Groupe de Recherches Musicales during 1959–61. He has continued to work for the network in executive positions, becoming music director in 1964.

PRINCIPAL COMPOSITIONS: *Piano Sonata* (1946, EFM); *Overture* for chamber orchestra (1948); *4 Mélodies sur des poèmes d'Apollinaire* for soprano, piano (1949); *Etudes Nos. 1–3*, musique concrète on tape (1952, 1958, 1962); *Piano Trio* (1953); *Variation* for 10 instruments (1957, Heugel); *3 Compositions* for piano (1958); *Ambiance Nos. 1–2*, musique concrète on tape (1959); *Composition* for string orchestra (1959, EFM); *Composition* for double orchestra (1959, EFM); *Pièce pour 10* for chamber ensemble (1962); *Transformations triangulaires* for 12 instruments (1962, EFM); *Pièce* for violin (1967, EFM).

PRINCIPAL WRITINGS: *Igor Stravinsky* (Paris 1965).

Phillips, Burrill (b. Omaha, Neb., 9 Nov 1907), studied at the Denver College of Music (1924–28) and the Eastman School (1928–33; composition with Howard Hanson, Edward Royce, Bernard Rogers). He has taught composition at Eastman (1933–49, 1965–66), the Univ. of Ill. (1949–64), and the Juilliard School (1968–69). He has written much music for the dance, the theater, and films, which, he notes, "has tended to make me compose in dramatic idioms," even when writing "in the most abstract forms." He prefers " 'hard edge' music, with clear harmonic content, clean lines, incisive rhythms." He particularly admires such composers as Mozart, Scarlatti, Soler, and Stravinsky.

PRINCIPAL COMPOSITIONS: *Selections from McGuffey's Reader*, suite for orchestra (1934, Fischer); *Piano Concerto* (1939–42); *Piano Sonatas Nos. 1–4* (1942, 49, 53, 60); *Tom Paine*, overture (1944, Hargail); *Don't We All*, 1-act chamber opera; libretto by Alberta Phillips (1948); *Partita* for piano, strings (1948); *Cello Sonata* (1949, Wash. Univ. Press); *Triple Concerto* for viola, clarinet, piano, orchestra (1953); *The Return of Odysseus* for chorus, orchestra; text by Alberta Phillips (1956, Galaxy); *String Quartet No. 2* (1958); *Perspectives in a Labyrinth* for 3 string orchestras (1962); *Organ Sonata* (1965); *Soleriana* for orchestra (1965); *Sonata in 2 Movements* for violin, harpsichord (1966); *That Time May Cease* for men's chorus, piano; text by Christopher Marlowe (1966); *Quartet* for oboe, strings (1967); *La*

Piñata, dance for chamber orchestra (1969); *Canzona III* for poet, violin, cello, flute, clarinet, trumpet, piano, percussion; text by Alberta Phillips (1970, Fischer).

BIBL.: "Saluting the American Composer: B. P., A Monograph," *National Federation of Music Clubs Magazine* (Jan 1971): 6, 8, 9, 18.

Phonograph, see Recording

Pijper, Willem (b. Zeist, Netherlands, 8 Sept 1894; d. Leidschendam, 19 March 1947), studied at the Utrecht Music School (composition with Johan Wagenaar, piano with Mme. H. J. van Lunteren-Hansen) and worked in Utrecht as a music critic. With Paul Sanders he edited the monthly periodical *De Muziek* (1926–33). He taught harmony and composition at the Amsterdam Conservatory (1925–30) and in the latter year became principal of the Rotterdam Music School, taking charge of the new conservatory there. Through his works and his influence as a teacher, he continues to be the seminal figure in contemporary Dutch music.

Pijper's compositions number just over 100. There are two dozen chamber and instrumental works, including four string quartets (a fifth was never finished); a few orchestral works, including three symphonies and concertos for piano, cello, and violin; many songs; some choral works (mostly a cappella); incidental music for five plays; and two operas. Pijper's style reflects the influence of Mahler, always strong in Holland, allied with equally strong French predilections and the fruits of a deep study of Dutch folk music. Technically he was given to combinative effects, both in harmony, where he was an early exponent of polytonality, and in rhythm, where he developed the use of constantly changing time signatures, often overlapping contrapuntally. His liking for structural coherence found expression in a germ-cell technique by which all the material in a work is derived from one or more small thematic units stated in either melodic or harmonic terms within the first few pages. The ingenious development of such units, enhanced in the orchestral music by bracing woodwind and brass sonorities, does much to camouflage the pedestrian melodic writing that is Pijper's only weakness.

PRINCIPAL COMPOSITIONS (published by Donemus unless otherwise noted): *Antigone*, incidental music for the play by Sophocles (1920–26);

Flute Sonata (1925, Oxford and Donemus); *Symphony No. 3* (1926); *Piano Concerto* (1927, Oxford); *6 Symphonic Epigrams* (1928); *Halewijn*, symphonic drama in 9 scenes (1932–34); *Violin Concerto* (1939); *6 Adagios for Orchestra* (1940). Complete list in Kloppenburg (see bibl.).

PRINCIPAL WRITINGS: *De Quintencirkel* (Amsterdam 1929); *De Stemvork* (Amsterdam 1930).

BIBL.: W. C. M. Kloppenburg, *Thematisch-Bibliografische Catalogus van de Werken van W. P.* (Assen 1960); Wouter Paap, *Music in Holland: Composers* (Amsterdam, n.d.) : 19–24.

Bernard Jacobson

SEE ALSO Netherlands.

Pinilla, Enrique (b. Lima, 3 Aug 1927), attended the Instituto Bach (1940–42), the Academia Sas-Rosay (1943–44), and the National Conservatory (1945–46) in Lima. In 1947 he studied composition with Nadia Boulanger in Paris. He then attended the Madrid Conservatory (1949–58; composition, orchestration with Conrado del Campo; piano, harmony with Angel Arias; counterpoint, fugue with Francisco Calés Otero), the Berlin Hochschule (1958–61; composition, orchestration with Boris Blacher; 12-tone techniques with Josef Rufer), and worked with Vladimir Ussachevsky at the Columbia-Princeton Electronic Music Center during 1966–67. He was music and ballet critic of the Lima daily *Expreso* (1962–70) and taught ethnomusicology at the National Conservatory (1963–66). Since 1964 he has been head of the department of music and film of the Casa de la Cultura del Perú. Pinilla has also held various positions at the Univ. of Lima: head of cultural activities (since 1964), manager of the university television station (since 1967), director of the school of television and film (1968–69), head of the department of communication sciences (since 1969), and professor in the art seminar (since 1969). He has composed numerous scores for films, television, and the theater.

PRINCIPAL COMPOSITIONS: *Sonatina* for flute (1950); *11 Canciones populares* for voice, piano (1952); *Theme and Variations* for piano (1954); *6 Pieces* for strings, woodwinds (1958); *Estudio sobre el ritmo de la marinera* for piano (1959); *String Quartet* (1960); *4 Pieces* for 14 winds (1960); *3 Movements* for percussion, piano (1961); *4 Pieces* for orchestra (1961); *Canto for Orchestra No. 1* (1963); *2 Villancicos* for chorus (1965); *Collages* for piano (1966); *Festejo* for orchestra (1966); *Evoluciones No. 1* for orchestra (1967); *Prisma* on tape (1967; Siglo XX record 502, Buenos Aires); *Canto for Orchestra No. 2* (1968). List to 1965: *Composers of the Americas* 11:85–90.

PRINCIPAL WRITINGS: *Al otro lado de la montaña*, a novel (printed privately in Madrid 1955); *La*

música en el Perú (Lima c.1971); *La etnomúsica de la selva peruana* (Lima c.1971).

Pinkham, Daniel (b. Lynn, Mass., 5 June 1923), studied organ and theory as a child. He attended Harvard Univ. (BA, 1943; MA, 1945; composition with Walter Piston, Aaron Copland), Tanglewood (composition with Arthur Honegger, Samuel Barber), and studied privately with Nadia Boulanger (composition), Wanda Landowska (harpsichord), and E. Power Biggs (organ). He was a concert organist and harpsichordist for many years and has lectured at colleges and music schools. In 1958 he became music director of King's Chapel, Boston. In 1959 he joined the faculty of the New England Conservatory. Pinkham's early works were in a neoclassic style. The recent works are largely 12-tone and strongly lyrical and often emphasize novel sonorities.

PRINCIPAL COMPOSITIONS (published by Peters unless otherwise noted): *Celesta and Harpsichord Concerto* (1954, Schirmer-E); *Christmas Cantata* for chorus, brass choir (1958, King); *Wedding Cantata* for chorus, optional soprano, tenor soloists (1959); *Easter Cantata* for chorus, organ or piano or orchestra (1961); *Symphony No. 1* (1961); *Concertante* for organ, celesta, 2 percussionists (1962); *The Reproaches* for chorus (1962, AMP); *Catacoustical Measures* for orchestra (1963); *Requiem* for alto, tenor, chorus (1963); *Concertante* for organ, brass, percussion (1964); *Symphony No. 2* (1964); *Signs of the Zodiac* for orchestra, optional speaker; poems by David McCord (1965); *Stabat Mater* for soprano, chorus (1965); *St. Mark Passion* for chorus, 4 soloists with organ or piano or small orchestra (1966); *Concertante* for guitar, harpsichord, strings or organ, 2 percussionists (1967); *Lamentations of Jeremiah* for chorus, organ or piano or small orchestra (1967); *Jonah* for chorus, 3 soloists, orchestra (1967, Schirmer-E); *Martyrdom of St. Stephen* for chorus, guitar (1967, Schirmer-E). List to 1966: *Composers of the Americas* 12:120–24.

BIBL.: Marlowe W. Johnson, "The Choral Writing of D. P.," *American Choral Review* 8/4:1–16.

SEE ALSO Liturgical Music: Christian.

Piños, Alois (b. Vyškov, Czechoslovakia, 2 Oct 1925), graduated from the College of Forestry of the Univ. of Brno in 1953 and studied music at the Brno Conservatory (1948–49, composition with Vilém Petrželka) and the Janáček Academy (1949–53, composition with Jaroslav Kvapil, theory with Theodor Schaefer). He attended the Darmstadt summer courses in 1965–66. In 1966 he also attended a seminar in Munich on electronic music, given by J. A. Riedl and M. Kagel, and a seminar in Prague on musique concrète, given by members of the Groupe de Recherches Musicales. Since 1953 he has taught composition and orchestration at the Janáček Academy, where he is director of the Studio of Experimental Music. Since 1965 he has been associated with the Studio for Electronic Music of the Czech Radio in Brno. In 1963 he and four colleagues founded the avant-garde composer's group Parasiti Apollinis, and in 1967 he organized a composer's group for the regular presentation of contemporary music. He has been chairman of the composer's section of the Union of Czech Composers in Brno since 1968. His musical development was influenced first by the traditions of Janáček and Bartók, in the late 50s by Schoenberg and Webern, and in the 60s by avant-garde techniques of the time. He is "interested in new relations between tones, between rhythmical units, between color schemes." The soloists in his *Double Concerto* quote Paganini over "atonal layers" in the orchestra; the *Chamber Concerto* allows the performers to choose from alternations in various parameters.

PRINCIPAL COMPOSITIONS: *Caricatures* for flute, bass clarinet (bassoon), piano (1962, SHV); *Abbreviations*, 10 miniatures for orchestra (1963, EM); *Conflicts* for violin, bass clarinet, piano, percussion (1963–64, Panton); *Concerto for Orchestra and Tape* (1964, Supraphon); *Double Concerto* for cello, piano, brass, percussion (1965–66, Panton); *Chamber Concerto* for string orchestra or string quartet (1967, Supraphon); *Ars amatoria* for soloists, men's chorus, orchestra (1967, Supraphon); *Gesta Machabaeorum* for chorus, flute, trumpet, harp, percussion (1967–68, ČHF); *Concerto on B-A-C-H* for cello, bass clarinet, piano, string orchestra, percussion (1968, ČHF); *Apollo 11*, symphony (1969).

PRINCIPAL WRITINGS: "Vyvážené intervalové řady" [Balanced Interval Series] in *Nové cesty hudby,* vol. 2 (Prague 1966); *Tónové skupiny* [Tone Groups] (Prague 1969).

BIBL.: Jindra Bártová, *A. P.* (Prague 1969); Miloš Štědroň, "Brněnská Musica nova" [New Music in Brno], *Acta musei Moraviae* (1966): 331–44; ——, "Participación del racionalismo e irracionalismo en la nueva música checca," *Sonda* (Madrid)1:27–30; ——, "Paradoxy řízené komposice" [Paradoxes of Controlled Composition], *Hudební rozhledy* 1968/24:730–34.

SEE ALSO Czechoslovakia.

Pipkov, Lubomir (Panayotov) (b. Lovech, Bulgaria, 6 Sept 1904), studied at the Sofia Music School (1918–23), the Bulgarian Music Academy in Sofia (1923–26, piano with I. Torchanov), and the Ecole Normale de Musique (1926–32; composition with Nadia Boulanger, Paul Dukas; piano with Yvonne Lefébure). During 1924–32 he concertized as an accompanist. He then joined the Sofia Opera House, first as an accompanist (1932–34), then as conductor of the chorus (1934–44), and finally as music director (1944–47). During 1948–70 he taught vocal interpretation in the opera department of the Sofia Music Academy. Since 1926 he has contributed articles on music, dramatic staging, and social problems to various Bulgarian newspapers and periodicals. His music has been influenced by the metric and rhythmic characteristics of Bulgarian folk music and by the work of Bartók and Stravinsky.

PRINCIPAL COMPOSITIONS (published by NI): *String Quartet No. 1*, Op. 3 (1928); *3 Ballades* for bass, piano, Op. 5 (1929); *Violin Sonata*, Op. 7 (1929); *Yaninite devet bratja* [Yana's 9 Brothers], opera; libretto by Vesselinov, Op. 17 (1932); *Symphony No. 1*, Op. 22 (1937–40); *Momchil*, opera, Op. 28; libretto by H. Radewsky (1939–44); *Patuvane iz Albania* [A Journey through Albania], variations for string orchestra, Op. 38 (1950); *Violin Concerto*, Op. 43 (1951); *Piano Concerto*, Op. 48 (1954); *Oratoria za nasheto vreme* [Oratorio for Our Time], Op. 61; text by Vladimir Bashev (1959); *Antigona 43*, opera; libretto by V. Bashev and P. Pantchev, Op. 63 (1961); *Pet pesni po stihove na chujdestranni poeti* [5 Songs on Verses of Foreign Poets] for voice, piano, Op. 64; texts by García-Lorca, Ronsard, Raphaël Alberti (1963–64); *Symphony No. 3* for string orchestra, 2 pianos, trumpet, percussion, Op. 65 (1965); *String Quartet No. 3* for strings, kettledrums, Op. 66 (1966); *4 Madrigals* for chorus, Op. 67 (1966–70); *Folksong Cycle* for chorus, Op. 71 (1968–69); *Sonata* for solo violin, Op. 72 (1969); *Symphony No. 4* for string orchestra, Op. 73 (1970).

BIBL.: L. Coen, *L. P.* (Sofia 1968); K. Iliev, *L. P.* (Sofia 1955). Several reviews of individual works have appeared in the periodical *Bulgarska musica.*

Pires, Filipe (b. Lisbon, 26 June 1934), studied at the Lisbon Conservatory (1946–54, composition with Croner de Vasconcelos, piano with Lucio Mendes) and at the College of Music and Theater in Hanover, Germany (1957–60, piano with Winfried Wolf, composition with Ernst-Lothar von Knorr). In 1960 he began teaching composition at the conservatory in Oporto, Portugal. Before 1960 Pires's works were tonal and atonal, but not 12-tone or serial. Since 1960 he has used 12-tone techniques and since 1964, serial techniques.

PRINCIPAL COMPOSITIONS: *Sonata* for piano (1954); *String Quartet* (1958, Gulbenkian); *Trio* for piano, violin, cello (1960, Curci); *Eternal Return* for baritone, orchestra (1961); *Akronos* for strings (1964); *Perspectives* for 3 groups, 19 players (1965); *Metronomie* for flute, viola, harp (1966); *Portugaliae Genesis* for baritone, choir, orchestra (1968).

PRINCIPAL WRITINGS: *Theoretical Elements of Counterpoint and Canon* (Lisbon 1968).

PRINCIPAL WRITINGS: with H. Ulrich, *History of Music and Musical Style* (New York 1964).

BIBL.: Thomas Collins, *The Instrumental Music of P. A. P.*, (PhD diss., Univ. of Mo., 1970); Kent Kennan, "P. A. P.," *ACA Bulletin* 9:7–16; Boris Kremenliev, "P. A. P.," *Music of the West Magazine* (Los Angeles, July 1952). Several articles on Pisk and a list of music and writings to 1963 are printed in John Glowacki, ed., *Essays in Honor of P. A. P.* (Austin, Texas, 1966).

Pisk, Paul A(madeus) (b. Vienna, 16 May 1893), attended the Univ. of Vienna (1911–14, 1916, 1918; musicology with Guido Adler) and the Vienna Conservatory (1912–13, 1919; piano with A. Epstein, conducting with F. Hellmesberger, composition with Franz Schreker). He also studied privately with Schoenberg for three years. He was chairman of the music department at the Volkshochschule, Vienna (1922–34) and has taught at the New Vienna Conservatory (1925–26), the Austro-American Conservatory near Salzburg (1931–33), the Univ. of Redlands in Calif. (1937–50), the Univ. of Texas (1950–63), and Washington Univ. in St. Louis (since 1963). From 1920 to 1928 he was coeditor of *Musikblätter des Anbruch* with Alban Berg and Paul Stefan. In both Europe and the U.S. he has lectured and written extensively on musicological subjects. He edited the Masses of Jacobus Gallus (Vienna 1935, 1959, 1967, 1969).

PRINCIPAL COMPOSITIONS: *Sänge eines fahrenden Spielmanns* for solo voice (1920–21, UE); *6 Concert Pieces* for piano (1922, UE); *Partita* for orchestra (1924, UE); *String Quartet* (1924, UE); *Der grosse Regenmacher*, ballet for narrator, orchestra (1931); *Campanella*, cantata for baritone, orchestra (1932); *Moresca Figures* for violin, clarinet, piano (1934, CFE); *Death Valley Sonatina* for piano (1942, Southern); *A Requiem for Gerald* for baritone, piano (1943); *Passacaglia* for orchestra (1944, Southern); *Bucolic Suite* for string orchestra (1946, Marks); *A Toccata of Galuppi's—Narration* for narrator, orchestra (1947); *Clarinet Sonata* (1947, CFE); *Quartet* for trumpets, horn, trombone (1951, CFE); *Horn Sonata* (1953, CFE); *Adagio and Fugue* for orchestra (1954); *6 Songs*, texts by Sara Henderson-Kay (1954); *4 Songs*, texts by Henderson-Kay (1957); *3 Ceremonial Rites* for orchestra (1957–58); *String Trio* (1958, CFE); *Woodwind Quintet* (1958, CFE); *God's Omnipotence* for chorus with organ or piano (1960); *9 Songs*, texts by Joyce (1960); *Music* for violin, clarinet, cello, bassoon (1962, CFE); *Envoy* for 6 instruments (1964); *In memoriam Carl Sandburg* for chorus (1967); *5 Songs* (1968); *Perpetuum mobile* for organ, brass instruments (1968); *13 Variations on an 8-Bar Theme* for piano (1968).

Piston, Walter (b. Rockland, Me., 20 Jan 1894), had Yankee ancestors except for his paternal grandfather, who was Italian (Antonio Pistone). His family moved to Boston, where Piston graduated from the Mechnical Arts High School and the Mass. Normal Art School. He turned from art to music in 1919, graduated in music from Harvard Univ. in 1924, and spent the next two years as a student of Nadia Boulanger in Paris. He taught at Harvard (1926–59) and has since devoted full time to composition.

The backbone of Piston's output is his set of eight symphonies. In addition to these and other orchestral works, there are many concerted pieces, including two concertos for violin and one each for viola, two pianos, and clarinet. He has written much chamber music for varied combinations, including five string quartets. There are two choral pieces and one ballet. Piston's style derives from a disciplined technique in harmony, counterpoint, and orchestration, and it emphasizes the manipulation of musical ideas, embracing both the contrapuntal patterns of Bach and the developmental practices of Mozart and Beethoven. He makes the important classical distinction between fast and slow movements: melodies are built from short motives in the fast movements and are long and lyrical in the slow ones. His harmony is essentially "common practice" with a free use of dissonance. His rhythms are always pulsating, whether "presto," "con brio," "perpetual motion," or in a slow tempo. His textures are transparent, and his understanding of the unique qualities of all instruments enables him to make each of them sound at its best whether in a solo or ensemble role. Dynamics in his writing are a part of the constructive action, not effects for their own sake. Above all, his musical ideas exist for their intrinsic beauty and are not intended to "represent" or delineate something outside music. His manipulation of these ideas uses techniques and structures derived from Bach, Beethoven, and

Stravinsky of the 1920s. Resisting many 20th-century trends, he has maintained his principles of composition with unusual consistency through more than 40 years.

PRINCIPAL COMPOSITIONS (published by AMP unless otherwise noted): *Suite No. 1* for orchestra (1928); *Concerto for Orchestra* (1933); *String Quartets Nos. 1–5* (1933; 1935, Schirmer-G; 1947, Boosey; 1951; 1962); *Piano Trios Nos. 1–2* (1935, 1966); *Concertino* for piano, chamber orchestra (1937); *Symphonies Nos. 1–8* (1937, Schirmer-G; 1943; 1947, Boosey; 1950; 1954; 1955; 1960; 1965); *The Incredible Flutist*, ballet (1938); *Violin Concertos Nos. 1–2* (1939, Boosey; 1960); *Sinfonietta* (1941, Boosy); *Quintet* for flute, strings, (1942); *Toccata* for orchestra (1948, Boosey); *Piano Quintet* (1949); *Wind Quintet* (1956); *Viola Concerto* (1957); *2-Piano Concerto* (1959); *String Sextet* (1964); *Variations* for cello, orchestra (1966); *Clarinet Concerto* (1967); *Ricercare* for orchestra (1968). List to 1959: *Composers of the Americas* 4:18–24.

PRINCIPAL WRITINGS: *Principles of Harmonic Analysis* (Boston 1933); *Harmony* (New York 1941, 3rd ed. 1962); *Counterpoint* (New York 1947); *Orchestration* (New York 1955); "More Views on Serialism," *Score* 23; "Problems of Intonation in the Performance of Contemporary Music," *Instrumental Music* ed. by D. Hughes (Cambridge, Mass., 1959).

BIBL.: William Austin, "P.'s Fourth Symphony," *Music Review* 16; Elliott Carter, "W. P.," *Musical Quarterly* 32; Peter Westergaard, "Conversation with W. P.," *Perspectives* 7/1.

G. Wallace Woodworth
SEE ALSO United States.

Pitch Class, a pitch without reference to a specific octave register. The term, which gained currency through the writings and teaching of Milton Babbitt, occurs most frequently in reference to 12-tone music and is used to separate the property of pitch from other properties of tones (timbre, volume, duration, etc.).

Pizzetti, Ildebrando (b. Borgo Strinato, near Parma, Italy, 20 Sept 1880; d. Rome, 13 Feb 1968), studied at the Parma Musical Academy (1895–1901; renaissance music with Giovanni Tebaldini; harmony, counterpoint with Telesforo Righi). He taught composition at the Parma Academy (1907–08); the L. Cherubini Institute in Florence (1908–17), where he was director during 1917–24; and the Accadèmia di S. Cecilia (from 1936). He was director of the Milan Conservatory during 1924–36.

PRINCIPAL COMPOSITIONS (published by Ricordi unless otherwise noted): *Fedra*, 3-act opera; libretto by Gabriele d'Annunzio (1909–12, Sonzogno); *Il clefta prigione* for voice, piano (1912, Forlivesi); *2 Canzoni corali* for chorus (1913); *Debora e Jaele*, 3-act opera (1915–21); *Violin Sonata in A* (1918–19, Chester); *Cello Sonata in F* (1921); *3 Sonetti del Petrarca* for voice, piano (1922); *Messa di Requiem* for 4–12 solo voices (1922); *Lo straniero*, 2-act opera (1922–25); *3 Canti* for cello (violin), piano (1924); *Piano Trio in A* (1925); *Fra Gherardo*, 3-act opera (1925–27); *Concerto dell'estate* for orchestra (1928); *Agamennone*, introduction for the play by Aeschylus for chorus, orchestra (1931); *Orscolo*, 3-act opera (1931–35); *String Quartet in D* (1932–33); *Cello Concerto in C* (1933–34); *L'oro*, 3-act opera (1938–42); *Epithalamium* for soprano, tenor, baritone, chorus, orchestra; text by Catullus (1939, unpub.); *Symphony in A* (1940); *Vanna Lupa*, 3-act opera (1942–47, unpub.); *Violin Concerto in A* (1944, S-Z); *3 Lyrics* for voice, piano (1944, Forlivesi); *Assassinio nella cattedrale*, 2-act opera after the play by T. S. Eliot (1957); *Il calzare d'argento*, 2-act opera; libretto by Riccardo Bacchelli (premiere 1961); *Clitennestra*, 2-act opera; libretto by the composer (premiere 1965).

PRINCIPAL WRITINGS: *La musica dei Greci* (Rome 1914); *Musicisti contemporanei* (Milan 1914); *Intermezzi critici* (Florence 1921); "La musica italiana dell'ottocento," *L'Italia a gli Italiani del secolo XIX* (Florence 1930) reprinted separately (Turin 1946); *Paganini* (Turin 1940); *Musica e dramma* (Rome 1945).

BIBL.: Guido Maria Gatti, *I. P.* trans. by D. Moore (London 1951); Gianandrea Gavazzeni, *3 Studi di P.* (Como 1937); ——, *Altri studi pizzettiani* (Bergamo 1956).

Plaetner, Jørgen (b. Copenhagen, 14 Feb 1930), studied at the Royal Danish Conservatory in Copenhagen (1948–51; theory with Bjørn Hjelmborg; form, analysis with Niels Viggo Bentzon; composition, orchestration with Vagn Holmboe). He also attended seminars in Darmstadt (1950, 1952, 1954), Hamburg (1951), and Bilthoven (1953). From 1957 to 1967 he taught music in a school for the blind in Kalundborg. Since 1967 he has been town composer for Hostebro, Denmark (the first Danish town to have such a position), where, in addition to writing music for civic occasions and performing groups of the city, he directs an electronic music studio (the first in Denmark) and music academy.

PRINCIPAL COMPOSITIONS: *Piano Sonatas Nos. 1–4*, Opp. 2, 3, 7, 9 (1951, 1952, 1954, 1956); *Piano Concerto No. 1*, Op. 8 (1954–56); *Relativités I–III* on 4 tape channels with live instrumental improvisation, Op. 19 (1960–62); *Beta* on tape, Op. 16b

(1962–63); *De elskende* on tape with slide projections, Op. 27a (1965); *Ødipus* for speaking chorus, 4 percussion groups (10 players), 2 pianos, flute, tape (1966); *Epos* on tape, Op. 34a (1968).

SEE ALSO Scandinavia.

Planchart, Alejandro Enrique (b. Caracas, 29 July 1935), studied at Yale Univ. (1954–60; composition with H. L. Baumgartner, Quincy Porter, Richard Donovan) and at Harvard Univ. (1964–67, musicology). He has conducted the Capella Cordina in New Haven since 1963 and has taught at Yale Univ. since 1967. His music is characterized by free atonality and is closer to the European serialists than to American 12-tone composers. After 1964 he became interested in complex, nonthematic polyphony inspired by 15th-century models, particularly Ockeghem.

PRINCIPAL COMPOSITIONS: *5 Solo Madrigals* for voice, piano (1958); *Serenade* for flute, cello, marimba, bongo drums (1958); *13 Ways of Looking at a Blackbird* for voice, flute, viola, xylophone, harpsichord, 2 percussionists (1959); *Japanese Lyrics* for voice, piano (1960–67); *Fantasia Sonata* for piano (1961); *Love Lyrics* for voice, piano (1962); *Clausulae* for piano (1964–67); *Lections* for oboe, double bass (1964–70); *Tropes* for orchestra (1968); *Seqventia cvm prosa* for voice, flute, celesta, cello, guitar (1970).

Pleskow, Raoul (b. Vienna, 12 Oct 1931), attended Queens College in New York (1952–56, composition with Karol Rathaus), and Columbia Univ. (1956–58, composition with Otto Luening). He has taught at C. W. Post College since 1959, where he is chairman of the music department. The music of Stefan Wolpe and Pleskow's friendship and association with him have been a great influence on his development.

PRINCIPAL COMPOSITIONS (available at ACA unless otherwise noted): *Movement for Flute, Cello, and Piano* (1962, Seesaw); *Music for 2 Pianos* (1965); *Movement for Oboe, Violin, and Piano* (1966); *Bagatelles* for violin (1967, McG-M); *Movement for 9 Players* for flute, clarinet, trumpet, violin, cello, double bass, piano, celesta, percussion (1967); *2 Movements for Orchestra* (1968); *For 5 Players and Baritone* for flute, clarinet, violin, cello, piano, baritone (1969); *Duo* for cello, piano (1970).

PRINCIPAL WRITINGS: "Piece for Piano," *Contemporary Music Newsletter* (New York, March 1969):4; program notes for the CRI recording of *Movement for Oboe, Violin, and Piano*.

BIBL.: Donald Chittum, "Current Chronicle," *Musical Quarterly* 55:403–05.

Podešva, Jaromír (b. Brno, 8 March 1927), studied at the Janáček Academy of Music in Brno (1947–54, composition with Jaroslav Kvapil) and at Tanglewood (1960, composition with Aaron Copland). He also studied composition privately in Paris with Henri Dutilleux (1960–61). During 1955–58 he was secretary of the Guild of Czechoslovak Composers in Prague. He was a free-lance composer during 1959–69, and he has taught composition at Ostrava Conservatory since then. In his music of the 1960s he has combined some principles of the "new" tonality with 12-tone techniques.

PRINCIPAL COMPOSITIONS: *String Quartet No. 1* (1950, Supraphon); *Kounicovy koleje* [Kounicovy College], symphonic poem (1952, Supraphon); *Violin Sonata* (1958, Panton); *String Quartet No. 4*, "From the Life of Contemporary Man" (1959–60, Panton); *Symphony No. 2* for flute, string orchestra (1960–61); *Symphonietta to Nature* for chorus (1962, ÚDLT); *Opustíš-li mne* [If You Leave Me], opera; libretto by the composer after Z. Pluhař (1962–66); *String Quartet No. 5* (1964); *Unséers* [Unheard] for children's chorus (1965, Supraphon); *Symphony No. 3*, "Culmination—The Pearl at the Bottom" (1966); *Symphony No. 4*, "Music from Soláň," for flute, string orchestra, harpsichord (1967, Supraphon); *Symphony No. 5* for voice, orchestra; texts by F. Halas and J. Yevtuschenko (1967); *Bambini di Praga*, opera buffa; libretto by the composer after Bohumil Hrabal (1968); *Suite* for viola, piano (1969); *Wind Quintet No. 1* (1969–70); *Symphony No. 6* (1970).

PRINCIPAL WRITINGS: *Současná hudba na Západě* [Western Contemporary Music] (Prague 1962); *Možnosti kadence v dvanáctitónovém poli* (*Základy tonální dodekafonie*) [The Possibilities of the Cadence in the Dodecaphonic Field (Foundation of Tonal Dodecaphony)] (Prague 1969–70). Since 1951 Podešva has also contributed musical articles to *Hudební rozhledy*.

BIBL.: Jan Trojan, "Tvůrčí profil J. P." [Creative Profile of J. P.], *Hudební rozhledy* 18/22:936–40; ———, "Symfonické paralely J. P." [Symphonic Parallels of J. P.], *Hudební rozhledy* 21/6:149–51; Jiří Válek, "Kapitola z české soudobé hudby" [A Principal in Czech Contemporary Music], *Hudební rozhledy* 13/19:792–96.

SEE ALSO Czechoslovakia.

Poetry, see Text Setting and Usage

Pointillism, a technique in painting, explored especially by Georges Seurat in the 1880s, in which colors are applied in a mosaic of dots or short strokes instead of in larger, solid fields; at a distance the dots merge into subtly vibrating areas of color and light. The term has been applied to some music of Anton Webern and others after him in which individual notes (or sparse chords), each with its own timbre, dynamic level, and articulation, are heard in relative isolation and in exact temporal relationships with other such events. The borrowing of the art term suggests that when these events are heard in the larger context of texture, they coalesce into coherent shapes of sound.

BIBL.: Pierre Boulez, "Schoenberg Is Dead," *Score* (May 1952): 18–22; H. Metzger, "Abortive Concepts in the Theory and Criticism of Music," *Die Reihe*, English ed., 5: 21–29; Karlheinz Stockhausen, "Structure and Experimental Time," *Die Reihe*, English ed., 2: 64–74.

Poland. Although Polish performers (especially pianists) were known throughout the world from the start of this century, composers did not gain worldwide fame until the 1960s. One must go back more than a century, to Chopin, to find a Polish composer whose international reputation is comparable to what Lutosławski, Penderecki, and others have achieved today. The main institutions of music life early in the century were the Warsaw Philharmonic (founded 1901 and still active today), the Grand Theater (also in Warsaw), and the opera house in Lvov. Performers in the early years were able to receive excellent training at the conservatories in Cracow, Lvov, and Warsaw. Composers generally studied abroad, Vienna, Berlin, and Prague being the main centers; thus a native Slavic tone found expression through an Austrian-German approach to instrumentation, harmony, and counterpoint. Most music of the period was in a postromantic vein, produced by contemporaries of Brahms, Tchaikovsky, and Bruckner. An infusion of newer thinking did occur when several composers known as Mloda Polska [Young Poland] appeared. They included Mieczysław Karłowicz (1876–1909), Grzegorz Fitelberg (1879–1953), Karol *Szymanowski (1882–1937), Ludomir Różycki (1884–1953), and Apolinary Szeluto (1884–1967). The most important was Szymanowski, who after 1910 relinquished a Brahms-Strauss orientation for the coloristic leanings and ecstatic lyricism of Debussy and Scriabin; his work became even more significant after the war.

Although World War I caused only a slackening, not a cessation, of composition and music making in Poland, it marked a break with the past, as it did in the rest of Europe. Postromanticism was replaced by neoclassicism, and the destination of composers studying abroad shifted to Paris and to the classes of Nadia Boulanger, Paul Dukas, Albert Roussel, and Florent Schmidt. In 1926 Piotr *Perkowski (b. 1901), Stanislaw Wiechowicz (1893–1963), and Felix *Labunski (b. 1892) formed the Association des Jeunes Musiciens Polonais à Paris and began giving monthly concerts of Polish music. In Poland itself a lively concert life developed. Orchestras now became active in Cracow, Lvov, and Poznań as well as Warsaw. Now, too, Poznań developed an important opera house. In 1927 the first International Chopin Competition was held in Warsaw. The Warsaw Conservatory became the foremost music school in the country, and beginning in 1927 several generations of composers were educated under Kazimierz Sikorski (b. 1895). Composition during the period was dominated by Szymanowsky, who reduced the excessive emotionalism of his earlier music, casting his ideas in a more disciplined and precise framework. He interested himself in folk music (mainly of the Tatra and Kurpie regions) and wrote articles on behalf of new Polish music. During 1930–32 he was rector of the Warsaw Conservatory. Another composer, Jozef Koffler (1906–43, killed by the Nazis), was probably the first Pole to cultivate 12-tone techniques; he was better known in Vienna during his lifetime than in his homeland, where dodecaphony was treated with hostility. The most original Polish music of the time was that of Roman Palester (b. 1910) whose dissonant harmony and aggressive rhythms first appeared in the 1930s. Witold *Lutosławski (b. 1913), Grayżna *Bacewicz (1913–69), and the mature works of Andrzej *Panufnik (b. 1914) came to light just before and during the early part of World War II.

Concerts and music teaching had to go underground during 1939–45. Young composers such as Panufnik and Lutosławski continued their creative work but necessarily at a slower pace. The whole structure of music life disintegrated and had to be rebuilt. In the fall of 1945 Poland's first music publishing house, Polskie Wydawnictwo Muzyczne (PWM) was founded in Cracow, and the Association of Polish Composers was organized. Also in 1945 the state took over the protection and cultivation of all artistic life, paralleling moves in other socialist countries of East Europe. New orchestras, new song and dance ensembles, and new amateur groups were organized. The collecting and classification of folklore began on a large scale. The first postwar Chopin Competition was held in 1949. Neoclassicism continued as the main compositional trend, extending as an active force into the mid-50s and dying out only with the passing of Miss Bacewicz in 1969.

Although music life in the postwar years grew in a healthy manner, composition from 1949 to 1956 suffered its most difficult period in Polish history. The doctrine of socialist realism, together with the official hostility toward innovation, separated the country from ongoing developments in the rest of Europe. A few socialist cantatas and songs for mass consumption from these years have a marginal worth, but it is the *Concerto for Orchestra* (1950–54) of Lutosławski, the *Concerto Grosso* (1954) of Bolesław Szabelski (b. 1896), and the *Piano Trio* (1953) of Artur Malawski (1904–57) that demonstrate that significant work was still being done.

SINCE 1956. In 1955–56 cultural change and political upheaval brought about a dramatic change in official policy. Kazimierz *Serocki (b. 1922) and Tadeusz *Baird (b. 1928), working through the Association of Polish Composers, organized the first Warsaw Autumn festival, thereby creating a forum (held annually since 1958) for the development of a Polish avant-garde. New trends were publicized in a monthly magazine published by PWM during 1957–59 and in a pioneering analysis of contemporary techniques, Bogusław Schäffer's *Nowa muzyka* [New Music] (Cracow 1958, 2nd ed. 1969). The young composers who had come to national attention in the 1949–56 period—including Serocki, Baird, Włodzimierz *Kotoński (b. 1925), Jan Krenz (b. 1927), and Andrzej Dobrowolski (b. 1921)—now became familiar with advanced European music and adopted 12-tone and serial writing. Simultaneously a new generation entered the arena, including some of the most promising composers of all: Henryk M. Górecki (b. 1933), Krzystof *Penderecki (b. 1933), Wojciech *Kilar (b. 1932), Witold *Szalonek (b. 1927), and the theorist and composer Bogusław *Schäffer (b. 1929). During the Warsaw Autumn festivals of 1964–66 a number of other composers were heard for the first time, among them Zbigniew *Rudziński (b. 1935), Tomasz *Sikorski (b. 1939), Edward *Bugusławski (b. 1940), and Krzysztof Meyer (b. 1943).

Today the major orchestras, opera houses, smaller ensembles, festivals, and conservatories are located in Warsaw, Cracow, Poznań, Wroclaw, Lodz, and the region of Upper Silesia. Another seven towns also have orchestras, and a few of these have occasional festivals. (All this activity, it should be noted, takes place among a population of only 30 million.) New Polish music is performed primarily at three festivals: the Warsaw Autumn, the Poznań Spring, and the Wroclaw Festival of Contemporary Polish Music. The National Philharmonic gives one-composer concerts of new Polish music, and two ensembles, the Music Workshops in Warsaw and Cracow, specialize in new music. One of the foremost electronic studios in Europe is located at the Polish Radio; here, electronic and concrete works are prepared along with film, stage, and radio music. PWM publishes a great deal of new music without favoring any particular stylistic trend. As elsewhere, however, new music in Poland does not usually reach a large part of the community. The overall economic position of the composer is similar to that of his colleagues in western Europe, except that in Poland the composer is generally more free of everyday cares, owing to various scholarship programs, royalties, and opportunities to travel abroad.

The spectrum of musical composition since 1956–58 is so variegated that it is difficult to speak of any "Polish" style. The leading figure is Lutosławski. Beginning with *Funeral Music* (1958), he developed his own method of relating the tones of the chromatic scale; it is primarily a system of consonances. Since *Venetian Games* (1960–61) he has also used aleatory devices and has employed many-colored blocks of sound as a basic compositional resource. Górecki used pointillistic textures and serial structures beginning about 1957–58. He then moved away from this orientation, and his concern today is to reduce music to its elemental sound forces. Repetitiveness and polyphony are examples of the simple structural designs he now uses. Somewhat akin to Górecki is Szalonek, who explores new sounds and new playing techniques. Schäffer incorporates aleatory processes, collage, and mixed-media theater in his music. He is the most outstanding of the composers at the Experimental Studio of the Polish Radio.

Less radical approaches are represented in the music of Baird and Penderecki. Baird has a lyric, romantic temperament and a great sensitivity to timbre. A dramatic sense was revealed in his opera *Jutro* (Tomorrow, 1966). Penderecki in recent years has been concerned with Christian themes: the *St. Luke's Passion* (1963–65) and *Utrenia* (1970–71), the latter a setting of the Eastern Orthodox matins. An example of a conservative orientation today is Perkowski, who uses classical formal schemes, an expanded tonal framework, and an approach to timbre that derives from impressionism. As for the youngest composers now on the scene, it seems that the upsurge of activity after 1956 has reached a plateau. For the time being at least, a new generation of composers of the caliber of Górecki, Penderecki, and Schäffer has not appeared.

BIBL.: J. M. Chomiński, *Muzyka polski ludowej* [The Music of People's Poland] (Warsaw 1968); S. Jarociński, ed., *Polish Music* (Warsaw 1965); *Polska współczesna kultura muzyczna* [Contemporary Polish Music Culture] (Cracow 1968).

Bohdan Pociej

(trans. from Polish by Ludwik Krzyzanowski)
SEE ALSO Israel.

Pololáník, Zdeněk (Alois) (b. Brno, Czechoslovakia, 25 Oct 1935), studied at the Brno State Conservatory (1952–57, composition with František Suchý, organ with Joseph Černocký) and the Janáček Academy in Brno (1957–61; composition with Vilém Petrželka, Theodor Schaeffer). He is a free-lance composer and has composed in addition to the works listed below over 100 scores for the theater, films, television, and radio. He uses a variety of freely adapted contemporary techniques for the purpose of achieving an "independent originality of sound." He composes "by visualizing" an instrumentation "and establishing the tempo. A musical idea appears immediately. In the case of programmatic music, it is an inner visual idea that immediately transforms itself into sound." His music has been somewhat influenced by folk music of the Brno region.

PRINCIPAL COMPOSITIONS: *Variations* for organ, piano (1956); *Sinfonietta* for orchestra (1958); *Sonata bravura* for organ (1959, SNKLHU); *Toccata* for double bass, chamber orchestra (1959); *Divertimento* for 4 horns, string orchestra (1960); *Nabuchodonosor* for chorus, 3 trumpets, timpani; text from the Vulgate (1961); *Symphonies Nos. 1–5*: No. 1 (1961); No. 2 for 11 winds (1962); No. 3 for organ, percussion, orchestra (1962); No. 4 for string orchestra (1963, General); No. 5 (1968); *Scherzo contrario* for xylophone (guitar), bass clarinet (clarinet), violin (1961, Zanibon); *Musica spingenta Nos. 1–3*: No. 1 for double bass, wind quintet (1961, Panton); No. 2 for string quartet, harpsichord (1962); No. 3 for bass clarinet, 13 percussion (1962, Panton); *Sonata laetitiae 2* for organ (1962, Panton); *3 Scherzi* for wind quintet (1963, Zanibon); *Zpěv mrtvých dětí* [Cantus liberorum mortuorom] for chorus, 3 trumpets, percussion (1963, Dům osvěty); *Musica concisa* for flute, bass clarinet, piano, percussion, harpsichord (1963, Panton); *Allegro affanato* for organ (1963); *Preludia dodici* for 2 pianos, organ (1963); *Vávra*

for children's chorus, piano (1964); *Concentus resonabilis* for 19 solo instruments, tape (1963, SNKLHU); *Mechanismus*, ballet; scenario by Rudolf Adler (1964, Dilia); *4 Sound Conversations and Finale*, musique concrète on tape (1965); *Concerto grosso* for guitar, flute, harpsichord, string orchestra (1966, Zanibon); *Cantus psalmorum* for bass, organ, harp, percussion (1966, De Santis); *Rumor letalis* for chorus (1966); *Popelka*, marionette ballet (1966); *Piano Concerto* (1966); *Oratio* for 9 instruments (1967); *Pulsazione* for percussion (1967); *Muscia trascurata* for bass clarinet, harpsichord (1968); *Sheer hush-sheereem* [The Song of Songs], opera-oratorio for 4 vocal soloists, chorus, orchestra; text in Hebrew (1969, ČHF); *Missa brevis* for children's chorus, organ (1970).

BIBL.: František Hrabal, notes for a recording of *Musica spingenta 3* (Supraphon SUA 18595, 1964).

SEE ALSO Czechoslovakia.

Polytonality, the use of more than one key center simultaneously, with the music stratified (by register, instrumentation, etc.) so that the separate identities of the different tonalities are maintained. The term is sometimes used in reference to short passages or even single chords, the pitch content of which can be analyzed (though not necessarily heard) in terms of more than one key.

Ponce, Manuel M. (b. Fresnillo, Mexico, 8 Dec 1886; d. Mexico City, 14 April 1948), studied at the National Conservatory in Mexico City (1901–02), the Liceo Rossini in Bologna (1904–06, composition with Enrico Rossi, counterpoint with Luigi Torchi), and the Stern Conservatory in Berlin (1906–08, piano with Martin Krause). He returned to Europe for the years 1925–33, living in Paris and coaching with Paul Dukas (while there he also founded and edited the journal *Gaceta músical*, 1928–29). He taught piano and music history at the National Conservatory (1909–15, 1917–22) and folk music at the Universidad Nacional Autónoma (1933–34). He was director for short periods of the Conservatory (1934–35) and of the University's music school (1945–c.47). In 1936–37 he founded and edited the journal *Cultura músical* in Mexico City. Ponce was the first Mexican composer to do research on creole and mestizo Mexican folklore. This material (along with the rhythms of Cuban music, which he assimilated during a stay in Havana, 1915–17) had an impact on his entire output. Dukas and other French composers (especially Debussy and Ravel) were also prominent influences. In addition to the works listed below, he composed more than 100 songs with piano and orchestral accompaniment and close to 100 salon pieces for piano.

PRINCIPAL COMPOSITIONS (most dates unavailable): ★ For guitar: *Folías de España*, 20 variations and a fugue (Schott); *24 Easy Preludes* (Schott); *Solo Sonatas Nos. 1–5* (Schott); *Sonata* with piano (Southern); *Pequeños preludios* (unpub.); *Concierto del sur* for guitar, orchestra (1941, Southern). ★ For chamber ensembles: *Cuarteto miniatura* for strings (Sénart); *Sonata a 2* for violin, viola (Sénart); *Violin Sonata* (Schirmer-G); *Trío romántico* for piano, violin, cello (J. Giralt, Havana). ★ For orchestra: *Chapultepec* (1929, revised 1934; Southern); *Ferial* (1940, Southern); *Poema elegíaco* (1935, Southern); *Suite en estilo antiguo* (1935, Southern). ★ For piano: *Álbum de amor* (Enrique Mungia, Mexico City); *Balada mexicana* (Wagner y Levien, Mexico City); *4 Mexican Dances* (Southern); *Fugue on a Theme of Bach* (Otto y Arzoy, Mexico City); *Légende* (Otto y Arzoy); *4 Pequeñas fugas para principiantes* (Southern); *Prelude and Fugue on a Theme of Handel* (Southern); *Rapsodias mexicanas Nos. 1–2* (Wagner y Levien); *Scherzino mexicano* (Enrique Mungia); *Suite cubana* (Enrique Mungia); *4 trozos romanticos* (Enrique Mungia); *Concertos Nos. 1–2* for piano, orchestra (Southern). ★ For violin: *Concerto* for violin, orchestra (1943, Southern). ★ Complete list: *Composers of the Americas* 1:62–70.

PRINCIPAL WRITINGS: *Nuevos escritos musicales* (Mexico City 1948).

[prepared with the help of Esperanza Pulido]
SEE ALSO Mexico.

Poniridy, Georges (b. Constantinople, 26 Sept 1892), studied at the Brussels Conservatory (technical studies with Michael Brusselmans, Paul Gilson; violin with Alfred Marchot) and the Schola Cantorum in Paris (1919–25; composition with Vincent d'Indy, Albert Roussel; Gregorian chant with Amédée Gastoué). He lived in Paris until World War II and was a conductor and violinist. During 1943–59 he was director of the music division of the Ministry of Education in Athens. He has also written criticism for European journals. He was brought up in the classic musical traditions, and his music has been influenced by this and by Greek folk and Byzantine music and Gregorian chant. He often uses what he refers to as "neo-Greek polyphony."

PRINCIPAL COMPOSITIONS: *6 Chants populaires grecs* for voice, piano (1915, Sénart); *2 Preludes* for piano (1916, Sénart); *Rythmes grecs* for piano (1924, Sénart); *3 Mélodies grecs* for voice, piano

(1924, Sénart); *Triptyque symphonique* for orchestra (1927, Enosis); *Cantate* on a Byzantine troparion, for mezzo-soprano, chorus, orchestra (1929); *3 Préludes symphoniques* for orchestra (1938, French Institute in Athens); *Antigone*, incidental music for Sophocles' drama (1939); *Suite lyrique* for orchestra (1941); *Symphony No. 2* (1942); *Petite symphonie* for string orchestra, percussion (1956); *Flute Sonata* (1956); *Variations No. 2* for piano (1956); *2 Recitations musicales* for voice, strings; texts by Seferis (1956); *4 Preludes* for piano (1957); *Poème symphonique* (1958); *String Quartet No. 1*, "de Noël" (1959); *String Quartet No. 2*, "de l'Epiphanie" (1959); *Lazaros*, 4-part tragedy after Homonyme de Prevelakis (1960–70); *Concertino* for horn, strings (1962); *Quartet* for flute, oboe, clarinet, bassoon (1962); *Clarinet Sonata* (1962); *Piano Sonata No. 2* (1962); *Violin Sonata No. 2* (1963); *String Trio* (1963); *3 Song Cycles*; texts by Prevelakis: No. 1 for voice, clarinet; No. 2 for voice, violin; No. 3 for voice, piano (1963); *Oboe Sonata* (1964); *Wind Quintet* (1966); *Eurythmiès No. 1* for piano (1966); *Viola Sonata* (1967); *Cello Sonata* (1967); *Piano Concerto* (1968); *Violin Concerto* (1969); *Eumolpiès No. 1* for piano (1969).

BIBL.: G. Bertouille, "G. P.," *Le Phare* (Brussels, 9 June 1963); Pierre Moulaert, "Musique grecque: G. P.," *Dernière Heure* (Brussels, June 1963).

Poot, Marcel (b. Vilvorde, Belgium, 7 May 1901), studied at the Royal Conservatories in Brussels (1916–20, harmony with M. Lunssens, piano with A. De Greef) and Antwerp (1921–23, counterpoint, fugue with L. Mortelmans). He also studied in Brussels with Paul Gilson (1921–23) and in Paris with Paul Dukas (1926). He was among the pupils of Gilson who founded Les Synthétistes in 1925. In that year he and Gilson founded the *Revue musicale belge*, to which he contributed until it ceased publication in 1938. During 1938–66 he taught at the Brussels Conservatory, becoming director in 1949.

PRINCIPAL COMPOSITIONS: *Piano Quartet* (1932, Eschig); *Ouverture joyeuse* (1934, UE); *Allegro symphonique* (1935, UE); *Camera*, 1-act ballet (1937, Eschig); *Triptyque symphonique* (1938, UE); *Suite* for wind instruments (1940, UE); *Le Dit du routier*, oratorio for narrator, soprano, tenor, orchestra; text by J. L. Weterings (1943, UE); *Sinfonietta* (1946, UE); *Octet* for clarinet, bassoon, English horn, 2 violins, viola, cello, double bass (1948, CBDM); *Symphony No. 3* (1952, CBDM); *Piano Concerto* (1962, Eschig); *Concertstück* for viola, orchestra (1962, Schott); *2 Symphonic Movements* (1963, UE); *Music for strings* (1963, Eschig); *Concerto grosso* for piano quartet, orchestra (1969, CBDM).

BIBL.: Richard De Guide, "M. P.," *Musica* (Paris, Nov 1955); Charles Van Den Borren, *M. P.* (Brussels 1953).

SEE ALSO Belgium.

Popular Music is that music which has come to be accepted for entertainment purposes by a majority of the total population, has gained wide dispersion through the mass media, and seems to reflect common taste in general. Popular pieces are usually common to many performers, who each seek to create a performance style that is unique and identifiable with themselves rather than with the composers of their repertory. The performer's personality thus takes precedence over the composer's. By contrast 20th-century concert pieces, with the exception of those by avantgarde composers, many of whom have been heavily influenced by jazz and popular music, tend to be performed the same at each repetition regardless of who the performer is. This is because the concert tradition maintains that the piece has an identity of its own which the performer must bring to life. At the present time popular music in the U.S. is virtually synonymous with most popular music in the rest of the Western world. For this reason and for reasons of space, this article will deal primarily with U.S. developments.

PITCH SYSTEMS. The roots of popular music stretch to cultures that are somewhat removed from the systems of traditional Western tonal organization (major and minor scales) or tuning (equal and just temperament). Tribal and non-Western music has brought to American popular music an enriched vocabulary of pitch systems. Chief among these is the blues scale (see Jazz for this and other jazz-related topics), whose intervals and melodic tendencies differ from those of the just and equal temperaments of concert music.

MELODY. Because popular music is primarily vocal, melody tends to be its most important element. Generally the melodies do not make use of a wide range or of a large number of different notes in one song. Melodic ornamentation is common and sometimes elaborate, especially in music related to folk and tribal music. In some cases melody is shaped by the language employed, especially in Afro-American types. In others it is shaped by the harmonic progressions in a song (e.g., Sigmund Romberg, "All the Things You Are") or the 19th-century European preference for symmetry and sequence (e.g., Frederick Loewe, "Almost Like Being in Love").

RHYTHM. Rhymically popular music tends to reflect either the structure of the language in which it is sung or the function it serves (as in dance music, work songs, etc.). Whereas irregular rhythmic patterns are common in non-Western folk and tribal music, regular patterns are common in the folklike and popular music of the West. Rhythm has been the most characteristic stylistic element in many American popular forms. Ragtime, popular during 1910–17, depended on the interplay between a syncopated treble and a regular pulsating bass. Dixieland, popularized by white musicians in the 1920s, was known as "two-beat" music. The big bands of the 30s featured a characteristic "four-beat" pattern, and the rock 'n' roll of the 1950s and early 60s used a heavily accented pulse known as a "big beat."

HARMONY. Harmony is frequently not present in the music of primitive or folk societies. Although blues, field hollers, and work songs stem from or are part of a monodic tradition, 20th-century popular and folklike music in America invariably makes use of harmonic accompaniment. Such homophonic music usually employs simple progressions (I–V–I, I–IV–V–I, and I–VI–IV–V–I are the most common) and has a distinct polarity of melody and bass. As any one popular type has developed, however, it has tended to become more sophisticated harmonically. An example is the development of rock 'n' roll from the early 1950s to the late 60s. Bill Haley's "Rock Around the Clock" (1953) merely repeated tonic, subdominant, and dominant triads, while the Beatles' "Eleanor Rigby" (1966) drew from a rich palette of chords and progressions.

FORM. The basic formal structure of popular music is most often short and simple; length is gained through devices such as repetition and variation. The strophic nature of most popular song texts is largely responsible for this phenomenon. Unity is often achieved by the insistent repetition of one melodic or rhythmic feature. In the case of boogiewoogie, a popular piano style of the 1930s, stylistic unity was achieved through the employment of an ostinato bass against a syncopated treble, while cohesion was gained through the use of functional harmonic levels and repeated melodic phrases.

The chaconne pattern of urban blues has provided schemata for much 20th-century American popular music. Most frequently used by jazz musicians through the 1950s, it was commonly employed by both black and white popular musicians in the 1960s and appears to be more popular than other forms. Another structure common to American popular music from the 1920s through the 60s is the AABA song or ballad form, which consists of an eight-bar statement, an eight-bar repeat, an eight-bar bridge, and an eight-bar reprise. With the advent of rock in the early 50s, the ballad began to disappear, even from the musical, in which for 50 years composers such as Kern, Gershwin, Porter, Rodgers, and Bernstein had used, elaborated, and even extended this form into complex, sophisticated structures.

Popular pieces from the 1920s through the 50s tended to be very short, approximately three minutes. The most likely explanation was the extramusical demand of the 78 rpm record, the principal means of popularizing music in America at that time. In the 1950s with the appearance of the long-play record, the old limit was extended to approximately 20 minutes, but the reluctance of radio stations to broadcast long pieces has kept the normal length at three minutes. Nevertheless, some of the popular groups of the 1960s began taking advantage of the new freedom (Iron Butterfly, "In-a-Gadda-da-Vida"), and a popular audience with a taste for more extended and complex forms began to appear.

TEXTURE. Folklike and popular music employs homophonic textures with vocal melody and instrumental, chordal accompaniment. Polyphony or monophony are rare. When polyphonic textures occur, the performers are often formally trained musicians with a knowledge of some concert repertory (e.g., the New York Rock and Roll Ensemble).

The favorite medium of popular music is the human voice. Most popular songs make use of instrumental accompaniment, and some use instrumental sonorities for the melody as well. Rhythm section, wind, and string instruments are all commonly used, and popular musicians of the 1960s have made extensive use of electronic instruments and apparatus. While most popular idioms are vocal, ragtime is an example of an American popular style that first emerged as an instrumental idiom and was adapted later to the voice.

PERFORMANCE PRACTICE. One prominent characteristic of folk and popular music is their oral tradition and guild system of education. This results in many versions of any given song, most of them "correct." Also the music is usually played and sung by non-professionals who do not feel constrained by the approved methods of concert performance. Twentieth-century American popular music began to acquire a concert tradition in the 1920s, but it still maintains most of the features of an oral tradition. Most Americans sing in the social settings of home, school, and church, and they have long danced to popular music. However, although publishers have supplied notated music and song texts for singing, and sound recordings and touring

dance bands have carried popular music to a dancing public, recordings, motion pictures, vaudeville, and concert performances of popular music have now created a nonparticipatory audience. The separate roles of composer, performer, and listener emerged during this century, and with the most recent electronic popular music (e.g., the Beatles, "Revolution 9," 1969), the public has been excluded altogether from participating in the performance of popular music. This contrasts with Paul Whiteman's efforts in the 1920s and 30s to make popular music more respectable through the creation of a "symphonic jazz"; in his case the music that became popular was that which was eminently singable.

The primitive oral tradition continues to the present day, and many professional popular singers are musically illiterate and must learn their repertory by rote (likewise, some successful popular composers cannot write musical notation). Many popular performers of the late 1960s adopted a life style indicating their desire not to be considered professional musicians but merely people who happened to sing and play music; as such they have been likened to itinerant minstrels of earlier ages.

An oral tradition has many ramifications upon performance practice features. Just as concert music has a variety of performance traditions that vocalists emulate (e.g., Italian dramatic opera style, *bel canto* style, Wagnerian dramatic opera style, Bach cantata aria style, etc.), popular music too has stereotyped sound ideals. The "natural" nasal twang of a "country-western" singer (Hank Snow, "I Don't Hurt Anymore") is a learned, not a natural technique. It is quite different from "natural" school-girl singing (Debbie Reynolds, "Tammy") or "natural" musical comedy singing (Judy Garland, "Over the Rainbow") or "natural" crooning (Bing Crosby, "Sweet Leilani"). The important feature in these supposedly natural styles is the belief by the public that popular singing is unlike learned concert styles and that one does not go to school to learn to sing popular music; it supposedly comes "naturally," and anyone can do it. Consequently many "natural" traditions exist that cannot be notated and are learned by and preserved only on recordings. Popular style, in fact, is a combination of the performer's personal idiosyncrasies, the public's expectations, and the total style's general rules of timbre, ornamentation, dynamics, vibrato, tempo, pronunciation, and other elements. The oral tradition is so strong that notated popular songs are little more than a rudimentary sketch of the music they represent.

FUNCTION. Popular music is often intended to serve a specific function in society. In the more primitive and folk communities, it is often tied to ritual, and this has carried into our more sophisticated society with activities relating to courtship. Popular music is action oriented and, at least until recently, has implied active participation. Even in periods when it is more fashionable to listen to popular music than to sing it, dance music has provided the public with an avenue of participation.

POPULAR MUSIC AND CONCERT MUSIC. Many concert composers have been attracted by popular music and have attempted to use popular styles. Some, writing a kind of gebrauchsmusik, attempted to communicate more directly to nonprofessionals and thereby enlarge the concert audience. Others sensed an inherent beauty in pop music and wished to incorporate it with their own. Several opera composers have made extensive use of jazz and popular techniques in their works. Krenek's opera *Jonny spielt auf* (1925–26), Weill's *Mahagonny* (1929), Blitzstein's *The Cradle Will Rock* (1936), and Bernstein's *West Side Story* (1957) are typical. Operas for school children were written by Hindemith, *Wir bauen eine Stadt* (1930); Copland, *Second Hurricane* (1937); and Weill, *Down in the Valley* (1945–48), but where the latter two sound like pop music, the Hindemith work is more typical of that composer's concert writing with its quartal harmony, symphonic forms, counterpoint, and other nonpopular features; it is, however, simple and has easily sung tunes. The best known popular or jazz opera is Gershwin's *Porgy and Bess* (1934–35). Although it blends popular and cultivated idioms successfully, it requires professional singers to handle the melodies and rhythms ("Bess, You Is My Woman" and "Little David Was Small"); it does not have what would be termed a "popular song" in the entire score. Gershwin's orchestral pieces (e.g., *Rhapsody in Blue*, 1924) have this same combination of jazz, popular, and concert materials.

Bartók derived material and inspiration from East European folk music. Among the most notable examples are the short piano pieces written early in his career, *15 Hungarian Peasant Songs* (1914–17). About the same time Hindemith was writing ragtime piano pieces, *Dance Suite* (1923). Other major composers who looked to ragtime and Dixieland for source material were Stravinsky, Milhaud, and Copland.

The achievement of men like Bartók, Kodály, and Hába was not the composition of folklike classical music but the enrichment of the Western musical language through the discovery and exploitation of East European folk sounds. Whereas Hába was unsuccessful in gaining followers for his microtonal innovations, Bartók was extremely influential. Latin Americans and Spaniards, too, have gone to their folk idioms for inspiration. The Mexican Chávez and the Brazilian Villa-Lobos command worldwide audiences, although their compositional styles seem to have advocates only in their own countries. Falla, whose *Harpsichord Concerto* (1923–26) blends folk and concert ideas, believed that folk music was the path to an international concert style; however, the pluralism of the 1960s speaks eloquently of the lack of any such synthesis.

Many Americans have used native music in their larger works. Ives, Cowell, Harris, Schuman, Thomson, and Riegger, in addition to those mentioned above, were strongly affected by jazz and popular music. The earliest, Ives, used ragtime, popular tunes, patriotic songs, hymns, band sonorities, and almost anything else he could lay his hands on. Cowell, Harris, and others have incorporated dances (reels, jigs, and the like) into large works.

Although many composers turned to popular materials in the spirit of nationalism, this, as a single cause, is less common in the 20th century than it was in the 19th. Sibelius and Vaughan Williams are notable examples.

A noticeable increase in interaction between concert and popular composers took place during the 1960s. Some observers even predicted a breakdown of the categories "serious" and "popular," because they saw concert musicians such as Ned Rorem, Cathy Berberian, and Leonard Bernstein praising the song writing efforts of popular groups such as the Beatles and saw popular groups such as the New York Rock and Roll Ensemble proclaim rock to be a kind of 20th-century chamber music. It is certainly true that the experimentation in popular music of the late 1960s made use of a wide range of stylistic materials; the most "advanced" group, the Beatles, incorporated sitar, baroquelike trumpet obbligatos, classical-style string-quartet writing, modal harmonies, and electronic apparatus. In addition the Beatles studied Luciano Berio, Karlheinz Stockhausen, Ravi Shankar, and others. Blood Sweat and Tears recorded their version of Satie's *Gymnopédies*. And The Mothers of Invention, even though they were reluctant to admit of outside influences, were known to listen to Ives, Bartók, Stravinsky, Stockhausen, and especially John Cage.

BIBL.: Gilbert Chase, *America's Music,* 2nd ed. (New York 1966); Arthur Cohn, *The Collector's 20th Century Music in the Western Hemisphere* (Philadelphia 1961); Jonathan Eisen, ed., *The Age of Rock: Sounds of the American Cultural Revolution* (New York 1969); David Ewen, *History of Popular Music* (New York 1961); ——, *Panorama of American Popular Music* (Englewood Cliffs, N. J., 1957); H. Wiley Hitchcock, *Music in the United States: A Historical Introduction* (Englewood Cliffs, N. J., 1970); Wilfrid Mellers, *Music in a New Found Land* (London 1964); Bruno Nettl, *An Introduction to the Folk Music of the United States* (Detroit 1962); Henry Pleasants, "Who's Afraid of Pierre Boulez?" *Encounter* (Feb 1969): 49–54; Charles A. Reich, *The Greening of America,* paperback ed. (New York 1971): 260–71; Ned Rorem, *Music and People* (New York 1968); Eric Salzman, "The Revolution of Music," *New American Review* 6: 76–96; ——, *20th-Century Music: An Introduction* (Englewood Cliffs, N.J., 1967); Nat Shapiro, ed., *Popular Music* (New York, 1964–68); Alec Wilder, *American Popular Song: The Great Innovators, 1900–1950* (New York 1972).

Frank Tirro and Roberta Newman

SEE ALSO Folk Resources; Jazz; Liturgical Music: Jewish; Mixed Media; Musical; Orchestration; Rhythm.

Porter, Quincy (b. New Haven, 7 Feb 1897; d. New Haven, 12 Nov 1966), studied at Yale Univ. (1915–20; composition with Horatio Parker, David S. Smith) and the Schola Cantorum in Paris (1920–21, composition with Vincent d'Indy, violin with Lucien Capet). He also studied composition in New York with Ernst Bloch (1921–22) and moved with Bloch to the Cleveland Institute, where Porter taught during 1922–28 and 1931–32 and played viola in the De Ribaupierre Quartet. During 1932–38 he taught at Vassar College; during 1938–46 he was dean and later director of the New England Conservatory; and during 1946–65 he taught at Yale Univ. From a close study of Orlando di Lasso motets "he derived his ideal of flowing, almost consistently stepwise melody, and very close knit continuity of sections." The opening of the *String Quartet No. 3* is characteristic in its "use of a strong 'head-motive' rather than a full-fledged theme of some bars' length, a bass pedal treated in a rhythmically significant way, many uses of the mordent figure (both alone and incorporated in scalewise groups of 16th-notes), and a vital sort of rhythmic counter-

point which creates tension by acting against the metrical character of the leading part" (Boatwright 1957:3–4; see bibl.).

PRINCIPAL COMPOSITIONS: *Violin Sonata No. 2* (1929, SPAM); *Piano Sonata* (1930, ACA); *Suite* for viola (1930, New Valley); *String Quartets Nos. 3, 6, 7, 8* (1930, SPAM; 1937, SPAM; 1943, New Valley; 1950, New Valley); *Poem and Dance* for orchestra (1932, ACA); *Symphonies Nos. 1–2* (1934, ACA; 1962, Peters); *Music for Strings* (1941, Mercury); *Horn Sonata* (1946, Music Publishers Holding Corp.); *Viola Concerto* (1948, AMP); *Concerto concertante* for 2 pianos, orchestra (1953, ACA); *Duo* for violin, viola (1954, ACA); *Concerto for Wind Orchestra* (1959, Peters); *Harpsichord Concerto* (1959, ACA); *Divertimento* for woodwind quintet (1960, Peters): *Oboe Quintet* (1966, Highgate). List to 1959: *Composers of the Americas* 4: 50–57.

BIBL.: Howard Boatwright, "Q. P.," *ACA Bulletin* 4/3 (1957): 2–9; ——, "Q. P.," *Perspectives* 5/2 (1967): 162–65.

[prepared with the help of Howard Boatwright and Alfred Kuhn]

Poulenc, Francis (b. Paris, 7 Jan 1899; d. Paris, 30 Jan 1963), studied piano during his teens with Ricardo Viñes and composition during 1921–24 with Charles Koechlin. His early writing was also influenced by the artistic climate of Paris in the late 1910s and early 20s. The first work that brought him celebrity, the *Rhapsodie nègre* (1917), is a tongue-in-cheek composition with a vocal interlude based on pseudo-African nonsense syllables; it was characteristic of the reaction against "phoney sublimity" in the arts, which was shared by the group of composers (including Poulenc) designated in 1920 as Les Six. After a pilgrimage to Rocamadour in southern France in August 1936, Poulenc reembraced the Catholic faith, which set the tone for many subsequent works. (He became, in fact, one of the 20th century's major composers of liturgical music.) In spite of this, he never lost his sense of humor and wit; he described himself once as having "a melancholic character . . . which likes to laugh like all melancholic characters." In 1944 he began to write operas, a genre to which he devoted much of his later career. He was working on his fourth opera, a setting of Cocteau's *La Machine infernale,* when he died.

Poulenc is considered by many as the greatest 20th-century exponent of the art song. He wrote more than 50 songs or song cycles. Other vocal works include some 19 choral works, three operas, and several miscellaneous theater pieces, such as *Le Bal masqué*. He also produced a large body of keyboard compositions, including concertos for organ, harpsichord, piano and two pianos, and works for solo piano. The rest of Poulenc's output consists mainly of chamber works, incidental music, ballets, and a few film scores. He never wrote more than one composition for any particular instrumental combination, and such standard genres as the symphony and the string quartet are entirely absent (although he did compose and later discard a quartet).

Poulenc's music exhibits a kind of classical (as opposed to neoclassical) simplicity and frequently emphasizes the unexpected (humor or buffoonery, deliberate vulgarity or banality, frequent contrasts, etc.). Although these traits can be found in music by Stravinsky, Ravel, and Satie (and, going further back, Emmanuel Chabrier), all of whom had some influence on Poulenc's style, they probably came to Poulenc more directly through the work of such writers as Guillaume Apollinaire, Paul Eluard (and the surrealists in general), and Jean Cocteau. Not only did these authors provide an esthetic with which Poulenc readily identified, they also furnished the texts for many of his best vocal pieces. Poulenc's opera, *Les Mamelles de Tirésias*, based on Apollinaire's play of 1917, is one of his most successful and characteristic works (it was also his favorite, along with the *Stabat Mater*). Besides the absurdity and hilarity of the text itself, it contains many popular elements, such as the "Boston" waltz that accompanies the upward flight of Thérèse's breasts, Spanish dances, polkas, and the like. At the same time, Poulenc gave depth to the opera's deliberately vulgar elements by setting them off against sections that are serious or pseudoserious in tone, such as the Prologue or the choral passage following the duel between Presto and Lacouf. This use of contrast to give relief to the musical and/or literary thought of a given work also manifests itself in frequent shifts between the major and minor modes, as in "Pablo Picasso" from *Le Travail du peintre*.

Melody is always the dominant element in Poulenc's music, and the songs often begin immediately with the voice. This same lyricism gives Poulenc's religious music an almost medieval quality of candor and naïveté, thus distinguishing it greatly from the romanticism of Florent Schmitt and the personal mysticism of Olivier Messiaen, two other major exponents of liturgical music in France. Poulenc's harmony is generally diatonic, and the texture homophonic; counterpoint is rare. He colored the diatonic idiom with modulations that are either pandiatonic (stemming particularly from Stravinsky) or chromatic, as in the opening of the *Piano Concerto*. He enriched his chord vocabulary with sevenths and especially added sixths, often in the bass. Also characteristic are occasional "wrong notes" and brief but strong dissonances used either for comic effect, as in the trumpet passage preceding the Presto-Lacouf duet in *Les Mamelles*, or dramatic relief, as in the opening of the *Organ Concerto*. In his later works, notably those with a religious orientation such as *Dialogues des Carmélites*, there are choralelike harmonic progressions. Form tends to be episodic, with the various sections in a given work or movement being fairly numerous and sharply contrasted. Even in works with such classical designations as concerto or sonata, repetition of themes or motives is based more on an internal logic than on an external pattern. Rarely does Poulenc develop a given theme or even vary it to any considerable extent. His last two operas contain the semblance of leitmotivs, but even here, these are used more to give emotional unity to the work than to symbolize a particular aspect or character. Like his harmonic idiom, Poulenc's rhythmic style is usually simple. There are many dance and music-hall patterns and rapid, "perpetual-motion" passages. Later (particularly from the *Stabat Mater* on) Poulenc's writing became somewhat more polished and serious. His last completed opera, *La Voix humaine*, has an unusually sumptuous orchestral scoring (but always transparent and subservient to the voice) and a conversational vocal style occasionally rising to semiarias in a manner recalling Debussy. If Poulenc has set an example for other composers, it has been more in his inherently modern esthetic than in his style and technique, which were conservative. His approach to music and to art in general was unsystematized and almost instinctive, and with his nondoctrinaire attitudes, he was not the type of composer to attract true disciples, although the name of Ned Rorem does come to mind.

PRINCIPAL COMPOSITIONS: *Rhapsodie nègre* for flute, clarinet, string quartet, piano, voice (1917, Chester); *3 Mouvements perpétuels* for piano (1918, Chester); *Sonata* for piano 4-hands (1918, Chester); *Le Bestiaire ou le cortège d'Orphée*, song cycle for medium voice with piano (string quartet), flute, clarinet, bassoon (1919, Eschig); *Le Gendarme incompris,* incidental music for the play by Cocteau-Radiquet (1921); *La Baigneuse de Trouville* and *Discours du général*, incidental music for Cocteau's *Les Mariés de la Tour Eiffel* (1921, Salabert);

Sonata for clarinet, bassoon (1922, Chester); *Sonata* for horn, trumpet, trombone (1922, Chester); *Les Biches*, ballet with songs (1923, Heugel); *Trio* for piano, oboe, bassoon (1926, Chester); *Concert champêtre* for harpsichord, (piano), orchestra (1927–28, Rouart-Lerolle); *3 Pièces* for piano (1938, Heugel); *Aubade*, choreographic concerto for piano, 18 instruments (1929, Rouart-Lerolle); *5 Poèmes de Max Jacob*, song cycle (1931, Rouart-Lerolle); *Le Bal masqué*, cantata for baritone, chamber orchestra; poems by Max Jacob (1932, Rouart-Lerolle); *Concerto in D Minor* for 2 pianos, orchestra (1932, Rouart-Lerolle); *Sextet* for piano, flute, oboe, clarinet, bassoon, horn (1932–39, Chester); *5 Poèmes de Paul Eluard*, song cycle (1935, Durand); *Litanies à la Vierge noire de Rocamadour* for children's (women's) chorus, organ (1936, Durand); *Tel Jour telle nuit*, song cycle; poems by Eluard (1936–37, Durand); *Mass in G* for chorus (1937, Rouart-Lorolle); *Concerto in G Minor* for organ, strings, timpani (1938, Salabert); *4 Motets pour un temps de pénitence* for 4 mixed voices (1938–39, Rouart-Lerolle); *Banalités*, song cycle; text by Apollinaire (1940, Eschig); *Les Animaux modèles*, ballet based on fables of La Fontaine (1940–41, Eschig); *Cello Sonata* (1940–48, Heugel); *Chansons villageoises* for voice, chamber orchestra or piano (1942, Eschig); *Violin Sonata* (1942–43, Eschig); *Figure humaine*, cantata for double chorus; poems by Eluard (1943, Rouart-Lerolle); *Les Mamelles de Tirésias*, opéra bouffe; text by Apollinaire (1944, Rouart-Lerolle); *Sinfonietta* (1947, Chester); *Calligrammes*, song cycle; text by Apollinaire (1948, Heugel); *Piano Concerto* (1949, Rouart-Lerolle); *La Fraîcheur et le feu*, song cycle; text by Eluard (1950, Eschig); *Stabat Mater* for soprano, chorus, orchestra (1950, Rouart-Lerolle); *Sonata* for 2 pianos (1952–53, Eschig); *Dialogues des Carmélites*, opera based on the play by Georges Bernanos (1953–55, Ricordi); *Le Travail du peintre*, song cycle; text by Eluard (1956, Eschig); *Flute Sonata* (1957, Chester); *La Voix humaine*, lyrical tragedy based on the play by Cocteau (1958, Ricordi); *Gloria* for soprano, chorus, orchestra (1959, Salabert); *La Dame de Monte Carlo*, monologue for soprano, orchestra; based on a text by Cocteau (1961); *7 Répons des Ténèbres* for boy soprano, children's and men's choruses, orchestra (1961, Ricordi); *Oboe Sonata* (1962, Chester); *Clarinet Sonata* (1962, Chester). List of works, 1918–56, in Hell; list, 1916–62, in Roy (see bibl.).

PRINCIPAL WRITINGS: "Feuilles américaines," *Table ronde* 30:66–75; *Entretiens avec Claude Rostand* (Paris 1954); "La Musique de piano d'Erik Satie," *Revue musicale* 214:23–26; *Emmanuel Chabrier* (Paris 1961); *Moi et mes amis* (Paris 1963); *Correspondance, 1915–63* (Paris 1967); *Journal de mes mélodies* (unpub.).

BIBL.: Henri Hell, *F. P.* trans. by Edward Lockspeiser (London 1959); Jean Roy, *F. P.* (Paris 1964).

Royal S. Brown

SEE ALSO Dance; France; Liturgical Music: Christian; Opera.

Pound, Ezra (b. Hailey, Idaho, 30 Oct 1884; d. Venice, 1 Nov 1972), studied at Hamilton College in Clinton, N. Y. (until 1905) and the Univ. of Pa. (until 1906). He taught English literature briefly at Wabash College (1906), then went to Italy (1908), London (1908–20), Paris (1920–24), and Italy again (1924–45). He was extradited to the U.S. in 1945 on charges of aiding fascism during World War II and was committed to a mental hospital (1946–58). In 1958 he returned to Italy. He was a prolific journalist in his early years and wrote for *Poetry* (1912–19), the *Dial* (1922), and the *Little Review*, of which he was editor during 1917–19. During 1917–21 he was music critic for *The New Age*. He promoted young artists in all the arts. His interest in music was closely allied to his theories of meter in poetry, which he derived in part from studying the work of the medieval troubadours, especially Arnaut Daniel, in which music and poetry are closely allied. His acquaintance with Arnold Dolmetsch and George Antheil inspired him to write an opera drawing on the linear compositional styles of the middle ages and early renaissance and deriving vocal and instrumental lines from a declamation of the text.

PRINCIPAL COMPOSITIONS: *Le Testament*, 1-act opera; libretto adapted from Villon (1920–21); *Homage à Froissart* for violin (premiere 1926); *Cavalcanti*, unfinished opera; libretto adapted from Guido and Sordello (late 1920s).

PRINCIPAL WRITINGS ON MUSIC: *Antheil and the Treatise on Harmony* (Paris 1924); *Guide to Kulchur* (London 1938).

BIBL.: R. Murray Schafer, "E. P. and Music," *Canadian Music Journal* 4:15–43.

Pousseur, Henri (b. Malmedy, Belgium, 23 June 1929), studied during 1947–53 at the Conservatories in Liège (where he worked with Pierre Froidebise) and Brussels (where he worked with André Souris and the pianist Marcelle Mercenier). He had his first contact with Webern's music in Liège in 1947. He met Pierre Boulez in 1951, Karlheinz Stockhausen in 1953 (composed his first electronic work in Cologne, 1954), and myself in 1956 (composed his second electronic work in Milan, 1957). He cofounded the Apelac electronic studio in Brussels in 1958. During 1950–60 he taught music in a secondary school in Brussels; since then he has taught at Darmstadt, in Basel, Cologne, the Univ. of N. Y. at Buffalo, and in Paris.

Pousseur was born and educated on the border between French and German culture, a fact which may explain the equilibrium in his development between ideology (one book and over two dozen articles) and action (some three dozen compositions). As with many other composers of his generation, contact with Webern's music was a decisive event in his life. He was attracted especially by the nondirectionality in Webern's chromaticism. During the period that ended in *Quintette à la mémoire de Webern* (1955), he avoided any direct consideration of form, treating it instead as an automatic result of pitch manipulation. New processes appeared in *Exercises pour piano* (1956), and thereafter the shape of a work was often based on an interaction of two opposites (for example, an extremely periodic harmony, such as an octave, interacting along a continuum with an extremely unperiodic harmony, such as a 12-tone cluster). Pousseur derived this process in part from those theories of perception that hold that experiences are defined according to how they fall between two extremes (hot and cold, fast and slow, etc.). In addition to extremes of harmonic periodicity in pitch relations, Pousseur's opposites include high vs. low speeds of instrumental activity; large vs. small ratios of register shifting, harmonic stability, or noise content; differences in articulation, timbre, etc. This way of thinking is a transformation of Webern's sound space into a phenomenological interpretation of the multidirectionality of all perceivable levels of musical structure (and not merely the four "serializable" parameters of pitch, duration, dynamics, and timbre).

In the electronic work *Scambi* (1957), perception is channeled through different modes of articulating bands of colored noise. The piece consists of a number of recorded sections of different lengths which can be interchanged and superimposed according to a "code" based on the initial and final characters of each section. The result is a discourse perpetually open, not a form but a process. *Mobile* for two pianos (1956–58) is a synthesis of the combined and developed experiences of *Exercises* and *Scambi*. A new and higher level of synthesis was reached in *Votre Faust* (1961–67), a variable "operatic fantasy" and an eloquent retrospective comment on the inner coherence of Pousseur's development. The work can follow several different courses, the direction supposedly determined by the audience (by voting) but in practice generally predetermined by the performers. The concept of a continuum between opposites is extended to associations of style (Wagner, for example, is quoted as an instance of evolving chromaticism); each continuum, in turn, is used to

typify something in the plot (chromaticism, for example, is often used in association with Henri, the composer). In reality, the main personage in *Votre Faust* is the history of music, not out of the old Faustian urge to use the past but out of the desire and need to deal with realities wherever they may be.

PRINCIPAL COMPOSITIONS: *Quintette*, in memoriam Anton Webern, for clarinet, bass clarinet, piano, violin, cello (1955, S-Z); *Mobile* for 2 pianos (1956–58, S-Z); *Scambi* on tape (1957, recorded by Philips); *Rimes* for various sound sources (1958–59, S-Z; recorded by RCA Victrola); *Répons* for flute, violin, cello, 2 pianists (playing piano, celesta, electric organ), harp, percussionist, actor (originally composed 1960 for 7 performers; recomposed 1965 in collaboration with Michel Butor); *Ode* for string quartet (1960–61, UE); *Caractères* for piano (1961, UE); *3 Visages de Liège* on tape (1961, UE; recorded by Columbia); *Votre Faust*, variable operatic fantasy for 5 speaking actors, vocal quartet, 12 musicians, tapes; composed in collaboration with Butor (1961–67, UE); *Madrigal III* for clarinet, violin, cello, piano, 2 percussionists (1962, UE); *Miroir de Votre Faust* for piano, soprano ad lib. (1964–65, UE); *Apostrophe et 6 réflexions* for piano (1964–66, UE); *Phonèmes couleurs croisées* for orchestra (1967, S-Z); *Mnemosyne 1–2*: No. 1, "Der Mnemosyne Anfang," monody for voice or instrument or unison chorus (1968, S-Z); No. 2, "Der Mnemosyne Entwicklung," a system of improvised developments on the preceding number for an undetermined number of performers (1969, S-Z); *Les Voyages de Votre Faust*, lyrical variations on 35-mm. color film; prepared in collaboration with Butor, Jean Antoine (1969); *Les Ephémérides d'Icare II* for a principal soloist, concertino (3 musicians), ripieno (16 musicians) (1970, S-Z).

PRINCIPAL WRITINGS: "Webern's Organic Chromaticism," *Die Reihe*, English ed., 2:51–61; "Da Schoenberg a Webern, una mutazione," *Incontri musicali* (Milan, 1956):3–39; "Entretiens avec H. P.," Maurice Faure, *Lettres nouvelles* (Paris) 29 (1962):111–30; "The Question of Order in New Music," *Perspectives* 5/1:93–111; "Calculation and Imagination in Electronic Music," *Electronic Music Review* (1968); "L'Apothéose de Rameau," *Les Musiques nouvelles* (Paris) 2–4 (1968):105–71. Several of Pousseur's essays are printed in *Fragments théoriques*, 2 vols. (Brussels 1970, 1972).

Luciano Berio

SEE ALSO Austria and Germany; Belgium; Liturgical Music: Christian; Mixed Media; Opera; Performance.

Powell, Mel (b. New York, 12 Feb 1923), played piano and arranged music for the Benny Goodman Band while still in his teens and for the Glenn Miller Air Force Band during World War II. He studied composition with Bernard Wagenaar and Joseph Schillinger in New York (1937–39) and with Ernst Toch in Los Angeles (1946–48), where he was doing recording and film work. During 1950–57 he lived in New York as a free-lance composer, pianist, and teacher (doing increasingly less work in the jazz and commercial fields), and in 1957 he joined the Yale Univ. composition faculty. He established one of the first U.S. electronic music studios at Yale in 1960. In 1969 he became dean of music at the Calif. Institute of the Arts.

Powell's output centers on vocal, chamber, orchestral, and taped electronic works. Most of the mature pieces are short (about five minutes), and their esthetic is one of delicate, quickly paced complexity within a miniaturized time world. His early pieces were molded in the image of Hindemith-Stravinsky neo-classicism (a strong influence on all American composers of the time). After 1955 he began to embrace a post-Webern total-chromatic (but nonserial) language. In *Filigree Setting* (1959) and later works he has used whatever pitches he feels are needed, maintaining an equalized pitch spectrum but allowing major seconds, minor thirds, and especially minor seconds to predominate. The most important determinant in his recent stylistic evolution is the notion of temporal articulation. Earlier total-chromatic pieces, such as *Filigree Setting* and *Haiku Settings*, embody series of quick changes, which replace the downbeat of tonal music as reference points. Later works, such as the *2nd Electronic Setting* and *Analogs*, tend toward less striated change and a more supple temporal flow. This is taken to an extreme in *Immobiles*, where the structure of each of the five pieces is based on the principles of nonchange and nondifferentiation. Even in his most recent works Powell has maintained strong ties with tradition. He is reluctant, for example, to use unusual playing techniques; the rare exceptions include *Filigree Setting* and *Immobile 2*, which employ finger drumming on string instruments. The bridging of past and present is also exemplified in his electronic music. He tends to use the medium as though it were a pitched instrument, and *Analogs*, one of the finest electronic works to date, is structured as a traditional four-movement symphony.

PRINCIPAL COMPOSITIONS (published by Schirmer-G unless otherwise noted): *Trio* for piano, violin, cello (1954, unpub.); *Divertimento* for violin, harp (1954, unpub.); *Divertimento* for flute, oboe, clarinet, bassoon, trumpet (1955, Fischer); *Stanzas* for orchestra (1957); *Filigree Setting* for string quartet (1959); *Haiku Settings* for high voice, piano (1961); *Setting* for cello,

orchestra (1961); *Improvisation* for clarinet, viola, piano (1962); *2nd Electronic Setting* on tape (1962, recorded by CRI); *Events* on tape (1963, recorded by CRI); *2 Prayer Settings* for tenor, oboe, violin, viola, cello (1963); *Analogs 1–4* on tape (1966); *Immobiles 1–4* for tape and/or orchestra (1967); *Immobile 5* for tape and orchestra (1969). List, 1948–67, in Thimmig (see bibl.); to 1964: *Composers of the Americas* 9:124–25.

PRINCIPAL WRITINGS: "A Note on Webern," *Juilliard Review* 4:3–5; a review of *The Musical Quarterly*'s special issue on "Problems of Modern Music" (April 1960), *Journal of Music Theory* 4:259–69; "A Volley for Varèse," *Saturday Review* (31 Dec 1960):34–35; "A Note on Rigor," *Perspectives* 1/2:121–24; "In Memoriam: Paul Hindemith (1895–1963)," *ibid.* 2/2:1; "Electronic Music and Musical Newness," *American Scholar* 35:290–91.

BIBL.: Joseph Machlis, "M. P.," *Introduction to Contemporary Music* (New York 1961):621–23; Harvey Sollberger, "M. P.'s *Haiku Settings*," *Perspectives* 3/1:147–55; Leslie Thimmig, "The Music of M. P.," *Musical Quarterly* 55:31–44.

Leslie Thimmig

Prado, José-Antonio (Almeida) (b. Santos, Brazil, 8 Feb 1943), studied piano until 1960 with Dinorá Carvalho and attended the Santos Conservatory (1960–64; harmony, counterpoint with Osvaldo Lacerda; piano with Italiano Tabarin). He studied composition in Santos with Camargo Guarnieri (1960–65) and in Paris with Nadia Boulanger (1969–70) and analysis in Paris with Olivier Messiaen (1969). He has taught piano at the Santos Conservatory (1965–69) and the Foundation of the Arts at São Caetano do Sul (1968–69). He has also appeared as a pianist in recitals of his music. Brazilian folk music, Villa-Lobos, and the serialism of Schoenberg and Webern have been major influences on his music.

PRINCIPAL COMPOSITIONS: *Variations 1963* for piano (1962–63, Vitale); *Toccata* for piano (1964, Vitale); *Variations* for piano, orchestra (1964); *Piano Sonata No. 1* (1965); *Missa da paz* for chorus (1965); *St. Mark Passion* for actors, soprano, alto, tenor, bass, 3 choruses, organ, piano (1967); *Recitative and Fugue* for piano (1968, Vitale); *Pequenos funerais cantantes* for mezzo-soprano, baritone, chorus, orchestra (1969); *Symphony No. 1* (1969).

SEE ALSO Brazil.

Pratella, Francesco (Balilla) (b. Lugo, Italy, 1 Feb 1880; d. Ravenna, 17 May 1955), studied at the Liceo Musicale in Pesaro until

1903 (composition with Pietro Mascagni and Giuseppe Cicognani). He was director of the Lugo Music Academy during 1910–c.1926 and of the Ravenna Liceo Musicale during c.1927–45. In 1910 he wrote a "Manifesto of Futurist Musicians," which "advocated such things as 'a single . . . atonal mode, the chromatic scale,' 'the realisation of the enharmonic mode' (i.e., microtonal scales), and 'a free, polyrhythmic manner' with continually changing time signatures. It ends with a typically futurist exhortation to bring into music the spirit of 'the crowd, of great factories, of trains, of transatlantic liners, of battleships, of motor-cars and aeroplanes' " (Waterhouse: 27; see bibl.). Pratella conceived his own music in terms of traditional instruments and achieved what Waterhouse has described as "tuneless Mascagni-with-wrong-notes, clogged with hamfisted whole-tone-scale patterns and dissonant block chords in parallel motion." It remained for another futurist, the painter Luigi *Russolo, to invent instruments and music capable of embodying the futurist esthetic. After 1915 Pratella lost interest in the movement and did research on Italian peasant music.

PRINCIPAL COMPOSITIONS: *Lilia*, opera (1903); *Musica futurista* for orchestra (1912, piano reduction published by Bongiovanni, Bologna); *L'aviatore dro*, 3-act opera (1915, Sonzogno); *Per un dramma orientale* for piano, string quartet (published 1938, Ricordi).

PRINCIPAL WRITINGS: "Manifesto of Futurist Musicians," *Revista musicale italiana* 17 (1910): 1007–11; "Technical Manifesto of Futurist Music," *ibid.* 18 (1911):486–90; *Musica italiana* (Bologna 1915); *Il terzo libro delle laudi spirituali* (Bologna 1916); *Evoluzione della musica*, 2 vols. (Milan 1918, 1919); *Cronache e critiche* (Bologna 1919); *Saggio di gridi, canzoni, cori e danze del popolo italiano* (Bologna 1919); *Appunti per lo studio dell'armonia* (Bologna 1930); *Appunti biografici e bibliografici* (Ravenna 1931); *Appunti per lo studio della storia dell'arte musicale* (Bologna 1931); *Scritti vari di pensiero, di arte, di storia musicale* (Bologna 1932); *Luci e ombre*, a book on V. Gnecchi ed. by Pratella (Rome 1933); *Etnofonia di Romagna* (Udine 1938); *Le arti e le tradizioni popolari d'Italia*, 2 vols. (Udine 1941); *Linee di storia della musica* (Milan 1946); *Il libro della musica e del canto in coro*, 3 vols. (Milan 1947).

BIBL.: Armando Gentilucci, "Il futurismo e lo sperimentalismo musicale d'oggi," *Studia et documenta historiae musiciae*, vol. 2 (Turin 1965); Alba Ghigi, *F. B. P., arti grafiche* (Ravenna 1930); Wilibald Nagel, "Musica futuristica," *Die Musik* (1914–15):3–25; F. K. Prieberg, *Musica ex machina* (Berlin 1960); J. C. Waterhouse, "A Futurist Mystery," *Music and Musicians* (April 1967):26–30.

SEE ALSO Futurism.

Precompositional refers to the plans and decisions a composer makes prior to the principal act of composition. In 12-tone and serial music, the precompositional steps may include the devising of basic set(s) and the determining of which set permutations are most likely to realize the composer's expressive intentions. Such traditional operations as choosing an instrumentation or experimenting with the developmental potentials of a melody might also be considered *precompositional*; however, the term is generally applied only to specifically 12-tone and serial decisions.

Prigozhin, Lucian (Abramovich) (b. Tashkent, U.S.S.R., 15 August 1926), studied at the Leningrad State Conservatory (1945–51, composition with Vladimir Shcherbatchev, piano with Stoliar). He teaches theory, instrumentation, and pedagogy at the Leningrad Conservatory and is chairman of the chamber and symphonic section of the composer's union in Leningrad. In his youth his musical development was influenced by Shostakovich and Stravinsky. In addition to the works listed below, he has composed scores for films, theater, and radio.

PRINCIPAL COMPOSITIONS: *Symphonietta* (1952, SC); *Symphonies Nos. 1–2* (1954; 1956, SC); *Nepokorennyi Promfei* [Indominable Prometheus], oratorio for chorus, orchestra (1959, SC); *Krug ada* [The Infernal Circle], ballet (1964, orchestral suite published by Muzyka); *Slovo o polku Igoreve* [The Legend of the Host of Igor], oratorio for mezzo-soprano, baritone, chorus of altos and basses, chamber ensemble (1966, Muzyka); *Sonata burlesque* for violin, orchestra (1967); *V'iuga* [Snowstorm], chamber oratorio after Alexander Blok for 2 vocal soloists, chorus, clarinet, piano, percussion (1968, SC); *Violin Sonata No. 2* (1969); *String Quartet* (1970).

BIBL.: A. Strupel', *Obraza mirovoi poezii v muzyke* [Images of World Poetry in Music] (Moscow-Leningrad 1965); M. Bialik, "Molodost' dukha zrelost' masterstva" [Young in Spirit, Mature in Artistry], *Neva* 1966/7; V. Gurevich, "Put' iskanii" [In Search], *Muzykal'naia zhizn'* 1969/2:10.

Printing, see Publishing

Probability Theory, see Mathematics, Theory

Prokofiev, Sergei (Sergeievich) (b. Sontzovka, Ukraine, 23 April 1891; d. Moscow, 5 March 1953), was born in a remote village where his ather was the manager of an estate. His earliest musical impressions were received from the piano playing of his mother, who taught him piano and encouraged him at a very early age to compose. During 1902–03 he studied harmony and composition with Reinhold Glière, which prepared him for entrance to the St. Petersburg Conservatory in 1904; there he studied composition and related subjects with Anatol Liadov, Rimsky-Korsakov, Joseph Wihtol, and Nicolas Tcherepnin until 1909 and then piano with Anna Esipova until 1914. By that time he had composed his first 15 opus numbers and published some of them, including two piano sonatas and the *Piano Concerto No. 1*, and was recognized as a notable member of the Petersburg avant-garde.

In the summer of 1914 Prokofiev spent a month in London, where he met Diaghilev, who commissioned the "Scythian" ballet *Ala and Lolly*, from which only an orchestral suite survives. On 7 May 1918, soon after the first performance of his *Classical Symphony*, he left Petrograd and traveled by way of Japan to the U.S., where he appeared as pianist and composer in New York and Chicago and composed the *Love for 3 Oranges* (1919, commissioned by the Chicago Opera, which produced it in 1921). In America he began another opera, *The Flaming Angel*, completed only in 1927 and never performed in his lifetime. He felt no more at home in capitalist America than in socialist Russia, and in 1920 he moved to Paris. Except for 18 months at Ettal, near Oberammergau (1922–23), he spent most of his time up to 1932 in Paris, though he made concert tours all over Europe and America and (beginning in January 1927) in the Soviet Union. He was an outstanding figure in the cultural world of Paris, with its ferment of ever-new ideas, and Diaghilev was on hand to encourage him to new ballets: *Le Pas d'acier* (1927) and *The Prodigal Son* (1929). (The latter yielded thematic material for the *Symphony No. 4*, 1930, just as *The Flaming Angel* had done for *No. 3*, 1928; however, *No. 3*, 1924, is even more markedly Parisian-of-the-20s.)

Prokofiev was increasingly conscious of his failure to strike roots in the West, and in 1933 he resettled in Moscow to teach composition. He could hardly have returned at a more unfortunate time. Whereas modernist tendencies in music had been tolerated ever since the Revolution, though attacked by "proletarian" musicians, the Communist Party had recently enunciated the doctrine of "socialist realism" in the arts. Like many others, Prokofiev did not realize the implications of this for music. Soon, however, modernism was equated with "formalism," art for art's sake, whereas socialist art must be art for the people, art with a positive "social content." For a time Prokofiev thought he would be able to go on writing "forward-looking music" side by side with "light-serious" music for the masses, but his first Soviet essay in "forward-looking" music, the *Symphonic Song* (1934), was received with extreme coldness, and his only real success was the music for the comic film *Lieutenant Kije* (1934). He had to learn to compromise. He found a congenial field for this in film and theater music; in one case, the score for Eisenstein's *Alexander Nevsky*, he was so successful that he could remould the music into a cantata (1939) that is one of his finest works. After World War II his *Symphony No. 6* (1947) was severely condemned and an opera, *The Story of a Real Man* (1948), in which he thought he had redeemed himself, fared no better at a preview, despite the simplicity of the musical language. It waited until 1960 for its production.

Although Prokofiev was a "Soviet composer" only during his last 20 years, his contribution to Soviet opera and ballet in particular has been unequalled. The scores of *Semyon Kotko* and *War and Peace* in the one field and *Romeo and Juliet* in the other attest to his supremacy, while his *Symphony No. 5* is a landmark in Soviet orchestral music. The young Prokofiev made his name by his dry wit, his sarcasm, his emotional coolness, his love of the grotesque, his pungent harmony. When these disappeared from his Soviet compositions or were limited to association with enemies and villains, the residue at first seemed rather insipid. It is not easy to determine, however, to what extent their exorcism was due to "socialist realism." Official pressure was probably responsible for Prokofiev's large production of diatonic marches, mass-songs, and celebration cantatas, though even some of these may have sprung from a genuine sense of obligation to the untutored masses of his fellow citizens. But the lyricism—and Russian musical lyricism is often cool and limpid—and the diatonic simplicity were always latent, even in the early Prokofiev. The pungent harmonies, the dislocations of melodic line or tonal sense, were not essential (as the complicated harmonies of late Scriabin are essential) but distortions of conceptions that, as surviving examples show, were originally quite simple, even commonplace. This is all obvious in the *Classical Symphony*, the

Violin Concerto No. 1 and *Piano Concerto No. 3*; the *Scythian Suite* is quite a different pagan Russia from *The Rite of Spring*. Back in his native land, he began in the *Violin Concerto No. 2* and *Romeo and Juliet* to shed those elements in his style that corresponded to contemporary fashion and allowed full play to the lyrical elements. In *Alexander Nevsky*, *Semyon Kotko*, *War and Peace*, and the *Symphony No. 5* he enriched his musical speech with Russian accents that remind one of the great 19th-century nationalists.

Prokofiev was at his best when inspired by visual images or human characters. A considerable proportion of his orchestral music, even of his piano music, originated in works for the stage. He was a true musical dramatist, a creator of characters in music. The characterization in *The Gambler* and the *Love for 3 Oranges* is necessarily external and superficial, but the demon-possessed Renata in *The Flaming Angel* is a remarkable creation, and *Semyon Kotko* contains a whole gallery of peasant characters, often in strongly dramatic situations, generally portrayed with power and subtlety. In *War and Peace*, of course, the scope was even greater—great to the point of impossibility. In both length and spectacle it is a throw-back to 19th-century grand opera, though the carrying out often reminds one of Mussorgsky, who also derived from grand opera. Indeed *War and Peace* stands in the great line of Russian opera and is Prokofiev's most convincing demonstration of the individuality possible within the conditions of "socialist realism."

PRINCIPAL COMPOSITIONS (available from Boosey or Mezhkniga as noted): *Piano Sonatas Nos. 1–9*, Opp. 1, 14, 28, 29, 38, 82, 83, 84, 103 (1909, 1912, 1917, 1917, 1923, 1940, 1942, 1944, 1947; Mezhkniga); *The Gambler*, opera, Op. 24; libretto by the composer after Dostoevsky (1915–16, revised 1927; Boosey); *Symphony No. 1*, "Classical," Op. 25 (1916–17, Mezhkniga); *Violin Concerto No. 1 in D*, Op. 19 (1917, Mezhkniga); *Piano Concerto No. 3 in C*, Op. 26 (1917–21; Boosey, Mezhkniga); *Love for 3 Oranges*, opera, Op. 33; libretto by the composer after Carlo Gozzi (1919, Boosey); *The Flaming Angel*, opera, Op. 37; libretto by the composer after Bryusov (1919, revised 1927; Boosey); *The Buffoon (Chout)*, ballet; choreography by Slavinsky, Larionov (1920, Boosey); *Symphony No. 2*, Op. 40 (1924, Boosey); *Le Pas d'acier*, ballet, Op. 41; choreography by Léonide Massine (1927, Boosey); *Symphony No. 3*, Op. 44 (1928, Boosey); *The Prodigal Son*, ballet, Op. 46; choreography by George Balanchine (1929, Boosey); *Symphony No. 4*, Op. 47 (1930, Boosey); *Piano Concerto No. 5 in G*, Op. 55 (1932, Boosey); *Cello Concerto No. 1*, Op. 58 (1938, Boosey); *Violin Concerto No. 2 in G*, Op. 63 (1935; Boosey, Mezhkniga); *Romeo and Juliet*, ballet, Op. 64; choreography by L. M. Lavrovsky (1936, Mezhkniga); *Alexander Nevsky*, cantata, Op. 78 (1939, Mezhkniga); *Violin Sonata No. 1*, Op. 80 (1938–46, Mezhkniga); *Semyon Kotko*, opera, Op. 81; libretto by J. Katanyev and the composer (1939, Mezhkniga); *The Duenna*, "Betrothal in a Monastery," opera, Op. 86; libretto by Mira Mendelson after Sheridan (1940, Mezhkniga); *Cinderella*, ballet, Op. 87; choreography by R. Zakharov (1944, Mezhkniga); *War and Peace*, opera, Op. 91; libretto by Mendelson after Tolstoy (1943, revised 1952; Mezhkniga); *Flute Sonata*, Op. 94 (1943, Mezhkniga; transcribed for cello, piano, Op 94b, 1944, Mezhkniga); *Symphony No. 5*, Op. 100 (1944, Mezhkniga); *Symphony No. 6*, Op. 111 (1947, Mezhkniga); *The Story of a Real Man*, opera, Op. 117; libretto by Mendelson (1948, Mezhkniga); *The Stone Flower*, ballet, Op. 118; choreography by Lavrovsky (1950, Mezhkniga); *Cello Sonata*, Op. 119 (1949, Mezhkniga); *Sinfonia concertante* for cello, orchestra, Op. 125 (1952, Mezhkniga); *Symphony No. 7*, Op. 131 (1952, Mezhkniga).

PRINCIPAL WRITINGS: *S. P.: Autobiography, Articles, Reminiscences* ed. by F. Shlifstein, trans. by Rose Prokofieva (Moscow 195–?).

BIBL.: Israel Nestyev, *P.* trans. by Florence Jonas (Stanford, Calif., 1961).

Gerald Abraham

SEE ALSO Dance, Harmony and Counterpoint, Opera, Soviet Union.

Proportionate (Proportional) Notation, a graphic method of indicating durations. Instead of employing the traditional system of open and blackened note-heads, stems, flags, rest signs, etc., the horizontal spacing of symbols is made to represent the intended length of durations. The concept is employed in most purely graphic scores and has sometimes been used in combination with traditional pitch notation (note-heads on staves).

SEE ALSO Notation.

Prose Music. In his *Philosophie der neuen Musik* (Tübingen 1949), T. W. Adorno speculated that one possible outgrowth of Schoenberg's dodecaphonic method of composition would be a form of music designed to be read in silence without the usual intermediate stage of performance. Although 12-tone music has led to nothing of the sort, other influences have combined to stimulate an interest in experimental forms of musical notation in which graphic layout or conceptual content generate a process of musical communication involving the eye or mind of the observer directly (i.e., independently of the conventional function of musical notation, which is to communicate instructions to a performer). The use of prose to communicate musical ideas is one such case, stimulated in part by the relative ease of publishing new ideas in a prose format and the relative difficulty of doing so with musical notation.

Mann, Proust, Joyce, Beckett, Burroughs, and other 20th-century writers have produced prose texts that can be regarded as music, but few are the composers who attempt to use the literary form as a vehicle for their music. The first to do so in a serious manner was perhaps John Cage, whose compositional methods as applied to literature have had a profound influence on artists in all fields. In 1960 La Monte Young produced a series of compositions in the form of short prose poems which could be construed as conventional music notation and used by a performer as instructions for realizing a work in sound and image; their message, however, can also be constructed by the imagination of the reader without the intervention of media for the excitement of the senses. An example is *Piano Piece for David Tudor # 2 (1960)*:

> Open the keyboard cover without
> making, from the operation, any
> sound that is audible to you.
> Try as many times as you like.
> The piece is over either when
> you succeed or when you decide
> to stop trying. It is not
> necessary to explain to the
> audience. Simply do what you
> do and, when the piece is over,
> indicate it in a customary way.

This piece may be understood either as music or as literature. In order to understand it fully, it may be necessary to carry out the instructions and physically perform them as is normally the case with music. But a partial understanding is possible from a mere reading, followed by the free exercise of fantasy on the theme of how one might go about performing the instructions.

Young's *Composition 1960 # 10 to Bob Morris* is a more complex example:

> Draw a straight line
> and follow it.

The average reader of prose, not accustomed as is the musician to reading scores as a collection of commandments, may take the command as a metaphor and translate it into the question, "What would happen *if* I were to draw a straight line and follow it?" A musician, on the other hand, might be inclined to take the instruction literally; Young himself spent several hours at a concert in March 1961 drawing lines across the floor with chalk. This difference in interpretation points up a salient (though not exclusive) feature of prose music, namely that the nature of a given composition depends largely on the reader.

In the early 1960s the Fluxus movement, founded by George Maciunas, stimulated the creation of a great many prose compositions by Maciunas himself, George Brecht, Yoko Ono, Nam June Paik, Benjamin Patterson, Terry Riley, and others. Some of these pieces are more or less fanciful instructions to performers; others abandon the imperative form in favor of pure images, as in Young's *Piano Piece for David Tudor # 3*:

> most of them
> were very old grasshoppers

Many of George Brecht's pieces consist of single words without further explanation. In performance, such texts may be treated as "mind-objects" by improvising musicians. An example is Cornelius Cardew's *Sextet—The Tiger's Mind* (1967), a two-part, 172-word score:

> The tiger fights the mind that loves the
>   circle that traps the tiger.
> The circle is perfect and outside time.
> The wind blows dust in tigers' eyes.
> Amy reflects, relaxes with her mind . . .

Such prose scores may refer to specific performing situations in which, however, the performer must choose from among a large number of possible interpretations, as in Christian Wolff's *Stones* (1968):

> Make sounds with stones, draw sounds
> out of stones, using a number of sizes
> and kinds (and colours); for the most
> part discretely; sometimes in rapid sequences. For the most part striking stones
> with stones, but also stones on other
> surfaces (inside the open head of a drum,
> for instance) or other than struck (bowed,
> for instance, or amplified). Do not break
> anything.

In Takehisa Kosugi's *Anima 7* the performer is instructed to take a long time executing any ordinary action, such as drawing a bow across a violin string in ten minutes or taking off his coat in 15. In Giuseppe Chiari's *Fuori* (1964) the performer is told to sit facing the audience with his head down and to describe in words what he hears. Such texts do not tell the performer exactly what to do; on the contrary, their purpose may be to quicken the mind by provoking questions: Describe what sounds? How often? In how many words? What kind of words? How fast? How long?

In group improvisation, prose is often used as a means of communicating basic performing techniques applicable to various unpredictable situations. A number of "improvisation rites" have been collected by members of the Scratch Orchestra of London and published as an anthology under the title *Nature Study Notes* (London 1969). Other uses of prose as a vehicle for improvisational ideas can be found in my *Plan for Spacecraft* (1967), in Karlheinz Stockhausen's *Aus den 7 Tagen* (1968), and in recent texts by Alvin Lucier, Robert Ashley, Gerald Shapiro, Pauline Oliveros, and other Americans. The example below is taken from my *Love Songs* (1968):

> Listen to all the sounds around you. Imitate as many of them as you can, combining them into a melody. This melody is a net which you throw over several people, drawing them together.

In the Musica Elettronica Viva's audience-participation *Sound Pool* (1968), the conventional format of the printed concert program was used to provide rudimentary information on the techniques of improvisation:

> . . . If somebody is playing something you don't like, stop what you are doing and listen to him for awhile, then try playing with him. If somebody seems to be playing too loudly, try to find another location in the room where you can hear better . . .

> If you are a strong musician, do mostly accompanying work; that is, help weaker players to sound better. Seek out areas where the music is flagging, and organize groups. Be a timekeeper: provide a basic pulse, without drowning out the others . . .

> Listen for the strongest, most prominent sounds in the total mass. If you wish to influence the music towards *order* (unity), play together with (simultaneously with) these sounds. If you wish to create *disorder* (variety) play in the *spaces in between* these sounds . . .

Finally words, letters, and typographical symbols have been used in their traditional function as texts for vocal music. John Cage's recent vocal music constitutes an encyclopedic *tour-de-force* in this area. *You blew it* (1971) by Christian Wolff is a simple and elegant example:

y   ou--b   lou   i   t

t-you   bl   ou   i

it-y   ou   blou

ou-it   y   ou-bl

lou   t-y   ou-b   b   l   ou-i   t-you

ou-blou   it

bl   ou-it

Frederic Rzewski

Prosody, see Text Setting and Usage

Publishing. The music publisher has traditionally been the link between the composer and the public. His activities are directed toward the exposure of the music in his catalog and the acceptance of it by the consumer. Music publishing in the concert field has been dominated by a few firms whose policies were determined by a handful of talented and forceful men. Among the most prominent were: Emil Hertzka of Universal Edition, Vienna, who was responsible for launching the careers of Arnold Schoenberg, Anton Webern, Alban Berg, Béla Bartók, Zoltán Kodály, Kurt Weill, and many others; Ralph Hawkes of Boosey and Hawkes, London, who is said to have "found" Benjamin Britten when he was a boy of 11; and August Durand and his son Jacques, who are credited with much of the success of many French composers, including Claude Debussy, Paul Dukas, and Maurice Ravel. Of the thousands of publishing companies in the U.S., only a handful are involved in concert music. It is this group that is examined here, although many of the principles, techniques, and problems are shared by the companies involved in popular and production (show and movie) music.

INCOME. The concert-music publishers depend on the income from works composed mainly for performance (solo, chamber music, symphonic, ballet, opera). The publishers find themselves in the 1970s confronted by problems stemming in large part from the economics of the time. Budgets of performing groups, already strained by climbing salaries and other costs, have been diminished by smaller audiences whose tastes are not oriented to contemporary concert music. The new music itself (serial, aleatory, graphic, electronic) does not readily lend itself to the established machinery of publishing staffs skilled in the techniques of another era. For economic reasons, too, a rash of mergers and takeovers in the late 1960s and early 70s has shrunk the whole industry as it struggles to survive and find new ways to fulfill its "middleman" function. Actually few of the large American publishers could stay alive if they depended solely on concert publishing; many rely on the comparative stability of the educational market to meet their daily overhead. The situation differs somewhat in Europe, where governmental subsidy of the arts in many countries has a side effect of supporting the efforts of publishers to promote new music.

Publishers derive their income from six main sources:

1. *Sales income*. The sale of printed music, formerly the most profitable part of a publisher's operation, has steadily declined since the peak periods earlier in this century when home performance was a major family activity. Although printed music still provides a considerable source of income, a diminishing number of dealers regularly stock concert publications. While composers understandably would like all their work to appear in print, an increasing number of contracts are being written that make the compositions available for rental only. (New production techniques could change this: it may soon be economically feasible to produce an edition for sale of 50–100 copies instead of the 500–1000 minimum which is now the rule.) Publication contracts differ from publisher to publisher, but the most usual royalty contract provides for payment of 10 percent of the list selling price on all copies sold and 50 percent of other revenues.

2. *Rental income*. Orchestral and musicodramatic works are most often made available on rental with the income divided between the publisher and the composer. In many agreements the division is made on a 50/50 basis provided that the materials are submitted to the publisher ready for use. If the publisher has to extract parts from the score or otherwise work over the materials, the percentage may be 75 percent for the publisher and 25 percent for the composer. Rental charges to performing organizations are usually based on the duration of the work, the number of performances scheduled, and the kind of performing group (the fee will often be higher for a major orchestra than for a community group, given the same work and number of performances).

3. *Performance income*. This is divided between *small rights* and *grand rights*. Small rights, which are fees for performing a copyrighted work in public (before a paying audience, over radio or television, etc.) are channeled through collection agencies such as ASCAP (American Society of Composers, Authors, and Publishers), BMI (Broadcast Music Incorporated), or SESAC, Inc., in the U.S. These have overseas ties to such organizations as PRS (Performing Right Society) in Britain, SACEM (Société des Auteurs, Compositeurs, et Editeurs de Musique) in France, GEMA (Gesellschaft für musikalische Aufführungs) in Germany and Austria, etc. These organizations grant blanket licenses to the radio and TV networks, major performing groups, individual stations, hotels, concert organizations, and even universities and colleges. Performances are logged by methods such as on-the-spot recordings, station logs, etc., supplemented by documented reports from the publishers. The money which the agencies collect from their licenses is then distributed among the publishers and composers using complicated formulas weighted to help concert music, which accounts for only a small percentage of overall income. Grand rights, which are fees for performing musicodramatic works, are not collected by the performing rights societies. Each performance is individually licensed by the publisher.

4. *Mechanical income*. This source of revenue comes primarily from phonograph records and tape recordings. The U.S. copyright law of 1909 specifies that a record company is to pay two cents per composition multiplied by the number of discs issued; this rate is often negotiated to a lower figure, and longer works are often paid for at the rate of a quarter cent per minute. After the premiere recording, permission for which is controlled by the publisher, the granting of a mechanical license is mandatory to all who wish to record the work. The Harry Fox organization, an arm of the National Music Publishers Association, handles the licensing of the major portion of these uses for the concert publisher, although some publishers prefer to handle these licenses individually. With the continuing

decline in the recording of the concert repertory by the major companies, this source of income has been diminished—this in a period when mechanical income from popular music has been steadily increasing.

5. *Synchronization rights.* Fees for the use of music with motion pictures, television, and replay devices are often licensed by the Harry Fox organization. In television, the first performance is considered "live" (even if on videotape) and therefore covered under the TV station's blanket performance licenses.

6. *Foreign rights.* Some publishers have their own foreign affiliates or agents abroad, while others make single arrangements for each work or deal directly with the user overseas.

These sources of income are influenced by public demand and acceptance of the product. In the 1970s the demand appears to be slackening. Expensive rentals and the heavy rehearsal requirements of new music tend to discourage performance groups from experimenting with this repertory, especially since audience tested-and-approved classics are already available in their libraries at no additional cost. An examination of the amount of American contemporary music performed by U.S. organizations shows it to be miniscule compared to the flood of Beethoven, Mozart, and Brahms. Unfortunately for the U.S. composer, performances of his works abroad are almost nonexistent and are far outnumbered by performances of contemporary foreign works in America.

PRINTING TECHNIQUES. There are various ways in which the composer's manuscript is made available to the public. The ideal, and the most costly, is engraved and printed music, which may then be offered for sale. The manuscript is first preedited or checked for error. The score and parts must agree in all details before the work goes to the note setter. Various processes are available, of which plate engraving is usually the best. This venerable art (Paul Revere was the first American music engraver) requires years of apprenticeship. The symbols are all cut or stamped into a soft pewter plate backward, that is from right to left. Reading-proofs are made by wiping the surface of the engraved plate with green ink so that when paper is applied to it the copy appears (left to right) white against a green background. These proofs are read against the manuscript. Any corrections must be made on the plate by stamping out the incorrect symbols, resurfacing the plate, and then engraving in the corrections. When the plate is finally correct, a black-and-white reproduction proof is made by filling the indents that have been cut into the plate with a mixture of beeswax and lampblack. The surface is then cleaned, and special paper is pressed against the plate, which is warmed so that the wax-base ink will transfer from the plate to the paper. There are many other processes for preparing the black-and-white reproduction copy. The most used among them are the music typewriter, which can produce most of the symbols except the connecting beams, slurs, and some of the very large symbols, which must then be finished by hand; and autographing, which is very sophisticated copying by hand. After the music pages are finished, title pages and prefatory material are set in type or a type substitute, such as varitype. The publication is then ready for the printer.

Music is normally printed by the offset lithography process. The finished black-and-white copy is photographed, then transferred from the photographic negative to a metal plate, which is then fastened to a cylinder of an offset press. Offset lithography printing itself is based on the principle that oil and water do not mix. The positive images on the metal plate accept ink (green) and repel water, which allows the image to transfer to a soft "blanket" fastened to another cylinder. It is the blanket with its negative images which touches the paper to produce the printed sheet of music.

DISTRIBUTION OF SALE COPIES. Publishers distribute sale copies through a network of retail dealers and wholesalers. There are approximately 1,000 major music dealers who purchase directly from the publishers, while perhaps 6,000 smaller outlets buy from one of the 20 or so wholesalers. Dealer discounts may be based on many factors, but those who gain the best discounts automatically accept the publishers' new issues, place one or two stock orders a year (to maintain a reserve on a cross-section of the publishers' catalogs) and achieve a prescribed minimum dollar volume of purchases from each publisher. The wholesaler receives the biggest discounts from the publisher, as he maintains a large reserve stock and services many stores with his own catalogs and special promotions; he also carries the credit risk of the smaller dealers, to whom he grants his own discount. Sales representatives are still used by the major publishers, although their ranks are being thinned by the rising costs of travel. The telephone and other alternate methods of communication with dealers are becoming more widely used.

New publications are promoted in a variety of ways. New-issue copies (probably not more than 200 of a contemporary music publication) are sent to those stores who subscribe. Review copies are sent to the major magazines, independent reviewers, and to conductors and performers who might be expected to program or perform the work. In the case of particularly important publications, news releases are sent to magazines and newspapers. The publisher must wait, sometimes for years, to know if his judgment and skills were sufficient to pay back the expenses or perhaps produce that rarity in the field of concert music, a "hit."

RENTAL MUSIC. This is seldom as carefully prepared as music printed for sale. The composer is usually responsible for the editorial accuracy, and, if his manuscript is legible and well laid out, it may be reproduced as is. Less legible manuscripts are copied out. Parts are extracted from scores by specialists. All these copies are made on translucent paper (Deshon paper) and are normally reproduced by the Ozalid or white-print process. Xerox and other copying processes are used as well. As there is seldom a need for many sets of a rental work, it is only necessary to have the master copy from which others may be easily reproduced.

Promotion of rental concert music requires a considerable number of scores for circulation to conductors and performers. For a prestigious work, these scores may be printed for sale as well (often in a miniature, study-score format). To service the orchestras, opera and ballet companies, music groups, and individual concert artists, the publisher maintains a specialized staff. Scores are circulated and promoted, material shipped, received, and checked to see that all parts are in usable condition with markings made for particular performances removed.

PROSPECTS. Music publishing is facing greater uncertainty than ever before. Synthesizers capable of producing any kind of sound open up infinite possibilities to composers. The challenge of adapting new methods of information storage and retrieval to the present printing and distribution methods will inevitably reshape all publishing, books as well as music. Tapes, cassettes, video cassettes, microfiche, and techniques still unknown but inherent in current electronic developments will cause changes that cannot be predicted. The threat to publishers' and composers' income by the illegal copying of printed matter and sound (as yet uncontrollable) have still to be met. New methods of operation will undoubtedly be devised to fulfill the function of the publisher in his task of identifying and exposing to the public the works of creative musical minds.

BIBL.: Arnold Broido et al., *Standard Music Engraving Practice* (Washington 1966); *The Music Industry, Markets and Methods for the 70's*, a conference report (New York 1970); Ernst Roth, *The Business of Music* (London 1969); Sidney Shemel and M. William Krasilovsky, *More about This Business of Music* (New York 1967).

Arnold Broido

SEE ALSO Recording; articles on individual countries.

Pulse Music, see Rhythm

Pylkkänen, Tauno (Kullervo) (b. Helsinki, 22 March 1918), attended the Sibelius Academy in Helsinki (composition with Leevi Madetoja, Selim Palmgren), and the Univ. of Helsinki (both 1937–41). He was on the musical staff of the Finnish Radio (1942–61) and was music critic for the newspaper *Uusi Suomi* (1942–69). During 1960–69 he was also artistic director of the Finnish National Opera and from 1958, chairman of the Association of Musical Artists of Finland. His special interest is opera, in which he has pursued a romantic, veristic approach.

PRINCIPAL COMPOSITIONS: *Batsheba Saarenmaalla* [Batsheba at Saarenmaa], 1-act opera for 3 vocal soloists, men's chorus, orchestra, Op. 10; libretto by Aino Kallas (1940, revised 1958); *Suden morsian* [The Wolf's Bride], radio opera, Op. 47; libretto by Kallas (1940); *Lapin kesä* [Summer in Lapland], symphonic poem, Op. 15 (1941); *Kullervon sotaanlähtö* [Kullervo Goes to War], symphonic poem, Op. 20 (1942); *Kuoleman joutsen* [The Swan of Death], song cycle for voice, piano or orchestra, Op. 21; texts by Kallas (1943, Fazer); *Mare ja hänen poikansa* [Mare and Her Son], 3-act opera, Op. 22; libretto by Kallas (1943); *Notturno* for violin, piano, Op. 23 (1943, Nordiska); *Sinfonietta*, Op. 25 (1944); *String Quartet*, Op. 27 (1945); *Symphony No. 1*, Op. 30 (1945); *Symphonic Fantasy,* Op. 40 (1948); *Ultima Thule*, tone poem for orchestra, Op. 46 (1949); *Cello Concerto*, Op. 48 (1950); *Symphonic Prelude*, Op. 54 (1952); *Varjo* [The Shadow], 1-act opera; libretto by Hjalmar Bergman (1952, Vera's Aria published by Fazer); *Kuunsilta* [Moon Bridge], song cycle for voice, piano, Op. 55; text by Yrjö Jylhä (1953, Westerlund); *Fantasia appassionata* for cello, piano, Op. 57 (1954); *Metropolis*, cantata for 3 narrators, chorus, orchestra, Op. 58; text by M. Kuusi (1955); *Opri and Oleksi,* 3-act opera, Op. 61; libretto by Kyllikki Mäntylä (1957);

Visioner, song cycle for voice, piano, Op. 63; text by Svea Kulvik (1958); *Maternità,* song cycle for women's chorus, Op. 65 (1958); *Kaarina Maununtytär,* ballet, Op. 66 (1960); *Songs* for voice, piano, Op. 68 (1963; "Satakieli" [The Nightingale] and "Venheessä" [In the Boat] published by Westerlund); *Vangit* [The Prisoners], 1-act opera, Op. 69; libretto by Arvi Kivimaa (1964).

PRINCIPAL WRITINGS: *Oopperavaeltaja* [The World of Opera] (Helsinki 1953).

BIBL.: Seppo Nummi, *Musica Fennica* (Helsinki 1964):84–86.

Q

Quadreny, Josep M. Mestres, see under Mestres-Quadreny

Quarter Tone, a pitch that lies midway between adjacent pitches of the chromatic scale as tuned in 12-tone equal temperament.

SEE ALSO Microtones.

Quinet, Marcel (b. Binche, Belgium, 6 July 1915; d. 1971), attended the Brussels Conservatory (1934–42, counterpoint with R. Moulaert, fugue with L. Jongen, piano with M. Maas) and studied composition and orchestration with Jean Absil (1940–45). He taught at the Brussels Conservatory from 1943 and at the Chapelle Musicale "Reine Elisabeth" during 1956–59 and 1968–71. In 1951 he became director of the Music School of St. Josse-ten-Noode/Schaerbeek. Quinet considered his compositions to be neoclassic in structure and atonal in language.

PRINCIPAL COMPOSITIONS (published by CBDM): *Croquis,* 8 little pieces for piano (1946); *8 Little Pieces* for wind quintet (1946); *String Trio* (1948); *2 Impromptus* for piano (1949); *Woodwind Quintet* (1949); *3 Pieces* for orchestra (1951); *Sonatina* for violin, piano (1952); *Sinfonietta* (1953); *4 Bluettes* for piano trio (1954); *Passacaille* for piano (1954); *Piano Concerto No. 1* (1955); *Serenade for Strings* (1956); *Variations* for orchestra (1956); *Piano Quartet* (1957); *Divertimento* for orchestra (1958); *String Quartet* (1958); *Improvisations* for piano (1958); *Enfantines* for piano (1959); *Concertino* for flute with piano or chamber orchestra (1959); *Suite* for 4 clarinets (1959); *Symphony* (1960); *Concertino* for oboe, clarinet, bassoon, string orchestra (1960); *Ballade* for clarinet, piano (or vibraphone, celesta, harp, strings) (1961); *Sonata* for trumpet, horn, trombone (1961); *Toccata* for piano (1961); *Hommage à Scarlatti* for piano (1962); *Ballade* for violin with wind quintet or piano (1962); *Viola Concerto* (1963); *Piano Concerto No. 2* (1964); *Sonata* for 2 violins, piano (1965); *Overture for a Festival*

for orchestra (1967); *Pochades* for saxophone quartet (1967); *La Nef des fous,* ballet (1969).

Quintanar, Hector (Prieto) (b. Mexico City, 15 April 1936), attended the Escuela Superior Nocturna de Música (1950–56) and the Conservatorio Nacional in Mexico City (1959–64; counterpoint with Blas Galindo; composition with Carlos Jiménez Mabarak, Carlos Chávez; harmony and analysis with Rodolfo Halffter). He studied electronic music with Andrés Lewin Richter in New York (1964) and concrete music with Jean-Etienne Marie at the studios of the French radio in Paris (1967) and in Mexico City (1968). He has directed the Composers' Workshop of the Conservatorio Nacional since 1965, and he supervised the installation of an electronic studio there in 1968. Since 1965 he has been head of the Secretaría Técnica for the music department of the Instituto Nacional de Bellas Artes and director of its contemporary music festivals. He was assistant coordinator for musical events at the Mexico City Olympics. Recently he has been active as an opera and operetta conductor. Quintanar has been especially influenced by the music of Debussy, Webern, and Penderecki.

PRINCIPAL COMPOSITIONS: *Sinfónia modal* (1962); *Sinfónia,* "in the style of Brahms" (1963); *El viejo y el mar,* symphonic poem (1963); *Symphony No. 3* (1964); *Fabula* for chorus, orchestra (1964); *Double Quartet* for string, wind quartets (1964–65, EMM); *String Trio* (1965–66, PAU); *Violin Sonata No. 1* (1967, EMM); *Aclamaciónes* for chorus, tape, orchestra (1967); Sonata for 3 trumpets (1967); *Galaxias* for orchestra (1968); *Sideral I* on tape (1968); *Solutio?* for soprano, piano (1969); *Simbolos* for violin, clarinet, alto saxophone, horn, trumpet, trombone, piano, tape, slides, lights (1969); *Sideral II* for orchestra (1969); *Ilapso* for clarinet, bassoon, trumpet, trombone, percussion, violin, double bass (1970). List to 1969: *Composers of the Americas* 15:178–80.

SEE ALSO Mexico.

R

Rääts, Jaan (b. Tartu, Estonia, 15 Oct 1932), attended the Tallin Conservatory (1952–57, composition with Heino Eller). He was music supervisor for Estonian radio during 1955–66 and has been music director for Estonian television since then. His first compositions show the influence of Shostakovich; his subsequent development has continued within a neobaroque orientation.

PRINCIPAL COMPOSITIONS: *Symphonies Nos. 1–6*, Opp. 3, 8, 10, 13, 28, 31 (1957; 1958; 1959; 1959; 1966, Muzyka; 1967); *Concerto for Chamber Orchestra*, Op. 16 (1961, Muzyka); *Violin Concerto*, Op. 21 (1963, Muzyka); *Karl Marx*, "declamatorio," Op. 18 (1963); *School Cantata*, Op. 32 (1968); *24 Preludes* for piano, Op. 33 (1969, Muzyka). Rääts has also composed 4 piano sonatas and 4 string quartets.

Rabe, Folke (Alvar Harald Reinhold) (b. Stockholm, 28 Nov 1935), studied at the Royal College of Music, Stockholm (1957–64, composition with Karl-Birger Blomdahl) and with György Ligeti (1961–64). He has been a jazz trombonist in several Swedish bands and is a member of the Culture Quartet, composed of four trombones. He has produced radio and television programs for the Swedish Broadcasting Corporation and contributed articles on music to Swedish publications. From 1964 to 1968 he was an assistant at the Royal College of Music in Stockholm, involved principally with composition seminars and sound engineering. In 1968 he became an advisor on educational methods and concert forms for the Institute for Nationwide Concerts. The dominate influence on his music has come from musicians around the San Francisco Tape Center and Ann Halprin's Dancers' Workshop, with whom he has been in contact since 1962. These include Pauline Oliveros, Morton Subotnick, Robert Erickson, and Terry Riley. Rabe spent the spring of 1965 in San Francisco and was musical director of the Dancers' Workshop both then and during the company's European tour later that year. His contacts with other Scandinavian composers and the central European avant-garde have had little influence on his music.

PRINCIPAL COMPOSITIONS (published by Hansen-W except for the electronic works): *Pièce* for speaking chorus; composed in collaboration with Lasse O'Månsson (1961); *Bolos* for 4 trombonists; includes special lighting, movement of the performers; composed in collaboration with Jan Bark (1962); *Rondes* for mixed or men's chorus (1964); *Polonaise*, stage piece for 4 trombones; in collaboration with Bark (1965); *Eh??* on 1-, 2-, or 4-track tape (1967, recorded by Wergo); *Smolensk Detyami* and *Intreytya* for TLLPA (an electronic tape-loop feedback system) and variable sound sources; in collaboration with Bark and Bo Hälphers (1968, 1969); *Pipelines*, collective work by the Culture Quartet for 4 trombones, drain pipes (1969).

PRINCIPAL WRITINGS: "Wahrheiten," *Begegnung* (Amriswil, Switzerland), 1967 special issue: 8–10; *Ljudverkstad* [Sound Workshop] (Stockholm: Rikskonserter, 1969); "Mikromusik und Makromusik," notes for the Wergo recording of *Eh??*; "Förkrossande serger för dragspelet?" [Annihilating Victory for the Accordion?], *Tonfallet* (Stockholm) 2 (1970): 1, 4.

BIBL.: Bernhard Lewkovitch, "Grat i grat" [Gray in Gray], *B. T.* (Copenhagen), 30 May 1964; Bo Wallner, *Vår tids musik i Norden* (Stockholm 1968):261–62, English trans. (London 1971).

SEE ALSO Scandinavia.

Rachmaninov, Sergey (Vassilievich) (b. Onega, Novgorod, 1 April 1873; d. Beverly Hills, Calif., 28 March 1943), entered the St. Petersburg Conservatory at an early age. He was sent to the Moscow Conservatory in 1885, where he studied piano until 1891 and composition until 1892 with Alexander Taneyev and Anton Arensky. His leaving exercise, the one-act opera *Aleko*, won him a gold medal and was produced in Moscow in 1893. He began concertizing as a pianist and later also as a conductor. The failure of his *Symphony No. 1* at its performance in 1897 produced a nervous crisis, and he was unable to compose for three years. He conducted at the Bolshoi

Theater during 1904–06, lived in Dresden for nearly two years, and was again in Moscow, 1910–17. The Revolution drove him into exile, and in 1918 he settled in the U.S. (where he had toured in 1909); later he bought a small estate on Lake Lucerne where he spent his summers during the 1930s. He became an American citizen shortly before his death. He was one of the great piano virtuosos of his time, and the piano is at the heart of his compositions. His songs depend very much on their accompaniments, and the texture of his orchestral music is often pianistic in origin.

PRINCIPAL COMPOSITIONS: *Piano Concertos Nos. 1–4* (1890–91, revised 1917, Foley; 1900–01, public; 1909, public; 1927, Foley); *Aleko*, 1-act opera after Pushkin (1892, Gutheil); *Prelude in C♯ Minor* for piano (1892, Augener); *Symphonies Nos. 1–3* (1897, Leeds; 1908, public; 1936, Foley); *10 Preludes* for piano, Op. 23 (1904, Gutheil); *The Miserly Knight*, opera, Op. 24 (premiere 1906, Gutheil); *Francesca da Rimini*, opera, Op. 25 (premiere 1906, Gutheil); *Piano Sonata No. 1 in D Minor*, Op. 28 (1907, Gutheil); *Isle of the Dead*, symphonic poem after the painting by Böcklin (1909, public); *13 Preludes* for piano, Op. 32 (1910, Gutheil); *Liturgy of St. John Chrysostom* for chorus, Op. 31 (1910, Boosey); *The Bells*, choral symphony after Poe (1913, Boosey); *Vesper Mass* for chorus, Op. 37 (1915, Novello); *9 Etudes-tableaux* for piano, Op. 39 (1916–17, ERM); *Rhapsody on a Theme of Paganini* for piano, orchestra (1934, Foley).

BIBL.: S. Bertenson and J. Leyda, *R.* (New York 1956); John Culshaw, *R.: The Man and His Music* (New York 1956); Oskar von Riesemann, *R.'s Recollections* (New York 1934); Victor Seroff, *R.* (New York 1950).

SEE ALSO Liturgical Music: Christian; Soviet Union.

Radić, Dušan (Milan) (b. Sombor, Yugoslavia, 10 April 1923), studied at the Belgrade Music Academy (1949–54, composition with Milenki Živković). He also studied in Paris during 1957–58 with Darius Milhaud and Olivier Messiaen. His music is largely neoclassic in style.

PRINCIPAL COMPOSITIONS: *Sinfonietta* for orchestra (1953, SKJ); *Opsednuta vedrina* [Beleaguered Calm] for women's chorus, 2 pianos (1954); *U očekivanju Marije* [Waiting for Mary], cantata for soloist, chorus, orchestra (1955); *Divertimento* for strings, vibraphone, percussion (1956); *Balada o mesecu lutalici* [Ballad of the Moon Wanderer], ballet (1957; suite from the ballet, SKJ); *Ćele-kula* [The Skull Tower], cantata for soloist, chorus, orchestra (1957, Prosveta); *Ljubav, to je glavna stvar* [Love's the Thing], musical comedy-ballet (1958–62); *Uspravna zemlja* [Earth Erect], cantata for narrator, chorus, chamber orchestra (1963); *Sinfonia* for orchestra (1965–67, UKS).

Radica, Ruben (b. Split, Croatia, Yugoslavia, 19 May 1931), attended the Zagreb Academy of Music (1951–57, composition with Milko Kelemen, conducting with Slavko Zlatić). He also studied composition with Vito Frazzi at the Siena Academy during the summers of 1958 and 1959 and with René Leibowitz in Paris, 1960–61. He taught at the Sarajevo Academy of Music during 1959–63, and since 1963 has been teaching theory at the Zagreb Academy. Radica's early works are based on extended tonality, "line and color being equally important"; since 1961 he has worked with 12-tone techniques. Beginning with his composition *19 and 10* he has tried to establish new kinds of relationships between musical parameters which would result in "a characteristic sonorous physiognomy."

PRINCIPAL COMPOSITIONS: *Concerto for Chamber Orchestra* (1956); *Concerto Grosso* (1957); *Dialogue* for 2 pianos (1958, UKH); *4 Dramatic Epigrams* for piano, string quartet (1959, SKJ); *Concerto abbreviato* for orchestra, cello obligato (1960); *Variations lyriques* for string orchestra (1961, SKJ); *19 and 10*, "interferences" for chorus, speaker, orchestra (1965); *Sustajanje* [Lassitude] for organ, orchestra (1967); *Composition* for chamber orchestra, ondes Martenot (1968).

Ragtime, see Jazz

Rajičić, Stanojlo (b. Belgrade, 16 Dec 1910), attended the Prague Conservatory (1930–36; composition with Rudolf Karel, Josef Suk; piano with Roman Veselý, Alois Šíma, and Karel Hoffmeister), and studied piano with Walter Kerschbaumer in Vienna (1936). He has been teaching composition at the Belgrade Music Academy since 1940. Whereas Rajičić's early works are expressionistic, his compositions of the 1940s reestablish tonal harmony and traditional forms and are often influenced by folklore. Since the late 50s he has worked with bolder harmonies, polytonality, and occasionally atonality.

PRINCIPAL COMPOSITIONS: *Pod zemljom* [Underground], ballet (1940); *Violin Concerto No. 2* (1946, Prosveta); *Cello Concerto* (1949, SANU); *Piano Concerto No. 3* (1950, SANU); *Na Liparu* [On Lipar] for voice, orchestra (1951, UKS); *Lisje žuti* [Yellowing Leaves] for voice, orchestra (1953); *Violin Concerto No. 3* (1953, Muzika); *Simonida*, opera (1957, UKS); *Symphony No. 5 in G* (1959, UKS); *Concerto No. 2* for clarinet, strings, piano, percussion (1962, SANU); *Magnovenja* [Quick Moments] for voice, orchestra (1965); *Symphony No. 6 in E* (1967).

BIBL.: D. Cvetko, "S. R.: Na Liparu," *Revija* (Belgrade) 1953/7:5; S. Djurić-Klajn, "Drugi koncert za violinu i orkestar S. R.," *Muzika* (Belgrade) 1949/2:62–75; Z. Kučukalić, " 'Simonida' S. R.," *Zvuk* (Belgrade) 13–14 (1957):139–43; V. Peričić, " 'Magnovenja', novi vokalni ciklus S. R.," *Zvuk* 68 (1966):352–58; ——, *Muzički stvaroaci u Srbiji* [Composers of Serbia] (Belgrade 1969):430–52; ——, *Stvaralački put S. R.* (Belgrade 1970); D. Skovran, "Simfonija in G, S. R.," *Zvuk* 51 (1961):72–81; P. Stefanović, "Novo delo S. R.," *Književnost* 1951/5–6:189–92.

Ramey, Phillip (b. Chicago, 12 Sept 1939), studied at De Paul Univ. (1959–62, composition with Alexander Tcherepnin) and Columbia Univ. (1962–65, composition with Jack Beeson). He also studied with Tcherepnin in 1959 at the International Academy of Music in Nice. He has assisted Aaron Copland and Leonard Bernstein on conducting tours and is a frequent contributor of liner notes for records. He began to work with 12-tone techniques in 1967. In his *Piano Sonata No. 4* "tonality, in effect, disappears, along with barlines; massive tone clusters and the extremes of the keyboard are used." In the *Piano Concerto* "extreme polytonality results in complex chord structures, tone clusters, and a tendency toward dissonant polyphony in separate choirs of the orchestra. The music, characterized by violent outbursts in the piano and orchestra, develops variationally from a few motives."

PRINCIPAL COMPOSITIONS: *Piano Sonatas Nos. 1–4* (1961, 1966, 1968, 1968); *Sonata* for 3 solo timpani (1961, Percus); *Concert Suite* for piano, orchestra (1962); *Seven, They Are Seven* for bass-baritone, orchestra; text by K. Balmont (1965); *Capriccio* for percussion (1966, Cole); *Orchestral Discourse* (1967); *Epigrams* for piano (1967, Boosey); *Commentaries* for flute, piano (1968); *Winter Music* for piano (1969); *Piano Concerto No. 1* (1969–71); *String Quartet No. 1* (1970–71); *Clarinet Sonata* (1971); *Incantations* for violin, piano (1971).

PRINCIPAL WRITINGS (unpublished): *The Music of Alexander Tcherepnin: A Survey and Analysis*; *A Survey of the Music of Robert Muczynski*; *Serial Techniques in the Recent Music of Aaron Copland*; *The Life and Music of Alexander Tcherepnin*.

Ramovš, Primož (b. Ljubljana, Yugoslavia, 20 March 1921), studied at the Ljubljana Music Academy (1935–41, composition with Slavko Osterc), at the Accàdemia Musicale Chigiana in Siena (1941, composition with Vito Frazzi), and privately in Rome with Alfredo Casella (1941–43). During 1948–64 he taught at the Ljubljana Conservatory. He has participated in contemporary music festivals in Warsaw and Zagreb, among others.

PRINCIPAL COMPOSITIONS: *Sinfonietta* (1951, DSS); *Musiques funèbres* for orchestra (1955, SKJ); *Concerto piccolo* for bassoon, strings (1958, DSS); *7 Pieces* for strings (1960); *Concerto* for violin, viola, orchestra (1961, DSS); *Kontrasti* for violin, cello, piano (1961, DSS); *Intrada* for orchestra (1962); *Enneafonia* for winds, strings, harp, piano, percussion (1963, DSS); *Apel* [Appeal] for flute, clarinet, horn, harp, strings (1963, DSS); *Transformaiions* for 2 violas, strings (1963); *Profili* for orchestra (1964); *Vzporedja* [Parallels] for piano, string orchestra (1964); *Odmevi* [Echoes] for flute, orchestra (1965); *Antiparalele* for piano, orchestra (1966); *Prolog—Dialog—Epilog* for flute, clarinet, bassoon (1966); *Preludij in vrnitve* [Prelude and Return] for piano (1966, Gerig); *Nihanja* [Oscillations] for flute, strings, harp, percussion (1967); *Impulzi* for oboe, harp (1967, Gerig); *Inventiones pastorales* for organ (1967, Gerig); *2 Nocturnes* for guitar (1967, Gerig); *Symphony 68* for orchestra (1968, DSS); *Portret* for harp, winds, strings, percussion (1968); *Nasprotja* [Oppositions] for string quartet (1969); *Con sordino* for trumpet, trombone, piano (1969); *Symphony* for piano, orchestra (1970).

BIBL.: Borut Loparnik, "P. R.," *15 dana* (Zagreb) 11:21–23; Ivo Petrić, "P. R.," *Sodobnost* (Ljubljana) 12:73–77; ——, "P. R.," program book of the Slovakian Philharmonic, 1969–70/7: 5–7.

Randall, James K. (b. Cleveland, 16 June 1929), studied at Columbia Univ. (BA, 1955), Harvard Univ. (MA, 1956), and Princeton Univ. (MFA, 1958). He has taught at the U.S. Naval School of Music (1951–54), Princeton Univ. (since 1957), and the Bennington Composers' Conference (summers, 1965–66).

PRINCIPAL COMPOSITIONS: *Slow Movement* for piano (1959); *Improvisation on a poem by e. e. cummings* (1960); *Pitch-derived Rhythm: 5 Demonstrations* (1961); *VI* (1963); *VII* (1964); *Mudgett: monologues by a mass murderer* (1965); *Lyric Variations* for violin, computer (1966–68).

PRINCIPAL WRITINGS: "Godfrey Winham's Composition for Orchestra," *Perspectives* 2/1: 102–13; "Haydn's String Quartet, Op. 76, No. 5," *Music Review* 21:94–105; "3 Lectures to Scientists," *Perspectives* 5/2:124–40; "Electronic Music and Musical Tradition," *Music Educators' Journal* 55/3:50–55, 163–67.

SEE ALSO Mathematics, Text Setting and Usage.

Rands, Bernard (b. Sheffield, England, 2 March 1935), attended the Univ. of Wales (1953–58, composition with Reginald Smith Brindle). He studied privately with Roman Vlad (Rome, 1958), Luigi Dallapiccola (Florence, 1959–60), and Luciano Berio (1960, 1962). He also attended composition classes of Boulez and Maderna (Darmstadt, summers, 1961–64). Rands taught at the Univ. of Wales (1961–66) and was a visiting composer at Princeton Univ. (1966–67) and the Univ. of Ill. (1967–68). He taught at the Univ. of York, England during 1969–70. Berio's approaches to the materials and craftsmanship of musical composition and to the nature and function of music have been the most important influence on Rands's development. He has also benefited from a close association with the duo-pianists Aloys and Alfons Kontarsky, the harpist Francis Pierre, the ensemble of the Domain Musical in Paris, and the composers John Cage and Earle Brown. The strongest nonmusical influences have come from the works of James Joyce.

PRINCIPAL COMPOSITIONS (published by UE): *3 Espressioni* for piano (1960); *Action for 6* for flute, viola, cello, harp, 2 percussionists (1962–63); *Espressione IV* for 2 pianos (1964); *Formants I*, "Les Gestes," for harp (1965); *Formants II*, "Labyrinthe," for harp (which plays *Formants I*), clarinet, trombone, viola, cello, piano, celesta, 2 percussionists (1966, revised 1969); *Metalepsis* for woman's voice, 3 percussionists, tape (1967, revised 1969); *Per esempio* for orchestra (1967); *Sound Patterns I* for voices, hands (1968, intended for use in classrooms with young players); *Sound Patterns II* for voices, miscellaneous instruments; for classroom use (1968); *Wildtrack I* for 30 players (1969).

Rathaus, Karol (b. Tarnopol, Austria—now Poland, 16 Sept 1895; d. New York, 21 Nov 1954), studied composition with Franz Schreker at the Vienna Academy of Music (1919, 1921–22) and the Berlin Hochschule für Musik (1920–21, 1922–23). He lived in Berlin (1922–32), Paris (1932–34), London (1934–38), Hollywood (1939) and New York. He taught composition at Queens College, New York, during 1940–54. Boris Schwartz (see bibl.) has pointed out that Rathaus's style evolved from the central European, postromantic heritage of the early 20th-century. His musical concept was essentially harmonic, not linear; his motoric rhythms give a characteristic vitality to his music. Although Polish and Jewish elements contributed to the shaping of his style, they never dominated his creative work.

PRINCIPAL COMPOSITIONS: *Piano Sonatas Nos. 3–4*, Opp. 20, 58 (1927, UE; 1946, Queens College); *Overture for Orchestra*, Op. 22 (1928, UE); *Suite* for violin, chamber orchestra, Op. 27 (1929, UE); *Suite for Orchestra*, Op. 29 (1930, UE); *Allegro concertante*, Op. 30 (1930, IMP); *Variations on a Hurdy-Gurdy Theme* for piano, Op. 40 (1936, Boelke); *String Quartets Nos. 3–5*, Opp. 41, 59, 72 (1936, Oxford; 1946, SPAM; 1954, UE); *Jacob's Dream*, nocturne for orchestra, Op. 44 (1938, UE); *Prelude and Gigue* for orchestra, Op. 44a (1939, Boosey); *Piano Concerto*, Op. 45 (1939, Boosey); *Music for Strings*, Op. 49 (1941, Boosey); *Requiem* for chorus, piano; text by Robert Louis Stevenson (c.1941, Boosey); *Rondo* for chorus, piano; text by Leigh Hunt (c.1941, Boosey); *3 Polish Dances* for piano, Op. 47 (1942, Boosey); *Symphony No. 3*, Op. 50 (1942–43, Boosey); *3 English Songs* for high or medium voice, piano, Op. 48 (1943, AMP); *Polonaise symphonique*, Op. 52 (1943, AMP); *Vision dramatique* for orchestra, Op. 55 (1945, Boosey); *4 Studies after Domenico Scarlatti* for piano, Op. 56 (1945–46, Presser); *Uriel Acosta Suite* for orchestra (1947, IMP); *Lament from "Iphigenia in Aulis" by Euripides* for chorus, horn, Op. 61 (1947, AMP); *Variations on a Theme by Georg Boehm* for piano, Op. 62 (1948, Queens College); *Rapsodia notturna* for viola (cello), piano, Op. 66 (1950, Boosey); *Diapason* for baritone, chorus, orchestra, Op. 67; texts by Dryden and Milton (1950, Queens College); *Sinfonia concertante*, Op. 68 (1950–51, Bärenreiter); *Trio Serenade* for piano, violin, cello, Op. 69 (1953, Queens College); *Prelude for Orchestra*, Op. 71 (1953, Boosey). Rathaus also revised and edited the orchestral score of Mussorgsky's *Boris Godunov* for the Metropolitan Opera (1953).

BIBL.: Boris Schwartz, "K. R.," *Musical Quarterly* (Oct 1955): 481–95.

[prepared with the help of the Karol Rathaus Memorial Assoc. and Gerta Rathaus]

Rautavaara, Einojuhani (b. Helsinki, 9 Oct 1928), studied literature and musicology at the Univ. of Helsinki (1948–53) and music at the Sibelius Academy (1948–54, composition with Aarre Merikanto), the Juilliard School (1955–56), the Berkshire Music Center (1955, 1956; composition with Vincent Persichetti, Aaron Copland, Roger Sessions), and at the Musik-hochschule in Cologne (1958, composition with Rudolf Petzold). He also studied composition privately with Wladimir Vogel in Ascona, Switzerland. During 1959–62 he was librarian of the City Symphony Orchestra in Helsinki; during 1965–67, director of the Käpylä Music School there; and since 1966, lecturer on theory at the Sibelius Academy.

PRINCIPAL COMPOSITIONS: *String Quartet No. 1* (1952); *A Requiem in Our Time* for brass, percussion (1953, King); *Symphonies Nos. 1–4* (1956,

1957, 1961, 1964); *Kaives* [The Mine], 3-act opera (1957–63); *String Quartet No. 2* (1958, Breitkopf); *5 Sonette an Orpheus* for voice, piano (or orchestra); texts by Rilke (1959, Fazer); *Die Liebenden* for voice, orchestra (1959); *Cantos I–II* for strings (1960); *Wind Octet* (1964); *String Quartet No. 3* (1965, Weinberger); *Quartet* for oboe, string trio (1965); *Soldier's Mass* for winds, percussion (1968); *Cello Concerto* (1968, Breitkopf); *Anadyomene* for orchestra (1968); *Piano Concerto* (1969); *Sonata* for solo cello (1969); *The Temptations*, ballet (1969).

PRINCIPAL WRITINGS: "Uttalanden om musikens framtid" [Day of Tomorrow], *Modern musik* ed. by Seppo Nummi (Stockholm 1967): 103–06.

Ravel, (Joseph) **Maurice** (b. Ciboure, France, 7 March 1875; d. Paris, 28 Dec 1937), was born in the Basque region but grew up in Paris. He evinced considerable musical talent as a child and, with parental encouragement, took both piano and composition lessons. His taste for exoticism was whetted by the international exposition of 1889, where he heard Javanese orchestras. In the same year he entered the Paris Conservatory, remaining for an unusually long apprenticeship of 16 years. During his student days he was part of a group of art enthusiasts who called themselves the Apaches. ("Apaches" are underworld hooligans. The group considered themselves "artistic outcasts," owing to their frequent support of controversial new works.) The group frequently met far into the night, declaiming poetry, discussing painting, and performing new music. At Apaches meetings Ravel met many of his future collaborators: the poet Tristan Klingsor, *Schéhérazade* (1903); the critic M. D. Calvocoressi, who commissioned the *5 Mélodies populaires grecques* and translated the Greek texts into French; and the pianist Ricardo Viñes, who introduced Ravel to the writings of Aloysius Bertrand and Evariste Parny, resulting in *Gaspard de la nuit* and the *Chansons madécasses.* Manuel de Falla and Stravinsky occasionally participated in the group.

In 1901 Ravel began competing for the Prix de Rome, France's highest award for composers. Even though his output included several major works by 1904, he continually failed to win first prize. Finally in 1905 his elimination in the preliminary round of the competition engendered a public scandal. He left the conservatory, and the following three years proved to be the most productive in his career. In 1907 his long-standing interest in Spanish music (stemming to some extent from his Basque mother) resulted in the *Rapsodie*

espagnole, L'Heure espagnole, and the *Vocalise en forme d'habanera.* 1912 proved to be his "ballet" year: *Daphnis et Chloé* (commissioned by the impressario, Sergei Diaghilev), *Ma Mère l'Oye* (adapted from the original version for piano four-hands), and *Adélaïde* (adapted from *Valses nobles et sentimentales*) were all first performed within a six-month period.

During World War I, Ravel served in the French army as a lorry driver and virtually ceased composing for three years. The death of his mother in January 1917 proved to be the deepest shock of his life. Between 1920 and 1932 he completed only 17 works. This small output was in part due to his delicate health, as well as an increasing number of concert tours, one of which brought him to the U.S. and Canada (1928). Upon returning to France he composed the remarkably popular *Bolero* for Ida Rubinstein's ballet company. Following his swan song *Don Quichotte à Dulcinée* (1932), he was virtually unable to notate his thoughts, owing to a rare brain disease. From 1933 until his death, he waited in vain for his faculties to return to normal.

There are little more than 50 published works by Ravel, written over a period of four decades, but few of them are insignificant. As a jeweler polishes and refines, he reconstructed and recast almost all of his music. He made important contributions to the literature of the piano, the orchestra, chamber music, and the French art song. He never composed a symphony, nor did he write any sacred music. He was particularly sensitive to the magical worlds of children (*Ma Mère l'Oye*) and animals (*Histoires naturelles*). His adaptation of *L'Enfant et les sortilèges* was a summation of the many styles and techniques he had previously utilized: bitonality, dance rhythms, orchestral wizardry, and talking animals, to name but a few.

Ravel once stated that his objective in composing was to achieve "technical perfection. I can strive unceasingly to this end since I am certain of never being able to attain it. The important thing is to get nearer to it all the time. Art, no doubt, has other *effects*, but the artist, in my opinion, should have no other aim" (Roland-Manuel 1956:53; see bibl.). Ravel revered Mozart as the composer who flawlessly achieved the clarity and perfection that he sought in his own compositions, and he remarked once that his own music was "quite simple, nothing but Mozart."[1]

In order to approach the goal of technical

1. Ursula Vaughan Williams, *Ralph Vaughan Williams* (London 1964):80.

perfection, Ravel suggested that composers submit to a rigorous academic training. His initial sketches consisted solely of a melody and figured bass, thus showing the influence of his training at the Paris Conservatory. He felt that composers should learn their craft like painters, by imitating good models. He himself studied throughout his career the scores of Mozart, Chopin, Liszt, Richard Strauss, Debussy, Satie, Chabrier, Fauré, and Saint-Säens, as well as the Russian composers, particularly Mussorgsky. Virtually all of his compositions were to some extent stylistic pastiches. He was equally at home writing "Spanish" music or adapting jazz (as in the two piano concertos), harmonizing Greek folk melodies, or writing an homage to 18th-century French music (*Le Tombeau de Couperin*). Two of his minor works for the piano were bona-fide imitations: *A la Manière de Borodine* and *A la Manière de Chabrier* (1913). In many works dance rhythms appear: pavane, malagueña, forlane, waltz, fox-trot, and bolero. In addition to the foregoing, Ravel utilized contemporary impressionistic techniques (*Jeux d'eau*).

Ravelian melody, be it vocal or instrumental, shows little of the wandering chromaticism of Franck or Fauré's favored enharmonic ambiguities. It is diatonic, often mixing modality with tonality, and it generally proceeds by repetition, sequence, and variation rather than by genuine development. When writing "Spanish" music, he often used the phrygian mode (e-f-g-a-b-c-d, *Rapsodie espagnole*). Likewise, pentatonic episodes (*Ma Mère l'Oye*) and the gapped scales of the East (for example, d-f-g-a-b-c) appear (*Daphnis et Chloé*). The melodic phrase is generally brief and unornamented, frequently outlining the interval of the seventh, which is important both melodically and harmonically.

Ravel's harmonies were considered audacious in their time. Without abandoning tonality, he extended its range, particularly by exploiting the chord of the major seventh (*Jeux d'eau*), chords of the ninth and eleventh, chords with unresolved appoggiaturas (*Valses nobles et sentimentales*), and those with multiple appoggiaturas over pedal points ("Scarbo" in *Gaspard de la nuit*). The use of bitonality (*Sonata* for violin and cello) and touches of atonality (*3 Poèmes de Stephane Mallarmé*) indicate a striking continuing harmonic curiosity. As Ravel's art unfolded, a slow but perceptible chastening occurred in his harmonic writing. With few exceptions the earlier period was a richer one harmonically, culminating in *Daphnis et Chloé*, than the

more austere harmonic style that followed, beginning with *Le Tombeau de Couperin* and continuing through the *Chansons madécasses*. The latter Ravel felt to be one of his finest works because it contained, in his opinion, a maximum of expression utilizing a minimum of notes. The prewar compositions favored homophonic writing while some of the postwar works emphasized linear motion (*Violin Sonata*).

Ravel's fastidious literary taste led him to select a wide variety of texts for musical adaptation, ranging from Marot to Colette, and encompassing the subtle prose of Jules Renard as well as Mallarmé's esoteric symbolism. Although he set poems with regular structures, he preferred free verse and poems in prose. He covered fresh ground in setting Renard's *Histoires naturelles* by frequently eliding the terminal mute *e* in order to approach the tone of everyday conversation as closely as possible. The critic Emile Vuillermoz, a close friend of Ravel, has pointed out that this "conversational" melodic style (which reappeared in *L'Heure espagnole*), with its characteristic fall of a fourth or fifth at the ends of phrases, resulted from the composer's own pronunciation when reading his texts (Vuillermoz: 59–60).

Ravel's art was essentially that of a miniaturist. His operas, each less than an hour, consist of brief contiguous scenes; *Daphnis et Chloé*, his longest work, was unified by a small number of recurring motives. Melodic repetition was used in order to unify song cycles (*Chansons madécasses*) or multimovement compositions (*Rapsodie espagnole*).

In contrast to his treatment of form, which was conservative, Ravel's extensions of instrumental virtuosity were bold. *Tzigane* was a spiritual descendant of Paganini, as *Jeux d'eau* was indebted to Liszt's keyboard writing. Ravel's orchestral technique was largely indebted to Rimsky-Korsakov and Richard Strauss. The former's *Capriccio espagnol* (1887) clearly influenced the *Rapsodie espagnole*, and the latter's tone poems (such as *Til Eulenspiegel*) were continually studied. In addition Ravel dutifully copied the "safe" and "dangerous" ranges for each instrument as given in Widor's *Technique de l'orchestre moderne*, although he deliberately sought the most "dangerous" possibilities of each instrument as well as novel combinations of timbre. When orchestrating, he felt the need to isolate the notes of each family of instruments at the keyboard, and observe for example what the woodwinds were doing at a particular moment. Indeed upon analyzing his complex orchestral scores in this way, one will detect an underlying Gallic clarity in the voice leading.

Although Ravel's output enjoys the respect of musicians, his influence on composers has declined since World War II. In 1938 Darius Milhaud acknowledged his strong influence on the younger composers at the Paris Conservatory (Milhaud: 40). In addition he influenced many of his contemporaries, including Debussy (whose *Estampes*, 1903, derived from *Jeux d'eau* and an unpublished *Habanera* of 1895) and Poulenc, whose song cycle *La Bestiaire* is an important successor of the *Histoires naturelles*. The music of Ravel's pupils, Maurice Delage, Roland-Manuel, Vaughan Williams, and Manuel Rosenthal, shows his imprint, and in the U.S. his orchestrations and harmonies have influenced innumerable jazz arrangers and film composers.

PRINCIPAL COMPOSITIONS (published by Durand unless otherwise noted): *Menuet antique* for piano or orchestra (1895, Enoch); *2 Epigrammes* for voice, piano; texts by Marot (1898, Demets-Eschig); *Pavane pour une infante défunte* for piano or orchestra (1899, Demets-Eschig); *Jeux d'eau* for piano (1901, Demets-Eschig); *String Quartet*, (1902–03); *Scéhérazade* for voice, orchestra (1903); *Sonatine* for piano (1905); *Miroirs* for piano (1905, Demets-Eschig); *5 Mélodies populaires grecques* for voice, piano (1904–06); *Introduction and Allegro* for harp, string quartet, flute, clarinet (1905–06); *Histoires naturelles* for voice, piano; text by Jules Renard (1906); *Rapsodie espagnole* for orchestra (1907); *L'Heure espagnole*, opera; libretto by Franc-Nohain (1907); *Ma Mére l'Oye* [Mother Goose] for piano 4-hands or orchestra (1908); *Gaspard de la nuit* for piano; based on 3 poems by Aloysius Bertrand (1908); *Valses nobles et sentimentales* for piano or orchestra (1911); *Daphnis et Chloé*, ballet; also 2 suites for orchestra (1909–12); *3 Poémes de Stephane Mallarmé* for voice, piano, string quartet, 2 flutes, 2 clarinets (1913); *Piano Trio* (1914); *2 Mélodies hébraïques* for voice, piano (1914); *3 Chansons* for chorus; texts by the composer (1915); *Le Tombeau de Couperin* for piano; partially orchestrated for ballet (1914–17); *La Valse* for orchestra (1919–20); *Sonata* for violin, cello (1920–22); *Tableaux d'une exposition* for orchestra; music by Mussorgsky, orchestration by Ravel (1922, Russe); *Tzigane* for violin, piano or orchestra (1924); *L'Enfant et les sortilèges*, opera; libretto by Colette (1920–25); *Chansons madécasses* for voice, piano, flute, cello; texts by Evariste Parny (1925–26); *Violin Sonata* (1923–27); *Bolero* for orchestra, ballet (1928); *Concerto* for piano left-hand, orchestra (1930–31); *Piano Concerto in G* (1930–31); *Don Quichotte à Dulcinée* for voice with piano or orchestra; text by Paul Morand (1932). Complete lists in Myers: 224–25; Roland-Manuel 1948:224–25 (see bibl.).

PRINCIPAL WRITINGS: Louis Laloy, "Wagner et les musiciens d'aujourd'hui—opinions de MM Florent Schmitt et M. R.," *Grande revue* 13/9:

160–64; "A Propos des Images de Claude Debussy," *Cahiers d'aujourd'hui* (Feb 1913):135–38; "Les Mélodies de Gabriel Fauré," *Revue musicale* 4 (1922):214–19; Bohdan Pilarski, "Une Conference de M. R. à Houston (1928)," *Revue de musicologie* 50:208–21; Roland-Manuel, "Une esquisse autcbiographique de M. R.," *Revue musicale* (Dec 1938):17–23; —— "Lettres de M. R. et documents inédits," *Revue de musicologie* 38:49–53; "Les nouveaux spectacles de la Saison Russe—*Le Rossignol*," *Comoedia illustré* 6/17:811–14. Partial list in Myers:230.

BIBL.: Jules van Ackere, *M. R.* (Brussels 1957); M. D. Calvocoressi, *Musicians Gallery: Music and Ballet in Paris and London* (London 1933); R. Chalupt and M. Gerar, *R. au miroir de ses lettres* (Paris 1956); Basil Deane, "Renard, R. and the 'Histoires naturelles,'" *Australian Journal of French Studies* 1:177–87; Madeleine Goss, *Bolero. The Life of M. R.* (New York 1940); Vladimir Jankélévitch, *R.* (English ed., New York 1959); Hélène Jourdan-Morhange, *R. et nous* (Geneva 1945); François Lesure, "L'Affaire Debussy-Ravel—lettres inédites," *Festschrift Friedrich Blume* (Kassel 1963):231–34; Darius Milhaud, "Homage à Ravel," *Revue musicale* (Dec 1938); Rollo H. Myers, *R.* (London 1960); Arbie Orenstein, "L'Enfant et les Sortilèges: correspondance inédite de R. et Colette," *Revue de musicologie* 52:215–20; ——, "M. R.'s Creative Process," *Musical Quarterly* 53:467–81; V. Perlemuter and H. Jourdan-Morhange, *R. d'après R.* (Lausanne 1953); Roland-Manuel, "Lettres de M. R. et documents inédits," *Revue de musicologie* (July 1956); ——, *M. R. et son oeuvre dramatique* (Paris 1928); ——, *A la Gloire de R.* (Paris 1938); ——, *R.* (Paris 1948); H. H. Stuckenschmidt, *M. R.* (English ed., Philadelphia 1968); E. Vuillermoz et al., *M. R. par quelques-uns de ses familiers* (Paris 1939).

Arbie Orenstein

SEE ALSO Dance, Form, France, Harmony and Counterpoint, Impressionism, Jazz, Melody, Opera, Text Setting and Usage.

Rawsthorne, Alan (b. Haslingden, Lancashire, England, 2 May 1905; d. Cambridge, 24 July 1971), studied at the Royal Manchester College (1926–30, composition with T. Keighley, piano with Frank Merrick, cello with Carl Fuchs). In 1930–31 he studied piano privately with Egon Petri. During 1932–35 he was music director of the School of Dance-Mime at Dartington Hall, since then he has been a free-lance composer.

PRINCIPAL COMPOSITIONS (dates are of first performance, all are published by Oxford): *Theme and Variations* for 2 violins (1938); *Symphonic Studies* (1939); *Violin Concertos Nos. 1–2* (1948, 1956); *Clarinet Quartet* (1948); *Cello Sonata* (1949); *Concerto for String Orchestra* (1949); *Symphonies Nos. 1–3* (1950, 1959, 1964); *Piano*

Concerto No. 2 (1951); *String Quartets Nos. 2–3* (1954, 1965); *Violin Sonata* (1959); *Quintet* for piano, oboe, clarinet, horn, bassoon (1963); *Carmen vitale* for soprano, chorus, orchestra; early English lyrics (1963); *Cello Concerto* (1966); *Ballade* for piano (1967); *Concerto* for 2 pianos, orchestra (1968); *Piano Quintet* (1968); *Oboe Quartet* (1970); *Quintet* for piano, clarinet, horn, violin, cello (1971).

SEE ALSO Great Britain.

Raxach, Enrique (b. Barcelona, 15 Jan 1932), studied music privately in Barcelona with Nuri Aymerich (1949–52) and at the Utrecht Conservatory (1962–65, conducting with Paul Hupperts). He became a Dutch citizen in 1969 and is a free-lance musician.

PRINCIPAL COMPOSITIONS: *Polifonias* for string orchestra (1954–56); *Métamorphose I–II* for orchestra (1956, 1958; Peters); *Prometheus* for orchestra (1958); *Fases* for string quartet (1961, Tonos); *Estrofas* for flute, clarinet, violin, cello, double bass, percussion (1962, Tonos); *Fluxión* for chamber orchestra (1962–63, Tonos); *The Looking Glass* for organ (1967); *Equinoxial* for orchestra (1967–68, Donemus and Peters); *Paraphrase* for alto, 11 instruments (1969, Donemus and Peters); *Inside Outside* for orchestra, tape (1969, Donemus).

PRINCIPAL WRITINGS: "Noten ohne Musik?" program book of the Gaudeamus Music Week (Sept 1962):7–11; "Selbstportrait," *Begegnung* (Amriswil, Oct 1965):24–25; "La ancrucijada musical holandesa," *Sonda* (Madrid, June 1968): 31–40.

BIBL.: Tomás Marco, *Música española de vanguardia* (Madrid 1970).

SEE ALSO Spain.

Read, Gardner (b. Evanston, Ill., 2 Jan 1913), attended the Eastman School (1932–37; composition and orchestration with Howard Hanson and Bernard Rogers, conducting with Paul White). He studied composition with Ildebrando Pizzetti in Italy and with Sibelius in Finland in 1939 and with Aaron Copland at Tanglewood in the summer of 1941. He headed the composition departments of the St. Louis Institute of Music (1941–43), the Kansas City Conservatory (1943–45), the Cleveland Institute of Music (1945–48), and Boston Univ. (1950–52). Since 1948 he has been professor of composition and theory at Boston Univ. He originated and served as host-commentator for the weekly radio series "Our American Music" in Boston (1953–60) and served as

editor of the Birchard-Boston Univ. Contemporary Music Series during 1950–60. Under the auspices of the U.S. State Department he lectured in Mexico on American music in the summers of 1957 and 1964.

PRINCIPAL COMPOSITIONS: *Sketches of the City*, symphonic suite, Op. 26 (1933, Kalmus); *Fantasy* for viola, orchestra, Op. 38 (1935, AMP); *Symphony No. 1*, Op. 30 (1936, AME); *Passacaglia and Fugue* for organ, Op. 34 (1936, Gray); *From a Lute of Jade* for mezzo-soprano, orchestra, Op. 36 (1936, CP and Southern); *Prelude and Toccata* for orchestra, Op. 43 (1937, Kalmus and Colombo); *The Golden Journey to Samarkand* for vocal soloists, chorus, orchestra, Op. 41 (1939); *Night Flight* for orchestra, Op. 44 (1942, Henmar); *Symphony No. 2*, Op. 45 (1942, AMP); *Cello Concerto*, Op. 55 (1945, AMP); *Sonata da chiesa* for piano, Op. 61 (1945); *Music for Piano and Strings*, Op. 47a (1946); *The Temptation of St. Anthony*, a dance symphony, Op. 56 (1947); *Pennsylvaniana*, symphonic suite, Op. 67 (1947, Colombo); *Symphony No. 3*, Op. 75 (1948, Colombo); *Sonata brevis* for violin, piano, Op. 80 (1948); *Suite for Organ*, Op. 81 (1949, Witmark); *Sound Piece* for brass, percussion, Op. 82 (1949, King); *Nine by Six* for flute/piccolo, oboe/English horn, clarinet/bass clarinet, trumpet, horn, bassoon, Op. 86 (1950); *Jesous Ahatonhia* for chorus, organ, Op. 87 (1950, S-B); *8 Preludes on Old Southern Hymns* for organ, Op. 90 (1950, Gray); *Arioso elegiaca* for strings, Op. 91 (1951); *The Golden Harp* for chorus, Op. 93 (1952, Fischer-J); *Toccata giocosa* for orchestra, Op. 94 (1953, Presser); *Vernal Equinox* for orchestra, Op. 96 (1955, Colombo); *String Quartet No. 1*, Op. 100 (1957); *Symphony No. 4*, Op. 92 (1958); *Sonoric Fantasia No. 1* for celesta, harp, harpsichord, Op. 102 (1959, Presser); *Los Dioses Aztecas* for 6 percussionists, Op. 107 (1959, Cole); *The Prophet* for alto, baritone, narrator, chorus, orchestra, Op. 110 (1960); *The Reveille* for chorus, winds, percussion, organ, Op. 89b (1962); *Sonoric Fantasy No. 2* for violin, orchestra, Op. 123 (1965, Presser); *Villon*, 3-act opera; libretto by James Forsyth, Op. 122 (1967). List to 1963: *Composers of the Americas* 8:127–39.

PRINCIPAL WRITINGS: *Thesaurus of Orchestral Devices* (New York 1953); "Imagination and Inspiration," *Boston Univ. Graduate Journal* 5/1: 3–6, reprinted in *Music Journal* (Nov 1956); "National Culture is in Jeopardy," *Music Journal* (Sept 1962):22–24, 66–67; "Mexico, Mission 2: 1964," *Music Clubs' Magazine* 44/2:10–11; *Music Notation—A Manual of Modern Practice* (Boston 1964, 1969); "The Artist-in-Residence: Fact or Fancy?" *Report of the National Council of the Arts in Education* (Sept 1964):31–39, reprinted in *Arts in Society* 3/4 (summer 1966); reprinted as "The Year of the Artist-in-Residence," *Music Journal* (July, Sept 1967); "Some Problems of Rhythmic Notation," *Journal of Music Theory* 9/1:162–69; *Twentieth-Century Notation* (in progress); *Orchestral Combinations* (in progress); *Style and Orchestration* (in progress).

Reck, David (b. Rising Star, Texas, 12 Jan 1935), studied at the Univ. of Houston (1952–56), the Univ. of Texas (1956–60; composition with Paul Pisk, Peter Phillips), the Princeton Seminars in Advanced Musical Studies (1959, 1960), and the Univ. of Pa. (1960–64, composition with George Rochberg). During 1964–67 he lived in New York, where he made several films and produced musical-theatrical happenings. He also lectured on new music at the New School for Social Research. Since 1968 he has lived in India, where he has studied improvisation in Karnatic music at the Central College of Karnatic Music in Madras and the veena with Tirukokarnam Ramachandra Iyer. He has traveled extensively in India to study traditional folk and classical forms.

PRINCIPAL COMPOSITIONS: *Number 1* for flute, clarinet, tenor saxophone, horn, viola, double bass, vibraphone, 3 percussionists, piano (1963, MJQ); *Number 2* for actress, flute, bass clarinet, violin, double bass, guitar, percussion, conductor (1965, Peters); *Blues & Screamer* for flute, alto saxophone, double bass, percussion, harmonium, amplified kitchen appliances, American flag, balloons, toy machine gun, TV set, transistor radio, sparklers, firecrackers, 16-mm. film (1967, published in *Source*, vol. 1); *MetaMusacke* for 5 players, 3 slide projectors, 16-mm. film, 2 tape recorders, composer-in-residence; a kit, meant to be continually in progress (1968–); *Asian Radio Nos. 1–3* on tape (1969–70); *Wood/Rock/Earth Musics*, involving digging, carving, and cutting trees, stone, and earth to make musical instruments; a work in progress (1970–).

Recording. During the three generations between Thomas A. Edison's invention of a crude tinfoil cylinder phonograph (4–6 Dec 1877) and the advent of combined audio-video record and playback systems for the home (late 1960s), recording grew from a primitive diversion to a prime experiential medium far surpassing in worldwide influence that of the actual hearing or seeing phenomenon itself. Edison's invention made use of a stylus attached to a vibrating diaphragm that was activated directly by sound waves. In its earliest form, the stylus made corresponding impressions on tinfoil wrapped around a pre-grooved cylinder. The vertical undulations of the groove floor were a record of the sound waves received by the diaphragm. Subsequently development of a carriage and feed-screw mechanism made possible the use of wax cylinder blanks. This system was the basis of patents owned by both the Edison Phonograph Co. (founded 1887) and the Columbia

Phonograph Co. (founded 1889). Mass production became possible when Emile Berliner in the U.S. developed techniques of flat disc recording by which a laterally actuated stylus cut a spiral groove embodying side-to-side deflections caused by sound waves. Using this innovation, as well as mechanical improvements by Eldridge Johnson in New Jersey, discs were mass produced by the Gramophone Co., Ltd., in London (established 1898) and the Victor Talking Machine Co. in the U.S. (established 1901 by Berliner and Johnson). Cylinders were not immediately abandoned, however; Edison continued to issue them exclusively through 1912, and Emil Pathé in France did the same through 1905. A major technical breakthrough occurred in the mid-20s with the application of vacuum tube audio amplification (already used in radio), which permitted an enormously broadened range of timbre and volume in recording and playback.

Until 1945 the American record market was dominated by three giants (RCA Victor, Columbia, and Decca), and there were only a few small independent concerns. Thereafter the number of companies increased to several hundred, owing to the introduction of the fine-groove long-playing record and of magnetic tape as a master recording medium (RCA Victor had tried to market a standard-groove long-playing record in 1931 but was frustrated by lack of suitable home playback equipment). In magnetic tape recording, the tape is coated with an iron oxide of magnetically conductive material and wound onto a supply reel. During the recording process, sound is converted into an electrical signal as in electrical disc recording. The signal produces a magnetomotive force that is stored by the particles along the tape coating. The differing directions and strengths of magnetization constitute the record of sound waves. The process in its basic principle was known both in America and in Europe from early in the century, but its potential in terms of ease of recording and distribution was not fully appreciated until Germany exploited the medium for propaganda purposes in World War II. Applied to the recording industry, the tape medium allowed anyone who could afford microphones and a professional tape recorder to make his own master tape and then have it transferred to disc masters and pressed into commercial records by an independent recording studio and disc manufacturing plant. It was no longer necessary for heavy lathes to be taken to a recording locale for direct cutting on master discs, and recording could be carried out in long rather than short segments (an hour of music could now be recorded for only a few hundred dollars). Furthermore several "takes" of a given work or part thereof could be combined by means of tape splicing into a note-perfect composite performance. In 1948 the long-playing disc was introduced by Columbia in America, making the recording of long works more practical, lowering the cost of recorded music per time unit, and lessening the space needed for the storage of a home record library. Such advantages as these, combined with increasing sound fidelity, created an upsurge in interest among the musical public. This interest was further increased by the advent of commercial stereophonic records in 1958.

REPERTORY: TECHNICAL FACTORS. The repertory of recorded music included 20th-century music almost from the beginning. The Gramophone Co. (London) and Victor (Camden, N. J.) pioneered the Red Seal celebrity recording idea and built up a substantial (though qualitatively crude) documentation of the great opera singers of the early 1900s. Rival firms, including Zonophone, Pathé, Odeon, and Fonotopia in Europe and Columbia and Edison in the U.S. were quick to sense the commercial potential in this idea. An early by-product of the celebrity idea was the documentation of composers' interpretations of their own works. Examples are Leoncavallo, who in 1904 accompanied Caruso in his song *Mattinata* (composed especially for the gramophone) and also conducted a substantially complete *Pagliacci*. Also in 1904 Debussy accompanied Mary Garden in a pair of songs, as well as in excerpts from *Pelléas et Mélisande*. However, it was not until recording and playback equipment improved substantially during the years around World War I, that 20th-century music entered the phonograph repertory in any significant way. Even the Richard Strauss tone poems, which were composed before 1900, were not recorded with the composer conducting until after World War I. Electrical recording, with its vastly improved sound fidelity, had an even greater impact on the 20th-century recorded repertory. Stravinsky, for instance, did not embark on a systematic program of recording his works until after the mid-20s, although *Petrouchka* (1910–11) had been recorded earlier in the decade.

The combination of magnetic tape and the long-playing record cut production costs to the point where companies dared to experiment with unknown repertory, including that of the 20th century. Sales, however, did not justify keeping many of the contemporary

works in print, and they were dropped from circulation in the late 1950s. Stereophonic recording reopened the record market, and by the mid-60s increased sales had come to include the 20th-century repertory. Both established companies and a number of new labels began reissuing either in monophonic format or in simulated stereo the recordings that had been dropped in the late 50s. Virtually the entire American Recording Society repertory (some 57 works recorded during 1951–52) turned up in 1965 on the newly established Desto label.

REPERTORY: ECONOMIC FACTORS. Commercial record companies, like book and music publishers, are in business to make a profit. If the end result of hopefully profit-making activity happens to have permanent artistic and/or documentary value, this is purely incidental. Such circumstances help to explain the fact that the bulk of 20th-century music represented in record manufacturers' catalogs throughout the world until the advent of the long-playing disc in 1948 was essentially the "safe" mainstream types, stemming from the European tonal classic and romantic tradition. The representation of controversial figures (Berg, Schoenberg, Webern, Varèse, Ives, Sessions, Riegger, and Messiaen) was miniscule compared with Ravel, Sibelius, Richard Strauss, Delius, Elgar, Falla, Kodály, Hindemith, and Copland. Though 20th-century-composer representation on discs available on the American market in mid-1969 surpassed the 700 mark, over two-thirds of the names represented could perhaps be described as post-Bartókian mainstream, the "safe" composers of the time. Of even these works, only a relative handful was commercially successful.

Subsidies of various sorts have alleviated commercial pressures. In the early 1930s the idea of an advanced subscription plan was introduced. Walter Legge of the Gramophone Co. in London brought out a Society series devoted to Hugo Wolf, Artur Schnabel's performance of the Beethoven *Piano Sonatas*, Edwin Fischer's performance of the *Well-Tempered Clavier*, Albert Schweitzer's Bach organ music, and issues of the living composers Sibelius, Kilpinen, Delius, and Bax. Henry Cowell in the U.S. was more adventurous. He founded the New Music Quarterly publishing and recording enterprise, which was also based on the subscription plan but which issued the first recordings of more controversial composers: Ives, Ruggles, and John J. Becker. Similar subscription plans have been adopted widely both during the 78 rpm and long-playing record eras: for example, Concert Hall Society (1947–53), the American Recording Society (1952–53), and the Louisville First Editions series (begun 1954).

Yet another form of subsidy for 20th-century music, though disguised, has emerged from within the commercial manufacturers themselves, usually thanks to the presence of a company official with an interest in contemporary music and a desire to see some of the firm's efforts devoted to educational enterprises. Such was the case with some of the early 1930s recordings by U.S. Columbia: Aaron Copland's own performance of his then controversial *Piano Variations*, and the *Clarinet Concerto* of the virtually unknown Roy Harris. With its introduction of the long-playing disc Columbia undertook such efforts on a far larger and more systematic scale, covering not only the works of American composers but the complete works of Stravinsky, Schoenberg, Webern, and Ives. In time the popularity of a particular composer may in effect subsidize new recordings. There is little doubt that proceeds from the sales of Stravinsky's pre-1931 works on records have subsidized the recording costs of the knottier post-1950 scores.

Outside the U.S., government subsidy has always played a significant role in the recording of works by the leading (or favored) composers within a given country. The British Council in England, the composers societies in the Scandinavian countries, Belgium, Switzerland, Argentina, Brazil, and the Netherlands, and most eastern European countries have all undertaken large-scale recording programs of this type, especially since 1948. Many such recordings made since 1960 have achieved international distribution either by way of direct export or through licensing arrangements with foreign manufacturers.

In the U.S., philanthropic foundations, such as the Rockefeller, Ford, Martha Baird Rockefeller, Alice M. Ditson Fund at Columbia Univ., and Serge Koussevitzky Music Foundation have played major roles since 1950 in subsidizing 20th-century music on American record labels. So too have subsidies or "revolving funds" established by individual patrons or under the auspices of universities and similar educational institutions. It should be noted that a number of American record labels specializing in 20th-century music are connected directly or indirectly with universities or university presses. (An expansion of such connections, including collaborations with commercial firms, could make out-of-print recordings again available.)

NONCOMMERCIAL RECORDING. The entire range of 20th-century music, from King Oliver-era jazz to the latest avant-garde works, exist not only on commercial phonograph records but on private and noncommercial tapes and transcription discs, embodying often unique performances otherwise undocumented. Many of these have been made from radio broadcasts and from live concerts, many of the latter originating at music schools and universities. Much of the work of Serge Koussevitzky and the Boston Symphony Orchestra and of Arturo Toscanini from the mid-30s to 1954 has been preserved on vinyl and acetate transcription discs or instantaneous acetate discs dating from before the days of magnetic tape. Since 1955 there has been considerable legitimate and *sub-rosa* circulation of copy tapes derived from all these sources, and it is not likely to decrease in the future despite efforts of copyright owners, performers unions, and some sectors of the broadcasting and recording industry to restrict this activity. The U.S. copyright law (adopted in 1909 before sound recording was a significant factor) does not provide for performance copyright as distinct from copyright of musical content. This has created severe difficulties in terms of developing ground rules whereby educational institutions and sound archives can engage legitimately in nonprofit exchanges of tapes and copies of rare commercial recordings for educational and archival purposes. As of 1971 some institutions were providing copy tapes for scholarly or study purposes while others were restricting audition to their own premises. (The introduction of cassette-cartridge tape-recorder–playback machines, which can be combined with radio receivers and used in conjunction with high-speed cassette duplicating equipment, has made even more urgent the need for U.S. legislation and for international agreement regarding rights and fair use.)

ESTHETIC CONSEQUENCES. An immediately obvious consequence of recordings is the synthetic "perfect" performance, created not by the performer "in hot blood" but rather by skillful tape editing. When one adds to this the alterations of dynamics, timbre, balance, localization, and perspective illusion that can be produced via multitrack, multimicrophone stereo recording, it becomes clear that pristine sonic documentation of performance is likely to become something of a rarity. Another consequence is that effects called for by composers but impossible of achievement under concert-hall conditions can be realized on recordings; for example, the church bells in

Charles Ives's *From the Steeples and the Mountains* and the cannons and carillons in Tchaikovsky's *1812 Overture*. Indeed multitrack recording techniques as used by the pop and rock groups of the 1960s have brought in their train a whole series of compositions by Karlheinz Stockhausen, John Cage, and others realizable only in recorded form. The fact that magnetic tape was found in the late 1940s to be amenable to infinite refinements of editing, speed-pitch fluctuation, and timbre alteration by means of filtering and artificial reverberation led to the early "tape music" of Otto Luening and Vladimir Ussachevsky, the tape "sonic montage" episodes of Varèse's *Deserts*, the musique concrète of Pierre Schaeffer and Pierre Henry at the ORTF studio in Paris, and the work in Cologne of Eimert, Stockhausen, and others. A further fruitful development in this area at the beginning of the 70s was the commissioning by record companies of electronic works. Elektra Records in the U.S. has commissioned and recorded for its Nonesuch label works by Eric Salzman, Morton Subotnick, Charles Wuorinen (whose *Time's Encomium* won the 1970 Pulitzer Prize for music), and others.

The impact of noncommercial recording among professionals is enormous. Performers, for instance, no longer have to piece together a new score at the piano prior to giving a regional first performance or making a commercial recording. They see to it that the composer or publisher supplies them with a broadcast or concert tape or previous commercial disc. Furthermore "world premieres" for most listeners take place on discs and tape rather than in a concert hall. Beginning with the Stokowski-Philadelphia Orchestra recording of the Shostakovich *Symphony No. 5* in 1938, it has been recordings that have created public demand for live concert performance, not vice versa.

Finally the musical experience of the listening generation from 1950 on has become a truly ecumenical one. The sonic repertory on commercial discs since then has expanded to include not only art music from every corner of the globe but ethnic and folk music that encompass virtually every rhythmic, harmonic, and textural combination possible to humankind.

RECORDINGS AS DOCUMENTS; ARCHIVES OF RECORDED SOUND. Stravinsky, who is the major instance in a long line of 20th-century composers who have recorded their own works, has said that the phonograph record is the only reliable means for objective documentation of the composer's views on tempo,

phrasing, and dynamics. Other significant composers of concert music who have also performed their works include Béla Bartók, Leonard Bernstein, Mark Blitzstein, Pierre Boulez, Benjamin Britten, Carlos Chávez, Aaron Copland, Henry Cowell, Edward Elgar, George Gershwin, Howard Hanson, Hans Werner Henze, Paul Hindemith, Aram Khatchaturian, Olivier Messiaen, Darius Milhaud, Harry Partch, Francis Poulenc, Sergey Rachmaninov, Dmitri Shostakovich, Karlheinz Stockhausen, Richard Strauss, Virgil Thomson, Ralph Vaughan Williams, Heitor Villa-Lobos, and William Walton. There are even more instances in which composers have remained in a supervisory rather than in an executant capacity, although documentation on the part of commercial recording companies as to the extent of such composer supervision or performance approval is spotty. We know that Vaughan Williams supervised the 78-rpm recording of his *Tallis Fantasia* by the Boyd Neel String Orchestra as well as all the British Decca (London in the U.S.) recordings of his orchestral works as conducted by Adrian Boult. Shostakovich was present at the Paris recording under André Cluytens of his *Symphony No. 11* and at the Philadelphia Orchestra recordings under Ormandy of his *Cello Concerto No. 1* and *Symphony No. 1*. The latter work is an especially significant example in view of the various tempos for the outer movements espoused by different conductors since the first recording of the work under Stokowski in the early 1930s.

Recordings, like motion pictures, are 20th-century additions to the historical record of civilization. For this and other reasons they need to be located, preserved, and cataloged, and they need to be made available for audition. One ultimate goal would seem to be a computerized union catalog capable of instant worldwide access. Presently, however, holdings are scattered among commercial record companies, broadcasters, composers and performing rights organizations, music publishers, educational institutions, specialty shops catering to collectors of rare recordings, and private collectors. Attempts have been made to gather information on these holdings and their availability. In some of the European countries national sound archives exist as part either of the national broadcasting or library agency. In the U.S. the situation is less systematically handled. The Library of Congress in Washington has the greatest quantity of archival sound recordings but limited means for public access at present. The Rodgers and

Hammerstein Archives at the New York Public Library has the only general research collection with a full range of audition and reference services. There are also specialized university archives covering such areas as jazz, Latin American music, ethnic music, and oral history. Major archives are being developed at Stanford Univ. in Calif., at the Boston Public Library, and elsewhere, and in the 1970s such audition and research facilities can be expected to increase.

BIBL.: Bob Auger, "From the Sound of the Cylinder to the Sight and Sound of Video," *Records and Recording* (London, Oct 1970): 26–32; Robert Bauer, *The New Catalogue of Historical Records, 1898–1908*, 2nd ed. (London 1947); H. Courtney Bryson, *The Gramophone Record* (London 1935); Francis F. Clough and G. J. Cuming, *The World's Encyclopedia of Recorded Music* (London 1952; supplements, 1953, 1957); Charles Delaunay, *New Hot Discography; the Standard Dictionary of Recorded Jazz* ed. by Walter E. Schaap and George Avakian (New York 1948); Robert M. W. Dixon and John G. Swansea, *Blues and Gospel Records, 1902–1942* (Swansea, Wales, 1963); Robert E. Dolan, *Music in Modern Media* (New York 1967); Roland Gelatt, *The Fabulous Phonograph*, revised ed. (New York 1965); Victor Girard and Harold M. Barnes, *Vertical-cut Cylinders and Discs, a Catalogue of all "Hill-&-Dale" Recordings of Serious Worth Made and Issued Between 1897–1932* (London 1964); Jorgen G. Jepsen, *Jazz Records 1942–1967* (Holte, Denmark, c.1968); Allen Koenigsberg, *Edison Cylinder Records, 1889–1912, with an Illustrated History of the Phonograph* (New York 1969); Ray McKinley Lawless, *Folksingers and Folksong in America* (New York 1960); Julian M. Moses, *Collectors' Guide to American Recordings 1895–1925* (New York c.1949); Kurtz Myers, comp., *Record Ratings. The Music Library Association's Index of Record Reviews* (New York c.1956); Andrew G. Pickett, *Preservation and Storage of Sound Recordings* (Washington 1959); Oliver Read and Walter L. Welch, *From Tin Foil to Stereo* (Indianapolis 1959); Helen P. Roach, *Spoken Records*, 3rd ed. (Metuchen, N. J., 1970); Brian A. L. Rust, *Jazz Records A–Z, 1932–1942* (Hatch End, England, 196–?); Joel Tall, *Techniques of Magnetic Recording* (New York 1958); Howard M. Tremaine, *Audio Encyclopedia,* 2nd ed. (Indianapolis 1969). Also important are two record catalogs: *The Gramophone Long Playing Classical Record Catalogue* (Kenton, England, since 1954); *Schwann Long Playing Record Catalog* (Boston, since 1949).

David Hall

SEE ALSO Dance, Orchestration, Publishing; articles on individual countries.

Reda, Siegfried (b. Bochum, Germany, 27 July 1916; d. Mülheim, 13 Dec 1968), studied church music at the Dortmund Conservatory and the Church Music School in Berlin-Spandau (graduated 1941; composition with Ernst Pepping, Hugo Distler). From 1941 until his death he taught Protestant church music, harmony, and organ at the Folkwang Hochschule für Musik, Theater, und Tanz in Essen; from 1953 he was also church-music director of the Altstadtgemeinde at St. Peter's Church in Mülheim. He was one of the leaders in the renaissance of evangelical church music in Germany and was an authority on 17th- and 18th-century organ building and performance practices.

PRINCIPAL COMPOSITIONS (with publication dates; music published by Bärenreiter): *Die alten Epistellesungen*, music for the church year for chorus (1947); *Chorale Concertos Nos. 1–3* for organ: No. 1, "O wie selig seid ihr doch, ihr Frommen" (1947); No. 2, "Gottes Sohn ist kommen" (1947); No. 3, "Christ unser Herr zum Jordan kam" (1949); *Organ Concertos Nos. 1–3* (1947, 1947, 1948); *Die beiden Schächer* for tenor, double chorus (1948); *Die Weihnachtsgeschichte* for soloists, chorus (1949); *Leidensverkündigung und Heilung eines Blinden* for chorus (1951); *Te Deum laudamus* for double chorus, brass (1951); *Das Psalmbuch*, music for the church year for chorus (1951); *Marienbilder* for organ (1952); *Amor Dei* for soprano, chorus, organ; text by Hans Thoma (1952); *Ecce homo*, passion motet for chorus (1952); *Das Graduallied*, music for the church year for chorus (1952); *Die Ostergeschichte* for 2 sopranos, chorus (1963); *Das Evangelium auf den 4. Advent* for chorus (1959); *Organ Sonata* (1963); *Requiem* for soprano, baritone, chorus, orchestra (1963); *Laudamus te* for organ (1964); *Psalm 8*, "Herr unser Herrscher," for soprano, baritone, chorus, organ (1965).

PRINCIPAL WRITINGS: "Selbstbildnisse Schaffender Kirchenmusiker II: S. R.," *Musik und Kirche* (1947):81–85; "Ein Selbstzeugnis von S. R.," ibid. (1969):249–50.

BIBL.: Helmut Bornefeld, "S. R. zum Gedächtnis," *Württembergische Blätter für Kirchenmusik* 1969/1:5–8; Klaus Kirchberg, "S. R.," *Musica* (Cassel, Jan 1969):54–55; ——, "Zum Tode S. R. in Dezember 1968," *Musik und Gottesdienst* 1969/4:89–97; Willem Mudde, "In memoriam S. R.," *Musica sacra* (Hilversum) 1969/3:41–43; Klaus Martin Ziegler, "S. R.," *Musik und Kirche* (Jan 1969).

[prepared with the help of Oskar Hülcker]

SEE ALSO Liturgical Music: Christian.

Reed, H(erbert) Owen (b. Odessa, Mo., 17 June 1910), studied at the Univ. of Mo. (1929–33; theory, composition with James Quarles and Scott Goldthwaite), Louisiana State Univ. (1933–37; theory, composition with Helen Gunderson), the Eastman School (1937–39; composition with Howard Hanson,

Bernard Rogers; conducting with Paul White), and at Tanglewood (1942, composition with Bohuslav Martinů). He also studied privately with Roy Harris in 1947. He spent several months in Mexico during 1948–49 and 1960 studying folk music. He has taught theory and composition at Mich. State Univ. since 1939. PRINCIPAL COMPOSITIONS (published by Mills unless otherwise noted): *Piano Sonata* (1934, unpub.); *String Quartet* (1937, unpub.); *A Psalm of Praise* for soprano, 2 flutes, oboe, 2 clarinets, bassoon, horn (1937, unpub.) or chorus (1939, Fox); *The Passing of John Blackfeather* for low voice, piano; text by Merrick F. McCarthy (1945); *Scherzo* for clarinet, piano (1947); *3 Nationalities* for piano (1947); *Dusk* for low voice, piano; text by Tom Boggs (1948); *Wondrous Love* for tenor, wind quintet (1948, unpub.); *Mountain Meditation* for low voice, piano; text by Marian Cuthbertson (1948); *Cello Concerto* (1949, Southern-S); *La fiesta mexicana*, Mexican folk-song symphony for band (1949) or orchestra (1964); *Nocturne* for piano (published 1953 in *Panorama*, a collection of American piano music); *Symphonic Dance* for piano, woodwind quintet (1954); *Michigan Dream*, 2-act folk opera; libretto by John Jennings (1955, revised 1959); *Ripley Ferry* for women's voices, wind septet; text by McCarthy (1958); *Renascence* for band (1959); *Che-ba-kun-ah* [Road of Souls] for string quartet, band (1959); *Earth Trapped*, chamber opera for alto, 15 instruments, 2 dancers; libretto after Hartley Alexander (1960); *Overture for Strings* (1961, unpub.); *El muchacho* for piano (revised 1962; scored for 7 hand bells, 3 percussion, 1965); *A Tabernacle for the Sun*, oratorio for alto, men's speaking chorus, singing chorus, orchestra; libretto by McCarthy (1963); *The Turning Mind* for orchestra (1968).

PRINCIPAL WRITINGS: *A Workbook in the Fundamentals of Music* (New York 1947); *Basic Music* (New York 1954); *Basic Contrapuntal Technique* with Paul Harder (New York 1964); *Scoring for Percussion* with Joel T. Leach (Englewood Cliffs, N.J., 1969).

Regamey, Constantin (b. Kiev, 28 Jan 1907), studied Indology at the Univ. of Warsaw (graduated 1936) and at L'Ecole des Hautes Etudes in Paris (1934–35). He is self-taught in composition. During 1935–39 he lectured on Sanskrit at Warsaw Univ. Since 1946 he has been professor of linguistics at the Univ. of Fribourg and since 1949, professor of Slavic and Oriental languages at the Univ. of Lausanne. He was president of the League of Swiss Musicians during 1963–68. During 1937–39 he was editor-in-chief of the journal *Muzyka Polska* (Warsaw) and during 1954–62, of *Feuilles musicales* (Lausanne). He has written over 300 articles on music, esthetics, and musicology for European journals. Since the mid-1960s he has aimed at a synthesis of tonal, dodecaphonic, and other musics, including Indian.

PRINCIPAL COMPOSITIONS: *Chansons persanes* for baritone, orchestra; text from the Rubaiyat of Omar Khayyam (1942); *Quintet* for clarinet, bassoon, violin, cello, piano (1944, PWM); *Sonatine* for flute, piano (1945); *Variazioni e tema* for orchestra (1948, Mills); *String Quartet* (1948); *Musique pour cordes* (1953, Mills); *5 Etudes* for female voice, piano (1955, Impero); *5 Etudes* for female voice, orchestra (1956, Impero); *Poèmes de Jean Tardieu* for chorus of 20 soloists (1962, PWM); *Autographe* for chamber orchestra (1962–66, PWM); *4 x 5*, concerto for 5 quintets (1963, PWM); *Symphonie des incantations* for soprano, baritone, orchestra (1967); *Alpha* for tenor, orchestra (1970); *Don Robott*, opera (in progress).

PRINCIPAL WRITINGS: *Treść i forma w muzyce* [Content and Form in Music] (Warsaw 1933); *Musiques du vingtième siècle* (Lausanne-Paris 1966).

BIBL.: Edmond Appia, "C. R.," *Revue musicale suisse* (May 1951); Henri Gagnebin, "C. R.," in *40 Contemporary Swiss Composers* (Amriswil 1956):141–46; R. A. Moser, *Panorama de la musique contemporaine* (Geneva 1953); ——, *Aspects de la musique contemporaine* (Geneva 1957); Bogusław Schäffer, *Klasycy dodekafonii* [Classics of Dodecaphony] (Cracow 1961).

Reibel, Guy (b. Strasbourg, 19 July 1936), studied electronics at the Institut Supérieur d'Electronique du Nord in Lille (1956–60) and physics at the Univ. of Lille (1956–61). He studied composition and electroacoustics at the Paris Conservatory with Olivier Messiaen, Serge Nigg, and Pierre Schaeffer (1963–65). He has been an assistant for Pierre Schaeffer's classes at the Paris Conservatory since 1968 and has been head of the teaching and research section at the Group de Recherches Musicales at the French Radio-Television Network since 1969.

PRINCIPAL COMPOSITIONS: *Durboth* for soprano, brass, percussion, tape (1965, recorded by Erato); *Antinote* on 4-track tape (1967); *Mouvances* for 6 singers, each with microphones, 6 loudspeakers (1967); *Variations en étoile* for percussion ad lib., tape (1967, recorded by Philips); *3 Pièces de rumeurs* ("Echappée," "Bloc choral," "Continuo") for 5 vocal soloists, 2 choruses of soloists, 6 ensemble choruses of 500 voices each, 4-track tape (1968, recorded by Erato); *Vertiges* for prepared electric guitar, 4-track tape (1969); *Carnaval* for narrator, 3 amateur choruses, 3 conductors, tape (c.1970, recorded by Erato); *Musiques en liesse*, musical spectacle for 2 soloists, tape, projections, recordings of African, American, and Asian music (c.1970); *Jeu d'échanges* for 3 orchestras (c.1971, EFM).

PRINCIPAL WRITINGS: "Rapport entre la hauteur et la fondamental d'un son musical," written with H. Chiarucci for the 5th International Conference on Acoustics in Liège (1965); "La Mise en oeuvre du temps," *Revue de l'Ecole Centrale des Arts* (Paris, 1968); "Pouvoir des machines, pouvoirs de l'oreille," *Conférences des Journées d'Etude* (Paris, 1969). Reibel also prepared the recorded musical examples for Pierre Schaeffer's *Solfège de l'objet sonore* (Paris 1966).

Reich, Steve (b. New York, 3 Oct 1936), studied philosophy, especially Wittgenstein, at Cornell Univ. (1953–57, BA) and composition at the Juilliard School (1958–61). He also attended Mills College in Oakland, Calif. (1962–63, MA; composition with Luciano Berio, Darius Milhaud). During 1964–65 he worked with the San Francisco Tape Music Center as a composer-performer. Subsequently he established his own electronic studio in New York, where he now lives. Some of the recent influences on his thinking have been the books *Studies in African Music* by A. M. Jones and *Music in Bali* by Colin McPhee. However, he is not interested in exoticism or improvisation but in "music which works exclusively with gradual changes in time. . . . A musical process happening so gradually that listening to it resembles watching the minute hand of a watch—you perceive it moving after you stay with it a little while."

PRINCIPAL COMPOSITIONS: *Pitch Charts* for any number of any instruments (1963); *Music* for 3 or more pianos or piano, tape (1964); *It's Gonna Rain* on tape (1965, Columbia record MS 7265); *Come Out* on tape (1966, recorded by Odyssey); *Melodica* on tape (1966); *Piano Phase* for 2 pianos (1967); *Violin Phase* for violin, tape, or for 4 violins (1967); *My Name Is* for 3 or more tape recorders, performers, audience (1967); *Pendulum Music* for microphones, loudspeakers, amplifiers, performers (1968); *Pulse Music* for phase shifting pulse gate, an instrument invented by the composer (1968–69); *4 Organs* for 4 electric organs, maracas (1969); *Piano Store* for a store full of pianos (1969–); *Phase Patterns* for 4 electric organs (1970); *Drumming* for 4 pairs of tuned bongo drums, 3 marimbas, 3 glockenspiels, male and female voices (1971).

PRINCIPAL WRITINGS: "Music as a Gradual Process," *Anti-Illusion Catalog of the Whitney Museum* (New York 1969):2.

BIBL.: Michael Nyman, "S. R.," *Musical Times* (March 1971).

SEE ALSO Mixed Media, Performance, Rhythm.

Reiner, Karel (b. Žatec, Czechoslovakia, 27 June 1910), studied at the Faculty of Law in Prague (1928–33). He studied music at Charles Univ. and the Academy of Music (1934–35) and composition privately with Alois Hába (1929–30) and Josef Suk (1930–31). A pianist, he gave concerts of contemporary music in Europe (1931–38, 1945–47) and worked with E. F. Burian's avant-garde theater in Prague (1935–38). He was in charge of music for the record company ESTA in Prague (1938–39) and a coach at the Opera of the Fifth of May, Prague (1945–47). He has written over 700 articles in Czech and foreign journals and was editor of *Rytmus* (1935–38, 1945–47), music editor of the weekly *Kulturní politika* (1945–49) and of the newspaper *Svobodné Československo* (1945–47). He has been head of the music department of the Folk Art Center in Prague (1951–61) and chairman of the Committee of the Czech Music Fund (1964–70). In his early music he experimented with 12-tone and quarter-tone writing. He now writes in a free atonal style with non-repeating developments and variations of melodic ideas built from primarily dissonant intervals (2nds, 7ths, 9ths).

PRINCIPAL COMPOSITIONS: *9 Merry Improvisations* for piano (1928–29, Hudebni Matice); *Piano Sonata No. 1* (1931, Panton); *String Quartet No. 1* (1931, Supraphon); *Dodici* [Twelve] for wind quintet (1931–63, Panton); *Overture and Dance* for 2 pianos or orchestra (1935, SHV); *7 Compositions,* "Minda-Minda," for piano (1937, Supraphon); *Piano Sonata No. 2* (1942, SHV); *Sonata brevis* for cello, piano (1946, Supraphon); *Suite concertante* for winds, percussion (1947, ČHF); *Divertimento* for clarinet, harp, strings, percussion (1947, ČHF); *2 Compositions* for horn with piano (1948, Orbis) or orchestra (unpub.); *4 Compositions* for clarinet, piano (1954–56, Supraphon); *Double Bass Sonata* (1957, Panton); *Violin Sonata No. 2* (1959, Supraphon); *Butterflies Don't Live Here,* suite for orchestra (1959–60, Panton); *Little Suite* for 9 winds (1960, ČHF); *Symphony* (1960, Panton); *Piano Sonata No. 3* (1961, Supraphon); *6 Bagatelles* for trumpet, piano (1962, Supraphon); *2 Compositions* for oboe, harp (1962, Panton); *3 Preludes* for organ (1963, Panton); *4 Compositions* for clarinet (1963, ČHF); *6 Studies* for flute, piano (1964, ČHF); *Suite* for harp (1964, CHF); *Symphonic Overture* (1964, Panton); *Trio* for flute, bass clarinet, percussion (1964, Supraphon); *3 Compositions* for piano (1964–65, Panton); *Piano Trio* (1965, ČHF); *Suite* for bassoon, piano (wind orchestra), percussion (1965, Panton); *Music for 4 Clarinets* (1965–66, ČHF); *Concerto* for bass clarinet, piano (1966, Panton) or strings, percussion (unpub.); *Sketches* for piano, string quartet (1966–67, Panton); *3 Songs on Words by F. Th. Csokor* for low voice, piano (1967, Doblinger); *3 Concert Studies* for cymbal (1967, ČHF); *2 Compositions* for alto, saxophone, piano (1967, ČHF); *Suite concertante* for orchestra (1967, Supraphon); *Sonata concertante* for percussion (1967, Panton); *Prolegomena* for string quartet

(1968, ČHF); *4 Abbreviations* for 2 trumpets, horn, 2 trombones (1968, ČHF); *Loose Leaves* for clarinet, cello, piano (1969, ČHF).

PRINCIPAL WRITINGS: "Poučení z Orientu" [Experiences in the Orient], *Klíč* 2:186–88; "Neue Notationsweise im Zwölfton und Viertleton (24-ton) System," *Der Auftakt* 12/11–12:224–25; "Technika hry na čtvrttónovém klavíru" [The Technique of Playing on the Quarter-Tone Piano], *Klíč* 3:22–23; "Interpretace nethematické hudby" [The Interpretation of Nonthematic Music], *Klíč* 4:46–48; "Soudobá hudba česká" [Contemporary Czech Music], *Československá vlastivěda* (Prague 1935) 8:539–58; "Sukův význam pro moderní českou hudbu" [The Significance of Suk for Modern Czech Music], *Josef Suk* (Prague 1935): 423–27; "La musica contemporánea en Checoslovaquia," *Boletin latino-americano de música* (Montevideo) 3:311–34; "Exotická hudba" [Exotic Music] (printed under Alois Hába's name), *Dějiny světové hudby* ed. by J. Brandberger (Prague 1939):720–33; "Czech Music After the War," *Keynote* (London) 2/6:16–17; *Pěvecký soubor* [The Vocal Ensemble] (Prague 1953).

BIBL.: Dragotin Cvetko, "Iz sodobnega glasbenega sveta (Razgovor s českim komponistom Reinerjom)" [From the Contemporary Musical World (A Talk with the Czech Composer R.)], *Piramida, neodvisna revija. Maribor* 1/5:144–46; Josef Kotek, "K. R. Rozhovor vlastně jubilejní" [K. R. A Conversation before a Jubilee], *Hudební rozhledy* 13:524–26; Milan Kuna, "Zrání umělce současnosti. K tvůrčí cestě K. R." [The Development of a Contemporary Artist. K. R.'s Way as a Composer], *Hudební rozhledy* 15:97–102; Vladimír Lébl, "Pínová tvorba K. R." [The Songs of K. R.], *Hudební rozhledy* 8:917–19.

Religious Music, see Liturgical Music: Christian; Liturgical Music: Jewish

Renosto, Paolo (b. Florence, 10 Oct 1935), studied at the Florence Conservatory (1949–62; piano with Paolo Rio Nardi; composition with Paolo Fragapane, Luigi Dallapiccola, and Roberto Lupi), the Accadèmia Musicale Chigiana in Siena (summer 1956, 1957; film music with Francesco Lavagnino), and the Salzburg Mozarteum (summer 1969, conducting with Bruno Maderna). He is a professional pianist and conductor and a consulting musician for the Italian Television Network; he has written for films, the theater, and television. Some works since 1965 use aleatory processes. *Du Côté sensible*, which he regards as his "best defined and most personal work," is concerned especially with the structural use of sound textures.

PRINCIPAL COMPOSITIONS (published by Ricordi unless otherwise noted): *Dinamica 1* for solo C or alto flute (1961); *Differenze* for 15 winds and strings (1963, unpub.); *Dissolvenza* for oboe, E♭ or B♭ clarinet (alto saxophone), bass clarinet, horn, viola, cello, double bass, 2 percussionists (1964, unpub.); *Mixage* for C flute, alto flute, piano (1965); *Avant d'Ecrire* for viola, piano (1965); *Scops*, structures and improvisations for viola, orchestra (1965–66); *Du Côté sensible* for 11 solo strings (1966–67); *The Al(do)us Quartet* for string quartet or trio (1967); *Ar-loth* for one player on oboe, English horn, musette, or oboe d'amore (1967); *Players* for any instrument(s) (1969); *Forma op 7* for orchestra (1968–69); *Nacht* for 2 orchestras, or string orchestra, or women's voice, string orchestra (1969); *Nacht* for woman's voice (1969); *Per Marisa T, pianista* for piano (1970); *Andante amoroso*, theater event for 3 actors, woman's voice, piano, percussion; text by Aldo Rosselli (1970).

Reutter, Hermann (Hart) (b. Stuttgart, 17 June 1900), studied music privately, 1907–20 (piano, cello with Eugen Uhlig; voice with Emma Rürkbed-Hiller), and attended the State Academy of Music, Munich (1920–23, composition with Walter Courvoisier, piano with Franz Dorfmüller). He taught composition at the Music Academy in Stuttgart during 1932–36; was director of the Music Academy in Frankfurt am Main, 1936–45; taught composition and lieder interpretation at the Stuttgart Academy, 1952–56; and became director of the Stuttgart Academy, 1956–66. Since 1966 he has held master classes in lieder interpretation at the Academy in Munich. Reutter has often appeared in concert as a piano soloist and lieder accompanist. Hearing Bruno Walter's Munich performances of operas by Schreker and Pfitzner made a deep impression on him. He was also influenced by Bartók, Berg, and Stravinsky and was among the early friends of Hindemith. In program notes for a concert of Reutter's songs, Alfred Frankenstein remarked on the "free-ranging and intensely expressive declamatory line in the voice and highly elaborated, often dissonant, but always tonal parts for the piano."

PRINCIPAL COMPOSITIONS: Reutter has written about 200 lieder; in addition to these are the following works (published by Schott unless otherwise noted): *Piano Concertos Nos. 1–7* (1925, 1929, 1938, 1944, 1947, 1952, 1963); *Saul*, opera (1928); *Der grosse Kalender* for chorus (1930–32); *Dr. Johannes Faust*, opera (1934–36); *Die Kirmes von Delft*, ballet (1936); *Gesang des Deutschen* for chorus (1938); *Chorfantasie* for chorus (1939); *Odysseus*, opera (1940–42); *Concerto* for 2 pianos, orchestra (1949); *Notturno Montmartre*, ballet (1951); *Tanz-Variationen* for orchestra (1952); *Die Witwe von Ephesus*, opera (1953); *Die Brücke von San Luis Rey*, opera (1954); *Prozession* for cello, orchestra (1956); *Symphony* for string orchestra (1960); *Der Tod des Empedokles*, opera (1965).

BIBL.: Heinrich Lindlar, *H. R.: Werk und Wirken* (Mainz 1965).

Revueltas, Silvestre (b. Santiago, Papasquiaro, Mexico, 31 Dec 1899; d. Mexico City, 5 Oct 1940), began violin lessons at age eight in Colima. In 1913 he moved to Mexico City, where he studied with local teachers. He attended the Chicago Musical College, 1918–20 and 1922–24, during the latter period studying with Vaslav Kochansky and Ottakar Sevcik. He was active as a free-lance violinist and conductor until 1928, when Carlos Chávez, with whom he had appeared in violin-piano recitals, appointed him assistant conductor of the Orquesta Sinfónica de México (founded that year by Chávez). He remained with the orchestra until 1935. He also taught violin and chamber music at Mexico's National Conservatory.

Revueltas had begun composing in 1917, following in his early works an impressionistic approach (*Elegía*, 1928). He taught himself mainly by conducting contemporary orchestral music and by listening to his own scores. Although he had less technical skill than Chávez (but perhaps because of this), he achieved a more picturesque portrayal of the Mexican character. Early in his career he discovered that the basso-ostinato device fitted the repetitive patterns of traditional Indian music, and he used it frequently. His good, sometimes caustic humor also adapted itself to Mexican traits. Beginning with *Esquinas* (1930) he began exploring atonalism and the structural use of instrumental tone coloring. In *Planos* (1934) the tonic is hidden among countless dissonances; clusters, pedals, and ostinato rhythms all appear here, and the folk element is hardly detectable.

PRINCIPAL COMPOSITIONS (published by Southern unless otherwise noted): *Cuauhnáhuac*, symphonic poem (1930, unpub.); *Esquinas*, symphonic poem (1930); *String Quartets Nos. 1–3*: No. 1 (1930); No. 2, "Magueyes" (1931); No. 3, "Musica de feria" (1932); *Dúo para pato y canario* for voice, piano or orchestra (1931); *Ranas* for voice, piano (1931); *El tecolote* for voice, piano or orchestra (1931); *3 Piezas* for violin, piano (1932); *Colorines*, symphonic poem for chamber orchestra (1932); *8 x Radio* for chamber orchestra (1933); *Janitzio*, symphonic poem (1933); *El renacuajo paseador*, ballet (1933–35); *Planos*, "danza geométrica" for

chamber orchestra (1934); *Caminos*, symphonic poem (1934–36); *Redes*, film score for chamber orchestra (1935); *Homenaje a García-Lorca* for chamber orchestra (1935–36); *2 Songs* for voice, various instruments; text by Nicolás Guillén (1937); *7 Songs* for voice, piano; text by García-Lorca (1938, Schirmer-G); *Sensemayá*, symphonic poem on an Indian snake-killing song (1938); *Música para charlar*, concert arrangement of the film scores "El Indio" and "Ferrocarriles de Baja California" (1938); *La coronela*, unfinished ballet (1939, completed by Blas Galindo and orchestrated by Candelario Huizar); *La noche de los Mayas*, film score (1939, unpub.); *Los de abajo*, film score (1939, unpub.); *Bajo el signo de la muerte*, film score (1939, unpub.). Complete list: *Composers of the Americas* 1: 73–76.

PRINCIPAL WRITINGS: *Cartas íntimas y escritos de S. R.* ed. by José Revueltas (Mexico City 1966). Revueltas also wrote many articles for the newspapers *El universal* and *Excelsior* and program notes for the Orquesta Sinfónica de México.

BIBL.: Otto Mayer-Serra, *Música y músicos de Latinoamerica* (Mexico City 1947); —— "S. R. and Music Nationalism in Mexico," *Musical Quarterly* (April 1941); Adolfo Salazar, *La música moderna* (Buenos Aires 1944).

Esperanza Pulido

SEE ALSO Mexico.

Reynolds, Roger (Lee) (b. Detroit, 18 July 1934), studied at the Univ. of Mich. (1952–61; composition with Ross Lee Finney, Roberto Gerhard) and at Tanglewood (1961, composition with Gerhard). He was a cofounder of the ONCE Group in Ann Arbor, Mich., and was associated with it during 1959–62. He worked at the Westdeutscher Rundfunk Electronic Music Studio in Cologne during 1962–63. In 1964 he coproduced concerts at the Centre de Musique in Paris, and during 1967–69 he organized the Cross Talk concerts, events, and festivals of Japanese and American music in Tokyo. He has taught at the Univ. of Calif. at San Diego since 1969. His music has been influenced by the work of Charles Ives and by his contacts with John Cage and Edgard Varèse.

PRINCIPAL COMPOSITIONS (published by Peters unless otherwise noted): *The Emperor of Ice Cream* for 8 vocal soloists, piano, percussion, double bass, staging (1962); *Fantasy for Pianist* (1963–64); *Gathering* for wind quintet (1964); *Quick Are the Mouths of Earth* for oboe, 3 flutes/piccolos, 3 cellos, trumpet, trombone, bass trombone, 2 percussionists, piano (1964–65); *Masks* for chorus, orchestra (1965); *Blind Men* for chorus, 3 trumpets, 2 trombones, bass trombone, tuba, 2 percussionists, piano (1966); *Threshold* for divided orchestra (1967); *Ping* for flute, piano, harmonium, bowed cymbal, tamtam, film, slides, tape, electronic equipment (1968,

CPE); *Traces* for piano solo, cello, flute, tape, electronic equipment (1968–69); *Again* for 2 flutes, 2 sopranos, 2 trombones, 2 double basses, 2 percussionists, amplification, 4-channel tape (1970, unpub.); *I/O* for 9 women's voices, 9 male mimes, 2 flutes, clarinet, projections, electronic equipment (1971, unpub.).

PRINCIPAL WRITINGS: "Indeterminacy, Some Considerations," *Perspectives* 4/1:136–40; "Happenings: Japan and Elsewhere," *Arts in Society* (Univ. of Wisc., fall 1968); "It (')s Time," *Electronic Music Review* 7; "John Cage: An Interview with R. R.," in *Contemporary Composers on Contemporary Music* ed. by B. Childs and E. Schwartz, (New York 1967):335–48.

BIBL.: Gilbert Chase, "The Scene in the '60s," *America's Music* (New York 1968); H. Wiley Hitchcock, "Current Chronicle," *Musical Quarterly* 48:247–48 and 51:539–40.

SEE ALSO Instrumental and Vocal Resources, United States.

Rhodes, Phillip (b. Forest City, N.C., 6 June 1940), studied at Duke Univ. (1958–62; composition, theory with Iain Hamilton) and at Yale Univ. (1963–66; composition with Donald Martino, Mel Powell; 20th-century theory with Gunther Schuller, George Perle). He was composer-in-residence for the public schools in Cicero-Berwyn, Ill., during 1966–68 and composer-in-residence for the city of Louisville, Ky., during 1969–71. He has taught at Amherst College (1968–69) and at the Univ. of Louisville (1969–71).

PRINCIPAL COMPOSITIONS: *4 Movements for Chamber Orchestra* (1962, UM); *3 Scenes* for voice, piano (1965, E-V); *3 Pieces* for cello (1966, Peters); *Kyrie* for women's chorus (1966, Peters); *Remembrance* for concert band (1966–67, CFE); *3 Pieces* for band (1967, Colombo); *Duo* for violin, cello (1968, CFE); *Autumn Setting* for soprano, string quartet (1969, CFE); *The Lament of Michal* for soprano, orchestra (1970, Peters).

PRINCIPAL WRITINGS: *Stravinsky's Progress Towards the 12-Tone System* (diss., Yale Univ., 1966).

BIBL.: *1969 Tanglewood Festival of Contemporary Music Report* (Chicago 1970); Robert Glidden, "Three Pieces for Band," *The National Band Association Journal* (Feb 1969):12; J. F. Goossen, "Current Chronicle," *Musical Quarterly* 50:519–20; F. W. Woolsey, "Occupation: Composer," *The Courier-Journal and Louisville Times Sunday Magazine* (29 March 1970):6–12.

Rhythm. Simultaneously with the dissolution of functional tonality in the late 19th and early 20th centuries came the dissolution of conventional rhythmic organization in the works of some composers. Just as changes in the organization of pitches reduced the predictability of harmonic and melodic progressions, so increasing irregularities renewed the rhythmic life of music by increasing the element of rhythmic surprise. New approaches to rhythmic organization have developed within two general contexts: 1) *metrical* organization, in which irregular groupings of short "counting" units were used; 2) *nonmetrical* organization, in which there is no perceptible unit of measurement and no tempo in the traditional sense (some writers prefer not to call nonmetrical organization rhythm but rather *duration* or *time*).

METRICAL RHYTHM. Most music in the first half of the century was essentially metrical; the differences in rhythmic styles depended upon the basic accent structure and the manner in which it was revealed (by means of duration and intensity patterns affirming and contradicting the basic accent structure). Thus in the music of Debussy the metrical structure is often veiled by subtle accentual contradictions, while in Schoenberg's music the contradictions tend to be more forceful. During Schoenberg's early atonal period (c. 1908–16), his rhythmic style was considerably more complex and less clearly metrical than in his previous and subsequent periods. His frequently changing tempos, greater use of changing time signatures, and tendency to use bar lines seemingly as a matter of convenience (without rhythmic significance) are evidences of the complexity of his rhythmic conception. When listening to Schoenberg's music of this period, the listener's attention is often drawn to a momentary metrical structure, only to be diverted by a constantly changing complex of subbeat units that tend to obscure the beat or by such a varied distribution of dynamic accents and durational patterns that there is little or no clarity of structure at the beatgroup level. During the same period, Stravinsky's music reveals a strikingly different rhythmic style in which the listener's attention is drawn to a clearly regular succession of subbeat units and to strong accents clearly defining irregular beats and sometimes irregular groups of beats. This style emerged gradually in *The Firebird*, *Petrouchka*, and *Le Sacre du printemps*, where it reached its climax in the "Danse sacrale." Stravinsky used frequently changing time signatures in this period, and the musical structures sometimes imply that he intended a traditional 19th-century interpretation of the measure as an abstract metrical unit. Frequently, however, such an interpretation is possible only for the score reader or the listener observing a conductor. Irregular groupings of regular units (as in types II–IV in the accompanying table) are found not only in most of Stravinsky's music but in Bartók and Hindemith as well and have become a part of the tradition of 20th-century music.

The technical procedures for the new rhythmic styles of the first half of this century are closely related to those of the 19th. Brahms and others had used a wide variety of syncopations, hemiolas, and temporary changes of meter without changing time signatures, while Mussorgsky and others had used changing time signatures for rhythmic irregularities; these procedures were all continued and intensified. On rare occasions in the 19th century and even more rarely in the 18th, different time signatures were simultaneously used to clarify polymetrical structures; the latter became increasingly prominent in the early 20th century, either with or without simultaneous time signatures.

The simplest type of metrical organization is found in music of the 18th and 19th centuries. The measures of this music were interpreted by 19th-century theorists as abstract skeletons of metrical weights (e.g., 4/4: 1″, 2, 3′, 4). Most rhythm in the music of that period may be termed *divisive* or *multiplicative*, as it is based on the systematic division or multiplication of a standard unit of time. Although some 20th-century composers have continued to use classic-romantic rhythmic style and its system of notation, irregular structures have become common, as has the tendency to use time signatures and bar lines without apparent aural significance. Twentieth-century writers about music often use the term *meter* to mean notated measures and their time signatures, regardless of whether the sounds and silences may be perceived in groups corresponding to the measure lengths; thus such terms as *changing meters*, *mixed meters*, *multimeters*, and *polymeters* usually mean either changing or simultaneous time signatures. Such complex "meters" exist for the score reader and possibly condition the manner of performance, but they may or may not be apparent to the listener. Thus in 20th-century music bar lines and time signatures are less reliable indications of perceived rhythmic structure than they were in the classic-romantic period; nevertheless, they sometimes correspond to perceived rhythmic structure.

In metrical rhythm the listener perceives one or more levels of regularity. Three of the possible levels of perceptible regularity are those of the beat, the subbeat or background,

and the group of beats. The beat level is that of the succession of accents (points of special attention) within the rhythmic flow that occur at intervals of time comparable to those designated by the beats of a conductor's hand. In 20th-century music, beats are regular or irregular, i.e., they occur at equal or unequal intervals of time; metrical rhythm at the beat level means that the beats recur regularly. The beat level is the most fundamental of the three in the sense that the listener feels the beat with greatest immediacy; even the most casual listener might tap his foot to the beat. At the level of the subbeat, the sounds occur at shorter intervals of time than at the beat level; the listener perceives them as a background or "lower stratum" of events; the subbeats are too fast for convenient muscular response, but when regular they are important as counting units for rhythm with irregular beats. When a succession of accents occurs in which the accents are farther apart than the individual beats, the group level of rhythmic structure comes into play. Groups may be either equal or unequal in duration; thus there may be either a regular (metrical) or an irregular rhythmic organization at the group level. Groups are often comparable in duration to measures and are sometimes so notated.

An assumption basic to the perception of metrical rhythm is that the listener will expect and actually perceive a regular pattern of accentuation that has been clearly established by sounds and silences, despite interruptions by unexpected rests, long notes, and dynamic accents, unless prolonged interruption or contradiction forces a change in the perceived pattern. Therefore the basic accent structure of a passage of music is an abstraction drawn from the organization of the sounds and silences and from the subjective continuation which they create.

Six types of metrical rhythm frequently employed in 20th-century music are illustrated in the accompanying table; the basic accent structures are drawn from specific musical examples. It should not be assumed, however, that the movements from which these examples are drawn use only the type illustrated; several types are sometimes employed in successive passages of a given composition, one subtly blending into another. (In the table, G = group level; B = beat level, S = subbeat level; R = regular, I = irregular, and A = absence of clear accent structure. The dots represent the basic accent structure; the curved lines represent groupings of subbeats into beats and of beats into groups of beats.)

METRICAL RHYTHM: SOME BASIC ACCENT STRUCTURES

TYPES

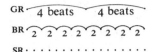

I Schoenberg, *String Quartet No. 3*, fourth movement, beginning

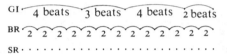

II Bartók, *String Quartet No. 5*, third movement, beginning

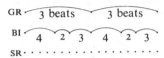

III Stravinsky, *Dumbarton Oaks Concerto*, first movement, rehearsal No. 2

GI 2 beats 3 beats 2 beats
BI 3 2 3 2 2 3 2
SR · · · · · · · · · · · · · · · · ·

IV Copland, *Short Symphony*, third movement, rehearsal No. 34

GA
BI 2 3 5 8 4 3 3 3
SR ·

V Blacher, *Ornamente No. 5*, beginning

VI Stravinsky, *L'Histoire du soldat*, "Petit concert," rehearsal No. 20

TYPE I is metrical at all levels and thus is divisive, as is most music of the classic-romantic period; this example is notated with a 4/4 signature. This is essentially a conservative type, but it is sometimes used in a complicated way with syncopations and interruptions of the basic structure; it forms the basis of popular music, jazz, and rock. TYPE II, with its regular grouping of irregular beats, is often used with irregular time signatures (5/8, 7/8, etc.); for this example the signature is $\frac{4 + 2 + 3}{8}$. This is *additive* rhythm, as the unequal beats are added together to form the groups that correspond in length to the measures. The example is metrical at the sub-beat and group levels. This type has become prominent in the 20th century, particularly among composers influenced by East European folk music. TYPE III is metrical at the two lower levels but irregular at the highest level, where there are groups of 4, 3, 4, and 2 beats. The composer represents the accent structure by changing time signatures: 4/4, 3/4, 4/4, 2/4. TYPE IV is metrical only at the lowest level. At the higher levels the accents form irregular beats and groups that are represented in the notation by changing time signatures: 5/8, 7/8, 5/8. TYPE V differs from TYPE IV only in the absence of a clear accent structure at the group level. (Stravinsky's "Danse sacrale" from *Le Sacre* fluctuates between TYPES IV and V.) In the Blacher composition, a higher, formal level of regularity is intended, however, and the composer reveals the extent of the formal group and its intended subdivision at the beginning of the composition: "2 3 5 13 8 5 3 ♪ " (Blacher uses the term *variable meters* for his rhythmic organization). The entire composition consists of repetitions of this pattern, and bar lines clarify the intended groupings. TYPE VI (polymetrical structure) simultaneously employs two or more different structures of regular accentuation. The level of the subbeat is the same for all four structures of this example; structures *b*, *c*, and *d* are entirely metrical (*c* exists only at the beat level), while structure *a* is irregular at the beat level and metrical only at the group level. The changing time signatures of this example relate to structure *a*: 3/4, 3/8, 3/4, 3/8. While the listener could easily perceive each metrical structure independently, the total ensemble of structures is difficult to grasp; his attention might follow only one of the structures or might shift from one to another. There is much music (Webern for instance) that seems to be on the borderline between types. The classification of such borderline rhythm depends upon the listener's ability to retain, subjectively, a regular accentuation.

The rhythm of jazz and rock is characteristically metrical at all levels of organization, and when notated it typically employs *alla breve* or 4/4 time signatures. The history of jazz shows a growing increase of rhythmic complexity in both the rhythm-section and the solo styles. In early New Orleans jazz the rhythm section tended to stress the first and third beats of four-beat groups and placed strong syncopated accents on beats two and four; in swing of the 1930s it tended to give the four beats more nearly equal stress; and in bop, cool, and "modern" jazz styles of the 1940s and 50s, and in rock of the 60s, the rhythm section often complicated the basic metrical structure by playing extremely complex beat subdivisions and syncopations, together with momentary polymetrical patterns. Jazz solo styles of such early performers as Jelly Roll Morton, Bix Biederbecke, and Louis Armstrong (in his early period), tend to use relatively few notes, and these clearly confirm the beat, despite the tendency to play slightly ahead or behind it. In performances during the 1930s of such men as Coleman Hawkins and Benny Goodman, jazz solos tended to use more notes than previously, but the beat was still strongly confirmed; in the 1940s, the music of Charlie Parker and Dizzy Gillespie is striking for its still greater number of notes (especially in quick tempos), irregular phrasing, and momentary groupings in conflict with the basic accent structure (producing polymetrical rhythm). Among the "modern" jazz and rock tendencies are the occasional use of traditional 6/8 meter and of irregular structures such as those identified with 5/8 and 5/4 time signatures.

NONMETRICAL RHYTHM. The second 20th-century rhythmic tendency, toward nonmetrical rhythm, is the more radical departure from past music. It begins musically at the point where fluctuating tempo, "metrical modulation" (E. Carter), "added values" (O. Messiaen), and "irrational" or "artificial" divisions of a notated measure or a theoretical counting unit totally obscure the perception of measurement. Nonmetrical rhythm is particularly common in electronic music and in music by John Cage and others that is conceived as "process," as nonstructured, random, or indeterminate activity.

The use of nonmetrical rhythm has roots in the 19th century. In parts of Wagner's *Tristan*, for example, harmonic and melodic ambiguity are sometimes combined with an elasticity of the conducted tempo to produce rhythm without a perceptible measuring unit. As early as 1907 Busoni affirmed the musical value of indeterminate duration when he said that the rest and the fermata most nearly approach the essential nature of music and that "the tense silence between two movements, in itself music," is more "elastic" than sound (*Sketch of a New Esthetic*: 23) (he seems to affirm the value of nonmetrical rhythm in recent music that is created by few sounds and much silence). An extremely active texture may also create nonmetrical rhythm; the roots of the more active style can be found in some of Schoenberg's early works (parts of *Pierrot lunaire*, 1912).

In the 1930s and 40s Messiaen began to develop a distinctive rhythmic style based on procedures set forth in his *Technique de mon langage musical* (1944). In that work he characterized his style as a refinement of that used by Stravinsky in *Le Sacre*, as it employs irregular groupings of short subbeat units; but here the similarity ceases in many of his works, for in Messiaen the unit is often so short and so seldom revealed to the listener as a clear measuring unit that the rhythmic organization sounds nonmetrical. Messiaen called this style "ametrical music"; among the rhythmic techniques explained in his treatise are the "added value," "augmented or diminished rhythms," "retrograde" and "nonretrogradable" rhythms, and "polyrhythm and rhythmic pedals." When his music employing these techniques is not nonmetrical in perception, it tends to fall within TYPES III–VI above.

Since the late 1940s nonmetrical rhythm has become increasingly prominent, particularly in serially organized works such as Milton Babbitt's *Composition for 12 Instruments* (1948), Messiaen's *Mode de valeurs et d'intensités* (1949–50), and Pierre Boulez's *Structures I* (1951–52), as well as in aleatory and electronic music. The rhythm of a work like *Structures* often seems so free as to be virtually indeterminate, despite the highly organized procedures employed: "Seen at close quarters, it is the factor of determinism, regularity, that stands out; but seen from a distance, the structure, being the result of many separate regularities, is seen to be something highly variable and chancy, comparable to the way the network of neon lights flashes on and off in a main street; the individual lamps are indeed exactly controlled by a mechanism, but as the separate lights flash on and off, they combine to form a statistical complex" (Ligeti:61; see bibl.). The nonmetrical rhythm of such music remains problematical for many listeners and musicians; Stravinsky, for example, preferred a sense of measured motion in music, and he considered works in which this is not made clear to be essentially "static": "Time . . . is a physical measure to me, and in music I must feel a physical here and there and not only a now, which is to say, movement from and toward. I do not always feel this sense of movement or location in, say, Boulez' *Structures* or those fascinating score-plans by Stockhausen . . ., and though every element in those pieces may be organized to engender motion, the result often seems to me like the essence of the static. . . ." (*Dialogues and a Diary*: 52).

Howard E. Smither

NONMETRICAL RHYTHM SINCE 1950. In Western music notated rhythms are usually expressed in terms of rational values, however complex the combinations may be; irrational or unmeasured values have been treated as aberrations, generally introduced spontaneously or by design for expressive purposes. The idea that an event may have its own duration and rhythm, not expressible in terms of some other yardstick-event, is absent from most Western music theory, which has concentrated on interpreting durations as multiples or fractions of real numbers (in this respect rhythmic theory has mirrored harmonic theory). A significant change has taken place in the last two decades in the understanding of musical rhythm, both through the increased use of technology to measure and control durations and through deliberate uncertainty in the measurement of time, as expressed in chance composition and collective improvisation. Consequently many composers are now interested in situations in which a perceivable meter is avoided. Periodic events, when present, are concealed, broken up, combined with one another in complex structures or made to change meters and tempos in such a way that they are but dimly perceived. The qualities of randomness and aperiodicity are prevalent characteristics of much recent music, which often appears to the casual listener to have no meter at all.

Two major influences, that of Webern and serialism on the one hand and of Asian music on the other, have provoked these changes. The application of serial techniques to the parameter of duration has led to increasing rationalization and complexity in the area of notated instrumental music. This development can best be seen in works by Karlheinz Stockhausen and John Cage of the early 1950s, as well as in music by Elliott Carter and Iannis Xenakis in the 60s. In addition the possibilities of precise realization afforded by electronics have encouraged composers to venture still further in the direction of the complex, especially in the last few years when they have had access to computers. On the other hand, some of the same composers who were responsible for introducing rhythms of unprecedented complexity into notated and tape music have also led the way in exploring a contrary direction, that of simplicity, chance, intuition, and spontaneous gesture, free of rational and conscious control.

Earle Brown, Cage, Morton Feldman, and Christian Wolff were among the first composers to introduce systems of rhythmic notation that departed from the traditional Western notation in meters. In early graphic compositions by Brown, such as *25 Pages* (1953) and *4 Systems*, events are distributed freely on the page and their duration, tempo, and even sequence are left to the interpreter. In Cage's *Music of Changes* (1951) durations and tempos are precisely notated, but the former are often expressed in terms of complex fractions of beats and the latter are subject to constant fluctuations in the form of retards and accelerandos. Meter thus becomes a highly subjective affair that influences the interpreter's activity but may not be evident to the listener. This technique was adopted, in a somewhat simpler form, by Stockhausen in his *Klavierstück VI* (1953). In other works by Cage in the 50s, such as *Music for Piano*, notes were placed wherever imperfections appeared on transparent paper or were chosen though other operations designed as alternatives to methods of composition dominated by tradition and taste. In these cases the decisions concerning the interpretation of tempo, duration, etc.—whether to apply some strict standard such as measuring distances and making inches equivalent to seconds, or to allow temporal intervals to be governed by the movement of the eye or some other criterion—were again left to the interpreter. In the *Concert for Piano and Orchestra* (1957–58) and in *Atlas Eclipticalis* (1961–62), a system of time keeping was devised in which a conductor describes a full circle with his outstretched arm, like the hand of a clock, moving faster or slower according to a part he prepares for himself; in the performers' parts, one system on a page is equivalent to one full revolution, and events are executed when the conductor's arm appears to have reached the appropriate point on the "clock." In most of Morton Feldman's music from the mid-50s on, durations are notated in nonmetrical form; in the few cases where meters occur the music is liberally sprinkled with fermatas and other remnants of the romantic tradition. Although rhythm for Feldman is not one of the essentials requiring precise notation (for him it belongs to oral rather than written tradition), anyone who has heard two different performances of a piece of his knows that his music retains a characteristic rhythmic identity. In certain compositions, such as those for two and four pianos in which the same material is read by several performers simultaneously but at freely varying speeds, interesting and apparently very complex rhythmic structures arise as a result of arbitrary juxtapositions. In most of Christian Wolff's music of the 50s, rhythms of single events and complexes of events are usually precisely defined. With *Duo for Pianists 2* (1958) he introduced a new concept of order by arranging the composed, more or less precisely notated material in fragments of greater or lesser duration, whose occurrence depended upon the hearing of cues, or trigger-events, present in the notated music but themselves contingent upon unpredictable combinations of events. In this he was undoubtedly influenced by Stockhausen's *Klavierstück XI* (1956) where, however, the contingency of events is limited by the implicit intention that each "version" be prepared in advance of the performance. Wolff also introduced the concept of "zero tempo" ($\rfloor$ = 0), interesting in that, within the rational framework of musical notation, the idea of tempo was abolished. Around 1960 he ceased to notate his music in terms of beats, seconds, or any standard relevant to traditional notions of meter and devised a simple method of notating durations as "short," "long," or dependent on unforeseeable events. In his recent improvisational pieces he has pursued this tendency still further. In the score for *Edges* (1968) graphic symbols are scattered around the page; they define extreme limits of multiple fields in which the performer "wanders," fixing his attention upon one or more parameters as the spirit moves him.

In Europe a surge of interest in experimental forms of notation in the late 50s and early 60s was instrumental in liberating the minds of many composers from the limitations imposed by traditional metric systems. Mauricio Kagel employed radically new methods of graphic notation in *Transición I* (1958–60)—also employed by Stockhausen in *Zyklus* (1959) and Sylvano Bussotti in *5 Pieces for David Tudor* (1959). In *Autumn '60* Cornelius Cardew

devised a system in which relatively conventional rhythmic notation was employed to determine whether a note was to be played on, just before, just after a beat, or between two beats given by a conductor, but avoiding reference to a regular or rational pulse. Dieter Schnebel, in *reactions* for soloist and audience (1960–61), was perhaps the first composer to systematically explore situations in which characteristic rhythms arise from spontaneous feedback generated by audience responses, audible or not, to indeterminate actions of a theatrical nature initiated by a performer. In the early 60s the Italian composer Giuseppe Chiari began to notate situations in which rhythm was determined by natural and spontaneous physical gesture, independent of rational order. Many of Chiari's notated compositions (from which counterpoint or simultaneous multiple ordering is excluded) have the character of lists or catalogs of seemingly unrelated events, sometimes of an acoustical, sometimes of a visual nature, in which each gesture, such as the whistling of a tune or the reading of a newspaper text, retains the natural rhythms it might have in a nonart, real-life situation. An example of this sort of "gestural" rhythm can be found in his *Strimpellare* (1966), in which a number of performers play on or with a random assortment of instruments in a deliberately absentminded fashion or concentratedly as if they had never touched the instruments before.

Around 1960 the influence of improvisational concepts as practiced in jazz and in the theater, as well as Asian ideas of time, began to be felt. Most of these influences were transmitted (sometimes indirectly via literature, visual art, or groups like the Living Theater) through John Cage. One of the most significant effects of such influence was the abandonment of rhythmic notation altogether or the use of simplified notation to express concepts that could be retained in the mind without reference to a score. Freed from rationally ordered time, the performer could now direct his undivided attention to the phenomenon of rhythm in an improvisational situation. Such freedom was, and still is, entirely new to the classically schooled Western musician. It is also quite different from the freedom familiar to musicians of Asian, African, jazz, or other improvising traditions, because it represents an attempt, totally modern in its anarchic premise, to create music out of nothing, beginning with a *tabula rasa* uncluttered by any limitations. Of the many examples of situations where rhythm has been "conceptualized" for application to pure improvisation (i.e., understood as an order that changes with the interpretation of each moment rather than as a structure standing within, yet withstanding time), I will cite one, my own *Ivan's piece* (1967). Here each performer in a group produces only one sound throughout and is instructed to focus his attention on the variations in amplitude of the total sound, determining entrances, exits, and changes of intensity with the intent of maintaining this composite sound, lending or withdrawing support proportionately as the general level falls or rises. Rhythm in this case becomes a non-rational process, comparable perhaps to automatic writing, a physical action that depends on what one hears or imagines one hears.

Another approach to the question of rhythm was introduced in 1960 in a series of compositions by La Monte Young characterized by an extreme simplicity with regard to informational content. An example is *Composition 1960 #7*, which consists of a perfect fifth, B and F♯, "to be held for a long time." During the following decade a style of music-making grew up in the U.S. whose most prominent exponents—Terry Riley, Steve Reich, and Philip Glass—have all been influenced to some extent by Young. They share a taste for qualities suggestive of Asian and other non-Western traditions: simplicity of material; a tendency to long durations, sometimes containing periodic repetitive figures; and the maintenance of a steady drone or pulse. One of the more interesting features of this "pulse music," as it is sometimes called, is that it provides the practiced listener with the opportunity to make his own rhythms. The ear, normally a relatively passive receiver of complex and constantly changing sensory data, is left alone in this music to focus on one or another detail that might pass unnoticed in other situations. This same object of involving the listener as an active rather than passive link in the communication process, thus enabling him to become conscious of a higher, relative form of rhythm which is in some way the product of a collective mind, has been pursued with the most varied means. One of these is to confront the listener with a barrage of complex information, forcing him to roam freely, in his own way, amidst a jungle of data, as in Cage's and Hiller's *HPSCHD* (1967–69); another has been to involve the listener directly in the process of sound production, as in Cage's *Musicircus* and in *Sound Pool* of the Musica Elettronica Viva group.

PROSPECTS. The process of expanding rhythmic consciousness has only begun—both outwardly toward greater knowledge of and control over the observable orderliness in the physical universe and inwardly toward greater understanding of the intuitive functions of perception and imagination. The frequency at which fluctuations in atmospheric pressure begin to be perceived as distinct pulses is around 20 hz. From there down to 1/6 hz. is the range within which most people are able to perceive and to execute fairly periodic rhythms; some Asian musicians are able to execute regular periods of a minute and more with precision. It is within this limited frequency band that it is usual to speak of musical rhythm. The concept of rhythm is, however, potentially extendable to astral, biological, and molecular phenomena that occur over a much broader frequency range not yet accessible to the unaided senses, although perhaps in some way to the imagination. It is reasonable to expect that some major breakthroughs in the understanding of many still obscure aspects of the phenomenon of rhythm may be achieved in the near future in the wake of new scientific and technological developments. Serious work has already been done by three American composers, Alvin Lucier, Richard Teitelbaum, and David Rosenboom, in brain waves and their controlled use in musical contexts. Technology may enable us to become aware of other elementary phenomena of this kind which have until now been ignored in Western music.

Frederic Rzewski

BIBL.: Milton Babbitt, "Twelve-Tone Rhythmic Structure and the Electronic Medium," *Perspectives* 1/1:49–79; Henri Bergson, *Introduction to Metaphysics*, trans. by T. E. Hulme (New York 1912); Boris Blacher, "Über variable Metrik," *Österreichische Musikzeitschrift* 6:219–22; Ferruccio Busoni, *Sketch of a New Esthetic of Music*, trans. by T. Baker (New York 1911); John Cage, *Silence* (Middletown, Conn., 1961); Elliott Carter, "The Rhythmic Basis of American Music," *Score* 12:27; Grosvenor W. Cooper and Leonard B. Meyer, *The Rhythmic Structure of Music* (Chicago 1960); Aaron Copland, *Copland on Music* (New York 1960); Paul Creston, *Principles of Rhythm* (New York 1964); Arnold Elston, "Some Rhythmic Practices in Contemporary Music," *Musical Quarterly* 42:318–29; Robert Erickson, "Time Relations," *Journal of Music Theory* 7:174–92; Philip Friedheim, "Rhythmic Structure in Schoenberg's Atonal Compositions," *Journal of the American Musicological Society* 19:59–72; Richard F. Goldman, "Current Chronicle" (a review of Elliott Carter's *Cello Sonata*), *Musical Quarterly* 37:83–89; Hans Keller, "Rhythm: Gershwin and Stravinsky," *Score* 20:19–31; David Lewin, "A Metrical Problem in Webern's Op. 27," *Journal of Music Theory* 6:125–32; György Ligeti, "Pierre Boulez: Decision and Automatism in Structure Ia," *Die Reihe* (English ed.) 4:36–62; Olivier Messiaen, *Technique of My Musical Language*, English ed. (Paris 1950); John M. Perkins, "Note Values," *Perspectives* 3/2:47–57; Alfred Pike, "The Time Set as a Rhythmic Agent for the Series," *Music Review* 24:168–75; Curt Sachs, *Rhythm and Tempo* (New York 1953); Howard E. Smither, "The Rhythmic Analysis of 20th-Century Music," *Journal of Music Theory* 8:54–88; Karlheinz Stockhausen, "Die Einheit der Musikalischen Zeit," *Texte zur elektronischen und instrumentalen Musik* (Cologne 1963):211–21; ——, "... How Time Passes...," *Die Reihe* (English ed.) 3:10–40; Igor Stravinsky and Robert Craft, *Dialogues and a Diary* (Garden City, N. J., 1963); Edgard Varèse, "Rhythm, Form and Content," *Contemporary Composers on Contemporary Music* ed. by Schwartz and Childs (New York 1967):201–04; Peter Westergaard, "Some Problems Raised by the Rhythmic Procedures in Milton Babbitt's *Composition for Twelve Instruments*," *Perspectives* 4/1:109–18.

H. E. S.

SEE ALSO Asian Music and Western Composition, Form, Jazz, Melody, Notation, Performance, Popular Music, Serialism, Text Setting and Usage, Texture, Theory.

Riadis, Émile (b. Salonica, Greece, 1 May 1886; d. Salonica, 17 July 1935), studied at the Munich Conservatory (1908–10, counterpoint with Felix Mottl, piano with B. Walbrunn) and privately in Paris with Gustave Charpentier and Maurice Ravel (1910–15). He taught piano at the Salonica Conservatory during 1916–35 and conducted a number of conferences on music history.

PRINCIPAL COMPOSITIONS: *Route verte*, fantasy opera (1912–32); *Jasmins et minarets*, 3 oriental songs for voice, piano (published 1913, Chapelier, Paris); *5 Chansons macédoniennes* (published 1914, Sénart); *Adagio in B* for cello (undated); *Désir* and *Vendange* for voice, clarinet, violin, viola, cello (undated); *Danse biblique* for piano, organ (undated); *13 Little Greek Songs*, 2 vols. (published 1921, Sénart); *Danse montagnarde* for orchestra (premiere 1925); *Hecuba*, incidental music to the play by Euripedes (c.1927); *Riquet à la houppe*, incidental music for the play by Théodore de Banville (c.1929); *Liturgie byzantine* for chorus (c.1931, Institute Français, Athens). Riadis also wrote many other vocal, chamber, and orchestral works.

[prepared with the help of George Leotsakos]
SEE ALSO Greece.

Ridout, Godfrey (b. Toronto, 6 May 1918), studied at the Toronto Conservatory (1937–40; composition with Healey Willan; counterpoint, form, organ with Charles Peaker; conducting with Ettore Mazzoleni; piano with Weldon Kilburn). He has been on the faculty of Toronto Univ. since 1948 and has been active for many years as a composer, arranger, and conductor of radio, TV, and film music. The British nationality and/or training of his teachers has given his music "a strong British bias." Jazz and North American folksong have also been an influence.

PRINCIPAL COMPOSITIONS: *Ballade* for viola, string orchestra (1938–39); *2 Etudes* for string orchestra (1946, Chappell); *Esther*, dramatic symphony for soprano, baritone, chorus, orchestra (1946–51); *Cantiones mysticae* for soprano, orchestra (1952–53, Harris); *Music for a Young Prince*, suite for orchestra (1959); *The Dance* for chorus, orchestra (1960, Novello); *Pange lingua* for chorus, orchestra without winds (1961, Waterloo); *Fall Fair* for orchestra (1961, Thompson); *The Ascension*, "Cantiones mysticae No. 2" for soprano, trumpet, string orchestra (1962); *La prima ballerina*, ballet (1966); *Partita accademica* for concert band (1969–70). Ridout also reconstructed Joseph Quesnel's *Colas et Colinette* (1788, the first North American opéra-bouffe) from vocal parts and a second violin part (1963, revised 1969; an overture newly composed 1964). List to 1965: *Composers of the Americas* 11:97–100.

PRINCIPAL WRITINGS: "Orpheus in Ecclesia, or The Riven Lute," *Canadian Journal of Theology* 15/3–4:165–76.

BIBL.: "G. R. — A Portrait," *Musicanada* 12:8–9; George Kidd, "G. R., Distinguished Composer and Teacher," *The Canadian Composer* 6:4, 40.

Riegger, Wallingford (b. Albany, Ga., 29 April 1885; d. New York, 2 April 1961), was born into a musical family (his mother played the piano, his father played the violin and directed a church choir), and he began music studies with the violin and later the cello. He entered Cornell Univ. in 1904 and transferred to the Institute of Musical Art in New York in 1905, graduating with the school's first class in 1907. Three years of study in Germany followed. He was at various times a cellist with the St. Paul Symphony, a conductor in Germany, and a teacher at Drake Univ. in Iowa (1918–22) and Ithaca Conservatory (1926–28). He then settled in New York, where he was active as a composer, participated in modern-music associations, had a part in the development of electronic instruments, and learned to play an electronic cello. He also taught at various schools in the area. In 1951–52 he was a visiting professor at Northwestern Univ.

Riegger composed 35 works for orchestra, string orchestra, and band, 32 chamber and piano pieces, and other works, including 14 for the dance. He also produced numerous arrangements of folksongs and anthems. He began composing in a 19th-century style. About 1920 he changed to an impressionistic style, later followed by compositions employing more contemporary techniques. For the most part his music is contrapuntally conceived and cast in the traditional formal schemes. Canons, fugues, passacaglias, etc., occur frequently, and only a few works are basically homophonic (*Blue Voyage, The Cry,* etc.). He tended to use similar intervals in succession (for melodies) or in stacks (for vertical structures): thirds predominate in the conservative works, fourths and fifths in the piano music, mixed intervals in the more radical compositions. Twelve-tone procedures were used in several works; in some cases an entire work is based on one or more sets, in others only part of a work is 12-tone. Tone clusters are infrequent. There is much rhythmic variety, often achieved by a fluctuation of agreement and disagreement between surface rhythms and the underlying meters. Some compositions have many meter changes and unusual meters, such as 2.5/4 or 11/16.

PRINCIPAL COMPOSITIONS (published by AMP unless otherwise noted): *La Belle Dame sans merci* for vocal soloists, chamber orchestra, Op. 4; text by Keats (1923, Peer); *Study in Sonority* for 10 violins or any multiple of 10, Op. 7 (1927, Schirmer-G); *Dichotomy* for chamber orchestra, Op. 12 (1931–32, New Music); *New Dance,* dance score arranged for 2 pianos, Op. 18a; choreography by Doris Humphrey (1935, Arrow); *The Cry,* dance score for orchestra, Op.22; choreography by Hanya Holm (1935, Peer); *String Quartets Nos. 1–3,* Opp. 30, 43, 42 (1938–39, Arrow; 1948, Arrow; 1945–47); *Canon and Fugue* for orchestra, Op. 33a (1941, Flammer); *New and Old,* 12 study pieces for piano, Op. 38 (1944, Boosey); *Symphony No. 3,* Op. 42 (1946–47); *Who Can Revoke?* for chorus, piano, Op. 44 (1948, Marks); *Music for Brass Choir,* Op. 45 (1948–49, Mercury); *In Certainty of Song,* cantata for vocal soloists, chorus, piano or chamber orchestra, Op. 46; text by Catherine Harris (1950, Peer); *Piano Quintet,* Op. 47 (1951); *Nonet* for brass, Op. 49 (1951–52); *Woodwind Quintet,* Op. 51 (1952); *Concerto* for piano, woodwind quintet, Op. 53 (1952); *Variations* for piano, orchestra, Op. 54 (1952–53); *Dance Rhythms* for orchestra, Op. 58 (1954–55); *The Dying of Light* for voice, piano, Op. 59, or orchestra, Op. 59a; text by Dylan Thomas (1954); *Variations* for violin, viola, Op. 57 (1956); *Symphony No. 4,* Op. 63 (1957); *Movement* for 2 trumpets, trombone, organ, Op. 66 (1957, Peer); *Festival Overture,* Op. 68 (1957); *Variations* for violin, orchestra, Op. 71 (1958–59); *Quintuple Jazz,* Op. 72 (1959, Leeds); *Duo* for piano, orchestra, Op. 75 (1960). Complete list: *Composers of the Americas* 7:75–82.

PRINCIPAL WRITINGS: "The Orchestra of the Future," *Eolus* (May 1926):20; "In Defense of Modernism: A Reply to D. C. Parker," *Musical America* (Sept 1932):12; "To the New Through the Old," *Magazine of Art* (August 1939):472–73; "Discovering the Orchestra Conductor," *American Composers Alliance Bulletin* 6:13–14; "For a Department of Fine Arts," *ibid.* 9:12.

BIBL.: John J. Becker, "W. R.," *ACA Bulletin* 9/3:13–14; Elliott Carter, "W. R.," *ibid.* 2/1:3–5; Henry Cowell, "A Note on W. R.," *Juilliard Review* 2/2:53–55; ——, "W. R.," *Musical America* (1 Dec 1948):9, 29; Paul Douglas Freeman, *The Compositional Technique of W. R. as Seen in Seven Major Twelve-Tone Works* (PhD diss., Eastman School of Music, 1963); Richard F. Goldman, "The Music of W. R.," *Musical Quarterly* 36:39–61; Joseph B. Schmoll, *An Analytical Study of the Principal Instrumental Compositions of W. R.* (PhD diss., Northwestern Univ., 1954); ——, "Dedicated Contemporary," *Musical America* (May 1955):8, 28.

Joseph Schmoll

SEE ALSO Dance, Popular Music, United States.

Rieti, Vittorio (b. Alexandria, Egypt, 28 Jan 1898), moved with his parents in 1917 to their native country, Italy, where he later studied piano with Giuseppe Frugatta in Milan and economics at the Univ. of Milan. In 1920 he moved to Rome, began to compose, and made contact with Alfredo Casella, Ottorino Respighi, and Gian Francesco Malipiero. Respighi gave him a few lessons in orchestration, but he was primarily self-taught. In 1924–25 he moved to Paris, attracted by the presence there of Igor Stravinsky, whom he acknowledges as a prime influence. While there he was commissioned by Diaghilev and others to write for the ballet; during the 1930s he also wrote for the theater and films of Louis Jouvet. He moved to the U.S. in 1940, where he has taught in several music schools in New York, Baltimore, and Chicago.

Rieti's large output includes five symphonies, three piano concertos, many stage works (including six operas), much chamber music, and songs. He is a highly rational man, and it is perhaps his elegant intellect that leads him to favor chamber music and, most recently, small orchestral ensembles. In all genres his music tends to be lean, though not dry. There is a great deal of dance in his work: a tarantella lurking in the last movement, lots of rhythmic motion, much play with modulations and key changes. Fugues are often present. There is often a strong, lyrical melodic line as well, one, however, that tends to be impressive more for its design than for the emotion it may convey.

PRINCIPAL COMPOSITIONS: *Concerto* for woodwind quintet, orchestra (1924, UE); *Barabau,* ballet with chorus; choreography by George Balanchine (1925, UE); *String Quartet No. 1* (1926, Salabert); *Le Bal,* ballet; choreography by Balanchine (1929, UE); *Concerto* for cello, 12 winds (1934, General); *Concerto du Loup* for small orchestra (1938, Eschig); *Night Shadow* (also called *Sonnambula*), ballet; choreography by Balanchine (1941, AMP); *Second Avenue Waltzes* for 2 pianos (1942, AMP); *Symphony No. 4,* "Sinfonia Tripartita" (1942, AMP); *Partita* for harpsichord, flute, oboe, string quartet (1945, Broude-B); *Symphony No. 5* (1945, AMP); *Trionfo di Bacco e Arianna,* cantata ballet on a 15th-century Italian text; choreography by Balanchine (1947, General); *Suite champêtre* for 2 pianos (1948, AMP); *Don Perlimplin,* 1-act opera; libretto by García-Lorca (1949, AMP); *Concerto* for 2 pianos, orchestra (1951, General); *String Quartet No. 3* (1951, General); *Viaggio d'Europa,* oratorio; text by Paola Masino (1954, General); *Harpsichord Concerto* (1955, General); *Dance Variations* for string orchestra (1956, Broude); *The Pet Shop,* 1-act musical farce; libretto by Claire White (1957, General); *String Quartet No. 4* (1960, General); *La Fontaine,* suite for orchestra (1968, General); *Violin Concerto* (1969, General); *Corale, variazioni e finale* for 2 pianos (1969, General); *Triple Concerto* for violin, cello, piano, orchestra (1971, General).

Paul Kapp

SEE ALSO Dance.

Riisager, Knudåge (b. Port Kunda, Estonia, 6 March 1897), studied political science at the Univ. of Copenhagen (1916–21). His musical training included studies in harmony with Peder Gram in Copenhagen (1915–18), orchestration with Albert Roussel and Paul Le Flem in Paris (1923–24), and counterpoint with Hermann Grabner in Leipzig (1932). From 1925 to 1947 he served with the Danish Ministry of Finance. He was chairman of the Danish Composers' League during 1937–62 and director of the Royal Danish Conservatory, 1956–67. Riisager's studies in Paris had a decisive impact on his music (which subsequently incorporated an intense rhythmic character, colorful orchestration, and polytonal techniques), and upon his return to Denmark he led the progressive movement there. A noted ballet composer, his works are in the repertory of major European companies and the American Ballet Theater.

PRINCIPAL COMPOSITIONS (published by Hansen-W unless otherwise noted): *Erasmus Montanus,* overture for orchestra, Op. 1 (1920, SUDM); *4 Epigrammes* for piano, Op. 11 (1921); *String Quartet No. 3,* Op. 3 (1922); *Violin Sonata No. 2,* Op. 5 (1923); *Variations on a Theme of Mezangeau* for orchestra, Op. 12 (1926); *Sonata* for flute, violin, clarinet, cello, Op. 15 (1927); *Benzin,* ballet, Op. 17; choreography by Elna Jørgen-Jensen (1928, unpub.); *Cocktails-Party,* "Ballet-bouffonnerie," Op. 19 (1929, unpub.); *Fastelavn* [Shrovetide], overture for orchestra, Op. 20 (1930); *Piano Sonata,* Op. 22 (1931); *Conversations* for oboe, clarinet, bassoon, Op. 26a (1932, Engstrøm); *Concertino* for 5 violins, piano, Op. 28a (1933); *Concertino* for trumpet, string orchestra, Op. 29 (1933); *2 Pieces* for piano (1933); *Lille Overture* for string orchestra (1934); *I Anledning Af* [For the Children's Party] for orchestra (1934); *Primavera,* concert overture, Op. 31 (1934, SUDM); *En glad Trompet og andre Klaverstykker* [A Funny Trumpet and Other Piano Pieces] (1935); *Valse lente* for chamber orchestra (1935); *Darduse,* orchestral suite from incidental music for a play by Johannes V. Jensen (1935–36, SUDM); *Serenade* for flute, violin, cello, Op. 26b (1936); *Slaraffenland* [Fools' Paradise], 2 orchestral suites, Op. 33 (1936, 1940; ballet with choreography by Harald Lander, 1940); *Partita* for orchestra, Op. 35 (1937); *Qarrtsiluni* for orchestra, Op. 36 (1938; ballet with choreography by Lander, 1942); *Tolv med Posten* [Twelve by the Mail], ballet after H. C. Andersen, Op. 37; choreography by Børge Ralov (1939); *Torgutisk Dans* for orchestra (1939, Lyche); *Wind Quartet,* Op. 40a (1941, SUDM); *Finalegalop* for orchestra (1941, SUDM); *Dansk Salme* for chorus, orchestra, Op. 41 (1942); *Sommer-Rhapsodi* on Danish folksongs for orchestra (1943); *Divertimento* for flute, oboe, horn, bassoon, Op. 42a (1944, Engstrøm); *Fugl Fønix,* ballet, Op. 44; choreography by Lander (1944–45, unpub.); *Bellman Variations* for small orchestra, Op. 45 (1945, Gehrman); *Sinfonietta,* Op. 46 (1947, Gehrman); *Etudes,* ballet; choreography by Lander (1947, unpub.); *Chaconne* for orchestra, Op. 50 (1948, Lyche); *Archaeopteryx* for orchestra, Op. 51 (1948, SUDM); *Sinfonia serena* (No. 5) for string orchestra, tympani, Op. 52 (1949–50, Peters); *Sonatina* for piano (1950, published by Gehrman in the collection Ny nordisk klavermusik); *Variations on a Sarabande of Charles, Duke of Orleans, 1415* for string orchestra, Op. 53 (1950, Peters); *Sonatina* for piano trio, Op. 55a (1951, Engstrøm); *Sonata* for 2 violins, Op. 55b (1951, Engstrøm); *Harlequinade,* suite for chamber orchestra from incidental music for the play De Usynlige (1951, Engstrøm); *Pro fistulis et fidibus* for winds, strings, Op. 56 (1952, SUDM); *Månerenen* [The Moon Reindeer], ballet, Op. 57; choreography by Birgit Cullberg (1956, SUDM); *Aandeligt Siungekor on a Theme of Kingo* for string orchestra (1956, Warny); *Fruen fra Havet* [The Lady from the Sea], ballet; choreography by Cullberg (1959, unpub.); *Sangen om det Uendelige* (*Canto dell'Infinito*) for chorus, orchestra, Op. 61; text by Giacomo Leopardi (1964, unpub.); *Stabat Mater* for chorus, orchestra, Op. 62 (1966, unpub.); *Galla Variations* for orchestra; pas de deux with choreography by Flemming Flindt (1966, unpub.); *Ballet Royal,* choreography by Flindt (1968, unpub.); *Svinedrengen* [The Swineherd], ballet after H. C.

Andersen; choreography by Flindt (1969, unpub.). Catalogue of compositions to 1966 published by Dansk Komponist-Forening (Copenhagen 1967).

PRINCIPAL WRITINGS: *Det usynlige Mønster* [The Invisible Pattern] (Copenhagen 1957).

BIBL.: Gerald Cockshoot, "K. R.," *Music and Education* (Sept/Oct 1966):237.

SEE ALSO Scandinavia.

Riley, Terry (Mitchell) (b. Colfax, Calif., 24 June 1935), studied at San Francisco State College (1955–57, composition with Robert Erickson, piano with Duane Hampton) and at the Univ. of Calif. at Berkeley (1960–61). He plays the soprano saxophone. Since 1963 he has been composing and giving concerts in the U.S. and Europe. In 1967 he organized programs of his music as a guest of the Swedish Radio and Academy of Music. He was a member of the Creative Associate program at the State Univ. of N. Y. in Buffalo in 1969. His music has been influenced by a variety of elements including Indian and African music, jazz, ragtime, and La Monte Young's "long durations and getting into a sound." His compositions "take the form of charts of repeated patterns and series, which must assume a form during rehearsal and performance." They are always based on a diatonic mode or series of modes. Through the use of ostinatos, tape loops, feedback systems during performance, and other devices, he creates a "musical hall of mirrors."

PRINCIPAL COMPOSITIONS: *In C* for any number of instruments (1964, recorded by Columbia); *The Keyboard Studies* for amplified or electronic keyboard instruments (1965–   ); *Dorian Reeds* for soprano saxophone, tape, time-lag and feedback system (1966, recorded by Massart Records); *Untitled Organ* for amplified reed organ (1966, Massart Records); *Poppy Nogood and the Phantom Band* for soprano saxophone, tape, time-lag and feedback system (1968, Columbia Records); *A Rainbow in Curved Air* for electronic keyboard instruments (1969, Columbia Records); *Music with Balls,* television film (1969).

SEE ALSO Indeterminacy, Mixed Media, Performance, Prose Music, Rhythm, United States.

Ring Modulator, an electronic device for combining signals so that the output consists of sums and differences of all the input frequency components. It is most often used to enhance or completely refashion the timbre of sounds that are already complex (e.g., with regard to rhythms and attacks).

SEE ALSO Electronic Music: Apparatus and Technology.

Ristić, Milan (Jovan) (b. Belgrade, 18 August 1908), studied at the Belgrade Academy of Music (1929–32, 1935–37; composition with Miloje Milojević, Josip Slavenski) and the Prague Conservatory (1937–39, composition with Alois Hába). He also studied with Gabriel Pierson in Paris (1927–29). He has worked in the music programing department of Radio Belgrade since 1950 and has been director since 1963. He describes the works listed below as neoclassic with nondogmatic applications of dodecaphonic procedures.

PRINCIPAL COMPOSITIONS: *Violin Concerto* (1944); *Symphonies Nos. 2–6* (1951, UKS; 1961, SANU; 1966, UKS; 1967; 1968); *Piano Concerto* (1954); *Symphonic Variations* (1957, SKJ); *7 Bagatelles* for orchestra (1959); *Concerto for Orchestra* (1963, SANU); *Clarinet Concerto* (1964); *Concerto for String Orchestra* (1969).

BIBL.: Marija Koren, "Simfonija u stvaralačkom opusu M. R." [The Symphony in the Creative Work of M. R.], *Zvuk* (1966):494–504; ——, *Monografija o M. R.* (Belgrade 1969); Zija Kučukalić, " M. R. — Stvaralački uspon i sazrevanje " [M. R. — Creative Progress and Maturation], *Zvuk* (1968):619–25; Vlastimir Peričić, *Muzički stvaraci u Srbiji* [Creators of Music in Serbia] (Belgrade 1969):453–73.

Rivier, Jean (b. Villemomble, France, 21 July 1896), attended the Paris Conservatory (1922–26, harmony with Jean Gallon, counterpoint and fugue with Georges Caussade, music history with Maurice Emmanuel). He taught composition there during 1948–66. He has been a member of the music committee of the French radio and served on the jury of several *concours,* including the Ville de Paris, Conseil Général de la Seine, and the Confédération des Travailleurs Intellectuels de France. He has been greatly interested in literature and architecture, especially the theories of Le Corbusier.

PRINCIPAL COMPOSITIONS (published by Salabert unless otherwise noted): *Ouverture pour un Don Quichotte* for orchestra (1929); *Symphony No. 1 in D* (1932); *Symphonie exotique* (1936, unpub.); *Vénitienne,* 1-act opéra-comique; libretto by René Kerdyk (1936, EMT); *Psalm 56* for soprano, chorus, orchestra (1937, unpub.); *Symphony No. 3 in G* for strings (1938); *Piano Concerto No. 1 in C* (1940, Billaudot); *Violin Concerto* (1942); *Symphony No. 5* (1950); *Requiem* for mezzo-soprano, bass, chorus, orchestra (1953, EMT); *Divertimento,* ballet (1958); *Musiques pour un ballet* (1958);

Symphony No. 6, "Les Présages" (1960); *Symphony No. 7,* "Les Contrastes" (1961); *Concerto for Brass, Tympani, and Strings* (1963); *Christus Rex* for alto, chorus, orchestra (1966).

SEE ALSO France.

Rochberg, George (b. Paterson, N. J., 5 July 1918), attended Montclair State Teachers College and the Mannes School of Music in New York (1939–41, theory and composition with Hans Weise and George Szell). After World War II, during which he served in Europe, he studied theory and composition at the Curtis Institute with Rosario Scalero and Gian-Carlo Menotti and received a B.Mus. degree in 1947. He began teaching at Curtis the following year and received an M.A. in composition from the Univ. of Penna. in 1949. In 1950 he went to Rome as a Fulbright and American Academy Fellow; there he met Luigi Dallapiccola and discovered the expressive potential of dodecaphony. In 1951 he returned to Philadelphia as music editor for the Theodore Presser Co. and resumed his teaching at Curtis. In 1960 he joined the music department of the Univ. of Penna., first as acting chairman, then as chairman. Since 1967 he has devoted himself exclusively to teaching and creative work.

Rochberg has written three symphonies, two string quartets, keyboard works, chamber music for small and large ensembles, songs with piano and chamber ensembles, a set of a cappella psalms, and miscellaneous pieces for orchestra and band. His early work shows the influence of Hindemith (in the somewhat mechanistic counterpoint of several discarded student pieces), followed by the Stravinsky of *Le Sacre du Printemps* (*cf.* the stark orchestral colors in *Night Music*) and Bartók (*cf.* the percussive ostinato effects of *Capriccio* and the dissonant chromatic polyphony of the *String Quartet No. 1*). Intensive study of Mahler and Schoenberg contributed much to Rochberg's full artistic maturation. The frequently performed *12 Bagatelles* (1952), Rochberg's first dodecaphonic essay, combines the emotional intensity and structural economy typical of Schoenberg's piano output. The broad melodic-rhythmic gestures of the *Symphony No. 2* (1956), on the other hand, were conceived in the spirit of Mahler as well as Schoenberg. Rochberg's subsequent preoccupation with Webern accounts no doubt for the relatively stationary interlacings of limited intervallic patterns in *Cheltenham Concerto* (1958) and *Time-Span* (1960, revised 1962).

From these experiments in what the composer has called "duration as process" it was a small step to the "projection of densities" (in late Varèse) that generated the sonorous feast of *Apocalyptica* (1964) and the closely related *Black Sounds* (1965), a choreographic piece for winds and percussion. Rochberg's most recent compositions incorporate Ivesian simultaneities of original and preexisting materials. The beautifully textured *Contra mortem et tempus* (1965) juxtaposes snatches from Boulez, Berio, Varèse, and Ives, as well as Rochberg's own somewhat Bergian *Dialogues* for clarinet and piano (1958).

Like Mahler, with whom he most readily identifies, Rochberg seeks to integrate the totality of human experience. And like Schoenberg, he does so in terms of his Jewish heritage as part of "the passionate people." This may explain why he has thus far steered clear of electronic media, concentrating increasingly on the sophisticated use of basically unmodified human voices: in his *Symphony No. 3* (1968) to represent man's inhumanity to man, and in the *Tableaux* (1968; on texts by the composer's son, who died at the age of 20) to convey man's sense of loneliness in a world he no longer controls.

PRINCIPAL COMPOSITIONS (published by Presser unless otherwise noted): *Book of Songs* for voice, piano (1937–69); *Night Music* for chamber orchestra (1949); *Symphony No. 1* (1949, revised 1957); *String Quartet No. 1* (1952); *12 Bagatelles* (1952; orchestral version, *Zodiac,* 1965); *Chamber Symphony* (1953); *3 Psalms* for chorus; Hebrew texts (1954); *David the Psalmist,* cantata for tenor, orchestra (1954); *Duo concertante* for violin, cello (1955); *Symphony No. 2* (1956); *Sonata-Fantasia* for piano (1956); *Dialogues* for clarinet, piano (1958); *Cheltenham Concerto* for chamber orchestra (1958); *La bocca della verità* for oboe, piano (1959; version for violin, piano, 1965, Impero); *String Quartet No. 2* with soprano (1959–61); *Time-Span* for orchestra (1960; revised 1962, Leeds); *Songs of Innocence and Experience* for voice, small ensemble; poems by William Blake (1961, Leeds); *Piano Trio* (1963); *Apocalyptica* for band (1964); *Music for the Magic Theater* for orchestra (1965); *Black Sounds* for winds, percussion (1965); *Contra mortem et tempus* for violin, flute, clarinet, piano (1965); *Tableaux* for soprano, 11 players (1968); *Symphony No. 3,* "A 20th-Century Passion," for orchestra, 4 solo voices, 8-part chamber chorus, double chorus (1968); *Songs of Krishna* for soprano, piano (1970); *Mizmor l'Piyus* [Song of Reconciliation] for bass-baritone, small orchestra (1970). List to 1964: *Composers of the Americas* 1c:87–90; list to 1966: *Musical Quarterly* 52:426–30.

PRINCIPAL WRITINGS: *The Hexachord and Its Relation to the Twelve-tone Row* (Bryn Mawr, Pa., 1955); "Tradition and Twelve-tone Music,"

Mandala 1:49–70; "Hugo Weisgall," *ACA Bulletin* 7:2–7; "The Harmonic Tendency of the Hexachord," *Journal of Music Theory* 3:208–30; "Indeterminacy in the New Music," *Score* 26:9–19; "Duration in Music," *The Modern Composer and His World* ed. by J. Beckwith and U. Kasemets (Toronto 1961):56–64; "Webern's Search for Harmonic Identity," *Journal of Music Theory* 7:109–22; "The New Image of Music," *Perspectives* 2/1:1–10; "Schoenberg's 'American' Period," *International Cyclopedia of Music and Musicians*, 9th ed.:1915–22.

BIBL.: Alexander L. Ringer, "Current Chronicle. Cleveland" and "Current Chronicle. St. Louis," *Musical Quarterly* 45:230–34 and 47:101–03; ——, "The Music of G. R.," *Musical Quarterly* 52:409–30.

Alexander L. Ringer

SEE ALSO Liturgical Music: Christian, United States.

Rock, see Popular Music

Rodrigo, Joaquín (b. Sagunto, Valencia, Spain, 22 Nov 1902), studied harmony and composition with Francisco Antich in Valencia (1920–23) and then attended the Ecole Normale de Musique in Paris (1927–32, composition with Paul Dukas). While in Paris he made the acquaintance of Manuel de Falla, whose friendship and advice was of great influence. In 1935 he studied music history with Maurice-Emmanuel at the Paris Conservatory and with André Pirro at the Sorbonne. He settled in Madrid in 1939, and since 1946 has been professor of music history at the Univ. of Madrid. He has made extensive tours as lecturer and pianist throughout Europe, North Africa, North and South America, Israel, etc., and in 1963 gave a course in music history at the Univ. of Puerto Rico. He has been musical advisor to the Spanish radio since 1944, head of the music division of the Spanish National Organization of the Blind, and vice-president of ISCM since 1954.

PRINCIPAL COMPOSITIONS: *Cantico de la esposa* for voice, piano; text by San Juan de la Cruz (1934); *Concierto de Aranjuez* for guitar, orchestra (1939); *Concierto heroico* for piano, orchestra (1942); *Concierto de estio* for violin, orchestra (1943, Billaudot); *4 Madrigales amatorios* for voice with piano or orchestra (1947, Chester); *Ausencias de Dulcinea* for bass, 4 sopranos, orchestra (1948, Eschig); *Concierto galante* for cello, orchestra (1949); *Concierto-Serenata* for harp, orchestra (1952, UME); *4 Villancicos* for voice, piano (1952, Nos. 1–3 published by Schott); *4 Villancicos*

(*Canciones de Navidad*) for chorus (1952); *Fantasia para un gentilhombre* for guitar, orchestra (1954, Schott); *Sonata pimpante in A* for violin, piano (1965–66, Eschig); *Concierto andaluz* for 4 guitars, orchestra (1967, Salabert); *Concierto-Madrigal* for 2 guitars, orchestra (1968).

PRINCIPAL WRITINGS: *Diez años de música en España*, in collaboration with Gerardo Diego and Federico Sopeña (Madrid 1949).

BIBL.: Antonio Iglesias, *La música para piano de J. R.* (Orense, Conservatory of Music, 1965); Federico Sopeña, *J. R.* (Madrid 1946).

SEE ALSO Spain.

Rogers, Bernard (b. New York, 4 Feb 1893; d. Rochester, 24 May 1968), attended the Institute of Musical Art in New York (1919–21, theory and composition with Percy Goetschius), and the Cleveland Institute (composition with Ernest Bloch). He studied privately in New York with Hans van den Berg, Arthur Farwell, and Ernest Bloch, and during 1927–29 with Frank Bridge in London and Nadia Boulanger in Paris. He was an editor and chief critic of *Musical America* from 1913 to 1924. He taught at the Hartt School of Music, Hartford, Conn., during 1926–27 and at the Eastman School from 1929 to 1967, when he retired as chairman of the composition department.

PRINCIPAL COMPOSITIONS (published by Presser unless otherwise noted): *3 Japanese Dances* for orchestra (1933, version for wind ensemble 1954); *Symphony No. 3* on a Thanksgiving song (1936, E-V); *Symphony No. 4 in G Minor* (1940, Southern); *The Passion*, oratorio (1942, E-V); *The Warrior*, opera; libretto by Norman Corwin (1944, unpub.); *A Letter from Pete*, cantata; text by Walt Whitman (1947, Southern); *The Prophet Isaiah*, cantata (1950, Southern); *The Veil*, opera; libretto by Robert Lawrence (1950, Southern); *Leaves from the Tale of Pinocchio* for narrator, chamber orchestra (1951, Southern); *Psalm 68* for baritone, orchestra (1952, Southern); *Portrait* for violin, orchestra (1952); *String Trio* (1953, Southern); *The Nightingale*, opera; libretto by the composer (1954, Southern); *The Musicians of Bremen* for narrator, 13 instruments (1958); *Symphony No. 5*, "Africa" (1959; version of 2nd movement, *Tribal Drums*, for wind ensemble, 1962); *Variations on a Song of Mussorgsky* for orchestra (1960); *Violin Sonata* (1962); *Apparitions* for orchestra or wind ensemble (1967, MCA); *Dirge for 2 Veterans* for chorus, piano; text by Walt Whitman (1967; version for piano, strings by Charles Fussell); *Psalm 114* for chorus, piano (1968). List to 1965: *Composers of the Americas* 10:93–97.

PRINCIPAL WRITINGS: *The Art of Orchestration* (New York 1951); "Teaching to Compose, an Inflamed Art," *Music Journal Anthology* (1963):25,

116–17; *"The Passion," The Composer's Point of View* ed. by Robert S. Hines (Norman, Okla., 1963):56–64. Reviews by Rogers appeared in *Modern Music* 21:246–48, 22:45–47, 22:262–63.

BIBL.: Arthur Cohn, "Rochester's Eleventh U.S.A. Festival," *Modern Music* 18:259–61; David Diamond, "B. R.," *Musical Quarterly* 33:207–27; ——, "B. R.," *Proceedings of the National Institute of Arts and Letters* (1968):119–20; Herbert Elwell, "B. R.," *Sunday Cleveland Plain-Dealer* (6 May 1962); Howard Hanson, "B. R.," *Modern Music* 22/5:170–74; ——, "The Rochester Group of American Composers," *American Composers on American Music* ed. by Henry Cowell (Stanford 1962):88–89.

SEE ALSO: Liturgical Music: Christian.

Rohwer, Jens (b. Neumünster, Germany, 7 July 1914), attended Bonn Univ. (1933–34), Berlin Univ. (1935–38), the Berlin Hochschule für Musik (1935–38), and Kiel Univ. (1956–58). He has taught composition at the Gaumusikschule in Posen (1943–45) and the Schleswig-Holstein Music Academy in Lübeck (since 1946), where he has been director since 1955. During 1948–56 he organized the Work Weeks for New Composition and Theory in Barsbüttel. The major influences on his music have come from folksong, the work of Hindemith, Stravinsky, and the German youth movement. In addition to the works listed below, he has composed over 400 songs for young people, which have been published in songbooks throughout Europe.

PRINCIPAL COMPOSITIONS (published by Möseler unless otherwise noted): *Das Wunschlied*, 60 songs for voice, piano; text by the composer (1944–46, Möseler and Voggenreiter in Godesberg); *Der Mond ist aufgegangen* for chorus (1947); *Little Phrygian Sonata* for piano (1947); *Ausgriffe* for piano (1948); *Quartet* for flute, string trio (1949); *Nun bitten wir den heiligen Geist* for chorus (1949); *Lydian Sonata* for violin, piano (1951); *3 Partitas* for solo violin (1951); *Sonatina* for violin, piano (1953, Heinr.); *Clarinet Sonata* (1954); *Waldkantaten* for tenor, chorus, recorders, string orchestra, percussion; text by Christian Morgenstern (1954–55); *Sonata* for harpsichord, viola da gamba (1955); *Harpsichord Sonata* (1955); *7 Gospel and Psalm Motets* for chorus (1956, Breitkopf); *7 Mädchenlieder*, cycle for chorus (1958, Schott); *Von dem Tode des Hühnchens*, a folk tale for chorus (1958, Fidula); *Trio* for oboe, violin, viola (1958); *Weinheberchansons*, 3 songs for chorus (1959); *Chamber Concerto* for 2 flutes, string orchestra (1959, Breitkopf); *Sonata concertante* for soprano recorder, piano (1959); *Wen der Tod trifft* for soprano, tenor, bass, chorus, chamber orchestra (1959–60); *4 Fantasias* for organ (1963); *Piano Concerto* (1963); *Duo Sonata* for 2 violins (1963); *Christus Triumphator* for soprano, alto, tenor, chorus, organ (1963); *Chelion*, ballet pantomime for dancers, actors, chorus, orchestra (1963–66); *Versuche mit Präludien und Fugen*, 12 pieces for piano (1964); *Concerto piccolo* for string orchestra (1966); *String Quartet* (1968); *Das Jüngste Gericht*, 7 chorales for organ (1968, Doblinger); *Flute Sonata* (1969).

PRINCIPAL WRITINGS: *Tonale Instruktionen und Beiträge zur Kompositionslehre* (Wolfenbüttel 1958); *Neueste Musik, Ein kritischer Bericht* (Stuttgart 1964); *Sinn und Unsinn in der Musik* (Wolfenbüttel 1969); *Die harmonischen Grundlagen der Musik* (Cassel 1970).

Roldán, Amadeo (b. Paris, 12 July 1900; d. Havana, 2 March 1939), studied at the Madrid Conservatory with Pablo Hernández (composition) and Agustín Soller (violin). He also studied composition privately with Conrado del Campo and violin with Antonio Fernández Bordas. He settled in Cuba c.1921, where he was active as a violist, violinist, and conductor. He taught harmony and composition at the Philharmonic and Municipal Conservatories in Havana. He was especially interested in the African influences on Cuban music and was the first composer to incorporate Afro-Cuban themes and rhythms in symphonic works.

PRINCIPAL COMPOSITIONS: *Fiestas galantes* for voice, piano; text by Paul Verlaine (1923); *Overture on Cuban Themes* for orchestra (1925); *3 Small Poems* for orchestra (1926); *La rebambaramba*, Afro-Cuban ballet; scenario by Alejo Carpentier (1928); *A changó* for lute quartet (1928); *Danza negra* for voice, 2 clarinets, 2 violas, percussion; text by F. Palés Mato (1928); *2 Cuban Folk Songs* for cello, piano (1928); *El milagro de Anaquillé*, 1-act ballet; scenario by Carpentier (1928–29, reorchestrated 1931); *Rítmicas I–IV* for wind quintet, piano (1930); *Rítmicas V–VI* for percussion (1930); *3 Toques* for orchestra (1931); *Curujey* for chorus, 2 pianos, percussion; text by Nicolás Guillén (1931); *Motivos de son* for soprano, chamber orchestra, percussion; text by Guillén (1934). Complete list: *Composers of the Americas* 1:80–83.

PRINCIPAL WRITINGS: "The Artistic Position of the American Composer," *American Composers on American Music* ed. by H. Cowell (Stanford, Calif., 1933):175–77.

BIBL.: León Argeliers, "Las obras para piano de A. R.," *Revista de música* (Havana) 1/4:112–23; Alejo Carpentier, *La música en Cuba* (Mexico City 1946):236–44; ——, "La música contemporánea de Cuba," *Revista musical chilena* (Dec 1947):9–16; Henry Cowell, "*Motivos de son*, a series of 8 songs for soprano with a small orchestra," *Musical Quarterly* 36:270–71; ——, "R. and Caturla of Cuba," *Modern Music* 18:98–99; Carmen Valdés de Guerra, "A. R., músico ejemplar," *Revista de musica* 1/3:72–89.

Rolón, José (b. Ciudad Guzmán, Jalisco, Mexico, 22 June 1883; d. Mexico City, 3 Feb 1945), studied piano with Mortiz Moskowski and fugue with André Gedalge in Paris (1903–07), after which he founded a music school in Guadalajara, which he directed until 1927. He returned to Paris during 1927–30, at which time he studied composition with Nadia Boulanger and Paul Dukas. He taught at the Mexico City Conservatory (1930–38) and during 1931–32 was also head of the music department of the Ministry of Public Education. His early works were in a romantic vein akin to Brahms. His second Paris sojourn stimulated an interest in Debussy and Ravel, and thereafter he combined many of the impressionist devices with a nationalist esthetic, including uses of folk and native Indian melodies.

PRINCIPAL COMPOSITIONS: *Zapotlán*, symphonic suite (1895, reorchestrated 1925); *Piano Quartet in E♭*, Op. 16 (1912); *Symphony* (1918–19); *El festín de los enanos*, ballet (1925, EMM); *String Quartet No. 3*, Op. 35 (192–?); *Cuauhtémoc*, symphonic poem (1929); *3 Danzas indígenas* for piano (1930, Eschig); *Piano Concerto* (1935). Rolón wrote a large number of other piano and vocal works, the dates of which are unknown.

PRINCIPAL WRITINGS: "La música autoctona mexicana y la tecnica moderna," *Música* (15 August 1930): 16–19; "Organización musical en México," *Boletín latino-americano de música* 3:77–80.

BIBL.: Otto Mayer-Serra, *Panorama de la música mexicana* (Mexico City 1941):153–57.

SEE ALSO Mexico.

Rorem, Ned (b. Richmond, Ind., 23 Oct 1923), grew up in Chicago, where he began formal training in harmony and composition in 1938 with Leo Sowerby at the American Conservatory. This was followed by studies in composition at Northwestern Univ. (1940–42), the Curtis Institute (1943), and the Juilliard School (1946, 1948). While attending Juilliard, he also studied with Virgil Thomson and Aaron Copland, his most influential teachers. In 1949 he took up residence in Morocco and in 1951 moved to Paris, where he remained until 1957 under the patronage of the Vicomtesse de Noailles (Marie Laure). Studies there with Arthur Honegger and friendships with Francis Poulenc, Georges Auric, and Darius Milhaud reinforced his basic musical directions. Since 1957 he has resided primarily in New York and has been composer-in-residence at the Univ. of Buffalo (1959–61) and the Univ. of Utah (1966–67).

Rorem is the foremost American composer of art songs. From *Doll's Boy* (1944) through the cycle *War Scenes* (1969) he has written 271, including 17 cycles. Poetic texts in the pre-1954 songs were drawn from all literary periods; since then Rorem has used primarily the poetry of 20th-century Americans (notably Paul Goodman, Theodore Roethke, Kenneth Koch, and Howard Moss) and of Walt Whitman. The 1944–57 songs were guided by traditional principles, concentrating on a smooth projection of the text by the voice in a lyric, diatonic modal style against a richly textured, chromatic accompaniment in the piano. The Whitman songs of 1957 exhibit greater use of angularity and dramatic timing in the vocal lines, while the fast-running, almost hysterical setting of *Visits to St. Elizabeths* (*Bedlam*), completed immediately after the Whitman, exhibits greater independence between vocal and piano lines. These two works presaged the dramatic songs of Rorem's "second period" when he returned to song writing in 1959. The lyrical songs since then are suffused with a simpler charm and build to clearer climaxes than do the earlier songs, while the piano parts, less chromatic, are leaner in texture. Vocal lines in the dramatic songs, sometimes completely unaccompanied, have rhythmic variety, are often highly melismatic, and employ wide leaps alternating with repeated-note passages. The piano parts contain extreme contrasts in dynamics and textures, often increasing the tension with clustered dissonances; they are no less important than the voice in expressing the text. Most vocal solo works since 1960 are cyclic.

Rorem's instrumental music was originally influenced by 20th-century French composers from Satie to Messiaen. This can be seen in the long tunes and in the play of string against wind timbres. Later developments show Rorem absorbed in coloristic possibilities of orchestral instruments and in expanding tonal vocabulary through altered chords, modality, and polytonality. Many compositions from the late 1960s are based on a modified serial technique. From the *Third Symphony* (1957) on, Rorem abandoned sonata structure in writing for orchestra, choosing instead to experiment with semiprogrammatic tone poems, variation forms, and multimovement pieces, molds more suited to his essentially vocal-inspired talents than the traditional devices used in the earlier instrumental works, which suffered from a lack of motivic development and rhythmic variety.

PRINCIPAL COMPOSITIONS (published by Boosey unless otherwise noted): *Alleluia* for voice, piano (1946, Hargail); *The Lordly Hudson* for voice, piano; poem by Paul Goodman (1947, Mercury); *Little Elegy* for voice, piano; poem by Elinor Wylie (1949, Hargail); *Rain in Spring* for voice, piano; poem by Goodman (1949); *Violin Sonata* (1949, Peters); *Flight for Heaven*, cycle for baritone, piano; poems by Robert Herrick (1950, Mercury); *6 Irish Poems* for voice, orchestra; poems by George Darley (1950, Southern); *Symphony No. 1* (1950, Southern); *Cycle of Holy Songs* for voice, piano; Biblical texts (1951, Southern); *A Childhood Miracle*, opera; libretto by Elliott Stein after Hawthorne (1952, Southern); *The Tulip Tree* for voice, piano; poem by Goodman (1953, Schirmer-E); *Sally's Smile* for voice, piano; poem by Goodman (1953, Peters); *Clouds* for voice, piano; poem by Goodman (1953); *Poèmes pour la paix*, cycle for voice, piano; medieval French texts (1953); *6 Songs for High Voice and Orchestra*; poems by John Dryden, Robert Browning (1953, Peters); *Design for Orchestra* (1953); *Youth, Day, Old Age and Night* for voice, piano; poem by Walt Whitman (1954, Peters); *4 Dialogues* for 2 voices, 2 pianos (1954); *The Poets' Requiem* for chorus, orchestra; various European authors (1955–56); *Look Down, Fair Moon* for voice, piano; poem by Whitman (1957); *Visits to St. Elizabeths (Bedlam)* for voice, piano (1957); *Symphony No. 3* (1957); *Eagles* for orchestra (1958); 4 songs for voice, piano; on poems by Theodore Roethke: *Root Cellar, Snake, Night Crow, My Papa's Waltz* (1959, Peters); *11 Studies for 11 Players* (1959); *King Midas*, cycle for voice, piano; text by Howard Moss (1960–61); *Trio* for flute, cello, piano (1960, Peters); *Poems of Love and the Rain*, cycle for voice, piano; 20th-century American authors (1962–63); *Lions* for orchestra (1963); *Lovers*, narrative in 10 scenes for harpsichord, oboe, cello, percussion (1964); *Miss Julie*, opera; libretto by Kenward Elmslie after Strindberg (1964–65); *Hearing*, cycle for voice, piano; poems by Kenneth Koch (1965–66); *Sun* for voice, orchestra (1966); *Letters from Paris* for chorus, orchestra; texts from Janet Flanner (1966); *Water Music* for violin, clarinet, chamber orchestra (1967); *Bertha*, opera; libretto by Koch (1968–69); *War Scenes* for voice, piano; texts by Whitman (1969); *3 Sisters Who Are Not Sisters*, opera; libretto by Gertrude Stein (1969); *Piano Concerto No. 3* (1969–70); *Fables*, 6 short chamber operas; texts by La Fontaine (1970); *Ariel* for voice, clarinet, piano; poems by Sylvia Plath (1971). List to 1965: *Composers of the Americas* 12:138–45; list to 1968: N. R., *Music and People*:235–42.

PRINCIPAL WRITINGS: *The Paris Diary of Ned Rorem* (New York 1966); *The New York Diary* (New York 1967); *Music from Inside Out* (New York 1967); *Music and People* (New York 1968); *Critical Affairs, A Composer's Journal* (New York 1970).

BIBL.: Garland Anderson, "The Music of N. R.," *Music Journal* (April 1963): 34, 71–72; Sharon A. Atack, *N. R. and His Songs* (MM thesis, Univ. of Neb., 1969); Marvin R. Bloomquist, *Songs of N. R. . . .* (DMA diss., Univ. of Mo., 1970); Bennie Middaugh, "The Songs of N. R., Aspects

of Musical Style," *NATS Bulletin* (May 1968): 36–39; William S. W. North, *N. R. as a 20th-Century Song Composer* (DMA diss., Univ. of Ill., 1965); L. G. Rickert, "Song Cycles for Baritone," *NATS Bulletin* (Nov 1967): 13–15.

James R. Holmes

SEE ALSO Liturgical Music: Christian.

Rosenberg, Hilding (b. Bosjökloster, Sweden, 21 June 1892), was educated primarily in Stockholm. He studied piano with Richard Andersson (1914–18) and composition, first with E. Ellberg at the Royal Academy of Music (1915–16) and later with Wilhelm Stenhammar. During 1920–21 Rosenberg continued his training in Germany, Vienna, and Paris (piano with Buchmayer in Dresden, conducting with Striegler in Dresden and Scherchen in Königsberg). In the earlier part of his life he was active as a pianist and organist and taught piano and theory at Richard Andersson's Music School in Stockholm (1916–30). During 1932–34 he was conductor of the Royal Swedish Opera in Stockholm and has been guest conductor of several European orchestras. From about 1950 Rosenberg taught composition privately; his pupils include Karl-Birger Blomdahl, Sven-Erik Bäck, and Ingvar Lidholm. Rosenberg's style was influenced first by Swedish national romanticism and Sibelius, and subsequently by his contact in Berlin with Schoenberg's music and with neoclassicism.

PRINCIPAL COMPOSITIONS (published by Nordiska unless otherwise noted): *Symphony No. 2* (1929; revised 1935, Gehrman); *Resa till Amerika* [Voyage to America], opera and orchestral suite (1932, Suecia); *Christmas Oratorio* (1936, unpub.); *Orfeus i stan* [Orpheus in Town], ballet and orchestral suite (1938); *Symphony No. 3* (1939); *Marionetter* [Marionettes], opera (1939); *Symphony No. 4*, "Johannes uppensarelse" [The Revelation of St. John] (1940); *Symphony No. 5*, "Hortulanus" (1944, Gehrman); *Lycksalighetens ö* [Island of Felicity], opera (1945); *Josef och hans bröder* [Joseph and his Brothers], opera-oratorio after Thomas Mann (1945–48, unpub.); *14 Chinese Poems* for soprano, piano (1945–51, Musikaliska Konstföreningen); *Concerto No. 1* for string orchestra (1946); *Motets* for chorus (1949); *String Quartet No. 5* (1949); *Piano Concerto* (1950); *Symphony No. 6*, "Sinfonia semplice" (1951); *Violin Concerto No. 2* (1951); *String Quartet No. 6* (1954); *String Quartet No. 7* (1956); *String Quartets Nos. 8–12* (1957); *Riflessioni 1–3* for string orchestra (1959–60); *Metamorfosi sinfoniche 1–3* (1964, Suecia); *Symphony* for wind orchestra (1968, unpub.); *Hus med dubbel ingång* [The House with Two Entrances], opera (1969, unpub.).

BIBL.: M. Pergament, "H. R.: A Journey in Modern Swedish Music," *Music and Letters* (July 1947):249–57; Alf Thoor, "Gösta Nystroem and H. R.," *Sweden in Music* (Stockholm: Musikrevy International, 1960):57–60; Nils L. Wallin, "H. R.'s The Revelation of St. John," *Music of the North* (Stockholm: Musikrevy International, 1951):17–24.

[prepared with the help of Per Olaf Lundahl]
SEE ALSO Scandinavia.

Rosenboom, David (b. Fairfield, Iowa, 9 Sept 1947), studied at the Univ. of Ill. (1965–67; composition with Gordon Binkerd and Salvatore Martirano, experimental and computer music with Lejaren Hiller). In 1970–71 he studied Indian music privately with Pandit Pran Nath. During 1967–68 he was composer-in-residence at the Center for the Creative and Performing Arts of the State Univ. of N. Y. at Buffalo. He was a lecturer at N. Y. Univ. during 1968–70 and since then has been director of computer and electronic media research at York Univ. in Toronto. In 1969 he helped found the Neurona Co. for research and development in electronics and multimedia production. Also in that year he was artistic director of the "Electric Ear" multimedia series in New York. He has been a freelance consultant to a number of electronics firms and universities on computer applications and mathematical modeling and has composed for films, radio, and television. He is currently involved in "research in brain activity as related to esthetic sets, neurological correlates of kinds of esthetic syntax, and an art-science marriage involved more with behavioral science than technological gadgetry."

PRINCIPAL COMPOSITIONS: *Contrasts* for violin, orchestra (1963); *Trio* for clarinet, trumpet, double bass (1966, Autograph); *Caliban upon Setebos* for orchestra, after Robert Browning (1966, Autograph); *Pocket Pieces* for flute, alto saxophone, viola, percussion (1966, Autograph); *The Thud, Thud, Thud of Suffocating Blackness* for 2 percussionists, alto saxophone, electric cello, piano/celesta, tape, lights (1966–67); *To That Predestined Dancing Place* for percussion quartet (1967); *Then We Wound Our Way through an Aura of Golden Yellow Gauze* for musicians, actress (1967, recorded by Columbia); *She Loves Me, She Loves Me Not*, theater piece for 4-channel tape, 2 actor-musicians, percussionists, witch doctor, 2 slide projectors, overhead projector, Crofon optic, SCR controllers (1968); *Urboui* for tape, 16-mm. film (1968); *And Come Up Dripping* for oboe, analog computer (1968, CPE and *Source*);6 *How Much Better if Plymouth Rock Had Landea on the Pilgrims* for live electronic and traditional instruments (1969–71); *Ecology of the Skin*, "a demonstration-performance-participation environment in biofeedback experience for performers and group dynamic brainwave encounters on the parts of members of the audience" (1970).

PRINCIPAL WRITINGS: "Saturation in Multi-Media," *The Continuum* 1/1 (1968); " . . . the future of art and power. For the Last Several Million Years," *The Composer* (Redondo Beach, Calif.) 1/4 (1970); *Systems Theoretical Approach to Art Media* (London, Pergamon Press, in preparation); *Information Concepts in Composing with Electronic Music Synthesizers*, an instructional method (Newton Highlands, Mass., Tonus, in preparation).

BIBL.: Barnard L. Collier, "A Composition for Cranium and Computer," *Washington Post* (7 Dec 1970); Edgar E. Coons, "Notes on 'Ecology of the Skin'," mimeographed program notes; David Cope, *New Directions in Music* (Dubuque, Iowa, 1971); Donal Henahan, "Music Draws Strains Direct from Brains," *New York Times* (25 Nov 1970); Carmen Moore, "The Sound of Mind," *Village Voice* (New York, 24 Dec 1970).

Rosenthal, Manuel (François) (b. Paris, 18 June 1904), attended the Paris Conservatory (1922–24, violin with Jules Boucherit) and studied composition and orchestration with Maurice Ravel (1926–30). He is a widely known symphonic and operatic conductor and has been teaching conducting at the Paris Conservatory since 1962.

PRINCIPAL COMPOSITIONS (published by Jobert unless otherwise noted): *Rayon des soieries*, 1-act opera bouffe; libretto by Nino (1926, Heugel); *Chansons du Monsieur Bleu* for medium voice, small orchestra (piano); poems by Nino (1934); *La Poule noire*, 1-act operetta; libretto by Nino (1934, Heugel); *Jeanne d'Arc*, orchestral suite, narrator ad lib.; text by Joseph Delterl (1936); *Gaîté parisienne*, ballet (for the Ballet Russe de Monte-Carlo) on themes of Offenbach (1938, unpub.); *St. François d'Assise*, oratorio for narrator, orchestra; text by Roland Manuel (1939); *Les Soirées du petit Juas*, 8 pieces for string quartet (1941); *La Piéta d'Avignon* for soprano, alto, tenor, bass, string orchestra, trumpet (1942); *La Belle Zélie*, suite for 2 pianos (1948); *Symphonies de Noël*, orchestral suite (1948); *Magic Manhattan*, symphonic poem (1949); *Symphony in C* (1950); *Missa Deo gratias* for vocal soloists, chorus, orchestra (1953, ORTF); *Les Femmes au tombeau*, 1-act opera; text by Michel de Ghelderode (1956, Meridian); *Hop Signor!*, 3-act opera; text by De Ghelderode, translated by Antoine Goléa (1957–58); *2 Etudes en camaïeu* for string orchestra, timpani (1969); *Aeolus* for wind quintet, string orchestra (1970).

SEE ALSO France.

Roussel, Albert (b. Tourcoing, France, 5 April 1869; d. Royan, 23 August 1937), began his career as a French navy officer but resigned in 1894 to undertake full-time musical study. In 1898, after working with Eugene Gigout, he entered the Schola Cantorum under Vincent d'Indy, where he continued as a pupil until 1909 and subsequently as professor of counterpoint until 1914. He served in the French army during World War I and thereafter devoted himself entirely to composition.

Roussel wrote orchestral and stage works, incidental theater music, choral, chamber, and piano works, and songs. The early large-scale works show the overwhelming influence of d'Indy; they are lengthy, cyclic in form, and melodically uninteresting. It was in the shorter works (*Divertissement* for wind and piano, Op. 6) that his personality began to declare itself, due in part to the liberating influence of impressionist techniques (with affinities to Ravel rather than Debussy). This liberation was finally completed in *Le Festin de l'Araignée* (1912), an "insect" ballet in which Roussel's forceful rhythms are allied to graceful melodic curves and delicate yet firm orchestral coloring. The influence of Indian music and legend, which he had come to know during his travels, appears in the scale formations (flat 2nd, raised 4th, flat 6th) used for the *Padmâvatî* ballet and *Evocations*. After the war Roussel developed his own version of neoclassicism, combining driving rhythms and harsh harmonies with expressive counterpoints and rich orchestral textures. This tendency culminated in the third and fourth symphonies and the ballets *Bacchus et Ariane* and *Aenéas*. The late orchestral works represent his most powerful expression, marred only occasionally by rhythmic rigidity. Despite his declared dislike in later years of program music, his ballet scores and his songs bear witness to a typically French ability to translate pictures and actions into musical terms. Owing to the eclectic and personal nature of his style, his influence has been slight, although he was a sympathetic teacher and numbered among his pupils such diverse musicians as Satie, Varèse, and Martinů.

PRINCIPAL COMPOSITIONS (published by Durand unless otherwise noted): *Divertissement* for wind quintet, piano, Op. 6 (1906, Rouart-Lerolle); *Le Festin de l'Araignée*, ballet, Op. 17 (1912); *Padmâvatî*, opera-ballet, Op. 18 (1914, orchestrated 1918); *Violin Sonata No. 2 in A*, Op. 28 (1924); *Serenade* for flute, harp, string trio, Op. 30 (1925); *Suite in F* for orchestra, Op. 33 (1926); *Psalm 80* for tenor, chorus, orchestra, Op. 37 (1928, S-B); *Petite Suite* for orchestra, Op. 39 (1929); *Trio* for flute, viola, cello, Op. 40 (1929); *Symphony No. 3 in G Minor*, Op. 42 (1930); *Bacchus et Ariane*, ballet, Op. 43 (1930); *String Quartet in D*, Op. 45 (1932); *Sinfonietta* for strings, Op. 52 (1934); *Symphony No. 4 in A*, Op. 53 (1934); *Aenéas*, ballet, Op. 54 (1935); *String Trio*, Op. 58 (1937). Complete list: *Catalogue de l'oeuvre d'A. R.* (Paris-Brussels 1947).

BIBL.: Basil Deane, *A. R.* (London 1961).

Basil Deane

Row, see Set; see also 12-Tone Techniques

Rozsa, Miklos (Budapest, 18 April 1907), studied during 1925–29 at the Leipzig Conservatory (composition with Hermann Grabner) and Leipzig Univ. (musicology with Theodor Kroyer). He lived in Paris during the early 30s, then in London, where he studied at the Trinity College of Music (1936–40, conducting with John Fry). During 1936–42 he was music director and composer for the film producer Alexander Korda. He emigrated to the U.S. in 1940 and was a composer for MGM films, 1948–62. During 1945–65 he taught at the Univ. of Southern Calif. A lasting influence on his music has been Hungarian folksong, which he collected as a young man.

PRINCIPAL COMPOSITIONS: *Theme, Variations, and Finale* for orchestra, Op. 13a (1933, Eulenberg and Peters); *For Everything There Is a Season*, Op. 21, motet for chorus, organ ad lib.; text from Ecclesiastes 3 (1946, Breitkopf and AMP); *Spellbound*, film score (1946); *Piano Sonata*, Op. 20 (1948, Breitkopf); *A Double Life*, film score (1948); *String Quartet*, Op. 22 (1950, AMP); *Violin Concerto*, Op. 24 (1953, Breitkopf); *Overture to a Symphony Concert*, Op. 26a (1956, Eulenberg and Peters); *Ben Hur*, film score (1959); *Sinfonia concertante* for violin, cello, orchestra, Op. 29 (1964, Breitkopf and AMP); *Piano Concerto*, Op. 31 (1965, Breitkopf and AMP); *The Vanities of Life*, motet for chorus, Op. 30; text from Ecclesiastes 1 (1966, Breitkopf and AMP); *Cello Concerto*, Op. 32 (1968, Breitkopf and AMP).

BIBL.: Ken Doeckel, "M. R. Composes as Thoughtfully for Films as for the Concert Stage," *Films in Review* (Nov 1965): 536–48.

Rubbra, Edmund (b. Northampton, England, 23 May 1901), studied at Reading Univ. (1920–21, composition with Gustav Holst, piano with Evelyn Howard-Jones) and at the Royal College of Music in London (1921–25; composition with Gustav Holst, R. O. Morris). He was pianist with the Rubbra-Gruenberg-Pleeth Trio during 1945–56. During 1947–68 he was senior lecturer in music at Oxford Univ., and since 1961 he has been professor of composition at the Guildhall School of Music in London.

PRINCIPAL COMPOSITIONS (published by Lengnick; the year given is date of publication): *Violin Sonata No. 2* (1932); *String Quartets Nos. 1–3* (1934, revised 1946; 1952; 1968); *Symphonies Nos. 1–8* (1937; 1938, revised 1951; 1939; 1942; 1949; 1955; 1957; 1968); *Missa cantuariensis* for double chorus (1946); *Cello Sonata* (1947); *Missa in honorem Sancti Dominici* for chorus (1949); *Piano Trio No. 1* (1950); *Viola Concerto* (1953); *In honorem Mariae Matris Dei*, cantata for soloists, chorus, children's chorus, orchestra (1957); *Missa a tre* for chorus (1958); *Oboe Sonata* (1959); *Piano Concerto* (1959); *Cantata di Camera* for tenor, chorus, flute, violin, cello, harp, organ (1961); *Violin Concerto* (1962); *Inscape*, suite for chorus, strings, harp; text by G. M. Hopkins (1965); *Veni, Creator Spiritus* for chorus, brass (1966); *8 Preludes* for piano (1967); *Violin Sonata No. 3* (1968); *Advent Cantata* for baritone, chorus, strings (1968); *Missa brevis* for chorus, organ (1969); *Piano Trio No. 2* (1970).

PRINCIPAL WRITINGS: *Holst: A Monograph* (Monaco 1947); *Counterpoint: A Survey* (London 1960); "Missa in Honorem Sancti Dominici," *The Composer's Point of View* ed. by R. S. Hines (Norman, Okla., 1963):103–10. Rubbra has also edited *The Evolution of Music* by Alfredo Casella (London 1963).

BIBL.: R. Murray Schafer, *British Composers in Interview* (London 1963):64–72.

SEE ALSO Great Britain.

Rudhyar, Dane (pseudonym of Daniel Chennevière) (b. Paris, 23 March 1895), studied at the Sorbonne (Bachelor of Philosophy, 1911) and the Paris Conservatory (1913) but was mainly self-taught as a composer. He emigrated to the U.S. in 1917 and has since earned his living as a free-lance composer, lecturer, and writer on many subjects. Since 1933 he has written a dozen books setting forth a "humanistic approach to astro-psychology." He also paints and writes poetry. He describes his music as having been influenced by Debussy, early Stravinsky (after 1913), Scriabin (after 1917), and the late piano works of Liszt (after 1920).

PRINCIPAL COMPOSITIONS: *3 Melodies* for flute, cello, piano (1919); *9 Tetragrams* for piano (in 3 series: 1920, 26, 27; 1925, 27, 29; 1924, 28, 67; CFE); *Syntony No. 1* for orchestra (1920–22); *Syntony No. 2* for orchestra (1921); *4 Pentagrams* for piano: "The Coming Forth," "The Enfolding," "The Release," "The Human Way" (1924, 1924, 1926, 1926; CFE; an earlier version of nos. 1–3 published by Birchard under the title "Moments");

Paeans for piano (1927, Presser); *5 Stanzas* for string ensemble (1927); *Syntony* for piano (1929, CFE); *Granites* for piano (1932, Presser); *Sinfonietta* (1937, New Music); *Emergence*, pentagram for string orchestra (1953); *Syntony No. 5* for orchestra (1954, not yet orchestrated).

PRINCIPAL WRITINGS: *Claude Debussy* (Paris 1913); "The Two Trends of Modern Music in Stravinsky's Works," *Musical Quarterly* (April 1919); "The Rise of the Musical Proletariat," *ibid.* (Jan 1919); "The Relativity of Our Musical Conceptions," *ibid.* (Jan 1922); "Claude Debussy and the Counterpoint of the Future," *Pearson's Magazine* (March 1925); "A New Conception of Music," *The Forum* (Dec 1926); *The Rebirth of Hindu Music* (Madras 1929); *World Music* (1936, unpub.).

BIBL.: Alfred Morand, *D. R., Pioneer in Creative Synthesis* (New York 1939); Paul Rosenfeld, "Musical Chronicle," *The Dial* (Dec 1925):525–28; James Shere, *D. R. 1895– , A Brief Biography With a Listing of Works* (privately printed 1972).

SEE ALSO Asian Music and Western Composition, Dance.

Rudziński, Witold (b. Siebież, Russia, 14 March 1913), attended the university in Vilna (1931–36) and the Vilna Conservatory (1928–37). During 1938–39 he studied at the Institut Grégorien in Paris and also worked with Nadia Boulanger and Charles Koechlin. He was head of the Stanisław Moniuszko School of Music in Święciany, Poland (1937–38) and taught at the conservatories of Vilna (1939–42) and Łodz (1945–47). He was head of the music department of the Ministry of Culture, Warsaw, during 1947–48 and directed the Warsaw opera and Philharmonic Orchestra, 1948–49. Since 1957 he has taught at the National Superior School of Music in Warsaw.

PRINCIPAL COMPOSITIONS: *Divertimento* for strings (1940); *Viola Sonata* (1940, PWM); *Pięć lat* [5 Years] for chorus; poem by Lesław M. Bartelski (1945, PWM); *Nonet* (1947); *Janko muzykant* [Janko the Fiddler], 3-act opera; libretto by T. Borowski and S. Wygodzki after H. Sienkiewicz (1951); *Chłopska droga* [Peasants' Road], cantata; texts by Krasicki, Lenartowicz, Wolski, Konopnicka (1952); *Quintet* for flute, strings (1954, PWM); *Komendant Paryża* [The Commandant of Paris], 3-act opera; libretto by T. Marek (1958); *Musique concertante* for piano, chamber orchestra (1959); *Dach świata* [The Roof of the World] for speaker, orchestra; poem by B. Ostromęcki (1960, PWM); *2 Portraits des femmes* for voice, string quartet; poems by Ronsard and Rimbaud (1961); *Odprawa posłów greckich* [The Dismissal of the Grecian Envoys], 1-act opera; libretto by Ostromęcki after Jan Kochanowski (1963, PWM); *Sulamith*, 1-act opera; libretto by

Ostromęcki (1964); *Les Images des Monts de la Sainte Croix* for orchestra (1965, PWM); *Gaude Mater Polonia*, oratorio; texts by Ostromęcki and Polish authors (1966, PWM); *Lipce*, oratorio; text from W. S. Reymont (1968).

PRINCIPAL WRITINGS: *Lekcje słuchania muzyki* [Lessons on Listening to Music] (Cracow 1948); *Muzyka dla wszystkich* [Music for Everybody] (Cracow 1948, 1967); *Warsztat kompozytorski Béli Bartóka* [Bartók's Musical Technique] (Cracow 1964); *Stanisław Moniuszko: Listy zebrane* [. . . Collected Letters] (Cracow 1954, 1957, 1970).

Rudziński, Zbigniew (b. Czechowice, Poland, 23 Oct 1935), attended the State College of Music in Warsaw (1956–62, composition with Piotr Perkowski). During 1960–67 he was music director of the Warsaw Documentary Film Studio. He currently works as a freelance composer in Warsaw.

PRINCIPAL COMPOSITIONS: *Sonata* for 2 string quartets, piano, tympani (1960); *4 Songs* for baritone, chamber orchestra (1961); *Epigrams* for flute, chorus, percussion (1962); *Contra fidem* for orchestra (1964, PWM); *String Trio* (1964, PWM); *Study in C* for ensemble ad lib. (1964, PWM); *Moments musicaux Nos. 1–3* for orchestra (1965, 66, 68; PWM); *Impromptu* for 2 pianos, 3 cellos, percussion (1966, PWM); *3 Songs* for tenor, 2 pianos; texts by Ezra Pound, James Joyce, William Rose Benét (1968); *Symphony* for bass chorus, orchestra; without text (1969); *Quartet* for 2 pianos, percussion (1969).

Ruggles, Carl (Charles Sprague) (b. Marion, Mass., 11 March 1876; d. Bennington, Vt., 24 Oct 1971), began lessons on a homemade violin at six. He went to Boston in his teens and earned his living in theater orchestras. He also attended rehearsals of the Boston Symphony and studied privately with Felix Winternitz (violin), Josef Claus (theory), and John Knowles Paine (composition). He enrolled as a special student at Harvard Univ. (where Paine taught) in the fall of 1903 and about this time adopted Carl as his first name. In 1907 he went to Winona, Minn., to teach at a local music school. He resigned a year later but remained in Winona as conductor of the local orchestra. When the orchestra's activity declined after 1912, he began to devote himself to composition. Following his return from Minn. in 1917, he divided his time between New York and Arlington, Vt. He was active in the International Composers Guild and the Pan American Assoc. of Composers; when in Vermont, aided by patrons, he was free to compose and paint (an avocation he took up in Winona). His most productive period extended from the late 1920s through the early 40s. After 1966 he lived in a nursing home in Bennington, Vt.

In general Ruggles worked with care at the expense of speed; he finished only a small number of compositions. His early efforts were predominantly vocal; most, including an opera, *The Sunken Bell* (on which he spent 13 years), have been lost or destroyed by the composer. The mature works are all instrumental: a set of piano pieces, a short piece for brass and a longer one for strings (both movements from uncompleted suites), and orchestral works. This music is essentially linear and chromatic with melodic tones frequently sustained to form harmonies, much in the manner of a piano's pedal. Like his Viennese contemporaries, Ruggles sought to avoid triadic tonality and, in its stead, to use the 12 tones of the chromatic scale as equally as possible. He was careful not to repeat a note (or any of its octave transpositions) until he was sure it would no longer be in the listener's consciousness. He worked intuitively, and the results are difficult to codify. Individual lines, however, can often be reduced to three-note "sets," of which the two intervening intervals (a fourth and minor second, for example) have been repeated, reversed, inverted, expanded into adjacent octaves, etc., to produce long passages that retain a feeling of consistency.

PRINCIPAL COMPOSITIONS (many of these works were first published in the periodical *New Music*; they are now available from AME unless otherwise noted): *Angels* for 5 trumpets, bass trumpet (1921, Curwen) or 4 trumpets (violins), 3 trombones (cellos) (1938); *Men and Mountains* for orchestra (1924); *Portals* for string orchestra (1926); *Sun-treader* for orchestra (1931–32); *Evocations* for piano (1937–44, revised 1954; transcribed for orchestra, unpub.); *Organum* for orchestra (1944–47).

BIBL.: Steven E. Gilbert, "C. R. and Total Chromaticism," *Yearbook for Inter-American Musical Research* 7; ——, "The 'Twelve-Tone System' of C. R.: A Study of the *Evocations* for Piano," *Journal of Music Theory* 14:68–91; Lou Harrison, "C. R.," *Score* (June 1955):15–26; John Kirkpatrick, "The Evolution of C. R., A Chronicle Largely in His Own Words," *Perspectives* 6/2:146–66; Charles Seeger, "C. R.," *Musical Quarterly* 18:578–92, reprinted in *American Composers on American Music* ed. by H. Cowell (New York 1961).

Steven E. Gilbert

SEE ALSO Expressionism, Form.

Russia, see Soviet Union

Russo, William (b. Chicago, 25 June 1928), studied English at Roosevelt Univ. in Chicago (1951–55) and composition privately with John J. Becker (1953–55) and Karel Jirák (1955–57). He founded and directed "An Experiment in Jazz," a Chicago rehearsal orchestra (1947–50), and was trombonist and later composer-arranger for the Stan Kenton Orchestra (1950–54). In New York he founded and directed the Russo Orchestra (1958–61), and in London he directed the London Jazz Orchestra (1962–65). He has been associated with the Center for New Music of Columbia College in Chicago since 1965, where he directs the Chicago Jazz Ensemble and, since 1968, the Free Theater. During 1969–70 he taught at the Peabody Institute, where he directed the Rock Theater.

PRINCIPAL COMPOSITIONS: *The English Suite* for jazz orchestra (1955); *Les Deux Errants*, ballet, choreography by Wolfgang Brunner (1955); *Symphony No. 1*, Op. 15 (1957); *Symphony No. 2 in C*, "The Titans," Op. 32 (1958); *Concerto Grosso* for band, Op. 37 (1960); *John Hooton*, 3-act opera, Op. 36; libretto by the composer (1961, EM); *Cello Concerto*, Op. 41 (1962); *The English Concerto* for violin, jazz orchestra, Op. 43 (1963); *In memoriam* for 2 soloists, chorus, jazz orchestra, Op. 47 (1966); *America 1966*, concerto grosso for jazz orchestra (1966); *The Civil War*, rock cantata for 3 soloists, chorus, rock band; composed with Irma Routen; text from poems by Paul Horgen (1968); *David*, rock cantata for 10 soloists, chorus, based on First and Second Samuel; composed with Robert Perrey (1968); *Liberation*, rock cantata for soloists, chorus, rock band, dancers; text by Naomi Lazard (1969).

PRINCIPAL WRITINGS: *Composing for the Jazz Orchestra* (Chicago 1961); *Jazz: Composition and Orchestration* (Chicago 1968).

Russolo, Luigi (b. Portogruaro, Italy, 1 May 1885; d. Cerro di Laveno, 4 Feb 1947), was trained as a painter and became a theorist of the futurist movement as well as one of its principal musical exponents. In 1913 he wrote *L'arte dei rumori*, in which he advocated the use of a variety of sounds and noises as materials for musical composition. Wishing to reach beyond the sounds obtainable from conventional instruments, he invented a series of *intonarumori* [noise intoners], beginning about 1912, which consisted of wooden boxes containing diaphragms and other mechanisms amplified by megaphones. By 1926 he had constructed prepared keyboard instruments, which he called *psofarmoni*. For these various instruments he developed a notation using graphics. None of the instruments or scores survive. According to Kirby (see bibl.), "not only did he seek a greater variety of quality, pitch, and rhythm in music, but he extended the concept of music itself to include sounds that never before were accepted. He made available for musical composition all the sounds of everyday life. With his own *intonarumori* and *psofarmoni*, he demonstrated that the practical limits of music were only those of technology and inventiveness. . . . He rejected the 'weak acoustical results' of traditional orchestras, and his emphasis on volume and intensity has now become widely accepted."

PRINCIPAL COMPOSITIONS: *Risveglio di una città* (premiere London 1914); *Convegno d'aeroplani e d'automobili* (premiere London 1914). Documentation of other compositions by Russolo is lacking.

PRINCIPAL WRITINGS: *L'arte dei rumori* (Milan, 7 March 1913) trans. into English by Robert Filliou, *The Art of Noise* (New York 1967); "Gl'intonarumori futuristi," *Lacerba* (1 July 1913):140–41; "Conquista totale dell'Enarmonismo mediante gl'intonarumori futuristi," *ibid.* (1 Nov 1913):242, 244–45; "Grafia enarmonica per gl'intonarumori futuristi," *ibid.* (1 March 1914):74–75.

BIBL.: Michael Kirby, *Futurist Performance* (New York 1971); Ignace Lilien, "Soniek anno 1914; *L'arte dei rumori* van L. R.," *Mens en melodie* (July 1963):203–06; F. K. Prieberg, "Der musikalische Futurismus," *Melos* 25:124–27; ——, *Musica ex machina* (Berlin 1960); J. C. Waterhouse "A Futurist Mystery," *Music and Musicians* (April 1967):26–30.

SEE ALSO Futurism.

Ruyneman, Daniel (b. Amsterdam, 8 August 1886; d. Amsterdam, 25 July 1963), studied at the Amsterdam Conservatory (1913–16, composition with Bernard Zweers). In 1918 he helped found the Netherlands Society for the Development of Modern Music, which later became a section of ISCM. During 1924–29 he was the conductor of Bragi, the student music society of the Univ. of Groningen. In 1930 he founded the Netherlands Society for Contemporary Music, which he led until 1962; he also edited the Society's journal, *Tijdschrift voor Hedendaagse Muziek*, during 1930–40, until it was suppressed by the Nazis. Through the 1930s he experimented with new sonorities: Gamelon-like sounds occur in *Hiëroglyphs*, and the choral works explore the color possibilities of phonemes (they do not use texts). He tended toward neoclassicism in his later music and in the 50s occasionally used serial techniques.

PRINCIPAL COMPOSITIONS (published by Donemus unless otherwise noted): *Hiëroglyphs* for 3 flutes, 2 mandolins, 2 guitars, celesta, harp, cup bells or vibraphone, piano (1918, Chester); *De Roep* for chamber chorus singing phonemes (1918, Alsbach); *Divertimento* for flute, clarinet, horn, viola, piano (1918, Chester); *Sonata for Chamber Choir* singing phonemes (1931, New Music); *4 Tempi* for 4 cellos (1937); *Violin Concerto* (1941); *Ouverture Amphitryon* (1943); *String Quartet* (1946); *Symphony 1953* (1953); *Reflexions IV* for wind quintet (1961); *Gilgamesj* for orchestra (1962).

PRINCIPAL WRITINGS: *De componist Jan Ingenhoven* (Amsterdam 1938); "De instrumentale koorstijl en zijn ontwikkelingsmogelijkheden" [Instrumental Choral Style and Its Potentials], *De Wereld der Muziek* 9 (1943):307–13.

BIBL.: Carol-Bérard, "D. R.," *The Chesterian* (1928):187–89; Arthur Hoérée, "D. R.," *Revue musicale* 25:30–32; Wouter Paap, "D. R.," *Mens en Melodie* 5:75–80; Willi Reich, "D. R.," *Musikblätter des Anbruch* 16:119–21; Jos Wouters, "D. R.," *Sonorum Speculum* 9:1–9.

[prepared with the help of P. M. Op de Coul]

Rydman, Kari (b. Helsinki, 15 Oct 1936), attended Helsinki Univ. and is self-taught in composition. He teaches music at a secondary school in Helsinki and at the Institute of Industrial Arts. Since 1964 he has been a music critic for the daily *Kauppalehti*; he is also an editor for the musical journal *Rondo*.

PRINCIPAL COMPOSITIONS: *3 Songs* for voice, piano; text by Elmer Diktonius (1957); *Sancta Maria ora pro nobis* for chorus (1957); *Composition* for piano (1959); *String Quartets Nos. 1–5* (1959, 1963, 1964, 1964, 1966; Nos. 2–4, Westerlund); *Piano Quintet* (1960); *Etude sur l'évolution tonale* for piano (1960); *Trio* for violin, cello, percussion (1961); *Declamatory Songs* for narrator, tape (1961); *Sonata No. 1* for 3 violins, viola, cello, piano, percussion (1962); *Sonata No. 2* for violin, viola, guitar, percussion (1962); *Suite* for narrator, 11 musicians; text by Tuomas Anhava (1962); *Sérénade à Djamila Boupacha* for orchestra (1963); *Sonata No. 4* for violin, clarinet, guitar, percussion (1963); *Dona nobis pacem* for chorus (1963); *O Crux ave spes unica* for chorus (1963); *Syrinx* for orchestra (1964); *Khoros 1* for 3 flutes, oboe, 2 percussion, harp, violin, viola, cello, double bass (1964); *Sonata No. 6* for cello, percussion ad lib. (1964); *Onnamai* for orchestra (1966); *Khoros 2* for orchestra (1966); *Rondeaux des nuits blanches d'été* for orchestra (1966); *Symphony of the Modern Worlds* for orchestra (1968); *Sonata No. 9* for 14 instruments (1969).

PRINCIPAL WRITINGS: Rydman has edited 3 books: *Sävelten maailma* [The World of Music] (1956), *Musiikin vaiheet* [Vicissitudes of Music] (1959), and *Mestarien musiikkia* [Music of the Masters] (1953).

Rzewski, Frederic (Anthony) (b. Westfield, Mass., 13 April 1938), attended Harvard Univ. (1954–58, counterpoint with Randall Thompson, orchestration with Claudio Spies) and Princeton Univ. (1958–60, music of Wagner with Oliver Strunk), where he also studied philosophy and Greek literature. Since 1960 he has performed professionally as a pianist. He taught at the Cologne Courses for New Music in 1963, 1964, and 1970. In 1966 he helped found the Musica Elettronica Viva studio in Rome, where he lived until moving to New York in 1971. Many of his musical ideas have been influenced by nonmusical disciplines, in particular the lectures of Herbert Marcuse, and by the music of John Cage, David Tudor, and Karlheinz Stockhausen.

PRINCIPAL COMPOSITIONS: *Preludes* for piano (1957); *Poem* for piano (1959); *Sonata* for 2 pianos (1960); *Study* for piano (1960); *Dreams* for piano (1961); *Octet* for flute, clarinet, trumpet, trombone, violin, double bass, piano, harp (1961–62); *For Violin* for solo violin (1962); *Requiem* for chorus, chamber ensemble (1963–67); *Composition for 2* for any 2 instruments (1964); *Speculum Dianae* for any 8 instruments (1964); *Self-portrait* for 1 person, any sounds (1964); *Nature morte* for winds, trumpet, horn, violin, cello, organ, piano, harp, 5 percussion (1965); *Zoologischer Garten* on tape (1965); *Impersonation* for 2 soloists, 4 stereo tape machines, mixer (1966); *Projector-Piece* for any 2 groups of musicians with dancers, slide projectors (1966); *Portrait* for actor, lights, slides, film, photoresistors, 6 tapes (1967); *Work Songs*, prose texts written for the Musica Elettronica Viva group (1967–69); *Les Moutons de Panurge* for any number of melody instruments (1969); *Last Judgment* for trombone (1969); *Monuments* for voice, piano (1970); *Old Maid* for soprano, chorus (1970); *Music for Children* on 2-track tape; *Falling Music* for piano, tape (1971); *Coming Together* for narrator, instruments; text from a 1971 letter by a prisoner at the Attica State Prison, N.Y., who was later murdered by law-enforcement officials (1972).

BIBL.: Henri Pousseur, *Fragments théoriques sur la musique expérimentale* (Brussels 1970):180f., 186.

SEE ALSO Mixed Media, Performance, Prose Music, Rhythm.

S

Sadaï, Yitzhak (b. Sofia, Bulgaria, 13 May 1935), studied at the Academy of Music in Tel Aviv (1951–56, composition and theory with Alexander Boskovitch, Öedöen Partos, and Roman Haubenstock-Ramati). He has taught theory at Rubin's Academy of Music in Jerusalem since 1960 and at the Univ. of Tel Aviv since 1966.

PRINCIPAL COMPOSITIONS (published by IMP): *Nuances* for chamber orchestra (1965); *Aria da capo* for 6 performers, 2 tape recorders (1966); *Prélude à Jérusalem* for chorus, orchestra (1968).

PRINCIPAL WRITINGS: *Metodologia shel hateosia hamusicalit* [Methodology of Music Theory] (Tel Aviv 1962); *Haaspectim hateosetim ve hafenoménologiim shel haharmonia hamusicalit* [Harmony and Its Theoretical and Phenomenological Aspects] (in prepararion).

BIBL.: Peter Gradenwitz, *Music and Musicians in Israel* (Tel Aviv 1959).

SEE ALSO Israel.

Saeverud, Harald (Sigurd Johan) (b. Bergen, Norway, 17 April 1897), studied at the Bergen Conservatory (1913–18) and the Berlin Hochschule für Musik (1921–22, composition with Franz E. Koch, orchestration with Emil von Rezniček). He also studied conducting in Berlin with Clemens Krauss (1935). During 1929–40 he was a music critic in Bergen. He has conducted the Bergen Harmonien orchestra (the fourth oldest in the world) in the premieres of all his orchestral works. He describes his music as much influenced by the natural grandeur of western Norway.

PRINCIPAL COMPOSITIONS (published by MH unless otherwise noted): *Overtura appassionata* for orchestra, Op. 2 (1920); *Symphonies Nos. 2–9:* No. 2, Op. 4 (1922); No. 3, Op. 5 (1926, unpub.); No. 4, Op. 11 (1937, unpub.); No. 5, "Quasi una fantasia," Op. 16 (1941, unpub.); No. 6, "Sinfonia dolorosa," Op. 19 (1942); No. 7, "Salme" [Psalm], Op. 27 (1944–45); No. 8, "Minnesota," Op. 40 (1959); No. 9, Op. 45 (1965, unpub.); *50 Variationi piccole* for chamber orchestra, Op. 8 (1931, Norsk); *Canto ostinato* for orchestra, Op. 9 (1934, Norsk); *Lucretia Suite* for orchestra, Op. 10 (1936); *Oboe Concerto*, Op. 12 (1938, unpub.); *Gjaetlevise-variasjoner* [Variations on a Shepherd

Tune] for chamber orchestra, Op. 15 (1941); *Siljnslåtten*, symphonic dance for orchestra, Op. 17 (1942, Norsk); 4 suites from the collection *Slåtter og stev fra Siljustöl* [Tunes and Dances from Siljustöl] for piano: Op. 21 (1942), Op. 22 (1943), Op. 24 (1944), Op. 25 (1967); *Kjempeviseslåtten* [The Ballad of Revolt] for orchestra, Op. 22 (1943); *Peer Gynt*, incidental music to Ibsen's play, Op. 28 (1947); *Peer Gynt Suite Nos. 1–2*, Op. 28 (1947); *Piano Concerto No. 2*, Op. 31 (1948–50); *Violin Concerto*, "Vade mors," Op. 37 (1956); *Entrata regale* for orchestra, Op. 41 (1960); *Bassoon Concerto*, Op. 44 (1963, unpub.); *Sonata giubilata* for orchestra, Op. 47 (1969); *Fanfare and Hymn* for orchestra, Op. 48 (1969); *String Quartet*, "Serenades for the 2 Rivals," Op. 49 (1969).

PRINCIPAL WRITINGS: "Peer Gynt-musikk—Salme," *Modern nordisk musik* (Stockholm 1957): 46–64; "H. S.," *Musicalske selvportretter* (Copenhagen 1966):279–84.

BIBL.: *H. S. 1897–1967* (Oslo 1967); S. Lind, "H. S.," *Nordisk Musikkultur* 4.

SEE ALSO Scandinavia.

Salas, Juan Orrego, see under Orrego-Salas

Salgado, Luis H. (b. Cayambe, Ecuador, 10 Dec 1903), studied at the Quito Conservatory (graduated 1928, composition with Francisco Salgado, piano with Sixto Durán). He has taught harmony, counterpoint, and fugue at the Quito Conservatory (1934–68) and at the Inter-American Institute for Sacred Music in Quito (since 1969). He has also written articles on music and literature for the Quito newspaper *El comercio*. His music has been influenced by the impressionists and by the 12-tone techniques of Schoenberg.

PRINCIPAL COMPOSITIONS: *Atahualpa*, symphonic suite for band (1933); *Sonfonía andina* (1943); *Cumandá*, 3-act opera (1944–47); *Suite ecuatoriana* for orchestra (1946); *Piano Sonatas Nos. 1–2* (1949, 1950); *Sinfonía sintética* (1953); *Symphonies Nos. 3–7* (1955, 1956, 1963, 1968, 1970; No. 6 is without winds). List to 1959: *Composers of the Americas* 4:142–51.

PRINCIPAL WRITINGS: *La música vernacular ecuatoriana* (Quito 1952).

Sallinen, Aulis (Heikki) (b. Salmi, Finland, 9 April 1935), studied at the Sibelius Academy (1955–60; composition with Aarre Merikanto, Joonas Kokkonen). During 1960–70 he was manager of the Finnish Radio Symphony Orchestra. He has taught at the Sibelius Academy since 1965.

PRINCIPAL COMPOSITIONS (published by Fazer unless otherwise noted): *Mauermusik* for orchestra (1962); *Metamorphoses* for piano, chamber orchestra (1964, unpub.); *Quattro per quattro* for oboe, violin, cello, harpsichord (1964–65, unpub.); *Cadenza* for violin (1965); *Variations on Mallarmé*, ballet (1967); *Violin Concerto* (1968); *String Quartet No. 3*, "Some Aspects of Peltoniomi Hendriks' Funeral March" (1969); *Chorali* for wind orchestra (1970); *Chaconne* for organ (1970, unpub.).

Salmenhaara, Erkki (b. Helsinki, 12 March 1941), studied at the Sibelius Academy in Helsinki (1957–64, composition with Joonas Kokkonen) and Helsinki Univ. (1960–65, musicology with Erik Tawaststjerna). He also studied composition privately with György Ligeti in Vienna during 1963. He has been a music critic for the *Helsingin Sanomat* since 1963 and since 1966, a lecturer in musicology at Helsinki Univ. He "started in the spirit of the post-Webern avant-garde" and began in the 1960s to use "tonal materials, triads, etc., in a new nonfunctional way. This includes a formal simplification of the musical texture and the use of musical quotations and collage techniques."

PRINCIPAL COMPOSITIONS: *Symphony No. 2* (1963–66, Finnish Broadcasting Co.); *Symphony No. 3* (1964); *Le Bateau ivre* for chamber orchestra (1965); *La Fille en mini-jupe*, poem for orchestra (1967); *Information Explosion*, electronic music (1967, Love Records, Finland); *Requiem profanum* for soprano, alto, baritone, organ, piano, string orchestra (1969).

PRINCIPAL WRITINGS: *Vuosisatamme musiikki* [The Music of Our Century] (Helsinki 1968); *Sointuanalyysi* [Harmonic Analysis] (Helsinki 1968); *Das musikalische Material und seine Behandlung bei Ligeti* (Helsinki-Regensburg 1969).

Salzedo, Carlos (b. Arcachon, France, 6 April 1885; d. Waterville, Me., 17 August 1961), studied at the Paris Conservatory (1896–1901, piano with Charles de Bériot, harp with Alphonse Hasselmans). He was solo harpist with the Association des Premiers Prix de Paris in Monte Carlo (1905–09), the Metropolitan Opera (1909–13), and the Trio de Lutèce (from 1913). In 1917 he organized the seven-member Salzedo Harp Ensemble. His work on behalf of contemporary music included the founding in 1921 of the *Eolian Review* (later called *Eolus* and discontinued in 1933) and of the International Composers Guild with Edgard Varèse. He organized a harp department at the Curtis Institute in 1924 and also taught at the Institute of Musical Art in New York and at the Juilliard School. In 1931 he established the Salzedo Harp Colony at Camden, Me.

PRINCIPAL COMPOSITIONS: *The Enchanted Isle*, symphonic poem for harp, orchestra (1918); *3 Poems by Sara Yarrow* for soprano, 6 harps, oboe, bassoon, horn (1919); *Bolmimerie* for 7 harps (1919); *Harp Sonata* (1922, Schirmer-G); *3 Poems by Mallarmé* for soprano, harp, piano (1924); *Concerto for harp*, 7 winds (1925–26); *Pentacle*, 5 pieces for 2 harps (1928); *Préambule et jeux* for harp, chamber orchestra (1928–29); *Scintillation* for harp (1936, E-V); *Suite*, 8 dances for harp (1943, Schirmer-G); *Prélude fatidique* for harp (1954, Schirmer-G).

PRINCIPAL WRITINGS: *Modern Study of the Harp* (New York 1921); *Method for the Harp* (New York 1929); *The Art of Modulating*, written with Lucile Lawrence (New York 1950); "Editing Mozart's Harp and Flute Concerto," *Musical America* (15 April 1952):23; "On Determining the Art of Working," *Harp News* (spring 1958): 2–3, and *Musical Courier* (9 Feb 1958); "Considerations on the Piano and the Harp," *Eolian Review* (June 1923) and *Harp News* (fall 1961): 10–11.

BIBL.: *Harp News*, memorial issue (fall 1961); R. Heylbut, "Modern Harp Technique: An Interview with C. S.," *Etude* (Jan 1952):9, 56.

Salzman, Eric (b. New York, 8 Sept 1933), studied at Columbia Univ. (1950–54; composition with Otto Luening, Vladimir Ussachevsky), Princeton Univ. (1954–56; composition with Roger Sessions, Milton Babbitt), and the Accadèmia di S. Cecilia (1956–58; composition with Goffredo Petrassi). During 1958–66 he was a music critic first for *The New York Times* and then for the *New York Herald Tribune*; he has been a contributing editor for *Stereo Review* since 1962. He has been music director of radio station WBAI in New York (1962–63, 1968–71), and during 1966–68 he taught at Queens College in New York. He has organized a number of concert series in New York to present new music, and in 1970 he organized a multimedia music theater ensemble, Quog. In his music he has drawn inspiration from such composers as Ives, Varèse, Ruggles, Cowell, and Cage.

Most of his music from the 1960s involves voices and/or electronic means, instrumental groups, and visual images. These works use "a wide variety of means and materials, cutting through various kinds of 'styles' and experiences" to create multilayered music theater.

PRINCIPAL COMPOSITIONS (published by MCA): *cummings set*, songs for voice with orchestra or piano (1953); *Inventions* for orchestra (1957–59); *The Owl and the Cuckoo* for soprano, guitar, chamber ensemble; texts by Shakespeare (1963–64); *Verses and Cantos* or *Foxes and Hedgehogs* for 4 voices, chamber ensemble, live electronics; text by John Ashbery (1963–67); *Queens Collage* on tape (1966); *Larynx Music* for voice, tape (1967); *The Peloponnesian War*, mime-dance-theater work with sound elements on tape; choreography by Daniel Nagrin (1967–68); *Feedback*, environmental work using live electronics; visuals by Stan Vanderbeek (1967–68); *Foxes and Hedgehogs*, antilecture for tape and live electronics (1967–); *The Nude Paper Sermon*, tropes for actor, ensemble of renaissance instruments, chorus, electronic apparatus, tape (1968–69, recorded by Nonesuch); *Can Man Survive?*, multitrack environmental tape work for an exhibition at the American Museum of Natural History, N. Y. (1969); *Strophe/Antistrophe* for harpsichord, tape (1969–71).

PRINCIPAL WRITINGS: "The New American Music," *The New American Arts* ed. by R. Kostelanetz (New York 1965):237–70; *Twentieth Century Music* (Englewood Cliffs, N. J., 1967); "The Revolution in Music," *New American Review* 6:76–96.

BIBL.: James Goodfriend, "E. S.," *Stereo Review* 23/1:104.

SEE ALSO Dance, Mixed Media, Recording, United States.

Saminsky, Lazare (b. Vale-Hotzulovo, near Odessa, Russia, 27 Oct 1882; d. Port Chester, N. Y., 30 June 1959), studied mathematics and philosophy at the Univ. of St. Petersburg (1906–09) and music at the St. Petersburg Conservatory (1906–10, composition and orchestration with Nicholas Rimsky-Korsakov). In 1908 he and some fellow students at the Conservatory founded the Society for Jewish Folk Music; in 1913 he took part in the Baron de Guinzburg Ethnological Expedition, collecting religious chants of the Georgian and Persian Jews in Transcaucasia. He was director of the Tiflis Conservatory during 1917–18, after which he left Russia, eventually settling in New York in 1920. He cofounded the League of Composers in 1923 and during 1924–58 was music director for Temple Emanu-El in New York, where he established the 3 Choirs Festival in 1936. As a composer he came to feel from 1913 on that biblical cantillation, certain old religious chants of both the Eastern and Western synagogue, and the mystical songs of the Hassidim were the most authentic and idiosyncratic elements on which to build new Jewish music. In the earlier years he sometimes quoted Jewish materials, but from 1918 on he more often reshaped and reassembled them. His liturgical works are landmarks in synagogue music.

PRINCIPAL COMPOSITIONS: *Hebrew Song Cycles Nos. 1–2* for voice, piano (1909, 1913–14; Fischer); *Vigiliae*, triad of poems for orchestra (1910–11, Muzyka); *Hebrew Rhapsody* for violin, piano (1911, Fischer); *4 Sacred Choruses* for chorus (1913, Boston Music Co.); *The Lament of Rachel*, biblical ballet in 1 act (1913, rewritten 1920; Salabert); *Symphonies Nos. 1–5:* No. 1, "Symphony of the Great Rivers" (1914); No. 2, "Symphony of the Summits" (1918, Salabert); No. 3, "Symphony of the Seas" (1924, UE); No. 4 (1926, UE); No. 5, "City of Solomon and Christ," with chorus (1929–30, Fischer); *The Vision of Ariel*, 1-act opera-ballet (1916, Bloch, N. Y.); *2 Pieces* for piano (1917, Salabert); *3 Pieces* for piano (1919, Salabert); *10 Hebrew Folk Songs and Folk Dances* for piano (1922, Fischer); *The Gagliarda of a Merry Plague*, 1-act opera-ballet (1924, Salabert); *The Songs of the 3 Queens* for soprano, piano or chamber orchestra (1924, Fischer); *Litanies of Women*, 5 songs for mezzo-soprano, piano or chamber orchestra (1925, Salabert); *6 Songs of the Russian Orient* for voice, piano or chamber orchestra (1925–26, UE); *Sabbath Eve Service* for cantor, chorus, organ (1925, revised 1947; Bloch); *Sabbath Morning Service* for cantor, chorus, organ (1925–28, Bloch); *Holiday Service* for cantor, chorus, organ (1927–29, Bloch); *The Daughter of Jephta*, cantata-pantomime in 3 scenes (1928, Salabert); *Ausonia, Italian Pages*, orchestral suite (1930, Salabert); *The Lord Reigneth* for soprano, baritone, chorus, piano, organ (1933, Fischer); *Defeat of Caesar Julian*, 3-act opera (1933–38, Chester); *3 Shadows*, poems for orchestra (1935, Chester); *Newfoundland Air* for chorus, piano; text by Thoreau (1935, Birchard); *Eon Hours*, 4 rondos for 4 voices, 4 instruments (1935); *Pueblo, a Moon Rhapsody* for orchestra (1936); *From Cynthia's Playnook*, 6 pieces for piano (1936, Fischer); *Out of the Deep* for tenor, chorus, organ ad lib. (c.1937, Birchard); *From the American Poets* for chorus, piano, percussion ad lib. (1940–48, Presser); *Rye Septet* for voice, 7 instruments (1942); *Requiem* for vocal soloists, chorus, orchestra (c.1946); *Anthology of Hebrew Sacred and Traditional Songs* for cantor, soloists, chorus, organ (1946, Bloch); *A Song Treasury of Old Israel* for voice, piano (1951, Bloch).

PRINCIPAL WRITINGS: *Jewish Music, Past and Present*, in Russian (St. Petersburg 1914); *Music of Our Day* (New York 1932, 2nd ed. 1939); *Music of the Ghetto and the Bible* (New York

1934); *Living Music of the Americas* (New York 1949); *Physics and Metaphysics of Music and Essays on the Philosophy of Mathematics* (The Hague 1957); *Essentials of Conducting* (London 1958); *Third Leonardo: Autobiography* (1959, unpub.).

BIBL.: Domenico de Paoli et al., *L. S., Composer and Civic Worker* (New York 1930); Albert Weisser, *The Modern Renaissance of Jewish Music, Events and Figures* (New York 1954).

Albert Weisser

SEE ALSO Liturgical Music: Jewish.

Santa Cruz, Domingo (b. La Cruz, Valparaíso, Chile, 5 July 1899), studied in Santiago at the Humanities Institute of Catholic Univ., the Colegio de los Sagrados Corazones, and the law school of the Univ. of Chile (graduated 1921). He studied music privately with Enrique Soro (c.1921) and in Madrid with Conrado del Campo (1921–23). During 1921–27 he occupied various foreign-office posts for the Chilean government in Europe and Santiago. He taught music history and analysis at the National Conservatory during 1928–53 and was dean from 1932. He also taught composition at the Univ. of Chile during 1942–48, where he was vice rector, 1944–49. He helped found many of Chile's most important musical institutions, including the Bach Society (1917–30), of which he was director; the National Association of Symphonic Concerts (1931); the National Association of Composers (1935); the Departamento de Extensión Artistica (1939), of which he was director until 1948; the Instituto de Extensión Musicale (1940); and the journal *Revista musical chilena* (1940). He also helped promote the plastic arts.

PRINCIPAL COMPOSITIONS: *Viñetas* for piano (1925–27, Casa Amarilla, Santiago); *Cantos de soledad* for voice, piano; texts by the composer (1927–28, Ricordi); *5 Poemas trágicos* for piano (1929, Casa Amarilla); *5 Pieces* for string orchestra (1936–37, IEM); *Cantata de los ríos de Chile* for chorus, orchestra; text by the composer (1941); *Variations in 3 Movements* for piano, orchestra (1942–43, IEM); *3 Dramatic Preludes* for orchestra (1946, IEM); *Égloga* for soprano, chorus, orchestra; text by Lope de Vega (1949, IEM); *6 Canciones de primavera* for chorus (1950, IEM); *Canciones del mar* for voice, piano; text by the composer (1952); *Endechas* for tenor, flute, clarinet, horn, violin, viola, cello, harp; text by Lope de Estúñiga (1960). List to 1960: *Composers of the Americas* 1:89–94.

PRINCIPAL WRITINGS: "Mis recuerdos sobre la Sociedad Bach," *Revista musical chilena* 6/40:8–62; "Transcendental aniversario en la vida musical chilena, La Facultad de Belles Artes de 1929," *ibid.* 8/67:5–16; "Antepasados de la *Revista*

musical chilena," *ibid.* 14/71:17–33; "¿Crisis en nuestro sistema de estímulo a la composición musical?" *ibid.* 14/69:12–19; "El Instituto de Extensión Musical, su orígen, fisonomía y objeto," *ibid.* 14/73:7–38; "El compositor Alfonso Letelier," *ibid.* 21/100:8–30.

BIBL.: René Amengual, "El sentido dramático de S. C. en sus obras para piano," *Revista musical chilena* 8/42:90–119; Gustavo Becerra, "Los Lieder de S. C.," *ibid.* 8/42:120–27; "Cincuentenario de la Sociedad Bach (1917–1967)," *ibid.* 21/101:3–4; Germán Ewart, "D. S. C.," *El mercurio* (Santiago, 5 Nov 1961):1; Alfonso Leng, "D. S. C.," *Revista musical chilena* 8/42:5–10; Alfonso Letelier, "Las composiciones corales de S. C.," *ibid.* 8/42:43–61; Juan Orrego-Salas, "Los cuartetos de cuerda de S. C.," *ibid.* 8/42:62–89; Eugenio Pereira-Salas, "La música chilena en los primeros cincuenta años del siglo XX," *ibid.* 6/40:63–78; Vicente Salas-Viú, *La creación musical en Chile 1900–1951* (Santiago de Chile, n.d.); ——, *Músicos modernos de Chile* (Washington 1944); Nicolas Slonimsky, *Music of Latin America* (New York 1945); Robert Stevenson, "Chilean Music in the S. C. Epoch," *Inter-American Music Bulletin* 68:1–18.

[prepared with the help of Samuel Claro]

SEE ALSO Chile.

Santoro, Claudio (b. Manaos, Brazil, 23 Nov 1919), studied at the Federal District Conservatory in Rio de Janeiro (violin with Edgardo Guerra, composition with Hans Koellreutter) and privately in Paris with Nadia Boulanger (composition) and Eugene Bigot (conducting). He has taught violin and harmony at the Federal District Conservatory, the Santos Conservatory (from 1953), the Univ. of Brasilia (from 1962), and the music seminars in Rio de Janeiro and Teresopolis (from 1963). He was the artistic director of radio for the Ministry of Education and Culture in the late 1950s. In 1962 he became music director of the Cultural Foundation of the Federal District of Brasilia. He performs as a violinist and has composed over 300 scores for radio and television and 15 for film.

PRINCIPAL COMPOSITIONS: *Symphony No. 1* for 2 string orchestras (1940); *Sonata* for solo violin (1940, Southern); *Violin Sonatas Nos. 1–5* (1940; 1941; 1947; 1950, Editora Cembra, São Paulo; 1957); *String Trio* (1941–42); *String Quartets Nos. 1–6* (1943; 1946–47; 1953; 1955, Ricordi; 1957; 1963–64); *Música 1944* for piano, orchestra (1944, Ricordi); *Variations* for orchestra (1945); *Symphonies Nos. 2–8* (1945; 1948; 1953, Ricordi; 1955, Ricordi; 1957–58, Ricordi; 1959–60; 1963); *Piano Sonatas Nos. 1–4* (1945; 1948; 1955, Ricordi; 1957, Ricordi); *Preludes* for piano, series 1–2 (1946–48; 1957–63, Ricordi); *Ode à Stalingrado* for narrator, chorus, orchestra; text by Rossini

Carmargo Guarnieri (1947); *Piano Concertos Nos. 1–3* (1951, 1958–59, 1960; Ricordi); *Violin Concertos Nos. 1–2* (1951, 1958); *Anticocos*, ballet; scenario by Silveira Sampaio (1951); *Danças brasileiras Nos. 1–2* (1951, Southern); *60 Corais infantis* for 2–4 voices (1951); *Brasiliana* for orchestra (1954, Ricordi); *Icamiabas*, ballet (1958–59, Ricordi); *12 Canções de amor* for voice, piano; texts by Vinicius de Maraes (1958–59, Ricordi); *Zuimaaluti*, ballet; scenario by Manuel Bandeira, choreography by Nina Verchinina (1960, Ricordi); *Berlin, 13th of August*, oratorio for narrator, chorus, orchestra (1961–62); *Introduction and Allegro* for string orchestra (1963, Ricordi). Santoro has also written a large number of songs for voice and piano. List to 1963: *Composers of the Americas* 9:128–43.

BIBL.: John Vinton, "Current Chronicle," *Musical Quarterly* 51:550–55.

SEE ALSO Brazil.

Santórsola, Guido (b. Canosa di Puglia, Italy, 18 Nov 1904), studied at São Paulo Conservatory in Brazil (1915–21; harmony, counterpoint with Agostino Cantu; music history with Mario de Andrade; piano with Zaccaria Autuori) and at the Trinity College of Music in London (1921–22, violin with Alfred Mitowski). During 1931–41 he studied conducting with Lamberto Baldi, Fritz Busch, and Erich Kleiber. He was violist with the Cuarteto Paulista and the São Paulo and Rio de Janeiro Symphonies during 1925–31 and with the orchestra and quartet of the Uruguayan Radio during 1931–41. He has been conductor of the Uruguayan Radio Symphony since 1942 and director of opera and ballet since 1955. Since 1941 he has also been director of the Escuela Normal de Música in Montevideo.

PRINCIPAL COMPOSITIONS: *Sonata* for violin, viola, piano (1928); *Viola Concerto* (1933); *Cancion trieste y danza Brasileña* for piano (1934); *Agonia* for alto, orchestra (1937, ECIC and Southern); *2 Inventions* for piano (1938); *Sonata-Fantasia* for viola, orchestra (1938); *Piano Sonata* (1939); *Concertino* for guitar, orchestra (1942, Southern); *Quintet* for 4 flutes, piano (1945); *Sinfonia No. 1* for string orchestra (1957); *String Quartet No. 1* (1957); *Bassoon Concerto* (1959, Southern); *Musica para "El juicio final,"* for actors, dancers, chorus, orchestra; text by Edgardo Genta (1960); *Quartet No. 2* for guitar, flute, viola, cello (1961, Southern); *Sonata a duo No. 1* for 2 guitars (1962, Southern); *Violin Concerto* (1962, Southern); *Concerto for Orchestra* (1964); *Trio* for flute or violin, clarinet, guitar (1964); *Cantata a Artigas* for speaker, chorus, orchestra; text by Alberto Reyes y Abel (1965); *Wind Quintet* (1966); *Concerto* for 2 guitars, orchestra (1966); *Os tres misterios da noite* for voice, speaker, orchestra; text by Herminio de Carvalho (1966); *Concerto for 10 Instruments* (1966); *Concerto* for 4 horns, orchestra (1967); *Concerto* for 4 violins, string orchestra (1969); *Trio* for flute, viola, piano (1969); *Guitar Sonata* (1969, Berben); *Sonata a duo No. 2* for 2 guitars (1969); *4 Tientos* for guitar (1970, Berben); *Diptico* for viola, guitar (1970). List to 1962: *Composers of the Americas* 8:142–48.

Satie, Erik (Alfred Leslie) (b. Honfleur, France, 17 May 1866; d. Paris, 1 July 1925), received his first piano lessons from a church organist in Honfleur. In 1878 he moved to Paris, where his family was living, and thereafter rarely left the city. He studied at the Paris Conservatory (1879?–86) with little success (he was dropped at one point and readmitted in 1885). His first works, two piano pieces, date from 1885, and these were soon followed by several other compositions, including three songs based on poems by his close friend J.-P. Contamine de Latour and the *Gymnopédies* (1888). During 1888 Satie also began to work as a second pianist in the Chat Noir cabaret in Montmartre.

In 1891, stimulated by his readings and probably by Contamine de Latour, Satie became associated with the Catholic Rosecrucian sect which, under the leadership of Joseph Péladan, was then known as the Rose Croix movement. Satie wrote several works associated with the sect, including three preludes for Péladan's play *Le Fils des étoiles* and his first ballet *Uspud*. The severe, Gothic-like style of Satie's Rose Croix works, however, was decidedly opposed to the Wagnerian esthetic espoused by Péladan and his associates. Leaving the Rose Croix movement, he set up his own "church," the short-lived Eglise Métropolitaine d'Art de Jésus Conducteur. In 1898 he moved to the Parisian suburb of Arcueil-Cachan, where he lived in self-imposed poverty (he later became a member of the Radical-Socialist party) for the rest of his life. About this time he also went into semiretirement, composing less than ten works over twelve years. However, being tired of reproaches for his "ignorance," he entered the Schola Cantorum in 1905 and obtained a diploma in counterpoint three years later. After this he found the artistic world much more receptive to his ideas. He met Jean Cocteau in 1915 and from this meeting grew a collaboration that led to *Parade*, produced by Diaghilev's Ballets Russes in 1917. During the remainder of his life, Satie turned increasingly to dramatic works. A contemplated opera (*Paul et Virginie*), with a libretto by Cocteau and Raymond Radiguet, was cut short by the composer's death.

Satie's output was limited to some 70 works, most of them short and none over a half hour. The largest single body of music is for piano (over 30 pieces), most of which bears programmatic or pseudoprogrammatic titles. The rest of his output is mainly songs and various dramatic compositions (ballets, incidental music, etc.). With few exceptions, such as the *Sarabandes*, *Passacaille*, *5 Nocturnes*, traditional designations are lacking. Because it lacks many of the elements that give musical and/or dramatic unity to the traditional Western musical styles, Satie's music often gives the impression of being simple and static. He typically used repetition to the point of monotony, whether it is the insistent F-minor accompaniment of the first *Gnossienne* or the numerous ostinato fragments of works such as *Parade* or *Socrate*. Most of his works, particularly those with well-defined melodies, have insistent rhythmic patterns that rarely change meter, tempo, or configuration within a given episode or, frequently, an entire piece.

Harmonically his musical language is characterized by frequent use of unresolved chords. Most important, historically, are the unresolved sevenths and ninths appearing in such early works as the *Sarabandes* and *Gymnopédies*. In spite of these occasional hints of impressionism, however, Satie's harmonic style is usually strongly opposed to that of the impressionists. There is, in fact, an archaic, choralelike quality to much of his writing (the openings of *Parade* and *Sports et divertissements*), in which there are chains of different chords (not parallel chords) that are either unrelated to one another or determined by quasimodal progressions. Much of the Rose Croix music contains chains of rather hollow 6/3 chords. There is also a fairly frequent use of superimposed fourth chords (prelude to the first act of *Le Fils des étoiles* and *Parade*). Open fourths and fifths are also used, particularly in Satie's later music (the ending of *Socrate*); rising or descending scales of parallel fourths are an earmark of his style. While Satie's melodies almost always maintain at least a tenuous relationship to the accompaniment, rarely do they determine the harmony, so that there is often a rather bizarre tension between the two elements. The melody of the first *Gnossienne*, for example, is written in an exotic, quasimodal scale that is not far from the F minor that dominates the accompaniment. One also finds the influence of Gregorian chant in certain melodies. While most of the

music is decidedly uncontrapuntal, several works after the Schola Cantorum period (notably *Parade* and *Socrate*) have passages where two independent lines (one usually an ostinato) are played simultaneously; *Parade* even contains a short fugal episode. Typical of Satie is his filling in of the harmony on the off-beat so that constant ONE-and-TWO-and patterns result. He often incorporated popular rhythms in his works, from marches (*Geneviève de Brabant*) to the charleston and ragtime (*Parade*), which appear particularly in the later music.

After he left the Schola Cantorum Satie began to compose for orchestra, although only a few works are for full orchestra (*Parade*, *Relâche*, etc.). Even in these he avoided tutti passages. *Socrate* is for chamber orchestra and is characterized by extremely lean scoring; *La Belle excentrique* uses a music-hall orchestra. Other nontraditional features are the use of noise and unpitched sound, such as the typewriter, steamship whistle, and siren in *Parade*.

Form in Satie is often described as cellular. In *Parade* this feature involves the juxtaposition of undeveloped, disparate cellules in a truly cubistic fashion. In other works themes are somewhat more developed and are frequently woven into smaller forms in which there is literal repetition. There are also many arch forms using a reverse recapitulation of various themes and motives. *Parade*, for example, gradually works back to the point from which it started, while the first *Gnossienne* follows the scheme AABBCCBB (repeated almost literally).

It is difficult to pinpoint the influences on Satie's work, which was greatly affected by extramusical considerations. Part of his early style probably grew out of the harmonic idiom of Chabrier and the piano writing of Fauré. His experience in improvisation at the Chat Noir perhaps prodded him to experiment with various unresolved dissonances, and he may also have been influenced by Debussy in this area (the problem of whether Satie's unresolved ninth chords influenced Debussy or vice versa is still unsolved). There is certainly no question of the impact his Schola Cantorum studies had on his later music. It was always difficult, however, for Satie to completely assimilate basic musical tenets, and it is highly significant that he turned this limitation into a positive esthetic that constitutes at least a partial revolt against the "sacred traditions" of music. One of Satie's major contributions to music was offering an alternative to the seriousness and complexity of

Wagner and the Germanic tradition in general. Some 30 years before *Le Coq et l'Arlequin* (1918), in which Cocteau more or less codified Satie's esthetic, Satie was proclaiming the necessity of a purely French music. Les Six (particularly Auric and Poulenc) and L'Ecole d'Arcueil followed in Satie's footsteps, and he was undoubtedly influential in steering Debussy away from Wagner. Satie's reaction against heaviness in music led him to attack serious traditions in a manner that foreshadowed the dadaist movement and, later on, the music of John Cage. His *Gnossiennes* (1890) is written without bar lines and contains incongruous verbal instructions that have no real relation to the music, a device Satie later used fairly often. The short *Vexations*, apparently written as early as 1892–93, is supposed to be played 840 times at each performance. Late in his life he even promulgated a deliberately unobtrusive *musique d'ameublement* (furniture music) intended to remain in the background. His score for the film entr'acte in *Relâche* (1924) is an example and also one of the earliest film scores. Satie's work was largely oriented towards a total-art esthetic, although in a non-Wagnerian way. His *Piège de Méduse* is actually a predadaist play written by the composer with accompanying incidental music. His major stage works are all ballets that brought together the talents of other important artists: *Parade* (Cocteau, Picasso, Massine), *Mercure* (Picasso, Massine), and *Relâche* (Francis Picabia and the filmmaker René Clair).

PRINCIPAL COMPOSITIONS: 3 *Sarabandes* for piano (1887, Salabert); 3 *Gymnopédies* for piano (1888, Salabert; Nos. 1 and 3 orchestrated by Debussy); 3 *Gnossiennes* for piano (1890, Salabert; No. 3 orchestrated by Poulenc); *Préludes* from *Le Fils des étoiles* for piano (1891, Salabert; orchestrated by Roland Manuel); *Uspud*, "Christian ballet in 3 acts" for piano (1892); *Vexations* for piano (c.1892–93); *Messe des pauvres* for voices, piano or organ (1894, Salabert; orchestrated by D. Diamond); *Geneviève de Brabant*, marionette opera (1899, UE; orchestrated by Désormière); *Jack-in-the-Box*, pantomime for piano (1899–1900, UE; orchestrated by Milhaud); 3 *Morceaux en forme de poire* for piano 4-hands (1893, 1903, Salabert; orchestrated by Désormière); *Aperçus désagréables* for piano 4-hands (1903, Eschig); *En Habit de cheval* for piano 4-hands or orchestra (1911, Salabert); *Le Piège de Méduse*, comedy with music for 4 actors, clarinet, trumpet, trombone, violin, cello, double bass, percussion (1913, Galerie Simon); 3 *Poèmes d'amour* for voice, piano; text by Satie (1914, Salabert); *Sports et divertissements* for piano (1914, Salabert); *Parade*, "realistic ballet" (1917, Salabert); *Sonatine bureaucratique* for piano (1917, Salabert); *Socrate*, symphonic drama for 4 sopranos, small orchestra;

based on Victor Cousin's translation of Plato's Dialogues (1919, Eschig); 5 *Nocturnes* for piano (1919, Salabert); *La Belle excentrique* for music-hall orchestra or piano 4-hands (1920, Eschig); *Ludions* for voice, piano; text by Farque (1923, Salabert); *Mercure*, "Plastic Poses," ballet (1924, UE); *Relâche*, "instantaneous ballet" (1924, Salabert). Lists of works in Myers: 145–46; Austin: 218–19; and Gowers (1965–66):24–25.

PRINCIPAL WRITINGS: *Le Piège de Méduse* (Paris 1931); *Mémoires d'un Amnésique* (Liège 1953). Extracts from Satie's various articles are in Myers: 109–23, 131–43; a list of sources in Shattuck: 373.

BIBL.: William Austin, "S. Before and After Cocteau," *Musical Quarterly* 48:216–33; John Cage, *Silence* (Middletown, Conn., 1961); Paul Collaer, *A History of Modern Music* (Cleveland 1961); J.-P. Contamine de Latour, "E. S. intime," *Comoedia* (5 August 1925); Laurence Davies, *The Gallic Muse* (London 1967); Peter Dickinson, "E. S. (1866–1926)," *Music Review* 23:139–46; David Drew, "Modern French Music," *European Music in the 20th Century* ed. by H. Hartog (New York 1957); Patrick Gowers, *E. S.: His Studies, Notebooks and Critics* (thesis, Cambridge Univ., 1966); ——, "S.'s Rose Croix Music (1891–1895)," *Proceedings of the Royal Musical Association* (1965–66):1–25; Rollo Myers, *E. S.* (London 1948); *La Revue musicale* (special issues March 1924 and June 1952); Roger Shattuck, *The Banquet Years, 1885–1918* (New York 1958); Harold C. Schonberg, "It Was a Long, Long Night (and Day) at the Piano," *New York Times* (11 Sept 1963); Pierre Daniel Templier, *E. S.* (Paris 1932).

Royal S. Brown

SEE ALSO Dance, Form, France, Instrumental and Vocal Resources, Jazz.

Sauguet, Henri (b. Bordeaux, 8 May 1901), studied piano and organ as a youth and began composition lessons with the composer-pianist Marie-Joseph Canteloube. He moved to Paris in 1922, studied there with Koechlin, and moved into the circle of artists, poets, and composers then in Paris. He and three other French composers became known as L'Ecole d'Arcueil, named after the suburb where their spiritual leader, Erik Satie, lived. During the mid-1920s Sauguet's reputation as a composer grew, and he was eventually able to turn from various office jobs and music and theater criticism to free-lance composing for films, radio, etc. He is currently president of the Société des Auteurs et Compositeurs Dramatiques and a member of various professional committees.

Sauguet's large output includes five operas, 25 ballets, symphonic, chamber, choral, and solo vocal works, as well as musique concrète and many functional scores. He shares the traditional French values of clarity and moderation as exemplified by a refined sense of tone color and a treatment of melody and harmony that usually emphasizes manipulations of the same component intervals (often thirds and fourths).

PRINCIPAL COMPOSITIONS: *La Chatte*, ballet; choreography by George Balanchine (1927, Salabert); *Piano Concerto No. 1* (1934, Eschig); *La Chartreuse de Parme*, 4-act opera; libretto by d'Armand Lunel after Stendhal (1936); *Les Mirages*, ballet; choreography by Serge Lifar (1943, Salabert); *Les Forains*, ballet; choreography by Roland Petit (1945, Salabert); *String Quartet No. 2* (1948, Heugel); *Les Saisons*, choreographic symphony (1949, EFM); *Le Cornette*, ballad for bass voice, orchestra; poem by Rilke (1951); *Concerto d'Orphée* for violin, orchestra (1953, Heugel); *Les Caprices de Marianne*, opéra-comique in 2 acts; libretto by Jean-Pierre Grédy after Alfred de Musset (1954, Ricordi); *Symphony No. 3*, "I. N. R." (1955, Salabert); *La Dame aux camélias*, ballet; choreography by Tatiana Gsovsky (1957, Ricordi); *L'Oiseau a vu tout celà*, cantata for baritone, strings; poem by Jean Cayrol (1960); *Piano Concerto No. 3* (1963, Salabert); *Mélodie concertante* for cello, orchestra (1964, CM); *Le Prince et le mendiant*, ballet-mime drama; choreography by Juan Corelli (1965, EFM); *Chant pour une ville meurtrie*, oratorio (1967).

France-Yvonne Bril
SEE ALSO Dance, France.

Savín, Francisco (Vazquez) (b. Mexico City, 18 Nov 1929), studied at the National Univ. of Mexico (1946–49, 1954–56; philosophy with Eduardo Nicol, esthetics with Justino Fernández) and at the Prague Music Academy (1957–59). He also studied music privately with José F. Velásquez (piano, 1935), Hermann Scherchen (conducting, 1951), Jean Giardino (conducting, 1956), and Rodolfo Halffter (composition, 1960). He was associate conductor of the National Symphony Orchestra of Mexico (1959–62), conductor of the Xalapa Orchestra in Veracruz (1963–67), conductor of the National Conservatory Orchestra in Mexico City (1960–62), and has been guest conductor of other orchestras. He has taught esthetics and art history at Veracruz Univ. (1963–67) and at the National Conservatory (1959–62, since 1967), where he has also been director since 1967. He was director of the Fine Arts School of Michocán Univ. in Morelia during 1962–63. In 1972 he became head of the music department of the National Institute of Fine Arts. He describes his style as "post-dodecaphonic," with emphasis on changing textures and timbres involving electronic instruments, glissandi, microtones, and tone clusters. Structural articulations tend to be very broadly spaced.

PRINCIPAL COMPOSITIONS (published by EMM): *Quetzalcoátl* for two reciters, orchestra (1957); *Metamorfosis* for orchestra (1963); *Formas plásticas* for wind quintet (1965); *3 Líricas* for medium voice, flute, clarinet, viola, piano, percussion (1966); *Concreción* for orchestra, electronic organ (1969); *Monología de las delicias* for 4 women's voices, orchestra (1969).

BIBL.: Guillermo Villegas Maldonado, "F. S., un dinamico," *Hoy en dia* (March 1967):62–64.
SEE ALSO Mexico.

Saygun, Ahmed Adnan (b. Izmir, Turkey, 7 Sept 1907), attended the Schola Cantorum in Paris (1928–31; composition with Vincent d'Indy, Eugène Borrel; organ with Edourd Souberbielle; Gregorian chant with Amédée Gastoué). During 1926–28 he taught at the Izmir Lyceum; during 1931–35, at the Ankara Music Teachers' School; during 1936–39, at Istanbul Conservatory; and since 1946, at the State Conservatory in Ankara, where he is chairman of the composition department. He was conductor of the Presidential Symphony Orchestra in Ankara during 1934–35, and during 1939–50 he was Counsellor for Music Education there.

PRINCIPAL COMPOSITIONS: *Divertimento* for orchestra, Op. 1 (1929–30, Southern); *Ağitlar* [Laments] for chorus, Op. 3 (1932); *Sezisler* [Intuitions] for 2 clarinets, Op. 4 (1932, Southern); *Çoban Armağani* [Shepherd's Offering] for chorus, Op. 7 (1933); *Inci'nin Kitabi* [Inci's Book] for small orchestra or piano, Op. 10 (1934, Southern); *Taş Bebek* [The Puppet], 1-act opera, Op. 13 (1934); *Duyuşlar* [Feelings] for chorus, Op. 11 (1935); *Cello Sonata*, Op. 12 (1935, Southern); *Anatolian Dance Suite No. 1*, Op. 14 (1937); *Piano Sonatina*, Op. 15 (1938, Southern); *Songs* for baritone, piano, Op. 16 (1939); *Bir Orman Masali* [A Forest Tale] for orchestra, Op. 17 (1939, Southern); *Dağlardan, Ovalardan* [From Mountains and Plains] for chorus, Op. 18 (1939); *Violin Sonata*, Op. 20 (1940); *Bir Tutam Kekik* [A Pinch of Thyme] for chorus, Op. 22 (1940); *Songs* for baritone, piano, Op. 21 (1941); *Anatolian Dance Suite No. 2* for orchestra, Op. 24 (1941); *Anadolu'dan* [From Anatolia] for piano, Op. 25 (1941); *Yunus Emre*, oratorio for soloists, chorus, orchestra, Op. 26 (1942, Southern); *String Quartet No. 1*, Op. 27 (1947, Southern); *Kerem*, 3-act opera, Op. 28 (1952, Southern); *Songs* for tenor, piano, Op. 32 (1953); *Symphony No. 1*, Op. 29 (1954, Southern); *Partita* for cello, Op. 31 (1954, Southern); *Symphony No. 2*, Op. 30 (1955, Southern); *Suite* for violin, piano, Op. 33 (1956, Southern); *Piano Concerto*, Op. 34 (1957, Southern); *String Quartet No. 2*, Op. 35 (1959, Southern); *Partita* for violin, Op. 36 (1959,

Southern); *Symphony No. 3*, Op. 39 (1961, Southern); *Songs* for bass, piano, Op. 41 (1962); *10 Etudes on Aksak Rhythms* for piano, Op. 38 (1966, Southern); *Violin Concerto*, Op. 44 (1967); *12 Preludes on Aksak Rhythms* for piano, Op. 45 (1967); *String Quartet No. 3*, Op. 46 (1967); *Gilgames*, ballet, for soloist, chorus, orchestra, Op. 42 (1968); *Wind Quintet*, Op. 46 (1968); *Tuo Mikum Hay* for string orchestra, Op. 47 (1969).

PRINCIPAL WRITINGS: *Türk Halk Musikisinde Pentatonism* [Pentatonicism in Turkish Folk Music] (Istanbul 1935); *Rize, Artvin ve Kars Türkü, Saz ve Oyunlari* [Folk Music of the Rize, Artvin, and Kars Districts] (Istanbul 1937); *Yedi Karadenis Türküsü ve bir Horon* [7 Folksongs and a Horon from the Black Sea] (Istanbul 1938); *Halkevlerinde Musiki* [Music Education in the Home] (Ankara 1940); *Karacaoğlan, Bir Rivayet, Türküler* [A Survey of the Turkish Troubadours] (Ankara 1952); *Musiki Temel Bilgisi* [A Theory of Music], vols. 1–4 (Ankara 1958–66); "La Musique turque," *L'Encyclopédie Pléiades*, vol. 1 (Paris 1960); "Le Genèse de la mélodie," *Zoltán Kodály octogenario sacrum* (Budapest 1961):281–300; *Töresel Solfej* [Modal Solfège] (Ankara 1962); "Sur l'Affinité des musiques turque et hongroise," *Studia musicologica* (Budapest)5:515–24; "The Classification of Premodal Melodies," *Folklore and Folk Music Archivist* (Bloomington, Ind.)7/1:15–28.

Scandinavia. Musical life at the beginning of the 20th century was mainly centered around the Danish and Swedish capitals, Copenhagen and Stockholm. Both cities had been cultural centers since the middle ages when they were made the seats of the Danish and Swedish courts. In Norway, which gained full national independence from Sweden only in 1905, the situation was different (see below). During this century cultural activity has spread from the old centers to nearly all parts of the area, and chamber music societies, theaters, orchestras, and music schools have been established in the major provincial cities. The founding of state radio corporations around 1930, together with the establishment of radio orchestras (the most active orchestras in terms of contemporary music), has had a powerful effect. Orchestras and concert associations in the capitals have decreased in number, but provincial activities not only survived World War II but expanded (mainly as a result of governmental subsidies). On the whole the governments have taken over nearly all the obligations formerly assumed by private patronage and sponsorship. In Denmark in 1970, for example, about 142,000 dollars was given to music by the Danish State Art Foundation; in addition, the Cultural Foundation gave somewhat over 200,000 dollars to regional orchestras and other institutionalized activities. A recent development in Sweden and Norway, with their vast northern territories, is the institution of State Public Concerts (*rikskonserter*) by means of which touring companies of all sorts and sizes reach even the remotest localities.

DENMARK. The Royal Conservatory of Music in Copenhagen, founded in 1867 by Niels W. Gade and others, was taken over by the state in 1949 and until recently has been the leading educational institution. Provincial conservatories have been founded at Århus (1926), Odense (1929), Ålborg (1932), and Esbjerg (1945). The two in Århus and Odense are now state conservatories, and the first has achieved an especially high standard. Performers, composers, and private music teachers are trained at the conservatories. Opera singers take a basic course there and then continue at the Opera Academy in Copenhagen. Music teachers for elementary schools train at teachers' colleges, and teachers for higher school levels train at the universities. Music schools for laymen, modeled after the *Volksmusikschulen* of Fritz Jöde in Germany, were started in Copenhagen in the late 1920s and have since spread to most parts of the country; since 1945 the Danish radio has also produced pedagogical programs for laymen.

The Royal Chapel, now the orchestra of the Royal Theater, traces its history to about 1500, when it performed polyphonic music in the court chapel. In addition to its present work in the theater (operas, ballets, incidental music), it gives concerts and occasionally makes recordings. Its high standard is shared by the orchestra of the Danish State Radio, founded 1932, which gives regular studio programs, weekly public concerts during the season, and occasionally makes records. The Music-Association orchestra (founded 1836) ceased activity in 1931; its principal conductor during 1915–27 was Carl Nielsen. Since its inception in 1843 the Tivoli amusement park has maintained an orchestra that gives daily concerts of "light" and "serious" music during the summer; since 1967 it has been the regional orchestra for the isle of Zealand during the winter. Provincial orchestras were founded at Århus in 1935, Ålborg in 1941, Odense in 1945, later in Sønderborg, Randers, and Esbjerg; in each case the group serves as a regional orchestra for its part of the country. Opera production was long the exclusive privilege of the Royal Theater in Copenhagen. Since 1946, however, operas have been performed at the theaters of Århus (where an opera company and training school are being established) and Odense and by the radio and television. Professional choirs are employed by both the radio and the Royal Theater. Chamber music is cultivated by numerous societies both within and without the capital; the best known are the Danish String Quartet, the Copenhagen String Quartet, and the Danish Wind Quintet.

In 1901 the Danish Concert Society was formed specifically to play new music. Another orchestra with the same goal, the Philharmonic Society, was active during 1920–34. After World War I the New Music society began promoting new currents. It became the Danish section of ISCM in 1923 and in 1930 was amalgamated with the Philharmonic Society and the Society of Young Musicians (founded 1920) into DUT (Det Unge Tonekunstnerselskab). DUT is still a leading forum for contemporary music, often working in collaboration with the radio, which since the 1950s has broadcast considerable new music. Since 1960 DUT, the Royal Theater, and the radio have occasionally commissioned works from Danish composers; apart from this, creative activities are financially supported by the Danish State Art Foundation. The major publishing houses include Wilhelm Hansen (founded 1857), Samfundet til Udgivelse af Dansk Musik (1871, a nonprofit organization subsidized by the state), Engstrøm & Sødring (1938), and Musikhøjskolens Forlag (1952).

The most important Danish composer in the first quarter of the century was Carl *Nielsen (1865–1931). Although he was a "national romantic" to some extent, he developed an antiromantic idiom in the sense that he reacted against the modern trends in German and French music (Strauss, Debussy, etc.) and followed instead a classic German line (Brahms). For the most part his major works are diatonic with modal inflections and rely heavily on counterpoint. After World War I Nielsen's harmony became even less dependent on tonality and his voice leading correspondingly freer. These changes, however, did not radically alter his simple, basically diatonic concept of music. His folklike songs have been widely used in schools and elsewhere, making his name known throughout the population as the composer of specifically Danish music. Almost all composers of the following generation, however individual their musical personalities, are indebted to him. Poul Schierbeck (1888–1949), who studied with Roussel in Paris, was an excellent orchestrator; his relatively small output is marked by high lyrical qualities. Finn *Høffding (b. 1899),

Jørgen Bentzon (1897–1951), Ebbe Hamerik (1898–1951), and Flemming Weis (b. 1898) form a "post-Nielsen" generation; the first two were active in the Volksmusikschule movement around 1930. Knudåge *Riisager (b. 1897) followed a more independent path, drawing inspiration from French neoclassicism. Herman D. *Koppel (b. 1908), Vagn *Holmboe (b. 1909), Svend Erik Tarp (b. 1908), Svend S. Schultz (b. 1913), and Jørgen Jersild (b. 1913) also followed neoclassic trends in the 1930s, influenced in part by Stravinsky and Bartók. In his later works Holmboe has developed a markedly epic quality. The late romantic Rued Langgaard (1893–1952) opposed these trends, especially Nielsen's music, in 16 symphonies and other orchestral works, an opera, six string quartets, many piano and organ pieces, and a large store of songs with piano and orchestral accompaniments; in the late 1960s his work was "rediscovered" and made known to a larger public.

NORWAY. In 1814, after the Napoleonic wars, Denmark ceded the territory of Norway to Sweden, and at that time Norway was given its own constitution (full independence came in 1905). During the 19th century Norway started to develop its own cultural institutions outside the Hanseatic trading and cultural city of Bergen. A conservatory was founded in Oslo in 1866 but failed after a few years. In 1883 L. M. Lindeman founded a school for organists there, which became the present Oslo Conservatory in 1894; it is a private institution supported by state subsidies. Several other private schools exist: the Bergen Conservatory was founded in 1905, the Trondheim Music School in 1911, the Stavanger Conservatory in 1945. There is also a conservatory in Drammen and municipal music schools exist in several other places; Oslo also has Barratt Due's Music Institute, the Piano Academy, and the Veitvedt Music School, the latter supported privately. Composers, performers, and private music teachers are trained at the conservatories. Most music teachers in the schools are trained at the faculties in Oslo, Bergen, and Trondheim; a special training program for elementary-school teachers was initiated in Bergen in 1958.

The Harmonien orchestra and chorus of Bergen, which date back to 1765, were reorganized in 1919 as the regional performing organization; since 1954 it has formed the nucleus of the annual Bergen Festivals. The orchestra of the National Theater, founded 1899, was reestablished after 1945 as the municipal orchestra of Oslo, and since 1959 it has been attached to the Norwegian Opera. The orchestra of the Philharmonic Society, founded 1846, was amalgamated in 1919 with the Music Society (founded 1871 by Grieg and others) and reorganized as a full symphony orchestra; it now serves the Norwegian State Radio and holds a leading position in Norwegian music life. Provincial orchestras were founded at Trondheim in 1909, at Stavanger in 1918, at Kristianssund and Drammen in 1919. State Public Concerts, which produce concerts throughout the country, were started in 1966. Opera production was sparse and irregular until the Opera Society (1950) founded the Norwegian Opera under the leadership of Kirsten Flagstad in 1958. Professional choirs are employed by the opera, by the Philharmonic Society, and by Harmonien in Bergen; a large number of semiprofessional choirs are active all over the country. The promotion of new music is largely due to the efforts of Pauline *Hall (1890–1969), who founded a New Music society in 1938 and had it incorporated as the Norwegian section of ISCM; it still plays a leading role in making contemporary music known in Norway, working in collaboration with the Norwegian Composers' Association. The major publishing houses are Lyche & Co. (founded 1851), Norsk Musikkforlag (1909), and Musikk-Huset A. M. Hancke (1939). The State Music Council gives financial support to composers and subsidizes performances of their works.

During the first half of the century cultural life in Norway was dominated by strong national feelings. The lyrical, national romanticism of Edvard Grieg (1843–1907) and Johan Svendsen (1840–1911) was worked out in a more grandiose and international style by Christian Sinding (1856–1941) and given a Wagnerian turn in the symphonic poems of Hjalmar Borgström (1864–1925) and Gerhard Schjelderup (1859–1933). After World War I the worldwide interest in authentic folk music was heartily embraced in Norway. A number of large-scale vocal and instrumental works ensued, inspired by the modal melodic turns and nonchromatic, often static harmony of Norwegian folk music. David Monrad Johansen (b. 1888), Arne Eggen (1881–1951), and Sparre Olsen (b. 1903) wrote large vocal works using old Nordic poetry, and Ludvig Irgens Jensen (b. 1894) wrote symphonic works in a similar vein. Part of Geirr Tveitt's (b. 1908) large production and all of the music of Eivind *Groven (b. 1901) resulted from serious folk-music study. Harald *Saeverud (b. 1897) started out in a more Germanic style but

turned in the 1930s and especially during World War II toward a more national idiom. In his youth Klaus *Egge (b. 1906) created a highly individual, free-atonal manner of expression based on folk dance; later he turned to a more international modern style. The influence of French impressionism made itself felt in Alf Hurum (b. 1882), Arvid Kleven (1899–1929), Harald Lie (1902–42), and Pauline Hall. A lonely figure in Norwegian— and in Scandinavian—music is Fartein *Valen (1887–1952). In the 1920s he developed an atonal, dissonant contrapuntal style with no trace of either folk music or impressionism. In later works he used 12-tone techniques, but without adhering to strict Schoenbergian dodecaphony. Rather long melodic lines, few contrasts, strict polyphony, transparent textures, and a lyrical refinement characterize his mature music.

SWEDEN. In 1864 the Swedish Academy of Music set up a regular conservatory in Stockholm, now called the Royal Higher School of Music; an opera school was attached in 1924. Malmö has a conservatory (founded 1907), Gothenburg an orchestral school (1916) and Music Institute (1932), Uppsala a music School (1930), and Lund a municipal music school (1948). In addition there are conservatories in other cities and several private music schools in Stockholm. Performers, composers, and teachers at all levels are trained at the Royal Higher School. Numerous music schools for laymen are sponsored by the Workers' Educational Foundation. The Swedish Broadcasting Corporation (SBC) has been particularly active in producing educational music programs. During the 1960s a "Radio Conservatory" was developed; its courses enable listeners to pass state examinations in theoretical disciplines at several levels.

The orchestra of the Royal Opera dates back to the 16th-century Court Chapel and, like its counterpart in Copenhagen, occasionally gives concerts and makes recordings. The SBC maintains an orchestra of equal stature, and public concerts are given regularly by the Stockholm Philharmonic (founded 1885). There are also orchestras in Gothenburg (1905), Malmö, Norrköping, Hälsingborg, and Gävle. The Swedish State Public Concerts (inaugurated 1964) arrange concerts all over the country, often more than 150 a week. Operas are performed primarily at the Royal Opera of Stockholm which, since 1863, has been concerned solely with opera and ballet. The old Drottningholm Court Theater, which is still as it was in the late 18th century, is an ideal setting for historical performances.

Opera is also performed at the Great Theater in Gothenburg and at the municipal theater in Malmö. Operettas have been given at Oscar's Theater in Stockholm since 1906. A large number of operatic performances are produced by the SBC over radio and television. Semiprofessional choirs exist all over the country. The best known chamber ensembles are the Frydén String Quartet, the Fresk String Quartet, and the Philharmonic Wind Quintet.

A Swedish section of the ISCM was formed in 1923. Until 1931 it was active in Stockholm, then at Lund in southern Sweden. In 1950 it was amalgamated with the chamber-music society Fylkingen [The Battle Cry], founded 1933, and from that time a breakthrough in favor of modern trends in music took place. Until the mid-60s, when Fylkingen gave up giving concerts and concentrated on the production of electronic music, it formed the most important forum for advanced music— so much so that in 1960 another society for the propagation of less extreme contemporary music, Samtida Musik, was founded. The functions of both societies were gradually taken over by the SBC. From 1954 monthly concerts of modern music have been given by the SBC and the Stockholm Concert Society, and from 1962 by the SBC alone. These events and the magazine *Nutida musik* (founded 1957), which furnishes program notes and articles, play a leading role in the expanding interest in new music. The SBC commissions new works (5–10 a year, including one large work) and operates one of the world's largest electronic studios (EMS), headed by Knut *Wiggen (b. 1927). Financial support in the field of music is distributed by the Royal Academy of Music. The Swedish Composers' Performing Rights Association operates a music information center (MIC) with scores, records, tapes, and printed information. The major publishing houses in the country are C. Gehrman (founded 1893), A. Lundquist (1838), Nordiska Musikförlaget (1915), and Eriks Musikhandel och Förlag.

Being less dominated by ideology than Denmark or Norway, Swedish music in the early part of the century embodied more facets of styles; on the other hand, it lacked the stamp of great personalities such as Grieg, Nielsen, or Valen. A Wagnerian late-romantic style was represented at the turn of the century by Wilhelm Peterson-Berger (1867–1942) and Hugo *Alfvén (1872–1960). Wilhelm Stenhammar (1871–1927) admired Nielsen but composed in a more traditional style and in a more introspective idiom. Ture Rangström

(1884–1947) was a most original composer of solo songs in a national romantic vein. Kurt *Atterberg (b. 1887) is known for his brilliant and effective symphonies. Austrian expressionism before 1914 is reflected in chamber and orchestral works by Edvin *Kallstenius (b. 1881). Gösta *Nystroem (1890–1966) combined a strong romantic feeling with a fondness for diatonic simplicity in his symphonies and vocal works. Moses Pergament (b. 1893) was the only proponent of Mahler's music in Scandinavia in the early part of the century. His own works began in a late-romantic style and moved toward German expressionism and Stravinsky; he used the 12-tone technique in several late concertos and chamber works. New music of the 20s was propagated in Sweden only in Hilding *Rosenberg (b. 1892), who has passed through many stylistic stages from an almost atonal style to neoclassicism in the 30s, a broadly epic style reminiscent of Hindemith in the 40s, and a serene and restrained manner of expression that has culminated in a cycle of six string quartets. Neoclassic traits, together with some aspects of Nielsen, are present in music by Dag *Wirén (b. 1905), Lars-Erik *Larsson (b. 1908), Hilding Hallnäs (b. 1903), Gunnar de Frumerie (b. 1908), and Erland von Koch (b. 1910).

SINCE 1945. Many of the composers mentioned above have continued their way of writing, and a number of younger composers pursue the artistic ideals of the 30s and 40s. What distinguishes recent development, however, is the adoption of international techniques of composition, first Viennese dodecaphony, second the so-called Darmstadt school (Stockhausen, Boulez, Nono), and most recently the various reactions against serialism. The traditional line among younger composers is followed by Leif Thybo (b. 1922), Svend Westergaard (b. 1922), Leif Kayser (b. 1919), and Ole Schmidt (b. 1928) in Denmark; Edvard Fliflet Braein (b. 1924) in Norway; and Göte Carlid (1920–53), Jan *Carlstedt (b. 1926), and Hans Eklund (b. 1927) in Sweden. Many other composers joined in the development of an international musical language after the war. The first wave was inspired by Hindemith's *Unterweisung im Tonsatz*, with its theories of extended tonality that corresponded to much of the music that had been written in the 30s and 40s. It inspired a further expansion as in the early works of Karl-Birger *Blomdahl (1916–68) in Sweden and Niels Viggo *Bentzon (b. 1919) in Denmark.

Serial composition was slow to manifest itself. The music of Schoenberg, Berg, and Webern was not introduced until the 50s, and it was not until about 1960 (when serial composition was already established in Germany, Belgium, France, and Italy) that Scandinavia experienced an avant-garde breakthrough. The summer courses at Darmstadt, the annual international festivals of the ISCM during the late 50s and early 60s, and several visits by Karlheinz Stockhausen to the Scandinavian capitals all helped pave the way for this development. The catalytic effect of serial composition revealed itself in many ways, different for each composer; seldom was the serial doctrine adopted without reservation. Pioneers of the new trend were particularly plentiful and active in Sweden. Bengt *Hambraeus (b. 1928) and Bo *Nilsson (b. 1937) are perhaps the most outstanding of the early "wild" modernists. Among the somewhat older composers who used serial techniques and gained inspiration from them are Blomdahl, whose mature works (e.g., the opera *Aniara*) are written in this manner, Ingvar *Lidholm (b. 1921), Sven-Erik *Bäck (b. 1919), and Siegfried Naumann (b. 1919) who, with his Musica Nova group, is also an excellent performer of new music. A more reserved attitude was taken by Gunnar *Bucht (b. 1927). Lars-Johan *Werle (b. 1926) represents an expressive, post-Webern lyricism. In Denmark the first serial compositions were written in 1954–56 by Jan *Maegaard (b. 1926) and Erik Jørgensen (b. 1912). Later the same influence made itself felt in works by Bernhard *Lewkovitch (b. 1927), whose vocal works are also strongly inspired by Stravinsky; Axel Borup-Jørgensen (b. 1924), who has never adhered to a strict serialism; Ib Nørholm (b. 1931); Per *Nørgård (b. 1932); and Poul Rovsing Olsen (b. 1922), whose studies in ethnomusicology are also discernible in several of his compositions. In Norway, somewhat later, similar changes occurred in the work of Knut *Nystedt (b. 1915), Finn *Mortensen (b. 1922), Finn Arnestad (b. 1915), Egil *Hovland (b. 1924), and Arne *Nordheim (b. 1931).

Electronic music has found especially fertile soil in Sweden, as evidenced in the works of many composers, e.g., Hambraeus, Folke *Rabe (b. 1935), and Jan Bark (b. 1934). The Norwegians Bjørn Fongaard (b. 1919) and Nordheim and the Danes Else Marie Pade (b. 1924) and Jørgen *Plaetner (b. 1930) have composed in this medium. The reaction against serialism during the second half of the 60s was inspired partly by György Ligeti, who has been a guest professor at the Royal Higher School of Music in Stockholm; partly by new theater movements, such as the hap-

pening; and partly by John Cage, who has visited Scandinavia several times. Happening and mixed media have attracted Henning Christiansen (b. 1932) and Eric Andersen (b. 1942) in Denmark and the Swede Karl-Erik *Welin (b. 1934), who is also an outstanding organist. A strong reaction against complex textures, sometimes labeled "new simplicity," is characteristic of the music of Pelle *Gudmundsen-Holmgreen (b. 1932), Christiansen, and the Swede Jan *Morthenson (b. 1940). Neoexpressionistic elements occur in music of Welin, Arne *Mellnäs (b. 1933), and Daniel Börtz (b. 1943) in Sweden; Norhølm, Nørgård, and Mogens Winkel Holm (b. 1936) in Denmark; and Björn Wilho Hallberg (b. 1938) and Alfred *Janson (b. 1937) in Norway. Two Danish composers stand somewhat apart: Bentzon's huge production covers all genres and nearly all styles and techniques from neoclassicism to happening; he is also a prominent pianist. Gunnar Berg (b. 1909), unlike most Scandinavian composers, received the greater part of his musical training abroad (with Honegger and Messiaen in Paris, where he lived during 1948–57). In complete solitude and without regard for outward success, he has written in an atonal, nonmotivic style.

BIBL.: Bo Wallner, *Music of Our Time in Scandinavia* (Stockholm-London 1971).

[prepared with the help of Jan Maegaard]

SEE ALSO Education for the Nonprofessional.

Schaeffer, Pierre (b. Nancy, France, 14 August 1910), was trained in radio broadcasting and has spent most of his professional life with the Radiodiffusion-Télévision Française in Paris (where he is now director of the Research Service). In 1948 he began to experiment with composition based on the concept of assembling and arranging recorded sounds. Others before him had used noise and noiselike sounds and/or electronic apparatus in "live" performances; the innovation that distinguished Schaeffer's work "was his isolation of the sound event (*'l'objet musical'*) by means of the recording process" (Cross: 41; see bibl.). He called his concept *musique concrète* to distinguish it from the "abstract" process of creating music on paper via notation. His first work, *Etude aux chemins de fer*, was assembled from train sounds that were part of the library of recorded sound effects at the radio station; the piece has a rondolike form. It and four other works, each lasting from two to five minutes, were broadcast over the French radio on 5 October 1948. The recorded sounds in the first work were not modified; in the other pieces Schaeffer began to discover and explore some of the possibilities for sound modification. In 1949 he began collaborating with the composer Pierre Henry (who remained at the radio's facility until 1958). In 1950 a sound engineer, Jacques Poullin, began building recording equipment for Schaeffer specifically for purposes of composition. In 1951 the radio established a studio under Schaeffer's direction, the first anywhere devoted to electronic music. Schaeffer "has been quite influential in establishing many of the techniques of transforming and manipulating sound for compositional purposes; he has actively promoted scientific research into the acoustical phenomena of musical events; and perhaps most importantly, he founded the first enduring 'school' of electronic music" (Cross:39). In recent years Schaeffer has been investigating the extent to which human communication (especially the mass media) can affect global problems.

PRINCIPAL COMPOSITIONS: *Etude aux chemins de fer*; *Etude aux tourniquets*; *Etude au piano 1*, "Etude violette"; *Etude au piano 2*, "Etude noire"; *Etude aux casseroles*, "Etude pathétique" (1948, these works constituted the 5 October broadcast over French radio); *Symphonie pour un homme seul*, composed in collaboration with Pierre Henry (1949–50, revised 1966); *Orphée 53* for violin, harpsichord, 2 singers, tape; composed with Henry (1951–53); *Le Capitaine Némo*; composed with Henry (1952); *Sahara d'aujourd'hui*; composed with Henry (1957); *Etude aux allures* (1958, revised 1960; recorded by Boite à musique); *Etudes aux objets*, using 2-track tape (1959; revised 1966, 1967; recorded by Philips).

PRINCIPAL WRITINGS: "Introduction à la musique concrète," *Polyphonie* 6:30ff.; "La Musique concrète," *La Vie musicale* 1:8ff.; *A la Recherche d'une musique concrète* (Paris 1952); *Traité des objets musicaux* (Paris 1966).

BIBL.: Lowell Cross, "Electronic Music, 1948–1953," *Perspectives* 7/1:32–65.

SEE ALSO Austria and Germany; Dance; Electronic Music: History and Development; Recording.

Schafer, R. Murray (b. Sarnia, Ontario, Canada, 18 July 1933), studied piano, harpsichord, and theory at the Royal Conservatory of Music, Toronto (1945–55) and attended the Univ. of Toronto (1954–55, composition with John Weinzweig, piano with Alberto Guerrero). In 1956 he went to Vienna to study medieval German and after a period of freelance work moved to England, where he composed under a Canada Council grant. He

returned to Canada in 1962, was president of the Ten Centuries Concerts (which he founded) in Toronto during 1962–63 and artist-in-residence at the Memorial Univ. of Newfoundland, 1963–65. In 1965 he became a resident in music at Simon Fraser Univ. and founded the Studio for Sonic Research and Electronic Music there. He credits the theoretical writings of Paul Klee, Ezra Pound, and Sergei Eisenstein as having had the most influence on his development.

PRINCIPAL COMPOSITIONS: *Canzoni for Prisoners* for orchestra (1960–61, unpub.); *Studies on Texts by Prudentius* for 4 flutes, soprano (1960–61, BMIC); *Loving/Toi*, TV opera (1964–65, unpub.); *Requiems for the Party Girl* for soprano, 9 instruments (1966, BMIC); *Gitā* for chorus, 8 brass instruments, tape (1967); *Threnody* for youth orchestra, chorus, 4 reciters, tape (1967, BMIC); *Son of Heldenleben* for orchestra, tape (1968); *Patria*, opera (1967–); *Sappho* for mezzo-soprano, harp, guitar, piano, percussion (1970); *Music for the Morning of the World* for mezzo-soprano, 4-track tape (1970); *String Quartet* (1970); *No Longer than Ten (10) Minutes* for orchestra (1970). List to 1965: *Composers of the Americas* 10:100–03.

PRINCIPAL WRITINGS: "Ezra Pound and Music," *Canadian Music Journal* 4:15–43; "Limits of Nationalism in Canadian Music," *Tamarack Review* (winter 1961):71–78; *British Composers in Interview* (London 1963); *The Composer in the Classroom* (Toronto 1965); *Ear Cleaning* (Toronto 1967); "The Future of Music in Canada," *Transactions of the Royal Society of Canada* (June 1967):37–43; "The Philosophy of Stereophony," *West Coast Review* (winter 1967):4–19; *The New Soundscape* (Toronto 1969).

SEE ALSO Canada.

Schäffer, Bogusław (Julian) (b. Lvov, Poland, 6 June 1929), studied at the State College of Music in Cracow (1949–53; composition with Artur Malawski, musicology with Z. Jachimecki). He has taught composition at the State Music College since 1963. He has been active as a writer on and theoretician of new music and is a member of the avant-garde artists group Grupa Krakowska. His music has been in the forefront of new developments in Poland: His *Music for Strings* (1953) was the first 12-tone work written there; *Tertium datur* (1958) is a graphic score; *Monosonata* (1959) uses space orchestration; *Equivalenze sonore* (1959) was the first Polish work for percussion.

PRINCIPAL COMPOSITIONS (published by PWM unless otherwise noted): *Music for Strings*, "Nocturne" (1953, Ahn & Sim); *Study in Diagram* for piano (1956); *Permutations* for 10 instruments (1956, Ahn & Sim); *Quattro movimenti* for piano, orchestra (1957); *Tertium datur* for harpsichord, orchestra (1958); *Monosonata* for 6 separated string quartets (1959); *Equivalenze sonore* for percussion (1959); *Non-stop*, 8 hours of music for piano (1960); *Mała symfonia* [Little Symphony], "Scultura" (1960); *Kody* [Codes] for chamber orchestra (1961); *Musica ipsa* for orchestra of low instruments (1962); *TIS MW2*, "audiovisual" music for voice, instruments, 2 actors, ballerina (1963); *S'alto* for alto saxophone, orchestra (1963); *Music for MI* for soprano, vibraphone, jazz ensemble, orchestra (1963); *Violin Concerto* (1963); *Scenariusz* [Scenario], indeterminate score for actor (1963, unpub.); *Collage and Form* for 8 jazz musicians, orchestra (1963); *String Quartet*, in ¼-tones (1964, Ahn & Sim); *Symphony—Electronic Music* on tape (1964, PWM); *Muzyka wizualna* [Visual Music] for 5 performers (1966); *4H/1P* for piano 4-hands (1966, Ahn & Sim); *Piano Concerto* (1967, unpub.); *Monodram* on 2-track tape (1968, unpub.); *Fragment* for 2 actors, cello (1968); *Heraklitiana* for 10 alternating performers, tape (1970, unpub.); *Synectics* for 3 performers (1970); *Comunicazione audiovisiva*, theater piece (1970); *Theme—Electronic Music* on tape (1970, unpub.).

PRINCIPAL WRITINGS: Editor, *Leksykon kompozytorów XX w.* [Dictionary of 20th-Century Composers], 2 vols. (Cracow 1963–65); *Klasycy dodekafonii* [12-Tone Classics], 2 vols. (Cracow 1964); *Nowa muzyka* [New Music], 2nd ed. (Cracow 1969); *Introduction to Composition* (Cracow, 1972).

BIBL.: J. Chomiński, *Polska współczesna kultura muzyczna* [Polish Contemporary Music Culture] (Cracow 1968); ——, *Polska muzyka* [Polish Music] (Warsaw 1968); B. Pociej, "Argument for the Existence of Music," *Poland* ed. by B. S. (Warsaw 1967); Z. Wachowicz, "Muzyka B. S." [The Music of B. S.] *Ruch muzyczny* (1960).

SEE ALSO Notation.

Schalit, Heinrich (b. Vienna, 2 Jan 1886), studied at the Vienna Academy (1902–06; composition with Robert Fuchs; piano with Theodor Leschetitzky; piano, theory with Josef Labor), and the Munich Academy (1908–09, organ with Ludwig Maier). He served as organist and music director of the Great Synagogues in Munich (1927–33) and Rome (1934–39) and of Temple B'rith Kodesh in Rochester, N. Y. (1940–43), Temple Beth-el in Providence, R. I. (1943–48), and Temple Israel in Hollywood. Since 1950 he has been living in Evergreen, Colo.

PRINCIPAL COMPOSITIONS: *Seelenlieder* for medium voice, piano (1916, UE); *Frühlingslieder* for high voice, piano (published 1917, Leuckart); *Liebeslieder* for high voice, piano (published 1923, UE); *In Ewigkeit*, hymn for 5-part chorus, organ,

harp, solo violin, strings (1928); *Eine Freitagabend-Liturgie* (1932, revised 1950 as *Sabbath Eve Liturgy*); *Hassidic Dances*, suite for string orchestra (1937); *Builders of Zion*, cantata (published by the composer 1944); *The Pilgrims*, cantata (published 1945); *98th Psalm* for high voice, chorus, organ (published 1952); *Sabbath Morning Liturgy* for cantor, chorus, organ (1952); *7 Sacred Songs* for medium voice, piano (1953); *Songs of Glory* for chorus, organ or piano (published 1963); *Hadrat kodesh* [The Beauty of Holiness], sacred service (1966); *Visions of Yehuda Halevi*, cycle for high voice, piano (published 1968).

PRINCIPAL WRITINGS: "H. S.," autobiographical sketch and bibliography, *Honoring 4 American Jewish Composers* (New York, National Jewish Music Council, 1964).

BIBL.: Israel Rabinowitch, *Of Jewish Music Ancient and Modern*, trans. by J. M. Klein (Montreal 1952):304; Aron Rothmüller, *The Music of the Jews* (South Brunswick, N. J., 1967): 233–34.

SEE ALSO Liturgical music: Jewish.

Schat, Peter (b. Utrecht, 5 June 1935), studied at the Utrecht Conservatory (composition with Kees van Baaren, piano with Jaap Callenbach) and privately with Mátyás Seiber in London and Pierre Boulez in Basel. His early works show the influence of the Bartók quartets and of Stravinsky's music from around 1950. Later influences include the music of Stockhausen and Webern's treatment of texture as an independent object. By 1970 he was moving in the direction of new theater forms, including political and "street" theater.

PRINCIPAL COMPOSITIONS (published by Donemus): *Septet* (1957); *Mozaiken* for orchestra (1959); *2 Pieces* for flute, violin, trumpet, percussion (1959); *Inscripties* for piano (1959); *Cryptogamen* for baritone, orchestra (1959); *Concerto da camera* for 2 clarinets, piano, strings, wooden percussion instruments, cymbals (1960); *Improvisations and Symphonies* for wind quintet (1960); *Entelechie No. 1* for 5 groups of instruments (1960–61); *Labyrinth*, theater piece (1960–65); *Entelechie No. 2* for 11 performers (1961); *Signalement* for 3 double basses, 6 percussionists (1961); *Collages* for 31-tone organ (1962); *First Essay on Electrocution* for violin, guitar, metal percussion (c.1966?); *On Escalation* (1968); *Reconstructie*, opera composed with Jan van Vlijmen, Louis Andriessen, Reinbert de Leeuw, Misha Mengelberg (1969); *Thema* for oboe, orchestra (1970).

BIBL.: Reinbert de Leeuw, "*Labyrinth*, an Opera of Sorts," *Sonorum Speculum* 27; Ernst Vermeulen, "On *Escalation*," *ibid.* 35.

[prepared with the help of Ernst Vermeulen]

SEE ALSO Netherlands.

Schibler, Armin (b. Kreuzlingen, Switzerland, 20 Nov 1920), studied music in Zurich (1940–45, piano with Walter Frey, composition with Willy Burkhard) and at the Darmstadt summer courses (1949–53; composition with René Leibowitz, Wolfgang Fortner, Ernst Krenek, Theodor Adorno). He has taught at the Kantonschule in Zurich since 1944. Schibler's music to 1945 was neobaroque. Free 12-tone writing for a few years beginning in 1950 added more chromaticism to his style. During 1953–60 he was especially concerned with rhythmic problems, uses of percussion instruments, and composing for dance. Music with recitation occupied more of his attention during the 60s.

PRINCIPAL COMPOSITIONS (published by Ahn & Sim unless otherwise noted): *String Quartets Nos. 1–4*: No. 1, Op. 14 (1945); No. 2, Op. 30 (1951); No. 3, Op. 57 (1958); No. 4, "Meerfahrt," with soprano, Op. 66; text by R. Jiménez (1959–60); *Symphonies Nos. 1–3*: No. 1, Op. 17 (1946); No. 2, Op. 35 (1952–53); No. 3, "Fantasia notturna," Op. 44 (1955–57); *Der spanische Rosenstock*, 3-act opera; libretto by Max Allenspach, Op. 20 (1947–50); *Passacaglia* for orchestra, Op. 24 (1949); *Die späte Sühne*, 1-act chamber opera, Op. 42; libretto by the composer (1953–54); *Lyrisches Konzert* for flute, orchestra, Op. 40 (1953); *Blackwood und Co.*, 2-act burlesque for singers, dancers, Op. 46; text by the composer and Alfred Goldmann (1955–58); *Media in vita*, oratorio for soloists, 2 choruses, orchestra; texts by C. F. Meyer, Op. 48 (1956–58, UE); *Der Gefangene*, ballet for 5 dancers, 7 instruments, Op. 52 (1957); *Ein Lebenslauf*, "Curriculum vitae," ballet for small dance group, 11 instruments, Op. 60 (1958); *Musik zu einem imaginären Ballett* for strings, Op. 56 (1958); *Antoine und Carmela*, musical play, Op. 81; text by Goldmann (1958–64, Bote); *Concerto 1959* for trumpet, horn, trombone, harp, piano, percussion, double string orchestra, Op. 59 (1959); *Violin Concerto*, Op. 61 (1959–60); *Selene und Endymion*, ballet for narrator, 12 strings, harpsichord, Op. 62 (1959–60); *Scènes fantastiques* for percussion, orchestra, Op. 63 (1959–60); *Concert pour le temps présent*, ballet, Op. 70 (1961, UE); *Gilgamesh*, dramatic oratorio; text by Goldmann (1962–); *Metamorphoses ebrietatis*, ballet, Op. 75 (1962–63); *Piano Concerto*, "Visions choréographiques," Op. 71 (1962–68, Eulenberg); *Huttens letzte Tage*, song cycle for bass, orchestra, Op. 84; texts by C. F. Meyer (1966–69, Eulenberg). In addition to the works listed, Schibler has written concertos for oboe, viola, cello, flute, horn, trombone, trumpet, woodwind quintet, flute and harp, and bassoon, as well as numerous chamber works, piano music, and instrumental pieces.

PRINCIPAL WRITINGS: *Neue Musik in dritter Generation* (Amriswil 1953); *Zum Werk Gustav Mahlers* (Lindau a.B. 1955); *Zur Oper der Gegenwart* (Amriswil 1956); *Mein Weg* (Amriswil 1969).

SEE ALSO Switzerland.

Schidlowsky, León (b. Santiago, Chile, 21 July 1931), began piano studies as a child at the National Conservatory and took liberal arts courses at the National Institute in Santiago (graduated 1948) and the Univ. of Chile (1948–52). He later studied music privately with Adolfo Allende and Free Focke in Santiago and composition in Germany during 1952–55. He taught music education at the Hebrew Institute in Santiago during 1955–61 and joined the Tonus group for new music, becoming its director in 1959. In 1961 he became director of the music archives of the Institute of Musical Extension of the Univ. of Chile, later director of the Institute and head of the composition department at the National Conservatory.

PRINCIPAL COMPOSITIONS (published by IEM unless otherwise noted): *5 Composiciones* for voice, piano; texts by Klee, Kandinsky, Morgenstern, Miguel Angel, and the composer (1954); *6 Japanese Songs* for soprano, clarinet, bass clarinet, trumpet, horn, violin, viola, cello, harp, piano; Haiku texts (1954); *Requiem* for soprano, chamber orchestra; text by Rilke (1954); *8 Structures* for piano (1955); *Cuarteto mixto* for flute, clarinet, violin, cello (1956); *Concerto for 6 Instruments* for clarinet, bass clarinet, trumpet, xylophone, piano, timpani (1957, PAU); *Cantata negra* for alto, piano, xylophone, 3 percussionists; text by Blaise Cendras (1957); *Caupolicán*, epic narrative for narrator, chorus, 2 pianos, celesta, percussion orchestra; text by Pablo Neruda (1958); *Epitafio a Vicente Huidobro* for soprano, flute, xylophone, vibraphone, percussion; text by Huidobro (1959); *Isla negra* for flute (1959); *Oda a la tierra* for 2 narrators, orchestra; text from Genesis 1 (1960); *La noche de cristal*, symphony for tenor, orchestra; liturgical text (1961); *Soliloquios* for clarinet, cello, guitar, piano, celesta, harp, vibraphone, 2 percussionists (1961); *Amatorias* for tenor, saxophone, guitar, harp, piano, celesta, xylophone, vibraphone, bells, percussion; text by Huidobro (1963); *De profundis* (Psalm 129) for soprano, alto, tenor, flute, oboe, bass clarinet, alto saxophone, trumpet, trombone, strings (1963, unpub.); *Eróstrato* for percussion orchestra (1963); *Invocación* for strings, percussion (1964); *Llaqui*, elegy for orchestra (1965); *Nueva York* for orchestra (1965). List to 1965: *Composers of the Americas* 10:106–09.

SEE ALSO Chile.

Schillinger, Joseph (b. Kharkov, Ukraine, 31 August 1895; d. New York, 23 March 1943), studied at the St. Petersburg Conservatory until 1918 (composition with Nikolai Tcherepnin). During 1918–22 he taught composition at the State Academy of Music in Kharkov and conducted the students' orchestra there. He also conducted the Ukrainian Symphony during 1920–21. During 1925–28 he was composer for the State Academic Theater in Leningrad. He emigrated to the U.S. in 1928 and taught in New York at the New School for Social Research, the American Institute, and Teachers' College of Columbia Univ. (where he taught mathematics and art history as well as music).

PRINCIPAL COMPOSITIONS: *March of the Orient* for orchestra, Op. 11 (1921); *Violin Sonata*, Op. 9 (1921–22); *Excentriade*, suite for piano (1924, Muzyka); *Symphonic Rhapsody* (1927); *Airphonic Suite* for aetherophone, orchestra (1929); *North Russian Symphony* for accordion, orchestra (1931).

PRINCIPAL WRITINGS: *Kaleidophone, New Resources of Melody and Harmony* (New York 1940); *The Schillinger System of Musical Composition* (New York 1946); *The Mathematical Basis of the Arts* (New York 1948).

BIBL.: Vernon Duke, "Gershwin, S., and Dukelsky," *Musical Quarterly* 33:102–15; Frances Schillinger, *J. S., A Memoir by His Wife* (New York 1949).

SEE ALSO Dance.

Schnebel, Dieter (b. Lahr, Germany, 14 March 1930), studied music at the Musikhochschule in Freiburg/Br. (1949–52); thereafter he studied theology and musicology at Tübingen (first theology exam in 1955, the second in 1959). He became a Lutheran curate at Kaiserslautern in 1957 and a vicar in 1960. Since 1963 he has been a teacher of religion in Frankfurt.

Schnebel challenges everything the word music includes, even the idea of sound itself. The source of his boldness lies in the *theologia crucis*, that rescue is possible only through abandonment. This concept, although close to Hegel's dialectic, differs from it in not ending with the "Here" but in pointing always to the "Utopia." As in *ki-no* it may result in abandoning the act of composing, in allowing sounds from both inside and outside the human body to become music themselves without being distorted by the composer and forced into music (*ki-no* consists of unrealizable drawings and of images such as ". . . the counterpoint of beating hearts . . . the heterophony of ticking watches . . .").

Versuche I–III, mostly instrumental compositions, grew out of analyses of Schoenberg, Webern, and Stockhausen. They go beyond their models, however, in isolating unconventional parameters such as vibratos.

für stimmen für and *glossolalie*, which are vocal works, continue the process of "denatured" singing that is apparent in *Versuche IIIa*, where a Rilke fragment is destroyed by means of post-Webern rests, leaps, and disjunct dynamic levels. In *für stimmen für* there is an uproar of sounds against words, of voices against language. The sacred texts used in the work are destroyed in order to free their primary meanings and expression (helplessness, moaning, stammering, shrieking, etc.). The phonetic materials, from various languages and times, join to form an ecstatic "speaking in tongues" as described in the Bible. The last section, :!, is a praise consisting of vocal noises (including animal noises) beyond speech. The music that arises from this frustrated attempt to articulate overflows in details of sound, and the expression approaches lunacy.

A third group of compositions, *Abfälle* and the *Schaustücke*, carries Schnebel's dialectic to its conclusion, the questioning of music itself. Music becomes a product of chance and at last disappears. In *réactions* an instrumentalist reacts upon audience noises (applause, stillness, uproar, etc.) even as the audience's noises are a reaction to what he does. In *visible music I (duo)* the duo consists of an instrumentalist and a silent conductor. In *nostalgie (visible music II)* the player is gone and the conductor celebrates a lonely, unhearable music of gestures.

PRINCIPAL COMPOSITIONS: ★ *Versuche I–III: Analysis* for string instruments, percussion (1953); *Stücke* for string quartet (1954–55); *Fragment* for chamber ensemble, voice (1955–56); *Compositio* for orchestra (1955–56, 1964–65). ★ *für stimmen für* (...*missa est*): *dt 31,6* for 12 vocal groups (1956–58); *amn* for 7 vocal groups (1966–68); *:! (madrasha II)* for 3 choirs (1958, 1964, 1967–68). ★ *Abfälle: réactions*, concerto for instrumentalist and audience (1960–61); *visible music I (duo)* for conductor and instrumentalist (1960–62). ★ *Schaustücke: nostalgie (visible music II)*, solo for conductor (1962); *espressivo (visible music III)* for instrumentalist (1963); *concert sans orchestre* for pianist and audience (1964); *fallout* for vocalist (1965); *anschläge-ausschläge*, staged variations for 3 instrumentalists on flute, cello, harpsichord (1965–66); *ki-no*, night music for projectors and listeners (1963–67); *mo-no, musik zum lesen* trans. by Margarete Rühle (1968–69; M. Dumont Schauberg, Cologne).

PRINCIPAL WRITINGS: *Studien zur Dynamik Arnold Schönbergs* (diss., Univ. of Tübingen, 1955); "Karlheinz Stockhausen," *Die Reihe* (English ed.) 4:121–35; "Abwege," *Neue Musik* (Munich) 5–6:3–6; "das musikalische material," *Collage* (Palermo) 3–4:35–36; "kommentar zu neuer musik," *Collage* 3–4:35–38; "Bericht von neuer Orgelmusik," *Festschrift Walter Gerstenberg* (Wolfenbüttel-Zurich 1964):151–61; "Mahlers Spätwerk als Neue Musik," *Collage* 6:13–16; "das formproblem in der neuen musik," *Collage* 6:17–21; "Sprache als Musik in der Musik,"

Schweizer Monatshefte (Sept 1966): 560–74; "Geist-liche Musik Heute," *Musik und Kirche* 3:109–18; "Musica sacra ohne Tabus," *Melos* 35:371–76; "sichtbare musik," *Collage* 8:8–18; *Mauricio Kagel: Musik Theater Film* (Cologne 1970).

Ernst-Jürgen Dreyer

SEE ALSO Austria and Germany, Rhythm, Text Setting and Usage.

Schneider, Urs Peter (b. Bern, 14 Feb 1939), studied at the Bern Conservatory (1958–63, composition with Sándor Veress, piano with Walter Lang), the Cologne Hochschule für Musik (1963–65, composition with Karlheinz Stockhausen, piano with Bruno Seidlhofer), the Vienna Academy (1965–66), and at the Darmstadt summer courses (1962, 1963). He has taught piano at the Bern Conservatory since 1966 and conducted the Ensemble Neue Horizonte Bern since 1968. He has concertized as a pianist throughout Europe. He has been influenced by a wide variety of literature and music, particularly Satie, Webern, Cage, Feldman, and pop music. His compositions have been compared with the theater pieces of Kagel and make use of unconventional sound sources: mouth pieces, a synthesizer, speaking voices, clock bells, radios, castinets, and a card table are among the sound sources in *20 Situationen*; they are to be used in many variable combinations simultaneously. Four optical and four acoustical "sources" are combined in *Abendfüllendes*.

PRINCIPAL COMPOSITIONS: *20 Situationen* for 1–4 performers using various sound sources (1960–69); *Babel* for 1–13 performers, each with several sound sources of his choice (1961–67, Howeg); *Kreuze* for xylophone, piano, flute, organ (1964–67); *Abendfüllendes* for 4 optical and 4 acoustical sources (1966–69); *Auf Anhieb* for 15 strings (1968); *Umkehr* for 32-piece orchestra, the sound of each instrument altered through electronic apparatus (1969–70); *Handwerk* for a pianist (1970).

BIBL.: Kjell Keller, "Theatralische Aspekte in der Musik von U. P. S.," *Dissonanz* (Zurich) 1970/1:16–18; Reinhard Oehlschlagel, "U. P. S. —ein Schweizer Kagel," *Neue Musikzeitung* 1970/2–3.

SEE ALSO Switzerland.

Schnitke, Alfred (b. Engels, U.S.S.R., 24 Nov 1934), studied at the Moscow Conservatory (1953–61, composition with E. Golubev, orchestration with N. Rakov). He has taught at the Moscow Conservatory since 1961. His music has been influenced by the work of Stravinsky, Orff, the 12-tone Viennese School, Stockhausen, and Cage, as well as by his acquaintance with Nono and his association with Philip Herschkowitz (a pupil of Webern). The young Soviet composers A. Karamanov and Arvo Pärt and Schnitke's correspondence with Pousseur and Ligeti have also affected his thinking. He has worked at the Moscow Electronic Music Studio.

PRINCIPAL COMPOSITIONS: *Nagasaki*, oratorio for mezzo-soprano, chorus, orchestra (1958); *Violin Concerto No. 1* (1957; revised 1962, SC); *Violin Sonata No 1* (1963, Muzyka); *Music for Piano and Chamber Orchestra* (1964); *3 Poems* for voice, piano; texts by Marina Tsvetaeva (1965); *Dialogue* for cello, flute, oboe, clarinet, trumpet, horn, piano, percussion (1965); *Violin Concerto No. 2* for chamber orchestra (1966); *String Quartet* (1966, UE); *Pianissimo* for orchestra (1968); *Violin Sonata No. 2* (1968); *Serenade for 5 Musicians* for clarinet, violin, double bass, piano, percussion (1968).

PRINCIPAL WRITINGS: "Zametki ob orkestrovoi polifonii v chetvyeortoi simphonii D. D. Shosta-kovicha" [Notes on the Orchestral Polyphony of D. D. Shostakovich's Fourth Symphony], *Muzyka i sovremennost'* 4 (Moscow 1966):127–61; "Oso-bennosti orkestrovogo golosovedeniia rannikh proizvedenii Stravinskogo" [Various Aspects of the Orchestral Voice Leading in the Early Works of Stravinsky], *ibid.* 5:209–61; "Nekotorie oso-bennosti orkestrovogo golosovedeniia v simfoni-cheskikh proizvedeniakh D. D. Shostakovicha" [Certain Aspects of Orchestral Voice Leading in the Symphonic Works of D. D. Shostakovich], *Dmitri Shostakovich* (Moscow 1967):499–532.

BIBL.: H. H. Stuckenschmidt, "Zwei Welten der Musik in Zagreb," *Melos* (1967):270; ——, "Holzknall und Röhrenglocken in Berliner Kon-zerten," *ibid.* (1970):106; Michail Tarakanov, "Novaia zhizn' staroii formy" [New Life of an Old Form], *Sovetskaia muzyka* 1968/6:60–62; ——, "Tri stilia ispolnenia" [Three Styles of Execution], *ibid.* 1970/3:83–84.

SEE ALSO Soviet Union.

Schoeck, Othmar (b. Brunnen, Switzerland, 1 Sept 1886; d. Zurich, 10 March 1957), studied at the Zurich Conservatory with Friedrich Hegar, Fritz Niggli, and Robert Freund (1905–07) and at the Leipzig Con-servatory with Max Reger (1907–08). He was mainly self-taught in composition. He per-formed professionally as a conductor and accompanist. During 1909–15 he directed the Men's Chorus of Aussersihl-Zurich; during 1911–17, the Zurich Lehrergesangverein; and during 1917–44, the St. Gallen Symphony Concerts. He is known chiefly for his vocal compositions, which follow in the tradition of Schubert and Hugo Wolf.

PRINCIPAL COMPOSITIONS: *Lieder nach Gedichten von Uhland und Eichendorff* for voice, piano, Op. 20 (1905–14, Breitkopf); *Der Postillon* for tenor, men's chorus, orchestra or piano, Op. 18; text by Lenau (1909, Hug); *Dithyrambe* for double chorus, orchestra, Op. 22; text by Goethe (1911, Hug); *Violin Concerto in Bb*, quasi una fantasia, Op. 21 (1911–12, Hug); *String Quartet in D*, Op. 23 (1912–13, Hug); *12 Eichendorfflieder* for voice, piano, Op. 30 (1917–18, Breitkopf); *Don Ranudo*, 4-act comic opera, Op. 27; libretto by Armin Rüeger after Holberg (1917–18, Breitkopf); *Venus*, 3-act opera, Op. 32; libretto by Rüeger after Merimée (1919–20, Breitkopf); *12 Hafislieder* for voice, piano, Op. 33 (1919–20, Breitkopf); *Der Gott und die Bajadere* for voice, piano, Op. 34; text by Goethe (1921, Breitkopf); *Elegie* for voice, orchestra, Op. 36; poems by Lenau and Eichendorff (1922–23, Breitkopf); *String Quartet in C*, Op. 37 (1923, Breitkopf); *Gaselen* for baritone, flute, oboe, bass clarinet, trumpet, piano, percussion, Op. 38; poems by Gottfried Keller (1923, Breitkopf); *Penthesilea*, incidental music for the play by Hermann von Kleist, Op. 39 (1924–25, Bärenreiter); *Lebendig begraben*, 14 songs for baritone, orchestra, Op. 40; poems by Keller (1926); *Vom Fischer un syner Fru*, dramatic cantata, Op. 43; text by P. O. Runge after Grimm (1928–30, Breitkopf); *Violin Sonata in E*, Op. 46 (1931, Hug); *Notturno*, 5 pieces for baritone, string quartet, Op. 47; poems by Lenau and Keller (1931–33, UE); *Präludium* for orchestra, Op. 48 (1932, UE); *Massimilla Doni*, 4-act opera, Op. 50; libretto by Rüeger after Balzac (1934–35, UE); *Wandsbecker Liederbuch* for voice, piano, Op. 52; poems by Matthias Claudius (1936–37); *Unter Sternen*, songs for medium voice, piano, Op. 54; poems by Keller (1941–43, UE); *Der Sänger*, songs for high voice, piano, Op. 57; poems by Heinrich Leuthold (1944–45, UE); *Sommernacht*, pastoral intermezzo for string orchestra, Op. 58 (1945, Hug); *Suite in Ab* for string orchestra, Op. 59 (1945, UE); *Das stille Leuchten*, songs for medium voice, piano, Op. 60; poems by C. F. Meyer (1946, UE); *Concerto* for cello, string orchestra, Op. 61 (1947, Hug); *Das holde Bescheiden*, songs for voice, piano, Op. 62; poems by Mörike (1947–50, UE); *Vision* for men's chorus, orchestra, Op. 63; poem by Keller (1949, Hug); *Festlicher Hymnus* for orchestra, Op. 64 (1950, Hug); *Concerto* for horn, string orchestra, Op. 65 (1951, Boosey); *Nachhall*, songs for medium voice, orchestra, Op. 70; poems by Lenau and Claudius (1954–55, UE).

BIBL.: Hans Corrodi, *O. S.*, 2nd ed. (Frauenfeld-Leipzig 1936); Willi Schuh, ed., *O. S., Festgabe der Freunde zum 50. Geburtstag* (Erlenbach-Zurich 1936); *Thematisches Verzeichnis der Werke von O. S.* (Zurich 1956); Werner Vogel, *Wesenzüge von O. S.s Liedkunst* (Zurich 1950).

[prepared with the help of the Othmar-Schoeck-Gesellschaft]

SEE ALSO Switzerland.

Schoenberg, Arnold (b. Vienna, 2 Sept 1874; d. Los Angeles, 13 July 1951), learned to play the violin and cello while a youth and almost immediately began composing pieces for these instruments. In 1894 he had his only formal composition lessons, counterpoint with Alexander von Zemlinsky. In 1897 his first major work, a string quartet in D, was publicly performed. He moved to Berlin in 1901, where a year later, through the influence of Richard Strauss, he obtained the Liszt stipend and a teaching position at the Stern Conservatory. Returning to Vienna in 1903, he joined an artistic circle around Gustav Mahler. As performances of his works increased, he attracted a group of gifted students, among whom were Alban Berg, Egon Wellesz, and Anton Webern. In 1910 he became a teacher of composition at the Vienna Academy, and the following year published his harmony text, *Harmonielehre*.

The following years produced radical advances in Schoenberg's style and saw more performances of his works throughout Europe. In 1918, as a result of critical attacks, he organized the Society for Private Musical Performances in Vienna; critics were excluded, programs were not announced in advance, and applause was forbidden. In 1925 Schoenberg began teaching again at Berlin, this time at the Prussian Academy of Arts. He was dismissed from his position in 1933 by the Nazi-dominated ministry of education, and he emigrated to the U.S. He settled in Hollywood and from 1936 taught at the Univ. of Calif. at Los Angeles.

Although Schoenberg's musical output was not exceptionally large, it included significant music for almost every medium. Excluding student works, there are over 40 lieder for voice and piano, ten with orchestral accompaniment, 16 pieces for chorus, 21 for piano, one work for organ, four operas, two concertos, two symphonies, one symphonic poem, and seven other orchestral compositions. Schoenberg also wrote many chamber works throughout his life, often for unusual instrumental combinations and some with voice. These include a solo for violin and piano, a string trio, four string quartets, one string sextet, and six other works utilizing varied instrumentation.

Schoenberg's earliest compositions, covering the years 1893–1903, were in the tradition of the great German romantic composers. They reflected the influence of Brahms and Wagner, even though these two composers were considered to hold irreconcilable positions during their own lifetimes. Brahms represented a conservative point of view with his classical forms and abstract structures, while Wagner, ostensibly writing "music of the future," represented a radical position with his freely constructed forms, continuous development of musical ideas, and programmatic allusions. When Schoenberg used traditional forms and structures, he showed the influence of Brahms; when he created an atmosphere of intense subjectivity and used a chromatic harmonic style, he revealed his debt to Wagner. *Verklärte Nacht*, Op. 4 (1899) is one of the best known works of this period. It is a tone poem for chamber ensemble (later arranged for string orchestra) based on a poem by Richard Dehmel. What appears on the surface as a long rhapsody freely following its own form turns out to be two interconnected symphonic movements, both in sonata-allegro form. The idea of writing a programmatic work within the confines of a string sextet shows Schoenberg's fresh approach to musical materials. *Gurrelieder* (1900–01), by contrast, is a long cantata utilizing one of the largest orchestras ever assembled. It requires 25 woodwind players (including eight flutes), 25 brass players (including ten horns), a large percussion section (including chains!), four harps, an eight-part chorus, three men's choirs, five vocal soloists, and a speaker-narrator. The quasi-Wagnerian subject matter, adapted from poems by Jens Peter Jacobsen, concerns a love that lives on after death and includes a wild ride of ghostly horsemen through the sky and lavish musical depictions of nature scenes. At the same time, rather than casting his semi-mythological story into a music drama, Schoenberg wrote it as an elaborate song cycle, suggesting again his attraction to traditional formal restrictions and the influence of Brahms.

Schoenberg's next works, 1903–07, continued to explore the romantic subjective elements found in his earlier compositions, while expanding the use of chromatic harmony to its furthest possible limits. In these works the basic harmonic and tonal structures became more and more tenuous and elusive, while the melodic invention became even more expressive. The most important compositions were the *String Quartet in D Minor*, Op. 7 (1905) and the first *Chamber Symphony* for 15 solo instruments (1906). In both works a wealth of melodic invention is coupled with an original approach to form whereby the traditional four movements are combined into one long uninterrupted work. In spite of their emotional surge, Schoenberg's works of the time were becoming increasingly difficult to follow. Coupled with the formal innovations

were highly chromatic harmonies in which chords never quite resolved to their expected goals, and a thick contrapuntal texture in which thematic material appeared in all inner voices and accompaniment figures.

In 1908, a landmark in the history of Western music, Schoenberg wrote his first atonal compositions, in which no keynote occupied a position of central importance and in which no given harmony needed to resolve to a more stable sonority. Although atonality may appear to have been unprecedented, it actually grew out of Schoenberg's previous experiments in chromatic harmony. As a result of what Schoenberg called "the emancipation of the dissonance," any note could be combined with any other, and any combination of tones could theoretically follow or precede any other. Schoenberg's free atonal compositions cover the period 1908–14. During this time he composed only nine works; they remain in many ways his most controversial music. The earliest atonal compositions were the song cycle *Das Buch der hängenden Gärten*, Op. 15, and the first two of the *3 Pieces* for piano, Op. 11, both completed in 1909 (the song cycle was begun the year before). In these works the musical structure is usually a simplified ABA form with some opening material returning more or less varied near the end. At the same time the thematic counterpoint and romantic atmosphere of the earlier works gives way to a static mood that stems from the lack of harmonic direction. The texture gets very thin and sparse, and the progression of musical ideas from bar to bar becomes more and more unclear. This fragmentary texture results from the fact that Schoenberg composed these works around short intervallic series rather than around thematic material. Finally, in the last of the *5 Pieces* for orchestra, Op. 16 (1909) and the third piano piece of Op. 11, Schoenberg arrived at a musical style that eliminated thematic repetition almost completely. These works are frantically emotional, and at the same time they verge on incoherence because the development of intervallic material is so fragmented.

Because of the extraordinary structural problems presented by this athematic style of writing, Schoenberg, beginning with the *6 Little Pieces* for piano, Op. 19 (1911), shortened the length of many of his compositions. Some of them last less than a minute in performance. This period of composition culminated in *Pierrot lunaire*, Op. 21 (1912), a work for reciter and small instrumental ensemble. In this work Schoenberg's use of sprechstimme (speaking voice) appeared in its most elaborate form. In this unusual vocal style the singer, according to Schoenberg's instructions, follows the notes and rhythms indicated but abandons the pitch immediately after it has been sung and slides up or down to the next pitch; the effect lies midway between singing and speaking. The continual use of the vocal glissando, which encompasses pitches that lie outside the well-tempered scales of Western music, accompanied by instruments that also exploit unusual sonorities (piano harmonics, extreme ranges, pizzicato glissandos in the strings, flutter-tonguing in the winds, etc.), creates a highly unstable texture that covers an emotional gamut from morbid depression to pathological hysteria. In *Pierrot lunaire* the emotional subjectivity characteristic of the romantic period reaches its ultimate extreme. At this point the problems of composing atonal or athematic music seem to have entangled Schoenberg excessively and he practically stopped composing. During 1913–16 he wrote only a few songs, and in 1917 started the oratorio, *Die Jakobsleiter*, which was never finished.

In 1921 Schoenberg started composing once again, and by 1923 some completed works appeared, introducing one last radical innovation, the 12-tone technique. As important in its own way as the use of atonality, this technique offered the composer an organized approach to the writing of atonal music. In addition to being Schoenberg's first 12-tone compositions, the music written 1921–27 also contained other unusual elements. Unlike his previous works, which were subjective and romantic, these are more objective and classical in structure. The *Suite* for piano, Op. 25 (1921–23), the first work written throughout in the 12-tone technique, contains a prelude, a gavotte with a musette, an intermezzo, a minuet and trio, and a gigue. In these works, Schoenberg used traditional forms more strictly than in any previous compositions. He even used repeat marks and da capo directions, producing his first works in which thematic material recurred in performance without alteration. In the *String Quartet No. 3*, Op. 30 (1927), one of the finest works of this period, the entire structure of a classical symphony (a first movement in sonata-allegro form, a set of variations for the slow movement, a scherzo with a trio, and a rondo finale) is sustained without any tonal reference, the entire edifice being supported solely through the repetition of thematic material.

Having tested his strength with a number of 12-tone compositions that were compara-

tively short, Schoenberg began his most ambitious work in 1930, the opera *Moses und Aron*. Convinced that the tone row was flexible enough to afford a composer as much thematic material as he needed, he set out to write the music for a three-act opera from a single row. Although only the first two acts were completed at his death, *Moses und Aron* remains Schoenberg's longest work written in the technique as well as one of his greatest achievements. The libretto was written by the composer following the style of a Wagnerian music drama, where mythological stories are incorporated and freely altered to support serious philosophical premises. The story concerns Moses' inability to reveal the essence of his vision of God to his people without distorting it beyond recognition; on another level, Moses becomes the symbol of the modern artist who, faithful only to his inner vision, finds he cannot communicate to his audience. The musical high points of the opera are the confrontation of Moses with the Voice from the burning bush (a scene full of mystery and awe), the meeting of Moses with Aron (where the two characters move on totally different levels both ideologically and musically), and, for the climax of the opera, the dance around the golden calf, an elaborate choreographic scene that stands among Schoenberg's most brilliant orchestral achievements.

In the years following Schoenberg's move to the U.S., his choice of subject matter for vocal works tended to exhibit a new social consciousness. At the same time he attempted to simplify his style to some extent. Many passages in these later works contain tonal implications, both those written in the 12-tone technique as well as occasional works written once again with key signatures. The *Kol Nidre*, Op. 39 (1938), a short cantata based on material taken from the Jewish Yom Kippur service, is written in G minor. The *Variations* for organ, Op. 40 (1941), while not written in the 12-tone technique, contains a principal theme suggesting a D-minor tonality which is treated in a serial manner. The *Ode to Napoleon*, Op. 41 (1942), written as a strict 12-tone work but not based on a specific tone row, once again incorporates tonal triads (the text, by Byron, was chosen because Schoenberg felt that it could be taken to refer to Hitler's dictatorship). The *Piano Concerto*, Op. 42 (1942), a strict 12-tone work, opens with one of his most lyric serial melodies. His final compositions were a set of choral pieces based on Jewish subject matter.

In addition to his musical compositions, Schoenberg wrote a large number of essays and some major theoretical works. Some of the essays, including his only explanation of the 12-tone technique, have been collected under the title *Style and Idea* (London 1950). His most important theoretical works are the *Harmonielehre* (Vienna 1911) and *Structural Functions of Harmony* (New York 1954). This last work goes beyond standard harmony textbooks in its attempts to show how different chord progressions affect the structure of a composition, with certain progressions tending to establish a key, others to dissolve a key, still others to harmonize a principal theme, to define a development section, to form a coda, etc.

Schoenberg's strongest influence can be felt in the music of his pupils Alban Berg and Anton Webern. Although each followed their master dutifully, writing tonal music at first, moving into atonal music around 1909 and to 12-tone music around 1924, each managed to maintain his individual style, a credit to Schoenberg's gifts as a teacher. After his death, following the discovery of Webern's music by American and European composers, the use of the 12-tone technique spread rapidly. In the early 1950s Stravinsky wrote his first 12-tone composition, and more conservative composers like Aaron Copland soon followed. The position of the mid-century European composer was perhaps best summarized by Pierre Boulez in his article "Schoenberg is Dead" (*Score*, May 1952:18–22), where he rejected Schoenberg's romantic esthetics along with the application of the 12-tone technique to classical forms. Boulez stated that while the technique was valid for modern composers, they would have to derive their own forms from it and not attempt to imitate Schoenberg's music itself.

Schoenberg's music has always had, and will probably always have, a circle of devoted admirers. In his own way he was a great melodist, and throughout his life he wrote some remarkably expressive lyric passages. In his early works he showed a consummate mastery of tonal harmony and orchestration. His ability to evoke on the instant any mood he chose seems almost to rival Wagner. The problem of his music seems to lie in its perpetual complexity and in his compulsion to push every element, including rhythm, form, and texture, to its furthest possible limits. His obsessive desire to make every moment count the most, to fill every bar with as much music as possible, to make every inner voice participate in the thematic content, to vary in some way every repetition, even of a single phrase, ultimately makes staggering demands on the listener. Many composers after Schoenberg wrote music in which the organizational principles must be known in advance if they are to be identified and understood. Schoenberg, however, expected listeners to hear everything in his works as they would hear every event in any serious music of the past. He was neither unmusical nor musically weak; if anything, he was in a strangely self-defeating way overly musical. The listener is sometimes bombarded with too much information too quickly; if he does not absorb it fast enough, the composition can become a nerve-wracking experience. Schoenberg's works may never find a large concert audience, although popularity might attach itself to some of his early works, where the harmony can be more easily absorbed, or the late ones, where a deep sense of humanity affords a foil to balance the complexity of the musical material.

PRINCIPAL COMPOSITIONS: *Verklärte Nacht* for string sextet, Op. 4; after the poem by Richard Dehmel (1899, Birnbach; arranged for string orchestra 1917, UE; revised 1943, AMP); *Gurrelieder*, cantata; text by Jens Peter Jacobsen (1900–01, UE); *String Quartet in D Minor*, Op. 7 (1905, Birnbach); *Chamber Symphony* for 15 solo instruments, Op. 9 (1906, UE; "new version for orchestra," Op. 9b, 1935, Schirmer-G); *String Quartet No. 2* with soprano solo, Op. 10 (1907–08, UE); *Das Buch der hängenden Gärten* for high voice, piano, Op. 15 (1908–09, UE); *3 Pieces* for piano, Op. 11 (1909, UE); *5 Pieces* for orchestra, Op. 16 (1909, Peters); *Erwartung*, monodrama for soprano, orchestra, Op. 17; libretto by Marie Pappenheim (1909, UE); *6 Little Pieces* for piano, Op. 19 (1911, UE); *Pierrot lunaire*, 21 melodramas for voice, instruments, Op. 21 (1912, UE); *Suite* for piano, Op. 25 (1921–23, UE); *String Quartet No. 3*, Op. 30 (1927, UE); *Moses und Aron*, opera (acts 1–2 completed 1930–32, Schott); *String Quartet No. 4*, Op. 37 (1936, Schirmer-G); *Kol Nidre* for reciter, chorus, orchestra, Op. 39 (1938, Boelke); *Variations on a Recitative* for organ, Op. 40 (1941, Gray); *Ode to Napoleon Buonaparte* for string quartet, piano, reciter, Op. 41 (1942, Schirmer-G; arranged for string orchestra, piano, reciter, Op. 41b); *Piano Concerto*, Op. 42, (1942, Schirmer-G). Complete list in Rufer.

PRINCIPAL WRITINGS: *Harmonielehre* (Vienna 1911; abridged English translation, New York 1948); *Style and Idea*, a collection of essays (London 1950); "My Evolution," *Musical Quarterly* 38; *Structural Functions of Harmony* ed. by H. Searle (New York 1954); *Schöpferische Konfessionen* ed. by W. Reich (Zurich 1964); *Letters* (New York 1965).

BIBL.: René Leibowitz, *S. and His School* (New York 1949); Dika Newlin, *Bruckner, Mahler, S.* (New York 1947); George Perle, *Serial Composition and Atonality* (Berkeley 1962); Josef Rufer, *The Works of A. S.* (New York 1963); Hans H. Stuckenschmidt, *A. S.* (New York 1960). Extensive bibl.: William Austin, *Music in the 20th Century* (New York 1966):620–26.

Philip Friedheim

SEE ALSO Asian Music and Western Composition; Austria and Germany; Dance; Debussy; Expressionism; Form; Harmony and Counterpoint; Liturgical Music: Jewish; Mathematics; Melody; Mixed Media; Opera; Orchestration; Performance; Rhythm; Text Setting and Usage; Texture; Theory; Tuning and Temperament; 12-Tone Techniques.

Schollum, Robert (b. Vienna, 22 August 1913), studied at the New Vienna Conservatory (1927–32, composition with Egon Lustgarten, piano with Carl Lafite) and at the Vienna State Academy of Music (1932–33, composition with Josef Marx, organ with Franz Schütz). He continued to study composition privately with Lustgarten until 1938. Since 1933 he has performed professionally as a conductor, organist, and choral director and has lectured on musicology. He has taught at the Vienna Hochschule für Musik since 1959. During 1964–69 he was president of the Austrian Composers' Union. Until about 1968 he followed Schoenberg's 12-tone techniques strictly, thereafter more freely. His use of timbres derived originally from Debussy and Milhaud. The later austerity in his style is related in part to his interest in the world's folk musics.

PRINCIPAL COMPOSITIONS (published by Doblinger unless otherwise noted): *Symphonies Nos. 1–5*: No. 1, Op. 50 (1953); No. 2, Op. 60 (1958); No. 3, Op. 67 (1963); No. 4, Op. 74 (1967); No. 5, Op. 77 (1969); *Kontraste* for orchestra, Op. 56 (1956); *Konturen* for string orchestra, Op. 59b (1958, Breitkopf); *Gespräche* for chamber orchestra, Op. 62 (1959); *Octet*, Op. 63, for flute, oboe, clarinet, bassoon, violin, viola, cello, double bass (1959); *Violin Concerto No. 2*, Op. 65 (1962); *Mosaik* for oboe, piano, percussion, Op. 75 (1968); *Psalmkomentare* for chorus, 2 pianos, percussion, Op. 80 (1970); *Spiele* for orchestra, Op. 81 (1970). Complete list of compositions and writings to 1968: *Biographisches Lexikon von Oberösterreich*, 6th ed. (Vienna-Leipzig 1960, supplement 1968).

PRINCIPAL WRITINGS: *Musik in der Volksbildung* (Vienna 1961); *Egon Wellesz* (Vienna 1964); *Die Wiener Schule* (Vienna 1968); *Singen als menschliche Kundgebung* (Vienna 1970); *Das kleine Wiener Jazzbuch* (Vienna 1970).

BIBL.: Erik Werba, "R. S.," *Österreichische Musikzeitschrift* (Nov 1961):3–4.

Schönbach, Dieter (b. Stolp, Pomerania, Germany—now Poland, 18 Feb 1931), attended the Nordwestdeutsche Musikakademie in Detmold (1949–57, composition with Günther Bialas) and the Staatliche Hochschule für Musik in Freiburg/Breisgau (1957–59, composition with Wolfgang Fortner). Since 1959 he has been music director of the Schauspielhaus in Bochum and director of the Bochum electronic and concrete music studio. Schönbach has done considerable work with experimental films. Through the influence of painting and sculpture he became involved with multimedia and musical environments, forming a multimedia team with Otto Piene and Edmund Kieselbach in 1967.

PRINCIPAL COMPOSITIONS: *String Quartet* (1957, Ahn & Sim); *Canticum psalmi resurrectionis* for soprano, 2 flutes, trumpet, 2 violas, guitar, percussion (1957, UE); *Orchestra Piece 1*, "Farben und Klänge" (1958, Peters and Litolff); *Piano Concerto* (1958); *Come Santo Francesco predico agli uccelli*, concerto for soprano, 16 instruments (1959, Peters and Litolff); *Kammermusik 1960* for 14 instruments (1960); *Orchestra Piece 2*, "Ritornelle" (1961, EM); *Lyrische Gesänge I* for soprano, chamber ensemble (1961, Peters and Litolff); *Orchestra Piece 3*, "Pour Varsovie" (1962, Peters and Litolff); *Lyrische Gesänge II* for soprano, 2 pianos (1963, Peters and Litolff); *Orchestra Piece 4*, "Entre" (1963, Peters and Litolff); *Hoquetus* for 8 winds (1964); *Canticum psalmi ad laudes* for soprano, chamber ensemble (1964, Peters and Litolff); *Chant liturgique* for chorus, orchestra (1964); *Canzona da sonar 1* for 16 solo strings (1965); *Canzona da sonar 2* for 13 instruments (1965); *Canzona da sonar 3* for soprano recorder, prepared piano, 2-track tape (1966, Moeck); *Canzona e strophi*, "54 mal Orgel," for organ (1966); *Concerto in D*, based on D. Scarlatti, for trumpet, chamber orchestra (1966, SM); *Canzona da sonar 4* for 2 lotus-flutes, clarinet, trumpet, trombone, violin, double bass (1967); *Die Geschichte von einem Feuer*, multimedia opera; text by Elisabeth Borchers (1967–68, Moeck); *Canzona* for soprano and an environment; multimedia piece in collaboration with Carla Henius and Otto Piene (1969).

SEE ALSO Austria and Germany.

Schroeder, Hermann (b. Bernkastel, Germany, 26 March 1904), studied at Innsbruck Univ. (1923–26) and the Cologne Musikhochschule (1926–30; composition with Heinrich Lemacher, Walter Braunfels). He has taught at the Musikhochschule in Cologne (1930–38, since 1946) and at the Univ. of Bonn (also since 1946). During 1938–45 he was organist at the Trier Cathedral. He also directed the Cologne Bach-Verein during 1942–62. He describes his style as atonal and dissonant and based on Hindemith's techniques. Primarily a composer of organ music, he has also written 11 orchestral works including seven concertos for various instruments, six string quartets and other chamber music, two piano sonatas, sacred and secular choral music, and an opera.

PRINCIPAL ORGAN COMPOSITIONS (published by Schott unless otherwise noted): *Prelude and Fugue on "Christ lag in Todesbanden"* (1930); *Toccata in C Minor*, Op. 5a (1930, Schwann); *Fantasia in E Minor*, Op. 5b (1931); *Little Preludes and Intermezzi* (1932); *6 Organ Chorales*, Op. 11 (1934); *Collected Preludes* (1935); *Prelude, Canzona, and Rondo* for violin, organ (1937); *Organ Concerto*, Op. 25 (1938); *4 Choral Preludes* (1948, Christoforus); *2 Chorale Preludes* (1952, Leuckart); *4 Marian Antiphons* (1953); *Preambles and Interludes* (1953); *Duet* for violin, organ (1954); *Fantasia on "O heiligste Dreifaltigkeit"* (1955, Schwann); *Sonatas Nos. 1–3* (1956, 1964, 1968); *Partita on "Veni creator Spiritus"* (1958); *Preludes* for the third mass of Christmas and the 23rd Sunday after Pentecost (1957, Christoforus); *Pezzi piccoli* (1959, McLaughlin); *3 Pieces* for organ manuals (1961, published by Carrara in Bergamo); *Organ Ordinary No. 4, "Cunctipotens Deus"* (1962); *Prelude in E* (1962, published by Adagio in Mecheln); *Organ Book for the Ulenberg Psalm Tunes* (1962, Schwann); *8 Chorales for the Church Year* (1963); *4 Chorale Preludes* (1965, published by Bieler in Cologne); *Gregorian Miniatures* (1965, Coppenrath); *Concertino* for oboe, violin, organ (1965); *Sonata* for cello, organ (1966); *Prelude in C Flat, Trio, Dialogue* (1967, Eulenberg); *Psalm 150*, antiphon with verse settings (1967, Orbis); *Duplum* for positive organ, harpsichord (1968); *Orgelmosaiken* (1969, Schwann); *3 Chorale Preludes* (1969, Concordia); *2 Chorale Preludes* (1970, Concordia); *Duo da chiesa* for violin, organ (1970, Orbis); *12 Chorales for Christmas* (1970, Concordia).

PRINCIPAL WRITINGS: *Kontrapunkt* (Mainz 1950); *Harmonielehre* (Dusseldorf 1953); *Generalbassübungen* (Dusseldorf 1954); *Musical Form* (New York 1967).

BIBL.: R. Keusen, *H. S.* (diss., Univ. of Bonn, 1971).

Schuller, Gunther (b. New York, 22 Nov 1925), is the son of a violinist who played in the New York Philharmonic. He had early formal training at the St. Thomas Choir School (1937–40), after which he was primarily self-taught. In addition to his work in composition, he has been extremely active as a performer, conductor, educator, jazz scholar, and champion of new music. His professional posts have included principal solo horn with the Cincinnati Symphony (1943–45) and Metropolitan Opera (1945–59), horn teacher at the Manhattan School of Music (1951–59), associate professor of music at Yale Univ.

(1964–67), and president of the New England Conservatory (since 1967). He has also been supervisor of contemporary-music activities at Tanglewood since 1965.

Schuller has written over 85 works, including over 25 orchestral and concerted works (including substantial concertos for double bass and tuba) and 40 pieces of chamber music for standard and ad hoc ensembles (e.g., *Lines and Contrasts* for 16 horns, *Fantasy Quartet* for 4 cellos). There is a song cycle, two operas, some didactic works for children, and many jazz-oriented compositions. An important facet of his self-training as a composer is the fact that he listens and studies and then relies on his ear and creative intelligence to make outside influences part of his own style. His early works (e.g., *Symphony* for brass and percussion, 1949–50), as appropriate to someone consciously or unconsciously using Mahler and Schoenberg for models, survey Viennese atonality and primitive 12-tone usage. Later (*Spectra*, 1958) there is a qualified immersion in the 12-tone technique and the large-scale formal solutions suggested by middle period Schoenberg of the *Orchestral Variations*, Op. 31; *Spectra*, unlike Schoenberg, uses acoustical and architectural probings as the basis for new sonic possibilities. In the late 1950s and early 60s (e.g., *Contrasts*, 1961) Schuller added techniques associated with the post-Webern European serial movement, which dealt with pitch, rhythmic, timbral, and registral parameters. Perhaps a more potent influence at this time was the combinatorial thinking of Milton Babbitt; Schuller's 1965 *Symphony* uses combinatorial permutations of sets to serve as surrogates for classical concepts of modulation and the dramatic balance of tonal weights. In addition to these influences, there are throughout the 60s isolated uses of metrical modulation as well as simultaneous strands, proportional notation, and electronically amplified or reproduced sound. Jazz, a central influence, is discussed below.

Schuller's approach to the orchestra is unstrained and instinctive, combining an intimate knowledge of the technical possibilities of the various instruments with an insight into the psychological makeup of orchestral players. He often treats the orchestra as a huge group of soloists capable of subtle and exquisite as well as grandiose and massive splotches of color and contour. (His chamber music makes even greater virtuoso demands on the players, including improvisation; e.g., *String Quartet No. 1*, 1957, and *Woodwind Quintet*, 1958). In this his music has roots both in jazz and in expressionistic, chamber-style orchestral music of the early 20th-century (though Stravinsky's orchestra has been a decided influence, too). He is fascinated by the sonic analogues of color and pictoriality and continually uses titles such as *Spectra, Shapes and Designs, 7 Studies on Themes of Paul Klee, American Triptych* (based on works of Jackson Pollock, Alexander Calder, and Stuart Davis). He does not transfer the visual into the audible in an atmospheric sense but literally, in a more evocative manner.

Schuller's music has been fertilized by jazz orchestration, the illusion of easy execution in jazz, the improvisation process as metaphor, improvisation itself, and the vocabulary of jazz articulation and sonority. The opening movement of his *Concerto for Orchestra* (1965–66) is unthinkable without the big-band brass-section sound in mind, and the most effective scenes of his opera *The Visitation* (1966–68) are those which parody American popular music habits or quote them directly. Concern in this direction had brought Schuller to the concept of a "third stream" (his term), which involves the interchangeability of concert and jazz techniques (e.g., *Symphonic Tribute to Duke Ellington*, 1955). He envisioned a breed of performer (which has largely come to pass) who could move effortlessly from style to style, thereby opening up new possibilities, i.e., a third stream. His own third-stream compositions require the artistry of jazz virtuosos on the order of the Modern Jazz Quartet or Ornette Coleman. In these pieces he fashions an appropriate music and setting, accompanying the whole with an established concert-music group, perhaps a string quartet or an orchestra. In *Conversations* for jazz quartet and string quartet (1959) there is a subtle interaction between the two groups which ultimately gives way to improvisation based on traditional chord-change procedures, after which the strings return to provide an atmospheric backdrop and epilogue. At the core of his first opera, *The Visitation*, is not only his typically virtuoso orchestra but also a highly effective conjunction of jazz and concert idioms. The use of a Bessie Smith recording, honky-tonk jazz, commercial string-ballad writing, and the like, compare favorably with such earlier juxtapositions of style as those of Milhaud in *La Création du monde*.

PRINCIPAL COMPOSITIONS (published by AMP unless otherwise noted): *Quartet* for 4 double basses (1947, MJQ); *Trio* for oboe, horn, viola (1948, MJQ); *Symphony* for brass, percussion (1949–50, Malcolm); *5 Pieces* for 5 horns (1952,

Bruzzichelli); *String Quartet No. 1* (1957, UE); *Music* for violin, piano, percussion (1957); *Spectra* for orchestra (1958, Schott); *Woodwind Quintet* (1958, AMP and Schott); *Concertino* for jazz quartet, orchestra (1959, MJQ); *7 Studies on Themes of Paul Klee* for orchestra (1959, UE); *Fantasy Quartet* for 4 cellos (1959, MJQ); *Capriccio* for tuba, orchestra (1960); *Variants* for jazz quartet of vibraphone, piano, double bass, piano, orchestra (1960); *Music* for brass quintet (1961); *Contrasts* for woodwind quintet, orchestra (1961); *Piano Concerto* (1962, Schott); *Symphony* (1965); *Concerto for Orchestra*, "Gala Music" (1965–66); *The Visitation*, 3-act opera; libretto by the composer (1966–68); *Colloquy* for 2 pianos, orchestra (1966); *Triplum* for orchestra (1967); *Double Bass Concerto* (1968); *Shapes and Designs* for orchestra (1968); *American Triptych* for orchestra (1969); *Museum Piece* for renaissance instruments, orchestra (1970); *The Fisherman and his Wife*, 1-act opera (1970). List to 1964: *Composers of the Americas* 10:112–16.

PRINCIPAL WRITINGS: *Horn Technique* (New York 1962); "American Performance and New Music," *Perspectives* 1/2:1–8; "Conversation with Steuermann," *ibid.* 3/1:22–35; "Conversation with Varèse," *ibid.* 3/2:32–37; *Early Jazz: Its Roots and Musical Development* (New York 1968).

Edwin London

SEE ALSO Jazz, Opera, Orchestration, Performance.

Schuman, William (Howard) (b. New York, 4 August 1910), had early musical training with Max Persin and Charles Haubiel, graduated from Columbia Univ., and during 1936–38 studied composition privately with Roy Harris. He taught at Sarah Lawrence College (1935–45) and was president of the Juilliard School (1945–62), where he completely reorganized the usual theory sequence into a comprehensive program known as "Literature and Materials of Music." He was president of Lincoln Center for the Performing Arts (1962–69) and since 1970 has been chairman of the board of the Videorecord Corp. of America.

Although he has composed extensively in all media, Schuman is primarily a composer of large-scale symphonic works. Together with Roger Sessions, he is the foremost American representative of that tradition which reaches through Mahler and Bruckner into the 19th century and earlier. By the sheer scope of their gestures and the largeness of their conception, his orchestral works, including the single-movement pieces and ballets, have a sweep and force that set them apart from most contemporary practices. The music is most often set in motion by melodic lines that are lyrically, if not vocally, conceived. The character of these melodies has changed during Schuman's career. The frenzied repeated notes and frequent leaps at the beginning of the *Symphony for Strings* (1943) are replaced by the subtler melodic arc at the opening of the *Symphony No. 6* (1948) or the motivically engendered horn solo in the first movement of the *Symphony No. 8* (1962). His melodies have also gradually moved away from what were tonally grounded diatonic lines to intense chromaticism, as in the *Symphony No. 7* (1960). Few melodies remain homophonic for long; most of them become strands in a contrapuntal web that functions not only structurally but provides rhythmic motion and variety. So strong is the melodic material that the listener tends to hear only moving lines and not the resultant simultaneities. The major-minor sound is rarely far away, and there is much parallelism in passages built of thirds, fourths, fifths, sevenths, or ninths. Such mannerisms are less obvious in the later works, where chromatic lines enrich the harmonic palette.

Most of Schuman's ideas are conceived in terms of a big sonic arsenal, capable of infinite variety and of producing huge blocks of identical sounds. The blocks are necessary in terms of Schuman's linear or parallel writing and to delineate harmonies that he does not want to mix. The opening of the *Symphony No. 6* is one of the few instances in which he has used the orchestra in chamber-music style, as do Mahler or Schoenberg. The vital rhythmic sense that is characteristic of much American music is exemplified at its best in Schuman, as in the opening of the third movement of the *Symphony for Strings*. Like Brahms, Schuman achieves whatever rhythmic variety he requires within symmetrically measured bars and not by changing meters. Sometimes in his single-movement works, the fast sections begin by a nervous twitching (usually two alternating tones that predictably result in a characteristic rhythmic outburst).

Schuman is clearly influenced by two factors: 1) American popular music, which invests his music with its particular individuality and rhythmic verve; and 2) an infatuation with orchestral sounds—something he learned to control very early and which has never ceased to fascinate him. The extent to which his style derives from that of Harris has always been a debatable matter. Though the earlier pieces, now mostly withdrawn, may have shown this influence strongly, his later technical proficiency, control of large forms, and the fire and drive of his musical imagination take him out of Harris's orbit. Although

Schuman has had few students, he has been a significant influence on many composers, especially those who were his early associates at Juilliard, notably Vincent Persichetti and Peter Mennin, as well as William Bergsma and Robert Ward.

PRINCIPAL COMPOSITIONS: *String Quartets Nos. 1–4* (1934; 1937, Boosey; 1939, Merion; 1950, Schirmer-G); *American Festival Overture* (1939, Schirmer-G); *Symphonies Nos. 3–9*: No. 3 (1941, Schirmer-G); No. 4 (1941, Schirmer-G); No. 5, "Symphony for Strings" (1943, Schirmer-G); No. 6 (1948, Schirmer-G); No. 7 (1960, Merion); No. 8 (1962, Merion); No. 9, "Le Fosse ardeatine" (1968, Merion); *A Free Song* for chorus, orchestra (1942); *Violin Concerto* (1947, revised 1954, 1959; Merion); *The Mighty Casey*, 1-act opera; libretto by Jeremy Gury after Ernest L. Thayer's poem (1953, Schirmer-G); *Credendum* for orchestra (1955, Merion); *New England Triptych* for orchestra (1956, Merion); *Carols of Death* for chorus (1958, Merion); *Song of Orpheus*, fantasy for cello, orchestra (1961, Merion); *String Trio*, "Amaryllis" (1964, Merion); *To Thee Old Cause* for orchestra (1968, Merion); *In Praise of Shawn* for orchestra (1969, Merion). ★ Dance scores: for Martha Graham: *Night Journey* (1947, Merion); *Judith* (1948, Schirmer-G); *Voyage for a Theater* (1953, Merion); *The Witch of Endor* (1965, Merion); for Antony Tudor: *Undertow* (1945, Schirmer-G). Schuman has also written numerous works for band and chorus.

PRINCIPAL WRITINGS: "On Teaching the Literature and Materials of Music," *Musical Quarterly* (April 1948).

BIBL.: Nathan Broder, "The Music of W. S.," *Musical Quarterly* (Jan 1945); Richard F. Goldman, "Current Chronicle," *Musical Quarterly* (April 1951); Flora Rheta Schreiber and Vincent Persichetti, *W. S.* (New York 1954).

Hugo Weisgall

SEE ALSO Dance, Education for the Professional, Popular Music, United States.

Schwartz, Elliot (b. Brooklyn, N. Y., 19 Jan 1936), studied at Columbia College (1953–57; composition with Otto Luening, Jack Beeson) and Columbia Teachers' College (1957–60). He also studied composition privately with Luening, Beeson, and Paul Creston and piano with Alton Jones and Thomas Richner. He has taught at the Univ. of Mass. (1960–64) and Bowdoin College (since 1964) and has been a visiting lecturer at the Trinity College of Music in London (1967) and the Univ. of Calif. at Santa Barbara (1970). He is co-director of the Bowdoin Music Press and director of the annual Bowdoin Contemporary Music Festival. He is also a professional pianist, specializing in the contemporary repertory. His own music has been influenced by his acquaintance with Henry Brant (and through him with the music of Ives), Barney Childs, and the painter John Goodyear. The work he heard during European visits in 1967 and 1969 of younger British composers (and some Dutch and Scandinavian ones) in pop-collage, quotation, music theater, and improvisation reinforced his own inclinations. Contact with such performers as double bassist Bertram Turetzky and trombonist Stuart Dempster has prompted him to write music designed for specific players and for the particular resources of their instruments. Many works, beginning with *Dialogue* (1966–67), exploit the spatial placement of sound sources, motion, and performer activity.

PRINCIPAL COMPOSITIONS: *Concert Piece* for wind quintet, 4 strings, percussion (1965, Broude-A); *Texture* for chamber orchestra (1966, Broude-A); *Dialogue* for double bass (1966–67, Fischer); *Signals* for trombone, double bass (1968); *Magic Music* for piano, orchestra (1967–68); *Music for Prince Albert* for piano, tapes (1969); *Music for Napoleon and Beethoven* for trumpet, piano, tapes (1969); *Septet* for voice, piano, any 5 instruments (1969); *Elevator Music* for performers on any instruments stationed at elevator doors while the audience rides up and down (1967); *Music for Soloist and Audience* for any instrument(s); the audience is divided into 4 groups, each with a conductor, and performs specified vocal and percussive sounds (1970); *Island* for orchestra (1970, Fischer).

PRINCIPAL WRITINGS: *Contemporary Composers on Contemporary Music*, coedited with Barney Childs (New York 1967); *The Symphonies of Ralph Vaughan Williams* (Amherst, Mass., 1965); "Current Chronicle: The Netherlands," *Musical Quarterly* 56:119–24; "Elevator Music," *The Composer* 2/2:49–54; *Electronic Music: A Listener's Guide* (New York 1971–72).

BIBL.: Meirion Bowen, "E. S.," *Music and Musicians* 16/7:24–27.

Schwertsik, Kurt (b. Vienna, 25 June 1935), attended the Vienna Academy of Music (1949–57; composition with Joseph Marx, Karl Schiske; French horn with Gottfried Freiberg). He worked with Stockhausen and Gottfried M. Koenig in the Electronic Music Studio of the Westdeutscher Rundfunk in Cologne (1959–60). He played French horn in the Wiener Tonkünstler Orchester during 1955–59 and 1962–68 and since 1968 has been a member of the Vienna Symphony. He participated in concerts with John Cage and David Tudor in Europe during 1959–61. Schwertsik has composed music for the Austrian Pavilion at Montreal's Expo '67, for the Austrian National Feiertag '67, and for the film *50 Jahre Republick*, 1968. The works listed below are written in "a very outspoken tonality (aggressive tonality). . . . I like a balance between moving and funny passages, and I most enjoy it if these elements are inextricably mixed."

PRINCIPAL COMPOSITIONS: *Liebesträume* for alto saxophone, trombone, double bass, piano, vibraphone, marimba, harmonium (1962–63, EM); *. . . Für Audifax und Abachum* for orchestra, Op. 8 (1962–64, EM); *Eichendorff-Quintett* for wind quintet (1963, UE); *Draculas Haus und Hofmusik*, "a Transylvanian symphony" for string orchestra, Op. 18 (1967–68, Doblinger); *Symphonie im Mob-Stil* (1968–69, UE).

SEE ALSO Austria and Germany.

Scriabin, Alexander (Nikolaevich) (b. Moscow, 6 Jan 1872; d. Moscow, 27 April 1915), the son of a civil functionary, was raised largely by relatives because of his father's absence on business and his mother's early death. His mother had been a gold medalist in piano under Leschetitsky at the St. Petersburg Conservatory, and the young Scriabin showed a prodigious musical talent. Following the family tradition he was enrolled in the Moscow Cadet School (where his uncle taught), but he was given time for musical pursuits. He became an adept pianist, studying with N. S. Zverev; he was unsuccessful at the guitar and violin. He had, during his more than eight years at the school, some instruction in musical materials from Georgii Konius and Sergei Taneyev. He entered the Moscow Conservatory in 1888 (piano with Vassily Safonov, composition with Taneyev and Anton Arensky) and graduated with a gold medal in piano. He left the composition class in 1892 without finishing.

A few early works had been published by the Jurgenson firm, but the future was not promising until these were heard by Mitrofan Belaiev, who became Scriabin's patron, publisher, and manager. In 1895, with Belaiev's help, he began to tour in Western Europe. In 1897 he married pianist Vera Isakovich, and in 1898 became professor of piano at the Moscow Conservatory. The next five years saw the birth of four children, a growing preoccupation with the Nietzchean concept of a superman and with his own ego, and an increasing dislike of the rigors of teaching. In 1903 a former student, Margarita Morozova, settled an annuity on him. He promptly left the conservatory and soon thereafter the country, going to Switzerland where he also abandoned his wife in favor of Tatiana Schloezer, the sister of a friend.

The years abroad were filled with composing, developing his philosophical ideas, concertizing, and raising a second family with Tatiana. A U.S. tour in 1906–07 was cut short when Scriabin's former teacher Safonov, now conducting in the U.S., revealed that Tatiana was not his lawful wife. Otherwise Scriabin thrived, for this was an era of Russian musical dominance. Koussevitzky had replaced Belaiev as publisher and patron when the latter died in 1904 and the firm Belaiev founded ceased to honor the financial arrangements so favorable to Scriabin. He moved back to Moscow in 1910. He had a falling out with Koussevitzky in 1911 but continued touring until his death (from septicaemia).

Scriabin's music is limited to piano pieces and a handful of orchestral works of substantial proportion. By 1903, the end of his first, Chopin-Lisztian period, he had written a number of short piano pieces, four of his ten sonatas, and his first two symphonies. With his *Symphony No. 3*, "The Divine Poem" (1903 or 1904), he began to express his highly personal notions. This work and a rash of piano pieces were written in a burst of activity following his resignation from the conservatory. The beginnings of harmonic experimentation lie here. He began to use chords built of fourths and sometimes seconds, although at first he maintained some tonal relationships. His formal departures are often overlooked or dismissed as naive or clumsy, yet time and the pacing of musical events were extremely important to him: For example, some of his etudes last but a few seconds while elsewhere a musical idea, slight in itself, is sustained for several minutes. His fourth chords, invented modes and scales, and harmonic motionlessness were synthesized into an impressionistic atonality. He verbalized very little about his "discoveries," but theorists have designated the "mystic" or "Promethean" chord (C-F♯-B♭-E-A-D) in his *Symphony No. 5* (1909–11) and elsewhere as a seminal harmony. (Among other analyses, the chord may be seen as the seventh through the twelfth partials of the overtone series.) Yet it is only typical of his usage in the last years. He often "horizontalized" such chords and added appoggiaturas and passing tones to form melodies. Scriabin's earlier orchestral *Poem of Ecstasy* (1908) had signalled the beginning of this final period, but even more telling in the progress to atonality and formal brevity are the late piano etudes. Of the last sonatas, Nos. 7 (1911)

and 9 (1913) are, respectively, a "white" and "black" mass.

By 1908 theosophy and mysticism had begun to dominate Scriabin's creative thinking. He had long contemplated a grandiose work uniting all arts, indeed all sensory experience. In this effort he showed deeply Russian leanings: toward the union of arts, the celebration of his own ego, and a Messianic or "Promethean" approach. He considered most of his works after 1908 to be preparatory to a final "Mystery," a "supreme, final ecstasy" which would accompany the ultimate cataclysm of the human race. It was to take place at a lake or on a mountain top in India or Tibet (the accounts do not concur), and Scriabin himself was to perish in a "suffocation of ecstasy." A scenario was prepared near Moscow in the summer of 1914, and a book of musical sketches exists, consisting of one chord after another, each consisting of ten and more notes with no apparent connection or relationship. They tend to support the belief that Scriabin, at the end, was not sane. His musical significance has been undervalued, owing partly to neglect after an earlier period of intense popularity, partly to a biographical concentration on the extramusical aspects of his life, and partly to the surface dazzle of his music, which, like that of Debussy, tends to obscure its orderliness and workmanship.

PRINCIPAL COMPOSITIONS (published by Belaiev unless otherwise noted): *Etudes* for piano: 3 Etudes, Op. 2 (1892, Jurgenson); 12 Etudes, Op. 8 (c.1892); 8 Etudes, Op. 42 (1903); 3 Etudes, Op. 65 (1912); *Piano Sonatas Nos. 1–10:* No. 1 in F minor, Op. 6 (1892); No. 2 in G♯ minor, "Sonata-Fantasy," Op. 19 (1892–97); No. 3 in F♯ minor, Op. 23 (1897); No. 4 in F♯ minor, Op. 30 (1903); No. 5 in F♯, Op. 53 (1908); No. 6 in G, Op. 62 (1911–12); No. 7 in F♯, "White Mass," Op. 64 (1911); No. 8 in A, Op. 66 (1913, Jurgenson); No. 9 in F, "Black Mass," Op. 68 (1913, Jurgenson); No. 10 in C, Op. 70 (1913, Jurgenson); *Piano Concerto in F♯ minor,* Op. 20 (1897–98); *Symphonies Nos. 1–5:* No. 1 in E, with chorus, Op. 26 (1900); No. 2 in C minor, Op. 29 (1901); No. 3 in C, "The Divine Poem," Op. 43 (1903 or 1904); No. 4, "The Poem of Ecstasy," Op. 54 (1908); No. 5, "Prometheus: The Poem of Fire," with chorus, light organ, Op. 60 (1909–11).

BIBL.: Gerald Abraham, "S.," *Masters of Russian Music* ed. by M. D. Calvocoressi, G. Abraham (London 1936):450–98; William W. Austin, *Music in the 20th Century* (New York 1966); Faubian Bowers, *S.* (Tokyo-Palo Alto 1969); D. Brook, *6 Great Russian Composers* (London 1946); Lev Vasil'evich Danilevich, *A.N.S.* trans. into German by M. Hoffmann (Leipzig 1954); E. Gunst, *S.* (Moscow 1915); A. E. Hull, *A*

Great Russian Tone-Poet: S. (London 1927); ——, "A Survey of the Pianoforte Works of S.," *Musical Quarterly* 2:601ff.; V. Karatygin, *S.* (Petrograd 1915); Alfred J. Swan, *S.* (London 1923; reissued New York 1969).

Stanley D. Krebs
SEE ALSO Asian Music and Western Composition, Impressionism, Mixed Media, Opera, Soviet Union.

Sculthorpe, Peter (Joshua) (b. Launceston, Tasmania, 29 April 1929), studied at the Univ. of Melbourne (1947–50) and Wadham College, Oxford (1958–60; composition with Edmund Rubbra, Egon Wellesz). He has taught at the Univ. of Sydney since 1963. The principal influences on his music have been Asian. He has "little interest in European music [but] identifies strongly with Australia and feels that the East can revitalize the music of the West."

PRINCIPAL COMPOSITIONS (published by Faber unless otherwise noted): *The Loneliness of Bunjil* for string trio (1954); *Sonatina* for piano (1954, Leeds); *Variations* for piano (1954); *Irkanda I* for solo violin (1955); *Sonata* for viola, percussion (1960); *Irkanda IV* for violin, strings, percussion (1961); *The Fifth Continent* for narrator, orchestra (1963); *String Quartet No. 6* (1965); *Sun Music I* for orchestra (1965); *Canto 1520* for chorus, percussion (1966); *Night Piece* for chorus (1966, Novello); *Teotihuacan* for string quartet (1966); *Morning Song* for chorus (1966); *Sun Music III* for orchestra (1967); *3 Haiku* for piano (1967); *Sun Music IV* for orchestra (1967); *Tabuh Tabuhan* for wind quintet, percussion (1968); *Autumn Song* for chorus (1968); *Sun Music II* for orchestra (1968); *Sun Music Ballet*, choreography by Robert Helpmann (1968); *Interlude* for brass, percussion (1968); *From Tabuh Tabuhan* for strings, percussion (1968); *Sea Chant* for unison voices, piano (1968); *Ketjak* for men's chorus (1969); *String Quartet Music* (1969); *Love 200* for 2 singers, pop group, orchestra (1970); *The Stars Turn* for medium voice, orchestra (1970); *Music for Japan* for orchestra (1970); *Music of Rain* for orchestra (1970). Sculthorpe has also written film, radio, television, and theater scores.

BIBL.: Roger Covell, *Australia's Music, Themes of a New Society* (Melbourne 1967).

SEE ALSO Australia.

Searle, Humphrey (b. Oxford, England, 26 Aug 1915), studied music (with George Dyson), classical and modern languages, and English literature at Winchester College (1928–33) and music (with Sydney Watson), philosophy, and languages at New College, Oxford (1933–37). He attended the Royal College of Music in 1937 (composition with John Ireland, counterpoint with R. O. Morris, orchestration and conducting with Gordon Jacob) and studied with Anton Webern in Vienna in 1937–38. Searle was a program producer in the BBC music department during 1938–40 and 1946–48. He was composer-in-residence at Stanford Univ., Calif., 1964–65, and has taught composition at the Royal College of Music since 1965. He was general secretary of the ISCM during 1947–49 and a member of the Sadler's Wells Ballet Advisory Panel, 1951–57. Since 1956, in addition to many concert works, he has been writing scores for theater, films, and television.

PRINCIPAL COMPOSITIONS (published by Schott unless otherwise noted): *Gold Coast Customs* for speakers, men's chorus, winds, 2 pianos, percussion (1947–49, Lengnick); *Poem* for 22 strings (1950, Galliard); *The Riverrun* for speaker, orchestra; text by James Joyce (1951); *The Shadow of Cain* for speakers, men's chorus, orchestra; text by Edith Sitwell (1952); *Symphonies Nos. 1–5* (1953, 1956–58, 1958–60, 1961–62, 1964); *Piano Concerto No. 2* (1955); *Noctambules*, ballet (1956); *The Great Peacock*, ballet (1957–58); *The Diary of a Madman*, opera; libretto after Gogol (1958); *Dualities*, ballet (1963); *The Photo of the Colonel*, opera; libretto after Ionesco (1963–64); *Hamlet*, opera (1964–68, Faber); *The Canticle of the Rose* for chorus; text by Sitwell (1965, Faber); *Oxus* for tenor, orchestra; text by Matthew Arnold (1967, Faber).

PRINCIPAL WRITINGS: *20th-Century Counterpoint* (London 1954); *Ballet Music: An Introduction* (London 1958); *Hector Berlioz: A Selection from his Letters* (London 1966); *The Music of Liszt* (New York 1966).

BIBL.: Martin Kingsbury, "H. S.'s Hamlet," *Musical Times* 110:369–71; Malcolm Rayment, "S.: Avant-Garde or Romantic?", *Musical Times* 105:430–32; R. Murray Schafer, *British Composers in Interview* (London 1963).

SEE ALSO Great Britain.

Seeger, Ruth Crawford, see under Crawford Seeger

Segerstam, Leif (b. Vaasa, Finland, 2 March 1944), attended the Sibelius Academy (1952–63; composition with Nils-Erik Fougstedt, Einar Englund, Joonas Kokkonen) and the Juilliard School (1963–65; composition with Hall Overton, Vincent Persichetti), where he was a teaching assistant during 1964–65. Since then he has been conductor at the Finnish Opera and director of orchestral courses at the Klemetti Institute of Music.

PRINCIPAL COMPOSITIONS: *String Quartets Nos. 1–4* (1962, arranged for string orchestra 1963; 1964; 1966; 1966); *Divertimento* for string orchestra (1963); *5 Pedagogical Duets* for 2 violins (1963, Fazer); *Morgonen* [The Morning] for chorus; text by Christer Kihlman (1963, Westerlund); *Missa piccola* for chorus (1964); *3 Sketches* for piano (1964); *3 Sketches* for 2 violins (1965, Fazer); *Myriasm* for 2 violins (1965); *Reincarnation* for soprano, women's chorus; text by Gunilla Josefsson (1965); *Improvisandum* for violin (1965); *3 Meditations* for piano (1965); *3 Songs* for voice, piano; texts by Viola Renwall (1965, orchestrated 1967); *3 Leaves of Grass* for soprano, piano; text by Walt Whitman (1966, Weinberger); *3 Songs* for voice, piano; texts by Gunnar Björling (1966, orchestrated 1967); *Violin Concerto* (1967); *Pandora*, essay for orchestra, 9 dancers (1967); *4 Songs* for voice, piano; text by Björling (1968); *3 Songs* for voice, piano; text by Björling (1969).

Sehlbach, Erich (b. Barmen, Germany, 18 Nov 1898), attended the Leipzig Conservatory (1919–24, voice with Wolfgang Geist, piano with Max Ludwig, theory with Stefan Krehl). He taught theory at the Folkwang Hochschule in Essen during 1928–67. The most important influences on his development came from Hindemith, Schoenberg, and Bartók.

PRINCIPAL COMPOSITIONS: *Die Stadt*, opera; libretto by the composer (1935, UE); *Galilei*, opera; libretto by the composer (1937, UE); *Signor Caraffa*, opera; libretto by the composer (1938, Schott); *Piano Sonatas Nos. 1–6* (1948–62); *Heitere Suite* for piano (1950); *Sinfonische Kantate* for 2 solo voices, chorus, orchestra (1950); *String Quartets Nos. 1–3* (1952, 1965, 1966); *Symphony in E Flat* (1953); *Piano Concerto* (1953, Möseler); *Symphony in G* (1958); *Violin Concerto* (1961, Möseler); *Toccata* for piano (1964); *Engramme*, 5 pieces for orchestra (1967, Möseler).

BIBL.: Alfred Brasch, *E. S.: Skizzen zu seiner Biographie* (Wolfenbüttel 1958); Gerhard Schuhmacher, *E. S.: Gedanken an sein Werk* (Wolfenbüttel 1968).

Seiber, Matyas György (Matthias Georg) (b. Budapest, 4 May 1905; d. Capetown, 24 Sept 1960), studied at the Academy of Musical Art in Budapest (cello with Adolf Schiffer, composition with Zoltán Kodály). Economic conditions in Hungary after World War I forced him to resettle in Germany, where he played in orchestras, conducted, and taught composition and jazz at the Frankfurt Conservatory. His courses in jazz were pioneering in the German system of music education. Because of the political situation in Germany, he moved in 1935 to London. There he became a successful composer of functional

music and a sought-after teacher of composition (the regard for craftsmanship he instilled in his students is perhaps his greatest legacy). During World War II he also taught at Morley College in London and became music director of the Dorian Singers. Together with some younger and then largely unknown musicians, he founded the Committee (now Society) for the Promotion of New Music c.1942. His increasing participation in ISCM contributed a great deal to his international reputation. His death resulted from an automobile accident.

The majority of Seiber's works are instrumental, mostly for chamber ensembles; however, the high quality of his vocal output gives it an equal importance. He was immensely fluent in all styles and idioms, so much so that in his earlier works he came near to having none of his own. One factor, however, stands out even in these: his technical facility allowed him to tailor all of his musical ideas to the essential qualities of their instrumental or vocal setting. This recalls the German tradition, personified in our days by a composer who left marks on Seiber's mind and music, Paul Hindemith. Another attribute that informs his entire output is a rhythmic imagination, expressed in the invention of memorable and effective schemes that give vitality to much of his music. This gift made him an outstanding composer for cartoon films, for which his music for *Animal Farm* (after Orwell's book) is his masterpiece. Seiber's ability to speak the languages of the masters of the past is clearly revealed in the *Missa brevis* (1924), in which a Kodály-like discipline of method is allied with ideas of Palestrinian inspiration. He could also write in the image of Bartók (*Sonata da camera*, 1925), the post-1918 generation of Wiemar Germany (*Serenade* for woodwinds, 1925), Debussy (*Pastorale and Burlesque*, 1941–42), and Schoenberg (*Fantasia concertante*, 1943–44). The serialism of the 1950s appears in *Permutazioni a 5* (1958) and the *Violin Sonata* (1960). The main inspiration of Seiber's late, mature music was literary: Joyce, Virgil, Goethe. He was increasingly occupied with an otherworldly melancholy, a reflective lyricism, although his rhythmic liveliness, as in *Permutazioni*, acquired a keener edge through the sharpening of thematic profiles.

PRINCIPAL COMPOSITIONS: *Missa brevis* for chorus (1924, Curwen); *String Quartets Nos. 1–3* (1924, S-Z; 1934–35, S-Z; 1948–51, Schott); *Sonata da camera* for violin, cello (1925, Chester); *Serenade* for 2 clarinets, 2 bassoons, 2 horns (1925, Hansen-W); *Pastorale and Burlesque* for flute, string orchestra (1941–42, Schott); *Fantasia concertante* for violin, string orchestra (1943–44, Ars Viva); *Ulysses*, cantata for tenor, chorus, orchestra (1946–47, Schott); *Faust* for soprano, tenor, chorus, orchestra (1949, S-Z); *Cantata secularis* for chorus, orchestra; text by Virgil (1949–51, Schott); *3 Fragments from "A Portrait of the Artist as a Young Man"* for chorus; text by Joyce (1956–57, Schott); *Improvisation* for oboe, piano (1957, Schott); *Violin Sonata* (1960, Schott); *Sonata* for flute, violin, piano (1960, Schott).

PRINCIPAL WRITINGS: "Jazz als Erziehungsmittel," *Melos* 7; "Jazz Instrumente, Jazz Klang und Neue Musik," *Melos* 9; "Rhythmic Freedom in Jazz?", *Music Review* 6; *The String Quartets of Béla Bartók* (London 1945).

BIBL.: Mosco Carner, "M. S. and his 'Ulysses'," *Music Review* 12; Hans Keller, "M. S. 1905–1960," *Tempo* 55–56; Colin Mason, "The Musical Personality of M. S.," *Listener* 57; John S. Weissmann, "M. S., Style and Technique," *Listener* 45; ——, "Die Streichquartette von M. S.," *Melos* 22, 23; Hugh Wood, "The Music of M. S.," *Musical Times* (Sept 1970): 888–90.

John S. Weissmann

SEE ALSO Great Britain.

Sender, Ramon (b. Madrid, 29 Oct 1934), studied piano with George Copeland and harmony with Elliott Carter in New York during 1948–51. He attended the San Francisco Conservatory (1959–62, composition with Robert Erickson) and Mills College (1962–65). He was cofounder and codirector of the San Francisco Tape Music Center during 1962–66 and in 1966 was codirector of the San Francisco Trips Festival. Since 1966 he has been living in communes in Sonoma County, Calif. He helped found the Open Land Church, is writing "song-chants" and other music for live, "para-professional" group performance, and is interested in "music as yoga, yoga as nature, nature as music." He has been attracted to the music of Carl Nielson, Lou Harrison, John Cage, Terry Riley, Steve Reich, Morton Subotnick, Pauline Oliveros, and others and to the writings of Sri Aurobindo Ghose, Buckminster Fuller, and Daniel Moore.

PRINCIPAL COMPOSITIONS: *4 Sanskrit Hymns* for 4 sopranos, 4 cellos, double bass, harp, piano, celesta, 3 percussionists, 3 tapes (1961); *Kronos* on tape (1962); *Korë* on tape (1962); *Time Fields* for any 6 instruments (1963); *Balances* for amplified string quintet with double bass (1963); *Desert Ambulance* for accordion, tape (1964); *In the Garden* for tape, clarinet, viola (1965); *World Food I–XII* for drone tapes (1965).

SEE ALSO Mixed Media.

Sequencer, an electronic device that permits the presetting of a succession of several sound events, along with modifications in each.

SEE ALSO Electronic Music: Apparatus and Technology.

Serebrier, José (b. Montevideo, Uruguay, 3 Dec 1938), studied at the Curtis Institute (1956–58, composition with Vittorio Giannini), Univ. of Minn. (1958–60, conducting with Antol Dorati), Tanglewood (1958, 1960; composition with Aaron Copland), and the Pierre Monteux School in Maine (1959, 60, 61; conducting). During 1962–64 he was music director of the American Shakespeare Festival. He taught at Eastern Mich. Univ. during 1966–68. He has conducted the American Symphony Orchestra (1962–66), the Plainfield, N. J., Symphony (since 1966), and the Cleveland Philharmonic Orchestra (since 1968). During 1968–70 he was composer-in-residence with George Szell's Cleveland Orchestra.

PRINCIPAL COMPOSITIONS (published by Southern unless otherwise noted): *Elegy for Strings* (1954, Peer); *Sonata* for solo violin (1954); *Sonata* for solo viola (1954); *Saxophone Quartet* (1955); *Pequeña música*, suite for woodwind quintet (1955); *Canción del destino* for chorus (1955); *Symphony No. 1* (1956); *Partita* for orchestra (1956–58); *Fantasia* for string orchestra (1960); *Symphony for Percussion* for 5 percussionists (1964); *Variations on a Theme from Childhood* for trombone with string quartet or string orchestra (1964); *Passacaglia and Perpetuum Mobile* for accordion, chamber orchestra (1967); *Erotica* for soprano, trumpet, woodwind quintet (1968); *Danza ritual* for accordion (1968, O. Pagani, New York); *Doce por doce* for woodwinds, brass, percussion (1969, Peters); *Nueve* for double bass, orchestra (1970).

PRINCIPAL WRITINGS: During 1960–68 Serebrier wrote many articles for *Music Journal* on conducting and on Latin American music.

BIBL.: Louis Chapin, "J. S.," *BMI Many Worlds of Music* (April 1967); Carole Farley, "J. S., Composer," *Music Journal* (March 1970).

Serialism is the compositional procedure by which an order of succession is established for the values appropriate to one or more parameters (components) of the musical process; these orders of succession or permutations of them are then repeated throughout the composition. The values include pitch (for tones of the tempered scale), loudness (for dynamic levels), units of time (for rhythm), etc. Because the parameter of pitch is readily suited to serialization, the serial concept was first applied here, producing the 12-tone method. Since the 1950s when the serialization of additional parameters became common, the term *serialism* has been used to designate the application of serial technique to more than the one parameter of pitch.

In predetermining the order of events in as many parameters as possible, a composer restricts his freedom of intuitive action to a high degree. (If he were to succeed in serially organizing all available aspects of the music, the composition would be completed before the first note is written down and intuition would be *entirely* excluded.) The composer is attracted by this working condition because the mechanism he has created will produce situations that he might not think of by relying on intuition alone. It is possible that these surprises will lead him to create events of particularly strong artistic impact.

Surprises in the serial system are caused by the built-in factor of unpredictability, which is only seemingly at variance with the concept of "total" predetermination. For instance, a tone row decrees in what order the pitches will enter the musical process, and the time series determines when those pitches will enter (analogous serial statements may also regulate the density and texture of the fabric). However, the resulting simultaneities (chords) will be unpredictable; they cannot be programmed serially, because this parameter has been preempted by operations in the other fields. Here the composer must accept what the mechanism he has created produces. The events in this sector will, for practical purposes, be highly unpredictable and thus assume the character of chance occurrences. It is possible, of course, for the composer to choose a different hierarchy of parameters so that, for instance, he could begin by setting up a sequence of simultaneities (chords). Their order of succession and its permutations would then form the initial invariant from which the serial statements for the remaining parameters would be derived according to suitable computations. Some of them would presumably again be left without a program and open to chance happenings.

In spite of the restrictions imposed upon intuition, the factor of inventive imagination, traditionally known as "inspiration," is not entirely eliminated. It operates in a phase of the creative process preliminary to the act of composition per se. In the province of serialism, inventive imagination is essentially concerned with conceiving a general comprehensive image of the music to be written and with preparing the tools for realizing this image by setting up the *modus operandi* in the divers parameters. These mechanisms can be tested by employing them for compositional experiments on a small scale. If their results do not sufficiently correspond to the overall image that the composer has conceived, he can return his serial apparatus to the drawing board and modify the rules until their application satisfies his idea of the music he wants to write.

PRECEDENTS. The concept of serialism underlies the isorhythmic and isometric techniques of the *ars nova* (14th century), where preestablished duration patterns were imposed upon the musical process. Another medieval precedent is the *cantus firmus* technique, where an already existing pitch sequence was employed as the foundation and often as the thematic model for a complex polyphonic fabric. Present-day serialism was hinted at for the first time by Olivier Messiaen in *Technique de mon langage musical* (1944), in which he discussed duration series. He elaborated on the serialization of rhythmic values in later writings. The characteristic integration of the dodecaphonic organization of pitches with equally invariant arrangements in other parameters is foreshadowed in Anton Webern's middle and late works, especially, for instance, in the second movement of his *Variations*, Op. 27 (1936), where the registral distribution of pitches and the distribution of time values among sound and silence evidently follows a preestablished serial plan. The earliest fully developed compositional manifestations of serialism are the *Composition* for four instruments (1948) by Milton Babbitt, Boulez's *Structures I* for two pianos (1951–52), and the electronic *Studies* (1954) by Karlheinz Stockhausen. By the mid-1950s the idea of serialism had caught the imagination of composers everywhere, and many works were being created in which the principles of serialism were applied in varying degrees of thoroughness.

COMPOSITIONAL METHODS. Works in which the total predetermination of all parameters has been attempted are relatively rare. More frequently composers have applied varying degrees of serial organization to various aspects of the musical process, ordering some of them more rigidly than others or not adhering to them with equal strictness at all points of the process. The composer may, for instance, set up a serial rule that will determine the number of tones to be sounded in any given time unit, but leave the exact timing of the tones within the unit to his own free decision or even to that of the performer at the time of performance. Likewise he may serially predetermine pitch succession and time relationships but reserve the registral placement of the preordered sounds to later free choice. Such loosening of serial ties makes the musical substance malleable and allows the composer to articulate the configurations brought about by the serial machinery to their best advantage. As long as the unfolding of the musical process is essentially ordered by premeditation, the balancing of strictly regulated and freely shaped parameters does not violate the principle of serialism.

The evolution of modern serial concepts began with the 12-tone method. Its basic tenet is that the sum total of a work and all its details should derive from a single germinating nucleus. This tenet was carried over into the newer way of thinking, and the tone row became the nucleus not only of the pitch succession but of other parameters as well. In order to use the tone row for the determination of values in other parameters, procedures were needed to transform the data of one field into the measuring systems of another. In the tone row the most obvious source from which precise measurements can be derived is the intervals between the consecutive tones of the row. The sizes of the intervals may be measured in terms of some linear scale, such as the number of half-steps, or by the ratios of the frequencies encompassing the intervals. If, for instance, the first step of the tone row ascends from A to E, the number of half-steps within the interval is seven; the ratio of frequencies is 440:660, or 2:3. Either of these magnitudes could constitute the first term of a row of numbers used in determining the sequence of values in other parameters. Not all parameters lend themselves to establishing series of distinct, precisely measurable terms. Thus, for instance, the dynamic range of a musical process is generally considered to be divisible into only a few zones of relative loudness, because the ear is not equipped to pinpoint degrees of dynamics as it is to discern pitches. The same is true for subtle differences in timbre. While we are able to locate accurately any nuance of color between infrared and ultraviolet, a similarly graded arrangement of tone colors is impossible. However, the parameter of time can be measured with as much precision as that of pitch; it is therefore in this realm that serialization has been applied most consistently and with the most far-reaching consequences.

An example of a fairly elementary rapport between a tone row and a corresponding series of time values may be found in Boulez's *Structures Ia* (1952). Here 12 progressively longer durations (from one 16th note to 12 16ths, or a dotted half) were associated with the pitch classes numbered one to 12 of the 12-tone row. Since these pitch classes in the 48 basic permutations of the tone row (original, inversion, retrograde, and retrograde inversion, each transposed to eleven different pitch levels) appear in 48 different orders of succession, there are an equal number of duration-row groupings. The overall structure of the work is the result of permanently combining these two serial systems (see György Ligeti, "Pierre Boulez," *Die Reihe* 4). A highly complex relationship of sizes of intervals and durations and subdivisions thereof has been described by Karlheinz Stockhausen ("wie die Zeit vergeht . . .," *Die Reihe* 3). Here the fraction representing the ratio of the interval, such as for instance $a:b$, is used to subdivide one time unit into a and the subsequent unit into b parts, while the relative durations of these units and their internal organization are determined by other computations based on the series of ratios contained in the tone row. Milton Babbitt has explained another way of deriving a time series from the sequence of intervals offered in the tone row, measuring these in terms of half-tone steps ("Twelve-tone Rhythmic Structure and the Electronic Medium," *Perspectives* 1/1). Here the smallest interval is identified with the smallest time unit (one 16th note), so that the sequence of durations in the time series reflects the sequence of the half-step groupings of the tone row. My *Sestina* (1957) illustrates another method of deriving time values from a tone row. Here the total expanse of the work is considered as consisting of a certain number of equal time segments. The first segment is assigned as many tones of the tone tow as the first interval of this row contains half steps. The individual durations of these tones are determined by dividing the number of the units by the sum of as many figures of the intervallic series as the number of tones contained in the segment indicates. The quotient thus obtained is then multiplied by the interval number and the result is the duration of the individual tone (the interval series is 4-3-1-6-2-etc.). The first segment is thus four units. The sum of the first four numbers in the series is 14. Four divided by 14 is 2/7. The durations of the tones are 8/7, 6/7, 2/7, and 12/7 of one-fourth of the entire segment (see "Extents and

Limits of Serial Techniques," *Musical Quarterly* 46). Many other ways of deriving a time series from a tone row could be devised. Much theoretical effort has been expended to demonstrate that such procedures should be expressive of the very nature of the sounding material and that therefore some procedures are more legitimate than others. If correspondences of this kind should exist, they leave little trace in the perceivable substance of the finished work. The fact is that the numbers arrived at through procedures of the type described above detach themselves from the musical elements of their origin and become objects of arithmetic operations, the results of which are then reapplied to the musical material. The composer may believe that the descendence of the numbers from the tone row makes the music orderly and artistically meaningful. But this is based more on mystique than on demonstrable fact.

When the electronic medium was opened for substantial compositional ventures, the numerical limitation of 12-tone technique became obsolete; not only any number of tempered scales, but also entirely irregular chains of frequencies without octave repetition could be constructed. It is now at least theoretically possible to establish series of pitches containing more than 11 intervals of varying sizes that are not necessarily multiples of the same unit, such as the half-tone step of the dodecaphonic idiom. Consequently from richly diversified tone rows, time series of extreme complexity can be derived. It is reasonable to assume that in pursuing this concept beyond certain limits one would reach a point of diminishing returns, for the internal organization of the final product would become so complicated that its outward appearance would be hardly distinguishable from that of unorganized chaos. This point has already been reached occasionally in dodecaphonic serialism (Boulez's *Structures*, Stockhausen's *Zeitmasse*, 1955–56, my *Quaestio temporis*, 1958–59). It must be borne in mind, however, that one of the motivations for turning to serialism was the general inclination of composers toward extreme complexity. Now composers have discovered that the organizational procedures of serialism, rather than the spontaneous efforts of intuition, actually do bring about the appearance of controlled chaos.

Since the principles of serial construction aim at a complete predetermination of all details of the work, they preclude the use of structural elements traditionally considered essential (e.g., themes and developments

thereof). Music is no longer visualized as a one-directional process moving through various stages to a quasilogical conclusion. Such a concept, characteristic of nearly all Western music, has given rise in the past to patterns closely associated with speech, patterns guided by logical reasoning and having a clearly defined subject matter. Analytical terms such as phrase, period, subject, answer, reveal the close relationship between music and speech. It is one of the outstanding properties of serial music that it cannot be heard with such assumptions in mind. Listeners steeped in the mode of perception appropriate to traditional music frequently feel frustrated. They criticize serial music for being static. This is true to the extent that it does not move along from point to point; rather, it exhibits musical objects that should be perceived in contexts other than the seemingly cause-effect relationships of older music. Since what ultimately transpires as the observable structure of a serial work is the unpremeditated result of comprehensive premeditation, it is neither possible nor necessary to identify and remember thematic substance, which in traditional music is necessary because of the variations, transformations, and restatements that follow. Thus the reception of serial music requires less intellectual effort than earlier music did, general opinion to the contrary notwithstanding.

PERSPECTIVES. By the end of the 60s some of the originators and early practitioners of serial techniques have developed manners of writing that may be called serial only in a loose sense. Indeed some of their verbal utterances seem to be critical of the concept (see Pierre Boulez, "Alea," *Perspectives* 3/1; Henri Pousseur, "The Question of Order in New Music," *Perspectives* 5/1). This is probably an inevitable development, because the characteristics of serial music, which at first were the startling, although desired results of new methods of compositional thinking, have now crystalized into objectively graspable ingredients of a new style. Such features as extended static complexes, improvisational and aleatoric passages, pointillistically scattered tones of widely contrasting dynamic levels, novel manners of articulation, and unusual sound qualities (many of which were inspired by experience in the electronic medium) are now available to composers without their having to repeat the serial operations that originally were required to generate them. Similar conditions existed when the 12-tone technique was completely assimilated, making it possible to produce an image of dodecaphonism without rigidly adhering to the methods of the technique. It may be presumed that the impact of serialism has not yet been exhausted by the compositional efforts of its first two decades, because these efforts have not only affected the basic principles of musical composition, but also revealed a radically new interpretation of the essence of music, its meaning, mode of perception, and social attitude.

BIBL.: Herbert Eimert, *Grundlagen der musikalischen Reihentechnik* (Vienna 1964); Paul Henry Lang, ed., *Problems of Modern Music* (New York 1962); George Perle, *Serial Composition and Atonality* (Berkeley 1962). Serialism has been frequently discussed in the following periodicals: *Contrepoint, Darmstädter Beiträge . . . , Gravesaner Blätter, Journal of Music Theory, Perspectives . . . ,* and *Die Reihe.*

Ernst Krenek

SEE ALSO Asian Music and Western Composition, Austria and Germany, Babbitt, Boulez, Form, Melody, Rhythm, Stockhausen, 12-Tone Techniques; articles on individual countries.

Series, see Set, 12-Tone Techniques

Serocki, Kazimierz (b. Torun, Poland, 3 March 1922), studied composition under Kazimierz Sikorski at the Hochschule in Lodz (1945–51) and with Nadia Boulanger in Paris (1947–48). In 1949 he, Tadeusz Baird, and Jan Krenz formed the Group 49. Serocki himself concertized as a pianist until 1952; since then he has been a free-lance composer. In 1956 he helped found the annual Warsaw Autumn festival of contemporary music, and during 1957–59 he took part in the summer courses at Darmstadt.

Until 1955 Serocki wrote mainly in the traditional genres with neoclassicism and a stylization of Polish folk music as prominent features. Since then he has used various kinds of serial and aleatory processes in which a taste for discipline and balance is combined with great sensitivity to timbre and texture. In the mid-1950s he began writing 12-tone music, stemming originally from Webern. Soon this developed toward the use of 12-tone "fields," in which differentiated textural settings of 12-tone material succeed one another. There is a strong sense of rhythmic gesture in his music, expressed through contrasts between quick and slow movement, clear and indistinct caesuras, periodic and fluid rhythms, etc. Indeterminacy operates chiefly on the rhythmic plane and within clearly defined limits (as in "glissandos" from one tempo to another). Proportions among blocks of time are often an important structural concern. His treatment of sound textures can be seen in the *Symphonic Frescos*, where emphasis is placed on highly differentiated articulations of sound. In other works clusters of various widths, durations, densities, pitch-movement speeds, etc., are also important. A speaking chorus in *Niobe* introduces clusters of phonemes, word aggregates, and variable blocks of spoken vocal sound. Throughout Serocki's music one finds a nondoctrinaire use of compositional techniques. This carries over to his notation as well; *Frescos*, for example, uses both precise and approximate rhythmic notations, including graphic signs to represent gradual changes in tempo.

PRINCIPAL COMPOSITIONS (published by PWM unless otherwise noted): *Symphony No. 1* (1952); *Suite of Preludes* for piano (1952); *Trombone Concerto* (1953); *Symphony No. 2* for soprano, baritone, chorus, orchestra (1953); *Piano Sonata* (1955); *Sinfonietta* for 2 string orchestras (1956); *Serce nocy* [Heart of the Night], song cycle for baritone, orchestra; text by K. I. Gałczyński (1956); *Oczy powietrza* [Eyes of the Air], song cycle for soprano, piano; text by J. Przyboś (1957; German edition for soprano, orchestra, 1958, Moeck); *Musica concertante* for orchestra (1958); *Epizody* [Episodes] for strings, 3 groups of percussion (1959); *Segmenti* for 19 instruments, 4 percussionists (1960–61, Moeck); *A piacere* [Propositions] for piano (1962–63); *Freski symfoniczne* [Symphonic Frescos] (1963–64); *Continuum*, sextet for percussion instruments (1965–66, PWM and Moeck); *Niobe* for 2 narrators, chorus, orchestra; text by Gałczyński (1966, PWM and Moeck); *Forte e piano* for 2 pianos, orchestra (1967, PWM and Moeck); *Poezje* [Poetry; in German: Gleichnisse] for soprano, chamber orchestra; text by T. Różewicz (1968–69, PWM and Moeck).

Michał Bristiger

Sessions, Roger (b. Brooklyn, N. Y., 28 Dec 1896), attended Harvard Univ. (1910–15) and Yale Univ. (1915–17, composition with Horatio Parker). He taught at Smith College during 1919–21, while studying privately with Ernest Bloch in New York, and became Bloch's assistant at the Cleveland Institute of Music, 1921–25. Between 1925 and 1933 he lived in Florence, Rome, and Berlin under various grants. He taught at Boston Univ. (1933–35), the New Jersey College for Women (1935–37), Princeton Univ. (1935–45), and the Univ. of Calif. at Berkeley (1945–51), and spent 1951–52 at the Accadèmia Luigi Cherubini in Florence on a Fulbright Fellowship. After one more year at Berkeley he returned to Princeton (1953–65). Following his retirement he taught for one year each at Berkeley (1966–67) and Harvard (1968–69). He has also been teaching at the Juilliard School in New York. He has been president (1934–42) and cochairman with Aaron Copland (since 1953) of the U.S. section of ISCM.

Sessions's principal works include many large orchestral and chamber works, two operas, and numerous other orchestral, choral, chamber, vocal, and solo compositions. His unique musical sensibility expresses itself in line, continuity, and the large gesture, a noteworthy fact since his development took place during a period when cellular structure, textural stratification, the piquancy of individual sonorities, ostinato, and folklorism were in fashion. All of his music has been characterized by a contrapuntal texture in which harmonic goals are typically established or approached through the elaboration of melodies. These melodies give the impression not of having been painfully constructed out of motivic cells, but rather of having been vocally conceived (sometimes in the ideal rather than in the literal sense). The motivic cells that do emerge seem almost to be byproducts of this conception; their development reveals a flexibility in the treatment of interval, rhythm, and accent that enables them to be readily accommodated, without loss of identity, to the demands of each new musical situation. Rhythm and accent are in general handled with resourcefulness and subtlety: although a pungent passage may remind the listener of jazz or some exotic dance pattern, such a detail is nevertheless clearly perceived as contributing to a larger design; it never becomes repetitive nor descends to the level of genre.

It is difficult to isolate aspects of Sessions's music for discussion, since the effect (whether of a single bold gesture or of a long development) depends on interaction. In studying this music, one should begin with the shapes of the phrases and the ways in which they are articulated, not with attempts to infer consistent stylistic traits from a mosaic of intervallic and rhythmic relations. Tones and rhythms are best regarded, at first, as means whereby phrases are formed or divided, energy is accrued or expended, harmonic structures are defined or contrasted. From such study one can begin to perceive more clearly the way in which certain harmonic ambiguities or oppositions established in opening phrases may have significance for the larger structure. For example, the B-minor/E♭-major conflict implicit in the opening of the fifth movement of the *String Quartet No. 2* is not only maintained throughout the movement by the prominent contours of the outer voices, but is concentrated and, as it were, sublimated in the kaleidoscopic shifting of harmonic color at the final cadence. What is remarkable is not that such correspondences exist (since they occur also in Beethoven, Stravinsky, and Bartók), but that they exist in a style that depends so little on the homophonic devices of chordal emphasis and reiteration. (Chords do, of course, frequently occur, but they tend to consist of voices-in-motion whose simultaneous sounding gives accentual impulsion without defining static harmonies.)

In speaking of such phenomena as E♭ major or B minor, one must guard against conceiving them in a conventionally narrow sense. Tonality in Sessions's music has always exerted its influence indirectly and progressively more so. Key signatures were used through the *Symphony No. 2* (1944–46). Beginning with the *Violin Sonata* (1953), he adopted the 12–tone technique. For Sessions, serial organization is a device for bestowing a certain cohesion and, to some extent, character upon the harmonic and melodic surface of the music. As his style became more chromatic, he found 12-tone technique helpful in solving problems of texture. He has never regarded it as a form-engendering principle. For him, the qualities of the intervals, as perceived by a listener who is experienced in music of both past and present, do not change for each new work and may be treated by the composer as inherent. Thus although triadic configurations with root functions are absent from Sessions's later works, "a fifth is still a fifth," and the tendency of the ear to follow stepwise motion is still recognized and exploited.

Sessions is neither a system builder nor a preserver of inherited values. One might call such earlier works as the *Symphony No. 1* (1927) "neoclassic," but even here the impulse toward sustained linear projection and extensive development places it apart from its contemporaries. Sessions's distrust of both systems and polemics has enabled him to respond to outside influence without becoming eclectic: The increasing influence of Schoenberg can combine with the diminishing influence of Stravinsky without either of them touching the essential quality of Sessions's own language. His influence on others has also been indirect. He has not been imitated, and in his teaching his concern has been to stress the superiority of craft over theory and to bring out the individual sensibility of each young composer.

PRINCIPAL COMPOSITIONS (published by Marks unless otherwise noted): *The Black Maskers*, incidental music for orchestra (1923); *Symphonies Nos. 1–8* (1927; 1944–46, Schirmer-G; 1957; 1958; 1964; 1966; 1967; 1968); *Piano Sonatas Nos. 1–3* (1930, 1946, 1965); *Violin Concerto* with orchestra including 5 clarinets and no violins (1935); *String Quartets Nos. 1–2* (1936, 1951); *Pages From a Diary* for piano (1939, published under the title *From My Diary*); *Duo* for violin, piano (1942); *The Trial of Lucullus*, 1-act opera; libretto by Bertolt Brecht (1947); *Sonata* for solo violin (1953); *Idyll of Theocritus* for soprano, orchestra; text translated by R. C. Trevelyan (1954); *Mass* for unison male chorus, organ (1955); *Piano Concerto* (1956); *String Quintet* (1958); *Divertimento for Orchestra* (1960); *Montezuma*, 3-act opera; libretto by G. A. Borghese (1941–62); *Psalm 140* for soprano with organ or orchestra (1963); *6 Pieces* for cello (1966); *When Lilacs Last in the Door-yard Bloom'd*, cantata for vocal soloists, chorus, orchestra (1970); *Rhapsody* for orchestra (1970). List to 1965: *R. S.* (New York, BMI, 1965).

PRINCIPAL WRITINGS: "Music in Crisis," *Modern Music* (Jan 1933); "Heinrich Schenker's Contribution," *ibid.* (May 1935); "New Musical Horizons," *ibid.* (Jan 1937); "Hindemith on Theory," *ibid.* (Nov 1937); "Exposition by Krenek," *ibid.* (Jan 1938); "Escape by Theory," *ibid.* (March 1938); "The Function of Theory," *ibid.* (May 1938); "The Composer and his Message," *The Intent of the Artist* ed. by A. Centeno (Princeton 1941); "The Scope of Music Criticism," *Music and Criticism: A Symposium* (Cambridge, Mass., 1948); *The Musical Experience of Composer, Performer, and Listener* (Princeton 1950); *Harmonic Practice* (New York 1951); "Song and Pattern in Music Today," *Score and I.M.A. Magazine* (Dec 1956); "To the Editor," *Perspectives* (spring 1957); "To the Editor," *Score* (July 1958); "Problems and Issues Facing the Composer Today," *Musical Quarterly* (April 1960); *Questions About Music* (Cambridge 1970).

BIBL.: Mark Brunswick, "R. H. S.," *Modern Music* (May 1933); Elliott Carter, "Current Chronicle," *re* the Violin Concerto, *Musical Quarterly* (July 1959); Edward Cone, "Conversation with R. S.," *Perspectives* (spring 1966); ——, review of the String Quartet No. 1, *Modern Music* (April 1941); ——, review of the String Quartet No. 2, *Musical Quarterly* (Jan 1957); Andrew Imbrie, "R. S.—In Honor of his 65th Birthday," *Perspectives* (fall 1962).

Andrew W. Imbrie

SEE ALSO Musicology and Composition, Opera, United States.

Set, an ordered collection of values within a compositional parameter. The term most often occurs in reference to ordered collections of pitch classes; it occurs less frequently in reference to other parameters, such as dynamic levels or durations. In composition, the set is used as the basis for the serial circulation of values within a parameter.

SEE ALSO Mathematics, Serialism, Theory, 12-Tone Techniques.

Seter, Mordecai (b. Novorosiysk, Russia, 26 Feb 1916), studied at the Ecole Normale de Musique in Paris (1932–37; composition with Nadia Boulanger, Paul Dukas; piano with Lazare Lévy). He has taught at the Israeli Academy of Music since 1952. His music has been influenced by liturgical chants of Middle Eastern Jewish communities, together with serial procedures.

PRINCIPAL COMPOSITIONS (published by IMI): *Sabbath Cantata* for soloists, chorus, string orchestra (1940–47); *Motets* for chorus (1941–51); *Ricercar* for solo strings, string orchestra (1953–56); *Variations* for orchestra (1959); *Judith*, symphonic chaconne after the dance for Martha Graham (1962); *Midnight Vigil*, oratorio for tenor, chorus, orchestra (1962); *Fantasy* for orchestra after the dance for Graham (1964); *The Daughter of Jephtah* for orchestra (1965); *Yemenite Suite* for voice, chamber orchestra (1966); *Jerusalem*, symphony for chorus, orchestra (1966).

BIBL.: Yehuda Cohen, "Werden und Entwicklung der Musik in Israel," *Die Musik Israels* by Max Brod, 2nd ed. (Cassel 1971); Alexander Ringer, "Musical Composition in Modern Israel," *Musical Quarterly* 51.

SEE ALSO Israel.

Shapero, Harold (b. Lynn, Mass., 29 April 1920), began piano lessons at seven and worked during his high-school years as a jazz pianist and arranger. He studied harmony for a time with Nicolas Slonimsky in Boston and attended Harvard Univ. (1937–41, composition with Walter Piston and Ernst Krenek). His most important musical education came from his two years of study with Nadia Boulanger and from his own analysis of Haydn, Mozart, and Beethoven. He has been teaching at Brandeis Univ. since 1952 and was chairman of the music department during 1966–69.

Shapero has composed primarily for the piano and for orchestra. His works are conceived in the so-called classical forms of the late 18th and 19th centuries. To these forms he brings a harmonic language inherited from Stravinsky and Copland, though some jazz influence is noticeable. His rhythms are characterized by wide ranging syncopations and cross accents. Melodic contours are most often disjunct with the leap of a diatonic seventh being a particular favorite. Often the seventh is filled in triadically. His technical command is extraordinary, and at his best (e.g., the *Arioso Variations*, 1948, or in the slow movement of the *Symphony*, 1947) he is capable of extraordinary expressive power within a context of subtle changes of texture and motion. In recent years he has been experimenting with the Buchla synthesizer and has completed several pieces on tape for synthesizer and piano. Despite the difference in sound surface, the power and energy that characterized his earlier music remains.

PRINCIPAL COMPOSITIONS (published by Southern unless otherwise noted): *3 Pieces for 3 Pieces* for woodwind trio (1939); *Trumpet Sonata* (1940); *9-Minute Overture* (1940, unpub.); *String Quartet* (1941); *Sonata* for piano 4-hands (1941, Mills); *Violin Sonata* (1942); *3 Piano Sonatas* (1944, Schirmer-G and Southern); *Serenade in D* for string orchestra (1945); *Symphony for Classical Orchestra* (1947); *Variations in C Minor* for piano (1947); *Piano Sonata in F Minor* (1948, 2nd movement also published separately as *Arioso Variations*); *Concerto for Orchestra* (1950, unpub.); *Hebrew Cantata*; on poems of Halevi (1954); *Credo for Orchestra* (1955); *On Green Mountain* for 13 jazz players (1957, unpub.); *Partita* for piano, small orchestra (1960); *3 Improvisations in B* for synthesizer, piano (1968, on tape); *4 Pieces* for synthesizer, piano (1970, on tape).

PRINCIPAL WRITINGS: "The Musical Mind," *Modern Music* 23:31–35; "Beethoven," *Atlantic Brief Lives—A Biographical Companion to the Arts* ed. by L. Kronenberger (Boston 1971).

Daniel L. Farber

SEE ALSO United States.

Shapey, Ralph (b. Philadelphia, 12 March 1921), studied violin with Emanuel Zetlin and composition with Stefan Wolpe. During 1938–42 he was assistant conductor of the Philadelphia National Youth Administration Orchestra. Since then he has conducted concerts of contemporary music throughout the U.S. He has taught at the Univ. of Pa. (1963–64) and the Univ. of Chicago (since 1964), where he directs the Contemporary Chamber Players. *Discourse* is a typical example of the cumulative form Shapey has used. It contains "large, contrasting, blocklike ideas set forth in broad planes and constantly returning in great overlapping phrased cycles. Within a static structure of balanced, inflexible, and immobile units, there is a kind of internal play of energies resulting from the continuous redefinition of a fixed material which remains set in a constant state of tension" (Salzman, see bibl.).

PRINCIPAL COMPOSITIONS: *String Quartets Nos. 2, 4, 5, 6* (1949; 1959; No. 5 with female voice, 1957–58; 1962); *Concerto* for clarinet with violin, cello, piano, horn, tom-tom, bass drum (1954); *Mutations* for piano (1956); *Duo* for viola, piano (1957); *Ontogeny* for orchestra (1958); *Violin Concerto* (1959); *Evocation* for violin, piano, percussion (1959); *Form* for piano (1959); *Rituals* for orchestra (1959); *Dimensions* for soprano, 23 instruments (1960); *Incantations* for soprano, 10 instruments (1961); *Discourse* for flute, clarinet, violin, piano (1961); *Convocation* for chamber group (1962); *Chamber Symphony* for 10 solo players (1962); *Seven* for piano 4-hands (1963); *Configurations* for flute, piano (1965); *String Trio* (1965); *Partita* for solo violin (1966); *Partita* for violin, 13 players (1966); *Partita-Fantasy* for cello, 16 players (1967); *Deux* for 2 pianos (1967); *Songs of Ecstasy* for soprano, piano, percussion, tape (1967).

BIBL.: Wilfrid Mellers, *Music in a New-Found Land* (London 1964); Eric Salzman, *Twentieth Century Music* (Englewood Cliffs, N. J., 1967):173. Detailed reviews of Shapey's music have appeared in the *Musical Quarterly* (1966–68).

SEE ALSO Performance, Text Setting and Usage, United States.

Shapiro, Gerald (b. Philadelphia, 14 May 1942), studied with Darius Milhaud at Mills College (where he was a technical assistant at the Tape Music Center during 1966–67), with Karlheinz Stockhausen at the Univ. of Calif. at Davis, and with Nadia Boulanger in Paris. Since 1967 he has taught at Brown Univ. and been director of its electronic-music studio. Since 1968 he has also been composer for the Zone theater group in Boston. He has been a jazz and danceband musician since he was a teenager. The composers Morton Subotnick and Ramon Sender (with whom he was associated at the Tape Music Center), Pauline Oliveros, John Cage, Alvin Lucier, and David Rosenboom have been major influences on his development (along with "lots of drugs, sailing, camping . . ."). The last three compositions listed below are participant (i.e., audience) activated electronic works, each incorporating a unique combination of custom-made listening and sound-producing apparatus. They are manifestations of Shapiro's conception of music "as a way of listening rather than the sound which is listened to, and of a piece of music as a process of interaction resulting in that special kind of listening we call music."

PRINCIPAL COMPOSITIONS: *Serenade* for 8 instruments, live electronics (1967); *From the Yellow Castle* (1968); *The Second Piece | The Piece About Finding Your Way in the Dark | The One for Ros and Harris* (1970); *Breath* (1971).

PRINCIPAL WRITINGS: "Functional Design of an Electronic Music Mixer," *Electronic Music Review* (1968).

SEE ALSO Instrumental and Vcoal Resources, Prose Music.

Shchedrin, Rodion (Konstantinovich) (b. Moscow, 16 Dec 1932), studied at the Moscow Conservatory (1950–55, composition with Yury Shaporin, piano with Jacob Fliez) and during 1964–69 taught composition there.

PRINCIPAL COMPOSITIONS (published by SC): *Piano Concertos Nos. 1–2* (1954, 1956); *Symphony No. 1* (1958); *Koniëk-gorbynok* [Little Humpback Horse], 4-act ballet (1959); *Ne tol'o linbov'* [Not Love Alone], 3-act opera (1961); *Ozornye tchastushky* [Naughty Limericks], concerto for orchestra (1963); *24 Preludes and Fugues* for piano (1963–70); *Symphony No. 2, "25 Preludes for Orchestra"* (1965); *Zvony* [The Chimes] for orchestra (1967); *Carmen Suite*, 1-act ballet; transcribed from Bizet's opera (1967); *Poetoria* for poet, woman's voice, chorus, orchestra; text by A. Vosnesensky (1968).

SEE ALSO Soviet Union.

Sheriff, Noam (b. Ramat-Gan, Israel, 7 Jan 1935), studied philosophy at the Hebrew Univ. in Jerusalem (1956–60) and music at the Berlin Hochschule für Musik (1960–62, composition with Boris Blacher). He also studied composition privately with Paul Ben-Haim (1949–57) and conducting with Igor Markevitch (1955). During 1952–54 he conducted the military orchestra in Israel and during 1955–59, the Hebrew Univ. Symphony, which he founded. He has taught orchestration at the Jerusalem Academy of Music since 1966 and at the National Academy in Tel Aviv since 1967. Since 1969 he has also been director of the Israkol recording studios. The early influences on his music came from Debussy and Stravinsky, later from Bartók. Most recently he has drawn inspiration from Oriental and Jewish music and has been using serial and heterophonic techniques.

PRINCIPAL COMPOSITIONS (published by IMI unless otherwise noted): *Festival Prelude* for orchestra (1957, IMP); *Songs of Degrees* for orchestra (1959, IMP); *Music* for woodwinds, trombone, double bass, piano (1960); *Ashrei* for alto, flute, 2 harps, percussion (1961); *Piano Sonata* (1962, Bote); *Heptaprisms* for chamber orchestra (1965); *Metamorphoses on a Galliard* for orchestra (1966); *2 Epigrams* for chamber orchestra (1968); *Chaconne* for orchestra (1968); *Cain*, choreographic drama; electronic music on tape (1969); *String Quartet* (1968–   ).

SEE ALSO Israel.

Shibata, Minao (b. Tokyo, 29 Sept 1916), studied botany (1936–39) and esthetics (1941–43) at Tokyo Imperial Univ. and composition privately with Saburo Moroi (1940–43). He has taught music theory and 20th-century music at Tokyo Univ. since 1959. His book *Inshōha-igo* [After Impressionism] was published in Tokyo in 1967. This was followed by a 3-volume history of music (1967–71).

PRINCIPAL COMPOSITIONS: *Kitazono katsue no mittsuno shi* [3 Poems on Katsue Kitazono] for soprano, chamber orchestra (1954–58); *Symphony* (1960, Ongaku); *Improvisation for Electronic Sounds* (1967–68, recorded by Philips); *Display '70* for electronic sounds, Japanese flute, marimba, percussion (1969–70).

BIBL.: Yasushi Togashi, *Nikon no Sakkyokuka* [Japanese Composers] (Tokyo c.1968):162–66.

SEE ALSO Japan.

Shifrin, Seymour (b. Brooklyn, N. Y., 28 Feb 1926), studied composition privately with William Schuman, at Columbia Univ. with Otto Luening, and in Paris with Darius Milhaud. He has taught at the Univ. of Calif. at Berkeley (1952–66) and at Brandeis Univ. (since 1966).

The main body of Shifrin's output is for various chamber ensembles; there are several pieces for solo voice and for chorus and also orchestral works. The roots of his compositional style are in neoclassicism, a fact made evident by the clear formal outlines of most of his music and by his use of certain pitch complexes as referential tonal centers. In Shifrin's case, however, these centers are almost always ambiguous in nature, a result of the chromatic character of the writing and the rapidity of the harmonic motion. They are thus constantly compromised through their association with adjacent pitches and by the tendency for subordinate pitches or pitch complexes to establish their own priority. The sense of ambiguity or conflict inherent in this tonal language may be viewed as one manifestation of what is perhaps Shifrin's most salient and pervasive stylistic trait: the superimposition of highly disparate and contrasting musical materials. This can be seen in all aspects of his work, from such large-scale factors as the juxtaposition of essentially lyric sections or movements with others that are virtually pointillistic in conception, to such details as the combination of short, explosive upbeat figures with long, sustained downbeats; mixtures of flowing principal lines and terse, fragmentary accompaniments; and the use of extreme registral relationships in the overall textural pattern. The tension that results from balancing such seemingly antithetical forces lends Shifrin's music a distinctly dramatic quality, accounting for both its difficulty for the average listener and its expressive power.

PRINCIPAL COMPOSITIONS: *String Quartets Nos. 1–4* (1949, Bote; 1961–62; 1965–66; 1967); *Fantasy for piano* (1950); *Chamber Symphony* (1953–54, Peters); *Serenade for 5 Instruments* for oboe, clarinet, viola, horn, piano (1954, Peters); *Cantata to Sophoclean Choruses* for chorus, orchestra (1956–57); *3 Pieces for orchestra* (1958, Peters); *Odes of Shang* for chorus, piano, percussion (1963); *Satires of Circumstance* for mezzo-soprano, flute, clarinet, violin, cello, double bass, piano (1964); *Duo* for violin, piano (1969).

PRINCIPAL WRITINGS: "Tomorrow's Theory Study," *College Music Symposium* (fall 1961):41–44; "A Note from the Underground," *Perspectives* 1/1:152–53.

BIBL.: Martin Boykan, "S. S.: Satires of Circumstance," *Perspectives* 5/1:163–69; David Lewin, "S. S.: Quartet No. 2," *ibid.* 2/2:169–75.

Robert P. Morgan

Shinohara, Makoto (b. Osaka, Japan, 10 Dec 1931), studied at the Tokyo Arts Univ. (1952–54, composition with Tomojiro Ikenouchi), the Paris Conservatory (1954–60, analysis with Olivier Messiaen), the Cologne State Conservatory (1964–65, composition with Karlheinz Stockhausen), and the Cologne Hochschule für Musik (electronic music with Gottfried Michael Koenig). During 1965–66 he was a technical assistant at the Electronic Music Studio of Utrecht Univ. He worked at the Columbia-Princeton Electronic Music Studio until 1972.

PRINCIPAL COMPOSITIONS: *Alternance* for 6 players on 70 percussion instruments (1961–62, Leduc); *Tendance* for piano (1963–69, Moeck); *Mémoires* on tape (1966); *Consonance* for flute, horn, cello, harp, vibraphone, marimba (1967, Moeck); *Visions II* for orchestra (1970).

SEE ALSO Japan.

Shostakovich, Dmitri (Dmitriovich) (b. St. Petersburg, 5 Sept 1906), is the son of a scientist. The family was originally Polish, the composer's grandfather having been exiled to Siberia. The young Shostakovich took piano lessons from his mother and later in the Glassor School in St. Petersburg. His first attempts at composition, which include a

Funeral March, were made there. He entered the Petrograd Conservatory in the fall of 1919 and studied piano with Leonid Nikolaev until 1923 and composition with Maximilian Steinberg. His graduation in 1925 was marked by his diploma work, the *Symphony No. 1 in F Minor*, the performance of which in 1926 brought him world attention. He began to seek ways to make his art serve the political needs of the time and under prompting from the conductor Nikolai Malko and the composer-musicologist Boris Asafiev, he turned to the stage. During the next decade several successful works appeared, including the opera *The Nose* (1927–28) and the ballet *The Golden Age* (1929–30), both in a parodistic, satirical vein. His first attempt at serious tragedy, the opera *Lady Macbeth of Mtsensk* (1930–31), was praised at its premiere in 1934 and in subsequent performances outside the Soviet Union but withdrawn in 1936 after being condemned by the Soviet government for its pessimistic libretto characterizing the masses as unhappy and for such musical features as discords, raucous brass writing, and naturalistic and sometimes erotic sound effects. As a "composer's reply to just criticism," he wrote the *Fifth Symphony* in 1937.

During 1937–41 Shostakovich taught orchestration and, later, composition at the Leningrad Conservatory. With the approach of German troops in 1941 he was evacuated to Moscow and then to Kuibyshev with other figures of the Moscow cultural world. By 1943 he was back in Moscow, teaching there and continuing to interpret the artist's political role in his own work. In 1948 his path, together with that of all his famous contemporaries, was condemned by the Communist Party as inimical to the interests of the Soviet peoples. He turned, as did many other composers, to motion-picture scoring and kept his more serious attempts under wraps until several years after Stalin's death in 1953, when the 1948 attack was officially rescinded. (The *Fourth Symphony* was finally released in the early 1960s.)

Except for Stravinsky, Shostakovich has probably been more highly honored throughout the world than any other 20th-century composer. On the other hand he has been sharply criticized in the Soviet Union for his pessimism (*Symphony No. 4*, the opera *Lady Macbeth*), for an overuse of "devices" such as percussive piano and string writing, for his "formalism" (an ideological concept) in favoring musical technique over drama, and for over-complexity of form (*Symphony No. 10*). His early works show traces of urban folk music and of Bartók's approach to folk material in general as well as the exploitation of orchestral color and instrumental effects of early Stravinsky. He has constantly used sarcasm, pastiche, the grotesque, and the imitation of natural sounds, although the sarcasm and grotesque naturalism that studded his early works is now so attenuated as to be indiscernible. Historically the most important part of his creative profile may be his career-long effort to accommodate extra-musical political phenomenon within his music. This extends even to accepting advice about creative direction from noncreative or at least nonmusical sources. As recently as 1968 he said, "Soviet music is a weapon in the international ideological battle . . . Soviet artists cannot remain indifferent observers in the struggle. . . ."

PRINCIPAL COMPOSITIONS (available from Mezhkniga unless otherwise noted): *Symphony No. 1,* Op. 10 (1924–25); *Aphorisms,* 10 pieces for piano, Op. 13 (1927); *Nos* [The Nose], 3-act opera, Op. 15; libretto by A. Price after Gogol (1927–28, unpub.); *Zoloti Vek* [The Golden Age], 3-act ballet, Op. 22 (1929–30); *Ledi Makbet Mtsenskogo Uezda* [Lady Macbeth of Mtsensk], later retitled *Ekaterina Izmailova,* 4-act opera, Op. 29; libretto by A. Price after Leskov (1930–31); *24 Preludes* for piano, Op. 34 (1932–33); *Concerto* for piano, trumpet, strings, Op. 35 (1933); *Cello Sonata,* Op. 40 (1934); *Symphony No. 5,* "A Composer's Answer to Just Criticism," Op. 47 (1937); *String Quartet No. 1,* Op. 49 (1938); *Piano Quintet,* Op. 57 (1940); an orchestration of Mussorgsky's *Boris Godunov,* Op. 58 (1939–40); *Symphony No. 7,* Op. 60 (1941); *6 Romances* for bass, orchestra, Op. 62; poems by Burns, Shakespeare, Raleigh (1942); *Symphony No. 8,* Op. 65 (1943); *String Quartet No. 2,* Op. 69 (1944); *Symphony No. 9,* Op. 70 (1945); *String Quartet No. 3,* Op. 73 (1946); *Violin Concerto No. 1,* Op. 78 (1947–48); *Iz Evreiskoi Narodnoi Poezii* [From Jewish Folk Poetry], song cycle for soprano, alto, tenor, piano, Op. 79 (1948); *Pesnia o Lesakh* [Song of the Forests], oratorio, Op. 81; text by E. Dolmatovsky (1949); *String Quartet No. 4,* Op. 83 (1949); *24 Preludes and Fugues* for piano, Op. 87 (1950–51); *String Quartet No. 5,* Op. 92 (1952); *Symphony No. 10,* Op. 93 (1953); *Violin Concerto No. 2,* Op. 99 (c.1956); *String Quartet No. 6,* Op. 101 (1957); *Piano Concerto No. 2,* Op. 102 (c.1957); *Symphony No. 11,* Op. 103 (1957); *Cello Concerto No. 1,* Op. 107 (1959); *Symphony No. 12,* Op. 112 (1961); *Symphony No. 13,* Op. 113 (1962); *String Quartet No. 9,* Op. 117 (c.1963); *Kazn' Stepana Razina* [The Execution of Stepan Razin], poem for bass, chorus, orchestra, Op. 119 (1964); *String Quartet No. 11,* Op. 122 (c.1967); *Cello Concerto No. 2,* Op. 126 (c.1969); *Symphony No. 14* (1970); *Symphony No. 15* (1971–72); *Violin Concerto No. 3,* Op. 129 (197–); *String Quartet No. 12.* Op. 133 (197–).

PRINCIPAL WRITINGS: an essay in *Russian Symphony: Thoughts About Tchaikovsky* (New York 1947).

BIBL.: Julian Herbage, "S.'s Eighth Symphony," *Musical Times* (July 1944); Stanley D. Krebs, *Soviet Composers and the Development of Soviet Music* (New York 1970); Ivan Martynov, *D. S.,* trans. by T. Guralsky (New York 1947); David Rabinovich, *S.,* trans. by G. Hanna (London 1949); Marina Sabinina, *D. S.* (Moscow 1959); Victor I. Seroff, *D. S.* (New York 1943); Nicolas Slonimsky, "D. S.," *Musical Quarterly* 28:415ff.

Larissa Janczyn

SEE ALSO Dance, Opera, Orchestration, Recording, Soviet Union.

Shrapnel, Hugh Michael (b. Birmingham, England, 18 Feb 1947), attended the Royal Academy of Music (1967–69, theory and composition with Norman Demuth) and Cornelius Cardew's class in experimental music at Morley College. He has been a member of The Scratch Orchestra since 1969 and of the Promenade Theatre Orchestra since 1970; both groups specialize in experimental music.

PRINCIPAL COMPOSITIONS (available from Experimental): *Space-Time Music* for any materials (1969); *Anthology* for any number of singers and instrumentalists (1969–70); *Bells* for tuned metal percussion (1970); *Cantation 1* for 1–3 keyboard instruments (1970); *Cantation 2* for any number of pianos (1970); *Tidal Wave* for any number of electric organs and other keyboard instruments (1970); *Chorale* for unspecified sound sources (1971).

Sibelius, Jean (Julius Christian) (b. Tavastehus, Finland, 8 Dec 1865; d. Järvenpää, 20 Sept 1957), studied law at the Univ. of Helsinki (1885) and music at the Helsinki Conservatory (1886–89; composition with Martin Wegelius, violin with Vasiliev Csillag). He also studied privately in Berlin with Albert Becker (1889–90) and in Vienna with Karl Goldmark and Robert Fuchs (1890–91). During 1892–97 he taught violin and theory at the Helsinki Music Institute, after which the Finnish government granted him a pension so that he could compose exclusively. In the 1880s he was influenced by the wave of romantic nationalism that affected all the arts in Finland (then under Russian rule). After 1905 he abandoned much of the romantic esthetic. His most adventurous work, the *Fourth Symphony,* dates from 1910–11: It "centers on the ambiguous interval of the augmented fourth, and from its opening measures until some point near the end, the tonal resolution of the piece is in doubt. The remarkable thing about this work, aside from its moody and dissonant character, is its strong conception of form generated organically out of the musical ideas. The ideas come in fragments, and the formal process—almost the reverse of traditional developmental conceptions—is one of gradual cohesion; the fragments merge and resolve into coherent tonal structures" (Salzman:90; see bibl.).

PRINCIPAL COMPOSITIONS: *Kullervo*, symphonic poem for soprano, baritone, men's chorus, orchestra, Op. 7 (1892, Breitkopf); *En Saga*, symphonic poem, Op. 9 (1892, revised 1901; Breitkopf); *Karelia Suite* for orchestra, Op. 11 (1893, Breitkopf); *Rakastava* for men's chorus, Op. 14 (1893, Ylioppilaskunnan Laulajat, Helsinki), revised for strings, timpani, triangle (1911, Breitkopf); *Lemminkainen Suite*, Op. 22 (Breitkopf): "Lemminkainen and the Maidens of Saari" (1895, revised 1897-39); "The Swan of Tuonela" (1893, revised 1897-1900); "Lemminkainen in Tuonela" (1895, revised 1897-1939); "Lemminkainen's Homeward Journey" (1895, revised 1897-1900); *Finlandia*, symphonic poem, Op. 26 (1899, revised 1900; Breitkopf); *Symphonies Nos. 1-7*, Opp. 39, 43, 52, 63, 82, 104, 105 (1898-99, Breitkopf; 1901-02, Breitkopf; 1904-07, Lienau; 1910-11, Breitkopf; 1915, revised 1916-19, Hansen-W; 1923, Hansen-W; 1924, Hansen-W); *Pelléas et Mélisande*, incidental music for the play by Maeterlinck, Op. 46 (1905, Lienau); *Violin Concerto*, Op. 47 (1903, revised 1905; Lienau); *Pohjola's Daughter*, symphonic fantasy, Op. 49 (1906, Lienau); *Svanevhit* [The White Swan], incidental music for the play by Strindberg, Op. 54 (1908, Leinau); *String Quartet*, "Voces intimae," Op. 56 (1909, Lienau); *2 Serenades* for violin, orchestra, Op. 69 (1912-13, Breitkopf); *Luonnotar*, poem for soprano, orchestra, Op. 70 (1913, Breitkopf); *Sonatina in E* for violin, piano, Op. 80 (1915, Hansen-W); *2 Humoresques* for violin, orchestra, Op. 87 (1917, Hansen-W); *4 Humoresques* for violin, orchestra, Op. 89 (1917, Hansen-W); *The Tempest*, incidental music for the play by Shakespeare, Op. 109 (1925, Hansen-W); *Tapiola*, symphonic poem, Op. 112 (1926, Breitkopf). Sibelius also composed over 100 songs.

PRINCIPAL WRITINGS: *Manuscripts*, commentary by Eino Roiha (Helsinki 1945).

BIBL.: Gerald Abraham, ed., *The Music of S.* (New York 1947); Karl Ekman, *J. S., His Life and Personality* (London 1936); (Harold E. Johnson, *J. S.: the Recorded Music* (Helsinki 1957); ——, *J. S.* (New York 1959); Simon Parmet, *The Symphonies of S.: a Study in Musical Appreciation*, trans. by K. A. Hart (London 1959); Nils-Eric Ringbom, *J. S.*, trans. by G. I. C. de Courey (Norman, Okla., 1954); Eric Salzman, *Twentieth-Century Music* (Englewood Cliffs, N. J., 1967):89-90.

SEE ALSO Popular Music.

Sicilianos, Yorgo (b. Athens, 29 August 1922), studied at the Athens Conservatory (1944-49; composition with Marios Varvoglis, harmony with George Sklavos), the Accadèmia di S. Cecilia in Rome (1951-53, composition with Ildebrando Pizzetti), the Paris Conservatory (1953-54), Harvard Univ. (spring 1955, composition with Walter Piston), Tanglewood (1955, composition with Boris Blacher), the Juilliard School (1955-56, composition with Vincent Persichetti). He wrote scores for the National Greek Theater during 1958-65 and was director of the music division of the Hellenic Broadcasting Network, 1960-62, and general secretary of the Greek Music Council, 1963-64. He has taught and directed the choir at Pierce College in Athens since 1967. His works of the mid and late 1950s are neoclassic. The *Cello Concerto* (1963) is 12-tone with some serial elements; the succeeding works are fully serial.

PRINCIPAL COMPOSITIONS: *Concerto for Orchestra*, Op. 12 (1953-54, Greek Ministry of Education); *String Quartets Nos. 2-4*, Opp. 13, 15, 28 (1955, 1957, 1967); *Bacchantes*, ballet for women's chorus, orchestra, Op. 19 (1959); *Cello Concerto*, Op. 22 (1963); *Variations on 4 Rhythmic Patterns* for orchestra, Op. 23 (1963); *Stasimen B!*, for mezzo-soprano, women's chorus, orchestra, Op. 24; text by Euripedes (1964); *Episodes* for chamber orchestra, Op. 27 (1967); *Epiklesis* for narrator, men's chorus, instruments, Op. 29 (1969).

PRINCIPAL WRITINGS: "O horós os ekfrastikó mésso sti synchroni moussikí" [Space as an Expressive Factor in Contemporary Music], *Chroniká Esthitikís* 2 (1963):91-102; "Merikés sképsis yíro apó ti sýnchroni moussikí ké tó kinó" [Some Thoughts on Contemporary Music] *Epochés* (June 1963):44-47; "Hemerológhio: Óro 24" [Calendar: 24 Hours] *ibid.* 20 (1964):23-26.

BIBL.: Nicolas Slonimsky, "New Music in Greece," *Musical Quarterly* 51:225-35.

SEE ALSO Greece.

Siegmeister, Elie (b. New York, 15 Jan 1909), grew up in Brooklyn and began piano lessons at the age of nine with Emil Friedberger. At 15 he entered Columbia Univ. where he studied composition with Seth Bingham; he also had private lessons in counterpoint with Wallingford Riegger. He lived in Paris during 1927-32, where he studied with Nadia Boulanger. After returning to the U.S., he studied conducting at the Juilliard School (1935-38) and became active in New York as a composer, conductor, author, pianist, and teacher. In the 1940s he organized the American Ballad Singers to promote American folk music and made several national tours as conductor of the group. Since 1949 he has taught at Hofstra Univ. near New York, where since 1966 he has been composer-in-residence.

Siegmeister's large output includes three symphonies, two concertos, and many other orchestral works; much chamber music; a dozen theater works, including four operas; more than 100 songs; and works for chorus, for band, and for piano, the last including many children's pieces. He has long been associated with works inspired by American music and folklore. Jazz elements appear in the last movement of the *Sextet* for brass and percussion (1965), blues elements can be heard in the melodic inflections and syncopations of the second movement of the *Clarinet Concerto* (1956). The influence of Western American folksong can be heard in *Wilderness Road* (1945), Southern American folksong in *Ozark Set* (1943). However, Siegmeister's works embrace a much broader range of musical ideas. An eclectic, he often combines traditional frameworks, such as sonata form, theme and variations, or fugue, with 20th-century devices: plucked strings or hammer blows in the *Piano Sonata No. 2* (1964) or the "Bartók pizzicato" in the *Violin Sonata No. 3* (1965). His melodic style ranges from the working out of taut germ motives (*String Quartet No. 2*) to the unfolding of long, winding themes (*American Sonata*, second movement). On the harmonic plane, his style has encompassed both bristling dissonance (*Strange Funeral in Braddock*, 1933; *The Face of War*, 1967–68) and folklike simplicity (*Darling Corie*, 1952; *American Harp Suite*, 1966).

PRINCIPAL COMPOSITIONS: *Strange Funeral in Braddock*, song for voice, piano; text by Michael Gold (1933, Presser); *String Quartet No. 1* (1935, AMC); *Sing Out, Sweet Land*, musical; text by Walter Kerr and Edward Eager (1944, MCA); *Symphony No. 1* (1947, AMC); *Darling Corie*, opera; libretto by Lewis Allan (1952, Chappell); *Clarinet Concerto* (1956, Fox); *The Mermaid in Lock No. 7*, musical play; text by Edward Mabley (1958, Henmar); *Flute Concerto* (1960, MCA); *String Quartet No. 2* (1960, AMC); *The Plough and the Stars*, opera; libretto by Sean O'Casey (1963, MCA); *Piano Sonata No. 2* (1964, MCA); *Madam To You*, 7 songs for voice, piano; texts by Langston Hughes (1964, AMC); *Sextet* for brass, percussion (1965, MCA); *Violin Sonata No. 3* (1965, AMC); *Songs of Experience* for voice, piano; poems by William Blake (1966, AMC); *The Face of War*, 5 songs for bass, orchestra; texts by Hughes (1967–68); *Symphony No. 4* (1969–70, MCA); *Violin Sonata No. 2* (1970, MCA); *Symphony No. 5* (1971, MCA).

PRINCIPAL WRITINGS: *Harmony and Melody* (Belmont, Calif., 1965–66); *The New Music Lover's Handbook* (New York 1972).

BIBL.: David Ewen, *The World of 20th Century Music* (New York 1968):752–56.

Alan Mandel

Sigurbjörnsson, Thorkell (b. Reykjavík, 16 July 1938), attended the Reykjavík School of Music (1948–57), Hamline Univ. in St. Paul (1957–59, theory and composition with Russell G. Harris), and the Univ. of Ill. (1959–61; composition with Kenneth Gaburo, acoustics and electronic music with Lejaren Hiller). In 1962 he attended lectures by Pierre Boulez and György Ligeti at Darmstadt. He has taught at the Reykjavík School since 1961 and was assistant head of music for the Iceland State Broadcasting Service during 1966–69. Since 1968 he has been a reviewer for *Morgunblaðið*. He has appeared frequently as a pianist and conductor, playing principally new music.

PRINCIPAL COMPOSITIONS: *Ballade* for tenor, flute, viola, guitar; text by Bertolt Brecht (1960); *Leikar* for chorus, orchestra (1961); *Composition in 3 Scenes*, chamber opera for soloists, chorus, 3 keyboard performers, 3 percussionists, guitar, alto saxophone; text by the composer (1963–64); *Cadenza and Dance* for violin, orchestra (1967); *String Quartet*, "Hässelby" (1968); *Ymur* for orchestra (1969); *Missa minuscula* for women's voices (1969); *Kisum* for clarinet, viola, piano (1970); *Laeti* for orchestra, tape (1971); *Fipur*, computer music (1971).

BIBL.: In 1971 the Swedish Institute for Nationwide Concerts published a brochure on Sigurbjörnsson written by Per Anders Hellquist.

Sikorski, Tomasz (b. Warsaw, 19 May 1939), studied at the Warsaw State College of Music (1956–62; composition with his father, Kazimierz Sikorski; piano with Zbigniew Drzewiecki). He concertizes as a pianist, specializing in contemporary music.

PRINCIPAL COMPOSITIONS: *Echoes II* for 1–4 pianos, chimes, 2 gongs, 2 tam-tams, tape (1963, PWM); *Antiphonies* for soprano, horn, piano, chimes, 2 gongs, 2 tam-tams, tape (1963); *Prologues* for women's chorus, 4 flutes, 4 horns, 2 pianos, 3 percussionists (1964, PWM); *Concerto breve* for piano, 24 winds, 4 percussionists (1965, PWM); *Sequenza I* for orchestra (1966, PWM); *Piano Sonata* (1967, PWM); *Homofonia* for 12 brass, piano, 2 gongs (1968); *Diafonia* for 2 pianos (1969).

BIBL.: Bohdan Pociej, " 'Echa' T. S." [T. S.'s "Echoes"], *Ruch muzyczny* (Feb 1964).

Silvestrov, Valentin (Vasilievich) (b. Kiev, 30 Sept 1937), studied engineering at the Kiev Engineering and Building Institute (1955–58) and music at the Kiev Evening Music School (1955–58, piano with Basil Mulov) and the Tchaikovsky Conservatory in Kiev (1958–64; composition with Boris Liatoshinsky; harmony, counterpoint with Levko Revutsky). He taught piano at the Music Studio of Kiev Univ. during 1963–65 and at the Music Studio of the Society of the Ukraine during 1965–69.

PRINCIPAL COMPOSITIONS: *2 Songs on the Words of Alexander Blok* for mezzo-soprano, piano (1961); *5 Pieces* for piano (1961); *Piano Quintet* (1961, Ukraine); *Quartetto piccolo* for string quartet (1961); *Triad* for piano (1961–62, Ukraine); *Trio* for flute, trumpet, celesta (1962); *Symphony No. 1* (1963); *Classical Overture* (1964); *Mystery* for alto flute, 6 percussion groups (1964); *Projections* for harpsichord, vibraphone, chimes (1965); *Monodia* for orchestra (1965); *Spectra* for chamber orchestra (1965); *Symphony No. 2* for chamber orchestra (1965); *Eschatophony* for orchestra (1966); *Elegy* for piano (1967); *Hymn* for 5 instrumental groups (1967); *Poem in memoriam Boris Liatoshinsky* for orchestra (1968).

PRINCIPAL WRITINGS: "To Go Out of Reserved Space," *Junost* (Moscow) 9:100–01; "The Mystery of V. S.," *Krugozor* (Moscow) 4:6.

BIBL.: Silvestrov's music has been discussed by Václas Kučera (*Hudební rozhledy*, 1969), Malina Mokrejewa (*Ruch muzyczny*, 1962), Luigi Pestalozza (*Rinascita*, 28 July 1967), Fred K. Prieberg (*Survey*, Jan 1963; *Zeit*, 29 Nov 1963), and Boris Schwarz (*Musical Quarterly*, 1965).

SEE ALSO Soviet Union.

Sims, Ezra (b. Birmingham, Ala., 16 Jan 1928), studied at Birmingham-Southern College (1944–47), the Birmingham Conservatory (1945–48; Hugh Thomas, G. Ackley Brower), Yale Univ. (1950–52, composition with Quincy Porter), and Mills College (1953–55; composition with Darius Milhaud, Leon Kirchner). Since 1958 he has been a cataloger for the Loeb Music Library of Harvard Univ. He is also American music director for the New England Dance Theater.

PRINCIPAL COMPOSITIONS (available from CFE unless otherwise noted): *Chamber Cantata on Chinese Poems* for tenor, chamber ensemble (1954, Presser); *Mass* for chorus (1955); *The Trojan Women* for chamber orchestra; score for the play by Euripedes (1955); *Masque* for chamber orchestra; dance score for the Halprin-Lathrop Co. (1955); *Brief Glimpses into Contemporary French Literature* for 4 countertenors, piano; text by David Stacton (1958); *Kubla Khan Nos. 1–2:* No. 1 for narrator, gamelan, chamber orchestra; No. 2 for narrator, tape; text by Coleridge (c.1958);

String Quartet (1959); *Sonate concertanti*, 1/4-tone music for oboe, viola, cello, double bass, string quartet (1961, Presser); *String Quartet No. 3* in 1/4-tones (1962); *A Passion*, 1/4-tone music for narrator, tenor, baritone, 4 clarinets, marimba 4-hands; text by Edward Gorey (1963); *Octet* for double string quartet using 1/4 and 1/6 tones (1964, Presser); *In memoriam Alice Hawthorne*, 1/4- and 1/6-tone music for narrator, tenor, baritone, 4 clarinets, horn, marimba 4-hands; text by Gorey (1967); *Antimatter, 3 Dances for Toby*, tape collage; choreography by Toby Armour (1968); *MacDowell's Fault or the 10th Sunday after Trinity*, tape collage; choreography by Armour (1968); *Alec*, musique concrète tape collage; choreography by Armour (1968); *Commonplace Book or A Salute to Our American Container Corp.*, musique concrète on tape (1969); *Real Toads*, musique concrète on tape; choreography by Cliff Keuter (1970); *Clément Wenceslas Lothaire Nepomucène, Prince Metternich, in memoriam* on tape; choreography by Armour (1970); *From an Oboe Quartet* for oboe, violin, viola, cello using 1/4 and 1/6 tones (1971).

PRINCIPAL WRITINGS: "Microtones," *The Harvard Dictionary of Music*, 2nd ed. (Cambridge, Mass. 1969).

[prepared with the help of John Herbert MacDowell]

Simultaneity, the simultaneous occurrence of musical events. Where such events are single pitches, the term may be used in place of *interval* or *chord* by those who wish to avoid the traditional functional connotations of those terms.

Sink, Kuldar (b. Tallin, Estonia, 14 Sept 1942), studied flute and composition at the Tallin Music School (1957–60) and composition with B. Drapov and A. Petrov at the Leningrad Conservatory. He is a flutist with the Estonian Radio Orchestra and a harpsichordist with the Tallin Chamber Orchestra. He also composes for films and theater. His compositions through 1962 were written within a neoclassic orientation. The first and fourth movements of his *Compositions for 2 Pianos* (1963–66) employ graphic notation, the second movement uses serial structures, and the third an open form. Subsequent works have continued to explore techniques of the international avant-garde.

PRINCIPAL COMPOSITIONS: *Flute Concertino* (1961); *Chamber Symphony No. 1* (1962); *Compositions for 2 Pianos* (1963–66); *The 4 Seasons*, cantata (1964); *Chamber Symphony No. 2* (1967); *Octet* (1968); *Diario degli accidenti musicali* for various chamber ensembles (1968–71).

Sitsky, Larry (b. Tientsin, China, 10 Sept 1934), studied piano and other musical subjects at the New South Wales State Conservatory in Australia (1952–58) and the San Francisco Conservatory (1959–61, piano with Egon Petri). He is self-taught as a composer. He has taught piano and lectured at the Queensland State Conservatory in Australia (1961–65) and the Canberra School of Music there (since 1966). He describes his style as "expressionistic (i.e., dealing with extreme emotional states)" and influenced by the music of Bartók, Berg, and Bloch and by the esthetics of Busoni, on whom he has done extensive research.

PRINCIPAL COMPOSITIONS: *Sonata* for solo flute (1960, Albert); *5 Improvisations* for chorus, piano (1961); *Fantasia in memoriam Egon Petri* for piano (1962); *Woodwind Quartet* (1963, Boosey); *Sinfonia* for 10 players (1964); *Fall of the House of Usher*, opera after Poe (1965, Ricordi); *Apparitions* for orchestra (1966, Boosey); *Concerto* for 2 pianos (1967, Boosey); *Homage to Stravinsky* for orchestra (1968); *Sonata* for 2 guitars (1968, Albert); *String Quartet* (1969); *Lenz*, opera after Büchner 1970); *Violin Concerto* (1970); *Concerto* for woodwind quartet, orchestra (1970–71).

PRINCIPAL WRITINGS: "Debunking Stockhausen & Co.," *Quadrant* (Sydney, May 1965):52–56; "Transcriptions and the Eunuch," *ibid.* (Sept 1966):30–35; "The Young Pianist and the Twentieth Century Idiom," *Australian Journal of Music Education* (Oct 1968):25–29; "Sitsky on Sitsky," *Music Now* (Sydney)1/4.

BIBL.: Roger Covell, *Australia's Music, Themes of a New Society* (Melbourne 1967); Andrew W. McCredie, *Musical Composition in Australia* (Canberra 1969):19–20.

SEE ALSO Australia.

Skalkottas, Nikos (b. Halkis, Eubea, Greece, 8 March 1904; d. Athens, 19 Sept 1949), began violin lessons at five with his father, continued with an uncle, then with Tony Schulze at the Athens Conservatory (1914–20) and with Willy Hess at the Berlin Hochschule für Musik (1921–23), where he also studied composition with P. Kahn. The first compositions he himself took seriously date from the winter of 1923–24, and they were followed by composition studies in Berlin with Kurt Weill (1924–25), Philipp Jarnach (1925–27), and Arnold Schoenberg (1927–31). He also played in chamber-music groups and conducted during these years. After 1931 his personality changed; he became more introspective and his rate of composition slackened. He returned to Athens in 1933, where his music met with indifference and even some hostility. He earned his living as an orchestral violinist and after 1935 began to compose feverishly but in secret. He married the pianist Maria Pangali in 1946. His exceedingly large output has begun to come to light only in the last decade. A Skalkottas Committee and, since 1961, a Society of Skalkottas's Friends in Athens has taken charge of a Skalkottas Archives there and of the publication and dissemination of his works.

Skalkottas's output exceeds 170 works (counting collections as one item) and consists mainly of chamber music (over 50 works), orchestral and concerted works (over 32), piano music, songs, and ballets. Composing mostly in his head and writing quickly, usually without error, he produced in 25 years almost as much music as Beethoven or Schubert. If the density of his 12-tone writing is taken into account, the quantity is still more impressive. His style evolved from a light, transparent, ironical sort of writing (until 1938) to more compactness and richness in works of 1939–45. During the last years folklike elements more frequently appeared, along with new virtuoso demands on performers. His *Piano Concerto No. 3*, lasting an hour, contains extremely complex polyphonic writing and is like an *Art of the Fugue* transferred to the concerto medium. The *Symphonic Suite No. 2* lasts some 75 minutes and is probably his magnum opus. By contrast, some works (such as the various sets of *Greek Dances*) use a simpler tonal or modal harmonic idiom and are much lighter in nature.

Skalkottas did not construct his music abstractly but fully heard the sounds involved and kept performance considerations in mind (even though solo parts reach the extreme registers and technical limits of their instruments). His 12-tone procedures went beyond "classical" Viennese practice in the use of matrices, coordinated dimensions, motivic dovetailing, and other technical details. They differ also in using 2–18 independent rows (depending on the size of the work) rather than one. He rejected inversion and transposition but used retrogrades extensively and transformations based on proximities within note groups in a set. Several works from 1938 on are freely atonal but resemble the 12-tone works in sound. Independently of other composers in Europe, he used variation procedures to secure both unity and variety, combined sonata form with 12-tone processes, and wrote long, lyric melodies that lend themselves to polyphonic treatment. He also evolved new sound concepts, including the superposition of multidimensional sound structures (each clearly defined), multiple-chord sound columns that succeed each other for the sole purpose of producing changing harmonic colors, and techniques of orchestration that anticipated recent developments, including some in electronic music. In spite of his highly personal and independent style, a few indirect influences can be detected: first, Schoenberg and Berg (but without their expressionistic elements); then Stravinsky and Busoni (through his teacher Jarnach), and sometimes Bartók, Scriabin, and Debussy.

PRINCIPAL COMPOSITIONS (published, where noted, by UE or by the Society of Skalkottas's Friends, SSF, in Athens): *String Quartet* (1923–24); *String Trio* (1923–24); *Greek Suite* for piano (1924); *Suite* for 2 pianos (1924); *Sonata* for solo violin (1925, UE); *Sonatina* for piano (1927); *15 Little Variations* for piano (1927, UE); *Sonatina No. 1* for violin, piano (1928; second movement published in *Moussiki Zoi*, Athens); *String Quartet No. 1* (1928); *Sonatina No. 2* for violin, piano (1929); *Violin Sonata No. 1* (1929); *Easy String Quartet* (1929); *String Quartet No. 2* (1929); *Symphonic Suite No. 1* in 6 movements (1929; revised 1935, SSF); *Concerto for Wind Orchestra* (1929); *The Unknown Soldier* for chorus, orchestra; poem by R. Stein (1929); *Concerto* for piano, violin, orchestra (1929–30); *Little Suite* for violin, orchestra (1929–30); *Octet* for 4 woodwinds, string quartet (1931, UE); *Piece* for 8 woodwinds or double string quartet (1931); *Piano Concerto No. 1* (1931); *36 Greek Dances* for orchestra (1933–36, some published by UE); *Sonatina No. 3* for violin, piano (1935); *Sonatina No. 4* for violin, piano (1935, SSF); *9 Greek Dances* for large wind orchestra; transcribed from the 36 Greek Dances (1936); *Piano Trio* (1936); *Piano Suite No. 1* (1936); *Scherzo* for piano, 3 strings (1936); *March of the Little Soldiers* for violin, piano (1936); *Rondo* for violin, piano (1936); *Little Chorale and Fugue* for violin, piano (1936); *10 Canons* for piano (1936); *Piano Concerto No. 2* (1937–38); *Cello Concerto* (1937–38); *Sometime* for voice, piano (1938, UE); *8 Variations on a Greek Theme* for piano, violin, cello (1938, UE); *The Maid and Death*, ballet suite (1938); *Violin Concerto* (1938, UE); *Suite* for cello, piano (1938); *Cello Sonata* (1938); *9 Greek Dances* for string quartet; transcribed from the 36 Greek Dances (1938–47); *Piano Concerto No. 3* for piano, 10 winds, percussion (1939, UE and SSF); *Concertino* for oboe, piano (1939); *Gavotta* for violin, piano (1939); *Scherzo and Menuetto cantato* for violin, piano (1939); *Duo* for violin, viola (1939–40, UE); *Concerto* for violin, viola, large wind orchestra (1939–40, SSF); *String Quartet No. 4* (1940, UE); *Violin Sonata No. 2* (1940, SSF); *10 Sketches* for string quartet or string orchestra (1940, UE); *Double Bass Concerto* (1940); *Largo* for cello, piano (1940, UE); *Music for Piano Solo*, 32 pieces (1940, some published by UE); *Piano Suite No. 2* (1940, UE); *The Moon* for voice, piano (1940); *Piano Suite No. 3* (1940, UE); *Piano Suite No. 4* (1940, UE);

4 Etudes for piano (1940); *16 Songs* for voice, piano; poems by Chrysos Evelpidis (1941); *Quartet No. 1* for piano, winds (1941–43, SSF); *Quartet No. 2* for piano, winds (1941–43, SSF); *Concertino* for trumpet, piano (1941–43, SSF); *Little Suite* for string orchestra (1942, UE); *Sonate concertante* for bassoon, piano (1943, SSF); *Symphonic Suite No. 2* in 6 movements (1942–44, UE and SSF); *6 Greek Dances* for violin, piano; transcribed from the 36 Greek Dances (1940–47); *The Mayday Spell*, fairy drama for narrator, soprano, dancers, orchestra (1944–49, UE); *The Return of Ulysses*, symphony in 1 movement (1944–45, SSF); *Concerto* for 2 violins, orchestra (1944–45); *Little Suite No. 1* for violin, piano (1946, UE); *5 Short Greek Dances* for orchestra (1946); *Echo*, short ballet for harp (1947); *Classical Symphony in A* for wind orchestra (1947); *Duo* for violin, cello (1947, UE); *Sinfonietta in B Flat* (1948); *Ballet Suite*, 4 rural scenes (1948); *Bolero* for cello, piano (1948–49, UE); *The Sea*, ballet in 11 scenes (1949); *Concertino in C* for piano, orchestra (1949); *Little Serenade* for cello, piano (1949); *Sonatina* for cello, piano (1949, UE); *Tender Melody* for cello, piano (1949, UE); *Little Suite No. 2* for violin, piano (1949, SSF); Complete list in Papaioannou 1969 (see bibl.).

PRINCIPAL WRITINGS: *The Technique of Orchestration* in Greek (1940, unpub.). There are also articles on musical life in Germany, published in various Greek journals (principally 1928–32), as well as program notes and introductions to the composer's own works.

BIBL.: G. Hadjinikos, "N. S., a Greek Composer," *Listener* (29 Jan 1966); Hans Keller, "N. S., an Original Genius," *Listener* (9 Dec 1954); F. Anoyanakis, "I Moussiki stin neoteri Hellada" [Music in Modern Greece], a supplement to *Historia tis Moussikis* [History of Music] by Karl Nef (Athens 1958):547–611; A. Orga, "S., Shadowy Figure of Greek Music," *Music and Musicians* (July 1969); John G. Papaioannou, "N. S.," *Archives of Eubean Studies* (1954); ——, "N. S.," *European Music in the Twentieth Century* ed. by H. Hartog (London 1957); ——, "N. S.'s Twentieth Anniversary," *Archives of Eubean Studies* (1969).

John G. Papaioannou

SEE ALSO Greece.

Skepton, Howard (While) (b. Chester, England, 31 Oct 1947), studied piano and composition privately with Thomas Wess (1964–66) and composition with Cornelius Cardew (1967–68). He attended Ealing Technical College (1967–70, music history with Donald Cashmore and Paul Davis) and Morley College (from 1968, experimental music with Cornelius Cardew). He has been particularly influenced by Anton Webern, Morton Feldman, the artist David Hockney, and the music programing of the BBC.

PRINCIPAL COMPOSITIONS (available from Experimental): *A Humming Song* for piano (1967); *For Strings* for any stringed instrument(s) (1969); *Waltz for Piano* (1970); *2 Highland Dances* for piano (1970).

SEE ALSO Great Britain.

Slavický, Klement (b. Tovačov, Moravia, Czechoslovakia, 22 Sept 1910), studied with his father, a pupil of Janáček, and attended the Prague Conservatory (1927–35; composition with Karel B. Jirák, Josef Suk; conducting with Pavel Dědeček, Václav Talich). During 1936–51 he was music director of the Czech Radio in Prague. Since 1951 he has taught theory privately and has worked as a free-lance composer.

PRINCIPAL COMPOSITIONS (published by Supraphon unless otherwise noted): *Fantasia* for piano, orchestra (1931, unpub.); *Moravian Dance Fantasies* for orchestra (1931); *Wind Trio* (1937); *Symphonietta* for orchestra (1940); *Zpěv rodné semě* [Songs of My Native Country] for tenor, piano (1942); *Lidice* for double men's chorus (1945); *3 Compositions* for piano (1947); *Rhapsodic Variations* for orchestra (1953); *Ej, srdenko moje* [O, My Heart], songs for voice, piano; Moravian folk texts (1954); *Frescos* for organ (1957); *Piano Sonata*, "Zamyšlení nad životem" [Contemplation of Life] (1958); *Suite* for oboe, piano (1959); *Madrigals* for chorus; folk texts (1959, Panton); *Symphonietta No. 2* for orchestra (1962, unpub.); *Invocation* for organ (1963, Panton); *Partita* for violin (1963, Panton); *Intermezzi mattutini* for flute, harp (1965, Panton); *Etudes and Essays* for piano (1965, Panton); *Trialogo* for violin, clarinet, piano (1966, Panton); *Capricci* for horn, piano (1967).

SEE ALSO Czechoslovakia.

Slonimsky, Nicolas (b. St. Petersburg, 27 April 1894), attended the St. Petersburg Conservatory (1908–15, piano with Isabelle Vengerova, theory with V. Kalafati, orchestration with M. Steinberg). He toured Europe as pianist and accompanist (1920–23) and then settled in the U.S. He was on the faculty of the Eastman School (1923–25), served as secretary to Serge Koussevitzky in Boston (1925–27), and directed the Boston Chamber Orchestra (1927–34) and the Harvard Univ. Orchestra (1928–30). He also conducted programs of modern music of the Americas in New York (1931–34), Paris (1931–32), Berlin, Budapest and Los Angeles (1932), Havana and Hollywood (1933), Rio de Janeiro (1941), and Guatemala City (1942), presenting orchestral

works (including premieres) by Ives, Cowell, Riegger, Varèse, Chávez, etc. He has taught at several schools including Simmons College in Boston (1947–49), the Peabody Conservatory (1956–57), and the Univ. of Calif. at Los Angeles (1964–67). In 1958 he was appointed a member of the music panel for the State Dept. Office of Cultural Exchange, and in 1962–63 he traveled and lectured under the auspices of the U.S. government in Russia, eastern Europe, Greece, and Israel. His early compositions show the influence of Russian romanticism and from about 1919, impressionism. His experimental music began in 1926. In his *Studies in Black and White* for piano (1928), he limited himself to "consonant intervals in unrelated harmonic systems, with the right hand playing on the white keys and the left on the black keys only, resulting in a species of polytonal atonality." He also developed a system of "tonal dodecaphony, using four mutually exclusive triads (e.g., C major, D minor, F♯ major, G♯ minor)," and introduced the term *pandiatonicism* to denote the free use of all seven diatonic scale degrees. *My Toy Balloon* (1942) calls for 100 balloons to be exploded in the final sforzando. *Möbius Strip Tease* is a "perpetual rondo in a linearly dodecaphonic, vertically consonant counterpoint, notated on Möbius bands to be rotated around the singers' heads."

PRINCIPAL COMPOSITIONS: *Russian Prelude* for piano (1914, Shawnee); *5 Advertising Songs* for voice, piano (1925); *Impressions* for voice, piano (1927, Shawnee); *I Owe a Debt to a Monkey* for voice, piano (1928, Shawnee); *Studies in Black and White* for piano (1928, New Music); *4 Picturesque Pieces for Ambitious Young Pianists* (1931, Shawnee); *Overture on an Ancient Greek Theme*, in an enharmonic mode (1933); *Aroma de Leyenda* for violin, piano (1934); *Silhouettes ibériennes* for piano (1934, Shawnee); *Moto perpetuo* for violin, piano (1936); *4 Russian Melodies* for clarinet, piano (1937, Leeds); *4 Simple Pieces for Small Orchestra* (1938, Coleman-Ross, N.Y.); *Little Suite* for flute, oboe, clarinet, percussion, portable typewriter, cat's meow (1941, Coleman-Ross); *My Toy Balloon*, variations on a Brazilian theme for orchestra, 100 balloons (1942, Shawnee); *Gravestones at Hancock, N. H.* for voice, piano (1945, Shawnee); *Suite* for cello, piano (1950); *Yellowstone Park Suite* for piano (1951, Shawnee); *Möbius Strip Tease* for soprano, tenor (1965). List to 1965: *Composers of the Americas* 15:210–13.

PRINCIPAL WRITINGS: *Music Since 1900* (New York 1937, 4th ed. 1971); *Music of Latin America* (New York 1945); *Thesaurus of Scales and Melodic Patterns* (New York 1947, 1969); *The Road to Music* (New York 1947); *Lexicon of Musical Invective* (New York 1953, 1969). Slonimsky has also edited the 5th–8th editions of *Oscar Thomp-son's International Encyclopedia of Music and Musicians* (1946–58) and the 5th edition of *Baker's Biographical Dictionary of Musicians* (1958, supplements 1965, 1971).

BIBL.: Henry Cowell, "N. S., Analysis of an Unfamiliar Modern Composer," *Singing and Playing* (August 1928); ——, "N. S.," *American Composers on American Music* (New York 1960): 107–09; David Ewen, *American Composers Today* (New York 1949); H. H. Stuckenschmidt, *Neue Musik* (Berlin 1951).

Slonimsky, Sergei (Mikhailovich) (b. Lenin-grad, 12 August 1932), studied at the Central Music School in Moscow (1943–45, compo-sition with Vissarion Shebalin), the Leningrad Music School (1945–50, composition with B. Arapov, piano with S. Savshinsky), and the Leningrad Conservatory (1950–55, compo-sition with O. Evlakhov, piano with V. N. Il'sen, choral techniques with M. Uspensky). He has taught composition at the Leningrad Conservatory since 1958 and has also lectured on contemporary music and folk music. His own music has been influenced by his folk-music collecting trips, especially the techniques of improvisation in folk music, by his parti-cipation in festivals of the U.S.S.R. Com-posers' Union and the Warsaw Autumn festi-vals (1962, 1966, 1969), and by the Moscow Dramatic Theater and the Theater on the Taganka, two contemporary theaters in Moscow.

PRINCIPAL COMPOSITIONS: *Carnival Overture* (1957, SC); *Symphony* (1958, SC); *Viola Sonata* (1959, SC); *Romances* for mezzo-soprano, piano; Japanese texts (1959, Muzyka); *Pesni vol'nitsy* [Songs of Free Men] for mezzo-soprano, baritone, orchestra; Russian folk texts (1960); *Sonata* for solo violin (1961, Muzyka); *Piano Sonata* (1962, Muzyka); *Golos iz khora* [A Voice from the Choir], cantata for vocal solosits, chamber orchestra, organ; text based on Alexander Blok (1962); *Pol'skie strofy* [Polish Verses], song cycle for soprano, flute; texts by Antonni Slonimsky (1963); *Khoreograficheskie miniatiury* [Choreographic Min-iatures] for orchestra, on motifs of Picasso, Rodin, and Botticelli (1963); *Liricheskie strofy* [Lyric Verses], song cycle for voice, piano; texts by Evgenii Rein (1964); *Dialogi* for woodwind quintet (1964); *Concerto buffo* (1965, Muzyka); *Proshchan'e s drugom v pustyne* [Parting from a Friend in the Desert], song cycle for voice, piano; text based on the Gilgamesh legend (1966, Muzyka); *Mono-logi*, song cycle for soprano, oboe, horn, harp; ancient Hebrew poem (1967); *Virineia*, 2-part opera; libretto by S. Tsenin after Lidya Seifullinoi (premiered 1967, Muzyka); *Antiphonies* for string quartet (1968); *Ikar* [Icarus], ballet; scenario by Iu. Slonimsky, choreography by Iu. Grigorovich

and V. Vasil'ev (1969); *Chromatic Poem* for organ (1969); *Romances* for soprano, piano; texts by Anna Akhmatova (1969).

PRINCIPAL WRITINGS: "Za tvorcheskuiu druzh-bu" [For Creative Friendship (on young com-posers)], *Sovetskaia muzyka* 1963/11; "Pesn' o semle Malera i voprosy oskestrovoi polifonii" [Mahler's "Songs of a Wayfarer" and Problems of Orchestral Polyphony], *Voprosy sovremennoi muzyki* [Problems in Contemporary Music] (Leningrad 1964); "Simfonii prokofeva," *ibid.*; "Pobeda 'Stenku Razina'" ["The Victory of Stenka Razin" (Shostakovich)], *Sovetskaia muzyka* 1965/4; "Iskusstvo divoe sovremennoe" [Art Magnificent and Contemporary (on Rimsky-Korsakov)], *ibid.* 1969/3; "Varshavakaia osen'" [Warsaw Autumn 1969], *ibid.* 1970/1.

BIBL.: M. Tapakanov, "Talant rasvitii" [Devel-oping Talent], *Sovetskaia muzyka* 1965/10.

SEE ALSO Soviet Union.

Smit, Leo (b. Philadelphia, 12 Jan 1921), attended the Curtis Institute (1930–32, piano with Isabelle Vengerova) and studied com-position with Nicolas Nabokov in 1935. He was pianist with George Balanchine's Ameri-can Ballet in 1936–37 and with the New York City Symphony in 1947–48. He made his piano debut at Carnegie Hall in 1939. He was administrator of artists and repertory for Concert Hall Society Records in 1947 and during 1947–49 taught at Sarah Lawrence College. From 1957 to 1963 he taught at the Univ. of Calif. at Los Angeles and during 1959–63, served on the board of directors for Monday Evening Concerts in Los Angeles. He has taught at the State Univ. of N. Y. at Buffalo since 1962. In 1967–68 he made a U.S. State Dept. tour of Latin America, playing American contemporary music. Of special significance to Smit has been his con-tact with Stravinsky (in 1936 when he was assisting George Balanchine), Copland, and the astronomer Fred Hoyle, with whom he collaborated on the opera *The Alchemy of Love*.

PRINCIPAL COMPOSITIONS (published by Mills unless otherwise noted): *Virginia Sampler*, ballet (1947); *A Choir of Starlings* for 4 solo voices, 10 instruments; text by A. Hecht (1951); *Symphony No. 1* (1956); *Academic Graffiti* for voice, clarinet, cello, piano, percussion; text by W. H. Auden (1959); *Symphony No. 2* (1965); *Piano Concerto* (1968, unpub.); *The Alchemy of Love*, 3-act opera; libretto by Fred Hoyle (1969, Belwin).

Smith, Julia (b. Denton, Texas, 25 Jan 1911), attended schools in Texas and later studied at the Juilliard School (1930–32, 1933–39;

piano with Lonny Epstein, Carl Friedberg; composition with Rubin Goldmark, Frederick Jacobi; orchestration with Bernard Wagenaar) and at New York Univ. (1932–33, 1947–52; composition with Marion Bauer). She taught theory and counterpoint at the Juilliard School (1940–42) and during 1944–46 was on the faculty of New Britain State Teachers' College in Conn. She was founder and head of the department of music education at Hartt College of Music (1941–46). She is now a free-lance composer, pianist, and author.

PRINCIPAL COMPOSITIONS: *American Dance Suite* for orchestra (1935–36; revised 1962–63, Presser) or 2 pianos (1938; revised 1964, Mowbray); *Episodic Suite* for piano (1935, Flammer and Mowbray) or orchestra (1936, Presser; chamber orchestra version for ballet, 1966, Presser); *Cynthia Parker*, 2-act opera (1935–38, revised 1943–45); *Piano Concerto* (1938–39; revised 1969–70, Presser); *Hellenic Suite* for orchestra (1940–41, Presser); *The Stranger of Manzano*, 1-act opera (1941–43); *Overture and Mexican Dances from the "Stranger of Manzano"* for orchestra (1942–43, Presser); *2 Pieces* for viola, piano (1944, Mowbray); *The Gooseherd and the Goblin*, 1-act opera (1945–46, Presser); *Sonatine in C* for piano (1943–44, Mowbray); *Folkways Symphony* (1947–48, Fischer); *Characteristic Suite* for piano (1949, Mowbray); *3 Love Songs*, poems by Karl Flaster (1953–55, Mowbray); *Cockcrow*, 1-act opera (1952–53, Presser); *Trio-Cornwall* for piano trio (1955, Mowbray); *Our Heritage* for chorus, piano (1956, Flammer; versions for chorus with large orchestra, small orchestra, or band, Flammer); *The Shepherdess and the Chimneysweep*, 1-act Christmas opera (1962–63, Presser); *String Quartet* (1962–64, Mowbray); *Remember the Alamo* for narrator, chorus, band; in collaboration with Cecile Vashaw (1964, Presser); *Sails Aloft*, overture for band; in collaboration with Cecile Vashaw (1965, Mowbray). She has also written *Work and Play*, a string method, in collaboration with Cecile Vashaw (begun 1959, Presser) and many other pieces for school use.

PRINCIPAL WRITINGS: *Aaron Copland* (New York 1955); "Composers' Lives," *Music Journal* 14/8: 19, 38; program notes on American composers for the National Association of American Composers and Conductors concerts (New York 1953, 1954); *Master Pianist: The Career and Teaching of Carl Friedberg* (New York 1963); *A Directory of American Women Composers* (Chicago, National Federation of Music Clubs, 1970).

BIBL.: Exie Burford, "Piano Keys Career—J. S.," *Music Clubs Magazine* (May 1956):17; M. Craig, "Composer and Ambassadress of U.S. Music," *Musical Courier* (July 1959):7.

Smith, Russell (b. Tuscaloosa, Ala., 23 April 1927), studied at Columbia Univ. (1948–53). He taught in New York at Queens College (1960–61) and at Hunter College (1962–64). He was editor and production manager at G. Ricordi in New York during 1961–65 and at H. W. Gray, 1965–66. Under grants from the Rockefeller Foundation, he has been composer-in-residence for the Cleveland Orchestra (1966–67) and the New Orleans Philharmonic (1969–70). During 1967–69 he taught at the Univ. of Ala. He has contributed articles and criticism to several newspapers and magazines. His works include over 20 songs and music for films and TV.

PRINCIPAL COMPOSITIONS: *Eclogue* for violin, piano (1949); *Duo and Fugue* for woodwind quintet (1949); *Antigone*, ballet for the Charles Weidman Dance Theater (1949); *Piano Concerto No. 1* (1953); *Anglican Mass* for chorus (1954, Ricordi; published under the title *Service in G*; *Gloria* also published separately); *The Unicorn in the Garden*, 1-act opera (1956, Schirmer); *Piano Concerto No. 2* (1957); *Tetrameron* for orchestra (1957, Peters); *Palatine Songs* for high voice, chamber orchestra; classical Greek texts (1956); *3 Chorale Preludes* for organ (1957, Gray); *Can-Can and Waltz* for orchestra (1958, Peters); *Divertimento* for orchestra (1958); *Piano Preludes* (1962); *Nocturne* for string choir (1967).

Smith Brindle, Reginald (b. Bamber Bridge, Lancaster, England, 5 Jan 1917), attended the Univ. College of North Wales in Bangor (1946–49) and the Accadèmia di S. Cecilia in Rome (1949–52, composition with Ildebrando Pizzetti). He studied composition privately with Luigi Dallapiccola in Florence in 1949 and 1952–53. During 1956–61 he worked for the Italian radio's third program. He taught at Bangor Univ. during 1967–70 and has since been professor at the Univ. of Surrey. He has been especially influenced in his composition by such Italian composers as Berio, Maderna, Nono, and Donatoni.

PRINCIPAL COMPOSITIONS (published by Peters): *Symphonic Variations* (1957); *Cosmos* for orchestra (1959); *Concerto* for flute, clarinet, vibraphone, harp, piano, percussion (1960); *Homage to H. G. Wells* for orchestra (1960); *Via Crucis* for string orchestra (1960); *Genesis Dream* for low or medium woman's voice, chamber orchestra; text by Dylan Thomas (1962); *Creation Epic*, choreographic suite for orchestra (1964); *Amalgam* for mezzo-soprano, piano, electronic organ, 4 percussion (1968); *Antigone*, chamber opera for narrator, mezzo-soprano, bass, flute, trombone, violin, viola, double bass, pianos, percussion (1969); *Apocalypse* for orchestra (1970).

PRINCIPAL WRITINGS: *Serial Composition* (London 1966); *Contemporary Percussion* (London

1970). Smith Brindle has also written articles for *Musical Quarterly*, *Musical Times*, *Rassegna musicale*, and other periodicals.

Solares, Enrique (b. Guatemala City, 11 July 1910), studied at the National Conservatory in Guatemala City (1933–35; piano with Salvador Ley, Raul Paniagua) and the Royal Conservatory in Brussels (1936, counterpoint with Raymond Moulaert). He also studied composition privately with Jaroslav Křička in Prague (1936–39) and Alfredo Casella in Rome (1939–42). During 1943–48 he taught piano both privately and at the National Conservatory in Guatemala City. He was music director of the Guatemala City radio station TGW from 1945 to 1946. Since 1948 he has been in the Guatemalan diplomatic service, serving in the embassies at Rome, Brussels, Madrid, and Paris. He eschews folk music as a source of musical inspiration, preferring instead the contemporary concert music of Europe. He did not compose during the mid-1960s but thereafter began working with 12-tone procedures (as evidenced in *Microtransparencia*).

PRINCIPAL COMPOSITIONS: *Suite miniatura* (1938, orchestrated 1943); *Ricercare sobre el nombre BACH* for string orchestra (1941); *Suite* for violin, piano (1941, 1946, 1948); *Te Deum* for 3 soloists, organ (1943); *Pater noster* for chorus (1944); *Toccatina* for guitar (1946, Metropolis); *Estudio en forma de marcha* for piano (1946, Marks); *Partita* for string orchestra (1946–47, revised 1957; PAU); *Partita clásica* for string orchestra (1947); *4 Preludes* for piano (1949–50); *5 Ricercari* for piano (1949–52); *Copok* for piano (1950, E-V); *Suite* for piano (1952–53); *4 Disparates* for piano (1953–55); *Suite* for cello, piano (1956?); *Cosecha de amistad*, 5 songs for voice, piano (1957); *Sonata* for solo violin (1958); *4 Piezas breves* for orchestra (1958–62); *Ofrenda a Fernando Sor* for guitar (1959, Metropolis); *Fantasia* for guitar (1959, Metropolis); *Quartet* for strings, bass voice; text by Miguel Angel Asturias (1959); *Idea con 15 deformaciones* for piano (1962); *7 Travesuras* for piano (1968–69); *12 Microtransparencias* for piano (1969–70); *Vals-Fantasía on Op. 66 of Chopin* for piano (1970). List to 1959: *Composers of the Americas* 4:155–64.

Sollberger, Harvey (b. Cedar Rapids, Iowa, 11 May 1938), attended the Univ. of Iowa (1956–60), where he studied composition and flute, and Columbia Univ., where he studied composition with Jack Beeson and Otto Luening (MA, 1964). He has been codirector of the Group for Contemporary Music, a performance group at Columbia, since 1962 and has taught at the University since 1965. He is active as a flutist and conductor.

Although many of Sollberger's works are not 12-tone, they have all been strongly affected by his contact with the 12-tone system as developed by Milton Babbitt. During the early 1960s he moved away from classically oriented 12-tone procedures. The cantata *Musica transalpina* (1964–70) and the song *To the Hawks* (1969) make use of a time-point system and of registral, timbral, and dynamic partitioning of set elements along lines familiar in Babbitt, Donald Martino, Peter Westergaard, and others. *Chamber Variations* (1964) and *Impromptu* for piano (1968) embody a less "systematic" approach and appear to be affected by contact with the gestural-contextual practices of Elliott Carter and Stefan Wolpe, in which types of musical activity (speeds, textures, phrase shapes, registral contours, timbral and articulative behavior, etc.) are the basic units of progression and often function on a par with pitch-unfolding in determining large form. The most recent works involve control of local pitch and durational events on the basis of the proportional relations embodied in the intervals of sets, which are extended over the duration of an entire work.

PRINCIPAL COMPOSITIONS: *2 Pieces for 2 Flutes* (1958, revised 1962; McG-M); *Grand Quartet for Flutes* (1962, McG-M); *Solos for Violin and 5 Instruments* (1962, McG-M); *Chamber Variations for 12 Players and Conductor* (1964, McG-M); *Music for Sophocles' "Antigone"* for narrator, electronic sounds on tape (1966, ACA); *Impromptu* for piano (1968, CFE); *For No Clear Reason* for soprano, piano (1969, CFE); *2 Motets from Musica transalpina* (1970, CFE); *Divertimento for Flute, Cello, and Piano* (1970, CFE); *As Things Are and Become* for string trio (1971, CFE).

PRINCIPAL WRITINGS: "Mel Powell: Haiku Settings," a review, *Perspectives* 3/1:147–55; "Footnote to Stravinsky," *Perspectives* 5/1:148–52; "A Flutist Looks at New Sounds for Woodwind by Bruno Bartolozzi," *Contemporary Music Newsletter* (New York, Oct 1968).

BIBL.: Kurt Stone, "Review of Records," re *Chamber Variations*, *Musical Quarterly* 52:541–43.

Charles Wuorinen

SEE ALSO Performance, United States.

Somers, Harry (Stewart) (b. Toronto, 11 Sept 1925), studied composition with John Weinzweig (Toronto 1945–49) and Darius Milhaud (Paris 1949–50) and piano with Reginald

Godden (Toronto 1942–43) and E. Robert
Schmitz (San Francisco 1947). In the early
1950s he taught himself guitar, and he has
occasionally played the instrument professionally. During the 1950s he earned his living
as a cab driver and later as a music copyist.
In the 1960s he was commentator on various
new-music series over CBC radio and television, and in 1968–69 he was composer-
consultant to the North York Board of
Education in suburban Toronto, working with
children and teenagers in classroom music
situations. Since about 1960 he has earned his
living primarily as a free-lance composer.

Somers's large output includes two operas,
three ballets, two symphonies, two concertos,
and other orchestral works, three string quartets, sonatas and other chamber music, many
songs, choral works, piano pieces, folk-music
arrangements, and incidental scores for stage,
radio, television, and films. He has worked in
the Univ. of Toronto electronic music studio,
but up to 1970 only one composition (the
opera *Louis Riel*) had incorporated tape
materials. Most of Somers's music uses 12-
tone procedures, but this aspect of his style
is less interesting than others. He feels that
12-tone techniques cannot convey lighter
qualities of expression in music, and in a
number of scores from the mid-1950s he juxtaposed tonal and dodecaphonic materials (opposing them on different planes simultaneously,
almost à la Charles Ives) in contexts that seem
to equate the tonal with good and the dodecaphonic with evil. Examples are the slow
movement of the *Violin Sonata No. 1* and a
passage from *Ballad*, a ballet about frontier
life in Alberta, in which the tonal factor is
represented by the 19th-century hymn tune,
"Abide With Me."

Somers's orchestral works of the early
1960s contain many original features, especially *Movement* (originally titled *Abstract for
Television* and written to a preconceived
scenario of TV camera shots showing orchestral musicians in performance), *5 Concepts*
(each movement being derived from a single
kind of orchestral treatment, such as ornamentation or opposed dynamic levels), and
Stereophony (in which the orchestra is seated
around a large hall on three levels). Two trade-
marks, traceable from the late 1940s, are a
nervous quirk (of pain?) consisting of a
motive of two short notes, the first accented,
that is often associated with the interval of
a falling semitone; and long-lined slow melodies that develop gradually into sustained
musical shapes, without closed or sectional
phrases. The latter are often associated with

a thin, even monophonic texture, but, as in
baroque music, they are frequently rich in
expressive melodic embellishment. In the later
1960s much of Somers's creative interest
shifted to the human voice. In *Louis Riel* there
is a fascination with intricate timbral effects
in often unaccompanied solo voices. His work
with young people has led him into more
improvisational areas of musical thought, and
in 1969 he expressed a wish to free himself
from the dictatorial role implied in conventional, precisely notated music.

PRINCIPAL COMPOSITIONS: *Piano Sonata No. 2*
(1946); *Scherzo* for string orchestra (1947, AMP);
Rhapsody for violin, piano (1948); *North Country*
for string orchestra (1948, Berandol); *Suite* for
harp, chamber orchestra (1949, Berandol); *String
Quartet No. 2* (1950); *Piano Sonata No. 3* (1950);
Piano Sonata No. 4 (1950); *Trio* for flute, violin,
cello (1950); *Symphony No. 1* (1951, Berandol);
12 × 12, 12 fugues for piano (1951, Berandol);
The Fool, opera in 2 scenes; libretto by Michael
Fram (1953); *Violin Sonata No. 1* (1953, Beran-
dol); *Passacaglia and Fugue* for orchestra (1954,
Berandol); *2 Songs for the Coming of Spring* for
chorus (1955, Berandol); *Violin Sonata No. 2*
(1955, Berandol); *5 Songs for Dark Voice* for alto,
chamber orchestra; text by Fram (1956); *Piano
Concerto No. 2* (1956); *The Fisherman and His
Soul*, ballet; choreography by Grant Strate (1956);
Piano Sonata No. 5 (1957); *Fantasia* for orchestra
(1958, Berandol); *Ballad*, ballet; choreography by
Strate (1958); *String Quartet No. 3* (1958); *Sonata*
for guitar (1959); *Lyric* for orchestra (1960,
Berandol); *Movement* for orchestra (1961, Ricordi); *5 Concepts for Orchestra* (1961, Berandol);
Stereophony for orchestra (1962); *The House of
Atreus*, ballet; choreography by Strate (1964);
12 Miniatures for soprano, flute, cello, harpsichord; Haiku texts translated by Henderson (1965,
Berandol); *Evocations* for mezzo-soprano, piano;
text by the composer (1966, Berandol); *Louis Riel*,
2-act opera; libretto by Mavor Moore and Jacques
Languirand (1967); *Kuyas* for soprano, flute, percussion; adapted from *Louis Riel* (1967); *Improvisation* for narrator with unspecified number of
strings, woodwinds, voices, piano, percussion
(1968); *Voiceplay* for singer-actor (male or female,
any range) (1971). Other (more complete) lists:
Composers of the Americas 5:80–84; *H. S.*
(Toronto: BMIC, 1969); *Musicanada* (1967); and
Olnick.

BIBL.: J. Beckwith, "Composers in Toronto and
Montreal," *Univ. of Toronto Quarterly* 26:47–69;
"Composer in the School: A Composer's View,"
Musicanada (May 1969):7–9, 13–16; "H. S.: A
Portrait," *Musicanada* (Sept 1967):8–9; E.
McLean, "*Riel* for Real—Important Début,"
Montreal Star (28 Oct 1967); H. Olnick, "H. S.,"
Canadian Music Journal (summer 1959):3–23;
H. Rosenthal, review of *Louis Riel*, *Opera* (London
Nov 1967):865–67.

John Beckwith

SEE ALSO Canada.

Sommer, Vladimír (b. Dolní Jeřetín, Czechoslovakia, 28 Feb 1921), attended the Prague Conservatory (1942–46, composition with Karel Janeček) and the Prague Academy of Music (1946–50, composition with Pavel Bořkovec). He was music director of Radio Prague during 1952–53 and secretary of the Guild of Czech Composers, 1953–56. He wrote music criticism for the journal *Kultura* during 1957–58 and has taught at Charles Univ. in Prague since 1960. In addition to the works listed below, he has composed several theater, film, and television scores. Honegger and Prokofiev were the principal influences on his early development.

PRINCIPAL COMPOSITIONS: *Sonata* for 2 violins (1948, Panton) or for violin, viola (1968); *Violin Concerto* (1950, Artia); *String Quartet No. 2* (1955, Artia; arranged as *Music for String Orchestra*, 1968); *Je nám dobře na zemi . . .* [We are doing fine . . .], 7 songs for children's chorus, piano or small orchestra (1955, ČMF); *Antigone*, overture for orchestra (1957, Artia); *Vocal Symphony* (Symphony No. 1) for mezzo-soprano, speaker, chorus, orchestra; texts by Kafka, Dostoevsky, Pavese (1958; revised 1963, Panton); *Cello Concerto* (1959); *Černý Muž* [The Black Man], tone poem for tenor, bass, orchestra; poem by Serge Jesenin (1964); *String Quartet No. 3* (1965); *Symphony No. 2*, "Anno mundi ardenti," for string orchestra, piano, tympani (1968); *Sinfonia concertante* (Symphony No. 3) for 2 violins, viola, cello, chamber orchestra (1969).

PRINCIPAL WRITINGS: "V. S. o hudbě těchto dní" [V. S. on Present-day Music], *Literární noviny* 49 (1958); "S. V. S. o hudbě a komponování" [With V. S. about His Music and Composing], *Hudební rozhledy* 1970/1:24–27. Sommer also prepared the official Czech translation of Honegger's *Je suis compositeur*.

BIBL.: Jaroslav Jiránek, "Od písňové momentky k symfonické konfliktnosti (z tvůrčí dílny V. S.)" [From Brief Songs to Conflicting Processes of Symphonic Development (From the Workshop of V. S.)], *Umění rozezpívat myšlenku—pokus o intonači analyzu* [The Art of Development of Musical Ideas] (Prague 1965):162–236; Ivan Vojtěch, "O dosavadní tvorbě V. S." [V. S.'s Music to Date], *Musikologie* 4 (1955):32–86.

SEE ALSO Czechoslovakia.

Sønstevold, Gunnar (b. Elverum, Norway, 26 Nov 1912), studied privately in Oslo while still young with Nils Larsen (piano), Oscar Holst (violin), and Johs. Hansen and Karl Andersen (theory). During 1941–43 he studied conducting at the Musilhögskolan and theory privately with Hilding Rosenberg in Stockholm. He attended the Vienna Music Academy during 1960–67 (sociology of music, 12-tone techniques), and during 1962–66 worked intermittently at the Studio for Electronic Music in Vienna. He has performed professionally in a variety of situations from night clubs to concert halls and has written many scores for films, radio, television, and theater. Since 1966 he has been head of the music division of Norwegian Television.

PRINCIPAL COMPOSITIONS (available from Norsk; dates are of first performance): *Sinfonietta* (1949); *Duo* for flute, oboe (1949); *Bendik og Årolilja*, ballet (1959); *String Quartets Nos. 1–2* (1960, No. 2 undated); *Saxophone Concerto* (1962); *Concerto for flute, bassoon, orchestra* (1964); *Ritual*, ballet; choreography by John Butler (1967); *Quadri* for harp, piano, 2 percussionists (1967); *Arnold*, a work for "beat" musicians (1970); *Intermezzo* for soprano, violin, tape (undated).

Soro, Enrique (b. Concepción, Chile, 15 July 1884; d. Santiago, 2 Dec 1954), studied piano with his father, José Soro-Sforza, until 1898, then attended the Milan Conservatory under a scholarship from the Chilean government (1898–1904), where he worked with Luigi Mapelli, Gaetano Coronaro, and Guglielmo Andreoli. He taught piano and composition and later harmony and counterpoint at the National Conservatory in Santiago (1905–28) and was its director during 1919–28 (he was deprived of his post when the Conservatory was reorganized). In 1942 he became a technical adviser to the board of directors of the Instituto de Extensión Musical of the Univ. of Chile, serving in that capacity until his death.

PRINCIPAL COMPOSITIONS: *String Quartet in A* (1903); *Andante appassionato* for orchestra (1915, Schirmer-G); *Danza fantástica* for orchestra (1916); *Impresiones líricas* for piano, orchestra (1919); *Piano Concerto in D* (1919, Ricordi); *Piano Quintet in B Minor* (1919, Evette); *Sinfonía romántica* (1920); *Piano Sonata No. 1 in C♯ Minor* (1920, Schirmer-G); *Violin Sonata No. 2 in A Minor* (premiere 1921, Schirmer-G); *Piano Trio in G Minor* (1926, Schirmer-G); *3 Symphonic Preludes* for orchestra (1936); *3 Chilean Airs* for orchestra (premiere 1942); *Piano Sonata No. 3 in D* (1942); *Suite en estilo antiguo* for orchestra (premiere 1943); *Cello Sonata in E Minor* (1947). Complete list: *Composers of the Americas* 1:97–103.

BIBL.: *Revista musical chilena* (August 1948); Vicente Salas-Viú, *La creación musical en Chile, 1900–1951* (Santiago c.1952); Robert Stevenson, "La música chilena en la época de Santa Cruz," *Boletín interamericano de música* (Sept 1968):7–8.

SEE ALSO Chile.

Sound, see Texture

Souris, André (b. Marchienne-au-pont, Belgium, 10 July 1899; d. Paris, 12 Feb 1970), studied at the Brussels Royal Conservatory (1911–18; harmony with Martin Lunssens; fugue, Léon Dubois; orchestration, Paul Gilson; music history, Ernest Closson; conducting, Hermann Scherchen). He was a free-lance composer. He also conducted the orchestra of the Belgian Radio-Television Network during 1937–46. He was director of the music studio of the Seminary of the Arts in Brussels (1944–48) and of the Marchienne-au-pont Academy of Music (1949). He taught harmony at the Conservatories of Charleroi and Brussels in 1949. In 1947 he founded the journal *Polyphonies* in Paris, with which he was associated until 1954. He was president of the Belgian section of ISCM, 1946–58.

PRINCIPAL COMPOSITIONS: *3 Japanese Poems* for voice, string quartet, piano (1916); *Berceuse* for violin, piano (1924); *Choral, Marche, et Galop* for 2 trumpets, 2 trombones (1925, CBDM); *Avertissement* for 3 narrators, percussion (1926); *Airs de Clarisse Juranville* for voice, instruments (1928); *Je le connais* for voice, piano; text by Paul Mougé (1928); *Renaissance Dances* for orchestra (1932); *Fatrasie* for violin, piano (1934, CBDM); *Hommage à Babeuf* for wind orchestra 1934); *Rengaines* for wind quintet (1937, Leduc); *Symphonies* for orchestra (1939); *Comptines pour enfants sinistres* for soprano, mezzo-soprano, clarinet, violin, piano; text by Fernard Marc (1942, S-Z); *Caprice No. 24 by Paganini* for violin, piano (1943, CBDM); *L'Autre Voix* for soprano, 5 instruments; text by Robert Guiette (1948, CBDM); *Le Marchand d'images*, cantata (1954–65); *4 Fantasies by Henry Purcell* for string orchestra (1960, CBDM); *Concert flamand* for wind trio (1965).

PRINCIPAL WRITINGS: "Le Fil d'Ariane," *Documents 34* I (Brussels, June 1934); "A la Trace des sons," lecture at the Palais des Beaux-Arts, Brussels (spring 1935); "Quelques définitions du rythme ou les avatars d'un concept" and "Notes sur le rythme concret," *Polyphonie* (Paris)2:3ff.; "Music in Belgium Today," *The Chesterian* (Jan 1949):64ff.; "Existe-t-il une musique expressioniste?", *Les Beaux-Arts* (Brussels, 29 Feb 1952); "Sur le Dodécaphonisme des origines à nos jours," *Jeunesses musicales* (Brussels, Oct 1953); "Problème d'analyse," *La Musique instrumentale de la renaissance* (Paris 1955):347ff.; "Debussy et la nouvelle conception de timbre," *Cahiers musicaux* (March 1956):23ff.; "Les Sources sensibles de la musique sérielle," *Visages et perspectives de l'art moderne* (Paris 1956):175ff.; "Debussy et Stravinsky," *Revue belge de musicologie* 16, fasc. 1/4:45ff. Souris also reviewed concert, film, and dance music for a number of Belgian and French journals.

BIBL.: P. Davay, "Hommage à A. S." *Clés pour la musique* (April 1970):6–10; A. Fraikin, "La Vie et l'oeuvre d'A. S.," *La Vie musicale*

belge (Jan 1970):40–42; *Music in Belgium* (Brussels 1964):125–26; R. Wangermée, *La Musique belge contemporaine* (Brussels 1959):82–99.
[prepared with the help of CBDM]
SEE ALSO Belgium.

Souster, Tim (Andrew James) (b. Bletchley, England, 29 Jan 1943), studied at New College, Oxford (1961–65; theory and music history with Bernard Rose, David Lumsden) and at the Darmstadt summer courses (1963, lectures by Stockhausen and Berio). He also studied composition in London with Richard Rodney Bennett in 1965. He was a music producer for the BBC during 1965–67 and composer-in-residence at King's College, Cambridge Univ., during 1969–71. In 1969 he cofounded a live-electronics group, Intermodulation, in which he performs as violist. His approach to music has been influenced by rock concerts (by the Soft Machine, the Who, etc.) and by the improvisations of Cornelius Cardew's AMM group in London.

PRINCIPAL COMPOSITIONS: *Metropolitan Games* for piano 4-hands (1966); *2 Choruses* for 2 sopranos, alto, 2 tenors, 2 basses, or 7-part chorus (1966, International); *Piano Piece I* (1966); *Study for Organ* (1966, Galliard); *Tsuwanonodomo* for soprano, 3 choruses, 3 orchestras, piano, prepared piano (jangle box), harp (1968); *Titus Groan Music* for wind quintet, tape, electronic apparatus (1969, Galliard); *Pelvic Loops* for 2-track tape (1969); *Chinese Whispers* for percussion, 3 electronic synthesizers (1970); *Triple Music II* for 3 orchestras (1970); *Music for Eliot's "Waste Land"* for piano, electronic organ, soprano saxophone, 3 miniaturized electronic synthesizers (1970).

PRINCIPAL WRITINGS: "Notes on Pop Music," *Tempo* (winter 1968–69):2–6. Souster has written many reviews for *Listener*, *Tempo*, and *The Observer*.
SEE ALSO Great Britain.

South America, see Argentina, Brazil, Chile

Soviet Union. On the eve of the 1905 revolution, Russia seemed to dominate the Western musical world. Tchaikovsky enjoyed an international popularity that no composer has since matched, and he was closely rivaled by Rimsky-Korsakov, Borodin, and Mussorgsky. Volumes of "little pieces" for piano abounded, composed by Russians whose names (some publisher's pseudonyms for composers of other nationalities) are now untraceable. Orchestras in theater and vaudeville pits everywhere delighted their audiences with short, highly flavored Russian works. Every major Western musical center boasted its Russian contingent in positions of musical prominence.

A large musical establishment existed in Russia as well. The Moscow and St. Petersburg Conservatories had been joined by schools in Kiev, Odessa, Saratov, Tbilisi (Tiflis), and elsewhere. The semiofficial Imperial Russian Music Society (IRMS) continued to pursue the objectives laid down by its founder, Anton Rubinstein, in 1859: "[to] develop musical training and taste in music in Russia and [to] stimulate the talent of the fatherland." To these ends the aforementioned schools were founded, and concerts, lectures, and contests were mounted by local IRMS chapters all over Russia. Private enterprises also abounded. In 1899 the Moscow Private (or Independent) Opera had become the Society for Private Opera, which in turn dissolved into the Zimin Opera Theater. The St. Petersburg Philharmonic Society, established 1802, still thrived. The Moscow Philharmonic Society listed Nikisch, Ziloty, Ippolitov-Ivanov, and Rachmaninov among its conductors and musical directors. The Russian Choral Society included Ippolitov-Ivanov and Vasilenko among its conductors. Jurgenson and Gutheil were established music publishers, joined by the Koussevitzky firm in 1908. All of these organizations—and many others—were intertwined with bureaucratic liaisons and levels that still characterize Russian establishment procedures.

Nicholas Rimsky-Korsakov (1844–1908) and Mily Balakirev (1836–1910), both members of the "Mighty Five," were still active; they were joined by Anton Arensky (1861–1906), Sergei Taneev (1856–1915), Anatolii Liadov (1855–1914), Alexander Glazunov (1865–1936), Mikhail Ippolitov-Ivanov (1859–1935), Sergey *Rachmaninov (1873–1943), Alexander Gretchaninov (1865–1956), Nikolai Tcherepnine (1873–1945), and Alexander *Scriabin (1871–1915). These men, Arensky excepted, all lived into or through the 1905–14 decade, which Maxim Gorky later characterized as the "most shameful" in Russian art. Although this period was a time of political repression, it was also one of proliferating styles in the arts, both in Russia and in western Europe. Rachmaninov, seemingly carrying on the tradition of Tchaikovsky, represented the direction of singing melody in music set off by effective harmonies. Scriabin, who always

thought in highly personal terms, sought through technical constructions such as his "mystic chord" (based on fourths instead of thirds) and extra-musical formal determinants to capture and use mystic musical powers. Both he and Rachmaninov toured as pianists and conductors, not only of their own works but of others as well. The decade also saw Igor *Stravinsky (1882–1971) move quickly from the orchestral colorism of the Firebird ballet and earlier works to The Rite of Spring —a work whose style gave rise to the term Scythianism (i.e., conveying the idea of primitive times and of proto-Russian peoples) in music. This was, musically, Russia's most Western moment. The best known conductors and performers became international figures. Rachmaninov, Scriabin, and Stravinsky spent much of the decade abroad. Building from a pre-1900 group calling itself The World of Art, the entrepreneur Sergei Diaghilev (1872–1929) began a series of "Russian Seasons" in Paris in 1907, later extended to London and other continental cities. Rimsky-Korsakov and Feodor Chaliapin (1873–1933) were among those featured on the first set of five concerts. Diaghilev soon focused his attention on stage productions, opera, and especially ballet, gathering artists from the Marinsky and Bolshoi companies, among them Nijinsky, Pavlova, and Stravinsky. Sergei *Prokofiev (1891–1953), who was 20 years old in 1911, followed Diaghilev abroad later.

World War I, Russia's faltering role therein, and the two revolutions (February and October) of 1917 with their aftermath, changed the course of Russian music in only one tangible aspect at first. There was a last, great diaspora of Russian musicians, including Rachmaninov, Stravinsky, and Prokofiev (who returned later), Serge Koussevitzky, Mischa Elman, Jascha Heifitz, and Efrem Zimbalist. The most significant composers who remained were Ippolitov-Ivanov, Glazunov, Reinhold *Glière (1875–1956), Sergei Vasilenko (1872–1956), and Nikolai Miaskovsky (1881–1950). (Composers of lesser talent such as these were characteristic of this, the end of the so-called "Silver Age" in Russian art.)

After the Revolution the structure of the musical establishment remained essentially the same. The machinery and remaining personnel of the IRMS was brought more or less intact into the new Peoples' Commissariat of Culture and Enlightenment, whose commissar, Anatole Lunacharsky, was sympathetic to and knowledgeable about the arts. Conservatories and theaters were nationalized and went on as before. The Jurgenson publishing house became the State Music Publishers with no change in personnel, location, or equipment. There was much theorizing about a new music for a new time, but what musicians and artists most welcomed was the apparent release from the pressure of a double censorship—that of the old Tsarist bureaucracy on the right and of the social critics on the left.

During the period of the Bolshevik's New Economic Policy (1921–27) new styles and ideas proliferated. Fed by ideological currents, there was a certain impatience with the past which even took the form of scorning the romanticism of Rachmaninov (labeled a "white bandit" in the 20s) and the mystic self-indulgence of Scriabin. Electronic musical means were pioneered by Lev (Leon) Theremin (1896–c.1938) in Petrograd-Leningrad, among others; Georgy Mikhailovich Rimsky-Korsakov (b. 1901), nephew of Nikolai, pioneered in the use of quarter tones. Composers experimented with unconventional sounds on conventional instruments. Some of these took the form of imitating folk instruments or even voices; others sought to imitate contemporary sounds as in the symphonic episode *The Factory* of Alexander Mosolov (b. 1900). Although traffic out of the Soviet Union was strictly curtailed, most musicians were aware of foreign events and trends in Vienna, Rome, Paris, Berlin, Boston, and New York through correspondents, many of them expatriates, whose articles appeared in the numerous musical journals of the 20s. The organizational base for the activity of the mid-20s was the Association of Contemporary Musicians, founded 1923 as a branch of ISCM. This organization provided the platform for the early successes of Dmitri *Shostakovich (b. 1906); his *Symphony No. 1*, actually a somewhat eclectic conservatory graduation piece, gave some definition to an emerging Soviet style and focused attention on the young generation in Soviet art. A second grouping of composers and musicians, the Russian Association for Proletarian Music (RAPM), was also founded in 1923 but was based largely on Moscow thinking (traditionally conservative). Its stated aim was to fight bourgeois "formalism" and to create a mass music, but until 1928 it remained small and attracted mostly those with inclinations more political than musical. Officially, the government appears to have been concerned but gingerly permissive: Art, as part of the Marxian social superstructure, must make its own way; as the economic base changed, the superstructure would follow, but there was to be no direct interference unless a tendency in art threatened

the Revolution. This was the view of political leaders, including Lunacharsky and, presumably, Lenin.

By 1928, with Joseph Stalin vigorously ascendant and the creators of the Revolution either dead (Lenin), discredited, or about to be discredited and/or liquidated, the notion of what threatened the Revolution was broadened. News of foreign ideas and events all but disappeared. The Communist Party now frowned on the Association of Contemporary Musicians, with its internationalist outlook, and supported RAPM by default. The latter became sufficiently noisy to scare Prokofiev abroad again after a visit in 1929. By 1932 the Party and government found RAPM (and like organizations in the other arts) to be unsuitable, and they were abolished. The new, government-connected organization for composers and music scholars was the Union of Soviet Composers. It was publically welcomed by Ippolitov-Ivanov, Glière, Miaskovsky, Boris Asafiev (1884–1949), and Shostakovich. Prokofiev endorsed it from Paris and found his eventual return (1936) made easier thereby.

During the 30s a number of new composers began making their names known in the Soviet Union. Yuri Shaporin (1887–1963) was the oldest, having started his creative career relatively late (which may explain his restrained idiom). Aram *Khachaturian (b. 1903) brought an Armenian name, if not a genuine Armenian flavor, into the Soviet musical scene. Dmitri *Kabalevsky (b. 1904) was—and still is—a major writer of music for the young, who sustained his piano students on pieces of his own during the difficult early years of the Soviet Union. Of the older composers, Glazunov had left the country in the late 20s and died in Paris in 1936; Ippolitov-Ivanov died in 1935. Glière was teaching (since 1920) at the Moscow Conservatory and made signal contributions to the musical stage, especially ballet. In 1938 he began a series of concertos that reawakened interest in that genre.

A superficial maturity—actually an organizational plateau—had been reached. Composer-musicologist Boris Asafiev began to develop an esthetic of musical meanings, his theory of "intonations" which was later to provide some of the vocabulary essential to the marriage of music and ideology. In 1934 Maxim Gorky supplied the term "socialist realism" for Soviet art, and Andrei Zhdanov, a high party leader and Stalin lieutenant, began a series of pronouncements on socialist creativity that soon took on a quasilegal force. The object against which the government first displayed its authority was the Shostakovich opera, *Lady Macbeth of Mtsensk* or *Ekaterina Izmailova*. Completed in 1932, it was immensely successful at its premiere in 1934. Nevertheless it was attacked in 1936 (probably because of its lewdness—Stalin epitomized Soviet puritanism), and from that date on codes of acceptable behavior and punishment were developed in the arts. Simultaneously redefinitions in political ideology were culminating in the Moscow trials of 1936–38. A system of rewards and prizes was developed, some with monetary value. Titles were initiated, ranging from the relatively modest "Honored Art Worker of the Armenian [for example] Republic" to the lofty "People's Artist of the U.S.S.R."

The Soviet alliance with Nazi Germany in 1939 severed even those Western musical contacts that had served the official Popular Front policy of the mid-30s. Prokofiev's plans for touring the West again were never realized. A musical exchange and especially trade in musical items was established with Nazi Germany, and for the first time since 1918 the nation's musical paraphernalia (instruments, strings, stands, rosin, etc.) could be refurbished and replaced. The Nazi invasion two years later naturally disrupted the idyll; it also reopened other Western contacts and halted Stalinist repression and control. In defending their country, composers shared in the Soviet Union's most patriotic period. The West hailed Shostakovich's *Symphony No. 7*, "Leningrad," and Prokoviev's *Symphony No. 5*. Others of the middle generation gained Western recognition, including Khachaturian, Kabalevsky, Shaporin, and Vissarion Shebalin (1902–63). They were writing in the straightforward, communicative style of the times and also experimenting along lines permitted under the relaxation of controls. Some atonality reappeared for the first time since the 20s and was generally reserved for depiction of evil or the enemy. Shortly after the war the ideological campaign resumed. Stalin appeared as the author of articles on linguistics, and the theses he developed for language were applied to music, which was also considered to be part of the historic superstructure. In 1948 the Party and government turned to Soviet music again and found its practitioners formalistic, dangerously cosmopolitan, nonideological, and anti-Party—a threat to the Revolution.

By mid-century it was clear that the structure of Soviet music life would continue to depend on the hierarchy and rank that had characterized pre-Revolutionary Russia. Musically the most important Soviet contributions were in the areas of orchestral color, unprepared tonal shifts, folklike melody, and vigorous folklike dance rhythms. Soviet composers were being encouraged to develop simple idioms and accessible styles and to use 19th-century techniques, all of which caused them to retain in their work much of the substance of the romantic period. The symphony and concerto were enjoying an active life long after their waning in the West. The cantata and oratorio, newly reborn, were serving as secular vehicles for the exaltation of the Party, its leaders, and the ideas and projects they supported. There was in theory a pervasive emphasis on folk idioms, but this may have been a somewhat spurious factor. By 1948 hundreds of "folk songs" about Stalin or about Stalin and Lenin were purported to have been found on various folklore expeditions. Certain popular urban, even Western, notions of Russian song were artificially emphasized. These were often Ukrainian, Jewish, or even 19th-century Italian borrowings. They tended, in usage by Soviet composers, to swamp the rather more subtle qualities of Russian song. The folk culture of the minority ethnic groups, especially in the peripheral republics, was encouraged, but with an effort to bring "imperfect" local musical developments abreast of the West. Although this approach was later corrected, the damage done by 1948 was considerable. Westerners have heard very little of the bulk of Soviet music; it is generally not intended for Western ears, and what is heard abroad is not at all representative.

Stanley D. Krebs

SINCE 1948. The Union of Soviet Composers is the most powerful organization in the country today in regulating contemporary music and the life of the Soviet composer. It is open to "composers of works of a high professional caliber possessing individual socio-artistic significance"[1] whose application for membership is accepted by a regional branch of the Union and confirmed by the Secretariat in Moscow. The scope of its regulatory powers is indicated by a provision of its charter, which specifies the task of giving "socio-creative advice to musical institutions and organizations which are connected with music, such as orchestras, radio, television, music publishing firms, musical educational institutions, clubs, palaces of culture, professional musical press and musical sections of

[1] *Charter of the Union of Composers of the U.S.S.R.*, trans. by Nicolas Slonimsky and printed in the 4th edition of his *Music Since 1900* (New York 1971).

the general press." Such advice is governed by other provisions, among them "the purpose of creating ideologically valid musical works of high artistic content which would contribute to the building of Communism in our country." The Union of Composers offers many services to its members, including help with publication and performance. It also offers an arena where disputes on urgent questions may be aired. For instance, at a conference in 1965 composers, performers, and musicologists discussed "Problems of Innovation in Contemporary Music." The Union also provides living accommodations and composers' colonies, called Houses of Creation, usually located outside the major cities and often in wooded areas. A member (composer, theoretician, or musicologist) may apply for space at a House of Creation when he wants to work uninterruptedly. Each of the 15 Soviet republics has its own Union of Composers, which is not only separate from the all-Union organization but enjoys some autonomy from it. Moscow, for example, is the home of two distinct organizations, the Union of Soviet Composers (a central organization) and the Union of Composers of the Russian Federated Republic.

Music education starts in the neighborhood music school, which offers elementary instrumental and theoretical instruction for all who desire it. The best students from these schools are selected to attend one of the musical colleges; these provide secondary (high-school level) and preprofessional music education. The best students here are selected to attend the various conservatories that exist throughout the country. Music education, like all forms of education, is state supported and hence tuition free. Capable students are offered stipends to defray the cost of room, board, and books. Unlike the universities, however, which are under the direction of the Ministry of Higher and Specialized Education, the music conservatories are the domain of the Ministry of Culture. Since the Revolution, when the capital was moved from Leningrad to Moscow and most of the major artists also moved there, the Tchaikovsky Conservatory in Moscow has been preeminent. The Conservatory in Leningrad, however, has maintained the high standards for which it was known before. Soviet universities do not offer a music program like those in American universities (which include performance instruction as in a conservatory). An interesting feature of Soviet music education is that most students are expected, after they finish at a conservatory, to leave the large urban centers

for three years and to serve in some capacity in the outlying provincial towns. During the last decade contacts between the Soviet Union and the West have permitted music students and composers to acquaint themselves with all trends and techniques in 20th-century music. Although scores and recordings of contemporary Western music are unavailable for purchase (owing to currency-exchange problems), they can be received as gifts from colleagues in Western countries.

Soviet composers enjoy a high status among their countrymen. Many are affiliated with conservatories and hold teaching posts. An equally large number are independent and earn a living through writing film music, television scores, and the like. A composer of light music may become quite wealthy through the collection of royalties. Performers who are chosen for concert careers are given a basic monthly salary plus an honorarium for every concert given (the honorarium based on their status). Musicologists receive approximately the same training as a performer and then proceed to graduate study at a university and possibly to work in a publishing house or research institute such as the State Research Institute of Music, Theater, and Cinematography in Leningrad or the Glinka Museum in Moscow. Each republic can confer a grade ("superior artist," "honored artist of the republic," etc.) on its artists, and the Soviet Union itself confers similar titles.

Efforts by the Communist Party to regulate Soviet music are unique in 20th-century music history. In 1948 Andrei Zhdanov, a prominent member of the Council of Ministers and a close associate of Stalin, took an active role in the condemnation of Soviet composers who, it was felt, had departed from the goals of socialist-realist art and been heavily influenced by the West. These included some of the most prominent Soviet composers of the day: Shostakovich, Prokofiev, Khatchaturian, Shebalin, and Miaskovsky. Also in 1948 Tikhon Khrennikov, General Secretary of the Union of Soviet Composers wrote in *Soviet Music* that "the antipopular formalistic direction of Soviet music is closely connected with the bourgeois decadent music of the contemporary West and modernistic music of pre-Revolutionary Russia. The present musical art of western Europe and America reflects the general morass and the spiritual abyss of bourgeois culture." Foreign composers accused of decadent tendencies were Stravinsky, Messiaen, Hindemith, Krenek, Berg, Britten, Menotti, and Schoenberg. Also in 1948 the Central Committee of the Communist Party published a series of decisions on music: 1) To condemn formalism in Soviet music as antipopular and leading to the liquidation of music. 2) To continue, via the directorate of the Central Committee of the Communist Party, to liquidate those deficiencies in Soviet music pointed out by the Central Committee and to guarantee the development of Soviet music in the direction of realism. 3) To call upon Soviet composers to adhere to those values that would bring the Soviet people to music and to abandon all that would weaken Soviet music and disrupt its development; furthermore, to guarantee a boom in creative work that would move Soviet musical culture ahead rapidly and lead to the creation of works of high quality. 4) To approve organizational measures that would enable Party and Soviet organs to improve musical work. It should be pointed out that purges of foreign influence in Russia date back at least to Ivan the Terrible and that the 1948 decrees were in character with the politcal, economic, and ideological isolation of the Soviet Union at that time. Also this was not the first time that the Soviet government had taken an interest in musical esthetics; Shostakovich's opera *Lady Macbeth of Mtsensk*, now called *Ekaterina Izmailovna*, was condemned when first offered to the Soviet public in 1936.

Immediately after the 1948 decrees there was an upsurge of patriotic works glorifying the peasantry, the working class, the motherland, the great Soviet state, the patriotic war (World War II), and extolling social progress, justice, etc. Much of this was an extension of 19th-century program music containing little in the way of unfamiliar harmonic dissonance, intricate rhythms, or abstract forms. Composers were urged to dip into the storehouse of the many national Soviet cultures. They were to strive to reflect the essence of the people, even though they did not necessarily have to quote folk material. Among the better known works of this time is *Song of the Forest* (1949) by Dmitri Shostakovich. It deals with the remaking of nature and bears such subtitles as "Let's Plant Woods All Over Our Country," "Recollection of the Past," "Young Pioneers Planting Woods," etc. Sergei *Prokofiev (1891–1953) followed suit with his oratorio *On Guard for Peace* (1950). Among the imitators of the Shostakovich is *A Day of My Country* (1954) by the Georgian composer Alexei Machavariani (b. 1913), which contains a series of tableaux utilizing songs, dances, and gay and lyrical scenes. The oratorio *In Memory of Sergei Yesenin* (1956) by Georgi *Sviridov (b. 1915) uses the poems of Yesenin

to help paint a picture of Russian winters, the Siberian mountains, and village life. The nationalist movement among the Soviet minorities is exemplified by the Georgian Otar Taktakishvilli (b. 1924), the Azerbaigianian Kara Karayev (b. 1918), and the Armenian Arno Babajanyan (b. 1921). While music of the first two uses folk material, it remains essentially close to the European symphonic school and is particularly influenced by Tchaikovsky. Taktakishvilli's *Piano Concerto* (1951), for example, is a four-movement, neo-romantic work that combines 20th-century orchestration and Oriental thematic material.

The musical situation began to change during the mid-1950s. A small group of musicians became interested in the works of Webern and Schoenberg, largely under the guidance of Philip Hershkovich (b. Rumania, 1906), a refugee from Hitler and a long-time resident of the Soviet Union who had been a student of Webern for five years. His *4 German Lieder* (1963), based on German texts of the Rumanian poet Paul Celan, contain a harmonic texture reminiscent of Schoenberg's Op. 19, while the melodic line recalls a style of declamation intended to accentuate the contours of German speech intonation. Hershkovich has done considerable research into the interconnections of form and harmony in works of the Viennese classicists, Mahler, and the new Viennese school. (Two recent studies are *The Tonal Sources of Dodecaphonic Music*, 1967, and *Mozartian Principles in the Structuring of the Sonata Cycle*, 1967). The earlier music of Andrei *Volkonsky (b. 1933), a pupil of Hershkovich, shows the influence of Hindemith and Stravinsky. His *Musica stricta* for piano (1957) is 12-tone. One of its movements is made up of small musical fragments separated by pauses of varying lengths that are intended to act as agogic accents. This device was expanded in *Lamentations of Shchaza* for soprano, violin, viola, English horn, percussion, and harpsichord (1962). Whereas one still senses a predeliction for neoclassic rhythms in *Musica stricta*, the latter piece abandons meter in favor of a fluid rhythmic organization akin to Boulez and Berio. Although it is not written in a purely graphic notation, note-heads are arranged on the page so as to indicate relative durations; the entire third movement is so arranged.

During the 1960s there was a move away from an exclusive adherence to socialist realism and toward a stylistic pluralism. Rodion* Shchedrin (b. 1932), for example, has composed works within the esthetic context of socialist realism well into the late 1960s and has not associated himself with avant-garde music. Yet his oratorio *Poetoria* for orchestra, chorus, and narrator (1968), which maintains the largess of traditional Russian and Soviet orchestral works, calls for orchestral techniques common among avant-garde composers in the West. Likewise the *Violin Sonata* (1963) of Alfred *Schnitke (b. 1934) adheres to neoclassic forms but uses serial structures as the souce of thematic material. The Soviet tours of Igor Stravinsky in 1963 and Pierre Boulez in 1966 indicated an official willingness to tolerate, if not endorse, new trends. Although the following brief remarks are sketchy, owing to the lack of documentation, they will at least indicate the range of progressive compositional activities.

Kiev, capital of ancient Russia, has long been a citadel of musical conservatism. In the carly 1960s, however, a group of composers thcrc began to produce music that reflected an awareness of musical developments in Poland. These composers include Vitali Gadsyatzky, Leonid *Grabovsky (b. 1935), and Valentin *Silvestrov (b. 1937). Silvestrov's *Spectri* (1965) uses graphic notation and builds orchestral textures and timbres through the fragmentation and combination of short motives. Grabovsky's *From Japanese Haiku* (1964) has piccolo and bassoon players at one point repeat small groups of notes in any order until the end of a vocal line in which a tenor soloist follows instructions to "scan with falsetto while holding one's nose and singing at the highest limit of one's range." Another example of the Kiev work is Gadsyatzky's musique-concrète piece *4 Studies for Tape Recorder* (1965).

In Moscow there are such composers as Herskovitz, Schnitke, Shchedrin, Volkonsky, and Edison *Denisov (b. 1929). Denisov was trained as a mathematician as well as a musician. He teaches composition at the Moscow Conservatory and has campaigned for new music in the Union of Composers. Most of his works from the mid-1960s are for chamber ensembles, often combining voice (especially soprano) with instruments. *Son of the Incas*, a cantata for soprano and 12 instruments (1964) contains a kaleidoscope of shadows reflecting such presences as Boulez, Mussorgsky, Ravel, and Schoenberg. It uses serial techniques and also mobile processes that allow the performers to choose the sequence of some passages during performance. An entire section of *Crescendo and Diminuendo* for harpsichord and strings (1965) permits each player to make such choices independently of his colleagues. *3 Pieces* for piano 4-hands

(1967) maintains a tighter control over rhythm and pitch but at some points allows pitches to be played in any order within a proportionally notated time span. Schnitke's *Music for Piano and Chamber Orchestra* (1964) has a vibraphone introduction and employs a technique of massing densities in layer-cake fashion; thickly sonorous intertwinings of row material continuously appear and disappear as though seen through a rotating prism. The final section utilizes jazz material in a way that brings to mind third-stream music of the 1950s. Many passages in the *Violin Sonata No. 2* (1966) use proportional rhythmic notation in both piano and violin parts. Also in Moscow is the Experimental Studio for Electronic Music founded 1966 by the Ministry of Culture. This studio uses the ANS synthesizer of Y. A. Murzin (ANS is taken from the initials of the composer A. N. Scriabin). The studio has been used for research into synthesized sound processes, for film scores, and to produce recordings. Both Denisov and Schnitke have produced music there for recordings and for live concert presentation.

In Leningrad, Sergei *Slonimsky (b. 1932) has employed many new devices. His song cycle *Farewell to a Friend in the Desert* for voice and piano (1966) directs the pianist to pluck the strings and to dampen them with his hand and has the singer perform quarter tones. Some passages employ cluster notations and others give the performers much rhythmic liberty. This work, together with 4 *Polish Verses* for soprano and flute (1964) and *Dialogi* for wind quintet (1964) demonstrate his interest in instrumental effects produced by modification of traditional performing techniques. The development of avant-garde techniques has been furthered in many of the smaller republics and most particularly in Estonia, where Arvo *Pärt (b. 1935) has been in a leading position. From the Baltic states, Vytautas *Montvila (b. 1935) has used both graphic notation and mobile processes in his *Skambesiai* for gongs, bells, and piano (1967). As in the West, contemporary music does not always find a ready outlet in performance. However, such organizations as the chamber orchestra of the Leningrad Philharmonic and the Borodin Quartet program new music, and new ensembles, such as Music of the Twentieth Century, have begun to appear. Performances also take place at conservatory seminars or meetings of the composers' unions.

Joel Spiegelman

BIBL.: Gerald Abraham, *8 Soviet Composers* (London 1943); *Istoriia Russk Sovetskoi muzyki* [History of Soviet Russian Music] ed. by a board under Lebedeva (Moscow 1956–63); Yuri Jelagin, *Taming of the Arts* trans. by Nicholas Wreden (New York 1951); Stanley Dale Krebs, *Soviet Composers and the Development of Soviet Music* (New York 1970); Andrei Olkhovsky, *Music under the Soviets* (New York 1955); Liudmilla Poliakova, *Soviet Music* (Moscow 1961).

S. D. K.

SEE ALSO Education for the Nonprofessional; Liturgical Music: Jewish; Opera.

Sowerby, Leo (b. Grand Rapids, Mich., 1 May 1895; d. Port Clinton, Ohio, 7 July 1968), was taken to Chicago in 1909, where he studied piano with Calvin Lampert (and briefly in 1917 with Percy Grainger) and composition with Arthur Olaf Anderson. He was self-taught as an organist. After three years in Italy as the first American Prix de Rome fellow for music (1921–24), he returned to Chicago to teach composition at the American Conservatory (1925–62) and later to become organist-choirmaster of St. James Episcopal Cathedral (1927–62). In 1962 he founded the College of Church Musicians at Washington Cathedral, where he was dean until his death. He wrote in all genres except opera, drawing on such diverse sources as American folk music, blues, liturgical music, and the classical concert traditions. His melodies and rhythms are sometimes sprightly, sometimes long-breathed and rhapsodic, underscored in the latter case by floating, contrapuntally derived harmonies with frequent modulations and enharmonic changes. Many of his compositions, particularly his numerous organ works, make use of passacaglia, canon, chaconne, and fugal textures and forms.

PRINCIPAL COMPOSITIONS: *Woodwind Quintet* (1916, SPAM); *Serenade* for string quartet (1917, SPAM); *Comes Autumn Time* for organ (1917, Boston); *Piano Concertos Nos. 1–2* (1917, revised 1919; 1932); *Trio* for flute, viola, piano (1919); *Cello Sonata* (1920); *Requiescat in Pace* for organ (1920, Gray); *The Edge of Dreams*, song cycle; text by Mark Turbyfill (1920, Gray); *Symphonies Nos. 1–5* (1921, 1928, 1940, 1947, 1964); *Violin Sonatas Nos. 1–2* (1921, UE; 1944); *From the North-land* for piano (1922, Boston; orchestrated 1925, SPAM); *Ballad of King Estmere* for 2 pianos, orchestra (1922); untitled 5-movement cantata based on the Psalms (1923–24); *Synconata* and *Monotony* for jazz orchestra (1924, 1925); *The Vision of Sir Launfal* for chorus, orchestra; poem by James Lowell (1925, Birchard); *Mediaeval Poem* for organ, orchestra (1926, Eastman); *Prairie*, symphonic poem (1929, Eastman); *Florida Suite* for piano (1929, Oxford); *Cello Concerto* (1929–34); *Organ Symphony* (1930, Oxford); *Passacaglia, Interlude, and Fugue* for orchestra (1931);

Organ Concertos Nos. 1–2 (1936, Gray; 1967); *Suite for organ* (1937, Oxford); *Theme in Yellow* for orchestra (1938); *Clarinet Sonata* (1938, SPAM); *Forsaken of Man*, cantata (1939, Gray); *Poem* for viola with organ or orchestra (1941, Gray); *Canticle of the Sun*, cantata; text by St. Francis of Assisi (1944, Gray); *Classic Concerto* for organ, strings (1944, Gray); *Trumpet Sonata* (1945, Remick); *Ballade* for English horn, organ (1949, Gray); *Canon, Chacony, and Fugue* for organ (1949, Gray); *Christ Reborn*, cantata (1950, Gray); *Whimsical Variations* for organ (1950, Gray); *Concert Piece* for organ, orchestra (1951 Gray); *Trio* for violin, viola, cello (1952); *All on a Summer's Day* for orchestra (1954); *Fantasy* for trumpet, organ (1954, Gray); *The Throne of God* for chorus, orchestra; text from Revelation (1957, Gray); *The Ark of the Covenant*, cantata (1959, Gray); *Bright, Blithe, and Brisk* for organ (1962, Gray); *Piano Sonata in D* (1964); *Solomon's Garden* for chorus, orchestra (1965, Gray); *Symphonia Brevis* for organ (1966, Gray); *Dialogue* for organ, piano (1967, Gray); *Organ Passacaglia* (1967). Sowerby also wrote more than 300 songs, and he prepared 23 settings of folk songs for Carl Sandburg's *American Songbag* (New York 1927). Complete list of organ and service works in Huntington.

PRINCIPAL WRITINGS: "The Folk Element: The Vitalizer of Modern Music," *Musical Scrapbook* (Chicago, Oct 1927): 1–2, 11; *Ideals in Church Music* (New York 1956); "The Throne of God," *The Composer's Point of View* ed. by R. S. Hines (Norman, Okla., 1963): 65–78.

BIBL.: John Tasker Howard, "L.S.," *Our Contemporary Composers* (New York 1941): 80–82; R.M. Huntington, *A Study of the Musical Contributions of L.S.* (MA thesis, Univ. of Southern Calif., 1957); Burnet C. Tuthill, "L.S.," *Musical Quarterly* 24: 249–64.

Francis Crociata

Spain. Composers in Spain face an unfortunate situation in that Spaniards interested in concert music have a negative attitude both toward their own country and toward the music of their own time (Wagner, for instance, remained a controversial figure in Spain until the 1920s). Noncreative musical life (concerts, amateur music making, governmental organizations, and other groups) are all in the hands of this stagnant social class. Recognized cultural achievements, such as those of Italy in the last century and of France and Germany afterwards, instead of inspiring new growth in Spain, are given preference over local endeavors and thereby stifle creative efforts.

From 1900 to 1936 (when the Civil War began) Spanish composers went to Paris to complete their education; Isaac Albéniz (1860–1909), Enrique Granados (1866–1916), and Manuel de Falla (1876–1946) are examples. Foreign training was necessary because then, as now, it was impossible for a student in Spain to become fully acquainted with contemporary music. The official theaters (Teatro Real in Madrid and the Teatro Liceo in Barcelona) rarely produced works by even these composers, although their compositions did appear with some regularity on programs of two Madrid orchestras, the Orquesta Filarmónica, founded 1915 and conducted by Bartolomé Pérez-Casas (1873–1956), and the Orquesta Sinfónica, founded 1917 and conducted by Enrique Fernández Arbós (1863–1939). There were few performances of contemporary Spanish music anywhere else in the country.

Among the progressive activities of the time were those of Felipe Pedrell (1841–1922), who taught many composers, including those mentioned above. His researches into Spanish music of the past helped create a Spanish nationalist movement. The critic Adolfo Salazar (1890–1958) helped bring Spanish and foreign music into closer contact. He published the first important works in Spain concerning contemporary music, he founded the Spanish section of the ISCM, and he brought the 1936 ISCM Festival to Barcelona. Musically his preference was for a neoclassicism based on Spanish music of the 15th–17th centuries, updated with Stravinskian harmony. In his later years his writing ranged over the entire history of music.

All contacts between new Spanish music and the outside world ceased during the Civil War. By its end many of Spain's most illustrious composers and performers had abandoned the country, and musical life had been largely destroyed. In place of the theaters and orchestras that had died, there rose the Orquesta Nacional de España in Madrid (founded 1940) and a municipal orchestra in Barcelona (founded 1944). Short opera seasons got underway in Bilbao, Oviedo, Valencia, and Malaga, but in all cases the official organisms remained dedicated to the standard, recognized repertory, and contemporary Spanish and foreign music continued to be neglected.

Composers themselves took the first steps to change this situation. In Barcelona beginning in 1949, a group who called themselves by the name "Manuel de Falla" sought new forms of expression by studying Bartók, Stravinsky (of the 1930s), Hindemith, and Some works of the Viennese school. The members of this group were Juan Comellas (b. 1913), Alberto Blancafort (b. 1928), Manuel Valls (b. 1928), Angel Cerdá (b. 1924), José Cercós (b. 1925), and José María Mestres-Quadreny (b. 1929). Their activities, lasting until about 1955, were supported by the French Institute and the Club 49, a group of private patrons, in Barcelona. Today only Mestres-Quadreny is still composing. The first concert of new music (Boulez, Nono, Stockhausen) to be held in postwar Spain took place in Barcelona in 1955. In 1958 the Grupo Nueva Música was created in Madrid. Its members included Ramón Barce (b. 1928) Cristóbal Halffter (b. 1930), Antón García-Abril (b. 1933), myself (b. 1930), Fernando Ember (b. 1931), Manuel Moreno Buendía (b. 1932), Enrique Franco (b. 1920), and Manuel Carra (b. 1931). The first four have continued to be active as composers. Their activities were held in Madrid in conjunction with the Juventudes Musicales Españolas and the Ateneo, then an independent association of artists now under the jurisdiction of the Ministry of Information and Tourism; their ideas were closer to the Viennese school than were those of the Barcelona group. In 1959 Juan Hidalgo (b. 1927) created the group Música Abierta in Barcelona with José Cercós, Mestres-Quadreny, Joaquím Homs (b. 1906), and myself. This group, aided by the Club 49, has presented many avant-garde works from North America, including those of John Cage (of whom Hidalgo is a follower). Also in 1959 I founded a chamber-music series, Tiempo y Música, at Madrid Univ., which still exists. In 1964 three important events took place: a Biennial for Contemporary Music, which I organized in collaboration with the National Service for Education and Culture (it was not held again); the first Festival of the Americas and Spain (held twice since), the Spanish section of which was organized by the Instituto de Cultura Hispánica (a pan-Hispanic cultural organization); and the Madrid ISCM Festival, the first ISCM festival to be held in Spain since 1936. All of these events brought new Spanish music to the attention of foreigners and strengthened the developing ties between us and our foreign colleagues. These events, however, were isolated offerings, and normal concert programing remains unaffected by them. Regular offerings of contemporary music continued to be held apart from the rest of Spain's musical life: ALEA, a privately financed Madrid Organization that I founded in 1965 and which houses an electronic studio and promotes new music largely through concerts; the KOAN group of Juventudes Musicales Españolas in Madrid promotes the youngest generation of composers and was founded in 1967 by Barce, Tomás Marco (b. 1942), and Arturo Tamayo (b. 1945); and a few similar groups. Festivals of contemporary music have been held during October in Barcelona since 1965; they are a joint project of the Juventudes Musicales Españolas and the city.

Whereas Spanish composers before the Civil War looked toward Paris for teachers, after 1950 they began looking to Germany, mainly to the summer courses at Darmstadt. This was not the only place, however. Hidalgo has studied with Bruno Maderna in Milan, I worked with Max Deutsch in Paris, and Carmelo Bernaola (b. 1929) has studied with Goffredo Petrassi in Rome. Spanish education in new music has taken place outside all official channels. The conservatories in Madrid, Pamplona, Seville, and Valencia may hold an occasional seminar on some aspect of new music, but there is no regular program anywhere devoted to (or incorporating) this music. Madrid Conservatory, however, is in the process of installing an electronic music laboratory (thus far only the ALEA group has a working studio).

In the dissemination of new music the Radio Nacional has played an important role. Although its orchestra (1948–52 and since 1965) does not regularly perform new Spanish music, the station does commission scores (four in 1970). In addition the chief of the radio's music division, Enrique Franco, is a lucid and positive spokesman for new music (he also writes for the Madrid newspaper *Arriba*). Spain does not have a major publishing house, and Spanish composers throughout the century have had to look elsewhere for this. Eschig in Paris and Chester in London published Albeniz, Falla, and Ernesto Halffter; UE in Vienna publishes Cristóbal Halffter; Salabert in Paris publishes Federico Mompou, myself, and Marco; Tonos in Darmstadt publishes Enrique Raxach and myself; Moeck in Celle publishes Mestres-Quadreny and Xavier Benguerel. The Spanish house Union Musical Española in Bilbao and Madrid, founded before the Civil War, confines its activities to nationalistic Spanish music. At the end of January 1971, the Commissariat of Music, an organization of the Ministry of Education and Science, began a campaign to promote Spanish music through commissions of works (more than five in 1971 alone) to be performed at the Festivals of Granada, Salamanca, Cuenca, Ávila, Segovia, and Madrid. They have also undertaken to distribute contemporary scores, both Spanish and foreign, to the universities.

In general the Spanish composer must earn his living through activities not strictly related to his profession. Many composers are lawyers, chemists, businessmen, etc. Others teach. Writing film music can be lucrative. Few composers can afford a totally creative life unless they possess an independent income, have a good contract with a publishing house, or are successful at managing concerts. Socially and economically the composer is still an unvalued member of Spanish society.

Spanish music in this century has experienced two sharp breaks with the past: The Falla generation rejected the folk-opera zarzuela tradition of its predecessors, and the progressive composers who gained prominence in the 1950s broke with the nationalism and neoclassicism of Falla's followers. These revolutionary (rather than evolutionary) changes are largely explained by the hidebound and isolated nature of Spain's musical life, which has made it impossible for Spanish composers to deal easily and smoothly with changing creative needs, styles, and tastes.

Folk materials gained prominence with the rise of Spanish nationalism in the mid-19th century. Zarzuelas from this period combined Italian opera formats with superficial native elements, notably Spanish dance rhythms and scale patterns (for instance, scales with raised second and sixth degrees). Pedrell combined a Wagnerian harmonic and orchestral language and native Spanish tunes in such operas as *La Celestina* (1902) and *El comte Arnau* (1904). The piano music of Isaac Albéniz (1860–1909) combined folk materials with audacious pianistic and harmonic effects (for instance, large numbers of unprepared dissonances and unresolved appoggiaturas). The phrase structure in his malagueñas, jotas, habaneras, and other dances reflects the spontaneous rhythmic and melodic invention of country people; however, popular (guitar) timbres, vocal techniques, and modal melodic inflections tend to be lost in a garb of traditional concert timbres and tonal harmonies. The best examples of folk usage in his music are in the *Suite Española* (1901) and *Iberia* (1909).

Enrique *Granados (1867–1916) was an early representative of neoclassicism. He drew on national elements, but they were from the past, especially from the 18th-century tonadilla, a genre of comic opera, Granados's phrase shaping and use of ornaments also testify to his love of the past. Manuel de *Falla (1876–1946) began as an unsuccessful zarzuela composer (for example, *Los amores* *de la Ines*, 1897), but he embraced neoclassicism and from his opera *La vida breve* (1904–05) through the 1920s carried the neoclassic movement in Spain to its apex. Drawing on Spanish traditions of the 16th–18th centuries, he developed an extremely concise manner of expression: he rarely doubled voices except for the purpose of achieving a new timbre; he barely sketched harmonic progressions and sometimes omitted traditional modulatory links; he sometimes eschewed formal links as well; and he never wrote any passages of mere filling. After his marionette opera *El retablo de Maese Pedro* (1919–23) he found a balance between past traditions and contemporary procedures, as can be seen in his use of polyphony, his search for new timbres, and his harmonic style, which often relied on appoggiaturas as axis points in a progression.

Until the 1950s most developments in Spanish music reflected the various aspects of Falla's output. His use of Andalusian melodies was taken up by Joaquín *Turina (1882–1949). Turina, however, orchestrated in a thick, 19th-century manner (without the skill of Dvořák or Rimsky-Korsakov) and was much less imaginative than Falla in his use of traditional forms and harmony; much of his music, in fact, sounds overly facile and decorative. Falla's Spanish neoclassicism inspired the initial efforts of Ernesto *Halffter (b. 1905), his brother Rodolfo *Halffter (b. 1900), Salvador Bacarisse (1898–1962), Joaquín *Rodrigo (b. 1902), and Oscar *Esplá (b. 1889). During the 1920s E. Halffter, as a follower of Falla, began to draw inspiration from Domenico Scarlatti, who had been at the Spanish court during the 18th century. The Scarlatti influence is particularly noticeable in the monothematic last movement of Falla's *Harpsichord Concerto* (1923–26) and in Halffter's ballet *Sonatina* (1928). Later Halffter worked with Ravel at Monfort l'Amaury, and the influence of this association can be heard in his *Portuguese Rhapsody* for piano and orchestra (1939). Whereas Rodrigo has remained a traditional (but skillful) melodist, R. Halffter and Esplá passed through neoclassicism, the first becoming in the late 1950s the first 12-tone composer in Spain, the second exploring various harmonic innovations, such as unusual scales, modes, and chord progressions. Jesús Guridi (1886–1962) tried to create a Basque style in imitation of Falla's use of Andalusian music. However, his harmonic language remained within the confines of late 19th-century European nationalism, and his main importance was as an organ teacher in Bilbao and later Madrid. José

María Usandizaga (1881–1915) was working toward an expressionistic style of melodrama, and had he lived longer he might have effectively countered the neoclassic movement (which I feel has been harmful to Spanish music). Roberto *Gerhard (1896–1970), the only Spanish student of Schoenberg, hesitated for many years between nationalism and the thinking of his teacher. He left Spain in 1939, and his eventual evolution toward serialism took place in England. Younger Spanish composers were thus deprived of one who could have been an inspiring leader.

After the Civil War the Falla tradition became dogma. Falla himself was exiled, along with Bacarisse, Esplá, and R. Halffter. Those who remained included Rodrigo, Joaquím *Homs (b. 1906), Federico *Mompou (b. 1893), Xavier de *Montsalvatge (b. 1912), and Gerardo *Gombau (b. 1906). During the 1940s their music tended to adhere to already familiar procedures. Mompou, who writes mainly for piano, combined impressionistic harmonies with idiomatic pianistic textures akin to those of Chopin. Montsalvatge combined Argentinian and Cuban creole elements with polytonality and a lightness and formal clarity akin to Poulenc and Milhaud. Later some of these composers explored more innovative means of expression. Homs, for instance, a student of Gerhard, now writes in a freely atonal idiom and is especially drawn to chamber music. Gombau, reacting to the work of younger composers, has moved towards serialism and aleatory procedures.

The generation born in the 1920s and 30s threw tradition aside, as Albeniz and Falla had done before them. Serialism and later indeterminacy are represented in Carmelo Bernaola (b. 1929) and Cristóbal *Halffter (b. 1930). Various aleatory procedures can be found frequently, including in my own music. Since 1967 I have been concerned with developing a musical language in which stylistic elements from all times and places can coexist. The influence of John Cage can be seen in the action music of Juan Hidalgo (b. 1927) and Ramon *Barce (b. 1928). A Webern-like use of timbres, serialism, and extreme brevity appear in Miguel Angel *Coria (b. 1937). Visual theater elements play an important role in Tomás *Marco (b. 1942). Arturo Tamayo (b. 1946) has moved from serialism toward collages of different styles and procedures. Electronic music is represented in the music of Eduardo Polonio (b. 1943).

BIBL.: *Enciclopedia Salvat de la música* (Barcelona 1967); Wolf-Eberhard von Lewinski, "Vier katalanische Komponisten in Barcelona," *Melos*

38:92–103; Tomás Marco, *La música española de vanguardia* (Madrid 1970); ——, "Luis de Pablo," *Ministerio de Educación y Ciencia* (Madrid 1971); Luis de Pablo, *Aproximación a una estética de la música contemporánea* (Madrid 1968); Federico Sopeña, *Historia de la música española contemporánea* (Madrid 1958); Manuel Valls, "La música española después de Manuel de Falla," *Revista de occidente* (Madrid 1962).

Luis de Pablo
(trans. from Spanish by Alcides Lanza)

Spatial Music, music in which a plan for the physical location of sound sources is an integral part of the structure, either explicit or implied. The sound sources, either live or recorded and heard via loudspeakers, may be stationary or in motion. An illusion of sound in motion is often achieved by transferring recorded sounds rapidly from one stationary speaker to another.

Henry Brant

SEE ALSO Orchestration.

Speech, see Instrumental and Vocal Resources, Text Setting and Usage

Spiegelman, Joel (Warren) (b. Buffalo, 23 Jan 1933), studied at Yale Univ. (1949–50), the Univ. of Buffalo (1950–53), the Longy School of Music in Cambridge, Mass. (1953–54, theory and harpsichord with Melville Smith), Brandeis Univ. (1954–56; composition with Harold Shapiro, Irving Fine; analysis with Arthur Berger), and the Paris Conservatory (1956–57, composition with Nadia Boulanger). He also studied privately with Boulanger during 1957–60. He has been resident composer and harpsichordist at Brandeis Univ. (1961–66) and Sarah Lawrence College (since 1966), where he also teaches music and directs the Studio for Electronic Music and Experimental Sound Media. He founded the New York Electronic Ensemble in 1970. Since 1964 he has worked with electronic composition and since 1969 devoted himself exclusively to the development of live electronic performance. His work has been influenced by the music of Stravinsky, Cage, and Berio and by his residence in the Soviet Union during 1965–66, when he rethought his musical values, "mainly the influence of neoclassicism," and

freed himself from all "doctrinaire modes of musical thought."

PRINCIPAL COMPOSITIONS: *Piano Sonata* (1956); *2 Movements* for orchestra (1957); *Serenade* for 2 flutes, 2 harps, piano, celesta (1958); *Fantasia* for string quartet (1963–64); *Medea*, electronic tape score for the play by Euripides (1964); *Kousochki* for piano 4-hands (1966, MCA); *Phantom of the Opera* for women's voices, crotales, wind chimes, candles (1967); *The 11th Hour*, ballet score on tape (1969); *Mystery of the Sabbath*, Jewish cantorial chants and electronic sounds, all on tape (1969); *They*, tape score for the NET production of the play by Marya Mannes (1970); *Symphony* for soprano, flute, double bass (all with contact microphones), synthesizers, tape using revised material from *The 11th Hour* (1971).

Spies, Claudio (b. Santiago, Chile, 26 March 1925), settled in the U.S. in 1942 and became an American citizen in 1966. He studied with Nadia Boulanger (Boston, 1943) and Harold Shapero (Boston, 1944–45) and at Harvard Univ. (1947–50; composition with Irving Fine, Paul Hindemith, Walter Piston; musicology with Otto Gombosi). He has taught at Harvard (1954–57), Vassar College (1957–58), Swarthmore College (1958–64), and Princeton Univ. (since 1970).

Approximately half of Spies's output consists of compositions for voice (solo and choral) with various instrumental combinations (from piano to orchestra). The remainder includes orchestral, piano, and chamber music. The earlier compositions are largely tonal but also make use of formal structures and voice-leading procedures that have more to do with contemporary than traditional practice (e.g., *3 Intermezzi* for piano, 1950–54; *Music for a Ballet*, 1955). This early music shows a strong influence of Stravinsky (whom Spies knew personally from the early 40s) not only in melodic and harmonic details but also in its concern for spacing, orchestration, and the Stravinskian value of craftsmanship and consistency. During the late 50s Spies's music became progressively less tonal and developed more in terms of its nontonal structural properties. This led to the use of 12-tone procedures, which first appeared in the *5 Psalms* (1959).

Spies's construction of sets for *Tempi* (1962) and *Viopiacem* (1965), two of his best works, reveals something of his thinking. In both pieces sets were chosen with a concern to control melodic and harmonic structures in terms of the composer's special compositional predilections and notions, rather than with a concern to maintain strict invariance, as in much Webern. In *Viopiacem*, for example, the end of a set statement often coincides with the beginning of another so that the last notes of one are the first notes of another. This is made into an interesting and important musical event by melodic similarities between the beginning and end of the basic set. In this way Spies creates a musical surface in which phrases are able to elide, coincide, and succeed each other in a musically challenging way. Spies also uses certain special melodic details of the basic set to form and interrelate large-scale structural events. As a result of such concerns, one is often aware of relations between large blocks of musical events. In a piece such as the *5 Psalms*, extremely effective rhythmic continuity is gained as a result of a great variety of rhythmic detail on the small and the large. Finally, Spies always makes his intentions most explicit by a great attention to detail (his compositions are full of subtle canonic and imitative structures). This is paralleled on the large by an equal concern for form and large-scale structure. In *Tempi*, for example, there are special relations between movements in terms of the overall pitch and rhythmic structure of the composition, and in *Il cantico di frate sole* and the *5 Psalms*, the multimovement structure has symmetrical properties that create a large-scale formal cohesiveness.

PRINCIPAL COMPOSITIONS: *In Paradisum*, motet for chorus (1950, E-V); *3 Intermezzi* for piano (1950–54, E-V); *Music for a Ballet* for orchestra (1955, Presser); *Descanso en jardín* for tenor, baritone, woodwind quartet; text by Jorge Guillén (1957); *Il cantico di frate sole* for bass-baritone, orchestra; text by St. Francis of Assisi (1958); *Music for Daniel Hoffman's "Taliesin"* for bassoon, horn, trombone, timpani, cello (1959); *7 Canons* for soprano, tenor, flute, bassoon, piano; text by Tibullus (1959); *Verses from the Book of Ruth* for women's voices, piano (1959, Presser); *5 Psalms* for soprano, tenor, flute, bassoon, horn, mandolin, viola, cello (1959, Boosey); *Canon for 4 Flutes* (1960, Boosey); *Canon for Violas* (1961); *Tempi*, music for 14 instruments (1962, E-V); *Impromptu* for piano (1963, E-V); *Ensembles for Orchestra* (1963–); *Proverbs on Wisdom* for men's chorus, organ, piano (1964, E-V); *Animula blandula, vagula* for chorus (1964, Boosey); *Viopiacem*, for viola, harpsichord/piano (1965, Boosey); *5 Orchestral Songs* for soprano, orchestra (1966–); *LXXXV*, "8s and 5s" for strings, clarinets; in honor of Stravinsky's 85th birthday (1967, Boosey); *Times 2* for 2 horns (1968, Boosey); *3 Songs on Poems by May Swenson* for soprano, piano (1969); *Bagatelle* for piano (1970). List to 1969: *Composers of the Americas* 15:216–18.

PRINCIPAL WRITINGS: "Notes on Stravinsky's *Abraham and Isaac*," *Perspectives* 3/2:104–26; "Notes on Stravinsky's *Variations*," *ibid.* 4/1:62–74; "Some Notes on Stravinsky's Requiem Settings," *ibid.* 5/2:98–123.

BIBL.: Donald Martino, "C. S., Tempi," *Perspectives* 2/2 112–24.

Paul Lansky

Sprechgesang, Sprechstimme ("spoken melody" or "speech-song") is a technique of vocal performance that lies between speech and song. It first appeared in Humperdinck's opera *Königskinder* (1897), in which most vocal lines were notated with X's instead of noteheads, indicating that the singers should approximate the pitches (however, the singers were doubled at all times by instruments playing exact pitches). Humperdinck abandoned the device and specified definite sung pitches when he revised the opera in 1910. Arnold Schoenberg applied the concept of approximation in a short section of his *Gurrelieder* (1900–01), used it again in *Die glückliche Hand* (1910–13), and applied it as a fully developed procedure in *Pierrot lunaire* (1912) and later works. For Schoenberg the device may have been an attempt to codify in notation, and thereby exploit in composition, an already existing performance convention. It is known that some singers of late-19th century lieder departed from traditional concepts of intonation and vocal production for dramatic effect; significantly, *Pierrot* deals with surreal images, for which such vocal procedures would be appropriate, and was composed not for a singer but for an actress.

Sprechgesang as a vocal technique is easier said than done. Detailed instructions appear in the forewords to *Die glückliche Hand*, *Pierrot lunaire*, and Alban Berg's *Wozzeck*, but considerable liberty in carrying out these instructions was apparently either allowed by the composers from the start or tacitly approved by them later on. Austin (pp. 196–202, see bibl.) outlines some of the difficulties and shows the deviations that occur in four recorded performances of *Pierrot*. Eduard Steuermann, Schoenberg's longtime friend and colleague, felt that "the emphasis must not be on singing. It seems to me many people sing the *Sprechstimme* too much" (*Perspectives* 3/1:25). The performance technique was widely used by composers of the second Viennese school and has been called for by many others as well.

BIBL.: William Austin, *Music in the 20th Century* (New York 1966):196ff., 310ff.; Hans Keller, "New Music: Two Schoenberg Problems," *Music*

Review 17:268–69; Erwin Stein, ed., *Orpheus in New Guises* (London 1953):86–89; Ralph Wood, "Concerning 'Sprechgesang'," *Tempo* 17:3–6.

SEE ALSO Instrumental and Vocal Resources, Performance, Schoenberg, Text Setting and Usage.

Srebotnjak, Alojz (b. Postojna, Slovenia, Yugoslavia, 27 June 1931), attended the Ljubljana Academy of Music (1953–58, composition with Lucijan M. Škerjanc) and summer courses of the Accadèmia Musicale Chigiana in Siena (1954–57, composition with Vito Frazzi, film music with Angelo Lavagnino). He studied composition privately in Rome with Boris Porrena (1958–59) and in London with Peter Racine Fricker (1960–61). During 1958–66 he composed scores for films in Yugoslavia. He taught harmony and counterpoint at the Pedagogical Academy of Ljubljana from 1964 to 1970 and since 1970 has been teaching composition at the Ljubljana Academy of Music. A major influence on Srebotnjak's development has been his association with the Pro Musica Viva group of composers in Ljubljana.

PRINCIPAL COMPOSITIONS (published by DSS unless otherwise noted): *Mati* [Mother] for voice, strings (1955); *Music for Strings* (1955, unpub.); *Pisma* [Letters] for voice, harp (1956); *Sonatina* for violin, piano (1957); *Vojne slike* [War Pictures] for voice, viola, piano, percussion (1957); *Sinfonietta in 2 Movements* (1959, unpub.); *Preludes* for harp (1960, Schirmer-G); *Invenzione variata* for piano (1961); *Serenata* for flute, clarinet, bassoon (1961); *Monologues* for flute, oboe, horn, timpani, string orchestra (1962); *6 Pieces* for bassoon, piano (1963); *Kraška suita* [The Lipizza Suite] for orchestra (1964, unpub.); *Antiphon* for orchestra (1964); *Microsongs* for voice, 13 instruments (1964, unpub.); *Ekstaza smrti* [The Ecstacy of Death] for baritone, chorus, orchestra (1965, unpub.); *6 Macedonian Love Songs* for chorus (1965, Tonger); *2 Macedonian Folksongs* for chorus (1966, Schirmer-G); *Sonatina No. 2* for violin, piano (1966); *Episodes* for orchestra (1967, unpub.); *Sonatina No. 3* for violin, piano (1968, unpub.).

Staempfli, Edward (b. Bern, 1 Feb 1908), studied composition with Wilhelm Maler and Philipp Jarnach at the Cologne Hochschule für Musik (1929–30) and with Paul Dukas at the Ecole Normale in Paris (1930–31). A professional pianist, he has performed his compositions in Europe, the U.S., and Israel and has given numerous lectures there on

contemporary music. Since 1954 he has resided in Berlin. His presence at the first performance in Barcelona of Berg's *Violin Concerto* in 1936 first stimulated Staempfli's interest in 12-tone techniques, which he has employed in his music since 1949.

PRINCIPAL COMPOSITIONS: *String Quartets Nos. 1–6* (1926, 1934, 1939, 1945, 1954, 1962); *Piano Concertos Nos. 1–4* (1932; 1933; 1954, Bote; 1963); *Violin Concertos Nos. 1–3* (1936; 1939; 1966, Gerig); *Symphonies Nos. 1–3* (1938, 1942, 1945); *Divertissement choreographique* for orchestra (1942); *Die Prinzessin und der Schweinehirt*, ballet after Anderson for flute, bassoon, trumpet, percussion, celesta, piano (1942); *Ein Traumspiel*, opera after Strindberg (1943); *Der Spiegel der Welt*, oratorio (1950); *Medea*, opera; libretto by the composer after Grillparzer (1954); *Flute Concerto* (1957, Bote); *Ornamente* for 2 flutes, celesta, percussion (1960); *Spannungen* for orchestra (1961, Bote); *Quartet* for clarinet, violin, cello, harp (1965); *Grosses Mosaik* for 2 pianos, 11 instruments (1966); *Wege des Wanderers*, cantata for soprano, 12 instruments; text by Hölderlin (1966); *Wenn der Tag leer wird*, oratorio; text by Nelly Sachs (1968, Gerig); *Tripartita* for 3 pianos, 23 winds (1969); *Zions Klage und Tröstung*, oratorio on texts from the book of Ezra (1970, IMP).

PRINCIPAL WRITINGS: "Musik, Wort und Sprache," *Melos* 34:339–43; "Strawinskys 'Symphonies pour instruments à vent'," *Melos* 36:509–12; "Schönbergs Streichtrio Op. 45," *Melos* 37:35–39.

Starer, Robert (b. Vienna, 8 Jan 1924), attended the Vienna Academy (1938–39, piano with Ebenstein), the Jerusalem Conservatory (1939–43, composition with Joseph Tal and Öedöen Partos), and the Juilliard School (1947–49, composition with Frederick Jacobi). He was staff pianist for the Palestine radio, 1941–43, and has been teaching at Juilliard since 1949 and at Brooklyn College since 1963.

PRINCIPAL COMPOSITIONS (published by MCA unless otherwise noted): *Piano Concerto No. 1* (1947); *Prelude and Dance* for orchestra (1949); *Symphony No. 1* (1950); *Symphony No. 2* (1951, IMP); *Kohelet* [Ecclesiastes] for soprano, baritone, chorus, orchestra (1952); *Piano Concerto No. 2* (1953); *Prelude and Rondo Giocoso* for orchestra (1953); *Concerto a tre* for clarinet, trumpet, trombone, string orchestra (1954; used for Martha Graham's dance *Secular Games*, 1962); *Ballade* for violin, orchestra (1955, Presser); *The Intruder*, 1-act opera (1956, Presser); *Concerto* for viola, strings, percussion (1958); *Ariel* (*Visions of Isaiah*) for soprano, baritone, chorus, orchestra (1959); *The Dybbuk*, dance; choreography by Herbert Ross and Nora Kaye (1960, suite published by MCA); *Samson Agonistes*, dance; choreography by Graham (1961; "symphonic portrait" of the same name, 1963); *Phaedra*, dance; choreography by Graham (1962, unpub.); *Mutabili*, variants for orchestra (1965); *Joseph and His Brothers* for narrator, soloists, chorus, orchestra (1966); *Concerto* for violin, cello, orchestra (1967); *Sabbath Eve Service* (1967); *On the Nature of Things* for chorus (1968).

PRINCIPAL WRITINGS: "Composer and Choreographer," *Dance Perspectives* (1963):11–17; *Rhythmic Training* (New York 1969).

BIBL.: Frederick Dorian, "Concerto for Violin, Cello, and Orchestra," Pittsburgh Symphony program notes (11 and 13 Oct 1968); Edward Downes, "Samson Agonistes," New York Philharmonic program notes (25–29 April 1968).

SEE ALSO Dance; Liturgical Music: Jewish.

Steuermann, Eduard (b. Sambor, near Lvov, Poland, 18 June 1892; d. New York, 11 November 1964), studied in Berlin (1911–14, piano with Ferruccio Busoni, theory with Arnold Schoenberg, composition briefly with Engelbert Humperdinck). He taught piano at the Paderewski School in Lvov and later at the Cracow Conservatory (1932–36). After his emigration to the U.S. in 1936 he taught piano at the Philadelphia Conservatory (1948–64) and at the Juilliard School (1952–64). From the time he was 20 he championed new music, especially Schoenberg's. He brought out piano scores of Schoenberg's orchestral works and premiered many of his piano pieces. In 1939–40 he gave a series of "Contemporary Concerts" of 12-tone music in New York. His own music has not often been performed. Writing about a memorial concert for Steuermann, Elliott Carter (see bibl.) described some aspects of his late work: The *Cantata* (1964) is a work "of delicate shadings, smooth transitions, with a mosaic of contrasting bits of material of much greater variety, character, and expressive scope than those of the late Webern cantatas, which it remotely resembles, although actually closer in character to the pre-12-tone Viennese works." The *Suite* for chamber orchestra (1964) "maintains an interesting flow of constantly evolving dialectical statements made of short strands (often three-note motifs) of contrasting intervallic, rhythmic, timbral, and dynamic content that in combination produce flexible phrases in a logical and expressive continuity."

PRINCIPAL COMPOSITIONS: 7 *Waltzes* for string quartet (1945); *Suite* for piano (1954); 3 *Choruses* for mixed voices, instruments (1956); *Auf der Galerie*, cantata; text by Franz Kafka (1964); *Suite* for chamber orchestra (1964). There are also: *Variations* for orchestra, 3 song cycles, 2 string quartets, and a number of piano works.

BIBL.: T. W. Adorno, "Nachruf auf einen Pianisten . . .," *Süddeutsche Zeitung* (28–29 Nov 1964); Elliott Carter, "Current Chronicle—New York," *Musical Quarterly* 52:93–101; Gunther Schuller, "A Conversation with S.," *Perspectives* 3/1:22–35.

Stevens, Halsey (b. Scott, N. Y., 3 Dec 1908), studied piano and theory privately (1917–26), after which he attended Syracuse Univ. (1926–31, 1935–37; composition with William H. Berwald, piano with George Mulfinger), and the Univ. of Calif. at Berkeley (1944, composition with Ernest Bloch). He taught at Dakota Wesleyan Univ. during 1937–41, then became a professor of music and director of the College of Music, Bradley Univ., 1941–46. He taught at the Univ. of Redlands during 1946 and became that year a professor and chairman of the composition department at the Univ. of Southern Calif., a post which he still holds. He has also been a visiting professor at several other colleges and universities in the U.S.

PRINCIPAL COMPOSITIONS (published by ACA unless otherwise noted): *17 Piano Pieces* (1933–66, Westwood); *Symphony No. 1* (1941–45); *Quintet* for flute, violin, viola, cello, piano (1945, Helios); *Suite* for clarinet (viola), piano (1945, Peters); *10 Short Pieces* for piano (1945–54); *Piano Sonata No. 3* (1947–48, AME); *Intermezzo, Cadenza, and Finale* for cello, piano (1948–49, Peer); *String Quartet No. 3* (1949; transcribed for string orchestra as *Adagio and Allegro*, 1955); 6 *Millay Songs* (1949–50, unpub.); *Viola Sonata* (1950); *Sonatinas Nos. 3–4* for piano (1950, 1952); 4 *Songs of Love and Death* (1951–53, unpub.); 6 *Preludes* for piano (1951–56); *Horn Sonata* (1952–53, King); *Adagio and Allegro* for orchestra (1953); *Triskelion* for orchestra (1953); *Partita* for harpsichord or piano (1953–54, Peer); *Trio No. 3* for violin, cello, piano (1953–54); *Trumpet Sonata* (1953–56, Peters); *Sonatina* for harp (1954, Peer); *Sonatina giocosa* for double bass, piano (1954); *Sonatina No. 5* for piano (1954, Westwood); *Suite* for violin (1954, Helios); 3 *Short Freludes* for organ (1954–56, Peer); *The Ballade of William Sycamore* for chorus, orchestra; text by Stephen Vincent Benét (1955, Highgate); *Sonatina piacevole* for alto recorder (flute), harpsichord (piano) (1955–56, Peer); *Sonetto del Petrarca* for voice, piano (1956); *Septet* for clarinet, bassoon, horn, 2 violas, 2 cellos (1956–57); *Sonata* for solo cello (1956–58, Peters); *11 Ukrainian Folksongs* for band (1957, Aberdeen); 5 *Pieces* for orchestra (1958, Peer; transcribed for band by Donald Bryce, 1958, Peer); *Symphonic Dances* for orchestra (1958, Peters); 2 *Shakespeare Songs* for voice, flute, clarinet (1958–59); *Divertimento* for 2 violins (1958–66); *A Testament of Life* for chorus, orchestra; Biblical texts (1959); *Sonatina No. 3* for violin, piano (1959,

Helios); *Sonatina No. 6* for piano (1959, West-wood); *Sonatina No. 2* for piano, second version (1959, Westwood); *Suite* for viola, piano (1959, Peer); *Trio* for winds and/or strings (1959); *Ritratti* for piano (1959-60, Westwood); *Sonatina* for tuba (trombone), piano (1959-60, Peer); *Fantasia* for piano (1961, Westwood); *4 Canciones* for voice; text by Antonio Machado (1961, unpub.); *The Rivals*, incidental music for the play by Richard B. Sheridan (1961); *Magnificat* for chorus, orchestra (1962, Mark Press); *3 Pieces* for organ (1962, Westwood); *12 Slovakian Folksongs* for 2 violins (1962, Highgate); *Cello Concerto* (1964); *7 Canciones* for voice; text by García-Lorca (1964, unpub.); *Cello Sonata* (1965, Peer); *Trombone Sonata* (1965, Peer); *8 Yugoslavian Folksongs* for piano (1966, Peer); *Melodic Studies* for solo clarinet (1966, Peer); *6 Slovakian Folksongs* for harp (1966, Peer); *Campion Suite* for chorus (1967, Westwood); *Chansons courtoises* for chorus (1967, Mark Press); *4 Duos* for double basses (1967); *Sonatina No. 1* for piano, second version (1967, Westwood); *Studies* for bassoon (1968); *Threnos* for orchestra (1968); *Concerto* for clarinet, string orchestra (1969); *8 Canons* for 2 violas or violin, viola (1969). List to 1966: *Composers of the Americas* 11:103-21.

PRINCIPAL WRITINGS: Program notes for concerts of the Los Angeles Philharmonic Orchestra (1946-51); "Contemporary Music and the Church," *Journal of the Choral Conductors Guild* 9/2:1-2 and 9/3:1-2; "Pótlás a Zenei Szemle decemberi számában megjelent Bartók-bibliográfiához," *Éneksző* 17/5:211-13; "On the Nature and Value of Theoretical Training for the Composer," *Journal of Music Theory* 3:32-37; "Youth and New Music," *Music Educators' Journal* (Sept 1963):49-51; "Bartók: Heretic Absolved," *Pavilion* (Los Angeles) 3/1:16-19; "Barok in skladatelji 20. stoletja," *Muzikološki zbornik* (Ljubljana) 2:101-15; "Some 'Unknown' Works of Bartók," *Musical Quarterly* 52:37-55; *The Life and Music of Béla Bartók* (1st ed., New York, 1953; paperback ed., 1967); program notes for Coleman Chamber Concerts (Pasadena, Calif., 1967); "Stravinsky: A Critical Decade," *Report of the 10th Congress, International Musicological Society* (New York 1967); "The Choral Music of Zoltán Kodály," *Musical Quarterly* 54:147-68.

BIBL.: Wallace Berry, "The Music of H. S.," *Musical Quarterly* 54:287-308; Paul A. Pisk, "H. S.," *ACA Bulletin* 4/2:2-11.

music (especially during 1945-57) was influenced by the esthetics, counterpoint, and motive development of Ferruccio Busoni and by correspondence with Percy Grainger. Since 1957 he has also been using Scottish folk materials. He said in a 1967 BBC interview that "my main interest in music is in the epic. This is an epic age it seems to me, and only epic forms can fully express its aspirations. I . . . absorb in my music elements from the East and from Africa, as well as from Western culture. In my future work I hope to find points of coalescence in world musics. . . . I'll use any techniques which will enable me to achieve these objectives."

PRINCIPAL COMPOSITIONS: *19 Songs of Innocence* for various voices, piano; texts by William Blake (1948-50); *Prelude, Fugue and Fantasy on Busoni's Faust* for piano (1949-59, Novello); *Jamboree for Grainger* for orchestra (1961); *Weyvers o' Blegburn* [Weavers of Blackburn] for boy's broken voice, weak amateur tenor, amateur chorus, piano; Lancashire dialect rhymes (1961); *Passacaglia on DSCH* for piano (1961-62, Oxford); *4 Meditations for String Quartet* (1964); *20 Songs to Poems by Hugh MacDiarmid* for various voices, piano (1964-66); *A Medieval Scottish Triptych* for chorus (1965, Novello); *Scots Dance Toccata* for orchestra (1965); *A Wheen Tunes for Bairns tae Spiel* [A Set of Tunes for Young Folks to Play], 4 Scottish pieces for piano (1967, Schott); *Harpsichord Sonata* (1968); *Anns an Airde, as an Doimhne* [In the Heights, from the Depths] for chorus; Scottish Gaelic poems by Sorley MacLean (1968). Stevenson has also edited the anthology, *The Young Pianist's Grainger* (1967, Schott).

PRINCIPAL WRITINGS: "Busoni and Mozart," *The Score* 13:25-38; "Busoni—The Legend of a Prodigal," *ibid.* 15:15-30; "Beethoven—The Concerted Works," *A Beethoven Symposium* (London 1970); *Western Music—An Introduction* (London 1970); *Busoni—A Bibliography of the Works* (1970, unpub.).

BIBL.: Ates Orga, "R. S.," *Music and Musicians* (Oct 1968):26-32; ——, "The Piano Music of R. S.," *Musical Opinion* (March 1969):292-95; Colin Scott-Sutherland, "The Music of R. S.," *Music Review* 26:118-28; Colin Wilson, *Colin Wilson on Music* (London 1967):178-80.

Stevenson, Ronald (b. Blackburn, England, 6 March 1928), studied at the Royal Manchester College of Music (1945-48) and at the Accàdemia de S. Cecilia in Rome (1955, composition with Guido Guerrini). He is a freelance composer and pianist. During 1963-65 he taught composition at the Univ. of Capetown, South Africa. Since 1967 he has been a monthly contributor to *The Listener*. His

Stibilj, Milan (b. Ljubljana, Yugoslavia, 2 Nov 1929), attended the Ljubljana Academy of Music (1956-61), the Zagreb Academy of Music (1962-64, composition with Milko Keleman), and the Univ. of Utrecht (1966-67, electronic music with Gottfried Michael Koenig). He lives as a free-lance composer in Ljubljana.

PRINCIPAL COMPOSITIONS (published by Bärenreiter unless otherwise noted): *Musique concertante* for horn, orchestra (1959, DSS); *The Nightingale and the Rose* for orchestra (1961, DSS); *Skladja* [Congruences] for piano, orchestra (1963, DSS); *Impressions* for flute, harp, string quintet or string orchestra (1963); *Epervier de ta faiblesse, domine* for speaker, 5 percussionists (1964); *Assimilation* for violin (1965); *Contemplation* for oboe, string quintet or string orchestra (1966); *Apokatastasis*, Slovenian requiem for tenor, chorus, orchestra (1967); *Condensation* for trombone, 2 pianos, percussion (1967); *Ekthesis* for orchestra (1968); *The Rainbow*, on 2- or 4-track tape (1968–69, DSS); *Zoom* for clarinet, bongos (1970).

PRINCIPAL WRITINGS: "Kasselski muzički dani" [Cassel's Musical Days], *Zvuk* 67 (1966):244–48; "Berlinske svečane nedelje" [The Berlin Festival Sundays], *ibid.* 82 (1967):115–20.

BIBL.: Andrej Rijavec, "Nove kompozicije M. S.," *Zvuk* 68:334–41; ———, "M. S.: Profil seines Schaffens," *Musica* 1969/1:45–47.

Still, William Grant (b Woodville, Miss., 11 May 1895), studied at Wilberforce Univ. (1911–15) and at the Oberlin Conservatory (1917–18, 1919–22; composition with George W. Andrews, theory with F. J. Lehmann, violin with Maurice Kessler). He studied privately with Edgard Varèse (1922–25) and with George W. Chadwick at the New England Conservatory (1922). In the 1920s and 30s he worked as an orchestrator (in which he was self-taught) of commercial and popular music and conducted for radio and Broadway shows. He has also played the violin, cello, and oboe in orchestras and conducted a number of symphonic groups in the U.S.

PRINCIPAL COMPOSITIONS: *Afro-American Symphony* (1930, Novello); *Sahdji*, choral ballet (1930, Fischer); *Kaintuck* for piano, orchestra (1935); *Lenox Avenue* for speaker, chorus, orchestra (1937); *Symphony in G Minor* (1937); *And They Lynched Him on a Tree* for speaker, double chorus, orchestra (1940); *Plain-Chant for America* for baritone, chorus, orchestra (1941); *Old California* for orchestra (1941); *Troubled Island*, opera (1941, Southern); *In Memoriam: The Colored Soldiers Who Died for Democracy* for orchestra (1943); *Festive Overture* (1944); *Poem for Orchestra* (1944, MCA); *Symphony No. 3*, "Western Hemisphere" (1945); *Archaic Ritual* for orchestra (1946); *Symphony No. 4*, "Autochthonous" (1947); *Danzas de Panama* for string quartet or string orchestra (1948, Southern); *The Little Song that Wanted to Be a Symphony* for speaker, women's trio, orchestra (1954); *The Peaceful Land* for orchestra (1960, AME); *Highway 1, U.S.A.*, opera (1962). List to 1958: *Composers of the Americas* 5:87–97.

PRINCIPAL WRITINGS: "Music, a Vital Factor in America's Racial Problems," *Australian Musical News* (1 Nov 1948); "The Composer Needs Determination and Faith," *Etude* (Jan 1949); "The Structure of Music," *Etude* (March 1950); "Interview," *Arts in Society* (summer-fall 1968); "The Negro Musician in America," *Music Educators' Journal* (Jan 1970).

BIBL.: Verna Arvey, *Studies in Contemporary American Music: W. G. S.* (Glenrock, N. J., 1939); Mariam Matthews, "Profile XXIII: W. G. S.," *Phylon* (Atlanta Univ., 1951); Mary D. Hudgins, "An Outstanding Arkansas Composer, W. G. S.," *Arkansas Historical Quarterly* (winter 1965).

Stochastic, a term derived from the Greek, meaning "point of aim" or "target," and first used by the 18th-century Swiss mathematician Jacques Bernoulli, the promulgator of the law of large numbers. Bernoulli's law states that the more numerous the phenomena, the more they tend toward a determinate end (i.e., a "target"). In music the term refers to a probabilistic compositional method, introduced by Iannis Xenakis, in which the overall contours of sound are specified but the inner details are left to random or chance selection. Xenakis might, for example, specify a range-band within which pitches may occur, along with changes in time of the height and width of the band; he would then leave the specific pitches and their small-scale temporal distribution to chance calculations (probably made with the aid of a computer). Other aspects of the sound contour, such as its timbre(s), articulations, etc., whether preselected or left to chance, would be plotted simultaneously with its pitches. Chance in stochastic music is restricted to the process of composition; the end result is fully notated.

SEE ALSO Mathematics, Xenakis.

Stock, David (Frederick) (b. Pittsburgh, 3 June 1939), studied at the Carnegie Institute of Technology (1956–63, composition with Nikolai Lopatnikoff, trumpet with Anthony Pasquarelli, musicology with Frederick Dorian), Brandeis Univ. (1965–68, composition with Arthur Berger), and the Ecole Normale de Musique (1960–61, composition with Andrée Vaurabourg-Honegger, conducting with Jean Fournet). He also studied composition privately with Nadia Boulanger during 1960–61. During 1961–63 he was a trumpeter with the Pittsburgh Symphony. He has taught theory at the Cleveland Institute (1964–65), Brandeis Univ. (1966–68), the New England Conservatory (1968–70), and Antioch College in Ohio (since 1970).

PRINCIPAL COMPOSITIONS: *Divertimento* for orchestra (1957); *String Quartet* (1960–62); *Capriccio* for chamber orchestra (1963); *Symphony in 1 Movement* (1963); *Serenade* for flute, clarinet, horn, viola, cello (1964); *Quintet* for clarinet, strings (1965–67); *Noro*, game piece using some rules based on 12-tone procedures; for any 2 instruments of similar range (1966); *Flashback* for chamber ensemble, harpsichord, percussion (1968); *3 Pieces* for violin, piano (1969); *Triple Play* for piccolo, double bass, percussion (1970).

PRINCIPAL WRITINGS: "Reports on New Music," *Perspectives* 7/1:143–44 and 8/1:141–43. Stock also wrote criticism for the *Boston Globe* (1966–68).

Stockhausen, Karlheinz (b. Mödrath, Germany, 28 August 1928), studied oboe, piano, and conducting as a youth. In 1947 he entered the Musikhochschule in Cologne and also began his studies of musicology and philosophy at the Univ. of Cologne. He studied theory with Hermann Schroeder and began composition studies in 1950 with Frank Martin. His early works, which exhibit the influence of Schoenberg, Stravinsky, Bartók, and early Webern, include a violin sonata and three songs with orchestra. Herbert Eimert, who later joined him as coeditor of *Die Reihe*, helped him to get performances of his music.

Stockhausen lived in Paris in 1952–53, where he studied with Messiaen and met Pierre Boulez, with whose name his is frequently linked. He worked in the musique concrète studio of the French radio and then became artistic director of the Studio for Electronic Music in Cologne, where he created *Studie I*, *Studie II*, *Gesang der Jünglinge*, *Kontakte*, and *Hymnen*. During 1954–56 he studied phonetics and communication theory, disciplines that have influenced his work, with Werner Meyer-Eppler at the Univ. of Bonn. Since 1957 he has given occasional composition seminars at the Darmstadt summer courses and at the Universities of Pa. and Calif. at Davis.

Stockhausen's point of departure was the music of Webern, in which he found powerful constructions, some fully developed, such as row technique and timbre composition, and some embryonic, such as rhythmic serialization and group composition. It was Webern's techniques rather than his esthetics or musical gestures that were important. As Stockhausen discovered the systematic control of independent elements in Webern's music, he realized that the traditional hierarchy of these elements might be challenged, and he embraced the idea that every sound is uniquely determined by five parameters or dimensions: pitch, intensity, duration, timbre, and position in space (the latter, of course, was not controlled by Webern). All other elements of music (tempo, rhythm, instrumentation, melody, density, harmony, register, meter, etc.) were derivable from the five basic parameters, and Stockhausen classified them as compositional parameters because their relevance in a musical context is controlled by the composer.

Stockhausen's early works, which extended the Webern principle of serialized pitches to every parameter, were often much longer than Webern's scores. He expanded Webern's proportions by creating a middle ground of durational units. The small units of Webern's music (the isolated point or the small motivic cell) he retained, but he organized these tiny cells into larger units. Unlike those of Webern, these larger units were smaller than the whole piece. This middle ground became the basis for what Stockhausen calls "group composition." A group is a segment of musical time, from a few seconds to a few minutes in duration (he calls the larger groups "moments"), the limits of which are defined by a self-contained process. For example, the character of a group might be that all or some pitches remain fixed in certain registers or that it is based exclusively on a single interval, or that the volume increases or decreases at a specified rate, or that extremely long or short durations (of notes, timbres, textures, etc.) prevail. The way various groups relate to one another defines the formal plan of the piece. The transition from Webernian point-music to group composition can be seen in *Klavierstücke I–IV* (1952–53); group composition reached its culmination in *Momente* (1962–64), a nearly two-hour piece whose basic idea is the juxtaposition of groups of different durations on several levels at once.

Since groups are carefully defined stretches of musical time, group composition led to a concern with proportions. Just as the relationship between various sizes and masses is crucial to the visual arts, the proportional lengths of groups became important in Stockhausen's music. More significantly, group composition led to the idea of mobility. Stockhausen saw that the order of self-contained groups could be varied so as to alter, but not destroy, the continuity of the music. He invented the multimeaningful form, which allowed different orderings of the sections of a given piece. Stockhausen's first mobile-form piece was *Klavierstück XI* (1956). It is printed on a single large sheet of paper on which groups are laid out separately so that they can be played in any order. The piece is so completely mobile that it loses its overall sense of direction, and the composer sought to correct this problem in *Zyklus* (1959). This work, for one percussionist, is circular: the performer may start at any of its 17 pages and proceed until he returns to his point of origin. The piece is both mobile and directional, and the processes by which the work moves are the same in every performance (actually there are two possible directions, for the performer may read from left to right or, turning over the score, from right to left).

Mobile form raised the question of direction in posttonal music. To explain how a work could be both mobile and directional and how a piece could acquire a sense of motion, Stockhausen formulated the concept of a process piece. In a process piece each parameter is subjected to a simple and obvious directional process, such as a diminuendo in some instruments, an accelerando in some instruments, the emergence of some pitches as prominent, or (as in *Kreuzspiel*, 1951) the gradual shift of pitches from one register to another. The complex sound of Stockhausen's music often results from the superimposition of several such processes, which generally take place at different rates and start, finish, or climax at different points. The mobility of *Zyklus* was accomplished, in part, by beginning a different process at each of the possible starting points of the piece, so that the performer would be in the middle of several processes but always at the beginning of one of them regardless of where he began.

Once Stockhausen had established for himself the independence and potential equality of parameters, he began to relate them in new ways. He worked by analogy, asking himself such questions as how would a major third of duration sound? or what is an octave of dynamics? Complete answers in the form of compositional constructions were not possible in instrumental music, since pitch is quantized, duration is on a continuum, and intensity can be controlled only approximately. Although some interesting relationships were possible, such as determining the ratios of the seven tempos used in *Kontra-Punkte* from the ratios of the frequencies of the seven opening pitches, the problem was ultimately best solved in the electronic medium. In *Studie II* (1954), for example, Stockhausen was able to treat timbre like the other parameters by using sine tones to structure the overtone spectrum of every sound; he was also able to make duration and intensity (amplitude) inversely proportional to frequency.

Electronic music gave Stockhausen his first opportunity to work with the spatial parameter. In *Gesang der Jünglinge* (1955–56), which mingles electronically produced sounds with altered sounds of a boy reciting, several loudspeakers produce the illusion of sounds traveling in space. Similar effects were subsequently tried in live music with *Gruppen* for three orchestras (1955–57) and *Carré* for four orchestras and four choruses (1959–60). Electronic technology made it possible for Stockhausen to work with thresholds, such as the pitch-noise threshold and the rhythm-pitch threshold. Since pitch and timbre are the result of rhythm accelerated to a rate within the audible frequency band, it is possible for the microworld of each sound to be structured. In *Telemusik* (1966) many of the sounds result from carefully composed long durations which were accelerated (and therefore raised in pitch) several thousand times so that the given duration became a single sound. The original pitches passed far above the audible frequency range; what was used were the combination tones. The sounds, resulting from inner structuring, are unique to *Telemusik*, for Stockhausen composed not only the piece but its sound materials. The idea of composing both the microstructure and the macrostructure of a piece in order to give it a unique sound context also led to the use of live electronic music in which the performed sounds are subjected to electronic transformation at the time of performance, as in *Solo* (1965–66).

With the advent of tape and live electronic music Stockhausen changed his idea of what a composer should specify in his music. Instead of the sounds themselves, he began to specify the procedures that would produce them and he thus embedded within a work the actual process of composition. In *Mikrophonie I* (1964), for example, a large tam-tam is set in vibration by a variety of means, the graphic and verbal instructions dealing with the manner of sound production rather than with the resulting music. The sound is picked up by two microphones moved by hand over the surface of the tam-tam. Thus the microphones become musical instruments, because the rhythms in which they are moved and their varying distances from the sound-producing parts of the tam-tam determine the final sounds.

The composer is not bothered by the loss of control implied in process composition and mobile form. Perhaps because electronic music allows for total control, Stockhausen is interested in the opposite, the collaboration between many musical minds. In *Carré*, for example, he determined the basic materials and forms of the work but allowed his assistant, Cornelius Cardew, to "realize" the details. The occasional struggle and occasional harmony between the two composers gives the work much of its interest, as does the interaction among the work's four conductors, who time their cues by interreaction rather than by referring to a clock or a metronome. In *Mikrophonie I* the performers react to one another to produce the musical form. They trade entrance cues back and forth, and they are instructed to make a given group either similar to, different from, or contrary to another group. Furthermore this relationship either remains constant, increases, or decreases for the duration of the group, and the ensuing group either supports, is neutral to, or destroys its predecessor. The result depends as much on the musicality of the performers as it does on that of the composer. This is true mobility on every level: the piece is multidirectional and multimeaningful, and it has infinite possibilities. Every performance is a unique event. Total mobility of composed segments reached an extreme in *Plus Minus* (1963), which consists of seven pages of musical figures and seven pages of reaction schemes, to be correlated by the performer(s), whose instrument(s) are not specified. In *Ensembles* (1967) Stockhausen assembled 12 student composers at Darmstadt, gave them each an instrumentalist, and prepared a piece in which each composer has his moment but in which each moment fits into a composed macrostructure. In recent works, such as *Prozession* (1968) and *Kurzwellen* (1969), the composer has found sufficient interest in the processes so that he designates very little, if any, of the musical elements that undergo the process.

Despite the elaborate constructions he has devised, despite the pages and pages of precompositional calculations, Stockhausen does use his intuition. He felt the need for last-minute changes in large structures: the tempo-interval correlation in *Kontra-Punkte* was an afterthought, as was the elimination of four sections in *Kontakte* (1959–60) and the addition of volume controls on the tape playback of live sounds in *Solo*. The elaborate calculations in *Studie II* all but disappeared when the composer played and rerecorded the tape in an acoustically live basement. His early works, totally serialized in every parameter, demonstrated what can be accomplished by means of a rigid system, but his freer later works, especially *Momente*, *Carré*, *Kontakte*, *Klavierstück X*, and *Mikrophonie I*, stand as his most significant compositions.

PRINCIPAL COMPOSITIONS (published by UE unless otherwise noted): *3 Lieder* for alto, chamber orchestra (1950); *Formel* for orchestra (1951–52); *Punkte* for orchestra (1952; revised 1962, 1967); *Kontra-Punkte* for 10 instruments (1952–53); *Klavierstücke I-XI*: I-IV (1952–53); V-VIII (1954–55); IX-X (1954–55, revised 1961); XI (1956); *Zeitmasse* for oboe, flute, English horn, clarinet, bassoon (1955–56); *Gruppen* for 3 orchestras (1955–57); *Gesang der Jünglinge* on tape (1955–56); *Zyklus* for percussionist (1959); *Carré* for 4 orchestras, 4 choruses (1959–60); *Kontakte* for piano, percussion, tape (1959–60); *Momente* for soprano, 4 choral groups, 13 instrumentalists (1962–64); *Telemusik* on tape (1966); *Prozession* for piano, electric viola, electronium, tam-tam, microphone, filters, potentiometer (1967); *Kurzwellen* for piano, electric viola, electronium, tam-tam, filters, potentiometer, 6 short-wave radio receivers (1968); *Stimmung* for 6 singers (1968); *Hymnen* for tape and/or 4 players and/or orchestra and/or colored lights (1969); *Mantra* for 2 pianos, electronics (1970); *Trans* for orchestra (1971).

PRINCIPAL WRITINGS: "...How Time Passes...," *Die Reihe*, English ed. 3:10–40; "2 Lectures," *ibid.* 5:59–82: "The Concept of Unity in Electronic Music," *Perspectives* I/1:39–48; *Texte zur elektronischen und instrumentalen Musik* ed. by D. Schnebel (Cologne 1963); "Une expérience électronique," *La Musique et ses problèmes contemporains* (Paris 1963):91–105; "Plus Minus auf 14 Notenblättern," *Melos* 33:144–45; "Mikrophonie I and II," *Melos* 33:354–58.

BIBL.: Cornelius Cardew, "Report on S.'s *Carré*," *Musical Times* (Oct 1961):619–22; Erhard Karkoschka, "S.'s Theorien," *Melos* 32:5–13; Dieter Schnebel, "K. S.," *Die Reihe*, English ed. 4:119–33; Roger Smalley, "S.'s *Gruppen*," *Musical Times* (Sept 1967):794–97; ——, "S.'s Piano Music," *Musical Times* (Jan 1969):30–32; Karl H. Wörner, ed., *K. S.: Werk und Wollen* (Rhein 1963).

Jonathan D. Kramer

SEE ALSO Asian Music and Western Composition; Austria and Germany; Electronic Music: History and Development; Electronic Music: Notation; Harmony and Counterpoint; Instrumental and Vocal Resources; Mathematics; Microtones; Mixed Media; Orchestration; Performance; Prose Music; Recording; Rhythm; Serialism; Text Setting and Usage; Texture.

Stout, Alan (b. Baltimore, 26 Nov 1932), studied at Johns Hopkins Univ. (1950–54), the Peabody Conservatory (1950–54, composition with Henry Cowell), and the Univ. of Wash. (1958–59, composition with John Verrall). He studied composition privately with Wallingford Riegger in New York (intermittently, 1951–56) and with Vagn Holmboe in Copenhagen (1954–55). He has taught composition and theory at Northwestern Univ.

since 1963. During 1968–69 he was a visiting lecturer at Johns Hopkins Univ.

PRINCIPAL COMPOSITIONS (published by CFE unless otherwise noted): *String Quartets Nos. 1, 7, 10* (1953, 1960, 1962); *Passion* for soloists, chorus, orchestra (1953–68, unpub.); *Symphonies Nos. 1, 2, 4* (1959; 1951–66; 1970, Peters); *Laudi* for soprano, baritone, orchestra (1961); *George Lieder* for baritone, orchestra (1962); *Movements* for violin, orchestra (1962, Peters); *Study in Densities and Durations* for organ (1965); *Cello Sonata* (1966); *Movements* for clarinet, string orchestra (1969).

Strang, Gerald (b. Claresholm, Alberta, Canada, 13 Feb 1908), studied at Stanford Univ. (1926–28), the Univ. of Calif. at Berkeley (1928–29), the Univ. of Southern Calif. (1935–36, composition with Arnold Schoenberg; 1946–48, composition with Ernst Toch). He also studied composition privately with Charles Koechlin in 1930. During 1936–38 he was a teaching assistant to Schoenberg in Los Angeles and during 1936–50 he was Schoenberg's editorial assistant. He has taught music at Long Beach City College (1938–58), San Fernando Valley State College (1958–65), Calif. State College at Long Beach (1965–69) and was lecturer in electronic music at the Univ. of Calif. at Los Angeles (1969–70). During 1935–40 he was editor of *New Music Edition*. He worked for the engineering department of the Douglas Aircraft Co. (1942–45) and since 1950 has been a consultant in building design and acoustics for several U.S. college and university music departments. He worked on electronic and computer music in 1964 and 1969 at the Bell Telephone Laboratories in N. J., and since 1964 at the Univ. of Calif. at Los Angeles.

PRINCIPAL COMPOSITIONS: *Percussion Music for 3 Players* (1935, New Music); *Overland Trail* for orchestra (1943, Mills); *Divertimento for 4 Instruments* (1948); *Concerto Grosso* (1951); *Cello Concerto* (1951); *Variations for 4 Instruments* (1956); *Composition Nos. 2–7* on tape (1963–69).

PRINCIPAL WRITINGS: "Educated Audio System," *Audio Magazine* (July 1965):26; "Case Study: Building a College Music Building," *Music Buildings, Rooms and Equipment* (Washington 1966):104; "The Computer in Musical Composition," *Computers and Automation* 15/8:16, reprinted *Cybernetics Serendipity* (London 1968):26; "Music and Computers," *The Man-Computer Team* (Los Angeles 1967):17; "The Problem of Imperfection in Computer Music," *Music by Computers* (New York 1969):133; "Ethics and Esthetics of Computer Music," *The Computer and Music* (Ithaca 1970).

Strauss, Richard (Georg) (b. Munich, 11 June 1864; d. Garmisch, 8 Sept 1949), was the son of a principal horn player in the Munich court opera. He began piano lessons at four and later studied violin; theory and composition followed with F. W. Meyer (1875–80). He read philosophy, art history, and esthetics at the Univ. of Munich (1882–83). He first conducted at Meiningen during 1885–86; then at Munich, 1886–89; Weimar, 1889–94; and Berlin, 1894–1918. During these years he also traveled widely, conducting his own and other music. He was director of the Vienna State Opera during 1919–24 and president of Hitler's Reichsmusikkamer, Nov 1933–June 1935.

From his first work (1876) to about 1888, Strauss composed in various genres. The years 1886–1903 were dominated by the tone poems, after which he concentrated on stage works. During his last years he returned to writing various concerted pieces. Songs and choral works appeared throughout his life. He was the only important 20th-century composer who, in a career spanning some 60 years, was able to work almost exclusively within the two major traditions of 19th-century German music and carry them forward successfully. After his earliest works (up to *Aus Italien*, 1886), which are derivative of Mendelssohn and Brahms, he turned to the second tradition, that of Wagner and Liszt, and developed their programmatic ideas, pushing their chromaticism to the point where it threatened to disintegrate into the kind of "atonality" then first being written by Schoenberg. He literally exhausted the Wagnerian potential in *Elektra*, then stopped short, and after some tentative steps in the direction of a protoneoclassicism (*Ariadne auf Naxos*, 1911–12), reverted to a grandiose, mellifluous, contrapuntal manner, which he continued to refine through his last works.

Strauss's natural lyricism is probably the key feature of his musical style. However important the Straussian orchestra may appear, his lyrical lines and the telling melodic shape of his motives are even more central. Melodies are astonishingly varied and carefully molded to each particular expressive situation. The motives have so clear a character that they are always easily recognizable no matter how much they are transformed in the course of a work. A characteristic passage occurs at the opening of *Don Juan*, where after seven furious 16th notes, eighth-note triplets take over the climbing theme to establish the heroic character of the Don; equally evocative is the upward line of the clarinet at the opening of *Salome*, where

Strauss sets the scene with less than a bar of music. More concentrated still are the opening motives of *Elektra* and *Rosenkavalier*. The impetuous quality of the love affair in *Rosenkavalier* is encapsulated in the violent horn leaps covering an octave and a major sixth with only a single whole-tone descent in its constant rise. The *Elektra* opening is significant in that it illustrates a typical Straussian procedure whereby a motive is derived from the rhythm of a spoken word. Although there are many quasi-Wagnerian melodies in the early pieces, such as the fanfare in *Macbeth*, melodies are used more for psychological or dramatic characterisation than for informing the audience about the plot or program. At times Strauss slipped in this respect, most notably in the Viennese waltzes that appear at such inappropriate times as in Salome's and Elektra's dances. He always admired the seemingly endless melodies Mozart produced and once confessed that no long melodies ever came to him fully formed. His melodies always required work. Two themes from opposite ends of his career are perhaps the best illustrations of his continuing lyricism: the long oboe tune in *Don Juan* (1888) and the lengthy violin solo in the third of the *4 Last Songs* (1948).

Tonality is a functioning force in most of Strauss's music. Though the rate of harmonic change is at times extravagantly rapid, there is more often than not a skeletal tonal framework that keeps the sounds in order and permits the spinning of inner moving lines, which Strauss himself called "nervous counterpoint." Sometimes the lines are so thick that they cannot be heard, nor do they always differ from each other significantly; this thickness continued into his latest works, such as *Metamorphosen* (1944–45). At times, especially in *Salome* and *Elektra*, he used every device to confuse harmonic clarity: multiple suspensions, free shifting triads and seventh chords, delays in the resolution of harmonic and melodic dissonances, enharmonic changes, frequent major-minor combinations, and, perhaps most disconcerting of all, the abrupt breaking off of ideas followed by totally new material. The use of these harmonic devices is always exceptional, however, and usually leads back to more normal sections where everything becomes solid and clear. Generally in the operas, these techniques serve to emphasize the more theatrical moments, such as the dissonant "Jewish quartet" in *Salome* and the saccharine unreality of the chromatic chords for harp and celesta at the end of *Rosenkavalier*.

Strauss's orchestration is that aspect of his music that has had the greatest effect on the popular culture of our time. For years all cinema "epics" were accompanied by a fat Straussian sound that in his early works frequently requires more than 100 musicians to produce. His orchestration is even richer than Wagner's, for he not only employed more unusual instruments, such as the heckelphone and viola d'amore, but devised new methods for playing traditional instruments (the great technical virtuosity he demanded is now part of standard technique). His naturalistic sounds —his imitation of such things as the bleating of sheep in *Don Quixote*—is another feature of his orchestration. The larger his orchestra grew, the more he employed it in chamber-music fashion, as did his contemporaries, Mahler and Schoenberg; examples are the effective subdivision of strings in *Elektra*, the numerous soloistic passages in *Die Frau ohne Schatten*, and the exquisite use of solo strings in *Capriccio*. Solo writing became more prominent midway in his career as he came to realize that he should not "kill" the singers. Some of his more notable solo passages are the solo viola in *Don Quixote*, the violin solo in *Die Frau ohne Schatten*, and, perhaps the best known, the horn solo in *Till Eulenspiegel*. He was as demanding of singers as of instrumentalists; his greatest vocal writing was for the soprano voice, influenced no doubt by the fact that his wife was a singer.

Although Strauss claimed that "new ideas must seek new forms" and that his own musical ideas became liberated by extramusical factors, his "new ideas" were executed in fairly traditional fashion. He employed rondo form in *Till*, variation form in *Don Quixote*, and a modified sonata allegro in *Don Juan*. His larger orchestral works, such as the *Alpensinphonie* or the *Sinfonia domestica*, are more complicated structurally because they are necessarily more multisectional. Among the operas, *Salome* and *Elektra* seem to have been the result of a single creative act of high, sustained energy. But even in these, certain "numbers" can be distinguished, if not for separate performance, at least for purposes of analysis. The different sections in his later works are more deliberately and clearly delineated and in fact sometimes suffer from too many sectional qualitative differences (a common problem in opera). There are some extraordinary ensembles in the operas, quite on a par with the best in opera literature: the "Jewish quartet" in *Salome*, the trio at the end of *Rosenkavalier*, the various ensembles in *Die schweigsame Frau*, and above all the "laughing" octet in *Capriccio*.

PRINCIPAL COMPOSITIONS (published by Boosey unless otherwise noted): *Burleske in D Minor* for piano, orchestra (1885–86, Steingräber); *Don Juan*, tone poem for orchestra, Op. 20 (1888, Peters); *Tod und Verklärung*, tone poem for orchestra, Op. 24 (1888–89, Peters); *Till Eulenspiegels lustige Streiche*, tone poem for orchestra, Op. 28 (1894–95, Peters); *Don Quixote*, tone poem for orchestra, Op. 35 (1896–97, Peters); *4 Songs* for voice, piano, Op. 36 (1897–98, UE); *Ein Heldenleben*, tone poem for orchestra, Op. 40 (1898, Leuckart); *5 Songs* for voice, piano, Op. 48; poems by Otto Julius Bierbaum, Karl Henckell (1900); *Salome*, 1-act opera, Op. 54; libretto from Oscar Wilde (1904–05); *Elektra*, 1-act opera, Op. 58; libretto by Hugo von Hofmannsthal (1906–08); *Der Rosenkavalier*, 3-act opera, Op. 59; libretto by Hofmannsthal (1909–10); *Ariadne auf Naxos*, 2-act opera, Op. 60; libretto by Hofmannsthal (1911–12, revised 1916); *Eine Alpensinfonie* for orchestra, Op. 64 (1911–15, Leuckart); *Die Frau ohne Schatten*, 3-act opera, Op. 65; libretto by Hofmannsthal (1914–17); *Arabella*, 3-act opera, Op. 79; libretto by Hofmannsthal (1930–32); *Die schweigsame Frau*, 3-act opera, Op. 80; libretto by Stefan Zweig after Ben Jonson (1932–35); *Capriccio*, "a conversation piece for music," Op. 85; libretto by Clemens Krauss and the composer (1940–41); *Metamorphosen*, study for 23 solo strings (1944–45); *4 Last Songs* for high voice, orchestra; poems by Hermann Hesse and Joseph von Eichendorff (1948). Complete list: Erich H. Muller von Asow, *R. S. Thematisches Verzeichnis* (Vienna 1959).

PRINCIPAL WRITINGS: A revision of the *Treatise on Instrumentation* by Hector Berlioz (1905, Peters); *Recollections and Reflections* (London 1953). ★ Correspondence: to his parents (Zurich 1954); to Joseph Gregor (Salzburg 1955); to Hugo von Hofmannsthal (London 1961); to Clemens Krauss (Munich 1963); to Stefan Zweig (Zurich 1955); to Hans von Bülow (London 1955); to Romain Rolland (Paris 1951).

BIBL.: Norman Del Mar, *R. S.: A Critical Commentary on his Life and Works*, 2 vols. (London, 1962, 1969); Ernst Krause, *R. S. Gestalt und Werk* (Leipzig 1956); William Mann, *R. S.: A Critical Study of the Operas* (London 1966); Richard Specht, *R. S. und sein Werk* (Leipzig 1921); Franz Trenner, *R. S.: Dokumente seins Lebens und Schaffens* (Munich 1954).

Hugo Weisgall

SEE ALSO Austria and Germany, Dance, Opera, Orchestration, Switzerland.

Stravinsky, Igor (Feodorovich) (b. Oranienbaum, Russia, 17 June 1882; d. New York, 6 April 1971), was the son of the bass Feodor Stravinsky. He read law and legal philosophy at St. Petersburg Univ. (1901–05) and studied composition with Nicolai Rimsky-Korsakov (1903–08). During 1909–29 he was associated with Serge Diaghilev and the Russian Ballet, and from 1928 he wrote for dance in association with George Balanchine (himself associated with several ballet groups). Stravinsky's international reputation was initiated by the scandal at the first performance of *The Rite of Spring* (1911–13). During World War I he lived in Switzerland, during 1920–39 in France, and from 1939 in the U.S. He concertized extensively as pianist and conductor, and from 1927 conducted recordings of his music. His first wife, Catherine Nossenko, whom he married in 1906, died in 1939; he married his second wife, Vera de Bosset, in 1940.

Stravinsky composed music in almost every genre. His stage music consists of 13 ballets and four operas; his music for the concert hall of four symphonies, 21 orchestral pieces, seven concertos, and seven works for voice and orchestra. There are 28 compositions for chamber and vocal ensembles, six for piano solo, two for two pianos, and nine religious works for voices and instruments. Stravinsky also made transcriptions of music by other composers, most notably Bach, Tchaikovsky, and Gesualdo. He and Robert Craft put together nine volumes of erudite autobiographical and musical reminiscence and comment.

In *Le Rossignol* (1908–14) and *The Firebird* (1909–10, Stravinsky's first ballet for the Russian Ballet), the influence of both Debussy and Rimsky-Korsakov are discernible, especially in the exoticism of the harmony and orchestral sonorities. These influences are still noticeable in some pages of the two succeeding ballets, *Petrouchka* (1910–11) and *The Rite of Spring* (1911–13), but such echoes are rare and sometimes coincidental, for early in his career Stravinsky achieved a unique voice. Beginning with *Scherzo fantastique* (1908), his characteristic mastery of orchestration became evident. Orchestration for him was the sonorous embodiment of his musical ideas; orchestral effects were used for the articulation of ideas and shapes and not merely for their own sake. So integral was his instrumentation to a whole composition that it is difficult to isolate examples of his command of instrumental resources from their context. However, a few examples may suggest the range of his imagination: the rocketing string harmonic glissandos in the Introduction to *The Firebird*; the straining of the bassoon in its highest register at the beginning of *The Rite*; the use of cimbalom and vocal falsetto in *Renard*; the soloistic use of percussion in *L'Histoire du soldat*; the beautifully pure scoring for strings in *Apollo*; and, a later example, the contrabass harmonics in the Introduction to *Agon*. After using large orchestras in the early orchestral music and the three early ballets, Stravinsky turned to smaller ensembles and orchestras and to a soloistic use of individual instruments. Such practice resulted in a range of differentiated instrumental color with emphasis on contrast and variety rather than on homogeneity.

The three early ballets are notable for their unique musical architecture. The Introduction to *The Firebird*, for example, is built on two contrasting groups of material, the first a slowly moving bass figure emphasizing the tritone, the second a fluttery movement in bassoons, clarinets, and trumpets. These materials are abruptly broken off, interchanged, and fragmented. The Introduction closes with a return of the first section. The composer's control over the temporal size of each section as well as over the contrast between these textures determined the shape of the section. Similar abrupt juxtapositions and terminations of material are heard frequently in the larger works, although the materials are not always contrasting in nature. In *Orpheus* (1947) the final movement is a brief fugato for horns and trumpet that is broken off at carefully planned points, allowing harp figures to be heard alone; the effect is of slowly dying away to the end. Such enjambment of materials occurs in almost every work, and Stravinsky's skill and judicious judgment kept the interlocking of materials from being merely discontinuous. In fact his ability to turn the essentially episodic nature of ballet music into an asset in shaping larger musical structures was a major factor in his success in this medium. His adaptation of the technique to nonballetic compositions can be seen in the *Symphony of Psalms* (1930), *Symphony in C* (1938–40), and *Symphony in 3 Movements* (1942–45), where it became a characteristic formal process. In these neoclassic works the superficial discontinuities coalesce into fresh and imaginative modes of handling traditional musical structures. Such a view contrasts with some initial criticisms of Stravinsky's neoclassicism, which pointed to the supposed gaps between the classic model and the subsequent composition. Now it can be seen that Stravinsky took both the procedures and the spirit of the model, dissected and examined them, and reassembled them to conform to his own sensibility.

Throughout his career Stravinsky's harmonic practice was deeply rooted in the relations inherent in triadic harmony and tonality. "Tonality is my discipline," he said in *Poetics of Music*. In this tonality "our chief concern is not so much with what is known as tonality as what one might term the polar attraction of sound, of an interval, or even of a complex of tones." The traditional dominant-tonic attraction of triadic tonality was not necessarily normative for him. What emerges from the harmonic relations in Stravinsky is a contextual tonality or pitch center defined by the harmonic and melodic movement of a specific composition. A straightforward example of contextual tonality is that of the *Serenade in A* (1925) for piano, in which the separate movements are not in any conventional sense in the key of A, but in which each movement converges on the pitch A as its final tonal goal.

The variety of chords in *Petrouchka* (1910–11) is paradigmatic of Stravinsky's harmonic practice. There are sections that are plainly triadic and tonal in the conventional sense (notably the parodistic dances like "Waltz for the Ballerina and Moor"). Other sections ("Russian Dance," for example) use extended triads and are less focused on conventional tonal centers; the "Russian Dance" pivots around the pitch G. Another device is the bi- or polytonality that results from the simultaneous unfolding of chords or melodic lines that represent two or more keys. This technique rarely results in two or more simultaneously heard keys but instead evolves into a new sound entity ("a complex of tones"). In the famous *Petrouchka* chord, first played by two clarinets as the unfolding of a C and an F♯ triad, the elements of importance are not the triads but rather the tritonal relation between C and F♯ and the relation between C and A♯ (which has ramifications later in the music). Other chords in *Petrouchka* include modal and chromatically altered chords and diatonic chord clusters; in every case they are derived from triads.

Vestigal triadic implications can be found even in a later, serial work, *Movements* for piano and orchestra (1958–59). The interval of the perfect fifth, which plays a large part in this composition, might have suggested the outline of a triad. However, the functional triadic implications of the interval are severely curtailed by the overall chromatic pitch context. The importance of triadically derived associations in *Agon* (1953–57), a partly serial work, is clearly audible; the C of the recurring fanfare introduction provides a point of departure and return for those weaker, less tonally centered portions of the score. Stravinsky's keen sense of the aural effects of the spacing of chord members and of the effects of doubling brought remarkable freshness to the sound of any chord, but especially to simple triads. The opening chord of *Symphony of Psalms* (1930), an E-minor triad with the third tripled, has an astonishingly dry and harsh effect because of the spacing and doubling.

However complex the harmonic relations in a particular work may have been, Stravinsky frequently summarized the basic movement in a concluding section; in such sections the melodic and rhythmic materials also may recur in a reduced form. The conclusion of *Les Noces* (1914–23) reduces instrumental sonorities to resonant bell-like sounds, at the same time condensing the harmonic structure to chords of fifths and seconds and the melodic shape to thirds and whole steps. The coda to the first movement of the *Symphony in C* reduces the pervasive rhythmic movement of the first group materials to a static movement in the lower instruments; the characteristic half-step melodic movement from the first group is radically simplified into single statements and finally incorporated into the concluding chords.

In the early Russian ballets, Stravinsky's melodic structures tended to be gnomish, folklike motifs that could be prolonged, proliferated, or expanded into longer melodies but only rarely were susceptible of development. Such melodic materials reflected the nature of the ballet's subject matter as well as Stravinsky's compositional allegiance to the investigation of the intervallic and rhythmic relationships of small melodic units. However, such melodic nuclei provided a springboard for the stratification of sections and their interlocking juxtapositions. The lessons learned from composition with such generative melodic techniques opened a flood of lyricism in Stravinsky's music after 1914, from such melodies as the theme of the variations in the *Octet* (1923) with its tightly controlled oscillations around major and minor thirds, to the beautifully molded Lacrimosa in *Requiem Canticles* (1964–66). The suavely poignant melody of "Air de Danse" in *Orpheus* depends upon the subtly irregular phrasing of its gracious ornamentation and the gentle harmonic movement from F minor to C minor for the coherence of its ABA structure. Here the scoring (two oboes and harp) contributes to the baroque-pastoral character of the melody.

Stravinsky's use of rhythm and irregular meters is perhaps the most immediately compelling aspect of his style. Sometimes rhythmic patterns are employed repetitiously to emphasize movement toward conclusion, as in the final chorus of *Oedipus Rex* (1926–27), where the repeated eighth-note pattern articulates the predominant minor third; or as in the *Symphony in C*, where the energetic eighth-note movement of the first group in the first movement is reduced to a static iteration of eighths in the coda. Sometimes ostinatos, or repetitions of rhythmic patterns, are used to build dense, polyphonic textures, such as those of the Introduction to part I of *The Rite of Spring* or those of the 12-part variations in the *Huxley Variations* (1964). Often, as in "Danse sacrale" in *The Rite* or in the march-like rhythms at no. 48 in *Danses concertantes* (1942), rhythmic patterns are not repetitive but serve to generate proliferating rhythmic patterns. Ostinatos occur frequently as rhythmic counterpoints to other parts moving irregularly, as in the March from *L'Histoire du soldat*, where the contrabass moves in regular duple meter while other parts unfold in irregular rhythmic and metrical movement against it.

Stravinsky's influence is incalculable. Irregular metrics and ostinatos, as well as ingenious and gorgeous instrumental sonorities, have seduced many who forgot that in Stravinsky these practices were not mechanical but generative. In Russia, due to the official disapproval of Stravinsky during the Stalinist era, his influence until recently was felt only indirectly through the music of such composers as Prokofiev. The brittle soloistic scoring and motoric rhythms of the fast movements in Shostakovich's *Symphony No. 1* reflect this influence. In Europe and the Americas, in addition to affecting instrumental practice, rhythmic procedures, harmonic construction and musical structure, Stravinsky's work influenced composers in two other areas: first, the revival of musical forms from the past (Poulenc's *Harpsichord Concerto*, Roger Sessions' *First Symphony*); second, the incorporation of jazz and other popular materials (Milhaud's *La Création du monde*, Copland's *Piano Concerto* and *Billy the Kid*). Stravinsky's espousal of serial techniques after 1952 helped bring about a renaissance of interest in serialism, especially in the U.S., where the simultaneous rise of exact theorizing about serialism by Milton Babbitt, George Perle, and others further encouraged serial composition. While Stravinsky did not compose electronic music, his influence is to be heard in the techniques of ostinato and sectional stratification in the electronic music of Mario Davidovsky, Morton Subotnick, Henri Pousseur, and others.

PRINCIPAL COMPOSITIONS (published by Boosey unless otherwise noted): *The Firebird* (L'Oiseau de feu), 1-act ballet; choreography by Michel Fokine (1909–10, Schott); *Petrouchka*, burlesque in 4 scenes; choreography by Fokine (1910–11); *The Rite of Spring* (Le Sacre du printemps), scenes of pagan Russia in 2 parts; scenario by Stravinsky, Nicolas Roerich; choreography by Vaslav Nijinsky (1911–13); *Renard*, 1-act opera-burlesque for chamber orchestra (1915–16, Chester); *The Wedding* (Les Noces), Russian choreographic scenes for vocal soloists, chorus, 4 pianos, percussion; choreography by Bronislava Nijinska (1914–23, Chester); *The Soldier's Tale* (L'Histoire du soldat) in 6 scenes for narrator, dancers, clarinet, bassoon, cornet, trombone, violin, double bass, percussion; libretto by C. F. Ramuz (1918, Chester); *Pulcinella*, ballet, for soprano, tenor, bass, chamber orchestra; choreography by B. Nijinska (1919–20); *Symphonies of Wind Instruments* (1920); *Octet* for flute, clarinet, 2 bassoons, 2 trumpets, 2 trombones (1922–23); *Concerto* for piano and wind instruments (1923–24); *Piano Sonata* (1924); *Oedipus Rex*, opera-oratorio; libretto by Jean Cocteau after Sophocles (1926–27); *Apollo musagetes*, ballet in 2 scenes for string orchestra; choreography by Adolph Bolm (Washington 27 April 1928), later by George Balanchine (Paris 12 June 1928) (1927–28); *The Fairy's Kiss* (Le Baiser de la fée), allegorical ballet in 4 scenes; choreography by B. Nijinska (1928); *Capriccio* for piano, orchestra (1928–29); *Symphony of Psalms* for chorus, orchestra without violins and violas (1930); *Violin Concerto in D* (1931, Schott); *Duo concertante* for violin, piano (1931–32); *Persephone*, melodrama in 3 scenes for narrator, tenor, chorus, children's chorus, orchestra; text by André Gide, choreography by Kurt Jooss (1933–34); *Concerto* for 2 pianos (1931–35, Schott); *Jeu de cartes* (Card Game), ballet in 3 deals; choreography by Balanchine (1936, Schott); *Dumbarton Oaks Concerto*, "Concerto in E♭" for chamber orchestra (1937–38, Schott); *Symphony in C* (1938–40, Schott); *Danses concertantes* for chamber orchestra (1941–42, Schott); *Symphony in 3 Movements* (1942–45, Schott); *Orpheus*, ballet in 3 scenes; choreography by Balanchine (1947); *Mass* for chorus, winds (1944–48); *The Rake's Progress*, 3-act opera; libretto by W. H. Auden (1948–51); *Cantata* for soprano, tenor, women's chorus, 2 flutes, oboe, English horn, cello (1951–52); *Septet* for clarinet, bassoon, horn, piano, violin, viola, cello (1952–53); *3 Songs from William Shakespeare* for mezzo-soprano, flute, clarinet, viola (1953); *Agon*, 1-act ballet; choreography by Balanchine (1953–57); *In Memoriam Dylan Thomas*, dirge-canons and song for tenor, string quartet, trombone quartet; text by Thomas (1954); *Canticum sacrum ad honorem Sancti Marci nominis* for tenor, baritone, organ, orchestra (1955); *Threni: id est Lamaentationes Jeremiae Prophetae* for soprano, alto, 2 tenors, 2 basses, orchestra (1957–58); *Movements* for piano, orchestra (1958–59); *A Sermon, a Narrative, and a Prayer*, cantata for speaker, alto, tenor, chorus, orchestra (1960–61); *The Flood*, biblical allegory based on Noah and the Ark for actors, tenor, 2 basses, chorus, orchestra (1961–62); *Abraham and Isaac*, sacred ballet for baritone, chamber orchestra; text from Genesis (1962–63); *Variations (Aldous Huxley in Memoriam)* for orchestra (1963–64); *Requiem Canticles* for alto, bass, chorus, orchestra (1964–66). List of compositions, 1903–65, in White (see bibl.).

PRINCIPAL WRITINGS: *An Autobiography* (New York 1936); *Poetics of Music* (Cambridge, Mass., 1947). ★ In collaboration with Robert Craft: *Avec S.* (Monaco 1958); *Conversations with I. S.* (New York 1959); *Memories and Commentaries* (New York 1960); *Expositions and Developments* (New York 1962); *Dialogues and a Diary* (New York 1963); *Themes and Episodes* (New York 1966); *Retrospectives and Conclusions* (New York 1969). List of writings to 1965 in White.

BIBL.: Benjamin Boretz and Edward T. Cone, eds., *Perspectives on Schoenberg and S.* (Princeton 1968); André Boucourechliev and others, *S.* (Paris 1968); Paul Henry Lang, ed., *S.: A New Appraisal of His Work* (New York 1963); Minna Lederman, ed., *S. in the Theatre* (New York 1949); André Schaeffner, *S.* (Paris 1931); *The Score and I. M. A. Magazine* 20 (June 1957); Alexander Tansman, *S.: The Man and His Music* (New York 1949); *Tempo* (summer 1948, spring-summer 1962, summer 1967); Roman Vlad, *S.* (New York 1960); Eric Walter White, *S.: The Composer and His Works* (Berkeley 1966).

Richard Swift

SEE ALSO Asian Music and Western Composition; Dance; Debussy; Folk Resources; Form; France; Harmony and Counterpoint; Instrumental and Vocal Resources; Jazz; Liturgical Music: Christian; Melody; Mixed Media; Musicology and Composition; Opera; Orchestration; Performance; Recording; Rhythm; Soviet Union; Switzerland; Text Setting and Usage; Texture; 12-Tone Techniques.

Stroe, Aurel (b. Bucharest, 5 May 1932), studied at the Bucharest Conservatory (1951–56; composition with M. Andrico; harmony, counterpoint, and fugue with M. Negrea) and at the Darmstadt summer courses (1966–69). He has taught composition and orchestration at the Bucharest Conservatory since 1962. His work has been influenced by his study of Byzantine and neo-Byzantine notation and by his collaboration with mathematicians at the Bucharest Computing Center in making algorithms for compositions and researching the logical bases of the compositional process. The latter activities were forwarded by a trip to the U.S. in 1968, when he observed applications of electronics to present-day music.

PRINCIPAL COMPOSITIONS: ★ *Démarche musicale I* (composed with the aid of computers): *Arcades* for 11 instrumental formations, organ, ondes Martenot (1962, Muzicală); *Signum* for winds (1963); *Musique de concert* for piano, brass, percussion (1964, Muzicală); *Only through Time, Time Is Conquered* for baritone, organ, trombones, gongs; text by T. S. Eliot (1965); *Laudes I* for 28 strings (1965–66); *Laudes II* for 12 instrumental formations, organ, ondes Martenot (1966–68); *Cantos I and II* for organ, orchestra (1967, 1970). ★ Other compositions: incidental music for Sophocles' *Oedipus at Colonos* for chorus, winds, percussion (1963, Ars Viva); *Ca n'aura pas le Prix Nobel*, opera and critique of opera in 3 parts for actors, vocal soloists, chorus, orchestra, tape, ballet; libretto by Paul Sterian (1965–69, Schott); *Son et écho* on 2-track tape (1969); *De Ptolemaeo*, miniopera on 2-track tape; texts by Nichita Stănescu (1970).

PRINCIPAL WRITINGS: "Compoziţii şi clase de compoziţii" [Compositions and Classes of Compositions], *Musica* 1970/4, 6, 11.

BIBL.: Georg Andrésen, "Rumaenskkomponist skaber elektroakustik i Holstebro" [Rumanian Composer Studies Electroacoustics in Holstebro], *Aarhus Stifstidende* (17 Sept 1969); Jacques Lonccchampt, "Au pays d'Enesco," *Le Monde* (16 Feb 1968); Wladyslaw Malinovski, "Rumania Nieznana," *Ruch muzyczńy* (March 1965).

Structure, see Form, Harmony and Counterpoint, Melody, Rhythm, Serialism, Theory, Text Setting and Usage, Texture, 12-Tone Techniques

Subotnick, Morton (b. 14 April 1933), attended Mills College (1957–59; composition with Darius Milhaud, Leon Kirchner) and then joined the Mills music faculty. He cofounded the Mills Performing Group and the San Francisco Tape Music Center (which later moved to Mills), directed music for the Dancer's Workshop of Ann Halprin, and was active in new-music performances. Moving to New York in 1967, he became music director of the Repertory Theater at Lincoln Center during its first season, was director of electronic music programs at the Electric Circus discotheque, taught in the Intermedia Program in the Arts at New York Univ. and one year at the Univ. of Md., and set up an electronic music studio at the Univ. of Pittsburgh. In 1969 he joined the Calif. Institute of the Arts in Los Angeles.

Subotnick's music since 1960 includes "sound" and "theater" works. The former includes *Serenade 3* for instruments and electronic sounds on tape and other pieces for instruments and tape. The purely tape works include *Realities 1–2*, prepared for the Electric Circus, *Touch*, and two commissions from Nonesuch Records: *Silver Apples of the Moon* (the first electronic work composed for records) and *The Wild Bull*. His mixed-media works combine instruments, tape, and films with abstract theatrical actions that extend the purely musical ideas. Subotnick feels that concerts today are decadent rituals unsuited to modern needs and sensibilities, and much of his mixed-media work involves direct audience participation, incorporating the spirit and activity of "play" as a compositional element. *Play! 4*, for instance, presents four successive games that can be won, lost, or stalemated with interaction among miniature societal groups determining detailed aspects of the performance.

Subotnick's electronic music exploits the modular electronic synthesizer designed for him by Donald Buchla of San Francisco and usually eschews concrete (i.e., natural) sounds. He balances certain traditional formal elements of repetition and continuity with poetic timbral content. He has developed new circuitry, exploring the spatial distribution of live electronic sound (sound not on tape but produced or altered in performance via electronics). A collaboration in 1968 with the New York Pro Musica, in which he enveloped older idioms with electronic music and visuals, led to *Misfortunes of the Immortals: A Concert*, in which extracts from traditional wind-quintet repertory are similarly engulfed, illustrating the predicament of live musicians forced to function in the "living museum" of the concert hall. Subotnick has also constructed electronic environments. At the New York toy store Creative Playthings he set up panels of buttons for shoppers to push, which control tape loops of rhythmic series, melodic patterns, and sound effects; these enable the instant creation of electronic works. For the office building at 77 Water St. in New York's financial district he devised a similar environment for the elevators, activated in this case by the floor-stop buttons.

PRINCIPAL COMPOSITIONS (published by MCA unless otherwise noted): *Serenade 1* for flute, clarinet, vibraphone, cello, piano, mandolin (1959, McG-M); *Mandolin* for viola, tape, film (1960); *Play! 1* for woodwind quintet, piano, tape, film (1962); *Music to "The Caucasian Chalk Circle"* for percussion, mandolin, narrator, solo voice, 3 choristers (1963); *Play! 2* for orchestra, conductor, tape (1963); *Play! 3* for mime, tape, film (1964); *Serenade 3* for flute, clarinet, violin, piano, tape (1965, Bowdoin); *The Tarot* for 10 instruments, tape, conductor (1965); *Prelude 4* for piano, electronic sounds (1966); *Play! 4* for 4 game players, 2 conductors, 4 musicians, tape, 2 films (1967); *Silver Apples of the Moon*, electronic sounds on tape (1967, recorded by Nonesuch); *The Wild Bull*, electronic sounds on tape (1968, recorded by Nonesuch); *Touch* on 4-channel tape (1969); *Misfortunes of the Immortals: A Concert* for wind quintet, tape, lights, 2 films, with additional music by Beethoven, Pergolesi, Rossini, Mozart (1969, unpub.); *Lamination 1* for orchestra, electronic sounds on tape (1969); *A Ritual Game Room* for electronic sounds on tape, lights, dancer, 4 game players, and no audience (1970).

PRINCIPAL WRITINGS: "Extending the Stuff Music Is Made Of," *Electronic Music* (Music Educators National Conference 1968):36–37.

BIBL.: Tod Dockstader, "Reviews of Records" (on *The Wild Bull*), *Musical Quarterly* 55:136–38; Richard Norton, "The Vision of M. S.," *Music Journal* (Jan 1970):35; John M. Perkins, "M. S.: Serenade No. 1," *Perspectives* 2/2:100–05; Elliott Schwartz, "Current Chronicle" re Serenade 3, *Musical Quarterly* 51:685–87.

David Bloch

SEE ALSO Electronic Music: History and Development; Mixed Media; Recording.

Suchoň, Eugen (b. Pezinok, Czechoslovakia, 25 Sept 1908), studied at the Bratislava Music School (1920–27, piano with Frico Kafenda), the Music and Drama Academy in Bratislava (1927–28, composition with Kafenda), and the Prague Conservatory (1931–33, composition with Vítězslav Novák). During 1931–48 he taught theoretical subjects and later composition at the Music and Drama Academy and during 1949–60, at the Teacher's Academy in Bratislava. He has also written textbooks on counterpoint, classical harmony, and 20th-century (primarily modal) harmony. The harmonic vocabulary in his music derives from the modality of Slovak folk music. His *Krútňava* is considered the first national Slovak opera.

PRINCIPAL COMPOSITIONS (published by SHV unless otherwise noted): *String Quartet*, Op. 2 (1930–31, unpub.); *Little Suite and Passacaglia* for piano, Op. 3 (1931, unpub.); *Serenade* for wind quintet, Op. 5 (1932–33, arrangement for string orchestra, SHV); *Piano Quartet*, Op. 6 (1932–33, SHF); *Burlesque concertante* for violin, orchestra, Op. 7 (1933); *From the Mountains*, songs for men's chorus, Op. 8 (1934); *Ballad Suite* for orchestra, Op. 9 (1935, UE); *Sonatina* for violin, piano, Op. 11 (1937); *Carpathian Psalm*, cantata for tenor, chorus, orchestra, Op. 12 (1937–38, UE and SHV); *Krútňava* [The Whirlpool],

opera in 6 scenes (1941–49, SHF and SHV); *Svatopluk*, 3-act music drama (1952–59, SHF and SHV); *Metamorphoses*, 5 variations for orchestra (1953); *Pictures of Slovakia*, 6 cycles of piano pieces (1956–57); *Ad astra*, 5 songs for soprano, orchestra (1961); *The Man*, cycle for chorus (1962); *Poème macabre* for violin, piano (1963, Panton); *Contemplations* for narrator, piano (1964); *Rhapsodic Suite* for piano, orchestra (1965).

SEE ALSO Czechoslovakia.

Sugár, Rezső (b. Budapest, 9 Oct 1919), studied at the Budapest Academy of Music (1937–42, composition with Zoltán Kodály). In 1949 he began teaching at the Bartók Conservatory in Budapest, and since 1969 he has taught composition at the Budapest Academy.

PRINCIPAL COMPOSITIONS (published by EMB): *Violin Sonata* (1946); *Divertimento* for string orchestra (1948); *String Quartet No. 2* (1950); *Heroic Song* for soloists, chorus, orchestra (1951); *Frammenti musicali* for piano, wind quintet (1958); *Rhapsody* for cello, piano (1959); *Concerto for Orchestra* (1963); *Metamorfosi* for orchestra (1965); *Partita* for string orchestra (1967); *String Quartet No. 3* (1969).

Suk, Joseph (b. Křečovice u Neveklova, Czechoslovakia, 4 Jan 1874; d. Benešov, 29 May 1935), studied at the Prague Conservatory (1885–92; composition with Karel Stecker, Antonín Dvořák, violin with Antonín Bennewitz; chamber music with Hanuš Wihan). He played second violin in the Czech Quartet during 1891–1933. During 1922–35 he taught composition at the Prague Conservatory. His early music was in the tradition of Dvořák and Brahms. After the death in 1905 of his wife Otilie (Dvořák's daughter), he developed a new style based on more complex harmonic and polyphonic designs and a greater variety of timbre.

PRINCIPAL COMPOSITIONS: *Serenade in Eb* for string orchestra, Op. 6 (1892, SHV); *Chant d'amour* for voice, piano: vol. 1, "Dumka" (1892, SHV); vol. 2, "Idylls" (1893, SHV); *String Quartet in Bb*, Op. 11 (1896, SHV); *Radúz and Mahulena*, incidental music for the fairy tale by Julius Zeyer, Op. 13 (1897–98, SNKLHU; suite for orchestra, *Pohádka*, Op. 16, 1899–1900, SHV); *10 Songs* for women's chorus, Op. 15; based on Slovak folksongs (1899, SHV); *4 Songs* for men's chorus, Op. 18; based on Serbian folksongs (1900, Mojmír Urbánek); *Pod jabloní*, incidental music for the play by Zeyer, Op. 20 (1900–01; suite for alto, chorus, orchestra, organ, 1911, Simrock); *Fantasia in G Minor* for violin, orchestra, Op. 24

(1902, SNKLHU); *Fantastické scherzo* for orchestra, Op. 25 (1903, Breitkopf); *Praga*, symphonic poem, Op. 26 (1904, SNKLHU); *Asrael*, symphony, Op. 27 (1905–06, SHV); *O matince* [About Mother], 5 songs for voice, piano, Op. 28 (1907, Orbis); *Pohádka léta* [A Summer's Tale], poem for orchestra, Op. 29 (1907–09, UE); *Životem a snem* [Life and Dreams] for voice, piano, Op. 30 (1909, SHV); *Zrání* [The Ripening], symphonic poem, Op. 34 (1912, Supraphon); *Svatý Václave* [Oh, St. Wenceslas], meditation on the old Czech chorale for string quartet (string orchestra), Op. 35 (1914, Orbis); *V nový život* [Toward a New Life], Sokol ceremonial march for orchestra, Op. 35c (1919–20, Hudební matice); *Epilogue* for soprano, baritone, bass, small and large choruses, orchestra, Op. 37; text from the bible and by Ladislav Vycpálek (1920–29, Hudební matice).

PRINCIPAL WRITINGS: *Živá slova J. S.* [In J. S.'s Own Words], ed. by J. M. Květ (Prague 1946).

BIBL.: Jiří Berkovec, *J. S. Život a dílo* [J. S. His Life and Work], 2nd ed. (Prague 1962); ——, *J. S.*, in English, French, German, Russian (Prague 1969); Jan M. Květ, *J. S.* (Prague 1936); ——, ed. *J. S.: Studie a vzpomínky* [J. S.: Studies and Reminiscences] (Prague 1935); Václav Štěpán, *Novák a S.* (Prague 1945).

[prepared with the help of the Czech Music Information Center]

SEE ALSO Czechoslovakia.

Šulek, Stjepan (b. Zagreb, 5 August 1914), studied at the Zagreb Academy of Music (1923–36, violin with Vaclav Huml). He has performed as a violinist and conductor since 1936 and has taught composition at the Zagreb Academy since 1945.

PRINCIPAL COMPOSITIONS: *Classical Concerto* for orchestra (1944, UE); *Symphony No. 2* (1949, Nakladni); *Piano Sonata* (1947, HGZ); *Violin Concerto* (1951, JAZU); *Coriolanus*, incidental music to Shakespeare's play (1957); *Viola Concerto* (1959, JAZU); *Zadnji Adam* [The Last Adam], cantata for bass, chorus, orchestra (1964, JAZU); *Symphony No. 6* (1966, JAZU); *The Tempest*, incidental music to Shakespeare's play (1969); *Piano Concerto No. 3* (1970).

BIBL.: Krešimir Kovačević, *Hrvatski kompozitori* [Croatian Composers] (Zagreb 1960): 465–84; Krešimir Sipus, *S. Š.* (Zagreb 1961); Ivo Supičić, "Estetika S. Š.," *Musicological annual of the Univ. of Ljubljana*, vol. 5: 101–09.

Surinach, Carlos (b. Barcelona, 4 March 1915), studied at the Barcelona Municipal Conservatory (1929–36, composition with Enrique Morera), the Robert Schumann Conservatory in Dusseldorf (1940–41), the Cologne Hochschule für Musik (1940–41, conducting with Eugen Papst), and the Prussian Academy of the Arts in Berlin (1941–43, composition with Max Trapp). During 1944–47 he was conductor of the Barcelona Philharmonic Orchestra and during 1946–49, of the Gran Teatro del Liceo Opera House. He also appeared throughout Europe as a guest conductor. In 1947 he moved to Paris and in 1951 to New York City, becoming a U.S. citizen in 1959. During 1966–67 he was visiting professor of composition at the Carnegie-Mellon Institute.

PRINCIPAL COMPOSITIONS (published by AMP unless otherwise noted): *Quartet* for piano, strings (1944, Peer); *Passacaglia Symphony* (1945, Peer); *El mozo que casó con mujer brava* [The Bridegroom Who Married a Wild Woman], 1-act opera (1948, unpub.); *Symphony No. 2* (1949, Eschig); *Flamenquerías* for 2 pianos (1951); *3 Cantos Bereberes* for chamber ensemble (1952, Peer); *Ritmo Jondo*, dance; choreography by Doris Humphrey (1953) *Sinfonietta flamenca* (1953); *Tientos* for harp (harpsichord), English horn, timpani (1953); *Doppio concertino* for violin, piano, chamber orchestra (1954, Rongwen); *Concertino* for piano, strings, cymbals (1956); *Sinfonia chica* (1957); *Embattled Garden*, dance; choreography by Martha Graham (1958); *Romance, oración y saeta* for voice, piano or orchestra (1958, Ricordi); *Concerto for Orchestra* (1958, Ricordi); *Paeans and Dances of Heathen Iberia* for wind symphony (1959, Peters); *Acrobats of God*, dance; choreography by Graham (1960); *A Place in the Desert*, ballet; choreography by Norman Morrice (1960); *Cantata of St. John* for chorus, percussion (1962); *Feast of Ashes*, ballet adapted from Ritmo Jondo and the Doppio Concertino (1962); *Symphonic Variations* for orchestra (1963, Peters); *Drama Jondo*, overture for orchestra (1964); *Songs of the Soul* for chorus (1965); *Flamenco Meditations* for voice, piano (1965); *Melorhythmic Dramas* for orchestra (1966); *Agathe's Tale*, ballet (1967); *The Missions of San Antonio*, symphonic canticle for men's chorus, orchestra (1968). ★ Orchestrations: 7 pieces from the *Iberia* suite by Albéniz (1955); *4 Spanish Tonadillas* (18th-century zarzuelas; 1965, Peer). List to 1963: *Composers of the Americas* 9: 144–54.

BIBL.: Gilbert Chase, *The Music of Spain* (New York 1959): 324–25; "C. S.," *Musique et radio* (Paris, June 1963): 81–89.

SEE ALSO Dance.

Suter, Robert (b. St. Gallen, Switzerland, 30 Jan 1919), studied at the Basel Conservatory (1937–43; composition with Walter Geiser; theory with Ernst Mohr, Gustav Güldenstein, Walter Müller von Kulm; piano with Paul Baumgartner). He also studied composition privately in Ansona with Wladimir Vogel in 1956. He has taught theory at the Bern Conservatory (1945–50) and theory and improvisation at the Basel Academy (since 1950).

PRINCIPAL COMPOSITIONS: *Musikalisches Tagebuch I* for alto, flute, oboe, bassoon, violin, viola, double bass; texts by Hofmannsthal and Trakl (1946–60, EM); *Musikalisches Tagebuch II* for baritone, flute, clarinet, bass clarinet, horn, viola, cello; texts by Rückert, Jacobsen, Hofmannsthal (1950, EM); *String Quartet No. 1* (1952, EM); *Heilige Leier, sprich, sei meine Stimme*, chamber cantata for soprano, flute, guitar; text based on classical Greek poetry (1960, Heinr.); *Die Ballade von des Cortez Leuten* for speaker, chorus, orchestra; text by Brecht (1960, EM); *Serenata* for flute, oboe, clarinet, harp, violin, viola, cello (1964, Heinr.); *Sonata per orchestra* (1967, Bärenreiter); *Epitaffio* for brass, strings, percussion (1968, Bärenreiter); *3 Nocturnes* for viola, orchestra (1969, Bärenreiter); *Capriccio* for 2 pianos, orchestra (1970, Gerig).

BIBL.: Dino Larese and Jacques Wildberger, *R. S.* (Amriswil 1967).

Sutermeister, Heinrich (Paul) (b. Feuerthalen, Switzerland, 12 August 1910), studied classics and philology at the Sorbonne (1930–31) and music at the Akademie der Tonkunst in Munich (1934–35; composition with Carl Orff, Walter Courvoisier). He has taught at the Staatliche Hochschule für Musik in Hanover since 1963. He regards the human pulse, the life-beat of the body, as "the life and soul of music," and he once objected to 12-tone music because it is not "based on the rhythm of the body." The music of Honegger, Prokofiev, and Verdi have been the principal influences on his development.

PRINCIPAL COMPOSITIONS (published by Schott): *Andreas Gryphius*, cantata for chorus (1934); *Divertimento No. 1* for string orchestra (1935); *Die schwarze Spinne*, 1-act opera; libretto by J. Gotthelf (1936); *Romeo und Julia*, 2-act opera; libretto after Shakespeare (1940); *Bergsommer* for piano (1941); *Die Zauberinsel*, 2-act opera; libretto after Shakespeare's *The Tempest* (1942); *Piano Concertos Nos. 1–3* (1942, 1953, 1960); *Capriccio* for clarinet (1948); *Raskolnikoff*, 2-act opera; libretto by Peter Sutermeister (1948); *Sonatine* for piano (1948); *Marche fantasque* for orchestra (1950); *Der rote Stiefel*, 2-act opera; libretto by W. Hauff (1951); *Missa da Requiem* for soprano, bass, chorus, orchestra (1951); *Cello Concerto* (1955); *Hommage à Arthur Honegger* for piano (1956); *Seraphine*, 1-act opera; libretto after Rabelais (1958); *Titus Feuerfuchs*, 2-act comic opera (1958); *Divertimento No. 2* for orchestra (1959); *Der Papagei aus Kuba*, fable of La Fontaine for chorus, chamber orchestra (1961); *Poème funèbre* for string orchestra (1965); *Erkennen und*

Schaffen, cantata for soloists, chorus, orchestra; text by Schiller (1965); *Omnia ad unum*, cantata for baritone, chorus, orchestra; text adapted by Wilhelm Totok from Wilhelm Leibnitz and Albrecht von Haller (1967); *Madame Bovary*, 2-act opera (1967); *Das Gespenst von Canterville*, 1-act opera; libretto after Oscar Wilde (1967).

PRINCIPAL WRITINGS: "Essentials of Opera," *Music* (London, March 1953):9–10; "Zeitgenössische Oper unzeitgemäss," *Musik der Zeit*, new series vol. 3.

BIBL.: "Zwei Komponisten geben auskunft" (H. S. and Pierre Boulez), *Melos* 28/3:65–68; *40 Compositeurs suisses contemporains* (Amriswil 1956); Hans Ehinger, "3 Gespräche mit H. S.," *Schweizerische Musikzeitung* 98/9; J. P. Liardet, "Un Entretien sur la musique avec H. S.," *Gazette Littéraire* (Lausanne, May 1962).

Sutherland, Margaret (b. Australia, 20 Nov 1897), studied briefly at Melbourne Univ. in 1925 (piano with Edward Goll) and also coached that year with Arnold Bax in London. During 1930–33 she taught at Melbourne Univ.

PRINCIPAL COMPOSITIONS (with approximate dates of composition; some information on publishers is not available): *Violin Sonata* (1925, L'Oiseau Lyre); *Suite on a Theme by Purcell* for orchestra (193–); *Clarinet Sonata*, also adapted for saxophone (194–); *Violin Concerto* (195–); *Quartet* for English horn, strings (195–, L'Oiseau Lyre); *Divertimento* for violin, viola, cello (195–); *Discussion* for string quartet (196–); *Haunted Hills*, symphonic poem (196–); *Concertante* for oboe, strings (196–); *Fantasy* for violin, orchestra (196–); *4 Symphonic Concepts* (196–); *3 Temperaments* for orchestra (196–); *Concertante* for violin, viola, harpsichord, strings (196–); *String Quartets Nos. 1–3* (196–); *6 Bagatelles* for violin, piano (1960); *Chiaroscuro Nos. 1–2* for piano (1969); *Voices Nos. 1–2* for piano (1969); *Extension* for piano (1969).

PRINCIPAL WRITINGS: *Young Days in Music* (Melbourne 1968).

Švara, Danilo (b. Ricmanje near Trieste, Yugoslavia, 2 April 1902), studied political science at the Univ. of Vienna (1920–22) and the Univ. of Frankfurt (1922–25) and music at the Frankfurt Hochschule (1926–30; composition with Bernhard Sekles; conducting with Hermann Scherchen, Hermann von Schmeidel. He has been conductor of the Ljubljana Opera during 1925–27 and since 1930 and has taught opera and conducting at the Ljubljana Academy since 1945. During 1948–59 he was music critic for *Delo* in Ljubljana. His musical tastes were influenced first (1920–22) by Strauss and Janáček and then (1923–29) by Hindemith, Krenek, Stravinsky, and Schoenberg.

PRINCIPAL COMPOSITIONS: *Piano Sonata* (1930); *String Quartet No. 1* (1931); *Symphonies Nos. 1–3* (1932, 1935, 1950); *Kleopatra*, 5-act opera (1940); *Veronika Deseniška*, 5-act opera (1946, SKJ); *Ouverture Borec* [Fighter Overture] (1947); *Slovo od mladosti* [Farewell to the Youth], 3-act opera (1948); *Suites Nos. 1–2* for violin, piano (1950); *Ouverture brillante* (1955); *Concerto grosso dodecáfonó* (1956); *Nina*, 3-act ballet (1962); *Violin Concerto* (1965); *Oboe Concerto* (1966); *Suites Nos. 1–2* for 6 winds, strings (1967); *Duo concertante* for flute, harpsichord (1967); *Clarinet Concerto* (1968); *Ocean*, 5-act opera (1968); *7 Arabesques* for orchestra (1969).

Sveinsson, Atli Heimer (b. Reykjavík, Iceland, 21 Sept 1938), studied at the Cologne Hochschule für Musik (1959–62; composition with Günther Raphael, Rudolf Petzold), the Cologne Courses for New Music (1963; composition with Henri Pousseur, Karlheinz Stockhausen), and the Electronic Music Studio at Bilthoven, Holland (1964, electronic composition with Gottfried Michael Koenig). He has taught theory at Reykjavík College since 1969. His music has been influenced mostly by the work of Webern, Stockhausen, and Cage.

PRINCIPAL COMPOSITIONS: *Hlými* [Sonant] for chamber orchestra (1963); *Klif* [Tautology] for flute, cello, piano (1968); *Seimur* [Soundings] for 2 pianos, orchestra (1968); *Spectacles* for percussion, tape (1969); *Tengsl* [Connections] for orchestra (1970); *Music* for viola, orchestra (1970); *Bizzarreries I* for flute, piano, tape (1970).

Sviridov, Georgy (Vasilyevich) (b. Fatezh, Kursk region, Russia, 12 Dec 1915), studied at the Kursk Elementary Music School, then the Central Music College in Leningrad (1932–36, composition with M. A. Yudin), and the Leningrad Conservatory (1936–41, composition with Dmitri Shostakovich). Since 1945 he has performed as a concert pianist. He became a secretary of the Union of Soviet Composers in 1962 and first secretary of the Union of Composers of the Russian Republic in 1968. His music has been influenced by Mussorgsky and Alexander Dargomyzhsky, as well as by Russian folksong and Orthodox church music.

PRINCIPAL COMPOSITIONS: *Shest' romansov na slova A. Pushkina* [6 Romances to Words by A. Pushkin] for voice, piano (1935, Muzyka); *Vosem' romansov na slova M. Lermontova* [8 Romances

to Words by M. Lermontov] for voice, piano 1938, SC); *Slobodskaia lirika* [Poems from a Workers' District], 7 songs for voice, piano; text by Alexander Prokofiev (1938, SC); *Piano Sonata* (1944, Muzyka); *Iz Shekspira* [From Shakespeare], 7 songs for voice, piano (1944, Muzyka); *Piano Trio* (1945, SC); *2 Partitas* for piano (1946, SC); *Detskii al'bom* [Children's Album] for piano (1948, SC); *Strana otsov* [The Country of Our Forefathers] for tenor, bass, piano; text by Avetik Isaacyan (1950, SC); *Pesni na slova Roberta Bernsa* [Songs to Words by Robert Burns] for bass, piano (1955, Muzfond); *Poema pamiati Sergeis Esenina* [Poem in Memory of Sergei Esenin] for tenor, chorus, orchestra; text by Esenin (1955–56, Muzyka); *U menia otets-krest'ianin* [My Father Is a Peasant] for tenor, baritone, piano; texts by Esenin (1956, SC); *Paticheskaia oratoriia* [Oratorio pathétique], text by Vladimir Mayakovsky (1959, Muzyka); *9 Unaccompanied Choruses* (1959–69); *5 Choruses* (1961, Muzyka); *Peterburgskie pesni* [St. Petersburg Songs] for vocal soloists, piano, violin, cello; texts by Alexander Blok (1961–63); *Grustnye pesni* [Sad Songs], cantata; text by Blok (1962–64); *Dereviamnaia Rus'* [Russia, the Wooden], cantata; text by Esenin (1964, Muzyka); *Music for Chamber Orchestra* (1964, Muzyka); *Kurskie pesni* [Kursk Songs], cantata (1964, Muzyka); *Malen'kii triptikh* [Miniature Triptych], for orchestra (1964, Muzyka); *Sneg idet* [Snow Is Falling], cantata; text by Boris Pasternak (1965); *Piat' pesen o Rossii* [5 Songs of Russia], oratorio; text by Blok (1967–69); *Vremia, vpered!* [Time, Forward March!], suite for orchestra (1967, Muzyka); *2 Choruses*, texts by Esenin (1970, Muzyka).

BIBL.: M.-R. Hofmann, *La Musique russe des origines à nos jours* (Paris 1968): 258–62; L. Polyakova, *Vokalnie tsikly G. V. S.* [G. V. S.'s Vocal Cycles] (Moscow 1961); ——, "Nekotorie voprosy tvorcheskogo stilia G. S." [Certain Problems in the Style of G. S.], *Muzyka i sovremennost* (Moscow 1962); A. Sokhor, *G. S.* (Moscow 1964); Yu. Yevdokimova, "Poet Rossii" [A Poet of Russia], *Sovietskaia muzyka* 1968/6; *G. S.*, a collection of articles by various authors (Moscow c.1971).

SEE ALSO Soviet Union.

Sweden, see Scandinavia

Swift, Richard (b. Middlepoint, Ohio, 24 Sept 1927), studied at the Univ. of Chicago (1953–56; composition with Leland Smith, Grosvenor Cooper). Since 1956 he has taught at the Univ. of Calif. at Davis and since 1963 has been chairman of the music department there. During 1958–64 he conducted the Univ. Symphony. He was pianist with the New

Music Ensemble during 1963–66. He describes his music as influenced by the Viennese 12-tone school; by the work and thought of Stravinsky, Babbitt, Perle, and Sessions; and by the analytical methods of Heinrich Schenker.

PRINCIPAL COMPOSITIONS: *A Coronal* for orchestra (1954); *String Quartet No. 1* (1955); *Clarinet Sonata* (1957); *Sonata* for solo violin (1957); *Stravaganza III* for clarinet, violin, piano (1959); *Concerto* for piano, chamber ensemble (1961, UCP); *Extravaganza* for orchestra (1962, Presser); *Domains I* for baritone, chamber ensemble (1963); *Domains III* for 4 groups of instruments (1963, Presser); *Bucolics* for harpsichord, clarinet, viola, percussion, celesta (1964); *String Quartet No. 3* (1964); *Summer Notes* for piano (1965); *Music for a While* for violin, viola, harpsichord (1965); *Tristia* for orchestra (1967); *Violin Concerto* (1968); *Music for a While II* for clarinet, viola, harpsichord (1969); *Stravaganza VII* for viola (1969).

PRINCIPAL WRITINGS: "The 'Demonstrations' of J. K. Randall." *Perspectives* 2/2:77–86; review of W. Austin's *Music in the Twentieth Century, Journal of Music Theory* 11/1:165–69; review of E. W. White's *Stravinsky, Journal of the American Musicological Society* (winter 1967):507–10.

BIBL.: Karl Kohn, "R. S.: 'Concerto'," *Perspectives* 2/1:90–102.

Swing, see Jazz

Switzerland. Political and social conditions in Switzerland encourage the attitudes of tolerance and neutrality. Perhaps because of this, 20th-century Swiss music has tended to strike a balance between the old and the new and between the various schools of modern musical thought. It has followed a steady, evolutionary course rather than an erratic or revolutionary one. There is also a feeling of middle-class solidity in the country, the influence of which was once summarized by Arthur Honegger: When asked what he owed to his Swiss origin, he stated that it was a rather sober idea of art and of himself as an artist, an emphasis on artistic honesty, and a distrust of everything resembling the vain and disreputable.

The country encompasses three main languages, French, German, and Italian, as well as a nearly equal distribution of Protestantism and Catholicism. Its small population (6 million) has absorbed not only these divergent influences but also many characteristics of the neighboring national cultures. Furthermore, having maintained a neutral position in international politics and having been spared the ravages of two world wars, it has been a haven for many foreign composers, some of them pioneers with radical tendencies. Ferruccio Busoni, who spent four years in Zurich during World War I, was one of the first to come. Wladimir Vogel, one of Busoni's pupils in Berlin, came to Switzerland in 1933 as a refugee from Nazism. He was one of many such refugees whose music was subsequently promoted by Hermann Scherchen, the German conductor who was active in Switzerland for over 25 years. The premieres of Berg's *Lulu* and Hindemith's *Mathis der Maler* which took place in Zurich in 1937 and 1938, respectively, are further testimony to the artistic tolerance in Swiss music life, even in the face of suppression next door.

The most important Swiss work of a foreign composer is *L'Histoire du soldat* of Stravinsky. It was created in collaboration with the French-Swiss poet, C. F. Ramuz, and was intended for performance by an itinerant theatrical group in the villages of French-speaking Switzerland. Its premiere in Lausanne, 1918, was financially supported by Werner Reinhart and Paul Sacher, the latter being one of the great patrons of 20th-century music. Ernest Ansermet, who conducted the premiere, had encouraged Stravinsky's interest in jazz as it appears in the work by bringing him examples of it from the U.S.

Richard Strauss's connection with Switzerland was less profound, although his *Metamorphoses* for 23 solo strings was commissioned by Sacher and first performed in Zurich in 1946. Hindemith, who taught at the Univ. of Zurich from 1951 to 1957, was not influenced by his Swiss years.

Among native Swiss composers, the predominant influence early in the century was German romanticism. Othmar *Schoeck (1886 –1957), who was born in the German-speaking central region of the country, was a lieder composer strongly influenced by Schumann and to a lesser extent by Schubert and Wolf. In choosing melodic shapes and harmonic underscoring, he adhered closely to the texts he set, reflecting perhaps the Swiss tendency to keep the imagination in check. Hermann Hesse, who lived in Switzerland for many years, once remarked that "nowhere in Schoeck's settings is there the slightest misunderstanding of the words. . . . Everywhere he lays his finger with an almost alarming certainty on the central experience of the poet as it was crystallized in a word or in the vibrations between words." Other German-influenced composers have included Volkmar

Andreae (1879–1962), Hans Huber (1852–1921), and Hermann Suter (1870–1926).

French music influenced Swiss composers during the heyday of impressionism. Such familiar impressionist images as sea, light, color, and clouds occur in the subjects and titles of works by Ernest *Bloch (1880–1959), Gustave Doret (1866–1943), Henri *Gagnebin (b. 1886), Conrad *Beck (b. 1901), and André-François *Marescotti (b. 1902). Italian impressionism appeared in the music of Othmar Nussio (b. 1902), who studied with Resphigi in Rome. All of these composers tended to combine the sensuous sounds and decorative harmonies of impressionism with such abstract Germanic procedures as sonata form and fugue. Gagnebin is a good example, along with the German-oriented works of Frank *Martin (b. 1890). The best known example of the interaction of cultures, however, is Arthur *Honegger (1892–1955), who was born of German-Swiss parents in Le Havre, France, and studied both in his father's native city of Zurich and in Paris.

Andres Briner

SINCE 1945. Willy *Burkhard (1900–55) played a particularly important role in the development of Swiss music after World War II. There is a strong feeling of structure in his own music, a reliance on baroque forms, and an expanded use of the tonal system. He was an active teacher, and his many students have come to represent a broad stylistic spectrum: Klaus *Huber (b. 1924), Giuseppe G. *Englert (b. Italy, 1927), Armin *Schibler (b. 1920), and Rudolf *Kelterborn (b. 1931). An important proponent of the 12-tone system in Switzerland is Wladimir *Vogel (b. Russia, 1896), among whose students have been Rolf *Liebermann (b. 1910) and Jacques *Wildberger (b. 1922).

Current Swiss musical life reflects the federal structure of the country: there is no real cultural center, and activities are distributed among the larger Swiss cities. Cultural associations, music societies, orchestras, etc., are largely independent of the government and merely receive financial support from this source. This is also true in the case of the Swiss Composers' Association (founded 1900), which is probably the most important organization in Switzerland's musical life. The Association represents the interests of composers, conductors, soloists, and music publishers, stresses in particular the cultivation of Swiss music, supports composers in their publishing activities, and takes an active interest in the recording of Swiss music. An objective sampling of Swiss music is sought in the annual festivals of the association, and compositions representative of all regions and styles in the country are included. The Composers' Association also represents the Swiss section of ISCM, which has branches in the larger cities and in whose concerts significant foreign compositions as well as new Swiss works are performed. RSR (the radio station of French-speaking Switzerland) plays an important role in exposing the public to new music in its yearly concert series, "Diorama de la Musique Contemporaine."

The younger and generally more radical composers, at least those whose reputations have reached beyond national boundaries, tend to be more strongly oriented than their predecessors to the new musical directions exemplified in ISCM. They can be divided into two main groups. The first is more or less a direct successor of Anton Webern, whose heritage in many instances has been transmitted by Pierre *Boulez (b. France, 1925). Basel, where Boulez has taught, is now a center of composition in its own right, with Klaus Huber as its dominating personality. The tendency there is to avoid rigid serialism. Great value is placed on craftsmanship, and there is only here and there (in Jürg *Wyttenbach, b. 1935, for example) a desire to break with traditional concepts of music. Huber himself uses serial techniques, employing shifts in dynamic level and tone color sparingly so as not to obscure the structure and polyphonic fabric of his music (*Tenebrae* for orchestra, 1967). His music often shows an affinity with religion and mysticism, as in *Soliloquia* (1959–62), a large-scale oratorio based on texts of St. Augustine. His constantly recurring application of mathematical principles of form is quite striking: in one section of *Tenebrae* the instrumental entrances are determined according to logarithmic progressions so that, even with the increasingly dense instrumentation, the entrances do not coincide until the end. Wyttenbach's music has a primeval drive. He does not, however, renounce the traditional forms. Thus in his cantata *De metalli* (1965) he has combined serial techniques within a format of a series of variations. In his most recent works Wyttenbach has tended to break increasingly out of a purely musical context and to include elements of a scenic or theatrical nature. Although most of the works of Heinz *Holliger (b. 1939) follow traditional principles, he has made subtle use of sound, including electronic distortions of live sound (*Siebengesang* for oboe, orchestra, voices, loudspeaker, 1967). *Noten* for organ (1964–66) by Hans Ulrich

*Lehmann (b. 1937) is a mobile score consisting of several short sections, which the performer assembles in an order of his own choosing. With most of the other composers in this group there is only a slight application of indeterminacy and other avant-garde techniques.

The other group of composers tends to make more of a break with tradition; they are closer to Stockhausen, Kagel, and the U.S, avant-garde. They do not adhere to the traditional categories of composer, interpreter, and listener and are concerned with solutions to new problems. Sociological reflections are drawn in; special emphasis and meaning are given to playful elements. Constant work and continuing experimentation in ensembles is of the utmost importance. Englert, probably the first antitraditional Swiss musician, gradually adopted the practices of John Cage, as in *Aria* for drums and several instruments (1965), in which each action to be performed is located in the notation by means of circular illustrations of the drumhead; the dynamic level and pitch (to be adjusted with the pedal) is determined simultaneously by a system of coordinates. *Fragment pour orchestre* (1964) is merely a torso and questions the possibility of a well-formed and complete work in today's world. It consists of several beginnings; when it is ready to begin a development, it ends. *Tarok* (1967) is scored for a loosely synchronized ensemble of three to six strings. One of the most daring musicians is Pierre *Mariétan (b. 1935), who has worked partly in collaboration with painters, sculptors, and architects. His belief is that music should issue from and merge with the environment; instead of finished pieces, he now composes mostly scores with verbal instructions that provide the impetus to musical action, rather than a finished product. Urs Peter *Schneider (b. 1939) strives for an unattainable goal, a totality of expression encompassing both artistic and nonartistic means. *Babel* (1961–67) is for a free choice of sound sources, and *Abendfüllendes* (1966–69) is for both visual and sound sources. In contrast to the "richness" of these works, Schneider also composes works in which a static periodicity is attained by means of an extreme reduction of musical material (*Kreuze*, 1964–67, for xylophone, piano, flute and organ; *Umkehr*, 1969–70, for orchestra with apparatus). Roland *Moser (b. 1943) tries to stimulate associations and thought participation among his listeners by means of contrasts. In *Harmonies . . . (. . . en conséquence d'une page de Franz Liszt)* for 2 pianos (1834/1969), he places different techniques of new

music in relief, ranging from serial and pseudoserial to aleatory processes.

Kjell H. Keller

BIBL.: *Festschrift des Schweiz* (Tonkünstlervereins 1950); *Jahrbuch 1968* der Neuhelvetischen Gesellschaft (Bern 1968); *Musik der Schweiz: Schweizer Komponisten* (Bonn 1955), *Österreichische Musikzeitschrift* (supplement, 1969); *Schweizer Musiker-Lexikon* (Zurich 1964); *40 Schwiezer Komponisten der Gegenwart* (Amriswel 1956). Articles on Swiss music frequently appear in the *Schweizerische Musikzeitung*.

A. B. and K. H. K.

Sydeman, William (Jay) (b. New York, 8 May 1928), studied at Duke Univ. (1944–45), the Mannes College (1946–51, 1953–55; theory and composition with Felix Salzer, Roy Travis), the Hartt College (1956–58, composition with Arnold Franchetti), and at Tanglewood (1955, 1956; composition with Roger Sessions, Goffredo Petrassi). He also studied privately with Sessions during 1954–55. He has taught composition at the Mannes College since 1959. In May 1966 he lectured on American music in Eastern Europe as part of a U.S. State Dept. Cultural Exchange Program. He describes himself as "a musical hybrid, split between the traditional urge to 'say something' and 20th-century materials, which have so long been associated with impersonality and abstraction."

PRINCIPAL COMPOSITIONS: *Songs* for soprano, flute, cello (1959, Ione); *Wind Quintet No. 2* (1959–61, McG-M); *Piano Sonata* (1961, Ione); *Homage to "L'Histoire du Soldat"* for clarinet, bassoon, trumpet, trombone, violin, double bass, percussion (1962, Okra); *Music* for flute, viola, guitar, percussion (1962, Peters); *Quartet* for flute, violin, clarinet, piano (1963, Okra); *Duo* for viola, harpsichord (1963, Okra); *Duo* for violin, piano (1963, Okra); *The Lament of Elektra* for alto, chorus, chamber orchestra; text by Sophocles (1964, Ione); *Oecumenicus*, concerto for orchestra (1964, Okra); *Study for Orchestra No. 3* (1965, AMP); *Concerto da camera No. 3* for violin, double bass, clarinet (bassoon), 2 trumpets in C, bass trumpet in F, trombone, 2 percussionists (1965, AMP); *Fantasy Piece* for harpsichord (1965, Okra); *In memoriam John F. Kennedy* for narrator, orchestra (1966, AMP); *Music* for viola, winds, percussion (1966, AMP); *Texture Studies* for wind quintet (1966, Okra); *Concerto* for piano 4-hands, chamber orchestra or electronic sounds on tape (1967, Ione); *Projections No. 1* for amplified violin, tape, slides (1968, Okra); *Texture Studies* for orchestra (1969, Okra); *Trio* for bassoon, bass clarinet, piano (1969, Okra).

BIBL.: "Composer on Wheels," *Time* magazine (19 Jan 1962):45–46; Nancy B. Reich, ed.,

Catalog of the Works of W. S., 2nd ed. (New York, N. Y. Univ., 1968); Kurt Stone, "Review of Records" [on *Music*] (1966), *Musical Quarterly* 50:546–50.

Symonds, Norman (Alec) (b. Nelson, B. C., Canada, 23 Dec 1920), studied during 1946–50 at the Toronto Conservatory and with Gordon Delamont (theory and counterpoint). He is primarily self-taught as a composer. Jazz has been a major influence on his music, first when he was a clarinet and saxophone player and later when he was a jazz arranger and composer. During the 1950s he wrote many chamber works for an experimental jazz octet in Toronto. For a while, as his interests led him to other areas of music, he was a "thirdstream" composer. "Prose shapes" appeal to his imagination, and he likes the "slow and measured rhythms of nature." He has conducted contemporary chamber ensembles in Toronto and composed for theater, television and films.

PRINCIPAL COMPOSITIONS: *Fugue for Reeds and Brass* for jazz orchestra (1952); *Concerto grosso* for jazz quintet, symphony orchestra (1957); *The Age of Anxiety*, suite for jazz orchestra; composed for a radio performance of W. H. Auden's work (1957); *Tensions*, television ballet for jazz quartet, chamber orchestra (1959); *The Nameless Hour* for improvised solo, string orchestra (1962, Leeds); *L'Age de Pierre (Man, Inc.)*, musical play (1967); *Impulse* for orchestra (1969). List to 1964: *Composers of the Americas* 11:124–26.

Synthesizer, a system of electronic instruments for the production and control of sound.

© *Music Educators Journal* (Nov 1968)
SEE ALSO Electronic Music: Apparatus.

Szabó, Ferenc (b. Budapest, 27 Dec 1902; d. 4 Nov 1969), studied at the Liszt Academy of Music in Budapest (1922–26; composition with Leó Weiner, Albert Siklós, Zoltán Kodály). In 1926 he became involved with the labor movement in Hungary and in 1932 was compelled to emigrate temporarily to Germany and the Soviet Union. During 1945–67 he was professor of composition at the Liszt Academy and during 1958–67 its director. He was also president of the Union of Hungarian Musicians during 1949–51. His music was influenced by his socialist concerns, and he composed many mass songs, marches, and folksong arrangements, as well as music for films.

PRINCIPAL COMPOSITIONS (published by EMB): *String Quartet No. 1* (1926); *Trio* for 2 violins, viola (1927); *Toccata* for piano (1928); *Sonata* for solo cello (1929); *Farkasok dala* [Song of the Wolves] for chorus (1929); *Sonatas Nos. 1–2* for solo violin (1930); *5 Small Pieces* for piano (1933); *Lyric Suite* for string orchestra (1936); *Concerto for Orchestra*, "Hazatérés" [Homecoming] (1948); *3 Small Choruses*, on poems by József Attila (1948); *Ludas Matyi Suite No. 1* for orchestra (1950); *Emlékezeto* [Momento], symphony (1952); *Föltámadott a tenger* [In Fury Rose the Ocean], oratorio (1955); *Ludas Matyi*, ballet (1960); *Ludas Matyi Suite No. 2* (1961); *String Quartet No. 2* (1962); *Elfelejett szerenád* [Sérénade oubliée] for orchestra (1964); *Beismerés* [Confession] for chorus (1967); *Be Good till Your Death*, opera (1969, unpub.).

PRINCIPAL WRITINGS: "Bartók nem alkuszik" [Bartók Doesn't Bargain], *Új Zenei Szemle* 1/4:3–12; "A II. Magyar Zenei Hétek" [The 2nd Huugarian Music Week], *Új Zenei Szemle* 4/11:13–22; "Élet és müvészet" [Life and Art], *Magyar Zene* 8/5:453–61.

BIBL.: János Maróthy, *S. F. indulása* [S. F.: The Beginning] (Budapest 1965); András Pernye, "S. F. fiatalkori kamaramüvei" [S. F.: Youthful Chamber Works], *Magyar Zene* 4/1:32–41; ———, *S. F.* (Budapest 1965).

[prepared with the help of the Musicology Institute, Hungarian Academy of Sciences]

SEE ALSO Hungary.

Szalonek, Witold (b. Czechowice, Poland, 2 March 1927), attended the State Academy of Music in Katowice (1949–56, piano with Wanda Chmielowska, composition with Bolesław Woytowicz). He has taught composition, analysis, and technical problems relating to contemporary music at the Katowice Academy since 1956 and was made a professor in 1967.

PRINCIPAL COMPOSITIONS (published by PWM unless otherwise noted): *Pastorale* for oboe with piano or orchestra (1952); *Suita polyphonica* for strings (1955, unpub.); *Suite de Kurpie* for alto-9 instruments (1955); *Symphonic Satire* for orchestra (1956, unpub.); *Cello Sonata* (1958); *Confessions*, triptych for speaker, chorus, chamber orchestra; text by K. Ittakowicz (1959, Moeck); *Concertino* for flute, chamber orchestra (1962); *Arabesques* for violin, piano (1964); *Les Sons* for orchestra (1965); *4 Monologhi* for oboe (1966); *Mutazioni* for orchestra (1966); *Proporzioni* for flute, viola, harp (1967); *Improvisations sonoristiques* for clarinet, trombone, cello, piano (1968); *Mutanza* for piano (1968); *1 + 1 + 1 + 1* for 1–4 strings (1969, unpub.); *Lovely Country . . .*, cantata for voice, orchestra (1969, unpub.).

PRINCIPAL WRITINGS: Program notes for the festivals at Darmstadt (1960) and Warsaw (1963, 1968) and for the ISCM festivals of 1959, 1966, and 1969.

BIBL.: Ulrich Dibelius, "Music Language—Sonority—Articulation," *Polish Music* 3/4:14–15; Eigel Kruttge, "The 42nd ISCM Festival and 12th Warsaw Autumn of 1968," *ibid.* 3/4:7–8; Tadeusz Marek, "Composer's Workshop, W. S.," *ibid.* 3/4:31–35; Kazimierz Nowacki, "W. S., *Quattro Monologhi . . .*," *ibid.* 3/3:13–14.

Szervánszky, Endre (b. Kistétény, Hungary, 27 Dec 1911), studied at the Liszt Academy in Budapest (1923–28, 1931–36; composition with Albert Siklós, clarinet with Franz Főrster). He has taught composition at the Budapest Conservatory (1942–48) and the Liszt Academy (since 1948).

PRINCIPAL COMPOSITIONS (published by EMB unless otherwise noted): *String Quartets Nos. 1–2* (1936–38, 1956–57); *Violin Sonata* (1945); *Serenade* for string orchestra (1947–48); *Ballet Suite* for orchestra (1950); *8 Petőfi Songs* for voice, piano (1952); *Wind Quintets Nos. 1–2* (1953, 1956); *Flute Concerto* (1953); *3 Petőfi Songs* for chorus (1954); *Concerto for Orchestra,* "In memoriam Atilla József" (1954); *3 Songs* for voice, piano (1957); *6 Pieces* for orchestra (1959, EMB and General); *3 Male Choruses* on ancient Chinese texts (1960, unpub.); *Sötét mennyország* [Gloomy Heaven], requiem for chorus, orchestra; text by János Pilinszky (1963, unpub.); *Variations* for orchestra (1964–65); *Clarinet Concerto* (1964–65).

BIBL.: István Barna, *S. E.* (Budapest 1965); Ferenc Halmy, "Hungarian Composers Today: E. S.," *Tempo* (spring 1969):2–5; Colin Mason, *Hungarian Music Since Bartók,* BBC lecture (28 April 1966).

SEE ALSO Hungary.

Szokolay, Sándor (b. Kunágota, Hungary, 30 March 1931), studied at the Budapest Academy of Music (composition with Ferenc Szabó and Ferenc Farkas). During 1951–57 he taught solfège at the Municipal Music School, and from then until 1961 he worked in the music department of the Hungarian Radio. Since 1961 he has been a free-lance composer.

PRINCIPAL COMPOSITIONS: *Children's Miniatures* for piano (1954); *Violin Concerto* (1956); *Sonata* for solo violin (1956); *2 Ballads* for chorus, 2 pianos, percussion (1957, EMB); *Orbán és az ördög* [Urban and the Devil], ballet (1958); *Piano Concerto* (1958); *Világok vetélkedése* [Rivalry of Worlds], cantata for chorus, orchestra (1959); *Az iszonyat balladája* [The Ballad of Horror], ballet (1960); *Istár pokolijárása* [Isthar's Descent to Hell], oratorio for chorus, orchestra (1960); *3 Miniature Ballads* for soprano, chamber ensemble (1960); *Néger kantáta* [Negro Cantata] for chorus, orchestra (1962, Leduc); *Vérnász* [Blood Wedding],

opera (1962–64); *Déploration,* in memory of F. Poulenc, for chorus, orchestra (1964); *Révélation* for chorus, orchestra; poem by Alfred Musset (1966); *Hamlet,* opera (1966–68); *Trumpet Concerto* (1969); *A zene hatalma* [The Power of Music] for children's and adult choruses, orchestra; poems by Mihály Babits (1969).

SEE ALSO Hungary.

Szymanowski, Karol (b. Tymoshovka, U-kraine, 6 Oct 1882; d. Lausanne, 28 March 1937), began his musical training with piano lessons and then during 1901–05 studied composition with Z. Noskowski. In 1905 his *9 Preludes* for piano were published in Berlin. The same year he founded the composers' group Young Poland in Music in Berlin with G. Fitelberg, L. Różycki, and A. Szeluto. He was in Berlin during 1906–08 and then in Warsaw, Italy, Vienna, Tymoshovka, and after 1920 in Warsaw again. He became director of the Warsaw Conservatory in 1927 and rector in 1930. From 1932 on he was also active as a pianist (he premiered his *Symphonie concertante* in Poznań in 1932) and writer.

The beginning of Szymanowski's output was marked by his study of other composers, particularly Brahms, Reger, Strauss, and Scriabin. Of the many compositions from this period, only a few (the opera *Hagith,* 1912–13; the *Hafiz* song cycle, 1914) give evidence of any individuality. Between 1914 and 1917, however, he composed perhaps his best music. Various technical features occur in these works —atonality, polytonality, ultrachromaticism with Oriental-like ornamentation, microtones, complex rhythms, declamatory passages (in both instrumental and vocal works) and improvisation—all of which create an intense and expressive music. The supposed influence of Debussy and Ravel at this time is a misconception, for Szymanowski had advanced independently of them in the use of polytonality and of orchestral color for its own sake.

After 1921 Szymanowski grew more conservative. He turned to folklore, at first by using texts (as in *Słopiewnie,* 1921), then simple tunes (as in the *Rymy dziecięce,* children's songs, 1923), and mazurkas (*20 Mazurków* for piano, 1924–26), in which he combined two contrasting folk elements (north Polish dances from Mazowsze and the Góral music and crude harmony of the mountain dwellers). His *Stabat Mater* (1926) draws on medieval liturgical music and folklorelike impulses. His *Symphony No. 4* (1932), a last major work, combines late romantic orchestration and emotionally charged melody with some folk elements.

Szymanowski was a romanticist par excellence, and in his time he dominated Polish music precisely because his compositions were easily understandable. After 1921 he avoided many of the progressive currents—neoclassicism, atonality, dodecaphony—and he tended to use folklore in a blunt manner by quoting tunes directly. He also orchestrated with a heavy hand. In spite of these shortcomings, however, he far outdistanced other Polish composers (who composed very little), and his influence has reached down to the present in such composers as Tadeusz Baird.

PRINCIPAL COMPOSITIONS: *9 Preludes* for piano (1900, Spółka Nakładowa); *3 Fragments* for voice, piano; text by J. Kasprowicz (1902, Gebethner i Wolff); *Variations* for piano (1903, Piwarski); *Piano Sonata No. 1* (1904, Piwarski); *Violin Sonata* (1904, Spółka Nakładowa); *Variations on a Polish Theme* for piano (1904, Spółka Nakładowa); *Concert Overture* for orchestra (1905, UE); *Symphony No. 1* (1907); *12 Songs* for voice, piano (1907, Spółka Nakładowa); *Symphony No. 2* (1910, PWM); *Piano Sonata No. 2* (1911, UE); *Love Songs of Hafiz* for voice, piano (1911, UE); *Hagith*, opera (1912–13, UE); *Love Songs of Hafiz* for voice, orchestra (1914, UE); *Symphony No. 3*, "Song in the Night," for tenor, chorus, orchestra (1914–16, UE); *Mity* [Myths], 3 poems for piano (1915, UE); *Songs of the Fairy Princess* for voice, piano (1915, UE); *12 Etudes* for piano (1916, UE); *Maski* [Masks], 3 pieces for piano (1916, UE);

Violin Concerto No. 1 (1916, UE); *Piano Sonata No. 3* (1917, UE); *Demeter* for alto, women's chorus, orchestra (1917, instrumentation revised 1924; UE); *String Quartet No. 1* (1917, UE); *Król Roger* [King Roger], opera (1918–24, UE); *Słopiewnie*, 5 songs for voice, piano (1921, UE); *Rymy dziecięce* [Children's Verses], 20 short songs for children (1923, PWM); *Harnasie*, ballet (1923–31, UE); *20 Mazurkas* for piano (1924–26, UE); *Stabat Mater* for soprano, alto, baritone, chorus, orchestra (1926, UE); *String Quartet No. 2* (1927, UE); *6 Kurpian Songs* for chorus (1929, PWM); *Veni Creator* for soprano, chorus, orchestra (1930); *12 Kurpian Songs* for voice, piano (1930–32, PWM); *Litania do Marii Panny*, 2 fragments for soprano, women's chorus, orchestra (1930–33, PWM); *Symphony No. 4*, "Symphonie concertante," for piano, orchestra (1932, Eschig); *Violin Concerto No. 2* (1932–33, Eschig); *2 Mazurkas* for piano (1934, Eschig). Complete list in K. Michałowski, *K. S., Thematic Catalogue of Works and Bibliography* (Cracow 1967).

PRINCIPAL WRITINGS: "Wychowawcza rola kultury muzycznej w społeczeństwie" [The Educational Role of Music in Society], *Pamiętnik Warszawski* 8 (1930). A novel, *Ephebe* (1918–19), was never published and has been lost.

BIBL.: J. Chomiński, ed., *K. S.* (Cracow 1960); T. Chylińska, *K. S.*, revised ed. (Cracow 1966); S. Golachowski, *K. S.* (Cracow 1956); Z. Lissa, *Polish Music* (Warsaw 1965); S. Łobaczewska, *K. S.* (Cracow 1950); B. Maciejewski, *K. S.* (London 1967).

Bogusław Schäffer

SEE ALSO Harmony and Counterpoint.

T

Takahashi, Yuji (b. Tokyo, 21 Sept 1938), studied at the Toho School of Music (1954–58; composition with Minao Shibata, Roh Ogura) and at Tanglewood (summers 1966–68). He also studied theory privately with Iannis Xenakis. He has performed as a professional pianist since 1961. During 1963–66 he participated in the Ford Foundation artist-in-residence program in West Berlin. Under a grant from the John D. Rockefeller III Fund, he composed computer music during 1966–68. He was affiliated with the Center of Creative and Performing Arts at the N. Y. State Univ. at Buffalo during 1968–69. He has taught piano at the San Francisco Conservatory since 1970. He uses stochastic procedures in his music and since 1971 has worked with the TENET 210 computer.

PRINCIPAL COMPOSITIONS (composed with the aid of a computer): *Chromamorphe II* for piano (1964, Peters); *Metatheses* for piano (1968, Peters); *Prajnâ Pâramitâ* for 4 ensembles, each consisting of mezzo-soprano, piccolo, bass clarinet, piccolo trumpet, bass trombone, violin, cello, harpsichord, 2 percussionists (1969); *Orphika* for orchestra (1969, Peters); *Yé-Guèn* for 3 recorded orchestras and resonating sculptures of various materials by François Bachet (1969); *Kaga-i* for piano, chamber orchestra (1971).

SEE ALSO Japan.

Takemitsu, Toru (b. Tokyo, 8 Oct 1930), is mostly self-educated except for a brief period of study with Yasuji Kiyose (1948–50). With painters and composers he organized in 1951 an experimental workshop in Tokyo, Jikken Kobo, and in 1958 joined the Institute for 20th-Century Music, which sponsored annual summer workshops in contemporary music. In 1966, with Toshi Ichiyanagi and Seiji Ozawa, he founded a biennial festival for contemporary music called Orchestral Space. For the 1970 World Exposition in Osaka he conceived and became artistic director for Space Theater, a concert hall equipped with laser beams and 800 loudspeakers.

Takemitsu's compositions in the 1950s include his major tape works and chamber music for various combinations. More recent works include several pieces for large orchestra and numerous film scores. The early music reflects not only the chromaticism of Schoenberg and Berg but also the melodic and chordal writing of Messiaen. The tape music is based on the techniques and esthetics of the musique concrète of Pierre Schaeffer. Since 1961 Takemitsu's music has used quasiserial combinations of small cells, and forms have evolved from perpetual variations of these cells (with the silence between musical events as important as the sound itself). The initial conception of a piece is often derived from a symbolic linguistic synthesis that suggests subsequent musical development. In *Asterism*, for example, the different meanings of the title word (a constellation; the star-shaped figure caused by the refraction of light in some crystals; a pyramid of three asterisks) determined the musical structure. Timbre is always an important concern, a tendency shared by Ligeti and the Polish school. The film scores are studies in unusual instrumentation and texture. His orchestration is colorful but never ostentatious, using divided strings, brasses with various mutes, novel effects on the harp, and many bell-like sounds. The rhythmic flow is nonmetric with an irregular pulsating effect. In his orchestral works, Takemitsu tries to realize a different time cycle for each instrumental group while simultaneously maintaining a delicate balance with the total movement. The ending of a piece is often evocative of the beginning of a simple melody.

PRINCIPAL COMPOSITIONS: *Relief statique* on tape (1955, recorded by Universal Recording); *Vocalism A-I* on tape (1956, recorded by RCA Victrola and Universal); *Requiem* for strings (1957, Peters); *Music of Tree* for orchestra (1961, Peters); *Ring* for flute, terz-guitar, lute (1961, Ongaku); *Coral Island* for soprano, orchestra (1962, Peters); *Harakiri*, film score (1962); *Woman in the Dunes*, film score (1964); *Kwaidan*, film score (1964); *The Dorian Horizon* for 17 strings (1966, Ongaku); *November Steps No. 1* for shakuhachi, biwa, orchestra (1967, Peters); *Green*, "November Steps

No. 2," for orchestra (1967, Peters); *Cross Talk* for 2 bandoneons, tape (1968); *Asterism* for piano, orchestra (1968, Peters).

Yuji Takahashi

SEE ALSO Asian Music and Western Composition, Japan.

Tal, Josef (b. Pinne, near Poznań, Poland, 18 Sept 1910), attended the Berlin Hochschule (1928–30; composition with Heinz Tiessen, piano with Max Trapp, harp with M. Saal). He was director of the Jerusalem Academy of Music (1948–52) and has been senior lecturer and chairman of the musicology department of Hebrew Univ. since 1965. During 1957–58 he held a UNESCO fellowship for research in electronic music and since 1961 has directed the Israel Center for Electronic Music. He has appeared as pianist and conductor in Europe, the U.S., South America, and Japan.

PRINCIPAL COMPOSITIONS: *Piano Concerto No. 1* (1944); *Yetziat Mitzrayim* [The Exodus from Egypt] for baritone, orchestra (1946, IMP); *6 Sonnets* for piano (1946); *Piano Sonata No. 1* (c. 1948, IMP); *Em habanim semeḥah* [A Mother Rejoices], symphonic cantata for chorus, clarinet, orchestra (1949, IMP); *Qinah* [Lament] for cello, harp (1950, IMP); *Mar'ot* [Reflections] for string orchestra (1950, UE); *Oboe Sonata* (1952); *Sukkot*, cantata (1952, IMI); *Piano Concerto No. 2* (1953, IMP); *Symphonies Nos. 1–2* (1953, 1960; IMP); *Viola Concerto* (1954, IMP); *Violin Sonata* (1955, IMP); *Piano Concerto No. 3*, with tenor solo (1956, IMP); *Sha'ul be En-Dor* [Saul at Endor], concert opera (1957, IMP); *Ḥizayon ḥagigi* [Festive Vision] for orchestra (1957, IMP); *Intrada* for harp (1959, IMP); *String Quartet No. 1* (1959, IMP); *Exodus*, electronic ballet (1960); *Viola Sonata* (1960); *Amnon veTamar*, short opera (1961, Impero); *Concerto* for cello, string orchestra (1962, IMI); *5 Instructive Compositions in Dodecaphonic Technique* for piano (1962, IMI); *Mivnim* [Structures] for harp (1962, IMI); *Piano Concerto No. 4* with tape (1962); *Dargot shel ozmah* [Ranges of Energy], electronic ballet (1963); *Harpsichord Concerto* with tape (1964, IMI); *Piano Concerto No. 5* with tape (1964, IMI); *Mot Mosheh* [The Death of Moses], requiem for vocal soloists, chorus, tape (c.1965, IMI); *Woodwind Quintet* (1966, IMI); *Duo* for viola, piano (1967, IMI); *Ashmedai*, opera (1968, IMI); *Misdar hanoflim* [Call of the Fallen Soldiers], cantata (1968, IMI).

BIBL.: Alexander Ringer, "Musical Composition in Modern Israel," *Musical Quarterly* (Jan 1965): 288–90; Eli Yarden, "The Israeli Composer and his Milieu," *Perspectives* 4/2: 137–39.

SEE ALSO Israel.

Talma, Louise (b. Arcachon, France, 31 Oct 1906), studied at the Institute of Musical Art in New York (1922–30, composition with Howard Brockway), Columbia Univ. (1923–33), New York Univ. (1930–31), and the Fontainebleau School of Music (summers 1926–39, 49, 51, 61; composition, organ with Nadia Boulanger; piano with Isidore Philipp). She has taught theory and ear training at the Manhattan School of Music (1926–28), solfège at the Fontainebleau School (summers 1936–39), and various musical subjects at Hunter College (since 2928). All of her works before 1953 are neoclassic in style; those after 1953, serial.

PRINCIPAL COMPOSITIONS: *4-Handed Fun* for piano 4-hands (1941; 2-piano version, Fischer); *Carmina Mariana* for 2 sopranos, piano (1943); *Piano Sonata No. 1* (1943, Fischer); *Terre de France*, song cycle for soprano, piano (1943–45); *Toccata for Orchestra* (1944, Fischer); *Alleluia in Form of Toccata* for piano (1944, Fischer); *Piano Sonata No. 2* (1944–55); *The Divine Flame*, oratorio for mezzo-soprano, baritone, chorus, orchestra (1946–48); *The Leaden Echo and the Golden Echo* for soprano, double chorus, piano; text by G. M. Hopkins (1950–51); *Let's Touch the Sky* for chorus, flute, oboe, clarinet; poems by e. e. cummings (1952); *6 Etudes* for piano (1953–54, Schirmer-G); *String Quartet* (1954); *La Corona* for chorus; 7 sonnets by John Donne (1954–55); *The Alcestiad*, 3-act opera; libretto by Thornton Wilder (1955–58); *Passacaglia and Fugue* for piano(1955–62); *Violin Sonata* (1962); *All the Days of My Life*, cantata for tenor, clarinet, cello, piano, percussion (1963–65); *Dialogues* for piano, orchestra (1963–64, Fischer); *A Time to Remember* for chorus, orchestra; text after John F. Kennedy and Arthur M. Schlesinger, Jr. (1966–67); *3 Dialogues* for clarinet, piano (1967–68, Musicus); *The Tolling Bell* for baritone, orchestra; texts by Shakespeare, Marlowe, Donne (1967–69).

Tansman, Alexandre (b. Lódź, Poland, 12 June 1897), studied at Warsaw Univ. (1915–19; composition with Adalbert Gawronski, Piotr Rytel; piano with S. Vas). In 1919 he emigrated to Paris, where he still lives. During 1941–46 he lived in the U.S. Since 1920 he has toured as a conductor and pianist.

PRINCIPAL COMPOSITIONS: *Symphonies Nos. 1–8*: No. 1 (1916); No. 2 (1925, Eschig); No. 3 (1931–32); No. 4 (1938, Eschig); No. 5 (1941, Eschig); No. 6 with chorus (1944, Eschig); No. 7 (1946, Eschig); No. 8, "Simfonia piccola" (1951, UE); *Triptyque* for string orchestra (1930, Eschig); *Poil de carotte*, film score (1932); *The Big City*, ballet, for 2 pianos (adapted originally, 1932, from *Sonatine transatlantique*) and later arranged for orchestra; choreography by Kurt Jooss (1933, Eschig); *Flesh and Fantasy*, film score (1941, Leeds); *Music for Orchestra* (1947, Eschig); *Isaiah the Prophet*, oratorio for chorus, orchestra (1947,

UE); *Le Serment*, opera (1954, UE); *Concerto for Orchestra* (1954, Eschig); *Sabbatai Zevi*, opera (1957–58, Eschig); *Psalms* for tenor, chorus, orchestra (1961, Eschig); *6 Etudes symphoniques* for orchestra (1962, EFM); *Resurrection* for orchestra (1962, Eschig); *6 Movements* for string orchestra (1963, EFM); *Il usignolo de Boboli*, opera (1964, Ricordi); *Concertino* for oboe, chamber orchestra (1966, Eschig); *4 Movements* for orchestra (1968, Eschig); *Concertino* for flute, chamber orchestra (1969, Eschig); *Hommage à Erasme de Rotherdam* for orchestra (1969, Eschig).

PRINCIPAL WRITINGS: *Igor Stravinsky*, English trans. (New York 1949).

BIBL.: Raymond Petit, "A. T.," *Revue musicale* (Feb 1929); Gdal Saleski, *Famous Musicians of a Wandering Race* (New York 1927); Irving Schwerke, *A. T., Compositeur polonais* (Paris 1930).

Tape Music, see Electronic Music: Apparatus and Technology; Electronic Music: History and Development.

Tăranu, Cornel (b. Cluj, Rumania, 20 June 1934), studied at the Cluj Conservatory (1951–57, composition with Sigismund Toduta), at the Darmstadt summer courses (conducting with Bruno Maderna), and privately in France with Nadia Boulanger (1966–67) and Olivier Messiaen (Feb 1967). He has taught at the Cluj Conservatory since 1957 and conducted the contemporary ensemble Ars Nova since 1968. Since 1958 he has contributed many articles about contemporary music to the Rumanian periodicals *Tribuna* and *Musica*. His music has been influenced by the work of Enescu, Varèse, and Xenakis.

PRINCIPAL COMPOSITIONS: *Secvente* [Sequences] for string orchestra (1960, Muzicală); *Flute Sonata* (1960, Muzicală) *Sonata ostinato* for piano (1961, Muzicală); *Simfonia brevis* (1962); *Contraste I–II* for piano (1962–63, Muzicală); *Piano Concerto* (1963–66); *Incantatii* [Incantations] for orchestra (1964–65, Leduc); *Simetrii* [Symmetries] for orchestra (1965, Muzicală); *Dialoguri I* [Dialogues] for flute, clarinet, trumpet (1966, Salabert); *Ebauche* for voice, clarinet, violin, viola, cello, piano (1966–68, Salabert); *Dialoguri II* for piano (1967, Gerig); *Alternante* [Antiphonies] for orchestra (1967–68); *Intercalari* [Interpolations] for piano, orchestra (1968–69); *Secretul lui Don Giovanni* [The Secret of Don Giovanni], chamber opera (1969–70).

PRINCIPAL WRITINGS: *Enescu in constiinta prezentului* [Enescu in the Consciousness of Our Time] (Bucharest 1969).

Tauriello, Antonio (b. Buenos Aires, 20 March 1931), studied composition with Alberto Ginastera at the Argentine National Conservatory and piano with Walter Gieseking. He is a production assistant and rehearsal coach, principally for the N. Y. City Opera, the American Opera Theater, and the Teatro Colón. He has also appeared elsewhere as a pianist and conductor.

PRINCIPAL COMPOSITIONS (published by Barry): *Obertura sinfónica* (1951); *Ricercari 1 à 6* for orchestra (1963); *Transparencias* for 6 instrumental groups (1965); *Musica III* for orchestra, piano (1966); *Serenata II* for 7 instruments or orchestra (1966); *Canti* for violin, orchestra (1967); *Piano Concerto* (1968); *Mansión de Tlaloc* for orchestra (1969); *Les guerras picorocholines*, opera after Rabelais (in progress 1970).

SEE ALSO Argentina.

Tavener, John (Kenneth) (b. London, 28 Jan 1944), studied at the Royal Academy of Music (1962–68, composition with Lennox Berkeley, piano with Guy Jonson). He also studied composition privately with David Lumsdaine (1965–67). He has been organist at St. John's in Kensington since 1960 and has taught composition at Trinity College since 1969. His development has been influenced by the music of Stravinsky, Richard Strauss, Messiaen, and Stockhausen and by the Roman Catholic liturgy.

PRINCIPAL COMPOSITIONS (published by Chester): *3 Holy Sonnets of John Donne* for baritone, chamber orchestra (1964); *The Cuppemakers*, religious drama for soloists, chamber ensemble (1964); *3 Sections from T. S. Eliot's "Quartets"* for voice, piano (1965); *Cain and Abel*, cantata for 4 vocal soloists, orchestra (1966); *Chamber Concerto* for orchestra (1966); *The Whale* for soloist, chorus, orchestra, tape (1967); *3 Surrealist Songs* for soloist, piano, bongo drums, tape (1967); *Introit for the Feast of St. John Damascene* for soloists, chorus, orchestra (1967–68); *Grandma's Footsteps* for 5 music boxes, chamber group (1967–68); *In alium* for soprano, orchestra, tape (1968); *Celtic Requiem* for adult and children's chorus, orchestra (1969); *Jesus* for narrator, soloists, 2 flutes, chamber organ (1969).

SEE ALSO Great Britain.

Taylor, (Joseph) **Deems** (b. New York, 22 Dec 1885; d. there, 3 July 1966), studied at New York Univ. until 1906 and then did editorial work and journalism. He was music critic for the *New York World* (1921–25), editor of *Musical America* (1927–29), and music critic of the *New York American* (1931–32). From 1931 he did considerable work as a music commentator on radio, reaching a nationwide audience. As a consultant on music for the CBS network (beginning in 1936), he initiated a program of commissions to American composers. He was president of ASCAP during 1942–48. His music is in the romantic and American nationalist traditions.

PRINCIPAL COMPOSITIONS (published by Fischer unless otherwise noted): *The Siren Song*, symphonic poem, Op. 2 (1912); *2 Studies in Rhythm* for piano, Op. 5 (1913?); *The Chambered Nautilus*, cantata for chorus, orchestra, Op. 7; poem by O. W. Holmes (1914, Ditson); *The Highwayman*, cantata for women's voices, orchestra, Op. 8; poem by Alfred Noyes (1914, Ditson); *Through the Looking Glass*, suite for chamber orchestra after Lewis Carroll, Op. 12 (1917–19, rescored for full orchestra 1921–22); *Traditional Airs* for woman's voice, piano, Op. 15 (1923?); *Jurgen*, symphonic poem, Op. 17 (1924?); *Circus Day*, suite for orchestra, Op. 18; scored for jazz orchestra by Ferde Grofé (1925); *The King's Henchman*, 3-act opera, Op. 19; libretto by Edna St. Vincent Millay (1926); *Peter Ibbetson*, 3-act opera, Op. 20; libretto by C. Collier (1930); *Ramuntcho*, 3-act opera, Op. 23; libretto by the composer (1941). Taylor also arranged many folksongs and instrumental pieces for chorus (principally woman's chorus).

PRINCIPAL WRITINGS: *Of Men and Music* (New York 1937); *The Well Tempered Listener* (New York 1940); *Music to My Ears* (New York 1949); *Some Enchanted Evenings: The Story of Rodgers & Hammerstein* (New York 1953).

BIBL.: John Tasker Howard, *D. T.*, 2nd ed. (New York 1940); J. F. Porte, "D. T., and American Hope," *Sackbut* 9:193–95.

SEE ALSO Dance, Opera.

Tchaikovsky, Boris, see under Chaikovsky

Tcherepnin, Alexander (b. St. Petersburg, 21 Jan 1899), is the son of the composer and conductor Nicolas Tcherepnin. He began playing the piano and composing at a young age and had produced many large works by the time he was 15. A strong early influence was Sergey Prokofiev, who studied conducting with Alexander's father and often played his latest compositions in the Tcherepnin home. In 1917 Alexander began study in harmony and piano at the St. Petersburg Conservatory; however, the Revolution soon forced the family to move to Georgia. The elder Tcherepnin became director of the conservatory in Tbilisi, and the son resumed his studies, at the same time absorbing a wealth of Georgian folk music

that was to have an influence on his later musical development. In 1921, when civil war reached the Caucasus, the Tcherepnins left Russia and settled in Paris. There Alexander completed his training (composition with Paul Vidal, piano with Isidor Philipp) and embarked on an international concert career as composer and pianist. In 1922 he made his Western debut in London playing his own works. In 1923 Anna Pavlova danced his *Ajanta's Frescos* at Covent Garden. In 1926 he made his first concert tour of the U.S., and in 1927 his *Symphony No. 1*, with its scherzo for percussion alone, caused a riot in Paris. During tours to the Orient, 1934–37, he taught young Chinese and Japanese composers and founded the Collection Tcherepnin in Tokyo for the publication of their music. In Shanghai he met the Chinese pianist Hsien Ming Lee, who later became his wife. During 1949–69 he taught composition and piano at De Paul Univ. in Chicago (and became a U.S. citizen). Since 1964 he has maintained residences in New York and Paris, continuing to compose and tour as pianist and conductor.

Tcherepnin has described his compositions to 1921 (mostly for piano) as "instinctive"; in general, they blend the romantic tradition of Rachmaninov and Scriabin with the grotesquerie of early Prokofiev (characteristic works are the *Bagatelles*, *Sonatine romantique*, *Sonata No. 1*, and *Concerto No. 1*). During 1921–33 he began to produce music of a more distinctive character in which is revealed a gift for variation techniques, along with a new concern for larger forms, polyphonic complexities, and experimentation; in the clarity and lightness of orchestral textures can be seen the influence of postimpressionist French composers and the neoclassic Stravinsky (the *Piano Concertos Nos. 2–3*, *Concerto da camera*, *Piano Quintet*, and *Symphony No. 1* are examples). His early fascination with the ambiguity of the major-minor triad and the modal possibilities suggested by it led to the formulation in these years of a nine-tone scale (C, D♭, E♭, E♮, F, G, A♭, A♮, B, [C]). It is most clearly viewed as being generated by the conjunction of two major-minor triads, the second built on the major mediant of the first, with the remaining notes (D♭, F, A) resulting from the inversion of the original six-note pattern. The harmonic possibilities of the scale are extensive, and many complex chord structures, particularly in scores after 1950, are directly attributable to it. Another development of the 1921–33 period is "interpoint," Tcherepnin's system of polyphony which presents rhythmic units used thematically. The principal thesis of vertical interpoint is that in a pair of contrapuntally linked lines, one progresses using the empty spaces of the other. A multipart edifice can be constructed with the displacement of the measure bar of each pair of vertical interpoints. This results in a horizontal species of interpoint.

During 1933–50 Tcherepnin generally abandoned intensely polyphonic writing and became preoccupied with both miniature forms and Russian (Georgian) and Oriental folklore. In scores such as the *Suite georgienne*, there is a new subtlety in textural conception and a more refined emotional atmosphere. However, other compositions (for example, the *Piano Concerto No. 4*) show less stylistic individuality due to overreliance on folk-derived melodic materials, an extensive use of pentatonic scales, and a considerable simplification of harmony.

Since 1950 Tcherepnin has consolidated and developed the previous aspects of his style. His recent music contains involved polytonal chord structures, often spaced so as to produce, in effect, tone clusters. Rhythms are most often regular but with occasional off-beat accents. Wide-ranging melodic contours sometimes flirt with atonality. There are contrasts between simple and complex part writing, a tendency toward freer forms, and extremely effective uses of orchestral tone color. A definite tonal foundation is always present, and though passages of serial writing occasionally occur, serial procedures are not made an integral part of Tcherepnin's musical personality.

PRINCIPAL COMPOSITIONS: *Bagatelles* for piano or piano, orchestra (strings), Op. 5 (1913–18, Heugel); *Sonatine romantique* for piano, Op. 4 (1918, Durand); *Piano Sonatas Nos. 1–2*, Opp. 22, 94 (1918, Heugel; 1961, Boosey); *Piano Concertos Nos. 1–3, 5–6*: No. 1, Op. 12 (1919–20, Chester); No. 2, Op. 26 (1923, Heugel; No. 3, Op. 48 (1931–32, Schott); No. 5, Op. 96 (1963, Belaieff); No. 6, Op. 99 (1965, Belaieff); *Rhapsodie georgienne* for cello, orchestra, Op. 25 (1922, Durand); *String Quartets Nos. 1–2*, Opp. 36, 40 (1922, Schott; 1926, Durand); *Ajanta's Frescos*, ballet, Op. 32 (1923, UE); *Concerto da camera* for flute, violin, chamber orchestra, Op. 33 (1924, Schott); *01–01*, opera, Op. 35; libretto by L. Andreyev (1924–25, UE); *Magna Mater* for orchestra, Op. 41 (1926–27, UE); *Symphonies Nos. 1–4*: No. 1, Op. 42 (1927, Durand); No. 2, Op. 77 (1947–51, AMP); No. 3, Op. 83 (1952, Templeton); No. 4, Op. 91 (1957, Boosey); *Piano Quintet*, Op. 44 (1927, UE); *Die Hochzeit der Sobeide*, opera, Op. 45; libretto by Hugo von Hofmannsthal (1929–30, UE); *Duo* for violin, cello, Op. 49 (1932, Bote); *Suite georgienne* for piano, string orchestra, Op. 57 (1938, Eschig); *Sonatine sportive* for saxophone, piano, Op. 63

(1939, Leduc); *Les Douze* for narrator, chamber orchestra, Op. 73 (1945, Belaieff); *Le Jeu de la Nativité*, cantata for vocal soloists, chorus, strings, percussion, Op. 74 (1945, Belaieff); *Showcase* for piano, Op. 75 (1946, Boosey); *The Farmer and the Nymph*, opera, Op. 72; libretto by Siao Yu (1952, Boosey); *12 Preludes* for piano, Op. 85 (1952–53, Marks); *Harmonica Concerto*, Op. 86 (1953, AMP); *Suite* for orchestra, Op. 87 (1953, Peters); *Divertimento* for orchestra, Op. 90 (1955–57, Boosey); *Symphonic Prayer* for orchestra, Op. 93 (1959, Belaieff); *Vom Spass und Ernst*, cantata for low voice, strings, Op. 97 (1964, Gerig); *Suite* for harpsichord, Op. 100 (1966, Peters); *Sonata da chiesa* for viola da gamba, organ, Op. 101 (1966, Simrock); *Mass* for 3-part chorus, Op. 102 (1966, Peters); *Ivan the Fool*, music for a BBC radio production of the Tolstoy play (1968). Complete list: *Music of the Tcherepnins* (London 1969): 7–14.

PRINCIPAL WRITINGS: "Autobiographisches," *Rheinische Musik- und Theater-Zeitung* (May 1928); *An Anthology of Russian Music* (Bonn 1966).

BIBL.: Victor Belaieff, "A. T. and Contemporary Music" (in Russian), *Sovremenneia muzyka* (Moscow) 11 (1925); Phillip Ramey, "T. at Seventy," Philharmonic Hall program booklet (New York, Feb 1969); ——, "Gespräch mit A. T.," *Boosey & Hawkes Verlagsnachrichten* (Bonn, July 1969); Willi Reich, "A. T.," *Chesterian* 102; ——, *A. T.* (Bonn 1959, Paris 1962); Nicolas Slonimsky, "A. T., Septuagenarian," *Tempo* 87; Gerhard Tischer, "A. T.," *Deutsche Musikzeitung* (Cologne) 12 (1933); Virgil Thomson, *American Music Since 1910* (New York 1971): 176–77.

Phillip Ramey

Temperament, see Tuning and Temperament

Tenney, James C. (b. Silver City, N. M., 10 August 1934), studied engineering at the Univ. of Denver (1952–54) and music at the Juilliard School (1954–55, piano with Eduard Steuermann), Bennington College (1956–58; composition with Lionel Nowak; conducting with Paul Boepple, Henry Brant), and the Univ. of Ill. (1959–61, composition with Kenneth Gaburo, electronic music with Lejaren Hiller). He also studied piano privately with Yi-an Chou in New York (1955–56) and composition informally with Carl Ruggles (1956–66), Edgard Varèse (1956–65), and John Cage (1961–66). He was on the technical staff of Bell Telephone Laboratories during 1961–64. He was a research associate in music theory at Yale Univ. (1964–66), and he has taught at the New School for Social Research (electronic music, 1965–66), the School of Visual Arts in New York (science and technology, 1968–69), the Polytechnic Institute of Brooklyn (electrical engineering, 1966–70), and the Calif. Institute of the Arts (since 1970). In 1963 he founded the Tone Roads Chamber Ensemble, for which he was a conductor and pianist.

PRINCIPAL COMPOSITIONS: *Seeds* for 6 instruments (1956–62); *13 Ways of Looking at a Blackbird* for tenor, 2 flutes, violin, viola, cello; text by Wallace Stevens (1958); *Monody for Solo Clarinet* (1959); *Collage No. 1*, "Blue Suede," concrete music on tape (1961); *Analog 1*, "Noise Study," computer-generated music on tape (1964, recorded by Decca); *Dialogue*, computer music on tape (1963); *Ergodos 1*, computer music for 2 tapes played together or separately, forward or backward, with or without the addition of *String Complement* or *Percussion Complement* or *Responses* (1963); *Phases*, computer music on tape (1963); *Music for Player Piano*, computer-organized piece on a player-piano roll (1964); *String Complement*, a score in indeterminant notation for any number of string instruments; to be played with *Erogdos I* or *II* or another ergodic (nonprogressive) sound source, such as traffic noise (1964, published in John Cage's Notations, New York 1968); *Erogodos II*, computer music on tape with or without *String Complement* or *Percussion Complement* or *Responses* (1964); *String, Woodwind, Brass, and Vocal Responses*, a set of scores for any number of vocal or instrumental sound sources; to be used like *String Complement* above (1964); *Fabric for Ché*, computer music on tape (1967); *For Anne (rising)* on tape (1969).

PRINCIPAL WRITINGS: "On the Discriminability of Differences in the Rise-Time of a Tone," *Journal of the Acoustical Society of America* 34/5:739; "Sound-Generation by Means of a Digital Computer," *Journal of Music Theory* 7/1:24–70; *Meta (+) Hodos: A Phenomenology of 20th-Century Music and an Approach to the Study of Form* (New Orleans 1964); "The Physical Correlates of Timbre," *Gravesaner Blätter;* 26:106–09; "Computer Study of Violin Tones," with Mathews, Miller, and Pierce, *Journal of the Acoustical Society of America* 38/5:912–13; "Computer Music Experiences 1961–64," *Electronic Music Reports* (Utrecht Univ.) 1:23–60.

SEE ALSO Form.

Terzakis, Dimitri (A.) (b. Athens, 12 March 1938), attended the Athens Conservatory (1960–65, composition with Yannis Papaïoannou) and the Cologne Musikhochschule (1965–67, composition with Bernd Alois Zimmermann, electronic music with Herbert Eimert). In 1966 he composed music for the Epidaurus Festival production of *The Suppliants* by Euripides. Terzakis was somewhat influenced initially by the Viennese School. Currently he combines atonal procedures with an untempered tuning system based on that of Byzantine music.

PRINCIPAL COMPOSITIONS: *Septet* for 7 flutes (1965); *Okeaniden* for orchestra (1966); *Ikos* for chorus (1968); *Chroniko* for flute, guitar (1968, UE); *String Quartet* (1969); *Chroai* for orchestra (1969); *Achos* for guitar, percussion (1970); *Nuances* for voice, viola, piano, percussion (1970).

Tetrachord, Tetrad, a collection of four pitch classes considered either as a simultaneity or as a succession. The terms occur most frequently in reference to segments of 12-tone sets. *Tetrachord* in this sense is unrelated to the ancient and medieval concepts to which the term is also applied.

Text Setting and Usage. Composers today who use texts are concerned with ways of using the voice itself and usually of using speech or speech sounds as part of their music. Traditionally, even in non-Western cultures with different standards of voice production, the voice is used in singing, recitative, or recitation to a musical accompaniment (melodrama), and the texts are organized for their connotative and denotative meanings. Although singing is still the predominant way of using the voice in the 20th century, other possibilities (e.g., humming, hissing, shouting, whispering) have been and are being explored and integrated into the act of composition; likewise texts may be chosen for their phonemic as well as for their morphemic content and may even be structured (or not structured) to produce a result whose "meaning" is nonverbal.

The interinfluence of text and music has changed throughout history, affecting fundamental decisions about the organization of the music. Where it clearly subserves the words (e.g., in recitative), the music moves according to the immediate demands of the text. Where the text serves as an impetus for specifically musical impulses (e.g., in Webern's vocal works), the music proceeds according to its own determinants; the text may help set the length of the piece and its parts, but specific words may fall, by and large, fortuitously.

PRE-20TH-CENTURY APPROACHES. Unlike the extremes above, most vocal works integrate text and music. In medieval and renaissance pieces, the texts usually dictated *a*) the ordering and lengths of the interior segments of the work (e.g., phrases, strophes); *b*) the rhythms (i.e., durations and accents) of at least the sung parts; and to some extent *c*) the melodic directions, based on the text's inflections. Although there are exceptions, composers generally considered the formal organization of a text more important than its semantic content.

From the late renaissance and early baroque on, a text's denotations became as primary a compositional concern as its form, rhythms, and inflections. Composers chose to *a*) highlight one idea or attitude at a time (as in the "galloping" accompaniment and changing dramatic situation in Schubert's *Der Erlkönig*); or *b*) project the general expressive qualities of the entire text or, in opera, the basic psychological traits of the characters. Except for the obvious use of formulas (e.g., diminished-seventh chords, tremolos) to evoke conditioned responses from listeners, *b* is generally achieved through creating a musically dramatic situation that parallels rather than "expresses" the text. This involves a set of choices: tempo; mode or even specific key; types of attack; phrasing; dynamics; style of singing (e.g., lyric, bravura, parlando); overall tessitura or details of registral placement; relation of the singer's line to the accompaniment; the rhythmic activity, density, and timbres of the total ensemble; the use of associative musical figures, either newly invented for the specific work (e.g., leitmotivs) or taken from the repertory of common practice (e.g., the baroque "affections"); types and relative predictability of both harmonic motion and melodic continuity; frequency of, placement of, and manner of resolving dissonances; the overall form of the song or aria; and, for the words, their metric placement, rhythms, and agogic accents, and stresses achieved through changes in direction. Except for the standardized usages of tonal music (i.e., mode and key, accepted definitions of consonance and dissonance, and expectations regarding chordal and linear successions), all these procedures have remained available to even the most radical of today's composers.

TRADITIONAL APPROACHES IN THE 20TH CENTURY. Quantitatively most 20th-century music is traditional in idiom and in ways of incorporating texts into musical works. Benjamin Britten's *War Requiem* (1961), for example, is a model of traditional musical prosody. The text is straightforward dramatic narrative, and the words are set simply, syllabically, stressing their normal accents and inflections, sometimes causing variable meters. Occasional illustrations occur (e.g., "wailing," "lachrymose") amid the general mood-settings (created by tempos, dynamics, timbre, etc.). There is also some Stravinsky-like chanting. The effectiveness of the music depends on its competent, craftsmanly use of known techniques, not on the development of new ones. Another traditional approach occurs in Charles Ives's songs, where there is direct tone painting and immediate, obvious associations: the music often imitates actions described or quotes tunes (e.g., hymns, popular songs) that the words suggest. (The presence of such devices may have only a little, and that not a crucial, bearing, compared with the other criteria available, on the total musicality of the works involved.) Hindemith, on the other hand, tried to substitute some kind of specifically musical symbolism for the common practice of overt musical parallelism when he revised his *Marienleben* (1922–23, revised 1936–48). He tried to associate specific concepts with selected "tonalities," a reapplication of the 18th-century practice of imbuing a key with certain "affections" (e.g., Mozart's "Turkish" key of A minor or his "vengeance" key of D minor).[1] But since Hindemith's "tonalities" are merely the prominence of selected pitches, mostly as basses of nontriadic, nontonal chords, and since the practice has severely limited application, it seems best to regard the idea as only a working method for the composer. None of the other musical elements seems to support the associations assigned to the "tonalities," and the listener's responses cannot correlate with them.

Qualitatively, Arnold Schoenberg's music is the most innovative and influential of the first half of the century; even so, his text settings exhibit some traditional features. He often expressed word meanings representationally or symbolically. In *Pierrot lunaire* (1912), for example, low slow notes evoke "night" in "Nacht," the activity imitates the gesture of "Raub," trills, glissando, and quick rhythms illustrate the words "Zerreisst die Priesterkleider" in "Rote Messe"; for a Kafkaesque, utterly prosaic setting of a gruesome event, there is "Zärtlich—einen Schädelbohrer!" in "Gemeinheit."[2] Schoenberg stated, however, in regard to his *4 Orchestral Songs*, Op. 22 (1913–14), that he was no longer illustrating words but the "meaning of the whole, creating opportunities for the singer to give the words their proper expression."[3] Nevertheless some word illustrations still occur, and some rather

[1] Paul Hindemith, Preface to *Marienleben*.

[2] See also the instances of tone painting cited by George Perle in the record notes for *The Music of Arnold Schoenberg* (Columbia Records) vol. 1.

[3] Arnold Schoenberg, "An Analysis of Arnold Schoenberg's *Four Orchestral Songs*, opus 22," trans. by Claudio Spies, record notes for *The Music of Arnold Schoenberg* (Columbia Records) vol. 3:21–28.

straightforward tone-painting is present in the later works, e.g., "light . . . into atoms" in *Kol Nidre*. This shows that when well done, such illustrations through imitative gesture are part of the work's compositional process, which may be interpreted as illustrations; but in other instances pictorializing may be merely superimposed on the musical material. Schoenberg was also carefully attentive to a text's prosody. Even in *Pierrot lunaire*, with its highly stylized adaptation of the elocutionary melodrama genre, the rhythms and inflections of the poems help determine the rhythms, directions, dynamics, metric placement, and phrasing of the vocal line. (Exceptions occur in his settings of English texts, where Schoenberg apparently gave an occasional English word the accentuation of the equivalent German one.) Also traditional is the fact that Schoenberg did not make compositional use of the intrinsic sounds of words. Even with Rilke's texts, where phonemes are an inherent part of the poem's organization, correspondences fall fortuitously. In Op. 22 "Alle, welche dich suchen" contains repetitive phonemes consistently set differently, and the sound-rich "Mach mich zum Wächter deiner Weiten," where the sounds must have rung in the composer's ear, shows concentration only on the morphemic content of the text. This approach may stem from Schoenberg's concept of continual variation and never-literal repetition, but in any case the phonemes do not seem to have dictated musical decisions. (The more advanced aspects of Schoenberg's text settings are discussed below under "New approaches.")

THE INFLUENCE OF THE NEW LITERARY STYLES. Most composers remain interested in realizing or complementing a text's form, rhythms, melodic possibilities, and morphemic content. Some, however, have rejected overt representationalism, and others have concluded that musical situations can be only generally expressive, that they can apply equally well to substitutable dramatic situations. That is, a quick descending scale followed by a low tremolo could represent a dive into wavy depths, vertigo, or "icy fingers down a spine" and the ensuing passion. Some composers, then, have recently become more aware of the phonemic organization of a text.

Poets, obviously, have been careful in varying degrees to choose words for their sounds as well as for their denotations and connotations, so that the phonemes may serve as elements in text organization, furthering also the semantic expressivity of the text. And composers, following the text's semantic and dramatic content, have created lines that to varying degrees correspond to or even express this phonemic organization.[4] Lately, however, some composers have begun to be less concerned with a text's morphemic content and to approach the words as a nondenotative sound source, relating, with varying rigor, the text's phonemic content to the music's organization. One impetus for such altered approaches derives from the changed attitudes of some late-19th- and early-20th-century writers toward choosing and organizing their material. G. M. Hopkins, for example, audacious in diction, syntax, and rhythm, did not just choose some words for rudimentary onomatopoeic reasons but had their evocative phonemes in mind, as Mallarmé did of his phonemic symbolism.[5] Even more carefully than previous poets, Hopkins organized the phonemic content into relationships more complex than the familiar rhyme schemes, alliteration, assonance, or even internal rhyme. Through his use of "sprung" rhythm,[6] he enriched meter and its numbering of syllabically determined feet by setting his words into diversified, semantically imitative, variably weighted rhythms.[7]

Other poets (e.g., Rilke, Pound, Yeats), in addition to using variable metric and rhythmic patterns and focusing on sounds per se, were also using richer imagery, suggestion, complex and highly personal associations, even to the use of private references, and, along with some novelists (e.g., Proust, James, Kafka, Joyce), intense psychological states as their material (i.e., "vocabulary"), with a resultant shift from denotation to connotation, while developing new novel and verse forms and new ways of creating continuity. Also although earlier playwrights like Ibsen or Shaw were effecting changes in the contents of plays, others like Brecht or Jarry were moving away as well from inherited esthetic attitudes, forms, and procedures.

The major internal evidence (i.e., beyond letters such as Schoenberg's to Richard Dehmel[8]) that these changes affected the

---

[4] Robert Cogan, "Toward a Theory of Timbre: Verbal Timbre and Musical Line in Purcell, Sessions, and Stravinsky," *Perspectives* 8/1:75–81.

[5] Robert Greer Cohn, *Toward the Poems of Mallarmé* (Berkeley-Los Angeles 1965):3–4, 7, 14–15 *et passim*.

[6] Abrupt rhythms, particularly those in which stresses occur on contiguous syllables.

[7] W. H. Gardner, *Gerard Manley Hopkins* (London 1944):42–49 *et passim*.

[8] Arnold Schoenberg, *Letters* ed. by Erwin Stein, trans. by Eithne Wilkins and Ernst Kaiser (New York 1965):35–36.

composers of the early 20th century is the fact (and the ways) that the composers chose to set texts of the advanced writers of their own and immediately preceding generations. The primary reason for all changes in musical approach, however, is the search by original composers for new musical possibilities. The major composers at this time were discarding tonality in favor of new means of organizing simultaneities, lines, and motion (all of which resulted in a diminution of predictability). This was accompanied by new ideas about rhythm, meter, and timbre. More important this new vocabulary required a new syntax and new forms, since it is not only the elements themselves that result in newness but their organization. Occasionally a composer's following of procedures in literature helped him to develop new processes.

NEW APPROACHES. The new attitudes toward and new ways of using texts and the voice were created by the same composers who broke new ground musically, Debussy, Schoenberg, Stravinsky, and Webern. Debussy reacted against the rather obvious emotionalism of the late German romanticists and adopted the esthetic of Mallarmé, whose *Afternoon of a Faun* he transformed into music. Mallarmé, like Hopkins, aspired toward the abstraction of music and was explicitly interested in the shaping of content, not in the content alone.[9] He chose words meticulously for their phonemes and activity-imitating rhythms and, like Debussy, conveyed not objects but sensations. In Debussy's songs the motion of the piano part sets off the usually syllabic vocal line, which intensifies the natural flow of the words. The length of the text determines the lengths of phrases and of the whole song. The form may follow either that of the poem or, as in the setting of Baudelaire's sonnet "Recueillement," the phonemic and morphemic content as well. In this song the music separates the octave with its acute "ē" rhyme from the sestet with its more open sounds, and it also divides the first eight lines, not into the two quatrains of the poetic form but into a semantically determined two (intimate tone), five (lofty tone), and one (intimate again). The concluding six lines are grouped again not in the couplets of the rhyme scheme, but in four, one, and one, with the slow rhythms of the last two lines particularly projecting the meaning of the words. Debussy's regard for text is further illustrated by his

setting of Maeterlinck's *Pelléas et Mélisande* (1893–95) as a continuous opera, using the entire play as written. Like many of his predecessors, he tied the singers' lines closely to the text, allowing them to dictate timing, inflection, and stress—but now to produce a flow emulating naturalistic rather than rhetorical speech.[10] A significant innovation in voice usage is Debussy's humming chorus, since ubiquitously imitated, in *Sirènes* (1899), and Ravel's use of composed vocalizations in song and in the *Daphnis and Chloë Suites* (1909–12). Both used the voice not in a narrative role but as an instrument, as one more available timbre, this one producing phonemes.

Stravinsky's reaction against the previous century's illustrations and excess sentimentality is evident, for example, in *Les Noces* (1914–23), which demonstrates a new way of conceiving melody. Stravinsky substituted ritualized speech, actual speaking, and quasishouting as well as singing with untraditional types of attack and linear movement for the bel-canto, legato line of, say, a Bellini or Puccini. Stravinsky thereby showed that any succession of notes could function as the melody, i.e., the prominent line of an ensemble. Further his was a new way of using the voice, solo or in chorus. To evoke archaic settings, he adapted archaisms to his composing techniques, using in the first part, for example, chantlike, syllabic, percussive, one-tessitura singing, insistent repetition and nondevelopment, severe constraint of range centered on one pitch (E), and the restriction of the pitch content within that range (B, D, E, with extensions forming a pentatonic scale, B, D, E, F$\sharp$, G). Stravinsky's objectivism is illustrated by his transferring of narration and indications of psychological process from the music to the words and miming, letting the story be told, like a parodied *chanson de geste*, to repetitive music.

Stravinsky's treatment of text is similar in his *Symphony of Psalms* (1930), where a general mood is set by the use of nonconnotative Latin, of a few pitches and one focal pitch,[11] chanting chorus, repetition, and syllabic setting following the word accents; only an occasional word, like "peregrinus," is illustrated. This attitude toward text setting was not altered in his later serial works, even those with highly potent texts. In the *In Memoriam Dylan Thomas* (1954) the vocal and

[9]Stephane Mallarmé, "Music and Literature," "Ideas on Poetry," *Mallarmé; Selected Prose Poems, Essays, and Letters* trans. by Bradford Cook (Baltimore 1956).

[10]Joseph Kerman, *Opera as Drama* (New York 1956):178–81.
[11]Eric Salzman, *Twentieth-Century Music . . .* (Englewood Cliffs .N. J., 1967):52–59.

instrumental lines are all built from linkages and overlappings of various forms of a five-note series, and the recurrent lines of the text are treated as refrains, ignoring the changing semantic function caused by their varied placement, the poem's grammar, and the cumulative repetition. Stravinsky allowed his music to unfold in its own way, so much so that he seemed occasionally either oblivious to the rhythms of the poem or else more interested in setting them against the vocal-line accentuations. He paid no heed to Thomas's luxuriant phonemes, although coincidental repetitions are unavoidable due to the restricted series of intervals. Accents occur here, as in other works,[12] through the use of dynamics, melodic direction, metric placement, registral placement, and (with the recurrent "Rage, rage" line) instrumental support, including pitch doubling. One possible relationship is suggested by the fact that the first notes of the second, third, and fourth stanzas are progressively one semitone higher and that the concluding one begins on the same pitch and uses the same series form as the fourth, seeming to create a connection between "Wild men" and "And you, my father." This is vitiated, however, by the similar connection of the fifth stanza's "Grave men" to the opening "Do not go gentle," and by the return to B♭ and B at the beginning of the fifth and sixth stanzas respectively. The text, then, seems to be an initiator and formal guideline for specifically musical concerns.[13] L'Histoire du soldat (1918), however, is an exception, for here the music is narrative: it serves as the composer's satiric commentary on what is portrayed on stage, achieved through distortions that burlesque well-known musical models, e.g., marches, dances, violin playing, tonality itself. (Since Stravinsky's variable-meter rhythms tend to follow the accentuations of the Russian language, it would be worth investigating the effect that performances in French and other languages have on his work. With all composers, it is worth investigating the effect of native language on rhythmic thinking; the case of Bartók is already documented, largely by the composer himself.)

Schoenberg's instrumental works, even many of the 12-tone ones, delineate forms and use formal procedures adapted from tonal practice; they do not develop from his new vocabulary. In his vocal works, however, he felt that by following the dramatic line of the text he was better able to substitute new processes for remembered forms.[14] Even in early works, such as the setting of Stefan George's Das Buch der hängenden Gärten (1908–09), he avoided the formal pedantry and the rhythmic and line-length rigidity of the poems and, like Debussy, followed the sense of the words. The results, as in later works like Erwartung (1909), are not conventional schemes (like ABA or rondo forms) but a "musical stream of consciousness."[15]

As noted above, many aspects of Schoenberg's text settings are traditional, including his general disregard for word sounds. In Moses und Aron (1930–32), however (for which he wrote his own text), he showed an awareness of and a compositional approach to the generative development of motivic phonemes. He set similar-sound words symbolizing conflicting forces against each other in each act.[16] Moreover as in the best coeval poetry, he used phonemes to express morphemes. In act I, scene I, for instance, the motivically repeated open, rolling vowels and voiced consonants of the Voice ("Vor ihren Ohren wirst du Wunder tun—ihre Augen werden sie anerkennen . . . fühlen, was ihrem Blut befohlen") contrast with the deliberately clumsy response of Moses ("Meine Zunge ist ungelenk: ich kann denken, aber nicht reden") with its glottal sounds ng, nk, ch, k stumbling against obstacles, tsung, st-ung, l-nk, ch-k-n, d-nk-n, n-cht-r-d-n, its inconsistency of vowel sounds, and the emphasis on the bland vowel e.

Schoenberg's inventiveness extended to his use of the voice. Most stunning is the use, in the influential Pierrot lunaire and later works, of sprechstimme, defined as "precisely rhythmed, contour-determined speech."[17] The technique is a development of the melodrama idea.[18] Schoenberg's later interest in sound as sound is shown by his use in Prelude for orchestra with chorus, Op. 44 (1945), of a choir singing only vowels. He also integrated other forms of nonsinging into his works (e.g., whispering in Die glückliche Hand; speaking singing, and sprechstimme in Moses und Aron; narration in Ode to Napoleon, 1942, and A

[12]Milton Babbitt, "Remarks on the Recent Stravinsky," Perspectives 2/2:40.

[13]Further investigations along the lines suggested by Cogan (see note 4) may modify this observation.

[14]See note 3.

[15]George Perle comments on Erwartung in the record notes for The Music of Arnold Schoenberg (Columbia Records) vol. 1.

[16]Allen Forte, "The Sonic Organization of the Text," record notes for Moses und Aron (Columbia Records):15.

[17]Milton Babbitt, "An Introduction to the Music," record notes for Moses und Aron (Columbia Records).

[18]H. H. Stuckenschmidt, Twentieth Century Music, English ed. (New York 1969):63.

Survivor from Warsaw, 1947). His use of counterpoint causes vocal parts to become an integral part of a total ensemble, like another instrument. Because of the range of his imagination and the quality of his music, Schoenberg has had probably the greatest influence on the use of texts in the 20th century.

Alban Berg's *Wozzeck* (1917–22) is another in the line of 20th-century sung plays. The main interest is not plot action, but character insight; therefore even when extended arialike solos occur, they do not stop the action, as in past operas: the probing of a character's inner state that they contain *is* the action. Characterization is achieved through the vocal lines (which individuate or caricature different manners of speech), some of the leitmotivs, some of the classical forms used, and through orchestral commentary. Vocal usages also include various types of nonsinging. Individual words, as in *Lulu* (1929–35) and Berg's songs, dictate the durations and accents of vocal lines, and their meanings determine inflections; the orchestra realizes overall textual connotations. In these ways some of the most probing and essential aspects of the traditional approach to text setting is adapted to contemporary theatrical, psychological, and, most important, musical content. In contrast to Berg, Anton Webern's settings are concerned with articulating musically the grammatical and formal organization of the texts, not the literal meanings of the words. Similarly, melodic lines reflect a sensitivity to word rhythms, not meanings. Webern used the voice as he did instruments—moving rapidly from one register to another—and this, like his attitude toward word meanings, has greatly influenced subsequent composers. Pierre Boulez's *Le Marteau sans maître* (1953–55) shows a similar attention paid to only the sounds and rhythms of the text. Overt representations, symbols, and parallel dramatic situations do not occur in the music, which proceeds according to its own operations. The poems themselves are "logical" in that each has a referent image; however, they are not prosaically progressive or connected in a sequential narrative. Boulez has complemented this situation apparently by giving a musical shape to his own responses to the poems. A more rigorous integration of text and music occurs in Milton Babbitt's *Spelt from Sybil's Leaves* (1955) to a sonnet of G. M. Hopkins. The rhythm of the music intensifies the rhythm of the poetry, a continuation of the traditional approach but applied here to a highly complex situation. As in the poetry, rhythm accumulates mo-

mentum within lines and rhythmic correspondences link rhymed lines. In addition pitch relationships articulate the poem's formal structure: *a* lines use the 4 forms of the source 12-tone set, which consists of 4 different trichord types, while *b*, *c*, and *d* lines use 4 forms of secondary sets, each of which is derived from a different trichord. (Babbitt's more advanced work, developing from such careful attention to text-music relationships, is discussed below.)

TEXT FRAGMENTATION; WORDS AS SOUND SOURCES. Superficially, eschewing literal meaning in compositions with texts might be related to the avoidance of forms and processes borrowed from tonal music. More convincing, however, is its derivation from the same impulse that makes, say, electronic sound sources attractive: the interest in new musical possibilities. A further relation is that electronic music, with its multiple speakers and their spread placement, offers newly precise modes of organization and seems to invite fragmentation of musical space and line. The newer literature, with either more tenuous or more complex associations and an increasing care for phonemic organization,[19] seems similarly to invite concentration on phonemes and a consequent fragmentation of the narrative line. Further since the expectations and associations afforded by tonality are no longer relied upon by advanced composers today, there is greater reliance on sounds per se, either on the effects of their mere succession or on the impact of their organized relatedness. The attitude toward sound as sound extends to the treatment of texts.

Luciano Berio's *Circles* (1962) occasionally uses the phonemes of its three e. e. cummings poems as a sound source, e.g., the *ng* sound of "stinging," imitated by the harp, connects to the harp accompaniment of "gold," the sforzando *g* of "dragging," and to some nasal (*n-m*) sounds, but does not connect with "ringing." In addition the setting sometimes attends to the morphemic, rhythmic, and articulating functions of the punctuation and spacing of the poem. For example, the separation of the lines at the end of *stinging* is realized musically through a reduced density, merged and split words in *n(o)w* are given appropriate rhythmic groupings (see "pounceupcrack" or "-visiblya mongban"), and capital letters receive stresses (see "THuNdeRB loSSo'M"). Sometimes, however, meanings are reflected, as in *n(o)w*, where "(Ghost)" and "(voiceless)," both in parentheses, are whispered. But sometimes, as

[19] Denise Levertov, "Work and Inspiration: Inviting the Muse," *Field* (Oberlin College) 1:24–40.

in *riverly is a flower*, the expected accentuation and the slowing down indicated by spacing of the text are disregraded (as are such tempting illustrative words as "softly" or "hushed "). Specifically the concentration on phonemes is most evident in the textual disarrangement that occurs the second time through *riverly's* third stanza, but here too, while the phonemes are the center of focus, no connections among them are made. The range of appeal in using phonemes separately is exemplified by Stefan Wolpe's use of it, since this is a telling departure from his earlier, traditional practice of attentiveness to word meanings. In the second part of his *Cantata* (1963–68), complete words (e.g., "smell," "fruit") and then parts of words (e.g., "ts," "dth," "t r" from "it is said that other trees") are set contrapuntally against the original text as a means of creating motivic variation of word sounds.

A more committed use of text fragmentation and more convincing evidence of the influence of composing with electronic means occur in works where vocalists talk, hiss, whistle, chant, do glissandos, howl, cry, breathe excitedly, and recurrently break up the words into their constituent phonemes. Frequently such works also use new modes of emitting instrumental sounds (e.g., Penderecki's *St. Luke Passion*, 1963–65, and Lutosławski's *3 Poèmes d'Henri Michaut*, 1963). Among the most inventive in this respect is Stockhausen's *Momente* (1962–64), which uses voices for aria-type singing and scat singing (the singing of morphemically meaningless syllables, a technique invented by Louis Armstrong and developed by Ella Fitzgerald) as well as for producing specifically evocative sounds, such as laughing, giggling, or screaming. Stockhausen uses these resources within a context of continuous change and shuffable continuity. Some works use similar approaches to text usage, but are based on the contrary esthetic premise of nonchange —a premise perhaps derived from such practices as Stravinsky's use of long-lasting ostinatolike, nondeveloping situations. Now, however, the idea has been extended into a principle of having nothing "happen" after the first act of invention. Examples include some works by the two Polish composers cited above. Sometimes the triggering concept may be potentially productive, as in Dieter Schnebel's multilingual a cappella choral work *Deuteronium 31.6*, which uses the phonemic similarities among four translations of the text as a means of combining them. Other radical approaches may be seen in Ralph Shapey's *Incantations* for soprano and instruments (1961), which uses only phonemes without

morphemic references, and in Luigi Nono's vocal works—for example, in his a cappella *Sarà dolce tacere* (1960), in which words disintegrate into their component sounds so that a word like "colline" is represented by only its vowels.

Sometimes minimal composition is combined with less original approaches to text setting, as in György Ligeti's a capella *Lux aeterna* (1966), which perhaps expresses eternal, continuous sound; or in Robert Ashley's *She Was a Visitor* (1967), where a speaker continuously repeats the title phrase with identical inflections while a chorus breaks the phrase down into its constituent phonemes. Here as in other recent works by other composers the performers choose the order of many events so that a great deal of responsibility for the work is theirs. The result is that occurrences and correspondences are superimposed as in much primitive music. John Cage used this approach in *Aria* (1958), in which he instructs the singer to use diverse singing styles previously restricted to disparate styles of music (e.g., jazz, opera, etc.). A more satisfying use of such procedures, owing to the range and attractiveness of the choices, occurs in George Crumb's *Night Music* (1963–64).

In contrast to the trend toward looser relationships, Milton Babbitt employs the most rigorous new means for advancing the traditional approach to text-music interdependence, for he makes the textual an integral part of the musical material. In his most recent works, he uses texts as nondenotative sound sources, or he uses individual phonemes (i.e., not connected to words), concentrating on the makeup of speech sounds. Investigators in speech acoustics had noted that vowels and continuous-sounding voiced consonants (e.g., l, m, n, r, v, z) can be spoken by differently pitched voices and sung on many specific pitches without losing their identifiability, that continuous-sounding unvoiced consonants (e.g., f, h, s, sh) can give a sense of general pitch, and that vowels cannot be pronounced above certain pitch levels. The phonemic identity of these pitched sounds depends on their respective *formants*. Formants are those frequency regions where, for a specific sound source, the amplitude of any wave whose frequency falls within that region is reinforced. For example, in contrast to a tuning fork, which produces a single frequency (perceived as a single pitch), a vowel sound, whether sung or spoken, consists also of co-occurring frequencies (*partials*) so that a complex and unique sound wave form results. Such a wave form can be analyzed into its constituent partials, and the partials themselves further investigated as to their amplitudes (i.e., perceived as loudness). Every vowel sound has its own individual pattern of formant distribution or areas of frequency within which any partial resonates more strongly. Thus its formants establish the phonemic identity of a vowel sound because they determine the makeup of its unique sound wave.[20] In a comparable but more complex way, the timbre of a sound produced by a traditional musical instrument is identifiable—regardless of the pitch being produced—because of the makeup of the transient partials occurring at the sound's attack and because of the sound's formants after it has settled into a specific pitch. Every musical instrument has a unique formant distribution functioning, again, as a filter that stresses the partials at certain frequencies and not others.

If each vowel or timbral sound is analyzed into its unique spectrum (a graph of its component partials and their respective amplitudes), one can observe relationships among speech spectra and timbral spectra. Babbitt, who customarily creates contexts of maximally organized relatedness, has used such relationships in his music. In *Vision and Prayer* for soprano and synthesized taped accompaniment (1961), he matched spectra by associating, for example, the formants of the *u* sound prominent in the poem's opening ("who," "you," "room," "womb") with electronically produced timbres. Similarly in *Composition for Tenor and 6 Instruments* (1960), he matched instrumental timbres with vowel sounds. In *Sounds and Words* (1960) and *Phonemena* (1969–70) again only nonmorphemic phonemes constitute the text, and formant as well as serial considerations influenced pitch and phoneme associations. Many composers who have studied or been otherwise relatively closely associated with Babbitt are concerned with investigating the possibilities for linking speech and other sounds in their work. Such linkage may be a relatively straightforward association, as in the third of my own *3 Images* for soprano and piano (1961), where the phonemic composition of the poem determined the choices of trichord types that generated derived 12-tone sets; or as in parts of Charles Wuorinen's masque *The Politics of Harmony* (1967),[21] where phonemes and their order determine the choice of specific pitch classes,

with word illustration one criterion for choosing register. More complex associations are apparent in Babbitt's own work[22] and in that of Godfrey Winham of Princeton Univ., who is investigating the construction and synthesis of speech sounds.

SUMMARY. Composers have been variously concerned throughout history with the text-music relationship. Their interest seems to have changed from a concern for the formal organization of a text to one including its denotations, then its connotations, and now toward speech sound as sound to the sonic structure of individual sounds, the relationships among them in a text, and the possible musical realizations of more complete text-music integrations. An indication of recent changes in attitude toward text-setting is the work of James K. Randall. His early *Improvisation on a poem of e. e. cummings* for voice and piano (1960) focused primarily on articulating musically the grammatical structure of the poem; his present work, much of which is computer assisted, is concerned with the makeup of speech sounds and the development of means whereby organized language sounds, co-functioning with the organization of other sound elements, can articulate a total musical structure using syntactical procedures specific to a nontonal vocabulary.

Edward Levy

SEE ALSO Asian Music and Western Composition, Jazz, Melody, Musicology and Composition, Opera, Prose Music.

Texture. The term *texture* is used here to refer to the quality of a sound or series of sounds that are generally, but not necessarily, from a musical composition. The texture of a sound is a product of the sound's component parts: pitch(es), timbre, and loudness. The texture of a succession of sounds also describes the way in which these elements are connected in time. Thus in a musical composition texture describes certain relations between voices (e.g., contrapuntal and homophonic textures) and the quality of the sound produced by a given combination of instruments in terms of their instrumental color and the way in which they produce pitches together. Some contemporary composers, especially in the electronic media, have used the texture of sounds as structural elements, as other composers have traditionally used pitches.

In the following discussion the term *harmonic texture* refers to those aspects of texture

[20]Peter Ladefoged, *Elements of Acoustic Phonetics* (Chicago 1962): 92 *et passim*.

[21]William Hibbard, "Younger American Composers: Charles Wuorinen: The Politics of Harmony," *Perspectives* 7/2: 155–56.

[22]See note 4.

that result from the pitch and rhythmic structure of a composition. Harmonic textures include 1) what have traditionally been called contrapuntal, polyphonic, homophonic, or chordal textures, or any such specific explication of the obvious aspects of the pitch and rhythmic structure; 2) any textural aspect of a composition that may be considered without reference to the means of sound production; and 3) any specific aspect of the ways in which pitches are used in a composition from the texture created by an accompaniment pattern (such as an Alberti bass) to that formed by details of voice leading. The term *sound texture* refers to those textures that are products of the orchestration of a piece or are related to a description of its sound apart from harmonic textures.

An important aspect of the textural problem is the extent to which these categories can be considered separable and the extent to which their identities are blurred by interaction and interdependence. The degree of separability between the two dimensions is a function of the difference in their importance. In piece *A*, for instance, if a change in the harmonic texture affected the values of the piece more than a commensurable change in the sound texture, the harmonic texture would be considered more important. The extent to which the commensurable changes affect the values of the piece would determine their separability (the greater the difference in affect, the greater the separability). In piece *B*, if the inverse were true, the sound textures would be more important. In piece *C*, if the two dimensions were equal in importance, their affect on the values of the piece being of equal weight, they would in effect be inseparable. (Perhaps it is necessary to speculate on the existence of a fourth type in which either dimension may be altered without affecting the values of the piece at all. They probably would be similar to piece *C*.) We will consider the texture of 20th-century music in three broad areas: 1) the affect of the dissolution of tonality on harmonic textures, and the harmonic textures of atonal and serial music (both categories to be subsumed under the classification *nontonal*); 2) the increased use of sound textures as generative and structural elements to reinforce and aid new kinds of harmonic textures; and 3) the abandonment of all constraints on harmonic textures and the total reliance on sound textures as a means of musical coherence.

THE DISSOLUTION OF TONALITY. Complex changes took place in the nature of harmonic textures following the dissolution of tonality and of music dependent on triadic prolonga-

tions and the hierarchical relationships of the diatonic scale. We will briefly examine the nature of these changes by means of comparison.

In tonal practice the function of a specific pitch is determined by its context. For example, a C that is the root of a triad has a different function from a C that is a seventh of a dominant seventh chord; a C that is a passing note has a different function from a C that is a point of arrival or departure. If the means of establishing this type of contextuality is removed, a note may still be contextually inflected, but its meaning and relations will be far more complex and less specific than in tonality. This makes the means of establishing contextuality often the unique property of a given piece, the structural norm governing the processes of only that one piece.

Traditional tonal music involves special distinctions and relations between its horizontal and vertical aspects. While what has traditionally been called a contrapuntal texture (requiring the existence of melodically independent parts) stresses the horizontal dimension to a greater extent than what has been called a homophonic texture (in which independent voices are less clearly delineated and the vertical dimension is more heavily emphasized), in both cases the same functional and generative relations between the vertical and horizontal operate. It is in fact a basic precept of Schenkerian theory that the horizontal dimension is created by an unfolding of a vertical phenomenon, the triad, according to the laws of counterpoint.[1] In nontonal music, when there are no specific procedures to establish a functional relation between the vertical and horizontal dimensions, new relations arise between them. The resultant texture can no longer be strictly identified with concepts of contrapuntal and homophonic texture since the factors that create these identities and their functional relations are no longer present. The extent to which one can speak of a horizontal or vertical dimension and texture and their interrelations has to be considered again in terms of a given piece and its own structural norm.

In traditional tonal music, hierarchies among sonorities and voice leading principles help to determine completion and goal and to direct the motion of the music, thereby contributing to both small- and large-scale coherence. These hierarchies give rise to normative procedures governing the progression of

[1]Heinrich Schenker, *Der Freie Satz*, rev. ed. (Vienna 1956); Felix Salzer, *Structural Hearing*, 2nd ed. (New York 1962); ——— and Carl Schachter, *Counterpoint in Composition* (New York 1969).

sonorities, the precedence of certain chords, their resolutions, the relations between sonorities and specific aspects of form, and the contextually determined rhythmic placement of a sonority according to its function. Given the lack of such constraints in nontonal music, questions of precedence, resolution, and formal implication, as well as the rhythmic unfolding of harmonic textures, are all left to the discretion of the composer. Thus one finds, for example, an enormous variety of means of rhythmic expression, ranging from relative periodicity with regularly recurring pulses (in late Webern works, such as the Op. 27 *Piano Variations* and the works of such present-day composers as Peter Westergaard) to extreme aperiodicity, in which it is difficult to perceive any regularly recurring pulse (Stockhausen's *Klavierstücke XI*).

In tonality part of the function of a given note has to be determined by considering its registral relation to other notes. Thus a C that is below an E and G has a different meaning from one that is above these two notes, though the three will always form a triad. Generally in tonal music, in situations where registers are delineated (as they generally are), the function of the lower register is different from that of the upper register. Given the absence of constraints that create this particular situation, register itself takes on a new role. First, the different registers of a piece can be more functionally equivalent than formerly. This means, for example, that the kind of thing that happens in the bass would not be as out of place in another register as it might be in tonal music. If a composer establishes any association between register and the kind of music that appears in it, such associations are likely to be the unique property of a given piece rather than a general nontonal characteristic. Second, the deployment of notes over several registers is often determined by the kind of sonority a composer wants at a given point; for example, the chord C, C♯, E will sound different in each of the wide variety of possible spacings. (A triad, such as C, E, G, would retain its identity more easily under such manipulation, as would symmetrical chords, such as C, E, G♯. However, symmetrical chords are used as vertical sonorities in nontonal music far less frequently than triads are in tonal music.) Finally, a composer may use register for structural purposes. In a serial piece, for example, he might state a prime set in an upper register and its inversion simultaneously in a lower register. The difference between the two registers would help clarify this event.

A byproduct of the new role of register is a decrease in what might be called transposability. For example, to transpose a Mozart piano sonata up a minor third would affect the values of the piece less than would a similar transposition of a composition such as Schoenberg's Op. 11. This is because simultaneities in nontonal music are determined more in terms of the sonority created by their registral deployment than is the case in tonal music. Although we can hear transpositions of pitches in nontonal music, other acoustic characteristics (e.g., the "quality" of the sound of a given group of pitches on a given instrument(s)) tend not to be transposable, and it is precisely these characteristics that have a higher structural value in nontonal music.

HINDEMITH, BARTÓK, STRAVINSKY. The gray area between tonality and nontonality is occupied by such figures as Hindemith, Bartók, and Stravinsky. The harmonic textures of their music look both forward and back. Except for Stravinsky's late music, their works retain the element of pitch centricity, in which one pitch or sonority is more important than others and in which a key is roughly defined. While pitch centricity is analogous to one of the most salient features of tonality, the general methods of organization used by these composers create textures that have less in common with each other than would the textures of three contemporaneous 18th- or 19th-century composers.

Hindemith outlined his system of composition in *Craft of Musical Composition*.[2] Invoking the numeric and acoustic properties of the overtone series, he established scales of values for individual pitches in relation to each other, as well as for intervals. He then created scales of melodic and harmonic values based on these and finally established a hierarchy of all possible sonorities. The value of each sonority is based on the "harmonic tension" it creates (the need to move on or not to move). On one end of the scale are sonorities without seconds, sevenths, or tritones (which leaves triads with or without thirds), and on the other, sonorities containing minor and/or major seconds plus a tritone. The former group creates the least possible harmonic tension, and the latter the most. Hindemith considered the vertical sonority to be devoid of horizontal implications. The progress of a piece is created by its "harmonic fluctuation," the motions from tension to release. The harmonic texture of Hindemith's music is a product of this careful consideration of the independent nature of

[2] English translation by Arthur Mendel (New York 1942).

vertical sonorities and of deliberate increases and decreases in tension. The intervalic and melodic profiles are carefully aligned to further these intentions.

The music of Bartók, while reflecting no such attempt at systematization, exhibits consistent characteristics that reveal much about his attitudes towards construction and tonal organization and how they effect the resultant harmonic textures of his music. He was, for example, often concerned with symmetrical relations among pitches so that a pitch or sonority that has hierarchical superiority over other notes occupies a symmetrically significant position (unlike tonal music where the tonic is not symmetrically placed in the scale). The value he placed on symmetry influenced his approach to vastly dissimilar situations. The opening movement of the *Music for Strings, Percussion, and Celesta*, for example, is a fugue; the texture is thus similar to that which in tonal music is called "contrapuntal." Bartók's pervasive concern for symmetrical relations, however, caused him both to alter the transposition levels at which fugal entries traditionally occur and to inform the harmonic and linear structure of the theme with symmetrical characteristics (the fourth and fifth notes, for example, are symmetrical contractions of the second and third notes). The voices enter alternately above and below the initial entry (on A) in a series of fifths; those entering above do so on the pitches E, B, F♯, etc., and those below, D, G, C, etc. The point at which the two entries equal each other is at E♭, a tritone as well as six fifths in either direction from A. This point, appropriately, is the structural center of the movement (bar 56). From here the procedure is reversed and the theme inverted so that the movement ends as it began, on A. The harmonic texture created by such symmetrical procedures emphasizes symmetrical pitch relations and collections such as the tritone, the diminished seventh chord, the augmented triad, the series of fifths, etc. (other examples of symmetrical relations may be seen in the fourth and fifth string quartets[3]).

The textural qualities of Stravinsky's music are more difficult to describe. The factors responsible for his "trademark" cannot be explained simply in terms of harmonic textures, for in all his work one is keenly aware of the difficulty in separating harmonic textures from sound textures. It is as though there are deep cause and effect relationships between the two

textural dimensions, which may be why Stravinsky is such a masterful orchestrator. His music thus approaches the hypothetical piece *C*, which implies that a transfer of a piece to a different sound medium would blur the meaning and value of the piece. Stravinsky's orchestrations of his *5 Doigts* for piano into *8 Instrumental Miniatures* and of the *3 Pieces for String Quartet* plus the *Etude for Pianola* into *4 Etudes for Orchestra* are interesting in this respect. In both cases the transfer was from a simple medium to a more complex one. The changes in the harmonic textures (mostly changes in pitches) are all meant to change the music to satisfy the larger resources of the orchestra (the long evolution of *Les Noces* to its final stage and the concomitant changes in the harmonic textures and sound textures is especially interesting in this respect). On the other hand, Stravinsky's reduction of *Agon* for two pianos is not nearly as satisfactory as the original orchestral version, and the interesting aspects of the piano reduction are the extent to which it succeeds in mimicking the original orchestration and the sidelights one receives on the composition itself by the mere change in scoring. It is obvious, however, that the composition suffers by the change.

One must also consider Stravinsky's music in relation to its occasional models and the effect the stylistic transformation into "Stravinsky" has on the texture.[4] Thus *Pulcinella* retains many textural qualities of the Pergolesi pieces it is based on (such as the harmonic progressions), while the orchestration and the changes in many pitches create an overall texture that is peculiar to Stravinsky's music.

Finally, the nature of local textures, unique to smaller groups of works, must be studied in relation to the similarly unique tonal structures and voice leading processes of these works. In the *Piano Concerto*, for example, the major-minor alteration at the opening establishes a collection of pitches that acts as a kind of referential collection and also implies relations between pitches that are superficially related to tonality but are much more specifically related to the sound-world of Stravinsky's music of this period and to the structure and voice leading of this piece (compare the opening with the music at nos. 5 and 11, for example). The same is true of the so-called "Petrouchka chord," which is polytonal only in a superficial sense and bears a

[3]George Perle, "Symmetrical Formations in the String Quartets of Béla Bartók," *Music Review* 16:300–12.

[4]Edward T. Cone, "The Uses of Convention: Stravinsky and His Models," *Musical Quarterly* 47:287–89.

deep relation to the harmonic textures of the work.[5] In the *Symphony of Psalms* an ostinato figure is derived from the harmonic material of the first movement (at no. 7) and is then transformed into the fugal opening of the second movement.[6] The textures of a piece such as *Le Sacre du printemps* are obviously created by specific kinds of voice-leading procedures, such as the parallel fourths of the clarinets at no. 1, the repetition of small motives to produce ostinatolike textures throughout the work, and simultaneous arpeggiations of different kinds of chords, such as at no. 42.

ATONALITY AND SERIALISM. Undoubtedly the most revolutionary and far reaching changes in harmonic texture in the 20th century have been caused by the advent of atonality. Early atonal music shared some harmonic textural qualities with tonal music. These included octave doublings for emphasis (for example, Schoenberg's Opp. 11 and 16 and Berg's *Altenberg Lieder*; the procedure is much less frequent in Webern) and occasional triadic formulations (bar 137 of Schoenberg's Op. 16, No. 2, and the Berg *Altenberg Lieder* at no. 35). The concept in tonality of the triad as a source of all musical material is seen in atonal music in the use of small cells, or groups of notes, as melodic and harmonic elements that unfold horizontally and vertically like a triad in tonal music; such cells, however, do not undergo the transformational procedures (passing and neighboring notes, etc.) used in tonal music to get from small to large or from vertical to horizontal[7] (for example, in Schoenberg's Op. 16, No. 1, the melodic motion of a third plus a second acts also as a harmonic element and is a pedal chord from bar 26 until the end, 102 bars later). An important factor responsible for the difference between the textures of early atonal music and tonal music is, in fact, the difference in functional relations between horizontal and vertical threads. In tonal music dissonant devices such as passing and neighboring motions generate melodic movement based on triadic prolongations; in atonal music, given the impossibility of contextually establishing consonance or dissonance, the vertical and horizontal dimensions become more functionally equivalent. As a result the literal horizontalization of simultaneities or the verticalization of linear elements becomes a significant aspect of the texture of atonal music and of 12-tone music later on.[8]

The kind of rhythmic framework necessary in tonality to establish the context and function of linear and horizontal elements is not necessary in atonal music. Rhythm, therefore, can be used with greater freedom to emphasize associations intended by the composer, to create impulse and motion through change in textural density and rhythmic complexity, or even to function as a motive.[9] One result of this is a decline both in the importance of meter as a structural element and of the need for a standard rhythmic unit, or beat. Though meters and beats continue to exist, they do so more as notational conveniences than as structural elements. Rhythm in atonal music thus becomes both more complex and freer, since it is constrained only by the imagination of the composer and the limits of human perception.

Several textural trends and tendencies in atonality point to the development of the 12-tone system and show that its seeds were present long before its conception. One such trend is the use of symmetrical pitch collections such as those mentioned above in connection with Bartók. In 12-tone music, however, the use of these symmetries was not accompanied by an emphasis on pitch centricity (see Schoenberg's orchestral pieces, Op. 16; the piano pieces, Op. 19; Webern's *String Quartet*, Op. 5; and Berg's clarinet and piano pieces, Op. 5, and *Wozzeck*). The greatest effect of pitch collections on harmonic texture is in delimiting the intervalic content of a composition (each symmetrical collection emphasizes the limited group of intervals created by its symmetries). This kind of thinking lead directly to the 12-tone method, whose transformations are necessarily always of a symmetrical nature.

The first four of Schoenberg's *5 Piano Pieces*, Op. 23 (the fifth is the first real 12-tone piece), expand the idea of cells as melodic and harmonic units to include the concept of an ordered succession of pitches, a fundamental principle of the 12-tone method.[10] In the works immediately preceeding this, the texture is marked by what becomes an early constraint of the 12-tone system (though not followed so strictly by Berg): an avoidance of octave relations and triadic or tonal formations.

An early attitude about the 12-tone method was that because of the intended equality of all 12 pitches, the inner life of the texture required

[5] Arthur Berger, "Problems of Pitch Organization in Stravinsky," *Perspectives* 2/1:22ff.
[6] *Ibid.*:32ff.
[7] George Perle, *Serial Composition and Atonality*, 2nd ed. (Berkeley 1968):9–15, 16–18.

[8] *Ibid.*:32ff.
[9] Wolfgang Martin Stroh, "Alban Berg's 'Constructive Rhythm'," *Perspectives* 7/1:18–31.
[10] Perle, *Serial Composition*:44–51.

a balanced statement of the "total chromatic." The lack of such "fulfillment" created the tension that impelled a piece onwards.[11] While it is true that a significant aspect of the harmonic texture of 12-tone music is the intentional lack of any tonal-type pitch hierarchies and that the textural color created by the "total chromatic" is a property shared by most 12-tone pieces, one must examine the structure of a specific set to understand how it generates the textures peculiar to a piece and affects the use of the set in the composition itself. (Similarly in tonal music one does not examine a piece merely to see how it exemplifies the tonal system but rather to uncover the unique use the piece makes of it.) Schoenberg hoped and intended that his method would do more than just generate a surface texture; he wanted it to control all the formal properties of a piece at the same levels at which tonality accomplished these goals.[12]

The specific effects of various sets on harmonic textures can be shown with several examples. The set of the Schoenberg *Wind Quintet*, Op. 26, is divided into two six-note groups, or hexachords, each of which contains five of the six notes of each of the two possible whole tone scales plus one note from the other scale. The intervalic profile of the piece is thus colored by the predominance of the intervals of a major second, major third, and tritone, all exclusively present in the whole-tone scale. The basic set of the Berg *Lyric Suite* for string quartet consists of two all-combinatorial hexachords,[13] which means that all possible 12-tone transformations can produce sets whose first six notes are different from the first six notes of the prime set (similarly for the last six of each). It is also an all-interval set, which means that each of the eleven intervals between the twelve members of the set is different. Finally, the content of each hexachord is equal to the first six notes of a major scale and also a series of six fifths. The affect of these properties on the texture of the first movement of the piece is seen in the choice of transpositions and transformations of the set to accomodate its combinatorial and special properties, in the harmonic textural qualities generated by the presence of all the 11 interval classes between members of the set, and in the special quality of the melodic contours created by the "diatonic" and "fifths" content of both hexachords. The set of the Webern *Concerto for 9 Instruments*, Op. 24, consists of four three-note groups related to each other in terms of the transformations of the 12-tone method (prime, retrograde, inversion, and retrograde inversion). Webern used this property to generate a texture in the first movement consisting almost exclusively of three-note statements in each of the instruments, rhythmically differentiated for additional clarity. In general Webern's textures are clean and sparse as compared with Schoenberg's, who was less careful to create textures in which there is little ambiguity about the set structure and its use in a piece. The use of a set, however, need not totally delimit the texture and form of a piece. For instance, "while certain harmonic formations in *Lulu* are serially derived, the texture in general is not dependent on serial procedures but on the assumption of a pervasive harmonic atmosphere based on the preferential employment of certain sonorities, a harmonic background that exists prior to any given series just as the triadic texture of tonality exists prior to any given melodic detail."[14]

After World War II composers began to consider the feasibility of organizing musical dimensions other than pitch with methods analogous to the 12-tone method. The progenitor of this effort was Webern,[15] whose concerns, however, were with amplifying and creating ". . . control of the interaction between characteristics of sound . . ."[16] rather than extending the logic of serial pitch organization to other dimensions. Milton Babbitt's efforts in this area have suggested several ways in which other elements, particularly rhythm, might be organized so as to coordinate the other musical dimensions according to the properties of the 12-tone method.[17]

NEW USES OF SOUND TEXTURES TO AID HARMONIC TEXTURES. The revolution in music in the areas of pitch and rhythmic structure necessarily affected orchestration and sound texture, as well as the relation of these areas to harmonic texture. Challenged in this respect is the notion of the separability of harmonic texture and sound texture, which brings the hypothetical piece *C* closer to reality. This challenge has come about because of the vulnerability of new harmonic textures and of

[11] Gunther Schuller, "Conversation with Steuermann," *Perspectives* 3/1:34.

[12] Arnold Schoenberg, *Style and Idea* (New York 1950):106–07.

[13] Milton Babbitt, "Some Aspects of 12-Tone Composition," *The Score and I.M.A. Magazine* 12 (1955).

[14] Perle, *Serial Composition*: 78.

[15] Peter Westergaard, "Webern and 'Total Organization': An Analysis of the Second Movement of the *Piano Variations*, Op. 27," *Perspectives* 1/2:107–20.

[16] *Ibid.*: 107.

[17] Milton Babbitt, "Twelve-Tone Rhythmic Structure and the Electronic Medium," *Perspectives* 1/1:49–79.

structural and functional relations to ambiguousness unless clearly defined by means not formerly assumed necessary. Orchestration is now called on to help define things by associating elements of the harmonic texture with specific timbral qualities, making associations easier and in some cases actually possible. Here again the fact that in nontonal music a structural norm is often defined for a single piece only may create the need to call all possible musical dimensions into play to assure coherence. Webern, for instance, used timbre, register, rhythm, and dynamics to delineate specific aspects of a serial structure. The first movement of the *Symphony*, Op. 21, is a double canon. In the first section (bars 1–25) each of the two canons consists of a prime set stated against its inversion. So that the contours of each of the canonic voices will be exactly the inversion of the opposite voice, each prime and its inversion is stationed symmetrically around A below middle C. In each of the two canons, in order to clarify the imitative structure between lines, which are divided among several instruments, Webern used classes of instruments to define the progression. For example, if the clarinet plays two notes in one voice (set statement), the clarinet or bass clarinet will play the two corresponding canonic notes at the corresponding place in the imitative voice. The strings similarly match each other as do the horns, while the harp matches itself. In this and other instances the succession of timbres deepens the meaning of a succession of pitches and, through the association of a class of timbres with itself, makes important connections for the listener. One must thus consider both textural dimensions to be interactive and interdependent.

Some composers have used sound textures to create large-scale structural identities. Stravinsky, for example, writes of his *Movements for Piano and Orchestra*: "The instruments are grouped according to timbre, by which I mean that each section of the piece is confined to a certain range of instrumental timbre. The interludes without piano, between the movements, are also confined each to a different range of timbre."[18]

Paul Lansky

SOUND TEXTURES. Music has to do with sound, all sounds and all aspects of sound. This is where many composers stand today: in the fullness of sound, not just traditional or concert-hall sounds but noises and singings of all kinds. Sound in this context is not merely

[18]Igor Stravinsky, program notes for a concert, Town Hall, New York, 10 Jan 1960.

pitch but also duration, loudness, timbre, articulation, and decay, and in the larger phrase-complex, varieties of energy level. Texture itself can be metaphorically defined as "the characteristic disposition or connection of threads in a woven fabric," or more directly as the relationships of sound in the context of time and space.

There is today a new awareness of sound as a physical phenomenon. Anyone who has heard a very low-cycle sine wave or a highly amplified group of instruments has experienced the tangible feeling of sound against the body, of sound as an atmospheric disturbance heard with the ears but also received with the whole body. Texture in this context can be thought of as an experience of energy structures. Some composers have experienced sound as a living phenomenon. Varèse, for instance, often quoted the definition by physicist Hoëne Wroński: music is the "corporealization of the intelligence that is in sounds." This awareness of sound and of its musical potentials has probably always been present in some degree, but today it has become more important than ever before. In the following discussion six compositions are explored in which this view of sound predominates.

Webern: No. 1 from *5 Pieces for Orchestra*, Op. 10 (1911–13). Heard traditionally (in terms of pitches and lines in counterpoint), this piece sounds discontinuous, like a series of pointillistic events or a counterpoint of seemingly unrelated lines. Heard in terms of texture, however, it blends together into a single melodic line, a *Klangfarbenmelodie* [tone-color melody] that expands and contracts again. The shape is apparent on all levels, e.g., pitch-registration

(as the music approaches its fullest expanse, the material in each of the individual instruments also becomes more and more expansive), dynamics

and general density contour

The piece contains four phrases (see Ex. 1). The importance of texture is evident at the outset in the simplicity of the first three pitches and the complexity of their orchestration. There is a gradually increased complexity of simultaneous rhythmic activities, the general momentum being toward greater animation later returning to repose. Complexity in terms of varieties of timbre reaches its peak with the clarinet, cello, and violin all in high registers against muted trumpet and trombone; the evolution is from a predominantly wind and bell-like (harp and celesta) sound to a complexity in which bowed strings predominate, followed by a return to the original timbres. The entire piece, 12 bars long, lasts about 30 seconds. Even its extreme concentration suggest that listening be transferred from notes to sounds.[19] Is it possible to hear the other four pieces in the set in a similar way—as melodic shapes defined by texture? Further, does the set as a whole have a textural shape?

Ives: "The Housatonic at Stockbridge" from *3 Places in New England* for orchestra (composed principally 1903–14). This piece presents a texture consisting of eddies and undulations that grow beyond themselves and overflow. Each instrument in Ex. 2 has its own rhythmic flow, creating a complex murmur. The 4/4 meter is merely a performance convenience. The first viola plays three phrases in a 7/4 meter. There are phrases in the first violin in which groups of ten 16ths are played in the time span of three 8ths. There are 3/8 groupings in violins 2 and 3. Various 16th-note phrases occur in violin 4. The pitch material in each line is more or less consistent but not rigidly so; the viola line, however, consists of exact repetitions. Once set in motion, the sound flow never repeats the original tonal or rhythmic relationships. Harmony and chords take on a new meaning: harmony becomes a fluid sonority, a vague shimmering of the resultant texture in which the violin and viola parts are a kind of overtone resonance over the fundamental C♯-G♯ in the bass. Thus the passage is an unfolding not of harmonies and chords but of a texture. An instance in which Ives transferred to texture a function traditionally performed by harmony occurs in Ex. 3. The fundamental C♯-G♯ in this passage is the same as in Ex. 2 (there had been a temporary excursion to other pitches), and on this return some of the quasi-overtones are new and the timbres are new (such as winds in place of strings). A kind of overtone, as

opposed to harmonic, transformation has taken place. The passage is also interesting because of other textural factors Ives had in mind. The piano part, he wrote, "was originally intended for two harps at a distance, outlining the two keys together. The figures need not be kept to the exact time relation indicated, but less than a 4/4 measure. The phrases are of uneven duration, as a kind of ebb and flow." One is reminded of his quotation of Thoreau in the fourth movement of the *Concord Sonata*: "At a distance over the woods the sound of the Concord bell acquires a certain vibratory hum as if pine needles in the horizon were the strings of a harp swept by the wind . . . a vibration of the universal lyre." Combined with the sound current of Ex. 2 is a hymn tune, beginning (unrecognizably) with the half notes of the cello part. It continues (from bar 6) in a dialogue between French horn and English horn, then in the violin, finally in the trumpets and horns. This occurs as the textural amalgam rises from a very soft string entrance (*pppp-ppp-pp*) to a full orchestral roar (*ffff*). When a massive textural activity has swelled up, it stops abruptly and there is a cadence that evokes an "amen."

Schoenberg: "Summer Morning by a Lake (Colors)," No. 3 from *5 Pieces for Orchestra*, Op. 16 (1909). Like the Webern example, this piece is an expansion and contraction of texture. In this case the *Klangfarbenmelodie* is a succession of chords, better referred to as simultaneously sounding pitch-timbres. "The change of chords in this piece," Schoenberg

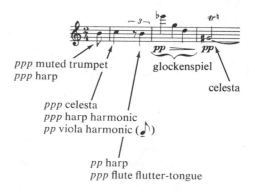

The clarinet begins the second phrase in a moderately
high register—a gently arching voice rising out of the
drone of the celesta, then holding back (zögernd)

and an
afterthought.

The flute, muted violin and viola, and harp play perhaps a transformation of the beginning of the piece
(melodic contour of the strings), perhaps a fleeting
accompaniment to the clarinet.

The last two pitches of the clarinet part overlap the
muted cello (using the penetrating timbre of the A
string); the cello begins haltingly after the return
to "a tempo."

(with the glockenspiel, *ppp*)

The violin enters, high,
delicate, using the ethereal
timbre of the E string.

The muted trumpet and trombone play perhaps a
further transformation of the beginning melodic
material, perhaps a condensed accompaniment.

The celesta trill is echoed and transformed by the flute (flutter-tongue),
which overlaps the end of the violin line above.

Wind timbres prepare
for a return to the
opening texture:

(celesta continuing)

muted trumpet

harp

The "holding back" resolves to the
"a tempo" downbeat played by
celesta and cello harmonic.

harp playing
"flute-like"
harmonics

flute
trumpet
celesta

(The transformation being of timbre,
rhythm, pitch, and pitch-contour—
though still related to the original contour)

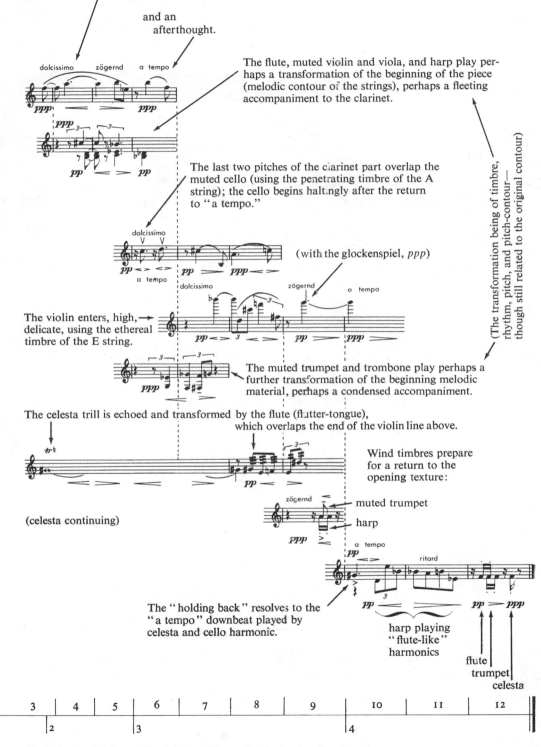

Ex. 1. Anton Webern, No. 1 from *5 Pieces for Orchestra*, Op. 10
Quoted by permission of Universal Edition and Theodore Presser

Ex. 2. Charles Ives, "The Housatonic at Stockbridge," No. 3 from *3 Places in New England*: 1–2

Ex. 3. Charles Ives, "The Housatonic at Stockbridge," No. 3 from *3 Places in New England*: 21–22

wrote in the score, "has to be executed with the greatest subtlety, avoiding accentuation of entering instruments so that only the difference in color becomes noticeable. The conductor need not try to polish sounds which seem unbalanced, but watch that every instrumentalist plays accurately the prescribed dynamic, according to the nature of his instrument. There are no motives in this piece which have to be brought to the fore."

At first there are pulsations on the same pitches, alternating between two timbre aggregates, each one sounding for about two seconds:

The subsequent shape of the piece is a subtle movement away from this sound core to a more agitated and complex texture and a return to a state of repose. The movement is defined by changes in pitch (the core moves up slightly and returns), dynamics (from *ppp* to *mp* and back, with the dynamic markings at one point applied to the whole ensemble as though it were one instrument), an increased variety in the timbral components of chords (which reach their greatest complexity in bars 26–29), and by interruptions in the pulse (e.g., the fermata in bars 11 and 30, the agitato complex in bars 26–30, and the fleeting triplet pulse in bar 31). Within this shape a number of other events also occur, among them: 1) subtle shifts of pitches within the aggregate so that, for example, the whole chord-mass descends a half step by the end of bar 4; 2) shifts in the bass fundamental, either as a passing phenomenon or (as in the D of bars 14–23) as a sustained change; 3) explorations of the bass register, as in the doublebass notes of bars 9, 27, 29, and 39; 4) rhythmic intrusions into the prevailing pulsations, as with the 16th- and 32nd-note entrances in bars 7, 9, and 20; 5) timbral intrusions into the homogeneous sound core, as with the use of violin harmonics in bars 20, 24, and 31, the string tremelo *ponticello* in bar 40, the cello and bass harmonics in bars 25 and 30, the occasional use of harp, celesta, and piccolo. After the agitato section there is a return to the original pulse and finally to the pitches of the opening chord. The timbres, however, are different, creating a different energy level. The bassoon playing in its high register and the English horn in its low register create a tension not present in the opening. This tension, created by means of texture rather than pitch harmony, leads the listener on to the next piece in the set.

Ives: *Symphony No. 4*, 2nd movement (composed principally 1910–16). Ives is dealing in this piece with a conception of musical experience that involves the interplay of foreground and background, space (placement and motion), and aural distance (a different phenomenon than loudness). Ives himself referred at various times to the placement of sections of a town band on various roof tops and in the bandstand, pianos being played in two different rooms, the sound of a French horn across a lake, two football bands playing as they march from either end of town through the center and past each other, separated ensembles playing at different tempos and with the possibility of speeding up and slowing down simultaneously. A detailed statement of related ideas is included in his "Conductor's Note" to this movement.

Ives's conception also involves collage as a fundamental compositional procedure: a seemingly continuous melodic line that is really bits and pieces, innuendoes and transformations (rhythmic and tonal) of a variety of musics—all this taking place in one instrumentalist's part as well as (sometimes) simultaneously in some or many other parts, sometimes with the source of the material clearly discernible, sometimes not, but always creating a new texture. In Ives, collage is more than a technique; it is a spiritual core of the music. It is a view of music as a spectrum of past and present, alive at all times and in different ways, without copyright of ideas. It is a view of individual compositions as one person's realization of the total sound complex, the particular sources transcended in the present moment of sounding. (It also creates an additional sense of foreground and background in the listener, a psychological one brought on by the evocation of situations and feelings that the listener associates with the material being used. He is thus free to move about the music in his own way and is not confined to a "correct" way of listening.) Using collage procedures, Ives arrived at techniques of transposition, loops (repeating rhythmic and/or melodic cells), multiple meters, keys and tempos, and counterpoints of sound masses (themselves products of independent lines) and momentums.

The form of this second movement consists of a succession of textures, and the overall shape, of a collage of various momentums and densities of activity. The following observations will indicate the variety of textures involved as well as some of the means used to produce them:

1. At rehearsal No. 7, two violin parts, played adagio and softly, have material unrelated to each other or to the 3/2 meter that is indicated. One or two of the first violins perform a hymn tune as harmonics. The other firsts play an embellished "Sweet Bye and Bye," then a transformed version (or perhaps it is a different tune), and then the original again. At the same time the cellos have a repeating 5/2 phrase in which quarter tones are used. Some of the percussion (gong, bass drum, Indian drum, together with an offbeat piano like a harp) perform the 3/2 meter as three half notes; the timpani, however, treats the same meter as two dotted halves. At rehearsal No. 8 there is a loud intrusion of woodwinds and brass playing allegro and evoking football games and marches; there is also a quotation on the piano from the "Hawthorne" movement of Ives's *Piano Sonata No. 2*. The allegro gets faster while the adagio remains constant. Then the allegro material collapses, and the adagio continues until rehearsal No. 10, where a more gradual overlap and transformation occurs. Again, though a 4/4 meter is indicated, there are multiple internal meters.

2. At rehearsal No. 36 a piano tuned a quarter-tone higher than the orchestra echoes *The Housatonic at Stockbridge*; after several bars it begins to gradually leave out "intermediary notes," in one of Ives's melodic transformation processes.

3. At rehearsal No. 23 the conductor is beating a 4/4 meter. A solo second violin has an allegro ragtime passage of 5/4 loops. A viola solo is playing "Sweet Bye and Bye" in an offbeat rhythmic pattern, also allegro but "slightly slower than the solo violin II."

4. In sections 33, 36, and 37 Ives suggests that "it is better if possible to have the celesta and solo violin at a distance or off the stage."

In playing collage textures such as these, performers should emphasize the bits and pieces and continual shiftings (whether in a subtle manner, if the material is a kind of innuendo, or with sudden contrasts of expression, articulation, tone color, etc., if this is called for). They should not play the lines as a blandly continuous flow. This is also clear on the first page of the *Violin Sonata No. 2*, where there is something different almost every bar.

It is not "too many ideas too close together" as a violinist once complained to Ives, but rather just enough ideas to create a new way of sounding.

Varèse: *Intégrales* for chamber orchestra (c.1924–25). This work is a succession of sound structures between which and within which there is an interplay of masses, densities, linear projections, articulations in time, loudnesses, etc. As Varèse himself pointed out, his music is based on "an internal structure, expanded and split into different shapes or groups of sound constantly changing in shape, direction, and speed, attracted and repulsed by various forces. The form of the work is the consequence of this interaction."[20]

The opening structure of *Intégrales* is an interplay of various elements, sounding like a gigantic mobile. There is a melodic configuration:

two pitch-timbre aggregates:

and some percussion timbres, including:

The melodic configuration is successively transformed in timbre and rhythm by the Eb clarinet, muted C trumpet, oboe, and D trumpet. There is a gradual expansion in the number of pitches, dynamics, and types of rhythm and phrasing. Large phrase shapes result from the play of such elements as the length of time each instrument sounds, the phrasing and breathing within each statement, the time relationships between entrances of different instruments, the dynamic interplay between these instruments and those of the opposing aggregate group. The two pitch-timbre aggregates are related to each other in time (sounding approximately together) yet unrelated in that specific details of articulation and duration and dynamics are independent. Thus there is a development arising from a kind of counterpoint of these masses, as well as from the juxtaposition of the combined

[20]Edgard Varèse, "Rhythm, Form and Content" ed. by Chou Wen-chung, *Contemporary Composers on Contemporary Music* ed. by E. Schwartz and B. Childs (New York 1967):203.

aggregates' energy weight against the linear, melodic energy. The orchestration of each aggregate is planned not only in regard to pitches played but also with consideration for the interaction of the overtone structure of the particular timbre registers indicated. And the percussion instruments are not just background for the pitches but are an integral part of the total sonority, following their own line of development parallel to winds and brass and becoming more and more complex. The structure comes to an end when there is a break in the pitch-timbre continuity, a crescendo of the full ensemble, and an abrupt halt.

The second sound structure is prepared for by the percussion. A new aggregate with a melodic (intervalic) configuration in the French horn:

recalls the melodic element of the first section. This time the contrasting aggregate also has a melodic shape:

which is coupled with a muted tenor trombone figure (a response to the French horn):

The percussion are grouped so that the tam-tam, bass drum, Chinese blocks, sleigh bells, and tenor drum are part of the Fench horn aggregate, and the crash cymbal and suspended cymbal are part of the tenor trombone aggregate. These units alternate back and forth, staccato, each block sounding a different length of time but generally short and very loud, creating a powerful tension. The overtones of the blocks (always an important factor) and the total register-spacing are more complex than in the aggregates of the first structure. The French horn, for example, is in its very low register and is combined with bass trombone tones (but with Chinese blocks providing a timbre contrast!). The tenor trombone is in its high register, forming part of a screaming soprano aggregate. The percussion not only contribute to each aggregate

but have internal contrasts of their own, for instance the hard staccato of the Chinese block and sleigh bells against the sustained tones of the gong, tam-tam, and cymbals. Again there is a break, and a new structure begins to form.

Cage: *Concert for Piano and Orchestra* for 1–13 parts (1957–58). This piece is "to be performed in whole or part, any duration, any number of the above performers, as a solo, chamber ensemble, symphony, concert for piano and orchestra, aria, etc." There is no master score, and there is no beginning or end except that someone starts playing an instrument and stops playing. What results in performance is a flux of activities, an interplay of noises, pitches, timbres, and silences. The texture is like an open field of possibilities in which Cage emphasizes the uniqueness of each sound. Because there is no directional structure to relate sounds in a preconceived way, the listener can only receive what there is to be heard. The individual parts "give specific directives and specific freedoms . . . to each player including the conductor. . . . As many various uses of the instruments as could be discovered were subjected to the composing means, which involved chance operations and the observation of imperfections in the paper upon which the music was written." Proceeding from a premise of nothingness, anything is free to happen.

Malcolm Goldstein

SEE ALSO Asian Music and Western Composition, Form, Indeterminacy, Jazz, Musicology and Composition, Notation, Orchestration, Performance, Popular Music, Serialism, Text Setting and Usage.

Theater, see Dance, Mixed Media, Musical, Opera. See also Indeterminacy, Performance.

Theory. At the beginning of the 20th century theories of music were largely determined by two important 19th-century developments: the rise of research techniques that permitted the systematic examination of acoustical micro-structures, and the trend in composition toward complex chromatic relationships lying outside traditional concepts of harmony, counterpoint, and form. In addition, two 19th-century beliefs were virtually axiomatic for early 20th-century theorists: that music follows an evolutionary development, and that it is founded in a phenomenon of nature, the overtone series.

At the onset of the century there was little new musical theory in the sense of systematic approaches to general problems of musical structure. Instead theory was generally only a classroom discipline, and theory textbooks were usually pastiches of 19th-century writings by A. B. Marx, Bellermann, Sechter, Reicha, Cherubini, and others. The subjects included harmony stemming from Rameau, species counterpoint stemming from Fux, fugue, and 18th- and 19th-century forms. The active theoretical field was dominated by Hugo Riemann (1849–1919). His study of rhythm (1903) attempted to classify rhythmic procedures (additive rhythms, polyrhythms, etc.), while his study of harmony (1887) was a further refinement of Rameau's ideas, its purpose being to increase pedagogical efficiency.

NEW THEORIES OF TONAL MUSIC. The static situation around 1900 was recognized by Heinrich Schenker (1868–1935), whose *Harmonielehre* (1906) was published under the anonym "an artist," signifying that Schenker did not want to be associated with the theory pedagogues. An evolutionist, he deplored certain late 19th- and early 20th-century composers and compositions that did not continue the masterwork tradition. As a natural-base theorist he gave deference to the chord of nature, the major triad derived from the overtone series. Among his achievements were his reevaluation of the role that harmony and counterpoint play in tonal compositions, his demonstration that protostructures (the *Urlinie* and *Ursatz*) exist in tonal music, and his description of the interactions between pitch configurations at distinct hierarchical levels of structure. The concept of structural levels was perhaps Schenker's most significant contribution (see Forte 1959 and Beach in the bibl.). Schenker's work has been particularly influential in the U.S. owing to the teaching and research of theorists who studied with him or with one of his students during the 1920s and 30s: Oswald Jonas, William J. Mitchell, Ernst Oster, Felix Salzer, and Hans Weisse.

Schenker influenced Ernst Kurth (1886–1946), whose books, however, embody methods and motivations quite different from those of Schenker. *Romantische Harmonik*, for instance, draws on several disciplines, including the psychology, philosophy, and history of music. Kurth was concerned with what he regarded as certain basic processes in music. His central notion was metaphysical and derived from Schopenhauer: tones are expressions of "tension events," which are expressions of the Will. He developed an elaborate and partially systematic study of late 19th-century harmony, identifying three "destructive" forces opposed to the "constructive" force, tonality. The most important of Kurth's tension events was the leading note, the attributes of which he extended to any chromatically altered note. Extended chromatic alterations, which tend to displace normative tonal progressions, were one of his "destructive" forces. Another was the suppression of tonic triads and triads in general by chords of more than three tones (as in the seventh and ninth chords in *Tristan*). His third destructive force was the use of harmonies for coloristic purposes, as in Debussy. Kurth saw in late romantic music, in *Tristan* particularly, "both a clinging to the basic paths of tonality and a striving for expansion and disintegration" (Kurth 1920:265). Kurth's evolutionary view, as well as his method of classifying harmonic procedures, undoutedly derived from the Belgian musicologist François Fétis, who invented the term "tonality" and who predicted as early as 1844 the technical development of harmony in the late 19th century. Kurth's influence was widespread, and he was probably responsible for the dissemination of the notion of tension and release in music. He also established the widely accepted (but probably erroneous) notion that atonality was an evolutionary outcome of the destructive processes he had identified.

Kurth's notion of extended tonality (the maintenance of basic tonal relationships over long spans of music despite chromatic excursions) stemmed from Schenker and was taken up in analyses of Wagner's music dramas by Alfred Lorenz (1868–1939). Lorenz's aim was to reveal and describe the *grosse Architektonik*, or form over the largest time-span (14 hours in the case of the *Ring*). Form for Lorenz was temporal in nature. It was a macrorhythm (*grosse Rhythmik*) consisting of time segments, generally equal in length, created by recurring melodic lines and by harmonic "waves" that departed from and returned to the tonic harmony. The synthesis of these components is found in the symphonic texture (*Gewebe*) made up of themes, which in turn are combinations of motives associated with the drama. From this basis Lorenz developed his concept of the hierarchical structure that characterizes the *grosse Architektonik* (he was undoubtedly indebted to Schenker for the notion of structural levels). He classified the patterns formed by successive thematic statement according to a small number of basic types exemplified both in short and long spans of music. Thus *Die Meistersinger* exhibits the medieval bar form, A-A-B, both in the smaller parts and in the opera as a whole. The analyses, however, are often incorrect. Furthermore Lorenz's argument was flawed by his failure to make explicit the connective transformations from level to level when he tried to form an all-inclusive concept of rhythm by combining the acoustical abstraction of a waveform with the idea of long- and short-range harmonic progressions.

THEORETICAL ASPECTS OF NONTRADITIONAL MUSIC. Schenker, Kurth, and Lorenz disregarded (or deplored in Schenker's case) nontraditional music of the early 20th century. Another group of authors systematically studied pitch organization and other aspects of structure relevant to newer music. Bernhard Ziehn (1845–1912) undertook a systematic treatment of chromatic harmonies (*Harmonie- und Modulationslehre*, 1888), including examples from recent works of Liszt, Wolf, Bruckner, and other contemporary composers. He displayed a remarkable grasp of the importance of linear motions in the formation of their harmonies. In his most important work, *Canonical Studies*, Ziehn applied the notion of symmetrical inversion, schematically represented as a one-octave chromatic scale ascending from D and matched by a one-octave chromatic scale descending from the same note. (Ziehn had introduced the idea in a piano exercise book published in 1876 and used it again in his 1888 work.) Although he evidently regarded symmetrical inversion as the fundamental relationship in terms of which scalar and chordal formations could be explained, his theoretical exposition is minimal, consisting mainly of notated examples. These examples, however, involve a number of nontraditional patterns, such as the whole-tone and other nondiatonic scales.

Ferruccio Busoni (1866–1924) admired Ziehn's innovations, particularly his treatment of the chromatic scale as a unit without reference to the diatonic scale. In "The New Harmony" Busoni envisioned a new key system synthesizing the 113 scales he had previously constructed along with Ziehn's concept of symmetrical inversion and Schoenberg's atonal experiments (Busoni 1907). To some extent this synthesis was realized around 1923 in Schoenberg's 12-tone method.

Ziehn's symmetric inversion was the point of departure for Hermann Schröder (1843–1909), who attempted in 1902 a more systematic investigation of the resources of the inversion process. His brief discussion of inter-

vallic relations (p. 16) included a tentative examination of the transformations that occur under inversion followed by transposition, an important compositional procedure in atonal and 12-tone music. Unlike Ziehn, Schröder regarded the chromatic scale as a combination of seven diatonic and five chromatic degrees. The scales he offered as compositional resources are the traditional modal scales and a new "major-minor" scale.

Georg Capellen (1869–1934) attacked Schröder for his espousal of the major-minor dualism in the form of the symmetric inversion concept (Capellen 1905). The issue of dualism versus monism, often confusing, was regarded as important at the time since it raised the acoustical problem of finding the minor triad in nature (that is in the overtone series) and the problem of explaining the complex chromatic harmonies of late 19th-century music. The standard, and evolutionary, explanation of chromatically inflected pitches was given in terms of the mixture of major and minor. This was essentially Schenker's explanation (Schenker 1906), for example, and reached an extreme form in Von der Null's treatise, where the major-minor mixture is advanced as the solution to the atonal harmonies of Schoenberg and others. Like Busoni, Capellen was interested in a new stock of musical materials. He was one of the first to appreciate the musical resources uncovered in field studies of non-Western music (Capellen 1906).

Arnold Schoenberg (1874–1951) dealt with many issues raised by the newer music, including the notions "consonance" and "dissonance." Rather than disregard the traditional distinction between them, he suggested that dissonances or more complex harmonies are derived from the upper partials of the overtone series (the explanation came to be known as "the emancipation of the dissonance"). Tonality in his view was but the simplest manifestation of the nature-given model, not an eternal law of music. Much more important for subsequent research in musical structures was Schoenberg's statement that in the future theoretical work would have to be based on the 12-note chromatic scale, not the seven-note diatonic scale (Schoenberg 1911: 434). This idea was greatly expanded in the 1922 edition of the *Harmonielehre*, where Schoenberg outlined the components of a 12-tone harmonic system. (The system appears to have little relation to the 12-tone method that he was developing at about the same time. The concept of the chromatic scale as a unit was also essential to Ziehn's contemporaneous work, as noted above.) Also novel in the 1911 edition were Schoenberg's discussions of the whole-tone scale and harmonies, chords featuring fourths instead of the conventional thirds, and the unusual harmonies composed of six or more different notes then being used for the first time in his compositions and in works by Webern, Berg, Bartók, and others (most traditional chords consist of only three or four different notes). Schoenberg did not try to assign functions to these newer harmonies, however.

NEW PITCH SYSTEMS. Schoenberg's brief consideration of new atonal harmonies inspired others to examine systematically the resources of the 12-tone method (the books by Lenormand and Hull are early examples). This in turn led to projections of other systems and resources. In *Neue Harmonielehre* (1927) Alois Hába (1893–1972) attempted to catalogue the chords available in the 12-pitch octave. He was ineffectual because criteria of similarity were not stated such that duplicate formations would be eliminated or identified (a similar problem besets Slonimsky's *Thesaurus* and other subsequent works). Hába's work was also inconsequential, because a mere inventory without any indication of structural functions proved useless. He is mainly known today for his exposition of the compositional possibilities offered by various microtonal systems, for example, the "bichromatic" system with 24 tones to the octave. It should be noted that multiple divisions of the octave have a long history, going back at least as far as the *De musica* (1577) of Francisco Salinas. Busoni discussed this possibility some years before Hába, and Charles Ives actually made use of it (see Boatwright).

The projection of new pitch systems was also undertaken by Joseph Yasser (b. 1893) in 1932. From a schematic analysis of the structure of the pentatonic ("infra-diatonic") and chromatic ("diatonic") scales he extrapolated a "supradiatonic" scale with 19 tones to the octave. Yasser regarded his effort as "organic" in contrast to the "mechanical" method of Hába, and he believed that his evolutionary theory explained the atonal and 12-tone music of Schoenberg as a transitional stage toward the ultimate supradiatonic period. Yasser's use of the concept "organic" reflects the influence and prestige of late 19th-century biology. He observed that the diatonic scale is a composite of the pentatonic scale (presumably a more primitive stage of human development) and two auxiliary degrees (4 and 7). Analogously the chromatic scale contains seven regular degrees (the diatonic scale) and five auxiliary

degrees (the pentatonic scale). By extending this process of inclusion, the projected supradiatonic scale contained the chromatic scale of 12 regular degrees and seven new auxiliary degrees, the latter corresponding to the diatonic scale. (A more convincing extension is made by Kraehenbuehl and Schmidt.)

Schoenberg's influence is evident in *New Musical Resources* (completed 1919, published 1930) by Henry Cowell (1897–1965). Cowell's purpose was "to point out the influence the overtone series has exerted on music throughout its history . . . [and to show] how by . . . applying its principles . . . a large palette of musical materials can be assembled" (Cowell: viii). Borrowing Schoenberg's idea that new tonal combinations derive from the higher overtones, Cowell proceeded to describe "toneclusters," chords composed of major and minor seconds. The most extraordinary part of the book, however, is that concerned with rhythm. By translating the ratios of the overtone series into durational ratios, he constructed scales of rhythm, meter, and tempo. He did not explain, however, how the correspondence is empirically meaningful or analytically useful. Cowell's procedure was reminiscent of Hauptmann (1853), who used the intervals octave, fifth, and third as a basis for analogies between meter and harmony and between rhythm and melody. (The construct *proportion*, as a basis of harmony, melody, meter, and rhythm goes back to ancient Greek times.)

It is not surprising that Cowell wrote the "Overture" to Joseph Schillinger's *System of Musical Composition* (1946). His apotheosis is no more remarkable than the claims of the editors of the volume: "The Schillinger System is a synthesis of musical theory and the most recent discoveries of modern physics, psychology, and mathematics." Actually "Schillinger's methods have no scientific or mathematical foundation" (Backus). Schillinger may have been influenced by the work of another Russian, Sergei Taneiev (1856–1915), who devised Schillinger-like formulas for constructing invertible counterpoint. Schillinger's fondness for drawing structural analogies between music and other phenomena has a little-known precedent in Victor Goldschmidt's treatise of 1901, which attempted to show an isomorphism of musical structure and the structure of crystals. Although Schillinger is usually credited with the notion of rhythmic "resultants" (the composite pattern formed by two or more distinct patterns within the same time span), the idea is merely an extension of Hugo Riemann's *Polyrhythmik* (Riemann 1903).

NUMBER AND PROPORTION. The work of Schillinger, Cowell, and Yasser involved the use of number and proportion, the ancient tools of the Greek theorists. This is also the case in the work of Ernő Lendvai, who has analyzed music in terms of the Golden Section, the proportion presumably used by the architects of classical antiquity, renaissance painters, and others. The simplest integral (whole number) representation of the Golden Section is provided by the numerical sequence known as the Fibonacci sequence. This is a sequence the first term of which is 1, the second 1, and each subsequent term the sum of the two preceding (1, 1, 2, 3, 5, etc.). According to Lendvai, the Golden Section accounts for the length of small and large sections in Bartók's music. For example, he divides the first movement of the *Music for Strings, Percussion and Celesta* into 55 plus 33 bars; since these two numbers are adjacent in the Fibonacci sequence, the proportional relation between them is an approximation of the Golden Section. Lendvai is not consistent in his application of the system, however, and it is unlikely that any such construct is relevant either to the esthetics or to the working methods of the composer (see Vinton). Lendvai's theory is interesting, however, in the attention it draws to the application of numbers and mathematics in theories since the 1950s.

The use of numerical sequences was basic to the work of Paul Hindemith (1895–1963). Hindemith attempted to construct an acoustically based system that would explain any musical structure employing the 12 notes of the equal-tempered scale as its vocabulary. His theory is based on two constructs: 1) an arrangement of the 12 scale degrees (called series 1) corresponding to the order in which they were derived by him from relationships in the overtone series; 2) an arrangement of the possible intervals according to the number of combination tones they yield (called series 2). Chords are classified hierarchically with reference to series 2, and the assertion is made that their functions are context-independent. (This, of course, is not true of traditional tonal harmonies; they are context-dependent because the intervallic structure of a chord in tonal music does not necessarily determine its function.) Hindemith described successions of chords according to patterns of "root progression," "guide tones," and "harmonic fluctuation," the last factor a Kurth-derived idea in which changes in tension are determined by intervallic content. He interpreted larger harmonic groups with reference to series 1, which serves as a measuring norm for the progression of assigned roots, called degrees. Corresponding to the degree-progression for larger harmonic groups is the "melody degree-progression," which is (or should be) essentially stepwise. The structure of Hindemith's system is problematic, as are his sample analyses, which cover a wide range of music (see Thomson, Landau, Cazden). Ernest Ansermet (1883–1969) represents the continuation of natural-base theory after Hindemith.

EXPLANATIONS OF NEWER MUSIC. Hindemith's conservatism did not provide an adequate basis for understanding nontraditional music. The problem of structural description and higher level theoretical formulations remained difficult. A novel effort toward solution was made by Felix Salzer, who presented analytical graphs of some quasitonal compositions (for example, Hindemith's *Piano Sonata No. 1*), using a reductive technique derived from Schenker, and showed some aspects of large-scale structure (Schoenberg, Berg, and Webern are not represented). Still a different approach was used by George Perle (1962). Taking the 12-tone method as a frame of reference, he regarded "free atonality" as an historically bounded corpus of works representing a stage in the development toward that system. Thus the organization of particular atonal works was explained in terms of melodic-harmonic cells transformed and combined in various ways to provide "a total interpenetration of harmonic and melodic elements" (Perle 1962:24). Although this approach leads to many significant analytical observations, it suffers from the lack of a general and systematic theoretical formulation that might elucidate the hierarchical structure of atonal music. Hubert Howe, Richard Teitelbaum, and Harold Oliver are among those who, in addition to Perle, have developed systematic theoretical tools for the study of atonal music.

12-TONE SET THEORY. The major writings of Milton Babbitt (b. 1916) are concerned with Schoenberg's 12-tone method (Babbitt 1955, 1960, 1961b, 1962). His work eclipses the earlier efforts of Leibowitz, Rufer, and others, including Schoenberg's own efforts to describe the system of relations underlying that music. (Mention should be made of Josef Hauer's method of organizing the 12 pitches according to "tropes"; see Eschman, Perle 1962, and especially Rochberg 1959.) Babbitt's approach to the 12-tone set system is by way of an abstract mathematical model, the group, which is used in mathematics to state or predict the general properties of a set of elements (see

Rothgeb 1966). Babbitt's use of the group has enabled him to make explicit a number of significant general properties of 12-tone compositions. In particular, he has elucidated the harmonic aspect of 12-tone music (a problem outlined in Perle 1953), the functions of melodic and rhythmic configurations, and the way components interact over various spans of music. The influence of Schenker's concept of structural levels is apparent, especially in the last named aspect of his work. Babbitt's studies have provided the basis for a number of significant research efforts in 12-tone set theory, including those reported by David Lewin (1962), Donald Martino (1961), John Rothgeb (1967), and Bauer-Mengelberg and Ferentz (1965).

MODELS: INFORMATION THEORY. A model can be described as a simplified representation of a complex process. If the model is analytical it provides information about the process; if it is synthetic it replicates the process. The adequacy and relevance of the model with respect to the process is therefore important. The distinction between a model and a theory is not entirely clear, even in the scientific fields where it is widely used. Often, however, "theory" is reserved for the larger and more general case and "model" for the smaller case.

Beginning in the 1950s efforts were made to show that a mathematical model developed for the study of communications systems was relevant to the study of musical structures. The model in question provides a quantitative measure of certain properties of a message (or of a composition in the musical application). The quantity *information* is of primary interest, and for this reason the model is also known as information theory. Computation of information involves the following considerations: A composition is regarded as a sequence of signs (notes) drawn from an alphabet (the 12 pitches) according to certain probabilities. These probabilities, which may be ascertained by sample frequency counts, reflect the degree to which rules or syntactic constraints are operative in the composition. If the probability of occurrence of the note C is greater than that of the note D, then the occurrence of C is said to have less *surprisal* or *self-information* than the occurrence of a D. Since surprisal and probability can be expressed as numerical quantities, it is possible to compute an average surprisal, called information, by weighting each surprisal with its probability over an entire system of signs (over an entire composition). If, for example, the signs occur with equal probability, the information quantity is high, in fact maximal. The greater

the information (sometimes called *entropy*), the less is the complementary quantity, called *redundancy*.

The statistical measures of the properties called information and redundancy have been interpreted in various ways with reference to music. For example, they may represent the fluctuation of information in terms of more or less stable sections during the course of a composition, or they may be used to provide an index of stylistic differences over various historical periods (see Hiller 1966). To date, studies have not gone beyond what is known as a *first-order Markov process*, that is, information computed on the basis of nondependent probabilities. For example, the notes preceding the note C are not taken into consideration when computing the probability of the occurrence of the C. The extension to Markov processes of higher order, in which such dependencies would be taken into account, entails a large amount of computation. Since there are no sophisticated studies of this kind yet, the potential of the model is uncertain. In fact, extension to higher-order Markov processes may never provide a basis for an adequate theory. (Some of the difficulties in applying the information-theoretic model to music are discussed in Slawson 1968.)

LINGUISTIC AND LOGICAL APPROACHES. Compared to the information-theoretic model, logical-linguistic models are nonstatistical (nonprobabilistic) and nonquantitative. One such model was used by Michael Kassler in an investigation of Schenker's theory of tonal music (Kassler 1967b). According to Kassler, Schenker's theory asserts that every tonal composition can be generated from a small number of primitive ("axiomatic" in the logical sense) compositions, namely Schenker's *Ursätze*. The *Ursätze* are subjected to a certain number of transformations (Schenker's prolongation techniques), which may be interpreted as rules. In like manner, syntactically correct English sentences could be generated from a set of rules of English grammar. The synthesis of a musical composition in this way necessarily means that the process is traceable since the rules applied and the order in which they were applied would have had to be specified. Although Schenker did not regard his theory as generative, but only as analytical, Kassler's study could provide a logical clarification of the theory, which Schenker specified only incompletely and informally (see also Regener).

John Rothgeb used a model of linguistic structure to examine the adequacy of traditional procedures described in some 18th-century treatises for the harmonization of given unfigured basses (Rothgeb 1968). These procedures, set out in the form of contextual rules, were interpreted by him as incipient theories of the structure of the tonal bass. As such they were found to be inadequate, and a method for constructing a formal grammar or general theory of structure of the tonal bass had to be outlined. (The difficulties that attend the rigorous utilization of a model to obtain insights into musical structures and theories of structure are described in Winograd.)

COMPUTATIONAL RESEARCH. It is significant that the studies of Kassler, Rothgeb, and Winograd all utilized digital computer programs, since this reflects changes in basic attitudes toward theoretical research in the late 1950s. Indeed the computer, because of its ability to manipulate complex symbolic data (which could represent musical compositions or theories) has had a marked effect on the kind of theoretical research undertaken and on the methods used (see Babbitt 1965b). Some current research is almost entirely embedded in computer programs (Erickson, Forte 1967), and it appears that if computer-controlled optical score readers can be developed, along with adjunct devices, work in this area will increase. With the improvement of sound-generation techniques by computer (Mathews, Tenney 1963; Slawson 1969) so that any specifiable sound can be produced instantaneously, a number of new possibilities arise, including "entry into the most refractory of areas, that of auditory perception" (Babbitt 1965b:82).

SOME PERSPECTIVES. The scope and variety of comtemporary musicotheoretical investigations, especially in the U.S. beginning in the 1950s, is remarkable. It appears now that the legacy of the 19th century, most of which was infertile, has largely been dissipated and that new approaches to musical problem solving are being developed. This is evident in certain of the studies cited above that use logic and mathematics and in those that have been influenced by the new computational sciences. Still a further dimension has been added by the recent philosophical considerations of the goals, methods, criteria, etc., of musical theory (see Boretz 1969, Clifton, Lewin 1969). There seems to be ample evidence that musical theory in the 20th century is once again what it has occasionally been in the past: a vital intellectual component of music.

BIBL. (The following abbreviations are used in this list: *JMT*, *Journal of Music Theory*; *MQ*, *Musical Quarterly*; *PNM*, *Perspectives of New Music*):

Ansermet, Ernest. *Les Fondements de la musique dans la conscience humaine* (Neûchatel 1961).

Babbitt, Milton
1955 "Some Aspects of Twelve-Tone Composition," *Score* 12.
1960 "Twelve-Tone Invariants as Compositional Determinants," *MQ* 46/2.
1961a "Past and Present Concepts of the Nature and Limits of Music," *Proceedings of the International Musicological Society Congress* (1961).
1961b "Set Structure as a Compositional Determinant," *JMT* 5/1.
1962 "Twelve-Tone Rhythmic Structure and the Electronic Medium," *PNM* 1/1.
1965a "The Structure and Function of Music Theory: I," *College Music Symposium* 5.
1965b "The Use of Computers in Musicological Research," *PNM* 3/2.

Backus, John
1960 "Pseudo-Science in Music," *JMT* 4/2.
1962 "*Die Reihe*: A Scientific Evaluation," *PNM* 1/1.

Barbaud, Pierre. *Initiation à la composition musicale automatique* (Paris 1966).

Basart, Ann. *Serial Music, A Bibliography* (Berkeley 1961).

Bauer-Mengelberg, Stefan, and Melvin Ferentz. "On Eleven-Interval Twelve-Tone Rows," *PNM* 3/2.

Beach, David. "A Schenker Bibliography," *JMT* 13/1.

Bengtsson, Ingmar. "Empirisk rytmforskning," *Swedish Journal of Musicology* 51 (1969).

Berger, Arthur. "New Linguistic Modes and the New Theory," *PNM* 3/1.

Boatwright, Howard. "Ives' Quarter-Tone Impressions," *PNM* 3/2.

Boretz, Benjamin
1963 "*Serial Composition and Atonality* by George Perle," *PNM* 1/2.
1966 "A Note on Discourse," *PNM* 4/2.
1969 "Meta-Variations: Studies in the Foundations of Musical Thought (I)," *PNM* 8/1.

Busoni, Ferruccio
1907 *Sketch of a New Esthetic of Music*, trans. by Th. Baker (New York 1911).
1921 *The Essence of Music and Other Papers*, trans. by R. Ley (New York 1957).

Capellen, Georg
1905 *Die Zukunft der Musiktheorie* (Leipzig 1905).
1906 *Ein neuer exotischer Musikstil* (Stuttgart 1906).

Cazden, Norman. "Hindemith and Nature," *Music Review* 15/3.

Clifton, Thomas. "Training in Music Theory: Process and Product," *JMT* 13/1.

Cohen, Joel. "Information Theory and Music," *Behavioral Science* 7/2.

Coons, Edgar, and David Kraehenbuehl. "Information as a Measure of Structure in Music," *JMT* 2/1.

Cone, Edward. "Beyond Analysis," *PNM* 6/1.

Cooper, Grosvener, and Leonard B. Meyer. *The Rhythmic Structure of Music* (Chicago 1960).

Cowell, Henry. *New Musical Resources* (New York 1930).

Erickson, Raymond. "A General-Purpose System for Computer Aided Musical Studies," *JMT* 13/2.

Forte, Allen
1955 *Contemporary Tone-Structures* (New York 1955).
1959 "Schenker's Conception of Musical Structure," *JMT* 3/1.
1964 "A Theory of Set-Complexes for Music," *JMT* 8/2.
1965 "The Domain and Relations of Set-Complex Theory," *JMT* 9/1.
1966 "A Program for the Analytic Reading of Scores," *JMT* 10/2.
1967 "Computer-Implemented Analysis of Musical Structure," *Computer Applications in Music* ed. by G. Lefkoff (Morgantown, W. Va., 1967).

Gamer, Carlton. "Some Combinational Resources of Equal-Tempered Systems," *JMT* 11/1.

Hába, Alois. *Neue Harmonielehre* (Leipzig 1927).

Hanson, Howard. *Harmonic Materials of Modern Music* (New York 1960).

Hauer, Josef. *Zwölftontechnik* (Vienna 1926).

Hauptmann, Moritz. *Die Natur der Harmonik und der Metrik zur Theorie der Musik* (Leipzig 1853).

Helmholtz, Hermann. *On the Sensations of Tone*, trans. by A. J. Ellis (London 1875).

Hiller, Lejaren
1959 *Experimental Music*, with Leonard Isaacson (New York 1959).
1966 "Information Theory Analyses of Four Sonata Expositions," with Calvert Bean, *JMT* 10/1.
1967 "Structure and Information in Webern's Symphonie, Op. 21," *JMT* 11/1.

Hindemith, Paul. *The Craft of Musical Composition*, trans. by A. Mendel (New York 1941).

Hull, A. Eaglefield. *Modern Harmony* (London 1915).

Howe, Hubert. "Some Combinational Properties of Pitch Structures," *PNM* 4/1.

Hsu, Dolores Menstell. "Ernst Kurth and His Concept of Music as Motion," *JMT* 10/1.

Johnston, Ben. "Proportionality and Expanded Musical Pitch Relations," *PNM* 5/1.

Jonas, Oswald. *Das Wesen des musikalischen Kunstwerks* (Vienna 1934).

Kassler, Michael
1963 "A Sketch of the Use of Formalized Languages for the Assertion of Music," *PNM* 1/2.
1967a "Toward a Theory that is the Twelve Note-Class System," *PNM* 5/2.
1967b *A Trinity of Essays* (PhD diss., Princeton Univ., 1967).

Kraehenbuehl, David, and Christopher Schmidt. "On the Development of Musical Systems," *JMT* 6/1.

Krenek, Ernst. "Extents and Limits of Serial Techniques," *MQ* 46/2.

Kurth, Ernst
1913 *Die Voraussetzungen der theoretischen Harmonik* (Vienna 1913).
1920 *Romantische Harmonik* (Bern 1920).

Landau, Victor. "Hindemith the System-Builder," *Music Review* 21/1.

Leibowitz, René. *Schoenberg and his School*, trans. by Dika Newlin (New York 1949).

Lendvai, Ernő. "Einführung in die Formen- und Harmoniewelt Bartóks," *Béla Bartók, Weg und Werk . . .* ed. by B. Szabolcsi (Budapest 1957).

Lenormand, René. *A Study of Modern Harmony*, trans. by H. Antcliffe (London 1915).

Lewin, David
1959 "Intervallic Relations between Two Collections of Notes," *JMT* 3/2.
1960 "The Intervallic Content of a Collection of Notes," *JMT* 4/1.
1962 "A Theory of Segmental Association in Twelve-Tone Music," *PNM* 1/1.
1968 "Some Applications of Communication Theory to the Study of Twelve-Tone Music," *JMT* 12/1.
1969 "Behind the Beyond," *PNM* 7/2.

Lorenz, Alfred. *Das Geheimnis der Form bei Richard Wagner* (Berlin 1924).

Martino, Donald. "The Source-Set and Its Aggregate Formations," *JMT* 5/2.

Mathews, M. V. "An Acoustic Compiler for Music and Psychological Stimuli," *Bell Systems Technical Journal* 40.

Meyer, Leonard B.
1956 *Emotion and Meaning in Music* (Chicago 1956).
1967 *Music, the Arts and Ideas* (Chicago 1967).

Mitchell, William J.
1962 "The Study of Chromaticism," *JMT* 6/1.
1968 "Ziehn, Bernhard," *Die Musik in Geschichte und Gegenwart*, vol. 14.

Moles, Abraham. *Information Theory and Aesthetic Perception* trans. by J. Cohen (Urbana, Ill., 1966).

Moser, Hans. *Bernhard Ziehn* (Bayreuth 1950).

Nüll, Edwin von der. *Moderne Harmonik* (Leipzig 1932).

Oster, Ernst. "Register and the Large-Scale Connection," *JMT* 5/1.

Palisca, Claude V. "American Scholarship in Western Music," *Musicology* ed. by R. Schlatter (Englewood Cliffs, N. J., 1963).

Perle, George
1953 "The Harmonic Problem in 12-Tone Music," *Music Review* 15.
1959 "Theory and Practice in Twelve-Tone Music," *Score* 25.
1962 *Serial Composition and Atonality* (Berkeley 1962).

Poland, William. "Theories of Music and Musical Behavior," *JMT* 7/2.

Pousseur, Henri. "The Question of Order in New Music," *PNM* 5/1.

Prieberg, Fred K. *Musica ex Machina* (Frankfurt 1960).

Randall, J. K. "Three Lectures to Scientists," *PNM* 5/2.

Regener, Eric. "Layered Music-Theoretic Systems," *PNM* 6/1.

Riemann, Hugo

1887 *Handbuch der Harmonielehre* (Leipzig 1887).

1903 *System der musikalischen Rhythmik und Metrik* (Leipzig 1903).

Rochberg, George

1955 *The Hexachord and its Relation to the Twelve-Tone Row* (Bryn Mawr 1955).

1959 "The Harmonic Tendency of the Hexachord," *JMT* 3/2.

Rogers, John. "Some Properties of Non-Duplicating Rotational Arrays," *PNM* 7/1.

Rothgeb, John

1966 "Some Uses of Mathematical Concepts in Theories of Music," *JMT* 10/2.

1967 "Some Ordering Relationships in the Twelve-Tone System," *JMT* 11/2.

1968 *Harmonizing the Unfigured Bass: A Computational Study* (PhD diss., Yale Univ., 1968).

Rufer, Josef. *Composition with 12 Notes Related Only One to Another* trans. H. Searle (London 1954).

Salzer, Felix. *Structural Hearing* (New York 1952).

Salzman, Eric. *Twentieth-Century Music* (New York 1967).

Sargeant, Winthrop. "Bernhard Ziehn, Precursor," *MQ* 19/2.

Schaeffer, Pierre. *Traité des objets musicaux* (Paris 1966).

Schenker, Heinrich

1906 *Harmony* ed. by O. Jonas, trans. by E. M. Borgese (Chicago 1954).

1910 *Kontrapunkt I* (Stuttgart 1910).

1922 *Kontrapunkt II* (Vienna 1922).

1935 *Der Freie Satz* (Vienna 1935).

Schillinger, Joseph. *The Schillinger System of Musical Composition* (New York 1946).

Schoenberg, Arnold

1911 *Harmonielehre* (Vienna 1911; second ed. with extensive revisions, 1922); the English trans. by R. D. W. Adams, *Theory of Harmony* (New York 1948) omits all of the material on atonal harmony as well as other important matter.

1950 *Style and Idea* (New York 1950).

Schröder, Hermann. *Die symmetrische Umkehrung in der Musik* (Leipzig 1902).

Seeger, Charles. "On the Moods of a Music-Logic," *Journal of the American Musicological Society* 13.

Shirlaw, Matthew. *The Theory of Harmony* (London 1917).

Slawson, A. W.

1968 Review of *Computer Applications in Music* ed. by G. Lefkoff (Morgantown 1967), *JMT* 12/1.

1969 "A Speech-Oriented Synthesizer of Computer Music," *JMT* 13/1.

Slonimsky, Nicholas. *Thesaurus of Scales and Melodic Patterns* (New York 1947).

Taneiev, Sergei. *Convertible Counterpoint* trans. by G. A. Brower (Boston 1963).

Teitelbaum, Richard. "Intervallic Relations in Atonal Music," *JMT* 9/1.

Tenney, James

1963 "Sound Generation by Means of a Digital Computer," *JMT* 7/1.

1964 *Meta (+) Hodos* (New Orleans 1964).

Thomson, William. "Hindemith's Contribution to Music Theory," *JMT* 9/1.

Vinton, John. "Bartók on his own Music," *Journal of the American Musicological Society* 19/2.

Winckel, Fritz. *Music, Sound and Sensation* trans. by T. Binkley (New York 1967).

Winograd, Terry. "Linguistics and the Computer Analysis of Tonal Harmony," *JMT* 12/1.

Xenakis, Iannis. *Musiques formelles* (Paris 1963).

Yasser, Joseph. *A Theory of Evolving Tonality* (New York 1932).

Ziehn, Bernhard

1888 *Harmonie- und Modulationslehre* (Berlin 1888).

1907 *Manual of Harmony* (Milwaukee 1907); corresponds to the 1888 work but has additional information as well.

1911 *Five- and Six-Part Harmonies* (Milwaukee 1911).

1912 *Canonical Studies, a New Technic in Composition* (Milwaukee 1912).

Allen Forte

SEE ALSO Austria and Germany, John Cage, Education for the Professional, Form, Indeterminacy, Charles Ives, Mathematics, Microtones, Harry Partch, Performance, Karlheinz Stockhausen, Texture, Tuning and Temperament, 12-Tone Techniques, Christian Wolff, Iannis Xenakis, La Monte Young.

Third Stream, a term invented in the mid-1950s by Gunther Schuller and referring to music in which traditional concepts of concert composition and performance are combined with those of jazz. In Schuller's third-stream works, the concert and jazz styles are generally confined to separate ensembles that are related to each other compositionally, sometimes in concerto-grosso fashion.

SEE ALSO Jazz, Gunther Schuller.

Thomson, Virgil (b. Kansas City, 25 Nov 1896), attended Harvard Univ. and also studied with Nadia Boulanger in Paris (1921–22) and Rosario Scalero in New York (1923–24). He began in these years to write music criticism for *Vanity Fair*, *The Boston Transcript*, and other periodicals. From 1925 until 1932 he lived primarily in Paris, where his principal contacts were among the circle around Les Six and around Gertrude Stein. He moved to New York permanently in 1940, where he was music critic for the *Herald Tribune* until 1954.

Since then he has devoted his time to composition, conducting, lecturing, and writing.

Debussy and Satie have been major influences on Thomson's style. Much of his music derives from visual and literary imagery (e.g., the stage works and incidental scores and the portraits of friends, which he has composed in various instrumental settings). The subject matter and tunes in some works are in the American nationalist tradition. Glanville-Hicks (see bibl.) has described the 1920s French influence on his development in terms of the "esthetic collages" of dada art: "moods, themes, styles were movable from context and from epoch; transposable—the form of the one into the idiom of another." Thomson has made such transpositions not only by quotation but by allusion. "A particularly effective and amusing use of inversion of custom in scoring comes at the end of the first movement [of the *Hymn Tune Symphony*] when the orchestra dwindles away to some trills and a cadenza on the trombone, in a style suggesting imitation of the behavior of a flute or piccolo." His harmonic vocabulary has made use of dissociated scales and triads, often resulting in polytonality and occasionally in atonality.

PRINCIPAL COMPOSITIONS: *Sonata da chiesa* for E♭ clarinet, D trumpet, viola, F horn, trombone (1926, Boosey); *La Valse grégorienne*, 4 songs for voice, piano; poems by Georges Hugnet (1927); *Capital Capitals* for 2 tenors, 2 baritones, piano; text by Gertrude Stein (1927, Boosey); *4 Saints in 3 Acts*, opera; libretto by Stein (1927–28, Mercury); *Symphony on a Hymn Tune* (1928, Southern); *Portraits*, 5 albums containing 40 pieces for piano (1929–45, Mercury); *Violin Sonata* (1930, Arrow); *Oraison funèbre* for tenor (baritone), piano (1930); *Stabat mater* for soprano, string quartet or string orchestra (1931, Cos Cob); *Symphony No. 2* (1931, MCA); *String Quartet No. 2* (1932, Arrow); *The Plough that Broke the Plains*, incidental score for the film by Pare Lorentz (1936; *Suite* for orchestra published by Schirmer-G); *The River*, incidental score for the film by Lorentz (1937; *Suite* for orchestra, Southern); *Filling Station*, ballet; choreography by Lew Christensen (1937, Arrow); *My Shepherd Will Supply My Need* for chorus; text by Isaac Watts (1937, Gray); *Sonata* for solo flute (1943, Schirmer-G); *10 Etudes* for piano (1943–44, Fischer); *9 Etudes* for piano (No. 1, 1940, Nos. 2–9, 1951, Fischer); *The Mother of Us All*, 2-act opera; libretto by Stein (1947, Mercury); *The Seine at Night* for orchestra (1947, Schirmer-G); *Louisiana Story*, incidental score for the film by Robert Flaherty (1948; *Suite* for orchestra, Schirmer-G); *A Solemn Music* for band (1949, Schirmer-G); *Cello Concerto* (1950, Ricordi); *4 Songs to Poems of Thomas Campion* for mezzo-soprano with piano or clarinet, viola, harp (1951, Boosey); *5 Songs from William Blake* for baritone, piano or orchestra (1951, Southern); *Sea Piece with Birds* for orches-

tra (1952, Schirmer-G); *Kyrie* for chorus (1953); *Concerto* for flute, strings, harp, percussion (1954, Ricordi); *Old English Songs* for soprano, piano (1955, Gray); *Old English Songs* for baritone, piano (1955, Southern); *Mass* for solo voice with piano or orchestra (1960, Schirmer-G); *Missa pro defunctis* for men's and women's choruses, orchestra (1960, Gray); *Praises and Prayers* for mezzo-soprano, piano (1963, Schirmer-G); *Autumn*, concertino for harp, strings, percussion (1964, Schirmer-G); *Lord Byron*, 3-act opera; libretto by Jack Larson (1968, Schirmer-G). List to 1956: *Composers of the Americas* 3:99–119; to 1957: Hoover-Cage (see bibl.).

PRINCIPAL WRITINGS: *The State of Music* (New York 1939); *The Musical Scene* (New York 1945); *The Art of Judging Music* (New York 1948); *Music, Right and Left* (New York 1951); *Virgil Thomson* (New York 1966); *Music Revisited: 1940–54* (New York 1967); *American Music Since 1910* (New York 1971).

BIBL.: Kathleen Hoover, John Cage, *V. T.* (New York 1959); Aaron Copland, *Our New Music* (New York 1941):187–201; Peggy Glanville-Hicks, "*V. T.*," *Musical Quarterly* 35:207–25.

SEE ALSO Dance, Mixed Media, Opera, Popular Music, United States.

Thorne, Francis (b. Bay Shore, N. Y., 23 June 1922), studied composition at Yale Univ. (1939–42; Paul Hindemith, Richard Donovan) and with Leo Smit (1956–58) and David Diamond (1959–61). During 1955–61 he was active as a jazz pianist, and in 1957 he helped found the Great South Bay Jazz Festival. He has been president of the Thorne Music Fund since 1965, executive director of the Naumburg Foundation since 1970, and has held a number of other directorial posts as well. His music is characterized by the strong influence of both modern jazz and 12-tone serialism.

PRINCIPAL COMPOSITIONS: *Elegy* for orchestra (1962–63, Marks); *Burlesque Overture* (1963–64, Marks); *Rhapsodic Variations* for piano, orchestra (1964–65); *Double Variations* for piano (1965); *Piano Concerto* (1965–66); *Lyric Variations* for orchestra (1966–67, Marks); *6 Set Pieces* for 13 players (1967, Marks); *Gemini Variations* for viola, double bass, orchestra (1967–68); *Song of the Carolina Low Country* for chorus, chamber orchestra (1968); *Sonar Plexus* for electric guitar, orchestra (1968, Marks); *Liebesrock* for 3 electric guitars, orchestra (1968–69, Marks); *Songs and Dances* for cello, keyboard instruments, percussion (1969, Opus One); *Symphony No. 3* for percussion, string orchestra (1969); *Antiphonies* for wind and percussion orchestra divided in 4 groups (1969–70); *Contra Band Music* for band (1970).

Tiessen, Heinz (b. Königsberg, Germany, 10 April 1887; d. Berlin, 29 Nov 1971), studied at the Stern Conservatory in Berlin (1905–14;

composition with Philipp Rufer, Wilhelm Klatte; conducting with Arno Kleffel) and the Univ. of Berlin (1905–14, philosophy and esthetics with Georg Simmel). During 1912–17 he was music critic for the *Allgemeine Musik-zeitung*. He assisted Richard Strauss in 1917 on the latter's Mozart opera tour in Switzerland, and during 1918–21 he was composer and kapellmeister at the Berlin Volksbühne. He taught composition at the Berlin Hochschule für Musik during 1925–46 and 1949–55; during 1946–49 he was director of the Municipal Academy (formerly the Stern Conservatory). In 1955 he helped organize the music section of the West Berlin Academy of the Arts, of which he was director until 1961. His music was much influenced by his acquaintance with Strauss, who persuaded him to change careers from music journalism to conducting and composition.

PRINCIPAL COMPOSITIONS (unless otherwise noted, dates are of first performance): *Symphony*, "Stirb und Werde," Op. 17 (1914, Ries & Erler); *Eine Natur-Trilogie* for piano, Op. 18 (1919, Leuckart); *Amsel Septett* for flute, clarinet, horn, string quartet, Op. 20 (1918, revised 1947; Ries & Erler); *3 Piano Pieces*, Op. 31 (1923, Leuckart); incidental music to Tagore's *Das Postamt*, Op. 32 (1924); *String Quartet*, Op. 32, of which the middle movement is based on *Das Postamt* (1924, UE; orchestrated as *Music for String Orchestra*, Op. 32a, 1931, UE); *Vorspiel zu einem Revolutionsdrama*, Op. 33 (1927, Ries & Erler); *Salambo*, ballet, Op. 34 (1929, UE); *2 Pieces from Salambo* for orchestra, Op. 34a, (1957, Ricordi); *Duo Sonate* for violin, piano, Op. 35 (1925, Bote); *6 Piano Pieces*, Op. 37 (composed 1924–28, UE); *Aufmarsch* for chorus, wind orchestra, Op. 40 (1931, Dt. Arb. Sängerbund); *Concert Variations* for piano, orchestra, Op. 60 (1962, Ries & Erler); *Die Amsel*, lyric rhapsody for soprano, orchestra, Op. 62 (1967, Ries & Erler).

PRINCIPAL WRITINGS: *Zur Geschichte der jüngsten Musik, 1913–28* (Mainz 1928); *Selbstzeugnis des Künstlers* (Cassel 1948); *Musik der Natur, über den Gesang der Vögel* . . . (Zurich 1953); "Wege eines Komponisten," *Die Rollen der Musik im Schauspiel* (Berlin 1962); *40 Jahre Berliner Singe-Gemeinschaft* (Berlin 1964); "Eduard Erdmann in seiner Zeit," *Begegnungen mit Eduard Erdmann* (Darmstadt 1967).

BIBL.: H. H. Stuckenschmidt, "Die Einfachheit des Komplizierten," *Melos* (May 1967).

SEE ALSO Austria and Germany.

Time, see Rhythm

Tippett, Michael (Kemp) (b. London, 2 Jan 1905), was largely self-taught but studied at the Royal College of Music (composition with Charles Wood, R. O. Morris; conducting with Adrian Boult, Malcolm Sargent). After pursuing various occupations, including schoolmaster, he devoted himself to conducting and music teaching. During 1940–51 he was director of music at Morley College in London. Public attention came first with the oratorio *A Child of Our Time* (1941). Since leaving Morley he has devoted full time to composition and to conducting choruses and orchestras, mainly in his own works.

Tippett's large-scale works—an oratorio, a cantata, two operas, and some orchestral compositions—are his most successful. He has usually disregarded traditional formal schemes. The music to 1945 reveals a fondness for the word-based rhythmic freedom and complex counterpoint of 16th- and 17th-century English madrigal and keyboard music. Progressive elements in the harmony (such as the semitone dissonances in the *Piano Sonata*) stemmed from Bartók, Hindemith, and even Fauré. Later on, folksong influences, as in the Negro spirituals used in *A Child of Our Time*, relaxed some of the harmonic and contrapuntal severity and made the music more immediately appealing. The *Piano Concerto* is representative of the post-1945 music, especially in its renewed emphasis on counterpoint and its brilliant, perhaps over-profuse, writing for the piano. In works of the 60s, such as the *Concerto for Orchestra*, there are wide skips and other gesticulative thematic elements as well as an occasional use of texture and sonority for their own sake.

PRINCIPAL COMPOSITIONS (published by Schott): *String Quartets Nos. 1–3* (1934–35, revised 1943; 1941–42; 1945–46); *Piano Sonatas Nos. 1–2* (1936–37, revised 1942; 1962); *Concerto for Double String Orchestra* (1938–39); *A Child of Our Time*, oratorio for soloists, chorus, orchestra; text by the composer (1939–41); *Symphonies Nos. 1–3* (1944–45; 1956–57; 1971); *Little Music* for strings (1946); *The Midsummer Marriage*, 3-act opera; text by the composer (1947–52; suite from the opera, *Ritual Dances*); *The Heart's Assurance* for voice, piano; poems by S. Keyes and A. Lewis (1950–51); *Fantasia concertante on a Theme of Corelli* for strings (1953); *Divertimento on "Sellinger's Round"* for chamber orchestra (1953–54); *Piano Concerto* (1953–55); *King Priam*, 3-act opera; text by the composer (1958–61); *Concerto for Orchestra* (1962–63); *Vision of St. Augustine* for baritone, chorus, orchestra (1965); *The Knot Garden*, 3-act opera; libretto by the composer (1967–70).

PRINCIPAL WRITINGS: *Moving into Aquarius* (London 1959); untitled article, *The Orchestral Composer's Point of View* ed. by R. S. Hines (Norman, Okla.):203–19.

BIBL.: Ian Kemp, ed., *M. T.: A Symposium on his 60th Birthday* (London 1965); Anthony Milner,

"The Music of M. T.," *Musical Quarterly* 50: 423–38; R. Murray Schafer, *British Composers in Interview* (London 1963).

John S. Weissmann

SEE ALSO Great Britain, Opera.

Toch, Ernst (b. Vienna, 7 Dec 1887; d. Los Angeles, 1 Oct 1964), studied medicine at the Univ. of Vienna, philosophy at the Univ. of Heidelberg (PhD 1921), and music at Zuschneid's Hochschule für Musik in Mannheim and the Hoch Conservatory in Frankfurt (1910–13, piano with Willy Rehberg). He was self-taught in composition. He taught composition at the Mannheim Hochschule during 1913–29 and privately in Berlin during 1929–32. He emigrated to the U.S. in 1934 and during 1934–36 taught composition at the New School for Social Research in New York. He then went to California, where he wrote a few film scores. In 1940 he joined the faculty of the Univ. of Calif. at Los Angeles.

PRINCIPAL COMPOSITIONS: *String Quartets Nos. 6–13*, Opp. 12, 15, 18, 26, 28, 34, 70, 74 (1905; 1905; 1911, Weinberger; 1919, Leuckart; 1920, Leuckart; 1924, Schott; 1946, Leeds; 1953, Mills); *The Chinese Flute* for soprano, chamber orchestra, Op. 29; poems by Hans Bethge (1922; revised 1949, Schott); *Cello Concerto*, Op. 35 (1925, Schott); *Piano Concertos Nos. 1–2*, Opp. 38, 61 (1927, 1932; Schott); *Die Prinzessin auf der Erbse*, 1-act opera, Op. 43; libretto by Benno Elkan (1927, Schott); *Piano Sonata* (1928, Schott); *Bunte Suite* for orchestra, Op. 48 (1929, Schott); *Geographical Fugue* for speaking chorus (1930, Mills); *Das Wasser*, cantata for narrator, vocal soloists, chorus, chamber orchestra, Op. 53 (1930, Schott); *Der Fächer*, 3-act opera, Op. 51 (1930, Schott); *50 Etudes* for piano (1931, Schott); *Big Ben*, variations for orchestra, Op. 62 (1934, Schott); *Piano Quintet*, Op. 64 (1938, Delkas); *Cantata of the Bitter Herbs* for narrator, vocal soloists, chorus, orchestra, Op. 65 (1941, Leeds); *Poems to Martha* for medium voice, strings, Op. 66 (1943, Leeds); *Symphonies Nos. 1–6*: No. 1, Op. 72 (1950–51, AMP); No. 2, Op. 73 (1953, AMP); No. 3, Op. 75 (1954–55, Mills); No. 4, Op. 80 (1957, Mills); No. 5, Op. 89 (1963); No. 6, Op. 91 (1963–64, Mills); *Peter Pan*, fairy tale for orchestra, Op. 76 (1956, Schott). Complete list: *Composers of the Americas* 7:83–95.

PRINCIPAL WRITINGS: *Melodielehre* (Berlin 1923); *The Shaping Forces in Music* (New York 1948).

BIBL.: E. Beninger, "Pianistische Probleme im Anschluss an die Klavierwerke von E. T.," *Melos* (Feb 1928):63–68; Frederick Dorian, "Current Chronicle," *Musical Quarterly* 42:395–96; Paul Pisk, "E. T.," *ibid.* 24:438–50; Hans Rutz, "E. T.," *Melos* (May 1952):139–42.

Togni, Camillo (b. Gussago, Italy, 18 Oct 1922), studied at the Accadèmia Musicale Chigiana in Siena (1939–42, composition,

piano with Alfredo Casella), the Univ. of Milan (1942–47, esthetics of music with Luigi Rognoni), and the Univ. of Pavia (1947–48), where he specialized in Benedetto Croce and earned a degree in philosophy. He also studied privately in Brescia (1935–40; composition with Franco Márgola, piano with Benedetti Michelangeli) and in Milan (1941–43, piano with Giovanni Anfossi). He performed contemporary piano music in Italy, Germany, and Switzerland during 1950–55 and taught at Florence Univ. for Foreigners during 1960–61. In 1961 he worked at the Electronic Music Studio of RIA in Milan. Since 1940 he has used the 12-tone techniques of Schoenberg.

PRINCIPAL COMPOSITIONS (published by S-Z unless otherwise noted): *6 Serenate* for piano (1940–44, unpub.); *Variations* for piano, orchestra (1946, unpub.); *Psalm 127* for soprano, alto, bass, violin, viola, cello (1949, unpub.); *3 Studies for "Morts sans sépulture" of J.-P. Sartre* for soprano, piano (1951, unpub.); *Coro di T. S. Eliot* for chorus, orchestra (1951); *Coro di T. S. Eliot* for chorus (1952); *Flute Sonata* (1953, UE); *Ricerca*, 6 studies for "La Nausée" of J.-P. Sartre, for baritone, flute, horn, viola, double bass, celesta (1953, unpub.); *Helian di Trakl*, 5 songs for soprano with piano (1954) or with chamber orchestra (1961); *3 Capriccios*, "A, B, C," for piano (1954, 1956, 1957); *Fantasia concertante* for flute, string orchestra (1957); *Recitativo* on tape (1961); *Gesang zur Nacht* for alto, chamber orchestra; text by Trakl (1962); *Rondeau per 10* for soprano, guitar, harp, harpsichord, celesta, glockenspiel, chimes, timpani, harmonium, double bass; text by Charles d'Orléans (1963–64); *Préludes et rondeaux* for soprano, harpsichord; text by Charles d'Orléans (1964); *Aubade* for flute/piccolo, clarinet, vibraphone, harp, harpsichord, cello (1965); *6 Notturni* for alto, clarinet, violin, 2 pianos; texts by Trakl (1966); *4 Capriccios*, "Ottave," for piano (1969).

PRINCIPAL WRITINGS: review of *L'Evolution de la musique de Bach à Schoenberg* by René Leibowitz, *Aut-Aut* (Milan) 7:72–75; "Luigi Dallapiccola," *Enciclopedia della Musica Ricordi* 2:4–5.

BIBL.: Mario Bartolotto, "La nuova musica a Palermo," *Il veltro* (Rome, April 1962):820–23; Reginald Smith Brindle, "The Lunatic Fringe III: Computational Composition," *Musical Times* (July 1956):354–56; Giancarlo Facchinetti, "C. T.," *Il bruttanome* (Brescia) 2/3:477–83; Roman Vlad, *Storia della dodecafonia* (Milan 1958):265.

Tomasi, Henri (Frédien) (b. Marseilles, 17 August 1901; d. Avignon, 13 Jan 1971), studied at the Paris Conservatory with Paul Vidal, Vincent d'Indy, and Philippe Gaubert. As a conductor he appeared throughout Europe in radio and live concerts. During 1930–35 he was music director of the colonial radio station in French Indochina, and during 1946–50 he directed the Monte Carlo Opera.

PRINCIPAL COMPOSITIONS: ★ Operas: *L'Atlantide* (1951, Lemoine); *Don Juan de Mañara*, libretto by O. V. de L. Milosz (1952, Leduc); *Sampiero Corso* (1953, Lemoine); *Le Triomphe de Jeanne* (1955, Lemoine); *Il poverello* (1957, Eschig); *Le Silence de la mer* (1959, Choudens); *Naissance de l'Odyssée* (1961, Eschig); *L'Elixir du R. P. Gaucher* (1963, Leduc); *L'Eloge de la folie* (1965, EFM). ★ Ballets: *Vocero* (1932, orchestral suite published by Lemoine); *La Grisi* (1935, Huegel); *Les Santons* (1936, Lemoine); *La Rosière du Village* (1939, Leduc); *Féerie Laotienne*, scenario by José Bruyr (1952, Leduc); *Noces de cendres*, scenario by Hubert Devillez (1953, Leduc; orchestral suite, 1954, Leduc); *Dassine, Sultane du Hoggar* (1959, Lemoine); *Jabadao* (1959, Leduc); *Nana* (1960); *Les Barbaresques* (1960). ★ Concertos (all with orchestra): flute (1945, Leduc); trumpet (1946, Leduc); saxophone (1949, Leduc); viola (1950, Leduc); clarinet (1954, Leduc); horn (1955, Leduc); trombone (1956, Leduc); oboe (1958, Leduc); violin (1963, Leduc); guitar (1966, Leduc); harp, "Highlands Ballad" (1966, Leduc); cello (1969, Eschig); double bass (1970, Choudens). ★ Other works: *Cyrnos* for orchestra (1929, Lemoine); *Tam Tam* for orchestra (1931, Lemoine); *5 Danses profanes et sacrées* for chamber orchestra, piano, percussion (1952, Leduc); *Fanfares liturgiques* for brass, timpani, percussion (1952, Leduc); *Lettres de mon Moulin* for orchestra (1957, Leduc); *Les Pastoureaux* for chorus (1957, Leduc); *Pâtres des Montagnes* for chorus (1957, Leduc); *12 Noëls de Saboly* for chorus (1962, Leduc); *La Chèvre de M. Seguin*, cantata for narrator, soprano, bass, children's or women's chorus, orchestra; text by Alphonse Daudet (1963, Leduc); *La Mort du petit dauphin*, chamber cantata (1965, Leduc); *M. le Sous-préfet aux champs*, chamber cantata (1965, Leduc); *Symphonie du Tiers Monds* for orchestra (1968, Leduc).

SEE ALSO France.

Tone Cluster, see Cluster

Tosar-Errecart, Héctor (b. Montevideo, 18 July 1923), studied privately in Montevideo with W. Kolischer (piano), T. Mujica (harmony and counterpoint), and L. Baldi (composition and orchestration). He attended Tanglewood (1946–48; composition with Aaron Copland, Arthur Honegger, and Darius Milhaud), and from 1948 to 1950 studied at the Paris Conservatory and at the Ecole Normale de Musique (composition with Darius Milhaud, Jean Rivier, Arthur Honegger; conducting with Jean Fournet and Eugène

Bigot). He taught music history at the Montevideo Conservatory during 1951–60 and harmony at the Instituto de Profesores in Montevideo, 1952–60. From 1961 to 1965 he served as acting dean and professor of analysis at the conservatory in San Juan, Puerto Rico. Since 1966 he has been professor of composition and orchestration at the Montevideo Conservatory and since 1967, professor of organology at the Univ. of Montevideo. He has directed the Montevideo Philharmonic since 1969 and has also been active as a pianist throughout South America and in the U.S.

PRINCIPAL COMPOSITIONS: *Toccata* for orchestra (1940, Ricordi); *Danza criolla* for piano (1941, Broude-B); *Symphony for Strings* (1951, Southern); *Sonatina No. 2* for piano (1956, Ricordi); *Sinfonia concertante* for piano, orchestra (1957); *Te Deum* for bass, chorus, orchestra (1959); *Stray Birds* for baritone, 11 instruments; poem by R. Tagore (1963). List to 1960: *Composers of the Americas* 6:103–06.

BIBL.: Gustavo Becerra, "Sinfonia No. 2 para cuerdas de H. T.," *Revista musical chilena* (Oct 1957):5–23.

Total Serialism, see Serialism

Total Theater, see Indeterminacy, Mixed Media

Touma, Habib (b. Nazareth, Israel, 12 Dec 1934), studied at the Israeli Academy of Music (1956–62, composition with Alexander Boscovitch), the Free Univ. of Berlin (1964–68, ethnomusicology with Kurt Reinhard), and the Darmstadt summer courses (1961, 65, 66; courses with Stockhausen, Messiaen, Boulez, Maderna, and Koenig). He taught music in the Nazareth public schools during 1962–63. Since 1968 he has been secretary for Asian and African Music Projects at the International Institute for Comparative Music Studies and Documentation. In the summer of 1970 he lectured on Near Eastern music at the Free Univ. in Berlin. His music has been much influenced by his studies of classical and oriental music, particularly the rhythms, forms, instrumentation, and melodic style of Arab music.

PRINCIPAL COMPOSITIONS (published by IMI unless otherwise noted): *Oriental Rhapsody* for 2 flutes, Arab drum (1956–57); *Study* for solo flute (1959); *Samai* for oboe, piano (1960); *Arabian Suite* for piano (1961); *Qasidah* for chorus with

piano or harp (1962, unpub.); *Study No. 2,*
"Combinations," for solo flute (1963); *Reflexus 1*
for 12 string instruments (1965); *Taqsim* for piano
(1966).

Travis, Roy (Elihu) (b. New York, 24 June
1922), studied composition with Bernard
Wagenaar at the Juilliard School (1947–50),
Otto Luening at Columbia Univ. (1950–51),
and Darius Milhaud at the Paris Conservatory (1951–52). He also studied privately with
Felix Salzer during 1947–50. He has taught at
Columbia Univ. (1952–53), the Mannes
College in New York (1952–57), and the Univ.
of Calif. at Los Angeles (since 1957), where
since 1969 he has also been working regularly
at the university's electronic music studio. He
has drawn inspiration from studies of Greek
drama (while an undergraduate) and African
tribal music (at the Institute of Ethnomusicology at UCLA).

PRINCIPAL COMPOSITIONS: *Symphonic Allegro*
(1951, Chappell); *Piano Sonata No. 1* (c.1954);
5 Preludes for piano (c.1956, Presser); *String
Quartet No. 1* (1958); *The Passion of Oedipus,* 2-act
opera (1965); *Songs and Epilogues,* 5 songs and 4
piano pieces for bass, piano; texts by Sappho
(1965, Oxford); *African Sonata* for piano (1966);
Duo concertante for violin, piano (1967, Univ. of
Calif. Press); *Septet* for flute, clarinet, violin,
cello, double bass, piano, percussion (1968); *Collage* for orchestra (1967–68, Oxford); *Piano Concerto* (1969); *Concerto* for flute, prerecorded
African instruments and synthesizer (1970–71).

PRINCIPAL WRITINGS: "Towards a New Concept
of Tonality?" *Journal of Music Theory* 3; "Directed Motion in 2 Brief Piano Pieces of Schoenberg and Webern," *Perspectives* 4/2; "Tonal Coherence in the First Movement of the Bartók
'Fourth String Quartet'," *Music Forum* (New
York) 2.

Tredici, David Del, see under Del Tredici

Tremblay, George (Amedée) (b. Ottawa, 14
Jan 1911), studied piano and organ with his
father and, in 1936, composition with Arnold
Schoenberg. In 1965 he founded in Los
Angeles the School for the Discovery and
Advancement of New Serial Techniques; the
school also serves as a center for consultation
about and experimental studies of music for
television and films. Tremblay has been influenced by American jazz and popular music,
as well as the classics, particularly Bach and

Mozart. His *Symphony No. 3* "is constructed
on an all-interval row and its definitive cycle of
288 permutations (3,456 notes). The form of
the work is shaped by the natural evolution of
the cycle. The result is total integration as
opposed to arbitrary serialism." He is working
on a monograph, *The Definitive Cycle of the
12-Tone Row and Its Application in All Fields of
Composition, Including the Computer.*

PRINCIPAL COMPOSITIONS: *Prelude and Dance* for
piano (1935, Pioneer); *String Quartet No. 1* (1936);
2 Sonatas for piano (1938, New Music); *Modes of
Transportation* for string quartet (1939, Polytone);
Chaparral Symphony (1939); *Wind Quintet* (1940);
In Memoriam for string quartet (1942); *Symphony
in 1 Movement* (1949, Pioneer); *Wind Quintet*
(1950, Pioneer); *Symphony* (1952); *Serenade* for
winds, strings, piano, percussion (1955, Pioneer);
Piano Sonata No. 3 (1957, Pioneer); *Piano Quartet*
(1958, Pioneer); *Piano Trio* (1959, Pioneer);
Epithalamium for winds, strings, piano, percussion
(1962); *String Quartet No. 3* (1962); *String Quartet
No. 4* (1963); *String Trio* (1964, Pioneer); *Quartet*
for oboe, clarinet, bassoon, viola (1964, Christ-
lieb); *Duo* for viola, piano (1966, Pioneer); *Double-
bass Sonata* (1967, Pioneer); *Fantasy and Fugue*
for bassoon, piano (1967, Pioneer); *Prelude, Aria,
Fugue, and Postlude* for concert band (1967);
Wind Sextet (1968, Pioneer); *Symphony No. 3*
(1970).

Tremblay, Gilles (b. Arvida, Quebec, 6 Sept
1932), after completing his studies at the
Montreal Conservatory with Claude Cham-
pagne (composition), he went to Paris, where
from 1954 to 1961 he studied with Oliver
Messiaen (analysis), Yvonne Loriod (piano),
Maurice Martenot (ondes Martenot), Andrée
Vaurabourg-Honegger (counterpoint) and at
the Studio for Experimental Music of the
French radio (electronic music techniques).
Since 1962 he has been professor of analysis and
composition at the Montreal Conservatory.

Tremblay shows a definite preference in his
music for winds and percussion; voices are
used only in *Kékoba* (1965), where they appear
towards the end of the work. Always present is
a poetic symbolism, which in *Champs II—
Souffle* (1968) manifests itself in an opposition
between *souffle* (duration) and *fulgurance* (the
instant). The opening of the work illustrates
the transition between wind and sound by in-
structing the players to breathe into their instruments, just touching the threshold of
sound before returning to wind. More often
than not Tremblay's music is monodic with an
extreme development of rhythmic and timbral
subtleties. Sometimes a rarified texture is used
to facilitate perception of such details as the

pitch of a cymbal resonance echoed by ondes Martenot. Formally the music is often a mosaic of sharp contrasts of pitch, dynamics, and density (an instrumental solo followed by a dense, improvised passage, for example). Distinctive textures also occur in the freer, aleatory sections, where within a total duration a network of pitches and a choice of rhythmic cells, attacks, dynamics, and pauses are specified. Another principle of coordination is the "reflex," which forces one player to react to musical signals from another. Notable in *Champs II* are the plainchantlike instrumental solos punctuated by staccato echoes and the three-layered textures with low chords in piano and double bass, a very soft choralelike passage in midrange in muted brass, and on top torrents of grace notes in xylophone, glockenspiel, and piano.

PRINCIPAL COMPOSITIONS: *Phases et réseaux* for piano (1956–58, BMIC); *Cantique de durées* for orchestra (1960); *Champs I* for piano, 2 percussion (1965, BMIC); *Kékoba* for ondes Martenot, percussion, soprano, alto, tenor; medieval hymn text (1965, BMIC); *Sonorisation*, electronic sounds on 24 tape channels, created for the Quebec pavillon at Expo '67 (1967); *Champs II—Souffle* for 2 flutes, oboe, clarinet, horn, 2 trumpets, 2 trombones, 2 percussion, piano, double bass (1968); *Champs III —Vers* for 3 violins, double bass, 2 flutes, clarinet, horn, trumpet, 3 percussion, piano (1969); *Dimension soleils*, electroacoustic music for a film of Raymond Brousseau (1970); "*. . . Le sifflement des vents porteurs de l'amour . . .*" for flute, percussion, 4 microphones (1971).

PRINCIPAL WRITINGS: "Les Sons en mouvements," *Liberté* (Montreal 1959); "Note pour *Cantique de durées*," *Revue d'esthétique* (1968); "Oiseau-nature, Messiaen, musique," *Les Cahiers canadiens de musique* (spring 1970).

Bruce Mather

SEE ALSO Canada.

Trichord, a collection of three pitch classes considered either as a simultaneity or as a succession. The term occurs most frequently in reference to segments of 12-tone sets; when applied to chords, it is sometimes used in place of "triad" by those who specifically wish to avoid the traditional connotations of the latter.

Trimble, Lester (Albert) (b. Bangor, Wis., 29 Aug 1923), was born into a musical family and studied violin as a child. He attended Carnegie-Mellon Univ. (1944–48, composition with Nikolai Lopatnikoff, musicology with Frederick Dorian, violin with Gosta Andreasson),

Tanglewood (summer 1947, composition with Darius Milhaud), and studied composition in Paris with Milhaud, Honegger, and Nadia Boulanger (1948). He taught at Chatham College, Pittsburgh, Pa. (1948–50) and was a music critic for the *New York Herald Tribune* (1951–59) and *The Nation* (1956–61). He has also been general manager of the American Music Center (1961–63), a professor of music at the Univ. of Md. (1963–67), composer-in-residence, New York Philharmonic (1967–68), and a composition instructor at the Juilliard School (since 1971). Trimble describes his style as "an American amalgamation of the Germanic (Beethovenian) concept of thematic, motivic, and formal unity, and the French sense of instrumental color (also harmonic color) and elegance of execution." He has used, but does not prefer, 12-tone procedures and is attracted to the use of polyrhythms, melodies, and harmonies in montagelike groupings.

PRINCIPAL COMPOSITIONS: *String Quartet No. 1* (1950, SPAM); *Symphony in 2 Movements* (1951, Peters); *String Quartet No. 2* (1956); *Sonic Landscape* for orchestra (1957–68, Duchess); *4 Fragments from the Canterbury Tales* (1958, Peters); *Boccaccio's "Nightingale"*, opera (1959–69); *5 Episodes* for orchestra (1961–62, Duchess); *Symphony No. 2* (1966–68, Duchess); *Duo concertante* for 2 violins, orchestra (1968, Peters). List to 1965: *Composers of the Americas* 10:119–21.

PRINCIPAL WRITINGS: "Serious Composer Gets Just the Crumbs, if Any," *New York Herald Tribune* (22 Sept 1959) IV:8; "The Special Woes of Opera Writing," *ibid.* (22 March 1959) IV:5; "Beneath the Quiet Surface," *New York Times* (27 August 1961) X:7; "Problems Confronting the American Composer," unpub. report used in the preparation of *The Performing Arts, Problems and Prospects* (New York: McGraw Hill, 1965).

Trope, a term used by Josef Matthais *Hauer (1883–1959) to refer to the 44 pairs of unordered hexachords (groups of six pitch classes), which form the basis for his method of 12-tone composition. *Trope* in Hauer's usage is not related to the medieval concepts to which the same term is applied.

BIBL.: Karl Eschmann, *Changing Forms in Modern Music* (Boston 1945); J. M. Hauer, *Zwölftontechnik: Die Lehre von den Tropen* (Vienna 1926); Walter Szmolyan, *J. M. Hauer* (Vienna 1965).

Tsouyopoulos, Georges S. (b. Athens, 11 Oct 1930), studied composition at the Athens Conservatory (1948–54, Phil. Economides) and at the Univ. of Zurich (1955–57, Paul Hindemith). Since 1955 his home has been Munich, where he has studied philosophy at the Univ. of Munich (1955–56, 1958) and architecture at the Munich Technical Univ. (1958–65). He works for an architectural firm. His earlier music (now withdrawn) was influenced by the works of Stravinsky, Shostakovich, Prokofiev, and Bartók, and contained some folklore elements. During the late 50s and early 60s he began working with a variety of avant-garde techniques, but without adopting any one approach exclusively.

PRINCIPAL COMPOSITIONS: *String Quartet No. 2* (1956); *Sinfonietta da camera* for oboe, clarinet, bassoon, horn, guitar, violin, viola, cello (1957); *Serenata* for woman's voice, flute, guitar, viola (1957, EM); *2 Madrigals* for woman's voice, chamber orchestra (1957, EM); *Sonata* for solo viola (1957); *3 Fragments* for chorus, orchestra (1958, EM); *Toccatas I–III* for piano (1958–65; No. 3, Gerig); *Music for Percussion* (1959, EM); *Music for Wind Quintet* (1965–66, Gerig).

PRINCIPAL WRITINGS: "Kritikó Schedíasma tis Hellenikis Mousikis Pragmatikótetas" [Critical Approach to Greek Music], *Skopiès* (Zurich, Jan–Feb 1960):7–12; an interview in Greek on the present situation of music, *Tachydromos* (Athens, 21 Dec 1963). Tsouyopoulos has also delivered lectures and been interviewed over the Cologne radio station Deutsche Welle (March–April 1965, April 1969).

SEE ALSO Greece.

Tsytovich, Vladimir (Ivanovich) (b. Leningrad, 6 August 1931), studied at the Leningrad Conservatory Music School (1949–53, composition with S. Ja. Vol'fenzon) and the Leningrad Conservatory (1953–61, composition with B. A. Arapov, piano with I. A. Braudo). Since 1961 he has taught composition at the Leningrad Conservatory, composed for television, and concertized in the U.S.S.R. as a pianist. In his recent compositions he has been combining some principles of serialism with tonal harmony.

PRINCIPAL COMPOSITIONS (published by Muzyka unless otherwise noted): *Konek-Gorbunok Suite* for orchestra (1956, SC); *5 Romances on Poems of A. Blok* for low voice, piano (1956, SC); *Sinfonietta* for orchestra (1957, unpub.); *Pohozhdeniia bravogo soldata Shveika* [The Adventures of the Good Soldier Schweik], sketches for narrator, orchestra (1959); *Piano Concerto* (1960); *Suite* for 2 pianos (1960); *Vesenniaia uvertiura* [Spring Overture] for orchestra (1961, unpub.); *2 Songs on Poems by I. Tul'en* for low voice, piano (1961, unpub.); *Triptych* for viola, piano (1962); *10 Preludes* for piano (1963); *Concerto* for viola, chamber orchestra (1965); *6 Concert Pieces* for piano (1966); *Dialogue and Scherzo* for violin, piano (1966);

Prikliucheniia Chipollino [The Adventures of Chip], 12 children's pieces for piano after the story by Rodari (1967); *Symphony* for chorus, orchestra; text by V. Kamensky (1969–70, unpub.).

PRINCIPAL WRITINGS: Tsytovich has written four articles on the structural implications of timbre in Bartók's music (scheduled for publication in Moscow, 1973–74), the subject on which he wrote his dissertation in Leningrad.

BIBL.: S. Ja. Vol'fenzon, "Iz pesnok Vinni-Pukha" [From the Hums of Pooh], *Sovetskaia muzyka* 1969/10:155.

Tudor, David (b. Philadelphia, 20 Jan 1926), studied in Philadelphia with H. William Hawke (organ, theory) and Josef Martin (piano) and in New York with Irma Wolpe (piano) and Stefan Wolpe (composition, analysis). He was organist at St. Mark's, Philadelphia (1938–43) and Swarthmore College (1944–48). During 1948 he taught piano at the Contemporary Music School in New York, a private conservatory that existed 1948–52. He has been on the summer faculties at Black Mountain College, N.C. (1951–53) and Darmstadt (1956, 58, 59, 61). Since 1953 he has been a musician with the Merce Cunningham Dance Co.

During 1948–49 Tudor began his associations with Morton Feldman and John Cage. The Cage-Tudor collaborations have been especially noteworthy. From 1951 to 1953 Tudor was a member of Cage's Project of Music for Magnetic Tape, the first American group organized for the production of electronic music. In the early 1960s he and Cage were influential in establishing the continuing trend of "live" (as distinct from prerecorded) electronic music in their performances of Cage's *Cartridge Music*, *Variations II*, and *Variations III*.

As a pianist Tudor has performed in the premieres of numerous works (many dedicated to him), including Cage's *Music of Changes* (in 1952), *Concert for Piano and Orchestra* (in 1958), and *Atlas Eclipticalis with Winter Music*, electronic version (in 1961), Sylvano Bussotti's *5 Piano Pieces for David Tudor* (in 1958), Karlheinz Stockhausen's *Kontakte* (in 1960), and the American premiere of Boulez's *Piano Sonata No. 2* (in 1950). He is also a self-taught player of the Argentine bandoneon, and he has performed works for this instrument by Mauricio Kagel, Gordon Mumma, and Pauline Oliveros, as well as his own large theater piece, *Bandoneon !*. He has given many performance seminars in colleges and universities, and in 1969–70 he was one of four Core Artists who oversaw the design of the Pepsi-Cola Pavilion for Expo '70 at Osaka.

Tudor's exceptional abilities as a pianist and as a performer of electronic music have given rise to many of the new freedoms and virtuoso demands in avant-garde music. Without his contributions, the collaborations in his catalog of works would not have come into existence. His creative realizations of music with indeterminate elements have not only been an important factor in removing the conventional distinctions between composer and performer but have also led him to discover the means for producing his own works.

Tudor possesses one of the world's largest collections of custom modular electronic devices, many of his own manufacture. His choices of specific electronic components, transducers, and their interconnections define both composition and performance in his works. His sound materials unfold through large gestures in time and space, and all of his compositions are associated with visual forces: light systems, dance, television, theatre, film, or laser projections. *Bandoneon !* (*Bandoneon Factorial*) exemplifies Tudor's use of multiple elements. It calls for programmed lighting and audio circuitry, moving loudspeakers, and projected video images, all actuated by the sounds of the bandoneon. He states that the work "uses no composing means; when activated it composes itself out of its own composite instrumental nature." In *Video III*, *Video/Laser I*, and *Video/Laser II* electronic signals simultaneously operate an audio system and multicolored visual displays generated on television screens and from krypton laser projections. The *Video/Laser* works are among the first to incorporate laser devices in musical performance. Tudor's innovations for producing live electronic music and technological events for theater have influenced many other composers, notably David Behrman, Toshi Ichiyanagi, Alvin *Lucier, Gordon *Mumma, and Frederic *Rzewski.

PRINCIPAL WORKS (with place and date of first production): *Fluorescent Sound*, produced for Robert Rauschenberg's *Shotput* and *Elgin Tie* (Stockholm, 13 Sept 1964); *Bandoneon!* with projected video images by Lowell Cross (New York, 14, 18 Oct 1966); *Reunion*, produced with David Behrman, John Cage, Cross, Marcel Duchamp, Teeny Duchamp, Gordon Mumma (Toronto, 5 March 1968); *RainForest*, produced for the Merce Cunningham dancework (Buffalo, N.Y., 9 March 1968); *Video III*, produced with Cross (San Diego, Calif., 10 May 1968); *Assemblage*, produced with Cage, Mumma for the KQED film group (San Francisco, Oct–Nov 1968); *Video/Laser I*, produced with Cross (Oakland, Calif., 9 May 1969); *Video/Laser II*, produced with Cross, Carson Jeffries (Berkeley, Calif., Jan–Feb 1970; Expo '70, Osaka, Japan, March–Sept 1970); *4 Pepsi Pieces* for the sound and light resources of the Pepsi-Cola Pavilion, Expo '70 (Osaka, March–April 1970). ★ Collaborative realizations: John Cage's *Solo for Piano for Indeterminacy* (Brussels, 9 Oct 1958); Richard Maxfield's *Piano Concert* (New York, 24 March 1961); Cage's *Variations II*, theater version with Jasper Johns, Robert Rauschenberg, Niki de Saint-Phalle, Jean Tinguely (Paris, 20 June 1961); Cage's *Variations II & III* (Berlin 1963); Cage's *Talk I* (Ann Arbor, Mich., 19 Sept 1965); Pauline Oliveros's *Light Piece for David Tudor* with visuals by Anthony Martin (San Francisco, 8 Nov 1965); "The Music of Conlon Nancarrow," performed with Cage, Viola Farber, Mumma, Peter Saul (New York, 18 Jan 1969). ★ Electronic versions and performance circuitry: Cage's *Variations II* (New York, 24 March 1961); Cage's *Winter Music* (Montreal, 3 August 1961); Cage's *Solo for Piano* (Minneapolis, 22 Jan 1962); Toshi Ichiyanagi's *Music for Piano #4* (San Francisco, 1 April 1964); Cage's *Solo(s) for Voice 2* (Buffalo, 21 Jan 1966); Michael von Biel's *Book for 3*, version for rotisseries and modulators (Buffalo, March 1966) and theater version with visuals by David Orcutt (Oakland, 16 April 1968); Cage's *Fontana Mix*, version for piano and electronic circuits (Davis, Calif., 6 Feb 1967) and version for bass drum and electronic circuits (Waltham, Mass., 1 April 1967); Ichiyanagi's *Activities for Orchestra* produced for Merce Cunningham's *Scramble* (Chicago, 25 July 1967).

BIBL.: John Cage, *Silence* (Middletown 1961); ——, *A Year from Monday* (Middletown, Conn., 1967); ——, *Notations* (New York 1969); Lowell Cross, "Audio/Video/Laser," *Source* 8:26–36; Carter Harmon, "Boulez' 2d Sonata Heard in Premiere," *New York Times* (18 Dec 1950); Harold Lawrence, "Of Mikes and Men," *Audio* (Nov 1963):64; *9 Evenings: Theatre & Engineering*, scores and program notes (New York, Experiments in Art and Technology, Inc., 1966); Harold C. Schonberg, "The Far-Out Pianist," *Harper's Magazine* (June 1960):49–54; Sogetsu Art Center program notes and articles (Tokyo 1962); Calvin Tomkins, "Onward and Upward with the Arts—E. A. T." *New Yorker* (3 Oct 1970):33ff; ——, "Profiles: John Cage—Figure in an Imaginary Landscape," *ibid.* (28 Nov 1964):64ff, revised version in Tomkins, *The Bride and the Bachelors* (New York 1965).

Lowell Cross

SEE ALSO Happening, Indeterminacy, United States.

Tuning and Temperament. In European musical theory, *tuning* refers to a system or scale of just intonation (tones related by simple whole numbers, as within the overtone series) first established around 600 B.C. *Temperament* refers to any adaptation that alters the acoustically correct system of just intervals by some practical but imperfect variant. (Tuning also commonly refers to what is done to bring an instrument into tune.)

The idea of a fixed scale of acoustically determined intervals appeared with the gradual recognition of the overtone series. Any scheme of tuning by just fifths will over-reach a just octave. To fit the scale within the octave, some intervals must be narrowed even though tempered tuning involves some pattern of discord. In some cultures the successive tones are obtained by a scheme of measurement not related to the overtone series. Present-day equal temperament, which divides the just octave by equally measured intervals, is a mensural scheme in an acoustic tradition, incorporating a body of theory which does not, intonationally, belong to it.

During the polyphonic period in Western music until around 1600, just intonation prevailed. To avoid discord with other voice parts, singers would adjust certain agreed-upon tones. Keyboard players, however, did not have this flexibility, and just intonation limited them to harmonization in only the one key in which their instrument was tuned. After 1600, as keyboard instruments were used with increasing frequency, composers devised a new and more flexible temperament, mean tone, based on a just major third and a narrow (and consequently discordant) fifth. Mean tone persisted until about 1800. The mean-tone pattern of mixed concordant and discordant intervals gave to each tonality a distinctive harmonic coloring by creating microtonal differences in the size of corresponding intervals in different keys. With mean tone, which allows no enharmonic tones, only eight keys are acceptable, up to and including either three sharps or three flats (the usual tuning, from C, ending either G♯ or A♭); beyond these eight keys the proportion of extremely discordant, or "wolf," tones becomes too great for acceptable harmonization. The distinctive coloration of each tonality and the strong consonance-dissonance contrasts of mean tone made modulation highly effective and favored the developing tonal-based and dramatic forms of 17th- and 18th-century music (sonata, rondo, etc.). In like manner, the system of equal temperament since 1800 has favored chromaticism and atonality.

Several composers explored variants of mean tone to extend the range of keys. One result was the so-called "well-tempered" tuning, a modified mean tone able to be played with full chords in all keys. The well-tempered system retains unequal intervals and therefore some change of color in modulation. The decisive change from mean-tone to equal temperament occurred around 1800 as the large orchestra, for which mean tone is impractical, came into prominence (other important changes included the rebuilding of violins for increased tension and the adoption of the Tourte bow). With equal temperament all intervals become equal and all tonalities equally accessible, all keys having the same interval structure. The acceptance of enharmonic and nonharmonic tones, the latter no longer so noticeably outside the tonality, enabled such composers as Chopin, Liszt, and Wagner to extend the idea of consonance to include tones previously considered dissonant. Chromatic dissonance, replacing the modulatory coloring of mean tone, reached its logical conclusion in 12-tone chromaticism. It is interesting that while theorists rationalized the systems of just intonation and mean tone within the unlike conditions of equal temperament, composers continued to move ahead: at the start of the 20th century Debussy was able to abandon traditional harmonic formulas, and Schoenberg was able to "emancipate the dissonance" by thinking in terms of a single "key" composed of all 12 tones. The fact that equally spaced tones can be thought of as equally spaced sounds "without any relation to harmonic questions" (Schoenberg) has influenced some composers to substitute for them any gamut of tones, sounds, or noises.

Some composers, notably Lou Harrison, have restored the 12-note gamut to just intonation ("tuning with the low-number ratios in predominance"). Others have adopted microtonal scales in just relationship (cf. the 43-tone compositions by Harry Partch). Some have followed John Cage in "emancipating music from its notes" with "prepared" instruments that produce unexpected pitches or sounds, with electronic systems, and with the computer as a composing instrument. Others have followed Edgard Varèse, Henry Cowell, and the Italian futurists in using extra-tonal, percussive, or noisemaking devices. Changing concepts of tuning, temperament, and of musically available sound mixtures are among the factors that have now opened the entire field of sound to musical composition.

BIBL.: J. Murray Barbour, *Tuning and Temperament* (East Lansing, Mich., 1951); Adriaan Fokker, *Just Intonation and the Combination of Harmonic Diatonic Melodic Groups* (The Hague 1949); Eivind Groven, a demonstration of Groven's organ with "Just Intonation" (a brochure accompanying Philips record No. 88.149DL); Wesley Kuhnle, *History of Tuning* (unpub. tape with examples; copies at the Univ. of Ill., Long Beach State College, Pomona College, Washington

Univ., Wesleyan Univ., Conn.); Ll. S. Lloyd and Hugh Boyle, *Intervals, Scales and Temperaments* (London 1963); Mayer J. Mandelbaum, *Multiple Division of the Octave and the Tonal Resources of 19-Tone Temperament* (Ann Arbor 1964); Harry Partch, *Genesis of a Music* (Madison, Wis., 1949); Curt Sachs, *History of Musical Instruments* (New York 1940).

Peter Yates

SEE ALSO Asian Music and Western Composition, Jazz, Microtones, Musicology and Composition, Popular Music, Theory.

Turina (y Pérez), **Joaquín** (b. Seville, 9 Dec 1882; d. Madrid, 14 Jan 1949), studied composition in Seville with E. García-Torres and piano with E. Rodriguez and attended the Madrid Conservatory (piano with José Tragó) and the Schola Cantorum in Paris (1905–13, composition with Vincent d'Indy). He was active as a pianist and conductor and directed performances of the Ballets Russes in Spain and of the Teatro Eslava Orchestra. He taught composition at the Madrid Conservatory from 1931 and directed the music section of the National Education Ministry from 1941. He also wrote criticism for the Madrid daily *El debate*.

PRINCIPAL COMPOSITIONS: *Sonata romántica* for piano, Op. 3 (1909, Eschig); *String Quartet*, Op. 4 (1911, Eschig); *3 Andalusian Dances* for piano, Op. 8 (1912, Rouart-Lerolle); *La procesión del rocío* for orchestra, Op. 9 (1912, Ricordi); *Navidad*, religious opera, Op. 19 (1916, UME); *Mujeres españoles* for piano, Op. 17 (1917, Rouart-Lerolle); *Danzas fantásticas* for orchestra, Op. 22 (1920, UME); *Sinfonia sevillana* for orchestra, Op. 23 (1920, UME); *El poema de una sanluqueña* for violin, piano, Op. 28 (1924, UME); *Jardines de Audalucia* for piano, Op. 31 (1924, Rouart-Lerolle); *La oración del torero* for string quartet (string orchestra), Op. 34 (1925, UME and Salabert); *Canto a Sevilla* for soprano, orchestra, Op. 37; text by Muñoz San Román (1927, UME); *Ritmos*, "choreographic fantasy" for orchestra, Op. 43 (1928, UME); *Violin Sonatas Nos. 1–2*, Opp. 51, 82 (1929, 1934); *3 Sonetos* for voice, piano, Op. 54; poems by Francisco Rodríguez Marín (1930); *Tarjetas postales*, 5 pieces for piano, Op. 58 (1930, Schott); *Siluetas*, 5 pieces for piano, Op. 70 (1932, Rouart-Lerolle); *Piano Trio No. 2*, Op. 76 (1933); *Piano Concerto*, Op. 88 (1935, UME); *Circulo* for piano trio, Op. 91 (1942).

PRINCIPAL WRITINGS: *Enciclopedia abreviada de la música* (Madrid 1917); *Tratado de composición musical*, vols. 1–2 (Madrid 1947, 1950).

BIBL.: Winton Dean, "J. T.," *Chesterian* (April 1949):92–98; Federico Sopeña, *J. T.* (Madrid 1956).

12-Tone Techniques. The 12-tone technique was developed gradually by Arnold Schoenberg (1874–1951) during the years after his uncompleted oratorio *Die Jakobsleiter* (composed 1915–17). It was first used by him in sections of his Op. 23 and Op. 24 and throughout his Op. 25 (all composed between July 1920 and March 1923). Schoenberg's method permits the composition of a work in which all pitches are related to a fixed ordering of the 12 chromatic tones, the order representing (in his words) a "basic shape" for the piece. The series (also called a row or set) established by the composer possesses a prime aspect designated P (or alternately O for original or S for set) which can be transposed to begin on any of the 12 pitches. The prime is only one of four guises under which the series may appear; the others are the retrograde (R), the inversion (I), and the retrograde inversion (RI). Since each of these may also be transposed, a total of 48 related pitch successions is available for each set. These series are conceived apart from any registral specification of their pitch elements and during the process of composition are capable of division into smaller units for purposes of isolating and stratifying individual lines (which in strict usage should always sum to the total chromatic collection).

While Schoenberg invented the specific guidelines of "classic" 12-tone composition, he was not the only one concerned with devising systematic means of using all 12 tones compositionally. Among others was J. M. Hauer (1883–1959), a composer of lesser stature whose work Schoenberg is reported to have known as early as 1916.[1] Hauer's 12-tone theories, which were developed independently of Schoenberg and presented in a series of theoretical writings published 1920–26, began with his discovery of a "12-tone law" in 1919 (arrived at through analysis of pitch content in his own recent compositions, as well as those of Schoenberg and Webern). Hauer considered the use of all 12 tones in a circulating fashion to be the richest resource available, and he first employed this principle in his Op. 19 *Nomos* (August 1919). Later developments in his theories include the classification of 44 different types of *tropes*, i.e., collections of the 12 tones, each divided into two 6-note units. The ordering of pitches with-

[1]Egon Wellesz, *The Origins of Schönberg's Twelve-Tone System* (Washington 1958):7–9; reprinted in *Lectures on the History and Art of Music* (New York 1968). Wellesz claims a parallel to the relation between Satie and Debussy in that Hauer's works suggested to Schoenberg a solution to his compositional problems, providing him with the principle of a 12-tone row.

in 6-note units, which were kept distinct from one another in his music, was a compositional rather than a precompositional decision. In Hauer's works, a composition does not restrict itself to a single trope, nor are there systematic bases for the choice of trope type and its transposition.

12-TONE SET OPERATIONS. Schoenberg called his procedure a "method of composing with 12 tones that are related only with one another." His principles, together with the compositional devices that he continued to explore throughout his life, actually have as a model a well-defined formal system of which the 12 tones, together with specific musical operations, can be considered an instance. A consideration of the principles of this system, rigorously formulated in the 1940s by Milton Babbitt (b. 1916), is worthwhile at this point because it will lead to a better understanding of the implications of Schoenberg's means. In discussing operations within the 12-tone system, numeric notation will be used as it allows the properties of sets to be inspected without the confusions that musical notation can cause.

The ordered succession of the 12 chromatic tones that constitute the set of a given composition or portion thereof can be represented by the integers 0–11. The number designating each element indicates the number of semitones distant that element is above the initial element, which is designated zero (e.g., 0, 2, 5, 4, 3, etc.). This set can be described more precisely by a succession of number couples in which the first number designates order position and the second number designates the pitch element in the manner already described: (0,0), (1,2), (2,5), (3,4), (4,3), etc. If zero were assigned to A in a composition, the pitch succession would be A, B, D, D♭, C, etc.

Twelve-tone procedures depend not only on the presence of a set as a precompositional proposition but on the notion of *octave equivalence*. Octave equivalence is a concept of congruence, a condition that obtains between numbers when their difference is divisible by the appropriate modulus; since there are 12 elements in the 12-tone system, the modulus here is 12. The numerals 3 and 15 or 3 and 27, which represent some pitch and *octave duplications* of it, are congruent because $15 - 3 = 12$ and $27 - 3 = 2(12)$. It follows that the numeral 3 represents not one element but a whole class of congruent elements. As an element in a set, the numeral 3 would be said to designate a *pitch class* rather than a pitch (the term *pitch* is properly reserved for a specific member of any class). The set above

thus describes a succession of pitch classes; the registral (octave) positions of elements in a compositional realization of the set are determined by other criteria.

Given a set considered prime and designating its initial element zero (these conditions represented by the symbol P_0), the various other forms of the set can be produced by simple operations. One such operation is complementation, which is the relation between two numbers such that their sum is congruent to zero for the given modulus. In a 12-element system, a and b are complements if $a + b = 0$ modulo 12. (Thus, 5 and 7 are complements, likewise 2 and 10, etc.). Complementation of pitch class number modulo 12 produces the inversion operation:

P_0: 0, 2, 5, 4, 3, etc. (A, B, D, D♭, C, etc.)

I_0: 0, 10, 7, 8, 9, etc. (A, G, E, F, F♯, etc.)

While inversion has been informally described as the *mirroring* of a set, this is a misleading analogy since the set is a succession of pitch classes, not pitches. The actual interval succession within the *I*-form consists of the complements of the *P*-form intervals. Were the interval succession of the *P* above to be represented by a series of positive numbers, the series would be 2, 3, 11, 11, etc. (i.e., $2 - 0$, $5 - 2$, $(4 + 12) - 5$, $(3 + 12) - 4$, etc.). The interval succession of the *I*-form is 10, 9, 1, 1, etc. Comparing the values of corresponding order positions in these interval series, we see that they are complements modulo 12. Such complements, as well as modulo 12 congruent intervals, can be considered members of interval classes; i.e., any interval class d can include d, $d + 12$, $d + 24$, etc., as well as $12 - d$, $24 - d$, etc. These classifications obviously differ from those of traditional theory; for example the intervals perfect 4th, 11th, etc. (which are congruent) and the complement of the 4th, the perfect 5th (along with its congruent 12th, etc.) are all members of the same interval class, 5; the same holds for major 3rd and minor 6th, major 2nd and minor 7th, etc. There are actually only six interval classes containing, respectively, 1, 2, 3, 4, 5 and 6 semitones. These classes include their respective complements 11, 10, 9, 8, and 7, and all respective congruent intervals.

The retrograde is produced when complementation is applied to the order numbers of the set. Each element of the prime is moved to the order position that is the complement of its order position in the prime set: The first element is sent to the last position, the second element to the penultimate position, etc. (the modulus for this operation is 11, since order positions 0 and 11 are exchanged, as are 1 and 10, 2 and 9, etc.).

While the I operation results in a complementation of the intervals of P, the RI operation, which is the complementation of both pitch-class numbers and order numbers, produces the retrograde of the interval succession of P (R is related to I in the manner just described for RI and P). Thus relations between set forms are concerned with more than pitch-class permutation; one must regard the affect upon intervallic properties as well. The final operation, transposition, is the addition of a constant value to all pitch-class elements of a set; while permuting pitch-class order, it does not affect interval succession.

The notation of set forms other than the P and I transpositions is not standardized. The most consistent method is one where the set-form name is given a numerical subscript designating its initial pitch-class element: P_0, R_0, I_0, and RI_0 are all sets beginning with pitch class 0. Note, however, that here I_0 and RI_0 are pitch-class complementations of P_0 and R_0, respectively, but R_0 is not the pitch-class retrograde of P_0 (since 0 occupies the initial position in each) nor is RI_0 so related to I_0. Another notation employs only the initial elements of P and I forms so that the retrograde-form symbols do not contain comparable information; in this case R_0 would denote an order number complementation of P_0, but the zero element would actually be the final element of R_0, not the first. The inconsistency of this method can be avoided by an alternative which maintains the identity of the P and I sets that are transformed by the R operation: P_0 and P_0R, I_0 and I_0R, etc., where the R denotes the retrograde operation applied to the specific P or I set.

SET USAGE: SCHOENBERG. All of the above operationally related set forms are permutations of the original set. Their usefulness in a composition depends upon the particular set involved and how the transformed sets relate to this prime. A basic relation concerns invariance, a situation where, for instance, order number or pitch number or both remain fixed under some operation. If the prime set (P_0) of Schoenberg's *Suite for Piano*, Op. 25, is inverted and transposed by six semitones (I_6), the adjacent pitch classes 3 and 9 are invariant:

P_0: 0, 1, $\boxed{3, 9,}$ 2, 11, 4, 10, 7, 8, 5, 6

I_6: 6, 5, $\boxed{3, 9,}$ 4, 7, 2, 8, 11, 10, 1, 0

These same two pitch classes, with their order

positions exchanged, remain adjacent in the P_6 and I_0 forms. The pitch-class letter names assigned to this set in Schoenberg's composition are as follows; the invariance here concerns pitch classes G and D♭ (the segmentation into units "a," "b," and "c" will be discussed later):

		┌─── a ───┐		┌─── b ───┐		
P_0:	E	F	$\boxed{\text{G}\quad\text{D}\flat}$		G♭	E♭	A♭	D
I_6:	B♭	A	$\boxed{\text{G}\quad\text{D}\flat}$		A♭	B	F♯	C
P_6:	B♭	C♭	$\boxed{\text{D}\flat\quad\text{G}}$		C	A	D	G♯
I_0:	E	E♭	$\boxed{\text{D}\flat\quad\text{G}}$		D	F	C	F♯

	┌─── c ───┐			
P_0:	B	C	A	B♭
I_6:	E♭	D	F	E
P_6:	F	F♯	D♯	E
I_0:	A	G♯	B	A♯

Other relations also exist among the 48 available set forms; however, Schoenberg used only these four forms and their retrogrades as the pitch material for this piece. The invariance described is exploited within the work, most prominently in the Musette, where G functions analogously to a tonal pedal, and its association with D♭ is explicitly projected.

The partitioning (subdivision into segments) of the set employed in Op. 25 is generally into the three four-note units (*tetrachords*) marked a, b, and c above; this type of partitioning is notated (4^3). Schoenberg often projected these tetrachords as distinct linear phenomena and also differentiated them by means of phrasing and modes of articulation. (There are many examples of such techniques in other works.) Since these set tetrachords are generally employed to realize some kind of "polyphony" of units, the presentation of the various set forms is usually successive and not simultaneous, the exceptions being the Trio to the Minuet, which is a two-part canon by inversion (in which the two lines consist of set forms related by inversion to each other), and the Prelude, which, according to existing records, appears to have been Schoenberg's first 12-tone piece. (The relatively simple techniques involved in the 12-tone sections of Opp. 23 and 24 suggest that they may have preceded the Prelude, but existing evidence does not confirm this. The Waltz, Op. 23, No. 5, cited by some as the first 12-tone piece, contains little technical sophistication, especially in comparison with the other pieces of Op. 23, some of which were composed in 1920. While not 12-tone, those pieces use techniques of transposition, inversion, retrogression, and multiple set statement characteristic of later 12-tone practice.)

As an example of consistency of set usage in projecting particular pitch relations through musical articulation, bars 22–24 of the Gavotte of Op. 25 (Ex. 1) are instructive. This

Ex. 1. Arnold Schoenberg, "Gavotte" from *Suite for Orchestra*, Op. 25: 22–24

is within the reprise of the material that opens the piece, now reduced to half the durational values of the opening. Each set within the succession P_0, I_6, P_6, I_0 is projected similarly. Corresponding tetrachords are associated with distinct means of articulation as follows: The first tetrachords (*a*) are themselves partitioned with the invariant G-D♭ adjacencies forming an "ostinato," the initial elements of which are staccato eighth-note values. The second tetrachords (*b*) are projected with one exception as dyads (two-note groups) sforzando; these tetrachords contain the other tritone adjacencies of the set forms, which are invariant between P_0 and P_6 (D-A♭) and I_0 and I_6 (F♯-C). The third tetrachords (*c*) are uniquely stated in 16th-note values, phrased by dyads. Of special note is the exchange of order of some dyads within tetrachords and the reordering within dyads for specifically musical reasons, a not uncommon device of Schoenberg at this point in a piece, pointing to the flexibility with which he regarded set order.

More sophisticated devices also appear in the Prelude of this *Suite*, but in an isolated fashion that affects local detail and does not contribute to long-range structure. One of these devices appears in bars 17–19, where the pitch-class elements of corresponding order numbers of P_0 and I_6 are stated as simultaneities (the invariant G-D♭ elements are telescoped and presented as a single dyad). Schoenberg's preoccupation with the intervals formed by this association of sets may have prompted his less rigorous adherence to order within the sets at this point; this illustrates the kind of interaction that can occur between a

set and its projection in a composition. The final two bars (Ex. 2) of the Prelude are more

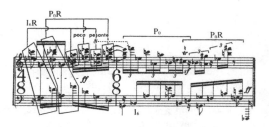

Ex. 2. Arnold Schoenberg, "Prelude" from *Suite for Orchestra*, Op. 25: 23–24

complexly disposed; here the simultaneously unfolding sets are interwoven, and three-note simultaneities and successions are drawn in most instances from the association of elements having corresponding order positions within the three tetrachords of each set. Deviations occur because of the isolation of pitch class G (which is associated with D♭, presaging its more obvious structural role in the Musette). The accompanying legend shows the tetrachordal disposition. The interpenetration of the two inversionally related set forms in bar 23 manifests itself as a pattern within which the corresponding units mirror each other. The more complicated bar 24 contains an interesting detail: the sforzando C♯-D trill not only projects the important C♯ but isolates the intersecting elements of P_0 and P_0R. Procedures in the rest of the work are more clearly devoted to projecting linear properties of the sets themselves and less concerned with permutational devices such as that just described. All of these means, however, illustrate the range of Schoenberg's search for ways by which the surface of a composition could reflect the properties of a set and its structural role in the piece.

Concurrent with Schoenberg's codification of 12-tone techniques appeared a formalization at the surface level of his compositions. Most obvious from the titles of the dance forms and their sectionalization within the *Suite*, Op. 25, this appropriation of tonal forms was continued in such works as the *Wind Quintet*, Op. 26 (whose first movement is a "Sonata Allegro"), and certain subsequent works. It is no accident that the arrival of Schoenberg's 12-tone thinking and his return to composing large-scale instrumental works coincided, for it was his discovery and innovations that enabled him to return to larger structures with renewed confidence. His use of structures dependent upon concepts from the tonal tradition has been criticized, but it must be emphasized that Schoenberg always conceived his music thematically, and that behind his apparent iconoclasm was a deep-rooted sense of being part of a classical continuity. What is important is that concomitant with this commitment to the preservation of a tradition, Schoenberg was able to use his 12-tone method in ways that operate at different levels of continuity and association and that point to the capacity of its devices to operate as autonomous principles.

A most important development was Schoenberg's discovery of the property of some sets in which the combined operations of inversion and transposition upon the first hexachord (the first six pitch classes) could produce a new hexachord whose pitch content was exclusive of the original (i.e., the combined pitch content of both hexachords would contain all 12 pitch classes). Specifically he described the condition where the inversion a fifth below of the first six tones of certain sets produces the other six tones of the chromatic scale (he did not, however, restrict himself to such sets). The general condition of which this is a specific instance is called *combinatoriality*, a property dependent upon the segmental pitch-class content but completely independent of the ordering of elements within those segments.

A comprehension of this concept is dependent on an understanding of the notion of *secondary set*, the principles of which were used by Schoenberg as one criterion governing set succession (the choices of what sets follow one another within a piece). An inspection of the pitch structure of the Theme from his *Variations* for orchestra, Op. 31 (1928), reveals the following succession of set forms: P_0, I_9R, P_0R, I_9. The prime and the inversion transposed nine semitones are ordered as follows:

$$\overbrace{\qquad Ha \qquad}\qquad \overbrace{\qquad Hb \qquad}$$

P_0: B♭ E F♯ E♭ F A D C♯ G G♯ B C
I_9: G C♯ B D C A♭ E♭ E B♭ A F♯ F

The hexachordal content is such that not only do the hexachordal pairs within each form sum to all 12 pitch classes but this same property obtains between the second hexachord (*Hb*) of P_0 and the first hexachord (*Ha*) of I_9R (and thus correspondingly between the remaining hexachords, as well as between those same hexachords of P_0R and I_9). The particular succession of set forms in the theme places these hexachords in adjacent positions, thereby creating secondary sets in addition to the

named forms. Collections of all 12 pitches within the theme are formed as indicated by the brackets:

$$\overbrace{P_0}\quad \overbrace{I_9R}\quad \overbrace{P_0R}\quad \overbrace{I_9}$$
$$Ha \quad Hb \quad Ha \quad Hb \quad Ha \quad Hb \quad Ha \quad Hb$$
$$\underbrace{\qquad\qquad \text{secondary sets} \qquad\qquad}$$

Secondary sets, then, are new orderings of the 12 pitch classes formed not by the operations of transposition, inversion, or retrogression but by the linear juxtaposition of sets within a composition in such a way that adjacent hexachords are mutually exclusive in content.

The set for the *Variations* possesses the property of *inversional hexachordal combinatoriality*, i.e., there is at least one inversional form of the set (here I_9) whose *Ha* content is exclusive of the *Ha* content of the prime and is therefore capable of forming a secondary set. This may be expressed as follows: $Ha + T_tIHa = A$, where the transposition T, at semitone level t from a designated zero, of the inversion of the given hexachord, when combined with the given hexachord, produces the aggregate A, a collection of all the elements of the system (here numbering 12) whose order is not defined.

This particular kind of I combinatoriality was the only type Schoenberg used in determining set succession. Other kinds of hexachordal combinatoriality exist, however. The simplest instance would be the relation between P_0 and P_0R, which exists for all sets. In addition there are RI combinatorial sets and also certain sets that possess both I- and RI-combinatorial properties (as well as P-combinatorial possibilities); these sets are *all combinatorial*. Since these properties are independent of order within the hexachords, the sets can be classified in terms of hexachordal content only. There are, for instance, only six such hexachords within the all-combinatorial category. It should be mentioned that combinatoriality is not limited to the pairing of hexachords as in Schoenberg's works but is also possible among three sets tetrachordally, four sets trichordally, etc., up to the instance of 12 set forms where each sum of corresponding order-number elements produces the aggregate (an example of the latter is contained in Babbitt's *Composition for 12 Instruments*, described below).

Returning to Schoenberg's *Variations*, the disposition of the chordal accompaniment to the theme reveals that the combinatorial relation between set pairs is also being used to unfold sets simultaneously. In this instance the fact that simultaneously occurring hexachords are mutually exclusive helps to stratify theme and accompaniment:

theme: P_0 I_9R P_0R I_9
accompaniment: I_9 P_0R I_9R P_0

The particular criterion used by Schoenberg in determining the density of the accompaniment is interesting: The number of pitches in each chord is in a $1:1$ correspondence with the partitioning of the theme sets into melodic phrases; for the opening of the theme, P_0 is partitioned into $5 + 4 + 3$ notes, a segmentation reflected in the accompaniment to those phrases.

The *Variations* is encyclopedic in its techniques, reflecting Schoenberg's increasing preoccupation with discovering means within his method and its materials that would suggest particular solutions to compositional problems. For example, within the time span in which a single statement of P_0 unfolds in the "thematic" line of variation 1, there are five statements of a complex of sets in the accompaniment; these sets are coupled in such a manner (P_0 with P_3, for instance) that the invariant intervals produced in their simultaneous unfolding reflect the particular transpositional relation at which the set of the piece is combinatorial (the "minor third" or, by complementation, the "major sixth"). Even the opening of the work (the Introduction) exposes a sonority (the "diminished seventh" chord) among whose pitch constituents are those dyads that remain invariant at the combinatorial transposition level: Bb-E and G-C♯ (see the P_0 and I_9 set forms as spelled out above).

The exploitation of inversionally combinatorial sets that appears in Schoenberg's *Klavierstück*, Op. 33a (1928), is notable for its use of particular characteristics of the set to impart specific identities to large formal components. The opening of the work, for example, exposes the harmonic properties of the set tetrachords, which remain even when the combinatorial sets are juxtaposed. The fact that the three opening set elements are related by distances of seven semitones allows the projection of the simultaneous sets to emphasize this as a group of "open fifths" harmonically, used by Schoenberg to delineate sections cadentially (bars 23–24 and, correspondingly, bar 34).

An example of stratification other than by hexachord occurs in the *Begleitungsmusik*, Op. 34 (1930). The phrasing of the oboe line (Ex. 3) is by hexachord, but the pacing of set elements

Ex. 3. Arnold Schoenberg, *Begleitungsmusik*, Op. 34, oboe part: 9–12

Quoted by permission of Heinrichshofen's Verlag

is by trichord. Labeling these trichords *a*, *b*, *c*, and *d*, their disposition is:

oboe: *a*   *b*   *c*   *d*

accompaniment: $\begin{cases} d & a & b & c \\ c & d & d & a \\ b & c & a & b \end{cases}$

For each oboe unit the accompaniment completes the aggregate, so that the aggregate pacing is also one per bar. The accompanimental trichords are each distinguished by their rhythmic and timbral projection (and partially by register as well). However, this situation is not a combinatorial one since not all the accompanimental lines form aggregates. A somewhat similar accompanimental situation occurs at the opening of the *String Quartet No. 4* (1936), where, in addition, the succession of trichords follows a specific rule of permutation. (This work, along with the later concertos for violin and piano, involves 12-tone concepts projected over a large time span, combined with certain procedures that attempt to forge analogies with the tonal practice in which the overall forms themselves had evolved.)

In some of Schoenberg's late works there is a relaxation from the strict concept of an ordered series toward a consideration of the specific pitch and intervallic possibilities of set segments whose internal order may vary in the course of the composition. Examples are the *Ode to Napoleon*, Op. 41 (1942), containing octave doublings, which Schoenberg had previously avoided, as well as specific triadic tonal references, and the *String Trio*, Op. 45 (1946). At the same time, such works exhibit types of formal organization that could stem only from the properties of the particular sets with regard to their potential for contributing structurally to formal differentiations.

SET USAGE: BERG AND WEBERN. As composers adopt 12-tone means, whether partially or wholly, to suit their own needs, a problem arises with "licenses," which, as Babbitt points out, "make it impossible to infer what stable properties the composer associates with the principles of the system."[2] It is thus impossible

[2]*Journal of the American Musicological Society* 3:266–67.

to speak of a "12-tone style" or "serial style," etc., not only because the system developed without having consistent and homogeneous stylistic traits associated with it, but because such limitations are in no way implied by it. An inspection of the 12-tone works of Schoenberg's foremost students, Alban Berg (1885–1935) and Anton Webern (1883–1945), reveals that not only do their works differ stylistically from those of their teacher but that they also differ in the specific uses made of 12-tone techniques and in the techniques themselves.

Much has been written of the tonal associations projected by some of Berg's compositions, particularly the *Violin Concerto*, an intention apparent from the structure of the set itself. His uses of 12-tone techniques display other idiosyncracies of his style, particularly his concern for thematic contour as something that can be imposed compositionally upon the set itself. Coexistent with this thematic association is Berg's reluctance to use retrograde operations unless whole sections of composed music are reversed, as in *Lulu* (1929–35) or in the third movement of the *Lyric Suite* (1925–26). This device, of course, is not unique to 12-tone music, for it had been used centuries earlier and appears even in Berg's pre-12-tone *Chamber Concerto* (1923–25).

More significant compositionally is Berg's attitude toward set order: Hexachords are often reordered to project different compositional ideas. At the opening of the first movement of the *Lyric Suite*, for example, the hexachords of the set (the thematic appearance of which is shown in Ex. 4) are ordered in

Ex. 4. Alban Berg, *Lyric Suite*, I: 2–4
Quoted by permission of Universal Edition and Theodore Presser

such a way as to project the "cycle of fifths" which they contain. Later in this movement the hexachordal elements are ordered as a series of whole and half steps, and their appearance in the music is within "scalar" passages. One such instance occurs in Ex. 5 (the overlapping lines are omitted in the ex.). Two other devices, previously described, are also present in Ex. 5: the "fifth" in the cello and the contour relation between that part of the first violin line (bars 36–37) which is projected as a thematic reference to bars 3–4 while retaining the "scalar" ordering within the hexachord.

Ex. 5. Alban Berg, *Lyric Suite*, I: 34–37
Quoted by permission of Universal Edition and Theodore Presser

The set of the *Lyric Suite* is an *all interval* set: the elements are ordered and fixed in register so that among the intervals between adjacent pitches each of the 11 possible intervals within the octave occurs precisely once. Not only are its hexachords symmetrically related (*Hb* is the retrograde of *Ha* transposed six semitones), it is also combinatorial, a property Berg did not exploit. Whereas Schoenberg would have used combinatoriality as a criterion for set succession, Berg does not, preferring generally to let terminal elements determine transpositional choice, as with the common B♮ between P_0 and I_6 at the end of Ex. 4. His criterion for simultaneously unfolding sets is more often a harmonic one; within this movement one encounters, for instance, juxtapositions of P_0, P_3, P_6, and P_9 (0, 3, 6, and 9 are the boundary elements of the P_0 hexachords) which project a series of "diminished seventh" chords (bars 15–16).

The more intricate procedures employed in *Lulu* are designed to project characterizations of and relations between individuals in the plot and to refer to particular events. The presence of several sets in this work is not a unique feature; the last movement of the earlier *Lyric Suite* incorporates two distinct sets, and the movements themselves are not all 12 tone.

With Webern's 12-tone works one is confronted with still other points of view, both technical and esthetic. Soon after his first essays with serial means (the songs of Op. 17, 1924), Webern produced a series of works remarkable for their rigor, clarity, economy, and self-generating form. Beginning with the *Symphony*, Op. 21 (1928), these works demonstrate a new attitude towards harmonic and polyphonic means within self-contained structures whose premises relate directly to the properties of their sets. While often outwardly reflecting traditional sectionalization ("sonata" movements or "song" forms, for instance), these works generally reject notions of musical growth and instead expose their inner relations within singularly original temporal concepts.

The *Symphony* has often been used to illustrate Webern's predeliction for imitation and symmetry: there are canons in both movements, and the symmetric nature of each variation within the second movement and of the movement as a whole reflects the hexachordal symmetry of the set. This work also illustrates his choices of transposition levels based on segmental invariance and the projection of those segments at the compositional foreground. In addition, the *Symphony* employs Webern's typical criterion of set succession: the closing element or elements of one set form is (are) duplicated by the beginning of the next set form, so that in the composition these sets overlap, with the pitches in question serving a "double function" in that they belong to two different sets. The presence of an invariant registral distribution of pitches is a striking characteristic of Webern's music and is responsible for the various degrees of harmonic staticity that occur in the three sections of the opening movement of the *Symphony*. (Expectedly, this distribution is at times symmetrically disposed with its center on A in the first section. A is the first element of the prime set.) While registral invariance is not unique to 12-tone music, its use by Webern is especially important to his style and its later influence.

Webern's preference for a limited intervallic vocabulary, noticeable in his pre-12-tone works as well, is reflected by many of his sets, which can be described as "derived sets" because they can be generated from some set segment by applying the operations of transposition, inversion, and retrogression to that segment. The set of the *Concerto for 9 Instruments*, Op. 24 (1934), for example, can be derived from the initial three-note segment. Considering the first segment prime (*P*), the four trichords stand in the relation:

P	*RI*	*R*	*I*
B Bb D	Eb G F#	G# E F	C C# A

The segmental similarity of derived sets necessarily limits their intervallic properties. While derived sets were occasionally used by Schoenberg and Berg, they are particularly pertinent to Webern. Not only do they suggest a harmonic consistency, they also possess properties of segmental invariance under the appropriate operations, a property important to Webern for projecting resemblances. They also suggest by their internal properties procedures for larger structuring.

At the opening of the *Concerto* the projection of each trichord is timbrally and rhythmically distinct, a procedure that anticipates the structuring of rhythm in later music by means analogous to pitch procedures. Rhythmic structure paralleling set segmentation is particularly evident in Webern's orchestral *Variations*, Op. 30 (1940). This is a piece, as Webern wrote in 1941, "whose twelve notes, that's to say the row, contain its entire content in embryo!"[3] In all these works the distinction between linear and harmonic planes is often practically obliterated. Webern's texture always clearly and consistently projects the intervallic properties of his material, and it is this characteristic, operating in a time continuum independent of any traditional sense of progression, that asserts the autonomy of the set.

SET USAGE: SOME LATER COMPOSERS. Perhaps the most significant among the "second-generation" composers to adopt 12-tone techniques is Ernst Krenek (b. 1900); his opera *Karl V* (1930–33) was the first of his works to use them. Later works incorporated methods of generating new sets within a work by a process of permutation that was dependent on a notion of hierarchy within set segments as notated within a single octave. The internal hierarchy was based on relative distances of pitches above the specified zero. The new sets were then composed successively from the "lowest" elements within the segments followed by the next "highest" group, etc. (Such a process is also evident in Berg's *Lulu*.) In his choral work *Lamentatio Jeremiae Prophetae* (1940–41) Krenek introduced a process of rotation within hexachords, which is essentially one of generating new hexachordal orderings by the addition of numerical constants to order numbers (modulo 6). Krenek later applied rotational methods to segments smaller than hexachords in such a manner that successive applications of the operation upon newly formed adjacencies ultimately reproduce the original ordering. This results in a "closed circuit" whose properties suggest certain large-scale formal devices.

Another European, Luigi Dallapiccola (b. 1904), developed a style that relies heavily on intricate canonic procedures with mensural relationships reminiscent of early renaissance

[3]Anton Webern, *Path to the New Music* ed. by W. Reich, trans. by Leo Black (Bryn Mawr 1963):62.

practice. While in one sense these procedures are an extension of Webern's use of canon, these works possess an individual harmonic vocabulary foreign to Webern's esthetic.

In the U.S., Babbitt and George Perle (b. 1915) have proposed various solutions to particular compositional problems. Perle developed a harmonic procedure that attempts to provide a rationale for harmonic structure other than the mere de-linearization of the set. First described by him in *Music Review* in 1941 and refined and employed intermittently in his works since then, Perle's theory depends on an "axis-tone" technique that recognizes the availability of certain modes of pitch progression from any given axis-tone, each of which can furnish consistently derived harmonic material.

The most far-reaching developments are contained in Babbitt's theoretical formulations and compositional applications. Beginning with the *3 Compositions for Piano* (1947) and the *Composition for 4 Instruments* (1947–48), Babbitt has explored and extended the principle of Schoenbergian combinatoriality and has employed the technique of derivation (producing derived sets similar to those used by Webern) as part of the form-generating process. In these works the techniques used to control pitch elements are also applied to the time domain in an attempt to relate the two dimensions. Dynamics and registral placement sometimes help stratify (or correlate) independent lines (sets) or create significant subsets within a set. The various means of differentiation, including timbre, are all systematically coordinated in projecting the pitch structure. In the *Composition for 12 Instruments* (1948), the technique of multiple set-unfolding is carried to the limits of combinatorial possibility: each of the 12 simultaneously unfolding instrumental parts contains a different set form, and combinatoriality obtains at several levels, including (1^{12}) where each group of correspondingly ordered elements within the 12 sets is aggregate forming. The work is further characterized by the presence of two simultaneously unfolding pitch canons, drawn from the 12 instrumental sets, the "voices" of which comprise derived sets. The continuity of these canonic "voices" is intended to be projected by the dynamics marked in the score. Finally, the work employs a different 12-element set (itself hexachordally combinatorial) that governs the distances between points of pitch attack.

In Babbitt's *Partitions* for piano (1957, Ex. 6a) four sets unfold simultaneously within non-intersecting registral areas, each encompassing

Ex. 6a. Milton Babbitt, *Partitions*: 9–12
Quoted by permission of Lawson-Gould

the octave A-G♯ in such a way that the union of corresponding trichords is aggregate forming. After the initial sets are presented, however, the remaining sets are exclusively derived sets generated from three-note subsets of the prime hexachord, whose content is 0, 2, 3, 4, 5, 7; the generators are 0, 1, 3; 0, 1, 4; 0, 1, 5; and 0, 2, 5. With the exception of 0, 1, 4 these trichords can themselves generate the prime hexachord content (i.e., for each trichord but 0, 1, 4, the hexachord can be partitioned into two operationally related trichords; for example, the 0, 2, 3 + 4, 5, 7 partitioning produces 0, 1, 3 types, the first an inversion, the second a prime). This feature is often reflected in the manner in which these derived sets unfold hexachordally, and the hexachords of the registrally "higher" and "lower" pairs of these sets can then form aggregates as well.

Ex. 6b illustrates a second device involving the registrally paired derived sets. Here the hexachordal content of the prime is produced by corresponding trichords, and adjacent hexachords form aggregates as indicated. (Within

Derived Sets:

025 generator

025 generator

013 generator

013 generator

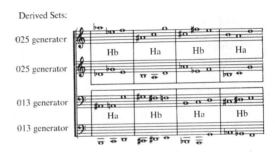

Ex. 6b.

each pair of sets, the ordering within the hexachords of the lower set can be seen to correspond to the ordering of the upper set hexachords with the same content.)

As the complexity of Ex. 6a indicates, Babbitt's synthesis and extension of the techniques of Schoenberg and Webern have produced works that make great and unusual demands on performers. His concern for controlling time has resulted in a theory of "time-points" as a means of governing rhythm by establishing analogies with the pitch domain. Compositionally, this concern has led him to the electronic medium by way of the RCA Synthesizer, which permits a control over musical dimensions beyond the capabilities of human performers. Electronic compositions such as *Ensembles* continue his investigation into methods of 12-tone organization. Although superficially similar, the extensions of serial controls to nonpitch elements that occurred in Europe in the 1950s are of an essentially different nature. Stemming initially from the innovations of Olivier Messiaen's *Modes de valeurs et d'intensités* for piano (1949), this movement does not display the consistency of interacting systematic relationships that characterizes corresponding developments in the U.S.

That the principles of 12-tone technique demand no specific commitments to a given musical style is amply evident in the work of Igor Stravinsky (1882–1971). Such pieces as *In Memoriam Dylan Thomas* of 1954 (which uses only a five-note set) and *Threni* of 1957–58 display the personal marks of their composer as surely as do his earlier works. In addition, the techniques they exhibit reflect Stravinsky's personal use of the available 12-tone resources.

SUMMARY. The origins of 12-tone music can be found in the music and theoretical speculations of those composers who attempted early in this century to establish procedures for musical organization whose foundations departed radically from those of tonal music as it had developed in the 19th century. Those procedures involved not only the dismissal of the traditional tonal hierarchies but encompassed a reassessment of how tones and intervallic properties might be made to function independently of tonal contexts. From this arose new concepts of what constitute precompositional materials, how they might function within a composition, and how decisions involving this material affect the structure and unfolding of a composition. Basic to this development is the concept of a limited pitch collection (or collections) with particular interval characteristics capable of generating both the melodic and the harmonic material of a piece. Such cells are found in works of late Scriabin and post-tonal Schoenberg, in the former functioning primarily harmonically with specific transposition levels as points of progression, in the latter more motivically. That these cells might be expanded to include all 12 tones upon which an ordering is imposed wherein each tone occurs but once and that the properties of this series might have implications for the building of musical forms as well as suggesting local musical connections were notions that arose as the concept of a 12-tone music evolved.

While characteristics of the 12-tone system suggest many powerful compositional devices, the extent to which any ostensibly 12-tone composition uses these resources is determined by each composer himself. This discussion has described a variety of possible compositional devices all drawn from the basic resources of the 12-tone system. It must be emphasized that this can provide only a skeletal basis for an understanding of how relationships might operate in a piece, for a composition exists as an interaction of many musical components. Indeed the means of coherence and continuity may be unique to a given work.

BIBL.: Milton Babbitt, "Some Aspects of Twelve-Tone Composition," *The Score and I.M.A. Magazine* (June 1955): 53–61; ——, "Set Structure as a Compositional Determinant," *Journal of Music Theory* 5: 72–94; René Leibowitz, *Schoenberg and His School* trans. by Dika Newlin (New York 1949); ——, *Introduction à la musique de douze sons* (Paris 1949); Ernst Krenek, "Extents and Limits of Serial Techniques," *Musical Quarterly* 46: 210–32; ——, "New Developments of the Twelve-Tone Technique," *Music Review* 4: 81–97; George Perle, *Serial Composition and Atonality*, 3rd ed. (Berkeley-Los Angeles 1971); Josef Rufer, *Composition with Twelve Notes*, trans. by Humphrey Searle (London 1954); Arnold Schoenberg, *Style and Idea* (London 1951); Walter Szmolyan, *Josef Matthias Hauer* (Vienna 1965).

Brian Fennelly

SEE ALSO Asian Music and Western Composition, Form, Melody, Notation, Serialism, Texture, Theory.

Uhl, Alfred (b. Vienna, 5 June 1909), graduated from the Vienna State Music Academy in 1932 (composition with Franz Schmidt). He has taught composition at the Vienna Academy since 1945.

PRINCIPAL COMPOSITIONS (published by Doblinger unless otherwise noted): *Kleines Konzert* for viola, clarinet, piano (1937); *48 Etudes* for clarinet (1938 Schott); *Divertimento* for 3 clarinets, bass clarinet (1942, Schott); *Symphonic March* for orchestra (1942, Schott); *Concertante sinfonie* for clarinet, orchestra (1943, UE); *Eine vergnügliche Musik* for 8 winds (1944, UE); *4 Capriccios* for orchestra (1944–45, UE); *String Quartet No. 1* (1945–46); *Introduction and Variations on a 16th-Century Melody* for string orchestra (1947, UE); *Gilgamesch*, oratorio for soloists, chorus, orchestra (1954–56, revised 1968–69); *Wer einsam ist der hat es gut*, cantata for soloists, chorus, orchestra (1960); *Jubiläumsquartett* for strings (1961); *Der mysteriöse Herr X*, opera (1962–65); *Concerto a ballo* for orchestra (1967); *Festlicher Auftakt* for chorus, organ, orchestra (1970).

BIBL.: Alexander Witeschnik, *A.U.* (Vienna 1966).

United States. As in the 19th century, most U.S. music until about 1920 imitated current European models. John K. Paine (1839–1906), strongly influenced by his training in Germany and the first professor of music at Harvard Univ., was the teacher of several prominent composers; among them Arthur W. Foote (1853–1937), Edward Burlingame *Hill (1872–1960), and Daniel Gregory Mason (1873–1953). They were all New Englanders who shared a devotion to the classic and romantic ideals. "Our whole view of music," wrote Mason "was based on the style of classic and romantic symphonists, beginning with Haydn and Mozart and ending with Mendelssohn and Schumann."[1] By 1900 Brahms and Wagner were also acceptable models. The New England group also included George W. Chadwick (1854–1931) and Horatio W. Parker (1863–1919), the latter a professor of music at Yale Univ. from 1895 until his death and the

former a teacher and later director at the New England Conservatory.

Although the dominant influence was that of Germany, French influence began to be felt even before the turn of the century. Homer Norris's *Practical Harmony on a French Basis* (Boston 1896) was a straw in the wind. Parker was attracted to César Franck, Mason went to Paris to study with Vincent d'Indy, and Hill developed a lifelong enthusiasm for French music, which he imparted to his students at Harvard from 1908 on. A more direct influence was that of Charles Martin Loeffler (1861–1935), an Alsatian musician who lived in the Boston area from 1881 on and composed impressionist works. Outside Boston, French influence was absorbed by the Chicagoan John Alden Carpenter (1876–1951); by the westerner Arthur Shepherd (1880–1958), who looked to Fauré and d'Indy for models; and by the New Yorker Charles T. *Griffes (1884–1920), who was drawn to Debussy as well as to Scriabin and Far Eastern music (the influence of Scriabin is especially evident in the *Piano Sonata*, 1918–19, which combines a condensed classic structure with exotic scale patterns, frequent chromatic inflections, and an extension of tonality that was bold for its time).

Some composers began to reach further. The adventurous instincts of Henry F. B. Gilbert (1868–1928), a New Englander who studied with Edward MacDowell in Boston, led him to absorb, as he said, "musical nutriment from many sources," especially "the folk tunes of the world, of all nationalities, races, and peoples."[2] He thus anticipated the ecumenical spirit that inspired such later composers as Henry *Cowell and Alan *Hovhaness. Gilbert drew on South American, American Indian, Celtic, and Negro sources: *Americanesque* (on minstrel tunes, 1903), *Comedy Overture* (on Negro themes, 1905), *The Dance in the Place Congo* (1906; arranged as a ballet, 1918), *American Dances in Ragtime Rhythm* (1915). Gilbert was the most eclectic

[1] Mason, *Music in My Time* (New York 1938):14.

[2] As quoted in Arthur Farwell, *Music in America* (New York 1915):408.

American composer in a period of rampant eclecticism. Mason summed it up when he said, "We are not only parrots, but polyglot parrots."

AMERICAN NATIONALISM. American Indian music had attracted American composers at least since 1870, and from about 1890 to 1920 it was a prominent phase of the "Americanist movement." The movement received strong impetus from Antonín Dvořák's sojourn in the U.S. (1892–95), during which he declared that Negro and Indian melodies offered "all that is needed for a great and noble school of music." Arthur Farwell (1872–1952) took his cue from Dvořák's challenge "to go after our folk music." Others who followed his example included Gilbert; Arthur Shepherd, who wrote a symphony on cowboy tunes, *Horizons* (1927); Charles Sanford Skilton (1868–1941), who used Indian tribal music; and John Powell (1882–1963), a Virginian attracted to Anglo-American folk music and to Negro life as sentimentalized by landed Southern whites (*Negro Rhapsody* for piano and orchestra, 1918; *Sonata Virginianesque* for violin and piano, 1919).

Musical Americanism acquired a different expression with Charles *Ives (1874–1954), a New Englander who studied with Parker at Yale but who remained aloof from both the Boston academics and the folklorists. He wrote a great deal of music dealing with American scenes, quoting American tunes, or alluding to traits of the American musical vernacular. He was not being a militant Americanist when he quoted well-known tunes, however. He regarded these tunes as part of the very substance of his musical thought. He used them not only for evocative or illustrative purposes but because they could be reworked and recombined in purely musical ways (he often chose a pair of tunes because they would work well together). Ives was the first composer to achieve a *substantially* independent and *essentially* American musical expression in the larger forms. With almost no one being aware of it at the time, he fulfilled Farwell's dream of "new and daring expressions of our own composers, sound-speech previously unheard." Ives was isolated from the mainstream of U.S. music, and his major works were unknown to the public (and to most musicians) until long after they were composed. His most productive period was 1895–1915, whereas his larger works began to be publicly performed (at wide intervals) only in 1930.

The important generation of American composers born around 1900 included Roy *Harris (b. 1898), Aaron *Copland (b. 1900), Virgil

*Thomson (b. 1896), Walter *Piston (b. 1894), Roger *Sessions (b. 1896), and George *Gershwin (1898–1937). Several of these composers added impetus to the Americanist movement, although they often gave the impression that they were actually initiating it. For instance, when Copland stated that around 1925 he "was anxious to write a work that would immediately be recognized as American in character,"[3] he was repeating what Farwell and Gilbert had said before him. During the 1920s the most prominent Americanism was jazz, which Copland and many others embraced. Copland's *Music for the Theatre* (1925) featured blues harmonies and jazz-dance rhythms. The *Piano Concerto* (1926), in two movements, exploited the contrast between the slow blues and "the snappy number." Copland limited the expressive possibilities of jazz to these two moods and stated that what interested him was not so much the spirit of jazz as its technical devices for enhancing rhythm, melody, harmony, and timbre.[4] Even the more academic composers such as Piston and Randall Thompson (b. 1899) made discreet allusions to jazz during the 1920s and 30s. Among those who used it more aggressively were George *Antheil (1900–59; *Jazz Symphonietta* for 22 instruments, 1926) and Louis *Gruenberg (1884–1964; *The Daniel Jazz* for voice and 8 instruments, 1924, and *Jazz Suite* for orchestra, 1925). Gershwin was a special case. His blend of tuneful themes and 1920s jazz with traditional, even hackneyed, elements of 19th-century romanticism helped to make him the first American composer to achieve both instant success and lasting popularity in the larger forms. His uniqueness also arises from the fact that he belonged basically to the world of popular music. The academically trained composer might dip into this world occasionally; only for Gershwin was it his own element.

Jazz and other vernacular elements have nourished a long line of stage works. During the Depression musical theater tended to take on "social significance" with a Leftist trend, a development for which the vernacular proved well suited. Gershwin pointed the way with two musicals, *Strike Up the Band* (1927, 1930) and *Let 'Em Eat Cake* (1933). Kurt *Weill (1900–50) followed this vein with *Johnny Johnson* (1936), an antiwar satire. The development is epitomized in the satirical opera, *The Cradle Will Rock* (1936) by Marc *Blitzstein (1905–64), which deals with corruption and

[3]Copland, *The New Music, 1900–1960* (New York 1968):158.
[4]*Ibid.*: 63.

hypocrisy in a labor union drive. In *Regina* (1948–49) Blitzstein combined the theme of moral corruption with an exploitation of vernacular elements, such as the use of a jazz band on stage, a Negro spiritual, a revival hymn, and a blues.

Copland eventually moved from jazz to the stylization of American folk and popular music, as in his dance scores *Billy the Kid* (1938), *Rodeo* (1942), and *Appalachian Spring* (1944). The first of these established some of the hallmarks of Copland's Americana: evocation of the open prairie with open fifths and widely spaced woodwinds, polyrhythmic and polyharmonic manipulation of cowboy tunes, sectional designs in rondo form, and expressive adaptation of familiar tunes ("The Dying Cowboy"). His *Lincoln Portrait* (1942) made use of the last device by drawing on the 18th-century ballad "On Springfield Mountain" and on Stephen Foster's "Camptown Races."

Among operatic composers of the older generation, none was more persistent or more successful than Douglas *Moore (1893–1969) in projecting Americana. His *The Ballad of Baby Doe* (1956) is one of the most widely performed American operas, the conventional harmonic idiom of which makes it acceptable to a wider public than is usually reached by contemporary opera. Thomson's *The Mother of Us All* (1947) is overt Americana in that it deals with the feminist leader Susan B. Anthony and is infused with the spirit of the American musical vernacular, although no specific tunes are quoted. As Thomson wrote, the music "is an evocation of 19th-century America, with its gospel hymns and cocky marches, its sentimental ballads, waltzes, darnfool ditties and intoned sermons. . . . It is a souvenir of all those sounds and kinds of tunes that were once the music of rural America and that are still the basic idiom of our country because they are the oldest vernacular still remembered here and used."[5] Thomson's *Four Saints in Three Acts* (1927–28) is American simply because it is inconceivable in terms of any other operatic tradition. Its recurrent tonic-dominants and frequent scale passages give it a down-to-earth quality even in the most mystical and symbolic passages, such as "Pigeons on the Grass, Alas!", which is a *locus classicus* of the American musical theater. Thomson's film scores, *The Plow that Broke the Plains* (1936), *The River* (1937), and *Louisiana Story* (1948) are also notable examples of musical Americana.

The symphony became a vehicle for musical Americana beginning with the *Symphony No. 2* (1897–1902) and *Orchestral Set No. 3*, "The Camp Meeting" (1904–11) of Ives and culminating in some of the symphonies of Harris, particularly *No. 4* (1939), which has five choral sections all based on American folk tunes; *No. 6* (1944) which is based on Lincoln's Gettysburg Address and dedicated to "the armed forces of Our Nation"; and *No. 9* (1951), inspired by the preamble to the Constitution and the poetry of Walt Whitman. Henry *Cowell (1897–1965) drew consistently on the American popular hymn-tune tradition, most conspicuously in the series called *Hymns and Fuguing Tunes* (1942–64). They were written for a variety of media from piano solo to large orchestra, and several were incorporated in his symphonies.

The Americanist movement reached its apogee around 1940. Harris, who has been much occupied both metaphysically and in terms of rhythm and harmony with the question of what is American in music, has argued that Americans have rhythmic impulses that are different from those of Europeans. Ours, he feels, is "less symmetrical" and more concerned with the smallest units of rhythm than with "its largest common denominator." He traces an alleged avoidance of definite cadence to "our national aversion to anything final."[6] In both his writings and in his music, he sums up one phase of the Americanist attitude.

THE ROMANTIC TRADITION. Romanticism is the musical outlook that has had the longest continuous history in the U.S. It began in the mid-19th century with William Henry Fry, reached its apogee with MacDowell, Paine, and Chadwick, and continues on a declining curve to the present time. Two different aspects of romanticism are represented by Thomson on the one hand and Howard *Hanson (b. 1896) and Samuel *Barber (b. 1910) on the other. Thomson championed what he called "the new romanticism," or "neo-romanticism," an esthetic of French origin (c.1930) seeking "spontaneity of sentiment," an international temper, elegance, together with "an infusion of warm personal feeling."[7] Hanson's five symphonies aimed at being "lyrical and romantic in temperament, and simple and direct in expression."[8] Neither Hanson nor Barber, however, could truthfully

[5]Thomson, "How 'The Mother of Us All' Was Created," *New York Times* (15 April 1956).

[6]As quoted in Henry Cowell, ed., *American Composers on American Music* (New York 1933):154.
[7]Virgil Thomson, *Virgil Thomson* (New York 1966):158.
[8]As quoted in Bagar and Biancolli, *The Concert Companion* (New York 1947):319.

echo the words of Thomson, "We are not out to impress, and we dislike inflated emotions."[9] When Thomson looked back, it was to Satie; when Hanson looked back, it was to Sibelius. After Hanson and Barber the most outspoken romanticist in the 1960s was Leon *Kirchner (b. 1919). He has urged the artist to "create a personal cosmos . . . in continuity with tradition . . . bringing new subtilization, vision and beauty to the elements of experience."[10] A pupil of Bloch, Schoenberg, and Sessions, Kirchner has blended a traditional harmonic framework with elements of chromaticism, Bartók-like rhythm, and rhapsodic expressionism.

Composers who may be regarded as neo-Schoenbergian romantics, believers in the Great Tradition with a 12-tone supplement, are Ben *Weber (b. 1916), George *Rochberg (b. 1918), and Ralph *Shapey (b. 1921). Their music tends to be expressionistic whether they use 12-tone, atonal, or tonally oriented procedures. Shapey has tried to reconcile the influences of Schoenberg and Varèse (music as "a pattern of processes in Time through which the inherent potentialities of sound proceed to be fully realized"[11]) in such works as Incantations for soprano and ten instruments (1961) in which the voice is used instrumentally. Even the early symphonic poems of Edgard *Varèse (1883–1965), particularly Amériques (1918?–21) and Offrandes (1921?–22), are as romantic in their own way as the music of Berlioz or Mahler. The composer's remarks about Déserts (1949–54) are instructive: "'Déserts' means to me not only the physical deserts of sand, sea, mountain, and snow, of outer space, of empty city streets . . . but also that remote inner space no telescope can reach, where man is alone in a world of mystery and essential loneliness."[12]

NEOCLASSICISM. Largely under the influence of Stravinsky and Hindemith, neoclassicism was an important trend from about 1925 to 1950. Based on the practice of American composers, the movement included the use of baroque forms and procedures (canon, fugue, passacaglia, chorale, etc.), as well as of classic structures. The strongholds of the movement were at Harvard, where Piston taught (1926–59), and at Yale, where Hindemith taught 1940–53). Its principal overseas outpost was the advanced composition class of Nadia Boulanger in Paris, where Copland, Thomson,

Harris, and Piston (of the older generation) studied, in addition to such younger men as Arthur *Berger (b. 1912), Irving *Fine (1914–62), John *Lessard, Paul Des *Marais, and Harold *Shapero (all b. 1920). The latter group were among those designated around 1950 as a "Stravinsky school" in the U.S. Many other composers went through a Stravinskian neoclassic phase in the 1940s, including Louise *Talma (b. 1906), Ingolf *Dahl (1912–70), and Andrew *Imbrie (b. 1921).

Of the older generation Piston has been the most consistently neoclassical. His Three Pieces for clarinet, flute, and bassoon (1926) stems from Stravinsky, but as he matured he developed an individuality marked by dissonant sharpness (especially in earlier works, such as the Symphony No. 1, 1937, which uses 12-tone procedures), an emphasis on counterpoint (especially fugal writing), diatonic and chromatic contrasts, asymmetrical rhythms, and polytonal writing. Sessions, like Thomson, Harris, and Copland, was only briefly attracted to neoclassicism, for example in his Symphony No. 1 (1927). Thomson's best neoclassical diversion was his Sonata da chiesa (1926). Harris emphasized baroque procedures, an inclination that was expanded by his pupil William *Schuman (b. 1910), particularly in the Symphony No. 3 (1940–41) whose four movements are Passacaglia, Fugue, Chorale, and Toccata. Many of the Stravinskians turned to 12-tone writings in the 1950s (as did Stravinsky himself) but without abandoning their allegiance to traditional forms and structural principles. Examples are Berger's Chamber Music for 13 Players (1956), Fine's String Quartet (1952), Dahl's Piano Quartet (1957), and Imbrie's Violin Concerto (1951–54).

Elliott *Carter (b. 1908) stands independently of all schools, but he does share the concern of neoclassicists and serialists for purely musical relationships and processes. A pupil of Piston and Boulanger, he attracted moderate attention with such early Ivesian works as the Symphony No. 1 (1942) and Holiday Overture (1944). During the 1940s he began to develop original compositional procedures, notably the device of "metric modulation," involving "the coordination of all the tempi of the work and their interrelation by notated changes of speed." The principle of "structurized tempi" was applied in String Quartets Nos. 1–2 (1951, 1958–59). In the second "the four instruments are individualized, each being given its own character embodied in a special set of melodic and harmonic intervals and rhythms that result in different

[9]Thomson, loc. cit.
[10]As quoted in Chase, America's Music (New York 1966):570.
[11]Ibid.:681.
[12]Ibid.:600.

patterns of slow and fast tempi with associated types of expression."[13] In the *Double Concerto* for harpsichord and piano with two chamber orchestras (1961) the solo instruments and their corresponding ensembles are treated antiphonally, their respective identities resulting from different repertories of melodic and harmonic intervals and different metronomic speeds. The whole is a "confrontation of diversified action-patterns and a presentation of their mutual interrelations."[14]

DODECAPHONY AND SERIALISM. Twelve-tone procedures were a major stylistic factor during the 1950s. The first American composer to study with Schoenberg in Berlin (1924–27) was Adolph *Weiss (1891–1971), who began to use the method with his *Chamber Symphony* (1927). Schoenberg's presence in the U.S. from 1933 until his death in 1951 (he taught composition at the Univ. of Calif. at Los Angeles, 1936–44) added impetus to the movement, as did the presence of Ernst *Krenek (b. 1900) and Stefan *Wolpe (1902–72).

Wallingford *Riegger (1885–1961) came to 12-tone writing gradually, after experimenting with various types of rows in his *Dichotomy* for orchestra (1931–32). In his *String Quartet No. 1* (1938–39) he applied the method according to the strictest Schoenbergian canon, each of the four movements presenting one of the basic forms of the row. His *Symphony No. 3* (1946–47) and later works used tone rows more freely. Although Ross Lee *Finney (b. 1906) studied briefly with Alban Berg during 1931–32, he did not turn to 12-tone writing until his *String Quartet No. 6* (1950). By then Finney had concluded that the method "is not actually in opposition to tonal functionalism but is a technique concerned with chromatic integration." George *Perle (b. 1915), author of *Serial Composition and Atonality* (Berkeley 1962), developed a "12-tone modal system" as a means to "rationalize harmonic events."[15] He first applied the system in such works as the *String Quartets Nos. 3–4* (1947, 1948). In other works he has used a free, atonal harmonic idiom. Roger Sessions came to 12-tone writing late in his career through an evolutionary process that can be observed in his symphonies: from the diatonic neoclassicism of the first (1927), through the high dissonant content of the second (1944–46), to the 12-tone organization of the third and fourth (1957, 1958). Sessions regards the method simply as

"a technical principle that a wide number and variety of composers have found useful for their own purposes."[16] Along with Piston and Copland he has been one of the most influential teachers of composition in America.

Milton *Babbitt (b. 1916), whose profession until the mid-1940s was mainly mathematics, has aimed at the "tonal structuralization" of a composition by applying "the pitch operations of the 12-tone system to nonpitch elements: durational rhythm, dynamics, phrase rhythm, timbre, and register."[17] This method, sometimes called total serialism, was applied first in Babbitt's *3 Compositions for Piano* (1947) and *Composition for 4 Instruments* (1947–48). He has set forth his views in a number of important theoretical articles that have influenced the thinking of what might be called the academic wing of the avant-garde, including such younger composers as Harvey *Sollberger and Charles *Wuorinen (both b. 1938). After 1960 Babbitt became increasingly involved with composition with electronic apparatus and with the highly complex serializations the medium permits. A director of the Columbia-Princeton Electronic Music Center, he has used its electronic synthesizer in such works as *Ensembles for Synthesizer* (1961–63) and *Philomel* (1964) for soprano, recorded soprano, and synthesized accompaniment. Describing the kind of musical composition he cultivates, Babbitt wrote in 1958, "This music employs a tonal vocabulary which is more 'efficient' than that of the music of the past or its derivatives. . . . Along with this increase of meaningful pitch materials, the number of functions associated with each component of the musical event also has been multiplied. In the simplest possible terms, each such 'atomic' event is located in a five-dimensional musical space, determined by pitch-class, register, dynamic, duration, and timbre. These five components not only together define the single event, but in the course of a work, the successive values of each component create an individually coherent structure, frequently in parallel with the corresponding structures created by each of the other components."[18]

THE RADICAL INNOVATORS. Revolutionary innovation in American music began with Charles Ives. Although he worked within the

[13]Carter, liner notes for recording of the *String Quartet No. 2*, quoted in Chase, *op. cit.*: 568.

[14]Carter, liner notes for recording of the *Double Concerto*, quoted in Chase, *loc. cit.*

[15]As quoted in Chase, *op. cit.*: 614.

[16]Sessions, "Problems and Issues Facing the Composer Today," *Musical Quarterly* 46:2; reprinted in Chase, *The American Composer Speaks* (Baton Rouge 1966): 278.

[17]Babbitt, liner notes for recording of *Composition for 4 Instruments* (CRI).

[18]Babbitt, in *High Fidelity Magazine* (2 Feb 1958): 39.

traditional genres (symphony, sonata, overture), he used sounds in a radically original manner, particularly through the use of polyrhythms and polytonalities, the concept of "spatial" music, use of tone-clusters, and the simultaneous occurrence of different musical events. By contrast composers such as Copland and Carter have made their innovations without undermining traditional values and techniques. The temporal continuity of the principal innovators is evident from their birthdates: Ives (1874), Cowell (1897), Henry *Partch (1901), and John *Cage (1912). Cowell introduced the systematic use of tone-clusters (aggregates of major and minor seconds), which he first employed publicly in *The Tides of Manaunaun* for piano (1912), and the direct manipulation of the piano strings with the fingers or with objects. Both devices appear in piano pieces of 1912–30. From about 1915 Cowell began to use tone-clusters orchestrally. He saw them as "a system of harmony based on the interval of a second instead of a third," for which his *New Musical Resources* (completed 1919, published 1930) offered theoretical justification. "His early works for piano," wrote Cage, "by their tone clusters and use of the piano strings, pointed towards noise and a continuum of timbre. Other works of his are indeterminate in ways analogous to those currently in use by Boulez and Stockhausen. For example Cowell's *Mosaic Quartet* [No. 3, 1934], where the performers, in any way they choose, produce a continuity from compositional blocks provided by him. These actions by Cowell are very close to current experimental compositions which have parts but no scores, and which are therefore not objects but processes providing experience not burdened by psychological intentions on the part of the composer."[19]

Cage was, of course, referring to some of his own conceptional innovations. "Indeterminate" compositional processes involve chance operations (tossing a coin, etc.), which Cage first applied to the tempos in *Music of Changes* for piano (1951). Here "at each small structural division . . . chance operations determined stability or change of tempo"; hence "it was not possible to know the total time-length of the piece until . . . the last toss of coins affecting the rate of tempo . . . ."[20] In *Music for Piano* (1953–56), "structure is no longer part of the compositional means."[21] This led to the

concept of "composition as process," an "essentially purposeless" activity outside the personal volition or "psychological intentions" of the composer. Chance operations became a means for enabling composers "to remove themselves from the activities of the sounds they make."[22] By the same token, an "experiment" to Cage is "an act of which the outcome is unknown," and its purpose is to free the "continuity" of a composition from "individual taste and memory (psychology)," as well as from "the literature and 'traditions' of the art."[23] Cage's influence in the U.S. was perhaps strongest during the 1950s when Earle *Brown, Morton *Feldman (both b. 1926), Christian *Wolff (b. 1934), and others gathered around him in New York.

Partch sought to break away from "the frame of an inherited keyboard and from inherited forms and instruments of Europe's 18th century"[24] by inventing his own theoretical system, a battery of instruments, and a notation. His ideas are set forth in *Genesis of a Music* (Madison, Wis., 1949; written about 20 years earlier). His music is "based on a monophonic system of acoustic intervals and an expandable source scale of more than 40 tones to the so-called octave."[25] One of his instruments, a reed organ called a chromelodeon (1945), uses a scale of 43 tones to the octave.

New kinds of musical theater emerged during the 1960s. In some cases the theatrical experience was an extension of the performance routine. Partch's instruments, for instance, are interesting as sculpture, and in "total theater" works, such as *Delusion of the Fury* (1963–66), the players are placed on stage, where they become part of the setting and action. Similarly Christopher Tree (b. 1932) has collected several dozen Eastern and Oriental gongs, bells, wind instruments, and the like, which he spreads out over the stage and improvises on. A more elaborate theater genre is multimedia, the synthesis of aural, visual, verbal, kinetic, plastic, electronic, and other elements, often within an aleatoric structure. This approach was pursued by the ONCE Group, an informal association of composers, performers, filmmakers, theatrical designers, architects, and other artists founded in 1960 at Ann Arbor, Mich. The composers included Robert *Ashley (b. 1930), Gordon

[19]Cage, "History of Experimental Music in the United States," *Silence* (Middletown, Conn., 1961):71.
[20]Cage, "Composition as Process," *ibid.*:20.
[21]*Ibid.*:22.

[22]Cage, "Experimental Music: Doctrine," *ibid.*:13.
[23]Cage, "Composition," *ibid.*:59.
[24]Partch, *Genesis of a Music* (Madison 1949):Preface.
[25]Partch, as quoted by Arthur Woodbury in *Source:Music of the Avant Garde* 1/2:92.

*Mumma (b. 1935), and Roger *Reynolds (b. 1934), whose setting of Wallace Stevens's poem, *The Emperor of Ice Cream* (1962), combines choreography, costumes, lighting, speech, music, and an elaborate time-space coordination of all movements by the performers. At the Univ. of Calif. at Davis, Larry *Austin (b. 1930) has composed multimedia works such as *The Maze* for three percussionists, dancer, tapes, machines, and projections (1965). During the 1960s Eric *Salzman (b. 1933) became a leading exponent of the new music theater and of multimedia. His works include *Verses and Cantos* (1963–67, texts by John Ashbery), a theater piece for voices, pop and non-pop groups, and electronics; and *The Nude Paper Sermon* for actor, renaissance consort, chorus in the audience and on stage, spatial amplification, and tape-and-electronic four-channel playback (1968–69, texts by Stephen Wade and John Ashbery).

Many facets of new musical theater involve electronic technology, which has become increasingly prevalent in all types of composition and performance since the 1950s. The first step was the use of magnetic tape as a compositional medium, a field in which Cage pioneered along with Otto *Luening (b. 1900) and Vladimir *Ussachevsky (b. 1911). Cage produced his first tape piece in January 1952 in collaboration with David *Tudor (b. 1926), *Imaginary Landscape No. 5*. This was followed later that year by *Williams Mix*, assembled from approximately 600 recordings of sounds. In both pieces the composing process involved chance operations utilizing the Chinese *I Ching*. Luening's first tape compositions (three pieces for flute on tape) date from the same year, as did the first concert of tape music by Luening and Ussachevsky, which took place in November at the Museum of Modern Art in New York. The combination of tape and live music became widespread during the 1960s. Varèse in *Déserts* alternated taped electronic sounds with live music played by conventional instruments. Wuorinen has combined media in such works as *Orchestral and Electronic Exchanges* (1965), "surrounding each section of the tape part with orchestral commentaries and variations"[26]; he has used structural procedures of Stravinsky and Varèse, as well as serial procedures derived from the 12-pitch-class system (especially as formulated by Babbitt). In *And on the Seventh Day Petals Fell in Petaluma* (1963–64, revised 1966), Partch used over-dubbing with magnetic tape

during performance to create complex instrumental combinations from the basic material of 23 one-minute duets and trios. Terry *Riley (b. 1935) and others have used tape loops to produce several-second delayed playbacks during their performances, which create canonlike effects. The capacities of conventional instruments have been extended through the use of contact microphones and loudspeakers to distribute sound throughout the concert environment. The former technique was used by Cage in *Atlas eclipticalis* (1961–62), the latter by Varèse in his *Poème électronique* (1957–58). One among many applications of these techniques is Austin's extension of the prepared piano, an instrument originally conceived by Cage in 1938. Cage inserted bolts, nuts, screws, wood, rubber, and other materials between certain strings to produce "a gamut of sounds moving from lower to high octaves without the correspondence of pitch characteristics of scales and modes."[27] Austin used contact microphones, guitar pickups, and phonograph cartridges to transmit the vibrations of objects lying on the strings to loudspeakers around the hall (e.g., *Accidents* for electronically prepared piano, ring modulator, mirrors, actions, black light, and projections, 1967).

By the late 1960s electronic equipment had become an easily accessible tool for composers. Electronic studios were in operation all over the U.S., mostly in universities, and equipment was being produced within the price range of private buyers. Lejaren A. *Hiller, Jr. (b. 1924), together with Leonard M. Isaacson, experimented with computer programs for producing music in the 1950s and composed the *Illiac Suite for String Quartet* (1957). In 1963 Hiller collaborated with Robert Baker on the *Computer Cantata*, which used music by Ives and Boulez as "models" or controls.[28] Other composers have used computers to produce synthetic sounds too complex in their makeup to be assembled by hand. James *Tenney (b. 1934) has used computer-generated sounds in several pieces, including *Ergodos II* (1964). The piece illustrates some of the technical syntheses being devised by younger composers: there is a "string complement" to be used by any number of strings in live performance with the taped sounds. "Each player responds to the sounds on the tape by producing sounds in opposition to

[26]Wuorinen, program notes of the New York Philharmonic Society (30 July 1965).

[27]Cage, program notes for 25-Year Retrospective Concert (New York, Town Hall, 15 May 1958).
[28]Hiller, *Music Composed with Computers—An Historical Survey* (Univ. of Ill., Experimental Music Studio, Technical Report No. 18):16.

these, by first locating a point in the space that is symmetrically disposed to the point that would represent the average or *clang* (a small group of sounds) according to the verbal and other indications found in the region of the point located."[29] These "verbal and other [graphic] indications" are found in an accompanying quadrisectional rectangular chart bisected by axes of pitch (high–low) and duration (short–long). "Thus, if the sounds on the tape are high and long (in the upper right quadrant), the instrumental sounds should be low and short (in the lower left quadrant), etc." *Ergodos II* is an example of the deployment of pitch and duration as the two "primary dimensions," vertical and horizontal, of a musical "space." The use of new space-time concepts and the graphic means to translate them into performing instructions or indications have revolutionized notation and scoring.

Although the musical avant-garde is flourishing in the U.S., it is only a very small part of the country's musical life. The most significant factor in musical composition in the U.S. today is its pluralism: neoromanticism, neoclassicism, nationalism, orientalism, ecumenical exoticism, dodecaphony, serialism, indeterminacy, minimalism, multimedia, rock, and the rapidly developing spectrum of electronic techniques.

BIBL.: John Cage, *Silence* (Middletown, Conn., 1961); Gilbert Chase, *America's Music* (New York 1966); ——, ed., *The American Composer Speaks* (Baton Rouge 1966); Aaron Copland, *The New Music, 1900–1960* (New York 1968); Henry Cowell, ed., *American Composers on American Music*, new ed. (New York 1962); —— and Sidney Cowell, *Charles Ives and His Music* (New York 1955); Lejaran A. Hiller and Leonard M. Isaacson, *Experimental Music: Composition with an Electronic Computer* (New York 1959); H. Wiley Hitchcock, *Music in the United States* (Englewood Cliffs, N.J., 1969); Wilfrid Mellers, *Music in a New-Found Land* (New York 1965); Harry Partch, *Genesis of a Music* (Madison, Wisc., 1949); Eric Salzman, "The New American Music," *The New American Arts* ed. by R. Kostelanetz (New York 1965): 237–70; Elliot Schwartz and Barney Childs, eds., *Contemporary Composers on Contemporary Music*, part 2 (New York 1967); *Source: Music of the Avant Garde* ed. by Larry Austin (Davis, Calif., 1967–); Virgil Thomson, *American Music Since 1910* (New York 1971); Peter Yates, *Twentieth Century Music*, part 2 (New York 1967).

Gilbert Chase

SEE ALSO Asian Music and Western Composition; Dance; Education for the Nonprofessional; Education for the Professional; Electronic Music: History and Development; Folk Resources; Jazz; Liturgical Music: Christian; Liturgical Music: Jewish; Mixed Media; Musical; Musicology and Composition; Opera; Orchestration; Performance; Popular Music; Publishing; Recording; Theory.

Ussachevsky, Vladimir (b. of Russian parents, Hailar, Manchuria, 21 Oct 1911), arrived in the U.S. in 1930 and studied general subjects at Pomona College in Calif. and music at the Eastman School (1935–39; composition with Bernard Rogers, Howard Hanson) and Columbia Univ. (1947–48, composition with Otto Luening). He has taught in the music dept., Columbia Univ., since 1947 and has been a codirector of the Columbia-Princeton Electronic Music Center since 1959. During 1970–71 he was composer-in-residence at the Univ. of Utah. He has lectured in the U.S., Europe, the U.S.S.R., and Latin America. His music before 1951 was neoromantic with a Russian flavor, clearly dependent on a tonal underpinning but with sudden shifts between diatonic and highly dissonant, occasionally polychordal, passages. Early influences included Russian Orthodox church music, Rachmaninov, and Stravinsky. In 1951 he began experimenting with composition via tape recorders. Since then both his instrumental and tape pieces have shared a preoccupation with highly varied timbres and a tight structural organization. The tape pieces, however, have evolved a generally more complex rhythmic style. In these Ussachevsky tends to select only a few sound sources and to subject these sounds to various electronic transformations (many of which he developed himself) to produce highly fragmented, rhythmically complex sound patterns. *Piece for Tape Recorder*, for example, is based primarily on an extensive timbre transformation of gong, cymbal, and piano sounds, altered through tape-speed and multiple-recording variation techniques. There is a "timbral thematicism" in this process in that all sound patterns have a common timbral origin. In 1968 he extended his work to the field of computer music.

PRINCIPAL COMPOSITIONS: *Jubilee Cantata* for narrator, baritone, chorus, orchestra (1938); *Sonic Contours* on tape (1952, recorded by Desto and Folkways); *Piece for Tape Recorder* (1956, recorded by CRI); *Linear Contrasts* on tape (1957); *Creation-Prologue* for 4 choruses, electronic sounds; Akkadian and Latin texts (1960–61); *No Exit*, tape score for the film by George Tabori of Sartre's play (1962); *Of Wood and Brass* on tape (1964–65); *Line of Apogee*, tape score for the film by Lloyd Williams (1967); *An Incredible Voyage*, tape score for the CBS television documentary (1968); *2 Images of a Computer Piece*, film score

[29]Tenney, *Computer Music Experience* (1961–64, unpublished report).

based on *Computer Piece No. 1* (1969); *We,* computer-synthesized tape score for the CBC radio production (1971). List to 1960: *Composers of the Americas* 9:157–60.

PRINCIPAL WRITINGS: "Sound Materials in the Experimental Media of Musique Concrète, Tape Music and Electronic Music," *Journal of the Acoustical Society of America* 29:768ff.; "The Processes of Experimental Music," *Journal of the Audio Engineering Society* 6/3:202ff.; "Music in the Tape Medium," *Juilliard Review* (spring 1959): 8ff.; "Columbia-Princeton Electronic Music Center," *Revue belge de musicologie* 13; "Notes on 'A Piece for Tape Recorder'," *Musical Quarterly* 46:202ff., and *Problems of Modern Music* ed. by P. H. Lang (New York 1962):64ff.; "Synthetic Means," *The Modern Composer and His World* ed. by J. Beckwith and U. Kasemets (Toronto 1961): 121ff.; "Electronic Music," *Tape Recording* (Dec 1966).

SEE ALSO Electronic Music: History and Development; Recording; United States.

Ustvol'skaia, Galina (Ivanovna) (b. Leningrad, 17 July 1919), studied at the Leningrad Conservatory (1940–50, composition with Maximilian Shtenberg and Dmitri Shostakovich). Since then she has taught film music at the Rimsky-Korsakov School of the Leningrad Conservatory.

PRINCIPAL COMPOSITIONS (available from Mezhkniga): *Piano Concerto* (1946); *San Stenkana Razina* [The Dream of Stenka Razin], legend for bass, orchestra (1948); *Piano Sonatas Nos. 1–3* (1948, 1950, 1952); *3 Suites* for orchestra (1950, 1952, 1958); *Trio* for clarinet, violin, piano (1949); *Octet* for 2 oboes, 4 violins, piano, timpani (1951); *Violin Sonata* (1952); *20 Preludes* for piano (1953); *Symphony No. 1* for 2 boy sopranos, orchestra (1955); *Grand Duo* for cello, piano (1959); *Duo* for violin, piano (1964); *Symphony No. 2* for voice, winds, percussion, piano (1967); *Composition* for flute/piccolo, tuba, piano (1970); *Composition* for piano, double bass (1971).

V

Valcárcel, Edgar (b. Puno, Peru, 4 Dec 1932), studied at the National Conservatory in Lima (1949–58, composition with Andrés Sas, piano with Inés Pauta), at the Catholic Univ. of Lima (1954–58), the Torcuato Di Tella Institute in Buenos Aires (1963–64; composition with Ginastera, Messiaen, R. Malipiero, Maderna, Dallapiccola, and José Vicente Azuar), Hunter College in New York (1961–62, composition with Donald Lybbert), and at the Laboratory of Electronic Music at Columbia Univ. (1966, 1968; electronic composition with Vladimir Ussachevsky, Alcides Lanza). He has taught at Hunter College (1966–68) and at the National Conservatory in Lima (1959, 1967–70). During 1969–70 he was assistant director of La Casa de la Cultura of Peru, and in 1967 and 1969 he was a music reviewer for *La prensa* in Lima.

PRINCIPAL COMPOSITIONS: *Variaciones* for piano (1963, Southern); *Espectros I* for flute, viola, piano (1964); *Canto coral a Tupac Amaru I* for soprano, baritone, chorus, orchestra (1965); *Dicotomías I–II* for piano (1966); *Dicotomías III* for chamber ensemble of brass, strings (1966, PAU and Peer); *Aleaciones* for orchestra (1966); *Invención*, electronic sounds on tape (1966); *Fisiones* for chamber ensemble of winds, strings (1967); *Hiwaña Uru*, "In memoriam Andrés Sas," for winds, strings, piano (1967); *Piano Concerto* (1968); *Canto coral a Tupac Amaru II* for chorus, electronic sounds on tape (1968); *Antaras* for flute, electronic sounds on tape (1968); *Checan I* for flute, oboe, clarinet, bassoon, horn, piano (1969); *Checan II* for orchestra (1970).

PRINCIPAL WRITINGS: "Una opera de Ginastera," *El comercio* (Lima, August 1964):9; "Estado actual de la composición musical en el Perú," *Cultura y pueblo* (Lima) 1965/7–8:44–45; "El 'Coordonome' y los problemas del multitempo," *El comercio* (4 Sept 1966):21; "Entrevista a Luis Herrera de la Fuente," *Cultura y pueblo* 1967/11–12:28–29; "Bomarzo," *El comercio* (28 April 1968):30–31.

BIBL.: Otto Mayer-Serra, "Conciertos," *Audiomúsica* (Mexico City) 187:17; Carman Moore, "Music:Columbia Composers," *The Village Voice* (New York, 3 Nov 1966):23; ———, "Music:Steiner-V.," *The Village Voice* (16 Feb 1967):17; Ernesto More, "E. V., reportaje con radar," *La crónica* (Lima, 18 May 1958):6.

Valdés, Miguel Francisco Letelier, see under Letelier-Valdés

Valen, Fartein (b. Stavanger, Norway, 25 August 1887; d. Valevaag, 14 Dec 1952), lived in Madagascar as a child. He studied philosophy and languages at Oslo Univ. (1906–09) and music at the Oslo Conservatory (1906–09) and the Berlin Hochschule für Musik (1909–13, composition with Max Bruch, piano with Hirschberg). During 1927–39 he was music librarian for Oslo Univ. Beginning in 1935 he received an annual stipend from the Norwegian government. He was greatly impressed by Schoenberg's *Quartet No. 2*, which he heard during his stay in Berlin. He spent 1913–23 in seclusion at Valevaag, where he studied Palestrina and Bach. The impact of 20th-century ideas and older polyphony were integrated in the *Piano Trio* (1924), his first atonal work.

PRINCIPAL COMPOSITIONS (published by Lyche unless otherwise noted): *Piano Sonata*, Op. 2 (1912, Norsk); *Piano Trio*, Op. 5 (1924, Norsk); *String Quartets Nos. 1–2*, Opp. 10, 13 (1929, Hansen-W; 1931, Norsk); *Pastorale* for orchestra, Op. 11 (1930, Norsk); *Sonette di Michelangelo* for orchestra, Op. 17, No. 1 (1932, Norsk); *Nenia* for orchestra, Op. 18, No. 1 (1932); *Cantico di ringraziamento* for orchestra, Op. 17, No. 2 (1933); *An die Hoffnung* for orchestra, Op. 18, No. 2 (1933); *Kirkegaarden ved havet* [Le Cimetière marin] for orchestra, Op. 20 (1934); *La isla de las calmas* for orchestra, Op. 21 (1934); *Variations* for piano, Op. 23 (1936); *Prelude and Fugue* for organ, Op. 33 (1939); *Pastoral* for organ, Op. 34 (1939); *Symphonies Nos. 1–5* (1939, unpub.; 1944; 1946; 1949, unpub.; No. 5, unfinished); *Violin Concerto*, Op. 37 (1940); *Piano Sonata No. 2*, Op. 38 (1941); *Serenade* for wind quintet, Op. 42 (1947); *Piano Concerto*, Op. 44 (1951).

BIBL.: Olav Gurvin, *F. V. En banebryter i nyere norsk musikk* [F. V., a Pioneer in Norwegian Music] (Oslo 1962); Bjarne Kortsen, *F. V., Life and Music* (Oslo 1965).

[prepared with the help of Kjell Skyllstad of the Valen Society]

SEE ALSO Scandinavia.

Valls, Manuel (b. Barcelona, 21 July 1920), studied at the Conservatorio del Liceo (1939–45, composition with P. Donostia) and the Univ. of Barcelona (1939–45). He describes his style as "free atonalism" in which the influence of Bartók, Roussel, and Stravinsky can be heard.

PRINCIPAL COMPOSITIONS: *Theme and Variations*, in memoriam Béla Bartók, for oboe, bassoon, string quartet (1946); *Piano Sonata* (1947); *Canciones del Alto Duero* for soprano, piano; text by Antonio Machado (1950, Clivis); *Trio* for flute, cello, piano (1951); *Cançons de la roda del tempo* for soprano, flute, oboe, clarinet, violin, cello, guitar; text by Salvador Espriu (1954); *Inventions* for violin, piano, or for chamber orchestra (1957); *Estudios concertantes* for piano, orchestra (1958); *Canciones sefardies* for soprano, flute, guitar (1962); *Movimientos* for orchestra (1964); *Guitar Concerto* (1965); *Les veus del carrer* for narrator, flute, clarinet, oboe; text by Espriu (1967); *Els preceptes* for soprano, flute, clarinet, bassoon (1967); *C A L 33 33 o El bon samaritá*, cabaret opera (1968); *Ciclo de fantasias* for guitar (1970); Valls has also written many additional songs.

PRINCIPAL WRITINGS: *La música catalana contemporania* (Barcelona 1960); *La música española despues de Manuel de Falla* (Madrid 1962); *Historia de la música catalana* (Barcelona 1970). He has also written 5 other books about Catalan music, a pocket music dictionary, and translations from French and English.

SEE ALSO Spain.

Vancea, Zeno (b. Vasiova, Rumania, 8 Oct 1900), studied at the Cluj Conservatory (1919–21; harmony with Gheorghe Dima, Augustin Bena) and the New Vienna Conservatory (1921–26, composition with Ernst Kanitz). He has taught harmony, counterpoint, and music history at the Conservatory of Targu Mures (1926–40), for which he was director during 1945–48; the Conservatory of Timisoara (1940–45); and the Bucharest Conservatory (1949–68). During 1948–50 he was director of music and education for the Ministry of Arts. He was editor of the journal *Muzica* during 1953–64. In his music he has worked toward a synthesis of Rumanian folk music and "pan-European" music (including the polyphony of neoclassicism and melodic formations derived by means of 12-tone techniques).

PRINCIPAL COMPOSITIONS: *Toccata* for piano (1926, Muzicală); *2 Psalms* for vocal soloists, chorus, orchestra (1927, 1930); *Priculiciul*, ballet; scenario by the composer (1932); *String Quartets Nos. 1–5* (1934, 1953, 1957, 1965, 1970); *Requiem* for vocal soloists, chorus, orchestra (1942); *2 Sinfoniettas* (1949, ES; 1960); *Symphonic Triptych* (1958, Muzicală); *Concerto for String Orchestra* (1961, Muzicală).

PRINCIPAL WRITINGS: "Locul şi rolui lui George Enescu in muzica romaneasca" [The Place and Role of George Enescu in Rumanian Music], *Muzica* 1955/5; "Grundlagen der rumänischen Kunstmusik," *Bericht über den Internationalen Musikwissenschaftlichen Kongress, Vienna 1956* (Cologne 1958); "Tradiţie şi inovaţie" [Tradition and Innovation], *Muzica* 1958/2; *Creaţia muzicală romaneasca din secolul XIX–XX* [Rumanian Music in the 19th and 20th Centuries] (Bucharest 1968).

BIBL.: Gheorghe Firca, " 'Concertul pentru orchestra' de Z. V.," *Muzica* 1962/8.

Van Vactor, David (b. Plymouth, Ind., 8 May 1906), studied premedical subjects and music at Northwestern Univ. (1924–28) and music at the Vienna Academy (1928–29, flute with Josef Niedermayr), the Paris Conservatory (1931, flute with Marcel Moyse), and the Ecole Normale (1931, composition with Paul Dukas). He also studied flute and conducting in the Chicago Symphony's training orchestra. During 1931–43 he was a flutist with the Chicago Symphony and from then until 1946, flutist and assistant conductor with the Kansas City Philharmonic. Since 1947 he has been conductor of the Knoxville Symphony and professor of music at the Univ. of Tenn.

PRINCIPAL COMPOSITIONS: *Gefunden* for voice, piano (1927); *Du bist wie eine Blume* for voice, piano (1927); *Due bist mein* for voice, piano (1927); *How Can I Sing Light Souled and Fancy Free* for voice, piano (1928, New Music); *Requiescat* for voice, piano (1928, New Music); *3 Rimas* for voice, piano (1928, New Music); *I Know a Maiden Fair* (1932, New Music); *Flute Quintet* (1932, Schirmer-G); *Suite* for 2 flutes (1934); *Nachtlied* for soprano, strings (1935); *Concerto grosso* for 3 flutes, harp, orchestra (1935, Fleischer); *Symphony in D* (1937, Fleischer); *5 Bagatelles* for strings (1938, Fleischer); *String Quartet in C* (1940); *Viola Concerto* (1940, Fleischer); *Overture to a Comedy No. 2* (1941, Fleischer and AME); *Variazioni solenne* for orchestra (1941, Fleischer); *Credo* for chorus, orchestra (1941, Fleischer); *Music for the Marines* for orchestra (1943, Fleischer); *Recitative and Salterello* for orchestra (1946); *Introduction and Presto* for string orchestra (1947, AME); *Cantata* for 3 treble voices, orchestra (1947); *Pastoral and Dance* for flute, strings (1947, Fleischer); *String Quartet No. 2* (1949); *Violin Concerto* (1950, Fleischer); *Prelude and March* for orchestra (1950, AME); *8 Choruses*, text from A. E. Housman's *Shropshire Lad* (1953, 4 choruses published by Galaxy); *The New Light*, Christmas cantata (1954, AME); *Fantasia, Chaconne, and Allegro* for orchestra (1957, Fleischer and AME); *Symphony No. 2 in C* (1958, AME); *Suite* for woodwind quintet (1959); *Christmas Songs for Young People* for chorus, orchestra (1961); *Brass Octet* (1963); *Suite on Chilean Folk Tunes*, ballet; choreography by Irma Witt (1963); *Passacaglia, Chorale, and*

Scamper for band (1964, S-B); *Sinfonia breve* (1964); *Economy Band No. 1* for trumpet, trombone, percussion (1966); *4 Etudes* for winds, percussion (1968); *Walden* for chorus, orchestra; text by Thoreau (1969). List to 1969: *Composers of the Americas* 9:163–71.

PRINCIPAL WRITINGS: "To Keep Going," *New York Times* (23 August 1953); *Every Child May Hear* (Knoxville 1960).

Varèse, Edgard (b. Paris, 22 Dec 1883; d. New York, 6 Nov 1965), was the son of an engineer who opposed a musical career and wanted Varèse to pursue engineering. He spent much of his childhood in the village of Villars in Burgundy, where his mother's family lived. He went to school in Paris until 1892 when the family moved to Turin, where about 1900 the director of the Turin Conservatory, Giovanni Bolzoni, gave Varèse lessons in harmony and counterpoint. In 1903 Varèse returned to Paris to study music. He was accepted at the Schola Cantorum in 1904 (composition with Vincent d'Indy, fugue with Albert Roussel, pre-18th-century music with Charles Bordes); later he studied in Charles Widor's masterclass at the Conservatory. During 1908–15 he lived primarily in Berlin, making frequent visits to Paris; at this time he met Debussy, Rodin, and, most importantly, Romain Rolland (whose Jean-Christophe bears many resemblances to Varèse), and Busoni. Through these friends he met Richard Strauss, Karl Muck, and Hugo von Hofmannsthal, all of whom helped further his career. Varèse himself was active as a conductor, founding a Symphonischer Chor (1909) that took part in several Max Reinhardt productions and conducting the Czech Philharmonic in Prague (1914) in a program of contemporary French music. The outbreak of war found him in Paris. In the spring of 1915 he was mobilized and then discharged for ill health. He left for New York, arriving in late December.

Varèse became active in New York artistic circles and, although never a dadaist himself, was close to Picabia, Duchamp, and the New York branch of dada. At this time he met Louise Norton, whom he later married and who became well-known as a translator of Rimbaud, Saint-John Perse, Bernanos, Michaux, and Simenon. (His first marriage, to the actress Suzanne Bing, ended in divorce.) In 1919 he founded and conducted the first concert of the New Symphony Orchestra. The program included Bartók, Casella, and Debussy; when Varèse was asked to conduct

more popular works, he resigned. In 1921 he founded the International Composers' Guild with Carlos Salzedo. This organization, one of the first anywhere devoted to the public performance of new music, lasted until 1927, and the following year Varèse helped found the Pan-American Association of Composers with Nicholas Slonimsky, Henry Cowell, Charles Ives, and Carlos Chávez.

During the Depression and Second World War, public interest in experimental music ebbed and Varèse became an increasingly isolated figure. He returned to Paris in 1928 but was back in the U.S. by 1932. In the late 30s he traveled in the western U.S., teaching at the Arsuna School of Fine Arts in Santa Fe in 1937 and visiting sound studios in Los Angeles in 1938 in an unsuccessful attempt to find audio facilities. (Since the late 20s he had been exploring the possibilities in "electric" instruments and media.) He returned to New York in 1940 and founded the New Chorus (later called the Greater New York Chorus), principally for the performance of early music. After the war his music began to be performed again and to exert an increasing influence on younger composers. In 1953 he was presented with an Ampex tape recorder anonymously and began working on the tape-electronic interpolations for *Déserts*, a work for which the instrumental parts were already completed. (He finished *Déserts* at the studios of the French radio in 1954.) His last two completed works were also on tape.

Varèse's mature works date from his emigration; it is not without significance that the first is entitled *Amériques*—literally "New Worlds." As in Debussy, texture and timbre are essential features which, along with rhythm and accent, become inseparable from the "harmonic" and "melodic" content. From Stravinsky Varèse perhaps learned something about block form—composition in static planes or levels within which repeated figures, harmonies, and rhythmic accents are laid out in flat, "cubist" juxtapositions. Varèse extended this idea to the creation of large overlapping cycles that constantly produce new juxtapositions out of old material, giving rise to the image of solid, unchanging figures rotating in space. Twelve-tone aggregates appear in *Intégrales* and elsewhere, although the use of such material in Varèse has little in common with Schoenberg's linear counterpoint. Varèse certainly owed something to the futurists, whose thought and ideas he knew quite well. Nevertheless he refuted the noise-machine ideal and asked in 1917, "Italian futurists, why have you slavishly produced only what is commonplace and boring in the bustle of our daily lives? I dream of instruments obedient to my thought and which, with their contribution of a whole new world of unsuspected sounds, will lend themselves to the exigencies of my inner rhythm." In the pursuit of this vision, Varèse was remarkably tenacious, and a certain progression in his work can be understood in the light of this search.

The early work, mostly lost or destroyed, was probably in a late-romantic idiom. The chamber-ensemble pieces of the 1920s not only create new instrumental forms but show an increasing use of the percussion, culminating in the all-percussion *Ionisation*. Later on, sounds free of the tempered system, sounds (such as noise) free from periodic pulsing, sounds synthesized through electronic technology, as well as sounds taken from contemporary life (i.e., "found" sound) all became logical and meaningful musical material. Electronic instruments and the human voice were introduced in *Equatorial*. The projected *L'Astronome*, with its theme of an astronomer who makes contact with another civilization, and *Espace*, with its plan for choruses from all over the world, beamed in by radio, singing in various languages, humming, yelling, chanting, mumbling, express a vision scarcely realized by the most "advanced" of recent musics. The late works make use of the tape and electronic media, but instruments and the human voice continued to play a role.

All of Varèse's innovations can be traced to his overthrow of the notions of linearity and directionality, which have dominated Western music for centuries. Far more than any of his European contemporaries, he approached the ideal of music as a sonorous object independent of notions of process or symbology. From *Amériques* on, he dispensed with contrapuntal and developmental forms. In *Hyperprism*, *Octandre*, *Intégrales*, and *Arcana*, melodic ideas are reduced to cycles of repeated notes and figures; the true "thematic" elements, as in *Ionisation*, are patterns of rhythm and accent. The harmonic elements merge into texture and become densities of sound and timbre. For *Espaces* he envisioned a "shifting play of planes, volumes, masses in space."

Varèse's three works involving tape are all based on recorded rather than synthesized sound; in effect they open up the external world as source material. These materials are, however, always transformed. In *Déserts* they alternate with brass and percussion music. In the *Good Friday Procession in Verges* (for Thomas Bouchard's film *Around and About Joan Miró*) they form a counterpoint to flickering images of a candlelight procession in Catalonia. In the *Poème électronique* they were sent spinning around the 425 loudspeakers on the inside surface of the Philips pavilion and accompanied by Le Corbusier's visual images. All three works employ recognizable sound images; the latter two make prominent use of the human voice as well as percussive sounds and pitched clusters. *Nocturnal* (completed by Chou Wen-chung in 1968) rounds off the last period of Varèse's work, in which the abstract play of volumes and planes evolves toward a larger spectrum of materials and a more dramatic form.

Varèse not only envisaged the development of the tape and electronic medium but composed some of the first masterpieces in the new idiom. He was the first to exploit percussion systematically and extensively. He deemphasized pitch as a fundamental factor in musical expression (although it is still important in all his work) and raised rhythm (including accent and dynamic) and timbre (including texture) to an equal plane. His forms, blocked out and spatial in effect, turn away from the traditional notion of developmental processes and seem to approach the contemporary ideal of sound experiences for themselves and not for their part in a larger process. Nevertheless, he never actually gave up the concepts of relatedness and "meaning," and his later works, including the tape compositions (for which he characteristically used the term "organized sound "), are highly dramatic in their juxtaposition of vocal, instrumental, and electronic elements. Finally, his use of tape and of a great variety of means suggest the enormous widening of perspective in which the range of material itself becomes a valid subject matter.

PRINCIPAL COMPOSITIONS (published by Colfrank unless otherwise noted): *Amériques* for orchestra (1918?–22); *Offrandes* for soprano voice, orchestra (1921?–22); *Hyperprism* for woodwinds, brass, percussion (1922?–23); *Octandre* for 7 winds, double bass (1923?–24); *Intégrales* for woodwinds, brass, percussion (1924?–25); *Arcana* for orchestra (1925–27); *Ionisation* for 13 percussion (1930–33); *Equatorial* for bass voice (bass chorus), piano, organ, 2 theremins, percussion (1933?–34); *Density 21.5* for flute (1936); *Etude pour espace* for chorus, 2 pianos, 6 percussionists (1947, unpub.); *Déserts* for wind, brass, percussion, tape (instrumental parts 1949–53, tape 1953–54); *Good Friday Procession in Verges*, tape music for Thomas Bouchard's film Around and About Joan Miró (1955–56); *Poème électronique* on 3 tapes (1957–58); *Nocturnal* for soprano, bass chorus, orchestra (begun 1960–61, completed 1968 by Chou Wen-chung).

PRINCIPAL WRITINGS: "The Liberation of Sound," excerpts from lectures of 1936–62 ed. by

Chou Wen-chung, *Contemporary Composers on Contemporary Music* ed. by E. Schwartz and B. Childs (New York 1967):196–208.

BIBL.: Chou Wen-chung, "Open Rather than Bounded" and "A Varèse Chronology," *Perspectives* 5/1:1–10; Henry Cowell, "The Music of E. V.," *Modern Music* 5; Gunther Schuller, "Conversation with V.," *Perpsectives* 3/2:32–37; James Tenney, *Meta* (+) *Hodos* (New Orleans 1964); Louise Varèse, *V.: A Looking-Glass Diary, 1883–1928* (New York 1972).

Eric Salzman

SEE ALSO Asian Music and Western Composition, Austria and Germany, Dance, Form, France, Instrumental and Vocal Resources, Melody, Mixed Media, Orchestration, Performance, Texture, Tuning and Temperament, United States.

Varvoglis, Mario (b. Brussels, 10 Jan 1885; d, Athens, 31 July 1967), studied painting at the Athens School of Fine Arts (1900–02) and music at the Paris Conservatory (1903–09, harmony with Xavier Leroux, counterpoint with Georges Caussade). He also studied composition with Vincent d'Indy at the Schola Cantorum. He remained in Paris until 1920, then taught at the Athens School of Music (1920–24) and the Hellenic School of Music (1924–67). He also wrote music criticism for various journals and periodicals, most notably the newspaper *Ta Nea* (1955–67).

PRINCIPAL COMPOSITIONS: *Evrikómi* for voice, piano; text by Dionyssios Solomos (1906, published in *Helleniká Tragoúdia*, UE); *To Tragoúdi toú Aghoyáti* [The Carter's Song] for voice, piano (1906); *To Panighíri* [The Fiesta], tone poem for orchestra (1909–19); *Aghía Varvára* [St. Barbara], symphonic prelude (1912); *Pimenikí Souíta* [Pastoral Suite] for string orchestra (1912, Enosis); *Hellenikó Capríccio* [Greek Capriccio] for cello with string orchestra or piano (1914); *Hommage à César Franck* for violin, piano (1922); *Sonatina* for piano (1927); *Stochasmós* [Meditation] for string orchestra (1936); *String Trio* (1938); *Laïkó Poíema* [Folk Poem] for violin, cello, piano (1943); *Tó Apóyema tis Agápis* [The Afternoon Agape], 1-act opera; libretto by the composer after T. Synodinos (1945); *Dháfnes ké Kyparíssia* [Laurels and Cypresses], symphonic contrasts (1950, Enosis); *Prelude and Fugue on a Byzantine Theme* for organ (1953). Varvoglis also wrote 14 children's pieces for piano, some dating from before 1920. ★ Incidental music: *O Órkos toú Pethaménou* [The Oath of the Departed] by Zacharias Papantoniou (1930); *Na Zi to Messolónghi* [Long Live Messolonghi] by Vassily Rotas (1930); *The Birds* by Aristophanes (1930); *Agamemnon* by Aeschylus (1932); *The Persians* by Aeschylus (1939); *Medea* by Euripides (1945).

PRINCIPAL WRITINGS: *Curriculum vitae* (Athens 1965).

[prepared with the help of George Leotsakos]
SEE ALSO Greece.

Vaughan Williams, Ralph (b. Down Ampney, England, 12 Oct 1872; d. London, 26 August 1958), came from a middle-class family of professional people. He studied at Cambridge Univ. (from 1892) and with Charles Parry and Charles Stanford at the Royal College of Music (1890, 1895). After a period as organist at St. Barnabas Church in South Lambeth, he went to Berlin and studied with Max Bruch (1897). He earned a Doctor of Music degree at Cambridge in 1901 and at about this time began his researches in English folk music. During 1908–10 he studied composition with Ravel in Paris. There, with the sponsorship of the Société Musicale Indépendante his *Norfolk Rhapsody* and *On Wenlock Edge* were performed in 1910. That year, too, his *Tallis Fantasia* was performed at the Gloucester Festival. In 1919 Vaughan Williams began teaching at the Royal Academy and became conductor of the London Bach Choir. He became increasingly active in Britain's music life and after Elgar's death in 1934 was acknowledged as the country's leading musician. From 1938 until his death, his time was devoted to composition, folksong research and publication, editing of music for church use, and the promotion of amateur musical activities.

Vaughan Williams was the fountainhead of the 20th-century English national school. Few British composers now alive have not been influenced by his style or by English folksong, which he helped restore to the national consciousness. His main contributions were his nine symphonies and his vocal works (mostly choral). Considering the paucity of good 20th-century operas, his five (really six) works are notable. The music of the earliest, *The Shepherds of the Delectable Mountains* (1922), was incorporated in the last, *The Pilgrim's Progress* (revised 1951–52), which was not successful dramatically. The others, though rarely performed, are stageworthy; in fact, *Sir John in Love* (1928) has a charming "Englishness" resulting from its broad tunes and general heartiness. Vaughan Williams was not adept at the virtuoso writing needed for solo concertos, although *The Lark Ascending* (revised 1920), a modest concerto for violin and orchestra, is attractive. His concerted works for unusual instruments (the *Tuba Concerto*, 1954, and *Romance* for harmonica and strings, 1951) provided an outlet for his boisterous humor and warm human sympathies. His few piano compositions are not noteworthy, and most of his chamber works were youthful compositions. The inflexible rhythmic pulse in most of his music tended to spoil the dance works.

Vaughan Williams's treatment of melody is the most conspicuous and typical aspect of his style. It is based on a tranquil, conjunct movement in which poetic allusions and more passionate accents are equally distributed. He often drew on folk sources, as in the *London* and *Pastoral Symphonies*, where street cries and country melodies appear. Later in his life, as his music exhibited an increasingly religious outlook, melodic turns borrowed from the church modes occurred more frequently. (The religious element can be traced back at least to the *Tallis Fantasia*, where hymn tunes were used.) His melodic-contrapuntal treatment was modeled on that of the Elisabethan era. Except for his use of the voice as an orchestral instrument, his treatment of sound resources was conventional. Although not attracted to the glittering elegance of Ravel, he seems to have gained much of Ravel's craft of orchestration. This shows up especially in his handling of the strings; their particular spacing gives his scores a typical spaciousness that is the source of a personal flavor. He tended to use woodwinds soloistically. The *Overture to the "Wasps"* and the *London* and *Pastoral Symphonies* give evidence of the fairly wide range of his orchestral treatment.

PRINCIPAL COMPOSITIONS (published by Oxford unless otherwise noted): *Norfolk Rhapsody No. 1 in E Minor* for orchestra (1905); *Symphonies Nos. 1–9*: No. 1, "Sea," for soprano, baritone, chorus, orchestra; text from Walt Whitman (1909; revised ed. published 1918 by Stainer); No. 2, "London" (1914, revised 1920, 1933; Stainer); No. 3, "Pastoral" (1920–21, revised 1950–51; Curwen); No. 4 (1931–34); No. 5 (1938–43, 1951); No. 6 (1944–47); No. 7, "Antarctica," for soprano, women's chorus, orchestra (1949–52); No. 8 (1953–55, finale revised 1956); No. 9 (1956–57, revised 1958); *On Wenlock Edge*, 6 songs for tenor, string quartet, piano; text by A. E. Housman (1909, Novello); *Fantasia on a Theme by Thomas Tallis* for strings (1910, revised 1913, 1919; Curwen); *Hugh the Drover*, 2-act ballad opera (1910–14, final revision 1956; Curwen); *5 Mystical Songs* for baritone, chorus, orchestra; text by George Herbert (1911, Stainer); *The Lark Ascending* for violin, orchestra (1914, revised 1920); *Sancta civitas* for chorus, orchestra (1923–25, Curwen); *Violin Concerto in D Minor* (1924–25); *Flos campi*, suite for viola, wordless chamber

chorus, orchestra (1925); *Piano Concerto in C* (1926, 1930–31; version for 2 pianos with revisions, 1946); *Riders to the Sea*, 1-act opera after J. M. Synge (1925–32); *The Pilgrim's Progress*, 4-act opera (composed principally 1925–36; revised principally 1944–49, 1951–52); *The Poisoned Kiss*, a "romantic extravaganza" (1927–29; revised 1934–35, 1936–37, 1956–57); *Sir John in Love*, 4-act opera after Shakespeare (1928); *Job*, a masque for dancing for orchestra (1930); *5 Tudor Portraits* for alto, baritone, chorus, orchestra (1935); *Serenade to Music* for 16 solo voices, orchestra; text from Shakespeare's *Merchant of Venice* (1938); *Hodie, A Christmas Cantata* for soprano, tenor, baritone, boys' chorus, chorus (1953–54); *Tuba Concerto* (1954). Complete list in Kennedy (see bibl.).

PRINCIPAL WRITINGS: *National Music and Other Essays*, an anthology (London 1963). Complete list in Kennedy.

BIBL.: Frank Howes, *The English Musical Renaissance* (London 1966); Michael Kennedy, *The Works of R. V. W.* (London 1964); Ursula Vaughan Williams, *R. V. W.* (London 1964).

John S. Weissmann

SEE ALSO Folk Resources; Great Britain; Liturgical Music: Christian; Popular Music; Recording.

de la Vega, Aurelio (b. Havana, 28 Nov 1925), studied humanities at De La Salle College in Havana (1939–45), law at the Univ. of Havana (1945–47), and music at the Instituto Musical Ada Iglesias, Havana (1950–55; orchestration, contemporary techniques with Harold Gramatges). He studied music privately during 1942–46 with Frederick Kramer in Havana (piano, harmony, counterpoint) and during 1947–49 with Ernst Toch in California. In Cuba, he was Dean of the Music School at the Univ. of Oriente in Santiago de Cuba (1953–59) and musical advisor of the National Institute of Culture, Havana (1953–59). He has since taught at the San Fernando Valley State College in Calif., where he is also director of the Electronic Music Studio. He was a music critic in Havana during 1950–57 and has written numerous articles on contemporary music for Latin American periodicals. His early music (1944–54) was influenced first by Szymanowski and later by Berg; the influence here was mainly in terms of instrumental textures and expressive melodic lines. From 1957 (the first serial works) to 1964, the main influences came from Boulez and Franco Evangelisti. De la Vega's most recent music reflects somewhat the use of instruments and new notation by the Polish avant-garde.

PRINCIPAL COMPOSITIONS: *The Death of Pan* for violin, piano (1948, ECM); *Piano Trio* (1949,

STA); *Overture to a Serious Farce* (1950, FE and Fleischer); *Soliloquy* for viola, piano (1950, FE); *Legend of the Creole Ariel* for cello, piano (1953, Peer); *Epigram* for piano (1953, FE); *Elegy* for string orchestra (1954; Cubanas, FE, Fleischer); *Toccata* for piano (1957); *String Quartet*, "In memoriam Alban Berg" (1957, FE); *Cantata* for 2 sopranos, alto, 21 instruments (1958, FE and Fleischer); *Woodwind Quintet* (1959, FE); *Symphony in 4 Parts* (1960, FE and Fleischer); *Trio* for flute, oboe, clarinet (1960); *Structures* for piano, string quartet (1962); *Vectors*, on monaural tape (1963); *Segments* for violin, piano (1964, FE); *Analigus* for orchestra (1965, FE and Fleischer); *Exametron* for flute, cello, percussion (1965); *Interpolation* for clarinet, tape (1965, STA); *Exospheres* for oboe, piano (1966, FE); *Antinomies* for piano (1967); *Labdanum* for flute, vibraphone, viola (1970). List to 1960: *Composers of the Americas* 7:98-102.

PRINCIPAL WRITINGS: *A Social Morality* (PhD diss., Univ. of Havana, 1946); *Arnold Schoenberg and the Atonalists* (Havana 1948); *The Negative Emotion* (Havana 1950); *The New Romanticism* (Havana 1951); "The Training of a Composer Today," *The Modern Composer and His World* ed. by J. Beckwith and U. Kasemets (Toronto 1961); "Mozart ahora," *Revista musical chilena* (April 1962):59-65; "El pianista y la música de hoy," *Boletín inter-americano de música* (Washington) 39:3-7; "New World Composers," *Inter-American Music Bulletin*, No. 43:1-6; "Regarding Electronic Music," *Tempo* (winter 1965-66):2-11; "Avant-Garde Music at the American Art Biennial of Córdoba," *Yearbook of the Inter-American Institute for Musical Research* (New Orleans 1967): 85-100.

BIBL.: Alice Ramsey, *A. de la V.: His Life and Works* (MA thesis, San Fernando Valley State College, 1963); John Ramsen Schortt, "A. de la V., un compositor de las Américas," *Revista musical chilena* (April 1963):62-68. De la Vega's music has also been discussed in the "Current Chronicle," *Musical Quarterly* 44/3, 47/1, 47/4, 50/4, 51/2, and 52/2.

Verbal Score, see Prose Music

Veress, Sándor (b. Kolozsvár, Hungary, 1 Feb 1907), studied at the Royal Academy of Music in Budapest (1924-30, piano with Béla Bartók, composition with Zoltán Kodály) and with László Lajtha at the folk-music department of the Hungarian Ethnographical Museum (1928-35). From 1936 to 1941 he assisted Bartók in the folk-music department at the Academy of Sciences, Budapest. He taught at the State Academy of Music in Budapest,

1943-48. In 1950 he began teaching at the Conservatory of Music in Bern. During 1965-67 he was visiting professor at the Peabody Conservatory, at Goucher College (Baltimore), and at the Univ. of Adelaide, Australia, and since 1968 he has been teaching at the Univ. of Bern.

PRINCIPAL COMPOSITIONS (published by S-Z unless otherwise noted): *String Quartet No. 1* (1931); *Sonatina* for violin, piano (1932); *Sonatina* for cello, piano (1933); *Erdélyi kantáta* [Transylvanian Cantata] for chorus (1935, unpub.); *Sonata* for solo violin (1935); *15 Gyermekkar* [15 Children's Choruses] (1936, MK); *2 Virágének* [2 Flower Songs] for women's chorus (1936, MK); *String Quartet No. 2* (1936-37); *Csodafurulya* [The Magic Flute], ballet (1937, UE; suite for orchestra, 1937, UE); *Violin Concerto* (1937-39); *Violin Sonata No. 2* (1939); *Rabaközi nóták* [Songs from the Raba-side] for men's chorus (1940, MK); *Symphony No. 1* (1940, Kigen); *Billegetőmuzsika* [Fingerlarks] for piano (1940-46; revised 1968); *Térszili Katica* [Kate of Terszil], ballet (1942-43); *Sancti Augustini Psalmus contra partem Donati* for bass, chorus, orchestra (1943-44); *4 Danze transilvane* for strings (1944); *Sirató ének: In Memoriam Béla Bartók* (1945); *József Attilla dalok*, 5 songs (1945, Cserépfalvi); *9 Cseremisz dal* [9 Tcheremis Songs] for solo voice (1945); *I Went Out A-Marketing* for women's chorus (1950, Gwynn); *Piano Concerto* (1950-52); *Hommage à Paul Klee* for 2 pianos, strings (1952); *Symphony No. 2* (1952-53); *String Trio* (1954); *Laudatio musicae* for soprano, chorus, chamber orchestra (1958); *Concerto* for string quartet, orchestra (1960-61); *Passacaglia concertante* for oboe, string orchestra (1961); *Mary Had a Little Lamb* for women's chorus (1961, Gwynn); *Elegy* for baritone string orchestra, harp (1964); *Musica concertante* for 12 strings (1965-66); *Sonata* for solo cello (1967); *Songs of the Seasons* for chorus (1967).

PRINCIPAL WRITINGS: "Népzenei gyüjtés a moldvai csángók között" [Folk Music Collecting Among the Csángós of Moldavia], *Ethnographia* (Budapest) 42/3; "Népdal, népzenegyüjtés" [Folksong, Folk Music Collecting], *Magyar muzsika könyve* (Budapest 1936); *Székely népballadák váltzatai Moldvában* [Variants of Transylvanian Folk Ballads] (Budapest 1941); "Goldolatok hangszertanitásunk reformjáról" [On Reforms in the Teaching of Instrumental Music], *Magyar zenei szemle* 1/4; "Folk Music in Musical and General Education," *Journal of the International Folk Music Council* 1.

BIBL.: Erich Doflein, "S. V.," *Melos* (March 1954); Denyse Hassid, "L'Avenir de la musique en Hongrie," *L'Art musical* 4:109; Pál Jardanyi, "Zenei figyelő" [Musical Observer], *Válasz* 8:3; György Ligeti, "Neue Musik in Ungarn," *Melos* 16:1; Colin Mason, "Music in Hungary: The Scene Since Bartók," *Manchester Guardian* (8 Jan 1949); John S. Weissmann, "The Contemporary Movement in Hungary," *Music Today* (London), vol. 1.

Vermeulen, Matthÿs (b. Helmond, Netherlands, 8 Feb 1888; d. Laren, 26 July 1967), studied theory with Daniel de Lange and composition with Alphons Diepenbrock. During 1909–56 he contributed numerous articles to Dutch, French, and East Indian newspapers and journals. He lived in Paris from 1921 to 1946. In his compositions he turned to medieval music for technical guideposts and developed a nonimitative, often nontonal contrapuntal style, usually over a cantus firmus of his own invention.

PRINCIPAL COMPOSITIONS (published by Donemus unless otherwise noted): *Symphonies Nos. 1–7*: No. 1, "Symphonia carminum" (1914); No. 2, "Prélude à la nouvelle journée" (1920); No. 3, "Thrène et Péan" (1922); No. 4, "Les Victoires" (1941); No. 5, "Les Lendemains Chantants" (1944); No. 6, "Les Minutes heureuses" (1958); No. 7, "Dithyrambes pour les tempes à venir" (1965, unpub.); *The Soldier* for mezzo-soprano, piano; text by Rupert Brooke (1916); *On ne passe pas* for soprano, piano (1917); *Les Filles de Roi d'Espagne* for mezzo-soprano, piano; text by Paul Fort (1917); *La Veille* for mezzo-soprano, piano; text by François Porché (1917, orchestrated 1929); *Cello Sonatas Nos. 1–2* (1918, 1938); *String Trio* (1924); *Violin Sonata* (1925); *De Vliegende Hollander* for orchestra (1930); *3 Salutations à Notre Dame* for soprano, piano (1942); *Le Balcon* for mezzo-soprano, piano; text by Baudelaire (1943); *String Quartet* (1961); *3 Chants d'amour* for mezzo-soprano, piano; texts by Li-tai-pei, Tou-fou, and Baudelaire (1962).

PRINCIPAL WRITINGS: *De Twee Muzieken* [2 Musics] (Amsterdam 1919); *Klankbord* [Sound Board] (Amsterdam 1929); *De Eene Grondtoon* [The Basic Fundamental] (Amsterdam 1931); *Het Avontuur van den Geest* [An Adventure of the Spirit] (Amsterdam 1948); *Princiepen der Europeesche Muziek* [Principles of European Music] (Amsterdam 1949); *De Myziek dat Wonder* [Music, a Miracle] (Amsterdam 1958).

BIBL.: Norbert Loeser, "M. V.," *Donemus* (June 1958); Wouter Paap, "M. V.," *Mens en Melodie* (June 1956); ——, "In memoriam M. V.," *ibid.* (Sept. 1967).

[prepared with the help of Th. Vermeulen-Diepenbrock]

Verrall, John (Weedon) (b. Britt, Iowa, 17 June 1908), attended the Minneapolis College of Music (1928–31, cello and composition with Englebert Roentgen), the Royal College of Music (1929–30; piano with Frank Merrick; composition, theory with R. O. Morris), the Liszt Conservatory, Budapest (1931–32; piano with Gabriel Zsigmondy, composition with Zoltán Kodály), and the Univ. of Minn. (1932–34, composition and piano with Donald

Ferguson). He also studied composition with Roy Harris at Colorado College (summer 1938), Aaron Copland (Tanglewood, summer 1941), and Frederick Jacobi (Institute of Musical Art, New York, 1946–47). He was an editor at G. Schirmer and the Boston Music Co., during 1946–48, after which he began teaching at the Univ. of Wash. The deepest influence on his development came from the criticism and support of Dmitri Mitropoulos during the years 1939–41.

PRINCIPAL COMPOSITIONS: *Concert Piece for Strings and Horn* (1940); *Sonata No. 1* for viola, piano (1942, Dow); *String Quartet No. 2* (1943, New Valley); *Serenade for 5 Wind Instruments* (1944, New Valley); *Ah, Come, Sweet Death* for chorus (1945, New Valley); *Prelude and Allegro* for string orchestra (1948, ACA-CFE); *String Quartet No. 3* (1949, Ditson); *Dark Night of St. John* for chamber orchestra (1949, ACA-CFE); *String Quartet No. 4* (1950, Ditson); *String Quartet No. 5* (1952, ACA-CFE); *Portrait of St. Christopher* for orchestra (1956, ACA-CFE); *Suite for Orchestra* (1958, ACA-CFE); *Concerto for Piano* for piano, orchestra (1960, ACA-CFE); *String Quartet No. 7* (1961, ACA-CFE); *Sonata No. 2* for viola, piano (1964, Peters); *Chamber Symphony* (1967, ACA-CFE); *Concerto for Viola* for viola, orchestra (1969, ACA-CFE).

PRINCIPAL WRITINGS: *Fugue and Invention in Theory and Practice* (Palo Alto, Calif., 1967).

BIBL.: James Beale, "The Music of J. V.," *ACA Bulletin 7/4*.

Vetter, Michael (b. Oberstdorf, Germany, 18 Sept 1943), is self-taught in music. He began by studying the recorder, and during 1964–68, while studying theology and philosophy at the Universities of Münster, Göttingen, and Tübingen, he wrote a method book for the recorder. He has taken part in premieres of works by Sylvano Bussotti, Henri Pousseur, Karlheinz Stockhausen, and others, and feels that his own music is especially close to that of Stockhausen. Many of his compositions involve some kind of audience participation, for "from active listening to acoustic participation is only a short step." In notating his music, he uses textual material and graphic notation.

PRINCIPAL COMPOSITIONS: *Reaktionen auf Revolutionäre*, "a musical mirror," duo for instrumentalist, amplifier (1968–69, UE); *New Incussions for 2* for up to 8 players, audience participation ad lib. (1968–69, UE); *Orzismus—Begeisterung wider Chöre* for audience, player, projections (1969); *Memorandum*, duo for 2 players "using different musical languages" (1969–70).

PRINCIPAL WRITINGS: *Il flauto dolce ed acerbo*: vol. 1 (Celle 1969); vol. 2, scheduled for publication in 1971, deals with extensions of instruments through electronic means and the use of vocalizations; vol. 3, 1973, *Aulodien*, is to contain material relating to the practice of composition. Other books in preparation include *Schule für den instrumentalen Umgang mit Gegenständen, Schule des Vokalen, Schule für die Blockflöte*, and *Musikalische Spiele—elementare Kompositions—lehre für Kinder*; these are scheduled for completion in 1972.

Vieru, Anatol (b. Iaşi, Rumania, 8 June 1926), attended the Bucharest Conservatory (composition with Leon Klepper, harmony with Paul Constantinescu, orchestration with Th. Rogalski, conducting with Constantine Silvestri) and the Moscow Conservatory (composition with Aram Khatchaturian, polyphony with Semion Bogatiriov, orchestration with Dm. Rogal-Levitzky). He conducted the National Theatre orchestra in Bucharest during 1947–49 and has taught at the Bucharest Conservatory since 1954.

PRINCIPAL COMPOSITIONS: *Struggle against Inertia* for tenor, mezzo-soprano, piano, clarinet, violin (1959, Muzicală); *Cello Concerto* (1962, Muzicală and Salabert); *Jeux* for piano, orchestra (1963, Salabert); *Nocturnal Scenes* for 2 choirs (1964, Schott); *Violin Concerto* (1964, Muzicală); *Steps of Silence* for string quartet, percussionist (1966, Salabert); *Ode to Silence* for orchestra (1967, Salabert); *Museum Music* for harpsichord (electric harpsichord), 12 strings (1968, Salabert); *Sanduhr* for orchestra (1969, Schott).

PRINCIPAL WRITINGS: "Music and about Music," *Secolul 20* (Bucharest) 1965/3:109–28; with L. Grigorovici, "11 Fragen an A/V.," *Melos* 35: 236–43.

BIBL.: Nicholas Slonimsky, "Modern Composition in Rumania," *Musical Quarterly* (Jan 1965): 242.

SEE ALSO Dance.

Villa-Lobos, Heitor (b. Rio de Janeiro, 5 March 1887; d. Rio de Janeiro, 17 Nov 1959), had his first music lessons from his father, a writer, cellist, and "man of the people." Other facts of Villa-Lobos's early life are difficult to establish, partly because of his own contradictory statements and anecdotes, some of which appear to be pure fantasy. After his father's death in 1899 he earned a meager living playing the cello in cafés. A rebellious lad, he had little formal education, musical or otherwise. In his youth he travelled to the north and interior of Brazil, where he developed a burning interest in folk music. Darius Milhaud's sojourn in Brazil (1917–18) may have fanned Villa-Lobos's

ambitions as a composer. Artur Rubinstein "discovered" him in 1919 and performed his works widely. Thanks to a travel grant from the Brazilian government, he spent 1923–30 in Europe, chiefly in Paris, then returned home where he held a series of official positions connected with music education. In 1942 he founded and became the director of the Conservatório Nacional de Canto Orfeónico, and in 1945 he established the Brazilian Academy of Music. His travels took him to other Latin-American countries, Europe, and (from 1944) the U.S., frequently as conductor of his own music. His last years were clouded by illness; only his native vitality and will power enabled him to keep going.

Villa-Lobos's enormous output (over 3,000 works) is marked by unevenness of quality and diversity of styles. A gifted musician who worked chiefly by instinct, he possessed a high degree of technical ability that enabled him to compose at great speed and almost automatically (while conversing, for instance). Self-criticism was not his strong point. He seldom revised his works extensively, and he did not discriminate carefully between his good and his inferior compositions. French influences in his music are sometimes patent, as in the impressionistic *Floral Suite* (1917), the Satie-like *Ironic and Sentimental Epigrams* (1921), or the Milhaud-derived harmonic style of the *Nonet* (1923). The sophisticated banalities of the fourth *Chôros* (1926) reflect the spirit of Milhaud's *Le Boeuf sur le toit* and the vogue for banal café music. Few pieces, however, are sheerly imitative.

While a Villa-Lobos style, as such, can scarcely be said to exist, there is nevertheless a personal quality, or "inflection," in his best music. In some instances it is the Brazilian flavor he imparted through the use of folk music traits (a predilection for syncopation, lush chords and chord progressions, broad melodies with a predominantly falling line, and the juxtaposition of sharply contrasting elements); in others it is more a question of atmosphere and feeling, especially the nostalgia that haunts Brazil and Brazilians and that can only be expressed by the word *saudades*, signifying a combination of longing, tenderness, and profound sadness as exemplified in the fifth *Chôros*, "Alma brasileira" [The Brazilian Soul]. The vigorous works, however, have an almost savage quality, verging at times on primitive kinetic energy, as in the finale, "Toccata," of the *Bachianas brasileiras No. 8*.

Except in choral settings and piano pieces, Villa-Lobos seldom quoted the rich repertory of Brazilian folk music, which ranges from primitive Indian chants and the languorous songs of the *sertão* in the northern interior to the "cowboy" songs of the south and the anonymous popular music of the cities. However, this music shaped many of his melodies and rhythms, as did such popular-music forms as the 19th-century *modinha*, a sentimental song, or the *chôros*, a highly rhythmic dance piece. Many works have local connotations (such as the four orchestral suites, 1937, entitled *The Discovery of Brazil*), others are full of local color (*3 Indigenous Poems*, 1926), and still others are programmatic (*Origin of the Amazon*, 1950). The most innovative aspect of Villa-Lobos's style was his lavish use of percussion instruments, many of them indigenous to Brazil.

Although he possessed an excellent contrapuntal technique, Villa-Lobos was a melodist par excellence. He was a thoroughgoing romanticist (he called himself a sentimentalist), who showed a cavalier disregard for theories and questions of style as such. There is, in fact, no direct line of development in his music; some of his most "radical" works were written in the 1920s, while many of his later works were "conservative." In some pieces, notably the *Bachianas brasileiras*, in which he envisaged a combination of Brazilian folk music and Bachian counterpoint, he sought a union of local and universal elements. In others (for example, the *String Quartet No. 5*, subtitled "Quarteto brasileiro") he set out to be purely Brazilian. He was the greatest of a long series of Latin-American nationalist-folklorist composers and the first to produce works that could hold their own in the international concert repertory. He founded no school, however, and his stylistic influence on younger composers has been slight.

PRINCIPAL COMPOSITIONS: ★ *String Quartets Nos. 1–16:* No. 1 (1915, Southern); No. 2 (1915, Eschig); No. 3 (1916, Eschig); No. 4 (1917, AMP); No. 5 (1930, AMP); No. 6 (1938, AMP); No. 7 (1942, Eschig); No. 8 (1944, Ricordi); No. 9 (1945, Southern); No. 10 (1946, Southern); No. 11 (1948, Southern); No. 12 (1950, AMP); No. 13 (1951); No. 14 (1953, Eschig); No. 15 (1954); No. 16 (1955). ★ *Symphonies Nos. 1–12:* No. 1 (1916, Eschig); No. 2 (1917, Ricordi); No. 3 (1919, Ricordi); No. 4 (1919, Ricordi); No. 5 (1920); No. 6 (1944, Ricordi); No. 7 (1945, Ricordi); No. 8 (1950); No. 9 (1951); No. 10 (1952); No. 11 (1955); No. 12 (1957). ★ *Bachianas brasileiras Nos. 1–9:* No. 1 for cellos (1930, AMP); No. 2 for orchestra (1930, Ricordi); No. 3 for piano, orchestra (1938, Ricordi); No. 4 for piano (1930–36) or orchestra (1941); No. 5 for voice, cellos (1938, AMP); No. 6 for flute, bassoon (1938, AMP); No. 7 for orchestra (1942, Eschig); No. 8 for orchestra (1944);

No. 9 for voices (1944). ★ *Chôros Nos. 1–14:* No. 1 for guitar (1920, Napoleão); No. 2 for flute, clarinet (1924, Eschig); No. 3 for 7 winds, men's chorus (1925, Eschig); No. 4 for 2 horns, trombone (1926, Eschig); No. 5 for piano (1926, Eschig); No. 6 for orchestra (1926, Eschig); No. 7 for flute, oboe, clarinet, saxophone, bassoon, violin, cello (1924, Eschig); No. 8 for 2 pianos, orchestra (1925, Eschig); No. 9 for orchestra (1929); No. 10 for orchestra, chorus (1925, Eschig); No. 11 for piano, orchestra (1928, AMP); No. 12 for orchestra (1929, AMP); No. 13 for 2 orchestras, band (1929); No. 14 for orchestra, band, chorus (1928). ★ Other works: *Amazonas* for orchestra, ballet (1917, Eschig); *Vidapura* for chorus, solo voices, orchestra (1919); *Canções típicas brasileiras* [Characteristic Brazilian Songs] for voice with piano or orchestra (1919–35, Eschig); *Lenda do caboclo* [Legend of the Caboclo] for piano (1920, Napoleão); *Prole do bebê*, "A familia do bebê" [The Baby's Family] No. 2 (1921, Eschig); *Rudepoema* for piano (1921–26) or orchestra (1932, both Eschig); *Fantasia de movimientos mixtos* for violin with orchestra or piano (1922, Southern); *Wind Quintet* in the form of a chôros (1928, Eschig); *Momoprecoce*, fantasia for piano with orchestra or band (1929, Eschig); *Modinhas e canções*, vol. 1 for voice with piano or orchestra (1933–42, Eschig), vol. 2 for voice, piano (1943); *New York Skyline Melody* for piano or orchestra (1939, AMP); *Fantasia* for cello with orchestra or piano (1945, AMP); *Erosão* [Erosion], symphonic poem (1950, Eschig). Complete list: *Composers of the Americas* 3:14–59.

BIBL.: C. Paula Barros, *O romance de V.-L.* (Rio de Janeiro, n.d.); David Ewen, ed., *The New Book of Modern Composers* (New York 1961); O. L. Fernandez, "A contribuição harmonica de V.-L. para a música brasileira," *Boletín latino-americano de música* 6; Everett Helm, "The Many-Sided Villa," *High Fidelity* 12/7:39; A. T. Luper, *The Music of Brazil* (Washington 1960); A. Magalhães de Giacomo, *V.-L.* (São Paulo 1960); Vasco Mariz, *H. V.-L., Brazilian Composer* (Gainesville, Fla., 1963; French ed., Paris 1967); Nicolas Slonimsky, *The Music of Latin America* (New York 1946); Carleton Sprague Smith, *H. V.-L.* (Washington 1960).

Everett Helm

SEE ALSO Brazil, Popular Music.

Villalpando, Alberto (b. La Paz, 21 Nov 1940), studied at the Torcuato Di Tella Institute in Buenos Aires (1959–64; composition with Alberto Ginastera; orchestration, 12-tone techniques with Riccardo Malipiero; dramatic music with Luigi Dallapiccola; Greek and Hindu rhythm with Oliver Messiaen; electronic music with Vincente Azuar, Bruno Maderna). During 1965–66 he composed film scores in association with the Bolivian Cinema Institute.

He has been national music director for the Ministry of Culture since 1967. His music has been influenced by the music of Bartók and Webern and by the general musical thought of Mahler.

PRINCIPAL COMPOSITIONS: *Cantata solar* for vocal soloists, chorus, chamber orchestra (1964); *Concertino semplice* for flute, orchestra (1965); *Mística No. 2* for string quartet (1966); *Inundación* musique concrète film score (1966); *Del amor, del miedo y del silencio* for piano, chamber orchestra (1967); *3 Sombras y la muerte* for 4 horns (1969); *Danzas para una imagen perdida*, ballet for chamber orchestra (1970); *Mística No. 3* for instruments with contact microphones, tape (1970); *Mística No. 4* for string quartet, piano, tape (1970).

PRINCIPAL WRITINGS (novels): *Un tren viajaba en los ojos de baní* (La Paz 1971); *Las joyas de las enanas* (in process).

Vincent, John (b. Birmingham, Ala., 17 May 1902), studied at the New England Conservatory (1922–27, composition with George Chadwick), George Peabody College (1930–33), Harvard Univ. (1933–35, composition with Walter Piston), the Ecole Normale de Musique (1935–37, composition with Nadia Boulanger), and Cornell Univ. (1941–42, composition with Roy Harris, musicology with Otto Kinkleday). He has taught composition at the Univ. of Calif. at Los Angeles since 1946. During 1953–65 he was director of the Huntington Hartford Foundation. He has conducted throughout the U.S. and South America and is a free-lance music reviewer for various U.S. publications. He describes his rhythmic style as "plastic polyrhythmic," derived in part from an interest in regular rhythmic elements in plainchant, medieval polyphony, and some folk musics. He is also attracted to the "clarity and strength" of 17th- and 18th-century forms.

PRINCIPAL COMPOSITIONS (published by Mills unless otherwise noted): *String Quartet in G* (1936–37); *The 3 Jacks*, ballet (1942–52; *Suite*, 1954); *Nude Descending a Staircase* for string orchestra (1950, revised most recently in 1962; MCA); *Symphony in D* (1954, revised 1956); *Incidental Music for "The Hallow'd Time"* (1954); *Symphonic Poem after Descartes* (1958); *Consort for Piano and Strings* for piano quintet (1960); *Benjamin Franklin Suite* for string orchestra (1962); *Rondo Rhapsody* for orchestra (1965); *The Phoenix*, symphonic poem (1965, MCA); *String Quartet No. 2* (1967, MCA); *Primeval Void*, 1-act opera buffa (1969, MCA); *Stabat Mater* for soprano, men's chorus (1969). List to 1962: *Composers of the Americas* 8:152–57.

PRINCIPAL WRITINGS: *The Diatonic Modes in Modern Music*, 2nd ed. (New York 1961). Vincent has also prepared sight-reading texts (New York 1948–49).

Vlad, Roman (b. Cernauti, Rumania, 29 Dec 1919), studied at the Cernauti Conservatory. In 1938 he moved to Rome, where he studied piano and composition with Alfredo Casella at the Accadèmia di S. Cecilia until 1941. He taught at the Dartington Hall summer school in England in 1954 and 1955. He has been artistic director of the Accadèmia Filarmonica Romana (1955–58) and of the Maggio Musicale Fiorentino (since 1964). He has been active as a critic and journalist and was co-founder of the journal *L'imagine* and music editor for the *Enciclopedia della Spettacolo* (1958–62). He has also performed as a pianist.

PRINCIPAL COMPOSITIONS: *La strada sul caffé*, ballet (1944, Leeds); *De profundis*, cantata for soprano, chorus, orchestra (1946, Leeds and S-Z); *Divertimento* for 11 strings (1948, Boosey); *Sinfonia all'antica* for orchestra (1947–48, Leeds and S-Z); *Storia di una mamma*, 1-act opera (1950–51, Leeds); *5 Elegie su testi biblici* for violin with strings or piano (1952, Leeds and S-Z); *Le Ciel est vide*, cantata (1954, Leeds and S-Z); *Variazioni concertanti sopra una serie di dodici note dal "Don Giovanni" di Mozart* for piano, orchestra (1954–55, Leeds and S-Z); *Sonetto a Orfeo*, "musica concertata" for harp, orchestra (1958, Leeds and S-Z); *Serenata* for 12 strings (1959, Leeds and S-Z); *Meloritmi*, music for strings (1958–59, Leeds); *Masques ostendais*, pantomime (1959, Leeds); *Il dottore di vetro*, opera in 6 scenes (1960, Leeds).

PRINCIPAL WRITINGS: *Modernita e tradizione nella musica contemporanea* (Turin 1955); *Luigi Dallapiccola* (Milan 1957); *Storia della dodecafonia* (Milan 1958); *Stravinsky* trans. by Frederick and Ann Fuller, 2nd ed. (London 1967).

BIBL.: Giorgio Graziosi, "R. V.," *Rassegna musicale* (Jan 1953): 6–18; Robert Stevenson, "An Introduction to the Music of R. V.," *Music Review* 22:124–35.

SEE ALSO Italy.

Van Vlijmen, Jan (b. Rotterdam, 11 Oct 1935), studied at the Utrecht Conservatory (1953–59, composition with Kees van Baaren, piano with Theo Bruins). During 1961–65 he was director of the Amersfoort School of Music. He taught theory at the Utrecht Conservatory during 1965–70 and has been assistant director of the Royal Conservatory in The Hague since 1967.

PRINCIPAL COMPOSITIONS (published by Donemus): *Morgenstern Songs* for mezzo-soprano, piano (1958); *Wind Quintet* (1959); *Costruzione* for 2 pianos (1960); *Gruppi per 20 strumenti e percussione* (1962); *Serenata I* for winds, brass (1964); *Serenata II* for flute, 4 instrumental groups (1965); *Sonata* for piano, orchestra in 3 groups (1966); *Dialogue* for clarinet, piano (1966); *Per dicia sette* for winds, brass (1967); *Prometheus*, incidental music for the play by Aeschylus (1967); *Interpolations* for orchestra, electronic sounds on tape (1968); *Reconstructie*, opera in collaboration with Louis Andriessen, Reinbert de Leeuw, Misja Mengelberg, Peter Schat (1969).

SEE ALSO Netherlands.

Vogel, Wladimir (b. Moscow, 29 Feb 1896), is the son of a German father and a Russian mother. His first studies occurred while he was part of a circle of musicians around Alexander Scriabin. He was interned (as a German citizen) during World War I and thereafter went to Berlin. There he studied with Heinz Tiessen and later with Ferruccio Busoni. He taught at the Klindworth-Scharwenka Conservatory in Berlin (1929–33), after which he moved to Switzerland, becoming a Swiss citizen in 1954.

Vogel has written about 80 compositions, of which the large-scale vocal works using speaking chorus and sprechstimme in addition to singing are especially noteworthy. His starting point in composition was Russian expressionism of the Scriabin type. In Berlin during the 1920s he came in contact with German expressionism. He felt the need to go beyond these approaches however, and, like Alban Berg in *Wozzeck*, he turned the means of expressionist style to more objective ends and fitted them into larger forms. On the one hand this led to the use of 12-tone procedures, beginning with the third and fourth movements of the *Violin Concerto* (1937), and on the other to the classicism of Busoni. In addition to his use of traditional formal schemes, Vogel's classicism is evident in his transparent textures and in the clear separation of voices in the 12-tone vocal works, achieved through the motivic development of different intervals within each. When he uses a speaking chorus, he divides it into four levels, high and low for both men's and women's voices, which he uses homophonically and polyphonically and in combination with solo speaking voices. Thus all sound resources can be orchestrated according to the needs of the dramatic situation.

PRINCIPAL COMPOSITIONS: *Sinfonia fugata* for orchestra (1924, Bote); *Etude-Toccata* for piano

(1926, Boosey); *Wagadu's Untergang durch die Eitelkeit* for soprano, alto, bass-baritone, speaking chorus, 5 saxophones/1 clarinet; text by Frobenius (1930, Ricordi); *4 Etudes for Orchestra* (1–2, 1930; 3–4, 1932; Bote); *Variétude* for piano (1932, Boosey); *Tripartita* for orchestra (1934, Bote); *Epitaffio per Alban Berg* for piano (1936, Ricordi); *Violin Concerto* (1937, Bote); *Madrigals* for chorus; texts by Aline Valangin (1938–39); *12 Variétudes* for violin, flute, clarinet, cello (1942, S-Z); *Thyl Claes, fils de Kolldrager* for soprano, 2 speaking voices, speaking chorus, orchestra (part 1, 1938–42; part 2, 1943–45; Ricordi); *7 Aspects d'une série de 12 sons* for orchestra (1950, Bote); *Spiegelungen* for orchestra (1952, UE); *Dal quaderno di Francine Settenne* for soprano, flute, piano (1952, S-Z); *Preludio, interludio lirico, postludio* for orchestra (1954, Ricordi); *Cello Concerto* (1954, S-Z); *Arpiade* for soprano, speaking chorus, flute, clarinet, viola, cello, piano; text by Hans Arp (1954, Ars Viva); *Goethe-Aphorismen* for soprano, strings (1955, S-Z); *Eine Gotthardkantate* for baritone, strings; text by Hölderlin (1956, Bote); *Jona ging doch nach Ninive* for baritone, speaker, speaking chorus, chorus, orchestra (1958, Bote);, *Alla memoria di G. B. Pergolesi* for tenor, strings (1958, Ricordi); *Das Lied von der Glocke* for speakers, speaking chorus (1959); *Meditazione sulla maschera di Amedeo Modigliani* for vocal soloists, speaker, chorus, orchestra; text by F. Filippini (1960, Ricordi); *Worte* for 2 women's sprechstimmen, 12 strings; text by Hans Arp (1962, Heinr.); *Flucht*, dramatic oratorio for vocal soloists, 4 sprechstimmen, speaking chorus, orchestra (1963–64, Bärenreiter); *Inspiré par Jean Arp* for flute, clarinet, violin, cello (1965, Heinr.). List to 1966: Oesch 1967: 207–12 (see bibl.).

PRINCIPAL WRITINGS: "Der moderne Sprechchor," *Neue Zeitschrift für Musik* (1960): 332–36; "Grundsätzliches zum Dramma-Oratorio," *W. V. Sein Weg zu einer neuen musikalischen Wirklichkeit* by H. Oesch (Bern-Munich 1967): 197–205; *The Orchestral Composer's Point of View* ed. by R. S. Hines (Norman, Okla., 1970).

BIBL.: Hans Oesch, *W. V.* (Bern-Munich 1967); ——, "W. V.s Werke für Klavier," *Schweizerische Musikzeitung* 97: 51–57; Luigi Rognoni, "Portrait W. V.," *Melos* 22: 165–67; Gerhard Schuhmacher, "Gesungenes und gesprochenes Wort in Werken W. V.s," *Archiv für Musikwissenschaft* 24: 64–80.

Hans Oesch
(trans. from German by Jeanne Wolf)

SEE ALSO Switzerland.

Voice, see Instrumental and Vocal Resources, Text Setting and Usage

Volkonsky, Andrei (Mikhailovich) (b. Geneva, 14 Feb 1933), studied at the Geneva Conservatory (1944–45, piano with Dinu Lipatti) and

the Paris Conservatory (1946–47, composition
with Nadia Boulanger) and had further training at the Tambovsky Musical College in
Moscow (graduated 1950) and the Moscow
Conservatory (1950–54, composition with
Yuri Shaporin). Since 1965 he has been artistic
director of Madrigal, an early-music ensemble
of the Moscow Philharmonic. The chief influences on his compositional development
have been Stravinsky, Webern, Boulez, Berio,
and music of Soviet Central Asia.

PRINCIPAL COMPOSITIONS: *Dead Souls*, cantata
for mezzo-soprano, chorus, organ, orchestra; text
by Gogol (1952); *Obraz mira*, cantata; text by Paul
Eluard (1953); *Concerto for Orchestra* (1953); *Piano
Quintet* (1954); *String Quartet* (1955); *Stepan
Kapitan*, film score (1955); *Piano Sonata* (1956);
Musica stricta for piano (1957); *2 Japanese Songs*
for chorus, electric instruments, percussion (1957);
Music for 12 instruments (1957); *Serenade to an
Insect* for chamber orchestra (1959); *Mirrors Suite*
for soprano, organ, flute, violin, guitar, percussion;
text by García-Lorca (1960); *Lamentations of
Shchaza* for soprano, violin, viola, English horn,
harpsichord, percussion (1962); *Jeux à 3* for flute,
violin, harpsichord, percussion (1963); *Wanderer
Concerto* for soprano, violin, percussion, orchestra;
text from the Rubaiyat of Omar Khayyám (1968).

PRINCIPAL WRITINGS: "Optimisticheskaya
Tragediya," *Sovetskaya musica* 1954/4.

[prepared with the help of Joel Spiegelman]
SEE ALSO Soviet Union.

Voormolen, Alexander (b. Rotterdam, 3
March 1895), studied first at the Utrecht
School of Music (composition with Johan
Wagenaar, piano with Willem Petri) and went
to Paris in 1916, where he worked with
Roussel and Ravel. From 1923 he lived in The
Hague. For many years he was music critic for
the *Nieuwe Rotterdamsche Courant* and later
librarian of the Royal Conservatory. He was
an early exponent of neobaroque tendencies,
and his music until the mid-20s was influenced
by the advanced French composers of the
time. Thereafter he became interested in
Dutch folksong and his harmonic style grew
more tonal.

PRINCIPAL COMPOSITIONS: *Tableaux des Pays Bas*
for piano, 2 vols. (1919–20, 1924; Rouart-Lerolle);
Beatrijs for narrator, piano; text by P. C. Boutens
(1921, Eck en Zoon); *Suite* for harpsichord (1921,
Alsbach); *Livre des enfants* for piano, 2 vols. (1923,
1925; Rouart-Lerolle); *Baron Hop Suites Nos. 1–2*
(1923–34, 1931; Donemus); *De drie Ruitertjes* [The
3 Little Horsemen], variations for orchestra (1927,
Alsbach); *Violin Sonata No. 2* (1934, Alsbach);
Oboe Concerto (1938, Basart); *Kleine Haagsche
Suite* for chamber orchestra (1939, Donemus);
String Quartet No. 2 (1942, Donemus); *Spiegel*

Suite for chamber orchestra (1943, Donemus);
Piano Sonata (1944, Alsbach); *Arethuza*, symphonic myth for orchestra (1947, Donemus); *3
Songs on British Verses* for voice, piano (1948,
Donemus); *Wanderers Nachtlied* for chorus; text
by Goethe (1949, Donemus); *Concerto* for 2
harpsichords, string orchestra (1950, Donemus);
Viola Sonata (1953, Donemus); *Chaconne en Fuga*
for orchestra (1958, Donemus).

BIBL.: Eduard Reeser, "A. V.," *Sonorum
speculum* 22–23.

Vostřák, Zbyněk (b. Prague, 10 June 1920),
studied composition in Prague with Rudolf
Karel (1938–43), at the Prague Conservatory
(1939–43, conducting with Pavel Dědeček),
and at the Darmstadt summer courses (1965–
66), where he attended lectures by Boulez,
Stockhausen, Ligeti, and Maderna. During
1943–45 he was a member of the Prague
Broadcasting Orchestra. He taught at the
Prague Music Academy and the Conservatory
during 1945–48. During 1959–60 he conducted
at the Zdeněk Nejedlý Opera Theater at Ústí-
on-the-Elbe, and since 1963 he has directed the
contemporary music ensemble Musica Viva
Pragensis. He has worked at the Electronic
Music Studio of Radio Prague since 1967. His
music since 1960 has been influenced by
Western contemporary composers, notably
Schoenberg, Webern, and Cage.

PRINCIPAL COMPOSITIONS: *Der zerbrochene Krug*,
comic opera, Op. 25; libretto by Heinrich von
Kleist (1960–61, Dilia); *3 Sonnets from Shakespeare*
for bass, chamber orchestra, Op. 33 (1963, ČHF
and Supraphon); *Kosmogonia* for string quartet in
quarter tones, Op 38 (1965, UE); *Zrození měsíce*
[The Birth of the Moon] for chamber orchestra,
Op. 39 (1966); *Kyvadlo času* [The Pendulum of
Time] for cello, winds, strings, percussion, electronic organ, Op. 40 (1966–67, UE); *Tao*, Op. 41, 12
cards for 9 players: flute, oboe, clarinet, bassoon,
violin, viola, cello, double bass, percussion (1967,
UE); *Váhy světla* [The Balance of Light] on 2-
track tape (1967); *Metahudba* [Metamusic] for
orchestra, Op. 43 (1968, UE); *Sextant* for wind
quintet, Op. 42 (1969, UE); *Dvě ohniska* [2 Focus]
on 2-track tape (1969).

PRINCIPAL WRITINGS: "Kapitoly z hudební
poetiky" [Chapters in Musical Poetics], *Konfrontace* (Prague) 1 (1969).

BIBL.: Eduard Herzog, "Avantgarde aus der
Tchechoslowakei," program booklet of the
Donaueschingen Musiktage (1968):6–7.
SEE ALSO Czechoslovakia.

Vycpálek, Ladislav (b. Prague, 23 Feb 1882; d.
there, 9 Jan 1969), studied at Charles Univ. in
Prague until 1906 and had private composition

lessons with Vítězslav Novák, 1908–12. During 1922–42 he was chief of the music division of the Charles Univ. Library. In contrast to the impressionist and Mahlerian atmosphere of pre-World War I Czech music, he preferred clear-cut forms and a linear style that often resulted in sharp dissonances. Partly because of the patriotism that the war engendered, he soon turned his attention to folk music and folk poetry and wrote a series of choral works on moral and social subjects.

PRINCIPAL COMPOSITIONS (published by Hudební Matice): *Festivities of Life*, 4 songs for voice, piano, Op. 8; poems by Richard Dehmel (1912–13); *The Vagabonds* for men's chorus, woodwinds, Op. 10; poem by K. Toman (1914); *War*, 10 folksongs for voice, piano, Op. 13 (1915); *Kantáta o posledních věcech člověka* [Cantata on the Final Affairs of Man] for vocal soloists, chorus, orchestra, Op. 16 (1920–22); *Sonata in D*, "In Praise of the Violin," for mezzo-soprano, violin, piano, Op. 19; text by S. Hanuš (1927–28); *Duet* for violin, viola, Op 20 (1929); Suite for viola, Op. 21 (1929); Suite for violin, Op. 22 (1930); *Blahoslavený ten člověk* [Blessed Is the Man], cantata for vocal soloists, chorus, orchestra, Op. 23; text from the Psalms (1933); *Czech Requiem* for vocal soloists, chorus, orchestra, Op. 24 (1940); *Vzhůru srdce!* [Up the Heart!], 2 fantasias on medieval folksongs for piano or orchestra, Op. 30 (1950).

BIBL.: Jaroslav Smolka, *Tvůrcí vývoj L. V.* [The Creative Development of L. V.] (Prague 1960).

Vyshnegradsky, Ivan, see under Wyschnegradsky

W

Wagenaar, Bernard (b. Arnhem, Netherlands, 18 July 1894; d. U.S., 18 May 1971), studied five years at the Utrecht Conservatory (composition with his father, Johan Wagenaar). He taught and conducted in the Netherlands before emigrating to the U.S. in 1920. During 1921–23 he was a violinist with the New York Philharmonic. He has taught composition at the Institute of Musical Art in New York (1925–37) and at the Juilliard School (1927–68).

PRINCIPAL COMPOSITIONS: *From a Very Little Sphinx* for voice, piano; texts by Edna St. Vincent Millay (1925); *Symphonies Nos. 1–4* (1926; 1931; 1935; 1949, Chappell); *Divertimento No. 1* for orchestra (1927, Fischer); *Violin Sonata* (1928, Schirmer-G); *Piano Sonata* (1928); *Sinfonietta* (1929, Boosey); *String Quartets Nos. 2–4* (1931, Boosey; 1936, Schirmer-G; 1960); *Sonatina* for cello, piano (1934, Fischer); *Triple Concerto* for flute, cello, harp, orchestra (premiere 1937); *Eclogue* for organ (1940, Gray); *Fantasietta on British-American Ballads* for chamber orchestra (1940); *Concertino* for 8 instruments (1942); *Feuilleton* for orchestra (1942); *El trillo* for chorus, 2 guitars, tambourine, snare drum, castanets (1942); *No quierotus Avellanas* for alto, women's chorus, flute, English horn, 2 guitars, tambourine, snare drum, castanets (1942); *Song of Mourning* for orchestra (premiere 1944, Fischer); *Pieces of 8*, 2-act chamber opera; libretto by Edward Eager (premiere 1944); *Ciacona* for piano (1948, Marks); *5 Tableaux* for cello, orchestra (1952); *Divertimento No. 2* for orchestra (1953); *Concert Overture* (premiere 1954, Shawnee); *Preamble* for orchestra (1956); *4 Vignettes* for harp (1965).

BIBL.: Donald Fuller, "B. W.," *Modern Music* 21:225–31.

Wagner, Joseph (Frederick) (b. Springfield, Mass., 9 Jan 1900), studied piano and organ privately in Providence (1919–21) and then attended the New England Conservatory (1921–23, composition with Frederick S. Converse) and Boston Univ. (1931–33). He studied composition privately with Alfredo Casella in Boston in 1928, and with Nadia Boulanger in Paris, 1934–35, at which time he

also studied conducting with Felix Weingartner and Pierre Monteux. He was assistant director of music and supervisor of instrumental music for the Boston public schools during 1923–44. He has taught at Boston Univ. (1920–40), Brooklyn College (1945–47), and elsewhere. During 1960–63 he was chairman of the theory department of the Los Angeles Conservatory, and became composer-in-residence at Pepperdine College in 1963. Wagner has also been active as a conductor. He founded the Boston Civic Symphony, which he conducted from 1925 to 1944. He conducted the Buffalo Philharmonic (1945), Duluth Symphony (1947–50), the St. Paul "Pop" Concerts (1947–48), and Orquesta Sinfonica Nacional de Costa Rica (1950–54), and other orchestras. Starting in 1936 he went through a decade of compositional experimentation. A "white period" and neoclassicism was followed by the use of polytonal concepts coupled with melodic lines having unusual intervalic relationships. This style became crystallized in the 1950s.

PRINCIPAL COMPOSITIONS (published by Southern unless otherwise noted): *Hudson River Legend*, ballet (1941, Brown); *Violin Sonata No. 2* (1941, Mills); *Sinfonietta No. 2* for string orchestra (1941); *Symphony No. 2* (1945, unpub.); *Piano Sonata in B Minor* (1946); *Concertino* for harp, orchestra (1947, Lyra); *Concerto grosso* for band (1949); *Northland Evocations* for orchestra (1949); *Symphony No. 3* (1951, unpub.); *Missa sacra* for soprano, chorus, orchestra or organ (1952, Ricordi); *Violin Concerto in C Minor* (1956, unpub.); *Serenade* for oboe, violin, cello (1958); *Sonata of Sonnets* for soprano, piano (1960); *Concerto* for organ, brass, percussion (1963); *Fantasy and Fugue* for wind quintet (1963); *Fantasy Sonata* for harp (1963, Lyra); *Merlin and Sir Boss* for band (1963); *New England Sampler*, 1-act opera (1964, orchestrated 1967; Southern); *Sonata With Differences* for 2 pianos (1963, unpub.); *3 Charades* for brass quintet (1964); *Preludes and Toccata* for harp, violin, cello (1964, Lyra); *Trio concertante* for piano, violin, cello (1969); *12 Concert Preludes* for organ (1970). List to 1966: *Composers of the Americas* 12:159–69.

PRINCIPAL WRITINGS: program notes for the Boston Civic Symphony, 1925–44; program notes for the Orquesta Sinfonica de Costa Rica, 1950–54; *Orchestration, A Practical Handbook and Workbook* (New York 1959); *Band Scoring and Workbook* (New York 1960); "Dilemma of Concert Band Programs," *Music Journal* (Jan 1969):38; "Band Scoring IS Composition," *ibid.* (Feb 1970):33.

PRINCIPAL WRITINGS: "Erhaltenes und Bewahrtes," aphorisms and notes, appendix to Härtwig (see bibl.); *Begegnungen*, correspondence with Caspar Neher (East Berlin 1969).

BIBL.: Dieter Härtwig, R. W.-R., *Der Opernkomponist: Leben und Werk* (East Berlin 1965).

[prepared with the help of Dieter Härtwig]

SEE ALSO Austria and Germany.

Wagner-Régeny, Rudolf (b. Szász-Régen in Transylvania, now Rumania, 28 August 1903; d. East Berlin, 18 Sept 1969), attended the Leipzig Conservatory (1919–20, piano with Robert Teichmüller), and the Berlin Musikhochschule (1920–23; harmony and counterpoint with F. E. Koch, orchestration with E. N. von Reznicek, opera with Franz Schreker, conducting with Rudolf Krasselt and Siegfried Ochs). He was a coach and chorus director at the Berlin Grosse Volksoper in 1923–25, and during 1927–30 was composer and music director for Rudolf von Laban's *Kammertanzbühne*. He also worked as pianist, free-lance composer, and consultant for films in Germany. He was director of the Musikhochschule in Rostock during 1947–50 and from 1950 to 1968 was professor of composition at the Hochschule and Academy of Arts in East Berlin. Wagner-Régeny was primarily an opera composer. In his earlier years he was influenced by Busoni, Schoenberg, Kurt Weill, and by his collaborations with Caspar Neher and Bertolt Brecht; his stage compositions of this period reflect a concern with social criticism, and they have a "didactic-epic" character. In about 1943 he began to work with 12-tone techniques and contrapuntal textures.

PRINCIPAL COMPOSITIONS (published by UE unless otherwise noted): *Der Günstling*, 3-act opera; libretto by Caspar Neher after Victor Hugo (1932–34); *Orchestermusik mit Klavier* (1935); *Die Bürger von Calais*, 3-act opera; libretto by Neher after Froissart (1936–38); *Der zerbrochene Krüg*, ballet after H. Kleist (1937); *Johanna Balk*, 3-act opera; libretto by Neher after a Transylvanian ballad (1938–40); *Persische Episode*, 4-act opera; libretto by Neher and Bertolt Brecht after the 1001 Nights (1940–50); *3 Movements for Orchestra* (1952, Bote); *Cantica Davidi Regis* for bass, boys' choir, small orchestra (1954, Bote); *Genesis* for alto, chorus, small orchestra (1955–56, Bote); *Prometheus*, staged oratorio (1957–58, Bote and Henschel); *Das Bergwerk zu Falun*, opera in 8 tableaux; text by von Hofmannsthal (1958–60, Bote and Henschel); *Schir haschirim* for alto, baritone, small women's chorus, small orchestra (1963–64, Bote); *Einleitung und Ode* for orchestra (1967, Peters-L); *8 Kommentare zu einer Weise des G. Machaut* for small orchestra (1968, Peters-L).

Walton, William (Turner) (b. Oldham, Lancashire, 29 March 1902), was first taught music by his father and then entered Christ Church Cathedral Choir School, Oxford. His precocious talents were soon recognized, enabling him to become an undergraduate at 16. He seemed to need little formal instruction in music, and after leaving Oxford a year or two later he received no further training apart from advice from Ernest Ansermet and Ferruccio Busoni.

A string quartet, performed at the first festival of the ISCM (Salzburg, 1923) and later withdrawn, brought his name before the public, but he first won fame with *Façade* (1923) to poems by Edith Sitwell. In this work all the features of Walton's mature style are present: the rhythmic vivacity, which owes something to Stravinsky and Prokofiev; the dissonant harmony; the pungent flavor of the instrumentation; the wit alternating with brooding melancholy. The melancholy strain recurs in the slow movement of the *Sinfonia concertante* (1927, revised 1943) and, more overtly, in the *Viola Concerto* (1929, revised 1962). In the latter work, probably Walton's masterpiece, the conflict in his music between romantic lyricism and rhythmic violence receives its finest expression. In his next work, *Belshazzar's Feast* (1931), the sufferings and jubilation of the Jewish captives in Babylon are depicted in savage orchestral colors and in choral writing of Handelian splendor. Equally powerful, if structurally less satisfying, is the *Symphony No. 1* (1934–35).

During World War II Walton wrote little except music for films, of which some (notably parts of the score for *Henry V*) have survived in the concert hall. His postwar works have shown him reluctant to extend the range of his style. Despite its many beauties, his first opera, *Troilus and Cressida* (1954), disappointed those who had hoped for more of the dramatic excitement of *Belshazzar's Feast*. Highly self-critical and a fastidious craftsman, Walton is not prolific and his reputation will probably continue to depend on a handful of works. These however include a few (the *Viola Concerto, Belshazzar's Feast*, and the *Symphony*

No. 1) which rank among the most original and best constructed essays in the major media by any British composer since Elgar.

PRINCIPAL COMPOSITIONS (published by Oxford): *Façade*, "entertainment" for reciter, 6 instruments; poems by Edith Sitwell (1923); *Portsmouth Point Overture* for orchestra (1926); *Sinfonia concertante* for piano, orchestra (1927, revised 1943); *Viola Concerto* (1929, revised 1962); *Belshazzar's Feast* for baritone, double chorus, orchestra, 2 optional brass bands; texts from the Old Testament (1931); *Symphonies Nos. 1–2* (1934–35, 1960); *In Honour of the City of London* for chorus, orchestra; poem by William Dunbar (1937); *Violin Concerto* (1939); *Scapino*, comedy overture for orchestra (1940); *Henry V*, film score (1944); *String Quartet* (1947); *Hamlet*, film score (1947); *Violin Sonata* (1950); *Troilus and Cressida*, opera; libretto by Christopher Hassall (1954); *Richard III*, film score (1955); *Cello Concerto* (1957); *Partita* for orchestra (1958); *Variations on a Theme by Hindemith* for orchestra (1963); *The Bear*, "extravaganza" in 1 act; libretto by Paul Dehn after Chekhov (1967).

BIBL.: Frank Howes, *The Music of W. W.*, revised ed. (London 1965); Peter J. Pirie, "Scapino: The Development of W. W.," *Musical Times* (April 1964):258–59; R. Murray Schafer, *British Composers in Interview* (London 1963).

Michael Graham-Dixon

SEE ALSO Great Britain.

Ward, Robert (Eugene) (b. Cleveland, 13 Sept 1917), studied at the Eastman School (1935–39; composition with Bernard Rogers, Howard Hanson) the Juilliard School (1939–46; composition with Frederick Jacobi; conducting with Albert Stoessel, Edgar Schenkman; orchestration with Bernard Wagenaar), and Tanglewood (1940, composition with Aaron Copland). He taught at Columbia Univ. (1946–48) and Juilliard (1946–56). During 1952–55 he was director of the Third Street Settlement Music School in New York. He was vice president and managing editor of Galaxy Music Corp. and the Highgate Press during 1956–67. Since then he has been president of the North Carolina School of the Arts in Winston-Salem. He has guest conducted numerous orchestras in the U.S. and Europe and has served on many boards and advisory committees of music and recording organizations. Ward has said that the "American quality" in his music since the 1950s stems "directly from an interest in American folksong and jazz." Even his early works, however, exhibit "the more basic penchants for austere contrapuntal writing, simple slow melodies with elaborate obbligato, and fast rhythmic dance tunes."

PRINCIPAL COMPOSITIONS (published by Highgate unless otherwise noted): *Symphonies Nos. 1–4* (1941, 1947, 1950, 1958); *Jubilation*, overture for orchestra (1946); *Violin Sonata* (1950, Peer); *Sacred Songs for Pantheists* for soprano, orchestra (1951); *Fantasia* for brass, timpani (1953); *Euphony* for orchestra (1954); *He Who Gets Slapped*, 3-act opera; libretto by Bernard Stambler after Andreyev (1956); *Earth Shall Be Fair* for soprano, children's chorus (or soprano solo), adult chorus, orchestra or organ (1960); *Divertimento* for orchestra (1960); *The Crucible*, 4-act opera; libretto by Stambler after Arthur Miller (1961); *Music for a Celebration* for orchestra (1963); *The Lady from Colorado*, 2-act operetta; libretto by Stambler (1964); *String Quartet* (1965); *Sweet Freedom's Song,* cantata for narrator, soprano, baritone, chorus, orchestra; text compiled by Mary and Robert Ward (1965); *Festive Ode* for orchestra (1966); *Piano Concerto* (1968). List to 1963: *Composers of the Americas* 9:174–79.

PRINCIPAL WRITINGS: "The Composer and the Music Business," *Juilliard Review* (winter 1955–56):45–49; "New Electronic Media," *ibid.* (spring 1958):17–22.

BIBL.: "R. W.," *ACA Bulletin* 4/4:3–12.

SEE ALSO Opera.

Ward-Steinman, David (b. Alexandria, La., 6 Nov 1936), studied at Florida State Univ. (1953–57, composition with John Boda), the Univ. of Ill. (1957–58, 1959–61; composition with Burrill Phillips), and Princeton Univ, (spring 1970, computer composition). He also studied with Nadia Boulanger in Paris (1958–59) and with Wallingford Riegger at Stockbridge, Mass. (summer 1954), Darius Milhaud at Aspen (summer 1956), and Milton Babbitt at Tanglewood (summer 1957). He has taught at San Diego State College (1961–70) and was composer-in-residence for the Tampa Bay, Fla., area under a Ford Foundation grant (1970–72).

PRINCIPAL COMPOSITIONS (published by Marks unless otherwise noted): *Piano Sonata* (1956–57, unpub.); *Symphony* (1959); *Prelude and Toccata* for orchestra (1962); *Fragments from Sappho* for soprano, flute, clarinet, piano (1962–65); *Song of Moses*, oratorio for narrator, soprano, 2 tenors, baritone, chorus, orchestra (1963–64, San Diego State College Press); *Western Orpheus*, ballet; choreography by Richard Carter (1964); *Cello Concerto* (1964–66); *These Three*, ballet for chorus, orchestra; choreography by Eugene Loring (1966); *Jazz Tangents* for wind ensemble or band (1966–67, MJQ); *The Tale of Issoubochi* for narrator, soprano, flute, clarinet, cello, piano interior, celesta, percussion; libretto by Susan Lucas from a Japanese fairy tale (1968); *Childs Play* for bassoon, piano, piano interior (1968, Highgate).

PRINCIPAL WRITINGS: *Serial Techniques in the Recent Music of Stravinsky* (DMA thesis, Univ. of Ill., 1961); "Beethoven—Composer for All Seasons," *Music Educators Journal* (Dec 1970).

BIBL.: Oliver Daniel, "D. W.-S.," *BMI: The Many Worlds of Music* (June 1970): 10. *San Diego Magazine* has published 3 articles on Ward-Steinman (Dec 1962, May 1964, April 1965).

Weber, Ben (b. 23 July 1916), studied voice, theory, and piano at De Pauw Univ. in Chicago but was not interested in a musical career until 1944, after a year of premedical training at the Univ. of Ill. Largely self-taught, he was encouraged in composition by the pianist Artur Schnabel and by Arnold Schoenberg, whom he visited in 1940. Since 1945 he has lived in New York, where he has taught composition and orchestration privately. He has also held executive posts in the ISCM, Composers Recordings, Inc., and the American Composers Alliance.

Weber was one of the first American composers to use 12-tone procedures, and since 1938 he has written in a basically contrapuntal 12-tone idiom, one that often has strong tonal implications. He generally uses forms associated with the diatonic tradition. His output includes over 30 chamber works, some with solo voice, and about half that number of orchestral works, including several concertos. There are also solo songs and song cycles, choruses, and pieces for piano solo. Two polarities exist in this music: The first, most noticeable in the works of the 1940s and early 50s, is characterized by declarative statements, jaunty rhythms, and an air of exuberance and wit. The second, appearing increasingly in more recent works, is characterized by greater emotional reserve. These latter works tend to be longer and to incorporate increased contrapuntal manipulation, denser harmonic textures, and larger instrumental forces.

PRINCIPAL COMPOSITIONS (published by ACA unless otherwise noted): *5 Pieces* for cello, piano, Op 13 (1941); *Episodes* for piano, Op. 26a (1950); *Symphony in 4 Movements on Poems of William Blake* for baritone, chamber ensemble, Op. 33 (1951); *Violin Concerto*, Op. 41 (1954); *Serenade* for strings, Op. 46 (1956, Boosey); *Piano Concerto*, Op. 52 (1961); *The Ways*, cycle for soprano or tenor, piano, Op. 54 (1964); *Dolmen* for winds, strings, Op. 58 (1966); *Concert Poem* for violin, orchestra, Op. 61 (1970). List to 1963: *Composers of the Americas* 9:182–86; list to 1967: Oliver Daniel, *B. W.* (New York: BMI, 1967).

Carl Sigmon

SEE ALSO United States.

Webern, Anton (Friedrich Wilhelm von) (b. Vienna, 3 Dec 1883; d. Mittersill, 15 Sept 1945), was the son of a mining engineer who took his family to Graz in 1890, thence to Klagenfurt in 1894. Webern's earliest instruction in music came from his mother, an amateur pianist. At Klagenfurt he studied piano and theory with Edwin Komauer. His earliest known music, 2 *Pieces* for cello and piano and some songs, dates from 1899.

Upon graduation from the Humanistisches Gymnasium at Klagenfurt in 1902, Webern traveled to the Wagner Festival at Bayreuth, and in the fall he entered the Univ. of Vienna, where he studied musicology with Guido Adler, harmony with Hermann Graedener, and counterpoint with Karl Navratil. He also sang in the chorus of the Akademische Wagner-Verein and met several leading conductors, including Gustav Mahler. After an unsuccessful attempt to study composition with Hans Pfitzner, he became in 1904 a pupil of Arnold Schoenberg. Before beginning his studies with Schoenberg, he had composed a number of songs and some instrumental music, including the idyll for orchestra *Im Sommerwind* (1904). In 1906 he received a doctorate from the Univ. of Vienna for an edition of part II of the *Choralis Constantinus* by the renaissance Netherlander Heinrich Isaac (the edition was published in 1909 in the *Denkmäler der Tonkunst in Österreich* series). He continued lessons with Schoenberg until 1908 and remained closely associated with him until 1925, when Schoenberg moved to Berlin. While a pupil he met Alban Berg, with whom he developed a warm friendship.

Beginning in 1908 Webern held a variety of conducting posts in theaters at such places as Bad Ischl (summer 1908), Teplitz (1910), Danzig (1910–11), Stettin (1911–12), and Prague (1917). Although the operetta type of repertory in these theaters was distasteful to him, it did give him the opportunity to develop his conducting craft. During 1918–22 he was active in Schoenberg's Society for Private Musical Performances, from 1922 to 1934 he conducted the Vienna Workers' Symphony Concerts, and, beginning in 1924, the Vienna Workers' Chorus. He became conductor and musical advisor for the Austrian Radio in 1927. On five occasions he conducted the BBC Orchestra in London (1929, 1932, 1933, 1935, 1936). Accounts of his conducting indicate that he was a meticulous craftsman, not given to dramatic gestures. In 1920 he began a life-long association with the publishers Universal Edition.

The only teaching position he held was with the Hebrew Institute for the Blind, but he did have several private composition students, including Ludwig Zenk, Karl Amadeus Hartmann, and Leopold Spinner. When the Social Democratic Party was dissolved in 1934, he lost his conducting posts with the Vienna Workers' organizations, and his work with the Austrian Radio terminated shortly after the Austrian Anschluss in 1938. During World War II he taught a diminishing number of private pupils in Vienna and did occasional work for Universal Edition. Performances of his music in Germany and Austria virtually ceased after it was proscribed by the Nazis. After the death of his only son early in 1945, Webern and his wife went to Mittersill to be with their remaining children (three daughters). While there he was accidentally shot by an American soldier.

After his death Webern's music gained increasing attention among the younger European composers. Those associated with the Kranichstein Summer School in Darmstadt and the first Electronic Studio in Cologne—Herbert Eimert (b. 1897), Karlheinz Stockhausen (b. 1928), and Pierre Boulez (b. 1925)—credited Webern with so much influence that the 1950s came to be called the "post-Webern" period. What was discovered in Webern's music at that time was a purity of conception and consistency of style that seemed to lead from a traditional base to a completely new sound world; it seemed to contain in its structure the roots of new levels of organization (i.e., serialism). His music known at that time consisted of only 31 opus numbers. Except for Opp. 1 and 2, all of the music was atonal and free of tonic-oriented harmony. The pieces were relatively short, generally sparsely scored, and imbued with a rigorous logic dependent upon individual intervallic relations. Appraisals of Webern's output changed during the 1960s owing to discoveries by Hans Moldenhauer of a large number of manuscripts, including previously unknown works of 1899–1925.

1899–1908. Compositions from this, Webern's tonal period, date from his student days in Klagenfurt through his early works under the tutelage of Schoenberg. The early *Avenarius Songs* (1903–04) are nondescript products of late romantic expression influenced by Wagner and Wolf. A more personal idiom emerged in the *Dehmel Lieder* (1906–08) and the *String Quartet* (1905); with the *Passacaglia*, Op. 1 (1908), and the a cappella chorus, Op. 2 (1908), there appeared such Webernian characteristics as symmetrical structures (Op. 1), canon (Op.

2), and interlocking structural units (both). Most works of this period were not brought to light until after Webern's death.

1908–27. A "free atonal" period began with the *5 Songs*, Op. 3 (1907–09), in which Webern abjured the process of developing key centers by traditional harmonic gravitation. However, experiments with key centers established by other means can be observed in Nos. 1 and 4 of *4 Pieces* for violin and piano, Op. 7 (1910), and other works. In the lieder to poems by Stefan George (Opp. 3, 4, and four posthumous songs), a delicate balance of vocal line and piano music produces an expression of fleeting beauty. Sections are set off by rests and changes of tempo, and the kinetic flow is directed in part by flexible ostinato structures. Few of the songs display formal outlines as in classic and early romantic songs, although occasional ABA patterns may be found (e.g., Op. 3, No. 1). In the string quartet music of this period, *5 Movements*, Op. 5 (1909), and the *Bagatelles*, Op. 9 (1913), individual movements are shortened to the point of aphorism. Special string sounds, such as *col legno*, *sul ponticello*, and *sul tasto*, combined with harmonics, pizzicato, and mute, are employed in a profusion that provides great variation of timbre from an otherwise homogeneous medium. In the orchestral music, *6 Pieces*, Op. 6 (1910), and *5 Pieces*, Op. 10 (1911–13), timbre variation functions in an ever more important way as a compositional determinant. *Klangfarbenmelodie* (melody of tone colors), discussed by Schoenberg in his *Harmonielehre* (1911), is applied to Webern's technique of orchestration in these and later works. Brevity of form, sometimes thought to be a weakness associated with atonality but really a concomitant of intensified expression, reached its furthest limits in Op. 10, the fourth piece of which consists of only six bars.

Between 1914 and 1926 Webern composed only lieder. Many aspects of his style crystallized in the Opp. 12–19 cycles (1915–26). Vocal lines contain larger intervals and greater contrasts of very high and very low notes, and instrumental lines continue to be fragmented. In the fifth song of Op. 15, "Fahr hin, O Seel'" (1917), Webern returned to canonic structures for the first time since Op. 2, using a strict double canon in contrary motion. The canonic lines are dispersed through the instruments in constantly varying timbres. The next cycle, Op. 16 (1923–24), consists entirely of two and three-voice canons, and in Op. 17, *3 Folk Texts* (1925), the 12-tone technique is applied.

Little change in musical style is evident in the *3 Folk Texts*. Chromatic proliferation is so nearly complete in all of the free atonal works, especially those from Op. 7 to Op. 17, that the music is almost a nonserial dodecaphony (the third piece of Op. 11 actually demonstrates a proto-serialism of pitches). Structural relations in this music are created through recurring and overlapping three-note motives consisting of one chromatic interval (major seventh or minor ninth) and one other interval (frequently a third or sixth). Integration of texture depends not so much on shape identification as on intervallic consistency. In the Opp. 17–19 song cycles, as in Webern's earliest known 12-tone piece (*Kinderstück* for piano, fall 1924), the method is employed in a limited and provisional fashion. However, in the *String Trio*, Op. 20 (1927), which closes the middle period in Webern's development, the method is more fully exploited, acting in conjunction with formal divisions (certain forms of the set are associated with certain sections of the rondo and sonata forms that make up the two movements).

1928–45. The third-period works are characterized by denser interrelations of musical materials along with generally sparser musical textures. Many of the 12-tone sets are structured so that one part is a transposed form of another (Opp. 21, 24, 28, 29, 30). The set of the *Concerto for 9 Instruments*, Op. 24 (1934), for example, consists of a three-note group followed by transpositions of its retrograde-inversion, its retrograde, and its inversion (B-Bb-D, Eb-G-F#, G#-E-F, C-C#-A). The *String Quartet*, Op. 28 (1938), consists of transformations of the B-A-C-H- (Bb-A-C-B♮) motive Webern's music reflects the relationships in these sets. The *Symphony*, Op. 21 (1928), the earliest work of this period, uses a set consisting of a six-note group and its transposed retrograde. The palindrome character of the set is reflected in the structure of the second movement, a set of variations, in which the theme and each variation are symmetrical. An important innovation appears in the first movement of the *Symphony* and reappears in the second movement of the *Piano Variations*, Op. 27 (1936): the restriction of the octave levels (registers) at which the various members of the set sound. Both movements are in sonata form, and in the exposition of the *Symphony* movement the musical space is frozen into a symmetrical chord centered on a *mese*, the note A′.

Only two cycles of songs were composed during this period, both with piano accompaniment. There are, however, three important works for chorus and orchestra: *Das Augenlicht*, Op. 26 (1935), and the cantatas Opp. 29

(1938–39) and 31 (1941–43). The poems, by Webern's close friend Hildegard Jone, have a mystical quality, a pantheism combining Christian theology with an adoration of all life. The choral writing combines many factors, including the 16th-century choral ideal, the properties of the sets used, and the changing sonorities of Webern's sound-world. The predominant textures can be characterized as 1) a polyphonic texture of two to four voices in free, direct imitation but with exact inversion, retrograde, or retrograde inversion of pitch classes, and 2) a homorhythmic texture in which the four voice parts consist of transpositions of forms of the series while forming varying simultaneities. The first procedure is developed to a highly abstract level in the final chorale of the Op. 31 cantata, where each part is related throughout to the other three by direct imitation, by inversion, and by retrograde.

Analyses of Webern's music have generally emphasized structural innovations that adumbrate later techniques, especially the incipient serialization of durations, registers, and dynamic levels in isolated areas of such works as Opp. 21, 24, and 27. What is also important in Webern's style is the manifestation of his concept of a continuing historical tradition in music. There is a romantic and lyric impulse behind much of his work, despite the presence of large intervals, melodic fragmentation, and extremes of range. A large number of the compositions are vocal, with texts by Goethe, Rilke, Stefan George, Georg Trakl, Hildegard Jone, and from folk and traditional sources; they contain frequent allusions to colors, atmospheres, plants, and childlike and mystical Christianity. Certain words are set pictorially (e.g., the settings of "Himmel" in Op. 15), but an even clearer manifestation of the lyric impulse is a melodic contour that recurs so often it might even be called a melodic signature. This contour, an expansion of the 16th-century cambiata figure, consists of two descending intervals (the second greater than the first) followed by an ascending interval, with at least one chromatic connection (major seventh or minor ninth). Another link to tradition is Webern's frequent adaptation of classical formal schemes (Opp. 1, 5, 20, 21, 27, 30) and the frequent use of canon (Opp. 2, 15, 16, 21, 22, 24, 31).

Webern's influence may be observed in most new music of the 1950s and 60s. More than his structural innovations or his use of classic forms, it is the sound of his music that most strongly affected composers, a sound in which each interval, even a single note, attains importance in itself and becomes a significant member of the glittering galaxy which is Webern's sound world. In 1962 a Webern Festival was held in Seattle, and the International Webern Society was formed. Most of his important manuscripts are housed in the Webern Archive, a division of the Moldenhauer Archives, a provisional catalog of which appears in *Anton von Webern: Perspectives*.

PRINCIPAL COMPOSITIONS (published by UE unless otherwise noted): *Im Sommerwind*, idyll for orchestra (1904, Fischer); *String Quartet 1905* (1905, Fischer); *Quintet* for string quartet, piano (1906, Boelke); *5 Songs* after poems by Richard Dehmel for voice, piano (1906–08, Fischer); *Passacaglia* for orchestra, Op. 1 (1908); *5 Songs* for voice, piano, Op. 3; poems from *Der Siebente Ring* by Stefan George (1907–09); *5 Movements* for string quartet, Op. 5 (1909); *6 Pieces* for orchestra, Op. 6 (1910); *2 Songs* for voice, 8 instruments, Op. 8; poems by Rilke (1910); *5 Pieces* for orchestra, Op. 10 (1911–13); *6 Bagatelles* for string quartet, Op. 9 (1913); *3 Orchestral Songs* (1913–14, Fischer); *4 Songs* for voice, orchestra, Op. 13 (1914–18); *6 Songs* for voice, clarinet, bass clarinet, violin, cello, Op. 14; poems by Georg Trakl (1917–21); *5 Canons after Latin Texts* for soprano, clarinet, bass clarinet, Op. 16 (1923–24); *Kinderstück* for piano (1924, Fischer); *3 Folk Texts* for voice, violin (viola), clarinet, bass clarinet, Op. 17 (1925); *Klavierstück* for piano (1925); *3 Songs* for voice, clarinet, guitar, Op. 18 (1925); *Movement for String Trio* (1925); *2 Songs* for chorus, celesta, guitar, violin, clarinet, bass clarinet, Op. 19; texts from Goethe's Chinesisch-Deutsche Jahres- und Tageszeiten (1926); *String Trio*, Op 20 (1927); *Symphony*, Op. 21 (1928); *Quartet* for clarinet, tenor saxophone, violin, piano, Op. 22 (1930); *3 Songs* for voice, piano, Op. 23; texts from *Viae inviae* by Hildegard Jone (1934); *Concerto for 9 Instruments* for flute, oboe, clarinet, horn, trumpet, trombone, violin, viola, piano, Op. 24 (1934); *Das Augenlicht* for chorus, orchestra, Op. 26; poems by Jone (1935); *Variations for Piano*, Op. 27 (1936); *String Quartet*, Op. 28 (1938); *Cantata No. 1* for soprano, chorus, orchestra, Op. 29; poems by Jone (1938–39); *Variations for Orchestra*, Op. 30 (1940); *Cantata No. 2* for soprano, bass, chorus, orchestra, Op. 31; poems by Jone (1941–43). Webern also made many arrangements, including the "Ricercar a 6 voci," No. 2 in the *Musical Offering* by J. S. Bach (1935).

PRINCIPAL WRITINGS: *Heinrich Isaac: Choralis Constantinus Part II* (*Denkmäler der Tonkunst in Österreich* 16/1, 1909); *The Path to the New Music* ed. by W. Reich, trans. by L. Black (Bryn Mawr, Pa., 1966); *Letters to Hildegard Jone and Josef Humplik* ed. by J. Polnauer, trans. by C. Cardew (Bryn Mawr 1967).

BIBL.: Herbert Eimert and Karlheinz Stockhausen, eds., *A. W.*, vol. 2 of *Die Reihe* trans. by L. Black and E. Smith (Bryn Mawr 1958); Walter Kolneder, *A. W.: An Introduction to His Works* trans. by H. Searle (Berkeley-Los Angeles 1968); Ernst Krenek, commentary to *A. v. W., Sketches* (*1926–1945*), foreword by Hans Moldenhauer (New York 1968); René Leibowitz, *Schoenberg and His School*, trans. by D. Newlin (New York 1949); Wallace McKenzie, *The Music of A. W.* (PhD diss., North Texas State Univ., 1960); Hans Moldenhauer, compiler, Demar Irvine, ed., *A. v. W.: Perspectives* (Seattle 1966); Hans Moldenhauer, *A. v. W., Chronicle of His Life and Works* (unpub.); ——, *The Death of A. W.: A Drama in Documents* (New York 1961); Claude Rostand, *A. W.* (Paris 1969); Friedrich Wildgans, *A. W.*, trans. by E. T. Roberts and H. Searle (London 1966).

Wallace McKenzie

SEE ALSO Asian Music and Western Composition, Austria and Germany, Dance, Form, Harmony and Counterpoint, Melody, Musicology and Composition, Performance, Rhythm, Text Setting and Usage, Texture, 12-Tone Techniques.

Weigl, Karl (b. Vienna, 6 Feb 1881; d. New York, 11 August 1949), attended the Vienna Academy (c.1898–1902, piano with Anton Door, composition with Robert Fuchs) and the Univ. of Vienna (1900–04, musicology with Guido Adler), receiving his PhD for a dissertation on E. A. Förster. He also studied composition with Alexander von Zemlinsky. From 1904 to 1906 he was assistant coach at the Vienna Hofoper under Gustav Mahler, who influenced and encouraged Weigl's compositional work. Weigl taught music theory and composition at the New Vienna Conservatory during 1918–28 and lectured at the Musicological Institute of the Univ. of Vienna from 1931 until his emigration to the U.S. in 1938. He taught theory and composition for the Committee on Musical Training and Scholarships of the New York Philharmonic Society and was on the faculties of the American Theatre Wing in New York, the Hartt Music Foundation, Hartford, Conn. (1941–42), Brooklyn College (1943–45), the Boston Conservatory (1945–48), and the Philadelphia Music Academy (1948–49).

PRINCIPAL COMPOSITIONS (unpublished chamber and vocal music available from ACA): ★ *8 String Quartets*: in C Minor (1903, Breitkopf); in D Minor with viola d'amore (1907); in A (1909, UE); in D Minor (1924, Joshua); in G (1933); in C (1939); in F Minor (1942, Joshua); in D (1949). ★ *6 Symphonies*: in E, Op. 5 (c.1908, UE); in D Minor, Op. 19 (1912, Schott); in B♭ (1931, Presser); in F Minor (1936, Presser); "Apocalyptic," in C Minor (1945, AMP); in A Minor (1947, Boosey). ★ *2 Violin Sonatas*: in C, Op. 16 (1922, Schott); in G (Joshua). ★ Other works: *Nachtphantasien* for piano, Op. 13 (1911, Joshua); *Weltfeier*, symphonic cantata for tenor, bass, chorus, orchestra, organ, Op. 17 (1912, Schott); *3 Intermezzi* for strings or string orchestra (1916, Presser); *Phantastisches Intermezzo* for orchestra, Op. 18 (1922, Schott); *Cello Sonata in G* (1923, John Markert, N. Y.); *Violin Concerto* (1928, Boosey); *Cello Concerto in G Minor* (1934); *5 Songs for Soprano and String Quartet*, Op. 40 (1934, Markert); *3 Songs for Alto and String Quartet* (1936); *Piano Concerto in F Minor*, Op. 21 (published 1937, UE); *Komödienouvertüre* for orchestra, Op. 32 (published 1937, UE); *Piano Trio* (1939, Joshua); *Viola Sonata* (1940, Markert).

PRINCIPAL WRITINGS: "E. A. Försters Leben," *Sammelbände der Internationalen Musikgesellschaft* 6; *Die Symphonien Gustav Mahlers* (Vienna c.1910); "Erinnerungen an Gustav Mahler," *Austria* 2/2 (Vienna-Graz, Nov 1947); "Mahler as I Remember Him," *Musical Courrier* (Jan 1948):5.

BIBL.: Ernst Bacon, "K. W.," *Musical America* (1 Jan 1950); Paul Frankl, "K. W. ist gestorben," *Österreichische Musikzeitschrift* 4 (1949); Rudolf Stefan Hoffmann, "K. W.," *Musikblätter des Anbruch* (Oct 1921); Rudolf List, "Ein österreichischer Musiker in Amerika," *Austria* 2/7 (July 1947).

Weill, Kurt (b. Dessau, 2 March 1900; d. New York, 3 April 1950), studied at the Berlin Hochschule für Musik (1918–19, composition with Engelbert Humperdinck) and privately in Berlin with Ferruccio Busoni (1921–24). During 1918–21 he was an opera coach at Dessau and a theater conductor at Lüdenscheid. He achieved his chief fame in the theater, first as an opera composer and then as a collaborator with Bertolt Brecht. In 1933 he left Germany and in 1935 settled in the U.S., where he wrote highly successful works for the Broadway stage. He was one of the first composers to successfully incorporate jazz elements in concert music and to deal in music-theater works with current social and political issues.

PRINCIPAL COMPOSITIONS: *String Quartet*, Op. 8 (1923, UE); *Quodlibet* for orchestra, Op. 9 (1923, AMP); *Concerto* for violin, winds, Op. 12 (1924, AMP); *Der neue Orpheus*, cantata for soprano, violin, orchestra, Op. 16 (1925, AMP); *Der Protagonist*, opera; libretto by Georg Kaiser (1925); *Der Lindberghflug*, radio cantata for tenor, baritone, bass, chorus, orchestra; text by Bertolt Brecht (1927, AMP); *Die Dreigroschenoper*, opera after John Gay's Beggar's Opera by Elisabeth Hauptmann; lyrics by Brecht (1927, UE); *Mahagonny*, singspiel; text by Brecht (1927–29, UE; reworked, 1929, into a 3-act opera, *Aufsteig und Fall der Stadt Mahagonny*); *Der Zar lässt sich photographiern*, opera; libretto by Kaiser (1928); *Der Jasager*, school opera after a Noh play (1930); *Die Bürgschaft*, 3-act opera; libretto by Caspar Neher (1930–31, UE); *Der Silbersee*, opera;

libretto by Kaiser (1932, UE); *Die sieben Todsünden* for soprano, men's chorus, orchestra (1933); *Johnny Johnson*, musical; libretto by Paul Green (1936); *Knickerbocker Holiday*, operetta; libretto by Maxwell Anderson (1938); *The Ballad of the Magna Carta*, cantata for vocal soloists, chorus, orchestra (1939, Chappell); *3 Walt Whitman Songs* for baritone, orchestra (1940, Chappell); *Lady in the Dark*, musical; libretto by Anderson (1940, Chappell); *One Touch of Venus*, musical; libretto by S. J. Perelman, Ogden Nash (1943); *Down in the Valley*, 1-act folk opera; libretto by Arnold Sundgaard (1945–48, Schirmer-G); *Street Scene*, musical; text by Elmer Rice (1946); *Lost in the Stars*, musical; libretto by Anderson (1949, Chappell).

PRINCIPAL WRITINGS: "Zeitoper," *Melos* 7:106–08; "Notiz zum Jazz," *Anbruch* 11:138; "Über den gestischen Charakter der Musik," *Die Musik* 21:419–23; "Aktuellas Theater," *Melos* 37:276–77.

BIBL.: Hans Curjel, "Erinnerungen am K. W.," *Melos* 37:81–85; Helmut Kotschenreuther, *K. W.* (Berlin 1962); Roberto Leydi, "Precisioni su 'Mahagonny' e altre questioni a proposito di K. W.," *La rassegna musicale* 32:195–209; John C. G. Waterhouse, "Weill's Debt to Busoni," *Musical Times* 105:897–99.

SEE ALSO Austria and Germany, Jazz, Musical, Opera, Popular Music, United States.

Weiner, Lazar (b. Kiev, 24 Oct 1897), attended the Kiev Conservatory (1910–14, piano and composition), and studied composition in New York with Robert Russell Bennett (1920–21), Frederick Jacobi (1923–24), and Joseph Schillinger (1935–40). He was conductor of the Workmen's Circle Chorus in New York from 1929 to 1964 and has been conducting the Choir of Central Synagogue there since 1930 and the "Message of Israel" program on WABC radio since 1935. Since 1953 he has also been on the faculty of the Hebrew Union College School of Sacred Music.

PRINCIPAL COMPOSITIONS: *Lag-B'Oimer*, ballet after Sholem Aleichem (1929); *Legend of Toil*, cantata (1933, TMP); *5 Yiddish Art Songs* (1936, TMP); *String Quartet* (1937); *5 Calculations* for piano (1938, Fischer); *Fugue and Postlude* for orchestra (1938); *Man in the World*, cantata (1939); *Fight for Freedom*, choral ballet (1943); *To Thee America*, cantata (1944); *11 Songs*, Yiddish texts (1948, TMP); *5 Yiddish Songs* (1953, TMP); *Likras Shabos*, sabbath service (1954, Mills); *Shiro Chadosho*, sabbath service (1956, Mills); *The Golem* opera (1958); *The Marred Passover*, ballet after Sholem Aleichem (1958); *5 Jewish Art Songs* (1961, Mercury); *Shir l'Shabat*, sabbath service (1963, Mills); *The Last Judgment*, cantata (1966, Mills); *6 Yiddish Art Songs* (1968, TMP).

BIBL.: Irene Heskes, "L. W.: in the Service of the Jewish Musical Heritage," *The Historic Contribution of Russian Jewry to Jewish Music* (supplement) (New York, National Jewish Music Council—National Jewish Welfare Board, 1968): 20–24; Israel Rabinovich, *Of Jewish Music* (Montreal 1952): 256–65; A. M. Rothmüller, *The Music of the Jews* (South Brunswick, N. J., 1967): 237–38; G. Salesky, *Famous Musicians of Jewish Origin* (New York 1949): 187–88; Albert Weisser, *The Modern Renaissance of Jewish Music* (New York 1954): 154, 157; ——, "L. W.—A Tribute," *Congress Bi-Weekly* (20 Nov 1967): 18.
SEE ALSO Liturgical Music: Jewish.

Weiner, Leo (b. Budapest, 16 April 1885; d. Budapest, 13 Sept 1960), studied at the Budapest Academy (1901–06, composition with János Koessler). For a short while he was a coach at the opéra comique (Vígopera) in Budapest. During 1908–60 he taught theory and chamber music at the Budapest Academy.

PRINCIPAL COMPOSITIONS: *String Quartets Nos. 1–3* (1906, Bote; 1921, EMB; 1938, Rózsavölgyi); *String Trio* (1908, Bote); *Violin Sonatas Nos. 1–2* (1911, Rózsavölgyi; 1918, EMB; arranged as *Violin Concertos Nos. 1–2*, 1950, 1957, No. 2 published by Mills); *Csongor és az ördögfiak* [Csongor and the Devil's Son] for orchestra (1913, Hansen-W); *Miniature Sketches* for piano (1917, Bárd); *Concertino* for piano, orchestra (1923, UE); *Divertimentos Nos. 1–5* for orchestra (1923, EMB; 1938, EMB; 1948, EMB; 1951, EMB; 1951); *Katonásdi* [Playing Soldiers] for orchestra or piano (1924, UE); *Hungarian Peasant Songs* for piano, 5 vols. (1932–50, EMB); *Ballad* for clarinet, orchestra (1949, Rózsavölgyi); *Romance* for cello, harp, orchestra (1949, EMB); *Variations on a Hungarian Folksong* for orchestra (1950, Rózsavölgyi); *Prélude, nocturne, et scherzo diabolico* for orchestra (1950, EMB); *Toldi*, symphonic poem (1952). Weiner also transcribed solo and chamber works by Bach, Beethoven, Schubert, Liszt, and Bartók for orchestra and prepared editions of Beethoven's piano sonatas and violin sonatas.

PRINCIPAL WRITINGS: *A zenei formák vázlatos ismertetése* [Outline of Musical Forms] (Budapest 1911); *Az összhangzattan előkészítő iskolája* [Preparatory Harmony Text] (Budapest 1917); *Elemző összhangzattan* [Analytic Harmony] (Budapest 1943); *A hangszeres zene formái* [The Forms of Instrumental Music] (Budapest 1954).

SEE ALSO Hungary.

Weinzweig, John (b. Toronto, 11 March 1913), received his training in traditional music at the Univ. of Toronto (1934–37) and then attended the Eastman School (1938, composition with Bernard Rogers), where impressions of Stravinsky's *Le Sacre du printemps* and Berg's *Lyric Suite* first opened the world of contemporary music to him. In 1934, while a student, he founded the Univ. of Toronto Orchestra and became its first conductor. He has taught composition and orchestration at the Royal Conservatory in Toronto (since 1939) and at the Univ. (since 1952). He was cofounder and first president (1951) of the Canadian League of Composers. Since 1941, in addition to the works listed below, he has written much radio and film music.

Weinzweig's special interest is orchestral composition, often in combination with a solo instrument. He was apparently the first person to use 12-tone techniques in Canada (*Suite No. 1*, 1939), and although his works usually have a tonal center and stand apart from the radical avant-garde and electronic techniques of the 1960s, they continue to reflect a boldness of thought and a quest for new sounds. Different stylistic goals pertain in individual works: polyphonic tension and a "free association" formal structure in the *String Quartet No. 3*, an extension of serial technique to nonpitch elements, such as timbre in the *Divertimento No. 4*, or silence as a primary experience in *Dummiyah*. Characteristic elements in other works include the repetition of short rhythmic figures with changing accents and added or subtracted notes; the use of Indian, Eskimo, and other folk motives; the use of jazz elements; and controlled improvisation. Weinzweig always strives for clarity of texture and form and to transmit human emotions to a responsive audience.

PRINCIPAL COMPOSITIONS: *Suite No. 1* for piano (1939); *Symphony* (1940); *Violin Sonata* (1941, Oxford); *Interlude in an Artist's Life* for strings (1943, Leeds); *To the Lands Over Yonder* for chorus (1945, Harris); *Divertimento No. 1* for flute, strings (1945–46, Boosey); *Edge of the World*, radio music for orchestra (1946, Leeds); *Divertimento No. 2* for oboe, strings (1948, Boosey); *Red Ear of Corn*, ballet suite for orchestra (1948–49); *Cello Sonata*, "Israel" (1948–50); *Suite No. 2* for piano (1949–50); *Violin Concerto* (1951–54); *Wine of Peace* for soprano, orchestra (1957); *Symphonic Ode* (1958, Leeds); *Divertimento No. 3* for bassoon, strings (1959–60, Leeds); *Divertimento No. 5* for trumpet, trombone, winds (1961); *String Quartet No. 3* (1962); *Woodwind Quintet* (1963–64); *Piano Concerto* (1965–66); *Harp Concerto* (1967, Leeds); *Divertimento No. 4* for clarinet, strings (1968); *Dummiyah* [Silence] for orchestra (1969); *Around the stage in 25 minutes during which a number of instruments are struck* for 1 percussionist (1970). List to 1959: *Composers of the Americas* 5: 105–07.

BIBL.: Andrée Desautels, "The History of Canadian Composition 1610–1967," *Aspects of Music in Canada* ed. by A. Walter (Toronto

1969):110–14; Udo Kasemets, "J. W.," *Canadian Music Journal* (summer 1960).

Helmut Kallmann

SEE ALSO Canada.

Weisgall, Hugo (b. Ivančice, Czechoslovakia, 13 Oct 1912), emigrated with his parents to the U.S. in 1920, settling in Baltimore. He attended the Peabody Conservatory (1928–31) and Johns Hopkins Univ. (1929–35, 1937–40); from the latter institution he received a doctorate in Germanics. He attended the Curtis Institute (1934–39), where he studied composition with Rosario Scalero and conducting with Fritz Reiner. He also studied composition privately with Roger Sessions in New York (1933–40). During World War II he was assistant military attaché at the American embassy in London, and in 1946 he became cultural attaché in Prague. He has been chairman of the music faculty of the Jewish Theological Seminary in New York since 1951 and has taught composition at the Juilliard School since 1956 and at Queens College since 1960.

Weisgall's primary concern has been with musical theater. He has composed three full-length operas, three one-act operas and three ballets. The major operatic works are *6 Characters in Search of an Author*, after the Pirandello play; *Athalia*, after the Racine tragedy; and *9 Rivers from Jordan*, after the novel by Denis Johnston. The one-act works are *The Tenor*, after Wedekind; *The Stronger*, after Strindberg; and *Purgatory*, a verbatim setting of Yeats. His other vocal works include songs and a cantata for solo voice and orchestra. There is also a series of chamber works for various instrumental combinations under the collective title *Graven Images*.

Whether literally, as in *9 Rivers*, or by indirection, as in *Athalia*, Weisgall's operas are intensely concerned with contemporary issues and thought. *6 Characters* exploits the Pirandellian theme of illusion versus reality. *Athalia* is a biblical drama in which the chorus plays a key role, functioning now as a participant, now as an observer from the sidelines. *9 Rivers* is a cinematically conceived saga of guilt and redemption set against the background of World War II. Themes in Weisgall's shorter operas range from a character study of a singer in *The Tenor*, to psychological monodrama (*The Stronger*), to the symbolic drama of a murder within a murder (*Purgatory*).

The music of these operas synthesizes the intense chromaticism of the second Viennese school with the clear textures and structures of mid-century neoclassicism. Although the constituent ingredients pose no radical departures or innovations in themselves, they blend together into a unique musical idiom. Weisgall's music is generally through composed and structured in large sections. Individual musical numbers (arias, ensembles, choruses) single themselves out from the ongoing fabric. Leitmotivic processes are in evidence as are intricate motivic development. There tends to be a consistent motion and texture within larger sections. Melodic lines are spun out into a widely arching continuum participated in by both instrumental and vocal forces. The rhythmic organization tends toward clearly defined, regularly recurring impulses, often evoking the calibrated rhythmic drive of baroque music. His use of a primary line with supportive chordal and contrapuntal configurations and extended areas of finely engineered polyphony has much in common with Hindemith. Weisgall's harmonic language is closely allied to some of the preserial atonal procedures of Schoenberg and Berg and to the later works of Sessions. The basic chordal material in *9 Rivers*, for instance, is derived from interlocking pairs of major sevenths or minor ninths. Although harmonic tension and chromaticism are maintained at a high level and serialism is sometimes used, the pull of tonal gravity is always present. Weisgall's intricate orchestration is for conventionally arrayed instrumental forces. He avoids percussion-section exoticisms and rarely calls attention to orchestration for its own sake. Sprechstimme and other areas between speech and song are avoided. Vocal lines are governed by natural declamation and make use of wide ranges controlled by diatonic degree-progressions; leaping Webernian pointillism is rarely in evidence.

PRINCIPAL COMPOSITIONS (published by Presser unless otherwise noted): *Overture in F* for orchestra (1942); *Soldier Songs* for baritone, orchestra (1946); *Outpost*, ballet (1947, unpub.); *The Tenor*, 1-act opera after Wedekind (1949); *The Stronger*, 1-act opera after Strindberg (1952, unpub.); *A Garden Eastward*, cantata for high voice, orchestra (1952); *2 Madrigals* for high voice, piano (1955); *6 Characters in Search of an Author*, opera; libretto by Denis Johnston (1956); *Purgatory*, 1-act opera; text by Yeats (1958); *Athalia*, opera; libretto by Richard Franko Goldman (1961); *Graven Images*, chamber works for various media (1966); *9 Rivers from Jordan*, opera; libretto by Denis Johnston (1968).

Harold Blumenfeld

SEE ALSO Opera.

Weiss, Adolph (b. Baltimore, 12 Sept 1891; d. Van Nuys, Calif., 20 Feb 1971), studied theory first with C. C. Mueller and Abraham Liliental and later with Cornelius Rybner and Frank Edwin Ward at Columbia Univ. During 1924–27 he studied with Arnold Schoenberg at the Akademie der Künste in Berlin, becoming the first American to learn the 12-tone technique. He played the bassoon during 1907–24 with the Russian Symphony, the New York Philharmonic, the New York Symphony, the Chicago Symphony, and the Rochester Symphony. During 1927–32 he was secretary of the Pan American Society of Composers in New York. He was conductor of the San Francisco Opera and Symphony (c.1933) and the Los Angeles Philharmonic (c.1951).

PRINCIPAL COMPOSITIONS (published by CFE unless otherwise noted): *Songs for Soprano* for soprano, piano (1916–18, unpub.); *Fantasie* for piano (1918, unpub.); *I segreti* for orchestra (1923, unpub.); *String Quartets Nos. 1–3* (1925, 1926, 1932, unpub.); *Chamber Symphony* for 10 instruments (1927, unpub.); *12 Preludes* for piano (1927, New Music); *American Life* for orchestra (1928, New Music); *7 Songs* for soprano, string quartet; poems by Emily Dickinson (1928, unpub.); *Sonata da camera* for flute, viola (1929, New Music); *The Libation Bearers*, choreographic cantata for vocal soloists, chorus, orchestra; choreography by Marjorie Hyder (1930); *Wind Quintet* (1931); *Piano Sonata* (1932, unpub.); *Theme and Variations* for orchestra (1933, unpub.); *Suite* for orchestra (1938); *Petite Suite* for flute, clarinet, bassoon (1939); *Violin Sonata* (1941); *Passacaglia* for horn, viola (1942); *10 Pieces* for low instrument, orchestra (1943); *Ode to the West Wind* for baritone, viola, piano (1945); *Protest*, dance score for 2 pianos; choreography by Janet Collins (1945, unpub.); *Sextet* for winds, piano (1947); *Trio* for clarinet, viola, cello (1948); *Concerto* for bassoon, string quartet (1949); *Pulse of the Sea*, etude for piano (1950); *Trumpet Concerto* (1952); *Trio* for flute, violin, piano (1955); *5 Fantasies* for violin, piano; based on gagaku (1956); *Tone Poem* for brass, percussion (1957); *Rhapsody* for 4 horns (1957); *Vade mecum*, a collection for various ensembles of wind instruments (1951, unfinished).

PRINCIPAL WRITINGS: "A. W., Autobiographical Notes," *ACA Bulletin* 7/3.

[prepared with the help of Virginio Majewski]

SEE ALSO Dance.

Welin, Karl-Erik (Vilhelm) (b. Genarp, Sweden, 31 May 1934), studied at the Berlin Hochschule für Musik (1955–56) and the Royal Academy of Music in Stockholm (1956–61, esthetics with Bo Wallner, piano with Sven Brandel, organ with Alf Linder). He studied composition privately in Stockholm with Gunnar Bucht (1958–60) and Ingvar Lidholm (1960–64) and piano with David Tudor in Darmstadt (1960–62). Since 1958 he has been a member of the Stockholm experimental arts group Fylkingen. He has concertized as a pianist and organist since 1962. During 1960–68 he was a member of the music department of the Swedish Broadcasting Corp., and in 1964 he was a visiting professor at the Universities of Freiberg and Utrecht. Since 1966 he has composed a number of scores for films and for the theater.

PRINCIPAL COMPOSITIONS: *4 Chinese Poems* for chorus (1956, Hansen-W); *Sermo modulatus* for flute, clarinet (1959); *Cantata* for children's chorus, violin, flute, harpsichord (1960, Hansen-W); *NO 3-61* for chamber ensemble (1961, Ahn & Sim); *Manzit* for clarinet, trombone, cello, piano (1962, Ahn & Sim); *Esservecchia* for horn, trombone, piano, electric guitar (1962); *Warum nicht?* for chamber ensemble (1963); *Pereo* for 36 strings (1966, Hansen-W); *Etwas für . . .* for wind quintet (1966, Hansen-W); *Eigentlich nicht* for string quartet (1967); *Ben fatto* for 1–100 instruments (1967); *Visoka 12* for string sextet (1967); *Glazba* for soprano, 3 flutes, bassoon (1969); *Incidental Music to Strindberg's "The Dream Play"* on 4-track tape (1969).

SEE ALSO Scandinavia.

Wellesz, Egon (b. Vienna, 21 Oct 1885), studied at the Univ. of Vienna (1895–1908, music history with Guido Adler) and the New Vienna Conservatory (1911–15). He attended performances and rehearsals by Gustav Mahler in Vienna and in 1905 and 1906 studied with Arnold Schoenberg. During 1913–38 he taught at the Univ. of Vienna. He emigrated to England and in 1939 joined the faculty of music at Oxford Univ., where he is a fellow of Lincoln College. As a musicologist, he has specialized in Byzantine music and Western plainchant; his books number about 18 and his articles about 230.

PRINCIPAL COMPOSITIONS: *3 Skizzen* for piano, Op. 6 (1911, Doblinger); *Vorfrühling* for orchestra, Op. 12 (1912, UE); *String Quartets Nos. 1, 2, 4, 5, 8, 9*: No. 1, Op. 14 (1912, Ahn & Sim); No. 2, Op. 20 (1915–16, Ahn & Sim); No. 4, Op. 28, (1920, UE); No. 5, Op. 60 (1943, Schott); No. 8, Op. 79 (1957, Sikorski); No. 9, Op. 97 (1966, Doblinger); *6 George Lieder* for mezzo-soprano, piano, Op. 22 (1917, UE); *Persisches Ballett*, Op. 30; choreography by Ellen Tels (1920, UE); *Achilles auf Skyros*, ballet, Op. 32; scenario by Hugo von Hofmannsthal (1921, UE); *Alkestis*, opera, Op. 35; libretto by Hofmannsthal after Euripedes (1922–23, UE); *Die Nächtlichen*, ballet, Op. 37; choreography by Max Terpis (1923, UE); *Die Opferung des Gefangenen*, opera-ballet, Op. 40; libretto by Eduard Stucken, choreography by Kurt Joos (1924–25, UE); *Scherz, List und Rache*, 1-act chamber opera, Op. 41; text from Goethe (c.1926–27, UE); *Die Bakchantinnen*, opera, Op. 44; libretto by the composer after Euripedes (1929–30, Bote); *Sonette der Elisabeth Barrett Browning* for soprano, string orchestra, Op. 52; translation by Rilke (1934, UE); *Prosperos Beschwörungen*, symphonic rhapsody, Op. 53 (1936, Doblinger); *Octet* for clarinet, bassoon, horn, string quintet, Op. 67 (1948–49, Lengnick); *Symphonies Nos. 4–8*: No. 4, "Symphonia Austriaca," Op. 70 (1950, Sikorski); No. 5, Op. 75 (1956, Sikorski); No. 6, Op. 95 (1965, Doblinger); No. 7, Op. 102 (1968, Doblinger); No. 8, Op. 110 (1970); *Lieder aus Wien*, 5 songs for baritone, piano, Op. 82; texts by H. C. Artmann (1959, Doblinger); *Violin Concerto* (1961, Heinr.); *4 Songs of Return* for soprano, chamber orchestra, Op. 85; texts by Elizabeth MacKenzie (1961, Heinr.); *String Trio No. 1*, Op. 86 (1962, Heinr.); *Duineser Elegie* for soprano, chorus, chamber ensemble, Op. 90; text by Rilke (1963, Doblinger); *5 Miniaturen* for violin, piano, Op. 93 (1965, Doblinger); *Mirabile mysterium*, Christmas cantata for soprano, baritone, chorus, orchestra, Op. 101 (1967, Doblinger); *Canticum sapientiae* for baritone, chorus, orchestra, Op. 104 (1968, Doblinger); *Studien in Grau*, 5 pieces for piano, Op. 106 (1969, Doblinger); *Symphonischer Epilog*, Op. 108 (1969–70, Doblinger); *String Quintet*, Op. 109 (1970, Doblinger).

PRINCIPAL WRITINGS: "Giuseppe Bonno (1710–1788)," *Sammelbände der Internationalische Musikgeschichte* 9 (Leipzig 1909):395–442; *Cavalli und der Stil der venezianischen Oper von 1640–1660* (Vienna 1913); "Zur Entzifferung der byzantinischen Notenschrift: Untersuchungen über die Bedeutung der byzantinischen Tonzeichen der mittleren und späten Epoche," *Oriens Christianus*, new series vol. 7:97–118; *Die Opern und Oratorien in Wein von 1660–1708* (Leipzig-Vienna 1919); *Arnold Schönberg* (Vienna 1921), English trans. by W. H. Kerridge (London-Toronto 1924); *Aufgaben und Probleme auf dem Gebiete der byzantinischen und orientalischen Kirchenmusik* (Münster 1923); *Arnold Schönberg, An appreciative monograph* (Oxford 1945); *Eastern Elements in Western Chant* (Boston 1947); "Early Byzantine Neumes," *Musical Quarterly* 38:68–79; "Early Christian Music," *New Oxford History of Music* 2 (London 1954):1–13; *A History of Byzantine Music and Hymnography* (Oxford 1963). Wellesz has also been coeditor and cotranscriber of Byzantine manuscripts (Copenhagen 1935, 1936; Boston 1957; Cologne 1959).

BIBL.: Wilfrid Mellers, "E. W. and the Austrian Tradition," *Studies in Contemporary Music* (London 1946); H. Redlich, "E. W.," *Musical Quarterly* 26/1; R. Reti, "E. W.," *Musical Quarterly* 42/1; R. Murray Schafer, *British Composers in Interview* (London 1963); Robert Schollum, *E. W.* (Vienna 1963).

SEE ALSO Dance.

Werder, Felix (b. Berlin, 24 Feb 1922), studied at the Shoreditch Polytechnicum in London (beginning in 1938), after which he settled in Australia and attended the Melbourne Teachers College (until 1946). He is primarily self-taught in composition. Since 1960 he has been music critic for *The Age* in Melbourne. He is also a free-lance conductor and lecturer. Werder was strongly influenced in his early years by Hebraic modes (as well as Persian and Sumerian); he has since discarded the modes but retained the speech rhythms. Sitsky (see bibl.) reports that Werder's "principal derivations come from Monteverdi (and much other early music, Gluck and the Gabrielis in particular), Mozart ('for content'), Handel and Bartók ('for technique')." Much of his orchestral music is concerned with some aspect of 12-tone technique.

PRINCIPAL COMPOSITIONS: *Flute Concerto*, Op. 15 (1954); *String Quartets Nos. 4, 6, 7, 9*, Opp. 16, 45, 66, 90 (1955, 1962, 1965, 1968); *Abstract* for 3 orchestral groups, Op. 27 (1958); *Quintet* for clarinet, horn, string trio, Op. 31 (1959); *Septet* for flute, clarinet, harp, string quartet, Op. 55 (1963); *Concert Music* for 5 winds, Op. 60 (1964); *Piano Quintet*, Op. 62 (1964); *Clarinet Quintet*, Op. 63 (1964); *Sonata* for solo violin, Op. 64 (1965); *Symphony No. 3*, "The Laocoön," Op. 67 (1965); *The General*, 1-act opera, Op. 69 (1966); *Violin Concerto*, Op. 71 (1966); *Agamemnon*, opera, Op. 76 (1967); *Radics Peace*, cantata, Op. 82 (1967); *Piano Sonata No. 3*, Op. 83 (1968); *Hölderlin Songs* for voice, piano, Op. 86 (1968); *Tower Concerto* for orchestra, Op. 91 (1968); *The Affair*, opera, Op. 99 (1969); *Sound Canvas* for orchestra, Op. 101 (1969); *Private*, opera, Op. 103 (1969); *Piano Trio*, Op. 106 (1969); *Symphony No. 4*, Op. 107 (1970); *The 5 Acts of Coriolanus* for orchestra, Op. 110 (1970); *Quartet Music*, Op. 114 (1970); *Divertimento* for guitar, string quartet, Op. 115 (1970).

PRINCIPAL WRITINGS: *A Sense of Style*, a collection of lectures given to adult education classes (unpub.).

BIBL.: Roger Covell, *Australia's Music, Themes of a New Society* (Melbourne 1967); Andrew McCredie, *Musical Composition in Australia* (Canberra 1969); Larry Sitsky, "F. W.," *Current Affairs Bulletin* (29 June 1970):43–44.

SEE ALSO Australia.

Werle, Lars Johan (b. Gävle, Sweden, 23 June 1926), attended Uppsala Univ. (1948–51, music history with Carl-Allan Moberg) and studied counterpoint privately with Sven-Erik Bäck in 1950. In 1958 he became a producer in the music department of the Swedish Radio in Stockholm, and since 1968 has been head of chamber music there.

PRINCIPAL COMPOSITIONS (published by Hansen-W unless otherwise noted): *Pentagram* for string quartet (1959–60, Nordiska); *Sinfonia da camera* (1961); *Drömmen om Thérèse* [The Vision of Thérèse], chamber opera-in-the-round; text by Lars Runsten after Zola's *Pour une Nuit d'amour* (1964); *Summer Music* for strings, piano (1965); *Zodiac*, ballet (1966); *Canzone 126 di Francesco Petrarca* for chorus (1967); *Resan* [The Journey], opera; text by Runsten after P. C. Jersild (1968).
SEE ALSO Scandinavia.

Wernick, Richard (b. Boston, 16 Jan 1934), studied composition at Brandeis Univ. (1952–55, with Irving Fine, Harold Shapero, Arthur Berger) and at Mills College (with Leon Kirchner). He also studied at Tanglewood (composition with Ernest Toch and Boris Blacher, conducting with Leonard Bernstein). In 1957–58 Wernick was music director and composer-in-residence for the Royal Winnipeg Ballet, Canada. From 1958 to 1964 he lived in New York and composed for documentary films, television, and the theater. He taught at the Universities of Buffalo (1964–65) and Chicago (1965–68) and has been at the Univ. of Pa. since 1968.
PRINCIPAL WORKS: *Music* for solo viola d'amore (1963); *Aevia* for orchestra (1965); *Stretti* for violin, clarinet, viola, guitar (1965, Mills); *Lyrics from IXI* for soprano, string bass, vibraphone, marimba (1966); *Haiku of Bashō* for soprano, flute, violin, string bass, tympani, clarinet, piano, tape (1967); *Cadenzas and Variations* for viola, piano (1968); *Moonsongs from the Japanese* for 1 or 3 sopranos with tape (1969).

Westergaard, Peter (b. Champaign, Ill., 28 May 1931), attended Harvard Univ. (1949–53, composition with Walter Piston, musicology with Otto Gombosi), and Princeton Univ. (1955–56, composition with Roger Sessions, theory with Milton Babbitt). He also studied composition with Darius Milhaud at the Aspen School (1951–52) and the Paris Conservatory (1953) and with Wolfgang Fortner in Detmold and Freiburg (1956–57). He was a Fulbright guest lecturer at the Freiburg Hochschule für Musik in 1958. He taught at Columbia Univ. (1958–66) and at Amherst College (1967–68). He has taught at Princeton Univ. (1966–67, since 1968), where he is director of the Princeton Univ. Orchestra. Westergaard has served on the boards of the ISCM (1961–63), the American Society of Univ. Composers (1965–67), *Perspectives* (since 1966), and the American Music Center (since 1969).

PRINCIPAL COMPOSITIONS: *Charivari*, chamber opera (1953); *The Plot against the Giant*, Cantata 1, for small women's chorus, clarinet, cello, harp (1956); *5 Movements* for small orchestra (1958, Bote); *A Refusal to Mourn the Death, by Fire, of a Child in London*, Cantata 2, for bass, 10 instruments; poem by Dylan Thomas (1958, Schott); *Quartet* for violin, vibraphone, clarinet, cello (1960, Schott); *Spring and Fall: to a Young Child* for voice, piano (1960) or voice, 5 instruments (1964); *Leda and the Swan*, Cantata 3, for mezzo-soprano, clarinet, viola, vibraphone, marimba (1961, Schott); *Trio* for flute, cello, piano (1962); *Variations for 6 Players* for flute, clarinet, violin, cello, percussion, piano (1963, Broude-A); *Mr. and Mrs. Discobbolos*, chamber opera after Edward Lear (1965, Broude-A); *Divertimento on Discobbolic Fragments* for flute, piano (1967, Broude-A); *Noises, Sounds, and Sweet Airs* for flute, clarinet, horn, trumpet, celesta, harpsichord, percussion, violin, viola, cello, bass (1968, Broude-A); *Tuckets and Sennets* for concert band (1969, Broude-A).
PRINCIPAL WRITINGS: "Some Problems in Rhythmic Theory," *Perspectives* 1/1:180–91; "Webern and 'Total Organization': An Analysis of the Second Movement of the Piano Variations, Op. 27," *ibid.* 1/2:107–20; "Some Problems Raised by the Rhythmic Procedures of Milton Babbitt's 'Composition for Twelve Instruments', " *ibid.* 4/1:109–18; "Toward a Twelve-Tone Polyphony," *ibid.* 4/2:90–112; "Conversation with Walter Piston," *ibid.* 7/1:3–17; "Sung Language," *Proceedings of the American Society of University Composers* (April 1967):9–36.
BIBL.: George Crumb, "P. W., 'Variations for Six Players', " *Perspectives* 3/2:152–59.
SEE ALSO Texture.

White, Michael (b. Chicago, 6 March 1931), studied at the Juilliard School (1953–58; composition with Peter Mennin, William Bergsma). During 1959–63 he was composer-in-residence on Ford Foundation grants in Seattle, Wash., and Amarillo, Texas. He taught at the Oberlin Conservatory during 1964–66 and since 1966, at the Philadelphia Musical Academy, where he is also an associate of the electronic music studio.
PRINCIPAL COMPOSITIONS: *The Dybbuk*, 3-act opera (1962–63); *Alice*, 2-act opera (1963–64); *Songs of Love* for high voice, piano (1964); *Metamorphosis*, 3-act opera for soloists, chamber orchestra, prerecorded electronic music (1967–68); *Tensions* for orchestra (1968); *Opposites* for wind ensemble, tape (1969); *My Lady Jessica*, songs and dances of the renaissance for tenor, chamber orchestra (1969); *A Child's Garden* for mezzo-soprano, viola, piano (1970); *The Trial and Death of Jesus Christ* for chorus, brass, percussion, tape (1970). List to 1962: *Composers of the Americas* 9:190–92.

BIBL.: Donald Chittum, "Current Chronicle: Philadelphia," *Musical Quarterly* (Jan 1969):91.

Whittenberg, Charles (b. St. Louis, 6 July 1927), attended the Eastman School (1944–48, composition and orchestration with Bernard Rogers). Since 1967 he has taught composition, theory, and analysis at the Univ. of Conn., where he also serves as artistic director of "The New Music" concert series. He has been a music reviewer for the Hartford *Times*. In 1962 he was associated with the Columbia-Princeton Electronic Music Center, and he is currently working at the Yale Electronic Studio. Whittenberg's teaching has been influenced especially by Heinrich Schenker and by research into the operations and properties of pitch-class sets as conducted by Milton Babbitt, George Perle, Donald Martino, and Hubert Howe. His compositions since 1965 have been concerned less with the "brilliant surface texture and idiomatic instrumental conception" of his earlier works than with "clarity, formal logic" and what he calls "12-tone classicism"—a "neoclassic attitude (of Stravinsky not Hindemith) within the strict applications of the 12 pitch class system." Important for his latest compositions have been the writings of Babbitt and Benjamin Boretz.

PRINCIPAL COMPOSITIONS: *Fantasy for Wind Quintet*, Op. 25 (1962, CFE); *Electronic Study No. 2 with Contrabass*, Op. 26 (1962, AMP); *Triptych for Brass Quintet*, Op. 27 (1962, Joshua); *3 Pieces for Clarinet Alone*, Op. 29 (1963, McG-M); *Event* for chamber orchestra, Op. 31b (1963, CFE); *Vocalise* for soprano, viola, percussionist, Op. 33 (1963, CFE); *Variations for 9 Players* for flute, oboe, clarinet, bassoon, trumpet, trombone, horn, violin, double bass, Op. 37 (1964–65, Peters); *String Quartet in 1 Movement*, Op. 38a (1965, CFE); *Polyphony for Solo C Trumpet*, Op. 38b (1965, McG-M); *4 Forms and an Epilogue* for harpsichord, Op. 39 (1965, CFE); *3 Compositions for Piano* (1967, Peters); *Conversations for Solo Double Bass*, Op. 41a (1967, Peters); *Games of Five* for wind quintet, Op. 45 (1968, Joshua); *Concerto for Brass Quintet*, Op. 47 (1968–69, AMP); *A due* for flute (piccolo or alto flute), percussionist, Op. 49 (1969, CFE); *From John Donne: A Sacred Triptych* for 8 solo voices (1970–71, CFE).

PRINCIPAL WRITINGS: "Richard Moryl's *Multiples*," *Perspectives* 8/1:126–32; "*Twentieth Century Music* by H. H. Stuckenschmidt," a review, *Yale Journal of Music Theory* 13:295–306.

BIBL.: Carman Moore, "Music," (review of the *Concerto for Brass Quintet*) *Village Voice* (New York, 27 March 1969).

Wienhorst, Richard (William) (b. Seymour, Ind., 21 April 1920), studied at Valparaiso Univ. in Ind. (1938–42), the American Conservatory in Chicago (1947–49, composition with Leo Sowerby, piano with Leo Heim), the Ecoles d'Art Americaines in Fontaincbleu (1951, composition with Nadia Boulanger), the Albert Ludwig Univ. in Freiburg (1951–52, composition with Harald Genzmer), and at the Eastman School (PhD 1961; composition with Bernard Rogers, Howard Hanson). Since 1946 he has taught theory and composition at Valparaiso Univ.; he became chairman of the music department in 1966 and director of the Studio for New Music in 1970.

PRINCIPAL COMPOSITIONS: *Missa brevis* for chorus (1953, AMP); *The 7 Words of Jesus Christ from the Cross* for solo voices, chorus (1954, Concordia); *Magnificat* for alto, chorus, orchestra (1960); *Domine in caelo* for vocal soloists, chorus, chamber orchestra (1965); *Percussion Matins* for chorus, percussion (1964); *2 Pieces for Synthesizer* (1970).

BIBL.: George Weller, "Composer for the Church: R. W.," *Church Music* 68/1:14–21.

Wiggen, Knut (b. Buvik, Norway, 13 June 1927), studied in Stockholm during 1950–53 with Karl-Birger Blomdahl (composition) and Hans Leygraf (piano) and at the Städtische Akademie für Tonkunst in Darmstadt (1953–55, piano with Hans Leygraf). During 1959–69 he was chairman of the Stockholm experimental music society, Fylkingen. He has been director of the Stiftelsen Electronic Music Studio in Stockholm since 1964 and is particularly interested in electronic music, musique concrète, and computer music.

PRINCIPAL COMPOSITIONS: *Musikmaskin* [Music Machine] Nos 1–2, which uses any sound source and produces music from it through loudspeakers (1961, 1962–   ). Wiggen's computer-music experiments (since 1962) have not been circulated.

PRINCIPAL WRITINGS: *Att spela piano* [To Play the Piano] (Stockholm 1966); *Elektronmusik* (Stockholm 1970).

Wildberger, Jacques (b. Basel, 3 Jan 1922), attended the Basel Conservatory (1940–45; piano with Eduard Ehrsam, Eduard Henneberger, Paul Baumgartner). He studied composition in Ascona, Switzerland with Wladimir Vogel (1949–53) and taught composition, orchestration, and analysis at the Karlsruhe Hochschule für Musik (1959–66). He began teaching part time at the Basel Musik-Akademie in 1963 and has been teaching there full time since 1966. The most important influences on his music have come from Arnold Schoenberg and Anton Webern.

PRINCIPAL COMPOSITIONS: *3 Mutazioni* for chamber orchestra (1953, EM); *Vom kommen und gehen des Menschen*, cantata for soprano, baritone, chorus, orchestra (1954); *Ihr meint, das Leben sei kurz*, cantata on Japanese poems for chorus, 10 instruments (1957, EM); *Intensio-Centrum-Remissio* for orchestra (1958, EM); *Epitaphe pour Evariste Galois* for soprano, baritone, speakers, speaking chorus, loudspeakers, orchestra (1959–62, EM); *Music for 22 Strings* (1960, Ahn & Sim); *Oboe Concerto* (1963, Ahn & Sim); *In My End Is My Beginning*, cantata for soprano, tenor, chamber orchestra; poem by T. S. Eliot (1963–64, Gerig); *Movements for Orchestra* (1964, Ahn & Sim); *La Notte* for tape, mezzo-soprano, 5 instruments; text by Michelangelo Buonarroti and Hans Magnus Enzensberger (1967, Gerig).

PRINCIPAL WRITINGS: "Freiheit von der rationalen Zeit," *Melos* 22:341–44; "Unser Adresset," *Melos* 24:281–83; "Dallapiccolas 'Cinque Canti'," *Melos* 26:7–10; Webern Gestern und Heute, program booklet, Donaueschingen Festival (1959); "Robert Suter. Schweizer Komponist," *Schweizerische Musikzeitung* 1967/6:320–30; "Der Komponist Robert Suter," *Robert Suter* by Dino Larese and J. W. (Amriswil 1967):16–24; "Verschiedene Schichten der musikalischen Wortbedeutung in den Liedern Franz Schuberts," *Schweizerische Musikzeitung* 1969/1:4–9.

BIBL.: Hansjörg Pauli, "Über J. W.," *Schweizerische Musikzeitung* 1960/1:5–8; Robert Suter, "Vom Avantgardisten zum Musiker. Bemerkungen über den Komponisten J. W.," *ibid.* 1968/3:157–67.

SEE ALSO Austria and Germany, Switzerland.

Wilder, Alec (b. Rochester, N. Y., 16 Feb 1907), studied at the Eastman School (composition with Edward Royce, counterpoint with Herbert Inch). In the late 1930s and early 40s he did jazz orchestrations, into which he introduced the innovation of woodwinds. He has written nearly 150 works, some for films and theatrical productions. Most of his chamber music has been written since 1945 and was conceived for specific performers.

PRINCIPAL COMPOSITIONS (dates not available): *Horn Sonata No. 3* (Wilder Music, Inc.); *Tuba Sonata No. 1* for tuba, piano or orchestra (Mentor); *Brass Quintet No. 3* (Wilder Music); *Entertainment No. 1* for band (Wilder Music); *Wind Quintets Nos. 3, 4, 6, 10* (No. 3, Schirmer-G; 4, 6, 10, Wilder Music); *Concerto* for wind quintet with baritone saxophone (Wilder Music); *Trio* for clarinet, flute, piano (Wilder Music); *Flute Sonata No. 2* (Wilder Music); *Bassoon Sonata No. 2*; *Trio* for clarinet, horn, piano (Wilder Music); *Ellen*, 2-act opera for wind quintet, string trio, double bass, percussion (Wilder Music); *Children's*

Plea for Peace for narrator, children's chorus, orchestra (Wilder Music); *Miss Chicken Little*, 1-act operetta (The Richmond Organization); *Viola Sonata* (Wilder Music); *Sand Castle*, film score; *Albert Schweitzer*, film score.

PRINCIPAL WRITINGS: "Artist and Creator," *Performing Arts Review* 1/2:3; *American Popular Song: The Great Innovators 1900–1950* (New York 1972).

[prepared with the help of John R. Barrows, Glenn Bowen, Harvey G. Phillips]

Willan, Healey (b. Balham, near London, 12 Oct 1880; d. Toronto, 16 Feb 1968), studied during 1899–1906 with William S. Hoyte (organ, theory) and Evelyn Howard-Jones (piano). He emigrated to Canada in 1913, where he began teaching theory at the Toronto Conservatory and was vice principal during 1920–36. He also taught at the Univ. of Toronto in 1914 and 1936–50 and was university organist beginning in 1932. During 1921–68 he was precentor of the Church of St. Mary Magdalene.

PRINCIPAL COMPOSITIONS: *Introduction, Passacaglia, and Fugue* for organ (1916, Oxford); *Apostrophe to the Heavenly Hosts* for double chorus (1921, Harris); *Symphonies Nos. 1–2* (1936, 1943–48, Berandol); *Piano Concerto in C Minor* (1944, Berandol); *Deirdre*, 3-act opera (1946, Berandol); *12 Chorale Preludes* for organ (1950–51, Concordia); *Coronation Suite* for chorus, orchestra (1953, Berandol). Willan's works for the Anglican Service include 14 settings of the *Missa brevis* for chorus (1932–63), and *11 Liturgical Motets* (1928–37). Complete list of compositions to 1953: *Composers of the Americas* 6:113–16.

PRINCIPAL WRITINGS: "Organ Playing in Its Proper Relation to Music in the Church," *Diapason* (Oct 1937); "Plainsong, the Earliest Song of the Church," *Canadian Churchman* (July 1963).

BIBL.: Charles Peaker, "Works for Organ by H. W.," *Canadian Music Journal* 1960/4:60; Godfrey Ridout, "H. W.," *ibid.* 1959/3:4ff.; Alec Wyton, "H. W.'s Musical London," *Music* (Dec 1967 and Jan 1968).

[prepared with the help of Giles Bryant]

SEE ALSO Liturgical Music: Christian.

Williamson, Malcolm (b. Sydney, Australia, 21 Nov 1931), studied at the Sydney Conservatory (1944–52) and in London with Elisabeth Lutyens and Erwin Stein (1950–55). He lives in England and performs professionally as a pianist and organist; he has also lectured at numerous universities and schools.

PRINCIPAL COMPOSITIONS (published by Weinberger): *Piano Concerto No. 3 in E Flat* (1961); *Organ Concerto* (1961); *The Display*, dance symphony; scenario and choreography by Robert Helpmann (1962); *Symphony for Voices* for chorus; texts by James McAuley (1962); *Our Man in Havana*, 3-act opera; libretto by Sidney Gilliat after Graham Greene (1962–63); *Elegy for J. F. K.* for organ (1963); *The Happy Prince*, 1-act opera for children's and women's voices, piano 4-hands, percussion, optional string quartet; libretto by the composer after Oscar Wilde (1964); *Violin Concerto* (1964); *Concerto* for wind quintet, 2 pianos 8-hands (1964–65); *The Violins of Saint-Jacques*, 3-act opera; libretto by William Chappell after P. L. Fermor (1964–66); *Julius Caesar Jones*, 2-act opera for 3 adults, children's voices, chamber orchestra; libretto by Geoffrey Dunn (1965–66); *Symphonic Variations* (1965–66); *2 Organ Epitaphs for Edith Sitwell* (1966); *Sinfonietta* (1966–67); *Dunstan and the Devil*, opera for piano 4-hands, 2 percussionists (1967); *Sonata* for 2 pianos (1967); *The Moonrakers*, cassation for audience, orchestra or piano (1967); *The Growing Castle*, 2-act chamber opera for soprano, mezzo-soprano, 2 baritones, piano, harpsichord, chime bars, percussion, actors; libretto by the composer after Strindberg (1967–68); *Piano Quintet* (1967–68); *From a Child's Garden* for high voice, piano; texts by Robert Louis Stevenson (1967–68); *Knights in Shining Armor*, cassation for audience, piano (1968); *The Snow Wolf*, cassation for audience, piano (1968); *Symphony No. 2* (1968–69).

[prepared with the help of Richard Toeman]
SEE ALSO Great Britain.

Wilson, George Balch (b. Grand Island, Neb., 28 Jan 1927), studied composition with Ross Lee Finney at the Univ. of Mich. (where he earned a DMA in 1963), with Jean Absil at the Royal Conservatory in Brussels (1953–54), with Roger Sessions at Tanglewood (1955), and with Nadia Boulanger in Paris (1955–56). He has taught composition at the Univ. of Mich. since 1961 and has been director of the Electronic Music Studio there since 1964. In 1966 he founded and became director of a university concert series, "Contemporary Directions." He worked at the Columbia-Princeton Electronic Music Center in 1970.

PRINCIPAL COMPOSITIONS: *String Trio* (1949); *String Quartet* (1950, SPAM); *Viola Sonata* (1952, Jobert); *Overture for Orchestra* (1953); *Fantasy* for violin, piano (1957); *6 Pieces* for orchestra (1960); *Fragment* on tape (1964); *The Flies*, incidental music on tape for the play by Sartre (1966); *Exigencies* on 4-track tape (1968, recorded by CRI); *Concatenations* for 12 instruments (1969, Jobert); *Polarity* for percussion, tape (1971).

Wimberger, Gerhard (b. Vienna, 30 August 1923), studied at the Mozarteum in Salzburg (1937–41, 1945–47; composition with Johann

Nepomuk David, conducting with Clemens Krauss). During 1947–48 he was a coach at the Vienna Volksoper. He was a conductor at the Salzburg Landestheater during 1948–51 and of the Mozarteum Akademie-orchester during 1957–67. Since 1963 he has taught composition and conducting at the Mozarteum.

PRINCIPAL COMPOSITIONS (published by Schott unless otherwise noted): *Schaubudengeschichte*, opera (1953–54); *Piano Concerto* (1955); *Figuren und Phantasien*, 3 pieces for orchestra (1956); *3 Lyrische Chansons* for voice, chamber orchestra; texts from Jacques Prévert (1957); *Heiratspostkantate* for chorus, harpsichord, double bass (1957); *La Battaglia, oder Der rote Federbusch*, opera (1959–60); *Etude dramatique* for orchestra (1961); *Stories* for winds, percussion (1962); *Hero und Leander*, dance drama (1963); *Dame Kobald*, musical comedy (1963–64); *Risonanze* for 3 orchestral groups (1965–66); *Ars amatoria*, cantata for soprano, baritone, chorus, combo, chamber orchestra; text from Ovid (1967); *Chronique* for orchestra (1968); *4 Songs* for medium voice, winds, percussion, electric guitar, 6 cellos, double bass (1969, unpub.); *Signum* for organ (1969, unpub.).

PRINCIPAL WRITINGS: "Mozart als Inbegriff des Humanen," *Musik und Szene* 4/13:152–55; "Der Komponist zwischen Elfenbeinturm und Kommerz," *Jahresbericht der Akademie Mozarteum* (1967–68): 29–36.

BIBL.: Eberhard Preussner, "G. W.," program booklet of the Nord-Deutscher Rundfunk (20–21 May 1962).

Wirén, Dag Ivar (b. Noraberg, Sweden, 15 Oct 1905), attended the Music Academy in Stockholm (1926–31; composition, orchestration, counterpoint with E. Ellberg; also studied organ). He studied in Paris on a state scholarship during 1932–34. Returning to Sweden, he became librarian of the Swedish Composers Society (1935–38) and music critic for *Svenska Morgonbladet* (1938–46). In 1939 he served on the board of directors of the Swedish performing rights society and since 1946 he has been a member of the Swedish Musical Academy. A variation procedure, which Wirén calls "metamorphosis technique," has dominated the composer's music since the *Symphony No. 3* (1944). The procedure involves the building of an entire work from a single musical cell or from a set of cells that are revealed as the piece unfolds. Similar procedures are found in the music of other Scandinavians, especially Lars-Erik Larsson, Karl-Birger Blomdahl, and Vagn Holmboe.

PRINCIPAL COMPOSITIONS (published by Gehrman unless otherwise noted): *Theme and Variations* for piano, Op. 5 (1933); *Piano Trio No. 1*, Op. 6

(1933); *Sinfonietta*, Op. 7 (1933–34, UE); *String Quartets Nos. 2–4*, Opp. 9, 18, 28 (1935, Nordiska; 1941–45, Nordiska; 1952–53); *Cello Concerto*, Op. 10 (1936); *Serenade for Strings*, Op. 11 (1937); *Symphonies Nos. 3–5*, Opp. 20, 27, 38 (1943–44, 1951–52, 1964); *Violin Concerto*, Op. 23 (1945–46); *Piano Concerto*, Op. 26 (1947–50); *Quartet* for flute, oboe, clarinet, cello, Op. 31 (1956); *Music for Strings*, Op. 40 (1965–66).

BIBL.: Göran Bergendal, "D. W. and Economy," *Musikrevy* (1969/2).

SEE ALSO Scandinavia.

Wiszniewski, Zbigniew (b. Lvov, Poland, 30 July 1922), studied at the Lódź Conservatory (1948–52, composition with Kasimierz Sikorski, viola with M. Szaleski) and the Univ. of Lódź (1948–51; classical philology, archeology). During 1955–57 he was a violinist in the Polish Dance Company Orchestra. He has been music director of the Polish Radio since 1957 and was a reader for the publishers B. Schott in Mainz, 1966–68.

PRINCIPAL COMPOSITIONS: *Neffru*, radio opera for 4 soloists, chorus, orchestra (1958–59); *Ad hominem*, ballet for chorus, orchestra (1962); *Dz, Hz, Sec.* on tape (1962); *3 Postludes* on tape (1963); *3 Pezzi della tradizione* for chamber orchestra (1964, PWM); *Kammermusik No. 1* for oboe, oboe d'amore, English horn, bassoon (c.1965, Schott); *Genesis*, oratorio for television for tenor, baritone, chorus, chamber orchestra (1967–68); *Tak jakby* [As if], radio opera for tenor, baritone, men's chorus, orchestra (1968–70).

Wohlgemuth, Gerhard (Friedrich Max) (b. Frankfurt, 16 March 1920), has studied at the Martin Luther Univ. in Halle (1946–49), the Ernst Moritz Arndt Univ. in Greisswald (1970) and piano with Bronislaw von Pozniak in 1952. He is self-taught in composition. During 1949–56 he was chief reader for the Hofmeister publishing house in Leipzig. He has taught theory at the Univ. of Halle since 1951.

PRINCIPAL COMPOSITIONS (published by Peters-L unless otherwise noted): *Concertino* for piano, orchestra (1948); *Heitere Musik* for orchestra (1952, Hofmeister); *Till*, opera in 4 scenes; libretto by E. Günther (1952, Henschel); *Suite* for orchestra (1953); *Provençalisches Liebeslied*, ballet; scenario after Paul Arène, choreography by Hinrich Köhn (1954, unpub.); *Symphony No. 1* (1955, International Musikleihbibliothek, Berlin); *Piano Sextet* (1955); *Violin Sonata* (1955); *Sinfonietta* (1956); *Concertino* for oboe, string orchestra (1957); *Händel Metamorphosen* for orchestra (1958); *Symphony No. 2* (1958–62, Neue Musik); *String Quartet* (1960); *Jahre des Wandlung*, oratorio for

vocal soloists, narrator, boys' chorus, chorus, orchestra; text by Friedrich Döppe (1960, unpub.); *Violin Concerto* (1963); *Telemann Variations* for orchestra (1964); *Allegria*, divertimento for orchestra (1965); *String Quartet No. 2*, "Dölauer" (1968–69).

PRINCIPAL WRITINGS: "Was er wartet der Komponist von der Musikwissenschaft," *Musik und Gesellschaft* (1955):315ff.; "Bemerkungen zum eigenen Violinkonzert," *ibid.* (1963):559ff.

BIBL.: Karla Damm, *Portrait G. W.* (diploma thesis, Univ. of Halle 1970); Rosemarie Lehmann, *Untersuchungen zur Rezeption einiger Werke G. W.s* (state examination thesis, Martin Luther Univ., 1965); Egon Rubisch, "G. W.," *Aus dem Leben und Schaffen unserer Komponisten* (Berlin 1969); Walther Stegmund-Schultze, "Neue Kammermusik von G. W.," *Musik und Gesellschaft* (1956): 362ff.

Wolff, Christian (b. Nice, France, 8 March 1934), studied classics and comparative literature at Harvard Univ. (1951–63). He has taught classics at Harvard since 1962 and has participated in avant-garde music performances in the U.S. and Europe and lectured on his esthetics in England.

Wolff has been associated with (and has learned from) John Cage, David Tudor, and Morton Feldman. He is, however, basically self-taught in composition. Influences on his development have included study of Webern's music, exposure to music of Varèse and Boulez (in the early 1950s), and later, the music of Cornelius Cardew and his improvisation group, AMM, in London. The pieces Wolff wrote before 1953 were conceived as single shapes of sound texture comprised of overlapping and simultaneously sounding pitches; the music tended to be static and nonlinear with the sense of passing time stayed. The music sometimes involved a restricted number of pitches (four or nine with no octave transpositions) and generous uses of silence. Since 1957 Wolff has been concerned with composition as material for performance: a composition "must make possible the freedom and dignity of the performers. It should have in it a persistent capacity to surprise (even the performers themselves and the composer). It should allow both concentration (precision in detail) and release (cheerful, joyful, or strong). No sound, noise, interval, etc., as such is preferable to any other sound, including the sounds always around us, provided that a) one is free to move away from them or towards them, and b) sounds are not used to bulldoze, dredge, or compel feelings deliberately. The listeners must be as free as the players." Also pertinent is the idea that "a given performance is a unique living organism passing through a stage of its life." The music itself may be intricately structured in composition, but it always allows the performers varying kinds of choice. Cueing (reactions to specified aspects in the sounds made by another performer) is used as a principal means of coordination. The variety of rhythmic effects caused by the unexpectedness of cues is noteworthy. Wolff has developed notational devices to facilitate this kind of performance (e.g., special uses of beams, differently shaped noteheads).

PRINCIPAL COMPOSITIONS (published by Peters unless otherwise noted): *For Prepared Piano* (1951, New Music); *Trio 1* for flute, trumpet, cello (1951); *Nine* for flute, clarinet, horn, trumpet, 2 cellos, celesta, piano (1951); *For Magnetic Tape* (1952, unpub.); *For Piano 1, 2* (1952, 1953); *Chance*, dance score for Merce Cunningham (1952, unpub.; *Suite* for prepared piano (1954); *Duo for Pianists 1, 2* (1957, 1958); *For Pianist* (1959); *For 6 or 7 Players* for flute, trumpet, trombone, violin, viola, cello, double bass, piano (1959, unpub.); *Rune*, dance score for Cunningham (1959, unpub.); *Duet 1* for piano 4 hands (1960); *Duet 2* for piano, horn (1961); *Trio 2* for piano 4 hands, percussion (1961); *Duo* for violinist, pianist (1961); *Summer* for string quartet (1961); *For 5 or 10 Players* on any instruments (1962); *For 1, 2, or 3 People* on any instruments (1964); *Septet* for any instruments (1964); *Electric Spring 1, 2, 3* for recorders, horn, trombone, violin, double bass, electric double bass, electric guitar (1966–68); *Pairs* for 2, 4, 6, or 8 players on any instruments (1968); *Edges* for any instrument(s) (1968, published in *Source* 5); *Prose Collection* for various combinations of players using, in many cases, any instruments or objects (1968–69, Experimental); *Tilbury 1, 2, 3* for keyboard or other instrument (1969); *Tread*, dance score for Cunningham (1970).

PRINCIPAL WRITINGS: "4 Musicians at Work," *Trans-formations* 1/3:172; "Movement [in Webern]," *Die Reihe*, English ed. 2:61–63; "New and Electronic Music," *Audience* (Cambridge, Mass.) 5/3; "On Form," *Die Reihe* 7:26–31; "Questions," *Collage* (Palermo) 3–4:16–17; "Electricity and Music," *Collage* 8:3–4.

BIBL.: David Behrman, "What Indeterminate Notation Determines," *Perspectives* 3/2:58–73; Mario Bortolotto, *Fase seconda; studi sulla nuova musica* (Turin 1969); Cornelius Cardew, "Notation—Interpretation . . .," *Tempo* (summer 1961): 23ff.; Gilbert Chase, *America's Music*, 2nd ed. (New York 1966):669–71; Henry Cowell, "Current Chronicle," *Musical Quarterly* 38:123–34.

SEE ALSO Indeterminacy, Microtones, Performance, Rhythm, United States.

Wolpe, Stefan (b. Berlin, 25 Aug 1902; d. New York, 4 April 1972), began serious study of theory and piano in 1917 and attended the Berlin Hochschule für Musik (1919–24). He has been most influenced by counseling he received from Ferruccio Busoni in 1920, studies with Hermann Scherchen at various times during 1920–35, association with Paul Klee, V. Schlemmer, and others at the Bauhaus in 1923 and with other artists (Tworkov, de Kooning) throughout his life, and studies with Anton Webern in 1933–34. He left Nazi Germany for Vienna in 1933 and went to Palestine the next year. In 1938 he moved to the U.S., first to New York (1938–52), then to Black Mountain College in N. C. (1952–56), and back to New York, where he lived from 1956. He was head of the music department at C. W. Post College of Long Island Univ. (1957–68) and continued to teach private students as well as students from the college and from the Mannes School. He developed Parkinson's disease in 1964. He was married three times: to Ola Okuniewska in 1927 (their daughter Katharina was born in 1931), to Irma Schoenberg in 1934, and to Hilda Morley in 1948.

Rather than being influenced by other composers, even those whom he studied closely (Schoenberg, Webern, Stravinsky, and Bartók), Wolpe developed parallel compositional concerns: developing variation, asymmetrical meters and rhythms, nontriadic chord constructs, contrapuntal textures, uneven phrases, the generation of material from intervallic relationships. Even his earliest pieces reflected these concerns: The textures are contrapuntal and the rhythms asymmetrical. The basic compositional principle is a concentrated variation technique with both simultaneities and lines used to project motivic intervals. The melodies are developmental and unornamented. The harmonic language is mostly diatonic with some contrasting chromaticism, using triadic and nontriadic chords but continuously progressing to distant rather than close relationships (creating "a decomposition of tonality" to use Wolpe's words). Always politically conscious, Wolpe simplified this atonal and dense style in the late 1920s in order to make it more readily performable by amateurs and more immediately accessible to relatively uninformed auditors. Also at this time he wrote some works influenced by quasi-jazz of the Paul Whiteman type, wrote some works satirizing social institutions, and took part in some dada performances. After the Nazis came into power, however, and his political world collapsed, he returned to his natural style and to his interest in music as art rather than as social commentary. He was greatly helped in this by Webern, with whom he also discussed composition and studied non-Debussy, non-R. Strauss, non-Stravinsky orchestration.

The music Wolpe wrote in Palestine reflected his involvement with his Jewish heritage. He absorbed traits of Semitic music (e.g., certain rhythmic impulses, typical pitch groupings, etc.) combining them with some longstanding preferences: the most frequent intervals are major seconds, minor sevenths, minor thirds, perfect and augmented fourths; chords are frequently first-inversion triads, various kinds of seventh chord, chords built in fourths; rhythms are declamatory, juxtaposing short against sustained notes; the use of pitch space opposes repeated notes and scalar circulations to large skips over many registers, and sets of block chords in the middle register to linear motion two or three octaves below or linear expansions two octaves above; dynamics contradict rather than reinforce the phrase gesture. The use of contiguous contrast typifies all of Wolpe's music.

This style culminated in the ballet suite *Man from Midian* (1942), but from about 1936 on a further refinement and development was also taking place. Wolpe composed many studies (often using serial techniques), much music which he discarded as unsatisfactory solutions to the problems, and much "didactic" music. The *Violin Sonata* (1949) evidences three main concerns: the distribution of space, the juxtaposition of contrasting activities, and the organization of harmonic areas. All are solved simultaneously through an application of his variation technique. Wolpe combined focal pitches and small groups of other pitches into motives; the variation of these motives focuses on intervallic rather than on rhythmic relationships; the variations set small against gradually growing or suddenly expanded registral distributions, so that the type of activity in which the lines are engaged (with stasis, slow rhythms, and long phrases being constantly set against contrasting types of activity) determines their spatial definition. Since the motives as they expand or contract either continually maintain a pitch field, incorporate new pitches into it, or omit pitches from it, the motivically created harmonic areas are either specifically defined or in a state of change with the rates of change ever changing. Again there is some parallel here with Schoenberg, specifically with his preserial music, for Wolpe's work is also largely contrapuntal, nontonal (using all 12 pitches in motivically determined combinations and constantly changing rates of circulation), and generally romantic in gesture, articulating sections by means of heightening,

climaxes, and liquidations. The difference derives mainly from Wolpe's leaner sound, chiseled lines, and use of irregular, contrasting rhythms within single phrases.

Wolpe's greatest work began with the monumental *Enactments* (1950–53), a work of immense density and equally immense clarity, for the shapes in which the variations occur are always tangible and finite. Later works are less dense and are marked by increasing care in nonserial pitch organization and transformation of motivic material. Bars 15–22 from the second movement of the *Trio* for flute, cello, and piano (1964) illustrate Wolpe's mature modulation and transformation procedures. In analogy to a classical tonal work, which would become increasingly chromatic before defining a new harmonic area, this passage starts with a focal field of five pitches (D♭, D, F, G♭, G); then carefully selected new pitches accrue to this field through motivic development until it becomes relatively undefined; following this, three of the new pitches (A, C, B) are selected to become the new harmonic area—the same one which opened the movement. This harmonic return marks a melodic restatement of the opening, a "second exposition," where both development and pitch accretion occur more slowly. In regard to transformation, the available pitches are formed into motives which develop nongradually, omitting the intervening steps of progressive development, i.e., they are transformed instantaneously into distantly related variants. The pitches are multiply engaged; the variants exist on various "levels of language," from the banal and deliberately quoted to the most newly invented, and in contrasting activities—isolated notes, brusque figures, trills, chords, or lines at various dynamic levels flashing out of and being absorbed back into the sound milieu. In this work, as elsewhere, the harmonic scheme and activities assigned to various pitch groups are planned precompositionally, but Wolpe allowed the form to unfold in its own way. He did not rely on forms borrowed from the past. His forms subsume contrast, are cumulative and unique. In addition his music has that freedom that comes only through exquisite discipline, that feeling of spontaneity that only rigor can achieve. It is this outlook that he passed on to a large number of students and other composers, and his influence will probably increase as more performances of his music become available on records.

PRINCIPAL COMPOSITIONS: *Hölderlin Lieder* for alto, piano (1924, revised 1935); *Schöne Geschichten* for actors, singers, marionettes, chorus, chamber orchestra (1927–29); *Zeus and Elide*, burlesque in 1 act for 5 voices, 3 saxophones, 2 trumpets, trombone, sousaphone, banjo, 12 violins, percussion (1928); *5 Characteristic Marches* for piano (1929–34); *March and Variations* for 2 pianos (1933); *4 Studies for Piano on Basic Rows* (including the "Passacaglia") (1935–36); *Songs from the Hebrew* for voice, piano (1936–39, Marx); *2 Palestinian Songs* for alto, piano (1936, Hargail); *Duo im Hexachord* for oboe, clarinet (1936); *2 Ancient Chinese Epitaphs* for chorus, drums (1937); *Oboe Sonata* (1938–41, Marx); *Zemach Suite* for piano (1939, Hargail); *Toccata in 3 Parts* for piano (1941); *The Man from Midian*, ballet suite for orchestra or 2 pianos (1942); *Encouragements and Battle Piece* for piano (1943–47); *2 Studies* for piano (1948, Marx); *Violin Sonata* (1949, Marx); *Quartet* for trumpet, tenor saxophone, percussion, piano (1950); *7 Pieces for 3 Pianos* (1950–51); *Enactments* for 3 pianos (1950–53); *Symphony No. 1* (1955–56, revised 1964); *Piece for Oboe, Cello, Percussion, and Piano* (1955); *Quintet with Voice* for baritone, clarinet, horn, cello, harp, piano (1957); *Form* for piano (1959, Tonos); *Piece in 2 Parts* for flute, piano (1960, Marx); *For Piano and 16 Players* for 2 flutes, oboe, clarinet, baritone saxophone, 2 trumpets, 2 horns, bass tuba, violin, viola, cello, harp, electric guitar, percussion, piano (1960–61); *In 2 Parts for 6 Players* for violin, cello, clarinet, trumpet, harp, piano (1962); *Street Music* for oboe, clarinet, cello, piano, baritone voice (1962, BCMA); *Piece for 2 Instrumental Units* for flute, cello, piano; oboe, violin, double bass, percussion (1962–63, BCMA); *Trio in 2 Parts* for flute, cello, piano (1964); *Piece in 2 Parts for Violin Solo* (1964, Marx); *Chamber Piece No. 1* for flute, oboe, English horn, clarinet, bassoon, trumpet, horn, trombone, piano, 2 violins, viola, cello, double bass (1964); *Chamber Piece No. 2* for the same 14 players (1965–66); *Solo Piece for Trumpet* (1966, Marx); *Second Piece for Violin Alone* (1966, Marx); *Cantata for Voice, Voices, and Instruments* for flute, clarinet, bassoon, trumpet, 2 violins, viola, double bass, 2 altos, soprano, mezzo-soprano, 2 speakers (1963–68); *From Here On Farther* for clarinet, bass clarinet, violin, piano (1969); *String Quartet in 2 Parts* (1969); *Piece for Trumpet and 7 Instruments* for trumpet, clarinet, bassoon, horn, violin, viola, cello, bass (1971). Complete list to 1969: Sucoff. During 1944–50 Wolpe also wrote composition exercises (which he calls "didactic music") in which he developed many of his mature compositional techniques.

PRINCIPAL WRITINGS: "Spatial Relations, Harmonic Structures, and Shapes," lecture, Yale Univ., 1951; "Thinking Twice," *Contemporary Composers on Contemporary Music* ed. by E. Schwartz and B. Childs (New York 1967):274–307; "Symmetrical Proportions" and "Asymmetrical Proportions," lectures, Darmstadt summer courses, 1962.

BIBL.: Edward Levy, *A Guide to Musical Analysis* (EdD diss., Columbia Univ., 1967):379–407; ——, "S. W.: for His Sixtieth Birthday," *Perspectives* 2/1:51–65; Frederick Prausnitz, "The Music of S. W.," *Listener* (Sept 1968); Paul

Rosenfeld, "S. W.," *New Republic* (6 Jan 1941); Abraham Skulsky, "S. W.," *Musical America* (1 Nov 1951):6, 29; Herbert Sucoff, *Catalogue and Evaluation of the Works of S. W.* (MA thesis, Queens College, N. Y., 1969).

Edward Levy

SEE ALSO Dance, Performance, Text Setting and Usage, United States.

Word Score, see Prose Music

Wuorinen, Charles (b. New York, 9 June 1938), studied composition with Otto Luening, Jack Beeson, and Vladimir Ussachevsky at Columbia Univ., where he earned an MA degree in 1963. He has taught at Columbia (1964–71) and the Mannes College (since 1971) and has lectured extensively in the U.S. and Europe. A pianist and conductor, he is codirector of the Group for Contemporary Music, which he cofounded with Harvey Sollberger in 1962. He is also an official in several organizations, including the American Composers Alliance, Composers Recordings, Inc., the American Society of University Composers, and the U.S. section of ISCM.

Influenced neither by folkloristic Americana music nor by aleatory efforts, the music of Wuorinen occupies a radical middle ground where the main tasks are the traditional ones of assimilation and extension through new works of a living musical tradition, in this case that growing from the work of Schoenberg and Stravinsky. His extensive output encompasses music in virtually all genres except opera and dance. The great bulk of it is chamber music ranging from solo pieces to concertos involving up to 12 musicians. The electronic works, while few in number, are significant as exemplars of his theory of the difference in kind between mechanically reproduced music and performed music.

The music to about 1960 has its roots in the tonal system and in Stravinsky's extensions of tonal practices. This is manifest particularly in its utilization of nondiatonic or modified diatonic pitch and interval centers and in the pronounced rhythmic periodicity and symmetry, which is less apparent in the later music. A new phase of development, first marked in 1961 by *Evolutio transcripta*, resulted from attempts to relate pitch and rhythmic structure more integrally than before and to find new bases for formal integration within works. Compositions of this period show the use of canonic (*Evolutio transcripta*) and retrograde

(*Chamber Concerto* for cello and 10 players) structures to achieve these ends. By 1962 Wuorinen was finding a more systematic basis for his work in the 12-tone system as formulated by Milton Babbitt, and most of his music composed until 1968 utilized the 12-tone timepoint system. Elliott Carter and Stefan Wolpe, in the contextually determined, nonsystematic aspects of their music, provided the impetus for such developments as Wuorinen's "fragment music," compositions based on the systematic but contextually conditioned mutation of source musical fragments (*Piano Variations, Exchanges*). Since about 1968 he has carried further his marriage of the systematic and the contextual, with the music being serial at deeper levels of structure and relatively undetermined at surface levels. Central to this has been the use of the intervals of a set to determine the temporal proportions of the various large-scale sections of a work and within these, those of subsections and, to some extent, of immediate note-to-note relationships.

PRINCIPAL COMPOSITIONS (published by Peters unless otherwise noted): *Symphony No. 3* (1959, CFE); *Turetzky Pieces* for flute, clarinet, double bass (1960, CFE); *Concertone* for brass quintet, orchestra (1960, CFE); *8 Variations* for violin, harpsichord (1960, CFE); *Symphonia sacra* for 3 men's voices, 2 oboes, 2 violins, double bass, organ (1961, CFE); *Evolutio transcripta* for chamber orchestra (1961, CFE); *Concert* for double bass (1961, McG-M); *Invention* for percussion quintet (1962, Percus); *Octet* for oboe, clarinet, horn, trombone, violin, cello, double bass, piano (1962, CFE); *Duuiensela* for cello, piano (1962, CFE); *The Prayer of Jonah* for chorus, strings (1962, CFE); *Second Trio* for flute, violin, piano (1962); *Chamber Concerto* for cello, 10 players (1963); *Piano Variations* (1963, McG-M); *Flute Variations 1* (1963, McG-M); *Composition* for violin, 10 instruments (1964); *Chamber Concerto* for flute, 10 players (1964); *Super salutem* for men's voices, instruments (1964); *Orchestral and Electronic Exchanges* (1965); *Chamber Concerto* for oboe, 10 players (1965); *Piano Concerto* (1966); *Janissary Music* for 1 percussion (1966); *Harpsichord Divisions* (1966); *Making Ends Meet* for piano 4-hands (1966); *Duo* for violin, piano (1966); *The Politics of Harmony*, a masque (1967); *String Trio* (1968); *Flute Variations 2* (1968); *Time's Encomium*, electronic music (1969, recorded by Nonesuch); *Adapting to the Times* for cello, piano (1969); *The Long and the Short* for violin (1969); *Contrafactum* for orchestra (1969); *Nature's Concord* for trumpet, piano (1969); *Piano Sonata* (1969); *Ringing Changes* for percussion ensemble (1970); *Chamber Concerto* for tuba, 12 winds, 12 drums (1970); *A Message to Denmark Hill*, cantata (1970); *Cello Variations* (1970); *String Quartet* (1971).

PRINCIPAL WRITINGS: "The Outlook for Young Composers," *Perspectives* 1/2:54–61; "Notes on the Performance of Contemporary Music," *ibid.* 3/1:10–21; review of *Music in the Twentieth Century* by William W. Austin, *ibid.* 5/1:142–47; "The Schooling of Young Composers in the U.S.," Yugoslav-American Seminar on Music held in Sveti Stefan, 1968; "Toward Good Vibrations," *Prose* 2 (1970).

Harvey Sollberger

SEE ALSO Performance, Recording, Text Setting and Usage, United States.

Wyner, Yehudi (b. Calgary, Canada, 1 June 1929), the son of naturalized American parents, was brought up in New York City, where his father, Lazar Weiner, was an active composer, pianist, and conductor, especially in the Jewish community. He received a diploma in piano in 1946 from the Juilliard School and then studied at Yale Univ. (piano with Bruce Simonds; composition with Richard Donovan, Paul Hindemith) and Harvard Univ. (composition with Randall Thompson, Walter Piston). From 1956 to 1967 he lived in New York City, accompanying singers, playing and recording chamber music (especially with the violinist Matthew Raimondi), directing music at a suburban synagogue, and teaching. He was music director of the Turnau Opera Co. in Woodstock, N. Y., 1962–64, and since 1964 has been teaching composition at Yale. He joined the Bach Aria Group in 1968 and is also music director of the New Haven Opera Society.

Chamber music, piano works, and liturgical music for the synagogue form the largest part of Wyner's output. All of his music shows a vivid consciousness of immediate effect, as befits one who has had an active career as a performer. Beginning with a straightforward, contrapuntal technique related to that of Hindemith, he came under the influence of Stravinsky and wrote some stylized neoclassic works; the *Partita* for piano (1952) contains neo-Bach mannerisms presented with a rhythmic verve that could only have been produced by a jazz-indoctrinated American.

With the *Concert Duo* for violin and piano (1955–57), Wyner discarded the veneer of neo-classic objectivity and spoke in what must be taken to be his true voice—expressive, improvisatory, rhapsodic, full of unexpected turns and playful fantasy. There is great emphasis on coloristic instrumental writing of a traditional virtuoso sort with a nervous, excited kind of melodic line filled with an individual type of extremely fast ornamentation. The harmonic language is freely chromatic but a simple and secure tonality is always evident, owing largely to the extensive use of repetition, particularly of accompaniment figures. Especially successful are the passages that derive from bop jazz style. The chamber works for several instruments, particularly the *Serenade* and the *Passover Offering*, feature low-pitched instruments, and their somber, slow, reflective passages are noteworthy. Although the composer seems most at home writing for one or two soloists, he has succeeded in adapting his flexible, improvisatory style to piano and orchestra in a still unfinished concerto, *Da camera*, which retains the romantic expressivity of the earlier pieces but is informed with a new lightness and grace. His religious works are mostly in an unpretentious style for practical use in liturgical services. The melodic writing is usually based on one or another of the Jewish chant traditions.

PRINCIPAL COMPOSITIONS: *7 Songs* for voice, piano (1950–55, AMP); *Partita* for piano (1952); *Psalm 143* for chorus (1952); *Piano Sonata* (1954); *Concert Duo* for violin, piano (1955–57, AMP); *Serenade* for flute, horn, trumpet, trombone, viola, cello, piano (1958); *Passover Offering* for flute, clarinet, trombone, cello (1959, AMP); *3 Informal Pieces* for violin, piano (1961, revised 1969); *Friday Evening Service* for cantor, chorus, organ (1963, AMP); *Short Fantasies* for piano (1963–66); *Torah Service* for chorus, four brasses, double bass (1966); *Da camera*, concerto for piano, orchestra (part 1, 1967); *Cadenza!* for clarinet, harpsichord or piano (1969–70).

                                    Billy Jim Layton

SEE ALSO Liturgical Music: Jewish.

Wyschnegradsky, Ivan (b. St. Petersburg, 4 May 1893), studied philosophy and law at the Univ. of St. Petersburg (1911–16) and composition and orchestration with Nicolas Sokoloff (1911–14). His early works were written under the influence of Tchaikovsky and Wagner. His interest in the music and philosophy of Scriabin, together with religious experiences of "cosmic consciousness" in 1916 and 1918, led him in 1918 to explore the use of microtones within a tonal framework (the extension of musical resources to include microtones had become for him symbolic of human consciousness expanding into the cosmic). He created and used "strictly determined ultrachromatic scales" (quarter-tone, sixth-tone, etc.), and gradually his compositions became "pantonal" (in the Scriabin sense). In 1919 he went to France in the hope of having a quarter-tone concert piano built by the Pleyel firm. This failing, he traveled to Germany, where he met Alois Hába and other musicians interested in microtonal music. He returned to France (where he still resides), and in 1929 Pleyel built a quarter-tone, three-manual piano to his design. After 1936 (and until very recently) Wyschnegradsky composed exclusively for pianos tuned a microtone (chiefly a quarter-tone) apart. He never adopted serial techniques, which he considers "totally alien to the spirit of the ultrachromatic revolution." In the 1950s he developed a "principle of nonoctavian spaces" with which he created a system of control over the extremes of ultrachromaticism as well as sixth and twelfth tones. His use of musical form has remained traditional.

PRINCIPAL COMPOSITIONS: *The Day of Existence* for narrator, orchestra; text by the composer (1916–17); *Le Soleil décline*, 3 songs for bass-baritone, piano, Op. 3; texts by Nietzsche (1918, Belaieff); *String Quartet No. 1* in 1/4-tones, Op. 13 (1924); *2 Choruses* for chorus, 4 pianos tuned in 1/4-tones, Op. 14; texts by A. Pomorsky (1927–36); *Ainsi parlait Zarathoustra* for orchestra, Op. 17; 1/4-tone scale (1929–30; arranged for 4 pianos tuned in 1/4-tones, 1936, L'Oiseau Lyre); *String Quartet No. 2* in 1/4-tones, Op. 18 (1931–32); *24 Preludes* for 2 pianos, Op. 22; using the 24 "tonalities" of a 13-tone "diatonicized" 1/4-tone scale (1934, revised 1950s); *Fragment symphonique No. 1* for orchestra in 1/4-tones, Op. 23 (1934); arranged for 4 pianos in 1/4-tones, 1936); *Fragment symphonique No. 2* for 4 pianos in 1/4-tones, Op. 24 (1937); *Linnita*, 1-act pantomime for 3 women's voices, 4 pianos in 1/4-tones, Op. 25; text by the composer's mother (1937); *Acte chorégraphique*, Op. 27, for bass-baritone, chorus, 4 pianos in 1/4-tones; text by the composer (1938–40, revised 1958–59); *5 Variations sans thème et conclusion* for orchestra in 1/4-tones, Op. 27 (1951–52, Belaieff); *Etude sur les movements rotatoire* for 2 pianos in 1/4-tones, 4-hands each, Op. 45 (1961, arranged for orchestra, 1964).

PRINCIPAL WRITINGS: "Quelques considérations sur l'emploi des quarts de ton en musique," *Monde musical* (Paris, 30 June 1927); "Quarter-tone Music, Its Possibilities and Organic Sources," *Pro Musica Quarterly* (New York, Oct 1927); "Musique et pansonorité," *Revue musicale* (Paris, Dec 1927); "Etude sur l'harmonie par quartes superposées," *Menestrel* (Paris; 12, 19 April 1935); "La musique à quarts de ton et sa réalisation pratique," *Revue musicale* (Jan 1937):26; "L'Enigme de la musique moderne," *Revue d'esthétique* (Paris; Jan, April 1949); "Préface à un traité d'harmonie par quartes superposées," *Polyphonie* 3 (Paris, 1949):56; "Problèmes d'ultrachromatisme," *Polyphonie* 9–10 (1954):129; "Continuum électronique et supression de l'interprète," *Cahiers d'études de radio-television* (Paris, 1958):43; "Ultrachromatisme et espaces nonoctaviant," *Polyphonie* (1971).

BIBL.: LeRoy B. Campbell, "W.'s Quarter-toned Piano," *The Musician* (New York, May 1937); H.-P. Coffy, "Un Musicien de l'espace,"

Inter-Hebdo (Paris, 28 May 1965); Serge Moreux, "I. W., ou le musicien ami des grandes nombres," *Les Arts* (Paris, Feb 1948); Boris de Schloezer, "La Musique," *Fontaine* (Paris, June 1949).

SEE ALSO Microtones.

Wyttenbach, Jürg (b. Bern, 2 Dec 1935), studied at the Conservatory in Bern (1948–55, composition with Sándor Veress, piano with Karl von Fischer), the Paris Conservatory (1955–57; Yvonne Lefébure, piano; Joseph Calvet, chamber music), and the Lower Saxony School of Music (1958–59; Karl Engle, piano). He has taught at the Biel Music School (1958–67), the Bern Conservatory (1960–67), and the Basel Academy of Music (since 1967). Wyttenbach is active as a pianist and conductor of contemporary music. His compositions use serial and aleatory tech-niques and have been influenced by the work of Pierre Boulez, Klaus Huber, and Heinz Holliger.

PRINCIPAL COMPOSITIONS (published by Ars Viva): *3 Pieces* for oboe, harp, piano (1963); *Piano Concerto* (1964); *Divisions* for piano, 9 strings (1964); *De metalli* for baritone, orchestra; text by Da Vinci (1965); *Anrufungen und Ausbruch* for winds (1966); *Nachspiel* for 2 pianos (1967); *Paraphrase* for flute, piano (1968); *Change* for 2–4 flutes (1969); *Contests* for musicians (1969, unpub.); *Exécution ajournée*, "gestes pour musi-cians" (1969–70, unpub.).

PRINCIPAL WRITINGS: notes for Pierre Boulez's *Sonatine*, program book of the Hessischer Rund-funk (15 Jan 1967); "Sutil und Laar," *Chordirigent* (Mainz) 31:12–16.

BIBL.: Josef Häusler, "J. W.," *Schweizerische Muzikzeitung* (May–June 1966):151–54; ——, "J. W.," program book of the Donaueschingen Festival (1966).

SEE ALSO Switzerland.

Xenakis, Iannis (b. Braïla, Rumania, of Greek parents, 29 May 1922), moved with his family to Greece in 1932. He began serious musical studies two years later under Aristotle Kundurov, a pupil of Ippolitov-Ivanov. A parallel interest in the sciences led to his graduation in 1947 from the Athens Polytechnic School with a degree in engineering. At the same time his activities in the anti-Nazi resistance had resulted in a severe face wound, imprisonment, and a death sentence. In 1947 he escaped to Paris where, after continuing his studies under Honegger and Milhaud, he became a pupil of Messiaen (1950–51). He also studied with Hermann Scherchen in Switzerland. During 1948–59 he earned his living by working with the architect Le Corbusier; they collaborated on the book *Modulor 2* and on several architectural projects, and Xenakis himself designed the Philips pavilion for the 1958 Brussels Exhibition. Since 1959 he has devoted himself almost entirely to music, though he is still intermittently active in the field of architecture. He became a French citizen in 1965, and in 1966 he established a School of Mathematical and Automated Music in Paris. Since 1967 he has divided his time between Paris and Indiana Univ., where he has set up a similar school.

Since *Metastaseis* (1953–54) Xenakis has written over 30 works. Except for five electronic works, their instrumentation is traditional: orchestra, chorus, chamber ensembles, solo instruments. They nevertheless embody a revolutionary concept, *stochastic* music; only a limited use of serialism in *Metastaseis* reveals the influence on Xenakis of other contemporary approaches.

The term *stochastic*, which Xenakis was the first to apply to music, is related to Jacques Bernoulli's Law of Large Numbers, which says that as the number of repetitions of a given chance trial (such as flipping a coin) increases, the probability that the results will tend to a determinate end approaches certainty. A stochastic process, then, is one that is probabilistic in the sense of tending toward a certain goal. Whereas John Cage and many other users of aleatory processes in music have sought to eliminate the primacy of the composer by pursuing the ideal of indeterminacy, Xenakis has maintained the dominance of the composer and of the principle of determinacy. His aim is nothing less than the expression in music of the unity he sees as underlying all activity, human and nonhuman, artistic and scientific. (The extent to which, in his mind, art and science interpenetrate is illustrated by his habitual use of "beautiful" to characterize scientific formulas and of "interesting" as a term of musical praise.) His method is to set the terms of the abstract structure of a work (the range and character of textural, dynamic, and pitch elements) by marshalling the concepts to be employed— whether Bernoulli's or some other large-numbers law, the Kinetic Theory of Gases, or any of a variety of formulations in symbolic and mathematical logic; then to calculate the actual musical events (the speeds of glissandos, for instance, or the densities of the "clouds" of sonorities that result from linking numerous individual "points" of sound originally plotted in graph form) either by himself or with the aid of a computer; and finally, to order the results of calculation and transcribe them into musical notation. In this third stage he applies the final "sheen" or "embellishment" by deciding what would be most "interesting" (making individual choices and rejecting what his ear disapproves, which determines at least 15 percent of the definitive formulation). The actual sound of his music, which is characterized by densely massed sonorities, systematic use of glissandi, and the writing of individual parts for every instrument in the orchestra (including each of the string players), makes for a sense of poetry and of drama on a cosmic scale. These characteristics have had a strong influence, especially on the work of contemporary Polish composers (Penderecki, Lutosławski, Gorecki, among others) and, partly through the agency of an informal pupil, Yuji Takahashi, from

Japan. His use of game theory in two works, *Duel* (1959) and *Strategie* (1959–62), has found many imitators, including Mauricio Kagel, though they have generally set the rules of their games far less stringently than Xenakis. Characteristically his mixed-media *Polytope*, realized for the French pavilion at the 1967 Montreal Exposition, was determined with full mathematical rigor, whereas most mixed-media works of the 1960s were not.

PRINCIPAL COMPOSITIONS (published by Boosey): *Metastaseis* for orchestra of 61 players (1953–54); *Pithoprakta* for orchestra of 50 players (1955–56); *ST/10* for 10 instruments (1956–62); *Duel*, game for 2 orchestras (1959); *Strategie*, game for 2 orchestras (1959–62); *Akrata* for 16 winds (1964–65); *Terretektorh* for orchestra of 88 players scattered among the audience (1965–66); *ST/4* for string quartet (1965–66); *Polytope* for 4 orchestras of 17 players each, distributed among the audience

(1967); *Nomos Gamma* for orchestra scattered among the audience (1967–68); *Kraanerg*, ballet for orchestra, prerecorded tape; choreography by Roland Petit (1968–69). Annotated list to 1967: *I.X.: The Man and His Music* (Boosey & Hawkes 1967).

PRINCIPAL WRITINGS: *Musiques Formelles* (Paris 1963); "Cosmic City," trans. by J. Ashberg, *Art and Literature* (Lausanne) No. 10; "La Voie de la recherche et de la question," *Preuves* (Paris, Nov 1965); "Towards a Metamusic," *Tempo* 93:2–19; a series of articles dealing mainly with stochastic music: *Gravesaner Blätter* (Switzerland) Nos. 1, 6, 11–12, 18–23, 26.

Bernard Jacobson

SEE ALSO Asian Music and Western Composition; Austria and Germany; Computer Applications; Dance; Electronic Music: History and Development; France; Instrumental and Vocal Resources; Mathematics; Melody; Microtones; Orchestration; Rhythm.

Yannai, Yehuda (b. Timisoara, Rumania, 26 May 1937), studied at the Israel Academy of Music (1960–64; composition with Alexander U. Boskovich; harmony, analysis with Mordecai Seter; conducting with Gary Bertini), Brandeis Univ. in Mass. (1964–66, composition with Arthur Berger, electronic composition with Ernst Krenek, theory with Harold Shapero), Tanglewood (1965, composition with Gunther Schuller), and the Univ. of Ill. (1968–70, composition with Salvatore Martirano, computer composition with Herbert Brun, musicology with Alexander Ringer). He has been teaching theory and composition privately since 1963. During 1966–68 he was dean of the Israel Conservatory of Music in Tel Aviv. *Permutations* is a mobile work in graphic notation. *Continuum* and *Houdini's Ninth* and other works are theater pieces involving visual as well as sound elements. Live electronics are used in *Coheleth*.

PRINCIPAL COMPOSITIONS: *Music for Piano* (1962, IMI); *Spheres* for soprano, flute, clarinet, bass clarinet, harp, prepared piano, 5 percussionists; text by Yehuda Amichay (1963); *Permutations* for 1 percussionist (1964); *Incantations* for medium voice, piano; text by W. H. Auden (1964, IMI); *Studies Nos. 1–3* on tape (1964–66); *Phonomontage pour Thérèse* on tape (1964–66); *Interconnections* for 14 solo winds and strings (1965); *2 Fragments for Violin and Piano* (1966, Media Press); *Continuum* for piano (1965); *Mirkamim*, sound textures for orchestra (1968); *Mutatis mutandis* for oboe, clarinet, horn, trumpet, viola, double bass (1968); *Wraphap*, theater piece for 5 participants, amplified aluminum sheet, Yannachord (1969); *Per se* for violin, English horn, tenor saxophone, tenor and bass trombones, viola, cello, double bass (1969); *Coloring Book for the Harpist*, a "do-it-yourself" score-kit for a harp player (1969); *Houdini's Ninth*, theater piece for double bass, escape artist, 2 hospital orderlies, record-player manipulator (1969); *Coheleth*, environment with mobile chorus, electronic apparatus (1970).

PRINCIPAL WRITINGS: "The Late A. U. Boskovich, profile of a creative artist," lecture at the Seventh Annual Conference of Israeli Music (3 Dec 1966).

SEE ALSO Israel.

Young, La Monte (b. Bern, Idaho, 14 Oct 1935), grew up in Los Angeles and Utah and studied at Los Angeles City College (1953–55), Los Angeles State College (1956–57), the Univ. of Calif. at Los Angeles (1957–58; theory, composition, ethnomusicology), and the Univ. of Calif. at Berkeley (1958–60, composition). He also studied privately in Los Angeles (saxophone, clarinet with William Green; counterpoint, composition with Leonard Stein), with Karlheinz Stockhausen at the Darmstadt summer courses (1959, when he was first extensively exposed to the music of John Cage), and with Richard Maxfield at the New School for Social Research in New York (fall-winter, 1960–61, electronic music). Since 1960 he has been a free-lance composer, performer, lecturer, and teacher. He was editor of *An Anthology* (1961–63), which he copublished with Jackson MacLow, and music editor of *S.M.S.*, a bimonthly published by The Letter Edged in Black Press (New York). In 1962 he founded a workshop, The Theatre of Eternal Music, with which he has developed and performed his music. In 1963 he married the painter and light artist Marian Zazeela. In March 1970 he became a disciple of Pandit Pran Nath, the Indian Kirana-style vocalist; however, his study and performance of Indian music have been kept separate from his own activities as a composer.

The first sound that made an impression on Young was the sustained, subtly varied sound of wind coming through chinks in the log house in Idaho where he was born. Other sustained sounds also made an impression on him: insects, motors, power plants, the resonance from valleys, lakes, plains and other geological configurations; the sound of telephone poles is embodied in *The Second Dream of the High-Tension Line Stepdown Transformer*, which is a sustained chord whose pitches, if the lowest is G, are G-C-C♯-D. His works of 1956–58 were in the Schoenberg 12-tone tradition; however, "his use of sustained notes, sparse textures, and the exclusion of certain combinations of pitches suggested directions he has since pursued" (Kostelanetz: 184; see bibl.). During this period he became aware of being "more interested in listening to chords than in listening to melodies" (Kostelanetz: 195). An example of this concern is the *Trio for Strings*, which consists entirely of sustained tones and chords. Simultaneously, elements of theater began to enter his work: *Composition 1960 #2* consists of building a fire in front of the audience, *#5* of releasing butterflies into the performance area. All of the *Composition 1961* pieces consist of the same activity, "Draw a straight line and follow it."

The Tortoise, His Dreams and Journeys, which Young began performing with his Theatre of Eternal Music workshop in 1964, is a crystallization of his ideas. It "is very long and comprehensive and unfolds through the performance of sections each day. . . . I hope it will be perpetuated through the establishment of Dream Houses designed especially for its continuous performance." It is composed of sustained intervals and chords that are preselected from frequencies that may be represented as integral multiples of a common fundamental. The performers predetermine which of these selected frequencies will be used and which combinations will be allowed. In some of the early realizations there were seven sound sources: an aquarium filter motor to provide the primary drone and voices and instruments for the other pitches. Public performances usually consisted of two sessions, each nearly two hours in length, within a room illuminated by projections of calligraphic light art by Marian Zazeela.

Young's interest in controlling the total harmonic structure of his music lead to the compositional theory formulated in *The Two Systems of Eleven Categories 1:07:40 AM 3 X 67– , first revision of 2–3 PM 12 XI 66– 3:43 AM 28 XII 66 for John Cage for Vertical Hearing or Hearing in The Present Tense*. This work "outlines a means for achieving graduated degrees of control over which frequencies will be present within a complex of concurrent generating frequencies and their associated combination frequencies." According to Swedish composer Christer Hennix, "in establishing a finite collection of frequencies and a finite set of recursive formation rules, this work represents the first attempt in music to outline a structure with a potentially infinite set of form-ordering elements that are all well-defined constituents. These rules combine with elements in a way very similar to the formal sentence formations that take place in grammars of Chomsky's type."

In 1966 Young began to work with only categories A1, B1, A2, B2, and X = 5, thereby developing a section of *The Tortoise*... entitled *Map of 49's Dream The Two Systems of Eleven Sets of Galactic Intervals Ornamental Lightyears Tracery*. He now uses electronically generated sine waves tuned to intervals and chords from this piece to maintain a periodic composite sound-wave environment in his studio and home. Concert performances consist of continuous frequency environments in sound and light, generally at least a week in duration, during which Young and Zazeela sing with the environment for several hours each day.

PRINCIPAL COMPOSITIONS: *for brass* for 2 trumpets, 2 horns, 2 trombones, 2 tubas (1957); *for guitar* (1958); *Trio for Strings* for violin, viola, cello or for string orchestra (1958); *Vision* for 11 instruments producing specified sounds (1959); *Untitled Works*, improvisations with live friction sounds produced by gong on cement, gong on wood floor, metal on wall (1959–); *Untitled Works*, improvisations within a specified structure for piano using a rhythmic-chordal drone style of the composer's invention (1959–62); *Poem for Chairs, Tables, Benches, Etc.* for the objects named, which are pushed or pulled along the floor within a time structure established for each performance according to a method described in the score; another version permits the use of any sound sources (1960–); *2 sounds*, 2 sounds (one made by scraping cans across window glass, the other by rotating a drum stick on a gong), each recorded on its own reel of tape; since 1964 this work has been used for the dance "Winterbranch" by Merce Cunningham (1960); *arabic numeral* (any integer) for gong or piano (1960); *Compositions 1960, #s 1–15*, word scores involving various objects and activities (1960, most of these pieces are published in *An Anthology*); *Compositions 1961, #s 1–29*, word scores for the same activity, "Draw a straight line and follow it" (1961); *Untitled Works*, improvisations on specific structures for sopranino saxophone/piano/gong, voice drone, guitar/violin/lute, viola (1962–64); *The Second Dream of the High-Tension Line Stepdown Transformer* (from *The 4 Dreams of China*) for bowed strings or other sustained-tone instruments that can be precisely tuned (1962); *Studies in the Bowed Disc* for a 4-foot steel gong made by the sculptor Robert Morris (1963); *The Well-Tuned Piano* for a specially tuned piano; 3 50-minute realizations of the work have been recorded on tape (1964); *The Tortoise, His Dreams and Journeys*, a continuing performance work initially for voice(s), string(s), drone(s) with microphones, mixers, amplifiers, and loudspeakers; projections by Marian Zazeela (1964–). Public performances of sections of this work have been given various titles, among them: "Prelude to The Tortoise" (first presented Oct 1964); "The Tortoise Droning Selected Pitches from The Holy Numbers for The Two Black Tigers The Green Tiger and The Hermit" (Nov 1964);

"The Tortoise Recalling The Drone of The Holy Numbers As They Were Revealed in The Dreams of The Whirlwind and The Obsidian Gong and Illuminated by The Sawmill, The Green Sawtooth Ocelot and The High-Tension Line Stepdown Transformer" (Dec 1964); "The Obsidian Ocelot, The Sawmill, and The Blue Sawtooth High-Tension Line Stepdown Transformer Refracting The Legend of The Dream of The Tortoise Traversing The 189/98 Lost Ancestral Lake Region Illuminating Quotients from The Black Tiger Tapestries of The Drone of The Holy Numbers" (Oct 1965); "The Ballad of The Tortoise" or "Pierced Earrings/Drone Ratios Transmitting The Manifestation of The Tortoise Center Drifting Obsidian Time Mists Through The Synaptic Stepdown Barrier" (Dec 1965); "7" (Feb 1966); "The Celebration of The Tortoise" (July 1966); "Tortoise" (August 1966). In 1966 a continuation of this work began under the title "Map of 49's Dream the Two Systems of Eleven Sets of Galactic Intervals Ornamental Lightyears Tracery." Many realizations have been recorded on tape. In addition to drones, voices, and continuously tunable sustaining instruments, the section uses sine waves. For subsequent sections, see the text above.

PRINCIPAL WRITINGS: *Selected Writings*, containing writings of Young and Zazeela from the years 1960–70 (Munich 1970); "Sound is God: The Singing of Pran Nath," *Village Voice* (New York, 30 April 1970).

BIBL.: Cornelius Cardew, "L. Y.," *New Departures* (1962):75–77; Howard Junker, "Johnny One-Note," *Newsweek* (4 March 1968):56; H. Wiley Hitchcock, "Current Chronicle," *Musical Quarterly* 51:538–39; Jill Johnston, "Music: L. Y.," *Village Voice* (New York, 19 Nov 1964); Richard Kostelanetz, *The Theatre of Mixed Means* (New York 1967); Folke Rabe, "Den illusionistiska Musiken," *Dagens Nyheter* (23 April 1967):4; Ron Rosenbaum, "L. Y.: Eternal Music in a Dreamhouse Barn," *Village Voice* (13 Feb 1970); Diane Wakoski, "The Theatre of Eternal Music," *Ikon* (fall 1967):15–19; Peter Yates, "Just Intonation," *Arts and Architecture* (Dec 1964):8–9.

SEE ALSO Indeterminacy, Microtones, Mixed Media, Performance, Prose Music, Rhythm.

Yuasa, Joji (b. Koriyama, Japan, 12 August 1929), was a premedical student at Keio Univ. (1948–51) and worked in composition at the Experimental Workshop in Tokyo (1951–57). He lectured in the U.S. and Europe in 1968 on a Japan Society Fellowship, and in 1969 helped organize the multimedia Japan Crosstalk Festival. In addition to the compositions listed below, he has written many radio, television, and film scores.

PRINCIPAL COMPOSITIONS: *Projection* for flute, oboe, clarinet, horn, trumpet, cello, piano (1955); *Cosmos Haptic* for piano (1957); *Projection Topologic* for piano (1959); *Projection Esemplastic* for 1 or more pianos (1961); *Aoi no Ue* [Princess Aoi], musique concrète (1961); *Interpenetration* for 2 flutes (1963, Ongaku); *Projection Esemplastic*, electronic score based on white noise (1964, Peters; recorded by Japan Victor); *Kansoku* for any number of voices (1965); *Icon*, 5-track electronic score based on white noise (1967); *Projection* for cello, piano (1967, Ongaku); *Projection*, "Flower, Bird, Wind, Moon," for 8 kotos, orchestra (1967); *Projection*, "The Arrogance of the Dead," for any number of electric guitars (1968); *Voices Coming* on tape (1969); *Music for Space Projection* on 6-track tape (1970); *Projection* for string quartet (1970); *Triplicity* for double bass (1970); *Questions* for chorus (1971).

SEE ALSO Asian Music and Western Composition, Japan.

Yun, Isang (b. Tongyoung, South Korea, 17 Sept 1917), received his first training in Western music in Korea and Japan. He studied cello and music theory at Osaka Conservatory (1935–37) and harmony and composition in Tokyo (1941–43). During 1946–52 he taught music at secondary schools in Tongyoung and Pusan and during 1952–56 was a lecturer in theory and composition at the universities of Pusan and Seoul. Under a grant from the city of Seoul, he studied in Europe at the Paris Conservatory (1956–57), at the Berlin Hochschule (1958–59; composition with Boris Blacher, Josef Rufer, and Reinhard Schwarz-Schilling), and for several summers in Darmstadt. He lived in Krefeld, Freiburg, and Cologne (1960–63), after which he made his home in Berlin. In 1967 he was one of several Koreans who were abducted by the government of South Korea and held in Seoul on a charge of spying. When this charge was proved unfounded in 1969, he was allowed to return to Berlin, where he is now teaching at the Hochschule für Musik.

Yun has withdrawn his earliest works (chamber music, songs, orchestral and film music), all of which were traditional in nature. In the *Piano Pieces* (1959) he used 12-tone procedures. The *Music for 7 Instruments* (1959) is based on comprehensive serial procedures in line with music then emanating from Darmstadt, where the piece was first performed. It also contains traces of Oriental music: the decoration of single tones in a melody by means of vibratos, crescendos, and decrescendos, and the use of accelerandos or rallentandos with a simultaneous lengthening or shortening of note values (as in the percussion parts of Korean court music). The attention that Messiaen and Boulez, and later

Stockhausen, paid to Eastern music encouraged Yun to further explore this stylistic path.
In the *String Quartet No. 3* (1959–60) he first
used pizzicatos followed by short glissandos,
which produces a sound similar to the Japanese
zuzumi (a small variable-pitch drum held
under the arm) and cymbals. The *Quartet* also
anticipated a device that Yun later developed
more fully in *Bara* (1960), *Colloides sonores*
(1961), and other works: a sound structure is
built up from tones that emerge from simultaneously sounding, independent, and highly
decorated melodic lines. The main tones are
held until the melodic lines reappear either as
they were before or transformed. *Bara* recalls
the solemn ceremonial atmosphere of a
Buddhist temple dance. *Colloides sonores*
reproduces the sound of Korean plucked
string instruments such as the gomungo,
hogum (Japanese: kokyu), or yangum (Chinese: yang-ch'in) by means of various glissandos
along with pizzicatos with glissandos and
vibratos. The most important work of this
period is *Loyang* (1962), named after the
ancient capital in East Central China. In this
work Yun contrasted chords with and without
vibrato and used percussion instruments to
accelerate or retard, divide or join together the
various sections of the composition.

The texture of sound complexes is the controlling element in such works as *Fluctuations*
(1964), *Réak* (1966), and *Tuyaux sonores* (1967).
Oriental features may be present, but they are
more varied than before. In general there are
no pulsating metrical rhythms or repeating
rhythmic patterns. The harmony consists
mainly of interchanges of various frictions, including clusters, with an occasional contrasting
flash of tonality. In works where voices are used,
a broad range of vocal techniques is called
for, ranging from nonverbal speech to song.

PRINCIPAL COMPOSITIONS (published by Bote):
Music for 7 Instruments for flute, oboe, clarinet,
bassoon, horn, violin, cello (1959); *Bara* for
orchestra (1960); *Colloides sonores* for string
orchestra (1961); *Loyang* for flute, oboe, clarinet,
bassoon, harp, percussion, vibraphone, violin,
cello (1962); *Gasa* for violin, piano (1963);
Fluctuations for orchestra (1964); *Om mani padme
hum*, oratorio for soprano, baritone, chorus,
orchestra; text from Gautama Buddha (1964); *The
Dream of Liu-tung*, 1-act opera; text from Ma
Chi-yuan in German translation (1965); *Réak*
for large orchestra (1966); *Shao Yang Yin* for
harpsichord (1966); *Tuyaux sonores*, a graphic
score for organ realized by Gerd Zacher (1967);
Butterfly Widow, 1-act opera; text by Harald Kunz
from a Chinese story (1967–68); *Riul* for clarinet,
piano (1968); *Images* for flute, oboe, violin, cello
(1968); *Geisterliebe*, 2-act opera; libretto by Kunz
(1969–70); *Namo* for 3 sopranos, orchestra; text
from Buddhist prayer formulas (1970); *Dimen-
sionen* for orchestra (1971); *Sim Tjong*, 2-act
opera; libretto by Kunz (1971–72).

BIBL.: "A Conversation with I.Y.," *Ford Foundation Berlin Confrontation: Artists in Berlin* (Berlin
1965): 64–69; Harald Kunz, "I. Y.," and Hans
Zender, "Zum musikalischen Denken I. Y.s,"
liner notes for Wergo record 60034 (1968).

Harald Kunz

SEE ALSO Asian Music and Western Composition.

Zacher, Gerd (b. Meppen, Germany, 6 July 1929), studied piano, organ, and composition privately in Lippstadt (1941–48) and attended the Detmold Academy (1949–52; composition with Günther Bialas; organ with Hans Heintze, Michael Schneider; conducting with Kurt Thomas). He also studied composition in Hamburg with Theodor Kaufmann (1952–54) and with Messiaen, Boulez, and Stockhausen at the Darmstadt summer courses. He was cantor and organist at the German Evangelical Church in Santiago, Chile (1954–57) and has been organist and church music director at the Luther Church in Hamburg (1957–70) and organist at the Immanuel Church in Wuppertal (since 1970). He has taught organ and Evangelical church music at the Lübeck Academy (1968–71) and the Folkwang Hochschule in Essen (since 1970). As an organist, he has concertized and recorded throughout Europe, premiering works by such composers as Mauricio Kagel, György Ligeti, Isang Yun, Juan Allende-Blin, and Dieter Schönbach.

PRINCIPAL COMPOSITIONS: *Prière pour aller au paradis avec les ânes* for baritone, 8 winds, piano (1952); *Transformationen* for piano (1954); *Diferencias* for organ (1961); *Das Gebet Jonas im Bauch des Fisches* for soprano, organ (1963); *Text* for organ (1964); *700,000 Tage später*, St. Luke passion for chorus (1968); *Szmaty* for organ (1968); *Ré* for organ (1969); *Die Kunst einer Fuge*, 10 interpretations of J. S. Bach's "Contrapunctus I" for organ (1969).

PRINCIPAL WRITINGS: "Werkzeug Orgel," *Der Kirchenmusiker* (Berlin) 1968/5; "Zur Orgelmusik seit 1960," *Orgel und Orgelmusik heute* (Stuttgart 1968); "Presentation av fyra orgelwerk," *Nutida musik* (Stockholm) 1968–69/2; "Interprète—compositeur—commissionaire," *Musique en jeu* (Paris) 1971/3.

BIBL.: "The Organ as Synthesizer," *Time* (8 June 1970); Heinz-Josef Herbert, "Die letzten Neuheiten auf der Kirchenorgel," *Die Zeit* (Hamburg, 3 April 1970); Norbert Linke, "Gespräch mit Organisten G. Z.," *Melos* (March 1968); André Manz, "Orgelmusik der Avantgarde," *Musica sacra* (Cologne, March 1970); Heinz-Klaus Metzger, "Play Bach," *Die Weltwoche* (Zurich, 22 Sept 1968).

Zeljenka, Ilja (b. Bratislava, Czechoslovakia, 21 Dec 1932), studied at the Univ. of Music and Performing Arts in Bratislava (1951–56; composition with Ján Cikker, esthetics with Otto Ferenczy, piano with Rudolf Macudzinski). During 1957–61 he was music editor for the Slovakian Philharmonic in Bratislava and during 1961–68, for the Czech Broadcasting Co. In 1961 he and Ivan Statdrucker established an electronic music studio at the Czech Television Network in Bratislava (the first in the country). He has been a free-lance composer since 1968. His music has been influenced by the work of Prokofiev, Stravinsky, and Webern. He has been affiliated with Czech and Slovak film companies since 1957 and has written over 200 film scores.

PRINCIPAL COMPOSITIONS: *Quintet* for clarinet, violin, viola, cello, piano (1958); *Oswiencym* for 2 narrators, chorus, orchestra; text by Kováč (1959–60, Supraphon); *String Quartet* (1963, Panton); *Štruktúry* [Structures] for orchestra (1964, SHF); *Hudba* [Music] for chorus, orchestra (1965); *Zaklínadlá* [Magic Formulas] for chorus, orchestra (1967); *Hry* [Plays], a "space mobile" for 13 singers playing drums (1969, Panton); *Zalm* [Psalm] for 4 string quintets (1970).

PRINCIPAL WRITINGS: "Starosti filmového skladateľa" [The Troubles of the Film Maker], *Slovenská hudba* 4:493.

BIBL.: Peter Faltin, "Nová hudba na Slovensku" [New Music in Slovakia], *Slovenská hudba* 11:341; Ivan Hrušovský, *Slovenská hudba v profiloch a rozboroch* [Slovak Music in Profile and Analysis] (Bratislava 1964):372–3; Peter Kolman, "Elektronická hudba na Slovensku" [Electronic Music in Slovakia], *Slovenská hudba* 11:348.

SEE ALSO Czechoslovakia.

Zemlinsky, Alexander von (b. Vienna, of Polish parents, 4 Oct 1872; d. Larchmont, N. Y., 16 March 1942), studied at the Vienna Conservatory (1884–90, piano with A. Door, composition with J. N. Fuchs). He was a prominent opera conductor, his most important posts being those of musical director in Prague (from 1911), where he was also rector of the German Music Academy (from 1920), and musical director of the Krolloper in Berlin (1927–32). He emigrated to the U.S. in 1934. His music is in the tradition of Richard Strauss, Franz Schreker, and Gustav Mahler; the latter's *Symphony No. 6* he arranged for piano 4-hands in 1906. His quartets stem from late Beethoven and contain frequent changes in tempo and overall character. He is perhaps best remembered today as the teacher of Arnold Schoenberg, who married his sister.

PRINCIPAL COMPOSITIONS: *Trio* for piano, clarinet (violin), cello, Op. 3 (published 1897, Simrock); *Sarema*, opera; libretto by Arnold Schoenberg after R. von Gottschall (premiere 1897, published by Berté, Vienna); *Songs* for voice, piano, Op. 5 (published 1898, Hansen-W); *String Quartets Nos. 1–3*, Opp. 4, 15, 19 (published 1898, Simrock; 1916, UE; 1925, UE); *Es war einmal*, opera; libretto by M. Singer (premiere 1900); *Kleider machen Leute*, opera; libretto by Leo Feld after G. Keller (premiere 1910, Bote); *23rd Psalm* for chorus, orchestra, Op. 14 (published 1911, UE); *6 Songs* for medium voice, orchestra, Op. 13; poems by Maurice Maeterlinck (published 1913, 1914; UE); *Eine florentinische Tragödie*, opera after Oscar Wilde (premiere 1917, UE); *Der Zwerg*, opera after Wilde (premiere 1921, UE); *Lyrische Symphonie* for soprano, baritone, orchestra, Op. 18; poems by Rabindranath Tagore (published 1926, UE); *Der Kreidekreis*, opera (premiere 1933, UE); *Sinfonietta*, Op. 23 (1935, UE). Zemlinsky also wrote three symphonies, all unpublished.

Zimmermann, Bernd Alois (b. Bliesheim, Germany, 20 March 1918; d. Cologne, 10 August 1970), studied philology beginning in 1937 at the Universities of Bonn, Cologne, and Berlin while earning his living as a laborer and as a dance-band musician. He studied composition with Heinrich Lemacher and Philipp Jarnach at the Cologne Hochschule für Musik and with Wolfgang Fortner and René Leibowitz at the Darmstadt summer courses. During 1950–52 he taught the history of music theory at the Univ. of Cologne; beginning in 1958 he taught composition and lead seminars in film and radio music at the Cologne Hochschule. He also wrote radio music for the WDR in Cologne. As H. H. Stuckenschmidt has observed, Zimmermann traversed the whole field of contemporary compositional technique: serialism and its disintegration, graphic notation, electronic resources, quotation and collage (*Melos* 37:349). The influence of Stravinsky is especially apparent in the *Oboe Concerto* (1952), that of Webern in *Perspectives* (1955). His collage techniques and eclectic approach to style found their best expression in the opera *Die Soldaten*, which calls for mixed-media production techniques (including a spherical distribution of sound sources), films, and loudspeakers. In addition to orchestral instruments and singing voices, the sounds include noise, sprechstimme, and electronic and concrete sound. The plot disregards linear concepts of time by sometimes shuffling events or presenting them simultaneously.

PRINCIPAL COMPOSITIONS (published by Schott): *Alagoana*, "Caprichos brasileiros," ballet; choreography for the first production, 1955, by Alfredo Bortoluzzi (1940, revised 1950); *Symphony in 1 Movement* (1947, revised 1953); *Concerto for String Orchestra* (1948, based on a string trio of 1943); *Lob der Torheit*, burlesque cantata for vocal soloists, chorus, orchestra; text after Goethe (1948); *Violin Concerto* (1950); *Violin Sonata* (1950); *Concerto* for oboe, chamber orchestra (1952); *Canto di speranza*, cantata for cello, chamber orchestra (1952, revised 1957); *Contrasts*, music for an imaginary ballet (after an idea by Fred Schneckenburger) for orchestra (1953); *Nobody Knows De Trouble I See*, concerto for trumpet in C, orchestra (1954); *Perspectives*, music for an imaginary ballet for 2 pianos (1955); *Die Soldaten*, 4-act opera after J. M. Reinhold Lenz (1958–60, revised 1963–64); *Dialogue*, concerto for 2 pianos, orchestra (1960, revised 1965; arranged for 2 pianos, *Monologue*, 1964); *Tempus loquendi* for 3 flutes (1963); *Cello Concerto* "in the form of a pas de trois" (1965–66); *Intercomunicazione* for cello, piano (1967); *Requiem für einen jungen Dichter*, "lingual" for speaking and singing choruses, vocal soloists, electronic sounds, orchestra, jazz combo, organ; text from various poetry and prose sources (1967–69); *Photoptosis*, prelude for orchestra (1968); *Stille und Umkehr*, sketches for orchestra (1970); *Ich wandte mich und sah an alles Unrecht, das geschah unter der Sonne*, "Ekklesiastische Aktion" for 2 narrators, bass, orchestra (1970). Complete list published by Schott.

BIBL.: Reinhold Schubert, "B. A. Z.," *Die Reihe*, English ed., 4:103–13; Ursula Stürzbecher, "Werkstattgespräch mit B. A. Z.," *Melos* 37:446–49.

[prepared with the help of Klaus Schöll]

SEE ALSO Austria and Germany.